Password

**English Dictionary for
Speakers of Portuguese
New Edition**

Tabela de pronúncia

Consoantes

[b]	but [bʌt]
[d]	dab [dæb]
[dʒ]	jam [dʒæm]; gem [dʒem]
[f]	fat [fæt]
[g]	go [gəʊ]
[h]	hat [hæt]
[j]	yet [jet]
[k]	cat [kæt]
[l]	lad [læd]
[m]	mat [mæt]
[n]	no [nəʊ]
[ŋ]	bang [bæŋ]
[p]	pat [pæt]
[r]	rat [ræt]
[(r)]	far [fɑ:(r)]
[s]	sat [sæt]
[ʃ]	sham [ʃæm]
[t]	tap [tæp]
[tʃ]	chat [tʃæt]
[θ]	thatch [θætʃ]
[ð]	that [ðæt]
[v]	vat [væt]
[w]	wall [wɔ:l]
[z]	zinc [zɪŋk]
[ʒ]	pleasure [pleʒə(r)]
[χ]	loch [lɒχ]

Vogais

[æ]	bat [bæt]
[ɑ:]	art [ɑ:t]
[e]	bet [bet]
[ɜ:]	curl [kɜ:l]
[ə]	amend [əˈmend]
[i:]	bee [bi:]
[ɪ]	bit [bɪt]
[ɒ]	wad [wɒd]
[ɔ:]	all [ɔ:l]
[ʊ]	put [pʊt]
[u:]	shoe [ʃu:]
[ʌ]	cut [kʌt]

Ditongos

[aɪ]	life [laɪf]
[au]	house [haʊs]
[eə]	there [ðeə(r)]
[eɪ]	date [deɪt]
[əʊ]	low [ləʊ]
[ɪə]	beer [brə(r)]
[ɔɪ]	boil [bɔɪl]
[ʊə]	poor [pʊə(r)]

Password

**English Dictionary for
Speakers of Portuguese
New Edition**

Tradução de Luciana Garcia

martins fontes
selo martins

Password: English Dictionary for
Speakers of Portuguese – New Edition

© 2018 Martins Editora Livraria Ltda., São Paulo, para a presente edição.
© 2009 Chambers Harrap Publishers Ltd.
www.chambersharrap.co.uk
Imagens reproduzidas com a autorização de QA International, www.qa-international.com
a partir do livro "The Visual Dictionary" QA internacional. 2009. Todos os direitos reservados.
Chambers® é uma marca registrada da Chambers Harrap Publishers Ltd. Todos os direitos reservados.
Chambers Publishing Ltd é uma empresa do grupo Hachette.

Publisher	*Evandro Mendonça Martins Fontes*
Coordenação editorial	*Vanessa Faleck*
Produção editorial	*Susana Leal*
Revisão	*Ellen Barros*
	Paula Piva
	Julio de Mattos
	Amanda Zampieri
	Bárbara Parente

**Dados Internacionais de Catalogação na Publicação (CIP)
(Câmara Brasileira do Livro, SP, Brasil)**

Password : English dictionary for speakers of portuguese – new edition / tradução de Luciana Garcia. – São Paulo : Martins Fontes – selo Martins, 2016.

Vários autores.
ISBN 978-85-8063-199-9

1. Inglês – Dicionários – Português 2. Português – Dicionários – Inglês.

	CDD-423.69
16-00909	-469.32

Índices para catálogo sistemático:
1. Inglês : Dicionários : Português   423.69
2. Português : Dicionários : Inglês   469.32

Todos os direitos desta edição para o Brasil reservados à
Martins Editora Livraria Ltda.
*Av. Dr. Arnaldo, 2076
01255-000 São Paulo SP Brasil
Tel. (11) 3116 0000
info@emartinsfontes.com.br
www.martinsfontes-selomartins.com.br*

Sumário

Prefácio	7
Como usar este dicionário	8-9
Indicações gramaticais	10
Gramática no dicionário	11
Uso especial de certas palavras	12
Inglês britânico e inglês americano	12
Collocations	13-14
Páginas de estudo	
Verbos modais	15-16
Pontuação	17-18
Construção das palavras	19-20
Artigos	21

Prefácio

Este é o primeiro dicionário de inglês semibilíngue, direcionado sobretudo aos falantes da língua portuguesa. *Password* possui um núcleo em inglês, isto é, a definição, os exemplos de uso corrente e as informações gramaticais correspondentes a cada verbete são fornecidos em inglês, e, ao final de cada definição ou exemplo de uso de derivado ou expressão idiomática, é dado o equivalente em português. Agora em nova edição revista e atualizada, ele contém todas as palavras importantes que você precisará para estudar, para trabalhar ou simplesmente para a vida, explicadas de um modo simples e claro, usando expressões que você já conhece.

Ao abrir o livro, você provavelmente notará o símbolo ⊞ em muitos verbetes. Esse sinal serve para mostrar um dos aspectos mais importantes da língua inglesa: certas associações comuns de palavras em um contexto (*collocation,* em inglês). A palavra *collocation* indica o modo como as palavras geralmente se combinam em determinada situação. Por exemplo, se há muitos carros na rua e o trânsito fica lento por esse motivo, dizemos que há "**heavy traffic**" (congestionamento), e se alguém faz alguma coisa ilegal, dizemos que essa pessoa "**committed a crime**" (cometeu um crime). Essas combinações frequentemente são impossíveis de concluir, mas aprendê-las é provavelmente a coisa mais importante que você pode fazer para tornar o seu inglês mais fluente e natural, e este dicionário o ajudará com isso.

Ao contrário de muitos dicionários, o *Password* não tem códigos gramaticais complicados, mas todas as palavras mais importantes e comuns têm exemplos que mostram claramente como usá-las. Pelo fato de este livro ter sido escrito por professores experientes, você também encontrará observações que o ajudarão a evitar erros comuns.

As informações deste dicionário são baseadas nas evidências fornecidas pela *Chambers Harrap Corpus*, uma coleção de milhões de palavras da língua inglesa provenientes de todos os tipos de linguagens, desde jornais e romances a conversas coloquiais. Isso nos ajuda a entender como as palavras são usadas na vida real e nos dá a certeza de que o dicionário está completamente atualizado.

Você também encontrará uma Seção de Estudo que fornece informações e ajuda com a gramática inglesa.

Esperamos que você faça um bom proveito deste dicionário em casa, nas aulas ou onde quer que esteja!

Como usar este dicionário

Os **verbetes** estão em ordem alfabética.

O **plural** de cada palavra é mostrado.

Todas as **formas verbais** são mostradas.

Os **phrasal verbs** são exibidos após o verbo principal do verbete.

lap /læp/ ▶ NOUN [plural **laps**]
1 the top part of a person's legs when they are in a sitting position □ *Jessie sat on her mother's lap.* (**colo**)
2 one complete journey around a race track □ *He crashed out on the first lap of the race.* (**volta**)
♦ IDIOM **in the lap of luxury** in a very comfortable situation, with expensive things around you (**no luxo**)
▶ VERB [**laps, lapping, lapped**]
1 to drink something with the tongue sticking out □ *The cat was lapping milk from a saucer.* (**beber a lambidas**)
2 if water laps, it moves gently against rocks or onto a beach □ *The waves were lapping at our feet.* (**marulhar**)
3 to pass someone more than once as you go round a race track (**dar volta de atraso**)
♦ PHRASAL VERB **lap something up** to enjoy experiencing or hearing something very much □ *She lapped up the compliments about her new dress.* (**escutar algo de bom**)

Toda palavra tem uma **indicação gramatical**, mostrando se é um substantivo, verbo, adjetivo etc.

As **expressões idiomáticas** comuns geralmente são mostradas.

Os números indicam os diferentes **significados** de uma palavra.

As palavras indicadas desta forma são as de **uso mais comum e útil**.

As palavras de uma **mesma família** são exibidas abaixo da palavra principal, em ordem alfabética.

eager /ˈiːgə(r)/ ADJECTIVE wanting very much to do or have something □ **+ to do something** *Imran seems eager to learn.* (**ansioso**)
● **eagerly** /ˈiːgəli/ ADVERB in an eager way (**ansiosamente**) ▣ *This is the eagerly awaited new film from the Spanish director.* (**ansiosamente aguardado**)
● **eagerness** /ˈiːgənɪs/ NOUN, NO PLURAL being eager □ *In his eagerness to get there, he fell over.* (**ânsia**)

Cada verbete apresenta a **pronúncia** com base no AFI*. Você pode encontrar a explicação dos símbolos na segunda página do dicionário.

Padrões gramaticais simples são apresentados para palavras comuns. São sempre seguidos de um exemplo, mostrando claramente como usar a palavra. Para uma explicação de todos os códigos gramaticais, ver página 11.

Este dicionário tem milhares de **exemplos de frases** mostrando os usos típicos dos verbetes.

---

* Alfabeto Fonético Internacional (International Phonetic Alphabet – IPA).

Como usar este dicionário

Os adjetivos e os advérbios nos graus **comparativo de superioridade e superlativo** são mostrados. Essas formas são usadas quando você quer dizer que alguma coisa ou alguém tem mais intensamente uma qualidade ao ser comparado com outros.

lonely /'ləʊnlɪ/ ADJECTIVE [**lonelier, loneliest**]
1 unhappy because you are alone, with no friends around you (**solitário**) ▫ *She suddenly* **felt** *very lonely.* (**sentiu-se solitária**) ▫ I **get lonely** *at the weekends.* (**me sinto solitário**)
2 far from other places and with very few people ▫ *He lived in a lonely cottage on the hillside.* (**isolado**)

Collocations (certas associações comuns de palavras) são uma característica muito importante deste dicionário. Para mais informações, ver página 13.

Este dicionário usa palavras simples em todos os verbetes, mas, quando há uma palavra mais difícil, é fornecida uma breve explicação.

duodenum /ˌdjuː'əʊ'diːnəm/ NOUN [*plural* **duodenums** *or* **duodena**] the first part of the small intestine (= tube that food goes into to be digested), just below the stomach. A biology word. (**duodeno**)

Uma vez que este dicionário foi projetado para ser usado na escola e em casa, palavras usadas nas **disciplinas escolares** de matemática, física, biologia, geografia e computação são identificadas.

Caso você precise identificar se uma palavra, por exemplo, é mais formal ou informal, isso será indicado. Para uma lista de palavras que descrevem essas características, ver página 12.

abeyance /ə'beɪəns/ NOUN (**inatividade, suspensão**) **in abeyance** not happening or not being used at present. A formal word. (**pendente, suspenso**)

Se uma palavra é sempre usada em determinada **expressão**, essa expressão é mostrada antes da explicação, e esta descreve a expressão completa.

picnic /'pɪknɪk/ ▶ NOUN [*plural* **picnics**] a meal that you take with you to eat outdoors (**piquenique**) ▫ *We had a picnic on the beach.* (**fizemos um piquenique**) ▫ *There's a beautiful picnic area in the forest.* (**área para piquenique**)

> ▸ Note that you **have** a picnic. You do not 'make' a picnic:
> ✓ We had a picnic in the park.
> ✗ We made a picnic in the park.

▶ VERB [**picnics, picnicking, picnicked**] to have a picnic (**fazer piquenique**)
• **picnicker** /'pɪknɪkə(r)/ NOUN [*plural* **picnickers**] someone who is having a picnic (**aquele que faz piquenique**)

Usage notes orientam sobre o uso de uma palavra. Elas ajudam você a evitar erros que os estudantes iniciantes de inglês cometem com frequência.

Algumas palavras podem ter mais de uma **grafia** possível.

lasagne *or* **lasagna** /lə'zænjə/ NOUN [*plural* **lasagnes** *or* **lasagnas**] an Italian food made up of layers of pasta, and layers of meat or vegetables with a white sauce and cheese (**lasanha**)

diaper /'daɪəpə(r)/ NOUN [*plural* **diapers**] the US word for **nappy** (**fralda**)

Este dicionário é escrito em inglês britânico. A grafia nas explicações e nos exemplos é britânica. Entretanto, grafias e palavras americanas comuns são identificadas.

Indicações gramaticais

Estas são as classificações gramaticais usadas neste dicionário.

abbreviation	forma simplificada das palavras, usando suas primeiras letras, abreviatura	l (litre), UK (United Kingdom)
adjective	palavra que descreve um substantivo, adjetivo	pretty, hot, uncomfortable
adverb	palavra que descreve um verbo ou um adjetivo, advérbio	slowly, extremely, well
auxiliary verb	verbos utilizados para formar tempos verbais, formas negativas e interrogativas, verbo auxiliar	be, do, have
conjunction	palavra que une partes de uma oração, conjunção	but, however
determiner	palavra usada antes de um substantivo para mostrar como ele está sendo usado, determinante	the, this, those
exclamation	alguma coisa que se diz de repente ou em voz alta, exclamação	hey, ouch
modal verb	um verbo usado para expressar ideias como: ser possível, necessário, correto etc., verbo modal	might, ought, will
noun	palavra que indica uma pessoa, coisa ou qualidade, substantivo	dog, table, car
noun no plural	substantivo que não pode ser usado no plural	air, happiness, ham
number	numeral	eleven, twenty, million
past participle	particípio passado	sung, watched, eaten
past tense	o verbo indicado no tempo passado	sang, watched, ate
plural noun	substantivo plural	trousers, outskirts
prefix	letras adicionadas no início de uma palavra para modificar seu significado, prefixo	anti-, eco-, hydro-
preposition	palavra usada para expressar noções como as de tempo, posição ou método, preposição	by, under, with
pronoun	palavra que pode substituir um substantivo, pronome	they, it, those
suffix	letras adicionadas no final de uma palavra para modificar seu significado, sufixo	-ful, -able
verb	palavra que indica ação ou estado de alguém ou de alguma coisa, verbo	speak, increase, allow

Gramática no dicionário

Para facilitar o uso deste dicionário, os códigos gramaticais são usados apenas para as palavras mais importantes ou mais comuns. A razão disso é porque essas são as palavras que você provavelmente mais usará.

Você verá que, onde houver um código gramatical, haverá também um exemplo mostrando seu significado.

Os códigos usados neste dicionário são:

+ ing	a palavra é seguida de um verbo usando a forma -ing	e.g. + ing: *I like playing computer games*
+ question word	a palavra é seguida de palavras como *who, what, why*	e.g. + question word: *I don't understand why he is so upset*
+ that	a palavra é seguida por parte de uma oração começando com *that*	e.g. + that: *I promise that I'll pay you back later*
+ to do something	a palavra é seguida por um verbo no infinitivo	e.g. + to do something: *I forgot to lock the door*
no plural	este sentido da palavra não pode ser usado na forma plural, mesmo que outros sentidos da mesma palavra possam	e.g. no plural: *all the hairs that grow on your head*
+ in/over/up etc.	esta palavra é seguida por uma preposição	e.g.: truth + about: *We're determined to learn the truth about his disapearance*

Uso especial de certas palavras

Algumas vezes, uma palavra que pode ser usada em determinada situação não é adequada para uma situação diferente (quando escrevemos um artigo, por exemplo, não usamos a mesma linguagem com que falamos com nossos amigos).

Essas diferenças são claramente mostradas nas explicações deste dicionário. Estas são as palavras que usamos para descrevê-las:

formal – palavras formais são adequadas para um texto escrito e situações oficiais. Elas parecerão ligeiramente estranhas se você usá-las em uma conversa comum.

> **longevity** /lɒnˈdʒevətɪ/ NOUN, NO PLURAL when someone lives for a long time. A formal word □ *Improvements in diet have led to an increase in longevity.* (**longevidade**)

informal – palavras informais não são adequadas para textos escritos ou para situações oficiais. É mais natural usá-las com pessoas as quais você conheça bem.

> **tubby** /ˈtʌbɪ/ ADJECTIVE [**tubbier, tubbiest**] an informal word meaning slightly fat (**rechonchudo**)

old-fashioned (antigo) – este dicionário não inclui palavras que não são mais usadas, mas existem algumas palavras que ainda estão em uso, embora não façam parte da linguagem comum dos jovens.

> **spinster** /ˈspɪnstə(r)/ NOUN [*plural* **spinsters**] an old-fashioned word for a woman who is not married (**solteira**)

literary (literário) – palavras normalmente encontradas em poemas ou romances.

> • **riches** /ˈrɪtʃɪz/ PLURAL NOUN a literary word meaning a lot of money and expensive things (**riquezas**)

Inglês britânico e inglês americano

Este dicionário é escrito em inglês britânico. A grafia e as palavras nas explicações e as frases de exemplos são britânicas. Entretanto, palavras americanas comuns também estão incluídas:

> **sidewalk** /ˈsaɪdwɔːk/ NOUN [*plural* **sidewalks**] the US word for **pavement** (**calçada**)

Algumas vezes, apenas um dos sentidos de uma palavra é americano. Por exemplo, o sentido do item de número 5:

> **after** /ˈɑːftə(r)/ ▶ PREPOSITION
> **1** when something has happened □ *I'll do it after dinner.* □ *It rained day after day.* (**após**)
> **5** used in US English to talk about the time when it is minutes past the hour □ *It's ten after eight.* (**depois**)

Muitas palavras têm grafias diferentes no inglês britânico e no inglês americano, e isto é explicado no dicionário:

> **sulfur** /ˈsʌlfə(r)/ NOUN, NO PLURAL the US spelling of **sulphur** (*ver* **sulphur**)

Collocations

O que são *collocations*?

Collocations são conhecidas como "palavras associadas", pois são palavras que se combinam em certas situações. Por exemplo, se está chovendo muito forte, podemos falar em "uma tromba d'água", e se duas pessoas se amam muito, podemos dizer que estão "loucamente apaixonadas".

Essas palavras aparecem juntas mais frequentemente do que apareceriam por acaso, ou simplesmente apenas por seus significados. Por exemplo, é correto dizer "roubou um carro", mas isso não é o que chamamos de *collocation*, porque o verbo roubar pode ser usado com muitos substantivos diferentes. Entretanto, se nos referirmos sobre alguém "cometendo um crime", estamos usando uma *collocation*, porque esse tipo de palavra se combina mais fortemente e, se você precisar de um verbo que combine com a palavra "crime", deve escolher "cometer" – um outro verbo como "fazer" não estaria correto.

Algumas vezes, conseguimos descobrir as *collocations* que queremos, mas geralmente é difícil. Por que nós "prestamos atenção", ou "chegamos a conclusões"? Por que "contamos mentiras" mas "fazemos promessas"?

É por essa razão que tivemos o cuidado de mostrar as *collocations* das palavras mais úteis do dicionário. As *collocations* são indicadas pelo símbolo ⊞ para que você veja as palavras que melhor combinam com aquela que você está pesquisando.

Por que é tão importante aprender as *collocations*?

As palavras geralmente não são usadas sozinhas. Além de aprender uma palavra, você precisa saber as palavras que se aproximam dela: as palavras que permitem a você usá-la de maneira clara e natural.

Saber as *collocations* ajudará você a falar e a escrever um inglês mais natural e fluente. Por exemplo, você deve saber o significado da palavra "exame", mas também é importante saber quais verbos usar com ela. Embora seja possível dizer: "Vou fazer um exame no final do ano", é muito mais natural dizer: "Vou prestar um exame no final do ano". Embora as pessoas entendam se você disser: "I was successful in my exam", um falante nativo inglês provavelmente não diria desse modo; ele diria "I passed my exam".

Conhecer as *collocations* tornará o seu inglês mais interessante e ajudará você a se expressar melhor. Por exemplo, está correto dizer "I was very disappointed", mas, se você souber dizer "I was bitterly disappointed", sua frase terá muito mais força e impressionará mais.

Conhecer as *collocations* ajudará você a evitar erros. Embora seja possível, algumas vezes, concluir quais palavras usar, ao mesmo tempo é fácil se enganar. Por exemplo, muitos estudantes de inglês dizem: "We decided to make a party for him". Isso não é o inglês correto; deve-se dizer "We decided to *have* a party for him", ou, ainda melhor, "We decided to *throw* a party for him".

Saber as *collocations* melhorará seus resultados nos exames. Muitos exames comuns de inglês testam o seu conhecimento sobre as *collocations*. Você perderá pontos se usar as incorretas e ganhará pontos se optar pelas corretas e interessantes.

14 Collocations

Encontrar e aprender as *collocations*

As ***collocations*** são uma parte muito importante do aprendizado do idioma, por isso é uma boa ideia aprendê-las corretamente desde o começo.

Vejas as seguintes frases simples, por exemplo, para entender quão importantes elas são, até mesmo para o tipo de ideias e atividades sobre as quais conversamos quase diariamente:

- *I **brush** my **teeth** every morning.*
- *I need to **do** my **homework**.*
- *He **watches TV** every evening.*
- *It was **raining heavily** yesterday.*
- *My sister **wears glasses**.*

Quando você pesquisar uma palavra no dicionário, tente verificar as ***collocations*** que se referem a ela e aprendê-las com a palavra.

Quais tipos de *collocations* existem?

adjective + noun	e.g. **strong accent, detailed account, heavy traffic**
verb + noun	e.g. **gain acceptance, open an account, commit a crime**
verb + adverb	e.g. **go abroad, chop finely**
noun + verb	e.g. **standards slip, war breaks out**
adverb + adjective	e.g. **hopelessly lost, pleasantly surprised**
verb + adjective	e.g. **fall asleep, get married**
noun + preposition + noun	e.g. **a sense of achievement, a piece of advice**
noun + noun	e.g. **travel arrangements, management skills**

Collocations adverbiais de intensidade

Se você pesquisar no dicionário, verá que há, frequentemente, modos muito mais interessantes de dizer "very" ou "extremely".

Por exemplo, se alguém estiver muito doente (very ill), poderemos dizer que está "seriously ill"; e, se alguém for muito tímido (very shy), poderemos dizer que é "painfully shy". Advérbios como "seriously" e "painfully" são chamados de advérbios intensificadores, pois deixam as palavras mais fortes ou intensas em seu significado. Essas são ***collocations*** bastante úteis porque podem deixar seu inglês mais interessante.

Páginas de Estudo

Verbos modais

Um verbo modal é um verbo extra usado antes do verbo principal. Um exemplo de um verbo modal é o verbo "can". "Can" vai diante de outro verbo e mostra que alguém é capaz de fazer alguma coisa. Por exemplo, na frase "Lucy can swin", mostra que Lucy é capaz de nadar. Os principais verbos modais são: *can, could, may, might, must, shall, will, would* e *should. Have to, have got to* e *need to* também são utilizados como verbos modais.

Alguns fatos sobre os verbos modais

1. São utilizados no "infinitivo" (forma primitiva) e sem "to":
- ✓ Julia *could go* instead of me.
- ✗ Julia *could to go* instead of me.

2. Não se usa 's' na 3ª pessoa do singular:
- ✓ She *must* get there early.
- ✗ She *musts* get there early.

3. O verbo modal "will" é muitas vezes abreviado para "ll", especialmente no discurso:
Don't worry – I'll help.

A seguir estão as principais formas de uso dos verbos modais:

1. Sugerir habilidade (verbos modais: can, could)
Usado para mostrar que alguém é capaz de fazer algo. (*Can* é usado para mostrar que alguém é capaz de fazer algo agora e *could* é usado para mostrar que alguém foi capaz de fazer alguma coisa no passado):

I can run faster than you.
I could run faster when I was a child.

2. Dizer o que é necessário (verbos modais: must, have to/have got to, need to)
Usado para dizer que é preciso fazer alguma coisa:

I must call my mum.
I have to finish my essay by tomorrow.
I have got to finish my essay by tomorrow.
I need to go now.

3. Dizer o que é possível (verbos modais: may, migh, could)
Usado para dizer que é possível que algo aconteça ou que é verdadeiro:

We may come if we've got time.
Jim might know what time it starts.
He could be right about that.

4. Dizer o que é provável (verbos modais: must, will, should)
Usado para dizer que algo provavelmente irá acontecer ou que algo provavelmente é verdade:

Here's Anna's coat so she must be here.
She will be here at the usual time.
He should call – he usually does at this time.

5. Pedir permissão (verbos modais: could, may, can)
Usado para perguntar se você pode fazer ou ter algo:

Could I borrow you pen, please?

May I have another biscuit, please?
Can I take this chair, please?

Note que *could* e *may* são mais formais do que *can*.

6. Fazer pedidos (verbos modais: could, can, would)
Usado para pedir a alguém para fazer algo:
Could you tell her to call me?
Can you write down any messages, please?
Would you give these to Louisa, please?

Note que *could* e *would* são mais formais do que *can*.

7. Dar conselhos e pedir conselhos (verbos modais: should)
Usado para fazer ou pedir sugestões:
You should complain to the manager.
Should I tell her?

8. Fazer ofertas (verbos modais: shall, will, can)
Usado para dizer que você vai fazer alguma oferta a alguém:
Shall I bring some food?
I'll help (= I will help).
I can take Juliana home if you'd like.

Pontuação

As letras maiúsculas (A, B, C etc.) são usadas:	• no início da frase	*The car came towards me.*
	• para nomes, títulos e organizações	*Jane, Mr Smith, Lord Jones, British Gas*
	• para os países e idiomas	*England, France, Chinese*
	• para dias e meses	*Monday, Saturday, July*
	• para a maioria das abreviaturas e siglas	*BBC, WHO*
	• para o pronome "I"	*I am tired.*
Pontos finais (.) são usados:	• no final da frase	*I read the letter.*
	• em e-mail e endereços de sites *(pronuncia-se o "ponto")*	*www.chambersharrap.co.uk*
	• em algumas abreviaturas, especialmente aquelas com palavras muito curtas	*Smith & Co., Dr. Smith*
Pontos de interrogação (?) são usados:	• no final de perguntas	*Do you know his name?*
Pontos de exclamação (!) são usados:	• para expressar surpresa, choque, raiva, ruídos altos etc.	*I've won! Get out of my house!*
Vírgulas (,) são usadas:	• para mostrar uma pausa em um longo período	*After a good night's sleep, I was ready for work.*
	• para dividir as informações de uma lista	*I bought eggs, milk, butter, and cheese.*
	• para adicionar informações extras em uma sentença	*My mother, who is nearly eight, enjoyed the show very much.*
	• para separar grupos de três números	*1,000, £234,500*
Apóstrofos (') são usados:	• para mostrar onde as letras estão em falta	*I'm, there'll*
	• para mostrar quem ou algo que pertence a	*Kate's dog, the car's engine*
Aspas – também chamadas de vírgulas invertidas (" ou " ") são usadas	• em torno de discurso	*"Go away", she said.*
	• em torno de pensamentos	*'I must phone John,' he thought.*
	• para mostrar algo que alguém disse ou escreveu	*He said that the work was 'not satisfactory'.*
	• para mostrar uma palavra nova, incomum ou interessante	*They play a style of music known as 'classical punk'.*

Pontuação

Os parênteses (( )) são usados:	• para adicionar informações e mantê-las separadas do resto de uma sentença	*I have many hobbies (e.g. sailing, jazz, cinema) and I go out a lot.*
Dois pontos (:) são usados:	• antes de listas	*You will need: cardboard, paint, glue.*
	• para mostrar que o leitor deve olhar para o que se segue	*Answer the following questions:*
Ponto e vírgula (;) são usados:	• dividir duas partes de uma sentença	*My mother hated birthday parties; we children loved them of course.*
	• para separar informações de uma lista na qual os itens são longos ou já incluem vírgulas	*Choose from the following: egg and chips; ham, egg and chips; sausage and chips.*
Hífens (-) são usados:	• em algumas palavras que existem a partir de duas palavras juntas	*Half-sister, one-sided.*
	• quando é preciso dividir uma palavra no final de uma linha	*I will give you my telephone number.*
Traços (–) são usados:	• para inserir uma parte adicional em uma frase	*I helped Ella – not that she really needs help – to wrap the presents.*
	• para adicionar um comentário ao final de uma frase	*She told me that Sara had been injured – it was a terrible shock.*
	• para mostrar que a frase foi interrompida	*We're expecting Louis to arrive at – oh, here he is!*

Construções das palavras

Esta página e a seguinte mostram de que maneira os grupos de letras são adicionados para a formação de diferentes palavras:

Prefixos

Muitas palavras são formadas pelo acréscimo de uma partícula *antes* de sua raiz. Esta partícula é chamada *prefixo*. Existem muitos prefixos. Alguns são bem comuns, como 'dis-', prefixo de *negação*, por exemplo, na palavra 'dishonest'; há também o prefixo 'inter-', que indica *relação entre*, por exemplo, 'international'.

A seguir, uma lista de prefixos: suas aplicações, seus significados e exemplos.

Prefixo	Significado	Palavras que contêm prefixo
anti-	oposição ou prevenção	*antisocial, antifreeze*
auto-	próprio, autossuficiente	*autobiography*
bi-	dois ou duas vezes	*bicycle, bilingual*
co-	em conjunto com ou trabalhar com	*co-star, cooperate*
de-	1. remoção de algo	*defrost*
	2. o oposto de	*decompose*
dis-	negação	*dislike*
eco-	meio ambiente, ecologia	*eco-friendly*
inter-	relação entre, entre	*international*
mini-	pequeno, curto	*minibus, miniskirt*
mis-	ruim ou mal, errado ou mau	*misbehave, misunderstand*
non-	não	*a non-smoker*
over-	demasiado, mais do que o normal	*overconfident, overcrowded*
post-	após	*postwar*
pre-	antes	*prehistoric*
re-	novamente, de novo	*reappear*
sub-	abaixo de, sob	*submarine*
super-	acima ou extremamente	*superhuman, superpower*
under-	1. abaixo	*underground*
	2. não suficiente	*undernourished*

Observe que alguns prefixos, como 'de-' e 'under-', têm mais de um significado.

Sufixos

Muitas palavras são formadas pelo acréscimo de uma partícula *depois* de sua raiz. Essa partícula é chamada *sufixo*. Os sufixos têm a função de modificar a categoria gramatical das palavras a que se aplicam. Isto é, um determinado sufixo será sempre aplicado a uma determinada categoria de palavra e resultará sempre em uma outra determinada categoria. Por exemplo, o sufixo '-ness', adicionado ao final de um adjetivo como 'happy', torna-se o substantivo 'happiness'.

Outro exemplo é o sufixo '-ful', o qual é aplicado ao substantivo 'hope' e torna-se o adjetivo 'hopeful', que significa 'having a lot of hope'.

Construção das palavras

A seguir, uma lista de sufixos: suas aplicações, seus significados e exemplos.

Sufixo	Significado	Palavras que contêm sufixo
-able	transforma verbos em adjetivos com o significado de "capaz de", "merecedor de"	*preventable*
-ful	forma adjetivos de substantivos, significando "full of" ("cheio de" ou "que tem")	*hopeful*
-ism	forma substantivos com o significado de "crenças" ou "atividade"	*communism, heroism*
-ist	1. forma substantivos que indicam "uma pessoa que estuda" ou se "aplica a"	*artist*
	2. forma substantivos que são usados para indicar "ideologia"	*communist*
-ize or -ise	formam verbos a partir de adjetivos	*computerize*
-less	usado com o sentido de "falta de", "ausência de", e pode vir ligado a substantivos para formar adjetivos	*hopeless, thoughtless*
-ment	adicionados ao final de verbos para formar substantivos que significam "a ação de" ou o "resultado da ação de"	*accomplishment*
-ness	adicionados ao final de adjetivos para formar substantivos abstratos	*sadness*
-proof	indica que algo é impermeável e não é afetado pelo substantivo que vem antes	*waterproof*
-ship	forma substantivos com o significado de "status", "domínio", "condição"	*friendship*

Artigos

As palavras 'a', 'an' e 'the' (um/uma e o(s)/a(s)) são artigos. Muitas vezes pode ser difícil saber quando usá-los e quando eles não são necessários, mas existem algumas regras que você deve seguir.

As palavras 'a' e 'an' (um/uma) são chamadas de artigos indefinidos. Usamos 'an' antes de palavras que começam com vogais (a, e, i, o, u) e 'a' antes de palavras que começam com consoantes (todas as outras letras).

Algumas palavras que começam com 'u' são pronunciadas /ju:/. Estas palavras são precedidas de artigo 'a' (usado antes de som de consoante), por exemplo, em *a ukulele*.

'The' (o(s)/a(s)) é chamado de artigo definido. Usamos 'the' para tratar de algo específico, como uma classe de pessoas ou de coisas. Veja os exemplos:

She went to buy a new coat.
The coat the bought was red.

No primeiro exemplo, não sabemos qual casaco ela saiu para comprar – só que ela iria comprar algum casaco. No segundo exemplo, estamos falando de um casaco *específico* – determinado, mencionado anteriormente, já definido pelo locutor.

Nós também usamos 'the' quando estiver definido o ouvinte ou o leitor do qual estamos falando. Veja estes exemplos:

Put your books on the table.
The doctor told me to drink plenty of water.

No primeiro exemplo, fica claro que você está próximo à mesa, que pode vê-la. No segundo exemplo, é evidente que você está falando sobre o médico de quem vocês conversaram a respeito.

Aa

A or **a** /eɪ/ (a primeira letra do alfabeto)

a ou **an** /ən/ DETERMINER
1 used before a noun to refer to one person or thing but not a particular person or thing □ *I need a pen.* □ *I'd love to have a baby.* (um, uma)
2 one □ *a hundred miles* (um, uma)
3 each or every □ *He gets £5 a week.* (por)

> Remember to use **an** (and not **a**) before a word that begins with a vowel, or a word that sounds as if it begins with a vowel: □ *a bag* □ *an apple* □ *an hour*

aback /ə'bæk/ ADVERB (para trás, trás) **taken aback** surprised or shocked □ *I was taken aback by the change in Dan.* (surpreso, espantado)

abacus /'æbəkəs/ NOUN [*plural* **abacuses**] a frame with small balls used for counting and calculations (ábaco)

abandon /ə'bændən/ VERB [abandons, abandoning, abandoned]
1 to leave someone or something, often not intending to go back □ *He abandoned the car and walked the rest of the way.* □ *How could she abandon her family like that?* (abandonar)
2 to stop something before it is finished □ *If it rains, we'll just abandon the whole trip.* (abandonar)

abashed /ə'bæʃt/ ADJECTIVE shy and embarrassed (embaraçado, envergonhado)

abate /ə'beɪt/ VERB [abates, abating, abated] a formal word meaning to become less strong □ *At last the storm abated.* (enfraquecer, abater)

abattoir /'æbətwɑː(r)/ NOUN [*plural* abattoirs] a place where animals are killed to make meat (abatedouro)

abbey /'æbɪ/ NOUN [*plural* abbeys]
1 the buildings where monks and nuns (= religious men and women) live (mosteiro, convento)
2 a church that monks or nuns use (abadia)

abbot /'æbət/ NOUN [*plural* abbots] a monk (= religious man) who is in charge of an abbey (abade)

abbreviate /ə'briːvɪeɪt/ VERB [abbreviates, abbreviating, abbreviated] to make a word or a phrase shorter □ *Everyone abbreviates Alistair James's name to A. J.* (abreviar)

• **abbreviation** /əˌbriːvɪ'eɪʃən/ NOUN [*plural* abbreviations] a short form of a word or phrase □ + **of** *UK is an abbreviation of United Kingdom.* (abreviação)

ABC /ˌeɪbiː'siː/ NOUN [*plural* **ABCs**] the alphabet □ *The children were learning their ABC.* (abecedário)

abdicate /'æbdɪkeɪt/ VERB [abdicates, abdicating, abdicated]
1 to decide to stop being king or queen (abdicar)
2 **abdicate responsibility for something** to stop being responsible for something you should be responsible for □ *He has abdicated all responsibility for the children.* (renunciar a toda responsabilidade)

• **abdication** /ˌæbdɪ'keɪʃən/ NOUN [*plural* abdications]
1 when a king or queen decides to stop being king or queen (abdicação)
2 when someone stops taking responsibility for something (renúncia)

abdomen /'æbdəmən/ NOUN [*plural* abdomens]
1 the part of an animal or person's body that contains the stomach (abdômen)
2 the end part of an insect's body. A biology word. (ventre)

• **abdominal** /æb'dɒmɪnəl/ ADJECTIVE to do with the abdomen. A biology word. □ *abdominal pain* (abdominal)

abduct /æb'dʌkt/ VERB [abducts, abducting, abducted] to take someone away by using force □ *Two more tourists have been abducted from their hotel room.* (raptar)

• **abduction** /æb'dʌkʃən/ NOUN [*plural* abductions] taking someone away using force □ *He faces charges of child abduction and murder.* (abdução)

aberration /ˌæbə'reɪʃən/ NOUN [*plural* aberrations] a situation or someone's behaviour that is different from usual, usually in a bad way. A formal word. (anomalia)

abeyance /ə'beɪəns/ NOUN (inatividade, suspensão) **in abeyance** not happening or not being used at present. A formal word. (pendente, suspenso)

abhor /əb'hɔː(r)/ VERB [abhors, abhorring, abhorred] to hate someone or something □ *I abhor violence.* (abominar)

• **abhorrence** /əb'hɒrəns/ NOUN, NO PLURAL very strong dislike (aversão)

- **abhorrent** /əbˈhɒrənt/ ADJECTIVE morally very bad □ *I find his views on immigration abhorrent.* (repugnante)

abide /əˈbaɪd/ VERB [abides, abiding, abided] (suportar) **can't abide something/someone** if you can't abide something or someone, you dislike them very much □ *I can't abide people who smoke in restaurants.* (não suportar algo/alguém)

♦ PHRASAL VERB **abide by something** to obey a rule or a decision □ *Please abide by the rules of the game.* (acatar algo)

- **abiding** /əˈbaɪdɪŋ/ ADJECTIVE lasting a long time (duradouro) *My abiding memory* of him is his loud laugh. (lembrança duradoura)

ability /əˈbɪləti/ NOUN [plural **abilities**] someone who has the ability to do something is able to do it or has the skill to do it □ + **to do something** *Not everyone has the ability to play a musical instrument.* (capacidade)

> Remember that **ability** is followed by the structure to do something:
> ✓ her ability to drive
> ✗ her ability of driving

abject /ˈæbdʒekt/ ADJECTIVE
1 abject failure/poverty, etc. when someone is extremely unsuccessful/poor, etc. (miserável)
2 abject behaviour shows that you are very afraid or ashamed □ *an abject coward* (desprezível)

- **abjectly** /ˈæbdʒektli/ ADVERB showing that you are very afraid or ashamed □ *He apologized abjectly.* (miseravelmente)

ablaze /əˈbleɪz/ ADJECTIVE, ADVERB
1 burning strongly □ *The bomb set several buildings ablaze.* (flamejante)
2 shining very brightly □ *The children's eyes were ablaze with excitement.* (brilhante)

able /ˈeɪbəl/ ADJECTIVE
1 able to do something if you are able to do something, you can do it □ *He wasn't able to run fast enough.* □ *Will you be able to help me?* (capaz de fazer alguma coisa)
2 an able person is good at doing something □ *an able student* (capaz)

-able /əbəl/ SUFFIX -able is added to the end of words to mean 'able to be' □ *manageable* □ *preventable* (-ável, -ível)

able-bodied /ˌeɪbəlˈbɒdɪd/ ▶ ADJECTIVE physically healthy (saudável)
▶ NOUN **the able-bodied** people who are physically healthy (pessoas saudáveis)

ably /ˈeɪbli/ ADVERB if you do something ably, you do it well □ *It is an unusual film, ably directed by George Clooney.* (habilmente)

abnormal /æbˈnɔːməl/ ADJECTIVE not normal, especially in way that worries you □ *This is abnormal behaviour for a five-year-old.* (anormal)

- **abnormality** /ˌæbnɔːˈmælɪti/ NOUN [plural **abnormalities**] something that is not normal (anormalidade)
- **abnormally** /æbˈnɔːməli/ ADVERB in a way that is not normal and which worries you □ *an abnormally fast heartbeat* (anormalidade)

aboard /əˈbɔːd/ PREPOSITION, ADVERB on or onto a bus, train, ship or aeroplane □ *He was one of the team aboard the shuttle.* □ *We all climbed aboard the boat.* (a bordo)

abode /əˈbəʊd/ NOUN [plural **abodes**] an old or formal word for the place where someone lives (residência) *He had no fixed abode* (= no permanent place to live) *and had to sleep on the street.* (sem residência fixa)

abolish /əˈbɒlɪʃ/ VERB [abolishes, abolishing, abolished] to get rid of a rule or a way of doing something □ *The school has abolished its uniform.* (abolir)

- **abolition** /ˌæbəˈlɪʃən/ NOUN, NO PLURAL getting rid of a law or a way of doing something □ *the abolition of slavery* (abolição)

abominable /əˈbɒmɪnəbəl/ ADJECTIVE very evil or unpleasant □ *He was an abominable man.* (abominável)

- **abominably** /əˈbɒmɪnəbli/ ADVERB in an evil or unpleasant way □ *She behaved abominably this evening.* (abominavelmente)

Aboriginal /ˌæbəˈrɪdʒənəl/ or **Aborigine** /ˌæbəˈrɪdʒəni/ NOUN [plural **Aboriginals** or **Aborigines**] one of the people who lived in Australia before anyone arrived from other countries (aborígine)

- **Aboriginal** /ˌæbəˈrɪdʒənəl/ ADJECTIVE to do with or belonging to Aboriginals □ *Aboriginal art* (aborígine)

abort /əˈbɔːt/ VERB [aborts, aborting, aborted] to abort a plan or process is to stop it □ *Severe storms forced NASA to abort the launch of the space shuttle.* (abortar)

- **abortive** /əˈbɔːtɪv/ ADJECTIVE an abortive plan or attempt is one that fails (fracassado, abortivo) *They made an abortive attempt to rescue the child.* (tentativa fracassada)

abound /əˈbaʊnd/ VERB [abounds, abounding, abounded] if things abound, there are a lot of them □ *Stories abound of girls forced to become servants.* (afluir)

about /əˈbaʊt/ ▶ PREPOSITION
1 on the subject of □ *a book about bats* □ *a talk about Spain* (sobre)
2 in different parts of a place □ *Clothes were scattered about the room.* (aqui e ali, por)
3 What about/How about something? used to make a suggestion □ *How about going for a walk?* (que tal alguma coisa?)
▶ ADVERB

1 not exactly but almost the number or amount given □ *about five years ago* □ *about four centimeters* (cerca de)

2 in or to different parts of a place □ *We started moving things about.* □ *They were running about all day.* (por ali/aqui)

3 about to do something if you are about to do something, you are going to do it very soon □ *I was about to leave when the phone rang.* □ *I think it's about to rain.* (estar prestes a fazer alguma coisa)

about-turn *or* **about-face** /əbaʊtˈfeɪs/ NOUN, NO PLURAL a complete change of plan or opinion (reviravolta)

above /əˈbʌv/ PREPOSITION, ADVERB

1 in a higher position than something else □ *the shelf above the sink* □ *clouds in the sky above* (cima, acima)

2 more than an amount or level □ *two degrees above zero* □ *in the class above me* (acima de)

3 earlier in a piece of writing □ *See instruction 5 above.* (acima)

4 above all more than anything else □ *Above all, I'm grateful to my parents.* (acima de tudo)

5 not above doing something if someone is not above doing something, they will do it, even if it is wrong or embarrassing □ *James was not above asking for his ten pence back.* (não titubear em)

above-board /əbʌvˈbɔːd/ ADJECTIVE fair and honest (honesto)

abrasion /əˈbreɪʒən/ NOUN [plural **abrasions**] an area where skin has been slightly cut by something rough (escoriação)

abrasive /əˈbreɪsɪv/ ADJECTIVE

1 abrasive substances scratch things that they rub against (abrasivo)

2 abrasive people are rude and seem as if they do not care about other people's feelings (abrasivo)

abreast /əˈbrest/ ADVERB

1 two/three, etc. abreast with two/three, etc. people or things moving next to each other □ *They were walking three abreast.* (lado a lado)

2 keep abreast of something if you keep abreast of information or changes, you make sure you know about them (ficar a par de algo)

abridge /əˈbrɪdʒ/ VERB [**abridges, abridging, abridged**] to make a book or story shorter (resumir)

• **abridgement** *or* **abridgment** /əˈbrɪdʒmənt/ NOUN [plural **abridgements** *or* **abridgments**] a book or story that has been made shorter (resumo)

abroad /əˈbrɔːd/ ADVERB in or to a foreign country □ *We always go abroad for our holidays.* □ *She's abroad at the moment.* (no exterior)

abrupt /əˈbrʌpt/ ADJECTIVE

1 sudden and unexpected □ *The driver made an abrupt change of direction.* (abrupto, repentino)

2 rude and unfriendly (abrupto, rude) □ *She has rather an abrupt manner* (maneira rude)

• **abruptly** /əˈbrʌptli/ ADVERB

1 suddenly and unexpectedly □ *He turned abruptly and walked out.* (repentinamente)

2 in a rude and unfriendly way (rudemente)

abscess /ˈæbsɪs, ˈæbses/ NOUN [plural **abscesses**] a painful swollen area on your body that is filled with pus (= white or yellow liquid) (abscesso)

abscond /əbˈskɒnd/ VERB [**absconds, absconding, absconded**]

1 a formal word meaning to leave a place without permission □ *He absconded from jail.* (fugir)

2 if someone absconds with something, they steal it and go away. A formal word. (evadir-se)

abseil /ˈæbseɪl/ VERB [**abseils, abseiling, abseiled**] to move down a rope with your feet against a wall or other surface (descer fazendo rapel)

• **abseiling** /ˈæbseɪlɪŋ/ NOUN, NO PLURAL the sport of moving down a rope with your feet against a wall or other surface (rapel)

absence /ˈæbsəns/ NOUN [plural **absences**] being away from a place □ *Your absence from the meeting was noticed.* (ausência)

• **absent** /ˈæbsənt/ ADJECTIVE not at a place where you are expected to be □ + *from* *She has been absent from school twice this week.* □ *Is anyone absent today?* (ausente)

• **absentee** /ˌæbsənˈtiː/ NOUN [plural **absentees**] a person who is absent (pessoa ausente)

• **absently** /ˈæbsəntli/ ADVERB without giving much attention to what you are doing □ *She picked up the book absently and put it down again.* (distraidamente)

absent-minded /ˌæbsəntˈmaɪndɪd/ ADJECTIVE an absent-minded person often forgets things (distraído)

absolute /ˈæbsəluːt/ ADJECTIVE complete (absoluto) □ *I have absolute trust in her.* □ *That's absolute rubbish!* (absolutamente)

• **absolutely** /ˈæbsəluːtli/ ADVERB

1 completely □ *Are you absolutely sure you locked the door?* (completamente)

2 extremely □ *This cake is absolutely delicious!* □ *That's absolutely ridiculous!* (absolutamente, extremamente)

3 used to agree or to give permission □ *'We should write and thank them.' 'Absolutely.'* (absolutamente)

> Absolutely meaning 'extremely' is only used before adjectives with very strong meanings:
> ✓ *That's absolutely crazy.*
> ✗ *That's absolutely silly.*
> ✓ *She's absolutely beautiful.*
> ✗ *She's absolutely pretty.*

absolute zero /ˈæbsəluːt ˈzɪərəʊ/ NOUN, NO PLURAL the lowest temperature that scientists think is possible. A physics word. (zero absoluto)

absolution /ˌæbsəˈluːʃən/ NOUN, NO PLURAL in the Christian Church, a statement that someone has been forgiven (absolvição)

absolve /əbˈzɒlv/ VERB [absolves, absolving, absolved] to say formally that someone is not guilty of something or responsible for something (absolver)

absorb /əbˈsɔːb/ VERB [absorbs, absorbing, absorbed]
1 to take up liquid and keep it inside ▢ *The bath mat will absorb the splashes.* (absorver)
2 be absorbed in something to be giving all your attention to something ▢ *We were so absorbed in our game, we didn't hear the bell.* (ficar entretido/entusiasmado)
• **absorbency** /əbˈsɔːbənsɪ/ NOUN, NO PLURAL how much liquid a substance can absorb (absorvência)
• **absorbent** /əbˈsɔːbənt/ ADJECTIVE an absorbent material is able to take up liquid and keep it inside ▢ *absorbent kitchen towels* (absorvente)
• **absorbing** /əbˈsɔːbɪŋ/ ADJECTIVE very interesting and taking all your attention ▢ *an absorbing puzzle* (cativante, interessante)
• **absorption** /əbˈsɔːpʃən/ NOUN, NO PLURAL when a substance absorbs liquid (absorção)

abstain /əbˈsteɪn/ VERB [abstains, abstaining, abstained] to choose not to vote yes or no (abster-se)
♦ PHRASAL VERB **abstain from something** to stop doing or having something that you enjoy. A formal word. ▢ *You will have to abstain from all forms of exercise.* (privar-se de algo)

abstemious /æbˈstiːmɪəs/ ADJECTIVE an abstemious person is careful not to eat or drink too much. A formal word. (moderado)

abstention /əbˈstenʃən/ NOUN [plural abstentions] when someone abstains (= does not vote yes or no) in a vote (abstenção)

abstinence /ˈæbstɪnəns/ NOUN, NO PLURAL when you do not do or have something that you enjoy (abstinência)

abstract /ˈæbstrækt/ ADJECTIVE
1 based on ideas and not real things or situations ▢ *Her writing is too abstract for me.* (teórico)
2 abstract art uses shapes and colours instead of pictures of real things (abstrato)

abstruse /æbˈstruːs/ ADJECTIVE an abstruse subject or argument is difficult to understand. A formal word. (confuso)

absurd /əbˈsɜːd/ ADJECTIVE very silly ▢ *What an absurd idea!* (absurdo)
• **absurdity** /əbˈsɜːdɪtɪ/ NOUN [plural absurdities] something that is very silly (absurdidade)
• **absurdly** /əbˈsɜːdlɪ/ ADVERB in a very silly way ▢ *The questions were absurdly easy.* (absurdamente, ridiculamente)

abundance /əˈbʌndəns/ NOUN, NO PLURAL
1 an abundance of something is a lot of it. A formal word. ▢ *There is an abundance of information on the subject.* (abundância)
2 in abundance if something exists in abundance, there is a lot of it ▢ *There was food in abundance.* (em abundância)
• **abundant** /əˈbʌndənt/ ADJECTIVE existing in large amounts ▢ *an abundant harvest* (abundante)
• **abundantly** /əˈbʌndəntlɪ/ ADVERB
1 in large amounts ▢ *Fruit grows abundantly in the area.* (abundantemente)
2 very ▢ *It is abundantly clear that he is lying.* (abundantemente)

abuse ▶ NOUN /əˈbjuːs/ [plural abuses]
1 using something the wrong way for a bad reason ▢ *This is an abuse of power.* ▢ *alcohol abuse* (= drinking too much alcohol) (abuso)
2 violence or bad treatment ▢ *child abuse* (maus-tratos)
3 insults ▢ *They shouted abuse at us.* (insulto, injúria)
▶ VERB /əˈbjuːz/ [abuses, abusing, abused]
1 to use something the wrong way for a bad purpose ▢ *She abused people's trust in order to steal money from them.* (abusar de)
2 to hurt someone or to treat them badly ▢ *He was abused in prison.* (abusar de, injuriar)
• **abusive** /əˈbjuːsɪv/ ADJECTIVE rude or insulting ▢ *abusive language* (injurioso)

> The noun **abuse** ends with an ss sound. The verb **abuse** ends with a z sound.

abysmal /əˈbɪzməl/ ADJECTIVE very bad ▢ *abysmal exam results* (péssimo)
• **abysmally** /əˈbɪzməlɪ/ ADVERB very badly ▢ *The team played abysmally.* (pessimamente)
abyss /əˈbɪs/ NOUN [plural abysses]
1 a very deep hole (abismo)
2 a very bad situation

academic /ˌækəˈdemɪk/ ▶ ADJECTIVE
1 to do with studying and education ▢ *academic qualifications* ▢ *the academic year* (acadêmico)
2 good at studying and learning ▢ *He loves school but he isn't very academic.* (erudito)
3 not having anything to do with a real situation ▢ *Whether she has the qualifications is academic – she can't take the job because she has to look after the children.* (teórico)
▶ NOUN [plural academics] a teacher at a college or university or someone who is paid to study there (acadêmico)
• **academically** /ˌækəˈdemɪkəlɪ/ ADVERB in a way that is to do with studying and learning ▢ *Not all students can succeed academically.* (academicamente)

academy /əˈkædəmɪ/ NOUN [plural academies]

accede

1 a school or college where you learn about a particular subject ☐ *a science academy* (**academia**)
2 an organization that supports a particular subject ☐ *the Academy of Ancient Music* (**academia**)

accede /æk'si:d/ VERB [accedes, acceding, acceded] a formal word meaning to agree to a plan or something you have been asked to do (**consentir**)

accelerate /ək'seləreɪt/ VERB [accelerates, accelerating, accelerated]
1 to drive faster ☐ *She accelerated round the corner.* (**acelerar**)
2 to happen faster or to make something happen faster ☐ *Air travel is accelerating global warming.* (**acelerar**)

• **acceleration** /ək,selə'reɪʃən/ NOUN, NO PLURAL when something moves faster or happens faster ☐ *You'll be pushed back into your seat during acceleration.* (**aceleração**)

• **accelerator** /ək'seləreɪtə(r)/ NOUN [plural accelerators] the part of a vehicle you press with your foot to make it go faster (**acelerador**)

accent ▶ NOUN /'æksent/ [plural accents]

1 the way people from a particular area pronounce words ☐ *I have a Scottish accent.* (**sotaque**) 🔳 *I speak German with a strong English accent* (**sotaque forte**)
2 a mark over a letter that shows how to pronounce it, for example in the word 'café' (**acento**)
3 the emphasis on part of a word or a note of music ☐ *Put the accent on the third syllable in the Word 'preparation'.* (**acento**)

▶ VERB /æk'sent/ [accents, accenting, accented] to put the emphasis on part of a word or a note of music ☐ *Make sure you accent the first syllable.* (**acentuar**)

accentuate /æk'sentjʊeɪt/ VERB [accentuates, accentuating, accentuated] to make something more obvious (**destacar**)

accept /ək'sept/ VERB [accepts, accepting, accepted]

1 to take something that someone offers you ☐ *+ from He accepted some food from us.* ☐ *She won't accept help from anyone.* (**aceitar**)
2 to say yes to an invitation ☐ *We've accepted his invitation to lunch.* (**aceitar**)
3 to agree that something is true ☐ *+ that I accept that I was wrong and I'm sorry.* (**concordar**)
4 to allow someone to join an organization ☐ *Raj has been accepted to study medicine.* (**admitir**)

• **acceptable** /ək'septəbəl/ ADJECTIVE good enough ☐ *This kind of behaviour just isn't acceptable!* ☐ *+ to The offer is not acceptable to families of the victims.* (**aceitável**)

• **acceptance** /ək'septəns/ NOUN, NO PLURAL
1 taking something that is given or offered to you ☐ *We are delighted about her acceptance of the job.* (**aceitação**)
2 when you agree that something is true, good or necessary (**aceitação**) 🔳 *His ideas on education never gained acceptance.* (**ganhou aceitação**)

• **accepted** /ək'septɪd/ ADJECTIVE agreed to by most people ☐ *Long hours are an accepted part of the job.* (**aceito**)

access /'ækses/ ▶ NOUN, NO PLURAL

1 when you are able to see or use something (**acesso**) ☐ *+ to They don't have access to a doctor.* 🔳 *Do you have Internet access?* (**acesso à internet**)
2 a way of getting to or entering a place ☐ *+ to The builders will need access to the house while you're out at work.* (**acesso**)

▶ VERB [accesses, accessing, accessed]
1 to be able to see or use something ☐ *This file was last accessed yesterday.* ☐ *I was able to access all the information I needed.* (**acessar**)
2 to be able to get to or enter a place ☐ *The castle is accessed by the sea.* (**acessar**)

• **accessible** /ək'sesəbəl/ ADJECTIVE
1 easy to get to ☐ *The house is not very accessible.* (**acessível**)
2 easy to see and use ☐ *We make the information accessible to the public.* (**acessível**)
3 easy to understand ☐ *Make sure you use clear, accessible language.* (**acessível**)

accession /æk'seʃən/ NOUN, NO PLURAL
1 the accession of a king or queen is the official start of their rule (**ascensão**)
2 when a country or organization becomes part of an international organization ☐ *the accession of Romania to the EU* (**adesão, consentimento**)

accessory /ək'sesəri/ NOUN [plural accessories]
1 an extra part that can be used with something ☐ *a hairdryer with lots of accessories* (**acessório**)
2 something like a bag or piece of jewellery, that goes with your clothes ☐ *a little black dress with bright pink accessories* (**acessório**)
3 a person who helps someone commit a crime ☐ *an accessory to murder* (**cúmplice**)

access provider /'ækses prə'vaɪdə(r)/ NOUN [plural access providers] a company that you pay so that you can use the Internet and e-mail. A computing word. (**provedor**)

accident /'æksɪdənt/ NOUN [plural accidents]

1 a bad thing that happens that is not intended 🔳 *Don's had an accident.* (**acidentou-se**) 🔳 *a serious/fatal accident* (**acidente sério/fatal**) ☐ *She was injured in a road traffic accident.* ☐ *I'm sorry I broke your clock – it was an accident.* (**por acidente**)
2 by accident if something happens by accident, it is not intended ☐ *I dropped the glass by accident and it smashed.* (**por acidente**)

A — Accident and Emergency — accordion

- **accidental** /ˌæksɪˈdentəl/ ADJECTIVE not intended (**acidental**) ▪ *There was a lot of accidental damage.* (**dano acidental**)
- **accidentally** /ˌæksɪˈdentəli/ ADVERB by accident ▪ *I accidentally shut the car door and locked my keys inside.* (**acidentalmente**)

Accident and Emergency /ˈæksɪdənt ənd ɪˈmɜːdʒənsi/ NOUN, NO PLURAL the hospital department that looks after people who have been injured or have suddenly become very ill (**pronto-socorro**)

acclaim /əˈkleɪm/ NOUN, NO PLURAL praise ▪ *international acclaim* (**aclamação, ovação**)
- **acclaimed** /əˈkleɪmd/ ADJECTIVE praised by many people ▪ *an acclaimed television show* (**consagrado**)

acclimatize or **acclimatise** /əˈklaɪmətaɪz/ VERB [**acclimatizes, acclimatizing, acclimatized**] to start to feel comfortable with a type of weather or a situation ▪ *It didn't take him long to acclimatize to Singapore's humidity.* (**aclimatizar**)

accommodate /əˈkɒmədeɪt/ VERB [**accommodates, accommodating, accommodated**]
1 to find someone a place to stay ▪ *The whole group can be accommodated in the same hotel.* (**acomodar**)
2 to be big enough for someone or something ▪ *This room could easily accommodate ten people.* (**acomodar**)
3 to provide what someone wants or needs (**acomodar**)
- **accommodating** /əˈkɒmədeɪtɪŋ/ ADJECTIVE helpful and willing to change your plans (**adaptável**)
- **accommodation** /əˌkɒməˈdeɪʃən/ NOUN, NO PLURAL somewhere to stay or live (**acomodação**) ▪ *She's staying in rented accommodation.* (**cômodo alugado**) ▪ *Does the college provide accommodation?* (**fornecer acomodação**)

> In UK English **accommodation** is never used in the plural:
> ✓ *Accommodation is very expensive.*
> ✗ *Accommodations are very expensive.*

accompaniment /əˈkʌmpənɪmənt/ NOUN [*plural* **accompaniments**]
1 the music that someone plays for a person to sing or play an instrument with ▪ *a love song with a guitar accompaniment* (**acompanhamento**)
2 food or drink that is good with another type of food or drink ▪ *This wine is the perfect accompaniment to fish.* (**acompanhamento**)

accompanist /əˈkʌmpənɪst/ NOUN [*plural* **accompanists**] someone who plays a musical accompaniment (**acompanhador**)

accompany /əˈkʌmpəni/ VERB [**accompanies, accompanying, accompanied**]
1 to go with someone ▪ + *to* *We accompanied him to the station.* (**acompanhar**)
2 to exist or come with something ▪ *The tickets were accompanied by a book on travel safety.* (**acompanhar**)
3 to play an instrument, especially the piano, while someone else sings a song or plays another instrument ▪ *Her sister usually accompanies her on the piano.* (**fazer-se acompanhar**)

accomplice /əˈkʌmplɪs/ NOUN [*plural* **accomplices**] someone who helps a person to do something bad (**cúmplice**)

accomplish /əˈkʌmplɪʃ/ VERB [**accomplishes, accomplishing, accomplished**] to manage to do something ▪ *Most children accomplished the task in a few minutes.* (**realizar**)
- **accomplished** /əˈkʌmplɪʃt/ ADJECTIVE having a lot of skill ▪ *an accomplished artist* (**talentoso**)
- **accomplishment** /əˈkʌmplɪʃmənt/ NOUN [*plural* **accomplishments**]
1 when you finish something successfully (**realização**)
2 something you are good at ▪ *Cooking is just one of her many accomplishments.* (**habilidade**)

accord /əˈkɔːd/ NOUN (**acordo**) **of your own accord** if you do something of your own accord, you do it without being asked or told ▪ *I was surprised that he thanked me of his own accord.* (**por iniciativa própria**)

accordance /əˈkɔːdəns/ NOUN, NO PLURAL (**conformidade**) **in accordance with something** obeying a rule, wish, etc. ▪ *He tries to live in accordance with Christian principles.* (**de acordo com, conforme**)

accordingly /əˈkɔːdɪŋli/ ADVERB
1 in a way that is suitable for a situation ▪ *The sun was shining and Jake dressed accordingly.* ▪ *They weigh the vegetables and we are paid accordingly.* (**de acordo**)
2 a formal word meaning for that reason ▪ *Their behaviour did not improve. Accordingly, I had to ask them to leave.* (**portanto, consequentemente**)

according to /əˈkɔːdɪŋ tuː/ PREPOSITION
1 as said or written by someone ▪ *Hannah's ill, according to Lucy.* ▪ *According to the dictionary, there are two m's in 'accommodation'.* (**de acordo com**)
2 using a particular measurement or system ▪ *You'll be paid according to how much work you have done.* (**de acordo com**) ▪ *Everything went according to plan* (= happened as intended). (**ocorreu de acordo com o plano**)

accordion /əˈkɔːdiən/ NOUN [*plural* **accordions**] a musical instrument that you play by pressing in and out a folding box with a small keyboard on its side (**acordeão**)

accost /əˈkɒst/ VERB [accosts, accosting, accosted] if you are accosted by someone, they come close to you and speak to you, often rudely (abordar)

account /əˈkaʊnt/ NOUN [plural accounts]
1 a description of something that has happened (prestar contas) 🔲 He gave a humorous *account* of his journey. 🔲 The report gives a *detailed account* of their work.
2 an arrangement with a bank to keep money there (conta) 🔲 I opened a savings *account*. (abrir uma conta bancária) □ Which account do you want to pay this cheque into?
3 an agreement with a shop to pay later for what you have bought (prestação de contas)
4 take something into account to consider something when you are thinking about a situation or a decision □ Will they take my age into account when they decide who can go? (levar algo em conta)
5 on no account certainly not □ On no account are you to stay out after ten o'clock. (sem chance)
⇨ go to accounts
◆ PHRASAL VERB [accounts, accounting, accounted] **account for something**
1 to be the reason for something □ The fact that it's her birthday accounts for all the visitors she's had today. (contar por algo)
2 to be a certain amount of a total □ Tourism accounts for over 50% of the country's income. (ser responsável por)

accountability /əˌkaʊntəˈbɪlɪti/ NOUN, NO PLURAL the state of being responsible for something (responsabilidade final)

accountable /əˈkaʊntəbəl/ ADJECTIVE
1 if you are accountable for something, you are responsible for it (responsável) 🔲 Employers should be *held accountable* for safety in their factories. (tornar responsável)
2 if you are accountable to someone, they judge and control what you do (responsável)

accountancy /əˈkaʊntənsi/ NOUN, NO PLURAL the job of keeping records of a person's or an organization's money (contabilidade)

• **accountant** /əˈkaʊntənt/ NOUN [plural accountants] someone whose job is to keep or examine records of a person's or an organization's money (contador)

• **accounting** /əˈkaʊntɪŋ/ NOUN, NO PLURAL the work of an accountant (contabilidade)

accounts /əˈkaʊnts/ PLURAL NOUN written records of the money received and spent by a person or organization (contas)

accrue /əˈkruː/ VERB [accrues, accruing, accrued] to increase over a period of time (resultar)

accumulate /əˈkjuːmjʊleɪt/ VERB [accumulates, accumulating, accumulated] to collect a number or amount of something, or to increase in number or amount □ Greenhouse gases are accumulating in the Earth's atmosphere. (acumular)

• **accumulation** /əˌkjuːmjʊˈleɪʃən/ NOUN [plural accumulations] when things have been accumulated □ the accumulation of knowledge (acumulação)

accuracy /ˈækjʊrəsi/ NOUN, NO PLURAL being exactly correct □ Please check the accuracy of this measurement. (precisão)

• **accurate** /ˈækjʊrət/ ADJECTIVE exactly correct (correto) 🔲 an *accurate description* (descrição correta) 🔲 *accurate measurements* (medidas corretas) 🔲 Their account of what happened was pretty accurate (muito correto).

• **accurately** /ˈækjʊrətli/ ADVERB in an accurate way □ Copy the shape as accurately as possible. (corretamente)

accusation /ˌækjuːˈzeɪʃən/ NOUN [plural accusations] a statement saying that someone has done something bad (acusação) 🔲 She has made some accusations against me. (fazer acusações contra alguém) 🔲 These are serious accusations. (acusação séria)

• **accuse** /əˈkjuːz/ VERB [accuses, accusing, accused] to say that someone has done something bad (acusar) □ + *of* He was accused of murder. □ Are you accusing me of lying?

• **accused** /əˈkjuːzd/ NOUN (acusado) **the accused** the person or people who are accused of a crime in court (o acusado)

• **accuser** /əˈkjuːzə(r)/ NOUN [plural accusers] a person who makes an accusation (acusador)

• **accusing** /əˈkjuːzɪŋ/ ADJECTIVE showing that you think someone has done something wrong □ She gave me an accusing stare. (acusador)

• **accusingly** /əˈkjuːzɪŋli/ ADVERB in an accusing way □ 'Look at that scratch on the door', she said accusingly. (acusadoramente)

accustom /əˈkʌstəm/ VERB [accustoms, accustoming, accustomed] (acostumar) **accustom yourself** to do or experience something often enough for it to become normal to you □ I'm gradually accustoming myself to the new software. (habituar-se)

• **accustomed** /əˈkʌstəmd/ ADJECTIVE having done or experienced something often enough for it to become normal to you □ I became accustomed to having to wait. (habituado)

ace /eɪs/ ▶ NOUN [plural aces]
1 a playing card with one symbol on it which has the highest or lowest value in games □ the ace of spades (ás)
2 when a tennis player hits their first shot and the other player cannot hit it back (ace)
3 an informal word for someone who is very good at something □ a Brazilian soccer ace (craque)
▶ ADJECTIVE an informal word that means very good □ an ace golfer (campeão)

ache /eɪk/ ▶ NOUN [plural **aches**] a pain which is not strong but continues for a long time (**dor**) ▣ *I started getting aches and pains.* (**dor e sofrimento**) □ *She could feel an ache in her back.*
▶ VERB [**aches, aching, ached**] to hurt for a long time, especially in a way which is not (**dor**) □ *My arm aches from playing too much tennis.* (**doer**)

achieve /ə'tʃiːv/ VERB [**achieves, achieving, achieved**] to succeed in doing or getting something good, especially by trying hard □ *We have achieved everything we set out to do.* □ *She has achieved a very high standard.* (**conquistar**)
• **achievement** /ə'tʃiːvmənt/ NOUN [plural **achievements**]
1 a success or a good result □ *Reaching the finals is a great achievement.* (**conquista**)
2 no plural having success generally (**realização**) ▣ *You get an enormous sense of achievement when you finish a project.* (**senso de realização**)

acid /'æsɪd/ NOUN [plural **acids**] a type of chemical. Strong acids can dissolve metals. A chemistry word. (**ácido**)
• **acidic** /ə'sɪdɪk/ ADJECTIVE
1 containing acid (**ácido**)
2 with a strong, sour taste (**ácido**)
• **acidity** /ə'sɪdəti/ NOUN, NO PLURAL how much acid a substance contains. A chemistry word. (**acidez**)

acid rain /'æsɪd 'reɪn/ NOUN, NO PLURAL rain that contains chemicals from air pollution (**chuva ácida**)

acid test /'æsɪd 'test/ NOUN [plural **acid tests**] something that will prove something, especially whether something works or not □ *The acid test for the system will be when the public start using it.* (**prova de fogo**)

acknowledge /ək'nɒlɪdʒ/ VERB [**acknowledges, acknowledging, acknowledged**]
1 to admit that something is true □ *I acknowledge that you were right.* (**admitir**)
2 to tell someone that you have got something they sent you □ *They never acknowledge my letters.* (**reconhecer**)
• **acknowledgement** /ək'nɒlɪdʒmənt/ NOUN [plural **acknowledgements**]
1 a message to tell someone that you have received something □ *I sent two letters but only got one acknowledgement.* (**reconhecimento**)
2 when you admit that something is true □ *There has been no acknowledgement of the mistake.* (**reconhecimento**)

acne /'ækni/ NOUN, NO PLURAL a skin problem that causes spots, usually on someone's face (**acne**)

acorn /'eɪkɔːn/ NOUN [plural **acorns**] a type of nut that grows on oak trees (**noz**)

acoustic /ə'kuːstɪk/ ADJECTIVE
1 to do with sound and hearing □ *an acoustic signal* (**acústico**)
2 an acoustic musical instrument does not need electricity to work (**acústico**) ▣ *an acoustic guitar* (**guitarra acústica**)
• **acoustics** /ə'kuːstɪks/ PLURAL NOUN the way a room can make music or speech sound better or worse □ *The concert hall has wonderful acoustics.* (**acústica**)

acquaint /ə'kweɪnt/ VERB [**acquaints, acquainting, acquainted**] to tell someone about something. A formal word. □ *Let me acquaint you with the facts.* (**comunicar**)
• **acquaintance** /ə'kweɪntəns/ NOUN [plural **acquaintances**]
1 someone you have met but do not know well □ *He was an acquaintance of the family.* (**conhecido**)
2 make someone's acquaintance to meet someone for the first time. A formal phrase. (**ser apresentado a alguém**)
• **acquainted** /ə'kweɪntɪd/ ADJECTIVE
1 be acquainted with someone to know someone □ *He became acquainted with several well-known writers.* (**conhecer alguém**)
2 be acquainted with something to know about something □ *I am not acquainted with her work.* (**saber de algo**)

acquiesce /ˌækwi'es/ VERB [**acquiesces, acquiescing, acquiesced**] a formal word meaning to agree to something, especially when you do not want to □ *He finally acquiesced to their demands.* (**consentir**)
• **acquiescence** /ˌækwi'esəns/ NOUN, NO PLURAL when you agree to something, especially when you do not want to. A formal word. (**condescendência**)

acquire /ə'kwaɪə(r)/ VERB [**acquires, acquiring, acquired**]
1 a formal word meaning to get or to buy something □ *I managed to acquire a copy of the tape.* □ *A Russian billionaire recently acquired a 25% stake in the company.* (**adquirir**)
2 to learn something or to develop something (**adquirir**) ▣ *He acquired some new skills.* (**adquiriu habilidades**) ▣ *She soon acquired a taste for Italian food.* (**adquiriu bom gosto para**)
• **acquisition** /ˌækwɪ'zɪʃən/ NOUN [plural **acquisitions**]
1 when you get, buy or learn something □ *People protested about the acquisition of land for industry.* □ *language acquisition* (**ganho, aquisição**)
2 something that you get or buy □ *The painting is one of the museum's newest acquisitions.* (**ganho, obtenção**)
• **acquisitive** /ə'kwɪzɪtɪv/ ADJECTIVE always wanting to get and own more things (**ganancioso**)

acquit /ə'kwɪt/ VERB [**acquits, acquitting, acquitted**] to decide in a court that someone did not commit a crime (**absolver**)
• **acquittal** /ə'kwɪtəl/ NOUN [plural **acquittals**] when someone is acquitted of a crime (**absolvição**)

acre /ˈeɪkə(r)/ NOUN [plural acres] a unit for measuring the area of land, equal to 4840 square yards (acre)

acrid /ˈækrɪd/ ADJECTIVE an acrid taste or smell is strong and unpleasantly bitter □ *The room began to fill with acrid smoke.* (acre)

acrimonious /ˌækrɪˈməʊniəs/ ADJECTIVE an acrimonious discussion or disagreement is full of anger and unfriendly feelings (mordaz)

• **acrimony** /ˈækrɪməni/ NOUN, NO PLURAL unfriendly feelings and disagreement between people □ *Their money discussions usually ended in acrimony.* (acrimônia, rudeza)

acrobat /ˈækrəbæt/ NOUN [plural acrobats] someone who performs skilful physical movements, like jumping and balancing, to entertain people (acrobata)

• **acrobatic** /ˌækrəˈbætɪk/ ADJECTIVE to do with skilful physical movements, especially jumping (acrobático)

• **acrobatics** /ˌækrəˈbætɪks/ PLURAL NOUN skilful physical movements like jumping and balancing (acrobacia)

acronym /ˈækrənɪm/ NOUN [plural acronyms] a word made from the first letters of other words □ *NATO is an acronym for North Atlantic Treaty Organization.* (acrônimo)

across /əˈkrɒs/ PREPOSITION, ADVERB
1 from one side of something to the other □ *a bridge across the river* □ *I ran across the road.* □ *Don't run, but walk across quickly.* □ *clouds moving across the sky* (de um lado para o outro)
2 on the opposite side □ *Their house is across the river from ours.* (do lado oposto)

acrylic /əˈkrɪlɪk/ ▶ NOUN, NO PLURAL a substance used for making some paints and different types of plastic materials (acrílico)
▶ ADJECTIVE made with acrylic □ *an acrylic sweater* (acrílico)

act /ækt/ ▶ VERB [acts, acting, acted]
1 to behave in a particular way (agir) ▣ *Stop acting like a baby!* (agir como) ▣ *Police thought the man was acting suspiciously.* (agindo de modo suspeito)
2 to do something (agir) ▣ *The hospital acted quickly to solve the problem.* (agir rapidamente) □ *We must act now to save the planet!* □ *+ on We were acting on medical advice.*
3 to perform in a film or in the theatre □ *+ in He has acted in more than 50 films.* (atuar)
♦ PHRASAL VERBS **act as something** to have a particular effect or to do a particular job (desempenhar a função de) □ *The security cameras act as a deterrent.* □ *Our local driver also acted as interpreter.* **act up** to behave badly (comportar-se de maneira volúvel) □ *Sam's been acting up at school.*
▶ NOUN [plural acts]
1 something that someone does (ato) ▣ *a terrorist act* (ato terrorista) ▣ *He was accused of committing a criminal act.* (ato criminoso) □ *+ of an act of kindness*
2 a law (ata, lei, decreto) ▣ *an act of parliament* (ata do parlamento)
3 a part of a theatre performance (ato) □ *He appears in the third act of the play.*
4 a short performance, or the people in the performance (ato) □ *a comedy act*
♦ IDIOM **get your act together** to start to do things better and achieve more (esforçar-se mais) □ *If you want to keep this job, you'd better get your act together.*

• **acting** /ˈæktɪŋ/ ▶ NOUN, NO PLURAL performing in films or in the theatre □ *There was some brilliant acting in the film.* (interpretação)
▶ ADJECTIVE doing someone else's job for a time while they are away □ *the acting headmaster* (interino)

action /ˈækʃən/ NOUN [plural actions]
1 something you do (ação) ▣ *We must take urgent action to prevent a disaster.* (agir) ▣ *They need to decide on a course of action* (= what to do). (modo de ação) □ *He has to take responsibility for his actions.*
2 no plural things which are happening □ *Let's see some action around here!* (ação)
3 a movement someone or something makes □ *Hit the ball with a swinging action.*
4 a legal process (ação) ▣ *She has threatened to take legal action.* (ação legal) □ *a libel action*
5 fighting in a war (combate, ação) ▣ *Both soldiers were killed in action.* (em combate) ▣ *the threat of military action* (ação militar)
6 the action what happens in the story of a film, book or theatre play □ *Most of the action takes place in America.* (a ação)
7 out of action not working □ *My car's out of action at the moment.* (quebrado)

action replay /ˈækʃən ˈriːpleɪ/ NOUN [plural action replays] when part of a film of a sports match is shown again, often more slowly (replay)

action stations /ˈækʃən ˈsteɪʃənz/ PLURAL NOUN used to tell people to get into positions ready to do something, especially soldiers getting ready to fight (estado de alerta)

activate /ˈæktɪveɪt/ VERB [activates, activating, activated] to make something start working □ *Someone activated the fire alarm.* (ativar)

active /ˈæktɪv/ ADJECTIVE
1 busy doing things or involved in an activity (ativo) □ *+ in Her mum's very active in the drama club.* ▣ *He remained politically active throughout his life.* (politicamente ativo) ▣ *Fathers are taking a more active role in childcare.* (papel ativo)
2 moving around a lot ▣ *She's still physically active.* (fisicamente ativo) ▣ *Try to keep active as you grow older.* (manter-se ativo)

3 in grammar, an active verb or sentence has a subject that performs the action of the verb, for example in the sentence 'The cat chased the mouse'. (ativo)

- **actively** /ˈæktɪvli/ ADVERB in a way that involves doing things and trying to have an effect (ativamente) ▸ *We actively encourage patients to ask questions.* (encorajamos ativamente) ▸ *I became actively involved in local politics.* (ativamente envolvido)

activist /ˈæktɪvɪst/ NOUN [plural **activists**]
someone who tries to change society by doing things that people notice □ *animal rights activists* (ativista)

activity /ækˈtɪvəti/ NOUN [plural **activities**]
1 something you do, especially something you do for fun, in an organized way (atividade) ▸ *Outdoor activities include sailing and waterskiing.* (atividades ao ar livre) ▸ *a variety of sporting activities* (atividades esportivas)

2 no plural being active or busy generally (atividade) ▸ *Children need regular physical activity.* (atividade física) ▸ *There was a flurry of activity* (= a lot of things happening) *for a few days.* (série de acontecimentos)

actor /ˈæktə(r)/ NOUN [plural **actors**]
someone who performs in a film or in the theatre (ator)

actress /ˈæktrɪs/ NOUN [plural **actresses**]
a woman who performs in a film or in the theatre (atriz)

actual /ˈæktʃuəl/ ADJECTIVE
1 really true or exact (real) ▸ *We guessed there were about 100 people but the actual number was 110.* (número real)

2 in actual fact used to emphasize the real situation □ *It may look easy, but in actual fact it takes a lot of hard work.* (na realidade)

> Actual means 'true' or 'exact'. It does not mean 'existing now'. Adjectives that mean 'existing now' are 'present' and 'current':
> ✓ *My current job involves a lot of travel.*
> ✗ *My actual job involves a lot of travel.*

- **actuality** /ˌæktʃuˈæləti/ NOUN, NO PLURAL
1 a formal word for what is real or a fact (realidade)
2 in actuality a formal phrase emphasizing that something is true □ *There are fewer cases of real poverty than you'd expect, in actuality.* (na realidade)

- **actually** /ˈæktʃuəli/ ADVERB
1 used to emphasize what is true □ *Actually, I haven't read any of his books.* □ *We haven't actually chosen a name yet.* (na verdade)
2 used to emphasize something surprising □ *Instead of improving, things have actually got worse.* (na verdade)

acumen /ˈækjumən/ NOUN, NO PLURAL someone's ability to judge a situation quickly and correctly and make the right decisions (perspicácia) ▸ *He has business acumen and can turn any idea into a business plan.* (perspicácia nos negócios)

acupuncture /ˈækjupʌŋktʃə(r)/ NOUN, NO PLURAL a treatment for illness where very thin needles are put into your skin at different places on your body (acupuntura)

- **acupuncturist** /ˈækjupʌŋktʃərɪst/ NOUN [plural **acupuncturists**] someone who does acupuncture (acupunturista)

acute /əˈkjuːt/ ADJECTIVE
1 an acute problem, especially an illness, is very bad □ *acute appendicitis* □ *an acute shortage of nurses* (agudo)
2 quick to notice or understand something □ *an acute mind* □ *acute eyesight* (aguçado)
3 an acute angle is less than 90°. A maths word. (agudo)

acute accent /əˌkjuːt ˈæksent/ NOUN [plural **acute accents**] a mark (´) put over a vowel in certain languages, such as French, showing pronunciation, as in 'début' and 'élite'. (acento agudo)

- **acutely** /əˈkjuːtli/ ADVERB extremely □ *I felt acutely embarrassed.* (intensamente)

AD /ˌeɪˈdiː/ ABBREVIATION used before or after a date to show that the date was after the birth of Jesus Christ □ *95 AD* (antes de Cristo)

ad /æd/ NOUN [plural **ads**] an informal short way to say or write *advertisement* (anúncio)

adamant /ˈædəmənt/ ADJECTIVE having a strong opinion or a fixed plan that you will not change □ *I told her it was a bad idea but she was adamant.* (inflexível)

- **adamantly** /ˈædəməntli/ ADVERB in an adamant way □ *She adamantly refused to move.* (inflexivelmente)

Adam's apple /ˈædəmz ˌæpəl/ NOUN [plural **Adam's apples**] the lump you can see at the front of a man's neck (pomo de Adão)

adapt /əˈdæpt/ VERB [**adapts, adapting, adapted**]
1 to change so that you become more happy or comfortable in a new situation □ *It didn't take long to adapt to the heat.* (adaptar)
2 to change something to make it more suitable □ *The design can be adapted for use in a variety of situations.* (ajustar)

- **adaptable** /əˈdæptəbəl/ ADJECTIVE able to deal with new or different situations (adaptável)

- **adaptation** /ˌædæpˈteɪʃən/ NOUN [plural **adaptations**] a film, TV programme, etc. that is made from a book □ *He is working on a television adaptation of a Roald Dahl novel.* (adaptação)

- **adaptor** /əˈdæptə(r)/ NOUN [plural **adaptors**] something that you attach to the plug (= object with metal pins) of a piece of electrical equipment that allows you to use that equipment in a different country, or allows you to connect many pieces of electrical equipment to one electrical supply (**adaptador**)

add /æd/ VERB [adds, adding, added]

1 to put things together □ + *to* *Add the sugar to the egg mixture.* (**adicionar**)

2 to put two or more numbers or amounts together □ *Add two and two.* (**somar**)

3 to say or write something more □ *'You could take the letter yourself – if you didn't mind?', he added.* □ + *that* *A police spokesman added that the two arrests weren't linked.* (**acrescentar**)

4 to make something better, bigger, stronger, etc. (**adicionar**) □ *The latest incident has added to an already nervous atmosphere.* *Having the baby has added a new dimension to my life.* (**adicionou uma nova dimensão**)

◆ PHRASAL VERBS **add up** to gradually increase to make a large amount (**aumentar aos poucos**) □ *All those little costs soon add up.* **add (something) up** to find the total of numbers put together (**somar**) □ *Can you add these numbers up in your head?*

adder /ˈædə(r)/ NOUN [plural **adders**] a poisonous snake which lives in the north of Europe and Asia (**víbora**)

addict /ˈædɪkt/ NOUN [plural **addicts**]
1 someone who cannot stop taking a drug (**viciado**) *a drug addict* (**viciado em drogas**)
2 someone who cannot stop doing or having something they enjoy □ *I'm a sugar addict.* (**viciado**)

• **addicted** /əˈdɪktɪd/ ADJECTIVE
1 not able to stop taking a drug □ *He became addicted to drugs.* (**viciado**)
2 not able to stop doing or having something you enjoy □ *I'm completely addicted to computer games.* (**viciado**)

• **addiction** /əˈdɪkʃən/ NOUN [plural **addictions**]
1 not being able to stop taking a drug □ *alcohol addiction* (**vício**)
2 not being able to stop doing or having something you enjoy (**vício**)

• **addictive** /əˈdɪktɪv/ ADJECTIVE if something is addictive, it makes you want to have it or do it more and more □ *an addictive computer game* (**viciante**)

addition /əˈdɪʃən/ NOUN [plural **additions**]

1 in addition (to something) extra or added to something □ *The schools offer extra subjects in addition to the core curriculum.* (**além de**)

2 no plural the process of adding numbers together □ *Pupils learn simple addition and subtraction.* (**adição**)

3 something that has been added or when something is added (**acréscimo**) *There are four new additions to our menu.* (**acréscimos a**) *The changes include the addition of a swimming pool.* (**acréscimo de**)

• **additional** /əˈdɪʃənəl/ ADJECTIVE extra □ *They requested additional information.* *There are no additional costs.* (**adicional**)

• **additionally** /əˈdɪʃənəli/ ADVERB as well as something else □ *Additionally, you have to pay to get in.* (**adicionalmente**)

additive /ˈædɪtɪv/ NOUN [plural **additives**] a substance that is added to food or drinks to make them taste better or stay fresh for longer □ *Our organic cheeses are free from additives.* (**aditivo**)

add-on /ˈædˌɒn/ NOUN [plural **add-ons**] a piece of software that is used with other software to make it able to do something extra. A computing word. (**complemento**)

address /əˈdres/ ▶ NOUN [plural **addresses**]

1 the details of the building, the street and the town where someone lives (**endereço**) □ *I'll give you my address and telephone number.* *Here is a list of the names and addresses of all the members.* (**nomes e endereços**)

2 the numbers, letters and symbols that are used to send e-mails or to find pages on the Internet. A computing word *What's your e-mail address?* (**endereço de e-mail**) *Our web address is in the brochure.* (**endereço web**)

3 a formal speech (**discurso**)

▶ VERB [addresses, addressing, addressed]
1 to write an address on an envelope (**endereçar**)
2 to deal with a problem (**tratar**) *The government has failed to address this problem.* (**tratar desse assunto**)
3 to speak to someone □ *Were you addressing me?* (**dirigir-se a alguém**)

address book /əˈdres ˌbʊk/ NOUN [plural **address books**]
1 a small book in which people's addresses are written (**agenda de endereços**)
2 a place on a computer where e-mail addresses are kept. A computing word. (**catálogo de endereços**)

adept /əˈdept/ ADJECTIVE very good or skilful at something □ *She'd become adept at hiding her feelings.* (**perito**)

adequate /ˈædɪkwət/ ADJECTIVE enough □ *Three rooms should be adequate for our family.* □ *There's na adequate supply of clean water.* (**adequado**)

• **adequately** /ˈædɪkwətli/ ADVERB in an adequate way □ *The staff were not adequately trained.* (**adequadamente**)

adhere /ədˈhɪə(r)/ VERB [adheres, adhering, adhered] a formal word meaning to stick firmly to something □ *This glue will adhere to any surface.* (**grudar, aderir**)

◆ PHRASAL VERB **adhere to something**
1 to obey a rule or to keep to a plan, arrangement, etc. □ *Visitors must adhere to a strict dress code.* (**seguir**)

2 to continue to have a belief, opinion, etc. (dedicar-se)

- **adherence** /əd'hɪərəns/ NOUN, NO PLURAL when you obey a rule or keep to a plan. A formal word. (lealdade)
- **adherent** /əd'hɪərənt/ NOUN [plural adherents] a loyal supporter of a political party, belief, etc. (partidário)

adhesive /əd'hi:sɪv/ ▶ NOUN [plural adhesives] a substance used to stick things together (adesivo)
▶ ADJECTIVE sticky ☐ adhesive tape (adesivo)

ad hoc /ˌæd'hɒk/ ADJECTIVE used only for a particular situation and not permanent or regular (ad hoc) ☐ The committee meets on an ad hoc basis to discuss issues which crop up. (para determinado fim)

adjacent /ə'dʒeɪsənt/ ADJECTIVE a formal word meaning next to ☐ There is a car park adjacent to the hospital. (adjacente, limítrofe)

adjective /'ædʒɪktɪv/ NOUN [plural adjectives] a word that tells you something about a noun. For example, difficult, good and stupid are adjectives. (adjetivo)

adjoin /ə'dʒɔɪn/ VERB [adjoins, adjoining, adjoined] a formal word that means to be joined to ☐ The bathroom adjoins the bedroom. (unir)

- **adjoining** /ə'dʒɔɪnɪŋ/ ADJECTIVE next to and joined to something (contíguo) ☐ an adjoining room (quarto contíguo)

adjourn /ə'dʒɜːn/ VERB [adjourns, adjourning, adjourned] to stop a meeting or a court trial which will continue at another time (adiar)

- **adjournment** /ə'dʒɜːnmənt/ NOUN [plural adjournments] when a meeting or a trial is adjourned (adiamento)

adjudicate /ə'dʒuːdɪkeɪt/ VERB [adjudicates, adjudicating, adjudicated]
1 a formal word meaning to be the official judge of a competition ☐ She was invited to adjudicate at the dancing championships. (julgar)
2 a formal word meaning to decide officially how a disagreement should be solved (sentenciar)

- **adjudicator** /ə'dʒuːdɪkeɪtə(r)/ NOUN [plural adjudicators] someone who makes official decisions (juiz)

adjust /ə'dʒʌst/ VERB [adjusts, adjusting, adjusted]
1 to change something slightly ☐ I adjusted the clock by two minutes. (ajustar)
2 to get used to a new situation ☐ It was difficult to adjust to living in a flat. (adaptar)

- **adjustable** /ə'dʒʌstəbəl/ ADJECTIVE able to be adjusted to fit something ☐ adjustable seat belts (ajustável)
- **adjustment** /ə'dʒʌstmənt/ NOUN [plural adjustments]
1 a slight change (ajuste) ☐ We've made a few adjustments to the schedule this week. (fizemos alguns ajustes)
2 when someone becomes familiar with a new situation ☐ You'll be fine after a short period of adjustment. (ajuste)

ad-lib /ˌæd'lɪb/ ▶ ADVERB done or said without preparation ☐ I admire people who can just get up and speak ad-lib in public. (de improviso)
▶ VERB [ad-libs, ad-libbing, ad-libbed] to speak without preparation, especially in a speech or performance ☐ I completely forgot my lines and had to ad-lib for a bit. (improvisar)

admin /'ædmɪn/ NOUN, NO PLURAL a shortway to say and write **administration** (= managing an organization) (administração)

administer /əd'mɪnɪstə(r)/ VERB [administers, administering, administered]
1 to manage a company, an organization or a project ☐ The free health care service is administered by the regional government. (administrar)
2 a formal word meaning to give a medicine to someone ☐ The drug should be administered by a doctor. (ministrar)

- **administration** /ədˌmɪnɪ'streɪʃən/ NOUN [plural administrations]
1 the work of planning, organizing and managing an organization ☐ So much of my time is taken up with administration, I hardly have time to actually do any work. (administração)
2 the politicians who govern a country ☐ the Bush administration (governo)
3 the process of giving something such as medicine to someone (tratamento)

- **administrative** /əd'mɪnɪstrətɪv/ ADJECTIVE to do with the administration of an organization ☐ He was hired to take on the administrative work. (administrativo)

- **administrator** /əd'mɪnɪstreɪtə(r)/ NOUN [plural administrators] someone who does administrative work (administrador)

admirable /'ædmərəbəl/ ADJECTIVE admirable behaviour is very good and respected by others ☐ The way he behaved was admirable. (admirável)

- **admirably** /'ædmərəblɪ/ ADVERB very well ☐ She coped admirably in a difficult situation. (admiravelmente)

admiral /'ædmərəl/ NOUN [plural admirals] one of the most important officers in the navy (almirante)

admiration /ˌædmə'reɪʃən/ NOUN, NO PLURAL a feeling of admiring someone or something ☐ + for I have the greatest admiration for her work. (admiração)

admire /əd'maɪə(r)/ VERB [admires, admiring, admired]
1 to like and respect someone or something very much ☐ He was someone I admired greatly. ☐ + for I admired her for her courage in speaking out. (admirar)

admissible / adulterate

2 to enjoy looking at something (**apreciar**) 🔁 *We stopped at the top of the hill to admire the view.* (**apreciar a vista**)

- **admirer** /əd'maɪərə(r)/ NOUN [plural **admirers**] a person who likes someone or something very much (**admirador**)
- **admiring** /əd'maɪərɪŋ/ ADJECTIVE showing admiration □ *admiring glances* (**admirador**)

admissible /əd'mɪsəbəl/ ADJECTIVE a formal word meaning acceptable or allowed □ *evidence that is admissible in a court of law* (**aceitável, admissível**)

admission /əd'mɪʃən/ NOUN [plural **admissions**]
1 when someone goes into a place or joins a club, university, etc. □ *A sign on the door said 'No admission'.* □ *the university admissions process* (**admissão**)
2 *no plural* the cost of going into a place □ *We don't charge admission here.* □ *Adult admission is £10.* (**ingresso**)
3 when you admit that something bad is true □ + *that* *We were surprised by his admission that he had done it.* (**confissão**) 🔁 *He had, by his own admission, played badly.* □ + *of* *They have made no admission of guilt.* (**por confissão própria**)

admit /əd'mɪt/ VERB [**admits, admitting, admitted**]
1 to agree that you have done something bad □ + *(that)* *I admit that I should have told you sooner.* □ + *to* *She admitted to cheating.* □ *He admitted his mistake.* (**confessar**)
2 to agree that something is true □ *I admit that this is a difficult exercise, but do your best.* (**reconhecer**)
3 to allow someone to go into a place or to take someone to hospital □ *They won't admit anyone wearing trainers.* □ + *to* *The next morning he was admitted to hospital.* (**permitir**)

- **admittance** /əd'mɪtəns/ NOUN, NO PLURAL being allowed to go into a place □ *No admittance for anyone under 18.* (**acesso**)
- **admittedly** /əd'mɪtɪdli/ ADVERB used to say that you agree that something is true □ *Admittedly, I wasn't there at the time, but I believe him.* (**reconhecidamente**)

admonish /əd'mɒnɪʃ/ VERB [**admonishes, admonishing, admonished**] a formal word meaning to tell someone that they have done something wrong □ *He was officially admonished for wasting the club's money.* (**advertir**)

ado /ə'duː/ NOUN (**confusão, barulho**) *without further/more ado* without waiting any longer (**sem demora**)

adolescence /ˌædə'lesəns/ NOUN, NO PLURAL the time between being a child and being an adult (**adolescência**)

- **adolescent** /ˌædə'lesənt/ ▶ NOUN [plural **adolescents**] someone older than a child, but not yet an adult (**adolescente**)

▶ ADJECTIVE to do with adolescents □ *adolescent girls/boys*

adopt /ə'dɒpt/ VERB [**adopts, adopting, adopted**]
1 to take someone else's child into your family and legally become their parent □ *I was ten before I knew I had been adopted.* (**adotar**)
2 to start doing something in a new way □ *We must adopt new methods of fighting crime.* (**adotar**)

- **adoption** /ə'dɒpʃən/ NOUN [plural **adoptions**]
1 when a child is adopted (**adoção**)
2 starting to use something new (**adoção**)
- **adoptive** /ə'dɒptɪv/ ADJECTIVE being a relation because of an adoption □ *my adoptive mother/parents* □ *an adoptive son/daughter* (**adotivo**)

adorable /ə'dɔːrəbəl/ ADJECTIVE if something or someone is adorable, they are very attractive and you like them very much □ *an adorable baby boy* (**adorável**)

adoration /ˌædə'reɪʃən/ NOUN, NO PLURAL loving someone or something very much □ *a look of adoration* (**adoração**)

adore /ə'dɔː(r)/ VERB [**adores, adoring, adored**] to love something or someone very much □ *She just adores her father.* (**adorar, idolatrar**)

- **adoring** /ə'dɔːrɪŋ/ ADJECTIVE showing great Love □ *Her adoring fans crowded the streets.* (**adorador**)

adorn /ə'dɔːn/ VERB [**adorns, adorning, adorned**] to decorate something □ *Their hair was adorned with flowers.* (**adornar**)

- **adornment** /ə'dɔːnmənt/ NOUN [plural **adornments**] a decoration, or the process of decorating something (**adorno**)

adrenalin or **adrenaline** /ə'drenəlɪn/ NOUN, NO PLURAL a chemical your body produces when you are afraid, angry or excited. A biology word. (**adrenalina**)

adrift /ə'drɪft/ ADJECTIVE, ADVERB a boat that is adrift is not tied up and is floating in the water □ *They spent three weeks adrift on the ocean.* (**à deriva**)

adulation /ˌædju'leɪʃən/ NOUN, NO PLURAL a lot of praise from people (**adulação**)

adult /'ædʌlt/ ▶ NOUN [plural **adults**]
1 someone who is no longer a child □ *The activity is suitable for adults and children.* (**adulto**)
2 an animal that is completely grown □ *adult rabbits* (**adulto**)

▶ ADJECTIVE to do with or for adults □ *adult sizes* □ *It's aimed at a more adult audience.* (**adulto**)

adulterate /ə'dʌltəreɪt/ VERB [**adulterates, adulterating, adulterated**] to make something, for example food or drink, less pure by adding something to it □ *The cooking oil had been adulterated with a poisonous substance.* (**adulterar**)

adulthood /'ædʌlthʊd/ NOUN, NO PLURAL the period of time in your life when you are an adult (**idade adulta, maioridade**)

advance /əd'vɑːns/ ▶ NOUN [plural **advances**]
1 in advance before something is needed or before a particular time □ I arrived in advance to make sure everything was ready. □ We prepared all the food in advance. (**adiantado**)
2 progress or new things □ technological advances □ We have to keep up with the latest advances in medicine. (**avanço**)
3 money paid before the usual time □ I asked for an advance of £50 on my salary. (**adiantamento**)
4 a movement towards a place by an army □ The troops continued their advance on the city. (**marcha**)
▶ VERB [**advances, advancing, advanced**]
1 to make progress □ Technology is advancing rapidly. (**progredir**)
2 to move forwards □ The crowd advanced towards us. □ The army is advancing on our borders. (**avançar**)
▶ ADJECTIVE happening before an event (**antecipado**) □ If you want to bring a friend, can you give us some advance warning? (**aviso antecipado**)

• **advanced** /əd'vɑːnst/ ADJECTIVE
1 the newest or most developed □ the most technologically advanced facilities (**desenvolvido**)
2 at a high academic level □ an advanced Spanish course □ advanced students (**avançado**)
3 if an illness is at an advanced stage, it is already very bad (**avançado**)

advantage /əd'vɑːntɪdʒ/ NOUN [plural **advantages**]
1 something good or helpful about a situation □ + **of** the advantages of working from home □ Being tall does have some advantages. (**vantagem**)
2 something that makes you more likely to succeed (**vantagem**) □ + **over** Max had an advantage over the others as he already spoke Italian. □ Her long legs give her an advantage in the high jump. (**dar vantagem**) □ an unfair advantage (**vantagem injusta**)
3 take advantage of something to use a situation well □ We took advantage of the sunshine to get the clothes dry. (**tirar vantagem de algo**)
4 take advantage of someone to get what you want from someone in an unfair way □ She's very generous and her children take advantage of her. (**aproveitar-se de alguém**)

• **advantageous** /ˌædvən'teɪdʒəs/ ADJECTIVE helping you to succeed □ It would not be advantageous for you to go abroad at this stage in your career. (**vantajoso, proveitoso**)

advent /'ædvent/ NOUN, NO PLURAL
1 the start of something □ the advent of television (**advento**)
2 Advent the four weeks before Christmas (**renascimento de Cristo**)

adventure /əd'ventʃə(r)/ NOUN [plural **adventures**] something exciting that happens to you □ A jungle visit would be a real adventure for us. (**aventura**)

• **adventurous** /əd'ventʃərəs/ ADJECTIVE an adventurous person likes to do exciting new things □ He's more adventurous than his brother. (**ousado**)

adverb /'ædvɜːb/ NOUN [plural **adverbs**] a word that you use to describe a verb or an adjective. For example, really, badly, abroad and often are adverbs. (**advérbio**)

adversary /'ædvəsəri/ NOUN [plural **adversaries**] a formal word for an enemy or someone you compete against (**adversário**)

adverse /'ædvɜːs/ ADJECTIVE negative or causing you problems (**adverso**) □ All this worry is likely to have an adverse effect on her health. (**efeito adverso**) □ It's amazing how the school children learn anything in such adverse conditions. (**condições adversas**)

• **adversely** /'ædvɜːsli/ ADVERB in a negative way □ I'm afraid their advertising campaign has affected our sales adversely. (**adversamente, contrariamente**)

adversity /əd'vɜːsəti/ NOUN, NO PLURAL a formal word for a very difficult situation (**adversidade**) □ She struggled on bravely in the face of adversity. (**diante das adversidades**)

advert /'ædvɜːt/ NOUN [plural **adverts**] a short word for an advertisement (**propaganda**)

advertise /'ædvətaɪz/ VERB [**advertises, advertising, advertised**]
1 to tell people about something in order to persuade them to buy it or use it □ They advertise their products in magazines. (**publicar**)
2 if you advertise for something, you put information in a newspaper, on the Internet, etc. to try to get something you want □ We decided to advertise for a gardener. (**anunciar**)

• **advertisement** /əd'vɜːtɪsmənt/ NOUN [plural **advertisements**] a picture, short article or film about something to persuade people to buy it or use it (**propaganda**) □ a television/newspaper advertisement (**propaganda de jornal ou televisão**) □ + **for** I saw an advertisement for a new chocolate bar.

• **advertiser** /'ædvətaɪzə(r)/ NOUN [plural **advertisers**] someone who advertises something (**anunciante**)

• **advertising** /'ædvətaɪzɪŋ/ NOUN, NO PLURAL the business of making advertisements □ She works in advertising. (**publicidade**) □ an advertising campaign (**campanha publicitária**)

advice /əd'vaɪs/ NOUN, NO PLURAL suggestions about what you think someone should do (conselho) 🔹 *She gave me some good advice.* (dar conselho) 🔹 *I decided to take Jane's advice and go to the doctor's.* (aceitar o conselho) 🔹 *May I offer a piece of advice?* (um conselho) ☐ + *on* *They provide expert advice on career development.*

➤ Remember that **advice** with a c is a noun and **advise** with an s is a verb: ☐ *Can you give me some advice?* ☐ *Can you advise me?*

➤ Remember also that you say any/some advice and not 'an advice':
✓ *Can I give you some advice?*
✗ *Can I give you an advice?*
➤ To talk about one particular suggestion, use **piece of advice**: ☐ *Can I give you a piece of advice?*

advisable /əd'vaɪzəbəl/ ADJECTIVE if something is advisable, it will avoid problems if you do it ☐ *It is advisable to book tickets early.* (recomendável)

advise /əd'vaɪz/ VERB [advises, advising, advised] to tell someone what you think they should do ☐ + *to do something* *They are advising motorists to drive carefully.* ☐ + *against* *We advise against all travel to the region.* ☐ + *on* *He advises us on financial matters.* (aconselhar)

• **adviser** or **advisor** /əd'vaɪzə(r)/ NOUN [plural advisers or advisors] someone whose job is to give advice about a particular subject ☐ *financial/security advisers* (conselheiro, consultor)

• **advisory** /əd'vaɪzəri/ ADJECTIVE to do with giving advice ☐ *an advisory body* (aconselhador)

advocate ▶ VERB /'ædvəkeɪt/ [advocates, advocating, advocated] to express support for an idea ☐ *We don't advocate giving up meat completely.* (defender)

▶ NOUN /'ædvəkət/ [plural advocates]
1 someone who supports an idea ☐ *He is an outspoken advocate of tax cuts.* (defensor)
2 in Scotland, a lawyer (advogado)

aerate /'eəreɪt/ VERB [aerates, aerating, aerated] to put air into something such as soil or a liquid. A biology word. (oxigenar)

aerial /'eəriəl/ ▶ NOUN [plural aerials] a piece of metal equipment for getting or sending radio or television signals (antena) 🔹 *a television aerial* (antena de televisão)

▶ ADJECTIVE from the air ☐ *an aerial photograph* (aéreo, atmosférico)

aero- /'eərə/ PREFIX aero- is added to the start of words to mean 'to do with air or flying' ☐ *aeroplane* (aero-)

aerobatics /ˌeərə'bætɪks/ PLURAL NOUN flying with skilful movements in an aeroplane (acrobacia)

aerobic /eə'rəʊbɪk/ ADJECTIVE
1 aerobic exercise makes your heart and lungs stronger (aeróbico)
2 using or needing oxygen. A biology word. (aeróbio)

aerobic respiration /eə'rəʊbɪk respə'reɪʃən/ NOUN, NO PLURAL when the body uses oxygen to make energy from food. A biology word. (respiração aeróbia)

aerobics /eə'rəʊbɪks/ PLURAL NOUN exercises for the whole body that make your heart and lungs work hard (aeróbico)

aerodrome /'eərədrəʊm/ NOUN [plural aerodromes] a small airport for private aeroplanes (aeródromo)

aerodynamic /ˌeərəʊdaɪ'næmɪk/ ADJECTIVE aerodynamic objects are able to move easily through the air. A physics word. ☐ *an aerodynamic design* (aerodinâmico)

• **aerodynamically** /ˌeərəʊdaɪ'næmɪkli/ ADVERB in a way that moves easily through the air. A physics word. (aerodinamicamente)

• **aerodynamics** /ˌeərəʊdaɪ'næmɪks/ PLURAL NOUN the study of the way objects move through the air. A physics word. (aerodinâmica)

aeroplane /'eərəpleɪn/ NOUN [plural aeroplanes] a flying vehicle that has wings and an engine ☐ *The aeroplane took off at midday.* (aeroplano)

aerosol /'eərəsɒl/ NOUN [plural aerosols] a container with a part that you press to let out very small drops of liquid (aerossol)

aesthetic /iːs'θetɪk/ ADJECTIVE to do with beauty, art and the appearance of things (estética)

• **aesthetically** /iːs'θetɪkəli/ ADVERB in a way that is to do with beauty and appearance ☐ *an aesthetically pleasing design* (esteticamente)

afar /ə'fɑː(r)/ ADVERB (longe) from afar a formal phrase meaning from a long distance away (de longe)

affair /ə'feə(r)/ NOUN [plural affairs]
1 affairs events or activities in a particular area of life, business, politics, etc. (negócios) 🔹 *He is very interested in foreign affairs* (= international politics). (negócios internacionais) 🔹 *She was responsible for the financial affairs of the club.* (negócios financeiros)

2 a situation or an event, especially a problem or something bad ☐ *Some people have criticized the way he handled the affair.* (questão)

3 a sexual relationship between two people, especially when one or both of them is married to someone else (romance, caso) 🔹 *She had an affair with an older man.* (ter um caso)

4 be someone's (own) affair used to say that something is personal and private ☐ *Her private life is her own affair.* (ser assunto particular)

affect

affect /əˈfekt/ VERB [affects, affecting, affected] to change, influence or cause harm to someone or something □ *The accident affected his eyesight.* □ *Were you affected by the floods?* (afetar)

> Be careful not to confuse **affect**, which is a verb, with **effect**, which is a noun: □ *One thing affects another.* □ *One thing has an effect on another.*

affectation /ˌæfekˈteɪʃən/ NOUN [plural affectations] behaviour that is not natural and is done only to impress other people □ *Her silly laugh is clearly an affectation.* (fingimento, simulação)

affection /əˈfekʃən/ NOUN, NO PLURAL a strong feeling of liking someone or something □ *I have great affection for the town.* □ *My father rarely showed his affection.* (afeição)

- **affectionate** /əˈfekʃənət/ ADJECTIVE showing that you like or love someone □ *Her mother gave her an affectionate kiss.* (carinhoso)
- **affectionately** /əˈfekʃənətli/ ADVERB in an affectionate way □ *Joe scratched the cat's head affectionately.* (afetuosamente)

affiliated /əˈfɪlieɪtɪd/ ADJECTIVE officially connected with another organization □ *The school is affiliated to the local college.* (associado)

- **affiliation** /əˌfɪliˈeɪʃən/ NOUN [plural affiliations] a connection between two or more organizations (associação)

affinity /əˈfɪnɪti/ NOUN [plural affinities] a feeling of close connection with someone or something □ *She had always felt a deep affinity with horses.* (afinidade)

affirm /əˈfɜːm/ VERB [affirms, affirming, affirmed] a formal word meaning to say clearly that something is true □ *He affirmed his continued support for the team's manager.* (afirmar, declarar)

- **affirmation** /ˌæfəˈmeɪʃən/ NOUN, NO PLURAL when you show that you agree with something □ *She signalled her affirmation with a nod.* (afirmação, declaração)

affirmative /əˈfɜːmətɪv/ ▶ ADJECTIVE an affirmative reply, word or gesture (= body movement) is one that says 'yes'. A formal word. (afirmativa)

▶ NOUN [plural affirmatives]
1 the word 'yes', or any word or gesture (= body movement) meaning 'yes'. A formal word. (afirmativa, confirmação)
2 in the affirmative by saying 'yes' or showing agreement □ *Peter answered in the affirmative.* (na afirmativa)

affix ▶ VERB /əˈfɪks/ [affixes, affixing, affixed] a formal word meaning to attach something □ *Affix stamp here.* (anexar)

afraid

▶ NOUN /ˈæfɪks/ [plural affixes] a part added to the beginning or the end of a word to give it an extra meaning (afixo)

afflict /əˈflɪkt/ VERB [afflicts, afflicting, afflicted] a formal word meaning to make someone suffer from something □ *This is a disease that can afflict anyone.* (afligir)

- **affliction** /əˈflɪkʃən/ NOUN [plural afflictions] an illness or problem that makes someone suffer (aflição)

affluence /ˈæfluəns/ NOUN, NO PLURAL having a lot of money to spend □ *There was greater affluence after the war.* (afluência)

- **affluent** /ˈæfluənt/ ADJECTIVE having a lot of money □ *an affluent area of the city* (afluente)

afford /əˈfɔːd/ VERB [affords, affording, afforded]
1 if you can afford something, you have enough money to pay for it □ *I can't afford a new dress.* □ + ***to do something*** *We couldn't afford to go abroad.* (dispor)
2 to be able to do something without it causing problems □ + ***to do something*** *We can't afford to make any mistakes.* □ *We can afford to wait a bit longer.* (causar)

- **affordable** /əˈfɔːdəbəl/ ADJECTIVE at a low enough price for most people □ *affordable accommodation* (disponível)

affront /əˈfrʌnt/ ▶ VERB [affronts, affronting, affronted] to offend someone □ *Brenda was affronted by his remark.* (ofender)
▶ NOUN [plural affronts] something that offends someone □ *They see the book as an affront to their culture.* (afronta, ofensa)

afield /əˈfiːld/ ADVERB **far/further afield** a long distance away ▣ *Some people had travelled from as far afield as Australia and South Africa.* (longe, no exterior)

afloat /əˈfləʊt/ ADVERB
1 floating on water (à tona) ▣ *He held on to a piece of wood to stay afloat.* (permanecer à tona)
2 with enough money to continue a business (em circulação) ▣ *He's struggling to keep his business afloat.* (manter em circulação)

afoot /əˈfʊt/ ADJECTIVE happening now or being planned □ *Plans are afoot for a concert in Beijing.* (em andamento)

afraid /əˈfreɪd/ ADJECTIVE
1 frightened or worried □ *There's no need to be afraid.* □ + ***of*** *Small children are often afraid of dogs.* □ + ***that*** *I was afraid that I'd fall.* □ + ***to do something*** *Don't be afraid to tell me if you don't understand.* (amedrontado)
2 I'm afraid used to tell someone in a polite way that you cannot do something or to give them bad news □ *I'm afraid I don't know.* □ *Helen can't come, I'm afraid.* □ + ***that*** *I'm afraid that I can't tell you any more now.* (recear que)

afresh /əˈfreʃ/ ADVERB once again □ *Throw that away and begin afresh.* (novamente)

African /ˈæfrɪkən/ ▶ ADJECTIVE belonging to or from Africa □ *an African country* (africano)
▶ NOUN [plural **Africans**] a person from Africa (africano)

Afro- /ˈæfrəʊ/ PREFIX Afro- is added to the start of words to mean 'from or to do with Africa' □ *Afro-Caribbean* (= with African and Caribbean origins) (afro-)

after /ˈɑːftə(r)/ ▶ PREPOSITION
1 when something has happened □ *I'll do it after dinner.* □ *It rained day after day.* (após)
2 after an hour/three days, etc. when an hour/three days, etc. have passed (depois de)
3 following in order □ *Your name's after mine on the list.* (seguinte)
4 following someone or something □ *We ran after the man.* (atrás)
5 used in US English to talk about the time when it is minutes past the hour □ *It's ten after eight.* (depois)
6 after all used to talk about something that happened or was true although you did not expect it to be □ *I decided to go to the party after all.* (afinal)
▶ ADVERB following in time □ *Can you come the week after?* (em seguida)
▶ CONJUNCTION when something has happened □ *Mrs Shaw died after we moved.* □ *After we'd said goodbye, we felt quite sad.* (logo que)

> ➤ Use the phrases **a week/month, etc. from now** or **in a week's/month's, etc. time** to talk about a time in the future that you are measuring from now. Do not say 'after a week/month, etc.' to mean this □ *A week from now my exams will all be finished.*
> ✓ *In a week's time my exams will all be finished.*
> ✗ *After a week my exams will all be finished.*

after- /ˈɑːftə(r)/ PREFIX after- is added to the start of words to mean 'after' or 'later' □ *afternoon* □ *afterthought* (pós-)

after-effects /ˈɑːftərɪˌfekts/ PLURAL NOUN bad things that happen after and because of something else (efeitos colaterais)

aftermath /ˈɑːftəmæθ/ NOUN, NO PLURAL **the aftermath** the situation that exists after something bad has happened (consequência) 🔊 *There was panic and confusion in the aftermath of the earthquake.* (em consequência de)

afternoon /ˌɑːftəˈnuːn/ ▶ NOUN [plural **afternoons**]
1 the time between the middle of the day and the evening □ *I saw him on Monday afternoon.* (tarde) □ *We finish at 4 o'clock in the afternoon.*
🔊 *What are you doing this afternoon?* (esta tarde)
2 Good afternoon used to say 'hello' when you meet someone in the afternoon (boa tarde)
▶ ADJECTIVE happening in the afternoon □ *afternoon classes* (período da tarde, vespertino)

aftershave /ˈɑːftəʃeɪv/ NOUN, NO PLURAL a liquid with a pleasant smell which men put on their skin after shaving (pós-barba)

aftershock /ˈɑːftəʃɒk/ NOUN [plural **aftershocks**] a small earthquake (= when the ground shakes) that happens after a larger earthquake (abalo secundário)

afterthought /ˈɑːftəθɔːt/ NOUN [plural **afterthoughts**] something you do or say later (reflexão tardia) 🔊 *'You could come too,' he suggested as an afterthought.* (como uma reflexão tardia)

afterwards /ˈɑːftəwədz/ ADVERB later or after something else □ *He's busy now but I'll speak to him afterwards.* □ *They moved to Paris and soon afterwards they got married.* (posteriormente)

again /əˈɡen/ ADVERB
1 once more □ *Do it again!* □ *Will I see you again?* (de novo)
2 in the sameplace or situation as before □ *Can we go home again now?* (de novo)
3 again and again many times □ *I've told you again and again to tidy your room!* (novamente)

> ➤ Remember that **again** meaning 'once more' usually comes after the object in a sentence:
> ✓ *I'd like to visit France again.*
> ✗ *I'd like to visit again France.*
> ✓ *We could have pizza again.*
> ✗ *We could have again pizza.*

against /əˈɡenst/ PREPOSITION
1 leaning on, touching or hitting something □ *She was throwing a ball against the wall.* □ *He was sitting with his back against a tree.* (contra)
2 competing or fighting with someone □ *Liverpool are playing against Barcelona.* □ *We all support the fight against racism.* (contra)
3 disagreeing with a plan or situation □ *I'm against the ban on hunting.* (contrário)
4 against the law/rules not allowed by the laws/rules □ *Smoking on the train is against the law.* (contra as regras/leis)

age /eɪdʒ/ ▶ NOUN [plural **ages**]
1 how old someone or something is (idade) 🔊 *Zoe will start school at the age of four.* (à idade de) 🔊 *He's 19 years of age.* (anos de idade) □ *+ of Do you know how old the age of the building?* 🔊 *It's suitable for children of all ages.* (de todas as idades) 🔊 *He reaches retirement age next year.* (atingiu a idade)
2 ages/an age an informal word meaning a very long time □ (longo período) *I haven't seen Alex*

for ages. 🔲 *You took ages to finish.* (levou muito tempo) □ *The tickets sold out ages ago.* □ *We had to wait an age for him to come out.*
3 a period of time in history □ *the Stone Age* (era)
4 under age not legally old enough to do something □ *You can't buy beer – you're under age.* (menor de idade)
5 come of age to become an adult (atingir a maioridade)
▶ VERB [**ages, aging** or **ageing, aged**] to become older or to look older □ *She's aged a lot recently.* (envelhecer)

- **aged** /eɪdʒd/ ADJECTIVE used to say how many years old someone is (com a idade de) □ *They have two children aged eight and three.* 🔲 *young people aged between 18 and 25* (com idades entre)
- **aged** /'eɪdʒɪd/ ▶ ADJECTIVE very old □ *She looks after her aged mother.* (idoso)
▶ NOUN **the aged** old people (idosos)
- **ageing** /'eɪdʒɪŋ/ ADJECTIVE becoming or looking older □ *an ageing actor* (idoso)
- **ageism** /'eɪdʒɪzəm/ NOUN, NO PLURAL treating old people unfairly because of their age (preconceito etário)

agency /'eɪdʒənsi/ NOUN [*plural* **agencies**]
1 a business that provides a particular service □ *an employment agency* □ *an advertising agency* (agência)
2 an organization that is part of a government or is controlled by a government □ *the UN refugee agency* (agência)
⇨ *go to* **travel agency**

agenda /ə'dʒendə/ NOUN [*plural* **agendas**]
1 a list of things to be discussed at a meeting (em pauta) 🔲 *What's on the agenda today?* (em pauta)
2 things that need to be done or discussed (em pauta) 🔲 *Getting more schools built is high on the country's agenda.* (prioridade na pauta do país)

agent /'eɪdʒənt/ NOUN [*plural* **agents**]
1 someone who does business for another person or company □ *Our overseas agents sell the books for us.* (representante)
2 someone who collects secret information for a government (agente) 🔲 *a secret agent* (agente secreto)
3 a substance that has a particular effect □ *a cleaning agent* (agente)
⇨ *go to* **travel agent, estate agent**

aggravate /'ægrəveɪt/ VERB [**aggravates, aggravating, aggravated**]
1 to make something worse □ *He aggravated the injury during training.* (agravar)
2 to annoy someone □ *He really aggravates me sometimes.* (irritar)

- **aggravation** /ˌægrə'veɪʃən/ NOUN, NO PLURAL annoying problems □ *That man has caused a lot of aggravation today.* (irritação)

aggregate /'ægrɪɡət/ NOUN [*plural* **aggregates**] a total (agregado)

aggression /ə'ɡreʃən/ NOUN, NO PLURAL behaviour that is angry and threatening (agressão)

- **aggressive** /ə'ɡresɪv/ ADJECTIVE angry and threatening (agressivo) 🔲 *aggressive behavior* (comportamento agressivo)
- **aggressively** /ə'ɡresɪvli/ ADVERB in a threatening way □ *He was shouting aggressively.* (agressivamente)
- **aggressor** /ə'ɡresə(r)/ NOUN [*plural* **aggressors**] someone who attacks someone else (agressor)

aggrieved /ə'ɡriːvd/ ADJECTIVE upset because someone has been unfair to you (aflito, prejudicado)

aghast /ə'ɡɑːst/ ADJECTIVE very surprised and shocked □ *She stared at him, aghast.* (espantado, chocado)

agile /'ædʒaɪl/ ADJECTIVE
1 good at moving about quickly and easily □ *He's an agile climber.* (ágil, rápido)
2 able to think quickly □ *an agile mind* (esperto)
- **agility** /ə'dʒɪləti/ NOUN, NO PLURAL being agile (agilidade)

aging /'eɪdʒɪŋ/ ADJECTIVE the US spelling of **ageing** (idoso)

agitate /'ædʒɪteɪt/ VERB [**agitates, agitating, agitated**]
1 to try to get social or political changes □ *We must agitate for a change in the law.* (debater)
2 to make someone nervous and upset (perturbar)
- **agitated** /'ædʒɪteɪtɪd/ ADJECTIVE nervous and upset □ *I started to get agitated when nobody answered the door.* (perturbar)
- **agitation** /ˌædʒɪ'teɪʃən/ NOUN, NO PLURAL a feeling of being nervous and upset □ *She tried to hide her agitation.* (agitação, perturbação)

AGM /ˌeɪdʒiː'em/ ABBREVIATION annual general meeting; an important meeting that an organization has once a year (**Annual General Meeting** – reunião geral anual)

agnostic /æɡ'nɒstɪk/ NOUN [*plural* **agnostics**] someone who believes nobody can know if God exists or not (agnóstico)

ago /ə'ɡəʊ/ ADVERB used to say how long in the past something happened (atrás) □ *I last saw Lily ten years ago.* 🔲 *That all seems a long time ago.* (muito tempo atrás)

agog /ə'ɡɒɡ/ ADJECTIVE excited and interested □ *The audience were agog with curiosity.* (impaciente, ansioso)

agonize or **agonise** /'æɡənaɪz/ VERB [**agonizes, agonizing, agonized**] to worry about making a difficult decision □ *She agonized over what to say to him.* (afligir-se)
- **agonizing** or **agonising** /'æɡənaɪzɪŋ/ ADJECTIVE

agony

1 extremely difficult or upsetting ☐ *an agonizing decision* (**aflito**)
2 extremely painful (**agonizante**)
agony /'ægənɪ/ NOUN, NO PLURAL very great pain ☐ *You could see he was in agony.* (**agonia, sofrimento**)
agoraphobia /ˌægərə'fəʊbɪə/ NOUN, NO PLURAL people who have agoraphobia are afraid of being in open spaces or of going outside (**agorafobia**)
• **agoraphobic** /ˌægərə'fəʊbɪk/ ADJECTIVE suffering from agoraphobia (**agorafóbico**)

agree /ə'griː/ VERB [agrees, agreeing, agreed]
1 to have the same opinion as someone else about something ☐ **+ with** *She never agrees with him about anything.* ☐ **+ about** *I'm glad we agree about something.* (**concordar**)
2 to say that you will do what someone has asked you to ☐ **+ to do something** *I only agreed to come if you came too.* (**concordar**)
3 to decide something together with someone ☐ **+ on** *They couldn't agree on a name for the baby.* ☐ *Doctors have agreed a pay deal.* (**concordar**)
• **agreeable** /ə'griːəbəl/ ADJECTIVE
1 possible to agree on ☐ *We need to find a solution that is agreeable to both sides.* (**adequado**)
2 pleasant ☐ *He was very agreeable.* (**agradável**)
• **agreeably** /ə'griːəblɪ/ ADVERB in a pleasant way ☐ *The holidays passed very agreeably.* (**agradavelmente**)
• **agreement** /ə'griːmənt/ NOUN [plural agreements]
1 a decision or a promise between two or more people (**acordo**) ☐ **+ between** *a trade agreement between Canada and the US* ☐ *We have an agreement with the local sports club.* ☐ *The two companies have reached an agreement.* (**chegaram a um acordo**)
2 *no plural* when people have the same opinion (**entendimento**) ☐ *There was no agreement about what to do.*
3 in agreement if people are in agreement, they agree with each other (**em concordância**)

agricultural /ˌægrɪ'kʌltʃərəl/ ADJECTIVE to do with farming ☐ *agricultural land* (**agrícola**)
agriculture /'ægrɪˌkʌltʃə(r)/ NOUN, NO PLURAL the work of farming (**agricultura**)
aground /ə'graʊnd/ ADJECTIVE, ADVERB if a ship is aground it is stuck because the water is not deep enough (**encalhado**) ☐ *The boat ran aground in stormy weather.* (**ficou encalhado**)

ahead /ə'hed/ ADVERB
1 in front ☐ *Run on ahead and tell them we're coming.* (**em frente**) ☐ *Our house is straight ahead.* (**bem em frente**)
2 in the future ☐ **+ of** *We've got a long journey ahead of us.* (**à frente**) ☐ *We're planning for the year ahead.* (**o ano à frente**)
3 in a better position in a race, competition, etc. ☐ **+ of** *They are four points ahead of their main rivals.* ☐ *Jones put United ahead with a goal in the first half.* (**à frente**)
4 before ☐ **+ of** *Everyone was nervous ahead of the first performance.* (**antes**)

AI /'eɪ'aɪ/ ABBREVIATION artificial intelligence; the use of computers that try to act like human brains (**inteligência artificial**)
aid /eɪd/ ▶ NOUN [plural aids]
1 help (**auxílio**) ☐ *He can walk with the aid of a stick.* (**com o auxílio de**) ☐ *Mr Oliver came to our aid* (= helped us). (**veio para auxiliar**)
2 money, food, etc. that is sent to places that need it ☐ *Many countries will send aid to the disaster area.* (**ajuda**)
3 in aid of someone/something in order to collect money for someone/something ☐ *a collection in aid of the crash victims* (**em auxílio de algo/alguém**)
4 something you use to help you do something ☐ *a teaching aid* (**apoio**)
▶ VERB [aids, aiding, aided] to help someone ☐ *Gentle exercise will aid your recovery.* (**ajudar**)
aide /eɪd/ NOUN [plural aides] someone whose job is to give help and advice, especially to a politician (**assistente**)
AIDS *or* **Aids** /eɪdz/ ABBREVIATION Acquired Immune Deficiency Syndrome; an illness that makes the body unable to fight disease (**aids**)
ailing /'eɪlɪŋ/ ADJECTIVE ill or weak ☐ *He knew he should visit his ailing mother.* ☐ *an ailing business* (**aflito, doente**)
ailment /'eɪlmənt/ NOUN [plural ailments] an illness (**doença**) ☐ *a minor ailment* (**uma doença secundária**)

aim /eɪm/ ▶ VERB [aims, aiming, aimed]
1 to intend or to hope to do something ☐ **+ to do something** *We aim to help all our customers.* ☐ **+ for** *She's aiming for a medal at the next Olympics.* (**almejar**)
2 be aimed at someone/something to be intended for a particular person, group or purpose ☐ *The magazine is aimed at 16 to 24-year-olds.* ☐ **+ ing** *The scheme is aimed at cutting traffic.* (**visar a algo/alguém**)
3 to point a weapon at someone or something ☐ **+ at** *Paul was aiming at the target but missed it completely.* (**apontar**)
▶ NOUN [plural aims]
1 what you are trying to achieve (**objetivo**) ☐ **+ of** *The aim of the project is to encourage healthy eating.* ☐ *My main aim is to get fit.* (**principal objetivo**) ☐ *We have achieved our aim.* (**alcançamos o objetivo**)
2 someone's ability to hit something when they throw, shoot, etc. ☐ *He has a good aim.* (**mira**)
3 take aim to point a weapon at someone or something ☐ **+ at** *He took aim at the open window.* (**visar**)

- **aimless** /ˈeɪmlɪs/ ADJECTIVE having no purpose □ *an aimless stroll* (**sem objetivo**)
- **aimlessly** /ˈeɪmlɪslɪ/ ADVERB without a reason □ *She walked aimlessly around the house.* (**sem rumo**)

ain't /eɪnt/ an informal short way to say and write 'am not', 'are not', 'is not', 'has not' or 'have not' □ *Ain't he clever?* □ *You ain't lived yet.* (*ver* **be**)

air /eə(r)/ ▶ NOUN
1 *no plural* the gases around us that we breathe in (**ar**) 🔁 *Kelly went outside to get some fresh air.* (**ar puro**) □ *The air carries the seeds for miles.*
2 *the air* the space above you □ *He put his hand in the air.* □ *Police fired into the air.* (**atmosfera**)
3 *no plural* travel in an aircraft (**ar**) □ *The food is transported by air.* 🔁 *air travel* (**viagem de avião**)
4 an appearance or quality □ + *of She has an air of mystery about her.* (**aparência**)
5 *on (the) air* being broadcast on radio or television (**no ar**)
♦ IDIOM *up in the air* not decided yet □ *Our holiday plans are still up in the air.* (**incerto, indeciso**)
▶ VERB [**airs, airing, aired**]
1 to broadcast something on television or radio □ *The show airs twice a week.* □ *The interview was aired on television.* (**transmitir**)
2 to tell people your opinion (**divulgar**) 🔁 *Everyone will have a chance to air their views.* (**divulgar suas opiniões**)
3 to hang clothes somewhere to make them completely dry (**ventilar**)
4 to let some fresh air into a room (**arejar**)

airbag /ˈeəbæg/ NOUN [*plural* **airbags**] a bag that fills with air to protect passengers in a car accident (**airbag**)

airbed /ˈeəbed/ NOUN [*plural* **airbeds**] a mattress (= soft thing to sleep on) filled with air (**colchão inflável**)

airborne /ˈeəbɔːn/ ADJECTIVE
1 when an aircraft is airborne, it is flying (**no ar, voando**) **2** moving in the air □ *airborne diseases* (**sendo transmitido, levado pelo ar**)

air-conditioned /ˈeəkənˌdɪʃənd/ ADJECTIVE air-conditioned vehicles or buildings have a system for keeping the air cool □ *an air--conditioned office* (**ar-condicionado**)
- **air conditioning** /ˈeəkənˌdɪʃənɪŋ/ NOUN, NO PLURAL a system for keeping the air cool in vehicles or buildings (**condicionador de ar**)

aircraft /ˈeəkrɑːft/ NOUN [*plural* **aircraft**] a vehicle that can fly (**aeronave**) 🔁 *a commercial aircraft* (**aeronave comercial**) 🔁 *a military aircraft* (**aeronave militar**)

aircraft carrier /ˈeəkrɑːft ˌkærɪə(r)/ NOUN [*plural* **aircraft carriers**] a military ship on which aircraft can take off and land (**porta-avião**)

airfield /ˈeəfiːld/ NOUN [*plural* **airfields**] a place used by private or military aircraft for taking off and landing (**campo de aviação**)

air force /ˈeə ˌfɔːs/ NOUN [*plural* **air forces**] a military organization that uses aircraft (**força aérea**)

air freshener /ˈeə ˌfreʃənə(r)/ NOUN [*plural* **air fresheners**] a substance that is used to get rid of bad smells from rooms, cars, etc. (**desodorizador de ambiente**)

airgun /ˈeəɡʌn/ NOUN [*plural* **airguns**] a gun that uses air pressure to fire bullets (**espingarda de ar comprimido**)

airing /ˈeərɪŋ/ NOUN [*plural* **airings**] when something is discussed in public or broadcast on television or radio □ *The film gets its first airing on British television this week.* (**radiodifusão**)

airing cupboard /ˈeərɪŋ ˌkʌbəd/ NOUN [*plural* **airing cupboards**] a heated cupboard for putting clean clothes in to dry completely (**armário ventilado**)

airless /ˈeəlɪs/ ADJECTIVE an airless room does not have enough fresh air (**malventilado**)

airlift /ˈeəlɪft/ ▶ VERB [**airlifts, airlifting, airlifted**] to take people or things somewhere by aircraft □ *The soldiers were airlifted to safety* (**transportar**)
▶ NOUN [*plural* **airlifts**] when goods or people are airlifted (**transporte**)

airline /ˈeəlaɪn/ NOUN [*plural* **airlines**] a company that takes people or goods to places by plane (**linha aérea**) 🔁 *a lowcost airline* (**linha aérea de baixo custo**) 🔁 *an airline ticket* (**passagem aérea**) 🔁 *an airline pilot* (**piloto de avião**)
- **airliner** /ˈeəlaɪnə(r)/ NOUN [*plural* **airliners**] a large aeroplane for passengers (**avião para transporte de passageiros**)

airmail /ˈeəmeɪl/ NOUN, NO PLURAL the system of sending letters and packages by aeroplane □ *I'll send you the book by airmail.* (**correio aéreo**)

airplane /ˈeəpleɪn/ NOUN [*plural* **airplanes**] the US word for an **aeroplane** (**avião**)

airport /ˈeəpɔːt/ NOUN [*plural* **airports**] a place where passengers get on and off aircraft □ *She arrived at the city's international airport.* (**aeroporto**)

air raid /ˈeə ˌreɪd/ NOUN [*plural* **air raids**] an attack by military aircraft (**ataque aéreo**)

airship /ˈeəʃɪp/ NOUN [*plural* **airships**] a large aircraft filled with a light gas for carrying things or people (**dirigível**)

airspace /ˈeəspeɪs/ NOUN, NO PLURAL the part of the sky over a particular country (**espaço aéreo**)

airtight /ˈeətaɪt/ ADJECTIVE made so that air cannot pass in or out (**hermético**) 🔁 *an airtight container* (**contêiner hermético**)

air-traffic control /ˈeə ˌtræfɪk kənˈtrəʊl/ NOUN, NO PLURAL the system of making sure

airwaves

aircraft can land or take off safely, or the people who do this (controle de tráfego aéreo)
• **air traffic controller** /'eə 'træfɪk kən'trəʊlə(r)/ NOUN [plural **air traffic controllers**] a person whose job is to do air traffic control (controlador de tráfego aéreo)

airwaves /'eəweɪvz/ PLURAL NOUN radio waves used for sending radio and television broadcasts □ *It's the only topic of debate on the nation's airwaves.* (ondas aéreas)

airy /'eərɪ/ ADJECTIVE [**airier, airiest**]
1 with a lot of space and air □ *The room is bright and airy.* (arejado)
2 showing that you are not worried about anything □ *an airy wave* (animado, alegre)

airy-fairy /'eərɪ 'feərɪ/ ADJECTIVE not based on real life or practical ideas (irreal, ilusório)

aisle /aɪl/ NOUN [plural **aisles**] the space that you can walk along between rows of seats or shelves in a church, supermarket, etc. (corredor)

ajar /ə'dʒɑː(r)/ ADJECTIVE, ADVERB slightly open □ *David left the door ajar on purpose.* (entreaberta)

aka /ˌeɪkeɪ'eɪ/ ABBREVIATION also known as; used before another name for someone □ *William H Bonney, aka Billy the Kid* (também conhecido como)

akimbo /ə'kɪmbəʊ/ ADVERB **with arms akimbo** with your hands on your hips and your elbows pointing out (com as mãos na cintura, cotovelos para fora)

alarm /ə'lɑːm/ ▶ NOUN [plural **alarms**]
1 a loud noise to warn people about something (alarme) 🔁 *the fire alarm* (alarme de incêndio) 🔁 *My alarm goes off at 7 o'clock.* (alarme toca) 🔁 *If the alarm sounds, leave the building.* (alarme tocar)
2 *no plural* a sudden feeling of fear and worry (temor) □ *He jumped back in alarm.* 🔁 *Everyone stay calm, there's no cause for alarm.* (motivo para temor)
3 raise/sound the alarm to warn people about something dangerous □ *His brother raised the alarm when he didn't return home last night.* (soar o alarme)
⇨ go to **false alarm**
▶ VERB [**alarms, alarming, alarmed**] to frighten and worry someone suddenly □ *It's okay, don't be alarmed.* (alarmado, assustado)

alarm clock /ə'lɑːm 'klɒk/ NOUN [plural **alarm clocks**] a clock that makes a noise to wake you up (relógio despertador) 🔁 *His alarm clock went off (= rang) at 6 am.* (o despertador tocou)

alarming /ə'lɑːmɪŋ/ ADJECTIVE frightening and making you worry □ *alarming reports* (alarmante)
• **alarmingly** /ə'lɑːmɪŋlɪ/ ADVERB in an alarming way □ *The floor shook alarmingly.* (alarmante)

alas /ə'læs/ EXCLAMATION a formal way of saying that you are sad □ *Alas, she didn't live that long.* (ai de mim!)

albatross /'ælbətrɒs/ NOUN [plural **albatrosses**] a large white sea bird (albatroz)

albeit /ˌɔːl'biːɪt/ CONJUNCTION although □ *It was her first success, albeit a modest one.* (embora)

albino /æl'biːnəʊ/ NOUN [plural **albinos**] a person or animal with no natural colour in their hair, skin or eyes. A biology word. (albino)

album /'ælbəm/ NOUN [plural **albums**]
1 a book for keeping photographs, stamps, etc. (álbum) 🔁 *a photo album* (álbum de fotografias)
2 a collection of songs or pieces of music on a CD, record, etc. □ *the band's new album* (disco)

albumen /'ælbjʊmɪn/ NOUN, NO PLURAL the colourless part of an egg that is white when cooked. A biology word. (albumina, clara de ovo)

alcohol /'ælkəhɒl/ NOUN, NO PLURAL
1 drinks like wine and beer that can make you drunk (álcool) 🔁 *He doesn't drink alcohol.* (ingerir álcool)
2 a substance in wine and beer that is also in some chemicals and medicines. A chemistry word. (álcool)
• **alcoholic** /ˌælkə'hɒlɪk/ ▶ ADJECTIVE containing alcohol (alcoólico) 🔁 *alcoholic drinks* (bebidas alcoólicas)
▶ NOUN [plural **alcoholics**] someone who regularly drinks too much alcohol (alcoólatra)
• **alcoholism** /'ælkəhɒlɪzəm/ NOUN, NO PLURAL the state of being an alcoholic (alcoolismo)

alcove /'ælkəʊv/ NOUN [plural **alcoves**] a space in a room where part of the wall is further back than the rest (alcova, quarto)

ale /eɪl/ NOUN [plural **ales**] a type of beer (cerveja "ale")

alert /ə'lɜːt/ ▶ ADJECTIVE quick to notice what is around you and to react to it □ *Stay alert – the enemy could attack at any time.* (alerta)
▶ VERB [**alerts, alerting, alerted**] to warn someone about a danger □ *If you see a suspicious package, alert the police at once.* □ *We should alert the public to the risks.* (alertar)
▶ NOUN [plural **alerts**]
1 a warning about something (alerta) 🔁 *Weather experts issued a flood alert.* (emitiu um alerta)
2 on alert ready to deal with problems (em alerta) 🔁 *Security forces are on full/high alert.* (em alerta total) 🔁 *Police are on the alert for another attack.* (em alerta para)

A level /'eɪ ˌlevəl/ NOUN [plural **A levels**] an exam that students in England, Wales and Northern Ireland take at about age eighteen in a particular subject □ *She's got (= has been successful in) 3 A levels.* (vestibular dos estudantes da Grã-Bretanha)

algae /'æld3i:/ PLURAL NOUN plants that grow near or in water and do not have stems, leaves or flowers (**algas**)

algebra /'æld31brə/ NOUN, NO PLURAL a type of mathematics that uses letters and signs instead of numbers (**álgebra**)

algorithm /'ælgərɪðəm/ NOUN [plural **algorithms**] a set of rules that are used for doing a calculation, especially in computing. A computing word. (**algoritmo**)

alias /'eɪlɪəs/ ▶ ADVERB also known as ☐ Norman Cook, alias Fatboy Slim (**também conhecido como**)
▶ NOUN [plural **aliases**] another name that someone uses (**pseudônimo**) ☐ She uses an alias when she travels abroad. (**usa um pseudônimo**)

alibi /'ælɪbaɪ/ NOUN [plural **alibis**] proof that someone could not have committed a crime, because they were somewhere else at the time (**álibi**)

alien /'eɪliən/ ▶ NOUN [plural **aliens**]
1 a creature from another planet (**alienígena**)
2 someone who is not from the country they are living in (**estrangeiro, imigrante**) ☐ an illegal alien (**imigrante ilegal**)
▶ ADJECTIVE
1 strange and not familiar ☐ The idea of taking orders from a woman was totally alien to him. (**discrepante**)
2 to do with creatures from another planet ☐ an alien spaceship (**alienígena**)

alienate /'eɪliəneɪt/ VERB [**alienates, alienating, alienated**]
1 to make someone start to dislike you ☐ She had alienated most of her former friends. (**indispor**)
2 to make someone feel that they do not belong somewhere ☐ We don't want to alienate older viewers. (**alienar**)

• **alienated** /'eɪliəneɪtɪd/ ADJECTIVE feeling that you do not belong ☐ Many young immigrants feel alienated. (**malquisto**)

• **alienation** /ˌeɪliəˈneɪʃən/ NOUN, NO PLURAL a feeling that you do not belong (**alienação**) ☐ a sense of alienation (**senso de alienação**)

alight /ə'laɪt/ ▶ ADJECTIVE burning ☐ The whole building was alight. (**ardente, aceso**)
▶ ADVERB burning (**em chamas**) ☐ They poured petrol over the car and set it alight. (**atearam fogo**)
▶ VERB [**alights, alighting, alighted**] a formal word meaning to get off a train or bus ☐ Alight here for the airport. (**descer**)

align /ə'laɪn/ VERB [**aligns, aligning, aligned**]
1 to put things in a straight line ☐ Align the words down the left side of the page. (**alinhar**)
2 be aligned with something/someone to support a political idea or group ☐ Many local police are aligned with the rebels. (**estar alinhado com algo/alguém**)

• **alignment** /ə'laɪnmənt/ NOUN, NO PLURAL the position of things in a straight line ☐ The wheels need to be in alignment. (**alinhamento**)

alike /ə'laɪk/ ▶ ADJECTIVE like one another ☐ The twins aren't at all alike in character. (**parecido**)
▶ ADVERB
1 in the same way ☐ Dad treats us both alike. (**da mesma maneira**)
2 used to refer to two people or things equally ☐ It's popular with adults and children alike. (**igualmente**)

alimentary canal /ˌælɪˈmentəri kəˈnæl/ NOUN [plural **alimentary canals**] the parts of the body (the oesophagus, stomach and intestines) that carry food through the body. A biology word. (**canal alimentar**)

alimony /'ælɪməni/ NOUN, NO PLURAL a mainly US word for money that is paid to a husband or wife you are no longer married to (**pensão alimentícia**)

alive /ə'laɪv/ ADJECTIVE
1 living ☐ He was seriously injured, but still alive. ☐ She didn't know whether he was alive or dead. (**vivo**)
2 still existing (**vivo**) ☐ They have to win to keep alive their chances of reaching the finals. (**manter vivas**)
3 full of activity (**animado**) ☐ The city really comes alive at night. (**fica animada**)

alkali /'ælkəlaɪ/ NOUN [plural **alkalis**] the type of chemical that behaves in the opposite way to an acid. A chemistry word. (**álcali**)

• **alkaline** /'ælkəlaɪn/ ADJECTIVE containing an alkali. A chemistry word. (**alcalino**)

all /ɔːl/ ▶ PRONOUN, DETERMINER
1 every one ☐ All the children stood up. ☐ I want to see them all. ☐ **+ of** All of the animals were healthy. (**todos**)
2 every part ☐ We ate all the cake. ☐ Don't spend it all. ☐ We've been working all day. (**todo**)
3 the only thing ☐ All he's interested in is football. (**tudo**)
4 at all used to emphasize a negative statement ☐ You haven't eaten anything at all. (**absolutamente**)
⇨ go to be **all talk** (and no action)
▶ ADVERB
1 completely ☐ His shirt was all dirty. (**totalmente**)
2 all over (a) in every place or part of something ☐ His clothes were all over the place. (**por todo**) (b) finished ☐ I'll be glad when it's all over. (**acabado**)

Allah /'ælə/ NOUN the Muslim name for God (**Alá**)

allay /ə'leɪ/ VERB [**allays, allaying, allayed**] a formal word meaning to reduce fears or worry (**tranquilizar**) ☐ The chairman tried to allay fears over job losses. (**tranquilizar, diminuir o receio**)

allegation /ˌælɪˈɡeɪʃən/ NOUN [plural

allege — allow

allegations] when you say that someone has done something wrong or illegal (**alegação**) □ *allegations of corruption* 🔁 *He denies all the allegations.* (**nega todas as alegações**)

allege /ə'ledʒ/ VERB [**alleges, alleging, alleged**] to say that someone has done something wrong or illegal □ *The boys allege that they are being bullied.* (**alegar**)

• **alleged** /ə'ledʒd/ ADJECTIVE said to exist or be true, but without proof □ *an alleged plot to bomb an airliner* (**suposto**)

• **allegedly** /ə'ledʒɪdli/ ADVERB if something is allegedly true, people say it but there is no proof □ *He allegedly stole money out of the till.* (**supostamente**)

allegiance /ə'li:dʒəns/ NOUN [plural **alliegances**] strong loyalty (**lealdade**) 🔁 *The soldiers all swear allegiance to their country.* (**jurou lealdade**)

allegory /'æligəri/ NOUN [plural **allegories**] a story, picture, etc. that represents an idea □ *His plays are mostly political allegories.* (**alegoria**)

allergic /ə'lɜ:dʒɪk/ ADJECTIVE having an allergy to something (**alérgico**) 🔁 *an allergic reaction* (**reação alérgica**) □ *I'm allergic to cats.*

allergy /'ælədʒi/ NOUN [plural **allergies**] a condition where your body reacts badly to something you touch, breathe, eat or drink (**alergia**) □ *a peanut allergy* 🔁 *I have an allergy to dairy products.* (**tenho alergia a**)

alleviate /ə'li:vieɪt/ VERB [**alleviates, alleviating, alleviated**] to make a problem, pain, etc. less serious □ *The medicine should alleviate the symptoms.* (**aliviar**)

alley /'æli/ or **alleyway** /'æliweɪ/ NOUN [plural **alleys**] a narrow passage between buildings (**ruela**)

alliance /ə'laɪəns/ NOUN [plural **alliances**] an agreement between organizations or countries to work together (**aliança**) 🔁 *The US car maker has formed an alliance with a Chinese manufacturer.* (**formou uma aliança**)

allied /'ælaɪd/ ADJECTIVE
1 Allied to do with countries joined by an agreement, especially Britain and other countries in the First and Second World Wars □ *the Allied invasion* (**Aliados**)
2 related or connected □ *They do say genius is closely allied to madness.* (**associados**)

alligator /'æligeɪtə(r)/ NOUN [plural **alligators**] a large reptile like a crocodile, with thick skin, a long body and a big mouth with sharp teeth (**jacaré**)

alliteration /ə,lɪtə'reɪʃən/ NOUN, NO PLURAL the use of the same sound repeated at the beginning of several words (**aliteração**)

allocate /'æləkeɪt/ VERB [**allocates, allocating, allocated**] to give someone something for them to use □ *Now we'll allocate the rooms you will be staying in.* □ *We need to allocate more money for schools.* (**alocar**)

• **allocation** /,ælə'keɪʃən/ NOUN [plural **allocations**]
1 giving or sharing something between people or things □ *the allocation of resources* (**alocação**)
2 something that has been given to someone □ *Both teams have the same allocation of tickets for the cup final.* (**distribuição**)

allot /ə'lɒt/ VERB [**allots, allotting, allotted**] to give someone a particular amount of something □ *It was hard to finish the exam in the time allotted.* (**repartir**)

• **allotment** /ə'lɒtmənt/ NOUN [plural **allotments**]
1 a small piece of land where someone can grow vegetables (**lote**)
2 the process of giving someone a particular amount of something (**cota**)

all-out /ˌɔːl 'aʊt/ ADJECTIVE complete □ *We want an all-out ban on smoking.* (**completo, total**)

allow /ə'laʊ/ VERB [**allows, allowing, allowed**]
1 to give permission for something □ + *to do something* *Will you allow me to come in now?* □ *We do not allow smoking in the house.* □ *Prisoners are allowed out to exercise.* (**permitir**)
2 to make something possible □ + *to do something* *The new technology allows them to stay in touch with their families.* □ *Social networking sites allow users to set up their own home pages.* (**permitir**)
3 to plan or give a certain amount of time, money, etc. for something □ *You should allow extra time for your journey.* (**conceder**)
4 to not stop something from happening □ *They allowed the grass to grow very long.* (**permitir**)
◆ PHRASAL VERB **allow for something** to include something in your plans or calculations □ *Add 5% to allow for inflation.* (**levar algo em conta**)

> Do not use the phrase **it is not allowed to do something** as this is not correct English. Instead use either of these phrases: □ *You are not allowed to talk in a written exam.* □ *Talking is not allowed in a written exam.*

• **allowable** /ə'laʊəbəl/ ADJECTIVE allowed according to a rule □ *Radiation was way above the allowable limit.* (**permitido**)

• **allowance** /ə'laʊəns/ NOUN [plural **allowances**]
1 an amount of money that someone is given regularly □ *Adam gets an allowance of £50 a month from his father.* (**pensão, mesada**)
2 the amount of something you are allowed □ *There's a baggage allowance that you mustn't go over.* (**tolerância**)
3 make allowances for someone/something to expect less from someone because you know

they have a problem, disadvantage, etc. ◻ *We'll make allowances for the fact that you've never done anything like this before.* (abrir concessão a alguém/algo)

alloy /ˈælɔɪ/ NOUN [plural **alloys**] a mixture of two or more metals. A chemistry word. (liga)

all-purpose /ˈɔːl ˈpɜːpəs/ ADJECTIVE designed or used for many different purposes ◻ *Aspirin became an all purpose remedy.* (para todos os fins)

all right /ˌɔːl ˈraɪt/ ▶ ADJECTIVE, ADVERB
1 quite good but not very good ◻ *The party was all right I suppose.* (bom)
2 safe or well ◻ *I'm all right. How are you?* ◻ *I'm glad you're all right – we heard there had been an accident.* (bem)
3 acceptable or not a problem ◻ *Is it all right if I go out tonight?* ◻ *It's all right – it wasn't your fault.* (tudo bem)
4 That's all right. used when someone has thanked you for something (tudo bem)
▶ EXCLAMATION used to agree to something ◻ *All right, I'll go then.* (tudo bem)

all-round /ˌɔːl ˈraʊnd/ ADJECTIVE good at or including a lot of different things ◻ *an all-round athlete* ◻ *a good all-round education* (em todos os lugares)
• **all-rounder** /ˌɔːl ˈraʊndə(r)/ NOUN [plural **all-rounders**] someone who is good at many different things (repleto de qualidades)

all-time /ˈɔːl ˌtaɪm/ ADJECTIVE if something is at an all-time best/high/low, etc., it is better/higher/ lower than it has ever been (de todos os tempos)

allude /əˈluːd/
♦ PHRASAL VERB [**alludes, alluding, alluded**] **allude to something** to refer to something without talking about it directly ◻ *'I'm moving much better now,' he said, alluding to his recent back problem.* (aludir a algo)

allure /əˈljʊə(r)/ NOUN, NO PLURAL something that you find attractive about something or someone ◻ *the allure of life at sea* (atração)
• **alluring** /əˈljʊərɪŋ/ ADJECTIVE attractive (atraente)

allusion /əˈluːʒən/ NOUN [plural **allusions**] when you refer to something without talking about it directly (alusão) ▣ *He made an allusion to the war.* (fez uma alusão)

alluvial /əˈluːvɪəl/ ADJECTIVE made from earth left by rivers or floods. A geography word. (aluvial)
• **alluvium** /əˈluːvɪəm/ NOUN, NO PLURAL earth left by rivers or floods. A geography word. (aluvião)

ally ▶ NOUN /ˈælaɪ/ [plural **allies**] a person or country that supports another (aliado) ▣ *He is one of the president's closest allies.* ◻ *Britain has been a strong political ally of the United States.* (aliados próximos)

▶ VERB /əˈlaɪ/ [**allies, allying, allied**] to support or work with another person, country, etc. ◻ *The rebels are allied to a local military group.* (aliar)

almighty /ɔːlˈmaɪti/ ▶ ADJECTIVE
1 very loud, strong, serious, etc. (poderoso) ▣ *We heard an almighty bang.* (barulho poderoso)
2 very powerful ◻ *almighty God* (onipotente)
▶ NOUN **the Almighty** God (Deus Todo-Poderoso)

almond /ˈɑːmənd/ NOUN [plural **almonds**] a long narrow nut (amêndoa)

almost /ˈɔːlməʊst/ ADVERB nearly but not quite or not completely (quase) ◻ *She is almost ten years old.* ▣ *Almost all the children go to state schools.* ◻ *(quase todos) He's almost as tall as his father.* ◻ *It's almost impossible to predict.* ◻ *I almost missed my flight.*

aloft /əˈlɒft/ ADVERB high up in the air (no alto) ▣ *Bernard held the cup aloft.* (moveu o troféu no alto)

alone /əˈləʊn/ ADJECTIVE, ADVERB
1 without anyone else (sozinho) ◻ *I live alone.* ▣ *I was all alone with no one to talk to.* (completamente sozinho) ◻ *A young woman sat alone in the waiting room.* ◻ *I felt completely alone.*
2 used to emphasize that only one person or thing is involved ◻ *The ticket alone will use up all my money.* (só)
3 leave something alone to not touch something ◻ *Leave my sweets alone!* (deixar em paz)
4 leave someone alone to not talk to or annoy someone ◻ *Leave her alone – she's had enough of your moaning.* (deixar alguém em paz)
5 not alone in something not the only person to be experiencing something bad ◻ *He's not alone in feeling disappointed.* (não ser o único a)

> Note that **alone** only means 'without anyone else'. It does not mean 'feeling sad because you are without other people'. The word for this is **lonely** ◻ *I was alone in the house.*

along /əˈlɒŋ/ ▶ PREPOSITION
1 from one part of something to another ◻ *Shona walked along the street.* (ao longo)
2 by the side of something long ◻ *Hari's house is somewhere along this street.* (ao longo)
▶ ADVERB
1 forwards ◻ *Move along, please.* ◻ *He was driving along, singing.* (para a frente)
2 with someone (ir junto com alguém) ▣ *We're going swimming – why don't you come along?* (acompanhar) ▣ *Adam brought a friend along.* (trouxe junto)
3 along with together with ◻ *We'd packed drinks along with the sandwiches.* (junto com)
4 be coming along to be making good progress ◻ *The building work is really coming along now.* (estar evoluindo)

alongside /əlɒŋˈsaɪd/ PREPOSITION, ADVERB
1 next to □ *A police car pulled up alongside us.* (ao lado de)
2 if you work alongside someone, you work together with them (lado a lado)

aloof /əˈluːf/ ADJECTIVE staying apart from other people or not friendly (indiferente) 🔁 *She remained aloof from the others.* (permaneceu indiferente)

aloud /əˈlaʊd/ ADVERB so that other people can hear (alto) 🔁 *She almost laughed aloud.* (riu alto) 🔁 *Edith read the letter aloud to the boys.* (leu em voz alta)

alphabet /ˈælfəbet/ NOUN [plural **alphabets**] all the written letters of a language (alfabeto) 🔁 *Z is the last letter of the alphabet.* (letra do alfabeto)

• **alphabetical** /ˌælfəˈbetɪkəl/ ADJECTIVE with the first letters in the order of the alphabet (alfabeto) 🔁 *The books are in alphabetical order.* (ordem alfabética) □ *an alphabetical index*

• **alphabetically** /ˌælfəˈbetɪkəli/ ADVERB with the first letters in the order of the alphabet □ *The list has been arranged alphabetically.* (alfabeticamente)

alphanumeric /ˌælfənjuːˈmerɪk/ ADJECTIVE using letters and numbers. A computing word. (alfanumérico)

alpine /ˈælpaɪn/ ADJECTIVE to do with high mountains □ *an alpine meadow* (alpino)

already /ɔːlˈredi/ ADVERB
1 before now or before a particular time □ *I had already gone when Bob arrived.* □ *We've already booked our summer holiday.* (já)
2 now, before the expected time □ *Is he here already?* □ *I'm already tired.* (já)

alright /ɔːlˈraɪt/ ADJECTIVE, ADVERB another spelling of **all right** (tudo bem)

alsatian /ælˈseɪʃən/ NOUN [plural **alsatians**] a large dog with short brown and black fur, often used by the police (cão policial)

also /ˈɔːlsəʊ/ ADVERB in addition □ *Bernie speaks French and also Italian.* □ *My sister also attends this school.* (também) 🔁 *The process is not only slow, but also very expensive.* (não só..., mas também)

altar /ˈɔːltə(r)/ NOUN [plural **altars**] a special table used for religious ceremonies in a church (altar)

alter /ˈɔːltə(r)/ VERB [**alters, altering, altered**] to change, or to change something □ *The town has altered a lot recently.* □ *Can you alter this skirt to fit me?* (alterar)

• **alteration** /ˌɔːltəˈreɪʃən/ NOUN [plural **alterations**] a change, or the process of being changed □ *There have been a few alterations to our plans.* □ *The museum is closed for alteration.* (alteração)

alternate¹ /ɔːlˈtɜːnət/ ADJECTIVE
1 happening on one day, week, etc. but not the next □ *I have to work on alternate Saturdays.* (alternado)
2 with one thing, then another, then the first thing again, in a repeated pattern □ *alternate stripes of red and green* (alternado)
3 a US word for **alternative** (alternative)

alternate² /ˈɔːltəneɪt/ VERB [**alternates, alternating, alternated**] if two things alternate, one happens or is used first, then the other, then the first again, etc. □ *She alternates between being too strict and being too soft.* □ *He alternates between the guitar and the violin.* (alternar)

alternative /ɔːlˈtɜːnətɪv/ ▶ ADJECTIVE
1 giving you another choice or possibility □ *If you cannot come on Tuesday you can suggest an alternative day.* □ *Drivers are advised to use an alternative route.* (alternativo)
2 not usual or traditional □ *an alternative lifestyle* (alternativo)
▶ NOUN [plural **alternatives**] another possibility or choice □ *Is there an alternative to chips on the menu?* □ *There are cheaper alternatives.* (alternativa)

• **alternatively** /ɔːlˈtɜːnətɪvli/ ADVERB used to offer another suggestion □ *Alternatively, we could go to the cinema.* (alternativamente)

alternative medicine /ɔːlˌtɜːnətɪv ˈmedsɪn/ NOUN, NO PLURAL treating diseases with methods which are different from usual Western medicine (medicina alternativa)

alternator /ˈɔːltəneɪtə(r)/ NOUN [plural **alternators**] a piece of equipment that produces an electric current that keeps changing its direction. A physics word. (alternador)

although /ɔːlˈðəʊ/ CONJUNCTION
1 despite the fact that □ *I did go to the show, although I'd said I wouldn't.* □ *Although he was a clever kid, he didn't do well in exams.* (embora)
2 but □ *He's retired from professional athletics, although he's still very fit.* (embora)

altitude /ˈæltɪtjuːd/ NOUN [plural **altitudes**] the height of a place above the level of the sea □ *We are flying at an altitude of 20,000 metres.* (altitude)

alto /ˈæltəʊ/ NOUN [plural **altos**] the lowest singing voice for a woman (contralto)

altogether /ˌɔːltəˈgeðə(r)/ ADVERB
1 completely □ *Finally, he stopped altogether.* (completamente) 🔁 *I'm not altogether happy.* (não completamente) □ *They're from altogether different cultures.*
2 in total □ *We raised £100 altogether.* □ *There are six of us altogether.* (no total)
3 in general □ *Altogether, it was a great holiday.* (em geral)

altruism /ˈæltruːɪzəm/ NOUN, NO PLURAL behaving in a way that shows you care more about others than yourself. A formal word. □ *an act of altruism* (altruísmo)

• **altruistic** /ˌæltruˈɪstɪk/ ADJECTIVE involving altruism. A formal word. □ *He did it for purely altruistic reasons.* (altruísta)

aluminium /ˌæljuˈmɪniəm/ NOUN, NO PLURAL a very light metal that is a silver colour (alumínio)

aluminum /əˈluːmɪnəm/ NOUN, NO PLURAL the US word for **aluminium** (alumínio)

alveolus /ælˈvɪələs/ NOUN [plural **alveoli**] alveoli are structures in the lungs like very small bags, that take oxygen into the blood. A biology word. (alvéolo)

always /ˈɔːlweɪz/ ADVERB
1 at all times □ *I always work hard.* (sempre) 🔁 *You look lovely, as always.* (como sempre)
2 at all times in the past □ *She's always lived in the same village.* (sempre) □ *He hasn't always been so successful.* (sempre)
3 forever □ *I'll always remember that day.* (sempre)
4 repeatedly □ *+ ing* *I'm always getting this wrong.* (sempre)

Alzheimer's disease /ˈælts.haɪməz dɪˌziːz/ NOUN, NO PLURAL a serious illness that affects the brain of older people, making them forget things and become confused (doença de Alzheimer)

am¹ /æm/ VERB the present tense of the verb be when it is used with I □ *I am happy.* (ver **be**)

> ➤ Note that instead of I **am**, people often say and write the short form **I'm** □ *I'm very pleased.*

am² /eɪˈem/ or **a.m.** ABBREVIATION used after the time to show that it is in the morning □ *My flight is at 6 am.* (manhã/abreviação de anti-meridian – antes do meio-dia)

amalgamate /əˈmælɡəˌmeɪt/ VERB [amalgamates, amalgamating, amalgamated] if two organizations amalgamate, they join together □ *The two firms amalgamated last year.* (unir)

• **amalgamation** /əˌmælɡəˈmeɪʃən/ NOUN, NO PLURAL the joining of two or more organizations □ *The new union is an amalgamation of three smaller unions.* (união)

amass /əˈmæs/ VERB [amasses, amassing, amassed] to collect a lot of something □ *The family has amassed a lot of furniture over the years.* (acumular)

amateur /ˈæmətə(r)/ ▶ NOUN [plural amateurs]
1 someone who does something because they enjoy it, not for money □ *The team is made up of enthusiastic amateurs.* (amador)
2 someone who is not very good at doing something □ *They're complete amateurs.* (amador)

▶ ADJECTIVE doing something for fun and not to be paid □ *an amateur photographer* □ *amateur athletics* (amador)

• **amateurish** /ˈæmətərɪʃ/ ADJECTIVE done or made without much skill □ *an amateurish video* (de amador)

amaze /əˈmeɪz/ VERB [amazes, amazing, amazed] to surprise someone very much □ *It amazes me how stupid you can be.* (surpreender)

• **amazed** /əˈmeɪzd/ ADJECTIVE very surprised □ *+ at* *We were all amazed at how easy it was.* □ *+ that* *I'm amazed that no one was hurt.* □ *Mum looked amazed when he walked in.* (surpreso)

• **amazement** /əˈmeɪzmənt/ NOUN, NO PLURAL great surprise (surpresa) 🔁 *To my amazement, Dad agreed with me.* □ *He shook his head in amazement.* (para minha surpresa)

• **amazing** /əˈmeɪzɪŋ/ ADJECTIVE
1 very surprising □ *an amazing sight* □ *It's amazing how quickly the weather can change.* (surpreendente)
2 very pleasant, exciting or enjoyable □ *We saw the most amazing sunset.* □ *It's a pretty amazing feeling.* (maravilhoso)

• **amazingly** /əˈmeɪzɪŋli/ ADVERB in a very surprising way □ *The cake was amazingly good.* □ *Amazingly, it didn't rain for our picnic.* (surpreendentemente)

ambassador /æmˈbæsədə(r)/ NOUN [plural ambassadors] someone who officially represents their government in a foreign country □ *the British ambassador to Japan* (embaixador)

amber /ˈæmbə(r)/ NOUN, NO PLURAL
1 a colour between yellow and orange □ *The traffic lights were on amber.* (cor de âmbar)
2 a clear yellow-brown substance that is used to make jewellery (âmbar)

ambi- /ˈæmbɪ/ PREFIX ambi- is added to the start of words to mean 'to do with both parts' or 'to do with two of something' □ *ambidextrous*

ambidextrous /ˌæmbɪˈdekstrəs/ ADJECTIVE able to use both of your hands equally well (ambidestro)

ambience /ˈæmbiəns/ NOUN, NO PLURAL the atmosphere of a place □ *The restaurant has a pleasant ambience.* (ambiente)

ambiguity /ˌæmbɪˈɡjuːətɪ/ NOUN [plural ambiguities] when something can have more than one meaning □ *We need to make sure there is no ambiguity in the contract.* (ambiguidade)

• **ambiguous** /æmˈbɪɡjuəs/ ADJECTIVE having more than one possible meaning □ *His comments on her performance were rather ambiguous.* (ambíguo)

• **ambiguously** /æmˈbɪɡjuəslɪ/ ADVERB in an ambiguous way □ *an ambiguously worded statement* (ambiguamente)

ambition /æmˈbɪʃən/ NOUN [plural ambitions]
1 something that you want to achieve (ambição)

ambivalence — amorous

I have an ambition to see the pyramids. (tenho uma ambição) *He achieved his ambition of performing on Broadway.* (alcançou a ambição) **2** *no plural* wanting to be very successful □ *He shows a lack of ambition.* (ambição)

- **ambitious** /æmˈbɪʃəs/ ADJECTIVE **1** wanting to be very successful in life □ *an ambitious and talented young player* (ambicioso) **2** difficult to achieve □ *an ambitious plan* (ambicioso)

ambivalence /æmˈbɪvələns/ NOUN, NO PLURAL when you have two different, often opposite, feelings about something □ *This shows the public's ambivalence about the monarchy.* (ambivalência)

- **ambivalent** /æmˈbɪvələnt/ ADJECTIVE having two different, often opposite, feelings about something □ *She had ambivalent feelings about marriage.* (ambivalente)

amble /ˈæmbəl/ VERB [ambles, ambling, ambled] to walk in a slow and relaxed way □ *They were ambling along, chatting.* (passear)

ambulance /ˈæmbjʊləns/ NOUN [plural ambulances] a vehicle for taking ill or injured people to hospital (ambulância)

ambush /ˈæmbʊʃ/ ▶ NOUN [plural ambushes] an attack by someone who was hidden □ *a deadly ambush* (emboscada, cilada)
▶ VERB [ambushes, ambushing, ambushed] to attack someone from a hidden position □ *Four masked men ambushed the security guard.* (emboscar)

ameba /əˈmiːbə/ NOUN [plural amebas or amebae] the US spelling of **amoeba** (ameba)

amen /ɑːˈmen/ EXCLAMATION something that is said by Christians at the end of a prayer (amém)

amend /əˈmend/ VERB [amends, amending, amended] to make changes to something written □ *We need to amend the guidelines.* (emendar)

- **amendment** /əˈmendmənt/ NOUN [plural amendments] a change to something written, for example a law (emenda)
- **amends** /əˈmendz/ PLURAL NOUN **make amends** to do something good to show you are sorry for something you did wrong □ *Now we'll see if he can make amends for letting in that goal.* (compensar)

amenity /əˈmiːnəti/ NOUN [plural amenities] something such as a shop or park that is available for people to use (conforto, facilidade) *Newlands has excellent local amenities.* (confortos locais)

American /əˈmerɪkən/ ▶ ADJECTIVE belonging to or from America, especially the United States of America □ *an American accent* (americano)
▶ NOUN [plural Americans] a person from America, especially the United States of America (norte-americano)

amethyst /ˈæmɪθɪst/ NOUN [plural amethysts] a valuable purple stone used in jewellery (ametista)

amiable /ˈeɪmiəbəl/ ADJECTIVE friendly and relaxed □ *a very amiable man* (amável)

- **amiably** /ˈeɪmiəbli/ ADVERB in a friendly, relaxed way □ *They chatted amiably.* (amavelmente)

amicable /ˈæmɪkəbəl/ ADJECTIVE friendly and without any argument (amigável) *an amicable agreement/settlement* (um acordo amigável)

- **amicably** /ˈæmɪkəbli/ ADVERB in a friendly way □ *This problem can be resolved amicably.* (amigavelmente)

amid /əˈmɪd/ or **amidst** /əˈmɪdst/ ADVERB a formal word meaning 'in the middle of' □ *It was a moment of calm amid great excitement.* (no meio de, entre)

amino acid /əˈmiːnəʊ ˈæsɪd/ NOUN [plural amino acids] one of the substances in the body that join together to make proteins. A biology word. (aminoácido)

amiss /əˈmɪs/ ADVERB if something is amiss, there is something wrong □ *He didn't notice anything amiss.* (errado, defeituoso)

ammonia /əˈməʊniə/ NOUN, NO PLURAL a substance that can be a gas or a liquid and has a very strong smell. A chemistry word. (amônia)

ammunition /ˌæmjʊˈnɪʃən/ NOUN, NO PLURAL bullets or bombs that you can fire from a weapon (munição)

amnesia /æmˈniːziə/ NOUN, NO PLURAL a medical condition that makes you forget things (amnésia)

amnesty /ˈæmnəsti/ NOUN [plural amnesties] a period of time when the usual punishments for people are stopped □ *The government announced an amnesty for political prisoners.* (anistia)

amniotic fluid /ˌæmniˈɒtɪk ˈfluːɪd/ NOUN, NO PLURAL the liquid that surrounds a baby in the mother's womb (= place where the baby grows). A biology word. (líquido amniótico)

amoeba /əˈmiːbə/ NOUN [plural amoebas or amoebae] a microorganism made from a single cell. A biology word. (ameba)

amok /əˈmɒk/ ADVERB **run amok** to behave in an uncontrolled way and do a lot of damage □ *Rioters ran amok in the city.* (correr em fúria/delírio)

among /əˈmʌŋ/ or **amongst** /əˈmʌŋst/ PREPOSITION **1** surrounded by or in the middle of □ *You are among friends.* (entre) **2** between people in a group □ *Divide the chocolate among yourselves.* (entre) **3** in a group of □ *The band is popular among teenagers.* (entre)

amoral /eɪˈmɒrəl/ ADJECTIVE not caring about moral principles (amoral)

amorous /ˈæmərəs/ ADJECTIVE full of love and sexual feeling □ *amorous behavior* (apaixonado, amoroso)

- **amorously** /'æmərəsli/ ADVERB in an amorous way □ *He clasped her hand amorously.* (amorosamente)

amount /ə'maʊnt/ NOUN [plural **amounts**] a quantity □ + *of* *a small amount of money* □ *These drinks contain large amounts of sugar.* (quantidade)

> Remember that 'large' and 'small' are used before the word amount but not 'big' or 'little' □ *A large amount of this food is wasted.* □ *A small amount of salt is necessary.*

◆ PHRASAL VERB [**amounts, amounting, amounted**]
amount to something
1 to be the same as something □ *Her lawyer said the behaviour amounted to blackmail.* (equivaler)
2 to add up to a total □ *What I've spent amounts to exactly $10.* (somar)

amp /æmp/ NOUN [plural **amps**]
1 the unit used to measure electric current. A physics word. (ampere)
2 a short informal way to say or write **amplifier** (amplificador)

ampere /'æmpeə(r)/ NOUN [plural **amperes**] a formal word for **amp**. A physics word. (ampere)

ampersand /'æmpəsænd/ NOUN [plural **ampersands**] the sign '&', which means **and** (e comercial)

amphibian /æm'fɪbiən/ NOUN [plural **amphibians**]
1 an animal that lives on land and in water. A biology word. □ *Frogs are amphibians.* (anfíbio)
2 a vehicle that can travel on land and on water (anfíbio)
- **amphibious** /æm'fɪbiəs/ ADJECTIVE able to go or live on land and in water (anfíbio)

amphitheatre /'æmfɪˌθɪətə(r)/ NOUN [plural **amphitheatres**] a large theatre with no roof that has seats in a circle around an area in the centre (anfiteatro)

ample /'æmpəl/ ADJECTIVE enough or more than enough □ *We had ample opportunity to ask questions.* □ *an ample supply of water* (amplo)

amplifier /'æmplɪfaɪə(r)/ NOUN [plural **amplifiers**] a piece of electrical equipment that makes sounds louder (amplificador)

amplify /'æmplɪfaɪ/ VERB [**amplifies, amplifying, amplified**]
1 to make something louder □ *The sounds are amplified.* (amplificar)
2 to make something stronger or clearer □ *The incident amplified concerns about safety.* (ampliar)

amply /'æmpli/ ADVERB very well or more than necessary □ *We were amply rewarded with tea and chocolate cake.* (amplamente, plenamente)

amputate /'æmpjuteɪt/ VERB [**amputates, amputating, amputated**] to cut off a part of the body in a medical operation □ *He had to have his left leg amputated.* (amputar)

- **amputation** /ˌæmpju'teɪʃən/ NOUN [plural **amputations**] when a part of the body is amputated (amputação)

amuse /ə'mju:z/ VERB [**amuses, amusing, amused**]
1 to make someone smile or laugh □ *He told jokes to amuse his classmates.* (divertir)
2 to keep someone happy and interested □ *Would you amuse the children for half an hour?* □ *She amused herself playing word games.* (distrair)
- **amused** /ə'mju:zd/ ADJECTIVE
1 finding something funny □ *He smiled, amused at John's silly mistake.* (divertido) □ *an amused expression* 🔂 *He was clearly not amused* (= he was annoyed) *by the decision.* (aborrecido)
2 happy and interested (entretido) 🔂 *Playing with the dog kept them amused for hours.* (manteve entretido)
- **amusement** /ə'mju:zmənt/ NOUN [plural **amusements**]
1 the feeling that makes you smile or laugh □ *He smiled with obvious amusement.* (diversão)
2 something you do for entertainment □ *What did you do for amusement?* □ *There were various amusements and food stalls.* (distração)
- **amusing** /ə'mju:zɪŋ/ ADJECTIVE making you want to smile or laugh □ *an amusing story* (divertido) 🔂 *She found the whole thing quite amusing.* (achou divertido)
- **amusingly** /ə'mju:zɪŋli/ ADVERB in an amusing way □ *It was an amusingly written article.* (divertidamente)

an /ən/ DETERMINER used instead of a before words beginning with a vowel, or before words beginning with 'h' when it is not pronounced □ *an apple* □ *an elephant* □ *an honest person* (um/uma)

anachronism /ə'nækrənɪzəm/ NOUN [plural **anachronisms**] something old-fashioned □ *Some view the Royal Family as an anachronism.* (anacronismo)
- **anachronistic** /əˌnækrə'nɪstɪk/ ADJECTIVE old-fashioned □ *His political views are anachronistic.* (anacrônico)

anaemia /ə'ni:miə/ NOUN, NO PLURAL a condition where someone does not have enough red blood cells and looks pale (anemia)
- **anaemic** /ə'ni:mɪk/ ADJECTIVE suffering from anaemia (anêmico)

anaerobic /ˌænə'rəʊbɪk/ ADJECTIVE not needing or using oxygen. A biology word. (anaeróbio)

anaerobic respiration /ˌænə'rəʊbɪk ˌrespə'reɪʃən/ NOUN, NO PLURAL respiration (= making energy) that uses little or no oxygen. A biology word. (respiração anaeróbia)

anaesthesia /ˌænɪs'θi:ziə/ NOUN, NO PLURAL giving someone a drug to stop them feeling pain or to make them unconscious (anestesia)
- **anaesthetic** /ˌænɪs'θetɪk/ NOUN [plural **anaesthetics**] a drug that stops you feeling pain

or makes you unconscious (**anestesia, anestésico**) 🔁 *The operation will be carried out under general anaesthetic* (= one which makes you unconscious). (**anestesia geral**) 🔁 *a local anaesthetic* (= one which stops pain in only one part of the body) (**anestesia local**)

- **anaesthetist** /əˈniːsθətɪst/ NOUN [plural **anaesthetists**] a doctor whose job is to give people anaesthetics (**anestesista**)
- **anaesthetize** or **anaesthetise** /æˈniːsθətaɪz/ VERB [**anaesthetizes, anaesthetizing, anaesthetized**] to give someone an anaesthetic before an operation (**anestesiar**)

anagram /ˈænəɡræm/ NOUN [plural **anagrams**] a word or phrase that has the same letters as another word or phrase, but in a different order □ *'Stone' is an anagram of 'notes'.* (**anagrama**)

analogous /əˈnæləɡəs/ ADJECTIVE similar in some way □ *The way the cells combine is analogous to how a key fits in a lock.* (**análogo**)

analogue /ˈænəlɒɡ/ ADJECTIVE
1 using a continuously changing signal, such as sound or electric current. A physics word. □ *The TV is capable of receiving both analogue and digital signals.* (**analógico**)
2 an analogue watch or clock has hands that move around a clock face to show the time (**analógico**)

analogy /əˈnælədʒi/ NOUN [plural **analogies**] a comparison with something similar that helps to explain something (**analogia**) 🔁 *To use a football analogy, it's like scoring the winning goal in extra time.* (**fazendo-se uma analogia**)

analysis /əˈnæləsɪs/ NOUN [plural **analyses**] when you examine something carefully in order to understand it (**análise**) 🔁 *a statistical analysis* (**análise estatística**) 🔁 *We carried out a detailed analysis of the project.* (**análise detalhada**)

- **analyst** /ˈænəlɪst/ NOUN [plural **analysts**]
1 someone who examines something carefully in order to understand it (**analista**) 🔁 *a political analyst* (**analista político**) 🔁 *a legal analyst* (**analista legal**)
2 someone whose job is talking to people to find out why they are unhappy (**analista, psicanalista**)

- **analytical** /ˌænəˈlɪtɪkəl/ or **analytic** /ˌænəˈlɪtɪk/ ADJECTIVE using a careful method to examine and understand something (**analítico**) 🔁 *an analytical mind* (**mente analítica**)

- **analytically** /ˌænəˈlɪtɪkəli/ ADVERB in an analytical way (**analiticamente**)

analyze or **analyse** /ˈænəlaɪz/ VERB [**analyzes, analyzing, analyzed**] to examine something carefully in order to understand it (**analisar**) 🔁 *We need to analyze the data.* (**analisar os dados**) □ *Researchers analyzed a thousand samples.*

anarchist /ˈænəkɪst/ NOUN [plural **anarchists**] someone who believes it is not necessary to have any government in a country (**anarquista**)

- **anarchy** /ˈænəki/ NOUN, NO PLURAL a situation where people do not obey normal rules or laws □ *There is a growing state of anarchy in the city.* (**anarquia**)

anathema /əˈnæθəmə/ NOUN, NO PLURAL a formal word for something you hate □ *Sitting in the sun was anathema to him.* (**anátema**)

anatomy /əˈnætəmi/ NOUN, NO PLURAL
1 the body of a person or animal (**anatomia**) 🔁 *a knowledge of human anatomy* (**anatomia humana**)
2 the study of the body and its structure □ *a professor of anatomy* (**anatomia**)

ancestor /ˈænsestə(r)/ NOUN [plural **ancestors**] a member of your family who lived in the past □ *His distant ancestors came from India.* (**ancestral**)

- **ancestral** /ænˈsestrəl/ ADJECTIVE belonging to your family in the past □ *the Duke's ancestral home* (**ancestral**)

- **ancestry** /ˈænsestri/ NOUN, NO PLURAL your family's past □ *We can trace our ancestry back to the twelfth century.* □ *a French citizen of Moroccan ancestry* (**linhagem**)

anchor /ˈæŋkə(r)/ ▶ NOUN [plural **anchors**]
1 a heavy piece of metal attached to a boat that is dropped into the water to stop it from moving away (**âncora**) 🔁 *The captain dropped anchor.* (**jogou a âncora**)
2 the main person who talks on a television news programme 🔁 *the CBS news anchor* (**âncora do jornal**)

▶ VERB [**anchors, anchoring, anchored**]
1 to drop the anchor of a boat to stop it moving away □ *The ship is anchored in Sydney harbour.* (**ancorar**)
2 to fix something firmly in a position □ *Steel rods anchor the statue in place.* (**fixar**)
3 to present a television news programme □ *Jennings was picked to anchor the evening news.* (**apresentar**)

- **anchorage** /ˈæŋkərɪdʒ/ NOUN [plural **anchorages**] a place where ships can stop (**ancoradouro**)

anchovy /ˈæntʃəvi/ NOUN [plural **anchovies**] a type of small fish with a very salty taste (**anchova**)

ancient /ˈeɪnʃənt/ ADJECTIVE
1 from a very long time ago (**antigo**) 🔁 *ancient history* (**História antiga**) 🔁 *the remains of an ancient civilization* (**civilização antiga**)
2 old □ *The building's ancient heating system had broken.* (**antigo**)

and /ænd/ CONJUNCTION
1 a word that is used to join parts of sentences □ *bread and butter* □ *I saw Alice and Peter.* □ *Go and get ready.* (**e**)
2 added to □ *Two and two make four.* (**mais**)

android /ˈændrɔɪd/ NOUN [plural **androids**] a robot (= machine that moves) that looks like a human being (**androide**)

anecdote /ˈænɪkdəʊt/ NOUN [plural **anecdotes**] a short story you tell about something that happened to you □ *He was full of amusing anecdotes.* (anedota, piada)

anemia /əˈniːmɪə/ NOUN, NO PLURAL the US spelling of anaemia (anemia)

• **anemic** /əˈniːmɪk/ ADJECTIVE the US spelling of anaemic (anêmico)

anemone /əˈnemənɪ/ NOUN [plural **anemones**] a type of flower that often grows in Woods (anêmona)

anesthesia /ˌænɪsˈθiːzɪə/ NOUN, NO PLURAL the US spelling of anaesthesia (anestesia)

• **anesthetic** /ˌænɪsˈθetɪk/ NOUN [plural **anesthetics**] the US spelling of anaesthetic (anestésico, anestesia)

• **anesthetist** /əˈniːsθətɪst/ NOUN [plural **anesthetists**] the US spelling of anaesthetist (anestesiador)

• **anesthetize** /æˈniːsθətaɪz/ VERB [**anesthetizes, anesthetizing, anesthetized**] the US spelling of anaesthetize (anestesiar)

anew /əˈnjuː/ ADVERB again from the beginning, usually in a different way (de novo, de nova maneira) 🔁 *This is an opportunity to* start anew*.* (começar de novo)

angel /ˈeɪndʒəl/ NOUN [plural **angels**]
1 a creature, usually shown like a person with wings, which is believed to bring messages from God (anjo)
2 a very good person □ *Thanks for doing all that – you're an angel!* (anjo)

• **angelic** /ænˈdʒelɪk/ ADJECTIVE very beautiful and good (angélico)

anger /ˈæŋɡə(r)/ ▶ NOUN, NO PLURAL the strong, bad feeling you get about someone or something that annoys you □ *The fans expressed their anger at the decision.* □ *There's a lot of anger and frustration among local people.* □ *He was shaking with anger.* (raiva)
▶ VERB [**angers, angering, angered**] to make someone feel angry □ *The plans have angered green campaigners.* (irritar)

angle /ˈæŋɡəl/ ▶ NOUN [plural **angles**]
1 the shape that is made at the point where two straight lines meet, measured in degrees □ *a 90-degree angle* (ângulo)
2 at an angle in a position that is not straight or normal □ *Slice the vegetables at an angle.* □ *His injured leg was at an awkward angle.* (inclinado)
3 a way of thinking about something (ângulo, ponto de vista) □ **+ on** *What's your angle on this?* 🔁 *We're* covering *all the* angles *of this story.* (cobrindo todos os ângulos)
4 the direction that something comes from □ *He looked at it from every angle.* □ *Wright shot from a narrow angle.* (ângulo, aspecto)
▶ VERB [**angles, angling, angled**]
1 to put something in a position or direction that is not straight □ *Angle your head back.* (curvar)
2 to try to get something without asking directly □ *Did you hear her angling to borrow my new coat?* (direcionar)

angler /ˈæŋɡlə(r)/ NOUN [plural **anglers**] someone who catches fish for sport or a hobby (pescador)

Anglican /ˈæŋɡlɪkən/ ▶ ADJECTIVE to do with or belonging to the Church of England (anglicano)
▶ NOUN [plural **Anglicans**] a member of the Church of England (anglicano)

angling /ˈæŋɡlɪŋ/ NOUN, NO PLURAL the sport or hobby of catching fish (pesca)

Anglo- /ˈæŋɡləʊ/ PREFIX Anglo- is added to the start of words to mean 'to do with to England' □ *the Anglo-French trade agreement* □ *She calls herself an Anglo-American.*

Anglo-Saxon /ˌæŋɡləʊˈsæksən/ ▶ NOUN [plural **Anglo-Saxons**]
1 one of the people who came to live in England in the 5th century (anglo-saxão)
2 the English language before about 1150 (anglo-saxão)
▶ ADJECTIVE belonging to or to do with the Anglo--Saxon people or their language (anglo-saxão)

angrily /ˈæŋɡrəlɪ/ ADVERB in an angry way □ *A young woman came in, shouting angrily.* □ *He reacted angrily.* (furiosamente)

angry /ˈæŋɡrɪ/ ADJECTIVE [**angrier, angriest**] very annoyed □ **+ about** *They're angry about the way they were treated.* (irritado) □ **+ with** *I'm not angry with you.* □ *an angry crowd* 🔁 *Then Mike got very* angry*.* (ficou irritado) 🔁 *That kind of thing makes me so* angry*.* (deixa irritado)

anguish /ˈæŋɡwɪʃ/ NOUN, NO PLURAL a strong feeling of unhappiness and suffering (agonia, angústia) □ *a cry of anguish* 🔁 *She suffered a lot of* mental anguish*.* (angústia mental)

• **anguished** /ˈæŋɡwɪʃt/ ADJECTIVE very unhappy and suffering □ *an anguished look* (angustiado)

angular /ˈæŋɡjʊlə(r)/ ADJECTIVE with straight lines and pointed □ *an angular face* (anguloso)

animal /ˈænɪməl/ NOUN [plural **animals**]
1 a living creature that is not a human (animal) 🔁 *a* wild animal (animal selvagem) 🔁 *a* farm animal (animal de fazenda) □ *The charity helps to protect endangered animals.*
2 any living creature that can feel and move □ *Humans and insects – we're all animals.* (animal)

animate /ˈænɪmət/ ADJECTIVE alive or having life (animado, vivo)

animated /ˈænɪmeɪtɪd/ ADJECTIVE
1 in an animated film, pictures or objects look as if they are moving (animado) 🔁 *a short* animated film (desenho animado)
2 behaving or talking in an interested and excited way □ *an animated conversation* □ *He had never seen them so animated.* (animado)

• **animatedly** /ˈænɪmeɪtɪdlɪ/ ADVERB in an

animosity

interested and excited way □ *The two men were talking animatedly.* (animadamente)

- **animation** /ˌænɪˈmeɪʃən/ NOUN [plural animations]
  1 the process of making a film in which pictures or objects look as if they are moving, or a film which is made like this (animação) ◘ *The film used computer animation.* (animação computadorizada)
  2 interest and excitement □ *She was talking with great animation.* (animação)
- **animator** /ˈænɪmeɪtə(r)/ NOUN [plural animators] someone who makes animated films (animador)

animosity /ˌænɪˈmɒsətɪ/ NOUN, NO PLURAL a feeling of strong dislike towards someone □ *There is deep animosity between the two men.* (animosidade)

aniseed /ˈænɪsiːd/ NOUN, NO PLURAL a seed with a strong taste, used in making sweets, drinks and medicines (semente de anis)

ankle /ˈæŋkəl/ NOUN [plural ankles] the place where your foot joins your leg □ *She fell over and sprained her left ankle.* (tornozelo)

annex[1] /ˈæneks/ or **annexe** NOUN [plural annexes] an extra part of a building that is added on to it (anexo)

annex[2] /æˈneks/ VERB [annexes, annexing, annexed] to take control of an area or country next to your own □ *After the war, the region was annexed by the Soviet Union.* (anexar)

annihilate /əˈnaɪəleɪt/ VERB [annihilates, annihilating, annihilated] to destroy someone or something completely (aniquilar)

- **annihilation** /əˌnaɪəˈleɪʃən/ NOUN, NO PLURAL destroying someone or something completely (aniquilação)

anniversary /ˌænɪˈvɜːsərɪ/ NOUN [plural anniversaries] a date when you celebrate something that happened on the same date in the past (aniversário) ◘ *a wedding anniversary* (aniversário de casamento) □ *+ of Today is the anniversary of the King's death.* ◘ *The celebrations will mark the 60th anniversary of the country's independence.* (marcar o aniversário)

annotated /ˈænəteɪtɪd/ ADJECTIVE an annotated text includes notes to help you understand it (notas)

announce /əˈnaʊns/ VERB [announces, announcing, announced] to tell people something, especially loudly or forcefully (anunciar) ◘ *The government has announced plans to build four new hospitals.* (anunciou planos) ◘ *Have they announced their engagement yet?* (anunciou o noivado) □ *+ that The minister has announced that he is retiring.*

- **announcement** /əˈnaʊnsmənt/ NOUN [plural announcements]
  1 something that people are told, especially publicly or officially (notificação) ◘ *I want to make an announcement.* ◘ *a formal/official announcement* (notificação formal/oficial)
  2 no plural when something is announced □ *We tried to delay the announcement of the news.* (anúncio)
- **announcer** /əˈnaʊnsə(r)/ NOUN [plural announcers] someone who introduces programmes on television or the radio (locutor)

annoy /əˈnɔɪ/ VERB [annoys, annoying, annoyed] to make someone angry □ *It really annoys me when she wastes food.* (irritar)

- **annoyance** /əˈnɔɪəns/ NOUN [plural annoyances]
  1 a feeling of being annoyed (aborrecimento) ◘ *She completely ignored him, much to his annoyance.* (principalmente pela amolação) □ *She gave him a look of annoyance.*
  2 something that annoys you (amolação)
- **annoyed** /əˈnɔɪd/ ADJECTIVE angry □ *+ with I could tell he was annoyed with me.* (irritado)
- **annoying** /əˈnɔɪɪŋ/ ADJECTIVE making you feel annoyed (irritado) ◘ *an annoying habit* (hábito irritante) □ *Jo can be so annoying!*

annual /ˈænjuəl/ ▶ ADJECTIVE
1 an annual event happens once every year □ *an annual meeting of shareholders* (anual)
2 measured over a period of one year □ *annual rainfall* □ *What is your annual income?* (anual)
▶ NOUN [plural annuals]
1 a book that is published every year (anuário)
2 a plant that lives for only one year (sazonal)
- **annually** /ˈænjuəlɪ/ ADVERB happening once every year (anualmente)

anode /ˈænəʊd/ NOUN [plural anodes] the negative electrode (= part where an electric current enters or leaves) in a battery. A physics word. (ânodo)

anomalous /əˈnɒmələs/ ADJECTIVE different from what is normal or expected. A formal word. (anômalo)

- **anomaly** /əˈnɒməlɪ/ NOUN [plural anomalies] something that is anomalous. A formal word. □ *Experts have spotted some anomalies in the data.* (anomalia)

anonymity /ˌænəˈnɪmətɪ/ NOUN, NO PLURAL when someone's name is kept secret □ *The police informant insisted on anonymity.* (anonimato)

- **anonymous** /əˈnɒnɪməs/ ADJECTIVE without giving a name □ *She started receiving anonymous phone calls.* (anônimo)
- **anonymously** /əˈnɒnɪməslɪ/ ADVERB by someone whose name is kept secret □ *The money has been given anonymously.* (anonimamente)

anorak /ˈænəræk/ NOUN [plural anoraks] a thick jacket with a hood (= part that goes over the head) (jaqueta grossa com capuz)

anorexia /ˌænəˈreksɪə/ NOUN, NO PLURAL an illness in which someone does not eat enough (anorexia)

- **anorexic** /ˌænəˈreksɪk/ ▶ ADJECTIVE suffering from anorexia and very thin (**anoréxico**)
▶ NOUN [*plural* **anorexics**] someone who is suffering from anorexia (**anoréxico**)

another /əˈnʌðə(r)/ DETERMINER, PRONOUN
1 one more person or thing □ *Have another piece of chocolate.* □ *He had two gold medals and now he has another.* (**outro**)
2 a different person or thing □ *We'll finish this game another time.* □ *If that pen's broken, use another one.* □ *I lost my coat and I haven't got another.* (**outro**)

answer /ˈɑːnsə(r)/ ▶ VERB [**answers, answering, answered**]
1 to reply when someone asks you a question or sends you a letter □ *I waited for him to answer.* □ *She tried to answer truthfully.* □ *I'm just going to answer his letter.* (**responder**)
2 to pick up the telephone when it rings, or to open the door when someone is there □ *A child answered the telephone.* □ *I knocked at the door and an old woman answered.* (**atender**)
3 to write or say the answer to a question in an exam or a competition □ *You have an hour to answer all four questions.* (**responder**)
◆ PHRASAL VERB **answer (someone) back** to reply rudely to someone who has criticized you □ *His teacher told him off for answering back.* (**replicar**)
▶ NOUN [*plural* **answers**]
1 a reply □ + **to** *I couldn't find an answer to my question.* (**resposta**) 🔁 *He gave a detailed answer.* (**deu resposta**)
2 the solution to a problem □ *If you can't afford a car, then a car sharing scheme could be the answer.* (**resposta**)
3 in answer to as a reply □ *In answer to my question, he handed me the document to read.* (**em resposta a**)
4 what you write or say to answer a question in an exam or a competition (**resposta**) 🔁 *the correct/wrong answer* (**resposta certa/errada**)

> ➤ Remember to use the preposition **to** after the noun **answer**:
> ✓ *What's the answer to question six?*
> ✗ *What's the answer for question six?*

- **answerable** /ˈɑːnsərəbəl/ ADJECTIVE **answerable to someone** if you are answerable to someone for something, you are responsible for it, and you will have to explain to them if anything goes wrong (**responsável por**)

answerphone /ˈɑːnsəˌfəʊn/ *or* **answering machine** /ˈɑːnsərɪŋ məˌʃiːn/ NOUN [*plural* **answerphones** *or* **answering machines**] a machine that automatically answers your telephone and records messages for you (**secretária eletrônica**)

ant /ænt/ NOUN [*plural* **ants**] a small, usually black, insect that lives in organized groups (**formiga**)

antagonism /ænˈtæɡənɪzəm/ NOUN, NO PLURAL a feeling of wanting to fight against a person or an idea □ *We couldn't understand their antagonism towards us.* (**antagonismo**)

- **antagonistic** /ænˌtæɡəˈnɪstɪk/ ADJECTIVE wanting to fight or argue against a person or an idea (**antagônico**)
- **antagonize** *or* **antagonise** /ænˈtæɡənaɪz/ VERB [**antagonizes, antagonizing, antagonized**] to make someone want to fight or argue with you (**antagonizar**)

Antarctic /ænˈtɑːktɪk/ ▶ NOUN **the Antarctic** the area of the world round the South Pole (**Antártica**)
▶ ADJECTIVE to do with the Antarctic □ *Antarctic exploration* □ *the Antarctic winter* (**antártico**)

ante- /ˌæntɪ/ PREFIX **ante-** is added to the beginning of words to mean 'before' □ *antenatal* (**anti-**)

antelope /ˈæntɪləʊp/ NOUN [*plural* **antelope** *or* **antelopes**] an animal like a deer, that has long horns and runs very fast (**antílope**)

antenatal /ˌæntɪˈneɪtəl/ ADJECTIVE to do with the time when a woman is pregnant, before the baby is born (**pré-natal**) 🔁 *antenatal classes* (**exames de pré-natal**)

antenna /ænˈtenə/ NOUN [*plural* **antennae** *or* **antennas**]
1 one of two long thin parts on the head of an insect or a sea animal, used for feeling (**antena**)
2 a thin piece of metal that is used for getting television or radio signals (**antena**)

anthem /ˈænθəm/ NOUN [*plural* **anthems**] a song that praises a country or an organization, for example a football team (**hino**)
⇨ go to **national anthem**

anthology /ænˈθɒlədʒɪ/ NOUN [*plural* **anthologies**] a book that is a collection of stories, poems or songs by different writers (**antologia**)

anthropologist /ˌænθrəˈpɒlədʒɪst/ NOUN [*plural* **anthropologists**] someone who studies the way humans live (**antropólogo**)

- **anthropology** /ˌænθrəˈpɒlədʒɪ/ NOUN, NO PLURAL the study of the way humans live (**antropologia**)

anti- /ˈæntɪ/ PREFIX **anti-** is added to the beginning of words to mean 'against' or 'preventing' □ *antisocial* □ *antifreeze* (**anti-**)

antibiotic /ˌæntɪbaɪˈɒtɪk/ NOUN [*plural* **antibiotics**] a medicine that kills bacteria that can cause infections □ *The doctor's put me on antibiotics.* (**antibiótico**)

antibody /ˈæntɪˌbɒdɪ/ NOUN [*plural* **antibodies**] a substance that is produced in your blood to fight disease. A biology word. (**anticorpo**)

anticipate /ænˈtɪsɪˌpeɪt/ VERB [anticipates, anticipating, anticipated] to expect something to happen, and often to prepare for it □ *We don't anticipate any problems.* (antecipar)
• **anticipation** /ænˌtɪsɪˈpeɪʃən/ NOUN, NO PLURAL
1 excitement about something that is going to happen □ *There was a sense of anticipation in the hall.* (expectativa)
2 in anticipation of something in order to prepare for something □ *The school has closed in anticipation of heavy snow.* (como prevenção de algo)

anticlimax /ˌæntiˈklaɪmæks/ NOUN [plural anticlimaxes] when something ends in a way that is less exciting than you expected or less exciting than what happened before it □ *After all the publicity, the show was a bit of an anticlimax.* (anticlímax)

anticlockwise /ˌæntiˈklɒkwaɪz/ ADJECTIVE, ADVERB going in the opposite direction to the hands (= parts that point) of a clock □ *Turn the top of the bottle anticlockwise.* (sentido anti-horário)

antics /ˈæntɪks/ PLURAL NOUN someone's antics are the funny or annoying things that they do (grotesco)

antidote /ˈæntidəʊt/ NOUN [plural antidotes]
1 an antidote to something something that stops the harmful effects of something else □ *Laughter is the best antidote to stress.* (um antídoto para)
2 a medicine that stops the effects of poison (antídoto)

antifreeze /ˈæntifriːz/ NOUN, NO PLURAL a chemical that you add to a liquid to stop it from freezing (anticongelante)

antigen /ˈæntɪdʒən/ NOUN [plural antigens] a substance that makes the body produce antibodies (= substances that fight disease). A biology word. (antígeno)

antihistamine /ˌæntiˈhɪstəmɪn/ NOUN [plural antihistamines] a medicine that is used to treat allergies (= bad reactions to something you have eaten or touched) (anti-histamínico)

anti-oxidant /ˌæntiˈɒksɪdənt/ NOUN [plural anti-oxidants] a substance, for example a vitamin from a healthy food, that removes harmful molecules (= groups of atoms) from your body (antioxidante)

antipathy /ænˈtɪpəθi/ NOUN, NO PLURAL a feeling of dislike □ *He had a deep antipathy towards the modern world.* (antipatia)

antiperspirant /ˌæntiˈpɜːspərənt/ NOUN [plural antiperspirants] a substance that stops you sweating (antitranspirante)

antiquated /ˈæntɪkweɪtɪd/ ADJECTIVE too old-fashioned □ *The factory was using antiquated machinery.* (antiquado)

antique /ænˈtiːk/ ▶ NOUN [plural antiques] an object that is old and valuable □ *a collector of antiques* (antiguidade)
▶ ADJECTIVE old and valuable □ *antique jewellery* (antigo)

> ➤ Remember that **antique** is used for old objects, such as furniture and jewellery. It is not used for old buildings. For buildings, use **old** or **ancient**. □ *They have a lot of very valuable antique furniture.* □ *We visited the ancient monuments.*

anti-Semitic /ˌæntisɪˈmɪtɪk/ ADJECTIVE showing hate towards Jewish people □ *anti-Semitic views* (antissemita)
• **anti-Semitism** /ˌæntiˈsemɪtɪzəm/ NOUN, NO PLURAL hate or unfair treatment of Jewish people (antissemitismo)

antiseptic /ˌæntiˈseptɪk/ NOUN [plural antiseptics] a substance that is used to clean injuries in order to prevent infections (antisséptico)

antisocial /ˌæntiˈsəʊʃəl/ ADJECTIVE
1 antisocial behaviour is unpleasant or harmful to other people (antissocial)
2 antisocial people do not enjoy being with other people (antissocial)

anti-spam /ˌæntiˈspæm/ ADJECTIVE anti-spam software stops you getting e-mails that you do not want, especially advertising. A computing word. (anti-spam)

antithesis /ænˈtɪθɪsɪs/ NOUN [plural antitheses] **the antithesis of something** the complete opposite of something. A formal word. □ *His new book is the antithesis of his previous gloomy, intellectual novels.* (antítese)

antivirus /ˈæntiˌvaɪrəs/ ADJECTIVE antivirus software stops other software from harming your computer. A computing word. (antivírus)

antler /ˈæntlə(r)/ NOUN [plural antlers] a horn that divides like branches and grows on the head of a deer (galhada)

antonym /ˈæntənɪm/ NOUN [plural antonyms] a word that means the opposite of another word (antônimo)

anus /ˈeɪnəs/ NOUN [plural anuses] the opening in your bottom through which you get rid of solid waste from your body (ânus)

anxiety /æŋˈzaɪəti/ NOUN [plural anxieties] a feeling of worry □ *The parents of these soldiers suffered a lot of anxiety.* (ansiedade)
• **anxious** /ˈæŋkʃəs/ ADJECTIVE
1 worried □ + **about** *He's anxious about missing his train.* □ *She gave me an anxious glance.* (aflito)
2 wanting very much to do something or wanting something to happen □ + **to do something** *We're anxious to make sure the work is finished on time.* (ansioso)

- **anxiously** /ˈæŋkʃəsli/ ADVERB in a worried way □ *He looked anxiously at his watch.* (**ansiosamente**)

any /ˈeni/ ▶ DETERMINER, PRONOUN

1 used in questions and negative statements to mean 'some' □ *Have we got any sweets?* □ *We had lots of food, but there isn't any left now.* (**algum, nenhum**)

2 one or a piece of something, but not a particular one □ *Let me know if you have any questions. Choose any colour you like.* □ *The children all know the answers – ask any of them.* (**qualquer**)

▶ ADVERB

1 at all □ *Are you feeling any better?* □ *Can't you walk any faster?* (**um pouco**)

2 any more if something does not happen any more, it has stopped happening □ *Ricky doesn't work here any more.* □ *The children don't get free milk any more.* (**não mais**)

anybody /ˈeniˌbɒdi/ PRONOUN

1 used in questions and negatives to mean 'a person' or 'people' □ *Has anybody seen my glasses?* □ *I didn't speak to anybody.* (**alguém**)

2 any person □ *Anybody is allowed to enter.* (**qualquer um**)

anyhow /ˈenihaʊ/ ADVERB

1 used to add another reason to what you have just said □ *I missed lunch but I wasn't hungry anyhow.* (**de qualquer maneira**)

2 despite that □ *Two of our players are injured, but anyhow we have a very good team.* (**de qualquer maneira**)

anyone /ˈeniwʌn/ PRONOUN

1 used in questions and negatives to mean 'a person' or 'people' □ *Has anyone got a mobile?* □ *There isn't anyone left.* (**alguém**)

2 any person □ *Anyone can bake a cake.* □ *He'll talk to anyone.* (**qualquer um**)

> Remember that 'anyone' is singular so the verb following it must be singular □ *If anyone calls, tell them I'll be back in ten minutes.* □ *Anyone is welcome to come.*

anyplace /ˈeniˌpleɪs/ ADVERB the US word for **anywhere** (**qualquer lugar**)

anything /ˈeniθɪŋ/ PRONOUN

1 used in questions and negative statements to mean 'something' □ *We didn't have anything to eat.* □ *Is there anything I can do to help?* (**algo**) □ *Is there anything else I should know?* (**algo mais**)

2 something of any type □ *He's capable of anything.* □ *We can do anything we like while our teacher is away.* (**qualquer coisa**)

anyway /ˈeniweɪ/ ADVERB

1 used to add another reason to what you have just said □ *I can give you a lift. I'm going that way anyway.* (**de qualquer maneira**)

2 despite that □ *Leon couldn't go with me but I enjoyed the party anyway.* (**de todo jeito**)

3 used to start a new part of a conversation □ *Anyway, how have you been lately?* (**de qualquer maneira**)

4 used to change something you have just said slightly □ *I'm not going to leave – not yet, anyway.* (**em todo caso**)

anywhere /ˈeniweə(r)/ ADVERB

1 in or to any place □ *I'm willing to travel anywhere.* □ *You can buy these anywhere in the world.* □ *Don't go anywhere near Dad – he's in a terrible mood.* (**qualquer lugar**)

2 used in questions and negative statements to mean 'a place' □ *Have you got anywhere to stay?* □ *There isn't anywhere to hide.* (**algum lugar**)

3 anywhere near used in questions and negative statements to mean 'almost in a particular state' □ *The building isn't anywhere near completion.* □ *Are you anywhere near finishing with the computer?* (**perto de**)

aorta /eɪˈɔːtə/ NOUN [plural **aortas**] the main tube that takes blood from your heart to the rest of your body. A biology word. (**aorta**)

apart /əˈpɑːt/ ADVERB

1 separated by distance or time □ *Stand with your feet apart.* □ *We had two classes, a week apart.* (**separado**)

2 into pieces (em pedaços) □ *The seams of this jacket have come apart.* (**romperam**) □ *We had to take the lamp apart to mend it.*

3 apart from except for □ *Apart from us, nobody's interested.* □ *I've had nothing to eat apart from a biscuit.* (**à parte de**)

4 tell apart if you cannot tell two people apart, you cannot see any differences in their appearance (**distinguir**)

apartheid /əˈpɑːtheɪt/ NOUN, NO PLURAL the system in the past in South Africa, where black and white people lived separately and were treated differently by law (**separação**)

apartment /əˈpɑːtmənt/ NOUN [plural **apartments**] a mainly US word for **flat** (= set of rooms on one level) □ *an apartment block* (**apartamento**)

apathetic /ˌæpəˈθetɪk/ ADJECTIVE not interested in anything (**apático**)

- **apathy** /ˈæpəθi/ NOUN, NO PLURAL being apathetic (**apatia**)

ape /eɪp/ ▶ NOUN [plural **apes**] a large animal like a monkey with no tail (**macaco**)

▶ VERB [**apes, aping, aped**] to copy the way someone else speaks or behaves (**imitar, arremedar**)

aperitif /əˌperəˈtiːf/ NOUN [plural **aperitifs**] an alcoholic drink that you have before a meal (**aperitivo**)

apex /ˈeɪpeks/ NOUN [plural **apexes** or **apices**] the top point of something, especially a triangle (**ápice, cume**)

aphid /ˈeɪfɪd/ NOUN [plural **aphids**] a small insect that eats plants (**pulgão**)

apiece /əˈpiːs/ ADVERB each □ *We bought five chairs at £30 a piece.* (**por peça**)

aplomb /əˈplɒm/ NOUN, NO PLURAL if you do something with aplomb, you do it well and with confidence □ *She delivered her speech with aplomb.* (**autoconfiança**)

apocryphal /əˈpɒkrɪfəl/ ADJECTIVE an apocryphal story is not true, although many people think it is (**apócrifo, falso**)

apolitical /ˌeɪpəˈlɪtɪkəl/ ADJECTIVE not interested in politics, or not connected to any political beliefs (**apolítico**)

apologetic /əˌpɒləˈdʒetɪk/ ADJECTIVE showing that you are sorry for doing something wrong □ *She gave me an apologetic smile.* (**apologético, apológico**)

apologize or **apologise** /əˈpɒlədʒaɪz/ VERB [**apologizes, apologizing, apologized**] to say sorry for doing something wrong □ + **for** *I had to apologize for being late.* (**desculpar-se**)

• **apology** /əˈpɒlədʒi/ NOUN [plural **apologies**] when someone apologizes (**desculpa, apologia**) ▣ *He made a public apology* (**apresentou uma desculpa**) ▣ *She demanded an apology from the newspaper's editor.* (**exigiu desculpa**) □ + **for** *I owe you an apology for forgetting your birthday again.*

apostle /əˈpɒsəl/ NOUN [plural **apostles**] one of the first twelve men who followed Jesus Christ (**apóstolo**)

apostrophe /əˈpɒstrəfi/ NOUN [plural **apostrophes**]
1 the symbol (') that shows where a letter or letters have been missed out □ *Jane's* (= Jane is) *late again.* □ *I think it'll* (= it will) *rain later.* (**apóstrofo**)
2 the symbol (') that is used before the letter s to show who something belongs to □ *I borrowed Ralf's bicycle.* (**apóstrofo**)

appal /əˈpɔːl/ VERB [**appals, appalling, appalled**] if you are appalled by something, you are shocked and upset by it □ *I was appalled by her language.* (**assustar**)

• **appalling** /əˈpɔːlɪŋ/ ADJECTIVE shocking and very bad □ *an appalling accident* □ *appalling weather* (**assustador**)

apparatus /ˌæpəˈreɪtəs/ NOUN, NO PLURAL the equipment that you need for a particular task □ *breathing apparatus* (**aparato, aparelho**)

apparent /əˈpærənt/ ADJECTIVE
1 easy to see (**aparente**) ▣ *Then, for no apparent reason, he began to cry.* (**sem motivo aparente**)
2 seeming to be true □ *We were shocked by his apparent lack of regret.* (**aparente**)

• **apparently** /əˈpærəntli/ ADVERB
1 used to tell people about something you have been told, although you are not sure if it is true □ *Apparently there's going to be an announcement later.* (**aparentemente**)
2 used to talk about something that seems to be true □ *The cause of the illness is apparently unknown.* (**aparentemente**)

apparition /ˌæpəˈrɪʃən/ NOUN [plural **apparitions**] a strange thing that someone sees, especially a ghost (= spirit of a dead person) (**aparição, fantasma**)

appeal /əˈpiːl/ ▶ VERB [**appeals, appealing, appealed**]
1 to ask for something, often forcefully or publicly □ *The police have appealed to the public for more information.* (**pedir**)
2 if something appeals to you, you think you would enjoy it □ *Diving doesn't appeal to me one bit.* (**agradar**)
3 to try to get a legal decision changed officially □ *They will appeal against the sentence.* (**apelar**)
▶ NOUN [plural **appeals**]
1 when someone appeals for something □ *Their appeals for calm were ignored.* □ *Their appeal raised £3,000 for the hospice.* (**apelo**)
2 the quality that makes something attractive □ *I don't understand the appeal of stamp collecting.* (**atração**)
3 when someone appeals against a legal decision □ *His appeal was rejected.* (**apelação**)

appear /əˈpɪə(r)/ VERB [**appears, appearing, appeared**]
1 to seem (**parecer**) □ + **that** *It appears that his wife knew nothing of his crimes.* □ + **to do something** *The man appeared to punch his victim.* ▣ *I appear to be the only one who has read the book.* □ *He appears determined to win.* (**pareço ser**)
2 to arrive or start to be able to be seen □ *Greta appeared round the corner.* □ *A car appeared in the distance.* (**aparecer**)
3 to start to exist □ *The first signs of the disease appeared in June.* (**aparecer, surgir**)
4 to be present somewhere, especially officially ▣ *He appeared in court charged with assault.* □ *Bax failed to appear at the meeting.* (**estar presente**)
5 if an actor appears in a film or a play, they are in it (**apresentar-se**)

• **appearance** /əˈpɪərəns/ NOUN [plural **appearances**]
1 the way someone or something looks □ *He was described as being of Asian appearance.* □ *We thought carefully about the appearance of the room.* (**aparência**)
2 when someone appears in public (**aparição**) ▣ *He is making his first appearance for AC Milan.* (**fazendo aparição**) ▣ *This is her first public appearance since her divorce.* (**aparição pública**)

He has already had several *court appearances*. (aparições no tribunal)
3 when someone or something arrives or starts to be seen □ *We were thrilled by the appearance of dolphins near our boat.* □ *The appearance of a police officer frightened the youths away.* (aparição)
4 the way something seems to be (aparência) □ *We like to give the appearance of efficiency.* *To all appearances* (= everyone thought) *they were the ideal couple.* (pela aparência) *We don't have much money, but we try to keep up appearances* (= make it seem that everything is good). (manter as aparências)

appease /əˈpiːz/ VERB [appeases, appeasing, appeased] to make someone feel less angry by doing what they want (apaziguar)

appendicitis /əˌpendɪˈsaɪtɪs/ NOUN, NO PLURAL an illness where your appendix becomes infected and has to be removed (apendicite)

appendix[1] /əˈpendɪks/ NOUN [plural appendixes] a small body part that has no purpose, just below the stomach. A biology word. (apêndice)

appendix[2] /əˈpendɪks/ NOUN [plural appendices] an extra part at the end of a book or document that gives more details about something (apêndice)

appetite /ˈæpɪtaɪt/ NOUN [plural appetites] the feeling of being hungry (apetite) *Elly has lost her appetite since she's been ill.* (perdeu o apetite) *You'll spoil your appetite if you eat all those biscuits.* (estragar o apetite)

• **appetizer** or **appetiser** /ˈæpɪtaɪzə(r)/ NOUN [plural appetizers] something small to eat before a meal (entrada)

• **appetizing** or **appetising** /ˈæpɪtaɪzɪŋ/ ADJECTIVE appetizing food smells or looks good (apetitoso)

applaud /əˈplɔːd/ VERB [applauds, applauding, applauded] to hit your hands together to show that you enjoyed something (aplaudir) □ *The audience applauded loudly.*

• **applause** /əˈplɔːz/ NOUN, NO PLURAL when people applaud (aplauso)

apple /ˈæpəl/ NOUN [plural apples] a hard, round fruit with red, green or yellow skin (maçã)

♦ IDIOM **the apple of someone's eyes** if someone is the apple of your eye, you love them and are very proud of them (a menina dos olhos de alguém)

appliance /əˈplaɪəns/ NOUN [plural appliances] a piece of electrical equipment (aparelho) *kitchen appliances* (equipamentos de cozinha)

applicable /əˈplɪkəbəl/ ADJECTIVE if something is applicable to a person or a situation, it is to do with them or affects them □ *Managers must understand the laws that are applicable to their companies.* (aplicável)

applicant /ˈæplɪkənt/ NOUN [plural applicants] someone who applies for something such as a job or university place (candidato)

application /ˌæplɪˈkeɪʃən/ NOUN [plural applications]
1 a written document asking for something such as a job (solicitação)
2 a computer program that does a particular job. A computing word. (aplicativo)
3 a particular use for something □ *This research could have several applications in medicine.* (uso)
4 *no plural* an effort to do something well □ *He could pass the exam with a little more application.* (dedicação)
5 when you put something such as paint or cream on a surface □ *Let the paint dry between applications.* (aplicação)

applicator /ˈæplɪkeɪtə(r)/ NOUN [plural applicators] a device that helps you put something in the right place □ *Spread the glue with the applicator on the top.* (aplicador)

applied /əˈplaɪd/ ADJECTIVE **applied maths/science** mathematics or science that has a practical use (aplicado)

apply /əˈplaɪ/ VERB [applies, applying, applied]
1 to officially ask for something, especially a job or a place on a course □ *+ for I've applied for a new job.* □ *+ to Maria's applying to university this year.* (requerer)
2 to spread a substance on a surface □ *Apply the cream to the affected skin three times a day.* (aplicar)
3 to affect a particular person or people □ *+ to Do these rules apply to all of us?* (aplicar)
4 apply yourself to work hard (esforçar-se)

appoint /əˈpɔɪnt/ VERB [appoints, appointing, appointed] to officially give someone a job □ *The committee has appointed Mark Burns as manager.* (nomear)

• **appointment** /əˈpɔɪntmənt/ NOUN [plural appointments]
1 a time when you have arranged to meet someone (compromisso) *I've made an appointment with the nurse.* (tenho um compromisso) *I have a doctor's appointment.* (consulta médica) *I've arranged a dental appointment.* (consulta odontológica)
2 choosing someone for a job □ *We hope to secure the appointment of a new music teacher this month.* (nomeação)
3 an important job □ *academic appointments* (compromissos)

> ➤ An **appointment** is an arranged meeting with a doctor, dentist, etc. It is not a meeting with a friend. To say that you are meeting a friend, say **I'm seeing x** or **I have arranged to see x**:
> ✓ *I'm seeing Maria this afternoon.*
> ✗ *I have an appointment with Maria this afternoon.*

appraisal

appraisal /əˈpreɪzəl/ NOUN [plural **appraisals**]
1 when you consider something and form an opinion about it (**apreciação**)
2 when you formally judge how well someone is doing their job (**avaliação**)

appraise /əˈpreɪz/ VERB [**appraises, appraising, appraised**] to consider something and form an opinion about it □ *She appraised the situation.* (**avaliar**)

appreciable /əˈpriːʃəbəl/ ADJECTIVE big or obvious enough to be noticed □ *The next day there was na appreciable drop in temperature.* (**apreciável**)
• **appreciably** /əˈpriːʃəblɪ/ ADVERB enough to be noticed (**apreciavelmente**)

appreciate /əˈpriːʃieɪt/ VERB [**appreciates, appreciating, appreciated**]
1 to feel grateful for something □ *I really appreciate all the time you've spent on this.* (**estimar**)
2 to enjoy or understand something that is of good quality □ *I bought Ava the more expensive perfume because I know she appreciates it.* (**apreciar**)
3 to understand that a situation is difficult □ *I appreciate that you have had a lot of problems to deal with.* (**reconhecer, entender**)
4 to become more valuable □ *The painting has appreciated in value over the years.* (**valorizar**)
• **appreciation** /əˌpriːʃiˈeɪʃən/ NOUN, NO PLURAL
1 when you are grateful to someone □ *Here's a little gift to show our appreciation of all your help.* (**agradecimento**)
2 when you enjoy or understand something that is of good quality □ *the appreciation of good food* (**apreciação**)
3 increasing value (**valorização**)
• **appreciative** /əˈpriːʃiətɪv/ ADJECTIVE
1 grateful to someone (**agradecido**)
2 showing enjoyment or understanding □ *an appreciative audience* (**apreciativo**)

apprehension /ˌæprɪˈhenʃən/ NOUN, NO PLURAL worry about something that is going to happen (**apreensão**)
• **apprehensive** /ˌæprɪˈhensɪv/ ADJECTIVE worried about something that is going to happen □ *She's a bit apprehensive about her interview.* (**apreensivo**)
• **apprehensively** /ˌæprɪˈhensɪvlɪ/ ADVERB in a worried way (**apreensivamente**)

apprentice /əˈprentɪs/ NOUN [plural **apprentices**] someone who is learning how to do a skilled job from someone who can already do it (**aprendiz**)
• **apprenticeship** /əˈprentɪʃɪp/ NOUN [plural **apprenticeships**] the time when someone is learning their job (**aprendizado**)

approach /əˈprəʊtʃ/ ▶ VERB [**approaches, approaching, approached**]
1 to come towards a place, person or thing (**aproximar-se**) □ *Approach the animals very slowly.* □ *The plane was approaching Paris from the south.*
2 to ask someone for something □ *If you want more money you'll have to approach your boss.* (**abordar**)
3 to deal with something □ *What's the best way to approach the problem?* (**abordar**)
▶ NOUN [plural **approaches**]
1 a way of trying to deal with something (**abordagem**) □ + **to** *It's a sensible approach to the problem.* **ⓘ** *We could take a different approach.* (**tentar uma abordagem**)
2 when something or someone gets closer □ *the approach of spring* □ *At the approach of the train, everyone pushed forward.* (**aproximação**)
3 a road or path that takes you to a building □ *a treelined approach* (**caminho**)
• **approachable** /əˈprəʊtʃəbəl/ ADJECTIVE an approachable person is easy to talk to (**acessível**)

appropriate /əˈprəʊpriət/ ADJECTIVE suitable □ *Please wear appropriate clothing.* (**apropriado**)
• **appropriately** /əˈprəʊpriətlɪ/ ADVERB in a suitable way □ *appropriately dressed* (**apropriadamente**)

approval /əˈpruːvəl/ NOUN, NO PLURAL
1 when someone thinks something is good □ *I've always wanted my father's approval.* (**aprovação**)
2 permission to do something □ *We need your approval before we can send the money.* (**aprovação, permissão**)

approve /əˈpruːv/ VERB [**approves, approving, approved**]
1 approve of something/someone to think something or someone is good □ *They don't approve of her boyfriend.* (**aprovar**)
2 to formally agree to something □ *Has he approved the proposal yet?* (**aprovar**)
• **approving** /əˈpruːvɪŋ/ ADJECTIVE showing that you think something or someone is good □ *He gave an approving nod.* (**aprovador**)
• **approvingly** /əˈpruːvɪŋlɪ/ ADVERB in an approving way (**aprovadoramente**)

approximate /əˈprɒksɪmət/ ADJECTIVE not exact but close □ *Can you tell me the approximate number of chairs we'll need?* □ *This is the approximate size of the rug.* (**aproximado**)
• **approximately** /əˈprɒksɪmətlɪ/ ADVERB not exactly although close to □ *There will be approximately sixty people there.* (**aproximadamente**)
• **approximation** /əˌprɒksɪˈmeɪʃən/ NOUN [plural **approximations**] a number or amount that someone has guessed and which is not exact □ *The number quoted was only an approximation.* (**aproximação**)

apricot

apricot /ˈeɪprɪkɒt/ ▶ NOUN [plural **apricots**] a small, light orange fruit with a soft skin and a stone inside (**damasco**)
▶ ADJECTIVE having a light orange colour, like an apricot (**adamascado**)

April /ˈeɪprəl/ NOUN the fourth month of the year, after March and before May □ *We're getting married in April.* (**abril**)

apron /ˈeɪprən/ NOUN [plural **aprons**] something that you wear over your normal clothes, especially when you are cooking, which keeps your clothes clean (**avental**)

apt /æpt/ ADJECTIVE
1 apt to do something if you are apt to do something, you often do it □ *He is apt to fly into a temper.* (**apto a fazer alguma coisa**)
2 suitable □ *an apt description* (**apto**)

aptitude /ˈæptɪtjuːd/ NOUN [plural **aptitudes**] a natural ability to do something □ *She never showed much aptitude for the piano.* (**aptidão**)

aptly /ˈæptlɪ/ ADVERB in a way that is suitable □ *They bought a house by the river, very aptly named 'River's Edge'.* (**adequadamente**)

aqua- /ˈækwə/ PREFIX aqua- is added to the start of words to mean 'to do with water' □ *aquarium* (**aqua-**)

aquamarine /ˌækwəməˈriːn/ ADJECTIVE having a pale, blue-green colour (**água-marinha**)

aquarium /əˈkwɛərɪəm/ NOUN [plural **aquariums**] a glass box or a building, for example in a zoo, for keeping fish or water animals (**aquário**)

aquatic /əˈkwætɪk/ ADJECTIVE to do with water □ *aquatic sports* □ *aquatic plants* (**aquático**)

aqueduct /ˈækwɪdʌkt/ NOUN [plural **aqueducts**] a bridge that carries a river or canal (= river made by men) across a valley (**aqueduto**)

Arabic numeral /ˈærəbɪk ˈnjuːmərəl/ NOUN [plural **Arabic numerals**] a number such as 0, 1, 2, 3, 4, 5, 6, 7, 8 or 9 (**algarismos arábicos**)
⇨ go to *Roman numeral*

arable /ˈærəbəl/ ADJECTIVE used for or to do with growing crops (**arável**)

arbiter /ˈɑːbɪtə(r)/ NOUN [plural **arbiters**] a person or an organization that acts as a judge, for example in a disagreement between people or countries (**árbitro**)

arbitrary /ˈɑːbɪtrərɪ/ ADJECTIVE an arbitrary decision or choice is one that you make without a good reason □ *Our choice of hotel was purely arbitrary.* (**arbitrário**)

arbitrate /ˈɑːbɪtreɪt/ VERB [**arbitrates, arbitrating, arbitrated**] to be a judge when people are arguing (**arbitrar**)

• **arbitration** /ˌɑːbɪˈtreɪʃən/ NOUN, NO PLURAL when someone official tries to solve an argument between other people (**arbitragem**)

arc /ɑːk/ NOUN [plural **arcs**] a curve that is like part of a circle (**arco**)

architect

arcade /ɑːˈkeɪd/ NOUN [plural **arcades**]
1 a place with a lot of machines that you can play games on (**fliperama**) 🔄 an *amusement árcade* (**salão de fliperama**)
2 a covered street with shops on both sides 🔄 a *shopping arcade* (**galeria de lojas**)

arch /ɑːtʃ/ ▶ NOUN [plural **arches**]
1 a curved structure that sometimes gives support to something, for example a bridge (**arco**)
2 the curved part on the under side of your foot (**arco**)
▶ VERB [**arches, arching, arched**] to make a curved shape □ *The cat arched its back.* (**arquear**)

archaeological /ˌɑːkɪəˈlɒdʒɪkəl/ ADJECTIVE to do with archaeology (**arqueológico**)

archaeologist /ˌɑːkɪˈɒlədʒɪst/ ADJECTIVE [plural **archaeologists**] someone who studies things from ancient societies that have been found (**arqueólogo**)

• **archaeology** /ˌɑːkɪˈɒlədʒɪ/ NOUN, NO PLURAL the study of ancient societies by looking at things from that time that have been found (**arqueologia**)

archaic /ɑːˈkeɪɪk/ ADJECTIVE very old, and often no longer used □ *archaic language* (**arcaico**)

archangel /ˈɑːkˌeɪndʒəl/ NOUN [plural **archangels**] a very important angel (= creature like a person with wings) (**arcanjo**)

archbishop /ɑːtʃˈbɪʃəp/ NOUN [plural **archbishops**] the most important priest in some Christian churches (**arcebispo**)

archeological /ˌɑːkɪəˈlɒdʒɪkəl/ ADJECTIVE the US spelling of **archaeological** (**arqueológico**)

archeologist /ˌɑːkɪˈɒlədʒɪst/ NOUN [plural **archeologists**] the US spelling of **archaeologist** (**arqueólogo**)

• **archeology** /ˌɑːkɪˈɒlədʒɪ/ NOUN, NO PLURAL the US spelling of **archaeology** (**arqueologia**)

archer /ˈɑːtʃə(r)/ NOUN [plural **archers**] someone who shoots arrows with a bow (= piece of curved wood with string attached) (**arqueiro**)

• **archery** /ˈɑːtʃərɪ/ NOUN, NO PLURAL the sport of shooting arrows with a bow (= piece of curved wood with string attached) (**tiro com arco e flecha**)

archetypal /ˌɑːkɪˈtaɪpəl/ ADJECTIVE very typical □ *an archetypal 1930s cinema* (**arquétipo**)

• **archetype** /ˈɑːkɪtaɪp/ NOUN [plural **archetypes**] a typical example of a particular type of person or thing □ *He seemed to me the archetype of an academic.* (**arquétipo**)

archipelago /ˌɑːkɪˈpelɪɡəʊ/ NOUN [plural **archipelagoes** or **archipelagos**] a group of small islands. A geography word. (**arquipélago**)

architect /ˈɑːkɪtekt/ NOUN [plural **architects**] someone whose job is to design buildings (**arquiteto**)

• **architectural** /ˌɑːkɪˈtektʃərəl/ ADJECTIVE to do with the design of buildings □ *architectural features* (**arquitetônico**)

archive — ark

- **architecturally** /ˌɑːkɪˈtektʃərəli/ ADVERB in a way that is to do with the design of buildings □ *Architecturally, the city is very interesting.* (arquitetonicamente)
- **architecture** /ˈɑːkɪtektʃə(r)/ NOUN, NO PLURAL
  1 designing buildings □ *He studied architecture.* (arquitetura)
  2 a style of building □ *modern architecture* (arquitetura)

archive /ˈɑːkaɪv/ ▶ NOUN [plural **archives**]
1 a collection of historical records about a place, organization, family, etc. □ *The information is kept in the company archives.* (arquivo)
2 a place on a computer where files that are not often used are stored. A computing word. (arquivo)
▶ VERB [**archives, archiving, archived**] to put paper or computer documents in an archive. A computing word. (arquivar)

archway /ˈɑːtʃweɪ/ NOUN [plural **archways**] an entrance or a passage with an arch (= curved structure) over it (arcada)

Arctic /ˈɑːktɪk/ ▶ NOUN **the Arctic** the area of the world around the North Pole (Ártico)
▶ ADJECTIVE
1 to do with the Arctic □ *the Arctic Ocean* (Ártico)
2 arctic extremely cold □ *They camped in arctic conditions.* (ártico)

ardent /ˈɑːdənt/ ADJECTIVE having strong feelings □ *an ardent football fan* (ardente)

arduous /ˈɑːdjuəs/ ADJECTIVE difficult or physically hard □ *an arduous journey/task* (árduo)

are /ɑː(r)/ VERB the present tense of the verb **be** when it is used with you, we and they □ *They are hungry.* □ *Are we late?* (ver **be**)

> Note that instead of **you are, we are** and **they are**, people often say or write the short forms, **you're, we're** and **they're** □ *You're late.* □ *We're here!* □ *They're over there.*

area /ˈeəriə/ NOUN [plural **areas**]
1 a part of a place □ *There are a lot of farms in this area.* □ *We work with children from deprived areas of the city.* (área)
2 a subject or activity □ *What area of medicine do you specialize in?* (área)
3 the size of a surface, that you measure in square units of measurement □ *A carpet that is 5 metres by 5 metres has an area of 25 square metres.* (área)
4 a part of a building or place used for a particular purpose □ *a children's play area* □ *a cooking area* (área)

arena /əˈriːnə/ NOUN [plural **arenas**] a large space for sports or concerts with seats all around it (arena)

aren't /ɑːnt/ a short way to say and write 'are not' □ *These aren't my boots.* (ver **be**)

- **arguable** /ˈɑːgjuəbəl/ ADJECTIVE if something is arguable, it is possible that it is true □ *It is arguable that prison was good for him.* (discutível)
- **arguably** /ˈɑːgjuəbli/ ADVERB something is arguably true if it is possible to believe it □ *He is arguably the best player we've ever had.* (discutivelmente)

argue /ˈɑːgjuː/ VERB [**argues, arguing, argued**]
1 to speak in an angry way with someone because you disagree with them □ + **with** *The children never stop arguing with each other.* □ + **about/over** *They were arguing about where to go on holiday.* (discutir)
2 to give reasons for thinking or believing something □ + **that** *The manager argued that the shop would have to close.* □ + **for** *They argued for an increase in their pay.* (sustentar, manifestar)

- **argument** /ˈɑːgjumənt/ NOUN [plural **arguments**]
  1 an angry discussion (discussão) □ *The kids were having an argument.* (brigando) □ *a heated argument* (= a very angry argument) (discussão acalorada) □ + **about** *an argument about money*
  2 a reason for having a particular point of view □ + **against** *My argument against the plan is that we just don't have the money.* (razão, argumento)
- **argumentative** /ˌɑːgjuˈmentətɪv/ ADJECTIVE an argumentative person often argues with other people (argumentativo, lógico)

aria /ˈɑːriə/ NOUN [plural **arias**] a song in an opera for one person to sing (ária)

arid /ˈærɪd/ ADJECTIVE very dry □ *arid regions* (árido)

arise /əˈraɪz/ VERB [**arises, arising, arose, arisen**] to happen □ *A small problem has arisen.* (surgir)

aristocracy /ˌærɪˈstɒkrəsi/ NOUN [plural **aristocracies**] people of a country's highest social class, often connected to royal families □ *Only members of the aristocracy are invited to these occasions.* (aristocracia)

- **aristocrat** /ˈærɪstəkræt/ NOUN [plural **aristocrats**] someone from a family of a very high social class, who often has a title like Lord or Lady (aristocrata)
- **aristocratic** /ˌærɪstəˈkrætɪk/ ADJECTIVE belonging to or typical of the aristocracy □ *an aristocratic family* (aristocrático)

arithmetic /əˈrɪθmətɪk/ NOUN, NO PLURAL mathematics that involves processes such as adding and multiplying □ *simple arithmetic* (aritmética)

- **arithmetical** /ˌærɪθˈmetɪkəl/ ADJECTIVE to do with calculating numbers □ *an arithmetical problem* (aritmético)

ark /ɑːk/ NOUN [plural **arks**] the boat that carried Noah, his family and two of every animal during the flood in the Bible story (arca)

arm¹ /ɑːm/ NOUN [plural **arms**]
1 the part of your body between your shoulder and your hand ◻ *I put my arm round his shoulder.* ▣ *She folded her arms* (= crossed one over the other close to her body). (**braço**)
2 the arm of a piece of clothing is the sleeve (**manga**)
3 the part of a chair that you rest your arms on (**braço**)
4 arm in arm holding someone's arm ◻ *They walked arm in arm along the beach.* (**de braços dados**)
⇨ go to **arms**

arm² /ɑːm/ VERB [**arms, arming, armed**] to give someone a weapon to fight with ◻ *The crowd was armed with sticks and knives.* (**armar-se**)

armaments /'ɑːməmənts/ PLURAL NOUN weapons and other military equipment (**armamentos**)

armchair /'ɑːmtʃeə(r)/ NOUN [plural **armchairs**] a comfortable chair with sides for resting your arms on (**poltrona**)

armed /ɑːmd/ ADJECTIVE carrying a weapon (**armado**) ▣ *heavily armed* (**fortemente armado**) ▣ *armed robbery/burglary* (**assalto à mão armada**)

armed forces /ɑːmd 'fɔːsɪz/ PLURAL NOUN the armed forces the military groups of a country, for example its army (**forças armadas**)

armistice /'ɑːmɪstɪs/ NOUN [plural **armistices**] an agreement between enemies to stop fighting in a war (**armistício, trégua**)

armor /'ɑːmə(r)/ NOUN, NO PLURAL the US spelling of armour (**armadura**)

• **armored** /'ɑːməd/ ADJECTIVE the US spelling of armoured (**blindado**)

armour /'ɑːmə(r)/ NOUN, NO PLURAL
1 metal covers worn by soldiers in the past to protect their bodies (**armadura**) ▣ *a suit of armour* (**conjunto de armadura**)
2 metal covers used to protect military vehicles (**blindagem**)

• **armoured** /'ɑːməd/ ADJECTIVE an armoured vehicle is protected by layers of metal (**blindado**)

armpit /'ɑːmpɪt/ NOUN [plural **armpits**] the part under your arm where it joins your body (**axila**)

arms /ɑːmz/ PLURAL NOUN weapons (**armas**) ▣ *the arms race* (= when countries try to get more and better weapons than each other) (**corrida armamentista**) ◻ *arms manufacturers*

◆ IDIOM **be up in arms** to be very angry about something and trying to stop it ◻ *Local people are up in arms over proposals for a nuclear power station.* (**estar em pé de guerra**)

army /'ɑːmɪ/ NOUN [plural **armies**]
1 an organization of soldiers (**exército**) ▣ *He joined the army after leaving school.* (**alistou-se ao exército**) ◻ *the US Army* ◻ *an army officer*
2 a large number of people ◻ *An army of decorators transformed the building.* (**multidão**)

aroma /ə'rəʊmə/ NOUN [plural **aromas**] a nice smell, especially of food (**aroma**)

aromatherapy /əˌrəʊmə'θerəpɪ/ NOUN, NO PLURAL using the oils of plants and flowers that have different smells to treat people who are not well (**aromaterapia**)

aromatic /ˌærə'mætɪk/ ADJECTIVE having a good smell ◻ *aromatic plants* (**aromático**)

arose /ə'rəʊz/ PAST TENSE OF **arise** (**surgido**)

around /ə'raʊnd/ PREPOSITION, ADVERB
1 on all sides ◻ *We were sitting around the table.* (**ao redor**)
2 in or to different parts of a place ◻ *We walked around the city.* ◻ *There were clothes lying around everywhere.* ◻ *The children are allowed to run around all over the place.* (**ao redor**)
3 to several different people ◻ *We passed the drinks around.* (**ao redor**)
4 about ◻ *They should arrive at around 4 o'clock.* ◻ *I weigh around sixty kilos.* (**aproximadamente**)
5 to face the opposite direction ◻ *He turned around and pointed the gun at me.* (**em direção oposta**)
6 in a circular movement ◻ *Twist the knife around in the hole.* (**em círculo**)
7 near ◻ *Is there a teacher around?* (**por perto**)

arouse /ə'raʊz/ VERB [**arouses, arousing, aroused**] to make someone have a particular feeling ◻ *His strange behaviour aroused my suspicion.* (**despertar**)

arrange /ə'reɪndʒ/ VERB [**arranges, arranging, arranged**]
1 to make plans or to prepare for something ◻ *Who is arranging the wedding?* ◻ *+ to do something He's arranged to go out with his mates tonight.* ◻ *+ for I've arranged for a taxi to pick him up later.* (**planejar**)
2 to put things in a particular order ◻ *Arrange the flowers in the vase.* ◻ *All his books are arranged in alphabetical order by author.* (**arrumar**)

• **arrangement** /ə'reɪndʒmənt/ NOUN [plural **arrangements**]
1 a plan that is made so that something can happen the way you want it to (**providência**) ▣ *They made arrangements to meet back at the car.* (**tomou providências**) ◻ *If he's not back in time, we'll have to make other arrangements.*
2 an agreement with someone (**acordo**) ▣ *We managed to come to an arrangement about who should do the cooking.* (**chegar a um acordo**) ◻ *I have an arrangement with my sister to look after the children on Fridays.*
3 a group of things that are in a particular order or position ◻ *a flower arrangement* (**arranjo**)

array /əˈreɪ/ NOUN [plural **arrays**] a large group of things □ *He owns a vast array of electronic equipment.* (**conjunto**)

arrears /əˈrɪəz/ PLURAL NOUN **in arrears** owing money on regular payments □ *He's in arrears with his rent.* (**em atraso**)

arrest /əˈrest/ ▶ VERB [**arrests, arresting, arrested**] if the police arrest someone, they take them to the police station because they may have committed a crime □ **+ for** *He was arrested for causing a disturbance.* (**prender**)
▶ NOUN [plural **arrests**]
1 when the police arrest someone (**prisão**) *Police have made three arrests in connection with the murder.* (**fazer prisões**)
2 under arrest someone is under arrest when the police are keeping them because they may have committed a crime (**detido**)

arrival /əˈraɪvəl/ NOUN [plural **arrivals**]
1 *no plural* when someone reaches a place □ *We are all looking forward to Alice's arrival.* (**chegada**)
2 on arrival when you arrive □ *On arrival, go straight to the meeting room.* (**no desembarque**)
3 a person or thing that has come to a place or started to exist □ *Come and meet the new arrivals.* □ *the arrival of spring* (**chegada**)

arrive /əˈraɪv/ VERB [**arrives, arriving, arrived**]
1 to reach a place □ **+ at** *Please arrive at the station by 5.30.* □ **+ in** *We arrived in Warsaw on Friday.* □ *If they don't arrive soon, we'll have to go without them.* (**chegar**)
2 to start to happen or exist □ *Would her birthday ever arrive?* (**chegar**)

> ➤ Remember that you **arrive** in a city or country:
> ✓ *We arrived in Madrid at 10 o'clock that night.*
> ✗ *We arrived to Madrid at 10 o'clock that night.*

◆ PHRASAL VERB **arrive at something** to manage to make an agreement, decision, etc. □ *We haven't really arrived at any conclusions.* (**chegar a uma decisão/acordo**)

arrogance /ˈærəgəns/ NOUN, NO PLURAL a feeling of being better or more important than other people (**arrogância**)

• **arrogant** /ˈærəgənt/ ADJECTIVE arrogant people think they are better or more important than other people □ *He's an extremely arrogant man.* (**arrogante**)

arrow /ˈærəʊ/ NOUN [plural **arrows**]
1 a pointed shape used to show a particular direction □ *Follow the red arrows to the X-ray department.* (**seta**)
2 a thin, pointed stick that is used as a weapon (**flecha**)

arsenal /ˈɑːsənəl/ NOUN [plural **arsenals**] a store for weapons (**arsenal**)

arsenic /ˈɑːsnɪk/ NOUN, NO PLURAL a strong poison (**arsênio**)

arson /ˈɑːsən/ NOUN, NO PLURAL the crime of setting fire to a building on purpose (**incêndio criminoso**)

• **arsonist** /ˈɑːsənɪst/ NOUN [plural **arsonists**] someone who sets fire to a building on purpose (**incendiário**)

art /ɑːt/ NOUN [plural **arts**]
1 *no plural* the beautiful things that people make and invent in painting, music, writing, etc. (**arte**)
2 a skill that you use to do or make something □ *the art of conversation* (**arte**)
3 the arts subjects that you can study that are not sciences (**Humanidades**)

artefact /ˈɑːtɪfækt/ NOUN [plural **artefacts**] a very old object that tells us something about history (**artefato**)

artery /ˈɑːtəri/ NOUN [plural **arteries**] a tube that takes blood from your heart to the rest of your body. A biology word. (**artéria**)

artful /ˈɑːtfʊl/ ADJECTIVE clever in a slightly dishonest way (**ardiloso**)

arthritic /ɑːˈθrɪtɪk/ ADJECTIVE swollen and painful because of arthritis □ *her arthritic hip* (**artrítico**)

arthritis /ɑːˈθraɪtɪs/ NOUN, NO PLURAL a disease that makes your joints (= knees, hips, etc.) swollen and painful (**artrite**)

artichoke /ˈɑːtɪtʃəʊk/ NOUN [plural **artichokes**] a round green vegetable with thick pointed leaves that you cook and eat the bottom part of (**alcachofra**)

article /ˈɑːtɪkəl/ NOUN [plural **articles**]
1 a piece of writing in a magazine or newspaper (**artigo**) *Maya wrote an article for the school magazine.* (**escreveu um artigo**) *I read an interesting article in the newspaper.* (**li um artigo**) □ **+ about/on** an article about farming
2 a thing (**item, peça**) *There were a few articles of clothing on the floor.* (**peça de roupa**)
3 in grammar, the words 'a' and 'the' (**artigo**)

articulate /ɑːˈtɪkjʊleɪt/ VERB [**articulates, articulating, articulated**] to express your ideas and feelings clearly in words. A formal word. □ *His books articulate his vision for a better world.* (**articular**)

articulated /ɑːˈtɪkjʊleɪtɪd/ ADJECTIVE an articulated truck has two parts which are joined together to make turning easier (**articulado**)

articulation /ɑːˌtɪkjʊˈleɪʃən/ NOUN, NO PLURAL how clearly someone speaks (**articulação**)

artifact /ˈɑːtɪfækt/ NOUN [plural **artifacts**] another spelling of **artefact** (**artefato**)

artificial /ˌɑːtɪˈfɪʃəl/ ADJECTIVE looking natural, but made by a person or machine □ *artificial snow* (**artificial**)

artificial intelligence /ˌɑːtɪˈfɪʃəl ɪnˈtelɪdʒəns/ NOUN, NO PLURAL the use of computers that try to act like human brains (**inteligência artificial**)

artificially /ˌɑːtɪˈfɪʃəli/ ADVERB not naturally □ *artificially sweetened drinks* (**artificialmente**)

artificial respiration /ˌɑːtɪˈfɪʃəl ˌrespəˈreɪʃən/ NOUN, NO PLURAL the process of blowing air into the nose or mouth of someone who has stopped breathing in order to make them start breathing again (**respiração artificial**)

artillery /ɑːˈtɪləri/ NOUN, NO PLURAL big guns that an army uses (**artilharia**)

artisan /ˌɑːtɪˈzæn/ NOUN [*plural* **artisans**] someone who is skilled at making something with their hands (**artesão**)

artist /ˈɑːtɪst/ NOUN [*plural* **artists**]
1 someone who paints or draws things □ *the well-known French artist, Claude Monet* (**pintor**)
2 a performer, for example a singer or a dancer (**artista**)

artiste /ɑːˈtiːst/ NOUN [*plural* **artistes**] a performer such as a dancer or a singer (**artista**)

artistic /ɑːˈtɪstɪk/ ADJECTIVE
1 to do with art □ *The ballet was one of his greatest artistic achievements.* (**artístico**)
2 good at art □ *Emma's very artistic.* (**artístico**)
• **artistically** /ɑːˈtɪstɪkəli/ ADVERB done in a way that is nice to look at □ *an artistically decorated room* (**artisticamente**)

artistry /ˈɑːtɪstri/ NOUN, NO PLURAL the skill of a painter, musician, poet, etc. (**talento artístico, vocação**)

as /əz/ CONJUNCTION, PREPOSITION
1 as ... as used to compare things □ *Are you as tall as me?* □ *This restaurant's not as cheap as the other one.* (**tão ... como**)
2 while □ *As we climbed, the air got colder.* (**conforme**)
3 used to talk about the purpose or job of something or someone □ *She works as a teacher.* □ *I use this room as my study.* (**como**)
4 as if/as though used to talk about how something seems □ *He looks as if he's going to faint.* □ *She cried as if her heart was broken.* (**como se**)
5 because □ *I went first as I was the youngest.* (**porque**)
6 in the same way □ *As I thought, most people had already left.* (**da mesma maneira**)

asap /ˌeɪeseɪˈpiː/ ABBREVIATION as soon as possible (**o mais rápido possível**)

asbestos /æsˈbestəs/ NOUN, NO PLURAL a grey poisonous material that does not burn (**amianto**)

ASBO /ˈæzbəʊ/ ABBREVIATION antisocial behaviour order; an official order from a court in the UK that says that someone must stop their bad behaviour or they will be punished (**abreviação de Antisocial Behaviour Order – Ordem do Comportamento Antissocial**)

ascend /əˈsend/ VERB [**ascends, ascending, ascended**]
1 a formal word that means to climb something □ *She began to ascend the narrow staircase.* (**ascender**)
2 a formal word that means to go up □ *a bird ascending into the sky* (**elevar-se**)
• **ascending** /əˈsendɪŋ/ ADJECTIVE **in ascending order** with the lowest, worst, etc. first and the highest, best, etc. last □ *Arrange the points in ascending order of importance.* (**em ordem ascendente**)
• **ascent** /əˈsent/ NOUN [*plural* **ascents**] a movement or climb up □ *The plane will now begin its ascent to 50,000 feet.* (**ascensão**)

ascertain /ˌæsəˈteɪn/ VERB [**ascertains, ascertaining, ascertained**] a formal word meaning to find something out □ *It should be possible to ascertain where he was born.* (**apurar**)

ascribe /əˈskraɪb/
♦ PHRASAL VERB [**ascribes, ascribing, ascribed**] **ascribe something to something/someone** to say that something is caused by something or someone □ *He ascribed the failure of his business to lack of trained staff.* (**atribuir algo a algo/alguém**)

asexual reproduction /eɪˌsekʃuəl ˌriːprəˈdʌkʃən/ NOUN, NO PLURAL when an animal or plant creates new animals or plants without sex. A biology word. (**reprodução assexuada**)

ash /æʃ/ NOUN [*plural* **ashes**]
1 the white powder that remains after something is burnt (**cinza**)
2 a tree with silver-grey bark (= hard outer covering) (**freixo**)

ashamed /əˈʃeɪmd/ ADJECTIVE feeling embarrassed or guilty about something □ + *of I am deeply ashamed of everything I said, and I apologize.* (**envergonhado**) 🔊 *You should be ashamed of yourself, behaving like that.* (**envergonhar-se de si mesmo**) □ + *that I felt ashamed that I had never visited him in hospital.*

ashore /əˈʃɔː(r)/ ADVERB onto the land at the edge of a sea, river, etc. □ *We went ashore for dinner and returned to the ship later.* (**na praia**)

ashtray /ˈæʃtreɪ/ NOUN [*plural* **ashtrays**] a small dish for the ash from people's cigarettes (**cinzeiro**)

Asian /ˈeɪʒən, ˈeɪʃən/ ▶ ADJECTIVE to do with Asia, or from Asia □ *Asian art* (**asiático**)
▶ NOUN [*plural* **Asians**] someone who comes from Asia (**asiático**)

aside

aside /əˈsaɪd/ ADVERB to or on one side (ao lado) 🔲 *Please stand aside and let us through.* (fique de lado)

ask /ɑːsk/ VERB [**asks, asking, asked**]
1 to say something as a question 🔲 *She asked how old I was.* 🔲 *+ about They asked us about our families.* (perguntar)
2 to say that you want someone to give you something 🔲 *+ for I asked Joanne for some food.* (pedir)
3 to say that you want someone to do something 🔲 *+ to do something He asked me to close the door.* (pedir)
4 to invite 🔲 *+ to We've asked twenty people to our party.* (convidar)

> Remember that you **ask someone**. You do not **ask to someone**:
> ✓ *He asked me the time.*
> ✗ *He asked to me the time.*

◆ PHRASAL VERBS **ask after someone** to ask about someone's health and what they are doing (perguntar como alguém está) 🔲 *Rob was asking after you.* **ask someone out** to invite someone to go somewhere, often as a way of starting a romantic relationship (convidar alguém para sair)

askew /əˈskjuː/ ADVERB not straight 🔲 *Dom's collar was open and his tie was askew.* (torto)

asleep /əˈsliːp/ ADJECTIVE
1 if you are asleep, you are sleeping 🔲 *Don't wake her if she's asleep.* (adormecido) 🔲 *The baby was fast asleep* (= deeply asleep) *in her pram.* (dormir profundamente) 🔲 *She got out of bed, still half asleep* (= very tired). (muito cansado)
2 fall asleep to start sleeping 🔲 *He fell asleep in front of the television.* (adormecer)

asparagus /əˈspærəɡəs/ NOUN. NO PLURAL a vegetable with long green stems (aspargo)

aspect /ˈæspekt/ NOUN [*plural* **aspects**] a part of a situation or subject 🔲 *Newspapers have examined every aspect of her life.* (aspecto)

aspersions /əˈspɜːʃənz/ PLURAL NOUN **cast aspersions on something/someone** to criticize something or someone 🔲 *Are you casting aspersions on my driving skills?* (difamar algo/alguém)

asphalt /ˈæsfælt/ NOUN, NO PLURAL a black substance used for making roads (asfalto)

asphyxiate /əsˈfɪksieɪt/ VERB [**asphyxiates, asphyxiating, asphyxiated**] if someone is asphyxiated, they die because air cannot get into their lungs (asfixiar, sufocar)
• **asphyxiation** /əsˌfɪksiˈeɪʃən/ NOUN, NO PLURAL when someone is asphyxiated (sufocamento)

aspiration /ˌæspəˈreɪʃən/ NOUN [*plural* **aspirations**] a hope that you will get or achieve something 🔲 *She has aspirations to be a lawyer.* (aspiração, desejo)

assert

aspire /əˈspaɪə(r)/ VERB [**aspires, aspiring, aspired**] **aspire to something/to do something** to hope that you will get or achieve something 🔲 *He aspires to be prime minister one day.* (aspirar a algo)

aspirin /ˈæsprɪn/ NOUN [*plural* **aspirin** or **aspirins**]
1 *no plural* a medicine that stops pain (aspirina) 🔲 *He takes aspirin every day.* (toma aspirina)
2 a pill that contains this medicine (aspirina) 🔲 *I've just taken a couple of aspirins for my headache.* (tomou aspirina)

ass /æs/ NOUN [*plural* **asses**] an old-fashioned word for a **donkey** (asno)

assailant /əˈseɪlənt/ NOUN [*plural* **assailants**] a formal word for someone who attacks someone (assaltante)

assassin /əˈsæsɪn/ NOUN [*plural* **assassins**] someone who kills an important person, for example a politician (assassino)
• **assassinate** /əˈsæsɪneɪt/ VERB [**assassinates, assassinating, assassinated**] to kill a famous person (assassinar)
• **assassination** /əˌsæsɪˈneɪʃən/ NOUN [*plural* **assassinations**] the murder of a famous person (assassinato)

assault /əˈsɔːlt/ ▶ NOUN [*plural* **assaults**] an attack (ataque) 🔲 *It was a violent assault on an elderly woman.* (ataque violento)
▶ VERB [**assaults, assaulting, assaulted**] to attack someone (atacar, agredir)

assemble /əˈsembəl/ VERB [**assembles, assembling, assembled**]
1 to bring several things or people together 🔲 *We've assembled a choir for the concert.* (reunir)
2 to come together in a group 🔲 *Please assemble in the hall after the show.* (agregar)
3 to make something by putting several parts together 🔲 *Where are the instructions for assembling the bookcase?* (construir, montar)
• **assembly** /əˈsemblɪ/ NOUN [*plural* **assemblies**]
1 making something by joining several parts together 🔲 *These are the assembly instructions.* (reunião, montagem)
2 a regular meeting for everyone in a school (assembleia)
3 a group of people who make decisions for a country or an organization 🔲 *the General Assembly of the United Nations* (assembleia)

assent /əˈsent/ ▶ NOUN, NO PLURAL a formal word that means agreement (assentimento, concordância)
▶ VERB [**assents, assenting, assented**] a formal word that means to agree (consentir, concordar)

assert /əˈsɜːt/ VERB [**asserts, asserting, asserted**]
1 assert yourself to behave in a very confident way (impor-se)
2 assert your authority/independence, etc. to show that you are in control/independent, etc. (impor sua autoridade/independência)

3 to say that something is true □ *He asserted that he had done nothing wrong.* (afirmar)

- **assertion** /əˈsɜːʃən/ NOUN [*plural* assertions] something that someone says is true □ *We know Nigel broke the TV in spite of his assertions to the contrary.* (afirmação)

- **assertive** /əˈsɜːtɪv/ ADJECTIVE confident and not afraid to say what you think (afirmativo, positivo)

assess /əˈses/ VERB [assesses, assessing, assessed] to examine something and make a judgment about it □ *One of our agents will assess the damage to your car.* (avaliar)

- **assessment** /əˈsesmənt/ NOUN [*plural* assessments] an opinion based on examining something □ *What is your assessment of the situation?* (avaliação)

asset /ˈæset/ NOUN [*plural* assets]

1 someone or something that helps you succeed □ *Sam is a tremendous asset to the team.* (recurso)

2 money or property that a person or a company owns (propriedade)

assiduous /əˈsɪdjuəs/ ADJECTIVE working very hard and carefully. A formal word. (assíduo)

assign /əˈsaɪn/ VERB [assigns, assigning, assigned]

1 to give someone a job or a responsibility □ *He had been assigned to work on the project.* (atribuir)

2 to give someone something or an amount of something □ *Each passenger was assigned a small amount of food.* (conceder)

- **assignment** /əˈsaɪnmənt/ NOUN [*plural* assignments] a job someone has given you to do □ *I've got three homework assignments to finish by Friday.* (tarefa)

assimilate /əˈsɪmɪleɪt/ VERB [assimilates, assimilating, assimilated]

1 to learn and understand new information, skills, etc. (assimilar)

2 to become part of a group or society □ *The immigrants were keen to assimilate into Dutch society.* (incorporar)

assist /əˈsɪst/ ▶ VERB [assists, assisting, assisted] to help □ *Villagers assisted in the search for the girl.* (auxiliar)

- **assistance** /əˈsɪstəns/ NOUN, NO PLURAL help (auxílio) 🔁 *The charity provides financial assistance to people in need.* (fornece auxílio, assistência) 🔁 *Can I be of any assistance* (= can I help)? (poder ajudar em algo)

- **assistant** /əˈsɪstənt/ NOUN [*plural* assistants]
1 someone whose job is to help someone else (assistente) 🔁 *She's a teaching assistant at the local school.* (assistente de sala de aula) 🔁 *You can speak to the assistant manager.* (assistente administrativo)

2 someone who works in a shop 🔁 *She worked as a shop assistant.* (vendedor)

associate ▶ VERB /əˈsəʊʃieɪt/ [associates, associating, associated]

1 to be related to or caused by something □ *Heavy pollution is associated with increased road travel.* (associar)

2 to connect two things in your mind □ *He has the manners that we associate with an English gentleman.* (associar)

◆ PHRASAL VERB **associate with someone** to spend time with someone (envolver-se com alguém)
▶ NOUN /əˈsəʊʃiət/ [*plural* associates] someone who you know from your work (sócio) 🔁 *business associates* (sócio nos negócios)

- **associated** /əˈsəʊʃieɪtɪd/ ADJECTIVE related □ *a disease with associated problems* (associado)

- **association** /əˌsəʊsiˈeɪʃən/ NOUN [*plural* associations]

1 an organization for people with similar interests □ *a professional association for teachers* (associação)

2 a connection □ *He stresses the association between obesity and early death.* (associação)

3 in association with working together with □ *They produced the programme in association with na American company.* (com a parceria de)

assonance /ˈæsənəns/ NOUN, NO PLURAL when parts of words have similar sounds (assonância)

assorted /əˈsɔːtɪd/ ADJECTIVE of different types □ *assorted flavours* (sortido)

- **assortment** /əˈsɔːtmənt/ NOUN [*plural* assortments] a mixture of different types □ *a strange assortment of people* (sortimento)

assume /əˈsjuːm/ VERB [assumes, assuming, assumed]

1 to think something is true, although you have no proof □ *Oh sorry, I assumed that you had met each other before.* (supor)

2 assume control/power/responsibility, etc. to take control/power/responsibility, etc. □ *Jones will assume responsibility for the Paris office.* (assumir o controle/poder/responsabilidade etc.)

- **assumed** /əˈsjuːmd/ ADJECTIVE an assumed name is a false one (fictício)

- **assuming** /əˈsjuːmɪŋ/ CONJUNCTION if □ *Assuming he's not too tired, we could take him out for a meal.* (pretensioso)

- **assumption** /əˈsʌmpʃən/ NOUN [*plural* assumptions]

1 something you think is true (suposição) 🔁 *You can't make any assumptions about the weather on the mountain.* (fazer suposição alguma)

2 when someone takes control, power, responsibility, etc. (pretensão)

assurance /əˈʃʊərəns/ NOUN [*plural* assurances]

1 a promise (promessa) 🔁 *He gave me an assurance that the work would be completed.* (fez uma promessa)

2 confidence □ *Tim plays tennis with complete assurance.* (confiança)

assure

assure /əˈʃʊə(r)/ VERB [assures, assuring, assured] to tell someone that something is certainly true or will certainly happen □ *Mr Harris has assured us that the car will be ready tomorrow.* (assegurar)

• **assured** /əˈʃʊəd/ ADJECTIVE
1 confident □ *an assured manner* (confiante)
2 be assured of something to be certain to get something □ *You can be assured of a warm welcome at the hotel.* (estar seguro quanto a algo)

asterisk /ˈæstərɪsk/ NOUN [plural **asterisks**] a mark (*), used in writing (asterisco)

asteroid /ˈæstərɔɪd/ NOUN [plural **asteroids**] a large piece of rock that moves around in space (asteroide)

asthma /ˈæsmə/ NOUN, NO PLURAL an illness that makes breathing difficult (asma)

• **asthmatic** /æsˈmætɪk/ ▶ ADJECTIVE suffering from asthma (asmático)
▶ NOUN [plural **asthmatics**] someone who has asthma (asmático)

astonish /əˈstɒnɪʃ/ VERB [astonishes, astonishing, astonished] to surprise someone very much □ *His arrest has astonished neighbours and friends.* (surpreender)

• **astonished** /əˈstɒnɪʃt/ ADJECTIVE very surprised □ *I was astonished at how much the place had changed.* (surpreso)

• **astonishing** /əˈstɒnɪʃɪŋ/ ADJECTIVE very surprising □ *Her mind worked with astonishing speed.* (surpreendente)

• **astonishment** /əˈstɒnɪʃmənt/ NOUN, NO PLURAL the state of being astonished □ *To my great astonishment, she agreed that I could stay.* □ *We stared in astonishment at the painting.* (surpresa)

astound /əˈstaʊnd/ VERB [astounds, astounding, astounded] to surprise or shock someone very much □ *The information astounded us all.* (assustar)

• **astounded** /əˈstaʊndɪd/ ADJECTIVE very surprised or shocked □ *He was astounded at the price.* (assustado, surpreso)

• **astounding** /əˈstaʊndɪŋ/ ADJECTIVE very surprising or shocking □ *Her knowledge of Chinese is astounding.* (espantoso, assustador)

astray /əˈstreɪ/ ADVERB
1 go astray to become lost □ *Too many letters are going astray in the post.* (extraviar-se)
2 lead someone astray to encourage someone to do bad things (incentivar mau comportamento)

astride /əˈstraɪd/ PREPOSITION with one leg on each side □ *sitting astride a horse* (a cavalo)

astro- /ˈæstrə/ PREFIX astro- is added to the start of words to mean 'to do with the stars or space' □ *astronomer* (astro-)

astrologer /əˈstrɒlədʒə(r)/ NOUN [plural **astrologers**] someone who tells people what may happen to them, by looking at the movement of stars (astrólogo)

atheism

astrology /əˈstrɒlədʒɪ/ NOUN, NO PLURAL the study of how the movement of stars may affect our lives (astrologia)

astronaut /ˈæstrənɔːt/ NOUN [plural **astronauts**] someone who travels into space (astronauta)

astronomer /əˈstrɒnəmə(r)/ NOUN [plural **astronomers**] someone who studies stars and planets (astrônomo)

astronomical /ˌæstrəˈnɒmɪkəl/ ADJECTIVE
1 very large □ *The cost was astronomical.* (astronômico)
2 to do with astronomy (astronômico)

• **astronomically** /ˌæstrəˈnɒmɪkəlɪ/ ADVERB very much □ *Prices have risen astronomically.* (astronomicamente)

astronomy /əˈstrɒnəmɪ/ NOUN, NO PLURAL the study of stars and planets (astronomia)

astute /əˈstjuːt/ ADJECTIVE quick to understand things and able to take advantage of them □ *His remarks were politically astute.* (astuto)

asylum /əˈsaɪləm/ NOUN, NO PLURAL when someone is allowed to stay in a country because they are in danger in their own country (asilo) 🔂 *Many people seek asylum in this country.* (procuraram asilo) 🔂 *He was granted asylum in 2006.* (recebeu asilo)

asylum seeker /əˈsaɪləm ˌsiːkə(r)/ NOUN [plural **asylum seekers**] someone who is trying to get asylum in a country (refugiado)

asymmetrical /ˌeɪsɪˈmetrɪkəl/ ADJECTIVE not the same shape on both sides (assimétrico)

at /ət/ PREPOSITION
1 used to show the position of something or something □ *Meet me at the station.* □ *The car is at Clara's house.* □ *He's still at work.* (em)
2 used to show the time or period that something happens □ *School finishes at 4 o'clock.* □ *Will you be here at the weekend?* □ *I always visit my parents at Christmas.* (em)
3 towards □ *He threw a bucket of water at me.* □ *Look at me!* □ *She drove the car straight at him.* (para)
4 bad/good at something used to show someone's level of ability □ *He's good at football.* (bom/ruim em algo)
5 used to show the price, speed, level, etc. of something □ *We bought four bottles at 75p each.* □ *The car was travelling at 70 miles an hour.* (a)
6 used to describe someone's reaction □ *He broke down at the news.* (por causa de)
7 at all used for emphasis, for example when talking about something that does not exist □ *Doesn't he have any friends at all?* □ *I'm not looking forward to the party at all.* (absolutamente)

ate /eɪt/ PAST TENSE OF **eat** (ver eat)

atheism /ˈeɪθɪɪzəm/ NOUN, NO PLURAL the belief that there is no god (ateísmo)

• **atheist** /ˈeɪθɪɪst/ NOUN [plural **atheists**] someone who does not believe in a god (ateu)

athlete

athlete /ˈæθliːt/ NOUN [plural **athletes**] someone who is good at sports such as running (atleta) ◧ *She is one of the country's* top athletes. (melhores atletas) ◧ *He was an Olympic athlete in 1928.* (atleta olímpico)

- **athletic** /æθˈletɪk/ ADJECTIVE
1 fit and good at sports (atlético)
2 to do with the sports of running, jumping and throwing ☐ *athletic events* (desportivo)

- **athletics** /æθˈletɪks/ NOUN, NO PLURAL the sports that include running, jumping and throwing ☐ *Lee is very good at athletics.* (atletismo)

atlas /ˈætləs/ NOUN [plural **atlases**] a book of maps (atlas)

ATM /ˌeɪtiːˈem/ ABBREVIATION automated teller machine; a machine, usually in the wall outside a bank, where you can get money using a small plastic card (caixa eletrônico)

atmosphere /ˈætməsfɪə(r)/ NOUN [plural **atmospheres**]
1 the feeling that a place or situation has (clima, atmosfera) ☐ *The atmosphere in the company was very friendly.* ☐ + *of Increased crime is creating an atmosphere of fear.* ◧ *We are trying to* create *a relaxed* atmosphere. (criar uma atmosfera)
2 the air around a planet ☐ *the Earth's atmosphere* (atmosfera)

- **atmospheric** /ˌætməsˈferɪk/ ADJECTIVE to do with the air or the atmosphere ☐ *atmospheric pressure* (atmosférico)

atoll /ˈætɒl/ NOUN [plural **atolls**] an island made from a ring of coral (= very small pink bones of sea creatures). A geography word. (atol)

atom /ˈætəm/ NOUN [plural **atoms**] the smallest part of a chemical element ☐ *Water contains two hydrogen atoms and one oxygen atom.* (átomo)

- **atomic** /əˈtɒmɪk/ ADJECTIVE
1 using the power that is created when atoms are broken (atômico) ◧ *an* atomic bomb (bomba atômica) ◧ atomic energy (energia atômica)
2 to do with atoms ☐ *the atomic structure of crystals* (atômico)

atomic mass /əˌtɒmɪk ˈmæs/ NOUN, NO PLURAL the amount of matter in an atom of a particular substance. A chemistry word. (massa atômica)

atomic number /əˌtɒmɪk ˈnʌmbə(r)/ NOUN, NO PLURAL the number of protons (= parts with a positive electrical charge) in the nucleus of a substance. A chemistry word. (número atômico)

atomic weight /əˌtɒmɪk ˈweɪt/ NOUN, NO PLURAL the amount of matter in an atom of a particular substance. A chemistry word. (peso atômico)

atone /əˈtəʊn/ VERB [**atones**, **atoning**, **atoned**] to do something to show that you are sorry for something bad you have done ☐ *She tried to atone for her rudeness by being extra helpful in the house.* (reparar)

atrium /ˈeɪtriəm/ NOUN [plural **atriums**]
1 a high space or an open space in the centre of a building (átrio, saguão)
2 one of the two upper spaces in your heart that push blood around your body. A biology word. (átrio)

atrocious /əˈtrəʊʃəs/ ADJECTIVE very bad ☐ *atrocious weather* (atroz, cruel)

- **atrocity** /əˈtrɒsəti/ NOUN [plural **atrocities**] a very cruel or violent event ☐ *The bombing was Britain's worst terrorist atrocity.* (atrocidade)

attach

attach /əˈtætʃ/ VERB [**attaches**, **attaching**, **attached**]
1 to join one thing to another thing ☐ + *to They attached a rope to the car.* (prender)
2 if you attach a document to an e-mail, you send the document with the e-mail. A computing word. (anexar)

- **attached** /əˈtætʃt/ ADJECTIVE **be attached to someone/something** to like someone or something very much ☐ *Teachers often become attached to their students.* (estar ligado a algo/alguém)

- **attachment** /əˈtætʃmənt/ NOUN [plural **attachments**]
1 a feeling of liking someone or something very much (ligação) ◧ *He felt an* emotional attachment *to the place.* (ligação emocional)
2 a document or picture that you send with an e-mail. A computing word. (anexo) ◧ *Don't* open an attachment *if you don't know who it's from.* (abrir um anexo)
3 an extra part that you can add to a machine to make it do something different (anexo)

attack

attack /əˈtæk/ ▶ VERB [**attacks**, **attacking**, **attacked**]
1 to suddenly try to hurt someone ☐ + *with He attacked her with a knife.* ☐ *A man was attacked and robbed on Friday.* (atacar)
2 to try to destroy a place using weapons ☐ *A violent crowd tried to attack the embassy.* (atacar)
3 to criticize someone or something ☐ *He attacked the government for failing to improve standards in schools.* (atacar)

▶ NOUN [plural **attacks**]
1 a violent act against a place or person (ataque) ◧ *The* attack *was* carried out *by four men.* (ataque realizado) ◧ Terrorist attacks *have killed thousands of people.* (ataques terroristas) ☐ + *on The attack on police officers began when an angry crowd started throwing bottles.*
2 strong criticism ☐ + *on He launched a personal attack on the President.* (ataque)
3 a sudden illness or bad feeling (ataque) ◧ *He had an* asthma attack. (ataque de asma) ☐ + *of I always get an attack of nerves before a performance.*

- **attacker** /əˈtækə(r)/ NOUN [plural **attackers**] a person who tries to hurt someone violently ☐ *Ravi was able to describe his attacker to police.* (agressor)

attain /əˈteɪn/ VERB [attains, attaining, attained] to achieve something □ *He attained a high level of fitness.* (atingir)

• **attainable** /əˈteɪnəbəl/ ADJECTIVE possible to achieve □ *Set yourself challenging but attainable goals.* (atingível)

• **attainment** /əˈteɪnmənt/ NOUN [plural attainments] achievement □ *Levels of educational attainment are low.* (capacidade)

attempt /əˈtempt/ ▶ VERB [attempts, attempting, attempted] to try to do something □ + *to do something He attempted to explain what he meant.* (tentar)

▶ NOUN [plural attempts] when you try to do something (tentativa) 🔊 *Doctors made a desperate attempt to save her life.* (fizeram uma tentativa) 🔊 *She made no attempt to escape.* (não fez tentativa para) □ + *to do something I will resist any attempts to force me to move.*

attend /əˈtend/ VERB [attends, attending, attended]
1 to go to an event. A formal word. □ *More than 100 people attended the meeting.* (comparecer)
2 to go regularly to a school, church, etc. A formal word. □ *James attended a private school.* (frequentar)

> People **attend** formal meetings but people usually **come to** or **go to** parties, friends houses, football matches, etc:
> ✓ *Did Jamie come to the wedding?*
> ✗ *Did Jamie attend the wedding?*

♦ PHRASAL VERB **attend to someone/something** to deal with someone or something □ *She was attending to the funeral arrangements.* (ocupar-se de/com)

• **attendance** /əˈtendəns/ NOUN, NO PLURAL
1 being present somewhere □ *She was given an award for 100% attendance at school.* (presença)
2 the number of people who go to an event or who go to a place regularly □ *Church attendance is declining.* (frequência)

• **attendant** /əˈtendənt/ NOUN [plural attendants] someone whose job is to help people in a public place □ *a parking attendant* (atendente)

attention /əˈtenʃən/ NOUN, NO PLURAL
1 pay attention to listen or watch carefully □ + *to He paid close attention to what was happening.* □ + *to Pay attention to what I'm saying, please.* (prestar atenção)
2 interest and thought that you give to something (atenção) 🔊 *The story attracted attention from all over the world.* (atraiu a atenção)
3 get someone's attention to make someone notice you □ *I waved at her to get her attention.* (atrair a atenção de alguém)
4 action to stop a problem (cuidado) 🔊 *If the symptoms continue, seek medical attention.* (cuidado médico)

• **attentive** /əˈtentɪv/ ADJECTIVE listening or watching carefully □ *an attentive student* (atencioso)

attest /əˈtest/ VERB [attests, attesting, attested] to give proof that something is true. A formal word. □ *As his many friends will attest, he was a quiet man.* (atestar, provar)

attic /ˈætɪk/ NOUN [plural attics] the space in the roof of a house (sótão)

attire /əˈtaɪə(r)/ NOUN, NO PLURAL a formal word for the clothes someone is wearing □ *casual attire* (traje)

• **attired** /əˈtaɪə(r)d/ ADJECTIVE wearing something. A formal word. □ *She was elegantly attired in a black dress.* (trajado, vestido)

attitude /ˈætɪtjuːd/ NOUN [plural attitudes] the way someone thinks about something (atitude) 🔊 *He has a very positive attitude.* (atitude positiva) 🔊 *He needs to change his attitude and start working hard.* (mudar de atitude) □ + *to/towards Jane has a relaxed attitude to life.*

attorney /əˈtɜːrni/ NOUN [plural attorneys] a lawyer (advogado)

attract /əˈtrækt/ VERB [attracts, attracting, attracted]
1 to make someone feel interested in or like someone or something □ *It was his smile that first attracted me.* □ + *to They were attracted to the idea of filming in Sydney because of the weather.* (atrair)
2 to make people come somewhere or do something □ *The museum attracts visitors from all around the world.* □ *The programme attracted 15 million viewers.* (atrair)
3 to make people have a particular reaction (atrair) 🔊 *The show attracted strong criticism.* (atraiu duras críticas) 🔊 *The painting will attract interest from private collectors.* (atraiu interesse)
4 to pull something towards something else using a natural force □ *A magnet attracts iron filings.* (atrair)

• **attraction** /əˈtrækʃən/ NOUN [plural attractions]
1 *no plural* a feeling of liking someone and finding them physically attractive □ + *between The attraction between them was immediate.* (atração)
2 something that people want to visit or do (atração) 🔊 *The Eiffel Tower is a popular tourist attraction.* (atração turística) 🔊 *The town's main attraction is its castle.* (principal atração)
3 a reason for liking something or wanting to do it (atração) □ + *of I can't see the attraction of fast cars.* 🔊 *One of the main attractions of the design is its simplicity.* (atração principal)
4 *no plural* the natural force that pulls things together (atração)

- **attractive** /əˈtræktɪv/ ADJECTIVE
1 nice to look at □ *She was an attractive woman in her late thirties.* □ *The hotel is set in attractive gardens.* (atraente)
2 interesting and worth having or doing (interessante) 🔹 *It's a very attractive offer.* (oferta interessante)
- **attractively** /əˈtræktɪvli/ ADVERB in a pleasant way □ *The house is attractively decorated.* (atrativamente)

attribute¹ /əˈtrɪbjuːt/
◆ PHRASAL VERBS [**attributes, attributing, attributed**] **attribute something to someone** to think that something was made, painted, written, etc. by a particular person □ *The statue had been wrongly attributed to Bernini.* (atribuir algo a alguém) **attribute something to something** to say that something is caused by something □ *He attributed his success to determination.* (atribuir algo a algo)

attribute² /ˈætrɪbjuːt/ NOUN [plural **attributes**] a quality or feature □ *He was chosen for his physical attributes rather than his acting ability.* (atributo)

attuned /əˈtjuːnd/ ADJECTIVE
1 if you are attuned to something, you understand it and know how to deal with it □ *They were very attuned to each other's moods.* (antenado)
2 if you are attuned to a sound, you hear and recognize it very quickly □ *Babies are attuned to the sound of their mother's voice.* (afinado)

aubergine /ˈəʊbəʒiːn/ NOUN [plural **aubergines**] a vegetable with a smooth, shiny, dark purple skin (berinjela)

auburn /ˈɔːbən/ ADJECTIVE auburn hair is reddish-brown (castanho-avermelhado, ruivo)

auction /ˈɔːkʃən/ ▶ NOUN [plural **auctions**] a sale in which the person who offers the most money buys something (leilão)
▶ VERB [**auctions, auctioning, auctioned**] to sell something to the person who offers the most money for it (oferecer em leilão)

- **auctioneer** /ˌɔːkʃəˈnɪə(r)/ NOUN [plural **auctioneers**] someone whose job is to sell things to the person who offers the most money for them (leiloeiro)

audacious /ɔːˈdeɪʃəs/ ADJECTIVE brave and taking risks □ *an audacious plan* □ *an audacious young man* (audacioso, audaz)
- **audacity** /ɔːˈdæsəti/ NOUN, NO PLURAL audacious behaviour (audácia)

audible /ˈɔːdəbəl/ ADJECTIVE able to be heard □ *His voice was barely audible.* (audível)

audience /ˈɔːdɪəns/ NOUN [plural **audiences**]
1 the people who listen to or watch a performance (plateia) 🔹 *My father was in the audience tonight.* (na plateia) 🔹 *Many audience members left before the end of the show.* (membros da plateia)
2 the people who watch a particular television programme, read a particular magazine, etc. (público) 🔹 *The programme attracted an audience of 13 million people.* (atraiu um público) 🔹 *The magazine's target audience is young women.* (público-alvo)

audio- /ˈɔːdɪəʊ/ PREFIX audio- is added to the start of words to mean 'to do with hearing' (audio-)

audio-visual /ˌɔːdɪəʊˈvɪʒjuəl/ ADJECTIVE to do with both hearing and seeing □ *The tour begins with an audio-visual presentation.* (audiovisual)

audit /ˈɔːdɪt/ ▶ NOUN [plural **audits**] an official examination of a company's financial records (auditoria)
▶ VERB [**audits, auditing, audited**] to officially examine a company's financial records (examinar)

audition /ɔːˈdɪʃən/ ▶ NOUN [plural **auditions**] a short performance that an actor, dancer, etc. does so that someone else can decide if they are good enough to be in a play, musical group, etc. (audição) 🔹 *They're holding auditions for the show next week.* (fazendo audições)
▶ VERB [**auditions, auditioning, auditioned**]
1 to do a short performance so that someone can see if you are good enough to be in a play, musical group, etc. (fazer um teste de audição)
2 to watch and listen to performers and try to choose the best ones for something like a play or musical group □ *We auditioned over 100 actors for the part.* (avaliar um teste de audição)

auditor /ˈɔːdɪtə(r)/ NOUN [plural **auditors**] someone who officially examines an organization's financial records (auditor)

auditorium /ˌɔːdɪˈtɔːrɪəm/ NOUN [plural **auditoriums**] the part of a theatre where the audience sits (auditório)

augment /ɔːgˈment/ VERB [**augments, augmenting, augmented**] a formal word that means to increase something (aumentar)

August /ˈɔːgəst/ NOUN the eighth month of the year, after July and before September □ *We'll visit you in August.* (agosto)

aunt /ɑːnt/ or **auntie** or **aunty** /ˈɑːnti/ NOUN [plural **aunts, aunties**]
1 the sister of one of your parents □ *My aunt and uncle live in Canada.* □ *Auntie Emily came to stay.* (tia)
2 your uncle's wife (tia)

au pair /ˌəʊˈpeə(r)/ NOUN [plural **au pairs**] someone who lives with a family in a foreign country and looks after their children (au pair)

aura /ˈɔːrə/ NOUN [plural **auras**] a quality that seems to surround a person, place or situation (aura) 🔹 *There was an aura of mystery around him.* (aura de mistério)

aural /ˈɔːrəl/ ADJECTIVE to do with your ears or hearing □ *an aural examination* (auricular)

auspices

auspices /ˈɔːspɪsɪz/ PLURAL NOUN **under the auspices of something** with the help and support of a particular organization. A formal phrase. (**sob os auspícios de**) □ *The 'Enjoy Reading' scheme was being run under the auspices of the British Council.*

auspicious /ɔːˈspɪʃəs/ ADJECTIVE showing signs that something is going to be successful □ *Their 5-0 win last weekend was an auspicious start to the season.* (**auspicioso**)

austere /ɒˈstɪə(r)/ ADJECTIVE
1 simple and not comfortable □ *an austere lifestyle* (**rigoroso**)
2 unfriendly and severe □ *He was an austere, private man.* (**severo**)
3 plain and with no decoration □ *an austere dining room* (**sóbrio**)
• **austerity** /ɒˈsterətɪ/ NOUN, NO PLURAL an austere quality (**austeridade**)

authentic /ɔːˈθentɪk/ ADJECTIVE real □ *an authentic wartime uniform* (**autêntico**)
• **authenticate** /ɔːˈθentɪkeɪt/ VERB [authenticates, authenticating, authenticated] to prove that something is real or true □ *They weren't able to authenticate the document.* (**autenticar**)
• **authenticity** /ˌɔːθenˈtɪsətɪ/ NOUN, NO PLURAL how real or true something is □ *It's difficult to prove the authenticity of this story.* (**autenticidade**)

author /ˈɔːθə(r)/ NOUN [plural **authors**] a writer □ *Atkinson is the author of four novels.* (**autor**)

authoritarian /ɔːˌθɒrɪˈteərɪən/ ▶ ADJECTIVE trying to control everything and stop people from making their own decisions □ *an authoritarian government* (**autoritário**)
▶ NOUN [plural **authoritarians**] someone who tries to control everything and stop people from making their own decisions (**autoritário**)

authoritative /ɔːˈθɒrɪtətɪv/ ADJECTIVE
1 based on information that is correct □ *It's an authoritative account of what happened.* (**autorizado**)
2 able to make people obey you □ *'Come here at once!', he said in an authoritative voice.* (**autoritário**)

authority /ɔːˈθɒrətɪ/ NOUN [plural **authorities**]
1 no plural power and control (**autoridade**) ▣ *People who are in a position of authority need to behave appropriately.* (**posição de poder**) □ **+ to do something** *As chairman, he has the authority to make decisions.* □ **+ over** *This law gives the government more authority over the police force.*
2 an official organization or government department that controls something (**autoridade**) ▣ *Some local authorities do not have enough money for repairing roads.* (**autoridades locais**)
3 the authorities the police and people who have the power to make people obey laws □ *The British authorities raised concerns over the deal* (**as autoridades**)
4 an expert □ **+ on** *She's a leading authority on climate change.* (**autoridade**)
• **authorization** or **authorisation** /ˌɔːθəraɪˈzeɪʃən/ NOUN, NO PLURAL official permission □ *We need to get authorization for the project.* (**autorização**)
• **authorize** or **authorise** /ˈɔːθəraɪz/ VERB [authorizes, authorizing, authorized] to give official permission for something □ *The government authorized the use of military force.* (**autorizar**)

autism /ˈɔːtɪzəm/ NOUN, NO PLURAL a medical condition in which someone finds it difficult to react to other people and communicate with them (**autismo**)
• **autistic** /ɔːˈtɪstɪk/ ADJECTIVE having autism (**autismo**)

auto /ˈɔːtəʊ/ ADJECTIVE to do with cars □ *the American auto industry* (**automóvel**)

auto- /ˈɔːtəʊ/ PREFIX (**auto-**)
1 auto- is added to the beginning of words to mean 'to do with yourself' □ *autobiography*
2 auto- is added to the beginning of words to mean 'on its own without human help' □ *automatic*

autobiographical /ˌɔːtəˌbaɪəˈɡræfɪkəl/ ADJECTIVE to do with someone's own life □ *Many of the events in Barrie's story are autobiographical.* (**autobiográfico**)
• **autobiography** /ˌɔːtəbaɪˈɒɡrəfɪ/ NOUN [plural **autobiographies**] the story of someone's own life (**autobiografia**)

autocrat /ˈɔːtəkræt/ NOUN [plural **autocrats**] a ruler with complete power (**autocrata**)
• **autocratic** /ˌɔːtəˈkrætɪk/ ADJECTIVE to do with or behaving like an autocrat □ *autocratic behaviour* (**autocrático**)

autograph /ˈɔːtəɡrɑːf/ ▶ NOUN [plural **autographs**] the name of a famous person, written by them (**autógrafo**) ▣ *Please can I have your autograph?* (**ter seu autógrafo**)
▶ VERB [autographs, autographing, autographed] to write your autograph on something □ *The whole team autographed the football.* (**autografar**)

automate /ˈɔːtəmeɪt/ VERB [automates, automating, automated] to use machines or computers to do something, and not people (**automatizar**) ▣ *Our bottle production is fully automated.* (**totalmente automatizado**)

automatic /ˌɔːtəˈmætɪk/ ▶ ADJECTIVE
1 an automatic machine works without a person operating it (**automático**) ▣ *automatic doors* (**portas automáticas**) ▣ *Our heating system is fully automatic.* (**totalmente automático**)
2 always happening because of a rule or a system □ *After two years, you get automatic promotion.* (**automático**)

3 an automatic action is something you do without thinking ◻ *My automatic response was to cover my face.* (**automático**)
▶ NOUN [plural **automatics**]
1 a car which changes gears itself (**automático**)
2 a gun that keeps firing bullets when you press the trigger (= device that causes bullets to fire) (**automático**)

• **automatically** /ˌɔːtəˈmætɪkəli/ ADVERB
1 without a person operating something ◻ *The doors open automatically.* (**automaticamente**)
2 because of a rule or a system ◻ *If you get caught speeding again, you will automatically lose your licence.* (**automaticamente**)
3 without thinking ◻ *When I saw the stone coming I automatically ducked.* (**automaticamente**)

automation /ˌɔːtəˈmeɪʃən/ NOUN, NO PLURAL using machines to do things instead of people (**automação**)

automobile /ˈɔːtəməbiːl/ ▶ NOUN [plural **automobiles**] a US word for car (**automóvel**)
▶ ADJECTIVE a US word meaning to do with cars ◻ *the automobile industry* (**automobilística**)

autonomous /ɔːˈtɒnəməs/ ADJECTIVE
1 an autonomous country, area or organization governs or controls itself (**autônomo**)
2 an autonomous person can make decisions and act without asking anyone else what to do (**independente**)

• **autonomy** /ɔːˈtɒnəmi/ NOUN, NO PLURAL
1 when a country, area or organization governs or controls itself ◻ *Many of the administrative regions are seeking more autonomy.* (**autonomia**)
2 the ability to make decisions and act without asking anyone else what to do (**autonomia**)

autopsy /ˈɔːtɒpsi/ NOUN [plural **autopsies**] an examination of a dead person's body to find out why they died (**necropsia**)

autumn /ˈɔːtəm/ NOUN [plural **autumns**] the season after summer, when the leaves change colour and fall ◻ *I love the colours of autumn leaves.* (**outono**)

autumnal /ɔːˈtʌmnəl/ ADJECTIVE typical of autumn ◻ *trees in their autumnal colours* (**outonal**)

auxiliary /ɔːgˈzɪljəri/ ▶ NOUN [plural **auxiliaries**]
1 an auxiliary verb (**auxiliar**)
2 someone whose job is to help and support another group of workers ◻ *He's a hospital auxiliary.* (**auxiliar**)
▶ ADJECTIVE helping and supporting another group of workers ◻ *auxiliary nurses/police officers* (**auxiliar**)

auxiliary verb /ɔːgˈzɪljəri ˈvɜːb/ NOUN [plural **auxiliary verbs**] a verb like be, have or do that you use to make tenses, negatives or questions (**verbo auxiliar**)

avail /əˈveɪl/ NOUN **to no avail** without success ◻ *Our attempt to hide was to no avail.* (**sem sucesso**)
◆ PHRASAL VERB [**avails, availing, availed**] **avail yourself of something** to make use of something ◻ *I availed myself of the opportunity to catch up on some sleep.* (**fazer uso de algo**)

availability /əˌveɪləˈbɪləti/ NOUN, NO PLURAL
1 how possible it is to get something ◻ *Please can you check the availability of tickets for Thursday?* (**disponibilidade**)
2 the times when someone is free to do something (**disponibilidade**)

available /əˈveɪləbəl/ ADJECTIVE
1 if something is available, you can get it or buy it (**disponível**) ▣ *Guns are readily available (= easy to get) here.* (**disponível**) ▣ *The government plans to make more college places available to poor students.* (**tornou disponível**) ◻ *Judging by the available information, the man died over a week ago.*
2 if someone is available, they are free to do something ◻ + **to do something** *I'm sorry, there's nobody available to help you at the moment.* (**disponível**)

avalanche /ˈævəlɑːnʃ/ NOUN [plural **avalanches**]
1 a large amount of snow and rocks sliding down the side of a mountain (**avalanche**)
2 a large amount of something ◻ *The paper received an avalanche of protests after its article on racism.* (**avalanche**)

avant-garde /ˌævɒŋˈgɑːd/ ADJECTIVE very modern and new ◻ *avant-garde paintings/theories* (**vanguarda**)

avarice /ˈævərɪs/ NOUN, NO PLURAL when someone wants more money and things than they need. A formal word. (**avareza**)

• **avaricious** /ˌævəˈrɪʃəs/ ADJECTIVE wanting more money and things than you need. A formal word. (**avarento**)

avatar /ˈævətɑː(r)/ NOUN [plural **avatars**] a picture that represents you in computer games, discussion websites, etc. A computing word. (**avatar**)

avenge /əˈvendʒ/ VERB [**avenges, avenging, avenged**] to do something bad to someone to punish them for something bad they did to you or someone else ◻ *She vowed to avenge her sister's death.* (**vingar-se**)

avenue /ˈævənjuː/ NOUN [plural **avenues**]
1 a wide street, usually with trees on both sides (**avenida**)
2 a way of achieving something (**possibilidade**) ▣ *If TV advertising doesn't work, there are other avenues we can explore.* (**possibilidades a explorar**)

average /ˈævərɪdʒ/ ▶ ADJECTIVE
1 usual or ordinary ◻ *How much do you earn in an average week?* (**normal**)

averse / aware

2 an average amount is the amount you get by adding amounts together and dividing by the number of amounts ☐ *average temperatures* ☐ *the average wage* **(média)**
3 not very good quality ☐ *The food was pretty average.* **(média)**
▶ NOUN [plural **averages**]
1 the amount you get by adding amounts together and dividing by the number of amounts. **(média)**
2 the normal amount ☐ *We spend an average of £100 a week on food.* **(média)**
3 on average usually, or based on an average amount ☐ *On average, adults in this country watch three hours of TV every day.* **(em média)**
4 above/below average more/less than the average amount ☐ *Temperatures are below average for the time of year.* **(acima/abaixo da média)**
▶ VERB [**averages, averaging, averaged**] to have a particular amount as an average ☐ *I usually average around 6 miles per hour when I run.* **(calcular a média)**

averse /əˈvɜːs/ ADJECTIVE
1 not averse to something not against doing or having something ☐ *We're not averse to lending the children money if it's for a worthwhile purpose.* **(não contrário a algo)**
2 averse to something not liking or wanting something ☐ *They are very averse to the idea of women priests.* **(contrário a algo)**
• **aversion** /əˈvɜːʃən/ NOUN **an aversion to something** a dislike of something **(aversão a algo)**

avert /əˈvɜːt/ VERB [**averts, averting, averted**]
1 to manage to stop something bad happening **(evitar, impedir)** *avert a crisis/war* **(evitar uma crise/guerra)**
2 to turn away **(desviar)** *avert your eyes/gaze* **(desviar o olhar)**

aviary /ˈeɪvjəri/ NOUN [plural **aviaries**] a large cage or building for keeping birds **(aviário)**

aviation /ˌeɪviˈeɪʃən/ NOUN, NO PLURAL making and flying aircraft **(aviação)** *the aviation industry* **(indústria da aviação)**

avid /ˈævɪd/ ADJECTIVE very enthusiastic **(ávido)** *an avid reader* **(ávido leitor)**

avocado /ˌævəˈkɑːdoʊ/ NOUN [plural **avocados**]
1 a fruit shaped like a pear, that is not sweet and has dark green skin and a large stone in the middle **(abacate)**
2 a light green colour **(cor de abacate)**

avoid /əˈvɔɪd/ VERB [**avoids, avoiding, avoided**]
1 to stay away from somewhere or someone ☐ *Have you been avoiding me?* ☐ *I left early to avoid the rush hour traffic.* **(evitar)**
2 to prevent something bad happening ☐ *I usually do the housework, just to avoid arguments.* ☐ *If you keep your joints supple, it can avoid problems in later life.* **(evitar)**
3 to manage not to do something ☐ + *ing It's hard to avoid offending her.* **(evitar)**

• **avoidable** /əˈvɔɪdəbəl/ ADJECTIVE able to be avoided ☐ *This was an avoidable tragedy.* **(evitável)**

await /əˈweɪt/ VERB [**awaits, awaiting, awaited**]
1 to wait for something or someone **(aguardar)** *He is in prison, awaiting trial for murder.* **(aguardando julgamento)**
2 to be going to happen to someone ☐ *She could never have imagined the triumph that awaited her in New York.* **(esperar)**

awake /əˈweɪk/ ▶ ADJECTIVE not sleeping **(acordado)** *I tried to stay awake.* **(ficar acordado)** *Stop talking – you're keeping me awake.* **(mantendo-me acordado)** *She's wide awake* (= completely awake) *by six every morning.* **(bem acordado)**
▶ VERB [**awakes, awaking, awoke, awoken**] to wake up or to make someone wake up. A formal word. ☐ *Gloria awoke early.* **(acordar)**

> **Awake** is used mainly as an adjective. The verb **awake** is formal and not often used. Instead, use the phrasal verb **wake up**:
> ✓ *I woke up early this morning.*
> ✗ *I awoke early this morning.*

• **awaken** /əˈweɪkən/ VERB [**awakens, awakening, awakened**]
1 to cause a feeling or emotion to start ☐ *The sight of the injured cat awakened a great tenderness in him.* **(despertar)**
2 to wake up or to make someone wake up. A formal word. ☐ *We were awakened by the bombs.* **(acordar)**
• **awakening** /əˈweɪkənɪŋ/ NOUN [plural **awakenings**]
1 when a feeling or an emotion starts **(despertar)**
2 a rude awakening a shock when someone discovers the truth about something **(consciência súbita)**

award /əˈwɔːd/ ▶ NOUN [plural **awards**]
1 a prize for someone who has achieved something **(prêmio)** *Joe won an award for his contribution to football.* **(ganhou um prêmio)**
2 an amount of money that is paid to someone because of a legal decision **(prêmio)**
▶ VERB [**awards, awarding, awarded**]
1 to give someone a prize or something good because of what they have achieved ☐ *She was awarded the Nobel Prize for literature.* **(premiar)**
2 to give someone money or something they want because of a legal decision **(conceder)** *She was awarded damages* (= money paid because she was harmed) *of £50,000.* **(concedida indenização)** *He was awarded custody of the children* (= allowed to have them living with him). **(concedida custódia)**

aware /əˈweə(r)/ ADJECTIVE if you are aware of something, you know about it **(ciente)** ☐ + *of*

Katya became aware of someone else in the room. 🔲 He's **well aware** (= very aware) of all the problems. (**bem ciente** 🔲 **+ that** I'm perfectly aware that you've been waiting a long time.
- **awareness** /əˈweənɪs/ NOUN, NO PLURAL being aware of something (**consciência**) 🔲 We are hoping to **raise awareness** of the disease. (**aumentar a consciência**)

awash /əˈwɒʃ/ ADJECTIVE

1 be awash with something to contain a lot of something 🔲 The village was suddenly awash with reporters. (**estar repleto de algo**)
2 covered with a liquid 🔲 The streets of Perth are awash tonight after heavy rain. (**inundado**)

away /əˈweɪ/ ▶ ADVERB

1 to a different place or in a different place 🔲 He walked away. 🔲 We'll be away for three weeks. (**fora**)
2 at a distance 🔲 How far away is the school? 🔲 The exam is only a week away. (**a distância**)
3 in the opposite direction 🔲 Peter turned away. (**em direção oposta**)
4 not at work or school 🔲 Tina was away today. (**fora**)
5 in the place where something is kept 🔲 Could you put the books away, please? (**de volta**)
6 continuously 🔲 They've been working away all night. (**sempre**)
▶ ADJECTIVE an away game or match is one a team has to travel to (**campo adversário**)

awe /ɔː/ NOUN, NO PLURAL

1 a feeling of great admiration and often fear 🔲 The children gazed at their hero in awe. (**reverência**)
2 be in awe of someone to admire someone and be slightly afraid of them (**reverenciar alguém**)

awe-inspiring /ˈɔːɪnˌspaɪərɪŋ/ ADJECTIVE if something is awe-inspiring, it is very surprising and you admire and respect it very much (**impressionante**)

awesome /ˈɔːsəm/ ADJECTIVE

1 if something is awesome, you admire and respect it, and are often slightly afraid of it 🔲 We were shocked by the awesome power of their weapons. 🔲 an awesome responsibility (**impressionante**)
2 an informal word meaning very good 🔲 Her show was awesome. (**legal**)

awestruck /ˈɔːstrʌk/ ADJECTIVE filled with feelings of admiration and often fear (**assombroso**)

awful /ˈɔːfʊl/ ADJECTIVE

1 very bad 🔲 an awful headache (**horrível**) 🔲 The food was absolutely awful. (**totalmente horrível**)
2 very great 🔲 There is an awful lot of ice on the roads. 🔲 Looking after their dogs is an awful nuisance. (**impressionante**)
- **awfully** /ˈɔːfli/ ADVERB

1 very 🔲 It's an awfully long way. 🔲 She's awfully shy. (**muito**)
2 very badly 🔲 We played awfully. (**terrivelmente**)

awkward /ˈɔːkwəd/ ADJECTIVE

1 difficult to manage or use 🔲 I find this keyboard a bit awkward. (**complicado**)
2 an awkward person causes difficulties for others 🔲 Just stop being awkward and say you'll come. (**desajeitado**)
3 embarrassed or embarrassing 🔲 I feel really awkward when she asks me for money. 🔲 an awkward silence (**desagradável**)
4 awkward movements are not easy and relaxed (**complicado**)
- **awkwardly** /ˈɔːkwədli/ ADVERB in an awkward way 🔲 He fell awkwardly and broke his leg. 🔲 They shuffled awkwardly when we asked them to tell the truth. (**desajeitadamente, embaraçosamente**)
- **awkwardness** /ˈɔːkwədnɪs/ NOUN, NO PLURAL being awkward 🔲 You soon get used to the awkwardness of using the headphones. (**inabilidade, embaraço**)

awoke /əˈwəʊk/ PAST TENSE OF **awake** (**acordado** – ver **awake**)

awoken /əˈwəʊkən/ PAST PARTICIPLE OF **awake** (**acordado** – ver **awake**)

awry /əˈraɪ/ ADJECTIVE, ADVERB

1 go awry to not happen in the way that was planned 🔲 We don't want the schedule to go awry again. (**errar, estragar**)
2 not in the correct position 🔲 Your skirt is a bit awry. (**fora do lugar**)

axe /æks/ C NOUN [plural **axes**]

1 a tool for cutting wood (**machado**)
2 the axe when someone or something is got rid of or stopped 🔲 Three hundred jobs are due to get the axe next week. (**encerrar**)
▶ VERB [**axes, axing, axed**] to stop a plan or a service, close a business or get rid of workers 🔲 Thousands of jobs were axed. (**despedir**)

axis /ˈæksɪs/ NOUN [plural **axes**]

1 the imaginary line that an object like a planet seems to turn around (**eixo**)
2 the line up the side or along the bottom of a graph used to show measurements and find positions. A maths word. (**eixo**)

axle /ˈæksəl/ NOUN [plural **axles**] a long metal bar that connects two wheels on a vehicle (**eixo**)

ayatollah /ˌaɪəˈtɒlə/ NOUN [plural **ayatollahs**] a Muslim religious leader in Iran (**aiatolá**)

aye /eɪ/ EXCLAMATION another word for **yes**, used especially in Scotland and the North of England (**sim**)

azure /ˈæʒʊər/ ADJECTIVE having a bright blue colour (**azul-celeste**)

B b

B or **b** /biː/ the second letter of the alphabet (a segunda letra do alfabeto)

babble /ˈbæbəl/ VERB [babbles, babbling, babbled]

1 to talk quickly in a way that is not easy to understand (balbuciar)

2 if a stream (= small river) babbles, it makes a nice, gentle sound (balbuciar)

babe /beɪb/ NOUN [plural babes]

1 a baby (bebê)

2 an informal word used for talking to someone □ Are you all right, babe? (baby)

baboon /bəˈbuːn/ NOUN [plural baboons] a type of large monkey with a long pointed nose and long teeth (babuíno)

baby /ˈbeɪbi/ ▶ NOUN [plural babies]

1 a very young child 🔲 Paola has had a baby. □ a baby boy (bebê)

2 an older child or an adult who is crying or behaving like a baby □ Don't be such a baby, it's only a little spider! (infantil)

▶ ADJECTIVE very young □ a baby elephant

• **babyish** /ˈbeɪbiɪʃ/ ADJECTIVE suitable for babies or younger children □ This game is probably too babyish for most ten-year-olds. (infantil)

babysit /ˈbeɪbiˌsɪt/ VERB [babysits, babysitting, babysat] to look after a baby or child when its parents are not in the house □ Could you babysit for me on Saturday? (cuidar como babá)

• **babysitter** /ˈbeɪbiˌsɪtə(r)/ NOUN [plural babysitters] someone who looks after a baby or a child when its parents are not in the house (babá)

bachelor /ˈbætʃələ(r)/ NOUN [plural bachelors] a man who has never married (solteiro)

back /bæk/ ▶ NOUN [plural backs]

1 the part of something that is furthest away from the front □ Nina hid her diary at the back of a drawer. (no fundo)

2 the part of the body that goes from the shoulders to the bottom □ I always sleep on my back. (costas)

3 in football and hockey, a player who tries to stop the other team scoring a goal (retornar)

4 in back of the American way of saying 'behind' □ She was sitting in back of me. (atrás)

♦ IDIOM **back to front** the wrong way, so that the part that should be at the back is now at the front □ You've got your sweater on back to front! (de trás para a frente)

▶ ADJECTIVE away from the front □ Ben's had one of his back teeth out. (de trás)

▶ ADVERB

1 to the place where a person or thing was before □ What time is he coming back? □ Could you give Maria her book back, please? (de volta)

2 in the direction that is the opposite of forwards □ I stood back to let her pass. □ She sat back in her chair. (para trás)

3 as a reply to something □ Can I call you back in an hour? (de volta)

4 to the condition someone or something was in before □ I went back to sleep. (de volta)

5 to an earlier time □ Thinking back to that day, she was obviously unhappy. (anteriormente)

▶ VERB [backs, backing, backed]

1 to support or help someone or something □ He is backing the female candidate in the election. (ajudar)

2 to move backwards, usually in a car □ She backed into the drive. (mover para trás)

♦ PHRASAL VERBS **back someone up** to support someone □ If you complain to the teacher, I'll back you up. (dar suporte para alguém) **back something up** to make an extra copy of information on a computer. A computing word. □ Are the files all backed up? (fazer uma cópia extra) **back down** to admit that you are wrong □ He backed down when I pointed out that his figures were wrong. (desistir)

backache /ˈbækeɪk/ NOUN, NO PLURAL pain in the back □ She suffers from backache. (dor nas costas)

backbench /ˈbækbentʃ/ ▶ ADJECTIVE a backbench MP (= member of the government) does not have an important job in the government (assento dos fundos)

▶ NOUN **the backbenches** the place where backbench MPs sit (os assentos)

• **backbencher** /ˌbækˈbentʃə(r)/ NOUN [plural backbenchers] a backbench MP (deputado)

backbiting /ˈbækˌbaɪtɪŋ/ NOUN, NO PLURAL when people say bad and unkind things about a person who is not there (calúnia)

backbone /ˈbækbəʊn/ NOUN [plural backbones] the row of bones down the middle of your back (coluna vertebral)

backbreaking /ˈbækˌbreɪkɪŋ/ ADJECTIVE backbreaking work is physically very hard and makes you tired (**árduo**)

backdate /ˌbækˈdeɪt/ VERB [backdates, backdating, backdated] if you backdate a cheque or a payment, you make it start from an earlier date □ *Claims for benefit can be backdated for up to 52 weeks.* (**antedatar**)

backdoor /ˈbækdɔː(r)/ ADJECTIVE backdoor activities are secret and not official □ *backdoor negotiations* (**ilícito**)

backdrop /ˈbækdrɒp/ NOUN [plural **backdrops**]
1 the situation that exists when something happens □ *The trial took place against a backdrop of political violence.* (**pano de fundo**)
2 the things you can see behind the main thing you are looking at □ *The hotel is set against a backdrop of stunning mountains.* (**pano de fundo**)
3 a cloth with a picture on it that is hung at the back of a stage in a theatre (**cenário**)

backer /ˈbækə(r)/ NOUN [plural **backers**] someone who supports a person, business or organization by giving them money (**patrocinador**)

backfire /ˌbækˈfaɪə(r)/ VERB [backfires, backfiring, backfired]
1 if a plan backfires, it goes wrong and has the opposite effect from what you wanted (**falhar**)
2 if a car backfires, its fuel burns too quickly, causing a sudden loud noise (**explodir**)

backgammon /ˈbækˌɡæmən/ NOUN, NO PLURAL a game where two playersmove pieces on a board with triangular patterns (**gamão**)

background /ˈbækɡraʊnd/ NOUN [plural **backgrounds**]
1 the part of a picture which is behind the main people or objects (**segundo plano**) 🔁 *Here's a photo of us with Ben Nevis in the background.* (**em segundo plano**)
2 a person's background is their family and the things they have done in the past □ *These children are from very poor backgrounds.* (**experiência**)
3 the background of an event is all the things that happened before it and caused it to happen □ + *to the background to the English civil war.* (**acontecimento**)

backhand /ˈbækhænd/ NOUN [plural **backhands**] in games like tennis, a way of hitting the ball by holding the racket (= round part with a stick) across the front of your body (**backhand**)

backing /ˈbækɪŋ/ NOUN, NO PLURAL
1 support or money for a person or plan in order to make them successful □ *Research of this type has the backing of industry.* (**patrocínio**)
2 music or singing that goes with amain singer's voice (**acompanhamento**) 🔁 *a backing singer* (**vocal de apoio**)

backlash /ˈbæklæʃ/ NOUN, NO PLURAL a sudden violent reaction to an event or situation □ *a backlash against the feminist movement* (**retrocesso**)

backlog /ˈbæklɒɡ/ NOUN, NO PLURAL a large amount of work that you have not done and must now do (**acúmulo**) 🔁 *We've got to work this weekend to try to clear the backlog.* (**eliminar o acúmulo**)

backpack /ˈbækpæk/ ▶ NOUN [plural **backpacks**] a large bag that you carry on your back □ *I was carrying the tent in my backpack.* (**mochila**)
▶ VERB [backpacks, backpacking, backpacked] to travel to a lot of different places carrying the things you need in a bag on your back (**excursionar**) 🔁 *I went backpacking when I was a student.* (**excursionei**)

backpedal /ˌbækˈpedəl/ VERB [backpedals, backpedalling/*US* backpedaling, backpedalled/*US* backpedaled] to try to change something that you have started doing or something that you said □ *They are backpedalling on promises for better funding.* (**mudar de ideia**)

backrest /ˈbækrest/ NOUN [plural **backrests**] the part of a piece of furniture that supports your back (**encosto**)

backslash /ˈbækslæʃ/ NOUN [plural **backslashes**] the symbol '\' (**barra invertida**)

backslide /ˌbækˈslaɪd/ VERB [backslides, backsliding, backslid] to start to do bad things again after a period of not doing them (**desviar-se**)

backspace /ˈbækspeɪs/ ▶ NOUN [plural **backspaces**] the key on a computer that you press to move back one space. A computing word. (**tecla de retrocesso**)
▶ VERB [backspaces, backspacing, backspaced] to move back one space by pressing a key on a computer. A computing word. (**voltar um espaço**)

backstage /ˌbækˈsteɪdʒ/ ADJECTIVE, ADVERB things that happen backstage in a theatre happen where the audience cannot see them, for example behind the stage □ *The play started late because of a problem backstage.* (**bastidores**)

backstroke /ˈbækstrəʊk/ NOUN, NO PLURAL a way of swimming in which you lie on your back and move your arms backwards over your shoulders (**nado de costas**)

backtrack /ˈbæktræk/ VERB [backtracks, backtracking, backtracked]
1 to say that you will not do something that you Said you would do earlier □ *He was accused of backtracking on promises to help them.* (**retroceder**)
2 to return to a subject you were talking about earlier (**regressar**)

backup /ˈbækʌp/ NOUN [plural **backups**]

backward

1 extra people or equipment that you can use if you need them (**substituto**)
2 an extra copy of information on a computer. A computing word. (**cópia extra**)

backward /'bækwəd/ ▶ ADJECTIVE
1 towards the back □ a backward look (**para trás**)
2 slow to learn or develop (**obtuso**)
▶ ADVERB backwards □ She was looking backward over her shoulder.

backwards /'bækwədz/ ADVERB
1 in the direction behind you □ I stepped backwards to give her some room. (**para trás**)
2 in the wrong position, with the back part at the front □ I think my skirt is on backwards. (**de trás para a frente**)
3 in the opposite way to the usual way □ Tom can say the alphabet backwards. (**de trás para a frente**)

bacon /'beɪkən/ NOUN, NO PLURAL thin pieces of salty meat from a pig (**bacon**)

bacteria /bæk'tɪərɪə/ PLURAL NOUN very small living things that sometimes cause disease in humans and animals (**bactéria**)

bad /bæd/ ADJECTIVE [**worse, worst**]
1 not of a good standard □ I've had a really bad haircut. □ The food was so bad I couldn't eat it. (**ruim**)
2 unpleasant, causing problems or worry □ Bad weather can spoil a holiday. □ I had some bad news this morning. (**ruim**)
3 not bad satisfactory or good enough □ We made over three hundred pounds so that's not bad. □ 'How are you doing, Maria?' 'Not bad, thanks.' (**nada mau**)
4 bad for someone harmful to your body, making you not healthy □ It's bad for you to eat too much sugar. (**mal para alguém**)
5 bad at something not able to do something well □ I'm very bad at maths. (**ruim em algo**)
6 food which is bad does not taste or smell good because it is old □ This meat is bad – throw it away. (**estragado**)
7 evil or cruel □ He's not a bad man. (**mau**)

> ➤ Remember that **bad** is an adjective and not an adverb. To describe the way that someone does something, use the adverb **badly**:
> ✓ He behaved very badly.
> ✗ He behaved very bad.

bade /bæd, beɪd/ PAST TENSE OF **bid**² □ I bade him goodbye. (**ver bid**²)

badge /bædʒ/ NOUN [plural **badges**] a small object with words or pictures that you put on your clothes to show something, for example your name (**crachá**)

badger /'bædʒə(r)/ NOUN [plural **badgers**] an animal with black and white stripes on its face, which lives underground (**texugo**)

badly /'bædli/ ADVERB [**worse, worst**]
1 seriously □ The car was badly damaged in the crash. (**seriamente**)
2 in a way that is not good □ Both children behaved badly. (**de modo ruim**)
3 very much (**muito**) 🔁 I badly wanted a new pair of trainers. (**queria muito**)

badly-off /ˌbædli'ɒf/ ADJECTIVE [**worse-off, worst-off**]
1 poor □ With my father in prison, we were fairly badly-off. (**pobre, em má situação**)
2 badly-off for something needing more of something □ We're quite badly-off for equipment. (**precisar repor algo**)

badminton /'bædmɪntən/ NOUN, NO PLURAL a sport in which two or four players hit a shuttlecock (= light object with feathers) across a net (**badminton**)

bad-tempered /ˌbæd'tempəd/ ADJECTIVE speaking or behaving angrily or rudely □ Perhaps you wouldn't be so bad-tempered in the morning if you got more sleep. (**mal-humorado**)

baffle /'bæfəl/ VERB [**baffles, baffling, baffled**] if you are baffled by a situation, you do not understand it □ Police were baffled by the crime. (**confundir**)
• **baffling** /'bæflɪŋ/ ADJECTIVE if a situation is baffling, you do not understand it □ a baffling problem (**desconcertante**)

bag /bæg/ ▶ NOUN [plural **bags**]
1 an object that you put things in and carry with you □ a leather bag □ a bag of crisps (**bolsa, saco**)
2 bags of an informal way of saying a lot of something □ We've got bags of time before the bus comes. (**muitos**)
▶ VERB [**bags, bagging, bagged**] to put things into a bag or bags □ We helped Dad bag all the garden rubbish. (**embolsar**)

bagel /'beɪgəl/ NOUN [plural **bagels**] a piece of hard bread in the shape of a ring (**rosca**)

bagful /'bægfʊl/ NOUN [plural **bagfuls**] the amount that a bag holds □ a bagful of sweets (**conteúdo de um saco**)

baggage /'bægɪdʒ/ NOUN, NO PLURAL the cases and bags that a person takes with them when they travel □ The baggage is stored in the back of the coach. (**bagagem**)

> ➤ Remember that the noun **baggage** is never used in the plural:
> ✓ I had so much baggage.
> ✗ I had so many baggages.

baggy /'bægi/ ADJECTIVE [**baggier, baggiest**] baggy clothes are too big for the person wearing them and hang loosely from their body □ a baggy sweater (**folgado**)

bagpipes /ˈbæɡpaɪps/ PLURAL NOUN a musical instrument made up of a bag with pipes attached. You play it by blowing down a pipe. (gaita de foles)

baguette /bæˈɡet/ NOUN [plural baguettes] a long, thin loaf of bread (baguete)

bail /beɪl/ ▶ NOUN, NO PLURAL money that must be paid to a court so that someone who has been arrested for a crime can leave a prison until their Trial (fiança) ▣ *He was released on bail.* (liberado sob fiança)

▶ VERB [bails, bailing, bailed] to let someone go free because bail has been paid (afiançar, pagar fiança)

◆ PHRASAL VERB **bail someone out** to help a person or organization by giving them money (doar dinheiro)

bailiff /ˈbeɪlɪf/ NOUN [plural bailiffs] someone whose job is to take away the things that belong to a person who has not paid money they owe (oficial de justiça)

bait /beɪt/ NOUN, NO PLURAL food that you use for catching a fish or an animal (isca)

bake /beɪk/ VERB [bakes, baking, baked]
1 to cook things like bread, cakes or biscuits in an oven ▢ *I baked a cake this afternoon.* ▢ *I love to bake with the children.* (assar)
2 to bake things that are soft is to make them hard in the sun or in an oven (assar)

baked beans /ˈbeɪkt ˈbiːnz/ PLURAL NOUN small white beans in a red tomato sauce, usually sold in tins (= metal containers) ▢ *baked beans on toast* (feijões cozidos)

baker /ˈbeɪkə(r)/ NOUN [plural bakers]
1 someone who bakes bread and cakes (padeiro)
2 baker's a shop that makes and sells bread and cakes (padaria)
• **bakery** /ˈbeɪkəri/ NOUN [plural bakeries] a shop or factory where bread and cakes are made (padaria)

balance /ˈbæləns/ ▶ NOUN, NO PLURAL
1 when you have the same amount of weight on each side of the body so that you do not fall over (equilíbrio) ▣ *I lost my balance and fell over.* (perder o equilíbrio) ▣ *I find it hard to keep my balance in high heels.* (manter o equilíbrio)
2 a good situation in which you have or do the right amount of two or more things ▢ *I try to achieve a balance between work and family life.* (equilíbrio)
3 the amount of money that is in a bank account (saldo)

▶ VERB [balances, balancing, balanced] to stay in a position where you do not fall to either side, or to put something in a position where it will not fall ▢ *Lisa balanced the book on her head.* (equilibrar)

balance sheet /ˈbæləns ˈʃiːt/ NOUN [plural balance sheets] a document that shows what a business has earned and what it has spent (balanço geral)

balcony /ˈbælkəni/ NOUN [plural balconies]
1 a part of a high building which is on the outside wall. You can sit or stand in it ▢ *We sat on the balcony and watched the sun go down.* (sacada)
2 in a theatre, the area upstairs where the seats are above the rest of the audience (camarote)

bald /bɔːld/ ADJECTIVE [balder, baldest]
1 with little or no hair on the head (careca) ▣ *He's going bald.* (ficando careca) ▣ *Dan has a bald patch.* (ponto calvo)
2 said clearly, in only a few words (trivial)

balding /ˈbɔːldɪŋ/ ADJECTIVE starting to lose the hair on your head ▢ *He was grey and balding.* (com queda de cabelo)
• **baldness** /ˈbɔːldnɪs/ NOUN, NO PLURAL being bald (calvície)

bale /beɪl/ NOUN [plural bales] a lot of something, for example cloth or hay (= dried grass), pressed and tied together tightly (fardo)
◆ PHRASAL VERB [bales, baling, baled] **bale out** to escape from a dangerous situation ▢ *The pilot had baled out of the burning aircraft.* (escapar)

balk /bɔːk/ VERB [balks, balking, balked] another spelling of **baulk** (evitar)

ball /bɔːl/ NOUN [plural balls]
1 a round object that you use for playing games like football, hockey and tennis (bola)
2 anything that has a round shape ▢ *a ball of string* ▢ *The hedgehog had rolled itself into a ball.* (bola)
3 a big formal party where people dance (baile)
◆ IDIOM **be on the ball** to be quick to understand what is happening (estar por dentro)

ballad /ˈbæləd/ NOUN [plural ballads] a slow song about Love (balada)

ballast /ˈbæləst/ NOUN, NO PLURAL any heavy substance such as sand or water which is put in ships to stop them turning over (lastro)

ball bearing /ˈbɔːl ˈbeərɪŋ/ NOUN [plural ball bearings] one of many small metal balls that are put between machine parts so that the parts move easily over each other (rolimã)

ballerina /ˌbæləˈriːnə/ NOUN [plural ballerinas] a female ballet dancer (bailarina)

ballet /ˈbæleɪ/ NOUN [plural ballets]
1 *no plural* a type of dancing that tells a story and uses smooth, attractive movements which are very difficult to do (balé) ▣ *a ballet dancer* (dançarina de balé) ▢ *Sarah does ballet and tap dancing.*
2 a story which is told using ballet ▢ *My favourite ballets are The Nutcracker and Swan Lake.* (balé)

ballistics

ballistics /bəˈlɪstɪks/ NOUN, NO PLURAL the study of the way that objects move through the air. A physics word. (**balística**)

balloon /bəˈluːn/ ▶ NOUN [plural **balloons**] a very large, round, rubber object that is filled with air or gas □ *The children were holding balloons.* (**balões**)
▶ VERB [**balloons, ballooning, ballooned**] to become larger and rounder □ *The sail ballooned out in the breeze.* (**inchar**)

ballot /ˈbælət/ ▶ NOUN [plural **ballots**] a way of voting in secret by marking a paper and putting it into a special box (**votação**) 🔲 *They held a ballot to decide who would be leader.* (**fizeram votação**)
▶ VERB [**ballots, balloting, balloted**] to ballot a group of people is to get votes from them by ballot □ *The workers were balloted and voted to strike.* (**votar**)

ballot box /ˈbælət ˈbɒks/ NOUN [plural **ballot boxes**] a box which people who have just voted put their ballot papers into (**urna de votos**)

ballot paper /ˈbælət ˈpeɪpə(r)/ NOUN [plural **ballot papers**] a piece of paper on which you make a mark to show who you are voting for (**cédula de votação**)

ballpark /ˈbɔːlpɑːk/ ADJECTIVE a ballpark amount or number has been guessed using the information available, but not calculated exactly (**estimado**) 🔲 *Do you have ballpark figures for the building costs?* (**números estimados**)

ballpoint pen /ˈbɔːlpɔɪnt ˈpen/ NOUN [plural **ballpoint pens**] a pen with a very small metal ball at the end where the ink comes out (**caneta esferográfica**)

ballroom dancing /ˈbɔːlrʊm ˈdɑːnsɪŋ/ NOUN, NO PLURAL a formal, old-fashioned type of dancing in which two people hold each other and do a pattern of steps (**dança de salão**)

balm /bɑːm/ NOUN, NO PLURAL oil or cream that you put on sore skin to make it feel better □ *lip balm* (**pomada**)

balmy /ˈbɑːmɪ/ ADJECTIVE [**balmier, balmiest**] describes weather than is warm and pleasant □ *a balmy evening* (**agradável**)

balsa /ˈbɔːlsə/ NOUN, NO PLURAL a very light, soft wood that people use for making model boats and aircraft (**balsa, jangada**)

bamboo /bæmˈbuː/ NOUN, NO PLURAL a tall Asian grass that has hard, round stems that are used to make furniture (**bambu**)

bamboozle /bæmˈbuːzəl/ VERB [**bamboozles, bamboozling, bamboozled**] to confuse or trick someone (**enganar, confundir**)

ban /bæn/ ▶ VERB [**bans, banning, banned**] to not allow people to do something □ *Cycling is banned in the park.* (**proibir**)
▶ NOUN [plural **bans**] an order that people are not allowed to do something □ *There's a ban on smoking in public places.* (**proibição**)

bang

banal /bəˈnɑːl/ ADJECTIVE boring and not original □ *She found his conversation rather banal.* (**banal**)
• **banality** /bəˈnælətɪ/ NOUN, NO PLURAL when something is banal (**banalidade**)

banana /bəˈnɑːnə/ NOUN [plural **bananas**] a long, curved, yellow fruit which is white inside (**banana**) 🔲 *I watched him peel a banana.* (**descascar uma banana**)

band /bænd/ NOUN [plural **bands**]
1 a group of musicians who play together □ *a rock band* (**banda**)
2 a long, thin piece of material used for putting round something 🔲 *a rubber band* (**elástico**)
3 a line of colour which is different from the colour around it □ *Her hat had a band of red around it.* (**faixa**)
4 a group □ *a band of robbers* (**bando**)
◆ PHRASAL VERB [**bands, banding, banded**] **band together** to join together as a group to do something □ *All the parents banded together to demand improvements in the school.* (**unir**)

bandage /ˈbændɪdʒ/ ▶ NOUN [plural **bandages**] a long piece of cloth that you put around a part of your body that has been cut or hurt □ *He had a bandage around his arm.* (**bandagem**)
▶ VERB [**bandages, bandaging, bandaged**] to put a bandage around a part of your body □ *The nurse bandaged his wrist.* (**enfaixar**)

bandit /ˈbændɪt/ NOUN [plural **bandits**] someone who attacks people who are travelling and takes money and possessions from them (**bandido**)

bandwagon /ˈbændwægən/ NOUN (**popularidade**)
◆ IDIOM **climb/jump on the bandwagon** to start to do something only because other people are doing it or it is fashionable □ *Once one company has a success with a product, other companies jump on the bandwagon and start producing a similar product.* (**fazer algo por imitação**)

bandwidth /ˈbændwɪdθ/ NOUN [plural **bandwidths**] a measurement of how much information an Internet connection can send in an amount of time. A computing word. (**banda larga**)

bandy /ˈbændɪ/ ADJECTIVE [**bandier, bandiest**] bandy legs curve out at the knees (**curvado**)

bane /beɪn/ NOUN **the bane of your life** something that causes you a lot of trouble □ *Hay fever is the bane of my life!* (**sua maldição**)

bang /bæŋ/ C NOUN [plural **bangs**]
1 a sudden loud noise □ *There was a loud bang and all the lights went out.* (**estrondo**)
2 when you knock part of your body against something □ *She's had a bang on the head and is feeling a bit dizzy.* (**pancada**)
▶ VERB [**bangs, banging, banged**]

1 to make a sudden loud noise by hitting against something □ *The door banged shut in the wind.* (bater)
2 to knock part of your body against something □ *Neil banged his head on the shelf.* (bater)

banger /'bæŋə(r)/ NOUN [*plural* bangers]
1 a type of very loud firework (= object that explodes in the sky and makes a noise and colours) (fogos de artifício)
2 an informal word for sausage (salsicha) 🔲 *bangers and mash* (= sausages and crushed potatoes) (salsichas e purê de batata)
3 an informal word for an old car that is in bad condition (calhambeque)

bangle /'bæŋgəl/ NOUN [*plural* bangles] a ring of metal, wood or plastic that you wear on your wrist (= part between hand and arm) (bracelete)

banish /'bænɪʃ/ VERB [banishes, banishing, banished]
1 to make someone leave their country or their home as a punishment (banir)
2 to make you stop thinking or feeling a particular way □ *You must banish all thoughts of revenge.* (expulsar)
• **banishment** /'bænɪʃmənt/ NOUN, NO PLURAL being banished (banimento, expulsão)

banisters /'bænɪstəz/ PLURAL NOUN a bar that you can hold as you walk up or down stairs and the poles that support the bar (corrimão)

banjo /'bændʒəʊ/ NOUN [*plural* banjos or banjoes] a musical instrument with strings, like a small guitar but with the main part round in shape (banjo)

bank /bæŋk/ ▶ NOUN [*plural* banks]
1 a business that looks after other people's money and also lends money (banco) 🔲 *I must go to the bank.* (ir ao banco)
2 a place where a lot of one thing is stored so that it can be used later □ *a blood bank* (banco)
3 an area of ground which is next to a river or lake □ *We camped on the banks of Loch Lomond.* (margem)
4 an area of ground which is raised □ *There's a steep wooded bank behind the house.* (ladeira, declive)
▶ VERB [banks, banking, banked] to have a bank account with a particular bank □ *I've banked with them for years.* (depositar no banco)
♦ PHRASAL VERB **bank on something** to depend on something □ *He might help you but don't bank on it.* (contar com algo)

bank account /'bæŋk ə'kaʊnt/ NOUN [*plural* bank accounts] an arrangement that you have with a bank for keeping money there, and for taking it out when you need it (conta bancária) 🔲 *I must open a bank account.* (abrir uma conta bancária)

bank balance /'bæŋk 'bæləns/ NOUN [*plural* bank balances] the amount of money you have in a bank account (saldo bancário)

bank card /'bæŋk 'kɑːd/ NOUN [*plural* bank cards] a small piece of plastic that you use to pay for things or to get money out of a machine (cartão magnético)

banker /'bæŋkə(r)/ NOUN [*plural* bankers] someone who has an important job in a bank (banqueiro)

bank holiday /'bæŋk 'hɒlɪdeɪ/ NOUN [*plural* bank holidays] a public holiday when the banks are closed (feriado bancário)

banking /'bæŋkɪŋ/ NOUN, NO PLURAL the business that banks do (negócio bancário)

banknote /'bæŋknəʊt/ NOUN [*plural* banknotes] a piece of paper money □ *a £20 banknote* (nota de banco)

bankrupt /'bæŋkrʌpt/ ADJECTIVE if a person or business is bankrupt, they are not able to pay the money they owe (falido) 🔲 *The business went bankrupt because costs rose.* (foi à falência)
• **bankruptcy** /'bæŋkrʌptsɪ/ NOUN [*plural* bankruptcies] being bankrupt (falência) 🔲 *The business is facing bankruptcy.* (enfrentando falência) □ *The number of bankruptcies went up last year.*

bank statement /'bæŋk 'steɪtmənt/ NOUN [*plural* bank statements] a list that your bank sends you, which shows all the money that you have put into your bank account, and the money you have taken out of your bank account during a particular period (extrato bancário)

banner /'bænə(r)/ NOUN [*plural* banners] a large piece of cloth with writing on it which people carry on poles □ *The anti-war protesters were carrying banners.* (faixa)

banquet /'bæŋkwɪt/ NOUN [*plural* banquets] a formal meal for a lot of people on an important occasion (banquete)

banter /'bæntə(r)/ NOUN, NO PLURAL talk in which people tell jokes and laugh at each other (brincadeira)

baptism /'bæptɪzəm/ NOUN [*plural* baptisms] a Christian ceremony in which some one has water put on their head to show that they are joining the Christian religion (batismo)

baptize /bæp'taɪz/ or **baptise** VERB [baptizes, baptizing, baptized] to make someone a member of the Christian religion by putting water on their head in a special ceremony (batizar)

bar /bɑː(r)/ ▶ NOUN [*plural* bars]
1 a place that sells alcoholic drinks □ *The city is full of café's and bars.* (bar)
2 a long narrow piece of metal □ *an iron bar* (barra)
3 a restaurant that serves a particular type of food □ *a burger bar* (bar)
4 a large piece of something such as chocolate or soap □ *+ of a bar of chocolate* (barra)

barb

5 a bar to something something that prevents something else from happening □ *The disease should not be a bar to success.* (uma barreira para algo)
6 one of the parts that a line of music is divided into □ *There were four beats in each bar.* (compasso)
▶ VERB [bars, barring, barred]
1 if someone is barred from a place or barred from doing something, they are not allowed in or are not allowed to do it □ **+ from** *Anyone over the age of 12 is barred from the competition.* (barrar)
2 to prevent someone from going somewhere by standing in their way □ *Over a hundred protestors barred the entrance to the building.* (barrar)
3 to lock a door or window by putting a metal bar across it (barrar)

barb /bɑːb/ NOUN [plural **barbs**] a curved point on an arrow or a fish hook (= used for catching fish) that makes it difficult to remove (gancho)

barbarian /bɑːˈbeərɪən/ NOUN [plural **barbarians**] someone who behaves badly and shows no respect for things like art and education (bárbaro)

barbaric /bɑːˈbærɪk/ ADJECTIVE cruel or violent □ *barbaric acts of terrorism* (bárbaro)

barbecue /ˈbɑːbɪkjuː/ ▶ NOUN [plural **barbecues**]
1 a piece of equipment used for cooking food outdoors (grelha) □ *She was trying to light the barbecue.* □ *Put some more sausages on the barbecue.*
2 a party or meal outdoors where food is cooked on a barbecue □ *We're having a barbecue tonight.* (fazendo um churrasco)
▶ VERB [barbecues, barbecuing, barbecued] to cook food on a barbecue (assar no espeto)

barbed wire /ˈbɑːbd ˈwaɪə(r)/ NOUN, NO PLURAL wire with sharp points on it, used to stop people getting into a place (arame farpado)

barber /ˈbɑːbə(r)/ NOUN [plural **barbers**]
1 a man whose job is to cut men's hair (barbeiro)
2 barber's a shop where men have their hair cut (barbearia)

bar chart /ˈbɑː(r) ˈtʃɑːt/ NOUN [plural **bar charts**] a graph (= picture in maths) which shows different amounts as thick lines of different lengths. A maths word. (diagrama de barras)

bar code /ˈbɑː(r) ˈkəʊd/ NOUN [plural **bar codes**] many printed black lines on a product, which a computer uses to get information, for example the price of the product (código de barras)

bare /beə(r)/ ADJECTIVE [barer, barest]
1 not covered with anything (nu) □ *It's too cold to go out with bare legs.* (pernas de fora) □ *The wall looks really bare without any pictures on it.*
2 basic and with nothing extra (limitado) □ *Her bag was packed with the bare essentials.* (noções

bar mitzvah

básicas limitadas) □ *We try to keep prices to a bare minimum.* (mínimo limitado)

bareback /ˈbeəbæk/ ADVERB if you ride bareback, you ride a horse without a saddle (= a leather seat) (sem sela)

barefaced /ˈbeəfeɪst/ ADJECTIVE done in a way that shows you are not embarrassed about behaving badly (audacioso) □ *a barefaced lie* (mentira audaciosa)

barefoot /ˈbeəfʊt/ ADJECTIVE, ADVERB not wearing any shoes or socks □ *barefoot children* □ *They were running barefoot on the beach.* (descalço)

barely /ˈbeəli/ ADVERB almost not □ *She was old and barely able to walk.* □ *They had barely arrived when they had to leave again.* (mal)

bargain /ˈbɑːɡɪn/ ▶ NOUN [plural **bargains**]
1 something that is cheap or cheaper than usual □ *These jeans were a real bargain.* (pechincha)
2 an agreement in which each person or group promises to do something (acordo) □ *She tried to strike a bargain with* (= make an agreement with) *him.* (fazer um acordo com)
▶ VERB [bargains, bargaining, bargained]
1 to try to persuade someone to sell something to you for less money (barganhar)
2 get more than you bargained for to be different from what you expected, especially in a way that is worse (diferente do esperado)

barge /bɑːdʒ/ ▶ NOUN [plural **barges**] a boat with a flat bottom, used on canals (= passages of water) and rivers (barcaça)
▶ VERB [barges, barging, barged] to go somewhere so quickly that you push people out of your way or hit things □ *Matt barged into the room knocking all the books over as he came.* □ *He barged past me to get to the front of the queue.* (irromper)

baritone /ˈbærɪtəʊn/ NOUN [plural **baritones**]
1 a male singing voice which is low but not the lowest (barítono)
2 a man with this singing voice (barítono)

barium /ˈbeərɪəm/ NOUN, NO PLURAL a softmetal element. A chemistry word. (bário)

bark /bɑːk/ ▶ NOUN [plural **barks**]
1 the short, loud sound that a dog makes (latido)
2 the rough wood on the outside of a tree (casca)
▶ VERB [barks, barking, barked]
1 when a dog barks, it makes a short, loud sound (latir)
2 to say something in a loud, angry voice □ *'Hurry up, you lot!' he barked.* (gritar)

barley /ˈbɑːli/ NOUN, NO PLURAL a grain used for food and for making beer (cevada)

barman /ˈbɑːmən/ NOUN [plural **barmen**] a man who serves drinks at a bar (barman)

bar mitzvah /ˌbɑː(r) ˈmɪtsvə/ NOUN [plural **bar mitzvahs**] a religious ceremony for a Jewish boy when he is 13. It marks the time when he starts to have the religious responsibilities of an adult. (bar mitzvah)

barmy /'bɑːmɪ/ ADJECTIVE an informal word meaning very silly or mad (**esquisito**)

barn /bɑːn/ NOUN [*plural* **barns**] a large building on a farm, for keeping crops or animals in (**celeiro**)

barnacle /'bɑːnəkəl/ NOUN [*plural* **barnacles**] a type of small shellfish (= sea creature) that sticks to rocks and the bottoms of boats (**cirrípede**)

barometer /bə'rɒmɪtə(r)/ NOUN [*plural* **barometers**] an instrument for measuring the pressure of air and showing changes in the weather (**barômetro**)

baron /'bærən/ NOUN [*plural* **barons**] a name given to some men who belong to the highest social class (**barão**)

baroness /'bærənɪs/ NOUN [*plural* **baronesses**] a female baron or a baron's wife ☐ *Baroness Thatcher* (**baronesa**)

baroque /bə'rɒk/ ADJECTIVE to do with the style of art, music and buildings used in Europe in the 17th and 18th centuries ☐ *baroque churches* (**barroco**)

barrack /'bærək/ VERB [**barracks, barracking, barracked**] to shout at someone who is speaking or performing in public, because you do not like what they are saying or doing ☐ *He was barracked by several members of the audience.* (**insultar**)

barracks /'bærəks/ PLURAL NOUN a group of buildings where soldiers live and work (**quartel**)

barracuda /ˌbærə'kuːdə/ NOUN [*plural* **barracudas**] a large fierce sea fish with big teeth, found in the Caribbean and other warm seas (**barracuda**)

barrage /'bærɑːʒ/ NOUN [*plural* **barrages**]
1 a continuous firing of guns (**fogo de barragem**)
2 a barrage of something a lot of questions or complaints said all at the same time by a lot of different people ☐ *He has faced a barrage of criticism.* (**artilharia de algo**)

barrel /'bærəl/ NOUN [*plural* **barrels**]
1 a wooden or metal container with curved sides, used for holding liquids such as beer (**barril**)
2 the barrel of a gun is the metal tube through which the bullet is fired (**cano**)

barren /'bærən/ ADJECTIVE barren land has very little or nothing growing on it (**árido**)

barricade /ˈbærɪˌkeɪd/ ▶ NOUN [*plural* **barricades**] something that is put across a road or door to stop people getting through ☐ *Police smashed barricades which had been erected by protesters.* (**barricada**)
▶ VERB [**barricades, barricading, barricaded**]
1 to put something across a road or door to stop people getting through (**barricar**)
2 barricade yourself somewhere to stay inside a place and put something across the door so that people cannot get in ☐ *They've barricaded themselves inside the house.* (**proteger-se em algum lugar**)

barrier /'bærɪə(r)/ NOUN [*plural* **barriers**]
1 a gate or fence used to stop people getting past ☐ *There is a barrier at the exit of the car park, and you need a ticket to get out.* (**barreira**)
2 something that stops you from making progress or stops you from being successful ☐ *Nowadays, being a woman isn't a barrier to a career in the navy.* (**barreira**)
3 something that prevents people from communicating or working well together (**barreira**) 🔗 *The* language barrier *can be a real problem when people go to live abroad.* (**barreira linguística**)

barring /'bɑːrɪŋ/ PREPOSITION unless something happens ☐ *Barring accidents, he should win the competition.* (**exceto, salvo**)

barrister /'bærɪstə(r)/ NOUN [*plural* **barristers**] a lawyer who works in a court (**advogado**)

barrow /'bærəʊ/ NOUN [*plural* **barrows**] a container on wheels that you push (**carroça**)

barter /'bɑːtə(r)/ VERB [**barters, bartering, bartered**] to exchange one thing for another thing, without using any money ☐ *They bartered crops for milk in nearby villages.* (**permutar**)

basalt /'bæsɔːlt/ NOUN, NO PLURAL a type of rock made from hot liquid rock from a volcano (= mountain that explodes). A geography word. (**basalto**)

base /beɪs/ c NOUN [*plural* **bases**]
1 the lowest part of something ☐ **+ of** *He broke a bone at the base of his spine.*
2 something which is under something else and which supports it ☐ *The shed stood on a concrete base.* (**base**)
3 the main place where someone works or stays ☐ **+ for** *The hotel is an ideal base for walking holidays.* (**base**)
4 a place where people in the army, navy, etc. live and work ☐ *a British military base in Germany* (**base**)
5 a situation or idea from which something can develop ☐ **+ for** *The conditions provide a good base for economic strength.* (**base**)
6 the number used as the most important unit in a system of counting, for example 10 in the decimal system. A maths word. (**base**)
▶ VERB [**bases, basing, based**] if a person or organization is based in a particular place, that is where they live or do their work ☐ *usually passive The company is based in Moscow.* ☐ *a London--based organization* (**base**)

◆ PHRASAL VERB **base something on something** to use an idea, situation, fact etc. as the thing that you develop something else from ☐ *often passive The court's decision was based on facts.* (**estabelecer**)

baseball

baseball /ˈbeɪsbɔːl/ NOUN [plural **baseballs**]
1 no plural a game for two teams who hit a ball with a long bat (= wooden stick) and run to four different (**beisebol**) ▣ *He taught me how to play baseball.* (**jogar beisebol**) ▣ *a baseball game*
2 a small ball used in the game of baseball (**bola de beisebol**)

baseless /ˈbeɪslɪs/ ADJECTIVE not based on facts or good reasons. A formal word. ▫ *baseless accusations* (**infundado**)

basement /ˈbeɪsmənt/ NOUN [plural **basements**] the lowest level of a building, under the ground ▫ *There is a restaurant in the basement.* ▫ *a basement flat* (**porão**)

bases /ˈbeɪsiːz/ PLURAL OF **basis** and **base** (**ver base, basis**)

bash /bæʃ/ ▶ VERB [**bashes, bashing, bashed**] an informal word meaning to hit something or someone very hard ▫ *The ball bashed him in the face.* (**golpear**)
▶ NOUN [plural **bashes**]
1 an informal word meaning a hard hit (**golpe**)
2 an informal word meaning a special party (**festa**)
3 an informal word meaning a try at something (**tentativa**) ▣ *The club allows members to have a bash at various sports.* (**fez uma tentativa**)

bashful /ˈbæʃfʊl/ ADJECTIVE shy and becoming embarrassed very easily ▫ *Lily, suddenly bashful, could think of nothing to say.* (**embaraçado**)

basic /ˈbeɪsɪk/ ADJECTIVE
1 being the main or most important part of something ▫ *He taught us the basic principles of karate.* ▫ *basic training/skills* (**básico**)
2 without any extra or special features ▫ *The cottage was pretty basic – it didn't even have a proper bath.* (**básico**)
• **basically** /ˈbeɪsɪkəli/ ADVERB used when you are stating the most important fact and not giving all the details ▫ *Joe's basically a good person.* ▫ *Basically, I was sick of the job.* (**basicamente**)
• **basics** /ˈbeɪsɪks/ PLURAL NOUN the most important things that you need ▫ *John taught her the basics of sailing.* ▫ *We spend most of our money on basics like food and clothes.* (**fundamentos**)

basil /ˈbæzəl/ NOUN, NO PLURAL a herb that is used in cooking with leaves that smell sweet (**manjericão**)

basin /ˈbeɪsən/ NOUN [plural **basins**]
1 a bowl with taps (= objects you turn to get water) for washing your hands and face in (**bacia**)
2 a bowl used in the kitchen for holding food ▫ *a pudding basin* (**travessa**)
3 an area of land from which water flows into a river ▫ *the Amazon basin* (**bacia**)

basis /ˈbeɪsɪs/ NOUN [plural **bases**]

bat

1 on a regular/part-time/unpaid, etc. basis used to express the method or system used for arranging or organizing something ▫ *The team meets on a weekly basis.* ▫ *I work there on a voluntary basis.* (**periodicamente, meio período etc.**)
2 on the basis of something used to show the reason why something is done in a particular way ▫ *Medical treatment should not be refused on the basis of age.* (**com base em algo**)
3 the thing on which something is based ▣ *Sweets can be eaten occasionally but should not form the basis of your diet.* (**compor a base de**)

bask /bɑːsk/ VERB [**basks, basking, basked**]
1 to sit or lie enjoying the warmth of the sun ▫ *We basked in the warm sunshine.* (**aquecer-se**)
2 if you bask in other people's praise or attention, you enjoy it ▫ *Amrish had scored the winning goal and was basking in the admiration of his friends.* (**deleitar-se**)

basket /ˈbɑːskɪt/ NOUN [plural **baskets**] a container for storing or carrying things, made of thin pieces of material such as wood or plastic (**cesto**) ▣ *a shopping basket* (**cesto de compras**) ▣ *a laundry basket* (**cestos de roupas**) ▫ + *of a basket of fruit*

basketball /ˈbɑːskɪtbɔːl/ NOUN [plural **basketballs**]
1 no plural a game played by two teams who try to throw a ball through a net (**basquetebol**)
2 a large ball used to play basketball (**bola de basquetebol**)

basmati /bæsˈmætɪ/ NOUN, NO PLURAL a type of rice that is often used in South Asian cooking (**basmati**)

bass /beɪs/ ▶ NOUN [plural **basses**]
1 the lowest range of notes in music (**baixo**)
2 an electric guitar that plays low notes (**baixo**)
3 a double bass (= very large instrument with strings) (**contrabaixo**)
4 a man with the lowest type of singing voice (**baixo**)
▶ ADJECTIVE of or making the lowest range of musical notes ▫ *singing the bass part* (**grave**)

bass clef /ˈbeɪs ˈklef/ NOUN [plural **bass clefs**] a sign [𝄢] used in music to show that the notes are in the lower range (**clave de fá**)

bassoon /bəˈsuːn/ NOUN [plural **bassoons**] a long wooden instrument that you play by blowing into it to make a low sound (**fagote**)

bastion /ˈbæstɪən/ NOUN [plural **bastions**] a place or organization that supports traditional beliefs or ways of doing things (**bastião**) ▣ *The college was Oxford University's last bastion of female-only education.* (**último bastião**)

bat /bæt/ ▶ NOUN [plural **bats**]
1 a piece of wood used for hitting the ball in sports such as cricket and baseball (**bastão**)
2 an animal that flies around at night, and looks like a mouse with wings (**morcego**)

▶ VERB [bats, batting, batted] to use the bat in games such as cricket and rounders □ It's Gary's turn to bat next. (bater)

batch /bætʃ/ NOUN [plural batches] several people or things that are dealt with as a group □ He stapled a batch of papers together. (grupo)

bated /ˈbeɪtɪd/ ADJECTIVE **with bated breath** feeling nervous or excited because you are waiting for something to happen □ I waited with bated breath as they announced the winner. (prender a respiração)

bath /bɑːθ/ ▶ NOUN [plural baths]

1 a long container that you fill with water and sit or lie in to wash yourself (banheira) □ Russell's in the bath. ▣ She went upstairs and ran a bath (= put water in it). (encheu a banheira)

2 when you sit or lie in a long container filled with water so that you can wash yourself ▣ I think I'll have a bath. (tomar um banho)

▶ VERB [baths, bathing, bathed] to wash someone in a bath (dar banho em)

bathe /beɪð/ VERB [bathes, bathing, bathed]

1 to wash your body □ They are forced to bathe in polluted water. (tomar banho)

2 to swim in a lake, a river, or the sea (tomar banho no mar, no rio, no lago)

3 to wash a cut or wash a sore part of your body □ I'm going to bathe my aching feet as soon as I get home. (lavar)

bathrobe /ˈbɑːθrəʊb/ NOUN [plural bathrobes] a soft piece of clothing that looks like a coat, that you wear before or after having a bath (roupão de banho)

bathroom /ˈbɑːθrʊm/ NOUN [plural bathrooms]

1 the room that you wash yourself in □ The hotel rooms all have a private bathroom. □ a bathroom mirror (banheiro)

2 go to the bathroom a US phrase meaning to go to the toilet (ir ao banheiro)

bathtub /ˈbɑːθtʌb/ NOUN [plural bathtubs] the US word for **bath** (= container that you sit in to wash yourself) (banheira)

bat mitzvah /ˌbæt ˈmɪtsvə/ NOUN [plural bat mitzvahs] a religious ceremony for Jewish girls when they are 12. It marks the time when they start having religious responsibilities. (bat mitzvah)

baton /ˈbætən/ NOUN [plural batons]

1 a stick, for example used by police to control crowds, or passed between runners in a race (bastão)

2 a thin stick used by the person conducting (= moving their arms to control) an orchestra (= large group of musicians) (batuta)

batsman /ˈbætsmən/ NOUN [plural batsmen] a man who is hitting the ball in cricket (batedor)

battalion /bəˈtæljən/ NOUN [plural battalions] a large group of soldiers (batalhão)

batten /ˈbætən/

♦ PHRASAL VERB [battens, battening, battened] **batten something down** to fix something with a long piece of wood to make sure it is tightly closed (consertar algo com tábua)

batter /ˈbætə(r)/ ▶ VERB [batters, battering, battered] to hit someone or something very hard several times □ He was battered to death with a hammer. □ Waves battered the shore. (espancar)

▶ NOUN, NO PLURAL a mixture of flour, milk and eggs, used for covering food before it is fried (massa)

• **battered** /ˈbætəd/ ADJECTIVE

1 damaged □ a battered leather suitcase (batido)

2 covered in batter □ battered cod (coberto por massa)

battering ram /ˈbætərɪŋ ˌræm/ NOUN [plural battering rams] a large heavy piece of wood or metal, used for breaking through a door (aríete)

battery /ˈbætrɪ/ NOUN [plural batteries] a device used to supply electrical power to things like watches, cameras and car engines (bateria) ▣ The car wouldn't start because the battery was flat (= the battery did not work). (bateria vazia)

battle /ˈbætəl/ ▶ NOUN [plural battles]

1 a fight between two armies □ the Battle of Hastings □ His father was killed in battle. (batalha)

2 a situation in which people compete or argue with each other (batalha) ▣ She won a bitter legal battle to get custody of their child. (batalha legal) □ **+ for** a battle for power □ **+ with** He was involved in a battle with his brother over some land.

3 a determined effort to deal with a difficult situation □ **+ against** the battle against crime (luta) ▣ She lost her battle against cancer. (perdeu a luta)

▶ VERB [battles, battling, battled] to try very hard to do something difficult □ **+ to do something** Surgeons battled to save her life. □ **+ against** Rescuers battled against strong winds and rough seas. □ **+ for** They are continuing to battle for compensation. (lutar)

battlefield /ˈbætəlfiːld/ NOUN [plural battlefields] a place where armies fight (campo de batalha)

battlements /ˈbætəlmənts/ PLURAL NOUN a wall around the top of a castle, with spaces for people to shoot weapons through (ameia)

battleship /ˈbætəlʃɪp/ NOUN [plural battleships] a very large ship that has big guns (couraçado)

batty /ˈbætɪ/ ADJECTIVE [battier, battiest] an informal word meaning slightly silly and strange □ a batty idea □ I can't remember where I put my keys. I must be going batty. (estranho)

bauble /ˈbɔːbəl/ NOUN [plural baubles] a round shiny decoration that you hang on a tree at Christmas (enfeite)

baulk /bɔːk/ VERB [baulks, baulking, baulked] to not want to do something because you think it is

bawdy

unpleasant or unreasonable ☐ *My father baulked at the cost of taking us all to Australia.* (**evitar**)

bawdy /ˈbɔːdɪ/ ADJECTIVE [**bawdier, bawdiest**] referring to sex in a funny way ☐ *bawdy jokes* (**desbocado**)

bawl /bɔːl/ VERB [**bawls, bawling, bawled**]
1 to shout loudly (**berrar**)
2 an informal word meaning to cry (**chorar**)

bay /beɪ/ NOUN [*plural* **bays**]
1 a piece of land on the coast that curves in ☐ *the Bay of Biscay* (**baía**)
2 an area that is used for a particular purpose (**local**) ☐ *The supermarket has promised to provide more disabled parking bays.* (**local para estacionamento**) ☐ *a loading bay* (= for taking goods on or off vehicles) (**local para carga e descarga**)
3 keep/hold something at bay to stop something bad from happening or affecting you ☐ *Treatment has kept the cancer at bay for the past five years.* (**manter algo a distância**)

bayonet /ˈbeɪənɪt/ NOUN [*plural* **bayonets**] a long knife fixed to the end of a gun (**baioneta**)

bay window /ˌbeɪ ˈwɪndəʊ/ NOUN [*plural* **bay windows**] a window that curves out from the wall of a house (**janela da sacada**)

bazaar /bəˈzɑː(r)/ NOUN [*plural* **bazaars**]
1 a market in Middle Eastern countries (**mercado, feira**)
2 an event where things are sold to make money for an organization (**bazar**)

BBC /ˌbiː biː ˈsiː/ ABBREVIATION British Broadcasting Corporation; the television and radio company paid for by the public in the UK (**BBC**)

BC /ˌbiː ˈsiː/ ABBREVIATION before Christ; used after a date to show that it was before the birth of Jesus Christ, for example, 450 BC. (**a.C. – antes de Cristo**)
⇨ *go to* **AD**

be /biː/ ▶ VERB
1 used for giving information about someone or something ☐ *He's French.* ☐ *Are you hungry?* ☐ *Her brother's an accountant.* (**ser, estar**)
2 there are/is/were, etc. used for saying that something exists or existed ☐ *There are a lot of people here.* ☐ *Is there anything else to eat?* (**há, houve, haverá etc.**)
▶ AUXILIARY VERB
1 used with the present participle of another verb to talk about actions that were or are continuous ☐ *I am enjoying my course.* ☐ *What are you doing?* ☐ *He is not doing very well at school*
2 used with the present participle of another verb to talk about actions in the future ☐ *He is going to London next week.* ☐ *They are opening a new shop.* ☐ *I am coming back again later.*
3 used with the past participle of another verb to make passive sentences ☐ *She was taken to hospital.* ☐ *They have been warned before.* ☐ *The animals will be kept in a zoo.*

beach /biːtʃ/ NOUN [*plural* **beaches**] an area of sand or stones at the edge of the sea ☐ *We spent the day on the beach.* (**praia**) ☐ *The town has a beautiful sandy beach.* (**praia arenosa**)

beacon /ˈbiːkən/ NOUN [*plural* **beacons**] a bright light that is used as a warning of danger or as a sign of something (**farol**)

bead /biːd/ NOUN [*plural* **beads**]
1 a small round piece of glass, plastic or wood with a hole through it, used for making jewellery (**conta**)
2 a round drop of liquid ☐ *There were beads of sweat on his forehead.* (**gota**)

beagle /ˈbiːɡəl/ NOUN [*plural* **beagles**] a type of dog with long ears (**beagle**)

beak /biːk/ NOUN [*plural* **beaks**] a bird's beak is its hard pointed mouth (**bico**)

beaker /ˈbiːkə(r)/ NOUN [*plural* **beakers**] a cup without a handle (**taça**)

beam /biːm/ ▶ NOUN [*plural* **beams**]
1 a line of light ☐ *the beam of the car's headlights* (**feixe de luz**)
2 a long thick piece of wood or metal that is used to support the weight of a building (**viga**)
3 a big smile (**sorriso**)
▶ VERB [**beams, beaming, beamed**]
1 to smile a big smile ☐ *Meg beamed at him gratefully.* (**sorrir**)
2 to send something using television or radio signals ☐ *The game was beamed around the world.* (**irradiar**)
3 if the sun beams, it shines brightly (**iluminar**)

bean /biːn/ NOUN [*plural* **beans**] a vegetable that is the large seed of some plants ☐ *kidney beans* (**vagem**)

beanbag /ˈbiːnbæɡ/ NOUN [*plural* **beanbags**] a large bag that is filled with very small objects like beans, used for sitting on (**pufe**)

bear /beə(r)/ ▶ VERB [**bears, bearing, bore, born or borne**]
1 to accept something unpleasant or painful (**suportar**) ☐ *I can't bear the thought of him suffering.* (**não consigo suportar**) ☐ *+ to do something* Stephen just can't bear to part with his old toys. ☐ *Can you bear to wait a bit longer for dinner?*
2 bear something in mind to remember that something is important ☐ *Please bear in mind that you only have an hour to write your essay.* (**ter em mente**)
3 bear a resemblance to someone/something to be similar to someone or something ☐ *She bears a striking resemblance to her sister.* ☐ *The language bears little resemblance to English.* (**parecer com algo/alguém**)

4 to carry something in your hand □ *Hassan appeared, bearing a cup of coffee.* (**carregar**)
5 to have or show a particular name, picture, or design □ *The plaque on the wall bore his name.* (**levar**)
6 to give birth to a baby or young animal (**dar à luz**)
▶ NOUN [plural **bears**] a large, strong animal with thick fur (**urso**)
• **bearable** /ˈbeərəbəl/ ADJECTIVE if something is bearable, you can accept it even though it is bad □ *The warmer weather made life a bit more bearable.* (**suportar**)

beard /bɪəd/ NOUN [plural **beards**] the hair that grows on a man's chin (**barba**) 🔊 *He wanted to grow a beard.* (**crescer a barba**) 🔊 *Dieter shaved off his beard.* (**raspou a barba**)
• **bearded** /ˈbɪədɪd/ ADJECTIVE having a beard □ *a tall bearded man* (**barbudo**)

bearer /ˈbeərə(r)/ NOUN [plural **bearers**] someone who brings or carries something (**portador**) 🔊 *I'm sorry to be the bearer of bad news.* (**portador de más notícias**)

bearing /ˈbeərɪŋ/ NOUN [plural **bearings**]
1 have a bearing on something to affect a situation □ *His age will have a bearing on how quickly He recovers from his illness.* (**ter relação com algo**)
2 get your bearings to find out where you are (**orientar-se**)
3 lose your bearings to get confused and not know where you are (**perder-se**)

beast /biːst/ NOUN [plural **beasts**]
1 an animal, especially a large one (**besta, animal selvagem**)
2 an old-fashioned word meaning a cruel person (**besta**)
• **beastly** /ˈbiːstlɪ/ ADJECTIVE [**beastlier**, **beastliest**] an old-fashioned word meaning cruel or unpleasant (**brutal**)

beat /biːt/ ▶ VERB [**beats**, **beating**, **beat**, **beaten**]
1 to defeat someone in a game or competition □ *England were beaten 3-0 by Italy.* □ **+ at** *She beat me at squash.* (**derrotar**)
2 to hit someone or something many times □ *He was beaten and robbed by two men.* (**bater**)
3 to make a regular sound or movement □ *He could hear his heart beating.* (**bater**)
4 to deal successfully with a bad situation or illness □ *Police are working with the community to try to beat crime.* □ *She beat cancer and went on to have a child.* (**combater**)
5 to mix food together very quickly □ *Beat the eggs.* (**bater**)
♦ IDIOM **off the beaten** track a long way from other people or houses (**fora do mapa**)
♦ PHRASAL VERB **beat someone up** to hit or kick someone until they are badly injured □ *He was beaten up by some boys in his class.* (**surrar**)
▶ NOUN [plural **beats**]

1 a regular sound or movement like that made by your heart □ **+ of** *I could hear the rapid beat of her heart.* (**batida**)
2 a regular rhythm in music (**ritmo**)
3 an area that a police officer walks around regularly □ *We want more police officers on the beat.* (**ronda**)

beautician /bjuːˈtɪʃən/ NOUN [plural **beauticians**] someone whose job is to make people look better by doing things such as painting their nails or putting make-up on them (**esteticista**)

beautiful /ˈbjuːtɪful/ ADJECTIVE
1 very attractive (**bonito**) □ *She was a very beautiful young woman.* 🔊 *She looked beautiful in her long blue dress.* (**estava bonita**) □ *beautiful countryside* □ *beautiful music*
2 very sunny and bright □ *It was a cold but beautiful day.* (**bonito**)
• **beautifully** /ˈbjuːtəfəlɪ/ ADVERB
1 in a beautiful way □ *The card was beautifully decorated.* (**com beleza**)
2 with great care and skill □ *a beautifully made jacket* (**muito bem feito**)
• **beautify** /ˈbjuːtɪfaɪ/ VERB [**beautifies**, **beautifying**, **beautified**] to make a place or person more attractive (**embelezar**)

beauty /ˈbjuːtɪ/ NOUN [plural **beauties**]
1 *no plural* the quality of being very attractive (**beleza**) 🔊 *The area is noted for its natural beauty.* (**beleza natural**) □ **+ of** *the beauty of her face*
2 the beauty of something a quality that makes something very good □ *The beauty of the software is that it is easy to use.* (**a beleza de algo**)
3 a thing you think is very good □ *Just look at the fish he caught. Isn't it a beauty?* (**beleza**)
4 a beautiful woman □ *She was a great beauty.* (**beleza**)
5 beauty products/treatments, etc. things to make people more attractive (**produtos/tratamentos de beleza etc.**)

beauty salon /ˈbjuːtɪ ˈsælɒn/ NOUN [plural **beauty salons**] a place where people go for treatments to make them more attractive (**salão de beleza**)

beauty spot /ˈbjuːtɪ ˈspɒt/ NOUN [plural **beauty spots**] a beautiful place in the countryside that a lot of people go to (**paisagem bela**)

beaver /ˈbiːvə(r)/ NOUN [plural **beavers**] an animal with brown fur and a large flat tail that builds dams (= walls) made from sticks across rivers (**castor**)
♦ PHRASAL VERB [**beavers**, **beavering**, **beavered**] **beaver away** to work very hard □ *Sanjay's been beavering away at his homework.* (**trabalhar duro**)

became /bɪˈkeɪm/ PAST TENSE OF **become** (**ver become**)

because /bɪˈkɒz/ CONJUNCTION
1 used for giving the reason for something □ *We chose the hotel because it was easy for everyone*

to get to. □ *You can't borrow my bike because there's something wrong with the brakes.* (**porque**)
2 because of as a result of □ *Because of your rudeness, we've lost the job.* □ *We decided not to go because of the rain.* (**por causa de**)
3 just because used for saying that although one thing is true, something else may not be true □ *Just because I'm younger than you doesn't mean I don't know anything.* (**o fato de**)

beckon /ˈbekən/ VERB [beckons, beckoning, beckoned] to signal with your hand that you want someone to come closer to you □ *Alice beckoned to the waiter.* (**aceitar**)

become /bɪˈkʌm/ VERB [becomes, becoming, became, become]
1 to begin to be something □ *She'd become old and frail.* □ *He became prime minister in 1997.* (**tornou-se**)
2 what became of someone/something used to ask what has happened to someone or something □ *Do you remember the woman with the pink coat? I wonder what became of her?* (**o que aconteceu com algo/alguém**)

becquerel /ˌbekəˈrel/ NOUN [plural becquerels] a unit used to measure radioactivity. A physics word. (**bequerel**)

bed /bed/ NOUN [plural beds]
1 a piece of furniture that you sleep on (**cama**) □ *He was ill and spent the day in bed.* 🔹 *I got out of bed and went downstairs.* (**acordo**) 🔹 *What time do you usually go to bed?* (**vai dormir**) 🔹 *I need to make the bed (= put the sheets on it).* (**fazer a cama**) 🔹 *The room had a double bed (= bed for two people) in it.* (**beliche**)
2 the bottom of a river, a lake or the sea 🔹 *the sea bed* (**leito do mar**)
3 an area in a garden that contains flowers and other plants □ *He was weeding the flower bed.* (**canteiro de flores**)

bed and breakfast /ˌbed ənd ˈbrekfəst/ NOUN [plural bed and breakfasts] a small hotel or someone's house where you can sleep and have breakfast (**pousada**)

bedclothes /ˈbedkləʊðz/ PLURAL NOUN things such as sheets that you use for covering a bed (**roupas de cama**)

bedding /ˈbedɪŋ/ NOUN, NO PLURAL
1 things such as sheets that you use for covering a bed (**roupas de cama**)
2 something soft that animals sleep on, for example hay (= dried grass) (**forragem**)

bedlam /ˈbedləm/ NOUN, NO PLURAL a situation or place in which there is a lot of noise and confusion □ *There was bedlam as everyone tried to get onto the train.* (**confusão, caos**)

bedlinen /ˈbedˌlɪnɪn/ NOUN, NO PLURAL things such as sheets that you use for covering a bed (**jogo de cama**)

bedraggled /bɪˈdrægəld/ ADJECTIVE untidy, wet and dirty (**desarrumado**)

bedridden /ˈbedˌrɪdən/ ADJECTIVE unable to get out of bed because you are too ill (**acamado, doente**)

bedrock /ˈbedrɒk/ NOUN [plural bedrocks] the main ideas and beliefs that something is based on □ *Free speech is the bedrock of democracy.* (**base, fundamento**)

bedroom /ˈbedrʊm/ NOUN [plural bedrooms] a room that you sleep in 🔹 *We have a spare bedroom so you can come and stay.* □ *bedroom furniture* (**quarto**)

bedside /ˈbedsaɪd/ NOUN, NO PLURAL the area next to a bed (**cabeceira**) 🔹 *a bedside table* (**mesa de cabeceira**)

bedsit /ˈbedˌsɪt/ or **bedsitter** /ˈbedˌsɪtə(r)/ NOUN [plural bedsits or bedsitters] a room where you can live, usually with a bed and a small kitchen area (**apartamento conjugado**)

bedspread /ˈbedspred/ NOUN [plural bedspreads] a cover that you put over a bed (**colcha**)

bedstead /ˈbedsted/ NOUN [plural bedsteads] the metal or wooden frame of a bed (**estrado**)

bedtime /ˈbedtaɪm/ NOUN [plural bedtimes] the time when you usually go to bed (**hora de dormir**) 🔹 *It's well past my bedtime.* (**passou de minha hora de dormir**) □ *a bedtime story*

bee /biː/ NOUN [plural bees] a black and yellow insect that makes honey (**abelha**)

beech /biːtʃ/ NOUN [plural beeches] a tree with grey, smooth bark (= wood on the outside of a tree) (**faia**)

beef /biːf/ NOUN, NO PLURAL meat from a cow (**carne**) 🔹 *We had roast beef for dinner.* (**carne assada**)

beefburger /ˈbiːfˌbɜːgə(r)/ NOUN [plural beefburgers] very small pieces of beef that have been pressed into a flat round shape and cooked (**hambúrguer**)

beefy /ˈbiːfi/ ADJECTIVE [beefier, beefiest] a beefy man is big and strong. An informal word. (**musculoso**)

beehive /ˈbiːhaɪv/ NOUN [plural beehives] a box where you keep bees to make honey (**colmeia**)

beeline /ˈbiːlaɪn/ NOUN
♦ IDIOM **make a beeline for something** to move quickly towards something □ *We made a beeline for the exit.* (**ir direto a algo**)

been /biːn/ PAST PARTICIPLE OF be □ *I have been thinking.* (**ver be**)

beep /biːp/ C VERB [beeps, beeping, beeped] if an electronic machine beeps, it makes a short, high sound □ *The microwave started to beep.* (**bipar**)

▶ NOUN [plural **beeps**] when a machine beeps □ *His watch gave a beep.* (**bipe**)

beer /bɪə(r)/ NOUN [plural **beers**]

1 *no plural* an alcoholic drink made from a type of grain (**cerveja**) 🔲 *He had a pint of beer in his hand.* (**copo de cerveja**) 🔲 *empty beer bottles* (**garrafas de cerveja**)

2 a glass of this drink □ *I'll have a beer please.* (**cerveja**)

beetle /ˈbiːtəl/ NOUN [plural **beetles**] a black insect with a hard back (**besouro**)

beetroot /ˈbiːtruːt/ NOUN [plural **beetroots**] a round, dark red vegetable that grows under the ground (**beterraba**)

befall /bɪˈfɔːl/ VERB [**befalls**, **befalling**, **befell**, **befallen**] if something befalls you, it happens to you. A formal word. (**acontecer**)

befit /bɪˈfɪt/ VERB [**befits**, **befitting**, **befitted**] to be suitable for someone or something. A formal word. (**condizer**) 🔲 *They were elegantly dressed as befitted the occasion.* (**como condizia**)

before /bɪˈfɔː(r)/ ▶ PREPOSITION

1 earlier than something (**antes**) 🔲 *He lost his job just before Christmas.* (**bem antes**) □ *I posted the letter the day before yesterday.* □ + **ing** *He tidied the house before going to bed.*

2 if one place is before another place, you get to that place first □ *Our house is just before the turning on the left.* (**antes de**)

3 before long soon □ *Before long, we became good friends.* (**logo**)

▶ ADVERB at an earlier time □ *I don't think we've met before.* (**anterior, anteriormente**) 🔲 *We had all been to the beach the day before.* (**o dia anterior**)

▶ CONJUNCTION

1 earlier than the time when something will happen □ *Wash your hands before you come to the table.* (**antes de**)

2 in order to prevent something bad from happening □ *Stop fighting before someone gets hurt.* (**até**)

3 until □ *It was a long time before I felt better.* (**antes**)

beforehand /bɪˈfɔːhænd/ ADVERB before the time when something else happens □ *I decided ten days beforehand that I would go.* (**de antemão**)

befriend /bɪˈfrend/ VERB [**befriends**, **befriending**, **befriended**] to become someone's friend, especially because they need your help. A formal word. (**fazer amizade com**)

beg /beg/ VERB [**begs**, **begging**, **begged**]

1 to ask someone for something in an eager or emotional way because you want it very much □ *I begged him to come home.* (**implorar**)

2 to ask people for money in the street because you are very poor (**mendigar**)

3 I beg your pardon (a) a formal way of saying sorry when you have made a mistake □ *Oh, I beg your pardon, I didn't realize this pen was yours.* (b) a formal way of asking someone to repeat what they have just said because you did not hear it □ *'I'm going now.' 'I beg your pardon.' 'I said, I'm going now.'* (**desculpar-se**)

began /bɪˈɡæn/ PAST TENSE OF **begin** (**ver** begin)

beggar /ˈbeɡə(r)/ NOUN [plural **beggars**] someone who asks people for money in the street (**mendigo**)

begin /bɪˈɡɪn/ VERB [**begins**, **beginning**, **began**, **begun**]

1 to start □ *The concert began at 7.30 and finished at 9.30.* □ + **to do something** *I was beginning to feel better.* □ + **ing** *She began walking towards the door.* □ + **by** *She began by apologizing.* □ + **with** *The year began with a big disappointment.* (**começar**)

2 to begin with at the start of something □ *Lorna didn't like her new school to begin with.*

• **beginner** /bɪˈɡɪnə(r)/ NOUN [plural **beginners**] someone who has just started to do or to learn something □ *a guitar class for beginners* (**novato, iniciante**)

• **beginning** /bɪˈɡɪnɪŋ/ NOUN [plural **beginnings**]

1 *no plural* the start of something or the first part of something (**começo**) 🔲 *My birthday is at the beginning of July.* (**no princípio de**) 🔲 *He led from the beginning of the race.* (**do começo**) 🔲 *In the beginning, I didn't like her very much.* (**no começo**)

2 the beginnings of something the first signs or stages of something □ *She had the beginnings of a bad headache.* (**os primeiros sintomas de algo**)

begrudge /bɪˈɡrʌdʒ/ VERB [**begrudges**, **begrudging**, **begrudged**] to feel jealous because someone has something good and you do not think they deserve it (**invejar**) 🔲 *I don't begrudge him his success.* (**eu não invejo**)

beguiling /bɪˈɡaɪlɪŋ/ ADJECTIVE a formal word meaning attractive and interesting □ *a beguiling smile* □ *a beguiling place* (**atraente**)

begun /bɪˈɡʌn/ PAST PARTICIPLE OF **begin** (**ver** begin)

behalf /bɪˈhɑːf/ NOUN **on someone's behalf/on behalf of someone** for someone else □ *Petra spoke on behalf of the other students.* (**em nome de**)

behave /bɪˈheɪv/ VERB [**behaves**, **behaving**, **behaved**]

1 to do things in a particular way (**comportar-se**) 🔲 *I'm sorry – I've behaved badly.* (**me comportei mal**) 🔲 *He was behaving like a child!* (**comportando-se como**)

2 to be polite and not do anything that you should not do (**comportar-se**) □ *Did the children behave?* 🔲 *I hope Harry behaved himself.* (**se comporte**)

behavior /bɪˈheɪvjə(r)/ NOUN, NO PLURAL the US spelling of **behaviour** (**comportamento**)

behead | 67 | **belligerent**

behaviour /bɪˈheɪvjə(r)/ NOUN, NO PLURAL the way you behave (**comportamento**) ◫ *Children should be rewarded for good behaviour.* (**bom comportamento**) ◫ *I've never seen such bad behaviour.* (**mau comportamento**) ☐ *+ towards His behaviour towards Sarah was appalling.*

> Remember that the noun **behaviour** is never used in the plural:
> ✓ *The children's behaviour was awful.*
> ✗ *The children's behaviours were awful.*

behead /bɪˈhed/ VERB [**beheads, beheading, beheaded**] to cut someone's head off (**decapitar**)

beheld /bɪˈheld/ PAST TENSE AND PAST PARTICIPLE OF **behold** (*ver* **behold**)

behind /bɪˈhaɪnd/ ▶ PREPOSITION
1 at the back of something or someone ☐ *Look behind the sofa.* ☐ *Rachel peeped out from behind the curtains.* ☐ *Shut the door behind you, please.* (**atrás de**)
2 making less progress than other people (**atrasado**) ◫ *Roberto's fallen behind the rest of the class.* (**está atrasado**)
3 supporting or encouraging someone or something (**em apoio a**) ◫ *The crowd really got behind him and cheered as he ran to the finishing line.* (**deram apoio a ele**)
4 responsible for something ☐ *So who was behind the robbery?* ☐ *What were the reasons behind your decision?* (**por trás**)
5 an experience is behind you when it happened in the past and does not affect you now ☐ *That's all behind him now.* (**para trás**)
6 behind someone's back without someone knowing ☐ *I don't like people talking about me behind my back.* (**pelas costas de alguém**)
▶ ADVERB
1 at the back (**atrás**) ◫ *The car was hit from behind.* (**por trás**)
2 late in doing something ☐ *I'm behind with my work.* (**atrasado**)
3 in the place where you were (**para trás**) ◫ *I stayed behind after the class to talk to my teacher.* (**ficou para trás**) ◫ *I left my bag behind.* (**deixou para trás**)
▶ NOUN [*plural* **behinds**] your bottom (**traseiro**)

behold /bɪˈhəʊld/ VERB [**beholds, beholding, beheld**] to see something. An old-fashioned word. (**contemplar**)

beige /beɪʒ/ ▶ ADJECTIVE having a light brown colour ☐ *They chose a beige carpet.* (**bege**)
▶ NOUN, NO PLURAL a light brown colour (**bege**)

being /ˈbiːɪŋ/ ▶ VERB the present participle of the verb **be** ☐ *Help! I'm being attacked!* (*ver* **be**)
▶ NOUN [*plural* **beings**] a person or creature ☐ *a being from another planet* (**ser**)

belated /bɪˈleɪtɪd/ ADJECTIVE happening late or arriving late ☐ *a belated birthday present* (**atrasado**)

belch /beltʃ/ ▶ VERB [**belches, belching, belched**] to let air from your stomach come out of your mouth with a noise (**arrotar**)
▶ NOUN [*plural* **belches**] the noise made when you let air from your stomach come out of your mouth (**arroto**)

beleaguered /bɪˈliːɡəd/ ADJECTIVE having a lot of problems. A formal word. (**sitiado**)

belfry /ˈbelfrɪ/ NOUN [*plural* **belfries**] a tower with a bell hanging in it (**campanário**)

belie /bɪˈlaɪ/ VERB [**belies, belying, belied**] to give you the wrong idea about something. A formal word. ☐ *Her obvious energy belies her age.* (**camuflar**)

belief /bɪˈliːf/ NOUN [*plural* **beliefs**] something you believe, especially something that you think is true or something that you think exists (**crença**) ◫ *religious beliefs* (**crenças religiosas**) ◫ *It's a mistaken belief that men are better drivers than women.* (**crença errônea**) ☐ *+ that There is a widespread belief that the economy will improve.* ☐ *+ in His belief in God remained with him all his life.*

believable /bɪˈliːvəbəl/ ADJECTIVE making you think that something is true or real ☐ *The story wasn't very believable.* (**possível**)

believe /bɪˈliːv/ VERB [**believes, believing, believed**]
1 to think that something is true ☐ *I believed his story.* ☐ *I found his excuses difficult to believe.* ☐ *+ that I can't believe that you did that!* (**acreditar**)
2 to think that something is true although you are not completely sure. A formal word. ☐ *+ that I believe that they're getting married.* (**acreditar**)
◆ PHRASAL VERB **believe in something 1** to think that something exists ☐ *I don't believe in ghosts.* (**acreditar em**) **2** to think that something is important or acceptable ☐ *I don't believe in hitting children.* (**acreditar em**)
• **believer** /bɪˈliːvə(r)/ NOUN [*plural* **believers**] someone who believes something, especially someone who believes in a particular religion (**crente**)

belittle /bɪˈlɪtəl/ VERB [**belittles, belittling, belittled**] to make someone or their achievements seem less important than they really are (**menosprezar**)

bell /bel/ NOUN [*plural* **bells**]
1 a hollow metal object that makes a ringing sound when it moves (**sino**) ◫ *The church bells were ringing.* (**sinos da igreja**)
2 a device that makes a ringing sound when you press it ☐ *a bicycle bell* ◫ *She walked up to the front door and rang the bell.* (**tocou a campainha**)

belligerent /bɪˈlɪdʒərənt/ ADJECTIVE wanting to argue or fight with people. A formal word. (**hostil**)

bellow /ˈbeləʊ/ ▶ VERB [bellows, bellowing, bellowed] to shout □ *He bellowed at us to stop what we were doing.* (urrar)
▶ NOUN [*plural* bellows] a shout (urro)

belly /ˈbeli/ NOUN [*plural* bellies]
1 an informal word for the stomach (barriga)
2 an informal word for the front part of your body between your chest and your legs (abdômen, ventre)

belly-button /ˈbeli ˈbʌtən/ NOUN [*plural* bellybuttons] an informal word for the small hollow mark on your stomach (umbigo)

belong /bɪˈlɒŋ/ VERB [belongs, belonging, belonged]
1 if something belongs in a particular place, that is where you usually keep it □ *That chair belongs in the kitchen.* (pertencer, ser parte de)
2 if you belong somewhere, you feel happy and comfortable there □ *She felt as if she didn't belong there.* (pertencer)

♦ PHRASAL VERBS **belong to someone** if something belongs to you, you own it (pertencer a alguém) □ *Who does this suitcase belong to?* **belong to something** to be a member of an organization □ *Peter belongs to the local tennis club.* (pertencer a algo)

• **belongings** /bɪˈlɒŋɪŋz/ PLURAL NOUN the things you own (pertences) 🔹 *They returned to the hotel to* collect *their* belongings. (recolher seus pertences) 🔹 *The bag contained a few* personal belongings. (pertences pessoais)

beloved /bɪˈlʌvɪd/ ADJECTIVE loved very much □ *I lost my beloved old teddy bear.* (amado)

below /bɪˈləʊ/ ▶ PREPOSITION
1 in a lower place or position □ *The plane was flying below the clouds.* □ *Simon was in the class below me in school.* (abaixo)
2 less than a particular amount or level (abaixo) □ *Audience numbers never fell below 1000.* 🔹 *The results were* below average. (abaixo da média)
▶ ADVERB at or to a lower place □ *We climbed to the top of the hill and looked down on the valley below.* □ *Write your name and address below.* (abaixo)

belt /belt/ ▶ NOUN [*plural* belts] a narrow piece of leather or cloth that you wear around your waist (cinto) 🔹 *Karim* undid *his* belt. (tirou o cinto)
▶ VERB [belts, belting, belted]
1 an informal word meaning to hit someone or something (bater)
2 belt along/down, etc. an informal word meaning to move very fast □ *They came belting down the road.* (correr)

bemoan /bɪˈməʊn/ VERB [bemoans, bemoaning, bemoaned] to say that you are not happy about something. A formal word. (lamentar)

bemused /bɪˈmjuːzd/ ADJECTIVE slightly confused □ *He was rather bemused by her attitude.* (confuso)

bench /bentʃ/ NOUN [*plural* benches] a long seat (banco) 🔹 *a* park bench (banco de praça)

benchmark /ˈbentʃmɑːk/ NOUN [*plural* benchmarks] something that acts as an agreed standard for comparing other things □ *These tests set the benchmark for educational achievement.* (nível de referência)

bend /bend/ ▶ VERB [bends, bending, bent]
1 to move the topart of your body to a lower position □ *She bent down to pick up some paper she'd dropped.* (inclinar-se)
2 to move a part of your body so that it is no longer straight (dobrar) 🔹 *Bend your knees slightly.* (dobrar os joelhos)
3 to curve □ *He bent the wire around the post.* □ *The road bends to the right up ahead.* (curvar-se)
♦ IDIOMS **bend over backwards** to try very hard to do something (esforçar-se ao máximo) □ *I've bent over backwards to be fair to you both.* **bend the rules** to allow someone to do something that is not usually allowed (quebrar as regras)
▶ NOUN [*plural* bends] a curve (curva) 🔹 *There was a* sharp bend *in the road.* (curva fechada)
♦ IDIOMS **be/go round the bend** to be/become mentally ill (enlouquecer) □ *I put my phone in the fridge – I must be going round the bend* **drive someone round the bend** to make someone very angry □ *Her constant chatter is* driving me round the bend. (tirar a paciência de alguém)

beneath /bɪˈniːθ/ PREPOSITION
1 below or under something □ *He lay on the ground beneath the tree.* □ *I hadn't realized there was a second layer of chocolates beneath.* (abaixo)
2 if something is beneath you, you think you are too good for it □ *She thinks it's beneath her to do her own housework.* (indigno)

benefactor /ˈbenɪfæktə(r)/ NOUN [*plural* benefactors] someone who gives money to a person or organization to help them (benfeitor)

beneficial /ˌbenɪˈfɪʃəl/ ADJECTIVE having a good effect on someone or something (benéfico) 🔹 *Improved diet had an extremely* beneficial effect *on patients.* (efeito benéfico)

beneficiary /ˌbenɪˈfɪʃəri/ NOUN [*plural* beneficiaries] someone who gets money or an advantage from a situation □ *Schools in southern Africa will be the main beneficiaries of the charity.* (beneficiário)

benefit /ˈbenɪfɪt/ ▶ NOUN [*plural* benefits]
1 an advantage that you get from something (benefício) 🔹 *Most patients* get *some* benefit *from the treatment.* (recebem benefício) 🔹 *The new system will* bring *enormous* benefits. (trará benefícios) 🔹 *The centre is run* for the benefit of (= in order to help) *the community.* (para benefício de)
2 money that you get from the government if you are ill or do not have a job (auxílio) 🔹 *He was*

claiming unemployment benefit. **(reivindicando auxílio-desemprego)** □ *The government wants to reduce the number of people who are on benefits.*

▶ VERB [**benefits, benefiting** or **benefitting, benefited** or **benefitted**] if you benefit from something, or if something benefits you, it helps you □ *+ from I think you'll benefit from the extra lessons.* **(beneficiar)**

benevolent /bɪˈnevələnt/ ADJECTIVE a formal word meaning kind and generous **(benévolo)**

benign /bɪˈnaɪn/ ADJECTIVE
1 a benign tumour (= growth in your body) will not cause you any harm **(benigno)**
2 a formal word meaning kind and gentle **(bondoso)**

bent /bent/ PAST TENSE AND PAST PARTICIPLE OF bend (ver **bend**)
▶ ADJECTIVE not straight □ *a bent pin*
♦ IDIOM **be bent on doing something** to be determined to do something **(estar determinado a fazer algo)**

benzene /ˈbenziːn/ NOUN, NO PLURAL a colourless liquid used for making plastics and other chemical products. A chemistry word. **(benzeno)**

bequeath /bɪˈkwiːð/ VERB [**bequeaths, bequeathing, bequeathed**] to bequeath your money or property to someone is to arrange for them to get it after you die **(passar por herança)**

• **bequest** /bɪˈkwest/ NOUN [*plural* **bequests**] money or property that is given by someone after their death **(herança)**

berate /bɪˈreɪt/ VERB [**berates, berating, berated**] to talk angrily to someone because they have done something wrong. A formal word. **(repreender)**

bereaved /bɪˈriːvd/ ▶ ADJECTIVE having someone in your family who has died recently □ *bereaved families* **(enlutado)**
▶ NOUN **the bereaved** the family of someone who has died recently □ *We had help from an organization offering counselling to the bereaved.* **(os enlutados)**

• **bereavement** /bɪˈriːvmənt/ NOUN [*plural* **bereavements**] when someone in your family dies **(luto)**

bereft /bɪˈreft/ ADJECTIVE
1 bereft of something completely without something. A formal word. □ *The refugees were bereft of hope or comfort.* **(privado de algo)**
2 a formal word meaning extremely sad **(desolado)**

beret /ˈbereɪ/ NOUN [*plural* **berets**] a flat round hat **(boina)**

berry /ˈberi/ NOUN [*plural* **berries**] a small soft fruit containing seeds □ *Holly has red berries.* **(fruto)**

berserk /bəˈzɜːk/ ADJECTIVE **go berserk** to become very angry or violent. An informal phrase. □ *Dad went berserk when he saw the damage to the car.* **(ficar louco de raiva)**

berth /bɜːθ/ ▶ NOUN [*plural* **berths**]
1 a bed on a boat or a train **(cabina, leito)**
2 a place in a port where a boat can stop **(ancoradouro)**
▶ VERB [**berths, berthing, berthed**] a ship berths when it stops and is tied up in a port **(ancorar)**

beseech /bɪˈsiːtʃ/ VERB [**beseeches, beseeching, besought** or **beseeched**] to ask someone to do something in a very urgent way. A literary word. **(implorar)**

beside /bɪˈsaɪd/ PREPOSITION
1 next to or at the side of someone or something □ *There was a chair beside the bed.* □ *Go and stand beside Billy.* **(ao lado de)**
2 compared with □ *Beside that tiny kitten the dog looks enormous.* **(comparado com)**
3 beside the point having nothing to do with what you are talking about □ *Yes, it was busy, but that's beside the point.* **(irrelevante)**
4 be beside yourself to be very upset or angry □ *Her parents are beside themselves with grief.* **(transtornado)**

besides /bɪˈsaɪdz/ ▶ PREPOSITION as well as □ *Besides playing the piano, she sings in a choir.* **(além de)**
▶ ADVERB also □ *It's too wet to go out. Besides, I'm really tired.* **(além disso)**

besiege /bɪˈsiːdʒ/ VERB [**besieges, besieging, besieged**]
1 if a place or person is besieged by people, they are surrounded by them □ *The headteacher was besieged by angry parents.* **(cercar)**
2 if you are besieged with something such as questions or complaints, you get a lot of them **(importunar)**
3 if an army besieges a place, they surround it **(sitiar)**

besotted /bɪˈsɒtɪd/ ADJECTIVE always thinking about someone because you love them so much **(estupefato)**

best /best/ ▶ ADJECTIVE better than everyone or everything else **(melhor)** ▣ *Mia is my best friend.* **(melhor amiga)** ▣ *What's the best way to cook this fish?* **(melhor modo)** □ *It is probably best to arrive a little early.*
▶ ADVERB
1 more than everything else **(mais)** ▣ *What food do you like best?* **(gosta mais)** ▣ *The area is best known for its wine.*
2 in the most satisfactory way □ *She performs best when she is slightly nervous.* **(melhor)**
3 as best you can as well as you can □ *I know it's difficult but just do it as best you can.* **(o melhor possível)**
▶ NOUN
1 the best the person or thing that is better than all others □ *Which of these computers is the best?* **(o melhor)**

2 do/try your best to do something as well as you can □ *It doesn't matter if you don't win, just do your best.* (fazer o seu melhor)

3 at best in the most satisfactory situation □ *At best, we can only hope to make £100 a week.* (na melhor das hipóteses)

4 for the best if a decision or an action is for the best, it will be the best thing for the future, even though it may seem unpleasant now □ *She's decided to get divorced. It's for the best really.* (para o melhor)

5 make the best of something to try to enjoy something or get an advantage from something even though the situation is not what you wanted (tirar o melhor partido de algo)

♦ IDIOM **the best of both worlds** if you have the best of both worlds, you have the advantages of two different situations (o melhor dos dois mundos) □ *He wants the best of both worlds – to be a father, but still to have plenty of free time.*

make the best of something to accept a situation and try to deal with it as well as possible (fazer o melhor possível)

best man /ˈbest ˈmæn/ NOUN, NO PLURAL the man at a wedding who helps the man who is getting married (padrinho)

bestow /bɪˈstəʊ/ VERB [bestows, bestowing, bestowed] a formal word meaning to give someone an important right or honour, or to give them something valuable (conferir)

bestseller /ˈbestˈselə(r)/ NOUN [plural bestsellers] a product that a lot of people buy (best-seller)

• **best-selling** /ˈbestˈselɪŋ/ ADJECTIVE bought by a lot of people □ *a best-selling novel* (que vende muito)

bet /bet/ ▶ VERB [bets, betting, bet or betted]

1 I bet (a) used for saying what you think will happen or what you think is true □ *I bet he'll forget to come.* □ *I bet Jane wasn't pleased about that.* (b) used for saying that you understand why someone feels the way they do □ *'I was really upset when he told me.' 'I bet you were!'* (apostar)

2 to try to win money by guessing the result of a competition, etc. □ *My uncle bets on horse races.* □ *I bet him 50p that I could climb the tree.* (apostar)

▶ NOUN [plural bets] money that you risk by trying to guess the result of a competition (aposta) 🔁 / *put a bet on* the winning horse. (fiz uma aposta)

betray /bɪˈtreɪ/ VERB [betrays, betraying, betrayed]

1 to do something which harms someone who trusts you □ *He betrayed me by telling everyone my secret.* (trair)

2 if you betray your emotions, you show them □ *Her voice betrayed no nervousness.* (denunciar)

• **betrayal** /bɪˈtreɪəl/ NOUN [plural betrayals] betraying someone (traição)

better /ˈbetə(r)/ ▶ ADJECTIVE

1 of a higher standard or more suitable or enjoyable □ *I want to buy a better computer.* (melhor) 🔁 *Is his work getting any better?* (melhorando) 🔁 *His French is much better than mine.* (bem melhor) □ *It's better to buy spices from an Asian shop.*

2 not as ill (melhor) 🔁 *I hope you get better soon.* (fique melhor) 🔁 *Are you feeling better now?* (sentindo-se melhor)

3 the bigger/faster, etc. the better the more big/fast, etc. something is, the more you will like it (quanto maior, mais rápido etc., melhor)

▶ ADVERB

1 in a more enjoyable or suitable way or to a higher standard □ *Which do you like better, the green one or the blue one?* □ *Try to do better next time.* □ *I wish I could swim better.* (mais)

2 I/he, etc. had better used to say that someone ought to do something □ *I'd better hurry, or I'll be late.* □ *I think you had better apologize.* (melhor)

3 better off (a) richer □ *We're better off now than we were ten years ago.* (b) in a better situation □ *You'd be better off hiring a car rather than buying one.* (em melhor situação)

4 know better to have enough experience to know that an action was not good □ *She should have known better than to try and trick him.* □ *I broke my leg jumping off a wall – I should have known better.* (saber melhor)

▶ NOUN, NO PLURAL

1 something that is better □ *I had hoped for better.* □ *She deserved better from her colleagues.* (mais)

2 for the better if a situation changes for the better, it improves □ *My fitness level has changed for the better.* (para melhor)

3 get the better of someone to trick or defeat someone (levar vantagem sobre alguém)

between /bɪˈtwiːn/ PREPOSITION, ADVERB

1 in the area that divides two people, things or places □ *What letter comes between Q and S in the alphabet?* □ *I had to stand between Dan and Shona.* □ *We were on the road between San Francisco and Los Angeles.* (entre)

2 in the period of time that separates two times □ *The shop is closed between 2 and 3.* □ *There was only a week between the wedding and their house move.* (entre)

3 used to show a range of amounts or measurements □ *We usually have between 2 and 4 centimetres of rainfall in January.* (entre)

4 used to show the people or groups involved in something □ *There was an interesting discussion between Angela and Kim.* □ *The match between Leeds and Arsenal has been cancelled.* □ *Between us, we cleaned the whole house.* (entre)

5 used to show the differences of two things, people or groups □ *Can you see the difference between the real jewels and the fakes?* (entre)

6 if you have to choose or decide between two things, you have to choose one of them ▫ *I can't decide between the soup or the fish.* (entre)
7 used to show how something is divided ▫ *Russell and Colin divided the work between them.* (entre)

beverage /ˈbevərɪdʒ/ NOUN [plural **beverages**] a formal word meaning a drink (bebida)

beware /bɪˈweə(r)/ VERB used for warning someone about something ▫ *The sign on the gate said 'Beware of the dog'.* (cuidado)

> The verb **beware** does not have different forms or tenses like other verbs, because it is only used when you are telling people what to do or giving them a warning.

bewilder /bɪˈwɪldə(r)/ VERB [**bewilders, bewildering, bewildered**] to confuse someone (confundir)
• **bewildering** /bɪˈwɪldərɪŋ/ ADJECTIVE confusing (confuso) ▣ *a bewildering array/variety* (ordem/variedade confusa)
• **bewilderment** /bɪˈwɪldəmənt/ NOUN, NO PLURAL being bewildered (confusão) ▫ *'What is this?', exclaimed Leo in bewilderment.*

bewitch /bɪˈwɪtʃ/ VERB [**bewitches, bewitching, bewitched**] to attract and interest someone so much that they cannot think about anything else (encantar)

beyond /bɪˈjɒnd/ PREPOSITION, ADVERB
1 on the other side of something ▫ *Turn right just beyond the bridge.* ▫ *She had never travelled beyond Europe.* ▫ *I stared out of the window at the hills beyond.* (além de)
2 after a particular time ▫ *The strike is likely to continue beyond Christmas.* (depois de)
3 more or greater than something ▫ *These prices are way beyond what we can afford.* (além)
4 if something is beyond someone, it is too difficult for them to do or understand ▫ *This modern technology is beyond me.* (fora de alcance)
5 beyond belief/doubt/recognition, etc. unable to be believed, doubted, recognized, etc. (acima da crença, dúvida, reconhecimento etc.)

bi- /baɪ/ PREFIX bi- is added to the start of words to mean 'two' or 'twice' ▫ *bicycle* ▫ *bilingual* (bi-)

bias /ˈbaɪəs/ NOUN [plural **biases**] when someone supports one person or thing in a way that is unfair ▫ *She felt there was a bias against female employees.* (preconceito)
• **biased** /ˈbaɪəst/ or **biassed** ADJECTIVE supporting one person or thing in an unfair way ▫ *He claimed that the report was biased.* (preconceituoso)

bib /bɪb/ NOUN [plural **bibs**] a piece of cloth that you put round a baby's neck to protect its clothes while it is eating (babador)

Bible /ˈbaɪbəl/ NOUN [plural **Bibles**] the holy book of the Christian religion (Bíblia)

• **biblical** /ˈbɪblɪkəl/ ADJECTIVE to do with the Bible, or in the Bible ▫ *a biblical character* (bíblico)

bibliography /ˌbɪbliˈɒɡrəfi/ NOUN [plural **bibliographies**]
1 a list of books on a particular subject (bibliografia)
2 a list of books that someone has used when writing something such as a book or an essay (bibliografia)

bicentenary /ˌbaɪsenˈtiːnəri/ NOUN [plural **bicentenaries**] the day or year that is 200 years after an important event ▫ *2009 is the bicentenary of Darwin's birth.* (bicentenário)

bicentennial /ˌbaɪsenˈtenjəl/ NOUN [plural **bicentennials**] the US word for **bicentenary** (bicentenário)

biceps /ˈbaɪseps/ NOUN [plural **biceps**] the big muscles at the top of your arms (bíceps)

bicker /ˈbɪkə(r)/ VERB [**bickers, bickering, bickered**] to argue about something that is not important ▫ *They were bickering about whether to go by train or bus.* (brigar)

bicycle /ˈbaɪsɪkəl/ NOUN [plural **bicycles**] a vehicle you sit on and turn the wheels by pressing the pedals (= parts your feet go on) ▣ *I learned to ride a bicycle when I was six.* (bicicleta)

bid¹ /bɪd/ ▶ NOUN [plural **bids**]
1 an amount of money that you offer to pay for something that a lot of people want to buy (lance) ▣ *The highest bid for the house was £300,000.* (lance para)
2 an attempt to do something ▣ *They made a bid for freedom.* (fizeram uma tentativa)
3 an offer to do a job for someone for an amount of money ▣ *We've put in a bid for the contract.* (fizemos uma proposta)
▶ VERB [**bids, bidding, bid**]
1 to offer to pay a particular amount of money for something (oferecer) ▣ *Will someone bid £5 for this beautiful old chair?* (oferecer por)
2 to offer to do a job for someone for an amount of money ▣ *Both companies have bid for the contract.* (oferecer por)

bid² /bɪd/ VERB [**bids, bidding, bid** or **bade, bidden** or **bid**] to say something such as 'good morning' or 'goodnight' to someone. An old-fashioned word. ▫ *He bade me goodnight.* (dizer)

bide /baɪd/ VERB [**bides, biding, bided**] **bide your time** to be patient and wait for an opportunity to do something (aguardar sua vez)

bidet /ˈbiːdeɪ/ NOUN [plural **bidets**] a low sink that you sit on to wash your bottom (bidê)

biennial /baɪˈeniəl/ ADJECTIVE happening every two years ▫ *a biennial event* (bienal)

bifocals /ˈbaɪfəʊkəlz/ PLURAL NOUN glasses that help you to see things which are close to you and things which are a long way from you (bifocal)

big

big /bɪg/ ADJECTIVE [**bigger, biggest**]
1 large in size (grande) □ *a big car* □ *It was the biggest fish he'd ever seen.* 🔁 *They live in a great big* (= very big) *house.* (**bem grande**)
2 important and having a large effect □ *a big decision* □ *a big mistake* □ *There's a big match on TV tonight.* (**grande**)
3 big brother/sister a brother or sister who is older than you □ *I've got a big sister and a little brother.* (**irmã/irmão mais velho**)
4 popular or famous □ *He's big in the US.* (**famoso**)

bigamy /'bɪgəmɪ/ NOUN, NO PLURAL when someone is married to two people at the same time (**bigamia**)

big bang /'bɪg 'bæn/ NOUN **the big bang** the very large explosion that many scientists think created the universe (**explosão cósmica**)

bighead /'bɪghed/ NOUN [plural **bigheads**] someone who thinks they are very clever and good at doing everything. An informal word. (**fanfarrão**)
• **bigheaded** /,bɪg'hedɪd/ ADJECTIVE thinking you are very clever and good at doing everything (**convencido**)

bigot /'bɪgət/ NOUN [plural **bigots**] someone who has strong, unpleasant opinions about subjects such as politics and religion and who does not accept different opinions (**intolerante**)
• **bigoted** /'bɪgətɪd/ ADJECTIVE having strong, unpleasant opinions about subjects such as politics and religion and not accepting different opinions (**intolerante**)
• **bigotry** /'bɪgətrɪ/ NOUN, NO PLURAL when someone is bigoted (**intolerância**)

bike /baɪk/ NOUN [plural **bikes**] a bicycle (**bicicleta**) 🔁 *Can you ride a bike?* (**andar de bicicleta**) 🔁 *We went on a bike ride.* (**passeio de bicicleta**) 🔁 *The road has a separate bike lane.* (**pista de bicicleta, ciclovia**)

bikini /bɪ'kiːnɪ/ NOUN [plural **bikinis**] a piece of clothing in two parts that women wear for swimming (**biquíni**)

bile /baɪl/ NOUN, NO PLURAL a liquid made in your liver that helps you to digest food (**bile**)

bilingual /baɪ'lɪŋgwəl/ ADJECTIVE speaking or using two languages □ *She's bilingual in French and German.* □ *a bilingual website* (**bilíngue**)

bilious /'bɪlɪəs/ ADJECTIVE feeling ill, as if you are going to vomit (**doente, bilioso**)

bill /bɪl/ NOUN [plural **bills**]
1 a piece of paper showing how much you must pay for something (**conta**) 🔁 *Have you paid the phone bill?* (**conta de telefone**) □ *a gas bill*
2 a suggestion for a new law that people in a government vote for or against (**lei**) 🔁 *The government have passed a bill* (= made a law) *which will restrict Internet gambling.* (**aprovou uma lei**)
3 the US word for **note** (= piece of paper money) □ *a $100 bill* (**nota**)
4 a bird's beak (**bico**)

billboard /'bɪlbɔːd/ NOUN [plural **billboards**] a large board with advertisements on it (**quadro de avisos, outdoor**)

billiards /'bɪljədz/ NOUN, NO PLURAL a game in which you use long sticks to hit balls into pockets at the edge of a table (**bilhar**)

billion /'bɪljən/ NUMBER [plural **billions**] the number 1,000,000,000 □ *The government gets billions of pounds a year from taxes.* (**bilhão**)

billionaire /,bɪljə'neə(r)/ NOUN [plural **billionaires**] someone who has a billion pounds or a billion dollars or more (**bilionário**)

billow /'bɪləʊ/ VERB [**billows, billowing, billowed**] to rise and be moved by the air □ *Smoke billowed from the chimney.* (**elevar-se**)

bin /bɪn/ C NOUN [plural **bins**] a container for putting rubbish in (**lata de lixo**) 🔁 *a rubbish bin* (**latão de entulho**) 🔁 *You should put paper in the recycling bin.* (**lixeira de recicláveis**)
▶ VERB [**bins, binning, binned**] to get rid of something by putting it in a bin. An informal word. (**guardar**)

binary number /'baɪnərɪ 'nʌmbə(r)/ NOUN [plural **binary numbers**] a number that is made up of the numbers 0 and 1 only. Computers use these numbers to operate. (**número binário**)

bind /baɪnd/ ▶ VERB [**binds, binding, bound**] to tie something together □ *The robbers bound his hands and feet with tape.* (**amarrar**)
▶ NOUN, NO PLURAL something you do that is boring or annoying □ *It was a bit of a bind having to take two buses to get to work.* (**combinar**)

binder /'baɪndə(r)/ NOUN [plural **binders**] a hard cover with metal rings inside, that you use for keeping pieces of paper in (**fichário**)

binge /bɪndʒ/ ▶ VERB [**binges, bingeing** or **binging, binged**] to eat or drink too much in a short time (**farrear**)
▶ NOUN [plural **binges**] a time when you eat or drink too much (**farrear**)

bingo /'bɪŋgəʊ/ NOUN, NO PLURAL a game in which you mark numbers on a card when someone shouts those numbers. You win if you are the first person to mark all the numbers on your card. (**bingo**)

binoculars /bɪ'nɒkjʊləz/ PLURAL NOUN a piece of equipment that you hold up to your eyes to help you see things that are a long way away □ *She was watching the birds with a pair of binoculars.* (**binóculos**)

bio- /'baɪəʊ-/ PREFIX bio- is added to the beginning of words to mean 'to do with life or living things' □ *biology* □ *biochemistry* (**bio-**)

biochemical /,baɪəʊ'kemɪkəl/ ADJECTIVE to do with biochemistry (**bioquímico**)

biochemistry /ˌbaɪəʊˈkemɪstrɪ/ NOUN, NO PLURAL the study of chemicals and chemical changes in living things (**bioquímica**)

biodegradable /ˌbaɪəʊdɪˈgreɪdəbəl/ ADJECTIVE a biodegradable substance does not harm the environment because it decays quickly and naturally ☐ *biodegradable packaging* (**biodegradável**)

biodiesel /ˈbaɪəʊˌdiːzəl/ NOUN, NO PLURAL diesel (= a type of fuel) that is made from plants (**biodiesel**)

biodiversity /ˌbaɪəʊdaɪˈvɜːsətɪ/ NOUN, NO PLURAL all the different living things that exist in an area (**biodiversidade**)

biofuel /ˈbaɪəʊfjʊəl/ NOUN, NO PLURAL a fuel made from plants (**biocombustível**)

biogas /ˈbaɪəʊgæs/ NOUN, NO PLURAL a gas that is produced by dead plants (**biogás**)

biographical /ˌbaɪəˈgræfɪkəl/ ADJECTIVE to do with a person's life ☐ *a biographical film* (**biográfico**)

biography /baɪˈɒgrəfɪ/ NOUN [plural **biographies**] a book about a real person's life ☐ + *of* She wrote a biography of Napoleon. (**biografia**)

biological /ˌbaɪəˈlɒdʒɪkəl/ ADJECTIVE to do with living things and the way they grow and behave ☐ *a biological process* (**biológico**)

biologist /baɪˈɒlədʒɪst/ NOUN [plural **biologists**] a person who studies biology (**biólogo**)

biology /baɪˈɒlədʒɪ/ NOUN, NO PLURAL the study of living things (**biologia**)

biometric /ˌbaɪəʊˈmetrɪk/ ADJECTIVE biometric information is taken from the human body, for example the pattern of the eye, to make sure that people are who they say they are (**biométrico**) 🔁 *biometric data* (**dados biométricos**)

biopsy /ˈbaɪɒpsɪ/ NOUN [plural **biopsies**] a medical test in which some cells are removed from your body to see if they are healthy (**biópsia**)

biosphere /ˈbaɪəʊˌsfɪə(r)/ NOUN, NO PLURAL **the biosphere** the area on and above the Earth where living things exist (**biosfera**)

biotechnology /ˌbaɪəʊtekˈnɒlədʒɪ/ NOUN, NO PLURAL the use of living cells in science and industry (**biotecnologia**)

birch /bɜːtʃ/ NOUN [plural **birches**] a type of tree with thin smooth branches (**bétula**)

bird /bɜːd/ NOUN a creature with wings and feathers that lays eggs ☐ *wild birds* ☐ *There was a bird's nest in the tree.* (**pássaro**)

bird of prey /ˈbɜːd əv ˈpreɪ/ NOUN [plural **birds of prey**] a bird that kills and eats small animals or birds (**ave de rapina**)

birdwatcher /ˈbɜːdˌwɒtʃɪŋ/ NOUN [plural **birdwatchers**] someone whose hobby is birdwatching (**observador de pássaros**)

• **birdwatching** /ˈbɜːdˌwɒtʃə(r)/ NOUN, NO PLURAL the hobby of looking at birds (**observação de pássaros**)

Biro /ˈbaɪrəʊ/ NOUN [plural **Biros**] a type of pen with a very small metal ball at the end where ink comes out. A trademark. (**marca de caneta esferográfica**)

birth /bɜːθ/ NOUN [plural **births**]
1 the time when someone is born (**nascimento**) ☐ *He was there at the births of all his children.* 🔁 *What is your date of birth* (= the date when you were born)? (**data de nascimento**)
2 give birth if a woman gives birth, a baby comes out of her body (**dar à luz**) ☐ *She gave birth to a healthy baby boy.*

birth control /ˈbɜːθ kənˌtrəʊl/ NOUN, NO PLURAL methods that are used to stop a woman becoming pregnant (**controle de natalidade**)

birthday /ˈbɜːθdeɪ/ NOUN [plural **birthdays**] the date you were born which happens each year (**aniversário**) ☐ *It's my mother's 60th birthday next week.* 🔁 *Happy Birthday, John!* (**feliz aniversário**) 🔁 *I'm going to his birthday party.* (**festa de aniversário**) 🔁 *Did you get a lot of birthday presents?* (**presentes de aniversário**)

birthmark /ˈbɜːθmɑːk/ NOUN [plural **birthmarks**] a mark on someone's skin that they have had since they were born (**marca de nascença**)

birthplace /ˈbɜːθpleɪs/ NOUN [plural **birthplaces**] the place where someone was born (**local de nascimento**)

birthrate /ˈbɜːθreɪt/ NOUN [plural **birthrates**] the number of babies who are born in a place in a particular period of time (**taxa de natalidade**)

biscuit /ˈbɪskɪt/ NOUN [plural **biscuits**] a flat hard cake (**biscoito**) ☐ *He was eating a chocolate biscuit.* 🔁 *a packet of biscuits* (**pacote de biscoitos**)

bisect /ˌbaɪˈsekt/ VERB [**bisects, bisecting, bisected**] a line bisects something when it divides it into two equal parts. A maths word. (**dividir em duas partes**)

• **bisector** /ˌbaɪˈsektə(r)/ NOUN [plural **bisectors**] a line that divides another line or angle into two equal parts. A maths word. (**bissetriz**)

bishop /ˈbɪʃəp/ NOUN [plural **bishops**] an important priest in some Christian churches (**bispo**)

bison /ˈbaɪsən/ NOUN [plural **bison** or **bisons**] a large animal that looks like a cow but has long hair (**bisão**)

bistro /ˈbiːstrəʊ/ NOUN [plural **bistros**] a small informal restaurant or bar (**bistrô**)

bit[1] /bɪt/ NOUN [plural **bits**]
1 a bit (a) slightly ☐ *I'm a bit tired today.* (**um pouco**) 🔁 *He looks a bit like David Beckham.* (**um pouco como**) (b) a short time ☐ *We had to wait a*

bit for the bus. 🔁 *I don't mind looking after her for a bit.* **(um pouco)** (c) a small amount ☐ *'Would you like some more fish?' 'Yes, just a bit, please.'* ☐ **+ of** *I need a bit of help with my homework.*
2 a piece or part of something bigger ☐ **+ of** *There were some bits of the book that I enjoyed.* **(parte)**
3 quite a bit a lot ☐ *He's quite a bit taller than his wife.* **(bem mais)**
4 the smallest unit of information in a computer. A computing word. **(bit)**

> The phrase **a bit** meaning 'slightly' is used a lot in spoken English but is too informal for formal written English. If you are writing an essay, it is better to use the words **slightly** or **a little**:
> ✓ Attitudes to this subject have changed slightly.
> ✗ Attitudes to this subject have changed a bit.

bitch /bɪtʃ/ NOUN [plural **bitches**] a female dog **(cadela)**
• **bitchy** /'bɪtʃɪ/ ADJECTIVE [**bitchier, bitchiest**] saying unkind things about someone. An informal word. ☐ *a bitchy remark* **(malicioso)**

bite¹ /baɪt/ ▶ VERB [**bites, biting, bit, bitten**]
1 to use your teeth to cut through something ☐ **+ into** *Guy bit into the apple.* **(morder)** 🔁 *A lot of people bite their nails.* **(roer as unhas)**
2 if an animal bites, it injures someone with its teeth ☐ *She was badly bitten by a dog.* **(morder)**
♦ IDIOM **bite the bullet** to decide to do something that you do not really want to do ☐ *In the end I had to bite the bullet and ask him for the money.* **(engolir o orgulho)**
▶ NOUN [plural **bites**]
1 when you bite food with your teeth **(morder)** 🔁 *Ali took a bite of the sausage.* **(dar uma mordida)**
2 an injury on your skin where an animal or insect has bitten you **(mordida)** 🔁 *an insect bite* **(picada de inseto)** ☐ *a mosquito bite*
• **biting** /'baɪtɪŋ/ ADJECTIVE a biting wind is very cold **(cortante)**
bite² /bɪt/ PAST TENSE OF **bite** (*ver* **bite**)

bitmap /'bɪtmæp/ NOUN [plural **bitmaps**] a computer image that is made up of a lot of small dots on the screen. A computing word. **(bitmap)**

bitten /'bɪtən/ PAST PARTICIPLE OF **bite** (*ver* **bite**)

bitter /'bɪtə(r)/ ADJECTIVE
1 angry because you feel someone has treated you badly ☐ *He turned into a bitter old man.* **(amargo)**
2 describes an argument in which there are a lot of bad, angry feelings ☐ *a bitter divorce battle* **(doloroso)**
3 making you feel very disappointed 🔁 *His career had been a bitter disappointment to him.* **(desgosto amargo)**
4 having a strong taste such as you find in strong coffee ☐ *Dark chocolate is too bitter for me.* **(amargo)**
5 if the weather is bitter, it is extremely cold ☐ *It's bitter out there!* **(congelante)**
• **bitterly** /'bɪtəlɪ/ ADVERB
1 extremely, in a way that is bad **(dolorosamente)** 🔁 *We were bitterly disappointed not to win.* **(dolorosamente desapontado)**
2 bitterly cold extremely cold **(muito frio)**
• **bitterness** /'bɪtənɪs/ NOUN, NO PLURAL when something or someone is bitter **(amargura)**

bitumen /'bɪtjumɪn/ NOUN, NO PLURAL a black substance used to make roads **(betume, asfalto)**

bizarre /bɪ'zɑː(r)/ ADJECTIVE very strange ☐ *bizarre behaviour* **(bizarro)**

black /blæk/ ▶ ADJECTIVE
1 having the colour of coal or complete darkness ☐ *I bought a black coat.* **(preto)**
2 black people are of a race that have dark brown skin ☐ *We need more black police officers.* **(negro)**
3 black tea or coffee has no milk in it **(preto)**
▶ NOUN, NO PLURAL the colour of coal or complete darkness **(preto)**
♦ PHRASAL VERB [**blacks, blacking, blacked**] **black out** to become unconscious **(desmaiar)**

blackberry /'blækbərɪ/ NOUN [plural **blackberries**]
1 a small black fruit that grows on a plant with sharp stems **(amora silvestre)**
2 Blackberry a very small computer that fits in your hand and does not have wires. A trademark. **(marca de telefone celular)**

blackbird /'blækbɜːd/ NOUN [plural **blackbirds**] a bird, the male having black feathers and a yellow beak **(melro)**

blackboard /'blækbɔːd/ NOUN [plural **blackboards**] a dark board that a teacher writes on in a classroom **(quadro-negro)**

blackcurrant /ˌblæk'kʌrənt/ NOUN [plural **blackcurrants**] a small, round, black fruit **(cassis)**

blacken /'blækən/ VERB [**blackens, blackening, blackened**]
1 to become black or to make something black ☐ *His face had been blackened by ash.* **(enegrecer)**
2 to make people think that someone is bad ☐ *They had blackened her name, she claimed.* **(difamar)**

black eye /ˌblæk 'aɪ/ NOUN [plural **black eyes**] an injury which makes the skin around your eye look black **(olho preto, machucado)**

black hole /ˌblæk 'həʊl/ NOUN [plural **black holes**] an area in outer space that pulls everything into it. Nothing can escape from a black hole. **(buraco negro)**

black ice /ˌblæk 'aɪs/ NOUN, NO PLURAL ice on a road that you cannot see and which is very dangerous **(camada fina de gelo)**

blacklist blast

blacklist /ˈblæklɪst/ ▶ VERB [blacklists, blacklisting, blacklisted] to put someone on a list because they are bad or dangerous and not allow them to do something (colocar na lista negra)
▶ NOUN [plural blacklists] a list of people or things who are bad or dangerous (lista negra)

black magic /ˌblæk ˈmædʒɪk/ NOUN, NO PLURAL magic which is used for bad purposes (magia negra)

blackmail /ˈblækmeɪl/ ▶ VERB [blackmails, blackmailing, blackmailed] to try to get money from someone by saying that you will tell people about their secrets (chantagear)
▶ NOUN, NO PLURAL the crime of blackmailing someone (chantagem)

• **blackmailer** /ˈblækˌmeɪlə(r)/ NOUN [plural blackmailers] a criminal who blackmails someone (chantagista)

black market /ˌblæk ˈmɑːkɪt/ NOUN, NO PLURAL if someone buys or sells something on the black market, they buy or sell it illegally (mercado negro)

blackout /ˈblækaʊt/ NOUN [plural blackouts]
1 a time when there is complete darkness because there is no electricity (blecaute)
2 when someone becomes unconscious for a short time (desmaio)

black sheep /ˌblæk ˈʃiːp/ NOUN [plural black sheep] a person in a family who does bad things and causes their family to be ashamed (ovelha negra)

blacksmith /ˈblækˌsmɪθ/ NOUN [plural blacksmiths] someone who makes and repairs things made of iron, especially shoes for horses (ferreiro)

bladder /ˈblædə(r)/ NOUN [plural bladders] the organ in your body where urine is collected. A biology word. (bexiga)

blade /bleɪd/ NOUN [plural blades]
1 the sharp part of a knife or tool which cuts (lâmina) ▣ a *razor blade* (lâmina afiada)
2 **a blade of grass** a long thin piece of grass (lâmina)

blame /bleɪm/ ▶ VERB [blames, blaming, blamed]
1 to say that something is someone's fault (culpar) □ + *for* He blamed me for the accident.
2 **be to blame** to be responsible for something bad that has happened (ser o responsável) □ Pilot error was to blame for the accident.
♦ IDIOM **I don't blame you** used for saying that you can understand someone's reasons for doing something □ I don't blame you for getting angry with him. (não é sua culpa)
▶ NOUN, NO PLURAL responsibility for something bad that has happened (culpa) ▣ Why do I always *get the blame for* everything? (levo a culpa) ▣ I'm not going to *take the blame for* someone else's mistake. (levar a culpa por)

• **blameless** /ˈbleɪmlɪs/ ADJECTIVE having done nothing wrong □ The victim was entirely blameless. (inocente)

bland /blænd/ ADJECTIVE [blander, blandest]
1 not interesting or exciting □ bland music (insípido)
2 bland food does not have a strong flavour (suave)

blank /blæŋk/ ▶ ADJECTIVE
1 with no writing on, or with no sound or pictures on (em branco) ▣ a *blank sheet of paper* (folha de papel em branco) □ a blank CD
2 showing no emotion or no understanding (vago) ▣ She gave me a *blank stare*. (olhar vago)
▶ NOUN [plural blanks] an empty space on a piece of paper (espaço em branco)

blank cheque /ˌblæŋk ˈtʃek/ NOUN [plural blank cheques] a cheque that has been signed but without an amount of money written on it (cheque em branco)

blanket /ˈblæŋkɪt/ NOUN [plural blankets]
1 a cover for a bed, usually made of wool □ a wool blanket (cobertor)
2 a layer that covers everything □ + *of* A blanket of snow covered the roads. (cobertor)

blankly /ˈblæŋkli/ ADVERB showing no emotion or understanding □ They stared at me blankly. (inexpressivamente)

blare /bleə(r)/ ▶ VERB [blares, blaring, blared] to make a very loud and unpleasant sound □ Music was blaring from the loudspeakers. (retumbar)
▶ NOUN, NO PLURAL a loud unpleasant sound □ the blare of a car's horn (estrondo)

blasé /ˈblɑːzeɪ/ ADJECTIVE not excited or not worried about something because you have done it many times before □ By the age of ten she was quite blasé about appearing on television. (indiferente, entediado)

blaspheme /blæsˈfiːm/ VERB [blasphemes, blaspheming, blasphemed] to say offensive things about God (blasfemar)

• **blasphemous** /ˈblæsfəməs/ ADJECTIVE offensive about God or about people's religious beliefs (blasfemo)

• **blasphemy** /ˈblæsfəmi/ NOUN [plural blasphemies] being blasphemous or a blasphemous word or phrase (blasfêmia)

blast /blɑːst/ ▶ NOUN [plural blasts]
1 an explosion (explosão) ▣ They were killed in a *bomb blast*. (explosão de bomba) □ Three people survived the blast.
2 **full blast** as loud, strong, energetic, etc. as possible □ They play their music full blast all night. (volume máximo)
3 a sudden strong movement of air □ The door opened, letting in a blast of freezing air. (rajada)
4 a loud sound from something such as a horn □ The lorry driver gave a couple of blasts on his horn. (toque)

blast-off

▶ VERB [blasts, blasting, blasted]
1 to make a lot of loud noise □ *Music was blasting out of the open windows.* (explodir)
2 to use explosives to break up something such as rock (explodir)
3 to criticize someone or something strongly □ *The mayor made a speech blasting his opponents.* (insultar)

◆ PHRASAL VERB **blast off** if a rocket (= type of spacecraft) blasts off, it starts to go up into the air (ser lançado, decolar)

blast-off /ˈblɑːst ˌɒf/ NOUN [plural **blast-offs**] the moment when a rocket (= type of spacecraft) goes up into the air (decolagem)

blatant /ˈbleɪtənt/ ADJECTIVE bad behaviour is blatant when it is very obvious and the person doing it does not seem to care (descarado) 🔁 *It was a blatant lie.* (mentira descarada)

blaze /bleɪz/ ▶ NOUN [plural **blazes**] a big fire (chama) 🔁 *Firefighters put out the blaze.* (lançaram as chamas)
▶ VERB [blazes, blazing, blazed] to burn or shine brightly □ *Her eyes were blazing with anger.* (brilhar)

blazer /ˈbleɪzə(r)/ NOUN [plural **blazers**] a type of jacket, often worn as part of a uniform (paletó)

blazing /ˈbleɪzɪŋ/ ADJECTIVE
1 burning very strongly □ *A blazing fire made the room very warm and cosy.* (flamejante)
2 very hot □ *We were sitting in the blazing sunshine.* (ardente)
3 a blazing row a very angry argument (discussão acalorada)

bleach /bliːtʃ/ ▶ NOUN, NO PLURAL a chemical used for cleaning things or making them more white (alvejante)
▶ VERB [bleaches, bleaching, bleached] to make something more white using bleach or because of being in the sun □ *Her hair was bleached blonde in the sun.* (alvejar)

bleak /bliːk/ ADJECTIVE [bleaker, bleakest]
1 without hope or happiness (desanimador) □ *The book paints a bleak picture of life in Victorian times.* 🔁 *a bleak future/outlook* (futuro desanimador)
2 a bleak place is cold, empty and not pleasant □ *a bleak winter landscape* (deserto)

bleary /ˈblɪəri/ ADJECTIVE [blearier, bleariest] if your eyes are bleary, you cannot see very well because you are tired (turvo)

bleat /bliːt/ ▶ VERB [bleats, bleating, bleated]
1 a sheep or goat bleats when it makes its usual sound (balir)
2 to complain in a weak or annoying way □ *She was bleating on about how unfair life was.* (choramingar)
▶ NOUN [plural **bleats**] the sound a sheep or goat makes (balido)

bleed /bliːd/ VERB [bleeds, bleeding, bled] when you bleed, blood comes out of a cut on your body (sangrar) □ *He was bleeding from a cut on his head.* 🔁 *My head was bleeding profusely* (= very much). (sangrando muito)

• **bleeding** /ˈbliːdɪŋ/ NOUN, NO PLURAL a flow of blood (sangramento) 🔁 *First try to stop the bleeding and then ring for an ambulance.* (estancar o sangramento)

bleep /bliːp/ ▶ NOUN [plural **bleeps**] a short sound made by an electronic device (som eletrônico)
▶ VERB [bleeps, bleeping, bleeped] if an electronic device bleeps, it makes a short sound (emitir som)

• **bleeper** /ˈbliːpə(r)/ NOUN [plural **bleepers**] an electronic device that makes a sound when someone wants to contact you (bipe)

blemish /ˈblemɪʃ/ NOUN [plural **blemishes**]
1 a mark that spoils something □ *an apple covered with blemishes* (defeito)
2 a bad action which damages someone's reputation □ *This is a serious blemish on his military record.* (mancha)

blend /blend/ ▶ VERB [blends, blending, blended] to mix things together completely □ *Blend the butter and the sugar.* (misturar)

◆ PHRASAL VERB **blend in** to look or seem the same as the other people or things that are around □ *The new houses blend in with the other houses in the area.* (combinar)
▶ NOUN [plural **blends**] a mixture of two or more things □ *Banana milkshake is a blend of milk, banana and ice cream.* (mistura)

• **blender** /ˈblendə(r)/ NOUN [plural **blenders**] a machine used for mixing food (liquidificador)

bless /bles/ VERB [blesses, blessing, blessed]
1 be blessed with something to be lucky enough to have something □ *They've been blessed with two beautiful children.* (ser abençoado)
2 to ask God to protect someone or to make something holy □ *The priest blessed the bread and the wine.* (abençoar)

◆ IDIOM **Bless you!** something you say when someone sneezes (saúde!)

• **blessing** /ˈblesɪŋ/ NOUN [plural **blessings**]
1 something good that improves a situation □ *It was a blessing that he didn't suffer for long.* (bênção)
2 your approval (aprovação) 🔁 *He gave his blessing to the plan.* (aprovou)
3 help and protection from God □ *They asked for God's blessing.* (bênção)

blew /bluː/ PAST TENSE OF **blow** (ver blow)

blight /blaɪt/ ▶ NOUN, NO PLURAL something which spoils something □ *He thought the new houses were a blight on the village.* (ruína)
▶ VERB [blights, blighting, blighted] to spoil something □ *His life was blighted by poor health.* (arruinar)

blind

blind /blaɪnd/ ▶ ADJECTIVE
1 not able to see (**cego**) ▣ *He went blind* (= became blind) *at the age of five.* (**ficou cego**)
2 blind panic/rage, etc. an emotion that is so strong that you cannot think clearly (**pavor, raiva etc. cega**)
3 be blind to something to be unable to notice something ▢ *She loved him so much, she was blind to his faults.* (**ignorar algo**)
♦ IDIOMS **turn a blind eye to something** to pretend not to notice something ▢ *The company turned a blind eye to thefts from its warehouse.* (**fazer vista grossa para algo**) **a blind spot** if someone has a blind spot about something, they do not notice it or they refuse to accept the truth about it ▢ *He has a real blind spot about money.* (**ponto cego**)
▶ VERB [**blinds, blinding, blinded**] to make someone blind ▢ *He was blinded in the war.* (**cegar**)
▶ NOUN [plural **blinds**]
1 the blind people who are blind (**os cegos**)
2 a covering that you pull down over a window (**cortina**)

blind date /ˌblaɪnd ˈdeɪt/ NOUN [plural **blind dates**] a romantic meeting that is arranged for two people who do not know each other (**encontro às cegas**)

blindfold /ˈblaɪndfəʊld/ ▶ NOUN [plural **blindfolds**] a cover put over someone's eyes to stop them seeing (**venda**)
▶ VERB [**blindfolds, blindfolding, blindfolded**] to put a blindfold on someone (**vendar**)

blinding /ˈblaɪndɪŋ/ ADJECTIVE
1 a blinding light is very bright and stops you seeing for a short time (**ofuscante**)
2 a blinding headache is very painful (**que cega**)
• **blindingly** /ˈblaɪndɪŋli/ ADVERB if something is blindingly clear, simple, etc., it is extremely clear, simple, etc. (**gritante**)

blindly /ˈblaɪndli/ ADVERB
1 without noticing what is around you ▢ *Claudia stared blindly out of the window.* (**cegamente**)
2 without considering all the facts or what might happen ▢ *You shouldn't blindly accept everything he says.* (**cegamente**)

blink /blɪŋk/ ▶ VERB [**blinks, blinking, blinked**] to close and open your eyes quickly ▢ *He was blinking in the strong sunlight.* ▢ *Emma tried to blink away the tears.* (**piscar**)
▶ NOUN [plural **blinks**] when you close and open your eyes quickly (**piscada de olhos**)

bliss /blɪs/ NOUN, NO PLURAL great happiness ▢ *The first few years of marriage were bliss.* (**felicidade**)
• **blissful** /ˈblɪsfʊl/ ADJECTIVE extremely happy ▢ *They spent a blissful week together.* (**feliz**)
• **blissfully** /ˈblɪsfʊli/ ADVERB happily (**extasiadamente**) ▣ *Pete was blissfully unaware of the problems ahead.* (**extasiadamente alheio**)

blister /ˈblɪstə(r)/ ▶ NOUN [plural **blisters**] a swollen area filled with liquid on your skin where it has been burned or rubbed (**bolha**)
▶ VERB [**blisters, blistering, blistered**] to form blisters (**empolar**)
• **blistering** /ˈblɪstərɪŋ/ ADJECTIVE
1 very hot (**causticante**) ▣ *blistering heat/ sunshine* (**calor causticante**)
2 criticizing someone or something very strongly (**furioso**) ▣ *a blistering attack* (**ataque furioso**)
3 very fast (**intenso**) ▣ *They set off at a blistering pace.* (**ritmo intenso**)

blithe /blaɪð/ ADJECTIVE ignoring or not caring about possible dangers or bad results ▢ *He drove with a blithe disregard for the rules of the road.* (**descuidado, negligente**)
• **blithely** /ˈblaɪðli/ ADVERB happily and without worrying or caring ▢ *Paul blithely imagines he can pass the exam without doing any work.* (**despreocupadamente**)

blitz /blɪts/ ▶ NOUN [plural **blitzes**]
1 when you do a lot of something in a short time ▢ *The company has launched an advertising blitz.* (**relâmpago**)
2 when a lot of bombs are dropped on a place (**ataque-relâmpago**)
▶ VERB [**blitzes, blitzing, blitzed**]
1 to do a lot of something in a short time ▢ *We got together and blitzed the housework.* (**agir subitamente**)
2 to drop a lot of bombs on a place (**atacar repentinamente**)

blizzard /ˈblɪzəd/ NOUN [plural **blizzards**] a storm with strong winds and snow (**nevasca**)

bloated /ˈbləʊtɪd/ ADJECTIVE swollen and too full ▢ *His stomach felt bloated after the huge meal.* (**inchado**)

blob /blɒb/ NOUN [plural **blobs**] a round lump of something soft ▢ *blobs of paint* (**bolha**)

bloc /blɒk/ NOUN [plural **blocs**] a group of countries that work together and have similar political aims ▢ *the Soviet bloc* (**bloco**)

block

block /blɒk/ ▶ NOUN [plural **blocks**]
1 a solid, usually square piece of something ▢ *Cut the wood into blocks.* ▢ *+ of a block of ice* (**bloco**)
2 a large building with a lot of offices or homes in it (**conjunto**) ▣ *a block of flats* (**conjunto de apartamentos**) ▣ *a fifteen-storey office block* (**conjunto comercial**)
3 a group of houses with roads on all four sides (**prédio**) ▣ *I went for a jog round the block.* (**ao redor do prédio**)
4 a US word for the distance from where one road crosses a street to the place where another road crosses it ▢ *He lives a few blocks from here.* (**quadra, quarteirão**)
▶ VERB [**blocks, blocking, blocked**]
1 to stop people or things from getting through (**bloquear**) ▢ *The road was blocked by an*

overturned lorry. 🔲 *A large police officer blocked our path/exit.* (bloqueou nossa passagem) ☐ + *up The channel was blocked up with sticks.* (paralisar)

2 to stop something from being done ☐ *The government threatened to block the deal.* (bloquear)

3 to be in front of someone so that they cannot see something or light cannot get to them 🔲 *A tall man in front was blocking my view.* (impedindo minha visão)

♦ PHRASAL VERBS **block something off** to close something such as a path or an entrance by placing something across it ☐ *The police had blocked off the road.* (bloquear algo) **block something out 1** to stop light or sound from reaching a place ☐ *Tall trees blocked out all the sunlight.* (bloquear) **2** if you block out thoughts or memories, you stop yourself thinking about them (evitar pensar em algo)

blockade /blɒˈkeɪd/ ▶ NOUN [plural blockades] when someone, usually soldiers, stops goods or people from getting in or out of a place (bloqueio) 🔲 *The blockade was lifted in August.* (bloqueio foi erguido)
▶ VERB [blockades, blockading, blockaded] to surround a place to stop people and goods getting in and out (bloquear)

blockage /ˈblɒkɪdʒ/ NOUN [plural blockages] something that blocks a tube, flow of water, etc. ☐ *Dead leaves had caused a blockage in the drains.* (entupimento)

block capitals /ˌblɒk ˈkæpɪtəlz/ PLURAL NOUN letters written as A, B, C, not a, b, c (letras maiúsculas)

blog /blɒg/ ▶ NOUN [plural blogs] a record of someone's activities and opinions that they put on the Internet for other people to read. A computing word. (blogue)
▶ VERB [blogs, blogging, blogged] to write a blog. A computing word. (escrever um blogue)
• **blogger** /ˈblɒgə(r)/ NOUN [plural bloggers] someone who writes a blog. A computing word. (blogueiro)

bloke /bləʊk/ NOUN [plural blokes] an informal word meaning man ☐ *He's a nice bloke.* (homem, sujeito)

blond or **blonde** /blɒnd/ ▶ ADJECTIVE [blonder, blondest]
1 blond hair is pale yellow ☐ *He had long blond hair.* (loiro)
2 having pale yellow hair ☐ *There was a blonde woman sitting next to him.* (loiro)
▶ NOUN [plural blonds or blondes] a person with pale yellow hair (loiro)

blood /blʌd/ NOUN, NO PLURAL the red liquid inside your body ☐ *Your heart pumps blood through your body.* (sangue) 🔲 *A blood test will show if you have an infection.* (exame de sangue)

bloodcurdling /ˈblʌdˌkɜːdlɪŋ/ ADJECTIVE very frightening (apavorante) 🔲 *a bloodcurdling scream* (grito apavorante)

blood donor /ˈblʌd ˌdəʊnə(r)/ NOUN [plural blood donors] someone who has blood taken from their body so that an ill person can have it (doador de sangue)

blood group /ˈblʌd ˌgruːp/ NOUN [plural blood groups] one of the types of human blood. A biology word. (grupo sanguíneo)

bloodhound /ˈblʌdˌhaʊnd/ NOUN [plural bloodhounds] a type of dog that finds things by smelling (cão de caça)

blood pressure /ˈblʌd ˌpreʃə(r)/ NOUN, NO PLURAL the pressure at which blood flows around your body. A biology word (pressão sanguínea) 🔲 *People with high blood pressure are more likely to have a heart attack.* (pressão alta)

bloodshed /ˈblʌdʃed/ NOUN, NO PLURAL violence in which many people are injured or killed (matança)

bloodshot /ˈblʌdʃɒt/ ADJECTIVE if your eyes are bloodshot, the white parts have red lines on them (injetado, vermelho)

bloodstream /ˈblʌdstriːm/ NOUN, NO PLURAL the blood moving round inside your body ☐ *If the infection gets into the bloodstream, it is carried quickly round the body.* (circulação sanguínea)

bloodthirsty /ˈblʌdˌθɜːstɪ/ ADJECTIVE wanting to kill people or animals, or liking to see them being killed (sanguinário)

blood transfusion /ˈblʌd trænsˌfjuːʒən/ NOUN [plural blood transfusions] when blood from someone else is put into the body of a person who is ill or injured (transfusão de sangue)

blood vessel /ˈblʌd ˌvesəl/ NOUN [plural blood vessels] one of the tubes that carries blood around the body. A biology word. (vasos sanguíneos)

bloody /ˈblʌdɪ/ ADJECTIVE [bloodier, bloodiest] covered in blood or full of blood ☐ *a bloody nose* (sangrento)

bloom /bluːm/ ▶ NOUN [plural blooms] a flower ☐ *The stems are covered in large white blooms.* (flor)
▶ VERB [blooms, blooming, bloomed] to produce flowers ☐ *A lot of plants have bloomed early this year.* (florescer)

blossom /ˈblɒsəm/ ▶ NOUN [plural blossoms] the flowers that appear on a fruit tree before the fruit grows (flor)
▶ VERB [blossoms, blossoming, blossomed]
1 to produce blossom (florescer)
2 a person blossoms when they become more successful or attractive ☐ *She has blossomed into a lovely young woman.* (desabrochar, desenvolver-se)

blot

blot /blɒt/ ▶ NOUN [plural **blots**]
1 a mark made by a small amount of ink (mancha)
🔹 *an ink blot* (mancha de tinta)
2 a blot on something something that makes people have a bad opinion about someone ☐ *It was a blot on his character.* (mancha em algo)
▶ VERB [**blots, blotting, blotted**]
1 to make a mark with a little ink (manchar)
2 to dry a wet surface by pressing something onto it (secar)
◆ PHRASAL VERB **blot something out** to make yourself stop thinking about something bad ☐ *I had blotted out the memory completely.* (apagar algo)

blotch /blɒtʃ/ NOUN [plural **blotches**] a spot or mark of a different colour ☐ *Maddy's skin was covered with red blotches.* (mancha, marca)
• **blotchy** /ˈblɒtʃi/ ADJECTIVE covered with blotches (manchado) 🔹 *blotchy skin* (pele manchada)

blotting paper /ˈblɒtɪŋ ˌpeɪpə(r)/ NOUN, NO PLURAL soft thick paper that you use for drying ink marks (mata-borrão)

blouse /blaʊz/ NOUN [plural **blouses**] a woman's shirt ☐ *a school blouse* (blusa)

blow /bloʊ/ ▶ VERB [**blows, blowing, blew, blown**]
1 wind blows when it moves around ☐ *A cold wind was blowing from the east.* (soprar)
2 to push out air from your mouth onto something or into something ☐ *Blow on your soup – it's hot.* (soprar)
3 to breathe into something such as a musical instrument in order to make a sound ☐ *When I blow this whistle, I want you all to stop.* (soprar)
4 blow your nose to get the liquid out of your nose by forcing air through it (assoar o nariz)
◆ PHRASAL VERBS **blow over** if an argument blows over, people forget about it (parar) **blow something up** to destroy something with an explosion ☐ *He was planning to blow up the aeroplane and all its passengers.* (explodir)
▶ NOUN [plural **blows**]
1 a hard knock ☐ + **to** *He suffered a blow to the face.* (soco)
2 something disappointing that happens ☐ *It was a blow not being able to go to the concert.* (golpe)

blow-dry /ˌbloʊ ˈdraɪ/ ▶ VERB [**blow-dries, blowdrying, blow-dried**] to dry your hair using a hairdryer (= piece of equipment that blows warm air at the hair) (secar os cabelos com um secador elétrico)
▶ NOUN, NO PLURAL when someone blow-dries your hair (secagem de cabelos com um secador) 🔹 *I made an appointment for a cut and blow-dry* (corte e secagem com um secador)

blowlamp /ˈbloʊlæmp/ NOUN [plural **blowlamps**] a tool that produces a very hot flame to heat things up or melt them (maçarico)

blunder

blown /bloʊn/ PAST PARTICIPLE OF **blow** (ver **blow**)

BLT /ˌbiː el ˈtiː/ ABBREVIATION bacon, lettuce and tomato; a type of sandwich (bacon, alface e tomate)

blubber /ˈblʌbə(r)/ NOUN, NO PLURAL the fat from whales (= large sea mammals) and other sea animals (gordura de baleia e outros animais marinhos)

bludgeon /ˈblʌdʒən/ VERB [**bludgeons, bludgeoning, bludgeoned**] to hit someone repeatedly with a heavy weapon ☐ *He had been bludgeoned to death.* (bater com porrete)

blue /bluː/ ▶ ADJECTIVE
1 having the colour of the sky (azul) 🔹 *She was wearing a dark blue dress.* (azul-escuro) 🔹 *He has a pale blue shirt on.* (azul-claro)
2 an informal word that means sad (triste)
▶ NOUN [plural **blues**] the colour of the sky ☐ *The sea was a deep blue.* (azul)
◆ IDIOM **out of the blue** not expected at all ☐ *Out of the blue, he announced that he was leaving.* (inesperado)
⇨ go to **blues**

bluebell /ˈbluːbel/ NOUN [plural **bluebells**] a plant with small flowers in the shape of bells (campânula)

blueberry /ˈbluːbəri/ NOUN [plural **blueberries**] a dark blue berry (= small fruit) that you can eat (mirtilo)

bluebottle /ˈbluːˌbɒtəl/ NOUN [plural **bluebottle**] a large flying insect with a shiny blue body (varejeira)

blue-collar /ˌbluːˈkɒlə(r)/ ADJECTIVE blue-collar workers do jobs involving physical work, not jobs in offices (operário)

blueprint /ˈbluːprɪnt/ NOUN [plural **blueprints**] a plan of work that needs to be done, often of something that is going to be built (planta, projeto)

blues /bluːz/ PLURAL NOUN
1 slow, sad jazz music originally sung and played by black Americans 🔹 *a blues Singer* (cantor de blues)
2 the blues unhappy feelings ☐ *I've just got the blues.* (tristeza)

bluff /blʌf/ ▶ VERB [**bluffs, bluffing, bluffed**] to pretend that you know something that you do not, or that you are going to do something that you will not (blefar)
▶ NOUN [plural **bluffs**] a time when you bluff (blefe)

blunder /ˈblʌndə(r)/ ▶ NOUN [plural **blunders**] a bad or embarrassing mistake (mancada)
▶ VERB [**blunders, blundering, blundered**]
1 to make a bad or embarrassing mistake (errar)
2 to move around in a heavy or awkward way ☐ *We blundered around in the dark.* (cambalear)

blunt /blʌnt/ ADJECTIVE [**blunter**, **bluntest**]
1 with an edge or point that is not sharp □ *This knife is blunt.* (**sem corte**)
2 saying what you think without trying to be polite □ *He can be quite blunt.* (**franco, direto**)
• **bluntly** /ˈblʌntli/ ADVERB without trying to be polite □ *'I hate it,' she said bluntly.* (**francamente, diretamente**)

blur /blɜː(r)/ NOUN, NO PLURAL
1 something that is difficult to see clearly (**borrão**) 🔄 *The cars raced past in a blur.* (**em um borrão**)
2 something that you cannot remember clearly (**borrão**) 🔄 *I don't know what happened next – it's all a blur.* (**em um borrão**)

blurt /blɜːt/
♦ PHRASAL VERB [**blurts**, **blurting**, **blurted**] **blurt something out** to say something suddenly without thinking (**falar sem pensar**)

blush /blʌʃ/ ▶ VERB [**blushes**, **blushing**, **blushed**] to start to have a red face because you are embarrassed □ *Everyone turned to look at Philip, who blushed.* (**corar**)
▶ NOUN [*plural* **blushes**] when your face turns red because you are embarrassed (**rubor**)

bluster /ˈblʌstə(r)/ VERB [**blusters**, **blustering**, **blustered**] to talk in a loud, angry way, especially when you are frightened or nervous (**vociferar**)

blustery /ˈblʌstəri/ ADJECTIVE with strong winds □ *It's quite blustery out there.* (**tempestuoso**)

boa constrictor /ˈbəʊə kənˈstrɪktə(r)/ NOUN [*plural* **boa constrictors**] a large South American snake that kills animals by wrapping itself around them and pressing hard (**jiboia**)

boar /bɔː(r)/ NOUN [*plural* **boars**]
1 a male pig (**porco**)
2 a wild pig (**javali**)

board /bɔːd/ ▶ NOUN [*plural* **boards**]
1 a flat piece of wood (**tábua**) 🔄 *Please use a bread board for cutting on.* (**tábua de pão**) 🔄 *I lifted the carpets to look at the floor boards.* (**tábuas do chão**)
2 a flat piece of wood or cardboard with marks on it, used to play a game □ *a chess board* (**tabuleiro**)
3 a surface on the wall of a classroom where the teacher writes □ *The answers are on the board.* (**quadro**)
4 a group of people who control a company or other organization (**conselho**) 🔄 *the board of directors* (**quadro de diretores**) 🔄 *a board meeting* (**conselho**)
5 no plural meals that you get in a hotel when you are staying there (**refeição**) 🔄 *Do we want full board* (= 3 meals a day)? (**pensão completa**)
6 on board on a ship, aircraft or other vehicle □ *There were 197 passengers on board.* (**a bordo**)
▶ VERB [**boards**, **boarding**, **boarded**]
1 to get on a ship or an aeroplane □ *Could all remaining passengers please board the plane.* (**embarcar, subir a bordo**)
2 if an aeroplane is boarding, people are getting onto it (**a bordo**)
• **boarder** /ˈbɔːdə(r)/ NOUN [*plural* **boarders**]
1 someone who pays in order to live in someone else's house with them (**aluno interno**)
2 a student who lives at his or her school □ *The school has day students and boarders.* (**interno**)

boarding house /ˈbɔːdɪŋ haʊs/ NOUN [*plural* **boarding houses**] a house which people can pay to live in for a short time (**pensão**)

boarding pass /ˈbɔːdɪŋ pɑːs/ or **boarding card** /ˈbɔːdɪŋ kɑːd/ NOUN [*plural* **boarding passes** or **boarding cards**] a card that you need to show someone before you can get on an aeroplane or a ship □ *Passengers are asked to have their boarding passes ready.* (**passagem**)

boarding school /ˈbɔːdɪŋ skuːl/ NOUN [*plural* **boarding schools**] a school in which students can live (**internato**)

boardroom /ˈbɔːdrʊm/ NOUN [*plural* **boardrooms**]
1 a room in which the managers of a company meet. (**sala de reunião**)
2 the people who control a company (**diretoria**)

boast /bəʊst/ ▶ VERB [**boasts**, **boasting**, **boasted**] to talk proudly about yourself in a way that other people find annoying □ *He's always boasting about the famous people he knows.* (**vangloriar-se**)
▶ NOUN [*plural* **boasts**] something you say when you boast □ *It was her proud boast that she never failed exams.* (**ostentação**)
• **boastful** /ˈbəʊstfʊl/ ADJECTIVE often boasting about the good things you have done or the expensive things you own (**orgulhoso**)

boat /bəʊt/ NOUN [*plural* **boats**] a vehicle for travelling over water □ *a fishing boat* (**barco**)
♦ IDIOM **in the same boat** having the same problems as other people □ *Don't worry, we're all in the same boat.* (**no mesmo barco**)

bob /bɒb/ VERB [**bobs**, **bobbing**, **bobbed**] to move up and down quickly □ *She watched the little boats bobbing on the lake.* (**agitar**)

bobbin /ˈbɒbɪn/ NOUN [*plural* **bobbins**] a round object which thread goes around (**bobina**)

bobble /ˈbɒbəl/ NOUN [*plural* **bobbles**] a small round piece of soft material, especially on top of a wool hat (**pompom**)

bobsleigh /ˈbɒbsleɪ/ NOUN [*plural* **bobsleighs**] a small vehicle that is used for travelling fast down slopes in the snow (**trenó**)

bode /bəʊd/ VERB [*plural* **bodes**]
1 bode well to show that something good will probably happen (**predizer coisas boas**)
2 bode ill to show that something bad will probably happen (**ser de mau agouro**)

bodice   81   bomb

bodice /ˈbɒdɪs/ NOUN [plural **bodices**] the part of a dress that fits tightly on the top part of the body (**espartilho**)

bodily /ˈbɒdɪli/ ▶ ADJECTIVE to do with the body (**corpóreo**) 🗋 *The virus is found in bodily fluids such as blood.* (**fluidos corpóreos**)
▶ ADVERB in a way that involves your whole body 🗆 *He was carried bodily out of the room.* (**completamente**)

body /ˈbɒdi/ NOUN [plural **bodies**]
1 the whole physical form of a person or animal 🗆 *I had red spots all over my body.* (**corpo**)
2 a dead person 🗆 *His body was never found.* (**corpo**)

body-building /ˈbɒdiˌbɪldɪŋ/ NOUN, NO PLURAL physical exercise such as lifting weights, that makes your muscles bigger and stronger. (**musculação**)

bodyguard /ˈbɒdigɑːd/ NOUN [plural **bodyguards**] someone whose job is to protect an important or famous person (**guarda-costas**)

bog /bɒg/ NOUN [plural **bogs**] an area of land that is very wet (**pântano**)
◆ PHRASAL VERB [**bogs, bogging, bogged**] **bog someone down** if you get bogged down in something, you spend so much time on it that you cannot make any progress 🗆 *Try not to get bogged down in details.* (**atolar-se**)

boggle /ˈbɒgəl/ VERB [**boggles, boggling, boggled**] **The mind boggles!** something you say when something is hard to imagine or understand. An informal phrase. 🗆 *Grandma's learning karate? The mind boggles!* (**espantoso**)

boggy /ˈbɒgi/ ADJECTIVE [**boggier, boggiest**] boggy ground is wet ground that you sink into when you step on it (**pantanoso**)

bogus /ˈbəʊgəs/ ADJECTIVE pretending to be real in order to trick people 🗆 *She was tricked by a bogus salesman.* 🗆 *bogus documents* (**falso**)

bohemian /bəʊˈhiːmiən/ C ADJECTIVE behaving and dressing in an informal way that is like artists, writers, etc. (**boêmio**)
▶ NOUN [plural **bohemians**] a person who lives in a bohemian way (**boêmio**)

boil /bɔɪl/ ▶ VERB [**boils, boiling, boiled**]
1 a liquid boils when it is heated until it produces bubbles and turns into gas 🗆 *Is the water boiling yet?* 🗆 *Boil some water in a pan and add the pasta.* (**ferver**)
2 to cook food in boiling water 🗆 *I'm going to boil some eggs.* (**ferver**)
3 to heat a container of liquid until it is boiling 🗆 *Shall I boil the kettle?* (**ferver**)
◆ PHRASAL VERBS **boil down to something** to be the reason for something 🗆 *She'll never be a successful pianist. It all boils down to lack of commitment.* (**resumir-se a algo**) **boil over 1** if a liquid that is being heated boils over, it comes up and over the sides of its container (**transbordar**) **2** if a violent situation or emotion boils over, it becomes impossible to control (**descontrolar-se**)
▶ NOUN [plural **boils**]
1 bring something to the boil to heat something until it boils 🗆 *Bring the water to the boil* (**fazer algo ferver**)
2 a painful red swollen area on your skin caused by an infection (**furúnculo**)

• **boiler** /ˈbɔɪlə(r)/ NOUN [plural **boilers**] a machine that heats water, especially for heating a building (**caldeira**)

• **boiling** /ˈbɔɪlɪŋ/ ADJECTIVE an informal word meaning very hot 🗆 *It's boiling in here!* (**fervente**)

boiling point /ˈbɔɪlɪŋ ˌpɔɪnt/ NOUN [plural **boiling points**] the temperature at which a particular liquid boils 🗆 *The boiling point of water is 100 degrees Celsius.* (**ponto de ebulição**)

boisterous /ˈbɔɪstərəs/ ADJECTIVE very active and full of energy 🗆 *a boisterous child* (**impetuoso**)

bold /bəʊld/ ADJECTIVE [**bolder, boldest**]
1 not afraid to take a risk (**corajoso**) 🗋 *Calling an election was a bold move* (= a brave thing to do) *for the president.* (**atitude corajosa**) 🗆 *It was rather bold of him to ask that question.*
2 with strong colours and shapes 🗆 *curtains with bold patterns* (**arrojado**)
3 bold type or print is thick dark letters like this 🗆 *Her name is clearly written in bold type at the top of the page.* (**negrito**)

• **boldly** /ˈbəʊldli/ ADJECTIVE in a brave, confident way 🗆 *Samuel walked boldly into the room, which was full of strangers.* (**corajosamente**)

bollard /ˈbɒlɑːd/ NOUN [plural **bollards**] a short post placed on a road to stop cars from driving somewhere (**moirão, poste**)

bolster /ˈbəʊlstə(r)/ VERB [**bolsters, bolstering, bolstered**] to make someone or something stronger or more confident 🗆 *We were bolstered up by the support of the crowds along the route.* (**reforçar**)

bolt /bəʊlt/ ▶ NOUN [plural **bolts**]
1 a metal bar that you push across a door to lock it 🗆 *She slid back the bolts and opened the door.* (**trinco**)
2 a metal object with small, raised lines that you use with a nut (= metal object with a hole in the middle) to fasten pieces of wood or metal together (**parafuso**)
3 bolt of lightning a flash of light in the sky during a storm (**raio, relâmpago**)
▶ VERB [**bolts, bolting, bolted**]
1 to lock a door using a bolt 🗆 *We bolted all the doors before we went to bed.* (**trancar**)
2 to run away very fast 🗆 *Beth's pony bolted when it heard the noise.* (**disparar**)

bomb /bɒm/ ▶ NOUN [plural **bombs**] a weapon that explodes to cause serious damage to

bombard

buildings, people, etc. (**bomba**) 🔲 *The bomb went off in a crowded market.* (**a bomba explodiu**)
▶ VERB [**bombs, bombing, bombed**]
1 to attack a place using bombs ☐ *Enemy aircraft bombed every town and village in the area.* (**bombardear**)

2 bomb along/through, etc. an informal word meaning to move very fast ☐ *He came bombing down the road on his new bike.* (**correr, andar a mil por hora**)

bombard /bɒmˈbɑːd/ VERB [**bombards, bombarding, bombarded**] to attack a place with bombs or guns (**bombardear**)

◆ PHRASAL VERB **bombard someone with something** to ask someone too many questions or to give them a large amount of something ☐ *They were bombarded with offers of cash.* (**assediar alguém com algo**)

bomber /ˈbɒmə(r)/ NOUN [*plural* **bombers**]
1 an aeroplane that carries and drops bombs (**bombardeiro**)
2 a person who causes a bomb to explode somewhere ☐ *The police are still searching for last Friday's bombers.* (**bombardeiro**)

bombing /ˈbɒmɪŋ/ NOUN [*plural* **bombings**] an attack using bombs (**bombardeio**)

bombshell /ˈbɒmʃel/ NOUN [*plural* **bombshells**] an informal word meaning a very surprising and usually bad piece of news (**bomba**) 🔲 *Mark dropped a bombshell this morning – he's moving to Australia.* (**lançou uma bomba**)

bond /bɒnd/ ▶ NOUN [*plural* **bonds**]
1 something that makes people feel connected to each other ☐ *a bond of friendship* (**laço**)
2 a financial document from a government or a company that shows that you have given them Money and they will pay it back with interest (= extra money) (**acordo, contrato**)
3 the strong force that holds two atoms together. A chemistry word. ☐ *a chemical bond* (**ligação**)
▶ VERB [**bonds, bonding, bonded**]
1 to make one thing stick firmly to another ☐ *Use glue to bond the two pieces together.* (**unir**)
2 if two people bond, they like each other and develop a strong relationship (**ligar**)

bondage /ˈbɒndɪdʒ/ NOUN, NO PLURAL **in bondage** in a situation where you have no freedom, for example being a slave (= servant that is not paid) (**escravidão**)

bone /bəʊn/ NOUN [*plural* **bones**] one of the hard parts that form the frame inside the body of an animal or person ☐ *Brian broke a bone in his arm.* (**osso**)

bone marrow /ˌbəʊn ˈmærəʊ/ NOUN, NO PLURAL the soft substance inside bones. A biology word. (**medula óssea**)

bonfire /ˈbɒnˌfaɪə(r)/ NOUN [*plural* **bonfires**] a large fire built outside (**fogueira**)

bookkeeper

bonkers /ˈbɒŋkəz/ ADJECTIVE an informal word meaning mad (**louco**) 🔲 *His constant chattering is driving me bonkers!* (**me deixando louco**)

bonnet /ˈbɒnɪt/ NOUN [*plural* **bonnets**]
1 the part at the front of a car that covers the engine (**capô**)
2 a woman's or child's hat that you tie under the chin (**gorro**)

bonus /ˈbəʊnəs/ NOUN [*plural* **bonuses**]
1 something good that you get in addition to something else good (**bônus**) 🔲 *The food is great, and has the added bonus of being healthy too.* (**bônus adicional**)
2 extra money that people sometimes get in addition to their usual payment ☐ *a Christmas bônus* (**bônus**)

bony /ˈbəʊni/ ADJECTIVE [**bonier, boniest**]
1 so thin that you can see the bones through the skin (**esquelético**)
2 full of bones ☐ *a bony piece of fish* (**ossudo**)

boo /buː/ ▶ VERB [**boos, booing, booed**] people in an audience boo when they make loud noises because they do not think the performance is good (**vaiar**)
▶ NOUN, EXCLAMATION [*plural* **boos**] a word that people in an audience shout when they do not think the performance is good (**vaia**)

booby prize /ˈbuːbi ˌpraɪz/ NOUN [*plural* **booby prizes**] a prize that is given to the person who has come last in a competition (**prêmio de consolação**)

booby trap /ˈbuːbi ˌtræp/ NOUN [*plural* **booby traps**] a bomb that is hidden in order to kill or injure someone who does not know it is there (**armadilha camuflada**)

book /bʊk/ ▶ NOUN [*plural* **books**] a set of pages joined together inside a *cover* ☐ *a library book* ☐ *Have you read Dan Brown's newbook?* ☐ *I'm reading a really interesting book about Mexico.* (**livro**)
⇨ go to **books**
▶ VERB [**books, booking, booked**]
1 to buy tickets for something or to arrange to have or use something in the future ☐ *I'd like to book a table for four, please.* ☐ *We've booked a family holiday in Majorca.* (**reservado**)
2 if the police book someone for something, they officially accuse them of that crime ☐ *She was booked for speeding.* (**registrado**)

bookcase /ˈbʊkkeɪs/ NOUN [*plural* **bookcases**] a piece of furniture with shelves for books (**estante de livros**)

booking /ˈbʊkɪŋ/ NOUN [*plural* **bookings**] an arrangement to buy something such as a ticket for a performance or a roomin a hotel 🔲 *to make a booking* (**fazer um agendamento**) 🔲 *an advance booking* (**reserva antecipada**)

bookkeeper /ˈbʊkˌkiːpə(r)/ NOUN [*plural* **bookkeepers**] a person whose job is to keep

booklet

records of all the money a business earns and spends (**contador**)

- **bookkeeping** /'bʊkˌkiːpɪŋ/ NOUN, NO PLURAL keeping a record of all the money a business earns and spends (**escrituração contábil**)

booklet /'bʊklɪt/ NOUN [plural **booklets**] a small book that gives information about something (**livreto**)

bookmaker /'bʊkˌmeɪkə(r)/ NOUN [plural **bookmakers**]
1 someone whose job is to take money from people who bet (= risk money) on things like horse races, and then to pay money to the people who have bet on the winner (**agenciador de apostas**)
2 bookmaker's a shop where people can make bets (= risk money to try to get more back) (**agência de apostas**)

bookmark /'bʊkmɑːk/ ▶ NOUN [plural **bookmarks**]
1 something that you put between the pages of a book so that you can find the place where you stopped reading (**marcador de páginas**)
2 a record on your computer of the address of a website that helps you find it again easily. A computing word. (**lista de endereços favoritos**)
▶ VERB [**bookmarks, bookmarking, bookmarked**] to make a record on your computer of the address of a website so that you can easily find it again. A computing word. (**listar endereços favoritos**)

books /bʊks/ PLURAL NOUN the written financial records of a business or an organization (**livro contábil**)

bookshelf /'bʊkʃelf/ NOUN [plural **bookshelves**] a shelf for holding books (**prateleira ou estante de livros**)

bookshop /'bʊkʃɒp/ NOUN [plural **bookshops**] a shop that sells books (**livraria**)

bookworm /'bʊkwɜːm/ NOUN [plural **bookworms**] someone who enjoys reading and reads a lot of books (**rato de biblioteca**)

boom /buːm/ ▶ NOUN [plural **booms**]
1 a situation in which a company or country sells a lot of products and makes a lot of money ▫ *an economic boom* (**crescimento**)
2 a time when something becomes very popular or successful ▫ *the boom in organic foods* (**crescimento**)
3 a loud noise like the sound of a big drum (**estrondo**)
▶ VERB [**booms, booming, boomed**]
1 if a business or the economy booms, it becomes very successful (**expandir-se**)
2 to make a loud noise like the sound of a drum (**estrondear**)

boomerang /'buːməræŋ/ NOUN [plural **boomerangs**] a curved piece of wood that comes back towards you when you throw it (**bumerangue**)

border

boon /buːn/ NOUN [plural **boons**] something that is very useful for you ▫ *These tax cuts are a real boon for poor families.* (**benefício**)

boor /bʊə(r)/ NOUN [plural **boors**] a person, usually a man, who behaves in a rude way (**ríspido**)
- **boorish** /'bʊərɪʃ/ ADJECTIVE rude ▫ *boorish behaviour* (**grosseiro**)

boost /buːst/ ▶ NOUN [plural **boosts**] something that makes something larger or more successful ▫ *The school funds got a boost from the money raised at the summer fair.* (**impulso**)
▶ VERB [**boosts, boosting, boosted**] to make something larger or more successful ▫ *Extra lessons will help to boost her confidence.* (**impulsionar**)

boot /buːt/ C NOUN [plural **boots**]
1 a type of shoe that covers the ankle and often part of the leg (**bota**)
2 the covered place at the back of a car for storing bags, etc. (**porta-malas**)
♦ IDIOM **get/be given the boot** to be told that you must leave your job. An informal phrase. (**ser demitido**)
▶ VERB [**boots, booting, booted**]
1 an informal word meaning to kick ▫ *She booted the ball over the fence.* (**chutar**)
2 to start the operating system (= program that controls all the other programs) of a computer. A computing word ▫ *I've booted (up) the server.* (**iniciar o computador**)
♦ PHRASAL VERB **boot someone out** to force someone to leave a place. An informal word. ▫ *Becky was booted out of the club for breaking the rules.* (**expulsar alguém**)

booth /buːð/ NOUN [plural **booths**] a small place with walls around it where you can do something privately, for example make a telephone call (**cabine**)

booty /'buːti/ NOUN, NO PLURAL
1 things that a thief has stolen (**roubo**)
2 an informal word for a large amount of things you have bought or received (**espólio**)

booze /buːz/ ▶ NOUN, NO PLURAL an informal word for alcoholic drink ▫ *He smelt of booze.* (**bebida alcoólica**)
▶ VERB [**boozes, boozing, boozed**] to drink a lot of alcoholic drinks. An informal word. ▫ *He used to go out boozing every evening.* (**embriagar-se**)

border /'bɔːdə(r)/ ▶ NOUN [plural **borders**]
1 the line which separates two countries or areas ▫ *They settled near the Canadian border.* (**fronteira**)
2 a strip around the edge of something, often for decoration ▫ *a pillowcase with a pretty lace border* (**borda**)
▶ VERB [**borders, bordering, bordered**]
1 to have a border with ▫ *Germany borders France in the West.* (**fazer fronteira**)

borderline

2 to form a line around the edge of something □ *The flowerbeds were bordered with small hedges.* (delimitar)

♦ PHRASAL VERB **border on something** to almost be something □ *His attention to detail borders on the ridiculous.* (chegar à beira de)

borderline /ˈbɔːdəlaɪn/ ▶ NOUN
1 the borderline the point at which one quality or state becomes another □ *The borderline between humour and rudeness can be very thin.* (a linha divisória)
2 on the borderline very close to being in a different group or having a different quality or state □ *He passed the exam, but he was on the borderline* (= he nearly failed). (no limite)
▶ ADJECTIVE very close to being in a different group or having a different quality or state □ *Your work is borderline. You might pass, but you might fail.* (limítrofe)

bore /bɔː(r)/ ▶ VERB [bores, boring, bored]
1 to make someone feel bored □ *The speech bored him.* (entediar)
2 to make a hole in something with a sharp tool (cavar)
▶ PAST TENSE OF **bear** (ver **bear**)
▶ NOUN [plural **bores**]
1 someone who makes you feel bored (chato)
2 a situation or a job that annoys you because it is difficult or boring □ *It's a real bore having to look after her dog.* (entediante)

• **bored** /bɔːd/ ADJECTIVE feeling that something is not interesting or that you have nothing to do (entediado) □ + *with* *I'm really bored with my clothes.* ▣ *The others enjoyed the show, but I was bored stiff* (= extremely bored). (muito entediado)

• **boredom** /ˈbɔːdəm/ NOUN, NO PLURAL the feeling of being bored (tédio)

• **boring** /ˈbɔːrɪŋ/ ADJECTIVE not at all interesting □ *My course is really boring.* (chato)

> Remember the difference between the words **boring** and **bored**. **Boring** means 'not interesting'. **Bored** is how you feel when something is not interesting □ *What a boring film!* □ *I was so bored during the film, I fell asleep.*

born /bɔːn/ ▶ VERB **be born** (a) a person or animal is born when it comes out of its mother's body □ *My sister was born in 1989.* □ *He was born with a heart problem.* (b) something is born when it starts to exist □ *The idea for the film was born over dinner at Jack's house.* (nascido)

> Remember that the verb is **be born** and not just **born**:
> ✓ *I was born in Germany.*
> ✗ *I born in Germany.*

▶ ADJECTIVE a born leader/performer, etc. is a very good leader/performer, etc. □ *Zoe's a born entertainer.* (nato)

bother

borne /bɔːn/ PAST PARTICIPLE OF **bear** (ver **bear**)

borough /ˈbʌrə/ NOUN [plural **boroughs**] a town or part of a city (município, vila)

borrow /ˈbɒrəʊ/ VERB [borrows, borrowing, borrowed] to use something that belongs to someone else and give it back to them later □ *Can I borrow your pencil for a minute, please?* □ + *from* *She borrowed £100 from her Dad.* (pegar emprestado)

> Remember that when you **borrow** something, you use something that belongs to someone else. When you give something to someone else to use, the verb is **lend** □ *I borrowed Dan's mobile.* □ *Dan lent me his mobile.*

• **borrower** /ˈbɒrəʊə(r)/ NOUN [plural **borrowers**] a person who borrows something, especially money from a bank (mutuário)

bosom /ˈbʊzəm/ ▶ NOUN [plural **bosoms**] a woman's chest (peito)
▶ ADJECTIVE a bosom friend is a very good friend (amigo do peito)

boss /bɒs/ NOUN [plural **bosses**] someone who is in charge of other people at work □ *I'm going to ask my boss for a pay rise.* (chefe)
♦ PHRASAL VERB [bosses, bossing, bossed] **boss someone around/about** to tell other people what to do, in a way that annoys them □ *I wish Amy would stop bossing us all around.* (mandar em alguém)

• **bossy** /ˈbɒsi/ ADJECTIVE always telling other people what to do □ *Stop being so bossy – you're not in charge here.* (mandão)

botanic /bəˈtænɪk/ or **botanical** /bəˈtænɪkəl/ ADJECTIVE to do with plants or the study of plants (botânico) ▣ *We visited the city's botanic gardens.* (jardins botânicos)

• **botanist** /ˈbɒtənɪst/ NOUN [plural **botanists**] someone who studies plants (botânico)

• **botany** /ˈbɒtəni/ NOUN, NO PLURAL the study of plants (botânica)

botch /bɒtʃ/ VERB [botches, botching, botched] to do something very badly □ *He botched his first attempt to score a goal.* (estragar)

both /bəʊθ/ PRONOUN, DETERMINER used for saying that the same thing is true for two people or things □ *She ate both cakes, and I didn't get one.* □ + *of* *Both of the boys are good at tennis.* □ *Both the men wore black suits.* □ *We both like classical music.* □ *The book is both interesting and informative.* (ambos)

bother /ˈbɒðə(r)/ ▶ VERB [bothers, bothering, bothered]
1 to do something that annoys or interrupts someone □ *Stop bothering me, I'm busy.* (incomodar)

bottle

2 can't be bothered if you can't be bothered to do something, you feel too lazy to do it ☐ *I can't be bothered to cook just for myself.* (**não estar com a mínima vontade**)
3 to make you feel unhappy or worried ☐ *He said that losing the match didn't bother him.* (**preocupar**)
4 to take the time or make an effort to do something ☐ *Don't bother tidying up yet.* (**não se dar ao trabalho**)
▶ NOUN, NO PLURAL effort or difficulty ☐ *The address book saves you the bother of having to remember email addresses.* ☐ *'I really appreciate your help.' 'It's no bother.'* (**incômodo, aborrecimento**)

bottle /ˈbɒtəl/ NOUN [plural **bottles**]
1 a glass or plastic container used for holding liquids, often with a narrow part at the top ☐ + *of a bottle of mineral water* ☐ *a wine bottle* (**garrafa**)
2 a plastic container used for feeding milk to a baby ☐ *Would you like to give the baby his bottle today?* (**mamadeira**)
◆ PHRASAL VERB [bottles, bottling, bottled] **bottle something up** to avoid talking about unpleasant memories or feelings, even though it would make you feel better if you did (**reprimir algo**)

bottle bank /ˈbɒtəl ˌbæŋk/ NOUN [plural **bottle banks**] a large container in a public place where you can put empty glass bottles so that the glass can be used again (**coleta seletiva de vidro**)

bottleneck /ˈbɒtəlnek/ NOUN [plural **bottlenecks**]
1 a problem in a process that causes the whole process to go more slowly ☐ *Strikes at the port are causing bottlenecks in delivery.* (**congestionamento**)
2 a place where a road is narrow or blocked so that traffic has to move through it slowly (**engarrafamento**)

bottom /ˈbɒtəm/ ▶ NOUN [plural **bottoms**]
1 the lowest part of something ☐ + *of He stood at the bottom of the stairs* ☐ *the bottom of the sea* (**fundo**)
2 the surface on the lowest part of something ☐ *There were holes in the bottom of his shoes.* (**fundo**)
3 the lowest level of success ☐ *My team is at the bottom of the league.* (**último**)
4 the part of something that is furthest away ☐ *the bottom of the road/garden* (**fundo**)
5 the part of your body that you sit on ☐ *Always keep your baby's bottom clean and dry.* (**traseiro**)
▶ ADJECTIVE
1 in the lowest position ☐ *Put the biggest books on the bottom shelf.* (**último**)
2 at the lowest level of success (**último**) ▣ *She came bottom in the exam.* (**ficou em último**)
• **bottomless** /ˈbɒtəmlɪs/ ADJECTIVE seeming to have no limits (**inesgotável**) ▣ *He seems to think there's a bottomless pit of money available.* (**fonte inesgotável**)

bottom line /ˈbɒtəm ˈlaɪn/ NOUN [plural **bottom lines**]
1 the amount of money that a business makes ☐ *Rises in oil prices will seriously affect our bottom line.* (**lucro líquido**)
2 the most important fact about something ☐ *The bottom line is that if you don't stop smoking, you could die.* (**ponto principal**)

bough /baʊ/ NOUN [plural **boughs**] one of the bigger branches that grows from the trunk (= main part) of a tree (**ramo**)

bought /bɔːt/ PAST TENSE AND PAST PARTICIPLE OF **buy** (*ver* **buy**)

boulder /ˈbəʊldə(r)/ NOUN [plural **boulders**] a very big stone (**rocha**)

bounce /baʊns/ VERB [**bounces, bouncing, bounced**]
1 to hit a hard surface and move away again ☐ *The ball bounced high into the air.* (**quicar**)
2 to jump up and down on a soft surface ☐ *The children were bouncing on the bed.* (**saltar**)
◆ PHRASAL VERB **bounce back**
1 to feel better again soon after a failure or disappointment (**recuperar-se**)
2 if an e-mail bounces back, it does not reach the person it was sent to (**retornar ao remetente**)

bouncer /ˈbaʊnsə(r)/ NOUN [plural **bouncers**] someone whose job is to keep out people who are not wanted in a club, bar, etc. (**segurança**)

bouncy /ˈbaʊnsi/ ADJECTIVE [**bouncier, bounciest**]
1 able to bounce easily ☐ *a bouncy Ball* (**pulante**)
2 a bouncy surface moves up and down when you move or jump on it (**flexível**)
3 happy and lively ☐ *a bouncy child* (**cheia de vida**)

bound /baʊnd/ ▶ ADJECTIVE
1 if something is bound to happen, it is certain to happen ☐ *It's bound to rain if we don't take our coats.* ☐ *He's bound to notice the damage.* (**evidente**)
2 be bound up with something to be closely connected with something ☐ *My feelings for the house are all bound up with memories of my childhood.* (**estar em estreita ligação a algo**)
3 having a formal duty to do something ☐ *I am bound by my contract not to talk to the press.* (**obrigado a**)
4 going in a particular direction ☐ *The trucks were bound for Warsaw.* ☐ *At last we are homeward bound.* (**com destino a**)
▶ VERB [**bounds, bounding, bounded**]
1 to run with long jumping steps ☐ *The dogs bounded into the room, barking excitedly.* (**pular**)
2 if an area is bounded by something, that thing is along its edge ☐ *The farm is bounded by a forest to the east.* (**limitar**)
▶ PAST TENSE AND PAST PARTICIPLE OF **bind** (*ver* **bind**)

boundary

▶ NOUN [plural **bounds**]
1 a jump ☐ *The deer was over the fence in a single bound.* (**salto**)
2 out of bounds if a place is out of bounds, you are not allowed to go there (**interditado**)

boundary /ˈbaʊndəri/ NOUN [plural **boundaries**]
1 a line that divides two places ☐ *We live on the boundary between the city and the countryside.* (**fronteira**)
2 a limit ☐ *This research will push back the boundaries of science.* (**limite**)

boundless /ˈbaʊndlɪs/ ADJECTIVE without limits (**ilimitado**) 🔁 *boundless energy* (**energia inesgotável**)

bounty /ˈbaʊnti/ NOUN [plural **bounties**]
1 good things that are provided ☐ *The harvest festival is a celebration of nature's bounty.* (**generosidade, abundância**)
2 money paid as a reward, especially for catching or killing someone (**recompensa**)

bouquet /bʊˈkeɪ/ NOUN [plural **bouquets**] flowers that have been tied together in an attractive way (**buquê**)

bourgeois /ˈbɔːʒwɑː/ ADJECTIVE typical of the middle class and their ideas (**burguês**)
• **bourgeoisie** /ˌbɔːʒwɑːˈziː/ NOUN **the bourgeoisie** the middle class, especially people who are too interested in money or their social position (**a burguesia**)

bout /baʊt/ NOUN [plural **bouts**] a period of something unpleasant, especially illness ☐ *a bout of flu* (**acometimento**)

boutique /buːˈtiːk/ NOUN [plural **boutiques**] a small shop that sells fashionable clothes (**butique**)

bow¹ /baʊ/ ▶ VERB [**bows, bowing, bowed**] to bend your head or the top part of your body forward to say hello to someone politely or to show them respect ☐ *Everyone bowed to the king and queen.* (**curvar-se**)
♦ PHRASAL VERB **bow to something** to be forced to do what someone wants ☐ *In the end I had to bow to their demands for foreign holidays.* (**render-se a algo**)
▶ NOUN [plural **bows**]
1 when you bow (**reverência**) 🔁 *The pianist came back on stage to take a bow.* (**fazer uma reverência**)
2 the pointed front part of a ship (**proa**)

bow² /boʊ/ NOUN [plural **bows**]
1 a knot with two circular ends, used to tie shoes or for decoration ☐ *Tie the ribbon in a bow.* (**laço**)
2 a weapon made from a long piece of wood, used for shooting arrows (**arco**)
3 a long, straight piece of wood with horse hair stretched along it, used for playing a musical instrument such as a violin (**arco**)

bowel /ˈbaʊəl/ NOUN [plural **bowels**] the long tube inside the lower part of your body that food goes through after leaving your stomach (**intestino**)

bowl /boʊl/ ▶ NOUN [plural **bowls**]
1 a round, open container, used for holding food ☐ *a soup bowl* ☐ *a bowl of cornflakes* (**tigela**)
2 in the US, used in the names of large areas where people go to watch sports such as baseball ☐ *Baker Bowl, Philadelphia* (**estádio**)
⇨ *go to* **bowls**
▶ VERB [**bowls, bowling, bowled**]
1 in sports such as cricket and baseball, to throw the ball towards a person who tries to hit it (**lançar a bola**)
2 to roll a large heavy ball along the ground in the game of bowls (**jogar a bola**)
♦ PHRASAL VERB **bowl someone over** to surprise someone very much with something good ☐ *Wendy was bowled over by their generosity.* (**impressionar alguém**)

bow-legged /ˌboʊˈlegɪd/ ADJECTIVE having legs that curve out at the knees. (**de pernas tortas**)

bowler /ˈboʊlə(r)/ NOUN [plural **bowlers**] the person who bowls in sports such as cricket and baseball (**lançador**)

bowler hat /ˌboʊlə(r) ˈhæt/ NOUN [plural **bowler hats**] a black hat with a hard round top, that was worn by businessmen in the past (**chapéu coco**)

bowling /ˈboʊlɪŋ/ NOUN, NO PLURAL a game in which players roll a large heavy ball along a track and try to knock over objects shaped like bottles (**boliche**)

bowls /boʊlz/ NOUN, NO PLURAL a game in which players roll heavy balls along a flat surface, and try to get them close to a smaller white ball (**partida de boliche**)

bow tie /ˌboʊ ˈtaɪ/ NOUN [plural **bow ties**] a piece of cloth tied in a bow that men wear round their necks for formal events (**gravata-borboleta**)

box /bɒks/ ▶ NOUN [plural **boxes**]
1 a container, sometimes with a lid, used for holding or storing things (**caixa**)
2 a small square on a page with information in it or with a space where you must write (**campo**) 🔁 *Tick the relevant box.* (**assinale o quadrado**)
▶ VERB [**boxes, boxing, boxed**] to take part in the sport of boxing (**lutar boxe**)
• **boxer** /ˈbɒksə(r)/ NOUN [plural **boxers**] someone who takes part in the sport of boxing (**boxeador**)

boxer shorts /ˈbɒksə(r) ˌʃɔːts/ PLURAL NOUN loose underwear for men that covers the bottom (**cueca samba-canção**)

boxing /ˈbɒksɪŋ/ NOUN, NO PLURAL a sport in which two people fight by hitting each other while wearing heavy gloves (= coverings for your hands) (**boxe**)

Boxing Day / branch

Boxing Day /'bɒksɪŋ ˌdeɪ/ NOUN the day after Christmas Day (**dia posterior ao Natal**)

box office /'bɒks ˌɒfɪs/ NOUN [plural **box offices**] the place at a theatre or cinema where you buy tickets (**bilheteria**)

boy /bɔɪ/ NOUN [plural **boys**] a male child ◻ *a six-year-old boy* ◻ *They've got two boys and a girl.* ◻ *When I was a little boy I wanted to be a train driver.* (**menino**)

boycott /'bɔɪkɒt/ ▶ VERB [**boycotts, boycotting, boycotted**] to refuse to take part in an activity or to buy a particular product (**boicotar**)
▶ NOUN [plural **boycotts**] a situation in which someone boycotts an activity or product (**boicote**)

boyfriend /'bɔɪˌfrend/ NOUN [plural **boyfriends**] a man or boy who you are having a romantic relationship with ◻ *Emily has got a new boyfriend.* (**namorado**)

boyhood /'bɔɪhʊd/ NOUN, NO PLURAL the period in your life when you are a boy (**juventude**)

boyish /'bɔɪɪʃ/ ADJECTIVE looking or behaving like a boy, especially in a good way ◻ *Even at forty, he still looks boyish.* (**infantil**)

bra /brɑː/ NOUN [plural **bras**] a piece of underwear that women wear to support their breasts (**sutiã**)

brace /breɪs/ NOUN [plural **braces**]
1 a piece of wire that you have on your teeth to pull them into a straight position (**braçadeira**)
2 a device that is used to hold part of the body in a straight position ◻ *a neck brace* (**suporte, atadura**)
⇨ go to **braces**

bracelet /'breɪslɪt/ NOUN [plural **bracelets**] a piece of jewellery that you wear around your arm ◻ *a diamond bracelet* (**bracelete, pulseira**)

braces /'breɪsɪz/ PLURAL NOUN a piece of clothing that consists of two narrow pieces of material that you stretch over your shoulders to hold your trousers up (**suspensórios**)

bracing /'breɪsɪŋ/ ADJECTIVE a bracing wind or a bracing walk is cold in a way that makes you feel healthy (**estimulante**) 🔎 *a bracing walk by the sea* (**caminhada estimulante**)

bracken /'brækən/ NOUN, NO PLURAL a wild plant with long, wide leaves that grows in forests and on hills (**samambaia**)

bracket /'brækɪt/ NOUN [plural **brackets**]
1 one of a pair of punctuation marks ( ) or [ ], used to separate information from the main text (**colchete, parênteses**) 🔎 *She added her own comments in brackets after each point.* (**entre parênteses**)
2 a group into which things are divided (**grupo**) 🔎 *Holidays to the Caribbean are in a much higher price bracket than holidays to Spain.* (**grupo de preços**)
3 a piece of metal that is used to attach a shelf to a wall (**suporte, cantoneira**)

brag /bræg/ VERB [**brags, bragging, bragged**] to talk about your achievements or possessions in a proud way that annoys people ◻ *Kate's always bragging about the expensive gifts he gives her.* (**gabar-se**)

braid /breɪd/ NOUN [plural **braids**]
1 a narrow woven (= made by twisting together) rope used for decorating military uniforms, furniture, etc. (**trança**)
2 the US word for **plait** (*ver* **plait**)

braille /breɪl/ NOUN, NO PLURAL a writing system for blind people which uses raised marks that they can read by touching them (**braile**)

brain /breɪn/ NOUN [plural **brains**]
1 the organ inside your head that controls all the other parts of your body, and that you think with ◻ *the human brain* (**cérebro**)
2 brains intelligence ◻ *Come on – use your brains!* (**cérebro**)

brainstorm /'breɪnstɔːm/ NOUN [plural **brainstorms**]
1 when you suddenly do something stupid that you cannot explain (**ideia súbita**)
2 the US word for **brainwave** (*ver* **brainwave**)

brainwash /'breɪnwɒʃ/ VERB [**brainwashes, brainwashing, brainwashed**] to make someone believe something by repeatedly telling them that it is true (**lavagem cerebral**)

brainwave /'breɪnweɪv/ NOUN **have a brainwave** to suddenly have a very good idea (**ter uma inspiração**)

brainy /'breɪni/ ADJECTIVE [**brainier, brainiest**] an informal word for clever ◻ *Cathy is brainy enough to be a doctor.* (**inteligente**)

brake /breɪk/ ▶ NOUN [plural **brakes**] the part in a vehicle that you press to stop the vehicle or make it go slower (**freio**) ◻ *Have you checked your brakes?* 🔎 *a brake pedal* (**pedal do freio**)
▶ VERB [**brakes, braking, braked**] to use a brake to stop a vehicle or make it go slower ◻ *Dad braked suddenly and we were all thrown forward.* (**frear**)

bramble /'bræmbəl/ NOUN [plural **brambles**] a plant on which blackberries (= small, black fruit) grow (**arbusto**)

bran /bræn/ NOUN, NO PLURAL the brown part on the outside of grain (**farelo de cereais**)

branch /brɑːntʃ/ ▶ NOUN [plural **branches**]
1 one of the smaller parts of a tree that grow out from the main straight part ◻ *Crows build their nests high in the branches of trees.* (**ramo**)
2 one of the shops or businesses that belong to a larger organization (**filial**) 🔎 *the local branch of the bank* (**filial local**) 🔎 *They're opening a new branch in Livingston.* (**abrindo filial**)
▶ VERB [**branches, branching, branched**] to separate into two or more parts like the branches

of a tree □ *The road branches to the north and west.* (ramificar)
♦ PHRASAL VERBS **branch off** to leave the main part of something □ *We left the main street and branched off up a hill* (desviar-se) **branch out** to develop in different ways □ *We're trying to branchout into selling on the Internet.* (expandir-se)

brand /brænd/ NOUN [*plural* **brands**] a product that has a particular name, and that is made by a particular company □ *This isn't my usual brand of shampoo, but it's just as good.* (marca)

brandish /ˈbrændɪʃ/ VERB [**brandishes, brandishing, brandished**] to hold up a weapon in your hand so that people can see it □*Three robbers burst in brandishing guns.* (brandir)

brand-new /ˌbrændˈnju:/ ADJECTIVE completely new □ *a brand-new car* (novo em folha)

brandy /ˈbrændi/ NOUN [*plural* **brandies**] a very strong alcoholic drink that people drink after a meal (conhaque)

brash /bræʃ/ ADJECTIVE speaking in a noisy, confident way that other people find annoying □ *I found her rather brash.* (insolente)

brass /brɑːs/ ▶ NOUN, NO PLURAL
1 a yellow metal used for making things such as musical instruments (latão)
2 musical instruments that are made of the metal brass, such as the trumpet or the trombone (instrumento de sopro)
▶ ADJECTIVE made of brass □ *a brass candlestick* (de latão)

brass band /ˌbrɑːs ˈbænd/ NOUN [*plural* **brass bands**] a group of musicians who play brass instruments such as the trumpet or the trombone (orquestra de instrumentos de sopro)

brassy /ˈbrɑːsi/ ADJECTIVE [**brassier, brassiest**] describes hair that is of a yellow colour that is not natural □ *a brassy blonde* (ouro)

brat /bræt/ NOUN [*plural* **brats**] an informal word for a child who behaves badly (moleque)

bravado /brəˈvɑːdəʊ/ NOUN, NO PLURAL behaviour that you think will make people believe that you are brave and confident, even when you are not (bravata)

brave /breɪv/ ADJECTIVE [**braver, bravest**] able to deal with danger without being afraid, or able to suffer pain without complaining □ + *of It was very brave of her to jump in the water and save the child.* □ *This might hurt a little – just try to be brave.* (valente)
♦ IDIOM **put a brave face on something** to behave as if you are not afraid or worried, although you feel afraid or worried (mostrar valentia perante algo)
▶ VERB [**braves, braving, braved**] to deal with a difficult situation so that you can do something □ *Over 8,000 people braved terrible weather conditions to see their team play.* (enfrentar)

• **bravely** /ˈbreɪvli/ ADVERB in a brave way □ *She smiled bravely, even though she was in pain.* (bravamente)
• **bravery** /ˈbreɪvəri/ NOUN, NO PLURAL being brave □ *an award for bravery* (bravura)

bravo /ˌbrɑːˈvəʊ/ EXCLAMATION a word used for saying that you liked a performance or that you think someone has done something well □ *There were calls of 'Bravo!' from the audience.* (bravo!)

brawl /brɔːl/ ▶ NOUN [*plural* **brawls**] a noisy fight, especially in a public place □ *He got involved in a brawl after the match.* (briga barulhenta)
▶ VERB [**brawls, brawling, brawled**] to fight noisily, especially in a public place (brigar)

brawn /brɔːn/ NOUN, NO PLURAL big, strong muscles (músculos fortes)
• **brawny** /ˈbrɔːni/ ADJECTIVE [**brawnier, brawniest**] having big, strong muscles □ *A brawny young man lifted the boxes out of the van.* (musculoso)

bray /breɪ/ ▶ NOUN [*plural* **brays**] the loud sound made by a donkey (= animal like a small horse) (zurro)
▶ VERB [**brays, braying, brayed**] a donkey brays when it makes a loud sound (zurrar)

brazen /ˈbreɪzən/ ▶ ADJECTIVE showing that you are not ashamed although you are doing something bad (insolente)
▶ VERB [**brazens, brazening, brazened**] **brazen it out** to deal with a difficult or embarrassing situation by pretending that you are not worried or upset (enfrentar descaradamente)
• **brazenly** /ˈbreɪzənli/ ADVERB in a brazen way (descaradamente)

brazier /ˈbreɪziə(r)/ NOUN [*plural* **braziers**] a metal container in which people burn coal to keep themselves warm when they are standing outside for a long time in cold weather (braseiro)

breach /briːtʃ/ ▶ NOUN [*plural* **breaches**]
1 the breaking of an agreement or a relationship □ *a breach of the peace agreement* (quebra)
2 a space or a hole in something solid like a wall □ *A breach in the dam caused flooding in the valley below.* (brecha)
▶ VERB [**breaches, breaching, breached**] to break something or make a hole in it □ *The explosion breached the castle wall.* (abrir uma brecha)

bread /bred/ NOUN, NO PLURAL a basic food made with flour and water that is baked in an oven. It is often sold in a large piece and then cut into smaller pieces. (pão) 🔁 *a loaf of bread (pão)* 🔁 *a slice of bread* (fatia de pão) 🔁 *brown/white bread* (pão preto/pão francês)

breadcrumbs /ˈbredkrʌmz/ PLURAL NOUN very small pieces of bread that can be used in cooking (migalhas de pão)

breadline /ˈbredlaɪn/ NOUN **on the breadline** very poor (muito pobre)

breadth /bredθ/ NOUN [plural **breadths**] the size of something measured from one side to the other □ *The teacher told us to measure the length and breadth of the room.* (**largura**)

breadwinner /'bredwɪnə(r)/ NOUN [plural **breadwinners**] the person or people in a family who earn money (**chefe de família**) □ *Janice is now the main breadwinner.*

break /breɪk/ ▶ VERB [**breaks, breaking, broke, broken**]
1 to separate into pieces or to make something separate into pieces □ *The vase fell to the floor and broke.* □ *Be careful, you'll break that glass.* □ *+ off I broke a piece off the biscuit.* □ *+ up The company was broken up and sold in several parts.* (**quebrar**)
2 to damage something or to become damaged □ *My camera broke.* □ *I've broken my umbrella.* (**quebrar**)
3 break your arm/leg, etc. to damage a bone so that it cracks (**quebrar o braço, a perna etc.**)
4 break the rules/the law/your promise, etc. to not do what you should do, for example because it is a rule or you have made a promise (**quebrar as regras**)
5 break the news to tell someone that something unpleasant has happened □ *I didn't want to break the bad news to them.* (**contar as novidades**)
6 break a record to do something better/faster, etc. than anyone has done it before (**quebrar um recorde**)
7 a boy's voice breaks when it gets deeper and becomes like a man's (**mudar**)
◆ IDIOMS **break someone's heart** to make someone very unhappy □ *It breaks my heart to see the children suffer.* (**partir o coração de alguém**) **break the ice** to make people who have only just met feel relaxed with each other □ *We played a game to break the ice.* (**quebrar o gelo**)
◆ PHRASAL VERBS **break down 1** if a machine or vehicle breaks down, it stops working □ *Sorry I'm late; the car broke down.* (**quebrar**) **2** if a relationship or an agreement breaks down, it stops being successful □ *Her marriage broke down under the strain.* (**falhar**) **3** to start to cry □ *When I mentioned her brother, she broke down and sobbed.* (**descontrolar-se**) **break in** to get into a place by using force □ *Thieves broke in using a hammer.* (**invadir**) **break off** to suddenly stop what you are doing or saying □ *She broke off to answer the phone.* (**parar de falar**) **break something off** to end a relationship (**romper**) ▣ *She broke off their engagement.* (**rompeu seu noivado**) **break out** to start suddenly (**começar, irromper**) ▣ *Fighting broke out during a match against Liverpool.* (**a luta de boxe começou**) ▣ *Fire broke out in the warehouse.* (**o incêndio começou**) **break up**
1 if two people break up, they end their relationship (**terminar**) □ *She's broken up with her boyfriend.*
2 a school breaks up when the term finishes and the holiday starts (**terminar**)

▶ NOUN [plural **breaks**]
1 a short period of time in which someone stops an activity (**intervalo**) ▣ *Shall we have/take a break?* (**fazer um intervalo**) ▣ *What time is your lunch break?* (**horário de almoço**) □ *+ from I need a break from the children.*
2 a time when something ends and something new begins □ *+ with The Queen's absence from this occasion marks a complete break with tradition.* (**mudança**)
3 an opening or crack in something □ *+ in a break in the clouds* □ *She suffered a nasty break in her leg.* (**abertura**)
4 a opportunity that gives you success □ *She's always been a great singer; she was just waiting for a lucky break* (**oportunidade**)
• **breakable** /'breɪkəbəl/ ADJECTIVE able to be broken easily (**quebrável**)
• **breakage** /'breɪkɪdʒ/ NOUN [plural **breakages**] when something is broken, or a thing that has been broken □ *You will have to pay for any breakages.* (**quebra**)

breakdown /'breɪkdaʊn/ NOUN [plural **breakdowns**]
1 when a machine or vehicle stops working □ *We had a breakdown on the motorway.* (**avaria**)
2 when something fails in a situation □ *a breakdown in communication* □ *Stress contributed to the breakdown of his marriage.* (**crise**)
3 a period of mental illness when someone is too upset or sad to deal with life (**colapso**) ▣ *She suffered a breakdown after her divorce.* (**sofreu um colapso**) ▣ *a nervous breakdown* (**colapso nervoso**)

breaker /'breɪkə(r)/ NOUN [plural **breakers**] a large wave that rolls onto the beach (**onda de arrebentação**)

breakfast /'brekfəst/ NOUN [plural **breakfasts**] the first meal that you eat in the morning □ *What do you usually have for breakfast?* (**café da manhã**)

break-in /'breɪkɪn/ NOUN [plural **break-ins**] when someone enters a house or other building illegally, usually to steal things (**arrombamento**)

breakneck /'breɪknek/ ADJECTIVE **at breakneck speed** very fast □ *He ran down the street at breakneck speed.* (**muito rápido**)

breakthrough /'breɪkθruː/ NOUN [plural **breakthroughs**] a discovery or a success that you have after working for a long time □ *This has been hailed as a breakthrough in the treatment of cancer.* (**grande avanço**)

break-up /'breɪkʌp/ NOUN [plural **break-ups**]
1 when a relationship or marriage fails □ *He blamed me for the break-up of his marriage.* (**separação**)
2 when a country or organization is divided into separate parts (**colapso**)

breast /brest/ NOUN [plural **breasts**]
1 one of the two organs on the front of a woman's body that produce milk when she has a

baby (seio) 🔲 breast milk (leite materno) 🔲 breast cancer (câncer de mama)

2 the front part of a bird's body, or the meat from this part (peito) 🔲 chicken breasts (peito de frango)

breastbone /'brestbəʊn/ NOUN [plural breastbones] the main bone on the front of your chest (esterno)

breastfeed /'brestfiːd/ VERB [breastfeeds, breastfeeding, breastfed] a woman breastfeeds a baby when she feeds it with milk from her breasts (amamentar)

breaststroke /'breststrəʊk/ NOUN, NO PLURAL a way of swimming in which you move your arms out to the sides and move your legs out to the sides while bending your knees (nado de peito)

breath /breθ/ NOUN [plural breaths]
1 when you fill your lungs with air and then let the air out again (respiração) 🔲 Take a deep breath. (respirar fundo)
2 the air that comes out of your mouth □ We could see our breath in the freezing air. (hálito)
3 be out of breath to be breathing fast because you have been running or working hard □ You shouldn't be out of breath after walking upstairs. (sem fôlego)
4 get your breath back to wait until you can breathe normally again after a period of effort (recuperar o fôlego)
5 hold your breath to breathe in but not breathe out again □ They have to hold their breath for a long time under the water. (prender a respiração)
6 under your breath if you say something under your breath, you say it very quietly (sussurrar)
◆ IDIOMS **a breath of fresh air** someone or something that is new and interesting (um sopro de ar fresco) □ She's a real breath of fresh air in the office. **take your breath away** to surprise you very much □ His generosity took my breath away. (deixar alguém boquiaberto)

breathalyze or **breathalyse** /'breθəlaɪz/ VERB [breathalyzes, breathalyzing, breathalyzed] the police breathalyze drivers when they ask them to breathe into a special bag that shows if they have been drinking alcohol (testar com bafômetro)
• **breathalyzer** or **breathalyser** /'breθəlaɪzə(r)/ NOUN [plural breathalyzers] a piece of equipment used for breathalyzing drivers (bafômetro)

breathe /briːð/ VERB [breathes, breathing, breathed] to take air into your lungs and let it out again □ He was so quiet, I thought he had stopped breathing. □ It feels good to breathe some clean air again. (respirar)
◆ PHRASAL VERBS **breathe in** to take air into your lungs (inspirar) □ Breathe in through your nose and count to ten. **breathe out** to let air out of your lungs □ Now breathe out through your mouth. (expirar)

> ► Remember that the verb **breathe** has an e at the end, while the noun **breath** does not. Be careful not to confuse the spellings of the verb **breathes** and the noun plural **breaths**.

breathless /'breθlɪs/ ADJECTIVE breathing fast because you have been running or working hard (sem fôlego, ofegante)

breathtaking /'breθˌteɪkɪŋ/ ADJECTIVE very beautiful, surprising or exciting □ The scenary was breathtaking. (espetacular)

breed /briːd/ ► VERB [breeds, breeding, bred]
1 when animals breed they produce young animals □ The birds breed across Europe and Asia. (reproduzir-se)
2 to produce young animals from dogs, cows, sheep, etc. □ These dogs are bred for hunting. (gerar)
3 to cause people to have bad feelings □ Lack of opportunity breeds despair in these young people. (gerar)
► NOUN [plural breeds] a particular type of animal □ The Aberdeen Angus is a famous Scottish breed of cattle. (raça)
• **breeder** /'briːdə(r)/ NOUN [plural breeders] someone who breeds animals □ a dog breeder (criador)

breeze /briːz/ NOUN [plural breezes] a light wind □ a cool/gentle breeze (brisa)
• **breezy** /'briːzɪ/ ADJECTIVE [breezier, breeziest]
1 with a light wind blowing □ a breezy day (ventilado)
2 lively and confident (alegre) 🔲 Shona's always bright and breezy in the mornings. (radiante e alegre)

brevity /'brevɪtɪ/ NOUN, NO PLURAL
1 when you use only a few words □ Aim for brevity when you are e-mailing people. (brevidade)
2 when something lasts for a short time only (brevidade)

brew /bruː/ VERB [brews, brewing, brewed]
1 to make beer (fazer cerveja)
2 to make tea or coffee, or to leave tea or coffee in hot water to develop its flavour (fazer café ou chá)
3 if a storm or trouble is brewing, it will begin soon (formar-se)
• **brewer** /'bruːə(r)/ NOUN [plural brewers] a person or business that makes beer (cervejeiro)
• **brewery** /'bruərɪ/ NOUN [plural breweries] a factory where beer is made (cervejaria)

bribe /braɪb/ ► NOUN [plural bribes] money that is offered to someone so that they will do something dishonest (suborno) 🔲 accept/take a bribe (aceitar um suborno)

bric-a-brac

▶ VERB [**bribes, bribing, bribed**] to offer someone a bribe ☐ *You were a fool to try to bribe the policeman.* (**subornar**)
• **bribery** /ˈbraɪbəri/ NOUN, NO PLURAL offering bribes (**suborno**)

bric-a-brac /ˈbrɪkəˌbræk/ NOUN, NO PLURAL small, often decorative objects that are not worth very much (**bugigangas**)

brick /brɪk/ NOUN [*plural* **bricks**] a block used for building walls (**tijolo**) ☐ *Someone had thrown a brick through the window.* 🆎 *a brick wall* (**parede de tijolos**)

bricklayer /ˈbrɪkˌleɪə(r)/ NOUN [*plural* **bricklayers**] a person whose job is to build things with bricks (**pedreiro**)

bridal /ˈbraɪdəl/ ADJECTIVE belonging to or used by a bride ☐ *a white bridal car* (**nupcial**)

bride /braɪd/ NOUN [*plural* **brides**] a woman who is getting married (**noiva**)

bridegroom /ˈbraɪdgrʊm/ NOUN [*plural* **bridegrooms**] a man who is getting married (**noivo**)

bridesmaid /ˈbraɪdzmeɪd/ NOUN [*plural* **bridesmaids**] a girl or woman who helps a bride on her wedding day (**dama de honra**)

bridge /brɪdʒ/ NOUN [*plural* **bridges**]
1 a structure that is built over a river or a road to allow people or vehicles to cross from one side to the other (**ponte**) ☐ *We drove across the bridge.* 🆎 *a railway bridge* (**ponte férrea**)
2 a card game for four people playing in pairs (**bridge**)

bridle /ˈbraɪdəl/ NOUN [*plural* **bridles**] the part of a horse's harness (= leather straps) that goes around its head (**rédea**)

brie /bri:/ NOUN, NO PLURAL a type of soft French cheese (**queijo brie**)

brief /bri:f/ ▶ ADJECTIVE [**briefer, briefest**] short ☐ *We had a brief telephone conversation.* ☐ *He wrote her a brief note.* (**breve**)
▶ VERB [**briefs, briefing, briefed**] to give someone information or instructions about something ☐ *Our football coach always briefs us before a match.* (**instruir**)
▶ NOUN [*plural* **briefs**] the information or instructions that someone needs to do their work (**síntese**)
⇨ *go to* **briefs**

briefcase /ˈbri:fkeɪs/ NOUN [*plural* **briefcases**] a flat case for carrying business documents (**pasta**)

briefing /ˈbri:fɪŋ/ NOUN [*plural* **briefings**] a meeting or a document that gives someone information or instructions ☐ *I give my boss regular briefings on our progress.* (**instrução, guia**)

briefly /ˈbri:fli/ ADVERB in or for a short amount of time ☐ *Tell us briefly what you want us to do.*

brim

☐ *They stopped briefly to get more petrol.* (**brevemente**)

briefs /bri:fs/ PLURAL NOUN underwear that you wear on your bottom (**cuecas**)

brigade /brɪˈgeɪd/ NOUN [*plural* **brigades**] a group of soldiers that forms part of a group in the army (**brigada**)
⇨ *go to* **fire brigade**

brigadier /ˌbrɪgəˈdɪə(r)/ NOUN [*plural* **brigadiers**] an army officer with a high rank (**brigadeiro**)

bright /braɪt/ ADJECTIVE [**brighter, brightest**]
1 producing a lot of light ☐ *We could see the bright lights of the city.* (**brilhante**)
2 full of light ☐ *This is a nice bright bedroom.* (**iluminado**)
3 a bright colour is strong and clear ☐ *His eyes were bright blue.* (**vivo**)
4 happy and healthy ☐ *Grandad was a lot brighter this morning.* (**radiante**)
5 clever ☐ *He was always the brightest child in our family.* (**inteligente**)
♦ IDIOM a **bright spot** a good part of a situation or event, usually one which is bad in general ☐ *His performance was the one bright spot of the evening.* (**ponto luminoso**)
• **brighten** /ˈbraɪtən/ VERB [**brightens, brightening, brightened**]
1 to become brighter or to make something brighter ☐ *The weather brightened up and we went out for a walk.* ☐ *A coat of paint would brighten the walls.* (**clarear**)
2 to become happier and more energetic or to make someone happier and more energetic ☐ *Jack brightened up a bit when I suggested a game of cricket.* (**animar**)
• **brightly** /ˈbraɪtli/ ADVERB
1 with a lot of light ☐ *The sun shone brightly.* (**brilhantemente**)
2 happily and with energy ☐ *'Let's play,'* she said brightly. (**alegremente**)
• **brightness** /ˈbraɪtnɪs/ NOUN, NO PLURAL the amount of light that something produces (**brilho**)

brilliance /ˈbrɪliəns/ NOUN, NO PLURAL
1 great skill ☐ *We had to admire the other team's brilliance.* (**inteligência**)
2 giving out strong light ☐ *the brilliance of the sunshine* (**esplendor**)
• **brilliant** /ˈbrɪliənt/ ADJECTIVE
1 very clever, or showing great skill ☐ *Fiona gave a brilliant speech.* (**brilhante**)
2 very bright (**brilhante**) 🆎 *brilliant sunshine* (**raio de sol brilhante**)
• **brilliantly** /ˈbrɪliəntli/ ADVERB
1 with great skill ☐ *Sanjay acted the bad--tempered king brilliantly.* (**brilhantemente**)
2 very brightly ☐ *The arena was brilliantly lit.* (**brilhantemente**)

brim /brɪm/ ▶ NOUN [*plural* **brims**]

1 the top edge of a container □ *His glass was filled right up to the brim.* (borda)
2 the lower part of a hat that sticks out □ *Val wore a big hat with a wide brim.* (aba do chapéu)
▶ VERB [**brims, brimming, brimmed**] to be full to the top □ *The bin is brimming over with empty cans.* □ *Her eyes were brimming with tears.* (estar cheio)

brine /braɪn/ NOUN, NO PLURAL water with salt in it, often used to keep food in (salmoura)

bring /brɪŋ/ VERB [**brings, bringing, brought**]
1 to take or carry a person or thing with you when you go somewhere □ **+ to** *You can bring all your friends to the party.* □ *He brought a couple of jigsaws downstairs.* □ **+ back** *He never brought back the book he borrowed.* (trazer)
2 to cause a feeling or a situation □ **+ to** *The new leaders brought peace to the area.* □ *Our grandchildren have brought us great happiness.* (trazer)
3 cannot bring yourself to do something to not be able to do something because you find it unpleasant □ *I couldn't bring myself to be polite to her.* (não ter coragem de fazer algo)

> Use **bring** when you are talking about taking a person or thing towards you (the person speaking). Use **take** when you are talking about taking a person or thing away from you (the person speaking), or away from the place where you are now. □ *Could you bring my mobile when you come?* □ *I'll take some flowers to the hospital.*

♦ PHRASAL VERBS **bring something about** to cause something to happen (provocar algo) □ *Motherhood had brought about enormous changes.* **bring something forward** to move the date or time of an event so that it happens earlier (adiantar algo) □ *They decided to bring forward their wedding.* **bring something in** to make people start using a new law or system (introduzir algo) □ *The government has brought in tax reforms.* **bring something off** to manage to do something successfully (conseguir algo) □ *They brought off the perfect crime.* **bring something on** to cause something bad, especially an illness (provocar algo) □ *Doctors think his heart attack was brought on by stress.* **bring something out** when companies bring out a new product, they make it available to be bought (produzir algo) □ *The band has brought out a new album.* **bring something up 1** to mention a subject (mencionar algo) □ *Did anyone bring up the subject of payment?* **2** to make food come up from your stomach and out of your mouth (vomitar) **bring someone up** to look after a child until they are old enough to look after themselves (criar alguém) □ *My parents brought me up to be polite and considerate.*

brink /brɪŋk/ NOUN **on the brink of something** if you are on the brink of something, it is going to happen very soon □ *Noreen was on the brink of tears.* (à beira de algo)

brisk /brɪsk/ ADJECTIVE [**brisker, briskest**] quick and energetic □ *We were walking at a brisk pace.* (ligeiro)
• **briskly** /'brɪskli/ ADVERB quickly and with energy □ *They walked briskly to keep warm.* (vivamente)

bristle /'brɪsəl/ NOUN [plural **bristles**] a short stiff hair on a man's face, or on a brush (pelo)
• **bristly** /'brɪsli/ ADJECTIVE [**bristlier, bristliest**] covered with bristles (peludo)

Brit /brɪt/ NOUN [plural **Brits**] a British person. An informal word □ *There are a lot of Brits in Majorca in the summer.* (britânico)

Britain /'brɪtən/ NOUN England, Scotland and Wales (Bretanha)

British /'brɪtɪʃ/ ▶ ADJECTIVE belonging to or coming from Britain □ *British industry* (britânico)
▶ NOUN **the British** the people who come from Britain (os britânicos)

Briton /'brɪtən/ NOUN [plural **Britons**] a person who comes from Britain □ *Several Britons were killed in the accident.* (britânico)

brittle /'brɪtəl/ ADJECTIVE a brittle material or object is hard but can be easily broken □ *brittle bones* (frágil)

broach /brəʊtʃ/ VERB [**broaches, broaching, broached**] to broach a subject or question is to Begin to talk about it (levantar) □ *I haven't broached the subject of payment yet.* (levantei a questão)

broad /brɔːd/ ADJECTIVE [**broader, broadest**]
1 wide (largo) □ *He was a tall man with broad shoulders.* (ombros largos) □ *She gave us a broad smile.*
2 including many different things (amplo) □ *We discussed a broad range of subjects.* (ampla gama)
3 general (geral) □ *The product has broad appeal across all ages.* (apelo geral) □ *She gave us a broad outline* (= told us about the main parts) *of her research.* (contornos gerais)
4 a broad accent is very strong (forte)
5 in broad daylight during the day, when people might be able to see □ *He was attacked in broad daylight.* (em plena luz do dia)

broadband /'brɔːdbænd/ NOUN, NO PLURAL an Internet connection that makes it possible to send and receive large amounts of information very quickly. A computing word. □ *We don't have broadband at home.* (banda larga)

broad bean /'brɔːd 'biːn/ NOUN [plural **broad beans**] a large, pale green bean that is eaten as a vegetable (feijão-fava)

broadcast /'brɔːdkɑːst/ ▶ NOUN [plural **broadcasts**] a programme sent out on television

broaden

or radio (**transmissão**) 🔊 *We watched a live broadcast of the World Cup Final.* (**transmissão ao vivo**)
▶ VERB [broadcasts, broadcasting, broadcast] to send out information or programmes on television or radio □ *The interview was broadcast on Sunday.* □ *The BBC broadcast the event live.* (**transmitir**)

- **broadcaster** /ˈbrɔːdkɑːstə(r)/ NOUN [*plural* broadcasters] someone whose job is to speak on television or radio programmes (**locutor**)

- **broadcasting** /ˈbrɔːdkɑːstɪŋ/ NOUN, NO PLURAL the work of television and radio companies (**radiodifusão**)

broaden /ˈbrɔːdən/ VERB [broadens, broadening, broadened]
1 to become wider, or to make something wider □ *They've broadened the road.* □ *Her smile broadened.* (**ampliar**)
2 to include more things or people □ *The socialist party will have to broaden its appeal.* (**ampliar**)
♦ IDIOM **broaden your mind** to give you more knowledge about the world and make you accept different people more □ *They say that travel broadens the mind.* (**ampliar a mente**)
⇨ *go to* **broaden your horizons**

broadly /ˈbrɔːdli/ ADVERB
1 in most ways □ *Your answer is broadly right, but it isn't detailed enough.* (**de modo geral**) 🔊 *Broadly speaking, we get on very well.* (**em linhas gerais**)
2 if you smile broadly, you give a very wide smile □ *He came out of the room smiling broadly.* (**amplamente**)

broad-minded /ˌbrɔːdˈmaɪndɪd/ ADJECTIVE willing to accept other people's opinions or behaviour, and not easily shocked (**tolerante**)

broadsheet /ˈbrɔːdʃiːt/ NOUN [*plural* broadsheets] a serious newspaper that is printed on large pieces of paper (**jornal**)

broccoli /ˈbrɒkəli/ NOUN, NO PLURAL a vegetable with a lot of very small green or purple flowers growing from a thick stem (**brócolis**)

brochure /ˈbrəʊʃə(r)/ NOUN [*plural* brochures] a small book containing information about particular products or services, often with pictures □ *a holiday brochure* (**folheto**)

broke /brəʊk/ ▶ PAST TENSE OF break (*ver* **break**)
▶ ADJECTIVE having very little or no money. An informal word □ *I can't afford a holiday; I'm completely broke.* (**sem dinheiro**)

broken /ˈbrəʊkən/ ▶ PAST PARTICIPLE OF break (*ver* **break**)
▶ ADJECTIVE
1 damaged, and often in several pieces (**quebrado**) 🔊 *broken glass* (**vidro quebrado**) 🔊 *a broken bone* (**osso quebrado**)

broom

2 if a machine is broken, it is not working □ *The washing machine is broken, I'm afraid.* (**quebrado**)
3 a broken home if a child comes from a broken home, its parents do not live together any more (**família separada**)
4 if someone's heart is broken, they are very sad, especially because someone they loved has gone away or died 🔊 *They say she died of a broken heart.* (**coração partido**)

broken-hearted /ˌbrəʊkənˈhɑːtɪd/ ADJECTIVE extremely sad, especially because someone you loved has gone away or died □ *I was broken-hearted when Robert left me.* (**com o coração partido**)

broker /ˈbrəʊkə(r)/ NOUN [*plural* brokers] someone whose job is to buy or sell goods or services for other people □ *an insurance broker* (**corretor**)

brolly /ˈbrɒli/ NOUN [*plural* brollies] an informal word for umbrella (**guarda-chuva**)

bromine /ˈbrəʊmiːn/ NOUN, NO PLURAL a dark red, usually liquid element. A chemistry word. (**bromo**)

bronchitis /brɒŋˈkaɪtɪs/ NOUN, NO PLURAL a disease that affects the lungs, making it difficult to breathe (**bronquite**)

bronze /brɒnz/ ▶ NOUN [*plural* bronzes]
1 a metal that is formed from a mixture of copper and tin □ *The statue was cast in bronze.* (**bronze**)
2 a bronze medal (= prize for coming third in a competition or race) □ *Williams came first, Miller came second, and Lewis got the bronze.* (**medalha de bronze**)
3 a red-brown colour (**bronze**)
▶ ADJECTIVE
1 made of bronze □ *a bronze medal* (**de bronze**)
2 having the colour of bronze (**cor de bronze**)
▶ **bronzed** /brɒnzd/ ADJECTIVE someone who is bronzed has dark skin because they have spent a lot of time in the Sun (**broze**)

brooch /brəʊtʃ/ NOUN [*plural* brooches] a piece of jewellery with a pin on the back that you fasten to the front of a dress or jacket (**broche**)

brood /bruːd/ ▶ NOUN [*plural* broods]
1 a group of young birds that come out of their eggs at the same time □ *a brood of chicks* (**ninhada**)
2 a group of young children from the same family. A humorous word □ *Michael was the youngest of their brood of five.* (**irmãos**)
▶ VERB [broods, brooding, brooded] to think a lot about something unpleasant □ *Gerry's brooding over the goal he missed.* (**remoer**)

- **broody** /ˈbruːdi/ ADJECTIVE
1 wanting to have a baby □ *I get all broody when I see other people's babies.* (**contemplativo**)
2 thinking and worrying about something unpleasant (**meditativo**)

broom /bruːm/ NOUN [*plural* brooms] a brush with a long handle, used for cleaning the floor (**vassoura**)

broomstick

broomstick /'bru:mstɪk/ NOUN [plural broomsticks]
1 a long stick with smaller sticks tied to one end that witches ride on in children's stories (vassoura)
2 a broom handle (cabo de vassoura)

broth /brɒθ/ NOUN, NO PLURAL thin soup often made with meat (caldo)

brother /'brʌðə(r)/ NOUN [plural brothers]
1 a boy or man who has the same parents as you (irmão) ▫ *I share a bedroom with my little brother.* (irmão mais novo) ▫ *Do you have any brothers and sisters?* (irmãos e irmãs)
2 a man who has the same opinions as you or is a member of the same organization as you ▫ *We call on our brothers abroad to end this dispute.* (irmão)

• **brotherhood** /'brʌðəhʊd/ NOUN [plural brotherhoods]
1 a friendly feeling between boys and men (irmandade)
2 an organization for men (fraternidade)

brother-in-law /'brʌðərɪnlɔː/ NOUN [plural brothers-in-law] your sister's husband or the brother of your husband or wife (cunhado)

brotherly /'brʌðəlɪ/ ADJECTIVE to do with the feelings such as love and loyalty that brothers often have for each other (fraternal) ▫ *brotherly love* (amor fraternal)

brought /brɔːt/ PAST TENSE AND PAST PARTICIPLE OF **bring** (ver bring)

brow /braʊ/ NOUN [plural brows]
1 the part of your face above your eyes ▫ *She wrinkled her brow in confusion.* (testa)
2 your brows are your eyebrows (= lines of hair above your eyes) (sobrancelha)
3 the top of a hill ▫ *He tried to overtake a car on the brow of a hill.* (cume)

browbeat /'braʊbiːt/ VERB [browbeats, browbeating, browbeat, browbeaten] to force someone to do something by talking to them in a threatening way (intimidar)

brown /braʊn/ ▶ ADJECTIVE
1 having the colour of soil or wood (marrom, castanho) ▫ *She has light brown hair.* (castanho-claro) ▫ *They painted the walls dark brown.* (castanho-escuro)
2 having dark skin because of being in the sun (bronzeado) ▫ *I went quite brown when we were in Spain.* (fiquei bronzeado)
▶ NOUN [plural browns] the colour of soil or wood ▫ *We chose a rich brown for the sofa.* (marrom)

browse /braʊz/ VERB [browses, browsing, browsed]
1 to look at information on the Internet. A computing word. ▫ *This mobile phone lets you send emails and browse the web.* (navegar)

brush

2 to look at things in a shop without buying them ▫ *'Can I help you?' 'I'm just browsing actually, thanks.'* (pesquisar)
3 to read parts of a newspaper or magazine ▫ *She was browsing through the Times when Angela came in.* (examinar)

• **browser** /'braʊzə(r)/ NOUN [plural browsers] a computer program that allows you to look at websites on the Internet. A computing word. (navegador)

bruise /bruːz/ ▶ NOUN [plural bruises]
1 a dark mark that you get on your skin if it is hit ▫ *Joe's got a big black bruise just under his eye.* (contusão)
2 a soft brown mark on a piece of fruit where it has been damaged (esmagamento)
▶ VERB [bruises, bruising, bruised]
1 to make a bruise on someone's skin ▫ *Daniel bruised his knee when he fell.* (machucar)
2 to damage a piece of fruit ▫ *Be careful not to bruise the peaches when you handle them.* (esmagar)

brunette /bruː'net/ ▶ NOUN [plural brunettes] a woman with brown hair (morena)
▶ ADJECTIVE having brown hair

brunt /brʌnt/ NOUN, NO PLURAL **bear/take the brunt of something** to take the worst part of something ▫ *The side of the bus bore the brunt of the impact.* ▫ *His wife bears the brunt of his bad temper.* (suportar o impacto de algo)

brush /brʌʃ/ ▶ VERB [brushes, brushing, brushed]
1 to make something tidy or clean using a brush (escovar) ▫ *Have you brushed your teeth?* (escovou seus dentes) ▫ *Make sure you brush your hair before you go out.* (escovar o cabelo)
2 to remove something from a surface using your hand or a brush ▫ + **off** *She brushed a hair off her skirt.* (limpar)
3 to put liquid on something using a brush ▫ + **with** *Brush the fish with oil before cooking it.* (pincelar)
4 to touch something lightly ▫ + **against** *She felt something brush against her shoulder.* (roçar)
♦ PHRASAL VERBS **brush something aside/off** to refuse to accept what people say ▫ *The minister brushed aside suggestions that he was planning to resign.* (fazer pouco caso de algo) **brush up (on) something** to practise a skill ▫ *I need to brush up my French before I go on holiday.* (praticar algo)
▶ NOUN [plural brushes]
1 an object with short hairs or thin pieces of plastic, wire, etc. fixed to a handle, used for tidying your hair, painting or cleaning ▫ *You'll need a stiff brush to get rid of the mud on those shoes.* ▫ *An artist needs a range of different brushes.* (escova)
2 **give something a brush** to clean or tidy something using a brush (escovar algo)

brusque 95 **Buddhism**

3 a short experience of something unpleasant (encontro) 🔲 *A brush with death* convinced him to give up the sport. (encontro com a morte)

brusque /bruːsk/ ADJECTIVE not patient or polite towards people □ *I was shocked by her brusque manner.* (brusco)

• **brusquely** /ˈbruːsklɪ/ ADVERB in a brusque way □ *'I'm sorry, I can't wait,' he said brusquely.* (bruscamente)

Brussels sprout /ˌbrʌsəlz ˈspraʊt/ NOUN [plural **Brussels sprouts**] a green vegetable that looks like a very small cabbage (couve-de-bruxelas)

brutal /ˈbruːtəl/ ADJECTIVE very cruel □ *a brutal murder* (brutal)

• **brutality** /bruːˈtælətɪ/ NOUN, NO PLURAL violent and cruel behaviour □ *We were shocked by the brutality of the attacks.* (brutalidade)

• **brutally** /ˈbruːtəlɪ/ ADVERB
1 in a brutal way □ *She had been brutally murdered.* (brutalmente)
2 brutally honest saying something that is true, even though you might upset people □ *I'm going to be brutally honest; I don't like your idea at all.* (extremamente honesto)

• **brute** /bruːt/ ▶ ADJECTIVE **brute force/strength** great physical strength □ *Football is a game of skill – not just brute strength.* (força bruta)
▶ NOUN [plural **brutes**] a big, strong man who behaves in a cruel way (brutamontes)

BSE /ˌbiːesˈiː/ NOUN, NO PLURAL a disease that affects cows' brains (doença da vaca louca)

BST /ˌbiːesˈtiː/ ABBREVIATION British Summer Time; a period in the summer when people in the UK put their clocks forward by one hour (horário de verão da Inglaterra)

BTW ABBREVIATION by the way; used in emails and text messages (a propósito)

bubble /ˈbʌbəl/ ▶ NOUN [plural **bubbles**] a very thin light ball of liquid filled with air (bolha) 🔲 *soap bubbles* (bolha de sabão) 🔲 *The children were blowing bubbles in the garden.* (fazendo bolhas)
▶ VERB [**bubbles, bubbling, bubbled**]
1 liquid bubbles when small balls of air form in it, usually because it is boiling □ *A big pot of soup was bubbling on the stove.* (borbulhar)
2 to feel an emotion very strongly □ **+ over** *She was bubbling over with happiness in her new home.* (transbordar)

bubble gum /ˈbʌbəl ˌɡʌm/ NOUN, NO PLURAL a type of sweet that you chew, and that you can blow to form bubbles (chiclete)

bubbly /ˈbʌbəlɪ/ ▶ ADJECTIVE [**bubblier, bubbliest**]
1 happy and full of energy □ *We'll miss her sense of humour and bubbly personality.* (alegre)
2 full of bubbles (borbulhante)
▶ NOUN, NO PLURAL an informal word for champagne (= pale wine with lots of bubbles) 🔲 *Let's open a bottle of bubbly.* (garrafa de espumante)

buck /bʌk/ NOUN [plural **bucks**]
1 an informal US word for an American dollar □ *It cost twenty bucks.* (dólares)
2 make a fast/quick buck an informal phrase meaning to make money quickly (ganhar dinheiro fácil)
◆ IDIOMS **pass the buck** to blame someone for something or to give them responsibility for something you should be responsible for yourself (passar a responsabilidade para outro) **the buck stops here** used to say that you will take responsibility for something (a responsabilidade é minha)
◆ PHRASAL VERB [**bucks, bucking, bucked**] **buck (someone) up 1** to become happier or to try to make someone happier □ *He bucked up a bit when the food arrived.* (alegrar, animar) **2 buck your ideas up** to start to try harder □ *We all need to get down to work and buck our ideas up.* (tentar com mais empenho)

bucket /ˈbʌkɪt/ NOUN [plural **buckets**] a round open container with a handle, used for carrying water, or substances such as soil or sand (balde) 🔲 *a bucket of water* (balde de água) □ *You'll need about four buckets of soapy water to wash the car.*

• **bucketful** /ˈbʌkɪtfʊl/ NOUN [plural **bucketfuls**] the amount that a bucket will hold □ *We'll need a couple more bucketfuls of cement to finish the path.* (baldada)

buckle /ˈbʌkəl/ ▶ NOUN [plural **buckles**] a metal object on the end of a belt or a strap, used for fastening it (fivela)
▶ VERB [**buckles, buckling, buckled**]
1 to bend or break under pressure □ *His knees buckled and he fell and hit the road.* □ *The roof buckled under the weight of the snow.* (dobrar)
2 to fasten something with a buckle □ *She buckled her belt tightly around her waist.* (afivelar)
3 to become weak and to stop trying to succeed □ *The team lost two goals, but they refused to buckle.* (ceder)
◆ PHRASAL VERB **buckle down** to start working hard or with determination □ *You'll have to buckle down to work when you go back to college.* (empenhar-se)

bud /bʌd/ NOUN [plural **buds**] the part of a plant from which a leaf or flower develops (broto)

Buddhism /ˈbʊdɪzəm/ NOUN, NO PLURAL a religion that is practised in many parts of the world, which follows the teaching of Buddha □ *He gave up politics, and went to Tibet to study Buddhism.* (budismo)

• **Buddhist** /ˈbʊdɪst/ ▶ NOUN [plural **Buddhists**] someone who practises Buddhism (budista)

▶ ADJECTIVE to do with Buddhism or Buddhists (budista) 🔲 *a Buddhist monk* (monge budista)

budding /'bʌdɪŋ/ ADJECTIVE in the early stages of something 🔲 *Henry's a budding scientist.* (em desenvolvimento)

buddy /'bʌdɪ/ NOUN [plural **buddies**] an informal word for a friend 🔲 *They've been buddies since high school.* (amigo)

budge /bʌdʒ/ VERB [**budges, budging, budged**]
1 if something will not budge, you cannot move it 🔲 *We tried to turn the key in the lock, but it wouldn't budge.* (mover)
2 to change your decision about something 🔲 *The managers are unwilling to budge from their position.* (ceder)
♦ PHRASAL VERB **budge up** to move along, so that there is space for someone to sit down. An informal word. (mover-se)

budgerigar /'bʌdʒərɪgɑː(r)/ NOUN [plural **budgerigars**] a small bird with brightly coloured feathers that is often kept as a pet (periquito)

budget /'bʌdʒɪt/ ▶ NOUN [plural **budgets**]
1 an amount of money that a person, company or government has available to spend 🔲 *We offer holidays to suit all budgets.* (orçamento) 🔲 *They were on a tight budget* (= *did not have much money*). (orçamento apertado) 🔲 *The company is cutting its marketing budget.* 🔲 *the education budget*
2 the Budget a plan for how the government will spend money over a certain period of time 🔲 *The Chancellor will submit the Budget to Parliament this afternoon.* (orçamento geral)
▶ VERB [**budgets, budgeting, budgeted**] to plan how you will spend a certain amount of money 🔲 *You'll have to budget very carefully to make your money last a month.* 🔲 *We've budgeted £1,000 for the website.* (planejar)
▶ ADJECTIVE cheap 🔲 *budget flights* (barato)
• **budgetary** /'bʌdʒɪtərɪ/ ADJECTIVE to do with a government's budget. A formal word. (orçamentário)

budgie /'bʌdʒɪ/ NOUN [plural **budgies**] a small bird with brightly coloured feathers that is often kept as a pet (periquito australiano)

buff /bʌf/ ▶ NOUN [plural **buffs**] someone who knows a lot about a particular subject 🔲 *a film buff* 🔲 *a computer buff* (aficionado)
▶ VERB [**buffs, buffing, buffed**] to rub a surface with a soft dry cloth to make it shiny (polir)
▶ ADJECTIVE [**buffer, buffest**] having a strong, attractive body. An informal word. (sarado)

buffalo /'bʌfələʊ/ NOUN [plural **buffalos** or **buffaloes**] a large African animal like a cow, with curved horns (búfalo)

buffer /'bʌfə(r)/ NOUN [plural **buffers**]
1 something that protects a person or thing from harm 🔲 *The grant money will provide us with a buffer for the first year.* (proteção)
2 one of two round pieces of metal on the front of a train or at the end of a train track which reduce the force if the train hits the end of the track (para-choque)
3 an area in a computer's memory where information can be stored for a short time. A computing word. (memória para armazenamento temporário)

buffet¹ /'bʊfeɪ/ NOUN [plural **buffets**] a meal where different types of food are put on a table from which people can choose what they want (bufê)

buffet² /'bʌfɪt/ VERB [**buffets, buffeting, buffeted**] to knock someone or something about roughly 🔲 *The little boat was buffeted by the storm.* (esbofetear)

buffet car /'bʊfeɪ ˌkɑː(r)/ NOUN [plural **buffet cars**] the part of a train where you can buy food and drink (vagão-restaurante)

bug /bʌg/ ▶ NOUN [plural **bugs**]
1 an informal word for an infectious illness (infecção) 🔲 *She's got a tummy bug.* (infecção na barriga) 🔲 *There's a nasty bug going round at the moment.*
2 a fault in a computer program (defeito) 🔲 *She is trying to fix a bug in the program.* (consertar um defeito)
3 a small insect (inseto)
4 a small piece of electronic equipment used for secretly recording what people say (grampo, escuta)
▶ VERB [**bugs, bugging, bugged**]
1 an informal word meaning to annoy someone 🔲 *Stop bugging me!* (irritar alguém)
2 to put a bug in a place in order to record what people say 🔲 *I think we're being bugged.* (grampear)

buggy /'bʌgɪ/ NOUN [plural **buggies**] a folding seat on wheels, used for pushing a small child around (carrinho de bebê)

build /bɪld/ ▶ VERB [**builds, building, built**]
1 to make something by putting materials or parts together 🔲 *He's planning to build his own house.* 🔲 *The walls are built of wood.* (construir)
2 to increase 🔲 + **up** *Excitement is building up as the World Cup approaches.* 🔲 *These exercises help to build upper body strength.* (aumentar)
3 to create and develop something 🔲 + **up** *She built up a chain of shoe shops.* (desenvolver)
▶ NOUN, NO PLURAL the shape of your body 🔲 *He had a strong, muscular build.* (estrutura física)
♦ PHRASAL VERBS **build something in/into (something)** to make something part of something else 🔲 *Make sure you build enough revision time into your schedule.* (incorporar algo) **build on something** to use an earlier success in order to develop further 🔲 *We must build on our successes of the past three years.*

building site

(partir da base de algo) **build up** to increase in amount □ *Resentment built up as she took more and more of the profits for herself.* (acumular)

- **builder** /'bɪldə(r)/ [*plural* **builders**] someone whose job is to build and repair houses and other structures (construtor)
- **building** /'bɪldɪŋ/ [*plural* **buildings**]

  1 a structure with walls and a roof, for example a house or a church □ *What's the tallest building in the world?* (edifício)

  2 *no plural* the activity of building houses and other structures □ *There is a lot of building going on in this street.* (construção)

building site /'bɪldɪŋ ˌsaɪt/ NOUN [*plural* **building sites**] an area where something is being built (canteiro de obras)

building society /'bɪldɪŋ səˈsaɪəti/ NOUN [*plural* **building societies**] an organization similar to a bank, from which people can borrow money to buy a house (sociedade do crédito)

build-up /'bɪldˌʌp/ NOUN [*plural* **build-ups**]

  1 a gradual increase in something □ *Doctors found a build-up of fluid in his lungs.* (aumento)

  2 a time of increasing excitement before an event □ *the build-up to the football World Cup* (empolgação, expectativa)

built /bɪlt/ PAST TENSE AND PAST PARTICIPLE OF build (*ver* **build**)

bulb /bʌlb/ NOUN [*plural* bulbs]

  1 a glass object that you put in an electric light to make it work □ *I need a new bulb for my bedside lamp.* (lâmpada elétrica)

  2 the round root of some plants □ *We planted some tulip bulbs at the weekend.* (bulbo)

bulbous /'bʌlbəs/ ADJECTIVE big and round (bulboso)

bulge /bʌldʒ/ ▶ VERB [**bulges, bulging, bulged**]

  1 if someone's eyes or muscles bulge, they stick out □ *His eyes bulged in horror.* (inchar)

  2 if a container is bulging, it is very full □ *His sack was bulging with presents.* (inchar)

  ▶ NOUN [*plural* **bulges**] a shape that curves out from a surface (saliência)

bulimia /buˈlɪmiə/ *or* **bulimia nervosa** /buˈlɪmiənɜːˈvəʊsə/ NOUN, NO PLURAL an illness in which people make themselves vomit after eating in order to control their weight (bulimia)

- **bulimic** /buˈlɪmɪk/ ADJECTIVE suffering from bulimia (bulímico)

bulk /bʌlk/ ▶ NOUN

  1 the bulk of something most of something □ *The bulk of his pocket money was spent on computer games.* (a maior parte)

  2 the large size of something □ *The massive bulk of Everest towered ahead.* (parte principal)

  3 in bulk you buy in bulk when you buy something in large quantities □ *It's much cheaper*

bully

to buy household goods in bulk. (em grande quantidade)

  ▶ ADJECTIVE to do with buying things in large quantities (volumoso) 🔲 *bulk buying* (compra volumosa)

- ◆ PHRASAL VERB [**bulks, bulking, bulked**] **bulk something out** to make something bigger by adding things to it □ *Bulk the soup out with some pasta.* (adicionar)

- **bulky** /'bʌlki/ ADJECTIVE [**bulkier, bulkiest**] large or difficult to carry □ *a bulky package* (volumoso)

bull /bʊl/ NOUN [*plural* bulls]

  1 an adult male cow (touro)

  2 the male of some other animals, such as the elephant (macho)

- ◆ IDIOMS **like a bull in a china shop** not very careful and often breaking things or upsetting people (como elefante em uma loja de cristais) **take the bull by the horns** to act in a firm way to deal with a difficult situation (enfrentar as dificuldades)

bulldog /'bʊldɒg/ NOUN [*plural* **bulldogs**] a dog with short legs, a strong body and loose folds of skin on its face (buldogue)

bulldozer /'bʊldəʊzə(r)/ NOUN [*plural* **bulldozers**] a large vehicle with a heavy metal container at the front, used for moving large amounts of earth and stones (escavadeira)

bullet /'bʊlɪt/ NOUN [*plural* bullets] a small piece of metal that is shot from a gun (bala) □ *a bullet wound* 🔲 *Several people were in the room when the bullets were fired.* (balas foram disparadas)

⇨ go to **bite the bullet**

bulletin /'bʊlətɪn/ NOUN [*plural* **bulletins**] a television or radio report of the most recent things in the news □ *The next bulletin will be at 6 p.m.* (comunicado)

bulletproof /'bʊlɪtˌpruːf/ ADJECTIVE made from a material that bullets cannot pass through (à prova de balas) 🔲 *a bulletproof vest* (colete à prova de balas)

bullfight /'bʊlfaɪt/ NOUN [*plural* **bullfights**] a type of entertainment that is traditionally performed in Spain, in which a man fights a bull (tourada)

- **bullfighter** /'bʊlˌfaɪtə(r)/ NOUN [*plural* **bullfighters**] a person who fights a bull in a bullfight (toureiro)

bullion /'bʊljən/ NOUN, NO PLURAL bars of gold or silver (barras de ouro ou prata)

bull's-eye /'bʊlzˌaɪ/ NOUN [*plural* **bull's-eyes**] the round red mark in the middle of a board that you aim at in sports like archery or darts (centro do alvo)

bully /'bʊli/ ▶ NOUN [*plural* **bullies**] a person who frightens or hurts people who are smaller or weaker than they are (valentão)

  ▶ VERB [**bullies, bullying, bullied**] to frighten or hurt smaller or weaker people (intimidar)

- **bullying** /'bʊliɪŋ/ NOUN, NO PLURAL when someone bullies another person (intimidação)

bumbag /'bʌmbæg/ NOUN [plural **bumbags**] a small bag attached to a belt. An informal word. (pochete)

bumblebee /'bʌmbəlbi:/ NOUN [plural **bumblebees**] a large bee (= flying insect with yellow and black stripes on its body) (abelhão)

bump /bʌmp/ ▶ VERB [**bumps, bumping, bumped**] to knock against something by accident ◻ *The baby bumped her head on the table.* ◻ *I bumped into the wall.* (bater)

◆ PHRASAL VERB **bump into someone** to meet someone by chance ◻ *I bumped into Sarah in town today.* (topar com alguém)

▶ NOUN [plural **bumps**]

1 a raised part on a surface ◻ *He had a nasty bump on the back of his head.* ◻ *There were a lot of bumps in the road.* (protuberância)

2 a knock ◻ *I felt a gentle bump against my leg.* (batida)

bumper /'bʌmpə(r)/ ▶ NOUN [plural **bumpers**] a long bar fixed to the front and back of a car that protects it if it hits something (para-choque)

▶ ADJECTIVE bigger than usual (abundante, farto) 🔲 *We had a bumper crop of tomatoes this year.* (colheita farta)

bumpy /'bʌmpi/ ADJECTIVE [**bumpier, bumpiest**]

1 covered in raised areas ◻ *a bumpy road* (acidentado)

2 a bumpy journey is uncomfortable because the surface of the road is rough (sacolejante)

3 full of problems (instável) 🔲 *Investors should prepare themselves for a a bumpy ride* (= a difficult time) *this year.* (caminho instável) 🔲 *We got off to a bumpy start* (= started badly). (tivemos um começo instável)

bun /bʌn/ NOUN [plural **buns**]

1 a small round sweet cake ◻ *a currant bun* (bolinho)

2 bread in the form of a round shape ◻ *a hamburger in a bun* (pãozinho)

3 a hairstyle in which the hair is twisted into a tight ball and fixed at the back of the head (coque)

bunch /bʌntʃ/ ▶ NOUN [plural **bunches**]

1 a group of things tied or held together (grupo, punhado) 🔲 *a bunch of flowers* (ramalhete de flores) ◻ *The caretaker has a big bunch of keys.*

2 a group of things that grow together ◻ *a bunch of grapes/bananas* (cacho)

3 a bunch of something an informal US phrase meaning a large number or amount of something ◻ *I've got a whole bunch of stuff to do.* (um monte de coisas)

▶ VERB [**bunches, bunching, bunched**] to be close together or to move people or things close together ◻ *Bunch up a bit so I can get you all in the photo.* ◻ *The runners all bunched together at the beginning of the race.* (agrupar)

bundle /'bʌndəl/ ▶ NOUN [plural **bundles**] a group of things fastened together ◻ *a bundle of newspapers* (maço)

▶ VERB [**bundles, bundling, bundled**]

1 to push someone roughly into a place ◻ *He was bundled into a taxi before the photographers could see him.* (empurrar)

2 to include an extra product when you sell something ◻ *Their software is bundled with games and movie clips.* (incluir)

bung /bʌŋ/ ▶ VERB [**bungs, bunging, bunged**] to put something somewhere quickly and without care. An informal word. ◻ *Bung it in the microwave.* (arremessar)

◆ PHRASAL VERB **bung something up** to cause something to become blocked. An informal word ◻ *The drains are bunged up with dead leaves.* ◻ *My nose is bunged up and I have a headache.* (tampar algo)

▶ NOUN [plural **bungs**]

1 something used to block a hole so that liquid does not get in or out (tampão)

2 an informal word for a bribe (= money paid illegally to make someone do what you want) ◻ *He told the BBC that he had never taken or received a bung.* (propina)

bungalow /'bʌŋgələʊ/ NOUN [plural **bungalows**] a house that is all on one level (bangalô)

bungee jumping /'bʌndʒi: 'dʒʌmpɪŋ/ NOUN. NO PLURAL a sport in which you jump from a high place with strong rubber ropes attached to your body (bungee-jump)

bungle /'bʌŋgəl/ VERB [**bungles, bungling, bungled**] to spoil something by doing it badly ◻ *The police have bungled this investigation from the beginning.* (estragar)

• **bungler** /'bʌŋglə(r)/ NOUN [plural **bunglers**] someone who bungles something (negligente)

• **bungling** /'bʌŋglɪŋ/ ADJECTIVE doing things badly ◻ *Bungling cops missed two chances to arrest a wanted man.* (incompetente)

bunk /bʌŋk/ NOUN [plural **bunks**] a narrow bed fixed to a wall (beliche)

◆ IDIOM **do a bunk** an informal phrase meaning to escape from a place (sumir)

bunk beds /'bʌŋk ˌbedz/ PLURAL NOUN two beds that are joined together with one above the other (beliche)

bunker /'bʌŋkə(r)/ NOUN [plural **bunkers**]

1 a strong underground room used to protect people from bombs during a war ◻ *a nuclear bunker* (abrigo)

2 a hole filled with sand on a golf course (buraco de areia)

3 a large container for storing coal (carvoeira)

bunny /'bʌni/ NOUN [plural **bunnies**] a child's word for rabbit (coelho)

Bunsen burner /ˌbʌnsən 'bɜːnə(r)/ NOUN [plural **Bunsen burners**] a piece of equipment that produces a flame, used by scientists to heat substances. A chemistry word. (bico de Bunsen)

bunting

bunting /ˈbʌntɪŋ/ NOUN, NO PLURAL a row of small triangular flags, used to decorate streets during celebrations (**bandeirolas para decoração**)

buoy /bɔɪ/ ▶ NOUN [plural **buoys**] a large object that floats in the sea, used to warn people or ships of danger (**boia**)

▶ VERB [**buoys, buoying, buoyed**]

1 if a company or other organization is buoyed by something, something has helped it to be more successful □ *The company was buoyed by strong profits last year.* (**apoiar**)

2 to make someone feel happier or more confident □ *The England players have been buoyed up by the return of their captain.* (**proteger**)

• **buoyant** /ˈbɔɪənt/ ADJECTIVE
1 if a business or the economy is buoyant, it is successful (**bem-sucedido**)
2 happy and confident □ *She was in a buoyant mood.* (**animado**)
3 able to float (**flutuante**)

burden /ˈbɜːdən/ ▶ NOUN [plural **burdens**]
1 something unpleasant or difficult that someone has to deal with (**fardo**) *The service will ease the burden on accident and emergency departments.* (**aliviar o fardo**) *He offered to share the burden of the work.* (**dividir o fardo**) □ *Running two homes is a big financial burden.*
2 if someone is a burden to you, you find it difficult to look after them or pay for their needs □ *I don't want to be a burden to you.* (**fardo**)
3 something heavy that someone is carrying (**carga**)

▶ VERB [**burdens, burdening, burdened**] to give someone something difficult or unpleasant to deal with □ *The country is already burdened with debt.* □ *I don't want to burden you with all my problems.* (**sobrecarregar**)

bureau /ˈbjʊərəʊ/ NOUN [plural **bureaux**]
1 an office or organization □ *the Graduate Recruitment Bureau* (**agência**)
2 a desk with drawers (**escrivaninha**)

• **bureaucracy** /bjʊəˈrɒkrəsɪ/ NOUN, NO PLURAL all the rules that organizations have to follow, especially those that are annoying because they seem unnecessary □ *We are hoping to reduce unnecessary bureaucracy.* (**burocracia**)

• **bureaucrat** /ˈbjʊərəkræt/ NOUN [plural **bureaucrats**] an official person in an organization who seems to follow rules too exactly (**burocrata**)

• **bureaucratic** /ˌbjʊərəˈkrætɪk/ ADJECTIVE involving a lot of complicated rules □ *bureaucratic delays* (**burocrático**)

bureau de change /ˌbjʊərəʊ də ˈʃɒndʒ/ NOUN [plural **bureaux de change** or **bureaus de change**] an office where you can buy foreign money (**departamento de câmbio**)

burette /bjʊˈret/ NOUN [plural **burettes**] a glass tube with a hole at the bottom, used for adding measured amounts of liquid. A chemistry word. (**bureta**)

burrow

burger /ˈbɜːɡə(r)/ NOUN [plural **burgers**] a type of flat round food made from small pieces of meat that have been pressed together □ *I'll have a burger with fries and a coke, please.* (**hambúrguer**)

burglar /ˈbɜːɡlə(r)/ NOUN [plural **burglars**] someone who illegally enters a building in order to steal things □ *The burglars broke in through a downstairs window.* (**ladrão**)

burglar alarm /ˈbɜːɡləˌrəˌlɑːm/ NOUN [plural **burglar alarms**] a piece of electronic equipment that makes a loud noise if someone tries to enter the building when it is switched on (**alarme contra roubo**)

burglary /ˈbɜːɡlərɪ/ NOUN [plural **burglaries**] the crime of going into a building and stealing things □ *He called the police to report a burglary.* (**roubo**)

burial /ˈberɪəl/ NOUN [plural **burials**] when a dead person is put in the ground (**enterro**)

burly /ˈbɜːlɪ/ ADJECTIVE [**burlier, burliest**] a burly man is big, strong and heavy □ *a burly security guard* (**corpulento**)

burn /bɜːn/ ▶ VERB [**burns, burning, burnt or burned**]
1 to destroy something by setting fire to it, or to be destroyed in this way (**queimar**) □ *We burn all our garden waste.* *Both houses burnt to the ground.* (**foram todas queimadas**)
2 to be on fire □ *We could see the grass burning from miles away.* (**queimar**)
3 to injure yourself by touching fire or heat □ *I burnt my hand on the cooker.* (**queimar**)
4 to cook food for too long so that it becomes black □ *You've burnt the toast!* (**carbonizar**)
5 to use fuel to make heat or energy (**incendiar**)
6 to put music, images or information on a CD-ROM (**gravar**)

♦ PHRASAL VERBS **burn down** if a building burns down, it is completely destroyed in a fire □ *The old school burnt down.* **burn out** if a fire burns out, it stops burning **burn up** to be destroyed by fire (**ser destruído**)

▶ NOUN [plural **burns**] an injury or mark left after touching fire or something very hot (**queimadura**)

• **burner** /ˈbɜːnə(r)/ NOUN [plural **burners**] an object that you use for burning things or for making heat □ *a wood burner* (**queimador**)

burp /bɜːp/ ▶ VERB [**burps, burping, burped**] to make a sound by letting air come out of your stomach through your mouth (**arrotar**)
▶ NOUN [plural **burps**] the sound that you make when you burp (**arroto**)

burrow /ˈbʌrəʊ/ ▶ VERB [**burrows, burrowing, burrowed**]
1 to make a hole or passage in the ground □ *They had managed to burrow deep into the hillside.* (**escavar**)
2 to move into or under something heavy or thick □ *She burrowed deep into her duvet again.* (**entocar-se**)

▶ NOUN [plural burrows] a hole or passage in the ground made by a small animal (toca)

bursary /ˈbɜːsəri/ NOUN [plural bursaries] an amount of money given to a student to allow them to study at college or university (bolsa de estudos)

burst /bɜːst/ ▶ VERB [bursts, bursting, burst]

1 to break or tear, especially from having too much pressure inside □ *The pipe had burst and water was running everywhere.* □ *He was bursting all the balloons with a pin.* (estourar)

2 burst into flames to suddenly start to burn a lot (irromper em chamas)

3 burst into tears to suddenly start to cry (irromper em lágrimas)

♦ PHRASAL VERBS **burst in/into (somewhere)** to enter a room suddenly and violently (irromper) □ *Both kids burst into our bedroom.* **burst out** to suddenly shout something □ *'Don't blame me!', he burst out.* (gritar) **burst out crying/laughing** to suddenly start to cry or laugh (desatar a rir/chorar)

▶ NOUN [plural bursts] a sudden, short period of something □ *a burst of applause* □ *a burst of energy* (salva, rajada)

bury /ˈberi/ VERB [buries, burying, buried]

1 to put something in the ground, especially a dead person □ *She was buried in the village where she was born.* □ *They buried the treasure.* (enterrar)

2 bury your face/head in something to cover your face or head with something, often because you are upset □ *She buried her face in her hands.* (cobrir a cabeça)

➪ go to **bury the** *hatchet*

bus /bʌs/ NOUN [plural buses] a large vehicle with a lot of seats for passengers (ônibus) 🔊 *I caught the bus into town.* (peguei o ônibus) 🔊 *Seven young men boarded the bus.* 🔊 *a school bus* (ônibus escolar) 🔊 *a bus driver* (motorista de ônibus)

bus conductor /ˈbʌs kənˌdʌktə(r)/ NOUN [plural bus conductors] a person whose job is to sell tickets to passengers on a bus (motorista de ônibus)

bush /bʊʃ/ NOUN [plural bushes]

1 a type of small tree □ *a rose bush* (arbusto)

2 the bush the wild part of some hot, dry countries where not many people live □ *the Australian bush* (mato)

• **bushy** /ˈbʊʃi/ ADJECTIVE [bushier, bushiest] growing in a thick mass □ *a long bushy tail* □ *a bushy beard* (espesso)

busily /ˈbɪzɪli/ ADVERB in a busy way, with a lot of effort and concentration □ *They were all busily working on their computers.* (ativamente)

business /ˈbɪznɪs/ NOUN [plural businesses]

1 *no plural* buying and selling, and the work of producing things that people will buy (negócios) 🔊 *He went into business* (= started buying and selling) *with his brother.* (fez negócios) 🔊 *In 2004 her company went out of business* (= ended because they had no money). (encerrou os negócios) 🔊 *They do a lot of business with Asia* (= They sell a lot to Asia). (fazem negócios com)

2 a company that makes and sells goods, or that sells services (negócios) 🔊 *He runs the business with his wife.* (controla os negócios)

3 on business working □ *He travels a lot on business.* (a negócios)

4 a type of business □ *the music business* □ *the fashion business* (negócio)

> ► Remember that you travel/go somewhere **on business**:
> ✓ I was recently in Paris on business.
> ✗ I was recently in Paris for business.

♦ IDIOM **Mind your own business!** used as a rude way of refusing to answer a personal question □ *'What's your boyfriend's name?' 'Mind your own business!'* (Cuide de sua vida!)

• **businesslike** /ˈbɪznɪslaɪk/ ADJECTIVE serious and effective □ *a businesslike manner* (profissional)

• **businessman** /ˈbɪznɪsmæn/ NOUN [plural businessmen] a man who works in business, usually in a high position (homem de negócios)

• **businesswoman** /ˈbɪznɪsˌwʊmən/ NOUN [plural businesswomen] a woman who works in business, usually in a high position (mulher de negócios)

busker /ˈbʌskə(r)/ NOUN [plural buskers] a musician who performs in the street for money (artista de rua)

bus stop /ˈbʌs stɒp/ NOUN [plural bus stops] a place where a bus stops to let passengers get on or off □ *I saw Fiona standing at the bus stop.* (ponto de ônibus)

bust /bʌst/ c NOUN [plural busts]

1 a woman's breasts (peito)

2 a model of a person's head and shoulders (busto)

▶ VERB [busts, busting, bust or busted]

1 an informal word that means to break something □ *I've gone and bust my zip.* (quebrar)

2 if a criminal is busted, they are arrested. An informal word. (prender)

▶ ADJECTIVE

1 go bust if a company goes bust, it has lost its money and cannot now operate (falir)

2 an informal word for broken (quebrado)

bustle /ˈbʌsəl/ NOUN, NO PLURAL noise and busy activity □ *She wanted to escape the bustle of the city.* (agitação, tumulto)

♦ PHRASAL VERB [bustles, bustling, bustled] **bustle about/around** to move around, doing a lot of different things ◻ *Melissa was bustling about in the kitchen.* (mover-se agitadamente)

• **bustling** /'bʌsəlɪŋ/ ADJECTIVE full of noisy activity ◻ *They walked through the bustling market.* (alvoroçado, agitado)

busy /'bɪzi/ ADJECTIVE [busier, busiest]
1 doing a lot of things ◻ + *with They're busy with wedding preparations.* ◻ + *doing something I was busy getting dinner ready.* (ocupado) ▣ *That report should keep him busy today.* (manter ocupado) ▣ *I've had a very busy day.* (dia cheio)
2 full of people or traffic (movimentado) ▣ *We live on a busy street.* (rua movimentada) ◻ *Were the shops busy this morning?*
3 if someone's telephone is busy, it is being used when you try to call ◻ *Her phone's been busy for nearly an hour.* (ocupado)

but /bʌt/ ▶ CONJUNCTION
1 used for joining two parts of a sentence which say different or opposite things ◻ *She eats fish but not meat.* ◻ *He's not very attractive but he's a nice guy.* ◻ *I can cycle but I can't drive.* ◻ *I'd like to come but I haven't got time.* (mas)
2 used after you have said 'excuse me' or 'I'm sorry' before you ask for something or give an explanation ◻ *I'm sorry, but I don't have time to help at the moment.* (mas)
3 used for showing surprise when someone has just told you something ◻ *'I don't like Nicole.' 'But I thought you were friends.'* (mas)
▶ PREPOSITION except ◻ *No one knows but you.* (exceto)
▶ NOUN [plural **buts**] **no buts** used for telling someone that they must do what you have told them to do ◻ *'But I'm too tired.' 'No buts! we're going!'* (sem desculpas)

butane /'bju:teɪn/ NOUN, NO PLURAL a type of gas in liquid form that is used as a fuel for cooking. A chemistry word. (butano)

butch /bʊtʃ/ ADJECTIVE a butch woman looks and behaves like a man (mulher com características masculinas, sapatão)

butcher /'bʊtʃə(r)/ NOUN [plural **butchers**]
1 someone whose job is to cut up and sell raw meat (açougueiro)
2 butcher's a shop that sells raw meat (açougue)

butler /'bʌtlə(r)/ NOUN [plural **butlers**] a male servant who looks after a rich person, or who is responsible for the other servants in a rich person's house (mordomo)

butt /bʌt/ ▶ NOUN [plural **butts**]
1 the part of a cigarette that remains when someone has finished smoking it (ponta) ▣ *a cigarette butt* (ponta de cigarro)
2 the wide end of the handle of a gun (coronha)

♦ IDIOM **be the butt of something** if you are the butt of people's jokes, you are the person they make jokes about (ser o alvo de alguma coisa)
▶ VERB [butts, butting, butted] to hit someone or something using your head ◻ *He walked back towards his opponent and butted his chest.* (dar cabeçada)

♦ PHRASAL VERB **butt in** to interrupt someone while they are talking ◻ *Sorry to butt in, but can I ask a question?* (interromper)

butter /'bʌtə(r)/ ▶ NOUN, NO PLURAL a yellow food made from milk, used for spreading on bread or for cooking (manteiga) ▣ *a slice of bread and butter* (pão com manteiga)
▶ VERB [butters, buttering, buttered] to spread butter on something such as bread ◻ *Butter the bread evenly.* (passar manteiga)

♦ PHRASAL VERB **butter someone up** to say nice things to someone so that they will do what you want them to do. An informal phrase. (bajular)

buttercup /'bʌtəkʌp/ NOUN [plural **buttercups**] a common wild flower with yellow petals (botão de ouro)

butterfly /'bʌtəflaɪ/ NOUN [plural **butterflies**] a type of insect with large brightly coloured wings (borboleta)

♦ IDIOM **get/have butterflies (in your stomach)** to have an uncomfortable feeling in your stomach because you are nervous (estar com frio na barriga)

buttocks /'bʌtəkz/ PLURAL NOUN your bottom (nádegas)

button /'bʌtən/ ▶ NOUN [plural **buttons**]
1 a small object that you press in order to make a machine work (botão) ▣ *I pressed the button to call the lift.* (pressionei o botão) ◻ *Press the start button.*
2 a small round object used for fastening clothes (botão) ▣ *He did/undid* (= fastened/unfastened) *up his buttons.* (abotoou/desabotoou)
▶ VERB [buttons, buttoning, buttoned] to fasten something with buttons ◻ *Button up your coat; it's cold out there.* ◻ *The dress buttons at the back.* (abotoar-se)

buttonhole /'bʌtənhəʊl/ NOUN [plural **buttonholes**] a hole that you push a button through to fasten your clothes (casa de botão)

buy /baɪ/ ▶ VERB [buys, buying, bought] to get something by giving money for it ◻ *I've bought the tickets.* ◻ *Have you bought him a present?* ◻ + *from We buy most of our food from the supermarket.* (comprar)

♦ PHRASAL VERBS **buy into something** to start believing in something ◻ *More consumers are buying into the idea of organic food.* (acreditar em alguma coisa) **buy something up** to buy large amounts of something ◻ *We bought up almost all the flowers in the shop.* (comprar muita coisa)

▶ NOUN [plural **buys**] **a good buy** something that is not expensive and is of good quality ◻ *At £11,000, this car is a really good buy.* (**compra**)

• **buyer** /'baɪə(r)/ NOUN [plural **buyers**] is someone who buys something ◻ *Have they found a buyer for their house?* (**comprador**)

buzz /bʌz/ C NOUN, NO PLURAL

1 an informal word that means excitement (**prazer**) ◻ *I get a real buzz from performing in public.* (**tive prazer**)

2 energy and interest that a group of people feel ◻ *There's a definite buzz about the office since Jane arrived.* (**burburinho**)

3 the continuous sound that a large flying insect makes ◻ *The constant buzz of insects disturbed his sleep.* (**zumbido**)

▶ VERB [**buzzes, buzzing, buzzed**]

1 to make a continuous sound like a large flying insect ◻ *Flies buzzed round our heads.* (**zumbir**)

2 to be full of noise and activity ◻ *The store was buzzing with activity.* (**zumbir**)

3 if your head or mind is buzzing, you have a lot of ideas and cannot relax ◻ *I left the meeting, my head buzzing with ideas.* (**zumbir**)

♦ PHRASAL VERB **buzz about/around** to move around, doing a lot of different things ◻ *Sylvie was buzzing about trying to organize everything.* (**mover-se de lá para cá**)

• **buzzer** /'bʌzə(r)/ NOUN [plural **buzzers**] a small piece of equipment that makes a continuous sound in order to get your attention ◻ *When the buzzer goes can you take the cake out of the oven?* (**campainha**)

buzzword /'bʌzwɜːd/ NOUN [plural **buzzwords**] a word that has become very popular, especially in newspapers, and on the radio and television (**jargão**)

by /baɪ/ ▶ PREPOSITION

1 shows who or what does something ◻ *a painting by Picasso* ◻ *The house was built by her grandfather.* ◻ *I was taught by nuns.* (**por**)

2 near or next to something ◻ *There's a café by the station.* (**perto de**)

3 using something ◻ *We came by train.* ◻ *All their clothes are made by hand.* ◻ *Can I pay by credit card?* ◻ **+ doing something** *By buying food from local shops you are supporting your community.* (**de, a, com**)

4 past ◻ *A tall boy ran by me.* (**por**)

5 by accident/chance without intending to ◻ *We met by chance.* ◻ *I only discovered it by accident.* (**por acaso**)

6 by 20%, £500, etc. shows how much something has increased or decreased ◻ *Prices have risen by 20 percent.* (**com**)

7 by the arm/coat, etc. shows which part of someone you take in your hand ◻ *She grabbed me by the hand.* (**por**)

8 before ◻ *I'll be home by 7.30.* (**antes de**)

9 used when giving measurements of length and width ◻ *The room is 5 metres by 3 metres.* (**por**)

▶ ADVERB past ◻ *A car went speeding by.* (**por aqui**)

♦ IDIOM **by the way** used before you say something that is not related to what you were saying before (**a propósito**)

bye /baɪ/ EXCLAMATION an informal word that means goodbye ◻ *Bye – see you later!* (**tchau**)

bye-bye /baɪ baɪ/ EXCLAMATION a word used by children that means goodbye (**adeus**)

by-election /'baɪ.ɪˌlekʃən/ NOUN [plural **byelections**] an election that takes place in a particular area in order to choose a new member of parliament (**eleição suplementar**)

bygone /'baɪɡɒn/ ADJECTIVE in the past (**passado, antigo**) ◻ *She seemed to belong to a bygone age/era.* (**era passada**)

by-law /'baɪˌlɔː/ NOUN [plural **by-laws**] a law made by local government (**estatuto**)

bypass /'baɪpɑːs/ ▶ NOUN [plural **bypasses**] a road around a town or city (**desvio**)

▶ VERB [**bypasses, bypassing, bypassed**] to avoid something ◻ *The thieves managed to bypass the security system.* (**evitar**)

by-product /'baɪˌprɒdʌkt/ NOUN [plural **byproducts**] something that is produced as a result of making something else (**subproduto**)

bystander /'baɪˌstændə(r)/ NOUN [plural **bystanders**] someone who sees an accident or crime happen, but who is not involved in it (**testemunha, espectador**) ◻ *She was an innocent bystander.* (**testemunha inocente**)

byte /baɪt/ NOUN [plural **bytes**] a unit for measuring the size of a computer file. A computing word. (**byte**)

byword /'baɪwɜːd/ NOUN [plural **bywords**] a byword for something that is known for a particular thing ◻ *The area soon became a byword for violence.* (**sinônimo de algo**)

Cc

C or **c¹** /si:/ the third letter of the alphabet (**a terceira letra do alfabeto**)

C² /si:/ ABBREVIATION
1 Celsius (**Celsius**)
2 centigrade (**centígrado**)

cab /kæb/ NOUN [plural **cabs**]
1 a taxi (**táxi**) ▣ *We took a cab to the airport.* (**peguei um táxi**)
2 the part at the front of a truck or bus where the driver sits ▢ *I climbed up into the cab next to Dad.* (**cabine**)

cabaret /'kæbəreɪ/ NOUN [plural **cabarets**] a performance, usually of dance, songs or comedy, at a restaurant or club (**cabaré**)

cabbage /'kæbɪdʒ/ NOUN [plural **cabbages**] a large round green vegetable formed of tight layers of leaves (**repolho**)

cabin /'kæbɪn/ NOUN [plural **cabins**]
1 a simple wooden house (**cabana**) ▣ *He built a log cabin in the forest.* (**cabana de madeira**)
2 a small room for sleeping in on a ship (**cabine**)
3 the part of an aeroplane which the passengers sit in (**cabine**)

cabin crew /'kæbɪn ˌkru:/ NOUN [plural **cabin crews**] the people whose job is to look after the passengers on an aeroplane (**tripulação**)

cabinet /'kæbɪnɪt/ NOUN [plural **cabinets**]
1 Cabinet a group of people with important government jobs who decide what the government will do ▢ *She became a member of the Cabinet in 1990.* ▢ *a Cabinet meeting* (**gabinete**)
2 a cupboard with shelves, used for storing things or for showing attractive objects ▢ *a bathroom cabinet* (**armário**)

cable /'keɪbəl/ NOUN [plural **cables**]
1 a tube containing wires that carry electricity or electronic signals ▢ *a telephone cable* (**cabo**)
2 thick, strong metal rope ▢ *Miles of cable were used to build the bridge.* (**cabo**)
3 no plural a television service in which programmes are sent along underground wires ▢ *We can't get cable or satellite here.* (**cabo**)

cable car /'keɪbəl ˌkɑː(r)/ NOUN [plural **cable cars**] a vehicle that hangs from a cable and is used to carry people up mountains (**bonde, teleférico**)

cable television /ˌkeɪbəl 'telɪvɪʒən/ NOUN, NO PLURAL a television service in which programmes are sent along underground wires (**televisão a cabo**)

cache /kæʃ/ NOUN [plural **caches**]
1 a supply of something that is hidden or stored somewhere ▢ *Police discovered a huge cache of weapons.* (**esconderijo**)
2 a place in a computer's memory where data that is often used is stored temporarily. A computing word. (**memória temporária**)

cackle /'kækəl/ ▶ NOUN [plural **cackles**] a loud and unpleasant laugh (**gargalhada**)
▶ VERB [**cackles, cackling, cackled**] to laugh in a loud and unpleasant way (**gargalhada**)

cacophony /kə'kɒfəni/ NOUN, NO PLURAL a loud and unpleasant mixture of sounds (**cacofonia**)

cactus /'kæktəs/ NOUN [plural **cactuses** or **cacti**] a plant with thick leaves and sharp points which grows in very dry places (**cacto**)

CAD /kæd/ ABBREVIATION computer-aided design; when computers are used to help draw plans for things like buildings or machines ▢ *We used a new CAD program.* (**programa de desenho**)

cadet /kə'det/ NOUN [plural **cadets**] a young person who is training to be in the police, army, etc. (**cadete**)

cadge /kædʒ/ VERB [**cadges, cadging, cadged**] to ask other people for money, food, etc. ▢ *He's always cadging drinks off people.* (**mendigar**)

caesarean /sɪ'zeəriən/ NOUN [plural **caesareans**] an operation in which a baby is taken out of its mother's body through a cut in her stomach (**cesariana**)

caesium /'siːzɪəm/ NOUN, NO PLURAL a soft, silverwhite element. A chemistry word. (**césio**)

café /'kæfeɪ/ NOUN [plural **cafés**] a small restaurant that serves drinks and things to eat (**café**)

cafeteria /ˌkæfɪ'tɪəriə/ NOUN [plural **cafeterias**] a restaurant where the customers buy food and drink and take it to a table to eat it (**cantina**)

cafetière /ˌkæfɪtɪ'eə(r)/ NOUN [plural **cafetières**] a container for making coffee with a part that you push down (**cafeteira**)

caffeine /'kæfiːn/ NOUN, NO PLURAL a substance in coffee and tea that makes you feel more awake (**cafeína**)

caftan /'kæftæn/ NOUN [plural **caftans**] a loose, light piece of clothing with long sleeves (**túnica**)

cage /keɪdʒ/ ▶ NOUN [plural **cages**] a box or an area with bars around it for keeping birds or animals in ▫ *The pet shop sells bird cages and hamster cages.* (**gaiola**)
▶ VERB [**cages, caging, caged**] to put an animal or bird in a cage (**engaiolar, enjaular**)
• **caged** /keɪdʒd/ ADJECTIVE kept in a cage ▫ *caged birds* (**engaiolado, preso**)

cagey /'keɪdʒi/ ADJECTIVE [**cagier, cagiest**] careful not to say much about something ▫ *She is very cagey about her family.* (**ressabiado**)

cagoule /kəˈguːl/ NOUN [plural **cagoules**] a light coat with a hood (= covering for the head) that protects you from the rain (**capa de chuva**)

cahoots /kəˈhuːts/ NOUN **in cahoots** if two or more people are in cahoots, they are planning something dishonest ▫ *The shop manager was in cahoots with the thieves.* (**em conluio**)

cajole /kəˈdʒəʊl/ VERB [**cajoles, cajoling, cajoled**] to persuade someone to do something by being nice to them or by making promises to them ▫ *He had been cajoled into going with them.* (**persuadir**)

cake /keɪk/ NOUN [plural **cakes**] a sweet food made from a baked mixture, usually of flour, sugar, butter and eggs (**bolo**) 🔳 *a birthday cake* (**bolo de aniversário**) 🔳 *He made a cake for the school fair.* (**fez um bolo**) 🔳 *Would you like another slice of chocolate cake?* (**fatia de bolo**)
♦ IDIOM **have your cake and eat it** to get all the advantages of a situation in a way that is unfair (**assobiar e chupar cana**)
⇨ go to **the icing on the cake, a piece of cake**
• **caked** /keɪkt/ ADJECTIVE **caked in something** covered in a thick, dry layer of something ▫ *His shoes were caked in mud.* (**coberto de algo**)

calamity /kəˈlæməti/ NOUN [plural **calamities**] something that causes a lot of damage or suffering (**calamidade**)

calcium /'kælsiəm/ NOUN, NO PLURAL a white chemical element in chalk (= soft white rock) and in bones and teeth. A chemistry word. (**cálcio**)

calculate /'kælkjʊleɪt/ VERB [**calculates, calculating, calculated**]
1 to find out an amount by using mathematics ▫ *One apple costs 13p. Calculate the cost of 174 apples.* ▫ *Do you understand how they calculate tax?* (**calcular**)
2 to guess something using all the facts that you have ▫ **+ that** *The teenagers had calculated that no one would be home for another two hours.* (**calcular**)
• **calculated** /'kælkjʊleɪtɪd/ ADJECTIVE
1 made or done after considering all the facts that you have (**calculado**) 🔳 *I decided to take a calculated risk.* (**risco calculado**)

2 calculated to do something intended to do something ▫ *His words had been calculated to hurt her.* (**programado para fazer algo**)
• **calculating** /'kælkjʊleɪtɪŋ/ ADJECTIVE carefully planning how to get what you want, without caring about other people (**calculista, sagaz**)
• **calculation** /ˌkælkjʊˈleɪʃən/ NOUN [plural **calculations**]
1 when you use mathematics to find out an amount (**cálculo**) 🔳 *I did some quick calculations to work out the total cost.* (**fiz cálculos**) ▫ *By my calculation, we should be finished by Tuesday.*
2 no plural when you plan carefully to get what you want, without caring about other people ▫ *an act of cold calculation*
• **calculator** /'kælkjʊleɪtə(r)/ NOUN [plural **calculators**] an electronic machine that you use for doing mathematical calculations (**calculadora**) 🔳 *a pocket calculator* (**calculadora de bolso**)

calendar /'kælɪndə(r)/ NOUN [plural **calendars**]
1 something that shows all the days, weeks and months of the year ▫ *She looked on the calendar to see what date it would be on Monday.* (**calendário**)
2 the Christian/Islamic, etc. calendar the way in which the days and special events of the year are arranged in the Christian/Islamic, etc. tradition (**calendário cristão, islâmico etc.**)
3 the school/political/sporting, etc. calendar the events which usually happen in a school, in politics, in a sport, etc. in a year ▫ *The race is one of the most exciting events in the sporting calendar.* (**calendário escolar, político, esportivo etc.**)

calf /kɑːf/ NOUN [plural **calves**]
1 the back part of your leg below the knee (**panturrilha**)
2 a young cow (**bezerro**)

caliber /'kælɪbə(r)/ NOUN the US spelling of **calibre** (**calibre**)

calibre /'kælɪbə(r)/ NOUN [plural **calibres**]
1 the quality or ability of something or someone ▫ *We need a manager of the highest calibre.* (**calibre**)
2 the width of a gun's barrel (= tube the bullet goes through) (**calibre**)

call /kɔːl/ ▶ VERB [**calls, calling, called**]
1 if a person or thing is called something, that is their name ▫ *He's called Jonathan James.* (**chamar**)
2 to describe someone in a particular way ▫ *How dare you call me a liar!* (**chamar**)
3 to shout ▫ *I heard him calling my name.* (**gritar**)
4 to ask someone to come to you ▫ *Call the children in from the garden.* (**chamar**)
5 to telephone someone ▫ *Have you called your mother yet?* (**ligar**)
6 to visit someone ▫ **+ in** *We called in to see Maria this morning.* ▫ **+ round** *My neighbour called round yesterday.* (**visitar**)

call centre

> Remember that the verb **call** meaning 'telephone' is used without 'to':
> ✓ I called my brother to wish him happy birthday.
> ✗ I called to my brother to wish him happy birthday.

◆ PHRASAL VERBS **I call for something** to demand that something happens □ Campaigners have called for changes to the law. (**requer algo**) **call for someone** to go to someone's house in order to go somewhere with them □ I'll call for you at seven. (**buscar alguém**) **call something off** to stop a plan or an activity □ The search has been called off. (**cancelar algo**) **call someone up** a US word meaning to telephone someone □ He called me up in the middle of the night. (**ligar para alguém**) **call something up** to find information on your computer screen □ He called up lots of information about horses. (**descobrir algo**)
▶ NOUN [plural **calls**]
1 when you contact someone by telephone 🔁 Give me a call tomorrow. (**fazer uma ligação**) 🔁 I'm sure I can find someone to fix you car – let me make a few calls. (**fazer ligações**)
2 a call for something a demand for something to happen □ The prime minister is facing calls for his resignation. (**demanda por algo**)
3 a shout □ They ignored his calls for help. (**grito**)
4 a short visit 🔁 I thought I might pay you a call tomorrow. (**fazer uma visita**)

call centre /ˈkɔːl ˌsentə(r)/ NOUN [plural **call centres**] a place where people work using the telephone to take orders or answer questions from customers (**central de atendimento**)

caller /ˈkɔːlə(r)/ NOUN [plural **callers**]
1 someone who makes a telephone call □ Several callers complained about the show. (**aquele que telefona**)
2 someone who visits your house for a short time (**visita**)

caller ID /ˌkɔːlər aɪˈdiː/ NOUN, NO PLURAL a system on a telephone that shows who is calling (**identificador de chamadas**)

calling /ˈkɔːlɪŋ/ NOUN [plural **callings**] a strong feeling that you should do a particular type of job □ He had felt a calling to become a teacher. (**vocação**)

callous /ˈkæləs/ ADJECTIVE cruel □ a callous thief (**cruel**)

calm /kɑːm/ ▶ ADJECTIVE [**calmer, calmest**]
1 not nervous, excited or upset □ Try to stay calm. □ "Yes," he said in a calm voice. (**calmo**)
2 if the sea is calm, it is flat with no big waves (**tranquilo**)
3 if the weather is calm, there are no storms (**tranquilo**)
▶ NOUN, NO PLURAL

1 a peaceful situation in which there is no fighting □ The President appealed for calm. (**tranquilidade**)
2 a state in which you are not nervous, excited or upset □ Impatience had replaced his usual calm. (**calma**)
3 when there is not much wind □ the calm of the early morning air (**tranquilidade**)
▶ VERB [**calms, calming, calmed**] to make someone feel calm □ They calmed the animal by stroking it gently. (**acalmar**)
◆ PHRASAL VERB **calm (someone) down** to stop someone being angry, excited or upset, or to stop being angry, excited or upset □ She took a couple of deep breaths to calm herself down. □ Just calm down! Nobody's going to hurt you. (**acalmar alguém**)

• **calmly** /ˈkɑːmlɪ/ ADVERB without seeming nervous or excited □ Grace walked calmly on to the stage. (**calmamente**)

• **calmness** /ˈkɑːmnɪs/ NOUN, NO PLURAL the quality of being calm □ We were impressed by his calmness under pressure. (**calma**)

calorie /ˈkælərɪ/ NOUN [plural **calories**] a unit used to measure how much energy food will produce (**caloria**)

calves /kɑːvz/ PLURAL OF **calf** (ver **calf**)

camcorder /ˈkæmkɔːdə(r)/ NOUN [plural **camcorders**] a type of camera that records moving pictures and sound (**filmadora portátil**)

came /keɪm/ PAST TENSE OF **come** (ver **come**)

camel /ˈkæməl/ NOUN [plural **camels**] a large animal that lives in the desert and has one or two humps (= tall rounded parts) on its back (**camelo**)

cameo /ˈkæmɪəʊ/ NOUN [plural **cameos**] a small part which a famous person has in a film (**participação**) 🔁 Tyson made a cameo appearance in the movie. (**participação especial**)

camera /ˈkæmərə/ NOUN [plural **cameras**] a device for taking photographs, or for making television programmes or films (**câmera**) 🔁 I have a digital camera. (**câmera digital**) 🔁 He's very confident in front of the television cameras. (**câmeras de televisão**)

camera crew /ˈkæmərə ˌkruː/ NOUN [plural **camera crews**] the people who operate the cameras which are used for making a film or a television programme (**equipe de câmeras**)

cameraman /ˈkæmərəmæn/ NOUN [plural **cameramen**] someone whose job is to operate a television camera or film camera (**cinegrafista**)

camisole /ˈkæmɪsəʊl/ NOUN [plural **camisoles**] a piece of women's underwear that covers the top part of the body (**camisola**)

camomile /ˈkæməmaɪl/ NOUN, NO PLURAL a plant with yellow flowers, used in drinks and medicines (**camomila**)

camouflage

camouflage /ˈkæməflɑːʒ/ ▶ NOUN, NO PLURAL a way of making something or someone difficult to see because they look similar to what is around them (**camuflagem**)
▶ VERB [**camouflages, camouflaging, camouflaged**] to make something or someone difficult to see because they look similar to what is around them □ *With its speckled coat, the leopard is perfectly camouflaged in the branches of a tree.* (**camuflar**)

camp /kæmp/ ▶ NOUN [*plural* **camps**] a place where people live in tents or temporary shelters, usually for a short time (**acampamento**) 🔊 *a holiday camp* (**acampamento de férias**) 🔊 *a refugee camp* (**acampamento de refugiados**) 🔊 *The boys set up camp in our field.* (**armaram acampamento**)
▶ VERB [**camps, camping, camped**] to stay somewhere for a short time in a tent or caravan (= vehicle for living in) □ *We camped next to the lake.* (**acampar**)

campaign /kæmˈpeɪn/ ▶ NOUN [*plural* **campaigns**]
1 a series of activities designed to achieve something □ *an advertising campaign* □ *an election campaign* (**campanha**)
2 a series of military attacks □ *Her dad fought in the Falklands campaign.* (**campanhas**)
▶ VERB [**campaigns, campaigning, campaigned**] to try to make something happen by organizing a series of activities □ *They've been campaigning for better street lighting.* (**fazer campanha**)
• **campaigner** /kæmˈpeɪnə(r)/ ▶ NOUN [*plural* **campaigners**] someone who campaigns for something (**defensor**)

camper /ˈkæmpə(r)/ ▶ NOUN [*plural* **campers**] someone who is staying in tent for a holiday (**pessoa que acampa**)

camper van /ˈkæmpər ˌvæn/ ▶ NOUN [*plural* **camper vans**] a vehicle that you can live in while you are on holiday (**trailer**)

camping /ˈkæmpɪŋ/ ▶ NOUN, NO PLURAL the activity of staying in a tent (**camping**) 🔊 *We went camping in France last summer.* (**fomos acampar**) 🔊 *The boys are on a camping trip.* (**viagem de camping**)

campsite /ˈkæmpsaɪt/ ▶ NOUN [*plural* **campsites**] a place where people stay in tents for a holiday □ *We found a good campsite near the river.* (**área para camping**)

campus /ˈkæmpəs/ ▶ NOUN [*plural* **campuses**] the land and buildings that form a university or college (**campus**)

can¹ /kæn/ MODAL VERB
1 to be able to do something □ *Can you swim? Yes, I can.* □ *Can you see my keys anywhere?* (**poder**)

cancer

2 to be allowed to □ *Can I go swimming? Yes, you can.* (**poder**)
3 used to ask someone to do something or give you something □ *Can you open the window, please?* □ *Can you lend me some money?* (**poder**)
4 used to talk about whether something is possible □ *Can you buy tickets here?* □ *Tiredness can cause accidents.* (**poder**)

> ➤ **Can** is the present tense form. Use **could** for the past tense.

> ➤ To ask for something politely, do not use **can** but instead use **could**: □ *Could I use this chair, please?*

can² /kæn/ ▶ NOUN [*plural* **cans**]
1 a closed metal container that keeps food or drink fresh (**lata**) 🔊 *a beer can* (**lata de cerveja**) 🔊 *Do you recycle your tin cans?* (**latas de alumínio**) 🔊 *She opened a can of beans.* (**lata de feijões**)
2 a container used for liquid or other substances □ *a paint can* (**lata**)
▶ VERB [**cans, canning, canned**] to pack food or drink in closed metal cans that keep it fresh (**enlatar**)

canal /kəˈnæl/ NOUN [*plural* **canals**]
1 a long passage filled with water, made for boats to travel along □ *the Panama Canal* (**canal**)
2 a tube in the body that something passes through. A biology word □ *the spinal canal* □ *The baby passes down the birth canal.* (**canal**)

canary /kəˈneəri/ NOUN [*plural* **canaries**] a small yellow bird that is often kept as a pet (**canário**)

cancel /ˈkænsəl/ VERB [**cancels, cancelling/US canceling, cancelled/US canceled**]
1 to say that a planned event will not happen □ *The match was cancelled because of the snow.* (**cancelar**)
2 to stop something from being done or paid, etc. □ *Please cancel my order.* □ *The cheque has been cancelled.* (**cancelar**)
◆ PHRASAL VERB **cancel something out** when two things cancel each other out, they stop each other from having any effect □ *What I saved in the price was cancelled out by the postage cost.* (**invalidar**)
• **cancellation** /ˌkænsəˈleɪʃən/ ▶ NOUN [*plural* **cancellations**] when something that was planned is now cancelled □ *the cancellation of train services* □ *You might get a seat on the flight if there are any late cancellations.* (**cancelamento**)

cancer /ˈkænsə(r)/ NOUN, NO PLURAL a serious disease in which some cells in the body start to grow very quickly □ *Smoking can cause lung cancer.* (**câncer**) 🔊 *Use sun cream – you don't want to get skin cancer.* (**desenvolver câncer**) 🔊

The drug is used to treat cancer patients. (pacientes com câncer)

• **cancerous** /'kænsərəs/ ADJECTIVE affected by cancer (cancerígeno) ▣ *cancerous cells* (células cancerígenas)

candid /'kændɪd/ ADJECTIVE honest ▢ *Sheena was very candid about the mistakes she'd made.* (sincero)

candidacy /'kændɪdəsɪ/ NOUN, NO PLURAL the state of being a candidate for something ▢ *She has announced her candidacy for mayor.* (candidatura)

candidate /'kændɪdət/ NOUN [plural **candidates**]
1 someone who is trying to get a job ▢ + **for** *There are three candidates for the job.* ▢ *The Democratic candidate for the US presidency is Barack Obama.* (candidato)
2 someone who is taking an exam ▢ *All our GCSE candidates were successful.* (candidato)

candidly /'kændɪdlɪ/ ADVERB in a way that tells the truth ▢ *He spoke candidly about what had gone wrong.* (francamente)

candle /'kændəl/ NOUN [plural **candles**] a stick of wax with a piece of string through the middle which produces a flame when you burn it (vela) ▣ *I must light the candles on the dinner table.* (acender velas) ▣ *Don't forget to blow out the candle.* (apagar as velas)

candlelight /'kændəllaɪt/ NOUN, NO PLURAL the light produced by a candle ▢ *They had to read by candlelight.* (luz de vela)

• **candlelit** /'kændəllɪt/ ADJECTIVE with light from candles (luz de vela) ▣ *a candlelit dinner* (jantar à luz de vela)

candlestick /'kændəlstɪk/ NOUN [plural **candlesticks**] an object which holds a candle (castiçal)

candor /'kændə(r)/ NOUN, NO PLURAL the US spelling of **candour** (candura)

candour /'kændə(r)/ NOUN, NO PLURAL the quality of speaking honestly, especially about something which is embarrassing or unpleasant ▢ *She spoke with surprising candour about her addiction.* (candura)

candy /'kændɪ/ NOUN [plural **candies**] the US word for **sweet** (= small piece of sweet food) (doce)

cane /keɪn/ NOUN [plural **canes**]
1 the hollow, hard stem of some plants (vara)
2 a stick that someone uses to help them walk (bengala)

canine /'keɪnaɪn/ ADJECTIVE
1 to do with dogs, or like a dog ▢ *She is an expert in canine behaviour.* (canino)
2 a canine tooth is sharp and pointed. A biology word. (canino)

canister /'kænɪstə(r)/ NOUN [plural **canisters**] a metal container for storing something (lata, vasilha) ▣ *The gas canisters exploded.* (botijões de gás)

cannibal /'kænɪbəl/ NOUN [plural **cannibals**] a person who eats other people (canibal)

• **cannibalism** /'kænɪbəlɪzəm/ NOUN, NO PLURAL eating other people (canibalismo)

cannon /'kænən/ NOUN [plural **cannons**] a large gun that fires cannonballs or other large explosives (canhão)

cannonball /'kænənbɔːl/ NOUN [plural **cannonballs**] a metal or stone ball that is fired from a cannon (bala de canhão)

cannot /'kænɒt/ MODAL VERB the negative form of **can** ▢ *I just cannot do it.* (forma negativa e não contraída de can)

> In spoken English, **can't** is usually used instead of 'cannot'. ▢ *I can't come tonight.*

canoe /kə'nuː/ ▶ NOUN [plural **canoes**] a light boat with pointed ends which you move through the water using a paddle (= stick with wide flat ends) (canoa)
▶ VERB [**canoes, canoeing, canoed**] to move on water in a canoe (navegar em canoa)

• **canoeing** /kə'nuːɪŋ/ NOUN, NO PLURAL the activity of using a canoe ▢ *a canoeing holiday* (canoagem)

can opener /'kæn ˌəʊpənə(r)/ NOUN [plural **can openers**] a device used in the kitchen for opening cans of food (abridor de lata)

canopy /'kænəpɪ/ NOUN [plural **canopies**]
1 a covering that is hung above something ▢ *a canopy over a bed* (dossel)
2 a covering layer that is formed by leaves and branches (abóbada) ▣ *the thick forest canopy* (abóbada da floresta)

can't /kɑːnt/ a short way to say and write **cannot** ▢ *I can't hear you.* (ver cannot)

cantankerous /kæn'tæŋkərəs/ ADJECTIVE bad tempered ▢ *He was a cantankerous old man.* (briguento)

canteen /ˌkæn'tiːn/ NOUN [plural **canteens**] a restaurant in a school or work place ▢ *I had lunch with my friends in the school canteen.* (cantina)

canter /'kæntə(r)/ ▶ VERB [**canters, cantering, cantered**] when a horse canters, it runs slowly (cavalgar a meio galope)
▶ NOUN, NO PLURAL the speed of a horse when it canters (meio galope)

canvas /'kænvəs/ NOUN [plural **canvases**]
1 a piece of strong cloth stretched on a frame for an artist to paint on (tela)
2 strong cloth used to make tents and sails (lona)

canvass /'kænvəs/ VERB [**canvasses, canvassing, canvassed**]

1 to try to persuade people to vote for you □ *He's canvassing for the Green Party.* (**angariar votos**)

2 to ask a lot of people for their opinions about something (**sondar**)

canyon /'kænjən/ NOUN [*plural* **canyons**] a deep valley with steep sides. A geography word. □ *the Grand Canyon* (**desfiladeiro**)

cap /kæp/ ▶ NOUN [*plural* caps]

1 a soft hat, often with a flat part that sticks out at the front (**boné, touca**) *The officer wore a peaked cap.* (**boné com ponta**) □ *a baseball cap*

2 a small top for a bottle, tube or pen *a bottle with a screw cap* (**tampa com pressão**) □ *The pen will dry up if you leave the cap off.*

▶ VERB [**caps, capping, capped**]

1 to set a top level or amount for something which you must not go above □ **+ at** *The interest rate has been capped at 2%.* (**superar**)

2 if a player is capped, they are asked to play for the country's national team in an international game of football, rugby or cricket □ *He's been capped eight times now.* (**convocar**)

3 be capped with something to have a layer of something on top □ *The mountains were capped with snow.* (**estar coberto com algo**)

♦ IDIOM **to cap it all** to be the worst thing that happens after a lot of other bad things have happened (**para completar**)

capability /ˌkeɪpəˈbɪləti/ NOUN [*plural* **capabilities**] ability or power to do something (**capacidade**) *The task is simply beyond his capabilities.* (**além de suas capacidades**) □ *The country wants to develop its nuclear capability.*

capable /'keɪpəbəl/ ADJECTIVE

1 if you are capable of something, you are able to do it □ *The old lady isn't capable of looking after herself any more.* (**capaz**)

2 able to do things and deal with problems without help □ *She's a very capable person.* (**capaz**)

> Note that the structure that comes after **capable** is **of doing something**:
> ✓ *She isn't* **capable of looking** *after a small child.*
> ✗ *She isn't capable to look after a small child.*

• **capably** /'keɪpəbli/ ADVERB in a capable way □ *Mary did the job very capably.* (**habilmente**)

capacitor /kəˈpæsɪtə(r)/ NOUN [*plural* capacitors] a device used to store electrical charge. A physics word. (**capacitor**)

capacity /kəˈpæsəti/ NOUN [*plural* **capacities**]

1 the total amount that a container or building will hold (**capacidade**) *The hall has a seating capacity of 300.* (**quantidade de assentos**) □ *Each barrel has a capacity of 100 litres.*

2 someone's ability to do or experience something □ *Flynn has the capacity to be a great leader.* □ *He obviously has a capacity for leadership.* (**capacidade**)

3 in your capacity as something as part of your job □ *Mrs Jones came to the meeting in her capacity as head teacher.* (**em sua qualidade de [algo]**)

cape /keɪp/ NOUN [*plural* **capes**]

1 a coat without sleeves that is tied at the neck (**capa**)

2 an area of land that goes out into the sea □ *the Cape of Good Hope* (**cabo**)

caper /'keɪpə(r)/ NOUN [*plural* **capers**] a silly activity that makes people laugh □ *He enjoyed the cartoon capers of Tom and Jerry.* (**travessura**)

capillary /kəˈpɪləri/ NOUN [*plural* **capillaries**] a very narrow tube in the body that carries blood. A biology word. (**vaso capilar**)

capital /'kæpɪtəl/ ▶ NOUN [*plural* capitals]

1 the city where the government of a state or country is □ **+ of** *London is the capital of England.* (**capital**)

2 a large letter such as B that you write at the beginning of a sentence, or at the beginning of a name (**maiúscula**) □ *Write your name in capitals at the top of the page.* *The notice was typed in capital letters.* (**letras maiúsculas**)

3 no plural money that can be used to make more money (**capital**) *My grandmother invested a lot of capital in the business.* (**investiu capital**)

▶ ADJECTIVE a capital crime is one for which the punishment is death (**capital**) *Murder is still a capital offence in some states.* (**crime capital**)

• **capitalism** /'kæpɪtəlɪzəm/ NOUN, NO PLURAL a system in which businesses are owned by business people and not by the government (**capitalismo**)

• **capitalist** /'kæpɪtəlɪst/ ▶ NOUN [*plural* **capitalists**] someone who supports capitalism (**capitalista**)

▶ ADJECTIVE a capitalist country or society has a system of capitalism (**capitalista**)

• **capitalize** or **capitalise** /'kæpɪtəlaɪz/ VERB [**capitalizes, capitalizing, capitalized**] to write or print a letter of the alphabet in its large form, for example *B* and not *b* (**escrever em iniciais maiúsculas**)

♦ PHRASAL VERB **capitalize on something** to use something that happens to get an advantage for yourself □ *With our best player injured, the other team will be keen to capitalize on the situation.* (**beneficiar-se de**)

capital punishment /ˌkæpɪtəl ˈpʌnɪʃmənt/ NOUN, NO PLURAL when someone is killed by the state as their punishment for a crime (**pena de morte**)

capitulate

capitulate /kəˈpɪtjuleɪt/ VERB [**capitulates, capitulating, capitulated**] to agree to something than you were fighting against before. A formal word. □ *They eventually capitulated to international pressure to release the prisoners.* (**render-se**)

cappuccino /ˌkæpʊˈtʃiːnəʊ/ NOUN [*plural* **cappuccinos**] coffee made with hot milk full of bubbles (**cappuccino**)

capricious /kəˈprɪʃəs/ ADJECTIVE often changing your opinions and behaviour suddenly (**inconstante**)

capsize /kæpˈsaɪz/ VERB [**capsizes, capsizing, capsized**] if a boat capsizes, it turns upside down (**virar, capotar**)

capsule /ˈkæpsjuːl/ NOUN [*plural* **capsules**]
1 a very small container with medicine inside (**cápsula**)
2 the part of a spacecraft in which the astronauts (= people who travel into space) live (**cápsula**)

captain /ˈkæptɪn/ ▶ NOUN [*plural* **captains**]
1 the person in charge of a ship or an aircraft □ *Everyone must obey the captain's orders.* (**capitão**)
2 the person in charge of a sports team 🔁 *He is the new England captain.* (**capitão**)
3 a person of middle rank in the army, high rank in the navy or high rank in the US police □ *Captain Jones* (**capitão**)
▶ VERB [**captains, captaining, captained**]
1 to be the captain of a team □ *Flint off will captain the English cricket team.* (**comandar**)
2 to be in charge of a ship or an aircraft (**comandar**)

• **captaincy** /ˈkæptɪnsɪ/ NOUN [*plural* **captaincies**] the job of being captain or someone's time as a captain (**capitania**)

caption /ˈkæpʃən/ NOUN [*plural* **captions**] words written near a picture to describe what is in it (**legenda**)

captivate /ˈkæptɪveɪt/ VERB [**captivates, captivating, captivated**] to interest or attract someone very much □ *He was captivated by her strength and beauty.* (**cativar**)

• **captivating** /ˈkæptɪveɪtɪŋ/ ADJECTIVE very attractive and interesting □ *a captivating smile* (**cativante**)

captive /ˈkæptɪv/ ▶ ADJECTIVE
1 kept in a prison or in a place you are not allowed to leave (**preso**) □ *a captive bird* 🔁 *He was held captive for five months.* (**mantido preso**)
2 a captive audience/market people who have to watch something or buy something because they have no choice (**público cativo**)
▶ NOUN [*plural* **captives**] a prisoner (**prisioneiro**)

• **captivity** /kæpˈtɪvətɪ/ NOUN, NO PLURAL when a person or animal is kept in a place which they are not allowed to leave □ *The bear spent its whole life in captivity.* (**cativeiro**)

captor /ˈkæptə(r)/ NOUN [*plural* **captors**] a person who is keeping someone a prisoner (**captor**)

capture /ˈkæptʃə(r)/ ▶ VERB [**captures, capturing, captured**]
1 to catch an animal or person and not allow them to escape □ *Many soldiers were captured by the enemy.* (**capturar**)
2 to succeed in getting something which other people are also competing for □ *They soon captured a large share of the toy market.* (**conquistar**)
3 to get control of a place or equipment by force □ *Armed soldiers have captured the airport.* (**conquistar**)
4 capture someone's imagination/attention, etc. to make someone feel very interested □ *Her stories captured the imagination of both parents and children.* (**prender a atenção/o interesse de alguém**)
5 to express something in a way that seems true and real □ *The description captures the beauty of the place.* (**apreende**)
▶ NOUN, NO PLURAL
1 when you catch someone or something (**captura**) 🔁 *How long can the killer avoid capture?* (**evitar a captura**)
2 when you take or get control of a place or equipment □ *the capture of enemy tanks* (**captura**)

car /kɑː(r)/ NOUN [*plural* **cars**]
1 a vehicle with an engine and seats for a small number of passengers (**carro**) □ *Many children travel to school by car.* 🔁 *You need a licence before you can drive a car.* (**dirigir um carro**) 🔁 *Where did you park the car?* (**estacionou o carro**) 🔁 *I've lost the car keys.* (**chaves do carro**)
2 the US word for a **train carriage** (**vagão**)

carafe /kəˈræf/ NOUN [*plural* **carafes**] a glass container with a wide opening at the top, used for serving wine or water (**jarro**)

caramel /ˈkærəmel/ NOUN [*plural* **caramels**]
1 a soft sweet made from sugar, butter and milk (**bala de caramelo**)
2 *no plural* sugar that has been heated until it goes brown (**caramelo**)

carapace /ˈkærəpeɪs/ NOUN [*plural* **carapaces**] the hard shell on the back of animals such as turtles and crabs. A biology word. (**carapaça**)

carat /ˈkærət/ NOUN [*plural* **carats**] a measurement used for weighing valuable stones such as diamonds, and for describing how pure gold is □ *18 carat gold* (**quilate**)

caravan /ˈkærəvæn/ NOUN [*plural* **caravans**] a vehicle for living in, especially on holiday, which can be pulled behind a car (**reboque, trailer**)

carbohydrate /ˌkɑːbəʊˈhaɪdreɪt/ NOUN [plural **carbohydrates**] a substance in foods such as potatoes and bread which gives your body energy (**carboidrato**)

carbon /ˈkɑːbən/ NOUN, NO PLURAL a chemical element which is in all living things and in substances such as coal and oil. A chemistry word. (**carbono**)

carbonated /ˈkɑːbəneɪtɪd/ ADJECTIVE a carbonated drink contains a lot of small bubbles (**gasoso**)

carbon copy /ˌkɑːbən ˈkɒpi/ NOUN [plural **carbon copies**] an exact copy of something or someone □ *Sarah is a carbon copy of her mother.* (**réplica**)

carbon cycle /ˈkɑːbən ˌsaɪkəl/ NOUN **the carbon** cycle the way carbon moves between living things and the air. A chemistry and biology word. (**ciclo do gás carbônico**)

carbon dioxide /ˌkɑːbən daɪˈɒksaɪd/ NOUN, NO PLURAL a gas that is produced when people and animals breathe out and when carbon is burned. A chemistry word. (**dióxido de carbono**)

carbon emissions /ˈkɑːbən ɪˌmɪʃənz/ PLURAL NOUN the amount of carbon that is released from the atmosphere from fuels such as coal and oil □ *Several countries agreed to reduce their carbon emissions.* (**emissões de gás carbônico**)

carbon footprint /ˈkɑːbən ˈfʊtprɪnt/ NOUN [plural **carbon footprints**] the amount of carbon produced by the way a person lives (**quantidade de gás carbônico emitido por uma atividade ou organização**)

carbon monoxide /ˌkɑːbən mɒˈnɒksaɪd/ NOUN, NO PLURAL a poisonous gas with no smell which is made when some types of fuel burn. A chemistry word. (**monóxido de carbono**)

carbon neutral /ˌkɑːbən ˈnjuːtrəl/ ADJECTIVE if an activity or an organization is carbon neutral, it saves as much carbon as it produces (**emissão zero de gás carbônico**)

carbon offsetting /ˌkɑːbən ˈɒfsetɪŋ/ NOUN, NO PLURAL activities such as planting trees that are intended to reduce carbon (**crédito por reduzir a emissão de gás carbônico**)

car boot sale /ˌkɑː ˈbuːt ˌseɪl/ NOUN [plural **car boot sales**] an event where people sell things from the back of their cars (**vendas informais de garagem**)

carburetor /ˌkɑːbəˈretə(r)/ NOUN [plural **carburetors**] the US spelling of **carburettor** (**carburador**)

carburettor /ˌkɑːbəˈretə(r)/ NOUN [plural **carburettors**] the part of a car engine which mixes air and fuel so that it burns and provides power (**carburador**)

carcass /ˈkɑːkəs/ NOUN [plural **carcasses**] a dead body of an animal (**carcaça**)

carcinogen /kɑːˈsɪnədʒən/ NOUN [plural **carcinogens**] a substance that can cause cancer (**carcinogênio**)

• **carcinogenic** /ˌkɑːsɪnəˈdʒenɪk/ ADJECTIVE causing cancer □ *carcinogenic chemicals* (**carcinogênico**)

card /kɑːd/ NOUN [plural **cards**]

1 a piece of stiff paper with a picture and a message (**cartão**) ▫ *a birthday/Christmas card* (**cartão de aniversário/Natal**) ▫ *I must send her a card.* (**enviar um cartão**)

2 *no plural* thick stiff paper □ *coloured card* (**cartão**)

3 a small flat piece of plastic that you can use in shops and machines to pay for things (**cartão**) □ *Can I pay by card?* ▫ *a bank card* (**cartão de banco**)

4 a small piece of stiff paper or plastic with information on it □ *a library card* □ *Here's my business card.* (**cartão**)

5 one of a set of rectangular pieces of card used for playing games (**carta**) ▫ *I bought a pack of cards.* (**baralho de cartas**)

6 cards games that are played with a set of cards (**baralho**) ▫ *Do you like playing cards?* (**jogar baralho**)

♦ IDIOMS **on the cards** if something is on the cards, it is probably going to happen (**provável**) **put/lay your cards on the table** to tell someone the truth about your situation or your plans (**colocar as cartas na mesa**)

cardboard /ˈkɑːdbɔːd/ NOUN, NO PLURAL very stiff thick paper used to make boxes and packages for goods (**papelão**) ▫ *a cardboard box* (**uma caixa de papelão**)

cardiac /ˈkɑːdiæk/ ADJECTIVE to do with the heart. A biology word. □ *a cardiac surgeon* (**cardíaco**)

cardiac arrest /ˌkɑːdiæk əˈrest/ NOUN [plural **cardiac arrests**] when someone's heart suddenly stops working (**parada cardíaca**)

cardigan /ˈkɑːdɪgən/ NOUN [plural **cardigans**] a piece of clothing for your upper body that is made from wool and fastens with buttons down the front (**cardigã**)

cardinal[1] /ˈkɑːdɪnəl/ NOUN [plural **cardinals**] a priest of high rank in the Roman Catholic Church (**cardeal**)

cardinal[2] /ˈkɑːdɪnəl/ ADJECTIVE

1 cardinal numbers are numbers like one, two, three, not first, second, third. A maths word. (**cardinal**)

2 very important or basic (**fundamental**) ▫ *One of the cardinal rules of travel is to make sure you have your tickets.* (**regras fundamentais**)

cardiologist /ˌkɑːdiˈɒlədʒɪst/ NOUN [plural **cardiologists**] a doctor who treats people with heart problems (**cardiologista**)

- **cardiology** /ˌkɑːdɪˈɒlədʒɪ/ NOUN, NO PLURAL the area of medicine that deals with the heart (**cardiologia**)

cardiovascular /ˌkɑːdɪəʊˈvæskjʊlə(r)/ ADJECTIVE to do with the heart and the tubes that carry blood around your body. A biology word. (**cardiovascular**)

care /keə(r)/ ▶ NOUN [plural **cares**]

1 no plural looking after someone (**cuidado**) 🔁 They need urgent medical care (**cuidados médicos**) 🔁 The care he received in hospital was excellent. (**recebeu cuidados**)

2 take care of someone/something to look after someone or something □ Their aunt took care of them after their parents died. (**cuidar de algo/alguém**)

3 no plural when you give something a lot of attention or effort (**cuidado**) 🔁 Meg does her work with great care. (**grande cuidado**) 🔁 She took a lot of care over her appearance. (**cuidou**)

4 take care to be careful not to have an accident or make a mistake □ You must take care to lock all the doors. □ Take care – the roads are very icy! (**tomar cuidado**)

5 something that makes you worried or unhappy (**preocupação**) 🔁 She was humming to herself as if she didn't have a care in the world. (**não se importasse com o mundo**)

6 in care children who are in care are being looked after by a local government department because their parents cannot look after them (**sob cuidado**)

▶ VERB [**cares, caring, cared**]

1 to think that something is interesting or important □ + **question word** He said he didn't care what happened. □ + **about** I don't care about your holiday plans – we've got work to do! (**preocupar-se**)

2 to feel love or affection for someone □ + **for** He really cares for his staff. (**importar-se**)

3 I/he/they, etc. couldn't care less an informal phrase used to show that you do not think something is at all interesting or important □ I couldn't care less what my dad will say. (**Eu, ele, eles não estamos nem aí**)

4 Who cares? an informal phrase used to show that you do not think something is at all interesting or important (**Quem se importa?**)

♦ PHRASAL VERB **care for someone/something** to look after a person or an animal □ Sarah wants to be a vet so that she can care for sick animals. (**cuidar de algo/alguém**)

career /kəˈrɪə(r)/ ▶ NOUN [plural **careers**] a job or type of work that you train for and continue doing for a long time □ + **in** a career in the police force □ a teaching career □ We both chose law as a career. (**carreira**)

▶ VERB [**careers, careering, careered**] to move very quickly and without control □ The car careered into a lamppost. (**sair em disparada**)

carefree /ˈkeəfriː/ ADJECTIVE having no worries □ a carefree attitude □ a carefree life (**despreocupado**)

careful /ˈkeəfʊl/ ADJECTIVE making sure that you do something correctly or safely (**cuidadoso**) 🔁 **Be careful** when you cross the road. (**Tome cuidado**) □ + **to do something** □ Dad is always careful to lock all the doors.

- **carefully** /ˈkeəfʊlɪ/ ADVERB without making mistakes or causing damage □ Greta wrapped up the glass carefully in tissue paper. (**cuidadosamente**)

careless /ˈkeəlɪs/ ADJECTIVE not being careful (**displicente**) 🔁 a careless mistake (**engano displicente**) 🔁 Alex is a bit careless with his money.

- **carelessly** /ˈkeəlɪslɪ/ ADVERB in a careless way □ He threw the letter aside carelessly. (**displicentemente**)

- **carelessness** /ˈkeəlɪsnɪs/ NOUN, NO PLURAL being careless (**descuido**)

carer /ˈkeərə(r)/ NOUN [plural **carers**] someone who looks after a child, an old person or an ill person (**tutor, guardião**)

caress /kəˈres/ ▶ VERB [**caresses, caressing, caressed**] to touch something or someone gently or with love □ Her hand caressed the child's face. (**acariciar**)

▶ NOUN [plural **caresses**] a gentle or loving touch (**carícia**)

caretaker /ˈkeəteɪkə(r)/ NOUN [plural **caretakers**] someone whose job is to look after a building □ a school caretaker (**zelador**)

cargo /ˈkɑːgəʊ/ NOUN [plural **cargoes**] the things that a vehicle is carrying □ The ship had a cargo of sugar and coffee. (**carga**)

caricature /ˈkærɪkəˌtʃʊə(r)/ ▶ NOUN [plural **caricatures**] a picture or a description of someone that makes their features stronger than they really are, often to make them seem funny (**caricatura**)

▶ VERB [**caricatures, caricaturing, caricatured**] to draw or describe someone in a way that makes their features stonger than they really are (**caricaturar**)

caring /ˈkeərɪŋ/ ADJECTIVE

1 kind and showing attention and affection □ a caring father (**cuidadoso**)

2 the caring professions jobs such as nursing that involve looking after people (**profissões humanitárias**)

carnage /ˈkɑːnɪdʒ/ NOUN, NO PLURAL when a lot of people are killed or injured □ a scene of absolute carnage (**carnificina**)

carnation /kɑːˈneɪʃən/ NOUN [plural **carnations**] a pink or white flower with a long stem (**cravo**)

carnival /ˈkɑːnɪvəl/ NOUN [plural **carnivals**] a celebration when people sing and dance outdoors wearing special clothes (**carnaval**)

carnivore /ˈkɑːnɪvɔː(r)/ NOUN [plural **carnivores**] an animal that eats meat. A biology word. (carnívoro)
- **carnivorous** /kɑːˈnɪvərəs/ ADJECTIVE eating meat. A biology word. ☐ *Tyrannosaurus rex was a huge carnivorous dinosaur.* (predador, carnívoro)

carol /ˈkærəl/ NOUN [plural **carols**] a song sung at Christmas ☐ *carol singing* (cântico alegre)

carotid artery /kəˌrɒtɪd ˈɑːtəri/ NOUN [plural **carotid arteries**] either of the two tubes in your neck that take blood from your heart to your head. A biology word. (artéria carótida)

carousel /ˌkærəˈsel/ NOUN [plural **carousels**] a moving surface from which you collect your bags in an airport (carrossel)

carp¹ /kɑːp/ NOUN [plural **carp**] a large fish that lives in lakes and rivers (carpa)

carp² /kɑːp/ VERB [**carps, carping, carped**] to complain a lot in a way that is annoying ☐ *He was carping about the cost of everything.* (reclamar)

car park /ˈkɑːr ˈpɑːk/ NOUN [plural **car parks**] a building or place where cars can be left ☐ *The car park was full.* (estacionamento)

carpel /ˈkɑːpəl/ NOUN [plural **carpels**] the female part of a flower. A biology word. (carpelo)

carpenter /ˈkɑːpəntə(r)/ NOUN [plural **carpenters**] someone whose job is to make things from wood (carpinteiro, marceneiro)
- **carpentry** /ˈkɑːpəntri/ NOUN, NO PLURAL making things from wood (carpintaria, marcenaria)

carpet /ˈkɑːpɪt/ ▶ NOUN [plural **carpets**]
1 a covering for a floor made of wool or a similar material ☐ *Don't get mud on the carpet.* (tapete)
2 a carpet of something a soft layer of something covering the ground ☐ *a carpet of leaves* (um tapete de algo)
▶ VERB [**carpets, carpeting, carpeted**] to cover an area with a carpet (atapetar)

carriage /ˈkærɪdʒ/ NOUN [plural **carriages**]
1 one of the long parts of a train where passengers sit (vagão)
2 a vehicle with wheels that is pulled by horses (carruagem)

carriageway /ˈkærɪdʒweɪ/ NOUN [plural **carriageways**] one of the two sides of a big road or motorway, that are each used by traffic travelling in one direction ☐ *There's heavy traffic on the North bound carriageway.* (pista)

carrier /ˈkærɪə(r)/ NOUN [plural **carriers**]
1 a vehicle or company which moves people or things from one place to another ☐ *British Airways is one of Britain's transatlantic carriers.* (transportador)
2 someone who can pass a disease to another person but does not have it themselves (portador)

carrier bag /ˈkærɪə ˌbæɡ/ NOUN [plural **carrier bags**] a plastic or paper bag with handles (saco)

carrot /ˈkærət/ NOUN [plural **carrots**] a long orange vegetable that grows under the ground (cenoura)

carry /ˈkæri/ VERB [**carries, carrying, carried**]
1 to pick something up and take it somewhere ☐ *This suitcase is too heavy for me to carry.* ☐ *You may only carry one bag onto the plane.* (carregar)
2 to have something with you in your hand, your pocket, etc. ☐ *The robber was carrying a gun.* ☐ *Why were you carrying so much cash on you?* ☐ + *around* *Do you have to carry that umbrella around with you?* (carregar)
3 to take something from one place to another ☐ *The ship was carrying over 3,000 soldiers.* ☐ *Water is carried to the buildings in huge pipes.* (carregar)
4 when sound carries, it can be heard from a long way away ☐ *His voice really carries.* (transmitir)
5 to support the weight of something ☐ *The bridge won't carry the weight of heavy lorries.* (suportar)
6 to have a particular result ☐ *Credit card fraud can carry heavy penalties* (= the punishment can be severe). ☐ *Skiing carries the risk of injury.* (resultar)
7 to be responsible for something ☐ *He had to carry the burden of his family's debts.* (carregar)
8 if a person or an animal carries a disease, they can pass it on to others ☐ *These insects carry malaria.* (transmitir)
♦ IDIOM **get carried away** to become too excited or enthusiastic ☐ *I got carried away and bought three new pairs of shoes.* (ficar entusiasmado)
♦ PHRASAL VERBS **carry something off** to do something successfully ☐ *The part of Lady Macbeth is a challenge, but she carried it off magnificently.* (sair-se bem em algo) **carry on 1** to continue ☐ + *with* *Carry on with your work while I go and see the headmaster.* ☐ + *ing* *When the noise stopped, our guide was able to carry on speaking.* (continuar) **2** to go further in the same direction ☐ *Carry on to the end of the road, then turn left.* (continuar) **3** to behave in a silly way ☐ *Do stop carrying on like children, you two, please!* (comportar-se mal) **carry out something 1** to do a task ☐ *carry out research/an experiment* (realizar) **2** to do something that you have said you will do (realizar) 🔁 *Will the terrorists manage to carry out their threat?* (fazer uma ameaça)

carrycot /ˈkærɪkɒt/ NOUN [plural **carrycots**] a small bed for a baby, with handles so that it can be carried (alcofa)

carry-on /ˈkæri ˌɒn/ NOUN, NO PLURAL an informal word meaning a lot of unnecessary worry or excitement ☐ *Really, what a carry-on! It's only her sister arriving, not the Queen.* (estardalhaço)

cart   113   cash

cart /kɑːt/ ▶ NOUN [plural **carts**]
1 a vehicle for goods which is pulled by a horse (**carroça**) ▫ *a horse and cart* (**um cavalo e carroça**)
2 the US word for **trolley** (= basket on wheels used in a supermarket) (**carrinho de supermercado**)
▶ VERB [**carts, carting, carted**] an informal word meaning to take someone or something somewhere ▫ *He fell and had to be carted off to hospital.* (**transportar**)

carte blanche /ˌkɑːt ˈblɑːʃ/ NOUN, NO PLURAL if you give someone carte blanche, you allow them to do what they want ▫ *The new sales manager was given carte blanche to reorganize the whole sales team.* (**carta branca**)

cartel /kɑːˈtel/ NOUN [plural **cartels**] a group of businesses who agree to sell something at the same price so they all make a profit (**cartel**)

cartilage /ˈkɑːtɪlɪdʒ/ NOUN, NO PLURAL a strong substance that bends, which is around bones in your knee, elbow, etc. A biology word. (**cartilagem**)

carton /ˈkɑːtən/ NOUN [plural **cartons**] a box for food or drink that is made of cardboard ▫ *a carton of milk* (**caixa de papelão**)

cartoon /kɑːˈtuːn/ NOUN [plural **cartoons**]
1 a funny drawing or series of drawings in a newspaper or magazine (**cartum**)
2 a film made from a long series of drawings ▫ *Mickey Mouse is a cartoon character.* (**personagem de desenho animado**)

• **cartoonist** /kɑːˈtuːnɪst/ NOUN [plural **cartoonists**] someone who draws cartoons (**cartunista**)

cartridge /ˈkɑːtrɪdʒ/ NOUN [plural **cartridges**]
1 a small container that fits inside a piece of equipment and contains something such as film or ink (**cartucho**) ▫ *Do you know how to replace the ink cartridge in the printer?* (**trocar o cartucho**)
2 a tube containing a bullet that goes inside a gun (**cartucho**)

cartwheel /ˈkɑːtwiːl/ NOUN [plural **cartwheels**] a movement in which you turn your body sideways onto your hands and your feet go up into the air, over your head (**movimento acrobático em forma de estrela**)

carve /kɑːv/ VERB [**carves, carving, carved**]
1 to make something by cutting wood, stone, etc. ▫ *There are angels carved out of stone.* (**entalhar**)
2 to cut meat into thin flat pieces using a sharp knife (**trinchar**)
3 to be successful in a particular job or activity ▫ *She carved out a successful career as a literary agent.* (**estabelecer**)

♦ PHRASAL VERB **carve something up** to divide something in a way that seems wrong ▫ *The countryside has been carved up for housing developers.* (**dividir algo**)

• **carving** /ˈkɑːvɪŋ/ NOUN [plural **carvings**]
1 an object made by cutting wood, stone, etc. (**entalhe**) ▫ *He does beautiful wood carvings.* (**entalhes de madeira**)
2 the activity or skill of making objects by cutting wood, stone, etc. (**escultura**)

carving knife /ˈkɑːvɪŋ ˌnaɪf/ NOUN [plural **carving knives**] a long, sharp knife used for cutting meat (**faca de trinchar**)

cascade /kæˈskeɪd/ ▶ VERB [**cascades, cascading, cascaded**] to flow down or hang down in large amounts ▫ *Water cascaded down the hillside.* (**cascatear**)
▶ NOUN [plural **cascades**] a large amount of something which hangs or flows down (**pequena cascata**)

case /keɪs/ NOUN [plural **cases**]
1 a situation or an example of a particular situation ▫ *Inspectors are examining several cases of cruelty to animals.* (**caso**) ▫ *This is a classic case of failure to communicate.* (**caso clássico**) ▫ *You haven't got any money? In that case, you'd better get a job.* (**naquele caso**)
2 the case the true situation ▫ *Is it the case that you have never owned a passport?* ▫ *If that's the case, you may as well sell it.* (**caso real**)
3 (just) in case because of the possibility of something ▫ *I don't think it's going to rain, but I'll take my umbrella just in case.* (**se por acaso**)
4 in my/his, etc. case according to someone's particular situation ▫ *Most people gave up the course through boredom, but in my case it was because I was too busy.* (**no meu/seu caso etc.**)
5 in any case whatever happens or whatever a situation is ▫ *Hopefully the game will be exciting, but in any case it will be a new experience for me.* (**de todo modo, em todo caso**)
6 a crime that the police are trying to solve ▫ *a murder case* (**caso**)
7 something that is being decided in a court (**caso**) ▫ *a court case* (**caso de tribunal**) ▫ *He won his case for unfair dismissal.* (**ganhou seu caso**)
8 when someone has a particular disease, or a person with that disease ▫ *Doctors are reporting an increase in the number of flu cases.* (**caso**)
9 a container for something ▫ *a violin case* ▫ *The crown jewels are in a glass case.* (**estojo, invólucro**)
10 a suitcase (= large container for carrying clothes on holiday) (**mala**) ▫ *Have you packed your case yet?* (**fez suas malas**)
11 facts that prove an opinion or support one side in an argument (**situação**) ▫ *He put the case for increased spending.* (**explicou a situação**) ▫ + *for* There is a strong case for allowing children more freedom. ▫ + *against* She argued the case against building a new road.

cash /kæʃ/ ▶ NOUN, NO PLURAL
1 money in the form of papermoney and coins ▫ *The gardener likes to be paid in cash.* (**dinheiro vivo**)

2 money (dinheiro) ▣ *I'm rather short of cash* (= I haven't got much money). (pouco dinheiro)
▶ VERB [**cashes, cashing, cashed**] to cash a cheque is to change it for paper money or coins (descontar)

◆ PHRASAL VERB **cash in on something** to make a profit from a situation, often in an unfair way ▢ *She quickly cashed in on her son's success by doing magazine articles and television interviews.* (lucrar com algo)

cashback /'kæʃbæk/ NOUN, NO PLURAL if you get cashback when you buy things in a shop, you get money as well as your shopping ▢ *Do you want any cashback?* (porcentagem de valor gasto devolvido em dinheiro)

cash card /'kæʃ ˌkɑːd/ NOUN [plural **cash cards**] a small plastic card that you use to buy things and to get money from machines (cartão de débito)

cash desk /'kæʃ ˌdesk/ NOUN [plural **cash desks**] a place where you go to pay for things in a shop (balcão de pagamento)

cashew /'kæʃuː/ NOUN [plural **cashews**] a curved nut that you can eat (caju)

cash flow /'kæʃ fləʊ/ NOUN [plural **cash flows**] the rate at which money is received and spent by a business or organization (fluxo de caixa)

cashier /kæ'ʃɪə(r)/ NOUN [plural **cashiers**] someone in a bank or shop whose job is to take and pay out money (operador de caixa, em banco ou loja)

cash machine /'kæʃ mə‚ʃiːn/ NOUN [plural **cash machines**] a machine, usually in the wall outside a bank, where you can get money using a small plastic card (caixa registradora)

cashmere /'kæʃmɪə(r)/ NOUN, NO PLURAL a very soft type of wool ▢ *a cashmere sweater.* (caxemira)

cashpoint /'kæʃpɔɪnt/ NOUN [plural **cashpoints**] a machine, usually in the wall outside a bank, where you can get money using a small plastic card (caixa eletrônico)

cash register /'kæʃ ˌredʒɪstə(r)/ NOUN [plural **cash registers**] a machine used in a shop to record and store the money paid by customers (caixa registradora)

casino /kə'siːnəʊ/ NOUN [plural **casinos**] a building where people play games in which they lose or win money (cassino)

casket /'kɑːskɪt/ NOUN [plural **caskets**]
1 a small decorated box for keeping things in (caixa de joias)
2 the US word for **coffin** (caixão)

casserole /'kæsərəʊl/ NOUN [plural **casseroles**]
1 a dish with a cover for cooking and serving food (caçarola)
2 a mixture of vegetables, meat, etc. cooked in a casserole ▢ *a beef casserole* (ensopado)

cassette /kə'set/ NOUN [plural **cassettes**] a plastic case that contains music or pictures recorded on a long magnetic strip (fita cassete)

cassette player /kə'set ˌpleɪə(r)/ or **cassette recorder** /kə'set rɪ'kɔːdə(r)/ NOUN [plural **cassette players** or **cassette recorders**] a machine for playing or recording sound using cassettes (toca-fitas)

cast /kɑːst/ C VERB [**casts, casting, cast**]
1 to choose the actors who will be in a play or a film ▢ *He was cast as Shylock in The Merchant of Venice.* (designar)
2 if something casts light or a shadow somewhere, it makes it go there ▢ *The lamp cast light onto the desk.* (lançar)
3 when you cast your vote, you vote for someone or something (dar o voto)
4 cast doubt/suspicion on someone/something to make people think that someone or something cannot be trusted (lançar suspeita sobre algo/alguém)
5 cast a spell on someone/something to use magic on someone or something (lançar feitiço sobre algo/alguém)
6 a formal word meaning to throw ▢ *They were cast into prison.* (jogar)

◆ IDIOM **cast a pall over something** to spoil an event or a situation ▢ *News of his death cast a pall over the celebrations.* (estragar algo)
▶ NOUN [plural **casts**]
1 *no plural* the actors in a play or a film ▢ *a member of the cast* (elenco)
2 a hard covering that is put on a broken arm or leg (molde)

castanets /ˌkæstə'nets/ PLURAL NOUN a musical instrument made of two pieces of wood or plastic that you hold in your hand to make a clicking sound (castanholas)

castaway /'kɑːstəweɪ/ NOUN [plural **castaways**] someone who has been left alone on an island, usually after a ship sinks (náufrago)

caste /kɑːst/ NOUN [plural **castes**] a social class in Hindu society (casta)

caster sugar /'kɑːstə ˌʃʊɡə(r)/ NOUN, NO PLURAL sugar with very small grains, used in cooking (açúcar branco muito refinado)

castigate /'kæstɪɡeɪt/ VERB [**castigates, castigating, castigated**] a formal word meaning to criticize someone severely ▢ *The minister responsible for the error was castigated by the prime minister.* (castigar, punir)

cast iron /ˌkɑːst 'aɪən/ NOUN, NO PLURAL a type of very hard iron (ferro fundido)
• **cast-iron** ADJECTIVE
1 made of cast iron ▢ *There were cast-iron bars on the windows.* (de ferro fundido, forjado)
2 very strong or impossible to doubt ▢ *This is not a cast-iron guarantee.* (forte)

castle

castle /ˈkɑːsəl/ NOUN [plural **castles**]
1 a large building with high walls and towers, which was built to protect people from attack □ *Edinburgh Castle stands high above the city.* □ *We visited a ruined castle built by the Normans.* (castelo)
2 a piece in the game of chess that looks like a castle (torre)

cast-offs /ˈkɑːstɒfs/ PLURAL NOUN clothes that people give away because they do not want them (refugo)

castor sugar /ˈkɑːstə ʃʊgə(r)/ NOUN, NO PLURAL another spelling of **caster sugar** (açúcar branco muito refinado)

castrate /kæˈstreɪt/ VERB [**castrates, castrating, castrated**] to remove the sexual organs from a male animal (castrar)
• **castration** /kæˈstreɪʃən/ NOUN, NO PLURAL the practice of castrating male animals (castração)

casual /ˈkæʒʊəl/ ADJECTIVE
1 not formal □ *casual clothes* □ *She runs the hotel in quite a casual and relaxed style.* (informal)
2 not serious □ *He has had several casual relationships since his divorce.* □ *I worry about Sarita's casual attitude to her work.* (casual)
3 not planned, or with no particular meaning or importance □ *It was just a casual remark – I shouldn't have said anything.* (casual)
4 not permanent (temporário) □ *casual work* □ *The factory uses a lot of casual labour* (= temporary workers). (trabalho temporário)
• **casually** /ˈkæʒʊəli/ ADVERB in a casual way □ *Most of the guests were casually dressed.* (casualmente)

casualty /ˈkæʒjʊəlti/ NOUN [plural **casualties**]
1 someone who has been injured or killed □ *Ambulances rushed the casualties to hospital.* (baixa)
2 the old name for **Accident and Emergency**; the hospital department that deals with people who have been injured or have suddenly become ill (pronto-socorro)
3 something that has been damaged or no longer exists because of something else □ *Our local library was a casualty of the government spending cuts.* (doente)

cat /kæt/ NOUN [plural **cats**]
1 an animal which people keep as a pet, which catches mice and birds □ *I stroked the cat and it purred happily.* (gato)
2 a wild animals such as a lion, that belongs to the same family as the cat (felino) □ *One of my favourite big cats is the snow leopard.* (grandes felinos)
➪ go to **let the cat out of the bag**

catalog /ˈkætəlɒg/ NOUN [plural **catalogs**], VERB [**catalogs, cataloging, cataloged**] the US spelling of **catalogue** (catálogo)

catalogue /ˈkætəlɒg/ ▶ NOUN [plural **catalogues**]
1 a book that shows the products you can buy from a company (catalogar) □ *Mum got me some jeans from a mail order catalogue.* (catálogo postal)
2 a list of all the books or objects in a collection (catálogo)
3 a catalogue of something a series of bad things □ *Their holiday seems to have been a catalogue of disasters.* (uma série de desastres)
▶ VERB [**catalogues, cataloguing, catalogued**] to make a list of all the things in a collection (catalogar)

catalyst /ˈkætəlɪst/ NOUN [plural **catalysts**]
1 a substance which makes a chemical reaction happen more quickly but which does not change itself. A chemistry word. (catalisador)
2 something that makes a change happen □ *a catalyst for social change* (estimulante)

catalytic converter /ˌkætəlɪtɪk kənˈvɜːtə(r)/ NOUN [plural **catalytic converters**] a device that stops harmful gases from a car's engine being released into the air (conversor catalítico)

catamaran /ˌkætəməˈræn/ NOUN [plural **catamarans**] a type of boat that looks like two boats joined together (catamarã)

catapult /ˈkætəpʌlt/ C VERB [**catapults, catapulting, catapulted**]
1 to throw something or someone forward forcefully □ *The bike hit a rock and Tom was catapulted over the handlebars.* (catapultar, impulsionar)
2 to suddenly put someone into a new situation (lançar) □ *The TV show catapulted her to fame.* (lançou para a fama)
▶ NOUN [plural **catapults**] a weapon for firing small stones, made from a stick and rubber which stretches (catapulta)

cataract /ˈkætərækt/ NOUN [plural **cataracts**] an eye condition in which someone gradually loses their ability to see (catarata)

catarrh /kəˈtɑː(r)/ NOUN, NO PLURAL the thick substance in your nose and throat when you have a cold (catarro)

catastrophe /kəˈtæstrəfi/ NOUN [plural **catastrophes**] an event that causes a lot of damage or suffering □ *The government has plans for dealing with floods and other natural catastrophes.* (catástrofe)
• **catastrophic** /ˌkætəˈstrɒfɪk/ ADJECTIVE causing a lot of damage or suffering □ *The plane suffered catastrophic engine failure.* (catastrófico)

catch /kætʃ/ ▶ VERB [**catches, catching, caught**]
1 to stop and hold something that is moving through the air □ *Throw the ball and I'll try to catch it.* (apanhar)
2 to stop a person or animal from escaping □ *James caught a huge fish.* □ *Police managed to catch the escaped prisoners.* (capturar)

3 to get an illness □ *Most people catch between two and four colds a year.* (**pegar**)
4 to get on a bus, train, etc. □ *I left early so that I could catch the 8.30 train.* (**pegar**)
5 to discover someone doing something, especially something that they should not do □ + **ing** *I caught him taking some money from my purse.* □ *You wouldn't catch me wearing a silly hat like that.* (**pegar**)
6 to become stuck on something, or to make something become stuck on something else □ *Sam caught his sleeve on the door handle.* (**prender**)
7 catch fire to start burning □ *The plane caught fire after its tyre burst on landing.* (**pegar fogo**)
8 catch sight of someone/something to see someone or something for a short time □ *I just managed to catch sight of the queen.* (**avistar algo/alguém**)
9 not catch something used as a polite way of saying that you did not hear what someone said □ *I'm sorry, I didn't catch your name.* (**não escutar algo**)
⇨ go to **catch someone's eye**

◆ PHRASAL VERBS **catch on** to become popular □ *The style never really caught on.* (**entrar na moda**) **catch someone out** to cause someone to make a mistake by tricking them (**apanhar alguém fazendo algo errado**) **catch (someone/ something) up**
1 to reach someone or something that is in front of you by moving faster than them □ *We ran to catch the others up.* (**alcançar**)
2 to get to the same level as someone or something □ *When children miss a lot of school, it can be difficult for them to catch up with the others.* (**alcançar**)

▶ NOUN [*plural* **catches**]
1 when someone stops and holds something that was moving through the air □ *That was a brilliant catch!* (**captura**)
2 a problem that is not obvious immediately □ *The holiday was supposed to be free, but there was a catch, of course.* (**cilada**)
3 the part on a door, chain, etc. that fastens it □ *The catch on my bracelet has broken.* (**trinco**)
4 the number of fish someone has caught (**safra de peixe**)

• **catching** /'kætʃɪŋ/ ADJECTIVE if an illness is catching, other people can get it from you □ *I hope that sore throat you have isn't catching.* (**contagioso**)

catchment area /'kætʃmənt ˌeəriə/ NOUN [*plural* **catchment areas**] an area from which a particular school gets its students (**área servida por escola**)

catchphrase /'kætʃfreɪz/ NOUN [*plural* **catchphrases**] a phrase that an entertainer uses repeatedly and that people remember (**dito popular**)

catchy /'kætʃi/ ADJECTIVE [**catchier, catchiest**] a catchy tune is one that you remember easily (**fácil de lembrar**)

categorical /ˌkætɪ'gɒrɪkəl/ ADJECTIVE clear and emphasizing what you mean □ *He gave a categorical assurance that no jobs would be lost.* (**categórico**)

• **categorically** /ˌkætɪ'gɒrɪkəli/ ADVERB in a clear way which emphasizes what you mean (**categoricamente**) □ *He categorically denied any involvement in the crime.* (**negou categoricamente**)

categorize or **categorise** /'kætəgəraɪz/ VERB [**categorizes, categorizing, categorized**] to group people or things together by their type, size, age, etc. (**categorizar**) □ *The plants are categorized according to their medical uses.* (**categorizados de acordo com**)

category /'kætəgəri/ NOUN [*plural* **categories**] a group of people or things of the same type (**categoria**) □ *Our members tend to fall into one of three categories.* (**cair em categorias**)

cater /'keɪtə(r)/ VERB [**caters, catering, catered**] to prepare and supply food □ *We are catering for 100 guests.* (**abastecer**)

◆ PHRASAL VERB **cater for someone/something** to provide what is wanted or needed □ *We try to provide courses that cater for every age group.* (**satisfazer algo/alguém**)

• **caterer** /'keɪtərə(r)/ NOUN [*plural* **caterers**] a person or business whose job is to prepare and supply food at an event □ *We hired a caterer for the wedding.* (**fornecedor**)

• **catering** /'keɪtərɪŋ/ NOUN, NO PLURAL the job of preparing and supplying food (**serviço de buffet**) □ *We hired someone to do the catering.* (**servir comida no buffet**) □ *Marcus is doing a catering course.*

caterpillar /'kætəpɪlə(r)/ NOUN [*plural* **caterpillars**] a small soft animal that eats, leaves and later becomes a butterfly (= insect with large colourful wings) (**lagarta**)

cat flap /'kæt ˌflæp/ NOUN [*plural* **cat flaps**] a small door for a cat to use (**passagem de gato**)

cathartic /kə'θɑːtɪk/ ADJECTIVE helping you to express feelings and feel better □ *a cathartic experience* (**catártico**)

cathedral /kə'θiːdrəl/ NOUN [*plural* **cathedrals**] a large and important church □ *St Paul's Cathedral in London* (**catedral**)

cathode /'kæθəʊd/ NOUN [*plural* **cathodes**] the positive electrode (= part where an electric current enters or leaves) in a battery. A physics word. (**cátodo**)

Catholic /'kæθlɪk/ ▶ ADJECTIVE to do with, or belonging to, the Roman Catholic Church □ *a Catholic priest* (**católico**)
▶ NOUN [*plural* **Catholics**] a member of the Roman Catholic Church (**católico**)

- **Catholicism** /kəˈθɒlɪsɪzəm/ NOUN, NO PLURAL the beliefs and practices of Catholics (Catolicismo)

Catseye /ˈkætsaɪ/ NOUN [plural **Catseyes**] a small object in the road surface which reflects light to help drivers at night. A trademark. (olho de gato)

cattle /ˈkætəl/ PLURAL NOUN male and female cows on a farm □ *cattle farmers* (gado)

catty /ˈkæti/ ADJECTIVE [**cattier, cattiest**] an informal word meaning deliberately unkind □ *catty remarks* (traiçoeiro)

catwalk /ˈkætwɔːk/ NOUN [plural **catwalks**] the path that models walk down at a fashion show (passarela)

caught /kɔːt/ PAST TENSE AND PAST PARTICIPLE OF **catch** (ver **catch**)

cauldron /ˈkɔːldrən/ NOUN [plural **cauldrons**] a big old-fashioned container for cooking over a fire □ *a witch's cauldron* (caldeirão)

cauliflower /ˈkɒlɪflaʊə(r)/ NOUN [plural **cauliflowers**] a round vegetable with green leaves around a hard white centre (couve-flor)

cause /kɔːz/ ▶ VERB [**causes, causing, caused**] to make something happen □ *Do they know what caused the accident?* □ *Strong winds caused problems on the roads.* □ *+ to do something Unfortunately the delay caused me to miss my appointment.* (causar)
▶ NOUN [plural **causes**]
1 what makes something happen □ *There are many causes of poverty.* □ *The engineer can't find the cause of the problem.* (causa)
2 something that people support because they believe it is good or useful (causa) ▣ *She collects money for many good causes.* (boas causas)
3 a reason (motivo) ▣ *Her behaviour has never been a cause for concern before.* (motivo de preocupação)

causeway /ˈkɔːzweɪ/ NOUN [plural **causeways**] a raised road over shallow water or wet ground (estrada pavimentada)

caustic /ˈkɔːstɪk/ ADJECTIVE
1 a caustic remark is unkind (cáustico, satírico)
2 a caustic substance can burn things (ácido, corrosivo)

caution /ˈkɔːʃən/ ▶ NOUN [plural **cautions**]
1 *no plural* when you take care to avoid danger or risk □ *Please drive with caution.* (atenção, cautela)
2 an official warning from the police □ *The police let him off with a caution.* (advertência)
▶ VERB [**cautions, cautioning, cautioned**]
1 a formal word meaning to warn someone □ *They cautioned us against swimming in the sea.* (prevenir)
2 if the police caution someone, they give them an official warning (advertir)

- **cautionary** /ˈkɔːʃənərɪ/ ADJECTIVE giving a warning about something bad which can happen (alerta cautelar) ▣ *Her experience is a cautionary tale of the potential dangers of the Internet.*

- **cautious** /ˈkɔːʃəs/ ADJECTIVE very careful to avoid danger or risk □ *He's very cautious with his money.* (cauteloso)

- **cautiously** /ˈkɔːʃəsli/ ADVERB in a cautious way □ *She stepped cautiously onto the ice.* (cautelosamente)

cavalier /ˌkævəˈlɪə(r)/ ADJECTIVE if you have a cavalier attitude to something, you do not treat it carefully or seriously (indiferente)

cavalry /ˈkævəlri/ NOUN, NO PLURAL soldiers who ride on horses (cavalaria)

cave /keɪv/ NOUN [plural **caves**] a large hole in a mountain or under the ground □ *The cave was dark and damp.* (gruta)
◆ PHRASAL VERB [**caves, caving, caved**] **cave in 1** if a roof caves in, it falls down to the ground (desabar) **2** to agree to something that you were against before □ *I've finally caved in to my daughter's pleas for a pet.* (ceder)

caveman /ˈkeɪvmæn/ NOUN [plural **cavemen**] someone who lived in a cave at the time when humans first existed (homem das cavernas)

cavern /ˈkævən/ NOUN [plural **caverns**] a large cave (caverna)

- **cavernous** /ˈkævənəs/ ADJECTIVE large and dark □ *a cavernous room* (cavernoso)

caviar /ˈkævɪɑː(r)/ NOUN, NO PLURAL an expensive food that is the eggs of a large fish (caviar)

caving /ˈkeɪvɪŋ/ NOUN, NO PLURAL the sport of climbing through caves under the ground (cavernismo)

cavity /ˈkævɪti/ NOUN [plural **cavities**]
1 a space inside something □ *the chest cavity* (cavidade)
2 a hole in a tooth, caused by decay (cárie)

cavort /kəˈvɔːt/ VERB [**cavorts, cavorting, cavorted**] to jump or dance in a noisy or excited way □ *The children were cavorting about on the beach.* (pular)

cc /ˌsiːˈsiː/ ABBREVIATION cubic centimetre; a unit for measuring the volume of something (centímetro cúbico)

CCTV /ˌsiːsiːtiːˈviː/ ABBREVIATION closed circuit television; a television system used in a building or area to prevent crime (sistema de televisão fechado que evita crimes)

CD /ˌsiːˈdiː/ ABBREVIATION **compact disc**; a disc with sound recorded on it □ *He bought a CD of Scottish folk songs.* (CD)

CD-ROM /ˌsiːdiːˈrɒm/ ABBREVIATION compact disc read-only memory; a type of CD that stores a lot of information which you play on a computer □ *The dictionary is available on CD-ROM.* (CD-ROM)

cease /siːs/ VERB [**ceases, ceasing, ceased**] a formal word meaning to stop (cessar)

ceasefire /ˈsiːsfaɪə(r)/ NOUN [plural **ceasefires**] an agreement between two armies to stop fighting for a period of time (**cessar-fogo**)

ceaseless /ˈsiːslɪs/ ADJECTIVE a formal word meaning never stopping □ *the ceaseless noise of traffic* (**constantemente**)

cedar /ˈsiːdə(r)/ NOUN [plural **cedars**] a large tree with red wood and small, thin leaves (**cedro**)

ceiling /ˈsiːlɪŋ/ NOUN [plural **ceilings**]
1 the surface at the top of a room □ *This house has very high ceilings.* (**teto**)
2 an upper limit □ *They set a ceiling of 7% on pay rises.* (**teto**)

celebrate /ˈselɪbreɪt/ VERB [**celebrates, celebrating, celebrated**] when you celebrate an event you have a party or do other special things because of it (**celebrar, comemorar**) ◨ *Dad took a day off work to celebrate his 50th birthday.* (**comemorar aniversário**) ◨ *We like to celebrate Christmas in a traditional way.* (**celebrar o Natal**) □ *Mark passed his driving test, so we're going out to celebrate!*
• **celebrated** /ˈselɪbreɪtɪd/ ADJECTIVE famous □ *He is a celebrated artist.* (**célebre**)
• **celebration** /ˌselɪˈbreɪʃən/ NOUN [plural **celebrations**]
1 a party or something special that is done to celebrate an event □ *a wedding celebration* (**celebração**)
2 *no plural* when you celebrate something (**comemoração**) ◨*They produced a book in celebration of his work.* (**em comemoração a**) □ *This ought to be a day of celebration.*
• **celebrity** /sɪˈlebrɪtɪ/ NOUN [plural **celebrities**] someone who is famous □ *Will there be any celebrities at the party?* (**celebridade**)

celery /ˈselərɪ/ NOUN, NO PLURAL a vegetable with long, pale green stems, usually eaten raw (**aipo**)

cell /sel/ NOUN [plural **cells**]
1 the smallest part of a living thing □ *cancerous cells* (**célula**)
2 a small room that a prisoner is kept in or that a monk (= religious man) lives in (**cela**)

cellar /ˈselə(r)/ NOUN [plural **cellars**] an underground room used for storing things (**porão, adega**)

cellist /ˈtʃelɪst/ NOUN [plural **cellists**] someone who plays the cello (**aquele que toca violoncelo**)

cello /ˈtʃeləʊ/ NOUN [plural **cellos**] a musical instrument like a large violin that you hold between your knees (**violoncelo**)

cellophane /ˈseləfeɪn/ NOUN, NO PLURAL a thin transparent material used to wrap things in. A trademark. (**celofane**)

cellphone /ˈselfəʊn/ NOUN [plural **cellphones**] the US word for **mobile phone** (**telefone celular**)

cellular /ˈseljʊlə(r)/ ADJECTIVE
1 to do with the cells of animals or plants. A biology word □ *cellular biology* (**celular**)
2 to do with mobile phones □ *a cellular network* (**celular**)

celluloid /ˈseljʊlɔɪd/ NOUN, NO PLURAL a type of plastic that film was made of in the past (**celuloide**)

cellulose /ˈseljʊləʊs/ NOUN, NO PLURAL a substance that forms the walls of plant cells. A biology word. (**celulose**)

Celsius /ˈselsɪəs/ ADJECTIVE measured using the temperature measurement at which water freezes at 0 degrees and boils at 100 degrees □ *57 degrees Celsius* (**Celsius**)

cement /sɪˈment/ ▶ NOUN, NO PLURAL a grey powder that is mixed with sand and water for use in building (**cimento**)
▶ VERB [**cements, cementing, cemented**]
1 to make a relationship stronger □ *It was a very special moment which cemented our friendship.* (**consolidar**)
2 to cover or stick things together with cement (**cimentar**)

cemetery /ˈsemɪtərɪ/ NOUN [plural **cemeteries**] a place where dead people are buried (**cemitério**)

censor /ˈsensə(r)/ ▶ VERB [**censors, censoring, censored**] to remove parts from books, films, etc. because they are offensive or not allowed (**censurar**) ◨ *Their letters were heavily censored.* (**severamente censurados**)
▶ NOUN [plural **censors**] someone whose job is to censor books, films, etc. (**censor, censurador**)

censure /ˈsenʃə(r)/ ▶ NOUN, NO PLURAL a formal word meaning severe criticism (**censura**)
▶ VERB [**censures, censuring, censured**] to criticize someone severely and in a formal way □ *The minister was censured for negligence.* (**censurar, repreender**)

census /ˈsensəs/ NOUN [plural **censuses**] an official process of finding out how many people are living in a particular country and getting information about them (**censo**)

cent /sent/ NOUN [plural **cents**] a unit of money worth 1/100 of a dollar (**centavo**)

cent- /sent/ PREFIX cent- is added to the beginning of words to mean a hundred □ *century* □ *centenary* (**cêntimo**)

centenary /senˈtiːnərɪ/ NOUN [plural **centenaries**] a date when people celebrate an event that happened one hundred years earlier □ *It is a special exhibition to mark the centenary of the artist's birth.* (**centenário**)

centennial /senˈtenɪəl/ NOUN [plural **centennials**] a US word for **centenary** (**centenário**)

center /ˈsentə(r)/ NOUN [plural **centers**] VERB [**centers, centering, centered**] the US spelling of **centre** (**centro**)

centi- / ceremonial

centi- /'sentɪ/ PREFIX centi- is added to the beginning of words to mean a hundred or 1/100 of something □ *centimetre* □ *centigrade* (**centi-**)

centigrade /'sentɪɡreɪd/ ADJECTIVE an old-fashioned word for Celsius □ *forty degrees centigrade* (**centígrado**)

centigram /'sentɪɡræm/ NOUN [plural **centigrams**] a unit for measuring weight. There are one hundred centigrams in a gram. This is often written cg. (**centigrama**)

centiliter /'sentɪliːtə(r)/ NOUN [plural **centiliters**] the US spelling of **centilitre** (**centilitro**)

centilitre /'sentɪliːtə(r)/ NOUN [plural **centilitres**] a unit for measuring liquid. There are one hundred centilitres in a litre. This is often written cl. (**centilitro**)

centimeter /'sentɪmiːtə(r)/ NOUN [plural **centimeters**] the US spelling of **centimetre** (**centímetro**)

centimetre /'sentɪmiːtə(r)/ NOUN [plural **centimetres**] a unit for measuring length, equal to 10 millimetres. This is often written cm. □ *The card measures eight centimetres across.* □ *These heels are 8 cm high.* (**centímetro**)

centipede /'sentɪpiːd/ NOUN [plural **centipedes**] an insect with a long body and lots of pairs of legs (**centopeia**)

central /'sentrəl/ ADJECTIVE

1 near or in the centre of an object or a place □ *He works in central London.* □ *Our school has a central courtyard.* (**central**)

2 being the main or most important part of an organization and controlling other parts of it □ *the central bank* □ *We have a system of central government.* (**central**)

3 most important (**principal**) ▣ *Love is the central theme of this film.* (**tema principal**) ▣ *She played a central role/part in the campaign.* (**papel principal**) □ *+ to This point is central to our religion.*

central heating /ˌsentrəl 'hiːtɪŋ/ NOUN, NO PLURAL a system used for heating houses where heated water goes through pipes to each room (**aquecimento central**)

centralization or **centralisation** /ˌsentrəlaɪ'zeɪʃən/ NOUN, NO PLURAL the process of centralizing something □ *We have seen increased centralization of our health services.* (**centralização**)

centralize or **centralise** /'sentrəlaɪz/ VERB [**centralizes, centralizing, centralized**] to have the main and controlling part of an organization, system or country in one place □ *The company plans to centralize its accounting systems.* (**centralizar**)

central nervous system /ˌsentrəl 'nɜːvəs ˌsɪstəm/ NOUN **the central nervous system** the brain and the spinal cord (= nerves in the spine that connect the body to the brain). A biology word. (**sistema nervoso central**)

centre /'sentə(r)/ ▶ NOUN [plural **centres**]

1 the middle point or part of something □ *It is difficult to park in the city centre.* □ *These chocolates have soft centres.* □ *+ of He stood in the centre of the field.* (**centro**)

2 the most important part of something □ *+ of The woman at the centre of the dispute is refusing to speak to journalists.* □ *The idea is at the centre of an ambitious project.* (**centro, cerne**)

3 the centre of attention if something or someone is the centre of attention, they are getting more attention than anything or anyone else (**o centro das atenções**)

4 a place or a building used for a particular activity □ *a sports centre* □ *The centre carries out research into breast cancer.* (**sede principal**)

5 the political position that is not extreme □ *The prime minister has moved further to the centre.* (**partido moderado**)

▶ VERB [**centres, centring, centred**] to put something in the centre □ *Centre the text underneath the image.* (**centralizar**)

◆ PHRASAL VERB **centre around/on something** to have something as its most important part □ *Talks centred on the need for international cooperation.* (**concentrar algo**)

century /'sentʃʊri/ NOUN [plural **centuries**] a hundred years □ *She lived in the fifteenth century.* □ *a twentieth-century building* (**século**)

ceramic /sɪ'ræmɪk/ ADJECTIVE made of clay that is baked in a hot oven to make it hard □ *a ceramic dish* (**cerâmica**)

• **ceramics** /sɪ'ræmɪks/ NOUN

1 the art of making objects with clay (**arte de fabricar louças**)

2 ceramic objects (**objetos de cerâmica**)

cereal /'sɪəriəl/ NOUN [plural **cereals**]

1 a plant such as wheat or rice, that is grown in order to use the grains for food (**cereal**)

2 food made from cereal crops, especially one eaten for breakfast (**cereais**) ▣ *breakfast cereals* (**cereais matinais**)

cerebral /'serɪbrəl/ ADJECTIVE

1 to do with the brain. A biology word. (**cerebral**)

2 cerebral people think a lot, and cerebral books, etc. are difficult and need a lot of thought to understand them. A formal word. (**racional**)

ceremonial /ˌserɪ'məʊniəl/ ADJECTIVE to do with a ceremony □ *Opening Parliament is one of the monarch's ceremonial duties.* (**cerimonial**)

• **ceremonious** /ˌserɪ'məʊniəs/ ADJECTIVE very formal and polite □ *He gave a ceremonious bow.* (**cerimonioso**)

- **ceremoniously** /ˌserɪˈməʊnɪəslɪ/ ADVERB in a grand and formal way □ *A huge cake was placed ceremoniously in the centre of the table.* (cerimoniosamente)
- **ceremony** /ˈserɪmənɪ/ NOUN [plural **ceremonies**]

1 a formal event where special or traditional words or actions are used (cerimônia) ▣ *a wedding ceremony* (cerimônia de casamento) ▣ *The graduation ceremony was held at the cathedral.* (a cerimônia aconteceu) ▣ *Who will be attending the award ceremony this year?* (apresentará a cerimônia)

2 *no plural* formal behaviour suitable for an important occasion □ *With great ceremony, the medals were brought forward.* (cerimônia)

certain /ˈsɜːtən/ ADJECTIVE

1 with no doubts □ + *about Dad wasn't certain about the time of the train.* □ + *question word I'm not certain how it works.* □ + *that I'm certain that I saw someone in the garden.* (certo)

2 sure to happen or be true □ + *that It seems certain that he will get the job.* (seguro) ▣ *Make certain that the rope is tight.* (Esteja certo) □ + *to do something She says you're certain to pass the exam.*

3 for certain without any doubt □ *I can't say for certain what will happen.* (com certeza)

4 used to talk about someone or something without saying exactly which person or thing you are talking about □ *There are certain rules which have to be obeyed.* □ *Certain people have been asked to leave.* (certo)

5 to a certain extent in some ways but not completely □ *I agree with you to a certain extent.* (até certo ponto)

- **certainly** /ˈsɜːtənlɪ/ ADVERB

1 used to show that there is no doubt about something □ *Joe certainly knows a lot about birds.* (certamente) ▣ *'Can I stay up until midnight?' 'Certainly not!'* (certamente não)

2 used to agree to something □ *'May I borrow your lawnmower?' 'Certainly.'* (com certeza)

- **certainty** /ˈsɜːtəntɪ/ NOUN [plural **certainties**]

1 *no plural* feeling or being certain □ *There is no certainty that the business will succeed.* (certeza)

2 something that is sure to happen □ *Since my husband's death, I feel there are no certainties in life.* (certeza)

certificate /səˈtɪfɪkət/ NOUN [plural **certificates**] an official document that shows something is true (certificado) ▣ *They asked to see my birth certificate.* (certidão de nascimento) □ *We each received a certificate for completing the course.*

- **certify** /ˈsɜːtɪfaɪ/ VERB [**certifies, certifying, certified**] to record in a formal way that something is true □ *Sign here to certify that this information is accurate.* □ *The product was certified as safe and nontoxic.* (certificar)

cervical /səˈvaɪkəl, ˈsɜːvɪkəl/ ADJECTIVE to do with the cervix. A biology word. □ *cervical cancer* (cervical)

cervix /ˈsɜːvɪks/ NOUN [plural **cervixes** or **cervices**] the small entrance to a woman's womb (= place where a baby grows). A biology word. (colo do útero)

cesarean /sɪˈzeərɪən/ NOUN [plural **cesareans**] the US spelling of **caesarean** (cesariana)

cesium /ˈsiːzɪəm/ NOUN, NO PLURAL the US spelling of **caesium** (césio)

cessation /seˈseɪʃən/ NOUN, NO PLURAL when something bad stops. A formal word. □ *The government has called for a total cessation of terrorist activity.* (suspensão)

CFC /ˌsiːefˈsiː/ ABBREVIATION **chlorofluorocarbon** (clorofluorcarbono)

cg /ˌsiːˈdʒiː/ ABBREVIATION **centigram** or **centigrams**

chafe /tʃeɪf/ VERB [**chafes, chafing, chafed**]

1 to rub your skin and make it sore □ *Toby's wellington boots were chafing his legs.* (esfolar)

2 to feel angry because you are not allowed to do what you want to do □ *He chafed against the rules of army life.* (irritar-se)

chaffinch /ˈtʃæfɪntʃ/ NOUN [plural **chaffinches**] a small bird (tentilhão)

chagrin /ˈʃæɡrɪn/ NOUN, NO PLURAL is a feeling of disappointment or anger when something does not happen the way you want it to □ *Much to his chagrin, he found that he had posted his application too late.* (pesar, desapontamento)

chain /tʃeɪn/ ▶ NOUN [plural **chains**]

1 metal rings that are connected in a line □ *He wore a gold chain around his neck.* □ *The chain came off my bicycle.* (corrente)

2 a group of similar shops, restaurants, etc. that have the same owner □ + *of She owns a chain of restaurants.* (cadeia)

3 a chain of events several events that happen one after the other (sequência de acontecimentos)

▶ VERB [**chains, chaining, chained**] to fasten something or someone with a chain □ *often passive The bicycle was chained to the fence.* (acorrentar)

chain mail /ˈtʃeɪn ˌmeɪl/ NOUN, NO PLURAL a type of armour (= metal pieces that protect the body in a fight) worn in the past, made of many small metal rings (tipo de armadura de corrente)

chain reaction /ˌtʃeɪn rɪˈækʃən/ NOUN [plural **chain reactions**]

1 a series of events where each event causes the next one (reação em cadeia)

2 a chemical change that makes something that causes another change. A chemistry word. (reação em cadeia)

chain saw /ˈtʃeɪn ˌsɔː/ NOUN [plural **chain saws**] a powerful tool with a motor and a chain with sharp parts in it, used for cutting wood (motosserra)

chain store /'tʃeɪn ˌstɔː(r)/ NOUN [plural **chain stores**] a shop that is part of a group of similar shops, all owned by the same company (**rede de lojas**)

chair /tʃeə(r)/ ▶ NOUN [plural **chairs**]
1 a piece of furniture that has a back and which one person sits on (**cadeira**)
2 the person who is in charge of a meeting, business or organization (**presidência**)
▶ VERB [**chairs, chairing, chaired**] to be officially in charge of a meeting (**presidir**)

chairlift /'tʃeəlɪft/ NOUN [plural **chairlifts**] a system of chairs hanging from thick wires, used for carrying people up mountains (**assentos de teleférico**)

chairman /'tʃeəmən/ NOUN [plural **chairmen**]
1 the person who is in charge of a company, group or organization □ *the chairman of the board* (**presidente**)
2 the person who is in charge of a meeting (**presidente**)
• **chairmanship** /'tʃeəmənʃɪp/ NOUN, NO PLURAL the job of being a chairman, or the time that someone is a chairman (**presidência**)

chairperson /'tʃeəpɜːsən/ NOUN [plural **chairpeople**] a male or female chairman (**presidente**)

chairwoman /'tʃeəwʊmən/ NOUN [plural **chairwomen**] a female chairman (**presidente**)

chalet /'ʃæleɪ/ NOUN [plural **chalets**] a small wooden house, often on a mountain (**chalé**)

chalk /tʃɔːk/ NOUN, NO PLURAL
1 no plural a type of soft white stone □ *crumbling chalk cliffs* (**giz**)
2 pieces of this stone that you use to draw with □ *She wrote on the blackboard with chalk.* (**giz**)
♦ IDIOM **as different as/like chalk and cheese** completely different from each other (**completamente diferente**)
• **chalky** /'tʃɔːki/ ADJECTIVE [**chalkier, chalkiest**] tasting or feeling like chalk (**calcário**)

challenge /'tʃælɪndʒ/ ▶ NOUN [plural **challenges**]
1 something that is difficult to do (**desafio**)
🔲 *The world faces a huge challenge in tackling climate change.* (**encarar o desafio**) 🔲 *We must ensure that these challenges are met* (= dealt with successfully). (**superados os desafios**) 🔲 *Crime poses/presents a serious challenge to our community.* (**apresenta desafio**)
2 when you try to change a rule, or do not accept a decision or someone's authority (**contestação**)
🔲 *There is likely to be a legal challenge to this ruling.* (**contestação legal**) 🔲 *We decided to mount a challenge against the president.* (**preparar uma contestação**)
3 when you ask someone to fight or compete with you □ *The approach of their army was a clear challenge.* (**desafio**)

▶ VERB [**challenges, challenging, challenged**]
1 to try to change a rule, or to say that you do not accept a decision or someone's authority □ *We will challenge this decision in the courts.* (**contestar**)
2 to ask someone to compete or fight □ *+ to He challenged his enemy to a duel.* (**desafiar**)
3 to ask someone if they have the right to be somewhere □ *The security guard challenged me and asked to see my identity card.* (**desafiar**)
4 if something challenges you, you find it difficult to do □ *This exam will challenge even our best pupils.* (**desafiar**)
• **challenger** /'tʃælɪndʒə(r)/ NOUN [plural **challengers**] someone who wants to try and beat another person in a game, election, etc. (**desafiante**)
• **challenging** /'tʃælɪndʒɪŋ/ ADJECTIVE difficult to do or understand □ *This book is very challenging for younger students.* (**desafiador**)

chamber /'tʃeɪmbə(r)/ NOUN [plural **chambers**]
1 a room for meetings or for a special purpose □ *the council chamber* □ *a burial chamber* (**câmara**)
2 one of the parts of a parliament □ *the upper/lower chamber* (**câmara**)
3 a space in a body, plant or machine □ *There was a blockage in one of the chambers of the heart.* (**cavidade**)
4 an old-fashioned word for a room or bedroom □ *the king's chamber* (**aposento**)

chambermaid /'tʃeɪmbəmeɪd/ NOUN [plural **chambermaids**] a woman who cleans bedrooms in a hotel (**camareira**)

chamber music /'tʃeɪmbə ˌmjuːzɪk/ NOUN, NO PLURAL classical music for a small group of players (**música de câmara**)

chameleon /kə'miːliən/ NOUN [plural **chameleons**] a small reptile that can change its colour to be the same as what is around it (**camaleão**)

champagne /ʃæm'peɪn/ NOUN, NO PLURAL a pale French wine with lots of bubbles, often drunk to celebrate something □ *Let's open a bottle of champagne.* (**champanhe**)

champion /'tʃæmpiən/ ▶ NOUN [plural **champions**]
1 a person or team that has beaten all the others in a competition □ *He became world boxing champion at twenty-six.* (**campeão**)
2 someone who strongly supports a particular belief or idea □ *Mrs Pankhurst was the champion of women's right to vote.* (**líder**)
▶ VERB [**champions, championing, championed**] to support a belief or idea strongly (**patrocinar**)
• **championship** /'tʃæmpiənʃɪp/ NOUN [plural **championships**] a competition to decide who is the champion (**campeonato**)

chance /tʃɑːns/ NOUN [plural chances]

1 a possibility that something will happen □ + *that* There is a good chance that she is still alive. □ + *of* Our school has no chance of winning the match. (**oportunidade**) 🔲 Our team doesn't *stand a chance* of winning. (**ter uma oportunidade**)
2 an opportunity □ + *to do something* I haven't had a chance to check yet. (**chance**) 🔲 You didn't *give* me *a chance* to answer. (**dar uma chance**) 🔲 This is your *last chance* to buy a ticket. (**última chance**)
3 by chance in a way that is not planned or expected □ I saw him quite by chance at the supermarket. (**por acaso**)
4 take a chance to take a risk □ I took a chance on the weather staying dry and left my coat at home. (**arriscar-se**)
5 no plural luck □ Roulette is a game of chance. (**sorte**)

> ➤ Note that **chance** meaning 'a possibility that something will happen' is followed by **that** or **of doing something**: □ *What are the chances that they will win?* □ *What are the chances of them winning?*

▶ VERB [chances, chancing, chanced] to take a risk □ The dog would probably have been fine at home, but I didn't want to chance it. (**arriscar**)
▶ ADJECTIVE happening by accident □ a chance meeting (**acidental**)

chancellor /ˈtʃɑːnsələ(r)/ NOUN [plural chancellors]

1 the British government official who is in charge of finance (**chanceler**)
2 the leader of the government of some European countries □ the German chancellor (**chanceler**)
3 the head of a university (**reitor**)

Chancellor of the Exchequer /ˌtʃɑːnsələr əv ðɪksˈtʃekə(r)/ NOUN [plural Chancellors of the Exchequer] the British government official who is in charge of finance (**ministro da Economia**)

chancy /ˈtʃɑːnsi/ ADJECTIVE [chancier, chanciest] involving a risk □ It was a bit chancy taking a route we didn't know. (**arriscado**)

chandelier /ˌʃændəˈlɪə(r)/ NOUN [plural chandeliers] a large light that hangs from the ceiling and is made from many small lights (**candelabro**)

change /tʃeɪndʒ/ ▶ VERB [changes, changing, changed]

1 to become different, or to make something different □ + *into* It has changed from a liquid into a gas. □ + *from* The leaves changed from green to gold. (**mudar**)
2 to stop having or using one thing and start having or using another instead □ We need to change the batteries. □ My daughter changed schools last term. (**mudar**) 🔲 Don't try to *change the subject* (= start talking about something else). (**mudar de assunto**) □ + *to* I'm changing to a new dentist.
3 to put on different clothes (**trocar**) 🔲 I must *get changed* (= change my clothes) for work. (**trocar de roupas**) □ + *into* I will just change into my jeans.
4 to get off a train, bus, etc. and get onto another one (**trocar**) 🔲 You have to *change trains* at York. (**trocar de trens**) □ Get a flight to Berlin and change there.
5 to exchange one type of money for another □ I need to change some dollars. (**trocar**)
6 change your mind to start to think or plan something different from before □ I've changed my mind – I'll have soup not pasta, please. (**mudar de ideia**)
7 change the bed to put clean sheets on a bed (**trocar a roupa de cama**)

▶ NOUN [plural changes]

1 a difference (**mudança**) 🔲 I have *made some changes* to the timetable. (**fazer algumas mudanças**) □ + *in* Let's wait until there is a change in the weather.
2 a change something that is enjoyable because it is new and different (**mudança**) 🔲 It will *make a change* to go out to eat. (**fazer uma mudança**) □ I didn't take my old job – I just fancied a change.
3 for a change instead of the usual thing □ Could you just stop complaining for a change? (**para variar**)
4 no plural money in the form of coins □ Have you got any change? (**trocado**)
5 no plural the extra money that is given back to you when you have paid for something (**troco**) 🔲 I told the taxi driver to *keep the change*. (**ficar com o troco**)
6 a change of clothes a different set of clothes to wear (**uma muda de roupa**)

• **changeable** /ˈtʃeɪndʒəbəl/ ADJECTIVE changing often □ The weather is rather changeable. (**instável**)

changing room /ˈtʃeɪndʒɪŋ ˌruːm/ NOUN [plural changing rooms]

1 a room where you can change your clothes before or after doing sport (**vestiário**)
2 a room in a clothes shop where you can try the clothes (**provador**)

channel /ˈtʃænəl/ ▶ NOUN [plural channels]

1 a television or radio station (**canal**) 🔲 May I *change channels*, or are you watching this? (**mudar de canal**) □ Let's turn over to the other channel.
2 channels the way something is communicated, given or received (**canais**) 🔲 You need to make your complaint through the *proper channels*. (**canais apropriados**) □ Our distribution channels have been affected by the war.
3 a passage for water or ships to travel along □ a shipping channel (**cano**)
4 a narrow piece of sea □ the English Channel (**canal**)

chant

▶ VERB [channels, channelling/US channeling, channelled/US channeled] to make water flow in a particular direction □ *This ditch channels water away from the campsite.* (canalizar)

◆ PHRASAL VERB **channel something into something** to use something for a particular purpose (**usar algo em algo**) 🔲 *They should channel their energies into something more useful.* (canalizar suas energias para)

chant /tʃɑːnt/ ▶ VERB [chants, chanting, chanted] to shout or sing something repeatedly (entoar)

▶ NOUN [plural **chants**] something that people shout or sing repeatedly (cântico)

Chanukah /'hɑːnəkə/ NOUN, NO PLURAL another spelling of **Hanukkah** (Hanucá)

chaos /'keɪɒs/ NOUN, NO PLURAL great confusion □ *There was chaos in town when the traffic lights stopped working.* (caos)

• **chaotic** /keɪ'ɒtɪk/ ADJECTIVE completely confused, with no organization □ *It was a chaotic scene with people running everywhere.* (caótico)

chap /tʃæp/ NOUN [plural **chaps**] an informal word for a man □ *He's a nice chap.* (sujeito)

chapel /'tʃæpəl/ NOUN [plural **chapels**] a small church, or a room used as a church □ *the hospital chapel* (capela)

chaplain /'tʃæplɪn/ NOUN [plural **chaplains**] a priest in the army or in a hospital, school or prison (capelão)

chapped /tʃæpt/ ADJECTIVE chapped skin is dry, red and sore □ *chapped lips* (rachado)

chapter /'tʃæptə(r)/ NOUN [plural **chapters**] one of the parts that a book is divided into □ *Turn to Chapter 3 in your history books.* □ *Can I just finish* (= finish reading) *this chapter?* (capítulo)

character /'kærəktə(r)/ NOUN [plural **characters**]

1 what someone or something is like and the qualities that they have □ *Can you describe her character? Is she reliable?* □ *It isn't in his character to stay angry for long.* (caráter)

2 a person in a story, film or play □ *Harry Potter is a fictional character.* □ *Who is your favourite character in the book?* (personagem)

3 an informal word for an unusual person □ *Her dad's a bit of a character, isn't he?* (figura)

4 a letter or symbol used in writing □ *Chinese characters* (letra)

• **characteristic** /ˌkærəktə'rɪstɪk/ ▶ NOUN [plural **characteristics**] the features or qualities that make someone or something what they are □ *Does he have any unusual characteristics?* (característica)

▶ ADJECTIVE a characteristic feature or quality is typical of a particular person or thing □ *Keith worked with his characteristic energy and enthusiasm.* (característica)

• **characterization** or **characterisation** /ˌkærəktəraɪ'zeɪʃən/ NOUN, NO PLURAL the way a writer creates and develops characters in a story (caracterização)

• **characterize** or **characterise** /'kærəktəraɪz/ VERB [characterizes, characterizing, characterized]

1 to be a typical part of someone or something □ *The disease is characterized by yellow skin and loss of appetite.* (caracterizar)

2 to describe someone in a particular way □ *He'd been characterized as a villain.* (caracterizar)

charade /ʃə'rɑːd/ NOUN [plural **charades**]

1 a situation that is false because people are not behaving sincerely □ *Their marriage is just a charade – it will never last.* (piada)

2 charades a game in which players have to act the title of a book, film or television programme (charada)

charcoal /'tʃɑːkəʊl/ NOUN, NO PLURAL wood that has been burnt until it is black and is used to draw with and as fuel (carvão)

charge

charge /tʃɑːdʒ/ ▶ C VERB [charges, charging, charged]

1 to ask a particular amount of money for something □ **+ for** *How much do you charge for a haircut?* □ *The shopkeeper charged me $20 too much.* (cobrar)

2 if the police charge someone with a crime, they accuse them officially □ **+ with** *He was charged with murder.* (acusar)

3 to move forward quickly and suddenly □ *The boys came charging into the room.* □ *We charged down the hill towards them.* (correr)

4 to attack someone or something by moving forward quickly □ *Their officer gave the order to charge.* (investir)

5 to fill a battery or piece of electrical equipment with electricity □ *Where can I charge my phone?* (carregar)

▶ NOUN [plural **charges**]

1 the amount of money that you have to pay (preço) 🔲 *You can have another cup of coffee free of charge* (= without paying). (de graça) □ *There will be a small charge for postage and packing.*

2 in charge controlling or managing something or someone □ *I am in charge while the boss is away.* □ *Ms Handy is in charge of the sales department.* (responsável por)

3 take charge to take control of something or someone □ *Can you take charge of the food preparation?* (tomar a direção)

4 when someone is accused of a crime (acusação) 🔲 *There was some evidence but not enough to bring charges against her.* (fazer acusações) □ *He was arrested on a charge of robbery.*

5 a sudden forward attacking movement □ *In the last minute of the match they made a charge for the line.* (ataque, acusação)

6 an amount of electricity in something (carga)

charge card /ˈtʃɑːdʒ ˌkɑːd/ NOUN [plural **charge cards**] a plastic card that you can use to buy things at a shop and pay for them later (**cartão de crédito**)

charger /ˈtʃɑːdʒə(r)/ NOUN [plural **chargers**] an electrical device that you use to charge (= put electricity into) something such as a mobile phone (**carregador**)

chariot /ˈtʃærɪət/ NOUN [plural **chariots**] an open vehicle with two wheels that is pulled by horses and was used in the past for racing and fighting (**biga**)

charisma /kəˈrɪzmə/ NOUN, NO PLURAL a personal quality that makes people attracted to you and interested in you ☐ *He was a politician with lots of charisma.* (**carisma**)
• **charismatic** /ˌkærɪzˈmætɪk/ ADJECTIVE having charisma ☐ *a charismatic leader* (**carismático**)

charitable /ˈtʃærətəbəl/ ADJECTIVE
1 a charitable organization, activity, etc. gives money or other help to people who need it (**caridade**)
2 a charitable person is kind and does not criticize others (**generoso**)

charity /ˈtʃærəti/ NOUN [plural **charities**]
1 an organization that gives money or other help to people who need it (**caridade**)
2 no plural being kind and generous to other people (**ato de caridade**)

charm /tʃɑːm/ ▶ NOUN [plural **charms**]
1 no plural a quality that makes someone pleasant and attractive to other people (**charme**)
2 an object that is believed to be lucky (**amuleto**)
▶ VERB [**charms, charming, charmed**] to attract and please someone very much (**encantar**)
• **charming** /ˈtʃɑːmɪŋ/ ADJECTIVE extremely pleasant ☐ *What a charming young man your son is.* (**charmoso**)

charred /tʃɑːd/ ADJECTIVE black from being burnt ☐ *We gazed at the charred remains of the hut.* (**chamuscado**)

chart /tʃɑːt/ ▶ NOUN [plural **charts**]
1 a drawing that shows information ☐ *This chart shows the population growth over the last fifty years.* (**gráfico**)
2 the charts a list of the most popular music ☐ *Their new record went straight to the top of the charts.* (**paradas de sucesso**)
3 a map of the sea used by sailors (**carta, mapa**)
▶ VERB [**charts, charting, charted**]
1 to record the progress or development of something (**registrar**) 🔁 *His book charts the progress of the reformers.*
2 to make a map of an area (**desenhar**)

charter /ˈtʃɑːtə(r)/ ▶ VERB [**charters, chartering, chartered**] to pay money to use a boat or an aeroplane (**fretar**)
▶ NOUN [plural **charters**] a written statement of an organization's principles and duties (**escritura**)

charter flight /ˈtʃɑːtə ˌflaɪt/ NOUN [plural **charter flights**] an aeroplane flight for which a travel company buys all the seats and sells them for a cheap price (**voo fretado**)

chase /tʃeɪs/ ▶ VERB [**chases, chasing, chased**]
1 to run after someone or something to try to catch them ☐ *A police officer chased the thief down the High Street.* ☐ *Our dog was chasing a rabbit.* (**perseguir**)
2 chase someone/something away/off, etc. to run after someone or something quickly to make them go away ☐ *He angrily chased the children off his land.* (**colocar algo/alguém para fora, afugentar**)
▶ NOUN [plural **chases**]
1 when someone or something is chased (**perseguição**) 🔁 *A man was arrested following a high-speed car chase.* (**perseguição de carro**)
2 give chase to run after someone or something to try and catch them (**dar busca**)

chasm /ˈkæzəm/ NOUN [plural **chasms**]
1 a very big difference between people ☐ *There is a chasm between rich and poor.* (**abismo**)
2 a deep narrow opening between rocks (**fenda**)

chassis /ˈʃæsi/ NOUN [plural **chassis**] the frame and wheels of a vehicle (**chassis**)

chastise /tʃæˈstaɪz/ VERB [**chastises, chastising, chastised**] to speak angrily to someone because they have done something wrong. A formal word. (**castigar**)

chat /tʃæt/ ▶ VERB [**chats, chatting, chatted**] to talk to someone in a friendly way ☐ *+ to She was chatting to her friend on the phone.* (**bater papo**)
♦ PHRASAL VERB **chat someone up** to talk to someone in a friendly way because you want to start a romantic relationship with them. An informal phrase. ☐ *This guy at the bar started chatting me up.* (**passar uma cantada**)
▶ NOUN [plural **chats**] a friendly talk (**bate-papo**) 🔁 *Come round later and we can have a chat.* (**bater um papo**)

chat room /ˈtʃæt ˌruːm/ NOUN [plural **chat rooms**] an area on the Internet where people can exchange messages. A computing word. (**sala de bate-papo**)

chatter /ˈtʃætə(r)/ VERB [**chatters, chattering, chattered**]
1 to talk about silly things that are not important ☐ *Stop chattering, you two, and get on with your work.* (**tagarelar**)
2 if your teeth chatter, they knock together because you are cold or frightened (**bater os dentes**)

chatterbox /ˈtʃætəbɒks/ NOUN [plural **chatterboxes**] an informal word for someone who likes to talk a lot (**tagarela**)

chatty /ˈtʃæti/ ADJECTIVE [**chattier, chattiest**] a chatty person likes to talk to other people ☐ *At first she was shy, but now she's quite chatty.* (**falador**)

chauffeur 125 cheek

chauffeur /ˈʃəʊfə(r)/ NOUN [plural **chauffeurs**] someone whose job is to drive a car for another person (**chofer, motorista**)

chauvinism /ˈʃəʊvɪnɪzəm/ NOUN, NO PLURAL
1 the belief of some men that men are better than women (**chauvinismo**)
2 the belief that your country is better than other countries (**chauvinismo**)

chauvinist /ˈʃəʊvɪnɪst/ NOUN [plural **chauvinists**]
1 a man who believes that men are better than women (**chauvinista**) ▣ *Clive is such a male chauvinist.* (**homem chauvinista**)
2 someone who believes that their country is better than other countries (**chauvinista**)
• **chauvinist** /ˈʃəʊvɪnɪst/ or **chauvinistic** /ˌʃəʊvɪˈnɪstɪk/ ADJECTIVE showing chauvinism ▣ *I hate her chauvinist attitude.* (**chauvinista**)

cheap /tʃiːp/ ▶ ADJECTIVE [**cheaper, cheapest**]
1 not costing a lot ▣ *a cheap air ticket* ▣ *It is cheaper to buy vegetables at the market.* (**barato**)
2 not charging high prices ▣ *a cheap restaurant* (**a preço reduzido**)
3 not good in quality ▣ *The handbag looks very cheap.* (**inferior**)
▶ ADVERB for a low price ▣ *I got these boots cheap in the sale.* (**barato**)
• **cheapen** /ˈtʃiːpən/ VERB [**cheapens, cheapening, cheapened**] to make someone or something seem less important or good ▣ *The dispute has cheapened their work.* (**depreciar**)
• **cheaply** /ˈtʃiːplɪ/ ADVERB for a low price ▣ *You can eat quite cheaply at these cafe´s.* (**barato**)

cheat /tʃiːt/ ▶ VERB [**cheats, cheating, cheated**] to behave dishonestly in order to succeed at something or get something ▣ *It's cheating to look at someone else's cards.* ▣ *Hey, you're cheating! That is against the rules.* ▣ + *out of* *They cheated the old lady out of her savings.* (**trapacear**)
▶ NOUN [plural **cheats**] someone who cheats (**trapaceiro**)

check /tʃek/ VERB [**checks, checking, checked**]
1 to make sure that something is correct ▣ *Please check your work carefully before you hand it in.* ▣ *I think my appointment is at 10.30, but I'll just check in my diary.* (**conferir**)
2 to find out ▣ + *question word* *Could you check whether the post has arrived?* ▣ *He is just checking how many copies we need.* (**verificar, checar**)
3 to make sure that something is working correctly ▣ *The engineer came to check the fire alarm.* (**verificar**)
4 to stop something bad from continuing ▣ *The ban on transporting cattle is intended to check the spread of the disease.* (**controlar**)
♦ PHRASAL VERBS **check in** to tell the people at a hotel or airport that you have arrived ▣ *Please check in two hours before the flight.* (**check-in**). **check out** to pay for your stay at a hotel and leave (**check-out**) **check something/someone out** an informal wordmeaning to find out what something or someone is like ▣ *Let's check out the clubs.* (**investigar algo ou alguém**) **check up on someone** to find out what someone is doing and how well they are doing it ▣ *Mum keeps coming in to check up on me.* (**investigar alguém**)
▶ NOUN [plural **checks**]
1 a test to see that something is correct or is working correctly (**verificação**) ▣ *a health/safety check* (**verificação de saúde/segurança**) ▣ *The police did fingerprint checks on the document.* (**fez verificação**)
2 a pattern of squares ▣ *black-and-white check* (**xadrez**)
3 hold/keep something in check to control something and prevent it from increasing ▣ *I must keep my emotions in check.* (**manter algo sob controle**)
4 the US spelling of **cheque** (**cheque**)
5 the US word for tick (sense 1) (**tique**)
6 the US word for a bill in a restaurant (**conta**)

checkbook /ˈtʃekbʊk/ NOUN [plural **checkbooks**] the US spelling of **chequebook** (**talão de cheques**)

checked /tʃekt/ ADJECTIVE having a pattern of squares ▣ *a checked shirt* (**xadrez**)

checkers /ˈtʃekəz/ PLURAL NOUN the US word for **draughts** (**damas**)

check-in /ˈtʃekɪn/ NOUN [plural **check-ins**]
1 a desk at an airport where passengers' tickets are checked (**check-in**)
2 no plural the process that happens when you arrive at an airport (**check-in**)

checkmate /ˈtʃekmeɪt/ NOUN [plural **checkmates**] a winning position in the game of chess (**xeque-mate**)

checkout /ˈtʃekaʊt/ NOUN [plural **checkouts**]
1 the place where you pay at a supermarket ▣ *There was a big queue at the checkout.* (**caixa**)
2 the place on a website where you pay for things you have bought. A computing word. (**caixa**)

checkpoint /ˈtʃekpɔɪnt/ NOUN [plural **checkpoints**] a place where soldiers or police stop vehicles or people (**posto de controle**)

check-up /ˈtʃekʌp/ NOUN [plural **check-ups**] an examination by a doctor or a dentist to see if you are healthy ▣ *I have to go for regular check-ups.* (**checape, exame médico completo**)

cheddar /ˈtʃedə(r)/ NOUN, NO PLURAL a type of hard british cheese (**cheddar**)

cheek /tʃiːk/ NOUN [plural **cheeks**]
1 one of the two areas on each side of your face below your eyes (**bochecha**) ▣ *She has lovely rosy cheeks.* (**bochechas rosadas**)

2 *no plural* rude behaviour that shows you do not respect someone (**atrevimento**) ◫ *He said I was the worst goalie he'd ever seen. 'What a cheek!'* (**que atrevimento!**) ◫ *She had the cheek to look in my bag.* (**teve o atrevimento de**)

- **cheekily** /'tʃiːkɪli/ ADVERB in a cheeky way □ *'Don't be stupid, sir', he replied cheekily.* (**atrevidamente**)

- **cheeky** /'tʃiːki/ ADJECTIVE [**cheekier, cheekiest**] a bit rude, often in a funny way □ *You cheeky boy!* □ *a cheeky grin* (**atrevido**)

cheer /tʃɪə(r)/ VERB [**cheers, cheering, cheered**] to shout loudly to praise or encourage someone □ *We cheered loudly when he came onto the stage.* □ *The spectators cheered each runner as they ran past.* (**ovacionar**)

♦ PHRASAL VERBS **cheer someone on** to shout loudly to encourage someone in a competition or race □ *The crowd was cheering him on.* (**torcer por alguém**) **cheer (someone) up** to feel happier, or to make someone feel happier □ *Cheer up! Don't look so miserable!* □ *I've got some news that will cheer you up.* (**animar alguém**)

▶ NOUN [*plural* **cheers**]

1 a loud shout to show that you are pleased □ *When he caught the ball there was a big cheer from the crowd.* (**ovação**)

2 *no plural* an old-fashioned word that means happiness □ *Christmas cheer* (**regozijo**)

- **cheerful** /'tʃɪəfʊl/ ADJECTIVE

1 happy □ *You're very cheerful this morning.* (**alegre**)

2 bright and pleasant □ *That's a lovely cheerful colour!* (**brilhante**)

- **cheerfully** /'tʃɪəfʊli/ ADVERB

1 in a happy way □ *He sang cheerfully as he worked.* (**alegremente**)

2 I could cheerfully do something used when you are annoyed with someone to joke that you would enjoy doing something bad to them □ *I could cheerfully strangle that boy sometimes, he is so lazy!* (**eu poderia fazer isso com muito prazer**)

- **cheering** /'tʃɪərɪŋ/ ADJECTIVE making you feel happier □ *There are some cheering signs of improvement in the weather.* (**aclamações, aplausos**)

cheerio /ˌtʃɪəri'əʊ/ EXCLAMATION an informal word meaning goodbye □ *Cheerio, see you tomorrow.* (**até logo!**)

cheers /tʃɪəz/ EXCLAMATION

1 a word used to express your good wishes to other people when you are drinking alcohol together □ *Cheers, everyone. Happy New Year!* (**saúde**)

2 an informal word meaning thank you □ *'Here's your book back.' 'Cheers.'* (**obrigado**)

cheery /'tʃɪəri/ ADJECTIVE [**cheerier, cheeriest**] happy □ *a cheery smile/wave* (**alegre**)

cheese /tʃiːz/ NOUN [*plural* **cheeses**] a solid white or yellow food made from milk (**queijo**) □ *cheese sauce* ◫ *Would you like some cheese and biscuits?* (**queijo e biscoitos**) ◫ *Sprinkle some grated cheese on the top.* (**queijo ralado**)

⇨ go to **as different as/like chalk and cheese**

cheesecake /'tʃiːzkeɪk/ NOUN [*plural* **cheesecakes**] a sweet food made with soft cheese on top of crushed biscuits (**torta de queijo**)

cheesy /'tʃiːzi/ ADJECTIVE [**cheesier, cheesiest**]

1 tasting or smelling of cheese (**parecido com queijo**)

2 an informal word meaning of low quality or not fashionable □ *a cheesy song* (**ordinário**)

3 a cheesy grin a big smile (**grande sorriso**)

cheetah /'tʃiːtə/ NOUN [*plural* **cheetahs**] a large, wild cat which runs very fast (**chita**)

chef /ʃef/ NOUN [*plural* **chefs**] someone whose job is to cook in a restaurant or a hotel □ *Please tell the chef that was delicious.* (**chefe de cozinha**)

chemical /'kemɪkəl/ ▶ NOUN [*plural* **chemicals**] a substance that is formed by or used in chemistry (**químico**) ◫ *The lorry contained dangerous chemicals.* (**produtos químicos perigosos**) □ *The hydrochloric acid and other chemicals are kept in the laboratory.*

▶ ADJECTIVE

1 involving or produced by chemistry (**químico**) ◫ *a chemical reaction* (**reação química**)

2 using or containing chemicals □ *a chemical solution* (**químico**)

chemical element /ˌkemɪkəl 'elɪmənt/ NOUN [*plural* **chemical elements**] a substance that cannot be divided into smaller chemical substances. A chemistry word. (**elemento químico**)

chemist /'kemɪst/ NOUN [*plural* **chemists**]

1 someone who prepares medicines □ *Could you ask the chemist if my prescription is ready?* (**farmacêutico**)

2 chemist's a shop where medicines and products for washing, etc. are sold (**farmácia**)

3 someone who studies chemistry (**químico**)

- **chemistry** /'kemɪstri/ NOUN, NO PLURAL

1 the study of chemical elements and how they react with each other □ *She studied physics and chemistry at a level.* (**química**)

2 when two people feel attracted to each other □ *There seems to be a bit of chemistry between those two!* (**química**)

chemotherapy /ˌkiːməʊ'θerəpi/ NOUN, NO PLURAL a treatment for cancer that uses powerful chemicals (**quimioterapia**)

cheque /tʃek/ NOUN [*plural* **cheques**] a piece of printed paper that you sign and use as a way of paying for things (**cheque**) 🔲 *I wrote him a cheque for £50.* (preenchi um cheque) 🔲 *Our last customer paid by cheque.* (pagou com cheque)

chequebook /'tʃekbʊk/ NOUN [*plural* **chequebooks**] a book of cheques for a particular person to use (talão de cheques)

cheque card /'tʃek ˌkɑːd/ NOUN [*plural* **cheque cards**] a small plastic card from your bank to show the person in a shop when you pay by cheque (cartão de banco)

cherish /'tʃerɪʃ/ VERB [**cherishes, cherishing, cherished**] to love and look after someone or something (estimar)

cherry /'tʃerɪ/ NOUN [*plural* **cherries**] a small round red fruit with a hard seed inside (cereja)

cherub /'tʃerəb/ NOUN [*plural* **cherubs** or **cherubim**] a type of angel (= creature with wings believed to live in heaven) that looks like an attractive fat baby (querubim)

chess /tʃes/ NOUN, NO PLURAL a game where two players move pieces on a board with black and white squares (**xadrez**) 🔲 *a chess board* (tabuleiro de xadrez) 🔲 *Tom plays chess almost every day.* (joga xadrez)

chest /tʃest/ NOUN [*plural* **chests**]
1 the front of your body between your neck and your stomach ▫ *a hairy chest* ▫ *chest pains* (peito)
2 a large box for storing things ▫ *a treasure chest* (arca)
♦ IDIOM **get something off your chest** to talk about something that has been worrying you or making you angry (desabafar)

chestnut /'tʃesnʌt/ ▶ NOUN [*plural* **chestnuts**] a shiny red-brown nut that has an outer shell covered with sharp points (castanha)
▶ ADJECTIVE having a red-brown colour ▫ *chestnut hair* (castanho)

chest of drawers /ˌtʃest əv 'drɔːz/ NOUN [*plural* **chests of drawers**] a piece of furniture with drawers for putting clothes in (cômoda)

chew /tʃuː/ VERB [**chews, chewing, chewed**]
1 to break up food inside your mouth with your teeth ▫ *My tooth is sore and it hurts to chew.* ▫ *He bit off a piece of bread and chewed it slowly.* (mastigar)
2 to bite something again and again without swallowing it ▫ + **on** *The dog was chewing on a bone.* (ruminar)
♦ PHRASAL VERB **chew something over** to think about something carefully, or to discuss it ▫ *I'll give you my answer later, after I've chewed it over.* (considerar, pensar cuidadosamente em algo)

chewing gum /'tʃuːɪŋ ˌɡʌm/ NOUN, NO PLURAL a sweet substance that you chew but do not swallow (chiclete)

chewy /'tʃuːɪ/ ADJECTIVE [**chewier, chewiest**] if food is chewy, you have to chew it a lot before you can swallow it (mastigável)

chick /tʃɪk/ NOUN [*plural* **chicks**] a baby bird (filhote de pássaro)

chicken /'tʃɪkɪn/ NOUN [*plural* **chickens**]
1 a bird that is kept on farms to produce eggs and to be eaten (**frango, galinha**) 🔲 *The farmer's wife keeps a few chickens.* (cria galinhas) 🔲 *This chicken has stopped laying* (= producing eggs). (galinha não põe mais ovos)
2 *no plural* the meat from this bird ▫ *roast chicken* (carne de frango)
3 an informal word meaning someone who is afraid ▫ *Jump! Don't be such a chicken.* (medroso)
♦ PHRASAL VERB [**chickens, chickening, chickened**] **chicken out** an informal word meaning to decide not to do something because you are afraid ▫ *Pete chickened out of singing, though he had brought his guitar.* (dar para trás)

chickenpox /'tʃɪkɪnpɒks/ NOUN, NO PLURAL an infectious disease which gives you spots on your skin that you want to scratch (catapora)

chickpea /'tʃɪkpiː/ NOUN [*plural* **chickpeas**] a large light brown pea (grão-de-bico)

chicory /'tʃɪkərɪ/ NOUN, NO PLURAL a green plant whose leaves are eaten in salads (chicória)

chief /tʃiːf/ ▶ ADJECTIVE
1 biggest or most important ▫ *the chief city of the region* ▫ *My chief worry is the cost.* (principal)
2 **chief adviser/correspondent**, etc. the person who has the highest rank in a particular job (chefe, líder)
▶ NOUN [*plural* **chiefs**]
1 a person in charge of a group or organization ▫ *We heard a speech by the new police chief.* ▫ *Industry chiefs met today in London.*
2 a ruler of a tribe (= large group of related people) ▫ *an African tribal chief*

chief executive /ˌtʃiːf ɪɡ'zekjʊtɪv/ NOUN [*plural* **chief executives**] the person who has the most important job in a company (presidente)

chiefly /'tʃiːflɪ/ ADVERB mainly ▫ *The programme is watched chiefly by women.* (principalmente)

chiffon /'ʃɪfɒn/ NOUN, NO PLURAL a thin transparent material (chiffon)

child /tʃaɪld/ NOUN [*plural* **children**]
1 a young human ▫ *When my dad was a child, he lived in New York.* ▫ *There are thirty children in my class.* (criança)
2 a son or daughter (**filho**) 🔲 *Sue never had* (= gave birth to) *any children.* (teve filhos) ▫ *Our children are grown up now.*

childbirth /'tʃaɪldbɜːθ/ NOUN, NO PLURAL the process of giving birth to a baby ▫ *His mother died in childbirth.* (parto)

childcare /ˈtʃaɪldkeə(r)/ NOUN, NO PLURAL when someone looks after children while their parents are working (**assistência à infância**)

childhood /ˈtʃaɪldhʊd/ NOUN, NO PLURAL the time in your life when you are a child □ *My memories of childhood are very happy.* (**infância**)

childish /ˈtʃaɪldɪʃ/ ADJECTIVE behaving in a silly way, like a child □ *Don't be so childish!* (**infantil**)
• **childishly** /ˈtʃaɪldɪʃli/ ADVERB in a childish way (**de maneira infantil**)

childlike /ˈtʃaɪldlaɪk/ ADJECTIVE simple and trusting like a child □ *childlike innocence* (**inocente**)

childminder /ˈtʃaɪldmaɪndə(r)/ NOUN [plural **childminders**] someone who looks after children when their parents are at work (**babá**)

childproof /ˈtʃaɪldpruːf/ ADJECTIVE if something is childproof, it is designed so that a child cannot open, use or damage it □ *a childproof lock* (**imune a crianças**)

children /ˈtʃɪldrən/ PLURAL OF **child** (**ver child**)

chili /ˈtʃɪli/ NOUN [plural **chilies**] the US spelling of **chilli** (**pimenta-malagueta**)

chill /tʃɪl/ ▶ VERB [**chills, chilling, chilled**]
1 to make food or drink cold □ *Chill the pudding in the fridge before serving.* (**resfriar**)
2 an informal word meaning to relax □ *I spent the afternoon chilling by the pool.* (**relaxar**)
◆ PHRASAL VERB **chill out** an informal phrase meaning to relax □ *We could just chill out with a couple of friends.* (**relaxar**)
▶ NOUN, NO PLURAL
1 if there is a chill in the air, it feels cold (**frio**)
2 an illness that gives you a fever (**resfriado**) *She caught a chill out in the rain.* (**pegou um resfriado**)

chilli /ˈtʃɪli/ NOUN [plural **chillies**]
1 a small, red or green vegetable which is put in food to give it a hot taste (**pimenta-malagueta**)
2 *no plural* spicy food containing red beans, tomatoes and usually meat (**pimenta mexicana**)

chilling /ˈtʃɪlɪŋ/ ADJECTIVE frightening □ *a chilling story* (**assustador**)

chilly /ˈtʃɪli/ ADJECTIVE [**chillier, chilliest**] cold □ *It's a bit chilly in here.* (**frio**)

chime /tʃaɪm/ ▶ NOUN [plural **chimes**] the sound of a bell or bells ringing (**toque**)
▶ VERB [**chimes, chiming, chimed**] to make a ringing sound (**soar**)

chimney /ˈtʃɪmni/ NOUN [plural **chimneys**] a pipe above a fire that allows smoke to escape □ *a factory chimney* (**chaminé**)

chimpanzee /ˌtʃɪmpænˈziː/ NOUN [plural **chimpanzees**] a small African ape (= large monkey) with black fur, a flat face and large brown eyes (**chimpanzé**)

chin /tʃɪn/ NOUN [plural **chins**] the part of your face that is below your mouth □ *The strap ties under your chin.* (**queixo**)

china /ˈtʃaɪnə/ NOUN, NO PLURAL
1 clay used for making things like cups and plates (**porcelana**)
2 cups, plates, etc. which are made from this clay (**porcelana**)

chink /tʃɪŋk/ NOUN [plural **chinks**]
1 a small opening □ *A shaft of sunlight came through a chink in the curtains.* (**fissura**)
2 a sound made when coins or other small metal objects hit each other (**tinido**)

chip /tʃɪp/ ▶ NOUN [plural **chips**]
1 a long thin piece of potato that is fried and eaten hot (**batata frita**) *fish and chips* (**peixe e batatas fritas**)
2 the US word for crisp (= a very thin piece of potato cooked in oil and eaten cold) □ *a bag of chips* (**fritas**)
3 a small piece broken off a hard object, or the place where a small piece has broken off □ *The plate had a chip in it.* (**rachadura**)
4 a very small part in a computer or other electronic equipment that contains a circuit (= system of wires) and stores information (**chip**)
◆ IDIOMS **a chip off the old block** someone who looks or behaves like one of their parents (**filho de peixe, peixinho é**) **have a chip on your shoulder** to have an angry attitude because you feel that you have not had advantages that other people have had □ *She has a real chip on her shoulder about not going to university.* (**ter complexo de inferioridade**)
▶ VERB [**chips, chipping, chipped**] to break a small piece off something □ *Roy chipped one of his teeth playing rugby.* (**rachar, lascar**)
◆ PHRASAL VERB **chip in** to say something in the middle of someone else's conversation □ *She chipped in with a couple of suggestions.* (**interromper uma conversa**)

chip and PIN /ˌtʃɪp ən ˈpɪn/ NOUN, NO PLURAL a system of paying for things in shops where you put a card into a machine and then press a secret combination of numbers into the machine (**tecnologia de cartão com chip e senha**)

chipmunk /ˈtʃɪpmʌŋk/ NOUN [plural **chipmunks**] a small North American animal with a long thick tail and stripes on its back (**esquilo listrado**)

chiropodist /kɪˈrɒpədɪst/ NOUN [plural **chiropodists**] someone whose job is to treat problems and diseases of people's feet (**quiropodista**)
• **chiropody** /kɪˈrɒpədi/ NOUN, NO PLURAL the care and treatment of people's feet (**quiropodia**)

chiropractor /ˈkaɪrəpræktə(r)/ NOUN [plural **chiropractors**] someone whose job is to reduce pain by pressing on joints (= places where bones meet) between bones in your body (**quiroprático**)

chirp /tʃɜːp/ or **chirrup** /ˈtʃɪrəp/ ▶ VERB [chirps, chirping, chirped or chirrups, chirruping, chirruped] to make a short high sound or sounds □ *birds chirping* (**gorjear**)

▶ NOUN [plural **chirps** or **chirrups**] a short high sound □ *the chirp of baby birds*

• **chirpy** /ˈtʃɜːpɪ/ ADJECTIVE [chirpier, chirpiest] an informal word meaning happy □ *You sound very chirpy this morning!* (**animado**)

chisel /ˈtʃɪzəl/ ▶ NOUN [plural **chisels**] a very sharp tool used for cutting pieces off wood, stone or metal (**cinzel**)

▶ VERB [chisels, chiselling/US chiseling, chiselled/US chiseled] to cut something using a chisel □ *Josh chiselled his name in the stone.* (**esculpir**)

chivalrous /ˈʃɪvəlrəs/ ADJECTIVE a chivalrous man is polite and shows respect towards women (**cavalheiresco**)

chive /tʃaɪv/ NOUN [plural **chives**] a herb with long thin leaves that taste slightly of onion (**cebolinha**)

chlorinate /ˈklɔːrɪneɪt/ VERB [chlorinates, chlorinating, chlorinated] to add chlorine to water in swimming pools to kill any bacteria (**clorar**)

chlorine /ˈklɔːriːn/ NOUN, NO PLURAL a gas with a strong smell which is used to kill bacteria in water. A chemistry word. (**cloro**)

chlorofluorocarbon /ˌklɔːrəflʊərəʊˈkɑːbən/ NOUN [plural **chlorofluorocarbons**] a chemical that harms the ozone layer (= layer of a type of oxygen that protects the Earth from the sun). A chemistry word. (**clorofluorcarbono**)

chlorophyll /ˈklɒrəfɪl/ NOUN, NO PLURAL a green substance in the leaves of a plant that allows it to use energy from the sun in a process called photosynthesis. A biology word. (**clorofila**)

chock-a-block /ˌtʃɒkəˈblɒk/ ADJECTIVE very full or crowded. An informal word. □ *The city centre was chock-a-block with tourists.* (**cheio, abarrotado**)

chocolate /ˈtʃɒkələt/ NOUN [plural **chocolates**]
1 *no plural* a sweet brown food made from the seeds of a tropical tree (**chocolate**) ▣ *milk/dark chocolate* (**chocolate ao leite/amargo**) ▣ *a bar of chocolate* (**barra de chocolate**)
2 one of many small sweets made with chocolate that are sold together (**chocolate**) ▣ *a box of chocolates* (**uma caixa de chocolates**)
3 a sweet drink made with chocolate (**chocolate**) ▣ *a hot chocolate* (**chocolate quente**)

choice /tʃɔɪs/ NOUN [plural **choices**]
1 when you can choose between different things (**escolha**) ▣ *If I had a choice, I'd work from home.* (**se eu tivesse escolha**) ▣ *I had to leave – I had no choice.* (**não tive escolha**)
2 a decision to choose a person or thing (**escolha**) ▣ *In the end I had to make a choice.* (**fazer uma escolha**) ▣ *It was a hard choice to make.* (**escolha difícil**)
3 the different things you can choose from (**escolha**) □ *+ of We were given a choice of meat or fish.* ▣ *The bag is available in a wide choice of colours.* (**escolha variada**)
4 out of choice if you do something out of choice, you do it because you want to do it □ *I wasn't there out of choice. My mother had sent me.* (**por decisão própria**)

choir /ˈkwaɪə(r)/ NOUN [plural **choirs**] a group of singers □ *She sings in the church choir.* (**coro**)

choke /tʃəʊk/ VERB [chokes, choking, choked] to not be able to breathe because something is blocking your throat □ *She choked on a fish bone.* (**sufocar, asfixiar**)

cholera /ˈkɒlərə/ NOUN, NO PLURAL a very infectious disease that affects the stomach and can kill people (**cólera**)

cholesterol /kəˈlestərɒl/ NOUN, NO PLURAL a substance in your body that can cause heart disease if there is too much of it. A biology word □ *My dad's got high cholesterol.* (**colesterol**)

chomp /tʃɒmp/ VERB [chomps, chomping, chomped] to chew noisily. An informal word. □ *She was chomping on a carrot.* (**mastigar**)

choose /tʃuːz/ VERB [chooses, choosing, chose, chosen] to take one particular thing or person from a group of people or things □ *Can you help me choose a present for grandma?* □ *Kitty chose a slice of chocolate cake.* □ *+ between I can't choose between the red one and the pink one.* □ *+ question word How do you choose which charity to give money to?* □ *+ to do something She chose to attend a university near home.* (**escolher**)

• **choosy** /ˈtʃuːzɪ/ ADJECTIVE [choosier, choosiest] wanting to find exactly the right thing. An informal word. (**exigente**)

chop /tʃɒp/ VERB [chops, chopping, chopped] to cut something into pieces □ *Chop the onion into large chunks.* □ *He was chopping wood for the fire.* (**picar**)

◆ PHRASAL VERBS **chop something down** to cut the main part of a tree or big plant so that it falls down (**cortar fora**) **chop something off** to remove a part of something by cutting it (**cortar a golpes**)
◆ IDIOM **chop and change** to keep changing a situation (**mudar de opinião a toda hora**)

▶ NOUN [plural **chops**] a piece of meat, usually with a bone □ *lamb chops* (**costeletas**)

• **chopper** /ˈtʃɒpə(r)/ NOUN [plural **choppers**] an informal word for **helicopter** (= aircraft with blades on top which turn round) (**helicóptero**)

choppy /ˈtʃɒpɪ/ ADJECTIVE [choppier, choppiest] a choppy sea has a lot of little waves caused by the wind (**agitado**)

chopsticks /ˈtʃɒpstɪks/ PLURAL NOUN two thin sticks used for eating with in places such as China and Japan (**palitos de madeira usados como talheres**)

choral /ˈkɔːrəl/ ADJECTIVE sung by or written for a large group of singers □ choral music (**coral**)

chord /kɔːd/ NOUN [plural **chords**] a musical sound made by playing several notes together □ *Andy can play a few chords on the guitar.* (**corda**)

chore /tʃɔː(r)/ NOUN [plural **chores**] something boring that you have to do often in your home □ *I find ironing a real chore.* (**tarefa**)

choreograph /ˈkɒriəɡrɑːf/ VERB [**choreographs, choreographing, choreographed**]
1 to make a dance by deciding the movements the dancers should make (**coreografar**)
2 to carefully organize an event or activity that has many parts (**planejar minuciosamente**)
- **choreographer** /ˌkɒriˈɒɡrəfə(r)/ NOUN [plural **choreographers**] someone whose job is to choreograph dances (**coreógrafo**)
- **choreography** /ˌkɒriˈɒɡrəfi/ NOUN, NO PLURAL the work of planning dance movements for a performance (**coreografia**)

chortle /ˈtʃɔːtəl/ VERB [**chortles, chortling, chortled**] to laugh (**gargalhar**)

chorus /ˈkɔːrəs/ ▶ NOUN [plural **choruses**]
1 the part of a song that you repeat several times □ *We all joined in with the chorus.* (**refrão**)
2 the performers in a show who perform as a group and are not the main characters (**coro**)
3 a large group of people who regularly sing together (**coral**)
▶ VERB [**choruses, chorusing, chorused**] to speak or to sing together. A formal word. □ *'Happy birthday to you', they chorused.* (**cantar em coro**)

chose /tʃəʊz/ PAST TENSE OF **choose** (**ver choose**)

chosen /ˈtʃəʊzən/ ▶ PAST PARTICIPLE OF **choose** (**ver choose**)
▶ ADJECTIVE being something that you have decided to do □ *Was that his chosen career?* (**escolhido**)

Christ /kraɪst/ NOUN Jesus Christ, the holy man that Christians believe is the Son of God (**Cristo**)

christen /ˈkrɪsən/ VERB [**christens, christening, christened**] to give a baby a name in a ceremony and make him or her a member of the Christian religion (**batizar**)
- **christening** /ˈkrɪsənɪŋ/ NOUN [plural **christenings**] a ceremony at which a a baby is christened (**batizado**)

Christian /ˈkrɪstʃən/ ▶ NOUN [plural **Christians**] someone who is a member of the religion that is based on the ideas of Jesus Christ and the Bible (**cristão**)
▶ ADJECTIVE to do with Christianity or Christians (**cristão**)
- **Christianity** /ˌkrɪstiˈænəti/ NOUN, NO PLURAL the religion that is based on the ideas of Jesus Christ and the Bible (**Cristianismo**)

Christian name /ˈkrɪstʃən ˌneɪm/ NOUN [plural **Christian names**] the first name of people from Western countries (**nome de batismo**)

Christmas /ˈkrɪsməs/ ▶ NOUN, NO PLURAL 25 December, the day Christians celebrate the birth of Christ each year □ *Happy Christmas!* (**Natal**)
▶ ADJECTIVE for or to do with Christmas □ *Christmas decorations/presents* (**decoração/presentes de Natal**)

Christmas Day /ˌkrɪsməs ˈdeɪ/ NOUN, NO PLURAL 25 December, the day on which Christmas is celebrated (**dia de Natal**)

Christmas Eve /ˌkrɪsməs ˈiːv/ NOUN, NO PLURAL 24 December, the day before Christmas Day (**véspera de Natal**)

Christmas tree /ˈkrɪsməs ˌtriː/ NOUN [plural **Christmas trees**] a tree that you cover with decorations and lights and put in your house during the Christmas period (**árvore de Natal**)

chromosome /ˈkrəʊməsəʊm/ NOUN [plural **chromosomes**] one of the very small parts in the centre of animal and plant cells that contain the genes (= parts that control what an animal or plant is like). A biology word. (**cromossomo**)

chronic /ˈkrɒnɪk/ ADJECTIVE
1 a chronic disease is one that continues for a long time (**crônico**)
2 an informal way of saying that something is very bad □ *The smell from the lab was really chronic.* (**crônico**)

chronicle /ˈkrɒnɪkəl/ c NOUN [plural **chronicles**] a record of things in the order that they happened (**crônica**)
▶ VERB [**chronicles, chronicling, chronicled**] to write down a record of events in the order that they happen (**narrar os fatos**)

chronological /ˌkrɒnəˈlɒdʒɪkəl/ ADJECTIVE in the order in which events happened □ *List your exam results in chronological order.* (**cronológico**)

chrysalis /ˈkrɪsəlɪs/ NOUN [plural **chrysalises**] an insect such as a moth or butterfly at the stage when it develops inside a hard covering. A biology word. (**crisálida**)

chrysanthemum /krɪˈsænθəməm/ NOUN [plural **chrysanthemums**] a large, brightly coloured flower with a lot of petals (**crisântemo**)

chubby /ˈtʃʌbi/ ADJECTIVE [**chubbier, chubbiest**] quite fat, but in an attractive way □ *the baby's chubby little legs* (**gorducho**)

chuck /tʃʌk/ VERB [**chucks, chucking, chucked**] an informal word meaning to throw something □ *He chucked a towel over to me.* (**atirar**)
◆ PHRASAL VERB **chuck something away/out** an informal phrase meaning to throw something away □ *I chucked out all the half-eaten food.* (**abandonar, deixar de lado**)

chuckle /ˈtʃʌkəl/ ▶ VERB [**chuckles, chuckling, chuckled**] to laugh quietly □ *The story made me chuckle to myself.* (**dar risinho**)

chuffed / circular

▶ NOUN [plural **chuckles**] a quiet laugh (**risadinha**)

chuffed /tʃʌft/ ADJECTIVE an informal word meaning very pleased □ *She's really chuffed about her exam results.* (**satisfeito**)

chug /tʃʌg/ VERB [**chugs, chugging, chugged**] to make a noise like an engine moving slowly, or to move along slowly □ *The little steam train came chugging up the hill.* (**produzir ruído**)

chum /tʃʌm/ NOUN [plural **chums**] an informal word for friend 🔄 *an old school chum* (**amigo**)

• **chummy** /'tʃʌmi/ ADJECTIVE friendly □ *Try not to get too chummy with your staff.* (**amigável**)

chunk /tʃʌŋk/ NOUN [plural **chunks**]
1 a thick piece of something □ *a chunk of cheese* □ *pineapple chunks* (**naco**)
2 a large part of something □ *We had to use quite a chunk of our savings to pay for the damage to the car.* (**bloco**)

• **chunky** /'tʃʌŋki/ ADJECTIVE [**chunkier, chunkiest**]
1 thick and heavy □ *a warm chunky sweater* (**espesso**)
2 a chunky person is short and heavy (**massudo**)

church /tʃɜːtʃ/ NOUN [plural **churches**] a building where people, especially Christians, go to pray (**igreja**) 🔄 *Do you go to church?* (**vai à igreja**)

churchyard /'tʃɜːtʃjɑːd/ NOUN [plural **churchyards**] the land around a church, where people are buried (**cemitério**)

churlish /'tʃɜːlɪʃ/ ADJECTIVE rude and not grateful □ *It would be churlish to refuse his generous offer.* (**rude**)

churn /tʃɜːn/ ▶ NOUN [plural **churns**] a machine for making butter from milk (**batedeira**)
▶ VERB [**churns, churning, churned**]
1 to mix something up so that the surface is rough □ *The ground was churned up by all the car tyres.* (**bater, mexer**)
2 if your stomach is churning, it feels uncomfortable because you are nervous (**agitar**)
3 to mix milk inside a churn to make it into butter (**fazer manteiga**)

♦ PHRASAL VERB **churn something out** to produce large quantities of something quickly and without much care □ *She manages to churn out a novel every six months.* (**produzir algo continuamente**)

chute /ʃuːt/ NOUN [plural **chutes**] a long, thin sloping structure that water, objects or people slide down □ *a laundry chute* (**tubo inclinado, rampa**)

chutney /'tʃʌtni/ NOUN [plural **chutneys**] a thick substance like jam, made from fruit or vegetables with vinegar (= sour brown liquid) and spices, which you eat with meat or cheese (**molho picante**)

CIA /ˌsiːaɪˈeɪ/ ABBREVIATION Central Intelligence Agency; the US organization that tries to get secret information about other countries (**CIA**)

ciabatta /tʃəˈbɑːtə/ NOUN [plural **ciabattas**] a type of quite flat Italian bread (**tipo de pão italiano**)

cider /'saɪdə(r)/ NOUN, NO PLURAL an alcoholic drink made from apples (**cidra**)

cigar /sɪˈgɑː(r)/ NOUN [plural **cigars**] a thick tube made from dried tobacco leaves that people smoke (**charuto**)

cigarette /ˌsɪgəˈret/ NOUN [plural **cigarettes**] a thin tube of paper filled with tobacco that people smoke (**cigarro**)

cinder /'sɪndə(r)/ NOUN [plural **cinders**] a small piece of wood, paper, etc. that has been burned (**cinza, brasa**)

cinema /'sɪnəmə/ NOUN [plural **cinemas**]
1 a place where you go to watch a film on a big screen □ *We went to the cinema last night.* (**cinema**)
2 no plural the art or industry of making films □ *a career in cinema* (**cinema**)

cinnamon /'sɪnəmən/ NOUN, NO PLURAL a brown spice used to give flavour to cakes and other food (**canela**)

circa /'sɜːkə/ PREPOSITION a word used before a date or a number to show that it is not exact □ *circa 1850* (**aproximadamente**)

circle /'sɜːkəl/ ▶ NOUN [plural **circles**]
1 a flat shape whose outside edge is a continuous curved line which is always the same distance away from a central point □ *Draw one circle for the head and another for the body.* □ *Form a circle in the centre of the room.* (**círculo**)
2 a group of people who know each other or do a particular activity together □ *a sewing circle* □ *He's not part of my circle of friends.* (**círculo**)
3 the circle the upper area of seats in a theatre or cinema (**balcão**)
▶ VERB [**circles, circling, circled**]
1 to move in a circle □ *Vultures circled overhead.* □ *Several planes were circling the airport.* (**cercar, rodear**)
2 to draw a circle around something □ *She circled the area on the map with a red pen.* (**circular**)

circuit /'sɜːkɪt/ NOUN [plural **circuits**]
1 a path, route or track that forms a circle □ *He drove five laps of the circuit.* (**circuito**)
2 the path that electricity goes along between two points (**circuito**)
3 a series of places or events regularly visited by people involved in a particular activity □ *the international golf circuit* (**circuito**)

circular /'sɜːkjʊlə(r)/ ▶ ADJECTIVE
1 in the shape of a circle □ *a circular window* (**circular**)
2 a circular journey or route finishes in the same place that it started (**circular**)
▶ NOUN [plural **circulars**] a letter or advertisement sent to a lot of different people (**circular**)

circulate

circulate /'sɜːkjuleɪt/ VERB [circulates, circulating, circulated]
1 to send something to all the members of a group □ *Details of the meeting will be circulated to all members of staff.* (**circular**)
2 if information, ideas, etc. circulate, they are passed to a lot of people (**circular, difundir**) 🔁 *Rumours are circulating that hundreds of jobs will be lost.* (**rumores estão circulando**)
3 to move around or through something □ *Water circulates in the central heating system.* (**circular**)

• **circulation** /ˌsɜːkjuˈleɪʃən/ NOUN, NO PLURAL
1 the movement of blood around your body. A biology word □ *I have very poor circulation.* (**circulação**)
2 movement around or through something □ *This system controls the circulation of air.* (**circulação**)
3 in circulation being passed from one person to another □ *These fake banknotes are still in circulation.* (**em circulação**)
4 the number of copies of a particular newspaper or magazine that are regularly sold □ *a fall in circulation* (**tiragem**)

circumcise /'sɜːkəmsaɪz/ VERB [circumcises, circumcising, circumcised] to cut away the loose skin covering the end of the penis, either for medical or for religious reasons (**circuncidar**)

• **circumcision** /ˌsɜːkəmˈsɪʒən/ NOUN [plural circumcisions] an operation to circumcise a man or a boy (**circuncisão**)

circumference /səˈkʌmfərəns/ NOUN [plural circumferences] the outside edge of a circle, or the length of the outside edge of a circle. A maths word. □ *Mark a point on the circumference of the circle and draw a line through it.* □ *What's the circumference of this coin?* (**circunferência**)

circumflex /'sɜːkəmfleks/ NOUN [plural circumflexes] the symbol (^) that is put over some letters in some languages (**circunflexo**)

circumspect /'sɜːkəmspekt/ ADJECTIVE a formal word meaning careful about what you do or say □ *She learnt to be more circumspect when talking to reporters.* (**circunspecto, prudente**)

circumstances /'sɜːkəmstənsɪz/ PLURAL NOUN
1 the events or conditions that affect or cause a particular situation (**circunstância**) 🔁 *His reaction was understandable under the circumstances* (= when you consider the situation). (**em tais circunstâncias**) 🔁 *Refunds of the fee are only allowed in exceptional circumstances.*
2 under no circumstances used for saying that something must not happen □ *Under no circumstances should you attempt to climb without a rope.* (**de jeito nenhum**)
3 the conditions you live in, especially how much money you have □ *You must notify the authorities of any change in your circumstances.* (**condições**)

• **circumstantial** /ˌsɜːkəmˈstænʃəl/ ADJECTIVE circumstantial evidence makes you believe something is true but does not prove it (**circunstancial**)

civil engineer

circumvent /ˌsɜːkəmˈvent/ VERB [circumvents, circumventing, circumvented] a formal word meaning to find a way of avoiding a law or a difficulty □ *She was accused of using her fame to circumvent the country's adoption rules.* (**evitar**)

circus /'sɜːkəs/ NOUN [plural circuses] a show performed in a big tent by people and often trained animals □ *We're taking the children to the circus tonight.* (**circo**)

cistern /'sɪstən/ NOUN [plural cisterns] a container for storing water, especially one connected to a toilet (**cisterna**)

citadel /'sɪtədəl/ NOUN [plural citadels] a strong castle inside a city where people went in the past if they were attacked (**citadela, fortaleza**)

cite /saɪt/ VERB [cites, citing, cited] to mention something as an example or as proof □ *Try to cite some examples of good environmental schemes in your essay.* (**citar, mencionar**)

citizen /'sɪtɪzən/ NOUN [plural citizens]
1 someone who lives in a particular town, state or country □ *citizens of Paris* (**cidadão**)
2 someone who has the right to live in a particular country permanently □ *He lives in Singapore but he's an Australian citizen.* (**cidadão, residente**)

• **citizenship** /'sɪtɪzənʃɪp/ NOUN, NO PLURAL
1 the legal right to live in a particular country □ *She's applied for Canadian citizenship.* (**cidadania**)
2 the responsibilities and duties you have as a citizen □ *Children should be taught good citizenship.* (**direitos e deveres do cidadão**)

citrus fruit /'sɪtrəs ˌfruːt/ NOUN [plural citrus fruits] a fruit with a thick skin and a lot of juice, for example an orange or a lemon (**frutas cítricas**)

city /'sɪti/ NOUN [plural cities] a large, important town (**cidade**) 🔁 *Paris is the capital city of France.* (**capital**) □ *the city streets*

civic /'sɪvɪk/ ADJECTIVE to do with a city or the people who live in it □ *civic pride* (**cívico**)

civil /'sɪvəl/ ADJECTIVE
1 to do with ordinary people, not people in military or religious organizations □ *civil life* □ *a civil marriage ceremony* (**civil**)
2 to do with private legal arguments, not criminal matters □ *a civil court* (**civil**)
3 talking or behaving in a polite way □ *He found it hard to be civil to his ex-boss.* (**gentil**)
4 involving the people who live in a country □ *They started a campaign of civil disobedience.* (**cívico**)

civil engineer /ˌsɪvəl endʒɪˈnɪə(r)/ NOUN [plural civil engineers] someone whose job is to plan and build public buildings and things like roads and bridges (**engenheiro civil**)

• **civil engineering** /ˌsɪvəl endʒɪˈnɪərɪŋ/ NOUN, NO PLURAL the work of a civil engineer (**engenharia civil**)

civilian /sɪˈvɪljən/ NOUN [plural **civilians**] a person who is not a member of a military organization or the police (**civil**)

civilization or **civilisation** /ˌsɪvɪlaɪˈzeɪʃən/ NOUN [plural **civilizations**]
1 a society that has its own culture and organizations □ *ancient civilizations* (**civilização**)
2 the process in which a society develops its own culture and organizations (**civilização**)

civilize or **civilise** /ˈsɪvɪlaɪz/ VERB [**civilizes, civilizing, civilized**]
1 to help a society to develop its culture or organizations (**civilizar**)
2 to teach someone how to behave more politely (**educar**)

• **civilized** or **civilised** /ˈsɪvɪlaɪzd/ ADJECTIVE
1 a civilized society or country has an advanced culture and organizations (**civilizado**)
2 behaving politely and reasonably, without arguing □ *Let's try and have a civilized discussion instead of all shouting at once.* (**educado**)
3 pleasant and comfortable □ *'This is all very civilized', he said, sipping his champagne.* (**civilizado**)

civil liberties /ˌsɪvəl ˈlɪbətiz/ PLURAL NOUN the basic rights you have to speak and behave in the way you want as long as you do not break the law (**liberdades civis**)

civil partnership /ˌsɪvəl ˈpɑːtnəʃɪp/ NOUN [plural **civil partnerships**] an arrangement like a marriage between people of the same sex (**sociedade civil**)

civil rights /ˌsɪvəl ˈraɪts/ PLURAL NOUN your basic rights to be treated fairly in society, to express yourself, and to practise your religion (**direitos civis**)

civil servant /ˌsɪvəl ˈsɜːvənt/ NOUN [plural **civil servants**] someone who works in the civil service of a country (**funcionário público**)

• **civil service** /ˌsɪvəl ˈsɜːvɪs/ NOUN **the civil service** all the departments of the government and the people who work in them (**serviço público**)

civil war /ˌsɪvəl ˈwɔː(r)/ NOUN [plural **civil wars**] a war between different groups within the same country (**guerra civil**)

CJD /ˌsiːdʒeɪˈdiː/ ABBREVIATION Creutzfeldt-Jakob Disease; a serious illness that destroys your brain cells and can kill you (**CJ; rara doença degenerativa cerebral**)

cl ABBREVIATION **centilitre** or **centilitres** (**cl**)

clad /klæd/ ADJECTIVE a formal word meaning dressed or covered □ *mountains clad in snow* (**coberto**)

claim /kleɪm/ ▶ VERB [**claims, claiming, claimed**]
1 to say that something is true, even though there is no clear proof □ *Marco claims he saw a flying saucer.* □ *The group claims to represent over a million workers.* (**afirmar**)

2 to officially ask for something as your right or to say that it is yours □ *You'll need to fill in this form to claim unemployment benefit.* □ *If no one claims any of the lost items they will be sold for charity.* (**reclamar**)
3 claim responsibility/victory, etc. to say that you have done something or achieved something □ *Raj did all the cooking – I can't claim any credit.* □ *A left-wing group has claimed responsibility for the attack.* (**reivindicar responsabilidade/vitória etc.**)
▶ NOUN [plural **claims**]
1 a statement that something is true although it has not been proved (**reclamação**) □ *The government has rejected claims that pensions will fall.* (**rejeitou reclamações**) □ *He denied claims of racism.* (**negou as reclamações**)
2 when you ask for something that you have a right to or that you say is yours (**reivindicação**) □ *He was convicted of making false insurance claims.* (**falsas reivindicações**) □ *compensation claims* (**reivindicação de compensação**)

• **claimant** /ˈkleɪmənt/ NOUN [plural **claimants**] someone who makes a claim for money (**reclamante**)

clairvoyant /kleəˈvɔɪənt/ ▶ ADJECTIVE able to see what will happen in the future (**vidente**)
▶ NOUN [plural **clairvoyants**] someone who says that they know what will happen in the future (**vidente**)

clam /klæm/ NOUN [plural **clams**] a small sea creature with two shells that are joined at one side, which can be eaten (**molusco**)
◆ PHRASAL VERB [**clams, clamming, clammed**] **clam up** to stop talking because you are embarrassed or want something to be a secret □ *When I asked him about his wife, he just clammed up.* (**perder a fala**)

clamber /ˈklæmbə(r)/ VERB [**clambers, clambering, clambered**] to climb up or over things using your hands and feet □ *They tried to clamber up the steep and slippery slope.* (**escalar**)

clammy /ˈklæmi/ ADJECTIVE [**clammier, clammiest**] slightly wet, in an unpleasant, sticky way □ *His hands became clammy with fear.* (**pegajoso**)

clamor /ˈklæmə(r)/ VERB [**clamors, clamoring, clamored**], NOUN, NO PLURAL the US spelling of **clamour** (**clamor**)

clamour /ˈklæmə(r)/ ▶ VERB [**clamours, clamouring, clamoured**] to try to get something by asking for it loudly □ *All the children were clamouring to see what was in the box.* (**clamar**)
▶ NOUN, NO PLURAL noisy shouts or demands (**clamor**)

clamp /klæmp/ ▶ NOUN [plural **clamps**]
1 a tool for holding things together tightly (**braçadeira**)
2 a piece of equipment attached tightly to something to stop it moving □ *a wheel clamp* (**cinta, fita**)

clampdown

▶ VERB [clamps, clamping, clamped] to put a clamp on something ☐ *Clamp the two pieces of Wood together until the glue dries.* (colar, firmar)

◆ PHRASAL VERB **clamp down** to try hard to stop something bad or illegal ☐ *We will have to clamp down on litter if we want to clean up the city.* (impor restrição a)

clampdown /ˈklæmpdaʊn/ NOUN [plural clampdowns] a strong effort to control or stop something bad or illegal ☐ *More police officers are being sent to the area as part of a clampdown on street crime.* (repressão)

clan /klæn/ NOUN [plural clans] a group of families that are related to each other, especially in Scotland (clã)

clandestine /klænˈdestɪn/ ADJECTIVE a formal word meaning secret or hidden, especially because something is not allowed ☐ *a clandestine meeting* (clandestino)

clang /klæŋ/ ▶ VERB [clangs, clanging, clanged] to make a loud ringing sound, like a heavy piece of metal hitting against something hard ☐ *The prison gate clanged shut behind them.* (retinir, ressoar)
▶ NOUN [plural clangs] a loud ringing sound (clangor)

clank /klæŋk/ ▶ VERB [clanks, clanking, clanked] to make a short loud sound, like metal hitting metal ☐ *Strange machines were clanking in the gloomy shed.* (retinir)
▶ NOUN [plural clanks] a short loud sound like metal hitting metal (ruído)

clap /klæp/ ▶ VERB [claps, clapping, clapped]
1 to hit your hands together, especially to show that you like or admire someone or something ☐ *The audience clapped and cheered.* ☐ *We all clapped in time to the music.* (aplaudir, bater palmas)
2 to hit someone lightly on their shoulder or back to show you are pleased with them ☐ *He clapped his brother on the back.* (dar tapas)
▶ NOUN [plural claps]
1 when you clap your hands (aplaudir) *Let's all give Adam a clap.* (dar uma salva de palmas)
2 a clap of thunder a sudden very loud sound made by thunder (trovoada)

clapped-out /ˌklæptˈaʊt/ ADJECTIVE an informal word meaning old and not working correctly ☐ *a clapped out car* (velho e quebrado)

claptrap /ˈklæptræp/ NOUN, NO PLURAL an informal word meaning nonsense ☐ *He described the report as utter claptrap.* (besteira)

clarification /ˌklærɪfɪˈkeɪʃən/ NOUN [plural clarifications] when someone makes something clearer or easier to understand ☐ *Do the rules require any further clarification?* (esclarecimento)

clarify /ˈklærɪfaɪ/ VERB [clarifies, clarifying, clarified] to make something clearer or easier to understand ☐ *I asked her to clarify her remarks.* (esclarecer)

classic

clarinet /ˌklærəˈnet/ NOUN [plural clarinets] a musical instrument shaped like a long tube that you play by blowing through it and pressing its keys with your fingers (clarinete)

• **clarinettist** /ˌklærəˈnetɪst/ NOUN [plural clarinettists] someone who plays the clarinet (clarinetista)

clarity /ˈklærətɪ/ NOUN, NO PLURAL how clear or easy to understand something is ☐ *the clarity of the image* (clareza)

clash /klæʃ/ ▶ VERB [clashes, clashing, clashed]
1 if two people or groups clash, they fight or disagree angrily with each other ☐ *Protesters clashed with the police.* (embater-se)
2 if two events clash, they happen at the same time ☐ *Unfortunately the meeting clashes with my piano exam.* (colidir)
3 if two colours clash, they do not look good together ☐ *The purple clashes with the red.* (não combinar)
4 if two metal objects clash, they make a loud sound as they hit each other (estrondear)
▶ NOUN [plural clashes]
1 an angry disagreement or fight ☐ *There were violent clashes between students and the police today.* (embate)
2 a sound made when two metal objects hit against each other (estrondo)

clasp /klɑːsp/ ▶ VERB [clasps, clasping, clasped] to hold something or someone tightly ☐ *Jenny was clasping a baby in her arms.* (segurar)
▶ NOUN [plural clasps]
1 a small metal object used to fasten a bag, belt, or piece of jewellery ☐ *The clasp's broken on this brooch.* (fivela, broche)
2 a way of holding something tightly (fecho, grampo)

class /klɑːs/ ▶ NOUN [plural classes]
1 a group of students who are taught together, or a period of time during which a particular subject is taught ☐ *Hannah's in my class at school.* ☐ *I'm going to my aerobics class tonight.* (aula)
2 one of the social groups into which people can be divided according to their family, income, job, etc. ☐ *the working class* (classe)
3 a division of things according to how good they are ☐ *Abby's a first class student.* ☐ *a second class degree* (categoria)
4 a group of animals or plants that are related to each other or have similar qualities (classe)
▶ VERB [classes, classing, classed] to put people or things in a group with others that have similar qualities ☐ *+ as Anyone under 16 is classed as a junior member.* (classificar)

classic /ˈklæsɪk/ NOUN [plural classics] a great book or other work of art that is admired for a long time after it was written or made ☐ *great film classics* (clássico)
⇨ go to **classics**
▶ ADJECTIVE

classical music

1 very good and popular for a long time □ *classic children's stories* (**clássico**)
2 a classic example of something is very typical □ *He made the classic mistake of thinking that he could do all his studying in the week before the exam.* (**clássico**)
3 traditional in a way that is of high quality □ *classic clothes* (**clássico**)

• **classical** /ˈklæsɪkəl/ ADJECTIVE
1 belonging to the style or culture of ancient Greece or Rome □ *classical architecture* (**clássico**)
2 traditional □ *classical ballet* (**clássico**)

classical music /ˌklæsɪkəl ˈmjuːzɪk/ NOUN,
NO PLURAL traditional, serious music written by people like Beethoven and Verdi (**música clássica**)

classics /ˈklæsɪks/ NOUN, NO PLURAL the study of the literature, languages and culture of ancient Greece and Rome (**clássicos, obras clássicas**)

classification /ˌklæsɪfɪˈkeɪʃən/ NOUN [*plural* **classifications**]
1 *no plural* the process of putting things into groups according to the qualities they have (**classificação**)
2 a group that includes people or things with the same qualities (**classificação**)

classified /ˈklæsɪfaɪd/ ADJECTIVE classified information is secret and known only by the government (**confidencial**)

classify /ˈklæsɪfaɪ/ VERB [**classifies, classifying, classified**] to put people or things into groups or classes according to what qualities they have □ *The books are classified by subject.* (**classificar**)

classmate /ˈklɑːsmeɪt/ NOUN [*plural* **classmates**] someone in your school or college class (**colega de classe**)

classroom /ˈklɑːsruːm/ NOUN [*plural*
classrooms] a room where students have lessons (**sala de aula**)

classy /ˈklɑːsi/ ADJECTIVE [**classier, classiest**] attractive, fashionable and expensive □ *a classy hotel* (**refinado**)

clatter /ˈklætə(r)/ ▶ VERB [**clatters, clattering, clattered**] to make a loud noise like hard objects falling or hitting each other □ *He came clattering downstairs in his ski boots.* (**retinir**)
▶ NOUN, NO PLURAL a sound made when hard objects fall or hit against each other (**ruído**) 🔊 *The plates fell to the floor with a clatter.* (**com um ruído**)

clause /klɔːz/ NOUN [*plural* **clauses**]
1 a group of words that makes up a sentence or part of a sentence □ *a relative clause* (**oração**)
2 a part of an official document or a law □ *clause 10 of the contract* (**cláusula**)

claustrophobia /ˌklɔːstrəˈfəʊbiə/ NOUN, NO PLURAL a fear of small, crowded or closed spaces (**claustrofobia**)

• **claustrophobic** /ˌklɔːstrəˈfəʊbɪk/ ADJECTIVE afraid of small, crowded or closed spaces (**claustrofóbico**)

claw /klɔː/ ▶ NOUN [*plural* **claws**]
1 one of the long pointed nails on the toes of some animals and birds (**garra**)
2 a long part at the end of the leg of some sea creatures and insects, that is used for holding things (**presa**)
▶ VERB [**claws, clawing, clawed**] to scratch something with claws or nails □ *The cat had been clawing at the sofa.* (**arranhar**)

clay /kleɪ/ NOUN, NO PLURAL a soft sticky
substance in the ground that goes hard when it is baked and is used for making cups and bowls □ *clay pots* (**barro**)

clean /kliːn/ ADJECTIVE [**cleaner, cleanest**]
1 not dirty □ *clean hands* □ *a clean kitchen* □ *clean air* □ *clean drinking water* (**limpo**) 🔊 *Everywhere looked clean and tidy.* (**limpo e arrumado**)
2 with no writing on □ *a clean sheet of paper* (**em branco**)
3 showing that you have done nothing bad or illegal (**limpo**) 🔊 *a clean driving licence* (= one that shows no driving crimes) (**carteira de habilitação limpa**)
4 honest □ *a clean election* (**honesto**)
♦ IDIOMS **come clean** to start to tell the truth about something (**confessar**) **make a clean breast of something** to tell someone the truth about something you had been keeping secret (**confessar**)
▶ VERB [**cleans, cleaning, cleaned**] to remove the dirt from something □ *I've just been cleaning the kitchen.* □ *Have you cleaned your teeth?* (**limpar**)
♦ PHRASAL VERBS **clean something out** to remove things from a place and clean it very well (**limpar, colocar em ordem**) □ *I've cleaned out the car.* **clean (something) up** to make a place clean and tidy, removing any rubbish □ *I'll start cleaning up this mess.* (**limpar**) **clean up after someone** to clean a place after someone has made it dirty □ *I'm sick of cleaning up after you!* (**limpar a bagunça feita por alguém**)
▶ ADVERB completely □ *I clean forgot I was supposed to meet her.* (**totalmente**)

• **cleaner** /ˈkliːnə(r)/ NOUN [*plural* **cleaners**]
1 someone whose job is to clean places □ *The cleaner comes in once a week.* (**limpador, faxineiro**)
2 a liquid for cleaning things □ *oven cleaner* (**limpador**)

• **cleaning** /ˈkliːnɪŋ/ NOUN, NO PLURAL the activity of making a place clean (**limpeza**) 🔊 *My mother does all the cleaning.* (**faz a limpeza**)

• **cleanliness** /ˈklenlɪnɪs/ NOUN, NO PLURAL the state of being clean or the process of keeping something clean (**limpeza**)

• **cleanly** /ˈkliːnli/ ADVERB if something breaks cleanly, it breaks completely and in a tidy way □ *The log split cleanly in half.* (**perfeitamente**)

cleanse /klenz/ VERB [cleanses, cleansing, cleansed] to clean your skin or a cut □ *Cleanse the wound with antiseptic.* (purificar)

- **cleanser** /'klenzə(r)/ NOUN [plural cleansers] a liquid or cream that cleanses your skin (produtos de limpeza)

clear /klɪə(r)/ ▶ ADJECTIVE [clearer, clearest]

1 easy to understand □ *I gave clear instructions.* □ *He drew a very clear map.* (claro)

2 obvious □ + *that* It was clear that she wasn't happy. (claro) 🔲 *Sally made her feelings very clear.* (deixou claro)

3 easy to see or hear □ *The recording wasn't very clear.* □ *The pictures were very clear.* (claro)

4 transparent □ *clear glass* (transparente)

5 not blocked or covered by anything □ *a clear sky* □ *a clear view of the stage* □ + *of* The road was clear of traffic. (desimpedido)

▶ VERB [clears, clearing, cleared]

1 to remove people or things from a place □ *I'll just clear these dishes.* □ *Police cleared the streets around the car bomb.* (desimpedir)

2 if the sky or the weather clears, it becomes brighter (clarear)

3 if a judge or other person in authority clears someone of a crime, the judge decides that person is not guilty □ + *of* He was cleared of all charges. (inocentar, absolver)

4 to jump over something without touching it □ *The pony cleared all the fences.* (transpor)

◆ IDIOM **clear the air** to improve a problem that you have with someone by talking to them about it □ *Yesterday's meeting helped to clear the air.* (esclarecer as coisas)

◆ PHRASAL VERBS **clear something away** to remove things that you have finished using in order to make a place tidy □ *I'll just clear away my papers.* (desobstruir) **clear (something) up** to make a place tidy □ *I helped to clear up after the party.* (colocar em ordem) **clear up** to get better □ *Her skin problem has cleared up.* □ *The weather has cleared up.* (melhorar)

▶ ADVERB not near something or not touching it (longe) 🔲 *Stand clear off the doors.* (longe)

▶ NOUN, NO PLURAL **in the clear** (a) not guilty of a crime or mistake (b) not in a bad situation any more □ *The goal put the team in the clear.* (livre de suspeita, fora de perigo)

- **clearance** /'klɪərəns/ NOUN [plural clearances]

1 no plural official permission to do something □ *The plane was given clearance to land.* (autorização)

2 no plural the amount of space between one thing and another that is moving past it (espaço livre)

3 the process of removing things that are not wanted (desimpedido)

clear-cut /ˌklɪə(r)'kʌt/ ADJECTIVE obvious and not causing doubt □ *This was a clear-cut case of abuse.* (claro)

clearing /'klɪərɪŋ/ NOUN [plural clearings] an area in a forest where there are no trees (clareira)

clearly /'klɪəli/ ADVERB

1 in a way that is easy to see, hear, or understand □ *You can see it quite clearly in the photo.* □ *She explained it very clearly.* (claramente)

2 obviously □ *Clearly, we can't do the job without enough people.* (claramente)

cleaver /'kliːvə(r)/ NOUN [plural cleavers] a knife with a large, square blade (cutelo)

clef /klef/ NOUN [plural clefs] a symbol used at the beginning of a piece of music to show how high or low the notes are (clave)

clemency /'klemənsi/ NOUN, NO PLURAL a decision that a king or leader makes not to punish someone severely. A formal word. (clemência)

clementine /'kleməntaɪn/ NOUN [plural clementines] a fruit like a small orange. (pequena laranja)

clench /klentʃ/ VERB [clenches, clenching, clenched] to close part of your body tightly or press it tightly together □ *Clenching his teeth, he jumped out of the plane.* (apertar, cerrar)

clergy /'klɜːdʒi/ PLURAL NOUN priests, especially in the Christian church (clero)

clergyman /'klɜːdʒɪmən/ NOUN [plural clergymen] a man who is a priest (clérigo, sacerdote)

clergywoman /'klɜːdʒɪwʊmən/ NOUN [plural clergywomen] a woman who is a priest (sacerdotisa)

cleric /'klerɪk/ NOUN [plural clerics] a member of the clergy (= priests) (clérigo)

- **clerical** /'klerɪkəl/ ADJECTIVE

1 involved in office work □ *a clerical assistant* (eclesiástico)

2 used by or to do with the clergy (= priests) □ *a clerical collar* (clerical)

clerk /klɑːk/ NOUN [plural clerks]

1 an office worker whose job is to write letters, store documents, or keep financial records (empregado de escritório)

2 the US word for *shop assistant* (vendedor)

clever /'klevə(r)/ ADJECTIVE [cleverer, cleverest]

1 good at learning and understanding things □ *He was a very clever boy.* (esperto)

2 showing good understanding and intelligence □ *a clever idea* (engenhoso)

3 skilful □ + *with* She's always been clever with her hands.* (habilidoso)

cliché /'kliːʃeɪ/ NOUN [plural clichés] a phrase that has been used so often it is not now interesting or original (clichê)

click /klɪk/ ▶ VERB [clicks, clicking, clicked]

1 to press a button on a computer mouse in order to make the computer do something. A com-

client   **clique**

puting word. ☐ *Just type your message and click 'Send'.* ☐ *+ on Click on the icon to open the program.* (**clicar**)

2 to make a short, sharp sound ☐ *We could hear her heels clicking on the stone floor.* (**estalar**)

▶ NOUN [*plural* **clicks**]

1 a short, sharp sound ☐ *The box closed with a click.* (**clique**)

2 when you press a button on a computer mouse to make the computer do something. A computing word. ☐ *You can place your order with just one click.* (**clique**)

client /ˈklaɪənt/ NOUN [*plural* **clients**] someone who pays someone else for a service (**cliente**)

cliff /klɪf/ NOUN [*plural* **cliffs**] the high, steep side of a piece of land, usually next to the sea (**penhasco**)

climactic /klaɪˈmæktɪk/ ADJECTIVE a climactic point or event is the most exciting or important one of a series (**relativo a clímax**)

climate /ˈklaɪmɪt/ NOUN [*plural* **climates**]

1 the type of weather that a country or area usually gets ☐ *These plants only grow in hot climates.* (**clima**)

2 the situation and opinions that exist at a particular time ☐ *It's a risky decision in the current political climate.* (**clima**)

climate change /ˈklaɪmɪt ˌtʃeɪndʒ/ NOUN, NO PLURAL the way the weather is changing and the Earth is getting warmer ☐ *a conference on climate change* (**mudanças climáticas**)

climax /ˈklaɪmæks/ NOUN [*plural* **climaxes**] the most important, most exciting or most interesting point in a story or situation ☐ *The climax of the show was a dazzling firework display.* (**clímax**)

climb /klaɪm/ ▶ VERB [**climbs, climbing, climbed**]

1 to go up or to go towards the top, often using your hands and feet ☐ *He likes to climb trees.* ☐ *It's a very difficult mountain to climb.* (**escalar**)

2 to get into or out of something ☐ *+ into He climbed into his car and drove off.* (**subir**)

3 to increase in number ☐ *By last year, the number of people without a job had climbed to 2 million.* (**subir**)

◆ PHRASAL VERB **climb down** to admit that your opinion was wrong, especially after an argument (**voltar atrás**)

▶ NOUN [*plural* **climbs**] an act of climbing or the distance you climb ☐ *We had a steep climb to the top.* (**escalada**)

• **climber** /ˈklaɪmə(r)/ NOUN [*plural* **climbers**]

1 someone who climbs, often as a hobby or sport ☐ *a very experienced climber* (**alpinista**)

2 a plant that grows upwards by attaching itself to things like walls and fences (**trepadeira**)

clinch /klɪntʃ/ VERB [**clinches, clinching, clinched**] to do one last thing to win an agreement, argument or game (**decidir, encerrar**) ▣ *That second goal has surely clinched it for United.* (**decidiu a favor de**)

cling /klɪŋ/ VERB [**clings, clinging, clung**]

1 to hold on to something tightly, usually because you are afraid ☐ *The child clung to her mother.* (**agarrar-se**)

2 to stick to or to fit something very tightly ☐ *His wet shirt clung to his body.* (**grudar, aderir**)

clingfilm /ˈklɪŋfɪlm/ NOUN, NO PLURAL a very thin sheet of plastic that is used to cover food (**papel-filme**)

clinic /ˈklɪnɪk/ NOUN [*plural* **clinics**] a place where people can see doctors to get treatment and advice (**clínica**)

• **clinical** /ˈklɪnɪkəl/ ADJECTIVE

1 involving working with people who are ill instead of doing tests in a laboratory (**médico**) ▣ *clinical trials* (**ensaios clínicos**)

2 not showing any emotion and not considering other people's feelings ☐ *a clinical approach* (**frio**)

clink /klɪŋk/ ▶ NOUN [*plural* **clinks**] a sharp ringing sound like the sound made when glasses or coins are hit together ☐ *the clink of glasses* (**tinido**)

▶ VERB [**clinks, clinking, clinked**] to make a clink sound (**tinir**)

clip /klɪp/ ▶ VERB [**clips, clipping, clipped**]

1 to cut small or short parts off something ☐ *He was busy clipping the hedge.* (**podar, tosquiar**)

2 to fasten something to something else with a pin ☐ *He had a badge clipped to his lapel.* (**prender**)

▶ NOUN [*plural* **clips**]

1 a small object that fastens something together or to something else (**clipe**) ▣ *a paper clip* (**clipe de papel**) ▣ *a hair clip* (**grampo de cabelo**)

2 a short piece from a film or television programme ☐ *I've seen a clip from his new film.* (**trailer**)

clip art /ˈklɪp ˌɑːt/ NOUN, NO PLURAL pictures that you can copy into your own computer documents. A computing word. (**clip art**)

clipboard /ˈklɪpbɔːd/ NOUN [*plural* **clipboards**]

1 a place on a computer for storing information so that you can copy it into another document. A computing word. (**área de transferência**)

2 a piece of strong card with a metal part at the top that you fasten paper to and write on as you move around (**quadro de edição**)

clippers /ˈklɪpəz/ PLURAL NOUN a tool used for cutting small bits from things ☐ *nail clippers* (**cortador**)

clique /kliːk/ NOUN [*plural* **cliques**] a small group of people who are friendly to each other but keep other people out of the group (**grupo**)

- **cliquey** /'kli:kɪ/ ADJECTIVE [cliquier, cliquiest] behaving like a clique (**referente a um grupo fechado**)

cloak /kləʊk/ ▶ NOUN [plural **cloaks**]
1 a loose coat without sleeves that hangs down from the shoulders (**capa**)
2 **a cloak of something** something that hides the truth. A literary phrase. □ *His business dealings were hidden under a cloak of secrecy.* (**um manto de algo**)
▶ VERB [**cloaks, cloaking, cloaked**] to cover or hide something. A literary word. □ *The hills were cloaked in mist.* (**esconder**)

cloakroom /'kləʊkru:m/ NOUN [plural **cloakrooms**] a room or area in a building where visitors can leave their coats, hats and bags (**vestiário**)

clobber /'klɒbə(r)/ VERB [**clobbers, clobbering, clobbered**]
1 to hit someone hard. An informal word. (**surrar**)
2 to defeat someone. An informal word. □ *The home team got clobbered.* (**derrotar**)

clock /klɒk/ NOUN [plural **clocks**] an object which shows the time □ *an alarm clock* □ *There's a clock on the kitchen wall.* (**relógio**)
♦ IDIOM **around/round the clock** during all of the day and all of the night □ *Emergency services have been working around the clock to find survivors.* (**24 horas por dia**)
♦ PHRASAL VERB [**clocks, clocking, clocked**] **clock up something** to get a particular number of something over a period of time □ *He clocked up over 100 goals for his country.* (**registrar ou acumular algo**)

clockwise /'klɒkwaɪz/ ADVERB, ADJECTIVE turning or moving in the same direction as the hands of a clock □ *a clockwise direction* □ *Turn the knob clockwise.* (**sentido horário**)

clockwork /'klɒkwɜ:k/ NOUN, NO PLURAL **go/run like clockwork** to happen correctly, with no stops or problems (**sair às mil maravilhas**)

clog /klɒg/ ▶ VERB [**clogs, clogging, clogged**] to block something or be blocked □ *The drains are clogged up with leaves.* (**entupir**)
▶ NOUN [plural **clogs**] a shoe with a wooden bottom (**tamanco**)

cloister /'klɔɪstə(r)/ NOUN [plural **cloisters**] a covered passage around the edge of a square garden in a religious building (**abóbada**)

clone /kləʊn/ ▶ NOUN [plural **clones**] an exact copy of a plant or animal, made by a scientist taking cells from that plant or animal (**clone**)
▶ VERB [**clones, cloning, cloned**] to make an exact copy of a plant or animal in this way □ *Scientists have successfully cloned a sheep.* (**clonar**)

close[1] /kləʊz/ ▶ VERB [**closes, closing, closed**]
1 to shut □ *Could you close the door, please?* □ *The door closed behind him.* □ *Close your eyes and go to sleep.* (**fechar**)
2 if a shop, restaurant, etc. closes, it stops serving people, for example at the end of a day □ *Supermarkets close around 8 o'clock.* (**fechar**)
3 to stop operating as a business, permanently □ *A lot of shops in this area have closed.* (**fechar**)
4 to finish something □ *I would like to close the meeting by thanking you all for coming.* (**terminar**)
5 to finish using a computer program or document and make it go off your screen. A computing word. (**fechar**)
♦ PHRASAL VERBS **close (something) down** to stop operating as a business, or make something stop operating as a business □ *A lot of small businesses are closing down.* (**encerrar**) **close in** to get nearer to someone so that you can catch or attack them □ *The troops are closing in on the rebels.* (**aproximar**) **close something off** to stop people from going into a place □ *Police closed off the streets around the theatre.* (**isolar**)
▶ NOUN, NO PLURAL the end of something □ *The pound was weak at the close of trading.* (**final**) 🔁 *She quickly brought the meeting to a close.* (**encerrar**)

close[2] /kləʊs/ ADJECTIVE [**closer, closest**]
1 near in distance or time □ + **to** *The flat is close to the shops.* □ *It was close to midnight when he got back.* (**perto**)
2 if you are close to someone, you know and like them well □ + **to** *I'm very close to my younger sister.* (**íntimo**) 🔁 *We invited a few close friends.* (**amigo íntimo**)
3 a close relation is someone such as your mother, father, sister or brother (**próximo**)
4 seeing or talking to someone often 🔁 *I'm still in close contact with my ex-colleagues.*
5 looking or listening carefully 🔁 *Pay close attention to what he says.* (**muita atenção**) 🔁 *I kept a close eye on the time.* (**ficar de olho**)
6 a close game or competition is one in which people score almost the same number of points (**apertado, justo**)
7 warm and with no fresh air □ *It was very close inside the tent.* (**abafado**)
♦ IDIOM **at close quarters** from very close to someone or something □ *I had never seen a lion at close quarters before.* (**nas imediações**)
⇨ go to **a close shave**
▶ ADVERB [**closer, closest**]
1 near □ *Her mother was standing close by.* (**perto**)
2 **be/come close to doing something** to almost do something □ *He came close to winning.* (**chegar perto de fazer algo**)

close[3] /kləʊs/ NOUN [plural **closes**] a street that cars can go into only at one end □ *They live at 16 Cathedral Close.* (**beco sem saída**)

closed /kləʊzd/ ADJECTIVE
1 not open □ *Laura kept her eyes closed.* (**fechado**)

2 not open for business □ *The banks are closed on Sundays.* (fechado)

close-knit /ˌkləʊsˈnɪt/ ADJECTIVE a close-knit group of people shares similar ideas and supports each other (estreitamente ligado)

closely /ˈkləʊslɪ/ ADVERB
1 carefully □ *Police are examining the scene closely.* (rigorosamente)
2 with little distance between two things (de perto) ▣ *He entered, closely followed by his parents.* (seguido de perto por)
3 if you work closely with someone, you work together, sharing information and ideas (estreitamente)
4 if two things are closely connected, they are very similar or have a strong connection □ *Humans are very closely related to apes.* (intimamente)

closet /ˈklɒzɪt/ NOUN [plural **closets**] the US word for cupboard (armário embutido)

close-up /ˈkləʊsʌp/ NOUN [plural **close-ups**] a photograph or part of a film that is taken from very close to something so that you can see all the details (close-up)

closure /ˈkləʊʒə(r)/ NOUN [plural **closures**]
1 when a business, organization, etc. stops operating □ *school closures* (fechamento)
2 when you have finished dealing with a bad experience and your life is not now spoilt by it (término)

clot /klɒt/ ▶ NOUN [plural **clots**] a solid mass that forms in liquids, especially in cream or blood (coágulo)
▶ VERB [**clots, clotting, clotted**] to form clots (coagular)

cloth /klɒθ/ NOUN [plural **cloths**]
1 *no plural* material made of wool, cotton, etc., used for making clothes, etc. □ *cotton cloth* □ *a cloth bag* (tecido)
2 a piece of cloth used for cleaning or drying □ *She wiped the table with a damp cloth.* (pano)

clothe /kləʊð/ VERB [**clothes, clothing, clothed**] to put clothes on someone or provide them with clothes □ *They need money to feed and clothe themselves.* (vestir-se)

• **clothes** /kləʊðz/ PLURAL NOUN the things people wear to cover their bodies (roupa) ▣ *She wears very interesting clothes.* (veste roupas) □ *baby clothes* □ *a clothes shop*

clothes peg /ˈkləʊðz ˌpeg/ NOUN [plural **clothes pegs**] a small object that you use to fasten wet clothes to a line while they dry (prendedor)

clothing /ˈkləʊðɪŋ/ NOUN, NO PLURAL clothes, especially for a particular activity □ *waterproof clothing* □ *Please bring a change of clothing* (roupa) ▣ *a piece of clothing* (peça de roupa)

cloud /klaʊd/ ▶ NOUN [plural **clouds**]
1 a white or grey mass of small water drops that is in the sky □ *rain clouds* □ *dark clouds* (nuvem)
2 a mass of smoke, dust, sand, etc. in the air □ *a cloud of flies* □ *Clouds of smoke were billowing from the factory.* (nuvem)
▶ VERB [**clouds, clouding, clouded**] to make something more difficult to see through □ *His eyes clouded with tears.* (anuviar, escurecer)
♦ PHRASAL VERB **cloud over** if the weather or the sky clouds over, the sky becomes full of clouds (fechar)

cloudburst /ˈklaʊdbɜːst/ NOUN [plural **cloudbursts**] when a lot of rain suddenly falls (aguaceiro)

cloudy /ˈklaʊdɪ/ ADJECTIVE [**cloudier, cloudiest**]
1 full of clouds (nublado) ▣ *a cloudy sky* (céu nublado)
2 not transparent □ *a cloudy liquid* (turvo)

clout /klaʊt/ ▶ NOUN [plural **clouts**]
1 influence and power □ *These organizations have a lot of political clout.* (poder)
2 a hard hit with the hand. An informal word. (bofetão)
▶ VERB [**clouts, clouting, clouted**] to hit someone with the hand. An informal word. (esbofetear)

clove /kləʊv/ NOUN [plural **cloves**]
1 a small dried flower, used in cooking as a spice (cravo)
2 one of the parts that makes up the root of some plants □ *a clove of garlic* (bulbo, dente)

clover /ˈkləʊvə(r)/ NOUN, NO PLURAL a small plant with leaves that have three parts (trevo)

clown /klaʊn/ NOUN [plural **clowns**] someone who wears funny clothes, has a painted face, and does silly things to make people laugh (palhaço)
♦ PHRASAL VERB [**clowns, clowning, clowned**] clown around to do silly things that make people laugh (fazer palhaçadas)

club /klʌb/ ▶ NOUN [plural **clubs**]
1 an organization of people who meet regularly to do a particular activity, or the place where they meet (clube) ▣ *She belongs to a golf club.* (pertence a um clube) ▣ *I've joined a tennis club.* (associar-se a um clube)
2 a place where people go at night to dance and drink (boate)
3 one of the sticks used in golf to hit the ball (taco)
4 a heavy piece of wood or metal used as a weapon (cassetete)
5 clubs one of the four types of playing card, which have the symbol (♣) printed on them □ *the four of clubs* (paus)
▶ VERB [**clubs, clubbing, clubbed**] **go clubbing** to go out dancing and drinking in clubs □ *She goes clubbing on Saturday night.* (ir à boate)
♦ PHRASAL VERB **club together** to share the cost of something □ *We all clubbed together to get her a present.* (dividir a conta)

cluck /klʌk/ ▶ VERB [clucks, clucking, clucked] when a chicken clucks, it makes a repeated low sound. (cacarejar)
▶ NOUN [plural clucks] the sound made by a chicken (cacarejo)

clue /kluː/ NOUN [plural clues] a sign or piece of information that helps solve a problem, mystery or crime □ a crossword clue □ The police are looking for clues. (chave, pista)
♦ IDIOM **not have a clue** an informal phrase meaning to know or understand nothing about something □ I didn't have a clue what she meant. (não ter a menor ideia)

clump /klʌmp/ NOUN [plural clumps] a group of plants growing close together □ a clump of trees (arvoredo)

clumsy /ˈklʌmzi/ ADJECTIVE [clumsier, clumsiest] a clumsy person is awkward in the way they move, often dropping things or knocking into things (desajeitado)

clung /klʌŋ/ PAST TENSE AND PAST PARTICIPLE OF cling (ver cling)

cluster /ˈklʌstə(r)/ NOUN [plural clusters] a group of similar things that are near each other □ a cluster of cottages (grupo)
♦ PHRASAL VERB [clusters, clustering, clustered] **cluster around (someone/something)** to form a group around someone or something □ The children clustered around the baby donkey. (agrupar-se ao redor de alguém/algo)

clutch /klʌtʃ/ ▶ VERB [clutches, clutching, clutched] to hold something tightly in your hand or hands □ She clutched her mother's hand. (apertar)
♦ PHRASAL VERB **clutch at something** to try to take hold of something □ I clutched at his arm as I fell. (agarrar-se a algo)
▶ NOUN [plural clutches]
1 the part of a car's engine that you operate by pressing with your foot to change gears (embreagem)
2 clutches when someone controls someone else □ He fell into the clutches of a criminal gang. (controle, influência)

clutter /ˈklʌtə(r)/ ▶ NOUN, NO PLURAL things that cover or fill a place so that it looks untidy □ I must get rid of some of this clutter. (desordem, tumulto)
▶ VERB [clutters, cluttering, cluttered] to fill a space with lots of things and make it untidy □ Books cluttered every surface. (amontoar, atravancar)

cm ABBREVIATION centimetre or centimetres (cm)

Co ABBREVIATION Company, used in the name of a business □ Smith, Jenkins and Co. (Cia.)

co- /kəʊ/ PREFIX co- is added to the beginning of words to mean 'together with' or 'working with' □ co-star □ cooperate (co-)

coach /kəʊtʃ/ ▶ NOUN [plural coaches]
1 a comfortable bus for long journeys □ a coach station (ônibus) ▣ a coach trip (viagem de ônibus)
2 someone who helps people to improve a skill, often a sport, or who gives extra teaching in a school subject □ a rugby coach □ a singing coach (treinador)
3 in the past, a vehicle that was pulled by horses (coche)
▶ VERB [coaches, coaching, coached] to help someone to improve a skill, often a sport, or to give extra teaching to someone in a school subject □ He's being coached by an ex-Olympic champion. (treinar)
• **coaching** /ˈkəʊtʃɪŋ/ NOUN, NO PLURAL teaching □ She has extra coaching in French. (treinamento)

coagulate /kəʊˈægjʊleɪt/ VERB [coagulates, coagulating, coagulated] if a liquid, especially blood, coagulates, it becomes thick and sticky. A biology word. (coagular)

coal /kəʊl/ NOUN, NO PLURAL a hard black substance that is dug out of the ground and burnt to give heat (carvão mineral)

coalition /ˌkəʊəˈlɪʃən/ NOUN [plural coalitions] a government formed from two or more political parties working together (coligação) ▣ a coalition government (coligação do governo)

coal mine /ˈkəʊl ˌmaɪn/ NOUN [plural coal mines] a place where coal is dug out of the ground (mina de carvão)

coarse /kɔːs/ ADJECTIVE [coarser, coarsest]
1 rough □ coarse cloth (áspero)
2 in large, irregular pieces □ coarse sea salt (grosso)
3 rude □ coarse language (rude, vulgar)

coast /kəʊst/ c NOUN [plural coasts] the area of land next to the sea □ It's a town on the west coast of Ireland. □ They've gone for a trip to the coast. (costa)
♦ IDIOM **the coast is clear** if the coast is clear, there is no one around to see you or stop you doing something (a barra está limpa)
▶ VERB [coasts, coasting, coasted]
1 to achieve something without making much effort □ + to United coasted to victory in the second half. (conquistar)
2 to travel in a vehicle without using any power □ Jack coasted down the hill on his bike. (locomover-se sem esforço)
• **coastal** /ˈkəʊstəl/ ADJECTIVE on or near a coast □ a coastal town (litorâneo)

coastguard /ˈkəʊstɡɑːd/ NOUN [plural coast-guards] someone whose job is to watch the sea near the coast to prevent illegal activities and to help ships in danger (guarda costeira)

coastline /ˈkəʊstlaɪn/ NOUN [plural coastlines] the edge of a coast □ the beautiful Northumberland coastline (litoral)

coat /kəʊt/ ▶ NOUN [plural **coats**]
1 a piece of clothing with sleeves that you wear over your other clothes when you go out □ *He was wearing a thick winter coat.* (casaco)
2 a layer of a substance (demão) 🔁 *a coat of paint* (demão de tinta)
3 the fur of an animal (pelagem)
▶ VERB [**coats, coating, coated**] to cover something with a thin layer of a substance □ *Their bodies were coated with mud.* (cobrir)

coat-hanger /ˈkəʊthæŋə(r)/ NOUN [plural **coat-hangers**] a piece of wood, plastic or metal with a curved part at the top, for hanging up clothes (cabide)

coating /ˈkəʊtɪŋ/ NOUN [plural **coatings**] a layer of a substance covering something □ *There was a thin coating of snow on the ground.* (camada, cobertura)

coax /kəʊks/ VERB [**coaxes, coaxing, coaxed**] to try to persuade someone to do something □ *He was finally coaxed into taking part in the game.* (persuadir)

cob /kɒb/ NOUN [plural **cobs**] a long round solid part of a maize plant that the seeds grow on (espiga de milho)

cobble /ˈkɒbəl/ NOUN [plural **cobbles**] a round stone used on the surface of a road (paralelepípedo)

• **cobbled** /ˈkɒbəld/ ADJECTIVE covered with cobbles (pavimentado com paralelepípedo)

cobbler /ˈkɒblə(r)/ NOUN [plural **cobblers**] someone whose job is making and repairing shoes (sapateiro)

cobblestone /ˈkɒbəlstəʊn/ NOUN [plural **cobblestones**] a round stone used on the surface of a road (paralelepípedo)

cobra /ˈkəʊbrə/ NOUN [plural **cobras**] a poisonous snake that makes its neck go flat before it attacks (cobra)

cobweb /ˈkɒbweb/ NOUN [plural **cobwebs**] a pattern of thin crossing threads that a spider makes to catch insects (teia de aranha)

coccyx /ˈkɒksɪks/ NOUN [plural **coccyxes** or **coccyges**] a small bone shaped like a triangle at the bottom of your spine (= line of bones down your back). A biology word. (cóccix)

cock /kɒk/ ▶ NOUN [plural **cocks**] a male bird (galo)
▶ VERB [**cocks, cocking, cocked**]
1 to move a part of your body (mover) 🔁 *He cocked his head to one side.* (moveu sua cabeça) □ *The dog suddenly cocked its ears.*
2 to make a gun ready to fire □ *The officer cocked his pistol.* (armar)

◆ PHRASAL VERB **cock (something) up** an informal word meaning to do something badly or wrong □ *I was supposed to book the hotel, but I cocked it up.* (estragar)

cockerel /ˈkɒkərəl/ NOUN [plural **cockerels**] a male chicken (galo)

cockle /ˈkɒkəl/ NOUN [plural **cockles**] a type of sea creature with a small round shell, that you can eat (molusco)

cockney /ˈkɒkni/ NOUN [plural **cockneys**]
1 someone who comes from East London (habitante da periferia de Londres)
2 the way cockneys speak □ *a cockney accent* (dialeto desses habitantes)

cockpit /ˈkɒkpɪt/ NOUN [plural **cockpits**] the area in an aeroplane where the pilot sits (cockpit)

cockroach /ˈkɒkrəʊtʃ/ NOUN [plural **cockroaches**] a large brown or black insect usually found in dirty places (barata)

cocktail /ˈkɒkteɪl/ NOUN [plural **cocktails**]
1 an alcoholic drink made with two or more types of drink mixed together (coquetel)
2 a mixture of substances or characteristics □ *a cocktail of drugs* (coquetel)

cocky /ˈkɒki/ ADJECTIVE [**cockier, cockiest**] confident in an annoying way (arrogante, convencido)

cocoa /ˈkəʊkəʊ/ NOUN, NO PLURAL
1 a brown powder made from the seeds of a tropical tree, used to make chocolate (cacau)
2 a hot drink made from cocoa powder mixed with milk (cacau)

coconut /ˈkəʊkənʌt/ NOUN [plural **coconuts**] a large nut with a brown outer part with hair on, and white flesh and liquid inside (coco) 🔁 *coconut milk* (leite de coco)

cocoon /kəˈkuːn/ NOUN [plural **cocoons**] a casemade by some insects inside which they change into their adult form (casulo)

cod /kɒd/ NOUN [plural **cod**] a large sea fish that you can eat (bacalhau)

coddle /ˈkɒdəl/ VERB [**coddles, coddling, coddled**] to protect someone too much (mimar)

code /kəʊd/ ▶ NOUN [plural **codes**]
1 a set of signs or letters used instead of normal writing to send a secret message □ *The letter was written in code.* (código) 🔁 *They managed to break the code* (= understand it). (quebrar o código)
2 a series of letters or numbers used to show what something is or to give information about it □ *a tax code* □ *Please enter your security code.* (código)
3 the first part of a telephone number that tells you the area or the country □ *What's the code for the UK?* (código)
4 a set of rules or laws (código, norma) 🔁 *The company has its own code of conduct.* (código de conduta) 🔁 *a strict dress code* (norma de vestuário)
5 a series of instructions used in computer software. A computing word. (código)
▶ VERB [**codes, coding, coded**]
1 to give something a code to show what it is or to give information about it □ *All the words are coded according to their subject area.* (codificar)

2 to put a message into code (codificar)
3 to write instructions for a computer. A computing word. (codificar)
- **coded** /'kəʊdɪd/ ADJECTIVE
1 written in code (codificado)
2 expressed in way that is not direct □ *The play contained coded criticism of the government.* (codificado)

coed /'kəʊed/ a short way to say and write coeducational (abreviação de *coeducacional*)

coeducation /ˌkəʊedʒʊ'keɪʃən/ NOUN, NO PLURAL the teaching of male and female students together (coeducação, educação mista)
- **coeducational** /ˌkəʊedʒʊ'keɪʃənəl/ ADJECTIVE teaching both male and female students □ *a coeducational school* (coeducacional)

coerce /kəʊ'ɜːs/ VERB [coerces, coercing, coerced] to force someone to do something that they do not want to do □ *None of our employees will be coerced into retiring.* (coagir)
- **coercion** /kəʊ'ɜːʃən/ NOUN, NO PLURAL forcing someone to do something they do not want to do □ *There were claims that they had used coercion.* (coerção)

coexist /ˌkəʊɪɡ'zɪst/ VERB [coexists, coexisting, coexisted] to live or exist together at the same time or in the same place □ *The two religions coexist peacefully in the region.* (coexistir)
- **coexistence** /ˌkəʊɪɡ'zɪstəns/ NOUN, NO PLURAL when two or more people or things coexist (coexistência) ▣ *They live in peaceful coexistence with their neighbours.* (coexistência pacífica)

coffee /'kɒfɪ/ NOUN [plural coffees]
1 no plural a drink made from the beans of a tropical plant □ *I don't drink coffee.* (café) ▣ *Let's have a cup of coffee.* (xícara de café) ▣ *black/white coffee* (= coffee without/with milk) (café puro ou com leite)
2 a cup of this drink □ *Two black coffees, please.* (xícara de café)

coffer /'kɒfə(r)/ NOUN [plural coffers]
1 coffers the money a company or organization has □ *This money will swell the government's coffers.* (cofre)
2 a large strong box used to store valuable things (caixa-forte)

coffin /'kɒfɪn/ NOUN [plural coffins] a long wooden box that a dead body is put into to be buried (caixão)

cog /kɒɡ/ NOUN [plural cogs] one of the pointed parts round the edge of a wheel in an engine or machine that helps it turn (roda de engrenagem)

cognac /'kɒnjæk/ NOUN, NO PLURAL a type of French brandy (= alcoholic drink) (conhaque)

cogwheel /'kɒɡwiːl/ NOUN [plural cogwheels] a metal disc with points around its edge, used to turn other cogwheels or parts inside a machine (engrenagem)

coherence /kəʊ'hɪərəns/ NOUN, NO PLURAL when something is coherent (coerência)
- **coherent** /kəʊ'hɪərənt/ ADJECTIVE
1 clear and easy to understand □ *He wasn't particularly coherent.* (coeso)
2 a coherent plan, argument, etc. is sensible and all the parts have been considered (coerente)
- **coherently** /kəʊ'hɪərəntlɪ/ ADVERB in a clear and sensible way □ *He argued forcibly and coherently against the changes.* (de modo coerente)

coil /kɔɪl/ C VERB [coils, coiling, coiled] to twist something long to form circles □ *The huge snake coiled itself round the branch.* (enrolar)
▶ NOUN [plural coils] a long piece of rope, wire, etc. twisted into circles □ *a coil of thin wire* (bobina)

coin /kɔɪn/ ▶ NOUN [plural coins] a round, flat piece of metal money (moeda) ▣ *a gold coin* (moeda de ouro) ▣ *a pound coin* (moeda de libra)
▶ VERB [coins, coining, coined]
1 to use a new word or phrase for the first time (inventar)
2 to coin a phrase something you say before using a phrase that is well known (cunhar uma expressão)

coincide /ˌkəʊɪn'saɪd/ VERB [coincides, coinciding, coincided] when events coincide with each other, they happen at the same time □ *The carnival will coincide with the beginning of the school holidays.* (coincidir)

coincidence /kəʊ'ɪnsɪdəns/ NOUN [plural coincidences] when two things happen at the same time by chance (coincidência) ▣ *It was pure coincidence that I was on the train that day.* (pura coincidência) □ *By coincidence, his father had also worked in China.*
- **coincidental** /kəʊˌɪnsɪ'dentəl/ ADJECTIVE happening at the same time by chance □ *It was completely coincidental that they arrived on the same day.* (coincidente)

coke /kəʊk/ NOUN, NO PLURAL a type of fuel made from coal (combustível de carvão)

cola /'kəʊlə/ NOUN [plural colas] a dark brown, sweet fizzy (= with bubbles) drink (coca)

colander /'kɒləndə(r)/ NOUN [plural colanders] a container with holes in the bottom used to remove water from food (coador)

cold /kəʊld/ ▶ ADJECTIVE [colder, coldest]
1 low in temperature □ *a cold drink* □ *She hated cold weather.* (frio) ▣ *It was a bitterly cold night.* (extremamente frio) ▣ *It's freezing cold outside.* (frio congelante) □ *His hands felt cold.*
2 unfriendly or not showing emotion □ *a cold stare* □ *She seemed so cold and uncaring.* (frio)
♦ IDIOM **have/get cold feet** to suddenly feel afraid to do something that you had planned to do □ *He was due to sing at the concert, but he got*

cold-blooded

cold feet at the last minute. (ter/ficar com medo)
▶ NOUN [plural colds]
1 a common illness that makes you cough and blocks your nose (resfriado) 🔊 *Hannah's got a cold.* (pegou um resfriado) 🔊 *I caught a cold while I was away.* (peguei um resfriado)
2 the cold cold weather or a low temperature ☐ *We waited around in the cold for an hour.* (frio)

cold-blooded /ˌkəʊldˈblʌdɪd/ ADJECTIVE
1 a cold-blooded person is cruel and shows no emotion ☐ *a cold-blooded killer* (sangue-frio)
2 a cold-blooded animal's temperature changes according to the temperature of the air or water around it. A biology word. (de sangue frio)

coldly /ˈkəʊldli/ ADVERB in an unfriendly way ☐ *She treated them coldly.* (friamente)

coldness /ˈkəʊldnɪs/ NOUN, NO PLURAL
1 being unfriendly and showing no emotion ☐ *Sarah heard the coldness in his voice.* (frieza, indiferença)
2 being cold ☐ *He was surprised by the coldness of the water.* (frio)

cold sore /ˈkəʊld ˌsɔː(r)/ NOUN [plural cold sores] a red, painful mark on your lip caused by a virus (herpes)

cold war /ˌkəʊld ˈwɔː(r)/ NOUN [plural cold wars] unfriendly political relations between countries, especially between the Soviet Union and the West after World War II (Guerra Fria)

coleslaw /ˈkəʊlslɔː/ NOUN, NO PLURAL a salad made from raw cabbage (= vegetable with green leaves) and mayonnaise (= sauce made from eggs and oil) (salada de repolho)

colic /ˈkɒlɪk/ NOUN, NO PLURAL a sudden bad pain in the stomach, especially in babies (cólica)

collaborate /kəˈlæbəreɪt/ VERB [collaborates, collaborating, collaborated]
1 to work together with someone else, sharing information and ideas ☐ *Dr Wallis collaborated with Japanese researchers on the study.* (colaborar)
2 to give information or help to an enemy ☐ *People who had collaborated with the former regime were imprisoned.* (cooperar)

• **collaboration** /kəˌlæbəˈreɪʃən/ NOUN, NO PLURAL
1 when people work together (colaboração) 🔊 *We work in close collaboration with local doctors.* (em colaboração próxima com)
2 when someone helps an enemy (cooperação)

• **collaborator** /kəˈlæbəˌreɪtə(r)/ NOUN [plural collaborators]
1 someone who works with other people (colaborador)
2 someone who helps an enemy (cooperador)

collage /ˈkɒlɑːʒ/ NOUN [plural collages] a picture made by sticking different pieces of paper, fabric, etc. on a surface (colagem)

collect

collagen /ˈkɒlədʒən/ NOUN, NO PLURAL a substance found in the skin and bones. A biology word. (colágeno)

collapse /kəˈlæps/ ▶ VERB [collapses, collapsing, collapsed]
1 if a building or structure collapses, it falls down because it is too weak ☐ *The bridge collapsed under the lorry's weight.* (ruir, desmoronar)
2 if a person collapses, they fall down because they are ill or very tired ☐ *He collapsed from exhaustion.* ☐ *I put down my bags and collapsed on the sofa.* (desmaiar)
3 to fail suddenly and completely ☐ *Workers were left jobless after the company collapsed.* (ruir)
4 to let your body fall onto a bed, chair, etc. because you are very tired (desfalecer)
5 if furniture or equipment collapses, it can be folded up to make it smaller ☐ *The table collapses so that it can be stored under the seat.* (dobrar)
▶ NOUN [plural collapses]
1 when a building, structure or person falls down ☐ *After her collapse, she went to Switzerland to recover.* (ruína)
2 when a business, government, plan, etc. fails ☐ *The country faces economic collapse.* (fracasso)

• **collapsible** /kəˈlæpsəbəl/ ADJECTIVE collapsible furniture or equipment can be folded so that it is smaller ☐ *a collapsible chair* (desmontável, dobrável)

collar /ˈkɒlə(r)/ ▶ NOUN [plural collars]
1 the piece of material on a shirt or jacket that fits round your neck ☐ *I unbuttoned my shirt collar.* (gola)
2 a piece of leather or other material fastened round an animal's neck (coleira)
▶ VERB [collars, collaring, collared]
1 an informal word meaning to stop someone to talk to them ☐ *A reporter collared him at a charity event.* (pegar pelo colarinho)
2 an informal word meaning to catch or arrest someone ☐ *He was collared by a security guard.* (capturar)

collarbone /ˈkɒləbəʊn/ NOUN [plural collarbones] one of two bones that go from your shoulder to the front of your neck (clavícula)

collate /kəˈleɪt/ VERB [collates, collating, collated] to bring together pieces of information or documents and arrange them in order (organizar)

colleague /ˈkɒliːɡ/ NOUN [plural colleagues] a person who you work with ☐ *A colleague of mine told me about it.* (colega)

collect /kəˈlekt/ VERB [collects, collecting, collected]
1 to get things from different places and put them together ☐ *The survey collected data from 500 people.* ☐ **+ up** *Could you collect up all the plates, please?* (coletar)
2 to get and keep things of a particular type as a

hobby □ *Ted collects unusual postcards.* (**colecionar**)

3 to go to a place to get someone or something □ *George collected me from the airport.* □ *The following items are collected for recycling.* (**apanhar**)

4 to receive money or a prize □ *She collected the award for Best Actress.* (**receber**)

5 to take money from people □ *I'm collecting donations for charity.* (**arrecadar**)

• **collection** /kəˈlekʃən/ NOUN [plural **collections**]

1 things that have been collected together (**colação**) 🔁 *a private art collection* (**coleção de arte**) □ + **of** *a collection of rare photographs* □ *The book is a collection of short stories.*

2 when you go to get something from a place □ *There cold-blooded 123 collect were two parcels waiting for collection.* □ *weekly rubbish collections* (**coleta**)

3 a number of clothes or products for sale by a company at the same time □ *Louis Vuitton's autumn/winter collection* (**coleção**)

4 money collected from different people □ *We had a collection for Bob's retirement.* (**coleta**)

• **collective** /kəˈlektɪv/ ADJECTIVE involving or done by several people or groups, not just one □ *a collective decision* (**coletiva**)

collective farm /kəˌlektɪv ˈfɑːm/ NOUN [plural **collective farms**] a large farm owned by the government and worked on by a group of people (**granja coletiva**)

collective noun /kəˌlektɪv ˈnaʊn/ NOUN [plural **collective nouns**] a word used to refer to a group of people or things. The words *family, team, staff, government, herd, luggage* and *furniture* are examples of collective nouns. (**substantivo coletivo**)

collectivize or **collectivise** /kəˈlektɪvaɪz/ VERB [**collectivizes, collectivizing, collectivized**] to join several small farms or businesses and control them together (**coletivizar**)

collector /kəˈlektə(r)/ NOUN [plural **collectors**]

1 someone who finds and keeps things of the same type in a collection □ *an art collector* (**colecionador**)

2 someone who collects something as a job □ *a tax collector* (**cobrador**)

college /ˈkɒlɪdʒ/ NOUN [plural **colleges**]

1 in the UK, a place where people go to learn after they have left school (**faculdade**) 🔁 *She went to college to do catering.* (**foi para a faculdade**)

2 a US word for university (**universidade**)

3 one of the parts that some universities are divided into □ *King's College, Cambridge* (**colégio**)

collide /kəˈlaɪd/ VERB [**collides, colliding, collided**] when moving objects collide, they hit each other □ *The bus collided with a car.* (**colidir**)

collie /ˈkɒli/ NOUN [plural **collies**] a type of dog that is used to control sheep (**cão pastor**)

colliery /ˈkɒljəri/ NOUN [plural **collieries**] a coalmine (**mina de carvão**)

collision /kəˈlɪʒən/ NOUN [plural **collisions**] a crash between moving vehicles or objects □ *A collision between two lorries has closed the road.* (**colisão, trombada**)

collocation /ˌkɒləˈkeɪʃən/ NOUN [plural **collocations**] two or more words that are often used together. *Commit a crime, heavy rain* and *fall ill* are examples of collocations. (**locução**)

colloquial /kəˈləʊkwɪəl/ ADJECTIVE colloquial language is used in normal conversation but not in formal speaking or writing □ *a colloquial term* (**coloquial**)

collude /kəˈluːd/ VERB [**colludes, colluding, colluded**] a formal word meaning to secretly do something dishonest with another person □ *He was accused of colluding with terrorists.* (**conspirar**)

• **collusion** /kəˈluːʒən/ NOUN, NO PLURAL when people collude (**conspiração**)

cologne /kəˈləʊn/ NOUN, NO PLURAL light perfume (= pleasant-smelling liquid that you put on your skin) (**colônia**)

colon /ˈkəʊlən/ NOUN [plural **colons**]

1 a punctuation mark (:) used to separate parts of a sentence or used before a list (**dois-pontos**)

2 part of your bowel. A biology word. (**cólon**)

colonel /ˈkɜːnəl/ NOUN [plural **colonels**] an officer with a high rank in the army or air force (**coronel**)

colonial /kəˈləʊnɪəl/ ADJECTIVE to do with a colony (= country controlled by another country) □ *colonial rule* (**colonial**)

colonist /ˈkɒlənɪst/ NOUN [plural **colonists**] someone who goes to another country to start a colony (= country controlled by another country) (**colonizador**)

colonize or **colonise** /ˈkɒlənaɪz/ VERB [**colonizes, colonizing, colonized**]

1 to send people to start living in another country and to take control of it □ *The area was colonized by Dutch immigrants.* (**colonizar**)

2 to start living or growing in a new place □ *Golden eagles have colonized the island.* (**colonizar**)

colony /ˈkɒləni/ NOUN [plural **colonies**]

1 a country or area that is controlled by another country (**colônia**) 🔁 *The French established a colony there in the 19th century.* (**estabeleceu uma colônia**)

2 a group of people, animals or plants of the same type living together □ *a colony of ants* (**colônia**)

3 a group of people with similar ideas or jobs who live together □ *a hippy colony* (**grupo**)

color

color /ˈkʌlə(r)/ NOUN [plural **colors**], ADJECTIVE, VERB [**colors, coloring, colored**] the US spelling of colour (ver **colour**)

color-blind /ˈkʌləblaɪnd/ ADJECTIVE the US spelling of **colour-blind** (ver **colour-blind**)

colored /ˈkʌləd/ ADJECTIVE the US spelling of **coloured** (ver **coloured**)

colorful /ˈkʌləfʊl/ ADJECTIVE the US spelling of **colourful** (ver **colourful**)

• **colorfully** /ˈkʌləfʊli/ ADVERB the US spelling of **colourfully** (ver **colourfully**)

coloring /ˈkʌlərɪŋ/ NOUN, NO PLURAL the US spelling of **colouring** (ver **colouring**)

colorless /ˈkʌləlɪs/ ADJECTIVE the US spelling of **colourless** (ver **colourless**)

colossal /kəˈlɒsəl/ ADJECTIVE extremely large □ *a colossal amount of energy* (**colossal**)

---

colour /ˈkʌlə(r)/ ▶ NOUN [plural **colours**]

1 red, blue, green, black, etc. (**cor**) □ + *of Look at the colour of the sky.* □ *What colour are your eyes?* □ *The sea was a lovely blue colour.* 🔁 *There is a range of designs in bright colours.* (**cores brilhantes**)

2 *no plural* using all colours, not just black and white □ *They printed the photos in colour.* (**colorido**)

3 the colour of someone's skin, because of their race □ *We oppose all discrimination on the grounds of colour.* (**cor**)

4 *no plural* interest or excitement □ *We aim to bring some colour back into politics.* (**ânimo**)

5 *off colour* feeling slightly ill □ *I'm feeling a bit off colour today.* (**indisposto**)

> ➤ When you say the colour of something or ask about the colour of something, remember to use the verb **be** and not **have**:
> ✓ *Your jacket is a lovely colour.*
> ✗ *Your jacket has a lovely colour.*
> ✓ *What colour is your coat?*
> ✗ *What colour has your coat?*

▶ ADJECTIVE having or using colour □ *a colour TV* □ *a colour photograph* (**colorido**)

▶ VERB [**colours, colouring, coloured**]

1 to make something a particular colour or to become a particular colour □ *Does she colour her hair?* □ *Jane's cheeks coloured and she looked away.* (**colorir, pintar**)

2 to use pens, pencils, etc. to add colour to a picture □ *Colour the sun yellow.* □ + *in Would you like to colour in your picture?* (**colorir**)

3 to affect how you think or feel about something □ *Her view of the city is coloured by those early bad experiences.* (**deturpar**)

colour-blind /ˈkʌləblaɪnd/ ADJECTIVE not able to see the difference between some colours (**daltônico**)

comb

coloured /ˈkʌləd/ ADJECTIVE having a colour or colours, not just black and white (**colorido**) 🔁 *a brightly coloured scarf* (**brilhantemente colorido**) □ *Use different coloured pens.*

colourful /ˈkʌləfʊl/ ADJECTIVE

1 having lots of bright colours □ *dancers in colourful costumes* □ *The garden was full of colourful flowers.* (**colorido**)

2 interesting or exciting (**interessante**) 🔁 *Her uncle's a colourful character.* (**pessoa interessante**)

• **colourfully** /ˈkʌləfʊli/ ADVERB in a colourful way □ *colourfully dressed children* (**de maneira colorida**)

colouring /ˈkʌlərɪŋ/ NOUN [plural **colourings**]

1 a substance used to give something a colour □ *red food colouring* (**pigmentação**)

2 the colour of your skin and hair □ *That shade of green suits her dark colouring.* (**coloração**)

3 *no plural* the activity of adding colour to a picture with pens, pencils, etc. □ *Would you like to do some colouring?* (**ato de colorir**)

colourless /ˈkʌləlɪs/ ADJECTIVE having no colour □ *Water is a colourless liquid.* (**incolor**)

colt /kəʊlt/ NOUN [plural **colts**] a young male horse (**potro**)

column /ˈkɒləm/ NOUN [plural **columns**]

1 a tall, thick post, usually made of stone □ *Huge marble columns support the roof.* (**coluna**)

2 a piece of writing in a newspaper that appears regularly and is usually written by the same person (**coluna**) 🔁 *He writes a weekly newspaper column.* (**coluna de jornal**)

3 numbers or words written one under the other on a page □ + *of a column of figures* □ *Add up the numbers in the right-hand column.* (**coluna**)

4 something with a long or tall narrow shape □ + *of Columns of smoke and dust rose from the erupting volcano.* (**coluna**)

5 a long line of people □ + *of a column of marching soldiers* (**fila**)

• **columnist** /ˈkɒləmnɪst/ NOUN [plural **columnists**] a person who writes a regular column in a newspaper □ *a columnist for the New York Times* (**colunista**)

coma /ˈkəʊmə/ NOUN [plural **comas**] when someone is unconscious for a long time □ *She was in a coma for ten days after the accident.* (**coma**)

• **comatose** /ˈkəʊmətəʊs/ ADJECTIVE in a coma or seeming to be in a coma (**estado de coma**)

---

comb /kəʊm/ ▶ NOUN [plural **combs**]

1 an object with a row of very narrow parts along one side that you use to tidy your hair (**pente**)

2 a part that stands up on the top of some birds' heads (**crista**)

▶ VERB [**combs, combing, combed**]

1 to tidy your hair using a comb □ *She combed her hair.* (**pentear**)
2 to search a place very carefully □ *Detectives were combing the area for clues.* (**vasculhar**)

combat /ˈkɒmbæt/ ▶ NOUN, NO PLURAL fighting, especially in a war □ *The two soldiers died in combat.* (**combate**)
▶ VERB [**combats, combatting, combatted**] to try to stop something bad or harmful □ *The government brought in new measures to combat terrorism.* □ *He will receive treatment to combat the infection.* (**combater**)

• **combative** /ˈkɒmbətɪv/ ADJECTIVE always willing to argue or fight □ *This latest interview shows the minister in a rather combative mood.* (**combativo**)

combination /ˌkɒmbɪˈneɪʃən/ NOUN [*plural* **combinations**]
1 several things that have been joined or mixed together □ **+ of** *The problem is due to a combination of factors.* (**combinação**)
2 *no plural* the process of joining or mixing things (**combinação**) ▣ *It's safe to use in combination with other drugs.* (**em combinação com**)
3 a series of numbers used to open a lock □ *Who knows the combination to the safe?* (**combinação**)

combination lock /ˌkɒmbɪˈneɪʃən ˌlɒk/ NOUN [*plural* **combination locks**] a lock that you open using a particular series of numbers (**fecho de segredo, combinação**)

combine /kəmˈbaɪn/ VERB [**combines, combining, combined**]
1 to join or mix things together □ *Combine all the ingredients in a mixing bowl.* □ **+ with** *Carbon dioxide combines with water to form an acid.* (**associar-se**)
2 to do or use two or more things at the same time □ **+ with** *You need to take regular exercise, combined with a healthy diet.* (**combinar**)

combine harvester /ˌkɒmbaɪn ˈhɑːvɪstə(r)/ NOUN [*plural* **combine harvesters**] a large farm machine that cuts crops and separates the grain from the stems (**ceifeira-debulhadora**)

combustible /kəmˈbʌstəbəl/ ADJECTIVE a combustible substance will burn or catch fire □ *a highly combustible gas* (**inflamável**)

combustion /kəmˈbʌstʃən/ NOUN, NO PLURAL burning □ *the combustion of gases* (**combustão, queima**)

come /kʌm/ VERB [**comes, coming, came, come**]
1 to move towards someone or a place □ *Come here!* □ *Here comes Julia.* □ *He came back to see me later.* □ *She came in and said hello.* (**vir**)
2 to go with someone □ **+ with** *Are you coming with us or not?* □ *We're going swimming – do you want to come?* (**vir**)
3 to arrive □ *Has my parcel come yet?* (**chegar**)
4 to move in a particular direction or to a particular level □ *Prices have come down.* □ *All the flowers have come up.* □ *We watched the sun come up.* (**baixar, desabrochar, nascer**)
5 come second/last/before, etc. to have a particular position in a competition or a list □ *P comes before Q in the alphabet.* □ *Philippe came first in the English exam.* (**vir em segundo, último, antes etc.**)
6 come apart/off, etc. to become separated from something □ *I picked up the jug and the handle came off.* (**desfazer-se**)
7 How come ...? used to ask for an explanation □ *How come Penny isn't here?* (**Por que...? Mas como...?**)

> Remember that the verb **come** means 'to move towards the speaker' or 'to move with the speaker'. For movements away from the speaker, use **go**: □ *Come here!* □ *Eva came to see us last night.* □ *Are you coming to the supermarket with me?*

♦ IDIOM **come clean** to tell the truth □ *I think it's time you came clean about your exam results.* (**falar a verdade**)
♦ PHRASAL VERBS **come about** to happen □ *How did the friendship come about?* (**aconteceu**) **come along**
1 to arrive □ *Luckily a police officer came along at that moment.* (**chegar**)
2 to go with someone □ *Do you mind if I come along?* (**vir também**) **come from somewhere** to be born somewhere or to live somewhere □ *She comes from Brazil.* (**ser de...**) **Come on!** used to encourage someone or to make them go faster □ *Come on, we're going to be late for school!* (**Vamos lá!**) **come out** to be available to buy or use □ *Their new CD comes out on Friday.* (**lançar, sair**) **come round** to become conscious again □ *When he came round, he could remember nothing about the accident.* (**voltar a si**) **come to something** to be a particular amount of money □ *Six bananas and a bag of apples – that comes to £2.80, please.* (**resultar**) **come up**
1 to happen □ *If the opportunity to travel comes up, you should take it.* □ *If any problems come up, just phone me.* (**surgir**)
2 to be discussed □ *The subject of Midori's birthday party came up.* (**a ser discutido**) **come up with** to produce □ *She came up with several good ideas.* (**produzir**)

comeback /ˈkʌmbæk/ NOUN [*plural* **comebacks**] when a performer starts to appear in public again after a period of not working (**retorno**) ▣ *She's made a comeback with a new album.* (**retornou**)

comedian /kəˈmiːdiən/ NOUN [*plural* **comedians**] a performer who tells jokes and funny stories (**comediante, humorista**)

comedienne

comedienne /kəˌmiːdɪˈen/ NOUN [plural **comediennes**] a female comedian (**comediante**)

comedy /ˈkɒmədi/ NOUN [plural **comedies**] entertainment that makes you laugh ◻ *His latest movie is a comedy.* ◻ *a comedy sketch* (**comédia**)

comet /ˈkɒmɪt/ NOUN [plural **comets**] a type of star that travels across the sky with a line of light behind it (**cometa**)

comfort /ˈkʌmfət/ ▶ NOUN [plural **comforts**]
1 *no plural* a feeling of being relaxed and without pain or other unpleasant feelings ◻ *I prefer to travel in comfort, flying first class.* ◻ *When I buy shoes, I choose comfort before fashion* (**conforto**) ▣ *People can now shop online in the comfort of their own home.* (**no conforto de**)
2 *no plural* a feeling of being less sad or worried (**conforto**) ▣ *I took some comfort from her words.* (**encontrei conforto em**) ▣ *We found comfort in the fact that we were not alone.* (**encontramos conforto**)
3 something or someone that makes you feel less sad or worried ◻ *My children are a great comfort to me.* (**consolo**)
4 *no plural* having enough money and other things to make your life easy and pleasant ◻ *They live in relative comfort.* (**conforto**)
5 comforts things that make your life easier or more pleasant ◻ + *of a hotel with all the comforts of home* (**conforto**)
▶ VERB [**comforts, comforting, comforted**] to make someone feel happier by saying or doing nice things ◻ *Last night she was being comforted by relatives.* (**consolar**)

• **comfortable** /ˈkʌmftəbəl/ ADJECTIVE
1 relaxed and without pain ◻ *Are you comfortable there?* (**confortável**) ▣ *I was in a lot of pain and couldn't get comfortable.*
2 feeling pleasant and not causing any pain ◻ *a comfortable chair* ◻ *They're the most comfortable shoes I've got.* (**confortável**)
3 not worried or nervous ◻ + *with I'm not really comfortable with the idea of being filmed.* (**à vontade**) ▣ *He immediately made me feel comfortable.* (**sentir-se à vontade**)
4 having enough money for the things you need ◻ *a comfortable lifestyle* ◻ *She had saved for a comfortable retirement.* (**cômodo**)
5 a comfortable win is when you win something easily (**cômodo**) ▣ *He started the tournament with a comfortable win over Murray.* (**vitória cômoda**) ▣ *a comfortable victory* (**vitória cômoda**)

• **comfortably** /ˈkʌmftəbli/ ADVERB
1 in a way that makes you feel pleasant and without pain ◻ *Are you all sitting comfortably?* (**confortavelmente**)
2 easily ◻ *They won comfortably.* (**comodamente**)

command

comfy /ˈkʌmfi/ ADJECTIVE [**comfier, comfiest**] an informal word for comfortable ◻ *a comfy chair* (**confortável**)

comic /ˈkɒmɪk/ ▶ ADJECTIVE
1 to do with comedy (**cômico**) ▣ *a comic actor* (**ator cômico**) ◻ *He has great comic timing.*
2 funny ◻ *His face had a really comic expression.* (**cômico**)
▶ NOUN [plural **comics**]
1 a magazine, especially for children, that has picture stories (**revista de quadrinhos**)
2 someone whose job is to tell jokes and make people laugh (**cômico**)

• **comical** /ˈkɒmɪkəl/ ADJECTIVE funny ◻ *The situation was almost comical.* (**cômico**)

comic strip /ˈkɒmɪk ˌstrɪp/ NOUN [plural **comic strips**] a series of pictures that tell a story (**cartum**)

coming /ˈkʌmɪŋ/ ADJECTIVE that will happen soon ◻ *There will be changes in the coming months.* (**próximo**)

comma /ˈkɒmə/ NOUN [plural **commas**] a punctuation mark (,) used to separate parts of a sentence (**vírgula**)

command /kəˈmɑːnd/ ▶ VERB [**commands, commanding, commanded**]
1 to be in control of someone or something, especially in a military organization ◻ *He eventually rose to command the regiment.* (**comandar**)
2 to order someone to do something ◻ *'Stand up straight!' he commanded.* ◻ + **to do something** *An officer commanded him to go back to his unit.* (**ordenar**)
3 to get respect, attention, etc. because you deserve it (**impor**) ▣ *He commands great respect from his colleagues.* (**impor respeito**)
4 to have a particular high price or value ◻ *Her paintings command huge prices.* (**merecer**)
▶ NOUN [plural **commands**]
1 an order to do something (**ordem**) ▣ *You must obey commands.* (**obedecer às ordens**) ▣ *He gave the command to shoot.* (**deu a ordem**)
2 *no plural* control of someone or something ◻ + *of He took command of the expedition.* (**controle**)
3 in command in control of a group of people ◻ *Who's the officer in command?* (**no comando**)
4 an instruction that you give to a computer to make it do something. A computing word. (**comando**)
5 knowledge of a particular subject ◻ + *of She had a poor command of English.* (**domínio**)

• **commandeer** /ˌkɒmənˈdɪə(r)/ VERB [**commandeers, commandeering, commandeered**] to take something, especially for military use ◻ *The troops commandeered several buses.* (**recrutar**)

- **commander** /kəˈmɑːndə(r)/ NOUN [plural **commanders**] someone who is in charge, especially in the police or a military organization (**comandante**)
- **commanding** /kəˈmɑːndɪŋ/ ADJECTIVE
  1 in a position where you are likely to win or succeed (**dominante**) ▫ *He has a commanding lead over his rivals.* (**liderança dominante**)
  2 powerful and getting respect and attention ▫ *He was a commanding figure.* (**imponente**)
- **commandment** /kəˈmɑːndmənt/ NOUN [plural **commandments**] one of the ten rules from God in the Bible (**mandamento**)

commando /kəˈmɑːndəʊ/ NOUN [plural **commandos** or **commandoes**] a soldier who is specially trained to do difficult or dangerous tasks (**comandante**)

commemorate /kəˈmeməreɪt/ VERB [**commemorates, commemorating, commemorated**] to do something to remember a special event or an important person, especially in a ceremony ▫ *There will be events to commemorate the 60th anniversary of independence.* (**comemorar**)

- **commemoration** /kəˌmeməˈreɪʃən/ NOUN [plural **commemorations**] something that is done to remember and celebrate a person or an event ▫ *the annual commemoration of the end of the war* (**comemoração**)

commence /kəˈmens/ VERB [**commences, commencing, commenced**] a formal word meaning to begin ▫ *The meeting will commence at 3 o'clock precisely.* (**iniciar**)

- **commencement** /kəˈmensmənt/ NOUN, NO PLURAL a formal word for the beginning of something (**início**)

commend /kəˈmend/ VERB [**commends, commending, commended**] a formal word meaning to praise someone or something ▫ *Mr Brown commended the work of the police.* (**aprovar**)

- **commendable** /kəˈmendəbəl/ ADJECTIVE deserving praise ▫ *commendable bravery* (**meritório**)
- **commendation** /ˌkɒmənˈdeɪʃən/ NOUN [plural **commendations**] an honour or praise given to someone who has done something well (**condecoração**) ▫ *He received a commendation for his actions.* (**recebeu uma condecoração**)

comment /ˈkɒment/ ▶ NOUN [plural **comments**]
1 something you say to give your opinion ▫ *I'd welcome any comments about the revised schedule.* (**comentário**) ▫ *He made the comments in a meeting.* (**fez os comentários**)
2 no comments something you say when you do not want to answer a formal question (**sem comentários**)
▶ VERB [**comments, commenting, commented**] to give your opinion about something ▫ *'That was a waste of time,' Sally commented.* ▫ *A spokesman refused to comment on the reports.* (**comentar**)

commentary /ˈkɒməntəri/ NOUN [plural **commentaries**] a description or explanation of an event as it happens ▫ *There will be live radio commentary of every match.* (**comentário**)

- **commentate** /ˈkɒmənteɪt/ VERB [**commentates, commentating, commentated**] to describe an event as it happens, especially on radio or television ▫ *He was commentating on the match for the BBC.* (**comentar**)
- **commentator** /ˈkɒmənteɪtə(r)/ NOUN [plural **commentators**] someone who gives a commentary ▫ *a football commentator* (**comentarista**)

commerce /ˈkɒmɜːs/ NOUN, NO PLURAL the buying and selling of goods and services ▫ *international commerce* (**comércio**)

- **commercial** /kəˈmɜːʃəl/ ▶ ADJECTIVE
  1 to do with business and selling things ▫ *commercial and residential buildings* ▫ *a commercial airline* (**comercial**)
  2 to do with making a profit ▫ *The decision was made on purely commercial grounds.* (**comercial**)
  ▶ NOUN [plural **commercials**] an advertisement for a product on television or radio (**comercial**)
- **commercialized** or **commercialised** /kəˈmɜːʃəlaɪzd/ ADJECTIVE only to do with making money ▫ *Christmas has become so commercialized.* (**comercializado**)

commiserate /kəˈmɪzəreɪt/ VERB [**commiserates, commiserating, commiserated**] to show sympathy about something that is making someone unhappy (**condoer-se**)

- **commiserations** /kəˌmɪzəˈreɪʃənz/ PLURAL NOUN sympathy for a disappointment or an unhappy situation ▫ *He offered his commiserations.* (**compaixão**)

commission /kəˈmɪʃən/ ▶ NOUN [plural **commissions**]
1 an official group of people who find out about and make decisions about something ▫ *the Commission for Racial Equality* ▫ *an independent commission of experts* (**comissão**)
2 when you ask someone to produce a piece of work for you ▫ *He was given a commission to paint her portrait.* (**comissão**)
3 money paid to someone according to how much they sell ▫ *He receives a commission of 5%.* (**comissão**)
▶ VERB [**commissions, commissioning, commissioned**] to ask someone to produce a piece of work ▫ *He'd been commissioned to write a book.* (**comissionar**)

commit /kəˈmɪt/ VERB [**commits, committing, committed**]
1 to do something bad or illegal (**cometer**) ▫ *He went on to commit more serious crimes.*

(cometer crimes) *What makes people commit murder?* (cometer assassinatos) *to commit suicide* (cometer suicídio)

2 to promise or to decide to do something □ + *to* *He doesn't want to commit to a fixed timetable.* (comprometer-se) *He has committed himself to the club for next season.* (se comprometer)

3 to give money, time, etc. for a particular purpose □ + *to* *The government needs to commit more money to redevelopment.* (depositar)

- **commitment** /kəˈmɪtmənt/ NOUN [*plural* **commitments**]

1 a promise to do something (compromisso) *Viran made a definite commitment to be there.* (prometeu compromisso) *The government has made a long-term commitment to the health service.* (compromisso de longo prazo)

2 *no plural* strong support, effort and enthusiasm for something (compromisso) *She has demonstrated great commitment to the job.* (demonstrou compromisso)

3 something that you must do or are responsible for (compromisso) *She couldn't come because of work commitments.* (compromissos de trabalho) *I don't want to take on more financial commitments.* (compromissos financeiros)

- **committed** /kəˈmɪtɪd/ ADJECTIVE having strong beliefs or support for something □ *a committed Christian* (comprometido, empenhado)

committee /kəˈmɪti/ NOUN [*plural* **committees**] a group of people chosen to do a particular job or to make decisions about something □ *I'm on the committee for the summer fair.* (comitê)

commodious /kəˈməʊdiəs/ ADJECTIVE a formal word meaning large, with a lot of space □ *a commodious hotel bedroom* (cômodo, confortável)

commodity /kəˈmɒdəti/ NOUN [*plural* **commodities**]

1 something that can be bought and sold □ *There were shortages of essential commodities.* (mercadoria)

2 something useful or necessary (objeto de utilidade) *Water is a precious commodity.* (bem de utilidade preciosa)

common /ˈkɒmən/ ▶ ADJECTIVE [**commoner, commonest**]

1 existing or happening often and in many places (comum) *Traffic jams are a common occurrence in cities.* (ocorrência comum) □ + *among* *The condition is common among older people.* □ *Chickenpox is one of the commonest childhood diseases.*

2 shared by several people (comum) *Their common goal was to make the event a success.* (objetivo comum) *We share a common language.* (mesma língua) *It's common knowledge (= everyone knows) that Ann's leaving.* (conhecimento geral)

3 ordinary □ *the common people* (ordinário)
▶ NOUN [*plural* **commons**]

1 **have something in common** to share the same idea, interest, characteristic, etc. as someone or something else □ *I didn't have anything in common with him.* □ *The two countries have a great deal in common.* (ter algo em comum)

2 **in common with someone/something** in the same way as someone or something else □ *In common with other airlines, they have introduced stricter safety measures.* (em comum com alguém/algo)

3 a piece of land that belongs to and can be used by everyone in an area □ *Wimbledon Common* (terra comum)

⇨ go to **Commons**

common denominator /ˌkɒmən dɪˈnɒmɪneɪtə(r)/ NOUN [*plural* **common denominators**]

1 a number that can be divided exactly by all the denominators (= numbers under the line) in a group of fractions. A maths word. (denominador comum)

2 something which is shared by everyone in a group (denominador comum)

common factor /ˌkɒmən ˈfæktə(r)/ NOUN [*plural* **common factors**] a number that two or more numbers can be divided by exactly. A maths word. (fator comum)

common fraction /ˌkɒmən ˈfrækʃən/ NOUN [*plural* **common fractions**] a fraction written with numbers above and below a line. A maths word. (fração comum)

common ground /ˌkɒmən ˈɡraʊnd/ NOUN, NO PLURAL interests or ideas which two or more people share or agree on □ *I believe we can find some common ground between us.* (ponto em comum)

common-law /ˌkɒmənˈlɔː/ ADJECTIVE your common-law husband or wife is a man or woman that you have lived with for a long time without being married (direito comum)

Common Market /ˌkɒmən ˈmɑːkɪt/ NOUN **the Common Market** the old name for the European Union (= political and economic organization of European countries) (Mercado Comum Europeu)

common multiple /ˌkɒmən ˈmʌltɪpəl/ NOUN [*plural* **common multiples**] a number that can be divided exactly by two or more other numbers. A maths word. (múltiplo comum)

commonplace /ˈkɒmənpleɪs/ ADJECTIVE not unusual □ *Wireless technology has become commonplace.* (lugar-comum)

common room /ˈkɒmən ˌruːm/ NOUN [*plural* **common rooms**] a room in a school or college where students can relax between classes (salão comunitário)

Commons /ˈkɒmənz/ NOUN **the Commons** one of the two parts of the British government, with elected members (Câmara dos Comuns)

common sense

common sense /ˌkɒmən ˈsens/ NOUN, NO PLURAL the ability to think and behave in a sensible, practical way (**bom senso**) 🔁 *Use your common sense.* (**use seu bom senso**) ▫ *He tries to take a common sense approach to his work.*

commonwealth /ˈkɒmənwelθ/ NOUN [plural **commonwealths**]
1 a group of countries or states that share political and economic interests (**comunidade**)
2 the Commonwealth Britain and the countries that were ruled by Britain in the past (**Comunidade Britânica de Nações**)

commotion /kəˈməʊʃən/ NOUN [plural **commotions**] noisy and confused activity ▫ *She heard a commotion outside.* (**tumulto, agitação**)

communal /ˈkɒmjunəl/ ADJECTIVE shared by several people ▫ *a communal garden* (**público, comunal**)

commune /ˈkɒmjuːn/ NOUN [plural **communes**] a group of people who live together sharing everything (**comunidade**)

communicable /kəˈmjuːnɪkəbəl/ ADJECTIVE a communicable disease can be passed from one person to another (**contagioso**)

communicate /kəˈmjuːnɪkeɪt/ VERB [**communicates, communicating, communicated**] to share information, opinions, feelings, etc. with other people by speaking, writing, etc. ▫ **+ with** *We are looking for new ways to communicate with our customers.* ▫ **+ by** *We communicate mainly by telephone and email.* ▫ *He failed to communicate important information.* (**comunicar**)

• **communication** /kəˌmjuːnɪˈkeɪʃən/ NOUN [plural **communications**]
1 *no plural* sharing of information (**comunicação**) 🔁 *Text messaging is a common form of communication.* (**meio de comunicação**) ▫ **+ with** *We want to improve communication with the public.* ▫ **+ between** *There was poor communication between departments.*
2 a formal word meaning a message ▫ *We've received an urgent communication from head office.* (**comunicado**)

• **communicative** /kəˈmjuːnɪkətɪv/ ADJECTIVE willing to talk to others and give them information (**comunicativo**)

Communion /kəˈmjuːnjən/ NOUN, NO PLURAL in the Christian Church, the ceremony in which people eat bread and drink wine to represent Christ's body and blood (**comunhão**)

communism /ˈkɒmjunɪzəm/ NOUN, NO PLURAL a political system in which the government owns all industry and everyone is treated equally (**comunismo**)

• **communist** /ˈkɒmjunɪst/ ▶ NOUN [plural **communists**] someone who believes in communism (**comunista**)
▶ ADJECTIVE believing in communism or to do with communists ▫ *a communist country* (**comunista**)

company

community /kəˈmjuːnətɪ/ NOUN [plural **communities**]
1 people living in a particular area (**comunidade**) 🔁 *The school serves the local community.* (**comunidade local**) ▫ *He grew up in a small fishing community.*
2 people who share the same interests, nationality, religion, job, etc. ▫ *the Jewish community in the UK* ▫ *He is respected within the scientific community.* (**comunidade**)

commute /kəˈmjuːt/ VERB [**commutes, commuting, commuted**]
1 to travel regularly between home and work ▫ *He commutes to London every day.* (**ir para o trabalho**)
2 to officially change a punishment to a less severe one ▫ *His death sentence was commuted to life in prison.* (**comutar**)

• **commuter** /kəˈmjuːtə(r)/ NOUN [plural **commuters**] someone who commutes to work (**pessoa que viaja diariamente**)

compact /kəmˈpækt/ ADJECTIVE small and taking up very little space ▫ *a compact camera* ▫ *The equipment is very compact and easy to carry.* (**compacto**)

compact disc /ˌkɒmpækt ˈdɪsk/ NOUN [plural **compact discs**] a disc with sound recorded on it (**CD**)

companion /kəmˈpænjən/ NOUN [plural **companions**]
1 someone who is with you ▫ *Who is her companion?* (**companheiro**)
2 someone who spends a lot of time with someone ▫ *She was his carer and devoted companion.* (**companheiro**)

• **companionable** /kəmˈpænjənəbəl/ ADJECTIVE friendly (**amigável**) 🔁 *We ate our meal in companionable silence.* (**silêncio amigável**)

• **companionship** /kəmˈpænjənʃɪp/ NOUN, NO PLURAL being with a friend or a group of friends and having a friendly relationship with them (**companheirismo**)

company /ˈkʌmpənɪ/ NOUN [plural **companies**]
1 a business organization ▫ *an insurance company* ▫ *He works for a small web design company.* (**companhia**)
2 *no plural* being with other people or the people you spend time with (**companhia**) 🔁 *He's very good company* (= fun to spend time with). (**boa companhia**) ▫ *She got into bad company and started going out late.*
3 keep someone company to stay with someone or go somewhere with them ▫ *Jon came along to keep me company.* (**fazer companhia a alguém**)
4 part company to leave each other ▫ *We parted company when we reached Paris.* (**separar-se**)
5 a group of actors, dancers, singers, etc. ▫ *the Royal Shakespeare Company* (**companhia**)

comparable /'kɒmpərəbəl/ ADJECTIVE similar in some way □ *The two games are comparable in difficulty.* (comparável)

comparative /kəm'pærətɪv/ ▶ ADJECTIVE
1 in grammar, a comparative adjective or adverb usually ends with -er or is used with more. For example better, happier and more dangerous are comparative forms. (comparativo)
2 when compared with something else □ *They reached the comparative safety of the camp.* (comparativo)
3 comparing similar things □ *a comparative analysis* (comparativo)
▶ NOUN [plural **comparatives**] a comparative form of an adjective or adverb (comparativo)
• **comparatively** /kəm'pærətɪvli/ ADVERB compared with something else □ *The house was noisy, and the garden was comparatively quiet.* (comparativamente)

compare /kəm'peə(r)/ VERB [**compares, comparing, compared**]
1 to consider how two or more things are similar or different, or which is better □ + **to** *The weather today is lovely compared to last week.* □ +**with** *The figure is slightly low compared with the national average.* (comparar) ▣ *Their prices compare favourably with those of their competitors.* (se compara favoravelmente) □ *Researchers compared the performance of the four groups.*
2 to describe someone or something as being like another person or thing □ + **to** *She compared him to a mad dog.* (comparar)
• **comparison** /kəm'pærɪsən/ NOUN [plural **comparisons**] when you compare things (comparação) ▣ *Many people have drawn a comparison between the two players.* (fizeram um comparativo) □ + **between** *Teachers were always making comparisons between me and my brother.* ▣ *There's no comparison between shop cakes and home made cakes (= home made cakes are much better).* (não há comparação) ▣ *Taxes are low in comparison with other countries.* (em comparação a)

compartment /kəm'pɑːtmənt/ NOUN [plural **compartments**]
1 a separate part within a container, piece of furniture, etc. □ *There was a secret compartment at the back of the desk.* (compartimento)
2 a separate area, especially in a train (cabine) ▣ *the first-class compartment* (cabine de primeira classe)

compass /'kʌmpəs/ NOUN [plural **compasses**]
1 a piece of equipment that shows the direction of north, which you can use to find your way (bússola)
2 compasses a piece of equipment used for drawing circles (compasso)

compassion /kəm'pæʃən/ NOUN, NO PLURAL a feeling of sympathy for someone's suffering □ *He showed compassion for the poor.* (compaixão)
• **compassionate** /kəm'pæʃənət/ ADJECTIVE showing compassion (compassivo)

compatibility /kəm,pætə'bɪlɪti/ NOUN, NO PLURAL the quality that allows people or things to work well together or have a good relationship (compatibilidade)

compatible /kəm'pætəbəl/ ADJECTIVE
1 compatible pieces of equipment can work together □ *Is the software compatible with your existing computer system?* (compatível)
2 if people are compatible, they are able to have a good relationship □ *We just weren't really compatible.* (compatível)
3 compatible ideas, beliefs or situations can exist together □ *Working such long hours isn't really compatible with family life.* (compatível)

compatriot /kəm'pætrɪət/ NOUN [plural **compatriots**] a formal word for someone who comes from the same country as you (compatriota)

compel /kəm'pel/ VERB [**compels, compelling, compelled**] a formal word meaning to force someone to do something (obrigar) ▣ *I felt compelled to get involved.* (Eu me senti obrigado)
• **compelling** /kəm'pelɪŋ/ ADJECTIVE
1 very interesting or exciting □ *It's a very dramatic and compelling story.* (irresistível)
2 compelling reasons or arguments are so strong that you cannot disagree with them (convincente) ▣ *There is compelling evidence of their guilt.* (evidência convincente) ▣ *There was no compelling reason to stay.* (motivo convincente)

compensate /'kɒmpənseɪt/ VERB [**compensates, compensating, compensated**]
1 to pay someone money in exchange for something they have lost or suffered □ *We were compensated for the extra hours we had to work.* (compensar)
2 to make a bad result or situation seem better □ *His ability to get on with people compensates for his lack of experience.* (compensar)
• **compensation** /,kɒmpən'seɪʃən/ NOUN, NO PLURAL
1 money given to someone for a loss or injury (indenização) ▣ *pay/receive compensation* (pagar/receber indenização) □ *He received £5,000 in compensation.*
2 something which makes a bad situation seem better □ *A win today would be some compensation for recent disappointments.* (compensação)

compère /'kɒmpeə(r)/ NOUN [plural **compères**] someone who introduces performers in a show (mestre de cerimônias, apresentador)

compete /kəm'piːt/ VERB [**competes, competing, competed**]
1 to take part in a race, competition, etc. □ + *in* *always dreamed of competing in the Olympics.* □

+ **against** We'll be competing against some top teams. □ + **for** Twenty-five players are competing for the title. □ He has the ability to compete at the highest level. (competir)
2 to try to be more successful than someone else □ + **with** The company can't compete with larger rivals. □ UK business needs to compete internationally. (competir)
3 to try to get something that other people also want □ + **for** Farmers and local people are competing for scarce water resources. (disputar) ▣ The three brothers were always competing for their mother's attention. (disputando atenção)

competence /ˈkɒmpɪtəns/ NOUN, NO PLURAL the ability to do something well (competência)
• **competent** /ˈkɒmpɪtənt/ ADJECTIVE able to do something well □ He's a very competent manager. (competente)
• **competently** /ˈkɒmpɪtəntli/ ADVERB effectively or skilfully □ She handled the situation competently. (competentemente)

competition /ˌkɒmpɪˈtɪʃən/ NOUN [plural competitions]
1 an event at which people try to win or to be better than the others (competição) ▣ She entered a competition to win a holiday. (entrou na competição) ▣ He won a singing competition. (venceu uma competição)
2 no plural trying to win or to be more successful than other people or organizations (disputa) ▣ There will be stiff competition for places. (disputa acirrada) ▣ There has always been fierce competition between Coca-Cola and Pepsi. (disputa feroz) ▣ Newspapers now face competition from the Internet. (encaram disputa)
3 the competition people or organizations you are competing against □ We have to keep ahead of the competition. (a concorrência)
• **competitive** /kəmˈpetɪtɪv/ ADJECTIVE
1 to do with or involving competition (competitivo) ▣ a competitive sport (esporte competitivo)
2 liking to compete and win □ I'm a very competitive person. (competitivo)
3 if businesses are competitive, they are able to be successful □ To remain competitive we have to cut costs. (competitivo)
4 cheaper than other similar products or services (competitivo) ▣ They offer high-quality products at competitive prices. (preços competitivos)
• **competitor** /kəmˈpetɪtə(r)/ NOUN [plural competitors]
1 someone taking part in a competition □ He's the oldest competitor in the race. (competidor)
2 a company selling the same thing as another □ The company has two main competitors. (concorrente)

compilation /ˌkɒmpɪˈleɪʃən/ NOUN [plural compilations]
1 a collection of pieces of writing, music or information □ The album is a compilation of the band's greatest hits. (coleção)
2 no plural the process of compiling something (compilação)

compile /kəmˈpaɪl/ VERB [compiles, compiling, compiled] to collect information together to make a book, list, etc. (compilar) ▣ The firm has compiled a list of candidates. (compilou uma lista de) ▣ The committee will compile a report on the event. (compilou um relatório)
• **compiler** /kəmˈpaɪlə(r)/ NOUN [plural compilers] someone who compiles something (compilador)

complacency /kəmˈpleɪsənsi/ NOUN, NO PLURAL the feeling that a situation is good enough, so you do not try very hard to improve it (complacência)
• **complacent** /kəmˈpleɪsənt/ ADJECTIVE when you think a situation is good enough, so you do not try very hard to improve it ▣ It's easy to become complacent about security. (complacente)

complain /kəmˈpleɪn/ VERB [complains, complaining, complained] to say that you are not happy or satisfied about something □ + **that** He complained that it was too hot. □ + **about** Our neighbours complained about the noise. (queixar-se)
◆ PHRASAL VERB **complain of something**
1 to say that you are ill □ She had complained of headaches. (queixar-se de algo)
2 to say that something bad has happened to you □ Several employees complained of discrimination. (queixar-se de algo)
• **complaint** /kəmˈpleɪnt/ NOUN [plural complaints]
1 when you complain about something □ + **about** We've received several complaints about his behaviour. (queixa, reclamação) ▣ I wish to make a complaint. (fazer uma reclamação) ▣ They filed a formal complaint with the police. (queixa formal)
2 an illness (doença) ▣ The nurse treats patients with minor complaints. (doenças secundárias)

complement ▶ NOUN /ˈkɒmplɪmənt/ [plural complements]
1 something that goes very well with another thing □ The sauce is a lovely complement to the meat. (complemento)
2 something that is added something else □ The software is a complement to existing applications. (complemento)
3 the total number or amount of something needed (complemento) ▣ The department is short of its full complement of 15 staff. (complemento total)
▶ VERB /ˈkɒmplɪment/ [complements, complementing, complemented] if two things complement each other, they go very well

together □ *Our online resources complement the printed books.* (completar, complementar)
- **complementary** /ˌkɒmplɪˈmentəri/ ADJECTIVE going well together □ *These approaches are complementary and work well in combination.* (complementar)

complementary medicine
/ˌkɒmplɪmentəriˈmedsɪn/ NOUN, NO PLURAL types of medical treatment not used by most ordinary doctors (medicina alternativa)

complete /kəmˈpliːt/ ▶ VERB [completes, completing, completed]
1 to finish something □ *You must complete the test in 15 minutes.* □ *She completed a 10-week English course.* □ *The work should be completed by the end of March.* (terminar)
2 to make something whole by adding all the parts □ *Complete the sentence using one word in each gap.* (completar)
3 to write all the information needed on a form or document (preencher) 🔒 *Each participant completes a questionnaire.* (preencher um questionário) □ *He had completed the necessary paperwork.*
▶ ADJECTIVE
1 including all parts □ *a complete set of golf clubs* □ *Here's the complete list of winners.* □ *+ with It's a 5-star hotel complete with indoor pool and spa.* (completo)
2 used to emphasize what you are saying □ *I felt a complete fool.* □ *It was a complete surprise to me.* (completo) 🔒 *She received a letter from a complete stranger.* (completo desconhecido)
3 finished □ *The building work is almost complete.* (finalizado)
- **completely** /kəmˈpliːtli/ ADVERB in every way or with every part finished □ *I agree completely.* □ *The whole day was completely ruined.* □ *This job is completely different from what I did before.* □ *They had completely cleaned the whole house.* (totalmente)

> ➤ Note that **completely** comes before adjectives that have strong meanings. Before adjectives that are less strong, use **very** or **extremely**: □ It's **completely** ridiculous. □ It's **very** silly. □ It's **completely** exhausting. □ It's **very** tiring.

- **completeness** /kəmˈpliːtnɪs/ NOUN, NO PLURAL the quality of being whole, with nothing missing □ *We check the data for accuracy and completeness.* (perfeição)
- **completion** /kəmˈpliːʃən/ NOUN, NO PLURAL when something is finished (término, finalização) 🔒 *The filming is nearing completion.* (próximo do término) □ *Payment is due on completion of the work.*

complex /ˈkɒmpleks/ ▶ ADJECTIVE with many different parts and difficult to understand □ *These are complex issues.* □ *The situation has become increasingly complex.* (complexo)
▶ NOUN [plural **complexes**]
1 a group of buildings all with the same use □ *a sports complex* (complexo)
2 a mental problem that makes someone very worried about something □ *She has a real complex about her weight.* (complexo)

complexion /kəmˈplekʃən/ NOUN [plural complexions] the colour and condition of your skin □ *She has blond hair and a fair complexion.* (tez, cútis)

complexity /kəmˈpleksɪti/ NOUN [plural complexities] the quality of being complicated or difficult (complexidade)

compliance /kəmˈplaɪəns/ NOUN, NO PLURAL obeying rules or someone else's wishes □ *All the work is carried out in compliance with safety standards.* (conformidade)
- **compliant** /kəmˈplaɪənt/ ADJECTIVE willing to do what another person wants (complacente, submisso)

complicate /ˈkɒmplɪkeɪt/ VERB [complicates, complicating, complicated] to make something more difficult to understand or to deal with (complicar) 🔒 *To complicate matters further, we could only film at night.* (para complicar ainda mais)
- **complicated** /ˈkɒmplɪkeɪtɪd/ ADJECTIVE difficult to understand or to deal with □ *a complicated calculation* □ *The situation has become more complicated.* (complicado)
- **complication** /ˌkɒmplɪˈkeɪʃən/ NOUN [plural complications] something that creates a problem or difficulty (complicação) 🔒 *The operation went well and there were no serious complications.* (complicações sérias)

complicit /kəmˈplɪsɪt/ ADJECTIVE involved with or knowing about something wrong or illegal □ *The company was complicit in the payment of bribes.* (cúmplice)
- **complicity** /kəmˈplɪsɪti/ NOUN, NO PLURAL being complicit in something wrong or illegal (cumplicidade)

compliment ▶ NOUN /ˈkɒmplɪmənt/ [plural compliments]
1 something that you say that praises someone (cumprimento, elogio) 🔒 *Otto paid me a compliment for once.* (fez um elogio)
2 compliments of someone used to say that something is from someone and you do not have to pay for it □ *We finished with a brandy, compliments of the chef.* (cortesia de alguém)
▶ VERB /ˈkɒmplɪment/ [compliments, complimenting, complimented] to praise someone □ *Leo complimented her on her good taste.* (cumprimentar)
- **complimentary** /ˌkɒmplɪˈmentəri/ ADJECTIVE
1 showing praise or admiration □ *The article she wrote was very complimentary.* (lisonjeiro)
2 given free □ *He sent us complimentary tickets for the show.* (grátis)

comply /kəmˈplaɪ/ VERB [**complies, complying, complied**] to obey a rule or to agree to do something □ *It is impossible to comply with such demands.* □ *We have changed our procedures to comply with the new regulations.* (**obedecer**)

component /kəmˈpəʊnənt/ NOUN [plural **components**] one of the parts of something □ *The company manufactures electronic components.* (**componente**) 🔲 *Exercise is a key component of the treatment programme.* (**componente chave**)

compose /kəmˈpəʊz/ VERB [**composes, composing, composed**]
1 to write a piece of music □ *He has composed the music for a number of movies.* (**compor**)
2 if something is composed of something, it is formed of it □ *The team is composed of three men and three women.* (**compor**)
3 to write something that you have to think about a lot □ *She sat down to compose a letter to Steven.* (**compor**)
4 compose yourself to control your feelings and become calm □ *She paused to compose herself.* (**acalme-se**)

• **composed** /kəmˈpəʊzd/ ADJECTIVE in control of your feelings □ *He remained calm and composed.* (**sereno**)

• **composer** /kəmˈpəʊzə(r)/ NOUN [plural **composers**] someone who writes music (**compositor**)

• **composite** /ˈkɒmpəzɪt/ ▶ ADJECTIVE made of several different parts or materials □ *It is made of a lightweight composite material.* (**compor**)
▶ NOUN [plural **composites**] something made of several different parts or materials □ *The picture was a composite of several old photographs.* (**composição, composto**)

• **composition** /ˌkɒmpəˈzɪʃən/ NOUN [plural **compositions**]
1 no plural the parts that something is made of □ + **of** *the chemical composition of the sample* □ *The culture reflects the city's ethnic composition.* (**composição**)
2 a piece of music (**composição**)
3 no plural the process of writing music □ *She studied composition.* (**composição**)
4 an essay □ *We had to write a composition on the nature of love.* (**redação**)

compost /ˈkɒmpɒst/ NOUN, NO PLURAL a mixture of decayed plants and leaves that is spread on soil to improve its quality (**adubo**) 🔲 *a compost heap* (= pile where compost is put) (**pilha de adubo**)

composure /kəmˈpəʊʒə(r)/ NOUN, NO PLURAL being in control of your feelings so that you are calm (**compostura**) 🔲 *He took a moment to regain his composure.* (**recuperar a compostura**)

compound ▶ NOUN /ˈkɒmpaʊnd/ [plural **compounds**]
1 a substance formed from two or more parts or substances. A chemistry word (**composto**) 🔲 *a chemical compound* (**composto químico**)
2 an area surrounded by a fence or wall □ *The troops were based in a walled compound.* (**recinto**)
3 a word made of two or more other words. The words airport and tape recorder are compounds. (**composto**)

▶ VERB /kəmˈpaʊnd/ [**compounds, compounding, compounded**] to make a problem worse by adding to it (**compor, formar**) 🔲 *Recent delays have compounded the problem.* (**agravar o problema**)

compound eye /ˌkɒmpaʊnd ˈaɪ/ NOUN [plural **compound eyes**] an eye, for example of an insect, that is made of many small parts. A biology word. (**olho facetado**)

comprehend /ˌkɒmprɪˈhend/ VERB [**comprehends, comprehending, comprehended**] a formal word meaning to understand □ *It's difficult to comprehend the scale of this disaster.* (**compreender**)

• **comprehensible** /ˌkɒmprɪˈhensəbəl/ ADJECTIVE able to be understood □ *Her words were barely comprehensible beneath the sobs.* (**compreensível**)

• **comprehension** /ˌkɒmprɪˈhenʃən/ NOUN, NO PLURAL understanding □ *a test of reading comprehension* (**compreensão**)

• **comprehensive** /ˌkɒmprɪˈhensɪv/ ▶ ADJECTIVE dealing with everything □ *a comprehensive report* (**amplo, abrangente**)
▶ NOUN [plural **comprehensives**] a comprehensive school (**inclusivo**)

comprehensive school /ˌkɒmprɪˈhensɪv ˌskuːl/ NOUN [plural **comprehensive schools**] a secondary school (= school for children aged around 11-16) run by the state where pupils of all abilities are educated in all subjects (**escola de Ensino Médio**)

compress /kəmˈpres/ VERB [**compresses, compressing, compressed**]
1 to make something fit into a smaller space □ *A diesel engine works by compressing the fuel.* (**comprimir**)
2 to use a computer program to make a computer file smaller. A computing word. (**compactar**)

comprise /kəmˈpraɪz/ VERB [**comprises, comprising, comprised**] a formal word meaning to contain or to be made of □ *The test will comprise two parts.* □ *The group was comprised of healthy individuals.* (**englobar, abranger**)

compromise /ˈkɒmprəmaɪz/ ▶ VERB [**compromises, compromising, compromised**]
1 to give up some part of what you want so that an agreement can be made □ *I'm not willing to compromise on this issue.* (**comprometer**)
2 to risk harming or losing something (**comprometer**) 🔲 *Releasing this information could compromise national security.* (**comprometer a segurança**)

▶ NOUN [plural **compromises**] an agreement in

compulsion

which each person or side gives up something they want (acordo) ⮕ We've finally reached a compromise on where to go on holiday. (chegamos a um acordo)

compulsion /kəmˈpʌlʃən/ NOUN [plural compulsions]
1 a feeling that you must do something □ She felt a sudden compulsion to leave the room. (compulsão)
2 being forced to do something □ There was no compulsion to take part. (imposição, obrigação)

• **compulsive** /kəmˈpʌlsɪv/ ADJECTIVE
1 not able to control something or not able to stop doing something (compulsivo) ⮕ a compulsive liar/gambler (mentiroso/jogador compulsivo)
2 so exciting or interesting that you cannot stop reading or watching (absorvente, fascinante) ⮕ The show has proved compulsive viewing. (vista fascinante)

• **compulsory** /kəmˈpʌlsəri/ ADJECTIVE if something is compulsory, you must do it or have it □ Subjects like Maths and English are compulsory. (obrigatório)

computer /kəmˈpjuːtə(r)/ NOUN [plural computers] an electronic machine that can store and deal with very large amounts of information (computador) ⮕ a personal computer (computador pessoal) ⮕ I mostly use my computer to send emails. (uso meu computador)

• **computerize** or **computerise** /kəmˈpjuːtəraɪz/ VERB [computerizes, computerizing, computerized] to use a computer to do something that was done in a different way before □ There is a plan to computerize medical records. (informatizar)

• **computerized** /kəmˈpjuːtəraɪzd/ ADJECTIVE stored in or dealt with by a computer □ computerized records of fingerprints (computadorizado)

• **computing** /kəmˈpjuːtɪŋ/ NOUN, NO PLURAL the use of computers or the skill of working with computers □ He studied computing. (informática)

comrade /ˈkɒmreɪd/ NOUN [plural comrades] a friend, especially in the army (camarada)

con /kɒn/ VERB [cons, conning, conned] an informal word meaning to trick someone into doing something or thinking that something is true □ I think we've been conned. □ People are being conned into paying for unnecessary software. (enganar)
▶ NOUN [plural cons] an informal word for a trick □ Ignore the email, it's just a con. (trapaça)
⇨ go to pros and cons

concave /ˈkɒnkeɪv/ ADJECTIVE curving in or down. A physics word. □ a concave lens (côncavo)

conceal /kənˈsiːl/ VERB [conceals, concealing, concealed] to hide something or to keep it secret □ She concealed herself behind a bush. □ He couldn't conceal his disappointment. (dissimular)

• **concealment** /kənˈsiːlmənt/ NOUN, NO PLURAL when something is concealed (dissimulado)

concede /kənˈsiːd/ VERB [concedes, conceding, conceded]
1 to admit that something is true even though you do not want to □ 'It may be possible,' he conceded. (admitir)
2 to allow someone you are competing against to win a point, goal, game, etc. (permitir) ⮕ They conceded a goal in the 89th minute. (permitir um gol)
3 concede defeat to accept that you have lost □ He finally conceded defeat when it became clear his rival had more votes. (reconhecer a derrota)

conceit /kənˈsiːt/ NOUN, NO PLURAL the quality of having a very good opinion of yourself and what you can do □ She was amazed at the actor's total lack of conceit. (presunção)

• **conceited** /kənˈsiːtɪd/ ADJECTIVE showing conceit □ He's a conceited young man. (presunçoso)

conceivable /kənˈsiːvəbəl/ ADJECTIVE possible to imagine or believe □ It's perfectly conceivable that it was lost in the post. □ She took photos from every conceivable angle. (concebível)

• **conceivably** /kənˈsiːvəbli/ ADVERB possibly □ She could conceivably become the first woman president. (de modo concebível)

conceive /kənˈsiːv/ VERB [conceives, conceiving, conceived]
1 to imagine something or to think of an idea □ He couldn't conceive how he was going to do it. (imaginar)
2 to think of an idea or a plan □ He conceived a plan to take over the company. (pensar)
3 if a woman conceives, she becomes pregnant (engravidar)

concentrate /ˈkɒnsəntreɪt/ VERB [concentrates, concentrating, concentrated]
1 to give all your attention to something □ + on Try to concentrate on one thing at a time. (concentrar) ⮕ I had to concentrate hard to understand what he said. (concentrar bastante) ⮕ The company is concentrating its efforts on the UK market. (concentrando seus esforços)
2 if things are concentrated in one place, they are all together in that place □ Most hotels are concentrated in the south of the island. (centralizar)

• **concentrated** /ˈkɒnsəntreɪtɪd/ ADJECTIVE
1 a concentrated liquid is stronger because some of the water has been removed from it □ concentrated orange juice (concentrado)
2 using a lot of effort to achieve something ⮕ We made a concentrated effort to finish the gardening. (concentrado)

• **concentration** /ˌkɒnsənˈtreɪʃən/ NOUN [plural

concentrations]

1 no plural when you give all your attention to something (**concentração**) 🔍 *I lost concentration and started making mistakes.* (**perdi a concentração**) □ *There was a look of concentration on her face.*

2 a large number or amount of something in one place (**concentração**) 🔍 *We found a high concentration of pollen in the air.* (**alta concentração**)

concentration camp /ˌkɒnsənˈtreɪʃən ˌkæmp/ NOUN [plural **concentration camps**] a prison where large numbers of people are kept, especially during a war (**campo de concentração**)

concentric /kənˈsentrɪk/ ADJECTIVE concentric circles are inside each other and have the same centre. A maths word. (**concentração**)

concept /ˈkɒnsept/ NOUN [plural **concepts**]
1 an idea or principle □ *the concept of democracy* □ *We teach some of the basic concepts of web design.* (**conceito, ideia**)

2 have no concept of something to not understand or be able to imagine something □ *He doesn't seem to have any concept of right and wrong.* (**não ter noção de algo**)

• **conception** /kənˈsepʃən/ NOUN [plural **conceptions**]
1 an understanding or belief about what something is like □ *He looked exactly like the popular conception of a scientist.* (**conceito, concepção**)

2 when a woman becomes pregnant (**ato de engravidar**)

concern /kənˈsɜːn/ ▶ VERB [**concerns, concerning, concerned**]
1 to worry someone □ *His disappearance was beginning to concern us.* □ *Which issue concerns you most right now?* (**preocupar-se**)

2 to affect or to be important to someone □ *Don't interfere in things that don't concern you.* (**interessar**)

3 to be about something □ *The research concerns the long-term effects of poor diet.* (**dizer respeito**)

4 concern yourself with something to become involved in doing something or to pay attention to something □ *You mustn't concern yourself with the travel arrangements.* (**envolver-se com algo**)

▶ NOUN [plural **concerns**]
1 something that worries you or a feeling of worry □ *If you have any concerns about the exam, speak to your teacher.* (**preocupação**) 🔍 *He expressed concern about the safety of the vehicle.* (**expressou preocupação**) 🔍 *There is widespread concern about fuel shortages.* (**preocupação vasta**)

2 something that affects you or is important to you (**preocupação**) 🔍 *My main concern is getting a job.* (**principal preocupação**)

3 when you care about something □ *They showed no concern for the law.* □ *There was genuine concern for her welfare.* (**preocupação**)

• **concerned** /kənˈsɜːnd/ ADJECTIVE
1 worried or caring about someone or something □ *concerned parents* □ *Many people are concerned about the environmental impact of flying.* (**preocupado**)

2 involved in or affected by something □ *He thanked everyone concerned.* (**envolvido**)

3 as far as I'm/he's, etc. concerned used to show someone's opinion □ *As far as I'm concerned, he can go ahead.* (**na opinião de alguém**)

4 as far as something is concerned used to show what you are talking about □ *As far as food's concerned, I'll eat anything.* (**no que diz respeito a algo**)

• **concerning** /kənˈsɜːnɪŋ/ PREPOSITION about or involving someone or something □ *There are serious allegations concerning his behaviour.* (**a respeito de**)

concert /ˈkɒnsət/ NOUN [plural **concerts**] a musical performance 🔍 *a rock concert* (**show**)

concerted /kənˈsɜːtɪd/ ADJECTIVE done with a lot of effort by a group of people working together (**em conjunto, combinado**) 🔍 *We must make a concerted effort to win this match.* (**esforços conjuntos**)

concertina /ˌkɒnsəˈtiːnə/ NOUN [plural **concertinas**] a musical instrument that you play by pushing the sides together while pressing buttons (**concertina, sanfona**)

concerto /kənˈtʃeətəʊ/ NOUN [plural **concertos**] a piece of music to be played by one instrument and an orchestra (= large group of musicians) (**concerto**) 🔍 *a piano concerto* (**concerto de piano**)

concession /kənˈseʃən/ NOUN [plural **concessions**] something that you agree to in order to end a disagreement (**concessão**) 🔍 *The company refused to make any concessions and the strike continued.* (**fazer concessão**)

conciliation /kənˌsɪliˈeɪʃən/ NOUN, NO PLURAL the process of reaching an agreement. A formal word. □ *Has there been any progress towards conciliation?* (**conciliação**)

concise /kənˈsaɪs/ ADJECTIVE short and containing all the information without unnecessary details □ *a concise summary* (**conciso**)

conclude /kənˈkluːd/ VERB [**concludes, concluding, concluded**]
1 to decide something after thinking carefully about it □ *He concluded that she was lying.* □ *The researchers concluded that the risk is very low.* (**concluir**)

2 a formal word meaning to end □ *The drama course concluded with a performance.* (**concluir**)

3 to complete something such as an agreement □ *We hope to conclude the deal by Friday.* (**concluir**)

- **concluding** /kənˈkluːdɪŋ/ ADJECTIVE last □ *the concluding chapter of the novel* (**último, derradeiro**)
- **conclusion** /kənˈkluːʒən/ NOUN [plural **conclusions**]
1 a decision you make after thinking carefully about something □ + *of What was the main conclusion of the study?* (**conclusão**) 🔁 *I've come to the conclusion that she just doesn't care.* (**cheguei à conclusão**) 🔁 *You can reach your own conclusion about that.* (**chegar à conclusão**) 🔁 *It's difficult to draw any conclusions from one small survey.* (**formular conclusões**)
2 the last part of something □ + *of I just have to write the conclusion of my essay.* □ *He spoke to reporters at the conclusion of the meeting.* (**fim**)
3 no plural when something is formally agreed or arranged □ + *of He was responsible for the conclusion of the peace treaty.* (**conclusão**)
4 jump to conclusions to make a decision about something too quickly, without knowing all the facts (**tirar conclusões antecipadas**)
- **conclusive** /kənˈkluːsɪv/ ADJECTIVE showing that something is certainly true (**conclusivo**) 🔁 *There is no conclusive evidence to support this claim.* (**evidência conclusiva**)
- **conclusively** /kənˈkluːsɪvlɪ/ ADVERB without any doubt □ *The videotape proved conclusively that he was the person who had broken in.* (**conclusivamente**)

concoct /kənˈkɒkt/ VERB [**concocts, concocting, concocted**]
1 to invent a story, plan, etc. which is not true (**inventar**) 🔁 *She concocted a story to get out of the trip.* (**inventou uma história**)
2 to make something unusual by mixing different things, usually foods, together (**misturar**)
- **concoction** /kənˈkɒkʃən/ NOUN [plural **concoctions**] something made by mixing different things, usually foods, together □ *The drink is a concoction of fruit juices.* (**mistura**)

concourse /ˈkɒŋkɔːs/ NOUN [plural **concourses**] a large room or area, for example at an airport or station □ *I'll meet you on the station concourse.* (**saguão, pátio**)

concrete /ˈkɒŋkriːt/ ▶ NOUN, NO PLURAL a strong, hard building material made by mixing sand, cement (= grey powder), small stones and water □ *a slab of concrete* (**concreto**)
⇨ go to **set in stone/concrete**
▶ ADJECTIVE
1 made of concrete □ *a concrete floor* (**feito de concreto**)
2 certain or based on facts (**concreto, real**) 🔁 *They found concrete evidence of fraud.* (**evidência concreta**) □ *There's a lack of concrete information.*
3 real or practical (**específico**) 🔁 *We are taking concrete steps to reduce crime.* (**passos específicos**) □ *Do you have any concrete proposals to make?*
4 able to be seen or touched □ *A table is a concrete object.* (**concreto**)
▶ VERB [**concretes, concreting, concreted**] to put concrete on something □ *Dan's going to concrete the driveway this weekend.* (**concretar**)

concur /kənˈkɜː(r)/ VERB [**concurs, concurring, concurred**] a formal word meaning to agree □ *The members concurred that a change of plan was needed.* (**concordar**)

concurrent /kənˈkʌrənt/ ADJECTIVE a formal word describing things which exist or happen at the same time □ *The system can support up to 5,000 concurrent users.* (**simultâneo**)
- **concurrently** /kənˈkʌrəntlɪ/ ADVERB a formal word meaning happening at the same time □ *It was decided that the two races couldn't be run concurrently.* (**simultaneamente**)

concussion /kənˈkʌʃən/ NOUN, NO PLURAL a slight injury to the brain caused by hitting your head (**concussão**)

condemn /kənˈdem/ VERB [**condemns, condemning, condemned**]
1 to say that someone or something is wrong or bad □ *The President has condemned the violence.* (**condenar, censurar**)
2 if someone is condemned to a serious punishment, they are given it by a court (**condenar, sentenciar**) 🔁 *He was condemned to death.* (**condenado à morte**)
3 to make someone experience a bad situation □ *His disability condemned him to a life of poverty.* (**condenar**)
4 to say that a building must be destroyed because it is not safe (**condenar, desapropriar**)
- **condemnation** /ˌkɒndemˈneɪʃən/ NOUN [plural **condemnations**] saying that something is wrong or bad □ *The attack provoked international condemnation.* (**condenação**)

condensation /ˌkɒndenˈseɪʃən/ NOUN, NO PLURAL drops of water that form when hot air or steam touches a cold surface such as a window (**condensação**)

condense /kənˈdens/ VERB [**condenses, condensing, condensed**]
1 to make something shorter □ *The report condenses the results into just ten pages.* (**comprimir, resumir**)
2 if steam or gas condenses, it becomes a liquid as it gets cooler. A chemistry word. (**condensar**)

condescending /ˌkɒndɪˈsendɪŋ/ ADJECTIVE showing that you think you are better than other people □ *a condescending attitude* (**condescendente**)

condiment /ˈkɒndɪmənt/ NOUN [plural **condiments**] things that you add to food to give it more flavour, for example salt and pepper (**condimento, tempero**)

condition /kənˈdɪʃən/ ▶ NOUN [plural conditions]

1 the state that someone or something is in □ *+ of There were concerns over the condition of the plane.* (condição) 🔳 *He was taken to hospital in a critical condition.* (condição crítica) 🔳 *The house was in a poor condition.* (condições lastimáveis)

2 something that has to happen before something else does, especially as part of an agreement □ *+ of He broke the conditions of his licence.* (condição) 🔳 *I'll go on the condition that you come too.* (na condição de que)

3 conditions the situation or things happening at a particular time or place (condições) 🔳 *The flight was cancelled due to bad weather conditions.* (condições do tempo) 🔳 *Our living conditions have improved.* (meios de vida)

4 an illness (problema) 🔳 *She was diagnosed with a serious medical condition.* (problema de saúde) 🔳 *He had a heart condition.* (problema cardíaco)

▶ VERB [conditions, conditioning, conditioned]

1 if you are conditioned to do something, you do it because you have been influenced by someone or something □ *Young troops are conditioned to obey orders.* □ *Our tastes are conditioned by fashion.* (condicionar)

2 to put conditioner on your hair (condicionar)

- **conditional** /kənˈdɪʃənəl/ ADJECTIVE
1 depending on something else happening □ *She has a conditional offer of a place at university.* □ *+ on The deal is conditional on official approval.* (condicional)
2 a conditional sentence usually starts with if and says that one thing must be true before another thing can be true (condicional)

- **conditionally** /kənˈdɪʃənəli/ ADVERB only if something else happens □ *They have conditionally approved the proposal.* (condicionalmente)

- **conditioner** /kənˈdɪʃənə(r)/ NOUN [plural conditioners] a substance you put on your hair to make it softer (condicionador)

- **conditioning** /kənˈdɪʃənɪŋ/ NOUN, NO PLURAL the way people and animals are influenced by what they have experienced or have been told (condicionamento)

condolences /kənˈdəʊlənsɪz/ PLURAL NOUN
something you say to show your sympathy when someone has died (pêsames, condolências) 🔳 *He expressed his deepest condolences to the family.* (expressou condolências)

condone /kənˈdəʊn/ VERB [condones, condoning, condoned]
to accept or allow something which is wrong □ *We don't condone violence in any form.* (tolerar)

conducive /kənˈdjuːsɪv/ ADJECTIVE
if one thing is conducive to another, it encourages it or makes it easier □ *The noisy atmosphere was not conducive to a romantic evening.* (condutivo)

conduct ▶ VERB /kənˈdʌkt/ [conducts, conducting, conducted]

1 to organize or do something (conduzir) 🔳 *Doctors are conducting further tests.* (conduzindo testes) □ *We are conducting a full investigation into the accident.*

2 conduct yourself to behave in a particular way □ *We expect you to conduct yourselves with dignity.* (comportar-se)

3 to stand in front of an orchestra (= large group of musicians) to control their performance □ *Sarah Hobbs conducted the orchestra.* (reger)

4 if a material conducts electricity or heat, it allows electricity or heat to flow through it. A physics word. (conduzir)

5 a formal word meaning to take someone somewhere □ *The butler conducted us into the library.* (conduzir)

▶ NOUN, NO PLURAL /ˈkɒndʌkt/

1 the way someone behaves □ *Their reckless conduct was the cause of the accident.* (conduta, comportamento) 🔳 *There is a strict code of conduct.* (código de conduta)

2 the way something is organized or done □ *An independent body is supervising the conduct of the election.* (condução)

- **conduction** /kənˈdʌkʃən/ NOUN, NO PLURAL the flow of electricity or heat through something. A physics word. (condução)

- **conductor** /kənˈdʌktə(r)/ NOUN [plural conductors]
1 someone who conducts an orchestra (regente)
2 an object that conducts electricity or heat. A physics word. □ *a lightning conductor* (condutor)

cone /kəʊn/ NOUN [plural cones]

1 a solid shape with a round base and sides that slope up to a point at the top, or an object with this shape (cone) 🔳 *a traffic cone* (cone de trânsito)

2 a fruit of a pine tree (pinha)

3 a cone-shaped container used to hold ice cream (casquinha de sorvete)

confectionery /kənˈfekʃənəri/ NOUN, NO PLURAL cakes and sweets (artigos de confeitaria)

confederate /kənˈfedərət/ NOUN [plural confederates] someone who helps you, especially to do something illegal (confederado, aliado)

- **confederation** /kənˌfedəˈreɪʃən/ NOUN [plural confederations] several groups or organizations that have joined together (confederação)

confer /kənˈfɜː(r)/ VERB [confers, conferring, conferred]

1 to discuss something with other people in order to make a decision □ *He turned to confer with his lawyer.* (conferenciar, deliberar)

2 a formal word meaning to give someone something □ *A government job confers status and opportunity.* (conceder, outorgar)

- **conference** /ˈkɒnfərəns/ NOUN [plural conferences]
1 a large meeting of people to discuss a particular subject □ *+ on a UN conference on climate change* (conferência) 🔳 *The union is holding its annual conference this week.* (realizando conferência)

confess

2 news/press conference a meeting at which someone gives information about something to newspapers, television, etc. (**entrevista coletiva**)

confess /kənˈfes/ VERB [confesses, confessing, confessed]
1 to admit to other people that you have done something wrong □ *He confessed to stealing the money.* (**confessar**)
2 to admit something you feel embarrassed or guilty about □ *I don't mind confessing that I was terrified.* □ *'I'd forgotten his name,' she confessed.* (**admitir, reconhecer**)

• **confession** /kənˈfeʃən/ NOUN [plural confessions]
1 when you confess that you are guilty of a crime or something wrong (**confissão**) 🔁 *I've got a confession to make.* (**uma confissão a fazer**) 🔁 *He made a full confession to the police.* (**confissão completa**)
2 when you tell a priest all the things you have done wrong (**confissão**) 🔁 *I haven't been to confession for years.* (**não me confessava**)

confetti /kənˈfeti/ NOUN, NO PLURAL very small pieces of coloured paper that people throw in the air at weddings (**confete**)

confidant or **confidante** /ˈkɒnfɪdænt/ NOUN [plural **confidants** or **confidantes**] a friend who you discuss personal things with (**confidente**)

confide /kənˈfaɪd/ VERB [confides, confiding, confided] to tell someone your secrets □ *She confided her secrets to her doctor.* (**confiar, contar segredos**)

♦ PHRASAL VERB **confide in someone** to tell someone your secrets (**fazer confidências a alguém**)

confidence /ˈkɒnfɪdəns/ NOUN [plural confidences]
1 *no plural* being sure of yourself and your abilities □ + *to do something* *It gave me the confidence to try again.* (**confiança**) 🔁 *We're growing in confidence.* (**aumentando a confiança**) 🔁 *I totally lost my confidence.* (**perdi a confiança**)
2 *no plural* trusting someone's ability to do something □ + *in* *I have every confidence in your abilities.* □ + *of* *He has the confidence of investors.* (**confiança**) 🔁 *We need to restore public confidence in the system.* (**restaurar confiança**) 🔁 *They have lost confidence in their manager.* (**perderam a confiança**)
3 *no plural* being sure about something □ *He expressed confidence that the project would go ahead.* (**convicção, segurança**)
4 a secret you tell someone □ *She's good at keeping confidences.* (**segredo, confidência**)
5 in confidence if you tell someone something in confidence, you expect them not to tell anyone else □ *Can I talk to you in confidence?* (**em particular**)

confidence trick /ˈkɒnfɪdəns ˌtrɪk/ NOUN [plural **confidence tricks**] a trick in which you persuade someone to trust you in order to get their money (**conto do vigário**)

confident /ˈkɒnfɪdənt/ ADJECTIVE
1 sure of yourself or your abilities □ + *in* *I'm confident in my own ability.* (**confiante**) 🔁 *I'm feeling pretty confident.* (**sentindo-me confiante**) □ *She's a very confident swimmer.*
2 sure that something will happen or be successful □ + *about* *We remain confident about the future.* □ + *of* *We're still confident of victory.* □ + *that* *I'm confident that we'll find the children safe and well.* (**confiante, seguro**)

confidential /ˌkɒnfɪˈdenʃəl/ ADJECTIVE secret or private (**confidencial, sigiloso**) 🔁 *He had access to confidential information.* (**informação confidencial**) 🔁 *highly/strictly confidential* (**altamente sigiloso**)

• **confidentiality** /ˌkɒnfɪdenʃiˈælɪti/ NOUN, NO PLURAL the state of being confidential □ *There has been a breach of confidentiality.* (**confiança, confidencialidade**)

• **confidentially** /ˌkɒnfɪˈdenʃəli/ ADVERB in a confidential way □ *The information will be treated confidentially.* (**confidencialmente**)

confidently /ˈkɒnfɪdəntli/ ADVERB
1 showing confidence in yourself □ *She walked confidently into the room.* (**confiantemente**)
2 showing you are sure about something □ *He confidently predicted a home win.* (**com segurança**)

confine /kənˈfaɪn/ VERB [confines, confining, confined] to keep someone or something within limits or shut inside a place □ *The soldiers were confined to barracks.* □ *Please confine your remarks to the subject under discussion.* (**confinar**)

• **confined** /kənˈfaɪnd/ ADJECTIVE a confined space is very small (**limitado**) 🔁 *a confined area/space* (**área limitada**)

• **confinement** /kənˈfaɪnmənt/ NOUN, NO PLURAL being locked up or confined (**confinamento, prisão**)

• **confines** /ˈkɒnfaɪnz/ PLURAL NOUN the outside edges or limits of something □ *Prisoners are not allowed beyond the confines of the prison.* (**limite**)

confirm /kənˈfɜːm/ VERB [confirms, confirming, confirmed]
1 to say or to make sure that something is correct or true □ *Police would not confirm the identity of the woman.* □ + *that* *A company spokesman confirmed that the director had resigned.* □ + *question word* *She refused to confirm whether the rumour was true.* □ + *as* *Robinson was confirmed as England captain yesterday.* (**confirmar**)
2 to say that something will happen as arranged □ + *that* *Please confirm that you will be able to come to the meeting.* □ *I'm writing to confirm the booking.* (**confirmar**)

confiscate

- **confirmation** /ˌkɒnfəˈmeɪʃən/ NOUN, NO PLURAL something that confirms an arrangement or the truth of something (confirmação) ▣ *We have not yet received official confirmation of the report.* (recebemos confirmação)

confiscate /ˈkɒnfɪskeɪt/ VERB [confiscates, confiscating, confiscated] to take something away from someone as a punishment □ *Police confiscated a number of illegal weapons.* □ *Teachers can confiscate mobile phones.* (confiscar, apreender)

- **confiscation** /ˌkɒnfɪˈskeɪʃən/ NOUN, NO PLURAL when something is confiscated (confisco, apreensão)

conflagration /ˌkɒnfləˈgreɪʃən/ NOUN [plural conflagrations] a formal word meaning a large fire that destroys a lot of things (incêndio destrutivo)

conflict ▶ NOUN /ˈkɒnflɪkt/ [plural conflicts]
1 an argument or a disagreement (conflito) ▣ *We help to resolve conflicts between neighbours.* (solucionar conflitos) ▣ *Money is often a source of conflict within families.* (motivo de conflito)
2 fighting or a war (combate) ▣ *There is an ongoing armed conflict in the region.* (conflito armado)
3 if there is a conflict between two things, they cannot exist together □ *There's often a conflict between economic development and conservation.* (conflito)
4 a conflict of interest a situation in which you cannot make a fair judgment because you will be affected by the result (conflito de interesse)
▶ VERB /kənˈflɪkt/ [conflicts, conflicting, conflicted] if two things conflict, they cannot both exist or be true at the same time □ *The eyewitness reports conflicted.* □ *Some of their actions seem to conflict with their policies.* (discordar, conflitar)

- **conflicting** /kənˈflɪktɪŋ/ ADJECTIVE two conflicting things are opposite or compete with each other (incompatível, conflitante) ▣ *There were conflicting reports of what happened.* (notícias conflitantes)

conform /kənˈfɔːm/ VERB [conforms, conforming, conformed]
1 to behave in a way that most other people behave □ *We all face pressure to conform.* (conformar-se)
2 if something conforms to a rule, it obeys it □ *All equipment has to conform to certain regulations.* (obedecer)

- **conformity** /kənˈfɔːməti/ NOUN, NO PLURAL
1 the quality of conforming □ *The study assessed men's conformity to traditional masculine roles.* (conformidade)
2 a formal word meaning conforming with a rule □ *Their religion demands conformity to a strict set of rules.* (submissão)

confuse

confound /kənˈfaʊnd/ VERB [confounds, confounding, confounded] if something confounds you, you are very surprised because you find it difficult to understand □ *He confounded doctors by recovering completely.* (confundir, desconcertar)

confront /kənˈfrʌnt/ VERB [confronts, confronting, confronted]
1 if you are confronted with a problem or a difficult situation, it appears and you have to deal with it □ *She was confronted with a difficult choice.* □ *How would you react if you were confronted by a real emergency situation?* (confrontar)
2 to try to do something about a problem or a difficult situation □ *We need to confront the challenge of climate change.* (enfrentar)
3 to try to make someone admit something you think they have done wrong □ *You should confront her and ask her about the missing money.* (confrontar)
4 to stand in front of someone in a threatening way □ *He turned and confronted his attackers.* □ *He tried to jump out of a window when confronted by police.* (enfrentar)

- **confrontation** /ˌkɒnfrʌnˈteɪʃən/ NOUN [plural confrontations] an angry argument or fight between two people or groups (confronto) ▣ *There was a violent confrontation between rival fans.* (confronto violento) ▣ *He's a man who avoids confrontation.* (evita confronto)

- **confrontational** /ˌkɒnfrʌnˈteɪʃənəl/ ADJECTIVE using strong methods that cause arguments or fights (confrontador) ▣ *The government has taken a confrontational approach towards the strikers.* (abordagem confrontante)

confuse /kənˈfjuːz/ VERB [confuses, confusing, confused]
1 to make someone unable to think clearly or to understand something □ *I think it will confuse people if we make changes.* (confundir)
2 to make something more difficult to understand ▣ *To confuse matters further, they use two different systems.* (para confundir ainda mais as coisas) □ *His comments have just confused the issue.* (confundir)
3 to think one thing or person is something or someone else □ *I think you're confusing the two brothers.* □ **+ with** *A podcast should not be confused with a webcast.* (confundir)

- **confused** /kənˈfjuːzd/ ADJECTIVE
1 unable to think clearly or understand something □ **+ about** *They seemed very confused about what was going on.* (confuso) ▣ *Angela looked confused.* (parecia confusa) □ *a confused expression*
2 not explained clearly or not easy to understand □ *We were getting confused messages.* (confuso)

- **confusing** /kənˈfjuːzɪŋ/ ADJECTIVE difficult to understand □ *It was a very confusing situation* (confuso) ▣ *Then things got very confusing.* (ficaram bem confusas)

- **confusion** /kənˈfjuːʒən/ NOUN
  1 no plural a feeling of being confused (**confusão**) 🔹 *The new rules caused confusion among tourists.* (**causou confusão**) ▫ *I saw the look of confusion on her face.*
  2 no plural a confusing situation ▫ *There was total confusion at the scene.* ▫ *The meeting ended in confusion.* (**desordem, balbúrdia**)
  3 when two people or things are confused with each other (**confusão**) 🔹 *We use different coloured text to avoid confusion.* (**evitar confusão**)

congeal /kənˈdʒiːl/ VERB [**congeals, congealing, congealed**] if a liquid congeals, it becomes thick and almost solid (**congelar-se, endurecer**)

congenial /kənˈdʒiːniəl/ ADJECTIVE a formal word meaning pleasant and friendly ▫ *We want to create a modern, congenial environment.* (**adequado, simpático**)

congenital /kənˈdʒenɪtəl/ ADJECTIVE congenital illnesses or problems are ones that a person is born with ▫ *congenital heart disease* (**congênito**)

congested /kənˈdʒestɪd/ ADJECTIVE crowded or blocked ▫ *The city's roads are badly congested.* (**congestionado**)

- **congestion** /kənˈdʒestʃən/ NOUN, NO PLURAL when something is congested (**congestão, congestionamento**) 🔹 *The scheme will ease traffic congestion in the city.* (**congestionamento de trânsito**) ▫ *Common symptoms are sneezing and nasal congestion.*

conglomerate /kənˈɡlɒmərət/ NOUN [plural **conglomerates**] a large business formed from several smaller companies (**conglomerado**)

congratulate /kənˈɡrætʃʊleɪt/ VERB [**congratulates, congratulating, congratulated**] to tell someone you are happy about their achievements or their good news ▫ *I congratulated her on her exam results.* (**parabenizar**)

- **congratulations** /kənˌɡrætʃʊˈleɪʃənz/ PLURAL NOUN something you say to congratulate someone (**parabéns, congratulações**) ▫ *Congratulations! That's great news.* ▫ *+ on Congratulations on passing your exams.* 🔹 *Simon called to offer his congratulations.* (**oferecer suas congratulações**)

> Remember that the preposition you use after the noun **congratulations** is on: ▫ *Congratulations on your marriage!*

congregate /ˈkɒŋɡrɪɡeɪt/ VERB [**congregates, congregating, congregated**] to come together somewhere in a group ▫ *Everyone had congregated around Ann's desk.* (**congregar-se**)

- **congregation** /ˌkɒŋɡrɪˈɡeɪʃən/ NOUN [plural **congregations**] all the people who are at a church service (**congregação**)

congress /ˈkɒŋɡres/ NOUN [plural **congresses**]
1 Congress the parliament of the United States, including the Senate and the House of Representatives (**Congresso**)
2 a meeting of many different people or organizations ▫ *the union's annual congress* ▫ *I attended an international congress to discuss refugees.* (**congresso**)

congruent /ˈkɒŋɡruənt/ ADJECTIVE congruent shapes are exactly the same size and shape. A maths word. (**congruente**)

conical /ˈkɒnɪkəl/ ADJECTIVE shaped like a cone (**cônico**)

conifer /ˈkɒnɪfə(r)/ NOUN [plural **conifers**] a type of tree with long thin leaves shaped like needles (**conífera**)

- **coniferous** /kəˈnɪfərəs/ ADJECTIVE coniferous trees grow cones (= hard, dry fruits). A biology word. (**conífero**)

conjecture /kənˈdʒektʃə(r)/ NOUN, NO PLURAL a formal word for the process of making opinions or judgments without having all the facts ▫ *The precise course of events remains a matter for conjecture.* (**suposição, hipótese**)

conjunction /kənˈdʒʌŋkʃən/ NOUN [plural **conjunctions**]
1 in grammar, a word that connects other words or parts of a sentence. For example, *and*, *but* and *or* are conjunctions. (**conjunção**)
2 in conjunction with happening, working or done with something or someone else ▫ *The work is being done in conjunction with the Department of Transport.* (**junto a**)

conjure /ˈkʌndʒə(r)/ VERB [**conjures, conjuring, conjured**] to make things appear or disappear as if by magic ▫ *She managed to conjure a meal out of nowhere.* (**conjurar, fazer aparecer**)
◆ PHRASAL VERB **conjure something up** to make you think of something ▫ *The smell of new hay conjured up a picture of the countryside.* (**fazer aparecer algo**)

- **conjuror** /ˈkʌndʒərə(r)/ NOUN [plural **conjurors**] someone who does magic tricks (**mágico**)

conker /ˈkɒŋkə(r)/ NOUN [plural **conkers**] a large brown seed of the horse chestnut tree (**castanha-da-índia**)

conman /ˈkɒnmæn/ NOUN [plural **conmen**] someone who tricks people, usually to get money (**vigarista**)

connect /kəˈnekt/ VERB [**connects, connecting, connected**]
1 to join two things together ▫ *The Channel Tunnel connects Britain and France.* ▫ *The two parts of the building are connected by a corridor.* (**conectar, ligar**)
2 to make it possible for people to communicate using a telephone, computer, etc. ▫ *+ to The number connects callers to voice mail.* (**estabelecer conexão**)

3 to see or understand how people or things are related to each other □ *The detective hadn't connected the two events in his mind.* (relacionar)

• **connected** /kəˈnektɪd/ ADJECTIVE
1 related to or involved with someone or something □ *He loves everything connected with football.* (ligado) 🔊 *I spoke to someone closely connected to the case.* (intimamente ligado)
2 joined to something □ *There's a small camera connected to each car.* (conectado)

• **connection** /kəˈnekʃən/ NOUN [plural connections]
1 the relationship between two people, things or events □ + *between* *They researched the connection between diet and certain diseases.* □ + *with* *There is a possible connection with corruption.* □ + *to* *I have a personal connection to the town.* (relação)
2 something that connects telephones, computers, etc. □ *a high-speed broadband connection* □ *a wireless Internet connection* (conexão)
3 something that joins two things together (conexão) 🔊 *a loose electrical connection* (conexão elétrica)
4 a train, bus or aeroplane that you need to catch to continue your journey (conexão) 🔊 *We missed our connection to Stansted because our train was late.* (perdemos nossa conexão)
5 in connection with to do with □ *He is wanted by the police in connection with a theft.* (com relação a)

connive /kəˈnaɪv/ VERB [connives, conniving, connived]
1 to secretly plan something bad or illegal □ *Apparently, he connived in a plot to kill the prime minister.* (conspirar)
2 to ignore something bad or illegal and to allow it to continue □ *There were those who said he had known of the crime and had connived at it.* (ser conivente)

connoisseur /ˌkɒnəˈsɜː(r)/ NOUN [plural connoisseurs] someone who knows a lot about something such as food or art □ *When it comes to wine, she's something of a connoisseur.* (perito, especialista)

connotation /ˌkɒnəˈteɪʃən/ NOUN [plural connotations] the feeling or extra meaning of a word or phrase in addition to its basic meaning (conotação) 🔊 *The word carries negative connotations.* (conotação negativa)

conquer /ˈkɒŋkə(r)/ VERB [conquers, conquering, conquered]
1 to take control of a country or an area, especially in a war □ *Napoleon tried to conquer Egypt.* (conquistar)
2 to succeed in controlling a strong emotion, difficult situation, etc. □ *Claire seems to have finally conquered her shyness.* □ *It helped me to conquer my fear of heights.* (superar)

• **conqueror** /ˈkɒŋkərə(r)/ NOUN [plural conquerors] someone who conquers a country or an area (conquistador)

• **conquest** /ˈkɒŋkwest/ NOUN [plural conquests] when someone conquers a country or an area □ *the Spanish conquest of Mexico* (conquista)

conscience /ˈkɒnʃəns/ NOUN [plural consciences]
1 your feeling of what is right and wrong □ *You should follow your conscience.* (consciência) 🔊 *Now I can relax with a clear conscience* (= without feeling guilty (consciência limpa) 🔊 *He clearly had a guilty conscience.* (consciência pesada)
2 on your conscience if something is on your conscience, you feel guilty about it □ *I must help her – I don't want her death on my conscience.* (consciência pesada)

• **conscientious** /ˌkɒnʃiˈenʃəs/ ADJECTIVE a conscientious person works hard and carefully to get things right □ *She was very conscientious about safety.* (cuidadoso)

• **conscientiously** /ˌkɒnʃiˈenʃəsli/ ADVERB in a conscientious way □ *They carried out their duties conscientiously.* (cuidadosamente)

conscientious objector /ˌkɒnʃiˈenʃəs əbˈdʒektə(r)/ NOUN [plural conscientious objectors] someone who refuses to fight in a war because they believe the war is wrong (pessoa que se recusa a tomar parte na guerra por questões de consciência)

conscious /ˈkɒnʃəs/ ADJECTIVE
1 aware of something □ + *of* *I'm conscious of the fact that we need to finish on time.* □ + *that* *I became increasingly conscious that people were watching me.* (ciente)
2 awake and aware of what is around you (consciente) 🔊 *He is now fully conscious following the operation.* (totalmente consciente) □ *He had to fight to remain conscious.*
3 a conscious choice, decision, etc. is one that you have thought about (consciente) 🔊 *He made a conscious decision to be more friendly towards them.* (decisão consciente) 🔊 *I've been making a conscious effort to eat more healthily.* (esforço consciente)

• **consciously** /ˈkɒnʃəsli/ ADVERB deliberately or being aware of what you are doing □ *They're consciously trying to change their image.* (conscientemente)

• **consciousness** /ˈkɒnʃəsnɪs/ NOUN, NO PLURAL
1 the state of being awake and aware of what is around you (consciência) 🔊 *She lost consciousness and woke up in hospital.* (perdeu a consciência) 🔊 *He never regained consciousness.* (readquiriu a consciência)
2 being aware of or knowing about something (consciência) 🔊 *We want to raise public consciousness about the issue.* (aumentar a consciência pública)

conscript

conscript ▶ VERB /kənˈskrɪpt/ [conscripts, conscripting, conscripted] to force someone by law to join the armed forces ☐ *The government conscripted young men.* (recrutar)
▶ NOUN /ˈkɒnskrɪpt/ [plural **conscripts**] someone who is conscripted (recruta)

• **conscription** /kənˈskrɪpʃən/ NOUN, NO PLURAL the process of conscripting people (recrutamento)

consecrate /ˈkɒnsɪkreɪt/ VERB [consecrates, consecrating, consecrated] to perform a ceremony to make something holy (consagrar)

• **consecration** /ˌkɒnsɪˈkreɪʃən/ NOUN, NO PLURAL the process of consecrating something (consagração)

consecutive /kənˈsekjʊtɪv/ ADJECTIVE one after the other ☐ *It snowed on three consecutive days.* ☐ *This is his fourth consecutive win.* (consecutivo)

consensus /kənˈsensəs/ NOUN, NO PLURAL agreement or a feeling shared by most people (consenso) 🔁 *We couldn't reach a consensus on a name for the group.* (chegar a um consenso) 🔁 *The general consensus is that we should change the date.* (consenso geral)

consent /kənˈsent/ ▶ VERB [consents, consenting, consented] to agree to something ☐ *He consented to be tested.* (consentir)
▶ NOUN, NO PLURAL when you agree to or allow something (consentimento) 🔁 *Patients must give their consent for the treatment.* (dar consentimento)

consequence /ˈkɒnsɪkwəns/ NOUN [plural **consequences**]
1 something that is the result of something else ☐ *She didn't realize the consequences of her actions.* (consequência) 🔁 *If you eat too much, you'll suffer the consequences.* (sofrerá as consequências) 🔁 *They could face serious health consequences if they don't change their lifestyles.* (encarar as consequências)
2 a formal word meaning importance ☐ *It was of no consequence.* ☐ *They achieved almost nothing of consequence.* (importância)

• **consequent** /ˈkɒnsɪkwənt/ ADJECTIVE happening as a result ☐ *He spoke about the problems in the fishing industry and the consequent loss of jobs.* (consequente)

• **consequently** /ˈkɒnsɪkwəntlɪ/ ADVERB as a result ☐ *He injured his ankle and, consequently, he had to withdraw from the match.* (consequentemente)

conservation /ˌkɒnsəˈveɪʃən/ NOUN, NO PLURAL
1 looking after something to prevent it being damaged or destroyed (conservação) 🔁 *nature conservation* (conservação da natureza)
2 being careful not to waste energy, water, etc. (conservação) 🔁 *We are encouraging energy conservation.* (conservação de energia)

consideration

• **conservationist** /ˌkɒnsəˈveɪʃənɪst/ NOUN [plural **conservationists**] someone who works to protect the environment (conservacionista)

Conservative /kənˈsɜːvətɪv/ NOUN [plural **Conservatives**] someone who supports the Conservative Party in the UK (Conservadorismo)

conservative /kənˈsɜːvətɪv/ ADJECTIVE
1 a conservative person does not like changes or new ideas ☐ *He's a very conservative dresser.* (conservador)
2 a conservative estimate or guess is usually less than the real amount (conservador) 🔁 *Many people believe this is a conservative estimate.* (estimativa conservadora)

conservatory /kənˈsɜːvətərɪ/ NOUN [plural **conservatories**] a room or building which has walls and a roof made of glass (conservatório)

conserve /kənˈsɜːv/ VERB [conserves, conserving, conserved]
1 to prevent something from being wasted or lost ☐ *Close the windows to conserve heat.* (conservar)
2 to prevent something from being damaged or destroyed ☐ *The country has to conserve its forests.* (proteger, preservar)

consider /kənˈsɪdə(r)/ VERB [considers, considering, considered]
1 to think about something carefully ☐ *I'll consider your idea.* ☐ *We're considering all the options.* ☐ *+ whether I'm considering whether to go or not.* ☐ *+ ing Have you considered hiring a car?* (considerar)
2 to have a particular opinion about someone or something ☐ *I consider him to be a true friend.* ☐ *We will delete anything we consider inappropriate.* ☐ *I consider myself to be very lucky.* (considerar)
3 to think about what other people want or need ☐ *He never considers other people's feelings.* (respeitar)

> ➤ Note that when **consider** (meaning 'to think about something carefully') is followed by a verb, that verb is in the -ing form:
> ✓ *She's considering leaving her job.*
> ✗ *She's considering to leave her job.*

considerable /kənˈsɪdərəbəl/ ADJECTIVE quite large or important ☐ *a considerable distance* ☐ *We've spent a considerable amount of money already.* (considerável)

• **considerably** /kənˈsɪdərəblɪ/ ADVERB quite a lot ☐ *John earns considerably more than I do.* (consideravelmente)

considerate /kənˈsɪdərət/ ADJECTIVE thinking of other people and what they want ☐ *It was considerate of you to help me.* (consideração)

consideration /kənˌsɪdəˈreɪʃən/ NOUN [plural **considerations**]

1 thinking carefully about things (atenção) ▸ *The idea deserves serious consideration.* (séria atenção) ▸ *We will give consideration to the request.* (dar atenção)
2 something that you have to think about when you are making a decision □ *His health is the most important consideration.* □ *There are practical considerations, such as childcare.* (consideração)
3 take something into consideration to think about something while you are making a decision or a plan □ *We will take all views into consideration.* (levar algo em consideração)
4 thinking about other people and what they want □ *We all want to be treated with consideration and respect.* □ *They showed little consideration for her privacy.* (consideração)

considering /kənˈsɪdərɪŋ/ PREPOSITION, CONJUNCTION used to show how something is affected by something else □ *Considering how clever you are, I think you should have done better.* □ *She played well considering she has been ill.* (considerando-se que)

consign /kənˈsaɪn/
◆ PHRASAL VERB [consigns, consigning, consigned]
consign something to something to put something somewhere as a way of getting rid of it. A formal phrase. □ *That old sweater should be consigned to the bin!* (entregar algo a algo)

• **consignment** /kənˈsaɪnmənt/ NOUN [plural consignments] several goods which are being sent together □ *It was part of a consignment of medicines imported from France.* (remessa)

consist /kənˈsɪst/
◆ PHRASAL VERB [consists, consisting, consisted]
consist of something to be made of two or more things □ *It was a simple meal, consisting of bread and cheese.* (consistir em) ▸ *His diet consists mainly of meat and potatoes.* (consiste principalmente em)

consistency /kənˈsɪstənsi/ NOUN [plural consistencies]
1 when something is always the same in quality □ *There is no consistency to his game.* (coerência)
2 how thick or smooth a substance is □ *The sauce should have the consistency of cream.* (consistência)

• **consistent** /kənˈsɪstənt/ ADJECTIVE always the same □ *The school has a consistent approach to dealing with bad behaviour.* (sólido)

consolation /ˌkɒnsəˈleɪʃən/ NOUN [plural consolations] something that makes a disappointment seem less bad □ *As a consolation for not getting the job, his girlfriend took him out to dinner.* (consolo)

consolation prize /ˌkɒnsəˈleɪʃən ˌpraɪz/ NOUN [plural consolation prizes] a prize given to someone who has come second in a competition (prêmio de consolação)

console¹ /kənˈsəʊl/ VERB [consoles, consoling, consoled] to make someone who is sad or disappointed feel better (consolar)

console² /ˈkɒnsəʊl/ NOUN [plural consoles]
1 a piece of equipment that you connect to a television to play video games on (console) ▸ *a games console* (um console de jogos)
2 a board that has the controls for a machine on it (painel de controle)

consolidate /kənˈsɒlɪdeɪt/ VERB [consolidates, consolidating, consolidated] to make your power or success stronger □ *The team consolidated its lead with two more goals.* (consolidar)

consonant /ˈkɒnsənənt/ NOUN [plural consonants] any letter of the alphabet except a, e, i, o, or u (consoante)
⇨ go to **vowel**

consort /kɒnˈsɔːt/
◆ PHRASAL VERB [consorts, consorting, consorted]
consort with someone to spend time with someone that other people do not approve of. A formal phrase. (associar-se a alguém)

consortium /kənˈsɔːtiəm/ NOUN [plural consortiums or consortia] a group of companies who are working together □ *The jet was developed by a consortium of companies.* (consórcio)

conspicuous /kənˈspɪkjuəs/ ADJECTIVE very easy to see □ *Beth felt very conspicuous in her bright red dress.* (evidente, visível)

conspiracy /kənˈspɪrəsi/ NOUN [plural conspiracies] a secret plan by a group of people to do something bad (conspiração)

• **conspirator** /kənˈspɪrətə(r)/ NOUN [plural conspirators] one of a group of people who are planning to do something bad (conspirador)

• **conspire** /kənˈspaɪə(r)/ VERB [conspires, conspiring, conspired]
1 to plan secretly with other people to do something bad □ *He had conspired to kill his business partner.* (conspirar)
2 conspire to do something if things that happen conspire to do something, they cause problems for you □ *Bad weather and injury had conspired to make him miss the game.* (conspirar a fazer algo)

constable /ˈkʌnstəbəl/ NOUN [plural constables] a police officer of low rank (guarda, policial)

constant /ˈkɒnstənt/ ADJECTIVE
1 never stopping □ *He was in constant pain.* □ *The city is under constant threat of attack.* (constante)
2 keeping at the same level □ *The thermostat keeps the house at a constant temperature.* (constante)

• **constantly** /ˈkɒnstəntli/ ADVERB all the time □ *It rained constantly for a week.* (constantemente)

constellation /ˌkɒnstəˈleɪʃən/ NOUN [plural constellations] a large group of stars (constelação)

constipated /ˈkɒnstɪpeɪtɪd/ ADJECTIVE finding it difficult to get rid of solid waste from your body (obstipado, com prisão de ventre)
• **constipation** /ˌkɒnstɪˈpeɪʃən/ NOUN, NO PLURAL being constipated (obstipação, prisão de ventre)

constituency /kənˈstɪtʃuənsi/ NOUN [plural constituencies] a part of a country that elects someone to a parliament (circunscrição eleitoral)
• **constituent** /kənˈstɪtʃuənt/ NOUN [plural constituents]
1 something that is a part of a larger thing □ *The main constituent of the human body is water.* (componente)
2 a person who lives in a particular constituency (eleitor)

constitute /ˈkɒnstɪtʃuːt/ VERB [constitutes, constituting, constituted] to be or to form something □ *Global warming constitutes a major threat to our planet.* (constituir)
• **constitution** /ˌkɒnstɪˈtʃuːʃən/ NOUN [plural constitutions]
1 a set of rules or laws that a country or organization has (constituição)
2 your health (estrutura, formação) ▣ *She has a very strong constitution.* (estrutura forte)
• **constitutional** /ˌkɒnstɪˈtʃuːʃənəl/ ADJECTIVE to do with a constitution (constitucional)

constrain /kənˈstreɪn/ VERB [constrains, constraining, constrained] to stop something from happening in the way someone wants it to □ *The research has been constrained by a lack of funding.* (limitar, restringir)
• **constraint** /kənˈstreɪnt/ NOUN [plural constraints] something that stops something from happening in the way someone wants it to (restrição, limite) ▣ *Financial constraints meant that staff were not given any training.* (restrição financeira)

constrict /kənˈstrɪkt/ VERB [constricts, constricting, constricted]
1 to become narrower or tighter, or to make something become narrower or tighter □ *Cold water makes your blood vessels constrict.* (contrair, comprimir)
2 to limit something □ *The new law constricts development along the coast.* (restringir)

construct /kənˈstrʌkt/ VERB [constructs, constructing, constructed] to build something □ *The building was constructed in 1974.* (construir)
• **construction** /kənˈstrʌkʃən/ NOUN [plural constructions]
1 the process of building something □ *The substance is used in road construction.* (construção)
2 a formal word meaning something that has been built □ *metal constructions* (construção)
• **constructive** /kənˈstrʌktɪv/ ADJECTIVE helpful (construtivo) ▣ *I offered her some constructive criticism.* (crítica construtiva)

construe /kənˈstruː/ VERB [construes, construing, construed] to think that what someone says or does has a particular meaning □ *She didn't want to say anything that could be construed as an insult.* (interpretar)

consul /ˈkɒnsəl/ NOUN [plural consuls] a government official who works in a foreign city and helps visitors from his or her own country □ *The British consul in Barcelona arranged for him to have a temporary passport.* (cônsul)
• **consulate** /ˈkɒnsjulət/ NOUN [plural consulates] the office of a consul □ *Protesters demonstrated outside the Mexican consulate in New York.* (consulado)

consult /kənˈsʌlt/ VERB [consults, consulting, consulted]
1 to speak to someone or to look at something in order to get information or advice □ *If symptoms persist, consult a doctor.* □ *Anna stopped to consult the map.* (consultar)
2 to speak to someone before you make a decision □ *The staff weren't consulted about any of the changes.* (consultar)
• **consultancy** /kənˈsʌltənsi/ NOUN [plural consultancies]
1 a business that offers advice and information about something (consultoria) ▣ *He set up a management consultancy.* (consultoria administrativa)
2 the job of offering advice and information about something □ *The company offers consultancy services.* (consultoria)
• **consultant** /kənˈsʌltənt/ NOUN [plural consultants]
1 someone whose job is to give advice on a subject □ *a marketing consultant* (consultor)
2 a hospital doctor who is an expert in a particular type of illness (clínico)
• **consultation** /ˌkɒnsəlˈteɪʃən/ NOUN [plural consultations] a meeting with an expert who can give you advice and information (consulta, conferência)

consume /kənˈsjuːm/ VERB [consumes, consuming, consumed]
1 to use something such as energy or time □ *Cities consume 75% of the world's energy.* (consumir)
2 a formal word meaning to eat or drink something □ *Once opened, milk should be consumed within three days.* (consumir)
3 if you are consumed by a feeling or thought, you cannot think about anything else □ *She was consumed by grief after the death of her daughter.* (consumir)
• **consumer** /kənˈsjuːmə(r)/ NOUN [plural consumers] someone who buys and uses things □ *Consumers want choice and competitive prices.* (consumidor)

consummate /ˈkɒnsəmət, kənˈsʌmət/ ADJECTIVE a formal word meaning very skilful (completo) 🔲 *She is the consummate professional.* (profissional completa)

consumption /kənˈsʌmpʃən/ NOUN, NO PLURAL
1 the use of things such as energy, fuel, water, etc. (consumo) 🔲 *The newer model of car offers better fuel consumption.* (consumo de combustível) □ *The leaflet suggests ways of reducing water consumption.*
2 a formal word meaning eating or drinking something □ *Most people need to increase their fruit and vegetable consumption.* (consumo)

contact /ˈkɒntækt/ ▶ NOUN [plural **contacts**]
1 *no plural* when you write to someone or speak to them by telephone □ *+ with* I've had no contact with my brother for over a year. (contato) 🔲 *I've lost contact with most of the people I went to school with.* (perdi contato) 🔲 *I keep in contact with all my ex-colleagues.* (mantenho contato)

2 in contact if you are in contact with someone, you write to them or speak to them by telephone □ *Have you been in contact with Adrian recently?* (em contato)

3 *no plural* when two things or people touch each other (contato) 🔲 *There was no physical contact between them.* (contato físico) 🔲 *She became ill after coming into contact with infected chickens.* (entrar em contato)

4 someone who you know who can help you (contato) 🔲 *He got the job through a business contact of his mother's.* (contato profissional)
▶ VERB [**contacts, contacting, contacted**] to write to someone or to speak to them on the telephone □ *Anyone with information about the fire should contact police.* (contatar)

contact lens /ˈkɒntækt ˌlenz/ NOUN [plural **contact lenses**] a thin piece of plastic that you wear on your eye to help you see better (lentes de contato)

contagious /kənˈteɪdʒəs/ ADJECTIVE a contagious disease can be spread between people if they touch each other (contagioso)

contain /kənˈteɪn/ VERB [**contains, containing, contained**]
1 to include something or have it as a part □ *The document contained important personal information.* □ *Oranges contain a lot of vitamin C.* (conter)
2 to have something inside □ *The bag contained some money.* (conter)
3 to stop something bad from spreading □ *Firefighters quickly managed to contain the fire.* (controlar, reter)
4 to control a feeling □ *Annie couldn't contain her excitement.* (controlar)

➤ Note that the verb **contain** (senses 1 and 2) is never used in the *-ing* form. It is always used in simple tenses:
✓ *The bag contained my passport.*
✗ *The bag was containing my passport.*

• **container** /kənˈteɪnə(r)/ NOUN [plural **containers**] something for putting things in, for example a box (recipiente) 🔲 *She put the food in a plastic container.* (recipiente plástico) □ *+ of* a container of milk

contaminate /kənˈtæmɪneɪt/ VERB [**contaminates, contaminating, contaminated**] to make something dirty or poisonous □ *The water was contaminated with chemicals.* (contaminar, poluir)
• **contamination** /kənˌtæmɪˈneɪʃən/ NOUN, NO PLURAL making something dirty or poisonous (contaminação)

contemplate /ˈkɒntəmpleɪt/ VERB [**contemplates, contemplating, contemplated**] to think seriously about something □ *We're contemplating moving to France.* (considerar, contemplar)
• **contemplation** /ˌkɒntəmˈpleɪʃən/ NOUN, NO PLURAL thinking in a quiet, serious way (contemplação)
• **contemplative** /kənˈtemplətɪv/ ADJECTIVE spending time thinking about something in a serious way (contemplativo, pensativo)

contemporary /kənˈtempərəri/ ▶ ADJECTIVE
1 belonging to the time now (contemporânea, moderna) 🔲 *an exhibition of contemporary art* (arte contemporânea)
2 existing or done at the same time as something else □ *This is the only contemporary account of the event that we have.* (simultâneo)
▶ NOUN [plural **contemporaries**] your contemporaries are people who are living at the same time as you (contemporâneo)

contempt /kənˈtempt/ NOUN, NO PLURAL a strong feeling that someone or something is bad and that you do not respect them □ *She made no effort to hide her contempt for him.* (desprezo)
• **contemptible** /kənˈtemptəbəl/ ADJECTIVE bad and deserving no respect. A formal word. □ *a contemptible act of violence* (desprezível)
• **contemptuous** /kənˈtemptʃuəs/ ADJECTIVE showing that you think someone or something is bad and that you do not respect them □ *She was contemptuous of most politicians.* (desdenhoso)

contend /kənˈtend/ VERB [**contends, contending, contended**]
1 to argue that something is true. A formal word. □ *Local people contend that new houses would mean an increase in traffic.* (discutir)
2 to compete for something □ *He is contending for a place in the team.* (disputar)
♦ PHRASAL VERB **contend with something** to deal with something difficult □ *Runners had to contend with rain and 52 mph winds.* (lutar contra algo)

- **contender** /kənˈtendə(r)/ NOUN [plural **contenders**] someone who is taking part in a competition (**competidor**)

content[1] /ˈkɒntent/ NOUN, NO PLURAL
 1 the subject or ideas that a magazine, television programme, etc. deals with □ *The content is not suitable for children.* (**conteúdo**)
 2 the amount of a substance that something contains (**quantidade**) ▣ *Pizzas have a very high fat content.* (**quantidade de gordura**)
 ➩ go to **contents**

content[2] /kənˈtent/ ADJECTIVE happy □ *Tatsuya was quite content to let Mai help him.* (**contente, satisfeito**)

- **contented** /kənˈtentɪd/ ADJECTIVE happy and satisfied □ *a contented smile* □ *Gemma was a contented baby.* (**contente**)

contention /kənˈtenʃən/ NOUN [plural **contentions**]
 1 an opinion that someone says during an argument. A formal word. (**alegação**)
 2 disagreement between people. A formal word. (**discussão**)

- **contentious** /kənˈtenʃəs/ ADJECTIVE a contentious subject is one that people disagree about (**controverso**) ▣ *a contentious issue* (**assunto controverso**)

contentment /kənˈtentmənt/ NOUN, NO PLURAL being happy and satisfied (**contentamento**)

contents /ˈkɒntents/ PLURAL NOUN
 1 the things that are inside something □ *She emptied the contents of her bag onto the table.* (**conteúdo**)
 2 the information and ideas that are in a piece of writing □ *The newspaper revealed the contents of the Prince's letter.* (**conteúdo**)

contest /ˈkɒntest/ NOUN [plural **contests**] a competition (**disputa**) ▣ *She entered a singing contest.* (**entrou em uma disputa**)

- **contestant** /kənˈtestənt/ NOUN [plural **contestants**] someone who is taking part in a contest (**disputante**)

context /ˈkɒntekst/ NOUN [plural **contexts**]
 1 the situation in which something happens and all the events that caused it (**contexto**) ▣ *These events need to be seen in the context of the decade in which they happened.* (**no contexto de**)
 2 the words before and after a word which help you to understand its meaning (**contexto**)
 3 take something out of context to repeat only a small part of what someone said so that the original meaning is changed (**frase fora do contexto**)

continent /ˈkɒntɪnənt/ NOUN [plural **continents**]
 1 one of the large areas that the Earth's land is divided into. The continents are Africa, Antarctica, North America, South America, Asia, Australia and Europe (**continente**)
 2 the Continent is a UK name for Europe but not including Britain □ *They drive on the right on the Continent.* (**o continente europeu**)

- **continental** /ˌkɒntɪˈnentəl/ ADJECTIVE
 1 to do with Europe but not including Britain □ *Continental holidays have become more popular.* (**continental**)
 2 to do with continents (**continental**)

continental crust /ˌkɒntɪnentəl ˈkrʌst/ NOUN, NO PLURAL the outer layer of the Earth including all the land and rocks. A geography word. (**crosta continental**)

continental plate /ˌkɒntɪnentəl ˈpleɪt/ NOUN [plural **continental plates**] one of the large pieces that the surface of the Earth is divided into. A geography word. (**placa tectônica**)

contingency /kənˈtɪndʒənsɪ/ NOUN [plural **contingencies**]
 1 something that might happen, especially something bad (**incerteza, eventualidade**)
 2 something that is done to prepare for the possibility of something bad happening (**contingência**) ▣ *The government is making contingency plans for war.* (**planos de contingência**)

continual /kənˈtɪnjuəl/ ADJECTIVE happening all the time without stopping □ *the continual noise of traffic* (**contínuo**)

- **continually** /kənˈtɪnjuəlɪ/ ADVERB all the time □ *Language is continually changing.* (**continuamente**)

continuation /kənˌtɪnjuˈeɪʃən/ NOUN [plural **continuations**]
 1 when something continues to exist or happen □ *Extra funding has guaranteed the continuation of our work.* (**sequência**)
 2 when something starts again in order to continue from what happened before □ *We will meet next week for a continuation of these discussions.* (**prosseguimento**)

continue /kənˈtɪnju:/ VERB [**continues, continuing, continued**]
 1 to keep happening, existing, or doing something without stopping □ *+ for This disagreement has continued for many years.* □ *+ to do something Jake continued to do well at school.* □ *+ ing She continued working past retirement age.* □ *+ with He said he would continue with his campaign.* (**continuar**)
 2 to start doing something again □ *Police will continue the search in the morning.* (**continuar**)
 3 to go further in the same direction □ *+ along They continued along the road until they reached the village.* (**continuar**)

- **continuity** /ˌkɒntɪˈnju:ətɪ/ NOUN, NO PLURAL when something does not stop □ *We try hard to ensure continuity of care for these patients.* (**continuidade**)

- **continuous** /kənˈtɪnjuəs/ ADJECTIVE
  1 existing or happening without stopping □ *There has been a continuous improvement in exam results.* (**contínuo**)
  2 in grammar, the continuous form of a verb shows that something is continuing to happen □ *The sentence 'They are playing football' is in the continuous form.* (**contínuo**)
- **continuously** /kənˈtɪnjuəslɪ/ ADVERB without stopping □ *Students are monitored continuously.* (**continuamente**)

contorted /kənˈtɔːtɪd/ ADJECTIVE twisted in a way that is not natural □ *His face was contorted with rage.* (**contorcido**)

contour /ˈkɒntʊə(r)/ NOUN [plural **contours**]
1 the shape of the outside of something □ *The car has very sleek contours.* (**contorno**)
2 a line on a map which joins places of the same height (**curva de nível**)

contra- /ˈkɒntrə/ PREFIX contra- is added to the beginning of words to mean 'against' or 'opposite to' □ *contradict* □ *contravene* (**contra-**)

contraception /ˌkɒntrəˈsepʃən/ NOUN, NO PLURAL preventing pregnancy □ *various methods of contraception* (**contracepção**)
- **contraceptive** /ˌkɒntrəˈseptɪv/ NOUN [plural **contraceptives**] something that is used to prevent a woman from becoming pregnant (**contraceptivo**)

contract¹ /ˈkɒntrækt/ NOUN [plural **contracts**] an official written agreement (**contrato**) 🔁 *She signed a contract to design clothes for a top store* (**assinou um contrato**) 🔁 *The company has won a contract to supply stationery to schools.* (**ganhou um contrato**)

contract² /kənˈtrækt/ VERB [**contracts, contracting, contracted**]
1 to get a disease □ *More than 400 people have contracted the virus.* (**contrair**)
2 to make an official agreement with someone to do something □ *The company has been contracted to do the cleaning.* (**contrair**)
3 to become smaller □ *Your stomach contracts if you don't eat for a long time.* (**contrair, encolher**)
- **contraction** /kənˈtrækʃən/ NOUN [plural **contractions**]
  1 a painful movement of muscles in a woman's womb (= place where a baby grows) when she is having a baby (**contração**)
  2 a word that is a short form of two other words □ *'I'm' is a contraction of 'I am'.* (**abreviação**)
  3 when something becomes smaller or less □ *There was a contraction of economic activity.* (**redução**)
- **contractor** /kənˈtræktə(r)/ NOUN [plural **contractors**] a company who provides goods or services for another company (**empreiteiro**)
- **contractual** /kənˈtræktʃuəl/ ADJECTIVE written in a contract □ *a contractual agreement/obligation* (**contratual**)

contradict /ˌkɒntrəˈdɪkt/ VERB [**contradicts, contradicting, contradicted**]
1 to say that what someone has said is not correct □ *Witnesses to the accident contradicted what the driver said.* (**contradizer**)
2 if one statement contradicts another, they are so different that they cannot both be true □ *The evidence seems to contradict the original report.* (**opor-se, discordar**)
- **contradiction** /ˌkɒntrəˈdɪkʃən/ NOUN [plural **contradictions**]
  1 something that makes a statement or fact seem not to be true because it shows the opposite (**contestação**)
  2 when someone says that what has been said is not correct (**contradição**)
- **contradictory** /ˌkɒntrəˈdɪktərɪ/ ADJECTIVE a contradictory statement is one that states the opposite of what has just been said (**contraditório**)

contraption /kənˈtræpʃən/ NOUN [plural **contraptions**] a machine that looks strange (**geringonça**)

contrary /ˈkɒntrərɪ/ ▶ ADJECTIVE completely different from something else □ *They have contrary views on the subject.* (**contrário**) 🔁 *Contrary to popular belief* (= although many people believe this), *hair does not grow quicker if you cut it.* (**contrário à crença popular**)
▶ NOUN, NO PLURAL
1 the contrary the opposite □ *He's not a nervous person. Quite the contrary, in fact.* (**o contrário**)
2 on the contrary used for emphasizing that the opposite is true □ *The situation isn't depressing. On the contrary, there's a new feeling of hope.* (**pelo contrário**)

contrast ▶ NOUN /ˈkɒntrɑːst/ [plural **contrasts**]
1 a big difference □ *The contrast between the two men could not be greater.* (**contraste**)
2 in contrast to something used when comparing two things and saying that they are very different □ *The team have played brilliantly this season which is in stark contrast to last season.* (**em comparação com algo**)
▶ VERB /kənˈtrɑːst/ [**contrasts, contrasting, contrasted**]
1 if two things contrast, they are very different from each other (**contrastar**) 🔁 *His comments contrast sharply with those of his colleagues.* (**contrastam acentuadamente**)
2 to compare two things and show the differences between them □ *She contrasted her experiences of working in China with her time spent in India.* (**comparar**)

contravene /ˌkɒntrəˈviːn/ VERB [**contravenes, contravening, contravened**] to not obey a law or rule □ *We believe the nuclear tests contravene international law.* (**violar**)
- **contravention** /ˌkɒntrəˈvenʃən/ NOUN [plural **contraventions**] not obeying a law or rule, or

contribute

something that does this □ *Their treatment of prisoners is in contravention of human rights laws.* (**contravenção, violação**)

contribute /kənˈtrɪbjuːt, ˈkɒntrɪbjuːt/ VERB [contributes, contributing, contributed]
1 to give something in order to buy or achieve something together with other people □ *We all contributed towards Paul's present.* □ *He contributed a lot to the discussion.* (**contribuir**)
2 to be one of the causes of something □ *Sunbathing has contributed significantly to the rise in skin cancer cases.* (**contribuir**)

• **contribution** /ˌkɒntrɪˈbjuːʃən/ NOUN [plural contributions] something that you give or do to help achieve something (**contribuição**) 🔍 *She has made a significant contribution to the project.* (**fez uma contribuição**)

• **contributor** /kənˈtrɪbjʊtə(r)/ NOUN [plural contributors]
1 someone who contributes something □ *He was a generous contributor to the party funds.* (**contribuinte**)
2 one of the causes of something □ *Transport is one of the biggest contributors to global emissions.* (**contribuinte**)

• **contributory** /kənˈtrɪbjʊtəri/ ADJECTIVE helping to cause something (**responsável, contributivo**) 🔍 *Late payments were a contributory factor in the firm's failure.* (**fator responsável**)

contrite /kənˈtraɪt/ ADJECTIVE very sorry about something bad you have done (**arrependido**)

• **contrition** /kənˈtrɪʃən/ NOUN, NO PLURAL being contrite (**arrependimento**)

contrive /kənˈtraɪv/ VERB [contrives, contriving, contrived] a formal word meaning to succeed in doing something or making something happen in a clever way □ *She contrived never to be in the office at the same time as Tony.* (**planejar**)

• **contrived** /kənˈtraɪvd/ ADJECTIVE false and not natural □ *The story seemed contrived.* (**inventado**)

control /kənˈtrəʊl/ ▶ NOUN [plural controls]
1 *no plural* the power to make decisions for a country, organization, etc. □ *+ of The companies are competing for control of the airline.* (**controle**) 🔍 *The army has taken control of the city.* (**assumiu o controle**)
2 **in control** having the power to make decisions in an organization, country etc. □ *He remains in control of the company.* (**no controle**)
3 *no plural* the ability to make someone or something do what you want □ *+ over He has no control over his children.* (**controle**) 🔍 *Brock lost control of the car and it hit a tree.* (**perdeu o controle**)
4 **under control** if something is under control, someone is dealing with it □ *The situation is under control.* □ *It took three hours to get the fire under control.* (**sob controle**)

convene

5 a rule or law that limits something □ *Australia has tightened gun controls.* □ *+ on The government has introduced tighter controls on spending.* (**fiscalização**)
6 **out of control** unable to be controlled □ *The situation is getting out of control.* (**fora de controle**)
7 controls the handles, buttons etc. you use to make a vehicle or machine work (**controle**)
▶ VERB [controls, controlling, controlled]
1 to have the power to make decisions □ *Congress was controlled by the Democrats.* (**controlar**)
2 to make someone or something do what you want □ *To be a good football player you must be able to control the ball.* (**controlar**)
3 to limit something □ *They tried to control the spread of the disease.* (**restringir, controlar**)
4 to behave calmly even if you feel angry or excited □ *He couldn't control his temper.* (**controlar**)

• **controller** /kənˈtrəʊlə(r)/ NOUN [plural controllers] a person or thing that controls something (**controlador**)

control tower /kənˈtrəʊl ˌtaʊə(r)/ NOUN [plural control towers] a tall building at an airport where people tell the pilots what to do (**torre de controle**)

controversial /ˌkɒntrəˈvɜːʃəl/ ADJECTIVE causing disagreement (**controverso, polêmico**) 🔍 *Nuclear power is a highly controversial issue.* (**altamente polêmico**)

• **controversy** /kənˈtrɒvəsi/ NOUN [plural controversies] disagreement about something (**controvérsia, polêmica**) 🔍 *The decision has caused controversy in the UK.* (**causou polêmica**)

conundrum /kəˈnʌndrəm/ NOUN [plural conundrums] a problem that is difficult to solve (**enigma**)

conurbation /ˌkɒnɜːˈbeɪʃən/ NOUN [plural conurbations] a city that is formed when towns are joined by building on the land between them (**conurbação**)

convalesce /ˌkɒnvəˈles/ VERB [convalesces, convalescing, convalesced] to rest after you have been ill so that your health improves (**convalescer, restabelecer**)

• **convalescence** /ˌkɒnvəˈlesəns/ NOUN, NO PLURAL the time when someone is convalescing (**convalescência**)

convection /kənˈvekʃən/ NOUN, NO PLURAL when heat moves through air or water as the hotter part rises. A physics word. (**convecção, difusão de calor**)

• **convector** /kənˈvektə(r)/ NOUN [plural convectors] a device that heats a room by blowing out hot air (**aquecedor**)

convene /kənˈviːn/ VERB [convenes, convening, convened] to come together for a meeting, or to bring people together. A formal word. □ *He convened a meeting.* □ *We all convened in the school hall.* (**reunir-se**)

convenience /kən'vi:njəns/ NOUN [plural **conveniences**]

1 no plural the state of being easy to use, reach or do □ *I like the convenience of living so close to the shops.* □ *For everyone's convenience, we will meet after school.* (**conveniência**)

2 something that makes people's lives easy or comfortable □ *The hotel has every modern convenience.* (**comodidade**)

• **convenient** /kən'vi:njənt/ ADJECTIVE

1 suitable and easy □ *Drinking fruit juice is a convenient way for children to get vitamin C.* (**conveniente**)

2 very close and easy to get to □ **+ for** *Our house is very convenient for the school.* (**cômodo, acessível**)

• **conveniently** /kən'vi:njəntlɪ/ ADVERB in a convenient way (**convenientemente**)

convent /'kɒnvənt/ NOUN [plural **convents**] a building where nuns (= religious women) live (**convento**)

convention /kən'venʃən/ NOUN [plural **conventions**]

1 a way of behaving that has become normal because people have been doing it for a long time (**convenção**)

2 a meeting of people to discuss a particular subject □ *a science-fiction convention* (**conferência, reunião**)

3 a formal agreement between governments (**acordo, tratado**)

• **conventional** /kən'venʃənəl/ ADJECTIVE

1 traditional and not at all unusual (**convencional**) 🔂 *Many people try homoeopathy if conventional medicine has not cured them.* (**medicina convencional**) □ *He uses conventional methods of teaching.*

2 conventional people are not willing to try new things (**comum, convencional**)

converge /kən'vɜ:dʒ/ VERB [**converges, converging, converged**]

1 to come together at a particular place □ *The two roads converge just beyond the bridge.* (**convergir**)

2 to come to a place and form a group there □ *Protesters converged on Trafalgar Square.* (**encontrar-se**)

conversant /kən'vɜ:sənt/ ADJECTIVE **conversant with something** knowing about something or having experience of it. A formal word. □ *Young people are so conversant with technology.* (**familiarizado com algo**)

conversation /ˌkɒnvə'seɪʃən/ NOUN [plural **conversations**] a talk between people (**conversa**) 🔂 *We had a long conversation about music.* (**tivemos uma conversa**) □ **+ with** *I had a nice conversation with my Dad last night.* 🔂 *I overheard a conversation between my brother and his girlfriend.* (**ouvi uma conversa**)

• **conversational** /ˌkɒnvə'seɪʃənəl/ ADJECTIVE to do with conversation (**conversacional**)

converse¹ /kən'vɜ:s/ VERB [**converses, conversing, conversed**] when people converse, they talk to each other. A formal word. (**conversar**)

converse² /'kɒnvɜ:s/ NOUN, NO PLURAL **the converse** the opposite of a statement, fact etc. (**inverso**)

• **conversely** /kən'vɜ:slɪ/ ADVERB in the opposite way, or from the opposite point of view (**inversamente**)

conversion /kən'vɜ:ʃən/ NOUN [plural **conversions**]

1 when you change something from one thing to another □ *the conversion from analogue to digital television* (**conversão**)

2 when someone changes to a different religion □ *her conversion from Christianity to Islam* (**conversão**)

convert ▶ VERB /kən'vɜ:t/ [**converts, converting, converted**]

1 to change something into something else □ *Convert this sum of money from pounds into dollars.* (**converter**)

2 to change from one religion to another one (**converter**)

▶ NOUN /'kɒnvɜ:t/ [plural **converts**] someone who has changed to a different religion or opinion (**convertido**)

• **convertible** /kən'vɜ:təbəl/ ▶ ADJECTIVE able to be changed from one thing to another (**mutável**)
▶ NOUN [plural **convertibles**] a car with a soft roof that you can fold back (**conversível**)

convex /kɒn'veks/ ADJECTIVE curving outwards (**convexo**)

convey /kən'veɪ/ VERB [**conveys, conveying, conveyed**]

1 to communicate information, ideas or feelings □ *What are you trying to convey in this poem?* (**expressar**)

2 a formal word meaning to take someone or something to a place □ *A bus conveyed us to the lecture theatre.* (**conduzir**)

conveyor belt /kən'veɪə ˌbelt/ NOUN [plural **conveyor belts**] a moving surface used to carry things from one place to another, especially in a factory (**esteira rolante**)

convict ▶ VERB /kən'vɪkt/ [**convicts, convicting, convicted**] to say in a court that someone is guilty of a crime □ *He was convicted of murder.* (**condenar**)

▶ NOUN /'kɒnvɪkt/ [plural **convicts**] someone who has been found guilty of a crime and sent to prison (**condenado**)

• **conviction** /kən'vɪkʃən/ NOUN [plural **convictions**]

1 a strong belief (**convicção**)

2 when a judge says that someone is guilty of a crime □ *Greene has had many convictions for theft.* (**condenação**)

convince

convince /kənˈvɪns/ VERB [convinces, convincing, convinced] to make someone believe that something is true □ *Vijay found it hard to convince his parents that he was too ill to go to school.* (convencer)

- **convinced** /kənˈvɪnst/ ADJECTIVE certain that something is true □ *David's convinced that he saw a ghost.* (convencido)
- **convincing** /kənˈvɪnsɪŋ/ ADJECTIVE
  1 making you believe that something is true or right □ *He gave a fairly convincing argument against nuclear weapons.* (convincente)
  2 a convincing win is one in which someone wins by a large amount (convincente)

convoluted /ˈkɒnvəluːtɪd/ ADJECTIVE complicated and difficult to understand □ *convoluted language* (enrolado, complicado)

convoy /ˈkɒnvɔɪ/ NOUN [plural convoys] a line of vehicles which are travelling together (comboio)

convulsion /kənˈvʌlʃən/ NOUN [plural convulsions] a sudden movement of your muscles, caused by illness (convulsão)

coo /kuː/ VERB [coos, cooing, cooed]
1 to make a soft gentle sound like that made by some birds such as a dove or pigeon (arrulhar)
2 to speak in a soft voice, especially in order to show that you like something □ *They were all cooing over the baby.* (falar de modo carinhoso)

cook /kʊk/ ▶ VERB [cooks, cooking, cooked]
1 to prepare and heat food so that it is ready to eat (cozinhar) ▣ *I offered to* cook a meal *for her.* (cozinhar uma refeição) ▣ *Ben* was cooking dinner. (está cozinhando o jantar) □ *Cook the pasta in a pan of boiling water.*
2 food cooks when it heats up and becomes ready to eat □ *While the potatoes are cooking, prepare the other vegetables.* (cozinhar)
▶ NOUN [plural cooks] someone who prepares and cooks food (cozinheiro) ▣ *Emma's a really* good cook. (boa cozinheira) □ *He works as a hospital cook.*

- **cooker** /ˈkʊkə(r)/ NOUN [plural cookers] a piece of kitchen equipment used for cooking food □ *a gas cooker* (fogão)

> Note that a **cook** is someone who prepares and cooks food and a **cooker** is a piece of equipment used for cooking food.

- **cookery** /ˈkʊkəri/ NOUN, NO PLURAL the skill or activity of cooking food □ *She's doing a cookery course.* (culinária)

cookie /ˈkʊki/ NOUN [plural cookies]
1 a biscuit □ *a chocolate chip cookie* (cookie, biscoito)
2 a piece of computer information about which websites you have looked at. A computing word. (cookie, grupo de dados)

coordination

cooking /ˈkʊkɪŋ/ ▶ NOUN, NO PLURAL
1 when someone cooks food □ *Cooking is my main interest.* (cozinha)
2 the type of food that is cooked □ *I love my grandma's cooking.* (comida)
▶ ADJECTIVE for use in cooking □ *cooking oil* (de cozinha)

cool /kuːl/ C ADJECTIVE [cooler, coolest]
1 slightly cold (fresco) ▣ *There was a* cool breeze. (brisa fresca) ▣ *I need a* cool drink. (bebida fria)
2 an informal word meaning great □ *He has a really cool haircut.* □ *'I've got a new mobile.' 'Cool!'* (legal)
3 calm (calmo) ▣ *Try to* stay cool *in a dangerous situation.* (ficar calmo)
4 not friendly □ *He gave a cool reply.* (indiferente)
▶ VERB [cools, cooling, cooled] to become cooler or to make something cooler □ *Have a drink to help you cool down.* (esfriar)

coop /kuːp/ NOUN [plural coops] a building for keeping chickens in (viveiro, gaiola)
◆ PHRASAL VERB [coops, cooping, cooped] **coop something/someone up** to keep a person or an animal in a small space □ *We've been cooped up indoors all day.* (manter alguém/algo preso)

cooperate /kəʊˈɒpəreɪt/ VERB [cooperates, cooperating, cooperated]
1 to work together with other people to achieve something □ *The two countries are cooperating with each other in the fight against terrorism.* (cooperar)
2 to help by doing something that someone wants you to □ *He refused to cooperate.* (cooperar, ajudar)

- **cooperation** /kəʊˌɒpəˈreɪʃən/ NOUN, NO PLURAL
  1 working with others so that something can be done or achieved (cooperação)
  2 doing what someone asks or tells you to do (cooperação)

- **cooperative** /kəʊˈɒpərətɪv/ ADJECTIVE
  1 willing to do what someone asks you to do (cooperativo)
  2 a cooperative business or organization is one that is managed or owned by everyone who works in it or uses it (cooperativo)

coordinate /kəʊˈɔːdɪneɪt/ VERB [coordinates, coordinating, coordinated] to organize all the different parts of something □ *He is coordinating the research project.* (coordenar)

coordinates /kəʊˈɔːdɪnəts/ PLURAL NOUN the two sets of numbers or letters that show the exact position of something on a map or graph (= mathematical picture) (coordenadas)

coordination /kəʊˌɔːdɪˈneɪʃən/ NOUN, NO PLURAL
1 the organization of people and activities so that they work well together (coordenação)

2 the ability to make different parts of your body work well together (**coordenação**) 🔲 *He has brilliant hand-eye coordination.* (**coordenação motora**)

cop /kɒp/ NOUN [plural **cops**] an informal word for a police officer □ *a New York cop* (**policial**)

cope /kəʊp/ VERB [**copes, coping, coped**] to be able to deal with something difficult □ *She said she couldn't cope with any more work.* □ *So many people came to the city that the transport system couldn't cope.* (**competir**)

co-pilot /ˈkəʊpaɪlət/ NOUN [plural **co-pilots**] the person who helps the main pilot on an aeroplane (**copiloto**)

copious /ˈkəʊpɪəs/ ADJECTIVE in large amounts (**copioso, abundante**) 🔲 *They drank copious amounts of beer.* (**quantidades abundantes**) 🔲 *He made copious notes during the interview.* (**notas abundantes**)

copper /ˈkɒpə(r)/ ▶ NOUN [plural **coppers**]
1 *no plural* a red-brown metal (**cobre**)
2 *no plural* a red-brown colour like this metal (**cobre**)
3 a brown coin that has a low value (**cobre**)
4 an informal word for **police officer** (**policial**)
▶ ADJECTIVE
1 made of copper □ *a copper kettle* (**de cobre**)
2 having the colour of copper □ *She had beautiful copper hair.* (**cor de cobre**)

copse /kɒps/ or **coppice** /ˈkɒpɪs/ NOUN [plural **copses** or **coppices**] a small group of bushes or trees (**matagal**)

copy /ˈkɒpɪ/ ▶ NOUN [plural **copies**]
1 something that is made so that it looks exactly the same as something else (**cópia**) 🔲 *Rick bought a CD and made a digital copy from that.* (**fez uma cópia**) □ *+ of He sent a copy of her death certificate.*
2 one book, magazine, etc. from many the same that have been produced □ *+ of I bought a copy of her new book.* (**exemplar**)
▶ VERB [**copies, copying, copied**]
1 to make something that is exactly the same as something else □ *She copied the file onto a CD.* (**copiar**)
2 to do the same things as someone else □ *Conrad copies everything his big brother does.* □ *He copied my idea.* (**copiar**)
3 to write down words or information that you have found somewhere □ *I copied the train times into my notebook.* □ *She tried to copy my answers in the exam.* (**copiar**)
◆ PHRASAL VERBS **copy something down** to write something that someone has told you or that is written somewhere □ *Copy down these questions and do them for homework.* **copy someone in** to send someone a copy of an email or a document □ *+ on Can you copy me in on your report?* (**copiar algo**)

copyright /ˈkɒpɪraɪt/ NOUN, NO PLURAL the legal right to copy or use a book, film, etc. (**direitos autorais**) 🔲 *The company owns the copyright to thousands of songs.* (**detém os direitos autorais**)

coral /ˈkɒrəl/ ▶ NOUN, NO PLURAL a hard pink or white substance formed from the bones of small sea creatures (**coral**)
▶ ADJECTIVE made of coral □ *a coral island* □ *a coral necklace* (**coral**)

coral reef /ˈkɒrəl ˌriːf/ NOUN [plural **coral reefs**] a large mass of coral under the sea (**recife de corais**)

cord /kɔːd/ NOUN [plural **cords**]
1 a piece of thick string □ *The prisoner's hands were tied with cord.* (**cordão**)
2 wire covered with plastic that connects a piece of equipment to an electrical supply (**fio**)

> ▶ Do not confuse the spellings of *cord* and *chord*, which have different meanings.

cordial /ˈkɔːdɪəl/ ▶ ADJECTIVE a formal word meaning friendly and polite □ *The two countries have a cordial relationship.* (**cordial**)
▶ NOUN [plural **cordials**] a sweet fruit drink that you mix with water □ *lime cordial* (**bebida refrescante**)

cordless /ˈkɔːdlɪs/ ADJECTIVE a cordless piece of electrical equipment does not have to be connected to an electricity supply all the time (**sem fio**) 🔲 *a cordless phone* (**telefone sem fio**)

cordon /ˈkɔːdən/ NOUN [plural **cordons**] a line of police or soldiers standing around an area to stop people getting in (**cordão de isolamento**) 🔲 *Protesters broke through a police cordon.* (**cordão de isolamento policial**)
◆ PHRASAL VERB [**cordons, cordoning, cordoned**] **cordon something off** to put something around a place so that people cannot get in □ *Police cordoned off the crime scene.* (**impedir o avanço**)

corduroy /ˈkɔːdərɔɪ/ NOUN, NO PLURAL cotton cloth with raised lines on it (**veludo**)

core /kɔː(r)/ ▶ NOUN [plural **cores**]
1 the most important part of something (**centro**) 🔲 *This area is at the core of the Chinese manufacturing industry.* (**no centro do**)
2 the hard part with seeds in the middle of fruit like apples or pears □ *an apple core* (**caroço**)
3 the centre of a planet (**núcleo**)
▶ ADJECTIVE most important (**principal**) 🔲 *core beliefs/values* (**crenças/valores principais**) □ *Our core business was not affected by the strike.*

corgi /ˈkɔːgɪ/ NOUN [plural **corgis**] a type of dog with short legs (**raça de cachorro Corgi**)

cork /kɔːk/ NOUN [plural **corks**]
1 *no plural* a light material from the outside part of a tree (**cortiça**)
2 a piece of cork, which is put inside the top of a wine bottle (**rolha**)

corkscrew /ˈkɔːkskruː/ NOUN [plural **corkscrews**] a device used for pulling corks out of wine bottles (**saca-rolhas**)

corn /kɔːn/ NOUN, NO PLURAL
1 a crop such as wheat that is grown for grain (**cereal**)
2 the US word for **maize** or **sweetcorn** (**milho**)

cornea /'kɔːnɪə/ NOUN [plural **corneas**] the transparent layer that covers your eye. A biology word. (**córnea**)

corner /'kɔːnə(r)/ ▶ NOUN [plural **corners**]
1 a point where two walls, edges or lines meet (**quina, canto**) 🔲 *It was a large room with a table in the corner.* (**no canto**) □ *+ of* The corner of the page was creased.
2 the point where two roads meet (**esquina**) 🔲 *There's a hairdresser's on the corner.* (**na esquina**) 🔲 *The school is just round the corner.* (**virando a esquina**) □ *+ of* I'll meet you at the corner of George Street and Alexander Road.
3 a place away from the main area or far away □ *He's travelled to the far corners of the world.* □ *We put the statue in a shady corner of the garden.* (**canto**)
4 a kick or hit from the corner of a sports field in some games such as football (**escanteio**)
▶ VERB [**corners, cornering, cornered**] to get someone into a position that it is not easy to escape from □ *He had been cornered and attacked with a baseball bat.* □ *He cornered meat the office party and suggested we should go out for dinner.* (**acossar**)

cornerstone /'kɔːnəstəʊn/ NOUN [plural **cornerstones**] the most important part of something, which everything else depends on □ *Voting is the cornerstone of democracy.* (**marco, pedra fundamental**)

cornet /'kɔːnɪt/ NOUN [plural **cornets**] a musical instrument that looks like a small trumpet (**corneta**)

cornflakes /'kɔːnfleɪks/ PLURAL NOUN flat, baked pieces of corn (= grain) that you eat with milk for breakfast □ *a bowl of cornflakes* (**flocos de milho**)

cornflour /'kɔːnflaʊə(r)/ NOUN, NO PLURAL a white powder made from corn (= grain), used in cooking, for example to make a sauce thicker (**maisena**)

cornflower /'kɔːnflaʊə(r)/ NOUN [plural **cornflowers**] a wild plant with bright blue flowers (**centáurea**)

corny /'kɔːnɪ/ ADJECTIVE [**cornier, corniest**] silly, or heard too many times before (**banal**) 🔲 *a corny joke* (**piada banal**)

coronary /'kɒrənərɪ/ ▶ ADJECTIVE to do with the heart. A biology word. □ *coronary disease* (**coronário**)
▶ NOUN [plural **coronaries**] when someone's heart suddenly stops working correctly (**coronária, trombose**)

coronation /ˌkɒrə'neɪʃən/ NOUN [plural **coronations**] a ceremony in which someone becomes a king or queen (**coroação**)

coroner /'kɒrənə(r)/ NOUN [plural **coroners**] someone whose job is to find out the cause of someone's death (**médico-legista**)

corporal /'kɔːpərəl/ NOUN [plural **corporals**] a soldier with a low rank (**cabo**)

corporal punishment /ˌkɔːpərəl 'pʌnɪʃmənt/ NOUN, NO PLURAL punishment which involves hitting someone (**castigo corporal**)

corporate /'kɔːpərət/ ADJECTIVE to do with a large company □ *The corporate headquarters are in Vancouver.* (**corporativo**)

corporation /ˌkɔːpə'reɪʃən/ NOUN [plural **corporations**] a large company (**corporação**)

corps /kɔː(r)/ NOUN [plural **corps**] a group in an army, especially one that does a special job □ *the Army Medical Corps* (**unidade militar**)

corpse /kɔːps/ NOUN [plural **corpses**] a dead body (**cadáver**)

corpulent /'kɔːpjʊlənt/ ADJECTIVE a formal word meaning fat □ *a corpulent old man* (**corpulento**)

corpuscle /'kɔːpʌsəl/ NOUN [plural **corpuscles**] a red or white cell in the blood. A biology word. (**corpúsculo**)

correct /kə'rekt/ ▶ ADJECTIVE
1 right, not wrong (**correto, certo**) 🔲 *The correct answer is 15.* (**resposta correta**) □ *What is the correct pronunciation of that word?*
2 behaving in a way that is socially acceptable □ *My father was always very correct.* (**correto**)
⇨ go to **politically correct**
▶ VERB [**corrects, correcting, corrected**]
1 to make something right □ *He had an operation on his ankle to correct the problem.* (**corrigir**)
2 to show someone the mistakes they have made in speaking or writing □ *He interrupted me to correct my grammar.* (**corrigir**)

• **correctly** /kə'rektlɪ/ ADVERB in a way that is correct □ *Make sure you enter your password correctly.* (**corrigir**)

• **correction** /kə'rekʃən/ NOUN [plural **corrections**] a change that makes something right (**correção**) 🔲 *They have made corrections to their earlier report.* (**fizeram correções**)

correlate /'kɒrəleɪt/ VERB [**correlates, correlating, correlated**] if two things correlate, one thing causes or influences the other thing. A formal word. □ *A mother's smoking in pregnancy correlates with low birth weight in her baby.* (**correlacionar**)

• **correlation** /ˌkɒrə'leɪʃən/ NOUN, NO PLURAL when one thing causes or influences another thing. A formal word. (**correlação**) 🔲 *Researchers found a strong correlation between poverty and ill health.* (**forte correlação**)

correspond /ˌkɒrɪ'spɒnd/ VERB [**corresponds, corresponding, corresponded**]
1 if two things correspond, they are the same □ *Let's see if what he told you corresponds with what he told me.* (**corresponder**)

2 if people correspond, they write to each other. A formal word. (**corresponder**)

• **correspondence** /ˌkɒrɪˈspɒndəns/ NOUN, NO PLURAL
1 letters that people write to each other, or the activity of writing letters (**correspondência**)
2 a connection between two things (**correspondência**)

• **correspondent** /ˌkɒrɪˈspɒndənt/ NOUN [plural correspondents] someone who writes news reports about a particular subject □ *a political correspondent* (**correspondente**)

• **corresponding** /ˌkɒrɪˈspɒndɪŋ/ ADJECTIVE relating to or similar to something else □ *Prices have risen with no corresponding increase in wages.* (**correspondente**)

corridor /ˈkɒrɪdɔː(r)/ NOUN [plural corridors] a passage in a building with doors on one or both sides (**corredor**) 🔁 *a long corridor* (**longo corredor**) □ *I was chatting to her in the corridor.*

corroborate /kəˈrɒbəreɪt/ VERB [corroborates, corroborating, corroborated] to give information that supports or proves what someone has said. A formal word. □ *Several witnesses corroborated her version of events.* (**corroborar**)

• **corroboration** /kəˌrɒbəˈreɪʃən/ NOUN, NO PLURAL information that supports or proves what someone has said. A formal word. (**corroboração**)

corrode /kəˈrəʊd/ VERB [corrodes, corroding, corroded] if metal corrodes, it is slowly destroyed by water or chemicals (**corroer**)

• **corrosion** /kəˈrəʊʒən/ NOUN, NO PLURAL when something corrodes (**corrosão**)

• **corrosive** /kəˈrəʊsɪv/ ADJECTIVE able to gradually destroy metal □ *a corrosive acid* (**corrosivo**)

corrugated /ˈkɒrəgeɪtɪd/ ADJECTIVE made in the shape of several folds (**ondulado**) 🔁 *a corrugated roof* (**telha ondulada**)

corrupt /kəˈrʌpt/ ▶ ADJECTIVE
1 being dishonest in order to get money or power □ *corrupt officials* (**corrupto**)
2 corrupt information has been spoiled so that it is no longer correct □ *The data was corrupt.* (**adulterado**)

▶ VERB [corrupts, corrupting, corrupted]
1 to make someone behave dishonestly in order to get money or power □ *People are easily corrupted by power.* (**corromper**)
2 to spoil information so that it is no longer correct □ *A virus corrupted all his data.* (**adulterar**)

• **corruption** /kəˈrʌpʃən/ NOUN, NO PLURAL dishonest behaviour by people in powerful jobs □ *There was widespread corruption among the police.* (**corrupção**)

corset /ˈkɔːsɪt/ NOUN [plural corsets] a piece of tight underwear that women in the past wore around their waists to make their waists look smaller (**espartilho**)

cosh /kɒʃ/ NOUN [plural coshes] a short heavy stick used for hitting people (**cassetete**)

cosine /ˈkəʊsaɪn/ NOUN [plural cosines] in a triangle with one angle of 90°, the cosine is the length of the side next to an angle of less than 90° divided by the hypotenuse (= longest side). A maths word. (**cosseno**)

cosmetic /kɒzˈmetɪk/ ADJECTIVE
1 designed to make you look more attractive □ *cosmetic products* (**cosmético**)
2 involving only small changes that are not important □ *The changes were merely cosmetic.* (**cosmético**)

• **cosmetics** /kɒzˈmetɪks/ PLURAL NOUN powders and creams that you put on your face to make you more attractive (**produtos de beleza**)

cosmetic surgery /kɒzˌmetɪk ˈsɜːdʒəri/ NOUN, NO PLURAL an operation that is done to make someone look more attractive (**cirurgia plástica**) 🔁 *She had cosmetic surgery to make her nose smaller.* (**fez cirurgia plástica**)

cosmic /ˈkɒzmɪk/ ADJECTIVE to do with the universe and outer space (**cósmico**)

cosmopolitan /ˌkɒzməˈpɒlɪtən/ ADJECTIVE including people or ideas from many parts of the world □ *cosmopolitan cities like London and New York* (**cosmopolita**)

cosmos /ˈkɒzmɒs/ NOUN, NO PLURAL **the cosmos** the universe (**cosmos**)

cosset /ˈkɒsɪt/ VERB [cossets, cosseting, cosseted] to give someone too much attention and care □ *It's not good to cosset your children.* (**mimar**)

cost /kɒst/ ▶ VERB [costs, costing, cost]
1 to have a particular price □ *The ticket cost £35.* □ *How much does a litre of milk cost?* □ *This coat cost me a lot of money.* □ *+ to do something It cost £10,000 to fix the roof.* (**custar**)
2 to cost someone something is to make them lose that thing □ *His brave actions cost him his life.* (**custar algo a alguém**)

▶ NOUN [plural costs]
1 the amount of money that you need in order to buy or do something □ *+ of The average cost of a house in this area is £350,000.* (**custo**) 🔁 *the high cost of fuel* (**alto custo**) 🔁 *There has been an increase in the cost of living (= the price of food, clothes, etc.).* (**custo de vida**)
2 damage that is done to someone or something □ *+ to There's a great cost to the environment when we burn carbon fuels.* (**custo**)

♦ IDIOM **at all costs** used for saying that you will do something even if it is difficult or even if people suffer □ *Yushi was determined to succeed at all costs.* (**a qualquer custo**)

• **costly** /ˈkɒstli/ ADJECTIVE
1 expensive □ *The building was costly to repair.* (**caro**)
2 causing a lot of problems (**dispendioso**) 🔁 *We made a few costly mistakes early in the game.* (**falhas onerosas**)

co-star

co-star /ˈkəʊstɑː(r)/ ▶ VERB [**co-stars, co-starring, co-starred**] to be in a film or play with another famous actor (**contracenar**)
▶ NOUN [plural **co-stars**] one of two famous actors in a film or play (**coadjuvante**)

costume /ˈkɒstjuːm/ NOUN [plural **costumes**]
1 a set of clothes that you wear to make you look like a different person or like an animal or other creature □ *The costumes in the film were beautiful.* □ *He was in a vampire's costume at Amy's party.* (**traje**)
2 in costume wearing a costume □ *Everyone at the party was in costume.* (**fantasia**)
3 the traditional clothes from a country or from a time in the past (**traje**) ▣ *The children were dressed in national costume for the parade.* (**trajes nacionais**) □ *Elizabethan costumes*

cosy /ˈkəʊzɪ/ ADJECTIVE [**cosier, cosiest**] warm and comfortable □ *a cosy little bedroom* □ *I'm nice and cosy sitting here by the fire.* (**aconchegante**)

cot /kɒt/ NOUN [plural **cots**] a bed with high sides that a baby sleeps in (**berço**)

cot death /ˈkɒt ˌdeθ/ NOUN [plural **cot deaths**] when a baby dies while it is sleeping and nobody knows why (**morte no berço**)

cottage /ˈkɒtɪdʒ/ NOUN [plural **cottages**] a small house in the countryside or in a village □ *They've bought one of the cottages in the village.* (**casa de campo**)

cotton /ˈkɒtən/ NOUN, NO PLURAL
1 a common type of cloth made from a plant □ *a white cotton shirt* □ *cotton sheets* (**algodão**)
2 a plant that produces a soft white substance, used for making cloth □ *cotton farmers* (**algodão**)

cotton wool /ˌkɒtən ˈwʊl/ NOUN, NO PLURAL a mass of soft cotton, used for cleaning cuts on your skin and for removing make-up (**algodão**)

couch /kaʊtʃ/ NOUN [plural **couches**] a long, comfortable chair that two or more people can sit on (**divã, sofá**)

couch potato /ˈkaʊtʃ pəˌteɪtəʊ/ NOUN [plural **couch potatoes**] a lazy person, especially one who sits watching television a lot. An informal phrase. (**pessoa preguiçosa e sedentária**)

cougar /ˈkuːgə(r)/ NOUN [plural **cougars**] a large wild animal of the cat family that lives in America (**puma**)

cough /kɒf/ ▶ VERB [**coughs, coughing, coughed**] to make a loud rough sound in your throat as air comes out of your lungs □ *He was coughing and sneezing.* (**tossir**)
▶ NOUN [plural **coughs**]
1 the noise you make when you cough (**tossida**) ▣ *She gave a little cough and looked up.* (**deu uma tossida**)

2 an illness that causes you to cough (**tosse**) ▣ *I have got a bad cough.* (**peguei uma tosse ruim**) ▣ *You need some cough medicine.* (**remédio para tosse**)

could /kʊd/ MODAL VERB
1 used as the past tense of **can** □ *We could see into the building.* □ *He could run very fast when he was young.* □ *He said we could go.* (**podia, poderia**)
2 used to ask for something or to ask someone to do something □ *Could I have a glass of water, please?* □ *Could you pass me the butter?* (**poderia**)
3 used to make a suggestion □ *You could try texting her.* □ *We could go for a walk.* (**poderia**)
4 used to say that something is possible □ *The weather could get better later.* □ *The disease could be prevented with good hygiene.* (**poderia**)

couldn't /ˈkʊdənt/ a short way to say and write *could not* (**não poderia**)

could've /ˈkʊdəv/ a short way to say and write *could have* (**poderia**)

council /ˈkaʊnsəl/ NOUN [plural **councils**]
1 a group of people who are elected to control a town or city (**conselho**) ▣ *Local councils are responsible for repairing roads.* □ *council leaders* (**conselhos locais**)
2 an official group of people who make decisions or give advice □ *a new business advisory council* (**conselho**)

• **councillor** /ˈkaʊnsələ(r)/ NOUN [plural **councillors**] a member of a town or city council (**conselheiro**)

▶ Be careful not to confuse the noun **council** with the noun and verb **counsel**.

council tax /ˈkaʊnsəl ˌtæks/ NOUN, NO PLURAL in Britain, a tax that you pay for local services such as schools and libraries, based on how much your house is worth (**taxa de conselho**)

counsel /ˈkaʊnsəl/ ▶ VERB [**counsels, counselling/US counseling, counselled/US counseled**]
1 to give someone advice and help with their problems □ *Students were counselled following the death of their classmate.* (**conselho**)
2 a formal word meaning to advise □ *He had been counselled by his lawyer to remain silent.* (**conselho**)
▶ NOUN [plural **counsels**]
1 a lawyer who speaks in a court □ *the counsel for the defence* (**advogado**)
2 a formal word meaning advice (**conselho**)

• **counselling** /ˈkaʊnsəlɪŋ/ NOUN, NO PLURAL giving advice and help to people with problems □ *the student counselling service* (**consulta**)

• **counsellor** /ˈkaʊnsələ(r)/ NOUN [plural **counsellors**] someone whose job is to give advice and help to people with problems (**conselheiro**)

counseling /ˈkaʊnsəlɪŋ/ NOUN, NO PLURAL the US spelling of **counselling** (consulta)

• **counselor** /ˈkaʊnsələ(r)/ NOUN [plural **counselors**] the US spelling of **counsellor** (conselheiro)

count /kaʊnt/ ▶ VERB [**counts, counting, counted**]

1 to find out the total of something ▫ *He was busy counting his money.* (contar)
2 to say numbers in order ▫ *Can you count backwards from 10?* (enumerar)
3 to think of someone or something in a particular way ▫ **+ as** *I counted him as one of my best friends.* (contar)
4 to be important ▫ *He played well when it counted.* (contar)

♦ PHRASAL VERBS **count against someone** to make it more difficult for someone to succeed ▫ *Lack of experience will count against him in the race.* (contar contra alguém) **count on someone** to depend on someone ▫ *I was counting on him to help.* (contar com alguém) **count out something** to say the numbers aloud while you are counting something ▫ *He counted out £500.* (enumerar) **count towards something** to form part of a total ▫ *This essay will count towards your final grades.* (contar no total) **count up something** to find out the total of something ▫ *She counted up how many people there were.* (contar o total)

▶ NOUN [plural **counts**]

1 the process of counting, or the total you get (contagem) ▫ *She did a quick count of the people present.* (fez uma contagem rápida)
2 keep count to know how many of something there is (manter contagem)
3 lose count to stop knowing how many of something there is (perder a conta)
4 on all/both counts in all or both ways ▫ *The claim is wrong on all counts.* (de qualquer modo)
5 a man of a high social rank (conde)

countable noun /ˌkaʊntəbəl ˈnaʊn/ NOUN [plural **countable nouns**] in grammar, a noun that can form a plural, e.g. dog, table or car (substantivos contáveis)

countdown /ˈkaʊntdaʊn/ NOUN, NO PLURAL
1 the time just before something important and exciting happens ▫ *The countdown to the World Cup has begun.* (contagem regressiva)
2 when people count backwards to zero before something happens (contagem regressiva)

counter /ˈkaʊntə(r)/ ▶ NOUN [plural **counters**]
1 the place where people are served in a shop or bank ▫ *She worked on the perfume counter.* (balcão)
2 a small plastic disc used in some games that are played on a board (ficha)
3 the US word for **work surface** (superfície plana)
▶ VERB [**counters, countering, countered**]

1 to reduce the bad effects that something has, or to prevent it from happening ▫ *We are doing everything we can to counter terrorism.* (conter)
2 to say something that disagrees with or criticizes what someone has said ▫ *'I can't do it,' she countered.* (opor)

counter- /ˈkaʊntə(r)/ PREFIX counter- is added to the beginning of words to mean 'the opposite of' ▫ *counteract* (contra-)

counteract /ˌkaʊntərˈækt/ VERB [**counteracts, counteracting, counteracted**] to reduce or remove the bad effect of something (neutralizar) ▫ *Massage may be able to counteract the harmful effects of stress.* (neutralizar efeitos)

counterattack /ˈkaʊntərətæk/ NOUN [plural **counterattacks**] an attack against someone who has attacked or criticized you first ▫ *The soldiers launched a counterattack.* (contra-ataque)

counterfeit /ˈkaʊntəfɪt/ ▶ ADJECTIVE not real, but made to look real ▫ *a counterfeit stamp* (falso)
▶ NOUN [plural **counterfeits**] a copy of something made to look as if it is real (imitação, falsificação)

counterfoil /ˈkaʊntəfɔɪl/ NOUN [plural **counterfoils**] the part of a ticket or cheque that is left when the main piece has been removed (recibo)

counterpart /ˈkaʊntəpɑːt/ NOUN [plural **counterparts**] the person who does the same job as you but in a different place ▫ *The British Prime Minister will be meeting his European counterparts.* (contraparte, duplicata)

countersign /ˈkaʊntəsaɪn/ VERB [**countersigns, countersigning, countersigned**] to sign a document that has already been signed by someone else (adicionar uma assinatura)

countess /ˈkaʊntɪs/ NOUN [plural **countesses**] a woman with a high social rank (condessa)

countless /ˈkaʊntlɪs/ ADJECTIVE very many ▫ *I've done this countless times.* (incontável)

count noun /ˈkaʊnt ˌnaʊn/ NOUN [plural **count nouns**] in grammar, a noun that can form a plural, e.g. dog, table or car (substantivo contável)

country /ˈkʌntri/ ▶ NOUN [plural **countries**]
1 an area of land with its own government and national borders ▫ *We don't have the death penalty in this country.* ▫ *Have you ever lived in a foreign country?* (país)
2 the country (a) areas that are away from towns and cities ▫ *I prefer living in the country.* (b) all the people who live in a nation ▫ *The President has lost the support of the country.* (interior)
3 no plural a particular type of land ▫ *He ran for miles across open country.* ▫ *the mountainous country of southern China* (campo)
▶ ADJECTIVE in or from the countryside ▫ *country lanes* ▫ *The Prime Minister's country house is located on Lake Mousseau.* (campo)

countryman

countryman /'kʌntrɪmən/ NOUN [plural **countrymen**] someone who comes from the same country as you □ *He beat countryman Healey 6–2, 7–5.* (**compatriota**)

countryside /'kʌntrɪsaɪd/ NOUN, NO PLURAL land that is away from towns and cities (**campo**) 🔲 *The hotel is surrounded by open countryside.* (**campo aberto**)

countrywoman /'kʌntrɪwʊmən/ NOUN [plural **countrywomen**] a woman who comes from the same country as you (**compatriota**)

county /'kaʊnti/ NOUN [plural **counties**] an area of a country or state that has its own local government □ *Yorkshire is a huge county.* (**condado**)

coup /kuː/ NOUN [plural **coups**]
1 when a group of people suddenly take control of a country without an election (**golpe**) 🔲 *a military coup* (**golpe militar**)
2 a great achievement □ *Signing Beckham was a real coup for the team.* (**vitória**)

couple /'kʌpəl/ ▶ NOUN [plural **couples**]
1 two or approximately two □ + **of** *I haven't seen him for a couple of months.* □ *She relaxed after the first couple of games.* □ *Who ate all the chocolates? I only had a couple.* (**par**)
2 a husband and wife, or two people who have a similar close relationship (**casal**) 🔲 *Most people on the holiday were married couples.* (**casais**) 🔲 *Many young couples can't afford to buy a house.* (**jovens casais**)
▶ VERB [**couples, coupling, coupled**] **coupled with** combined with □ *A high-fat diet coupled with a lack of exercise is causing many people to become obese.* (**combinado com**)

coupon /'kuːpɒn/ NOUN [plural **coupons**] a piece of paper that you can use to get something free or at a cheaper price than usual (**cupom**)

courage /'kʌrɪdʒ/ NOUN, NO PLURAL the ability to do difficult or frightening things (**coragem**) 🔲 *He didn't have the courage to tell her what he really thought.* (**ter a coragem de**) 🔲 *John showed great courage throughout his ordeal.* (**grande coragem**) 🔲 *I haven't plucked up the courage (= found the courage) to leave my job yet.* (**encontrou coragem**)

• **courageous** /kəˈreɪdʒəs/ ADJECTIVE brave □ *a courageous decision* (**corajoso**)

courgette /kɔːˈʒet/ NOUN [plural **courgettes**] a long green vegetable that you cook and eat (**abobrinha**)

courier /'kʊrɪə(r)/ ▶ NOUN [plural **couriers**] someone who takes packages from one place to another □ *a courier company* (**mensageiro**)
▶ VERB [**couriers, couriering, couriered**] to send something using a courier (**enviar encomenda**)

courteous

course /kɔːs/ NOUN [plural **courses**]
1 of course (a) used for saying yes □ *'Can I borrow your pen?' 'Of course you can.'* (b) used for saying that what happened was what you expected □ *We went on holiday and of course it rained the whole time.* (**evidentemente, obviamente**)
2 of course not used for emphasizing the word no □ *'Did you leave the keys in the car?' 'No, of course not.'* (**claro que não**)
3 a set of lessons on a particular subject (**curso**) 🔲 *I'm doing a French course.* (**curso de francês**) 🔲 *There was a four-year training course to become a teacher.* (**treinamento**) □ + **in** *a part-time course in business studies*
4 one of the parts of a meal (**prato**) 🔲 *For the main course we had roast chicken.* (**prato principal**)
5 the direction that a vehicle is travelling in (**curso**) 🔲 *The pilot had to change course and land in Berlin.* (**mudar o curso**)
6 the things that you do in a particular situation (**modo**) 🔲 *He advised me on the best course of action.* (**modo de ação**)
7 a piece of land that a race is run on or a game of golf is played on □ *a golf course* (**pista**)
8 during/in the course of while something is happening □ *During the course of the evening, I started to feel unwell.* (**no decurso de**)

> ▶ Remember that **course** (sense 3) is followed by the preposition in: □ *She's doing a four-day course in travel writing.*

court /kɔːt/ ▶ NOUN [plural **courts**]
1 the room where legal trials take place (**tribunal**) 🔲 *He will appear in court charged with murder.* (**comparecer ao tribunal**)
2 the court the people who make a legal judgment about whether someone is guilty of a crime □ *He told the court that he had never met the woman before.* (**a corte**)
3 an area where you play sports such as tennis or basketball □ *an indoor tennis court* (**quadra**)
4 the home of a king or queen and the people who live with them (**corte**)
▶ VERB [**courts, courting, courted**]
1 to do things to try to get someone's support □ *The party is attempting to court young voters.* (**cortejar, atrair**)
2 to do something that brings a particular result □ *He has courted controversy with offensive statements about the chairman.* (**provocar**)

courteous /'kɜːtɪəs/ ADJECTIVE polite □ *His manner was always courteous.* (**cortês, polido**)

• **courtesy** /'kɜːtɪsi/ NOUN [plural **courtesies**]
1 no plural polite behaviour (**cortesia**) 🔲 *She didn't even have the courtesy to explain.* (**teve a cortesia**)

2 something polite that you do □ *As a courtesy, she phoned before she visited him.* (cortesia)
3 courtesy of (a) as a result of □ *The team went into the lead courtesy of a brilliant goal from Miller.* (b) used for saying who provided or paid for something □ *Politicians travel all around the world courtesy of taxpayers.* (cortesia de)

courthouse /'kɔ:thaʊs/ NOUN [plural **courthouses**] a US word for a building with legal courts in it (corte judicial)

courtier /'kɔ:tɪə(r)/ NOUN [plural **courtiers**] someone who works or spends a lot of time at a king or queen's home (cortesão)

court-martial /ˌkɔ:t'mɑ:ʃəl/ ▶ NOUN [plural **court-martials** or **courts-martial**] a military trial (corte marcial)
▶ VERB [**court-martials, court-martialling, court-martialled**] to judge a soldier in a military court (submeter a julgamento)

courtroom /'kɔ:tru:m/ NOUN [plural **courtrooms**] the room where a trial takes place (sala de audiência)

courtship /'kɔ:tʃɪp/ NOUN [plural **courtships**] the time when you have a romantic relationship with someone before you get married (namoro)

courtyard /'kɔ:tjɑ:d/ NOUN [plural **courtyards**] an open area that is surrounded by walls, usually next to a building (pátio)

cousin /'kʌzən/ NOUN [plural **cousins**] the son or daughter of your aunt or uncle □ *Clare and I are cousins.* (primo)

cove /kəʊv/ NOUN [plural **coves**] a part of the coast where the sea is partly surrounded by land (enseada)

covenant /'kʌvənənt/ NOUN [plural **covenants**] a formal written agreement (pacto)

cover /'kʌvə(r)/ ▶ VERB [**covers, covering, covered**]
1 to put something over something else to hide or protect it □ + *with* *Mum had covered the table with a clean cloth.* □ + *up* *We covered up the broken window with a board.* □ *Cover your mouth when you cough, please.* (cobrir)
2 to form a layer on the surface of something □ *The mountains were covered in snow.* □ *The carpets are covered in mud.* (cobrir)
3 to deal with or to include a subject or some information □ *The local newspaper covered the story.* □ *The course covers every aspect of childcare.* □ *This law only covers UK residents.* (tratar)
4 to travel a particular distance □ *We covered ten miles in three hours.* (percorrer)
5 to be a particular size □ *The farm covers an area of over a hundred square miles.* (abranger)
6 to be enough to pay for something □ *£100 should cover our expenses.* (cobrir)
7 to provide protection from financial problems caused by a particular situation □ *Our insurance covers accidental damage.* □ *I'm covered for loss of earnings if I'm ill.* (cobrir)
◆ PHRASAL VERBS **cover for someone** to do someone's work while they are not there □ *I'm covering for Jenny while she's on holiday.* (substituir alguém) **cover something up** to stop people from discovering something bad you have done □ *He set fire to the house in an attempt to cover up his crime.* (encobrir algo)
▶ NOUN [plural **covers**]
1 something that you put on top of or around something to protect it □ *a duvet cover* (coberta)
2 the outer part of a book or magazine (capa) 🔲 *There was a photograph of him on the front cover.* (capa)
3 no plural protection so that you get money if something bad happens □ *Make sure you have enough insurance cover if you are going on holiday.* (cobertura)
4 no plural protection from attack or bad weather (cobertura) 🔲 *We took cover in an old church.* (encontramos abrigo)

• **coverage** /'kʌvərɪdʒ/ NOUN, NO PLURAL when a newspaper or a television programme reports an event 🔲 *The channel showed live coverage of the game.* (cobertura)

• **covering** /'kʌvərɪŋ/ NOUN [plural **coverings**]
1 something that you use to cover something □ *The shop has a wide range of floor coverings.* (revestimento)
2 a layer which covers something □ + *of* *There was a light covering of snow on the hills.* (cobertura)

covering letter /ˌkʌvərɪŋ 'letə(r)/ NOUN [plural **covering letters**] a letter that you include with something to give more information about it (carta explicativa)

covert /'kəʊvɜ:t, 'kʌvət/ ADJECTIVE done secretly □ *a covert military operation* (secreto)

covet /'kʌvɪt/ VERB [**covets, coveting, coveted**] to want something very much. A formal word. (cobiçar)

• **covetous** /'kʌvɪtəs/ ADJECTIVE wanting something very much. A formal word. (cobiçoso)

cow /kaʊ/ NOUN [plural **cows**] a large animal kept on farms for its milk or meat (vaca) 🔲 *The farmer had a large herd of cows.* (manada de vacas)

coward /'kaʊəd/ NOUN [plural **cowards**] someone who has no courage (covarde)

• **cowardice** /'kaʊədɪs/ NOUN, NO PLURAL being a coward (covardia)

• **cowardly** /'kaʊədli/ ADJECTIVE behaving like a coward (covarde)

cowboy /'kaʊbɔɪ/ NOUN [plural **cowboys**] a man who rides a horse and looks after cows in the US (caubói, vaqueiro)

cower /'kaʊə(r)/ VERB [**cowers, cowering, cowered**] to move your body away from someone because you are frightened (esconder-se)

cowgirl /ˈkaʊgɜːl/ NOUN [plural **cowgirls**] a woman who rides a horse and looks after cows in the US (**vaqueira**)

coy /kɔɪ/ ADJECTIVE [**coyer, coyest**]
1 pretending to be shy ◻ *a coy smile* (**tímido**)
2 not willing to give information about something ◻ *She's very coy about her age.* (**reservado**)

coyote /kɔɪˈəʊti/ NOUN [plural **coyotes**] a wild dog that lives in North America (**coiote**)

cozy /ˈkəʊzi/ ADJECTIVE [**cozier, coziest**] the US spelling of cosy (**aconchegante**)

CPU /ˌsiːpiːˈjuː/ ABBREVIATION central processing unit; a part of a computer that controls what it does. A computing word. (**CPU**)

crab /kræb/ NOUN [plural **crabs**] a sea creature with a round shell and ten legs, whose pink meat is eaten (**caranguejo**)

crack /kræk/ ▶ VERB [**cracks, cracking, cracked**]
1 to break something so that a line appears on the surface, or to break in this way ◻ *I'm sorry, I've cracked this cup.* ◻ *The ice had started to crack.* (**rachar**)
2 if you crack an egg or a nut, you break it open (**quebrar**)
3 to hit part of your body hard against something ◻ *He fell and cracked his head on the pavement.* (**bater**)
4 to solve something ◻ *We hope this will help us crack the mystery.* (**solucionar**)
5 **crack a joke** to make a joke (**contar uma piada**)
◆ PHRASAL VERBS **crack down** to start dealing with someone or something in a more severe way ◻ *The government is cracking down on illegal fishing.* (**tomar medidas severas**) **crack up** an informal word meaning to become mentally ill (**ter um colapso**)
▶ NOUN [plural **cracks**]
1 a narrow break ◻ *This mug has a crack in it.* ◻ *The ceiling had lots of cracks in it.* (**rachadura**)
2 a narrow space between two parts of something ◻ *The sun was coming in through a crack in the curtain.* (**fresta**)
3 a sudden short sound ◻ *the crack of a whip* (**estalo**)
◆ IDIOM **have a crack at something** to try to do something. An informal phrase. (**sofrer um estalo**)

crackdown /ˈkrækdaʊn/ NOUN [plural **crackdowns**] when you start dealing with someone or something more severely ◻ *a crackdown on illegal street traders* (**sanção severa**)

cracker /ˈkrækə(r)/ NOUN [plural **crackers**]
1 a paper tube with a toy inside that you pull apart at Christmas (**embrulho em forma de tubo, presenteado no Natal**)
2 a plain, dry biscuit that you eat with cheese (**bolacha**)

crackle /ˈkrækəl/ ▶ VERB [**crackles, crackling, crackled**] to make several short cracking noises ◻ *The fire crackled in the grate.* (**crepitar**)
▶ NOUN, NO PLURAL several short cracking noises ◻ *the crackle of twigs underfoot* (**crepitação**)

cradle /ˈkreɪdəl/ ▶ NOUN [plural **cradles**] a baby's bed that can move from side to side (**berço**)
▶ VERB [**cradles, cradling, cradled**] to hold someone or something carefully and gently ◻ *She cradled the baby in her arms.* (**embalar**)

craft[1] /krɑːft/ ▶ NOUN [plural **crafts**] a skill in which you make something with your hands ◻ *They teach traditional crafts such as pottery and sewing.* (**artesanato**)
▶ VERB [**crafts, crafting, crafted**] to make something using skill ◻ *The statues were crafted from marble.* (**elaborar**)

craft[2] /krɑːft/ NOUN [plural **craft**] a boat (**barco**)

craftsman /ˈkrɑːftsmən/ NOUN [plural **craftsmen**] a man who is skilled at making things with his hands (**artesão**)
• **craftsmanship** /ˈkrɑːftsmənʃɪp/ NOUN, NO PLURAL the skill of a craftsman or craftswoman (**artesanato**)

craftswoman /ˈkrɑːftswʊmən/ NOUN [plural **craftswomen**] a woman who is skilled at making things with her hands (**artesã**)

crafty /ˈkrɑːfti/ ADJECTIVE [**craftier, craftiest**] good at getting what you want by tricking people (**esperto**)

crag /kræg/ NOUN [plural **crags**] a high steep rock that sticks up from the area around it (**penhasco**)
• **craggy** /ˈkrægi/ ADJECTIVE [**craggier, craggiest**]
1 with a lot of crags ◻ *We could see the craggy peaks of the island.* (**escarpado**)
2 a craggy face is strong with a lot of lines (**áspero**)

cram /kræm/ VERB [**crams, cramming, crammed**]
1 to push people or things into a small space ◻ *Elizabeth tried to cram everything into her bags.* ◻ *We all crammed into the car.* (**abarrotar**)
2 an informal word meaning to study a lot before an exam (**estudar muito**)
• **crammed** /kræmd/ ADJECTIVE completely full ◻ *The shelves were absolutely crammed with books.* (**estufado**)

cramp /kræmp/ NOUN [plural **cramps**] a sudden pain in a muscle that makes it feel tight (**câimbra**)
• **cramped** /kræmpt/ ADJECTIVE a cramped space is uncomfortable because it is too small (**apertado**)

cranberry /ˈkrænbəri/ NOUN [plural **cranberries**] a small red fruit with a sour taste ◻ *cranberry juice* (**amora**)

crane /kreɪn/ ▶ NOUN [plural **cranes**]
1 a tall machine used to lift and move heavy things (**guindaste**)
2 a large bird with a long neck and long thin legs (**grande garça azul**)

▶ VERB [cranes, craning, craned] to stretch your neck up to see something (estender o pescoço)

cranium /'kreɪniəm/ NOUN [plural **crania** or **craniums**] your skull (= bone in your head). A biology word. (crânio)

crank /kræŋk/ NOUN [plural **cranks**]
1 someone who has strange ideas or behaves in a strange way (excêntrico)
2 a handle that you turn to make an engine or a piece of machinery start (manivela)

• **cranky** /'kræŋki/ ADJECTIVE [crankier, crankiest] bad-tempered □ *The baby was getting cranky.* (mal-humorado)

cranny /'kræni/ NOUN [plural **crannies**] a narrow opening, especially in a rock or wall (rachadura)
⇨ *go to* every nook and cranny

crash /kræʃ/ ▶ VERB [crashes, crashing, crashed]
1 if a vehicle crashes, or you crash it, it hits something by accident □ *A plane had crashed into the mountain.* □ *Jane crashed her car last night.* (colidir)
2 to make a loud noise, often by hitting something □ *The crystal vase crashed to the floor.* □ *The waves were crashing against the rocks.* (espatifar-se)
3 if a computer crashes, it suddenly stops working. A computing word. (pifar)
4 if the stock market (= the buying and selling of parts of businesses) crashes, it loses value suddenly (quebrar)
♦ PHRASAL VERB **crash out** an informal phrase meaning to go to sleep when you are very tired □ *We crashed out on Emma's floor.* (dormir)
▶ NOUN [plural **crashes**]
1 an accident in which a vehicle hits something □ *Her parents were killed in a plane crash.* (acidente)
2 a loud noise made when something breaks or falls □ *the crash of breaking glass* (estrondo)
3 when a computer suddenly stops working. A computing word. (travamento)
4 when the value of a country's businesses suddenly falls □ *the stock market crash of 1987* (quebra)
▶ ADJECTIVE done in a short time to get results quickly (intensivo) 🔷 *a crash diet* (dieta intensiva) 🔷 *I took a crash course in French.* (curso intensivo)

crash helmet /'kræʃ ˌhelmɪt/ NOUN [plural **crash helmets**] a hard hat worn by motorcycle riders to protect their head (capacete)

crash-land /ˌkræʃ 'lænd/ VERB [crash-lands, crash-landing, crash-landed] to land an aeroplane suddenly in an emergency, sometimes causing damage or injuries (fazer pouso de emergência)

• **crash-landing** /ˌkræʃ 'lændɪŋ/ NOUN [plural **crash-landings**] when you have to land an aeroplane in an emergency (pouso de emergência) 🔷 *The pilot had to make a crash-landing in a field.* (fazer um pouso de emergência)

crass /kræs/ ADJECTIVE stupid and not showing respect for other people's feelings □ *a crass remark* (grosso)

crate /kreɪt/ NOUN [plural **crates**] a wooden or plastic box used for carrying or storing things, especially bottles (engradado)

crater /'kreɪtə(r)/ NOUN [plural **craters**]
1 a large hole in the ground □ *The bomb left a crater 10 metres wide.* (buraco)
2 the round hole at the top of a volcano (= mountain that explodes). A geography word. (cratera)

cravat /krə'væt/ NOUN [plural **cravats**] a wide strip of thin cloth that is folded and tied under the collar of a man's shirt (gravata)

crave /kreɪv/ VERB [craves, craving, craved] to want something very much (suplicar) 🔷 *Disruptive children often crave attention.* (suplicam atenção)

• **craving** /'kreɪvɪŋ/ NOUN [plural **cravings**] a strong feeling that you need or want something □ *When she was pregnant she developed a craving for salty foods.* (desejo)

crawl /krɔːl/ ▶ VERB [crawls, crawling, crawled]
1 to move on your hands and knees □ *The baby has just learnt to crawl.* (engatinhar)
2 insects crawl when they move around on their legs □ *There's a spider crawling up the wall behind you.* (rastejar)
3 if vehicles crawl, they move very slowly □ *The traffic was crawling along at about 2 miles per hour.* (mover-se lateralmente)
♦ PHRASAL VERB **crawl with something** or **be crawling with something** (a) to be too full of people □ *The country was crawling with spies.* (b) to be covered with insects □ *The meat was crawling with flies.* (coberto de algo)
▶ NOUN, NO PLURAL
1 a very slow speed □ *We were moving forward at a crawl.* (passo de tartaruga)
2 a way of swimming in which you kick your legs and move one arm and then the other over your head (nado crawl)

crayon /'kreɪɒn/ NOUN [plural **crayons**] a stick of coloured wax or a coloured pencil for drawing with (lápis de cor)

craze /kreɪz/ NOUN [plural **crazes**] something that is very popular for a short time □ *the craze for Japanese puzzles* (moda)

crazed /kreɪzd/ ADJECTIVE behaving in a wild, uncontrolled way □ *a crazed gunman* (insano)

crazy /'kreɪzi/ ADJECTIVE [crazier, craziest]
1 mad or stupid (louco) □ *a crazy idea* 🔷 *Have you gone crazy?* (ficou louco)
2 angry (louco) 🔷 *Mum will go crazy when she finds out.* (vai ficar louca) 🔷 *His stupid questions drives me crazy.* (me deixa louco)

3 be crazy about someone/something to like someone or something very much □ *As a child, she was crazy about horses.* (**ser louco por alguém/algo**)

creak /kriːk/ ▶ VERB [creaks, creaking, creaked] if a door or a piece of wood creaks, it makes a long low sound □ *The floorboards creaked as he crossed the room.* (**ranger**)
▶ NOUN [plural creaks] a long low sound (**rangido**)
• **creaky** /ˈkriːkɪ/ ADJECTIVE [creakier, creakiest] making long low sounds □ *a creaky gate* (**rangedor**)

cream /kriːm/ ▶ NOUN [plural creams]
1 *no plural* a thick yellow-white liquid that forms on top of milk □ *strawberries and cream* (**nata**)
2 a soft substance that you put on your skin or hair □ *suntan cream* (**creme**)
3 *no plural* a yellow-white colour (**cor de creme**)
▶ ADJECTIVE having a yellow-white colour □ *a cream leather sofa* (**creme**)
♦ PHRASAL VERB [creams, creaming, creamed] **cream something off** to take the best part of something □ *He showed no interest in the business – he just creamed off all the profits.* (**selecionar algo**)
• **creamy** /ˈkriːmɪ/ ADJECTIVE [creamier, creamiest] containing cream or like cream □ *a creamy dessert* (**cremoso**)

crease /kriːs/ ▶ NOUN [plural creases] a line on cloth or paper where it has been folded or crushed □ *With this fabric you can shake out the creases.* (**prega, dobra**)
▶ VERB [creases, creasing, creased] to get creases or make something get creases □ *Linen creases very easily.* (**vincar**)

create /kriːˈeɪt/ VERB [creates, creating, created] to make something happen or exist □ *We are hoping to create an environmentally friendly building.* □ *Snow created problems for drivers today.* □ *He hoped to create a good impression by arriving on time.* (**criar**)
• **creation** /kriːˈeɪʃən/ NOUN [plural creations]
1 *no plural* the act or process of creating something □ *He opposed the creation of a new department.* (**criação**)
2 something that has been made □ *This plastic dress is one of the designer's latest creations.* (**criação**)
3 the Creation the time when some people believe that God made the universe (**a Criação**)
• **creative** /kriːˈeɪtɪv/ ADJECTIVE
1 good at imagining and making new things, especially works of art □ *She's a very creative artist.* (**criativo**)
2 to do with creating things □ *the creative process* (**criativo**)
• **creativity** /ˌkriːeɪˈtɪvətɪ/ NOUN, NO PLURAL the ability or imagination to make or invent things (**criatividade**)

• **creator** /kriːˈeɪtə(r)/ NOUN [plural creators] someone who creates something □ *She was the creator of some of TV's most popular characters.* (**criador**)

creature /ˈkriːtʃə(r)/ NOUN [plural creatures] any living thing that is not a plant (**criatura**)

crèche /kreʃ/ NOUN [plural crèches] a place where very young children are looked after while their parents are somewhere else (**creche**)

credentials /krɪˈdenʃəlz/ PLURAL NOUN
1 the qualities and experience that make you suitable for a particular job or activity or make you seem good in a particular way □ *The company has worked hard to establish its green credentials.* (**referência**)
2 official documents that prove someone is who they say they are □ *Did you ask to see his credentials?* (**credencial**)

credibility /ˌkredəˈbɪlətɪ/ NOUN, NO PLURAL a quality that makes people believe and respect someone (**credibilidade**) *The government has lost all credibility over the war.* (**perdeu credibilidade**)

credible /ˈkredəbəl/ ADJECTIVE able to be believed □ *a credible story* (**crível**)

credit /ˈkredɪt/ ▶ NOUN [plural credits]
1 *no plural* a way of buying goods or services and paying for them later □ *I bought the car on credit.* (**crédito**) *We offer interest-free credit on all goods over £200.* (**crédito sem juros**)
2 *no plural* praise that people give you for something you have done *We all worked hard but Ben got most of the credit.* (**ficou com o crédito**) *I can't take all the credit for the success of the film.* (**levar o crédito**)
3 to someone's credit if behaviour is to someone's credit, they have done something good □ *To her credit, she never gave away Tammy's secret.* (**a favor de alguém**)
4 be a credit to someone to do something that makes someone proud of you □ *Your children really are a credit to you.* (**dar o devido crédito a alguém**)
5 in credit your bank account is in credit when you have money in it (**saldo bancário positivo**)
6 an amount paid into a bank account (**empréstimo**)
⇨ *go to* **credits**
▶ VERB [credits, crediting, credited]
1 to put some money into a bank account (**creditar**)
2 to believe something (**confiar**) *We could scarcely credit their cheek!* (**confiar vagamente**)
♦ PHRASAL VERBS **credit something to something** to say that something was the reason for something good □ *They credited their success to a happy working environment.* (**creditar algo a algo**) **credit someone with something**
1 to say that someone is responsible for achieving something good □ *He was credited with saving many lives.* (**atribuir o mérito a alguém**)

2 to say that someone has a particular quality □ *Credit me with a bit of common sense!* (**creditar**)

- **creditable** /ˈkredɪtəbəl/ ADJECTIVE good enough to deserve praise □ *a very creditable performance* (**digno**)

credit card /ˈkredɪt ˌkɑːd/ NOUN [plural credit cards] a small plastic card that allows you to buy things when you want them and to pay for them later □ *Can I pay by credit card?* (**cartão de crédito**)

credit crunch /ˈkredɪt ˌkrʌntʃ/ NOUN [plural credit crunches] a time when it is difficult to borrow money, and people have less money to spend (**contração de crédito**)

credits /ˈkredɪts/ PLURAL NOUN **the credits** the list at the end of a film or television programme that shows who worked on it (**créditos**)

creed /kriːd/ NOUN [plural creeds] something that you believe in, especially religious beliefs (**crença**)

creek /kriːk/ NOUN [plural creeks]
1 a small river (**riacho**)
2 a narrow area of sea that flows into the land (**pequena baía**)

creep /kriːp/ ▶ VERB [creeps, creeping, crept] to move slowly and quietly so that nobody hears you □ *He crept downstairs in the middle of the night.* (**rastejar**)

♦ PHRASAL VERB **creep up on someone**
1 to walk up very quietly behind someone to surprise them (**escalar**)
2 if something creeps up on you, it happens gradually so you do not notice it happening □ *My retirement date just seemed to creep up on me.* (**rastejar**)

▶ NOUN [plural creeps]
1 someone who is nice to people only so that they will like them (**pessoa aproveitadora**)
2 someone who is unpleasant □ *What a creep!* (**pessoa desagradável**)

♦ IDIOM **give someone the creeps** to make someone feel frightened or disgusted □ *Her new boyfriend really gives me the creeps.* (**dar arrepios em alguém**)

- **creeper** /ˈkriːpə(r)/ NOUN [plural creepers] a plant that grows over the ground or up a wall (**trepadeira**)
- **creepy** /ˈkriːpi/ ADJECTIVE [creepier, creepiest] making you feel nervous or frightened □ *a creepy old churchyard* (**sinistro, arrepiante**)

cremate /krɪˈmeɪt/ VERB [cremates, cremating, cremated] to burn a dead body instead of burying it (**cremar**)

- **cremation** /krɪˈmeɪʃən/ NOUN [plural cremations] the burning of a dead body or dead bodies (**cremação**)
- **crematorium** /ˌkreməˈtɔːriəm/ NOUN [plural crematoriums or crematoria] a building where cremations take place (**crematório**)

creosote /ˈkriːəsəʊt/ NOUN, NO PLURAL a type of dark brown paint used to stop wood decaying (**creosoto**)

crept /krept/ PAST TENSE AND PAST PARTICIPLE OF **creep** (*ver* **creep**)

crescendo /krɪˈʃendəʊ/ NOUN [plural crescendos] when music or another sound gradually gets louder (**crescendo**)

crescent /ˈkresənt/ NOUN [plural crescents]
1 a curved shape that is pointed at each end and is wider in the middle □ *a crescent moon* (**crescente**)
2 used in the names of some curved streets □ *21 Chestnut Crescent* (**rua em formato de semicírculo**)

cress /kres/ NOUN, NO PLURAL a small plant with very small green leaves that are used in salads □ *an egg and cress sandwich* (**agrião**)

crest /krest/ NOUN [plural crests]
1 the highest point of a hill or wave (**topo, cume**)
2 the feathers that point upwards on the top of some birds' heads (**crista**)
3 a design that is used as the symbol of a family or organization (**cocar**)

crestfallen /ˈkrestfɔːlən/ ADJECTIVE sad or disappointed (**desapontado**)

crevasse /krɪˈvæs/ NOUN [plural crevasses] a deep crack in rock or ice (**rachadura**)

crevice /ˈkrevɪs/ NOUN [plural crevices] a thin crack or opening in rock □ *a crevice between the rocks* (**fenda**)

crew /kruː/ ▶ NOUN [plural crews]
1 a group of people who work together on a ship, aeroplane or train □ *The lifeboat has a crew of five.* (**bando**)
2 a team of skilled people who work together □ *The film crew were busy setting up lights and cameras.* (**equipe**)

▶ VERB [crews, crewing, crewed] to crew a boat or ship is to work as a member of its crew (**ser tripulante**)

▶ PAST TENSE OF **crow**

crib /krɪb/ NOUN [plural cribs] the US word for cot (**berço**)

cricket /ˈkrɪkɪt/ NOUN [plural crickets]
1 *no plural* a game played outdoors between two teams of eleven players who score points by hitting a ball □ *a cricket bat* (**críquete**)
2 a small insect that lives in grass and makes a noise by rubbing its wings together (**grilo**)

- **cricketer** /ˈkrɪkɪtə(r)/ NOUN [plural cricketers] someone who plays cricket (**jogador de críquete**)

cried /kraɪd/ PAST TENSE AND PAST PARTICIPLE OF cry (*ver* **cry**)

crime /kraɪm/ NOUN [plural crimes]
1 *no plural* illegal activities □ *a life of crime* (**crime**) ▣ *The government is introducing new*

crimson 183 **croak**

measures to fight crime. (combater o crime) 🗨 Violent crime is increasing. (crimes violentos)
2 an illegal activity (crime) ☐ minor crimes like shoplifting 🗨 Have you ever committed a crime? (cometeu um crime) 🗨 The police never managed to solve the crime (= discover who did it). (solucionar o crime)

> ➤ Note that a person **commits** a crime. A person does not **make** or **do** a crime.

• **criminal** /ˈkrɪmɪnəl/ ➤ NOUN [plural criminals] someone who has committed a crime ☐ a dangerous criminal (criminoso)
➤ ADJECTIVE
1 to do with crime or criminals (criminal) 🗨 He has a criminal record. (recorde criminal)
2 illegal or very wrong ☐ a criminal act (criminoso)

crimson /ˈkrɪmzən/ ➤ ADJECTIVE having a dark red colour ☐ She turned crimson with embarrassment. (carmesim)
➤ NOUN, NO PLURAL a dark red colour (carmesim)

cringe /krɪndʒ/ VERB [cringes, cringing, cringed]
1 to move away from something because you are frightened ☐ The young soldier was found cringing behind a wall. (encolher-se)
2 to feel very embarrassed ☐ These old photos really make me cringe. (envergonhar)

crinkle /ˈkrɪŋkəl/ VERB [crinkles, crinkling, crinkled] to make something have a lot of small folds or lines ☐ He crinkled his eyes against the sun. (ruga, dobra)
• **crinkly** /ˈkrɪŋkli/ ADJECTIVE [crinklier, crinkliest] having lots of crinkles ☐ a crinkly skirt (enrugado)

cripple /ˈkrɪpəl/ VERB [cripples, crippling, crippled]
1 to damage someone's body so that they cannot walk or move in a normal way ☐ She was crippled by arthritis. (mutilar)
2 to damage something badly so that it cannot work effectively ☐ Rising oil prices are crippling the economy. (incapacitar)
• **crippling** /ˈkrɪplɪŋ/ ADJECTIVE
1 causing a lot of damage or having a very bad effect (incapacitante) 🗨 crippling debts (dívida incapacitante)
2 crippling pain is so bad that you cannot move (paralisante)

crisis /ˈkraɪsɪs/ NOUN [plural crises]
1 a very difficult or dangerous time or event ☐ a financial crisis ☐ the growing crisis in the housing market (crise)
2 in crisis in a very difficult or dangerous situation ☐ The government is in crisis. (em crise)

crisp /krɪsp/ ➤ ADJECTIVE [crisper, crispest]
1 crisp food is pleasantly hard or fresh ☐ crisp salad leaves ☐ crisp pastry (fresco)
2 clean and looking new ☐ a crisp uniform (impecável)
3 crisp weather is cold and dry ☐ a crisp spring morning (fresco)
4 a crisp image is very clear (nítido)
➤ NOUN [plural crisps] a very thin piece of potato that is cooked in oil and eaten cold (batata frita) 🗨 a bag of crisps (um saco de batatas fritas)
• **crispness** /ˈkrɪspnɪs/ NOUN, NO PLURAL the quality of being crisp ☐ Chopped celery adds crispness to salads. (crocância)
• **crispy** /ˈkrɪspi/ ADJECTIVE [crispier, crispiest] pleasantly hard ☐ cod in crispy batter (crocante)

criss-cross /ˈkrɪskrɒs/ VERB [criss-crosses, criss-crossing, criss-crossed] to cross an area several times in different directions ☐ The park is criss-crossed with a network of footpaths. (entrelaçar-se)

criterion /kraɪˈtɪəriən/ NOUN [plural criteria] a standard you use when you have to make a choice or decision ☐ He failed to meet the criteria for a university place. (critério)

critic /ˈkrɪtɪk/ NOUN [plural critics]
1 someone who says that someone or something is bad ☐ a critic of the government (crítico)
2 someone whose job is to give their opinion of new books, films, plays, etc. ☐ He was the film critic for the Times. (crítico)
• **critical** /ˈkrɪtɪkəl/ ADJECTIVE
1 saying that you think something is bad or wrong (crítico) 🗨 The report was highly critical of her work (altamente crítico) ☐ critical remarks/comments
2 very important ☐ The talks have reached a critical stage. ☐ Good hygiene is of critical importance. (importante)
3 very serious (sério, crítico) 🗨 The patient is in a critical condition. (numa condição crítica)
• **critically** /ˈkrɪtɪkəli/ ADVERB
1 in a way that shows disapproval ☐ She looked critically at the children. (criticamente)
2 very or seriously (crítico) 🗨 critically ill (doença crítica) ☐ a critically important decision
• **criticism** /ˈkrɪtɪsɪzəm/ NOUN [plural criticisms]
1 no plural when you say what is bad about someone or something (crítica) 🗨 Her actions drew criticism from colleagues. (atraíram críticas) 🗨 There has been widespread criticism of the new laws. (crítica difundida) 🗨 The company has faced criticism from environmental campaigners. (encarou a crítica)
2 a statement about what you think is bad about someone or something ☐ My only criticism is the story is too long. (crítica)
• **criticize** or **criticise** /ˈkrɪtɪsaɪz/ VERB [criticizes, criticizing, criticized] to say what you think is bad about someone or something ☐ It always hurts when you criticize me. ☐ + for They were criticized for leaving the children alone. (criticar)

croak /krəʊk/ ➤ VERB [croaks, croaking, croaked]
1 to speak in a rough voice because your throat is sore or dry (falar com voz rouca)

2 a frog (= small green animal that lives near water) croaks when it makes its deep sound (**coaxar**)
▶ NOUN [plural **croaks**]
1 the sound made by a frog (**coaxo**)
2 a low rough voice (**voz rouca**)
- **croaky** /'krəʊki/ ADJECTIVE [**croakier, croakiest**] a croaky voice is deep and rough (**rouquidão**)

crochet /'krəʊʃeɪ/ VERB [**crochets, crocheting, crocheted**] to make clothes, etc. by using wool and a needle with a curved piece at the end (**fazer crochê**)

crockery /'krɒkəri/ NOUN, NO PLURAL plates, bowls, cups, etc. (**louça**)

crocodile /'krɒkədaɪl/ NOUN [plural **crocodiles**] a large reptile with a long tail and a big mouth that lives in rivers and lakes (**crocodilo**)

crocus /'krəʊkəs/ NOUN [plural **crocuses**] a small white, purple or yellow spring flower □ *a bowl of crocuses* (**açafrão**)

croissant /'kwæsã/ NOUN [plural **croissants**] a type of soft bread in a curved shape that you eat for breakfast (**croissant**)

crony /'krəʊni/ NOUN [plural **cronies**] one of a group of friends who help each other, especially in a way that is not fair □ *The best jobs will go to his cronies.* (**camarada**)

crook /krʊk/ NOUN [plural **crooks**]
1 an informal word for a criminal or someone who tricks people (**ladrão**)
2 the crook of your arm is the part on the inside where it bends (**curva**)
- **crooked** /'krʊkɪd/ ADJECTIVE
1 not straight or even □ *crooked teeth* □ *That picture's crooked.* (**torto**)
2 an informal word meaning not honest □ *crooked cops* (**desonesto**)

crop /krɒp/ ▶ NOUN [plural **crops**]
1 a plant that is grown for food □ *They grow crops such as corn and maize.* (**produto agrícola**)
2 the amount of vegetables, fruit, etc. that is produced in a place at one time □ *Our apple trees produced a good crop this year.* (**colheita**)
3 a group of things or people □ *This year's crop of novels is an extraordinary one.* (**grupo**)
▶ VERB [**crops, cropping, cropped**]
1 to cut something very short □ *She cropped his hair very short.* (**cortar rente**)
2 to cut the edges off a picture in order to make it fit somewhere, especially using a computer (**recortar**)
◆ PHRASAL VERB **crop up** if something crops up, it happens when you are not expecting it □ *Something cropped up and I couldn't get to the meeting.* (**surgir**)
- **cropped** /'krɒpt/ ADJECTIVE cropped hair is cut very short (**cortado**)

cropper /'krɒpə(r)/ NOUN, NO PLURAL
◆ IDIOM **come a cropper**
1 to fall over or have an accident □ *She came a cropper on some slippery steps.* (**tombar**)
2 to fail or make a mistake □ *His team came a cropper in the first round.* (**fracassar**)

croquet /'krəʊkeɪ/ NOUN, NO PLURAL a game played on grass, in which you use long wooden hammers to hit balls through curved wires in the ground (**croquê**)

cross /krɒs/ ▶ NOUN [plural **crosses**]
1 a shape made when two straight lines go over each other at a point in the middle (**cruz**)
2 a symbol used in the Christian religion to represent the cross on which Christ died (**cruz**)
3 the symbol 'x', used to show when an answer is wrong, or used to show someone where to write something on a document (**sinal de erro**)
4 a mixture of two different things □ **+ between** *The film is a cross between Short Cuts and Love, Actually.* (**cruzamento, mistura**)
5 a kick or hit of the ball across the field in sports such as football (**passe**)
▶ VERB [**crosses, crossing, crossed**]
1 to go from one side of something to the other (**atravessar**) 🔊 *Find a safe place to* cross the road. (**atravessar a rodovia**) □ *A bridge crosses the river at that point.* □ *Troops crossed the border at dawn.*
2 if two things cross, they go across each other □ *The accident happened where the road and railway line cross.* (**cruzar**)
3 **cross your arms/fingers/legs** to put one arm/finger/leg over the top of the other □ *She was sitting quietly, with her arms crossed.* (**cruzar os braços/dedos/pernas**)
4 to make two different animals or plants breed together □ *They crossed this rose with a more disease free variety.* (**cruzar**)
5 to kick or hit the ball across the field in sports such as football □ *He crossed the ball into the penalty box.* (**cruzar**)
◆ IDIOM **cross your mind** to come into your mind □ *It never crossed my mind that she'd believe me.* (**passar pela cabeça**)
⇨ go to **cross paths (with someone)**
◆ PHRASAL VERBS **cross something off** to remove something from a list by drawing a line through it □ *Karen's crossed her name off the list for the quiz.* (**cancelar**) **cross something out** to draw a line through something, usually because it is wrong □ *He crossed out his answer and started again.* (**riscar**)
▶ ADJECTIVE [**crosser, crossest**] angry □ **+ with** *I got very cross with him for not doing his homework.* (**zangado, irritado**)

crossbar /'krɒsbɑː(r)/ NOUN [plural **crossbars**]
1 the piece of wood over the top of a goal in games such as football □ *Spurs have hit the crossbar again!* (**trave**)
2 the piece of metal that joins the front and back of a bicycle (**barra**)

cross-country /ˌkrɒsˈkʌntri/ ADJECTIVE across fields and countryside instead of a road or track □ *cross-country skiing* (**por bosques e trilhas**)

cross-examination /ˈkrɒsɪɡˌzæmɪˈneɪʃən/ NOUN [plural **cross-examinations**] a series of questions asked to check that what someone has said is true (**interrogatório minucioso**)

• **cross-examine** /ˌkrɒsɪɡˈzæmɪn/ VERB [**cross-examines, cross-examining, cross-examined**] to ask someone a lot of questions to check that what they have said is true (**interrogar**)

cross-eyed /ˌkrɒsˈaɪd/ ADJECTIVE a cross-eyed person has eyes that look towards their nose (**estrábico**)

crossfire /ˈkrɒsfaɪə(r)/ NOUN, NO PLURAL a situation in which guns are being fired from different directions (**fogo cruzado**) 🔲 *Two soldiers were caught in the crossfire.* (**pegos no fogo cruzado**)

crossing /ˈkrɒsɪŋ/ NOUN [plural **crossings**]
1 a place where you can cross a road or a river □ *Be sure to cross at the crossing.* (**travessia**)
2 a journey from one side of an area of water to the other □ *It's a short ferry crossing from Mull to Iona.* (**viagem**)

cross-legged /ˌkrɒsˈleɡɪd/ ADJECTIVE, ADVERB sitting on the floor with your legs bent so that your knees are wide apart and one ankle is on top of the other □ *The children sat cross-legged in a circle.* (**pernas cruzadas**)

crossly /ˈkrɒsli/ ADVERB angrily □ *'Leave me alone,' she said, crossly.* (**de modo rabugento**)

cross purposes /ˌkrɒs ˈpɜːpəsɪz/ PLURAL NOUN at **cross purposes** if two people are at cross purposes, they are talking about different things but they do not know this □ *We seem to be talking at cross purposes here.* (**mal-entendido**)

cross-reference /ˌkrɒsˈrefərəns/ NOUN [plural **cross-references**] a note in a book that tells you to look somewhere else for more information (**referência cruzada**)

crossroads /ˈkrɒsrəʊdz/ NOUN [plural **crossroads**] a place where two roads meet and cross each other □ *Turn left at the crossroads up ahead.* (**encruzilhada**)

cross-section /ˈkrɒssekʃən/ NOUN [plural **cross-sections**]
1 a small group of people or things that represents all the different types in a large group □ *a cross-section of the public* (**amostragem**)
2 a cut made through a solid object so that you can see the structure inside, or a picture of this □ *a cross-section of the eye* (**corte transversal**)

crosswalk /ˈkrɒswɔːk/ NOUN [plural **crosswalks**] the US word for **pedestrian crossing** (**faixa de pedestres**)

crossword /ˈkrɒswɜːd/ NOUN [plural **crosswords**] a game in which you write words that are the answers to questions into square spaces □ *Dad loves doing crosswords.* (**palavras cruzadas**)

crotch /krɒtʃ/ NOUN [plural **crotches**] the area of your body or of your trousers where your legs join your body (**virilha**)

crouch /kraʊtʃ/ VERB [**crouches, crouching, crouched**] to bend your legs and back so that your body is close to the ground □ *She crouched down to tie her shoe lace.* (**agachar-se**)

crow /krəʊ/ ▶ NOUN [plural **crows**] a large black bird that makes a loud, rough sound (**corvo**)
▶ VERB [**crows, crowing, crowed**]
1 if a cock (= male chicken) crows, it makes a loud sound, especially early in the morning (**cacarejar**)
2 to talk a lot about something good that you have done in a way that annoys other people (**gritar de alegria**)

crowbar /ˈkrəʊbɑː(r)/ NOUN [plural **crowbars**] a heavy metal bar with a curved end that is used for forcing things open (**pé-de-cabra**)

crowd /kraʊd/ ▶ NOUN [plural **crowds**] a large number of people or things together in one place □ *a football crowd* □ *crowds of shoppers* (**multidão**) 🔲 *A crowd had gathered at the scene.* (**multidão se juntou**)
▶ VERB [**crowds, crowding, crowded**] if a large number of people crowd somewhere, they fill that place □ *Onlookers crowded the streets.* (**lotar, abarrotar**)

• **crowded** /ˈkraʊdɪd/ ADJECTIVE full of people □ *crowded shops* (**lotado, abarrotado**)

crown /kraʊn/ ▶ NOUN [plural **crowns**]
1 a circle made of gold and valuable stones that a king or queen wears on their head at formal occasions (**coroa**)
2 the top of something such as your head or a hill (**cabeça**)
▶ VERB [**crowns, crowning, crowned**] to make someone the king or queen of a country in a ceremony where a crown is put on their head (**coroar**)

crucial /ˈkruːʃəl/ ADJECTIVE very important □ *The talks are now at a crucial stage.* □ *crucial information* (**crucial**)

crucifix /ˈkruːsɪfɪks/ NOUN [plural **crucifixes**] a cross with a model of Christ on it, used as a symbol of the Christian religion (**crucifixo**)

• **crucifixion** /ˌkruːsɪˈfɪkʃən/ NOUN [plural **crucifixions**] the punishment of fastening someone's hands and feet to a large wooden cross and leaving them there to die (**crucificação**)

• **crucify** /ˈkruːsɪfaɪ/ VERB [**crucifies, crucifying, crucified**] to punish someone by crucifixion (**crucificar**)

crude /kruːd/ ADJECTIVE [cruder, crudest]
1 made or done in a simple, rough way showing little skill ☐ *I had a rather crude map that Josh had quickly drawn.* (cru)
2 rude ☐ *a crude joke* (rude)

cruel /kruəl/ ADJECTIVE [crueller, cruellest] causing pain or suffering to people or animals without caring ☐ + **to do something** *It's cruel to keep an animal in such a small cage.* ☐ + **to** *He was cruel to his children.* (cruel)
• **cruelly** /ˈkruəlɪ/ ADVERB in a cruel way ☐ *The dog had been treated cruelly.* (cruelmente)
• **cruelty** /ˈkruəltɪ/ NOUN, NO PLURAL when someone is cruel ☐ *They were accused of cruelty to animals.* (crueldade)

cruise /kruːz/ ▶ VERB [cruises, cruising, cruised] to travel in a car, boat, etc. at the same speed (viajar)
▶ NOUN [plural **cruises**] a holiday spent on a ship, travelling to a lot of different places (cruzeiro)
• **cruiser** /ˈkruːzə(r)/ NOUN [plural **cruisers**] a large, fast ship used in wars (cruzador)

crumb /krʌm/ NOUN [plural **crumbs**]
1 a very small piece of bread, cake, or biscuit (migalha de pão)
2 a crumb of something a very small amount of something ☐ *The late goal gave England a crumb of comfort.* (um pouco de algo)

crumble /ˈkrʌmbəl/ VERB [crumbles, crumbling, crumbled] to break into very small pieces ☐ *The walls of the old house were crumbling.* ☐ *Crumble the biscuit on top of the fruit.* (despedaçar, fazer em migalhas)
• **crumbly** /ˈkrʌmblɪ/ ADJECTIVE [crumblier, crumbliest] breaking down easily into very small pieces ☐ *dry crumbly soil* (esmigalhado, despedaçado)

crumple /ˈkrʌmpəl/ VERB [crumples, crumpling, crumpled] to crush something so that it has a lot of folds in it, or to become crushed and folded in this way ☐ *He crumpled up the letter and threw it in the bin.* ☐ *a crumpled jacket* (amassar)

crunch /krʌntʃ/ ▶ VERB [crunches, crunching, crunched]
1 to make a noise as you bite and eat something hard ☐ *She was crunching on a carrot stick.* (mastigar ruidosamente)
2 to make the sound of something being crushed ☐ *The snow crunched under our feet.* (ranger)
▶ NOUN, NO PLURAL the sound of something being crushed ☐ *the crunch of feet on the gravel path* (ruído)
♦ IDIOM **if/when it comes to the crunch** if or when you are in a difficult situation and you must make an important decision ☐ *When it came to the crunch, she knew she couldn't leave him.* (decisão final)
• **crunchy** /ˈkrʌntʃɪ/ ADJECTIVE [crunchier, crunchiest] crunchy food is pleasantly hard and makes a noise when you bite it ☐ *a crunchy biscuit* (crocante)

crusade /kruːˈseɪd/ NOUN [plural **crusades**] a determined effort, over a period of time, to change or achieve something ☐ *a crusade for free health care* (cruzada)
• **crusader** /kruːˈseɪdə(r)/ NOUN [plural **crusaders**] someone who takes part in a crusade (guerreiro)

crush /krʌʃ/ ▶ VERB [crushes, crushing, crushed] to press something so that it is broken or in small pieces ☐ *His leg was crushed by a falling rock.* ☐ *Crush two cloves of garlic.* (esmagar)
▶ NOUN [plural **crushes**] a crowd of people forced to stand close together in a small space ☐ *Some fans were trampled in the crush.* (multidão)
♦ IDIOM **have a crush on someone** to feel very attracted to someone, usually for a short time (estar apaixonado por alguém)
• **crushed** /krʌʃt/ ADJECTIVE
1 broken up or made flat by a heavy weight ☐ *crushed peppercorns* (comprimido)
2 disappointed and sad ☐ *Maya felt crushed by their criticism.* (triste)
• **crushing** /ˈkrʌʃɪŋ/ ADJECTIVE causing someone to be completely defeated (esmagador) ▣ *a crushing defeat* (derrota esmagadora)

crust /krʌst/ NOUN [plural **crusts**]
1 the hard surface on the outside of bread or some other baked foods ☐ *Cut the crusts off two slices of bread.* (crosta)
2 the Earth's crust is its outside layer (crosta terrestre)
• **crusty** /ˈkrʌstɪ/ ADJECTIVE [crustier, crustiest]
1 having a pleasantly hard crust (crostoso) ▣ *crusty bread* (pão com crosta)
2 an informal word meaning bad-tempered and unfriendly ☐ *a crusty old professor* (ríspido)

crutch /krʌtʃ/ NOUN [plural **crutches**] a stick you put under your arm to help you walk if your leg or foot is hurt (muleta, bengala) ▣ *Poor Wayne came to watch the match on crutches.* (de muletas)

crux /krʌks/ NOUN, NO PLURAL **the crux of something** the most important or difficult part of a problem ☐ *The crux of the matter is lack of money.* (o xis da questão)

cry /kraɪ/ ▶ VERB [cries, crying, cried]
1 to produce liquid from your eyes because you are sad or in pain ☐ *I could hear a baby crying in the next room.* (chorar)
2 to shout ☐ + **out** *She cried out in pain.* (chorar convulsivamente)
♦ IDIOM **cry your eyes out** to cry a lot (chorar amargamente)
♦ PHRASAL VERB **cry out for something** if something is crying out for something, it needs it very much ☐ *This kitchen is crying out for a coat of paint.* (clamar por algo)
▶ NOUN [plural **cries**]

crypt

1 *no plural* an act of crying (choro) 🔲 *She had a little cry on my shoulder.* (chorou)
2 a shout 🔲 **+ for** *No one heard her cries for help.* (súplica)

♦ IDIOM **be a far cry from something** to be very different from something 🔲 *United's performance was a far cry from their usual magic.* (estar a uma grande distância de algo)

crypt /krɪpt/ NOUN [*plural* **crypts**] a room built under a church, where bodies were sometimes buried (cripta)

cryptic /ˈkrɪptɪk/ ADJECTIVE having a hidden meaning that is difficult to understand (cifrado) 🔲 *a cryptic remark* (declaração cifrada)

crystal /ˈkrɪstəl/ NOUN [*plural* **crystals**]
1 a small regular shape that some substances form when they become solid, for example salt, ice, or a mineral 🔲 *sugar crystals* (cristal)
2 *no plural* a type of high quality glass 🔲 *crystal wine glasses* (cristal)

cub /kʌb/ NOUN [*plural* **cubs**] a baby animal, for example a lion or bear (filhote)

cube /kjuːb/ NOUN [*plural* **cubes**]
1 a solid shape with six equal square sides 🔲 *sugar cubes* (cubo)
2 the number you get if you multiply a number by itself twice. A maths word. 🔲 *The cube of 4 is 64.* (cubo)

• **cubed** /kjuːbd/ ADJECTIVE multiplied by itself twice. A maths word. 🔲 *3 cubed is 27.* (ao cubo)

cube root /ˌkjuːb ˈruːt/ NOUN [*plural* **cube roots**] the cube root of a number is the number which equals it when it is multiplied by itself twice. A maths word. 🔲 *The cube root of 125 is 5.* (raiz cúbica)

cubic /ˈkjuːbɪk/ ADJECTIVE a cubic measurement is one used to measure volume. For example, a cubicmetre is a space onemetre long, onemetre wide and one metre high. (cúbico)

cubicle /ˈkjuːbɪkəl/ NOUN [*plural* **cubicles**] a small space with walls around it that is separate from the rest of a room 🔲 *Get changed in the cubicle.* (cubículo)

cuboid /ˈkjuːbɔɪd/ NOUN [*plural* **cuboids**] a solid shape with six sides that are all rectangular. A maths word. (cuboide)

cuckoo /ˈkʊkuː/ NOUN [*plural* **cuckoos**] a bird that makes the sound 'cuckoo' (cuco)

cucumber /ˈkjuːkʌmbə(r)/ NOUN [*plural* **cucumbers**] a long vegetable with a green skin that you eat raw in salads (pepino)

cuddle /ˈkʌdəl/ ▶ VERB [**cuddles, cuddling, cuddled**] to hold someone in your arms to show that you love them 🔲 *They were kissing and cuddling on the sofa.* (aconchegar)

♦ PHRASAL VERB **cuddle up** to sit or lie very close together 🔲 *The baby panda cuddled up to its mother.* (aconchegar-se)

▶ NOUN [*plural* **cuddles**] when you put your arms around someone and hold them closely (abraço) 🔲 *Come and give me a cuddle.* (me dê um abraço)

• **cuddly** /ˈkʌdli/ ADJECTIVE [**cuddlier, cuddliest**] soft and pleasant to cuddle 🔲 *a cuddly teddy bear* (fofo)

cue /kjuː/ NOUN [*plural* **cues**]
1 a signal to a performer to start doing something 🔲 *He missed his cue to go on stage.* (sinal)
2 something that lets you know it is time to do or say something 🔲 *Charles yawned and said he was tired which was my cue to leave.* (dica)
3 on cue if something happens on cue, it happens at exactly the right moment 🔲 *Right on cue, the telephone rang.* (no momento certo)
4 a long thin stick used to hit the balls on the table in games like snooker and pool (taco de bilhar)

cuff /kʌf/ NOUN [*plural* **cuffs**] the end part of a sleeve near your hand (pulso)

♦ IDIOM **off the cuff** if you speak off the cuff, you speak without planning what you are going to say 🔲 *I can't give you a precise answer off the cuff.* (de improviso)

cufflinks /ˈkʌflɪŋks/ PLURAL NOUN a pair of small objects used instead of buttons to fasten shirt cuffs (abotoaduras)

cuisine /kwɪˈziːn/ NOUN [*plural* **cuisines**] a particular style of cooking 🔲 *Mediterranean cuisine* (culinária, cozinha)

cul-de-sac /ˈkʌldəsæk/ NOUN [*plural* **cul-de-sacs**] a street that is blocked at one end (beco sem saída)

culinary /ˈkʌlɪnəri/ ADJECTIVE a formal word meaning to do with cooking 🔲 *culinary skills* (culinária)

cull /kʌl/ ▶ VERB [**culls, culling, culled**] to kill some of a particular animal so that there will not be too many animals of that type (caça para controle populacional de certas espécies de animais selvagens)

▶ NOUN [*plural* **culls**] when animals are culled 🔲 *a badger cull* (seleção para abate)

culminate /ˈkʌlmɪneɪt/ VERB [**culminates, culminating, culminated**]

♦ PHRASAL VERB **culminate in/with something** to finish with a particular event or result 🔲 *The celebrations culminated in a fireworks display.* (culminar em algo)

• **culmination** /ˌkʌlmɪˈneɪʃən/ NOUN, NO PLURAL the final event or result of a series of events or actions 🔲 *His promotion was the culmination of all his hard work.* (culminação)

culpable /ˈkʌlpəbəl/ ADJECTIVE responsible for something bad. A formal word. (culpado)

culprit /ˈkʌlprɪt/ NOUN [*plural* **culprits**] someone who has done something wrong (réu, acusado)

cult /kʌlt/ ▶ NOUN [*plural* **cults**]
1 a religion or a religious group, especially one with secret or strange beliefs (culto, ritual)

2 someone or something that becomes very popular or fashionable (**adorado, cultuado**)
▶ ADJECTIVE very popular or fashionable with a particular group of people (**moda**) 🔲 *a cult hero* (**herói da moda**)

cultivate /'kʌltɪveɪt/ VERB [**cultivates, cultivating, cultivated**]
1 to prepare land so that you can grow crops on it □ *Peasants used to cultivate the land.* (**cultivar**)
2 to grow a crop to eat or to sell □ *Rice is cultivated in India.* (**cultivar**)
3 to make something develop or improve □ *She has tried hard to cultivate her own style.* (**desenvolver, melhorar**)
• **cultivation** /ˌkʌltɪ'veɪʃən/ NOUN, NO PLURAL
1 the process of preparing land to grow crops (**cultivo**)
2 the process of growing crops (**cultivo**)
3 the process of developing or improving something (**melhoria**)

cultural /'kʌltʃərəl/ ADJECTIVE to do with culture, especially art, music and literature □ *cultural activities* (**cultural**)

culture /'kʌltʃə(r)/ NOUN [plural **cultures**]
1 the customs and beliefs of a particular group or society that make it different from other people or societies □ *The school has students from many different cultures.* (**cultura**)
2 *no plural* music, literature, art, etc. (**cultura**)
• **cultured** /'kʌltʃəd/ ADJECTIVE well educated and knowing about things like art, music and literature (**culto**)

cumbersome /'kʌmbəsəm/ ADJECTIVE
1 large and awkward to carry or wear □ *a cumbersome diving suit* (**embaraçoso**)
2 slow and difficult to deal with □ *a cumbersome legal process* (**enfadonho**)

cunning /'kʌnɪŋ/ ▶ ADJECTIVE clever in a dishonest way □ *I have a cunning plan.* (**astuto**)
▶ NOUN, NO PLURAL the ability to get what you want by dishonest and clever planning (**engenhoso**)

cup /kʌp/ ▶ NOUN [plural **cups**]
1 a small container with a handle that you drink from □ *cups and saucers* □ *Let's have a cup of tea.* (**xícara**)
2 a metal cup given as a prize in a competition, or the competition itself □ *the World Cup* (**taça**)
◆ IDIOM **not be someone's cup of tea** if something is not your cup of tea, you do not like it or are not interested in it □ *Graphic novels aren't my cup of tea.* (**não fazer o gênero de alguém**)
▶ VERB [**cups, cupping, cupped**] to put your hands together and bend them to form the shape of a cup (**fazer com as mãos o formato de copo**)

cupboard /'kʌbəd/ NOUN [plural **cupboards**] a piece of furniture with shelves and a door, used to store things in □ *a kitchen cupboard* □ *The plates are in the cupboard.* (**armário**)

cupful /'kʌpfʊl/ NOUN [plural **cupfuls**] the amount a cup will hold □ *Add a cupful of flour.* (**copo cheio**)

curable /'kjʊərəbəl/ ADJECTIVE a curable disease can be cured (**curável**)

curate /'kjʊərət/ NOUN [plural **curates**] a priest in the Church of England whose job is to help a more important priest (**cura, vigário**)

curator /kjʊə'reɪtə(r)/ NOUN [plural **curators**] someone whose job is to look after the things in a museum (**curador**)

curb /kɜːb/ ▶ VERB [**curbs, curbing, curbed**] to control something, especially something bad □ *He tried hard to curb his spending.* (**conter**)
▶ NOUN [plural **curbs**] the US spelling of kerb (**ver kerb**)

curdle /'kɜːdəl/ VERB [**curdles, curdling, curdled**] if a liquid curdles it forms lumps, often because it has become sour □ *The milk has curdled.* (**coalhar**)

cure /kjʊə(r)/ ▶ VERB [**cures, curing, cured**]
1 to make someone with an illness healthy again □ + *of The treatment cured her of her insomnia.* (**curar**)
2 to make an illness end or go away □ *Nothing seemed to cure his migraines.* (**curar**)
3 to solve a problem □ *The government is determined to cure the problem of inflation.* (**consertar**)
▶ NOUN [plural **cures**] something that makes an illness end or go away □ + *for a cure for cancer* (**cura**)

curfew /'kɜːfjuː/ NOUN [plural **curfews**]
1 a law that says that people must stay in their houses after a particular time (**toque de recolher**)
2 a time when there is a curfew (**hora de recolher**)

curiosity /ˌkjʊərɪ'ɒsɪti/ NOUN [plural **curiosities**]
1 *no plural* the feeling of wanting to discover facts about something □ *Children have a natural curiosity about the world.* (**curiosidade**)
2 a strange and interesting object (**curiosidade**)

curious /'kjʊərɪəs/ ADJECTIVE
1 wanting to know something □ + *about He was very curious about my past.* □ + *to do something I was curious to hear her side of the story.* (**curioso**)
2 strange or unusual □ *Her style is a curious mixture of jazz and country.* (**estranho**)
• **curiously** /'kjʊərɪəsli/ ADVERB
1 in a way that shows that you are curious □ *The children peered curiously in through the window.* (**curiosamente**)
2 in a strange or unusual way □ *curiously shaped rocks* (**estranhamente**)

curl /kɜːl/ ▶ NOUN [plural **curls**] a piece of hair that forms a curved shape □ *blonde curls* (**cacho**)
▶ VERB [**curls, curling, curled**]

1 to form curves or to make something form curves □ *Do you curl your hair or is it natural?* (enrolar)
2 to move in a curving shape □ *Smoke curled up from the chimneys.* (espiralar)
◆ PHRASAL VERB **curl up** to sit or lie with your arms and legs close to your body □ *Jenny curled up on the sofa and fell asleep.* (enrolar)
• **curly** /'kɜːlɪ/ ADJECTIVE [**curlier, curliest**] shaped like a curl or with a lot of curls (cacheado) 🔹 *curly hair* (cabelo cacheado) □ *a curly tail*

currant /'kʌrənt/ NOUN [*plural* **currants**] a small, black, dried soft fruit used especially in cakes (groselha)

currency /'kʌrənsɪ/ NOUN [*plural* **currencies**] the money used in a particular country (moeda) 🔹 *foreign currency* (moeda estrangeira) □ *The euro is the European currency.*

current /'kʌrənt/ ▶ ADJECTIVE existing or happening now □ *The current situation is not acceptable.* (atual, corrente)
▶ NOUN [*plural* **currents**]
1 a flow of water or air going in one direction (corrente) 🔹 *Strong currents swept them out to sea.* (correntes fortes)
2 a flow of electricity through a wire (corrente)

current account /ˌkʌrənt əˈkaʊnt/ NOUN [*plural* **current accounts**] a bank account that allows you to take money out at any time (conta-corrente)

current affairs /ˌkʌrənt əˈfeəz/ PLURAL NOUN important political events that are happening at the present time (atualidades)

currently /'kʌrəntlɪ/ ADVERB at the present time □ *We are currently experiencing problems with our website.* (presentemente)

curriculum /kəˈrɪkjʊləm/ NOUN [*plural* **curriculums** or **curricula**] a course of study or all the courses of study at a school or college (currículo)

curry /'kʌrɪ/ NOUN [*plural* **curries**] a type of food cooked with spices □ *chicken curry* (curry)

curse /kɜːs/ ▶ NOUN [*plural* **curses**]
1 magic words which are intended to make someone have bad luck (maldição) 🔹 *She put a curse on the family.* (lançou uma maldição em)
2 a rude word (blasfêmia)
3 something that causes problems for a long time □ *Pollution is the curse of this city.* (desgraça, maldição)
▶ VERB [**curses, cursing, cursed**]
1 to use rude words (maldizer)
2 to say angry things about someone or something □ *I was cursing him for leaving the car so dirty.* (praguejar)

cursor /'kɜːsə(r)/ NOUN [*plural* **cursors**] a flashing mark on a computer screen that shows you where you are working. A computing word. (cursor)

cursory /'kɜːsərɪ/ ADJECTIVE quick and short, without looking at the details (superficial) 🔹 *The border guards gave our passports a cursory glance and waved us through.* (olhada superficial)

curt /kɜːt/ ADJECTIVE short and sounding unfriendly □ *a curt reply* (brusco, rude)

curtail /kɜːˈteɪl/ VERB [**curtails, curtailing, curtailed**] a formal word meaning to limit something or to make something shorter □ *Her tennis career was abruptly curtailed by a back injury.* (reduzir)

curtain /'kɜːtən/ NOUN [*plural* **curtains**] a long piece of material that can be pulled across a window (cortina) 🔹 *Could you draw the curtains (= open or close the curtains), please?* (abrir as cortinas)

curtsy or **curtsey** /'kɜːtsɪ/ ▶ VERB [**curtsies, curtsying, curtsied** or **curtseys, curtseying, curtseyed**] a woman or girl curtsies when she bends her knees with one leg behind the other to show respect to a royal person □ *All the girls curtsied to the princess.* (fazer reverência)
▶ NOUN [*plural* **curtsies** or **curtseys**] the movement a girl or woman makes when she curtsies (reverência)

curve /kɜːv/ ▶ NOUN [*plural* **curves** or **curtseys**] a line that bends (curva)
▶ VERB [**curves, curving, curved**] to form a curve or make something form a curve □ *The wall curves round the end of the garden.* (virar)

cushion /'kʊʃən/ ▶ NOUN [*plural* **cushions**]
1 a cloth bag filled with something soft that you sit on or rest against to be comfortable □ *There were some cushions on the sofa.* (almofada)
2 something that protects something or keeps something off a hard surface □ *The hovercraft moves along on a cushion of air.* (amortecedor)
▶ VERB [**cushions, cushioning, cushioned**]
1 to make something less unpleasant □ *A large divorce settlement cushioned the impact on his family.* (amortecer)
2 to provide a soft surface to protect something or someone if they fall or are hit □ *The snow cushioned her fall.* (amortecer)

cushy /'kʊʃɪ/ ADJECTIVE [**cushier, cushiest**] an informal word meaning very easy □ *a cushy job* (fácil)

custard /'kʌstəd/ NOUN, NO PLURAL a thick, sweet sauce made from eggs, milk or cream, and sugar (pudim)

custodial /kʌˈstəʊdɪəl/ ADJECTIVE a custodial sentence is a punishment of being sent to prison (privativas de liberdade)

custody /'kʌstədɪ/ NOUN, NO PLURAL
1 when someone is kept in prison until their trial for a crime (custódia) 🔹 *He was held in custody for several weeks.* (preso sob custódia)

2 the legal right to have a child living with you, especially after parents separate (**guarda**) ⬛ *She lost/won custody of the children.* (**perdeu/ganhou a guarda**)

custom /ˈkʌstəm/ NOUN [plural **customs**]

1 something that people usually do or that is a tradition □ *Japanese customs* □ *It is my custom to walk to the station each morning.* (**costume**)
2 no plural you give a shop your custom when you buy things from it (**hábito**)

• **customary** /ˈkʌstəməri/ ADJECTIVE something that is customary is what usually happens □ *He tackled the job with his customary efficiency.* (**habitual**)

• **customer** /ˈkʌstəmə(r)/ NOUN [plural **customers**] a person who buys things or services from a shop or business □ *The business attracts customers from all over the country.* □ *This office handles customer complaints.* (**cliente**)

• **customize** or **customise** /ˈkʌstəmaɪz/ VERB [**customizes, customizing, customized**] to make changes to something so that it is suitable for a particular person □ *The company customizes cars for disabled people.* (**personalizar**)

• **customs** /ˈkʌstəmz/ NOUN, NO PLURAL the place at an airport or port where officials check your bags to make sure they do not contain anything illegal □ *a customs officer* (**alfândega**)

cut /kʌt/ ▶ VERB [**cuts, cutting, cut**]

1 to use a knife or a sharp tool to divide something or remove a piece from something □ *Cut the cake into six pieces.* □ *Ben tried to cut the plank in two.* □ + **off** *She's cut off all her hair.* □ + **up** *Shall I help you cut up your food?* (**cortar**)
2 to injure yourself by rubbing or hitting your skin with something sharp □ *I cut my finger on the can lid.* (**cortar**)
3 to be able to cut □ *This knife doesn't cut very well.* (**cortar**)
4 to reduce the amount or level of something □ *Mum and Dad have cut my allowance.* (**cortar**)
5 to remove an amount of text from a computer document (**cortar**)

♦ IDIOMS **cut someone short** to prevent someone from finishing what they were saying **cut something short** to stop something before it is finished □ *We had to cut short our visit to Zak's.* (**interromper alguém**)

♦ PHRASAL VERBS **cut across something** to go across a space instead of around the edge □ *We cut across the park to get home in time.* (**atravessar**) **cut back (something)** to reduce the amount of money spent on something □ *We need to cut back on our heating bills.* (**reduzir consideravelmente**) **cut down (on something)** to reduce the amount or number of something or to do something less □ *The doctor told her to cut down on red meat.* (**reduzir algo**) **cut someone off** if you are cut off on the telephone, the connection is broken before the call ends (**cortar a ligação**) **cut someone/something off**

1 to stop people from leaving a place □ *The whole town was cut off by the flooding.* (**ficar isolado**)
2 to stop the supply of something □ *If you don't pay your bill, the electricity will be cut off.* (**cortar algo**) **cut something out**
1 to stop eating or drinking something □ *I feel much better since I cut meat out of my diet.* (**cortar algo**)
2 cut it out an informal phrase used to tell someone that you want them to stop doing something (**parar algo**)
3 not be cut out to do something to not have the suitable qualities to do something □ *She decided she wasn't cut out to be a teacher.* (**não ser feito para algo**)

▶ NOUN [plural **cuts**]

1 an opening or injury made by something sharp □ *She's got a nasty cut on her forehead.* □ *He made two cuts in the fabric.* (**corte**)
2 a reduction in something □ *a price cut* □ *job cuts* (**corte, redução**)
3 an informal word meaning a share of something □ *He's hoping for a cut of the profits.* (**corte, redução**)
4 when someone's hair is cut, or the way hair looks when it has been cut □ *a cut and blow-dry* (**corte**)

cut-and-dried /ˌkʌtənˈdraɪd/ ADJECTIVE clearly decided, so there can be no change or argument (**feito conforme o planejado**)

cutback /ˈkʌtbæk/ NOUN [plural **cutbacks**] a reduction in something, for example the amount of money an organization spends □ *The government announced cutbacks in defence spending.* (**redução**)

cute /kjuːt/ ADJECTIVE [**cuter, cutest**]

1 attractive or pretty □ *a cute little puppy* (**gracioso**)
2 clever in a way that does not show any respect □ *Don't try to be cute with me.* (**esperto**)

cutlery /ˈkʌtləri/ NOUN, NO PLURAL knives, forks and spoons (**faqueiro**)

cutlet /ˈkʌtlɪt/ NOUN [plural **cutlets**] a small piece of meat with a bone □ *lamb cutlets* (**costeleta**)

cut-price /ˈkʌtpraɪs/ ADJECTIVE cut-price goods are sold more cheaply than usual (**preço reduzido**)

cutting /ˈkʌtɪŋ/ ▶ NOUN [plural **cuttings**]

1 an article cut out of a newspaper or magazine (**recorte**)
2 a piece cut off a plant that you use to grow a new plant (**muda**)

▶ ADJECTIVE meant to hurt someone's feelings □ *a cutting remark* (**sarcástico**)

cutting-edge /ˌkʌtɪŋˈedʒ/ ADJECTIVE very modern and advanced □ *cutting-edge technology* (**moderno**)

CV /ˌsiː'viː/ ABBREVIATION curriculum vitae; a list of your qualifications and the jobs you have done, that you show to someone you want to work for □ *She has an impressive CV.* (**CV – abreviação de curriculum vitae**)

cwt ABBREVIATION **hundredweight** (**cem libras**)

cyanide /'saɪənaɪd/ NOUN, NO PLURAL a strong poison (**cianeto**)

cyber- /'saɪbə(r)/ PREFIX cyber- is added to the beginning of words to mean 'to do with electronic communication or the Internet' (**ciber-**)

cybercafé /'saɪbəkæfeɪ/ NOUN [*plural* **cybercafés**] a place where you can buy something to eat or drink and use the Internet (**cibercafé**)

cyberspace /'saɪbəspeɪs/ NOUN, NO PLURAL the Internet, where electronic messages pass from one computer to another. A computing word. (**ciberespaço**)

cycle /'saɪkəl/ ▶ NOUN [*plural* **cycles**]
1 a series of things that happen one after the other and then start again □ *He seems to be trapped in a cycle of stealing and prison.* (**ciclo**)
2 a bicycle (**bicicleta**)
▶ VERB [**cycles, cycling, cycled**] to ride a bicycle □ *I always cycle to school.* (**pedalar**)
• **cyclical** /'saɪklɪkəl/ ADJECTIVE happening in a cycle □ *We are experiencing a cyclical increase in prices.* (**cíclico**)
• **cyclist** /'saɪklɪst/ NOUN [*plural* **cyclists**] someone who rides a bicycle (**ciclista**)

cyclone /'saɪkləʊn/ NOUN [*plural* **cyclones**] a large storm that happens in tropical countries, with strong winds moving in a circle (**ciclone**)

cygnet /'sɪgnɪt/ NOUN [*plural* **cygnets**] a baby swan (= large white bird) (**filhote de cisne**)

cylinder /'sɪlɪndə(r)/ NOUN [*plural* **cylinders**] a solid shape with a circular top and bottom and long straight sides (**cilindro**)
• **cylindrical** /sɪ'lɪndrɪkəl/ ADJECTIVE shaped like a cylinder (**cilíndrico**)

cymbals /'sɪmbəlz/ PLURAL NOUN a musical instrument made of two metal circles that you hit together (**chocalhos, címbalos**)

cynic /'sɪnɪk/ NOUN [*plural* **cynics**]
1 someone who believes that people are only interested in themselves and are not honest or sincere (**cínico**)
2 someone who does not believe that something will be successful (**cético**)
• **cynical** /'sɪnɪkəl/ ADJECTIVE
1 behaving in a way that is not honest or kind in order to get an advantage □ *This was a cynical attempt to gain votes.* (**cínico**)
2 believing that people are only interested in themselves and are not honest or sincere □ *He has such a cynical outlook on life.* (**cínico**)
3 not believing that something will be successful □ *He was rather cynical about the new working system.* (**cético**)
• **cynicism** /'sɪnɪsɪzəm/ NOUN, NO PLURAL cynical beliefs (**cinismo**)

cyst /sɪst/ NOUN [*plural* **cysts**] a hard raised part filled with liquid in the body or under the skin (**cisto**)

cytoplasm /'saɪtəʊplæzəm/ NOUN, NO PLURAL the substance a cell is made of, except for the nucleus. A biology word. (**citoplasma**)

czar /zɑː(r)/ NOUN [*plural* **czars**] another spelling of tsar (**czar**)

Dd

D or **d** /diː/ the fourth letter of the alphabet (**a quarta letra do alfabeto**)

dab /dæb/ ▶ VERB [**dabs, dabbing, dabbed**] to touch something lightly □ *She took out a tissue and dabbed her eyes.* (**tocar levemente**)
▶ NOUN [*plural* **dabs**] a light touch of something □ *She put a dab of face cream on each cheek.* (**toque leve**)

dabble /ˈdæbəl/ VERB [**dabbles, dabbling, dabbled**] to do an activity for a short time and not seriously □ *He dabbled in photography for a while.* (**praticar algo por pouco tempo**)

dachshund /ˈdækshʊnd/ NOUN [*plural* **dachshunds**] a dog with short legs and a long body (**Dachshund, cão-salsicha**)

dad or **Dad** /dæd/ NOUN [*plural* **dads** or **Dads**] an informal word that you use for talking to your father □ *Hey Dad, I scored a goal today!* □ *It was really nice of your dad to help.* (**papai**)

daddy or **Daddy** /ˈdædi/ NOUN [*plural* **daddies** or **Daddies**] a word that children use for talking to or about their father □ *Read me another story, Daddy!* □ *I gave my daddy a big hug.* (**papai**)

daffodil /ˈdæfədɪl/ NOUN [*plural* **daffodils**] a yellow flower that appears in spring (**narciso**)

daft /dɑːft/ ADJECTIVE [**dafter, daftest**] silly □ *What a daft thing to do.* □ *Don't be daft – you can't do that!* (**ridículo**)

dagger /ˈdægə(r)/ NOUN [*plural* **daggers**] a small knife that is used as a weapon (**punhal**)

daily /ˈdeɪli/ ▶ ADJECTIVE
1 happening or done every day (**diária**) 🔁 *Exercise is part of my daily routine.* (**rotina diária**) □ *Two tablets is the correct daily dose.*
2 a daily newspaper is produced every day (**jornal produzido diariamente**)
▶ ADVERB every day □ *We have fresh bread delivered daily.* (**diariamente**)

dainty /ˈdeɪnti/ ADJECTIVE [**daintier, daintiest**] small and delicate □ *a dainty little girl* (**delicado**)

dairy /ˈdeəri/ ▶ ADJECTIVE
1 to do with keeping cows to produce milk (**leiteria**) 🔁 *a dairy farmer* (**fazenda produtora de leite**)
2 dairy foods contain milk or are made from milk (**laticínio**) 🔁 *She can't eat dairy products.* (**produtos de laticínio**)
▶ NOUN [*plural* **dairies**] a place where foods such as butter and cheese are made from milk (**fábrica de laticínios**)

dais /ˈdeɪɪs/ NOUN [*plural* **daises**] a raised area of floor at one end of a room □ *The speakers sat behind a table on the dais.* (**palco**)

daisy /ˈdeɪzi/ NOUN [*plural* **daisies**] a small white flower with a yellow centre (**margarida**)

dale /deɪl/ NOUN [*plural* **dales**] a valley □ *I love the Yorkshire Dales.* (**vale**)

dally /ˈdæli/ VERB [**dallies, dallying, dallied**] to take too much time doing something □ *We really mustn't dally over lunch.* (**demorar-se**)
◆ PHRASAL VERB **dally with something** to consider doing something but not seriously □ *I dallied with the idea of teaching abroad.* (**brincar com algo**)

Dalmatian /dælˈmeɪʃən/ NOUN [*plural* **Dalmatians**] a large dog that is white with dark spots (**Dálmata**)

dam /dæm/ ▶ NOUN [*plural* **dams**] a wall across a river that holds a lot of the water back (**represa**)
▶ VERB [**dams, damming, dammed**] to build a dam across a river (**represar**)

damage /ˈdæmɪdʒ/ ▶ NOUN [*plural* **damages**]
1 *no plural* harm that is done by something (**dano**) 🔁 *The storm caused a lot of damage.* (**causou danos**) □ **+ to** *The storm did some damage to the roof.* □ *He suffered brain damage in the accident.*
2 damages money that a law court decides someone will get because they have been harmed (**indenização**) 🔁 *She was awarded damages of £5000.* (**recebeu indenização**)

> Note the verbs that are used with the noun **damage** (sense 1). Something **causes** damage or **does** damage:
> ✓ *The fire caused a lot of damage.*
> ✗ *The fire made a lot of damage.*

▶ VERB [**damages, damaging, damaged**] to spoil or break something □ *The book was damaged in the post.* (**danificar**) *men were injured in the accident.*

> Note that the verb **damage** is used for things and not people. For people, use **hurt** or **injure**: □ *The car was badly damaged in the accident.*

- **damaging** /ˈdæmɪdʒɪŋ/ ADJECTIVE causing damage (**daninho, nocivo**) 🔊 We all know about the *damaging effects* of the sun on our skin. (**efeitos nocivos**)

dame /deɪm/ NOUN [plural **dames**] a title that is given to a woman because she has done some important work ☐ *Dame Judi Dench* (**dama**)

damn /dæm/ ▶ EXCLAMATION an informal word that people use when they are angry ☐ *Damn! I forgot my umbrella.* (**droga!, maldição!**) 🔊 *Damn it! Why isn't this machine working?* (**droga!**)

▶ ADJECTIVE, ADVERB an informal word people say when they are angry ☐ *This damn machine won't work!* ☐ *You knew damn well I wasn't going!* (**maldito, droga de**)

▶ NOUN **not give a damn (about something)** to not be interested in something. An informal phrase. ☐ *I don't give a damn what she thinks of me!* (**não dar a mínima**)

▶ VERB [**damns, damning, damned**]

1 *Damn you/him, etc.!* used to show that you are angry with someone. An informal phrase. ☐ *Damn him! Why is he always late?* (**maldito seja!**)

2 to criticize someone very strongly (**condenar**)

- **damned** /dæmd/ ADJECTIVE, ADVERB an informal word that people use when they are angry ☐ *Look what that damned cat has done!* (**maldito**)

♦ IDIOM **I'm damned if I'll do something** used when you are angry to say that you will certainly not do something ☐ *Well I'm damned if I'll help him again!* (**Estou frito se não fizer algo**)

- **damning** /ˈdæmɪŋ/ ADJECTIVE

1 showing strong criticism of someone or something (**crítico, desfavorável**) 🔊 *a damning report* (**notícia desfavorável**)

2 showing clearly that a person has done something wrong (**condenatório**) 🔊 *The police found some very damning evidence at the scene.* (**provas condenatórias**)

damp /dæmp/ ▶ ADJECTIVE [**damper, dampest**] slightly wet ☐ *Wipe with a damp cloth.* (**úmido**)

> Note that **damp** is usually used for objects and buildings and means 'slightly wet and unpleasant or cold'. When the air is slightly wet and warm, the word to use is **humid**: ☐ *The walls of the house were cold and damp.* ☐ *In summer it is hot and humid.*

▶ NOUN, NO PLURAL when something is damp ☐ *There is a patch of damp on the wall.* (**umidade**)

- **dampen** /ˈdæmpən/ VERB [**dampens, dampening, dampened**] to make something slightly wet ☐ *Dampen the brush before using it.* (**umedecer-se**)

dance /dɑːns/ ▶ VERB [**dances, dancing, danced**] to move your feet and body to music ☐ *Let's dance!* ☐ *She danced with her boyfriend all evening.* ☐ *Will you teach me how to dance the tango?* (**dançar**)

▶ NOUN [plural **dances**]

1 when you dance (**dança**) 🔊 *Why don't you have a dance with your dad?* (**dançar**)

2 a particular set of steps that you do to music ☐ *The first dance we learnt was the waltz.* (**dança**)

3 *no plural* a type of dancing ☐ *Louise teaches modern dance.* (**dança**)

4 a party for dancing (**baile**)

- **dancer** /ˈdɑːnsə(r)/ NOUN [plural **dancers**] someone who dances (**dançarino**)

- **dancing** /ˈdɑːnsɪŋ/ NOUN, NO PLURAL the activity of moving your feet and body to music ☐ *I love dancing.* (**dança**)

dandelion /ˈdændɪlaɪən/ NOUN [plural **dandelions**] a common wild flower with lots of thin yellow petals (**dente-de-leão**)

dandruff /ˈdændrʌf/ NOUN, NO PLURAL small dry pieces of dead skin in your hair ☐ *an anti-dandruff shampoo* (**caspa**)

danger /ˈdeɪndʒə(r)/ NOUN [plural **dangers**]

1 a situation where something may harm you ☐ *Danger! Keep out!* (**perigo**)

2 *in danger* in a situation where something could harm you ☐ *He wasn't in danger at any point.* (**em perigo**)

3 something or someone that may harm you ☐ + *of the dangers of smoking* ☐ + *to This man is a serious danger to the public.* (**perigo**)

4 *danger of something* a chance that something bad might happen ☐ *Is there danger of flooding?* ☐ *We were in danger of missing our flight.* (**correr o risco de algo**)

- **dangerous** /ˈdeɪndʒərəs/ ADJECTIVE

1 likely to harm you ☐ *a dangerous substance* (**nocivo**)

2 likely to have a bad effect ☐ *It would be dangerous to ignore his opinions.* (**perigoso**)

- **dangerously** /ˈdeɪndʒərəslɪ/ ADVERB in a dangerous way ☐ *He was driving dangerously close to the edge.* (**perigosamente**)

dangle /ˈdæŋgəl/ VERB [**dangles, dangling, dangled**] to hang down loosely or to make something do this ☐ *We sat with our legs dangling in the water.* ☐ *He dangled the key on a string in front of me.* (**balançar**)

dank /dæŋk/ ADJECTIVE [**danker, dankest**] a dank place is wet and cold (**frio e úmido**)

dapper /ˈdæpə(r)/ ADJECTIVE a dapper man is very tidy and wears good quality clothes (**agradável**)

dappled /ˈdæpəld/ ADJECTIVE with light and dark areas ☐ *a dappled horse* ☐ *dappled sunlight through the trees* (**manchado**)

dare

dare /deə(r)/ VERB [dares, daring, dared]
1 dare (to) do something to be brave enough to do something □ Rachel wouldn't dare argue with the boss. □ I never thought I'd dare to jump out of a plane. (ousar fazer algo)
2 to ask someone to do something dangerous or frightening (desafiar) 🔊 I dare you to climb to the top. (eu o desafio)
3 How dare you/he, etc. do something! something you say when someone has done something that upsets you very much □ How dare you speak to me like that! (Como se atreve a fazer algo)
4 Don't you dare! used to tell someone that if they do something you will be very angry with them □ Don't you dare throw that at me! (Não se atreva!)

daredevil /'deədevəl/ ▶ NOUN [plural daredevils] someone who enjoys doing dangerous things (valente)
▶ ADJECTIVE dangerous □ Eddie performed many daredevil stunts. (audacioso)

daren't /deənt/ a short way to say and write dare not

daring /'deərɪŋ/ ADJECTIVE
1 brave □ a daring rescue attempt (audacioso)
2 quite shocking □ a daring outfit (ousado)

dark /dɑːk/ ▶ ADJECTIVE [darker, darkest]
1 without light (escuro) 🔊 When we looked outside it was getting dark. (ficando escuro) 🔊 All of a sudden it went dark. (ficou escuro)
2 not light in colour and nearer to black than to white □ dark blue □ Ruth has dark hair. (escuro)
3 a dark person has hair that is black or almost black □ Both my children are dark. (moreno)
4 a formal word for sad □ dark thoughts (triste)
▶ NOUN, NO PLURAL
1 where there is no light □ I'm not afraid of the dark. (escuridão)
2 the time when it becomes dark outside (anoitecer) 🔊 Don't go out after dark without a torch. (depois do anoitecer)

• **darken** /'dɑːkən/ VERB [darkens, darkening, darkened] to get darker, or to make something darker □ The sky darkened and it began to rain. □ It helps if you darken the room a little. (escurecer)

• **darkness** /'dɑːknɪs/ NOUN, NO PLURAL where there is no light (escuridão)

darkroom /'dɑːkruːm/ NOUN [plural darkrooms] a room that is kept dark and that people use when they develop photographs (= make photographs from film) (quarto escuro)

darling /'dɑːlɪŋ/ NOUN [plural darlings] a word used for talking to someone you love □ What's the matter, darling? (querido)

darn /dɑːn/ VERB [darns, darning, darned] to mend a hole in something made of wool using a needle (costurar) 🔊 She was darning his socks. (costurando suas meias)

dart /dɑːt/ ▶ NOUN [plural darts]
1 darts a game where you throw small arrows at a round board called a dartboard (dardos)
2 a little arrow that can be used as a weapon or in the game of darts (dardo)
▶ VERB [darts, darting, darted] to move somewhere fast □ A child darted out of the door as I came in. (disparar)

dartboard /'dɑːtbɔːd/ NOUN [plural dartboards] a round board that you throw darts at in the game of darts (alvo)

dash /dæʃ/ ▶ VERB [dashes, dashing, dashed]
1 to hurry somewhere □ I've got to dash to the shops. □ Mary came in but then she dashed off again. (apressar-se)
2 a formal word that means to hit against something hard □ The boat was dashed against the rocks. (bater)
3 dash someone's hopes to take away what someone was hoping for □ My hopes were dashed again when the examiner said I'd failed. (acabar com as esperanças de alguém)
♦ PHRASAL VERB **dash something off** to write something quickly □ Mum dashed off two more letters while she was waiting. (rabiscar algo apressadamente)
▶ NOUN [plural dashes]
1 a line (–) that is sometimes used in writing between parts of a sentence (travessão)
2 a small amount of a liquid that you add to food or drink □ Add a dash of vinegar. (pingo)
3 when you hurry to get somewhere (corrida rápida) 🔊 The two boys made a dash for the door. (correram) 🔊 In our mad dash to catch the plane we forgot the presents. (corrida maluca)

dashboard /'dæʃbɔːd/ NOUN [plural dashboards] the area in a car in front of the driver where you see information such as the speed and petrol level (painel)

dashing /'dæʃɪŋ/ ADJECTIVE an old-fashioned word that means attractive and dressed well □ You look very dashing in that hat. (elegante)

data /'deɪtə/ NOUN, NO PLURAL information (informações) 🔊 The hospital keeps a lot of personal data on its patients (dados pessoais) □ We collected data over a five year period.

database /'deɪtəbeɪs/ NOUN [plural databases] information that is stored on a computer in an organized form □ Details of known criminals are stored on a national computer database. (banco de dados)

data processing /ˌdeɪtə 'prəʊsesɪŋ/ NOUN, NO PLURAL the use of a computer to organize and store information. A computing word. (processamento de dados)

date /deɪt/ ▶ NOUN [plural dates]
1 the number of the day of the month, the month and the year □ The date today is 30 July. (data)

daub

2 a particular day of a particular month and year (**data**) 🔳 *What is your date of birth?* (**data de nascimento**) 🔳 *Shall we fix/set a date for our next meeting?* (**marcar uma data**) 🔳 *We can decide all the details at a later date.* (**em uma data posterior**)
3 an arrangement to meet someone that you are having a romantic relationship with or who you may start a romantic relationship with □ *Polly's got another date with Chris tonight.* (**encontro**)
4 a small, brown, sticky fruit (**tâmara**)
▶ VERB [dates, dating, dated]
1 to write a date on a letter or other document □ *The letter was dated 3rd May.* (**datar**)
2 to decide how old something is □ *The ring's very old but I couldn't date it exactly.* (**datar**)
3 to become old-fashioned □ *Shoes always date very quickly.* (**ficar ultrapassado**)
4 to have a romantic relationship with someone and meet them regularly □ *How long have you and Kelly been dating?* (**namorar**)
◆ PHRASAL VERBS **date back to something** to have existed for a particular length of time or since a particular time □ *Our involvement with horses dates back to the sixteenth century.* (**remeter a algo**) **date from something** to have existed since a particular time □ *These silver items date from the 13th century.* (**datar de algo**)
• **dated** /ˈdeɪtɪd/ ADJECTIVE old-fashioned □ *My mobile phone looks rather dated now.* (**fora de moda**)

daub /dɔːb/ VERB [daubs, daubing, daubed] to put a thick liquid such as paint roughly onto something □ *The car was daubed with red paint.* (**manchar**)

daughter /ˈdɔːtə(r)/ NOUN [plural daughters] someone's female child □ *She was the daughter of a poet.* □ *Dave and Maria have a new baby daughter.* (**filha**)

daughter-in-law /ˈdɔːtərɪnˌlɔː/ NOUN [plural daughters-in-law] your son's wife □ *Have you met my daughter-in-law, Sandra?* (**nora**)

daunt /dɔːnt/ VERB [daunts, daunting, daunted] if you are daunted by something you are going to do, you are worried because it is difficult or a lot of work □ *I was a bit daunted by the size of the project.* (**assombrar, amedrontar**)
• **daunting** /ˈdɔːntɪŋ/ ADJECTIVE so difficult or needing so much work that you are worried (**desencorajador**) 🔳 *Now we face the daunting task of playing against the champions.* (**tarefa desencorajadora**) 🔳 *Moving house is a daunting prospect* (= makes you worry before you do it). (**esperança desencorajadora**)

dawdle /ˈdɔːdəl/ VERB [dawdles, dawdling, dawdled] to walk slowly □ *Ralph was dawdling along behind everyone else.* (**vadiar**)

dawn /dɔːn/ C NOUN [plural dawns] the beginning of the day, when it gets light (**alvorada**)
▶ VERB [dawns, dawning, dawned] a formal word that means to start □ *A new age has dawned.* (**despontar**)
◆ PHRASAL VERB **dawn on someone** if something dawns on you, you suddenly understand it □ *Then it dawned on me that she was his daughter.* (**tornar-se claro para alguém**)

daze

day /deɪ/ NOUN [plural days]
1 the twenty-four hours between one midnight (= 12 am) and another □ *There are 365 days in a year.* □ *I do five hours' work a day.* (**dia**) 🔳 *I try to do some exercise every day.* (**todo dia**)
2 the time when there is light from the sun, or when you are awake □ *We spent the whole day on the beach.* □ *I spent all day cleaning the house.* □ *Did you have a good day at work?* (**dia**)
3 a time or period □ *In my grandfather's day* (**tempos**) 🔳 *In those days we didn't have computers.* (**naquele tempo**)
4 one day used to talk about something that happened in the past or something that will happen in the future □ *One day I came home to discover my car had been stolen.* □ *I hope to have my own business one day.* (**algum dia**)
5 the other day a few days ago □ *I saw Julio the other day.* (**outro dia**)
6 these days used to talk about what things are like now □ *These days I don't play much tennis.* (**hoje em dia**)

daybreak /ˈdeɪbreɪk/ NOUN, NO PLURAL when light first appears in the sky in the morning □ *He left before daybreak.* (**aurora**)

daydream /ˈdeɪdriːm/ ▶ VERB [daydreams, daydreaming, daydreamed] to think about things that you would like to happen □ *I used to daydream about being rich.* (**devanear**)
▶ NOUN [plural daydreams] something pleasant that you daydream about (**devaneio**)

daylight /ˈdeɪlaɪt/ NOUN, NO PLURAL
1 the light that comes from the sun during the day □ *In the daylight she looked pale.* (**luz do dia**)
2 the part of the day when there is light □ *I'd like to get home in daylight.* (**de dia**)

daytime /ˈdeɪtaɪm/ NOUN, NO PLURAL the part of the day when there is light □ *Don't waste electricity by having the lights on in the daytime.* □ *daytime television* (**dia, de dia**)

day-to-day /ˌdeɪtəˈdeɪ/ ADJECTIVE happening or done regularly, every day (**diário**) 🔳 *These attacks now happen on a day-to-day basis* (= every day). (**diário**) 🔳 *Diane is in charge of the day-to-day running of the department.* (**corrida diária**)

day trip /ˈdeɪ ˌtrɪp/ NOUN [plural day trips] a visit to an interesting or attractive place that you go to and come back from in one day □ *We went on a day trip to the Pyramids.* (**excursão de um dia**)

daze /deɪz/ ▶ NOUN **in a daze** confused or unable to think clearly □ *I stood there in a daze, not knowing what to do.* (**confuso**)

dazzle

▶ VERB [dazes, dazing, dazed] to shock and confuse someone ☐ *The knock on the head dazed him for a minute.* (aturdir)

- **dazed** /deɪzd/ ADJECTIVE shocked and confused ☐ *The survivors of the crash were dazed but unhurt.* (estupefato)

dazzle /ˈdæzəl/ VERB [dazzles, dazzling, dazzled]
1 if you are dazzled by a light, it is so bright that you cannot see well ☐ *I was dazzled by the car headlights.* (ofuscar)
2 if you are dazzled by something or someone you think they are very exciting and special (deslumbrar)

- **dazzling** /ˈdæzlɪŋ/ ADJECTIVE
1 a dazzling light is so bright that you cannot see well (ofuscante)
2 very exciting and special (deslumbrante) ☐ *It was a truly dazzling performance.* (espetáculo deslumbrante)

de- /diː/ PREFIX
1 de- is added to the beginning of words that are to do with removing something ☐ *decaffeinated* ☐ *defrost* (des-)
2 de- is added to the beginning of words to mean 'the opposite of' ☐ *decompose* ☐ *decode* (de-)
3 de- is found at the beginning of words that are to do with going down ☐ *descend* ☐ *decline* (de-)

dead /ded/ ADJECTIVE
1 not now living ☐ *I could see he was dead.* (morto) ☐ *He dropped dead (= died suddenly) on the tennis court.* (morreu) ☐ *a dead body*
2 no longer working ☐ *My phone's gone dead.* ☐ *The batteries are dead.* (inerte, inativo)
3 complete (completo, total) ☐ *There was dead silence in the room.* (silêncio total) ☐ *They came to a dead stop.*
▶ ADVERB
1 stop dead to stop suddenly and completely (completamente)
2 exactly ☐ *They were standing dead in the centre of the circle.* (exatamente)
3 an informal word meaning very ☐ *dead boring/easy* (muito)
▶ NOUN, NO PLURAL
1 the dead people who have died (os mortos)
2 the dead of night the darkest and quietest part of the night (plena noite)

- **deaden** /ˈdedən/ VERB [deadens, deadening, deadened] to stop you feeling or hearing something so much ☐ *They gave him an injection to deaden the pain.* (aliviar)

dead end /ˌded ˈend/ NOUN [plural dead ends] a road that does not lead to any other road ☐ *You'll have to turn around – this is a dead end.* (beco sem saída)

dead heat /ˌded ˈhiːt/ NOUN [plural dead heats] when two people finish a race at exactly the same time (empate)

deadline /ˈdedlaɪn/ NOUN [plural deadlines] the time when something must be finished (prazo final) ☐ *You'll miss the deadline if you delay.* (você perderá o prazo final)

deadlock /ˈdedlɒk/ NOUN, NO PLURAL when people cannot agree and will not change what they think (impasse) ☐ *They talked all night in an effort to break (= end) the deadlock.* (acabar com o impasse)

deadly /ˈdedli/ ADJECTIVE [deadlier, deadliest] able to kill (mortal) ☐ *a deadly weapon* (arma mortal) ☐ *a deadly poison* (veneno mortal)

deaf /def/ ▶ ADJECTIVE [deafer, deafest] not able to hear, or not able to hear well ☐ *Grandma is getting a bit deaf.* (surdo)
▶ PLURAL NOUN the deaf people who are deaf (os surdos)

- **deafen** /ˈdefən/ VERB [deafens, deafening, deafened] to make someone deaf for a short time ☐ *The explosion deafened us for a moment.* (ensurdecer)

- **deafening** /ˈdefənɪŋ/ ADJECTIVE unpleasantly loud ☐ *The music was deafening and we had to leave.* (ensurdecedor)

- **deafness** /ˈdefnɪs/ NOUN, NO PLURAL being deaf (surdez)

deal /diːl/ ▶ NOUN [plural deals]
1 an agreement, especially in business or politics (transação) ☐ *make/strike a deal* (fazer uma transação) ☐ *We are about to sign a deal with a major record producer.* (assinar uma transação) ☐ *I got a good deal (= a cheap price) on my new car.* (boa quantia)
2 the way someone is treated or the amount of something that they get (contrato) ☐ *Teachers always seem to get a raw/rough deal (= a bad deal) when it comes to pay.* (contrato ruim) ☐ *We are campaigning for a better deal for mental health patients.*
3 a great deal a large amount ☐ *We spent a great deal of money on solar panels.* (uma boa quantia)
4 when cards are given to players in a game ☐ *It's your deal.* (vez de jogar)
▶ VERB [deals, dealing, dealt] to give cards to players in a game ☐ *You deal the cards this time.* (embaralhar as cartas do jogo)

◆ PHRASAL VERBS **deal in something** to buy and sell something ☐ *They deal in luxury fabrics.* (comercializar algo) **deal with something/someone** (lidar com algo/alguém)
1 to take action, especially to solve a problem or to get something done ☐ *New houses were built to deal with the problem of homelessness.* ☐ *You take the boy to another room – I'll deal with his father.* ☐ *I need to deal with all these letters.* (resolver algo)
2 to learn to accept a difficult situation ☐ *I'm finding it hard to deal with his death.* (lidar com algo)

3 to be about a particular subject □ *The programme deals with the true cost of cheap labour.* (tratar de)
- **dealer** /ˈdiːlə(r)/ NOUN [plural **dealers**] someone who buys and sells things □ *an antiques dealer* (negociante)
- **dealings** /ˈdiːlɪŋz/ PLURAL NOUN contact with other people, especially to do business (negócios) 🔲 *I have never had any dealings with his company.* (fiz nenhum negócio)

dear /dɪə(r)/ ▶ ADJECTIVE [**dearer, dearest**]
1 Dear the word you use with a name or title at the beginning of a letter □ *Dear Max* □ *Dear Sir* (caro/prezado)
2 loved 🔲 *a very dear friend* (estimado/querido amigo)
3 expensive □ *The shoes were beautiful but very dear.* (caro)
▶ NOUN [plural **dears**] a word used for talking to someone that you like □ *Sorry, dear, what did you say?* (querido)
▶ EXCLAMATION **Oh dear!** something you say when something slightly bad has happened □ *Oh dear! I'm late again.* (Ó, meu Deus!)
- **dearly** /ˈdɪəli/ ADVERB very much 🔲 *You know I love him dearly.* (eu o amo muito)

dearth /dɜːθ/ NOUN, NO PLURAL when there is not enough of something. A formal word. □ *There's a dearth of good maths teachers.* (escassez)

death /deθ/ NOUN [plural **deaths**]
1 the time when a person or animal stops living □ *He wrote this just before his death in 1875.* (morte) □ + *from The number of deaths from cancer is decreasing all the time.* 🔲 *The cause of death was unknown.* (causa da morte)
2 to death until you are dead □ *Most of these people starved to death.* □ *He choked to death.* (até a morte)
3 frightened, worried, etc. to death extremely frightened or worried, etc. □ *I was frightened to death when I saw the gun.* (morrer de medo)
♦ IDIOM **be at death's door** to be so ill that you are almost dead (estar à beira da morte, entre a vida e a morte)

deathbed /ˈdeθbed/ NOUN **be on your deathbed** to be so ill that you are going to die soon (estar em seu leito de morte)

deathly /ˈdeθli/ ▶ ADJECTIVE extreme and unpleasant (mortal) 🔲 *There was a deathly silence.* (silêncio mortal)
▶ ADVERB in a way that is extreme and unpleasant (mortalmente) 🔲 *She went deathly pale.* (mortalmente pálida)

death penalty /ˈdeθ ˌpenəlti/ NOUN [plural **death penalties**] when someone is killed as a legal punishment for a crime (pena de morte)

debacle /deˈbɑːkəl/ NOUN [plural **debacles**] an embarrassing failure □ *The show was a complete debacle.* (desastre, fracasso)

debase /dɪˈbeɪs/ VERB [**debases, debasing, debased**] to make something less valuable or respected □ *He criticized the debasing effect of mass culture.* (humilhar)

debatable /dɪˈbeɪtəbəl/ ADJECTIVE if something is debatable, some people believe that it is true and some people do not □ *It's debatable whether animal fats are really bad for you.* (discutível)

debate /dɪˈbeɪt/ ▶ NOUN [plural **debates**] a big or formal discussion about something □ *a parliamentary debate* (debate)
▶ VERB [**debates, debating, debated**] to have a debate about something (debater)

debilitating /dɪˈbɪlɪteɪtɪŋ/ ADJECTIVE making someone weak. A formal word. (que enfraquece) 🔲 *He suffers from a debilitating illness* (doença debilitadora)

debit /ˈdebɪt/ ▶ NOUN [plural **debits**] an amount of money that is taken out of a bank account (débito)
▶ VERB [**debits, debiting, debited**] to take money out of a bank account □ *The sum will be debited from your account on the first of every month.* (debitar)

debit card /ˈdebɪt ˌkɑːd/ NOUN [plural **debit cards**] a small plastic card for buying things by taking money immediately from your bank account (cartão de débito)

debonair /ˌdebəˈneə(r)/ ADJECTIVE describes an attractive, confident man. An old-fashioned word. (encantador)

debris /ˈdeɪbriː/ NOUN, NO PLURAL the parts of something that has broken into pieces □ *Debris from the crashed aircraft lay all around.* (escombros)

debt /det/ NOUN [plural **debts**]
1 an amount of money that one person owes to another (dívida) 🔲 *I always pay off my debts.* (pago minhas dívidas)
2 in debt owing someone money (em dívida)
- **debtor** /ˈdetə(r)/ NOUN [plural **debtors**] a person who owes someone else money (devedor)

debug /ˌdiːˈbʌɡ/ VERB [**debugs, debugging, debugged**] to remove mistakes from a computer program. A computing word. (depurar)
- **debugger** /ˌdiːˈbʌɡə(r)/ NOUN [plural **debuggers**] a computer program that debugs other programs. A computing word. (depurador)

debunk /ˌdiːˈbʌŋk/ VERB [**debunks, debunking, debunked**] to prove that an idea or someone's opinion is wrong or silly (desmascarar)

début /ˈdeɪbjuː/ NOUN [plural **débuts**] the first time an actor or performer performs in public (estreia) 🔲 *She made her début at the King's Theatre in 1999.* (fez sua estreia)

dec- /dek/ or **deca-** /ˈdekə/ PREFIX dec- or deca- is found at the beginning of words to do with the number ten □ *decagon* □ *decimal* (dec-)

decade /ˈdekeɪd/ NOUN [plural **decades**] a period of ten years □ *This is the second decade of the twenty-first century.* (década)

decadence /ˈdekədəns/ NOUN, NO PLURAL morally bad behaviour, especially when people only do things for pleasure (decadência)

• **decadent** /ˈdekədənt/ ADJECTIVE when people are morally bad, only doing things for pleasure (decadente)

decaff /ˈdiːkæf/ NOUN, NO PLURAL an informal word for decaffeinated coffee □ *Have you got any decaff?* (café descafeinado)

decaffeinated /ˌdiːˈkæfɪneɪtɪd/ ADJECTIVE describes coffee which has no caffeine (= a substance that makes you feel more awake) (descafeinado)

decagon /ˈdekəɡən/ NOUN [plural **decagons**] a flat shape with ten straight sides (decágono)

decapitate /dɪˈkæpɪteɪt/ VERB [**decapitates, decapitating, decapitated**] to cut off a person's head (decapitar)

decathlon /dɪˈkæθlɒn/ NOUN [plural **decathlons**] a sports competition in which you do ten different types of sports like running, jumping and throwing (decatlo)

decay /dɪˈkeɪ/ ▶ NOUN, NO PLURAL when something becomes rotten or breaks into pieces (deterioração) 🔁 *This toothpaste helps prevents gum disease and tooth decay.* (deterioração dos dentes)

▶ VERB [**decays, decaying, decayed**] to go rotten or break into pieces □ *The bins were full of decaying food.* (deteriorar)

deceased /dɪˈsiːst/ ▶ ADJECTIVE a formal word that means dead (falecido)

▶ NOUN **the deceased** the particular person who has recently died □ *We believe that the deceased knew his attacker.* (o falecido)

deceit /dɪˈsiːt/ NOUN, NO PLURAL when you lie to or trick people (desonestidade)

• **deceitful** /dɪˈsiːtfʊl/ ADJECTIVE lying or tricking people □ *He is very deceitful.* (desonesto, mentiroso)

deceive /dɪˈsiːv/ VERB [**deceives, deceiving, deceived**] to make someone believe something that is not true □ **+ by** *Don't be deceived by his friendly manner.* □ **+ into** *She was deceived into thinking she'd won a holiday.* □ *If she thinks Keith actually loves her, she's deceiving herself.* (enganar, falsear)

decelerate /ˌdiːˈseləreɪt/ VERB [**decelerates, decelerating, decelerated**] to become slower (desacelerar)

December /dɪˈsembə(r)/ NOUN the twelfth month of the year, after November and before January □ *Her birthday is in December.* (dezembro)

decency /ˈdiːsənsi/ NOUN, NO PLURAL behaviour that is good and of a high moral standard (decência) 🔁 *She didn't even have the decency to tell me the news herself.* (teve a decência)

• **decent** /ˈdiːsənt/ ADJECTIVE

1 acceptable or good enough □ *Is there a decent butcher's near here?* (decente) 🔁 *After a decent interval* (= an amount of time considered acceptable) *he married again.* (intervalo decente) 🔁 *I think they have a decent chance of winning.* (chance decente)

2 good, honest and of a high moral standard □ *He's a very decent bloke.* (decente)

decentralization or **decentralisation** /ˌdiːsentrəlaɪˈzeɪʃən/ NOUN, NO PLURAL when something is decentralized (descentralização)

decentralize or **decentralise** /ˌdiːˈsentrəlaɪz/ VERB [**decentralizes, decentralizing, decentralized**] to change an organization so that the work is done in several places instead of one central place (descentralizar)

deception /dɪˈsepʃən/ NOUN [plural **deceptions**] when you trick or lie to people □ *an act of deliberate deception* (trapaça, engano)

• **deceptive** /dɪˈseptɪv/ ADJECTIVE making you believe something that is not true □ *That photo is quite deceptive – it makes me look a lot younger than I am.* (enganoso)

• **deceptively** /dɪˈseptɪvli/ ADVERB in a way that is different from what you expect or think □ *The apartment was deceptively spacious.* (enganosamente)

decibel /ˈdesɪbel/ NOUN [plural **decibels**] a unit that is used for measuring how loud a sound is. A physics word. (decibel)

decide /dɪˈsaɪd/ VERB [**decides, deciding, decided**]

1 to choose what you are going to do □ **+ to do something** *Greg decided to buy a computer.* □ **+ that** *She decided that she would go with him.* □ *I can't decide what to do.* (decidir)

2 to form an opinion after thinking about something □ **+ that** *I decided that the coat was too short for me.* (decidir)

3 to choose what to have or buy □ **+ between** *I can't decide between the blue one and the green one.* □ **+ on** *I decided on the duck in the end.* (decidir)

4 to cause a result in a competition □ *Amrish's goal decided the match.* (decidir)

• **decided** /dɪˈsaɪdɪd/ ADJECTIVE certain or obvious (claro) 🔁 *This essay is a decided improvement on your last effort.* (melhora evidente)

• **decidedly** /dɪˈsaɪdɪdli/ ADVERB in a way that is certain and obvious □ *He was looking decidedly unhappy.* (decididamente)

deciduous /dɪˈsɪdjuəs/ ADJECTIVE a deciduous tree does not have leaves in the winter. A biology word. (efêmero, transitório)

decimal /ˈdesɪməl/ ▶ ADJECTIVE

1 a decimal system is a way of counting based on the number ten (decimal)

decimal place / decorate

2 using or to do with a decimal system (**decimal**) 🔊 *Britain changed to decimal currency* (= money in decimal units) *in 1971.* □ *a decimal number* (**moeda decimal**)

▶ NOUN [*plural* **decimals**] a fraction (= number that is less than a whole number) written as a decimal point followed by the number of tenths and hundredths. A maths word. □ *A half, written as a decimal, is 0.5.* (**decimal**)

decimal place /ˌdesɪməl ˈpleɪs/ NOUN [*plural* **decimal places**] a particular number or position after the decimal point in a decimal. A maths word. □ *3.846 rounded off* (= reduced) *to two decimal places is 3.85* (**casa decimal**)

decimal point /ˌdesɪməl ˈpɔɪnt/ NOUN [*plural* **decimal points**] a point (.) used in a decimal after the whole units and before the tenths. A maths word. □ *To multiply by ten, move the decimal point one place to the right.* (**vírgula decimal**)

decimate /ˈdesɪmeɪt/ VERB [**decimates, decimating, decimated**] to spoil or destroy a large part of something □ *Their crops have been decimated by the floods.* (**dizimar, destruir**)

• **decimation** /ˌdesɪˈmeɪʃən/ NOUN, NO PLURAL when something is decimated

decipher /dɪˈsaɪfə(r)/ VERB [**deciphers, deciphering, deciphered**] if you decipher something that is difficult to read, you discover what it says □ *Philip's handwriting is almost impossible to decipher.* (**decifrar**)

decision /dɪˈsɪʒən/ NOUN [*plural* **decisions**]
1 when you decide something (**decisão**) 🔊 *I will let you know when I have made my decision.* (**tomei minha decisão**) 🔊 *Finally we took the difficult decision to sell the house.* (**decisão difícil**) 🔊 *Most of us think the directors came to the right decision.* (**chegaram à decisão**)
2 *no plural* the ability to decide about things □ *He acted with great decision.* (**decisão**)

• **decisive** /dɪˈsaɪsɪv/ ADJECTIVE
1 showing the ability to make decisions □ *I wish he'd be more decisive.* (**decidido**)
2 completely certain and important (**decisivo**) 🔊 *Our college won a decisive victory over Queen's on Saturday.* (**vitória decisiva**)

deck /dek/ NOUN [*plural* **decks**]
1 the flat part that you walk on on the outside of a boat □ *Let's take a walk up on deck.* (**convés**)
2 one of the levels of a boat or bus (**piso**) 🔊 *There are more seats on the upper deck.* (**piso superior**)
3 the US word for a pack of cards (**conjunto**)

◆ PHRASAL VERB [**decks, decking, decked**] **deck something out** if something is decked out with something, it has been decorated with it (**enfeitar algo**)

deckchair /ˈdektʃeə(r)/ NOUN [*plural* **deckchairs**] a folding chair with a wooden frame that is used outdoors (**espreguiçadeira**)

declaration /ˌdekləˈreɪʃən/ NOUN [*plural* **declarations**] an announcement □ *a declaration of war* (**declaração**)

declare /dɪˈkleə(r)/ VERB [**declares, declaring, declared**]
1 to announce something firmly or officially (**declarar**) 🔊 *England declared war on Germany.* (**declarou guerra**) □ *She suddenly declared that she was leaving.*
2 have something to declare to have goods that you should pay tax on □ *Do you have anything to declare, Madam?* (**ter algo a declarar**)
3 to tell the tax authority about money you receive □ *Have you declared all your earnings?* (**declarar**)

decline /dɪˈklaɪn/ VERB [**declines, declining, declined**]
1 to become weaker or smaller □ *His popularity has declined sharply.* (**declinar**)
2 a formal word that means to refuse □ *I'm afraid I must decline your kind invitation.* □ *The minister declined to comment.* (**recusar**)

decode /ˌdiːˈkəʊd/ VERB [**decodes, decoding, decoded**] to find out the secret meaning of something (**decodificar**)

decompose /ˌdiːkəmˈpəʊz/ VERB [**decomposes, decomposing, decomposed**] to decay (**decompor**)

• **decomposition** /ˌdiːkɒmpəˈzɪʃən/ NOUN, NO PLURAL the process of decaying (**decomposição**)

decor /ˈdeɪkɔː(r)/ NOUN, NO PLURAL the style of decoration and furniture in a room □ *It's a lovely house, but I hate the decor.* (**decoração**)

decorate /ˈdekəreɪt/ VERB [**decorates, decorating, decorated**]
1 to put things on or around something to make it look more attractive □ *We'll decorate the cake with sugar roses.* (**decorar**)
2 to put paint or paper on the inside walls of a room □ *We've just decorated the dining room.* (**decorar**)
3 if someone is decorated, they are given a medal (= metal disc) for doing something brave or good □ *He was decorated for bravery in the war.* (**condecorar**)

• **decoration** /ˌdekəˈreɪʃən/ NOUN [*plural* **decorations**]
1 when you add something to make something more attractive, or the thing you add (**decoração**) 🔊 *Christmas/party decorations* (**decoração de Natal/festas**)
2 *no plural* putting paint or paper on the inside walls of a room □ *The whole house is in need of decoration.* (**decoração**)

• **decorative** /ˈdekərətɪv/ ADJECTIVE intended to make something look more attractive □ *The brass buttons are purely decorative* (= not for a real purpose). (**decorativo**)

decoy

- **decorator** /'dekəreɪtə(r)/ NOUN [plural **decorators**] someone whose job is to decorate rooms (decorador)

decoy /'di:kɔɪ/ NOUN [plural **decoys**] a thing or person used to trick and catch someone (isca)

decrease ▶ VERB /dɪ'kri:s/ [**decreases, decreasing, decreased**] to make something less or to become less ▢ A healthy diet helps to decrease the risk of heart disease. ▢ Josh's interest in football decreased as he got older. (diminuir)
▶ NOUN /'di:kri:s/ [plural **decreases**] an amount by which something is smaller ▢ + **in** There was a decrease in violent crime in the area. ▢ + **of** They saw a decrease of 5% in sales. (diminuição)

decree /dɪ'kri:/ ▶ NOUN [plural **decrees**] an official order that something should happen (decreto)
▶ VERB [**decrees, decreeing, decreed**] to announce publicly that something should happen. A formal word. (decretar)

decrepit /dɪ'krepɪt/ ADJECTIVE old and in bad condition (gasto)

dedicate /'dedɪkeɪt/ VERB [**dedicates, dedicating, dedicated**] to spend a particular amount of time doing something ▢ She dedicated her whole life to music. (dedicar)
♦ PHRASAL VERB **dedicate something to someone** to say at the beginning of a book, song, etc. that it is for a person that you love or admire ▢ This song is dedicated to my friends at home. (dedicar algo a alguém)

- **dedicated** /'dedɪkeɪtɪd/ ADJECTIVE spending a lot of time and effort on what you do ▢ She is a very dedicated nurse. (dedicado)

- **dedication** /ˌdedɪ'keɪʃən/ NOUN [plural **dedications**]
  1 when you use a lot of time and effort to do something ▢ He praised the dedication of the nurses. (dedicação)
  2 words used to dedicate a song, book, etc. to someone ▢ The dedication read 'For Bill, for being so understanding.' (dedicatória)

deduce /dɪ'dju:s/ VERB [**deduces, deducing, deduced**] to think that something is true from the information you have (deduzir)

deduct /dɪ'dʌkt/ VERB [**deducts, deducting, deducted**] to take an amount away from a larger number ▢ Tax has already been deducted from your earnings. (deduzir)

- **deduction** /dɪ'dʌkʃən/ NOUN [plural **deductions**]
  1 an amount that you deduct (dedução)
  2 something that you deduce from the information you have (dedução)

deed /di:d/ NOUN [plural **deeds**]
1 a formal word meaning something that someone has done (proeza)
2 an official document that shows who owns something ▢ Here are the deeds of the house. (certificado)

deep-seated

deem /di:m/ VERB [**deems, deeming, deemed**] a formal word meaning to have a particular opinion about something ▢ I leave you to take whatever action you deem suitable. (considerar)

deep /di:p/ ▶ ADJECTIVE [**deeper, deepest**]
1 going a long way down from the top ▢ Is the pond very deep? ▢ The sea was 30 metres deep at that point. (profundo)
2 deep feelings and emotions are very strong ▢ I have a deep dislike of dogs. (profundo)
3 deep colours are strong and dark ▢ I painted the walls deep blue. (intenso)
4 a deep sound is very low (grave) 🔊 a deep voice (voz grave)
5 going a long way from the front to the back ▢ a deep cupboard (fundo)
6 a deep sleep when someone is sleeping so much that it is difficult to wake them (sono profundo)
7 a deep breath a big breath that fills your lungs ▢ Take a deep breath then jump into the water. (uma respiração profunda)
♦ IDIOM **in deep trouble** in a very bad situation ▢ He'll be in deep trouble if his Dad finds out he's been stealing. (em uma grande confusão)
▶ ADVERB [**deeper, deepest**]
1 a long way from the top of something ▢ They swam deep beneath the ocean. (profundamente)
2 a long way from the edge of something ▢ They travelled deep into the mountains. (profundamente)
3 three/five, etc. deep in three/five, etc. rows ▢ The soldiers were standing four deep. (fileira)

- **deepen** /'di:pən/ VERB [**deepens, deepening, deepened**]
  1 to become deeper or to make something deeper ▢ The river deepens here to more than 2 metres. (aprofundar)
  2 to become worse or to make something worse ▢ A deepening gloom spread across the country. (agravar)

deep freeze /ˌdi:p 'fri:z/ ▶ NOUN [plural **deep freezes**] a large container for storing frozen foods (congelador, freezer)
▶ VERB [**deep-freezes, deep-freezing, deep--froze, deep-frozen**] to freeze food in order to store it (congelar)

deep-fry /ˌdi:p'fraɪ/ VERB [**deep-fries, deep--frying, deep-fried**] to cook food in hot oil that completely covers it ▢ deep-fried fish (fritar em imersão)

deeply /'di:pli/ ADVERB
1 very much ▢ I deeply regret my actions. (muitíssimo)
2 if you breathe deeply, you take a lot of air into your lungs (profundamente)

deep-seated /ˌdi:p'si:tɪd/ ADJECTIVE deep--seated feelings are strong and difficult to change (arraigado)

deer /dɪə(r)/ NOUN [plural **deer**] a large wild animal that has antlers (= parts like branches) on the head of the males (**veado**)

deface /dɪˈfeɪs/ VERB [**defaces, defacing, defaced**] to spoil the way something looks □ *Someone defaced the statue with paint.* (**desfigurar**)

default /dɪˈfɔːlt/ NOUN [plural **defaults**]
1 the way that something is or will be if nothing is done to make it different □ *The default setting on my computer is for American English.* (**padrão**)
2 by default if something happens by default it only happens because something else does not happen □ *She got the job by default as nobody else applied.* (**por não comparecimento**)
♦ PHRASAL VERB [**defaults, defaulting, defaulted**] **default on something** to fail to pay or do something in the way that has been agreed □ *If you default on the rent you will have to leave.* (**deixar de cumprir algo**)

defeat /dɪˈfiːt/ ▶ VERB [**defeats, defeating, defeated**]
1 to beat someone in a war or competition (**derrotar**) 🔲 *We shall defeat the enemy and restore peace.* (**derrotar o inimigo**) □ *The visiting team were defeated 3–0.* (**vencer**)
2 to prevent something from succeeding □ *The plan was defeated in a public vote.* (**vencer**)
3 if something defeats you, you cannot do it or understand it □ *Do you know what this means? It defeats me.* (**vencer**)
▶ NOUN [plural **defeats**]
1 a game, fight, war, etc. that you have lost (**derrota**) 🔲 *The king suffered a humiliating defeat by the rebel army.* (**sofreu derrota**) 🔲 *England had another heavy defeat in the cricket.* (**grande derrota**)
2 *no plural* when you have been defeated (**derrota**) 🔲 *After a long argument, I was forced to admit defeat.* (**admitir a derrota**)

defect[1] /ˈdiːfekt/ NOUN [plural **defects**] a fault that stops something from working correctly □ *He has a serious heart defect.* (**defeito**)

defect[2] /dɪˈfekt/ VERB [**defects, defecting, defected**] to leave a country or organization and go to live or work in an enemy country or organization □ *The spy defected to the United States.* (**desertar**)
• **defection** /dɪˈfekʃən/ NOUN [plural **defections**] when someone defects □ *There were three more defections when the athletes were in Canada.* (**deserção**)

defective /dɪˈfektɪv/ ADJECTIVE not working well because of a fault (**defeituoso**)

defector /dɪˈfektə(r)/ NOUN [plural **defectors**] someone who leaves their country or organization to live or work in an enemy country or organization (**desertor**)

defence /dɪˈfens/ NOUN [plural **defences**]
1 *no plural* the act of protecting someone or something from attack, harm, criticism, etc. (**defesa**) 🔲 *His bodyguards leaped to his defence.* (**lançaram-se à defesa**) 🔲 *The prime minister spoke out in defence of the chancellor.* (**na defesa de**)
2 something that protects something or someone from attack, harm, criticism, etc. □ *They have built massive defences against the tide.* (**defesa**) 🔲 *For him, humour is a defence mechanism* (= way of protecting himself) *that he uses when he feels criticized.*
3 *no plural* the military organizations that protect a country □ *There have been cuts in defence spending.* (**defesa**)
4 the defence lawyers who are trying to prove in court that someone is not guilty (**a defesa**)
5 in sport, the members of a team who try to stop the other team from scoring (**defesa**)
• **defenceless** /dɪˈfensləs/ ADJECTIVE defenceless people or animals are unable to protect themselves □ *a defenceless baby seal* (**indefeso**)

defend /dɪˈfend/ VERB [**defends, defending, defended**]
1 to protect someone or something from attack, harm, criticism, etc. □ + ***against*** *Heavy armour on the tanks defends them against gunfire.* □ *Kim always defends his brother if people say he's too quiet.* (**defender**)
2 to try to prove to a court that someone is not guilty □ *He was defended by a top barrister.* (**defender**)
3 in sport, to try to stop the other team scoring □ *Leeds United defended well.* (**defender**)
• **defendant** /dɪˈfendənt/ NOUN [plural **defendants**] a person that is accused of committing a crime in a court (**acusado, réu**)
• **defensive** /dɪˈfensɪv/ ADJECTIVE
1 showing that you are angry if you think someone is criticizing you □ *He's very defensive about his work.* (**defensivo**)
2 designed to protect somewhere from an attack (**defensivo**) 🔲 *defensive weapons* (**armas defensivas**)

defense /dɪˈfens/ NOUN [plural **defenses**] the US spelling of **defence** (**defesa**)
• **defenseless** /dɪˈfensləs/ ADJECTIVE the US spelling of **defenceless** (**indefeso**)

defer /dɪˈfɜː(r)/ VERB [**defers, deferring, deferred**] to arrange to do something later than planned □ *The meeting was deferred until more people could come.* (**protelar, adiar**)

deference /ˈdefərəns/ NOUN, NO PLURAL a formal word meaning behaviour that shows that you respect someone and will obey them (**consideração**) 🔲 *We were expected to show deference to our teachers.* (**mostrar consideração**)
• **deferential** /ˌdefəˈrenʃəl/ ADJECTIVE showing deference (**respeitador**) 🔲 *Try to behave in a deferential manner towards customers.* (**modos respeitadores**)

defiance

defiance /dɪˈfaɪəns/ NOUN, NO PLURAL
deliberately not obeying someone or something (**desafio**) 🔂 *Pamela went out, in defiance of her parents' instructions.* (**em desafio a**)

- **defiant** /dɪˈfaɪənt/ ADJECTIVE showing defiance ☐ *a defiant child* (**desafiador**)
- **defiantly** /dɪˈfaɪəntli/ ADVERB in a defiant way (**desafiadoramente**)

deficiency /dɪˈfɪʃənsi/ NOUN [plural **deficiencies**]
1 when your body does not have enough of something it needs ☐ *You have a vitamin B deficiency.* (**deficiência**)
2 a fault or a missing quality that means that something is not good enough ☐ *Her deficiencies as a mother were obvious to everyone.* (**falta**)

- **deficient** /dɪˈfɪʃənt/ ADJECTIVE
1 not having enough of something ☐ *Your diet is deficient in protein.* (**deficiente**)
2 a formal word meaning not good enough ☐ *The standard of care was seriously deficient.* (**deficiente**)

deficit /ˈdefɪsɪt/ NOUN [plural **deficits**] how much less money you have than you need or expect ☐ *The accounts show a deficit of several hundred pounds.* (**déficit**)

define /dɪˈfaɪn/ VERB [**defines, defining, defined**]
1 to show or explain exactly what something is ☐ *Researchers have defined three classes of offender.* ☐ *The scope of the project was poorly defined.* (**definir**)
2 to give the exact meaning of a word or phrase (**definir**)
3 to show the shape of something ☐ *The parking spaces are clearly defined by white lines.* (**delimitar**)

definite /ˈdefɪnɪt/ ADJECTIVE certain ☐ *It's not definite, but the wedding will probably be in August.* ☐ *I've noticed a definite improvement in his condition.* (**definitivo**)

definite article /ˌdefɪnɪt ˈɑːtɪkəl/ NOUN [plural **definite articles**] the name used in grammar for the word *the* (**artigo definido**)

> There are two kinds of article in English grammar: *the* is the *definite article* and *a* or *an* is the *indefinite article*.

definitely /ˈdefɪnɪtli/ ADVERB certainly ☐ *We'll definitely be back by 10 o'clock.* ☐ *'Do you think she'll pass the exam?' 'Oh yes, definitely.'* ☐ *I definitely want to go back there.* (**definitivamente**)

definition /ˌdefɪˈnɪʃən/ NOUN [plural **definitions**]
1 an explanation of the meaning of a word or phrase ☐ *Look up the definition of 'magic' in your dictionary.* (**definição**)
2 how clear an image is (**definição**) 🔂 *high definition television* (= television that gives a very clear image) (**televisão de alta definição**)

defuse

definitive /dɪˈfɪnɪtɪv/ ADJECTIVE
1 very certain and not likely to change (**definitivo, final**) 🔂 *a definitive answer* (**resposta final**)
2 better than any others ☐ *You should read Sherwin's definitive book on this subject.* (**final**)

- **definitively** /dɪˈfɪnɪtɪvli/ ADVERB in a definitive way ☐ *I can't say definitively that this treatment will work.* (**de modo decisivo**)

deflate /dɪˈfleɪt/ VERB [**deflates, deflating, deflated**]
1 to let the air out of a tyre, balloon, etc. (**esvaziar**)
2 to make someone feel less confident ☐ *He felt deflated after losing the match.* (**diminuir**)

deflect /dɪˈflekt/ VERB [**deflects, deflecting, deflected**]
1 deflect attention/blame, etc. to direct attention/blame, etc. away from yourself ☐ *The government is trying to deflect attention away from its recent failures.* (**desviar atenção, culpa etc.**)
2 to change the direction that something is moving in ☐ *Craig deflected the ball into the net.* (**desviar**)

deforestation /diːˌfɒrɪˈsteɪʃən/ NOUN, NO PLURAL cutting down the trees in an area (**desmatamento**)

deform /dɪˈfɔːm/ VERB [**deforms, deforming, deformed**] to spoil the shape of something ☐ *He had a disease that deforms your bones.* (**deformar**)

- **deformed** /dɪˈfɔːmd/ ADJECTIVE not shaped in a normal way ☐ *He was born with a deformed arm.* (**deformado**)
- **deformity** /dɪˈfɔːmɪti/ NOUN [plural **deformities**] when something is deformed ☐ *a physical deformity* (**deformidade**)

defraud /dɪˈfrɔːd/ VERB [**defrauds, defrauding, defrauded**] to get money from a business or organization by dishonest actions ☐ *She defrauded the company of $40,000.* (**defraudar**)

defrost /ˌdiːˈfrɒst/ VERB [**defrosts, defrosting, defrosted**]
1 to make frozen food become no longer frozen ☐ *Remember to defrost the chicken for tomorrow's lunch.* (**descongelar**)
2 to remove the ice from a fridge or freezer (= place where frozen food is kept) (**descongelar**)

deft /deft/ ADJECTIVE [**defter, deftest**] quick and skilful ☐ *With a few deft movements she created a paper flower.* (**hábil**)

- **deftly** /ˈdeftli/ ADVERB quickly and skilfully ☐ *Hannah deftly flicked the ball over the net.* (**habilmente**)

defunct /dɪˈfʌŋkt/ ADJECTIVE a formal word that means no longer existing or working ☐ *The company that made this product is now defunct.* (**extinto**)

defuse /ˌdiːˈfjuːz/ VERB [**defuses, defusing, defused**]

defy

1 if you defuse a bomb you remove part of it so that it cannot explode (desarmar)
2 if you defuse a difficult situation you make it more relaxed (acalmar)

defy /dɪˈfaɪ/ VERB [defies, defying, defied]
1 to refuse to obey someone or something □ *Defying his mother, he left the house.* (desafiar)
2 defy gravity to stay up in the air in a way that is not natural □ *These huge planes seem to defy gravity.* (desafiar a gravidade)
3 defy belief/description, etc. to be impossible to believe/describe, etc. □ *It's a story that defies belief.* (desafiar a crença, descrição etc.)
4 defy someone to do something to say that you do not think it is possible for someone to do something □ *I defy you to do that again!* (desafiar alguém a fazer algo)

degenerate ▶ VERB /dɪˈdʒenəreɪt/ [degenerates, degenerating, degenerated] to get worse □ *The situation soon degenerated into chaos.* (degenerar, decair)
▶ ADJECTIVE /dɪˈdʒenərət/ morally bad □ *a degenerate lifestyle* (degenerado)

• **degenerative** /dɪˈdʒenərətɪv/ ADJECTIVE a degenerative disease is one that gradually makes you more and more ill (degenerativo)

degradation /ˌdegrəˈdeɪʃən/ NOUN, NO PLURAL very bad conditions that make people feel ashamed (degradação)

degrade /dɪˈgreɪd/ VERB [degrades, degrading, degraded]
1 to make someone feel that they are not respected □ *She felt dirty and degraded.* (degradar)
2 to change something into a worse state (rebaixar)

• **degrading** /dɪˈgreɪdɪŋ/ ADJECTIVE making a person feel degraded □ *a degrading job* (degradante)

degree /dɪˈgriː/ NOUN [plural **degrees**]
1 a unit for measuring temperature, shown by the symbol ° □ *It's 30° (degrees) here today.* (grau)
2 a unit for measuring angles, shown by the symbol ° □ *An angle of 90° (degrees) is a right angle.* (grau)
3 an amount of something □ *You will have to accept a small degree of hardship.* (parte) ▣ *I agree with her to some degree* (= in part). (em partes) ▣ *Their success depends to a large degree on the teenage market.* (em grande parte)
4 a qualification that students can study for at a university or college □ *He's got a degree in German.* (diploma) ▣ *He did his degree at Cambridge.* (tirou seu diploma)

dehydrate /ˌdiːhaɪˈdreɪt/ VERB [dehydrates, dehydrating, dehydrated] to remove the water from something (desidratar)

• **dehydrated** /ˌdiːhaɪˈdreɪtɪd/ ADJECTIVE
1 weak and ill because you have not had enough water to drink □ *He was severely dehydrated.* (desidratado)

deliberate

2 a dehydrated substance no longer contains water □ *dehydrated food* (desidratado)

• **dehydration** /ˌdiːhaɪˈdreɪʃən/ NOUN, NO PLURAL being dehydrated □ *He was suffering from dehydration.* (desidratação)

deign /deɪn/ VERB [deigns, deigning, deigned] if you deign to do something, you do it although you do not want to □ *He hardly ever deigned to come to my school concerts.* (condescender)

deity /ˈdiːɪti/ NOUN [plural **deities**] a formal word that means a god or goddess (= female god) □ *Jupiter and Juno are Roman deities.* (divindade)

déjà vu /ˌdeɪʒɑːˈvuː/ NOUN, NO PLURAL the feeling that you have experienced exactly the same thing before (déjà-vu)

dejected /dɪˈdʒektɪd/ ADJECTIVE unhappy and disappointed (abatido, desanimado)

• **dejection** /dɪˈdʒekʃən/ NOUN, NO PLURAL when you are dejected (abatimento)

delay /dɪˈleɪ/ ▶ NOUN [plural **delays**] the extra time you have to wait if something happens later than expected □ *There was a delay of half an hour before take-off.* (atraso) ▣ *Please return to your seats without delay.* (sem atraso)
▶ VERB [delays, delaying, delayed]
1 to do something or make something happen later than was planned or expected □ *We delayed our holidays until after the strike.* □ *Buy now! Don't delay!* (atrasar)
2 to make someone or something late □ *I was delayed by the arrival of an unexpected visitor.* (atrasar)

delegate ▶ VERB /ˈdelɪgeɪt/ [delegates, delegating, delegated] to give a job to someone else to do for you (delegar)
▶ NOUN /ˈdelɪgət/ [plural **delegates**] someone who goes to a meeting to represent someone else (delegado, representante)

• **delegation** /ˌdelɪˈgeɪʃən/ NOUN [plural **delegations**] a group of delegates (delegação)

delete /dɪˈliːt/ VERB [deletes, deleting, deleted]
1 to remove something from a piece of writing □ *Someone has deleted your name from the list.* □ *I think we should delete the last paragraph.* (suprimir)
2 to remove something such as a file that is stored on a computer □ *I've accidentally deleted all their addresses.* (excluir)

• **deletion** /dɪˈliːʃən/ NOUN [plural **deletions**] something that has been deleted or the act of deleting something (supressão, eliminação)

deli /ˈdeli/ NOUN [plural **delis**] a short way to say and write **delicatessen** (delicatéssen)

deliberate[1] /dɪˈlɪbərət/ ADJECTIVE done on purpose □ *He said it was an accident, but I'm sure it was deliberate* (deliberado) ▣ *It was a deliberate attempt to confuse his opponent.* (atentado deliberado)

deliberate

deliberate² /dɪˈlɪbəreɪt/ VERB [deliberates, deliberating, deliberated] to think carefully about something □ *They deliberated for three hours over their decision.* (deliberar)

deliberately /dɪˈlɪbərətli/ ADVERB on purpose □ *You deliberately dropped that so that you wouldn't have to eat it!* (deliberadamente)

delicacy /ˈdelɪkəsi/ NOUN [plural delicacies]
1 something to eat that is unusual or expensive □ *These eggs are regarded as a great delicacy here.* (iguaria)
2 *no plural* when something is easy to damage (fragilidade)
3 *no plural* when a flavour, smell, etc. is not strong (delicadeza)
4 *no plural* when a situation needs to be dealt with using great skill in order to avoid making people upset or angry (cortesia)

delicate /ˈdelɪkət/ ADJECTIVE
1 easily damaged □ *This china is very delicate.* (frágil)
2 not strong (suave) 🔲 *a delicate flavour* (sabor suave) 🔲 *a delicate fragrance* (fragrância suave)
3 needing to be treated or done very carefully (delicado) 🔲 *a delicate operation* (uma operação delicada) 🔲 *We must respect the delicate balance between humans and nature.* (equilíbrio delicado) 🔲 *After some delicate negotiations an agreement was reached.* (negociações delicadas)
4 small and attractive □ *delicate fingers* (fino)
5 a delicate person is often ill (sensível)

• **delicately** /ˈdelɪkətli/ ADVERB
1 skilfully (cuidadosamente) 🔲 *She handled the situation very delicately.* (lidou cuidadosamente)
2 delicately balanced in a situation that could easily be damaged (delicadamente equilibrado)
3 carefully and politely □ *She sipped her tea delicately.* (delicadamente)
4 not strongly □ *delicately flavoured* (suavemente)

delicatessen /ˌdelɪkəˈtesən/ NOUN [plural delicatessens] a shop that sells cooked meat, cheese, etc. (delicatéssen)

delicious /dɪˈlɪʃəs/ ADJECTIVE tasting very good (delicioso) 🔲 *Mum's homemade soup tastes absolutely delicious.* (é delicioso) □ *That was a delicious meal.*

• **deliciously** /dɪˈlɪʃəsli/ ADVERB in a delicious way □ *a deliciously creamy dessert* (deliciosamente)

delight /dɪˈlaɪt/ ▶ NOUN [plural delights] great pleasure □ *The baby squealed with delight when he saw his mother.* □ *It was such a delight to see her.* (deleite)
▶ VERB [delights, delighting, delighted] to please someone very much (deleitar)

♦ PHRASAL VERB **delight in something** to get a lot of pleasure from something □ *He seems to delight in pointing out my mistakes.* (ter prazer em fazer algo)

• **delighted** /dɪˈlaɪtɪd/ ADJECTIVE very pleased (encantado) 🔲 *That's great news – I'm absolutely delighted!* (absolutamente encantado) □ *+ to do something We'd be delighted to come to the party.*

• **delightful** /dɪˈlaɪtfʊl/ ADJECTIVE very pleasant □ *What a delightful surprise!* (encantador)

• **delightfully** /dɪˈlaɪtfʊli/ ADVERB in a delightful way □ *a delightfully funny book* (encantadoramente, deliciosamente)

delinquency /dɪˈlɪŋkwənsi/ NOUN, NO PLURAL bad and illegal behaviour (delinquência) 🔲 *juvenile delinquency* (delinquência juvenil)

delinquent /dɪˈlɪŋkwənt/ ▶ NOUN [plural delinquents] someone who behaves badly and illegally (delinquente)
▶ ADJECTIVE behaving badly and illegally □ *a delinquent teenager* (delinquente)

delirious /dɪˈlɪriəs/ ADJECTIVE
1 thinking or speaking in a confused way because you are ill (delirante)
2 extremely happy □ *When he scored the final goal the fans were delirious.* (delirante)

• **deliriously** /dɪˈlɪriəsli/ ADVERB in an extremely happy way (delirantemente) 🔲 *We were deliriously happy.* (muito felizes)

deliver /dɪˈlɪvə(r)/ VERB [delivers, delivering, delivered]
1 to take something, especially letters, packages or something you have bought, to a place □ *We're delivering leaflets to all the houses in this area.* □ *Our new washing machine is being delivered next week.* (entregar)
2 to provide a service □ *Our company delivers training for managers.* (fazer)
3 to do something that you have promised to do (cumprir) 🔲 *The government has failed to deliver the tax cuts it promised.* (falhou em cumprir)
4 if someone delivers a baby, they help the baby to be born (parto)

• **delivery** /dɪˈlɪvəri/ NOUN [plural deliveries]
1 *no plural* when something is delivered (entrega) 🔲 *We took delivery of our new car on Friday.* (recebemos a entrega de) 🔲 *The price includes free delivery.* (entrega grátis)
2 something that has been delivered or will be delivered □ *We are expecting a delivery of bricks.* (entrega)
3 *no plural* the process of providing a service □ *They are responsible for the delivery of healthcare in the region.* (distribuição)
4 when a baby is born □ *It was a straight forward delivery.* (parto)

delta /ˈdeltə/ NOUN [plural deltas] an area of land where a river divides into separate parts before it reaches the sea. A geography word. (delta)

delude /dɪˈluːd/ VERB [deludes, deluding, deluded] to make someone believe something that is not true □ *If he thinks he looks good, he's deluding himself.* (iludir)

• **deluded** /dɪˈluːdɪd/ ADJECTIVE believing

deluge

something that is not true □ *Poor deluded fool!* (**iludido**)

deluge /ˈdeljuːdʒ/ ▶ NOUN [plural **deluges**]
1 a very large amount of something □ *We've had a deluge of complaints.* (**abundância**)
2 a flood or a large amount of rain (**dilúvio**)
▶ VERB [**deluges, deluging, deluged**] if you are deluged with things, you receive a very large number of them □ *We were deluged with entries for our last competition.* (**transbordar**)

delusion /dɪˈluːʒən/ NOUN [plural **delusions**] something that you believe that is not true (**ilusão, desilusão**) 🔁 *She's under the delusion* (= believes wrongly) *that I'm rich.* (**tem a ilusão**)

delve /delv/ VERB [**delves, delving, delved**]
1 to try to find information about something, or to study something carefully □ *This book delves into the details of their business activities.* (**investigar**)
2 to put your hand in a container to try to find something □ *Nan was delving into her handbag for her purse.* (**procurar dentro**)

demand /dɪˈmɑːnd/ ▶ VERB [**demands, demanding, demanded**]
1 to ask for something in a forceful way that shows you do not expect to be refused □ *They are demanding the release of all political prisoners.* (**exigir**) 🔁 *He demanded an apology from the journalist.* (**exigiu desculpas**) □ *+ to do something* *I demanded to see the manager.* □ *+ that* *The group is demanding that the law should be changed.*
2 to need something □ *Her career demands total commitment.* □ *The sport demands a high level of fitness.* (**ter necessidade de, necessitar**)
▶ NOUN [plural **demands**]
1 when someone asks for something in a very forceful way □ *+ for* *I gave in to his demands for a new computer.* (**exigência**) 🔁 *Employers say they can't meet the union's demands.* (**atendeu às exigências**)
2 *no plural* a need or wish for goods or services (**demanda**) □ *+ for* *There is not much demand for sun cream at this time of year.* (**demanda**) 🔁 *We do not have enough stock to meet the demand.* (**atender às demandas**)
3 in demand wanted by a lot of people □ *His legal skills are in demand all over the world.* (**muito procurado**)
4 make demands on someone/something to be difficult for someone, or to use up a lot of something □ *Her charity work makes great demands on her time.* □ *The growing number of elderly people is making huge demands on the health service.* (**exigir grande quantidade de algo/alguém**)
5 on demand when you want or need something □ *She thinks the drug should be available on demand.* (**a pedido**)

• **demanding** /dɪˈmɑːndɪŋ/ ADJECTIVE

demolish

1 needing a lot of time or effort □ *a very demanding job* (**exigente**) 🔁 *The sport is physically demanding.* (**fisicamente exigente**)
2 wanting or needing a lot of attention □ *She has a demanding job in the city.* □ *Toddlers can be extremely demanding.* (**exigente**)

demean /dɪˈmiːn/ VERB [**demeans, demeaning, demeaned**] **demean yourself** to behave in a way that makes people respect you less □ *I would not demean myself by arguing about money.* (**rebaixar-se**)

• **demeaning** /dɪˈmiːnɪŋ/ ADJECTIVE making you feel that people do not respect you □ *a demeaning job* □ *The new TV show is demeaning to women.* (**degradante**)

demeanor /dɪˈmiːnə(r)/ NOUN, NO PLURAL the US spelling of **demeanour** (**conduta**)

demeanour /dɪˈmiːnə(r)/ NOUN, NO PLURAL the way someone looks and behaves □ *Something in his demeanour made me suspicious.* (**conduta**)

demented /dɪˈmentɪd/ ADJECTIVE mad or mentally ill □ *Her poor mother was demented with worry.* (**demente**)

dementia /dɪˈmenʃə/ NOUN, NO PLURAL a medical condition, especially in old people, in which they gradually lose their memory and mental abilities □ *She is suffering from dementia.* (**demência**)

demise /dɪˈmaɪz/ NOUN, NO PLURAL the death of a person or the end of something □ *Are we seeing the demise of the health service?* (**fim, falência**)

democracy /dɪˈmɒkrəsi/ NOUN [plural **democracies**]
1 *no plural* a form of government where people elect their leaders □ *The allies plan to introduce democracy to the country.* (**democracia**)
2 a country that has this form of government □ *We live in a democracy.* (**democracia**)

• **democrat** /ˈdeməkræt/ NOUN [plural **democrats**]
1 someone who believes in democracy (**democrata**)
2 Democrat someone who supports the Democratic Party in the US (**democrata**)

• **democratic** /ˌdeməˈkrætɪk/ ADJECTIVE
1 based on the system of democracy □ *democratic elections* (**democrático**)
2 based on a system where everyone has an equal right to make a decision □ *It was a democratic decision to move abroad.* (**democrático**)

demolish /dɪˈmɒlɪʃ/ VERB [**demolishes, demolishing, demolished**]
1 to destroy something, especially a building □ *The flats will be demolished immediately.* (**demolir**)
2 to show that someone's opinions are wrong □ *She demolished all their arguments.* (**destruir**)
3 to defeat someone completely □ *They absolutely demolished their opponents.* (**arruinar**)

- **demolition** /ˌdeməˈlɪʃən/ NOUN, NO PLURAL when something is demolished □ *We watched the demolition of the old sports centre.* (demolição)

demon /ˈdiːmən/ NOUN [plural **demons**] an evil spirit (demônio)

demonstrable /dɪˈmɒnstrəbəl/ ADJECTIVE that can be proved or shown □ *Sadly, Susan has made no demonstrable progress this year.* (demonstrável)

- **demonstrably** /dɪˈmɒnstrəblɪ/ ADVERB in a way that can be shown or proved □ *The old teaching method is demonstrably better.* (demonstravelmente, demonstrativamente)

demonstrate /ˈdemənstreɪt/ VERB [**demonstrates, demonstrating, demonstrated**]
1 to show that something exists or is true (demonstrar) □ *Katie's exam results clearly demonstrate the importance of good preparation.* □ *Her success demonstrates that women can do well in business.* (demonstra claramente)
2 to show someone how to do something or how something works □ *Can you demonstrate how the ice cream maker works?* (mostrar)
3 to show that you have a particular feeling, quality or skill □ *Ben has demonstrated no interest in the project.* □ *She demonstrates a total lack of respect for authority.* (manifestar)
4 to march or stand with a group of other people to show that you support or disagree with something □ *They are demonstrating against the war.* (manifestar-se)

- **demonstration** /ˌdemənˈstreɪʃən/ NOUN [plural **demonstrations**]
1 an event where a group of people stand or march together to show that they support or disagree with something (manifestação) □ *Supporters of the prisoners held a demonstration outside the court* (fizeram uma manifestação) □ *Over 5,000 people took part in the demonstration.* (participaram da manifestação) □ + *against They organized a peaceful demonstration against the war.*
2 when someone shows you how to do something or how something works □ *a cookery demonstration* (demonstração) □ *The sales assistant gave us a demonstration of the phone's features.* (deu uma demonstração)
3 proof that something exists or is true □ *This attack is a clear demonstration of the need for stricter laws.* (prova)

- **demonstrative** /dɪˈmɒnstrətɪv/ ADJECTIVE a demonstrative person is happy to show and express their feelings (expansivo)

- **demonstrator** /ˈdemənstreɪtə(r)/ NOUN [plural **demonstrators**]
1 someone who takes part in a demonstration for or against something □ *Demonstrators marched through the city.* (protestante)
2 someone who shows people how something works or how to do something □ *She works as a demonstrator in the kitchen department.* (demonstrador)

demoralize or **demoralise** /dɪˈmɒrəlaɪz/ VERB [**demoralizes, demoralizing, demoralized**] to make someone feel less confident about doing something □ *The defeat had completely demoralized the team.* (desmoralizar)

demote /diːˈməʊt/ VERB [**demotes, demoting, demoted**] to give someone a less important and usually worse paid job (degradar, rebaixar)

- **demotion** /diːˈməʊʃən/ NOUN [plural **demotions**] when someone is demoted (rebaixamento)

demure /dɪˈmjʊə(r)/ ADJECTIVE quiet and shy (reservado)

den /den/ NOUN [plural **dens**]
1 the home of a wild animal □ *a lion's den* (covil)
2 a place like a room that children make or find to play in □ *We've made a den in the woods.* (toca)

denial /dɪˈnaɪəl/ NOUN [plural **denials**]
1 when you say that something is not true □ *He repeated his denial of his guilt.* (recusa)
2 in denial when you refuse to accept that something unpleasant has happened □ *He's still in denial about his wife's death.* (em negação)
3 when someone is not allowed to do or have something □ *Keeping him in prison without trial is a denial of natural justice.* (renúncia)

denim /ˈdenɪm/ NOUN, NO PLURAL a strong cotton cloth, usually blue, that is used to make clothes □ *Joe was wearing a denim jacket.* (brim)

denominator /dɪˈnɒmɪneɪtə(r)/ NOUN [plural **denominators**] the number below the line in a fraction. A maths word. (denominador)

denounce /dɪˈnaʊns/ VERB [**denounces, denouncing, denounced**] to say publicly that something is bad or that someone has done something bad □ *He was denounced as a liar.* (denúncia)

dense /dens/ ADJECTIVE [**denser, densest**]
1 containing a lot of people or things very close together □ *a dense forest* (denso)
2 thick and difficult to see through □ *Dense fog filled the valley.* (denso)
3 an informal word meaning stupid □ *Are you being deliberately dense?* (estúpido)

- **densely** /ˈdenslɪ/ ADVERB densely inhabited/populated having a lot of people living there (densamente populoso/habitado)

- **density** /ˈdensɪtɪ/ NOUN [plural **densities**]
1 the number of people or things in a place □ *Population densities are low in this area.* (densidade)
2 how thick something is (espessura)
3 a measurement of a solid, gas or liquid which measures its mass compared to its volume. A physics word. (densidade)

dent /dent/ ▶ NOUN [plural **dents**]
1 a hollow in a hard surface where it has been hit □ *There's a dent in the car bumper.* (cavidade)
2 a reduction in the amount of something □ *These wind farms could make a big dent in our carbon emissions.* (redução)

dental

▶ VERB [dents, denting, dented]
1 to damage something or to reduce the amount of something □ *The injury has really dented her confidence.* (danificar)
2 to make a dent in something □ *I'm sorry but I think I've dented your car.* (amassar)

dental /ˈdentəl/ ADJECTIVE to do with teeth □ *Children get free dental care.* (dental)

dentist /ˈdentɪst/ NOUN [plural **dentists**] someone whose job is to look after people's teeth (dentista)

• **dentistry** /ˈdentɪstri/ NOUN, NO PLURAL
1 the work of a dentist (odontologia)
2 the study of teeth and the mouth □ *a degree in dentistry* (odontologia)

dentures /ˈdentʃəz/ PLURAL NOUN a set of artificial teeth (dentadura)

deny /dɪˈnaɪ/ VERB [denies, denying, denied]
1 to say that something is not true □ + *that Nina denied that she had stolen the bag.* □ + *ing He denies doing anything wrong.* □ *She denied any involvement in the crime.* (negar)
2 to not allow someone to have something or do something □ *She has been denied access to her children.* (recusar)

deodorant /diːˈəʊdərənt/ NOUN [plural **deodorants**] a substance that you put on your body to stop unpleasant smells (desodorante)

depart /dɪˈpɑːt/ VERB [departs, departing, departed] to leave a place, especially to start a journey □ *Flight BA123 is now departing.* □ + *from The Oxford train departs from platform 8.* (partir)

department /dɪˈpɑːtmənt/ NOUN [plural **departments**] a part of a school, shop, business or government that deals with a particular subject or area of work □ *the sales department* □ *The college has a very fine modern languages department.* (departamento)

• **departmental** /ˌdiːpɑːtˈmentəl/ ADJECTIVE to do with a department □ *our departmental secretary* (departamental)

department store /dɪˈpɑːtmənt ˌstɔː(r)/ NOUN [plural **department stores**] a large shop that has different departments which sell different types of product (loja de departamentos)

departure /dɪˈpɑːtʃə(r)/ NOUN [plural **departures**]
1 when someone or something leaves a place □ *All departures are shown on the left of the timetable.* □ *We were shocked by her sudden departure from the school.* (partida)
2 a change from what is usual □ *This novel is a complete departure from his normal style.* (mudança)

depend /dɪˈpend/ VERB [depends, depending, depended] **it/that depends** used to say that you are not certain because something else affects the situation □ *'Do you want to come to the film?' 'It depends how late it goes on.'* □ *'Are you going to invite Rick?' 'That depends. I think he's still angry with me.'* (depender)

◆ PHRASAL VERB **depend on someone/something**
1 to need the help of someone or something □ *Millions of children depend on charity for their education.* □ *The farm depends on government subsidies.* (contar com)
2 if what happens depends on something else, it is affected by it and may change because of it □ *A lot will depend on how well you do in your exams.* □ *The outcome of the election depends on which party wins the voters' trust.* (depender de)
3 to be able to trust someone to do what you want or need □ *I know I can depend on my family to help me.* (confiar em)

• **dependable** /dɪˈpendəbəl/ ADJECTIVE able to be trusted to do what you want or need □ *Our staff are very dependable.* (de confiança)

• **dependant** /dɪˈpendənt/ NOUN [plural **dependants**] someone whose food, clothes, house, etc. you have to pay for □ *Fill in the names of all your dependants.* (dependente)

• **dependence** /dɪˈpendəns/ or **dependency** /dɪˈpendənsi/ NOUN, NO PLURAL when someone cannot live or manage without something □ *Our society needs to reduce its dependence on fossil fuels.* □ *alcohol dependency* (dependência)

• **dependent** /dɪˈpendənt/ ▶ ADJECTIVE
1 needing something or someone to live or exist □ *She's totally dependent on her car to get around.* (dependente)
2 dependent on something if something is dependent on something else, it is affected by it and may be changed by it □ *Getting into university is totally dependent on my exam results.* (dependente de algo)
▶ NOUN [plural **dependents**] the US spelling of dependant (dependente)

depict /dɪˈpɪkt/ VERB [depicts, depicting, depicted] to show or describe something in a picture or story □ *The novel depicts the struggle to survive in Victorian London.* (representar)

deplete /dɪˈpliːt/ VERB [depletes, depleting, depleted] to reduce the amount of something, so that little is left □ *Our food stocks were being depleted.* (esgotar)

deplorable /dɪˈplɔːrəbəl/ ADJECTIVE very bad and shocking □ *Some families are still living in deplorable conditions.* (deplorável)

deplore /dɪˈplɔː(r)/ VERB [deplores, deploring, deplored] to say or think that something is very bad or shocking □ *The President said he deplored the use of violence.* (deplorar)

deploy /dɪˈplɔɪ/ VERB [deploys, deploying, deployed] if soldiers or weapons are deployed, they are sent to a place to be used □ *Troops have* been deployed along the border. (**dispor em formação de combate**)

- **deployment** /dɪˈplɔɪmənt/ NOUN, NO PLURAL when soldiers or weapons are deployed (**disposição em formação de combate**)

deport /dɪˈpɔːt/ VERB [**deports, deporting, deported**] to force a foreign person to leave a country □ *He will be deported when he finishes his prison sentence.* (**deportar, expulsar**)

- **deportation** /ˌdiːpɔːˈteɪʃən/ NOUN [*plural* **deportations**] when a foreign person is forced to leave a country □ *Several refugees now face deportation.* (**deportação**)

depose /dɪˈpəʊz/ VERB [**deposes, deposing, deposed**] to remove the leader of a country from their position □ *The president has been deposed.* (**destituir**)

deposit /dɪˈpɒzɪt/ ▶ NOUN [*plural* **deposits**]
1 part of the price of something that you pay before you buy the thing, and that you will lose if you do not buy it (**depósito, sinal**) 🔲 *We've put down a deposit on a flat.* (**fizemos um depósito**)
2 an amount of money that you pay into a bank account (**depósito**) 🔲 *He made several large deposits.* (**fez depósitos**)
3 an amount of money that you pay when you rent something, that you get back if you return the thing without any damage (**depósito, sinal**)
4 a layer of a substance that has developed naturally or in a chemical process □ *coal deposits* □ *deposits of natural gas* (**sedimento**)
▶ VERB [**deposits, depositing, deposited**]
1 to put something down or to leave something or someone somewhere □ *They were fed up with people depositing rubbish in their garden.* □ *We deposited the children with my mother.* (**deixar**)
2 to put money into a bank account □ *I'm hoping to deposit £50 a month into a savings account.* (**depositar**)
3 to leave a layer of a substance behind □ *The overflowing river deposited a thick layer of mud in the village.* (**sedimentar**)

deposit account /dɪˈpɒzɪt əˌkaʊnt/ NOUN [*plural* **deposit accounts**] a bank account that you use to save money in (**conta poupança**)

depot /ˈdepəʊ/ NOUN [*plural* **depots**]
1 a place where vehicles like buses or trains are kept when they are not being used (**garagem**)
2 a building where goods are stored □ *a weapons depot* (**armazém**)
3 a US word for a bus or train station (**estação ferroviária/rodoviária**)

depraved /dɪˈpreɪvd/ ADJECTIVE morally bad □ *The judge described the book as the work of a depraved mind.* (**depravado, corrompido**)

- **depravity** /dɪˈprævəti/ NOUN, NO PLURAL the state of being morally bad (**depravação, corrupção**)

depreciate /dɪˈpriːʃieɪt/ VERB [**depreciates, depreciating, depreciated**] to become less valuable □ *New cars depreciate very quickly.* (**depreciar**)

- **depreciation** /dɪˌpriːʃiˈeɪʃən/ NOUN, NO PLURAL when something depreciates (**depreciação**)

depress /dɪˈpres/ VERB [**depresses, depressing, depressed**]
1 to make someone feel unhappy □ *It depresses me to think of how much work we still have to do.* (**deprimir**)
2 to make a business or the economy less successful or prices lower □ *Poor sales have depressed the value of the company's shares.* (**decrescer**)
3 a formal word meaning to press something down □ *Depress the brake gently.* (**comprimir, pressionar**)

- **depressed** /dɪˈprest/ ADJECTIVE
1 unhappy □ *I felt a bit depressed about how much weight I'd put on.* (**deprimido**)
2 suffering from depression □ *After my son was born I was depressed.* (**deprimido**)
3 a depressed area or economy does not have enough businesses or jobs □ *In recent months the housing market has become depressed.* (**rebaixado**)

- **depressing** /dɪˈpresɪŋ/ ADJECTIVE making a person feel unhappy □ *This dull weather is so depressing.* (**deprimente**)

- **depression** /dɪˈpreʃən/ NOUN [*plural* **depressions**]
1 *no plural* an illness where you feel unhappy for a long time (**depressão**) 🔲 *He was suffering from depression at the time.* (**sofrendo de depressão**)
2 a period when the economy is in a bad state and a lot of people do not have a job □ *There is no hope of a quick end to the economic depression.* (**depressão**)
3 a formal word for a hollow area of a surface □ *Water was collecting in the depressions in the path.* (**fenda, depressão**)

deprivation /ˌdeprɪˈveɪʃən/ NOUN, NO PLURAL when someone does not have the basic things that they need □ *They live in conditions of extreme deprivation.* (**privação**)

deprive /dɪˈpraɪv/ VERB [**deprives, depriving, deprived**] to take something important or necessary away from someone □ *She's been deprived of sleep for days.* (**privar**)

- **deprived** /dɪˈpraɪvd/ ADJECTIVE not having all the things that are necessary for a normal life □ *They are working in the most deprived areas of the city* (**carente, desprovido**)

depth /depθ/ NOUN [*plural* **depths**] (**deprimente**)
1 the distance from the top to the bottom of something □ *This instrument measures the depth of the water.* □ **+ of** *We dug down to a depth of around 2 metres.* □ *The swimming pool was only 2 metres in depth.* (**profundidade**)
2 the distance from the front to the back of something □ *We need to increase the depth of the shelves.* (**largura**)

deputize

3 *no plural* how much someone knows or feels about something □ *He surprised the examiners with the depth of his knowledge.* (**profundidade**)
4 in depth in a lot of detail □ *We discussed the situation in great depth.* (**a fundo**)
5 the depths of something (a) a position that is very deep or very far from the edge of something □ *Divers cannot explore the depths of the ocean.* (b) the worst part of an emotion (**em profundo**) 🔹 *He is in the depths of despair about his job.* (**em profundo desespero**)
6 your depth the level of water that is not too deep for you to stand up in □ *Don't go out of your depth.* (**sua altura**)

◆ IDIOM **out of your depth** not having the knowledge or experience to understand or deal with a situation □ *He had looked after animals before, but he was out of his depth with lions.* (**fora de sua capacidade**)

deputize *or* **deputise** /ˈdepjʊtaɪz/ VERB [deputizes, deputizing, deputized] to do someone's job for a short time while they are away □ *Mrs Henderson was deputizing for the Principal that week.* (**substituir alguém**)

deputy /ˈdepjʊti/ NOUN [plural **deputies**] someone who has the job that is next in importance to another job □ *He is deputy sales manager.* (**substituto**)

derail /dɪˈreɪl/ VERB [derails, derailing, derailed] if a train derails or is derailed, it comes off the track (**descarrilar**)

• **derailment** /dɪˈreɪlmənt/ NOUN [plural **derailments**] when a train comes off the track (**descarrilamento**)

deranged /dɪˈreɪndʒd/ ADJECTIVE not normal in your behaviour, suggesting that you are mentally ill (**demente, louco**)

derby /ˈdɑːbi/ NOUN [plural **derbies**] a sports match between two teams from the same town or area (**clássico**) 🔹 *a local derby* (**um clássico local**)

deregulate /diːˈregjʊleɪt/ VERB [deregulates, deregulating, deregulated] to remove rules, especially in business □ *The industry has been deregulated.* (**desregulamentar**)

• **deregulation** /ˌdiːregjʊˈleɪʃən/ NOUN, NO PLURAL when something, especially a business, is deregulated (**desregulamentação**)

derelict /ˈderəlɪkt/ ADJECTIVE not now used and in bad condition □ *a derelict factory* (**abandonado**)

deride /dɪˈraɪd/ VERB [derides, deriding, derided] to show you think that someone or something is stupid and does not deserve respect. A formal word. □ *The film was derided by critics.* (**menosprezar, ridicularizar**)

• **derision** /dɪˈrɪʒən/ NOUN, NO PLURAL laughter or remarks which deride someone or something □ *At this comment there were shouts of derision from the crowd.* (**menosprezo**)

describe

derive /dɪˈraɪv/
◆ PHRASAL VERB [derives, deriving, derived] **derive something from something**
1 to get something, especially a good feeling, from something □ *He derives a lot of pleasure from his grandchildren.* (**tirar algo**)
2 to be developed from something or made from a part of something □ *The substance is derived from corn.* (**obter**)

dermis /ˈdɜːmɪs/ NOUN, NO PLURAL the layer of skin that is just under the outer layer. A biology word. (**derme**)

derogatory /dɪˈrɒɡətəri/ ADJECTIVE saying something bad about someone or something (**depreciativo**) 🔹 *a derogatory comment* (**comentário depreciativo**) 🔹 *a derogatory term* (**termo depreciativo**)

derrick /ˈderɪk/ NOUN [plural **derricks**]
1 a crane (= machine for lifting heavy things), especially at a port (**guindaste**)
2 a tower over an oil well that lifts equipment (**torre de perfuração**)

descend /dɪˈsend/ VERB [descends, descending, descended]
1 a formal word meaning to go or climb down □ *They descended the stairs.* □ *The road descended steeply.* (**descer**)
2 a formal word meaning to start to exist or happen (**sobrevir**) 🔹 *A silence descended on the room.* (**silêncio sobreveio**) 🔹 *As darkness descended, it grew colder.* (**escuridão sobreveio**)

◆ PHRASAL VERBS **descend from someone** if you are descended from someone, you come after them in the same family □ *He was descended from an Irish farming family.* (**descender de alguém**)
descend into something to become worse and end in a bad state □ *The country is descending into civil war.* (**transformar em algo**)

• **descendant** /dɪˈsendənt/ NOUN [plural **descendants**] someone who is descended from a person who lived in the past □ *a direct descendant of Genghis Khan* (**descendente**)

• **descending** /dɪˈsendɪŋ/ ADJECTIVE in order from the highest or most important to the lowest or least important (**decrescente**) 🔹 *They were arranged in descending order of height.* (**em ordem decrescente**)

• **descent** /dɪˈsent/ NOUN [plural **descents**]
1 a movement down □ *the descent of the mountain* □ *The plane started its descent.* (**descida**)
2 the origin of your family □ *a Frenchman of North African descent* (**descendência**)
3 a slow change to a bad state or situation □ *the country's descent into anarchy* (**declínio**)

describe /dɪˈskraɪb/ VERB [describes, describing, described] to say what happened or what someone or something is like □ *A reporter described the scene in detail.* □ *+ question word*

Can you describe what you saw? □ **+ as** *He described his daughter as kind and caring.* (**descrever**) 🔁 *She describes herself as a feminist.* (ela se descreve como)

- **description** /dɪˈskrɪpʃən/ NOUN [*plural* **descriptions**]

1 when you describe someone or something □ **+ of** *There's a description of the hotel.* (**descrição**) 🔁 *She gave a detailed description of the man.* (**fez uma descrição**) 🔁 *He fitted the general description of the attacker* (= his appearance was the same as what was described). (**encaixa-se na descrição**) 🔁 *a job description* (**descrição do trabalho**)

2 a type (**tipo**) 🔁 *Goods of all descriptions can be bought there.* (**de todos os tipos**)

- **descriptive** /dɪˈskrɪptɪv/ ADJECTIVE describing someone or something □ *a descriptive poem* (**descritivo**)

desert¹ /dɪˈzɜːt/ VERB [**deserts, deserting, deserted**] to go away and leave someone or something, especially the army □ *The soldier was shot for deserting.* □ *She deserted her young family.* (**desertar**)

desert² /ˈdezət/ NOUN [*plural* **deserts**] an area of land where it rains very little so the ground is very dry □ *the Sahara desert* (**deserto**)

desert island /ˌdezət ˈaɪlənd/ NOUN [*plural* **desert islands**] a tropical island where nobody lives (**ilha deserta**)

deserve /dɪˈzɜːv/ VERB [**deserves, deserving, deserved**] if you deserve something, you should have it because of your behaviour □ *I'm pleased Molly won the prize – she deserves it.* □ **+ to do something** *Samir deserves to be promoted.* (**merecer**)

- **deservedly** /dɪˈzɜːvɪdli/ ADVERB in a way which is deserved □ *It has become very popular and deservedly so.* (**merecidamente**)

- **deserving** /dɪˈzɜːvɪŋ/ ADJECTIVE worth supporting or helping 🔁 *a deserving cause* (**merecedor, digno**)

desiccated /ˈdesɪkeɪtɪd/ ADJECTIVE dried □ *desiccated coconut* (**desidratado**)

design /dɪˈzaɪn/ ▶ VERB [**designs, designing, designed**]

1 to plan something before it is built or made □ *The concert hall was designed by architect Frank Gehry.* □ *She designs clothes for a top fashion store.* □ *We design software to control robots.* (**projetar**)

2 if something is designed for a particular purpose, it is made to do that thing □ **+ to do something** *The paths are designed to encourage people to walk more.* □ **+ for** *The equipment is designed for use in schools.* (**planejar**)

▶ NOUN [*plural* **designs**]

1 the way in which something is planned before it is made □ **+ of** *We have improved the design of the aircraft.* □ *She has won awards for her innovative designs.* (**projeto**)

2 *no plural* the process of designing something new (**projeto**) 🔁 *The company specializes in interior design.* (**projeto interior**) 🔁 *She studied art and graphic design.* (**projeto gráfico**)

3 a plan or drawing of something that could be made □ **+ for** *a design for a new racing car* (**desenho, modelo**)

4 a pattern □ *They wore dresses in bright floral designs.* (**padrão**)

designate /ˈdezɪgneɪt/ VERB [**designates, designating, designated**] to choose someone or something for a particular purpose. A formal word. (**designar**) □ *The area is designated as a wildlife reserve.*

designer /dɪˈzaɪnə(r)/ ▶ NOUN [*plural* **designers**] someone whose job is to design things (**projetista, desenhista**) 🔁 *a fashion designer* (**desenhista de moda**) □ *a web designer*
▶ ADJECTIVE expensive and fashionable and made by a famous company □ *designer clothes* □ *designer sunglasses* (**designer**)

desirable /dɪˈzaɪərəbəl/ ADJECTIVE very good or attractive and wanted by many people □ *They live in a very desirable area.* (**agradável**)

desire /dɪˈzaɪə(r)/ ▶ NOUN [*plural* **desires**] a strong feeling of wanting something (**desejo**) 🔁 *He had a burning desire* (= very much wanted) *to become a doctor.* (**grande desejo**) □ *We respect his desire for privacy.*

▶ VERB [**desires, desiring, desired**]

1 a formal word meaning to want something very much □ *You can have any model you desire.* (**desejar**)

2 if desired if you want □ *Add more salt if desired.* (**se desejar**)

- **desired** /dɪˈzaɪəd/ ADJECTIVE wanted or intended (**desejado**) 🔁 *His approach had the desired effect.* (**efeito desejado**) □ *Turn the water to the desired temperature.*

desk /desk/ NOUN [*plural* **desks**]

1 a table for writing or working at (**mesa de trabalho, escrivaninha**) 🔁 *Andrew sat at his desk.* (**em sua mesa**) □ *There was a big pile of papers on her desk.*

2 a place in a building where you can get information or a service (**balcão**) 🔁 *We went to the reception desk.* (**balcão de recepção**) 🔁 *a check-in desk* (**balcão de check-in**)

desktop /ˈdesktɒp/ NOUN [*plural* **desktops**] a computer screen that shows the icons (= small pictures) for programs you can use. A computing word. (**computador de mesa**)

desolate /ˈdesələt/ ADJECTIVE

1 a desolate place has no people in it □ *a desolate landscape* (**abandonado**)

2 very unhappy □ *She looked utterly desolate.* (**desolado**)

despair 211 **destroy**

- **desolation** /ˌdesəˈleɪʃən/ NOUN, NO PLURAL
1 a feeling of great sadness □ *She felt a sense of grief and desolation.* (desolação)
2 the quality of being completely empty (desolado)

despair /dɪˈspeə(r)/ ▶ NOUN, NO PLURAL a feeling of having no hope (desespero) 🔲 *We were in deep despair.* (profundo desespero) 🔲 *There's a growing sense of despair among local people.* (sensação de desespero)
▶ VERB [despairs, despairing, despaired] to feel that you have no hope □ *He despaired of ever seeing his son again.* (desesperar-se)

- **despairing** /dɪˈspeərɪŋ/ ADJECTIVE feeling despair □ *She gave me a despairing look.* (desesperador)

despatch /dɪˈspætʃ/ VERB [despatches, despatching, despatched] another spelling of dispatch (despachar)

desperate /ˈdespərət/ ADJECTIVE
1 feeling very worried and that you will do anything to improve your situation □ *She was becoming increasingly desperate.* (desesperado) 🔲 *He made a last desperate attempt to escape.* (tentativa desesperada)
2 needing something very much □ *Farmers are desperate for workers.* □ *He was desperate to win.* (desesperado)
3 extremely bad or serious (desesperador) 🔲 *a desperate situation* (situação desesperadora) 🔲 *They are in desperate need of financial assistance.* (necessidade desesperadora)

- **desperately** /ˈdespərətli/ ADVERB
1 extremely or very much □ *a desperately difficult situation* □ *We're all desperately disappointed.* (excessivamente)
2 showing that you feel desperate □ *She searched desperately for hours.* (desesperadamente)

- **desperation** /ˌdespəˈreɪʃən/ NOUN, NO PLURAL a feeling that you will do anything to improve your situation □ *In desperation, she called the doctor.* (desespero)

despicable /dɪˈspɪkəbəl/ ADJECTIVE very bad or cruel □ *a despicable crime* □ *His behaviour was absolutely despicable.* (desprezível)

despise /dɪˈspaɪz/ VERB [despises, despising, despised] to hate someone or something very much □ *The two men despised each other.* (desprezo)

despite /dɪˈspaɪt/ PREPOSITION used to say that something happens or is true, even though something else makes it seem unlikely □ *Despite the rain, we enjoyed the picnic.* (apesar de) 🔲 *I think that she'll be very good, despite the fact that she doesn't have much experience.* (apesar do fato de) □ *+ ing The team remained positive, despite losing their first two games.*

despondency /dɪˈspɒndənsi/ NOUN, NO PLURAL a feeling of being unhappy and having no interest or enthusiasm □ *There was an air of despondency at home.* (desânimo)

- **despondent** /dɪˈspɒndənt/ ADJECTIVE feeling despondency □ *He became despondent about the future.* (desanimado)

despot /ˈdespɒt/ NOUN [plural **despots**] a leader who keeps all the power for himself or herself and who behaves cruelly (tirano)

dessert /dɪˈzɜːt/ NOUN [plural **desserts**] sweet food eaten at the end of a meal □ *We had ice cream for dessert.* (sobremesa)

dessertspoon /dɪˈzɜːtspuːn/ NOUN [plural **dessertspoons**]
1 medium-sized spoon used for eating (colher de sobremesa)
2 the amount that a dessertspoon can hold □ *Add three dessertspoons of sugar.* (colher de sobremesa)

destination /ˌdestɪˈneɪʃən/ NOUN [plural **destinations**] the place someone is travelling to (destino) 🔲 *We were very tired when we finally reached our destination.* (chegamos ao nosso destino) 🔲 *The town is a popular tourist destination.* (destino de turistas)

destined /ˈdestɪnd/ ADJECTIVE if something is destined, it will certainly happen □ *She is destined to become a star.* (destinado)

- **destiny** /ˈdestɪni/ NOUN [plural **destinies**]
1 what will happen to someone in the future □ *I believe we can control our own destinies.* (destino)
2 a power that some people believe controls what happens to you (destino)

destitute /ˈdestɪtjuːt/ ADJECTIVE with no money, food or a place to live □ *The family were left destitute.* (necessitado)

- **destitution** /ˌdestɪˈtjuːʃən/ NOUN, NO PLURAL the state of being destitute (privação)

destroy /dɪˈstrɔɪ/ VERB [destroys, destroying, destroyed]
1 to damage something so badly that it no longer exists or cannot be used □ *Thousands of homes were destroyed by the earthquake.* □ *A fire destroyed dozens of paintings at the museum.* (destruir)
2 to kill an animal □ *Cattle on the infected farm had to be destroyed.* (exterminar)

- **destroyer** /dɪˈstrɔɪə(r)/ NOUN [plural **destroyers**]
1 someone who destroys something (destruidor)
2 a fast military ship (destróier)

- **destruction** /dɪˈstrʌkʃən/ NOUN, NO PLURAL when something is destroyed □ *+ of We need to stop the destruction of the rainforest.* □ *The storms caused widespread destruction.* (destruição)

- **destructive** /dɪˈstrʌktɪv/ ADJECTIVE doing a lot of damage or harm □ *The next storm was even more destructive.* □ *Jealousy can be very destructive within a marriage.* (destrutivo)

detach /dɪˈtætʃ/ VERB [detaches, detaching, detached] to separate one thing from another □ *You can detach the hood from the jacket.* (separar)

• **detached** /dɪˈtætʃt/ ADJECTIVE
1 a detached house is not joined to another building (isolado)
2 a detached person is not involved or interested in something □ *He felt a bit detached from what was going on.* (imparcial)

• **detachment** /dɪˈtætʃmənt/ NOUN [plural detachments]
1 a feeling that you are not involved in something (imparcialidade)
2 a group of soldiers doing a particular job □ *a small detachment of troops* (destacamento)

detail /ˈdiːteɪl/ ▶ NOUN [plural details]
1 a small part, fact or piece of information about something □ + *of* *They provided details of the plans.* □ + *about* *We learnt more details about the incident.* (detalhe) 🔲 *For further details, see our website.* (para mais detalhes) 🔲 *She didn't give any details.* (deu detalhes)
2 in detail including all the information or facts about something □ *She described in detail what had happened.* □ *We need to examine it in detail.* (detalhadamente)
3 go into detail to mention all the facts or information about something □ *I can't go into detail at the moment.* (entrar em detalhes)
▶ VERB [details, detailing, detailed] to list all the details of something □ *The invoice detailed everything he spent on materials.*

• **detailed** /ˈdiːteɪld/ ADJECTIVE including all the facts or the smallest parts of something (detalhar) 🔲 *Can you send me detailed information about the trip?* (informações detalhadas) 🔲 *a detailed description* (descrição detalhada) □ *a detailed drawing*

detain /dɪˈteɪn/ VERB [detains, detaining, detained]
1 to make someone stay somewhere □ *He was detained by the police for 24 hours.* (deter)
2 a formal word meaning to delay someone □ *I'm sorry to have detained you.* (reter)

detect /dɪˈtekt/ VERB [detects, detecting, detected]
1 to discover something that is difficult to find □ *The dogs are trained to detect explosives.* □ *The test can detect cancer at an early stage.* (detectar)
2 to notice something □ *I detected a hint of annoyance in his voice.* (perceber)

• **detection** /dɪˈtekʃən/ NOUN, NO PLURAL finding or noticing things □ *Early detection of this illness is very important.* (descoberta)

• **detective** /dɪˈtektɪv/ NOUN [plural detectives] someone whose job is to try to find out information about a crime (detetive) 🔲 *a private detective* (detetive particular) 🔲 *a retired police detective* (detetive de polícia) □ *She told detectives that she'd seen a man leaving the building.*

• **detector** /dɪˈtektə(r)/ NOUN [plural detectors] a piece of equipment that is used to detect something (detector) 🔲 *a smoke detector* (detector de fumaça)

detention /dɪˈtenʃən/ NOUN [plural detentions]
1 when someone is kept in a place and not allowed to leave □ *He is being held in detention for questioning.* (detenção, prisão)
2 when a student has to stay at school at the end of the day as a punishment (detenção)

deter /dɪˈtɜː(r)/ VERB [deters, deterring, deterred] to make someone less likely to do something □ *Alcohol should be more expensive to deter youngsters from buying it.* (dissuadir)

detergent /dɪˈtɜːdʒənt/ NOUN [plural detergents] a chemical used for cleaning things □ *washing detergent* (detergente)

deteriorate /dɪˈtɪəriəreɪt/ VERB [deteriorates, deteriorating, deteriorated] to get worse □ *Joe's health is deteriorating rapidly.* (deteriorar)

• **deterioration** /dɪˌtɪəriəˈreɪʃən/ NOUN, NO PLURAL the process of deteriorating □ *There's been a deterioration in her condition.* (deterioração)

determination /dɪˌtɜːmɪˈneɪʃən/ NOUN, NO PLURAL a strong feeling that you want to do something, even when it is difficult □ *They showed great determination.* □ + *to do something* *He has a determination to win.* (determinação)

• **determine** /dɪˈtɜːmɪn/ VERB [determines, determining, determined]
1 to discover the truth or facts about something □ *The police are still trying to determine exactly how she died.* □ *They are using a new method for determining the age of stars.* (determinar)
2 to control or influence what happens □ *The weather will determine how long the event lasts.* □ *This issue could determine the outcome of the election.* (controlar)

• **determined** /dɪˈtɜːmɪnd/ ADJECTIVE having or showing determination □ + *to do something* *The team was determined to finish first if they possibly could.* □ *She's a very determined young woman.* (determinado) 🔲 *He's made a determined effort to lose weight.* (esforço determinado)

determiner /dɪˈtɜːmɪnə(r)/ NOUN [plural determiners] a word that is used before a noun to show how that noun is being used. For example, the, this and some are determiners. (determinante)

deterrent /dɪˈterənt/ NOUN [plural deterrents] something that makes someone less likely to do something □ *Is prison an effective deterrent?* (impedimento)

detest /dɪˈtest/ VERB [detests, detesting, detested] to hate someone or something very much □ *He detests violence in any form.* □ *She detested him or what he had done.* (detestar)

detonate

detonate /ˈdetəneɪt/ VERB [detonates, detonating, detonated] to explode or to make something explode ◻ *The bomb was detonated from across the street.* (**detonar**)

• **detonator** /ˈdetəneɪtə(r)/ NOUN [plural detonators] the part of a bomb which makes it explode (**detonador**)

detour /ˈdiːtʊə(r)/ NOUN [plural detours] a different and longer way of getting somewhere than usual (**desvio**) ▣ *I took a detour on the way home to visit my sister.* (**peguei um desvio**)

detox /ˈdiːtɒks/ ▶ NOUN, NO PLURAL treatment to get rid of harmful substances such as drugs and alcohol from your body (**desintoxicação**)
▶ VERB [detoxes, detoxing, detoxed] to have treatment to remove harmful substances from your body (**desintoxicar**)

detract /dɪˈtrækt/
♦ PHRASAL VERB [detracts, detracting, detracted] **detract from something** to make something seem less good ◻ *The last-minute problems did not detract from the overall achievement.* (**depreciar algo**)

• **detractor** /dɪˈtræktə(r)/ NOUN [plural detractors] someone who criticizes something publicly (**caluniador**)

detrimental /ˌdetrɪˈmentəl/ ADJECTIVE damaging (**prejudicial**) ▣ *Large classes can have a detrimental effect on children's education.* (**efeito prejudicial**)

devalue /ˌdiːˈvæljuː/ VERB [devalues, devaluing, devalued]
1 to reduce the value of a country's money. An economics word. (**desvalorizar**)
2 to make something seem less important ◻ *His enemies have tried to devalue his achievements.* (**desvalorizar**)

devastate /ˈdevəsteɪt/ VERB [devastates, devastating, devastated]
1 to destroy something or damage it very badly ◻ *The storm devastated much of the city.* (**arrasar**)
2 to make someone very upset ◻ *His death has devastated our family.* (**devastar**)

• **devastated** /ˈdevəsteɪtɪd/ ADJECTIVE
1 very shocked and upset ◻ *We were absolutely devastated by the news.* (**arrasado**)
2 completely destroyed ◻ *The minister visited the devastated area.* (**destruído, arruinado**)

• **devastating** /ˈdevəsteɪtɪŋ/ ADJECTIVE
1 making someone very shocked and upset ◻ *devastating news* (**devastador**)
2 causing a lot of damage ◻ *devastating floods* (**devastador**)

• **devastation** /ˌdevəˈsteɪʃən/ NOUN, NO PLURAL
1 when something has been destroyed or badly damaged ◻ *There were scenes of devastation after the explosion.* (**devastação, destruição**)
2 a feeling of being very shocked and upset (**desolação**)

develop

develop /dɪˈveləp/ VERB [develops, developing, developed]
1 to grow or change, or to make something grow bigger, better or more advanced ◻ *The young animals develop very quickly.* ◻ **+ into** *The eggs develop into adult insects.* ◻ *There are plans to develop tourism in the area.* ◻ *The process has developed over time.* (**evoluir**)
2 to design and create something new ◻ *Researchers are developing new technologies.* ◻ *We need to develop strategies to deal with this problem.* (**desenvolver**)
3 to start to have an illness, problem, feeling, etc. ◻ *Smokers are more likely to develop cancer.* ◻ *He developed an interest in art.* ◻ *The equipment developed some technical problems.* (**desenvolver**)
4 to start to happen or exist ◻ *The disease develops gradually.* ◻ *A close friendship developed between the two women.* (**desenvolver**)
5 to make a photograph on a film into a picture (**revelar**)
6 to build new buildings on land ◻ *This land is to be developed.* (**crescer**)

• **developed** /dɪˈveləpt/ ADJECTIVE a developed country has an advanced economy, social structure, etc. (**desenvolvido**) ▣ *Developed nations must cut carbon emissions.* (**nações desenvolvidas**)

• **developer** /dɪˈveləpə(r)/ NOUN [plural developers]
1 a person whose job is to build new buildings on land (**incorporador**)
2 someone whose job is to design and create new products (**desenvolvedor**) ▣ *a software developer* (**desenvolvedor de softwares**)

• **developing** /dɪˈveləpɪŋ/ ADJECTIVE
1 a developing country is quite poor and its economy is not very advanced (**em desenvolvimento**)
2 in the process of happening or growing ◻ *We're reporting on two developing news stories.* (**em desenvolvimento**)

• **development** /dɪˈveləpmənt/ NOUN [plural developments]
1 when something becomes bigger, better or more advanced (**desenvolvimento**) ▣ *There has been rapid economic development.* (**desenvolvimento econômico**) ◻ **+ of** *The condition affects the normal development of the brain.*
2 when something new is created ◻ **+ of** *This research may aid the development of new treatments.* ◻ *The project is still in the early stages of development.* (**avanço**) ▣ *New developments in mobile phone technology have made communication easier.* (**novos avanços**)
3 when something begins to happen or exist ◻ **+ of** *Several factors affect the development of the disease.* (**progresso**)
4 a new event in a story or situation (**incremento**) ▣ *They met to discuss the latest developments in the case.* (**últimos incrementos**)

5 an area of land with new buildings on it □ *a housing development* (**urbanização**)

- **developmental** /dɪˌveləpˈmentəl/ ADJECTIVE to do with the development of a person □ *The centre is for children with developmental disabilities.* (**do desenvolvimento**)

deviate /ˈdiːvɪeɪt/ VERB [**deviates, deviating, deviated**] to do something different from what is normal or expected □ *We had to deviate from the original plan.* (**desviar-se**)

- **deviation** /ˌdiːvɪˈeɪʃən/ NOUN [plural **deviations**] something that is different from what is normal (**divergência**)

device /dɪˈvaɪs/ NOUN [plural **devices**]
1 a tool or piece of equipment □ *a device for cleaning keyboards* (**instrumento**)
2 a bomb (**bomba**) ▣ *The police found an explosive device.* (**bomba**)

♦ IDIOM **leave someone to their own devices** to leave someone to do what they want to do □ *Left to his own devices, he'd eat chips every day.* (**deixar alguém fazer o que quiser**)

devil /ˈdevəl/ NOUN [plural **devils**]
1 The Devil the most powerful evil spirit in some religions (**Diabo**)
2 an evil spirit (**demônio**)
3 an informal word for someone who behaves badly □ *The boys can be little devils sometimes.* (**malvado**)

devil's advocate /ˌdevəlz ˈædvəkət/
♦ IDIOM **play devil's advocate** to pretend to disagree with someone in order to test their argument (**ser o advogado do diabo**)

devious /ˈdiːvɪəs/ ADJECTIVE clever in a way which is not honest □ *a devious plan* (**evasivo**)

devise /dɪˈvaɪz/ VERB [**devises, devising, devised**] to design a plan or way of doing something (**inventar, tramar**) ▣ *We need to devise a plan.* (**bolar um plano**) ▣ *He devised a method of measuring earthquakes.* (**inventou um método**)

devoid /dɪˈvɔɪd/ ADJECTIVE **devoid of something** a formal word meaning not having something □ *The village was completely devoid of life.* (**destituído de algo**)

devolution /ˌdiːvəˈluːʃən/ NOUN, NO PLURAL the process of giving some government power to smaller areas (**descentralização**)

- **devolve** /dɪˈvɒlv/ VERB [**devolves, devolving, devolved**] to give some government power to a smaller area (**descentralizar**)

devote /dɪˈvəʊt/
♦ PHRASAL VERB [**devotes, devoting, devoted**]
devote something to something/someone
1 to give time, space, energy, etc. to something (**dedicar algo a algo/alguém**) ▣ *I want to devote more time to my family.* (**dedicar mais tempo a**) □ *We are devoting increased resources to training.*

2 devote yourself to someone/something to give all your time and interest to someone or something □ *She devoted herself to helping the poor.* (**dedicar-se a algo/alguém**)

- **devoted** /dɪˈvəʊtɪd/ ADJECTIVE loving or caring about someone or something very much □ *He was a devoted husband and father.* □ *a devoted football fan* (**devotado, dedicado**)

- **devotee** /ˌdevəˈtiː/ NOUN [plural **devotees**]
1 someone who is very interested in something □ *She's a passionate devotee of the theatre.* (**fanático**)
2 someone who follows a particular religion □ *a Hindu devotee* (**devoto**)

- **devotion** /dɪˈvəʊʃən/ NOUN, NO PLURAL
1 great love or loyalty □ *I remember her devotion to her husband.* (**dedicação**)
2 a very strong belief in something □ *religious devotion* (**devoção, crença**)

devour /dɪˈvaʊə(r)/ VERB [**devours, devouring, devoured**]
1 to eat something very quickly □ *He devoured a huge breakfast.* (**devorar**)
2 to read or listen to something with a lot of interest □ *As a child, I devoured books.* (**devorar**)

devout /dɪˈvaʊt/ ADJECTIVE very religious □ *a devout Muslim* (**devoto, religioso**)

dew /djuː/ NOUN, NO PLURAL very small drops of water that form on the ground at night (**orvalho**)

dexterity /dekˈsterətɪ/ NOUN, NO PLURAL skill, especially using your hands □ *I admired her dexterity with a needle.* (**destreza, habilidade**)

- **dextrous** or **dexterous** /ˈdekstrəs/ ADJECTIVE skilful at using your hands (**hábil**)

dhoti /ˈdəʊtɪ/ NOUN [plural **dhotis**] a long piece of cloth that Hindu men wear wrapped around the lower half of their bodies (**vestimenta masculina indiana**)

di- /daɪ/ PREFIX di- is added to the beginning of words to mean 'two' □ *a dialogue* (**di-**)

diabetes /ˌdaɪəˈbiːtiːz/ NOUN, NO PLURAL a serious illness in which your body cannot control the amount of sugar in your blood (**diabetes**)

- **diabetic** /ˌdaɪəˈbetɪk/, ▶ ADJECTIVE having diabetes or to do with diabetes □ *a diabetic patient* (**diabético**)
▶ NOUN [plural **diabetics**] a person with diabetes (**diabético**)

diabolical /ˌdaɪəˈbɒlɪkəl/ ADJECTIVE
1 an informal word meaning very bad □ *The service was absolutely diabolical.* (**diabólico**)
2 very evil (**diabólico**)

diagnose /ˈdaɪəɡnəʊz/ VERB [**diagnoses, diagnosing, diagnosed**] to decide what is wrong with a person or a piece of equipment □ *She was diagnosed with cancer last year.* □ *It's important to diagnose the disease early.* □ *An engineer diagnosed the problem and fixed it.* (**diagnosticar**)

- **diagnosis** /ˌdaɪəɡˈnəʊsɪs/ NOUN [plural **diagnoses**] a decision about what is wrong with

someone ▫ *The doctor made a diagnosis from one look at the patient.* (**diagnóstico**)
- **diagnostic** /ˌdaɪəgˈnɒstɪk/ ADJECTIVE to do with diagnosing an illness or problem (**diagnóstico**) 🔲 *a diagnostic test* (**exame diagnóstico**)

diagonal /daɪˈægənəl/ ADJECTIVE going from one corner of something straight to the opposite corner (**diagonal**) 🔲 *a diagonal line* (**linha diagonal**)
- **diagonally** /daɪˈægənəli/ ADVERB in a diagonal direction ▫ *Cut it into slices diagonally.* (**diagonalmente**)

diagram /ˈdaɪəgræm/ NOUN [plural **diagrams**] a drawing that explains something (**diagrama**) 🔲 *He drew a diagram of the building.* (**desenhou um diagrama**)

dial /ˈdaɪəl/ ▶ NOUN [plural **dials**]
1 the round part on a clock or a machine that shows the time or a measurement (**mostrador**)
2 a round control on a radio or other machine that you turn to operate it ▫ *I turned the radio dial.* (**mostrador**)
3 the round part of an old telephone that you turn to make a call (**discador**)
▶ VERB [**dials, dialling/US dialing, dialled/US dialed**] to call a telephone number (**discou**) 🔲 *She picked up the phone and dialled the number.* (**discou o número**) ▫ *In an emergency, dial 999.*

dialect /ˈdaɪəlekt/ NOUN [plural **dialects**] the form of a language that is used by people who live in a particular area and has some words that are not used by other speakers of the same language (**dialeto**)

dialog /ˈdaɪəlɒg/ NOUN [plural **dialogs**] the US spelling of **dialogue** (**diálogo**)

dialog box /ˈdaɪəlɒg ˌbɒks/ NOUN [plural **dialog boxes**] a box that appears on a computer screen to ask you what you want to do next (**caixa de diálogo**)

dialogue /ˈdaɪəlɒg/ NOUN [plural **dialogues**]
1 formal discussion between two people or groups ▫ *We are hoping to open a dialogue with the government.* (**diálogo**)
2 the words or conversation of characters in a book, film, etc. (**diálogo**)

dial-up /ˈdaɪəlʌp/ ADJECTIVE using a telephone connection. A computing word. ▫ *dial-up access* (**acesso discado**)

dialysis /daɪˈælɪsɪs/ NOUN, NO PLURAL treatment to remove harmful substances from the blood of a person whose kidneys do not work well enough (**diálise**)

diameter /daɪˈæmɪtə(r)/ NOUN [plural **diameters**] a straight line from one side of a circle to the other through its centre, or this measurement. A maths word ▫ *the diameter of the pipe* (**diâmetro**)

diamond /ˈdaɪəmənd/ NOUN [plural **diamonds**]
1 a very hard, clear stone that is very valuable ▫ *a diamond ring* (**diamante**)
2 a four-sided pointed shape (♦) (**ouro**)
3 diamonds one of the four types of playing card, with a diamond symbol printed on them ▫ *the eight of diamonds* (**ouros**)

diaper /ˈdaɪəpə(r)/ NOUN [plural **diapers**] the US word for **nappy** (**fralda**)

diaphragm /ˈdaɪəfræm/ NOUN [plural **diaphragms**] a layer of muscle that separates your stomach from your chest. A biology word. (**diafragma**)

diarrhea /ˌdaɪəˈrɪə/ NOUN, NO PLURAL the US spelling of **diarrhoea** (**diarreia**)

diarrhoea /ˌdaɪəˈrɪə/ NOUN, NO PLURAL an illness which causes you go to the toilet very often and makes the solid waste from your body more liquid than usual (**diarreia**)

diary /ˈdaɪəri/ NOUN [plural **diaries**]
1 a book with spaces for all the dates of the year where you can write things down ▫ *I've put the appointment in my diary.* ▫ *I'll check my diary.* (**diário**)
2 a book where you write down your experiences each day (**diário**) *He kept a diary.* (**escreve um diário**)

dice /daɪs/ ▶ NOUN [plural **dice**]
1 a small object with six square sides with different numbers of small round marks on each side that you use in games (**dado**) 🔲 *Each player rolls the dice.* (**joga os dados**)
2 small square pieces of food ▫ *Cut the tomato into small dice.* (**cubo**)
▶ VERB [**dices, dicing, diced**] to cut food into dice ▫ *Finely dice the carrot.* (**cortar em cubos**)
♦ IDIOM **dice with death** to do something very dangerous where you might be killed (**brincar com a morte**)

dictate /dɪkˈteɪt/ VERB [**dictates, dictating, dictated**]
1 to influence or control what happens ▫ *The timing will be dictated by the weather conditions.* ▫ *The market will dictate whether these airlines succeed.* (**impor**)
2 to tell someone exactly what to do ▫ *I will not be dictated to by head office.* (**dar ordens**)
3 to say words for someone to write down ▫ *I have to type the letters that my boss dictates.* (**ditar**)
- **dictation** /dɪkˈteɪʃən/ NOUN [plural **dictations**] a piece of text that a teacher dictates for students to write down, or the process of doing this (**ditado**)
- **dictator** /dɪkˈteɪtə(r)/ NOUN [plural **dictators**] a person who has complete power over a country ▫ *a fascist dictator* (**ditador**)
- **dictatorial** /ˌdɪktəˈtɔːriəl/ ADJECTIVE to do with or behaving like a dictator ▫ *a dictatorial style of management* (**ditatorial**)
- **dictatorship** /dɪkˈteɪtəʃɪp/ NOUN [plural **dictatorships**]
1 government by a dictator (**ditadura**)

dictionary /ˈdɪkʃənəri/ NOUN [plural **dictionaries**] a book that gives words in alphabetical order and their meanings □ *a French dictionary* □ *+ of a dictionary of medical terms* (dicionário)

did /dɪd/ PAST TENSE OF **do** (*ver* do)

didn't /ˈdɪdənt/ a short way to say and write **did not** (*ver* do)

die /daɪ/ VERB [**dies, dying, died**]
1 to stop living □ *Her father died suddenly at the age of 56.* □ *Six people died in the crash.* □ *+ of He died of heart failure.* □ *+ from He was taken to hospital, but died from his injuries.* (morrer)
2 to disappear or stop existing □ *My love for him will never die.* (desaparecer)
♦ IDIOM **be dying for something/to do something** an informal phrase meaning you want to have something or do something very much and you do not want to wait □ *I'm dying for a cold drink.* □ *The kids were dying to get outside.* (morrer de vontade de ter ou fazer algo)
♦ PHRASAL VERBS **die away** to gradually become quieter or weaker and then stop □ *The noise of the siren gradually died away.* (desvanecer) **die down** to gradually become quieter or less active □ *She waited until the applause had died down.* □ *All the attention seems to have died down now.* (diminuir gradualmente) **die off** if a group dies off, the members die over a period of time until there are none left □ *The trees began to die off.* (morrer um após o outro) **die out to** gradually disappear or stop existing □ *More and more species of animal are dying out.* □ *The tradition died out decades ago.* (extinguir-se)

diesel /ˈdiːzəl/ NOUN, NO PLURAL a heavy type of oil that is used as fuel (diesel)

diet /ˈdaɪət/ ▶ NOUN [plural **diets**]
1 the food that a person eats (dieta) 🖸 *Do you have a healthy diet?* (dieta saudável) 🖸 *You need to eat a balanced diet.* (dieta equilibrada) □ *+ of They live on a basic diet of rice and beans.*
2 a limited amount or range of foods that someone eats, for example to lose weight (regime) 🖸 *Maybe you need to go on a diet.* (fazer regime) 🖸 *She began to follow a strict diet.* (seguiu um regime estrito)
▶ VERB [**diets, dieting, dieted**] to eat less food in order to lose weight □ *I've never dieted, but I do do a lot of exercise.* (fazer dieta)

differ /ˈdɪfə(r)/ VERB [**differs, differing, differed**]
1 to not be the same as something else □ *+ from His working methods differ from other TV producers.* □ *+ in The males and females differ in size.* (ser diferente) 🖸 *The eyewitness accounts differ.* (os relatos diferem)
2 to disagree with someone about something □ *+ over They differ over just about everything.* □ *+ on Experts differ on how high the levels are.* (diferir) 🖸 *Opinions differ widely over its real value.* (as opiniões diferem)

• **difference** /ˈdɪfrəns/ NOUN [plural **differences**]
1 the way in which two people or things are not the same □ *+ between Is there a difference between male and female players?* □ *+ in There was a noticeable difference in the children's behaviour.* (diferença) 🖸 *There are big differences between the two cultures.* (grandes diferenças) 🖸 *They don't know the difference between right and wrong.* (sabem a diferença)
2 the amount by which one thing is different from another □ *+ between The difference between 6 and 10 is 4.* (diferença) 🖸 *The two sisters get on well, despite their age difference.* (diferença de idade)
3 a disagreement □ *Differences remain between the two sides.* (diferença) 🖸 *I'm sure we can resolve our differences.* (resolver nossas diferenças) □ *+ over They've had their differences over politics.* 🖸 *There were some serious differences of opinion.* (diferenças de opiniões)
4 make a difference to have an effect on something □ *+ to This will make a difference to people's lives.* □ *Working harder didn't make any difference – we still couldn't manage.* (fazer a diferença)

• **different** /ˈdɪfrənt/ ADJECTIVE
1 not the same as someone or something else □ *+ from He seems quite different from the rest of the boys.* □ *+ in The two girls are very different in appearance and personality.* (diferente) 🖸 *Each case is completely different.* (completamente diferente) □ *We listen to different types of music.*
2 used to talk about separate things of the same type □ *She teaches at several different schools.* □ *There are three different terminals at the airport.* (diferente)

• **differently** /ˈdɪfrəntli/ ADVERB in a different way □ *Our new boss does everything differently.* (diferentemente)

differentiate /ˌdɪfəˈrenʃieɪt/ VERB [**differentiates, differentiating, differentiated**]
1 to see or show the difference between two things □ *Many people don't differentiate between different types of fat.* □ *Children must be taught early to differentiate right from wrong.* (distinguir)
2 to be the quality or feature that makes something different from something else □ *What differentiates their product from their competitors'?* (diferenciar)

• **differentiation** /ˌdɪfərenʃiˈeɪʃən/ NOUN, NO PLURAL when people or things are different from each other, or making them different □ *There is little differentiation between the rival candidates.* (diferenciação)

difficult

difficult /ˈdɪfɪkəlt/ ADJECTIVE
1 not easy to do or understand □ *That's a very difficult question.* □ + *to do something* *It's becoming increasingly difficult to find a parking space.* □ + *for* *It's difficult for anyone to understand.* (**difícil**) 🔁 *Many people are finding it difficult to get jobs.* (**achando difícil**)
2 causing a lot of problems or unhappiness (**difícil**) 🔁 *It's been a difficult time for us.* (**tempo difícil**) 🔁 *He was faced with a difficult situation.* (**situação difícil**)
3 not friendly or easy to please □ *a difficult customer* (**problemático**)

• **difficulty** /ˈdɪfɪkəlti/ NOUN [plural **difficulties**]
1 *no plural* when something is difficult to do or understand □ *You should be able to do this without difficulty.* □ + *ing* *She was having difficulty sleeping.* □ + *in* *He was having difficulty in breathing.* □ + *with* *My grandmother now has difficulty with everyday tasks.* (**dificuldade**) 🔁 *With great difficulty, he managed to pull himself out of the water.* (**grande dificuldade**)
2 something that causes a problem 🔁 *We had a few difficulties at the beginning of the day.* (**tivemos dificuldades**)

diffidence /ˈdɪfɪdəns/ NOUN, NO PLURAL the quality of being shy and nervous (**desconfiança**)
• **diffident** /ˈdɪfɪdənt/ ADJECTIVE shy and nervous (**desconfiado**)

diffraction /dɪˈfrækʃən/ NOUN, NO PLURAL when light or sound waves are broken up by being passed over something or through a small space. A physics word. (**difração**)

diffuse /dɪˈfjuːz/ VERB [**diffuses, diffusing, diffused**] to spread or make something spread over a wide area □ *The light diffused through the mist.* (**difundir**)
• **diffusion** /dɪˈfjuːʒən/ NOUN, NO PLURAL
1 when light spreads over a wide area. A physics word. (**difusão**)
2 when a substance gradually mixes with gas or liquid. A physics word. (**dispersão**)

dig /dɪg/ ▶ VERB [**digs, digging, dug**]
1 to make a hole, especially in the ground (**cavar**) 🔁 *They dug a hole in the snow.* (**cavaram um buraco**) □ *They're digging a tunnel.*
2 to lift up and turn over soil with a spade (= tool with a flat, metal part that you push into the soil) □ *He's digging in the garden.* (**cavoucar**)
♦ PHRASAL VERBS **dig (something) into something** to press or make something press hard into something □ *The cat dug its claws into the chair.* (**cravar algo em algo**) **dig something out** to find something that you have not seen for a long time □ *I dug out some old school photos.* (**retirar algo**)
dig something up
1 to break or turn over the ground or a surface by digging □ *They were digging up the road.* (**arrancar algo da terra**)
2 to remove something from under the ground by digging □ *We dug up some vegetables.* (**desenterrar algo**)
3 to find information about someone or something □ *Journalists are trying to dig up stories from his past.* (**encontrar algo**)
♦ IDIOMS **dig the dirt** to discover bad information about a famous person that the person is trying to keep secret (**encontrar más notícias**) **dig your heels in** to refuse to do something or to change your opinion □ *I dug my heels in and insisted that we go back.* (**bater os pés no chão**)
▶ NOUN [plural **digs**]
1 a remark that you make to annoy someone deliberately □ *He couldn't resist a dig at his rival.* (**pontada**)
2 a quick, hard push □ *She gave him a dig in the ribs.* (**empurrão**)
3 a place where people dig in the ground to look for ancient objects (**escavação**) 🔁 *an archaeological dig* (**escavação arqueológica**)

digest /daɪˈdʒest/ VERB [**digests, digesting, digested**]
1 when the body digests food, it changes it into substances that it can use (**digestão**) 🔁 *Bacteria in the stomach help to digest food.* (**digerir a comida**)
2 to read or hear new information and understand it □ *It took time to digest the news.* (**assimilar**)
• **digestion** /daɪˈdʒestʃən/ NOUN, NO PLURAL the process of digesting food (**digestão**)
• **digestive** /daɪˈdʒestɪv/ ADJECTIVE to do with digesting food □ *It can cause digestive problems.* (**digestivo**)

digestive system /daɪˈdʒestɪv ˌsɪstəm/ NOUN [plural **digestive systems**] the system of body parts and processes that digest food. A biology word. (**sistema digestório**)

digger /ˈdɪgə(r)/ NOUN [plural **diggers**] a machine that can move or break up large amounts of soil (**escavadeira**)

digit /ˈdɪdʒɪt/ NOUN [plural **digits**]
1 a number from 0 to 9 □ *a six-digit number* (**dígito**)
2 a formal word for finger or toe (**digital**)

digital /ˈdɪdʒɪtəl/ ADJECTIVE
1 storing information, sounds and pictures as sets of numbers or electronic signals (**digital**) 🔁 *a digital camera* (**câmera digital**) 🔁 *a digital radio* (**rádio digital**) 🔁 *There's been a growth in digital music sales.* (**música eletrônica**)
2 a digital clock or watch shows the time as numbers (**relógio digital**)
• **digitally** /ˈdɪdʒɪtəli/ ADVERB using digital equipment □ *The photos are digitally enhanced.* (**digitalmente**)

digital television /ˌdɪdʒɪtəl ˈtelɪvɪʒən/ NOUN, NO PLURAL a method of broadcasting that uses electronic signals (**televisão digital**)

digitize or **digitise** /ˈdɪdʒɪtaɪz/ VERB [**digitizes, digitizing, digitized**] to change data into a digital form (= as sets of numbers) so that it can be used by computers (**digitalizar**)

dignified /ˈdɪɡnɪfaɪd/ ADJECTIVE behaving in a calm, controlled way that makes people respect you □ *I think she handled the situation in a very dignified way.* (**digno**) 🔁 *She kept a dignified silence throughout the trial.* (**silêncio digno**)

dignitary /ˈdɪɡnɪtəri/ NOUN [plural **dignitaries**] someone with an important official job or position □ *The President is having lunch with foreign dignitaries.* (**dignitário**)

dignity /ˈdɪɡnəti/ NOUN, NO PLURAL
1 calm, controlled behaviour, especially in a difficult situation □ *She showed great dignity through a difficult period.* □ *I tried to maintain my dignity.* (**dignidade**)
2 respect for someone or for yourself (**dignidade**) 🔁 *This is a violation of human dignity.* (**dignidade humana**)

digress /daɪˈɡres/ VERB [**digresses, digressing, digressed**] if you digress from the subject you are talking about, you start talking about something else □ *But I digress. Let me get back to the story.* (**divagar**)

• **digression** /daɪˈɡreʃən/ NOUN [plural **digressions**] when you digress □ *He told us tales of his travels, with frequent digressions.* (**divagação**)

dike /daɪk/ NOUN [plural **dikes**] another spelling of **dyke** (**represa, dique**)

dilapidated /dɪˈlæpɪdeɪtɪd/ ADJECTIVE old and in bad condition □ *a dilapidated old car* □ *a dilapidated building* (**decadente**)

dilate /daɪˈleɪt/ VERB [**dilates, dilating, dilated**] to become larger or wider, or to make something larger or wider □ *The pupils of your eyes dilate in the dark.* (**dilatar-se**)

dilemma /dɪˈlemə/ NOUN [plural **dilemmas**] when you have to decide which of two or more things to do and you are finding this decision difficult (**dilema**) 🔁 *I'm in a dilemma over whether to go or not.* (**em um dilema**) 🔁 *a moral dilemma* (**dilema moral**)

dilettante /ˌdɪlɪˈtænti/ NOUN [plural **dilettantes**] someone who is interested in subjects such as art or literature, but not in a very serious way (**apreciador, diletante**)

diligence /ˈdɪlɪdʒəns/ NOUN, NO PLURAL a serious and careful attitude to work □ *He has a reputation for honesty and diligence.* (**diligência**)

• **diligent** /ˈdɪlɪdʒənt/ ADJECTIVE showing diligence □ *a diligent student* (**diligente, aplicado**)

dilute /daɪˈluːt/ ▶ VERB [**dilutes, diluting, diluted**] to add water to a liquid so that it is weaker □ *Try diluting the juice with water.* (**diluir**)
▶ ADJECTIVE a dilute liquid has been diluted. A chemistry word □ *a dilute solution* (**diluição**)

• **dilution** /daɪˈluːʃən/ NOUN, NO PLURAL the process of diluting something (**diluição**)

dim /dɪm/ ▶ ADJECTIVE [**dimmer, dimmest**]
1 not bright or clear (**fraco, tênue**) 🔁 *We couldn't see much in the dim light.* (**luz fraca**) □ *I made my way along the dim corridor.*
2 not clear or not well remembered (**turvo, vago**) 🔁 *I only have a dim memory of my great-grandfather.* (**memória vaga**)
3 an informal word meaning not quick to understand things (**estúpido**)
◆ IDIOM **take a dim view of something** to not approve of something □ *We take a very dim view of such behaviour.* (**desaprovar algo**)
▶ VERB [**dims, dimming, dimmed**] to become less bright, or to make something less bright (**diminuir**) 🔁 *The lights dimmed and the performance began.* (**luzes diminuíram**)

dime /daɪm/ NOUN [plural **dimes**] a US or Canadian coin worth ten cents (**moeda de 10 centavos**)
◆ IDIOM **a dime a dozen** very common (**a preço de bananas**)

dimension /dɪˈmenʃən/ NOUN [plural **dimensions**]
1 a part of a situation or subject (**dimensão**) 🔁 *There is a moral dimension to the work we do.* (**dimensão moral**) 🔁 *Ashley will add another dimension to the team.* (**adicionar dimensão**)
2 a measurement such as the length, width or area of something □ *Please give the dimensions of the doorway.* (**dimensão, tamanho**)

diminish /dɪˈmɪnɪʃ/ VERB [**diminishes, diminishing, diminished**] to become less or smaller, or to make something less or smaller □ *I don't want to diminish the importance of this meeting.* □ *Recently, their power has diminished.* (**reduzir**)

diminutive /dɪˈmɪnjʊtɪv/ ▶ ADJECTIVE a formal word meaning very small □ *She appeared in the doorway, a diminutive figure.* (**reduzido, diminuto**)
▶ NOUN [plural **diminutives**] a word formed with a suffix such as **-let** (e.g. booklet) or **-ette** (e.g. statuette), used to refer to a small type of something (**diminutivo**)

dimly /ˈdɪmli/ ADVERB
1 not clearly or brightly (**fracamente**) 🔁 *a dimly lit room* (**fracamente aceso**) □ *It was only dimly visible through the smoke.*
2 not clearly understood or remembered □ *She dimly remembered someone telling her about it.* (**vagamente**)

dimple /ˈdɪmpəl/ NOUN [plural **dimples**] a small hollow place on the skin of your chin or cheek □ *Harry has dimples when he smiles.* (**covinha**)

dim-witted /ˌdɪmˈwɪtɪd/ ADJECTIVE stupid (**idiota**)

din /dɪn/ NOUN, NO PLURAL a lot of very loud noise □ *The house was filled with the constant din of children.* (**algazarra**)

dine

dine /daɪn/ VERB [dines, dining, dined] a formal word meaning to eat dinner (= main meal) □ *They regularly dine at the best restaurants.* (jantar)

• **diner** /ˈdaɪnə(r)/ NOUN [plural diners] someone who is eating dinner (= main meal), especially in a restaurant (comensal)

dinghy /ˈdɪŋɡi/ NOUN [plural dinghies] a small boat for rowing or sailing (pequeno barco)

dingy /ˈdɪndʒi/ ADJECTIVE [dingier, dingiest] dark, unpleasant and often dirty □ *a small, dingy room* (lúgubre)

dining room
/ˈdaɪnɪŋ ˌruːm/ NOUN [plural dining rooms] the room in a house or hotel where you have your meals (sala de jantar)

dinner
/ˈdɪnə(r)/ NOUN [plural dinners]
1 a main meal in the evening or in the middle of the day □ *We had fish for dinner.* (jantar) ▣ *We sat down to eat dinner.* (jantar) ▣ *Alice is cooking dinner.* (preparando o jantar)
2 a formal evening meal arranged for a lot of people □ *There's a dinner on the last night of the conference.* (ceia, jantar)

dinner jacket /ˈdɪnə ˌdʒækɪt/ NOUN [plural dinner jackets] a formal jacket worn by a man, that is usually black or white (paletó)

dinosaur /ˈdaɪnəsɔː(r)/ NOUN [plural dinosaurs] a very large type of animal that lived millions of years ago and no longer exists (dinossauro)

diode /ˈdaɪəʊd/ NOUN [plural diodes] a piece of electronic equipment that allows electricity to move through it in one direction only. A physics word. (diodo)

dip /dɪp/ ▶ VERB [dips, dipping, dipped]
1 to put something in and out of a liquid quickly □ *Dip the clothes in the dye.* □ *She dipped a toe into the water.* (mergulhar)
2 to become lower in amount or level □ *At night temperatures dip below freezing.* □ *Sales dipped slightly last month.* (abaixar)

◆ PHRASAL VERB **dip into something**
1 to take a small amount of money from an amount saved □ *I had to dip into my savings.* (resgatar uma pequena quantia)
2 to read or watch small parts of something at different times (folhear)

▶ NOUN [plural dips]
1 a fall in the level or amount of something □ *The company reported a 2% dip in profits.* (queda)
2 an informal word meaning a quick swim □ *Do you fancy a dip in the pool?* (mergulho)
3 a place in a surface or the ground that is lower than the part around it □ *There was a dip in the road.* (buraco, depressão)
4 a soft food that you eat by dipping things in it □ *a cheese dip* (molho)

diploma
/dɪˈpləʊmə/ NOUN [plural diplomas] a qualification that someone can study for in a particular subject □ + *in She has a postgraduate diploma in Journalism Studies.* (diploma)

diplomacy /dɪˈpləʊməsi/ NOUN, NO PLURAL
1 the job or skill of keeping friendly relationships between countries (diplomacia) ▣ *He is in New York for three days of international diplomacy at the UN.* □ *If diplomacy fails, we will have to consider other options.* (diplomacia internacional)
2 the ability to deal with people without offending them □ *The job requires enormous tact and diplomacy.* (diplomacia)

• **diplomat** /ˈdɪpləmæt/ NOUN [plural diplomats] someone whose job is to keep good relationships and communications between countries □ *a British diplomat* (diplomata)

• **diplomatic** /ˌdɪpləˈmætɪk/ ADJECTIVE
1 to do with the relationships between countries (diplomático) ▣ *This could damage diplomatic relations between the two countries.* (relações diplomáticas) ▣ *She led the diplomatic effort to end the crisis.* (esforços diplomáticos)
2 showing diplomacy in dealing with people □ *You're being very diplomatic.* (diplomático)

• **diplomatically** /ˌdɪpləˈmætɪkəli/ ADVERB
1 in a way that does not offend anyone □ *'Both were very good,' she answered diplomatically.* (diplomaticamente)
2 by using diplomacy □ *We want to resolve this issue diplomatically.* (diplomaticamente)

dire /ˈdaɪə(r)/ ADJECTIVE very bad, serious or extreme (perigoso) ▣ *a dire warning* (aviso perigoso) ▣ *These people are in dire need of help.* (necessidade perigosa) ▣ *If these spending cuts go ahead, they will have dire consequences.* (consequências perigosas)

direct
/dɪˈrekt/ ▶ ADJECTIVE
1 straight from one place to another (direto) ▣ *It's the shortest, most direct route.* (rota direta) ▣ *a direct flight between London and Beijing* (voo direto)
2 involving two people or things with nothing else between (direto) ▣ *We had no direct contact with Mr Ellis.* (contato direto) ▣ *They found a direct link between computer usage and back pain.* (ligação direta)
3 honest and saying what you think □ *He's very direct in his approach.* □ *He asked some pretty direct questions.* (sincero, direto)

▶ ADVERB
1 going straight from one place to another □ *They fly daily direct from Glasgow to New York.* (diretamente)
2 in a way that involves two people or things only □ *We buy direct from the manufacturer.* (diretamente)

▶ VERB [directs, directing, directed]
1 to intend something for a particular person or purpose □ *His remarks were directed at me.* □

Many of the attacks are directed against civilians. (direcionar)
2 to tell the actors in a film or play what to do (dirigir) 🔲 *The film was directed by Clint Eastwood.* (o filme foi dirigido) ▫ *She directed the new Broadway production of the musical.*
3 to tell someone how to get somewhere ▫ *Could you direct me to the post office, please?* (orientar)
4 to control or organize the way something is done ▫ *The police direct the traffic when it's busy.* (controlar)

direct debit /dɪˌrekt ˈdebɪt/ NOUN [plural **direct debits**] an instruction to your bank to pay money regularly to a person or organization 🔲 *We pay our bills by direct debit.* (débito automático)

direction /dɪˈrekʃən/ NOUN [plural **directions**]
1 the place or point a thing or person is going or facing towards ▫ *In which direction was she going – towards town or away?* ▫ **+ of** *He pointed in the direction of the kitchen.* (direção) 🔲 *The bus was travelling in the opposition direction.* (direção oposta) 🔲 *They all headed off in different directions.* (direções diferentes) 🔲 *The wind has changed direction.* (mudou a direção)
2 directions instructions for getting somewhere or doing something (instruções) 🔲 *I followed his directions as we headed out of town.* (segui suas instruções) ▫ *Make sure you read the directions for use carefully.*
3 the way something develops or changes (direção) 🔲 *We are taking the company in a new direction.* (novas direções)
4 no plural controlling or organizing things ▫ *The dock was built under the direction of Brunel in the 1850s.* (direção, comando)
5 no plural the feeling of having a clear purpose ▫ *I had no real direction in my life.* (objetivo)

directly /dɪˈrektli/ ADVERB
1 with no other person or thing between or involved ▫ *It plugs directly into your computer.* ▫ *Did you talk directly to him?* (diretamente) 🔲 *He wasn't directly involved in the project.* (diretamente envolvido) 🔲 *She wasn't directly responsible for the error.* (responsável direto)
2 straight from one place to another ▫ *We went directly to the station.* (diretamente)
3 exactly (imediatamente, precisamente) 🔲 *Chloe sat directly behind him.* (imediatamente atrás) 🔲 *He stood directly in front of me.* (imediatamente em frente)
4 saying exactly what you think in a clear, honest way ▫ *He didn't directly address the issue.* (claramente)
5 immediately ▫ *We spoke directly after the meeting.* (imediatamente)

direct object /dɪˌrekt ˈɒbdʒɪkt/ NOUN [plural **direct objects**] the noun or pronoun that is affected by the action of a verb. For example, in *He gave the boy a pound*, the direct object is a pound. (objeto direto)

director /dɪˈrektə(r)/ NOUN [plural **directors**]
1 the manager of a business, organization or department ▫ **+ of** *the director of the CIA* (diretor) 🔲 *the institute's executive director* (diretor executivo) 🔲 *the supermarket's finance director* (diretor financeiro)
2 someone who makes a film or organizes a stage show (diretor) 🔲 *a Hollywood film director* (diretor de cinema) 🔲 *She's the artistic director of the Sydney Theatre Company.*

directory /dɪˈrektəri/ NOUN [plural **directories**]
1 a book containing an alphabetical list of names, numbers or other information (catálogo, lista) 🔲 *a telephone directory* (catálogo telefônico)
2 a computer file where other files, documents, etc. are stored. A computing word. (diretório)

direct speech /dɪˌrekt ˈspiːtʃ/ NOUN, NO PLURAL in a story or report, the exact words that a person said (discurso direto)

dirt /dɜːt/ ▶ NOUN, NO PLURAL
1 any substance that is not clean or that makes something become not clean ▫ *Rinse under water to remove any dirt.* ▫ *She brushed the dirt from the surface.* (sujeira)
2 soil ▫ *a mound of dirt* (lama, terra) 🔲 *We drove up a dirt track to the farm.* (caminho de lama)
▶ ADVERB **dirt cheap/poor** extremely cheap or poor ▫ *I got it dirt cheap at the market.* (extremamente barato/pobre)

• **dirty** /ˈdɜːti/ ADJECTIVE [**dirtier, dirtiest**]
1 not clean (sujo) ▫ *dirty hands* ▫ *I cleared all the dirty dishes.* 🔲 *Try not to get your clothes dirty.* (sujar suas roupas) 🔲 *a pile of dirty laundry* (roupa suja)
2 to do with sex in a way that is not polite 🔲 *a dirty joke* (piada suja)
3 not fair or not honest (sujo, baixo) 🔲 *This is another of his dirty tricks.* (truques sujos)
♦ IDIOM **do someone's dirty work** to do something unpleasant or dishonest for someone else ▫ *He pays other people to do his dirty work for him.* (fazer o trabalho sujo de alguém)
▶ VERB [**dirties, dirtying, dirtied**] to make something dirty ▫ *I don't want to dirty my shoes.* (sujar)

dis- /dɪs/ PREFIX
1 dis- is added to the beginning of words to mean 'not' ▫ *dislike*
2 dis- is added to the beginning of words to mean 'to do with separating and moving apart' ▫ *disjointed* (des-)

disability /ˌdɪsəˈbɪləti/ NOUN [plural **disabilities**] a physical or mental problem that makes some parts of life difficult (invalidez, deficiência) 🔲 *a physical disability* (deficiência física) ▫ *Buildings should be accessible to people with disabilities.*

disadvantage — disapproval

- **disable** /dɪsˈeɪbəl/ VERB [disables, disabling, disabled]
  1 to stop a piece of equipment from working □ *The men disabled the security system.* (**desativar**)
  2 to cause someone to have a disability □ *She has been disabled by a back injury.* (**incapacitar**)

- **disabled** /dɪsˈeɪbəld/ ▶ ADJECTIVE having a disability (**inválido**) ▣ *We provide support for disabled people.* (**pessoas inválidas**) ▣ *Our son is severely disabled.* (**gravemente inválido**)
  ▶ NOUN **the disabled** people who are disabled (**os deficientes**)

disadvantage /ˌdɪsədˈvɑːntɪdʒ/ ▶ NOUN [plural disadvantages] something that makes something less attractive, less successful or more difficult □ *+ of The only disadvantage of the plan is that it could be too expensive.* □ *The advantages outweigh the disadvantages.* (**desvantagem**)
▶ VERB [disadvantages, disadvantaging, disadvantaged] to cause someone to have a disadvantage □ *The schedule unfairly disadvantages players who have long matches.* (**tirar vantagem**)

- **disadvantaged** /ˌdɪsədˈvɑːntɪdʒd/ ADJECTIVE poor and without many opportunities (**desprotegido, desfavorecido**) ▣ *He comes from a disadvantaged background.* (**passado desfavorecido**)

- **disadvantageous** /ˌdɪsædvɑːnˈteɪdʒəs/ ADJECTIVE causing a disadvantage □ *The new tax arrangements will be disadvantageous to people on low incomes.* (**desvantajoso**)

disaffected /ˌdɪsəˈfektɪd/ ADJECTIVE very disappointed and no longer supporting something □ *He hopes to win back disaffected voters.* (**descontente**)

- **disaffection** /ˌdɪsəˈfekʃən/ NOUN, NO PLURAL being disaffected □ *There is growing disaffection with the President.* (**descontentamento**)

disagree /ˌdɪsəˈɡriː/ VERB [disagrees, disagreeing, disagreed] to have a different opinion from someone else about something □ *+ with I completely disagree with you about that.* □ *+ about Doctors disagree about how effective the treatment is.* □ *+ over Ministers disagree over who is to blame.* □ *+ on They disagree on almost everything.* (**discordar**)
♦ PHRASAL VERBS **disagree with something** to not approve of something □ *Many people disagree with the death penalty.* (**discordar de algo**)
disagree with someone an informal word meaning to make you feel ill □ *Something I ate disagreed with me.* (**fazer mal a alguém**)

- **disagreeable** /ˌdɪsəˈɡriːəbəl/ ADJECTIVE unpleasant □ *a disagreeable smell* □ *She's being very disagreeable this morning.* (**desagradável**)

- **disagreement** /ˌdɪsəˈɡriːmənt/ NOUN [plural disagreements] when people have different opinions or argue (**discordância**) ▣ *We've had several disagreements on this subject.* (**várias discordâncias**) □ *There are still some areas of disagreement.* □ *+ between There was some disagreement between John and Robert.* □ *+ over There are also disagreements over finances.*

disallow /ˌdɪsəˈlaʊ/ VERB [disallows, disallowing, disallowed] to officially say that something cannot be accepted □ *Our next shot was disallowed by the referee.* (**rejeitar**)

disappear /ˌdɪsəˈpɪə(r)/ VERB [disappears, disappearing, disappeared]
1 if someone or something disappears, they go somewhere where they cannot be seen or found □ *+ from The woman disappeared from her home in April.* □ *He turned and disappeared into the crowd.* □ *The car disappeared down the street.* (**sumir, desaparecer**)
2 to stop existing □ *The symptoms usually disappear within a couple of days.* □ *Finally the light disappeared altogether.* (**desaparecer**)

- **disappearance** /ˌdɪsəˈpɪərəns/ NOUN [plural disappearances] when something or someone disappears □ *The police are investigating the disappearance of the businessman.* (**desaparecimento**)

disappoint /ˌdɪsəˈpɔɪnt/ VERB [disappoints, disappointing, disappointed] to make someone feel unhappy because something is not how they had hoped or expected □ *I'm sorry to disappoint you, but I can't come to your party.* □ *We don't want to disappoint our fans.* (**desapontamento**)

- **disappointed** /ˌdɪsəˈpɔɪntɪd/ ADJECTIVE unhappy because something is not how you had hoped or expected □ *+ that I'm disappointed that he can't come.* □ *+ with I'm very disappointed with the result.* (**desapontado, decepcionado**) ▣ *I feel bitterly disappointed.* (**amargamente desapontado**)

- **disappointing** /ˌdɪsəˈpɔɪntɪŋ/ ADJECTIVE not as good as you hoped or expected ▣ *It was a disappointing performance by the team.* □ *It's extremely disappointing that we haven't made any progress.* (**decepcionante**)

- **disappointingly** /ˌdɪsəˈpɔɪntɪŋli/ ADVERB in a disappointing way □ *Progress is disappointingly slow.* (**de modo decepcionante**)

- **disappointment** /ˌdɪsəˈpɔɪntmənt/ NOUN [plural disappointments] a feeling of being disappointed or something that makes you disappointed □ *It was a disappointment to find that all the tickets had already been sold.* (**decepção**) ▣ *The hotel was a big disappointment.* (**grande decepção**) ▣ *She expressed her disappointment at the decision.* (**expressou sua decepção**)

disapproval /ˌdɪsəˈpruːvəl/ NOUN, NO PLURAL when you think something is bad, wrong or not suitable □ *+ of Her decision earned her the disapproval of her family* (**desaprovação**) ▣ *His*

parents *expressed their disapproval* of the planned marriage. (expressaram sua desapovação)

- **disapprove** /ˌdɪsəˈpruːv/ VERB [**disapproves, disapproving, disapproved**] to think that something or someone is bad, wrong or not suitable □ + *of* My parents definitely disapproved of my new friend. □ We were wearing short skirts and he clearly disapproved. (desaprovar)
- **disapproving** /ˌdɪsəˈpruːvɪŋ/ ADJECTIVE showing that you disapprove □ a *disapproving tone of voice* (desaprovador)

disarm /dɪsˈɑːm/ VERB [**disarms, disarming, disarmed**]
1 to take a weapon away from someone □ *A security guard managed to disarm the intruder.* (desarmar)
2 to get rid of weapons that you have (desarmar)
3 to make someone feel less angry □ *His positive attitude disarmed many.* (acalmar, abrandar)

- **disarmament** /dɪsˈɑːməmənt/ NOUN, NO PLURAL the process of getting rid of weapons (desarmamento) 🔹 *He campaigned for nuclear disarmament.* (desarmamento nuclear)
- **disarming** /dɪsˈɑːmɪŋ/ ADJECTIVE making people feel less angry or unfriendly by your behaviour □ *a disarming smile* (afável)

disarray /ˌdɪsəˈreɪ/ NOUN, NO PLURAL
1 **in disarray** very untidy □ *The kitchen was in complete disarray.* (em desordem)
2 a situation in which things are confused or not organized □ *The troops were thrown into disarray by the death of their leader.* (confusão)

disaster /dɪˈzɑːstə(r)/ NOUN [plural **disasters**]
1 something that causes a lot of damage, injuries or deaths (desastre) 🔹 *They help victims of natural disasters such as earthquakes.* (desastre natural) 🔹 *The flight had just taken off when disaster struck.* (ocorreu um desastre)
2 a very bad situation or failure □ *The whole day was an absolute disaster.* □ *This could be a disaster for the tourist industry.* (um desastre)

- **disastrous** /dɪˈzɑːstrəs/ ADJECTIVE extremely bad (desastroso) 🔹 *The plans could have disastrous consequences for wildlife.* (consequências desastrosas) □ *They made a disastrous start to the championship.*

disband /dɪsˈbænd/ VERB [**disbands, disbanding, disbanded**] a formal word meaning to stop working together as a group □ *The government has promised to disband the armed militias.* (dissolver-se)

disbelief /ˌdɪsbɪˈliːf/ NOUN, NO PLURAL not believing something □ *She shook her head in disbelief.* □ *He had an expression of complete disbelief.* (descrença)

- **disbelieve** /ˌdɪsbɪˈliːv/ VERB [**disbelieves, disbelieving, disbelieved**] to think someone is lying or that something is not true □ *I have no reason to disbelieve him.* (não acreditar)
- **disbelieving** /ˌdɪsbɪˈliːvɪŋ/ ADJECTIVE showing disbelief □ *He gave me a disbelieving look.* (descrente)

disc /dɪsk/ NOUN [plural **discs**]
1 something flat and round □ *a small metal disc* □ *a disc of yellow plastic* (disco)
2 a record (= flat plastic object with music recorded on it) or CD (= small flat metal object with music or information recorded on it) (disco)
3 a round piece of cartilage (= strong substance in the body) between the bones in your back (disco)

discard /dɪˈskɑːd/ VERB [**discards, discarding, discarded**] to throw something away □ *a discarded wrapper* □ *Discard the herbs before serving.* (descartar)

discern /dɪˈsɜːn/ VERB [**discerns, discerning, discerned**] a formal word meaning to see or recognize something □ *It is often difficult to discern the difference between the two.* □ *She could just discern shapes in the darkness.* (discernir, perceber)

- **discernible** /dɪˈsɜːnəbəl/ ADJECTIVE able to be seen, heard or recognized (discernível, perceptível) 🔹 *There was no discernible difference.* (diferença perceptível) □ *His voice was barely discernible above the noise.*
- **discerning** /dɪˈsɜːnɪŋ/ ADJECTIVE good at judging the quality of things □ *She was a discerning judge of character.* (perspicaz)

discharge ▶ VERB /dɪsˈtʃɑːdʒ/ [**discharges, discharging, discharged**]
1 to allow someone to leave prison, a hospital or a military organization □ *She was discharged from hospital yesterday.* (receber alta)
2 if something discharges a substance, the substance comes out □ *The sewage is discharged into the river.* (despejar)
3 a formal word meaning to do something you should (cumprir) 🔹 *He had failed to discharge his official duties.* (cumprir deveres)
4 a formal word meaning to fire a weapon □ *Police say that no firearm was discharged.* (descarregar)
▶ NOUN /ˈdɪstʃɑːdʒ/ [plural **discharges**]
1 when someone is allowed to leave a hospital, prison or a military organization □ *He received an honourable discharge from the army.* (dispensa)
2 a substance that comes out of something □ *They were fined over illegal discharges of industrial waste.* (emissão)

disciple /dɪˈsaɪpəl/ NOUN [plural **disciples**]
1 a person who follows and believes in someone else's ideas (discípulo)
2 one of the first people to follow Jesus Christ (apóstolo)

disciplinarian /ˌdɪsɪplɪˈneərɪən/ NOUN [plural **disciplinarians**] someone who is very severe and punishes people who do not obey them □ *His father was a strict disciplinarian.* (disciplinador)

disciplinary /dɪsɪplɪnəri/ ADJECTIVE to do with punishment for breaking rules (**disciplinador**) 🔲 *The investigation led to disciplinary action against several staff members.* (**ação disciplinar**)

discipline /ˈdɪsɪplɪn/ ▶ NOUN [*plural* **disciplines**]

1 *no plural* when people are made to obey rules and behave in a particular way 🔲 *We're concerned about the lack of discipline in the school.* (**disciplina**) 🔲 *He couldn't maintain discipline in the classroom.* (**manter a disciplina**)

2 *no plural* the ability to control your own behaviour 🔲 *Martial arts require concentration and physical discipline.* (**disciplina**)

3 a formal word meaning a subject of study (**disciplina**) 🔲 *an academic discipline* (**disciplina acadêmica**)

▶ VERB [**disciplines, disciplining, disciplined**]

1 to punish someone 🔲 *Parents are asked how they discipline their children.* (**punir**)

2 to teach someone to control their behaviour 🔲 *I disciplined myself to train every day.* (**disciplinar**)

• **disciplined** /ˈdɪsɪplɪnd/ ADJECTIVE behaving in a controlled and organized way 🔲 *We need to take a more disciplined approach.* (**disciplinado**)

disc jockey /ˈdɪsk ˌdʒɒki/ NOUN [*plural* **disc jockeys**] someone who plays recorded music on the radio or at a club (**disc-jóquei**)

disclaim /dɪsˈkleɪm/ VERB [**disclaims, disclaiming, disclaimed**] a formal word meaning to say that you are not responsible for something, or that you do not know about it 🔲 *She disclaimed all responsibility for the mistake.* (**negar**)

• **disclaimer** /dɪsˈkleɪmə(r)/ NOUN [*plural* **disclaimers**] a written statement saying that someone does not accept responsibility for something (**carta de renúncia/repúdio**)

disclose /dɪsˈkləʊz/ VERB [**discloses, disclosing, disclosed**] to tell someone something new or secret (**revelar**) 🔲 *I'm not authorized to disclose that information.* (**revelar informação**) 🔲 *She didn't want to disclose her name.*

• **disclosure** /dɪsˈkləʊʒə(r)/ NOUN [*plural* **disclosures**] when information is disclosed 🔲 *Police are investigating an unauthorized disclosure of classified information.* (**revelação**)

disco /ˈdɪskəʊ/ NOUN [*plural* **discos**] a place or party where people dance to recorded music (**discoteca**)

discolor /dɪsˈkʌlə(r)/ VERB [**discolors, discoloring, discolored**] the US spelling of **discolour** (**descolorir, manchar**)

• **discolored** /dɪsˈkʌləd/ ADJECTIVE the US spelling of **discoloured** (**descolorido, desbotado, manchado**)

discolour /dɪsˈkʌlə(r)/ VERB [**discolours, discolouring, discoloured**] to become an unpleasant colour or to make something an unpleasant colour (**descolorir, manchar**)

• **discoloured** /dɪsˈkʌləd/ ADJECTIVE changed in colour in a way that is not attractive 🔲 *He had crooked, discoloured teeth.* (**descolorido, manchado**)

discomfort /dɪsˈkʌmfət/ NOUN, NO PLURAL

1 a feeling of being uncomfortable 🔲 *The doctor asked if I had felt any discomfort.* (**desconforto**)

2 a feeling of being nervous or embarrassed 🔲 *Some people have expressed discomfort with the decision.* (**incômodo**)

disconcert /ˌdɪskənˈsɜːt/ VERB [**disconcerts, disconcerting, disconcerted**] to make someone feel nervous or confused 🔲 *Grace was clearly disconcerted by his unexpected arrival.* (**perturbar, desconcertar**)

• **disconcerting** /ˌdɪskənˈsɜːtɪŋ/ ADJECTIVE making you feel nervous or confused 🔲 *I found his attitude a bit disconcerting.* (**perturbador, desconcertante**)

disconnect /ˌdɪskəˈnekt/ VERB [**disconnects, disconnecting, disconnected**]

1 to stop the supply of something such as gas or electricity 🔲 *The phone has been disconnected.* (**cortar**)

2 to separate things that were joined together 🔲 *His harness became disconnected from the safety rope.* (**desconectar**)

disconsolate /dɪsˈkɒnsələt/ ADJECTIVE unhappy or disappointed (**desconsolado**)

• **disconsolately** /dɪsˈkɒnsələtli/ ADVERB in a disconsolate way 🔲 *The golfers waited disconsolately as the rain poured down.* (**desconsoladamente**)

discontent /ˌdɪskənˈtent/ NOUN, NO PLURAL a feeling of not being happy or satisfied with a situation (**descontentamento**) 🔲 *There is widespread discontent with the government.* (**descontentamento geral**)

• **discontented** /ˌdɪskənˈtentɪd/ ADJECTIVE not happy or satisfied 🔲 *They grew discontented with their work.* (**descontente**)

discontinue /ˌdɪskənˈtɪnjuː/ VERB [**discontinues, discontinuing, discontinued**] to stop making or selling a product 🔲 *That model has been discontinued.* (**interromper, descontinuar, suspender**)

discord /ˈdɪskɔːd/ NOUN, NO PLURAL disagreement between people 🔲 *The pay system in this office has always been a cause of discord.* (**discórdia**)

discount ▶ NOUN /ˈdɪskaʊnt/ [*plural* **discounts**] a reduction in the price of something 🔲 *+ on There's a 10% discount on all goods.* (**desconto**) 🔲 *I got a £5 discount.* (**obtive desconto**) 🔲 *The company offers discounts to students.* (**oferece descontos**)

▶ VERB /ˈdɪskaʊnt, dɪsˈkaʊnt/ [**discounts, discounting, discounted**]

1 to believe that something is not likely, possible

or important □ *We can't discount the possibility of further legal action.* (**descartar**)
2 to reduce the price of something □ *Many shops discount their prices just after Christmas.* (**descontar**)

discourage /dɪˈskʌrɪdʒ/ VERB [discourages, discouraging, discouraged]
1 to try to stop something happening or to persuade someone not to do something □ *They introduced new measures to discourage smoking.* □ *We want to discourage people from driving into the city centre.* (**desencorajar**)
2 to make someone feel less confident or enthusiastic about something □ *Don't be discouraged by what he said.* (**desanimar**)

• **discouragement** /dɪˈskʌrɪdʒmənt/ NOUN, NO PLURAL
1 the process of discouraging something or something that discourages □ *This shouldn't be a discouragement to other families.* (**desencorajamento**)
2 a feeling of disappointment that stops you continuing with something (**desânimo**)

• **discouraging** /dɪˈskʌrɪdʒɪŋ/ ADJECTIVE making you feel less enthusiastic or confident about something □ *discouraging news* (**desanimador**)

discourteous /dɪsˈkɜːtɪəs/ ADJECTIVE rude and not showing respect (**rude, indelicado**)

discover /dɪˈskʌvə(r)/ VERB [discovers, discovering, discovered] to find information, a place or an object, especially for the first time □ *The settlers discovered gold in the mountains.* □ *The man's body was discovered yesterday.* □ *She finally discovered the truth.* □ **+ that** *We discovered that the paint wouldn't mix with water.* □ **+ question word** *Scientists hope to discover why numbers of the birds have dropped.* (**descobrir**)

• **discoverer** /dɪˈskʌvərə(r)/ NOUN [plural discoverers] a person who finds something for the first time (**descobridor**)

• **discovery** /dɪˈskʌvəri/ NOUN [plural discoveries] when someone discovers something, or the thing they discover □ **+ of** *the discovery of America* (**descoberta**) □ *He made a surprising discovery.* (**fez uma descoberta**)

discredit /dɪsˈkredɪt/ ▶ VERB [discredits, discrediting, discredited]
1 to prove that something is wrong or not true □ *As each slimming product is discredited a new one comes along.* (**desacreditar**)
2 to damage someone's reputation so they lose respect □ *Her rivals have tried to discredit her.* (**desacreditar**)
▶ NOUN, NO PLURAL loss of respect or damage to someone's reputation □ *Some pupils have brought discredit on the school by misbehaving on the buses.* (**descrédito, má reputação**)

discreet /dɪˈskriːt/ ADJECTIVE careful not to say or do things that attract attention or that could cause trouble □ *I wish you'd be a little more discreet.* (**discreto**)

• **discreetly** /dɪˈskriːtli/ ADVERB in a discreet way □ *He left discreetly.* (**discretamente**)

discrepancy /dɪˈskrepənsi/ NOUN [plural discrepancies] a difference between things that should be the same □ *The auditors discovered discrepancies in the accounts.* (**discrepância**)

discretion /dɪˈskreʃən/ NOUN, NO PLURAL
1 the quality of being careful not to embarrass or cause trouble for others □ *Please behave with discretion in all matters concerning his financial affairs.* (**discrição**)
2 the right or skill to make judgments and decisions □ *Increases in salary are at the discretion of the Board.* (**critério**)

• **discretionary** /dɪˈskreʃənəri/ ADJECTIVE (a) based on what someone decides, not on a rule or a right (b) discretionary payments (**arbitrário, discricionário**)

discriminate /dɪsˈkrɪmɪneɪt/ VERB [discriminates, discriminating, discriminated]
1 to treat someone unfairly because of their colour, religion, sex, etc. □ *Some employers were accused of discriminating against women.* (**discriminar**)
2 to recognize differences between things □ *They asked the children to discriminate between different shapes.* (**distinguir**)

• **discriminating** /dɪsˈkrɪmɪneɪtɪŋ/ ADJECTIVE able to make good judgments about the quality of something □ *Our more discriminating clients tend to choose the organic meat.* (**perspicaz**)

• **discrimination** /dɪsˌkrɪmɪˈneɪʃən/ NOUN, NO PLURAL
1 treating people unfairly because of their colour, religion, sex, etc. (**discriminação**) 🔲 *racial discrimination* (**discriminação racial**) 🔲 *They have suffered discrimination.* (**sofreram discriminação**)
2 the ability to judge the quality of something (**discernimento**)

• **discriminatory** /dɪsˈkrɪmɪnətəri/ ADJECTIVE treating people unfairly because of their colour, religion, sex, etc. □ *These rules are discriminatory.* (**discriminatório, discriminador**)

discus /ˈdɪskəs/ NOUN [plural discuses] a heavy disc that is thrown as a sport (**disco**)

discuss /dɪsˈkʌs/ VERB [discusses, discussing, discussed] to talk about something □ *You should try to discuss these issues with your wife.* □ **+ question word** *We have been discussing whether or not to replace them.* (**discutir**)

> ▶ Note that when you use the verb **discuss**, you must say what you are discussing:
> ✓ I must discuss the problem with Angela.
> ✗ I must discuss with Angela.

• **discussion** /dɪsˈkʌʃən/ NOUN [plural discussions] when people discuss something □ **+ about** *We got into a discussion about politics.* □

disdain

+ between *There have been weeks of discussion between US and Chinese officials.* (discussão) ▣ *The two sides have agreed to hold discussions next week.* (continuar as discussões) □ *There are three options under discussion.*

disdain /dɪsˈdeɪn/ NOUN, NO PLURAL a feeling that you do not like or respect someone or something □ *He could not hide his disdain for Thomas.* (desdém)

- **disdainful** /dɪsˈdeɪnfʊl/ ADJECTIVE showing disdain □ *a disdainful expression* (desdenhoso)

disease /dɪˈziːz/ NOUN [plural **diseases**]
1 an illness □ **+ of** *Multiple sclerosis is a disease of the nervous system.* (doença) ▣ *He developed heart disease.* (doença cardíaca) ▣ *The infection can cause liver disease.* (causar doença)
2 no plural illness generally □ *Poor hygiene leads to the spread of disease.* □ *Thousands died of disease and hunger.* (doença)

- **diseased** /dɪˈziːzd/ ADJECTIVE not healthy because of an illness □ *He had surgery to remove the diseased tissue.* (doente, enfermo)

disembark /ˌdɪsemˈbɑːk/ VERB [**disembarks, disembarking, disembarked**] a formal word meaning to get off a boat or an aircraft (desembarcar)

disenchanted /ˌdɪsɪnˈtʃɑːntɪd/ ADJECTIVE if you are disenchanted with something, you are no longer as enthusiastic about it as you were before (desiludido)

- **disenchantment** /ˌdɪsɪnˈtʃɑːntmənt/ NOUN, NO PLURAL when you become disenchanted with something □ *Life in Russia added to his disenchantment with communism.* (desilusão)

disfigure /dɪsˈfɪgə(r)/ VERB [**disfigures, disfiguring, disfigured**] to spoil the look of something □ *Her face was disfigured by the attack.* (desfigurar)

disgrace /dɪsˈgreɪs/ ▶ NOUN, NO PLURAL
1 when someone loses respect because of something they have done □ *It's no disgrace to come last if you tried hard.* □ *You have brought disgrace to your family.* (desgraça)
2 in disgrace if you are in disgrace, other people are angry with you □ *Debbie's in disgrace for staying out all night.* (em desgraça)
3 someone or something very bad or unacceptable (desgraça) ▣ *I think it's an absolute disgrace that this has taken so long.* (desgraça absoluta) □ *He's a disgrace to his profession.*
▶ VERB [**disgraces, disgracing, disgraced**] to lose other people's respect because of your behaviour □ *I disgraced myself and my family.* (envergonhar)

- **disgraceful** /dɪsˈgreɪsfʊl/ ADJECTIVE very bad or shocking (desgraça) ▣ *I think their behaviour was absolutely disgraceful.* (absolutamente vergonhoso) □ *There were disgraceful scenes at the end of the evening.*

disheartened

- **disgracefully** /dɪsˈgreɪsfʊli/ ADVERB very badly □ *They treated him disgracefully.* (desgraçadamente)

disgruntled /dɪsˈgrʌntəld/ ADJECTIVE disappointed, unhappy or angry about something (desapontado)

disguise /dɪsˈgaɪz/ ▶ NOUN [plural **disguises**] something you wear to change your appearance so that people do not recognize you □ *He left the hotel in disguise.* (disfarce)
▶ VERB [**disguises, disguising, disguised**]
1 to hide something such as your feelings or the truth □ *She couldn't disguise the fact that she was disappointed.* (disfarçar)
2 to put a disguise on someone □ *She disguised herself as a tourist.* (disfarçar)
3 to make something look, sound or seem like something else □ *He had an explosive device disguised as a laptop computer.* (disfarçar)

disgust /dɪsˈgʌst/ ▶ NOUN, NO PLURAL a strong feeling that you do not like or approve of something □ *The sight of the worms filled Luisa with disgust.*
▶ VERB [**disgusts, disgusting, disgusted**] to make someone feel disgust □ *They were disgusted by what they saw.* □ *It disgusts me that people can behave that way.* (repugnância, repulsa)

- **disgusted** /dɪsˈgʌstɪd/ ADJECTIVE feeling disgust □ *Alan gave her a disgusted look.* (nojento)
- **disgusting** /dɪsˈgʌstɪŋ/ ADJECTIVE
1 extremely unpleasant □ *a disgusting mess* (repugnante, nojento) ▣ *It looked absolutely disgusting.* (absolutamente nojento)
2 very bad or shocking □ *disgusting behaviour* (desagradável)

dish /dɪʃ/ NOUN [plural **dishes**]
1 a plate or bowl for food □ *Cover the dish with a lid.* (prato, travessa) ▣ *a pile of dirty dishes* (pratos sujos) ▣ *I'll wash the dishes.* (lavar os pratos)
2 food that has been prepared for eating (prato) □ *a fish dish* ▣ *The restaurant serves traditional dishes.* (serve pratos)
3 a round piece of equipment that receives television signals (antena parabólica) ▣ *a satellite dish* (antena parabólica via satélite)
◆ PHRASAL VERBS [**dishes, dishing, dished**] **dish something out**
1 an informal word meaning to give or say things to people without much thought or care □ *My job's not just about dishing out pills.* □ *He's always dishing out advice.* (distribuir algo)
2 to serve food □ *I began dishing the rice out.*
dish something up to serve food □ *She dished up some hot soup.* (servir algo)

dishcloth /ˈdɪʃklɒθ/ NOUN [plural **dishcloths**] a small cloth you use in the kitchen for washing dishes (pano de prato)

disheartened /dɪsˈhɑːtənd/ ADJECTIVE feeling less hope or confidence about something □ *Don't get disheartened.* (desanimado)

- **disheartening** /dɪsˈhɑːtənɪŋ/ ADJECTIVE making you feel less hope or confidence □ *The results are disheartening.* (desencorajado)

disheveled /dɪˈʃevəld/ ADJECTIVE the US spelling of **dishevelled**

dishevelled /dɪˈʃevəld/ ADJECTIVE with untidy hair and clothes □ *He looked slightly dishevelled.* (desalinhado)

dishonest /dɪsˈɒnɪst/ ADJECTIVE not telling the truth, or doing things that are wrong or illegal □ *I didn't do anything dishonest.* □ *It would be dishonest to hide it from him.* (desonesto)

- **dishonestly** /dɪsˈɒnɪstli/ ADVERB in a dishonest way □ *He obtained the money dishonestly.* (desonestamente)

- **dishonesty** /dɪsˈɒnɪsti/ NOUN, NO PLURAL being dishonest □ *There were accusations of dishonesty and corruption.* (desonestidade)

dishonor /dɪsˈɒnə(r)/ NOUN, NO PLURAL the US spelling of **dishonour** (desonra)

- **dishonorable** /dɪsˈɒnərəbəl/ ADJECTIVE the US spelling of **dishonourable** (desonroso)

- **dishonorably** /dɪsˈɒnərəbli/ ADVERB the US spelling of **dishonourably** (desonrosamente)

dishonour /dɪsˈɒnə(r)/ NOUN, NO PLURAL when someone loses people's respect because of their bad behaviour □ *They brought dishonour on the whole army.* (desonra)

- **dishonourable** /dɪsˈɒnərəbəl/ ADJECTIVE not honest and not deserving respect □ *He would do nothing dishonourable, even to save himself.* (desonroso)

- **dishonourably** /dɪsˈɒnərəbli/ ADVERB in a dishonourable way □ *You acted dishonourably.* (desonrosamente)

dishwasher /ˈdɪʃwɒʃə(r)/ NOUN [plural **dishwashers**] a machine for washing things such as plates, cups, etc. after a meal (lava-louças)

disillusion /ˌdɪsɪˈluːʒən/ VERB [**disillusions, disillusioning, disillusioned**] to make you disappointed in something that you liked or approved of before □ *I'm sorry to disillusion you, but he's not really an actor.* (decepcionar)

- **disillusioned** /ˌdɪsɪˈluːʒənd/ ADJECTIVE disappointed in something you liked or approved of before □ *I was feeling disillusioned with university and wondering whether to leave.* (desiludido)

- **disillusionment** /ˌdɪsɪˈluːʒənmənt/ NOUN, NO PLURAL the feeling of being disillusioned □ *He shared my disillusionment with the present government.* (desilusão)

disinfect /ˌdɪsɪnˈfekt/ VERB [**disinfects, disinfecting, disinfected**] to clean something with a substance that destroys bacteria that might cause disease □ *All surfaces should be disinfected regularly.* (desinfetar)

- **disinfectant** /ˌdɪsɪnˈfektənt/ NOUN [plural **disinfectants**] a substance that kills bacteria (desinfetante)

disintegrate /dɪsˈɪntɪgreɪt/ VERB [**disintegrates, disintegrating, disintegrated**]

1 to break into pieces □ *The plane disintegrated on impact.* (desintegrar)

2 to become much worse or to fail □ *The country disintegrated into civil war.* □ *Her marriage had disintegrated.* (desfazer-se, fragmentar)

- **disintegration** /dɪsˌɪntɪˈgreɪʃən/ NOUN, NO PLURAL the process of disintegrating (desintegração)

disinterested /dɪsˈɪntrəstɪd/ ADJECTIVE not being involved in something, and so able to make a fair judgment □ *A disinterested judge will make a fair decision.* (desinteressado)

disjointed /dɪsˈdʒɔɪntɪd/ ADJECTIVE confused and not in a clear order □ *She could only give a very disjointed account of what had happened.* (incoerente)

disk /dɪsk/ NOUN [plural **disks**]

1 a round flat object that computers use to store information on. A computing word □ *Insert a disk into drive D.* (disco) □ *It requires at least 600MB of disk space.* (espaço em disco)

2 the US spelling of **disc** (disco)

disk drive /ˈdɪsk ˌdraɪv/ NOUN [plural **disk drives**] the part of a computer that reads information from disks. A computing word. (unidade de disco)

dislike /dɪsˈlaɪk/ ▶ VERB [**dislikes, disliking, disliked**] to not like someone or something □ *She disliked the idea of the children travelling alone.* □ *He disliked dentists intensely.* □ + **ing** *I dislike having to get up early.* (detestar)

▶ NOUN [plural **dislikes**] something you dislike or the feeling of disliking something or someone □ *He had a dislike of crowds* (aversão) □ *They took an instant dislike to each other.* (sentiram aversão)

dislocate /ˈdɪsləkeɪt/ VERB [**dislocates, dislocating, dislocated**] to move a bone in your body out of its correct position (deslocar) □ *Tom dislocated his shoulder in a rugby match.* (deslocou o ombro)

dislodge /dɪsˈlɒdʒ/ VERB [**dislodges, dislodging, dislodged**] to move something which was fixed in a position □ *The strong wind dislodged tiles from the roof.* (deslocar)

disloyal /dɪsˈlɔɪəl/ ADJECTIVE not loyal to someone you should support □ *She felt it would be disloyal to her brother.* (desleal)

- **disloyalty** /dɪsˈlɔɪəlti/ NOUN, NO PLURAL when someone is disloyal (deslealdade)

dismal /ˈdɪzməl/ ADJECTIVE

1 not bright or attractive, and making you feel unhappy □ *dismal weather* (triste, sombrio)

2 very bad or disappointing □ *the team's dismal performance* □ *They have a dismal record on safety.* (péssimo)

dismantle / dispense

dismantle /dɪsˈmæntəl/ VERB [dismantles, dismantling, dismantled] to separate something into several pieces □ *They dismantled the equipment and packed it into the van.* (desmontar)

dismay /dɪsˈmeɪ/ NOUN, NO PLURAL an unpleasant feeling of surprise and worry □ *We watched in dismay as Ted fell into the water.* (consternação) 🔁 *To her dismay, she found her foot was stuck.* (para sua consternação) 🔁 *Campaigners expressed dismay at the decision.* (expressou consternação)

- **dismayed** /dɪsˈmeɪd/ ADJECTIVE feeling dismay □ *I was dismayed when I heard the news.* (consternado)

dismiss /dɪsˈmɪs/ VERB [dismisses, dismissing, dismissed]

1 to refuse to think about or accept an idea (dispensar) 🔁 *He dismissed suggestions that he was planning to leave.* (dispensou sugestões) □ *She dismissed the idea as too expensive.*
2 to make someone leave their job □ *She was dismissed for misconduct.* □ *He was dismissed from the army.* (demitir)
3 to officially decide that a court case should not continue (dispensar) 🔁 *The judge dismissed the case because of lack of evidence.* (dispensou o caso)
4 to send someone away □ *The class were dismissed by the teacher early today.* (dispensar)

- **dismissal** /dɪsˈmɪsəl/ NOUN [plural dismissals]
1 when someone is dismissed from their job (demissão) 🔁 *He is claiming unfair dismissal.* (demissão injusta)
2 when someone dismisses an idea (repúdio)

- **dismissive** /dɪsˈmɪsɪv/ ADJECTIVE not treating something or someone as important □ *He made a dismissive gesture with his hand.* (desdenhoso)

- **dismissively** /dɪsˈmɪsɪvli/ ADVERB in a dismissive way □ *She spoke dismissively of her rival's work.* (desdenhosamente)

dismount /ˌdɪsˈmaʊnt/ VERB [dismounts, dismounting, dismounted] to get off a bicycle or a horse (desmontar)

disobedience /ˌdɪsəˈbiːdiəns/ NOUN, NO PLURAL when someone does not do what they are told to do (desobediência)

- **disobedient** /ˌdɪsəˈbiːdiənt/ ADJECTIVE not doing what you are told to do □ *a disobedient dog* □ *He's rude and disobedient.* (desobediente)
- **disobey** /ˌdɪsəˈbeɪ/ VERB [disobeys, disobeying, disobeyed] to not do what you are told to do □ *How dare you disobey me!* (desobedecer)

disorder /dɪsˈɔː(r)də(r)/ NOUN [plural disorders]
1 an illness □ *This could help to treat sleep disorders.* (doença, enfermidade)
2 when something is confused or badly organized □ *The meeting broke up in disorder.* (desordem)
3 violent, uncontrolled behaviour by groups of people □ *There have been two nights of disorder in the city.* (tumulto, motim)

- **disorderly** /dɪsˈɔː(r)dəli/ ADJECTIVE
1 behaving badly (desordeiro, indisciplinado) 🔁 *disorderly conduct* (comportamento desordeiro)
2 untidy or badly organized □ *a disorderly house* (desarrumado, desordenado)

disorganized or **disorganised** /dɪsˈɔːɡənaɪzd/ ADJECTIVE
1 not tidy or not well organized □ *Her clothes lay in a disorganized heap.* (desorganizado)
2 bad at making plans or doing things in an efficient way □ *I found him a very disorganized person to work with.* (desorganizado)

disorientated /dɪsˈɔːriənteɪtɪd/ or **disoriented** /dɪsˈɔːrientɪd/ ADJECTIVE confused about where you are or what is happening (desorientado)

- **disorientation** /dɪsˌɔːriənˈteɪʃən/ NOUN, NO PLURAL when you are disorientated □ *She experienced feelings of panic and disorientation.* (desorientação)

disown /dɪsˈəʊn/ VERB [disowns, disowning, disowned] to say that you do not want to have any connection with someone, especially your children □ *Her parents disowned her when she left the religion.* (rejeitar, renegar)

disparage /dɪˈspærɪdʒ/ VERB [disparages, disparaging, disparaged] to say that someone or something is not very good □ *His comments were not intended to disparage the staff.* (depreciar)

- **disparagement** /dɪˈspærɪdʒmənt/ NOUN, NO PLURAL when someone disparages someone or something □ *There's so much disparagement of charitable work these days.* (depreciação)
- **disparaging** /dɪˈspærɪdʒɪŋ/ ADJECTIVE criticizing someone or something □ *We can do without your disparaging comments.* (depreciativo)
- **disparagingly** /dɪˈspærɪdʒɪŋli/ ADVERB in a disparaging way □ *He wrote disparagingly about modern poetry.* (de modo depreciativo)

disparity /dɪˈspærəti/ NOUN [plural disparities] a difference between two things, for example amounts of money □ *There is a huge disparity in their incomes.* (disparidade)

dispassionate /dɪˈspæʃənət/ ADJECTIVE able to form opinions and make judgments without becoming emotionally involved (imparcial)

dispatch /dɪˈspætʃ/ VERB [dispatches, dispatching, dispatched] a formal word meaning to send something or someone somewhere □ *The parcel was dispatched on the 29th.* □ *The navy dispatched a helicopter to help in the search.* (despachar)

dispel /dɪˈspel/ VERB [dispels, dispelling, dispelled] to get rid of an idea or a feeling □ *He acted quickly to dispel investors' fears.* (afastar)

dispensable /dɪˈspensəbəl/ ADJECTIVE not necessary □ *Some of these items can be regarded as dispensable extras.* (dispensável)

dispense /dɪˈspens/ VERB [dispenses, dispensing, dispensed]

1 to give something to people □ *The vending machines dispense cold drinks.* (distribuir)
2 to give people medicines □ *Only trained pharmacists can dispense the drug.* (ministrar, aviar medicamentos)
◆ PHRASAL VERB **dispense with someone/something** to stop using or to get rid of someone or something □ *He has dispensed with the services of his coach.* (dispensar algo/alguém)
• **dispenser** /dɪˈspensə(r)/ NOUN [plural dispensers] a machine that dispenses something □ *a cash dispenser* □ *a water dispenser* (distribuidor, dispensador)

dispersal /dɪˈspɜːsəl/ NOUN, NO PLURAL the action of dispersing people or things (dispersão)

disperse /dɪˈspɜːs/ VERB [disperses, dispersing, dispersed] to separate people or things and make them go in different directions, usually to get rid of them, or to separate in this way □ *The crowd is now beginning to disperse.* (dispersar)

displace /dɪsˈpleɪs/ VERB [displaces, displacing, displaced]
1 to make someone leave their home or country □ *Thousands of people were displaced during the war.* (deslocar)
2 to take the place of someone or something □ *Their party hopes to displace the military government.* (substituir)
• **displacement** /dɪsˈpleɪsmənt/ NOUN, NO PLURAL when someone or something is displaced (deslocamento, destituição)

display /dɪˈspleɪ/ ▶ NOUN [plural displays]
1 things which are arranged or presented for people to look at □ + *of* *a display of the children's work* (exibição) □ *a fireworks display* (uma exibição de fogos de artifício)
2 on display arranged for people to look at □ *The painting is on display at the National Gallery.* (em exposição)
3 when someone shows a particular feeling or quality □ + *of* *It was a very public display of affection.* □ *They were impressed by her display of courage.* (manifestação)
4 the way you see things on a computer screen □ *You can change the display so that it's bigger.* (tela)
▶ VERB [displays, displaying, displayed]
1 to arrange things for people to look at □ *The treasure will be displayed in the museum for two months.* □ *All offices must display no smoking signs.* (expor)
2 to show a particular feeling or quality □ *The men displayed great courage.* □ *She displayed an early talent for driving.* (mostrar)
3 to show something on a computer screen □ *The pictures were displayed on a big screen.* (exibir)

displease /dɪsˈpliːz/ VERB [displeases, displeasing, displeased] a formal word meaning to annoy someone □ *He was displeased with their performance.* (desagradar)

• **displeasure** /dɪsˈpleʒə(r)/ NOUN, NO PLURAL when someone is displeased (desprazer, desagrado)

disposable /dɪˈspəʊzəbəl/ ADJECTIVE a disposable product is meant to be used and then thrown away □ *disposable nappies* □ *a disposable razor* (descartável)

disposal /dɪˈspəʊzəl/ NOUN, NO PLURAL
1 getting rid of something (descarte) □ *We are using new methods of waste disposal.* (descarte de lixo) □ *There are strict regulations about the disposal of chemicals.*
2 at your disposal available for you to use □ *There will be a car at your disposal.* (à disposição)

dispose /dɪˈspəʊz/
1 PHRASAL VERB [disposes, disposing, disposed] **dispose of something** to get rid of something □ *Where can I dispose of my old fridge?* (dispor de algo)

disposition /ˌdɪspəˈzɪʃən/ NOUN, NO PLURAL someone's character and the way they usually behave □ *This ride is not for those of a nervous disposition.* (disposição)

disproportionate /ˌdɪsprəˈpɔːʃənət/ ADJECTIVE bigger or smaller than is right or reasonable when compared with something else □ *We feel we are paying a disproportionate share of the costs.* (desproporcional)
• **disproportionately** /ˌdɪsprəˈpɔːʃənətli/ ADVERB in a disproportionate way □ *Poorer households will be disproportionately affected by the price rises.* (desproporcionalmente)

disprove /dɪsˈpruːv/ VERB [disproves, disproving, disproved] to prove that something is not true □ *This new evidence seems to disprove his theory.* (contestar)

dispute /dɪˈspjuːt/ ▶ NOUN [plural disputes] a serious disagreement about something □ *They went on strike in a dispute over pay.* (disputa) □ *They are trying to resolve their dispute.* (resolver sua disputa)
▶ VERB [disputes, disputing, disputed] to say that something is not true or correct □ *They dispute that they have been treated fairly.* (disputar)

disqualification /dɪsˌkwɒlɪfɪˈkeɪʃən/ NOUN, NO PLURAL when someone is stopped from doing something because they have done something wrong □ *Students could face disqualification if caught with mobile phones in exams.* (desqualificação, exclusão)

disqualify /dɪsˈkwɒlɪfaɪ/ VERB [disqualifies, disqualifying, disqualified] to stop someone from doing something because they have done something wrong □ *Two athletes were disqualified for a false start.* (desqualificar, excluir)

disregard /ˌdɪsrɪˈɡɑːd/ VERB [disregards, disregarding, disregarded] to ignore or show no interest in something □ *They have completely disregarded my instructions.* (ignorar)

disrepair /ˌdɪsrɪˈpeə(r)/ NOUN, NO PLURAL a bad state or condition (**mau estado**) ◻ *The building had fallen into disrepair.* (**caiu em mau estado**)

disreputable /dɪsˈrepjutəbəl/ ADJECTIVE not respected or not honest ☐ *I had heard of his disreputable business activities.* (**infame, de má reputação**)

• **disrepute** /ˌdɪsrɪˈpjuːt/ NOUN, NO PLURAL **bring something into disrepute** a formal phrase meaning to spoil the reputation of something ☐ *This sort of thing brings the club into disrepute.* (**desacreditar, desprestigiar**)

disrespect /ˌdɪsrɪˈspekt/ NOUN, NO PLURAL when someone behaves without respect towards someone or something ☐ *He showed complete disrespect for the local culture.* (**desrespeitar**)

• **disrespectful** /ˌdɪsrɪˈspektfʊl/ ADJECTIVE not showing respect towards someone or something ☐ *disrespectful behaviour* (**desrespeitoso**)

disrupt /dɪsˈrʌpt/ VERB [**disrupts, disrupting, disrupted**] to stop something continuing as usual ☐ *Traffic was disrupted because of the march.* (**perturbar**)

• **disruption** /dɪsˈrʌpʃən/ NOUN [*plural* **disruptions**] when something is disrupted ☐ *There was disruption in the town centre caused by a burst water pipe.* (**perturbação**)

• **disruptive** /dɪsˈrʌptɪv/ ADJECTIVE causing disruption ☐ *Disruptive pupils will be excluded.* (**perturbador**)

dissatisfaction /ˌdɪssætɪsˈfækʃən/ NOUN, NO PLURAL when you are not pleased because something is not good enough ☐ *Public dissatisfaction with the government is growing.* (**insatisfação**)

• **dissatisfied** /ˌdɪsˈsætɪsfaɪd/ ADJECTIVE not pleased because something is not good enough ☐ *She was becoming increasingly dissatisfied with her job.* (**descontente**)

dissect /dɪˈsekt/ VERB [**dissects, dissecting, dissected**] to cut a dead body into pieces so that you can examine it (**dissecar**)

• **dissection** /dɪˈsekʃən/ NOUN, NO PLURAL when someone dissects something (**dissecação**)

dissent /dɪˈsent/ ▶ NOUN, NO PLURAL disagreement with an opinion or decision ☐ *Within the party there was dissent on some key issues.* (**discordância**)
▶ VERB [**dissents, dissenting, dissented**] to disagree with an opinion or decision. A formal word. (**discordar**)

• **dissenter** /dɪˈsentə(r)/ NOUN [*plural* **dissenters**] someone who disagrees with something ☐ *Political dissenters were imprisoned.* (**discordante**)

dissertation /ˌdɪsəˈteɪʃən/ NOUN [*plural* **dissertations**] a long piece of writing on a particular subject, especially done for a university degree (**dissertação**)

disservice /dɪsˈsɜːvɪs/ NOUN, NO PLURAL **do someone a disservice** to do something that harms someone or to say something that makes other people's opinion of someone worse ☐ *By forbidding debate on the issue, he is doing a great disservice to the country.* (**prestar um mau serviço a alguém**)

dissident /ˈdɪsɪdənt/ NOUN [*plural* **dissidents**] someone who publicly criticizes their country's government (**dissidente**)

dissimilar /dɪˈsɪmɪlə(r)/ ADJECTIVE different ☐ *These are two very dissimilar cultures.* (**diferente**)

dissolve /dɪˈzɒlv/ VERB [**dissolves, dissolving, dissolved**]
1 to melt or be melted in liquid ☐ *Keep stirring until the sugar dissolves completely.* ☐ *Stir to dissolve the sugar.* (**dissolver**)
2 to officially end something such as a government, organization or legal arrangement ☐ *Parliament was dissolved in 2002.* ☐ *Their marriage was dissolved.* (**dissolver, acabar**)

dissuade /dɪˈsweɪd/ VERB [**dissuades, dissuading, dissuaded**] to persuade someone not to do something ☐ *She tried to dissuade her son from joining the army.* (**dissuadir**)

distance /ˈdɪstəns/ NOUN [*plural* **distances**]
1 the space between things ☐ + *between* Measure the distance between the lines. ☐ + *from* The hotel is only a short distance from the city centre. (**distância**) ◻ *He doesn't like driving long distances.* (**longas distâncias**)
2 in the distance if you see or hear something in the distance you see or hear it but it is a long way away ☐ *I could hear the sound of a train in the distance.* (**a distância**)
3 at/from a distance at or from a place that is not close ☐ *I watched him from a distance.* (**de longe**)
4 keep your distance (a) to not get close to something so that you are safe ☐ *They kept their distance from the bears.* (b) to not become involved with someone or something ☐ *He was advised to keep his distance from the media.* (**mantenha distância**)

• **distant** /ˈdɪstənt/ ADJECTIVE
1 far away in space or time ☐ *He heard distant voices which were getting closer.* (**distância**) ◻ *The holiday seems like a distant memory now.* (**lembrança distante**) ◻ *the distant past* (**passado distante**)
2 related to you but not closely (**distante**) ◻ *She's a distant relative of my husband.* (**parente distante**)
3 not paying attention, and thinking about other things ☐ *He seemed a bit distant.* (**distante, ausente**)

• **distantly** /ˈdɪstəntli/ ADVERB
1 from far away ☐ *lights glimmered distantly* (**a distância**)
2 distantly related belonging to the same family, but not close relations (**parente distante**)
3 without showing much emotion or interest, often because you are thinking about something

else □ *She smiled distantly.* (**friamente, reservadamente**)

distaste /dɪsˈteɪst/ NOUN, NO PLURAL a feeling of dislike □ *He had a distaste for any kind of gossip.* (**aversão**)

• **distasteful** /dɪsˈteɪstfʊl/ ADJECTIVE unpleasant □ *She found the idea very distasteful.* (**detestável, repugnante**)

distil /dɪˈstɪl/ VERB [**distils, distilling, distilled**] to make a liquid pure by boiling it until it becomes a gas and then cooling it. A chemistry word. (**destilar**) ▣ *distilled water* (**água destilada**)

• **distillery** /dɪˈstɪləri/ NOUN [*plural* **distilleries**] a factory that makes strong alcoholic drinks like whisky and brandy (**destilaria**)

distinct /dɪˈstɪŋkt/ ADJECTIVE
1 certain (**evidente, nítido**) ▣ *Winning the race remains a distinct possibility.* (**possibilidade nítida**) ▣ *He had a distinct advantage over his rivals.* (**vantagem evidente**)
2 easy to see, hear, smell etc. □ *Green tea has a distinct flavour.* (**claro, inconfundível**)
3 different □ *The two languages are quite distinct.* (**distinto**)

• **distinction** /dɪˈstɪŋkʃən/ NOUN [*plural* **distinctions**]
1 a difference (**distinção**) ▣ *The terrorists made no distinction between military and civilian targets.* (**não fizeram distinção**)
2 something that makes someone or something different (**honra**) ▣ *She had the distinction of being the first female airline pilot.* (**teve a honra de**)

• **distinctive** /dɪˈstɪŋktɪv/ ADJECTIVE different and easy to recognize □ *She has a very distinctive voice.* (**distinto**)

distinguish /dɪˈstɪŋgwɪʃ/ VERB [**distinguishes, distinguishing, distinguished**]
1 to see a difference between things □ *If you're colour blind, you have difficulties distinguishing green from red.* (**distinguir, diferenciar**)
2 to be the quality that makes someone or something different □ *It's his intelligence as an actor that distinguishes him from other actors of his generation.* (**caracterizar**)
3 to be able to hear or see something. A formal word. □ *In the dark I could just distinguish the shape of a man outside the window.* (**discernir**)

• **distinguished** /dɪˈstɪŋgwɪʃt/ ADJECTIVE successful and respected □ *a distinguished professor* (**distinto, ilustre**) ▣ *He had a long and distinguished career in the army.* (**carreira ilustre**)

distort /dɪˈstɔːt/ VERB [**distorts, distorting, distorted**]
1 to change information so that it is not correct □ *He accused the government of distorting the facts.* (**distorcer**)
2 to change the shape or sound of something so that it seems strange □ *The microphone distorted his voice.* (**distorcer**)

• **distortion** /dɪˈstɔːʃən/ NOUN, NO PLURAL distorting something □ *This is a deliberate distortion of the truth.* (**distorção**)

distract /dɪˈstrækt/ VERB [**distracts, distracting, distracted**] to take someone's attention away from something □ *Advertisements at the side of the road can distract drivers.* (**distrair**)

• **distracted** /dɪˈstræktɪd/ ADJECTIVE not able to think about something because you are thinking about something else □ *He looked distracted.* (**distraído**)

• **distraction** /dɪˈstrækʃən/ NOUN [*plural* **distractions**] something that takes your attention away from something □ *I can't work with all these distractions.* (**distração**)

distraught /dɪˈstrɔːt/ ADJECTIVE extremely upset □ *They showed the distraught parents on television.* (**consternado**)

distress /dɪˈstres/ ▶ NOUN, NO PLURAL when someone is upset □ *I didn't want to cause them any distress.* (**aflição**)
▶ VERB [**distresses, distressing, distressed**] to upset someone (**afligir, angustiar**)

• **distressed** /dɪˈstrest/ ADJECTIVE upset □ *He was too distressed to talk about it.* (**aflito**)

• **distressing** /dɪˈstresɪŋ/ ADJECTIVE making someone feel very upset □ *It has been a very distressing time for me and my family.* (**angustiante**)

distribute /dɪˈstrɪbjuːt/ VERB [**distributes, distributing, distributed**]
1 to give something to a lot of people □ *Please distribute the leaflets to your friends.* (**distribuir**)
2 to supply something to shops and companies □ *The company manufactures and distributes drinks.* (**distribuir**)

• **distribution** /ˌdɪstrɪˈbjuːʃən/ NOUN, NO PLURAL
1 the process of giving something to a group of people □ *He organized the distribution of food among the refugees.* (**distribuição**)
2 the way that something is shared or exists among a group of people □ *The distribution of wealth is not equal.* (**distribuição**)
3 the process of supplying things to shops and companies □ *He is involved in the marketing and distribution of new products.* (**distribuição**)

• **distributor** /dɪˈstrɪbjuːtə(r)/ NOUN [*plural* **distributors**] a company that supplies goods to shops or companies (**distribuidor, distribuidora**)

district /ˈdɪstrɪkt/ NOUN [*plural* **districts**] a part of a country or city □ *Shanghai's business district* (**distrito, bairro**)

distrust /dɪsˈtrʌst/ ▶ NOUN, NO PLURAL a feeling that you cannot trust someone □ *Many people have a deep distrust of the government.* (**desconfiança**)
▶ VERB [**distrusts, distrusting, distrusted**] to not trust someone or something

disturb

disturb /dɪˈstɜːb/ VERB [**disturbs, disturbing, disturbed**]
1 to interrupt what someone is doing □ *I'm sorry to disturb you, but I need to ask you a question.* (**incomodar**)
2 to upset or worry someone □ *The incident had disturbed him.* (**perturbar**)
3 to move something and change its position □ *I knew that someone had been at my desk because the papers had been disturbed.* (**desarranjar**)

- **disturbance** /dɪˈstɜːbəns/ NOUN [plural **disturbances**]
1 an occasion when people fight or shout in a public place □ *There was a disturbance in the street last night.* (**perturbação**)
2 something that interrupts what you are doing □ *We hope that the event won't cause any disturbance to local residents.* (**distúrbio**)
3 a change in the way your mind or a part of your body works □ *The drug can cause visual disturbances.* (**perturbação**)

- **disturbed** /dɪˈstɜːbd/ ADJECTIVE
1 upset or worried □ *He was deeply disturbed by the news.* (**perturbado**)
2 having serious mental or emotional problems □ *a disturbed child* (**perturbado**)

- **disturbing** /dɪˈstɜːbɪŋ/ ADJECTIVE making you feel upset or worried □ *She found the violence in the film disturbing.* (**perturbador, inquietante**)

disused /ˌdɪsˈjuːzd/ ADJECTIVE not used any more □ *a disused railway station* (**abandonado**)

ditch /dɪtʃ/ ▶ NOUN [plural **ditches**] a long narrow hole at the side of a field or road (**valeta**)
▶ VERB [**ditches, ditching, ditched**] an informal word meaning to get rid of something or someone (**livrar-se de**)

dither /ˈdɪðə(r)/ VERB [**dithers, dithering, dithered**] to be unable to make a decision □ *He was dithering over what to do.* (**hesitar**)

ditto /ˈdɪtəʊ/ ▶ ADVERB used for saying that something else is also true, to avoid repeating words □ *You can recycle empty cans and ditto bottles.* (**como anteriormente**)
▶ NOUN [plural **dittos**] the mark (") that you write under a word in a list to show that you want to repeat that word (**idem**)

dive /daɪv/ ▶ VERB [**dives, diving, dived**]
1 to jump into water with your arms and head first □ *+ into Sasha dived into the pool.* (**mergulhar**)
2 to swim under water using special equipment (**mergulhar**)
3 to go down quickly through the air □ *She saw the plane suddenly dive.* (**mergulhar**)
4 to quickly move somewhere □ *He dived behind the door when she came in.* □ *I went home and dived into the shower.* (**precipitar-se**)
▶ NOUN [plural **dives**]
1 a jump into water with your arms and head first (**mergulho**)

divide

2 a time when you swim under water using special equipment (**mergulho**)
3 when something moves quickly down through the air □ *The plane went into a steep dive.* (**deu um mergulho**)
4 a sudden movement towards something (**mergulho**) □ *The robbers made a dive for the open window.* (**mergulharam**)

- **diver** /ˈdaɪvə(r)/ NOUN [plural **divers**] someone who swims under water using special equipment (**mergulhador**)

diverge /daɪˈvɜːdʒ/ VERB [**diverges, diverging, diverged**] to become different □ *Accounts of what happened after this point diverge dramatically.* (**divergir**)

- **divergence** /daɪˈvɜːdʒəns/ NOUN [plural **divergences**] when two things become different □ *a divergence of opinion* (**divergência**)

diverse /daɪˈvɜːs/ ADJECTIVE of very different types □ *He has appeared in a diverse range of films.* (**diverso**)

- **diversify** /daɪˈvɜːsɪfaɪ/ VERB [**diversifies, diversifying, diversified**] to start to sell different products or offer different services □ *Many farms have diversified into holiday accommodation.* (**diversificar-se**)

diversion /daɪˈvɜːʃən/ NOUN [plural **diversions**]
1 something that is intended to take your attention away from something (**desvio**) □ *The younger boys created a diversion while the older ones stole the bike.* (**criaram um desvio**)
2 a change in the way that something, especially money, is used □ *This has resulted in a diversion of funds to other projects.* (**desvio**)
3 a different route for traffic because the usual one is closed (**desvio**)
4 something you do so that you are not bored. A formal word. □ *Exploring the museum is a pleasant diversion for a rainy day.* (**distração**)

diversity /daɪˈvɜːsɪti/ NOUN, NO PLURAL when there are many different types of people or things □ *Australia's cultural diversity* (**diversidade**)

divert /daɪˈvɜːt/ VERB [**diverts, diverting, diverted**]
1 to make something go in a different direction □ *Traffic was diverted because of an accident.* (**desviar**)
2 to use something for a different purpose □ *The government should divert the money into education.* (**desviar**)
3 **divert attention from** to take someone's attention away from something that you do not want them to notice □ *The country is keen to divert attention from its nuclear programme.* (**desviar a atenção de**)

divide /dɪˈvaɪd/ VERB [**divides, dividing, divided**]
1 to separate into parts, or to separate something into parts □ *+ into Divide the class into teams of five.* □ *The cell divides and becomes two cells.* (**dividir, separar**)

2 to separate something and give a part of it to several people □ **+ up** They divided up the money. □ **+ between** She divided the cake between the children. (**dividir, separar**)
3 to keep two areas separate □ **+ from** A high wall divides our garden from theirs. (**dividir**)
4 to make a lot of people disagree □ The decision has divided the community. (**dividir**)
5 to find how many times one number contains another number. A maths word. □ **+ by** If you divide 12 by 3, you get 4. □ 12 divided by 3 is 4. (**dividir**)

• **divided** /dɪˈvaɪdɪd/ ADJECTIVE if a group of people are divided, they do not agree about something □ Experts are divided over the cause of the disease. (**dividido**) 🔁 The country is deeply divided. (**profundamente dividido**)

dividend /ˈdɪvɪdend/ NOUN [plural **dividends**] an amount of money that you get regularly if you own shares in a company (**dividendo**)

divine /dɪˈvaɪn/ ADJECTIVE coming from God, or to do with God □ divine punishment (**divino**)

diving /ˈdaɪvɪŋ/ NOUN, NO PLURAL
1 the sport of swimming under water with special equipment (**mergulho**)
2 the sport of jumping into water with your arms and head first (**salto**)
⇨ go to **scuba diving**

divisible /dɪˈvɪzəbəl/ ADJECTIVE able to be divided exactly □ 12 is divisible by 2, 3, 4 and 6. (**divisível**)

division /dɪˈvɪʒən/ NOUN [plural **divisions**]
1 no plural the process of separating people or things into groups or parts □ cell division (**divisão**)
2 no plural the way something is shared between people □ **+ of** We need a more equal division of power between governments. (**divisão**)
3 disagreement □ **+ between** This created divisions between the police and the military. (**divisão**) 🔁 There are deep divisions within the Democratic Party. (**divisões profundas**)
4 no plural when you calculate how many times one number contains another. A maths word. (**divisão**)
5 a group within a large organization □ He heads the company's sales and marketing division. (**seção, departamento**)
6 one of several groups that sports teams or players are divided into (**divisão**) 🔁 The football team is in the top division. (**divisão principal**)

divisive /dɪˈvaɪsɪv/ ADJECTIVE causing disagreement (**desagregador**) 🔁 a divisive issue (**questão desagregadora**)

divisor /dɪˈvaɪzə(r)/ NOUN [plural **divisors**] a number by which another number is divided. A maths word. (**divisor**)

divorce /dɪˈvɔːs/ ▶ NOUN [plural **divorces**] the legal ending of a marriage (**divórcio**) 🔁 We're getting a divorce. (**entrando em um divórcio**)

▶ VERB [**divorces, divorcing, divorced**] to legally end your marriage □ His parents divorced when he was six. □ Julia is divorcing her husband. (**divorciar-se**)

• **divorced** /dɪˈvɔːst/ ADJECTIVE
1 get divorced to legally end your marriage □ My parents got divorced when I was six. (**divorciar-se**)
2 having ended your marriage legally □ Holmes is a divorced father of three. (**divorciado**)

• **divorcee** /dɪvɔːˈsiː/ NOUN [plural **divorcees**] someone whose marriage has legally ended (**divorciado**)

divulge /daɪˈvʌldʒ/ VERB [**divulges, divulging, divulged**] to tell someone secret information □ He refused to divulge any details of the agreement. (**revelar, divulgar**)

DIY /ˌdiːaɪˈwaɪ/ ABBREVIATION do-it-yourself; when you make or repair things in the home yourself □ DIY stores (**faça você mesmo**)

dizzy /ˈdɪzi/ ADJECTIVE [**dizzier, dizziest**] feeling as if everything around you is moving and you are going to fall (**tonto, vertiginoso**) 🔁 You'll get dizzy if you spin round like that. (**ficará tonto**) 🔁 She's been suffering from dizzy spells. (**ataques vertiginosos**)

DJ /ˌdiːˈdʒeɪ/ ABBREVIATION disc jockey; someone who plays music in a club or on the radio (**DJ**)

DNA /ˌdiːenˈeɪ/ ABBREVIATION deoxyribonucleic acid; the substance in the cells of living things that controls what they are like. A biology word. (**DNA**)

do /duː/ ▶ AUXILIARY VERB [**does, doing, did, done**]
1 used with another verb to make questions and negative sentences □ Do you want another drink? □ I don't (= do not) like her husband. □ She doesn't (= does not) play tennis.
2 used to avoid repeating a verb □ 'I love chocolate.' 'So do I.' □ They spent a lot more money than I did.
3 used to emphasize the main verb □ I do love Paris. □ She does want to come, but she's very busy.
4 used at the end of a sentence to make it into a question □ Lucy goes to this school, doesn't she?

> ▶ Notice that instead of **do not**, people often say or write the short form **don't** and instead of **does not**, people often say or write the short form **doesn't**.

▶ VERB [**does, doing, did, done**]
1 to perform an action □ What are you doing? □ Make sure you do your homework. □ What does your mother do (= what is her job)? □ **+ with** What have you done with the map (= where is it)? (**fazer**)
2 to make something or to provide a service □ Do you do picture framing? □ They do great cakes. (**fazer**)
3 to study a subject □ I'm doing English and French. (**estudar**)

4 do badly/well to make bad/good progress □ *Oleg's doing well with his swimming.* **(ir bem/mal)**
5 How are you doing? an informal way of asking someone about their health and situation □ *Hi Carlos – how are you doing?* **(como você está?)**
6 something will do something will be enough or be suitable □ *If you haven't got walking boots, trainers will do.* **(algo vai dar certo)**
7 to do with something connected with something □ *He's writing a book – something to do with astronomy.* **(diz respeito a)**
8 someone could do with something someone needs something. An informal phrase. □ *I could do with a hot drink.* **(bem que alguém gostaria de algo)**

◆ PHRASAL VERBS **do away with something** to get rid of something □ *The school has done away with its uniform.* **(desfazer-se de algo) do something up**
1 to fasten a piece of clothing □ *Do your jacket up.* **(abotoar)**
2 to repair or decorate a room or building **do without (something)** to manage without something **(fechar algo)**
▶ NOUN [*plural* **dos**] an informal word for a party □ *The wedding's at three and there's an evening do afterwards.* **(festa)**

DOB ABBREVIATION date of birth **(abreviação de** *date of birth* **– data de nascimento)**

docile /ˈdəʊsaɪl/ ADJECTIVE a docile person or animal is quiet and easy to control **(dócil, calmo)**

dock /dɒk/ ▶ NOUN [*plural* **docks**]
1 the place where ships stop so goods can be taken on and off **(doca)**
2 the dock the place in a court where the person who is accused of a crime sits **(banco dos réus)**
▶ VERB [**docks, docking, docked**]
1 a ship docks when it goes into a dock **(atracar)**
2 a spacecraft docks when it joins another spacecraft during a flight **(acoplar-se)**
3 to reduce the amount of money, points, etc. that someone gets, as a punishment □ *They dock your wages if you're late.* **(reduzir, cortar)**
• **docker** /ˈdɒkə(r)/ NOUN [*plural* **dockers**] someone who works at a dock and takes goods onto and off a ship **(estivador)**

dockyard /ˈdɒkjɑːd/ NOUN [*plural* **dockyards**] a place where ships are built or repaired **(estaleiro)**

doctor /ˈdɒktə(r)/ ▶ NOUN [*plural* **doctors**]
1 someone whose job is to treat people who are ill **(médico)** 🔲 *You should see a doctor if your symptoms don't improve.* □ *Could I make an appointment with Doctor Kennedy, please?*
2 the doctor's the place where a doctor works □ *Go to the doctor's if your cough isn't any better.* **(clínica médica)**
3 someone who has a university qualification of the highest level □ *Doctor Smith is the head of our physics department.* **(doutor)**

▶ VERB [**doctors, doctored, doctoring**] to change something, especially in order to trick people □ *The photo had been doctored to make her look slimmer.* **(adulterada)**
• **doctorate** /ˈdɒktərət/ NOUN [*plural* **doctorates**] a university qualification of a very high level **(doutorado)**

doctrine /ˈdɒktrɪn/ NOUN [*plural* **doctrines**] a set of religious or political beliefs □ *Catholic doctrine* **(doutrina)**

document ▶ NOUN /ˈdɒkjumənt/ [*plural* **documents**]
1 a paper with official information on it □ *Make sure you have all your travel documents with you.* **(documento)** 🔲 *She had to sign some legal documents.* **(assinar documentos)**
2 something that you write and keep on a computer. A computing word. **(documento, arquivo)** 🔲 *How do I open a new document?* **(abrir um arquivo)**
▶ VERB /ˈdɒkjument/ [**documents, documenting, documented**] to write about something or film it in order to record information about it □ *The events have been documented in many books.* **(documentar)**
• **documentary** /ˌdɒkjuˈmentəri/ ▶ NOUN [*plural* **documentaries**] a film or television programme about real people or real events □ *They made a documentary on global warming.* **(documentário)**
▶ ADJECTIVE
1 a documentary programme or film is about real people or real events **(documentário)** 🔲 *It's a new documentary series set in a school.* **(série de documentário)**
2 documentary evidence or proof is in the form of a document □ *You'll need to provide documentary proof of your age before you can buy alcohol.* **(documental)**
• **documentation** /ˌdɒkjumenˈteɪʃən/ NOUN, NO PLURAL
1 the documents you need to prove something □ *I bought the car legally, and I have all the documentation.* **(documentação)**
2 instructions for how to make a computer or software work **(documentação)**

doddle /ˈdɒdəl/ NOUN **be a doddle** an informal phrase meaning to be very easy □ *The exam was a doddle.* **(ser muito fácil)**

dodge /dɒdʒ/ ▶ VERB [**dodges, dodging, dodged**]
1 to move quickly to avoid something □ *Graeme managed to dodge out of the way before the ball hit him.* **(esquivar)**
2 to avoid doing something or talking about something **(esquivar)** 🔲 *He dodged questions about his private life.* **(esquivou-se de perguntas)**
▶ NOUN [*plural* **dodges**] a dishonest way of avoiding something. An informal word. **(trapaça)** 🔲 *a tax dodge* **(trapaça fiscal)**
• **dodgy** /ˈdɒdʒi/ ADJECTIVE [**dodgier, dodgiest**] an informal word meaning not honest or not of good

quality □ I've got a dodgy knee. □ He's known for his dodgy deals. (**desonesto**)

doe /dəʊ/ NOUN [plural **does**] a female rabbit or deer (**corça**)

does /dʌz/ VERB the form of the verb do that is used with he, she and it (**ver do**)

doesn't /'dʌzənt/ a short way to say and write **does not** (**ver do**)

dog /dɒg/ ▶ NOUN [plural **dogs**] an animal with four legs that is kept as a pet, for hunting or for guarding buildings (**cão, cachorro**) 🗨 The dog barks whenever anyone comes to the house. (**cão late**) 🗨 He walks the dog every evening. (**passeia com o cachorro**)
▶ VERB [**dogs, dogging, dogged**] if something dogs you, it causes problems for a long time □ He was dogged by ill health throughout his life. (**perseguir**)

dog-eared /'dɒgɪəd/ ADJECTIVE a dog-eared book or page has been used so much that the corners are bent (**dobras em folhas de livros, cadernos**)

dogged /'dɒgɪd/ ADJECTIVE very determined (**obstinado, teimoso**) 🗨 Only her dogged determination kept her going. (**determinação obstinada**)

dogma /'dɒgmə/ NOUN [plural **dogmas**] a belief or a set of beliefs that people are expected to believe without questioning them □ religious dogma (**dogma**)
• **dogmatic** /dɒg'mætɪk/ ADJECTIVE certain that you are right and expecting other people to accept this without questioning you □ He had dogmatic views about the game. (**dogmático**)

dogsbody /'dɒgz,bɒdɪ/ NOUN [plural **dogsbodies**] someone who has to do all the small and boring jobs (**servente, criado**)

doldrums /'dɒldrəmz/ PLURAL NOUN **the doldrums** a situation in which something is not very successful □ The industry has been in the doldrums for the last five years. (**estagnação**)

dole /dəʊl/ NOUN, NO PLURAL **be on the dole** to get money from the government because you do not have a job (**receber seguro-desemprego**)
◆ PHRASAL VERB [**doles, doling, doled**] **dole something out** to give something such as money or food to people □ The company doled out free chocolates to angry customers. (**distribuir algo**)

doll /dɒl/ NOUN [plural **dolls**] a toy in the shape of a person (**boneca, boneco**)

dollar /'dɒlə(r)/ NOUN [plural **dollars**] the unit of money in many countries including the US, Canada, Australia and New Zealand. The written symbol is $. □ They've spent millions of dollars on the project. (**dólar**)

dollop /'dɒləp/ NOUN [plural **dollops**] an amount of soft food that you have dropped from a spoon □ Serve the cake with a dollop of cream. (**bocado**)

dolphin /'dɒlfɪn/ NOUN [plural **dolphins**] an intelligent sea mammal that has grey skin and a long pointed mouth (**golfinho**)

domain /də'meɪn/ NOUN [plural **domains**] a particular subject or activity that someone is involved in or responsible for (**domínio**) 🗨 The information was already in the public domain. (**domínio público**) □ The kitchen is my husband's domain.

domain name /də'meɪn ˌneɪm/ NOUN [plural **domain names**] an address on the Internet. A computing word. (**nome de domínio**)

dome /dəʊm/ NOUN [plural **domes**] a raised round roof on a building (**cúpula**)

domestic /də'mestɪk/ ADJECTIVE
1 to do with your home, or happening in your home □ I hate domestic tasks like cleaning and cooking. (**doméstico**) 🗨 She was the victim of domestic violence. (**violência doméstica**)
2 to do with one particular country and not international □ the government's domestic policies (**doméstico**) 🗨 At Boston, he hoped to take a domestic flight to Seattle. (**voo doméstico**)
3 a domestic animal is kept as a pet or on a farm (**doméstico**)
• **domesticated** /də'mestɪkeɪtɪd/ ADJECTIVE
1 a domesticated animal is one that lives with people (**doméstico**)
2 a domesticated person likes looking after their home and family (**doméstico, caseiro**)

dominance /'dɒmɪnəns/ NOUN, NO PLURAL when someone has more influence, power, and control than other people □ The company's dominance of the home phone market is starting to wane. (**dominância**)
• **dominant** /'dɒmɪnənt/ ADJECTIVE
1 more important, powerful or noticeable than others □ The issue of relationships is the dominant theme of the book. (**dominante**)
2 wanting to control other people □ He had a very dominant father. (**dominante, autoritário**)
3 a dominant gene gives a child a particular characteristic even if only one parent has it. A biology word. (**dominante**)

dominate /'dɒmɪneɪt/ VERB [**dominates, dominating, dominated**]
1 to have more influence, power, or success than others □ It's a company which has dominated the insurance market. (**dominar**)
2 to be the most important or most noticeable feature □ The castle dominates the landscape. □ The plane crash dominated the news. (**dominar**)
• **domination** /ˌdɒmɪ'neɪʃən/ NOUN, NO PLURAL control or power over people or things □ The country had ambitions of world domination. (**dominação**)

domineering /ˌdɒmɪ'nɪərɪŋ/ ADJECTIVE wanting to control people □ She was very domineering. (**dominante**)

dominoes /ˈdɒmɪnəʊz/ NOUN, NO PLURAL a game played with small rectangular blocks that have spots on them (**dominó**)

donate /dəˈneɪt/ VERB [**donates, donating, donated**] to give something, especially money, to someone who needs it ▫ *He donated money to a local charity.* (**doar**)

• **donation** /dəˈneɪʃən/ NOUN [*plural* **donations**] something, especially money, that you give to help a person or an organization (**doação**) ▫ *She made generous donations to various charities.* (**fez doações**)

done /dʌn/ PAST PARTICIPLE OF **do** (*ver* **do**)

donkey /ˈdɒŋki/ NOUN [*plural* **donkeys**] an animal that looks like a small horse with long ears (**burro**)

donor /ˈdəʊnə(r)/ NOUN [*plural* **donors**]
1 someone who gives part of their body for someone else to use (**doador**) ▫ *Blood donors are urgently needed.* (**doadores de sangue**)
2 someone who gives money to help a person or organization (**doador**) ▫ *An anonymous donor has offered £5,000 to help find the girl's killer.* (**doador anônimo**)

don't /dəʊnt/ a short way to say and write **do not** (*ver* **do**)

doodle /ˈduːdəl/ ▶ NOUN [*plural* **doodles**] a drawin that you do while you are thinking about something else (**rabiscos**)
▶ VERB [**doodles, doodling, doodled**] to draw a doodle (**fazer um rabisco**)

doom /duːm/ ▶ NOUN, NO PLURAL when something bad is certain to happen (**destruição, ruína**) ▫ *I felt a sense of doom.* (**sensação de destruição**)
▶ VERB if someone or something is doomed to something unpleasant, that thing is certain to happen (**condenar, fadar**) ▫ *The project was doomed to failure.* (**fadado ao fracasso**)

• **doomed** /duːmd/ ADJECTIVE certain to have a bad end ▫ *Investigators say the doomed flight may have been on the wrong runway.* (**condenado**)

door /dɔː(r)/ NOUN [*plural* **doors**]
1 the thing you open to get into a building, room, cupboard or vehicle (**porta**) ▫ *Janie opened the door and went in.* (**abriu a porta**) ▫ *She quickly closed the door.* (**fechou a porta**) ▫ *There was a bell by the front door.* (**porta da frente**) ▫ *Just go and knock on the door.* (**bata na porta**) ▫ *She closed the car door.*
2 the space in a wall where you go into a building or room ▫ *He was so fat he could barely get through the door.* (**porta**)
3 at the door if there is someone at the door, someone is waiting for you to open the door so they can come inside ▫ *Mum, there's someone at the door.* (**à porta**)

doorbell /ˈdɔːbel/ NOUN [*plural* **doorbells**] a button on the door of a building that you press to ring a bell to tell the people inside that you are there (**campainha**)

doorknob /ˈdɔːnɒb/ NOUN [*plural* **doorknobs**] a round handle that you use to open or close a door (**maçaneta**)

doormat /ˈdɔːmæt/ NOUN [*plural* **doormats**]
1 a piece of rough material by a door, which you clean your shoes on (**capacho**)
2 someone who allows other people to treat them badly. An informal word. (**capacho**)

doorstep /ˈdɔːstep/ NOUN [*plural* **doorsteps**]
1 the step in front of the door of a house ▫ *There was a parcel on the doorstep when I got home.* (**soleira**)
2 on someone's doorstep very close to someone's house ▫ *There are some great parks right on your doorstep.* (**a um passo da casa de alguém**)

doorway /ˈdɔːweɪ/ NOUN [*plural* **doorways**] the entrance to a room or building ▫ *He was standing in the doorway.* (**vão da porta**)

dormant /ˈdɔːmənt/ ADJECTIVE not active now but possibly active later ▫ *a dormant volcano* (**inativo, latente**) ▫ *The virus can lie dormant for several years.* (**permanecer dormente**)

dormitory /ˈdɔːmətəri/ NOUN [*plural* **dormitories**] a bedroom for several people, especially in a school (**dormitório coletivo**)

DOS /dɒs/ ABBREVIATION disk operating system; the software that makes all the different parts of a computer work together. A computing word. (**DOS**)

dosage /ˈdəʊsɪdʒ/ NOUN [*plural* **dosages**] the amount of a medicine that you should take (**dosagem**) ▫ *Doctors put him on a high dosage of the drug.* (**alta dosagem**)

dose /dəʊs/ NOUN [*plural* **doses**]
1 an amount of medicine that you take at one time (**dose**) ▫ *You get side effects if you take a high dose of the drug.* (**dose alta**)
2 a dose of something an amount of a quality ▫ *The debate badly needs a dose of realism.* (**uma dose de algo**)

dossier /ˈdɒsieɪ/ NOUN [*plural* **dossiers**] a set of papers with information about someone or something (**dossiê**) ▫ *The police have compiled a dossier on key gang members.* (**compilou um dossiê**)

dot /dɒt/ ▶ NOUN [*plural* **dots**]
1 a small round mark (**ponto**)
2 the symbol (.) in an Internet or email address ▫ *Is it 'al dot wood?' (= Is it 'al.wood?')* (**ponto**)
3 on the dot at exactly the time mentioned. An informal phrase. ▫ *Matilda arrived at three o'clock on the dot.* (**na hora exata**)
▶ VERB [**dots, dotting, dotted**] if a large area is dotted with things, there are a lot of them with

spaces between each thing □ *The hillside was dotted with sheep.* (pontilhada)

dote /doʊt/
♦ PHRASAL VERB [dotes, doting, doted] **dote on someone** to love someone very much □ *She dotes on her grandchildren.* (adorar alguém)
• **doting** /ˈdoʊtɪŋ/ ADJECTIVE loving someone very much □ *doting parents* (devotado)

double /ˈdʌbəl/ ▶ ADJECTIVE

1 twice as much or twice as many □ *He was given a double dose of medicine.* (duplo)
2 having or involving two parts or things which are the same □ *double doors* □ *She's a double Olympic medallist.* (duplo)
3 suitable for two people (duplo) 🔁 *It costs £100 a night for a double room.* (quarto duplo)
4 used when you are saying that a particular number or letter is repeated □ *You spell 'marry' m-a-double r-y.* (duplo)

▶ NOUN [plural **doubles**]

1 twice as much □ *She gets paid double for doing the same job.* (duas vezes)
2 a room for two people in a hotel □ *I've booked a double and two singles.* (duplo)
3 doubles a tennis game played between two pairs of players (duplas)
4 your double someone who looks like you very much □ *I saw your double in the street yesterday.* (sua réplica)

▶ VERB [doubles, doubling, doubled] to become twice as big, or to make something become twice as big □ **+ in** *The shares have doubled in value.* □ *The drug doubles your risk of having a heart attack.* (duplicar)

♦ PHRASAL VERBS **double as something/someone** to have another use or job □ *The hall doubles as a dining room.* (fazer as vezes de) **double over/up** to bend at your waist because you are in pain or laughing a lot □ *He doubled up in pain.*
DETERMINER twice as big or twice as much □ *She earns double the amount I do.* (o dobro)

double bass /ˌdʌbəl ˈbeɪs/ NOUN [plural **double basses**] a musical instrument that looks like a very large violin which you play standing up (contrabaixo)

double bed /ˌdʌbəl ˈbed/ NOUN [plural **double beds**] a big bed for two people (cama de casal)

double-check /ˌdʌbəlˈtʃek/ VERB [double-checks, double-checking, double-checked] to check something again so that you are completely sure □ *He called the airport to double-check what time the flight leaves.* (dupla verificação)

double-click /ˌdʌbəlˈklɪk/ VERB [double-clicks, double-clicking, double-clicked] to click twice with a computer mouse. A computing word. (duplo clique)

double-decker /ˌdʌbəlˈdekə(r)/ NOUN [plural **double-deckers**] a bus with two levels (ônibus de dois andares)

double figures /ˌdʌbəl ˈfɪɡəz/ PLURAL NOUN numbers which are between 10 and 99 □ *Their score didn't even reach double figures.* (dois dígitos)

double glazing /ˌdʌbəl ˈɡleɪzɪŋ/ NOUN, NO PLURAL windows with two layers of glass in them (janela com vidro duplo)

double helix /ˌdʌbəl ˈhiːlɪks/ NOUN [plural **double helixes**] the shape of a DNA molecule. A biology word. (estrutura helicoidal)

double standard /ˌdʌbəl ˈstændəd/ NOUN [plural **double standards**] a way of treating people which is unfair (código moral)

doubly /ˈdʌblɪ/ ADVERB extra □ *He went back to make doubly sure that the door was locked.* (duplamente)

doubt /daʊt/ ▶ NOUN [plural **doubts**]

1 a feeling of not being certain about something (dúvida) 🔁 *Leo had serious doubts about the plan.* (teve dúvidas) 🔁 *I have no doubt that you will succeed.* (não tive dúvidas) 🔁 *This raises doubts about (= makes me not certain about) his reliability.* (gera dúvidas)
2 without (a) doubt certainly □ *She was without doubt the best singer of her generation.* (sem dúvida)
3 be in doubt if something is in doubt, it is not certain whether it will succeed or continue to exist □ *His future at the club is in doubt.* (estar em dúvida)
4 no doubt used for emphasizing that something seems very certain □ *No doubt he'll be late as usual.* (sem dúvida)

▶ VERB [doubts, doubting, doubted] to think that something is probably not true or will probably not happen □ **+ that** *I doubt that he will agree* (duvidar) 🔁 *'Do you think Rebecca will come?' 'I doubt it.'* (duvido)

• **doubtful** /ˈdaʊtfʊl/ ADJECTIVE

1 probably not true, or probably not going to happen (duvidoso) 🔁 *It's doubtful whether she'll take the job.* (é duvidoso se)
2 not certain about something □ *I asked Jim whether he would be here but he seemed doubtful.* (incerto)

dough /doʊ/ NOUN, NO PLURAL a mixture of flour and water for making bread (massa)

doughnut /ˈdoʊnʌt/ NOUN [plural **doughnuts**] a small round cake, often with a hole in the middle (sonho)

dour /dʊə(r)/ ADJECTIVE [dourer, dourest] serious and not friendly □ *a dour expression* (sério)

dove /dʌv/ NOUN [plural **doves**] a white bird, used as a sign of peace (pomba)

dowdy /ˈdaʊdɪ/ ADJECTIVE [dowdier, dowdiest] not attractive and not fashionable □ *a dowdy woman* (desleixado)

down

down /daʊn/ ▶ ADVERB
1 towards or in a lower position □ *He was sitting down.* □ *She bent down to speak to the child.* □ *I'll put the box down here.* (**para baixo**)
2 to a smaller size, amount or level □ *He cut the picture down to fit the frame.* □ *Can you turn the television down, please?* (**para baixo**)
3 along □ *I'm just going down to the post office.* (**ao longo de**)
4 in or towards the south □ *We're driving down from Edinburgh tonight.* (**ao sul**)
▶ PREPOSITION
1 towards or in a lower part □ *There were tears running down his face.* (**para baixo**)
2 along □ *Rachel was walking down the road.* (**ao longo de**)
▶ ADJECTIVE
1 an informal word meaning unhappy □ *You seem a bit down.* (**triste**)
2 if a computer or website is down, it is not working. A computing word □ *I can't book the tickets because the website's down.* (**pane**)
▶ VERB [**downs, downing, downed**] to drink something very quickly. An informal word. □ *He downed a whole litre of milk.* (**entornou**)
▶ NOUN, NO PLURAL soft feathers

downcast /'daʊnkɑːst/ ADJECTIVE
1 sad (**abatido**)
2 if your eyes are downcast, you are looking down (**cabisbaixo**)

downfall /'daʊnfɔːl/ NOUN, NO PLURAL when someone suddenly loses their power and stops being successful □ *The scandal eventually led to the president's downfall.* (**queda, derrocada**)

downhearted /ˌdaʊn'hɑːtɪd/ ADJECTIVE feeling sad because you have not achieved something (**desanimado**)

downhill /ˌdaʊn'hɪl/ ▶ ADVERB
1 down a slope □ *The car rolled downhill.* (**em declive**)
2 go downhill to become worse □ *The school's gone downhill since I was there.* (**ir de mal a pior**)
▶ ADJECTIVE going down a slope □ *a downhill skiing race* (**morro abaixo**)

download /'daʊnləʊd/ ▶ VERB [**downloads, downloading, downloaded**] to copy information, such as pictures or music, onto your computer from the Internet or another computer. A computing word. □ *You can download music for free.* □ *The file is downloading now.* (**baixar, descarregar arquivo**)
▶ NOUN [*plural* **downloads**] something that you have downloaded. A computing word. (**o arquivo baixado, descarregado**)
• **downloadable** /ˌdaʊn'ləʊdəbəl/ ADJECTIVE able to be downloaded. A computing word. □ *downloadable games* (**que pode ser baixado**)

downmarket /ˌdaʊn'mɑːkɪt/ ADJECTIVE low in quality and price □ *downmarket shops* (**popular**)

downpour /'daʊnpɔː(r)/ NOUN [*plural* **downpours**] a lot of rain that falls in a short period of time (**aguaceiro**)

downright /'daʊnraɪt/ ADJECTIVE, ADVERB used for emphasizing something bad □ *Some of the ideas were downright silly.* (**absolutamente**)

downstairs ▶ ADVERB /ˌdaʊn'steəz/ to or on a lower level of a building (**andar de baixo**) ▣ *He went downstairs to get breakfast.* (**foi para o andar de baixo**) □ *The kids were all downstairs.*
▶ ADJECTIVE /'daʊnsteəz/ on a lower level in a building □ *a downstairs bathroom* (**no andar de baixo**)

downstream /ˌdaʊn'striːm/ ADVERB further down a river in the direction it is flowing in (**rio abaixo**)

downtime /'daʊntaɪm/ NOUN, NO PLURAL time when a computer is not working. A computing word. (**tempo ocioso**)

down-to-earth /ˌdaʊntə'ɜːθ/ ADJECTIVE someone who is down-to-earth accepts the true facts of their situation and does not pretend to be something that they are not (**realista**)

downturn /'daʊntɜːn/ NOUN [*plural* **downturns**] a time when there is less business than usual □ *There has been a downturn in the housing market.* (**queda**)

downward /'daʊnwəd/ ADJECTIVE towards a lower place or position □ *a downward slope* (**para baixo**)
• **downwards** /'daʊnwədz/ or **downward** /'daʊnwəd/ ADVERB towards a lower place or position □ *The path winds downwards to the lake.* (**para baixo**)

dowry /'daʊəri/ NOUN [*plural* **dowries**] money and property that a woman's family gives to her husband's family when they marry (**dote**)

doze /dəʊz/ ▶ VERB [**dozes, dozing, dozed**] to sleep lightly for a short time (**dormitar**)
◆ PHRASAL VERB **doze off** to start to sleep □ *He dozed off in his armchair.* (**cochilar**)
▶ NOUN [*plural* **dozes**] a short sleep (**soneca**) ▣ *I had a doze after lunch.* (**tirei uma soneca**)

dozen /'dʌzən/ NOUN [*plural* **dozens**]
1 twelve □ *a dozen eggs* (**dúzia**) ▣ *There were about two dozen (= 24) people at the party.* (**duas dúzias**) ▣ *I read half a dozen (= 6) pages.* (**meia dúzia**)
2 dozens of something an informal phrase meaning a lot of something □ *He's been in dozens of films.* (**dúzias de algo**)

dozy /'dəʊzi/ ADJECTIVE [**dozier, doziest**]
1 feeling as if you want to sleep □ *The heat was making me dozy.* (**sonolento**)
2 an informal word meaning stupid (**estúpido**)

Dr ABBREVIATION **doctor**. The abbreviation is used in writing. □ *Dr Smith* (**Dr.**)

drab /dræb/ ADJECTIVE [drabber, drabbest] not interesting and not bright in colour ▢ She was wearing a drab grey cardigan. (sem graça)

draft /drɑːft/ ▶ NOUN [plural drafts]
1 a piece of writing that is not in its final form (rascunho, esboço) ▣ This is just the first draft of my essay. (primeiro rascunho)
2 the US spelling of **draught**
▶ VERB [drafts, drafting, drafted] to write something that you will change before you finish it ▢ He was drafting a letter to his boss. (esboçar)

draftsman /'drɑːftsmən/ NOUN [plural draftsmen] another spelling of **draughtsman** (desenhista)

drag /dræg/ ▶ VERB [drags, dragging, dragged]
1 to pull something along the ground ▢ Thomas came out of school, dragging his school bag behind him. (puxar)
2 to pull someone or something strongly or violently ▢ The police dragged him out of the car. (puxar)
3 to make someone go somewhere when they do not want to ▢ Mum dragged me round the shops all morning. (arrastar)
4 if time or an event drags, it seems to pass very slowly because you are bored (passar lentamente)
5 to move words or pictures on a computer screen by pulling them with a mouse. A computing word. (arrastar)
♦ PHRASAL VERBS **drag someone into something** to make someone become involved in an unpleasant situation ▢ I wish you two wouldn't drag me into your arguments. (envolver alguém desnecessariamente em algo) **drag on** to continue for too long ▢ The play seemed to drag on for hours. (arrastar-se)
▶ NOUN, NO PLURAL an informal word for something that is annoying or boring ▢ Choir practice was always such a drag. (chatice)

drag and drop /ˌdræɡ ən 'drɒp/ VERB [drags and drops, dragging and dropping, dragged and dropped] to move words or pictures on a computer screen by pulling them with a mouse. A computing word. (arrastar e soltar)

dragon /'dræɡən/ NOUN [plural dragons] a big imaginary animal with wings, that breathes fire from its mouth (dragão)

dragonfly /'dræɡənflaɪ/ NOUN [plural dragonflies] an insect with a thin colourful body and long wings (libélula)

drain /dreɪn/ ▶ VERB [drains, draining, drained]
1 to make the liquid in something flow away ▢ They had to drain the tank ▢ Drain the pasta and serve with the sauce. (escoar, escorrer)
2 if a liquid drains, it flows away ▢ She watched the water drain down the sink. (drenar)
3 if you drain a cup or a glass, you drink all the liquid in it (beber)
4 to make someone feel very tired ▢ The work had drained him. (esgotar)
▶ NOUN [plural drains]
1 a pipe or hole that allows waste water to flow away ▢ The drain was blocked. (canal de escoamento)
2 a drain on something something that uses a lot of your money ▢ Childcare is a big drain on our finances. (consumir algo)
♦ IDIOM **down the drain** an informal phrase meaning wasted ▢ If I quit the course, that's six hundred pounds down the drain. (desperdício)
• **drainage** /'dreɪnɪdʒ/ NOUN, NO PLURAL removing waste water by systems of pipes and rivers (drenagem)
• **drained** /dreɪnd/ ADJECTIVE extremely tired ▢ After being in court all day, I felt completely drained. (exaurido, esgotado)

draining board /'dreɪnɪŋ ˌbɔːd/ NOUN [plural draining boards] a surface next to a kitchen sink where you put wet dishes when you have washed them (escorredor de louça)

drainpipe /'dreɪnpaɪp/ NOUN [plural drainpipes] a pipe on the outside of a building, that takes waste water down into the ground (cano de esgoto)

drama /'drɑːmə/ NOUN [plural dramas]
1 a play at the theatre or on television (drama) ▣ a TV drama (drama de TV) ▣ an Australian drama series (séries de drama)
2 no plural plays and acting in general ▢ Dan studied drama at Birmingham University. (arte dramática) ▣ She went to drama school. (escola de arte dramática)
3 something exciting which happens (acontecimento) ▣ They watched the drama unfold (= happen) from her bedroom window. (desenrolar do acontecimento)
• **dramatic** /drə'mætɪk/ ADJECTIVE
1 sudden and unexpected (espetacular, incrível) ▣ There has been a dramatic increase in the number of exam passes. (aumento incrível) ▣ Computers have led to dramatic changes in work habits. (mudanças incríveis)
2 exciting and involving activity and danger ▢ He described his dramatic rescue from the sinking boat. (dramático)
3 to do with plays and the theatre ▢ the dramatic works of an author (dramático)
4 dramatic behaviour is done to make other people notice you ▢ Anna spread her hands in a dramatic gesture. (dramático)
• **dramatically** /drə'mætɪkəli/ ADVERB in a dramatic way ▢ Prices rose dramatically last month. (dramaticamente)
• **dramatist** /'dræmətɪst/ NOUN [plural dramatists] someone who writes plays (dramaturgo)
• **dramatization** or **dramatisation** /ˌdræmətaɪ'zeɪʃən/ NOUN [plural dramatizations] a

play which is based on a book or real event □ *She won a prize for her dramatization of Edith Wharton's novel.* (dramatização)

• **dramatize** or **dramatise** /'dræmətaɪz/ VERB [**dramatizes, dramatizing, dramatized**]
1 to make a theatre or television play from a book or real event (dramatizar)
2 to make a story or report more exciting than the real event (dramatizar)

drank /dræŋk/ PAST TENSE OF **drink** (*ver* **drink**)

drape /dreɪp/ VERB [**drapes, draping, draped**]
1 to put cloth loosely over or around something □ *Sue draped the shawl around her shoulders.* (cobrir)
2 if something is draped in or with a piece of cloth, it is covered by it □ *The coffin was draped in the Australian flag.* (cobrir)

drapes /dreɪps/ PLURAL NOUN a US word for **curtains** (cortinas)

drastic /'dræstɪk/ ADJECTIVE having a very big effect (drástico) ▣ *Drastic action is needed to reduce pollution levels.* (ações drásticas)
• **drastically** /'dræstɪkəli/ ADVERB in an extreme and sudden way □ *The place has changed drastically since I was last there.* (drasticamente)

draught /drɑːft/ NOUN [*plural* **draughts**]
1 a movement of air in a room which feels cold (corrente de ar)
2 draughts a game for two people who move flat, round pieces on a board that has black and white squares on it (jogo de damas)

draughtsman /'drɑːftsmən/ NOUN [*plural* **draughtsmen**] someone whose job is to draw plans for something such as a machine or building (desenhista)

draughty /'drɑːfti/ ADJECTIVE [**draughtier, draughtiest**] a draughty building or room is cold because cold air blows into it (frio)

draw /drɔː/ ▶ VERB [**draws, drawing, drew, drawn**]
1 to make a picture with a pencil or pen (desenhar) □ *Ellie was drawing.* ▣ *She drew a lovely picture of a horse.* (fez um desenho)
2 to attract people □ *The programme drew 13 million viewers.* (atrair) ▣ *The festival draws crowds of up to 30,000 people.* (atraiu multidões) □ + *to He was drawn to Australia because of the weather.*

3 draw (someone's) attention to someone/something to make someone notice someone or something □ *I was trying not to draw attention to myself.* (chamar a atenção de alguém para algo/alguém)

4 to get a particular reaction (provocar) ▣ *The policy drew criticism from many people.* (provocou críticas)

5 to score the same number of points as someone else in a game □ *We drew 2-2.* (empatar)

6 draw closer/near to move closer in time or distance □ *As they drew closer she saw a path.* □ *Election day is drawing near.* (mover-se)

7 draw the curtains to pull curtains so that they cover a window or do not cover a window (puxar as cortinas)

8 to pull something from somewhere or pull something in a particular direction. A literary word. □ *He drew a small piece of paper from his pocket.* (jogar)

♦ IDIOM **draw the line** to not do something because you think it is wrong or too much □ *I love sweet food, but even I draw the line at her chocolate cake.* (passar dos limites)

⇨ go to **draw lots**

1 PHRASAL VERBS **draw someone into something** to involve someone in a conversation or argument □ *I won't be drawn into their dispute.* (envolver alguém em algo) **draw on something** to use your knowledge for a particular purpose □ *He had a lot of experience to draw on.* (fazer uso de algo) **draw something up** to write something such as a plan or document (redigir algo) ▣ *They've drawn up a list of the best candidates.* (redigiu uma lista) **draw up** if a vehicle draws up, it stops □ *A taxi drew up outside the house.* (estacionar)

▶ NOUN [*plural* **draws**]
1 a game that ends with both players or teams having the same score (empate) ▣ *The game ended in a draw.* (acabou em empate)
2 when a winner or two teams who will play each other in a competition are chosen by chance (loteria) ▣ *They won a car in a prize draw.* (loteria)

drawback /'drɔːbæk/ NOUN [*plural* **drawbacks**] a disadvantage (desvantagem) ▣ *The only drawback is the cost.* (a única desvantagem)

drawer /drɔː(r)/ NOUN [*plural* **drawers**] a part of a piece of furniture that you pull out and keep things in (gaveta) ▣ *He opened the drawer and got out some paper.* (abriu a gaveta) ▣ *The pens are in the top drawer.* (gaveta de cima)

drawing /'drɔːɪŋ/ NOUN [*plural* **drawings**]
1 a picture done with a pencil or pen (desenho) ▣ *She did a few drawings.* (fez alguns desenhos) □ + *of a drawing of a house*
2 no plural making pictures using a pencil or pen □ *Most children like drawing.* (desenho)

drawing pin /'drɔːɪŋ ˌpɪn/ NOUN [*plural* **drawing pins**] a short pin with a wide, round top that you use for fixing paper to a wall (tachinha)

drawl /drɔːl/ ▶ VERB [**drawls, drawling, drawled**] to speak slowly with long vowel sounds □ *'I don't know,' he drawled.* (falar com lentidão)
▶ NOUN, NO PLURAL a slow way of speaking with long vowel sounds (fala arrastada)

drawn /drɔːn/ PAST PARTICIPLE OF **draw** (*ver* **draw**)

dread /dred/ ▶ VERB [**dreads, dreading, dreaded**]
1 to feel worried or frightened about something that is going to happen □ *We're all dreading the exams.* (temer)

dreadful

2 I dread to think used for saying that something that might happen is too unpleasant to think about ☐ *If children had found the tablets, I dread to think what might have happened.* (eu temo em pensar)
▶ NOUN, NO PLURAL a feeling of fear ☐ *The thought of flying fills me with dread.* (temor, pavor)

dreadful /'dredfʊl/ ADJECTIVE very bad ☐ *dreadful news* ☐ *a dreadful film* (terrível, pavoroso)
• **dreadfully** /'dredfʊli/ ADVERB
1 very badly ☐ *I thought he behaved dreadfully towards her.* (terrivelmente)
2 very ☐ *I'm dreadfully sorry.* (muito)

dreadlocks /'dredlɒks/ PLURAL NOUN hair that is in long twisted pieces (dreadlocks, cabelo rastafári)

dream /dri:m/ ▶ NOUN [plural **dreams**]
1 the things you think and see in your mind while you sleep (sonho) 🔹 *I had a very strange dream last night.* (tive um sonho) ☐ + *about* *I had a dream about you.* 🔹 *a bad dream* (pesadelo)
2 something you hope will happen ☐ *It was always her dream to go to Hollywood.* (sonho)
3 in a dream not noticing what is happening around you because you are thinking of other things (em devaneio)
4 of your dreams that is perfect for you ☐ *She met the man of her dreams while working in New York.* (dos sonhos)
▶ VERB [**dreams, dreaming, dreamt** or **dreamed**]
1 to think about and see something in your mind while you sleep ☐ + *that* *Last night I dreamt that I was lying on a beach.* ☐ + *about* *I often dream about flying.* (sonhar)
2 to imagine something that you would like to happen ☐ + *of* *I've always dreamt of moving to the coast.* (sonhar)
3 wouldn't dream of doing something used for saying that you would never do something because you think it is bad ☐ *I would never dream of telling your secrets to anyone.* (não fazer algo nem em sonhos)

> Note that sense 2 of the verb **dream** is followed by **of** + the ing-form of the verb:
> ✓ *I've always dreamt of owning a restaurant.*
> ✗ *I've always dreamt to own a restaurant.*

◆ PHRASAL VERB **dream something up** to think of something, especially something clever or unusual ☐ *Eliza dreamt up the scheme.* (sonhar com algo)
▶ ADJECTIVE a dream house, wedding etc. is one that is perfect or exactly what you want ☐ *Working in a chocolate factory would be my dream job.* (dos sonhos)
• **dreamy** /'dri:mi/ ADJECTIVE [**dreamier, dreamiest**] thinking about pleasant things and not what is happening around you ☐ *She was a dreamy child.* (sonhador)

dreary /'drɪəri/ ADJECTIVE [**drearier, dreariest**] boring ☐ *He'd had a dreary day at the office.* (chato)

dredge /dredʒ/ VERB [**dredges, dredging, dredged**] to remove mud and sand from the bottom of a lake or river (dragar)
◆ PHRASAL VERB **dredge something up** to talk about something bad that happened in the past (lembrar de algo ruim)

dregs /dregz/ PLURAL NOUN the bits that are sometimes left in the bottom of a cup or glass after you have finished drinking something (sujeira, borra)

drench /drentʃ/ VERB [**drenches, drenching, drenched**] if you are drenched in something, you are completely wet ☐ *Ben was drenched in sweat.* (ensopar)

dress /dres/ ▶ NOUN [plural **dresses**]
1 a piece of clothing for girls or women like a top and skirt joined together ☐ *She was wearing a black dress.* (vestido) 🔹 *a wedding dress* (vestido de noiva)
2 *no plural* clothes of a particular type (roupas) 🔹 *The dancers were wearing traditional Highland dress.* (roupa tradicional)
▶ VERB [**dresses, dressing, dressed**]
1 to put clothes on yourself or someone else (vestir) 🔹 *She got dressed and had breakfast.* (vestiu-se) ☐ *I'll dress the children.*
2 to wear a particular style of clothes ☐ *She always dresses smartly.* (vestir)
3 if you dress a cut or injury, you cover it (colocar curativos)

> Note that when you put clothes on yourself, you **get dressed**:
> ✓ *I get dressed in the dark.*
> ✗ *I dress myself in the dark.*

◆ PHRASAL VERB **dress up**
1 to put on clothes that make you look like someone else ☐ *Oliver is going to dress up as a pirate.* (fantasiar-se)
2 to wear clothes that are more formal than the clothes you usually wear ☐ *Can I go in jeans, or do I need to dress up?* (arrumar-se)
• **dressed** /drest/ ADJECTIVE
1 wearing clothes ☐ *Are you dressed yet?* (vestido)
2 wearing a particular type of clothes ☐ + *in* *Ali was dressed in jeans and a T-shirt.* ☐ *He's always well dressed.* (arrumado)
• **dresser** /'dresə(r)/ NOUN [plural **dressers**] a piece of furniture with a cupboard at the bottom and shelves above for keeping plates on (armário de cozinha)
• **dressing** /'dresɪŋ/ NOUN [plural **dressings**]
1 a sauce for a salad (tempero) 🔹 *a salad dressing.* (tempero de salada)

2 something you use to cover a cut or injury on your skin (**curativo**)

dressing-gown /'dresɪŋgaʊn/ NOUN [plural **dressing-gowns**] a piece of clothing that looks like a long coat, which you wear in your house when you are not dressed (**roupão**)

dress rehearsal /,dres rɪ'hɜːsəl/ NOUN [plural **dress rehearsals**] the final practice for a play or show, using all the clothes (**ensaio geral**)

drew /druː/ PAST TENSE OF **draw** (ver **draw**)

dribble /'drɪbəl/ VERB [dribbles, dribbling, dribbled]

1 to let liquid come out of your mouth □ *The baby was dribbling.* (**babar**)

2 if a liquid dribbles somewhere, it flows slowly □ *Blood was dribbling from a cut on his neck.* (**escorrer**)

3 to move a ball along in front of you as you run □ *He dribbled past a couple of players.* (**driblar**)

dried /draɪd/ ▶ PAST TENSE AND PAST PARTICIPLE OF **dry** □ *Jill dried the glasses with a soft cloth.* (ver **dry**)

▶ ADJECTIVE dried food or flowers have had the water taken out of them (**seco**) 🔁 *dried fruit* (**frutas secas**) □ *dried herbs*

drier /'draɪə(r)/ NOUN [plural **driers**] another spelling of **dryer** (ver **drier**)

drift /drɪft/ ▶ VERB [drifts, drifting, drifted]

1 to move with a current of water or air □ *Smoke drifted over the city.* (**flutuar**)

2 to slowly move somewhere □ *It was late and people were starting to drift away.* (**ser levado**)

3 to start to do something without having planned it □ *I just drifted into teaching.* (**fazer algo por acaso**)

◆ PHRASAL VERBS **drift apart** if two people drift apart, they gradually stop being friends (**separar--se**) **drift off** to gradually start to sleep (**adormecer**) 🔁 *Tom drifted off to sleep.* (**adormeceu**)

▶ NOUN [plural **drifts**]

1 a slow and gradual change or movement □ *There has been a drift away from religion, particularly among young people.* (**mudança gradual**)

2 a pile of snow or sand that has been blown by the wind (**monte, duna**) 🔁 *a snow drift* (**monte de neve**)

3 get/catch someone's drift to understand the general meaning of what someone says □ *I think I get your drift.* (**entender o que foi dito**)

drill /drɪl/ ▶ NOUN [plural **drills**]

1 a tool for making holes in something hard, such as stone □ *an electric drill* (**broca, furadeira**)

2 a practice so that people know what to do in a particular situation (**treinamento**) 🔁 *We have a fire drill every month at school.* (**treinamento contra incêndio**) □ *a military training drill*

3 a way of teaching something by making students repeat something several times (**exercício**)

▶ VERB [drills, drilling, drilled]

1 to make a hole in something hard (**perfurar**) 🔁 *She drilled a hole in the wall.* (**fez um buraco**) □ *They had to drill through rock.*

2 to teach someone something by making them do it several times □ *All staff are drilled in emergency procedures.* (**treinar**)

drink /drɪŋk/ ▶ VERB [drinks, drinking, drank, drunk]

1 to swallow a liquid □ *I drink a lot of coffee.* (**beber, tomar**) 🔁 *I'll get you something to drink.* (**algo para beber**)

2 to drink alcohol □ *Mark doesn't drink.* (**bebe álcool**)

◆ PHRASAL VERB **drink to someone/something** to hold your glass up before you drink something, in order to wish someone good health, success etc. □ *Let's drink to your good health!* (**beber à saúde de alguém/algo**)

▶ NOUN [plural **drinks**]

1 a liquid that you swallow (**bebida**) 🔁 *Can I have a drink, please?* (**tomar uma bebida**) □ **+ of** *Would you like a drink of water?*

2 no plural drinks in general □ *We hadn't had any food or drink all day.* (**bebida**)

3 an alcoholic drink □ *They went out for a few drinks to celebrate.* (**bebidas alcoólicas**)

4 no plural alcoholic drinks □ *Please do not bring drink into the hostel.* (**bebidas alcoólicas**)

• **drinker** /'drɪŋkə(r)/ NOUN [plural **drinkers**]

1 someone who regularly drinks alcohol (**bêbado**) 🔁 *He used to be a heavy drinker* (= someone who regularly drinks a lot of alcohol). (**bêbado inveterado**)

2 someone who drinks a particular type of drink □ *coffee drinkers* (**bebedor**)

• **drinking** /'drɪŋkɪŋ/ NOUN, NO PLURAL when someone drinks alcohol □ *His drinking was becoming a problem.* (**consumo de álcool**)

drip /drɪp/ ▶ NOUN [plural **drips**]

1 a drop of liquid □ *We're trying to catch the drips in a bucket.* (**pingo**)

2 a series of falling drops of liquid □ *I could hear the drip of the bathroom tap all night.* (**gotejamento**)

3 a piece of hospital equipment for putting liquids into someone's body □ *He was on a drip for a week.* (**tubo para soro**)

▶ VERB [drips, dripping, dripped]

1 if a liquid drips, it falls in drops □ *Water was dripping from the trees.* (**pingar**)

2 to produce drops of liquid □ *I can hear a tap dripping somewhere.* (**gotejar**)

drive /draɪv/ ▶ VERB [drives, driving, drove, driven]

1 to make a car, bus, etc. move and control where it goes and how fast it moves □ *Can you drive?* □ *I had to drive my mother's car.* □ *We drove to Spain.* □ *She drove me to the airport.* (**dirigir**)

2 drive someone mad/crazy to annoy someone very much □ *He was driving me mad with all his questions.* (enlouquecer alguém)

3 to make someone leave a place □ **+ away/out of** *Police fired tear gas to drive away the crowd.* (afugentar, repelir)

4 to strongly influence someone or something □ *The big banks are driving the market.* □ *He was driven by greed.* (forçar, influenciar)

⇨ go to **drive someone round the bend, drive someone up the wall**

▶ NOUN [*plural* **drives**]

1 a journey in a car (passeio de carro) 🔁 *We went for a drive in the country.* (saímos para um passeio de carro) 🔁 *He began the long drive home.* (longo passeio de carro) □ *It's a two-hour drive to the coast.*

2 an area in front of a house where you can put your car □ *There were two cars on the drive.* (entrada da garagem)

3 a part of a computer that stores information. A computing word. □ *The PC has a standard DVD drive.* (unidade de disco)

4 an effort by a government or organization to do something □ *It's part of a recruitment drive for new nurses.* (campanha)

5 *no plural* the wish to achieve things that makes you try hard (impulso)

6 Drive used in the names of some roads □ *My address is 13 Bishop's Drive.* (estrada)

drive-by /ˈdraɪvbaɪ/ ADJECTIVE a drive-by shooting is done by someone driving past in a car (feito às pressas)

drivel /ˈdrɪvəl/ NOUN, NO PLURAL nonsense □ *He's talking drivel.* (baboseira)

driven /ˈdrɪvən/ PAST PARTICIPLE OF **drive** (ver **drive**)

driver /ˈdraɪvə(r)/ NOUN [*plural* **drivers**] a person who drives a car, etc. □ *a taxi driver* □ *She's a good driver.* (motorista)

driveway /ˈdraɪvweɪ/ NOUN [*plural* **driveways**] an area in front of a house where you can put your car □ *There was a car parked in the driveway.* (garagem)

driving /ˈdraɪvɪŋ/ NOUN, NO PLURAL when you drive a car, etc. or the way that you drive (direção) 🔁 *Jane's having driving lessons.* (aulas de direção) □ *He was arrested for dangerous driving.*

driving licence /ˈdraɪvɪŋ ˌlaɪsəns/ NOUN [*plural* **driving licences**] an official document that shows you are allowed to drive □ *He didn't have a driving licence.* (carteira de motorista) 🔁 *A clean driving licence (= showing that you have never done anything wrong while driving) is essential for the job.* (carteira de motorista sem pontuação)

drizzle /ˈdrɪzəl/ ▶ NOUN, NO PLURAL very light rain ▶ VERB [**drizzles, drizzling, drizzled**] to rain very lightly (garoa, chuvisco)

• **drizzly** /ˈdrɪzli/ ADJECTIVE drizzly weather is when it is raining very lightly (garoar, chuviscar)

drone /drəʊn/ ▶ VERB [**drones, droning, droned**] to make a continuous low sound □ *Helicopters droned above us.* (zumbir)

♦ PHRASAL VERB **drone on** to talk a lot about something boring □ *I had to listen to Nate droning on about work.* (falar com monotonia)

▶ NOUN, NO PLURAL a continuous low sound □ *She could hear the drone of traffic outside.* (zumbido)

drool /druːl/ ▶ VERB [**drools, drooling, drooled**] to let liquid come out of your mouth □ *The dog was drooling.* (babar)

♦ PHRASAL VERB **drool over someone/something** to admire someone or something too much, in a way that is silly □ *We stood drooling over the dresses in the window.* (babar por alguém/algo)

droop /druːp/ VERB [**droops, drooping, drooped**] to hang down □ *The flowers were starting to droop.* □ *Her head drooped slightly forwards.* (pender)

drop /drɒp/ ▶ VERB [**drops, dropping, dropped**]

1 to fall to the ground, or to let something fall to the ground □ *She tripped and dropped her glass.* □ *The ball dropped into the hole.* (cair)

2 to change to a lower level or amount □ *The temperature drops at night.* □ **+ from** *The exam pass rate has dropped from 75% to 60%.* (cair)

3 to stop doing something or stop continuing with something (abandonar, largar) 🔁 *He dropped everything and went to help his mother in France.* (abandonou tudo) □ *They've had to drop their plans.*

4 to decide not to include someone in a team □ **+ from** *Davis was dropped from the team.* (excluir)

5 if you drop someone somewhere, you take them there in your car, and then drive somewhere else yourself □ *I'll drop you at the doctor's on my way to the supermarket.* (deixar alguém/dar carona)

♦ PHRASAL VERBS **drop by/in/round** to visit someone for a short time □ *Why don't you drop round for a coffee later?* (dar um pulo) **drop off** to start sleeping. An informal phrase. □ *Jim dropped off in front of the TV.* (dormir) **drop someone/something off** to take someone or something to a place □ *I've got to drop this bag off at my Mum's house.* (deixar algo/alguém em algum lugar) **drop out** to stop doing something before you have finished □ *She dropped out of school at the age of fifteen.* (desistir, desligar)

▶ NOUN [*plural* **drops**]

1 a very small amount of a liquid □ **+ of** *Was that a drop of rain?* □ *There were some drops of blood on the floor.* (gota)

2 *no plural* a decrease (queda) 🔁 *There has been a sharp drop (= big drop) in profits.* (grande queda) □ **+ in** *There was a small drop in the number of tourists last year.*

drop-down menu | dual

3 *no plural* the distance down from a high place to the ground (declive) ◘ *She leant over the wall, gazing down at the steep drop below.* (declive íngreme)

4 *no plural* a small amount of drink ◘ *Would you like a drop more tea?* (dose)

drop-down menu /ˈdrɒpdaʊn ˌmenjuː/ NOUN [*plural* **drop-down menus**] a list of things to choose from on a computer screen that appears when you click on it (menu suspenso)

drought /draʊt/ NOUN [*plural* **droughts**] a time when very little rain falls (seca) ◘ *The country is currently suffering from a severe drought.* (forte seca)

drove /drəʊv/ PAST TENSE OF **drive** (ver drive)

drown /draʊn/ VERB [**drowns, drowning, drowned**]
1 to die because of being under water and not able to breathe ◘ *Three soldiers drowned when their truck fell into a river.* (afogar-se)
2 to kill someone by holding them under water (afogar)
◆ PHRASAL VERB **drown out something** to stop something from being heard by making a louder sound ◘ *Her voice was drowned out by the sound of the music.* (abafar o som)

drowsy /ˈdraʊzi/ ADJECTIVE [**drowsier, drowsiest**] tired and almost asleep ◘ *The heat was making me drowsy.* (sonolento)

drudgery /ˈdrʌdʒəri/ NOUN, NO PLURAL boring, hard work (trabalho monótono)

drug /drʌɡ/ ▶ NOUN [*plural* **drugs**]
1 a medicine (remédio, fármaco) ◘ *Doctors usually prescribe the drug for children.* (receitou o remédio)
2 an illegal substance that people take to change the way they feel (droga) ◘ *He was on drugs* (= regularly taking drugs) (usando drogas) ◘ *I've never taken drugs.* (usei drogas) ◘ *a drug addict* (viciado em drogas)
▶ VERB [**drugs, drugging, drugged**] to give someone a drug that will make them unconscious (drogar)

drugstore /ˈdrʌɡstɔː(r)/ NOUN [*plural* **drugstores**] the US word for **chemist's** (farmácia)

drum /drʌm/ ▶ NOUN [*plural* **drums**]
1 an instrument that is round and has a skin stretched over it that you hit to make a rhythm (tambor) ◘ *He plays the drums in a band.* (bateria) ◘ *a drum kit* (= a set of drums) (conjunto de bateria)
2 a tall round container for liquids ◘ *an oil drum* (tambor de óleo)
▶ VERB [**drums, drumming, drummed**]
1 to hit something in a regular rhythm ◘ *Rain was drumming on the roof.* (tamborilar)
2 to hit your fingers against something several times ◘ *He was drumming impatiently on the steering wheel.* (batucar)

◆ PHRASAL VERBS **drum something into someone** to make someone understand that something is important by saying it to them many times ◘ *My parents drummed it into me that I had to be brave.* (martelar algo na cabeça de alguém) **drum something up** to try to get people to support you or buy things from you ◘ *He went to China to try to drum up new business.* (lutar para conseguir algo)

• **drummer** /ˈdrʌmə(r)/ NOUN [*plural* **drummers**] someone who plays the drums (baterista)

drunk /drʌŋk/ ▶ PAST PARTICIPLE OF **drink** (ver drink)
▶ ADJECTIVE having drunk too much alcohol (bêbado) ◘ *He got drunk at the party.* (ficou bêbado)

• **drunken** /ˈdrʌŋkən/ ADJECTIVE having drunk too much alcohol, or involving people who have drunk too much alcohol ◘ *a drunken brawl* (bêbado)

dry /draɪ/ ▶ ADJECTIVE [**drier, driest**]
1 not wet ◘ *Are the clothes dry yet?* (seco)
2 with little rain (seco) ◘ *dry weather* (tempo seco) ◘ *a hot, dry summer*
3 dry hair or skin does not have enough natural oils in it ◘ *a shampoo for dry hair* ◘ *My skin gets very dry in the winter.* (seco)
4 boring to read or listen to ◘ *I find her writing rather dry.* (árido)
5 dry humour is funny in a way that is not obvious (irônico)
6 dry wine is not sweet (seco)
▶ VERB [**dries, drying, dried**] to make something dry, or to become dry ◘ *He dried his hands on the towel.* ◘ *She hung the clothes out to dry.* (secar)
◆ PHRASAL VERBS **dry (someone/something) off** to become dry, or to make someone or something dry ◘ *He went swimming and then dried off in the sun.* (enxugar) **dry up**. **1** if something dries up, there is no more available ◘ *Work often dries up for models when they reach 35.* (tornar-se raro)
2 if a river or lake dries up, there is no water in it **dry (something) up** to dry plates, bowls, etc. after someone has washed them (secar)

dry-clean /ˌdraɪˈkliːn/ VERB [**dry-cleans, dry-cleaning, dry-cleaned**] to clean clothes with chemicals instead of water (lavar a seco)

• **dry cleaner's** /ˌdraɪ ˈkliːnəz/ NOUN, NO PLURAL a shop where clothes are dry-cleaned (tinturaria, lavanderia)

• **dry cleaning** /ˌdraɪ ˈkliːnɪŋ/ NOUN, NO PLURAL
1 clothes that are dry-cleaned (lavagem a seco)
2 cleaning clothes using a chemical instead of water (lavagem a seco)

dryer /ˈdraɪə(r)/ NOUN [*plural* **dryers**] a machine that dries wet clothes or hair (secador)

dual /ˈdjuːəl/ ADJECTIVE having two parts (dupla) ◘ *Hening has dual Belgian/French nationality.* (dupla nacionalidade)

dual carriageway

dual carriageway /ˌdjuːəl ˈkærɪdʒweɪ/ NOUN [plural **dual carriageways**] a road with two lines of traffic going in each direction (**autoestrada, rodovia**)

dub /dʌb/ VERB [**dubs, dubbing, dubbed**]
1 to give someone or something a different name that describes them in some way □ *The ceremony was dubbed 'The invisible wedding' by Italian newspapers.* (**apelidar**)
2 to change the language in a film or television programme into a different language □ *The film has been dubbed into Russian.* (**dublar**)

dubious /ˈdjuːbiəs/ ADJECTIVE
1 not sure about something □ *I'm a bit dubious about his ability to do the job.* (**incerto**)
2 probably dishonest or not true □ *He knows some very dubious people.* (**suspeito**)

duchess /ˈdʌtʃɪs/ NOUN [plural **duchesses**] the title of a woman who has a very high social rank (**duquesa**)

duck /dʌk/ ▶ NOUN [plural **ducks**]
1 a water bird with short legs and a wide, flat beak □ *wild ducks* (**pato**)
2 *no plural* the meat from a duck □ *roast duck* (**pato**)
▶ VERB [**ducks, ducking, ducked**]
1 to lower your head or body so that you are not hit or seen (**esquivar-se**) 🔁 *Hamish ducked his head to get through the low doorway.* (**esquivou sua cabeça**) □ + **behind** *He ducked behind a car when the shooting began.*
2 to avoid something difficult such as a question, subject or responsibility (**evitar, livrar-se**) 🔁 *The Prime Minister ducked questions on whether taxes would be increased.* (**evitou questões**)

duckling /ˈdʌklɪŋ/ NOUN [plural **ducklings**] a baby duck (**patinho, filhote de pato**)

duct /dʌkt/ NOUN [plural **ducts**]
1 a tube in your body that carries liquid □ *The tear duct is in the corner of the eye.* (**canal**)
2 a pipe in a building □ *heating ducts* (**tubo**)

dud /dʌd/ ▶ NOUN [plural **duds**] someone or something that is not good. An informal word. □ *His next film was a dud.* (**fracasso**)
▶ ADJECTIVE not working correctly □ *a dud light bulb* (**defeituoso**)

due /djuː/ ▶ ADJECTIVE
1 expected to arrive or happen □ + **at** *The train is due at 10:15.* □ + **in** *Their baby is due in March.* □ + **to do something** *The project is due to start next month.* (**esperado**)
2 needing to be paid □ *The rent is due at the beginning of the month.* (**devido**)
3 **due to something** because of something □ *The plane was delayed due to bad weather.* (**devido a**)
4 if something is due to you, you deserve it or someone owes it to you □ *He paid the money that was due to her.* (**devido**)
5 **be due for something** if you are due for something, it is time for you to have that thing □ *I'm due for a pay rise.* (**merecer algo**)
6 a formal word meaning suitable and correct □ *He gave the matter due consideration.* (**justo, exato**)
▶ ADVERB directly □ *London is due south of here.* (**diretamente**)

duel /ˈdjuːəl/ NOUN [plural **duels**] in the past, a fight using weapons between two men who have argued (**duelo**)

duet /djuːˈet/ NOUN [plural **duets**] a piece of music sung or played by two people (**dueto**)

dug /dʌɡ/ PAST TENSE AND PAST PARTICIPLE OF **dig** (ver **dig**)

duke /djuːk/ NOUN [plural **dukes**] a title for a man with a very high social rank (**duque**)

dull /dʌl/ ▶ ADJECTIVE [**duller, dullest**]
1 boring □ *It was the dullest job you could imagine.* □ *Life is never dull when John's around.* (**maçante**)
2 not bright □ *It was a dull, grey day.* (**sombrio**)
3 a dull sound is low and not clear □ *His head hit the door with a dull thud.* (**abafado**)
4 a dull pain is not strong but continues for a long time (**crônica**) 🔁 *She felt a dull ache in her stomach.* (**dor crônica**)
▶ VERB [**dulls, dulling, dulled**] to make a feeling or sound less strong □ *He took a tablet to dull the pain.* (**aliviar**)

duly /ˈdjuːli/ ADVERB a formal word meaning at the correct time, in the correct way, or as expected □ *The new car was duly admired by friends and colleagues.* (**devidamente**)

dumb /dʌm/ ADJECTIVE [**dumber, dumbest**]
1 an informal word meaning stupid □ *He kept asking me dumb questions.* (**idiota**)
2 not able to speak (**mudo**)
◆ PHRASAL VERB [**dumbs, dumbing, dumbed**] **dumb (something) down** to make something so simple or easy to understand that it makes it less good □ *Television companies have been accused of dumbing down programmes.* (**empobrecer**)

dumbfounded /dʌmˈfaʊndɪd/ ADJECTIVE extremely surprised (**chocado**)

dummy /ˈdʌmi/ ▶ NOUN [plural **dummies**]
1 a model of a person □ *The cars are tested for crashes with dummies in them.* (**manequim**)
2 a rubber object that a baby sucks for comfort (**chupeta**)
3 something that is made to look like something real, but is not real □ *There were two pills but one of them was a dummy.* (**imitação**)
▶ ADJECTIVE made to look real, but not real □ *a dummy bomb* (**falso**)

dump /dʌmp/ ▶ VERB [**dumps, dumping, dumped**]
1 to put something somewhere quickly □ *He dumped his bag in the hall and ran upstairs.* (**largar**)

2 to leave something somewhere because you do not want it □ *It is not acceptable to dump toxic waste in the sea.* (**despejar**)
3 an informal word meaning to end a relationship with your boyfriend or girlfriend □ *Dan's upset because his girlfriend's dumped him.* (**terminar um relacionamento**)
▶ NOUN [plural **dumps**]
1 a place where people can leave things they do not want □ *I'm going to take the old sofa to the dump.* (**despejo, depósito de lixo**)
2 an informal word for a dirty or untidy place □ *This flat is such a dump.* (**espelunca**)

dumpling /'dʌmplɪŋ/ NOUN [plural **dumplings**] a mixture of fat and flour in the shape of a ball, that you cook in a boiling liquid (**bolinho de massa cozido**)

dumpy /'dʌmpɪ/ ADJECTIVE [**dumpier, dumpiest**] an informal word meaning short and fat (**atarracado**)

dune /dju:n/ NOUN [plural **dunes**] a hill of sand (**duna**)

dung /dʌŋ/ NOUN, NO PLURAL the solid waste of animals (**esterco**)

dungarees /ˌdʌŋgə'ri:z/ PLURAL NOUN trousers with a square part attached that covers your chest and pieces that go over your shoulders (**jardineira**)

dungeon /'dʌndʒən/ NOUN [plural **dungeons**] a dark underground room, used as a prison in the past (**masmorra**)

duo /'dju:əʊ/ NOUN [plural **duos**] two people who perform together (**dupla**) ▣ *a comedy duo* (**dupla de comediantes**)

duodecimal /ˌdju:əʊ'desɪməl/ ADJECTIVE using units of 12 as the base for a system of counting. A maths word. (**duodecimal**)

duodenum /ˌdju:əʊ'di:nəm/ NOUN [plural **duodenums** or **duodena**] the first part of the small intestine (= tube that food goes into to be digested), just below the stomach. A biology word. (**duodeno**)

dupe /dju:p/ VERB [**dupes, duping, duped**] to trick someone □ *The tourists were duped into handing over their money.* (**enganar**)

duplex /'dju:pleks/ NOUN [plural **duplexes**] the US word for **semi** (**duplo, de dois andares**)

duplicate¹ /'dju:plɪkeɪt/ VERB [**duplicates, duplicating, duplicated**]
1 to make a copy of something □ *Many entries in the database have been duplicated.* (**copiar, duplicar**)
2 to repeat something in exactly the same way □ *He is hoping to duplicate that success at the Olympic Games.* (**duplicar**)

duplicate² /'dju:plɪkət/ ▶ NOUN [plural **duplicates**] an exact copy □ *She sent a duplicate of the photo.* (**cópia, duplicata**)
▶ ADJECTIVE exactly the same □ *a duplicate key* (**duplicada**)

duplication /ˌdju:plɪ'keɪʃən/ NOUN, NO PLURAL
1 when something has the same purpose or effect as another thing so it is not necessary □ *To avoid duplication, each team will be assigned a particular task.* (**duplicação**)
2 copying something exactly □ *the duplication of images* (**cópia**)

durability /ˌdjʊərə'bɪlɪtɪ/ NOUN, NO PLURAL the ability to stay in a good condition for a long time □ *The material is known for its durability.* (**durabilidade**)

durable /'djʊərəbəl/ ADJECTIVE staying in a good condition for a long time □ *durable building materials* (**durável**)

duration /djʊ'reɪʃən/ NOUN, NO PLURAL the length of time that something continues. A formal word. (**duração**) ▣ *Hotel guests are offered a car for the duration of their stay.* (**pela duração de**)

duress /djʊ'res/ NOUN, NO PLURAL **under duress** if you do something under duress, you do it because someone forces you to, and not because you want to. A formal phrase. □ *The contract was signed under duress.* (**sob coação**)

during /'djʊərɪŋ/ PREPOSITION
1 at one point in a period of time □ *My great-grandfather was killed during the war.* (**durante**)
2 through the whole of a period of time □ *The garden looks beautiful during the summer.* (**durante**)

> ➤ Remember that **during** is not used to talk about how long something happens. Use **for** for this:
> ✓ I studied English **for** three years.
> ✗ I studied English during three years.

dusk /dʌsk/ NOUN, NO PLURAL the time in the evening when it starts to get dark (**penumbra**) ▣ *Dusk was falling.* (**a penumbra estava chegando**)

dust /dʌst/ ▶ NOUN, NO PLURAL a powder of dirt on a surface or in the air (**pó**) ▣ *A thin layer of dust covered the desk.* (**camada de pó**) ▣ *The horses kicked up a cloud of dust.* (**nuvem de pó**) ▣ *The books were gathering dust in his attic.* (**acumulando poeira**)
▶ VERB [**dusts, dusting, dusted**] to clean dust from something using a cloth □ *I've dusted the shelves.* (**tirar o pó, desempoeirar**)
◆ PHRASAL VERB **dust something off** to get something ready to use when you have not used it for a long time □ *She dusted off her dancing shoes in preparation for the ball.* (**tirar o pó de algo, deixar algo pronto para uso**)

dustbin /'dʌstbɪn/ NOUN [plural **dustbins**] a container for rubbish, which is outside your house □ *She threw the empty boxes in the dustbin.* (**lata de lixo**)

duster /'dʌstə(r)/ NOUN [plural **dusters**] a cloth for removing dust from surfaces (**espanador**)

dustman /'dʌstmən/ NOUN [plural **dustmen**] someone whose job is to collect rubbish from people's houses (**lixeiro**)

dustpan /'dʌstpæn/ NOUN [plural **dustpans**] a flat container with a handle, that you brush dust and waste into (**pá de lixo**) ◨ *a dustpan and brush* (**pá e escova**)

dusty /'dʌsti/ ADJECTIVE [**dustier**, **dustiest**] covered with dust □ *a dusty floor* □ *Children played in the dusty streets.* (**poeirento**)

dutiful /'dju:tɪfʊl/ ADJECTIVE a dutiful person does what other people think they should do. A formal word. □ *Amir tried to be a dutiful son.* (**obediente**)

duty /'dju:ti/ NOUN [plural **duties**]
1 something that you do because other people expect you to do it or because it is morally right to do it (**dever**) ◨ *He felt he had a moral duty to help her.* (**dever moral**) □ + **to do something** *Society has a duty to protect children.*
2 duties the things that you have to do in your job (**deveres**) ◨ *The President has a number of official duties next week.* (**deveres oficiais**) □ *My duties include producing reports.*
3 on/off duty if someone such as a doctor, police officer etc. is on duty, they are working, and if they are off duty, they are not working □ *Which doctor is on duty tonight?* (**estar/não estar de plantão**)
4 a tax □ + **on** *The government will raise the duty on imports.* (**taxa, imposto**)

duty-free /ˌdju:tɪ'fri:/ ADJECTIVE duty-free products are cheaper because you can bring them into a country without paying tax □ *duty-free perfume* (**isento de taxa**) ◨ *We went to the duty-free shop at the airport.* (**loja duty-free**)

duvet /'du:veɪ/ NOUN [plural **duvets**] a thick warm cover for your bed □ *He pulled the duvet over his head.* (**acolchoado**) ◨ *a duvet cover* (**coberta acolchoada**)

DVD /ˌdi:vi:'di:/ ABBREVIATION digital versatile disk; a type of disk with pictures and sound recorded on it □ *The movie is available on DVD.* (**DVD**) ◨ *a DVD player* (**aparelho de DVD**) ◨ *The children were watching a DVD.* (**assistindo a um DVD**)

dwarf /dwɔ:f/ ▶ NOUN [plural **dwarfs** or **dwarves**] an imaginary creature in children's stories, which looks like a very smallman (**gnomo, duende**)
▶ ADJECTIVE dwarf plants are much smaller than the usual type □ *dwarf apple trees* (**anão**)
▶ VERB [**dwarfs, dwarfing, dwarfed**] to make something else look small in comparison □ *The new hotel dwarfs the buildings around it.* (**tornar menor**)

dwell /dwel/ VERB [**dwells, dwelling, dwelt**] a literary word meaning to live somewhere (**residir, morar**)
◆ PHRASAL VERB **dwell on something** to think or talk for too long about something unpleasant □ *There's no point in dwelling on your mistakes now.* (**insistir em algo, estender-se sobre algo**)
• **dwelling** /'dwelɪŋ/ NOUN [plural **dwellings**] a formal word for home □ *The region will have 2,000 new dwellings in the next 10 years.* (**residência**)

dwindle /'dwɪndəl/ VERB [**dwindles, dwindling, dwindled**] to become less □ *Church membership has dwindled.* (**diminuir, reduzir**)
• **dwindling** /'dwɪndlɪŋ/ ADJECTIVE becoming less □ *Australia is facing dwindling water supplies.* (**reduzido**)

dye /daɪ/ ▶ NOUN [plural **dyes**] a substance used for changing the colour of cloth or hair (**tintura**)
▶ VERB [**dyes, dyeing, dyed**] to use a substance to change the colour of cloth or hair □ *Emma dyed her hair red.* (**tingir**)

dyke /daɪk/ NOUN [plural **dykes**]
1 a wall that stops water from flooding the land (**represa**)
2 a narrow passage in the ground, that takes water away from fields (**canal**)

dynamic /daɪ'næmɪk/ ADJECTIVE
1 full of energy and new ideas □ *a dynamic young manager* (**dinâmico**)
2 changing continuously □ *a dynamic situation* (**dinâmico**)
3 to do with movement. A physics word. (**dinâmico**)
• **dynamics** /daɪ'næmɪks/ NOUN, NO PLURAL
1 the way in which things and people affect each other □ *Serious illness can change the dynamics of a family.* (**dinâmica**)
2 the part of physics that is to do with movement. A physics word. (**dinâmica**)

dynamite /'daɪnəmaɪt/ NOUN, NO PLURAL
1 a powerful explosive (**dinamite**)
2 something which could cause a lot of excitement or arguments □ *The immigration issue is political dynamite.* (**bomba, dinamite**)

dynasty /'dɪnəsti/ NOUN [plural **dynasties**] a family whose members rule a company, are in charge of a business, etc. for a long time (**dinastia**)

dyslexia /dɪs'leksiə/ NOUN, NO PLURAL a brain problem which makes it difficult for someone to read and spell (**dislexia**)
• **dyslexic** /dɪs'leksɪk/ ADJECTIVE having dyslexia (**disléxico**)

Ee

e- /iː/ PREFIX e- is added to the beginning of words to mean 'electronic' or to do with the Internet □ *e-commerce* (**e-**)

E¹ *or* **e** /iː/ the fifth letter of the alphabet (**a quinta letra do alfabeto**)

E² /iː/ ABBREVIATION east (**L – abreviação de leste**)

each /iːtʃ/ DETERMINER, PRONOUN

1 every separate person or thing □ *We had to pay £5 each.* □ **+ of** *Each of the soldiers was given a gun.* □ *He had a heavy suitcase in each hand.* (**cada**)

2 each other used to show that each person or thing in a group of two or more does something to the others □ *The team all hugged each other.* □ *The cat and dog don't like each other much.* (**mutuamente, um ao outro, uns aos outros**)

> Remember that **each** is followed by a singular noun: □ *Each person starts the game with five cards.*

eager /ˈiːgə(r)/ ADJECTIVE wanting very much to do or have something □ **+ to do something** *Imran seems eager to learn.* (**ansioso**)

• **eagerly** /ˈiːgəli/ ADVERB in an eager way (**ansiosamente**) ▣ *This is the eagerly awaited new film from the Spanish director.* (**ansiosamente aguardado**)

• **eagerness** /ˈiːgənɪs/ NOUN, NO PLURAL being eager □ *In his eagerness to get there, he fell over.* (**ânsia**)

eagle /ˈiːgəl/ NOUN [*plural* **eagles**] a large bird with a curved beak that hunts small birds and animals (**águia**)

ear /ɪə(r)/ NOUN [plural ears]

1 one of the two parts on each side of your head that you hear with □ *He whispered something in my ear.* (**orelha**)

2 the part at the top of the stem of some plants where the grains grow □ *an ear of corn* (**espiga**)

♦ IDIOMS **couldn't believe their ears** used to say that someone was very surprised when they were told something □ *I couldn't believe my ears when she said she was going to marry Ben.* (**não acreditei quando ouvi**) **fall on deaf ears** to be ignored □ *Her pleas for help fell on deaf ears.* (**ser ignorado**) **have an ear for something** to be able to recognize and repeat sounds □ *Ann has an ear for languages.* (**ter habilidade para reconhecer e repetir sons**) **keep your ears open** to try to get information about something by listening to what people say **play it by ear** to decide how to act as a situation develops instead of having a plan at the beginning □ *We don't have any firm instructions, so you'll have to just play it by ear.* (**agir de improviso**) **play something by ear** to play a piece of music without reading the notes (**tocar algum trecho de música sem ler as notas**)

earache /ˈɪəreɪk/ NOUN, NO PLURAL pain inside your ear (**dor de ouvido**)

eardrum /ˈɪədrʌm/ NOUN [*plural* **eardrums**] a thin, tight skin inside your ear that allows you to hear sounds (**tímpano**)

earl /ɜːl/ NOUN [*plural* **earls**] a British man with a high social rank □ *Earl Spencer* □ *the Earl of Warwick* (**conde**)

earlobe /ˈɪələʊb/ NOUN [*plural* **earlobes**] the soft round part that hangs down at the bottom of your ear (**lóbulo da orelha**)

early /ˈɜːli/ ADJECTIVE, ADVERB [earlier, earliest]

1 happening or arriving before others or before the expected or normal time □ *Nick had taken an earlier train.* □ *I'm tired so I'm going to bed early tonight.* (**cedo**)

2 near the beginning of something □ *It's so quiet here in the early morning.* □ *She showed musical talent early in life* (**no início**) ▣ *The police were in the early stages of the investigation.* (**nos estágios iniciais**)

3 early on in the first part of something □ *He defended really well early on in the match.* (**no começo**)

4 at the earliest used to say that something will not happen or be done before a particular time □ *The new house won't be ready until August at the earliest.* (**não antes de**)

5 the early hours the time between 12 o'clock at night and the beginning of the morning □ *The robbery must have taken place in the early hours.* (**de madrugada**)

earmark /ˈɪəmɑːk/ VERB [**earmarks, earmarking, earmarked**] to decide to use something, especially money, for a particular purpose □ *That money's been earmarked for a new car.* (**destinar**)

earn /ɜːn/ VERB [earns, earning, earned]

1 to get money for work that you do □ *He earns about £45,000 a year.* (**ganhar**) 🔲 *Does she earn her living* (= get all the money she needs to live) *as an artist?* (**ganhou sua vida**)

2 to get something good, such as praise, because you have done something well □ *He worked hard and earned the respect of his colleagues.* (**merecer**)

3 to get money as interest on an amount you have in a bank or have lent to someone □ *Your savings can earn 5.5% in our high-interest account.* (**render**)

> Remember that you **earn** money for work that you do. You win money in a competition □ *He earns a very good salary.* □ *He won a million pounds on the lottery.*

earnest /'ɜːnɪst/ ▶ ADJECTIVE serious and honest □ *The three men were in earnest conversation.* (**sério**)

▶ NOUN, NO PLURAL **in earnest** (a) speaking honestly about what you want to do □ *Was he in earnest when he said he wanted to leave?* (b) if something happens in earnest, it happens more seriously than before □ *The war began in earnest that May.* (**de verdade, a sério**)

earnings /'ɜːnɪŋz/ PLURAL NOUN money that you get from working (**rendimentos, vencimentos**)

earphones /'ɪəfəʊnz/ PLURAL NOUN a piece of electronic equipment that you wear in or on your ears so that you can listen to music, radio, etc. (**fones de ouvido**)

earplugs /'ɪəplʌgz/ PLURAL NOUN small pieces of a soft material that you put in your ears to keep out noise (**protetores auriculares**)

earring /'ɪərɪŋ/ NOUN [plural **earrings**] a piece of jewellery for the ear □ *a pair of earrings* □ *diamond earrings* (**brincos**)

earshot /'ɪəʃɒt/ NOUN, NO PLURAL

1 out of earshot too far away to hear (**longe dos ouvidos**)

2 in/within earshot close enough to hear (**perto dos ouvidos**)

ear-splitting /'ɪəˌsplɪtɪŋ/ ADJECTIVE extremely loud □ *An ear-splitting scream came from the attic.* (**extremamente alto**)

earth /ɜːθ/ NOUN [plural earths]

1 Earth the planet we live on (**Terra**) 🔲 *life on Earth* (**na Terra**) □ *The Earth rotates around the sun.*

2 NO PLURAL soil □ *a pile of earth* (**terra**)

3 NO PLURAL the surface of our planet □ *The earth shook with the explosion.* (**solo, terra**)

4 a wire that makes electrical equipment safer by taking the electric current into the ground (**fio terra**)

♦ IDIOMS **cost the earth** to cost a lot of money. An informal phrase. □ *Their new house must have cost the earth.* (**custar uma fortuna**) **how/what/where/why on earth?** used to emphasize a question, usually when you are very surprised □ *How on earth did that happen?* □ *What on earth was he wearing?* (**como/o que/onde/por que diabos?**)

• **earthly** /'ɜːθli/ ADJECTIVE

1 used to emphasize a question or a negative statement (**possível**) 🔲 *There is no earthly reason why you shouldn't go.* (**razão possível**)

2 to do with life on Earth and not life in heaven. A literary word. (**terreno, terrestre**)

earthquake /'ɜːθkweɪk/ NOUN [plural **earthquakes**] when the ground suddenly moves, often causing serious damage to buildings (**terremoto**)

earthworm /'ɜːθwɜːm/ NOUN [plural **earthworms**] a small, long, thin animal that lives in the soil (**minhoca**)

ease /iːz/ ▶ NOUN, NO PLURAL

1 with ease easily □ *She won the race with ease.* (**com facilidade**)

2 at ease relaxed □ *He's never completely at ease talking to strangers.* (**sentir-se à vontade**)

▶ VERB [eases, easing, eased]

1 to become less difficult or painful, or to make something less difficult or painful (**aliviar**) 🔲 *These tablets should ease the pain.* (**aliviar a dor**) □ *Tensions in the area have gradually eased.*

2 to move something somewhere gradually □ *They eased the last big block into position.* (**mover**)

♦ PHRASAL VERB **ease off** to gradually stop □ *The rain seems to be easing off now.* (**parar aos poucos**)

easel /'iːzəl/ NOUN [plural **easels**] a frame used to hold a picture while someone is painting it (**cavalete**)

easily /'iːzɪli/ ADVERB

1 with no effort or difficulty □ *Chelsea won easily.* (**facilmente**)

2 certainly □ *She's easily the most successful female pop singer today.* (**certamente**)

3 very possibly □ *It could easily be two weeks before you get a replacement.* (**possivelmente**)

east /iːst/ ▶ NOUN, NO PLURAL

1 the direction that you look towards to see the sun rise □ *Which way is east?* □ *York is to the east of Harrogate.*

2 the countries in Asia □ *We do a lot of business in the East.* (**Leste**)

3 the part of a country that is in the east □ *There has been heavy rain in the east today.* (**leste**)

Easter

▶ ADJECTIVE, ADVERB in or towards the east □ *the east coast* □ *East London* □ *We headed east.* (**para leste, sentido leste**)

Easter /'i:stə(r)/ NOUN, NO PLURAL a Christian holiday in March or April to celebrate when Christ came back to life from the dead □ *the Easter holidays* □ *Easter Sunday* (**Páscoa**)

Easter egg /'i:stə(r) ‚eg/ NOUN [*plural* **Easter eggs**] a chocolate egg, given as a present at Easter. (**ovo de Páscoa**)

easterly /'i:stəli/ ADJECTIVE
1 towards the east □ *They set off in an easterly direction.* (**para leste**)
2 coming from the East □ *an easterly breeze* (**oriental**)

eastern /'i:stən/ ADJECTIVE
1 in or from the east part of a country or area □ *the eastern coast of America* □ *Eastern England* (**oriental**)
2 to do with the countries of Asia □ *She's studying Eastern philosophy.* (**oriental**)

eastward /'i:stwəd/ or **eastwards** /'i:stwədz/ ADVERB to or towards the east □ *We were sailing eastwards.* (**em direção ao leste, para o leste**)

easy /'i:zi/ ▶ ADJECTIVE [**easier, easiest**]
1 not difficult to do □ *an easy exam paper* (**fácil**)
2 I'm easy said when someone offers you a choice and you are happy to have or do any of the things offered □ *'Shall we order a pizza or a curry?' 'I'm easy, you choose.'* (**para mim, tanto faz**)
▶ ADVERB [**easier, easiest**] **take it easy** to relax and not work hard □ *Grandad's taking it easy in the garden.* (**pegar leve**)
♦ IDIOMS **Easier said than done.** used to say that something is difficult to do □ *I know I should get the kids to help but that's easier said than done.* (**falar é facil, difícil é fazer**) **go easy on someone** to treat someone more gently □ *Go easy on Matt, he's having a hard time at the moment.* (**ir devagar com alguém**) **go easy on something** to eat or use only a little of something □ *My doctor said I should go easy on the red meat.* (**ir devagar com algo**)

easy-going /,i:zi'gəʊɪŋ/ ADJECTIVE relaxed and not often upset or angry (**tolerante**)

eat /i:t/ VERB [**eats, eating, ate, eaten**]
1 to put food in your mouth and swallow it □ *We've eaten all the bread.* □ *He ate a huge meal.* (**comer**) 🗣 *Do you fancy something to eat?* (**algo para comer**)
2 to have a meal □ *What time would you like to eat?* (**comer**)
♦ PHRASAL VERBS **eat away at someone** if a bad memory or feeling eats away at you, you cannot forget it and it makes you feel bad **eat away at something** to gradually destroy something □ *The acid eats away at the tooth enamel.* (**destruir,** **corroer alguém**) **eat into something** to use more of your money, time, etc., than you had planned □ *The journey to work really eats into my day.* (**destruir pouco a pouco**) **eat out** to have a meal in a restaurant □ *We eat out about twice a month.* (**comer fora**) **eat something up 1** to eat all of an amount of food □ *Eat up your vegetables, Maisie.* (**comer tudo**) **2** to use all of something valuable □ *The repairs had eaten up all of their savings.* (**consumir tudo**)
• **eater** /'i:tə(r)/ NOUN [*plural* **eaters**]
1 someone who eats in a particular way □ *She's not a big eater.* □ *a fussy eater* (**comedor**)
2 a person or animal that eats a particular thing □ *It's a good restaurant for meat eaters.* (**comedor**)

eaves /i:vz/ PLURAL NOUN the edges of a roof that stick out over the walls (**calha**)

eavesdrop /'i:vzdrɒp/ VERB [**eavesdrops, eavesdropping, eavesdropped**] to listen to other people's conversations without them knowing □ *I think Tony was eavesdropping on our conversation.* (**ouvir escondido**)

eBay /'i:beɪ/ NOUN, NO PLURAL a website where you can buy and sell things. A trademark. (**eBay**)
🗣 *She buys a lot of clothes on eBay.* (**no eBay**)

ebb /eb/ ▶ VERB [**ebbs, ebbing, ebbed**]
1 to gradually get less and less □ *Her enthusiasm for the project has slowly ebbed away.* (**diminuir**)
2 when the tide ebbs, the sea flows away from the land (**baixar**)
▶ NOUN, NO PLURAL **be at a low ebb** if a good feeling is at a low ebb, there is very little of it at a particular time □ *Morales was at a low ebb after the strike.* (**estar em maré baixa**)

ebony /'ebəni/ NOUN, NO PLURAL a very hard black wood from an African tree (**ébano**)

eccentric /ɪk'sentrɪk/ ADJECTIVE behaving in a way that is strange or different from most people □ *an eccentric millionaire* (**excêntrico**)
• **eccentricity** /,eksen'trɪsəti/ NOUN [*plural* **eccentricities**] eccentric behaviour (**excentricidade**)

ECG /,i:si:'dʒi:/ ABBREVIATION electrocardiogram or electrocardiograph; a medical test in which you are connected to a machine that measures how well your heart is beating (**ECG – abreviação de eletrocardiograma**)

echo /'ekəʊ/ ▶ VERB [**echoes, echoing, echoed**]
1 a sound echoes when it comes back and you hear it again □ *Their laughter echoed in the empty concert hall.* (**ecoar**)
2 to repeat what someone has said or thought □ *The minister echoed the Foreign Secretary's view.* (**repetir**)
▶ NOUN [*plural* **echoes**] a sound that you hear again after it is sent back off a surface such as a wall (**eco**)

eclectic /ɪ'klektɪk/ ADJECTIVE including a lot of different styles or types of things (**eclético**) 🗣

There's an eclectic mix of musical instruments. (mistura eclética)

eclipse /ɪ'klɪps/ NOUN [plural **eclipses**] when the sun disappears behind the moon or the moon is covered by the Earth's shadow □ *a total eclipse of the sun* (eclipse)

eco- /'i:kəʊ/ PREFIX eco- is added to the beginning of words to mean 'to do with the environment' □ *eco-friendly* (eco-)

eco-friendly /ˌi:kəʊ'frendli/ ADJECTIVE not harmful to the environment □ *eco-friendly detergents* (ecologicamente correto)

ecological /ˌi:kə'lɒdʒɪkəl/ ADJECTIVE to do with ecology □ *an ecological disaster* (ecológico)

ecology /ɪ'kɒlədʒi/ NOUN, NO PLURAL the study of how plants and animals exist together and how their environment affects them (ecologia)

e-commerce /'i:kɒmɜːs/ NOUN, NO PLURAL the business of buying and selling goods on the Internet (comércio eletrônico)

economic /ˌi:kə'nɒmɪk/ ADJECTIVE

1 to do with money, business and industry (econômico) ⧫ More *economic growth* is predicted. (crescimento econômico) ⧫ *economic development* (desenvolvimento econômico) □ *an economic forecast*
2 making a profit □ *The business was no longer economic and closed down.* (rentável)

• **economical** /ˌi:kə'nɒmɪkəl/ ADJECTIVE costing only a little money □ *It's a very economical car to run.* (econômico)

• **economics** /ˌi:kə'nɒmɪks/ NOUN, NO PLURAL the study of how money, business and industry are organized □ *a degree in economics* (economia)

• **economist** /ɪ'kɒnəmɪst/ NOUN [plural **economists**] someone who studies economics (economista)

• **economize** or **economise** /ɪ'kɒnəmaɪz/ VERB [**economizes, economizing, economized**] to save money by using less of something or buying something cheaper (economizar)

economy /ɪ'kɒnəmi/ NOUN [plural economies]

1 all the money a country or area creates through producing and selling goods and services, and the way that money is used □ *Canada's economy grew fast.* □ *Tourism benefits the local economy.* (economia)
2 when someone is careful not to waste something such as money, time or fuel □ *We're looking for a car that offers both performance and economy.* (economia) ⧫ *The company will have to make economies to survive.* (fazer economias)

ecosystem /'i:kəʊˌsɪstəm/ NOUN [plural **ecosystems**] all the plants and animals in an area and the way they depend on each other and on their environment to live (ecossistema)

ecotourism /'i:kəʊˌtʊərɪzəm/ NOUN, NO PLURAL holidays that are organized so that they help local people and do not damage the environment (ecoturismo)

• **ecotourist** /'i:kəʊˌtʊərɪst/ NOUN [plural **ecotourists**] someone who takes a holiday like this (ecoturista)

ecstasy /'ekstəsi/ NOUN, NO PLURAL a feeling of great happiness or pleasure (êxtase)

• **ecstatic** /ek'stætɪk/ ADJECTIVE extremely happy (extasiado)

eczema /'eksɪmə/ NOUN, NO PLURAL a disease in which your skin develops dry, red areas (eczema, dermatite)

edge /edʒ/ ▶ NOUN [plural edges]

1 the outer part or end of something □ *We stood on the edge of the cliff.* □ *I live on the outer edge of the city.* □ *Trim off all the rough edges.* (beira)
2 a side of something that is sharp enough to cut (gume)
3 an advantage that makes someone or something more successful than others □ *+ over This technology gives us a competitive edge over our rivals.* (em vantagem)
4 on edge nervous and slightly bad-tempered (nervoso, impaciente)

◆ IDIOM **take the edge off something** to make a pain, bad emotion, etc. slightly less strong (aviar, reduzir algo)

▶ VERB [**edges, edging, edged**]

1 to move slowly and carefully □ *Harry edged along the narrow ledge.* (mover aos poucos)
2 to put something round the edge of something, usually as decoration □ *The pillowcases were edged with lace.* (delimitar, margear)

edgeways /'edʒweɪz/ ADVERB

◆ IDIOM **not get a word in edgeways** to not have the chance to speak because other people are talking too much □ *You can't get a word in edgeways once he starts.* (não conseguir participar das conversas)

edging /'edʒɪŋ/ NOUN [plural **edgings**] something that goes round the edge of something else, usually as decoration (enfeite, bainha)

edgy /'edʒi/ ADJECTIVE [**edgier, edgiest**]
1 nervous and slightly bad-tempered (nervoso)
2 fashionable in an unusual and exciting way (mordaz)

edible /'edɪbəl/ ADJECTIVE
1 safe to eat □ *edible mushrooms* (comestível)
2 good enough to eat □ *Her chocolate cake was barely edible.* (comestível)

edifice /'edɪfɪs/ NOUN [plural **edifices**] a very large building □ *The town hall is an imposing edifice.* (edifício)

edit /'edɪt/ VERB [**edits, editing, edited**]
1 to prepare a book, document, film, etc. by correcting mistakes and making any changes that are needed (editar)
2 to be the editor of a newspaper, magazine, etc. (editar)

- **edition** /ɪˈdɪʃən/ NOUN [plural **editions**]
1 the copies of a book, newspaper, etc. that are printed at the same time □ *The story was in the early editions of the newspaper.* □ *I bought the hardback edition of her first novel.* (**edição**)
2 one of a series of television or radio programmes □ *I saw her on Saturday's edition of the talk show.* (**edição**)

- **editor** /ˈedɪtə(r)/ NOUN [plural **editors**]
1 someone whose job is to prepare a book, document, newspaper, etc. to be published by correcting mistakes and making any changes that are needed □ *He thanked his editor for all her help.* (**editor, organizador**)
2 someone who is in charge of a newspaper, magazine, etc. or someone who writes or talks about a particular subject for a newspaper, television show, etc. □ *He is the arts editor of The Guardian.* (**editor**)

- **editorial** /ˌedɪˈtɔːriəl/ ▶ ADJECTIVE to do with editing or editors □ *the editorial staff* □ *She questioned my editorial judgement.* (**editorial**)
▶ NOUN [plural **editorials**] an article in a newspaper or magazine that expresses the opinion of the editor or the owner (**editorial**)

educate /ˈedjʊkeɪt/ VERB [educates, educating, educated]
1 to teach someone □ *He was educated at the local school.* (**educar, ensinar, instruir**)
2 to give people information about something so that they understand it more □ + *about* *We need to educate people about the importance of exercise.* (**educar**)

- **educated** /ˈedjʊkeɪtɪd/ ADJECTIVE an educated person knows a lot because they have had a good education □ *a highly educated workforce* (**instruído, educado**)

- **education** /ˌedjʊˈkeɪʃən/ NOUN, NO PLURAL the process of teaching, especially in schools or colleges □ *Our students receive a good standard of education.* □ *secondary education* (**educação, instrução, formação**)

- **educational** /ˌedjʊˈkeɪʃənəl/ ADJECTIVE to do with teaching and learning (**educacional**) 🔲 *She organized an educational visit to the museum.* (**visita educacional**) □ *He works for a company manufacturing educational toys.*

-ee /iː/ SUFFIX
1 -ee is added to the end of words to mean 'someone who is having something done to them' □ *interviewee* □ *employee*
2 -ee is added to the end of words to mean 'someone who has done a particular thing' □ *escapee* (= someone who has escaped)

eel /iːl/ NOUN [plural **eels**] a type of fish that has a long thin body like a snake (**enguia**)

eerie /ˈɪəri/ ADJECTIVE [**eerier, eeriest**] strange in a frightening way □ *a dark and eerie old house* (**misterioso**)

- **eerily** /ˈɪərɪli/ ADVERB in an eerie way □ *The forest suddenly became eerily silent.* (**misteriosamente**)

effect /ɪˈfekt/ NOUN [plural **effects**]
1 if one thing has an effect on another, it influences it or causes something to happen to it □ + *on* *His asthma has no effect on his ability as a footballer.* □ *She was suffering from the effects of a long plane journey.* (**efeito**)
2 **come into effect** to start to be used □ *The law came into effect in July.* (**entrar em vigor**)
3 **bring/put something into effect** to start to use knowledge, a plan, a law, etc. □ *We will put our training into effect as soon as we get back to work.* (**colocar algo em funcionamento**)
4 **take effect** to start to have results or to produce changes □ *It will be a few minutes before the drugs take effect.* (**surtir efeito**)
5 the way something has been made to look or sound, or the reaction that people have to it □ *Soft lighting creates a romantic effect in this room.* 🔲 *They added the sound effects later.* (**efeitos sonoros**)
6 **in effect** used to explain in a short way what the true situation is □ *In effect, they were unable to work again.* (**na realidade**)

> ➤ Be careful not to confuse effect, which is a noun, with affect, which is a verb: □ *One thing has an effect on another.* □ *One thing affects another.*

- **effective** /ɪˈfektɪv/ ADJECTIVE
1 working well or producing the results you want □ *This claims to be an effective treatment for the common cold.* □ *Do you know of an effective way of removing chewing gum from a carpet?* (**eficaz**)
2 if a law, plan, etc. is effective from a particular time, that is when it starts to be used □ + *from* *The new system will be effective from January 1st.* (**efetivo, útil**)
3 used to talk about what the real situation is □ *Troops have taken effective control of the region.* (**efetivo**)

- **effectively** /ɪˈfektɪvli/ ADVERB
1 in a successful way □ *He dealt with the problem very effectively.* (**eficazmente**)
2 used to talk about what the real situation is □ *We were effectively without food or water.* (**efetivamente**)

effeminate /ɪˈfemɪnət/ ADJECTIVE an effeminate man behaves like a woman (**afeminado**)

effervescent /ˌefəˈvesənt/ ADJECTIVE
1 an effervescent liquid is full of bubbles of gas (**efervescente**)
2 someone with an effervescent personality has a lot of enthusiasm and energy (**agitado**)

efficiency /ɪˈfɪʃənsi/ NOUN, NO PLURAL when someone or something works well and does not waste time or energy □ *Increased efficiency has cut their costs.* (eficiência)

efficient /ɪˈfɪʃənt/ ADJECTIVE working well and not wasting any time or energy □ *The questionnaire was an efficient method of collecting information.* □ *This is not an efficient use of resources.* (eficiente)

• **efficiently** /ɪˈfɪʃəntli/ ADVERB in an efficient way □ *She organised the show very efficiently.* (eficientemente)

effort /ˈefət/ NOUN [plural **efforts**]
1 the physical or mental energy that you need to do something (esforço) ▣ *She made a real effort to be friendly.* (fez um esforço) ▣ *You must put some more effort into your school work.* (esforçar-se mais) □ + **to do something** *It takes a lot of effort to be an athlete.*
2 an attempt □ *That was a really good effort, Sonia.* (tentativa)

• **effortless** /ˈefətlɪs/ ADJECTIVE not needing a lot of effort □ *A good ballet dancer makes it look effortless.* (sem esforço, fácil)

• **effortlessly** /ˈefətlɪsli/ ADVERB in an effortless way (facilmente)

eg or **e.g.** /ˌiːˈdʒiː/ ABBREVIATION for example □ *The zoo specializes in African animals, eg the lion and the giraffe.* (p. ex., abreviação de por exemplo)

egalitarian /ɪˌɡælɪˈteəriən/ ADJECTIVE giving everyone the same rights and opportunities. A formal word □ *an egalitarian society* (igualitário)

egestion /iːˈdʒestʃən/ NOUN, NO PLURAL the way waste food comes out of the body. A biology word. (evacuação)

egg /eɡ/ NOUN [plural **eggs**]
1 an oval object with a shell or case, in which a baby bird, reptile or fish develops (ovo) ▣ *The cuckoo lays its eggs in another bird's nest.* (bota seus ovos)
2 an oval object with a shell produced by a chicken or similar bird that we eat as food (ovo) ▣ *a boiled/fried egg* (ovo cozido/frito) ▣ *Beat two egg yolks with a little milk.* (gemas de ovos)
3 a special cell stored inside the body of a female mammal which can grow into a baby (óvulo)

♦ IDIOMS **have egg on your face** to be very embarrassed because of something silly you have done (ficar com cara de bobo) **put all your eggs in one basket** to put all your money or effort into one thing, so that if it fails you lose everything (arriscar todo o dinheiro em apenas um objetivo)

♦ PHRASAL VERB [**eggs, egging, egged**] **egg someone on** to encourage someone to do something, usually something bad □ *He hit the man again, as his friends egged him on.* (incitar alguém a fazer algo)

eggplant /ˈeɡplɑːnt/ NOUN [plural **eggplants**] the US word for **aubergine** (berinjela)

eggshell /ˈeɡʃel/ NOUN [plural **eggshells**] the hard thin shell covering an egg (casca do ovo)

ego /ˈiːɡəʊ/ NOUN [plural **egos**] the opinion you have of yourself □ *All the attention and praise was good for her ego.* (ego)

Eid /iːd/ NOUN, NO PLURAL either of two Muslim celebrations, especially Eid-ul-Fitr which is held each year to celebrate the end of Ramadan, when there is a big meal and people give each other presents (Eid)

eiderdown /ˈaɪdədaʊn/ NOUN [plural **eiderdowns**] a warm covering for a bed, filled with feathers or some other light material (edredom)

eight /eɪt/ NUMBER [plural **eights**] the number 8 (oito)

eighteen /ˌeɪˈtiːn/ NUMBER the number 18 (dezoito)

eighteenth /ˌeɪˈtiːnθ/ NUMBER 18th written as a word (décimo oitavo)

eighth /eɪtθ/ ▶ NUMBER 8th written as a word □ *the eighth book in the series* □ *Our team finished eighth.* (oitavo)
▶ NOUN [plural **eighths**] 1/8; one of eight equal parts of something (oito avos)

eightieth /ˈeɪtiəθ/ NUMBER 80th written as a word (octogésimo)

eighty /ˈeɪti/ NUMBER [plural **eighties**]
1 the number 80 (octogésimo)
2 the eighties the years between 1980 and 1989 (anos oitenta)

either /ˈaɪðə(r)/ ▶ ADVERB used in negative sentences to mean 'as well' □ *If you don't go, I won't go either.* □ *Dan doesn't like cheese either.* (também não)
▶ CONJUNCTION **either ... or** used to show a choice □ *You can have either a video game or a CD.* (ou... ou)
▶ DETERMINER, PRONOUN
1 one or the other □ *She can write with either hand.* □ + **of** *I can't afford either of them.* (um ou outro, nem um, nem outro)
2 both (ambos, tanto um quanto outro) ▣ *They stood on either side of the Queen.* (em ambos os lados)

eject /ɪˈdʒekt/ VERB [**ejects, ejecting, ejected**]
1 to push or throw someone or something out of a place □ *He was ejected from the nightclub.* (expulsar)
2 to remove something from a machine, usually by pressing a button □ *How do you eject the CD?* (ejetar)
3 to escape from an aircraft in an emergency by operating a special seat which is thrown out of the plane (lançar, ejetar)

eke /iːk/
♦ PHRASAL VERB [**ekes, eking, eked**] **eke something out** to not use much of something that you have a small amount of, in order to make it last longer

☐ *We had to eke out our supplies of water for ten days.* (usar com parcimônia)

elaborate ▶ ADJECTIVE /ɪˈlæbərət/ involving complicated detail or decoration ☐ *an elaborate plan* ☐ *elaborate costumes* (complexo, complicado)

▶ VERB /ɪˈlæbəreɪt/ [**elaborates, elaborating, elaborated**] to explain something in more detail ☐ *Would you like to elaborate on that statement?* (elaborar)

elapse /ɪˈlæps/ VERB [**elapses, elapsing, elapsed**] when time elapses, it passes ☐ *Three years elapsed before I saw her again.* (decorrer)

elastic /ɪˈlæstɪk/ ▶ ADJECTIVE able to stretch and then go back to its original size (elástico, flexível)
▶ NOUN, NO PLURAL a type of material with rubber or a similar substance in it to make it stretch (elástico)

elastic band /ɪˌlæstɪk ˈbænd/ NOUN [**plural elastic bands**] a small thin circle of rubber used for holding things together (elástico)

elated /ɪˈleɪtɪd/ ADJECTIVE very pleased and excited ☐ *They were elated after winning the cup.* (exultante)
• **elation** /ɪˈleɪʃən/ NOUN, NO PLURAL the state of being elated (exultação, euforia)

elbow /ˈelbəʊ/ ▶ NOUN [**plural elbows**] the part in the middle of your arm where it bends (cotovelo)
▶ VERB [**elbows, elbowing, elbowed**] to push someone with your elbow, especially to get past them (acotovelar) ☐ *She managed to elbow her way to the front of the queue.* (acotovelar para abrir caminho)

elder /ˈeldə(r)/ ▶ ADJECTIVE older ☐ *She has an elder brother.* (o mais velho)
▶ NOUN [**plural elders**]
1 the elder the older of two people ☐ *He's the elder of two brothers.* (o mais velho)
2 your elders people who are older than you ☐ *We were taught to respect our elders.* (os mais velhos)
• **elderly** /ˈeldəli/ ▶ ADJECTIVE old ☐ *an elderly lady* (idoso, velho)
▶ NOUN the elderly people who are old ☐ *Sarah works in a care home for the elderly.* (os idosos)

eldest /ˈeldɪst/ ▶ ADJECTIVE oldest ☐ *Alex is my eldest child.* (o mais velho)
▶ NOUN the eldest the person who is the oldest ☐ *Fiona is the eldest of three sisters.* (o mais velho)

elect /ɪˈlekt/ VERB [**elects, electing, elected**] to choose someone for a particular job or position in an organization by voting ☐ *The committee has to elect a chairperson.* ☐ *The president was elected in 2004.* (eleger)
• **election** /ɪˈlekʃən/ NOUN [**plural elections**] when people choose someone by voting (eleição) ☐ *Nobody knows when he will decide to hold the election.* (aguardar as eleições) ☐ *Her party won the election.* (venceu as eleições)

• **elector** /ɪˈlektə(r)/ NOUN [**plural electors**] someone who votes in an election (eleitor)
• **electoral** /ɪˈlektərəl/ ADJECTIVE to do with elections or electors (eleitoral) ☐ *electoral reform* (reforma eleitoral)
• **electorate** /ɪˈlektərət/ NOUN [**plural electorates**] all the people who can vote in an election ☐ *His policies are popular with the electorate.* (eleitorado)

electric /ɪˈlektrɪk/ ADJECTIVE
1 made or worked by electricity ☐ *an electric spark* ☐ *an electric light* ☐ *electric current* (elétrico, de eletricidade)
2 very exciting ☐ *In the hall, the atmosphere was electric.* (eletrizante)
• **electrical** /ɪˈlektrɪkəl/ ADJECTIVE to do with electricity ☐ *She's studying electrical engineering.* ☐ *The shop sells small electrical appliances like kettles and irons.* (elétrico)

electrician /ɪlekˈtrɪʃən/ NOUN [**plural electricians**] someone whose job is to put in or repair electrical equipment (eletricista)

electricity /ɪlekˈtrɪsəti/ NOUN, NO PLURAL a type of energy used to make light and heat and to make machines work ☐ *We're trying to save electricity by turning off our computers at night.* (eletricidade)

electrify /ɪˈlektrɪfaɪ/ VERB [**electrifies, electrifying, electrified**]
1 to make people very excited ☐ *His performance in Othello has been electrifying audiences.* (eletrizar)
2 to supply electricity to machines or equipment to make them work (eletrificar)

electro- /ɪˈlektrəʊ/ PREFIX electro- is added to the beginning of words to mean 'to do with electricity' ☐ *electromagnet* (eletro-)

electrocute /ɪˈlektrəkjuːt/ VERB [**electrocutes, electrocuting, electrocuted**] if someone is electrocuted, they are killed by a strong electric current which passes through their body ☐ *He was electrocuted while he was trying to fix the lights.* (eletrocutar)
• **electrocution** /ɪˌlektrəˈkjuːʃən/ NOUN, NO PLURAL when someone is electrocuted (eletrocução)

electrode /ɪˈlektrəʊd/ NOUN [**plural electrodes**] a small metal device that allows electricity to pass from a source of power, such as a battery, to a piece of equipment. A physics and chemistry word. (eletrodo)

electrolysis /ɪlekˈtrɒləsɪs/ NOUN, NO PLURAL when electricity is passed through a substance to cause chemical change. A physics and chemistry word. (eletrólise)

electromagnet /ɪˈlektrəʊˌmægnɪt/ NOUN [**plural electromagnets**] a magnet that works when electricity passes through it. A physics word. (eletromagneto)

- **electromagnetic** /ɪˌlektrəʊmæɡˈnetɪk/ ADJECTIVE using an electric current to make something magnetic. A physics word. (eletromagnético)

electron /ɪˈlektrɒn/ NOUN [plural **electrons**] one of the parts of an atom that move around the nucleus and have a negative electrical charge. A chemistry and physics word. (elétron)

electronic /ɪlekˈtrɒnɪk/ ADJECTIVE
1 using electricity and very small electrical parts to work (eletrônico) 🔁 *an electronic device* (aparelho eletrônico) 🔁 *They sell computers and other electronic equipment.* (equipamento eletrônico)
2 using electronic equipment □ *electronic communications* □ *electronic music* (eletrônica)
3 to do with electronics □ *electronic engineering* (eletrônico)

- **electronics** /ɪlekˈtrɒnɪks/ NOUN, NO PLURAL the study of how electricity flows and how it can be used in machinery (eletrônica)

elegance /ˈelɪɡəns/ NOUN, NO PLURAL the quality of being attractive and having good style □ *The city has an air of elegance about it.* (elegância)

- **elegant** /ˈelɪɡənt/ ADJECTIVE attractive and having good style □ *an elegant lady* □ *an elegant house* (elegante)
- **elegantly** /ˈelɪɡəntli/ ADVERB in an elegant way □ *She dances very elegantly.* □ *an elegantly dressed woman* (elegantemente)

element /ˈelɪmənt/ NOUN [plural **elements**]
1 a part of something (elemento) □ *They are unhappy about some elements of the course.* □ *His work has a political element.* 🔁 *There is an element of truth in her accusations.* (um elemento de verdade)
2 a substance that cannot be divided into smaller chemical substances, for example hydrogen, oxygen and carbon. A chemistry word. (corpo simples, átomo)
3 the part of a piece of electrical equipment that produces heat. A physics word. (componente)
4 **the elements** the weather □ *They were stuck on a bare hillside, completely exposed to the elements.* (fenômenos atmosféricos)
5 **in your element** doing the things that you are best at or that you enjoy the most □ *She was in her element bossing all the soldiers around.* (em seu fundamento)

- **elementary** /ˌelɪˈmentəri/ ADJECTIVE
1 basic □ *You have forgotten the elementary principles of journalism.* □ *He is making too many elementary mistakes.* (básico, elementar)
2 to do with the first stages of studying a subject □ *elementary maths* □ *elementary classes/students* (básico, elementar)
3 to do with the education that very young children receive □ *elementary education/teachers* (básico, elementar)

elementary particle /ˌelɪmentəri ˈpɑːtɪkəl/ NOUN [plural **elementary particles**] one of the very small pieces of matter that make up a subatomic particle. A physics word. (partícula elementar)

elementary school /ˌelɪˈmentəri ˌskuːl/ NOUN [plural **elementary schools**] the US word for primary school (ensino fundamental)

elephant /ˈelɪfənt/ NOUN [plural **elephants**] a very large animal with a long nose, large ears and thick grey skin (elefante)

elevate /ˈelɪveɪt/ VERB [**elevates, elevating, elevated**]
1 a formal word meaning to move something to a higher position or level □ *Elevate the patient's feet slightly.* (elevar)
2 a formal word meaning to give something a more important position □ *These roles have elevated her international status.* (elevar)

- **elevation** /ˌelɪˈveɪʃən/ NOUN, NO PLURAL
1 the height of something above sea level (elevação)
2 when something is elevated (altitude)
- **elevator** /ˈelɪveɪtə(r)/ NOUN [plural **elevators**] the US word for lift (= for carrying people up and down in a tall building) (elevador)

eleven /ɪˈlevən/ NUMBER [plural **elevens**] the number 11 (onze)

eleventh /ɪˈlevənθ/ NUMBER 11th written as a word (décimo primeiro)

elf /elf/ NOUN [plural **elves**] an imaginary creature like a very small person which often causes trouble in stories (elfo)

- **elfin** /ˈelfɪn/ ADJECTIVE like an elf, especially with small, attractive features □ *an elfin face* (duende)

elicit /ɪˈlɪsɪt/ VERB [**elicits, eliciting, elicited**] a formal word meaning to get information, an answer or a reaction from someone (produzir, obter) 🔁 *The suggestions elicited a positive response.* (produziu uma resposta) □ *He tried to elicit a bit more detailed information.*

eligible /ˈelɪdʒəbəl/ ADJECTIVE
1 suitable for or allowed to do something □ *Am I eligible for a payment?* □ *There are 6 million eligible voters in the country.* (ter direito a)
2 an eligible man is someone who would be suitable to marry (qualificado)

eliminate /ɪˈlɪmɪneɪt/ VERB [**eliminates, eliminating, eliminated**]
1 to get rid of something completely □ *We aim to eliminate poverty.* (eliminar, erradicar) 🔁 *The new technology eliminates the need for ID cards and passwords.* (elimina a necessidade)
2 to remove someone from a competition, for example by beating them □ *The team was eliminated from the World Cup in the quarter finals.* (eliminar, expulsar)

3 to decide that someone or something is not involved in something, so you can ignore them □ *The man has been eliminated from police enquiries.* (eliminar)

• **elimination** /ɪˌlɪmɪˈneɪʃən/ NOUN, NO PLURAL
1 when someone or something is eliminated (eliminação)
2 a process of elimination when you decide an answer by getting rid of all possible answers until only one is left (processo eliminatório)

elite /ɪˈliːt/ ▶ NOUN [plural **elites**] the best, most important or most powerful people in a society or group □ *the country's ruling elite* □ *the sporting elite* (elite)
▶ ADJECTIVE of very high quality □ *an elite athlete* (de elite)

• **elitism** /ɪˈliːtɪzəm/ NOUN, NO PLURAL when rich, powerful or well educated people have more power or advantages than everyone else □ *There is still some elitism in the world of classical music.* (elitismo)

• **elitist** /ɪˈliːtɪst/ ADJECTIVE to do with elitism □ *The university still has a rather elitist image.* (elitista)

elk /elk/ NOUN [plural **elk** or **elks**] a type of very large deer that is found in northern Europe and Asia (alce)

ellipse /ɪˈlɪps/ NOUN [plural **ellipses**] an oval shape. A maths word. (elipse)

• **elliptical** /ɪˈlɪptɪkəl/ ADJECTIVE shaped like an oval. A maths word. (elíptico)

elm /elm/ NOUN [plural **elms**] a type of tall tree with wide round leaves (olmo)

elocution /ˌeləˈkjuːʃən/ NOUN, NO PLURAL the skill of speaking correctly and clearly (elocução)

elongate /ˈiːlɒŋɡeɪt/ VERB [**elongates, elongating, elongated**] to get longer or to make something longer (alongar)

• **elongated** /ˈiːlɒŋɡeɪtɪd/ ADJECTIVE long and narrow, especially more than usual □ *It has an elongated neck, like a giraffe.* (alongado)

elope /ɪˈloʊp/ VERB [**elopes, eloping, eloped**] to run away secretly with someone to get married □ *He eloped with the Earl's daughter.* (fugir para se casar)

• **elopement** /ɪˈloʊpmənt/ NOUN, NO PLURAL when someone elopes (fuga)

eloquence /ˈeləkwəns/ NOUN, NO PLURAL the ability to talk and express yourself well □ *She spoke with such eloquence.* (eloquência)

• **eloquent** /ˈeləkwənt/ ADJECTIVE able to talk and express yourself well □ *an eloquent speech* (eloquente)

• **eloquently** /ˈeləkwəntli/ ADVERB in an eloquent way □ *He spoke eloquently.* (eloquentemente)

else /els/ ADVERB
1 as well as the thing or person that has been talked about (mais, outro) 🔊 *Promise not to tell anyone else.* (mais ninguém) 🔊 *You must wait in the queue, the same as everybody else.* (outros) 🔊 *There's something else I need to tell you.* (algo mais)
2 different from something or someone (mais, outro) 🔊 *I had to leave. What else could I have done?* (o que mais) 🔊 *I hate swimming. Can't we do something else instead?* (outra coisa) 🔊 *He must have been angry. Why else would he have reacted like that?* (por que outro motivo)
3 or else (a) used to say that a bad thing will happen if another thing does not happen □ *Put on a jumper or else you'll get cold.* (b) used to talk about two different situations, actions or possibilities □ *Our students are usually young adults, or else older people wanting a change of career.* (c) used to say that something must be true because something different would have happened if it was not □ *She must have been ill, or else I'm sure she would have come.* (ou então)

elsewhere /elsˈweə(r)/ ADVERB in or to another place □ *It's too expensive here, we'll have to look elsewhere.* (em outro lugar)

elude /ɪˈluːd/ VERB [**eludes, eluding, eluded**]
1 to avoid being caught □ *He managed to elude the police for weeks.* (escapar)
2 if something eludes you, you are not able to achieve it □ *An effective treatment has long eluded scientists.* (escapar, ficar fora do alcance)
3 if a word or an idea eludes you, you cannot remember it □ *The phrase he wanted eluded him.* (fugir à memória)

• **elusive** /ɪˈluːsɪv/ ADJECTIVE difficult to see or find □ *They are searching for the rare and elusive snow leopard.* (esquivo)

elves /elvz/ PLURAL OF **elf** (plural de *elf*)

emaciated /ɪˈmeɪʃieɪtɪd/ ADJECTIVE very thin and weak because of illness or not eating enough (definhado)

e-mail or **email** /ˈiːmeɪl/ ▶ NOUN [plural **e-mails** or **emails**]
1 NO PLURAL the system for sending messages between computers □ *They keep in touch by email.* □ *Are you on email?* (e-mail) 🔊 *What's your email address?* (endereço de e-mail)
2 a written message sent between computers (e-mail, mensagem eletrônica) 🔊 *He sends me an email every day.* (me enviou um e-mail)
▶ VERB [**e-mails, e-mailing, e-mailed** or **emails, emailing, emailed**] to send someone an email □ *I'll email you the address.* (enviar um e-mail)

emanate /ˈeməneɪt/ VERB [**emanates, emanating, emanated**] a formal word meaning to come from something or somewhere □ *Loud music emanated from the upstairs flat.* (emanar)

emancipate /ɪˈmænsɪpeɪt/ VERB [**emancipates, emancipating, emancipated**] a formal word meaning to give someone freedom and political rights □ *Emancipating the working classes no* *longer seems to be the party's principal aim.* (emancipar)

- **emancipation** /ɪˌmænsɪˈpeɪʃən/ NOUN, NO PLURAL when a group of people are emancipated □ *the emancipation of women* (emancipação)

embankment /ɪmˈbæŋkmənt/ NOUN [plural **embankments**] a slope of soil built along the sides of a railway, river or road (dique)

embargo /emˈbɑːɡəʊ/ NOUN [plural **embargoes**] an official order stopping trade with another country (proibição, embargo) 🗨 *There are no signs that the arms embargo will be lifted.* (o embargo será suspenso)

embark /ɪmˈbɑːk/ VERB [**embarks, embarking, embarked**] to get on a ship or an aircraft at the beginning of a journey (embarcar)

◆ PHRASAL VERB **embark on something** to start doing something new □ *We're about to embark on an exciting new project.* (envolver-se em algo)

embarrass /ɪmˈbærəs/ VERB [**embarrasses, embarrassing, embarrassed**] to make someone feel ashamed or stupid □ *Stop it! You're embarrassing me!* □ *The information could embarrass the president if it gets out.* (embaraçar, envergonhar)

- **embarrassed** /ɪmˈbærəst/ ADJECTIVE looking or feeling ashamed or stupid □ *an embarrassed silence* (constrangido) 🗨 *Quinn felt embarrassed.* (sentiu-se constrangido) □ + **about** *They're very embarrassed about what's happened.* □ + **by** *She looked a little embarrassed by all the attention.*

- **embarrassing** /ɪmˈbærəsɪŋ/ ADJECTIVE making you feel embarrassed □ *It was one of those embarrassing moments.* (constrangedor) 🗨 *a highly embarrassing photo* (uma foto muito constrangedora) □ + **for** *The incident was very embarrassing for the government.*

- **embarrassingly** /ɪmˈbærəsɪŋli/ ADVERB in an embarrassing way □ *Things have gone embarrassingly wrong.* (embaraçoso, vergonhoso)

- **embarrassment** /ɪmˈbærəsmənt/ NOUN, NO PLURAL
  1 a feeling of being embarrassed (vergonha, constrangimento) 🗨 *Check the price in advance to avoid embarrassment.* (evitar constrangimento) 🗨 *I don't want to cause her any embarrassment.* (causar nenhum constrangimento)
  2 someone or something that makes you feel embarrassed □ *The case is a huge embarrassment for the authorities.* (vergonha)

embassy /ˈembəsi/ NOUN [plural **embassies**] a group of officials who represent their government in a foreign country, or the building where they work □ *the Australian embassy in Washington* (embaixada)

embedded /ɪmˈbedɪd/ ADJECTIVE
1 fixed firmly in the surface of something □ *The boat had become embedded in the mud.* (cravado)
2 being a very important part of something and difficult to change □ *Hunting is deeply embedded in their culture.* (enraizado)

embellish /ɪmˈbelɪʃ/ VERB [**embellishes, embellishing, embellished**] to add details to something to make it more interesting or more decorated % *He had embellished the story a bit.* □ *The boxes are embellished with gold and silver.* (embelezar)

- **embellishment** /ɪmˈbelɪʃmənt/ NOUN [plural **embellishments**] something added to embellish something □ *The story is so amazing, it needs no embellishment.* (ornamentação)

embers /ˈembəz/ PLURAL NOUN the small hot pieces left when coal or wood is burnt in a fire (brasas)

embezzle /ɪmˈbezəl/ [**embezzles, embezzling, embezzled**] to steal money that belongs to someone you work for □ *He embezzled money from his clients.* (usurpar, desfalcar)

- **embezzlement** /ɪmˈbezəlmənt/ NOUN, NO PLURAL the crime of embezzling money (desfalque)

emblem /ˈembləm/ NOUN [plural **emblems**] an object or image that is used as a symbol to represent something □ *The thistle is the emblem of Scotland.* (emblema)

embodiment /ɪmˈbɒdɪmənt/ NOUN, NO PLURAL **the embodiment of something** when somebody embodies something □ *She is the embodiment of good health.* (a personificação de algo)

embody /ɪmˈbɒdi/ [**embodies, embodying, embodied**] to represent or to be a good example of an idea or a quality □ *She embodies the spirit of the Olympic games.* (personificar)

embrace /ɪmˈbreɪs/ ▶ VERB [**embraces, embracing, embraced**]
1 to put your arms around someone and hold them as a sign of love or being friends □ *The two friends embraced warmly.* (abraçar)
2 to accept an idea or activity with enthusiasm (agarrar) 🗨 *They've embraced the idea of distance learning.* (agarrou a ideia) □ *Small businesses have embraced the new technology.*
3 a formal word meaning to include something □ *The subject embraces both maths and science.* (abraçar)
▶ NOUN [plural **embraces**] when you put your arms round someone □ *They parted with an embrace.* (abraço)

embroider /ɪmˈbrɔɪdə(r)/ VERB [**embroiders, embroidering, embroidered**] to sew patterns or pictures with coloured threads on a piece of cloth □ *a silk scarf embroidered with flowers* (bordar)

- **embroidery** /ɪmˈbrɔɪdəri/ NOUN [plural **embroideries**]
  1 the activity of embroidering (bordado)
  2 a piece of cloth that has been embroidered (bordado)

embryo

embryo /ˈembrɪəʊ/ NOUN [plural **embryos**] a groups of cells that will form a baby or animal inside its mother's womb. A biology word. (embrião)

emerald /ˈemərəld/ ▶ NOUN [plural **emeralds**] a valuable green stone used in jewellery □ *an emerald ring* (esmeralda)
▶ ADJECTIVE having a bright green colour like an emerald (verde-esmeralda)

emerge /ɪˈmɜːdʒ/ VERB [**emerges, emerging, emerged**]
1 to come out of something or from behind something □ *The baby crocodiles emerge from the eggs.* □ *Al emerged from the tent.* (emergir)
2 to become known or recognized □ *More details have emerged about the accident.* (surgir)
• **emergence** /ɪˈmɜːdʒəns/ NOUN, NO PLURAL when something appears or becomes recognized □ *the emergence of a new virus* □ *China's emergence as a world power* (emergência)

emergency /ɪˈmɜːdʒənsi/ ▶ NOUN [plural **emergencies**] a sudden, unexpected and usually dangerous event that needs immediate action (emergência) 🔊 *In an emergency, call my husband's number* (em uma emergência) 🔊 *I always take my mobile with me in case of emergencies.* (em caso de emergência) 🔊 *a medical emergency* (emergência médica)
▶ ADJECTIVE to do with an emergency □ *emergency surgery* □ *The plane made an emergency landing.* (de emergência)

emergency services /ɪˈmɜːdʒənsi ˌsɜːvɪsɪz/ PLURAL NOUN organizations that deal with accidents, fire, crime, etc. such as the police and fire service (serviços de emergência)

emigrant /ˈemɪɡrənt/ NOUN [plural **emigrants**] someone who leaves the country where they were born to live in a different country (imigrante)
• **emigrate** /ˈemɪɡreɪt/ VERB [**emigrates, emigrating, emigrated**] to leave the country where you were born in order to live in a different country □ *The family emigrated to Australia in 1954.* (imigrar)

eminent /ˈemɪnənt/ ADJECTIVE famous and respected □ *an eminent lawyer* (eminente)

emission /ɪˈmɪʃən/ NOUN [plural **emissions**]
1 something that goes out into the air, such as smoke from a factory (emissão) 🔊 *We must reduce carbon emissions.* (emissão de gás carbônico) □ *emissions of greenhouse gases*
2 the process of going out into the air (emissão)

emit /ɪˈmɪt/ VERB [**emits, emitting, emitted**] to send light, heat, gas or a sound out into the air. A formal word. □ *The substance emits light.* □ *The machine emitted a high-pitched screech.* (emitir)

emoticon /ɪˈməʊtɪkɒn/ NOUN [plural **emoticons**] a sideways image of a face made with keyboard symbols. People put emoticons in e-mails to show that they are joking, or pleased, etc. A computing word. (emoticon)

employ

emotion /ɪˈməʊʃən/ NOUN [plural **emotions**] a feeling, such as love, hate, fear or anger (emoção, sentimento) 🔊 *He showed no emotion throughout the trial.* (mostrou emoção) □ *Anya struggled to control her emotions.* 🔊 *I've got mixed emotions* (= good and bad feelings) *about the place.* (emoções diversas)
• **emotional** /ɪˈməʊʃənəl/ ADJECTIVE showing or having strong feelings (emotivo) □ *an emotional speech* 🔊 *I get emotional just talking about it.* (fiquei emotivo) □ *He was in a highly emotional state.*
• **emotionally** /ɪˈməʊʃənəli/ ADVERB
1 in a way that is to do with someone's emotions □ *He is still emotionally fragile.* (emocionalmente)
2 in an emotional way □ *He spoke very emotionally.* (emocionalmente)

empathize or **empathise** /ˈempəθaɪz/ VERB [**empathizes, empathizing, empathized**] to understand how someone feels because you have experienced the same things they have □ *I can empathize with the family's situation.* (mostrar empatia)
• **empathy** /ˈempəθi/ NOUN, NO PLURAL the ability to understand how someone feels (empatia)

emperor /ˈempərə(r)/ NOUN [plural **emperors**] the ruler of an empire (imperador)

emphasis /ˈemfəsɪs/ NOUN [plural **emphases**]
1 special importance or attention you give to something (ênfase) 🔊 *Schools put too much emphasis on exams.* (dão ênfase em) 🔊 *We need a greater emphasis on English today.* (ênfase maior)
2 extra force or strength you give to a word or sound when you are speaking □ + *on You say it with the emphasis on the second syllable.* (ênfase)
• **emphasize** or **emphasise** /ˈemfəsaɪz/ VERB [**emphasizes, emphasizing, emphasized**] to give special importance or attention to something (enfatizar) 🔊 *I want to emphasize the importance of road safety.* (enfatizar a importância) □ *She emphasized that she had been treated very well.*
• **emphatic** /ɪmˈfætɪk/ ADJECTIVE strong and clear □ *The answer is an emphatic yes.* □ *an emphatic victory* (enfático)
• **emphatically** /ɪmˈfætɪkəli/ ADVERB in a strong, clear way □ *He emphatically denied any connection.* (enfaticamente)

empire /ˈempaɪə(r)/ NOUN [plural **empires**]
1 a group of countries governed by one leader or government □ *the Roman Empire* (império)
2 a group of companies controlled by one person or organization □ *a global media empire* (império)

employ /ɪmˈplɔɪ/ VERB [**employs, employing, employed**]
1 to pay someone to work for you □ *The company employs skilled workers.* □ + *as He was employed*

empower

as a design consultant. □ **+ to do something** *We employed a local builder to do the work.* (empregar)

2 a formal word meaning to use something □ *Police employed DNA techniques to solve the crime.* (aplicar)

• **employee** /ɪmˈplɔɪiː/ NOUN [*plural* **employees**] someone who works for a company or another person (empregado) *The company has 16 full-time employees.* (empregados em tempo integral) □ **+ of** *We spoke to a former employee of the firm.*

• **employer** /ɪmˈplɔɪə(r)/ NOUN [*plural* **employers**] a company or person who employs people □ *It's a chance for students to meet potential employers.* □ *The factory is the area's largest employer.* (empregador)

• **employment** /ɪmˈplɔɪmənt/ NOUN, NO PLURAL
1 paid work for a company or person (emprego) *Are you in full-time employment?* (emprego de período integral) *He found employment as a security guard.* (encontrou emprego)

2 a formal word meaning the use of something (uso, emprego)

empower /ɪmˈpaʊə(r)/ VERB [**empowers, empowering, empowered**]
1 to give someone the skills, confidence, etc. to control their life □ *We aim to empower people with disabilities.* (autorizar)

2 be empowered to do something to have the power or authority to do something □ *The police are not empowered to break up peaceful demonstrations.* (ter o poder de fazer algo)

empress /ˈemprɪs/ NOUN [*plural* **empresses**] a female ruler of an empire (imperatriz)

emptiness /ˈemptɪnɪs/ NOUN, NO PLURAL
1 a feeling of having no meaning, emotion or purpose □ *There was an emptiness in his eyes.* (vazio)

2 the state of being empty □ *the emptiness of outer space* (vazio)

empty /ˈempti/ ▶ ADJECTIVE [**emptier, emptiest**]
1 containing nothing or no one □ *an empty box* (vazio) *There was an empty space between the two buildings.* (espaço vazio) □ *The restaurant was almost empty.* □ **+ of** *The streets were empty of traffic.*

2 with no emotion or purpose □ *Without Tom her life felt empty.* (vazio)

3 not sincere or likely to be effective (vazio) *This is just another empty promise.* (promessa vazia)

▶ VERB [**empties, emptying, emptied**] to become empty, or to make something empty □ *Empty your pockets.* □ *The theatre slowly emptied.* (esvaziar)

emu /ˈiːmjuː/ NOUN [*plural* **emus**] a very large Australian bird that cannot fly (emu)

enclose

emulate /ˈemjuleɪt/ VERB [**emulates, emulating, emulated**] a formal word meaning to copy someone or something because you admire them □ *We hope to emulate the success of such schemes in other countries.* (emular)

emulsion /ɪˈmʌlʃən/ NOUN [*plural* **emulsions**]
1 a type of paint that produces a surface that is not shiny (emulsão)

2 a smooth mixture of two or more liquids. A chemistry word. (emulsão)

en- /en-/ PREFIX **en-** is added to the beginning of words to mean 'into' □ *enclose* (= put something into something)

enable /ɪˈneɪbəl/ VERB [**enables, enabling, enabled**] to make it possible for someone to do something □ *The software enables users to download music.* (possibilitar)

-enabled /-ɪˈneɪbəld/ SUFFIX **-enabled** is added to the end of words to mean 'having the technology or equipment to do a particular thing' □ *a WiFi-enabled phone* (habilitado)

enact /ɪˈnækt/ VERB [**enacts, enacting, enacted**]
1 a formal word meaning to make something law □ *They have little chance of enacting this bill.* (realizar)

2 to perform a story as a play □ *Children from the Sunday school enacted Jesus's life.* (representar)

• **enactment** /ɪˈnæktmənt/ NOUN, NO PLURAL when something is enacted. A formal word. □ *the enactment of new legislation* (decreto, lei)

enamel /ɪˈnæməl/ ▶ NOUN, NO PLURAL
1 a hard shiny substance used to cover metal to protect or decorate it (esmalte)

2 the hard white substance that covers teeth (esmalte)

▶ ADJECTIVE made of or covered with enamel □ *an enamel plate*

encapsulate /ɪnˈkæpsjuleɪt/ VERB [**encapsulates, encapsulating, encapsulated**] to say the main facts about something in a short, clear way. A formal word. □ *It's difficult to encapsulate a lifetime's work in a single lecture.* (encapsular)

enchanted /ɪnˈtʃɑːntɪd/ ADJECTIVE
1 finding someone or something very attractive and interesting. A formal word. □ *I was enchanted by the children.* (encantado)

2 affected by magic □ *an enchanted forest* (enfeitiçado)

• **enchanting** /ɪnˈtʃɑːntɪŋ/ ADJECTIVE very attractive. A formal word. □ *an enchanting smile* (encantador)

enclose /ɪnˈkləʊz/ VERB [**encloses, enclosing, enclosed**]
1 to put something in an envelope with a letter □ *I'm enclosing a copy of the certificate.* (incluir)

2 to be all around something □ *The children's play area is enclosed by a wooden fence.* (cercar)

• **enclosed** /ɪnˈkləʊzd/ ADJECTIVE surrounded by something (cercado) *an enclosed space* (espaço cercado)

encompass — endeavour

- **enclosure** /ɪnˈkləʊʒə(r)/ NOUN [plural **enclosures**]

  1 an area of land with a wall or fence around it ☐ *the penguin enclosure at the zoo* (**cerca**)

  2 something you put in an envelope with a letter. A formal word. (**anexo**)

encompass /ɪnˈkʌmpəs/ VERB [**encompasses, encompassing, encompassed**] to include many things, ideas, etc. A formal word. ☐ *The course encompasses all aspects of painting.* (**abarcar**)

encore /ˈɒŋkɔː(r)/ NOUN [plural **encores**] an extra song etc. at the end of a performance because the audience wants more (**bis**)

encounter /ɪnˈkaʊntə(r)/ ▶ VERB [**encounters, encountering, encountered**]

1 to experience something bad (**deparar-se**) 🔲 *We didn't encounter any problems.* (**nos deparamos com problemas**) ☐ *The troops encountered fierce resistance.*

2 a formal word meaning to meet someone by chance (**encontrar-se por acaso**)

▶ NOUN [plural **encounters**] a meeting that happens by chance ☐ *I had a chance encounter with a ski instructor from the same resort.* (**encontro por acaso**)

encourage /ɪnˈkʌrɪdʒ/ VERB [**encourages, encouraging, encouraged**]

1 to support someone and make them feel confident about doing something ☐ **+ *to do something*** *We encourage students to work together.* ☐ *My parents encouraged me to write.* ☐ *We have been encouraged by recent successes.* (**incentivar**)

2 to make something more likely to happen ☐ *The school aims to encourage healthy eating.* (**estimular**)

- **encouragement** /ɪnˈkʌrɪdʒmənt/ NOUN, NO PLURAL when you encourage someone or something ☐ *The crowd shouted encouragement to the team.* (**incentivo**) 🔲 *They offered her words of encouragement.* (**palavras de incentivo**) ☐ **+ *to do something*** *She needed no encouragement to dive into the pool.*

- **encouraging** /ɪnˈkʌrɪdʒɪŋ/ ADJECTIVE giving you confidence or hope (**incentivador, encorajador**) 🔲 *an encouraging sign* (**sinal encorajador**) ☐ *The results are highly encouraging.*

- **encouragingly** /ɪnˈkʌrɪdʒɪŋli/ ADVERB in an encouraging way ☐ *He smiled encouragingly at her.* (**de modo incentivador, encorajador**)

encroach /ɪnˈkrəʊtʃ/ VERB [**encroaches, encroaching, encroached**] to take away or use up something. A formal word. ☐ *The job began to encroach on my family life.* (**prejudicar**)

encyclopedia or **encyclopaedia** /ɪnˌsaɪkləˈpiːdiə/ NOUN [plural **encyclopedias** or **encyclopaedias**] a book with information about many subjects, or on a particular subject ☐ *an encyclopedia of art* (**enciclopédia**)

- **encyclopedic** or **encyclopaedic** /ɪnˌsaɪkləˈpiːdɪk/ ADJECTIVE giving or having a lot of facts and information about many things (**enciclopédico**)

end /end/ ▶ NOUN [plural **ends**]

1 the last part of something ☐ *The end of the book is very sad.* ☐ *I'll come back at the end of the week.* (**fim**)

2 the part of something that is furthest away from the middle ☐ *He poked me with the end of a stick.* (**fim, extremidade, último**) 🔲 *There is a church at the other end of this street.* (**no fim de**) 🔲 *We sat at opposite ends of the table.* (**extremidades opostas a**)

3 when something does not exist any more (**fim**) 🔲 *We were sad when our holiday came to an end.* (**chegou a um fim**) 🔲 *I hope this agreement will put an end to the fighting.* (**colocou um fim em**)

4 in the end after a long period of time ☐ *The train was delayed, but we got there in the end.* (**por fim**)

5 an aim or purpose ☐ *They used their power for their own private ends.* (**finalidade, propósito**)

6 for days/weeks, etc. on end for many days/ weeks, etc. ☐ *In the hospital, they kept us waiting for hours on end.* (**por dias/semanas etc.**)

▶ VERB [**ends, ending, ended**] to finish ☐ *Our holiday ends tomorrow.* ☐ **+ *with*** *He ended his speech with a joke.* ☐ *The word cough ends with a 'f' sound.* (**terminar**)

♦ PHRASAL VERB **end up somewhere/doing something** to have to do something or to finish in a bad situation ☐ *I knew he'd end up in prison.* ☐ *I ended up catching a later train.* (**acabar fazendo algo/ir parar em**)

endanger /ɪnˈdeɪndʒə(r)/ VERB [**endangers, endangering, endangered**] to cause someone to be in a dangerous situation (**pôr em perigo**) 🔲 *His actions could have endangered the lives of people nearby.* (**pôr em perigo as vidas**) ☐ *These chemicals could endanger public health.*

- **endangered** /ɪnˈdeɪndʒəd/ ADJECTIVE an endangered type of animal or plant may soon stop existing because there are very few still alive (**ameaçada**) 🔲 *an endangered species* (**espécies ameaçadas**) ☐ *a list of endangered animals*

endear /ɪnˈdɪə(r)/ VERB [**endears, endearing, endeared**] to make someone like you ☐ *He also endeared himself to staff with his sense of humour.* (**tornar querido**)

- **endearing** /ɪnˈdɪərɪŋ/ ADJECTIVE making people like you ☐ *Her honesty is very endearing.* (**afetuoso**)

endeavour /ɪnˈdevə(r)/ ▶ VERB [**endeavours, endeavouring, endeavoured**] a formal word meaning to try hard ☐ *We endeavour to meet the highest possible standards.* (**empenhar-se**)

▶ NOUN [plural **endeavours**]

1 a formal word meaning the effort or energy people put into doing things □ *human endeavour* (**empenho**)

2 a formal word meaning an attempt to do something □ *I wish you luck in all your endeavours.* (**esforço**)

ending /ˈendɪŋ/ NOUN [plural endings]

1 the last part of a story (**final**) 🔹 *The story had a happy ending.* (**final feliz**) □ **+ of** *I don't want to spoil the ending of the film.*

2 NO PLURAL when something ends □ **+ of** *This contributed to the ending of the Cold War.* (**fim**)

3 letters added to the end of a word □ *an irregular past tense ending* (**terminação de uma palavra**)

endless /ˈendlɪs/ ADJECTIVE seeming to never finish □ *The task seemed endless.* (**sem fim, interminável**) 🔹 *There's an endless supply of cheap workers.* (**fornecimento interminável de**)

- **endlessly** /ˈendlɪsli/ ADVERB in a way that continues for a long time or distance □ *They argued endlessly about it.* (**infinitamente, interminavelmente**)

endocrine gland /ˈendəʊkraɪn ˌɡlænd/ NOUN [plural endocrine glands] an organ in the body that produces hormones (= chemicals that control how the body grows). A biology word. (**glândula endócrina**)

endorse /ɪnˈdɔːs/ VERB [endorses, endorsing, endorsed] to give your support to something or someone publicly □ *The UN has endorsed the plan.* □ *He refused to endorse any of the candidates.* (**aprovar**)

- **endorsement** /ɪnˈdɔːsmənt/ NOUN [plural endorsements] public support for someone or something □ *He welcomed the union's endorsement of the new plan.* (**aprovação**) 🔹 *This was a ringing endorsement* (= very enthusiastic support). (**aprovação entusiasmada**)

endow /ɪnˈdaʊ/ VERB [endows, endowing, endowed]

1 be endowed with something to have a particular quality or ability. A formal phrase. □ *She was endowed with a beauty that most women dream of.* (**ser dotado de algo**)

2 to give a large amount of money to a hospital, college, etc. (**doar**)

- **endowment** /ɪnˈdaʊmənt/ NOUN [plural endowments]

1 money given to an organization □ *The college receives several endowments from private individuals.* (**doação**)

2 a natural quality or ability that someone has. A formal word. (**dom**)

endurance /ɪnˈdjʊərəns/ NOUN, NO PLURAL the ability to do something physically difficult for a long time □ *a test of endurance* □ *We do fitness work to improve endurance.* (**resistência**)

endure /ɪnˈdjʊə(r)/ VERB [endures, enduring, endured]

1 to suffer something unpleasant, especially for a long time □ *He endured long periods of loneliness.* □ *She endured terrible pain.* (**suportar, resistir**)

2 to last for a long time □ *Our friendship endured until his death.* (**perdurar**)

- **enduring** /ɪnˈdjʊərɪŋ/ ADJECTIVE continuing to exist (**duradouro, eterno**) 🔹 *How can you explain the enduring appeal of this film?* (**apelo duradouro**)

enemy /ˈenɪmi/ ▶ NOUN [plural enemies]

1 someone who is against you and wants to harm you (**inimigo**) 🔹 *He made a few enemies while he was there.* (**fez inimigos**) □ **+ of** *They are viewed as enemies of the regime.*

2 the enemy in a war, the people or country you are fighting against □ *We will defend ourselves and defeat the enemy.* (**o inimigo**)

♦ IDIOM **be your own worst enemy** to do things which harm you more than other people □ *Sometimes he's his own worst enemy.* (**ser seu próprio inimigo**)

▶ ADJECTIVE to do with the enemy □ *enemy troops*

energetic /ˌenəˈdʒetɪk/ ADJECTIVE very active and full of energy □ *an energetic dance* □ *I feel a lot more energetic.* (**enérgico**)

energy /ˈenədʒi/ NOUN [plural energies]

1 the strength or power you have to work or to be active □ *Young children have loads of energy.* □ *My boss has tremendous energy and enthusiasm.* □ **+ to do something** *I didn't have the energy to walk home.* (**energia**)

2 a form of power, such as heat or electricity (**enegia**) 🔹 *Turn off lights to save energy.* (**poupar energia**) 🔹 *nuclear energy* (**energia nuclear**) 🔹 *renewable sources of energy* (**fontes de energia**) □ *energy efficiency*

enforce /ɪnˈfɔːs/ VERB [enforces, enforcing, enforced]

1 to make sure people obey a law or rule (**cumprir**) 🔹 *It is the job of the police to enforce the law.* (**cumprir a lei**) □ *Airlines must ensure the rules are enforced.*

2 to make sure that something happens □ *He tried to enforce discipline in the team.* (**reforçar**)

- **enforcement** /ɪnˈfɔːsmənt/ NOUN, NO PLURAL when something is enforced (**aplicação**) 🔹 *law enforcement* (**aplicação da lei**) 🔹 *the enforcement of public health rules*

engage /ɪnˈɡeɪdʒ/ VERB [engages, engaging, engaged]

1 to make someone interested and get their attention □ *A good speaker will engage their audience.* (**prender a atenção**)

2 a formal word meaning to start to employ someone □ *She engaged a top lawyer to represent her.* (**contratar**)

engine — enlarge

3 engage someone in conversation to start a conversation with someone (envolver alguém na conversa)

◆ PHRASAL VERB **engage in something** to take part in an activity. A formal phrase. □ *Are they willing to engage in discussions?* (dedicar-se a algo, envolver-se com algo)

• **engaged** /ɪnˈgeɪdʒd/ ADJECTIVE
1 if two people are engaged, they have promised to marry each other □ + **to** *She's engaged to actor Alex Donovan.* (comprometido) 🔊 *The couple got engaged last month.* (ficaram noivos)
2 if a telephone or toilet is engaged, it is being used (ocupado)

• **engagement** /ɪnˈgeɪdʒmənt/ NOUN [plural **engagements**]
1 a promise to marry someone (noivado) 🔊 *They announced their engagement in September.* (anunciaram seu noivado)
2 an arrangement to meet someone or to do something (compromisso) 🔊 *He has a lot of social engagements.* (compromissos sociais) □ *The prince was forced to cancel several official engagements.*

engine /ˈendʒɪn/ NOUN [plural **engines**]
1 a part of a machine that uses energy to produce movement □ *a car with a diesel engine* (motor) 🔊 *He closed the door and started the engine.* (ligou o motor)
2 the part at the front of a train that pulls it along □ *a steam engine* (locomotiva)

engineer /ˌendʒɪˈnɪə(r)/ ▶ NOUN [plural **engineers**]
1 someone who designs and makes things like bridges, roads or machines (engenheiro)
2 someone who works with and repairs engines and machines □ *a telephone engineer* (mecânico)
▶ VERB [engineers, engineering, engineered] to make something happen by clever planning □ *He tried to engineer a meeting between the two sides.* (maquinar, construir)

• **engineering** /ˌendʒɪˈnɪərɪŋ/ NOUN, NO PLURAL the study or work of designing and making machines, roads, bridges, etc. (engenharia) 🔊 *He graduated in mechanical engineering.* (engenharia mecânica)

English /ˈɪŋglɪʃ/ ▶ ADJECTIVE
1 belonging to or from England □ *the English countryside* (inglês)
2 to do with the English language □ *an English translation* (inglês)
▶ NOUN
1 NO PLURAL the main language of Britain, North America and Australia, and an official language in some other countries □ *She speaks English very well.* (língua inglesa)
2 the English people from England (os ingleses)

Englishman /ˈɪŋglɪʃmən/ NOUN [plural **Englishmen**] a man who comes from England, or who has English parents (inglês)

engrave /ɪnˈgreɪv/ VERB [engraves, engraving, engraved] to cut a pattern or letters into a hard surface □ *The trophy is engraved with the names of previous winners.* (gravar, esculpir)

• **engraving** /ɪnˈgreɪvɪŋ/ NOUN [plural **engravings**]
1 a picture made by engraving (gravura)
2 the process or skill of engraving (gravação)

engrossed /ɪnˈgrəʊst/ ADJECTIVE if you are engrossed in something, it takes all your attention or interest □ *I sat engrossed in a book.* (absorto)

engulf /ɪnˈgʌlf/ VERB [engulfs, engulfing, engulfed]
1 to surround something and cover it completely □ *Fire engulfed the building.* (engolfar, engolir)
2 if fighting or violence engulfs a place, it affects all of it □ *Violence is threatening to engulf the entire city.* (subjugar)

enhance /ɪnˈhɑːns/ VERB [enhances, enhancing, enhanced] to improve something □ *The swimmer claims he has never used drugs to enhance his performance.* (melhorar, aumentar)

• **enhancement** /ɪnˈhɑːnsmənt/ NOUN [plural **enhancements**] when something is improved, or the improvement itself □ *There were a number of security enhancements put in place at the airport.* (melhora)

enigma /ɪˈnɪgmə/ NOUN [plural **enigmas**] someone or something mysterious that no one understands □ *Their sudden disappearance remains an enigma.* (enigma)

• **enigmatic** /ˌenɪgˈmætɪk/ ADJECTIVE mysterious and impossible to understand □ *an enigmatic smile* (enigmático)

enjoy /ɪnˈdʒɔɪ/ VERB [enjoys, enjoying, enjoyed]
1 to like doing something □ *They seemed to enjoy the concert.* □ *Enjoy your meal!* □ + **ing** *I enjoy playing tennis.* (gostar de, apreciar)
2 enjoy yourself to have a good time doing something □ *We enjoyed ourselves at the party.* □ *He was clearly enjoying himself.* (divertir-se)
3 to experience something good or an advantage. A formal word. □ *He has enjoyed some success as an author.* (desfrutar de)

• **enjoyable** /ɪnˈdʒɔɪəbəl/ ADJECTIVE fun and giving you pleasure □ *The whole trip was a really enjoyable experience.* (agradável)

• **enjoyment** /ɪnˈdʒɔɪmənt/ NOUN, NO PLURAL when you enjoy something (prazer) 🔊 *I get tremendous enjoyment out of the sport.* (tive prazer) □ + **of** *I don't let the illness affect my enjoyment of life.*

enlarge /ɪnˈlɑːdʒ/ VERB [enlarges, enlarging, enlarged] to make something bigger □ *Click here to enlarge the image.* (ampliar)

◆ PHRASAL VERB **enlarge on/upon something** a formal word meaning to give more information about something (fornecer mais informações)

• **enlargement** /ɪnˈlɑːdʒmənt/ NOUN [plural **enlargements**]
1 when something is enlarged □ *the enlargement of the European Union* (expansão)

2 a larger photograph made from a smaller one (ampliação)

enlighten /ɪnˈlaɪtn/ VERB [enlightens, enlightening, enlightened] a formal word meaning to explain something to someone (esclarecer)

• **enlightened** /ɪnˈlaɪtənd/ ADJECTIVE having good, modern ideas and beliefs about something (erudito, esclarecido) ▫ *We now have a more enlightened attitude towards disability.* (atitude esclarecida)

• **enlightening** /ɪnˈlaɪtənɪŋ/ ADJECTIVE giving you new information about something ▫ *an enlightening conversation* (esclarecedor)

enlist /ɪnˈlɪst/ VERB [enlists, enlisting, enlisted]

1 to join the army, navy or air force ▫ *He enlisted in the Marines.* (alistar-se)

2 to ask someone to help or support you (inscrever-se) ▫ *He enlisted the help of his brother.* (inscreveu-se para ajudar)

enmity /ˈenmɪti/ NOUN, NO PLURAL a feeling of strong dislike towards someone. A formal word. (inimizade)

enormity /ɪˈnɔːmɪti/ NOUN, NO PLURAL how large or important something is ▫ *We are aware of the enormity of the problem.* (enormidade)

enormous /ɪˈnɔːməs/ ADJECTIVE very big or great ▫ *an enormous tree* (enorme, imenso) ▫ *It cost an enormous amount of money.* (imensa quantia) ▫ *The staff were under enormous pressure.*

• **enormously** /ɪˈnɔːməsli/ ADVERB very much or extremely ▫ *They all enjoyed themselves enormously.* ▫ *We are enormously grateful.* (enormemente)

enough /ɪˈnʌf/ ▶ DETERMINER, PRONOUN

1 as much or as many as you need or want ▫ *Have you all had enough to eat?* ▫ *We need some more oil – there isn't enough here.* ▫ *I've got enough problems without this!* (suficiente)

2 have had enough of something if you have had enough of something, you do not want to have it or do it any more ▫ *I've had enough of cooking every day!* (estar farto de algo)

▶ ADVERB as much as is needed or wanted ▫ *She's not pretty enough to be a model.* ▫ *Stop when you think you've written enough.* (o suficiente)

enquire /enˈkwaɪə(r)/ VERB [enquires, enquiring, enquired] another spelling of **inquire** (ver inquire)

• **enquiry** /enˈkwaɪəri/ NOUN [plural enquiries] another spelling of **inquiry** (ver inquiry)

enrage /ɪnˈreɪdʒ/ VERB [enrages, enraging, enraged] to make someone very angry ▫ *The referee's decision enraged Chelsea fans.* (enfurecer)

enrich /ɪnˈrɪtʃ/ VERB [enriches, enriching, enriched] to improve something by adding something to it ▫ *Art enriches people's lives.* ▫ *The nutrients enrich the soil.* (enriquecer)

enrol /ɪnˈrəʊl/ VERB [enrols, enrolling, enrolled] to put your name or someone else's name on a list to become a member of a course, club, college, etc. ▫ *Jackie's just enrolled at a stage school.* ▫ *It costs £50 to enrol a child in the activities programme.* (matricular, inscrever)

• **enrolment** /ɪnˈrəʊlmənt/ NOUN [plural enrolments] the process of enrolling or the number of people enrolled ▫ *There's been an increase in international student enrolments.* (matrícula)

enroll /ɪnˈrəʊl/ VERB [enrolls, enrolling, enrolled] the US spelling of **enrol** (ver enrol)

• **enrollment** /ɪnˈrəʊlmənt/ NOUN [plural enrollments] the US spelling of **enrolment** (ver enrolment)

ensue /ɪnˈsjuː/ VERB [ensues, ensuing, ensued] a formal word meaning to happen after something, often caused by that thing ▫ *Hundreds of people came into the shop and chaos ensued.* (resultar, seguir-se)

• **ensuing** /ɪnˈsjuːɪŋ/ ADJECTIVE happening after something, often caused by that thing ▫ *Police shot one of the protesters and 12 more people were injured in the ensuing battle.* (posterior, subsequente)

ensure /ɪnˈʃʊə(r)/ VERB [ensures, ensuring, ensured] to make certain of something. A formal word. ▫ *Please ensure you have all your belongings with you when you leave the train.* (assegurar)

entail /ɪnˈteɪl/ VERB [entails, entailing, entailed] to involve something or to make it necessary ▫ *Can you tell me what the job will entail?* (exigir)

entangled /ɪnˈtæŋgəld/ ADJECTIVE

1 twisted together and difficult to separate ▫ *The animals get entangled in the fishing nets.* (emaranhado)

2 involved in a difficult situation that you cannot escape from ▫ *The company has become entangled in a legal battle.* (envolvido)

enter /ˈentə(r)/ VERB [enters, entering, entered]

1 to go into a place ▫ *A tall man entered the room.* ▫ *He entered hospital at 3pm.* ▫ *The bullet entered his skull.* ▫ *They entered the country illegally.* (entrar em)

2 to put information in a book, document, computer, etc. ▫ *Enter your name here.* ▫ *The data is entered in a special computerized system.* (registrar)

3 to get to a particular period of time ▫ *We are entering a new era of prosperity.* ▫ *Talks have entered their fourth week.* (ingressar)

4 to start to take part in a job or an activity ▫ *He entered parliament at the age of forty.* ▫ *Our company entered the Chinese market in 1996.* (iniciar)

5 to take part in a competition or an exam ▫ *My mum agreed to enter the mother's race.* (inscrever-se)

6 enter a plea to tell a court that you are guilty or not guilty ☐ *She entered a plea of not guilty.* (apresentar uma declaração)

◆ PHRASAL VERB **enter into something** to become involved with something ☐ *France has agreed to enter into discussions with other countries.* (iniciar algo)

enterprise /ˈentəpraɪz/ NOUN [plural **enterprises**]

1 a business or organization ☐ *a large commercial enterprise* (empresa)

2 a large or difficult plan or activity ☐ *The research project is a joint enterprise between UCLA and the University of California.* (empreendimento)

3 the ability to think of new ideas and to make them happen (espírito empreendedor)

• **enterprising** /ˈentəpraɪzɪŋ/ ADJECTIVE able to think of new ideas and not frightened of taking risks ☐ *Some enterprising individuals are already using the technology to create their own TV channels.* (empreendedor)

entertain /ˌentəˈteɪn/ VERB [**entertains, entertaining, entertained**]

1 to do something which people find interesting and enjoyable ☐ *Emily entertained us by telling a few jokes.* ☐ *A band entertained the crowd.* (entreter)

2 to invite people as your guests for a meal or a drink ☐ *Tom tends to cook when we're entertaining.* (receber)

3 a formal word meaning to consider an idea (cogitar) ☐ *He had entertained thoughts of leaving his job.* (cogitou pensamentos)

• **entertainer** /ˌentəˈteɪnə(r)/ NOUN [plural **entertainers**] someone who performs to entertain people ☐ *He's one of Britain's most popular entertainers.* (artista de variedades)

• **entertaining** /ˌentəˈteɪnɪŋ/ ADJECTIVE interesting and enjoyable ☐ *She gave an entertaining account of her trip.* ☐ *It was a highly entertaining match.* (divertido)

• **entertainment** /ˌentəˈteɪnmənt/ NOUN [plural **entertainments**] something that entertains people ☐ *There's live entertainment every night.* (espetáculo, entretenimento) ☐ *Traditional dancers provided the entertainment.* (fizeram o espetáculo) ☐ *There are new forms of entertainment developing on the Internet.* (formas de entretenimento)

enthral /ɪnˈθrɔːl/ VERB [**enthrals, enthralling, enthralled**] to interest you and hold your attention completely (cativar, fascinar)

• **enthralled** /ɪnˈθrɔːld/ ADJECTIVE very interested by something and giving it all your attention ☐ *an enthralled audience* (fascinado)

• **enthralling** /ɪnˈθrɔːlɪŋ/ ADJECTIVE very interesting and taking all your attention ☐ *an enthralling contest* (fascinante)

enthuse /ɪnˈθjuːz/ VERB [**enthuses, enthusing, enthused**] to speak or write about how much you like something in an excited way ☐ *'Great dance!' she enthused, smiling at him.* (entusiasmar-se)

enthusiasm /ɪnˈθjuːziæzəm/ NOUN, NO PLURAL when you are very interested in something or want to do it very much ☐ + **for** *Her enthusiasm for her subject remains as strong.* (entusiasmo) ☐ *There was a general lack of enthusiasm for the project.* (falta de entusiasmo)

• **enthusiast** /ɪnˈθjuːziæst/ NOUN [plural **enthusiasts**] someone who is very interested or involved in a particular thing ☐ *a cycling enthusiast* (entusiasta)

• **enthusiastic** /ɪnˌθjuːziˈæstɪk/ ADJECTIVE showing enthusiasm ☐ + **about** *Not everyone is enthusiastic about the idea.* ☐ *You don't sound very enthusiastic.* (entusiasmado)

• **enthusiastically** /ɪnˌθjuːziˈæstɪkəli/ ADVERB in an enthusiastic way (entusiasmadamente)

entice /ɪnˈtaɪs/ VERB [**entices, enticed, enticing**] to persuade someone to do something by promising them something good ☐ *Companies offer bonuses to entice young mothers back to work.* (atrair)

entire /ɪnˈtaɪə(r)/ ADJECTIVE all of something ☐ *He lived his entire life in the same town.* (inteiro)

• **entirely** /ɪnˈtaɪəli/ ADVERB completely ☐ *It was my fault entirely.* ☐ *The two things are entirely different.* (completamente)

• **entirety** /ɪnˈtaɪərəti/ NOUN, NO PLURAL the whole of something ☐ *I haven't seen the finished film in its entirety.* (totalidade)

entitle /ɪnˈtaɪtəl/ VERB [**entitles, entitling, entitled**]

1 to give someone the right to have or to do something ☐ *You are entitled to five weeks' holiday per year.* (dar direito a)

2 to give something a title ☐ *The book is entitled 'A Soldier's Tale'.* (intitular)

• **entitlement** /ɪnˈtaɪtəlmənt/ NOUN [plural **entitlements**] something you are entitled to ☐ *holiday entitlement* (direito)

entity /ˈentəti/ NOUN [plural **entities**] a formal word for a complete, separate thing (entidade) ☐ *The two companies have the same owner but they operate as separate entities.* (entidades separadas)

entrance /ˈentrəns/ NOUN [plural **entrances**]

1 the part of a building where you go into it (entrada) ☐ *I'll meet you outside the main entrance.* (entrada principal) ☐ + **of** *There are security staff at the entrance of the building.* ☐ + **to** *There were clear signs at the entrance to the tunnel.*

2 when you go into a place (entrada) ☐ *Everyone looked round as the singer made her entrance.* (fez sua entrada)

3 the right to go into a place or to become a member of an organization ☐ *a university*

entrance exam (admissão) ◧ There's an entrance fee of £8. (taxa de admissão)
- **entrant** /ˈentrənt/ NOUN [plural **entrants**] someone who enters a competition or exam □ Competition entrants must be 16 or over. (participante)

entreat /ɪnˈtriːt/ VERB [**entreats, entreating, entreated**] to ask someone for something in an eager or emotional way because you want it very much. A formal word. □ She entreated him to leave the gun behind. (rogar, suplicar)
- **entreaty** /ɪnˈtriːtɪ/ NOUN [plural **entreaties**] when you entreat someone to do something. A formal word. □ He left that day, despite Anna's passionate entreaties. (súplica)

entrepreneur /ˌɒntrəprəˈnɜː(r)/ NOUN [plural **entrepreneurs**] a person who starts a business using their own ideas and usually their own money □ China's young entrepreneurs (empreendedor)
- **entrepreneurial** /ˌɒntrəprəˈnɜːrɪəl/ ADJECTIVE to do with entrepreneurs (empreendedor) ◧ an entrepreneurial spirit (espírito empreendedor)

entrust /ɪnˈtrʌst/ VERB [**entrusts, entrusting, entrusted**] to give someone the responsibility of dealing with or looking after something □ I wouldn't entrust my child's education to these people. (confiar)

entry /ˈentrɪ/ NOUN [plural **entries**]
1 when you go into a place (entrada) ◧ They were refused entry into the country (recusaram a entrada) ◧ We gained entry (= got in) through an open window. (conseguiram entrada) □ + to This card gives you free entry to most museums. □ + into They were allowed entry into the area.
2 no entry a phrase used on signs to show that you must not go into a place. (proibida a entrada)
3 a piece of information that is written in a book, document, computer system, etc. □ I checked my diary entry for that day. (apontamento)
4 something that you have done to try to win a competition (inscrição) ◧ The winning entries will be announced next week. (inscrições vencedoras) □ The competition attracted thousands of entries.
5 when you become a member of an organization or start to take part in a job or activity □ + into The year 2001 saw their entry into the European Union. □ Many people opposed their entry into the war. (inscrito)

envelop /ɪnˈveləp/ VERB [**envelops, enveloping, enveloped**] to surround and cover something completely □ A thick fog enveloped the hills. (envolver)

envelope /ˈenvələʊp/ NOUN [plural **envelopes**] a folded paper cover for a letter, especially one that is sent by post □ a brown A4 envelope (envelope) ◧ You haven't opened the envelope. (abriu o envelope)

envious /ˈenvɪəs/ ADJECTIVE wanting something that someone else has □ He was rather envious of his brother's success. (invejoso)

environment /ɪnˈvaɪərənmənt/ NOUN [plural **environments**]
1 the environment all the things, such as air, land, sea, animals and plants, that make up the natural world around us (o ambiente) ◧ Our main aim is to protect the environment. (proteger o ambiente)
2 the things that surround you where you live, work or do something (ambiente) ◧ We want to create a positive working environment. (criar um ambiente) □ It provides a safe environment for young children to play.
- **environmental** /ɪnˌvaɪərənˈmentəl/ ADJECTIVE to do with the environment □ an environmental group □ environmental concerns (ambiental)
- **environmentalist** /ɪnˌvaɪərənˈmentəlɪst/ NOUN [plural **environmentalists**] someone who tries to protect the environment from damage (ambientalista)
- **environmentally** /ɪnˌvaɪərənˈmentəlɪ/ ADVERB in a way that is to do with the environment □ These chemicals are environmentally damaging. (pelo lado ambiental)

environmentally friendly /ɪnˌvaɪərənˌmentəlɪ ˈfrendlɪ/ ADJECTIVE not harmful to the environment (inofensivo ao meio ambiente)

envisage /ɪnˈvɪzɪdʒ/ VERB [**envisages, envisaging, envisaged**] to imagine something or to think it is likely to happen in the future □ I tried to envisage a life without Lily. □ We don't envisage taking on more staff. (imaginar)

envoy /ˈenvɔɪ/ NOUN [plural **envoys**] a government official sent to another country to meet with a foreign government □ the United Nations envoy to Bosnia (enviado)

envy /ˈenvɪ/ ▶ NOUN, NO PLURAL
1 a feeling of wanting what someone else has □ I felt a little envy at her success. (inveja)
2 be the envy of someone to be something that other people would very much like to have □ Our health system was once the envy of the world. (ser invejado por alguém)
▶ VERB [**envies, envying, envied**] to want what someone else has □ We envied him because he didn't have to go to school. (invejar, cobiçar)

enzyme /ˈenzaɪm/ NOUN [plural **enzymes**] a chemical substance made in both animals and plants, which causes chemical changes. A biology word. (enzima)

ephemeral /ɪˈfemərəl/ ADJECTIVE lasting only for a short time. A formal word. (efêmero)

epic /ˈepɪk/ ▶ NOUN [plural **epics**] a long story, poem or film about great events or exciting adventures □ His new film is a historical epic. (épico, epopeia)
▶ ADJECTIVE like an epic □ an epic journey

epicenter /ˈepɪsentə(r)/ NOUN [plural **epicenters**] the US spelling of **epicentre** (**epicentro**)

epicentre /ˈepɪsentə(r)/ NOUN [plural **epicentres**] the point on the ground just above the strongest part of an earthquake (= when the earth shakes) (**epicentro**)

epidemic /ˌepɪˈdemɪk/ NOUN [plural **epidemics**] a situation in which a disease spreads quickly and many people become ill at the same time □ *a flu epidemic* (**epidemia**)

epidermis /ˌepɪˈdɜːmɪs/ NOUN, NO PLURAL the outer layer of skin. A biology word. (**epiderme**)

epidural /ˌepɪˈdjʊərəl/ NOUN [plural **epidurals**] a medical treatment in which a drug is put into the lower part of your back in order to stop you feeling pain (**peridural**)

epiglottis /ˌepɪˈɡlɒtɪs/ NOUN [plural **epiglottises**] a small part at the back of your tongue which stops food from going into the pipe that is for air. A biology word. (**epiglote**)

epilepsy /ˈepɪlepsi/ NOUN, NO PLURAL an illness that affects the brain, making someone shake in an uncontrolled way, or become unconscious for short periods (**epilepsia**)

• **epileptic** /ˌepɪˈleptɪk/ ▶ ADJECTIVE
 1 caused by epilepsy □ *an epileptic fit* (**epilético**)
 2 affected by epilepsy □ *She's epileptic.* (**epilético**)
 ▶ NOUN [plural **epileptics**] someone who suffers from epilepsy (**epilético**)

episode /ˈepɪsəʊd/ NOUN [plural **episodes**]
 1 one separate part of a story that is broadcast on the radio or television over a period of time (**episódio**)
 2 an event □ *It was one of the most embarrassing episodes of his life.* (**episódio**)

epitaph /ˈepɪtɑːf/ NOUN [plural **epitaphs**] a short piece of writing on a dead person's grave (**epitáfio**)

epitome /ɪˈpɪtəmi/ NOUN, NO PLURAL **the epitome of something** a typical example of something □ *Slim and dressed all in black, she is the epitome of elegance.* (**ser a mais pura expressão de algo**)

• **epitomize** or **epitomise** /ɪˈpɪtəmaɪz/ VERB [**epitomizes, epitomizing, epitomized**] to be a typical example of something. A formal word. □ *His lack of skill epitomizes everything that is wrong with the team.* (**epitomar, ser um exemplo perfeito**)

epoch /ˈiːpɒk/ NOUN [plural **epochs**] a period of time in history (**época**)

equal /ˈiːkwəl/ ▶ ADJECTIVE
 1 of the same size, value or amount □ *Cut the cake into four roughly equal slices.*
 2 having or deserving the same rights as other people □ *Men and women were finally regarded as equal.* (**igual**) 🔁 *equal rights for all* (**direitos iguais**)
 ▶ VERB [**equals, equalling/US equaling, equalled/US equaled**]
 1 to be the same in size, value or amount □ *Two plus two equals four.* (**igualar**)
 2 to achieve as much as someone else □ *She equalled the world record in training.* (**igualar**)
 ▶ NOUN [plural **equals**] someone who has the same rights or importance as another person □ *The women quite rightly expect to be treated by the men as equals.*

• **equality** /iːˈkwɒləti/ NOUN, NO PLURAL when everyone has the same rights and importance (**igualdade**) 🔁 *racial equality* (**igualdade racial**) 🔁 *sexual equality* (**igualdade sexual**)

• **equalize** or **equalise** /ˈiːkwəlaɪz/ VERB [**equalizes, equalizing, equalized**]
 1 to win a point that gives you the same score as a team you are playing against □ *Rooney equalized just before half-time.* (**empatar**)
 2 to make two or more things equal □ *When you swallow, it equalizes the pressure in your ears.* (**igualar**)

• **equalizer** or **equaliser** /ˈiːkwəlaɪzə(r)/ NOUN [plural **equalizers**] a goal that makes two teams' scores the same (**gol de empate**)

• **equally** /ˈiːkwəli/ ADVERB
 1 to the same level □ *The two drivers were equally to blame for the accident.* □ *He works hard but Tom works equally hard.* (**igualmente**)
 2 in amounts or parts that are the same □ *Share the sweets out equally.* (**igualmente**)
 3 in a way that gives the same rights and importance to everyone □ *I try to treat the children equally.* (**igualmente**)

equal opportunities /ˈiːkwəl ˌɒpəˈtjuːnətɪz/ PLURAL NOUN the set of ideas which states that people of all races, sexes, ages, etc. must have the same chances to do things, especially at work □ *They have been fighting for an equal opportunities policy.* (**oportunidades iguais**)

equation /ɪˈkweɪʒən/ NOUN [plural **equations**] a mathematical statement that shows that two sets of numbers are equal (**equação**)

equator /ɪˈkweɪtə(r)/ NOUN, NO PLURAL **the equator** the line drawn on maps that goes around the middle of the Earth □ *Kampala is just north of the equator.* (**equador**)

equilateral /ˌiːkwɪˈlætərəl, ˌekwɪˈlætərəl/ ADJECTIVE an equilateral triangle has three equal sides. A maths word. (**equilateral**)

equilibrium /ˌiːkwɪˈlɪbriəm, ˌekwɪˈlɪbriəm/ NOUN, NO PLURAL equal balance between two things (**equilíbrio**)

equip /ɪˈkwɪp/ VERB [**equips, equipping, equipped**]
 1 to provide something or someone with all the machines, furniture, etc. that are needed for a particular purpose □ *a fully equipped hospital* (**equipar**)
 2 to provide someone with the skills they need in order to do something □ *The aim of the course is*

to equip young people for the business world. (preparar)

- **equipment** /ɪˈkwɪpmənt/ NOUN, NO PLURAL the machines, furniture, etc. that you need in order to do a particular activity or job □ *camping equipment* □ *office equipment* (**equipamento**) 🔁 *a piece of equipment* (**um equipamento**)

> Remember that **equipment** is never used in the plural:
> ✓ *We need more equipment.*
> ✗ *We need more equipments.*

equivalent /ɪˈkwɪvələnt/ ▶ NOUN [plural **equivalents**] something that has the same value, use, meaning or effect as something else □ *The Internet has become the modern equivalent of a telephone or a daily newspaper.* □ *Children eat the equivalent of almost twelve bags of sugar every year.*
▶ ADJECTIVE having the same value, use, meaning or effect □ *The average temperature of Mars is roughly equivalent to the temperature in Antarctica.* (**equivalente**)

-er /-ər/ SUFFIX
1 -er is added to the end of words to mean 'a person or thing that does something' □ *teacher*
2 -er is added to the end of some adjectives to make a comparative form □ *brighter*

era /ˈɪərə/ NOUN [plural **eras**] a period of time (**era**) 🔁 *The country is entering a new era of peace and prosperity.* (**nova era**)

eradicate /ɪˈrædɪkeɪt/ VERB [**eradicates, eradicating, eradicated**] to get rid of something bad completely. A formal word. □ *The government aims to eradicate poverty by 2015.* (**erradicar**)
- **eradication** /ɪˌrædɪˈkeɪʃən/ NOUN, NO PLURAL when you eradicate something. A formal word. (**erradicação**)

erase /ɪˈreɪz/ VERB [**erases, erasing, erased**]
1 to remove information or files from a computer □ *The file had somehow been erased.* (**apagar**)
2 to get rid of something completely. A formal word. □ *She had erased the memory.* (**apagar**)
- **eraser** /ɪˈreɪzə(r)/ NOUN [plural **erasers**] a small piece of rubber used to remove pencil marks from paper (**borracha**)

erect /ɪˈrekt/ ▶ VERB [**erects, erecting, erected**]
1 to build something. A formal word. □ *They erected a monument to their leader.* □ *A barrier was erected around the area.* (**erigir**)
2 to put the parts of a tent together. A formal word. □ *We had to erect the tent in the dark.* (**erguer**)
▶ ADJECTIVE standing up straight □ *an erect posture*
- **erection** /ɪˈrekʃən/ NOUN, NO PLURAL the act of erecting something. A formal word. (**ereção**)

erode /ɪˈrəʊd/ VERB [**erodes, eroding, eroded**]
1 if something erodes or is eroded, its surface is gradually removed by wind or water, for example □ *Houses are falling into the sea as the coastline erodes.* (**erodir**)
2 to gradually make a quality less strong. A formal word. □ *The recent scandal has eroded public confidence in the government.* (**desgastar-se**)
- **erosion** /ɪˈrəʊʒən/ NOUN, NO PLURAL when something is eroded □ *soil erosion* (**erosão**)

erotic /ɪˈrɒtɪk/ ADJECTIVE to do with sex □ *an erotic painting* (**erótico**)

errand /ˈerənd/ NOUN [plural **errands**] run an errand to do a small job that involves going somewhere (**fazer serviço de rua**)

erratic /ɪˈrætɪk/ ADJECTIVE changing often and when you do not expect it □ *Her increasingly erratic behaviour is causing concern.* (**irregular**)
- **erratically** /ɪˈrætɪkəli/ ADVERB in an erratic way □ *Police said he had been driving erratically.* (**irregularmente**)

error /ˈerə(r)/ NOUN [plural **errors**] a mistake (**erro, falha**) 🔁 *He admits making some errors.* (**cometer erros**) 🔁 *The report blamed human error for the air crash.* (**falha humana**)

error message /ˈerə ˌmesɪdʒ/ NOUN [plural **error messages**] a message that appears on a computer screen when there is a problem. A computing word. (**mensagem de erro**)

erupt /ɪˈrʌpt/ VERB [**erupts, erupting, erupted**]
1 violence or fighting erupts when it starts suddenly □ *Violence erupted at the demonstration.* (**explodir**)
2 a volcano erupts when hot rocks, flames and dust suddenly come out of it (**entrar em erupção**)
- **eruption** /ɪˈrʌpʃən/ NOUN [plural **eruptions**] when something erupts □ *a volcanic eruption* (**erupção**)

escalate /ˈeskəleɪt/ VERB [**escalates, escalating, escalated**] to make or become worse or more serious □ *The violence has escalated in recent weeks.* (**subir, escalar**)
- **escalator** /ˈeskəleɪtə(r)/ NOUN [plural **escalators**] a set of moving stairs for carrying people between the levels of a building (**escada rolante**) 🔁 *Shall we take the escalator?* (**subir de escada rolante**)

escapade /ˌeskəˈpeɪd/ NOUN [plural **escapades**] an exciting and dangerous adventure (**aventura**)

escape /ɪˈskeɪp/ ▶ VERB [**escapes, escaping, escaped**]
1 to get away from a place where you are being kept □ + *from* *The lion had escaped from its cage.* (**escapar, fugir**)
2 to get away from a dangerous place or situation □ + *from* *He escaped from the country hidden in a lorry.* □ *When fire broke out, we managed to escape through the window.* (**safar-se de**)
3 to avoid something unpleasant (**livrar-se de**) 🔁 *You're lucky to have escaped punishment.*

(livrou-se da punição) 🔁 *They escaped injury by wrapping themselves in blankets.* (**evitaram ferir-se**)

4 if something escapes attention, notice, etc. nobody notices it (**passar despercebido**) 🔁 *It has not escaped my attention that you have been late every day this week.* (**passou despercebido**) ☐ *This software uses advanced technology to escape detection.*

5 if something escapes you, you cannot remember it ☐ *I've met her before, but her name escapes me.* (**escapar**)

6 if a substance escapes from a container, it comes out of it (**vazar**)

▶ NOUN [*plural* **escapes**]

1 when someone gets away from a place or a bad situation ☐ **+ from** *He wrote a book about his daring escape from prison.* (**fuga**)

2 when someone avoids something unpleasant (**fuga**) 🔁 *Our car was balanced on the edge of the mountain – we had a very lucky escape.* (**escapar por um triz**) 🔁 *The family had a narrow escape* (= could have been killed) *when their house was bombed.*

3 something that makes you forget about the problems of your life ☐ *Dancing is a means of escape for me.* (**válvula de escape**)

• **escaped** /ɪˈskeɪpt/ ADJECTIVE an escaped prisoner or animal has got away from the place where they were being kept (**em fuga**)

• **escapee** /ɪˌskeɪˈpiː/ NOUN [*plural* **escapees**] someone who has escaped, for example from prison (**fugitivo**)

escape key /ɪˈskeɪp ˌkiː/ NOUN [*plural* **escape keys**] the key on a computer keyboard with 'Esc' on it, which allows you to leave a screen. A computing word. (**tecla Esc**)

escort ▶ VERB /ɪˈskɔːt/ [**escorts, escorting, escorted**] to go somewhere with someone in order to look after them ☐ *Airport staff will escort your child to the boarding gate.* (**acompanhar, escoltar**)

▶ NOUN /ˈeskɔːt/ [*plural* **escorts**] someone who escorts another person (**acompanhante, escolta**) 🔁 *The players needed a police escort to get to the bus.* (**escolta policial**)

esophagus /iːˈsɒfəgəs/ NOUN [*plural* **esophaguses**] the US spelling of **oesophagus** (**esôfago**)

especially /ɪˈspeʃəli/ ADVERB
1 very, more than anything or anyone else ☐ *I was especially impressed by the food.* ☐ *He wasn't especially clever.* ☐ *The children, especially the younger ones, were tired.* (**especialmente**)

2 for one person or purpose only ☐ **+ for** *I bought it especially for you.* ☐ **+ to do something** *I came here especially to see you.* (**especialmente**)

espionage /ˈespiəˌnɑːʒ/ NOUN, NO PLURAL the activity of trying to find out another country's or company's secrets (**espionagem**)

espresso /eˈspresəʊ/ NOUN [*plural* **espressos**] a strong black coffee that you drink in small amounts (**espresso**)

-ess /es/ SUFFIX **-ess** is added to the end of words to make a female form ☐ *lioness*

essay /ˈeseɪ/ NOUN [*plural* **essays**] a piece of writing by a student about a particular subject (**ensaio, redação**) ☐ **+ on** *Students are required to write a 4,000-word essay on a topic of their choice.*

essence /ˈesəns/ NOUN, NO PLURAL
1 the essence of something the most important part of something, or its true character ☐ *The film captures the essence of life in 18th-century Paris.* (**a essência de algo**)

2 a liquid that contains the very strong taste of the plant it has come from ☐ *vanilla essence* (**essência**)

essential /ɪˈsenʃəl/ ADJECTIVE if something is essential, you must do it or have it ☐ **+ that** *It is essential that we all stay together.* (**essencial**) 🔁 *Fat is an essential part of our diet.* (**parte essencial**) ☐ *A car is useful, but not essential.*

• **essentially** /ɪˈsenʃəli/ ADVERB
1 used for saying that something is mostly true ☐ *He looked a little older, but essentially the same.* (**essencialmente**)

2 used for emphasizing the most important part of what you are saying ☐ *Essentially, he's her father, and that is what matters.* (**basicamente**)

• **essentials** /ɪˈsenʃəlz/ PLURAL NOUN things that you must have (**princípios básicos**) 🔁 *Just bring the bare essentials; your wallet, your passport and your ticket.* (**o essencial**)

-est /-ɪst/ SUFFIX **-est** is added to the end of some adjectives to make a superlative form ☐ *neatest*

establish /ɪˈstæblɪʃ/ VERB [**establishes, establishing, established**]
1 to start an organization or business ☐ *He established a small bakery.* (**fundar, estabelecer**)

2 to make something start to exist ☐ *Police have established a good relationship with the community.* ☐ *We are trying to establish trade links with the area.* (**estabelecer**)

3 to discover the truth about something ☐ *We managed to establish that he was born in Cambridge.* ☐ *Police have not established the cause of death.* (**determinar**)

4 to become successful at something ☐ *He established himself as the leading expert on Mozart.* (**estabelecer**) 🔁 *She established her reputation as an international artist.* (**estabeleceu sua reputação**)

• **established** /ɪˈstæblɪʃt/ ADJECTIVE having existed successfully for a long time ☐ *an established business* (**sólido**)

• **establishment** /ɪˈstæblɪʃmənt/ NOUN [*plural* **establishments**]

1 when something is started □ *The report recommends the establishment of a new committee.* (fundação)
2 the educational/medical/scientific, etc. establishment the people who control a particular activity or job (estatuto educacional, médico, científico etc.)
3 the establishment the most important and powerful people in a country □ *She uses her art to challenge the establishment.* (as autoridades)
4 an organization or business □ *a research establishment* (instituição)

estate /ɪˈsteɪt/ NOUN [plural **estates**]
1 a large area with a lot of buildings on it (loteamento, propriedade) 🔹 *an industrial estate* (propriedade industrial) 🔹 *a housing estate* (propriedade residencial)
2 a large area of land that belongs to one person or family (loteamento, propriedade)
3 all the things that a person owns, especially when they die (patrimônio)
4 a large type of car with a lot of space behind the seats for carrying things □ *a Volvo estate* (veículo tipo perua)

estate agent /ɪˈsteɪt ˌeɪdʒənt/ NOUN [plural **estate agents**] someone whose job is to help people to buy and sell houses and apartments (corretor de imóveis)

estate car /ɪˈsteɪt ˌkɑː(r)/ NOUN [plural **estate cars**] a large type of car with a lot of space behind the seats for carrying things (veículo tipo perua)

esteem /ɪˈstiːm/ NOUN, NO PLURAL respect and admiration for someone. A formal word. (estima)
⇨ go to **self-esteem**

• **esteemed** /ɪˈstiːmd/ ADJECTIVE respected and admired by a lot of people □ *an esteemed author* (estimado)

esthetic /iːsˈθetɪk/ ADJECTIVE the US spelling of **aesthetic** (estético)

• **esthetically** /iːsˈθetɪkəli/ ADVERB the US spelling of **aesthetically** (esteticamente)

estimate ▶ VERB /ˈestɪmeɪt/ [**estimates, estimating, estimated**] to try to judge the size, amount or value of something, using the information that you have □ *The government estimated the cost at over £5 million.* □ *Experts estimate that thousands of deaths every year are caused by unhealthy diets.* (estimar)
▶ NOUN /ˈestɪmət/ [plural **estimates**]
1 when you estimate something (estimativa)
2 a statement telling a customer how much a service will cost (orçamento)

• **estimated** /ˈestɪmeɪtɪd/ ADJECTIVE approximate □ *An estimated 650,000 people have died as a result of the war.* (estimado)

• **estimation** /ˌestɪˈmeɪʃən/ NOUN **in my estimation** in my opinion or judgment □ *She's really gone up in my estimation* (= I admire her more now than I did before). (na minha opinião)

estranged /ɪˈstreɪndʒd/ ADJECTIVE
1 no longer living with your husband or wife (estar separado) 🔹 *his estranged wife* (esposa separada) 🔹 *her estranged husband* (marido separado)
2 no longer seeing or speaking to your family or friends □ *In the 1990s, he became estranged from his family.* (estar brigado)

estrogen /ˈiːstrədʒən/ NOUN, NO PLURAL the US spelling of **oestrogen** (estrogênio)

estuary /ˈestjʊəri/ NOUN [plural **estuaries**] the wide part of a river where it flows into the sea. A geography word. (estuário)

etc or **etc.** /ɪtˈsetərə/ ABBREVIATION used after a list to show that there are other similar things that you have not mentioned □ *The art shop sells paints, canvases, brushes, etc.* (etc.)

etch /etʃ/ VERB [**etches, etching, etched**] to cut writing or images into a hard surface such as stone or metal (entalhar)
♦ IDIOM **be etched on your memory/mind** if something bad is etched on your memory or mind, you cannot forget it (estar gravado na memória)

• **etching** /ˈetʃɪŋ/ NOUN [plural **etchings**] a picture made using a print from a piece of metal that has the picture cut into it (entalhe)

eternal /ɪˈtɜːnəl/ ADJECTIVE
1 lasting forever, or seeming to last forever □ *the eternal cycle of the seasons* (eterna) 🔹 *the secret of eternal youth* (juventude eterna)
2 always being a particular type of person □ *Max is the eternal optimist.* (eterno)

• **eternally** /ɪˈtɜːnəli/ ADVERB forever (eternamente) 🔹 *I'm eternally grateful to you for all your help.* (eternamente grato)

• **eternity** /ɪˈtɜːnəti/ NOUN, NO PLURAL
1 all of time, that never ends (eternidade)
2 a very long time □ *After what seemed an eternity, she spoke.* (eternidade)

ethic /ˈeθɪk/ NOUN [plural **ethics**]
1 ethics rules about what is right and wrong □ *Journalists must follow a code of ethics.* (ético)
2 a belief or principle that affects the way someone behaves (ética) 🔹 *I admire her work ethic.* (ética profissional)

• **ethical** /ˈeθɪkəl/ ADJECTIVE
1 involving rules about what is right and wrong □ *ethical standards* (ético)
2 morally right □ *ethical consumers* (ético)

ethnic /ˈeθnɪk/ ADJECTIVE to do with a group of people who have the same race and culture (étnico) 🔹 *The Pashtuns form the main ethnic group of Afghanistan.* (grupo étnico)

ethnic minority /ˌeθnɪk maɪˈnɒrəti/ NOUN [plural **ethnic minorities**] a group of people who all have the same race or culture, living in a place where most people have a different race or culture (minoria étnica)

etiquette

etiquette /ˈetɪket/ NOUN, NO PLURAL a set of rules to do with polite behaviour (**etiqueta**)

EU /ˌiːˈjuː/ ABBREVIATION the EU the European Union; a political and economic organization of European countries (**abreviação de European Union – União Europeia**)

eucalyptus /ˌjuːkəˈlɪptəs/ NOUN [plural **eucalyptuses** or **eucalypti**] a tree with leaves containing oil that has a strong smell, used in medicines (**eucalipto**)

euphemism /ˈjuːfəmɪzəm/ NOUN [plural **euphemisms**] a polite word or phrase that you use instead of a more direct one, to talk about something unpleasant □ He never talked about dying, preferring the euphemism 'pass away'. (**eufemismo**)

euphoria /juːˈfɔːriə/ NOUN, NO PLURAL a feeling of great excitement and happiness (**euforia**)
- **euphoric** /juːˈfɒrɪk/ ADJECTIVE feeling very excited and happy (**eufórico**)

euro /ˈjʊərəʊ/ NOUN [plural **euros**] the main unit of money in many European countries □ There are 100 cents in a euro. (**euro**)

European /ˌjʊərəˈpiːən/ ▶ ADJECTIVE belonging to or from Europe (**europeu**)
▶ NOUN [plural **Europeans**] a person from Europe (**europeu**)

European Union /ˌjʊərəˌpiːən ˈjuːnjən/ NOUN, NO PLURAL the European Union a political and economic organization of European countries (**União Europeia**)

euthanasia /ˌjuːθəˈneɪziə/ NOUN, NO PLURAL when someone helps a very old or ill person to die, so that they will not suffer any longer (**eutanásia**)

evacuate /ɪˈvækjueɪt/ VERB [**evacuates, evacuating, evacuated**] to leave a place because it is dangerous, or to make people leave a place because it is dangerous □ Hundreds of people had to evacuate their homes during the floods. □ Residents were evacuated from the areas affected by the fires. (**evacuar**)
- **evacuation** /ɪˌvækjuˈeɪʃən/ NOUN [plural **evacuations**] the act of evacuating people or a place (**evacuação**)
- **evacuee** /ɪˌvækjuˈiː/ NOUN [plural **evacuees**] someone who has been evacuated from a place, especially during a war (**evacuado**)

evade /ɪˈveɪd/ VERB [**evades, evading, evaded**]
1 to avoid being caught or noticed. A formal word. □ He managed to evade capture for 13 months before the police found him. (**evitar**)
2 to avoid dealing with something that you should deal with. A formal word. □ The opposition have accused him of evading responsibility. (**esquivar-se**)

evening

evaluate /ɪˈvæljueɪt/ VERB [**evaluates, evaluating, evaluated**] to decide how good or useful something is. A formal word. □ Studies will evaluate the performance of the new drug. (**avaliar**)

evaporate /ɪˈvæpəreɪt/ VERB [**evaporates, evaporating, evaporated**] if liquid evaporates, it turns into gas or steam. A chemistry word. (**evaporar**)
- **evaporation** /ɪˌvæpəˈreɪʃən/ NOUN, NO PLURAL when liquid evaporates. A chemistry word. (**evaporação**)

evasion /ɪˈveɪʒən/ NOUN [plural **evasions**] when someone tries to avoid dealing with something, or being caught (**evasão**) 🔁 He was charged with tax evasion. (**evasão de tributos**)
- **evasive** /ɪˈveɪsɪv/ ADJECTIVE not answering questions directly or honestly □ She became evasive when I asked her why she had left the job. 🔁 He gave a rather evasive answer. (**evasivo**)
- **evasively** /ɪˈveɪsɪvli/ ADVERB in an evasive way □ 'I can't remember,' said Phil evasively. (**evasivamente**)

eve /iːv/ NOUN [plural **eves**]
1 the day or evening before a particular day □ He died on the eve of his 80th birthday. (**véspera**)
2 Eve used in the names of some days that come before an important day □ Christmas Eve □ New Year's Eve (**véspera**)

even /ˈiːvən/ ▶ ADVERB
1 used to emphasize another word □ It was even colder the next morning. □ Max is even better than Adam at football. □ Even Pia seemed to be enjoying herself. (**até**)
2 even though although □ She still tried to help him, even though he was so rude to her. (**ainda que, mesmo que**)
3 even if used to say that what you are going to say next would not change anything □ Grandad wouldn't go on holiday even if we paid for it. (**mesmo que**)
▶ ADJECTIVE
1 an even surface is level and smooth (**liso**)
2 equal □ The scores were even. (**quite**)
3 regular and not changing □ The wine must be stored at an even temperature. (**constante**)
4 an even number is one that can be divided by 2 (**par**)
◆ PHRASAL VERB [**evens, evening, evened**] **even (something) out**
1 to become level □ The track evened out once we got over the hill. (**nivelar**)
2 to become equal □ Sometimes she works more and sometimes I do – it evens out in the end. (**igualar**)

evening /ˈiːvnɪŋ/ NOUN [plural **evenings**] the last part of the day, before the night begins (**noite**) 🔁 What are you doing this evening? (**esta noite**) 🔁 We're going to the cinema on Friday evening.

(sexta-feira à noite) 🗣 *They usually watch TV in the evening.* (à noite) 🗣 *What time do you usually have your evening meal?* (jantar)

evenly /ˈiːvənli/ ADVERB
1 in an even or smooth way □ *Spread the icing evenly over the top of the cake.* (de maneira uniforme)
2 in a way that is equal □ *The two teams were evenly matched.* (equitativamente)

event /ɪˈvent/ NOUN [plural **events**]
1 something that happens (evento, acontecimento) 🗣 *These events occurred in the 19th century.* (eventos) 🗣 *Recent events have made it necessary to introduce new rules.* (acontecimentos recentes) 🗣 *Millions of people watched the events unfold (= happen) on TV.* (desenrolar dos eventos)
2 something such as sport or entertainment that is organized □ *The next event is the men's relay.* (evento) 🗣 *This is the biggest event ever staged in the city.* (evento encenado) 🗣 *The main event this evening is a display of horse riding.* (evento principal)
3 in the event of a formal phrase meaning if something happens □ *In the event of an emergency, follow these instructions.* (na eventualidade)
4 in any event whatever happens □ *The train was late, but in any event we'd never have got there on time.* (em todo caso)

• **eventful** /ɪˈventfʊl/ ADJECTIVE full of interesting events □ *She's led an eventful life.* (memorável)

eventual /ɪˈventʃuəl/ ADJECTIVE happening at the end of a period of time or as a result of a process □ *They lost the match to the eventual winners, Liverpool.* (final)

• **eventuality** /ɪˌventʃuˈæləti/ NOUN [plural **eventualities**] something bad that might happen. A formal word. □ *We need to be prepared for every eventuality.* (eventualidade)

• **eventually** /ɪˈventʃuəli/ ADVERB at the end of a period of time or as a result of a process □ *The bus eventually arrived, half an hour late.* (finalmente)

ever /ˈevə(r)/ ADVERB
1 at any time or at all □ *Have you ever been to France?* □ *Nobody ever offers to help me.* □ *It was the most delicious meal ever.* □ *If you are ever in Edinburgh, do come and see me.* (jamais)
2 bigger/happier, etc. than ever bigger/happier, etc. than at any time before □ *The music was louder than ever.* (maior, mais feliz etc. do que nunca)
3 ever since since the time when □ *He's been unhappy ever since he started at his new school.* (desde então)
4 ever so/ever such a very □ *It's ever so hot in here.* □ *He's ever such a nice boy.* (muito)
5 for ever for all future time □ *I'm sure we'll be friends for ever.* (sempre)

evergreen /ˈevəɡriːn/ ▶ ADJECTIVE evergreen plants and trees do not lose their leaves in the winter. A biology word. (perene)
▶ NOUN [plural **evergreens**] an evergreen plant or tree (sempre-viva)

everlasting /ˌevəˈlɑːstɪŋ/ ADJECTIVE lasting for ever □ *everlasting love* (eterno)

every /ˈevri/ DETERMINER
1 all the people or things □ *Every runner will get a medal for taking part.* □ *There were eight cakes on the plate, and she ate every one.* (tudo, todos)
2 every day/week/three hours, etc. used to show how often something happens □ *He does 200 pressups every day.* (a cada dia, semana, três horas etc.)
3 every so often/every now and then sometimes □ *He comes to visit us every now and then.* (às vezes)
4 every other day/evening, etc. on one of each two days/evenings, etc. □ *I only have to work every other day.* (a cada...)

➤ Remember that every is followed by a singular noun: □ *Every student in the group owns a mobile phone.*

everybody /ˈevriˌbɒdi/ PRONOUN everyone □ *I thought everybody liked ice cream.* □ *Could everybody listen, please?* (todo mundo)

everyday /ˈevrideɪ/ ADJECTIVE normal and happening often (dia a dia, rotina) 🗣 *Acts of violence are an everyday occurrence for these people.* (acontecimentos de rotina) 🗣 *Mobile phones have become part of everyday life for many children.* (vida de rotina)

everyone /ˈevriwʌn/ PRONOUN
1 every person □ *Everyone likes Jonathan.* □ *I knew everyone at the party.* (todos) 🗣 *Everyone else (= all other people) had left by this point.* (todos os outros)
2 people generally □ *Surely everyone likes chocolate.* □ *Everyone wants to be liked.* (todo mundo)

everything /ˈevriθɪŋ/ PRONOUN
1 all the things in a place or situation □ *Everything in the room was covered in dust.* (tudo) 🗣 *We kept the books, and threw everything else in the bin.* (tudo mais)
2 life in general □ *Is everything okay?* □ *Everything seems worse when you're tired.* (tudo)

everywhere /ˈevriweə(r)/ ADVERB in or to every place □ *We looked everywhere but couldn't find it.* □ *They go everywhere together.* (em todo lugar, por toda parte)

evict /ɪˈvɪkt/ VERB [**evicts, evicting, evicted**] to force someone to leave a home or an area of land □ *Fourteen families were evicted from land they had farmed for generations.* (expulsar)

- **eviction** /ɪˈvɪkʃən/ NOUN [plural **evictions**] when someone is evicted from their home or land (**expulsão**)

evidence /ˈevɪdəns/ NOUN, NO PLURAL
1 facts or objects that help to prove something □ *His body was examined and no evidence of the disease found.* (**evidência, prova**)
2 facts or statements that help people in a court of law to decide if someone has committed a crime or not □ *Mr Gleeson was the only witness to give evidence yesterday.* (**evidência**)

- **evident** /ˈevɪdənt/ ADJECTIVE obvious or easy to understand □ *It was evident that she was unhappy.* (**evidente**)

- **evidently** /ˈevɪdəntlɪ/ ADVERB
1 obviously □ *Howard was evidently confused by her answer.* (**evidentemente**)
2 used for saying that something is probably true, based on the information that you have □ *Evidently, there had been some sort of argument.* (**evidentemente**)

evil /ˈiːvəl/ ▶ ADJECTIVE morally very bad and cruel □ *an evil man* □ *This was an evil act.* (**mau**)
▶ NOUN, NO PLURAL evil actions generally □ *So are we all capable of evil?* (**mal**)

evoke /ɪˈvəʊk/ VERB [**evokes, evoking, evoked**] to make a particular memory or feeling come into your mind. A formal word. (**evocar, incitar**) *This place evokes so many memories.* (**evoca memórias**)

evolution /ˌiːvəˈluːʃən/ NOUN, NO PLURAL the process by which animals and plants change over many thousands of years in order to suit their environment (**evolução**)

- **evolve** /ɪˈvɒlv/ VERB [**evolves, evolving, evolved**]
1 animals and plants evolve when they change very gradually over many thousands of years (**evoluir**)
2 if something evolves, it gradually changes over time (**evoluir**)

ewe /juː/ NOUN [plural **ewes**] an adult female sheep (**ovelha**)

ex- /eks/ PREFIX
1 ex- is added to the beginning of words to mean 'outside' □ *exterior* (**ex-**)
2 ex- is added to the beginning of words to mean 'former' □ *an ex-president* □ *his ex-girlfriend* (**ex-**)

exacerbate /ɪɡˈzæsəbeɪt/ VERB [**exacerbates, exacerbating, exacerbated**] to make something worse. A formal word. □ *Bad weather only exacerbated the problem.* (**exacerbar**)

exact /ɪɡˈzækt/ ADJECTIVE accurate in every way □ *Those were his exact words.* □ *I don't recall the exact date.* □ *The exact amount of money was never stated.* □ *This is an exact copy of the document.* (**exato**)

- **exactly** /ɪɡˈzæktlɪ/ ADVERB
1 used when saying prices, amounts, the time, etc. that are completely accurate □ *That comes to £10 exactly.* □ *It's five o'clock exactly.* (**exatamente**)
2 in every way □ *That's exactly what I was thinking.* □ *He looks exactly like his father.* (**exatamente**) *The coats look exactly the same to me.* (**exatamente o mesmo**)
3 used for agreeing strongly with what someone has said □ *'She should be pleased she's got a job.' 'Exactly.'* (**exatamente**)
4 not exactly used for saying that what someone says is not completely right □ *'You're a nurse, aren't you?' 'Well, not exactly; I work in an old people's home.'* (**não exatamente**)

exaggerate /ɪɡˈzædʒəreɪt/ VERB [**exaggerates, exaggerating, exaggerated**] to say that something is more extreme than it really is □ *He's not that fat – you're exaggerating!* □ *The media have exaggerated the scale of the problem.* (**exagerar**)

- **exaggeration** /ɪɡˌzædʒəˈreɪʃən/ NOUN [plural **exaggerations**] when you exaggerate □ *It's a slight exaggeration to call them enemies – they just don't especially like each other.* (**exagero**)

exam /ɪɡˈzæm/ NOUN [plural **exams**] an important test of someone's knowledge or ability (**exame**) *I'm taking my final exams in June* (**fazer exames**) *She passed her exams.* (**passou nos exames**) *What if he fails his exams?* (**reprovou nos exames**)

- **examination** /ɪɡˌzæmɪˈneɪʃən/ NOUN [plural **examinations**]
1 a formal word that means exam (**exame**)
2 when a doctor looks carefully at your body to see if there is anything wrong (**exame**)
3 NO PLURAL when someone looks carefully at something □ *On closer examination, the painting turned out to be a copy.* (**investigação**)

- **examine** /ɪɡˈzæmɪn/ VERB [**examines, examining, examined**]
1 to look at something carefully □ *The sample was examined under a microscope.* (**examinar**)
2 if a doctor examines you, he or she looks carefully at your body to see if there is anything wrong □ *The doctor examined her throat and ears.* (**examinar**)
3 to consider something carefully □ *Police are examining the possibility that the driver may have fallen asleep.* (**investigar**)

- **examiner** /ɪɡˈzæmɪnə(r)/ NOUN [plural **examiners**] someone whose job is to test people's knowledge or ability (**examinador**)

example /ɪɡˈzɑːmpəl/ NOUN [plural **examples**]
1 something which has all the features or qualities of the type of thing that you are talking about □ *This is a typical example of a building from this period.* (**exemplo**) *Let me give you an example of what I mean.* (**dar um exemplo**)
2 for example used for giving an example of something □ *People drive unnecessarily. Jo, for example, drives to her friend's house which is 10 minutes' walk away.* (**por exemplo**)

3 good behaviour that other people should copy (exemplo) ▸ *You should set an example to the younger children (= behave in a good way that they can copy).* (**servir de exemplo**)

exasperate /ɪɡˈzɑːspəreɪt/ VERB [**exasperates, exasperating, exasperated**] to make you feel annoyed because you cannot do what you want to do (**exasperar**)

- **exasperated** /ɪɡˈzɑːspəreɪtəd/ ADJECTIVE annoyed because you cannot do what you want to do ▸ *She gave an exasperated sigh.* (**exasperado**)

- **exasperating** /ɪɡˈzɑːspəreɪtɪŋ/ ADJECTIVE making you feel exasperated ▸ *It's so exasperating when she won't listen to you.* (**exasperante**)

- **exasperation** /ɪɡˌzɑːspəˈreɪʃən/ NOUN, NO PLURAL when you feel exasperated (**exasperação**)

excavate /ˈekskəveɪt/ VERB [**excavates, excavating, excavated**] to dig in the ground in order to find things from the past ▸ *They are currently excavating the site.* (**escavar**)

- **excavation** /ˌekskəˈveɪʃən/ NOUN [plural **excavations**] when people excavate in order to find things from the past (**escavação**)

exceed /ɪkˈsiːd/ VERB [**exceeds, exceeding, exceeded**]
1 to be greater than a particular limit or amount ▸ *He exceeded the speed limit by 30 kilometres per hour.* (**exceder**)
2 exceed your expectations to be better than you expected ▸ *This year's profit exceeded our expectations.* (**superar as expectativas**)

- **exceedingly** /ɪkˈsiːdɪŋli/ ADVERB a formal word that means extremely ▸ *Both men played exceedingly well.* (**extremamente**)

excel /ɪkˈsel/ VERB [**excels, excelling, excelled**] to be extremely good at something. A formal word. ▸ *He excels in sport and music.* (**destacar-se**)

- **excellence** /ˈeksələns/ NOUN, NO PLURAL the quality of being excellent ▸ *educational excellence* (**excelência**)

- **excellent** /ˈeksələnt/ ADJECTIVE
1 extremely good or of a very high standard ▸ *Her work is excellent.* (**excelente**)
2 used for showing that you are pleased about something ▸ *'I've finished writing the report.' 'Excellent!'* (**excelente**)

except /ɪkˈsept/ PREPOSITION, CONJUNCTION not including something ▸ *He works every day except Sunday.* ▸ *+ that I feel better now, except that my head still hurts a bit.* ▸ *+ for Everyone stayed, except for the children.* (**exceto**)

- **exception** /ɪkˈsepʃən/ NOUN [plural **exceptions**]
1 something that is not the same as the others in a group, and so cannot be included in a statement about them ▸ *With a few exceptions, the people were very friendly.* ▸ *There is one exception to this rule.* (**exceção**)
2 make an exception to say that one person does not have to follow a particular rule ▸ *You're not really supposed to leave the room during the lesson, but I'll make an exception for you.* (**abrir uma exceção**)

- **exceptional** /ɪkˈsepʃənəl/ ADJECTIVE
1 very good or special ▸ *She showed exceptional courage.* (**excepcional**)
2 not likely to happen often ▸ *Surgery can be considered only in exceptional circumstances.* (**excepcional**)

- **exceptionally** /ɪkˈsepʃənəli/ ADVERB extremely or in a way that is unusual ▸ *You've all done exceptionally well.* (**excepcionalmente**)

excerpt /ˈeksɜːpt/ NOUN [plural **excerpts**] a short piece that has been taken from a book, film, piece of music etc. (**excerto**)

excess ▸ NOUN /ɪkˈses/ [plural **excesses**]
1 too much of something ▸ *There was an excess of fat in his blood.* (**excesso**)
2 in excess of more than a particular amount ▸ *The football club has debts in excess of £10 million.* (**ultrapassar**)
3 to excess if you do something to excess, you do it too much ▸ *Chips and ice cream were top of the list of items which children eat to excess.* (**exagerar**)
4 excesses bad or harmful things which someone does too much ▸ *She was trying to lose weight after the excesses of the holiday.* (**excessos**)
▸ ADJECTIVE /ˈekses/ more than you want, or more than is allowed (**excesso**) ▸ *Many airlines charge you for excess baggage.* (**excesso de bagagem**)

- **excessive** /ɪkˈsesɪv/ ADJECTIVE too much or too great ▸ *Police officers are not allowed to use excessive force when arresting someone.* (**excessivo**)

exchange /ɪksˈtʃeɪndʒ/ ▸ VERB [**exchanges, exchanging, exchanged**]
1 to give someone something and take something from them ▸ *We exchanged rings as a sign of our friendship.* ▸ *They exchanged phone numbers.* ▸ *We only exchanged a few words (= spoke for a short time).* ▸ *This website enables us to exchange information.* (**trocar**)
2 to take something back to a shop and get something else instead ▸ *+ for I'd like to exchange these trousers for a smaller size.* (**trocar**)
3 to do something to someone who does the same to you ▸ *They exchanged amused glances.* ▸ *During the argument, blows were exchanged (= they hit each other).* (**trocar**)
4 to change money to the money of another country ▸ *I want to exchange these dollars for euros.* (**trocar**)
▸ NOUN [plural **exchanges**]
1 in exchange for something if you do something or give something in exchange for something, you do it or give it to get that thing ▸ *He took bribes in exchange for passing on information.* (**em troca de algo**)

2 when you give something to someone and take something from them □ **+ of** *The exchange of food is a symbol of our community.* (troca)

3 a conversation, often an angry one (discussão) 🔳 *He had a heated exchange* (= angry conversation) *with his boss.* (discussão acalorada)

excite /ɪkˈsaɪt/ VERB [**excites, exciting, excited**] to make someone feel excited (excitar)

- **excited** /ɪkˈsaɪtɪd/ ADJECTIVE feeling very happy and not calm because something good is going to happen (empolgado) 🔳 *He was getting excited about the party.* (ficando animado) □ **+ about** *It was my first trip to the US and I was really excited about it.* □ **+ to do something** *I'm excited to be part of the team.*

- **excitedly** /ɪkˈsaɪtɪdli/ ADVERB in an excited way □ *The dog jumped around excitedly.* (excitadamente)

- **excitement** /ɪkˈsaɪtmənt/ NOUN, NO PLURAL the feeling of being excited (excitação) 🔳 *The news caused great excitement.* (grande excitação) □ *In her excitement, she had forgotten something important.* □ **+ of** *I still remember the excitement of winning the competition.*

- **exciting** /ɪkˈsaɪtɪŋ/ ADJECTIVE making you feel excited □ *an exciting opportunity* □ **+ to do something** *The game was exciting to watch.* (excitante)

> ▶ Remember the difference between the words **excited** and **exciting**. If you are **excited**, you are very happy because something good is going to happen. Something that is **exciting** makes you feel excited: □ *I was so excited during that game.* □ *It was such an exciting game.*

exclaim /ɪkˈskleɪm/ VERB [**exclaims, exclaiming, exclaimed**] to say something suddenly and loudly because you are surprised, angry, etc. □ *'What a wonderful surprise!' she exclaimed.* (exclamar)

- **exclamation** /ˌekskləˈmeɪʃən/ NOUN [plural **exclamations**] something you say suddenly or loudly because you are surprised, angry, etc. □ *Vicky gave an exclamation of delight.* (exclamação)

exclamation mark /ˌekskləˈmeɪʃən ˌmɑːk/ NOUN [plural **exclamation marks**] a punctuation mark (!) that you write after an exclamation (ponto de exclamação)

exclude /ɪkˈskluːd/ VERB [**excludes, excluding, excluded**]

1 to not allow someone to take part in something or go into a place □ *Paul was excluded from school for a week as a punishment.* (excluir, expulsar)

2 to deliberately not include something □ *The figures exclude children under the age of twelve.* (excluir)

3 to decide that something cannot be possible (eliminar) 🔳 *He had blood tests to exclude the possibility of an infection.* (excluir a possibilidade)

- **excluding** /ɪkˈskluːdɪŋ/ PREPOSITION not including someone or something □ *The hotel costs £70 a night excluding meals.* (sem, que não inclui)

- **exclusion** /ɪkˈskluːʒən/ NOUN [plural **exclusions**]

1 when someone is not allowed to take part in something or go into a place □ *If found guilty, he risks exclusion from the team.* (exclusão)

2 something that is deliberately not included □ *Insurance policies usually contain some exclusions.* (exclusão)

3 to the exclusion of if you do something to the exclusion of something else, you do it so much that you do not have time for the other thing. A formal phrase. □ *His obsession with golf to the exclusion of his family was the reason his wife divorced him.* (à exclusão de, deixar de lado)

- **exclusive** /ɪkˈskluːsɪv/ ▶ ADJECTIVE

1 available only for one person or for one group of people □ *On Wednesdays, women are given exclusive access to the spa.* (exclusivo)

2 expensive, and designed for people who have a lot of money □ *an exclusive restaurant* (exclusivo)

3 published in only one newspaper, or shown on only one television station (exclusivo) 🔳 *Kewell did an exclusive interview with Channel Nine.* (entrevista exclusiva)

4 exclusive of not including something □ *It costs £20, exclusive of postage.* (sem inclusão de)

▶ NOUN [plural **exclusives**] a story that is published by only one newspaper or magazine, or reported by only one television station (reportagem ou entrevista exclusiva)

- **exclusively** /ɪkˈskluːsɪvli/ ADVERB only □ *The stadium is used exclusively for big international events.* (exclusivamente)

excrement /ˈekskrɪmənt/ NOUN, NO PLURAL a formal word meaning the solid waste from a person's or animal's body (excremento)

excrete /ekˈskriːt/ VERB [**excretes, excreting, excreted**] to get rid of waste from your body. A biology word. □ *The drug causes the kidneys to excrete water and salt.* (evacuar)

- **excretion** /ekˈskriːʃən/ NOUN [plural **excretions**] excreting something, or something that is excreted. A biology word. (excreção, evacuação)

excruciating /ɪkˈskruːʃieɪtɪŋ/ ADJECTIVE

1 extremely painful (doloroso)

2 used for emphasizing how bad something is □ *He told us about his holiday in excruciating detail.* (excruciante)

excursion /ɪkˈskɜːʃən/ NOUN [plural **excursions**] a short visit to a place □ *They were on a school excursion to the theatre.* (excursão)

excusable /ɪkˈskjuːzəbəl/ ADJECTIVE if something bad is excusable, you can understand why someone did it, and forgive them □ *His behaviour was excusable because he was tired.* (perdoável)

excuse

excuse ▶ NOUN /ɪk'skju:s/ [plural **excuses**]
1 a reason you give to explain why you did something wrong or did not do something (desculpa) ▣ *I'm sick of you making excuses about your work.* (dando desculpas) ▣ *He's late again – he'd better have a good excuse this time!* (boa desculpa) ☐ **+ for** *There's no excuse for this sort of behaviour.*
2 a reason to do or have something that you want (desculpa) ▣ *She was just looking for an excuse to stop working.* ☐ *His promotion was a good excuse for a party.* (procurando uma desculpa)
▶ VERB /ɪk'skju:z/ [**excuses, excusing, excused**]
1 excuse me (a) something that you say to get someone's attention ☐ *Excuse me, could you tell me the way to the library?* ☐ *Excuse me, Susan, there's someone on the phone for you.* (b) used to say sorry ☐ *Oh, excuse me, I didn't realize this seat was taken.* (com licença)
2 to forgive someone for doing something, especially something that is not serious ☐ *Please excuse the mess in here.* ☐ *I hope you'll excuse us being late.* (desculpar)
3 to be a reason why someone does something bad ☐ *Having a headache doesn't excuse her rudeness.* (justificar)
4 if you are excused something, you are allowed not to do it ☐ **+ from** *Could I be excused from tennis today, as I don't feel well?* (dispensar)

execute /'eksɪkju:t/ VERB [**executes, executing, executed**]
1 to kill someone as an official punishment ☐ *Many of the prisoners were executed.* (executar)
2 a formal word meaning to do something that has been ordered or planned ☐ *We continue to execute our business plan.* (executar)
• **execution** /,eksɪ'kju:ʃən/ NOUN [plural **executions**]
1 killing someone as an official punishment ☐ *He is facing execution for his role in the terrorist bombings.* (execução)
2 when someone does something that has been ordered or planned. A formal word. ☐ *They tried to block the execution of a High Court order.* (execução)
• **executioner** /,eksɪ'kju:ʃənə(r)/ NOUN [plural **executioners**] someone whose job is to kill criminals as an official punishment (carrasco)

executive /ɪg'zekjutɪv/ ▶ NOUN [plural **executives**] someone who has an important job in a company ☐ *senior executives of British Airways*
▶ ADJECTIVE
1 to do with making important decisions in a company ☐ *the executive committee* (executivo)
2 designed for rich people who have important jobs ☐ *an executive jet* (executivo)

exemplary /ɪg'zemplərɪ/ ADJECTIVE a formal word which describes something that is so good that other people should copy it ☐ *Ralf carried out his duties in an exemplary manner.* (exemplar)

exemplify /ɪg'zemplɪfaɪ/ VERB [**exemplifies, exemplifying, exemplified**] to be a typical example of something. A formal word. ☐ *He exemplified many qualities which people admire.* (exemplificar)

exempt /ɪg'zempt/ ▶ ADJECTIVE allowed not to do something such as obey a law or pay for something ☐ *Non-UK residents are exempt from the tax.* (isento)
▶ VERB [**exempts, exempting, exempted**] to give someone permission not to do something that other people must do ☐ *Teachers were exempted from military service.* (isentar)
• **exemption** /ɪg'zempʃən/ NOUN [plural **exemptions**] being exempt from something ☐ *tax exemptions* (isenção)

exercise

exercise /'eksəsaɪz/ ▶ NOUN [plural **exercises**]
1 NO PLURAL physical activities done to keep your body strong and healthy (exercício) ▣ *We should all take more exercise.* (fazer exercício) ▣ *Regular exercise will help to control your weight.* (exercícios regulares)
2 a particular movement done to make your body strong and healthy ☐ *We did some stretching exercises.* ☐ *This exercise works the stomach muscles.* (exercício)
3 a piece of written work you do when you are studying ☐ *Please do exercise 4 in your grammar book.* ☐ *This exercise deals with prepositions.* (exercício)
4 an activity that is intended to achieve something (exercício) ▣ *The object of the exercise was to impress his boss.* (o objetivo do exercício) ☐ *Our staff see this as an exercise in cutting costs.*
5 an activity done by a military organization to prepare for war ▣ *Their forces have been conducting* (= doing) *joint exercises for about ten years.* (conduzindo exercícios)
▶ VERB [**exercises, exercising, exercised**]
1 to do exercises to make you strong and healthy (exercitar, fazer exercício) ▣ *I try to exercise regularly.* (exercitar regularmente) ☐ *You should try to exercise the damaged joints.*
2 to use something (exercer) ▣ *Travellers have been told to exercise caution* (= be careful) *in the region* (exercer cautela) ▣ *I intend to exercise my right to vote in the election.* (exercer meu direito)

exert /ɪg'zɜ:t/ VERB [**exerts, exerting, exerted**]
1 to use your influence or power to make something happen ☐ *Government leaders are exerting pressure on the country to stop its military operations.* (exercer)
2 exert yourself to use a lot of effort and energy (esforçar-se)
• **exertion** /ɪg'zɜ:ʃən/ NOUN [plural **exertions**] when you use a lot of physical or mental energy ☐ *I stood there, breathless with exertion.* (esforço)

exhale /eks'heɪl/ VERB [exhales, exhaling, exhaled] a formal word meaning to breathe air out through your nose or mouth (**exalar**)

exhaust /ɪg'zɔːst/ ▶ VERB [exhausts, exhausting, exhausted]
1 to make someone very tired ☐ *Normally that jog would have exhausted me.* (**esgotar**)
2 to use all of something ☐ *They have exhausted all their legal options.* ☐ *The city is exhausting its supply of water.* (**esgotar**)
▶ NOUN [plural exhausts]
1 the pipe on a vehicle which waste gas come out of (**escapamento**)
2 the waste gas that comes out of a vehicle (**escapamento**) 🔵 *exhaust fumes* (**fumaça de escapamento**)

• **exhausted** /ɪg'zɔːstɪd/ ADJECTIVE extremely tired ☐ *She was completely exhausted by the time she got home.* (**exausto**)

• **exhausting** /ɪg'zɔːstɪŋ/ ADJECTIVE making you feel extremely tired ☐ *It was an exhausting climb.* (**esgotante**)

• **exhaustion** /ɪg'zɔːstʃən/ NOUN, NO PLURAL a feeling of extreme tiredness ☐ *The singer cancelled his tour because of stress and exhaustion.* (**exaustão**)

• **exhaustive** /ɪg'zɔːstɪv/ ADJECTIVE done very carefully and completely ☐ *Police made an exhaustive search of the area.* (**exaustivo**)

exhibit /ɪg'zɪbɪt/ ▶ NOUN [plural exhibits] something that people go to see in a place such as a museum ☐ *The sculpture is the newest exhibit at London's National Gallery.* (**objeto em exposição**)
▶ VERB [exhibits, exhibiting, exhibited]
1 a formal word meaning to show a quality or feeling ☐ *She began to exhibit symptoms of poisoning.* (**demonstrar**)
2 to show something in a place such as a museum ☐ *Julia exhibits her paintings at a small local gallery.* (**expor**)

• **exhibition** /ˌeksɪ'bɪʃən/ NOUN [plural exhibitions]
1 a show where people go to see paintings, photographs, etc. (**exposição**) 🔵 *an art exhibition* (**exposição de arte**) ☐ + *of The museum will be holding an exhibition of works by Monet.*
2 on exhibition if things such as paintings or photographs are on exhibition, people can go to see them ☐ *This remarkable jewellery was recently on exhibition in Paris.* (**em exposição**)
3 an exhibition of something when someone or something shows a particular skill, feeling, etc. ☐ *The rescue had been an exhibition of pure courage.* (**uma exibição de algo**)

• **exhibitor** /ɪg'zɪbɪtə(r)/ NOUN [plural exhibitors] someone who exhibits their work (**expositor**)

exhilarated /ɪg'zɪləreɪtɪd/ ADJECTIVE feeling excited and full of energy ☐ *You could see the experience had left him exhilarated.* (**estimulado**)

• **exhilarating** /ɪg'zɪləreɪtɪŋ/ ADJECTIVE making you feel exhilarated ☐ *We had an exhilarating ride across the fields.* (**estimulante**)

• **exhilaration** /ɪgˌzɪlə'reɪʃən/ NOUN, NO PLURAL a feeling of excitement and energy (**euforia**)

exile /'eksaɪl/ ▶ NOUN [plural exiles]
1 someone who has been forced to leave their country, usually for political reasons (**exílio**)
2 in exile if someone is in exile, they have been forced to live in a country that is not their own, for political reasons ☐ *The former leader is now living in exile in Japan.* (**em exílio**)
▶ VERB [exiles, exiling, exiled] if you are exiled, you are forced to leave your own country and live somewhere else, for political reasons (**exilar**)

exist /ɪg'zɪst/ VERB [exists, existing, existed]
1 to be real, or to happen ☐ *Does God really exist?* ☐ *Similar problems exist in Britain.* (**existir**)
2 to stay alive, especially in difficult conditions ☐ *It's possible to exist without food for a few days.* ☐ + *on He seems to exist on a diet of burgers and chips.* (**sobreviver**)

• **existence** /ɪg'zɪstəns/ NOUN, NO PLURAL
1 when someone or something exists ☐ *The rule was in existence for almost 40 years.* ☐ + *of We can no longer deny the existence of global warming.* (**existência**)
2 the type of life that someone has ☐ *She had a lonely and miserable existence.* (**existência**)

• **existing** /ɪg'zɪstɪŋ/ ADJECTIVE happening or present now ☐ *The existing rules apply to anyone over 18.* ☐ *Existing customers are being offered a discount.* (**existente**)

exit /'eksɪt/ ▶ NOUN [plural exits]
1 a door you go through to leave a public building or vehicle (**saída**) 🔵 *The bus has an emergency exit at the back.* (**saída de emergência**)
2 when someone leaves a place (**saída**) 🔵 *He made a quick exit.* (**saiu apressadamente**)
3 a road you use to leave a motorway or round about (= circle that vehicles drive around) (**saída**) 🔵 *Take the next exit.* (**pegue a saída**)
4 when someone leaves something such as a competition or type of work ☐ + *from The team had a shock early exit from the tournament.* ☐ *The defeat marked his exit from politics.* (**saída**)
▶ VERB [exits, exiting, exited]
1 a formal word meaning to leave a place ☐ *They exited the stadium by the west gate.* (**sair**)
2 a formal word meaning to leave something such as a competition or business ☐ *She exited the competition after losing to Lindsay Davenport.* (**abandonar, sair**)
3 to stop using a computer program ☐ *How do I exit?* (**sair**)

exodus /'eksədəs/ NOUN, NO PLURAL when a lot of people leave a place at the same time (**êxodo, retiro**) 🔵 *The lack of jobs has led to a mass exodus of young people from the area.* (**êxodo em massa**)

exonerate /ɪgˈzɒnəreɪt/ VERB [exonerates, exonerating, exonerated] to officially say that someone should not be blamed for something □ *The investigation into the accident exonerated him entirely.* (**exonerar**)

exorbitant /ɪgˈzɔːbɪtənt/ ADJECTIVE unreasonably expensive □ *Exorbitant house prices are preventing many young people from buying a house.* (**exorbitante**)

exotic /ɪgˈzɒtɪk/ ADJECTIVE interesting and unusual, and often to do with a foreign country □ *exotic animals* □ *exotic holidays* (**exótico**)

expand /ɪkˈspænd/ VERB [expands, expanding, expanded] to become bigger, or to make something become bigger □ *Many cities are expanding very rapidly.* □ *The company plans to expand its range of products.* (**expandir**)

⇨ go to **expand your horizons**

expanse /ɪkˈspæns/ NOUN [plural expanses] a large area of land, sea or sky (**extensão**) ▣ *She looked out of the window at the* vast expanse *of sky.* (**vasta extensão**)

expansion /ɪkˈspænʃən/ NOUN, NO PLURAL when something increases in size or amount □ *The rapid expansion of the airline industry has led to cheap flights.* (**expansão**)

expect /ɪkˈspekt/ VERB [expects, expecting, expected]
1 to think that something will happen or be true □ *We're expecting an announcement soon.* □ *I expect he's forgotten the meeting.* □ *I didn't expect anything like this to happen.* □ *+ to do something Sales are expected to fall next month.* □ *+ that I expect that it will be hot in Portugal.* (**esperar, acreditar**)
2 to think that something or someone will arrive □ *I'm expecting a phone call from Mary.* (**esperar**)
3 to think that something ought to happen or that you have a right to it □ *+ to do something I expect you to behave better than this.* □ *Our customers expect a first class service.* (**esperar**)
4 if you are expected to do something, you have to do it □ *We are expected to do 3 hours homework a day.* (**esperar**)
5 a woman who is expecting a baby is pregnant (**esperar**)

• **expectant** /ɪkˈspektənt/ ADJECTIVE
1 thinking that something good will happen (**expectante**)
2 an expectant mother is a pregnant woman (**expectante**)

• **expectation** /ˌekspekˈteɪʃən/ NOUN [plural expectations]
1 how you think something will be, especially when you think it will be good (**expectativa**) ▣ *We had very* high/low expectations *of our builders.* (**altas/baixas expectativas**) ▣ *The job didn't really* live up to *my* expectations. (**estava de acordo com as expectativas**) ▣ *It will be impossible to* meet *their* expectations. (**corresponder às expectativas**) ▣ *The company's profits* exceeded expectations. (**superaram as expectativas**)
2 when you expect something to happen or to be true □ *My expectation was that I would be paid for the work.* □ *He had no expectation of winning.* (**expectativa**)

expedition /ˌekspɪˈdɪʃən/ NOUN [plural expeditions] a long journey, especially to a dangerous place or to a place that has not been visited before □ *The group went on an expedition to the South Pole.* (**expedição**)

expel /ɪkˈspel/ VERB [expels, expelling, expelled]
1 to make someone leave a school, country or organization because they have done something wrong □ *John was expelled from school for hitting a teacher.* (**expulsar**)
2 a formal word meaning to force a liquid or gas out of something (**expelir**)

expend /ɪkˈspend/ VERB [expends, expending, expended] a formal word meaning to use time, energy or money □ *He didn't want to expend any more energy on the problem.* (**empregar**)

• **expendable** /ɪkˈspendəbəl/ ADJECTIVE not necessary, and possible to get rid of □ *The company had decided that 20 of its employees were expendable.* (**dispensável**)

expenditure /ɪkˈspendɪtʃə(r)/ NOUN, NO PLURAL
1 a formal word meaning the amount of money that a government, organization or person spends □ *Government expenditure on education has risen.* (**gasto**)
2 a formal word meaning the use of money, energy or time □ *The process has improved and there's now less expenditure of fuel.* (**gasto**)

expense /ɪkˈspens/ NOUN [plural expenses]
1 the money that you pay for something (**despesa**) ▣ medical/legal expenses (**despesas médicas/legais**) ▣ *The money he gave me will* cover the expense *of the transport.* (**cobrir as despesas**) ▣ *We have to* pay *our own travelling* expenses. (**pagar as despesas**)
2 the high cost of something (**custo**) ▣ *I didn't want to* go to the expense of *hiring a car.* (**arcar com os custos de**) ▣ *They repaired the painting* at great expense. ▣ *No* expense was spared (= a lot of money was spent) *to make the palace perfect.* (**custo poupado**)
3 expenses money that you spend while you are doing your job, that your employer will pay back to you (**gastos, conta**) ▣ *I can* put *the meal* on my expenses. (**colocar na minha conta**)
4 at the expense of something if one thing happens or exists at the expense of another, the second thing is damaged or destroyed by it □ *Academic achievement came at the expense of her health.* (**à custa de algo**)

• **expensive** /ɪkˈspensɪv/ ADJECTIVE costing a lot

experience

of money □ *These clothes are too expensive for me.* □ *expensive gifts/equipment* (caro)
• **expensively** /ɪkˈpensɪvli/ ADVERB in an expensive way □ *expensively dressed* (de maneira cara)

experience /ɪkˈspɪəriəns/ ▶ NOUN [plural **experiences**]

1 NO PLURAL knowledge and skill that you get by doing something or by something happening to you (experiência) 🔹 *The players have been gaining experience over the last four years.* (ganhando experiência) 🔹 *She had no experience of looking after children.* (nenhuma experiência) □ + **of** *The company is looking for someone with experience of managing budgets.*

2 in my experience used for saying what you think is true because of what life has taught you □ *In my experience, most children enjoy watching television.* (a meu ver)

3 something that happens to you (experiência) 🔹 *We had a bad experience on holiday.* (tivemos experiência) 🔹 *The whole experience was terrifying.* (toda a experiência) □ *Watching a baby being born was an amazing experience.*

▶ VERB [**experiences, experiencing, experienced**] if you experience something, it happens to you or you feel it □ *Many customers were experiencing problems with Internet access.* □ *He had never experienced such pain.* (experimentar)

• **experienced** /ɪkˈspɪəriənst/ ADJECTIVE having skill and knowledge because you have done something for a long time □ *an experienced teacher* (experiente)

experiment /ɪkˈsperɪmənt/ ▶ NOUN [plural **experiments**]

1 a scientific test to discover or prove something (experiência, experimento) 🔹 *Two experiments were conducted, using children suffering from heart problems.* (experiências conduzidas) 🔹 *The experiment shows that lack of sleep affects people's performance of basic tasks.* (experiência mostra)

2 something new which you try, to discover whether it is successful □ *This soup is a bit of an experiment.* (experimento)

▶ VERB [**experiments, experimenting, experimented**]

1 to try different things to find out what they are like □ + **with** *He experimented with various ingredients until he came up with the perfect recipe.* (fazer experiência)

2 to do scientific tests to discover or prove something □ + **on** *The team had experimented on rats.* (fazer experiência)

• **experimental** /ɪkˌsperɪˈmentəl/ ADJECTIVE
1 using new ideas and methods that have not been tested yet □ *an experimental school* (experimental)
2 to do with scientific tests □ *experimental data* (experimental)

explode

expert /ˈekspɜːt/ ▶ NOUN [plural **experts**]
someone who knows a lot about something □ *legal/health experts* □ + **on/in** *She's an expert on Middle East politics.* (perito, especialista)

▶ ADJECTIVE

1 very good at something, or knowing a lot about something □ *expert skiers* (especializado)

2 expert help or advice is given by someone who knows a lot about something (especializado) 🔹 *We took expert advice.* (conselho especializado)

• **expertise** /ˌekspɜːˈtiːz/ NOUN, NO PLURAL special skill or knowledge □ *technical expertise* (perícia)

expire /ɪkˈspaɪə(r)/ VERB [**expires, expiring, expired**] if an official document or agreement expires, the time when you can use it ends □ *Your passport expired last month.* (expirar)

• **expiry** /ɪkˈspaɪəri/ NOUN, NO PLURAL the end of the time in which you can use something (vencimento) 🔹 *The contract's expiry date is 2012.* (data de vencimento do contrato)

explain /ɪkˈspleɪn/ VERB [**explains, explaining, explained**]

1 to give someone more or simpler information so that they can understand something □ + **question word** *Could you explain what you mean?* □ + **to** *She explained the rules of the game to me.* (explicar)

2 to give or to be a reason for something □ *He was asked to explain his absence.* □ *Having a bad childhood can explain the behaviour of some criminals.* □ + **that** *She explained that she had lost her keys.* (explicar)

> ► Note that you cannot explain someone something. You must explain something to someone:
> ✓ She explained the rules to me.
> ✗ She explained me the rules.

• **explanation** /ˌekspləˈneɪʃən/ NOUN [plural **explanations**]

1 something you say or write to make something easy to understand (explicação) 🔹 *She gave an explanation of how to do it.* (deu uma explicação) □ + **of** *The teacher started with an explanation of why plants are green.*

2 a reason for something (explicação) 🔹 *The research offers several explanations for this behaviour.* (oferece explicações) □ + **for** *Is there a scientific explanation for this?*

• **explanatory** /ɪkˈsplænətəri/ ADJECTIVE explaining something □ *an explanatory note* (explicativo)

explicit /ɪkˈsplɪsɪt/ ADJECTIVE clear and exact □ *Michael gave me explicit instructions about how to do it.* (explícito)

explode /ɪkˈspləʊd/ VERB [**explodes, exploding, exploded**]

1 to burst (= break suddenly so the parts fly out) and make a very loud noise (**explodir**) 🖼 *A bomb exploded in the centre of the city.* (**bomba explodiu**) □ *The car exploded, killing two police officers.* □ *Fireworks exploded in every direction.* **2** to suddenly start shouting because you are very angry □ *He exploded with rage.* (**explodir, estourar**)

> Note that a bomb explodes. When people make a bomb explode in a building, aeroplane, etc. they blow up that building, aeroplane, etc: □ *The bomb exploded in the centre of the building.* □ *They blew up the building.*

exploit ▶ VERB /ɪkˈsplɔɪt/ [**exploits, exploiting, exploited**]
1 to use someone unfairly to help you get what you want □ *These people are often exploited as they will work for very little money.* (**explorar**)
2 to use something so that you get as much advantage as possible □ *He was keen to exploit new opportunities.* (**explorar**)
▶ NOUN /ˈeksplɔɪt/ [*plural* **exploits**] a brave or exciting thing that someone has done □ *He told us about his war time exploits.* (**proeza**)
• **exploitation** /ˌeksplɔɪˈteɪʃən/ NOUN, NO PLURAL exploiting someone or something □ *the exploitation of foreign workers* (**exploração**)

exploration /ˌekspləˈreɪʃən/ NOUN [*plural* **explorations**]
1 going to a place to find out about it □ *space exploration* (**exploração**)
2 a careful study or discussion of a subject □ *The report provides a thorough exploration of how the new law will affect schools.* (**investigação**)

explore /ɪkˈsplɔː(r)/ VERB [**explores, exploring, explored**]
1 to travel around a place and find out what it is like □ *The hotel is a good base for exploring the region.* □ *Radar technology will help us to explore the planet Mars.* (**explorar**)
2 to think about and discuss something (**investigar**) 🖼 *I'm exploring the possibility of working abroad.* (**investigando a possibilidade**) 🖼 *The charity is exploring new ways of raising money.* (**investigando novas maneiras**)
• **explorer** /ɪkˈsplɔːrə(r)/ NOUN [*plural* **explorers**] someone who travels to places that people have not been to before □ *a Polar explorer* (**explorador**)

explosion /ɪkˈspləʊʒən/ NOUN [*plural* **explosions**]
1 when something such as a bomb explodes □ *The explosion happened inside the building* (**explosão**) 🖼 *Two soldiers were killed in a roadside bomb explosion.* (**explosão de bomba**) 🖼 *He was seriously injured in a gas explosion.* (**explosão de gás**)
2 a sudden large increase in something (**explosão**) 🖼 *The population explosion was caused by immigration.* (**explosão populacional**) □ *+ of There has been an explosion of interest in American football.*
• **explosive** /ɪkˈspləʊsɪv/ ▶ ADJECTIVE
1 able to cause an explosion □ *a highly explosive gas* (**explosivo**) 🖼 *an explosive device* (**dispositivo explosivo**)
2 possibly making people become angry or violent (**explosivo**) 🖼 *a potentially explosive situation* (**potencialmente explosiva**)
▶ NOUN [*plural* **explosives**] a substance that can cause an explosion

exponent /ɪkˈspəʊnənt/ NOUN [*plural* **exponents**]
1 someone who tries to persuade other people that a principle or idea is right. A formal word. □ *He was an early exponent of women's rights.* (**expoente**)
2 a small, raised number that shows how many times an amount must be multiplied by itself. A maths word. (**expoente**)
• **exponential** /ˌekspəˈnenʃəl/ ADJECTIVE
1 an exponential increase is a very large increase. A formal word. (**exponencial**)
2 connected to a number's exponent. A maths word. (**exponencial**)

export ▶ VERB /ɪkˈspɔːt/ [**exports, exporting, exported**]
1 to sell goods to another country □ *India exports rice and wheat to many countries.* (**exportar**)
2 if you export computer information, you copy it to another place. A computing word. (**exportar**)
▶ NOUN /ˈekspɔːt/ [*plural* **exports**]
1 a product that a country sells to another country □ *Syria's main export is oil.* (**produto de exportação**)
2 the process of selling goods to another country □ *The country relies on the export of wool.* (**exportar**)
• **exporter** /ekˈspɔːtə(r)/ NOUN [*plural* **exporters**] a country or company which exports goods □ *They are the world's biggest exporter of coal.* (**exportador**)

expose /ɪkˈspəʊz/ VERB [**exposes, exposing, exposed**]
1 to show something that was covered or hidden □ *He pulled up his shirt to expose his stomach.* (**expor**)
2 to tell the public about bad or dishonest things that someone important has done □ *Journalists exposed widespread corruption in the government.* (**revelar**)
3 if someone is exposed to something harmful, they are in a place or situation where they experience it □ *He had been exposed to the virus.* (**expor**)
4 to let someone experience something □ *The idea was to expose the students to modern art.* (**expor**)

- **exposure** /ɪkˈspəʊʒə(r)/ NOUN [plural exposures]
1 being in a situation in which you experience something □ *He'd had little exposure to foreign cultures.* □ *Too much exposure to the sun is bad for the skin.* (**exposição**)
2 when something bad that someone important has done is reported in a newspaper or on television □ *He was forced to resign after the exposure of his affair.* (**revelação**)
3 a medical problem that is caused by being outside in cold weather for too long □ *The climbers were found suffering from exposure.* (**exposição**)

express /ɪkˈspres/ ▶ VERB [expresses, expressing, expressed] to show or tell people what you are thinking or feeling (**expressar**) 🔁 *He expressed his concerns about the safety of the equipment.* (**expressou preocupações**) 🔁 *She expressed strong views about education.* (**expressou opiniões**) 🔁 *Amy expressed surprise at his comments.* (**expressou surpresa**) □ *He was unable to express himself clearly.*
▶ ADJECTIVE
1 travelling fast from one place to another (**expresso**) 🔁 *an express train* (**trem expresso**) □ *The package arrived express delivery.*
2 an express wish or purpose is one that is very clear and certain. A formal word. □ *The plan cannot be carried out without the express approval of the President.* (**expresso**)
▶ NOUN [plural expresses] a train or bus that is fast because it does not stop at many places □ *We caught the express to Leeds.* (**expresso**)

- **expression** /ɪkˈspreʃən/ NOUN [plural expressions]
1 a look on your face that shows what you are thinking or feeling (**expressão**) 🔁 *I could tell by the expression on his face that he didn't believe me* (**expressão em seu rosto**) 🔁 *I couldn't read her facial expression.* (**expressão facial**) □ + *of* *Bindi put on an expression of great surprise.*
2 a word or phrase (**expressão**) 🔁 *Dieter always uses very old fashioned expressions.* (**utiliza expressões**)
3 something that you do or say as a way of showing what you feel or think □ + *of* *He wore the clothes as an expression of his faith.* (**demonstração**)

- **expressive** /ɪkˈspresɪv/ ADJECTIVE clearly showing what someone's feelings are □ *Kate has one of those expressive faces.* (**expressivo**)

- **expressly** /ɪkˈspresli/ ADVERB
1 a formal word meaning clearly and certainly (**expressamente**) 🔁 *Doctors had expressly forbidden him from flying.* (**proibiram expressamente**)
2 a formal word meaning for one particular purpose □ *I went to school expressly to talk to his teacher.* (**exclusivamente**)

expulsion /ɪkˈspʌlʃən/ NOUN [plural expulsions] being ordered to leave a place □ *He was depressed following his expulsion from university.* (**expulsão**)

exquisite /ɪkˈskwɪzɪt/ ADJECTIVE very beautiful and delicate □ *exquisite pink roses* (**refinado**)

extend /ɪkˈstend/ VERB [extends, extending, extended]
1 to make something bigger □ *We're having our kitchen extended.* □ *The airport has plans to extend the runway.* (**ampliar**)
2 to make something continue for longer □ *The contract was extended by three months.* (**prorrogar**)
3 to make something include or affect more people □ *The ban has been extended to schools.* (**estender**)
4 to cover a distance or area □ *The wall extended for about a mile.* (**estender, prolongar**)
5 a formal word meaning to stretch out your arm, hand or leg □ *She extended a hand towards me.* (**estender**)

- **extended** /ɪkˈstendɪd/ ADJECTIVE a formal word meaning continuing for a long time (**extenso, prolongado**) 🔁 *He often missed school for extended periods because of ill health.* (**período prolongado**)

- **extension** /ɪkˈstenʃən/ NOUN [plural extensions]
1 a part added to a building □ *They're building an extension at the side of the house.* (**extensão**)
2 the process of making something bigger □ *the extension of the rail network* (**ampliação**)
3 the process of making something include more people or things □ *Ministers have called for an extension of anti-terror laws.* (**anexo**)
4 extra time that is added to something □ *Can I have an extension to finish my project?* □ *a two-year contract extension* (**prorrogação**)
5 a telephone line to a particular person in an office □ *Can I have extension 4321, please?* (**extensão**)

- **extensive** /ɪkˈstensɪv/ ADJECTIVE large in size or amount (**extenso, grande**) 🔁 *The fire caused extensive damage.* (**grandes danos**) 🔁 *He has an extensive collection of rare books.* (**grande coleção**)

- **extent** /ɪkˈstent/ NOUN, NO PLURAL
1 the size or degree of something □ *What's the extent of the damage?* (**extensão**)
2 **to some extent/to a certain extent** in some ways □ *The situation has improved to some extent.* (**até certo ponto**)

exterior /ɪkˈstɪəriə(r)/ ▶ NOUN [plural exteriors]
1 the outside of something □ *The house had a very impressive exterior.* (**exterior**)
2 someone's behaviour which hides their real character □ *Behind that tough exterior is a very shy girl.* (**aspecto**)
▶ ADJECTIVE on or for the outside of something □ *exterior walls* (**exterior**)
⇨ go to **interior**

exterminate /ɪkˈstɜːmɪneɪt/ VERB [**exterminates, exterminating, exterminated**] to kill all of a particular group of animals or people (**exterminar**)

external /ɪkˈstɜːnəl/ ADJECTIVE
1 on the outside of a person or thing □ *The building has external lighting.* (**externo**)
2 from outside a particular country, organization etc. □ *The university applied for external funding.* (**externo**)

extinct /ɪkˈstɪŋkt/ ADJECTIVE
1 a type of animal or plant which is extinct no longer exists □ *Many types of frog have already become extinct.* (**extinto**)
2 an extinct volcano (= mountain that explodes) no longer erupts (= sends out smoke and hot rocks) (**extinto**)
• **extinction** /ɪkˈstɪŋkʃən/ NOUN, NO PLURAL being extinct (**extinção**) *A lot of mammals are facing extinction.* (**enfrentando extinção**)

extinguish /ɪkˈstɪŋɡwɪʃ/ VERB [**extinguishes, extinguishing, extinguished**] a formal word meaning to make a fire stop burning or to make a light stop shining □ *Firefighters tried to extinguish the flames.* (**apagar**)
• **extinguisher** /ɪkˈstɪŋɡwɪʃə(r)/ NOUN [*plural* **extinguishers**] a piece of equipment for stopping small fires (**extintor**) *Public buildings have fire extinguishers.* (**extintor de incêndio**)

extortionate /ɪkˈstɔːʃənət/ ADJECTIVE very expensive □ *Fans complain about extortionate ticket prices.* (**extorsivo**)

extra /ˈekstrə/ ▶ ADJECTIVE more or more than usual □ *The extra money will be used to buy books.* □ *The teacher gives Raj extra help with maths.* □ *The room is £70 but meals are extra* (= meals are not included in the price). (**adicional**)
▶ ADVERB more than usual □ *I get paid extra for working at weekends.* □ *I bought an extra large box of chocolates.* (**extra**)
▶ NOUN [*plural* **extras**]
1 something you can choose to have that is not included in the price of something (**adicional**) *Optional extras on the car include air conditioning and heated seats.* (**adicionais extras**)
2 an actor in a film or television programme who does not say anything but is one of a crowd of people (**figurante**)

extra- /ˈekstrə/ PREFIX **extra-** is added to the beginning of words to mean 'more' or 'further away than' □ *extraordinary* □ *extraterrestrial* (**extra-**)

extract ▶ VERB /ɪkˈstrækt/ [**extracts, extracting, extracted**]
1 a formal word meaning to remove something from a place □ *No dentist will extract a tooth that could be saved.* (**extrair**)
2 to get something such as information or money from someone who does not want to give it to you. A formal word □ *Police tried to extract a confession from him.* (**arrancar**)
▶ NOUN /ˈekstrækt/ [*plural* **extracts**]
1 a short piece from a book or film □ *He read an extract from the book.* (**passagem**)
2 a substance that has been removed from a plant □ *vanilla extract* (**extrato, essência**)
• **extraction** /ɪkˈstrækʃən/ NOUN [*plural* **extractions**]
1 when something is extracted □ *oil extraction* (**extração**)
2 of Irish/European/Jewish etc. extraction having parents or grandparents etc. who were Irish, European etc. (**ter antepassados irlandeses, europeus, judeus etc.**)

extraneous /ɪkˈstreɪniəs/ ADJECTIVE a formal word meaning not directly related to something □ *extraneous details* (**estranho**)

extraordinarily /ɪkˈstrɔːdənrəli/ ADVERB extremely and in a surprising way □ *She was extraordinarily beautiful.* (**extraordinariamente**)

extraordinary /ɪkˈstrɔːdənri/ ADJECTIVE very special, unusual or surprising □ *Ann told me the most extraordinary story.* (**extraordinário**) *He knew he had seen something quite extraordinary* (= very extraordinary). (**muito extraordinário**) □ + *that* It's extraordinary that he survived the accident.

extraterrestrial /ˌekstrətəˈrestriəl/ ▶ ADJECTIVE from a planet or place that is not Earth (**extraterrestre**)
▶ NOUN [*plural* **extraterrestrials**] a creature from another planet

extravagance /ɪkˈstrævəɡəns/ NOUN [*plural* **extravagances**]
1 spending a lot of money or using a lot of something (**extravagância**)
2 something that you spend too much money on □ *My only extravagance was handbags.* (**extravagância**)

extravagant /ɪkˈstrævəɡənt/ ADJECTIVE
1 spending or costing too much money, or using too much of something □ *an extravagant lifestyle* □ *Don't be too extravagant with the paper – we haven't much left.* (**gastador, extravagante**)
2 extreme and probably unreasonable □ *The advertisement makes some extravagant claims.* (**exagerado**)

extravaganza /ɪkˌstrævəˈɡænzə/ NOUN [*plural* **extravaganzas**] a big and exciting show or event which has cost a lot of money □ *a Hollywood wedding extravaganza* (**obra espetacular**)

extravert /ˈekstrəvɜːt/ NOUN [*plural*] another spelling of **extrovert** (**extrovertido**)

extreme /ɪkˈstriːm/ ▶ ADJECTIVE **extraverts**
1 very great (**extremo**) *The roads are icy, and motorists should drive with extreme caution.* (**extremo cuidado**) □ *We were working under extreme pressure.*
2 very unusual or severe (**extremo**) *Planes cannot take off or land in extreme weather*

extricate / **eye-opener**

conditions. (condições de tempo extremas) ▣ *In extreme cases, the illness can cause death.* (casos extremos)

3 extreme opinions, beliefs etc. are very strong and unreasonable (**radical**) ▣ *She was often ridiculed for her extreme views.* (opiniões radicais)

4 at the furthest edge of something ▢ *My mother is on the extreme right of the picture.* (extremo)

▶ NOUN [*plural* **extremes**]

1 something that is much greater, much more severe etc. than usual ▢ + *of The crops cannot survive extremes of temperature.* (extremo)

2 the other/opposite extreme used when comparing two things that are as different as possible ▢ *Some of the holidays on offer cost just £99 per person. At the other extreme, they have world cruises costing £20,000.* (no extremo oposto/outro extremo)

3 go to extremes to do something much more than is usual or reasonable ▢ *She went to extremes to change her image, even having cosmetic surgery.*

- **extremely** /ɪkˈstriːmli/ ADVERB very ▢ *He found it extremely difficult to relax.* ▢ *Education is extremely important.* ▢ *Ben did extremely well in the test.* (chegar ao extremo)

> - *Extremely* is not used before adjectives which have a strong meaning:
>   ✓ *It was extremely difficult to hear.*
>   ✗ *It was extremely impossible to hear.*
> - If you are using an adjective with a strong meaning, put an adverb such as completely or absolutely before it: ▢ *It was absolutely impossible to hear.*

extricate /ˈɛkstrɪkeɪt/ VERB [**extricates, extricating, extricated**] **extricate yourself** a formal word meaning to manage to stop being involved in a difficult situation ▢ *He was trying to extricate himself from this embarrassing situation.* (livrar-se)

extrovert /ˈɛkstrəvɜːt/ NOUN [*plural* **extroverts**] a confident person who enjoys being with other people (extrovertido)

exuberant /ɪɡˈzjuːbərənt/ ADJECTIVE happy, excited and full of energy ▢ *He was young and exuberant.* (exuberante)

eye /aɪ/ ▶ NOUN [*plural* **eyes**]

1 one of the two things on your face which you see with ▢ *I have blonde hair and blue eyes.* (olho) ▣ *John closed his eyes and tried to sleep.* (fechou os olhos) ▣ *When she opened her eyes again, he'd gone.* (abriu os olhos)

2 the hole in a needle that you put the thread through (buraco)

⇨ go to **black eye**

◆ IDIOMS **catch someone's eye** (a) if something catches your eye, you notice it ▢ *A sudden movement caught my eye.* (b) if you catch someone's eye, you look at them to get their attention ▢ *I tried to catch Penny's eye.* (chamar a atenção) **have your eye on something** to want something and think that you will get it ▢ *I've got my eye on a velvet coat.* (estar de olho em algo) **keep an eye on someone/something** to look after someone or something to make sure they are safe ▢ *Could you keep an eye on the children for me?* (ficar de olho em alguém) **keep an eye out for something/someone** to watch so that you see something or someone ▢ *Keep an eye out for any mistakes.* (ter cuidado com algo/alguém) **keep your eyes open** to watch carefully for something ▢ *Keep your eyes open for signs of the illness.* (prestar atenção) **lay/set eyes on something/someone** to see something or someone for the first time ▢ *As soon as I laid eyes on the house, I knew I wanted to live there.* (ser apresentado a algo/alguém) **not see eye to eye** to disagree with someone about something ▢ *We don't see eye to eye about religion.* (não concordar plenamente) **take your eye/eyes off someone/something** to stop looking at something or someone ▢ *I only took my eye off her for a minute and she'd gone.* ▢ *She can't take her eyes off him!* (desviar os olhos de alguém/algo) **be up to your eyes in something** to have too much of something ▢ *I'm up to my eyes in work at the moment.* (estar muito ocupado com algo)

▶ VERB [**eyes, eyeing, eyed**] to look at someone or something ▢ *They eyed our bags suspiciously.* (olhar)

◆ PHRASAL VERB **eye someone/something up** to look at someone or something in a way that shows that you like them or want them ▢ *I could see him eyeing up my CD collection.* (cobiçar alguém/algo)

eyeball /ˈaɪbɔːl/ NOUN [*plural* **eyeballs**] the round part that makes up your whole eye (globo ocular)

eyebrow /ˈaɪbraʊ/ NOUN [*plural* **eyebrows**] one of the two lines of hair above your eyes (sobrancelha)

eye-catching /ˈaɪˌkætʃɪŋ/ ADJECTIVE if something is eye-catching, it looks unusual and attractive so you notice it ▢ *an eye-catching display* (vistoso)

eyelash /ˈaɪlæʃ/ NOUN [*plural* **eyelashes**] one of the many hairs round the edges of your eyes (cílios)

eyelid /ˈaɪlɪd/ NOUN [*plural* **eyelids**] one of the pieces of skin that cover your eyes when your eyes are closed (pálpebra)

eyeliner /ˈaɪˌlaɪnə(r)/ NOUN [*plural* **eyeliners**] makeup that you use to draw a line around your eyes (delineador de olhos)

eye-opener /ˈaɪˌəʊpənə(r)/ NOUN [*plural* **eyeopeners**] something which shows you what someone or something is really like and surprises you ▢ *The film of his life is quite an eye-opener.* (uma revelação)

eyeshadow /ˈaɪˌʃædəʊ/ NOUN [plural **eyeshadows**] coloured make-up that you put on your eyelids (= skin over your eyes) **(sombra)**

eyesight /ˈaɪsaɪt/ NOUN, NO PLURAL the ability to see ☐ *Her eyesight is poor so she wears contact lenses.* **(visão)**

eyesore /ˈaɪsɔː(r)/ NOUN [plural **eyesores**] something ugly that spoils a view ☐ *The new building is an eyesore.* **(algo desagradável, feio)**

eyewitness /ˌaɪˈwɪtnɪs/ NOUN [plural **eyewitnesses**] someone who has seen a crime or accident happen ☐ *Police are appealing for eyewitnesses.* **(testemunha ocular)**

F f

F¹ *or* **f** /ef/ the sixth letter of the alphabet (**a sexta letra do alfabeto**)

F² /ef/ ABBREVIATION Fahrenheit (**abreviação de Fahrenheit**)

fable /ˈfeɪbəl/ NOUN [*plural* **fables**] a story that teaches a lesson about how people should behave (**fábula**)

fabric /ˈfæbrɪk/ NOUN [*plural* **fabrics**] cloth □ *They are made of natural fabrics such as cotton or linen.* (**tecido**)

fabricate /ˈfæbrɪkeɪt/ VERB [**fabricates, fabricating, fabricated**] to invent information to trick people □ *It was later proved that the police had fabricated evidence.* (**fabricar**)

• **fabrication** /ˌfæbrɪˈkeɪʃən/ NOUN [*plural* **fabrications**] an invented story or piece of information □ *Her explanations were pure fabrication.* (**invenção**)

fabulous /ˈfæbjʊləs/ ADJECTIVE extremely good □ *The weather was fabulous.* □ *You look fabulous in that dress.* (**fabuloso**)

façade /fəˈsɑːd/ NOUN [*plural* **façades**]

1 the front of a building □ *The library has a glass façade.* (**fachada**)

2 a false appearance which hides what someone or something is really like □ *His happiness was just a façade.* (**fachada**)

face /feɪs/ ▶ NOUN [*plural* **faces**]

1 the front of your head where your eyes, nose, and mouth are □ *She had a huge smile on her face.* (**rosto**)

2 pull/make a face to twist your face into a strange expression (**fazer careta**)

3 the part of a clock or watch where the numbers are (**mostrador**)

4 the vertical side of a mountain or cliff (= steep side of high land next to the sea) (**face, lado**)

⇨ go to **keep a straight face**

▶ VERB [**faces, facing, faced**]

1 to be in a particular direction □ *My house faces the park.* □ *She turned to face him.* (**dar de frente para**)

2 to have to deal with a difficult situation □ *She has faced many difficulties in her life.* (**enfrentar**)

3 can't face doing something if you can't face doing something, it is too unpleasant for you to do □ *I just can't face cooking this evening.* (**não aguentar algo**)

◆ PHRASAL VERB **face up to something** to accept and deal with a problem □ *You must face up to your responsibilities.* (**enfrentar algo**)

facecloth /ˈfeɪsklɒθ/ NOUN [*plural* **facecloths**] a small square cloth for washing yourself (**toalha de rosto**)

facelift /ˈfeɪslɪft/ NOUN [*plural* **facelifts**]

1 a medical operation to make someone's face look younger by making the skin tighter (**cirurgia plástica para rugas**)

2 work to make a building or place look more attractive □ *The building has had a £2 million facelift.* (**reforma**)

facet /ˈfæsɪt/ NOUN [*plural* **facets**] a part or a feature of a situation or of a person's character □ *I had not known about this facet of her personality before.* (**faceta**)

facetious /fəˈsiːʃəs/ ADJECTIVE trying to say something funny in a way that is annoying or not suitable □ *Let's have no more facetious suggestions.* (**alegre, brincalhão, faceiro**)

• **facetiously** /fəˈsiːʃəsli/ ADVERB in a facetious way □ *I didn't mean that facetiously.* (**alegremente**)

facial /ˈfeɪʃəl/ ▶ ADJECTIVE to do with your face (**facial**) ▣ *a facial expression* (**expressão facial**)
▶ NOUN [*plural* **facials**] a beauty treatment for your face (**limpeza facial**)

facilitate /fəˈsɪlɪteɪt/ VERB [**facilitates, facilitating, facilitated**] a formal word meaning to make a task or process easier □ *Nowadays students have access to all sorts of visual aids that facilitate the learning process.* (**facilitar**)

facility /fəˈsɪləti/ NOUN [*plural* **facilities**]

1 facilities buildings, rooms or equipment that you can use for doing something (**instalação**) ▣ *The university has excellent sports facilities.* (**instalações de esporte**) □ *The company provides childcare facilities for employees.*

2 a feature of a machine, system, etc. that makes it able to do something □ *I want a mobile phone with an Internet facility.* (**acesso**)

3 a building used for a particular purpose (**serviço**) ▣ *The injured were taken to the nearest medical facility.* (**serviço médico**)

4 an ability □ **+ for** *He has a great facility for solving problems.* (**facilidade**)

fact /fækt/ NOUN [plural facts]

1 something that you know is true □ + *about* We don't yet know all the facts about the accident. (fato) 🔹 You need to face facts (= accept the truth) – you'll never be a successful ballet dancer. (encarar os fatos) 🔹 You should get your facts straight (= be sure you know the truth) before you make accusations like that. (entender bem os fatos) 🔹 I know for a fact (= I'm certain) that he was in London last week. (tenho certeza) 🔹 The fact is, I'm too scared to talk to him. (o fato é) 🔹 The fact that she's ill means she can't work full-time. (o fato de que)

2 in fact/as a matter of fact used to give more information about something (de fato) □ They know each other well; in fact they went to school together.

3 in fact used to say what is really true □ He said he was ill, when in fact he was at the football match. (na verdade)

4 NO PLURAL real things, not things that are imagined □ The movie is based on fact. □ She doesn't seem able to separate fact from fiction. (realidade)

5 the facts of life information about sex and how babies are born (fatos sobre sexo e como os bebês nascem)

faction /ˈfækʃən/ NOUN [plural factions]
a group that is part of a larger group but has different opinions from others in that group (facção)

factor /ˈfæktə(r)/ NOUN [plural factors]

1 something that causes or influences a situation □ The weather is often one of the main factors in choosing where to go for a holiday. (fator) 🔹 Price is an important factor for many people. (fator importante) 🔹 Blood pressure is a key risk factor for heart disease. (fator de risco)

2 a number that a larger number can be divided by exactly. A maths word. (coeficiente)

factory /ˈfæktəri/ NOUN [plural factories]
a building where something is made in large quantities □ a chocolate factory (fábrica)

factual /ˈfæktʃuəl/ ADJECTIVE
based on facts □ factual information □ The report contains factual errors. (baseado em fatos)

faculty /ˈfækəlti/ NOUN [plural faculties]

1 a natural ability that someone has, especially to see, hear, speak, think, etc. □ the faculty of speech □ He's 95 but he still has all his faculties. (faculdade)

2 a department of a university □ the Faculty of Law (faculdade)

fad /fæd/ NOUN [plural fads]
something that is popular or fashionable for a short time □ a passing fad for skateboarding (moda, mania)

fade /feɪd/ VERB [fades, fading, faded]

1 to disappear or become less strong gradually □ Hopes of finding him were starting to fade. □ His smile faded. □ Their voices faded into the background. (enfraquecer)

2 to lose colour and become less bright □ These jeans have faded. □ The light was fading. (enfraquecer)

faeces /ˈfiːsiːz/ PLURAL NOUN
a formal word for solid waste from people's or animal's bodies (fezes)

Fahrenheit /ˈfærənˌhaɪt/ NOUN, NO PLURAL
a system for measuring temperature in which water freezes at 32 degrees and boils at 212 degrees (Fahrenheit)

fail /feɪl/ ▶ VERB [fails, failing, failed]

1 to not be successful □ + *in* They failed in their attempt to sail round the world. □ + *to do something* The business failed to attract enough customers. □ After four years, the marriage failed. (fracassar, falhar) 🔹 We failed miserably in our efforts to cheer him up. (falhamos miseravelmente)

2 if you fail an exam or test, you do not pass it □ My brother failed his driving test. (reprovar)

3 to not do something that is expected or needed □ + *to do something* The parcel failed to arrive. □ Yesterday's announcement failed to address the main problems. □ They failed to provide adequate food for the animals. (fracassar)

4 if a part of a machine or part of your body fails, it stops working □ The brakes failed. □ My eyesight is beginning to fail. (falhar)

5 to not help someone □ Our society is failing the poor. (falhar)

6 never fail to do something to always do something □ His rudeness never fails to amaze me. (nunca deixar de fazer algo)

▶ NOUN [plural fails]

1 a result in a test or an exam that is not successful (reprovação)

2 without fail (a) used to show that something always happens in a particular way or at a particular time □ He visits me every day, without fail (b) used to emphasize that something must be done □ I want your homework in tomorrow, without fail! (sem falta)

• **failed** /feɪld/ ADJECTIVE not successful (fracassado) 🔹 He had two failed attempts at climbing Everest. (tentativas fracassadas) □ a failed marriage

• **failing** /ˈfeɪlɪŋ/ ▶ NOUN [plural failings] a bad quality or fault □ Her worst failing is being late all the time. (fraqueza)

▶ PREPOSITION **failing that** if that is not possible □ We can get a lift from my Dad, or failing that, there's always the bus. (se aquilo não for possível)

• **failure** /ˈfeɪljə(r)/ NOUN [plural failures]

1 when something is not successful (fracasso) 🔹 Their first attempt ended in failure. (terminou em fracasso) □ + *of* After the failure of his business, he went to live abroad.

faint

2 when you do not do something that is wanted or needed □ **+ to do something** *The hospital's failure to give her the correct drugs contributed to her death.* (**fracasso**)
3 someone or something that is not successful □ *She felt like a failure.* □ *The party was a complete failure.* (**fracasso**)
4 when something stops working □ *a power failure* (**falha**) 🔎 *He died of heart failure.* (**parada cardíaca**)

faint /feɪnt/ ▶ ADJECTIVE [fainter, faintest]
1 difficult to see, hear or smell □ *There's a faint mark on the carpet.* □ *the faint sound of footsteps* □ *He gave a faint smile.* (**fraco**)
2 if you feel faint, you feel as though you might become unconscious (**fraco**) 🔎 *I suddenly felt faint.* (**me senti fraco**)
3 very slight (**pequeno, vago**) 🔎 *She still holds out a faint hope of finding it.* (**vaga esperança**)
4 not have the faintest idea used to emphasize that you do not know something □ *I don't have the faintest idea where it is.* (**não ter a menor ideia**)
5 the faintest used to emphasize that something is very slight □ *There wasn't the faintest chance he'd be chosen.* □ *He only has the faintest hint of an accent.* (**mínimo**)
▶ VERB [faints, fainting, fainted] to suddenly become unconscious and fall to the ground □ *Richard fainted when he saw the blood.* (**desmaiar**)

• **faintly** /ˈfeɪntli/ ADVERB
1 in a way that is difficult to see, hear or smell □ *'Yes,' she said faintly.* □ *The room smelled faintly of smoke.* (**ligeiramente**)
2 slightly □ *He looked faintly ridiculous.* (**vagamente**)

fair /feə(r)/ ▶ ADJECTIVE [fairer, fairest]
1 treating everyone in the same, reasonable way (**justo**) 🔎 *It's not fair! Ella got more cake than me.* (**não é justo**) 🔎 *a fair trial/election* (**julgamento/eleição justa**) 🔎 *Make sure Patsy does her fair share of the work.* (**divisão justa**)
2 acceptable and reasonable □ **+ on** *It's not fair on my family to go away so often.* (**justo**) 🔎 *Make sure you get a fair price for the jewellery.* (**preço justo**) 🔎 *To be fair, Mohon has been working very hard recently.* (**para ser justo**)
3 fair skin or hair is light in colour (**loiro**)
4 quite large (**grande**) 🔎 *There's a fair amount of food left.* (**grande montante**) 🔎 *We have a fair bit of work still to do* (**grande parte**) 🔎 *There's a fair chance that they will win.* (**grande chance**)
5 fair weather is pleasant, with no rain (**bom, claro**)
6 quite good but not very good □ *Joe's work is only fair.* (**mediano**)
7 fair enough used to say that you accept what has been said □ *'I couldn't help because I had to visit my grandma.' 'Oh, fair enough then.'* (**é justo**)
◆ IDIOM **be fair game** to be something or someone that people feel they can criticize or use in a bad way □ *For journalists, the private lives of politicians are fair game.* (**ser um alvo justificado para críticas**)
▶ NOUN [plural fairs] an event held outdoors, where you can ride on machines, play games, etc. (**feira, evento**)

• **fairly** /ˈfeəli/ ADVERB
1 quite a lot, but not extremely □ *He is fairly well paid.* □ *It's fairly obvious that she is lying.* (**bastante**)
2 in a fair way □ *They treat their staff fairly.* □ *The money was divided fairly between them.* (**imparcialmente**)

• **fairness** /ˈfeənɪs/ NOUN, NO PLURAL being fair □ *They treated us with fairness.* (**imparcialidade**)

fairy /ˈfeəri/ NOUN [plural fairies] an imaginary creature which looks like a small person with wings (**fada**)

fairy lights /ˈfeəri laɪts/ PLURAL NOUN coloured lights for decoration, especially on a Christmas tree (**luzes de decoração, geralmente natalina**)

fairy story /ˈfeəri ˌstɔːri/ or **fairy tale** /ˈfeəri ˌteɪl/ NOUN [plural fairy stories or fairy tales] a traditional story in which magic things happen (**conto de fadas**)

faith /feɪθ/ NOUN [plural faiths]
1 great trust and belief in someone or something (**fé, confiança**) 🔎 *I have a lot of faith in him.* (**tenho fé**) 🔎 *I've lost faith in the whole system.* (**perdi a confiança**)
2 a religion □ *the Christian faith* □ *people of different faiths* (**fé**)
3 religious belief generally □ *He was a man of deep faith.* (**fé**)
4 good faith a belief that what you are doing is good, honest or legal □ *He acted in good faith.* (**boa-fé**)

• **faithful** /ˈfeɪθfʊl/ ADJECTIVE loyal and keeping your promises □ *a faithful friend* □ *He was faithful to his wife.* (**fiel**)

• **faithfully** /ˈfeɪθfʊli/ ADVERB
1 in a loyal, honest way □ *She promised faithfully to come.* (**fielmente**)
2 Yours faithfully something you write at the end of a formal letter that begins with 'Dear Sir' or 'Dear Madam' (**atenciosamente**)

fake /feɪk/ ▶ ADJECTIVE not real, but copying something else □ *fake fur* □ *He was travelling on a fake passport.* (**falso**)
▶ NOUN [plural fakes] a copy of something instead of the real thing □ *It's hard to spot a fake.* (**falsificação**)
▶ VERB [fakes, faking, faked]
1 to make a copy of something and pretend it is real □ *Roberts admitted he had faked the documents.* (**falsificar**)

2 to pretend something in order to trick someone □ *He faked an injury to avoid playing.* (**fingir**)

falcon /ˈfɔːlkən/ NOUN [plural **falcons**] a bird that kills other animals for food (**falcão**)

fall /fɔːl/ VERB [falls, falling, fell, fallen]

1 to drop down to the ground □ *The apples fell from he tree.* □ *Snow fell all morning.* (**cair**)

2 to suddenly go down to the ground by accident □ *Ben fell downstairs.* □ **+ off** *He fell off a fence and broke his arm.* (**cair**)

3 fall apart/off/out, etc. to become separated □ *The doll's arms fell off.* □ *All his hair fell out.* (**desprender**)

4 if an amount, price or temperature falls, it goes down □ **+ by** *The temperature has fallen by several degrees.* □ **+ to** *Prices fell to their lowest levels since June.* (**cair**)

5 to start being in a particular state (**ficar**) 🔁 *They fell in love.* (**ficaram apaixonados**) 🔁 *I often fall asleep at the cinema.* (**fico com sono**) 🔁 *He fell ill on holiday.* (**ficou doente**)

⇨ go to **fall on deaf ears**

♦ PHRASAL VERBS **fall for someone** to start to love someone (**apaixonar-se por alguém**) **fall for something** to be tricked by something □ *I told her I'd give her the money later and she fell for it!* (**deixar-se enganar**) **fall over** to fall to the ground or onto one side □ *I fell over and cut my knee.* (**cair no chão**) **fall out** to stop being friends □ *Carlos and Sergei have fallen out.* (**romper a amizade**) **fall through** to fail or not happen □ *Their plans for a holiday have fallen through.* (**fracassar**)

▶ NOUN [plural **falls**]

1 when someone falls by accident □ *My grandmother had a serious fall last week.* (**queda**)

2 a decrease in a price, amount or temperature □ **+ in** *There has been a fall in unemployment.* (**queda**)

3 the US word for **autumn** (**outono**)

fallacy /ˈfæləsi/ NOUN [plural **fallacies**] an idea that is not true although many people think it is □ *It's a fallacy that cutting your hair makes it grow faster.* (**falácia**)

fallible /ˈfæləbəl/ ADJECTIVE not perfect and likely to be wrong or to make mistakes □ *Even teachers are fallible.* (**falível**)

fallopian tube /fəˌləʊpiən ˈtjuːb/ NOUN [plural **fallopian tubes**] one of the two tubes that carry a woman's eggs to the womb (= place where the baby grows). A biology word. (**tuba uterina**)

fallout /ˈfɔːlaʊt/ NOUN, NO PLURAL

1 radioactive dust from a nuclear explosion (**partículas radioativas**)

2 the bad results of something that has happened □ *We are still dealing with the fallout of last year's financial crisis.* (**efeito colateral**)

false /fɔːls/ ADJECTIVE

1 not true or based on information that is not correct □ *He made a false statement to the police.* □ *These claims are completely false.* (**falso**) 🔁 *We had a false sense of security.* (**falsa sensação**) 🔁 *We don't want to give people false hope.* (**falsa esperança**)

2 not real or natural (**postiço**) 🔁 *false teeth* (**dentes postiços**) □ *a false passport*

3 not showing your real feelings (**falso**) □ *a false smile* (**sorriso falso**)

♦ IDIOM **under false pretences** if you do something under false pretences, you do it by tricking someone □ *He admitted he had married her under false pretences.* (**sob falsas pretensões**)

false alarm /ˌfɔːls əˈlɑːm/ NOUN [plural **false alarms**] when you believe something bad or dangerous is going to happen, but it does not □ *Someone thought there was a fire, but it was a false alarm.* (**alarme falso**)

falsely /ˈfɔːlsli/ ADVERB not correctly □ *I was falsely accused of theft.* (**falsamente**)

• **falseness** /ˈfɔːlsnɪs/ NOUN, NO PLURAL being false (**falsidade**)

falsification /ˌfɔːlsɪfɪˈkeɪʃən/ NOUN, NO PLURAL when someone falsifies something □ *the falsification of documents* (**falsificação**)

falsify /ˈfɔːlsɪfaɪ/ VERB [**falsifies, falsifying, falsified**] to change information in order to trick people □ *He had falsified the firm's accounts.* (**falsificar**)

falter /ˈfɔːltə(r)/ VERB [falters, faltering, faltered]

1 to pause or have difficulty when you are moving or speaking □ *He walked steadily beside me and only faltered occasionally.* □ *His voice faltered slightly.* (**titubear**)

2 to become less confident, strong or effective □ *Once we were sure of what we were doing we never faltered.* (**vacilar**)

fame /feɪm/ NOUN, NO PLURAL the state of being known by a lot of people (**fama**) 🔁 *She found fame in a hit TV series.* (**encontrou fama**) 🔁 *He achieved international fame as a novelist.* (**fama internacional**) 🔁 *Young actors go to Hollywood seeking fame and fortune* (= fame and money). (**fama e fortuna**)

familiar /fəˈmɪliə(r)/ ADJECTIVE

1 known to you □ *His voice sounded familiar.* (**familiar**) 🔁 *It looked vaguely familiar.* 🔁 *There were a few familiar faces* (= people you know) *at the party.* (**rostos familiares**)

2 be familiar with something to have seen or used something before □ *I'm not familiar with this software.* □ *If you're familiar with the area, it's just next to the big park.* (**estar familiarizado com algo**)

3 common and happening often (**familiar**) 🔁 *Electric cars are becoming a more familiar sight.* (**visão familiar**) □ *This is a sadly familiar story.*

family

4 behaving in a friendly and informal way □ *I thought he was too familiar.* (**familiar**)

- **familiarize** or **familiarise** /fəˈmɪljəraɪz/ VERB [**familiarizes, familiarizing, familiarized**] familiarize yourself with something to make sure you know something □ *Try to familiarize yourself with the rules.* (**familiarizar-se**)

family /ˈfæmli/ NOUN [plural **families**]

1 a group of people who are related to each other (**família**) 🔊 *I invited my whole family to the wedding.* (**toda a família**) 🔊 *I met her parents and several other family members.* (**parentes**) 🔊 *She discussed the decision with family and friends.* (**família e amigos**) □ *The minister met the families of the victims.*
2 the children in a family (**filhos**) □ *I have a wife and family at home.* 🔊 *He wants to marry and start a family* (= have children). (**ter filhos**)
3 a group of animals, plants or languages that are related to each other (**família**)

> Family can be used with a singular or plural verb in British English: □ *The family next door has a dog.* □ *The family next door have a dog.*

family tree /ˌfæmli ˈtriː/ NOUN [plural **family trees**] a picture which shows the relationships within a family (**árvore genealógica**)

famine /ˈfæmɪn/ NOUN [plural **famines**] a situation in which many people in an area do not have enough food and may die □ *The country was hit by a severe drought and famine.* (**fome, escassez**)

famished /ˈfæmɪʃt/ ADJECTIVE very hungry (**faminto**)

famous /ˈfeɪməs/ ADJECTIVE known by a lot of people □ *a famous actor* □ *a famous painting* □ + *for* *She is most famous for her role in Star Wars.* □ + *as* *He later became famous as a children's writer.* (**famoso, célebre**)

fan /fæn/ ▶ NOUN [plural **fans**]

1 someone who likes or admires a person or thing very much □ *football fans* □ *She's a big fan of Madonna.* (**fã**)
2 a machine with thin blades that turn round and make the air cooler □ *There was a ceiling fan in our room.* (**ventilador**)
3 something that you move in front of your face to make you feel cooler (**leque**)
▶ VERB [**fans, fanning, fanned**]
1 to move something in front of your face to make you feel cooler □ *He fanned himself with his cap.* (**abanar**)
2 to make a fire burn more strongly □ *Strong winds fanned the flames.* (**atiçar**)
◆ PHRASAL VERB **fan out** to spread in different directions □ *Rescue teams fanned out across the area.* (**espalhar-se**)

fantasize

fanatic /fəˈnætɪk/ NOUN [plural **fanatics**]
1 someone who has very extreme political or religious beliefs (**fanático, fervoroso**) 🔊 *a religious fanatic* (**fanático religioso**)
2 someone who likes something very much and spends a lot of time doing it □ *a cycling fanatic* (**fanático**)

- **fanatical** /fəˈnætɪkəl/ ADJECTIVE
1 having very extreme political or religious beliefs □ *a fanatical preacher* (**fanático**)
2 liking something very much and spending a lot of time doing it □ *He's fanatical about football.* (**fanático**)

- **fanaticism** /fəˈnætɪˌsɪzəm/ NOUN, NO PLURAL very strong religious or political beliefs that can make people behave unreasonably (**fanatismo**)

fancy /ˈfænsi/ ▶ VERB [**fancies, fancying, fancied**]
1 an informal word meaning to want to have or do something □ *Do you fancy going to the cinema?* □ *I really fancy a curry.* (**ter vontade de**)
2 an informal word meaning to be attracted to someone □ *My friend fancies you.* (**deseja**)
3 to think that something or someone will be successful (**imaginar**) 🔊 *They fancy their chances of winning tomorrow.* (**imaginam suas chances**) □ *Whitaker is strongly fancied for the best actor award.*
4 fancy yourself (as something) to think you are or could be a particular type of person, often wrongly □ *He fancies himself as a poet.* (**achar-se algo**)
▶ ADJECTIVE [**fancier, fanciest**]
1 fashionable or expensive □ *fancy clothes* □ *We went for a meal at a fancy restaurant.* (**na moda, extravagante**)
2 clever or complicated □ *We don't use any fancy equipment.* (**exagerado**)
3 decorated and not plain □ *fancy cakes* (**luxuoso**)
▶ NOUN, NO PLURAL
1 take your fancy to make you want to have or do something □ *Do any of these dresses take your fancy?* (**ser de seu interesse**)
2 take a fancy to someone an informal phrase meaning to be attracted to someone □ *I think he's taken a fancy to you.* (**estar interessado em alguém**)

fancy dress /ˌfænsi ˈdres/ NOUN, NO PLURAL clothes that you wear to a party to make you look like someone or something else (**fantasia**) 🔊 *a fancy dress party* (**festa à fantasia**) □ *Are you going in fancy dress?*

fanfare /ˈfænfeə(r)/ NOUN [plural **fanfares**] a short, loud piece of music played on a trumpet (**fanfarra**)

fang /fæŋ/ NOUN [plural **fangs**] a long, pointed tooth of an animal or a snake (**presa**)

fantasize or **fantasise** /ˈfæntəsaɪz/ VERB [**fantasizes, fantasizing, fantasized**] to imagine something good happening to you that is not

fantastic

likely □ *He used to fantasize about being a famous actor.* (fantasiar)

fantastic /fæn'tæstɪk/ ADJECTIVE

1 an informal word meaning extremely good □ *We had a fantastic time in Rome.* □ *This is a fantastic opportunity for us.* (fantástico) 🔊 *You look fantastic!* (está fantástico)
2 an informal word meaning very large (grande, muito) 🔊 *They've spent a fantastic amount of money.* (grande quantia)
3 not real or not true □ *a fantastic tale* (fantástico)

fantasy /'fæntəsɪ/ NOUN [plural fantasies]

1 something good that you imagine but that probably will not happen □ *I often think about going to live somewhere warm and sunny but it's just a fantasy.* (fantasia)
2 a story about imaginary things □ *The film is a futuristic fantasy.* (fantasia)

FAQ /ˌefeɪˈkjuː/ ABBREVIATION frequently asked questions; a list of questions about a particular subject (perguntas frequentes)

far /fɑː(r)/ ▶ ADVERB [farther or further, farthest or furthest]

1 a long distance □ *Don't go too far.* □ + *away Is the hotel very far away?* □ + *to It's not far to Paris.* □ + *from He lives not far from the church.* (longe)
2 a long time in the past or the future □ *Records go as far back as the 16th century.* □ *We can't tell you the exact number of guests this far in advance.* (muito)
3 an amount of progress (longe) 🔊 *I haven't got very far with my homework.* (foi muito longe)
4 much □ *She's a far better swimmer than I am.* □ *He's far more interested in football.* (muito) 🔊 *These trousers are far too small for me.* (muito)
5 as far as I know/can remember, etc. used to say what you think is true □ *As far as I can remember, there aren't any very steep hills.* (até/tanto quanto sei/lembro etc.)
6 as far as something is concerned used to talk about a particular thing □ *As far as food is concerned, I'm happy with a sandwich.* (no que se refere)
7 as far as I'm/he's, etc. concerned used to talk about someone's opinion □ *As far as I'm concerned, you can take all the money.* (a meu ver)
8 as far as possible as much as possible □ *I try to avoid sugar as far as possible.* (tanto quanto possível)
9 by far used to emphasize the quality you are talking about □ *He's by far the most talented of our dancers.* (de longe)
10 far from not at all □ *The problem is still far from being sorted out.* (até agora, por enquanto)
11 so far until now □ *So far, there haven't been any accidents.* (até agora)

➤ Note that **far**, meaning 'a long distance', is mainly used in questions and in negative sentences: □ *How far is it to the town centre?* □ *It's not far from the town centre.*
➤ In positive sentences, we usually say **a long way**: □ *It's a long way from the town centre.*

▶ ADJECTIVE

1 the far part of something is the part that is the greatest distance from you (distante) 🔊 *The house is on the far side of the lake.* (lado distante)
2 the far left/right the people with the most extreme political opinions (extrema esquerda/direita)

farce /fɑːs/ NOUN [plural farces]

1 a situation that is silly because it is so confused or badly organized □ *The trial has become a complete farce.* (absurdo)
2 a theatre play in which funny and unlikely things happen (farsa, pantomima)

fare /feə(r)/ ▶ NOUN [plural fares]

1 the price of a journey by bus, train, aeroplane, etc. (tarifa, passagem) 🔊 *The train fare to London is £33.* (passagem de trem) 🔊 *Cheap air fares make travel much easier.* (passagens de avião)
2 a formal word for a type of food □ *They serve hearty German fare.* (comida)
▶ VERB [fares, faring, fared] used to say how well or badly someone does in a situation (sentir-se bem/mal) 🔊 *Companies are faring better than they did last year.* (sentindo-se melhor) 🔊 *The party fared poorly in the elections.* (sentiu-se indisposto)

Far East /ˌfɑːr ˈiːst/ NOUN, NO PLURAL the countries of East and Southeast Asia, including Japan and China (Oriente)

farewell /ˌfeəˈwel/ ▶ EXCLAMATION an old--fashioned word for goodbye. (adeus)
▶ NOUN [plural farewells] an old-fashioned word for a goodbye □ *We said our farewells.* □ *a farewell speech* (despedida)

far-fetched /ˌfɑːˈfetʃt/ ADJECTIVE very unlikely to be true □ *a far-fetched story* □ *That's not such a far-fetched idea.* (absurdo)

farm /fɑːm/ ▶ NOUN [plural farms] an area of land where crops are grown and animals are kept (fazenda) 🔊 *a dairy farm* (= which keeps cows for milk) (fazenda de gado leiteiro) 🔊 *a farm animal* (animal de fazenda) □ *He works on a farm.*
▶ VERB [farms, farming, farmed] to use land for growing crops or keeping animals for meat □ *They have farmed the land here for generations.* (cultivar)

• **farmer** /'fɑːmə(r)/ NOUN [plural farmers] someone who owns and works on a farm □ *a local sheep farmer* (fazendeiro, agricultor)

farmhouse

farmhouse /'fɑːmhaʊs/ NOUN [plural **farmhouses**] a house on a farm where the farmer lives (**casa de fazenda**)

farming /'fɑːmɪŋ/ NOUN, NO PLURAL the activity or business of working on and managing a farm □ *The organization promotes organic farming.* (**agricultura, lavoura**) ▣ *He grew up in a small farming community.* (**comunidade da fazenda**)

farmland /'fɑːmlænd/ NOUN, NO PLURAL land that is used for farming (**gleba de terra cultivada**)

farmyard /'fɑːmjɑːd/ NOUN [plural **farmyards**] an area surrounded by buildings on a farm (**celeiro**)

far-reaching /ˌfɑːˈriːtʃɪŋ/ ADJECTIVE having an important effect or affecting many people (**poderoso**) ▣ *The new rules are bound to have far-reaching consequences for schools.* (**consequências poderosas**)

fascinate /'fæsɪneɪt/ VERB [**fascinates, fascinating, fascinated**] to interest and attract someone very much □ *The story of Tutankhamun has fascinated people for many years.* □ *The thing that fascinates me is the variety of shapes and colours.* (**fascinar**)

• **fascinated** /'fæsɪneɪtɪd/ ADJECTIVE very interested and attracted by something □ *As a kid I was fascinated by the stars.* □ *She watched the fascinated expressions of the children.* (**fascinado**)

• **fascinating** /'fæsɪneɪtɪŋ/ ADJECTIVE very interesting (**fascinante**) ▣ *a fascinating story* (**uma história fascinante**) □ *It's the island's wildlife that I find fascinating.*

• **fascination** /ˌfæsɪˈneɪʃən/ NOUN, NO PLURAL a great interest in something □ *I've always had a fascination for unusual animals.* □ *the public's fascination with celebrities* □ *She watched in fascination.* (**fascinação**)

fascism /'fæʃɪzəm/ NOUN, NO PLURAL a political system in which the state has strong control over all areas of society (**fascismo**)

• **fascist** /'fæʃɪst/ ▶ NOUN [plural **fascists**]
1 someone who supports fascism (**fascista**)
2 someone who tries to control other people and ignores their opinions (**fascista**)
▶ ADJECTIVE to do with fascism (**facista**) ▣ *a fascist regime* (**regime fascista**) ▣ *The country was ruled by a fascist dictator.* (**ditador fascista**)

fashion /'fæʃən/ NOUN [plural **fashions**]
1 something, especially a piece of clothing, that is very popular at a particular time □ + **for** *There was a fashion for tight jeans.* □ *Short skirts were in fashion then.* (**moda**) ▣ *She wears all the latest fashions.* (**última moda**)
2 NO PLURAL the business of making and selling clothes (**moda**) ▣ *a fashion designer* (**estilista**) ▣ *a fashion magazine* (**revista de moda**)
3 the way someone does something □ *The second half began in a similar fashion.* (**forma**)

fat

• **fashionable** /'fæʃənəbəl/ ADJECTIVE popular with many people at a particular time □ *a fashionable restaurant* (**na moda**) ▣ *The area has become fashionable with students.* (**ficou na moda**) □ + **to do something** *It's fashionable to play team sports again.*

fast¹ /fɑːst/ ▶ ADJECTIVE [**faster, fastest**]
1 quick □ *a fast car* □ *He was the fastest runner.* (**rápido**)
2 if a clock or watch is fast, it shows a time that is later than the correct time (**adiantado**)
▶ ADVERB [**faster, fastest**]
1 quickly □ *She can run very fast.* □ *We're working as fast as we can.* □ *The population has grown faster than in any other region.* (**depressa**)
2 fast asleep completely asleep □ *The boys are fast asleep.* (**profundamente adormecido**)
3 firmly or tightly (**firme**) ▣ *The door was stuck fast.* (**preso firme**)

fast² /fɑːst/ ▶ VERB [**fasts, fasting, fasted**] to not eat any food for a period of time, often for religious reasons □ *I am fasting because it is Ramadan.* (**jejuar**)
▶ NOUN [plural **fasts**] a time when you fast (**jejum**)

fasten /'fɑːsən/ VERB [**fastens, fastening, fastened**] to join or fix two things or parts together (**apertar, firmar**) ▣ *Please fasten your seat belts.* (**apertem os cintos**) □ + **to** *The phone was fastened to the wall.* □ *She fastened the papers together with a stapler.* □ *The dress fastens at the back.*

• **fastener** /'fɑːsənə(r)/ NOUN [plural **fasteners**] something that is used to join two things together (**prendedor, fecho**)

fast food /ˌfɑːst 'fuːd/ NOUN, NO PLURAL food that is prepared and served quickly in a restaurant, such as a hamburger (**refeição rápida, fast-food**)

fastidious /fəˈstɪdiəs/ ADJECTIVE wanting everything to be tidy, clean and perfect (**meticuloso**)

fat /fæt/ ▶ ADJECTIVE [**fatter, fattest**]
1 a fat person has too much flesh, usually because they eat too much (**gordo**) ▣ *George is getting fat, isn't he?* (**engordando**) ▣ *Do these jeans make me look fat?* (**parecer gordo**) □ *Fat children are often teased.*
2 thick or large □ *a big, fat book* (**gordo**)

> It is not polite to describe someone as fat. To sound less rude, use the words **big** or **overweight**: □ *She's quite big at the moment and unhappy about it.*

♦ IDIOM **fat chance** used to mean you think something is very unlikely. An informal phrase. □ *Will he tidy up? Fat chance!* (**sem chance**)
▶ NOUN [plural **fats**]

1 a soft white substance that forms a layer under your skin (gordura) ▫ *Can exercise reduce body fat?* (gordura corporal)
2 a substance like oil that is in food or used in cooking ▫ *Limit the amount of fat you eat.* (gordura) ▫ *Hard cheese has a higher fat content.* (índice de gordura)

fatal /ˈfeɪtəl/ ADJECTIVE
1 causing someone's death (fatal, mortal) ▫ *a fatal accident* (acidente fatal) ▫ *The disease is potentially fatal.* (potencialmente mortal)
2 causing serious problems ▫ *a fatal mistake* (fatal)
- **fatality** /fəˈtæləti/ NOUN [plural **fatalities**] a death in an accident ▫ *We want to reduce the number of fatalities and injuries in road accidents.* (fatalidade, morte trágica em acidente)
- **fatally** /ˈfeɪtəli/ ADVERB in a way which causes someone's death ▫ *He was fatally wounded.* (fatalmente)

fate /feɪt/ NOUN, NO PLURAL
1 the things that happen to someone, especially bad things (destino) ▫ *I hope that the others don't suffer the same fate.* (tenham o destino) ▫ *The High Court will decide the fate of the three men.* (decidir o destino)
2 a power that seems to control what happens ▫ *She believes that fate brought them together.* (destino, sorte)
- **fated** /ˈfeɪtɪd/ ADJECTIVE likely to happen because of fate ▫ *We were fated to meet.* (determinado)
- **fateful** /ˈfeɪtfʊl/ ADJECTIVE having an important, usually bad, effect on future events (fatal, fatídico) ▫ *It turned out to be a fateful decision.* (decisão fatídica) ▫ *We look back on that fateful day in 2001.* (dia fatídico)

father /ˈfɑːðə(r)/ ▶ NOUN [plural **fathers**]
1 your male parent ▫ *I'll speak to my father.* (pai)
2 Father the title of some priests ▫ *Father Anthony* (padre)
3 the father of something the man who first started something ▫ *Sigmund Freud is known as the father of psychoanalysis.* (o pai de algo)

> **Father** is a formal way of speaking or referring to your male parent. Most young people use the word Dad instead and young children often use the word Daddy.

▶ VERB [**fathers, fathering, fathered**] a formal word meaning to be the father of a child ▫ *He had four wives and fathered many children.* (gerar, procriar)

Father Christmas /ˌfɑːðə ˈkrɪsməs/ NOUN an imaginary old man with a white beard and a red coat who children believe brings presents on Christmas Eve (Papai Noel)

fatherhood /ˈfɑːðəhʊd/ NOUN, NO PLURAL being a father ▫ *the joys of fatherhood* (paternidade)

father-in-law /ˈfɑːðərɪnˌlɔː/ NOUN [plural **fathers-in-law**] the father of your wife or husband (sogro)

fatherly /ˈfɑːðəli/ ADJECTIVE like a kind father ▫ *a fatherly hug* (paternalmente)

fathom /ˈfæðəm/ VERB [**fathoms, fathoming, fathomed**] to understand something after thinking about it ▫ *I still can't fathom why he didn't tell me.* (entender)

fatigue /fəˈtiːɡ/ NOUN, NO PLURAL extreme tiredness ▫ *The condition can cause fatigue and shortness of breath.* (fadiga)

fatten /ˈfætən/ VERB [**fattens, fattening, fattened**] to make an animal fatter so it can be eaten ▫ *The pigs are being fattened up for sale.* (engordar)
- **fattening** /ˈfætənɪŋ/ ADJECTIVE making you fatter (engorda) ▫ *fattening foods* (alimentos que engordam) ▫ *Chocolate is very fattening.*

fatty /ˈfæti/ ADJECTIVE [**fattier, fattiest**] containing a lot of fat (gorduroso) ▫ *Try to avoid fatty foods.* (alimentos gordurosos)

faucet /ˈfɔːsɪt/ NOUN [plural **faucets**] the US word for a **water tap** (torneira)

fault /fɔːlt/ ▶ NOUN [plural **faults**]
1 the fact of being responsible for something bad or wrong ▫ *Sorry, that's my fault – I left it unlocked.* ▫ *+ of This is not the fault of the teachers.* ▫ *The driver was not at fault.* (culpa) ▫ *I believe the fault lies with the government.* (a culpa é do)
2 a mistake, problem or bad feature ▫ *The plane developed a technical fault.* ▫ *+ with There was a fault with the design.* ▫ *For all his faults, he's always been good to me.* (defeito)
3 find fault (with someone/something) to criticize someone or something ▫ *He always seems to find fault with her work.* (ter algo para criticar)
4 a long crack in the Earth's surface which causes earthquakes (= when the earth shakes) (falha) ▫ *fault line* (uma falha)
▶ VERB [**faults, faulting, faulted**] to criticize someone or something ▫ *I can't fault his effort.* (criticar)
- **faultless** /ˈfɔːltlɪs/ ADJECTIVE perfect ▫ *a faultless performance* (impecável)
- **faulty** /ˈfɔːlti/ ADJECTIVE not working correctly ▫ *a faulty computer* (defeituoso)

fauna /ˈfɔːnə/ NOUN, NO PLURAL the animals, birds and insects that live in an area. A biology word. (fauna)

favor /ˈfeɪvə(r)/ NOUN [plural **favors**], VERB [**favors, favoring, favored**] the US spelling of **favour** (favor)
- **favorable** /ˈfeɪvrəbəl/ ADJECTIVE the US spelling of **favourable** (favorável)
- **favorably** /ˈfeɪvrəbli/ ADVERB the US spelling of **favourably** (favoravelmente)

favorite

favorite /ˈfeɪvrɪt/ ADJECTIVE, NOUN [plural **favorites**] the US spelling of **favourite** (favorito)

- **favoritism** /ˈfeɪvrɪtɪzəm/ NOUN, NO PLURAL the US spelling of **favouritism** (favoritismo)

favour /ˈfeɪvə(r)/ ▶ NOUN [plural **favours**]

1 something you do for someone to help them (favor) ▢ Could you *do me a favour* and check my homework? (me fazer um favor) ▢ I need to *ask you a favour*. (pedir-lhe um favor) ▢ As a *special favour*, Bill's fixing my car. (favor especial)

2 in favour of something supporting something as a good idea ▢ I'm in favour of higher pay for nurses. ▢ Workers have voted in favour of strike action. (a favor de algo)

3 in someone's favour giving someone an advantage ▢ The exchange rate is in our favour at the moment. (a favor de alguém)

4 in/out of favour popular/not popular ▢ This sort of music has gone out of favour. (a favor/contra)

5 NO PLURAL a formal word meaning when people like or approve of something (graça) ▢ These reforms have *found favour* with the public. (caiu nas graças)

▶ VERB [**favours, favouring, favoured**]

1 to treat one person or group better than others ▢ The legal system seems to favour the wealthy. (favorecer)

2 to use, like or support something ▢ Many people favour the death penalty. ▢ She favoured tight-fitting dresses. (preferir)

- **favourable** /ˈfeɪvrəbəl/ ADJECTIVE

1 making someone like and approve of someone or something, or showing that you like and approve of someone or something (favorável) ▢ The tidy room created a *favourable impression*. ▢ Inspectors wrote a very favourable report. (impressão favorável)

2 good and suitable ▢ We're hoping for favourable weather conditions. (favorável)

3 giving agreement ▢ We're hoping for a favourable reply. (a favor)

4 giving someone an unfair advantage ▢ They were accused of giving some people favourable treatment. (favorável)

- **favourably** /ˈfeɪvrəblɪ/ ADVERB in a favourable way (favoravelmente) ▢ Her exam results *compare favourably* with (= are better than) those of her friends. (são melhores) ▢ We were *favourably impressed* by (= liked) their work. (favoravelmente impressionados)

favourite /ˈfeɪvrɪt/ ▶ ADJECTIVE your favourite person or thing is the one you like best ▢ My favourite colour is purple. ▢ Who's your favourite player? (preferido, favorito)

▶ NOUN [plural **favourites**]

1 the person or thing you like best ▢ I love all cheese, but brie is my favourite. (favorito)

2 someone who is treated better than others by a teacher, parent, etc. (preferido)

fear

3 the person or animal that most people think will win a competition (favorito) ▢ Jones is *firm/hot favourite* to win the 100 m. (firme/forte favorito)

- **favouritism** /ˈfeɪvrɪtɪzəm/ NOUN, NO PLURAL when someone is treated better than others in a way that is not fair. (favoritismo)

fawn /fɔːn/ ▶ NOUN [plural **fawns**] a young deer (cervo)

▶ ADJECTIVE having a pale brown colour

◆ PHRASAL VERB [**fawns, fawning, fawned**] **fawn over someone** to praise someone too much to try to make them like you (adular, bajular)

fax /fæks/ ▶ NOUN [plural **faxes**]

1 a written message that is sent by a machine over a telephone line (fax) ▢ I *sent a fax* to the bank. (enviei um fax)

2 a machine used for sending a fax message (aparelho de fax)

▶ VERB [**faxes, faxing, faxed**] to send someone a fax

FBI /ˌefbiːˈaɪ/ ABBREVIATION Federal Bureau of Investigation; the national police of the US (FBI)

fear /fɪə(r)/ ▶ NOUN [plural **fears**]

1 NO PLURAL the feeling of being very frightened ▢ She was shaking with fear. (temor, medo) ▢ They live in *constant fear* of attack. (medo constante)

2 a feeling of being frightened or worried about a particular thing ▢ + **of** John has a fear of spiders. ▢ + **about** He has raised fears about the future of the company. ▢ + **for** She expressed fears for their safety. (medo) ▢ The news confirmed her *worst fears*. (pior medo)

3 for fear of something because you are worried about something bad happening ▢ She didn't complain for fear of losing her job. (por medo de algo)

▶ VERB [**fears, fearing, feared**]

1 to be afraid of or worried about someone or something ▢ Experts fear the virus could spread. ▢ + **that** She feared that she was already too late. ▢ + **for** He feared for his safety. (ter medo de, temer) ▢ She *feared for her life* (= thought she might die). (temeu por sua vida)

2 fear the worst to be worried that something very bad has happened or will happen (temer pelo pior)

- **fearful** /ˈfɪəfʊl/ ADJECTIVE

1 feeling frightened or worried about something ▢ The villagers are fearful of another attack. (temeroso)

2 very bad ▢ He woke up with a fearful headache. (terrível)

- **fearfully** /ˈfɪəfʊlɪ/ ADVERB

1 showing fear ▢ She looked up fearfully. (medrosamente)

2 a formal word that means extremely ▢ It was fearfully hot. (terrivelmente)

- **fearless** /ˈfɪəlɪs/ ADJECTIVE not frightened by anything □ *a fearless fighter* (destemido)
- **fearlessly** /ˈfɪəlɪsli/ ADVERB not showing any fear □ *He spoke out fearlessly against the regime.* (destemidamente)
- **fearsome** /ˈfɪəsəm/ ADJECTIVE very frightening □ *The gang have a fearsome reputation.* (terrível)

feasibility /ˌfiːzəˈbɪləti/ NOUN, NO PLURAL the state of being feasible □ *We're investigating the feasibility of the project.* (viabilidade)

feasible /ˈfiːzəbəl/ ADJECTIVE possible to be done or achieved □ *Cycling to work isn't feasible for many people.* (viável)

feast /fiːst/ NOUN [plural **feasts**] a large meal for a special occasion (banquete)

feat /fiːt/ NOUN [plural **feats**]
1 something someone does that needs a lot of skill, strength or courage □ *a feat of strength and endurance* (proeza) 🔖 *He achieved the remarkable feat of staying on the bestseller list for 237 weeks.* (conseguiu a proeza)
2 be no mean feat to be difficult to achieve □ *Getting four young children ready for school is no mean feat.* (não ser tarefa fácil)

feather /ˈfeðə(r)/ NOUN [plural **feathers**] one of the long light things that cover a bird's body (pena)
- **feathery** /ˈfeðəri/ ADJECTIVE soft and light like a feather (leve)

feature /ˈfiːtʃə(r)/ ▶ NOUN [plural **features**]
1 a part or quality of something □ + **of** *One of the key features of the system is its flexibility.* (característica) 🔖 *The phone's other features include a camera, radio and MP3 player.* (características incluem) 🔖 *The school buses have special safety features.* (características de segurança)
2 a part of your face, such as your eyes, nose or mouth (traços faciais) 🔖 *She described the man's hair colour and facial features.* (traços faciais)
3 a special article in a newspaper or magazine about something □ *The magazine ran a feature on highly paid women.* (artigo, reportagem)
▶ VERB [**features, featuring, featured**] to have someone or something as an important part □ *The film features some exotic locations.* □ + **in** *The same woman features in several of his paintings.* (contar com)

February /ˈfebruəri/ NOUN the second month of the year, after January and before March □ *I started my new job in February.* (fevereiro)

fed /fed/ PAST TENSE AND PAST PARTICIPLE OF **feed** (ver **feed**)

federal /ˈfedərəl/ ADJECTIVE
1 to do with a group of states which make some of their own laws but also have a national government □ *a federal system* (federal)
2 to do with the national government of a country made up of states, like the US □ *a federal court* □ *the Italian football federation* (federal)
- **federation** /ˌfedəˈreɪʃən/ NOUN [plural **federations**] a group of states or organizations which have joined together (federação)

fed up /ˌfed ˈʌp/ ADJECTIVE annoyed or bored with something that has been happening for a long time □ *I've been peeling potatoes all morning and I'm fed up now.* □ *We're fed up with your moaning.* (farto, cheio)

fee /fiː/ NOUN [plural **fees**] an amount of money that you pay for a service □ + **for** *They charge a monthly fee for unlimited Internet access.* (honorário, pagamento) 🔖 *Companies pay a fee to advertise on the site.* (pagam uma taxa)

feeble /ˈfiːbəl/ ADJECTIVE [**feebler, feeblest**]
1 very weak □ *He looked feeble and ill.* □ *a feeble voice* (débil)
2 not good or effective (débil, fraco) 🔖 *a feeble excuse* (desculpa fraca) 🔖 *He made a feeble attempt to protest.* (fraca tentativa)
- **feebly** /ˈfiːbli/ ADVERB in a feeble way □ *She struggled feebly.* (debilmente)

feed /fiːd/ ▶ VERB [**feeds, feeding, fed**]
1 to give food to a person or an animal □ *Dad was feeding the baby.* □ *I don't earn enough money to feed my family.* □ *Can you feed my cat while I'm on holiday?* (alimentar)
2 to eat food □ + **on** *Rabbits feed on grass.* □ + **off** *The caterpillars feed off the leaves.* (comer)
3 to provide something to a person or a machine, often continuously □ + **into** *The information is fed into a computer.* (alimentar)
▶ NOUN [plural **feeds**]
1 food for animals or babies □ *cattle feed* (alimento, ração)
2 the fast movement of information, pictures, etc. to a computer or other equipment □ *You can watch a live feed of the debate on the website.* (alimentador)

feedback /ˈfiːdbæk/ NOUN, NO PLURAL opinions from people about work you are doing or have done, intended to help you do it better (retorno) 🔖 *It's always good to get feedback from customers.* (receber retorno)

feel /fiːl/ ▶ VERB [**feels, feeling, felt**]
1 to have an emotion or to be in a particular state □ *I feel tired.* □ *Do you feel better today?* □ *How are you feeling?* □ *I don't feel any anger towards them.* (sentir)
2 to experience something touching you or happening to you □ *Suddenly, she felt a hand on her shoulder.* □ *He could feel himself falling.* □ *I felt a pain in my leg.* (apalpar)
3 if something feels a certain way, that is how it seems to you □ *Your forehead feels hot.* □ *It*

feels strange to be back here. □ *It feels as though nobody is interested.* (**parecer**)
4 to touch something with your fingers to see what it is like □ *Feel how soft her fur is!* (**sentir**)
5 to think or believe something □ *I feel he should have asked my opinion first.* (**achar**)
6 feel like something to want something or want to do something □ **+ ing** *Do you feel like going for a swim?* (**estar com vontade de**)
▶ NOUN, NO PLURAL the way something is when you touch it □ *I love the feel of these silk sheets.* (**sensação**)

• **feeler** /ˈfiːlə(r)/ NOUN [plural **feelers**] one of the two long parts on an insect's head (**antena**)

• **feeling** /ˈfiːlɪŋ/ NOUN [plural **feelings**]
1 an emotion □ *There was a feeling of excitement amongst the children.* (**sentimento**)
2 something that you experience physically, or the ability to experience it □ *I don't like the feeling of being under water.* (**sensibilidade**) 🔁 *I lost the feeling in my toes.* (**perdi a sensibilidade**)
3 a belief that something is true (**sensação**) 🔁 *I have the feeling that she's avoiding me.* (**tenho a sensação**)
4 opinion □ *My feeling is that they should pay for the damage.* (**opinião**)
⇨ go to **hurt someone's feelings**

feet /fiːt/ PLURAL OF **foot** (**pés**)

feign /feɪn/ VERB [**feigns, feigning, feigned**] to pretend to be experiencing a feeling, an illness, etc. □ *She feigned illness to avoid going to school.* (**fingir**)

feline /ˈfiːlaɪn/ ADJECTIVE to do with cats (**felino**)

fell¹ /fel/ PAST TENSE OF **fall** (*ver* **fall**)

fell² /fel/ VERB [**fells, felling, felled**] if you fell a tree, you cut it down (**derrubar**)

fellow /ˈfeləʊ/ ▶ NOUN [plural **fellows**]
1 an old-fashioned word for a boy or man □ *He's an unusual fellow.* (**sujeito, companheiro**)
2 a person whose job is to teach or study at a university □ *He's a fellow of Trinity College, Cambridge.* (**membro**)
▶ ADJECTIVE used to refer to a person who is similar to you in someway □ *He chatted with fellow passengers.* (**do mesmo tipo**)

• **fellowship** /ˈfeləʊʃɪp/ NOUN [plural **fellowships**]
1 the position of being a fellow at a university (**congregação, sociedade**)
2 a feeling of being friends between people who have similar interests (**companheirismo**)
3 a club or organization (**associação**)

felony /ˈfeləni/ NOUN [plural **felonies**] a US word meaning a serious crime such as murder □ *He could face felony charges.* (**crime**)

felt¹ /felt/ NOUN, NO PLURAL a type of cloth made of rolled and pressed wool (**feltro**)

felt² /felt/ PAST TENSE AND PAST PARTICIPLE OF **feel** (*ver* **feel**)

felt-tip pen /ˌfelt tɪp ˈpen/ NOUN [plural **felt-tip pens**] a pen with a writing point made of soft material (**caneta hidrográfica**)

female /ˈfiːmeɪl/ ▶ ADJECTIVE belonging to the sex which can give birth or lay eggs □ *a female athlete* □ *She won the award for best female artist.* □ *A female lion is called a lioness.* (**fêmea, do sexo feminino**)
▶ NOUN [plural **females**] a female animal or person □ *We saw an adult female with three cubs.* (**fêmea**)

feminine /ˈfemɪnɪn/ ADJECTIVE
1 to do with women, or having qualities that are typical of a woman □ *a feminine voice* □ *This outfit feels more feminine.* (**feminino**)
2 in English grammar, feminine forms of words refer to females. For example, she is a feminine pronoun. (**feminino**)

• **femininity** /ˌfemɪˈnɪnəti/ NOUN, NO PLURAL being like a woman (**feminilidade**)

• **feminism** /ˈfemɪnɪzəm/ NOUN, NO PLURAL the belief that women should have the same rights and opportunities as men (**feminismo**)

• **feminist** /ˈfemɪnɪst/ NOUN [plural **feminists**] someone who supports feminism (**feminista**)

fence /fens/ ▶ NOUN [plural **fences**] a wooden or metal structure that goes around or separates land □ *He put up a fence around the garden.* (**cerca**)
▶ VERB [**fences, fencing, fenced**] to put a fence around or across an area □ *They fenced off the end of their garden.* (**cercar**)
♦ IDIOM **be/sit on the fence** to not make a choice between two possibilities or opinions □ *I'm sitting on the fence on this and waiting to find out a bit more.* (**estar indeciso, em cima do muro**)

fencing /ˈfensɪŋ/ NOUN, NO PLURAL
1 a sport in which people fight with thin swords (= long metal blades) (**esgrima**)
2 fences or the wood or metal that is used to make them (**cercas**)

fend /fend/ VERB [**fends, fending, fended**] **fend for yourself** to look after yourself without help from other people □ *She was left to fend for herself in a strange city.* (**cuidar de si mesmo**)
♦ PHRASAL VERB **fend someone/something off** to defend yourself against an attack or criticism □ *The minister tried to fend off the accusations.* (**defender-se de alguém/algo**)

fender /ˈfendə(r)/ NOUN [plural **fenders**] the US word for **bumper** (**para-choque**)

ferment /fəˈment/ VERB [**ferments, fermenting, fermented**] when beer or wine ferments, the sugar becomes alcohol (**fermentar**)

• **fermentation** /ˌfɜːmənˈteɪʃən/ NOUN, NO PLURAL the process of fermenting (**fermentação**)

fern /fɜːn/ NOUN [plural **ferns**] a plant with long leaves like feathers (**samambaia**)

ferocious

ferocious /fəˈrəʊʃəs/ ADJECTIVE extremely violent, strong or dangerous □ *a ferocious dog* □ *a ferocious storm* (feroz)

- **ferociously** /fəˈrəʊʃəsli/ ADVERB in a ferocious way □ *They fought ferociously.* (ferozmente)

- **ferocity** /fəˈrɒsɪti/ NOUN, NO PLURAL being ferocious □ *She was shocked by the ferocity of his anger.* (ferocidade)

ferret /ˈferɪt/ ▶ NOUN [*plural* **ferrets**] a small animal with a long body, used to hunt rabbits (furão)

▶ VERB [**ferrets, ferreting, ferreted**] to look for something somewhere □ *She was ferreting around in her bag for her keys.* (procurar)

♦ PHRASAL VERB **ferret something out** to look for something that is difficult to find □ *Reporters are trying to ferret out the names of those* (desenterrar) *involved.*

ferry /ˈferi/ ▶ NOUN [*plural* **ferries**] a boat that carries people and vehicles (balsa) a *passenger ferry* (balsa de passageiros) *We took a ferry to a smaller island.* (pegamos uma balsa)

▶ VERB [**ferries, ferrying, ferried**] to take people regularly from one place to another □ *A shuttle bus ferries tourists between the hotel and the airport.* (transportar)

fertile /ˈfɜːtaɪl/ ADJECTIVE
1 fertile land is good for growing crops on □ *fertile soil* (fértil)
2 a fertile person or animal is able to produce children or young animals (fértil)
3 producing a lot of new ideas □ *You have a fertile imagination.* (fértil)
4 fertile ground a situation which encourages something □ *Spying is fertile ground for authors and film-makers.* (produtivo)

- **fertility** /fɜːˈtɪlɪti/ NOUN, NO PLURAL being fertile □ *She is having fertility treatment.* (fertilidade)

- **fertilization** or **fertilisation** /ˌfɜːtɪlaɪˈzeɪʃən/ NOUN, NO PLURAL the act of fertilizing something (fertilização)

- **fertilize** or **fertilise** /ˈfɜːtɪlaɪz/ VERB [**fertilizes, fertilizing, fertilized**]
1 to add a substance to soil so that plants grow better (adubar)
2 to put male and female cells together to produce a baby or a young plant or animal (fertilizar)

- **fertilizer** or **fertiliser** /ˈfɜːtɪlaɪzə(r)/ NOUN [*plural* **fertilizers**] a substance you put on soil to make plants grow better (fertilizante)

fervent /ˈfɜːvənt/ ADJECTIVE very enthusiastic and sincere □ *He was a fervent admirer of Picasso.* (ardente)

- **fervour** /ˈfɜːvə(r)/ NOUN, NO PLURAL a strong enthusiasm for or belief in something □ *A wave of religious fervour swept the country.* □ *He spoke with fervour about the need for reform.* (fervor)

fervor /ˈfɜːvə(r)/ NOUN, NO PLURAL the US spelling of fervour (fervor)

festival /ˈfestɪvəl/ NOUN [*plural* **festivals**]
1 a series of special events of a particular type (festival) a *film festival* (festival de filmes) a *five-day music festival* (festival de música) □ + *of an annual festival of traditional music*
2 a special time or day when people celebrate something (festa) a *religious festival* (festa religiosa) □ + *of the Muslim festival of Eid*

- **festive** /ˈfestɪv/ ADJECTIVE to do with happy celebrations □ *a festive occasion* □ *a festive atmosphere* (festivo) *We spent the festive season* (= Christmas) *with my family.* (época festiva)

- **festivities** /feˈstɪvətiz/ PLURAL NOUN the things you do to celebrate a special event □ *the Independence Day festivities* (festividades)

festoon /feˈstuːn/ VERB [**festoons, festooning, festooned**] to decorate a place with colourful decorations □ *The city was festooned with flags.* (adornar)

fetch /fetʃ/ VERB [**fetches, fetching, fetched**]
1 to go somewhere and bring something or someone back with you □ *Could you fetch the newspaper for me, please?* □ *I'll come and fetch you.* □ *The women fetch water from the river.* (ir buscar)
2 to be sold for a particular amount of money (atingir) *The painting fetched a record price.* (atingiu um preço) □ *It is expected to fetch £100,000 at auction.*

fête /feɪt, fet/ NOUN [*plural* **fêtes**] a special event held outside with games and things for sale □ *a school fête* (feira, quermesse)

fetus /ˈfiːtəs/ NOUN [*plural* **fetuses**] the US spelling of foetus (feto)

feud /fjuːd/ ▶ NOUN [*plural* **feuds**] a serious argument between two people or groups that continues for a long time (rixa)

▶ VERB [**feuds, feuding, feuded**] to have a feud with someone (rixa)

fever /ˈfiːvə(r)/ NOUN [*plural* **fevers**] if you have a fever, your body temperature is higher than normal because you are ill (febre) *He had a high fever* (febre alta)

- **feverish** /ˈfiːvərɪʃ/ ADJECTIVE feeling very hot because you are ill (febril)

few /fjuː/ DETERMINER, PRONOUN [**fewer, fewest**]
1 a small number □ *I packed a few apples and some bread.* □ *A few people tried to help him.* □ *I visit her every few days.* □ *The past few weeks have been very difficult.* (alguns)
2 some but not many □ *We only had a few replies to our advert.* □ *Few of the children had seen a cow before.* (poucos) *Very few people know her real name.* (muito poucos)

3 quite a few quite a lot ☐ *There were quite a few mistakes in his work.* (**muitos**)

fiancé /fɪˈɒnseɪ/ NOUN [*plural* **fiancés**] a woman's fiancé is the man she has promised to marry ☐ *She will marry her fiancé in April.* (**noivo**)

fiancée /fɪˈɒnseɪ/ NOUN [*plural* **fiancées**] a man's fiancée is the woman he has promised to marry ☐ *Tom's fiancée is a teacher.* (**noiva**)

fiasco /fiˈæskəʊ/ NOUN [*plural* **fiascos**] a situation that is a complete and embarrassing failure (**fiasco, fracasso**)

fib /fɪb/ ▶ NOUN [*plural* **fibs**] an informal word meaning a lie about something which is not important (**mentira**) 🔄 *Many young children tell fibs.* (**contam mentiras**)
▶ VERB [**fibs, fibbing, fibbed**] to tell a lie about something that is not important (**mentir**)

fibre /ˈfaɪbə(r)/ NOUN [*plural* **fibres**]
1 a substance in food which your body cannot digest, and which helps your bowels work well ☐ *Brown bread is high in fibre.* (**fibra**)
2 a cloth made up of threads (**fibras**) 🔄 *Try to wear clothes made from natural fibres, such as cotton.* (**fibras naturais**)
3 a thin thread of something ☐ *Fibres from the girl's clothing were found in his car.* (**fibra**)

fibreglass /ˈfaɪbəɡlɑːs/ NOUN, NO PLURAL a strong, light material made from very small pieces of glass or plastic (**fibra de vidro**)

fibre optics /ˌfaɪbər ˈɒptɪks/ NOUN, NO PLURAL the use of small threads of glass to send information in the form of light. A physics word. (**fibras óticas**)

fickle /ˈfɪkəl/ ADJECTIVE always changing your opinion about people or things (**volúvel**)

fiction /ˈfɪkʃən/ NOUN, NO PLURAL
1 books about imaginary people and situations (**ficção**) ☐ *He enjoys reading crime fiction.* (**crimes de ficção**) 🔄 *JK Rowling is one of the most famous children's fiction writers.* (**escritores de ficção**)
2 something that is not true or real (**ficção**) 🔄 *Her excuses were pure fiction.* (**pura ficção**)
• **fictional** /ˈfɪkʃənəl/ ADJECTIVE from a book or story, and not real (**fictício**) 🔄 *Harry Potter is a well-known fictional character.* (**personagem fictício**)
• **fictitious** /fɪkˈtɪʃəs/ ADJECTIVE not true, or not real ☐ *a fictitious name* (**fictício**)

fiddle /ˈfɪdəl/ ▶ VERB [**fiddles, fiddling, fiddled**]
1 to touch something repeatedly with small movements ☐ *She was fiddling with her hair.* (**brincar com**)
2 to move something slightly in order to improve it or make it work ☐ *He was fiddling with the wires at the back of the computer.* (**remexer**)
3 to change something in a way that is not honest in order to get money or an advantage ☐ *He fiddles his taxes.* (**alterar**)
▶ NOUN [*plural* **fiddles**]
1 an informal word for a violin (= musical instrument) (**violino**)
2 an informal word meaning a dishonest way of getting money (**fraude**)
• **fiddly** /ˈfɪdli/ ADJECTIVE difficult to do or use because very small parts are involved ☐ *Changing the battery in a watch can be quite fiddly.* (**complicado**)

fidget /ˈfɪdʒɪt/ VERB [**fidgets, fidgeting, fidgeted**] to keep moving because you are nervous or bored (**impacientar-se**)

field /fiːld/ ▶ NOUN [*plural* **fields**]
1 an area of land used for growing crops or keeping animals on ☐ *There were lots of cows in the field.* ☐ **+ of** *We saw a lovely field of poppies.* (**campo**)
2 an area of grass used for playing sport on (**campo**) 🔄 *a football field* (**campo de futebol**)
3 a subject that people study, or the type of work they do ☐ *These charts are widely used by experts in the medical field.* ☐ *This is a new and exciting field of research.* (**campo**)
▶ VERB [**fields, fielding, fielded**]
1 to be the team that throws and catches the ball instead of hitting it, in games such as cricket or baseball (**apanhar a bola**)
2 to send a team of people to take part in a game or election ☐ *They fielded a very strong team.* (**formar**)
3 to deal with a lot of something such as questions or telephone calls ☐ *The Prime Minister fielded questions on a range of subjects.* (**receber e responder**)
• **fielder** /ˈfiːldə(r)/ NOUN [*plural* **fielders**] someone who is in the sports team that is fielding (**jogador que intercepta a bola**)

fiend /fiːnd/ NOUN [*plural* **fiends**] an evil person (**demônio**)

fierce /fɪəs/ ADJECTIVE [**fiercer, fiercest**]
1 violent and angry ☐ *a fierce animal* ☐ *fierce fighting* (**feroz**)
2 very powerful or strong (**intenso**) 🔄 *The company faces fierce competition.* (**competição intensa**) ☐ *Fierce winds brought down power lines.*
• **fiercely** /ˈfɪəsli/ ADVERB in a fierce way ☐ *She defended her cubs fiercely.* ☐ *He is fiercely opposed to the new airport.* (**ferozmente**)

fiery /ˈfaɪəri/ ADJECTIVE
1 full of strong or angry feelings ☐ *He has a fiery temper.* ☐ *a fiery speech* (**furioso**)
2 like fire ☐ *a fiery orange light* (**flamejante**)

fifteen /ˌfɪfˈtiːn/ NUMBER the number 15 (**quinze**)

fifteenth /ˌfɪfˈtiːnθ/ NUMBER 15th written as a word (**décimo quinto**)

fifth /fɪfθ/ ▶ NUMBER 5th written as a word ☐ *Today is their fifth wedding anniversary.* (**quinto**)
▶ NOUN [*plural* **fifths**] 1/5; one of five equal parts of something ☐ *A fifth of the money is mine.* (**quinto**)

fiftieth /ˈfɪftɪəθ/ NUMBER 50th written as a word (**quinquagésimo**)

fifty /ˈfɪfti/ NUMBER [plural **fifties**]
1 the number 50 (**cinquenta**)
2 the fifties the years between 1950 and 1959 (**anos cinquenta**)

fig /fɪɡ/ NOUN [plural **figs**] a fruit with a lot of seeds in it, which is often eaten dried (**figo**)

fight /faɪt/ ▶ VERB [**fights, fighting, fought**]
1 to use your body or weapons to try to defeat someone ☐ *They started fighting.* ☐ *My great grandfather fought in the second world war.* ☐ *Troops fought a fierce battle in the desert.* (**lutar**)
2 to argue with someone ☐ + *about They're fighting about who should do the washing up.* ☐ + *over They're fighting over her money* (= arguing about who should have it). (**brigar, discutir**)
3 to try to stop something (**combater**) 🔁 *fight crime/infection.* (**combater o crime/infecção**) ☐ + *against We are fighting against plans for a new airport.*
4 to try to achieve something ☐ + *for They were fighting for the right to vote.* ☐ + *to do something He is fighting to get his job back.* (**lutar**)

♦ PHRASAL VERB **fight back**
1 to fight against someone who has attacked you (**resistir**)
2 to argue against or try to stop someone who has criticized you or harmed you ☐ *After years of poor treatment, the workers are starting to fight back.* (**responde**)
3 fight back tears to try not to cry (**segurar as lágrimas**)

▶ NOUN [plural **fights**]
1 when people use physical force to hurt each other ☐ + *between There was a fight between local gangs.* (**luta**)
2 when people argue with each other ☐ *I had a fight with my Mum about staying out late.* (**briga, discussão**) 🔁 *Josh is always trying to pick a fight* (= start an argument). (**começar uma briga**)
3 when people try to stop something ☐ + *against We need everyone to help in the fight against racism.* (**luta**)
4 when people try hard to achieve something ☐ + *for His book describes the long fight for justice.* (**luta**)
5 a boxing (= sport where people hit each other) competition (**luta**)

• **fighter** /ˈfaɪtə(r)/ NOUN [plural **fighters**]
1 someone who is fighting (**lutador**)
2 a fast military aeroplane used for attacking (**avião de caça**)

• **fighting** /ˈfaɪtɪŋ/ NOUN, NO PLURAL when people are fighting, especially in a war (**batalha, luta**) 🔁 *fierce/heavy fighting* (**combate feroz/pesado**)

figment /ˈfɪɡmənt/ NOUN [plural **figments**] a figment of someone's imagination something that someone imagines is real, but that does not really exist (**produto da imaginação de alguém**)

figurative /ˈfɪɡərətɪv/ ADJECTIVE a figurative use of a word has a meaning that has developed from its main meaning. For example, 'She was glued to the television all day' is a figurative use of 'glued'. (**figurativo**)

figure /ˈfɪɡə(r)/ ▶ NOUN [plural **figures**]
1 a number that tells you an amount, especially in official documents (**soma**) 🔁 *official/government figures* (**números oficiais/do governo**) 🔁 *The latest unemployment figures were released* (= told to the public) *today.* (**números divulgados**) 🔁 *Figures show that obesity has increased.* (**números mostram**)
2 a number ☐ *He paid a four figure sum* (= over £1,000). (**dígito, número**) 🔁 *The number of deaths has reached double figures* (= is at least 10). (**dois dígitos**)
3 the shape of your body ☐ *She's got a lovely figure.* (**silhueta**)
4 a person of a particular type (**figura**) 🔁 *He is a leading/senior figure in the government.* (**figura de liderança/sênior**) ☐ *Privacy is difficult for public figures.*
5 a person that you do not know or cannot see clearly ☐ *There was a shadowy figure in the doorway.* (**contorno, vulto**)
6 a shape. A maths word. ☐ *a three-sided figure* (**figura**)

▶ VERB [**figures, figuring, figured**]
1 to be part of something ☐ + *in Babies don't figure in her plans for the future.* (**fazer parte**)
2 to think that something is true ☐ + *that I figured that we could manage without him.* (**imaginar**)
3 it/that figures used to say that you are not surprised about something bad ☐ *Casey's given up college? That figures.* (**isso faz sentido**)

♦ PHRASAL VERBS **figure something out** to understand something complicated ☐ *I can't figure out how to open this cupboard.* (**entender algo**) **figure someone out** to understand someone's character or behaviour ☐ *She says she wants to be alone, then complains that nobody visits her – I just can't figure her out.* (**entender alguém**)

figure of speech /ˌfɪɡər əv ˈspiːtʃ/ NOUN [plural **figures of speech**] a word or phrase used in a different way from usual to create a particular idea. For example, if you say someone is a lion, you mean that they are as brave or fierce as a lion. (**figura de linguagem**)

file /faɪl/ ▶ NOUN [plural **files**]
1 a place for storing information on a computer. A computing word. ☐ *I've created a new file for the accounts.* ☐ *I downloaded some image files.* (**arquivo**)
2 a collection of information about something or someone (**arquivo**) 🔁 *We keep files on all our employees.* (**mantemos arquivos**)

file extension   297   **final**

3 on file if information is on file, it is recorded and kept somewhere ▫ *We'll keep your details on file.* (**arquivado**)
4 a piece of folded card for keeping documents in (**fichário**)
5 a tool with a rough edge for making things smooth (**lima**)
6 in single file if people walk in single file, they walk with one person behind another (**em fila única**)
▶ VERB [**files, filing, filed**]
1 to put documents into a file ▫ *Please file these application forms under 'rejects'.* (**arquivar**)
2 to take official, especially legal action (**protocolar**) ▣ *She decided to file for divorce.* (**protocolar divórcio**)
3 to walk somewhere, one person behind another ▫ *The children filed into the hall.* (**andar em fila, desfilar**)
4 to make something smooth using a file (**limar**)

file extension /ˈfaɪl ɪkˌstenʃən/ NOUN [plural **file extensions**] three letters at the end of a computer document's name that show the type of document (**extensão de arquivo**)

filename /ˈfaɪlneɪm/ NOUN [plural **filenames**] the name that you give to a computer file. A computing word. (**nome do arquivo**)

filing cabinet /ˈfaɪlɪŋ ˌkæbɪnɪt/ NOUN [plural **filing cabinets**] a piece of furniture for an office, which has big drawers for keeping papers in. (**fichário**)

filings /ˈfaɪlɪŋz/ PLURAL NOUN very small pieces of metal that have been cut from a larger piece ▫ *iron filings* (**limalhas**)

fill /fɪl/ VERB [**fills, filling, filled**]
1 to make a container or space full ▫ + **with** *The waiter filled our glasses with wine.* ▫ *The room was filled with smoke* ▫ + **up** *She filled up the pan with water.* (**encher**)
2 to become full ▫ + **with** *The concert hall quickly filled with people.* ▫ + **up** *The room had filled up by the time we got back.* (**encher-se**)
3 if a sound, smell, etc. fills a place, you easily notice it (**encher**) ▣ *The sound of laughter filled the air.* (**encheu o ar**)
4 to make someone have a feeling very strongly ▫ + **with** *The idea filled her with excitement.* ▫ *He was filled with hate.* (**encher**)
5 to provide something that people need or want (**satisfazer**) ▣ *The service will fill a gap in healthcare provision.* (**satisfazer um vazio**)
6 to do a job, or find someone to do a job (**preencher**) ▣ *Many positions are filled by doctors from overseas.* (**cargos foram preenchidos**)

♦ PHRASAL VERB **fill something in/out** to write information in the spaces on an official document (**preencher algo**) ▣ *To apply for a place on the course, you need to fill in this form.* (**preencher este requerimento**)

fillet /ˈfɪlɪt/ ▶ NOUN [plural **fillets**] a piece of meat or fish with no bones in it (**filé**)
▶ VERB [**fillets, filleting, filleted**] to remove the bones from meat or fish (**cortar em filés**)

filling /ˈfɪlɪŋ/ ▶ NOUN [plural **fillings**]
1 a substance used to fill a hole in your tooth ▫ *Ben hasn't got any fillings.* (**obturação**)
2 food that is put inside things such as cakes or sandwiches (= pieces of bread with food between) ▫ *pancakes with a chocolate filling* (**recheio**)
▶ ADJECTIVE food that is filling makes your stomach feel full

filling station /ˈfɪlɪŋ ˌsteɪʃən/ NOUN [plural **filling stations**] a place where you buy petrol (**posto de gasolina**)

film /fɪlm/ ▶ NOUN [plural **films**]
1 a story that you watch in a cinema or on television (**filme**) ▣ *Have you seen this James Bond film?* (**viu o filme**) ▣ *He was watching a film on television.* (**assistindo ao filme**) ▣ *They made a film about his life.* (**fizeram um filme**) ▣ *a film star* (= a famous actor who has been in many films) (**estrela do filme**)
2 something you put inside a camera so you can take photographs (**filme**) ▣ *I need a new roll of film.* (**rolo de filme**)
3 a film of something a thin layer of something on a surface ▫ *The glass was covered with a film of dirt.* (**uma película de algo**)
▶ VERB [**films, filming, filmed**] to make a film of something ▫ *They were filming scenes for her new movie.* ▫ *'Brokeback Mountain' was filmed in Canada.* (**filmar**)

filter /ˈfɪltə(r)/ ▶ NOUN [plural **filters**] a device that you put a liquid or gas through in order to remove solid substances ▫ *a water filter* (**filtro**)
▶ VERB [**filters, filtered, filtering**]
1 to put something through a filter (**filtrar**)
2 if light or sound filters into a place, small amounts of it reach there ▫ *Light was filtering into the bedroom through a gap in the curtains.* (**infiltrar-se**)
3 if news or information filters somewhere, people gradually hear about it ▫ *News of his resignation filtered through the college.* (**infiltrar-se**)

filth /fɪlθ/ NOUN, NO PLURAL
1 dirt (**imundície**)
2 rude words or pictures (**obscenidade**)

• **filthy** /ˈfɪlθi/ ADJECTIVE [**filthier, filthiest**]
1 very dirty ▫ *His clothes were filthy.* (**imundo**)
2 very rude ▫ *filthy language* (**obsceno**)

fin /fɪn/ NOUN [plural **fins**] one of the two parts on a fish that help it to balance and swim (**barbatana**)

final /ˈfaɪnəl/ ▶ ADJECTIVE
1 coming at the end ▫ *I'm reading the final chapter of the book.* ▫ *On the final day of his tour, the Prime Minister visited a school.* (**final, último**)

2 a final decision, offer, agreement etc. cannot be changed (**final**) ▣ We haven't made a *final decision* yet. (**decisão final**) ▢ They're waiting for final approval of the plans.

▶ NOUN [*plural* **finals**] the last game in a competition, which decides who will win ▢ Federer will play Henman in the final. ▢ The team are through to the finals. (**final**)

finale /fɪˈnɑːlɪ/ NOUN [*plural* **finales**] the last part of a show or piece of music (**ato final**)

finalist /ˈfaɪnəlɪst/ NOUN [*plural* **finalists**] a person or team who is in the last part of a competition (**finalista**)

finalize or **finalise** /ˈfaɪnəlaɪz/ VERB [**finalizes, finalizing, finalized**] to decide the last details of something, such as a plan or journey ▢ The deal was finalized on Monday. (**finalizar**)

finally /ˈfaɪnəli/ ADVERB
1 after a long time ▢ When he finally arrived, it was after midnight. (**finalmente**)
2 used to introduce the last in a list of things ▢ Finally, I would like to thank everyone who has helped. (**finalmente**)

finance ▶ NOUN /ˈfaɪnæns/ [*plural* **finances**]
1 NO PLURAL things that are to do with money, especially in a government or company ▢ John is an expert in finance. (**finanças**) ▣ She's the company's *finance director*. (**diretor de finanças**)
2 NO PLURAL the money needed for something in business ▢ They're struggling to raise the finance for a new theatre. (**renda**)
3 finances the money that an organization or person has ▢ Our finances are in a healthy state (**finanças**) ▣ He *handles the finances* of several charities. (**gerencia as finanças**)

▶ VERB /faɪˈnæns/ [**finances, financing, financed**] to provide the money for something, especially in business ▢ They took out a loan to finance the project. (**financiar**)

• **financial** /faɪˈnænʃəl/ ADJECTIVE to do with money (**financeiro**) ▣ banks and other *financial institutions* (**instituições financeiras**) ▣ Many companies are facing *financial difficulties*. (**dificuldades financeiras**)

• **financially** /faɪˈnænʃəli/ ADVERB in a way that is to do with money ▢ He is financially secure. (**financeiramente**)

finch /fɪntʃ/ NOUN [*plural* **finches**] a small bird with a short beak (**tentilhão**)

find /faɪnd/ ▶ VERB [**finds, finding, found**]
1 to discover or see something or someone you have been looking for ▢ I can't find my pencil case. ▢ The murderer was never found. (**encontrar**)
2 to discover something by chance ▢ A jogger found the body by the river last night. ▢ I found a beetle in my soup. (**achar**)
3 to discover that something has happened or that something is true ▢ The survey found a link between birth weight and intelligence. ▢ + *that* I find that it is best to call her in the mornings. ▢ I found I had forgotten my phone. (**descobrir**)
4 to discover an answer, a reason or a way of doing something (**descobrir**) ▣ We *found a way* to stop the leak. (**descobrir um modo**) ▣ We are trying to *find a solution* to the problem of litter. (**descobrir uma solução**)
5 to have a particular experience of someone or something ▢ I found him very rude. ▢ I found it difficult to lift the rocks. (**achar**)
6 to get something (**encontrar**) ▣ She *found work* in a local hospital. (**encontrou trabalho**) ▢ I managed to find somewhere to live.
7 to manage to have enough of something (**encontrar**) ▣ I don't know how she *finds the time* to go running every day. (**encontra tempo**) ▢ Somehow, he found the courage to speak his mind.
8 find yourself doing something to become aware that you are doing something without intending to ▢ I found myself feeling sorry for her. (**pegar-se fazendo algo**)
9 find your way to get to a place ▢ Can you find your way to the station? (**encontrar o caminho**)
10 find someone guilty/not guilty to say that someone is guilty/not guilty in a court ▢ He was found guilty of murder and sentenced to life in prison. (**considerar alguém culpado/ inocente**)

◆ PHRASAL VERB **find out (something)** to discover information or the truth about something ▢ + *that* We found out that they had been stealing from us. ▢ + *about* She used the Internet to find out about bees. ▢ I need to find out how to set up a website. (**descobrir algo**)

▶ NOUN [*plural* **finds**] something or someone useful, good or valuable that has been found ▢ The baker's in Hope Street was a real find! (**achado, descoberta**)

• **finding** /ˈfaɪndɪŋ/ NOUN [*plural* **findings**] information that is got by studying a subject (**achado**) ▣ The scientists *published their findings* in the journal 'Nature'. (**publicaram achados**)

fine /faɪn/ ADJECTIVE [**finer, finest**]
1 good or acceptable ▢ 'Let's meet at seven.' 'OK, that sounds fine.' ▢ 'Is the water hot enough?' 'Yes, it's fine, thanks.' (**ótimo**)
2 healthy or happy ▢ 'How are you?' 'I'm fine, thanks.' (**bem**) ▣ Don't worry, I'm *absolutely fine*. (**completamente bem**)
3 of a very good quality ▢ The museum has many fine examples of Japanese art. ▢ It was a fine performance. (**ótimo**)
4 very thin, or made of very small pieces ▢ a fine needle ▢ fine powder (**fino**)
5 sunny, with no rain (**ensolarado**) ▣ The *fine weather* brought many people to the coast. (**tempo ensolarado**)

> Note that the adjective **fine**, meaning 'healthy or happy' never has the word 'very' before it:
> ✓ 'How are you, Lilia?' 'I'm fine, thanks.'
> ✗ 'How are you, Lilia?' 'I'm very fine, thanks.'

▶ ADVERB an informal word meaning well ☐ *I get on fine with my parents.* ☐ *The system works fine.* (bem) 🔁 *Leaving a bit later suits me just fine.* (simplesmente bem)

▶ NOUN [plural **fines**] money that someone must pay as a punishment (multa) 🔁 *He was given a parking fine.* (multa de estacionamento) 🔁 *She was ordered to pay a fine of £60 for speeding.* (pagar uma multa)

▶ VERB [**fines, fining, fined**] to make someone pay a fine ☐ *He was fined for dropping litter.* (multar)

• **finely** /ˈfaɪnli/ ADVERB
1 into very thin small pieces (finamente) 🔁 *Chop the onion finely.* (corte finamente)
2 in a beautiful way that impresses people ☐ *The palace was finely decorated.* (otimamente)
3 very exactly ☐ *a finely tuned machine* (exatamente)

finesse /fɪˈnes/ NOUN, NO PLURAL if you do something with finesse, you do it with skill and style (sutileza)

finger /ˈfɪŋɡə(r)/ ▶ NOUN [plural **fingers**] one of the five long parts at the end of your hand (dedo) 🔁 *Sam had a cut on his little finger* (= smallest finger). (mindinho)
⇨ go to **index finger**

◆ IDIOMS (**keep your**) **fingers crossed** used for saying that you hope something will happen ☐ *We're keeping our fingers crossed that he passes the exam.* ☐ *Fingers crossed the train arrives on time.* (cruzar os dedos) **put your finger on something** to understand exactly what is wrong, different etc. ☐ *Something wasn't right but I couldn't put my finger on it.* (apontar algo)

▶ VERB [**fingers, fingering, fingered**] to touch something with your fingers ☐ *She fingered the necklace she was wearing.* (apontar)

fingernail /ˈfɪŋɡəneɪl/ NOUN [plural **fingernails**] the hard part at the top of each finger ☐ *He bites his fingernails.* (unha)

fingerprint /ˈfɪŋɡəprɪnt/ NOUN [plural **fingerprints**] the mark that your finger leaves when you touch something ☐ *The police took his fingerprints.* (impressão digital)

fingertip /ˈfɪŋɡətɪp/ NOUN [plural **fingertips**]
1 the top end of each finger (ponta do dedo)
2 **have something at your fingertips** to have something easily available and ready to use ☐ *He had all the latest facts at his fingertips.* (ter algo na ponta dos dedos)

finish /ˈfɪnɪʃ/ ▶ VERB [**finishes, finishing, finished**]
1 to complete something ☐ *Have you finished your homework?* ☐ + *ing* *I've finished cleaning the bathroom.* (terminar)
2 to come to an end ☐ *What time did the film finish?* (acabar)
3 to use, eat or drink all of something ☐ *I've finished the last of the bread.* (acabar)
4 to have a particular position at the end of a race, competition, etc. ☐ *He finished third in the long jump.* ☐ *They finished five points ahead of their nearest rivals.* (terminar)

◆ PHRASAL VERBS **finish something off**
1 to complete the last part of something ☐ *I just need to finish off the housework.* (completar) **2** to eat, drink or use the last part of something ☐ *The children finished off all the sausages.* (terminar) **finish with something** to stop using or needing something ☐ *Have you finished with the bread knife?* (acabar de usar algo) **finish up** to end by being in a particular place or situation ☐ *We finished up having to apologize to our neighbours.* (acabar)

▶ NOUN [plural **finishes**]
1 the end of a race (final) 🔁 *It was a close finish.* (final apertado)
2 the last part of something (chegada) 🔁 *The course was badly planned from start to finish.* (do início à chegada)

• **finished** /ˈfɪnɪʃt/ ADJECTIVE
1 completed (completo) 🔁 *the finished product* (produto completo)
2 if you are finished, you have completed what you are doing ☐ *I'll be finished in a moment.* (pronto)

finite /ˈfaɪnaɪt/ ADJECTIVE having a limit or an end (limitado) 🔁 *Oil and coal are finite resources.* (recursos limitados)

fir /fɜː(r)/ NOUN [plural **firs**] a type of tree with very thin, sharp leaves that keeps those leaves in winter (aberto)

fire /ˈfaɪə(r)/ ▶ NOUN [plural **fires**]
1 NO PLURAL flames and heat that are caused by something burning ☐ *The building was destroyed by fire.* (fogo)
2 when something burns in a way that is not intended (fogo) 🔁 *Fire broke out* (= started) *in the warehouse.* (o fogo começou) 🔁 *We used buckets of water to put out the fire.* (acabar com o fogo) 🔁 *The curtains caught fire* (= started to burn). (pegaram fogo)
3 on fire burning ☐ *Soon the whole building was on fire.* (em chamas)
4 **set fire to something** to make something burn (colocar fogo em algo)
5 a pile of wood, coal, etc. that is burned to provide heat (fogueira) 🔁 *I lit a fire in the bedroom.* (acendi uma fogueira)
6 a device that heats a room using gas or electricity ☐ *Put the fire on if you're cold.* (lareira)

7 when guns are shot (disparo) ◻ *The troops came under heavy fire.* (disparos pesados)

♦ IDIOM **come under fire** to be criticized ◻ *Company bosses have come under fire for giving themselves huge salaries.* (ser muito criticado)

▶ VERB [**fires, firing, fired**]

1 to fire a gun is to shoot a bullet from it (atirar)

2 an informal word meaning to tell someone that they must leave their job ◻ *She was fired for bullying her colleagues.* (ser demitido)

♦ PHRASAL VERBS **fire something off** to quickly send a letter, message or instructions to do something ◻ *He fired off a letter to the editor.* (enviar algo apressadamente) **fire someone up** to make someone enthusiastic or angry ◻ *We were all fired up and ready for the match.* (empolgar alguém)

fire alarm /ˈfaɪər əˌlɑːm/ NOUN [*plural* **fire alarms**] a bell that rings to warn you of a fire in a building (alarme de incêndio)

firearm /ˈfaɪərɑːm/ NOUN [*plural* **firearms**] a formal word meaning a gun (arma de fogo)

fire brigade /ˈfaɪə brɪˌɡeɪd/ NOUN [*plural* **fire brigades**] the group of people whose job is to stop fires burning (corpo de bombeiros)

fire engine /ˈfaɪər ˌendʒɪn/ NOUN [*plural* **fire engines**] a vehicle that carries firefighters and their equipment (carro de bombeiros)

fire escape /ˈfaɪər ɪˌskeɪp/ NOUN [*plural* **fire escapes**] stairs on the outside of a building, which people use if there is a fire (escada de incêndio)

firefighter /ˈfaɪəˌfaɪtə(r)/ NOUN [*plural* **firefighters**] someone whose job is to stop fires burning ◻ *Firefighters battled for two hours to get the blaze under control.* (bombeiro)

fireman /ˈfaɪəmən/ NOUN [*plural* **firemen**] a man whose job is to stop fires burning (bombeiro)

fireplace /ˈfaɪəpleɪs/ NOUN [*plural* **fireplaces**] a place for a fire in the wall of a room, or the frame around this space (lareira)

fire station /ˈfaɪə ˌsteɪʃən/ NOUN [*plural* **fire stations**] a building where firefighters and their vehicles and equipment wait until they are needed (quartel de bombeiros)

firewall /ˈfaɪəwɔːl/ NOUN [*plural* **firewalls**] software that protects your computer when you are on the Internet. A computing word. (firewall, sistema de segurança)

firewood /ˈfaɪəwʊd/ NOUN, NO PLURAL wood for burning (lenha)

firework /ˈfaɪəwɜːk/ NOUN [*plural* **fireworks**] something which explodes and makes bright lights in the sky for entertainment (fogo de artifício) ◻ *The festival ended with a spectacular fireworks display.* (show de fogos de artifício)

firing squad /ˈfaɪərɪŋ ˌskwɒd/ NOUN [*plural* **firing squads**] a group of soldiers whose job is to shoot and kill a prisoner (pelotão de fuzilamento)

firm /fɜːm/ ▶ ADJECTIVE [**firmer, firmest**]

1 not soft ◻ *a firm bed* (firme)

2 certain and not changing ◻ *He has very firm views on education.* ◻ *There was no firm evidence linking him to the crime.* (firme)

3 showing that you are in control and that you mean what you say ◻ *She spoke in a quiet but firm voice.* ◻ *She is a very firm leader.* ◻ + **with** *You should be more firm with the children.* (firme)

4 tight, strong and not going to move ◻ *Betsy took a firm hold on the tray.* (firme)

▶ NOUN [*plural* **firms**] a company ◻ *Sally works for a law firm.* ◻ *a software firm* (firma, empresa)

• **firmly** /ˈfɜːmli/ ADVERB in a firm way (firmemente) ◻ *I firmly believe he's innocent.* (acredito firmemente) ◻ *'No I won't,' he said firmly.* ◻ *Raj pressed the lid down firmly.*

first /fɜːst/ ▶ DETERMINER, NUMBER

1 coming before everyone or everything else ◻ *His was the first name on the list.* ◻ *The first time I went skiing, I hated it.* ◻ *Take the first road on the left.* (primeiro)

2 1st written as a word (primeiro)

3 best in a competition, exam, etc. ◻ *first place/ prize* (primeiro)

4 at the beginning of something ◻ *The first few months of college were tough.* (primeiro)

▶ ADVERB

1 before anyone or anything else ◻ *You can phone Josh, but eat your dinner first.* ◻ *First you need to dig the foundations.* (primeiro)

2 for the first time ◻ *We first met at university.* ◻ *I first became aware of the problem last week.* (pela primeira vez)

3 doing better than everyone else in a competition, exam, etc. (em primeiro) ◻ *Philip came first in the cookery competition.* (chegou em primeiro)

4 at first at the beginning ◻ *At first I couldn't speak French at all.* (a princípio)

5 more important than anything or anyone else (em primeiro lugar) ◻ *I have to put my children's happiness first.* (colocar em primeiro lugar) ◻ *It's obvious that money comes first for her.* (vem em primeiro lugar)

▶ PRONOUN, NOUN, NO PLURAL

1 the person or thing that comes before all others ◻ *She was the first to realise how the drug could be used.* ◻ *This is the first in a series of Beethoven concerts.* ◻ *The doctor's ready now. Who's first?* (primeiro)

2 a first something that has never happened before ◻ *Everyone's here on time today – I think that must be a first.* (o primeiro)

3 the best result in a UK university exam (primeiro lugar) ◻ *He got a first in economics.* (conseguiu o primeiro lugar)

first aid /ˌfɜːst ˈeɪd/ NOUN, NO PLURAL simple medical treatment that you give to an injured or ill person as soon as you can (primeiros socorros) ▣ a *first aid course* (curso de primeiros socorros)

first-class /ˌfɜːstˈklɑːs / ▶ ADJECTIVE
1 used about travel when you pay more for a better seat etc., and about post when you pay more for a quicker service ▢ *a first-class train ticket* ▢ *a first-class stamp* (primeira classe)
2 extremely good ▢ *It was a first-class game of football.* (de primeira classe)
▶ ADVERB using the best or most expensive type ▢ *Len always travels first-class.*

first-hand /ˌfɜːstˈhænd / ADJECTIVE learned because you have done something yourself and not because someone else has told you (experiência própria) ▣ *I know from first-hand experience how difficult skiing is.* (experiência própria)

firstly /ˈfɜːstli/ ADVERB used for introducing the first of several things ▢ *Firstly, I'd like to welcome everybody.* (em primeiro lugar)

first name /ˈfɜːst ˌneɪm/ NOUN [plural **first names**] the name that comes before your family name ▢ *Her first name's 'Jane' and her surname is 'Smith'.* (prenome)

first person /ˌfɜːst ˈpɜːsən/ NOUN, NO PLURAL in grammar, the form of words used when people are talking or writing about themselves ▢ *'I' and 'we' are first person pronouns.* (primeira pessoa)

first-rate /ˌfɜːstˈreɪt / ADJECTIVE excellent ▢ *a first rate doctor* (excelente)

fish /fɪʃ/ ▶ NOUN [plural **fish** or **fishes**]
1 an animal that lives and swims in water (peixe) ▣ *They were trying to catch fish in the stream.* (pegar peixe)
2 NO PLURAL the meat from this animal eaten as food ▢ *We had fish for dinner.* (peixe)

> Note that the plural form of fish is usually fish. Fishes is not common but is sometimes used when talking about different types of fish:
> ✓ *We caught a lot of fish.*
> ✗ *We caught a lot of fishes.*

▶ VERB [fishes, fishing, fished]
1 to try to catch fish ▢ + **for** *The men were fishing for salmon.* (pescar)
2 to look for something in a bag, drawer, etc. ▢ *Amy was fishing in her bag for her key.* (procurar)
◆ PHRASAL VERB **fish something out** to pull something out from somewhere. An informal phrase. ▢ *She fished the papers out of the bin.* (atirar algo para fora)

fisherman /ˈfɪʃəmən/ NOUN [plural **fishermen**] someone who catches fish as a job or sport (pescador)

fishing /ˈfɪʃɪŋ/ NOUN, NO PLURAL the sport or job of catching fish (pesca) ▣ *We're going fishing at the weekend.* (vamos pescar) ▣ *the fishing industry* (indústria da pesca)

fishing rod /ˈfɪʃɪŋ ˌrɒd/ NOUN [plural **fishing rods**] a long stick used for catching fish (vara de pesca)

fishmonger /ˈfɪʃˌmʌŋɡə(r)/ NOUN [plural **fishmongers**]
1 someone who sells fish (peixeiro)
2 fishmonger's a shop that sells fish (peixaria)

fission /ˈfɪʃən/ NOUN, NO PLURAL dividing an atom so that energy is given out. A physics word. (fissão)

fist /fɪst/ NOUN [plural **fists**] your hand when it is closed tightly ▢ *Don't shake your fist at me!* (punho)

fit /fɪt/ VERB [fits, fitting, fitted]
1 to be the right shape or size for someone or something ▢ *The dress fits you perfectly.* ▢ *The cupboard will fit in the corner.* (ajustar-se)
2 to have enough room to put something or someone somewhere, or to be small enough to go somewhere ▢ *I can't fit any more documents in this file.* ▢ *We tried to get the piano up the stairs, but it wouldn't fit.* (caber)
3 to fix something in a place ▢ *We're having new kitchen units fitted next week.* ▢ + **with** *He was fitted with a pacemaker.* (equipar)
4 to be what someone describes or asks for (ajustar-se) ▣ *He certainly fits the description issued by the police.* (ajusta-se à descrição)
5 to be suitable for something ▢ *Bright colours don't really fit our image.* ▢ *The services on offer don't fit the needs of our clients.* (ajustar-se)
◆ PHRASAL VERBS **fit in**
1 to become accepted by a group of people ▢ *They were all very sporty, and I didn't really fit in.*
2 to be a part of something ▢ *We need to update our online business, and that's where your skills fit in.* (ajustar-se, adaptar-se) **fit someone/ something in** to have time to see someone or do something ▢ *We can fit you in to see the doctor at ten.* (encaixar alguém ou algo)
▶ ADJECTIVE [**fitter, fittest**]
1 healthy, especially because of doing exercise (em forma) ▣ *I'm trying to get fit.* (ficar em forma)
2 suitable or good enough ▢ + **to do something** *This food isn't fit to eat.* (pronto) ▣ *I wasn't in a fit state to work.* (pronto)
▶ NOUN [plural **fits**]
1 whether or not something is the right size and shape for something or someone ▢ *The jacket was a perfect fit.* (ajuste)
2 a sudden period of doing something or feeling a particular way ▢ *I cleaned the whole house in a fit of enthusiasm.* ▢ *He collapsed in a fit of laughter.* (acesso)
3 a period of illness where someone's body makes sudden movements they cannot control (convulsão, espasmo)

- IDIOM **have a fit** to become very angry. An informal phrase. (ter um ataque)
- **fitness** /ˈfɪtnɪs/ NOUN, NO PLURAL
  1 how healthy someone is □ *I'm hoping to improve my fitness.* (boa forma) 🔁 *physical fitness* (boa forma física)
  2 how suitable someone or something is □ *Many people doubt his fitness to govern.* (aptidão)
- **fitting** /ˈfɪtɪŋ/ ADJECTIVE suitable (adequado) 🔁 *The award is a fitting tribute to a great actor.* (tributo adequado)

five /faɪv/ NUMBER [plural **fives**] the number 5 (cinco)

fix /fɪks/ ▶ VERB [**fixes, fixing, fixed**]
1 to attach something to something else □ + *to* *She fixed the shelves to the wall.* (fixar)
2 to repair something □ *He's trying to fix the roof.* (consertar) 🔁 *I need to get the car fixed.* (consertar)
3 to solve a problem (resolver) 🔁 *All our staff are working to fix the problem.* (resolver o problema)
4 to decide something (marcar) 🔁 *Have you fixed a date for the wedding?* (marcou uma data)
- PHRASAL VERB **fix something up**
  1 to arrange something such as a meeting or visit □ *They fixed up a meeting for the following week.* (marcar algo)
  2 to repair and improve something such as a building □ *Taxpayers money was used to fix up the Opera House.* (consertar)
  ▶ NOUN [plural **fixes**] something which solves a problem (conserto) 🔁 *The problem is a long-term one and there are no quick fixes.* (consertos rápidos)
- **fixation** /fɪkˈseɪʃən/ NOUN [plural **fixations**] a very strong interest in something, which other people think is not normal □ *He had a fixation with knives.* (fixação)
- **fixed** /fɪkst/ ADJECTIVE not changing □ *He had a fixed smile on his face.* □ *He works for a fixed number of hours each week.* (fixo)

fizz /fɪz/ VERB [**fizzes, fizzing, fizzed**] if liquid fizzes, it makes the noise of bubbles breaking (efervescer)
- **fizzy** /ˈfɪzi/ ADJECTIVE [**fizzier, fizziest**] a fizzy drink has bubbles in it (gasoso)

flabbergasted /ˈflæbəˌgɑːstɪd/ ADJECTIVE an informal word meaning extremely surprised (surpreso)

flabby /ˈflæbi/ ADJECTIVE [**flabbier, flabbiest**] fat, and having skin that is not tight □ *flabby arms* (flácido, mole)

flag /flæg/ ▶ NOUN [plural **flags**] a piece of cloth with a pattern on it, used as the symbol of a country or organization □ *The American flag has stars and stripes on it.* (bandeira) 🔁 *Hundreds of people were waving flags as the Queen arrived.* (agitando bandeiras) 🔁 *Flags across the country were flying at half-mast when the President died.* (bandeiras estavam sendo agitadas)
  ▶ VERB [**flags, flagging, flagged**] to become tired or weak (fraquejar)
- PHRASAL VERB **flag someone/something down** to wave at the driver of a car to make them stop □ *I tried to flag down a taxi.* (acenar para alguém/algo)

flagpole /ˈflæɡpəʊl/ NOUN [plural **flagpoles**] a pole that you hang a flag from (mastro)

flagrant /ˈfleɪɡrənt/ ADJECTIVE obvious, and showing that you do not care that you are doing something bad □ *He showed a flagrant disregard of the speed limit.* (flagrante)

flagstone /ˈflæɡstəʊn/ NOUN [plural **flagstones**] a flat piece of stone used for making a path or floor (pedra de pavimentação)

flail /fleɪl/ VERB [**flails, flailing, flailed**] to move your arms or legs in a violent and uncontrolled way □ *She flailed around in the water, and screamed for help.* (agitar-se)

flair /fleə(r)/ NOUN, NO PLURAL
1 a natural ability to do something well □ *He has a flair for cooking.* (talento)
2 when you do something in an interesting and skilful way □ *We need a designer with plenty of flair.* (estilo)

flake /fleɪk/ ▶ NOUN [plural **flakes**] a small thin piece of something □ *A few flakes of snow began to fall.* (floco)
  ▶ VERB [**flakes, flaking, flaked**] to come off in small flat pieces □ *Paint was flaking off the door.* (descascar)
- **flaky** /ˈfleɪki/ ADJECTIVE [**flakier, flakiest**] breaking up easily into small thin pieces □ *flaky pastry* (quebrável, separável em flocos)

flamboyant /flæmˈbɔɪənt/ ADJECTIVE
1 very confident and behaving in a way that attracts attention □ *a flamboyant actor* (vistoso)
2 bright and colourful □ *flamboyant clothes* (chamativo)

flame /fleɪm/ ▶ NOUN [plural **flames**]
1 the hot orange gas you see in a fire (chama) 🔁 *Flames leapt from the roof.* (as chamas saltaram) 🔁 *Firefighters tried to put out the flames.* (apagaram as chamas)
2 in flames burning □ *The building was in flames.* (em chamas)
3 burst into flames/go up in flames to suddenly start burning □ *The plane skidded off the runway and burst into flames.* (explodir em chamas)
4 an angry or rude e-mail. A computing word. (e-mail ofensivo)
  ▶ VERB [**flames, flaming, flamed**] to send someone an angry or rude e-mail. A computing word. (enviar e-mail ofensivo)
- **flaming** /ˈfleɪmɪŋ/ ADJECTIVE burning □ *Flaming debris fell from the plane before it crashed.* (queimado)

flamenco

flamenco /fləˈmeŋkəʊ/ NOUN [plural **flamencos**] an energetic Spanish dance (**flamenco**)

flamingo /fləˈmɪŋgəʊ/ NOUN [plural **flamingoes** or **flamingos**] a large pink bird with long legs (**flamingo**)

flammable /ˈflæməbəl/ ADJECTIVE something that is flammable burns easily (**inflamável**) 🔹 *The gas is highly flammable.* (**altamente inflamável**)

> ➤ **Inflammable** means the same as **flammable**.

flan /flæn/ NOUN [plural **flans**] a circle of pastry that has something inside it □ *a lemon flan* (**flan**)

flank /flæŋk/ ▶ VERB [**flanks, flanking, flanked**] if you are flanked by two people, you have one of them on each side of you □ *She left the courtroom flanked by police officers.* (**flanquear**)
▶ NOUN [plural **flanks**] the side of an animal's body, especially a horse's (**flanco**)

flannel /ˈflænəl/ NOUN [plural **flannels**]
1 a piece of cloth used for washing yourself
2 a type of cloth, warm cloth, used especially for night clothes (**toalhinha**)

flap /flæp/ ▶ VERB [**flaps, flapping, flapped**]
1 if a bird flaps its wings, it moves them up and down (**bater asas, adejar**)
2 if a piece of cloth flaps, it moves backwards and forwards □ *The flags were flapping in the wind.* (**agitar**)
▶ NOUN [plural **flaps**]
1 a piece of something that hangs down over an opening □ *He closed the tent flaps.* (**aba**)
2 a movement up and down, like that of a bird's wings (**batida de asas**)

flare /fleə(r)/ ▶ VERB [**flares, flaring, flared**]
1 to suddenly start to burn or shine brightly □ *The fire had flared up again overnight.* (**explodir**)
2 if something such as anger or violence flares, it suddenly starts or becomes worse □ *Violence flared in several towns.* (**rebentar**)
3 if an illness or injury flares, it comes back again or becomes worse □ *His knee injury flared up after the game.* (**reaparecer**)
▶ NOUN [plural **flares**] something that produces a bright light to show that you need help (**clarão**)

flash /flæʃ/ ▶ VERB [**flashes, flashing, flashed**]
1 if a light flashes, it goes on and off quickly □ *The warning light was flashing.* (**lampejar**) 🔹 *a flashing light* (**luz lampejante**)
2 to make a light go on and off quickly □ *He flashed his car lights to warn other drivers of the danger.* (**piscar**)
3 to appear for a short time and then disappear □ *Some important news suddenly flashed up on the screen.* (**mostrar rapidamente**)
4 to move very quickly (**passar**) □ *+ by The cars flashed by.* 🔹 *A bullet flashed past his head.* (**passou raspando**)

flat

5 to show something to someone quickly □ *Mary flashed her card to the man on the door.* (**mostrar rapidamente**)
6 if you flash a smile or look at someone, you smile at them or look at them for a short time □ *He flashed a cheeky grin for the camera.* (**sorrir ou olhar rapidamente**)
▶ NOUN [plural **flashes**]
1 a sudden bright light (**lampejo**) 🔹 *a flash of lightning* (**lampejo de luz**)
2 a light on a camera that you use when you are taking photographs indoors (**flash**)
3 a sudden feeling □ *+ of He had a flash of guilt.* (**instante**)
4 in a flash an informal phrase meaning very quickly □ *She was out of the door in a flash.* (**em um piscar de olhos**)
▶ ADJECTIVE
1 happening very suddenly (**repentino**) 🔹 *a flash flood* (**enchente repentina**)
2 expensive and designed to make people notice you. An informal word. □ *Rick drives around in a really flash car.* (**vistoso**)

flashback /ˈflæʃbæk/ NOUN [plural **flashbacks**]
1 part of a film or book which shows you what happened earlier (**volta ao passado**)
2 a sudden clear memory of something that happened to you in the past □ *She experienced flashbacks and nightmares after the accident.* (**flashback**)

flashlight /ˈflæʃlaɪt/ NOUN [plural **flashlights**] the US word for **torch** (= small electric light) (**lanterna**)

flashy /ˈflæʃi/ ADJECTIVE [**flashier, flashiest**] expensive, and designed to make people notice you □ *a flashy car* (**ostentoso**)

flask /flɑːsk/ NOUN [plural **flasks**]
1 a container for keeping drinks hot or cold (**garrafa térmica**)
2 a glass bottle with a wide base, used in science for holding liquids (**frasco**)

flat /flæt/ ▶ ADJECTIVE [**flatter, flattest**]
1 level, smooth and not sloping □ *a flat roof* □ *Place the box on a flat surface.* □ *I'd like to have a flatter stomach.* (**plano, raso**)
2 lying on a surface □ *She lay flat on the floor.* (**estendido**)
3 a flat tyre does not have enough air in it (**vazio**)
4 a flat battery has no more power in it (**descarregado**)
5 a flat drink does not have enough bubbles in it (**que perdeu o gás, choco**)
6 without emotion or enthusiasm □ *She spoke in a flat voice.* (**monótono**)
7 a flat rate or amount is always the same (**único**) 🔹 *He charges a flat fee of £50 per hour.* (**preço único**)
8 in music, lower by half a note (**desafinado**)
9 flat shoes do not have high heels (= parts at the back) (**rasteiro**)

▶ ADVERB

1 in a way that is level, smooth and not sloping □ *I spread the carpet flat on the floor.* (horizontalmente)

2 stretched out on a surface □ *Omar was lying flat on his back.* (planamente)

3 in 10 minutes/2 seconds, etc. flat in only 10 minutes/2 seconds, etc. □ *I did my homework in five minutes flat.* (exatamente)

4 flat out as fast or with as much effort as possible □ *We worked flat out to get it finished.* (a toda)

▶ NOUN [plural **flats**]

1 a set of rooms that someone lives in, which are part of a larger building (apartamento)

2 in written music, a sign (♭) that makes a note lower by half a note (bemol)

- **flatly** /ˈflætli/ ADVERB

1 in a determined way (completamente) 🔊 *He flatly refused to do it.* (recusou completamente) 🔊 *She flatly denied taking the money.* (negou completamente)

2 without emotion or enthusiasm (sem graça)

- **flatten** /ˈflætən/ VERB [**flattens, flattening, flattened**]

1 to destroy something completely □ *A tornado flattened the village.* (arrasar)

2 to make something become flat (aplanar-se)

flatter /ˈflætə(r)/ VERB [**flatters, flattering, flattered**]

1 to say nice things to someone because you want to please them, especially when you are not being sincere □ *I'm sure he's just flattering me when he said he enjoyed reading my article.* (adular)

2 if clothes flatter you, they make you look attractive when you wear them □ *That dress really flatters you.* (favorecer)

3 flatter yourself to believe that your abilities or achievements are better than they are □ *Don't flatter yourself. He talks to everyone.* (iludir-se)

- **flattered** /ˈflætəd/ ADJECTIVE feeling pleased because someone has shown that they like you □ *I was really flattered that they invited me to the wedding.* (satisfeito)

- **flattering** /ˈflætərɪŋ/ ADJECTIVE

1 making you look attractive □ *a flattering photo* □ *a flattering skirt* (lisonjeiro)

2 making you feel special or important □ *It was very flattering to be asked to join the school council.* (lisonjeiro)

3 praising someone and making them feel pleased □ *He made some flattering remarks about my work.* (agradável)

- **flattery** /ˈflætəri/ NOUN, NO PLURAL nice things you say to someone because you want to please them, especially when you are not being sincere (lisonja)

flavor /ˈfleɪvə(r)/ NOUN [plural **flavors**], VERB [**flavors, flavoring, flavored**] the US spelling of flavour (sabor)

- **flavored** /ˈfleɪvəd/ ADJECTIVE the US spelling of flavoured (aromatizado)

- **-flavored** /ˈfleɪvəd/ SUFFIX the US spelling of -flavoured (com sabor de)

- **flavoring** /ˈfleɪvərɪŋ/ NOUN [plural **flavorings**] the US spelling of flavouring (aromatizante)

flavour /ˈfleɪvə(r)/ ▶ NOUN [plural **flavours**]

1 the taste that something has □ *Chocolate is my favourite ice cream flavour.* □ *Brown rice has a wonderful nutty flavour.* (sabor)

2 NO PLURAL a good or strong taste (sabor) 🔊 *The herbs add flavour to the salad.* (adiciona sabor)

3 NO PLURAL a special quality that something has □ *The big cities have a much more international flavour.* (sabor)

▶ VERB [**flavours, flavouring, flavoured**] if food is flavoured with something, that thing has been added to give the food a particular taste □ *pasta flavoured with garlic* (aromatizar)

- **flavoured** /ˈfleɪvəd/ ADJECTIVE with something added to give a particular taste □ *flavoured water* (com sabor)

- **-flavoured** /ˈfleɪvəd/ SUFFIX added to the end of a word to show what something tastes of □ *chocolate flavoured milk* (aromatizado)

- **flavouring** /ˈfleɪvərɪŋ/ NOUN [plural **flavourings**] something added to food to give it a particular taste (aromatizante)

flaw /flɔː/ NOUN [plural **flaws**] a fault in someone or something □ *The building is prone to leaks because of design flaws.* (defeito)

- **flawed** /flɔːd/ ADJECTIVE having faults or mistakes □ *The system is seriously flawed.* (defeituoso)

- **flawless** /ˈflɔːlɪs/ ADJECTIVE perfect, with no faults □ *a flawless performance* (invicto)

flea /fliː/ NOUN [plural **fleas**] a very small insect that jumps and bites people or animals (pulga)

fleck /flek/ NOUN [plural **flecks**] a very small mark or spot of a colour or a substance □ *Her black hair had flecks of grey in it.* (partícula, pingo)

- **flecked** /flekt/ ADJECTIVE marked with flecks □ *green eyes flecked with gold* (pequena mancha)

fled /fled/ PAST TENSE AND PAST PARTICIPLE OF **flee** (ver **flee**)

fledgling /ˈfledʒlɪŋ/ ADJECTIVE new and still developing □ *Her fledgling career in fashion was going well.* (iniciante)

flee /fliː/ VERB [**flees, fleeing, fled**] a formal word meaning to run away or to escape □ *Nina turned and fled.* (fugir)

fleece /fliːs/ NOUN [plural **fleeces**]

1 the wool on a sheep (tosão)

2 a type of soft, warm, artificial material (lã)

3 a jacket made from fleece (jaqueta)

fleet /fliːt/ NOUN [plural **fleets**] a group of ships or vehicles □ *a fleet of boats* (frota)

fleeting /ˈfliːtɪŋ/ ADJECTIVE lasting for only a short time □ *a fleeting smile* (passageiro)

flesh

flesh /fleʃ/ NOUN, NO PLURAL
1 the part of a person's or animal's body between the skin and the bones □ *The salmon's flesh should be pink and firm.* (**carne**)
2 a person's skin □ *her pale flesh* (**pele**)
3 the soft inside part of fruit and vegetables □ *Cut the avocado in half and scoop out the flesh.* (**polpa**)

flew /fluː/ PAST TENSE OF **fly** (*ver* **fly**)

flex /fleks/ ▶ NOUN [*plural* **flexes**] a piece of wire covered in plastic, which carries electricity to a piece of equipment (**fio elétrico**)
▶ VERB [**flexes, flexing, flexed**] to bend part of your body so that the muscle becomes tight (**flexionar**)

flexibility /ˌfleksəˈbɪlɪtɪ/ NOUN, NO PLURAL the quality of being flexible (**flexibilidade**)

flexible /ˈfleksəbəl/ ADJECTIVE
1 able to change to suit different people or situations □ *flexible arrangements* (**flexível**)
2 easy to bend □ *flexible wires* (**flexível**)

flick /flɪk/ ▶ VERB [**flicks, flicking, flicked**]
1 to send something through the air quickly and suddenly, often with your fingers □ *She flicked the fly off her coat.* □ *He flicked the ball back to me.* (**jogar algo para o alto**)
2 to move quickly and suddenly, or to make something move quickly and suddenly □ *Leah flicked her hair back confidently.* (**fazer um movimento rápido**)
3 if you flick a switch, you press it to make something start working (**pressionar de leve**)
♦ PHRASAL VERB **flick through something** to look quickly at each page in a magazine, book, etc. (**folhear algo rapidamente**)
▶ NOUN [*plural* **flicks**] a sudden quick movement □ *He passed the ball with a deft flick.* (**movimento rápido**)

flicker /ˈflɪkə(r)/ ▶ VERB [**flickers, flickering, flickered**]
1 if a light or flame flickers, it changes several times from bright to weak □ *The light flickered and went out.* (**tremeluzir**)
2 to last for a very short time and then disappear □ *A faint smile flickered across my father's face.* (**vacilar**)
3 to make a sudden small movement □ *Her eyelids flickered.* (**piscar**)
▶ NOUN [*plural* **flickers**]
1 when a light or flame is sometimes bright and sometimes weak □ *The kitchen was dark apart from the flicker of a candle.* (**centelha**)
2 a flicker of something a feeling or expression that lasts for a very short time □ *He felt a flicker of hope.* (**lampejo**)

flight /flaɪt/ NOUN [*plural* **flights**]
1 a journey in an aircraft □ + **from** *a direct flight from Heathrow to Singapore* (**voo**) 🔁 *He boarded a flight to Tokyo.* (**subir a bordo de um voo**)

flipper

2 a set of stairs (**lance**) 🔁 *We walked up several flights of stairs.* (**lances de escada**) 🔁 *a flight of steps* (**andar**) □ *She climbed the five flights to her apartment.*
3 NO PLURAL the action of flying □ *a flock of birds in flight* (**voo**)
♦ IDIOM **a flight of fancy/imagination** something you imagine which is fun or exciting, but very unlikely □ *He dismissed the idea as a flight of fancy.* (**coisas da imaginação**)

flight attendant /ˈflaɪt əˌtendənt/ NOUN [*plural* **flight attendants**] a person whose job is to look after passengers while they are on an aeroplane (**comissário de bordo**)

flimsy /ˈflɪmzɪ/ ADJECTIVE [**flimsier, flimsiest**]
1 thin or light and likely to break or tear □ *We sat on flimsy plastic chairs.* □ *a flimsy summer dress* (**fraco, fino**)
2 difficult to believe and not able to be trusted □ *He was arrested on flimsy evidence.* (**fraco**)

flinch /flɪntʃ/ VERB [**flinches, flinching, flinched**] to move part of your body suddenly, because you are frightened or in pain □ *The boys flinched at the sound of gunfire.* (**recuar**)
♦ PHRASAL VERB **flinch from something** to avoid doing something difficult □ *She didn't flinch from asking tough questions.* (**esquivar-se diante de algo**)

fling /flɪŋ/ VERB [**flings, flinging, flung**] to throw or move something using a lot of force □ *He flung his racket down.* □ *She flung her arms round him.* □ *She flung herself down in the chair, completely exhausted.* (**arremessar**)

flint /flɪnt/ NOUN [*plural* **flints**] a hard, grey stone that can produce a flame and was used in the past to make tools (**pedra de isqueiro**)

flip /flɪp/ VERB [**flips, flipping, flipped**]
1 to turn over quickly or to make something turn over quickly □ *The car ran off the road and flipped over.* □ *After a couple of minutes, flip the fish over to cook the other side.* (**virar**)
2 to change the position of something with a quick movement □ *Someone flipped the light switch.* □ *She took the box and flipped the lid open.* (**virar**)
♦ PHRASAL VERB **flip through something** to look quickly at the pages of a book or magazine □ *She sat in the waiting room flipping through a magazine.* (**ler rapidamente**)

flippant /ˈflɪpənt/ ADJECTIVE not serious and not suitable for the situation □ *a flippant remark* (**irreverente**)
• **flippantly** /ˈflɪpəntlɪ/ ADVERB in a flippant way □ *He replied rather flippantly.* (**de maneira irreverente**)

flipper /ˈflɪpə(r)/ NOUN [*plural* **flippers**]
1 one of the large flat feet that some sea animals have to help them swim (**barbatana, nadadeira**)
2 a wide, long, flat shoe that you wear to help you swim under water (**pé de pato**)

flirt /flɜːt/ ▶ VERB [**flirts, flirting, flirted**] to behave as though you think someone is attractive □ *Emma was flirting with her sister's boyfriend.* (**flertar**)

♦ PHRASAL VERB **flirt with something**
1 to think about doing something, but not in a serious way □ *He's flirting with the idea of becoming a monk.* (**ter interesse passageiro em algo**)
2 flirt with danger/disaster, etc. to take a serious risk (**flertar com o perigo**)
▶ NOUN [*plural* **flirts**] someone who often flirts with people (**namorador, conquistador**)

• **flirtation** /flɜːˈteɪʃən/ NOUN, NO PLURAL
1 when you flirt with someone (**flerte**)
2 when you become interested in something for a short time □ *He had a brief flirtation with politics.* (**namorico**)

• **flirtatious** /flɜːˈteɪʃəs/ ADJECTIVE flirting a lot (**galanteador**)

flit /flɪt/ VERB [**flits, flitting, flitted**] to move quickly and lightly from one place to another □ *His eyes flitted round the room.* □ *The butterfly flitted from flower to flower.* (**esvoaçar**)

float /fləʊt/ ▶ VERB [**floats, floating, floated**]
1 to move slowly or to stay on the surface of a liquid and not sink □ *Leaves were floating on the surface of the lake.* □ *The boat floated slowly down the river.* (**flutuar, boiar**)
2 to stay in the air or to move slowly through the air □ *He let go of the balloon and it floated away.* □ *Voices floated down the stairs.* (**flutuar**)
3 to start selling shares (= parts of a company that people buy and sell) in a company □ + *on The company was floated on the stock exchange last year.* (**flutuar**)
4 to suggest an idea for people to think about (**propor**) □ *I floated the idea at yesterday's meeting.* (**propus uma ideia**) □ *They floated plans to build new offices.*
▶ NOUN [*plural* **floats**] an object that is designed to float on water, for example to help someone swim (**boia**)

flock /flɒk/ ▶ NOUN [*plural* **flocks**] a group of sheep or birds (**bando, rebanho**)
▶ VERB [**flocks, flocking, flocked**] to move or come together in large numbers □ *Thousands of tourists flock to the town every summer.* □ *Fans have flocked to see him.* (**agrupar-se**)

flog /flɒg/ VERB [**flogs, flogging, flogged**]
1 to hit someone repeatedly with something as a punishment (**açoitar**)
2 an informal word meaning to sell something (**vender algo**)

flood /flʌd/ ▶ NOUN [*plural* **floods**]
1 a lot of water covering a place that is usually dry □ *Two days of heavy rain caused floods.* (**inundação**)
2 a large number of people or things that appear suddenly in a place □ + *of They received a flood of complaints.* (**enxurrada**)
3 floods of tears a lot of crying □ *The little boy was in floods of tears.* (**mar de lágrimas**)
▶ VERB [**floods, flooding, flooded**]
1 if water floods a place or if a place floods, it becomes covered in a lot of water □ *Large parts of the town were flooded.* □ *The river has flooded its banks.* (**inundar**)
2 to arrive somewhere in large numbers □ *Demonstrators flooded the streets.* □ *The newspaper has been flooded with complaints.* (**encher, transbordar**)

floodgates /ˈflʌdgeɪts/ PLURAL NOUN **open the floodgates** to suddenly let a lot of people do something □ *If we give one person permission, we'll open the floodgates to hundreds of similar requests.* (**abrir as comportas**)

flooding /ˈflʌdɪŋ/ NOUN, NO PLURAL when an area that is usually dry is covered with water □ *The storms caused severe flooding.* (**inundação**)

floodlight /ˈflʌdlaɪt/ NOUN [*plural* **floodlights**] a bright light used at night for lighting outside areas □ *The match was played under floodlights.* (**holofote**)

• **floodlit** /ˈflʌdlɪt/ ADJECTIVE lit by floodlights (**iluminado com holofote**)

floor /flɔː(r)/ ▶ NOUN [*plural* **floors**]
1 the surface that you stand on in a room □ *There were toys all over the kitchen floor.* □ *The hall has a wooden floor.* (**piso, assoalho**)
2 one of the levels in a building □ *Which floor is your apartment on?* □ *Our office is on the top floor of the building.* (**andar**)
3 the ground at the bottom of a particular area □ *the forest/ocean floor* (**nível**)
▶ VERB [**floors, flooring, floored**]
1 to hit someone so hard that they fall down □ *He floored his opponent in the sixth round.* (**derrubar ao chão**)
2 to surprise someone so much that they do not know how to react □ *I was slightly floored by the question.* (**desconcertar**)

floorboard /ˈflɔːbɔːd/ NOUN [*plural* **floorboards**] one of the long narrow boards which form a wooden floor (**tábua**)

flop /flɒp/ ▶ VERB [**flops, flopping, flopped**]
1 to fall or sit down suddenly in a heavy way □ *She flopped into the nearest armchair.* □ *I flopped down on the bed.* (**despencar, cair**)
2 to hang or fall loosely □ *His hair flopped over his eyes.* (**cair**)
3 if an event, product, etc. flops, it is not successful. An informal word □ *His last few films have flopped.* (**fracassar**)
▶ NOUN [*plural* **flops**]
1 an informal word for something that is not successful □ *The film was a box office flop.* (**fracasso**)

2 a sudden, heavy movement (**golpe**)

• **floppy** /ˈflɒpɪ/ ADJECTIVE [**floppier, floppiest**] soft and hanging down loosely ☐ *She wore a big, floppy summer hat.* ☐ *a dog with floppy ears* (**frouxo**)

floppy disk /ˌflɒpɪ ˈdɪsk/ NOUN [plural **floppy disks**] a disk inside a flat piece of plastic that is used for copying information from a computer. A computing word. (**disco flexível**)

flora /ˈflɔːrə/ NOUN, NO PLURAL the trees and plants that grow in an area. A biology word. 🔹 *He's an expert on the local flora and fauna* (= plants and animals). (**flora**)

floral /ˈflɔːrəl/ ADJECTIVE
1 made of flowers ☐ *a floral arrangement* (**floral**)
2 decorated with pictures of flowers ☐ *floral wallpaper* (**floral**)

florid /ˈflɒrɪd/ ADJECTIVE
1 a florid face is red or pink ☐ *florid cheeks.* (**corado, rosado**)
2 too decorated or complicated ☐ *a florid description* (**floreado**)

florist /ˈflɒrɪst/ NOUN [plural **florists**]
1 someone who sells flowers (**florista**)
2 florist's a shop that sells flowers (**floricultura**)

floss /flɒs/ ▶ NOUN, NO PLURAL thread you use for cleaning between your teeth (**fio dental**) 🔹 *dental floss* (**fio dental**)
▶ VERB [**flosses, flossing, flossed**] to clean your teeth using floss (**passar fio dental**)

flotation /fləʊˈteɪʃən/ NOUN [plural **flotations**] when a company sells shares on the stock market ☐ *the successful flotation of the company* (**lançamento de ações**)

flounce /flaʊns/ VERB [**flounces, flouncing, flounced**] to walk away suddenly, because you are angry or upset ☐ *Kat flounced out of the room and slammed the door.* (**precipitar-se**)

flounder /ˈflaʊndə(r)/ VERB [**flounders, floundering, floundered**]
1 to fail or experience difficulties ☐ *The economy continued to flounder.* (**chafurdar**)
2 to not know what to say or do in a situation ☐ *I felt I was floundering in the interview.* (**atrapalhar-se**)
3 to move in an awkward way, especially because you are trying not to sink in water (**debater-se**)

flour /ˈflaʊə(r)/ NOUN, NO PLURAL powder made from wheat (= grain), used for making bread and cakes (**farinha**)

flourish /ˈflʌrɪʃ/ ▶ VERB [**flourishes, flourishing, flourished**]
1 to develop quickly and well ☐ *Her new business is flourishing.* ☐ *Wildlife is once again flourishing in the area.* (**florescer, prosperar**)
2 to wave something in the air ☐ *The tour guide flourished her umbrella.* (**agitar**)

▶ NOUN [plural **flourishes**] a special, skilful or large movement ☐ *He removed his hat with a flourish.* (**floreio**)

flout /flaʊt/ VERB [**flouts, flouting, flouted**] if you flout a law or rule, you intentionally do not obey it ☐ *Drivers who flout the rule face a fine.* (**desprezar**)

flow /fləʊ/ ▶ VERB [**flows, flowing, flowed**]
1 if a liquid flows, it moves along ☐ + *through The River Thames flows through London.* ☐ + *into The water flows into the sea.* ☐ *Tears flowed down her face.* (**correr**)
2 to move continuously and easily without stopping (**fluir**) 🔹 *The traffic was flowing freely.* (**fluindo livremente**) ☐ *Foreign investment flowed into the country.*
3 if ideas, conversation, etc. flow, they continue in an easy, relaxed way ☐ *His words flowed easily.* ☐ *The conversation flowed smoothly.* (**fluir**)
▶ NOUN [plural **flows**] a continuous movement of something ☐ + *of We used bandages to stop the flow of blood.* (**fluxo**) 🔹 *a steady flow of tourists* (**fluxo estático**)

flow chart /ˈfləʊ tʃɑːt/ NOUN [plural **flow charts**] a picture showing the different stages in a process (**fluxograma**)

flower /ˈflaʊə(r)/ ▶ NOUN [plural **flowers**] the coloured part of a plant ☐ *Tulips are my favourite flower.* (**flor**) 🔹 *We picked some wild flowers.* (**flores silvestres**) 🔹 *They gave her a bunch of flowers.* (**buquê de flores**)
▶ VERB [**flowers, flowering, flowered**] to produce flowers ☐ *Bluebells usually flower in May.* (**florescer, dar flores**)

flowerbed /ˈflaʊəbed/ NOUN [plural **flowerbeds**] a piece of ground in a garden, park, etc. where flowers are grown (**canteiro de flores**)

flowerpot /ˈflaʊəpɒt/ NOUN [plural **flowerpots**] a round clay or plastic container for growing plants in (**vaso de flores**)

flown /fləʊn/ PAST PARTICIPLE OF **fly** (**ver fly**)

fl oz ABBREVIATION fluid ounce or fluid ounces (**onça fluida**)

flu /fluː/ NOUN, NO PLURAL an illness like a very bad cold which makes you feel hot and tired (**gripe**) 🔹 *Last month she caught flu.* (**pegar gripe**) ☐ *I had a bad bout of flu.*

fluctuate /ˈflʌktʃueɪt/ VERB [**fluctuates, fluctuating, fluctuated**] to keep changing in amount, level or character (**variar**) 🔹 *House prices fluctuated wildly over the next few months.* (**variaram loucamente**)

• **fluctuating** /ˈflʌktʃueɪtɪŋ/ ADJECTIVE often changing ☐ *fluctuating temperatures* (**instável**)

• **fluctuation** /ˌflʌktʃuˈeɪʃən/ NOUN [plural **fluctuations**] when something fluctuates ☐ *There are daily fluctuations in oil prices.* (**instabilidade**)

flue /fluː/ NOUN [plural **flues**] a metal tube that takes air or smoke away from a fire (cano de chaminé)

fluent /ˈfluːənt/ ADJECTIVE able to speak a language easily and well □ She speaks fluent German. (fluente)

• **fluently** /ˈfluːəntli/ ADVERB easily and well □ Hannah speaks Italian fluently. (fluentemente)

fluff /flʌf/ ▶ NOUN, NO PLURAL small, soft pieces from wool or other material □ You've got a bit of fluff on your sleeve. (felpa)
▶ VERB [**fluffs**, **fluffing**, **fluffed**]
1 an informal word meaning to do something badly or to make a mistake □ She was so nervous, she fluffed her lines. (fracassar, errar)
2 to shake something to make it bigger, softer and more full of air □ Polly fluffed up her hair. (afofar)

• **fluffy** /ˈflʌfi/ ADJECTIVE [**fluffier**, **fluffiest**] very soft or covered in fur or soft material □ a fluffy toy □ a pile of fluffy towels (felpudo, peludo)

fluid /ˈfluːɪd/ ▶ NOUN [plural **fluids**] a liquid □ Runners should drink plenty of fluids. (fluido, líquido)
▶ ADJECTIVE
1 able to flow like a liquid □ Blood is a fluid substance. (fluido)
2 changing often □ It's a very fluid situation. (instável)
3 moving in a smooth and easy way □ Their moves were fluid and well-rehearsed. (solto)

fluid ounce /ˌfluːɪd ˈaʊns/ NOUN [plural **fluid ounces**] a unit for measuring liquid, equal to 1/20 pint. This is often written fl oz. (onça fluida)

fluke /fluːk/ NOUN [plural **flukes**] a lucky or unusual thing that happens by chance □ It was just a complete fluke that I won. (sorte)

flume /fluːm/ NOUN [plural **flumes**] a tube with water in the bottom that you can slide down into a swimming pool (canal, calha)

flung /flʌŋ/ PAST TENSE AND PAST PARTICIPLE OF **fling** (ver fling)

fluorescent /flʊəˈresənt/ ADJECTIVE
1 a fluorescent light is an electric light in the shape of a tube that produces a very bright light (fluorescente)
2 very brightly coloured and easy to see □ fluorescent yellow socks □ Workers wear fluorescent jackets. (brilhante)

fluoride /ˈflʊəraɪd/ NOUN, NO PLURAL a chemical added to toothpaste (= substance for cleaning your teeth) or water to protect your teeth. A chemistry word. (fluoreto)

flurry /ˈflʌri/ NOUN [plural **flurries**]
1 a short period of activity or emotion □ There's been a recent flurry of interest in the sport. (lufada, alvoroço)
2 a small amount of sn ow or rain □ snow flurries (nevada, pancada)

flush /flʌʃ/ ▶ VERB [**flushes**, **flushing**, **flushed**]
1 to press or pull a handle to make water go down a toilet (dar descarga) □ I can't flush the toilet. (dar a descarga)
2 to get rid of something by moving it somewhere with a strong flow of water □ Plastic objects shouldn't be flushed down the toilet. □ The chemicals are flushed into the canal. (esguichar, afluir)
3 to become red in the face □ He flushed with embarrassment. (corar)
▶ NOUN [plural **flushes**]
1 when your face becomes red and sometimes hot □ Side effects may include hot flushes. (rubor)
2 a sudden feeling or emotion for a short time □ a flush of pride (jorro)
3 when you flush a toilet (descarga)
▶ ADJECTIVE
1 if two surfaces are flush, they are exactly level with each other □ The edge of the pool is flush with the ground. (plano, reto)
2 an informal word meaning having more money than usual (rico, abundante)

fluster /ˈflʌstə(r)/ VERB [**flusters**, **flustering**, **flustered**] to make someone feel nervous and confused □ Nothing seemed to fluster her. (aturdir)

• **flustered** /ˈflʌstəd/ ADJECTIVE feeling nervous and confused □ I got a bit flustered. (aturdido)

flute /fluːt/ NOUN [plural **flutes**] a musical instrument you play by holding it sideways against your mouth and blowing into it (flauta)

flutter /ˈflʌtə(r)/ ▶ VERB [**flutters**, **fluttering**, **fluttered**]
1 to move quickly up and down or from side to side □ Her eyelids fluttered. □ The flags fluttered in the breeze. (agitar)
2 to move lightly and quickly through the air □ Leaves fluttered down and covered the ground. (esvoaçar)
▶ NOUN [plural **flutters**]
1 a short, quick, gentle movement □ a flutter of wings (abano)
2 a sudden, short feeling or emotion □ I felt a little flutter of excitement. (agitação)

flux /flʌks/ NOUN, NO PLURAL a state of continuous change (fluxo) □ Our plans are in a state of flux. (em um estado de fluência)

fly /flaɪ/ ▶ VERB [**flies**, **flying**, **flew**, **flown**]
1 to travel in an aircraft □ + to He flew to Miami. □ She flew in by helicopter. (voar)
2 to move through the air using wings □ A robin flew across the garden. □ A plane flew overhead. (voar)
3 to take someone or something somewhere in an aircraft □ His body was flown back to Australia. (voar)

flyer

4 to control an aircraft □ *She learned to fly a helicopter.* (**pilotar**)
5 to move very quickly □ *A bullet flew past my head.* (**mover-se rapidamente**) *The door flew open.* (**abrir-se de repente**)
6 send someone/something flying to knock someone or something and make them fall □ *He stood up quickly and the chess pieces went flying.* (**fazer alguém/algo voar**)
7 if time flies, it goes by quickly (**passar rápido**)
8 fly into a temper/rage to suddenly become very angry (**ficar nervoso**)
* IDIOMS **with flying colours** if you pass an exam with flying colours, you get a very high mark **fly off the handle** to suddenly become very angry □ *I only asked when he would be ready and he flew off the handle.* (**com notas altas**)
▶ NOUN [*plural* **flies**] a small insect that flies (**mosca**)

flyer /ˈflaɪə(r)/ NOUN [*plural* **flyers**] a small piece of paper that advertises something (**folheto**)

flying saucer /ˌflaɪɪŋ ˈsɔːsə(r)/ NOUN [*plural* **flying saucers**] a round object in the sky, which some people believe is a spacecraft from another planet (**disco voador**)

flyover /ˈflaɪˌəʊvə(r)/ NOUN [*plural* **flyovers**] a road that crosses over another road like a bridge (**viaduto**)

flywheel /ˈflaɪwiːl/ NOUN [*plural* **flywheels**] a heavy wheel in a machine or engine that moves a part of it (**volante**)

foal /fəʊl/ NOUN [*plural* **foals**] a young horse (**potro**)

foam /fəʊm/ ▶ NOUN, NO PLURAL
1 a mass of small bubbles on top of a liquid □ *I like to eat the foam off my coffee with a spoon.* (**espuma**)
2 a thick substance containing lots of small bubbles (**espuma**) *shaving foam* (**espuma de barbear**)
3 a soft material that is full of small holes, often used in furniture □ *a foam mattress* (**espuma**)
▶ VERB [**foams, foaming, foamed**] to produce foam □ *The horse was foaming at the mouth.* (**espumar**)

fob /fɒb/
* PHRASAL VERB [**fobs, fobbing, fobbed**] **fob someone off** to try to stop someone asking questions or complaining by telling them something that is not true □ *She fobbed him off with excuses.* (**iludir, pregar uma peça**)

focus /ˈfəʊkəs/ ▶ VERB [**focuses, focusing, focused**]
1 to concentrate on one particular thing □ *The report focused on the need to improve standards.* (**concentrar**) *She wants to focus attention on the problem.* (**concentrar a atenção**)
2 if your eyes focus, they change to let you see something clearly □ *It took a while for my eyes to focus.* (**enfocar**)
3 to make small changes to equipment such as a camera so that you get a clear picture (**focalizar**)
▶ NOUN, NO PLURAL
1 when you focus on one thing, or the thing you focus on (**foco**) *My main focus is to play well.* (**foco principal**) *She soon became the focus of media attention.* (**tornou-se o foco**)
2 in focus if an image is in focus, it can be seen clearly □ *Make sure the faces are in focus.* (**em foco**)
3 out of focus if an image is out of focus, it cannot be seen clearly □ *Some of the photos were out of focus.* (**fora de foco**)

fodder /ˈfɒdə(r)/ NOUN, NO PLURAL food for horses or farm animals (**forragem**)

foe /fəʊ/ NOUN [*plural* **foes**] a formal word for an enemy □ *The two men are old foes.* (**adversário**)

foetus /ˈfiːtəs/ NOUN [*plural* **foetuses**] a baby before it is born. A biology word. (**feto**)

fog /fɒg/ NOUN, NO PLURAL thick, low cloud that makes it difficult to see (**neblina, névoa**) *The flight was delayed due to thick fog.* (**névoa espessa**) □ *The fog had lifted slightly.*
* **foggy** /ˈfɒgi/ ADJECTIVE [**foggier, foggiest**] having a lot of fog □ *a foggy day* □ *foggy weather* (**enevoado**)
* IDIOM **not have the foggiest (idea)** used to emphasize that you do not know anything about something □ *I haven't got the foggiest idea where he is.* (**não ter a mínima ideia**)

foghorn /ˈfɒghɔːn/ NOUN [*plural* **foghorns**] equipment that makes a loud noise to warn ships when it is foggy (**buzina**)

foil /fɔɪl/ NOUN, NO PLURAL metal in very thin sheets, used for wrapping food (**papel-alumínio**)

foist /fɔɪst/
* PHRASAL VERB [**foists, foisting, foisted**] **foist something on/onto/upon someone** to force someone to take, accept or deal with something they do not want to □ *The extra work was just foisted upon us.* (**obrigar alguém a aceitar algo**)

fold /fəʊld/ ▶ VERB [**folds, folding, folded**]
1 to bend one part of something so that it covers another part □ *Dan folded the letter and put it in the envelope.* □ *He folded the clothes neatly.* (**dobrar**)
2 to make something smaller by bending parts of it □ **+ up** *He folded up his laptop and put it in his bag.* □ *The back seats fold down to give more luggage space.* (**dobrar**)
3 fold your arms to cross your arms over your chest (**cruzar os braços**)
4 if a business folds, it stops because it is not successful (**fechar**)
▶ NOUN [*plural* **folds**]
1 a line or mark where something is folded (**dobra**)
2 a thick piece of cloth, skin, etc. that hangs in a loose way □ *He reached inside the folds of his coat.* (**prega**)

folder /ˈfəʊldə(r)/ NOUN [plural **folders**]
1 a cardboard or plastic cover for holding papers (**pasta**)
2 a place where you keep documents on a computer. A computing word. (**pasta**)

foliage /ˈfəʊliɪdʒ/ NOUN, NO PLURAL the leaves on a tree or plant (**folhagem**)

folk /fəʊk/ ▶ PLURAL NOUN people □ *He has more money than most folk around here.* (**povo**) 🔁 *Babies and old folk are most at risk.* (**pessoas de idade**)
▶ ADJECTIVE to do with the traditions and culture of the people of a country or area (**popular, folclórico**) 🔁 *an Irish folk song* (**música popular**) 🔁 *Russian folk tales* (**contos populares**)

folklore /ˈfəʊklɔː(r)/ NOUN, NO PLURAL the customs, beliefs, stories and traditions of a particular country or group of people □ *The story has become part of the folklore of the area.* (**folclore**)

folk music /fəʊk ˌmjuːzɪk/ NOUN, NO PLURAL traditional music from a particular country or area (**música popular**)

follicle /ˈfɒlɪkəl/ NOUN [plural **follicles**] a small hole in the skin where a hair grows. A biology word. (**folículo**)

follow /ˈfɒləʊ/ VERB [**follows, following, followed**]
1 to go behind someone or something and go where they go □ *He followed her down the street.* (**seguir**)
2 to happen after something □ *The meal was followed by a dance.* (**seguir**)
3 to be next in size, quality, importance, etc. (**seguir**) 🔁 *Our team won, followed closely by the London team.* (**seguido de perto**)
4 to be interested in something and continue to get information about it 🔁 *We have been following the baby elephant's progress.*
5 to do what a person or a rule, law, etc. says you should do (**seguir**) 🔁 *We decided to follow his advice and catch the train.* (**seguir seu conselho**) 🔁 *Just open the letter and follow the instructions in it.* (**seguir as instruções**)
6 follow someone's example to act in the same way as someone else □ *I'm going to follow my brother's example and get up earlier.* (**seguir o exemplo de alguém**)
7 if you follow a road, you go along it □ *Follow the path to the end and turn right.* (**seguir**)
8 to understand what someone is saying □ *Do you follow me?* (**acompanhar**)
♦ PHRASAL VERB **follow something up** to take further action or to get more information about something □ *Detectives are following up reports that the child has been seen in France.* (**acompanhar algo**)

• **follower** /ˈfɒləʊə(r)/ NOUN [plural **followers**] someone who supports or admires a person or particular ideas (**seguidor**)

• **following** /ˈfɒləʊɪŋ/ ADJECTIVE
1 the following day, week, year, etc. is the next one □ *I finished work on Friday and we went on holiday the following Wednesday.* (**seguinte**)
2 used to introduce what you are going to say or write about next □ *The following people should come with me.* (**seguinte**)
▶ PREPOSITION after something has happened □ *Following his arrest, police made a thorough search of his office.* (**após**)
▶ NOUN, NO PLURAL a group of people who support or admire someone or something □ *The band has a large following in Germany.* (**os seguidores**)

folly /ˈfɒli/ NOUN [plural **follies**] something you think is silly or dangerous □ *It's absolute folly to drive as fast as that in the fog.* (**tolice, estupidez**)

fond /fɒnd/ ADJECTIVE [**fonder, fondest**]
1 fond of someone/something liking someone or something □ + **ing** *We're very fond of walking in the countryside.* 🔁 *He is particularly fond of chocolate.* (**amigo, apreciador**) 🔁 *I've grown very fond of the children.* (**cresci muito amigo de**)
2 causing or expressing happy or friendly feelings (**carinhoso, querido**) 🔁 *I have fond memories of my time at university.* (**lembranças queridas**)

fondle /ˈfɒndəl/ VERB [**fondles, fondling, fondled**] to touch a person or animal in a way which shows affection □ *He fondled the dog's ears.* (**acariciar**)

fondly /ˈfɒndli/ ADVERB in a way that shows you like someone or something □ *Miss Price is fondly remembered at the school.* (**carinhosamente**)

fondness /ˈfɒndnɪs/ NOUN, NO PLURAL when you like someone or something □ *She has a fondness for designer shoes.* (**afeição, carinho**)

font /fɒnt/ NOUN [plural **fonts**]
1 a style of letters used in printing or computer documents (**fonte**)
2 a large stone bowl in a church for holding water during a baptism (= when someone becomes a member of the Christian religion) ceremony (**pia**)

food /fuːd/ NOUN [plural **foods**]
1 NO PLURAL things that people and animals eat □ *They didn't have enough food.* □ *We often eat Chinese food.* (**comida**) 🔁 *pet food* (**comida para animais**)
2 a particular type of food □ *Try to avoid processed foods.* (**comida, alimento**)

> ➤ Note that food is not usually used in the plural. Foods is sometimes used when talking about different types of food but is not common:
> ✓ *I buy most of our food at the supermarket.*
> ✗ *I buy most of our foods at the supermarket.*

food chain /fuːd tʃeɪn/ NOUN **the food chain** a series of living things where each thing is eaten by the next thing in the series. A biology word. (**a cadeia alimentar**)

foodie /'fu:di/ NOUN [plural **foodies**] a person who loves food and eats only the best food (**gourmet**)

food miles /'fu:d maɪlz/ PLURAL NOUN how far food travels from the place where it is grown to the place where people eat it (**distância que o alimento percorre do produtor ao consumidor final**)

food processor /,fu:d 'prəʊsesə(r)/ NOUN [plural **food processors**] an electric machine for cutting or mixing food (**processador de alimentos**)

foodstuff /'fu:dstʌf/ NOUN [plural **foodstuffs**] any substance used as food □ They lack basic foodstuffs such as bread and cheese. (**gênero alimentício**)

fool /fu:l/ ▶ NOUN [plural **fools**]
1 a stupid or silly person □ I'm not a complete fool. □ I didn't want to look a fool. (**tolo**)
2 make a fool of yourself to do something that makes people think you are silly □ They're going to make fools of themselves. (**fazer papel de bobo**)
3 make a fool (out) of someone to try to make someone look silly (**fazer alguém de bobo**)
▶ VERB [**fools, fooling, fooled**] to trick someone □ His story didn't fool anyone. □ Don't be fooled by cheap copies. (**lograr**)
♦ PHRASAL VERB **fool about/around** to behave in a silly way or to have fun □ He was fooling around on his bike. (**perder tempo**)

foolhardy /'fu:l,hɑ:di/ ADJECTIVE taking silly and unnecessary risks □ It would be foolhardy to sell now. (**imprudente**)

foolish /'fu:lɪʃ/ ADJECTIVE silly or stupid □ a foolish mistake □ He didn't want to appear foolish. (**idiota, tolo**)

foolproof /'fu:lpru:f/ ADJECTIVE a foolproof plan, method, etc. is one that cannot go wrong □ I've got a foolproof recipe for bread. (**infalível**)

foot /fʊt/ NOUN [plural **feet**]
1 one of the parts of your body that you stand on □ He has a broken foot. (**pé**) ▣ We got to our feet (= stood up) when she came in. (**ficamos de pé**) ▣ I've been on my feet (= standing up) all day. (**em pé**)
2 a unit for measuring length, equal to 12 inches. This is often written ft. (**pé**)
3 the foot of the bottom of something □ We camped at the foot of the mountain. (**pé, base**)
4 on foot if you travel on foot, you walk (**a pé**)
5 set foot in/on somewhere to go to a place □ She'd never set foot in a casino. (**pisar, pôr os pés em algum lugar**)
♦ IDIOMS **put your feet up** to rest and relax (**descansar**) **put your foot down** to say in a forceful way what you want or what you want to happen (**bater o pé**) **put your foot in it** to say something by accident that upsets or annoys someone. An informal phrase. (**dar um fora**)
⇨ go to **get cold feet, sweep someone off their feet**

footage /'fʊtɪdʒ/ NOUN, NO PLURAL a filmed record of an event □ We bring you live footage of the ceremony. (**filmagem**)

football /'fʊtbɔ:l/ NOUN [plural **footballs**]
1 NO PLURAL a sport played by two teams who try to kick a ball into a goal (**futebol**) ▣ The boys are playing football outside. (**jogando futebol**) ▣ a football match (**partida de futebol**) ▣ a game of football (**jogo de futebol**) ▣ a football team (**time de futebol**)
2 the ball used for playing football □ Some kids were kicking a football about. (**bola de futebol**)
• **footballer** /'fʊtbɔ:lə(r)/ NOUN [plural **footballers**] someone who plays football, especially as their job (**jogador de futebol**)

footbridge /'fʊtbrɪdʒ/ NOUN [plural **footbridges**] a narrow bridge for people to walk across (**passarela**)

foothills /'fʊthɪlz/ PLURAL NOUN hills at the bottom of a high mountain (**região montanhosa**)

foothold /'fʊthəʊld/ NOUN [plural **footholds**]
1 a place where you can put your foot when you are climbing (**apoio para os pés**)
2 a strong position from which you can make progress (**posição segura**) ▣ The company has gained a foothold in the Asian market. (**obteve uma posição segura**)

footing /'fʊtɪŋ/ NOUN, NO PLURAL
1 when you are standing in a firm position (**equilíbrio**) ▣ I lost my footing and fell. (**perdi meu equilíbrio**)
2 someone's position or situation (**situação**) ▣ We're on a sound financial footing. (**situação financeira**)
3 the relationship between two people or groups (**relacionamento**) ▣ The two groups are on an equal footing. (**em um relacionamento igual**)

footnote /'fʊtnəʊt/ NOUN [plural **footnotes**] a note at the bottom of a page, which adds information about something in the text above (**nota de rodapé**)

footpath /'fʊtpɑ:θ/ NOUN [plural **footpaths**] a path you can walk on, especially in the countryside (**trilha**)

footprint /'fʊtprɪnt/ NOUN [plural **footprints**]
1 a mark that your foot leaves on the ground □ footprints in the snow (**pegada**)
2 the amount of the Earth's energy that each person or business uses □ I'm trying to reduce my footprint by using the car less. (**impacto**)

footstep /'fʊtstep/ NOUN [plural **footsteps**] the sound of someone walking □ I could hear footsteps. (**passo, ruído de passos**)

footwear /'fʊtweə(r)/ NOUN, NO PLURAL things such as shoes and boots that you wear on your feet □ Wear sensible footwear. (**calçados**)

for /fɔː(r)/ PREPOSITION

1 to be received or used by someone, or to help someone □ *There's a letter for you.* □ *She made a cake for her Mum.* □ *I did all the ironing for Peter.* (**para**)

2 in order to do something or to get something □ *He asked me for money.* □ *Let's go for a walk.* □ *I went to the supermarket for some eggs.* (**por**)

3 used to show a reason or what something is intended to do □ *What's this switch for?* □ *He was arrested for shoplifting.* □ *I gave her a necklace for her birthday.* (**para**)

4 used to show an amount of time, distance, money, etc. □ *I've lived here for eight years.* □ *We walked for two miles.* □ *I got these trainers for £30.* (**por**)

5 meaning something □ *What's the word for 'girl' in French?* (**para**)

6 supporting or agreeing with someone or something □ *I voted for her.* □ *Are you for or against the new airport?* (**a favor de**)

> When you are explaining why someone does something, remember to use the infinitive **to do something**. Do not use for:
> ✓ *I went home to see my mother.*
> ✗ *I went home for seeing my mother.*

forbid /fəˈbɪd/ VERB [forbids, forbidding, forbade, forbidden] to tell someone that they must not do something □ + *to do something* *They forbade their daughter to see Henry any more.* □ + *from* *He is forbidden from discussing the case.* □ *The school rules forbid the use of mobile phones in class.* (**proibir**)

- **forbidden** /fəˈbɪdən/ ADJECTIVE not allowed □ *Smoking is forbidden throughout the hospital.* (**proibido**) ▣ *Alcohol is strictly forbidden.* (**estritamente proibido**)
- **forbidding** /fəˈbɪdɪŋ/ ADJECTIVE looking frightening or unfriendly □ *She gave me a forbidding stare.* (**amedrontador**)

force /fɔːs/ ▶ NOUN [plural forces]

1 NO PLURAL power or physical strength □ *The force of the explosion damaged many buildings.* (**força**)

2 *by force* by violent physical action □ *They took the land by force.* (**à força**)

3 a group of people, such as police or soldiers, who are trained to work together (**força**) ▣ *the armed forces* □ *A defence force was sent into the region.* (**forças armadas**)

4 something or someone with power or influence (**força**) ▣ *market forces* (**força de mercado**) □ *Their new leader is felt to be a force for good.*

5 *come into force* if a rule or law comes into force, it starts being used (**começar a usar**)

6 *in force* (a) if a law or rule is in force, it is being used and must be obeyed (b) if people do something in force, a lot of them are involved □ *Police arrived in force to stop the demonstration.* (**em vigor**)

▶ VERB [forces, forcing, forced]

1 to make someone do something □ + *to do something* *He forced me to give him money.* □ often passive □ *She was forced to move house.* (**forçar, obrigar**)

2 to make something move by using your strength □ *The police had to force the door open.* (**forçar**)

- **forced** /fɔːst/ ADJECTIVE a forced smile or laugh is not sincere (**forçado**)
- **forceful** /ˈfɔːsfʊl/ ADJECTIVE forceful opinions are very strong, and forceful people express their opinions in a strong way (**forte**) ▣ *She has a forceful personality.* (**personalidade forte**) ▣ *a forceful argument* (**argumento forte**)
- **forcefully** /ˈfɔːsfʊli/ ADVERB in a forceful way □ *He insisted forcefully that he was innocent.* (**fortemente**)

forceps /ˈfɔːseps/ PLURAL NOUN a piece of medical equipment with two narrow parts, used for holding things firmly (**fórceps**)

forcible /ˈfɔːsəbəl/ ADJECTIVE done using physical force □ *He protested about the forcible removal of the children from their families.* (**à força**)

- **forcibly** /ˈfɔːsəbli/ ADVERB using physical force □ *I was forcibly detained for three hours at the police station.* (**energicamente**)

ford /fɔːd/ NOUN [plural fords] a part of a river that is not deep where you can drive across (**vau**)

fore- /fɔː(r)/ PREFIX fore- is added to the beginning of words to mean 'before' or 'at the front of' □ *forename* (= the name before your family name)

forearm /ˈfɔːrɑːm/ NOUN [plural forearms] the part of your arm that is below your elbow (**antebraço**)

foreboding /fɔːˈbəʊdɪŋ/ NOUN, NO PLURAL a feeling that something bad is going to happen (**mau pressentimento**) ▣ *As he entered the house, he had a sense of foreboding.* (**ter mau pressentimento**)

forecast /ˈfɔːkɑːst/ ▶ NOUN [plural forecasts] a statement about what is likely to happen in the future, based on information (**previsão**) ▣ *a weather forecast* (**previsão do tempo**) □ + *of* *We had a forecast of heavy rain.*

▶ VERB [forecasts, forecasting, forecast] to make a forecast □ *Rain is forecast for the weekend.* □ *The company has forecast record profits.* (**prever**)

- **forecaster** /ˈfɔːkɑːstə(r)/ NOUN [plural forecasters] someone whose job is to forecast something (**quem faz previsões**) ▣ *a weather forecaster* (**homem do tempo**) □ *Forecasters say that prices are likely to rise.*

forecourt /ˈfɔːkɔːt/ NOUN [plural forecourts] an open area with a hard surface in front of a building □ *a garage forecourt* (**pátio**)

forefather

forefather /ˈfɔːˌfɑːðə(r)/ NOUN [plural **forefathers**] someone in your family who lived a long time ago (**antepassado**)

forefinger /ˈfɔːˌfɪŋɡə(r)/ NOUN [plural **forefingers**] the finger that is next to your thumb (**indicador**)

forefront /ˈfɔːfrʌnt/ NOUN, NO PLURAL the forefront an important or leading position ◻ His team of scientists was at the forefront of research into breast cancer. (**vanguarda**)

forego /fɔːˈɡəʊ/ VERB [**foregoes, foregoing, forewent, foregone**] another spelling of **forgo** (**anteceder**)

foregone conclusion /ˌfɔːɡɒn kənˈkluːʒən/ NOUN, NO PLURAL a result that is certain before it happens ◻ The election seemed like a foregone conclusion. (**conclusão antecipada**)

foreground /ˈfɔːɡraʊnd/ NOUN, NO PLURAL the foreground the part of a view or a picture that is nearest to you ◻ There's a group of children in the foreground, with the sea behind them. (**primeiro plano**)

forehand /ˈfɔːhænd/ NOUN [plural **forehands**] in games such as tennis, a way of hitting the ball with your arm out on the side that you hold the racket (= thing you hit the ball with) (**golpe de jogo de tênis**)

forehead /ˈfɔːhed/ NOUN [plural **foreheads**] the top part of your face above your eyes (**testa**)

foreign /ˈfɒrən/ ADJECTIVE
1 from a country that is not your country (**estrangeiro**) 🔁 a foreign language (**uma língua estrangeira**) ◻ a group of foreign tourists
2 to do with other countries (**estrangeiro**) 🔁 foreign policy (**política estrangeira**) 🔁 the foreign minister (**ministro estrangeiro**)
3 strange and not familiar ◻ + **to** The whole situation was completely foreign to me. (**estranho**)

• **foreigner** /ˈfɒrənə(r)/ NOUN [plural **foreigners**] someone who comes from a country that is not your country (**estrangeiro**)

foreleg /ˈfɔːleɡ/ NOUN [plural **forelegs**] one of the front legs of an animal that has four legs (**pata dianteira**)

foreman /ˈfɔːmən/ NOUN [plural **foremen**] someone who is in charge of a group of workers (**capataz**)

foremost /ˈfɔːməʊst/ ADJECTIVE the most famous or important ◻ He is one of the country's foremost experts on the disease. (**principal**)

forename /ˈfɔːneɪm/ NOUN [plural **forenames**] a formal word for the name or names that come before your family name (**prenome**)

forensic /fəˈrensɪk/ ADJECTIVE to do with using science to solve crimes ◻ forensic medicine (**forense, perícia técnica**) 🔁 There was no forensic evidence. (**evidência forense**)

forget

• **forensics** /fəˈrensɪks/ PLURAL NOUN the use of science to solve crimes (**ciência forense**)

foresee /fɔːˈsiː/ VERB [**foresees, foreseeing, foresaw, foreseen**] to expect that something will happen ◻ We didn't foresee this problem. (**prever**)

• **foreseeable** /fɔːˈsiːəbəl/ ADJECTIVE the foreseeable future as far in the future as you can reasonably know about ◻ The situation will remain as it is for the foreseeable future. (**futuro previsível**)

• **foresight** /ˈfɔːsaɪt/ NOUN, NO PLURAL when you know or guess what will happen in the future ◻ There was a lack of foresight by the company. (**previsão**)

forest /ˈfɒrɪst/ NOUN [plural **forests**] a place where a lot of trees are growing together ◻ We stayed at a camp deep in the forest. (**floresta**)

• **forested** /ˈfɒrɪstɪd/ ADJECTIVE covered in forest ◻ a thickly forested area (**florestal**)

• **forestry** /ˈfɒrɪstri/ NOUN, NO PLURAL planting and looking after trees and forests (**área florestal**)

forever /fəˈrevə(r)/ ADVERB
1 for all future time ◻ You can't stay in your room forever. ◻ Their lives have been changed forever. (**para sempre**)
2 an informal word meaning 'for a very long time' ◻ It took forever to get there. (**muito tempo**)
3 used to mean that something happens often ◻ + **ing** They're forever arguing. (**constantemente**)

foreword /ˈfɔːwɜːd/ NOUN [plural **forewords**] an introduction at the start of a book (**prefácio**)

forfeit /ˈfɔːfɪt/ VERB [**forfeits, forfeiting, forfeited**] to have something taken away from you because of something you have done ◻ If someone commits a serious crime, they forfeit their right to vote. (**perder**)

forgave /fəˈɡeɪv/ PAST TENSE OF **forgive** (**ver forgive**)

forge /fɔːdʒ/ ▶ VERB [**forges, forging, forged**]
1 to make an illegal copy of something ◻ He was sent to prison for forging passports. (**falsificar**)
2 to develop a good relationship with someone or something ◻ The Chinese have forged trade links around the world. (**estabelecer**)
◆ PHRASAL VERB **forge ahead** to make good progress with something ◻ She's forging ahead with her acting career. (**progredir com rapidez**)
▶ NOUN [plural **forges**] a place where metal is heated and shaped to make things (**forja**)

• **forgery** /ˈfɔːdʒəri/ NOUN [plural **forgeries**]
1 the crime of making an illegal copy of something ◻ He faces charges of forgery. (**falsificação**)
2 an illegal copy of something ◻ The painting turned out to be a forgery. (**falsificação**)

forget /fəˈɡet/ VERB [**forgets, forgetting, forgot, forgotten**]
1 to be unable to remember something ◻ I've forgotten her name. ◻ + **that** I forgot that you had

been there before. □ **+ about** *I had forgotten about the heat here.* (esquecer)

2 to not remember to do something or that something is happening □ **+ to do something** *I forgot to feed the dog.* □ **+ that** *He forgot that Milo was coming.* (esquecer) 🔁 *Don't forget to lock the door.* (não esqueça) 🔁 *I completely forgot her birthday.* (esqueci completamente)

3 to not remember to bring something □ *Val's forgotten her umbrella.* (esquecer)

4 to stop thinking or caring about something □ *Forget about your exams and come to the party.* (esquecer)

• **forgetful** /fəˈgetful/ ADJECTIVE often forgetting things (esquecido, distraído)

forgivable /fəˈgɪvəbəl/ ADJECTIVE if something is forgivable, you can understand it and so forgive it □ *It was a forgivable error.* (perdoável)

forgive /fəˈgɪv/ VERB [forgives, forgiving, forgave, forgiven] to stop being angry with someone for something they have done □ **+ for** *Have you forgiven him for breaking the window?* □ *His family can never forgive the killers.* □ *If anything happens to her, I'll never forgive myself.* (perdoar)

• **forgiveness** /fəˈgɪvnɪs/ NOUN, NO PLURAL when you forgive someone (perdão) 🔁 *I want to ask your forgiveness.* (pedir seu perdão)

• **forgiving** /fəˈgɪvɪŋ/ ADJECTIVE willing to forgive □ *Others might not be quite so forgiving.* (complacente)

forgo /fɔːˈgəʊ/ VERB [forgoes, forgoing, forwent, forgone] a formal word meaning to decide not to have or do something you would like □ *We might have to forgo a holiday this year.* (abrir mão)

forgot /fəˈgɒt/ PAST TENSE OF **forget** (ver forget)

forgotten /fəˈgɒtən/ ▶ PAST PARTICIPLE OF **forget** (ver forget)

▶ ADJECTIVE not remembered by anyone □ *forgotten heroes* (esquecidos)

fork /fɔːk/ ▶ NOUN [plural forks]

1 an object with a handle and points that you use for lifting food to your mouth (garfo) 🔁 *a knife and fork* (garfo e faca)

2 a place where a road or river divides and goes in two different directions □ *We came to a fork in the road.* (bifurcação)

3 a tool with a long handle and points that you use for digging (garfo)

▶ VERB [forks, forking, forked] if a road or a river forks, it divides into two parts going in different directions □ *Just after the bridge, the road forks.* (bifurcar)

♦ PHRASAL VERB **fork out** an informal word meaning to pay for something, especially when you do not want to □ *Students have to fork out £3,000 a year in tuition fees.* (pagar para algo)

• **forked** /fɔːkt/ ADJECTIVE divided into two parts at one end (bifurcado) 🔁 *a forked tongue* (língua bifurcada)

fork-lift truck /ˌfɔːklɪft ˈtrʌk/ NOUN [plural fork-lift trucks] a vehicle with two flat parts on the front for lifting and moving heavy things (caminhão empilhadeira)

forlorn /fəˈlɔːn/ ADJECTIVE looking lonely and unhappy □ *He looked so forlorn.* □ *a forlorn figure* (miserável)

form /fɔːm/ ▶ NOUN [plural forms]

1 a type of something □ *What form of transport do you use?* □ *I have tried various forms of exercise.* □ *You need to use some form of wrist support.* (tipo)

2 a document with questions and spaces to write your answers (formulário) 🔁 *You have to fill in a form to get a passport.* (preencher um formulário) □ *Can you sign this form, please?*

3 the way that something is □ *He gets most of his calories in the form of sugar.* (forma) 🔁 *In its current form, the programme is not effective.* (forma atual) 🔁 *My stress takes the form of frequent headaches.* (pega a forma de)

4 the shape of someone or something □ *I saw his lifeless form on the floor.* (forma)

5 a class at school □ *Which form are you in?* (série)

6 how well or badly someone is doing (forma) 🔁 *Our team was on top form* (= very good) *today.* (ótima forma)

▶ VERB [forms, forming, formed]

1 to start to exist or to make something start to exist □ *How was the Earth formed?* □ *An idea formed in his mind.* □ *I formed a good impression of his work.* □ *His party is likely to form the next government.* (tomar forma)

2 to be something or the thing that something is made of □ *This article could form the basis of a book.* □ *The area forms part of a safari park.* (constituir)

3 to make a particular shape □ *The children held hands and formed a circle.* (formar, constituir)

formal /ˈfɔːməl/ ADJECTIVE

1 following rules about what is polite and correct, not friendly and relaxed □ *a formal dinner party* □ *The atmosphere was very formal.* (formal)

2 public or official, or following official rules or methods (formal) 🔁 *A formal announcement is expected tomorrow.* (anúncio formal) 🔁 *I wish to make a formal complaint.* (reclamação formal)

3 formal education or training involves study at a school or college (convencional) 🔁 *She received little formal education.* (educação formal) 🔁 *He has no formal qualifications.* (qualificações convencionais)

• **formality** /fɔːˈmælɪti/ NOUN [plural formalities]

1 something that must be done because of rules or the law □ *There are certain legal formalities to go through.* (trâmite)

2 formal, polite behaviour □ *There's a lack of formality that I really like.* (formalidade)

format   315   **fortune**

- **formally** /ˈfɔːməlɪ/ ADVERB
1 officially □ *They have formally announced their engagement.* (**oficialmente**)
2 in a way that follows rules about what is polite and correct □ *They were formally dressed for the occasion.* (**formalmente**)

format /ˈfɔːmæt/ ▶ NOUN [plural **formats**] the way something is designed or arranged □ *Please send two photographs in digital format.* □ *There are plans to change the format of the tournament.* (**formato**)
▶ VERB [**formats, formatting, formatted**]
1 to prepare a computer disk so that you can store information on it. A computing word. (**formatar**)
2 to arrange the design of information on a page or document (**formatar**)

formation /fɔːˈmeɪʃən/ NOUN [plural **formations**]
1 when something is formed □ *the formation of a new government* □ *They believe it is a new planet in the process of formation.* (**formação**)
2 a shape made by the way people or things are arranged □ *a huge rock formation* (**formação**)

former /ˈfɔːmə(r)/ ▶ ADJECTIVE existing or true in the past but not now □ *the former President* □ *In former times, people did not travel so much.* (**passado, ex-, anterior**)
▶ NOUN, NO PLURAL **the former** the first of two people or things you mention □ *We visited America and Canada but stayed longer in the former.* (**os primeiros**)

- **formerly** /ˈfɔːməlɪ/ ADVERB in the past but not now □ *Their house was formerly a shop.* (**antigamente, outrora**)

formidable /ˈfɔːmɪdəbəl/ ADJECTIVE difficult to deal with or frightening □ *a formidable task* □ *He proved a formidable opponent.* (**difícil**)

formula /ˈfɔːmjʊlə/ NOUN [plural **formulas** or **formulae**]
1 in maths or chemistry, a set of letters, numbers or symbols that represent a rule, structure, etc. □ *What's the formula for calculating the area of a circle?* (**fórmula**) 🔁 *a mathematical formula* (**fórmula matemática**)
2 a method or plan for achieving something (**receita**) 🔁 *There is no magic formula* (= simple, easy method) *to solve the problem.* (**receita mágica**)
3 the combination of substances used to make something (**fórmula**)

- **formulate** /ˈfɔːmjʊleɪt/ VERB [**formulates, formulating, formulated**] to invent and develop a plan or idea □ *We didn't have much time to formulate a plan.* (**formular, inventar**)

- **formulation** /ˌfɔːmjʊˈleɪʃən/ NOUN [plural **formulations**]
1 the process of formulating something □ *the formulation of government policy* (**formulação**)
2 the combination of substances used to make something (**fórmula**)

fort /fɔːt/ NOUN [plural **forts**] a strong building used by soldiers to defend a place from attack (**forte**)

forth /fɔːθ/ ADVERB
1 back and forth in one direction then in the opposite direction □ *They threw the ball back and forth.* □ *He goes back and forth between Canada and the US.* (**de um lado para outro**)
2 a formal word meaning forwards, out of or away from a place □ *They went forth into the desert.* (**para a frente, avante**)

forthcoming /ˌfɔːˈkʌmɪŋ/ ADJECTIVE happening soon □ *forthcoming events* □ *They played some tracks from their forthcoming album.* (**futuro**)

forthright /ˈfɔːθraɪt/ ADJECTIVE very honest and saying what you think □ *John was forthright in his criticism.* (**direto**)

fortieth /ˈfɔːtɪɪθ/ NUMBER 40th written as a word (**quadragésimo**)

fortifications /ˌfɔːtɪfɪˈkeɪʃənz/ PLURAL NOUN strong walls or buildings that are built to defend a place from attack (**fortificações**)

fortify /ˈfɔːtɪfaɪ/ VERB [**fortifies, fortifying, fortified**]
1 to make someone or something stronger □ *I had a big breakfast to fortify myself for the journey.* (**fortalecer**)
2 to build strong walls, etc. around a place to protect it against attack □ *a fortified compound* (**fortificar**)

fortnight /ˈfɔːtnaɪt/ NOUN [plural **fortnights**] a period of two weeks □ *We're going to Greece for a fortnight.* □ *I've been very busy over the past fortnight.* □ *He visits her once a fortnight.* (**quinzena**)

- **fortnightly** /ˈfɔːtnaɪtlɪ/ ADVERB, ADJECTIVE happening every two weeks □ *They're paid fortnightly.* □ *a fortnightly magazine* (**quinzenalmente**)

fortress /ˈfɔːtrɪs/ NOUN [plural **fortresses**] a strong building used to defend a place from attack (**fortaleza**)

fortunate /ˈfɔːtʃənət/ ADJECTIVE lucky □ *We were fortunate to catch our train, we were so late.* □ *It's extremely fortunate that no one was hurt.* □ *We should help people who are less fortunate than ourselves.* (**afortunado**)

- **fortunately** /ˈfɔːtʃənətlɪ/ ADVERB used to say that something lucky has happened □ *Fortunately, nobody was injured.* (**felizmente**)

fortune /ˈfɔːtʃuːn/ NOUN [plural **fortunes**]
1 a very large amount of money □ *His uncle died and left him a fortune.* (**fortuna**) 🔁 *He made his fortune in the oil industry.* (**fez sua fortuna**)
2 an informal word used to mean a lot of money (**fortuna**) 🔁 *They spent a fortune on it.* (**gastaram uma fortuna**)
3 fortunes the good and bad things which happen to someone □ *It was a year of mixed fortunes for the party.* (**casualidades**)

4 good luck (**sorte**) ▣ *Sue had the good fortune to win first prize.* (**boa sorte**)

fortune-teller /ˈfɔːtʃuːnˌteɪlə(r)/ NOUN [*plural* **fortune-tellers**] a person who says they can tell people what is going to happen to them in the future (**cartomante**)

forty /ˈfɔːtɪ/ NUMBER [*plural* **forties**]
1 the number 40 (**quarenta**)
2 the forties the years between 1940 and 1949 (**anos quarenta**)

forum /ˈfɔːrəm/ NOUN [*plural* **forums**] a place or situation in which people can discuss things and express their opinions ▢ *an online forum* ▢ *The programme is intended to be a forum for public debate.* (**fórum**)

forward /ˈfɔːwəd/ ▶ ADJECTIVE

1 in the direction that is in front of you ▢ *a forward movement* (**para a frente**)
2 thinking about or planning for the future (**para o futuro**) ▣ *It just takes a little forward planning.* (**planos para o futuro**)

▶ VERB [**forwards, forwarding, forwarded**] to send a letter or e-mail you have received to someone else ▢ *He forwarded the e-mail to several colleagues.* (**expedir, enviar**)

▶ NOUN [*plural* **forwards**] a player in some team sports whose main job is to attack and to try to score (**atacante**)

• **forward** /ˈfɔːwəd/ or **forwards** /ˈfɔːwədz/ ADVERB
1 in the direction that is in front of you ▢ *The car moved slowly forwards.* ▢ *Amy leaned forward.* (**para a frente**) ▣ *He rocked backwards and forwards.* (**para trás e para a frente**)
2 towards a better or more developed state or situation (**adiante**) ▣ *This is a big step forward.* (**grande avanço adiante**) ▢ *We hope the political process can move forward.*
3 towards the future ▢ *We want to look forwards, not backwards.* (**para o futuro**)

forward slash /ˈfɔːwəd ˌslæʃ/ NOUN [*plural* **forward slashes**] the symbol '/', often used in Internet addresses (**barra**)

fossil /ˈfɒsəl/ NOUN [*plural* **fossils**] a dead animal or plant that has been kept in a piece of rock for thousands of years (**fóssil**)

fossil fuel /ˈfɒsəl ˌfjuːəl/ NOUN [*plural* **fossil fuels**] a fuel such as coal or oil that is formed from animals and plants that lived thousands of years ago (**combustível fóssil**)

fossilize or **fossilise** /ˈfɒsəlaɪz/ VERB [**fossilizes, fossilizing, fossilized**] to become a fossil (**fossilizar**)

foster /ˈfɒstə(r)/ VERB [**fosters, fostering, fostered**]
1 to look after a child as part of your family for a period of time while their parents cannot look after them (**acolher**)
2 to encourage an idea or a feeling to develop ▢ *Sports can foster teamwork.* (**fomentar**)

foster child /ˈfɒstə(r) ˌtʃaɪld/ NOUN [*plural* **foster children**] a child who is looked after by another family for a period of time when its parents cannot look after them (**criança acolhida**)

foster parent /ˈfɒstə(r) ˌpeərənt/ NOUN [*plural* **foster parents**] someone who looks after children that are not their own (**pai ou mãe de acolhimento**)

fought /fɔːt/ PAST TENSE AND PAST PARTICIPLE OF **fight** (*ver* **fight**)

foul /faʊl/ ADJECTIVE [**fouler, foulest**]
1 very dirty or with a bad smell or taste ▢ *The tea tasted foul.* (**nojento**)
2 very unpleasant (**abominável**) ▣ *foul weather* (**tempo abominável**) ▣ *He's in a foul mood.* (**humor abominável**)
3 against the rules of a sport or game ▢ *a foul shot* (**faltoso**)

♦ IDIOMS **fall foul of someone/something** to have problems because you have not obeyed a rule or someone in authority ▢ *She soon fell foul of the law.* (**desentender-se com alguém/por causa de algo**) **foul play** dishonest behaviour, especially causing someone's death ▢ *Police said there were no signs of foul play.* (**crime violento**)

▶ NOUN [*plural* **fouls**] an action that is against the rules of a sport ▢ *He was sent off for a foul on another player.* (**falta**)

▶ VERB [**fouls, fouling, fouled**]
1 a formal word meaning to make something dirty ▢ *Do not allow your dogs to foul the play area.* (**sujar**)
2 to do something that is against the rules of a sport (**cometer falta**)

found¹ /faʊnd/ VERB [**founds, founding, founded**] to start an organization ▢ *The college was founded in 1950.* (**fundar**)

found² /faʊnd/ PAST TENSE AND PAST PARTICIPLE OF **find** (*ver* **find¹**)

foundation /faʊnˈdeɪʃən/ NOUN [*plural* **foundations**]
1 an idea or principle that something is based on ▢ *Literacy is one of the basic foundations of education.* ▢ *This new technology forms the foundation of all our products.* ▢ *Her accusations have no foundation in truth.* (**fundação**)
2 a situation from which something else can develop ▢ *Jealousy and suspicion are not a good foundation for a happy marriage.* (**base**) ▣ *His government laid the foundations for better human rights.* (**lançou as bases**)
3 when an organization, business or country is started ▢ *She has worked here since the company's foundation in 1997.* (**fundação**)
4 an organization that provides money for a particular purpose ▢ *a scientific/educational foundation* (**fundação**)
5 foundations the part of a building that is under the ground and which supports it (**fundação**) ▣ *They have dug the foundations for our new home.* (**escavaram as fundações**)

founder /ˈfaʊndə(r)/ NOUN [plural **founders**] someone who starts an organization (**fundir**)

foundry /ˈfaʊndrɪ/ NOUN [plural **foundries**] a factory where metal or glass is melted and made into things (**fundição**)

fountain /ˈfaʊntɪn/ NOUN [plural **fountains**] a structure that pushes water up into the air for decoration in a garden or park (**fonte**)

fountain pen /ˈfaʊntɪn ˌpen/ NOUN [plural **fountain pens**] a pen that you fill with ink (**caneta-tinteiro**)

four /fɔː(r)/ NUMBER [plural **fours**] the number 4 (**quatro**)

fourteen /ˌfɔːˈtiːn/ NUMBER the number 14 (**catorze**)

fourteenth /ˌfɔːˈtiːnθ/ NUMBER 14th written as a word (**décimo quarto**)

fourth /fɔːθ/ ▶ NUMBER 4th written as a word □ *You are fourth on the list.* □ *Mario finished fourth in the race.* (**quarto**)
▶ NOUN [plural **fourths**] a US word for quarter

fowl /faʊl/ NOUN [plural **fowl** or **fowls**] a bird that is kept for its meat and eggs, for example a chicken (**ave**)

fox /fɒks/ NOUN [plural **foxes**] a wild animal that looks like a dog, with red fur and a thick tail (**raposa**)

foxglove /ˈfɒksɡlʌv/ NOUN [plural **foxgloves**] a tall plant with purple flowers shaped like bells (**dedaleira**)

foyer /ˈfɔɪeɪ/ NOUN [plural **foyers**] the area inside the entrance to a large building such as a theatre or a hotel (**hall de entrada**)

fracas /ˈfrækɑː/ NOUN, NO PLURAL a noisy argument or fight □ *He got involved in a fracas outside a nightclub.* (**rixa, tumulto**)

fraction /ˈfrækʃən/ NOUN [plural **fractions**]
1 an amount, such as 1/2 or 3/8, that is part of a whole number (**fração**)
2 a small amount or part of something □ *It lasted only a fraction of a second.* □ *This is a tiny fraction of total government spending.* (**fração**)
• **fractionally** /ˈfrækʃənəlɪ/ ADVERB by a very small amount □ *This one is fractionally higher.* (**fracionariamente**)

fracture /ˈfræktʃə(r)/ ▶ VERB [**fractures, fracturing, fractured**] to crack or break something, especially a bone in your body □ *Emma's fractured her arm.* (**fraturar**)
▶ NOUN [plural **fractures**] a crack or break in something, especially a bone in your body (**fratura**)

fragile /ˈfrædʒaɪl/ ADJECTIVE
1 not very strong and likely to be broken, damaged or destroyed □ *The bones become fragile and more likely to break.* □ *a fragile peace* (**frágil**)

2 thin and weak □ *Her mother looked so fragile.* (**delicado**)
• **fragility** /frəˈdʒɪlətɪ/ NOUN, NO PLURAL the state of being fragile (**fragilidade**)

fragment ▶ NOUN /ˈfræɡmənt/ [plural **fragments**] a small piece that has broken off something □ *There were fragments of glass on the floor.* (**fragmento, pedaço**)
▶ VERB /fræɡˈment/ [**fragments, fragmenting, fragmented**] to break into small pieces or parts (**fragmentar**)
• **fragmentary** /ˈfræɡməntərɪ/ ADJECTIVE consisting of small pieces or parts which are not well connected □ *The accounts we have are fragmentary and inconclusive.* (**fragmentado, incompleto**)

fragrance /ˈfreɪɡrəns/ NOUN [plural **fragrances**]
1 a pleasant smell □ *the sweet fragrance of jasmine flowers* (**fragrância**)
2 a pleasant-smelling liquid which people put on their bodies (**perfume**)
• **fragrant** /ˈfreɪɡrənt/ ADJECTIVE smelling pleasant □ *fragrant flowers* (**perfumado**)

frail /freɪl/ ADJECTIVE [**frailer, frailest**] thin and weak □ *a frail old man* (**frágil**)
• **frailty** /ˈfreɪltɪ/ NOUN [plural **frailties**] physical, mental or moral weakness □ *He's still very active despite his frailty.* (**fragilidade**) 🔁 *We are all subject to human frailties.* (**fragilidade humana**)

frame /freɪm/ ▶ NOUN [plural **frames**]
1 a structure that fits around the edge of something, for example a picture or a window (**moldura**)
2 a structure that supports something, and around which the thing is built □ *My bike has a lightweight frame.* (**armação**)
3 frames the part that holds the glass parts in a pair of glasses (**armação**)
4 the shape of someone's body □ *a muscular frame* (**armação**)
5 frame of mind the way someone is feeling □ *He's in a very positive frame of mind.* (**estado de espírito**)
▶ VERB [**frames, framing, framed**]
1 to put something such as a picture in a frame □ *I'm going to get this photo framed.* (**emoldurar**)
2 to form an edge around something □ *Her face was framed with golden curls.* (**emoldurar**)
3 to develop a plan or a law □ *New legislation is being framed.* (**formular**)
4 a formal word meaning to express or show something in a particular way □ *They have framed their argument in legal terms.* (**formular**)
5 to make it look as though someone who is not guilty has committed a crime □ *He claims he was framed.* (**incriminar**)

framework /ˈfreɪmwɜːk/ NOUN [plural **frameworks**]
1 the basic ideas or principles that something is based on □ *We operate within a legal framework.*

☐ *This provides a framework for sustainable development.* (**sistema**)
2 the structure that supports something such as a building ☐ *the framework of the building* (**estrutura**)

franchise /'fræntʃaɪz/ NOUN [plural **franchises**] the right to sell the goods or services of a particular company using the company's name ☐ *He's the manager of a fast food franchise.* (**franquia**)

frank /fræŋk/ ADJECTIVE [**franker, frankest**] honest and saying what you think (**franco**) 🔁 *We had a fairly frank discussion.* (**discussão franca**) 🔁 *To be quite frank, I don't think it'll work.* (**para ser franco**)

• **frankly** /'fræŋkli/ ADVERB
1 used to give an honest opinion ☐ *Frankly, I don't think he's good enough for the job.* (**francamente**)
2 in a direct, honest way ☐ *She spoke frankly about her experiences.* (**francamente**)

• **frankness** /'fræŋknɪs/ NOUN, NO PLURAL the quality of being frank ☐ *She was surprised at the General's frankness.* (**franqueza**)

frantic /'fræntɪk/ ADJECTIVE
1 done with a lot of energy and activity, by people who are very worried ☐ *They joined in the frantic search for survivors.* (**frenético**)
2 extremely worried ☐ *His mother was frantic with worry.* (**desesperado**)

• **frantically** /'fræntɪkəli/ ADVERB in a frantic way ☐ *We've been working frantically to get finished in time.* (**freneticamente**)

fraternal /frə'tɜːnəl/ ADJECTIVE to do with brothers ☐ *fraternal loyalty* (**fraternal**)

• **fraternity** /frə'tɜːnəti/ NOUN [plural **fraternities**]
1 a feeling of being friends and having shared interests (**fraternidade**)
2 in the US, a club or group for male students at a college (**fraternidade**)

fraternization or **fraternisation** /ˌfrætənaɪ'zeɪʃən/ NOUN, NO PLURAL when people fraternize. A formal word. (**fraternização**)

fraternize or **fraternise** /'frætənaɪz/ VERB [**fraternizes, fraternizing, fraternized**] a formal word meaning to meet with people as friends, especially people from a different group ☐ *Muslims and Christians fraternized with each other without apparent tension.* (**fraternizar**)

fraud /frɔːd/ NOUN [plural **frauds**]
1 the crime of tricking people to get money ☐ *He was found guilty of credit card fraud.* (**fraude**)
2 someone who tricks other people by pretending to be something they are not (**impostor**)

• **fraudulent** /'frɔːdjʊlənt/ ADJECTIVE deliberately dishonest or intended to trick people. A formal word. ☐ *Her claims were fraudulent.* (**fraudulento**)

• **fraudulently** /'frɔːdjʊləntli/ ADVERB in a fraudulent way. A formal word. ☐ *He obtained the money fraudulently.* (**fraudulentamente**)

fraught /frɔːt/ ADJECTIVE
1 nervous and worried, or making you feel nervous and worried ☐ *She looked fraught.* ☐ *The preparations were fraught.* (**preocupante**)
2 fraught with something full of danger or problems ☐ *The journey was fraught with danger.* ☐ *The strategy is fraught with risk.* (**cheio de algo**)

fray /freɪ/ VERB [**frays, fraying, frayed**]
1 if cloth frays, the threads along the edge become loose (**desfiar-se**)
2 if your temper or nerves fray, you gradually become more angry or less calm (**desgastar-se**) 🔁 *Tempers were fraying on both sides.* (**os temperamentos foram se desgastando**)

• **frayed** /freɪd/ ADJECTIVE with loose threads along the edge ☐ *frayed jeans* (**desfiado**)

freak /friːk/ ▶ NOUN [plural **freaks**]
1 a very strange person or a person who looks very strange (**estranho, esquisito**)
2 an informal word for someone who is very interested in something ☐ *a health freak* (**maluco**)
▶ ADJECTIVE extremely unusual (**bizarro**) 🔁 *a freak accident* (**acidente bizarro**) 🔁 *a freak storm* (**tempestade bizarra**)
▶ VERB [**freaks, freaking, freaked**] an informal word meaning to suddenly become very angry or upset about something ☐ *She'll freak when she sees what they've done to her car.* (**irritar-se**)

freckle /'frekəl/ NOUN [plural **freckles**] a small brown mark on your skin, especially your face (**sarda**)

• **freckled** /'frekəld/ ADJECTIVE covered in freckles ☐ *She has pale, freckled skin.* (**sardento**)

free /friː/ ▶ ADJECTIVE
1 not costing any money ☐ *It's free to get into the museum.* ☐ *I've got two free tickets for the show.* (**gratuito**)
2 not controlled by people or laws ☐ *We were given free access to all the files.* ☐ *The country needs to hold free and fair elections.* ☐ **+ to do something** *You are free to leave whenever you wish.* (**livre**)
3 not a prisoner ☐ *He is once more a free man.* (**livre**) 🔁 *They broke into the compound and set the prisoners free.* (**libertaram**)
4 available to be used ☐ *Is this seat free?* (**livre**)
5 not busy ☐ *Are you free this evening?* (**livre**)
6 free time time when you are not busy and can do what you want (**tempo livre**)
7 free from/of something not containing or having a particular unpleasant thing ☐ *All our cakes are free from additives.* (**livre de algo**)
8 feel free to something you say when you are saying that someone can do something or have something ☐ *Feel free to help yourself from the drinks machine.* (**esteja à vontade para algo**)
▶ ADVERB
1 without any payment ☐ *Children under 5 travel free.* (**livre**)

free enterprise   319   French horn

2 out of a place where a person or animal is being kept or tied up ☐ *They struggled to get free.* **(livre)** ▣ *They managed to break free of their chains.* **(ficar livre)**

3 without being controlled ☐ *All their children were allowed to roam free.* **(livremente)**

▶ VERB [**frees, freeing, freed**]

1 to let a person or animal out of a prison or place where they were being kept ☐ *The remaining hostages were freed this morning.* **(libertar)**

2 to manage to get someone out of a place ☐ *A man was freed from the burning wreckage.* **(livrar)**

3 to take away something, for example work or problems, that makes someone's life difficult ☐ *The inheritance has freed her from the strain of supporting five children.* **(libertar)**

4 to make something available to be used ☐ **+ up** *Having the motorbike will free up the car for my wife to use.* **(libertar)**

- **-free** /friː/ SUFFIX **-free** is added to the end of words to mean 'without' ☐ *fat-free* **(livre de)**
- **freedom** /ˈfriːdəm/ NOUN, NO PLURAL
1 the right to do what you want **(liberdade)** ▣ *freedom of speech/movement* **(liberdade de expressão/movimento)**
2 the state of not being a prisoner **(liberdade)**
3 **freedom from something** not having something unpleasant ☐ *freedom from fear* **(imunidade contra algo)**

free enterprise /ˌfriː ˈentəpraɪz/ NOUN, NO PLURAL a system where businesses operate with little government control. An economics word. **(livre-iniciativa)**

freehand /ˈfriːhænd/ ADJECTIVE, ADVERB a freehand drawing is done without the help of things such as a ruler **(à mão livre)**

free kick /ˌfriː ˈkɪk/ NOUN [plural **free kicks**] when a football player is allowed to kick the ball without anyone from the other team trying to stop them **(tiro livre)**

freelance /ˈfriːlɑːns/ ADJECTIVE, ADVERB working for yourself and not working as a part of a company or organization ☐ *a freelance journalist* ☐ *Sally works freelance as a writer.* **(autônomo)**

freely /ˈfriːli/ ADVERB
1 without being limited or controlled **(livremente)** ▣ *The information is freely available.* **(disponíveis livremente)** ☐ *You can speak freely to me.*
2 in a willing way **(livremente)** ▣ *I freely admit I was wrong.* **(admito livremente)**

free market /ˌfriː ˈmɑːkɪt/ NOUN [plural **free markets**] a system where the price of goods depends on how much there is of something and how many people want it. An economics word. **(mercado livre)**

free-range /ˌfriːˈreɪndʒ/ ADJECTIVE to do with animals that are allowed to move around a farm **(criação extensiva de animais)** ▣ *free-range eggs* **(ovos de galinha caipira)**

free speech /ˌfriː ˈspiːtʃ/ NOUN, NO PLURAL the right to express your opinions without being punished **(liberdade de expressão)**

freeway /ˈfriːweɪ/ NOUN [plural **freeways**] the US word for **motorway** **(autoestrada)**

freewheel /ˌfriːˈwiːl/ VERB [**freewheels, freewheeling, freewheeled**] to ride a bicycle without turning the pedals (= parts you push with your feet) **(andar no embalo)**

freeze /friːz/ ▶ VERB [**freezes, freezing, froze, frozen**]

1 to become very cold and hard, or to turn into ice ☐ *The lake freezes in winter.* ☐ **+ over** *The river froze over* (= became covered in ice). **(congelar)**

2 to store food at a very cold temperature so it keeps for a long time ☐ *We'll eat some and freeze the rest.* **(congelar)**

3 if someone freezes they become very cold ☐ *You'll freeze if you go out without a coat!* **(congelar)**

4 to stop moving suddenly, usually because you are afraid ☐ *He froze when he saw the dog.* **(paralisar)**

5 to stop the level or amount of something increasing ☐ *University tuition fees have been frozen for the next two years.* **(congelar)**

▶ NOUN [plural **freezes**]

1 when the level of something is fixed **(congelamento)** ▣ *Doctors have accepted a pay freeze for this year.* **(congelamento de pagamento)**

2 when a process is suddenly stopped ☐ *We need a freeze on all new airport expansion.* **(congelamento)**

3 a period of very cold weather **(frio intenso)**

- **freezer** /ˈfriːzə(r)/ NOUN [plural **freezers**] a machine for keeping food very cold **(congelador)**
- **freezing** /ˈfriːzɪŋ/ ADJECTIVE very cold ☐ *It's freezing in here!* **(muito frio)** ▣ *It was freezing cold outside.* **(gelado)**

freezing point /ˈfriːzɪŋ ˌpɔɪnt/ NOUN [plural **freezing points**] the temperature at which a liquid becomes solid. A chemistry word. **(ponto de congelamento)**

freight /freɪt/ NOUN, NO PLURAL goods that are being carried by a truck, ship or plane **(carga)**

- **freighter** /ˈfreɪtə(r)/ NOUN [plural **freighters**] a large ship or plane for carrying goods **(navio cargueiro)**

French fries /ˌfrentʃ ˈfraɪz/ PLURAL NOUN long thin pieces of potato, fried in oil ☐ *a burger with French fries* **(batatas fritas)**

French horn /ˌfrentʃ ˈhɔːn/ NOUN [plural **French horns**] a large musical instrument made of a curved metal tube which is wide at one end, played by blowing into it **(trompa francesa)**

French window /ˌfrentʃ ˈwɪndəʊ/ NOUN [plural French windows] a tall glass door that opens onto a garden (**porta envidraçada**)

frenetic /frəˈnetɪk/ ADJECTIVE involving a lot of excitement and quick activity (**frenético**) ▫ They work at such a *frenetic pace*. (**passo frenético**) ▫ The announcement was followed by a week of *frenetic activity*. (**atividade frenética**)

frenzied /ˈfrenzid/ ADJECTIVE very excited and uncontrolled (**enlouquecido**) ▫ a *frenzied attack* (**ataque enlouquecido**) ▫ *frenzied activity* (**atividade enlouquecida**)

frenzy /ˈfrenzi/ NOUN, NO PLURAL a state or period of great excitement, activity and emotion (**frenesi**) ▫ a *frenzy of activity* (**frenesi de atividade**) ▫ Their engagement has generated *a media frenzy*. (**um frenesi dos meios de comunicação**)

frequency /ˈfriːkwənsi/ NOUN [plural frequencies]
1 how often something happens ▫ Global warming may increase the frequency of severe hurricanes. (**frequência**)
2 the number of times sound or radio waves pass the same point in one second. A physics word. (**frequência**) ▫ Many animals can hear *higher frequencies* than we can. (**frequências mais altas**)

• **frequent** /ˈfriːkwənt/ ADJECTIVE happening often ▫ Dave makes frequent visits to his grandmother. ▫ His e-mails are becoming more frequent. (**frequente**)

• **frequently** /ˈfriːkwəntli/ ADVERB often ▫ Lee is frequently late for work. ▫ She frequently appears in women's magazines. (**frequentemente**)

fresh /freʃ/ ADJECTIVE [fresher, freshest]
1 fresh food is not old, and has not been dried, frozen, etc. (**fresco**) ▫ *fresh fruit/vegetables* (**frutas/vegetais frescos**) ▫ This salad will stay fresh for a day or two.
2 new and different (**novo**) ▫ They hope to make a *fresh start* in Australia. (**recomeço**) ▫ I'll put some fresh sheets on the bed.
3 fresh air is clean air in outside areas (**fresco**) ▫ I'm going for a walk to get some *fresh air*. (**ar fresco**)
4 fresh water does not contain salt (**água doce**)
5 made or done recently ▫ A layer of fresh snow lay on the ground. (**recente**)
6 having a pleasant, clean smell ▫ a fresh, floral fragrance (**fresco**)

• **freshen** /ˈfreʃən/ VERB [freshens, freshening, freshened] to make something fresher ▫ I use a mouthwash to freshen my breath. (**refrescar**)

• **freshly** /ˈfreʃli/ ADVERB only just made or done (**recentemente**) ▫ *freshly baked* bread (**recentemente assado**)

• **freshness** /ˈfreʃnɪs/ NOUN, NO PLURAL the quality of being fresh (**fresco, frescor**)

freshwater /ˈfreʃˌwɔːtə(r)/ ADJECTIVE a freshwater fish lives in rivers and lakes, not in the sea (**água doce**)

fret /fret/ VERB [frets, fretting, fretted] to feel worried and unable to relax ▫ If he's late coming home she starts to fret. (**preocupar-se**)

friction /ˈfrɪkʃən/ NOUN, NO PLURAL
1 when one surface rubs against another surface, making movement more difficult. A physics word. ▫ Oil is used to reduce friction. (**atrito**)
2 disagreement or arguing ▫ The rumours have caused friction within the band. (**atrito, conflito**) ▫ Housework is a common *source of friction* between couples. (**motivo de conflito**)

Friday /ˈfraɪdi/ NOUN [plural Fridays] the day of the week after Thursday and before Saturday ▫ It's my birthday on Friday. (**sexta-feira**)

fridge /frɪdʒ/ NOUN [plural fridges] a machine that you store food or drink in to keep it cold and fresh ▫ He opened the fridge to get some milk. ▫ There's some chocolate in the fridge. (**refrigerador**)

fried /fraɪd/ ▶ PAST TENSE AND PAST PARTICIPLE OF **fry** ▫ She fried the fish in butter. (**ver fry**)
▶ ADJECTIVE cooked in hot oil or fat ▫ a *fried egg*

friend /frend/ NOUN [plural friends]
1 someone who you know well and like ▫ + *of* She's a friend of mine (**amigo**) ▫ Lindsay is my *best friend* (**melhor amiga**) ▫ They only told their family and *close friends*. (**amigos íntimos**)
2 friends if two people are friends, they know and like each other ▫ + *with* I'm friends with her sister. ▫ They remained *good friends* after university. (**amigos**) ▫ The boys soon *became friends*. (**tornaram-se amigos**)
3 make friends (with someone) to meet and become friends with someone ▫ She soon made friends. ▫ I made friends with Alex at college. (**fazer amizade com alguém**)

• **friendliness** /ˈfrendlɪnɪs/ NOUN, NO PLURAL
1 being friendly towards people (**simpatia**)
2 the quality of not harming something ▫ They rate products in terms of their environmental friendliness. (**cordialidade**)

• **friendly** /ˈfrendli/ ▶ ADJECTIVE [friendlier, friendliest]
1 kind and pleasant towards someone ▫ + *to* She's friendly to everyone. ▫ a *friendly smile* ▫ The staff are friendly and helpful. (**simpático, amável**)
2 being friends with someone ▫ + *with* I've been friendly with the family for years. (**amigável**) ▫ He *became friendly* with Richard. (**tornou-se amigável**)
3 to do with a game that is played for fun, not as part of a competition ▫ a *friendly match* (**amistoso**)
▶ NOUN [plural friendlies] a game played for fun, not as part of a competition ▫ He's in the team for tomorrow's friendly against Spain.

• **-friendly** /ˈfrendli/ SUFFIX **-friendly** is added to the end of words to mean 'not harming

frieze

something' or 'welcoming a particular type of people' □ *eco-friendly* (= not harming the environment) *packaging* □ *a child-friendly restaurant* (**inofensivo, convidativo**)

• **friendship** /'frendʃɪp/ NOUN [plural **friendships**] the relationship you have with a friend (**amizade**) 🗣 *We have a close friendship.* (**amizade íntima**) 🗣 *She formed a lifelong friendship with Ellis.* (**amizade duradoura**)

---

frieze /fri:z/ NOUN [plural **friezes**] a long narrow strip of decorated paper that you put on a wall (**friso**)

frigate /'frɪɡət/ NOUN [plural **frigates**] a small military ship (**fragata**)

fright /fraɪt/ NOUN [plural **frights**] a sudden feeling of fear (**pavor, susto**) 🗣 *You gave me a fright, jumping out like that!* (**me assustou**) 🗣 *I got a fright when I saw it.* (**levei um susto**) 🗣 *She took fright* (= felt suddenly afraid) *and ran off.* (**sentiu pavor**)

• **frighten** /'fraɪtən/ VERB [**frightens, frightening, frightened**] to make someone feel afraid or worried □ *A sudden noise frightened the horses.* □ *You'll frighten the baby!* (**amedrontar**)

♦ PHRASAL VERB **frighten someone away/off** to make a person or animal so nervous that they move or run away □ *We lit a fire to frighten away wild animals.* □ *Too much technology might frighten customers off.* (**afugentar, espantar**)

• **frightened** /'fraɪtənd/ ADJECTIVE afraid or very worried □ **+ of** *He's frightened of dogs.* □ **+ to do something** *He was too frightened to tell his parents.* (**assustado, apavorado**) 🗣 *I felt very frightened.* (**fiquei apavorado**) □ *a frightened expression*

• **frightening** /'fraɪtənɪŋ/ ADJECTIVE making you feel afraid or very worried □ *a frightening experience* □ *They look very frightening.* □ *That's a frightening thought!* (**assustador**)

• **frighteningly** /'fraɪtənɪŋlɪ/ ADVERB in a way that frightens or worries you □ *He's frighteningly fast.* (**assustadoramente**)

frill /frɪl/ NOUN [plural **frills**]
1 a narrow strip of cloth pulled into folds that is attached to something as a decoration (**babado**)
2 frills extra things which are added to something to make it more attractive, special, etc. (**adorno, enfeite**) 🗣 *It's a basic hotel with no frills.* (**simples, sem enfeites**)

• **frilly** /'frɪlɪ/ ADJECTIVE decorated with frills □ *a frilly skirt* (**com babados**)

fringe /frɪndʒ/ ▶ NOUN [plural **fringes**]
1 hair that hangs down over the top part of your face (**franja**)
2 the outside edge of something □ *There's a lot of poor housing on the fringes of the city.* (**margem**)
3 loose threads that hang down from the edge of something as decoration (**franja**)

front

▶ ADJECTIVE not belonging to the main part, group or activity (**à margem**) 🗣 *They're a fringe group and don't represent the views of the main party.* (**grupo à margem**)

▶ VERB [**fringes, fringing, fringed**] if a place or thing is fringed with something, it has that thing along its edge □ *The lake is fringed by trees.* (**estar cercado**)

frisky /'frɪskɪ/ ADJECTIVE [**friskier, friskiest**] lively and full of energy □ *a frisky puppy* (**brincalhão**)

fritter /'frɪtə(r)/
♦ PHRASAL VERB [**fritters, frittering, frittered**]
fritter something away to waste time or money on silly things (**esbanjar algo**)

frivolous /'frɪvələs/ ADJECTIVE fun and not serious or necessary (**frívolo, supérfluo**)

frizzy /'frɪzɪ/ ADJECTIVE [**frizzier, frizziest**] frizzy hair has very small tight curls (**frizado**)

fro /frəʊ/ ADVERB **to and fro** backwards and forwards □ *The mast swayed to and fro.* (**para a frente e para trás**)

frog /frɒɡ/ NOUN [plural **frogs**] a small brown or green animal that can jump and swim and lives near water (**sapo**)

frogman /'frɒɡmən/ NOUN [plural **frogmen**] someone whose job is to swim under water wearing special clothes and using breathing equipment □ *police frogmen* (**mergulhador**)

frogmarch /'frɒɡmɑːtʃ/ VERB [**frogmarches, frogmarching, frogmarched**] if two people frogmarch someone somewhere, they force the person to alk there by holding each arm firmly (**obrigar**)

frolic /'frɒlɪk/ VERB [**frolics, frolicking, frolicked**] to play in a lively and happy way □ *Lambs were frolicking in the fields.* (**brincar, divertir-se**)

from /frəm/ PREPOSITION

1 used to show where or when something started or where it was before □ *She's driving up from London.* □ *The shops are open from nine to five.* □ *He took a photograph from the drawer.* □ *You can get batteries from the shop over the road.* □ *He stole some money from his parents.* (**de**)
2 used to show who gave or sent something □ *I had a lovely card from Julie.* (**de**)
3 used to show where someone was born or lives □ *I'm from Taiwan.* (**de**)
4 used to show what something is made of or what has caused something □ *Yogurt is made from milk.* □ *He was shivering from the cold.* (**de**)
5 used to show how far something is □ *Do you live far from here?* □ *We are 15 miles from the nearest supermarket.* (**de**)
6 from now on starting now and continuing into the future □ *From now on I'll be much more careful about locking the house.* (**de agora em diante**)

front /frʌnt/ ▶ NOUN [plural **fronts**]
1 the part of something that faces forwards, or the part that is furthest forwards □ *The house*

has a red front. □ *The front of the car was badly damaged.* (**frente**)

2 in front of someone/something (a) next to the front part of something □ *Please don't park in front of the gates.* □ *He stood right in front of me.* □ *She jumped in front of the moving train.* (b) where someone can see or hear you □ *He hit the children in front of their parents.* □ *She loves performing in front of a large audience.* (**diante de alguém/algo**)

3 in front further forward than someone or something □ *I was driving along when the car in front suddenly stopped.* (**em frente**)

4 an area where fighting takes place during a war (**o fronte**)

▶ ADJECTIVE at the front of something (**da frente**) ▣ *I knocked on the front door.* (**porta da frente**) ▣ *We sat in the front row.* (**fileira da frente**)

frontier /ˈfrʌntɪə(r)/ NOUN [plural frontiers]

1 a dividing line between two countries □ *Pakistan's western frontier* □ **+ of** *He extended the frontiers of his empire.* □ **+ with** *The mountains mark Nepal's frontier with India.* (**fronteira**)

2 the newest or most advanced ideas or the limits of our knowledge □ *We aim to advance the frontiers of biotechnology.* (**fronteira**)

frost /frɒst/ NOUN [plural frosts]

1 NO PLURAL a very thin layer of white ice that forms on surfaces outside when the weather is cold □ *There's frost on the ground.* (**geada**)

2 a time when frost forms (**geada**) ▣ *There was a hard frost last night.* (**grande geada**)

frostbite /ˈfrɒstbaɪt/ NOUN, NO PLURAL an injury to parts of the body, especially the fingers and toes, caused by extreme cold (**ulceração**)

frosted /ˈfrɒstɪd/ ADJECTIVE frosted glass has a surface that you cannot see through (**congelado**)

frosty /ˈfrɒsti/ ADJECTIVE [frostier, frostiest]

1 when it is frosty, everything is covered in frost (= a thin, white layer of ice) □ *a frosty morning* (**coberto de geada**)

2 not friendly □ *Relations between the two countries have been frosty for some time.* (**frio**)

froth /frɒθ/ ▶ NOUN, NO PLURAL a lot of small bubbles on top of a liquid □ *She stirred the thick froth on her cappuccino.* (**espuma**)

▶ VERB [froths, frothing, frothed] to form froth (**espumar**)

• **frothy** /ˈfrɒθi/ ADJECTIVE [frothier, frothiest] with froth on the top □ *a frothy milkshake* (**espumante**)

frown /fraʊn/ ▶ VERB [frowns, frowning, frowned] to look as if you are angry, worried or thinking a lot by moving your eyebrows (= lines of hair above your eyes) down □ *She frowned when I suggested it.* (**franzir a testa**)

◆ PHRASAL VERB **frown on/upon something/someone** to disapprove of something or someone □ *Smoking is frowned on.* (**desaprovar algo/alguém**)

▶ NOUN [plural frowns] when you frown

froze /froʊz/ PAST TENSE OF **freeze** □ *The milk froze in the fridge.* (**ver freeze**)

frozen /ˈfroʊzən/ ▶ PAST PARTICIPLE OF **freeze** □ *It was so cold that the lake had frozen.* (**ver freeze**)

▶ ADJECTIVE frozen food is stored at a very cold temperature to make it last for a long time □ *a packet of frozen peas* (**congelado**)

fructose /ˈfrʌktoʊs/ NOUN, NO PLURAL a type of sugar found in some types of fruit. A biology word. (**frutose**)

frugal /ˈfruːɡəl/ ADJECTIVE careful with your money and saving it instead of spending a lot (**econômico**)

fruit /fruːt/ NOUN

1 NO PLURAL a food such as an apple or a banana which grows on a plant and contains the seeds of the plant (**fruta**) ▣ *fruit and vegetables* (**frutas e legumes**) ▣ *We eat plenty of fresh fruit* (**frutas frescas**) ▣ *I usually have a piece of fruit for breakfast.* (**pedaço de fruta**)

2 the fruits of something the good results of something, especially work □ *We're now seeing the fruits of our labour.* (**os frutos de algo**)

> Note that fruit is not usually used in the plural. Sometimes the plural **fruits** is used, meaning 'types of fruit' but it is not common:
> ✓ *You should eat more fruit.*
> ✗ *You should eat more fruits.*

fruitcake /ˈfruːtkeɪk/ NOUN [plural fruitcakes] a cake containing dried fruits (**bolo de frutas**)

fruitful /ˈfruːtfʊl/ ADJECTIVE having good results □ *a fruitful meeting* (**proveitoso**)

fruition /fruːˈɪʃən/ NOUN, NO PLURAL a formal word for the result you have been trying to achieve □ *This is the fruition of five years' work.* (**realização**) ▣ *The plan never came to fruition.* (**teve realização**)

fruitless /ˈfruːtlɪs/ ADJECTIVE not producing the result you wanted □ *a fruitless search* (**infrutífero**)

fruit salad /ˌfruːt ˈsæləd/ NOUN [plural fruit salads] a dish of small pieces of different fruit (**salada de frutas**)

frumpy /ˈfrʌmpi/ ADJECTIVE [frumpier, frumpiest] wearing old-fashioned clothes that do not make you look attractive (**desmazelada**)

frustrate /frʌˈstreɪt/ VERB [frustrates, frustrating, frustrated]

1 to make you feel annoyed because you cannot do or achieve what you want □ *It frustrates me that we can't get started sooner.* □ *Call centres often frustrate customers.* (**frustrar**)

2 to prevent someone from doing something □ *Bad weather frustrated efforts to rescue the men.* (**frustrar**)

- **frustrated** /frʌˈstreɪtɪd/ ADJECTIVE annoyed because you cannot do or achieve what you want □ *He became increasingly frustrated at the lack of progress.* □ *frustrated passengers* (frustrado)
- **frustrating** /frʌˈstreɪtɪŋ/ ADJECTIVE making you feel frustrated □ *frustrating delays* □ *It's very frustrating for everyone concerned.* (frustrante)
- **frustration** /frʌˈstreɪʃən/ NOUN [plural **frustrations**] a feeling of being frustrated or something that causes this feeling □ *She expressed frustration at the authorities.* □ *We all moan about the frustrations of office life.* (frustração)

fry /fraɪ/ VERB [**fries, frying, fried**] to cook something in hot oil or fat □ *Fry the onions in a little olive oil.* (fritar)

frying pan /ˈfraɪɪŋ ˌpæn/ NOUN [plural **frying pans**] a flat pan with a long handle for frying food □ *Heat the oil in a large frying pan.* (frigideira)

♦ IDIOM **out of the frying pan into the fire** used for saying that someone has left one bad situation but is now in a different and much worse situation (sair da lama e cair no atoleiro)

ft /ˌefˈtiː/ ABBREVIATION **foot** (= measurement) or **feet** (pé, pés)

fudge /fʌdʒ/ ▶ NOUN, NO PLURAL a soft sweet made from butter and sugar (doce)
▶ VERB [**fudges, fudging, fudged**] to avoid giving a clear answer or details □ *The final report fudged the issue.* (camuflar)

fuel /fjuəl/ ▶ NOUN [plural **fuels**] a substance such as gas, wood or coal that burns to give heat, light or power □ *The trains run on diesel fuel.* (combustível) ▣ *fuel consumption* (consumo de combustível)
▶ VERB [**fuels, fuelling/US fueling, fuelled/US fueled**]
1 to make something stronger, worse, etc. □ *His comments have fuelled speculation that he might resign.* □ *The riots were fuelled by anger and frustration.* (fortalecer)
2 to use or to put fuel into a vehicle, machine, etc. □ *The power station is fuelled by coal.* (abastecer)

fugitive /ˈfjuːdʒətɪv/ NOUN [plural **fugitives**] someone who has escaped from the police (fugitivo)

-ful /fʊl/ SUFFIX
1 -ful is added to the end of words to mean 'full of' □ *joyful* (pleno de)
2 -ful is added to the end of words to mean 'the amount that something holds' □ *spoonful* (pleno de)

fulfil /fʊlˈfɪl/ VERB [**fulfils, fulfilling, fulfilled**]
1 to do a particular job or something you are expected to do (cumprir) ▣ *He fulfils a vital role within the team.* (cumpre um papel) ▣ *He failed to fulfil his financial obligations.* (cumprir suas obrigações)
2 to achieve something you wanted to do (realizar) ▣ *It was a chance to fulfil a childhood dream.* (realizar um sonho)
3 to have the qualities or standard needed for something (preencher) ▣ *Only those who fulfil very strict criteria are accepted.* (preenchi os critérios)

- **fulfilling** /fʊlˈfɪlɪŋ/ ADJECTIVE making you feel that you have achieved something good □ *Being a youth worker is a fulfilling job.* (realizador)
- **fulfilment** /fʊlˈfɪlmənt/ NOUN, NO PLURAL
1 a feeling of having achieved something good □ *It gives you a sense of fulfilment.* (realização)
2 when you do something that you have always wanted to do or have promised to do □ *This is the fulfilment of a dream for me.* □ *the fulfilment of their duties* (realização)

fulfill /fʊlˈfɪl/ VERB [**fulfills, fulfilling, fulfilled**] the US spelling of **fulfil** (cumprir, realizar)

- **fulfillment** /fʊlˈfɪlmənt/ NOUN, NO PLURAL the US spelling of **fulfilment** (realizar)

full /fʊl/ ADJECTIVE [**fuller, fullest**]
1 containing as much as possible □ *The train was full.* □ *He gave me a full bottle of milk.* □ *The jug was only half full.* (cheio)
2 containing a lot of something □ *Your work is full of mistakes.* □ *My socks are full of holes.* (cheio)
3 complete (completo) ▣ *He told me the full story.* (história completa) ▣ *She made a full recovery.* (recuperação completa)
4 having eaten enough □ + **up** *No more cake for me, thanks – I'm full up.* (cheio)
5 **full speed/volume**, etc. as fast/loud, etc. as possible (velocidade/volume máximo etc.)
6 **in full** in a complete form □ *The interview was published in full.* (completamente)
⇨ go to **give full rein to something**

full moon /ˌfʊl ˈmuːn/ NOUN [plural **full moons**] the moon when it is a complete circle (lua cheia)

full stop /ˌfʊl ˈstɒp/ NOUN [plural **full stops**] the mark (.) used for showing where a sentence ends (ponto final)

full-time /ˌfʊlˈtaɪm/ ADJECTIVE, ADVERB working for all the hours of a normal job, not part of the time (em tempo integral) ▣ *a full-time job* (trabalho em tempo integral) ▣ *a full-time employee* (empregado de tempo integral) ▣ *We both work full-time.* (trabalhamos em tempo integral)

fully /ˈfʊli/ ADVERB completely □ *He hasn't fully recovered from the accident.* □ *We are fully aware of the problem.* □ *The hotel is fully booked.* (completamente)

fumble /ˈfʌmbəl/ VERB [**fumbles, fumbling, fumbled**] to use your hands in an awkward way, often to try to find something □ *Raj fumbled in his pocket for the key.* (**tatear**)

fume /fju:m/ VERB [**fumes, fuming, fumed**] to be very angry about something □ *She's absolutely fuming over the decision.* (**irritar**)

• **fumes** /fju:mz/ PLURAL NOUN smoke or gas that is unpleasant to breathe in (**fumaça**) ▣ *the smell of exhaust fumes* (**fumaça do escapamento**) □ *He was overcome by the fumes from the fire.*

fun /fʌn/ NOUN, NO PLURAL

1 enjoyment and pleasure (**divertimento**) ▣ *Skateboarding is really good fun.* (**bom divertimento**) ▣ *It was great fun!* (**grande divertimento**) ▣ *We had a lot of fun at the party.* (**nos divertimos**) □ *That sounds like fun.*

2 make fun of someone/something to make jokes about someone or something, in a way that is not kind □ *They're always making fun of my accent.* (**caçoar de alguém/algo**)

function /ˈfʌŋkʃən/ ▶ NOUN [*plural* **functions**]

1 the purpose of someone or something (**função**) ▣ *Proteins perform different functions in the body.* (**desempenham funções**) ▣ *The operating system controls the basic functions of a computer.* (**funções básicas**)

2 a large social event (**cerimônia**) ▣ *a social function* (**cerimônia formal**) ▣ *The hotel often hosts private functions such as weddings.* (**cerimônia particular**)

▶ VERB [**functions, functioning, functioned**] to work in the correct way ▣ *In some patients these cells don't function properly.* □ *The system seems to be functioning normally.*

• **functional** /ˈfʌŋkʃənəl/ ADJECTIVE

1 practical and useful □ *a functional design* (**funcional**)

2 working correctly □ *The ship has been repaired and is now fully functional.* (**funcional**)

function key /ˈfʌŋkʃən ˌki:/ NOUN [*plural* **function keys**] one of the keys at the top of a computer keyboard that has an F and a number on it. A computing word. (**tecla de função**)

fund /fʌnd/ ▶ NOUN [*plural* **funds**]

1 an amount of money for a particular purpose □ *a pension fund* □ *We set up a fund for victims of the earthquake.* (**fundo**)

2 funds money available to spend (**fundos**) ▣ *Should we spend public funds on such projects?* (**fundos públicos**) ▣ *The event was to raise funds for charity.* (**levantar fundos**)

▶ VERB [**funds, funding, funded**] to provide money for a particular purpose □ *The research was funded by the Medical Research Council.* (**financiar**)

fundamental /ˌfʌndəˈmentəl/ ADJECTIVE basic and important □ *the fundamental rules of management* □ *This raises some fundamental questions.* (**fundamental**)

• **fundamentalism** /ˌfʌndəˈmentəˌlɪzəm/ NOUN, NO PLURAL a belief that traditional religious rules should be followed exactly (**fundamentalismo**)

• **fundamentalist** /ˌfʌndəˈmentəlɪst/ NOUN [*plural* **fundamentalists**] someone who believes that traditional religious rules should be followed exactly □ *religious fundamentalists* (**fundamentalista**)

• **fundamentally** /ˌfʌndəˈmentəli/ ADVERB in a basic and important way □ *I fundamentally disagree.* □ *They have fundamentally different views of the world.* (**fundamentalmente**)

• **fundamentals** /ˌfʌndəˈmentəlz/ PLURAL NOUN the basic parts, rules, etc. of something □ *They learn the fundamentals of website design.* (**fundamentos, princípios**)

funding /ˈfʌndɪŋ/ NOUN, NO PLURAL money for a particular purpose, especially from a government (**financiamento**) ▣ *public funding* (**financiamento público**) ▣ *The council provides funding for the homeless shelter.* (**fornece financiamento**)

funeral /ˈfju:nərəl/ NOUN [*plural* **funerals**] a ceremony for a person who has recently died in which the body of the dead person is buried or burned ▣ *I didn't go to her funeral.* (**funeral**)

funfair /ˈfʌnfeə(r)/ NOUN [*plural* **funfairs**] an event at which people can enjoy themselves going on rides (= large machines you ride on for fun) and playing games (**parque de diversões**)

fungus /ˈfʌŋgəs/ NOUN [*plural* **fungi**] a plant with no leaves or flowers, for example a mushroom (**fungo**)

funnel /ˈfʌnəl/ NOUN [*plural* **funnels**]

1 a tube that is wide at the top and narrow at the bottom, used for pouring liquid into a container (**funil**)

2 a large tube through which smoke leaves a ship (**chaminé**)

funnily /ˈfʌnɪli/ ADVERB in a way that seems strange or surprising (**comicamente**) ▣ *Funnily enough, we were born on exactly the same day.* (**cômico o suficiente**)

funny /ˈfʌni/ ADJECTIVE [**funnier, funniest**]

1 making you laugh □ *a funny story* □ *I don't find him very funny.* □ *They looked so funny that she had to smile.* (**engraçado**) ▣ *Luckily, he saw the funny side of the situation.* (**lado engraçado**)

2 strange, surprising or unusual □ *There was a funny noise coming from the engine.* (**esquisito**) ▣ *The funny thing is, I was just about to call him when he called me.* (**o esquisito é**)

> ➤ Do not confuse the adjective **funny** with the noun **fun**. Something that is funny makes you laugh. Something that you describe as fun is very enjoyable although it may not make you laugh: □ *That was such a funny film – I laughed all the way through.* □ *Skating is fun.*

funny bone

funny bone /ˈfʌnɪ ˌbəʊn/ NOUN [plural **funny bones**] a part of your elbow that hurts when you hit it against something (osso do cotovelo)

fur /fɜː(r)/ NOUN, NO PLURAL
1 the soft hair on some animals ☐ *a rabbit with soft, brown fur* (pelo de alguns animais)
2 the skin and fur of an animal when it is removed or material made to look like this ☐ *a fur hat* (pele)

furious /ˈfjʊərɪəs/ ADJECTIVE
1 extremely angry ☐ *We're absolutely furious about this.* ☐ *I had a furious row with Charlotte.* (furioso)
2 done with a lot of energy, activity or speed ☐ *He set off at a furious pace.* (violento)
• **furiously** /ˈfjʊərɪəslɪ/ ADVERB
1 in a way that shows you are very angry ☐ *Clive reacted furiously.* (furiosamente)
2 very fast or with a lot of energy ☐ *They worked furiously to get everything clean.* (violentamente)

furnace /ˈfɜːnɪs/ NOUN [plural **furnaces**] a large, very hot oven used in some industrial processes (caldeira)

furnish /ˈfɜːnɪʃ/ VERB [**furnishes, furnishing, furnished**] to put furniture in a house or room ☐ *The six large rooms are furnished with antiques.* (mobiliar)

♦ PHRASAL VERB **furnish someone with something** to give something to someone, especially information. A formal phrase. (prover algo a alguém)

• **furnishings** /ˈfɜːnɪʃɪŋz/ PLURAL NOUN the furniture, carpets and curtains in a house or room (mobília)

furniture /ˈfɜːnɪtʃə(r)/ NOUN, NO PLURAL objects such as beds, tables and chairs that you put in a room (mobília) ☐ *A small bed and an old wardrobe were the only pieces of furniture in the room.* (peças de mobília)

> Remember that **furniture** is an uncountable noun:
> ✓ We don't have any furniture.
> ✗ We don't have any furnitures.

furor /ˈfjʊrɔːr/ NOUN, NO PLURAL the US spelling of **furore** (furor, exaltação)

furore /fjʊˈrɔːrɪ/ NOUN, NO PLURAL general excitement or anger in reaction to something (furor, exaltação) ☐ *Her appointment caused a furore.* (causou furor)

furrow /ˈfʌrəʊ/ ▶ NOUN [plural **furrows**]
1 a long narrow cut made in the ground by a plough (= farm equipment) (ranhura)
2 a deep line in the skin of your face, especially above your eyes ☐ *He gazed out of the window with a slight furrow of his brow.* (sulco, ruga)
▶ VERB [**furrows, furrowing, furrowed**] to make a furrow in your skin when you are worried, concentrating etc. ☐ *His brow furrowed in concentration.* (sulcar, enrugar)

furry /ˈfɜːrɪ/ ADJECTIVE [**furrier, furriest**] covered in fur ☐ *a small furry animal* (peludo)

further /ˈfɜːðə(r)/ ▶ ADJECTIVE, ADVERB
1 at or to a greater distance away ☐ + *from Which is further from here, London or Aberdeen?* ☐ + *up Santa Monica is a few miles further up the coast.* ☐ *I walked further than I needed.* ☐ *We travelled further north.* (mais longe)
2 more or extra (mais) ☐ *If you need further information, please ask.* (mais informações) ☐ *He refused to comment further* (= say more). ☐ *Prices may rise even further.* (ainda mais)
▶ VERB [**furthers, furthering, furthered**] to help something be successful ☐ *These qualifications will help further your career.* (avançar)

further education /ˈfɜːðə(r) ˌedjʊˈkeɪʃən/ NOUN, NO PLURAL education or training for people who have left school but do not go to university (ensino supletivo)

furthermore /ˌfɜːðəˈmɔː(r)/ ADVERB a formal word used when you are adding something to what you have already said ☐ *His plans will be very expensive. Furthermore, they will cause a lot of disruption.* (além disso)

furthest /ˈfɜːðəst/ ADVERB, ADJECTIVE at or to the greatest distance or amount ☐ *Who can throw the ball the furthest?* ☐ + *from They sat in the corner furthest from the door.* ☐ *We reached the furthest point south.* (o mais longe)

furtive /ˈfɜːtɪv/ ADJECTIVE done secretly to avoid being seen ☐ *a furtive glance* (furtivo)
• **furtively** /ˈfɜːtɪvlɪ/ ADVERB in a furtive way ☐ *He whispered furtively.* (furtivamente)

fury /ˈfjʊərɪ/ NOUN, NO PLURAL a very strong feeling of anger ☐ *The announcement sparked fury from unions.* (fúria)

fuse /fjuːz/ ▶ NOUN [plural **fuses**]
1 a wire inside a piece of electrical equipment that makes it stop working if too much electricity passes through it (fusível) ☐ *I think the fuse has blown.* (fusível queimou)
2 the part of a bomb or firework that starts the explosion (pavio) ☐ *Light the fuse and stand well back.* (acenda o pavio)

♦ IDIOM **a short fuse** if someone has a short fuse, they become angry very easily ☐ *Tom has a very short fuse.* (pavio curto)
▶ VERB [**fuses, fusing, fused**]
1 if two things fuse or are fused, they join together to form one thing ☐ *The broken bones will eventually fuse back together.* (fundir-se)
2 if a piece of electrical equipment fuses, the fuse stops it working (queimar)

fuselage /ˈfjuːzəlɑːʒ/ NOUN [plural **fuselages**] the main part of an aeroplane (fuselagem)

fusion /ˈfjuːʒən/ NOUN, NO PLURAL

1 when two or more things are combined □ *He experimented with a fusion of styles, mixing flamenco with jazz.* (**fusão**)
2 when the nuclei (= centre parts) of atoms are combined to produce nuclear energy. A physics word. (**fusão**) ▫ *nuclear fusion* (**fusão nuclear**)

fuss /fʌs/ ▶ NOUN, NO PLURAL
1 unnecessary worry, excitement or anger about something □ *I don't know what all the fuss is about.* (**preocupação exagerada, escarcéu**) ▫ *I don't want to make a fuss about it.* (**fazer escarcéu**)
2 make a fuss of someone to give someone a lot of attention □ *He made a great fuss of her when she visited.* (**dar atenção exagerada a alguém**)
▶ VERB [**fusses, fussing, fussed**] to worry too much about something or give it too much attention □ *She fusses over her pet dog.* (**preocupar-se**)

• **fussy** /'fʌsi/ ADJECTIVE [**fussier, fussiest**]
1 worrying too much about small details that are not important (**caprichoso, meticuloso**)
2 only liking particular things □ *Children can be so fussy about food.* (**exigente**) ▫ *a fussy eater* (**comilão exigente**)

futile /'fju:taɪl/ ADJECTIVE having no effect or result (**inútil**) ▫ *He made a futile attempt to escape.* (**tentativa inútil**) □ *Their efforts proved futile.*

• **futility** /fju:'tɪləti/ NOUN, NO PLURAL when something is not likely to have any effect or result □ *the futility of war* (**inutilidade**)

futon /'fu:tɒn/ NOUN [*plural* **futons**] a simple bed on a wooden frame or on the floor that can also be folded to use as a seat (**colchão japonês**)

future /'fju:tʃə(r)/ ▶ NOUN [*plural* **futures**]
1 the future the time to come after now □ *You can't know what will happen to you in the future.* (**futuro**) ▫ *We expect a decision in the near future.* (**futuro próximo**) ▫ *We won't be moving, at least for the foreseeable future.* (**futuro próximo**)
2 what will happen to someone or something in the future □ + *of Digital technology is threatening the future of the music industry.* (**futuro**) ▫ *He has a bright future in management.* (**futuro brilhante**)
3 in future in the time from now on □ *In future, please be more careful.* (**no futuro, doravante**)
▶ ADJECTIVE happening or existing in a time after now □ *future plans* □ *We need to preserve the planet for future generations.* (**futuro**)

future tense /ˌfju:tʃə 'tens/ NOUN [*plural* **future tenses**] the form of a verb that you use when you are talking about what will happen in the future (**tempo futuro**)

futuristic /ˌfju:tʃə'rɪstɪk/ ADJECTIVE seeming to belong in the future, or about events in the future □ *futuristic buildings* (**futurístico**)

fuzz /fʌz/ NOUN, NO PLURAL thin, light hair or feathers (**penugem**)

• **fuzzy** /'fʌzi/ ADJECTIVE [**fuzzier, fuzziest**]
1 not clear □ *a fuzzy image* (**borrado**)
2 covered in soft short hair (**felpudo, peludo**)

Gg

G or g /dʒiː/ the seventh letter of the alphabet (a sétima letra do alfabeto)

g /dʒiː/ ABBREVIATION gram or grams (abreviação de grama)

gab /gæb/ NOUN, NO PLURAL
♦ IDIOM **have the gift of the gab** to be good at talking □ *A salesman needs to have the gift of the gab.* (ter muita lábia)

gabble /ˈgæbəl/ VERB [gabbles, gabbling, gabbled] to talk so quickly that it is difficult for other people to understand what you are saying (tagarelar)

gable /ˈgeɪbəl/ NOUN [plural gables] a side of a building where the wall and the roof form a triangular shape (cumeeira)

gadget /ˈgædʒɪt/ NOUN [plural gadgets] a tool or small piece of equipment □ *I've got a gadget to unblock the sink.* (dispositivo)

gaffe /gæf/ NOUN [plural gaffes] when someone says or does something that upsets or embarrasses people, often without meaning to □ *His first gaffe was asking my mother her age.* (gafe)

gag /gæg/ ▶ NOUN [plural gags]
1 something put over someone's mouth to stop them speaking (mordaça)
2 an informal word meaning a joke (piada)
▶ VERB [gags, gagging, gagged]
1 to put a gag over someone's mouth to stop them speaking (amordaçar) 🔲 *The bank manager was found, bound and gagged, in an office.* (amarrado e amordaçado)
2 to stop someone talking about something □ *The government took steps to gag the media.* (silenciar)
3 to feel as if you are going to vomit □ *The smell of raw meat made her gag.* (nausear)

gaggle /ˈgægəl/ NOUN [plural gaggles] a group of noisy people □ *a gaggle of young girls* (grupo de pessoas barulhentas)

gaily /ˈgeɪli/ ADVERB
1 in a happy way □ *She laughed gaily.* (alegremente)
2 with bright colours □ *gaily coloured banners* (vistosamente)

gain /geɪn/ ▶ VERB [gains, gaining, gained]
1 to get or achieve something □ *You gain twenty extra points for that move.* (ganhar, obter) 🔲 *We could not gain access (= get in) to the building.*
(obter acesso) 🔲 *Rebel soldiers have fought to gain control of the area.* (ganhar controle)
2 to increase in amount, speed, weight, etc. □ *I gained over 20 kilos when I was pregnant.* (ganhar, engordar)
3 to get something good from a situation □ *It's wrong that criminals should gain from their crimes by writing books.* (beneficiar-se, lucrar) 🔲 *There's nothing to be gained by waiting any longer.* (nada para se beneficiar)
♦ IDIOM **gain ground** to become more successful when compared to someone or something else □ *They are gaining ground on the larger companies.* (ganhar terreno)
♦ PHRASAL VERB **gain on someone** to get closer to someone in a race or competition (aproximar-se de alguém)
▶ NOUN [plural gains]
1 something that you get or achieve that is more than you had before □ *Her loss was my gain.* □ *The party made big gains in the local elections.* (ganho)
2 money or advantages that someone gets □ *personal/political gain* (lucro)

gait /geɪt/ NOUN, NO PLURAL the way someone walks □ *His gait was unsteady, and he seemed confused.* (modo de andar, passo)

gala /ˈgɑːlə/ NOUN [plural galas] a special public event or entertainment □ *a swimming gala* □ *a gala dinner* (gala, luxo)

galaxy /ˈgæləksi/ NOUN [plural galaxies] a very large group of stars in the universe □ *Our galaxy is the Milky Way.* (galáxia)

gale /geɪl/ NOUN [plural gales] a very strong wind □ *The old apple tree blew down in a gale.* (vendaval)

gall /gɔːl/ ▶ VERB [galls, galling, galled] if something galls you, it annoys you □ *What really galls me is that she never apologized.* (atormentar)
▶ NOUN, NO PLURAL **have the gall to do something** to be rude enough to do something □ *He wouldn't have the gall to say something like that.* (ter a audácia de fazer algo)

gallant /ˈgælənt/ ADJECTIVE
1 brave □ *It was a gallant effort to win the title.* (valente)
2 very polite and showing respect, especially to women □ *a gallant young man* (galante)

- **gallantry** /ˈgæləntrɪ/ NOUN, NO PLURAL being gallant ☐ *He won an award for gallantry in battle.* (bravura, coragem)

gall bladder /ˈgɔːl ˌblædə(r)/ NOUN [plural **gall bladders**] an organ near your liver where a substance that helps you digest food is stored. A biology word. (vesícula biliar)

galleon /ˈgælɪən/ NOUN [plural **galleons**] a large Spanish sailing ship used in the sixteenth and seventeenth centuries (galeão)

gallery /ˈgæləri/ NOUN [plural **galleries**]
1 a large building or a shop where works of art are shown to the public (galeria de arte)
2 an open floor high up at the back or side of a large room, for example a theatre ☐ *Seats in the gallery are usually much cheaper.* (galeria)

galley /ˈgælɪ/ NOUN [plural **galleys**]
1 a kitchen on a boat or aeroplane (cozinha)
2 a type of ship used by the Ancient Greeks and Romans (galé)

gallon /ˈgælən/ NOUN [plural **gallons**] a unit for measuring liquids, equal to 8 pints (galão)

gallop /ˈgæləp/ ▶ VERB [**gallops, galloping, galloped**] a horse gallops when it runs at its fastest speed with all four feet off the ground at the same time (galopar)
♦ PHRASAL VERB **gallop through something** to do something very quickly ☐ *We seem to be galloping through the work today.* (fazer um trabalho rapidamente)
▶ NOUN [plural **gallops**]
1 a fast run ☐ *She set off at a gallop.* (galopada)
2 a ride on a horse going at this speed (galope)

gallows /ˈgæləʊz/ NOUN [plural **gallows**] a high wooden frame where criminals were killed in the past by hanging them ☐ *He was sent to the gallows for murder.* (forca)

galore /gəˈlɔː(r)/ ADJECTIVE used after a noun to emphasize that there is a large number of that thing ☐ *There were goals galore in this afternoon's match.* (abundante)

galvanize or **galvanise** /ˈgælvəˌnaɪz/ VERB [**galvanizes, galvanizing, galvanized**]
1 to shock someone and make them suddenly decide to do something (estimular, chocar) ☐ *His father's death galvanized him into action.* (estimulou-o a agir)
2 to cover metal with a layer of zinc (= blue-white metal) to stop it being damaged by water (galvanizar)

gamble /ˈgæmbəl/ ▶ VERB [**gambles, gambling, gambled**] to risk money on the result of a game, race or competition ☐ *He enjoyed gambling on horse races.* (jogar, apostar)
♦ PHRASAL VERB **gamble on something** to take a risk that something will happen ☐ *We've decided to gamble on the rain stopping before we have our barbecue.* (apostar em algo)
▶ NOUN [plural **gambles**] something you decide to do that is a risk (risco) ☐ *We took a gamble on the weather.* (nós apostamos) ☐ *Their gamble paid off* (= was successful). (risco valeu a pena)
- **gambler** /ˈgæmblə(r)/ NOUN [plural **gamblers**] someone who gambles money on the result of a race or game (jogador, apostador)
- **gambling** /ˈgæmblɪŋ/ NOUN, NO PLURAL the activity of risking money on the result of a game, race or competition (jogo de azar)

game /geɪm/ NOUN [plural **games**]
1 an activity that people do for enjoyment, that has rules, often needs skill, and is usually won or lost ☐ *a computer game* (jogo, partida) ☐ *After dinner, we all played games.* (brincamos com jogos) ☐ *a game of tennis/chess*
2 in some sports, a game is one of the parts of a complete match ☐ *He won the first set 7 games to 5.* (jogo, partida)
3 games when people do sport at school or at an organized event ☐ *the Olympic Games* (jogos, educação física)
4 no plural wild animals and birds that are hunted for their meat (caça)
5 something that someone is not serious about ☐ *Running a business is just a game to her.* (peça)
♦ IDIOM **give the game away** to let someone know something that spoils a surprise or a secret (revelar um segredo)

gamekeeper /ˈgeɪmˌkiːpə(r)/ NOUN [plural **gamekeepers**] someone whose job is to look after wild animals and birds on private land where they are going to be hunted (guarda de caça)

gamer /ˈgeɪmə(r)/ NOUN [plural **gamers**] someone who plays a lot of computer games (jogador)

game show /ˈgeɪm ˌʃəʊ/ NOUN [plural **game shows**] a television programme where people play games (programa de televisão de jogos)

gamete /ˈgæmiːt/ NOUN [plural **gametes**] a cell that joins with a cell of the opposite sex to form a cell that grows into a person, animal or plant. A biology word. (gameta)

gamma globulin /ˌgæmə ˈglɒbjʊlɪn/ NOUN, NO PLURAL a substance in the blood that gives protection against some diseases. A biology word. (glóbulo branco)

gamma radiation /ˌgæmə ˌreɪdiˈeɪʃən/ NOUN, NO PLURAL rays that are produced by some radioactive substances. A physics word. (radiação gama)

gander /ˈgændə(r)/ NOUN [plural **ganders**] a male goose (ganso)

gang /gæŋ/ NOUN [plural **gangs**]
1 a group of young people who spend time together and often cause trouble ☐ *Her son's got involved in a gang in town.* (gangue, bando)
2 an organized group of criminals ☐ *Police have arrested a gang of bank robbers.* (gangue, quadrilha)

gangling

3 an informal word meaning a group of friends who meet regularly □ *I'm meeting up with the gang tonight.* (**equipe**)

◆ PHRASAL VERB [gangs, ganging, ganged] **gang up on someone** to form a group to attack or criticize someone □ *She felt that the other girls were ganging up on her.* (**juntar-se contra alguém**)

gangling /ˈɡæŋɡlɪŋ/ or **gangly** /ˈɡæŋɡli/ ADJECTIVE tall and thin □ *a gangling youth* (**esbelto**)

gangrene /ˈɡæŋɡriːn/ NOUN, NO PLURAL a medical condition where a part of the body dies because blood is not flowing through it (**gangrena**)

gangster /ˈɡæŋstə(r)/ NOUN [plural **gangsters**] a member of a group of criminals (**gângster**)

gangway /ˈɡæŋweɪ/ NOUN [plural **gangways**]
1 a narrow passage where people can walk between rows of seats, for example on an aeroplane or in a cinema (**corredor**)
2 a narrow bridge used to get on and off a ship (**passadiço**)

gaol /dʒeɪl/ NOUN [plural **gaols**] another spelling of **jail** (**cadeia**)
• **gaoler** /ˈdʒeɪlə(r)/ NOUN [plural **gaolers**] another spelling of **jailer** (**carcereiro**)

gap /ɡæp/ NOUN [plural **gaps**]
1 an opening or space in the middle of something or between things □ *The fox got through a gap in the wall.* □ *He has a gap between his front teeth.* (**brecha**)
2 a difference between two things □ *The gap between rich and poor is widening.* (**diferença**) ◘ *There's a big age gap between her two children.* (**diferença de idade**)
3 something missing □ *There's a gap in his memory around the time of the accident.* (**lacuna, vazio**)
4 a period of time when something stops □ *He's going back to university after a three-year gap.* (**intervalo**)

gape /ɡeɪp/ VERB [gapes, gaping, gaped]
1 to look at someone or something with your mouth open, usually because you are very surprised or impressed □ *We all gaped at her in amazement.* (**olhar boquiaberto**)
2 to be wide open □ *Her dressing gown was gaping open.* (**abrir-se**)
• **gaping** /ˈɡeɪpɪŋ/ ADJECTIVE wide open (**aberto**) ◘ *a gaping hole/wound* (**uma ferida/buraco aberto**)

gap year /ˈɡæp jɪə(r)/ NOUN [plural **gap years**] a year between school and university that some students spend working or travelling □ *She took a gap year and went to Australia.* (**ano sabático**)

garage /ˈɡærɑːʒ, ˈɡærɪdʒ/ NOUN [plural **garages**]
1 a small building that you keep your car in (**garagem**)
2 a place where vehicles are repaired, or a shop selling petrol (**oficina**)

garbage /ˈɡɑːbɪdʒ/ NOUN, NO PLURAL the US word for **rubbish** (**lixo**)

329

gaseous

garbled /ˈɡɑːbəld/ ADJECTIVE not clear and not correct □ *I heard a garbled version of what happened.* (**confuso**)

garden /ˈɡɑːdən/ NOUN [plural **gardens**]
1 a piece of land next to a house where flowers, trees and vegetables are grown (**jardim**) ◘ *The front garden is mainly lawn.* (**jardim da frente**)
2 gardens a large area of grass, trees, flowers, etc. for the public to use or around a big house (**jardim**)
• **gardener** /ˈɡɑːdnə(r)/ NOUN [plural **gardeners**] someone who works in a garden (**jardineiro**)
• **gardening** /ˈɡɑːdnɪŋ/ NOUN, NO PLURAL the activity of working in and taking care of a garden (**jardinagem**)

gargle /ˈɡɑːɡəl/ VERB [gargles, gargling, gargled] to move a liquid around in your mouth without swallowing in order to clean your mouth (**fazer gargarejo**)

garish /ˈɡeərɪʃ/ ADJECTIVE garish colours or patterns are too bright □ *He was wearing a hideous jacket in garish green stripes.* (**berrante, extravagante**)

garland /ˈɡɑːlənd/ NOUN [plural **garlands**] flowers or leaves twisted together into a circle □ *Christmas garlands of holly and ivy* (**guirlanda**)

garlic /ˈɡɑːlɪk/ NOUN, NO PLURAL a plant like a small onion with a strong taste and smell used in cooking to add flavour (**alho**) ◘ *Crush two cloves of garlic with the spices.* (**dentes de alho**)

garment /ˈɡɑːmənt/ NOUN [plural **garments**] a formal word meaning a piece of clothing (**roupa**)

garnish /ˈɡɑːnɪʃ/ ▶ VERB [garnishes, garnishing, garnished] to decorate food with something such as herbs or pieces of fruit or vegetables □ *Garnish the fish with slices of cucumber.* (**decorar, enfeitar**)
▶ NOUN [plural **garnishes**] something used to garnish food □ *The chicken was served with a garnish of parsley.* (**guarnição**)

garrison /ˈɡærɪsən/ NOUN [plural **garrisons**] a group of soldiers living in and guarding a town or building (**guarnição**)

garrulous /ˈɡærələs/ ADJECTIVE garrulous people talk too much (**tagarela, falador**)

gas /ɡæs/ ▶ NOUN [plural **gases** or **gasses**]
1 a substance that is not liquid or solid and that moves about like air □ *Oxygen and carbon dioxide are two of the gases that make up air.* (**gás**)
2 no plural a gas or mixture of gases that burns easily and is used for cooking or heating □ *a gas fire* (**gás**)
3 no plural the US word for **petrol** (**gasolina**)
▶ VERB [gasses, gassing, gassed] to kill a person or animal using poisonous gas (**asfixiar com gás**)

gaseous /ˈɡæsɪəs, ˈɡeɪsɪəs/ ADJECTIVE to do with gas or in the form of gas. A chemistry and physics word. (**gasoso**)

gash /gæʃ/ ▶ NOUN [plural **gashes**] a deep open cut ☐ *She had a gash in her leg.* (corte profundo)
▶ VERB [**gashes, gashing, gashed**] to make a long deep cut in something (cortar profundamente)

gas mask /ˈgæs ˌmɑːsk/ NOUN [plural **gas masks**] a cover for your nose and mouth that protects you from poisonous gas (máscara de gás)

gasoline /ˈgæsəliːn/ NOUN, NO PLURAL the US word for petrol (gasolina)

gasp /gɑːsp/ ▶ VERB [**gasps, gasping, gasped**]
1 to take a short sudden breath in through your open mouth because you are shocked or surprised ☐ *They all gasped in horror.* (engasgar)
2 to find it hard to breathe (arfar) 🔂 *He slumped to the floor, gasping for breath.* (arfar em busca de ar)
▶ NOUN [plural **gasps**] the sound of a sudden short breath (arfada)

gastric /ˈgæstrɪk/ ADJECTIVE to do with the stomach ☐ *a gastric ulcer* (gástrico)

gastroenteritis /ˌgæstrəʊˌentəˈraɪtɪs/ NOUN, NO PLURAL a painful stomach illness caused by a virus or by bacteria in food (gastrenterite)

gastropod /ˈgæstrəpɒd/ NOUN [plural **gastropods**] an animal with a soft body and often a shell, for example a snail. A biology word. (gastrópode)

gastropub /ˈgæstrəʊpʌb/ NOUN [plural **gastropubs**] a pub which sells good quality food (bar, lanchonete)

gate /geɪt/ NOUN [plural **gates**]
1 the part of a fence, wall etc. that opens and closes like a door ☐ *Please close the gate.* (porteira, cancela)
2 the place where passengers get on or off a plane at an airport ☐ *Flight BA123 to Rome is now boarding at Gate 12.* (portão)

gateau /ˈgætəʊ/ NOUN [plural **gateaus** or **gateaux**] a large cake made in layers, usually decorated with cream, chocolate or fruit ☐ *a chocolate gateau* (tipo de bolo)

gatecrash /ˈgeɪtkræʃ/ VERB [**gatecrashes, gatecrashing, gatecrashed**] to go to a party or other private event without being invited ☐ *A gang of youths had gatecrashed the party.* (entrar sem ser convidado)

• **gatecrasher** /ˈgeɪtkræʃə(r)/ NOUN [plural **gatecrashers**] someone who goes to a party without being invited (penetra)

gateway /ˈgeɪtweɪ/ NOUN [plural **gateways**]
1 an opening in a fence or wall with a gate in it (entrada, portão)
2 the way to get somewhere or to achieve something ☐ *This invention is the gateway to the future.* (passagem)
3 a connection between two computer systems that allows information to be passed between them. A computing word.

gather /ˈgæðə(r)/ VERB [**gathers, gathering, gathered**]
1 if people gather or are gathered, they come together or are brought together in a group (aglomerar-se) 🔂 *A crowd gathered at the airport.* (uma multidão aglomerou-se) ☐ *The teachers gathered all the children together in the dining hall.*
2 to collect things or bring them together ☐ *Police are gathering as much information as they can about the attacker.* ☐ *The lecturer gathered together all her papers.* (reunir, juntar)
3 to understand something because you hear or read about it ☐ *From what I can gather, she lives with her parents.* ☐ *'He's a keen gardener.' 'So I gathered.'* (deduzir, compreender)
4 gather speed/support, etc. to gradually get faster/get more support, etc. (ficar mais rápido/receber mais ajuda etc.)

• **gathering** /ˈgæðərɪŋ/ NOUN [plural **gatherings**] a party or occasion where a lot of people get together (encontro) 🔂 *We usually have a big family gathering at Christmas.*

gaudy /ˈgɔːdi/ ADJECTIVE [**gaudier, gaudiest**] having very bright colours ☐ *gaudy Hawaiian shirts* (chamativo)

gauge /geɪdʒ/ ▶ NOUN [plural **gauges**]
1 a piece of equipment for measuring things such as temperature or amounts ☐ *a fuel gauge* (medidor)
2 a fact or method that you can use to judge a situation ☐ *Exports are an important gauge of economic activity.* (medidor)
▶ VERB [**gauges, gauging, gauged**]
1 to make a judgment about a situation ☐ *I can never gauge what his reaction will be.* (julgar)
2 to measure something such as a temperature or amount (medir, calcular)

gaunt /gɔːnt/ ADJECTIVE a gaunt person is very thin, often because they are ill (abatido)

gauntlet /ˈgɔːntlɪt/ NOUN [plural **gauntlets**] a thick glove that protects your hand and lower arm (luvas de proteção)

♦ IDIOM **throw down the gauntlet** to invite someone to fight or compete with you (desafiar)

gauze /gɔːz/ NOUN, NO PLURAL a very thin cloth that is used to cover injuries (gaze)

gave /geɪv/ PAST TENSE OF **give** (ver give)

gawky /ˈgɔːki/ ADJECTIVE [**gawkier, gawkiest**] tall and awkward ☐ *a gawky teenage boy* (desengonçado, desajeitado)

gawp /gɔːp/ VERB [**gawps, gawping, gawped**] to look at something with your mouth open because you are shocked or surprised ☐ *I was carried out on a stretcher with everybody gawping at me.* (ficar boquiaberto)

gay /geɪ/ ▶ ADJECTIVE [**gayer, gayest**]
1 homosexual or to do with homosexuals ☐ *a gay bar* ☐ *a gay marriage* (homossexual)
2 an old-fashioned word meaning happy and excited (alegre)

gaze

3 an old-fashioned word meaning brightly coloured □ *gay banners* (**chamativo**)
▶ NOUN [*plural* **gays**] someone who is homosexual (**gay, homossexual**)

gaze /geɪz/ ▶ VERB [**gazes, gazing, gazed**] to look at something or someone for a long time, especially because they are interesting or attractive □ *The children gazed longingly at the toys in the window.* (**fitar**)
▶ NOUN, NO PLURAL a long look (**olhar fixo**)

gazelle /gəˈzel/ NOUN [*plural* **gazelles**] a type of African or Asian animal that looks like a small deer with long, delicate legs (**gazela**)

GB /ˌdʒiːˈbiː/ ABBREVIATION Great Britain (**abreviação de Grã-Bretanha**)

GCSE /ˌdʒiːsiːesˈiː/ ABBREVIATION General Certificate of Secondary Education; an exam taken by students in England and Wales at around the age of 16 □ *He's doing GCSE maths.* (**abreviação de General Certificate of Secondary Education**)

gear /gɪə(r)/ NOUN [*plural* **gears**]
1 the set of parts in a car or bicycle that controls how fast the wheels turn □ *Our new car has five gears.* (**marcha**)
2 a particular position of the gears on a vehicle (**marcha**) ▣ *She still finds it hard to* change gear. (**trocar de marcha**) ▣ *Put the car into* first gear *and move off.* (**primeira marcha**)
3 the clothes and equipment you use for a particular sport or job □ *tennis gear* (**equipamento**)
◆ PHRASAL VERBS [**gears, gearing, geared**] **gear something to/towards someone/something** to arrange something so that it is suitable for a particular group, situation or purpose □ *The course is geared to more advanced students.* (**adaptar algo a algo/alguém**) **gear (someone/something) up for something** to get ready or make someone or something ready for something □ *Everything's geared up for the exams at the moment.* (**preparar algo/alguém para algo**)

gearbox /ˈgɪəbɒks/ NOUN [*plural* **gearboxes**] the part of a motor vehicle that contains a set of gears (**câmbio**)

geek /giːk/ NOUN [*plural* **geeks**] a person who is very interested in a particular hobby, for example computers, but is not good at making friends. An informal word. (**pessoa geralmente tímida e que entende muito de computadores**)

geese /giːs/ PLURAL OF **goose** (**ver goose**)

gel /dʒel/ ▶ NOUN [*plural* **gels**] a thick clear substance that is between a liquid and a solid (**gel**) ▣ *shower gel* (**gel para banho**) ▣ *Do you use* hair gel*?* (**gel para cabelo**)
▶ VERB [**gels, gelling, gelled**]
1 if an idea gels, it becomes clearer (**tornar-se claro**)
2 if a group of people gels, the people begin to form a good relationship (**fazer amizade**)

generalization

gelatine /ˈdʒeləti:n/ NOUN, NO PLURAL a clear substance used in cooking to make liquids thick or firm (**gelatina**)

gem /dʒem/ NOUN [*plural* **gems**]
1 a valuable stone that is used in jewellery (**pedra preciosa**)
2 someone or something that you like or admire very much □ *This is an absolute gem of a museum.* (**joia**)

gender /ˈdʒendə(r)/ NOUN [*plural* **genders**]
1 the state of being male or female (**gênero, sexo**)
2 the form of a noun, pronoun or adjective, which can be masculine, feminine or neuter (**gênero**)

gene /dʒi:n/ NOUN [*plural* **genes**] a part of a living cell that is passed on from parents to children and that controls things like hair or skin colour. A biology word. (**gene**)

genealogy /ˌdʒi:niˈælədʒi/ NOUN [*plural* **genealogies**] the history of how past and present members of a family are related (**genealogia**)

genera /ˈdʒenərə/ PLURAL OF **genus** (**ver genus**)

general /ˈdʒenərəl/ ▶ ADJECTIVE
1 involving or affecting most people or things □ *There was a general feeling of gloom.* (**geral**) ▣ *Sales to* the general public (= ordinary people) *will begin on July 11.* (**o público geral**)
2 not detailed or exact, but giving the most important information □ *Can you give me a general idea of what it will cost?* (**geral**) ▣ *I understand the principles of economics* in general terms. (**em termos gerais**) ▣ *As a general rule* (= in most situations) *I use two eggs for every 125g flour.* (**como regra geral**)
3 in general (a) considering the whole of something or someone □ *Schools are achieving better results in general.* □ *There is agreement among the population in general.* (b) in most situations □ *In general, I think it's better to travel by train.* (**em geral**)
4 dealing with a lot of activities, subjects or parts of a subject □ *He does general household repairs.* □ *I'm looking for a general introduction to Western art.* (**geral**)
▶ NOUN [*plural* **generals**] an important army officer (**general**)

general anaesthetic /ˌdʒenərəl ænɪsˈθetɪk/ NOUN [*plural* **general anaesthetics**] a drug that makes you not conscious while you have a medical operation (**anestesia geral**)

general election /ˌdʒenərəl ɪˈlekʃən/ NOUN [*plural* **general elections**] an election in which all the people in a country vote to choose the people who will be in the next government (**eleição geral**)

generalization or **generalisation** /ˌdʒenərəlaɪˈzeɪʃən/ NOUN [*plural* **generalizations**] a general statement based on a few facts that is usually but not always true (**generalização**) ▣ *I shouldn't* make generalizations *but Italians are very creative.* (**fazer generalização**)

generalize or **generalise** /ˈdʒenərəlaɪz/ VERB [generalizes, generalizing, generalized] to state an opinion about a group of people or things that is true for most of them but may not be true for all □ *It's impossible to generalize about marriage.* (generalizar)

general knowledge /ˌdʒenərəl ˈnɒlɪdʒ/ NOUN, NO PLURAL what someone knows about a lot of different things in the world, instead of about one particular subject (conhecimentos gerais)

generally /ˈdʒenərəli/ ADVERB
1 by most people or in most cases □ *She's generally considered Britain's greatest actoress.* □ *They were generally well dressed.* (em geral)
2 usually □ *Children generally start school at about the age of five.* (geralmente)
3 in a way that states basic facts but not details □ *She spoke very generally about life in the UK.* (geralmente)

general practitioner /ˌdʒenərəl prækˈtɪʃənə(r)/ NOUN [plural general practitioners] a doctor who looks after people from a particular area and treats them for a lot of different illnesses (clínico geral)

generate /ˈdʒenəreɪt/ VERB [generates, generating, generated]
1 to create something □ *His work generated a lot of interest.* □ *We generate more profit from the training side of our business.* (gerar)
2 to produce energy □ *The house uses solar power to generate electricity.* (gerar)

• **generation** /ˌdʒenəˈreɪʃən/ NOUN [plural generations]
1 all the people in a family or society who were born at about the same time (geração) ▭ *the younger generation* (geração mais jovem) □ *There were four generations of the family at the wedding.*
2 the average time it takes for a child to become an adult, usually considered to be about 25 years □ *His family have been farmers for generations.* (geração)
3 the production of something, especially energy □ *the generation of electricity* (produção)
4 a product that is produced at a particular time, usually more developed than it was before □ *A new generation of environmentally friendly vehicles is available.* (geração)

• **generator** /ˈdʒenəreɪtə(r)/ NOUN [plural generators] a machine that produces electricity (gerador)

generosity /ˌdʒenəˈrɒsəti/ NOUN, NO PLURAL the quality of being generous (generosidade)

generous /ˈdʒenərəs/ ADJECTIVE
1 giving a lot of money, presents or time to others □ *The locals are kind and generous people.* (generoso)
2 bigger or more than usual or expected □ *He made a generous donation to the appeal fund.* □ *She took a generous helping of pasta.* (abundante)

• **generously** /ˈdʒenərəsli/ ADVERB in a generous way □ *Please give generously.* (generosamente)

genetic /dʒɪˈnetɪk/ ADJECTIVE to do with genes or genetics. A biology word □ *a genetic defect* (genético)

genetically modified /dʒɪˌnetɪkəli ˈmɒdɪfaɪd/ ADJECTIVE genetically modified plants or animals have had one or more of their genes changed so that their natural characteristics are improved □ *genetically modified crops* (geneticamente modificado)

genetic engineering /dʒɪˌnetɪk ˌendʒɪˈnɪərɪŋ/ NOUN, NO PLURAL the science of changing how living things develop by changing the information in their genes (engenharia genética)

genetics /dʒɪˈnetɪks/ NOUN, NO PLURAL the scientific study of how living things develop as a result of the qualities children take from their parents in their genes (genética)

genial /ˈdʒiːniəl/ ADJECTIVE pleasant and friendly □ *a genial man* (cordial)
• **geniality** /ˌdʒiːniˈæləti/ NOUN, NO PLURAL the quality of being genial (cordialidade)
• **genially** /ˈdʒiːniəli/ ADVERB in a genial way (cordialmente)

genie /ˈdʒiːni/ NOUN [plural genies or genii] in magical stories, a spirit who can give someone what they wish for □ *The genie granted Aladdin three wishes.* (gênio)

genitals /ˈdʒenɪtəlz/ PLURAL NOUN the sexual organs. A biology word. (genitália)

genius /ˈdʒiːnjəs/ NOUN [plural geniuses]
1 someone who is extremely clever or skilful (gênio)
2 the quality of being extremely clever or skilful □ *the genius of Shakespeare* (gênio, talentoso)

genocide /ˈdʒenəsaɪd/ NOUN, NO PLURAL when a lot of people from one race, religion or country are intentionally killed (genocídio)

genome /ˈdʒiːnəʊm/ NOUN [plural genomes] the set of genes that make up a cell or living thing. A biology word □ *the human genome* (genoma)

genre /ˈʒɑːrə/ NOUN [plural genres] a particular type or style of literature, music, etc. □ *Hitchcock was a master of the horror genre.* (gênero)

genteel /dʒenˈtiːl/ ADJECTIVE behaving very politely, like people from a high social class □ *She was drinking her tea in genteel sips.* (refinado)

gentle /ˈdʒentəl/ ADJECTIVE [gentler, gentlest]
1 careful not to hurt or upset anyone or anything □ *He was a gentle man.* □ *She gave him a gentle tap on his shoulder.* (delicado)
2 not strong, severe or violent □ *a gentle breeze* (suave)
3 a gentle slope is not steep (suave)

gentleman /ˈdʒentəlmən/ NOUN [plural gentlemen]
1 a word used to refer politely to a man □ *Good morning, gentlemen.* (senhor, cavalheiro)

Ladies and gentlemen, welcome to the show. (senhoras e senhores)
2 a man who is polite and treats people with respect □ *Her husband's a real gentleman.* (cavalheiro)

• **gentlemanly** /ˈdʒentəlmənli/ ADJECTIVE polite (cortês, polido)

gentleness /ˈdʒentəlnɪs/ NOUN, NO PLURAL the quality or state of being gentle □ *I was surprised at the gentleness of his touch.* (amabilidade)

gently /ˈdʒentli/ ADVERB in a gentle way □ *He picked the injured bird up gently.* (suavemente)

gentry /ˈdʒentri/ NOUN, NO PLURAL **the gentry** an old-fashioned word for people from a high social class (nobreza)

gents /dʒents/ NOUN, NO PLURAL **the gents** a public toilet for boys and men □ *Where is the gents, please?* (sanitário público masculino)

genuine /ˈdʒenjuɪn/ ADJECTIVE
1 real or true □ *a genuine work of art* (autêntico)
2 honest and not pretending □ *Her sympathy was genuine.* (sincero)

• **genuinely** /ˈdʒenjuɪnli/ ADVERB really or honestly □ *I was genuinely impressed.* (genuinamente)

genus /ˈdʒenəs/ NOUN [plural **genera**] a group of animals or plants which have the same characteristics. A biology word. (gênero)

geo- /ˈdʒiːəʊ/ PREFIX **geo-** is added to the beginning of words to mean 'to do with the Earth' □ *geology* (geo-)

geographic /ˌdʒiːəˈɡræfɪk/ or **geographical** /ˌdʒiːəˈɡræfɪkəl/ ADJECTIVE to do with geography and where things are on the Earth's surface (geográfico)

geography /dʒiˈɒɡrəfi/ NOUN, NO PLURAL the study of the Earth's surface and the countries, weather and people of the world □ *human geography* (geografia)

geological /ˌdʒiːəˈlɒdʒɪkəl/ ADJECTIVE to do with geology or the surface of the earth (geológico)

geologist /dʒiˈɒlədʒɪst/ NOUN [plural **geologists**] someone who studies geology (geólogo)

geology /dʒiˈɒlədʒi/ NOUN, NO PLURAL the study of the Earth's rocks and soil (geologia)

geometric /ˌdʒiːəˈmetrɪk/ or **geometrical** /ˌdʒiːəˈmetrɪkəl/ ADJECTIVE (geométrico)
1 made up of straight lines and angles □ *a geometric pattern* (geométrico)
2 to do with geometry (geométrico)

geometry /dʒiˈɒmətri/ NOUN, NO PLURAL a type of maths in which you study angles, lines and shapes (geometria)

geranium /dʒəˈreɪniəm/ NOUN [plural **geraniums**] a garden plant that has a lot of red, pink and white flowers (gerânio)

gerbil /ˈdʒɜːbɪl/ NOUN [plural **gerbils**] a small animal similar to a large mouse that is often kept as a pet (gerbo)

geriatric /ˌdʒeriˈætrɪk/ ADJECTIVE to do with old people and the illnesses they suffer from □ *a geriatric care unit* (geriátrico)

• **geriatrics** /ˌdʒeriˈætrɪks/ NOUN, NO PLURAL the medical care and treatment of old people (geriatria)

germ /dʒɜːm/ NOUN [plural **germs**] a very small living thing that can cause disease □ *This disinfectant kills most germs.* (germe)

German measles /ˌdʒɜːmən ˈmiːzəlz/ NOUN, NO PLURAL a disease children sometimes get which causes red spots on the skin (rubéola)

germinate /ˈdʒɜːmɪneɪt/ VERB [**germinates, germinating, germinated**] a seed germinates or is germinated when it begins to grow. A biology word. (germinar)

• **germination** /ˌdʒɜːmɪˈneɪʃən/ NOUN, NO PLURAL the process of germinating. A biology word. (germinação)

gestation /dʒeˈsteɪʃən/ NOUN, NO PLURAL the time when a baby human or animal is growing inside its mother. A biology word. (gestação)

gesticulate /dʒeˈstɪkjuleɪt/ VERB [**gesticulates, gesticulating, gesticulated**] to wave your hands or arms to express something □ *The officer shouted and gesticulated towards the car.* (gesticular)

gesture /ˈdʒestʃə(r)/ ▶ NOUN [plural **gestures**]
1 a movement made with your hand, arm or head to express what you think or feel (gesto) 🔾 *The driver made a rude gesture out of the car window.* (fez um gesto)
2 something you do to show how you feel about someone or something (gesto) 🔾 *It was a nice gesture to send the flowers.* (um gesto de bondade)
▶ VERB [**gestures, gesturing, gestured**] to point at something or express something by moving your hand, arm or head □ *She gestured towards the garden.* (gesticular)

get /ɡet/ VERB [**gets, getting, got**]
1 to take, receive or buy something □ *Isabel got lots of birthday presents.* □ *Did you get my letter?* □ *I got a new dress today.* (ganhar, alcançar, comprar)
2 to go somewhere and then bring something back □ *Could you get me a drink?* □ *I'll go and get the money.* (conseguir)
3 get away/in/out, etc. to move in a particular direction □ *We managed to get over the wall.* □ *All the chickens have got out.* □ *Catch a bus, and get off near the cathedral.* (sair, escapar, chamar)
4 to become □ *The baby's getting bigger every day.* □ *I got wet in the rain.* □ *If I mention money, he always gets angry.* □ *The wine glasses got broken.* (tornar-se)

5 if you get somewhere, you arrive there ☐ *We got to New York at 5 o'clock in the morning.* ☐ *What time will you get home?* ☐ *The train gets in at three thirty.* (**chegar em algum lugar**)

6 if you get a bus, train, etc., that is how you travel. ☐ *I usually get the train to work.* (**pegar**)

7 to become ill with a particular illness ☐ *They had an injection to stop them getting measles.* (**contrair**)

8 if you get something done, you make sure it is done genteel ☐ *We got our house painted.* ☐ *I need to get the washing done.* (**ter algo pronto**)

◆ PHRASAL VERBS **get something across** to explain something ☐ + *to The government is struggling to get its message across.* (**comunicar algo**) **get along** if two people get along, they are friendly ☐ + *with She gets along really well with her cousins.* (**dar-se bem**) **get around to doing something** to do something that you have been intending to do ☐ *We finally got around to decorating the bathroom.* (**ter intenção de fazer algo**) **get at someone** to criticize someone ☐ *I felt that the teacher was getting at me.* (**pegar no pé de alguém**) **get at something** if someone is getting at something, they are trying to express it ☐ *He kept mentioning the past, but I wasn't sure what he was getting at.* (**insinuar algo**) **get away with something** to avoid being punished or criticized ☐ *I'm hoping to miss the next meeting, if I can get away with it.* (**escapar impunemente**) **get on 1** to make progress ☐ + *with I need to get on with my work.* ☐ *How are you getting on in your new job?* (**progredir**) **2** to be friendly ☐ *Pierre and Alex don't really get on.* (**entender-se com**) **get out of something** to avoid doing something ☐ *He'll do anything to get out of the washing up.* (**evitar**) **get over something** to feel better after being ill or unhappy ☐ *He never really got over his wife's death.* (**recuperar-se de**) **get round to doing something** to do something that you have been intending to do ☐ *I'd like to do more exercise, but I never seem to get round to it.* (**conseguir**) **get through** to manage to talk to someone on the telephone ☐ *I tried to ring her, but I couldn't get through.* (**conseguir falar**) **get through something** to reach the end of a difficult situation ☐ *It was a terrible illness, but his determination helped to get him through it.* (**superar**) **get (someone) up** to wake up and get out of bed ☐ *I always get up early.* ☐ *My Dad gets me up in the morning.* (**fazer alguém acordar**) **get up to something** to do something, often something wrong ☐ *Sent to the head teacher? What's she been getting up to now?* (**meter-se em algo**)

geyser /ˈgiːzə(r)/ NOUN [plural **geysers**] a strong stream of hot water that comes up out of the ground (**gêiser**)

ghastly /ˈɡɑːstli/ ADJECTIVE [ghastlier, ghastliest] very unpleasant or ugly ☐ *a ghastly smell* ☐ *There's been a ghastly accident.* (**medonho**)

ghetto /ˈɡetəʊ/ NOUN [plural **ghettos**] a poor area in a town where a lot of people of the same race, religion, etc. live (**gueto**)

ghost /ɡəʊst/ NOUN [plural **ghosts**] the spirit of a dead person which some people think they can see ☐ *Do you believe in ghosts?* (**fantasma**)

• **ghostly** /ˈɡəʊstli/ ADJECTIVE [ghostlier, ghostliest] making you think of ghosts ☐ *a ghostly light* (**fantasmagórico**)

ghoul /ɡuːl/ NOUN [plural **ghouls**]
1 in stories, an evil spirit that steals and eats dead bodies (**demônio**)
2 someone who is too interested in death, accidents, etc. (**mórbido**)

• **ghoulish** /ˈɡuːlɪʃ/ ADJECTIVE too interested in death, accidents etc. ☐ *A crowd of ghoulish onlookers stood round the ambulance.* (**mórbido**)

giant /ˈdʒaɪənt/ ▶ NOUN [plural **giants**]
1 in stories, a man who is extremely tall and strong (**gigante**)
2 a very large company or organization ☐ *the software giant, Microsoft* (**gigante**)
▶ ADJECTIVE much bigger than usual ☐ *a giant crane* ☐ *a giant tortoise* (**gigante**)

gibberish /ˈdʒɪbərɪʃ/ NOUN, NO PLURAL language that has no meaning, or language that you cannot understand ☐ *He was talking absolute gibberish.* (**bobagem**)

giddy /ˈɡɪdi/ ADJECTIVE [giddier, giddiest] if you feel giddy, you feel as if everything around you is moving and you cannot stay standing (**zonzo**)

gift /ɡɪft/ NOUN [plural **gifts**]
1 a present (**presente**) ▣ *a wedding gift* (**presente de casamento**) ▣ *Many children give gifts to their teacher at the end of term.* (**dão presentes**) ▣ *a gift shop* (**loja de presentes**) ☐ + *from The necklace had been a gift from her boyfriend.*
2 a natural ability ☐ + *for Adam has a gift for languages.* (**dom**)

• **gifted** /ˈɡɪftɪd/ ADJECTIVE having a natural ability to do something extremely well ☐ *a gifted child* ☐ *a gifted writer* (**talentoso**)

gig /ɡɪɡ/ NOUN [plural **gigs**] an informal word for a pop music concert (**apresentação**)

gigabyte /ˈɡɪɡəbaɪt/ NOUN [plural **gigabytes**] a unit used to measure computer information, equal to approximately a thousand megabytes. A computing word. (**gigabyte**)

gigantic /dʒaɪˈɡæntɪk/ ADJECTIVE extremely big ☐ *a gigantic statue* (**gigantesco**)

giggle /ˈɡɪɡəl/ ▶ VERB [giggles, giggling, giggled] to laugh in a silly or nervous way (**dar risadinha**)
▶ NOUN [plural **giggles**] a silly or nervous laugh (**risadinha**)

gills /ɡɪlz/ PLURAL NOUN a fish's gills are the openings at each side of its body, which it breathes through (**guelra**)

gilt /ɡɪlt/ ADJECTIVE decorated with a thin layer of gold ☐ *a gilt frame* (**dourado**)

gimmick /ˈgɪmɪk/ NOUN [plural **gimmicks**] something that is done to get people's attention, but is not useful □ *The policy is just a political gimmick.* (**truque**)

gin /dʒɪn/ NOUN, NO PLURAL a strong alcoholic drink (**gim**)

ginger /ˈdʒɪndʒə(r)/ ▶ NOUN, NO PLURAL a root that has a spicy taste and is used in cooking (**gengibre**)
▶ ADJECTIVE ginger hair is a reddish-brown colour (**amarelo-avermelhado**)

• **gingerly** /ˈdʒɪndʒəlɪ/ ADVERB if you do something gingerly, you do it slowly and carefully because you are nervous about what will happen □ *She stepped gingerly onto the wobbly bridge.* (**cuidadosamente**)

giraffe /dʒɪˈrɑːf/ NOUN [plural **giraffes**] an African animal with a very long neck and long legs (**girafa**)

girder /ˈgɜːdə(r)/ NOUN [plural **girders**] a long piece of metal used for supporting a bridge or building (**viga**)

girl /gɜːl/ NOUN [plural **girls**] a female child or young woman □ *Police are searching for a missing 10-year old girl.* (**menina**) 🔁 *a teenage girl* (**adolescente**) 🔁 *There were two little girls (= very young girls) playing in the garden.* (**menininhas**)

girlfriend /ˈgɜːlfrend/ NOUN [plural **girlfriends**]
1 a girl or woman that you are having a romantic relationship with □ *Dan has a new girlfriend.* (**namorada**)
2 a female friend that a girl or woman has □ *I go out with my girlfriends once a week.* (**amiga**)

gist /dʒɪst/ NOUN, NO PLURAL **the gist** the main points of something that someone says or writes □ *Pam told me the gist of their conversation.* (**essencial**)

give /gɪv/ VERB [**gives, giving, gave, given**]
1 to let someone have something □ *Give your bags to the porter.* □ *Make sure you give back all the books you borrowed.* □ *Let me give you some advice.* □ *This news gives us hope.* □ *He gave us permission to visit the temple.* □ *Could you give us some information about hotels?* (**dar**)
2 to make someone have something □ *They were given a severe punishment.* □ *Our boss gives us too much work.* □ *The sudden noise gave me a fright.* (**dar**)
3 give evidence/a performance/a speech, etc. to say something or to perform in public □ *She gave evidence at his trial.* □ *He gave a wonderful performance of Beethoven's Moonlight Sonata.* (**dar evidência/desempenho/palestra etc.**)
4 to make a sound or a movement □ *He gave a shout of joy.* □ *She gave her brother a kick.* (**dar**)
5 if something gives, it bends or breaks when too much weight is put on top of it □ *The rotten floorboard gave under him.* (**ceder**)
6 give way if you give way to another vehicle, you stop to allow it to drive before you (**dar passagem**)
◆ PHRASAL VERBS **give something away 1** to let someone have something without paying for it □ *I gave away all my old toys.* (**desfazer-se de**) **2** to tell a secret □ *The party was meant to be a surprise, but Billy gave it away.* (**deixar escapar**)
give in to agree to something you did not want to agree to □ *I kept asking for the new computer game, and eventually Dad gave in and bought it for me.* (**ceder**) **give something out** to give something to a group of people □ *Can you give out the reading books please, Kazuo?* (**distribuir**)
give up to stop trying to guess an answer □ *'How many beans are there in this jar?' 'Three hundred? A thousand? I give up.'* (**desistir**) **give up (something) 1** if you give up a habit, you stop doing it □ *She's managed to give up smoking.* (**abandonar um hábito**) **2** to stop doing something before it is finished, because it is too difficult □ *I've given up trying to keep this room tidy.* □ *Don't give up – only another mile to go!* (**desistir, largar**)

• **given** /ˈgɪvən/ ▶ ADJECTIVE decided or agreed □ *You have a given time to complete each question.* □ *On any given day, there are several dozen accidents.* (**dado**)
▶ PREPOSITION considering the fact that □ *Given that they don't have much money, their offer is extremely generous.* (**dado**)
▶ PAST PARTICIPLE OF **give** (*ver* **give**)

glaciation /ˌgleɪsɪˈeɪʃən/ NOUN, NO PLURAL when land becomes covered in glaciers. A geography word. (**glaciação**)

glacier /ˈglæsɪə(r)/ NOUN [plural **glaciers**] a large mass of ice that moves slowly down a mountain valley (**geleira**)

glad /glæd/ ADJECTIVE [**gladder, gladdest**]
1 pleased and happy because of something □ *+ that I'm just glad that the exams are over.* □ *+ to do something I'm so glad to see you.* (**feliz, alegre**)
2 willing and happy □ *+ to do something I'd be glad to help if you need me.* (**contente**)
3 be glad of something a formal phrase meaning to be grateful for something □ *He was glad of an excuse to leave.* (**estar grato por algo**)

gladiator /ˈglædɪˌeɪtə(r)/ NOUN [plural **gladiators**] in ancient Rome, a man who fought other men or animals to entertain people (**gladiador**)

gladly /ˈglædlɪ/ ADVERB happily or with pleasure □ *She offered him some coffee which he gladly accepted.* (**com prazer**)

glamorous /ˈglæmərəs/ ADJECTIVE attractive, fashionable and exciting □ *She was looking very glamorous in a black dress.* □ *a glamorous lifestyle* (**glamuroso**)

glamour /ˈglæmə(r)/ NOUN, NO PLURAL a special quality that makes someone or something seem attractive, fashionable and exciting ☐ *She will add some glamour to the show.* **(glamour, sedução)**

glance /glɑːns/ ▶ VERB [glances, glancing, glanced]

1 to look at something or someone for a very short time ☐ **+ at** *Anselm glanced nervously at his watch.* ☐ **+ around** *He glanced around to see if anyone was looking.* **(dar uma olhadela, lançar um olhar)**

2 glance at/over something to read something very quickly ☐ *He glanced at his notes before he spoke.* **(dar uma olhada em algo)**

▶ NOUN [*plural* **glances**]

1 a quick look **(olhadela)** 🔁 *He cast a nervous glance at Yvonne.* **(olhada nervosa)** 🔁 *Richard and I exchanged glances* (= we looked at each other for a short time). **(trocamos rápidos olhares)**

2 at a glance if you see or understand something at a glance, you see or understand it immediately ☐ *She could tell at a glance that her father was upset.* **(uma rápida olhada)**

gland /glænd/ NOUN [*plural* **glands**] an organ in your body that produces a substance that your body needs. A biology word. **(glândula)**

• **glandular** /ˈɡlændjʊlə(r)/ ADJECTIVE to do with a gland or glands. A biology word. **(glandular)**

glandular fever /ˌɡlændjʊlə(r) ˈfiːvə(r)/ NOUN, NO PLURAL an infectious illness which makes you feel tired and weak for a very long time **(mononucleose infecciosa)**

glare /gleə(r)/ ▶ VERB [glares, glaring, glared]

1 to look at someone in a way that shows you are very angry ☐ *Mia glared at him.* **(fulminar com o olhar)**

2 if a light glares, it is bright and makes your eyes hurt ☐ *The setting sun glared in her eyes.* **(ofuscar)**

▶ NOUN [*plural* **glares**]

1 *no plural* very strong bright light that makes your eyes hurt ☐ *He stood in the harsh glare of the car's headlights.* **(brilho ofuscante)**

2 *no plural* when someone gets a lot of attention from newspapers, television, etc., especially when they do not want it ☐ *The singer even changed hotels to avoid the media glare.* **(olhar penetrante)**

3 an angry look **(olhar furioso)**

• **glaring** /ˈɡleərɪŋ/ ADJECTIVE

1 very obvious **(flagrante)** 🔁 *a glaring mistake* **(erro flagrante)**

2 very bright, and making your eyes hurt ☐ *the glaring sun* **(ofuscante)**

glass /ɡlɑːs/ ▶ NOUN [*plural* **glasses**]

1 *no plural* a hard transparent material, used for making bottles, windows, etc. **(vidro)** 🔁 *There was broken glass all over the pavement.* 🔁 *She stepped on a piece of glass and cut her foot.*

2 a container made of glass, which you drink from ☐ *a tall glass* **(copo)** 🔁 *a wine glass* **(taça de vinho)** ☐ **+ of** *She drank three glasses of milk.* 🔁 *Betsy poured a glass of juice.* **(serviu um copo de)**

3 glasses something you wear to help you see better, which consists of two pieces of plastic or glass in a frame **(óculos)** 🔁 *I need a new pair of glasses.* **(par de óculos)** 🔁 *My Dad wears glasses.* **(usa óculos)**

▶ ADJECTIVE made of glass ☐ *a glass bowl* **(de vidro)**

• **glassy** /ˈɡlɑːsi/ ADJECTIVE [glassier, glassiest]

1 shiny like glass, or transparent like glass ☐ *the glassy surface of the water* **(vítreo)**

2 if someone's eyes are glassy, they show no feeling, usually because the person is ill **(opaco)**

glaze /ɡleɪz/ ▶ VERB [glazes, glazing, glazed]

1 if your eyes glaze, you start to look bored or tired ☐ *Riley's eyes glazed over.* **(tornar-se vítreo)**

2 to cover clay objects with a substance that makes them shiny **(envernizar)**

3 to put glass into the frame of a window **(envidraçar)**

▶ NOUN [*plural* **glazes**] a liquid you put on something to make it look shiny **(verniz)**

• **glazier** /ˈɡleɪziə(r)/ NOUN [*plural* **glaziers**] someone whose job is to put glass in the frame of a window **(vidraceiro)**

gleam /ɡliːm/ ▶ VERB [gleams, gleaming, gleamed]

1 to shine ☐ *A light gleamed in the distance.* **(brilhar, reluzir)**

2 if your eyes or face gleam, they show a good feeling very strongly ☐ *Her eyes were gleaming with pride.* **(vislumbrar, cintilar)**

▶ NOUN [*plural* **gleams**]

1 a light ☐ *He saw the first gleam of sunrise on the horizon.* **(lampejo)**

2 a good feeling that someone shows in their eyes or face ☐ *There was a gleam of satisfaction in her eyes.* **(vislumbre)**

• **gleaming** /ˈɡliːmɪŋ/ ADJECTIVE clean and shiny ☐ *a gleaming black sports car* **(reluzente)**

glean /ɡliːn/ VERB [gleans, gleaning, gleaned] to find out information by asking questions and listening carefully ☐ *I tried to glean as much information as I could from him.* **(obter informações)**

glee /ɡliː/ NOUN, NO PLURAL a feeling of pleasure because something good has happened to you or because something bad has happened to someone else ☐ *Ray told them about my accident with a certain amount of glee.* **(regozijo, euforia)**

• **gleeful** /ˈɡliːfʊl/ ADJECTIVE showing glee ☐ *a gleeful smile* **(eufórico)**

glib /ɡlɪb/ ADJECTIVE [glibber, glibbest] said with little thought, and having little meaning ☐ *a glib answer* **(improvisado)**

glide /ɡlaɪd/ VERB [glides, gliding, glided] to move smoothly and quietly ☐ *The waiters glide effortlessly between the tables.* **(deslizar)**

glimmer · glory

- **glider** /ˈɡlaɪdə(r)/ NOUN [plural **gliders**] an aeroplane with no engine which moves on air currents (**planador**)
- **gliding** /ˈɡlaɪdɪŋ/ NOUN, NO PLURAL the activity of flying a glider (**ato de pilotar um planador**)

glimmer /ˈɡlɪmə(r)/ ▶ NOUN [plural **glimmers**]
1 a glimmer of hope/interest etc. a small amount of something good, especially hope or interest (**um vislumbre de esperança/interesse etc.**)
2 a weak light □ *We could see the glimmer of torches inside the tent.* (**luz trêmula**)
▶ VERB [**glimmers, glimmering, glimmered**] to shine with a weak light □ *Something glimmered in the dark.* (**luzir fracamente**)

glimpse /ɡlɪmps/ ▶ NOUN [plural **glimpses**] when you see someone or something only for a very short time (**vislumbre, lampejo**) 🔹 *People climbed on fences, hoping to catch a glimpse of (= see) the princess.* (**conseguir um vislumbre**)
▶ VERB [**glimpses, glimpsing, glimpsed**] to see someone or something only for a very short time, or to see only part of them □ *Through the trees he glimpsed a woman on the path.* (**vislumbrar**)

glint /ɡlɪnt/ ▶ VERB [**glints, glinting, glinted**]
1 to shine brightly with flashes of light □ *The knife was glinting in the sun.* (**reluzir**)
2 if someone's eyes glint, they seem to shine, often because someone is excited about something, especially something bad (**brilhar**)
▶ NOUN [plural **glints**]
1 a flash of very bright light (**lampejo**)
2 a light that seems to shine in someone's eyes when they are excited, especially about something bad □ *There was a wicked glint in his eye as he said it.* (**brilho**)

glisten /ˈɡlɪsən/ VERB [**glistens, glistening, glistened**] to shine because of being wet or covered in something such as oil □ *Her eyes glistened with tears.* (**reluzir**)

glitter /ˈɡlɪtə(r)/ ▶ VERB [**glitters, glittering, glittered**] to shine with small flashes of light □ *His eyes glittered in the light.* (**cintilar**)
▶ NOUN, *no plural*
1 when something shines with small flashes of light □ *the glitter of the jewels* (**brilho**)
2 very small shiny pieces of metal, used for decorating things (**glitter**)
3 an exciting and attractive quality that something has □ *the glitter of Hollywood* (**brilho**)
- **glittering** /ˈɡlɪtərɪŋ/ ADJECTIVE
1 very exciting and successful (**brilhante**) 🔹 *a glittering career* (**uma carreira brilhante**)
2 shining with small flashes of light □ *glittering silver trophies* (**resplandecente**)

gloat /ɡləʊt/ VERB [**gloats, gloating, gloated**] to show too much pleasure at your own success or at someone else's failure □ *He always beat me at tennis but he never gloated over his victories.* (**envaidecer-se**)

global /ˈɡləʊbəl/ ADJECTIVE
1 to do with or involving the whole world □ *Global sales rose by 20%.* □ *global climate change* (**global**)
2 involving everyone or everything □ *a global increase in pay* (**global**)
- **globalization** *or* **globalisation** /ˌɡləʊbəlaɪˈzeɪʃən/ NOUN, NO PLURAL the way that all the countries of the world are becoming similar, especially because of big companies selling the same thing in many countries (**globalizaçao**)
- **globally** /ˈɡləʊbəli/ ADVERB around the whole world □ *The company operates globally.* □ *Globally, 2.6 billion people lack access to clean water supplies.* (**globalmente**)

global warming /ˌɡləʊbəl ˈwɔːmɪŋ/ NOUN, NO PLURAL the gradual increase in the Earth's temperature caused by pollution (**aquecimento global**)

globe /ɡləʊb/ NOUN [plural **globes**]
1 a large ball with a map of the Earth printed on it (**globo terrestre**)
2 the globe the world □ *The company has offices around the globe.* (**planeta**)

gloom /ɡluːm/ NOUN, NO PLURAL
1 a feeling of sadness and no hope □ *News of the accident added to her gloom.* (**tristeza, pessimismo**)
2 darkness □ *A man appeared out of the gloom.* (**penumbra**)
- **gloomy** /ˈɡluːmi/ ADJECTIVE [**gloomier, gloomiest**]
1 suggesting that a situation is bad and will get worse □ *There were gloomy predictions of a rise in unemployment.* (**pouco promissor**)
2 sad and without hope □ *He was in a gloomy mood.* (**deprimido**)
3 unpleasantly dark □ *a gloomy passageway* (**escuro**)

glorify /ˈɡlɔːrɪfaɪ/ VERB [**glorifies, glorifying, glorified**]
1 to make something bad seem to have good qualities □ *It was said that the films glorified violence.* (**exaltar**)
2 to praise someone, especially God (**glorificar**)

glorious /ˈɡlɔːriəs/ ADJECTIVE
1 extremely beautiful or good □ *glorious sunshine* □ *The hotel is surrounded by glorious countryside.* (**glorioso**)
2 deserving or receiving praise □ *a glorious victory* (**esplêndido**)

glory /ˈɡlɔːri/ NOUN [plural **glories**]
1 praise and admiration □ *His moment of glory came when he won the championship.* (**glória**)
2 great beauty (**esplendor**) 🔹 *The house has been restored to its former glory.* (**restaurou seu antigo esplendor**)
♦ PHRASAL VERB [**glories, glorying, gloried**] **glory in something** to enjoy something and be proud of it

□ *They gloried in their unexpected victory.* (orgulhar-se de algo)

gloss /glɒs/ NOUN, NO PLURAL
1 a type of paint that produces a shiny surface □ *a tin of gloss* (tinta brilhante)
2 shine on a surface (brilho)
♦ PHRASAL VERB [**glosses, glossing, glossed**] **gloss over something** to say little about a problem because you do not want to make it seem important (tratar de algo por alto)

glossary /ˈglɒsəri/ NOUN [*plural* **glossaries**] a list of words and their meanings, at the end of a book (glossário)

glossy /ˈglɒsi/ ADJECTIVE [**glossier, glossiest**]
1 smooth and shiny (lustroso) 🔸 *glossy hair* (cabelo lustroso) □ *a glossy surface*
2 glossy magazines are printed on shiny paper and have a lot of pictures in them (reluzente)

glove /glʌv/ NOUN [*plural* **gloves**] something you wear to cover your hand (luva) 🔸 *a pair of gloves* (par de luvas) 🔸 *I wear gloves in the winter.* (uso luvas) 🔸 *It's a good idea to wear rubber gloves when you're cleaning.* (luvas de borracha)

glow /gləʊ/ ▶ NOUN, NO PLURAL
1 warm or soft light □ *the glow of the fire* (incandescência)
2 a healthy colour that someone's face has □ *Her skin still has a youthful glow.* (brilho)
3 a glow of satisfaction/pride etc. a good feeling of being satisfied, proud, etc. □ *He felt a glow of satisfaction when he looked at his work.* (sensação de satisfação, orgulho etc.)
▶ VERB [**glows, glowing, glowed**]
1 to burn or shine with a soft light □ *A fire glowed in the corner of the room.* (irradiar)
2 to look warm and healthy □ *Her cheeks were glowing.* (corar)
3 glow with pride/satisfaction/confidence, etc. to show that you are very proud, satisfied, etc. □ *She was glowing with pride as she watched her son accept the award.* (irradiar de orgulho, satisfação, confiança etc.)

glower /ˈglaʊə(r)/ VERB [**glowers, glowering, glowered**] to look at someone in an angry way (olhar com raiva)

glowing /ˈgləʊɪŋ/ ADJECTIVE
1 burning or shining with a soft light □ *the glowing lights of the village* (incandescente)
2 praising someone a lot (entusiasmado) 🔸 *He got a glowing report from his teachers.* (relato entusiasmado)

glucose /ˈgluːkəʊs/ NOUN, NO PLURAL a type of sugar (glicose)

glue /gluː/ ▶ NOUN [*plural* **glues**] a substance used for sticking things together □ *Use glue to stick the fabric onto the paper.* (cola)
▶ VERB [**glues, gluing** or **glueing, glued**]
1 to stick something using glue (colar) 🔸 *He glued the two pieces of wood together.* (colou)
2 if you are glued to a television or computer screen, you are looking at it all the time. An informal phrase. □ *The kids are just glued to the TV all day.* (colar, grudar)
• **gluey** /ˈgluːi/ ADJECTIVE covered with glue, or sticky like glue (pegajoso)

glum /glʌm/ ADJECTIVE [**glummer, glummest**] unhappy (carrancudo, mal-humorado)

gluten /ˈgluːtən/ NOUN, NO PLURAL a sticky substance in wheat and some other grains (glúten)

glutton /ˈglʌtən/ NOUN [*plural* **gluttons**]
1 someone who eats too much (glutão)
2 a glutton for punishment someone who seems to enjoy doing things that are unpleasant or difficult (pessoa que gosta de sofrer)
• **gluttony** /ˈglʌtəni/ NOUN, NO PLURAL eating too much (glutonaria)

GM /ˌdʒiːˈem/ ABBREVIATION **genetically modified** (abreviação de geneticamente modificado)

GMT /ˌdʒiːemˈtiː/ ABBREVIATION Greenwich Mean Time; the time in Greenwich, England that is used to calculate the time in other parts of the world (abreviação de meridiano de Greenwich)

gnarled /nɑːld/ ADJECTIVE twisted and rough □ *gnarled trees* (retorcido, nodoso)

gnat /næt/ NOUN [*plural* **gnats**] a small flying insect that bites (mosquito)

gnaw /nɔː/ VERB [**gnaws, gnawing, gnawed**] to keep biting a hard object □ *The dog was gnawing at a bone.* (roer)

gnome /nəʊm/ NOUN [*plural* **gnomes**]
1 in stories, a little man with a pointed hat who can do magic (gnomo)
2 a model of a little man with a pointed hat, used as a garden decoration (gnomo)

go /gəʊ/ ▶ VERB [**goes, going, went, gone**]
1 to travel or move somewhere □ *I'm going home now.* □ + **to** *We're going to France for our holiday.* □ *He went into the other room.* □ *I wish she'd go away.* □ *He left home at 18 and never went back.* (ir)
2 to travel or move somewhere so that you can do something □ + **to** *She goes to school in the next village.* □ + **for** *Shall we go for a swim?* □ *We all went cycling.* (ir)
3 to leave or disappear □ *It's six o'clock, so I'll have to go soon.* □ *I'm sure I left my coat here, but it's gone.* □ *The food all went very quickly.* (sumir, partir)
4 if a road or path goes somewhere, it leads there □ *Does this road go to Edinburgh?* (ir)
5 the place where something goes is where it fits or is kept □ *That piece of the jigsaw goes at the top.* □ *The cups go on the top shelf.* (ser)
6 to become □ *Her face went pale.* □ *Your soup's gone cold.* (tornar-se)
7 to happen in a particular way □ *The concert went well.* □ *How's your new job going?* (transcorrer)

goad

8 be going to do something (a) to intend to do something ☐ *I'm going to write to Molly.* ☐ *What were you going to say?* (b) to be expected to happen ☐ *I think it's going to rain.* (**ir fazer algo**)
⇨ go to **go to great lengths to do something**
◆ PHRASAL VERBS **go about something** to do something in a particular way ☐ *I'm not sure how to go about slicing this chicken.* (**ter intenção de fazer algo**) **go ahead** to start to do something ☐ *+ with They're going ahead with the new airport.* (**seguir**) **go around 1** to be enough for everyone ☐ *Are there enough books to go around?* (**ser suficiente para todos**) **2** if someone goes around doing something, they often do something that upsets other people ☐ *You can't go around telling lies about him.* (**sair fazendo algo desagradável**) **go by** if time goes by, it passes (**passar**) **go down** to become lower in level ☐ *His temperature has gone down a bit.* (**cair**) **go down with something** to get an illness ☐ *She's gone down with a tummy bug.* (**cair de cama**) **go for something** to choose something ☐ *I'm going to go for the curry.* (**escolher alguma coisa**) **go into something 1** to talk about something in detail ☐ *She told me a lot about her marriage, though I won't go into that now.* (**entrar em detalhes sobre algo**) **2** to start working in a particular type of job ☐ *After university, he went into banking.* (**entrar em algo**) **go off 1** if food goes off, it becomes rotten (**estragar**) **2** to explode ☐ *A bomb has gone off in a busy London street.* (**explodir**) **go off someone/something** to stop liking someone or something ☐ *I've gone off spicy food.* (**desistir de alguém/algo**) **go on 1** to continue for a period of time ☐ *His speech went on for hours.* (**continuar**) **2** to continue doing something ☐ *+ ing He went on singing, despite the noise.* ☐ *+ with Go on with your work.* (**continuar**) **3** if something is going on, it is happening ☐ *What's going on?* (**acontecer**) **go out** to leave your house, especially for a social activity ☐ *Are you going out tonight?* (**sair**) **go round 1** to be enough for everyone ☐ *Is there enough bread to go round?* (**ser suficiente**) **2** if someone goes round doing something, they often do something that upsets other people ☐ *She goes round complaining to anyone who'll listen.* (**continuar**) **go through something** to experience something ☐ *She went through agony during the illness.* (**passar por algo**) **go through with something** to do something even though it is difficult ☐ *They persuaded her to go through with the operation.* (**prosseguir com algo**) **go up** to become higher in level ☐ *Prices have gone up again.* (**subir**)
▶ NOUN [plural **goes**]
1 an attempt (**tentativa, chance**) 🔲 *It doesn't matter if you can't climb to the top – just have a go.* (**faça uma tentativa**) 🔲 *She asked me if I'd go to dancing lessons with her, so I decided to give it a go.* (**dar uma chance**)

2 when it is your turn to do something, especially in a game ☐ *Pick up a card, Adam – it's your go.* (**vez**)
◆ IDIOMS **have a go at someone** to criticize someone ☐ *He had a go at me for not doing my homework.* (**dar uma bronca em alguém**) **on the go** active or busy ☐ *I'm on the go from the moment I wake up.* (**estar atarefado**)

goad /gəʊd/ VERB [**goads, goading, goaded**] to make someone do something by annoying them until they do it ☐ *He had tried to goad them into fighting.* (**provocar alguém**)

go-ahead /ˈgəʊəˌhed/ NOUN, NO PLURAL **get/give the go-ahead** to get or give permission to do something ☐ *The government has given the go-ahead for a new power station.* (**dar permissão**)

goal /gəʊl/ NOUN [plural **goals**]
1 something that you want to achieve (**objetivo, meta**) 🔲 *If she works hard, she should achieve her goal* (**atingir seu objetivo**) 🔲 *The government's long-term goal is to reduce the number of people in prison.* (**objetivo de longo prazo**)
2 a point scored when a ball goes into the net in a game such as football or hockey (**gol**) 🔲 *Cahill scored the first goal.* (**marcou um gol**) 🔲 *Giggs scored the winning goal.* (**o gol da vitória**)
3 the area where the ball must go to score a point in a game such as football or hockey ☐ *He was standing in front of the goal.* (**gol**)

goalie /ˈgəʊli/ NOUN [plural **goalies**] an informal word for a **goalkeeper** (**goleiro**)

goalkeeper /ˈgəʊlˌkiːpə(r)/ NOUN [plural **goalkeepers**] the player who stands in front of the net in a game such as football and who tries to stop the ball going into the net (**goleiro**)

goat /gəʊt/ NOUN [plural **goats**] an animal with horns and long hair under its chin ☐ *The cheese is made from goat's milk.* (**bode**)

gobble /ˈgɒbəl/ VERB [**gobbles, gobbling, gobbled**] to eat something very quickly ☐ *He gobbled down the burger in three bites.* (**devorar**)

go-between /ˈgəʊbɪˌtwiːn/ NOUN [plural **go-betweens**] someone who takes messages between people who cannot meet or who do not want to meet (**intermediário**)

goblin /ˈgɒblɪn/ NOUN [plural **goblins**] in stories, a small ugly creature who tricks people (**duende**)

god /gɒd/ NOUN [plural **gods**]
1 God no plural the spirit that Christians, Muslims and Jews pray to (**Deus**) 🔲 *Do you believe in God?* (**acredita em Deus**)
2 a spirit that some people believe controls nature or represents a particular quality ☐ *Greek and Roman gods* ☐ *+ of Thor was the Viking god of thunder.* (**deus**)

godchild /ˈgɒdtʃaɪld/ NOUN [plural **godchildren**] your godchild is a child whose parents have asked you to support their child and make sure that the child learns about Christianity (**afilhado**)

god-daughter /ˈgɒddɔːtə(r)/ NOUN [plural **god-daughters**] a female godchild (**afilhada**)

goddess /ˈgɒdɪs/ NOUN [plural **goddesses**] a female god (**deusa**)

godfather /ˈgɒdfɑːðə(r)/ NOUN [plural **godfathers**] a child's godfather is a man who has agreed to make sure that the child learns about Christianity (**padrinho**)

godmother /ˈgɒdmʌðə(r)/ NOUN [plural **godmothers**] a child's godmother is a woman who has agreed to make sure that the child learns about Christianity (**madrinha**)

godparent /ˈgɒdpeərənt/ NOUN [plural **godparents**] a godfather or godmother (**padrinho ou madrinha**)

godsend /ˈgɒdsend/ NOUN, NO PLURAL someone or something that is very helpful when you are having problems (**dádiva do céu**)

goes /gəʊz/ VERB the present tense of the verb **go** when it is used with 'he', 'she', or 'it' ▢ *He goes to work at eight o'clock.* (**ver go**)

goggles /ˈgɒglz/ PLURAL NOUN something you wear to protect your eyes when you are swimming or working with things that might damage your eyes ▢ *a pair of swimming goggles* (**óculos de natação**)

going /ˈgəʊɪŋ/ ▶ NOUN, NO PLURAL
1 how easy, difficult or slow something is (**indicador de quão fácil, difícil, lento algo é**) 🔁 *She found the course very hard going* (= difficult). (**difícil**)
2 when someone leaves ▢ *What were the reasons for his going?* (**saída, partida**)
▶ ADJECTIVE **the going rate/price** the amount you usually have to pay for a particular thing ▢ *£150 is about the going rate for a hotel room round here.* (**a tarifa/o preço atual**)

go-kart /ˈgəʊkɑːt/ NOUN [plural **go-karts**] a small low car with no roof, used for racing (**kart**)

gold /gəʊld/ ▶ NOUN [plural **golds**]
1 *no plural* a valuable pale yellow metal, used to make jewellery ▢ *bars of gold* (**ouro**)
2 a gold medal (= prize for coming first in a competition or race) ▢ *He won gold in the long jump.* (**ouro**)
▶ ADJECTIVE
1 made of gold ▢ *a gold ring* (**ouro**)
2 having the colour of gold ▢ *a gold leather handbag* (**ouro**)
• **golden** /ˈgəʊldən/ ADJECTIVE
1 made of gold ▢ *a golden crown* (**de ouro**)
2 having the colour of gold ▢ *golden hair* (**dourado**)

golden wedding /ˌgəʊldən ˈwedɪŋ/ NOUN [plural **golden weddings**] the day that is exactly fifty years after someone's wedding (**bodas de ouro**)

goldfish /ˈgəʊldfɪʃ/ NOUN [plural **goldfish**] a small orange fish that people keep as a pet (**peixinho dourado**)

golf /gɒlf/ NOUN, NO PLURAL a game in which you have to hit a small ball into holes in the ground (**golfe**) 🔁 *a golf ball* (**bola de golfe**) 🔁 *My Dad plays golf.* (**joga golfe**) 🔁 *an 18-hole golf course* (**campo de golfe**) 🔁 *Professional golfers have someone to carry their golf clubs* (= sticks used for hitting the ball). (**tacos de golfe**)
• **golfer** /ˈgɒlfə(r)/ NOUN [plural **golfers**] someone who plays golf (**jogador de golfe**)

gone /gɒn/ PAST PARTICIPLE OF **go** (**ver go**)

gong /gɒŋ/ NOUN [plural **gongs**] a large round piece of metal that you hit with a stick to make a loud sound (**gongo**)

good /gʊd/ ▶ ADJECTIVE [**better, best**]
1 suitable or of a high standard ▢ *That's a good idea.* ▢ *I've got some good news for you.* ▢ *She has been a good friend to me.* ▢ *I know a good way to cook rice.* (**bom**)
2 enjoyable or pleasant ▢ *Did you have a good holiday?* ▢ *We had a good time in Moscow.* (**bom, agradável**)
3 able to do something well ▢ + **at** *Mark's very good at fixing cars.* ▢ *Ben's a pretty good cook.* (**bom**)
4 something you say to show you are pleased ▢ *Oh, good – Harry's arrived.* (**bom**)
5 good for you something that is good for you makes you healthy or makes your life better ▢ *Eat your vegetables – they're good for you.* (**bom para você**)
6 kind and helpful ▢ *My grandparents are very good to me.* (**bom**)
7 a good child or animal behaves well ▢ *The children have been very good.* (**bom, bonzinho**)
♦ IDIOMS **it's a good job** it is lucky ▢ *It's a good job you had an umbrella with you.* (**é muita sorte**)
⇨ go to **have a good mind to do something**

> ➤ Remember that good is an adjective and not an adverb. Use the adverb well to say that someone does something in a way that is good: ▢ *She is a good cook.*
> ✓ *She cooks very well.*
> ✗ *She cooks very good.*

▶ NOUN, NO PLURAL
1 something that produces an advantage (**bom, proveitoso**) 🔁 *Cleaning it with water won't do any good – you need soap.* (**não fará diferença**) 🔁 *I know this medicine tastes bad, but it's for your own good.* (**é para seu próprio bem**)
2 no good/not any good not of good quality, or not helpful ▢ *These gloves are no good – they're too thin.* ▢ *It's no good phoning her – she never has her phone switched on.* (**inútil**)
3 do someone good to make someone feel better or to make their life better ▢ *Have a day off work – it will do you good.* (**bem**)

good afternoon

4 what is morally right □ *We recognize the difference between good and evil.* (bem) **for good** forever □ *I left home for good when I was 18.* (para sempre)

good afternoon /gʊd ˌɑːftəˈnuːn/ EXCLAMATION something that you say when you meet someone in the afternoon (boa tarde)

goodbye /gʊdˈbaɪ/ EXCLAMATION something you say when you are leaving or when other people are leaving □ *Goodbye, Anna. See you next week.* (até logo, adeus) 🔁 *I felt sad when it was time to say goodbye.* (dizer adeus)

good evening /gʊd ˈiːvnɪŋ/ EXCLAMATION a formal way of saying 'hello' when you see someone in the evening □ *Good evening ladies and gentlemen, and welcome to the show.* (boa noite)

good-looking /gʊdˈlʊkɪŋ/ ADJECTIVE someone who is good-looking has an attractive face □ *Amy's new boyfriend is really good-looking.* (bonito, de boa aparência)

good morning /gʊd ˈmɔːnɪŋ/ EXCLAMATION a formal way of saying 'hello' when you see someone in the morning □ *Good morning, everyone.* (bom dia)

goodness /ˈgʊdnɪs/ NOUN, NO PLURAL
1 being good and kind (bondade)
2 things in food that will make you healthy when you eat it □ *Tomatoes are full of goodness.* (valor nutritivo)
♦ IDIOMS **for goodness' sake** something you say when you are annoyed □ *For goodness sake, Dave, just open the door!* (pelo amor de Deus) **Goodness (me)!** something you say when you are surprised □ *Goodness me, it's five o'clock already.* (minha nossa!) **goodness (only) knows** used for emphasizing that you do not know something □ *Goodness knows how long it will take us to get there.* (só Deus sabe)

good night /gʊd ˈnaɪt/ EXCLAMATION
1 something you say to someone just before you go to sleep at night □ *Good night, Mum.* (boa noite) 🔁 *He's upstairs saying good night to the children.* (dando boa noite)
2 a formal way of saying 'goodbye' to people late in the evening □ *Good night. Thanks for coming.* (boa noite)

goods /gʊdz/ PLURAL NOUN things that have been made to sell □ *electrical goods* □ *cars, jewellery and other luxury goods* (artigos) 🔁 *Sales of household goods have fallen.* (artigos para casa)

goodwill /gʊdˈwɪl/ NOUN, NO PLURAL good feelings towards someone, especially kindness and wanting to help (boa vontade) 🔁 *As a gesture of goodwill he offered to pay for my coat which he'd ruined.* (gesto de boa vontade)

got

gooey /ˈguːɪ/ ADJECTIVE [gooier, gooiest] an informal word meaning soft and sticky □ *a lovely gooey chocolate cake* (grudento)

google /ˈguːgəl/ VERB [googles, googling, googled] to look for something on the Internet using the Google (trademark) search engine (= program which looks for words that you have typed). A computing word. □ *I googled the company and found out all about them.* (fazer busca no Google)

goose /guːs/ NOUN [plural **geese**] a large white or grey bird (ganso)

gooseberry /ˈgʊzbəri/ NOUN [plural **gooseberries**] a small round green fruit which is sour (groselha-espinhosa)

goosebumps /ˈguːsbʌmps/ or **goosepimples** /ˈguːsˌpɪmpəlz/ PLURAL NOUN very small lumps on your skin that you get when you are cold (pele arrepiada)

gore /gɔː(r)/ ▶ NOUN, NO PLURAL lots of blood □ *The film contains a lot of gore.* (sangue)
▶ VERB [gores, goring, gored] if an animal gores someone, it injures them with its horns (chifrar)

gorge /gɔːdʒ/ NOUN [plural **gorges**] a deep narrow valley (garganta)
♦ PHRASAL VERB [gorges, gorging, gorged] **gorge (yourself) on something** to eat too much of something □ *They gorged themselves on chocolate cake.* (fartar-se com algo)

gorgeous /ˈgɔːdʒəs/ ADJECTIVE very beautiful or pleasant □ *The baby's absolutely gorgeous.* □ *gorgeous weather* (muito bonito, agradável)

gorilla /gəˈrɪlə/ NOUN [plural **gorillas**] an animal that looks like a very large monkey (gorila)

gory /ˈgɔːri/ ADJECTIVE [gorier, goriest] with a lot of blood and often violence □ *a gory film* (sangrento, muito violento)

gosling /ˈgɒzlɪŋ/ NOUN [plural **goslings**] a baby goose (filhote de ganso)

gospel /ˈgɒspəl/ NOUN [plural **gospels**]
1 the gospel the life of Jesus Christ and the things he taught (o evangelho)
2 one of the four parts in the Bible that describe Jesus Christ's life (evangelho)

gossip /ˈgɒsɪp/ ▶ NOUN [plural **gossips**]
1 informal talk about other people, often about their private lives □ *She told me all the latest gossip.* □ *Tim loves a good gossip.* (fofoca)
2 someone who enjoys talking about other people's lives, in a way that you disapprove of (fofoqueiro)
▶ VERB [gossips, gossiping, gossiped] to talk about other people, often about their private lives (mexericar, fofocar)

got /gɒt/ PAST TENSE AND PAST PARTICIPLE OF **get** (ver get)

▶ In North America the past participle of 'get' is **gotten** and not 'got'. □ *She'd gotten mad at him.*

gouge /gaʊdʒ/ VERB [**gouges, gouging, gouged**] to make a deep hole or cut in something □ *The explosion had gouged a huge hole in the ground.* (furar)

♦ PHRASAL VERB **gouge something out** to remove something by digging or cutting it out of something □ *Be careful, you almost gouged my eye out with that pen!* (arrancar algo)

gourmet /ˈɡʊəmeɪ/ ▶ ADJECTIVE involving very good food □ *a gourmet meal* □ *a gourmet restaurant* (gourmet)

▶ NOUN [*plural* **gourmets**] someone who likes good food (conhecedor de gastronomia, gourmet)

govern /ˈɡʌvən/ VERB [**governs, governing, governed**]

1 to officially control a country or area □ *The country was governed by the Republicans.* □ *the governing party* (governar)

2 to control the way that something happens or is done □ *The gene governs cell division.* □ *There are laws governing the disposal of toxic waste.* (dirigir)

• **governess** /ˈɡʌvənɪs/ NOUN [*plural* **governesses**] a woman who taught children in their home in the past (governanta)

• **government** /ˈɡʌvənmənt/ NOUN [*plural* **governments**]

1 the group of people who control a country or area (governo) ▣ *The party will form the next government.* (formar governo) □ *The government has announced an increase in taxes.* ▣ *government officials* (oficiais do governo) ▣ *a government department* (departamento do governo) ▣ *He criticized government policies.* (políticas de governo)

2 *no plural* the process or way of controlling a country or area □ *We need a new style of government.* (governo)

3 in government controlling a country □ *The Labour Party has been in government for more than ten years.* (no governo)

• **governor** /ˈɡʌvənə(r)/ NOUN [*plural* **governors**] someone who is in charge of a place or organization □ *the governor of Arkansas* □ *a school governor* (governador)

gown /ɡaʊn/ NOUN [*plural* **gowns**]

1 a long formal dress that women wear on special occasions (vestido longo)

2 a loose piece of clothing worn in hospital □ *a hospital gown* (avental)

GP /ˌdʒiːˈpiː/ ABBREVIATION **general practitioner**; a doctor who looks after people from a particular area and treats them for a lot of different illnesses (abreviação de clínico geral)

grab /ɡræb/ VERB [**grabs, grabbing, grabbed**]

1 to take something suddenly or violently □ *He grabbed my bag and ran away.* □ *She grabbed my arm as I fell.* (agarrar)

2 grab someone's attention to get someone's attention □ *It was his unusual tie which grabbed my attention.* (chamar a atenção de alguém)

3 an informal word meaning to get some food or sleep quickly because you are busy □ *Let's stop and grab a sandwich.* (pegar)

4 if you grab a chance or opportunity, you take it in an eager way (agarrar) ▣ *Tom grabbed the chance to join the team.* (agarrou a oportunidade)

grace /ɡreɪs/ ▶ NOUN, NO PLURAL

1 a smooth and attractive way of moving □ *He kicks the ball with effortless grace.* (graça, elegância)

2 polite and pleasant behaviour □ *She dealt with the situation with grace and humour.* (graça)

3 with good grace in a willing way, and without complaining □ *Ben accepted the decision with good grace.* (de boa vontade)

4 a prayer that some people say before a meal □ *Dad said grace.* (prece)

▶ VERB [**graces, gracing, graced**] to be somewhere and make it more attractive □ *Her photo has graced the cover of many magazines.* (enfeitar)

• **graceful** /ˈɡreɪsfʊl/ ADJECTIVE

1 smooth and attractive in shape or in the way you move □ *He watched her graceful movements.* □ *the graceful curve of the dome* (gracioso)

2 polite and pleasant (delicado)

• **gracefully** /ˈɡreɪsfʊli/ ADVERB in a graceful way (graciosamente)

gracious /ˈɡreɪʃəs/ ADJECTIVE polite and kind □ *It was very gracious of you to apologize.* (delicado, cortês)

grade /ɡreɪd/ ▶ NOUN [*plural* **grades**]

1 a number or letter that shows how good a student's work is (nota) ▣ *She got a grade A in her English exam.* (obteve nota) ▣ *He achieved top grades in his exams.* (notas altas)

2 a level of quality or importance □ *The jewellery is made from a lower grade of gold.* □ *He had been promoted to a higher grade at work.* (categoria)

3 the US word for **form** (= school class) (série, ano escolar)

4 make the grade to be successful, or to achieve the necessary standard □ *She was a singer who failed to make the grade.* (atingir a média)

▶ VERB [**grades, grading, graded**]

1 to separate things into groups of similar size or quality □ *Hotels are graded according to the facilities they offer and their cleanliness.* □ *a grading system* (classificar)

2 to judge the quality of a student's work by giving it a particular letter or number □ *Students' work is graded from A–E.* (dar nota)

gradient /ˈɡreɪdiənt/ NOUN [*plural* **gradients**] a measure of how steep a slope is (gradiente)

gradual /ˈɡrædʒuəl/ ADJECTIVE happening slowly over a long period □ *There has been a gradual improvement in his work.* □ *Recovery will be a very gradual process.* (**gradual**)
- **gradually** /ˈɡrædʒuəlɪ/ ADVERB slowly over a long period □ *His health has gradually improved.* □ *Gradually, her life began to return to normal.* (**gradualmente**)

graduate ▶ NOUN /ˈɡrædʒuət/ [*plural* **graduates**] someone who has a degree (= qualification) from a university or college □ *George is a graduate of Edinburgh University.* (**graduado, diplomado**)
▶ VERB /ˈɡrædʒueɪt/ [**graduates, graduating, graduated**] to get a degree (= qualification) from a university or college (**graduar**)
- **graduation** /ˌɡrædʒuˈeɪʃən/ NOUN, NO PLURAL when you finish a university course and get a degree (= qualification) □ *a graduation ceremony* (**graduação**)

graffiti /ɡrəˈfiːtɪ/ NOUN, NO PLURAL writing or pictures which people have written or drawn illegally on walls, trains, etc. (**grafite, pichação**)

graft /ɡrɑːft/ ▶ VERB [**grafts, grafting, grafted**] to take something such as skin or bone from a healthy part of someone's body and use it to repair a damaged part □ *He had skin grafted from his leg onto his arm.* (**enxertar**)
▶ NOUN [*plural* **grafts**] a piece of skin or bone taken from a healthy part of someone's body and used to repair a damaged part (**enxerto**) 🔁 *The burns were so bad that she needed a skin graft.* (**enxerto de pele**)

grain /ɡreɪn/ NOUN [*plural* **grains**]
1 *no plural* the seeds of crops such as wheat or rice □ *They export grain to Russia.* (**grão**)
2 a seed from a crop such as wheat or rice □ + *of a grain of rice* (**grão**)
3 one of the very small pieces of something such as sugar, salt, etc. □ + *of grains of sand* (**grão**)
4 the pattern of lines on the surface of wood (**veio, fibra**)

gram /ɡræm/ NOUN [*plural* **grams**] a unit for measuring weight, equal to one thousandth of a kilogram. This is often written **g**. (**grama**)

grammar /ˈɡræmə(r)/ NOUN [*plural* **grammars**]
1 *no plural* the rules of a particular language, for example how words are formed and how words are put together in a sentence □ *French grammar*
2 a book of grammar rules (**gramática**)

grammar school /ˈɡræmə(r) ˌskuːl/ NOUN [*plural* **grammar schools**] in Britain, a school for children from 11–18 who have passed a special exam (**escola de ensino fundamental**)

grammatical /ɡrəˈmætɪkəl/ ADJECTIVE
1 to do with grammar □ *grammatical rules* □ *a grammatical error* (**gramatical**)
2 correct according to the rules of grammar □ *That sentence isn't grammatical, is it?* (**gramaticalmente correto**)
- **grammatically** /ɡrəˈmætɪkəlɪ/ ADVERB according to the rules of grammar (**gramaticalmente**) 🔁 *Is that grammatically correct?* (**gramaticalmente correto**)

gramme /ɡræm/ NOUN [*plural* **grammes**] another spelling of **gram** (**grama**)

gran /ɡræn/ NOUN [*plural* **grans**] an informal word for grandmother (**vovó**)

grand /ɡrænd/ ADJECTIVE [**grander, grandest**] very large, expensive or special, making you feel admiration □ *The house itself was very grand.* (**grandioso**)

grandad /ˈɡrændæd/ NOUN [*plural* **grandads**] an informal word for grandfather (**vovô**)

grandchild /ˈɡrændtʃaɪld/ NOUN [*plural* **grandchildren**] a child of your son or daughter □ *We've got three grown-up children and five grandchildren.* (**neto**)

granddaughter /ˈɡrændɔːtə(r)/ NOUN [*plural* **granddaughters**] the daughter of your son or daughter (**neta**)

grandfather /ˈɡrændfɑːðə(r)/ NOUN [*plural* **grandfathers**] the father of your mother or father (**avô**) 🔁 *my paternal grandfather* (= father's father) (**avô paterno**) 🔁 *my maternal grandfather* (= mother's father) (**avô materno**) □ *He recently became a grandfather.* (**avô**)

grandly /ˈɡrændlɪ/ ADVERB in a way that looks or sounds important, or tries to do this □ *'I'm the senior consultant,'* he said rather grandly. (**grandiosamente**)

grandma /ˈɡrænmɑː/ NOUN [*plural* **grandmas**] an informal word for grandmother □ *At the weekend I usually visit my grandma.* (**vovó**)

grandmother /ˈɡrænmʌðə(r)/ NOUN [*plural* **grandmothers**] the mother of your mother or father (**avó**) 🔁 *my maternal grandmother* (= mother's mother) (**avó materna**) 🔁 *my paternal grandmother* (= father's mother) (**avó paterna**) □ *We called in to see my grandmother.* (**avó**)

grandpa /ˈɡrænpɑː/ NOUN [*plural* **grandpas**] an informal word for grandfather □ *My grandpa loved singing.* (**vovô**)

grandparent /ˈɡrænpeərənt/ NOUN [*plural* **grandparents**] a parent of your father or your mother □ *I went to stay with my elderly grandparents.* (**avô ou avó**)

grandson /ˈɡrænsʌn/ NOUN [*plural* **grandsons**] the son of your son or daughter (**neto ou neta**)

grandstand /ˈɡrændstænd/ NOUN [*plural* **grandstands**] a large structure for people watching a sports event with rows of seats (**tribuna**)

granite /ˈɡrænɪt/ NOUN, NO PLURAL a very hard grey or red rock (**granito**)

granny /ˈɡrænɪ/ NOUN [plural **grannies**] an informal word for grandmother (**vovó**)

grant /ɡrɑːnt/ ▶ VERB [**grants, granting, granted**]
1 to officially allow someone to have or to do something they have asked for (**conceder**) ◻ *The judge granted him permission to appeal.* (**deu-lhe permissão**) ◻ *His request was granted.*
2 take something/someone for granted to expect something or someone to be there as usual and to forget that you are lucky to have them ◻ *We take our health for granted.* (**não dar valor a algo/alguém**)
3 take something for granted to expect something to happen without checking or thinking much about it ◻ *You can't take anything for granted.* (**dar por certo**) ◻ *She took it for granted that I would agree.* (**deu por certo**)
4 a formal word meaning to admit that something is true ◻ *It's very difficult, I grant you.* (**admitir**)
▶ NOUN [plural **grants**] an amount of money that has been given to you for a special purpose (**subvenção**) ◻ *The college received a grant of £20,000 to improve computer facilities.* (**recebeu uma subvenção**) ◻ *She applied for a research grant.*

granule /ˈɡrænjuːl/ NOUN [plural **granules**] a very small grain or part ◻ *sugar granules* (**grânulo**)

grape /ɡreɪp/ NOUN [plural **grapes**] a small, pale green or dark red fruit that grows in groups and is used to make wine (**uva**) ◻ *a bunch of grapes* (**cacho de uvas**)

grapefruit /ˈɡreɪpfruːt/ NOUN [plural **grapefruit** or **grapefruits**] a round fruit with thick yellow skin and yellow or pink flesh and a sour taste (**toranja**)

grapevine /ˈɡreɪpvaɪn/ NOUN [plural **grapevines**]
1 a plant that grapes grow on (**videira**)
2 the grapevine an informal word used to talk about how information spreads quickly in conversations between people (**boato**) ◻ *I heard on the grapevine that she's planning to leave.* (**ouvi boatos**)

graph /ɡrɑːf/ NOUN [plural **graphs**] a picture with lines drawn between different points, used to show how things compare to each other or how something changes (**gráfico**)

graphic /ˈɡræfɪk/ ADJECTIVE
1 showing or giving a lot of detail, often in a way which is shocking (**vívido**) ◻ *He went into graphic detail about the operation.* (**detalhes vívidos**) ◻ *a graphic description of the attack*
2 to do with drawing, painting or text and its design (**gráfico**) ◻ *graphic design* (**projeto gráfico**)
• **graphically** /ˈɡræfɪkəli/ ADVERB including a lot of detail, so very clear and sometimes shocking ◻ *The film graphically demonstrates the horrors of war.* (**graficamente**)
• **graphics** /ˈɡræfɪks/ PLURAL NOUN pictures, drawings and text, especially those on a computer screen ◻ *The game has very realistic graphics.* (**imagens gráficas**)

graphics card /ˈɡræfɪks ˌkɑːd/ NOUN [plural **graphics cards**] a part inside a computer that allows the computer to show pictures and video. A computing word. (**unidade de processamento gráfico**)

graphite /ˈɡræfaɪt/ NOUN, NO PLURAL a black soft form of the mineral carbon, used in pencils (**grafite**)

graph paper /ˈɡrɑːf ˌpeɪpə(r)/ NOUN, NO PLURAL paper covered in very small squares (**papel quadriculado**)

grapple /ˈɡræpəl/ VERB [**grapples, grappling, grappled**] to hold someone and fight with them ◻ *The bodyguard tried to grapple him to the floor.* (**lutar**)
♦ PHRASAL VERB **grapple with something** to try hard to understand or to deal with something difficult (**atracar-se com alguém**)

grasp /ɡrɑːsp/ ▶ VERB [**grasps, grasping, grasped**]
1 to take hold of something tightly ◻ *She saw the dog and grasped my hand.* ◻ *He grasped the rope and began to climb.* (**agarrar**)
2 to understand an idea ◻ *I still couldn't grasp what he was trying to tell me* (**compreender**) ◻ *It might be difficult for children to grasp this concept.* (**compreender este conceito**)
3 to take advantage of an opportunity (**aproveitar**) ◻ *She grasped the opportunity to speak to Dr. Williams alone.* (**aproveitou a oportunidade**)
♦ IDIOM **grasp the nettle** to deal directly with something difficult or unpleasant ◻ *We've got to grasp the nettle and get rid of polluting cars.* (**encarar o problema**)
▶ NOUN, NO PLURAL
1 when you understand or know about something ◻ *He has a fairly good grasp of the language.* ◻ *I have to get a grasp on what's happening here.* (**conhecimento**)
2 when you take hold of something firmly ◻ *He held her wrist in a firm grasp.* (**controle**)
3 the ability to achieve something ◻ *A deal was within our grasp.* (**alcance**)

grass /ɡrɑːs/ NOUN, NO PLURAL a plant with very thin green leaves which covers gardens and fields ◻ *I cut the grass at the weekend.* (**capim, grama**) ◻ *a blade of grass* (= one leaf) (**capim**)
♦ IDIOM **the grass is (always) greener on the other side** the situation somewhere else or for someone else always seems better than your own (**o jardim do vizinho é sempre mais verde**)

grasshopper /ˈɡrɑːsˌhɒpə(r)/ NOUN [plural **grasshoppers**] a brown or green insect with long back legs that can jump (**gafanhoto**)

grass roots /ˌgrɑːs ˈruːts/ PLURAL NOUN the ordinary people in a society or organization, not its leaders □ *He's lost touch with the grass roots of the party.* (bases)

grassy /ˈgrɑːsɪ/ ADJECTIVE [grassier, grassiest] covered with grass □ *a grassy field* (gramado)

grate¹ /greɪt/ VERB [grates, grating, grated]
1 to cut food into small, thin pieces by rubbing it against a grater (= kitchen tool) □ *grated cheese* (ralar)
2 to make an unpleasant noise by rubbing against something □ *The two surfaces grated against each other.* (ranger)
3 to annoy someone □ *His attitude has started to grate.* (irritar)

grate² /greɪt/ NOUN [plural grates] a frame of metal bars which holds the wood, coal, etc. in a fireplace (= space for a fire in the wall of a room) (grelha)

grateful /ˈgreɪtfʊl/ ADJECTIVE pleased with someone and wanting to thank them because they have done something for you □ + *for I'm very grateful for all your kindness.* □ + *to I felt so grateful to him for stopping to help.* □ *She gave me a grateful smile.* (grato)

• **gratefully** /ˈgreɪtfʊlɪ/ ADVERB in a grateful way □ *We gratefully accepted the offer.* (com gratidão)

grater /ˈgreɪtə(r)/ NOUN [plural graters] a kitchen tool with a lot of small holes with sharp edges on its surface, used for cutting food into small bits (ralador)

grating /ˈgreɪtɪŋ/ NOUN [plural gratings] a cover for something with holes in it so that water or air can pass through (rede)

gratitude /ˈgrætɪtjuːd/ NOUN, NO PLURAL a feeling of being grateful to someone □ *She expressed her gratitude to the hospital* (gratidão) 🔊 *I owe a debt of gratitude to my parents for their support.*

grave¹ /greɪv/ NOUN [plural graves] a place where a dead body is buried (túmulo)

grave² /greɪv/ ADJECTIVE [graver, gravest]
1 very serious □ *a grave mistake* (grave, sério) 🔊 *You are in grave danger.* (grave perigo) 🔊 *He expressed grave concern about the situation.* (séria preocupação)
2 looking serious □ *She looked grave for a moment.* (sério, preocupado)

gravel /ˈgrævəl/ NOUN, NO PLURAL small stones used to cover roads, paths, etc. (cascalho)

gravestone /ˈgreɪvstəʊn/ NOUN [plural gravestones] a piece of stone with writing on it which says who is buried in a grave (lápide)

graveyard /ˈgreɪvjɑːd/ NOUN [plural graveyards] a place where dead bodies are buried (cemitério)

gravitate /ˈgrævɪteɪt/ VERB [gravitates, gravitating, gravitated] to be attracted to someone or something, or to gradually move towards something □ *People tend to gravitate towards her at a party because she's such good fun.* (gravitar)

gravity /ˈgrævətɪ/ NOUN, NO PLURAL
1 the force that pulls things towards the earth and makes them fall to the ground (gravidade)
2 a formal word meaning how serious something is □ *We appreciate the gravity of the situation.* (gravidade)

gravy /ˈgreɪvɪ/ NOUN, NO PLURAL a hot sauce made from the juices that come out of meat while it is cooking (molho)

gray /greɪ/ ADJECTIVE, NOUN [plural grays] the US spelling of **grey** (cinza)

graze /greɪz/ ▶ VERB [grazes, grazing, grazed]
1 if animals graze, they move around eating grass and other plants (pastar)
2 to hurt your skin by rubbing it against something hard and rough □ *I fell and grazed my knees.* (esfolar)
3 to touch the surface of something lightly □ *His hand grazed mine as he held the door open.* (roçar)
▶ NOUN [plural grazes] a mark on your skin where it has been grazed (arranhão)

grease /griːs/ ▶ NOUN, NO PLURAL
1 a substance such as fat or thick oil □ *a grease stain* (gordura)
2 a substance like thick oil used to make parts of machines move smoothly (graxa lubrificante)
▶ VERB [greases, greasing, greased] to rub grease on something □ *Grease the pan well.* (engraxar, lubrificar)

• **greasy** /ˈgriːsɪ/ ADJECTIVE [greasier, greasiest]
1 covered in or containing grease □ *greasy food* □ *He wiped his greasy fingers on his jeans.* (engordurado)
2 containing a lot of natural oil □ *greasy hair* (gorduroso, ensebado)

great /greɪt/ ADJECTIVE [greater, greatest]
1 very good □ *This is a great opportunity for you to travel.* □ *Our builders have done a great job.* □ *Your hair looks great like that.* □ *I've had a great idea!* (grande)
2 very large in size, amount or level □ *The elephant lifted one of its great feet.* (grande) 🔊 *We had a great deal of* (= a lot of) *trouble getting the information we needed.* (grande quantidade de) 🔊 *His dinner party was a great success.* (grande sucesso) □ *They were in great danger.*
3 very good and skilled □ *He was one of the greatest scientists of all time.* □ *She's a great player.* (grande)
4 important and powerful □ *great armies* □ *a great nation* (grande, magnífico)
5 a slightly informal word meaning very enjoyable □ *It was a great film.* □ *We had a great time in Venice.* (ótimo)
6 a slightly informal way of expressing pleasure or agreement □ *'We'll meet you at seven.' 'Great – see you then!'* (ótimo)

Great Britain /ˌgreɪt ˈbrɪtən/ NOUN England, Scotland and Wales (Grã-Bretanha)

great-grandchild /ˌgreɪtˈgrændtʃaɪld/ NOUN [plural **great-grandchildren**] your grandson's or granddaughter's child (**bisneto, bisneta**)

great-granddaughter /ˌgreɪtˈgrændɔːtə(r)/ NOUN [plural **great-granddaughters**] your grandson's or granddaughter's daughter (**bisneta**)

great-grandfather /ˌgreɪtˈgrændfɑːðə(r)/ NOUN [plural **great-grandfathers**] your grandmother's or grandfather's father (**bisavô**)

great-grandmother /ˌgreɪtˈgrænmʌðə(r)/ NOUN [plural **great-grandmothers**] your grandmother's or grandfather's mother (**bisavó**)

great-grandparent /ˌgreɪtˈgrænpeərənt/ NOUN [plural **great-grandparents**] a parent of your grandmother or grandfather (**bisavô ou bisavó**)

great-grandson /ˌgreɪtˈgrænsʌn/ NOUN [plural **great-grandsons**] your grandson's or granddaughter's son (**bisneto**)

greatly /ˈgreɪtlɪ/ ADVERB very much □ The effects can vary greatly. □ I greatly admire what he's done. □ Your help is greatly appreciated. □ Smoking greatly increases your risk of developing cancer. (**muito**)

greatness /ˈgreɪtnɪs/ NOUN, NO PLURAL when someone is very important, respected or skilled □ He has achieved greatness as a player. (**grandeza**)

greed /griːd/ NOUN, NO PLURAL when you want more of something than you need, especially food or money □ Big businesses are often accused of greed and selfishness. (**ganância, gula**)

• **greedily** /ˈgriːdɪlɪ/ ADVERB in a greedy way (**gananciosamente**)

• **greediness** /ˈgriːdɪnɪs/ NOUN, NO PLURAL the quality of being greedy (**cobiça**)

• **greedy** /ˈgriːdɪ/ ADJECTIVE [**greedier, greediest**] wanting more of something than you need □ You greedy pig! You've eaten it all. (**guloso**)

green /griːn/ ▶ ADJECTIVE

1 having the colour of leaves or grass □ He's wearing a green coat. □ The curtains were dark green. (**verde**)

2 to do with protecting the environment □ She's involved in green politics. □ We're trying to be green by cycling to work. (**ecológico, ecologicamente correto**)

3 green spaces places with grass and plants (**espaços verdes**)

▶ NOUN [plural **greens**]

1 the colour of leaves and grass (**verde**)

2 an area of short grass on a golf course (**gramado**)

green belt /ˈgriːn ˌbelt/ NOUN, NO PLURAL an area of green fields around a city where you are not allowed to build (**cinturão verde**)

greenery /ˈgriːnərɪ/ NOUN, NO PLURAL plants with green leaves (**folhagem**)

green fingers /ˌgriːn ˈfɪŋɡəz/ PLURAL NOUN someone who has green fingers is good at making plants grow (**dedos verdes**)

greengrocer /ˈgriːnˌgrəʊsə(r)/ NOUN [plural greengrocers]

1 someone who sells fruit and vegetables (**verdureiro, quitandeiro**)

2 greengrocer's a shop selling fruit and vegetables (**quitanda**)

greenhouse /ˈgriːnhaʊs/ NOUN [plural **greenhouses**] a building with glass walls and a glass roof that stays warm and is used for growing plants in (**estufa**)

greenhouse effect /ˈgriːnhaʊs ɪˌfekt/ NOUN, NO PLURAL the heating of the Earth's surface caused by pollution which stops heat from leaving the atmosphere (**efeito estufa**)

greenhouse gas /ˈgriːnhaʊs ˌgæs/ NOUN [plural **greenhouse gases**] a gas that stops heat from leaving the atmosphere, causing the temperature of Earth to increase □ Greenhouse gases include carbon dioxide and methane. (**gás de estufa, um dos tipos de gases considerados como os causadores do aquecimento global**)

greens /griːnz/ PLURAL NOUN green vegetables such as cabbage □ Be sure to eat all your greens. (**verduras**)

greet /griːt/ VERB [greets, greeting, greeted]

1 to say something to someone when they arrive or when you meet them □ She went outside to greet her visitors. □ He was greeted by a crowd of fans at the airport. (**cumprimentar, saudar**)

2 to react to something in a particular way □ + **with** The announcement was greeted with enthusiasm. (**acolher, receber**)

• **greeting** /ˈgriːtɪŋ/ NOUN [plural **greetings**] something polite or friendly that you say when you meet someone or send a message to someone □ They exchanged friendly greetings. □ John sends his warmest greetings. (**cumprimentos, saudações**)

grenade /grəˈneɪd/ NOUN [plural **grenades**] a small bomb that explodes a few seconds after someone throws it (**granada**)

grew /gruː/ PAST TENSE OF **grow** (**ver grow**)

grey /greɪ/ ▶ ADJECTIVE

1 having the colour you get when you mix black and white □ The sheets were grey with dirt. (**cinza, cinzento**)

2 grey hair has become grey or white as someone gets older (**grisalho**) 🔁 At what age did you go grey? (**ficou grisalho**)

3 if the weather is grey, there are lots of clouds and it seems as though it will rain (**nublado**)

♦ IDIOM **a grey area** a subject or situation which people are not sure about because there are no clear rules □ We are not allowed to accept money, but other gifts are a bit of a grey area. (**área sombria**)

▶ NOUN [plural **greys**] the colour that you get when you mix black and white (**cinza**)

greyhound — grindstone

greyhound /'greɪhaʊnd/ NOUN [plural **greyhounds**] a type of dog with a thin body and narrow head which can run very fast (**galgo**)

grid /grɪd/ NOUN [plural **grids**]
1 a pattern of lines that cross each other to form squares (**grade**)
2 a system of wires which carry electricity to a large area □ *the Australian electricity grid* (**rede**)
3 a map with a set of numbered lines to help you find places (**linhas coordenadas**)
4 metal bars that cross each other to form squares (**grade**)

grid reference /'grɪd ˌrefrəns/ NOUN [plural **grid references**] a set of numbers or letters used to show a place on a map (**coordenada**)

grief /griːf/ NOUN, NO PLURAL a feeling of great sadness, especially when someone has died □ *He expressed his grief at his baby daughter's death.* □ *His death prompted an outpouring of grief.* (**pesar**)
♦ IDIOM **come to grief** to fail or to have an accident □ *Drivers often come to grief on the mountain roads.* (**sofrer um acidente, fracassar**)

grievance /'griːvəns/ NOUN [plural **grievances**] something you complain about because you think it is wrong or unfair (**queixa**) ▣ *People will get a chance to air their grievances (= say what is making them angry) at the meeting.* (**expor suas queixas**)

grieve /griːv/ VERB [**grieves, grieving, grieved**] to feel very sad, especially because someone has died □ *She was still grieving for her dead son.* (**estar de luto**)

grievous /'griːvəs/ ADJECTIVE a formal word meaning very serious □ *He suffered grievous injuries.* □ *a grievous error* (**sério, doloroso**)
• **grievously** /'griːvəsli/ ADVERB in a very serious way □ *He was grievously wounded.* (**seriamente**)

grill /grɪl/ ▶ VERB [**grills, grilling, grilled**]
1 to cook food by putting it close to direct heat □ *Grill the fish for a couple of minutes on each side.* (**grelhar**)
2 to ask someone a lot of questions □ *Detectives grilled him about his recent movements.* (**interrogar**)
▶ NOUN [plural **grills**]
1 a piece of kitchen equipment which cooks food under a direct heat (**grelha**)
2 metal bars which food can be cooked on over a fire (**grelha**)

grille /grɪl/ NOUN [plural **grilles**] a cover for a door, window, etc. made of wire or metal bars (**grade**)

grilling /'grɪlɪŋ/ NOUN [plural **grillings**] when someone asks you a lot of difficult questions □ *The minister faced a grilling by journalists about the new plans.* (**interrogatório**)

grim /grɪm/ ADJECTIVE [**grimmer, grimmest**]
1 very unpleasant, worrying or shocking □ *The situation looked pretty grim.* (**sinistro**) ▣ *The pictures illustrate the grim reality of life in the refugee camps.* (**realidade sinistra**)
2 serious and unfriendly □ *The men wore grim expressions.* (**carrancudo**)

grimace /'grɪmɪs/ ▶ VERB [**grimaces, grimacing, grimaced**] to twist your face into an expression of pain, dislike, etc. □ *She tried to get up and grimaced in pain.* □ *He grimaced at the memory.* (**fazer caretas**)
▶ NOUN [plural **grimaces**] when you grimace (**careta**)

grime /graɪm/ NOUN, NO PLURAL dirt that has been on a surface for a long time □ *He wiped away a thick layer of grime.* (**sujeira**)

grimly /'grɪmli/ ADVERB
1 in a serious, unfriendly way □ *He nodded grimly.* (**severamente**)
2 showing determination □ *In the second half, the team hung on grimly.* (**inflexivelmente**)

grimy /'graɪmi/ ADJECTIVE [**grimier, grimiest**] covered with dirt □ *a grimy window* (**encardido**)

grin /grɪn/ ▶ VERB [**grins, grinning, grinned**] to give a big smile □ *Ben was grinning broadly as he came out.* (**dar um grande sorriso**)
♦ IDIOM **grin and bear it** to accept a difficult situation without complaining □ *You'll just have to grin and bear it.* (**aguentar firme**)
▶ NOUN [plural **grins**] a big smile □ *His face broke into a broad grin.*

grind /graɪnd/ ▶ VERB [**grinds, grinding, ground**]
1 to crush something solid into a powder □ *ground pepper* □ *The rocks are ground into dust.* (**moer, triturar**)
2 grind your teeth to make a noise when you rub your teeth together (**ranger os dentes**)
3 grind to a halt to gradually become slower and stop moving or working □ *The traffic ground to a halt.* (**parar aos poucos**)
4 to make something smooth or sharp by rubbing it against a hard surface (**afiar**)
♦ PHRASAL VERB **grind someone down** to make someone lose their confidence and energy □ *He was ground down by weeks of illness.* (**ficar abatido**)
▶ NOUN, NO PLURAL something that is difficult and boring to do (**rotina**) ▣ *the daily grind of work* (**rotina diária**)
• **grinder** /'graɪndə(r)/ NOUN [plural **grinders**] a machine that grinds things such as coffee beans (**moedor**)
• **grinding** /'graɪndɪŋ/ ADJECTIVE
1 used to emphasize that something is very bad and continues without stopping (**opressivo**) ▣ *These people live in grinding poverty.* (**pobreza opressiva**)
2 a grinding halt when something stops moving or working completely □ *The whole city came to a grinding halt.* (**paralisação gradual**)

grindstone /'graɪndstəʊn/ NOUN [plural **grindstones**] a circular stone that turns on top of another stone and is used to grind corn (**pedra de amolar**)

♦ IDIOM **have/keep your nose to the grindstone** to be working very hard, especially for a long time ◻ *He kept his nose to the grindstone.* (enfiar o nariz no trabalho)

grip /ɡrɪp/ ▶ VERB [grips, gripping, gripped]
1 to hold something tightly ◻ *Martha gripped his arm.* ◻ *I gripped the steering wheel tighter.* (segurar)
2 to hold your attention completely ◻ *The story has gripped the public imagination.* (absorver)
3 to feel an emotion very strongly and suddenly ◻ *Panic gripped him suddenly.* ◻ *The small community was gripped by fear.* (dominar)
▶ NOUN [plural **grips**]
1 when someone holds something tightly (aperto) 🔼 *He tightened his grip on her shoulder.* (apertou com força)
2 control over something (controle) 🔼 *He has further tightened his grip on power.* (firmou seu controle) ◻ *They have a firm grip on the market.*
3 in the grip of something in a difficult situation ◻ *The south is in the grip of a severe drought.* (em situação difícil)
4 get a grip (on something) to try to control your emotions ◻ *You need to calm down and get a grip.* (controlar suas emoções)
5 a small U-shaped piece of wire used to keep hair in place (grampo)
♦ IDIOM **come/get to grips with something** to understand and to start to deal with something ◻ *I had to get to grips with the fact that I couldn't walk.* (lidar com algo)
• **gripping** /ˈɡrɪpɪŋ/ ADJECTIVE holding your attention completely ◻ *a gripping film* (fascinante)

grisly /ˈɡrɪzli/ ADJECTIVE unpleasant and frightening, often involving blood or death ◻ *a grisly story* (apavorante)

gristle /ˈɡrɪsəl/ NOUN, NO PLURAL a hard substance that is sometimes found in meat (cartilagem)
• **gristly** /ˈɡrɪsli/ ADJECTIVE containing pieces of gristle (cartilaginoso)

grit /ɡrɪt/ ▶ NOUN, NO PLURAL
1 very small sharp pieces of stone or sand ◻ *He brushed the grit off his trousers.* (areia)
2 bravery and determination ◻ *She showed true grit to hang on and win the second set.* (coragem, determinação)
▶ VERB [grits, gritting, gritted] to put grit onto a road to stop vehicles sliding on ice (cobrir uma estrada com areia)
♦ IDIOM **grit your teeth**
1 to hold your teeth tightly together, for example when you are angry or in pain ◻ *She gritted her teeth against the pain.* ◻ *He replied through gritted teeth.* (cerrar os dentes)
2 to show bravery and determination ◻ *I gritted my teeth and plunged into the water.* (tomar coragem)

• **gritty** /ˈɡrɪti/ ADJECTIVE [**grittier**, **grittiest**]
1 feeling rough like grit (áspero, arenoso)
2 brave and determined ◻ *He had a gritty determination to succeed.* (corajoso, determinado)
3 showing unpleasant details about life ◻ *a gritty television drama* (áspero)

grizzly /ˈɡrɪzli/ NOUN [plural **grizzlies**] a **grizzly bear** (urso cinzento)

grizzly bear /ˈɡrɪzli ˌbeə(r)/ NOUN [plural **grizzly bears**] a type of large brown bear found in parts of the United States and Canada (urso cinzento)

groan /ɡrəʊn/ ▶ VERB [groans, groaning, groaned]
1 to make a long deep sound to express pain, unhappiness, etc. ◻ *He groaned in pain.* (gemer)
2 to say something in a way that shows you are unhappy ◻ *'Not again!' Matt groaned.* (queixar-se)
3 to make a sound like a groan ◻ *The trees creaked and groaned.* (ranger)
▶ NOUN [plural **groans**]
1 when you groan ◻ *She got slowly to her feet with a groan.* (gemido)
2 a complaint (queixa) 🔼 *There are always a few moans and groans.* (gemidos e queixas)

grocer /ˈɡrəʊsə(r)/ NOUN [plural **grocers**]
1 grocer's a shop selling food and things for the house (mercearia)
2 someone who runs a shop selling food and things for the house (merceeiro)
• **groceries** /ˈɡrəʊsəriz/ PLURAL NOUN food and things for the house that you buy regularly ◻ *a bag of groceries* ◻ *More people now buy their groceries online.* (secos e molhados, comestíveis)
• **grocery** /ˈɡrəʊsəri/ ADJECTIVE to do with groceries or a grocer's ◻ *grocery shopping* ◻ *a grocery list* (relativo a produtos de mercearia)

groggy /ˈɡrɒɡi/ ADJECTIVE [**groggier**, **groggiest**] slightly weak, tired and not able to think clearly ◻ *They were still groggy from their long flight.* (tonto, zonzo)

groin /ɡrɔɪn/ NOUN [plural **groins**] the place where your legs join your body (virilha)

groom /ɡruːm/ ▶ VERB [grooms, grooming, groomed]
1 to look after an animal, especially by brushing its fur ◻ *She groomed and exercised the horses.* (escovar)
2 to prepare someone for a particular position or job ◻ *She's being groomed for an important role.* (preparar)
3 to make yourself look clean and tidy ◻ *He has carefully groomed hair.* (cuidar)
4 when animals groom each other, they clean each other's fur (limpar)
▶ NOUN [plural **grooms**]
1 someone whose job is to look after horses (cavalariço)
2 a bridegroom (= man who is getting married) (noivo)

- **grooming** /ˈgruːmɪŋ/ NOUN, NO PLURAL the things that people do to keep clean and make themselves look good ☐ *They sell men's grooming products.* (**cuidados com a aparência**)

groove /gruːv/ NOUN [*plural* **grooves**] a long narrow line cut into a surface ☐ *Deep grooves had been cut into the stone.* (**ranhura**)

grope /grəʊp/ VERB [**gropes, groping, groped**]
1 to feel with your hand to try to find something you cannot see ☐ *I groped around for my glasses.* ☐ *She groped in her pocket for her ticket.* (**tatear**)
2 to try to think of a word or an answer ☐ *I groped for an answer.* (**procurar**)

gross /grəʊs/ ▶ ADJECTIVE [**grosser, grossest**]
1 a gross amount is the total amount without anything being taken away, especially tax (**bruto**) ◘ *monthly gross income* (**rendimento bruto**)
2 very bad or serious (**grosseiro**) ◘ *He was dismissed for gross misconduct* (= very bad behaviour). (**comportamento grosseiro**) ◘ *His death was a result of gross negligence by his employer.* (**negligência grosseira**)
3 an informal word meaning very unpleasant or offensive ☐ *It tastes pretty gross.* (**grosseiro, vulgar**)
▶ VERB [**grosses, grossing, grossed**] to earn a particular amount of money before tax, etc. is taken away ☐ *The film has grossed £13.5 million.* (**totalizar, atingir**)

- **grossly** /ˈgrəʊsli/ ADVERB to a great level ☐ *The claim is grossly exaggerated.* (**extremamente**)

grotesque /grəʊˈtesk/ ADJECTIVE very ugly or unpleasant ☐ *grotesque masks* (**grotesco**)

- **grotesquely** /grəʊˈteskli/ ADVERB in a grotesque way ☐ *His face was grotesquely distorted.* (**grotescamente**)

grotty /ˈgrɒti/ ADJECTIVE [**grottier, grottiest**] an informal word meaning unpleasant or of bad quality ☐ *He lived in a grotty little apartment.* (**desagradável**)

ground¹ /graʊnd/ ▶ NOUN [*plural* **grounds**]
1 the Earth's surface ☐ *The damaged satellite is expected to fall to the ground next week.* ☐ *These plants thrive on higher ground.* (**solo**)
2 earth or soil ☐ *The ground is frozen.* ☐ *fertile ground* (**solo, terreno**)
3 an area where a particular sport is played ☐ *a football ground* (**campo**)
4 an area of information (**assunto**) ◘ *We have covered a lot of ground in this lesson.* (**preenchemos o assunto**) ◘ *Every time we talk, we go over the same ground* (= talk about the same things). (**voltamos ao mesmo assunto**)
⇨ go to **grounds**

♦ IDIOMS **get (something) off the ground** to start something successfully ☐ *I tried to set up a football club, but it never really got off the ground.* (**iniciar com êxito**) **gain/lose ground** to become more/less popular or successful **stand your ground** to refuse to change your opinion about something (**ceder/perder terreno**)

⇨ go to **suit someone down to the ground**
▶ VERB [**grounds, grounding, grounded**] to stop an aircraft from leaving the ground (**impedir a decolagem**)

ground² /graʊnd/ PAST TENSE AND PAST PARTICIPLE OF **grind** (*ver* **grind**)

grounded /ˈgraʊndɪd/ ADJECTIVE
1 sensible and not too emotional ☐ *She has remained grounded despite her fame.* (**com os pés no chão**)
2 be grounded in/on something to be based on something ☐ *Their work is grounded in street culture.* (**estar aterrado em algo**)

ground floor /ˌgraʊnd ˈflɔː(r)/ NOUN, NO PLURAL the floor of a building at the level of the ground outside ☐ *The electrical department is on the ground floor.* (**andar térreo**)

grounding /ˈgraʊndɪŋ/ NOUN, NO PLURAL knowledge of the basic facts or skills relating to something (**base, fundamento**) ◘ *The job should give her a good grounding in management technique.* (**dar-lhe fundamento**)

grounds /graʊndz/ PLURAL NOUN
1 the area of land that surrounds and belongs to a large house or building ☐ *They attended a party in the grounds of the castle.* (**jardins, terrenos**)
2 reasons for doing something ☐ *There are some grounds for optimism.* ☐ *He had to retire on health grounds.* (**motivos, razões**)

group /gruːp/ ▶ NOUN [*plural* **groups**]
1 a number of people or things that are together or that belong together ☐ **+ of** *There was a small group of people waiting outside.* ☐ *We split the samples into three different groups.* ☐ *Environmental groups have opposed the plans.* (**grupo**)
2 a number of people who perform music together (**grupo, banda**) ◘ *a pop group* (**banda de música pop**)
▶ VERB [**groups, grouping, grouped**] to put people or things together in a group or groups ☐ *The children were grouped according to age.* (**agrupar**)

grouse¹ /graʊs/ NOUN [*plural* **grouse**] a type of fat bird that lives on open land and is hunted for sport (**galo silvestre**)

grouse² /graʊs/ ▶ VERB [**grouses, grousing, groused**] to complain about something ☐ *People always grouse about ticket prices.* (**queixar-se**)
▶ NOUN [*plural* **grouses**] a complaint

grove /grəʊv/ NOUN [*plural* **groves**] a small group of trees growing close together ☐ *an olive grove* (**arvoredo**)

grovel /ˈgrɒvəl/ VERB [**grovels, grovelling**/US **groveling, grovelled**/US **groveled**]
1 to show someone too much respect in order to try to make them like you or forgive you ☐ *I wish he wouldn't grovel to the boss like that.* (**humilhar-se, rebaixar-se**)

2 to move close to the ground on your hands and knees, usually in order to look for something (arrastar-se, rastejar)

grow /grəʊ/ VERB [grows, growing, grew, grown]
1 if a person, animal or plant grows, it becomes bigger or taller □ *He's grown as tall as his father.* □ *The grass has grown a lot this week.* (crescer)
2 if you grow plants, you put seeds in the ground and look after them □ *We grow vegetables in our garden.* □ *organically grown produce* (crescer)
3 if your hair or nails grow, they become longer (crescer)
4 to increase in amount or size □ *The world's population is growing rapidly.* □ *Since he changed schools, his confidence has grown.* (crescer)
5 to become □ *It was growing dark.* □ *The sound grew louder.* (crescer)

◆ PHRASAL VERBS **grow on someone** if something grows on you, you start to like it □ *I must admit that the yellow walls are growing on me.* (tornar--se mais atraente a alguém) **grow out of something 1** if a child grows out of clothes, they become too big for them (crescer a ponto de as roupas ficarem pequenas para alguém) **2** to stop liking or doing something as you become older □ *I used to take a doll to bed, but I grew out of it in the end.* (passar da idade para algo) **grow up 1** to become older or to become an adult (crescer) **2** to stop behaving like a child □ *I wish you'd grow up and take some responsibility!* (crescer) **3** to develop □ *An unpleasant atmosphere grew up in the office.* (desenvolver-se)

• **grower** /'grəʊə(r)/ NOUN [plural growers] someone who grows crops to sell (cultivador)

• **growing** /'grəʊɪŋ/ ADJECTIVE increasing (crescente) 🔲 *Growing grotesque numbers of nurses are leaving their jobs.* (números crescentes) □ *There are growing fears for his safety.*

growl /graʊl/ ▶ VERB [growls, growling, growled]
1 if an animal such as a dog growls, it makes a deep threatening noise in its throat □ *Two black guard dogs growled.* (rosnar)
2 if a person growls, they talk in a deep voice, often because they are angry (resmungar)
▶ NOUN [plural growls] a deep threatening sound □ *The dog let out a low growl.* (rosnado)

grown /grəʊn/ PAST PARTICIPLE OF grow (ver grow)

grown-up /'grəʊnʌp/ ▶ NOUN [plural grown--ups] an adult □ *The grown-ups enjoyed themselves as much as the children.* (adulto)
▶ ADJECTIVE adult □ *We have three grown-up children.* (adulto)

growth /grəʊθ/ NOUN [plural growths]
1 no plural when something **grows**, develops or gets bigger □ + **of** *the rapid growth of computer technology* □ + **in** *The company reported a growth in sales.* □ *economic growth* □ *Warmth brings about growth in the garden.* (crescimento)
2 a lump that grows on the body □ *A growth developed on his hand.* (tumor)

grub /grʌb/ NOUN [plural grubs]
1 a form of an insect with a soft body because it has just come out of an egg (larva)
2 an informal word for food (boia)

grubby /'grʌbɪ/ ADJECTIVE [grubbier, grubbiest] slightly dirty □ *Go and wash those grubby hands!* (sujo)

grudge /grʌdʒ/ ▶ VERB [grudges, grudging, grudged]
1 to feel that someone does not deserve something □ *We did not grudge them their good fortune, after all their problems.* (invejar)
2 to give your time, money, etc. unwillingly □ *I grudged the months I had spent with them.* (fazer algo com má vontade)
▶ NOUN [plural grudges] a feeling of anger or dislike for someone because of something they have done in the past (ressentimento, rancor) 🔲 *I don't* **bear a grudge** *against them.* (guardo ressentimento)

• **grudging** /'grʌdʒɪŋ/ ADJECTIVE given unwillingly □ *In spite of his bad temper, his courage had earned him the grudging respect of his men.* (conceder de má vontade)

• **grudgingly** /'grʌdʒɪŋlɪ/ ADVERB in a grudging way □ *'I suppose she could stay with us,' Tina offered, grudgingly.* (de má vontade)

grueling /'gruəlɪŋ/ ADJECTIVE the US spelling of gruelling (cansativo, duro)

gruelling /'gruəlɪŋ/ ADJECTIVE very difficult and making you very tired □ *It was a gruelling climb to the summit of the mountain.* (cansativo, árduo)

gruesome /'gru:səm/ ADJECTIVE very unpleasant, violent and upsetting □ *a gruesome murder* (medonho, horrível)

gruff /grʌf/ ADJECTIVE [gruffer, gruffest] a gruff voice is deep and sounds unfriendly (áspero, brusco)

grumble /'grʌmbəl/ ▶ VERB [grumbles, grumbling, grumbled] to complain in an unhappy way, especially about small things □ *She was grumbling about the food.* (resmungar, queixar-se)
▶ NOUN [plural grumbles] a complaint □ *There were some grumbles about scheduling.* (queixa)

grumpily /'grʌmpɪlɪ/ ADVERB in a grumpy way □ *'Oh, all right then.' he said, grumpily.* (irritadamente)

grumpy /'grʌmpɪ/ ADJECTIVE [grumpier, grumpiest] bad-tempered □ *He's grumpy in the morning.* (mal-humorado)

grunt /grʌnt/ ▶ VERB [grunts, grunting, grunted] to make a deep noise like a pig □ *He only grunted in response.* (grunhir)
▶ NOUN [plural grunts] a deep noise like a pig (grunhido)

guarantee /ˌgærən'ti:/ ▶ NOUN [plural guarantees]

guard · guide

1 a promise that something will certainly be done or will happen (garantia) 🔹 *I give a guarantee that we will do everything we can.* (garantia) ☐ *Simply having talent is no guarantee of success.*
2 a promise that a product will be repaired or replaced if there is something wrong with it ☐ *a money-back guarantee* ☐ *The equipment has a one-year guarantee.* (garantia)
▶ VERB [guarantees, guaranteeing, guaranteed]
1 to make a promise that something will happen or be done ☐ *We couldn't guarantee his safety.* (garantir)
2 to give a guarantee for a product that is sold (garantir)

guard /gɑːd/ ▶ NOUN [plural guards]

1 someone whose job is to protect a person or place, or to make sure that prisoners do not escape (guarda)
2 under guard being protected or prevented from escaping ☐ *He was taken to the prison under armed guard.* (sob guarda)
3 keep/stand guard to protect a person or place, or to make sure that prisoners do not escape ☐ *I stood guard over the money.* (vigiar/montar guarda)
4 a group of soldiers or police who are protecting a person or place ☐ *the presidential guard* (guarda)
5 an object that protects or covers something ☐ *a mouth guard* ☐ *a fire guard* (protetor)
6 on guard (a) responsible for protecting a person or place ☐ *There were no soldiers on guard that night.* (b) ready to deal with a difficult situation ☐ *You need to be on guard for suspicious phone calls.* (prevenido, em alerta)
7 off guard not ready to deal with a difficult situation ☐ *She caught me off guard and I agreed to help her.* (desprevenido)
8 drop/lower you guard to stop being careful ☐ *If you lower your guard for a minute, he'll start asking you personal questions.* (baixar a guarda)
▶ VERB [guards, guarding, guarded]
1 to make sure that someone does not escape ☐ *You guard the back entrance.* (guardar, resguardar)
2 to protect someone or something ☐ *I guarded the children while he went for help.* (guardar)
♦ PHRASAL VERB **guard against something** to try to make sure that something does not happen ☐ *I take regular breaks to guard against tiredness.* (evitar algo)

• **guarded** /ˈgɑːdɪd/ ADJECTIVE careful not to show your emotions or give too much information (cauteloso, precavido) 🔹 *a guarded response* (resposta cautelosa)

• **guardian** /ˈgɑːdɪən/ NOUN [plural guardians]
1 someone who is legally responsible for a child when its parents have died (guardião, tutor)
2 someone who protects something ☐ *We see ourselves as guardians of democracy.* (guardião, protetor)

guerrilla /gəˈrɪlə/ NOUN [plural guerrillas] a fighter who is a member of a small or unofficial army fighting for political reasons (guerrilha)

guess /ges/ ▶ VERB [guesses, guessing, guessed]

1 to give an answer or opinion without knowing all the facts ☐ **+ question word** *Guess how old she is.* (adivinhar)
2 to give a correct answer or correct information without knowing all the facts ☐ **+ that** *He guessed that we were hiding something from him.* (adivinhar) 🔹 *You'll never guess what I've done!* (você nunca vai adivinhar)
3 I guess a slightly informal phrase used to say that you think something is true ☐ *I guess we'll have to sell the car.* (eu acho)
▶ NOUN [plural guesses] an answer or opinion made by guessing (palpite, chute) 🔹 *At a rough guess, I'd say he's forty.* (chute aproximado)

guest /gest/ NOUN [plural guests]

1 someone you invite to your house or to a party ☐ *a wedding guest* ☐ *She was one of 200 guests at the party.* (convidado)
2 someone staying in a hotel ☐ *Hotel guests can use the gym for free.* (hóspede)
3 a famous person who appears on a television or radio show (convidado) 🔹 *Let me introduce our special guest.* (convidado especial)

guesthouse /ˈgesthaʊs/ NOUN [plural guesthouses] a small hotel (pensão)

guffaw /gʌˈfɔː/ ▶ VERB [guffaws, guffawing, guffawed] to laugh loudly (gargalhar)
▶ NOUN [plural guffaws] a loud laugh (gargalhada)

GUI /ˌdʒiː juː ˈaɪ/ ABBREVIATION Graphical User Interface; a way of showing information on a computer screen using pictures and symbols. A computing word. (abreviação de interface de uso gráfico)

guidance /ˈgaɪdəns/ NOUN, NO PLURAL advice about how you should do something ☐ *We provide guidance on environmental management.* (orientação)

guide /gaɪd/ ▶ NOUN [plural guides]

1 someone whose job is to show places to people who are visiting ☐ *A guide showed us around the cathedral.* (guia)
2 something that helps you make a correct judgment about something (guia) 🔹 *As a rough guide, I cook 50 g rice for each person.* ☐ *If house prices are any guide, this area is becoming more popular.* (guia, referência)
3 a book that gives information about a place or tells you how to do something (guia)
▶ VERB [guides, guiding, guided]
1 to go with someone to show them where to go or tell them about a place (guiar)
2 to help someone or something move in the right direction ☐ *Metal tracks guide the missiles into place.* (orientar)
3 to show someone how to behave or how to do something ☐ **+ through** *My parents helped to*

guide me through a difficult time in my life. □ His religion is the guiding principle of his life. (influenciar)

guidebook /'gaɪdbʊk/ NOUN [plural guidebooks] a book which contains information for people visiting a particular place (guia)

guide dog /'gaɪd ˌdɒg/ NOUN [plural guide dogs] a specially trained dog used by a blind person to help them get around (cão-guia)

guidelines /'gaɪdlaɪnz/ PLURAL NOUN advice or rules about how to do something □ Our company has strict guidelines on safety at work. (diretrizes)

guild /gɪld/ NOUN [plural guilds] an organization for people with the same job, especially a skilled job □ the writer's guild (associação)

guile /gaɪl/ NOUN, NO PLURAL the quality of being clever, often in a dishonest way (fraude)

guillotine /'gɪləˌtiːn/ NOUN [plural guillotines]
1 a piece of equipment with a blade that falls very quickly, which was used in the past to cut off criminals' heads (guilhotina)
2 a machine with a very sharp blade used for cutting paper (guilhotina)

guilt /gɪlt/ NOUN, NO PLURAL
1 an unpleasant feeling you get when you know you have done something wrong □ a sense of guilt □ She felt no guilt at what she had done. (culpa)
2 the fact that you have done something wrong □ He admitted his guilt and accepted the punishment. (culpa)
• **guiltily** /'gɪltɪli/ ADVERB in a way that shows you feel guilty □ We looked at each other guiltily. (com culpa)
• **guilty** /'gɪlti/ ADJECTIVE [guiltier, guiltiest]
1 ashamed because you have done something wrong (culpado) 🔲 I felt guilty about lying to them. (me senti culpado) □ I had a guilty conscience. (consciência culpada)
2 having committed a crime □ + of They are guilty of war crimes. (culpado) 🔲 He pleaded guilty to manslaughter. (declarou-se culpado) 🔲 He was found guilty of drug smuggling. (considerado culpado)
3 responsible for doing something wrong □ + of She's guilty of neglecting her duties as a mother. (culpado)

guinea pig /'gɪni ˌpɪg/ NOUN [plural guinea pigs]
1 a small animal with fur and no tail that children often keep as a pet (porquinho-da-índia)
2 an informal word for someone who is used as part of an experiment, for example to test a new medicine (cobaia)

guitar /gɪ'tɑː(r)/ NOUN [plural guitars] an instrument with strings that you play with your fingers or a small piece of plastic (violão) 🔲 an electric guitar (guitarra)
• **guitarist** /gɪ'tɑːrɪst/ NOUN [plural guitarists] someone who plays the guitar, especially as their job (guitarrista)

gulf /gʌlf/ NOUN [plural gulfs]
1 a large area of sea almost surrounded by land □ the Gulf of Taranto (golfo)
2 a very big difference between two situations or between the way two groups of people live (abismo) 🔲 The gulf between the rich and the poor is widening. (o abismo está aumentando)

gull /gʌl/ NOUN [plural gulls] a white or grey sea bird (gaivota)

gullible /'gʌləbəl/ ADJECTIVE a gullible person believes what they are told and is easily tricked □ Gullible pensioners were paying far too much to handymen. (crédulo)

gully /'gʌli/ NOUN [plural gullies] a deep narrow valley that was made by rain or a fast stream (vale)

gulp /gʌlp/ ▶ VERB [gulps, gulping, gulped]
1 to eat or drink something quickly □ He gulped down his tea. (engolir em seco)
2 to swallow loudly because you are nervous, afraid or surprised □ Mum gulped when she saw the bill. (engolir)
▶ NOUN [plural gulps]
1 the sound made when you gulp □ 'Don't leave me', she said with a gulp. (soluço)
2 an amount of food or drink that is being eaten or drunk quickly □ He finished the beer in two gulps. (gole)

gum /gʌm/ ▶ NOUN [plural gums]
1 the hard pink part in your mouth that your teeth grow from (gengiva) 🔲 gum disease (doença da gengiva)
2 no plural a soft sweet substance that you chew but do not swallow □ a stick of gum (chiclete, goma de mascar)
3 a type of fruit sweet that you can chew □ fruit gums (goma)
4 no plural a type of glue used to stick paper or card (goma, resina)
▶ VERB [gums, gumming, gummed] to stick something with gum (colar)
• **gummy** /'gʌmi/ ADJECTIVE [gummier, gummiest] sticky like gum □ The baby's hands were gummy with jam. (grudento)

gun /gʌn/ NOUN [plural guns] a weapon that fires bullets from a metal tube (arma de fogo) 🔲 The soldier quickly loaded his gun. (carregou sua arma)
⇨ go to **jump the gun**, **stick to your guns**
♦ PHRASAL VERB [guns, gunning, gunned] **gun someone down** to shoot someone (atirar em alguém)

gunfire /'gʌnfaɪə(r)/ NOUN, NO PLURAL when guns are fired or the sound that this makes □ They suddenly heard gunfire in the distance. (tiroteio)

gunge /gʌndʒ/ NOUN, NO PLURAL any unpleasant sticky substance □ There was a layer of black gunge on the inside of the oven. (limo, lodo)

gunman /'gʌnmən/ NOUN [plural gunmen] a man who uses a gun to steal from people or kill them

☐ *Two masked gunmen attacked him in his own home.* (**pistoleiro**)

gunpoint /'gʌnpɔɪnt/ NOUN, NO PLURAL **at gunpoint** when someone is pointing a gun at you ☐ *Customers were held at gunpoint while the men emptied the tills.* (**sob a mira de uma arma**)

gunpowder /'gʌnˌpaʊdə(r)/ NOUN, NO PLURAL an explosive powder, used in bombs and fireworks (= objects that explode in the sky with bright colours) (**pólvora**)

gunshot /'gʌnʃɒt/ NOUN [plural **gunshots**] when a gun is fired, or the noise this makes (**disparo, tiro**) 🔂 *We're seeing more gunshot wounds in the hospital nowadays.* (**feridas por disparos**)

gurgle /'gɜːɡəl/ ▶ VERB [**gurgles, gurgling, gurgled**]
1 to make a sound like water flowing through a narrow space (**gorgolejar**)
2 if a baby gurgles, it makes quiet, happy sounds (**gorjear**)
▶ NOUN [plural **gurgles**] a gurgling sound ☐ *We could hear the gurgle of water in the pipes.* (**gorgolejo**)

guru /'ɡʊruː/ NOUN [plural **gurus**]
1 a Hindu or Sikh religious leader and teacher (**guru, mestre espiritual**)
2 a teacher or leader whose ideas or opinions you respect ☐ *a tennis guru* (**guru**)

gush /ɡʌʃ/ ▶ VERB [**gushes, gushing, gushed**]
1 if liquid gushes, it flows out suddenly and in large amounts ☐ *Blood was gushing from a wound on her forehead.* (**jorrar**)
2 to praise someone or something so much that it does not seem sincere ☐ *'What an absolutely fabulous meal,' she gushed.* (**falar com ímpeto**)
▶ NOUN [plural **gushes**] a large amount of a liquid that suddenly flows ☐ *Suddenly a gush of water poured out of the tap.* (**torrente, fluxo**)

gust /ɡʌst/ NOUN [plural **gusts**] a sudden strong wind ☐ *A gust of wind blew her hat off.* (**rajada**)

gusto /'ɡʌstəʊ/ NOUN, NO PLURAL **with gusto** with great enthusiasm and enjoyment ☐ *He ate his spaghetti with gusto.* (**com entusiasmo**)

gusty /'ɡʌsti/ ADJECTIVE [**gustier, gustiest**] gusty weather has sudden strong winds (**tempestuoso**)

gut /ɡʌt/ ▶ NOUN [plural **guts**]
1 the tube that takes food from your stomach to be passed out of your body as waste (**intestino**)
2 guts (a) courage and determination (**coragem**) 🔂 *It took guts to stand up to his father.* ☐ *He didn't have the guts to tell me he was leaving.* (**foi preciso coragem**) (b) the organs inside an animal's body

3 a fat stomach ☐ *His gut was hanging over his trousers.* (**barriga**)
◆ IDIOM **hate someone's guts** to hate someone very much (**detestar alguém**)
▶ VERB [**guts, gutting, gutted**]
1 to destroy or remove everything inside a place ☐ *The building was gutted by fire.* (**destruir por dentro, implodir**)
2 to remove the organs from inside the body of a dead fish or animal (**estripar**)
▶ ADJECTIVE based on your feelings and emotions (**instintivo**) 🔂 *My gut reaction was to run away.* (**reação instintiva**) 🔂 *I just had a gut feeling that she was lying.* (**sensação instintiva**)

gutter /'ɡʌtə(r)/ NOUN [plural **gutters**]
1 a long, curved piece of plastic or metal that is fastened to the edge of a roof to carry away the water when it rains (**calha**)
2 the curved edge of a road where water can flow away (**sarjeta**)

guy /ɡaɪ/ NOUN [plural **guys**]
1 an informal word for a man (**sujeito, rapaz**)
2 guys used in informal situations to talk to or about two or more people ☐ *Do any of you guys want some chips?* (**pessoal**)

guzzle /'ɡʌzəl/ VERB [**guzzles, guzzling, guzzled**] to eat or drink something quickly ☐ *Did you guzzle all the chocolate?* (**empanturrar-se**)

gym /dʒɪm/ NOUN [plural **gyms**]
1 a room or building with equipment for doing exercises ☐ *I go to the gym three times a week.* (**academia de ginástica**)
2 exercises that you do inside, especially at school ☐ *We have gym on Wednesday.* (**ginástica**)

gymnasium /dʒɪm'neɪziəm/ NOUN [plural **gymnasiums** or **gymnasia**] a large room or building with equipment for doing exercises (**ginásio**)

gymnast /'dʒɪmnæst/ NOUN [plural **gymnasts**] someone trained to do gymnastics (**ginasta**)

• **gymnastics** /dʒɪm'næstɪks/ NOUN, NO PLURAL a sport in which people use their bodies to bend, jump, etc. in a beautiful way (**ginástica**)

gynaecologist /ˌɡaɪnɪ'kɒlədʒɪst/ NOUN [plural **gynaecologists**] a doctor who treats medical problems that only affect women (**ginecologista**)

• **gynaecology** /ˌɡaɪnɪ'kɒlədʒi/ NOUN, NO PLURAL the study and treatment of medical problems that only affect women (**ginecologia**)

gynecologist /ˌɡaɪnɪ'kɒlədʒɪst/ NOUN [plural **gynecologists**] the US spelling of **gynaecologist** (**ginecologista**)

• **gynecology** /ˌɡaɪnɪ'kɒlədʒi/ NOUN, NO PLURAL the US spelling of **gynaecology** (**ginecologia**)

H*h*

H or **h** /eɪtʃ/ the eighth letter of the alphabet (**a oitava letra do alfabeto**)

ha /hɑː/ ABBREVIATION **hectare** or **hectares** (**abreviação de hectare**)

habit /'hæbɪt/ NOUN [plural **habits**]
1 something that you do regularly, especially without thinking about it □ **+ of** *We want to get kids into the habit of regular exercise.* (**hábito**) ▣ *Tommy has a bad habit of grinding his teeth.* (**péssimo hábito**) ▣ *We asked people about their eating habits.* (**hábitos alimentares**)
2 a long, simple dress worn by some religious people □ *a nun's habit* (**hábito**)
♦ IDIOMS **change/break the habit(s) of a lifetime** to change the way you have always done something (**mudar hábitos**) **old habits die hard** used to mean that it is difficult to change your behaviour (**mudar antigos hábitos é difícil**)

habitable /'hæbɪtəbəl/ ADJECTIVE in good enough condition for people to live in □ *Some of the flats were barely habitable.* (**habitável**)

habitat /'hæbɪtæt/ NOUN [plural **habitats**] the place where an animal or a plant lives or grows (**hábitat**) ▣ *We wanted to study the otters in their natural habitat.* (**hábitat natural**)

habitual /hə'bɪtʃuəl/ ADJECTIVE
1 usual or done regularly, as a habit □ *She had her habitual morning cup of coffee.* (**habitual**)
2 used to describe a particular habit or activity □ *a habitual criminal* □ *a habitual liar* (**habitual**)
• **habitually** /hə'bɪtʃuəli/ ADVERB regularly or usually □ *She looked in the old handbag that she habitually carried.* (**habitualmente**)

hack /hæk/ ▶ VERB [**hacks, hacking, hacked**]
1 to cut something roughly □ *They hacked their way through the thick jungle.* □ *She hacked off chunks of hair.* (**picar**)
2 to get into someone's computer illegally to look at information stored there. A computing word □ *He hacked into military computer systems.* (**acessar ilegalmente um computador**)
▶ NOUN [plural **hacks**] an informal word for someone who writes for money, often poor quality writing □ *a newspaper hack* (**amador**)
• **hacker** /'hækə(r)/ NOUN [plural **hackers**] someone who illegally hacks into other people's computers. A computing word. (**ciberpirata**)

hacksaw /'hæksɔː/ NOUN [plural **hacksaws**] a tool with a thin blade (= cutting part), used to cut metal (**serra de arco**)

had /hæd/ PAST TENSE AND PAST PARTICIPLE OF **have** (*ver* **have**)

haddock /'hædək/ NOUN [plural **haddock** or **haddocks**] a type of sea fish with firm, white flesh that is eaten as food (**hadoque**)

hadn't /'hædənt/ a short way to say and write had not □ *Laura hadn't expected to win.* (*ver* **have**)

haemoglobin /ˌhiːmə'gləʊbɪn/ NOUN, NO PLURAL a red substance in blood that carries oxygen around the body. A biology word. (**hemoglobina**)

haemorrhage /'hemərɪdʒ/ ▶ NOUN [plural **haemorrhages**] when someone suddenly loses a lot of blood (**hemorragia**)
▶ VERB [**haemorrhages, haemorrhaging, haemorrhaged**] to suddenly lose a lot of blood (**ter hemorragia**)

hag /hæg/ NOUN [plural **hags**] an ugly old woman (**mulher muito feia e velha**)

haggard /'hægəd/ ADJECTIVE a haggard person looks thin and tired, worried or ill □ *Cho looked haggard.* (**abatido**)

haggis /'hægɪs/ NOUN [plural **haggises**] a Scottish food made from the organs of a sheep that are cut into small pieces and mixed with grains and herbs (**prato de miúdos de carneiro**)

haggle /'hægəl/ VERB [**haggles, haggling, haggled**] to argue about the details of something, especially to try to get a lower price for something you want to buy □ *He haggled with the taxi driver over a fare to the temple.* (**pechinchar, barganhar**)
• **haggling** /'hæglɪŋ/ NOUN, NO PLURAL when you haggle with someone (**barganha**)

haiku /'haɪkuː/ NOUN [plural **haikus**] a poem in a Japanese style with three lines and 17 syllables (= parts of words) (**haicai**)

hail /heɪl/ ▶ VERB [**hails, hailing, hailed**]
1 to say publicly that someone or something is good or important □ *The pilot was hailed as a hero.* □ *Scientists around the world hailed the breakthrough.* (**aclamar**)
2 to shout or to wave to someone to get their attention □ *I hailed a taxi on the main road.* (**chamar atenção**)

hailstones

3 if it hails, small white balls of frozen ice fall from the sky (**chover granizo**)
◆ PHRASAL VERB **hail from somewhere** to come from a particular place □ *He hailed from a small village in the mountains.* (**vir de algum lugar**)
▶ NOUN, NO PLURAL
1 small white balls of frozen ice that fall from the sky □ *a hail storm* (**granizo**)
2 a hail of something a large number of things that are fired or thrown □ *He was gunned down in a hail of bullets.* (**uma saraivada de algo**)

hailstones /ˈheɪlstəʊnz/ PLURAL NOUN small white balls of frozen water that fall from the sky (**pedras de granizo**)

hair /heə(r)/ NOUN [*plural* **hairs**]
1 *no plural* all the thin threads that grow on your head (**cabelo**) ▣ *long/short hair* (**cabelo comprido/curto**) ▣ *straight/curly hair* (**cabelo liso/encaracolado**) ▣ *She's tall with shoulder-length blonde hair.* (**cabelo loiro**) ▣ *I need to get my hair cut.* (**cortar o cabelo**)
2 one of the thin hairs that grow on the surface of the skin of animals and humans □ *It made the hairs on my arms stand up.* (**pelo**)
◆ IDIOMS **Keep your hair on!** a slightly rude phrase used to tell someone to stop being so angry □ *Keep your hair on! I'll pay for the damage.* (**fique calmo!**) **make someone's hair stand on end** to make someone very frightened or shocked □ *The thought of finding a snake makes my hair stand on end.* (**deixar alguém de cabelo em pé**)

> Remember that 'hair' meaning 'all the hair on your head' is never used in the plural:
> ✓ *She has short hair.*
> ✗ *She has short hairs.*

⇨ go to **split hairs, let your hair down, not turn a hair**

hairbrush /ˈheəbrʌʃ/ NOUN [*plural* **hairbrushes**] a brush for brushing your hair (**escova de cabelo**)

haircut /ˈheəkʌt/ NOUN [*plural* **haircuts**]
1 when someone cuts your hair □ *You need a haircut.* (**corte de cabelo**)
2 the style in which your hair is cut □ *She's got a new haircut.* (**corte de cabelo**)

hairdo /ˈheəduː/ NOUN [*plural* **hairdos**] the style in which your hair has been cut and arranged (**penteado**)

hairdresser /ˈheədresə(r)/ NOUN [*plural* **hairdressers**]
1 someone whose job is to cut, arrange and colour people's hair (**cabeleireiro**)
2 hairdresser's a place where a hairdresser works (**salão de cabeleireiro**)
• **hairdressing** /ˈheədresɪŋ/ NOUN, NO PLURAL the skill or work of a hairdresser (**arte de cortar/pentear os cabelos**)

hairdryer or **hairdrier** /ˈheədraɪə(r)/ NOUN [*plural* **hairdryers** or **hairdriers**] a piece of electrical equipment that dries your hair by blowing hot air over it (**secador de cabelo**)

hairgrip /ˈheəgrɪp/ NOUN [*plural* **hairgrips**] a narrow piece of bent metal that you can push into your hair to keep it in place (**grampo de cabelo**)

hairline /ˈheəlaɪn/ NOUN [*plural* **hairlines**] the line along the top of your face where your hair starts to grow (**linha do cabelo**)

hair-raising /ˈheəˌreɪzɪŋ/ ADJECTIVE very frightening or dangerous □ *It was a hair-raising ride.* (**apavorante**)

hairstyle /ˈheəstaɪl/ NOUN [*plural* **hairstyles**] the style in which your hair has been cut and arranged □ *She showed off her new hairstyle.* (**penteado**)

hairy /ˈheəri/ ADJECTIVE [**hairier, hairiest**]
1 covered with hair □ *a hairy chest* (**peludo, cabeludo**)
2 an informal word meaning very frightening or dangerous □ *If it is stormy, the ferry crossing can get a bit hairy.* (**perigoso, arriscado**)

halal /həˈlɑːl/ ADJECTIVE halal meat is from animals killed and prepared according to the laws of Islam (**halal, carne preparada conforme as leis do Islamismo**)

half /hɑːf/ ▶ NOUN, DETERMINER [*plural* **halves**]
1 1/2; one of two equal parts of something □ *He ate half and I ate the other half.* □ *You have an hour and a half to play.* (**metade, meio**) ▣ *Meet us here in half an hour.* (**meia hora**)
2 in half if you break, cut, etc. something in half, you divide it into two equal parts □ *We cut the cake in half.* (**metade, meio**)
3 half past one/two, etc. 30 minutes after one o'clock/two o'clock, etc. □ *He left at half past six.* (**uma, duas, três... e meia**)
▶ ADVERB
1 to the amount of a half □ *This glass is only half full.* □ *She is half Spanish* (= one of her parents is Spanish). (**meio**)
2 partly, but not completely □ *I was half asleep.* (**meio**)

half-baked /ˌhɑːfˈbeɪkt/ ADJECTIVE not well considered or planned □ *He's full of half-baked ideas.* (**mal-planejado, incompleto**)

half board /ˌhɑːf ˈbɔːd/ NOUN, NO PLURAL when a hotel provides breakfast and an evening meal, but not a meal in the middle of the day □ *The cost is £250 per night, half board.* (**meia-pensão**)

half-brother /ˈhɑːfˌbrʌðə(r)/ NOUN [*plural* **half-brothers**] a male relation with either the same father or the same mother as you (**meio-irmão**)

half day /ˌhɑːf ˈdeɪ/ NOUN [*plural* **half days**] a day when people work for only the morning or the afternoon (**meio período**)

half-hearted /ˌhɑːfˈhɑːtɪd/ ADJECTIVE without much enthusiasm or effort (**pouco entusiasmado**) 🔹 *He made a rather half-hearted attempt to apologize.* (**tentativa pouco entusiasmada**)
- **half-heartedly** /ˌhɑːfˈhɑːtɪdlɪ/ ADVERB in a halfhearted way (**com pouco entusiasmo**)

half-life /ˈhɑːflaɪf/ NOUN [plural **half-lives**] the time it takes for a substance to become half as radioactive as it was at the beginning. A physics word. (**meia-vida**)

half-mast /ˌhɑːfˈmɑːst/ NOUN, NO PLURAL if a flag is at half-mast, it is in a position halfway up the pole, usually because someone has died (**meio mastro**)

half moon /ˌhɑːfˈmuːn/ NOUN [plural **half moons**] the moon when it looks like half a circle (**meia-lua**)

half-price /ˌhɑːfˈpraɪs/ ADJECTIVE, ADVERB costing only half the usual price □ *half-price goods* □ *We bought the furniture half-price in a sale.* (**metade do preço**)

half-sister /ˈhɑːfsɪstə(r)/ NOUN [plural **half-sisters**] a female relation with either the same father or the same mother as you (**meia-irmã**)

half-term /ˌhɑːfˈtɜːm/ NOUN [plural **half-terms**] a short holiday from school about halfway through the school term (**curto período de férias no ano letivo**)

half-time /ˌhɑːfˈtaɪm/ NOUN, NO PLURAL in some sports, a break from play in the middle of the game □ *They led 2-0 at half-time.* (**meio-tempo**)

halfway /ˌhɑːfˈweɪ/ ADVERB, ADJECTIVE in the middle between two places, or in the middle of a period of time □ *At the halfway point of my journey, I stopped for a break.* □ *I had to leave halfway through the lesson.* (**a meio caminho, na metade**)

hall /hɔːl/ NOUN [plural **halls**]
1 an area just inside the entrance to a house that you go through to get to other rooms or to the stairs □ *She checked her hair in the mirror in the hall.* (**saguão**) 🔹 *The front door opens into a small entrance hall.* (**saguão de entrada**)
2 a large building or room where meetings, concerts and other events are held (**salão**) 🔹 *a concert hall* (**salão de concertos**) 🔹 *a meeting at the village hall* (**salão da cidade**)

hallelujah /ˌhælɪˈluːjə/ EXCLAMATION a shout or exclamation of praise to God (**aleluia**)

hallmark /ˈhɔːlmɑːk/ NOUN [plural **hallmarks**]
1 a mark on things made of gold or silver to show their quality (**marca característica**)
2 a quality that is typical of something □ *The hallmark of a good writer is the ability to hold the reader's attention.* (**marca de qualidade**)

hallo /həˈləʊ/ EXCLAMATION another spelling of **hello** (**oi, olá**)

Halloween /ˌhæləʊˈiːn/ NOUN, NO PLURAL the night of October 31st, when children dress to look like ghosts, witches, etc. (**dia das bruxas**)

hallucinate /həˈluːsɪneɪt/ VERB [**hallucinates, hallucinating, hallucinated**] to see things that are not really there □ *The fever made him hallucinate.* (**alucinar**)
- **hallucination** /həˌluːsɪˈneɪʃən/ NOUN [plural **hallucinations**] something you see that is not really there (**alucinação**)

hallway /ˈhɔːlweɪ/ NOUN [plural **hallways**] a small room inside the entrance of a house or building with doors going into other rooms □ *She walked down the long, narrow hallway.* (**corredor**)

halo /ˈheɪləʊ/ NOUN [plural **haloes**] a circle of light round the head of a holy person in religious pictures (**auréola, halo**)

halogen /ˈhælədʒen/ NOUN [plural **halogens**] any of five chemical elements that combine with hydrogen to form salts. A chemistry word. (**halogênio**)

halt /hɔːlt/ ▶ VERB [**halts, halting, halted**]
1 to stop happening or developing or to stop something happening or developing □ *The government is taking measures to halt the spread* (**parar**) *of the disease.* □ *These attacks should halt immediately.*
2 to stop moving or to make something stop moving □ *Traffic suddenly halted.* (**parar**)
▶ NOUN [plural **halts**]
1 when something stops happening or developing (**parada**) 🔹 *He called a halt to the press conference and walked out.* (**pediu uma parada**)
2 when something stops moving (**parada**) 🔹 *The car came to an abrupt halt.* (**deu uma parada**)

halter /ˈhɔːltə(r)/ NOUN [plural **halters**] a rope you put over a horse's head, so that you can hold it or lead it (**cabresto**)

halting /ˈhɔːltɪŋ/ ADJECTIVE pausing often when you are speaking because you are nervous or not certain □ *She addressed us in a shy, rather halting voice.* (**hesitante, vacilante**)
- **haltingly** /ˈhɔːltɪŋlɪ/ ADVERB in a halting way □ *He spoke haltingly as he described his experience.* (**com hesitação**)

halve /hɑːv/ VERB [**halves, halving, halved**]
1 to divide or cut something into two equal parts □ *Halve the mushrooms.* (**cortar ao meio**)
2 to reduce something to half its original size or amount □ *We aim to halve the number of deaths in road accidents.* □ *The investment has almost halved in value.* (**reduzir à metade**)
- **halves** /hɑːvz/ PLURAL OF **half** (**ver half**)

ham /hæm/ NOUN, NO PLURAL meat from the leg of a pig which has been cooked using salt or smoke (**presunto defumado**)

hamburger /ˈhæmbɜːgə(r)/ NOUN [plural **hamburgers**] a round flat shape made from very small pieces of meat that is fried and usually eaten between pieces of bread (**hambúrguer**)

hamlet /ˈhæmlɪt/ NOUN [plural **hamlets**] a small village (**aldeia, vilarejo**)

hammer

hammer /'hæmə(r)/ ▶ NOUN [plural **hammers**]
a tool with a heavy metal or wooden part at the end of a handle, used for hitting nails, etc. (**martelo**)

▶ VERB [**hammers, hammering, hammered**]
1 to hit something with a hammer □ *Hammer the nails in one by one.* (**martelar**)
2 to hit something hard □ **+ on** *He was hammering on the door with his fists.* □ *The region was hammered by powerful storms.* (**martelar**)
3 an informal word meaning to beat someone completely or easily □ *We hammered the other team 10–0.* (**arrasar**)

♦ IDIOM **hammer something home** to tell someone something forcefully so that they understand it □ *We really need to hammer this message home.* (**convencer alguém**)

♦ PHRASAL VERB **hammer something out** to discuss or argue about something until everyone agrees □ *The two sides tried to hammer out a deal.* (**insistir sobre algo até alguém concordar**)

hammock /'hæmək/ NOUN [plural **hammocks**] a bed made of a long piece of material hung from ropes at either end (**rede**)

hamper¹ /'hæmpə(r)/ VERB [**hampers, hampering, hampered**] to make it difficult for someone or something to make progress □ *Rescue efforts were hampered by rain.* (**estorvar**)

hamper² /'hæmpə(r)/ NOUN [plural **hampers**] a large basket (= container made from very thin pieces of wood) with a lid, often used for carrying food (**cesta**)

hamster /'hæmstə(r)/ NOUN [plural **hamsters**] a small animal with soft fur and a short tail, often kept as a pet (**hamster, cobaia**)

hand /hænd/ ▶ NOUN [plural **hands**]

1 the part of your body at the end of your arm □ *I took her by the hand.* (**mão**) ⊡ *They walked hand in hand* (= with their hands joined together). (**de mãos dadas**) ⊡ *Hold hands with me while we cross the road.* (**me dê as mãos**) ⊡ *He refused to shake hands with my father.* (**apertar as mãos**)
2 by hand (a) if something is made or done by hand, it is made or done by a person, not a machine (b) if a letter is delivered by hand, someone brings it to you without posting it (**à mão**)
3 help (**mão, ajuda**) ⊡ *Can I give you a hand with those bags?* (**ajudar**) ⊡ *Do you need a hand with the washing up?* (**precisa de ajuda**)
4 at/on/onto hand near and ready to be used □ *Make sure you keep plenty of clean water to hand.* (**à mão, perto**)
5 in hand being dealt with □ *The party arrangements are all in hand.* (**disponível, sob controle**)
6 at someone's hands if you are harmed at someone's hands, they harm you □ *He died at the hands of terrorists.* (**pelas mãos de alguém**)
7 be in someone's hands if something is in someone's hands, they are responsible for it □ *The matter is in the hands of my legal team.* (**estar nas mãos de alguém**)
8 the part of a watch or clock that points to the time (**ponteiro**)

♦ IDIOMS **get/lay your hands on something** to be able to get something □ *I've managed to lay my hands on a lovely piece of velvet.* (**pegar algo**)
have your hands full to be very busy □ *With four small children, she's really got her hands full.* (**estar muito ocupado**) **on the one hand … on the other hand** used to compare the advantages and disadvantages of something □ *On the one hand, working at home saves me a lot of time, on the other hand it can be rather lonely.* (**por um lado … por outro lado**)

▶ VERB [**hands, handing, handed**] to give something to someone □ *Could you hand me a plate?* (**dar, entregar**)

♦ PHRASAL VERBS **hand something back** to give something back to the person who gave it to you □ *I handed back the keys.* (**devolver algo**) **hand something down** to give something to someone younger than you □ *These traditions have been handed down over the centuries.* (**passar adiante, para alguém mais novo/outra geração**) **hand something in** to give something to someone, for example a teacher □ *Have you handed in your homework?* (**entregar algo**) **hand something out** to give something to everyone in a group □ *Can you hand out the textbooks?* (**distribuir algo**) **hand something over** to give something to someone □ *Hand over all your money.* (**entregar algo**)

handful

handbag /'hændbæg/ NOUN [plural **handbags**] a woman's bag for carrying things like money and keys □ *a black leather handbag* (**bolsa de mão**)

handbook /'hændbʊk/ NOUN [plural **handbooks**] a book of instructions on how to do something □ *I bought an illustrated handbook on first aid.* (**manual, guia**)

handbrake /'hændbreɪk/ NOUN [plural **handbrakes**] a brake (= part that makes a vehicle stop) in a vehicle that you operate using your hand (**freio de mão**)

handcuffs /'hændkʌfs/ PLURAL NOUN a pair of metal rings joined by a chain which police use to lock around a prisoner's wrists (= parts of the arms next to the hands) (**algemas**)

handful /'hændfʊl/ NOUN [plural **handfuls**]
1 an amount that you can hold in your hand □ *a handful of rice* (**punhado**)
2 a handful of something a small number of something □ *Only a handful of people turned up.* (**um punhado de algo**)
3 a handful an informal word for a child or an animal whose behaviour makes them difficult to deal with □ *Greta can be quite a handful.* (**insuportável**)

hand-held /ˈhændheld/ ADJECTIVE small enough to hold in your hand during use □ *It was filmed using a hand-held video camera.* (**portátil**)

handicap /ˈhændɪkæp/ ▶ NOUN [plural **handicaps**]
1 an old-fashioned word for a physical or mental injury or disability that prevents someone from living normally □ *A school for children with mental and physical handicaps.* (**deficiência**)
2 a disadvantage that prevents you doing something easily or as well as other people □ *Lack of qualifications can be a major handicap.* (**desvantagem**)
▶ VERB [**handicaps, handicapping, handicapped**] to cause someone to have a disability or a disadvantage (**ter ou impor desvantagem**)
• **handicapped** /ˈhændɪkæpt/ ADJECTIVE an old-fashioned word meaning having a disability (**deficiente**)

handicraft /ˈhændɪkrɑːft/ NOUN [plural **handicrafts**] an activity such as sewing or working with wood that involves making something using your hands, using artistic skill (**artesanato**)

handiwork /ˈhændɪwɜːk/ NOUN, NO PLURAL something that you have made or done yourself □ *He put down the paintbrush and stepped back to admire his handiwork.* (**trabalho manual**)

handkerchief /ˈhæŋkətʃɪf/ NOUN [plural **handkerchiefs**] a small piece of cloth or thin, soft paper used for drying your nose or eyes (**lenço**)

handle /ˈhændəl/ ▶ NOUN [plural **handles**]
1 the part of an object that you use to pick it up and hold it □ *a brush with a long handle* (**cabo**)
2 the part of a door that you hold when you open and close it (**maçaneta**) 🔑 *a door handle* (**maçaneta da porta**)
♦ IDIOM **get/have a handle on something** to start to understand or to control something □ *We need to get a better handle on the problem.* (**começar a entender algo**)
⇨ go to **fly off the handle**
▶ VERB [**handles, handling, handled**]
1 to deal with something □ *Mr Peters is handling all the arrangements for the trip.* (**negociar, lidar**) 🔑 *I would have handled the situation differently.* (**lidar de modo diferente com a situação**)
2 to touch something or to hold it with your hands □ *Try not to handle the fruit too much.* (**manipular**)
3 to buy or sell something, often illegally (**negociar, manusear**) 🔑 *He was arrested on suspicion of handling stolen goods* (**manusear produtos roubados**)

handlebars /ˈhændəlbɑːz/ PLURAL NOUN the curved part at the front of a bicycle that you hold with your hands (**guidons**)

handler /ˈhændlə(r)/ NOUN [plural **handlers**] someone who trains or controls an animal □ *Several police dogs arrived with their handlers.* (**treinador, domador**)

handmade /ˌhændˈmeɪd/ ADJECTIVE made by a person, not a machine □ *handmade silk scarves* (**artesanal**)

handout /ˈhændaʊt/ NOUN [plural **handouts**]
1 money, food or clothing that is given free to poor people (**donativo**)
2 a document containing information that is given to people at a class, a talk, etc. (**declaração**)

handrail /ˈhændreɪl/ NOUN [plural **handrails**] a long, narrow bar that people can hold on to, for example when going up and down stairs (**corrimão**)

handset /ˈhændset/ NOUN [plural **handsets**] the part of a telephone that you hold in your hand and talk or listen through □ *Lift the handset and dial the number you want.* (**telefone**)

handshake /ˈhændʃeɪk/ NOUN [plural **handshakes**] the action of taking someone's right hand in yours and moving it up and down when you meet them or leave them, or to make an agreement with them □ *He greeted me with a handshake.* (**aperto de mãos**)

handsome /ˈhænsəm/ ADJECTIVE [**handsomer, handsomest**]
1 attractive, especially used about a man □ *a handsome young actor* □ *He looked so handsome in his uniform.* (**bonito, atraente**)
2 large in size or amount □ *They made a handsome profit.* (**generoso**)

hands-on /ˌhændzˈɒn/ ADJECTIVE involving doing something yourself instead of reading about it or watching others do it (**prático**) 🔑 *I want to get more hands-on experience* (**experiência prática**)

handstand /ˈhændstænd/ NOUN [plural **handstands**] a movement in which you balance on your hands, holding your body and legs straight up in the air (**parada de mãos**)

handwriting /ˈhændraɪtɪŋ/ NOUN, NO PLURAL
1 writing done with a pen or a pencil, not printed □ *The speech is written in a notebook in Dr King's own handwriting.* (**letra manuscrita, escrita**)
2 the way someone's writing looks □ *He has neat handwriting.* (**escrita**)
• **handwritten** /ˌhændˈrɪtən/ ADJECTIVE written with a pen or pencil, not printed □ *a handwritten note* (**escrito à mão**)

handy /ˈhændi/ ADJECTIVE [**handier, handiest**]
1 useful and easy to use □ *It's a handy size for carrying in your pocket.* (**prático**)
2 come in handy an informal phrase meaning to be useful □ *Bring the torch, it might come in handy.* (**acessível**)
3 near and easy to reach □ *The house is handy for the station.* (**ser acessível, prático**)

handyman /ˈhændimæn/ NOUN [plural **handymen**] someone who does small building and repair jobs (**faz-tudo**)

hang

hang /hæŋ/ VERB [hangs, hanging, hung]

1 to attach something so that the top part is fixed and the lower part is able to move ☐ *Hang your jackets on the pegs.* ☐ *Joe was hanging upside down by his feet.* ☐ *The branches hung down to the ground.* (**pendurar**)

2 to kill someone by tying a rope around their neck and making them drop so that the rope is tight ☐ *He hanged himself in his prison cell.* (**enforcar**)

◆ PHRASAL VERBS **hang about/around** to stay in a place, doing nothing ☐ *There was a group of boys hanging round outside our house.* (**vadiar**) **hang back** to stay behind other people because you are shy or do not want to do something (**retrair-se**) **hang on 1** to hold something tightly ☐ *Hang on tight and we'll pull you up.* (**segurar-se**) **2** an informal word meaning to wait ☐ *Hang on a minute!* (**esperar**) **hang onto/on to something** an informal word meaning to keep something ☐ *You should hang onto those records – they might be worth something one day.* (**manter algo**) **hang something up** to put something such as clothing in a place where it can hang ☐ *We hung up our coats in the hall.* (**pendurar algo**)

▶ NOUN, NO PLURAL

◆ IDIOM **get the hang of something** to learn how to do something or use something ☐ *I can't get the hang of this camera.* (**pegar o jeito de algo, aprender a usar algo**)

hangar /'hæŋə(r)/ NOUN [plural **hangars**] a large building where aeroplanes are kept (**hangar**)

hangdog /'hæŋdɒg/ ADJECTIVE looking sad or ashamed (**envergonhado**) ☐ *He wore a hangdog expression.* (**semblante envergonhado**)

hanger /'hæŋə(r)/ NOUN [plural **hangers**] a shaped piece of metal, wood or plastic used to hang clothes on (**cabide**)

hang-glider /'hæŋglaɪdə(r)/ NOUN [plural **hanggliders**] a large frame covered in cloth which a person hangs from to fly through the air (**asa-delta**)

• **hang-gliding** /'hæŋglaɪdɪŋ/ NOUN, NO PLURAL the sport of flying in hang-gliders (**voo de asa-delta**)

hangman /'hæŋmən/ NOUN [plural **hangmen**] someone whose job is to kill criminals by hanging them (**carrasco**)

hangover /'hæŋəʊvə(r)/ NOUN [plural **hangovers**]

1 a feeling of being ill, especially having a headache, that people sometimes get after they have drunk too much alcohol (**ressaca**)

2 something that remains after an event or period of time is over ☐ *The system is a hangover from the Soviet era.* (**remanescente**)

hang-up /'hæŋʌp/ NOUN [plural **hang-ups**] something about your body, behaviour, etc. that makes you feel worried or embarrassed ☐ *She's always had a hang-up about her nose.* (**complexo**)

happy

hanker /'hæŋkə(r)/

◆ PHRASAL VERB [hankers, hankering, hankered] **hanker after/for something** to want something very much ☐ *He was soon hankering for a career in Hollywood.* (**ansiar por algo**)

• **hankering** /'hæŋkərɪŋ/ NOUN, NO PLURAL a feeling of wanting something very much ☐ *I've got a hankering for a chicken sandwich.* (**desejo**)

hankie or **hanky** /'hæŋki/ NOUN [plural **hankies**] an informal word meaning handkerchief (= piece of cloth or paper used for drying the nose or eyes) (**lenço**)

Hanukkah /'hɑːnəkə/ NOUN, NO PLURAL a Jewish celebration lasting for eight days in November or December (**Chanucá**)

haphazard /ˌhæpˈhæzəd/ ADJECTIVE with no organization or planning ☐ *The market stalls are set up in a rather haphazard way.* (**ao acaso, de qualquer maneira**)

happen /'hæpən/ VERB [happens, happening, happened]

1 if something happens, it takes place, usually without being planned ☐ *The accident happened last week.* ☐ *I pressed the button but nothing happened.* (**acontecer**) ☐ *He'll be pleased, whatever happens.* (**o que quer que aconteça**)

2 to be the result of something ☐ + to *Do you know what's happened to the front door key?* ☐ *Whatever happened to your coat? It's covered in paint.* ☐ *What happens if you forget to log off?* (**ocorrer, acontecer**)

3 happen to do something to do something by chance ☐ *She just happened to be there and saw the whole thing.* (**acontecer algo ao acaso**)

• **happening** /'hæpənɪŋ/ NOUN [plural **happenings**] a strange or unusual event (**acontecimento**)

happily /'hæpɪli/ ADVERB

1 feeling, showing or expressing happiness ☐ *The girls were smiling happily.* (**alegremente**) ☐ *They're happily married.* (**alegremente casados**)

2 in a willing way ☐ *She happily agreed to help.* (**com satisfação**)

3 with a lucky result ☐ *Happily, it all turned out well.* (**felizmente**)

happiness /'hæpɪnɪs/ NOUN, NO PLURAL the state of being happy (**felicidade**) ☐ *He has finally found happiness in his personal life.* (**encontrou felicidade**) ☐ *My children are my greatest source of happiness.*

happy /'hæpi/ ADJECTIVE [happier, happiest]

1 pleased and feeling that a situation is good ☐ *It was the happiest day of her life.* ☐ *He looked really happy.* (**feliz**) ☐ *More money won't make her happy.* (**fazê-la feliz**)

2 making you feel happy ☐ *I had a very happy childhood.* ☐ *The story has a happy ending.* (**feliz**)

3 satisfied □ **+ with** *My teacher wasn't happy with my performance.* □ *I'm more than happy with our progress so far.* (contente)
4 happy to do something very willing to do something □ *I'd be happy to drive you there.* (feliz por fazer algo)
5 Happy Birthday/Christmas, etc. used to say that you hope someone will be happy on a special day (feliz aniversário, feliz Natal etc.)

happy-go-lucky /ˌhæpɪ-gəʊ-ˈlʌkɪ/ ADJECTIVE happy and enjoying life, and not worrying about the future □ *He's a happy-go-lucky youngster.* (despreocupado)

harangue /həˈræŋ/ ▶ VERB [harangues, haranguing, harangued] to express your opinion or to criticize someone strongly and loudly □ *Several players harangued the referee.* (criticar)
▶ NOUN [plural harangues] when you harangue someone (crítica)

harass /ˈhærəs, həˈræs/ VERB [harasses, harassing, harassed] to repeatedly annoy or upset someone □ *She was constantly harassed by journalists and photographers.* (atormentar, assediar)
• **harassed** /ˈhærəst, həˈræst/ ADJECTIVE feeling worried, often because you have too much to do □ *She looked tired and harassed.* (atormentado)
• **harassment** /ˈhærəsmənt, həˈræsmənt/ NOUN, NO PLURAL harassing someone or being harassed (assédio, tormento)

harbor /ˈhɑːbə(r)/ VERB [harbors, harboring, harbored], NOUN [plural harbors] the US spelling of harbour (abrigar, porto)

harbour /ˈhɑːbə(r)/ ▶ NOUN [plural harbours] a safe area of water near the coast, usually protected by big walls, where ships come so that people can go onto the land □ *The ship sailed into Sydney harbour.* (porto)
▶ VERB [harbours, harbouring, harboured]
1 to keep a feeling in your mind for a long time □ *She'd harboured a grudge against them for years.* □ *He harboured ambitions to become an actor.* (nutrir)
2 to protect a criminal from being found by the police (proteger, abrigar)

hard /hɑːd/ ▶ ADJECTIVE [harder, hardest]
1 firm and solid and not easy to bend or break □ *This bread is a bit hard.* □ *The ball will only bounce on a hard surface.* (duro)
2 difficult to do □ **+ to do something** *It was hard to concentrate with all the noise.* □ *The exam was really hard.* (difícil)
3 needing a lot of effort (duro, cansativo) 🔲 *hard work* (trabalho duro)
4 unpleasant or full of problems (difícil) 🔲 *They had a hard life* (uma vida difícil) 🔲 *He had a hard time in the army.* (tempos difíceis)
5 be hard on someone (a) to criticize someone or be unkind to someone □ *You shouldn't be so hard on your children – they are trying their best.*
(b) to be a difficult situation for someone □ *It's hard on her family when she's ill.* (ser duro com alguém, estar em situação difícil)
♦ IDIOM **a hard line** a very forceful and severe way of dealing with something □ *The club has taken a hard line against racism.* (linha-dura)
▶ ADVERB [harder, hardest]
1 with a lot effort (intensamente) 🔲 *They always work hard.* (trabalham intensamente) 🔲 *You need to try harder.* (tentar mais intensamente)
2 with a lot of force □ *It was raining hard when we got there.* (forte)

hardback /ˈhɑːdbæk/ NOUN [plural hardbacks] a book that has a hard cover (livro de capa dura)

hardboard /ˈhɑːdbɔːd/ NOUN, NO PLURAL thin strong board made from small pieces of wood pressed together (quadro de madeira)

hard-boiled /ˌhɑːdˈbɔɪld/ ADJECTIVE a hard-boiled egg has been boiled in its shell until the inside is solid (escaldado)

hard copy /ˌhɑːd ˈkɒpɪ/ NOUN [plural hard copies] information printed from a computer onto paper (cópia impressa)

hardcover /ˈhɑːdkʌvə(r)/ NOUN [plural hardcovers] an especially US word for a book that has a hard cover (livro de capa dura)

hard disk /ˈhɑːd ˌdɪsk/ or **hard drive** /ˈhɑːd ˌdraɪv/ NOUN [plural hard disks or hard drives] a part inside a computer where information is stored. A computing word. (disco rígido)

harden /ˈhɑːdən/ VERB [hardens, hardening, hardened]
1 to become hard or solid □ *The mixture hardens into a solid gel.* (endurecer)
2 to become less gentle, kind or willing to change □ *Both sides have hardened their positions.* (insensibilizar-se)

hard-fought /ˌhɑːdˈfɔːt/ ADJECTIVE using a lot of effort against someone who is determined to win □ *a hard-fought election* (luta difícil)

hard-hearted /ˌhɑːdˈhɑːtɪd/ ADJECTIVE not caring about other people's feelings or problems (coração de pedra)

hardline /ˈhɑːdlaɪn/ ADJECTIVE having strong or extreme opinions and refusing to change them □ *He's known for his hardline stance on immigration.* (inflexível, intransigente)

hardly /ˈhɑːdlɪ/ ADVERB
1 only just or almost not □ *I hardly know him.* □ *He hardly spoke a word of English.* (apenas, mal) 🔲 *There were hardly any people there.* (mal havia alguém) 🔲 *We hardly ever saw her.* (nunca) □ *He'd hardly put the key in the door when down came the rain.*
2 used for emphasis to mean not at all □ *She's hardly likely to want him at the party after the way he insulted her.* □ *She could hardly be described as beautiful!* (mal, quase)

> Notice that the word **hardly** does not mean 'with a lot of effort' or 'with a lot of force'. For these two meanings, use the word **hard**:
> ✓ She works so hard.
> ✗ She works so hardly.
> ✓ It's raining hard.
> ✗ It's raining hardly.

hardship /ˈhɑːdʃɪp/ NOUN [plural **hardships**] something that makes your life difficult, especially not having enough money or comfort (**dificuldade**) 🔄 *They are in severe financial hardship.* (**dificuldade financeira**) □ *Rising prices are causing widespread hardship.*

hard shoulder /ˌhɑːd ˈʃəʊldə(r)/ NOUN, NO PLURAL the strip of road at either side of a motorway for use in an emergency (**acostamento**)

hard up /ˌhɑːd ˈʌp/ ADJECTIVE an informal word meaning poor □ *His family is too hard up to be able to afford the fees.* (**sem dinheiro**)

hardware /ˈhɑːdweə(r)/ NOUN, NO PLURAL
1 the machines and equipment that make up a computer system. A computing word □ *We need to update our computer hardware and software.* (**hardware**)
2 tools and equipment used in the house and garden (**ferramentas**) 🔄 *a hardware store* (**loja de ferramentas**)
3 equipment, machines, vehicles, etc. especially used by the military (**armamentos**) 🔄 *They are a leading supplier of military hardware.* (**armamentos militares**)

hard-wearing /ˌhɑːdˈweərɪŋ/ ADJECTIVE well made and able to last a long time □ *The fabric is hardwearing and waterproof.* (**resistente**)

hardy /ˈhɑːdɪ/ ADJECTIVE [**hardier**, **hardiest**] strong and able to deal with difficult conditions □ *a hardy plant* (**robusto, resistente**) 🔄 *A few hardy souls* (= people) *jumped into the icy cold water.* (**pessoas resistentes**)

hare /heə(r)/ ▶ NOUN [plural **hares**] an animal similar to a rabbit that has very large ears and runs very quickly (**lebre**)
▶ VERB [**hares, haring, hared**] to run somewhere very quickly □ *She hared off to get a ladder.* (**correr**)

hare-brained /ˈheəbreɪnd/ ADJECTIVE silly and not likely to be successful (**tolo**) 🔄 *a hare-brained scheme* (**esquema tolo**)

hark /hɑːk/ VERB [**harks, harking, harked**] an old-fashioned or literary word meaning to listen □ *Hark, the nightingale is singing.* (**ouvir, escutar**)
♦ PHRASAL VERB **hark back to something** to remember or to return to something that happened in the past □ *The style harks back to the 1960s.* (**referir-se a algo dito anteriormente**)

harm /hɑːm/ ▶ VERB [**harms, harming, harmed**] to hurt, damage or cause problems for someone or something □ *You might harm your eyes if you sit too close to the TV.* □ *She believes that violent video games can harm children.* □ *We know that air travel harms the environment.* (**fazer mal**)
▶ NOUN, NO PLURAL
1 damage, injury or problems (**mal, dano**) 🔄 *The knife wasn't sharp enough to cause much harm.* (**causar dano**) 🔄 *If you stay with me, you won't come to any harm.* (**não vai acontecer nada de mal**) 🔄 *It wouldn't do any harm to ask for advice.* (**causar mal algum**)
2 there's no harm in doing something used to say that an action will not cause problems and may help a situation □ *I don't think you'll be able to persuade him to come, but there's no harm in trying.* (**não há mal algum em fazer algo**)

• **harmful** /ˈhɑːmfʊl/ ADJECTIVE causing damage, injury or problems □ *Use a cream to protect your skin from the sun's harmful rays.* (**prejudicial**)

• **harmless** /ˈhɑːmlɪs/ ADJECTIVE
1 not causing any damage, injury or problems □ *This substance is harmless to animals.* (**inofensivo**)
2 not intended to offend or upset people □ *harmless fun* (**inocente**)

harmonica /hɑːˈmɒnɪkə/ NOUN [plural **harmonicas**] a small musical instrument that you hold to your mouth and play by blowing air through it (**gaita de boca**)

harmonious /hɑːˈməʊnɪəs/ ADJECTIVE
1 having a friendly relationship without disagreements □ *The atmosphere at work was generally harmonious.* (**harmonioso**)
2 fitting well together in an attractive way □ *The architecture is varied, but the overall effect is harmonious.* (**concordante**)
3 pleasant to listen to (**sonoramente agradável**)

• **harmoniously** /hɑːˈməʊnɪəslɪ/ ADVERB in a harmonious way □ *People of different faiths live together harmoniously in this area.* (**harmoniosamente**)

harmonize *or* **harmonise** /ˈhɑːmənaɪz/ VERB [**harmonizes, harmonizing, harmonized**]
1 to look attractive together □ *The buildings harmonize with their surroundings.* (**harmonizar**)
2 to make systems, rules, etc. more similar so that they work well together □ *We want to harmonize the regulations in different European countries.* (**conciliar**)
3 to sing or play music in harmony, or to provide a harmony for a main tune □ *He harmonized the melody with violins and cellos.* (**harmonizar**)

harmony /ˈhɑːmənɪ/ NOUN [plural **harmonies**]
1 when people live in a peaceful and friendly way □ *We live in harmony with our neighbours.* (**harmonia**)
2 a combination of musical notes that sound pleasant together □ *complex vocal harmonies* (**harmonia**)
3 when things look attractive together □ *The building is in complete harmony with its surroundings.* (**harmonia**)

harness /ˈhɑːnɪs/ ▶ NOUN [plural **harnesses**]
1 a set of leather straps that attach a horse to something it is pulling (**arreios**)
2 a set of straps for attaching someone to something (**equipamento**) ▣ *He climbs without a safety harness.* (**equipamento de segurança**)
▶ VERB [**harnesses, harnessing, harnessed**]
1 to control something in order to use it for a particular purpose (**atrelar**) ▣ *We need to harness the power of the sea to provide energy.* (**atrelar a energia**)
2 to put a harness on a horse or a person □ *The dancers are harnessed to wires.* (**arrear**)

harp /hɑːp/ NOUN [plural **harps**] a musical instrument with strings stretched across an open triangular frame (**harpa**)
◆ PHRASAL VERB [**harps, harping, harped**] **harp on (about something)** to keep talking about something in an annoying way □ *Will you stop harping on about dinner?* (**falar repetidamente sobre algo**)
• **harpist** /ˈhɑːpɪst/ NOUN [plural **harpists**] someone who plays the harp (**harpista**)

harpoon /hɑːˈpuːn/ NOUN [plural **harpoons**] a spear (= long, sharp weapon) with a rope attached that is used for hunting large fish (**arpão**)

harpsichord /ˈhɑːpsɪkɔːd/ NOUN [plural **harpsichords**] a musical instrument similar to a small piano, often used in old music (**espineta**)

harrowing /ˈhærəʊɪŋ/ ADJECTIVE very upsetting or unpleasant □ *a harrowing experience* □ *There were harrowing scenes of badly injured children.* (**angustiante**)

harsh /hɑːʃ/ ADJECTIVE [**harsher, harshest**]
1 very cold, uncomfortable or difficult, etc. □ *a harsh climate* □ *a harsh winter* □ *The poor lived in very harsh conditions.* (**severo**)
2 cruel, severe and often unfair □ *a harsh punishment* (**severo**) ▣ *harsh criticism* (**crítica severa**) ▣ *He had harsh words for his teammate.* (**palavras severas**)
3 unpleasantly strong or loud □ *harsh light* □ *the harsh cry of a bird* (**estridente**)
• **harshly** /ˈhɑːʃli/ ADVERB in a harsh way □ *'Stand up,' he said harshly.* □ *The report was harshly critical.* □ *They were treated harshly.* (**severamente**)
• **harshness** /ˈhɑːʃnɪs/ NOUN, NO PLURAL the quality of being harsh □ *She was surprised by the harshness of his tone.* (**estridentemente**)

harvest /ˈhɑːvɪst/ ▶ NOUN [plural **harvests**]
1 the activity of collecting crops □ *Heavy rains delayed the harvest.* (**colheita**)
2 the amount of a crop that is collected □ *The price rise is due to poor wheat harvests.* (**colheita**)
▶ VERB [**harvests, harvesting, harvested**] to collect a crop □ *The apples are harvested in late summer.* (**colher**)

has /hæz/ VERB the present tense of the verb **have** when it is used with he, she and it □ *He has brown eyes.* (**ver have**)

has-been /ˈhæzbiːn/ NOUN [plural **has-beens**] an informal word for someone who was famous or successful in the past, but who is no longer important or interesting (**fora de moda**)

hash /hæʃ/ NOUN [plural **hashes**] the sign '#' that is used on telephones (**sustenido**)
◆ IDIOM **make a hash of something** an informal phrase meaning to spoil something by doing it badly (**estragar algo**)

hasn't /ˈhæzənt/ a short way to say and write has not □ *Anne hasn't arrived yet.* (**ver have**)

hassle /ˈhæsəl/ ▶ NOUN [plural **hassles**] something that annoys you or causes problems for you. An informal word. □ *Avoid the hassle of finding a parking space: take the bus.* (**discussão**)
▶ VERB [**hassles, hassling, hassled**] to repeatedly ask someone something in a way that annoys them □ *We were continually hassled by journalists.* (**perturbar**)

haste /heɪst/ NOUN, NO PLURAL when someone hurries, especially when this causes them to make mistakes □ *In her haste she almost dropped the basket.* □ *He has criticized the government for acting in haste.* (**pressa**)
• **hasten** /ˈheɪsən/ VERB [**hastens, hastening, hastened**]
1 to cause something to happen sooner □ *The shock hastened his death.* (**acelerar**)
2 I hasten to add used when you want to explain something quickly to avoid someone getting the wrong opinion about what you have just said □ *I couldn't believe it. Not, I hasten to add, that I thought he was lying.* (**eu me apressei em dizer**)
• **hastily** /ˈheɪstɪli/ ADVERB very quickly, often without enough planning □ *We hastily packed our bags and caught the next plane home.* (**apressadamente**)
• **hasty** /ˈheɪsti/ ADJECTIVE [**hastier, hastiest**] done quickly, often without enough planning □ *I scribbled a hasty note.* □ *You shouldn't make any hasty decisions about something so important.* (**apressado**)

hat /hæt/ NOUN [plural **hats**] a covering you wear on your head □ *a straw hat* □ *a fur hat* (**chapéu**)

hatch[1] /hætʃ/ VERB [**hatches, hatching, hatched**]
1 to make a plan, especially in secret □ *They're hatching a plot to give Fiona a surprise birthday party.* (**tramar algo**)
2 an egg hatches when a baby bird or reptile breaks out of it □ *The eggs hatch after about ten days.* (**chocar**)
3 baby birds or reptiles hatch when they break out of their eggs □ *We watched the chicks hatch.* (**chocar**)

hatch[2] /hætʃ/ NOUN [plural **hatches**]

hatchback

1 an opening in a wall, especially one through which food can be passed (**abertura**)
2 an opening or a door in a ship or an aircraft □ *an escape hatch* (**portinhola**)

hatchback /'hætʃˌbæk/ NOUN [*plural* **hatchbacks**] a type of car with a large door at the back that opens upwards (**hatchback**)

hatchet /'hætʃɪt/ NOUN [*plural* **hatchets**] a small axe (= tool for cutting wood) (**machadinha**)
♦ IDIOM **bury the hatchet** to become friends again after an argument (**fazer as pazes**)

hate /heɪt/ ▶ VERB [**hates, hating, hated**]
1 to dislike someone or something very much □ + *ing I hate being late.* □ *I hate the idea of wasting all that money.* (**odiar, detestar**)
2 I hate to do something used to say sorry when you are going to say or do something that someone will not like □ *I hate to say this, but I think you're going to miss your plane.* (**odeio fazer isso**)
▶ NOUN [*plural* **hates**]
1 *no plural* a very strong feeling that you do not like someone or something □ *There was a look of real hate in his eyes.* (**ódio**)
2 something that you hate (**ódio**) 🔁 *Lateness is one of his pet hates.* (**coisas que odeia**)
• **hateful** /'heɪtfʊl/ ADJECTIVE very unkind or unpleasant □ *What a hateful thing to say!* (**detestável, odioso**)
• **hatred** /'heɪtrɪd/ NOUN, NO PLURAL a very strong feeling that you do not like someone or something □ *I have a hatred of dogs* (**ódio**) 🔁 *He was accused of promoting racial hatred.* (**ódio racial**)

hat-trick /'hæt,trɪk/ NOUN [*plural* **hat-tricks**] when a team or a player is successful three times in a game, for example by scoring three goals (**três pontos em um mesmo jogo**)

haughty /'hɔːtɪ/ ADJECTIVE [**haughtier, haughtiest**] behaving as though you think you are better or more important than other people □ *She gave him a haughty look.* (**arrogante**)

haul /hɔːl/ ▶ VERB [**hauls, hauling, hauled**]
1 to pull someone or something using a lot of effort □ *He managed to haul himself up on to a narrow ledge.* (**puxar**)
2 to force someone to go somewhere □ *He was hauled off the train by a security guard.* (**arrastar**)
▶ NOUN [*plural* **hauls**] an amount of something that someone manages to get, often something illegal □ *Police claimed that the thieves' total haul was worth about $155,000.* □ *He returned home with his haul of fish.* (**ganho**)
• **haulage** /'hɔːlɪdʒ/ NOUN, NO PLURAL the business of carrying goods from one place to another □ *a haulage company* (**frete**)

haunt /hɔːnt/ ▶ VERB [**haunts, haunting, haunted**]
1 if a ghost (= dead person's spirit) haunts a place, people think it appears there □ *People claim that the castle is haunted by the ghost of the young prince.* (**assombrar**)

363

have

2 if a bad feeling or memory haunts you, you often think about it □ *The image of that face haunted his dreams.* (**atormentar**)
▶ NOUN [*plural* **haunts**] a place where you often go □ *This club is one of my old haunts.* (**lugar preferido**)
• **haunted** /'hɔːntɪd/ ADJECTIVE
1 visited by ghosts (= spirits of dead people) □ *Some people believe that this room is haunted.* □ *a haunted castle* (**assombrado**)
2 looking very frightened or worried □ *She always seemed to have a haunted look.* (**atormentado**)
• **haunting** /'hɔːntɪŋ/ ADJECTIVE sad and beautiful in a way that you cannot forget □ *a haunting melody* (**marcante**)

haute couture /ˌəʊt kuːˈtʊə(r)/ NOUN, NO PLURAL very expensive and fashionable clothes (**alta-costura**)

haute cuisine /ˌəʊt kwɪˈziːn/ NOUN, NO PLURAL cooking of a very high standard (**culinária gourmet**)

have /hæv/ AUXILIARY VERB used with the past participle of another verb to form the present perfect tense or the past perfect tense □ *I have bought a new car.* □ *Have you fed the rabbit?* □ *She has been feeling tired recently.* □ *They had opened a restaurant in Athens.* (**ter**)
▶ VERB [**has, having, had**]
1 used for describing someone or something □ *He has got black hair.* □ *The room had patches of damp on the walls.* □ *The soup had a delicious flavour.* (**ter**)
2 to own something □ *He has a house in Spain.* □ *I have got three brothers.* □ *She has the determination to win.* (**ter**)
3 used for saying that someone has something with them □ *Do you have a towel I could use?* □ *He had a large dog with him.* (**ter**)
4 to have an illness is to suffer from it □ *She has cancer.* □ *I had a terrible headache.* (**ter**)
5 have a look/shower/walk, etc. to do a particular thing (**dar uma olhada, tomar um banho, dar uma caminhada etc.**)
6 to have food or drink is to eat it or drink it □ *You'll have lunch with us, won't you?* □ *I had a huge curry last night.* (**comer, beber**)
7 to experience something □ *We've had a lot of problems.* □ *I hope you have a great time in Mexico.* (**ter**)
⇨ go to **have your cake and eat it**
▶ MODAL VERB

> ► Notice that **have** and **have got** (sense 2) are both used to mean 'to own something'. It is normal, especially in spoken English, to use the short forms of have got and has got: □ *I've got a dog.* (= I have got a dog). □ *She's got a dog.* (= She has got a dog).

1 have to do something if you have to do something, you must do it □ *I have to go away for*

a few days. ☐ *You'll have to give him the money.* 🔒 *I don't have to go to work tomorrow.* (**ter de**)
2 used for telling someone how to do something ☐ *You have to press the green button.* (**ter de**)

> Notice that have to (sense 1) is negative, the negative form is usually made with **do**: ☐ *I don't have to go.* ☐ *He doesn't have to work.*
> The question form of have to is also made with do: ☐ *Do you have to tell him?* ☐ *Do we have to come?*

haven /ˈheɪvən/ NOUN [plural **havens**] a place where people or animals can be safe (**refúgio**) 🔒 *The families were moved to a safe haven in the mountains.* (**refúgio seguro**)

haven't /ˈhævənt/ a short way to say and write **have not** ☐ *I haven't seen the film yet.* (**ver have**)

havoc /ˈhævək/ NOUN, NO PLURAL a state of damage, destruction or confusion (**devastação, destruição**) 🔒 *Heavy rain has caused havoc on the roads.* (**causou destruição**) 🔒 *Spicy food plays havoc with my digestion.* (**causa devastação**)

hawk /hɔːk/ NOUN [plural **hawks**] a bird that can see very well and hunts small animals for food (**falcão**)

hawthorn /ˈhɔːθɔːn/ NOUN [plural **hawthorns**] a small tree with thorns (= sharp points), pink or white flowers and red berries (= small fruits) (**espinheiro**)

hay /heɪ/ NOUN, NO PLURAL grass that has been cut and dried, used to feed animals (**feno**)

hay fever /ˌheɪ ˈfiːvə(r)/ NOUN, NO PLURAL a medical condition caused by pollen (= powder produced by flowers) which makes you feel as if you have a cold (**alergia alérgica**)

haystack /ˈheɪstæk/ NOUN [plural **haystacks**] a large pile of hay that is left in a field until it is needed (**monte de feno**)

haywire /ˈheɪwaɪə(r)/ ADJECTIVE **go haywire** to stop working correctly and to start behaving in an uncontrolled way ☐ *The virus causes the human body to go haywire.* (**enlouquecer**)

hazard /ˈhæzəd/ ▶ NOUN [plural **hazards**] something that could cause harm or damage (**risco**) 🔒 *Undercooked food is a potential health hazard.* (**risco para a saúde**) 🔒 *a fire hazard* (**risco de incêndio**) 🔒 *Industrial waste poses a hazard to the environment.* (**traz risco**)
▶ VERB [**hazards, hazarding, hazarded**] **hazard a guess** to risk making a guess about something ☐ *'How many people were there?' 'I don't know, but I'd hazard a guess at about two thousand.'* (**arriscar um palpite**)

• **hazardous** /ˈhæzədəs/ ADJECTIVE dangerous ☐ *Hazardous driving conditions led to several accidents this afternoon.* (**perigoso**)

haze /heɪz/ NOUN [plural **hazes**] air that is difficult to see through because of heat, smoke, dust, etc. (**neblina**)

hazel /ˈheɪzəl/ ▶ NOUN [plural **hazels**] a small tree on which nuts grow (**aveleira**)
▶ ADJECTIVE having a light green-brown colour ☐ *hazel eyes*

hazelnut /ˈheɪzəlnʌt/ NOUN [plural **hazelnuts**] a nut that you can eat, that grows on a hazel tree (**avelã**)

hazy /ˈheɪzi/ ADJECTIVE [**hazier, haziest**]
1 not clear because of heat, smoke, dust, etc. in the air ☐ *The sea was blue under a hazy sky.* (**nebuloso**)
2 hazy memories are not clear ☐ *He has only hazy memories of his father.* (**vago**)

he /hiː/ PRONOUN used to talk or write about a man, boy or male animal that has already been mentioned ☐ *Everyone likes Ted because he is so funny.* ☐ *Don't worry – he won't bite.* (**ele**)

head /hed/ ▶ NOUN [plural **heads**]
1 the part of the body that contains the brain, eyes, mouth, etc. ☐ *She suffered serious head injuries.* ☐ *He turned his head to look at the clock.* (**cabeça**) 🔒 *nod/shake your head* (**balançar a cabeça**) 🔒 *She was dressed in black from head to toe.* (**da cabeça aos pés**)
2 your mind ☐ *The idea just popped into my head.* (**cabeça, mente**)
3 the person who is in charge of an organization or a group of people ☐ *He is the former head of the prison service.* (**cabeça, chefe**)
4 the top or front of something ☐ *Put your name at the head of each page.* ☐ *I went straight to the head of the queue.* (**topo, cabeceira**)
⇨ go to **heads**
♦ IDIOMS **be over someone's head** to be too difficult for someone to understand ☐ *The stuff about economics was right over my head.* (**estar acima da compreensão de alguém**) **can't make head nor tail of something** to not be able to understand what something means or how something works ☐ *I can't make head nor tail of these instructions.* (**não conseguir entender algo**) **come to a head** if a situation comes to a head, it becomes so much worse that it must be dealt with (**atingir o ponto culminante**) **go to someone's head** if success, praise, etc. goes to someone's head, they become too proud (**subir à cabeça de alguém**) **head over heels 1** if you fall head over heels, you fall in a sudden and forceful way ☐ *He slipped on the ice and went head over heels.* (**de pernas para o ar**) **2** if you are head over heels in love, you love someone very much (**perdidamente**) **keep your head** to stay calm ☐ *She kept her head in a crisis.* (**manter a calma**) **laugh/scream, etc. your head off** an informal phrase meaning to laugh/shout, etc. a lot (**gritar, rir muito**) **lose your head** to become very frightened or excited and behave in a way that is not calm (**perder a cabeça**)
⇨ go to **off the top of your head**

▶ VERB [heads, heading, headed]
1 to go towards a particular place □ *It's time for us to head home.* □ *We were heading north along the motorway.* (rumar para)
2 to be in charge of an organization or a group of people □ *She heads the development team.* (chefiar)
3 to hit a ball with your head (cabecear)

headache /ˈhedeɪk/ NOUN [plural headaches]
1 a pain in your head (dor de cabeça) 🔂 *I've got a splitting headache.* (terrível dor de cabeça) 🔂 *That noise is giving me a headache.*
2 something that gives you a lot of problems (dor de cabeça) 🔂 *The new rule has created a major headache for airport security staff.* (enorme dor de cabeça)

header /ˈhedə(r)/ NOUN [plural headers] when you hit the ball with your head in a game of football □ *Doyle sent a powerful header towards the goal.* (cabeçada)

headfirst /ˌhedˈfɜːst/ ADVERB moving forwards with your head in front of the rest of your body □ *I fell headfirst down the stairs.* (de cabeça)

heading /ˈhedɪŋ/ NOUN [plural headings] a title at the beginning of a piece of writing (título)

headland /ˈhedlənd/ NOUN [plural headlands] a piece of land that sticks out into the sea (cabo)

headlight /ˈhedlaɪt/ NOUN [plural headlights] one of the two big lights at the front of a vehicle (farol dianteiro)

headline /ˈhedlaɪn/ NOUN [plural headlines]
1 the words that are printed in large letters at the top of a newspaper article (título)
2 headlines the most important news stories that are reported at the beginning of a news programme on the television or radio □ *Here is Charlotte Green with today's headlines.* (manchete)

headlong /ˈhedlɒŋ/ ADVERB
1 with your head in front of the rest of your body □ *She plunged headlong down the stairs.* (de ponta-cabeça)
2 rush/plunge headlong into something to start to do something too quickly, before you have had enough time to think carefully about it □ *We must not rush headlong into this war.* (fazer algo apressadamente)

headmaster /ˌhedˈmɑːstə(r)/ NOUN [plural headmasters] a male teacher who is in charge of a school (diretor)

headmistress /ˌhedˈmɪstrɪs/ NOUN [plural headmistresses] a female teacher who is in charge of a school (diretora)

head-on /ˌhedˈɒn/ ▶ ADVERB
1 if two cars hit each other head-on, the front parts of both cars hit each other (de frente)
2 without trying to avoid unpleasant things □ *We need to tackle these problems head-on.* (de frente)

▶ ADJECTIVE describes a car accident in which two cars moving towards each other hit each other (frontal) 🔂 *a head-on collision* (colisão frontal)

headphones /ˈhedfəʊnz/ PLURAL NOUN a piece of equipment with two parts that you wear over your ears, so that you can listen to music, etc. and other people do not hear it (fones de ouvido)

headquarters /ˌhedˈkwɔːtəz/ PLURAL NOUN
1 the central office from which a large business or organization is controlled □ *Our company headquarters are in London.* (sede)
2 a place from which an army or police force is controlled (quartel-general)

headroom /ˈhedrʊm/ NOUN, NO PLURAL
1 the space between someone's head and a ceiling □ *For a small car, the Micra gives you plenty of headroom.* (altura livre)
2 used on road signs to show how much space there is under a bridge □ *Maximum headroom 2.3 metres.* (altura livre)

heads /hedz/ PLURAL NOUN the side of a coin that has a picture of a head on it □ *Heads or tails?* (cara)

headscarf /ˈhedskɑːf/ NOUN [plural headscarves] a woman's thin scarf (= piece of cloth), worn over the head (lenço de cabeça)

headset /ˈhedset/ NOUN [plural headsets] a piece of equipment with two parts that you wear over your ears for listening, and a part near your mouth that you speak into (fones de ouvido)

headstand /ˈhedstænd/ NOUN [plural headstands] a position in which your body is upside down, with your head and hands on the ground and your feet pointing upwards (parada de cabeça)

head start /ˌhed ˈstɑːt/ NOUN, NO PLURAL an advantage that you have over other people, especially by starting before them (vantagem inicial) 🔂 *Nursery French classes give your children a great head start in their schooling.* (dá vantagem inicial)

headstone /ˈhedstəʊn/ NOUN [plural headstones] a piece of stone with writing on it which says who is buried in a grave (lápide)

headstrong /ˈhedstrɒŋ/ ADJECTIVE determined to do what you want to do, and unwilling to take advice from other people (teimoso)

heads-up /ˌhedzˈʌp/ NOUN, NO PLURAL a warning that something will happen, usually so that someone can prepare (alerta) 🔂 *Dan gave me a heads-up that Judy would be there.* (me deu um alerta)

headteacher /ˌhedˈtiːtʃə(r)/ NOUN [plural headteachers] a teacher who is in charge of a school (diretor escolar)

headway /ˈhedweɪ/ NOUN, NO PLURAL **make headway** to make progress □ *The discussions continued for hours, but we made little headway.* (progredir, avançar)

headwind /ˈhedwɪnd/ NOUN [plural **headwinds**] a wind that blows towards you and slows you down (**vento contrário**)

heady /ˈhedi/ ADJECTIVE [**headier, headiest**]
1 making you feel excited and confident ☐ *We thought we could do everything back in those heady days of the 1960s.* (**estonteante**)
2 having a pleasant and strong effect on you ☐ *The room was filled with the heady aroma of spices.* (**inebriante**)

heal /hiːl/ VERB [**heals, healing, healed**] to become healthy again, or to make a person or part of the body healthy again ☐ *The wound needs time to heal.* ☐ *The substance is used for healing cuts and injuries generally.* ☐ *With time, the body will heal itself.* (**curar**)
• **healer** /ˈhiːlə(r)/ NOUN [plural **healers**] someone who makes ill people better, especially a person who does not use modern medical methods ☐ *She went to a spiritual healer for help.* (**curandeiro**)

health /helθ/ NOUN, NO PLURAL
1 how well your body is ☐ *Her health has been very poor recently.* (**saúde**) *Too much red meat is bad for your health.* (**ruim para sua saúde**) *He appeared to be in good health.* (**em boa saúde**) *She was forced to leave due to ill health.* (**saúde debilitada**)
2 the work of looking after ill people and of preventing illness generally ☐ *The government spends a huge amount on health.* (**saúde**) *The country lacks trained health workers.* (**trabalhadores da saúde**)
3 how successful a business, industry or economy is ☐ *The growth of tourism has been good for the health of the economy.* (**vitalidade, saúde**)

health care /ˈhelθ ˌkeə(r)/ NOUN, NO PLURAL the organizations that look after people's health ☐ *private health care* (**assistência médica**)

health centre /ˈhelθ ˌsentə(r)/ NOUN [plural **health centres**] a place where people from a particular area can go to see a doctor or a nurse (**centro médico**)

health club /ˈhelθ ˌklʌb/ NOUN [plural **health clubs**] a place where people who are members can go to do activities such as swimming and exercise classes (**clube médico**)

health food /ˈhelθ ˌfuːd/ NOUN [plural **health foods**] food that is believed to be good for your health (**alimentação saudável**)

healthily /ˈhelθɪli/ ADVERB in a way that is good for your health ☐ *I eat healthily.* (**de maneira saudável**)

healthiness /ˈhelθɪnɪs/ NOUN, NO PLURAL being healthy (**saúde**)

health service /ˈhelθ ˌsɜːvɪs/ NOUN [plural **health services**] an organization that provides medical care for everyone (**serviço médico**)

health visitor /ˈhelθ ˌvɪzɪtə(r)/ NOUN [plural **health visitors**] a nurse who visits people in their homes (**enfermeiro que atende em domicílio**)

healthy /ˈhelθi/ ADJECTIVE [**healthier, healthiest**]
1 physically well and not ill in any way ☐ *Exercise and a good diet can help you stay healthy.* ☐ *She seems perfectly healthy.* (**saudável**)
2 having a good effect on your health (**saudável**) *healthy eating* (**alimentação saudável**) *She has a very healthy lifestyle.* (**estilo de vida saudável**)
3 showing a good attitude and likely to have a good result ☐ *A certain level of competition between companies is healthy.* (**saudável**)
4 something that is healthy is successful and likely to stay successful (**saudável**) *a healthy economy* (**economia saudável**)
5 a healthy amount of money is a large amount ☐ *She now has a good career and a healthy bank balance.* (**saudável**)

heap /hiːp/ ▶ NOUN [plural **heaps**]
1 an untidy pile of things ☐ *I found a heap of dirty clothes at the top of the stairs.* (**monte**) *His clothes were in a heap in the bottom of the wardrobe.* (**em um monte**)
2 heaps of something a lot of something. An informal phrase. ☐ *There's heaps of time before the match starts.* (**um monte de algo**)
▶ VERB [**heaps, heaping, heaped**]
1 to make a big untidy pile of things ☐ *His plate was heaped with food.* (**empilhar algo**)
2 heap praise/criticism on someone to praise or criticize someone a lot (**elogiar/criticar muito alguém**)

hear /hɪə(r)/ VERB [**hears, hearing, heard**]
1 to be aware of sounds through your ears ☐ *Can you hear that clicking noise?* ☐ *I heard the sound of an explosion.* ☐ *She screamed, but nobody heard her.* (**ouvir**)
2 to be told something ☐ **+ that** *I heard that she was unhappy in her job.* ☐ *The court heard that the men both used false passports.* ☐ **+ about** *Did you hear about Rob's accident?* (**ouvir**)
3 I hear used to talk about something you have been told ☐ *I hear you're getting married.* (**soube que...**)
4 have heard of someone/something to know that someone or something exists ☐ *I'd never heard of him before.* (**ouvir falar de alguém/algo**)
♦ PHRASAL VERB **hear from someone** to receive a letter, email, telephone call, etc. from someone ☐ *Have you heard from Joss recently?* (**ter notícias de alguém**)
• **hearing** /ˈhɪərɪŋ/ NOUN [plural **hearings**]
1 your ability to hear ☐ *My hearing was affected by the constant noise.* (**audição**)
2 in your hearing if something is said in your hearing, you hear it (**em sua frente**)

3 an official meeting where a judge or a group of people hear the facts about something □ *a court hearing* (audiência)
4 a chance to give your explanation or opinions (audiência) 🔲 *I don't feel that I had a fair hearing.* (audiência justa)

hearing aid /ˈhɪərɪŋ ˌeɪd/ NOUN [plural **hearing aids**] a small piece of equipment that is fitted onto a person's ear in order to help them hear better (aparelho auditivo)

hearsay /ˈhɪəseɪ/ NOUN, NO PLURAL things other people have told you for which you have no proof □ *His evidence was nothing more than hearsay.* (boato)

hearse /hɜːs/ NOUN [plural **hearses**] a large black car used for carrying the dead body to a funeral (carro funerário)

heart /hɑːt/ NOUN [plural **hearts**]
1 the organ that sends blood around your body (coração) 🔲 *My heart was beating very fast.* (coração batendo) 🔲 *He suffers from heart disease.* (doença cardíaca)
2 the centre of something □ + **of** *She lives in the heart of the city.* (centro)
3 the most important part of something □ + **of** *Jealousy is at the heart of their problems.* (centro) 🔲 *I really tried to get to the heart of what was upsetting her.* (chegar ao centro de)
4 at heart used to say what someone's real character is □ *He's a conventional man at heart.* (coração)
5 someone's feelings or character □ *She captured the hearts of the audience.* □ *Ken has a kind heart.* (coração)
6 a shape (♥) that represents the human heart and human love (coração)
7 hearts one of the four types of playing card, which have the symbol (♥) printed on them (copas)

♦ IDIOMS **know/learn something (off) by heart** to know or learn something so well that you do not have to read it □ *I learned the whole poem off by heart.* (saber algo de cor) **not have the heart to do something** to be too kind to do something □ *I didn't have the heart to tell him his story was rubbish.* (não ter peito para) **someone's heart sinks** if someone's heart sinks, they are disappointed or expect that something bad will happen □ *My heart sank when I saw how dirty the holiday cottage was.* (perder ânimo ou coragem)
⇨ go to **break someone's heart**

heartache /ˈhɑːteɪk/ NOUN, NO PLURAL great sadness (pesar, tristeza)

heart attack /ˈhɑːt əˌtæk/ NOUN [plural **heart attacks**] when someone's heart suddenly stops working □ *He died of a heart attack.* (ataque cardíaco)

heartbeat /ˈhɑːtbiːt/ NOUN [plural **heartbeats**] the regular sound or movement that your heart makes (batimento cardíaco)

heartbreak /ˈhɑːtbreɪk/ NOUN, NO PLURAL great sadness (sofrimento)
• **heartbreaking** /ˈhɑːtbreɪkɪŋ/ ADJECTIVE making you feel extremely sad □ *a heartbreaking story* (de partir o coração)
• **heartbroken** /ˈhɑːtbrəʊkən/ ADJECTIVE feeling extremely sad because something very bad has happened □ *Kay was heartbroken when he left her.* (de coração partido)

hearten /ˈhɑːtən/ VERB [**heartens, heartening, heartened**] to make someone feel happier about a situation □ *I was heartened to see so many people at the meeting.* (animar)
• **heartening** /ˈhɑːtənɪŋ/ ADJECTIVE making you feel happier about a situation (animador)

heartfelt /ˈhɑːtfelt/ ADJECTIVE completely sincere (sincero) 🔲 *a heartfelt apology* (desculpas sinceras)

hearth /hɑːθ/ NOUN [plural **hearths**] the area in front of a fireplace (= the space for a fire in the wall of a room) (lareira)

heartily /ˈhɑːtɪli/ ADVERB
1 loudly and with enthusiasm □ *They all laughed heartily at all his jokes.* (animadamente)
2 sincerely or completely (completamente) 🔲 *I'm heartily sick of their constant complaints.* (completamente enjoado de)

heartless /ˈhɑːtləs/ ADJECTIVE unkind and cruel (desumano, cruel)

heart-rending /ˈhɑːtrendɪŋ/ ADJECTIVE making you feel great sympathy and sadness for someone □ *heart-rending scenes of poverty* (de cortar o coração)

heart-throb /ˈhɑːtθrɒb/ NOUN [plural **heart-throbs**] an informal word for a very attractive man, especially one who is famous (homem atraente)

heart-to-heart /ˌhɑːttəˈhɑːt/ NOUN [plural **heart-to-hearts**] a conversation between two people in which they talk about their private feelings (conversa franca)

hearty /ˈhɑːti/ ADJECTIVE [**heartier, heartiest**]
1 loud, enthusiastic and friendly □ *He gave a hearty laugh.* (expansivo)
2 a hearty meal is a large meal □ *a hearty breakfast* (abundante)

heat /hiːt/ ▶ NOUN [plural **heats**]
1 *no plural* the quality of being hot or how hot something is □ *The panels use heat from the sun.* □ *Turn up the heat until the soup is boiling.* (calor)
2 the heat very hot weather □ *I can't stand the heat in summer.* (o calor)
3 *no plural* anger or strong feelings □ *She tried to calm them down and take the heat out of the situation.* (irritação)
4 a game or a race to decide who goes on to the next stage of a competition □ *Ian won his heat*

and went through to the semi-final. (prova eliminatória)

♦ IDIOM **in the heat of the moment** when you are very angry or excited and not controlling your words or behaviour □ *Some very nasty things were said in the heat of the moment.* (no calor do momento)

▶ VERB [**heats, heating, heated**] to make something hot or hotter □ *We use solar energy to heat our water.* □ *Heat the oven to medium.* (aquecer)

♦ PHRASAL VERB **heat (something) up** to become hotter or to make something hotter □ *We heated up the soup over the fire.* (aquecer algo)

• **heated** /ˈhiːtɪd/ ADJECTIVE full of anger or strong feelings (inflamado) 🔳 *a heated debate* (um debate inflamado)

• **heater** /ˈhiːtə(r)/ NOUN [*plural* **heaters**] a piece of equipment that heats water or a place □ *I'll turn this heater on.* (aquecedor)

heath /hiːθ/ NOUN [*plural* **heaths**] an area of wild land covered with grass and low bushes. A geography word. (charneca)

heather /ˈheðə(r)/ NOUN, NO PLURAL a plant with small purple or white flowers, that grows close to the ground on hills and mountains (urze)

heating /ˈhiːtɪŋ/ NOUN, NO PLURAL the system or machinery used to heat a building (calefação)

heatwave /ˈhiːtweɪv/ NOUN [*plural* **heatwaves**] a period of time when the weather is much hotter than usual (onda de calor)

heave /hiːv/ VERB [**heaves, heaving, heaved**] to lift, pull or throw something heavy using a lot of effort □ *We spent the morning heaving boxes of books into the van.* □ *Both teams heaved on the rope.* (arrastar, levantar)

♦ IDIOM **heave a sigh of relief** to feel happy because something unpleasant or worrying has not happened or has ended □ *We'll all heave a sigh of relief when the project is finished.* (respirar aliviado)

heaven /ˈhevən/ NOUN [*plural* **heavens**]

1 *no plural* in some religions, the place where God lives and where good people go when they die (céu, paraíso)

2 *no plural* something that is very pleasant □ *I had no work and no children for three whole days – it was heaven.* (paraíso)

3 the heavens the sky □ *The heavens opened and the rain came lashing down.* (o céu)

• **heavenly** /ˈhevənli/ ADJECTIVE

1 to do with heaven □ *a heavenly choir of angels* (celestial)

2 very pleasant □ *It was heavenly just lying in the sunshine.* (divino)

heavily /ˈhevɪli/ ADVERB

1 a lot or to a large degree □ *The soldiers were heavily armed.* □ *His wife is heavily pregnant.* (bem, muito)

2 with a lot of force or weight □ *It was snowing heavily when we left.* □ *She fell heavily, twisting her ankle.* (pesadamente)

heaviness /ˈhevɪnəs/ NOUN, NO PLURAL when something is heavy (peso)

heavy /ˈhevi/ ADJECTIVE [**heavier, heaviest**]

1 something that is heavy weighs a lot □ *The bags were too heavy for me to carry.* (pesado)

2 if you say how heavy something is, you say how much it weighs □ *How heavy are these bricks?* (pesado)

3 large in amount or degree (intenso, abundante, pesado) 🔳 *heavy traffic* (trânsito pesado) 🔳 *heavy rain/snow* (chuva/neve abundante) 🔳 *There was heavy fighting in the region.* (luta pesada)

4 a heavy smoker/drinker someone who smokes a lot/drinks a lot of alcohol (alguém que fuma/bebe muito)

5 a heavy burden/load/responsibility, etc. something that is difficult for someone to manage to deal with (uma carga/responsabilidade etc. muito pesada)

6 using a lot of force □ *a heavy blow* (muito forte)

heavy-handed /ˌhevi ˈhændɪd/ ADJECTIVE using more force than is necessary when dealing with a situation □ *I think the police response was a bit heavy-handed.* (opressivo)

heavy industry /ˌhevi ˈɪndʌstri/ NOUN [*plural* **heavy industries**] an industry or industries that use large machinery to produce coal, metal, ships etc. (indústria pesada)

heckle /ˈhekəl/ VERB [**heckles, heckling, heckled**] to interrupt a speaker or performer with loud remarks or questions □ *Someone started to heckle from the back of the hall.* (perturbar um orador)

• **heckler** /ˈheklə(r)/ NOUN [*plural* **hecklers**] someone who heckles a speaker or performer (perturbador)

hectare /ˈhekteə(r)/ NOUN [*plural* **hectares**] a unit for measuring area equal to 10,000 square metres. This is often written **ha**. (hectare)

hectic /ˈhektɪk/ ADJECTIVE very busy, with a lot of activity □ *We've had a rather hectic week.* (frenético)

he'd /hiːd/ a short way to say and write **he had** or **he would** □ *He'd never been there before.* □ *He'd do it for me if I asked him.* (ver **have**)

hedge /hedʒ/ ▶ NOUN [*plural* **hedges**] a line of bushes or trees growing close together that separates one piece of land from another □ *A thick hedge surrounds the garden.* (sebe)
▶ VERB [**hedges, hedging, hedged**] to avoid answering a question (esquivar-se)

hedgehog /ˈhedʒhɒg/ NOUN [*plural* **hedgehogs**] a small wild animal with sharp points all over its body (ouriço)

hedgerow

hedgerow /ˈhedʒrəʊ/ NOUN [plural **hedgerows**] a line of bushes and small trees growing close together along the side of a road or field (**sebe**)

heed /hiːd/ ▶ VERB [**heeds, heeding, heeded**] to pay attention to advice or a warning (**prestar atenção**) 🔳 *He didn't heed the warning.* (**prestar atenção ao aviso**)
▶ NOUN, NO PLURAL **pay/take heed** to pay attention to something ☐ *Drivers are taking heed of antidrinking advice.* (**dar atenção**)

• **heedless** /ˈhiːdlɪs/ ADJECTIVE paying no attention to possible danger or difficulty ☐ *He dived in and saved her, heedless of the risk to himself.* (**descuidado, insensato**)

heel /hiːl/ NOUN [plural **heels**]
1 the back part of your foot ☐ *She was getting a blister on her heel.* (**calcanhar**)
2 the part of a shoe under the back of your foot (**salto**) 🔳 *She was wearing high heels.* (**salto alto**)
3 the part of a sock that covers your heel (**soquete**)

hefty /ˈhefti/ ADJECTIVE [**heftier, heftiest**]
1 large and strong or fat ☐ *She's a fairly hefty woman.* (**robusto**)
2 large in amount (**pesado**) 🔳 *I got a hefty fine for driving in a bus lane.* (**multa pesada**)

height

height /haɪt/ NOUN [plural **heights**]
1 how tall or high someone or something is ☐ *He's of average height.* ☐ *I'd say the wall's about six feet in height.* (**altura**)
2 no plural the fact of being tall ☐ *I remarked on his height.* (**altura**)
3 how far above the ground something is ☐ *We are now flying at a height of 11,000 metres.* (**altitude**)
4 no plural the strongest or most extreme point that something reaches or can reach ☐ *He was at the height of his fame.* ☐ *It is the height of stupidity to throw a lit firework.* (**auge**)
5 heights high places ☐ *I'm afraid of heights.* ☐ *A coach took us up to the heights of Machu Picchu.* (**altura**)

• **heighten** /ˈhaɪtən/ VERB [**heightens, heightening, heightened**] to increase or be increased ☐ *The film's music heightens the tension.* ☐ *Passive smoking heightens the risk of lung cancer.* (**intensificar, aumentar**)

heinous /ˈheɪnəs/ ADJECTIVE very bad and shocking. A formal word. (**abominável**) 🔳 *He has been accused of a heinous crime.* (**crime abominável**)

heir /eə(r)/ NOUN [plural **heirs**] the person who has a legal right to someone's money or property when they die ☐ *He is the heir to a large fortune.* (**herdeiro**)

heiress /ˈeərɪs/ NOUN [plural **heiresses**] a girl or woman who has a legal right to someone's money or property when they die (**herdeira**)

heirloom /ˈeəluːm/ NOUN [plural **heirlooms**] something valuable that is given by parents or grandparents to their children or grandchildren (**relíquia**) 🔳 *That clock was a family heirloom.* (**relíquia de família**)

held /held/ PAST TENSE AND PAST PARTICIPLE OF **hold** ☐ *She held my hand* ☐ *We had held the meeting in David's office.* (ver **hold**)

helicopter

helicopter /ˈhelɪkɒptə(r)/ NOUN [plural **helicopters**] a small aircraft without wings that is lifted into the air by long thin parts on top which turn round very fast (**helicóptero**)

helium /ˈhiːliəm/ NOUN, NO PLURAL a gas that is lighter than air. A chemistry word. (**hélio**)

he'll /hiːl/ a short way to say and write **he will** ☐ *He'll be here soon.* (ver **will**)

hell

hell /hel/ NOUN, NO PLURAL
1 in some religions, the place where bad people go when they die (**inferno**)
2 a very unpleasant experience ☐ *The last few months of the relationship were hell.* (**inferno**)

hello

hello /həˈləʊ/ EXCLAMATION something you say when you meet someone or begin talking to someone on the telephone ☐ *Hello, Sophie. How are you?* ☐ *Hello, it's Mark.* (**olá, oi**)

helm /helm/ NOUN [plural **helms**]
1 the wheel or handle used to change direction on a ship or boat (**timão, leme**)
2 the helm used for saying that someone is in charge of a company or organization ☐ *He took over the helm 14 months ago.* (**na direção**)

helmet /ˈhelmɪt/ NOUN [plural **helmets**] a hard hat worn to protect your head ☐ *a cycling helmet* ☐ *a fireman's helmet* (**capacete**)

help

help /help/ ▶ VERB [**helps, helping, helped**]
1 to do something to make a situation or activity easier for someone ☐ **+ to do something** *I helped him to find somewhere to stay.* ☐ *I find a warm bath helps me to relax me.* ☐ **+ with** *My Mum helped me with my homework.* (**ajudar**)
2 to make a situation better or easier ☐ *If you've got a cold, eating oranges might help.* ☐ *It helps if you put the heavier items at the bottom.* ☐ *I took some painkillers, but they didn't help much.* (**ajudar**)
3 can't help (doing) something if you can't help something, you cannot stop yourself from doing it or stop it happening ☐ *She couldn't help laughing when she saw his face.* (**deixar de, evitar**)
4 help yourself to take something without waiting for someone to give it to you ☐ *Help yourself to some food.* (**servir-se de**)

◆ PHRASAL VERB **help (someone) out** to help someone by doing work for them or giving them money ☐ *My parents help out with the rent.* (**dar uma mão, sustentar**)

▶ NOUN [plural helps]
1 *no plural* when someone does something to make a situation or an activity easier for someone (ajuda) 🔁 *He needs help with his garden.* (precisa de ajuda) 🔁 *I was in debt, but I didn't know where to get help.* (conseguir ajuda) 🔁 *He tried to seek help for his depression.* (procurar ajuda) 🔁 *These children get extra help with their reading.* (ajuda extra)
2 someone or something that helps someone (ajuda) 🔁 *Thanks for the advice. It was a great help.* ☐ *I couldn't work out how to use the system, and the instructions weren't much help.*
3 part of a computer system that tells you how to deal with problems or questions. A computing word. (ajuda)
▶ EXCLAMATION **Help!** used to shout for help in a serious situation (socorro)

help desk /'help ˌdesk/ NOUN [plural **help desks**] a person or people who give advice to people who are having problems with a computer system. A computing word. (suporte técnico)

helper /'helpə(r)/ NOUN [plural **helpers**] someone who helps another person (ajudante)

helpful /'helpfʊl/ ADJECTIVE
1 useful ☐ *helpful advice* (útil)
2 willing to help ☐ *There was a lot of tidying up, but the children were very helpful.* (útil)
• **helpfully** /'helpfʊli/ ADVERB in a helpful way ☐ *She helpfully suggested that I might get information at the library.* (de modo útil)

helping /'helpɪŋ/ NOUN [plural **helpings**] an amount of food put on a plate for one person ☐ *Who'd like a second helping?* (porção)

helpless /'helpləs/ ADJECTIVE not able to do anything for yourself, or to help other people in trouble ☐ *How could anyone rob a helpless old man?* (desamparado)
• **helplessly** /'helpləsli/ ADVERB in a helpless way ☐ *We had to watch helplessly while our daughter died.* (desamparadamente)

helpline /'helplaɪn/ NOUN [plural **helplines**] a telephone number that you can call for advice on a particular subject ☐ *Ring our 24-hour free helpline.* (disque-ajuda)

hem /hem/ ▶ NOUN [plural **hems**] the edge of a piece of cloth that has been folded over and sewn down ☐ *I could let down the hem on that skirt for you.* (bainha)
▶ VERB [**hems, hemming, hemmed**] to sew a hem on the edge of a piece of cloth (fazer a bainha)
♦ PHRASAL VERB **hem someone in** to surround someone and stop them moving in any direction ☐ *A line of policemen hemmed the marchers in.* (encurralar, cercar alguém)

hemisphere /'hemɪsfɪə(r)/ NOUN [plural **hemispheres**]
1 one half of the Earth ☐ *the northern hemisphere* (hemisfério)
2 a shape which is like half of a ball. A maths word. (hemisfério)

hemoglobin /ˌhiːməˈgləʊbɪn/ NOUN, NO PLURAL the US spelling of **haemoglobin** (hemoglobina)

hemorrhage /'hemərɪdʒ/ NOUN [plural **hemorrhages**], VERB [**hemorrhages, hemorrhaging, hemorrhaged**] the US spelling of **haemorrhage** (hemorragia)

hemp /hemp/ NOUN, NO PLURAL a plant that is used to make ropes and rough cloth (cânhamo)

hen /hen/ NOUN [plural **hens**] a female chicken (galinha)

hence /hens/ ADVERB
1 for this reason ☐ *He's just had some bad news, hence his gloomy expression.* (daí, portanto)
2 from this time or from this place ☐ *five years hence* (daqui a, desde já)

henna /'henə/ NOUN, NO PLURAL a reddish-brown dye (= substance that adds colour) that you can use to colour your hair or decorate your body (hena)

hen party /'hen ˌpɑːti/ or **hen night** /'hen ˌnaɪt/ NOUN [plural **hen parties** or **hen nights**] a party for a group of women, especially one held just before a woman gets married (festa de despedida de solteiras)

hepatitis /ˌhepəˈtaɪtɪs/ NOUN, NO PLURAL a disease of the liver that can be very serious (hepatite)

her /hɜː(r)/ ▶ PRONOUN used as the object of a sentence to talk or write about a woman, girl or female animal that has already been mentioned ☐ *I'm looking for Mrs Peters. Have you seen her?* ☐ *I gave the letter to her.* (ela, a)
▶ DETERMINER belonging to or to do with a woman, girl or female animal ☐ *Her hair is blonde.* ☐ *That's her problem, not mine.* (dela)

herald /'herəld/ ▶ VERB [**heralds, heralding, heralded**] to be a sign that something is going to happen or come soon ☐ *The treaty heralded the birth of a new Europe.* (anunciar)
▶ NOUN [plural **heralds**] a sign that something is going to happen or come soon ☐ *Snowdrops are a herald of spring.* (arauto, anunciador)

herb /hɜːb/ NOUN [plural **herbs**] a plant that is used for giving flavour to food and for making medicines ☐ *herbs and spices* ☐ *a herb garden* (erva)
• **herbal** /'hɜːbəl/ ADJECTIVE made with herbs ☐ *herbal medicines* ☐ *herbal tea* (herbáceo)

herbivore /'hɜːbɪvɔː(r)/ NOUN [plural **herbivores**] an animal that eats only grass and plants. A biology word. (herbívoro)
• **herbivorous** /hɜːˈbɪvərəs/ ADJECTIVE eating only grass and plants. A biology word ☐ *Deer are herbivorous.* (herbívoro)

herd /hɜːd/ ▶ NOUN [plural **herds**] a large group of animals of one type that live as a group ☐ *a herd of cattle* (rebanho, manada)

here

▶ VERB [**herds, herding, herded**] to make animals or people come together and go somewhere in a group ☐ *We were herded into a small room at the back.* (**conduzir**)

here /hɪə(r)/ ADVERB
1 in or to this place ☐ *I like it here.* ☐ *Come here!* ☐ *You can leave your shoes here.* ☐ *He's American, but he's lived over here for years.* (**aqui**)
2 used to say that someone or something has arrived or has been found ☐ *Here's Tom at last.* ☐ *Here's the house we are looking for.* (**aqui**)
3 used when you give someone something ☐ *Here, put on this jacket.* ☐ *Here you are – we saved some food for you.* (**aí**)
4 at a particular place in a talk or a piece of writing ☐ *There were so many people involved, I can't list them all here.* (**aqui**)
5 in the present time, or at the present point in an activity ☐ *How shall we proceed from here?* ☐ *Wait until summer is here.* (**daqui**)
6 here and there in a few different places ☐ *There were a few mistakes here and there.* (**aqui e ali**)

hereafter /ˌhɪərˈɑːftə(r)/ ▶ ADVERB used in legal documents to mean after this or from this time on. A formal word. (**daqui por diante**)
▶ NOUN, NO PLURAL **the hereafter** life after death (**a vida após a morte**)

hereby /ˌhɪəˈbaɪ/ ADVERB used in legal documents to say what you are going to do and how it will be done. A formal word. ☐ *We hereby promise to abide by this agreement.* (**por este meio**)

hereditary /hɪˈredɪtəri/ ADJECTIVE passed on from parent to child ☐ *a hereditary disease* (**hereditário**)

• **heredity** /hɪˈredɪti/ NOUN, NO PLURAL the way in which qualities and features are passed from a parent to a child before the child is born (**hereditariedade**)

heresy /ˈherəsi/ NOUN [plural **heresies**] an opinion or belief, especially a religious one, that is different from what most people in a group or society believe and is considered wrong ☐ *Galileo was charged with heresy for his beliefs.* (**heresia**)

heritage /ˈherɪtɪdʒ/ NOUN, NO PLURAL the buildings, customs, culture, etc. of a country that are important because they have existed for a long time ☐ *Spain's cultural heritage* (**herança**)

hermaphrodite /hɜːˈmæfrədaɪt/ NOUN [plural **hermaphrodites**] an animal or a plant with both male and female sex organs. A biology word. (**hermafrodita**)

hermit /ˈhɜːmɪt/ NOUN [plural **hermits**] someone who lives alone and does not see other people (**eremita**)

• **hermitage** /ˈhɜːmɪtɪdʒ/ NOUN [plural **hermitages**] a place where a hermit lives (**habitação do eremita**)

hero /ˈhɪərəʊ/ NOUN [plural **heroes**]
1 someone who people admire because of the brave or difficult things they have done ☐ *Nelson Mandela is a hero to many of us.* (**herói**)
2 the most important male character in a story or film ☐ *The hero of the book is a New York detective.* (**herói**)

• **heroic** /hɪˈrəʊɪk/ ADJECTIVE very brave ☐ *He threw himself in front of her in a heroic attempt to save her.* (**heroico**)

• **heroine** /ˈherəʊɪn/ NOUN [plural **heroines**]
1 a woman or girl who people admire because of the brave or difficult things she has done (**heroína**)
2 the most important female character in a story or film (**heroína**)

• **heroism** /ˈherəʊɪzəm/ NOUN, NO PLURAL very brave behaviour ☐ *He won a medal for his heroism in battle.* (**heroísmo**)

heron /ˈherən/ NOUN [plural **herons**] a bird with long legs and a long neck that lives near water and catches fish in its long sharp beak (**garça**)

herring /ˈherɪŋ/ NOUN [plural **herring** or **herrings**] a small, silver, sea fish that is eaten as food (**arenque**)

hers /hɜːz/ PRONOUN used to talk or write about things belonging to or to do with a woman or girl that has already been mentioned ☐ *I gave Sandra my phone number and she gave me hers.* ☐ *'Was it your idea, or Ann's?' 'It was hers.'* (**dela, o/a dela**)

> Notice that there is no apostrophe between the **r** and the **s** in **hers**.

herself /hɜːˈself/ PRONOUN
1 the reflexive form of her ☐ *Did Barbara hurt herself when she fell down?* ☐ *She sang to herself as she worked.* (**ela mesma**)
2 used to show that she does something without any help from other people ☐ *She always answers every fan letter herself* (**ela mesma**) ☐ *She's only 3 but she can get dressed all by herself.* (**sozinha**)
3 used to emphasize the pronoun she ☐ *I wanted to speak to Gina herself.* (**ela mesma**)
4 by herself not with or near other people ☐ *She always sits by herself.* (**sozinha**)
5 to herself without having to share with anyone else ☐ *She had the whole flat to herself.* (**consigo mesma**)

he's /hiːz/ a short way to say and write he is or he has ☐ *He's my brother.* ☐ *He's done all the work.* (*ver* **be, have**)

hesitant /ˈhezɪtənt/ ADJECTIVE slow to do something and showing that you are are nervous or not sure that you should do it ☐ *She gave a rather hesitant answer.* (**hesitante, indeciso**)

• **hesitate** /ˈhezɪteɪt/ VERB [**hesitates, hesitating, hesitated**]
1 to pause before you say or do something because you are not sure you should say or do it ☐ *She hesitated before answering his question.* (**hesitar**)

2 not hesitate to do something to do something immediately because you know you should □ *If you need any help, don't hesitate to call me.* (**fazer algo sem hesitar**)

- **hesitation** /ˌhezɪˈteɪʃən/ NOUN [plural hesitations] when you pause before saying or doing something because you are not sure you should say or do it □ *He accepted without hesitation.* □ *There was a brief hesitation before she answered.* (**hesitação, dúvida**)

hexagon /ˈheksəgən/ NOUN [plural hexagons] a shape with six sides. A maths word. (**hexágono**)

- **hexagonal** /hekˈsægənəl/ ADJECTIVE in the shape of a hexagon. A maths word. (**hexagonal**)

hey /heɪ/ EXCLAMATION an exclamation used to get someone's attention or show you are surprised □ *Hey, stop that!* □ *Hey, look at this!* (**ei**)

heyday /ˈheɪdeɪ/ NOUN, NO PLURAL the time when someone or something was most famous or successful (**auge, apogeu**) 🔒 *In her heyday she was the highest paid star on Broadway* (**seu auge**)

HGV /ˌeɪtʃdʒiːˈviː/ ABBREVIATION heavy goods vehicle; a large vehicle such as a truck (**abreviação de caminhão para cargas pesadas**)

hi /haɪ/ EXCLAMATION hello □ *Hi, Charlotte!* □ *Hi, how are you?* (**oi, olá**)

hiatus /haɪˈeɪtəs/ NOUN [plural hiatuses] a period of time in which nothing happens. A formal word. □ *After a two-year hiatus the band are back on tour.* (**hiato, lacuna**)

hibernate /ˈhaɪbəneɪt/ VERB [hibernates, hibernating, hibernated] if an animal hibernates, it sleeps all winter □ *Her tortoise was hibernating in a box in the shed.* (**hibernar**)

- **hibernation** /ˌhaɪbəˈneɪʃən/ NOUN, NO PLURAL when an animal hibernates (**hibernação**) 🔒 *Bears go into hibernation in the winter.* (**entram em hibernação**)

hiccup /ˈhɪkʌp/ ▶ NOUN [plural hiccups]
1 a sudden repeated noise in your throat that you cannot control (**soluço**) 🔒 *Fizzy drinks often give me hiccups.* (**me deram soluços**) 🔒 *She laughed so much she got the hiccups.* (**teve soluços**)
2 a small problem that causes a delay □ *There were a few hiccups at the start of the project.* (**problema**)

▶ VERB [hiccups, hiccupping, hiccupped] to make repeated noises in your throat that you cannot control (**soluçar**)

hide¹ /haɪd/ VERB [hides, hiding, hid, hidden]
1 to put or keep something or someone in a place where people cannot see or find them easily □ *I hid her presents under my bed.* □ *He kept his money hidden from his wife.* (**esconder-se**)
2 to go to a place where people cannot see you □ *Eva was hiding and the other children were looking for her.* □ *He hid behind a tree.* (**esconder-se**)
3 to not let other people know about your feelings or some information □ *Sarah didn't try to hide her disappointment at losing.* □ *I've got nothing to hide.* (**esconder**)

hide² /haɪd/ NOUN [plural hides] the skin of an animal (**pele, couro**)

hide-and-seek /ˌhaɪdənˈsiːk/ NOUN, NO PLURAL a game in which one child hides and the other players look for him or her (**esconde-esconde**)

hideous /ˈhɪdiəs/ ADJECTIVE extremely ugly □ *I thought the dress was hideous.* (**horrendo**)

hideout /ˈhaɪdaʊt/ NOUN [plural hideouts] a place where someone hides, especially from the police □ *The gang had a secret hideout in the mountains.* (**esconderijo**)

hiding /ˈhaɪdɪŋ/ NOUN, NO PLURAL when someone stays in a secret place or changes their appearance so that no one will find them (**esconderijo**) 🔒 *The ex-spy is believed to be in hiding in London.* (**em um esconderijo**) 🔒 *He knew he would be arrested so he went into hiding.* (**foi para um esconderijo**)

hierarchy /ˈhaɪəˌrɑːki/ NOUN [plural hierarchies] a system or organization in which people are arranged according to their rank or importance □ *It is mostly men at the top of the political hierarchy.* (**hierarquia**)

hieroglyphics /ˌhaɪərəˈɡlɪfɪks/ PLURAL NOUN a system of writing used in Ancient Egypt in which little pictures represent letters and words (**hieróglifos**)

hi-fi /ˈhaɪˌfaɪ/ NOUN [plural hi-fis] a piece of electronic equipment for playing music (**som de alta fidelidade**)

high /haɪ/ ▶ ADJECTIVE [higher, highest]
1 a large distance above the ground □ *The apples were too high to reach.* □ *It's best to keep medicines on a high shelf.* (**alto**)
2 a long distance from the bottom to the top □ *It is a very high building.* □ *They built a high wall around the house.* (**alto**)
3 having a particular height □ *The fence is 4 metres high.* □ *How high is Snowdon?* (**de altura**)
4 large in amount or level (**alto**) 🔒 *The temperature was unusually high.* (**temperatura estava alta**) 🔒 *We drove at high speed through the town.* (**velocidade alta**) 🔒 *We were shocked at the high cost of housing.* (**custo alto**) 🔒 *They found high levels of radiation in the area.* (**altos níveis**)
5 very good (**alto**) 🔒 *high quality* (**alta qualidade**) 🔒 *We expect a very high standard of work.* (**alto padrão**)
6 important □ *He had a high rank in the army.* (**importante**)
7 a high sound or musical note is near the top of the range of sounds □ *We could hear the children's high voices.* (**agudo**)

♦ IDIOM **it's high time** used to emphasize that something should happen or be done very soon □ *It's high time Leo got a job.* (**está bem na hora**)

highbrow | hijack

> Remember that people who are big in height are described as tall and not high:
> ✓ *Her father is very tall.*
> ✗ *Her father is very high.*

▶ ADVERB [**higher, highest**]
1 at or to a large distance above the ground □ *She threw the ball high in the air.* □ *Dirty clothes were piled high in her bedroom.* □ *The village is perched high above the sea.* (**alto**)
2 at or to a large amount or level □ *The temperature rose higher and higher.* □ *Prices remain high.* (**alto**)
▶ NOUN [*plural* **highs**]
1 the largest amount or level that something reaches □ *Confidence was at an all-time high.* (**pico**) ⚎ *Temperatures reached a high of 25 degrees.* (**atingiram o pico**)
2 a feeling of happiness □ *We were all on a high after winning the match.* (**alegria**)

highbrow /ˈhaɪbraʊ/ ADJECTIVE highbrow books, programmes, discussions, etc. are serious and enjoyed by intelligent, well educated people □ *They have very highbrow conversations over dinner.* (**erudito, intelectual**)

high chair /ˈhaɪ ˌtʃeə(r)/ NOUN [*plural* **high chairs**] a chair with long legs for a baby or young child to sit in while they are eating (**cadeira alta para bebês**)

higher education /ˌhaɪə(r) ˌedjuˈkeɪʃən/ NOUN, NO PLURAL education at a university or college □ *They have two children, both now in higher education.* (**ensino superior**)

high jump /ˈhaɪ ˌdʒʌmp/ NOUN, NO PLURAL a sport in which people try to jump over a horizontal bar that gets higher as the competition continues (**salto em altura**)

highland /ˈhaɪlənd/ ADJECTIVE to do with an area that has a lot of mountains □ *a highland cottage* (**região montanhosa**)
• **highlands** /ˈhaɪləndz/ PLURAL NOUN an area of a country that has a lot of mountains □ *the Scottish Highlands* (**regiões montanhosas**)

highlight /ˈhaɪlaɪt/ ▶ VERB [**highlights, highlighting, highlighted**]
1 to emphasize something □ *These figures highlight a growing problem.* (**destacar**)
2 to mark words on a page with a different colour so that people give them more attention □ *I've highlighted the important quotations in green.* (**realçar**)
▶ NOUN [*plural* **highlights**]
1 the best part of an event or period of time □ *His singing was the highlight of the concert.* (**ponto alto**)
2 highlights lines of a lighter colour that are put in your hair (**luzes**)
• **highlighter** /ˈhaɪlaɪtə(r)/ NOUN [*plural* **highlighters**] a pen with brightly coloured transparent ink that you use to mark words in a piece of writing (**marca-texto**)

highly /ˈhaɪli/ ADVERB
1 very □ *highly qualified teachers* □ *This seems highly unlikely.* (**altamente, muito**)
2 highly paid paid a lot of money □ *highly paid executives* (**muito bem pago**)
3 highly regarded/respected admired by a lot of people □ *a very highly regarded politician* (**altamente respeitado**)
4 speak/think highly of someone to admire someone □ *Martin's always spoken very highly of you.* (**ter alguém em alta conta**)

highly-strung /ˌhaɪliˈstrʌŋ/ ADJECTIVE very nervous and easily made upset (**tenso, irritadiço**)

high-maintenance /ˌhaɪˈmeɪntənəns/ ADJECTIVE needing a lot of effort and attention □ *a high-maintenance hairstyle* (**de muita manutenção**)

Highness /ˈhaɪnɪs/ NOUN [*plural* **Highnesses**] **Your/Her/His Highness** a title you use when you are speaking about or to a member of a royal family (**Sua/Vossa Alteza**)

high-pitched /ˌhaɪˈpɪtʃt/ ADJECTIVE a high-pitched voice or sound is high and sometimes unpleasant (**agudo, voz aguda**)

high-powered /ˌhaɪˈpaʊəd/ ADJECTIVE very powerful and responsible □ *high-powered jobs in industry* □ *a high-powered executive* (**poderoso**)

high-rise /ˈhaɪraɪz/ ▶ ADJECTIVE high-rise buildings are tall and narrow with a lot of levels (**com muitos andares, arranha-céu**)
▶ NOUN [*plural* **high-rises**] a very tall building (**edifício alto**)

high school /ˈhaɪ ˌskuːl/ NOUN [*plural* **high schools**] in the US, a school for children aged between 14 and 18 (**ensino médio**)

high street /ˈhaɪ ˌstriːt/ NOUN [*plural* **high streets**] the main street of a town, where the shops and banks are □ *Most of the high street banks will be raising their interest rates.* (**rua principal**)

high-tech /ˌhaɪˈtek/ ADJECTIVE using the most modern technology □ *high-tech security equipment* □ *high-tech computer graphics* (**de alta tecnologia**)

highway /ˈhaɪweɪ/ NOUN [*plural* **highways**] a US word for a road between towns and cities (**estrada**)

Highway Code /ˌhaɪweɪ ˈkəʊd/ NOUN, NO PLURAL **the Highway Code** a set of official rules that tells you how to use the roads (**código de trânsito**)

hijack /ˈhaɪdʒæk/ VERB [**hijacks, hijacking, hijacked**] to take control of an aeroplane by force □ *Two students hijacked the plane in Thailand.* (**sequestrar**)
• **hijacker** /ˈhaɪdʒækə(r)/ NOUN [*plural* **hijackers**] someone who hijacks an aeroplane □ *The hijackers were arrested by Australian police.* (**sequestrador**)

- **hijacking** /'haɪdʒækɪŋ/ NOUN [plural **hijackings**] the crime of taking control of an aeroplane by force (**sequestro**)

hike /haɪk/ ▶ NOUN [plural **hikes**]
1 a long walk in the countryside (**caminhada**)
2 a sudden increase in the level of something □ *a hike in interest rates* (**aumento**)
▶ VERB [**hikes, hiking, hiked**]
1 to go for a long walk in the countryside (**fazer uma caminhada**)
2 to increase the level of something □ *Retailers have hiked up the price of many household goods.* (**aumentar o nível**)

- **hiker** /'haɪkə(r)/ NOUN [plural **hikers**] someone who goes for long walks in the countryside (**caminhante**)
- **hiking** /'haɪkɪŋ/ NOUN, NO PLURAL the activity of taking long walks in the countryside (**caminhada**)

hilarious /hɪ'leərɪəs/ ADJECTIVE very funny □ *The film was hilarious.* (**hilariante, hilário**)

- **hilarity** /hɪ'lærɪtɪ/ NOUN, NO PLURAL when people think something is very funny and laugh loudly □ *His comments caused great hilarity.* (**hilaridade**)

hill /hɪl/ NOUN [plural **hills**] a raised or high area of land, smaller than a mountain □ *We went walking in the Tuscan hills.* (**colina**)
♦ IDIOM **over the hill** if someone is over the hill, they are too old to do something (**estar velho demais para fazer algo**)

hillside /'hɪlsaɪd/ NOUN [plural **hillsides**] the side of a hill (**encosta**)

hilly /'hɪlɪ/ ADJECTIVE [**hillier, hilliest**] a hilly area has a lot of hills (**montanhoso**)

hilt /hɪlt/ NOUN [plural **hilts**] the handle of a knife or sword (**punho de espada, cabo de faca**)
♦ IDIOM **to the hilt** very much or as much as you possibly can □ *I'd defend his character to the hilt.* (**incondicionalmente**)

him /hɪm/ PRONOUN used as the object of a sentence to talk or write about a man, boy or male animal that has already been mentioned □ *I'm looking for Mr Peters. Have you seen him anywhere?* □ *She threw the book at him.* (**ele, o**)

himself /hɪm'self/ PRONOUN
1 the reflexive form of him □ *He poked himself in the eye by mistake.* □ *The old man was muttering to himself.* (**ele mesmo, se**)
2 used to show that he does something without any help from other people □ *I was surprised he did all the cooking himself.* (**ele mesmo**) 🔲 *Jack can tie his shoelaces all by himself already.* (**sozinho**)
3 used to emphasize the pronoun him □ *He's never been to London himself.* (**ele mesmo**)
4 by himself not with or near other people □ *He stood by himself in a corner.* (**sozinho**)

5 to himself without having to share with anyone else □ *He enjoyed having his mother to himself.* (**apenas para ele**)

hind /haɪnd/ ADJECTIVE **hind leg/foot** the back leg or foot of an animal □ *The horse reared up on its hind legs.* (**perna/pé traseiro**)

hinder /'hɪndə(r)/ VERB [**hinders, hindering, hindered**] to make it more difficult to do something □ *Lack of money has hindered research into the disease.* (**retardar, atrapalhar**)

- **hindrance** /'hɪndrəns/ NOUN [plural **hindrances**] something that makes it difficult to do something (**impedimento**)

hindsight /'haɪndsaɪt/ NOUN, NO PLURAL understanding of an event or situation that you have after it has happened (**retrospectiva**) 🔲 *With hindsight I can see I was a fool to trust him.* (**em retrospectiva**)

Hindu /'hɪnduː/ ▶ NOUN [plural **Hindus**] a person whose religion is Hinduism (**hindu**)
▶ ADJECTIVE to do with Hinduism □ *The main Hindu gods are Brahma, Vishnu and Shiva.* (**hindu**)

- **Hinduism** /'hɪnduːɪzəm/ NOUN, NO PLURAL a religion of India and parts of South East Asia, which has many gods and teaches that after people die they will return to life in another body (**hinduísmo**)

hinge /hɪndʒ/ NOUN [plural **hinges**] a piece of metal or plastic which attaches a door to its frame, and allows the door to open and close (**dobradiça**)
♦ PHRASAL VERB [**hinges, hinging, hinged**] **hinge on something** if one thing hinges on another, it depends on it □ *Whether he gets into university hinges on his A level results.* (**depender de algo**)

hint /hɪnt/ ▶ NOUN [plural **hints**]
1 something that suggests what you think or want but not in a direct way (**dica, pista**) 🔲 *She dropped a hint that something exciting was about to happen.* (**deixou uma dica**) 🔲 *He kept yawning but no one took the hint and went home.* (**pegou a dica, se tocou**)
2 a helpful piece of advice □ *Can you give me any hints on how to learn vocabulary?* (**dica, pista**)
3 a small amount of something □ *fizzy water with a hint of lemon* (**indício**)
▶ VERB [**hints, hinting, hinted**] to suggest something in a way that is not clear or direct □ *Laura hinted that she might be leaving.* (**insinuar**)

hip /hɪp/ NOUN [plural **hips**] each of the two parts at the side of your body, below your waist and above your leg □ *Gran fell and broke her hip.* (**quadril**)

hip-hop /'hɪphɒp/ NOUN, NO PLURAL a type of pop music in which the words are about social problems and are spoken not sung □ *hip-hop groups* (**hip-hop**)

hippie

hippie /ˈhɪpɪ/ NOUN [plural **hippies**] a long-haired person in the 1960s who believed in peace and love and was against war and tradition (**hippie**)

hippo /ˈhɪpəʊ/ NOUN [plural **hippos**] an informal word for a **hippopotamus** (**hipopótamo**)

hippopotamus /ˌhɪpəˈpɒtəməs/ NOUN [plural **hippopotamuses** or **hippopotami**] a large African animal with a heavy body, small ears and short legs, that lives near or in rivers (**hipopótamo**)

hippy /ˈhɪpɪ/ NOUN [plural **hippies**] another spelling of **hippie** (**hippie**)

hire /ˈhaɪə(r)/ ▶ VERB [**hires, hiring, hired**]
1 to pay to use something for a period of time, especially a short period, and then return it □ *We hired bikes while we were on holiday.* (**alugar**)
2 to begin to employ someone □ *I've decided to hire a cleaner.* (**contratar**)

> Notice that in British English you hire things usually for a short time, only paying once to use them. You rent, usually for a longer period, a house or an office, etc., paying every month or many times. In American English you always rent things. The verb hire is not used.

▶ NOUN, NO PLURAL when you pay to use something for a period of time □ *The holiday price includes the hire of a car.* (**aluguel**) 🔳 *There are boats for hire on the lake.* (**de aluguel**)

his /hɪz/ ▶ DETERMINER belonging to or to do with him □ *Julian has left his coat behind.* □ *Blame Harry. It was his idea.* (**dele, seu, sua**)
▶ PRONOUN used to talk or write about things belonging to or to do with to a man, boy or male animal that has already been mentioned □ *I didn't have an umbrella so Grandad lent me his.* (**o/a dele**)

hiss /hɪs/ ▶ VERB [**hisses, hissing, hissed**]
1 to make a noise like a long 's' sound □ *a hissing snake* (**silvar**)
2 to say something quietly and angrily □ *'I said be quiet!' he hissed.* (**sibilar**)
▶ NOUN [plural **hisses**] a sound like that made by a snake □ *We could hear the hiss of gas escaping from the pipe.* (**silvo, assobio**)

histogram /ˈhɪstəɡræm/ NOUN [plural **histograms**] a diagram in which amounts are shown using thick lines of different heights. A maths word. (**histograma**)

historian /hɪˈstɔːrɪən/ NOUN [plural **historians**] someone who studies history □ *a local historian* (**historiador**)

• **historic** /hɪˈstɒrɪk/ ADJECTIVE important and likely to be remembered for a long time □ *a historic victory* (**histórico**)

• **historical** /hɪˈstɒrɪkəl/ ADJECTIVE to do with history □ *historical records* (**histórico**)

> Notice the difference between **historic** and **historical**. Historic means 'important in history'. Historical means 'to do with history': □ *This was a historic moment.* □ *She writes historical novels.*

• **history** /ˈhɪstərɪ/ NOUN [plural **histories**]
1 *no plural* all the things that happened in the past, or the study of things that happened in the past □ *local history* □ *modern European history* □ *He studied history at university.* □ *history books* (**história**)
2 the series of events or things that happened or relate to someone or something in the past (**histórico**) 🔳 *We didn't know the patient's medical history.* (**histórico médico**) □ + *of He has a history of mental illness.*

hit /hɪt/ ▶ VERB [**hits, hitting, hit**]
1 to move against someone or something with force □ *Stop hitting your brother!* □ *The plane hit the ground and burst into flames.* □ *I hit my head on the cupboard door.* □ *She hit him with a baseball bat.* □ *Storms hit the west coast last night.* (**bater**)
2 to have a bad effect on someone □ *The business was hit by big rent rises.* (**afetar**) 🔳 *The area was hard hit by unemployment.* (**duramente afetada**)
3 to reach a particular level □ *Temperatures hit record levels today.* (**acertar**) 🔳 *The sales team managed to hit their target.* (**acertar seu alvo**)
4 if the truth about something hits you, you suddenly become aware of it □ *It suddenly hit me that we could die.* (**dar-se conta**)
◆ IDIOM **hit it off** to like each other quickly □ *We met in Spain, and hit it off straight away.* (**dar-se bem rapidamente**)
◆ PHRASAL VERBS **hit back** to attack or criticize someone who has attacked or criticized you □ *The singer hit back at critics who accused her of being too sentimental.* (**revidar**) **hit on/upon something** to have a good idea about something □ *He'd hit on the perfect solution to the problem.* (**ter uma boa ideia sobre algo**)
▶ NOUN [plural **hits**]
1 something or someone that is very popular □ *The show was an instant hit.* □ *He's a big hit with the old ladies.* (**sucesso**)
2 when you touch against something with force □ *I got a hit on my arm.* (**golpe**)
3 a record of someone looking at a document on the Internet. A computing word. □ *Our website gets over three thousand hits a week.* (**número de acessos da internet**)
▶ ADJECTIVE popular and successful □ *a hit song* (**de sucesso**)

hit-and-miss /ˌhɪtənˈmɪs/ or **hit-or-miss** /ˌhɪtəˈmɪs/ ADJECTIVE not planned or organized well, so sometimes successful and sometimes not □ *Their methods are pretty hit-and-miss.* (**aleatório**)

hit-and-run

hit-and-run /ˌhɪtənˈrʌn/ ▶ ADJECTIVE to do with an accident in which a driver hits someone but does not stop to help the injured person □ *a hit-and-run driver* (atropelamento e fuga)
▶ NOUN [*plural* **hit-and-runs**] a hit-and-run accident (atropelamento)

hitch /hɪtʃ/ ▶ VERB [**hitches, hitching, hitched**]
1 to get a free ride in a vehicle by standing at the side of the road and waiting for someone to stop and take you with them □ *We couldn't afford the train ticket so we decided to hitch.* (pegar carona) 🔊 *I hitched a lift out of town.* (peguei uma carona)
2 to fasten one thing to another □ *He hitched the caravan to the back of the car.* (acoplar, engatar)
♦ PHRASAL VERB **hitch something up** to pull up a piece of your clothing □ *She hitched her skirt up and climbed over the wall.* (arregaçar)
▶ NOUN [*plural* **hitches**] a small difficulty (problema) 🔊 *The school show went off without a hitch.* (sem nenhum problema)

hitchhike /ˈhɪtʃhaɪk/ ▶ VERB [**hitchhikes, hitchhiking, hitchhiked**] to get a free ride in a vehicle by standing at the side of the road and waiting for someone to stop and take you with them □ *We hitchhiked around Europe.* (pedir carona)
• **hitchhiker** /ˈhɪtʃhaɪkə(r)/ NOUN [*plural* **hitchhikers**] someone who hitchhikes (pessoa que viaja de carona)

hi-tech /ˌhaɪˈtek/ ADJECTIVE another spelling of **high-tech** (alta tecnologia)

hitherto /ˌhɪðəˈtuː/ ADVERB until now. A formal word. □ *Hitherto the librarian had always been in charge of the keys.* (até agora)

HIV /ˌeɪtʃaɪˈviː/ ABBREVIATION human immunodeficiency virus; the virus that causes the disease AIDS (HIV)

hive /haɪv/ NOUN [*plural* **hives**] a container that bees live in and where they store their honey (colmeia)
♦ IDIOM **a hive of activity** a place where everyone is busy doing something (local onde muitas pessoas trabalham arduamente)

HMS /ˌeɪtʃemˈes/ ABBREVIATION His or Her Majesty's Ship used in the names of British Royal Navy ships □ *HMS Victory* (abreviação de Sua Majestade nas embarcações da realeza britânica)

hoard /hɔːd/ ▶ VERB [**hoards, hoarding, hoarded**] to collect things and store them away in large quantities □ *He started hoarding food because he thought there was going to be a war.* (acumular)
▶ NOUN [*plural* **hoards**] a large store of things that you have collected and kept □ *a hoard of Roman coins* (acúmulo)
• **hoarder** /ˈhɔːdə/ NOUN [*plural* **hoarders**] someone who likes saving and keeping a lot of things (colecionador, acumulador)

hold

hoarding /ˈhɔːdɪŋ/ NOUN [*plural* **hoardings**] a large board in the street where advertisements are put up (outdoor, placa publicitária)

hoarse /hɔːs/ ADJECTIVE [**hoarser, hoarsest**] if you are hoarse, your voice sounds rough, often because your throat is sore □ *He was hoarse from cheering on the team.* (rouco)

hoax /həʊks/ NOUN [*plural* **hoaxes**] a trick in which someone tells people something bad that is not true, for example by saying that there is a bomb somewhere (trote) 🔊 *He was accused of making hoax calls to the fire brigade.* (trotes)

hob /hɒb/ NOUN [*plural* **hobs**] the top surface of a cooker where you heat food in pans (placa de aquecimento)

hobble /ˈhɒbəl/ VERB [**hobbles, hobbling, hobbled**] to walk with difficulty because your foot or leg hurts □ *He was hobbling around the pitch.* (mancar)

hobby /ˈhɒbɪ/ NOUN [*plural* **hobbies**] something you like doing in your free time (passatempo) 🔊 *My Dad's favourite hobby is birdwatching.* (passatempo favorito) 🔊 *It's my new hobby.* (novo passatempo) 🔊 *She didn't really have any hobbies.* (tem algum passatempo)

hockey /ˈhɒkɪ/ NOUN, NO PLURAL a game in which two teams use curved sticks to hit a ball into a net (hóquei) 🔊 *We play hockey at school.* (joga hóquei) 🔊 *a hockey stick* (taco de hóquei) □ *a hockey team*

hoe /həʊ/ ▶ NOUN [*plural* **hoes**] a garden tool used for turning soil (enxada)
▶ VERB [**hoes, hoeing, hoed**] to use a hoe to turn soil in a garden (carpir)

hog /hɒɡ/ ▶ VERB [**hogs, hogging, hogged**] to use something yourself which stops other people from using it. An informal word. □ *He had parked badly and was hogging two parking spaces.* (monopolizar)
▶ NOUN [*plural* **hogs**] a pig (porco)

hoist /hɔɪst/ ▶ VERB [**hoists, hoisting, hoisted**] to lift something □ *He hoisted his bag over his shoulder.* (levantar, içar)
▶ NOUN [*plural* **hoists**] a piece of equipment for lifting heavy things (guindaste)

hold /həʊld/ ▶ VERB [**holds, holding, held**]
1 to have something in your hand or hands □ *He was holding a big wooden box.* (segurar) 🔊 *Hold tight – we're going over some rough ground.* (segure firme)
2 to support something or to stop something moving □ *The pieces of wood are held together with nails.* (segurar) 🔊 *Use glue to hold the cardboard in place.* (segure no lugar)
3 to keep a part of your body in a particular position □ *Hold your hands in the air.* (manter)
4 to organize an event □ *We held the meeting in our office.* (realizar) 🔊 *The government will never*

holdall — holiday

hold talks with terrorists. (**manter conversa**) The general has promised to *hold an election*. (**realizar uma eleição**)

5 to have space for something □ *The room holds 300 people.* (**acomodar**)

6 to contain something □ *This rack holds my wine collection.* (**conter**)

7 to keep someone as a prisoner □ *He is being held in a Russian jail.* (**manter**) *The three women were held hostage for over an hour.* (**mantidas prisioneiras**)

8 to keep information or documents □ *All his papers are held at the bank.* □ *The police hold records on all the suspects.* (**manter**)

9 to have a particular job or position in an organization □ *She holds the post of director.* (**ocupar**)

10 to have a particular opinion □ *He holds the view that women should stay at home.* (**considerar**)

11 hold your breath to deliberately not breathe (**prender a respiração**)

12 hold hands to curve your hand around someone else's hand (**apertar as mãos**)

13 hold a record to be the person or thing that is the best, biggest, fastest, etc. □ *He holds the world record for the 400 m.* (**ter o recorde**)

⇨ go to **hold your own**

◆ PHRASAL VERBS **hold something against someone** to continue to feel angry with someone about something they did in the past □ *I got the job he wanted and he's always held it against me.* (**ter algo contra alguém**) **hold something/someone back** to stop someone or something making progress □ *A lack of formal education did not hold her back.* (**conter algo/alguém**) **hold something down 1** to keep prices, amounts, etc. at a low level □ *The company has tried to hold down wages.* (**segurar algo**) **2** if you hold down a job, you manage to continue doing it □ *He's held down a steady job for two years now.* (**manter algo**) **hold off** to wait for a period of time before doing something □ *He decided to hold off contacting her.* (**refrear temporariamente**) **hold on 1** to hold something tightly □ *Hold on tight! We're coming to get you.* (**segurar-se**) **2** to wait □ *Hold on a minute – I just need to check my email.* (**esperar**) **hold out 1** to continue to be enough □ *I don't know how long our supplies will hold out.* (**durar**) **2** to continue to manage in a difficult situation □ *The soldiers started firing at us, but we held out until our comrades arrived.* (**aguentar**) **hold someone/something up** to make something or someone slow or late □ *We got held up by the traffic.* □ *All these regulations are holding up progress.* (**deter alguém/algo**)

▶ NOUN [plural **holds**]

1 when you hold something, or the way something is held (**segurar, agarrar-se a**) □ *I got hold of the handle and pulled it hard.* (**agarrei**) *Try to catch hold of the rope.* (**segurar**) *My hands were so wet, I couldn't keep hold of the rail.* (**segurar**)

2 get hold of something to manage to get something □ *Do you know where I can get hold of some cheap bricks?* (**conseguir algo**)

3 get hold of someone to manage to speak to someone □ *I've been trying to get hold of her all morning.* (**contatar alguém**)

4 on hold (a) if an activity is on hold, it has been stopped until a later time (b) if someone puts you on hold on the telephone, they leave you waiting to speak to someone (**em espera**)

5 power that someone can use to control someone **+ over** *He had a strong hold over all his pupils.* (**influência, controle**)

6 the place in a ship or an aeroplane where goods or bags are stored (**porão**)

holdall /ˈhəʊldɔːl/ NOUN [plural **holdalls**] a large soft bag (**sacola de viagem**)

holder /ˈhəʊldə(r)/ NOUN [plural **holders**]
1 someone who has something (**titular, portador**) *Ticket holders are entitled to a refund if the concert is cancelled.* (**portadores de ingresso**) *He's the world record holder for the 100 m.* (**titular do recorde**)
2 something used for holding something else □ *a toothbrush holder* (**suporte**)

hold-up /ˈhəʊldʌp/ NOUN [plural **hold-ups**]
1 a delay □ *The train conductor apologized for the hold-up.* (**atraso**)
2 when someone uses a gun to try to steal money from a shop or bank (**assalto**)

hole /həʊl/ NOUN [plural **holes**]
1 a space in the surface of something □ **+ in** *He had a hole in his sock.* □ *She drilled a hole in the wall.* (**buraco, orifício**)
2 a space dug in the ground (**buraco**) *They dug a deep hole in the ground to plant the rose bush in.* (**cavaram um buraco**) □ *a rabbit hole*
3 in golf, one of the places in the ground that you try to hit the ball into (**buraco**)

holiday /ˈhɒlɪdeɪ/ NOUN [plural **holidays**]
1 a time when you do not have to work or go to school (**férias**) *What are you doing in the summer holidays?* (**férias de verão**) *The museum is very busy during school holidays.* (**férias escolares**)
2 on holiday if you are on holiday, you are not working or not at school for a period □ *I'm on holiday next week.* (**de férias**)
3 a period of time when you stay in a different place to enjoy yourself (**férias**) *We're going on holiday next week.* (**estamos de férias**) □ *a skiing holiday* *Spain is a popular holiday destination for British travellers.* (**destino de férias**)
4 an official day when many people in a country do not have to go to work (**feriado**) *1st August is a national holiday in Switzerland.* (**feriado nacional**)

> The word **holiday** is used by British speakers of English. North American speakers of English use the word **vacation**.

holiness /ˈhəʊlɪnɪs/ NOUN, NO PLURAL
1 being holy (**santidade**)
2 His/Your Holiness a title used for the Pope, and some other religious leaders (**Sua Santidade**)

hollow /ˈhɒləʊ/ ▶ ADJECTIVE [**hollower, hollowest**]
1 having an empty space inside □ *hollow chocolate eggs* □ *a hollow tube* (**oco**)
2 having no real meaning or emotion □ *a hollow promise* □ *a hollow victory* (**falso**)
3 hollow cheeks and eyes have a surface that curves in (**fundo**)
▶ NOUN [*plural* **hollows**] an empty space in something or an area that is lower than the area around it □ *There were cracks and hollows in the rock.* (**depressão, buraco**)

holly /ˈhɒli/ NOUN, NO PLURAL a tree with sharp leaves and red berries (= small fruit) (**azevinho**)

holocaust /ˈhɒləkɔːst/ NOUN [*plural* **holocausts**]
1 the Holocaust the murder of many Jewish people by the Nazis in the 1930s and 1940s (**o Holocausto**)
2 an event in which many people are killed and many things are damaged □ *a nuclear holocaust* (**holocausto**)

hologram /ˈhɒləɡræm/ NOUN [*plural* **holograms**] a type of picture that does not look as if it is flat, especially when you move it (**holograma**)

holster /ˈhəʊlstə(r)/ NOUN [*plural* **holsters**] a container for a gun that someone wears on a belt (**coldre**)

holy /ˈhəʊli/ ADJECTIVE [**holier, holiest**]
1 to do with God or religion □ *The Koran is the Muslim holy book.* □ *The Golden Temple is a holy site in Punjab.* (**sagrado**)
2 having strong religious feelings □ *a holy man* (**santo**)

homage /ˈhɒmɪdʒ/ NOUN, NO PLURAL **pay homage to something/someone** to do or say something to show your respect for someone or their achievements □ *He paid homage to the artist by writing a book about her.* (**prestar homenagem a algo/alguém**)

home /həʊm/ ▶ NOUN [*plural* **homes**]
1 the place where you live or where you lived when you were a child □ *I left my watch at home.* (**lar, casa**) 🔁 *He left home at the age of twenty.* (**saiu de casa**) 🔁 *Cambridge is my home town.* (**cidade natal**)
2 a building that people live in □ *We can't afford to buy our own home.* □ *Hundreds of new homes will be built in the city.* (**casa**)
3 the place where something started or where a lot of something exists or is done □ *Mumbai is the home of the Indian film industry.* (**berço**)
4 a place where people or animals who need care live □ *a children's home* □ *an old people's home* (**abrigo**)
5 the place where a sports team is based □ *The home side is favourite to win.* (**casa**)
◆ IDIOMS **be/feel at home** to be very relaxed and confident in a place (**sentir-se em casa**) **make yourself at home** to be relaxed in a place as if it was where you live (**sentir-se à vontade**)
▶ ADVERB **1** to the place where you live (**para casa**) 🔁 *It's time to go home.* (**ir para casa**) 🔁 *Thousands of soldiers are returning home this week.* (**voltando para casa**) □ *I met Freddie on my way home.* **2** at the place where you live □ *Will you be home tomorrow?* (**em casa**)

> Notice that you **go home** or **get home**. You do not 'go to home' or 'get to home':
> ✓ *I usually get home later.*
> ✗ *I usually get to home later.*

◆ PHRASAL VERB [**homes, homing, homed**] **home in on something** to give a lot of attention to a particular part of something □ *He homed in on the sales figures.* (**prestar atenção em algo**)

homeless /ˈhəʊmləs/ ▶ ADJECTIVE having nowhere to live □ *Thousands of people have been made homeless by the earthquake.* (**sem lar**)
▶ NOUN **the homeless** people who have nowhere to live □ *The charity provides meals for the homeless.* (**os sem-teto**)
• **homelessness** /ˈhəʊmləsnəs/ NOUN, NO PLURAL when people have nowhere to live □ *Homelessness is a problem in many big cities.* (**falta de moradia**)

homely /ˈhəʊmli/ ADJECTIVE [**homelier, homeliest**] pleasant and comfortable □ *The hotel is quiet and homely.* (**simples, despretensioso**)

homemade /ˌhəʊmˈmeɪd/ ADJECTIVE made in someone's home and not in a factory □ *homemade cakes* (**caseiro**)

homeopath /ˈhəʊmiəʊpæθ/ NOUN [*plural* **homeopaths**] someone who uses homeopathy to treat people (**homeopata**)
• **homeopathic** /ˌhəʊmiəʊˈpæθɪk/ ADJECTIVE to do with homeopathy □ *homeopathic remedies* (**homeopático**)
• **homeopathy** /ˌhəʊmiˈɒpəθi/ NOUN, NO PLURAL treating diseases by giving someone a very small amount of a substance that in large amounts would cause the illness (**homeopatia**)

home page /ˈhəʊm ˌpeɪdʒ/ NOUN [*plural* **home pages**] the first page on a website. A computing word. (**página inicial**)

homesick /ˈhəʊmsɪk/ ADJECTIVE feeling unhappy because you are away from home and your family □ *A lot of children feel homesick when they first spend time away from their parents.* (**ter saudade de casa**)

- **homesickness** /ˈhəʊmsɪknɪs/ NOUN, NO PLURAL the feeling of being homesick (o sentimento de ter saudades de casa)

homeward /ˈhəʊmwəd/ ADJECTIVE, ADVERB towards home □ his homeward journey (para casa)

homework /ˈhəʊmwɜːk/ NOUN, NO PLURAL school work that you have to do at home (lição de casa) 🔁 Have you done your maths homework yet? (fez a lição de casa) 🔁 The teacher gives us too much homework. (nos deu lição de casa)

homicidal /ˌhɒmɪˈsaɪdəl/ ADJECTIVE wanting to murder someone (homicida)

homicide /ˈhɒmɪsaɪd/ NOUN [plural homicides] a US or legal word for murder (= the crime of killing someone) (homicídio)

homoeopath /ˈhəʊmiəʊˌpæθ/ NOUN [plural homoeopaths] another spelling of homeopath (homeopata)

- **homoeopathic** /ˌhəʊmiəʊˈpæθɪk/ ADJECTIVE another spelling of homeopathic (homeopático)

- **homoeopathy** /ˌhəʊmiˈɒpəθi/ NOUN, NO PLURAL another spelling of homeopathy (homeopatia)

homograph /ˈhɒməɡrɑːf/ NOUN [plural homographs] a word that has the same spelling as another word but has a different meaning and often a different pronunciation □ 'Lead' meaning 'guide', and 'lead' meaning 'a type of metal' are homographs. (homógrafo)

homonym /ˈhɒmənɪm/ NOUN [plural homonyms] a word that has the same spelling or pronunciation as another word, but has a different meaning (homônimo)

homophone /ˈhɒməfəʊn/ NOUN [plural homophones] a word that has the same pronunciation as another word but has a different spelling and meaning □ 'See' and 'sea' are homophones. (homófono)

homosexual /ˌhɒməˈsekʃuəl/ ▶ ADJECTIVE attracted to people of the same sex (homossexual) ▶ NOUN [plural homosexuals] someone who is attracted to people of the same sex (homossexual)

- **homosexuality** /ˌhɒməˌsekʃuˈælətɪ/ NOUN, NO PLURAL being attracted to people of the same sex (homossexualidade)

hone /həʊn/ VERB [hones, honing, honed] to improve a skill that you already have (afiar, melhorar)

honest /ˈɒnɪst/ ADJECTIVE
1 an honest person can be trusted and does not lie, cheat or steal □ You can trust her – she's very honest. (honesto)
2 sincere and telling the truth (sincero) 🔁 The honest answer is I'm not sure what I'm going to do. □ If you want my honest opinion, I don't like him very much. (resposta sincera) □ + about You need to be honest about your own abilities. □ + with I'm afraid I haven't been completely honest with you.
3 to be honest used before you say what you really think □ To be honest, I don't really want to go. (para ser honesto)

- **honestly** /ˈɒnɪstlɪ/ ADVERB
1 in an honest way □ Martin told me honestly what he thought. □ He behaved very honestly and handed the money in to the police. (honestamente)
2 used for emphasizing that what you are saying is true even though it is surprising □ I honestly didn't realize you were all waiting for me. (honestamente)
3 something you say to show that you are annoyed □ Honestly, I wish you'd listen to what I tell you. (francamente)

- **honesty** /ˈɒnɪstɪ/ NOUN, NO PLURAL
1 being honest □ Thanks for telling me. I appreciate your honesty. (honestidade)
2 in all honesty used for saying what you really think □ In all honesty, it's been quite a difficult experience. (com toda franqueza)

honey /ˈhʌnɪ/ NOUN, NO PLURAL
1 a sweet food that bees make (mel)
2 a word you use when talking to someone you love □ Are you OK, honey? (querido/a)

honeycomb /ˈhʌnɪkəʊm/ NOUN [plural honeycombs] a structure with many small holes where bees store honey (favo de mel)

honeymoon /ˈhʌnɪmuːn/ NOUN [plural honeymoons] a holiday that a man and woman go on just after their wedding □ Rob and Sarah went to Mexico for their honeymoon. (lua de mel)

honk /hɒŋk/ ▶ VERB [honks, honking, honked] to make a loud, short sound with a car horn (buzinar) ▶ NOUN [plural honks] a loud, short sound made by a car horn (buzina)

honor /ˈɒnə(r)/ VERB [honors, honoring, honored], NOUN [plural honors] the US spelling of honour (honra)

- **honorable** /ˈɒnərəbəl/ ADJECTIVE the US spelling of honourable (honrável)

- **honorably** /ˈɒnərəblɪ/ ADVERB the US spelling of honourably (honravelmente)

honorary /ˈɒnərərɪ/ ADJECTIVE given to show respect and admiration for someone □ The footballer was given an honorary degree from Edinburgh University. (honorário)

honour /ˈɒnə(r)/ ▶ NOUN [plural honours]
1 NO PLURAL when someone behaves in a way that is honest and good □ I felt that he was questioning my honour. (honra)
2 NO PLURAL the respect that people have for someone who has behaved well or achieved something that people admire □ I am fighting for my family's honour. (honra)
3 in someone's honour/in honour of someone in order to show respect to someone □ I wrote the book in honour of my father. (em homenagem a)

4 something that makes you proud □ *It was an honour to meet him.* □ *It is a great honour to be here today.* (honra)

5 a reward that someone is given in public because they have achieved something □ *She received an honour from the Queen.* (condecoração)

6 guest of honour the most important guest at an event (convidado de honra)

▶ VERB [honours, honouring, honoured]

1 to show respect to someone who has behaved in a good way or achieved something that people admire □ *They built a monument to honour the dead.* (honrar)

2 to behave in a way that does not go against an agreement, principle, someone's wish, etc. □ *All the countries have honoured the treaty.* (respeitar)

• **honourable** /'ɒnərəbəl/ ADJECTIVE honest and morally good □ *He is an honourable man.* (honrável)

• **honourably** /'ɒnərəblɪ/ ADVERB in an honourable way □ *I have no doubt she behaved honourably.* (honravelmente)

---

hood /hʊd/ NOUN [plural **hoods**]

1 the part of a coat, etc. which you can pull up to cover the back of your head (capuz)

2 the US word for **bonnet** (= part of a car) (capô)

• **hooded** /'hʊdɪd/ ADJECTIVE having or wearing a hood □ *a hooded sweatshirt* □ *a hooded gunman* (encapuzado)

-hood /hʊd/ SUFFIX -hood is added to the end of words to mean 'the state of being something' or 'the time when someone is something' □ *childhood*

hoody /'hʊdɪ/ NOUN [plural **hoodies**] a piece of clothing for the top half of the body with a hood (= part that covers the back of the head) (agasalho com capuz)

hoof /huːf/ NOUN [plural **hooves**] the hard foot on an animal such as a horse or a cow (casco, pata)

hook /hʊk/ ▶ NOUN [plural **hooks**]

1 a bent piece of metal or plastic that you hang things on □ *Hang your coats on the hook.* (gancho)

2 a bent piece of metal used for catching fish (anzol)

3 off the hook if a telephone is off the hook, the part you speak into has not been put back correctly, so nobody can call you (telefone fora do gancho)

♦ IDIOM **let/get someone off the hook** to allow someone to avoid a duty or avoid an unpleasant situation □ *I'm not going to let you off the hook just yet.* (tirar alguém do aperto)

▶ VERB [hooks, hooking, hooked] to hang or catch something using a hook (enganchar)

♦ PHRASAL VERB **hook someone/something up** to connect someone or something to a piece of equipment □ *He was hooked up to a heart monitor.* (conectar alguém/algo)

hook and eye /ˌhʊk ən 'aɪ/ NOUN [plural **hooks and eyes**] a small metal hook (= curved metal part) and ring, used for fastening clothes (colchete)

hooked /hʊkt/ ADJECTIVE

1 liking something very much and wanting to do it a lot (ficar viciado) □ *I played the game with Ian a couple of times and I got hooked.* (fiquei viciado)

2 curved □ *a hooked nose* (curvado)

hooligan /'huːlɪgən/ NOUN [plural **hooligans**] someone who is violent and noisy in a public place (torcedor fanático que pratica vandalismo)

• **hooliganism** /'huːlɪgənɪzəm/ NOUN, NO PLURAL the behaviour of hooligans (vandalismo)

hoop /huːp/ NOUN [plural **hoops**] a ring of metal, plastic or wood (aro)

hooray /hʊ'reɪ/ EXCLAMATION used for showing that you are pleased when something good has happened □ *We've won! Hooray!* (viva!)

hoot /huːt/ ▶ NOUN [plural **hoots**]

1 the sound made by an owl (= bird) or a car horn (pio)

2 a sound you make when you think something is funny or stupid □ *His comments were met with hoots from the audience.* (vaia)

3 someone or something that that makes you laugh. An informal word. □ *Maria's an absolute hoot.* (engraçado)

▶ VERB [hoots, hooting, hooted]

1 to make a sound that shows you think something is funny or stupid □ *The crowd whistled and hooted.* (assobiar)

2 to make a sound with a car horn □ *Another driver hooted at him.* (buzinar)

3 if an owl (= bird) hoots, it makes a noise (piar)

• **hooter** /'huːtə(r)/ NOUN [plural **hooters**] a device that makes a loud sound, for example as a warning □ *the ship's hooter* (buzina, sirene)

Hoover /'huːvə(r)/ NOUN [plural **Hoovers**] a machine that cleans floors by sucking up small bits. A trademark. (aspirador)

• **hoover** VERB [hoovers, hoovering, hoovered] to clean a floor using a machine that sucks up small bits □ *He hoovered up the salt he'd spilt.* (passar o aspirador)

hooves /huːvz/ PLURAL OF **hoof** (ver hoof)

hop /hɒp/ ▶ VERB [hops, hopping, hopped]

1 to jump on one leg (pular em um pé só)

2 if a bird or animal hops, it moves by jumping □ *A little bird hopped onto the arm of the chair.* (saltitar)

3 an informal word meaning to move somewhere quickly, especially to get in or out of a vehicle quickly □ *Hop in and I'll take you to the station.* (pular)

▶ NOUN [plural **hops**] a jump, especially on one leg (um pulo, um salto)

⇨ go to **hops**

hope

hope /həʊp/ ▶ VERB [hopes, hoping, hoped] to think that something is possible and to wish for it to happen or be true ☐ + *that* I hope that David manages to get home for Christmas. ☐ + *to do something* I hope to set up my own business next year. ☐ + *for* I'm hoping for a new bike for my birthday. (esperar) 🔲 'Will the bank still be open?' *'I hope so!'* (espero que sim) 🔲 'Is he coming with us?' *'I hope not.'* (espero que não) ▶ NOUN [plural **hopes**]
1 *no plural* a feeling that the future will be good or that something good will happen (esperança) 🔲 We're not *giving up hope* of finding her. (oferecendo esperança) 🔲 The new centre *offers hope* to people with cancer. (oferece esperança) 🔲 We knew it would be difficult to succeed, but we never *lost hope*. (perdemos a esperança)
2 something that you wish will happen or be true ☐ My hope is that he will agree to lend us the money. (esperança) 🔲 News of the president's interest really *raised our hopes*. (aumentou nossas esperanças)
3 something that gives you a chance of success (esperança) 🔲 Going to court is our *only hope* of getting justice. (única esperança) 🔲 There is *little hope* of finishing the work on time. (pouca esperança)
4 in the hope of something in order to try to get something or make something happen ☐ I left work early in the hope of meeting Tom. (na esperança de algo)
• **hopeful** /ˈhəʊpfʊl/ ▶ ADJECTIVE
1 feeling that the future will be good or that something good will happen ☐ I'm very hopeful that we can find a suitable house. (esperançoso, otimista)
2 making you feel that something good will happen ☐ The fact that he's contacted you is a very hopeful sign. (promissor, de esperança)
▶ NOUN [plural **hopefuls**] someone who is hoping to be successful, especially in entertainment ☐ Hundreds of young hopefuls queued all night for the chance of a part in the musical. (esperançoso)
• **hopefully** /ˈhəʊpfʊli/ ▶ ADVERB
1 used to say that you hope something will happen ☐ Hopefully she'll have forgotten about our homework. (tomara que)
2 showing hope ☐ 'Is there any more?' she asked hopefully. (esperançosamente)
• **hopeless** /ˈhəʊplɪs/ ADJECTIVE
1 without any hope of succeeding ☐ We tried to put out the flames, but it was hopeless. (inútil)
2 an informal word meaning very bad ☐ Chris was hopeless in goal. (sofrível)
• **hopelessly** /ˈhəʊplɪsli/ ADVERB extremely (extremamente) 🔲 We got *hopelessly lost*. (extremamente perdidos)

hops /hɒps/ PLURAL NOUN the flowers used for making beer (lúpulos)

horrific

horde /hɔːd/ NOUN [plural **hordes**] a large crowd ☐ Hordes of tourists wandered around the town. (horda, multidão)
horizon /həˈraɪzən/ NOUN
1 the horizon the line where the land and sky seem to meet (o horizonte)
2 on the horizon probably going to happen soon ☐ There are more changes on the horizon. (no horizonte)
♦ IDIOM **broaden/expand your horizons** to increase the experiences that you have had ☐ The job gave him the opportunity to broaden his horizons. (expandir seus horizontes)

horizontal /ˌhɒrɪˈzɒntəl/ ADJECTIVE straight and parallel to the ground (horizontal) 🔲 a *horizontal line* (linha horizontal) ☐ She was wearing a T-shirt with horizontal stripes.

hormonal /hɔːˈməʊnəl/ ADJECTIVE to do with or caused by hormones ☐ a hormonal problem (hormonal)
hormone /ˈhɔːməʊn/ NOUN [plural **hormones**] a chemical that your body makes, which controls things such as how the body grows. A biology word. (hormônio)

horn /hɔːn/ NOUN [plural **horns**]
1 one of the two pointed things made of bone on the heads of some animals, such as a goat ☐ a bull's horns (chifre)
2 a device in a vehicle that you press to make a loud noise (buzina) 🔲 He heard a *car horn* outside. (buzina de carro) 🔲 Drivers *sounded their horns* as the men ran into the road. (buzinaram)
3 a musical instrument made of metal that you blow into ☐ the French horn (corneta, trompa)
• **horned** /hɔːnd/ ADJECTIVE with horns on the head ☐ horned animals (chifrudo)

horoscope /ˈhɒrəskəʊp/ NOUN [plural **horoscopes**] a description of what might happen to you, which is based on the position of stars when you were born (horóscopo)
horrendous /hɒˈrendəs/ ADJECTIVE extremely bad or shocking ☐ a horrendous crime (horrendo)

horrible /ˈhɒrəbəl/ ADJECTIVE very unpleasant ☐ It was a horrible feeling to think I wouldn't see him again. ☐ a horrible situation ☐ Why are you being so horrible to everyone? (horrível)
• **horribly** /ˈhɒrəbli/ ADVERB in a horrible way (horrivelmente) 🔲 The plan *went horribly wrong*. (saiu horrivelmente errado) ☐ He had been horribly injured in the accident.

horrid /ˈhɒrɪd/ ADJECTIVE an old-fashioned word meaning very unpleasant ☐ a horrid place ☐ a horrid man (horrível, antipático)
horrific /hɒˈrɪfɪk/ ADJECTIVE extremely bad, often involving death or injuries ☐ a horrific car crash ☐ horrific scenes of violence (horroroso)

horrified /ˈhɒrɪfaɪd/ ADJECTIVE extremely shocked and upset ☐ He was horrified at the suggestion that he had cheated. (**horrorizado**)

horrify /ˈhɒrɪfaɪ/ VERB [**horrifies, horrifying, horrified**] to shock and upset someone ☐ It's a story that will horrify any parent. (**horrorizar**)

• **horrifying** /ˈhɒrɪfaɪɪŋ/ ADJECTIVE shocking and upsetting ☐ horrifying pictures of starving children (**tenebroso, horripilante**)

horror /ˈhɒrə(r)/ ▶ NOUN [plural **horrors**]
1 a strong feeling of shock and upset ☐ I watched in horror as the car went up in flames. (**horror**)
2 something that is extremely shocking and upsetting ☐ He had witnessed such horrors while fighting. (**horror**)
3 to someone's horror used when saying that something makes you feel shocked and upset ☐ To my horror, I realized it was a dead body. (**para surpresa de alguém**)
▶ ADJECTIVE a horror film or story is very frightening and often unpleasant (**terror**)

horse /hɔːs/ NOUN [plural **horses**] a large animal which people ride or use for pulling things (**cavalo**) 🔊 Have you ever ridden a horse? (**andou a cavalo**) 🔊 The horse galloped (= ran) across the field. (**cavalo galopou**)

horseback /ˈhɔːsbæk/ NOUN, NO PLURAL **on horseback** riding a horse (**montaria a cavalo**)

horse-chestnut /ˌhɔːsˈtʃesnʌt/ NOUN [plural **horse-chestnuts**] a tree which has smooth brown nuts that children play with (**castanheira**)

horsepower /ˈhɔːspaʊə(r)/ NOUN, NO PLURAL a unit for measuring the power of engines (**potência**)

horseriding /ˈhɔːsraɪdɪŋ/ NOUN, NO PLURAL the activity of riding on a horse ☐ My hobbies are reading and horseriding. (**andar a cavalo**)

horseshoe /ˈhɔːsʃuː/ NOUN [plural **horseshoes**] a curved piece metal fastened to a horse's foot (**ferradura**)

horticulture /ˈhɔːtɪkʌltʃə(r)/ NOUN, NO PLURAL the science or activity of growing plants (**horticultura, jardinagem**)

hose /həʊz/ NOUN [plural **hoses**] a long tube used for putting water on fires or gardens (**mangueira**)

hosiery /ˈhəʊzɪəri/ NOUN, NO PLURAL a formal word for socks and tights (= thin coverings for legs) (**meias e roupas íntimas**)

hospice /ˈhɒspɪs/ NOUN [plural **hospices**] a hospital for people who are dying (**hospital para pacientes terminais**)

hospitable /hɒˈspɪtəbəl/ ADJECTIVE friendly to visitors, liking to provide food and a pleasant place to stay ☐ It's a beautiful country and the people are very hospitable. (**hospitaleiro**)

hospital /ˈhɒspɪtəl/ NOUN [plural **hospitals**] a building where people go for medical treatment when they are ill or injured ☐ Jane is in hospital having an operation. (**hospital**) 🔊 She was taken to hospital after being stabbed. (**levada ao hospital**) 🔊 He's recovered and is coming out of hospital tomorrow. (**ter alta do hospital**) ☐ a psychiatric hospital 🔊 Many hospital wards (= rooms where people stay) have been closed. (**alas/seções do hospital**)

hospitality /ˌhɒspɪˈtælɪti/ NOUN, NO PLURAL
1 being friendly to visitors, liking to provide food and a pleasant place to stay ☐ The hotel is known for its warm hospitality. (**hospitalidade**)
2 food, drink and entertainment that a company gives to people ☐ the hospitality industry (**hospitalidade**)

hospitalize or **hospitalise** /ˈhɒspɪtəlaɪz/ VERB [**hospitalizes, hospitalizing, hospitalized**] if someone is hospitalized, they are in a hospital for treatment ☐ He was hospitalized for two months following his accident. (**hospitalizar**)

host /həʊst/ ▶ NOUN [plural **hosts**]
1 someone who introduces the guests on a television show ☐ He's a well-known game show host. (**apresentador**)
2 a place that provides the equipment and space for a big event (**sede**) 🔊 London will play host to the Olympic Games in 2012. ☐ the host nation (**sediou**)
3 the person at a party or meal who has invited you and arranged everything (**anfitrião**)
4 a host of something a lot of people or things ☐ The player has struggled with a host of injuries. (**grande número de**)
▶ VERB [**hosts, hosting, hosted**]
1 to be the host of a big event ☐ The city of Athens hosted the Olympics in 2004. (**ser a sede**)
2 to provide the systems that allow a website to operate. A computing word. (**hospedar**)

hostage /ˈhɒstɪdʒ/ NOUN [plural **hostages**] someone who is kept as a prisoner until the people holding them get what they want (**refém**) 🔊 He was taken hostage by a group of militants. (**feito refém**)

hostel /ˈhɒstəl/ NOUN [plural **hostels**] a cheap place for people to stay ☐ a youth hostel ☐ He was staying in a hostel for homeless people. (**albergue, alojamento**)

hostess /ˈhəʊstɪs/ NOUN [plural **hostesses**]
1 the woman at a party or meal who has invited you and arranged everything (**anfitriã**)
2 a woman who introduces the guests on a television show (**apresentadora**)

hostile /ˈhɒstaɪl/ ADJECTIVE
1 unfriendly or showing strong dislike ☐ a hostile reaction ☐ Hostile crowds booed and jeered at the Prime Minister. (**inimigo**)
2 difficult to live in ☐ Not many plants can survive in the hostile mountain conditions. (**adverso**)

hot

3 to do with an enemy in a war □ *hostile territory* (**hostil**)

• **hostility** /hɒˈstɪlətɪ/ NOUN, NO PLURAL

1 unfriendly behaviour □ *Immigrants have faced a lot of hostility.* (**hostilidade**)

2 when people show that they disagree with something very strongly □ *There was widespread hostility to the plan.* (**resistência**)

3 hostilities a formal word that means fighting in a war □ *We hope the deal will end the hostilities.* (**estado de guerra**)

hot /hɒt/ ADJECTIVE [**hotter, hottest**]

1 having a high temperature □ *Don't touch the oven. It's very hot.* □ *Is there any hot water left?* □ *It was a very hot summer.* (**quente**) 🔲 *It was a boiling hot day.* (**quente e fervente**)

2 spicy □ *hot curries* (**picante**)

3 if someone has a hot temper, they get angry very easily (**temperamento forte**)

4 a hot topic a subject that people are very interested in at the moment (**assunto da moda**)

♦ PHRASAL VERB [**hots, hotting, hotted**] **hot up** if a situation hots up, it becomes more exciting □ *Things hotted up a bit when the band arrived.* (**esquentar**)

hot chocolate /ˌhɒt ˈtʃɒkələt/ NOUN, NO PLURAL a drink made from hot milk mixed with chocolate powder (**chocolate quente**)

hotdog /ˈhɒtdɒg/ NOUN [*plural* **hotdogs**] a sausage in a long piece of bread (**cachorro-quente**)

hotel /həʊˈtel/ NOUN [*plural* **hotels**] a building that you pay to stay in when you are travelling or on holiday (**hotel**) 🔲 *We stayed in a five-star hotel.* (**ficamos em um hotel**) 🔲 *Our hotel room didn't even have a television.* (**quarto de hotel**) 🔲 *Hotel guests have free use of the swimming pool.* (**hóspedes de hotel**)

hotline /ˈhɒtlaɪn/ NOUN [*plural* **hotlines**] a special telephone number that you can call to get information (**central de atendimento**) 🔲 *Call our hotline for more information about special offers.* (**ligue para nossa central de atendimento**)

hotly /ˈhɒtlɪ/ ADVERB

1 in an angry way (**energicamente**) 🔲 *He hotly denied that he'd cheated.* (**negou energicamente**)

2 hotly contested if a competition is hotly contested, people are competing very strongly against each other (**disputado com afinco**)

hot spot /ˈhɒt ˌspɒt/ NOUN [*plural* **hot spots**]

1 a place where a lot of bad activity happens □ *Police have published a list of crime hot spots.* (**local de crime**)

2 a place where there is a lot of fighting and violence □ *He has reported from many of the world's hot spots.* (**local de tensão**)

3 a very popular place □ *This is a hot spot for fine dining.* (**local popular**)

hot-water bottle /ˌhɒtˈwɔːtə ˌbɒtəl/ NOUN [*plural* **hot-water bottles**] a rubber container that you fill with hot water and use for making your bed warm (**bolsa de água quente**)

hound /haʊnd/ ▶ NOUN [*plural* **hounds**] a dog used for hunting (**cão de caça**)

▶ VERB [**hounds, hounding, hounded**] to follow someone everywhere they go, asking them a lot of questions or taking a lot of photographs of them □ *Many celebrities are hounded by the press.* (**acossar**)

hour /aʊə(r)/ NOUN [*plural* **hours**]

1 a period of time that lasts 60 minutes. □ *There are 24 hours in one day* □ *Each lesson lasts an hour.* □ *An hour later, they had all gone.* □ *I do an hour's exercise every day.* (**hora**) 🔲 *I'll be about half an hour.* (**meia hora**)

2 the period of time when something happens □ *What hours do you work?* (**horário**) 🔲 *Our opening hours are 9–5.* (**horário de expediente**) 🔲 *Shall we meet up in the lunch hour?* (**horário de almoço**)

3 hours an informal word meaning a long time (**horas**) 🔲 *We spent hours talking on the phone.* (**passamos horas**)

• **hourly** /ˈaʊəlɪ/ ADJECTIVE, ADVERB

1 happening every hour □ *The trains run hourly from here.* (**de hora em hora**)

2 for each hour (**por hora**) 🔲 *an hourly rate/wage* (**porcentagem por hora**)

house /haʊs/ ▶ NOUN [*plural* **houses**]

1 a building in which people, especially one family, live □ *Our house is the one with the yellow door.* (**casa**) 🔲 *We moved house last year.* (**mudamos de casa**)

2 the people who live in a house □ *Their party kept the whole house awake.* (**morador**)

3 the place where a particular activity or business happens □ *an opera house* □ *a software house* (**sala de espetáculo, teatro, loja**)

♦ IDIOMS **get on like a house on fire** to like each other very much □ *I introduced her to my mother, and they got on like a house on fire.* (**dar-se bem um com o outro**) **on the house** if you are given food or drinks on the house in a restaurant, bar, etc., you do not have to pay for them (**cortesia da casa**)

▶ VERB /haʊz/ [**houses, housing, housed**]

1 to provide someone with a place to live □ *They were housed in old army barracks.* (**alojar**)

2 to keep something in a particular place □ *The collection is housed in a pleasant old building.* (**acomodar**)

houseboat /ˈhaʊsbəʊt/ NOUN [*plural* **houseboats**] a boat on a river that you can live in (**casa flutuante**)

housebound /ˈhaʊsbaʊnd/ ADJECTIVE unable to leave your house because you are too ill or old (**confinado à casa**)

household /ˈhaʊshəʊld/ ▶ NOUN [*plural* **households**] all the people who live in the same

house □ *Most UK households have access to the Internet.* (**lar, grupo domiciliar**)
▶ ADJECTIVE to do with your home □ *household chores* □ *household bills* (**de arranjos domésticos**)
• **householder** /ˈhaʊsˌhəʊldə(r)/ NOUN [plural **householders**] someone who owns or rents a house (**proprietário**)

household name /ˌhaʊshəʊld ˈneɪm/ NOUN [plural **household names**] someone or something that is very famous (**nome famoso**)

housekeeper /ˈhaʊskiːpə(r)/ NOUN [plural **housekeepers**] someone whose job is to cook and clean in someone else's house (**governanta**)

houseplant /ˈhaʊsplɑːnt/ NOUN [plural **houseplants**] a plant that you grow in your house (**planta cultivada em casa**)

house-trained /ˈhaʊstreɪnd/ ADJECTIVE a housetrained pet has learnt to be clean inside the house (**treinado**)

housewarming /ˈhaʊswɔːmɪŋ/ NOUN [plural **housewarmings**] a party in your new house to celebrate moving into it □ *We're having a housewarming next week.* (**festa de inauguração da casa nova**)

housewife /ˈhaʊswaɪf/ NOUN [plural **housewives**] a woman who stays at home to look after her family and house, and does not have a paid job □ *She tried to be the perfect housewife.* (**dona de casa**)

housework /ˈhaʊswɜːk/ NOUN, NO PLURAL the work you do to keep your house clean and tidy (**serviço doméstico**) 🔂 *She hated doing the housework.* (**fazer serviço doméstico**)

▶ Remember that **housework** is not used in the plural:
✓ *Who does most of the housework?*
✗ *Who does most of the houseworks?*

housing /ˈhaʊzɪŋ/ ▶ NOUN, NO PLURAL homes for people to live in □ *There is a shortage of affordable housing.* (**habitação**)
▶ ADJECTIVE to do with houses □ *a housing project* (**imobiliário**) 🔂 *The housing market* (= buying and selling houses) *has slowed down.* (**mercado imobiliário**)

hovel /ˈhɒvəl/ NOUN [plural **hovels**] a small, dirty and untidy place that someone lives in □ *The family lived in a two-room hovel.* (**cabana**)

hover /ˈhɒvə(r)/ VERB [**hovers, hovering, hovered**]
1 to stay still in the air □ *Police helicopters hovered overhead.* (**pairar**)
2 to stand somewhere because you are waiting to do something □ *The waiter hovered, ready to take our order.* (**rondar**)

hovercraft /ˈhɒvəkrɑːft/ NOUN [plural **hovercrafts**] a vehicle that travels across water or land, and has a cushion (= soft bag) of air under it (**veículo anfíbio**)

how /haʊ/ ADVERB
1 used for asking or talking about the way something is done □ **+ to do something** *I'll show you how to tie a reef knot.* □ *How will we get there?* □ *Do you know how to turn the oven on?* (**como**)
2 used for asking or talking about size, amount, level or age □ *I don't know how old Maurice is exactly.* □ *How strong do you like your tea?* (**quanto, quão**) 🔂 *How much is that DVD player?* (**quanto custa**) 🔂 *How many brothers and sisters have you got?* (**quantos**)
3 used for asking or talking about what something is like or what form or condition it is in □ *How do you want this money – cash or cheque?* □ *How's work?* □ *How's the new extension coming on?* (**como**)
4 used for asking or talking about someone's health (**como**) 🔂 *Hello, how are you today?* (**como vai você**) □ *How's your leg now?*
5 How about ...? used for making a suggestion □ *How about asking the children to help?* (**que tal...?**)
6 used to emphasize an adjective or an adverb □ *How odd that she didn't phone.* □ *He died? Oh, how sad.* (**que**)

▶ Remember that **how** is not used with **like** to ask someone to describe someone or something. The correct phrase for this is **what is someone/something like?**:
✓ *What is your new teacher like?*
✗ *How is your new teacher like?*

however /haʊˈevə(r)/ CONJUNCTION, ADVERB
1 used for saying that something does not affect a situation □ *However hard he tried, he couldn't do it.* (**por mais que**) □ *She wanted to travel to Australia however much it cost.* (**por mais que**) □ *Your donation, however small, will make an important difference.*
2 despite what has just been said □ *The business had been successful. Over the past few years, however, sales had started to fall.* □ *People were saying that the school was going to close. However, the school denied the rumours.* (**no entanto**)
3 used for asking how something is done when you are surprised. A formal word □ *However did you find this place?* (**como é que**)
4 in any way □ *Do it however you want to.* (**como**)

howl /haʊl/ ▶ VERB [**howls, howling, howled**]
1 if a dog or wolf howls, it makes a long, high noise (**uivar**)
2 to shout or cry loudly □ *He was howling with pain.* (**gritar**)
3 if the wind howls, it makes a lot of noise □ *The wind howled in off the sea.* (**uivar**)
▶ NOUN [plural **howls**]

how's — 385 — **humanitarian**

1 a long, loud sound made by a wolf or dog (uivo)
2 a loud shout of pain or laughter (grito)

how's /haʊz/ a short way to say or write how is or how has ☐ *How's your mother?* (como é/está)

HQ /ˌeɪtʃˈkjuː/ ABBREVIATION **headquarters** (abreviação de quartel-general)

HTML /ˌeɪtʃtiːemˈel/ ABBREVIATION hypertext markup language; a system used for writing things on the Internet. A computing word. (HTML)

hub /hʌb/ NOUN [*plural* **hubs**]
1 the most important place where something happens ☐ *Mumbai is the financial hub of India.* (centro)
2 the central part of a wheel (centro)

hubbub /ˈhʌbʌb/ NOUN, NO PLURAL the noise made by a lot of people talking at the same time (algazarra)

huddle /ˈhʌdəl/ ▶ VERB [**huddles, huddling, huddled**] if people or animals huddle, they stay very close to each other, for example because they are cold or frightened ☐ *The children huddled together under the blanket.* (aconchegar-se)
▶ NOUN [*plural* **huddles**] a group of people standing or sitting very close to each other ☐ *They stood in a huddle on the pavement.* (aglomerado)

hue /hjuː/ NOUN [*plural* **hues**] a literary word meaning colour (matiz)

huff /hʌf/ ▶ NOUN, NO PLURAL **in a huff** annoyed with someone and showing this by your behaviour. An informal phrase. ☐ *He walked off in a huff.* (com raiva)
▶ VERB [**huffs, huffing, huffed**]
1 to say something in a way that shows you are annoyed ☐ *'I'm not coming here again,' he huffed.* (estar com raiva)
2 huff and puff (a) to breathe noisily, for example because you have been running ☐ *He ran past huffing and puffing.* (b) to behave in a way that shows you are annoyed ☐ *He was in a terrible mood, huffing and puffing about how he had lost all his work.* (soprar e bufar)

hug /hʌɡ/ ▶ VERB [**hugs, hugging, hugged**] to put your arms around someone and hold them ☐ *My mother was always hugging and kissing us.* ☐ *Everyone was crying and hugging each other.* (abraçar)
▶ NOUN [*plural* **hugs**] the action of putting your arms around someone and holding them (abraço) ☐ *I could see she was upset so I gave her a hug.* (deu um abraço)

huge /hjuːdʒ/ ADJECTIVE very big ☐ *The school has spent a huge amount of money on the project.* ☐ *The film was a huge success.* ☐ *I'm a huge fan of his music.* ☐ *The house was huge.* (enorme)
• **hugely** /ˈhjuːdʒli/ ADVERB very or very much ☐ *hugely popular* (enormemente)

hulk /hʌlk/ NOUN [*plural* **hulks**]
1 a very large and heavy person or thing ☐ *the towering hulk of the new building* (pesado)
2 an old ship, car, etc. that is not used any more ☐ *She saw the rusting hulk of an old bus.* (casco de navio, carro etc.)
• **hulking** /ˈhʌlkɪŋ/ ADJECTIVE very large and heavy ☐ *He noticed a hulking figure in the doorway.* (volumoso, maciço)

hull /hʌl/ NOUN [*plural* **hulls**] the bottom part of a boat that goes in the water (casco)

hullabaloo /ˌhʌləbəˈluː/ NOUN, NO PLURAL an informal word for a lot of excitement or anger about something ☐ *There was a big hullabaloo when three members of staff were fired.* (tumulto)

hullo /həˈləʊ/ EXCLAMATION another spelling of **hello** (olá, oi)

hum /hʌm/ ▶ VERB [**hums, humming, hummed**]
1 to sing with your mouth closed ☐ *She hummed quietly to herself as she worked.* (cantarolar)
2 to make a low continuous noise like someone humming ☐ *He turned the key and the engine hummed into life.* (zumbir)
▶ NOUN, NO PLURAL a low continuous sound ☐ *We could hear the hum of conversation.* (zumbido, murmúrio)

human /ˈhjuːmən/ ADJECTIVE
1 to do with people and the way that people behave (humano) ☐ *They appeared to have no respect for human life.* (vida humana) ☐ *Everyone wants to win: it's human nature.* (natureza humana)
2 to do with people's bodies (humano) ☐ *The human brain can process huge amounts of information.* (cérebro humano) ☐ *The human body is designed for physical activity.* (corpo humano)
3 be only human if you say that someone is only human, you mean that it is not reasonable to expect them to be better, stronger, etc. ☐ *You can't do everything; you're only human.* (apenas humano)
• **human** or **human being** /ˌhjuːmən ˈbiːɪŋ/ NOUN [*plural* **humans** or **human beings**] a person ☐ *Is there a vaccine to protect humans from the disease?* ☐ *Technology has enabled human beings to survive longer.* (ser humano)

humane /hjuːˈmeɪn/ ADJECTIVE kind to people and animals and causing as little suffering as possible ☐ *Ministers called for the humane treatment of war prisoners.* (humanitário, humano)
• **humanely** /hjuːˈmeɪnli/ ADVERB in a humane way ☐ *The animals are killed quickly and humanely.* (humanamente)

humanitarian /hjuːˌmænɪˈteəriən/ ADJECTIVE
1 to do with reducing the suffering of people who have been affected by problems such as floods or war (humanitário) ☐ *The trucks were carrying humanitarian aid like food and cooking fuel.* (ajuda humanitária)

2 to do with a situation, such as war, that causes great suffering to many people □ *The government was accused of creating a humanitarian crisis.* (humanitário)

humanities /hjuːˈmænətɪz/ PLURAL NOUN **the humanities** subjects that are not sciences, for example history and languages (humanidades)

humanity /hjuːˈmænəti/ NOUN, NO PLURAL
1 all the people in the world □ *We must act now to save humanity.* (humanidade)
2 kindness towards other people □ *He always showed humanity to his students.* (humanidade)

humankind /ˌhjuːmənˈkaɪnd/ NOUN, NO PLURAL people in general □ *He has committed some of the worst crimes in the history of humankind.* (raça humana)

humanly /ˈhjuːmənli/ ADVERB **humanly possible** possible for a person to do □ *They did all that was humanly possible to save his life.* (humanamente)

human resources /ˌhjuːmən rɪˈsɔːsɪz/ NOUN, NO PLURAL the department in a company that is responsible for looking after the people who work there (recursos humanos)

human rights /ˌhjuːmən ˈraɪts/ PLURAL NOUN basic rights such as freedom and fair treatment, especially by a government □ *The organization promotes human rights for all.* (direitos humanos)

humble /ˈhʌmbəl/ ▶ ADJECTIVE [**humbler, humblest**]
1 not believing that you are important (humilde)
2 having a low social position □ *He comes from a humble background.* (humilde)
3 in my humble opinion used humorously when you are giving your opinion about something (em minha humilde opinião)
▶ VERB [**humbles, humbling, humbled**] to make someone feel humble □ *I was humbled by their generosity.* (sentir-se humilde)

humdrum /ˈhʌmdrʌm/ ADJECTIVE boring and ordinary □ *a humdrum existence* (monótono)

humid /ˈhjuːmɪd/ ADJECTIVE humid air or weather is hot and slightly wet (úmido)
• **humidity** /hjuːˈmɪdəti/ NOUN, NO PLURAL how humid the air is □ *Humidity levels were high.* (umidade)

humiliate /hjuːˈmɪlieɪt/ VERB [**humiliates, humiliating, humiliated**] to make someone feel stupid or ashamed □ *His wife accused him of humiliating her in public.* (humilhar)
• **humiliating** /hjuːˈmɪlieɪtɪŋ/ ADJECTIVE making you feel stupid or ashamed □ *The team has suffered yet another humiliating defeat.* (humilhante)
• **humiliation** /hjuːˌmɪliˈeɪʃən/ NOUN, NO PLURAL when you feel humiliated □ *She has tried, unsuccessfully, to avoid more public humiliation.* (humilhação)

humility /hjuːˈmɪləti/ NOUN, NO PLURAL a way of behaving that shows that you do not believe that you are better or more important than other people □ *She should show a bit of humility and admit that she was wrong.* (humildade)

humor /ˈhjuːmə(r)/ NOUN, NO PLURAL, VERB [**humors, humoring, humored**] the US spelling of **humour** (humor, graça)
• **humorless** /ˈhjuːmələs/ ADJECTIVE the US spelling of **humourless** (sem graça)

humorous /ˈhjuːmərəs/ ADJECTIVE funny (engraçado) 🔲 *He told us a humorous story about a man on his wedding day.* (história engraçada) 🔲 *The President made a humorous remark.* (observação engraçada)

humour /ˈhjuːmə(r)/ ▶ NOUN, NO PLURAL
1 the quality that makes something funny □ *She suddenly saw the humour in the situation and laughed loudly.* (cômico)
2 the ability to know when something is funny, or to say things that make people laugh □ *He loved her for her humour and her quiet determination.* (humor) 🔲 *We share the same sense of humour.* (senso de humor)
3 your mood □ *There was a lot of ill humour in the office.* (humor)
▶ VERB [**humours, humouring, humoured**] to pretend to agree with someone in order to please them (fazer a vontade de alguém)
• **humourless** /ˈhjuːmələs/ ADJECTIVE not funny, or not showing that you think things are funny □ *He was a small, humourless man in his fifties.* (sem graça)

hump /hʌmp/ NOUN [*plural* **humps**]
1 a rounded part that sticks out from a surface, especially the ground □ *They have installed speed humps in our street.* (corcova, montículo)
2 a rounded lump on the back of a camel (= desert animal) (corcunda)
3 a rounded lump at the top of someone's back (corcunda)

hunch /hʌntʃ/ ▶ NOUN [*plural* **hunches**] a feeling you have that something might be true (palpite) 🔲 *She had a hunch that something was wrong.* (tinha um palpite)
▶ VERB [**hunches, hunching, hunched**] to sit or stand with the top part of your body bent forward □ *He hunched over his books.* (curvar-se)

hundred /ˈhʌndrəd/ NUMBER [PLURAL **hundreds**]
1 the number 100 (cem)
2 hundreds a large number. An informal word □ **+ of** *There were hundreds of people queuing for tickets.* (centenas)

hundredth /ˈhʌndrədθ/ ▶ NUMBER 100th written as a word (centésimo)
▶ NOUN [*plural* **hundredths**] 1/100; one of a hundred equal parts of something □ *He lost the race by two hundredths of a second.* (centésimos)

hundredweight

hundredweight /'hʌndrədweɪt/ NOUN [plural **hundredweight**] a unit for measuring weight, equal to 8 stone (**cem libras**)

hung /hʌŋ/ PAST TENSE AND PAST PARTICIPLE OF **hang** (**ver hang**)

hunger /'hʌŋgə(r)/ ▶ NOUN, NO PLURAL
1 a feeling that you want to eat □ *It seemed that nothing would satisfy his hunger.* (**fome**)
2 not having enough food □ *These children are dying of hunger.* (**fome**)
3 a very strong feeling of wanting something □ **+ for** *He has a real hunger for success.* (**ânsia**)
▶ VERB [**hungers, hungering, hungered**] to want something very much □ **+ for** *He hungered for excitement in his life.* (**ansiar**)
• **hungrily** /'hʌŋgrɪli/ ADVERB in a way that shows you are hungry □ *She took a slice of the cake and ate it hungrily.* (**com fome**)
• **hungry** /'hʌŋgri/ ADJECTIVE [**hungrier, hungriest**]
1 having a feeling of wanting to eat □ *The children were starting to get hungry.* (**faminto, esfomeado**)
2 go hungry to not have enough to eat □ *If you don't eat your fish, you'll have to go hungry.* (**com fome**)
3 wanting something very much □ **+ for** *The team is hungry for success this season.* (**ansioso, desejoso**)

hunk /hʌŋk/ NOUN [plural **hunks**] a big, rough piece of something such as bread or cheese □ *Jake tore a hunk of bread from the loaf.* (**naco, pedaço grande**)

hunt /hʌnt/ ▶ VERB [**hunts, hunting, hunted**]
1 to chase and kill animals for food or for sport □ *The men hunt seals and the women fish.* □ **+ for** *They were out hunting for rabbits.* (**caçar**)
2 to try to find someone or something □ **+ for** *More than 40 officers are hunting for the killer.* □ *Investigators are hunting for more clues.* (**caçar**)
♦ PHRASAL VERB **hunt someone/something down** to look for someone or something until you find them □ *Police are determined to hunt the killer down.* (**perseguir até capturar**)
▶ NOUN [plural **hunts**]
1 when people search for someone or something (**busca**) ▣ *Police launched a hunt for the child when they failed to return home.* (**começou uma busca**)
2 when people chase and kill animals for food or for sport (**caça**) ▣ *People attended fox hunts across the country today.* (**caça às raposas**)
• **hunter** /'hʌntə(r)/ NOUN [plural **hunters**] a person or animal that hunts (**caçador**)
• **hunting** /'hʌntɪŋ/ NOUN, NO PLURAL the activity of chasing and killing animals for food or for sport □ *She wants a ban on hunting.* (**caça**)

hurdle /'hɜːdəl/ ▶ NOUN [plural **hurdles**]
1 a problem that needs to be solved in order to make progress (**obstáculo**) ▣ *Finding enough* money was a major hurdle for our business (**maior obstáculo**) ▣ *He had to face many hurdles on the road to recovery.* (**encarar obstáculos**)
2 a bar or frame that people or horses jump over in a race □ *She won the 400-metre hurdles in the Olympic Games.* (**barreira, obstáculo**)
▶ VERB [**hurdles, hurdling, hurdled**] to jump over something such as a fence □ *The police officer hurdled the wooden gate, and went after the man.* (**saltar**)
• **hurdler** /'hɜːdlə(r)/ NOUN [plural **hurdlers**] a competitor in a hurdles race (**saltador**)

hurl /hɜːl/ VERB [**hurls, hurling, hurled**]
1 to throw something with great force □ *A brick was hurled through her window.* (**arremessar**)
2 hurl abuse/insults, etc. to shout rude things at someone (**proferir insultos**)

hurrah /hʊ'rɑː/ EXCLAMATION used for showing that you are pleased when something good has happened □ *Hurrah! We've won!* (**viva**)

hurricane /'hʌrɪkən/ NOUN [plural **hurricanes**] a storm with very strong winds (**furacão**)

hurried /'hʌrid/ ADJECTIVE done quickly □ *We ate a hurried breakfast, and left the house.* (**rápido**)
• **hurriedly** /'hʌrɪdli/ ADVERB quickly □ *The boy hurriedly hid something under his jacket.* (**rapidamente**)

hurry /'hʌri/ ▶ VERB [**hurries, hurrying, hurried**]
1 to go somewhere quickly □ *She turned and hurried back along the path.* □ *The streets were full of people hurrying home to their families.* (**apressar-se**)
2 to do something more quickly □ *You'll have to hurry if you want to leave at six.* (**apressar-se**)
♦ PHRASAL VERB **hurry up** to start moving somewhere or doing something more quickly □ *Hurry up! We're going to be late.* □ *I wish he'd hurry up in the bathroom.* (**apressar-se**)
▶ NOUN, NO PLURAL
1 in a hurry doing something or going somewhere quickly, because you do not have much time □ *We had to finish the job in a hurry.* □ *I can't talk now – I'm in a hurry.* (**com pressa**)
2 there's no hurry used for telling someone that they do not need to do something quickly because you have a lot of time □ *Call me back when you're ready; there's no hurry.* (**não há pressa**)
3 not be in a hurry to do something to not need to do something quickly or to not want to do it soon □ *I'm in no hurry to get married.* (**não ter pressa para fazer algo**)
4 the need to do something quickly □ *What's the hurry? She won't be back for hours.* (**pressa**)

hurt /hɜːt/ VERB [**hurts, hurting, hurt**]
1 to cause pain or injury to someone □ *She fell and hurt her ankle.* □ *Will the injection hurt?* (**ferir, machucar**)

2 to be painful □ *My shoulder hurts.* (**doer**)
3 to make someone feel upset □ *The truth can hurt sometimes.* □ *His criticism really hurt her.* (**magoar**)
4 to harm something □ *This publicity won't hurt her chances of being elected.* □ *This political crisis could well hurt the economy.* (**ferir**)
◆ IDIOM **hurt someone's feelings** to make someone feel upset □ *If you don't visit her, you'll hurt her feelings.* (**ferir, magoar alguém**)
▶ ADJECTIVE
1 injured (**ferido, machucado**) ▣ *Be careful – someone could get hurt.* (**se machucar**)
2 upset (**magoado**) ▣ *I was deeply hurt by his lack of appreciation.* (**profundamente magoado**)
▶ NOUN, NO PLURAL when someone is upset □ *Her remarks have caused a lot of hurt.* (**mágoa**)
• **hurtful** /ˈhɜːtfʊl/ ADJECTIVE making someone feel upset □ *His comments were very hurtful.* (**ofensivo**)

hurtle /ˈhɜːtəl/ VERB [**hurtles, hurtling, hurtled**] to move very fast, often in a dangerous or uncontrolled way □ *The car hurtled down a slope and crashed into a tree.* (**lançar**)

husband /ˈhʌzbənd/ NOUN [plural **husbands**] the man that a woman is married to □ *Her husband died five years ago.* (**marido**)

hush /hʌʃ/ ▶ VERB [**hushes, hushing, hushed**] to tell someone to be quiet □ *She hushed the children.* (**calar**)
◆ PHRASAL VERB **hush something up** to stop people from knowing something □ *There were several accidents at the hospital, but it was all hushed up.* (**manter algo em segredo**)
▶ NOUN, NO PLURAL a sudden silence □ *A sudden hush fell over the crowd.* (**silêncio**)
• **hushed** /hʌʃt/ ADJECTIVE very quiet □ *'I must speak with you,' he said in a hushed voice.* (**abafado, baixo**)

husky[1] /ˈhʌski/ ADJECTIVE a husky voice is deep and rough (**rouco**)

husky[2] /ˈhʌski/ NOUN [plural **huskies**] a type of large dog that is used to pull heavy things over snow (**cão esquimó que puxa trenós, husky**)

hustle /ˈhʌsəl/ ▶ VERB [**hustles, hustling, hustled**] to make someone go somewhere quickly, often by pushing them □ *The protesters were hustled out of the hotel by ten police officers.* (**empurrar**)
▶ NOUN, NO PLURAL **hustle and bustle** busy and noisy activity □ *The hotel is ideal for those who like the hustle and bustle of the city.* (**corre-corre**)

hut /hʌt/ NOUN [plural **huts**] a small, simple building made of wood, mud or metal (**cabana**)

hutch /hʌtʃ/ NOUN [plural **hutches**] a wooden box with a wire front and a door, in which small pets such as rabbits are kept (**tipo de gaiola**)

hyacinth /ˈhaɪəsɪnθ/ NOUN [plural **hyacinths**] a plant with a lot of small, sweet-smelling flowers growing on one stem (**jacinto**)

hybrid /ˈhaɪbrɪd/ NOUN [plural **hybrids**]
1 an animal or plant that has been produced from two different types of animal or plant (**híbrido**)
2 a mixture of different types of things □ *This is an unusual hybrid of classical and jazz styles.* (**híbrido**)
3 a type of car that uses both petrol and another type of energy, especially electricity (**híbrido, flexível**)

hydrant /ˈhaɪdrənt/ NOUN [plural **hydrants**] a pipe in the street that is connected to the main water supply, used for getting water to put out fires (**hidrante**)

hydraulic /haɪˈdrɒlɪk/ ADJECTIVE operated by liquid moving with pressure □ *hydraulic brakes* (**hidráulico**)

hydro- /ˈhaɪdrəʊ/ PREFIX hydro- is added to the beginning of words to mean 'water' □ *hydrogen* □ *hydroelectric* (**hidro-**)

hydrocarbon /ˌhaɪdrəˈkɑːbən/ NOUN [plural **hydrocarbons**] one of several chemical substances found in coal and oil. A chemistry word. (**hidrocarbono**)

hydrochloric acid /ˌhaɪdrəˌklɒrɪk ˈæsɪd/ NOUN, NO PLURAL a type of acid used in a strong form in industry and found in a weak form in the stomach for digesting food. A chemistry word. (**ácido clorídrico**)

hydroelectric /ˌhaɪdrəʊɪˈlektrɪk/ ADJECTIVE to do with electricity produced using the power of water (**hidroelétrico**)
• **hydroelectricity** /ˌhaɪdrəʊɪlekˈtrɪsəti/ NOUN, NO PLURAL electricity produced using the power of water (**hidroeletricidade**)

hydrofoil /ˈhaɪdrəfɔɪl/ NOUN [plural **hydrofoils**] a type of boat that rises slightly above the surface of the water when it is moving fast (**hidrofólio**)

hydrogen /ˈhaɪdrədʒən/ NOUN, NO PLURAL the lightest gas that exists, which combines with oxygen to make water. A chemistry word. (**hidrogênio**)

hydrogenated /haɪˈdrɒdʒɪneɪtɪd/ ADJECTIVE hydrogenated fats and oils have hydrogen added, usually to make them more solid. A chemistry word. (**hidrogenado**)

hyena /haɪˈiːnə/ NOUN [plural **hyenas**] a wild animal similar to a dog, that lives in Asia and Africa, and makes a noise that sounds like laughter (**hiena**)

hygiene /ˈhaɪdʒiːn/ NOUN, NO PLURAL keeping yourself and the things around you clean, so that you stay healthy □ *The best way to avoid infection is to practise good hygiene.* (**higiene**) ▣ *Poor food hygiene can cause disease.* (**higiene alimentar**)
• **hygienic** /haɪˈdʒiːnɪk/ ADJECTIVE without any dirt or bacteria □ *Viruses can spread even in the most hygienic situations.* (**higiênico**)

hymn / hysteria

hymn /hɪm/ NOUN [plural **hymns**] a song sung by Christians to praise God (hino, canto de louvor)

hype /haɪp/ ▶ NOUN, NO PLURAL when something is talked about a lot, especially on television or in newspapers, to make it seem good or interesting □ *There has been a lot of media hype surrounding the movie.* (propaganda)
▶ VERB [**hypes, hyping, hyped**] to talk about or advertise something a lot in order to make people interested in it □ *They were hyped as the best Brazilian team of all time.* (exagerar os fatos)

hyped up /ˌhaɪpt ˈʌp/ ADJECTIVE behaving in a very excited way. An informal word. □ *The children were all hyped up after the party.* (excitado)

hyper /ˈhaɪpə(r)/ ADJECTIVE behaving in an excited and uncontrolled way. An informal word. □ *The kids always go hyper just before bedtime.* (excitado)

hyper- /ˈhaɪpə(r)-/ PREFIX **hyper-** is added to the beginning of words to mean 'more than normal' or 'bigger than normal' □ *hyperactive* □ *hypermarket* (hiper)

hyperactive /ˌhaɪpərˈæktɪv/ ADJECTIVE much more active than most people, and often finding it difficult to concentrate (hiperativo)

hyperlink /ˈhaɪpəlɪŋk/ NOUN [plural **hyperlinks**] a connection on a website or other computer document that you can click on in order to move to another website or document. A computing word. (hyperlink)

hypermarket /ˈhaɪpəmɑːkɪt/ NOUN [plural **hypermarkets**] a very large supermarket (hipermercado)

hypertext /ˈhaɪpətekst/ NOUN, NO PLURAL computer text containing words and images that you can click on in order to move to a related document, image or piece of text. A computing word. (hipertexto)

hyphen /ˈhaɪfən/ NOUN [plural **hyphens**] the short line (-) used for joining two words together, or for showing that a word has been divided and part of it is on the next line (hífen)

• **hyphenate** /ˈhaɪfəneɪt/ VERB [**hyphenates, hyphenating, hyphenated**] to use a hyphen to join two words, or to divide a word at the end of a line (hifenizar)

hypnosis /hɪpˈnəʊsɪs/ NOUN, NO PLURAL a state in which you seem to be in a deep sleep, but in which you can be influenced, or a treatment using this state □ *I tried hypnosis to give up smoking.* □ *Under hypnosis, she was able to remember more about the incident.* (hipnose)

• **hypnotic** /hɪpˈnɒtɪk/ ADJECTIVE making you feel as if you have been hypnotized □ *They danced to the hypnotic beat of the African drums.* (hipnótico)

• **hypnotism** /ˈhɪpnətɪzəm/ NOUN, NO PLURAL the practice of hypnotizing people (hipnotismo)

• **hypnotist** /ˈhɪpnətɪst/ NOUN [plural **hypnotists**] someone who hypnotizes people (hipnotista)

• **hypnotize** or **hypnotise** /ˈhɪpnətaɪz/ VERB [**hypnotizes, hypnotizing, hypnotized**] to put someone into a state of hypnosis (hipnotizar)

hypochondriac /ˌhaɪpəˈkɒndriæk/ NOUN [plural **hypochondriacs**] someone who worries a lot about their health, and often thinks that they are ill (hipocondríaco)

hypocrisy /hɪˈpɒkrəsi/ NOUN, NO PLURAL when someone pretends to have strong moral beliefs, but does not behave according to these beliefs (hipocrisia)

• **hypocrite** /ˈhɪpəkrɪt/ NOUN [plural **hypocrites**] someone who pretends to have strong moral beliefs, but does not behave according to those beliefs (hipócrita)

• **hypocritical** /ˌhɪpəˈkrɪtɪkəl/ ADJECTIVE showing hypocrisy □ *It's a bit hypocritical to accuse him of greed when you've just eaten a whole chocolate cake.* (hipócrita)

hypodermic needle /ˌhaɪpəˌdɜːmɪk ˈniːdəl/ or **hypodermic syringe** /ˌhaɪpəˌdɜːmɪk sɪˈrɪndʒ/ NOUN [plural **hypodermic needles** or **hypodermic syringes**] a medical instrument with a sharp, hollow needle, used for putting drugs into someone's body through their skin (agulha de injeção)

hypotenuse /haɪˈpɒtənjuːz/ NOUN [plural **hypotenuses**] in a triangle with one angle of 90°, the hypotenuse is the longest side, which is opposite that angle. A maths word. (hipotenusa)

hypothermia /ˌhaɪpəʊˈθɜːmiə/ NOUN, NO PLURAL a medical condition in which someone's body temperature becomes dangerously low because they are very cold (hipotermia)

hypothesis /haɪˈpɒθɪsɪs/ NOUN [plural **hypotheses**] a theory or idea that is suggested as a possible explanation for something, but that has not yet been proved □ *They carried out a series of experiments to test their hypothesis.* (hipótese)

• **hypothesize** or **hypothesise** /haɪˈpɒθɪsaɪz/ VERB [**hypothesizes, hypothesizing, hypothesized**] to form a hypothesis about something □ *Scientists have hypothesized that this type of activity may have health benefits.* (formular hipóteses)

• **hypothetical** /ˌhaɪpəˈθetɪkəl/ ADJECTIVE based on what can be imagined, instead of on facts □ *Imagine a hypothetical situation in which you're rich and famous.* (hipotético)

hysterectomy /ˌhɪstəˈrektəmi/ NOUN [plural **hysterectomies**] a medical operation to remove a woman's womb (= part where a baby grows) (histerectomia)

hysteria /hɪsˈtɪəriə/ NOUN, NO PLURAL when people cannot control their actions because of extreme fear, excitement, etc. □ *The media were accused of arousing public hysteria over the incident.* (histeria)

• **hysterical** /hɪsˈterɪkəl/ ADJECTIVE

1 reacting to something in an uncontrolled way, because of extreme fear, excitement, etc. □ *She burst into hysterical tears.* □ *He was absolutely hysterical with excitement.* (**histérico**)
2 very funny. An informal word. □ *Have you seen his new film? It's absolutely hysterical.* (**hilariante**)

- **hysterically** /hɪsˈtɛrɪkəlɪ/ ADVERB
1 in a hysterical way □ *She screamed hysterically, tearing at her hair.* (**histericamente**)
2 something that is hysterically funny is extremely funny (**hilariante**)

- **hysterics** /hɪsˈtɛrɪks/ PLURAL NOUN
1 behaviour that is extremely emotional and uncontrolled □ *He was in hysterics, screaming and shouting at everyone.* (**crise de histeria**)
2 uncontrolled laughter □ *The audience was in hysterics.* (**ataque de riso**)

I i

I[1] *or* **i** /aɪ/ the ninth letter of the alphabet (**a nona letra do alfabeto**)

I[2] /aɪ/ PRONOUN used to talk or write about yourself □ *I live near Edinburgh.* □ *I didn't forget your birthday, did I?* (**eu**)

-ible /-əbəl/ SUFFIX **-ible** is added to the end of words to mean 'able to be' □ *accessible* □ *visible* (**-ível**)

-ic /-ɪk/ *or* **-ical** /-ɪkəl/ SUFFIX **-ic** or **-ical** is added to the end of words to mean 'to do with a particular thing' □ *historic* □ *political* (**-ico**)

ice /aɪs/ ▶ NOUN, NO PLURAL frozen water □ *The ice melted and the water began to rise.* (**gelo**) 🔁 *Her hand felt like a block of ice.* (**bloco de gelo**)
⇨ go to **break the ice**
▶ VERB [**ices, icing, iced**] to cover a cake with icing (= sweet substance) □ *Finally, ice the cake and decorate it with sweets.* (**cobrir com glacê**)
◆ PHRASAL VERB **ice over/up** to become covered in ice □ *The lake iced over in January this year.* (**ficar coberto de gelo**)

Ice Age /aɪs ˌeɪdʒ/ NOUN **the Ice Age** a period of time in the past when a large part of the Earth was covered with ice (**Era do Gelo**)

iceberg /ˈaɪsbɜːg/ NOUN [*plural* **icebergs**] a large mass of ice floating in the sea (**iceberg**)

ice cap /ˈaɪs ˌkæp/ NOUN [*plural* **ice caps**] a layer of ice that permanently covers the land and the sea at the North and South Pole (**calota glacial**)

ice cream /ˌaɪs ˈkriːm/ NOUN [*plural* **ice creams**]
1 *no plural* a sweet frozen food made from milk or cream □ *I'll have some strawberry ice cream, please.* (**sorvete**)
2 an amount of ice cream for one person □ *Would you like an ice cream?* (**sorvete**)

ice cube /ˈaɪs ˌkjuːb/ NOUN [*plural* **ice cubes**] a small block of ice that you put in a drink to make it cold (**cubo, pedra de gelo**)

ice hockey /ˈaɪs ˌhɒki/ NOUN, NO PLURAL a sport played on ice in which two teams use curved sticks to try to hit a small round object into a net (**hóquei**)

ice lolly /ˌaɪs ˈlɒli/ NOUN [*plural* **ice lollies**] a piece of sweet, fruit-flavoured ice on a stick (**picolé**)

ice rink /ˈaɪs ˌrɪŋk/ NOUN [*plural* **ice rinks**] a large area of ice, often in a building, where you can skate (= move over ice wearing special boots with blades on the bottom) (**pista de gelo**)

ice skate /ˈaɪs ˌskeɪt/ NOUN [*plural* **ice skates**] a boot with a metal blade on the bottom, that you wear for moving over ice (**patim de esqui**)
• **ice-skating** /ˈaɪsˌskeɪtɪŋ/ NOUN, NO PLURAL the activity of moving over ice wearing ice skates □ *We go ice-skating every Sunday.* (**patinação no gelo**)

icicle /ˈaɪsɪkəl/ NOUN [*plural* **icicles**] a long thin piece of ice that hangs from something (**pingente de gelo**)

icing /ˈaɪsɪŋ/ NOUN, NO PLURAL a substance made from sugar and water that you use for decorating cakes (**glacê**)
◆ IDIOM **the icing on the cake** something that makes a good situation even better □ *It was great to get the job, but being able to work with Renate is the icing on the cake.* (**a cereja do bolo**)

icing sugar /ˈaɪsɪŋ ˌʃʊɡə(r)/ NOUN, NO PLURAL sugar in the form of a powder, used for making icing (**açúcar para glacê**)

icon /ˈaɪkɒn/ NOUN [*plural* **icons**]
1 a person or thing that is famous or that represents a particular idea (**ícone**) 🔁 *a fashion icon* (**ícone da moda**) □ *The Eiffel Tower is Paris's most famous icon.*
2 a small symbol on a computer screen that represents a program or a file. A computing word □ *Click on the browser icon on your desktop.* (**ícone**)
• **iconic** /aɪˈkɒnɪk/ ADJECTIVE very famous and representing a particular idea □ *She was an iconic figure in the pop world.* (**icônico**)

ICT /ˌaɪsiːˈtiː/ ABBREVIATION information and communication technology; a school subject to do with computers and electronic forms of communication (**abreviação de tecnologia da informação e comunicação**)

icy /ˈaɪsi/ ADJECTIVE [**icier, iciest**]
1 covered with ice □ *Drivers lost control of their cars on the icy roads.* (**gelado**)
2 extremely cold □ *An icy wind was blowing.* □ *She threw off her jacket and jumped into the icy water.* (**gelado**)
3 extremely unfriendly □ *She gave him an icy look.* (**hostil, frio**)

ID /ˌaɪˈdiː/ ABBREVIATION identification; an official document that proves who you are □ *We'll need some form of ID.* (**identidade**)

I'd /aɪd/ a short way to say and write I would or I had □ *I'd like another drink, please.* □ *I'd just gone to bed when the phone rang.* (ver **have, would**)

idea /aɪˈdɪə/ NOUN [plural **ideas**]
1 a thought or plan about something you could do (**ideia**) 🔲 *It was a good/brilliant idea to look online.* (**ideia boa/brilhante**) 🔲 *Taking six children swimming was a bad idea.* (**má ideia**) 🔲 *I've had an idea about how to fix the fence.* (**tive uma ideia**) □ **+ to do something** *It was Kate's idea to buy a van.*
2 *no plural* knowledge about something (**ideia**) 🔲 *I had no idea what was happening.* (**não tenho ideia**) □ *Can you give us some idea of how many people are coming?* □ *Do you have any idea how to switch the heating on?*
3 a belief □ **+ about** *He has some strange ideas about food.* (**ideia**) 🔲 *I don't want you to get the wrong idea about our relationship.* (**tenha a ideia errada**)
4 *no plural* a plan or purpose □ **+ of** *What's the idea of keeping the rabbits in separate hutches?* □ *The idea is to see if we like camping before we buy a tent.* (**sugestão**)
5 *no plural* the way you think something is or would be □ **+ of** *The idea of giving a speech in front of all those people terrifies me.* □ *Rock climbing isn't my idea of fun.* (**ideia**)

ideal /aɪˈdɪəl/ ▶ ADJECTIVE
1 exactly right for a particular purpose □ *It's an ideal house for a family.* (**ideal**) 🔲 *The meeting was an ideal opportunity to make my announcement.* (**oportunidade ideal**)
2 in an ideal world used for talking about what you would like, even if this is not possible □ *In an ideal world, all the costs would be shared.* (**no mundo perfeito**)
3 not ideal used for saying that an arrangement or plan is not very convenient for you □ *'Can you come on Thursday evening?' 'Well, it's not ideal, but I'll try.'* (**não é o ideal**)
▶ NOUN [plural **ideals**]
1 an idea about what is good and right that you try to follow in the way that you behave □ *He seems to have trouble living up to his ideals.* (**ideal**)
2 someone or something that you believe is a perfect example of something □ *Garbo was everyone's ideal of beauty.* (**ideal, perfeição**)

• **idealism** /aɪˈdɪəlɪzəm/ NOUN, NO PLURAL the belief that it is possible to achieve something good or perfect, even if this is unlikely (**idealismo**)
• **idealist** /aɪˈdɪəlɪst/ NOUN [plural **idealists**] someone who believes that something good or perfect can be achieved, even if this is unlikely (**idealista**)
• **idealize** or **idealise** /aɪˈdɪəlaɪz/ VERB [**idealizes, idealizing, idealized**] to believe that someone or something is perfect, or better than they really are □ *We often idealize our parents when we are children.* (**idealizar**)

• **ideally** /aɪˈdɪəlɪ/ ADVERB
1 used for talking about what you would like to do or have, even if this is not possible □ *Ideally, I'd like to finish this by tomorrow.* (**de preferência**)
2 in a way that is exactly right, or just what you want □ *The hotel is ideally situated for the beach.* (**idealmente**)

identical /aɪˈdentɪkəl/ ADJECTIVE exactly the same (**idêntico**) 🔲 *She gave birth to identical twins.* (**gêmeos idênticos**) □ *The room was identical to his own.*

identification /aɪˌdentɪfɪˈkeɪʃən/ NOUN, NO PLURAL
1 an official document that gives details such as your name and your date of birth, sometimes with a photograph of you on it, to prove who you are □ *The men wore their uniforms and carried official identification.* (**identificação**)
2 the process of finding out who someone is or what something is (**identificação**)

identify /aɪˈdentɪfaɪ/ VERB [**identifies, identifying, identified**]
1 to recognize someone or something and to say who or what they are □ *She had to identify the body.* □ *Maps helped them identify the buildings.* □ *We were taught how to identify the signs of mental illness.* (**identificar**)
2 to find something □ *Scientists have identified the gene that is responsible for the disease.* □ *We are trying to identify suitable buildings to rent.* (**identificar**)
3 to be a sign that shows what someone or something is □ *Her uniform identified her as a member of the armed forces.* (**identificar**)

♦ PHRASAL VERBS **identify with someone** to understand someone and to share their feelings □ *The author does not intend us to identify with the main character.* (**identificar-se com alguém**)
be identified with someone/something to be considered to be connected to or involved with someone or something □ *She is identified with left-wing politics.* (**ter ligações com alguém/algo**)

identity /aɪˈdentətɪ/ NOUN [plural **identities**]
1 who someone is □ *Police are trying to discover the identity of the thief.* (**identidade**) 🔲 *Can you confirm your identity?* (**confirmar sua identidade**)
2 the qualities that make a person or an organization what they are, and different from others □ *We are losing our sense of national identity.* (**identidade**)

identity card /aɪˈdentətɪ ˌkɑːd/ NOUN [plural **identity cards**] an official document showing details of who someone is (**documento de identidade**)

identity theft /aɪˈdentətɪ ˌθeft/ NOUN, NO PLURAL stealing information about someone in order to pretend to be them, for example to get money from their bank account (**ladrão de identidade**)

idiocy /ˈɪdɪəsɪ/ NOUN, NO PLURAL being stupid □ *I couldn't believe the idiocy of his suggestion.* (**idiotice**)

idiom /ˈɪdɪəm/ NOUN [plural **idioms**] a phrase that has a meaning that you cannot understand simply by knowing the meaning of the separate words □ *The idiom 'once in a blue moon' means 'very rarely'.* (**expressão idiomática**)
- **idiomatic** /ˌɪdɪəˈmætɪk/ ADJECTIVE
  1 expressed in a natural way □ *He speaks fluent, idiomatic French.* (**idiomático**)
  2 containing idioms □ *idiomatic language* (**idiomático**)

idiot /ˈɪdɪət/ NOUN [plural **idiots**] a stupid person □ *I felt like a complete idiot.* (**idiota**)
- **idiotic** /ˌɪdɪˈɒtɪk/ ADJECTIVE extremely stupid □ *That's an idiotic idea.* (**estúpido**)

idle /ˈaɪdəl/ ADJECTIVE
1 without a particular purpose (**vão, inútil**) *Let's not waste time in idle chatter.* (**conversa inútil**)
2 lazy (**preguiçoso**) *Those children are just bone idle* (= very lazy). (**muito preguiçosas**)
3 if a machine is idle, it is not being used (**inativo, ocioso**)
- **idly** /ˈaɪdlɪ/ ADVERB not doing anything, or without a particular purpose □ *She sat, idly looking through a magazine.* (**inutilmente**)

idol /ˈaɪdəl/ NOUN [plural **idols**]
1 someone you admire very much, or someone very famous and admired by many people □ *The show is hosted by former pop idol, Donny Osmond.* (**ídolo**)
2 a picture or object that people pray to (**ídolo**)
- **idolize** *or* **idolise** /ˈaɪdəlaɪz/ VERB [**idolizes, idolizing, idolized**] to admire someone or something very much □ *He idolizes David Beckham.* (**idolatrar**)

idyllic /ɪˈdɪlɪk, aɪˈdɪlɪk/ ADJECTIVE extremely pleasant or beautiful □ *It sounds like you had an idyllic childhood.* □ *The cottage is in an idyllic spot.* (**idílico**)

if /ɪf/ CONJUNCTION
1 used to say that something must happen before something else can happen or be true □ *If we leave now, we should catch the train.* □ *If you do your homework now, you can go out later.* (**se**)
2 used to say that something will be the result of something that might happen or be true □ *He will have to go into hospital if his condition gets worse.* (**se**) *I hope the bricks will arrive tomorrow. If not, the builders won't be able to work.* (**se não**) *Will you be at home tomorrow? If so* (= if you are), *would you mind taking in a parcel for me?* (**se sim**)
3 whether □ *I don't know if I can come on Thursday.* □ *He asked me if I minded him smoking.* (**se**)
4 used for talking about a situation you are imagining □ *You wouldn't behave like that if your father were still alive.* (**se**)
5 every time □ *I always call in at his house if I'm passing.* (**quando, sempre que**)
6 **if only** used to talk about something you wish would happen or be true □ *If only he'd listen to your advice!* (**se apenas**)
7 **What if ...?** used to ask what will happen if something else happens or is true □ *What if I miss the phone call?* (**E se...?**)

i.e. /ˌaɪˈiː/ ABBREVIATION used for giving more information to show what you mean □ *The whole trip, i.e. food, travel and hotel, cost £500.* (**isto é**)

igloo /ˈɪgluː/ NOUN [plural **igloos**] a round house made from blocks of snow (**iglu**)

igneous /ˈɪgnɪəs/ ADJECTIVE igneous rock is formed from hot liquid rock from a volcano (= mountain that explodes). A geography word. (**ígneo, magmático**)

ignite /ɪgˈnaɪt/ VERB [**ignites, igniting, ignited**]
1 to start to burn or to make something start to burn □ *The fuel ignited, causing a massive blaze.* □ *Lightning and high winds ignited the dry wood.* (**inflamar**)
2 to cause strong feelings such as anger □ *The attack has ignited fury throughout the country.* (**provocar, despertar**)
- **ignition** /ɪgˈnɪʃən/ NOUN, NO PLURAL the place where you put your key to start a vehicle's engine (**ignição**)

ignorance /ˈɪgnərəns/ NOUN, NO PLURAL not knowing about a subject or a situation □ *The report suggests that there is widespread ignorance about the disease.* (**ignorância**) *They were living in blissful ignorance of the outside world.* (**feliz ignorância**)
- **ignorant** /ˈɪgnərənt/ ADJECTIVE
  1 not knowing about something □ *Many people are ignorant of the dangers.* (**ignorante**) *Ministers still appear to be blissfully ignorant of this fact.* (**completamente ignorantes**)
  2 stupid and rude □ *What an ignorant thing to say!* (**grosseiro**)

ignore /ɪgˈnɔː(r)/ VERB [**ignores, ignoring, ignored**]
1 to not pay attention to someone or something □ *He ignored all my advice.* □ *The sport has been generally ignored by the media.* (**ignorar**)
2 to pretend not to notice someone □ *I said hello, but she just ignored me.* (**ignorar**)

iguana /ɪˈgwɑːnə/ NOUN [plural **iguanas**] a large reptile with sharp points on its back, that lives mainly in South America (**iguana**)

il- /ɪl/ PREFIX il- is added to the beginning of words to mean 'not' □ *illogical* □ *illegal* (**il-**)

ileum /ˈɪlɪəm/ NOUN [plural **ilea**] the last part of the small intestine. A biology word. (**íleo**)

I'll /aɪl/ a short way to say and write I will □ *I'll be back next week.* □ *I'll carry these things for you.* (ver **will, shall**)

ill /ɪl/ ADJECTIVE

1 suffering from an illness (**doente**) ◘ *Do you feel ill?* (**sente-se doente**) ◘ *She fell ill after eating chicken that was not cooked properly.* (**ficou doente**) ◘ *He is seriously ill with cancer.* (**seriamente doente**)

2 bad or harmful (**ruim, mau**) ◘ *He seemed to be suffering no ill effects from his accident.* (**efeitos colaterais**) ◘ *We have no ill feelings towards her.* (**sentimentos ruins**)

▶ Notice that you use seriously ill and not 'badly ill' to describe someone with a very bad illness.

ill- /ɪl/ ADVERB bad or badly ◘ *ill-treat* ◘ *ill-tempered* (**mal**)

illegal /ɪˈliːgəl/ ADJECTIVE not allowed by the law
◘ *It is illegal to sell alcohol to children.* ◘ *They are involved in illegal activitites.* (**ilegal**)

- **illegality** /ˌɪlɪˈgælɪti/ NOUN, NO PLURAL being illegal (**ilegalidade**)
- **illegally** /ɪˈliːgəli/ ADVERB in an illegal way ◘ *Your car is parked illegally.* ◘ *He was found guilty of illegally possessing a firearm.* (**ilegalmente**)

illegible /ɪˈledʒɪbəl/ ADJECTIVE impossible to read
◘ *His handwriting is almost illegible.* (**ilegível**)

illegitimate /ˌɪlɪˈdʒɪtɪmət/ ADJECTIVE having parents who are not married to each other ◘ *He believes he is the illegitimate child of a princess.* (**ilegítimo**)

illicit /ɪˈlɪsɪt/ ADJECTIVE

1 not allowed by law ◘ *They were involved in forgery and other illicit activities.* (**ilícito, proibido**)
2 disapproved of by most people (**ilícito**)

illiterate /ɪˈlɪtərət/ ADJECTIVE unable to read or write (**analfabeto**)

ill-mannered /ˌɪlˈmænəd/ ADJECTIVE not polite
◘ *She felt that she had been ill-mannered, and was ashamed of herself.* (**grosseiro**)

illness /ˈɪlnɪs/ NOUN [plural illnesses]

1 a disease (**doença**) ◘ *He is suffering from a serious illness.* (**doença séria**) ◘ *Measles was once a common childhood illness.* (**doença de criança**) ◘ *The illness is caused by a virus.*
2 NO PLURAL bad health ◘ *Illness prevented him from competing in the championship.* (**doença**)

illogical /ɪˈlɒdʒɪkəl/ ADJECTIVE not based on clear or sensible thought ◘ *Offering plastic bags to online shoppers is totally illogical.* (**ilógico**)

ill-tempered /ˌɪlˈtempəd/ ADJECTIVE speaking or behaving angrily or rudely ◘ *ill-tempered remarks* (**mal-humorado**)

ill-treat /ˌɪlˈtriːt/ VERB [ill-treats, ill-treating, ill-treated] to treat a person or an animal in a cruel way ◘ *Some of the older residents had been ill-treated.* (**maltratar**)

- **ill-treatment** /ˌɪlˈtriːtmənt/ NOUN, NO PLURAL when a person or an animal is treated in a cruel way ◘ *There was clear evidence of abuse and ill-treatment by staff.* (**maus-tratos**)

illuminate /ɪˈluːmɪneɪt/ VERB [illuminates, illuminating, illuminated]

1 to make a dark place brighter with light, or to shine lights on something ◘ *Fires illuminated the night sky.* (**iluminar**)
2 to make something easier to understand. (**esclarecer**)

- **illuminated** /ɪˈluːmɪneɪtɪd/ ADJECTIVE made bright using lights ◘ *An illuminated sign informed us that there were traffic queues ahead.* (**iluminado**)
- **illuminating** /ɪˈluːmɪneɪtɪŋ/ ADJECTIVE giving information that makes something easier to understand ◘ *Well, that was a very illuminating discussion.* (**esclarecedor**)
- **illumination** /ɪˌluːmɪˈneɪʃən/ NOUN, NO PLURAL the use of light to make something brighter ◘ *The light from behind the door provided the only illumination.* (**iluminação**)

illusion /ɪˈluːʒən/ NOUN [plural illusions]

1 a false idea or belief (**ilusão**) ◘ *He's under the illusion that it's easy to get a job.* (**sob a ilusão**) ◘ *She had no illusions about her son's abilities.* (**nenhuma ilusão**)
2 something that is not really what it seems to be (**ilusão**) ◘ *Try using mirrors to create an illusion of space.* (**criar uma ilusão**)

illustrate /ˈɪləstreɪt/ VERB [illustrates, illustrating, illustrated]

1 to give an example or to be an example that explains something (**ilustrar**) ◘ *He told us a story to illustrate his point.* (**ilustrar o argumento**) ◘ *Her case illustrates the importance of using a good lawyer.*
2 to draw pictures to go in books, magazines, etc. ◘ *She illustrated several books for children.* (**ilustrar**)

- **illustration** /ˌɪləˈstreɪʃən/ NOUN [plural illustrations]

1 a picture in a book, magazine, etc. (**ilustração**)
2 an example that shows that something is true or what something is like ◘ *That was a perfect illustration of why the safety harness is essential.* ◘ *To give you an illustration: if you invest £3,000 a year, you could end up with a sum of £50,000 at the end of the period.* (**exemplo**)

- **illustrator** /ˈɪləstreɪtə(r)/ NOUN [plural illustrators] someone who draws pictures for books, magazines, etc. (**ilustrador**)

illustrious /ɪˈlʌstriəs/ ADJECTIVE admired and respected by many people. A formal word ◘ *The book charts Churchill's illustrious political career.* (**ilustre**)

ill-will /ˌɪlˈwɪl/ NOUN, NO PLURAL bad feelings towards someone because of something that has happened in the past (**maus sentimentos**) ◘ *We*

bear them no ill-will, and wish them the best of luck. (não lhe desejamos nenhum mal)

I'm /aɪm/ a short way to say and write I am □ *I'm hungry.* □ *I'm going to New York tomorrow.* (ver **be**)

im- /ɪm/ PREFIX im- is added to the beginning of words to mean 'not' □ *immature* □ *immoral* (i-)

image /ˈɪmɪdʒ/ NOUN [plural images]

1 an idea or opinion that people have about someone or something (imagem) 🔁 *She likes to project an image of confidence.* (projetar uma imagem) 🔁 *The agency is aiming to create an image of a dynamic, modern city.* (criar uma imagem)

2 a picture, especially one on television, film or on a computer □ *We have new images of accident.* (imagem) 🔁 *A special camera was used to capture images of the child in its mother's womb.* (capturar imagens)

3 a picture that you have in your mind □ *Disturbing images filled his head.* (imagem)

4 be the image of someone to look exactly like someone □ *Jessica is the image of her mother.* (ser a imagem de alguém)

• **imagery** /ˈɪmɪdʒəri/ NOUN, NO PLURAL

1 pictures or objects that represent an idea □ *The movie is full of striking visual imagery.* (imagens)

2 pictures □ *Satellite imagery shows us the effects of global warming.* (imagens)

3 in literature, words that produce pictures in your mind □ *We discussed Shakespeare's use of imagery in 'Hamlet'.* (imagens)

imaginary /ɪˈmædʒɪnəri/ ADJECTIVE existing in your mind but not real □ *It is perfectly normal for children to have imaginary friends.* (imaginário)

• **imagination** /ɪˌmædʒɪˈneɪʃən/ NOUN, NO PLURAL

1 your ability to think of new ideas or to form interesting pictures and stories in your mind. (imaginação) 🔁 *Rory has a very vivid imagination.* (imaginação vívida) 🔁 *Reading encourages children to use their imagination.* (usar a imaginação)

2 when someone believes something that is not true or real □ *She thinks people hate her, but it's all in her imagination.* (imaginação)

• **imaginative** /ɪˈmædʒɪnətɪv/ ADJECTIVE

1 using new and interesting ideas □ *That's an imaginative design.* (imaginativo)

2 using the imagination □ *Imaginative play is important for children.* (imaginativo)

• **imagine** /ɪˈmædʒɪn/ VERB [imagines, imagining, imagined]

1 to form a picture of someone or something in your mind □ **+ question word** *I tried to imagine what he would look like.* □ **+ that** *Imagine that you're the manager of a large company.* □ **+ ing** *Imagine having your own aeroplane!* (imaginar)

2 to think that something is probably true □ *I imagine he'll want some food.* (imaginar)

3 to think that something exists or is true when it does not or is not □ *I keep imagining I can hear voices.* (imaginar)

imam /ɪˈmɑːm/ NOUN [plural **imams**] a Muslim priest or leader (imame)

imbalance /ɪmˈbæləns/ NOUN [plural **imbalances**] when things are not arranged fairly or equally □ *There is an imbalance between the amount they eat and the amount of calories they use up.* (desequilíbrio)

imbecile /ˈɪmbɪsiːl/ NOUN [plural **imbeciles**] a stupid person □ *I felt like a complete imbecile!* (imbecil)

imitate /ˈɪmɪteɪt/ VERB [imitates, imitating, imitated]

1 to copy someone or something because you like them or it □ *He tries to imitate the style of famous artists.* (imitar)

2 to copy the way someone speaks or behaves as a joke □ *He's always imitating my friend's voice.* (imitar)

• **imitation** /ˌɪmɪˈteɪʃən/ NOUN [plural **imitations**]

1 when you copy the way someone speaks or behaves as a joke □ *He does a good imitation of his English teacher.* (imitação)

2 a copy of something □ *He threatened them with an imitation gun.* (cópia, reprodução) 🔁 *Their records are a pale imitation* (= not as good) *of their live performances.* (imitação barata)

• **imitator** /ˈɪmɪteɪtə(r)/ NOUN [plural **imitators**] someone who copies someone or something else □ *As a successful politician, he has many imitators.* (imitador)

immaculate /ɪˈmækjʊlət/ ADJECTIVE

1 extremely clean and tidy □ *The house looked immaculate.* (imaculado)

2 completely perfect □ *With immaculate timing, he arrived just as we were starting.* (impecável)

immature /ˌɪməˈtjʊə(r)/ ADJECTIVE

1 behaving in a silly way that is typical of a younger person □ *I was too immature to be a father.* (imaturo)

2 not yet completely developed □ *Her immature lungs struggled for oxygen.* (não desenvolvido)

• **immaturity** /ˌɪməˈtjʊərəti/ NOUN, NO PLURAL being immature or behaving in an immature way (imaturidade)

immediate /ɪˈmiːdɪət/ ▶ ADJECTIVE

1 happening now, and without delay (imediato) 🔁 *I can't give you an immediate response.* (resposta imediata) □ *They demanded the immediate withdrawal of troops.*

2 existing now (imediato) 🔁 *We are in no immediate danger.* (perigo imediato) 🔁 *Her immediate concern is for her children.* (preocupação imediata)

3 closest to someone or something (mais próximo) 🔁 *Police evacuated the immediate area.* (área próxima) 🔁 *I'm only inviting my immediate family.* (familiares mais próximos)

4 the immediate future the next period of time □ *I certainly don't plan to change jobs in the immediate future.* (o futuro próximo)

immense

- **immediately** /ɪˈmiːdiətli/ ▶ ADVERB
  1 now or without delay □ *Come here immediately!* □ *I rang the doctor immediately.* (imediatamente)
  2 immediately before/after something in the period just before/after something □ *Immediately before the bomb went off, they were talking on the balcony.* (imediatamente antes/depois de algo)
  3 with no space between □ *Immediately in front of the church you will see a signpost.* (imediatamente)
  ▶ CONJUNCTION as soon as □ *Immediately I got the message, I ran to tell father.*

immense /ɪˈmens/ ADJECTIVE extremely large in size, amount or degree □ *Some children are under immense pressure to succeed.* □ *He used his immense wealth to help a lot of people.* (imenso)

- **immensely** /ɪˈmensli/ ADVERB extremely □ *He's immensely popular.* (imensamente, extremamente)

immerse /ɪˈmɜːs/ VERB [immerses, immersing, immersed]
  1 to put something in a liquid so that it is completely covered □ *The cloth is then immersed in dye.* (imergir)
  2 immerse yourself in something/be immersed in something to give all of your attention to something □ *After the divorce, Brian immersed himself in his work.* □ *She was too immersed in her magazine article to notice me.* (ficar absorto em algo)

- **immersion** /ɪˈmɜːʃən/ NOUN, NO PLURAL
  1 when you put something into a liquid (imersão)
  2 when you spend most of your time doing something or in a particular situation □ *His immersion in Spanish culture influenced his art deeply.* (imersão, dedicação)

immigrant /ˈɪmɪgrənt/ NOUN [plural **immigrants**] someone who has come to live in a country from another country (imigrante)

immigration /ˌɪmɪˈgreɪʃən/ NOUN, NO PLURAL
  1 when people come to live in a foreign country □ *Immigration rose sharply in 2007.* (imigração) ▣ *The government has announced new immigration laws.* (leis de imigração)
  2 the place where a person's documents are checked when they come into a country □ *She was stopped at immigration and questioned for hours.* (imigração)

imminent /ˈɪmɪnənt/ ADJECTIVE something that is imminent is going to happen very soon (iminente) ▣ *Her life is in imminent danger.* (perigo iminente) ▣ *There is no imminent threat to health.* (ameaça iminente)

immobile /ɪˈməʊbaɪl/ ADJECTIVE not moving or not able to move □ *He lay immobile on the floor.* (imóvel)

- **immobilize** or **immobilise** /ɪˈməʊbɪlaɪz/ VERB [immobilizes, immobilizing, immobilized] to prevent someone or something from moving □ *The ankle needs to be immobilized to give it a chance to heal.* (imobilizar)

impact

immoral /ɪˈmɒrəl/ ADJECTIVE morally wrong □ *He accused her of immoral conduct.* (imoral)

- **immorality** /ˌɪməˈrælɪti/ NOUN, NO PLURAL immoral behaviour (imoralidade)

immortal /ɪˈmɔːtəl/ ADJECTIVE
  1 living for ever □ *This type of accident makes you realize you're not immortal.* (imortal)
  2 very famous, and likely to be remembered for a long time □ *Who said the immortal words 'You ain't seen nothing yet'?* (imortal, eterno)

- **immortality** /ˌɪmɔːˈtælɪti/ NOUN, NO PLURAL being immortal □ *He wants to achieve immortality through his work.* (imortalidade)

- **immortalize** or **immortalise** /ɪˈmɔːtəlaɪz/ VERB [immortalizes, immortalizing, immortalized] to make someone or something famous for a long time □ *She was immortalized in Betjeman's poem.* (imortalizar)

immune /ɪˈmjuːn/ ADJECTIVE
  1 not affected by something □ *I am not immune to criticism.* (imune)
  2 unable to be infected by a particular disease. A biology word □ *Some people are naturally immune to the virus.* (imune)
  3 not affected by a law □ *Diplomats are immune from prosecution.* (imune)

immune system /ɪˈmjuːn ˌsɪstəm/ NOUN [plural **immune systems**] the system in your body that protects it from disease. A biology word. (sistema imunológico)

immunity /ɪˈmjuːnɪti/ NOUN, NO PLURAL
  1 your ability to avoid getting a particular disease. A biology word □ *Catching chickenpox gives lifelong immunity against the virus.* (imunidade)
  2 when you cannot be punished for something □ *As President, he enjoys immunity from prosecution.* (imunidade) ▣ *She has diplomatic immunity.* (imunidade diplomática)

immunization or **immunisation** /ˌɪmjʊnaɪˈzeɪʃən/ NOUN [plural **immunizations**] when a substance is put into someone's body, usually through their skin, to prevent them from getting a particular disease in the future □ *Has your daughter had all her immunizations?* (imunização)

- **immunize** or **immunise** /ˈɪmjʊnaɪz/ VERB [immunizes, immunizing, immunized] to put a substance into someone's body, usually through their skin, to prevent them from getting a particular disease in the future □ *Has he been immunized against measles?* (imunizar)

imp /ɪmp/ NOUN [plural **imps**]
  1 an imaginary creature that looks like a small man and behaves badly (diabinho)
  2 a child who behaves badly in a way that is not very serious (criança endiabrada)

impact ▶ NOUN /ˈɪmpækt/ [plural **impacts**]
  1 the effect that something has □ *The changes will have a significant impact on schools.* (impacto)

impair / imperious

2 the force of one thing hitting another thing □ *The car is designed to absorb the impact of a crash.* (**choque**)
▶ VERB /ɪmˈpækt/ [**impacts, impacting, impacted**] to have an effect on something □ *A long journey could impact on the team's performance.* (**causar impacto**)

impair /ɪmˈpeə(r)/ VERB [**impairs, impairing, impaired**] to make something less good, especially by damaging it □ *Even a small amount of alcohol can impair your ability to drive.* (**prejudicar, deteriorar**)
• **impairment** /ɪmˈpeəmənt/ NOUN [*plural* **impairments**] when part of your body does not work correctly □ *His stroke caused some visual impairment.* (**deterioração**)

impale /ɪmˈpeɪl/ VERB [**impales, impaling, impaled**] to push a sharp object through something □ *His leg was impaled on a piece of broken railing.* (**empalar**)

impart /ɪmˈpɑːt/ VERB [**imparts, imparting, imparted**]
1 to give someone information or your opinions □ *She was desperate to impart the great news.* (**revelar, propagar**)
2 to give a particular quality to something □ *The leaves impart a spicy flavour to the dish.* (**conferir**)

impartial /ɪmˈpɑːʃəl/ ADJECTIVE not influenced by one particular person or group □ *Phone this number for free and impartial advice.* (**imparcial**)
• **impartiality** /ɪmˌpɑːʃiˈælɪti/ NOUN, NO PLURAL being impartial (**imparcialidade**)

impassable /ɪmˈpɑːsəbəl/ ADJECTIVE if a road or path is impassable, you cannot travel along it (**intransitável**)

impasse /æmˈpɑːs/ NOUN, NO PLURAL a situation in which no more progress is possible (**impasse**) 📖 *Our discussion seems to have reached an impasse.* (**chegou a um impasse**)

impassive /ɪmˈpæsɪv/ ADJECTIVE not showing any emotion □ *Her face was totally impassive.* (**impassível**)
• **impassively** /ɪmˈpæsɪvli/ ADVERB in an impassive way □ *He listened impassively to my story of childhood hardship.* (**impassivamente**)

impatience /ɪmˈpeɪʃəns/ NOUN, NO PLURAL being impatient □ *He never showed any sign of impatience.* (**impaciência**)
• **impatient** /ɪmˈpeɪʃənt/ ADJECTIVE
1 wanting something to happen soon □ *She was impatient to get started on the job.* (**impaciente**)
2 annoyed because you have to wait or because someone is making mistakes □ *Flights were delayed and passengers were becoming impatient.* (**impaciente, aborrecido**)
• **impatiently** /ɪmˈpeɪʃəntli/ ADVERB in a way that shows you are impatient □ *'Hurry up!' she said impatiently.* (**impacientemente**)

impeccable /ɪmˈpekəbəl/ ADJECTIVE perfect □ *The car is still in impeccable condition.* □ *The children's behaviour was impeccable.* (**impecável**)
• **impeccably** /ɪmˈpekəbli/ ADVERB perfectly □ *The dogs were impeccably groomed.* (**impecavelmente**)

impede /ɪmˈpiːd/ VERB [**impedes, impeding, impeded**] to delay the progress of someone or something □ *Snow impeded their progress.* (**impedir, retardar**)
• **impediment** /ɪmˈpedɪmənt/ NOUN [*plural* **impediments**]
1 something that delays progress or prevents something from happening □ *Lack of time is a major impediment to getting exercise.* (**obstáculo**)
2 a speech impediment a problem that affects someone's ability to speak (**problema na fala**)

impel /ɪmˈpel/ VERB [**impels, impelling, impelled**] to force someone to do something. A formal word. □ *Curiosity impelled me to visit her one more time.* □ *I felt impelled to protest.* (**impelir**)

impending /ɪmˈpendɪŋ/ ADJECTIVE an impending event is going to happen very soon □ *They failed to warn us of the impending disaster.* (**iminente**)

imperative /ɪmˈperətɪv/ ▶ ADJECTIVE extremely important or necessary □ *It is absolutely imperative that we take this opportunity now.* (**imprescindível**)
▶ NOUN, NO PLURAL **the imperative** a verb form that you use to tell someone to do something (**modo imperativo**)

imperceptible /ˌɪmpəˈseptəbəl/ ADJECTIVE too small or quiet to be noticed □ *His nod was almost imperceptible.* (**imperceptível**)

imperfect /ɪmˈpɜːfɪkt/ ADJECTIVE having some faults □ *We live in an imperfect world.* (**imperfeito**)
• **imperfection** /ˌɪmpəˈfekʃən/ NOUN [*plural* **imperfections**] a fault □ *Avoid jokes that relate to people's physical imperfections.* (**imperfeição**)

imperial /ɪmˈpɪəriəl/ ADJECTIVE
1 to do with an empire (= a number of countries governed by one ruler) □ *It's a book about Britain's imperial past.* (**imperial, real**)
2 to do with a system of measuring or weighing that uses units such as feet for measuring length and pounds for measuring weight (**imperial**)
• **imperialism** /ɪmˈpɪəriəlɪzəm/ NOUN, NO PLURAL
1 when one country rules several other countries (**imperialismo**)
2 when one country has a lot of influence over other countries □ *American cultural imperialism* (**imperialismo**)
• **imperialist** /ɪmˈpɪəriəlɪst/ ADJECTIVE to do with imperialism (**imperialista**)

imperious /ɪmˈpɪəriəs/ ADJECTIVE showing that you think people should obey you. A formal word. □ *'Bring me a clean glass,' she said in an imperious voice.* (**dominador, arrogante**)

impermeable /ɪmˈpɜːmɪəbəl/ ADJECTIVE impermeable substances do not allow liquid or gas to pass through them. A biology or physics word. (impermeável)

impersonal /ɪmˈpɜːsənəl/ ADJECTIVE intended for people generally but not showing interest in separate people and not friendly □ Big hotels can be a bit impersonal. (impessoal)

impersonate /ɪmˈpɜːsəneɪt/ VERB [impersonates, impersonating, impersonated] to copy the way someone talks and behaves, especially to entertain people (personificar)

• **impersonation** /ɪmˌpɜːsəˈneɪʃən/ NOUN [plural impersonations] an attempt to impersonate someone □ Ben can do a brilliant impersonation of the Prime Minister. (personificação)

• **impersonator** /ɪmˈpɜːsəneɪtə(r)/ NOUN [plural impersonators] someone who impersonates people (ator, imitador)

impertinence /ɪmˈpɜːtɪnəns/ NOUN, NO PLURAL a formal word meaning rude behaviour that shows you do not respect someone (impertinência)

• **impertinent** /ɪmˈpɜːtɪnənt/ ADJECTIVE a formal word meaning behaving in a rude way and not showing respect □ an impertinent child (impertinente)

impervious /ɪmˈpɜːvɪəs/ ADJECTIVE
1 a formal word meaning not affected by something □ He seems impervious to the cold. (insensível)
2 an impervious material does not let water pass through it □ impervious surfaces (impermeável)

impetuous /ɪmˈpetʃʊəs/ ADJECTIVE doing things without thinking about what might happen as a result □ He was young and impetuous. (impetuoso)

impetus /ˈɪmpɪtəs/ NOUN, NO PLURAL
1 an influence which helps something to happen □ Sometimes it takes a tragedy to provide the impetus for change. (ímpeto)
2 the force which makes something move. A physics word. (impulso)

impinge /ɪmˈpɪndʒ/
◆ PHRASAL VERB [impinges, impinging, impinged] **impinge on someone/something** to affect someone or something, especially in a bad way □ Having a bad neighbour can really impinge on your life. (afetar alguém/algo)

implant ▶ VERB /ɪmˈplɑːnt/ [implants, implanting, implanted] to put something into someone's body to make it work or look better □ A device is implanted in the heart which regulates the heartbeat. (implantar)
▶ NOUN /ˈɪmplɑːnt/ [plural implants] something that is implanted in someone's body to make it work or look better □ dental implants (implante)

implausible /ɪmˈplɔːzəbəl/ ADJECTIVE difficult to accept as true or real □ It seemed an implausible excuse. (inverossímil)

implement ▶ VERB /ˈɪmplɪment/ [implements, implementing, implemented] to start using a new plan, law, system, etc. □ The new rules will be implemented next year. (aplicar, executar)
▶ NOUN /ˈɪmplɪmənt/ [plural implements] a formal word for a tool □ sharp implements (instrumento)

• **implementation** /ˌɪmplɪmenˈteɪʃən/ NOUN, NO PLURAL implementing something □ the implementation of new laws (aplicação, execução)

implicate /ˈɪmplɪkeɪt/ VERB [implicates, implicating, implicated] to suggest that someone is involved in something bad such as a crime □ He was implicated in the murder of his neighbour. (envolver alguém em algo)

• **implication** /ˌɪmplɪˈkeɪʃən/ NOUN [plural implications]
1 a possible effect or result □ What are the implications of the President's announcement? (consequência)
2 something that is suggested and not said directly □ He rejected the implication that the project was a waste of money. (sugestão, inferência)

implicit /ɪmˈplɪsɪt/ ADJECTIVE
1 suggested or shown but not said directly □ implicit criticism (implícito)
2 complete, without any doubts □ I have implicit faith in her abilities. (absoluto)

implore /ɪmˈplɔː(r)/ VERB [implores, imploring, implored] a formal word meaning to ask someone in a strong and emotional way to do something □ He tearfully implored her not to leave. (implorar)

imply /ɪmˈplaɪ/ VERB [implies, implying, implied] to suggest that something is true without saying it directly □ Are you implying that he lied? (insinuar)

impolite /ˌɪmpəˈlaɪt/ ADJECTIVE a formal word meaning rude □ It seemed impolite to ask how old she was. (rude, indelicado)

import ▶ VERB /ɪmˈpɔːt/ [imports, importing, imported]
1 to bring a product from another country into your country in order to sell it □ + into The cars had been imported into the UK. □ + from Many electrical goods are imported from Japan. (importar)
2 to copy computer information from another place. A computing word. (importar)
▶ NOUN /ˈɪmpɔːt/ [plural imports]
1 a product that is brought from another country into your country in order to sell □ The country is dependent on oil imports. (importação)
2 no plural the process of bringing a product into a country to sell □ + of There's a ban on the import of wild birds. □ import restrictions (importação)
⇨ go to **export**

importance

importance /ɪmˈpɔːtəns/ NOUN, NO PLURAL
1 when something is important ☐ *+ of This just shows the importance of education.* (**importância**) 🔁 *She stressed the importance of eating healthily.* (**enfatizou a importância**)
2 of great/utmost/vital importance extremely important ☐ *The industry is of vital importance to the UK economy.* (**vital/grande importância**)

• **important** /ɪmˈpɔːtənt/ ADJECTIVE
1 necessary or having a big effect on something ☐ *Books are an important part of our culture.* (**importante**) *+ to do something* 🔁 *It's important to listen to what the teacher is saying.* (**é importante**) ☐ *+ that It's important that people are given this information.* ☐ *+ to Amy's career is very important to her.* 🔁 *For me, the most important thing is to be happy.* (**a coisa mais importante**)
2 an important person has a lot of power or influence ☐ *The Prime Minister is the most important person in government.* (**importante**)

> Remember that something is important to someone and not important for someone:
> ✓ *My family is very important to me.*
> ✗ *My family is very important for me.*

• **importantly** /ɪmˈpɔːtəntli/ ADVERB more/most importantly used before saying something that is more important or the most important thing ☐ *I love it here in Hong Kong and more importantly, the children love it too.* (**o mais importante**)

impose /ɪmˈpəʊz/ VERB [**imposes, imposing, imposed**]
1 to force someone to accept something new such as a rule or punishment ☐ *The government imposed a new tax.* (**impor**)
2 to make someone do something for you in a way that is not convenient for them ☐ *They said I could stay with them but I didn't like to impose on them.* (**abusar**)

• **imposing** /ɪmˈpəʊzɪŋ/ ADJECTIVE an imposing person or thing is big in a way that makes you admire them ☐ *an imposing building* (**imponente**)

impossibility /ɪmˌpɒsəˈbɪləti/ NOUN [*plural* **impossibilities**] something that is not possible (**impossibilidade**) 🔁 *Searching every home for the missing girl would be a physical impossibility.* (**impossibilidade física**)

impossible /ɪmˈpɒsəbəl/ ▶ ADJECTIVE
1 not possible (**impossível**) 🔁 *an impossible task* (**tarefa impossível**) *+ to do something* 🔁 *It's impossible to explain.* (**é impossível**) 🔁 *Ink stains are almost impossible to get rid of.* (**quase impossível**) 🔁 *Rain made it impossible for the game to continue.* (**tornou impossível**)
2 an impossible situation is very difficult ☐ *The new rules have put teachers in an impossible position.* (**insuportável**)

improbable

3 someone who is impossible is unreasonable and annoying (**insuportável**)
▶ NOUN, NO PLURAL **the impossible** something that is not possible ☐ *You're asking me to do the impossible.* (**o impossível**)

• **impossibly** /ɪmˈpɒsəbli/ ADVERB extremely ☐ *She was impossibly beautiful.* (**extremamente**)

impostor /ɪmˈpɒstə(r)/ NOUN [*plural* **impostors**] someone who pretends to be someone else in order to trick people (**impostor**)

impoverished /ɪmˈpɒvərɪʃt/ ADJECTIVE very poor ☐ *impoverished countries* (**empobrecido**)

impractical /ɪmˈpræktɪkəl/ ADJECTIVE
1 not sensible or able to be done or used easily ☐ *an impractical suggestion* ☐ *Their clothes are very pretty but rather impractical.* (**impraticável**)
2 an impractical person is not good at doing normal, useful things, such as planning or repairing things (**pouco prático**)

imprecise /ˌɪmprɪˈsaɪs/ ADJECTIVE not exact or not correct ☐ *imprecise measurements* (**impreciso**)

impress /ɪmˈpres/ VERB [**impresses, impressing, impressed**] to make someone feel admiration ☐ *He was trying to impress his friends in his new car.* ☐ *Her attitude impressed me.* (**impressionar**)

• **impressed** /ɪmˈprest/ ADJECTIVE admiring someone or something very much ☐ *The teacher didn't look very impressed when she saw my work.* ☐ *I was impressed at how quickly they dealt with the problem.* (**impressionado**)

• **impression** /ɪmˈpreʃən/ NOUN [*plural* **impressions**]
1 an idea or feeling that you get about someone or something (**impressão**) 🔁 *I got the impression that he wasn't happy.* (**tive a impressão**) 🔁 *She gives the impression of not really caring.* (**dá a impressão**)
2 the effect that someone or something has on you (**impressão**) 🔁 *The film made a big impression on me* (**fez grande impressão**)
3 when someone copies the way someone else talks and behaves in order to entertain people (**imitação**) 🔁 *She does a great impression of Juan.* (**faz uma grande imitação**)

• **impressive** /ɪmˈpresɪv/ ADJECTIVE making you feel admiration ☐ *an impressive performance* ☐ *She's a very impressive woman.* (**impressionante**)

imprison /ɪmˈprɪzən/ VERB [**imprisons, imprisoning, imprisoned**] to put someone in prison or in a place they cannot escape from ☐ *He was imprisoned for fraud.* (**encarcerar, aprisionar**)

• **imprisonment** /ɪmˈprɪzənmənt/ NOUN, NO PLURAL when someone is imprisoned ☐ *She was sentenced to 20 years' imprisonment.* (**encarceramento, prisão**)

improbable /ɪmˈprɒbəbəl/ ADJECTIVE unlikely to happen or unlikely to be true ☐ *a highly improbable story* (**improvável**)

impromptu /ɪmˈprɒmptjuː/ ADJECTIVE not planned □ *an impromptu speech* (**improvisado**)

improper /ɪmˈprɒpə(r)/ ADJECTIVE a formal word meaning not suitable, not right or not honest □ *It would be improper for me to comment before the court case.* (**impróprio, inconveniente**)

improper fraction /ɪmˌprɒpə(r) ˈfrækʃən/ NOUN [plural **improper fractions**] a fraction where the number above the line is bigger than the number below the line. A maths word. (**fração imprópria**)

improve /ɪmˈpruːv/ VERB [**improves, improving, improved**]

1 to become better □ *I hope the weather improves soon.* □ *The situation has slowly improved.* (**melhorar**)

2 to make something better □ *Exercise can improve your health.* □ *The new law is intended to improve road safety.* □ *This treatment will improve the quality of life for many cancer sufferers.* (**aperfeiçoar**)

• **improvement** /ɪmˈpruːvmənt/ NOUN [plural **improvements**]

1 no plural the process of becoming better or of making something better (**aperfeiçoamento**) 🔲 *His test results have shown a great improvement.* (**mostrou aperfeiçoamento**) 🔲 *We have seen no improvement in the health service.* (**vimos aperfeiçoamento**) 🔲 *There has been a significant improvement in living standards.* (**aperfeiçoamento significativo**) □ + *in an improvement in behaviour*

2 a change that makes something better □ *improvements to the home* (**melhoria**)

improvise /ˈɪmprəˌvaɪz/ VERB [**improvises, improvising, improvised**]

1 to decide what to say or do at the time when you are saying or doing it and not before □ *I had forgotten the notes for my talk so I had to improvise.* (**improvisar**)

2 to make something using the things that are available because you do not have the correct equipment □ *We improvised a shelter from some old blankets.* (**improvisar**)

impudence /ˈɪmpjʊdəns/ NOUN, NO PLURAL a formal word meaning rude behaviour or remarks (**atrevimento, insolência**)

• **impudent** /ˈɪmpjʊdənt/ ADJECTIVE a formal word meaning rude and showing no respect (**atrevido, insolente**)

impulse /ˈɪmpʌls/ NOUN [plural **impulses**]

1 a sudden feeling that makes you want to do something □ *He resisted the impulse to hit the man.* (**impulso**)

2 on impulse without thinking first □ *On impulse, he put his arm around her.* (**sem pensar**)

• **impulsive** /ɪmˈpʌlsɪv/ ADJECTIVE doing things suddenly without thinking first □ *Jane is very impulsive.* (**impulsivo**)

impunity /ɪmˈpjuːnəti/ NOUN, NO PLURAL **with impunity** without any risk of being punished. A formal phrase. □ *Some companies ignore the rules with impunity.* (**com impunidade**)

impure /ɪmˈpjʊə(r)/ ADJECTIVE not pure □ *impure hydrogen* (**impuro**)

• **impurity** /ɪmˈpjʊərəti/ NOUN [plural **impurities**] something in a substance that makes it dirty or not pure □ *impurities in water* (**impureza**)

in- /ɪn/ PREFIX

1 in- is added to the beginning of words to mean 'not' □ *inaccurate* □ *informal* (**in-**)

2 in- is added to the beginning of words to mean 'in', 'into' or 'towards' □ *in land*

in¹ /ɪn/ ▶ PREPOSITION

1 inside something □ *He keeps his keys in the drawer.* □ *The books are in my bedroom.* (**em**)

2 at a place □ *They live in Nottingham.* (**em**)

3 being part of something □ *There's a hole in my trousers.* □ *There was a strange smell in the air.* (**em**)

4 at a particular time □ *It's my birthday in May.* (**em**)

5 after a period of time □ *I'll be back in a few minutes.* (**em**)

6 wearing particular clothes □ *Who's the woman in the red dress?* (**em**)

7 shown as part of something □ *I looked in the dictionary to find the spelling of 'weird'.* (**em**)

8 using a particular thing □ *They were speaking in Japanese.* □ *The letter was written in purple ink.* (**em**)

▶ ADVERB

1 into a place or towards the inside of something □ *Come in and sit down.* □ *Push the needle in.* □ *A wide belt will hold your tummy in.* (**para dentro**)

2 at your home or place of work □ *I'm sorry, Dad's not in. Can I take a message?* (**em, aqui, aí**) 🔲 *I usually get in at around eight.* (**chego aí**)

3 having arrived (**aqui**) 🔲 *What time does your train get in?* (**chega aqui**)

▶ ADJECTIVE fashionable □ *Pilates seems to be the in thing to do these days.* (**na moda**)

in² /ɪn/ ABBREVIATION **inch** or **inches** (**abreviação de polegada**)

inability /ˌɪnəˈbɪləti/ NOUN, NO PLURAL the fact of not being able to do something □ *He criticized the government's inability to deal with the problem.* (**inabilidade**)

inaccessible /ˌɪnəkˈsesəbəl/ ADJECTIVE impossible to reach □ *The forest is inaccessible by road.* (**inacessível**)

inaccuracy /ɪnˈækjʊrəsi/ NOUN [plural **inaccuracies**] when a statement or detail is not correct or exact □ *The report was full of inaccuracies.* □ *He criticized the book for its inaccuracy.* (**imprecisão**)

• **inaccurate** /ɪnˈækjʊrət/ ADJECTIVE not exact or correct □ *inaccurate information* (**impreciso**)

inaction /ɪnˈækʃən/ NOUN, NO PLURAL when someone is not doing anything to solve a problem ▫ *He blamed the government's inaction for the increasing crime rate.* (**inatividade**)

• **inactive** /ɪnˈæktɪv/ ADJECTIVE not doing anything ▫ *Being overweight and inactive has a bad effect on your health.* (**inativo**)

• **inactivity** /ˌɪnækˈtɪvəti/ NOUN, NO PLURAL when someone or something is not doing anything ▫ *physical inactivity* (**inatividade**)

inadequacy /ɪnˈædɪkwəsi/ NOUN [plural **inadequacies**] not being good enough or not being enough ▫ *She suffered from feelings of inadequacy.* (**insuficiência, imperfeição**)

• **inadequate** /ɪnˈædɪkwət/ ADJECTIVE not enough, or not good enough ▫ *inadequate water supplies* (**inadequado, insuficiente**)

inadvertent /ˌɪnədˈvɜːtənt/ ADJECTIVE a formal word meaning done by accident ▫ *inadvertent damage* (**acidental, involuntário**)

• **inadvertently** /ˌɪnədˈvɜːtəntli/ ADVERB a formal word meaning by accident ▫ *I had inadvertently left the door unlocked.* (**sem querer, involuntariamente**)

inadvisable /ˌɪnədˈvaɪzəbəl/ ADJECTIVE not sensible and likely to have bad results ▫ *It is highly inadvisable for children to watch television all day.* (**desaconselhável**)

inane /ɪˈneɪn/ ADJECTIVE stupid and annoying ▫ *inane questions* (**idiota, fútil**)

inanimate /ɪnˈænɪmət/ ADJECTIVE not alive (**inanimado, involuntário**) ▫ *inanimate objects such as chairs and books* (**objetos inanimados**)

inapplicable /ˌɪnəˈplɪkəbəl/ ADJECTIVE a formal word meaning not able to be used or not suitable for a particular situation ▫ *Old laws often seem inapplicable to the modern world.* (**inaplicável**)

inappropriate /ˌɪnəˈprəʊpriət/ ADJECTIVE not suitable for a particular situation or occasion ▫ *inappropriate behaviour* (**inadequado**)

inarticulate /ˌɪnɑːˈtɪkjʊlət/ ADJECTIVE not able to express clearly what you want to say (**inarticulado**)

inaudible /ɪˈnɔːdɪbəl/ ADJECTIVE not loud enough to hear ▫ *His reply was inaudible.* (**inaudível**)

inaugural /ɪˈnɔːɡjʊrəl/ ADJECTIVE first, and marking the beginning of something important ▫ *the President's inaugural speech* ▫ *the airline's inaugural flight* (**inaugural, de posse**)

• **inaugurate** /ɪˈnɔːɡjʊreɪt/ VERB [**inaugurates, inaugurating, inaugurated**] to mark the beginning or opening of something important with a ceremony ▫ *The research centre was inaugurated in 1998.* (**inaugurar**)

• **inauguration** /ɪˌnɔːɡjʊˈreɪʃən/ NOUN [plural **inaugurations**] a ceremony to mark the beginning or opening of something important ▫ *Bush's inauguration as president* (**inauguração**)

in-box /ˈɪnbɒks/ NOUN [plural **in-boxes**] the place on a computer which stores email messages that people have sent to you. A computing word. ▫ *I was looking through my in-box for Bret's e-mail.* (**caixa de entrada**)

incapable /ɪnˈkeɪpəbəl/ ADJECTIVE not able to do something ▫ *He seems incapable of making any kind of decision.* (**incapaz**)

incapacitate /ˌɪnkəˈpæsɪteɪt/ VERB [**incapacitates, incapacitating, incapacitated**] if you are incapacitated by something, it makes you too ill or weak to live in a normal way. A formal word ▫ *He was incapacitated by ill health.* (**incapacitar**)

• **incapacity** /ˌɪnkəˈpæsəti/ NOUN, NO PLURAL **1** when you are not able to do something. A formal word. ▫ *The problem is his incapacity to recognize the truth.* (**incapacidade**) **2** when you cannot live in a normal way because you are ill or weak. A formal word. (**incapacidade**)

incendiary /ɪnˈsendiəri/ ADJECTIVE an incendiary bomb is designed to start a fire when it explodes (**incendiário**) ▫ *Police discovered several incendiary devices.* (**equipamentos incendiários**)

incense /ˈɪnsens/ NOUN, NO PLURAL a substance that smells nice when you burn it, often used in religious ceremonies (**incenso**)

incentive /ɪnˈsentɪv/ NOUN [plural **incentives**] something that encourages you to do something ▫ *Praise gives students an incentive to work harder.* (**incentivo**)

incessant /ɪnˈsesənt/ ADJECTIVE continuous, in a way that is annoying ▫ *incessant rain* (**incessante**)

inch /ɪntʃ/ NOUN [plural **inches**] a unit for measuring length, equal to about 2.5 centimetres ▫ *The ruler was 12 inches long.* (**polegada**)

incidence /ˈɪnsɪdəns/ NOUN [plural **incidences**] how often something happens, especially something bad, such as illness or crime ▫ *This country has one of the highest incidences of breast cancer.* (**incidência**)

• **incident** /ˈɪnsɪdənt/ NOUN [plural **incidents**] something that happens, especially something bad such as a crime. A formal word. ▫ *a violent incident* ▫ *She reported the incident to the police.* (**incidente**)

• **incidental** /ˌɪnsɪˈdentəl/ ADJECTIVE happening in connection with something else but less important than it ▫ *These details are incidental to the story.* (**sem importância, secundário**)

• **incidentally** /ˌɪnsɪˈdentəli/ ADVERB something you say when you are going to talk about a new subject or add some more information ▫ *Incidentally, did you know Jack was getting married?* (**a propósito**)

incinerate /ɪnˈsɪnəreɪt/ VERB [**incinerates, incinerating, incinerated**] to burn waste (**incinerar**)

• **incinerator** /ɪnˈsɪnəreɪtə(r)/ NOUN [plural **incinerators**] a container for burning waste (**incinerador**)

incision /ɪnˈsɪʒən/ NOUN [plural **incisions**] a cut made in something, especially during a medical operation. A formal word. (**incisão**)

incisive /ɪnˈsaɪsɪv/ ADJECTIVE showing that you are intelligent and understand something very well □ *incisive comments* (**incisivo, mordaz**)

incisor /ɪnˈsaɪzə(r)/ NOUN [plural **incisors**] one of the teeth at the front of your mouth that you use to cut food. A biology word. (**dente incisivo**)

incite /ɪnˈsaɪt/ VERB [**incites, inciting, incited**] to encourage people to be violent or do something bad □ *He denied that his speech had incited violence.* (**incitar**)

inclination /ˌɪnklɪˈneɪʃən/ NOUN [plural **inclinations**] a feeling that makes you want to do something (**disposição**) 🔁 *He showed no inclination to help.* (**não mostrou disposição**)

incline ▶ VERB /ɪnˈklaɪn/ [**inclines, inclining, inclined**] if you incline your head, you move it down. A formal word. (**inclinar**)
▶ NOUN /ˈɪnklaɪn/ [plural **inclines**] a slope (**declive**)

• **inclined** /ɪnˈklaɪnd/ ADJECTIVE
1 be inclined to agree/think something to have an opinion although you are not completely certain □ *I must say I'm inclined to agree with her.* (**estar propenso a concordar, pensar em algo**)
2 be inclined to do something (a) to want to do something, although you are not completely certain □ *I'm inclined to tell him the truth.* (**estar disposto a fazer algo**) (b) to often do something □ *He's inclined to make silly mistakes.* (**fazer algo com frequência**)

include /ɪnˈkluːd/ VERB [**includes, including, included**]
1 if one thing includes another thing, the second thing is part of the first thing □ *The price of the ticket includes dinner.* □ *The guest list included many famous people.* □ *Ryan's films include 'Sleepless in Seattle' and 'Against the Ropes'.* (**incluir**)
2 to allow someone to be part of a group □ **+ in** *Students are included in making decisions.* (**incluir**)

• **including** /ɪnˈkluːdɪŋ/ PREPOSITION a word used to show that a person or thing is part of a larger group □ *We went to all the museums, including the new one.* □ *Seven people, including two young girls, died in the accident.* (**inclusive**)

• **inclusion** /ɪnˈkluːʒən/ NOUN, NO PLURAL when you include someone or something as part of a larger group □ *His inclusion in the team was a surprise.* (**inclusão**)

• **inclusive** /ɪnˈkluːsɪv/ ADJECTIVE
1 an inclusive price includes everything □ *A three-day course costs £700, fully inclusive.* (**incluído**)
2 used for saying that the first and last thing you mention is included □ *From Tuesday to Thursday inclusive is three days.* (**inclusive**)
3 including all types of people □ *We need a more inclusive government.* (**inclusive**)

incoherent /ˌɪnkəʊˈhɪərənt/ ADJECTIVE not clear, and difficult to understand □ *He had left an incoherent message on my answerphone.* (**incoerente**)

income /ˈɪŋkʌm/ NOUN [plural **incomes**]
1 the amount of money you earn (**rendimento**) 🔁 *He had an annual income of £35,000.* (**rendimento anual**) 🔁 *The average household income has increased.* (**rendimento do lar**) □ **+ from** *She has had income from the sale of two houses.*
2 on a high/low income earning a lot/not much money □ *There aren't enough houses for people on low incomes.* (**com rendimento alto/baixo**)

income tax /ˈɪŋkʌmˌtæks/ NOUN, NO PLURAL tax that you have to pay on the money you earn (**imposto sobre a renda**)

incoming /ˈɪnkʌmɪŋ/ ADJECTIVE
1 just starting an important job □ *the incoming director* (**novo**)
2 coming into a place □ *The airport was shut and incoming flights were diverted.* (**chegada, entrada**)

incompatible /ˌɪnkəmˈpætɪbəl/ ADJECTIVE
1 if people are incompatible, they are so different that they cannot have a good relationship (**incompatível**)
2 too different to exist or be used together □ *The software is incompatible with the operating system.* (**incompatível**)

incompetence /ɪnˈkɒmpɪtəns/ NOUN, NO PLURAL when someone is incompetent (**incompetência**)

• **incompetent** /ɪnˈkɒmpɪtənt/ ADJECTIVE not doing your job well □ *an incompetent government* (**incompetente**)

incomplete /ˌɪnkəmˈpliːt/ ADJECTIVE not finished, or not having all the necessary parts □ *an incomplete jigsaw puzzle* (**incompleto**)

incomprehensible /ɪnˌkɒmprɪˈhensəbəl/ ADJECTIVE impossible to understand □ *The article was completely incomprehensible.* (**incompreensível**)

inconceivable /ˌɪnkənˈsiːvəbəl/ ADJECTIVE extremely surprising and so impossible to imagine □ *In the past, it was inconceivable that a woman would ever become Prime Minister.* (**inconcebível**)

inconclusive /ˌɪnkənˈkluːsɪv/ ADJECTIVE not giving you certain proof of something □ *The test results were inconclusive.* (**inconclusivo**)

incongruous /ɪnˈkɒŋgruəs/ ADJECTIVE a formal word meaning different from the things or people in a particular situation and so not suitable □ *He looked rather incongruous in his suit when everyone else was wearing jeans.* (**incongruente**)

inconsiderate /ˌɪnkənˈsɪdərət/ ADJECTIVE not thinking about other people's feelings □ *It was very inconsiderate of him not to tell you he was going to be late.* (**sem consideração**)

inconsistency /ˌɪnkənˈsɪstənsi/ NOUN [plural **inconsistencies**]
1 something that cannot be true if something else is also true □ *The report contained several inconsistencies.* (**inconsistência**)

2 failing to behave in the same way each time in the same situation □ *The government has been accused of inconsistency in the way it treats refugees.* (incoerência)

• **inconsistent** /ˌɪnkənˈsɪstənt/ ADJECTIVE
1 if two reports, statements, etc. are inconsistent, they cannot both be true □ *inconsistent statements* (inconsistente)
2 sometimes of good quality and sometimes of bad quality □ *Her work is very inconsistent.* (inconsistente)
3 not showing the same principles as something else □ *His behaviour was inconsistent with his religious beliefs.* (incoerente)

inconsolable /ˌɪnkənˈsəʊləbəl/ ADJECTIVE too upset for anyone to comfort you (inconsolável)

inconspicuous /ˌɪnkənˈspɪkjuəs/ ADJECTIVE not easy to see □ *I'm too tall to be inconspicuous.* (pouco visível)

inconvenience /ˌɪnkənˈviːniəns/ ▶ NOUN [plural **inconveniences**] problems that something or someone causes you □ *We apologize for the delay and for any inconvenience caused.* (incômodo)

▶ VERB [**inconveniences, inconveniencing, inconvenienced**] to cause problems for someone (incomodar)

• **inconvenient** /ˌɪnkənˈviːniənt/ ADJECTIVE causing problems □ *Have I called at an inconvenient time?* (inconveniente, inoportuno)

incorporate /ɪnˈkɔːpəreɪt/ VERB [**incorporates, incorporating, incorporated**] to include something □ *The television incorporates all the latest technology.* (incorporar)

incorrect /ˌɪnkəˈrekt/ ADJECTIVE wrong □ *The answer to number three is incorrect.* □ *He'd been given incorrect information.* (errado, incorreto)

• **incorrectly** /ˌɪnkəˈrektli/ ADVERB in a way that is wrong □ *The packets were incorrectly labelled.* (incorretamente)

increase ▶ VERB /ɪnˈkriːs/ [**increases, increasing, increased**]
1 to become bigger in size or amount (aumentar) 🔊 *The number of students has increased dramatically over the last ten years.* (aumentou enormemente) □ + *in The house has increased in value.* □ + *by Their wages will increase by 4%.*
2 to make something become bigger in size or amount (aumentar) 🔊 *Being overweight increases the risk of heart disease.* (aumenta o risco) 🔊 *The government plans to increase the number of police officers.* (planeja aumentar)

▶ NOUN /ˈɪnkriːs/ [plural **increases**]
1 a rise in amount or size □ *price increases* □ + *in There's been a big increase in sales.* (aumento)
2 on the increase happening more often than before, or becoming bigger in amount □ *Violent crime is on the increase.* □ *House prices are on the increase.* (em alta)

• **increasing** /ɪnˈkriːsɪŋ/ ADJECTIVE becoming bigger in amount or size □ *An increasing number of people have a computer in their house.* (crescente)

• **increasingly** /ɪnˈkriːsɪŋli/ ADVERB more and more □ *The need to reduce car use is becoming increasingly important.* (cada vez mais)

incredible /ɪnˈkredəbəl/ ADJECTIVE
1 extremely good or great □ *To reach the finals is an incredible achievement.* □ *He showed incredible strength.* (incrível)
2 difficult to believe □ *It's incredible that he didn't realize he was so ill.* (incrível)

• **incredibly** /ɪnˈkredəbli/ ADVERB
1 used for saying that something is difficult to believe □ *Incredibly, no one was injured in the accident.* (inacreditavelmente)
2 extremely □ *She's incredibly beautiful.* (inacreditavelmente, extremamente)

incredulous /ɪnˈkredjuləs/ ADJECTIVE unable to believe something □ *Don't sound so incredulous* (incrédulo, cético)

increment /ˈɪŋkrɪmənt/ NOUN [plural **increments**] one of a series of increases, especially in the money you earn for doing a job (acréscimo)

incriminate /ɪnˈkrɪmɪneɪt/ VERB [**incriminates, incriminating, incriminated**] to show that someone has taken part in a crime □ *All the evidence incriminated her.* (incriminar)

incubator /ˈɪŋkjubeɪtə(r)/ NOUN [plural **incubators**]
1 a piece of hospital equipment that a premature (= born too early) or ill baby lives in while it has medical treatment (incubadora)
2 a piece of equipment that keeps eggs warm until a baby bird comes out (incubadora)

incur /ɪnˈkɜː(r)/ VERB [**incurs, incurring, incurred**] to get something unpleasant because of what you have done. A formal word. □ *Any member of the team who breaks the rules will incur a penalty.* (incorrer)

incurable /ɪnˈkjʊərəbəl/ ADJECTIVE an incurable illness cannot be cured (incurável)

indecency /ɪnˈdiːsənsi/ NOUN, NO PLURAL behaviour that shocks and offends people (indecência)

• **indecent** /ɪnˈdiːsənt/ ADJECTIVE shocking and offensive □ *indecent pictures* (indecente)

indeed /ɪnˈdiːd/ ADVERB
1 used to emphasize what you are saying □ *He was driving very fast indeed.* □ *It was indeed a mistake.* (mesmo)
2 a formal word used to add something which supports what you have just said □ *The Internet has become very popular. Indeed most people now have Internet access at home.* (de fato)
3 used when someone has said something annoying or surprising □ *'Mum, James said he*

wasn't going to do his homework.' 'Did he, indeed?' (mesmo)

indefensible /ˌɪndɪˈfensəbəl/ ADJECTIVE too bad to be excused □ *His behaviour was completely indefensible.* (injustificável)

indefinite /ɪnˈdefɪnɪt/ ADJECTIVE not having a fixed limit □ *He was jailed for an indefinite period.* (indefinido)

indefinite article /ɪnˌdefɪnɪt ˈɑːtɪkəl/ NOUN [*plural* **indefinite articles**] the word *a* or the word *an* (artigo indefinido)

> ➤ There are two types of article in English grammar: *a* or *an* is the indefinite article and *the* is the definite article.

indefinitely /ɪnˈdefɪnɪtlɪ/ ADVERB for a period of time with no fixed limits □ *The game was postponed indefinitely.* (indefinidamente, por tempo indeterminado)

indelible /ɪnˈdeləbəl/ ADJECTIVE impossible to remove or forget □ *indelible ink* □ *indelible memories* (indelével)

independence /ˌɪndɪˈpendəns/ NOUN, NO PLURAL
1 when a country is not controlled by another country (independência) 🔁 *East Timor gained independence in 2002.* (conquistou independência)
2 when someone does not depend on other people for help □ *financial independence* (independência)

• **independent** /ˌɪndɪˈpendənt/ ADJECTIVE
1 not controlled by another government or organization □ *independent companies* □ **+ from** *Mozambique became independent from Portugal in 1975.* □ **+ of** *The council will be independent of the government.* (independente)
2 fair because of not being influenced by anyone or anything (independente) 🔁 *The business was valued by an independent expert.* (perito independente) 🔁 *An independent inquiry was launched after a man died while being arrested.* (investigação independente)
3 not depending on other people for help □ *My greatgrandmother's 90 but she's very independent.* (independente) 🔁 *Some students are financially independent.* (financeiramente independentes)

indestructible /ˌɪndɪˈstrʌktəbəl/ ADJECTIVE too strong to be destroyed (indestrutível)

index /ˈɪndeks/ NOUN [*plural* **indexes** or **indices**]
1 an alphabetical list in a book that tells you what page you can find information on □ *Look up 'wild flowers' in the index.* (índice)
2 a system that is used to compare things, especially prices, and to record changes □ *The Nikkei stock market index has risen by 40%.* (indicador)

index finger /ˈɪndeks ˌfɪŋɡə(r)/ NOUN [*plural* **index fingers**] the finger that is next to your thumb (dedo indicador)

indicate /ˈɪndɪkeɪt/ VERB [**indicates, indicating, indicated**]
1 to show that something is true or that something exists □ *The study indicates that 70% of road accidents happen on country roads.* (indicar)
2 to show an intention or opinion, though not directly □ *He has indicated a willingness to help.* (indicar, sinalizar)
3 to show someone what they should look at or where they should go □ *There was an arrow indicating where to go.* (indicar)
4 to show which way you are going to turn in a vehicle □ *Always indicate before turning.* (sinalizar)

• **indication** /ˌɪndɪˈkeɪʃən/ NOUN [*plural* **indications**] a sign of something □ *This comment was an indication of his state of mind at the time.* (indicação) 🔁 *Did he give you any indication when it would be finished?* (deu algum indício)

• **indicative** /ɪnˈdɪkətɪv/ ADJECTIVE **indicative of something** showing that something is true or that something exists. A formal phrase. □ *These symptoms could be indicative of a more serious illness.* (indicativo)

• **indicator** /ˈɪndɪkeɪtə(r)/ NOUN [*plural* **indicators**]
1 something which shows you how successful or healthy something is (indicador) 🔁 *Your resting heart rate is a good indicator of your general fitness.* (bom indicador)
2 a flashing light on a car that shows which way the car is going to turn (pisca-pisca)

indifference /ɪnˈdɪfərəns/ NOUN, NO PLURAL when someone shows no interest in someone or something and does not care about them □ *He showed complete indifference to their suffering.* (indiferença)

• **indifferent** /ɪnˈdɪfərənt/ ADJECTIVE
1 not interested in something or someone and not caring about them □ *Clare was indifferent to his feelings.* (indiferente)
2 not good but not bad □ *The hotel was nice but the food was fairly indifferent.* (medíocre)

indigenous /ɪnˈdɪdʒɪnəs/ ADJECTIVE having always existed in a place and not coming to it from somewhere else □ *The domestic cat isn't actually indigenous to Europe.* (indígena)

indigestion /ˌɪndɪˈdʒestʃən/ NOUN, NO PLURAL an uncomfortable feeling in your stomach after you have eaten (indigestão)

indignant /ɪnˈdɪɡnənt/ ADJECTIVE angry because you think you have been treated unfairly □ *The company received letters of complaint from indignant customers.* (indignado)

• **indignation** /ˌɪndɪɡˈneɪʃən/ NOUN, NO PLURAL being indignant (indignação)

indignity /ɪnˈdɪɡnətɪ/ NOUN [*plural* **indignities**] a situation that makes you feel ashamed, usually in front of other people (humilhação) 🔲 *They suffered the indignity of a 6-0 defeat.* (sofreram a humilhação de)

indigo /ˈɪndɪɡəʊ/ ▶ ADJECTIVE having a dark, purple blue colour 🔲 *an indigo sweater* (cor de anil)
▶ NOUN, NO PLURAL a dark, purple-blue colour (índigo, anil)

indirect /ˌɪndɪˈrekt/ ADJECTIVE
1 not directly caused by something, or not directly related to something 🔲 *indirect effects* (indireto)
2 not saying something in an obvious and clear way 🔲 *She made an indirect reference to her father.* (indireto)
3 not going the shortest way 🔲 *an indirect route* (indireto)

indirect object /ˌɪndɪrekt ˈɒbdʒɪkt/ NOUN [*plural* **indirect objects**] in grammar, the person that something is given to, done to, etc. 🔲 *In the sentence 'I bought my mother a watch.', 'mother' is the indirect object.* (objeto indireto)

indirect speech /ˌɪndɪrekt ˈspiːtʃ/ NOUN, NO PLURAL reporting what someone said without repeating their exact words 🔲 *'He said he would come with me' is an example of indirect speech.* (discurso indireto)

indiscreet /ˌɪndɪˈskriːt/ ADJECTIVE talking about subjects which should be private, often when the subject relates to other people 🔲 *She can be very indiscreet.* (indiscreto)

indiscriminate /ˌɪndɪˈskrɪmɪnət/ ADJECTIVE done to everyone or everything, without thinking about who or what will be harmed 🔲 *indiscriminate attacks* (indiscriminado)

indispensable /ˌɪndɪˈspensəbəl/ ADJECTIVE someone or something that is indispensable is so useful that you cannot manage without them 🔲 *The Internet is an indispensable tool for businesses.* (indispensável)

indistinct /ˌɪndɪˈstɪŋkt/ ADJECTIVE not easy to see, hear or remember 🔲 *indistinct images* (confuso, pouco claro)

individual /ˌɪndɪˈvɪdʒuəl/ ▶ ADJECTIVE
1 for or relating to one person only 🔲 *The choice you make depends on your individual circumstances.* (individual)
2 considered separately from other things or people (distinto) 🔲 *We do not comment on individual cases.* (casos distintos) 🔲 *Each individual school has its own rules.*
3 unusual and different in a way that is interesting 🔲 *She is known for her highly individual designs.* (particular, próprio)
▶ NOUN [*plural* **individuals**] one person rather than a group 🔲 *The medical study included 100 healthy individuals.* (indivíduo)

• **individuality** /ˌɪndɪˌvɪdʒuˈælətɪ/ NOUN, NO PLURAL a quality that makes someone or something different from others (individualidade)

• **individually** /ˌɪndɪˈvɪdʒuəlɪ/ ADVERB separately from other things or people 🔲 *Wrap each glass individually.* 🔲 *He talked to each student individually.* (individualmente)

indoctrinate /ɪnˈdɒktrɪneɪt/ VERB [**indoctrinates, indoctrinating, indoctrinated**] to try to make someone have particular beliefs and not consider any others 🔲 *Some religious groups were accused of indoctrinating children.* (doutrinar)

indoor /ˈɪndɔː(r)/ ADJECTIVE inside a building 🔲 *an indoor swimming pool* 🔲 *indoor activities* 🔲 *indoor plants*

• **indoors** /ˌɪnˈdɔːz/ ADVERB into or inside a building 🔲 *It was cooler indoors.* (dentro, no interior) 🔲 *Police warned people to stay indoors.* (permanecerem no interior) 🔲 *We went indoors because it started to rain.* (fomos para dentro)

induce /ɪnˈdjuːs/ VERB [**induces, inducing, induced**]
1 a formal word meaning to persuade someone to do something 🔲 *Nothing would induce him to move back to the city.* (induzir)
2 a formal word meaning to cause a particular feeling or state 🔲 *The drug is used to induce sleep.* (induzir)

• **inducement** /ɪnˈdjuːsmənt/ NOUN [*plural* **inducements**] something that is offered to someone as a way of persuading them to do something 🔲 *financial inducements* (incentivo, persuasão)

induction course /ɪnˈdʌkʃən ˌkɔːs/ NOUN [*plural* **induction courses**] a training course for a company's new employees (curso de indução)

indulge /ɪnˈdʌldʒ/ VERB [**indulges, indulging, indulged**]
1 to allow yourself to do or have something because you enjoy it 🔲 *He regularly indulged in his favourite breakfast of pancakes and syrup.* (dar-se ao capricho de)
2 to allow someone to do or have anything they want 🔲 *Indulging children by buying them everything they want is not good.* (satisfazer)

• **indulgence** /ɪnˈdʌldʒəns/ NOUN [*plural* **indulgences**]
1 indulging yourself or someone else 🔲 *He led a life of indulgence.* (vício)
2 something expensive or special that you have because you want it and not because you need it 🔲 *I didn't need a new bike – it was a complete indulgence.* (capricho)

• **indulgent** /ɪnˈdʌldʒənt/ ADJECTIVE allowing someone to do or have everything they want 🔲 *indulgent parents* (indulgente)

industrial /ɪnˈdʌstrɪəl/ ADJECTIVE
1 relating to industry and factories 🔲 *industrial laws* 🔲 *Industrial production fell last month.* 🔲 *Pollution is caused by industrial processes.* (industrial)
2 an industrial place has a lot of industries in it 🔲 *industrial towns* (industrial)

industrious

- **industrialization** or **industrialisation** /ɪnˌdʌstrɪəlaɪˈzeɪʃən/ NOUN, NO PLURAL the process of developing industries in a country □ *China's rapid Industrialization* (**industrialização**)
- **industrialized** or **industrialised** /ɪnˈdʌstrɪəlaɪzd/ ADJECTIVE an industrialized country or area has a lot of industries in it (**industrializado**)

industrious /ɪnˈdʌstrɪəs/ ADJECTIVE working very hard □ *an industrious student* (**trabalhador**)

industry /ˈɪndəstri/ ▶ NOUN [plural **industries**]
1 *no plural* the production of goods, especially in a factory □ *The chemical is widely used in industry.* (**indústria**) ▣ *Heavy industry* (= production of large goods) *has almost disappeared from the area.* (**indústria pesada**)
2 all the companies involved in one particular type of trade or service □ *She had a successful career in the music industry.* □ *The violence has damaged the country's tourism industry.* □ *Electricity and gas industries are facing rising costs.* (**indústria**)
▶ ADJECTIVE to do with industry or a particular industry (**da indústria**) ▣ *Industry experts have predicted an increase in online fraud.* (**especialistas da indústria**) ▣ *Industry leaders met to discuss the new proposals.* (**líderes da indústria**)

inedible /ɪnˈedɪbəl/ ADJECTIVE too bad to eat □ *The meal was completely inedible.* (**não comestível**)

ineffective /ˌɪnɪˈfektɪv/ ADJECTIVE not achieving the result you want □ *The drug is ineffective against this form of the disease.* (**ineficiente**)

ineffectual /ˌɪnɪˈfektʃuəl/ ADJECTIVE
1 achieving very little □ *The government's response to the disaster was largely ineffectual.* (**ineficaz**)
2 not able to do something well □ *an ineffectual leader* (**inútil, ineficiente**)

inefficiency /ˌɪnɪˈfɪʃənsi/ NOUN [plural **inefficiencies**] being inefficient, or something that is inefficient □ *the inefficiency of the government* (**ineficiência**)
- **inefficient** /ˌɪnɪˈfɪʃənt/ ADJECTIVE not using energy, time, money, etc. in the most effective way □ *an inefficient heating system* □ *The project is an inefficient use of taxpayers' money.* (**ineficiente, incompetente**)

ineligible /ɪnˈelɪdʒəbəl/ ADJECTIVE not allowed to have or do something because of a rule or law □ *You are ineligible to vote until you are 18.* (**não ter direito a**)

inept /ɪˈnept/ ADJECTIVE having or showing no skill □ *an inept performance* (**inepto**)

inequality /ˌɪnɪˈkwɒləti/ NOUN [plural **inequalities**] when some people have more power, money, opportunities, etc. than other people □ *We need to tackle social inequality.* (**desigualdade**)

infancy

inert /ɪˈnɜːt/ ADJECTIVE
1 not moving □ *He lay inert on the floor.* (**inerte**)
2 inert substances do not produce a reaction with other substances. A chemistry word. (**inerte**)

inertia /ɪˈnɜːʃə/ NOUN, NO PLURAL
1 when nobody does anything and nothing changes (**inércia**)
2 the force that keeps something in the same position, or makes something continue moving until something else stops it. A physics word. (**inércia**)

inevitable /ɪnˈevɪtəbəl/ ▶ ADJECTIVE certain to happen and not possible to avoid □ *Further conflict in the region is inevitable.* (**inevitável**)
▶ NOUN, NO PLURAL **the inevitable** something which is certain to happen □ *Then one day, the inevitable happened, and he was called to the headteacher's office.* (**o inevitável**)

inexcusable /ˌɪnɪkˈskjuːzəbəl/ ADJECTIVE too bad to be excused □ *inexcusable behaviour* (**imperdoável**)

inexpensive /ˌɪnɪkˈspensɪv/ ADJECTIVE cheap □ *The shop has a wide selection of inexpensive kitchen equipment.* (**barato**)

inexperience /ˌɪnɪkˈspɪəriəns/ NOUN, NO PLURAL not having much experience of something □ *His mistake was put down to youthful inexperience.* (**inexperiência**)
- **inexperienced** /ˌɪnɪkˈspɪəriənst/ ADJECTIVE not having much experience or knowledge of something □ *Insurance premiums are high for inexperienced young drivers.* (**inexperiente**)

inexplicable /ˌɪnɪkˈsplɪkəbəl/ ADJECTIVE impossible to explain □ *Daisy felt an inexplicable urge to scream.* (**inexplicável**)

inextricably /ˌɪnɪkˈstrɪkəbli/ ADVERB if things are inextricably connected, you cannot separate them □ *In the book, fact and fiction are inextricably linked.* (**inextricavelmente, de modo insolúvel**)

infallible /ɪnˈfæləbəl/ ADJECTIVE
1 never making a mistake □ *Like most of my friends, I assumed our teachers were infallible.* (**infalível**)
2 certain to work or be successful □ *I have an infallible method for making jam.* (**infalível**)

infamous /ˈɪnfəməs/ ADJECTIVE famous for doing something bad (**infame**)
- **infamy** /ˈɪnfəmi/ NOUN, NO PLURAL being famous for doing something bad (**infâmia**)

infancy /ˈɪnfənsi/ NOUN, NO PLURAL
1 the time when someone is a baby or a very young child (**infância**)
2 in its infancy only just beginning to exist or develop □ *This technology is still in its infancy.* (**primeiros passos**)
- **infant** /ˈɪnfənt/ NOUN [plural **infants**] a baby or a very young child (**criança pequena**)
- **infantile** /ˈɪnfəntaɪl/ ADJECTIVE behaving in a silly way, like a young child □ *I'm sick of his infantile jokes.* (**infantil**)

infantry /'ɪnfəntri/ NOUN, NO PLURAL soldiers who fight on foot (**infantaria**)

infatuated /ɪn'fætʃueɪtɪd/ ADJECTIVE loving someone very much in a way that seems silly because you do not know them very well □ *She's completely infatuated with him.* (**vidrado, apaixonado**)

infect /ɪn'fekt/ VERB [**infects, infecting, infected**]
1 to give someone an illness □ + *with Several patients were infected with the virus.* (**infectar, contaminar**)
2 if a computer is infected with a virus (= harmful program), it is damaged because of it. A computing word. (**infectar**)
3 if a place, cut or substance is infected, it contains bacteria that cause disease □ *The wound had become infected.* (**infectar**)
4 to make other people have the same feeling as you □ *She infected us all with her enthusiasm.* (**contaminar**)

• **infection** /ɪn'fekʃən/ NOUN [plural **infections**]
1 a disease that is caused by bacteria, a virus, etc. □ *an ear infection* (**infecção**)
2 no plural the process of becoming infected □ *The hospital has taken steps to prevent infection.* (**infecção, contágio**)

• **infectious** /ɪn'fekʃəs/ ADJECTIVE
1 an infectious disease can be passed from one person to another (**contagioso**) 🔊 *The virus is highly infectious.* (**altamente contagioso**)
2 infectious feelings or laughter quickly spread to other people □ *You have such an infectious laugh.* □ *His enthusiasm was infectious.* (**contagioso**)

infer /ɪn'fɜː(r)/ VERB [**infers, inferring, inferred**] to form an opinion from information you already know □ *I inferred from our conversation that she was unhappy at home.* (**inferir**)

• **inference** /'ɪnfərəns/ NOUN [plural **inferences**] something that you think is true because of information you already know (**inferência, conclusão**)

inferior /ɪn'fɪəriə(r)/ ▶ ADJECTIVE not as good as someone or something else □ *Amy often felt inferior to the other women in the office.* □ *This cake was made with inferior ingredients.* (**inferior**)
▶ NOUN [plural **inferiors**] someone who is less important than or not as good as someone else □ *She treated him like a social inferior.* (**inferior**)

• **inferiority** /ɪn,fɪəri'ɒrəti/ NOUN, NO PLURAL being or feeling inferior to someone or something else □ *Charles commented on the inferiority of the wine.* (**inferioridade**)

inferno /ɪn'fɜːnəʊ/ NOUN [plural **infernos**] a large and dangerous fire (**inferno**)

infertile /ɪn'fɜːtaɪl/ ADJECTIVE
1 infertile land does not produce good crops (**infértil**)
2 an infertile person or animal cannot have babies (**estéril**)

• **infertility** /ˌɪnfə'tɪləti/ NOUN, NO PLURAL when a person, animal or piece of land is infertile (**infertilidade**) 🔊 *Doctors have suggested infertility treatment* (= medical treatment to help a woman become pregnant). (**tratamento contra a infertilidade**)

infest /ɪn'fest/ VERB [**infests, infesting, infested**] if animals, insects or plants that you do not want infest a place, there are a lot of them there □ *The whole house was infested with mice.* (**infestar**)

infiltrate /'ɪnfɪltreɪt/ VERB [**infiltrates, infiltrating, infiltrated**] to join an organization or group secretly in order to get information about it □ *The journalist had infiltrated the gang to get a story.* (**infiltrar**)

infinite /'ɪnfɪnət/ ADJECTIVE
1 without any limits or end □ *The universe is infinite.* (**infinito**)
2 very great □ *My maths teacher had infinite patience with me.* (**infinito**)

• **infinitely** /'ɪnfɪnətli/ ADVERB very much □ *This computer is infinitely better than the last one.* (**infinitamente**)

infinitive /ɪn'fɪnətɪv/ NOUN [plural **infinitives**] the basic form of a verb that can be used to make all the other forms, for example *to play* or *to eat* (**infinitivo**)

infinity /ɪn'fɪnəti/ NOUN, NO PLURAL
1 space or time that has no end or limit (**infinito**)
2 the largest possible number. A maths word. (**infinito**)

infirm /ɪn'fɜːm/ ADJECTIVE weak, especially because of being old or ill (**enfermo, doente**)

• **infirmary** /ɪn'fɜːməri/ NOUN [plural **infirmaries**] used in the name of some hospitals □ *Sunderland Eye Infirmary* (**enfermaria**)

• **infirmity** /ɪn'fɜːməti/ NOUN [plural **infirmities**] an illness, or when someone is weak because of being old or ill (**enfermidade**)

inflamed /ɪn'fleɪmd/ ADJECTIVE red and swollen because of an infection □ *Her eyes were inflamed and sore.* (**inflamado**)

inflammable /ɪn'flæməbəl/ ADJECTIVE inflammable substances burn very easily □ *Paper is highly inflammable.* (**inflamável**)

inflammation /ˌɪnflə'meɪʃən/ NOUN [plural **inflammations**] swelling, pain and sometimes red skin in part of your body □ *The drug will reduce the inflammation in your joints.* (**inflamação**)

inflatable /ɪn'fleɪtəbəl/ ADJECTIVE an inflatable object must be filled with air before you use it □ *They crossed the river in an inflatable dinghy.* (**inflável**)

inflate /ɪn'fleɪt/ VERB [**inflates, inflating, inflated**] to fill something with air □ *The tyres need to be inflated.* (**encher de ar, inflar**)

• **inflation** /ɪn'fleɪʃən/ NOUN, NO PLURAL
1 when prices increase or the rate at which they

increase □ *The priority is to keep inflation low.* (inflação)

2 when something is filled with air (inflação, repleto de ar)

inflect /ɪnˈflekt/ VERB [inflects, inflecting, inflected]

1 when a word inflects, it changes its ending to show number, tense etc. so that it is suitable for the words it is with (flexionar, declinar)

2 to change the way your voice sounds, for example to show you are asking a question (modular, variar o tom de voz)

• **inflection** /ɪnˈflekʃən/ NOUN [plural **inflections**]

1 a change in the form of a word to show its tense, number, etc. so that it is suitable for the words it is with (flexão)

2 a word that has been changed in this way. For example, finds, finding and found are inflections of the verb find (inflexão)

3 when you change the way your voice sounds, for example to show you are asking a question

inflexible /ɪnˈfleksəbəl/ ADJECTIVE

1 unwilling to change or impossible for someone to change □ *an inflexible attitude* □ *inflexible rules* (inflexível)

2 stiff and unable to bend □ *inflexible plastic* (inflexível)

inflict /ɪnˈflɪkt/ VERB [inflicts, inflicting, inflicted] to make someone suffer something unpleasant or painful □ *The home team inflicted a heavy defeat on the visitors.* (infligir)

in-flight /ˈɪnˌflaɪt/ ADJECTIVE happening or provided during a flight □ *The standard of in--flight meals has improved greatly.* (em voo, durante o voo)

influence /ˈɪnfluəns/ ▶ NOUN [plural **influences**]

1 the power to affect other people or things □ + **over** *He has considerable influence over his colleagues.* □ + **on** *Exchange rates have a big influence on our business.* (influência) 🔁 *He was found guilty of driving under the influence of alcohol.* (sob influência de)

2 someone or something that has an effect on other people or things □ *Ann is a good influence on you.* □ *Her films reflect her diverse cultural influences.* (influência)

▶ VERB [influences, influencing, influenced] to have an effect on someone or something □ *His advice influenced my decision.* □ *My early work was influenced by Samuel Beckett.* (influenciar)

• **influential** /ˌɪnfluˈenʃəl/ ADJECTIVE having a lot of influence (influente) 🔁 *He was one of the most influential figures in Hollywood at that time.* (figuras influentes)

influenza /ˌɪnfluˈenzə/ NOUN, NO PLURAL a formal word for **flu** (= illness like a very bad cold) (gripe)

influx /ˈɪnflʌks/ NOUN [plural **influxes**] when a lot of people or things come to a place □ *There has been an influx of tourists from the mainland.* (afluxo)

info /ˈɪnfoʊ/ NOUN, NO PLURAL an informal word for **information** (info, informação)

inform /ɪnˈfɔːm/ VERB [informs, informing, informed] to tell someone about something, especially officially □ *If you trespass again I'll inform the police.* □ + **that** *We were informed that our luggage had been lost.* □ + **of** *I'll inform you of my decision.* (informar, levar ao conhecimento) 🔁 *Please keep me informed of your whereabouts.* (me mantenha informado)

informal /ɪnˈfɔːməl/ ADJECTIVE

1 relaxed and friendly, or suitable for relaxed occasions □ *The meeting was an informal affair.* □ *We can wear informal clothes to the office at weekends.* (informal)

2 informal language and words can be used when you are speaking to your friends, but they are not as suitable for writing (informal)

informant /ɪnˈfɔːmənt/ NOUN [plural **informants**] someone who gives information to someone else (informante)

information /ˌɪnfəˈmeɪʃən/ NOUN, NO PLURAL facts about someone or something □ + **on** *Have you got any information on things to do in the area?* □ + **about** *I gave him some information about our services.* (informações) 🔁 *The report provides a lot of information about medical errors.* (fornece informações) 🔁 *For further information visit our website.* (mais informações) 🔁 *That is a very interesting piece of information.* (informação)

> ➤ Remember that bad is an adjective and not an adverb. To describe the way that someone does something, use the adverb badly:
> ✓ *He behaved very badly.*
> ✗ *He behaved very bad.*
> ➤ To talk about one fact about a subject and not many facts, use the phrase piece of information: □ *Here's a useful piece of information.*

information technology /ˌɪnfəˌmeɪʃən tekˈnɒlədʒɪ/ NOUN, NO PLURAL the study or use of computers to store, send or use information (tecnologia da informação)

> ➤ You will often see the abbreviation for information technology, which is IT.

informative /ɪnˈfɔːmətɪv/ ADJECTIVE giving you a lot of useful information □ *I found her article very informative.* (informativo)

informed /ɪnˈfɔːmd/ ADJECTIVE having enough information or knowledge about something (instruído, informado) 🔁 *Parents should be able to make an informed decision about their children's education.* (decisão instruída)

informer /ɪnˈfɔːmə(r)/ NOUN [plural **informers**] someone who secretly gives information about a crime to the police (delator, informante)

infrared /ˌɪnfrəˈred/ ADJECTIVE infrared light cannot be seen but gives out heat (infravermelho)

infrastructure /ˈɪnfrəˌstrʌktʃə(r)/ NOUN, NO PLURAL the basic systems and services, such as transport, communications, water and power, that a country or organization needs to operate (infraestrutura)

infrequent /ɪnˈfriːkwənt/ ADJECTIVE not happening very often □ *an infrequent bus service* (infrequente, raro)
• **infrequently** /ɪnˈfriːkwəntlɪ/ ADVERB not often (raramente)

infringe /ɪnˈfrɪndʒ/ VERB [**infringes, infringing, infringed**]
1 to limit someone's rights or freedom □ *People see the introduction of identity cards as infringing on their civil liberties.* (infringir)
2 to break a law or rule □ *Their policies may infringe EU law.* (violar)
• **infringement** /ɪnˈfrɪndʒmənt/ NOUN [plural **infringements**]
1 when someone's rights or freedom are limited □ *This is a serious infringement on public freedom.* (infração)
2 the act of breaking a law or rule □ *an infringement of building regulations* (violação)

infuriate /ɪnˈfjʊərieɪt/ VERB [**infuriates, infuriating, infuriated**] to make someone very angry (enfurecer)
• **infuriated** /ɪnˈfjʊərieɪtɪd/ ADJECTIVE extremely angry (furioso)
• **infuriating** /ɪnˈfjʊərieɪtɪŋ/ ADJECTIVE making you extremely angry □ *I find his behaviour absolutely infuriating.* (de dar raiva)

ingenious /ɪnˈdʒiːniəs/ ADJECTIVE clever and involving new ideas □ *He came up with an ingenious scheme to make money.* (engenhoso)
• **ingenuity** /ˌɪndʒɪˈnjuːətɪ/ NOUN, NO PLURAL skill at inventing things or solving problems □ *The size of the building was a challenge to the architects' ingenuity.* (engenhosidade)

ingot /ˈɪŋgət/ NOUN [plural **ingots**] a block of metal, especially gold or silver (lingote)

ingrained /ɪnˈgreɪnd/ ADJECTIVE
1 if behaviour or opinions are ingrained, they have existed for a long time and are difficult to change □ *Texting has become ingrained in our culture.* (arraigado)
2 ingrained dirt has been rubbed in and is difficult to get out (impregnado)

ingratitude /ɪnˈgrætɪtjuːd/ NOUN, NO PLURAL when someone is not grateful (ingratidão)

ingredient /ɪnˈgriːdiənt/ NOUN [plural **ingredients**]
1 one of the things you use to make a particular food □ *Mix the dry ingredients in a bowl.* (ingrediente)
2 one of the qualities something needs to be successful □ *Music is an essential ingredient of most teenagers' lives.* (ingrediente)

inhabit /ɪnˈhæbɪt/ VERB [**inhabits, inhabiting, inhabited**] to live in a particular place □ *The series looks at the creatures that inhabit our planet.* (habitar)
• **inhabitant** /ɪnˈhæbɪtənt/ NOUN [plural **inhabitants**] someone who lives in a place □ *There are differences between the inhabitants of the two islands.* (habitante, morador)
• **inhabited** /ɪnˈhæbɪtɪd/ ADJECTIVE with people living there □ *The south-east is the most densely inhabited area of England.* (habitado)

inhale /ɪnˈheɪl/ VERB [**inhales, inhaling, inhaled**] to breathe air, smoke, etc. into your lungs □ *She inhaled deeply.* (respirar, inalar)
• **inhaler** /ɪnˈheɪlə(r)/ NOUN [plural **inhalers**] a small tube which contains medicine to help you breathe more easily if you have asthma (= an illness that makes it difficult to breathe) (inalador)

inherent /ɪnˈhɪərənt, ɪnˈherənt/ ADJECTIVE being a basic and permanent part of something □ *We cannot ignore the risks inherent in gambling.* (inerente)
• **inherently** /ɪnˈhɪərəntlɪ, ɪnˈherəntlɪ/ ADVERB in a basic and permanent way □ *The scheme is inherently flawed.* (inerentemente)

inherit /ɪnˈherɪt/ VERB [**inherits, inheriting, inherited**]
1 to receive money or other possessions from someone who has died □ *Imogen inherited the house from her father.* (herdar)
2 to get a particular characteristic from one of your parents □ *I inherited my fair hair from my mother.* (herdar)
3 to be left with a particular situation or problem by someone who has been in your position before you □ *The new government has inherited a failing transport system.* (herdar)
• **inheritance** /ɪnˈherɪtəns/ NOUN [plural **inheritances**]
1 money or possessions that you receive from someone who has died □ *She lived on a small inheritance from her grandmother.* (herança)
2 when you receive a characteristic from one of your parents □ *They are carrying out research into the inheritance of certain diseases.* (herança)

inhibit /ɪnˈhɪbɪt/ VERB [**inhibits, inhibiting, inhibited**]
1 to prevent something from happening or to make it happen more slowly □ *The drug may inhibit the growth of bacteria.* (impedir)
2 to make someone feel nervous or embarrassed so that they do not behave in a natural way □ *He was inhibited by the presence of TV cameras.* (inibir)
• **inhibited** /ɪnˈhɪbɪtɪd/ ADJECTIVE not feeling relaxed or confident enough to do or say what you want □ *Teenagers often feel inhibited in adult company.* (inibido)

inhospitable

- **inhibition** /ˌɪnhɪˈbɪʃən/ NOUN [plural **inhibitions**] a feeling of being nervous or embarrassed that stops you doing or saying what you want (**inibição**) 🔁 The children soon *lost their inhibitions* and joined in the dancing. (**perderam a inibição**)

inhospitable /ˌɪnhɒˈspɪtəbəl/ ADJECTIVE
1 an inhospitable place is not pleasant to live in because it is too hot, cold, dangerous, etc. □ The jungles of South America are the most inhospitable places on earth. (**inóspito**)
2 not friendly and welcoming □ When we arrived, Guy was most inhospitable. (**inospitaleiro**)

inhuman /ɪnˈhjuːmən/ ADJECTIVE extremely cruel □ His treatment of the prisoners was inhuman. (**desumano, cruel**)

inhumane /ˌɪnhjuːˈmeɪn/ ADJECTIVE treating people or animals in an extremely cruel way □ They campaigned against inhumane methods of rearing chickens. (**desumano**)

inhumanity /ˌɪnhjuːˈmænəti/ NOUN, NO PLURAL extremely cruel behaviour □ They were shocked by the inhumanity of prison life. (**desumanidade**)

initial /ɪˈnɪʃəl/ ▶ ADJECTIVE at the beginning (**inicial**) 🔁 *Initial reports* suggest the crash was caused by engine failure. (**relatos iniciais**) 🔁 My *initial reaction* was horror. (**reação inicial**)
▶ NOUN [plural **initials**] the first letter of a word, especially someone's name □ His initials are J.C. (**inicial**)

- **initially** /ɪˈnɪʃəli/ ADVERB in the beginning □ Initially, things were very difficult. (**no início, inicialmente**)

initiate /ɪˈnɪʃieɪt/ VERB [**initiates, initiating, initiated**]
1 to start something □ Max initiated the conversation. (**iniciar**)
2 to accept someone into a group or organization with a special ceremony □ He was initiated into the priesthood at the age of 25. (**iniciar**)
3 to teach someone about something they know nothing about □ I was initiated into the art of making jam. (**iniciar**)

- **initiation** /ɪˌnɪʃiˈeɪʃən/ NOUN [plural **initiations**]
1 when something is started by someone □ He is responsible for the initiation and design of new wind farms. (**iniciação**)
2 when someone is accepted into a group or organization □ an initiation ceremony (**iniciação**)
3 when someone is taught something new □ That was my initiation into the world of drug companies. (**iniciação**)

- **initiative** /ɪˈnɪʃətɪv/ NOUN [plural **initiatives**]
1 a new plan or process to solve a problem or improve a situation □ The government has introduced an initiative to keep teenagers in school (**iniciativa**)
2 the ability to do something without waiting for someone else to tell you what to do □ He showed great initiative when dealing with customers' complaints. (**iniciativa**) 🔁 Eventually Mia *took the initiative* (= decided what should be done) *and called a taxi*. (**tomou a iniciativa**)

inject /ɪnˈdʒekt/ VERB [**injects, injecting, injected**]
1 to put a substance into someone's body using a needle □ She has to inject herself with insulin every day. (**dar injeção**)
2 to add a particular quality to a situation □ Leah tried to inject some enthusiasm into her voice. (**acrescentar**)
3 to provide money for something □ Local businesses have agreed to inject cash into the club. (**injetar**)

- **injection** /ɪnˈdʒekʃən/ NOUN [plural **injections**]
1 when a substance is injected into someone's body □ insulin injections (**injeção**)
2 when money is provided □ They need a huge injection of funds. (**injeção**)
3 when a quality is added to a situation □ These people need an injection of reality. (**acréscimo**)

injure /ˈɪndʒə(r)/ VERB [**injures, injuring, injured**]
1 to hurt someone or something □ Matt injured his knee in a skiing accident. (**machucar**)
2 to harm something □ The fall injured her pride. (**ferir**)

- **injured** /ˈɪndʒəd/ ADJECTIVE hurt □ Fiona was badly injured in a road accident. (**machucado, ferido**)
▶ NOUN, NO PLURAL **the injured** people who are injured □ The injured were rushed to hospital. (**os feridos**)

- **injury** /ˈɪndʒəri/ NOUN [plural **injuries**] damage to part of your body (**lesão, ferimento**) 🔁 *a serious head injury* (**uma lesão séria**) 🔁 He was lucky to suffer only *minor injuries* in the crash. (**pequenas lesões**)

injustice /ɪnˈdʒʌstɪs/ NOUN [plural **injustices**] when people are treated unfairly or an action that is unfair □ I was hurt by the injustice of her criticism. (**injustiça**)

ink /ɪŋk/ NOUN [plural **inks**] a coloured liquid used for writing or printing (**tinta**)

inkling /ˈɪŋklɪŋ/ NOUN, NO PLURAL a slight idea that something might happen or be true □ Sheila had no inkling of what awaited her. (**suspeito**)

inland ▶ ADJECTIVE /ˈɪnlənd/ not by the sea □ Britain's inland waterways (**interior**)
▶ ADVERB /ɪnˈlænd/ in a direction away from the sea □ The people fled inland to escape the tsunami. (**para o interior**)

in-laws /ˈɪnlɔːz/ PLURAL NOUN the relations of your husband or wife □ I'm spending Christmas with my in-laws. (**parentes da família do cônjuge**)

inlet /ˈɪnlet/ NOUN [plural **inlets**] a narrow area of water that flows into the land from the sea (**enseada**)

inmate /ˈɪnmeɪt/ NOUN [plural **inmates**] someone who is being kept in a prison (**presidiário**)

inn /ɪn/ NOUN [plural **inns**] a small hotel or pub, especially in the countryside (**albergue**)

innate /ɪˈneɪt/ ADJECTIVE innate qualities and abilities are ones that you are born with, or ones that are very natural for you □ *He had an innate sense of justice.* (**inato**)

inner /ˈɪnə(r)/ ADJECTIVE
1 on the inside or close to the centre of something □ *She kept her purse in the inner pocket of her bag.* (**interno**)
2 near the centre of a city □ *inner London* (**interno**)
3 inner feelings or thoughts are private and secret (**íntimo**)

inner city /ˌɪnə ˈsɪti/ NOUN [plural **inner cities**] an area in the centre of a large city, often with social problems □ *We are failing the children in our inner cities.* (**área central da cidade**)
• **inner-city** ADJECTIVE from or to do with an inner city □ *inner-city schools/neighbourhoods* (**central**)

innermost /ˈɪnəməʊst/ ADJECTIVE your innermost thoughts and feelings are private and secret (**mais profundo**)

innings /ˈɪnɪŋz/ NOUN [plural **innings**] the period of time when one player or team is hitting the ball in cricket (**ciclo**)

innocence /ˈɪnəsəns/ NOUN, NO PLURAL
1 when someone is not guilty of a crime □ *New evidence proved his innocence.* (**inocência**)
2 when someone does not have much experience of life □ *The bully took advantage of Billy's innocence.* (**inocência**)
• **innocent** /ˈɪnəsənt/ ADJECTIVE
1 not guilty of a crime □ *An innocent man had been hanged in error.* □ *She claims she is innocent of the crime.* (**inocente**)
2 used to emphasize that someone who is hurt, injured or killed had done nothing wrong □ *Several innocent bystanders were caught in the crossfire.* (**inocente**)
3 not intended to hurt or upset someone □ *It was a perfectly innocent remark but he was furious about it.* (**inocente**)
4 not having much experience of life □ *The film is not suitable for innocent children.* (**inocente**)
• **innocently** /ˈɪnəsəntli/ ADVERB
1 in a way that is not intended to hurt or upset anyone □ *He acted quite innocently.* (**inocentemente**)
2 in a way that is intended to make people think you are not guilty □ *I smiled innocently at her.* (**inocentemente**)

innovation /ˌɪnəˈveɪʃən/ NOUN [plural **innovations**] something completely new, especially a new method of doing something □ *He keeps up with all the latest innovations in medicine.* (**inovação**)
• **innovative** /ˈɪnəvətɪv/ ADJECTIVE using new and original ideas □ *His book is an innovative approach to reducing stress.* (**inovador**)

innuendo /ˌɪnjuːˈendəʊ/ NOUN [plural **innuendos** or **innuendoes**] a remark that is intended to express something rude or unpleasant in a way that is not direct (**insinuação**)

inoculate /ɪˈnɒkjʊleɪt/ VERB [**inoculates, inoculating, inoculated**] to protect someone from a disease by injecting (= putting a substance into the body with a needle) them with a substance containing a very small amount of the disease □ *Babies are inoculated against measles.* (**vacinar**)
• **inoculation** /ɪˌnɒkjʊˈleɪʃən/ NOUN [plural **inoculations**] when someone is inoculated (**vacinação**)

inoffensive /ˌɪnəˈfensɪv/ ADJECTIVE not likely to offend or upset anyone □ *His type of humour is very inoffensive.* (**inofensivo**)

inordinate /ɪnˈɔːdɪnət/ ADJECTIVE much greater than is usual or reasonable □ *She spends an inordinate length of time in the bathroom every morning.* (**exagerado, desmedido**)
• **inordinately** /ɪnˈɔːdɪnətli/ ADVERB much more than is usual or reasonable □ *Their goods are inordinately expensive.* (**exageradamente, desmedidamente**)

inorganic /ˌɪnɔːˈgænɪk/ ADJECTIVE not a living thing or not made from living things. A chemistry word. □ *inorganic materials* (**inorgânico**)

in-patient /ˈɪnpeɪʃənt/ NOUN [plural **in-patients**] someone who is staying in a hospital for treatment (**hospitalizado**)

input /ˈɪnpʊt/ ▶ NOUN, NO PLURAL
1 energy, ideas or money that you put into something to make it succeed □ *I had very little input in the project.* (**contribuição**)
2 information that is put into a computer. A computing word. (**entrada**)
▶ VERB [**inputs, inputting, input or inputted**] to put information into a computer. A computing word □ *We paid someone to input all the names and addresses.* (**inserir dados no computador**)

inquest /ˈɪnkwest/ NOUN [plural **inquests**] a legal process to find out how someone died (**inquérito**) 🔁 *An inquest will be held to establish the cause of death.* (**inquérito será feito**)

inquire /ɪnˈkwaɪə(r)/ VERB [**inquires, inquiring, inquired**] to ask for information about something □ *He inquired how to get to the library.* □ *I'm inquiring about the job advertised in the paper.* (**indagar, perguntar**)
◆ PHRASAL VERB **inquire after someone** to ask how someone is or what they are doing, to be polite □ *Kevin inquired after your father.* (**saber de alguém**)
• **inquiry** /ɪnˈkwaɪəri/ NOUN [plural **inquiries**]
1 a question you ask in order to get information □ *We've had a number of inquiries about hybrid cars.* (**interrogatório**)
2 an official process to find out why something happened □ *There was an inquiry into the*

children's deaths. □ *He's helping police with their inquiries.* (investigação)

inquisitive /ɪnˈkwɪzətɪv/ ADJECTIVE wanting to know about a lot of different things, and often asking a lot of questions □ *an inquisitive child* (curioso)

- **inquisitively** /ɪnˈkwɪzətɪvli/ ADVERB in an inquisitive way □ *She could see several neighbours peering inquisitively out of their windows.* (curiosamente)

insane /ɪnˈseɪn/ ADJECTIVE
1 having a serious mental illness (louco)
2 very silly □ *Her work schedule is just insane.* (insensato)

- **insanity** /ɪnˈsænəti/ NOUN, NO PLURAL
1 when someone has a serious mental illness (demência)
2 when something is very silly □ *Deciding to build our own house was just insanity.* (insanidade)

insatiable /ɪnˈseɪʃəbəl/ ADJECTIVE always wanting more of something (insaciável) □ *She seems to have an insatiable appetite for celebrity gossip.* (apetite insaciável)

inscribe /ɪnˈskraɪb/ VERB [**inscribes, inscribing, inscribed**] to cut or write words on the surface of something □ *We had her name inscribed on the back of the bracelet.* (gravar)

- **inscription** /ɪnˈskrɪpʃən/ NOUN [*plural* **inscriptions**] words that are cut or written on something □ *We could not read the inscription on the medal.* (inscrição)

insect
/ˈɪnsekt/ NOUN [*plural* **insects**] a small creature with six legs and often wings, for example a bee or a fly (inseto)

insecure /ˌɪnsɪˈkjʊə(r)/ ADJECTIVE
1 not feeling confident □ *After her mother's death she became increasingly insecure.* (inseguro)
2 not safe or protected □ *Many jobs in banking are now insecure.* (inseguro)

- **insecurity** /ˌɪnsɪˈkjʊərəti/ NOUN [*plural* **insecurities**]
1 when someone is not confident □ *He suffers all the usual teenage insecurities* (insegurança)
2 when something is not safe or protected □ *They were concerned about the insecurity of the building.* (insegurança)

insensitive /ɪnˈsensətɪv/ ADJECTIVE
1 not noticing other people's feelings □ *She was always making insensitive remarks about her sister.* (insensível)
2 not affected by physical things such as pain or cold □ *He seemed to be insensitive to the noise around him.* (imune, insensível)

- **insensitively** /ɪnˈsensətɪvli/ ADVERB in an insensitive way (insensivelmente)
- **insensitivity** /ɪnˌsensəˈtɪvəti/ NOUN, NO PLURAL the state of being insensitive (insensibilidade)

inseparable /ɪnˈsepərəbəl/ ADJECTIVE not able to be separated or kept apart □ *At school we were inseparable.* (inseparável)

insert /ɪnˈsɜːt/ VERB [**inserts, inserting, inserted**] to put something into something else □ *He inserted some coins into the meter.* □ *You need to insert a few more examples.* (inserir, introduzir)

- **insertion** /ɪnˈsɜːʃən/ NOUN [*plural* **insertions**] when something is inserted into something else, or the thing that is inserted □ *He made several insertions in my text.* (inserção)

inside
▶ PREPOSITION /ɪnˈsaɪd/
1 in or into a building, container or area □ *She put the book inside her bag.* □ *Draw a cross inside the box.* (dentro de)
2 in an organization, group of people, etc. □ *People inside the company know the truth.* (dentro de)
3 in less than a particular amount of time □ *We'll be there inside an hour.* (dentro de)
▶ ADVERB /ɪnˈsaɪd/
1 in or into a building □ *Come inside – you'll get cold.* (dentro)
2 in or into a container or an area □ *Has that tin got anything inside?* (dentro)
3 in someone's mind □ *I may have looked confident, but I was terrified inside.* (por dentro)
▶ ADJECTIVE /ˈɪnsaɪd/
1 in or facing the middle of something □ *Keep it in an inside pocket.* (interno, de dentro)
2 provided by someone who is a member of an organization, group, etc. and knows about it (interno) □ *She gave us some inside information about how the company works.* (informação interna)
▶ NOUN /ɪnˈsaɪd/ [*plural* **insides**]
1 the inside the part that is in the middle and not on the outside □ *The inside of his jacket was torn.* (o interior)
2 inside out if clothes are inside out, the part that should be on the inside is on the outside □ *You've got your socks on inside out.* (do avesso)

insight /ˈɪnsaɪt/ NOUN [*plural* **insights**]
1 the ability to understand something clearly □ *Her book on depression showed great insight into the illness.* (perspicácia)
2 the chance to understand something clearly □ *The book offers an insight into the mind of a killer.* (percepção)

insignificant /ˌɪnsɪɡˈnɪfɪkənt/ ADJECTIVE not at all important □ *He spends too much time describing insignificant details.* (insignificante)

insincere /ˌɪnsɪnˈsɪə(r)/ ADJECTIVE pretending to feel something that you do not really feel □ *an insincere compliment* (falso)

- **insincerely** /ˌɪnsɪnˈsɪəli/ ADVERB in an insincere way □ *The waiter smiled insincerely at us.* (falsamente)

insipid / installment

- **insincerity** /ˌɪnsɪnˈserəti/ NOUN, NO PLURAL when someone is insincere (**falsidade**)

insipid /ɪnˈsɪpɪd/ ADJECTIVE boring, not strong or bright, or without much flavour ▫ *She served up a rather insipid lamb stew.* (**insípido, sem sabor**)

insist /ɪnˈsɪst/ VERB [**insists, insisting, insisted**]
1 to say firmly that something must happen or be done ▫ + *on* *I always insist on a single room.* ▫ + *on* *Fay insisted on paying.* ▫ + *that* *The school insists that all students must wear full uniform.* (**insistir**)
2 to keep saying firmly that something is true ▫ + *that* *Mark insists that he hasn't done anything wrong.* (**insistir**)
- **insistence** /ɪnˈsɪstəns/ NOUN, NO PLURAL
1 when you insist that something must happen or be done ▫ *At the chairman's insistence, another meeting was arranged.* ▫ *He soon rebelled against his mother's insistence on good manners.* ▫ *Some schools ignored the government's insistence that all children should learn a foreign language.* (**insistência**)
2 when you insist that something is true ▫ *Despite his insistence that he was innocent, he was charged with murder.* (**insistência**)
- **insistent** /ɪnˈsɪstənt/ ADJECTIVE insisting that something must happen or be done ▫ *Sarah was insistent that we should visit her.* (**insistente**)

insolence /ˈɪnsələns/ NOUN, NO PLURAL behaviour that shows no respect or politeness (**insolência**)
- **insolent** /ˈɪnsələnt/ ADJECTIVE rude and not showing respect ▫ *The headmaster will not tolerate insolent behaviour.* (**insolente**)

insoluble /ɪnˈsɒljʊbəl/ ADJECTIVE
1 an insoluble substance cannot be dissolved (**insolúvel**)
2 an insoluble problem, mystery, etc. is impossible to solve (**insolúvel, sem solução**)

insomnia /ɪnˈsɒmniə/ NOUN, NO PLURAL when you are not able to sleep ▫ *He has suffered from insomnia since he was a child.* (**insônia**)
- **insomniac** /ɪnˈsɒmniæk/ NOUN [*plural* **insomniacs**] someone who regularly suffers from insomnia (**insone**)

inspect /ɪnˈspekt/ VERB [**inspects, inspecting, inspected**]
1 to look very carefully at someone or something ▫ *He inspected our documents closely.* (**inspecionar**)
2 to officially visit a place to make sure that everything there is the way it should be ▫ *The school is to be inspected next week.* (**vistoriar**)
- **inspection** /ɪnˈspekʃən/ NOUN [*plural* **inspections**]
1 when you look very carefully at someone or something (**inspeção**) ▫ *On close inspection, I realized the note wasn't in Josh's handwriting.* (**em uma inspeção detalhada**)
2 an official visit to inspect a place (**vistoria**) ▫ *Public health officers carry out regular inspections of restaurants.* (**fazem vistorias regulares**)
- **inspector** /ɪnˈspektə(r)/ NOUN [*plural* **inspectors**]
1 someone whose job is to inspect a place such as a school or restaurant (**inspetor**)
2 a police officer with quite a high rank (**inspetor**)
3 someone whose job is to check tickets on a bus or train (**fiscal**)

inspiration /ˌɪnspəˈreɪʃən/ NOUN [*plural* **inspirations**]
1 someone or something that encourages you and gives you new ideas ▫ *I use the countryside as inspiration for my paintings.* (**inspiração**)
2 a sudden good idea (**inspiração**) ▫ *Newton had a flash of inspiration when he saw the apple fall from the tree.* (**um momento de inspiração**)
3 be an inspiration to someone to be someone or something that everyone admires and would like to copy ▫ *Her courage is an inspiration to us all.* (**ser uma inspiração para alguém**)
- **inspirational** /ˌɪnspəˈreɪʃənəl/ ADJECTIVE giving you ideas and enthusiasm ▫ *She is an inspirational teacher.* (**inspirador**)

inspire /ɪnˈspaɪə(r)/ VERB [**inspires, inspiring, inspired**] to give someone ideas and enthusiasm ▫ *My mother inspired me to write stories.* (**inspirar**)
- **inspired** /ɪnˈspaɪəd/ ADJECTIVE showing a lot of ability and special qualities ▫ *He gave an inspired performance of the Schubert.* (**inspirado**)

instability /ˌɪnstəˈbɪləti/ NOUN, NO PLURAL
1 when a situation keeps changing ▫ *The country went through a long period of economic instability.* (**instabilidade**)
2 when someone's mental state keeps changing (**instabilidade**)

install *or* **instal** /ɪnˈstɔːl/ VERB [**installs** *or* **instals, installing, installed**]
1 to put a piece of equipment in place and make it ready to use ▫ *We have installed central heating.* (**instalar**)
2 to put software on to a computer to be used. A computing word ▫ *I installed the software and began the work.* (**instalar**)
3 to give someone an important job or position ▫ *She was installed as Prime Minister in May.* (**nomear**)
- **installation** /ˌɪnstəˈleɪʃən/ NOUN [*plural* **installations**]
1 when equipment or software is installed ▫ *They paid for the installation of a new kitchen.* (**instalação**)
2 when someone is installed in a job or position (**instalação**)
3 a building with equipment for a particular purpose, for example for the army or a large business ▫ *a military installation* (**nomeação**)

installment /ɪnˈstɔːlmənt/ NOUN [*plural* **installments**] the US spelling of **instalment** (*ver* **instalment**)

instalment /ɪnˈstɔːlmənt/ NOUN [plural **instalments**]
1 one of a number of payments that you make for something □ *I paid the last instalment on the car today.* (**prestação**)
2 one of several parts of a story in a magazine, on television, etc. □ *Don't miss next week's thrilling instalment!* (**fascículo, capítulo**)

instance /ˈɪnstəns/ NOUN [plural **instances**]
1 for instance for example □ *Some birds, penguins for instance, cannot fly at all.* (**por exemplo**)
2 an example of something □ *In some instances, legal action was taken.* (**caso**)

instant /ˈɪnstənt/ ▶ ADJECTIVE
1 happening immediately □ *The film was an instant success.* (**instantâneo**)
2 able to be prepared very quickly □ *instant coffee* (**instantâneo**)
▶ NOUN [plural **instants**]
1 a very short time □ *The doctor will be with you in an instant.* (**instante**)
2 a particular moment in time □ *At that very instant, the phone rang.* (**instante**)
• **instantaneous** /ˌɪnstənˈteɪnɪəs/ ADJECTIVE done or happening immediately or very quickly □ *The search results are almost instantaneous.* (**instantâneo**)
• **instantly** /ˈɪnstəntlɪ/ ADVERB immediately □ *I recognized him instantly.* (**instantaneamente**)

instant messaging /ˌɪnstənt ˈmesɪdʒɪŋ/ NOUN, NO PLURAL communicating by using the Internet in a way where you can reply to someone immediately when they send you a message. A computing word. (**mensagem instantânea**)

instead /ɪnˈsted/ ADVERB in place of someone or something else □ *Bob was ill so Joe went instead.* □ + **of** *You could use a pencil instead of a pen.* □ *Instead of moaning you could actually help.* (**em vez disso**)

> Notice that when you put a verb after instead, you need the preposition of before the verb. Also, the verb must be in the -ing form: □ *Instead of lying in bed all day, you could work.*

instep /ˈɪnstep/ NOUN [plural **insteps**] the raised top part of your foot (**peito do pé**)

instigate /ˈɪnstɪgeɪt/ VERB [**instigates, instigating, instigated**] to make something happen, especially an official process □ *The committee has instigated an inquiry into the affair.* (**instigar**)
• **instigation** /ˌɪnstɪˈgeɪʃən/ NOUN, NO PLURAL when something is instigated □ *A thorough investigation of the claims is being carried out at the instigation of the local MP.* (**instigação**)
• **instigator** /ˈɪnstɪgeɪtə(r)/ NOUN [plural **instigators**] the person who instigates something (**instigador**)

instil /ɪnˈstɪl/ VERB [**instils, instilling, instilled**] to make someone think or feel something □ *We are trying to instil some confidence in these youngsters.* (**incutir algo**)

instill /ɪnˈstɪl/ VERB [**instills, instilling, instilled**] the US spelling of **instil** (**incutir algo**)

instinct /ˈɪnstɪŋkt/ NOUN [plural **instincts**] the natural way you react or behave without thinking or being taught □ *These animals have a strong survival instinct.* □ *My first instinct was to run away.* (**instinto**)
• **instinctive** /ɪnˈstɪŋktɪv/ ADJECTIVE behaving or reacting by instinct □ *Parents have an instinctive urge to protect their children.* (**instintivo**)
• **instinctively** /ɪnˈstɪŋktɪvlɪ/ ADVERB in an instinctive way □ *I knew instinctively that something was wrong.* (**instintivamente**)

institute /ˈɪnstɪtjuːt/ ▶ NOUN [plural **institutes**] an organization where people study a particular subject □ *We have a training institute in Florida.* (**instituto**)
▶ VERB [**institutes, instituting, instituted**] to start a new system, process, rule, etc. □ *The company has instituted a smoking ban.* (**instaurar, instituir, estabelecer**)

institution /ˌɪnstɪˈtjuːʃən/ NOUN [plural **institutions**]
1 a large organization □ *I have worked for several banks and other financial institutions.* (**instituição**)
2 the act of starting a system, process, rule, etc. □ *We have seen the institution of new rules governing social work.* (**instituição**)
3 a place where people are sent to be looked after, for example a prison or a hospital □ *Her aunt had spent years in a mental institution.* (**instituição**)
4 a tradition or social custom that has lasted for a long time □ *the institution of marriage* (**instituição**)

instruct /ɪnˈstrʌkt/ VERB [**instructs, instructing, instructed**]
1 to tell someone to do something □ *I instructed her to go straight home.* (**instruir**)
2 to teach someone □ *Staff will be instructed in the correct use of the machinery.* (**instruir**)
• **instruction** /ɪnˈstrʌkʃən/ NOUN [plural **instructions**]
1 instructions printed information about how to do something □ *Read the instructions before you begin.* (**instrução**) 🔂 *Make sure you* **follow the instructions**. (**siga as instruções**)
2 something you are told to do □ *She stood there shouting instructions at us.* (**instrução**)
3 no plural when you are taught something □ *I had a day's golf instruction.* (**instrução, aula**)
• **instructive** /ɪnˈstrʌktɪv/ ADJECTIVE providing a lot of useful information □ *It was a very instructive talk.* (**instrutivo**)
• **instructor** /ɪnˈstrʌktə(r)/ NOUN [plural **instructors**] someone who teaches a sport or a skill □ *a driving instructor* (**instrutor, professor**)

instrument /ˈɪnstrəmənt/ NOUN [plural **instruments**]
1 something used for making music, for example a violin or a piano (**instrumento**) 🔁 *She plays several musical instruments.* (**instrumentos musicais**)
2 a tool for doing a particular task □ *surgical instruments* (**instrumento**)
3 a piece of equipment that is used for measuring speed, fuel, height, etc. □ *He showed us the plane's instrument panel.* (**instrumento**)
• **instrumental** /ˌɪnstrʊˈmentəl/ ADJECTIVE
1 instrumental music is written for musical instruments and not singers (**instrumental**)
2 helpful in making something happen □ *His wife was instrumental in his success.* (**providencial**)

insufficient /ˌɪnsəˈfɪʃənt/ ADJECTIVE not enough □ *There was insufficient evidence to make an arrest.* (**insuficiente**)
• **insufficiently** /ˌɪnsəˈfɪʃəntli/ ADVERB not enough □ *We were insufficiently prepared for the climate.* (**insuficientemente**)

insulate /ˈɪnsjʊleɪt/ VERB [**insulates, insulating, insulated**] to cover something with a material that does not let electricity, heat or sound through □ *Make sure your loft is adequately insulated.* (**isolar**)
• **insulation** /ˌɪnsjʊˈleɪʃən/ NOUN, NO PLURAL the process of insulating something, or the material used to do this (**isolamento**)

insulin /ˈɪnsjʊlɪn/ NOUN, NO PLURAL a chemical produced in your body that controls the amount of sugar in your blood. A biology word. (**insulina**)

insult ▶ VERB /ɪnˈsʌlt/ [**insults, insulting, insulted**] to say or do something rude that offends someone □ *He was fired for insulting his line manager.* (**insultar**)
▶ NOUN /ˈɪnsʌlt/ [plural **insults**] a remark or action that is rude and offends someone □ *The crowd were hurling insults at the referee.* □ *To sell the jewellery is an insult to her memory.* (**insulto**)
• **insulting** /ɪnˈsʌltɪŋ/ ADJECTIVE rude and offensive □ *I found her patronizing attitude insulting.* (**insultante**)

insurance /ɪnˈʃɔːrəns/ NOUN, NO PLURAL an arrangement in which you pay a company money and they pay the costs if you have an accident or are ill, or if something you own is damaged or stolen □ *car insurance* (**seguro**) 🔁 *I've taken out health insurance.* (**contratei seguro**)

insure /ɪnˈʃɔː(r)/ VERB [**insures, insuring, insured**] to pay money to a company who will pay the costs if you have an accident or are ill, or if something you own is damaged or stolen □ + *for She insured her jewellery for £50,000.* □ + *against Are you insured against loss of earnings?* (**segurar**)

insurgent /ɪnˈsɜːdʒənt/ NOUN [plural **insurgents**] someone who is fighting against the government or army of their country (**insurgente**)

intact /ɪnˈtækt/ ADJECTIVE not broken or damaged □ *One of the mosaic floors has been preserved intact.* (**intacto**)

intake /ˈɪnteɪk/ NOUN [plural **intakes**]
1 the amount of something that you eat, drink or take into your body □ *Doctors advise cutting down our daily intake of salt.* (**consumo**)
2 an intake of breath a sudden breath in, often caused by shock □ *There was a sharp intake of breath when the result was announced.* (**respiração profunda**)
3 the group of people who start at a school, university, company, etc. at the same time (**admissão**)

integer /ˈɪntɪdʒə(r)/ NOUN [plural **integers**] a whole number. A maths word. (**inteiro**)

integral /ˈɪntɪɡrəl/ ADJECTIVE forming a necessary and important part of something □ *Sport is an integral part of my life.* (**integral**)

integrate /ˈɪntɪɡreɪt/ VERB [**integrates, integrating, integrated**]
1 to become part of a group of people □ *Women have been fully integrated into the regiment.* (**integrar**)
2 to combine two or more things so that they work well together □ *Transport planning should be integrated with energy policy.* (**integrar**)

integrated circuit /ˌɪntɪˌɡreɪtɪd ˈsɜːkɪt/ NOUN [plural **integrated circuits**] a microchip (= small computer part) with a large number of electronic parts instead of several separate parts. A computing word. (**circuito integrado**)

integration /ˌɪntɪˈɡreɪʃən/ NOUN, NO PLURAL when people or things are integrated □ *She is studying the integration of minority groups into society.* (**integração**)

integrity /ɪnˈteɡrəti/ NOUN, NO PLURAL the quality of being honest and having high moral standards □ *Colleagues praised his integrity and devotion to his patients.* (**integridade**)

intellect /ˈɪntəlekt/ NOUN [plural **intellects**]
1 your ability to think about things and understand them (**inteligência, intelecto**)
2 a very intelligent person □ *He was one of the great intellects of the 20th century.* (**intelectual**)
• **intellectual** /ˌɪntəˈlektjuəl/ ▶ ADJECTIVE
1 to do with the ability to think about things and understand them □ *intellectual development* (**intelectual**)
2 intellectual activities involve using your brain to understand complicated ideas (**intelectual**)
3 intelligent and interested in complicated ideas □ *He's very intellectual.* (**inteligente**)
▶ NOUN [plural **intellectuals**] someone who is intelligent and likes thinking about complicated ideas (**intelectual**)

intelligence /ɪnˈtelɪdʒəns/ NOUN, NO PLURAL
1 your ability to learn and understand things □ *No one is questioning your son's intelligence.* (**inteligência**)

2 secret information about other countries □ *During the war she worked in military intelligence.* (inteligência)

- **intelligent** /ɪnˈtelɪdʒənt/ ADJECTIVE
1 clever and able to understand things quickly (inteligente) 🔂 *These students are highly intelligent.* (altamente inteligente)
2 showing intelligence □ *The report was an intelligent analysis of the prison system.* (inteligente)

- **intelligently** /ɪnˈtelɪdʒəntli/ ADVERB in an intelligent way □ *He spoke intelligently about politics.* (inteligentemente)

intelligible /ɪnˈtelɪdʒəbəl/ ADJECTIVE clear enough to understand □ *His handwriting was barely intelligible.* □ *This kind of explanation is simply not intelligible to a young child.* (inteligível)

intend /ɪnˈtend/ VERB [intends, intending, intended]
1 to plan to do something □ + *to do something* I *intend to visit Will when I'm in Seattle.* □ + *ing They intended staying longer but their money ran out.* (tencionar, ter intenção de)
2 be intended for someone/something to be designed or made for a particular person or purpose □ *This course is intended for people who already have a basic knowledge of Spanish.* □ *This furniture is intended for outdoor use.* (destinado a alguém/algo)

intense /ɪnˈtens/ ADJECTIVE very great or strong □ *intense heat* □ *He came under intense pressure to resign.* (intenso)

- **intensely** /ɪnˈtensli/ ADVERB very much □ *She is intensely interested in Chinese politics.* (intensamente)

- **intensify** /ɪnˈtensɪfaɪ/ VERB [intensifies, intensifying, intensified] to become greater or stronger, or to make something greater or stronger □ *Fighting has intensified since the elections.* □ *We intensified our efforts to find new staff.* (intensificar)

- **intensity** /ɪnˈtensɪti/ NOUN, NO PLURAL the strength of something □ *The battle went on with new intensity.* □ *The heat increased in intensity.* (intensidade)

- **intensive** /ɪnˈtensɪv/ ADJECTIVE
1 involving a lot of effort or activity in a short time □ *an intensive language course* (intensivo)
2 intensive farming tries to produce as much as possible from the land (intensivo)

intensive care /ɪnˌtensɪv ˈkeə(r)/ NOUN, NO PLURAL a part of a hospital that looks after people who are very ill or badly injured □ *One of the victims was still in intensive care last night.* (unidade de terapia intensiva)

intent /ɪnˈtent/ ▶ ADJECTIVE
1 if you are intent on doing something, you are determined to do it □ *Lorna was intent on winning the athletics' trophy.* (com intenção ou intento)
2 giving a lot of concentration to something □ *The inspector looked at him with intent curiosity.* □ *Gary didn't hear her, intent on his gardening magazine.* (atento)
▶ NOUN, NO PLURAL when you intend to do something □ *It was not my intent to offend him.* (intenção)

- **intention** /ɪnˈtenʃən/ NOUN [plural **intentions**] the thing you plan to do □ + *to do something It is my intention to finish before 5 o'clock.* (intenção) 🔂 *He had no intention of obeying his father.* (ele não teve intenção)

- **intentional** /ɪnˈtenʃənəl/ ADJECTIVE done deliberately □ *Do you think his rudeness was intentional?* (intencional)

- **intentionally** /ɪnˈtenʃənəli/ ADVERB deliberately □ *Did he intentionally deceive the police?* (intencionalmente, de propósito)

- **intently** /ɪnˈtentli/ ADVERB with a lot of concentration □ *She examined the document intently.* (atentamente)

inter- /ˈɪntə(r)/ PREFIX inter- is added to the beginning of words to mean 'between' or 'among' a group of people or things □ *international* □ *interfaith* (inter-)

interact /ˌɪntərˈækt/ VERB [interacts, interacting, interacted]
1 to talk to other people and do things with them □ *Joe always interacted well with other children.* (interagir)
2 if two things interact, they have an effect on each other □ *The drug is thought to interact with chemicals in the brain.* (interagir)

- **interaction** /ˌɪntərˈækʃən/ NOUN [plural **interactions**]
1 when people interact with each other □ *We looked at the interaction between doctor and patient.* (relacionamento)
2 when two or more things have an effect on each other □ *There is a possibility of interaction between the medicines.* (interação)

- **interactive** /ˌɪntərˈæktɪv/ ADJECTIVE
1 involving communication between two people □ *interactive teaching methods* (interativo)
2 interactive computer programs, electronic games, etc. react to the instructions that you give them (interativo)

intercept /ˌɪntəˈsept/ VERB [intercepts, intercepting, intercepted] to stop and take something that is going from one place to another □ *The police intercepted the parcel before it arrived at its destination.* (interceptar)

interchangeable /ˌɪntəˈtʃeɪndʒəbəl/ ADJECTIVE when two things are interchangeable, you can use either of them in the same situations with the same result □ *The strap and the handle are interchangeable.* (trocável, intercambiável)

intercom /ˈɪntəkɒm/ NOUN [plural **intercoms**] a system that allows you to talk to people who are in a different part of a building or vehicle (interfone, comunicação interna) 🔊 *The pilot spoke to us over the intercom.* (por meio de comunicação interna)

interest /ˈɪntrəst/ ▶ NOUN [plural interests]

1 *no plural* the feeling of wanting to know about something or give your attention to something □ + **in** *I have no interest in cricket* (interesse) 🔊 *I try to take an interest in my husband's work.* (ter interesse) 🔊 *He expressed an interest in learning Chinese.* (mostrou interesse) 🔊 *In the end, I lost interest in my studies.* (perdi interesse)

2 something that you enjoy doing or learning about □ *My main interests are sport and reading.* (passatempo)

3 *no plural* extra money that you have to pay back when you have borrowed money, or that a bank pays you for having your money □ + **on** *The interest on the car payments was huge.* (juros) 🔊 *I had to pay interest on the loan.* (pagar juros) 🔊 *They charge 10% interest.* (10% de juros)

4 interests the things that give someone an advantage or make their life good (os interesses) 🔊 *I have to protect the interests of my family.* (proteger os interesses) □ *We look after the interests of our members.*

5 be in someone's interest(s) to be something that will give someone an advantage or make their life better □ *It's not in my interests to give you the information.* □ *It is in the national interest to publish these documents.* (ser de interesse de alguém)

6 in the interest(s) of something in order to achieve or protect something □ *In the interests of peace, I gave all the children a bar of chocolate.* (pelo bem de algo)

▶ VERB [interests, interesting, interested] to make someone want to know about something or do an activity □ + **in** *I'm trying to interest him in ancient music.* □ *Can I interest you in a boat ride?* (interessar)

• **interested** /ˈɪntrəstɪd/ ADJECTIVE
1 having or showing interest □ + **in** *Dan is very interested in old cars.* □ + **to do something** *I'd be interested to hear her side of the story.* (interessado)

2 wanting to do something □ + **in** *I'm not interested in making money.* □ *I'm interested in buying a bike.* (interessado)

• **interesting** /ˈɪntrəstɪŋ/ ADJECTIVE making you feel interested □ *It was a very interesting story.* □ *It is interesting to note that he had never been to Egypt.* (interessante)

> Remember the difference between the words **interesting** and **interested**. **Interesting** means 'making you feel interested'. **Interested** is how you feel when something is interesting: □ *It's a very interesting subject.* □ *I'm very interested in the subject.*

interest rate /ˈɪntrəst ˌreɪt/ NOUN [plural **interest rates**] the amount of extra money that you have to pay back when you borrow money, or that a bank pays you for having your money (taxa de juros) 🔊 *Interest rates rose by 1.5% last month.* □ *Banks announced a cut in interest rates.* (a taxa de juros subiu)

interface /ˈɪntəfeɪs/ NOUN [plural **interfaces**] the place in a computer system where information goes from one part to another, or the way the person using the computer sees the information on it. A computing word. (interface)

interfaith /ˈɪntəfeɪθ/ ADJECTIVE involving people from different religions □ *an interfaith service* (inter-religioso)

interfere /ˌɪntəˈfɪə(r)/ VERB [**interferes, interfering, interfered**] to get involved in a situation where you are not wanted □ *Many teenagers feel their parents interfere too much in their lives.* (interferir)

♦ PHRASAL VERB **interfere with something** to affect something in a bad way □ *The illness doesn't interfere with my ability to do the job.* (dificultar algo)

• **interference** /ˌɪntəˈfɪərəns/ NOUN, NO PLURAL
1 when someone interferes in something □ *political interference* (intromissão)
2 electronic signals that spoil the sound or picture on a television or radio (interferência)

interim /ˈɪntərɪm/ ▶ ADJECTIVE temporary □ *an interim government* (provisório)
▶ NOUN, NO PLURAL **in the interim** in the time between two events (nesse ínterim)

interior /ɪnˈtɪəriə(r)/ ▶ NOUN [plural **interiors**] the inside of something □ *The interior of the house was perfectly maintained.* (interior)
▶ ADJECTIVE on or for the inside of something □ *an interior wall* (interior)
⇨ go to **exterior**

interjection /ˌɪntəˈdʒekʃən/ NOUN [plural **interjections**] a word or phrase used to express a strong feeling like surprise, shock or anger. For example, **Oh!** and **Hooray!** are interjections. (interjeição)

interlude /ˈɪntəluːd/ NOUN [plural **interludes**] a short period of time between two events or situations □ *He lived in London all his life except for a brief interlude in New York.* (intervalo)

intermediate /ˌɪntəˈmiːdiət/ ADJECTIVE

1 between a basic and advanced level in a subject □ *an intermediate English course* (intermediário) 🔊 *The book is for students studying maths at an intermediate level.* (nível intermediário)

2 between two stages, places, levels, etc. □ *It's an intermediate step in the process.* (intermediário)

intermission /ˌɪntəˈmɪʃən/ NOUN [plural **intermissions**] a short pause in the middle of a play or concert (intervalo)

intermittent /ˌɪntəˈmɪtənt/ ADJECTIVE
happening some of the time but not continuously □ *intermittent rain* (intermitente)

internal /ɪnˈtɜːnəl/ ADJECTIVE
1 inside your body □ *internal injuries* □ *internal organs* (interno)
2 within an organization or country □ *an internal investigation* □ *internal flights* (interno)

international /ˌɪntəˈnæʃənəl/ ADJECTIVE
involving several countries □ *international law* □ *an international conference* □ *international trade* (internacional)

• **internationally** /ˌɪntəˈnæʃənəli/ ADVERB in many parts of the world □ *the internationally acclaimed author* (internacionalmente)

Internet /ˈɪntənet/ NOUN, NO PLURAL **the Internet** a computer system that allows people around the world to share information □ *I found this hotel on the Internet.* (internet)
▶ ADJECTIVE to do with the Internet (internet) ▣ *Most homes now have Internet access.* (acesso à internet) ▣ *Internet users* (usuários de internet)

interpret /ɪnˈtɜːprɪt/ VERB [**interprets, interpreting, interpreted**]
1 to understand something in a particular way □ + *as I interpreted his silence as shyness.* □ *Legal experts are divided over how to interpret the law.* (interpretar)
2 to change what someone has said into a different language □ *If you don't speak French, we can provide someone to interpret for you.* (interpretar, traduzir)

• **interpretation** /ɪnˌtɜːprɪˈteɪʃən/ NOUN [plural **interpretations**]
1 a way of explaining or understanding something □ *a literal interpretation of the text* (interpretação)
2 the way someone performs a piece of music, a play, etc. □ *He was famous for his interpretations of Mozart's music.* (interpretação)

• **interpreter** /ɪnˈtɜːprɪtə(r)/ NOUN [plural **interpreters**] someone whose job is to change what someone says into a different language (intérprete)

interrogate /ɪnˈterəgeɪt/ VERB [**interrogates, interrogating, interrogated**] to ask someone a lot of questions in order to get information, especially in a forceful or threatening way □ *The terrorist suspects were interrogated.* (interrogar)

• **interrogation** /ɪnˌterəˈgeɪʃən/ NOUN, NO PLURAL when someone is interrogated □ *the interrogation of prisoners* (interrogatório)

• **interrogator** /ɪnˈterəgeɪtə(r)/ NOUN [plural **interrogators**] someone who interrogates another person (interrogador)

interrupt /ˌɪntəˈrʌpt/ VERB [**interrupts, interrupting, interrupted**]
1 to stop someone when they are in the middle of saying or doing something □ *I'm sorry to interrupt, but what time do we have to leave?* □ *Could I just interrupt you for a moment?* (interromper)
2 to stop a process or activity for a short time □ *She interrupted the meeting to make a phone call.* □ *His career was interrupted by World War II.* (interromper)

• **interruption** /ˌɪntəˈrʌpʃən/ NOUN [plural **interruptions**]
1 something that stops you doing or saying something □ *I can't work with all these interruptions.* (interrupção)
2 when something stops for a period of time □ + *in an interruption in oil supplies* (interrupção)

intersect /ˌɪntəˈsekt/ VERB [**intersects, intersecting, intersected**] if lines or roads intersect, they cross each other (cruzar)

• **intersection** /ˌɪntəˈsekʃən/ NOUN [plural **intersections**] a place where lines or roads cross each other (interseção)

intersperse /ˌɪntəˈspɜːs/ VERB [**intersperses, interspersing, interspersed**] to put one type of thing among another type of thing, in various different places □ *Fruit trees were interspersed with shrubs.* (entremear, intercalar)

interval /ˈɪntəvəl/ NOUN [plural **intervals**]
1 a period of time between two things □ *Her husband died in 1990, and after a decent interval, she married again.* (intervalo) ▣ *After a short interval the police arrived.* (curto intervalo) □ + *of an interval of two weeks*
2 at weekly/monthly etc. intervals used for saying how often something happens □ *Meetings are held at regular intervals.* □ *You should have a dental check-up at six month-intervals.* (a cada semana, mês etc.)
3 at 5m/3m etc. intervals used to describe the distance between objects □ *There were bins placed at regular intervals along the road.* (a intervalos de 5 m, 3 m etc.)
4 a short pause in the middle of a concert or play □ *I bought an ice cream during the interval.* (intervalo)

intervene /ˌɪntəˈviːn/ VERB [**intervenes, intervening, intervened**]
1 to do something to try to stop an argument, fight or problem □ *The government intervened in the dispute.* (intervir)
2 if something intervenes, it happens, and stops or delays something else □ *He was the favourite to win the game until injury intervened.* (interpor-se)
3 to say something which interrupts someone □ *'Shut up both of you!' she intervened swiftly.* (intervir)

• **intervening** /ˌɪntəˈviːnɪŋ/ ADJECTIVE **the intervening period/years/months etc.** the time,

interview

- **intervention** /ˌɪntəˈvenʃən/ NOUN [plural **interventions**] when someone intervenes in something □ *military intervention* (**intervenção**)

interview /ˈɪntəvjuː/ ▶ NOUN [plural **interviews**]
1 a meeting in which someone asks you a lot of questions to find out if you are suitable for a job or a place on a course (**entrevista**) 🔹 *I have got an interview this afternoon.* (**terei uma entrevista**) 🔹 *I wear this suit for job interviews.* (**entrevista de emprego**) □ + *for I didn't even get an interview for the job.*
2 a meeting in which someone asks a famous person questions (**entrevista**) 🔹 *Most reporters are nervous if they do an interview with the Queen.* (**fazem uma entrevista**) 🔹 *The singer doesn't give interviews very often.* (**dá entrevistas**) 🔹 *In an exclusive interview with this paper, she talks openly about her marriage.* (**entrevista exclusiva**)
3 a meeting in which the police ask someone questions (**interrogatório**) 🔹 *A tape of the police interview was played in court.* (**interrogatório policial**)

▶ VERB [**interviews, interviewing, interviewed**] to ask someone questions at an interview □ *The driver was interviewed by police.* (**entrevistar**)

- **interviewer** /ˈɪntəvjuːə(r)/ NOUN [plural **interviewers**] the person who asks the questions at an interview (**repórter**)

intestines /ɪnˈtestɪnz/ PLURAL NOUN the tubes that take food from your stomach. A biology word. (**intestinos**)

intimate /ˈɪntɪmət/ ADJECTIVE
1 having a very close relationship with someone (**íntimo**) 🔹 *intimate friends* (**amigos íntimos**)
2 relating to private and personal things (**íntimo**) 🔹 *intimate details of their relationship* (**detalhes íntimos**)
3 an intimate place is friendly and relaxed and usually small □ *We found a nice, intimate restaurant where we could chat.* (**íntimo**)
4 an intimate knowledge of something is a very good and detailed knowledge (**profundo**) 🔹 *I don't have an intimate knowledge of the area.* (**conhecimento profundo**)

intimidate /ɪnˈtɪmɪdeɪt/ VERB [**intimidates, intimidating, intimidated**] to frighten someone, especially by threatening them □ *He won't let his attackers intimidate him into moving away from the area.* (**intimidar**)

- **intimidated** /ɪnˈtɪmɪdeɪtɪd/ ADJECTIVE frightened or not confident □ *Try not to feel intimidated by a large audience.* (**intimidado**)
- **intimidating** /ɪnˈtɪmɪdeɪtɪŋ/ ADJECTIVE making you feel frightened or less confident □ *He can be quite intimidating.* (**intimidante**)
- **intimidation** /ɪnˌtɪmɪˈdeɪʃən/ NOUN, NO PLURAL when someone is intimidated (**intimidação**)

intrigue

into /ˈɪntu/ PREPOSITION
1 towards the inside of a room, container, area, etc. □ *We went into the house.* □ *I got into bed.* □ *He shovelled earth into the hole.* (**dentro**)
2 towards the lower part of a substance □ *Our feet sank into the soft sand.* □ *He fell into the water.* (**dentro**)
3 hitting against something □ *I drove into a wall.* (**contra**)
4 used for saying how something or someone changes □ *She cut the pizza into four pieces.* □ *The caterpillar changed into a butterfly.* (**em**)
5 towards a particular thing □ *He looked into my eyes.* □ *She gazed into the mirror.* (**em**)
6 to do with a particular subject or situation □ *How did we get into this mess?* □ *We are holding an investigation into child poverty.* (**em, dentro**)
7 used when talking about dividing one number by another □ *2 into 4 goes twice.* (**em**)

intolerable /ɪnˈtɒlərəbəl/ ADJECTIVE so bad that you cannot continue □ *The situation became intolerable.* (**intolerável, insuportável**)

intolerance /ɪnˈtɒlərəns/ NOUN, NO PLURAL being intolerant (**intolerância**)

- **intolerant** /ɪnˈtɒlərənt/ ADJECTIVE refusing to accept behaviour and ideas that are different from your own (**intolerante**)

intonation /ˌɪntəˈneɪʃən/ NOUN, NO PLURAL the way that your voice goes up and down, showing your feelings and intentions, when you speak (**entonação**)

intranet /ˈɪntrənet/ NOUN [plural **intranets**] a system of connected computers in an organization which allows the people in that organization to read the same information. A computing word. □ *You'll find the sales figures on the Intranet.* (**intranet**)

intransitive /ɪnˈtrænsətɪv/ ADJECTIVE an intransitive verb does not have an object □ *In the sentence 'He fell.', the verb 'fall' is intransitive.* (**intransitivo**)

intravenous /ˌɪntrəˈviːnəs/ ADJECTIVE into a vein (= tube that carries blood) □ *an intravenous injection* (**intravenoso**)

intrepid /ɪnˈtrepɪd/ ADJECTIVE showing no fear and willing to do dangerous things □ *Our intrepid reporter is at the scene of the crime.* (**intrépido**)

intricate /ˈɪntrɪkət/ ADJECTIVE having a lot of small parts or details □ *an intricate pattern* (**complicado, intrincado**)

intrigue ▶ VERB /ɪnˈtriːg/ [**intrigues, intriguing, intrigued**] to interest someone and make them want to know more □ *The whole subject has always intrigued me.* (**intrigar**)

▶ NOUN /ˈɪntriːg/ [plural **intrigues**] secret plans to do something bad □ *It was a fascinating story of intrigue.* (**intriga**)

- **intriguing** /ɪnˈtriːgɪŋ/ ADJECTIVE very interesting and unusual □ *The house was an intriguing mixture of old and new.* (**fascinante**)

intrinsic

intrinsic /ɪnˈtrɪnsɪk/ ADJECTIVE part of the basic features of something or someone (**intrínseco**) *Computers are an intrinsic part of modern life.* (**parte intrínseca**)

introduce /ˌɪntrəˈdjuːs/ VERB [**introduces, introducing, introduced**]

1 if you introduce two people who do not know each other, you tell each of them the other person's name □ **+ to** *He introduced me to his sister.* □ *Have you two been introduced?* (**apresentar**)

2 to make something start to happen or be used □ *The new law was introduced in 1999.* (**introduzir**)

3 to tell an audience the name of someone who is going to speak or perform to them □ *It gives me great pleasure to introduce tonight's speaker.* (**apresentar**)

♦ PHRASAL VERB **introduce someone to something** to give someone the chance to experience something new □ *She introduced me to tap dancing.* (**apresentar alguém a algo**)

• **introduction** /ˌɪntrəˈdʌkʃən/ NOUN [plural **introductions**]

1 *no plural* when something is started or begins to be used □ *They opposed the introduction of identity cards.* (**introdução**)

2 the first part of a book, speech or piece of music (**prólogo**)

3 a book, course, etc. that teaches you the basic facts about a subject □ *She wrote an introduction to Chinese painting.* (**apresentação**)

4 when two people are introduced □ *After the introductions, we all sat down.* (**apresentação**)

• **introductory** /ˌɪntrəˈdʌkətəri/ ADJECTIVE

1 intended to explain what will come later or give the basic facts about a subject □ *I attended his introductory lectures on Greek philosophy.* (**introdutório**)

2 given when a product or service begins in order to encourage people to buy it (**de lançamento**) *an introductory offer* (**oferta de lançamento**)

introvert /ˈɪntrəvɜːt/ NOUN [plural **introverts**] someone who is quiet and shy (**introvertido**)

intrude /ɪnˈtruːd/ VERB [**intrudes, intruding, intruded**] to become involved in a situation where you are not wanted □ *She had no wish to intrude on his life.* (**intrometer-se**)

• **intruder** /ɪnˈtruːdə(r)/ NOUN [plural **intruders**] someone who goes into a place where they should not be, especially to steal something □ *Intruders stole all her jewellery.* (**intruso**)

• **intrusion** /ɪnˈtruːʒən/ NOUN [plural **intrusions**] someone or something that is not wanted in a situation (**invasão, intromissão**) *Stella's arrival was an unwelcome intrusion.* (**invasão indesejável**)

• **intrusive** /ɪnˈtruːsɪv/ ADJECTIVE becoming involved in a situation that should be private, in a way that is wrong □ *He found the media's interest in his private life intrusive.* (**intruso**)

intuition /ˌɪntjuːˈɪʃən/ NOUN [plural **intuitions**] an idea that something is true, based on your feelings instead of knowledge □ *Intuition can tell a mother that her child is ill.* (**intuição**)

• **intuitive** /ɪnˈtjuːɪtɪv/ ADJECTIVE based on intuition □ *intuitive judgements* (**intuitivo**)

inundate /ˈɪnʌndeɪt/ VERB [**inundates, inundating, inundated**] if you are inundated with something, you receive so much of it that you cannot deal with it all □ *The office has been inundated with offers of help.* (**inundar**)

invade /ɪnˈveɪd/ VERB [**invades, invading, invaded**]

1 to enter a country with an army, and try to take control of it □ *7000 troops invaded the country.* (**invadir**)

2 invade someone's privacy to become involved in someone's private life when they do not want this (**invadir a privacidade de alguém**)

3 if a lot of people invade a place, they go there □ *Every summer, the island is invaded by tourists.* (**invadir**)

• **invader** /ɪnˈveɪdə(r)/ NOUN [plural **invaders**] someone who invades another country (**invasor**)

invalid¹ /ɪnˈvælɪd/ ADJECTIVE

1 not acceptable because of a law or rule □ *an invalid bus pass* (**inválido**)

2 not correct or not based on facts □ *an invalid excuse* (**inválido, nulo**)

invalid² /ˈɪnvəlɪd/ NOUN [plural **invalids**] someone who is ill or unable to look after themselves (**doente**)

invaluable /ɪnˈvæljuəbəl/ ADJECTIVE extremely useful □ *an invaluable piece of advice* (**inestimável**)

invariably /ɪnˈveəriəbli/ ADVERB always □ *Dean is invariably late for everything.* (**invariavelmente**)

invasion /ɪnˈveɪʒən/ NOUN [plural **invasions**]

1 an attack on a country by an army entering it □ **+ of** *The government decided to launch an invasion of the country.* (**invasão**)

2 when a lot of people go to a place □ *The town is preparing for its biggest invasion of the year – the annual pop festival.* (**invasão**)

3 an invasion of privacy involvement in someone's private life which is not wanted □ *Publishing the photos was an invasion of privacy.* (**invasão de privacidade**)

invent /ɪnˈvent/ VERB [**invents, inventing, invented**]

1 to design or create a new type of thing □ *Thomas Edison invented the electric light bulb.* □ *There was a lot of argument about who had invented the word.* (**inventar**)

2 to think of a story or excuse that is not true (**inventar**) *She invented an excuse not to go to his house.* (**inventou uma desculpa**)

- **invention** /ɪnˈvenʃən/ NOUN [plural **inventions**]
1 a new type of thing which someone has designed or created □ The washing machine was a brilliant invention. (**invento**)
2 NO PLURAL when someone designs or creates a new type of thing □ **+ of** The invention of the computer would change the world forever. (**invenção**)
3 a story or excuse that is not true □ Is crime increasing, or is it just an invention of the media? (**invenção**)

- **inventive** /ɪnˈventɪv/ ADJECTIVE using new and interesting ideas □ He has an inventive mind. □ an inventive solution (**imaginativo**)

- **inventor** /ɪnˈventə(r)/ NOUN [plural **inventors**] someone who has invented something new (**inventor**)

inverse /ɪnˈvɜːs/ ADJECTIVE an inverse relationship between two amounts is one in which one amount becomes bigger at the same rate as the other one becomes smaller (**inverso, contrário**)

invert /ɪnˈvɜːt/ VERB [**inverts, inverting, inverted**] a formal word meaning to turn something upside down (**inverter**)

invertebrate /ɪnˈvɜːtɪbrət/ NOUN [plural **invertebrates**] an animal that does not have a bone in its back, for example an insect or worm. A biology word. (**invertebrado**)

inverted /ɪnˈvɜːtɪd/ ADJECTIVE turned upside down (**invertido**)

inverted commas /ɪnˌvɜːtɪd ˈkɒməz/ PLURAL NOUN the symbols ' ' or " ", used in writing to show what someone says (**aspas**)

invest /ɪnˈvest/ VERB [**invests, investing, invested**] to put money in a bank or business in order to make more money □ My Dad has invested some money in the business. (**investir**)

◆ PHRASAL VERB **invest in something** to buy something expensive that will be useful □ I think we need to invest in a new printer. (**investir em algo**)

investigate /ɪnˈvestɪɡeɪt/ VERB [**investigates, investigating, investigated**] to try to find out about something such as an accident or crime □ Police are investigating his death. (**investigar**)

- **investigation** /ɪnˌvestɪˈɡeɪʃən/ NOUN [plural **investigations**] an attempt to find out about something such as an accident or a crime (**investigação**) ▣ Officials have launched an investigation into allegations of corruption. (**lançou uma investigação**)

- **investigator** /ɪnˈvestɪɡeɪtə(r)/ NOUN [plural **investigators**] someone who is investigating something (**investigador**)

investment /ɪnˈvestmənt/ NOUN [plural **investments**]
1 when you use money to get a profit or to make a business successful □ The country hopes to attract foreign investment in its telephone network. (**investimento**)
2 something that you spend a lot of money on because it will be very useful (**investimento**) ▣ A warm coat is a good investment. (**bom investimento**)

investor /ɪnˈvestə(r)/ NOUN [plural **investors**] someone who gives money to a bank or business in order to get a profit (**investidor**)

invigorating /ɪnˈvɪɡəreɪtɪŋ/ ADJECTIVE making you feel full of energy □ We went for an invigorating walk by the sea. (**revigorante, estimulante**)

invincible /ɪnˈvɪnsəbəl/ ADJECTIVE impossible to defeat or destroy □ Young people often feel invincible. (**invencível**)

invisibility /ɪnˌvɪzəˈbɪləti/ NOUN, NO PLURAL being impossible to see (**invisibilidade**)

invisible /ɪnˈvɪzəbəl/ ADJECTIVE impossible to see □ The star is almost invisible. (**invisível**)

invitation /ˌɪnvɪˈteɪʃən/ NOUN [plural **invitations**]
1 when someone asks you if you would like to go somewhere or do something □ **+ to** We've had an invitation to William and Charlotte's wedding. □ **+ to do something** He accepted an invitation to meet the President. (**convite**)
2 a card or piece of paper that you use for inviting someone to something (**convite**) ▣ I've bought some party invitations. (**convites da festa**) ▣ Those are pretty wedding invitations. (**convites de casamento**)
3 something that encourages something bad to happen □ **+ to** Leaving your car door open is an invitation to thieves. (**convite**)

invite ▶ VERB /ɪnˈvaɪt/ [**invites, inviting, invited**]
1 to ask someone if they would like to do something or go somewhere □ **+ for** We've invited some friends round for dinner. □ **+ to** Raj has invited me to his birthday party. □ **+ to do something** Beth was invited to speak at the conference. (**convidar**)
2 to encourage something bad to happen □ Using those words is likely to invite criticism. (**pedir**)

◆ PHRASAL VERBS **invite someone in** to ask someone to come into your house □ When we got to her house, she invited me in. (**convidar alguém para entrar**) **invite someone over/round** to ask someone to come to your house, for example to have a meal with you □ I've invited Ann round tonight. (**convidar alguém para sua casa**)

▶ NOUN /ˈɪnvaɪt/ [plural **invites**] an informal word meaning an invitation □ Have you had an invite to the wedding? (**convite**)

- **inviting** /ɪnˈvaɪtɪŋ/ ADJECTIVE attractive and pleasant, making you want something or want to go somewhere □ an inviting smell □ an inviting restaurant (**convidativo, tentador**)

invoice

invoice /ˈɪnvɔɪs/ ▶ NOUN [plural **invoices**] a piece of paper showing you the goods or services that you have bought and how much you must pay for them (**fatura**)
▶ VERB [**invoices, invoicing, invoiced**] to send someone an invoice (**enviar uma fatura**)

involuntary /ɪnˈvɒləntəri/ ADJECTIVE an involuntary movement or action is one you cannot control □ *Sneezing is an involuntary action.* (**involuntário**)

involve /ɪnˈvɒlv/ VERB [**involves, involving, involved**]
1 if an activity or situation involves something, that thing is a part of it □ *The treatment involves a slight risk.* □ *+ ing The job involves selling Internet space to companies.* (**acarretar, implicar**)
2 to affect someone or something □ *Crimes involving children are very rare.* □ *Five vehicles were involved in the accident.* (**envolver**)
3 to allow someone to take part in something □ *+ in The school tries to involve students in decision-making.* (**envolver**)
• **involved** /ɪnˈvɒlvd/ ADJECTIVE
1 get/be involved to take part in something □ *I don't want to get involved in an argument.* □ *He's been involved in politics for 30 years.* (**ser implicado**)
2 an involved story or explanation is long and complicated (**complicado**)
3 be/get involved with someone to have a relationship with someone □ *He's not the sort of man you want to get involved with.* (**estar envolvido com alguém**)
• **involvement** /ɪnˈvɒlvmənt/ NOUN, NO PLURAL when someone takes part in something (**envolvimento, participação**) *He doesn't have any direct involvement in the company.* (**envolvimento direto**) □ *+ in He denies any involvement in the killing.* □ *+ of The project was carried out with the full involvement of local people.*

inward /ˈɪnwəd/ ADJECTIVE
1 in your mind and not shown to other people □ *inward satisfaction* □ *an inward smile* (**interior, íntimo**)
2 towards the inside or middle of something □ *the natural inward curve of your lower back* (**para dentro**)
• **inwardly** /ˈɪnwədli/ ADVERB in your own mind but not shown to other people □ *Inwardly, she felt very scared.* (**por dentro**)
• **inwards** /ˈɪnwədz/ ADVERB towards the inside of something □ *The door swung inwards.* (**para dentro**)

iodine /ˈaɪədiːn/ NOUN, NO PLURAL a chemical element, sometimes used to clean cuts on the body. A chemistry word. (**iodo**)

ion /ˈaɪən/ NOUN [plural **ions**] an atom with an electrical force. A chemistry and physics word. (**íon**)

ironing

iota /aɪˈəʊtə/ NOUN, NO PLURAL a very small amount □ *Anyone with an iota of intelligence could see he was lying.* (**um pouquinho**)

IOU /ˌaɪəʊˈjuː/ ABBREVIATION I owe you; a note that you sign to say that you owe someone money (**abreviação de eu devo a você**)

IQ /ˌaɪˈkjuː/ ABBREVIATION intelligence quotient; how intelligent someone is, measured by a special test (**QI**) *She has a very high IQ.* (**QI elevado**)

ir- /ɪr/ PREFIX ir- is added to the beginning of words to mean 'not' □ *irreversible* □ *irresponsible* (**ir-**)

irascible /ɪˈræsəbəl/ ADJECTIVE often becoming angry. A formal word. (**irascível**)

irate /aɪˈreɪt/ ADJECTIVE extremely angry □ *Hundreds of irate customers have complained about the company.* (**irado, colérico**)

iris /ˈaɪrɪs/ NOUN [plural **irises**]
1 the coloured circle in your eye. A biology word. (**íris**)
2 a tall plant with purple, white or yellow flowers (**íris**)

Irish /ˈaɪrɪʃ/ ▶ ADJECTIVE belonging to or from Ireland (**irlandês**)
▶ NOUN, NO PLURAL **the Irish** people from Ireland (**os irlandeses**)

irk /ɜːk/ VERB [**irks, irking, irked**] to annoy someone □ *It irks me that she never thanked us.* (**irritar, provocar**)

iron /ˈaɪən/ ▶ NOUN [plural **irons**]
1 *no plural* a hard strong metal that is used to make steel and is also found in small amounts in your blood and some food □ *The railings were made from iron.* □ *Spinach contains vitamin C and iron.* (**ferro**)
2 a piece of electrical equipment that you press on clothes to make them smooth □ *Have you switched the iron off?* (**ferro de passar**)
▶ ADJECTIVE made from iron □ *iron gates* (**ferro**)
▶ VERB [**irons, ironing, ironed**] to make clothes smooth using an iron □ *Ben was ironing some shirts.* (**passar a ferro**)

ironic /aɪˈrɒnɪk/ ADJECTIVE
1 an ironic situation is surprising, often because it is the opposite of what you expected □ *It's ironic that a man who spent his life treating heart disease should die of a heart attack.* (**irônico**)
2 saying the opposite of what you really mean □ *Were you being ironic when you described her as 'lovely'?* (**irônico**)

ironing /ˈaɪənɪŋ/ NOUN, NO PLURAL
1 the activity of making clothes smooth by pressing them with a piece of electrical equipment (**ato de passar roupas**) *Mum always watches television while she's doing the ironing.* (**passando as roupas**)
2 clothes which you are going to iron, or which you have just ironed □ *There was a pile of ironing on the chair.* (**roupas passadas a ferro**)

ironing board · isle

ironing board /ˈaɪənɪŋ ˌbɔːd/ NOUN [plural **ironing boards**] a flat board that you iron clothes on (tábua de passar roupas)

irony /ˈaɪərəni/ NOUN [plural **ironies**]
1 a situation that is surprising because it is the opposite of what you expected (ironia) 🔁 *The irony is that the man who cooks all this marvellous food can no longer taste it.* (a ironia é)
2 using words that are the opposite of what you really mean in order to be funny (ironia)

irregular /ɪˈregjələ(r)/ ADJECTIVE
1 having a different amount of time or space between separate things (irregular) 🔁 *an irregular heartbeat* (batidas cardíacas irregulares) □ *The trees had been planted at irregular intervals.*
2 not smooth or even □ *irregular shapes* (irregular, assimétrico)
3 not following the usual rules of grammar □ *irregular verbs* (irregular)
4 a formal word meaning not following the usual moral or legal rules (irregular, excepcional)
• **irregularity** /ɪˌregjʊˈlærəti/ NOUN [plural **irregularities**]
1 a situation in which the usual moral or legal rules have not been followed (irregularidade) 🔁 *The company was investigated for financial irregularities.* (irregularidades financeiras)
2 when things have a different amount of time or space between each one □ *heartbeat irregularity* (irregularidade, assimetria)
3 when something is not smooth or even (irregularidade, assimetria)

irrelevance /ɪˈreləvəns/ NOUN [plural **irrelevances**] something that is not related to a particular situation or subject and is not important □ *It's a mistake to view the local media as an irrelevance.* (irrelevância)
• **irrelevant** /ɪˈreləvənt/ ADJECTIVE not related to a particular situation or subject so not important □ *His comments were completely irrelevant to the discussion.* (irrelevante)

irreplaceable /ˌɪrɪˈpleɪsəbəl/ ADJECTIVE too special or valuable to be replaced □ *irreplaceable documents* (insubstituível)

irresistible /ˌɪrɪˈzɪstəbəl/ ADJECTIVE
1 if something is irresistible, it is so attractive that you want it □ *The offer of a cool swim on a hot day was irresistible.* (irresistível)
2 too strong to ignore or control □ *She had an irresistible urge to scream.* (irresistível)

irrespective /ˌɪrɪˈspektɪv/ ADJECTIVE **irrespective of something** not influenced by a particular fact □ *Workers should be treated the same, irrespective of their sex or age.* (independentemente de algo)

irresponsible /ˌɪrɪˈspɒnsəbəl/ ADJECTIVE behaving in a silly way without thinking about the bad things that might happen □ *It was completely irresponsible to leave a six-year-old at home alone.* (irresponsável)

irreversible /ˌɪrɪˈvɜːsəbəl/ ADJECTIVE lasting forever (irreversível) 🔁 *Pollution has caused irreversible damage to the environment.* (danos irreversíveis)

irrigate /ˈɪrɪgeɪt/ VERB [**irrigates, irrigating, irrigated**] to supply land or crops with water (irrigar)
• **irrigation** /ˌɪrɪˈgeɪʃən/ NOUN, NO PLURAL supplying land or crops with water (irrigação)

irritable /ˈɪrɪtəbəl/ ADJECTIVE becoming annoyed very easily □ *Jamal is irritable if he doesn't get enough sleep.* (irritável)

irritate /ˈɪrɪteɪt/ VERB [**irritates, irritating, irritated**]
1 to make someone feel annoyed □ *It irritates me that he never helps with the washing up.* (irritar)
2 to make something such as your skin or eyes sore □ *Some sun creams can irritate your skin.* (irritar)
• **irritated** /ˈɪrɪteɪtɪd/ ADJECTIVE annoyed (irritado) 🔁 *I was starting to get irritated.* (ficar irritado)
• **irritating** /ˈɪrɪteɪtɪŋ/ ADJECTIVE making you feel annoyed □ *He had an irritating habit of repeating everything I said.* (irritante)
• **irritation** /ˌɪrɪˈteɪʃən/ NOUN [plural **irritations**]
1 feeling annoyed about something □ *She couldn't hide her irritation.* (irritação)
2 something that annoys you □ *His constant complaints are an irritation.* (irritação)
3 a sore feeling on your skin or in your eyes □ *Smoke causes eye irritation.* (irritação)

is /ɪz/ VERB the present tense of the verb be when it is used with he, she, or it □ *He is tall.* □ *It is too hot.* (ver **be**)

> ► Note that instead of he is, she is and it is, people often say and write the short forms, **he's**, **she's** and **it's**: □ *He's here.* □ *She's tall.* □ *It's great.*

-ise /aɪz/ SUFFIX another way of spelling **-ize** (ver **-ise**)

-ish /ɪʃ/ SUFFIX **-ish** is added to the end of words to mean 'slightly' □ *reddish* (= slightly red) (sufixo - levemente)

Islam /ˈɪzlɑːm/ NOUN, NO PLURAL the Muslim religion that was started by Mohammed (Islã)
• **Islamic** /ɪzˈlæmɪk/ ADJECTIVE to do with Islam □ *Islamic law* □ *the Islamic faith* (islâmico)

island /ˈaɪlənd/ NOUN [plural **islands**] an area of land surrounded by sea □ *There are lots of unusual plants on the island.* □ *the Caribbean island of Trinidad* (ilha) 🔁 *a remote island in the Pacific Ocean* (ilha remota) □ *the Channel Islands*

isle /aɪl/ NOUN [plural **isles**] a word meaning 'island', used in poems or in the name of an island □ *the Isles of Scilly* (ilha)

-ism /-ɪzəm/ SUFFIX **-ism** is added to the end of words to make nouns to do with beliefs or qualities ◻ *communism* ◻ *heroism* **(-ismo)**

isn't /'ɪzənt/ a short way to say and write is not ◻ *It isn't fair.* **(ver be)**

isobar /'aɪsəbɑː(r)/ NOUN [plural **isobars**] a line on a weather map that joins places with the same air pressure. A geography word. **(linha isobárica)**

isolate /'aɪsəleɪt/ VERB [**isolates, isolating, isolated**] to separate someone or something from other people or things ◻ *The infected animals were isolated in a field.* **(isolar)**

• **isolated** /'aɪsəleɪtɪd/ ADJECTIVE
1 feeling alone and sad that you do not meet other people ◻ *Old people often feel isolated.* **(isolado)**
2 far away from other places ◻ *an isolated farmhouse* **(isolado)**
3 happening only once and not related to other events **(isolado)** 🔂 *This theft was an isolated incident.* **(incidente isolado)**

• **isolation** /ˌaɪsə'leɪʃən/ NOUN, NO PLURAL
1 when a person, place or thing is separate from others ◻ *The deal should end the country's economic isolation.* **(isolamento)**
2 a feeling of being alone and sad because you do not meet other people ◻ *Working from home can lead to isolation.* **(isolamento, solidão)**
3 in isolation separately from other people or things ◻ *Each incident must be considered in isolation.* **(isolado)**

isosceles /aɪ'sɒsəliːz/ ADJECTIVE an isosceles triangle has two sides of the same length. A maths word. **(isósceles)**

isotope /'aɪsətəʊp/ NOUN [plural **isotopes**] one of the forms of a chemical element with the same number of protons but a different number of neutrons. A chemistry word. **(isótopo)**

ISP /ˌaɪes'piː/ ABBREVIATION Internet Service Provider; a company that sells you a connection to the Internet. A computing word. **(PSI)**

issue /'ɪʃuː/ ▶ NOUN [plural **issues**]
1 a subject that people discuss or that causes problems ◻ + *of We discussed the issue of funding.* **(assunto)** 🔂 *Polly raised the issue of transport* **(levantou o assunto)** 🔂 *We are trying to address the issue* (= deal with the issue) *of truancy.* **(lidar com o assunto)** 🔂 *The environment is a key issue in this election campaign.* **(assunto chave)** 🔂 *The issue arose because one of the children made a complaint.* **(assunto surgiu)**
2 at issue being discussed or causing arguments ◻ *The matter at issue is whether the centre should open at the weekend.* **(em discussão)**
3 a newspaper or magazine that is one of a number printed and sold at the same time ◻ *Have you seen this week's issue of the magazine?* **(número)**
4 no plural the act of supplying someone with something ◻ *She organized the issue of warm bedding.* **(provisão)**

▶ VERB [**issues, issuing, issued**]
1 to say something to the public in an official way **(publicar)** 🔂 *issue a statement/warning* **(publicar uma declaração)**
2 to supply someone with something ◻ + *with We were all issued with pens.* **(distribuir)**

-ist /ɪst/ SUFFIX
1 -ist is added to the end of words to make nouns to do with people who do a particular thing ◻ *artist* **(-ista)**
2 -ist is added to the end of words to make nouns to do with people who have particular beliefs ◻ *communist* **(-ista)**

isthmus /'ɪsməs/ NOUN [plural **isthmuses**] a narrow piece of land with water on each side that goes between two larger pieces of land. A geography word. **(istmo)**

IT /ˌaɪ'tiː/ ABBREVIATION **information technology** **(TI)**

it /ɪt/ PRONOUN **(isso, isto, aquilo, o, a)**
1 used to talk or write about something that has already been mentioned ◻ *I've lost my book. Have you seen it?* ◻ *It was a great day.*
2 used to talk about a fact or opinion ◻ *It's expensive to travel by train.* ◻ *It's very quiet here, isn't it?* ◻ *What's it like in Spain?*
3 used to talk about the weather, time and dates ◻ *It rained yesterday.* ◻ *What time is it?* ◻ *It's 3 o'clock.*
4 used to talk about distance ◻ *It's a long way to the coast.* ◻ *How far is it to your house?*
5 used to tell someone who is there, on the telephone, etc. ◻ *Hello, it's Pat here.* ◻ *It's your brother at the door.*
6 used as the object of a sentence ◻ *I liked it when he sang that song.* ◻ *I considered it to be rude.*
7 used as the subject of a sentence ◻ *It made me happy to see him laugh.* ◻ *It seems as though he's forgotten us.*

italics /ɪ'tælɪks/ PLURAL NOUN a style of writing in which the letters slope to the right. The examples given in this book are in italics. **(itálico)**

itch /ɪtʃ/ ▶ VERB [**itches, itching, itched**] if part of your body itches, it feels uncomfortable and makes you want to scratch it **(coçar)**

◆ IDIOM **be itching to do something** an informal phrase meaning to want to do something very much ◻ *I was itching to play football again.* **(estar louco para fazer algo)**

▶ NOUN [plural **itches**] an uncomfortable feeling on part of your body that makes you want to scratch it ◻ *I've got an itch on my back.* **(coceira)**

• **itchy** /'ɪtʃi/ ADJECTIVE an itchy part of your body feels uncomfortable and makes you want to scratch it **(que coça, coceira)**

it'd /'ɪtəd/ a short way to say and write it would or it had ◻ *It'd be good if you could come.* ◻ *It'd been raining all day.* **(ver have, would)**

item /ˈaɪtəm/ NOUN [plural **items**]
  1 one thing which is part of a group or is on a list ◻ *There were several items on the list.* (**item, peça, objeto**) 🔁 *He left his mobile phone and other personal items in the car.* (**objetos pessoais**) 🔁 *She had some very expensive items of clothing in her wardrobe.* (**peças de roupas**)
  2 a piece of news in a newspaper, magazine or on television (**notícia**) 🔁 *I saw an interesting news item.* (**notícias**) ◻ + *on/about* There was an item on famous painters.
  • **itemize** or **itemise** /ˈaɪtəmaɪz/ VERB [**itemizes, itemizing, itemized**] to give things separately in a list, with details about each thing ◻ *Phone companies usually itemize your calls.* (**detalhar, registrar**)

itinerary /aɪˈtɪnərəri/ NOUN [plural **itineraries**] a list of the places you will visit when you are travelling ◻ *France, Germany and Italy are on the President's itinerary.* (**itinerário**)

it'll /ˈɪtəl/ a short way to say and write it will ◻ *It'll be nice to see you.* (ver **will**)

it's /ɪts/ a short way to say and write it is or it has ◻ *It's snowing.* ◻ *It's been a long time since I saw you.* (ver **be, have**)

> ➤ Try not to confuse the spellings of its and it's. **Its** is the possessive form of it, and tells you something belongs to it: *The bird built its nest.* **It's** is a short form of two words put together: *I think it's going to rain.*

its /ɪts/ ADJECTIVE belonging to or to do with it ◻ *Keep the hat in its box.* (**seu, sua, seus, suas**) 🔁 *The school has its own tennis courts.* (**seu próprio**)

itself /ɪtˈsɛlf/ PRONOUN
  1 the reflexive form of **it** ◻ *The school has transformed itself.* ◻ *Australia has found itself in a difficult position.* (**si mesmo, si mesma**)
  2 used to show that a thing or animal does something without any help from anyone or anything else ◻ *The cut soon healed itself.* (**sozinho, por si só**) 🔁 *The dog managed to get free all by itself.* (**sozinho**)
  3 used to emphasize the pronoun it ◻ *I don't dislike the building itself.* (**em si**)
  4 by itself not with or near other things ◻ *The cottage stood by itself on a hillside.* ◻ *Talent by itself is not enough to make you successful.* (**ele mesmo**)

I've /aɪv/ a short way to say and write I have ◻ *I've finished my homework.* ◻ *I've got six cats.* (ver **have**)

ivory /ˈaɪvəri/ NOUN, NO PLURAL the hard white substance that an elephant's tusks (= long teeth) are made of (**marfim**)

ivy /ˈaɪvi/ NOUN, NO PLURAL a plant with dark green leaves which grows up walls (**hera**)

-ize or **-ise** /-aɪz/ SUFFIX **-ize** or **-ise** is added to the end of words to make verbs to do with making something become a particular way ◻ *computerize* (**-izar, -isar**)

Jj

J or **j** /dʒeɪ/ the tenth letter of the alphabet (a décima letra do alfabeto)

jab /dʒæb/ ▶ VERB [**jabs, jabbing, jabbed**] to push something sharp quickly and hard into something ▫ *He jabbed me in the arm with his pen.* (espetar)

▶ NOUN [*plural* **jabs**]

1 when you quickly push something sharp into or towards something ▫ *She gave him a jab in the ribs with her elbow.* (cutucão, pontada)

2 when you put a substance into someone's body with a needle, in order to stop them getting a disease (injeção) 🔁 *a flu jab* (injeção contra a gripe)

jack /dʒæk/ NOUN [*plural* **jacks**]

1 a playing card with a picture of a young man, that comes between the ten and the Queen in value ▫ *the jack of hearts* (valete)

2 a tool used to raise something heavy off the ground, especially a car (macaco)

jackal /ˈdʒækəl/ NOUN [*plural* **jackals**] a wild animal that looks like a dog and hunts in groups (chacal)

jacket /ˈdʒækɪt/ NOUN [*plural* **jackets**] a short coat, usually with long sleeves ▫ *a leather jacket* ▫ *a denim jacket* (jaqueta, casaco)

jacket potato /ˌdʒækɪt pəˈteɪtəʊ/ NOUN [*plural* **jacket potatoes**] a potato baked in the oven in its skin (batata assada)

jack-knife /ˈdʒæknaɪf/ VERB [**jack-knifes, jack-knifing, jack-knifed**] if a truck jack-knifes, it loses control and bends so that the back moves round towards the front (dobrar-se ao meio)

jackpot /ˈdʒækpɒt/ NOUN [*plural* **jackpots**] the largest prize in a game or competition (sorte grande, grande prêmio)

◆ IDIOM **hit the jackpot** to be very successful, usually winning a lot of money (ser vencedor, ganhador)

Jacuzzi /dʒəˈkuːzi/ NOUN [*plural* **Jacuzzis**] a warm bath or pool with a lot of bubbles in the water. A trademark. (jacuzzi, banheira)

jade /dʒeɪd/ NOUN, NO PLURAL a green stone used in jewellery (jade)

jaded /ˈdʒeɪdɪd/ ADJECTIVE feeling tired and bored, especially because you have been doing the same thing for a long time (entediado)

jagged /ˈdʒægɪd/ ADJECTIVE with sharp, edges or points ▫ *a jagged rock* ▫ *a jagged edge* (pontiagudo)

jaguar /ˈdʒægjuə(r)/ NOUN [*plural* **jaguars**] a large wild cat with black spots, that comes from South and Central America (jaguar)

jail /dʒeɪl/ ▶ NOUN [*plural* **jails**] a building where criminals are kept ▫ *She was sentenced to 12 months in jail.* (cadeia) 🔁 *He's just been released from jail.* (foi solto da cadeia)

▶ VERB [**jails, jailing, jailed**] to put someone in a jail ▫ *Peters was jailed for 30 months for assaulting a neighbour.* (prender)

• **jailer** /ˈdʒeɪlə(r)/ NOUN [*plural* **jailers**] someone who guards people while they are in prison (carcereiro)

jam /dʒæm/ ▶ NOUN [*plural* **jams**]

1 a sweet, sticky food made of fruit and sugar that you spread on bread ▫ *strawberry jam* (geleia)

2 a line of vehicles that are not moving or are moving very slowly (engarrafamento) 🔁 *I got stuck in a traffic jam.* (engarrafamento de trânsito)

▶ VERB [**jams, jamming, jammed**]

1 to push something into a space so that it fits very tightly ▫ *She jammed the clothes into her suitcase.* (apinhar)

2 to become or to make something become unable to move or work ▫ *I tried to open the door but it was jammed.* (emperrar)

3 to fill a place completely with people or things ▫ **+ with** *The M6 was jammed with traffic after an accident.* (amontoar) 🔁 *All the cupboards were jammed full of clothes.* (amontoado de)

4 to send out a signal that stops a radio from being heard (interferir)

jammy /ˈdʒæmi/ ADJECTIVE [**jammier, jammiest**]

1 filled or covered with jam (= sweet food made with fruit) ▫ *jammy doughnuts* (coberto com geleia)

2 an informal word meaning lucky (sorte)

jangle /ˈdʒæŋɡəl/ ▶ VERB [**jangles, jangling, jangled**] to make the ringing sound of metal hitting against metal ▫ *He walked up the path, jangling his keys.* (soar de modo estridente)

▶ NOUN [*plural* **jangles**] the ringing sound of metal hitting against metal ▫ *She could hear the*

janitor   jerk

janitor /'dʒænɪtə(r)/ NOUN [plural **janitors**] the US word for **caretaker** (**zelador**)

January /'dʒænjuəri/ NOUN the first month of the year, after December and before February □ *My birthday is in January.* (**janeiro**)

jar /dʒɑː(r)/ ▶ NOUN [plural **jars**] a glass container with a wide neck and a lid, used for storing food □ *a jam jar* □ *a jar of coffee* (**pote**)
▶ VERB [**jars, jarring, jarred**]
1 to hurt or damage something from a sudden hit or movement □ *He fell awkwardly, jarring his spine.* (**ferir**)
2 to make you feel slightly annoyed □ *Her voice just starts to jar after a while.* (**irritar**)

jargon /'dʒɑːgən/ NOUN, NO PLURAL special words and phrases used by people working in a particular job, which are difficult for other people to understand □ *computer jargon* (**jargão**)

jasmine /'dʒæzmɪn/ NOUN [plural **jasmines**] a bush or climbing plant with white or yellow flowers with a sweet smell (**jasmim**)

jaundice /'dʒɔːndɪs/ NOUN, NO PLURAL an illness that makes your skin and the whites of your eyes become yellow, usually caused by your liver not working correctly (**icterícia**)

• **jaundiced** /'dʒɔːndɪst/ ADJECTIVE
1 not expecting good things to happen because of your bad experiences in the past □ *Her mother had a very jaundiced view of men.* (**amargurado, despeitado**)
2 suffering from jaundice □ *The baby was slightly jaundiced.* (**amarelado**)

jaunt /dʒɔːnt/ NOUN [plural **jaunts**] a short journey made for pleasure □ *a jaunt to the seaside* (**viagem curta**)

• **jaunty** /'dʒɔːnti/ ADJECTIVE [**jauntier, jauntiest**] happy and confident (**alegre**)

javelin /'dʒævəlɪn/ NOUN [plural **javelins**]
1 a long light stick with a pointed end that you throw in a sports event (**dardo**)
2 the javelin the sports event in which you throw a javelin as far as you can (**jogo de atirar dardos**)

jaw /dʒɔː/ NOUN [plural **jaws**] the lower part of your face made up of two bones that your teeth grow in (**maxilar**)

♦ IDIOM **someone's jaw drops** if someone's jaw drops, they show with their face that they are extremely surprised □ *She told us what she earned and our jaws dropped.* (**deixar alguém de queixo caído**)

jazz /dʒæz/ NOUN, NO PLURAL a type of music with a strong beat that is often changed or added to as it is played □ *modern jazz* (**jazz**)

♦ PHRASAL VERB [**jazzes, jazzing, jazzed**] **jazz something up** to make something brighter and more colourful. An informal phrase. □ *You can jazz up an old sofa with some bright cushions.* (**animar algo**)

• **jazzy** /'dʒæzi/ ADJECTIVE [**jazzier, jazziest**] an informal word meaning bright and colourful □ *That's a very jazzy tie you have on.* (**espalhafatoso**)

JCB /ˌdʒeɪsiːˈbiː/ NOUN [plural **JCBs**] a large machine used for digging and moving earth and stones. A trademark. (**JCB**)

jealous /'dʒeləs/ ADJECTIVE
1 feeling angry and unhappy because someone has something you want or because you want to be like someone else □ **+ of** *He's jealous of his brother's success.* (**ciumento**) 🔂 *She made me jealous by going out with her other friends.* (**me deixou com ciúme**)
2 feeling upset and angry because you think someone you love is in love with someone else □ *a jealous wife* (**ciumento**)

• **jealousy** /'dʒeləsi/ NOUN, NO PLURAL jealous feelings (**ciosamente, com ciúme**)

jeans /dʒiːnz/ PLURAL NOUN trousers made of denim (= thick, usually blue, cotton) (**jeans**)

Jeep /dʒiːp/ NOUN [plural **Jeeps**] a small, strong vehicle that can travel over rough ground. A trademark. (**jipe**)

jeer /dʒɪə(r)/ ▶ VERB [**jeers, jeering, jeered**] to shout rude remarks at someone and laugh at them □ *The crowd jeered as the team left the pitch.* (**vaiar**)
▶ NOUN [plural **jeers**] an angry shout or laugh □ *The speaker was greeted with jeers from the gallery.* (**vaia**)

Jell-o /'dʒeləʊ/ NOUN, NO PLURAL the US word for **jelly**. A trademark. (**gelatina**)

jelly /'dʒeli/ NOUN [plural **jellies**]
1 a soft, sweet food with a fruit flavour that shakes when you move it and is eaten cold □ *a bowl of jelly and ice cream* (**gelatina**)
2 a US word for **jam** (**geleia**)

jellyfish /'dʒelifɪʃ/ NOUN [plural **jellyfish** or **jellyfishes**] a sea animal with a soft transparent body that can sting you (= hurt you by putting poison into your skin) (**água-viva**)

jeopardize or **jeopardise** /'dʒepədaɪz/ VERB [**jeopardizes, jeopardizing, jeopardized**] to harm something or put something in danger □ *The injury could jeopardize her chances of winning a medal.* (**colocar em perigo**)

• **jeopardy** /'dʒepədi/ NOUN, NO PLURAL **in jeopardy** in a situation where something risks being lost or damaged □ *Her life is in jeopardy.* (**em perigo**)

jerk /dʒɜːk/ ▶ VERB [**jerks, jerking, jerked**]
1 to make a short sudden movement □ *The driver started the engine and the old bus jerked forward.* (**mover-se aos trancos**)

jersey

2 to pull something with a sudden rough movement ☐ *He jerked his hand away.* (sacudir)
▶ NOUN [plural **jerks**]
1 a short sudden movement (solavanco)
2 an informal word for a stupid person (idiota)
• **jerky** /ˈdʒɜːkɪ/ ADJECTIVE jerky movements are short and quick (sacudido)

jersey /ˈdʒɜːzɪ/ NOUN [plural **jerseys**]
1 a warm piece of clothing with sleeves that you pull on over your head and wear on the top half of your body (casaco de lã)
2 a soft cotton or wool cloth used for making clothes ☐ *a black dress in soft jersey* (tecido)

Jesus /ˈdʒiːzəs/ or **Jesus Christ** /ˌdʒiːzəs ˈkraɪst/ NOUN the man who Christians believe to be the son of God and on whose teachings Christianity is based (Jesus Cristo)

jet /dʒet/ ▶ NOUN [plural **jets**]
1 a fast plane with powerful engines ☐ *a passenger jet* (avião a jato)
2 a strong fast flow of liquid or gas forced through a small hole ☐ *The printer releases jets of coloured ink.* (jato)
▶ VERB [**jets, jetting, jetted**] to fly somewhere ☐ *Dan's jetting off to New York this Saturday.* (pilotar)

jet-black /ˌdʒetˈblæk/ ADJECTIVE very dark black ☐ *jet-black hair* (preto intenso)

jet lag /ˈdʒet ˌlæɡ/ NOUN, NO PLURAL a tired feeling that you get after a long journey by plane to a place where the time is different (fadiga de viagem)

Jet Ski /ˈdʒet ˌskiː/ NOUN [plural **Jet Skis**] a small vehicle like a motorcycle for one or two people to ride on water. A trademark. (jet ski)
• **jet-skiing** /ˈdʒetˌskiːɪŋ/ NOUN, NO PLURAL the sport of riding on jet skis (pilotar jet ski)

jetty /ˈdʒetɪ/ NOUN [plural **jetties**] a wooden structure at the edge of a lake or the sea where small boats can stop (cais)

Jew /dʒuː/ NOUN [plural **Jews**] someone whose religion is Judaism or whose family originally came from the ancient Hebrew people of Israel (judeu)

jewel /ˈdʒuːəl/ NOUN [plural **jewels**] a valuable stone, used to make jewellery ☐ *a ring set with precious jewels* (pedra preciosa)
• **jeweler** /ˈdʒuːələ(r)/ NOUN [plural **jewelers**] the US spelling of **jeweller** (joalheiro)
• **jeweller** /ˈdʒuːələ(r)/ NOUN [plural **jewellers**] someone whose job is making or selling jewellery (joalheiro)
• **jewellery** /ˈdʒuːəlrɪ/ NOUN, NO PLURAL things that you wear to decorate your body and clothes, often made of metal and valuable stones ☐ *She wears a lot of gold jewellery.* (joias) ☐ *a beautiful piece of jewellery* (peça de joias)
• **jewelry** /ˈdʒuːəlrɪ/ NOUN, NO PLURAL the US spelling of **jewellery**

job

Jewish /ˈdʒuːɪʃ/ ADJECTIVE to do with Jews or Judaism ☐ *a Jewish religious festival* ☐ *Jewish history* (judaico)

jibe /dʒaɪb/ NOUN [plural **jibes**] a rude or insulting remark ☐ *I'm sick of her jibes about my age.* (zombaria)

jig /dʒɪɡ/ NOUN [plural **jigs**] a lively dance in which people jump about ☐ *an Irish jig* (jiga)

jiggle /ˈdʒɪɡəl/ VERB [**jiggles, jiggling, jiggled**] to quickly move from side to side, or up and down many times, or to make something do this ☐ *I tried jiggling the key in the lock.* (ziguezaguear)

jigsaw /ˈdʒɪɡsɔː/ NOUN [plural **jigsaws**] a picture cut up into a lot of pieces that you have to fit together again (quebra-cabeça) ☐ *The children were doing a jigsaw on the floor* (montando um quebra-cabeça)

jingle /ˈdʒɪŋɡəl/ ▶ VERB [**jingles, jingling, jingled**] to make the ringing sound of light pieces of metal hitting against each other ☐ *Bells were jingling in the background.* (tilintar)
▶ NOUN [plural **jingles**]
1 a short song used to advertise a product on the television or radio (anúncio cantarolado)
2 a ringing sound made when light pieces of metal hit against each other ☐ *She heard the jingle of keys as he walked up the path.* (tilintar)

jinx /dʒɪŋks/ NOUN [plural **jinxes**] bad luck, or a person or thing that brings bad luck (azarado)
• **jinxed** /dʒɪŋkst/ ADJECTIVE having bad luck and not able to stop it ☐ *I was beginning to think the whole project was jinxed.* (amaldiçoado)

jittery /ˈdʒɪtərɪ/ ADJECTIVE nervous ☐ *Katie was very jittery before her driving test.* (tenso, nervoso)

job /dʒɒb/ NOUN [plural **jobs**]
1 the work someone does regularly for money (emprego) ☐ *He needs to get a job* (conseguir um emprego) ☐ *They offered me a job in the shop.* (me ofereceram um emprego) ☐ *He lost his job because of the illness.* (perdeu o emprego) ☐ + *as She got a job as a chef.* ☐ *a part-time/full-time job* (emprego de meio período/período integral)
2 a piece of work ☐ *There are plenty of jobs to do about the house.* (trabalho)
3 a good/bad, etc. job the standard of work someone has done ☐ *You've made a good job of that painting.* ☐ *The builders did a great job.* (bom trabalho/mau trabalho etc.)
4 something that is your responsibility ☐ *It's my job to make sure there's enough food.* (dever, responsabilidade)
5 have a job an informal phrase meaning to find something difficult ☐ *I had a job finding her house.* (ter trabalho, ter dificuldade)

> If you want to ask someone what type of job they do, the usual question is *What do you do?* Or *What do you do for a living?* People do not usually ask '*What is your job?*'

jobshare

⇨ go to **it's a good job**

- **jobless** /ˈdʒɒblɪs/ ▶ ADJECTIVE not having a job, or to do with people who do not have jobs □ *The jobless rate has fallen.* (desempregado)
  ▶ PLURAL NOUN **the jobless** people who do not have a job (os desempregados)

jobshare /ˈdʒɒbʃeə(r)/ VERB [jobshares, jobsharing, jobshared] to divide the duties and pay of one job between two people who work at different times □ *I've jobshared with Anna for 5 years now.* (dividir o turno de trabalho)

- **jobsharing** /ˈdʒɒbʃeərɪŋ/ NOUN, NO PLURAL when two or more people jobshare (divisão do turno de trabalho)

jockey /ˈdʒɒki/ NOUN [plural jockeys] someone who rides a horse in races □ *a champion jockey* (jóquei)

jocular /ˈdʒɒkjʊlə(r)/ ADJECTIVE intended to be funny □ *a jocular remark* (jocoso, cômico)

jodhpurs /ˈdʒɒdpəz/ PLURAL NOUN trousers that you wear for riding a horse (culote)

jog /dʒɒɡ/ ▶ VERB [jogs, jogging, jogged]
1 to run slowly, especially for exercise □ *She jogs around the park every morning.* (praticar cooper, correr)
2 to push or knock something gently by mistake □ *You jogged my elbow and made me spill my tea!* (empurrar)
- IDIOM **jog someone's memory** to make someone remember something □ *Police reconstructions are designed to jog people's memories about crimes.* (refrescar a memória de alguém)
  ▶ NOUN [plural jogs] a slow run for exercise □ *They've gone for a jog along the beach.* (cooper, corrida leve)
- **jogger** /ˈdʒɒɡə(r)/ NOUN [plural joggers] someone who jogs for exercise (corredor)
- **jogging** /ˈdʒɒɡɪŋ/ NOUN, NO PLURAL running slowly for exercise (cooper, corrida)

join /dʒɔɪn/ VERB [joins, joining, joined]
1 to become a member of a group or organization □ *I've joined a rowing club.* □ *He joined the army last year.* □ *I joined the company in 1999.* (associar-se a)
2 to connect things together □ *+ to You have to join the metal part to the wood.* (ligar)
3 to come together at a particular point □ *The track joins the main road just around this corner.* (juntar-se a)
4 to come together with other people □ *Please welcome Jill Smith, who joins us from London.* □ *Would you like to join us for lunch?* (juntar-se a)
5 **join hands** to hold someone's hand with your hand (dar as mãos)
- IDIOM **join forces with someone** to work together with someone to achieve something □ *Our school joined forces with the girls' school to put on a play.* (trabalhar em conjunto com alguém)

jostle

- PHRASAL VERB **join in** to take part in an activity with other people □ *He didn't join in with the singing.* (participar) NOUN [plural joins] a place where two things are joined together (junta)

joint /dʒɔɪnt/ ▶ NOUN [plural joints]
1 a place in your body where two bones meet □ *painful hip joints* (articulação)
2 a large piece of meat that is cooked whole □ *a joint of beef* (carne com osso)
3 a place where two or more things join □ *Water was leaking from a joint in the pipe.* (junta)
▶ ADJECTIVE done or owned together (conjunto)
🔳 *The project was a joint effort between Tom and Sue.* (esforço conjunto) 🔳 *Some married couples have a joint account.* (conta conjunta)
- **jointly** /ˈdʒɔɪntli/ ADVERB together □ *They're applying jointly for a mortgage.* (juntos, em conjunto)

joke /dʒəʊk/ ▶ NOUN [plural jokes]
1 something that someone says or does to make people laugh (piada, brincadeira) 🔳 *Matt is always telling jokes.* (contando piadas)
2 something that you cannot respect or be serious about because it is so bad □ *The whole company has become a bit of a joke.* (piada)
- IDIOMS **be no joke** to be difficult and to need a lot of work or effort □ *It's no joke managing a team that size.* (ser sério) **go beyond a joke** if a bad situation goes beyond a joke, it becomes very serious (tornar-se sério)
  ▶ VERB [jokes, joking, joked]
1 to make a joke □ *The kids were laughing and joking about him missing the goal.* (caçoar)
2 **Just/Only joking!** something you say meaning that what you have just said is not true and was intended to be funny □ *There's a big rip in your trousers. Only joking!* (É brincadeira!)
3 **You're joking!** something you say when someone says something extremely surprising □ *'She's only twenty.' 'You're joking! I thought she was nearer forty!'* (Você está brincando!)
- **joker** /ˈdʒəʊkə(r)/ NOUN [plural jokers]
1 someone who likes telling jokes or making people laugh (brincalhão, palhaço)
2 one of two cards in a set of playing cards that can be used as any card in some games (curinga)

jolly /ˈdʒɒli/ ADJECTIVE [jollier, jolliest] happy □ *a man with a jolly face* (jovial)

jolt /dʒəʊlt/ ▶ NOUN [plural jolts]
1 a sudden, forceful movement □ *The train stopped with a jolt.* (sacudida)
2 an unpleasant shock □ *The news gave Liama bit of a jolt.* (susto)
▶ VERB [jolts, jolting, jolted] to make a sudden, forceful movement □ *The roller coaster jolted to a stop.* (sacudir)

jostle /ˈdʒɒsəl/ VERB [jostles, jostling, jostled] to push roughly against someone in a crowd □ *The* *prime minister was jostled by an angry mob.* (empurrar, acotovelar)

jot /dʒɒt/
- PHRASAL VERB [jots, jotting, jotted] **jot something down** to write a small amount quickly □ *He quickly jotted down the car number plate.* (anotar algo)

joule /dʒuːl/ NOUN [plural **joules**] a unit of measurement of work or energy. A physics word. (joule)

journal /ˈdʒɜːnəl/ NOUN [plural **journals**]
1 a magazine about a particular subject □ *He subscribes to several political journals.* (revista)
2 a book in which someone writes what they have done each day (diário)

- **journalism** /ˈdʒɜːnəlɪzəm/ NOUN, NO PLURAL the work of writing articles for newspapers, magazines, television or radio □ *a career in journalism* (jornalismo)

- **journalist** /ˈdʒɜːnəlɪst/ NOUN [plural **journalists**] someone who works in journalism (jornalista)

journey /ˈdʒɜːni/ NOUN [plural **journeys**] when you travel from one place to another, especially a long distance □ *He has a two-hour journey to work each day.* □ *The train journey was very pleasant.* (viagem)

> Note that when you visit a place and come back again, you usually call this a trip and not a journey: □ *Dan has just come back from a trip to Paris.*

jovial /ˈdʒəʊviəl/ ADJECTIVE happy and friendly □ *David was in a very jovial mood.* (alegre, contente)

joy /dʒɔɪ/ NOUN [plural **joys**]
1 a feeling of being very happy □ *She finally experienced the joy of holding her child.* (alegria)
2 something that makes you very happy □ *The new model is a joy to drive.* (alegria)

joyful /ˈdʒɔɪfʊl/ or **joyous** /ˈdʒɔɪəs/ ADJECTIVE very happy □ *the joyful occasion of their wedding* (alegre)

joypad /ˈdʒɔɪpæd/ NOUN [plural **joypads**] the thing with buttons on that you hold in your hand and press when you play a computer game (controle de video game)

joyride /ˈdʒɔɪraɪd/ NOUN [plural **joyrides**] a fast drive for pleasure in a stolen car (dar um passeio em um carro roubado)

- **joyrider** /ˈdʒɔɪraɪdə(r)/ NOUN [plural **joyriders**] someone who steals a car and drives it for pleasure (ladrão que rouba carros para dar um passeio)

- **joyriding** /ˈdʒɔɪraɪdɪŋ/ NOUN, NO PLURAL the crime of stealing a car and driving it fast for pleasure (roubo de carros para passeios)

joystick /ˈdʒɔɪstɪk/ NOUN [plural **joysticks**] a vertical handle used to control movement in an aircraft or used when playing a computer game (alavanca de controle de avião ou *video game*)

JP /ˌdʒeɪˈpiː/ ABBREVIATION Justice of the Peace; a judge in a local law court (abreviação de Justiça da Paz)

JPEG /ˈdʒeɪpeɡ/ NOUN [plural **JPEGs**] a type of computer file that contains pictures. A computing word. (jpeg)

Jr ABBREVIATION Junior; used after someone's name to Show they are the younger of two men in a family with the same name □ *John Willis Jr* (abreviação de júnior)

jubilant /ˈdʒuːbɪlənt/ ADJECTIVE very happy, usually because of achieving a success □ *Jubilant supporters surrounded their team.* (jubiloso)

- **jubilation** /ˌdʒuːbɪˈleɪʃən/ NOUN, NO PLURAL great happiness because of achieving a success (júbilo)

jubilee /ˈdʒuːbɪliː/ NOUN [plural **jubilees**] a celebration of an important event that happened on a particular day many years ago □ *The Queen celebrated her golden jubilee in 2002.* (jubileu)

Judaism /ˈdʒuːdeɪɪzəm/ NOUN, NO PLURAL the Jewish religion which is based on the Old Testament of the Bible (judaísmo)

judge /dʒʌdʒ/ ▶ VERB [**judges, judging, judged**]
1 to form an opinion about someone or something □ + **on** *I tend to judge books on their story rather than their use of language.* □ + **by** *It's wrong to judge people by what clothes they wear.* □ *They judged it necessary to hire a bodyguard.* □ *The event was judged a success.* (julgar)
2 to decide who or what is the winner of a competition □ *I was asked to judge the jam making competition.* (julgar)
3 to try to guess the amount, size, etc. of something □ *I failed to judge the distance correctly and drove into a wall.* (calcular)
4 to have a bad opinion of a person or their behaviour □ *I try not to judge other people.* (julgar)
▶ NOUN [plural **judges**]
1 someone who is in charge of a trial in court and decides what punishments should be given (juiz)
2 someone who judges a competition (árbitro, jurado)
3 **a good/bad, etc. judge of something** someone who is good/bad, etc. at forming the correct opinion of something □ *He is a poor judge of character.* (bom/mau etc. julgador de algo)

- **judgement** or **judgment** /ˈdʒʌdʒmənt/ NOUN [plural **judgements** or **judgments**]
1 the ability to make good decisions or form correct opinions (discernimento) □ *When it comes to education, I trust her judgement.* (confio no discernimento) □ *I can't tell you exactly how much salt to add – just use your judgement.* (use discernimento)
2 an opinion about someone or something (opinião) □ *In my judgement, it wouldn't be a very sensible thing to do.* (na minha opinião)

judicial

You will have to make a judgement *about whether or not to trust her.* (**formar uma opinião**) **3** the decision made by a judge in a court (**julgamento**) ▣ *He is due to* pass judgment *on Wednesday.* (**julgar**)

• **judgemental** *or* **judgmental** /dʒʌdʒˈmentəl/ ADJECTIVE quick to form a bad opinion of a person or someone's behaviour (**crítico**)

judicial /dʒuːˈdɪʃəl/ ADJECTIVE to do with judges or a court of law ▢ *a judicial review* (**judicial**)

judiciary /dʒuːˈdɪʃəri/ NOUN [plural **judiciaries**] **the judiciary** the part of a country's government that is responsible for its legal system and is made up of all its judges (**o Judiciário**)

judicious /dʒuːˈdɪʃəs/ ADJECTIVE sensible and showing good judgment ▢ *Many dishes are improved by a judicious use of spices.* (**judicioso**)

judo /ˈdʒuːdəʊ/ NOUN, NO PLURAL a sport from Japan in which two people fight and try to throw each other to the ground (**judô**)

jug /dʒʌg/ NOUN [plural **jugs**] a container with a handle used for pouring liquids ▢ *a milk jug* ▢ *a jug of cream* (**jarra**)

juggernaut /ˈdʒʌgənɔːt/ NOUN [plural **juggernauts**] a very long truck (**carreta pesada**)

juggle /ˈdʒʌgəl/ VERB [**juggles, juggling, juggled**] **1** to keep several balls, etc. in the air by repeatedly throwing them up and catching them (**fazer malabarismo**)
2 to deal with several jobs or activities at the same time ▢ *A lot of women juggle a job with looking after their home and their family.* (**conciliar família e trabalho**)

• **juggler** /ˈdʒʌglə(r)/ NOUN [plural **jugglers**] someone who juggles to entertain people (**malabarista**)

juice /dʒuːs/ NOUN [plural **juices**]
1 the liquid in fruit or vegetables, often used as a drink ▢ *a glass of orange juice* (**suco**)
2 the liquid that comes out of a piece of meat while it is being cooked (**caldo**)

• **juicy** /ˈdʒuːsi/ ADJECTIVE [**juicier, juiciest**]
1 full of juice ▢ *a nice juicy peach* (**suculento**)
2 describes information about another person's private life that is interesting and slightly shocking ▢ *a juicy bit of gossip* (**interessante, suculento**)

jukebox /ˈdʒuːkbɒks/ NOUN [plural **jukeboxes**] a machine that plays music when you put money in it and press buttons (**jukebox, fonógrafo**)

July /dʒuːˈlaɪ/ NOUN the seventh month of the year, after June and before August ▢ *Clara will be 11 in July.* (**julho**)

jumble /ˈdʒʌmbəl/ ▶ VERB [**jumbles, jumbling, jumbled**] to mix things up so that they are untidy ▢ *His clothes are all jumbled up in his drawers.* (**misturar**)

jumpy

▶ NOUN, NO PLURAL a lot of things that have been mixed up in an untidy way ▢ *It's hard to find anything in the jumble on Pam's desk.* (**bagunça**)

jumble sale /ˈdʒʌmbəl ˌseɪl/ NOUN [plural **jumble sales**] a sale where old things or things you do not want are sold to get money for an organization (**bazar**)

jumbo /ˈdʒʌmbəʊ/ ▶ ADJECTIVE very big ▢ *a jumbo crossword* (**tamanho gigante**)
▶ NOUN [plural **jumbos**] a jumbo jet (**avião gigante, Boeing**)

jumbo jet /ˌdʒʌmbəʊ ˈdʒet/ NOUN [plural **jumbo jets**] a very big plane that can carry hundreds of passengers (**avião gigante, Boeing**)

jump /dʒʌmp/ ▶ VERB [**jumps, jumping, jumped**]
1 to push yourself off the ground or other surface with your legs ▢ *We jumped up and down in excitement.* ▢ **+ over** *The dog jumped over the wall.* ▢ *He jumped down from the tree.* (**pular, saltar**)
2 to go over something by pushing yourself into the air with your legs ▢ *The horse jumped the fence.* (**saltar**)
3 to move or go somewhere quickly ▢ *As soon as I heard the news, I jumped on a train to Scotland.* ▢ *He jumped to his feet when she came in.* (**pular**)
4 to increase suddenly in amount or value ▢ *Shares jumped more than 20%.* ▢ *Property prices have jumped dramatically.* (**subir, saltar**)
5 to make a movement because you are suddenly afraid (**pular**) ▣ *The noise of the bell* made *me* jump. (**me fez pular**)
6 jump the queue to go to the front of a queue (= line of people waiting) (**furar a fila**)

♦ IDIOM **jump the gun** to start doing something too soon ▢ *Asking her to marry you after 3 weeks was jumping the gun a bit, wasn't it?* (**colocar a carroça na frente dos bois**)

♦ PHRASAL VERB **jump at something** to accept an opportunity in a very eager way (**agarrar uma oportunidade com unhas e dentes**) ▣ *He* jumped at the chance *to work in Africa.* (**agarrou a oportunidade**)
▶ NOUN [plural **jumps**]
1 when you push yourself off the ground with your legs ▢ *Do three more jumps.* (**pulo**)
2 something to be jumped over, or a distance that must be jumped (**salto**)
3 a sudden increase ▢ **+ in** *There has been a jump in the unemployment numbers.* (**alta**)

jumper /ˈdʒʌmpə(r)/ NOUN [plural **jumpers**] a warm piece of clothing with sleeves that you pull on over your head and wear on the top half of your body (**blusão**)

jumpy /ˈdʒʌmpi/ ADJECTIVE [**jumpier, jumpiest**] an informal word for nervous ▢ *Adam was getting jumpy about his exam results.* (**nervoso**)

junction /'dʒʌŋkʃən/ NOUN [plural **junctions**] a place where roads or railway lines meet and cross □ *Turn right at the junction ahead.* (**entroncamento**)

juncture /'dʒʌŋktʃə(r)/ NOUN [plural **junctures**] a particular point in a series of events. A formal word. □ *We can't possibly give up at this juncture.* (**ponto, momento, conjuntura**)

June /dʒuːn/ NOUN the sixth month of the year, after May and before July □ *We're moving house in June.* (**junho**)

jungle /'dʒʌŋgəl/ NOUN [plural **jungles**] a thick forest in a hot country □ *the Peruvian jungle* (**selva**)

junior /'dʒuːniə(r)/ ▶ ADJECTIVE
1 having a lower position in an organization □ *junior staff* □ *She's a junior minister at the Foreign Office.* (**subalterno, hierarquicamente inferior**)
2 of or for younger people □ *junior members of the tennis club* □ *junior classes* (**júnior, mais novo**)
▶ NOUN [plural **juniors**]
1 be 5, 10 etc. years someone's junior to be 5/10 etc. years younger than someone □ *His brother is 3 years his junior.* (**ser 5, 10 etc. anos mais novo do que alguém**)
2 someone who has a low position in an organization □ *an office junior* (**subalterno**)
3 a child in a junior school (**aluno de Ensino Fundamental**)

junior high school /,dʒuːniə haɪ 'skuːl/ NOUN [plural **junior high schools**] a school in the US for young people between 12 and 14 years old (**escola de Ensino Fundamental II**)

junior school /'dʒuːniə ,skuːl/ NOUN [plural **junior schools**] a school in Britain for children between 7 and 11 years old (**escola de Ensino Fundamental I**)

junk /dʒʌŋk/ NOUN, NO PLURAL old things with little use or value □ *Most of this is junk and we can just get rid of it.* (**ferro-velho, traste**)

junk food /'dʒʌŋk ,fuːd/ NOUN, NO PLURAL food that is not good for your health but that you can eat or prepare quickly (**comida sem valor nutritivo, fast-food**)

junk mail /'dʒʌŋk ,meɪl/ NOUN, NO PLURAL advertisements that are sent to you by post although you did not ask for them (**correspondências de publicidade não solicitadas**)

jurisdiction /,dʒʊərɪs'dɪkʃən/ NOUN, NO PLURAL the power of an official organization to make legal decisions □ *Libraries come under the jurisdiction of the local authority.* (**jurisdição**)

juror /'dʒʊərə(r)/ NOUN [plural **jurors**] one of the members of a jury (**jurado**)

• **jury** /'dʒʊəri/ NOUN [plural **juries**]
1 a group of people in a court of law who listen to the facts and decide whether someone is guilty of a crime or not (**júri**)
2 a group of people who decide who will win a competition (**júri**)

♦ IDIOM **the jury is (still) out** used for saying that no one has yet decided for sure whether something is a good thing or not □ *The jury is still out on whether these vitamins help prevent the disease.* (**ainda não é certo, ainda não foi decidido**)

just /dʒʌst/ ▶ ADVERB
1 at this time, or at a particular time in the past □ *I'm just getting dressed.* □ *We were just sitting down to dinner.* (**justamente**) 🔁 *Just then, a man came in.* (**justamente então**) 🔁 *I can't talk to you just now.* (**neste momento, agora mesmo**)
2 a very short time ago □ *I've just finished work.* □ *The clock's just struck five.* (**há pouco**)
3 only □ *I'll just have a sandwich.* □ *It was just a joke.* □ *I just want to go home.* (**só, apenas**)
4 almost not (**apenas**) 🔁 *I could only just see him.* (**apenas**) □ *We just managed to swim to the shore.* □ *She was just ahead of me.*
5 used to emphasize what you are saying □ *I was just devastated by the news.* □ *A cold drink was just what I needed.* (**simplesmente**)
6 just about almost □ *I've just about finished here.* (**quase**)
7 be just about to do something to be going to do something very soon □ *I was just about to phone you.* (**estar para fazer algo**)
8 just as at the same time as □ *Just as we got there, the fire alarm went off.* (**exatamente**)
▶ ADJECTIVE
1 fair □ *a just decision* (**justo**)
2 deserved □ *a just reward* (**justo**)

justice /'dʒʌstɪs/ NOUN [plural **justices**]
1 *no plural* fair treatment of people by the law □ *The group is fighting for justice for all.* (**justiça**)
2 *no plural* the quality of being fair when dealing with people and their problems (**justiça**)
3 *no plural* the system of laws which judges and punishes people □ *the criminal justice system* (**justiça**)
4 a US word for **judge** (**juiz**)

justifiable /'dʒʌstɪ,faɪəbəl/ ADJECTIVE acceptable because of having a good reason □ *His reaction was completely justifiable in the circumstances.* (**justificável**)

• **justifiably** /'dʒʌstɪ,faɪəbli/ ADVERB in a justifiable way □ *She was justifiably annoyed.* (**justificadamente**)

• **justification** /,dʒʌstɪfɪ'keɪʃən/ NOUN [plural **justifications**] a good reason for doing something □ *There is no justification for that sort of behaviour.* (**justificativa**)

• **justify** /'dʒʌstɪfaɪ/ VERB [**justifies, justifying, justified**] to be a good reason for something or to give a good reason for something □ *I couldn't justify spending all that money on myself.* (**justificar**)

justly /'dʒʌstli/ ADVERB
1 in a way that is right or reasonable □ *She is justly proud of her son's achievements.* (**com razão**)

2 fairly □ *The headmaster dealt with the matter justly in my opinion.* (**justamente**)

jut /dʒʌt/ VERB [**juts, jutting, jutted**] to stick out from the surrounding surface or edge □ *The peninsula juts out into the Irish Sea.* (**sobressair**)

juvenile /'dʒu:vənaɪl/ ▶ ADJECTIVE
1 for or to do with young people □ *a juvenile court* (**juvenil**)
2 behaving in a silly way like a child □ *a juvenile sense of humour* (**pueril**)
▶ NOUN [*plural* **juveniles**] a young person

juvenile delinquent /ˌdʒu:vənaɪl dɪˈlɪŋkwənt/ NOUN [plural **juvenile delinquents**] a young person who commits a crime (**delinquente juvenil**)

juxtapose /ˌdʒʌkstəˈpəʊz/ VERB [**juxtaposes, juxtaposing, juxtaposed**] to put two people or things together, often to show how different they are. A formal word. (**justapor**)

• **juxtaposition** /ˌdʒʌkstəpəˈzɪʃən/ NOUN [*plural* **juxtapositions**] when people or things are juxtaposed. A formal word. □ *The artist uses fascinating juxtapositions of colours and textures.* (**justaposição**)

K*k*

K¹ *or* **k** /keɪ/ the 11th letter of the alphabet (a décima primeira letra do alfabeto)

K² /keɪ/ ABBREVIATION
1 one thousand □ *She earns £30K a year.* (mil)
2 kilobyte (kilobyte)

kaleidoscope /kə'laɪdəskəʊp/ NOUN [plural kaleidoscopes] a tube that you look into, with small pieces of coloured glass that make different patterns when you turn the tube (caleidoscópio)

kangaroo /ˌkæŋgə'ru:/ NOUN [plural kangaroos] an Australian animal that moves by jumping, and carries its baby in a pouch (= a pocket at the front of its body) (canguru)

karaoke /ˌkærɪ'əʊkɪ/ NOUN, NO PLURAL a type of entertainment in which members of the audience sing popular songs while recorded music is played (caraoquê)

karate /kə'rɑ:tɪ/ NOUN, NO PLURAL a type of Japanese fighting in which you use your hands and feet (caratê)

kayak /'kaɪæk/ NOUN [plural kayaks] a type of long narrow boat for one person that you move using a paddle (= long piece of wood) with two flat ends (caiaque)

Kb *or* **KB** /ˌkeɪ'bi:/ ABBREVIATION **kilobyte** (kilobyte)

kebab /kɪ'bæb/ NOUN [plural kebabs] pieces of meat cooked on a long thin stick (espetinho)

keel /ki:l/ NOUN [plural keels] a long piece of wood or metal attached under a ship, used for balancing it (quilha)

♦ IDIOM **on an even keel** continuing calmly, without problems or sudden changes □ *The company has had a difficult few months but we're back on an even keel now.* (calmo, calmamente)

♦ PHRASAL VERB [keels, keeling, keeled] **keel over** to fall because you are ill or tired □ *He suddenly just keeled over.* (desmaiar)

keen /ki:n/ ADJECTIVE [keener, keenest]

1 interested in or enjoying a particular activity very much □ *Jim's a keen swimmer.* □ + on *She's very keen on riding.* (entusiasmado) 🔲 *She has a keen interest in art.* (interesse entusiasmado)
2 wanting to do something □ + to do something *Everyone seemed very keen to help.* (com vontade)
3 a keen sense of smell or hearing is a very good sense of smell or hearing □ *Mice have a keen sense of smell.* (aguçado)

• **keenly** /'ki:nlɪ/ ADVERB strongly □ *The government is keenly aware of the problem.* (profundamente)
• **keenness** /'ki:nnɪs/ NOUN, NO PLURAL when someone is keen (entusiasmo)

keep /ki:p/ ▶ VERB [keeps, keeping, kept]

1 to make someone or something stay in a particular state □ *Keep the door closed.* □ *The noise kept me awake.* □ *Keep still!* □ *Keep your mouth shut!* (permanecer)
2 to prevent someone or something going to a particular place □ *Keep the children away from the fire.* □ *I tried to keep the sun off my face.* □ *A high fence kept out strangers.* (manter)
3 **keep doing something** to continue to do something, or to do something repeatedly □ *It's hard to keep going when you're so tired.* □ *I keep forgetting to lock the door.* (continuar, prosseguir)
4 to continue to have or own something □ *You can keep the book.* □ *The company has promised that they will keep their jobs.* (conservar)
5 to put something in a particular place when you are not using it □ *I keep my diary in a drawer.* (guardar) 🔲 *This ring is valuable – make sure you keep it in a safe place.* (mantenha em lugar seguro)
6 to make someone stay in a particular place □ *They're keeping him in hospital for a few more days.* □ *She was kept in after school.* (reter, manter)
7 to have a written record of something (escrever, manter) 🔲 to *keep notes/records* (escrever ou manter notas/registros) □ *I kept a diary for years.*
8 **keep a promise** to do what you have promised to do (manter uma promessa)
9 **keep a secret** to not tell anyone a secret (guardar um segredo)

⇨ go to **keep an eye on someone/something, keep an eye out for someone/something, keep your eyes open, keep your ears open, keep a straight face, keep your hair on**

♦ PHRASAL VERB **keep something down**
1 to make an amount or level of something stay low □ *We have managed to keep our prices down.* (manter algo em um nível baixo)
2 to eat something without vomiting □ *He hasn't kept anything down today.* (ficar sem vomitar)

keep on doing something to continue to do something, or to do something repeatedly □ *He*

ignored the cries and kept on walking. (**continuar fazendo algo**) □ *They keep on waking me up.*
keep to something
1 to stay in an area □ *Keep to the marked path.* (**permanecer**) □ to do what you have said you will do □ *We decided to keep to our original plan.* (**seguir algo**) **keep up**
1 to move at the same speed as someone else □ *She walks so fast I can hardly keep up.* (**acompanhar**)
2 to make the same amount of progress as someone or something else □ *Their rivals invested in new technology, and they failed to keep up.* (**acompanhar**)
3 to know and understand something □ *We need to keep up with all the latest research.* (**atualizar-se**) **keep up something** to continue to do something □ *I've been keeping up my exercise programme.* (**continuar, prosseguir**)
▶ NOUN, NO PLURAL the money that you need in order to live (**sustento**) 🔲 *I earn my keep by doing housework.* (**tiro meu sustento**)

• **keeper** /ˈkiːpə(r)/ NOUN [*plural* **keepers**] a person who looks after something, especially animals in a zoo (**zelador, guarda**)

• **keeping** /ˈkiːpɪŋ/ NOUN, NO PLURAL
1 in keeping with something in the same style as something, and suitable to be with or near it □ *The new building is not in keeping with its surroundings.* (**em harmonia com algo**)
2 in someone's keeping being kept by someone (**sob os cuidados de alguém**)

kennel /ˈkenəl/ NOUN [*plural* **kennels**] a small shelter for a dog (**casinha de cachorro**)

kept /kept/ PAST TENSE AND PAST PARTICIPLE OF **keep** (**ver keep**)

kerb /kɜːb/ NOUN [*plural* **kerbs**] the edge of a pavement (= the path along the side of a road) (**meio-fio**)

kernel /ˈkɜːnəl/ NOUN [*plural* **kernels**] the soft part in the shell of a nut or inside the stone of a fruit (**semente de noz ou caroço**)

kerosene *or* **kerosine** /ˈkerəsiːn/ NOUN, NO PLURAL the US word for **paraffin** (**querosene**)

ketchup /ˈketʃəp/ NOUN, NO PLURAL a thick red sauce made from tomatoes (**ketchup**)

kettle /ˈketəl/ NOUN [*plural* **kettles**] a container with a lid and a handle, used for boiling water (**chaleira**) 🔲 *I've put the kettle on* (= I am heating water in a kettle) *for a cup of tea* (**levei a chaleira ao fogo**)

kettledrum /ˈketəldrʌm/ NOUN [*plural* **kettledrums**] a large metal drum in the shape of a bowl (**tímpano, tipo de tambor**)

key /kiː/ ▶ NOUN [*plural* **keys**]
1 a small metal object used for locking something like a door or window, or for starting the engine of a vehicle (**chave**) 🔲 *I switched the light off and turned the key in the lock.* (**girei a chave**) 🔲 *Have you seen my car keys?* (**chaves do carro**) 🔲 *a bunch of keys* (**molho de chaves**)
2 a button on a computer keyboard or a telephone (**tecla**) 🔲 *Use the arrow keys to move from one image to the next.* (**teclas de seta**) □ *Press any key to continue.*
3 the main thing that helps you to achieve something □ + *to Confidence is the key to success in this business.* (**chave**)
4 one of the white or black parts you press on a piano or a similar instrument to make a sound (**tecla**)
5 a set of musical notes □ + *of This piece is played in the key of D minor.* (**clave**)
6 a list of signs with their meanings □ *The key is printed on the back of the map.* (**legenda**)
7 a list of answers to questions in an exercise or test (**solução, resposta**)
▶ ADJECTIVE most important (**essencial, muito importante**) 🔲 *He played a key role in the campaign* (**papel essencial**) 🔲 *Dean is one of the team's key players.* (**jogadores mais importantes**) □ + *to Their support is key to the success of the project.*
▶ VERB [**keys, keying, keyed**] to put data into a computer or other piece of electronic equipment using a keyboard □ + *in Please key in your personal number.* (**digitar, teclar**)

keyboard /ˈkiːbɔːd/ NOUN [*plural* **keyboards**]
1 a piece of computer equipment with keys (= buttons) on it that you press to put information into the computer (**teclado**)
2 the set of keys on a musical instrument such as a piano □ *a piano keyboard* (**teclado**)
3 an electronic musical instrument that is similar to a piano (**teclado**)

• **keyboarder** /ˈkiːbɔːdə(r)/ NOUN [*plural* **keyboarders**] someone whose job is to enter information on a computer (**teclado**)

keyhole /ˈkiːhəʊl/ NOUN [*plural* **keyholes**] the part of a lock that you put a key into (**buraco de fechadura**)

keypad /ˈkiːpæd/ NOUN [*plural* **keypads**] a small keyboard on a telephone, for example (**teclado numérico**)

key ring /ˈkiː rɪŋ/ NOUN [*plural* **key rings**] a metal ring for keeping keys on (**chaveiro**)

kg /ˌkerˈdʒiː/ ABBREVIATION **kilogram** or **kilograms** (**abreviação de quilograma**)

khaki /ˈkɑːkɪ/ ▶ ADJECTIVE having a green-brown colour □ *a khaki uniform* (**cáqui**)
▶ NOUN, NO PLURAL a green-brown colour (**cáqui**)

kHz ABBREVIATION **kilohertz** (**abreviação de quilo-hertz**)

kick /kɪk/ ▶ VERB [**kicks, kicking, kicked**]
1 to hit someone or something with your foot □ *Jane kicked the ball over the fence.* □ *He kicked me in the leg.* (**dar um pontapé em**)

2 to move your legs quickly and with force ◻ *She was carried, kicking and screaming, to the car.* (chutar)

◆ PHRASAL VERBS **kick in** to start to have an effect ◻ *You'll feel better when the painkillers kick in.* (agir, fazer efeito) **kick (something) off** to start something ◻ *We kicked off the session with a discussion about love.* (iniciar algo) **kick someone out** to make someone leave a place ◻ *He was kicked out of the army for laziness.* (expulsar alguém)

▶ NOUN [*plural* **kicks**]

1 when you kick, or kick something ◻ *I gave him a kick in the shins.* (pontapé, chute)

2 an informal word meaning a feeling of pleasure or excitement (prazer, emoção) 🔲 *He gets a kick out of driving fast.* (tem o prazer em)

kick-off /ˈkɪk ɒf/ NOUN [*plural* **kick-offs**] the start of a football game (pontapé inicial)

kick-start /ˈkɪk stɑːt/ VERB [**kick-starts, kick-starting, kick-started**] to make something start working or start being successful, especially after a less successful period ◻ *That television appearance kick-started her career.* (alavancar)

kid /kɪd/ ▶ NOUN [*plural* **kids**]

1 an informal word meaning child ◻ *Have they got any kids?* ◻ *You can't expect him to look after the baby – he's just a kid.* (garoto)

2 a young goat (cabrito)

▶ VERB [**kids, kidding, kidded**]

1 to say something that is not true, as a joke. An informal word. ◻ *Don't worry; I'm only kidding.* (brincar)

2 kid yourself to try to believe something that is not true ◻ *She says she's happy but I think she's just kidding herself.* (enganar-se)

3 Are you kidding? an informal way of saying that you think something someone has said is not true or not sensible ◻ *'She's 40.' 'Are you kidding? She looks about 60!'* (você está brincando?)

kidnap /ˈkɪdnæp/ VERB [**kidnaps, kidnapping, kidnapped**] to take someone away using force, and to ask their family or the government for something such as money in exchange for their safe return ◻ *The journalist was kidnapped three weeks ago.* (sequestrar, raptar)

• **kidnapper** /ˈkɪdnæpə(r)/ NOUN [*plural* **kidnappers**] a person who kidnaps someone ◻ *The kidnappers have demanded a ransom of £2 million.* (sequestrador, raptor)

• **kidnapping** /ˈkɪdnæpɪŋ/ NOUN [*plural* **kidnappings**] when someone is kidnapped ◻ *There have been several kidnappings in this part of the world recently.* (sequestro, rapto)

kidney /ˈkɪdni/ NOUN [*plural* **kidneys**] one of the two organs in your body that clean your blood and remove waste from it. A biology word. (rim)

kill /kɪl/ VERB [**kills, killing, killed**]

1 to make a person or animal die ◻ *Two people were killed in the crash.* ◻ *The explosion killed six people.* ◻ *He tried to kill himself.* (matar)

2 if part of your body is killing you, it hurts a lot ◻ *My feet are killing me.* (matar)

• **killer** /ˈkɪlə(r)/ NOUN [*plural* **killers**] a person who kills someone ◻ *Police have appealed for more information to help catch the killer.* (assassino, matador)

• **killing** /ˈkɪlɪŋ/ NOUN [*plural* **killings**] when someone is killed ◻ *Police are investigating the killing.* (assassinato, morte)

◆ IDIOM **make a killing** to make a lot of money (ganhar muito dinheiro)

kiln /kɪln/ NOUN [*plural* **kilns**] a large oven for baking clay things such as bricks (forno para fazer tijolos)

kilo /ˈkiːləʊ/ NOUN [*plural* **kilos**] a short way to say and write kilogram (quilo)

kilo- /ˈkɪləʊ/ PREFIX kilo- is added to the beginning of words to mean 'one thousand' ◻ *kilogram* ◻ *kilometre* (quilo-)

kilobyte /ˈkɪləbaɪt/ NOUN [*plural* **kilobytes**] a unit for measuring computer memory or data, equal to 1024 bytes. This is often written Kb. A computing word. (kilobyte)

kilogram or **kilogramme** /ˈkɪləgræm/ NOUN [*plural* **kilograms** or **kilogrammes**] a unit for measuring weight, equal to 1000 grams. This is often written kg. ◻ *Katherine weighs 60 kilograms.* (quilograma)

kilohertz /ˈkɪləhɜːts/ NOUN [*plural* **kilohertz**] a unit for measuring radio waves. This is often written kHz. A physics word. (quilo-hertz)

kilometre /ˈkɪləmiːtə(r), kɪˈlɒmɪtə(r)/ NOUN [*plural* **kilometres**] a unit for measuring distance, equal to 1000 metres. This is often written km. ◻ *We live 20 kilometres from the coast.* (quilômetro)

kilowatt /ˈkɪləwɒt/ NOUN [*plural* **kilowatts**] a unit for measuring electrical power, equal to 1000 watts. This is often shortened to kW. (quilowatt)

kilt /kɪlt/ NOUN [*plural* **kilts**] a traditional Scottish piece of clothing that looks like a skirt and is worn especially by men (*kilt*, saiote escocês masculino)

kimono /kɪˈməʊnəʊ/ NOUN [*plural* **kimonos**] a traditional Japanese piece of clothing that looks like a long coat, and is tied round the waist (quimono)

kin /kɪn/ NOUN, NO PLURAL a formal word that means all your family (família)
⇨ go to **next of kin**

kind /kaɪnd/ ▶ NOUN [*plural* **kinds**]

1 a type of person or thing ◻ + *of What kind of dog have you got?* (espécie, tipo) 🔲 *Encourage*

children to try different kinds of fruit. (**diferentes tipos de**) 🔊 There are all kinds of styles to choose from. (**todos os tipos de**)
2 kind of an informal phrase that means slightly □ It's kind of like Sara's dress. (**de certo modo**)
▶ ADJECTIVE [**kinder, kindest**] behaving in a way that shows you care about people and want to make them happy □ She's the kindest person I know. □ **+ to** You've all been very kind to me. □ **+ of** It was kind of you to help us. □ Thank you for your kind offer. (**gentil**)

kindergarten /ˈkɪndəˌɡɑːtən/ NOUN [plural **kindergartens**]
1 in the UK, a school for children under five (**jardim de infância**)
2 in the US, the first year of school education for children aged five or six (**jardim de infância**)

kind-hearted /ˌkaɪndˈhɑːtɪd/ ADJECTIVE kind towards other people (**bondoso, de bom coração**)

kindly /ˈkaɪndli/ ▶ ADVERB
1 in a kind way □ Charlotte has very kindly offered to help. (**amavelmente**)
2 used for politely asking someone to do something when you are angry □ Would you kindly be quiet! (**por favor**)
3 not take kindly to something to be annoyed by something □ I do not take kindly to being called a liar. (**não gostar de algo**)
▶ ADJECTIVE [**kindlier, kindliest**] an old-fashioned word that means kind □ a kindly old lady (**amável**)

kindness /ˈkaɪndnɪs/ NOUN, NO PLURAL when someone is kind □ What I like most about him is his kindness. (**gentileza**) 🔊 This small act of kindness made a great impression on her. (**ato de gentileza**)

kinetic /kɪˈnetɪk, kaɪˈnetɪk/ ADJECTIVE to do with movement. A physics word. (**cinética**)

king /kɪŋ/ NOUN [plural **kings**]
1 a man who rules a country, being the most important male member of its royal family □ He's the future king of Great Britain. (**rei**)
2 a man who is considered to be the best at a particular thing □ **+ of** Elvis, the king of rock. (**rei**)
3 a playing card with a picture of a king on it (**rei**)
4 in the game of chess, the most important piece that each player has one of and that can move in any direction (**rei**)
• **kingdom** /ˈkɪŋdəm/ NOUN [plural **kingdoms**] a country ruled by a king or queen □ the United Kingdom □ the kingdom of Denmark (**reino**)

kingfisher /ˈkɪŋˌfɪʃə(r)/ NOUN [plural **kingfishers**] a bird that eats fish and has an area of bright blue on it (**martim-pescador**)

king-size /ˈkɪŋˌsaɪz/ or **king-sized** /ˈkɪŋˌsaɪzd/ ADJECTIVE larger than the usual size □ We've bought a king-size bed. (**tamanho grande**)

kink /kɪŋk/ NOUN [plural **kinks**] a curve or twist in something, often something that should be straight □ The water won't flow if there's a kink in the tube. (**dobra, curva**)

kiosk /ˈkiːɒsk/ NOUN [plural **kiosks**] a small shop that sells things such as newspapers, drinks and sweets (**quiosque**)

kipper /ˈkɪpə(r)/ NOUN [plural **kippers**] a herring (= type of fish) that has been treated with smoke (**arenque defumado**)

kiss /kɪs/ ▶ VERB [**kisses, kissing, kissed**] to touch someone with your lips, especially on their mouth or face, to show that you feel love or affection for them (**beijar**) 🔊 He kissed her goodbye and got into the car. (**deu um beijo de despedida**) □ She leaned towards him and kissed his cheek.
▶ NOUN [plural **kisses**] when you kiss someone (**beijo**) 🔊 He gave her a kiss. (**deu um beijo**) □ **+ on** a kiss on the lips

kit /kɪt/ NOUN [plural **kits**]
1 the clothes that you need for a particular activity (**material**) 🔊 I brought my football kit home for washing. (**material de futebol**)
2 a set of tools or equipment that you need for a particular activity □ a first aid kit □ a bicycle repair kit (**material**)
3 a set of parts that you can put together to make something □ I got a model boat kit for my birthday. (**kit**)

kitchen /ˈkɪtʃɪn/ NOUN [plural **kitchens**] a room where you prepare and cook food, and sometimes eat food □ John is in the kitchen. (**cozinha**) 🔊 I sat at the kitchen table and drank my coffee. (**mesa de cozinha**)

kite /kaɪt/ NOUN [plural **kites**] a toy made of a light material with a long string attached to it that you hold while it flies in the air (**pipa**)

kitten /ˈkɪtən/ NOUN [plural **kittens**] a young cat (**gatinho**)

kitty /ˈkɪti/ NOUN [plural **kitties**] an amount of money that is collected by a group of people and used for a particular purpose (**vaquinha**)

kiwi /ˈkiːwiː/ NOUN [plural **kiwis**] a bird from New Zealand that cannot fly (**kiwi**)

kiwi fruit /ˈkiːwiː fruːt/ NOUN [plural **kiwi fruit**] a small fruit with bright green flesh, black seeds and skin with small hairs (**kiwi, quiuí**)

km ABBREVIATION **kilometre** or **kilometres** (**abreviação de quilômetro**)

knack /næk/ NOUN, NO PLURAL a skill □ Gina has a knack for making people do what she wants. (**jeito**) 🔊 They seem to have lost the knack of winning. (**perderam o jeito**)

knead /niːd/ VERB [**kneads, kneading, kneaded**] to press dough (= the soft substance that you cook to make bread) repeatedly with your hands before you cook it (**amassar**)

knee /niː/ NOUN [plural **knees**]
1 the part in the middle of your leg where the leg bends □ *a knee injury* (**joelho**)
2 the part of a pair of trousers that covers your knee (**joelheira**)

kneecap /ˈniːkæp/ NOUN [plural **kneecaps**] the bone at the front of your knee (**rótula**)

kneel /niːl/ VERB [**kneels, kneeling, knelt**] to move into a position in which your knees and lower legs are on the ground, or to be in this position □ + ***down*** *She knelt down beside me and stroked my hair.* □ *He was kneeling by the bed, praying.* (**ajoelhar**)

knelt /nelt/ PAST TENSE AND PAST PARTICIPLE OF **kneel** (*ver* **kneel**)

knew /njuː/ PAST TENSE OF **know** (*ver* **know**)

knickers /ˈnɪkəz/ PLURAL NOUN a piece of underwear for women or girls, which covers the bottom (**calcinha**)

knick-knack /ˈnɪknæk/ NOUN [plural **knick-knacks**] a small decorative object that is usually not expensive (**quinquilharia, enfeite**)

knife /naɪf/ ▶ NOUN [plural **knives**]
1 a tool with a blade and a handle, used especially for cutting food (**faca**) 🔹 *Have we got enough knives and forks?* (**garfos e facas**) 🔹 *a sharp knife* (**faca afiada**)
2 a similar tool with a sharp blade, used as a weapon (**faca**) 🔹 *She was injured in a knife attack.* (**ataque com faca**)
▶ VERB [**knifes, knifing, knifed**] to attack someone using a knife □ *He was knifed in the back.* (**esfaquear**)

knight /naɪt/ NOUN [plural **knights**]
1 in the past, a soldier of a high social class who rode a horse (**cavaleiro**)
2 a man who has been given an honour by a British king or queen that allows him to use the title 'Sir' (**cavaleiro**)
3 in the game of chess, a piece which looks like a horse's head (**cavalo**)
• **knighthood** /ˈnaɪthʊd/ NOUN [plural **knighthoods**] an honour given by a British king or queen that allows a man to use the title 'Sir' (**título de cavaleiro**)

knit /nɪt/ VERB [**knits, knitting, knitted**] to make something, for example a piece of clothing, using two long knitting needles (= pointed metal or wooden sticks) and wool □ *I'm knitting a scarf.* (**tricotar**)
• **knitting** /ˈnɪtɪŋ/ NOUN, NO PLURAL the activity of making things using wool and long needles □ *a knitting pattern* (**trabalho de tricô**)

knives /naɪvz/ PLURAL OF **knife** (*ver* **knife**)

knob /nɒb/ NOUN [plural **knobs**]
1 a round handle on a door or a drawer (**maçaneta, puxador**) 🔹 *a door knob* (**maçaneta da porta**)
2 a round button used for controlling a piece of equipment such as a radio □ *Keep turning the knob until the sound is clear.* (**botão**)
3 a small lump of something □ *a knob of butter* (**calombo, monte**)

knock /nɒk/ ▶ VERB [**knocks, knocking, knocked**]
1 to hit someone or something so that it moves or falls □ + ***over*** *The cat knocked over the vase.* □ *The blast knocked us off our feet.* □ *I fell and knocked my tooth out.* (**derrubar**)
2 to hit a hard surface, especially a door, with your hand in order to get attention □ *Knock before you come in.* □ + ***on*** *I knocked on the door but nobody answered.* (**bater**)
3 if someone's confidence is knocked, they become less confident (**derrubar**)
4 an informal word meaning to criticize someone or something □ *It's a very generous offer, so don't knock it.* (**criticar**)
♦ PHRASAL VERBS **knock off something** to take an amount away from a price □ *She knocked off £5 because there was a button missing.* (**terminar algo**) **knock someone out 1** to make someone become unconscious (**nocautear**) **2** to defeat a person or a team in a competition □ + ***of*** *Liverpool have been knocked out of the cup.* (**eliminar**)
▶ NOUN [plural **knocks**]
1 a hit □ *He's had a nasty knock on the head.* (**pancada, golpe**)
2 the sound of someone or something knocking on a hard surface □ *There was a knock at the door.* (**batida**)
3 when someone or something is criticized or damaged (**crítica**) 🔹 *The economy has taken a knock.* (**ganhou uma crítica**)
• **knocker** /ˈnɒkə(r)/ NOUN [plural **knockers**] a metal object on a door, which you knock with (**aldrava**)

knockout /ˈnɒkaʊt/ ▶ NOUN [plural **knockouts**] a competition in which a player or team stops being in the competition if they lose a game □ *They went out in the third round of the knockout.* (**eliminatórias**)
▶ ADJECTIVE *a knockout blow/punch* a hit in a boxing match that makes someone unconscious (**um soco de nocaute**)

knot /nɒt/ ▶ NOUN [plural **knots**]
1 a join made by tying two ends of string, rope or cloth together (**nó**) 🔹 *to tie a knot* (**dar um nó**)
2 a mass of untidy, twisted threads of hair, string, etc. that are difficult to separate □ *Let's comb these knots out of your hair.* (**nó**)
3 a unit for measuring how fast a ship is travelling (**nó**)
▶ VERB [**knots, knotting, knotted**] to tie something with a knot □ *A scarf was knotted around his neck.* (**atar**)

know /nəʊ/ VERB [knows, knowing, knew, known]
1 to have information or knowledge about something □ I didn't know the answer to her questions. (saber, conhecer) 🗨 'What's the capital of Hungary?' 'I don't know.' (eu não sei) □ + **question word** Do you know where he lives? □ She knows how to make me happy. □ + **about** I didn't know about the course.
2 to be familiar with a person □ I didn't know anyone at the party. (conhecer) 🗨 I got to know her when I was a student. (conhecia) 🗨 I don't know him very well. (conheço bem)
3 to be familiar with a place or a thing because you have been there, seen it, used it, etc. □ Do you know Berlin well? □ I know his work. (conhecer)
4 let someone know to tell someone something □ I'm going to be late – could you let John know, please? (avisar alguém)
5 be known as something to be called something □ Cromwell's supporters were known as Roundheads. (ser conhecido como)

> Remember that to know something means to have knowledge about something. To find out something is to get knowledge about something:
> ✓ I called Annie to find out when she was leaving.
> ✗ I called Annie to know when she was leaving.

• **knowing** /'nəʊɪŋ/ ADJECTIVE showing that you know something that is supposed to be secret □ He gave me a knowing look. (de cumplicidade, compreensivo)

knowledge /'nɒlɪdʒ/ NOUN, NO PLURAL the information that you know about something (conhecimento) 🗨 Candidates need to show that they have a basic knowledge of English. (conhecimento básico) 🗨 It's common knowledge (= everyone knows) that he has health problems. (senso comum) □ + **of** She has a good knowledge of sport.

• **knowledgeable** /'nɒlɪdʒəbəl/ ADJECTIVE knowing a lot about something □ She's very knowledgeable about Greek history. (versado)

known /nəʊn/ ▶ PAST PARTICIPLE OF **know** (ver know)
▶ ADJECTIVE
1 that people know about □ There is no known cure for the disease. (conhecido)
2 famous □ She is known for her performance in the film 'The Red Shoes'. (conhecido, famoso)

knuckle /'nʌkəl/ NOUN [plural **knuckles**] one of the parts of your fingers where they bend or where they join your hand (nós dos dedos)

koala /kəʊ'ɑːlə/ NOUN [plural **koalas**] an Australian animal that looks like a small bear, climbs trees and eats leaves from the eucalyptus tree (coala)

Koran /kə'rɑːn/ NOUN **the Koran** the holy book of the Islamic religion (Corão)

kosher /'kəʊʃə(r)/ ADJECTIVE describes food which is prepared according to Jewish law (kosher, lei judaica para preparo de alimentos)

kung-fu /ˌkʌŋ'fuː/ NOUN, NO PLURAL a type of Chinese fighting using the hands and feet (kung fu)

kW ABBREVIATION **kilowatt** or **kilowatts** (abreviação de quilowatt)

L or **l¹** /el/ the 12th letter of the alphabet (a décima segunda letra do alfabeto)

l² /el/ ABBREVIATION **litre** (abreviação de litro)

lab /læb/ NOUN [plural **labs**] a short way to say and write **laboratory** (abreviação de laboratório)

label /ˈleɪbəl/ ▶ NOUN [plural **labels**]
1 a small piece of paper or cloth that is fixed to something and gives information about it □ *The washing instructions are on the label.* □ *I looked at the ingredients on the label.* (rótulo, etiqueta)
2 a company that records and sells music (selo) ▣ *a record label* (selo de gravadora)
3 a company that makes fashionable clothes, or the clothes they make (marca) ▣ *Her wardrobe is full of designer labels.* (marcas famosas)
4 a word or phrase that is used to describe someone or something □ *With his next novel, he shed the label of science fiction writer.* (rótulo)
▶ VERB [**labels, labelling**/US **labeling, labelled**/US **labeled**]
1 to fix a label to something □ *All the boxes have been carefully labelled.* □ *Manufacturers should label their products more clearly.* (rotular, etiquetar)
2 to describe someone or something using a particular word or phrase □ *Take care not to label a child a troublemaker.* (rotular)

labor /ˈleɪbə(r)/ ▶ NOUN, NO PLURAL the US spelling of **labour** (trabalho, mão de obra, parto)
▶ VERB [**labors, laboring, labored**] the US spelling of **labour** (trabalhar)
• **laborer** /ˈleɪbərə(r)/ NOUN [plural **laborers**] the US spelling of **labourer** (trabalhador)

laboratory /ləˈbɒrətrɪ/ NOUN [plural **laboratories**] a room containing equipment for scientific work □ *a laboratory experiment* □ *Further tests were carried out at a laboratory.* (laboratório)

laborious /ləˈbɔːrɪəs/ ADJECTIVE difficult, boring and taking a lot of hard work □ *a laborious task* □ *We had to go through a long, laborious process.* (cansativo, laborioso)
• **laboriously** /ləˈbɔːrɪəslɪ/ ADVERB in a laborious way □ *He laboriously copied it all by hand.* (cansativamente)

labour /ˈleɪbə(r)/ ▶ NOUN, NO PLURAL
1 workers, especially in a particular country or type of work (mão de obra) ▣ *There is a shortage of skilled labour.* (mão de obra qualificada) □ *the rising cost of labour* ▣ *the labour market* (mercado de mão de obra)
2 work, especially hard, physical work (trabalho) ▣ *He was used to hard, manual labour.* (trabalho manual)
3 the process of giving birth to a baby (trabalho de parto) ▣ *She went into labour this morning.* (entrou em trabalho de parto)
4 a labour of love work you do because you want to, not for money (trabalho por prazer)
▶ VERB [**labours, labouring, laboured**] to work hard, especially doing physical work □ *Farm workers were labouring in the fields.* (trabalhar pesado)
• **labourer** /ˈleɪbərə(r)/ NOUN [plural **labourers**] a person who does hard physical work □ *a farm labourer* (trabalhador)

Labour Party /ˈleɪbə(r) ˈpɑːtɪ/ NOUN, NO PLURAL in the UK, one of the main political parties (Partido trabalhista)

labrador /ˈlæbrədɔː(r)/ NOUN [plural **labradors**] a large black or cream-coloured dog with short fur (labrador)

labyrinth /ˈlæbərɪnθ/ NOUN [plural **labyrinths**] a complicated system of paths that is difficult to find your way through □ *an underground labyrinth of tunnels* (labirinto)

lace /leɪs/ ▶ NOUN [plural **laces**]
1 a decorative cloth with delicate patterns of many holes □ *a collar trimmed with lace* (renda)
2 a piece of string for tying up shoes or other clothing (cadarço) ▣ *He bent down to tie his shoe laces.* (cadarços do sapato)
▶ VERB [**laces, lacing, laced**] to put laces in something or to tie laces □ *He laced up his boots.* (amarrar)

lace-ups /ˈleɪsʌps/ PLURAL NOUN shoes that are tied with laces (sapatos com cadarço)

lack /læk/ ▶ VERB [**lacks, lacking, lacked**] to be without something or not to not have enough of something □ *Audrey lacks a sense of humour.* □ *We lack the resources to deal with all the requests.* (ter falta de)
▶ NOUN, NO PLURAL when you do not have something, or you do not have enough of something □ **+ of** *He was suffering from lack of sleep.* (falta, ausência) ▣ *He shows a complete lack of understanding.* (total falta)

lackluster   lament

- **lacking** /ˈlækɪŋ/ ADJECTIVE if something is lacking, there is not enough of it □ *He is lacking in confidence.* (ausente, deficiente) 🔁 *Support for the leader has been sadly lacking in recent months.* (tristemente ausente)

lackluster /ˈlækˌlʌstə(r)/ ADJECTIVE the US spelling of **lacklustre** (apagado, sem brilho)

lacklustre /ˈlækˌlʌstə(r)/ ADJECTIVE not exciting or energetic □ *a lacklustre performance* (apagado, sem brilho)

lacquer /ˈlækə(r)/ ▶ NOUN [*plural* **lacquers**] a clear liquid which is put on a surface to make it hard and shiny (verniz)
▶ VERB [**lacquers, lacquering, lacquered**] to cover something with lacquer (laquear, envernizar)

lactate /lækˈteɪt/ VERB [**lactates, lactating, lactated**] to produce milk from the breasts. A biology word. (produzir leite materno)

- **lactation** /ˌlækˈteɪʃən/ NOUN, NO PLURAL when milk is produced from the breasts (lactação)

lactose /ˈlæktəʊs/ NOUN, NO PLURAL a type of sugar that is found in milk. A biology word. (lactose)

lacy /ˈleɪsɪ/ ADJECTIVE
1 made of or containing lace (= cloth with a delicate pattern of holes) □ *a lacy blouse* (rendado)
2 like lace (rendado)

lad /læd/ NOUN [*plural* **lads**] an informal word for a boy or young man □ *He's a nice lad.* (rapaz)

ladder /ˈlædə(r)/ NOUN [*plural* **ladders**]
1 a set of steps that you use for climbing up to high places and can move around to different places □ *He had to climb a ladder to reach the top cupboard.* (escada)
2 a situation in which there are different levels of importance and people repeatedly try to reach a higher level, especially by working (escala) 🔁 *She hopes to make her way up the career ladder.* (escala na carreira)
3 a long hole in someone's tights (= underwear that covers a woman's legs) □ *There's a ladder in your tights.* (fio puxado, desfiado)

laden /ˈleɪdən/ ADJECTIVE carrying or holding a lot of something □ *He was laden with bags of shopping.* □ *The tree is laden with fruit.* (carregado)

ladies /ˈleɪdɪz/ PLURAL NOUN a public toilet for women and girls □ *Where is the ladies, please?* (banheiro feminino)

ladle /ˈleɪdəl/ ▶ NOUN [*plural* **ladles**] a large spoon for serving liquids, especially soup (concha)
▶ VERB [**ladles, ladling, ladled**] to serve something with a ladle □ *Mrs Moore was busy ladling soup into bowls.* (servir com concha)

lady /ˈleɪdɪ/ NOUN [*plural* **ladies**]
1 a polite word for a woman □ *Ask that lady if the seat by her is free.* (senhora, mulher) 🔁 *Good evening ladies and gentlemen.* (senhoras e senhores)
2 in the UK, a title for a woman with a high social rank (madame)

ladybird /ˈleɪdɪbɜːd/ NOUN [*plural* **ladybirds**] a small insect that is usually red with black spots (joaninha)

ladylike /ˈleɪdɪlaɪk/ ADJECTIVE behaving in a polite, controlled way that some people think is suitable for a woman (elegante, refinado)

ladyship /ˈleɪdɪʃɪp/ NOUN [*plural* **ladyships**] a title you use when you are speaking about or to a woman of high social rank who has the title of 'Lady' (senhoria)

lag /læg/ ▶ VERB [**lags, lagging, lagged**]
1 to make progress more slowly than something else □ *The company is lagging a long way behind its rivals.* (ficar para trás)
2 to move more slowly than someone or something else □ *One child lagged behind the rest of the group.* (atrasar-se)
▶ NOUN [*plural* **lags**] the period of time or delay between two things happening (defasagem) 🔁 *There's a slight time lag between receiving the request and sending it to the warehouse.* (defasagem no tempo)

lager /ˈlɑːɡə(r)/ NOUN [*plural* **lagers**] a light--coloured beer (cerveja leve e clara)

lagoon /ləˈɡuːn/ NOUN [*plural* **lagoons**] an area of water separated from the sea by sand or rocks. A geography word. (lagoa)

laid /leɪd/ PAST TENSE AND PAST PARTICIPLE OF **lay** □ *She laid the baby on the blanket.* (ver **lay**)

laid-back /ˌleɪdˈbæk/ ADJECTIVE relaxed and not worrying about things □ *He's pretty laid-back.* (relaxado, descontraído)

lain /leɪn/ PAST PARTICIPLE OF **lie**² (= put your body in a flat position) □ *I had lain down for a moment and fallen fast asleep.* (ver **lie**)

lake /leɪk/ NOUN [*plural* **lakes**] a large area of water with land all around it □ *Lake Como* (lago)

lamb /læm/ NOUN [*plural* **lambs**]
1 a young sheep (cordeiro)
2 *no plural* meat from a young sheep □ *roast lamb* □ *lamb chops* (de cordeiro)

lame /leɪm/ ADJECTIVE [**lamer, lamest**]
1 not able to walk well because of an injury □ *a lame horse* (manco)
2 difficult to believe or respect (pouco convincente) 🔁 *He made up some lame excuse.* (desculpa esfarrapada)

◆ IDIOM **lame duck** someone who is weak and not likely to succeed □ *The minister is looking increasingly like a lame duck.* (incapaz, fraco)

- **lamely** /ˈleɪmlɪ/ ADVERB in a way that is difficult to believe □ *'My bus was late,' she said lamely.* (de modo não convincente)

lament /ləˈment/ ▶ NOUN [*plural* **laments**] a sad song or poem, especially about someone's death (lamento)

laminated

▶ VERB [laments, lamenting, lamented] a formal word meaning to feel or to express sadness about something □ *He was lamenting the passing of the old days.* (lamentar)

• **lamentable** /ˈlæməntəbəl/ ADJECTIVE extremely bad, in a way that makes you feel upset □ *a lamentable waste of money* (lamentável)

laminated /ˈlæmɪneɪtɪd/ ADJECTIVE
1 covered with thin, clear plastic (laminado)
2 made by sticking layers together □ *laminated flooring* (laminado, feito por camadas)

lamp /læmp/ NOUN [plural **lamps**] a light, especially one which stands on a table □ *a table lamp* □ *a bedside lamp* □ *an old oil lamp* (lampião)

lamppost /ˈlæmppəʊst/ NOUN [plural **lampposts**] a tall pole in the street with a light at the top (poste)

lampshade /ˈlæmpʃeɪd/ NOUN [plural **lampshades**] a cover placed over a light (abajur)

LAN /læn/ ABBREVIATION local area network; a system connecting the computers of people who are in the same building. A computing word. (LAN, rede local)

land /lænd/ ▶ NOUN [plural **lands**]
1 no plural an area of ground □ *an acre of land* (terra) 🔁 *agricultural land* (terra agrícola)
2 no plural the part of the Earth not covered by water (terra) 🔁 *It's good to be back on dry land.* (na terra seca)
3 a word for a country used especially in stories (terra) 🔁 *He talked of his adventures in foreign lands.* (terras estrangeiras)

▶ VERB [lands, landing, landed]
1 when an aircraft lands, it arrives on the ground after a flight □ *The plane landed around 3pm.* □ *The flight landed safely at Glasgow airport.* (aterrissar)
2 to stop somewhere after flying or falling □ *The bird landed on a branch.* □ *The book fell off the table and landed heavily on the floor.* □ *I slipped but managed to land on my feet.* (pousar)
3 to get something you want, especially a job □ *He landed a job with the local paper.* (conseguir)
4 to cause someone to be in a difficult situation or to have problems □ *He's always landing me in trouble.* □ *I found myself landed with a huge phone bill.* (causar)

• **landing** /ˈlændɪŋ/ NOUN [plural **landings**]
1 the process of moving a plane down to the ground (aterrissagem, desembarque) 🔁 *The helicopter made an emergency landing.* (aterrissagem de emergência)
2 when someone or something reaches the ground after flying or falling □ *He had a soft landing in some leaves.* (pouso)
3 the floor at the top of some stairs or the floor between two sets of stairs □ *She reached the second floor landing.* (patamar)

landfill /ˈlændfɪl/ NOUN [plural **landfills**] a large hole in the ground where waste is put (aterro sanitário) 🔁 *a landfill site* (local de aterro sanitário)

landlady /ˈlændˌleɪdi/ NOUN [plural **landladies**]
1 a woman who owns a house that someone else pays to live in (senhoria)
2 a woman who runs a pub or a small hotel (proprietária)

landline /ˈlændlaɪn/ NOUN [plural **landlines**] a phone with wires which is not a mobile phone □ *Have you tried his landline?* (linha fixa)

landlord /ˈlændlɔːd/ NOUN [plural **landlords**]
1 a man who owns a house that someone else pays to live in □ *Her landlord raised the rent.* (senhorio)
2 a man who runs a pub or a small hotel (proprietário) 🔁 *a pub landlord* (proprietário do bar)

landmark /ˈlændmɑːk/ NOUN [plural **landmarks**]
1 a place, especially a building, that helps you know where you are because you can easily recognize it □ *The tower is one of the city's most famous landmarks.* □ *He spotted a familiar landmark.* (marco)
2 an important event or achievement □ *The speech is viewed as a landmark in American history.* (ponto de referência)

landmine /ˈlændmaɪn/ NOUN [plural **landmines**] a bomb that is put under the ground and explodes if someone walks or drives over it (minas terrestres)

landscape /ˈlændskeɪp/ NOUN [plural **landscapes**]
1 a view of a large area of land □ *He looked out at the beautiful landscape.* □ *a snowy landscape* (paisagem)
2 when a piece of paper is arranged so that it is wider than it is tall (formato paisagem)

landslide /ˈlændslaɪd/ NOUN [plural **landslides**]
1 when a large amount of the ground slides down the side of a hill □ *Heavy rain triggered landslides.* (desabamento)
2 when one person or political party wins very easily in an election (vitória esmagadora) 🔁 *He won a landslide victory in 2000.* (vitória esmagadora)

lane /leɪn/ NOUN [plural **lanes**]
1 a narrow road □ *We drove along narrow country lanes.* (caminho)
2 a strip of a road separated by painted lines (pista) 🔁 *She pulled out into the fast lane.* (pista rápida) □ *The northbound lane of the motorway was closed after an accident.*
3 a route that ships or aircraft use in the sea or air (raia, faixa) 🔁 *a busy shipping lane* (rota marítima)

language

language /ˈlæŋɡwɪdʒ/ NOUN [plural **languages**]
1 *no plural* communication using speech and writing □ *formal language* (**linguagem**) □ *He was warned for using foul language* (= offensive words). (**linguagem obscena**) □ *He used some interesting language to describe the scene.* (**utilizou linguagem**) □ *+ of the language of diplomacy*
2 the words used by a particular group, especially the people that live in one country □ *the English language* □ *All children should learn a foreign language.* (**língua estrangeira**) □ *Do you speak any other languages?* (**idioma**)
3 a system of symbols that represent instructions, used to program computers □ *a programming language* (**linguagem**)

languid /ˈlæŋɡwɪd/ ADJECTIVE doing things slowly and without energy □ *a languid voice* (**lânguido**)

languish /ˈlæŋɡwɪʃ/ VERB [**languishes, languishing, languished**] to stay in an unhappy or difficult situation □ *Political activists languished in prison for years.* (**definhar, sofrer**)

lanky /ˈlæŋki/ ADJECTIVE [**lankier, lankiest**] tall and thin, sometimes in a way that is not attractive □ *a lanky 15-year-old boy* (**magricela**)

lantern /ˈlæntən/ NOUN [plural **lanterns**] a light inside a clear container that you can carry (**lanterna**)

lap /læp/ ▶ NOUN [plural **laps**]
1 the top part of a person's legs when they are in a sitting position □ *Jessie sat on her mother's lap.* (**colo**)
2 one complete journey around a race track □ *He crashed out on the first lap of the race.* (**volta**)
◆ IDIOM **in the lap of luxury** in a very comfortable situation, with expensive things around you (**no luxo**)
▶ VERB [**laps, lapping, lapped**]
1 to drink something with the tongue sticking out □ *The cat was lapping milk from a saucer.* (**beber a lambidas**)
2 if water laps, it moves gently against rocks or onto a beach □ *The waves were lapping at our feet.* (**marulhar**)
3 to pass someone more than once as you go round a race track (**dar volta de atraso**)
◆ PHRASAL VERB **lap something up** to enjoy experiencing or hearing something very much □ *She lapped up the compliments about her new dress.* (**escutar algo de bom**)

lapel /ləˈpel/ NOUN [plural **lapels**] the front part of the collar of a coat or jacket □ *He had a flower pinned to his lapel.* (**lapela**)

lapse /læps/ ▶ NOUN [plural **lapses**]
1 a failure to work or to happen for a short period of time □ *a lapse of concentration* □ *There was a serious lapse in security.* (**erro, deslize**)
2 a period of time between two things happening □ *After a lapse of ten years, he started to play football again.* (**lapso, intervalo**)

▶ VERB [**lapses, lapsing, lapsed**] if an agreement or an arrangement lapses, it finishes after a period of time □ *His insurance policy had lapsed.* (**expirar**)
◆ PHRASAL VERB **lapse into something** to gradually become quieter or less active □ *They both lapsed into silence.* (**silenciar gradualmente**)

laptop /ˈlæptɒp/ NOUN [plural **laptops**] a small computer that can be carried easily. A computing word. (**laptop**)

lard /lɑːd/ NOUN, NO PLURAL a hard, white fat that is used in cooking and that comes from a pig (**banha de porco**)

larder /ˈlɑːdə(r)/ NOUN [plural **larders**] a large cupboard where food is kept □ *a well-stocked larder* (**despensa**)

large

large /lɑːdʒ/ ADJECTIVE [**larger, largest**] big or bigger than normal in size or amount □ *a large house* □ *A large number of people were waiting.* □ *Large parts of the country are without power.* (**grande**)
◆ IDIOMS **at large 1** generally □ *This is a problem, not just for parents, but for the community at large.* (**em geral**) **2** if a dangerous animal or a criminal is at large, they are free and have not been caught □ *The suspects may still be at large.* (**à solta**) **by and large** mostly or in most situations □ *The situation was by and large peaceful.* □ *Americans, by and large, support the policy.* (**de modo geral**)

large intestine /lɑːdʒ ɪnˈtestɪn/ NOUN [plural **large intestines**] the lower part of the body's system for digesting food, where food that is not digested is made into solid waste. A biology word. (**intestino grosso**)

largely /ˈlɑːdʒli/ ADVERB mainly or mostly □ *The church has been largely rebuilt.* □ *The report was largely positive.* (**em grande parte**)

lark /lɑːk/ NOUN [plural **larks**]
1 a singing bird that flies high in the sky (**cotovia**)
2 something you do for fun. An informal word. □ *We were just having a lark.* (**brincadeira**)
◆ PHRASAL VERB **lark about** to do something for fun or as a joke. An informal phrase. □ *We were larking about at the back of the class.* (**fazer gracejos**)

larva /ˈlɑːvə/ NOUN [plural **larvae** /ˈlɑːviː/] an insect in its first stage after coming out of the egg. A biology word. (**larva**)

laryngitis /ˌlærɪnˈdʒaɪtɪs/ NOUN, NO PLURAL an illness that makes your throat sore and makes it difficult for you to talk (**laringite**)

larynx /ˈlærɪŋks/ NOUN [plural **larynxes**] the part at the top of the throat that contains the vocal cords (= the parts that make your voice). A biology word. (**laringe**)

lasagne or **lasagna** /ləˈzænjə/ NOUN [plural **lasagnes** or **lasagnas**] an Italian food made up of layers of pasta, and layers of meat or vegetables with a white sauce and cheese (**lasanha**)

laser /ˈleɪzə(r)/ NOUN [plural **lasers**] a very narrow, powerful beam of light (**laser**) ◨ *a laser beam* (**um raio laser**) □ *The surgery uses lasers.*

laser printer /ˈleɪzə prɪntə(r)/ NOUN [plural **laser printers**] a fast printer for a computer, that uses light from a laser (**impressora a laser**)

lash /læʃ/ ▶ NOUN [plural **lashes**]

1 when someone is hit with a whip (= a long thin piece of leather) as a punishment □ *ten lashes of the whip* (**chicotada**)

2 an **eyelash** (= one of the many hairs round the edges of your eyes) (**cílio**)

▶ VERB [**lashes, lashing, lashed**]

1 to hit someone or something with force □ *Rain lashed against the tent.* (**atacar alguém com violência**)

2 to tie something up with rope or string □ *The banners were lashed to the walls of the buildings.* (**prender**)

3 to hit someone with a whip (**chicotear**)

◆ PHRASAL VERB **lash out 1** to suddenly hit or attack someone □ *He suddenly lashed out, knocking me to the ground.* (**lançar-se**) **2** to criticize someone very strongly □ *Yesterday he lashed out at his critics.* (**atacar**)

lass /læs/ NOUN [plural **lasses**] a girl or a young woman (**moça**)

lasso /læˈsuː/ ▶ NOUN [plural **lassoes** or **lassos**] a long rope with a circle that gets tighter when the rope is pulled, used especially for catching wild horses (**laço**)

▶ VERB [**lassoes, lassoing, lassoed**] to throw a lasso around something to catch it (**laçar**)

last /lɑːst/ ▶ ADJECTIVE, DETERMINER

1 most recent □ *We moved house last October.* □ *In the last few months we have been very busy.* □ *On my last birthday, he gave me a necklace.* □ *The last time I ate fish, I was ill.* □ *Their last album was a huge success.* (**último**)

2 coming after all the others □ *We caught the last train to Cambridge.* □ *This is the last time I will ever help you.* □ *That was her last public appearance.* (**último**)

3 the last moment/minute the latest possible time before something □ *Our flight was cancelled at the last moment.* □ *Don't leave it to the last minute to book a hotel.* (**último momento/minuto**)

4 the final one remaining □ *She ate my last toffee.* (**último**)

5 used to emphasize that someone or something is not wanted or not suitable □ *She's the last person I'd ask for help.* □ *The last thing he needs is more work.* (**último**)

⇨ *go to* **be on its last** *legs*

▶ ADVERB

1 after all the others □ *She arrived last.* □ *Make sure you add the sugar last.* (**por último**) ◨ *I came last in the swimming race.* (**cheguei por último**)

2 most recently □ *When did you last see Anna?* (**última vez**)

▶ VERB [**lasts, lasting, lasted**]

1 to continue for a period of time □ *The lesson seemed to last for ever.* □ *The film lasted over three hours.* (**durar**)

2 to remain in good condition □ *These boots have lasted well.* (**durar**)

3 to manage to stay safe, stay alive, or stay in a job □ *Without shelter, I wasn't sure we'd last the night.* (**durar**) ◨ *She won't last long in a job like that.* (**não vai durar muito**)

4 to be enough □ *The food lasted for three days.* (**ser suficiente**)

▶ NOUN, PRONOUN

1 the person or thing that comes after all the others □ *You are always the last to finish.* □ *Am I the last?* (**último**)

2 the final person or thing remaining □ *+ of I've eaten the last of the apples.* (**último**)

3 at last after a long period of time □ *I've found a job at last.* (**finalmente**)

• **lasting** /ˈlɑːstɪŋ/ ADJECTIVE continuing to exist for a long time □ *They hope to achieve a lasting peace.* □ *His book made a lasting impression on me.* (**duradouro, durável**)

• **lastly** /ˈlɑːstli/ ADVERB after all other people or things □ *Lastly, I just want to thank my wife.* (**por fim**)

latch /lætʃ/ NOUN [plural **latches**]

1 a piece of wood or metal that you lift or lower to open or fasten a door (**tranca**)

2 a type of lock that needs a key to be opened from the outside (**trinco**)

◆ PHRASAL VERBS [**latches, latching, latched**] **latch on** to start to understand or to be interested in something (**compreender**) **latch onto something/someone** to hold tightly onto someone or something or to follow them closely (**agarrar-se, segurar-se**)

late /leɪt/ ADJECTIVE, ADVERB [**later, latest**]

1 after the time that is expected or necessary □ *The bus was late.* □ *+ for If you don't hurry, you'll be late for work.* □ *I was too late to help him.* □ *I'm coming to the meeting, but I might be a bit late.* (**atrasado**)

2 near the end of the day (**tarde**) ◨ *The children stayed up late to watch a movie.* (**ficaram acordadas até tarde**) ◨ *Will the party go on late?* (**terminar tarde**) ◨ *It's getting late – we should leave.* (**está ficando tarde**)

3 near the end of a period of time □ *the late 18th century* □ *It was late afternoon by the time we arrived.* (**no final**)

4 recent, or happening or produced towards the end of a period of time □ *Her late work was more*

latecomer — launch

experimental. □ *The late editions all had the news.* (**último, antigo**)

5 a formal word meaning dead □ *This house belonged to the late Mrs Edwards.* (**finado, falecido**)

• **lately** /ˈleɪtlɪ/ ADVERB recently □ *I haven't been to many parties lately.* (**ultimamente**)

• **lateness** /ˈleɪtnəs/ NOUN, NO PLURAL being late □ *She apologized for her lateness.* (**atraso, tarde**)

• **later** /ˈleɪtə(r)/ ADJECTIVE, ADVERB
1 after the time you have been talking about □ *Later, he married an artist.* □ *She rang me later to apologize.* □ *Two years later I received a letter from him.* □ *Is there a later train?* (**mais tarde**)
2 more recent, or happening or produced towards the end of a period □ *Later versions of the software include that feature.* □ *I am a great admirer of his later novels.* (**últimas, recentes**) 🔲 *In later life*, he became very deaf. (**no fim da vida**)

• **latest** /ˈleɪtɪst/ ▶ ADJECTIVE most recent □ *I regularly check the Internet for the latest news.* □ *We stock all the latest fashions.* (**mais recente**)
▶ NOUN
1 the latest the most recent example of something □ *This is the latest in a series of mistakes.* (**o mais recente, o mais novo**)
2 at the latest used to emphasize that something must happen or be done before a particular time □ *You must be home by seven at the latest.* (**no máximo**)

latecomer /ˈleɪtˌkʌmə(r)/ NOUN [*plural* **latecomers**] someone who is late for an event (**retardatário**)

lather /ˈlɑːðə(r)/ NOUN, NO PLURAL small bubbles that you get when you mix soap in water □ *Rinse off the lather.* (**espuma**)
♦ IDIOM **in a lather** very upset or worried about something (**em estado de agitação**)

Latin /ˈlætɪn/ NOUN, NO PLURAL the language of the ancient Romans (**latim**)

latitude /ˈlætɪtjuːd/ NOUN [*plural* **latitudes**] the position of a place along imaginary lines around the Earth north and south of the equator (= line around the middle of the Earth). It is measured in degrees north and south. (**latitude**)

latte /ˈlæteɪ/ NOUN [*plural* **lattes**] a drink made with strong coffee and hot milk (**café com leite**)

latter /ˈlætə(r)/ ▶ ADJECTIVE nearer the end of a period of time than the beginning (**final**) 🔲 *the latter part* of the 19th century (**a parte final**)
▶ NOUN, NO PLURAL the second one of two people or things mentioned □ *If I'm offered tea or coffee, I'll always take the latter.* (**este último**)

• **latterly** /ˈlætəlɪ/ ADVERB a formal word that means recently (**recentemente**)

laudable /ˈlɔːdəbəl/ ADJECTIVE deserving praise. A formal word □ *This is a laudable first attempt at portrait painting.* (**louvável**)

laugh /lɑːf/ ▶ VERB [**laughs, laughing, laughed**] to make a sound of enjoyment when you think something is funny □ + **at** *She laughed at my jokes.* □ + **about** *We can laugh about the whole thing now.* (**rir**) 🔲 *It really made me laugh.* (**me fez rir**) 🔲 *They burst out laughing* (= suddenly laughed loudly). (**começaram a rir**)
♦ PHRASAL VERBS **laugh at someone/something** to laugh or say something rude because you think someone or something is stupid □ *Wallis just laughed at the suggestion.* (**rir de algo/alguém**)
laugh something off to make a joke about something to show that it is not important to you □ *She laughed off the criticisms.* (**tratar como algo de pouca importância**)
▶ NOUN [*plural* **laughs**]
1 when you laugh, or the sound that you make when you laugh (**riso, risada**) 🔲 *He gave a nervous laugh.* (**deu uma risada**) □ *He has a very loud laugh.*
2 a (good) laugh an informal phrase that means a person or an activity that is fun □ *John's a good laugh.* (**uma piada**)
3 have a laugh an informal phrase that means to have fun and enjoy yourself □ *We all have such a laugh together.* (**dar risada**)
4 for a laugh an informal phrase that means for fun or as a joke □ *I only did it for a laugh.* (**por diversão**)

• **laughable** /ˈlɑːfəbəl/ ADJECTIVE very bad and deserving to be laughed at □ *a laughable suggestion* (**risível**)

laughing stock /ˈlɑːfɪŋ ˌstɒk/ NOUN [*plural* **laughing stocks**] someone or something that everyone thinks is silly and does not deserve respect (**fazer pouco caso**)

laughter /ˈlɑːftə(r)/ NOUN, NO PLURAL when someone laughs or the sound that they make when they laugh □ *I could hear laughter in the next room* (**risada, gargalhada**) 🔲 *We were in fits of laughter.* (**em uma gargalhada**)

launch /lɔːntʃ/ ▶ VERB [**launches, launching, launched**]
1 to start an important piece of work (**lançar**) 🔲 *We are launching an investigation into the incident.* (**iniciar uma investigação**)
2 to start to sell a new product □ *The latest model will be launched next month.* (**lançar**)
3 to send a rocket or a spacecraft into the sky □ *The first Sputnik satellite was launched into space in 1957.* (**lançar**)
4 to put a boat or ship in the water for the first time (**lançar**)
♦ PHRASAL VERB **launch into something** to start saying something with enthusiasm or anger □ *He then launched into a great long speech on the subject.* (**dar início a algo**)
▶ NOUN [*plural* **launches**]
1 when a spacecraft, ship, etc. is launched □ *a shuttle launch* (**lançamento**)

2 when an important piece of work is started □ *the campaign launch* (**lançamento**)
3 when a new product starts to be sold □ *This month sees the launch of the latest version.* (**lançamento**)

launch pad /'lɔːntʃ ˌpæd/ NOUN [plural **launch pads**] a place that a spacecraft is launched from (**plataforma de lançamento**)

launder /'lɔːndə(r)/ VERB [**launders, laundering, laundered**]
1 to put money into legal businesses to hide the fact that it was made illegally (**lavar dinheiro**)
2 to wash or clean clothes so that they are ready to wear again. A formal word. (**lavar**)

• **launderette** /ˌlɔːndəˈret/ NOUN [plural **launderettes**] a shop full of washing machines that you can pay to use (**lavanderia automática**)

• **laundry** /'lɔːndri/ NOUN, NO PLURAL clothes that are going to be washed, or have just been washed □ *a pile of dirty laundry* □ *a laundry basket* (**roupa lavada, roupa para lavar**) 🔊 *I've done the laundry.* (**lavei as roupas**)

laundry detergent /'lɔːndri dɪˈtɜːdʒənt/ NOUN, NO PLURAL the US phrase for **washing powder** (= a powder used for washing clothes) (**sabão para lavar roupa**)

lava /'lɑːvə/ NOUN, NO PLURAL the hot liquid rock that comes out of a volcano (= mountain that explodes) and becomes solid as it cools down. A geography word. (**lava**)

lavatory /'lævətri/ NOUN [plural **lavatories**] a formal word for toilet □ *a public lavatory* (**sanitário**)

lavender /'lævəndə(r)/ ▶ NOUN [plural **lavenders**] a plant with small purple flowers with a strong, sweet smell (**lavanda**)
▶ ADJECTIVE having a pale purple colour (**de tonalidade azulada**)

lavish /'lævɪʃ/ ▶ VERB [**lavishes, lavishing, lavished**] to give someone a lot of, or too much of something □ *Her parents had always lavished gifts on her.* (**dar em abundância**)
▶ ADJECTIVE very generous, with more than enough of everything □ *a lavish dinner* □ *a lavish lifestyle* (**gastador**)

• **lavishly** /'lævɪʃli/ ADVERB in a lavish way □ *a lavishly decorated room* (**em abundância**)

law /lɔː/ NOUN [plural **laws**]
1 the law an official set of rules that everyone in a country or state must obey (**lei**) 🔊 *They have broken the law.* (**desrespeitaram a lei**)
2 be against the law to not be allowed by law □ *Driving at the age of 13 is against the law.* (**ser contra a lei**)
3 an official rule in a country or state that everyone must obey □ + *against* *laws against discrimination* (**lei**)
4 the law as a subject for studying or a job □ *He studied law at university.* (**direito**)
5 by law if you have to do something by law, there is an official rule which says that you must do it □ *You are required by law to provide this information.* (**pela lei**)
6 a scientific rule that explains why something always happens in the same way □ + *of* *the laws of gravity* (**lei**)

• **lawful** /'lɔːfʊl/ ADJECTIVE allowed by the law □ *The strike was not lawful.* (**legal, permitido**)

lawn /lɔːn/ NOUN [plural **lawns**] an area of short grass in a garden (**gramado**) 🔊 *I need to mow the lawn* (= cut the grass with a machine). (**cortar o gramado**)

lawnmower /'lɔːnˌməʊə(r)/ NOUN [plural **lawnmowers**] a machine for cutting grass (**cortador de grama**)

lawsuit /'lɔːsuːt/ NOUN [plural **lawsuits**] a disagreement between two people that a court of law is asked to make a decision about (**processo, ação**)

lawyer /'lɔːjə(r)/ NOUN [plural **lawyers**] someone whose job is to advise people about the law and to act for other people in legal situations (**advogado**) 🔊 *a defence lawyer* (**advogado de defesa**) □ *His lawyer said he would appeal against the sentence.*

lax /læks/ ADJECTIVE [**laxer, laxest**] not carefully controlled □ *Lax security at the airport was to blame.* (**frouxo, relaxado**)

laxative /'læksətɪv/ NOUN [plural **laxatives**] a drug or food that makes you pass solid waste from your body (**laxante**)

lay /leɪ/ VERB [**lays, laying, laid**]
1 to put something down carefully □ + *on* *She laid the book on the table.* □ + *down* *Slowly, he laid down the gun.* □ *I went to lay flowers on his grave.* (**pousar**)
2 to put something into its correct position □ *to lay bricks* □ *A railway track was laid between the cities.* (**assentar**)
3 if a bird lays an egg, it produces it (**botar**)
4 lay the table to put knives, forks, etc. on a table to prepare for a meal (**pôr a mesa**)
5 lay the blame/responsibility (for something) on someone to say that it is someone's fault that something has happened (**jogar a culpa/responsabilidade em alguém**)
6 lay the foundations to do what is necessary for something to develop □ *They are trying to lay the foundations for a lasting peace.* (**estabelecer a base**)

⇨ go to **lay eyes on something/someone**

◆ PHRASAL VERBS **lay something down** to say officially how something should be done □ *lay down rules/standards* (**estipular, estabelecer**) **lay into someone** to attack or criticize someone (**atacar, criticar alguém**) **lay someone off** to stop employing someone (**demitir alguém**) **lay**

lay-by

something on to provide something, for example food or a service □ *They laid on buses to take all the guests to the hotel.* (**prover algo**) **lay something out** to explain something □ *The article lays out her vision for the future.* (**explicar algo**)

> Try not to confuse the verbs **lay** and **lie**. To lay something somewhere is to put something down. To lie somewhere is to be in a flat position: □ *She looked for a place to lay the baby.* □ *Why don't you lie on the sofa and watch TV?*

▶ ADJECTIVE
1 involved in religious activities but not an official employee of the church □ *a lay preacher* (**amador**)
2 not having a detailed knowledge of a particular subject □ *I was speaking to a lay audience.* (**leigo**)
▶ PAST TENSE OF **lie²** (*ver* **lie**)

lay-by /'leɪbaɪ/ NOUN [*plural* **lay-bys**] an area at the side of a road where drivers can stop for a short time (**acostamento**)

layer /'leɪə(r)/ ▶ NOUN [*plural* **layers**]
1 an amount of a substance that covers something or is between other things □ *+ of The grass was covered with a layer of snow.* (**camada**) ▣ *Remove the outer layers of the onion.* (**camadas externas**) □ *Wear several layers of clothing.* □ *Dust had settled in a thin layer over everything.*
2 a level of an organization or system □ *This just adds another layer of bureaucracy.* (**nível, camada**)
▶ VERB [**layers, layering, layered**] to arrange something in layers □ *The dessert is made by layering fruit and ice cream.*

layman /'leɪmən/ NOUN [*plural* **laymen**] a person who has no special knowledge or training in a subject (**leigo**) ▣ *Can you explain that in layman's terms?* (**em linguagem de leigo**)

layoff /'leɪɒf/ NOUN [*plural* **layoffs**] when a company stops employing people because there is no work for them to do □ *The company blamed the layoffs on the recession.* (**demissão**)

layout /'leɪaʊt/ NOUN [*plural* **layouts**] the way things are arranged □ *The diagram shows the layout of the rooms.* (**layout, esboço**)

laze /leɪz/ VERB [**lazes, lazing, lazed**] to be lazy and to do very little □ *I just like to laze around in the holidays.* (**vadiar**)
• **laziness** /'leɪzɪnɪs/ NOUN, NO PLURAL when someone is lazy (**preguiça**)
• **lazy** /'leɪzi/ ADJECTIVE [**lazier, laziest**]
1 not liking to work hard or to exercise □ *At school they say he's very lazy.* □ *She's far too lazy to walk to work.* (**vadio**)
2 relaxing, involving little effort □ *I've had a very lazy morning in bed with the papers.* (**preguiçoso**)

lb ABBREVIATION **pound** (= weight) (**abreviação de libra**)

lead¹ /li:d/ ▶ VERB [**leads, leading, led**]
1 to show someone where to go by going first or going with them □ *You lead and I'll follow on my bike.* □ *She led me into a large room.* (**conduzir**)
2 if a road, path, etc. leads somewhere, that is where it goes □ *+ to This road leads to London.* (**levar a algum lugar**)
3 to be winning in a race or competition, or to be the most successful at something □ *Liverpool were leading 2-0 at the end of the first half.* □ *+ by They are leading by three goals to nil* (**estar à frente**) ▣ *Our company leads the world in aviation technology.* (**está à frente do mundo**)
4 to direct or control an activity or a group of people □ *The team should be led by someone with a lot of experience.* □ *A new officer has been brought in to lead the investigation.* (**conduzir**)
5 to cause someone to do something □ *+ to do something His expression led me to think he was lying.* (**levar**) ▣ *I was led to believe that he was a doctor.* (**levado a acreditar**) □ *The long hours led me to give up my career in law.*
6 lead a comfortable/full/normal, etc. life to live in a particular way (**levar uma vida completa, confortável, plena etc.**)
7 lead the way to be the first to do something □ *This university led the way in introducing schemes to attract poorer students.* (**mostrar o caminho**)
◆ PHRASAL VERBS **lead to something** to cause something to happen or exist □ *Long hours at work led to the breakdown of his marriage.* □ *Using the mouse too much can lead to wrist problems.* (**causar algo**) **lead up to something** to happen before something □ *He took part in the talks that led up to the deal.* □ *We were very busy in the weeks leading up to the election.* (**levar a algo**)

▶ NOUN [*plural* **leads**]
1 the position in a race or competition where you are winning □ *Jenkins has been in the lead for most of the race.* (**liderança**) ▣ *Juventus took the lead after 23 minutes.* (**tomou a liderança**)
2 when you show someone where to go or what to do (**conduzir, guiar**) ▣ *I didn't know what to do, so I just followed Ted's lead.* (**seguir o exemplo**)
3 a wire that connects a piece of electrical equipment to an electricity supply (**fio**)
4 a long, narrow piece of leather attached to a dog's collar in order to hold it. (**coleira**) ▣ *All dogs must be kept on a lead.* (**mantidos em coleira**)
5 a piece of information that may help police solve a crime □ *The police are following up several new leads.* (**pista**)
6 the main actor in a play, film, etc. (**papel principal**) ▣ *He plays the lead in Miller's new production.* (**faz o papel principal**)

lead² /led/ NOUN [plural **leads**]
1 a soft, dark grey metal (**chumbo**)
2 the dark grey inside part of a pencil (**grafite**)

leader /ˈliːdə(r)/ NOUN [plural **leaders**]
1 a person who is in charge of a group of people □ + **of** the leader of the expedition (**líder, chefe**) 🔲 a religious leader (**líder religioso**) 🔲 the country's political leaders (**chefes políticos**) □ the Republican Party leader
2 the person, team, etc. that is winning a race or competition at a particular time □ He's now just three points behind the leader. (**líder**)
3 the company that sells most of a particular type of product, or the best-selling product itself □ a brand leader (**líder**)
• **leadership** /ˈliːdəʃɪp/ NOUN, NO PLURAL
1 being a leader □ The club has done well under Will's leadership. (**liderança**)
2 the ability to be a good leader □ He's a good worker but he lacks leadership. (**liderança**)

leading /ˈliːdɪŋ/ ADJECTIVE
1 most important or most successful □ He is one of Scotland's leading playwrights. □ the team's leading scorer (**principal, mais importante**)
2 in first position in a race or competition at a particular time □ She was in the leading group with three miles to go. (**principal**)

leaf /liːf/ NOUN [plural **leaves**]
1 a flat green part of a plant or tree that grows out from a stem or a branch □ The sun shone through the leaves. □ a plate of salad leaves (**folha**)
2 a page of a book (**folha, página**)
♦ IDIOMS **take a leaf out of someone's book** to copy someone's behaviour because it is good or successful (**seguir o exemplo de alguém**) **turn over a new leaf** to change your life by starting to behave in a better way (**mudar de vida**)
♦ PHRASAL VERB [**leafs, leafing, leafed**] **leaf through something** to look quickly through the pages of a book, a magazine, etc. □ She sat in the waiting room, leafing through a magazine. (**folhear rapidamente**)

leaflet /ˈliːflɪt/ NOUN [plural **leaflets**] a piece of paper that gives printed information about something □ a leaflet about recycling (**folheto**)

leafy /ˈliːfi/ ADJECTIVE [**leafier, leafiest**]
1 with a lot of leaves □ green leafy vegetables (**coberto de folhas**)
2 with a lot of plants or trees □ a leafy suburb (**frondoso**)

league /liːɡ/ NOUN [plural **leagues**]
1 a group of teams that play sports matches against each other □ the professional basketball league (**liga**) 🔲 I'm still hoping we can win the league this season. (**ganhou a liga**) 🔲 They're top of the league table. (**tabela da liga**)
2 a group of people or things of the same quality (**classe, categoria**) 🔲 She's a good enough actress, but not in the same league as (= definitely not as good as) Katherine Hepburn. (**não na mesma categoria de**) 🔲 The car's in a league of its own (= better than any other) when it comes to fuel economy. (**o melhor em sua categoria**)
3 a group of people or countries who agree to work together (**liga**)
4 be in league with someone to work or plan with someone else, especially to do something bad (**estar em conluio com alguém**)

leak /liːk/ ▶ NOUN [plural **leaks**]
1 a hole that liquid or gas can escape or enter through, or the gas or liquid that escapes □ There could be a leak in the pipe. (**vazamento**) 🔲 a gas leak (**vazamento de gás**)
2 when someone tells people secret information □ There have been too many leaks of classified information. (**divulgação de informações**)
▶ VERB [**leaks, leaking, leaked**]
1 if gas or liquid leaks, it escapes from or enters something and if an object leaks, gas or liquid escapes from or enters it through a hole □ Gas was leaking from somewhere under the floor. □ My boots leak. (**vazar**)
2 to tell people secret information □ This news was leaked to a newspaper yesterday. (**vazar**)
♦ PHRASAL VERB **leak out** if secret information leaks out, it becomes known publicly (**tornar público**)
• **leakage** /ˈliːkɪdʒ/ NOUN [plural **leakages**] when gas, a liquid or information leaks □ We lost a lot of oil through leakage. □ the leakage of private memos (**vazamento**)
• **leaky** /ˈliːki/ ADJECTIVE [**leakier, leakiest**] having small holes or cracks which a gas or liquid can leak out of □ a leaky roof (**furado**)

lean /liːn/ ▶ VERB [**leans, leaning, leant** or **leaned**]
1 to move your body in a particular direction by bending at the waist □ + **forward** He leaned forward to kiss her. □ + **back** She leaned back in her chair. □ + **over** Could you lean over and get the salt for me? □ + **out** She leaned out of the window. (**inclinar-se**)
2 to put something against something so that it is supported by it, or to be in this position □ + **on** She leaned her head on his shoulder. □ + **against** A bike was leaning against the wall. (**apoiar-se**)
3 to be in a position that is not exactly vertical □ The tree leans slightly to one side. (**pender**)
▶ ADJECTIVE [**leaner, leanest**] with no fat or little fat □ I only buy lean meat. (**magro, sem gordura**)

leap /liːp/ ▶ VERB [**leaps, leaping, leapt** or **leaped**]
1 to move suddenly and quickly □ She leapt up and ran to the door. □ I leapt out of bed. (**pular**)
2 to jump high or a long distance □ We saw dolphins leaping out of the water. □ The dancer leapt into the air. (**saltar**)
♦ PHRASAL VERB **leap at something** to accept an offer or to take an opportunity with enthusiasm

□ *I leapt at the chance to meet them.* (agarrar algo)

▶ NOUN [*plural* **leaps**]

1 a big and sudden increase or improvement □ *This is a huge leap forward for us.* □ *a 45% leap in profits* (**pulo**)

2 a big jump □ *He took an impressive leap over the fence.* (**salto**)

◆ IDIOM **in/by leaps and bounds** used to say that someone or something is making progress quickly □ *The team's coming along in leaps and bounds.* (**com grande velocidade**)

leap year /ˈliːp jɪə(r)/ NOUN [*plural* **leap years**] a year that happens every four years and has 366 days. The extra day is February 29. (**ano bissexto**)

learn /lɜːn/ VERB [**learns, learning, learnt** *or* **learned**]

1 to get to know about something or get to knowhow to do something □ *+ to do something* *He's learning to drive.* □ *She wanted to learn English.* □ *+ question word* *I learned how to cook from my mother.* □ *+ about* *We learnt about the local culture.* □ *+ from* *I've learnt from my mistakes.* (**aprender**)

2 to find out some news or information □ *+ that* *I was surprised to learn that she'd already left.* □ *+ of* *I was saddened to learn of his death.* □ *+ whether* *Today he will learn whether he needs surgery.* (**ficar sabendo**)

3 learn your lesson to not do something wrong or silly again because of your past experiences (**aprender a lição**)

• **learned** /ˈlɜːnɪd/ ADJECTIVE a formal word meaning having a lot of knowledge about academic subjects □ *a learned man* (**instruído, erudito**)

• **learner** /ˈlɜːnə(r)/ NOUN [*plural* **learners**] a person who is learning something □ *It's a book for young language learners.* (**aprendiz**) 🔁 *He was a quick learner.* (**um aprendiz veloz**)

• **learning** /ˈlɜːnɪŋ/ NOUN, NO PLURAL

1 the process of learning something □ *He had no aptitude for language learning.* (**aprendizagem**)

2 knowledge, especially from studying □ *a man of great learning* (**saber**)

lease /liːs/ ▶ NOUN [*plural* **leases**] an agreement to rent a flat or a house to someone (**arrendamento, aluguel**) 🔁 *He signed a lease on a two-bedroom apartment.* (**assinou um contrato de aluguel**)

◆ IDIOM **a new lease of life** a new feeling of enthusiasm, happiness or health □ *Since the move he's had a new lease of life.* (**começar uma vida nova**)

▶ VERB [**leases, leasing, leased**] to rent something to someone □ *They lease the land from the local council.* (**arrendar, alugar**)

leash /liːʃ/ NOUN [*plural* **leashes**] a long piece of leather, etc. attached to a dog's collar to control or to lead it (**correia, trela**)

least /liːst/ ▶ ADVERB

1 less than anyone or anything else in size, amount or degree □ *She chose the least expensive trousers.* □ *He always turns up when you least expect him.* □ *These price rises will affect those who are least able to afford them.* (**menos**)

2 at least (a) not less than □ *She must be at least 50.* □ *It will take at least two hours to get there.* (b) used before you add a positive statement after talking about something bad □ *She was very late, but at least she phoned to let us know.* (c) used to correct what you have just said or to make it less certain □ *I saw her in the library – at least, I think it was her.* (**pelo menos**)

3 not least used to emphasize the importance of something □ *I try to avoid her – not least because she's always asking me for money.* (**até porque, mesmo porque**)

▶ DETERMINER, PRONOUN

1 the smallest amount, size or degree □ *The person who had the least difficulty was the tallest.* □ *Of everyone here, I know least about the subject.* □ *He is the richest, but he gave the least.* (**o mínimo**)

2 at the (very) least used to show that this is the smallest amount or degree possible □ *At the very least, you could have offered to help.* (**no mínimo**)

3 not in the least (bit)/not the least bit not at all □ *He wasn't the least bit sorry for all the trouble he caused.* (**de maneira alguma**)

leather /ˈleðə(r)/ NOUN, NO PLURAL a strong material for making shoes, bags and clothes that is made from the skin of an animal □ *a leather jacket* □ *a pair of black leather boots* (**couro**)

leave /liːv/ ▶ VERB [**leaves, leaving, left**]

1 to go away from a place □ *I left the office early.* □ *The train leaves at two.* □ *I left work at four thirty.* (**sair, partir**) 🔁 *I left home when I was 18.* (**saí de casa**)

2 to not take something with you when you go away □ *Maria left her umbrella on the bus.* □ *+ behind* *I left all my books behind.* (**deixar**)

3 to put something or someone somewhere □ *Leave your shoes by the back door.* □ *I left the children with a neighbour.* (**deixar**)

4 to allow something to be in a particular position or state □ *Leave the conditioner in your hair for five minutes.* □ *She left the door unlocked.* (**deixar**)

5 to end a relationship with someone you live with □ *His wife left him.* (**deixar, abandonar**)

6 to cause a situation or an emotion □ *The illness left me without a job.* □ *High crime rates have left people afraid to go out after dark.* (**deixar**)

7 to not use all of something □ *Is there any milk left?* (**de sobra**)

8 to not do something but do it later or let someone else do it □ *I'll leave the washing up* and do it in the morning. □ + to I left all the driving to her. (deixar)

9 to give something to someone after your death □ Her grandmother left Joy all her jewellery. (legar)

10 leave someone/something alone to stop touching something or talking to someone □ Journalists wouldn't leave her alone. □ Leave my clothes alone. (deixar em paz)

⇨ go to **leave someone to their own** *devices*, **leave a bad/bitter/nasty, etc.** *taste* **in your mouth**

♦ PHRASAL VERBS **leave someone/something out** to not include someone or something □ I told him what she said, but I left out the rude bits. (omitir, excluir) □ Some of our members felt left out because they could not do the activities. (sentiram-se excluídas) **leave something over** if something is left over, it is what remains when the rest of something has been used □ There was a lot of food left over from the party. (de sobra)

▶ NOUN, NO PLURAL a period of holiday from work □ I had a week's leave. □ He committed the crime while he was on leave from the army. (licença)

leaves /liːvz/ PLURAL OF **leaf** (ver **leaf**)

lecture /ˈlektʃə(r)/ ▶ NOUN [plural **lectures**]

1 a talk by someone to a group of people to teach them about something □ + on a lecture on economics (conferência) □ He was due to give a lecture at Leeds University. (participar de uma conferência) □ He attended a lecture by Carl Jung. (participou de uma conferência)

2 a long, serious talk which criticizes someone for their behaviour □ He got a lecture from the coach about punctuality. (repreensão)

▶ VERB [**lectures, lecturing, lectured**]

1 to give a lecture or lectures about a particular subject □ He lectured on history at Cambridge University. (dissertar, dar aula)

2 to give someone a long serious talk about their behaviour □ She's always lecturing me about my diet. (repreender)

• **lecturer** /ˈlektʃərə(r)/ NOUN [plural **lecturers**] a person who gives lectures, especially to college and university students (palestrante)

led /led/ PAST TENSE AND PAST PARTICIPLE OF **lead**¹ □ Connor led a wild life for many years. □ Where have you led us? (ver **lead**¹)

ledge /ledʒ/ NOUN [plural **ledges**] a narrow shelf under a window, or a part of a vertical surface that sticks out (borda, aba) □ a window ledge (borda da janela) □ Both birds were perched on a ledge halfway up the cliff.

leek /liːk/ NOUN [plural **leeks**] a long green and white vegetable that tastes like an onion (alho-poró)

leeway /ˈliːweɪ/ NOUN, NO PLURAL freedom to do what you want or to change your plans □ Individual schools now have greater leeway to plan spending. (liberdade, tolerância)

left¹ /left/ ▶ ADJECTIVE, ADVERB on or towards the side of your body that is to the west if you are facing north (esquerdo, à esquerda) □ Can you write with your left hand? (mão esquerda) □ You stand on the left side of him. (lado esquerdo) □ Now turn left. (vire à esquerda) □ Click on the link in the top left corner of the screen.

▶ NOUN, NO PLURAL

1 the left side or direction □ Stop just here on the left. □ Diana is standing to the left of Robert. (esquerda)

2 the left people or groups with political opinions that support ideas about sharing money and power equally (esquerda)

left² /left/ PAST TENSE AND PAST PARTICIPLE OF **leave** □ She left early. □ I've left my book at home. (ver **leave**)

left click /ˌleft ˈklɪk/ VERB [**left clicks, left clicking, left clicked**] to press the left button on a computer mouse so that the computer will do something. A computing word. (clicar com o botão esquerdo do mouse)

left-hand /ˈlefthænd/ ADJECTIVE on the left side of something (à esquerda, do lado esquerdo) □ Look at the numbers on the left-hand side of the page. (no lado esquerdo) □ The ball flew into the bottom left-hand corner of the net. (no canto à esquerda)

left-handed /ˌleftˈhændɪd/ ADJECTIVE using your left hand to do things, especially to write □ Are you lefthanded? □ a left-handed batsman (canhoto)

leftovers /ˈleftəʊvəz/ PLURAL NOUN food that has not been eaten at a meal □ Shall I put the leftovers in the fridge? (sobras, restos de comida)

left wing /ˌleft ˈwɪŋ/ NOUN **the left wing** the members of a political party that believe most strongly in ideas about sharing money and power equally □ the left wing of the Labour Party (ala esquerda)

• **left-wing** /ˈleftˌwɪŋ/ ADJECTIVE supporting the ideas of the political left □ left-wing politicians (ala esquerdista)

leg /leg/ NOUN [plural **legs**]

1 one of the parts of the body that animals and humans stand and walk on □ I broke my leg skiing. □ How many legs do spiders have? □ Try standing on one leg. (perna, pata)

2 the part of a pair of trousers that covers one leg (perna)

3 one of the pieces that support a table, chair, etc. (pé)

4 one part in a journey or a competition □ This is the second leg of the race across Europe. (trecho, caminho)

♦ IDIOMS **not have a leg to stand on** to not have any proof that you are right in an argument □ He'll never win his claim for compensation – he

legacy | length

doesn't have a leg to stand on. (**não ter base, argumento**) **be on its last legs** if something is on its last legs, it is in such a bad condition that it will soon stop working or continuing to exist □ My washing machine's on its last legs. (**estar nas últimas**) **pull someone's leg** to trick someone as a joke □ He didn't really grow the bananas – he's only pulling your leg. (**passar trote em alguém**)

legacy /'legəsɪ/ NOUN [plural **legacies**]
1 something that still exists as a result of things that happened in the past □ Hatred and mistrust are the legacies of war. (**legado**) As a writer he has left a lasting legacy. (**deixou um legado**)
2 something that you receive from someone after their death (**herança**)

legal /'li:gəl/ ADJECTIVE
1 allowed by the law □ Is it legal to ride your bike on the pavement? (**legal, válido**)
2 to do with the law □ the legal profession □ Consult your legal advisor. (**legal**)
• **legalize** or **legalise** /'li:gəlaɪz/ VERB [**legalizes, legalizing, legalized**] to make something allowed by law (**legalizar**)
• **legally** /'li:gəlɪ/ ADVERB in a way that is legal □ He acquired the business legally. (**legalmente**)

legend /'ledʒənd/ NOUN [plural **legends**]
1 an old traditional story that is usually not true □ the legend of St George and the dragon (**lenda**)
2 a very famous person □ Formula One legend, Ayrton Senna (**mito**)
• **legendary** /'ledʒəndrɪ/ ADJECTIVE
1 to do with old stories □ legendary knights (**lendário**)
2 very famous □ His goal-scoring skills were legendary. (**lendário, famoso**)

leggings /'legɪnz/ PLURAL NOUN thin, tight women's trousers made of a material that stretches (**calça legging**)

legible /'ledʒəbəl/ ADJECTIVE legible writing can be read (**legível**)

legion /'li:dʒən/ NOUN [plural **legions**]
1 a very big number □ He still has legions of fans. (**multidão**)
2 in the past, a group of many thousand Roman soldiers (**legião**)

legislate /'ledʒɪsleɪt/ VERB [**legislates, legislating, legislated**] to make a new law or laws □ The government has legislated against smoking in public places. (**legislar, elaborar leis**)
• **legislation** /ˌledʒɪs'leɪʃən/ NOUN, NO PLURAL
1 a set of laws □ The government brought in legislation to improve food labelling. (**leis**)
2 the process of making laws (**legislação**)

legitimate /lɪ'dʒɪtɪmət/ ADJECTIVE
1 allowed by law □ the legitimate government (**legítimo**)
2 having a good reason and so able to be accepted or understood □ In my opinion she has a legitimate complaint. (**legítimo**)

• **legitimately** /lɪ'dʒɪtɪmətlɪ/ ADVERB according to the law □ a legitimately elected government (**legitimamente**)

leisure /'leʒə(r)/ NOUN, NO PLURAL time when you do not have to work □ Families are spending more on leisure. (**lazer**) What do you do in your leisure time? (**período de lazer**)
◆ IDIOM **at your leisure** when you have time □ Take the brochure home and read it at your leisure. (**quando lhe convier**)

leisure centre /'leʒə(r) ˌsentə(r)/ NOUN [plural **leisure centres**] a public building where you can swim and play sports (**centro de lazer**)

leisurely /'leʒəlɪ/ ADVERB without hurrying □ We walked at a leisurely pace. (**vagarosamente**)

lemon /'lemən/ NOUN [plural **lemons**] an oval fruit with a hard, yellow skin and very sour juice □ tea with a slice of lemon □ Add the juice of a lemon. (**limão**)

lemonade /ˌlemə'neɪd/ NOUN [plural **lemonades**]
1 a cold drink with a lemon flavour and a lot of bubbles □ a bottle of lemonade (**limonada**)
2 a cold drink made from fresh lemon juice, water and sugar □ a glass of homemade lemonade (**limonada**)

lend /lend/ VERB [**lends, lending, lent**] to let someone use something or have some money for a short time □ Could you lend me £5, Mum? □ + **to** Adam has lent his MP3 player to Andy. □ The bank no longer lends to first-time buyers. (**emprestar**)
◆ IDIOM **lend a hand** to help someone (**dar uma mão**)

> Remember that when you **lend** something, you give something to someone else to use. When you use something that belongs to someone else, the verb is **borrow** □ Dan lent me his mobile. □ I borrowed Dan's mobile.

length /leŋθ/ NOUN [plural **lengths**]
1 how long something is from one end to the other end □ Measure the table's length. □ The pieces of wood were all different lengths. (**comprimento, extensão**)
2 how long something is in time □ The average length of a stay in hospital is four days. (**duração**)
3 how long a speech or piece of writing is □ Quotes from other authors added to the length of the essay. (**extensão**)
4 at length if you talk at length, you talk for a long time □ The doctor explained the different treatments at length. (**detalhadamente**)
5 a piece of something long and thin such as a rope or pipe □ I need a length of plastic piping. (**pedaço, seção**)

♦ IDIOM **go to great lengths to do something** to make a lot of effort and do a lot of things in order to try to achieve something □ *They went to great lengths to ensure his safety.* (fazer todo o possível para realizar algo)

• **lengthen** /ˈleŋθən/ VERB [lengthens, lengthening, lengthened] to become longer or to make something longer □ *I think you should lengthen that skirt.* □ *Shadows lengthened as the sun went down.* (encompridar)

lengthways /ˈleŋθweɪz/ or **lengthwise** /ˈleŋθwaɪz/ ADVERB in the direction along the length of something □ *Fold the sheet of paper lengthways.* (no sentido do comprimento)

lengthy /ˈleŋθi/ ADJECTIVE [lengthier, lengthiest] taking a long time □ *Getting a passport was a lengthy process.* (comprido)

lenient /ˈliːniənt/ ADJECTIVE
1 not giving severe punishments □ *The judge was too lenient.* (tolerante, indulgente)
2 describes a punishment that is not severe □ *a lenient sentence* (leniente, brando)

lens /lenz/ NOUN [plural lenses]
1 a curved piece of glass that you look through in glasses, cameras and scientific instruments □ *a zoom lens* □ *Adjust the lens in the telescope.* (lente)
2 a part of your eye behind your pupil (= black hole at the front) that helps you see clearly (cristalino)

Lent /lent/ NOUN, NO PLURAL the forty days before Easter when some Christians do not eat something that they like □ *Anna's given up chocolate for Lent.* (quaresma)

lent /lent/ PAST TENSE AND PAST PARTICIPLE OF **lend** □ *I lent him a book.* □ *I've lent her some money.* (ver **lend**)

lentil /ˈlentɪl/ NOUN [plural lentils] a small orange, brown or green seed that is dried and cooked □ *lentil soup* (lentilha)

leopard /ˈlepəd/ NOUN [plural leopards] a large animal of the cat family with yellow fur and dark spots (leopardo)

leotard /ˈliːətɑːd/ NOUN [plural leotards] a tight piece of clothing covering your body from the neck to the top of the legs that you wear for doing exercises or dancing (roupa de malha para ginástica ou dança)

leper /ˈlepə(r)/ NOUN [plural lepers] someone who suffers from leprosy (leproso)

• **leprosy** /ˈleprəsi/ NOUN, NO PLURAL a serious infectious disease that affects the skin and nerves and can damage parts of the body (lepra)

less /les/ ▶ DETERMINER, PRONOUN a smaller amount of □ *We'll have to spend less money.* □ *I have less time than Patrick.* □ *I had less on my plate than you.* □ *+ of He spends less of his time with his children.* (menos)

▶ Notice that **less** is used with uncountable nouns, for example *time* and *money*. With the plural form of countable nouns, for example *cars* and *people*, use **fewer**: □ *I have less money than I used to.* □ *I have fewer problems than I used to.*

▶ ADVERB
1 used to make comparative forms of adjectives and adverbs, with the meaning 'not as much' □ *My clothes are less expensive.* (menos) ▣ *I'm less patient than you.* (menos do que) ▣ *These instructions are a lot less complicated.* (bem menos) ▣ *I'm less and less interested in TV.* (cada vez menos)
2 to a smaller degree □ *I exercise less these days.* ▣ *I eat less than I used to.* (menos do que) ▣ *I see her less and less.* (cada vez menos)
▶ PREPOSITION taking away a particular amount □ *The cost will be £100 less the discount.* (menos)

• **lessen** /ˈlesən/ VERB [lessens, lessening, lessened] to become less or to make something less □ *The drugs should lessen the pain.* (diminuir, reduzir)

-less /lɪs/ SUFFIX **-less** is added to the end of words to mean 'without' □ *hopeless* □ *thoughtless* (sem, desprovido de)

lesser /ˈlesə(r)/ ADJECTIVE not so large or important as other things you are considering □ *Auden, Eliot and a few lesser poets* □ *He had been involved in burglary and other lesser crimes.* (inferior, menor) ▣ *Bill is also guilty but to a lesser extent* (= not as much). (menor extensão)
♦ IDIOM **the lesser of two evils** the less bad or harmful of two bad or harmful things □ *He regarded the Nationalist party as the lesser of two evils.* (o menor dos problemas)

lesson /ˈlesən/ NOUN [plural lessons]
1 a period of time in which you learn something or teach someone something □ *When's your next lesson?* □ *a driving lesson* (aula) ▣ *I'm taking swimming lessons.* (fazendo aulas)
2 something that you learn from life and experiences □ *The war has taught us some valuable lessons.* (lição)
♦ IDIOM **teach someone a lesson** to punish someone so that they will not do something again (dar uma lição em alguém)

let /let/ VERB [lets, letting, let]
1 to allow someone to do something or something to happen □ *He won't let anyone use his tools.* □ *This card lets me travel free.* (deixar)
2 to allow someone or something to go somewhere □ *+ in They won't let him in the building.* □ *She won't let the children out of her sight.* □ *These windows let in the rain.* (deixar)
3 let's used to make a suggestion about what to do □ *Let's go swimming.* □ *Let's get out of here.* (vamos)

4 let go to stop holding something □ *He grasped my hand and wouldn't let go.* □ *Now you can let go of the rope.* (largar)
5 let someone know to tell someone something □ *Could you let Mick know I'll be late?* □ *I want to let everyone know why I acted the way I did.* (informar alguém)
6 Let's see/Let me see used when you are thinking about something or trying to remember something □ *I've worked here for – let me see – over twenty years.* (deixe-me ver)
7 let alone used to emphasize that one thing is even more impossible than another □ *I can't even run for the bus, let alone run a marathon!* (quanto mais, muito menos)
8 to rent a room, building, etc. to someone (alugar)
♦ IDIOMS **let the cat out of the bag** to tell someone something secret, often by mistake □ *We were planning a surprise party, but Alex let the cat out of the bag.* (dar com a língua nos dentes) **let your hair down** to relax and have a good time □ *Come to the party with us – let your hair down for once!* (relaxar e curtir o momento)
⇨ go to **let something** *slip*
♦ PHRASAL VERBS **let someone down** to upset someone by behaving badly or not doing something they expected you to do □ *Our suppliers have let us down.* □ *You've let yourself down and you've let your family down.* (decepcionar, desapontar alguém) **let someone off** to not punish someone for something bad they have done (dispensar) **let on** to tell someone something secret (revelar)

-let /let/ SUFFIX **-let** is added to the end of words to mean 'very small' □ *piglet* (pequeno, diminuto)

lethal /ˈliːθəl/ ADJECTIVE causing or able to cause death □ *a lethal weapon* □ *a lethal dose of the drug* (letal, mortal)

lethargic /ləˈθɑːdʒɪk/ ADJECTIVE having no energy and feeling that you do not want to do anything □ *After my big lunch I felt very lethargic.* (letárgico, apático)
• **lethargy** /ˈleθədʒi/ NOUN, NO PLURAL a feeling of being lethargic (apatia, letargia)

letter /ˈletə(r)/ NOUN [*plural* **letters**]
1 a message that you write and send by post to another person (carta) 🔂 *Why don't you write a letter?* (escreve uma carta) 🔂 *I got a letter from Laura this morning.* (recebi uma carta de)
2 one of the written shapes that you combine to write words, like a, b or c □ *the letters of the alphabet* (letra)

letterbox /ˈletəbɒks/ NOUN [*plural* **letterboxes**]
1 a thin hole in a door or wall through which letters are delivered to a building (caixa de correio)
2 a large metal container with a hole in the front, where people can post letters (caixa de correio)

lettuce /ˈletɪs/ NOUN [*plural* **lettuces**] a vegetable with large green leaves that are used in salads (alface)

leukaemia /luːˈkiːmɪə/ NOUN, NO PLURAL a type of cancer that affects the body's white blood cells (leucemia)

leukemia /luːˈkiːmɪə/ NOUN, NO PLURAL the US spelling of **leukaemia** (leucemia)

level /ˈlevəl/ ▶ ADJECTIVE
1 flat or horizontal □ *a piece of level ground* □ *Add a level tablespoonful of flour.* (raso, plano)
2 at the same height as something else □ **+ with** *The picture needs to be level with the mirror next to it.* (nivelado)
3 having the same score as someone else □ *The two teams were level at half-time.* (uniforme, igual)
▶ NOUN [*plural* **levels**]
1 the amount, size or number of something (nível) 🔂 *Sudoku puzzles need a high level of concentration.* (alto nível) 🔂 *Low levels of contamination were recorded.* (baixos níveis) □ *Unemployment has stayed at the same level for over three years.*
2 a particular height or distance above or below the ground □ *She hung the pictures at eye level.* □ *The water level was rising.* (nível)
3 the particular ability or standard of someone or something □ *It's best to start at beginners' level.* □ *He played squash at international level.* (nível)
4 one of the floors that a building has (nível)
▶ VERB [**levels, levelling/US leveling, levelled/US leveled**]
1 to make something flat, smooth or horizontal □ *The ground will have to be levelled before they can build on it.* (nivelar)
2 to make things equal □ *Gray scored again to level the scores.* (equiparar, comparar)
♦ PHRASAL VERBS **level something at someone**
1 to accuse someone of something □ *Charges of corruption have been levelled at the government.* (acusar alguém de fazer algo)
2 to point a gun at someone or something (apontar arma para alguém) **level off/out** to become flat, equal or level □ *House prices have begun to level off.* □ *The plane levelled out at 2000 feet.* (estabilizar)

level crossing /ˌlevəl ˈkrɒsɪŋ/ NOUN [*plural* **level crossings**] a place where a road crosses a railway line (passagem de nível)

lever /ˈliːvə(r)/ ▶ NOUN [*plural* **levers**]
1 a handle that operates a machine or an engine □ *Push the lever up to start the engine.* □ *a gear lever* (alavanca)
2 a strong bar that you press on in order to move something heavy (alavanca)
▶ VERB [**levers, levering, levered**] to move something by forcing a bar under or behind it □ *He tried to lever the lid off with a knife.* (erguer com alavanca)

levy /ˈlevi/ ▶ VERB [**levies, levying, levied**] to officially take money as a tax □ *VAT is levied on all goods sold.* (**arrecadar**)
▶ NOUN [*plural* **levies**] an amount of money that must be paid, especially a tax □ *The government plan to introduce an extra levy on fuel.* (**arrecadação**)

liability /ˌlaɪəˈbɪləti/ NOUN [*plural* **liabilities**]
1 legal responsibility for something □ *The driver of the other car has admitted liability for the crash.* (**responsabilidade**)
2 a person or thing that causes serious problems for you (**obrigações, encargos**)

liable /ˈlaɪəbəl/ ADJECTIVE
1 liable to do something often doing something, especially something bad □ *She's liable to lose her temper.* (**propenso a fazer algo**)
2 legally responsible for something □ *You are liable for any damage you cause.* (**responsável por**)

liaise /liˈeɪz/ VERB [**liaises, liaising, liaised**] to exchange information regularly with other people so that you can work together effectively □ *You will need to liaise with staff in other departments.* (**estabelecer ligação**)
• **liaison** /liˈeɪzɒn/ NOUN, NO PLURAL communication between different groups or organizations that work together □ *We need better liaison between the departments.* (**contato, ligação**)

liar /ˈlaɪə(r)/ NOUN [*plural* **liars**] someone who tells lies (**mentiroso**)

libel /ˈlaɪbəl/ NOUN [*plural* **libels**] the printing of a statement about someone that is not true and that damages people's opinion of them □ *He sued the newspaper for libel.* (**calúnia, difamação**)

liberal /ˈlɪbərəl/ ADJECTIVE
1 accepting different ideas and types of behaviour □ *It's a very liberal society.* (**liberal, tolerante**)
2 liberal political parties believe in greater personal freedom and a more equal society (**liberal**)

liberally /ˈlɪbərəli/ ADVERB in large amounts or generously □ *Pour the sauce liberally over the dish.* (**liberalmente**)

liberate /ˈlɪbəreɪt/ VERB [**liberates, liberating, liberated**] to set someone free □ *The hostages were eventually liberated by the army.* (**liberar**)
• **liberation** /ˌlɪbəˈreɪʃən/ NOUN, NO PLURAL being set free from someone else's control □ *the liberation of France in 1945* (**liberação**)

liberty /ˈlɪbəti/ NOUN [*plural* **liberties**] freedom to do or say what you want, or go where you want □ *Prisoners are deprived of their liberty.* (**liberdade**)

librarian /laɪˈbreərɪən/ NOUN [*plural* **librarians**] someone who works in a library □ *the school librarian* (**bibliotecário**)
• **library** /ˈlaɪbrəri/ NOUN [*plural* **libraries**] a building or room that has a lot of books, CDs or DVDs that you can borrow (**biblioteca**) 🔁 *library books* (**livros da biblioteca**)

lice /laɪs/ PLURAL OF **louse** (*ver* **louse**)

licence /ˈlaɪsəns/ NOUN [*plural* **licences**] an official document that gives someone permission to do or have something □ *a driving licence* □ *a licence to sell alcohol* (**licença**)

license /ˈlaɪsəns/ ▶ VERB [**licenses, licensing, licensed**] to give someone official permission to do something □ *The restaurant is licensed to serve alcohol.* (**autorizar**)
▶ NOUN the US spelling of **licence** (**licença**)

lichen /ˈlaɪkən, ˈlɪtʃən/ NOUN [*plural* **lichens**] a type of very small plant that grows on surfaces like rocks and trees (**líquen**)

lick /lɪk/ ▶ VERB [**licks, licking, licked**] to move your tongue over something □ *The cat was licking its paws.* □ *She licked her lips nervously.* (**lamber**)
▶ NOUN [*plural* **licks**]
1 a movement of your tongue over something □ *Can I have a lick of your lolly?* (**lambida**)
2 a lick of paint a layer of paint □ *A lick of paint and this room will be fine.* (**demão de tinta**)

licorice /ˈlɪkərɪs/ NOUN, NO PLURAL the US spelling of **liquorice** (**licor**)

lid /lɪd/ NOUN [*plural* **lids**] a cover that fits the top of a container □ *Can you get the lid off this jar?* (**tampa**)

lie¹ /laɪ/ ▶ VERB [**lies, lying, lied**] to say something that you know is not true □ **+ about** *He lied about his age.* □ **+ to** *Did you lie to me?* (**mentir**)
▶ NOUN [*plural* **lies**] something that you say that is not true when you know that it is not true (**mentira**) 🔁 *He's always telling lies.* (**contando mentiras**)

> ▶ Notice that people **tell lies**. They do not 'say lies':
> ✓ *Don't tell lies, Oliver.*
> ✗ *Don't say lies, Oliver.*

lie² /laɪ/ VERB [**lies, lying, lay, lain**]
1 to be in a flat position, for example on the floor or on a bed, or to put your body in this position □ *She's been lying on a beach all day.* □ *Lie flat on your back.* □ *Go and lie on the couch.* (**deitar**)
2 to be on a surface □ *There were clothes lying all over the floor.* □ *Snow lay on the hills.* (**ficar**)
3 to be in a particular position □ *The town lies to the east of Geneva.* (**encontrar-se**)
♦ PHRASAL VERBS **lie down** to put your body in a flat position, especially to rest □ *I don't feel well – I'm going to lie down for a while.* (**deitar-se**) **lie in** to stay in bed in the morning later than usual □ *I usually lie in on Sundays.* (**ficar na cama até tarde**)

> ▶ Notice that the past tense of **lie** when it means 'to say something that you know is not true' is **lied**. The past tense of **lie** when it means 'to be in a flat position' is **lay**.

lieutenant

lieutenant /lɛfˈtɛnənt/ NOUN [plural **lieutenants**] an officer in the army or navy (**tenente**)

life /laɪf/ NOUN [plural **lives**]

1 the time between being born and dying (**vida**) ▣ He *spent* his *life* helping others. (**passou sua vida**) ▣ I've had these problems my *whole life*. (**vida toda**) ▣ He lived in Glasgow *all his life*. (**toda sua vida**) □ Our lives have been ruined by this disease.

2 the way someone lives (**vida**) ▣ They *live a simple life*. (**levam uma vida simples**) ▣ We *lead a quiet life*. (**levamos uma vida**) ▣ This course will *change your life*. (**mudar sua vida**)

3 the existence of a person (**vida**) ▣ I'm not prepared to *risk* my *life* to save your dog. ▣ He saved my *life*. ▣ Hundreds of soldiers have *lost their lives* in this conflict.

4 no plural the state of being alive □ I kept feeling her pulse for any sign of life. (**vida**)

5 real life the way things are in the real world □ You see all these rich people on TV, but real life isn't like that. (**vida real**)

6 someone's personal/professional/social, etc. life a particular part of someone's existence (**a vida pessoal/profissional/social de alguém**)

7 no plural L living things □ Is there human life anywhere else in the universe? □ plant life (**vida, existência**)

8 the period of time that something exists or works (**período/duração**) ▣ This table *started life* as part of a railway track. (**iniciou o período**) □ Using this feature will extend the life of your batteries.

9 energy and enthusiasm □ Try to put a bit more life into your singing. (**vida**) ▣ He's always *full of life*. (**cheio de vida**)

lifeboat /ˈlaɪfboʊt/ NOUN [plural **lifeboats**] a boat used for saving people from dangerous situations at sea □ the lifeboat crew (**barco salva-vidas**)

life coach /ˈlaɪf ˌkoʊtʃ/ NOUN [plural **life coaches**] someone who is employed to give someone advice about how to get what they want in life (**conselheiro pessoal**)

life-cycle /ˈlaɪfˌsaɪkəl/ NOUN [plural **life-cycles**] the different forms that a living thing changes into during its life (**ciclo de vida**)

life expectancy /ˈlaɪf ɪkˈspɛktənsi/ NOUN [plural **life expectancies**] how long someone is likely to live (**expectativa de vida**)

lifeguard /ˈlaɪfɡɑːd/ NOUN [plural **lifeguards**] someone who works at a swimming pool or on a beach, helping people who are in dangerous situations in the water (**guarda-costas**)

life jacket /ˈlaɪf ˌdʒækɪt/ NOUN [plural **life jackets**] a jacket filled with air that will float and stop someone from sinking in water (**colete salva-vidas**)

light

lifeless /ˈlaɪflɪs/ ADJECTIVE

1 dead or seeming dead □ Her brother lay lifeless in the corner. (**sem vida, morto**)

2 with no energy or emotion □ a lifeless performance (**inerte**)

lifelike /ˈlaɪflaɪk/ ADJECTIVE looking like a real thing or person □ a lifelike doll (**semelhante, natural**)

lifeline /ˈlaɪflaɪn/ NOUN [plural **lifelines**] something that you depend on, usually because it is your only way of communicating when you need help □ The telephone is her lifeline. (**único meio de contato**)

lifelong /ˈlaɪflɒŋ/ ADJECTIVE lasting the whole of your life (**para a vida toda, vitalício**) ▣ They were *lifelong friends*. (**amigos para a vida toda**)

life-size /ˈlaɪfˌsaɪz/ ADJECTIVE being the same size as the real person or thing □ a life-size model of James Bond (**do tamanho natural**)

lifespan /ˈlaɪfspæn/ NOUN [plural **lifespans**] the length of time someone lives or something lasts □ A lot of modern appliances have a short lifespan. (**expectativa de vida**)

lifestyle /ˈlaɪfstaɪl/ NOUN [plural **lifestyles**] the way that someone lives □ We try to have a healthy lifestyle. (**estilo de vida**)

lifetime /ˈlaɪftaɪm/ NOUN [plural **lifetimes**] the length of time that a particular person is alive □ These children will see such technological advances in their lifetime. (**vida**)

lift /lɪft/ ▶ VERB [**lifts, lifting, lifted**]

1 to move something upwards or raise it □ She lifted the baby out of his cot. □ He was so weak that he couldn't lift his head. (**erguer**)

2 to move upwards and disappear □ The fog seems to be lifting. (**levantar, subir**)

3 to officially end a rule that says something is not allowed □ The ban on imports was lifted last month. (**suspender, revogar**)

▶ NOUN [plural **lifts**]

1 a machine like a large box that carries people or things between floors in a tall building (**elevador**) ▣ *Take the lift* to the sixth floor. (**pegue o elevador**)

2 a ride in someone's car (**carona**) ▣ Could you *give me a lift* home? (**me dar uma carona**)

3 when you move something or someone upwards □ Try to do ten lifts with each leg. (**levantamento**)

lift-off /ˈlɪftɒf/ NOUN [plural **lift-offs**] the time when a spacecraft leaves the ground (**lançamento**)

ligament /ˈlɪɡəmənt/ NOUN [plural **ligaments**] a band of strong tissue in the body that joins bones together. A biology word □ He has torn a ligament in his thigh. (**ligamento**)

light /laɪt/ ▶ NOUN [plural **lights**]

1 no plural brightness from something such as the sun or a piece of electrical equipment □ There isn't enough light to read. (**luz**) ▣ A ray of *light shone through the curtains.* (raio de luz) ◻ *The room was filled with bright light.* (luz brilhante)

2 a piece of equipment that produces light (luz) ◻ *Don't forget to switch off the light.* (apagar a luz) ◻ *I turned on the light.* (acendi a luz) ◻ *Where is the light switch?* (interruptor)

3 set light to something to make something burn (colocar fogo em algo)

4 a flame that you use to make a cigarette burn (isqueiro) ◻ *Have you got a light?* (tem isqueiro)

♦ IDIOMS **bring something to light** if facts are brought to light, they are discovered ◻ *Investigation of the company's accounts brought to light the scale of the fraud.* (descobrir algo) **come to light** if facts come to light, people discover them ◻ *The mistake only came to light a year later.* (tornar-se conhecido) **shed/throw light on something** to provide information that helps people understand something ◻ *I was wondering if you could shed any light on the matter of the missing documents?* (explicar algo)

▶ ADJECTIVE [**lighter, lightest**]

1 bright or not dark ◻ *It's still light enough to read.* (claro) ◻ *Mike got up as soon as it began to get light.* (ficar claro)

2 pale in colour ◻ *light blue* ◻ *You can make colours lighter by adding white to them.* (claro)

3 not heavy ◻ *My bike has a very light frame.* ◻ *This bag feels light.* (leve)

4 not strong or in large amounts (leve, suave) ◻ *Light winds reduced the temperature.* (brisa suave) ◻ *Traffic is light around London tonight.* (o trânsito está leve) ◻ *I felt a light touch on my arm.*

5 not serious or difficult ◻ *I did a little light housework.* ◻ *I want some light reading for my holiday.* (fácil)

♦ IDIOM **make light of something** to act or talk as if something is not serious ◻ *She makes light of her problems.* (não ligar algo a sério)

▶ VERB [**lights, lighting, lit**]

1 to make something start to burn (acender) ◻ *Let's light the fire.* (acender o fogo)

2 to start burning ◻ *Why won't the cooker light?* (acender)

3 to light a place is to make it brighter ◻ *The stage was lit with candles.* (iluminar)

♦ PHRASAL VERB **light up** if your face or eyes light up, you suddenly look happy (iluminar-se)

light bulb /laɪt bʌlb/ NOUN [plural **light bulbs**] a hollow glass object that contains a wire which produces light when electricity passes through it ◻ *energy-saving light bulbs* (lâmpada)

lighten /ˈlaɪtən/ VERB [**lightens, lightening, lightened**]

1 if a situation lightens or is lightened, it becomes less serious (aliviar) ◻ *He tried to lighten the mood by making a few jokes.* (animar o ambiente)

2 to make something brighter ◻ *The white walls certainly lighten the room.* (tornar-se claro)

3 to reduce the amount of work that must be done ◻ *Having an assistant has lightened my workload.* (aliviar)

♦ PHRASAL VERB **lighten up** to become less serious. An informal phrase. ◻ *You've got to learn to lighten up a bit.* (descontrair)

lighter /ˈlaɪtə(r)/ NOUN [plural **lighters**] a small object that produces a flame to make a cigarette start burning ◻ *Do you have a lighter I could use?* (isqueiro)

light-hearted /ˌlaɪtˈhɑːtɪd/ ADJECTIVE for fun and not serious ◻ *a light-hearted remark* (alegre, despreocupado)

lighthouse /ˈlaɪthaʊs/ NOUN [plural **lighthouses**] a tall, narrow building next to the sea with a flashing light at the top to tell ships of danger or to show them where to go (farol)

light industry /laɪt ˈɪndəstri/ NOUN, NO PLURAL factories that produce small goods such as electrical parts for machines in the home (indústria leve)

lighting /ˈlaɪtɪŋ/ NOUN, NO PLURAL the lights used in a room ◻ *soft lighting* (iluminação)

lightly /ˈlaɪtli/ ADVERB

1 gently ◻ *She touched me lightly on the arm and smiled.* (levemente)

2 not much ◻ *a lightly boiled egg* ◻ *She was lightly tanned.* (ligeiramente)

3 not in a serious way ◻ *I did not take this decision lightly* (= I thought about it very seriously). (impensadamente)

♦ IDIOM **get off lightly** to be punished less than you expected or have less trouble than you expected ◻ *Brown got off lightly with a yellow card for the foul.* (receber castigo leve)

lightning /ˈlaɪtnɪŋ/ ▶ NOUN, NO PLURAL a bright flash of electricity in the sky that sometimes happens in a storm ◻ *a flash of lightning* (raio, relâmpago) ◻ *thunder and lightning* (raios e trovões) ◻ *The church steeple was struck by lightning in the storm.* (atingida por um raio)

▶ ADJECTIVE very fast or sudden (rápido, de surpresa) ◻ *The firemen called a lightning strike.* (golpe rápido)

lightweight /ˈlaɪtweɪt/ ADJECTIVE

1 not heavy ◻ *a lightweight raincoat* (leve)

2 not important or serious ◻ *a lightweight comedy* (leve)

light year /laɪt jɪə(r)/ NOUN [plural **light years**] the distance that light travels in a year, which is 6 billion miles (ano-luz)

likable /ˈlaɪkəbəl/ ADJECTIVE another spelling of **likeable** (agradável, amável)

like¹ /laɪk/ ▶ PREPOSITION

1 similar to ◻ *Geraldine looks just like her mother.* (como)

2 in a similar way to ◻ *She dances like a professional.* (como)

3 if you ask what someone or something is like, you want someone to describe them □ *What's your new teacher like?* (**como**)
4 typical of □ *It's not like you to be late.* (**típico de**)
5 used to give examples □ *I love sports like tennis and badminton.* (**como**)
◆ IDIOM **look/feel like death warmed up** to look or feel very ill (**sentir-se muito mal**)
▶ CONJUNCTION
1 as if □ *You look like you've seen a ghost.* (**como**)
2 in the same way as. An informal word □ *Tie the knot like I showed you.* (**como**)

like² /laɪk/ VERB [likes, liking, liked]
1 to think that something or someone is pleasant or enjoyable □ *I like pizza.* □ *I don't like football.* (**gostar de**) 🔁 *I like this house better than our old house.* (**gosto mais**) 🔁 *I don't like the idea of eating raw fish.* (**não gosto da ideia**) 🔁 *He liked the way she talked.* (**gostou do jeito**) □ *+ ing I don't like coming home after dark.* □ *+ to do something I like to get up early.*
2 Would you like …? used to offer someone something □ *Would you like a biscuit?* □ *Would you like to come with us?* (**Você gostaria de…?**)
3 would like if you would like something, you want it □ *I'd like a cup of tea.* (**querer**)
4 would like to do something if you would like to do something, you want to do it □ *I'd like to go home now.* (**gostaria de fazer algo**)
5 if you like (a) used when you make an offer □ *I'll come with you if you like.* (b) used to say yes when someone suggests doing something □ *'Shall I bring some food?' 'Yes, if you like.'* (**se quiser**)

> Notice that would like meaning 'want to do something' (sense 4) is followed by the verb form to do something:
> ✓ *I would like to go home.*
> ✗ *I would like that I go home.*

likeable /'laɪkəbəl/ ADJECTIVE a likeable person is nice and easy to like (**agradável, amável**)
likelihood /'laɪklɪhʊd/ NOUN, NO PLURAL how likely it is that something will happen □ *There's a strong likelihood of rain today.* (**probabilidade**)

likely /'laɪklɪ/ ADJECTIVE
1 expected to happen □ *+ to do something People are more likely to come if the weather is good.* □ *+ that It's very likely that nobody will come.* (**é provável que**)
2 probably true □ *That seems the most likely explanation.* (**provável**)

like-minded /,laɪk'maɪndɪd/ ADJECTIVE having similar opinions and enjoying the same things □ *She set up the film club with a group of like-minded friends.* (**com as mesmas ideias**)
liken /'laɪkən/ VERB [likens, likening, likened] to say that two people or things are like each other □ *Her writing has been likened to J. K. Rowling's.* (**assemelhar**)
likeness /'laɪknɪs/ NOUN [plural likenesses]
1 when two people or things are similar in appearance (**semelhança**) 🔁 *There is a strong likeness between the girls.* (**forte semelhança**)
2 something that looks very similar to the real thing or person □ *It's a good likeness of your father.* (**semelhança**)
likewise /'laɪkwaɪz/ ADVERB in the same way. A formal word. (**do mesmo modo, igualmente**) 🔁 *Peter has left and I suggest we do likewise.* (**fazermos do mesmo modo**)
liking /'laɪkɪŋ/ NOUN, NO PLURAL
1 when you enjoy something (**preferência**) 🔁 *Most children have a liking for chocolate.* (**têm preferência por**)
2 for your liking if something is too big/bright etc. for your liking, it is bigger/brighter, etc. than you want it to be □ *The bed was too soft for my liking.* (**para seu gosto**)
3 take a liking to someone to start to like someone that you have just met (**simpatizar com alguém**)
4 to be to someone's liking if something is to someone's liking, it is how they like it. A formal phrase. □ *Is the room to your liking, Madam?* (**estar do gosto de alguém**)
lilac /'laɪlək/ ▶ NOUN [plural lilacs]
1 a bush or tree with groups of white or purple flowers that hang down (**lilás**)
2 a pale purple colour (**lilás**)
▶ ADJECTIVE pale purple (**lilás**)
lily /'lɪlɪ/ NOUN [plural lilies] a tall plant with large white or coloured flowers that smell very sweet (**lírio**)
limb /lɪm/ NOUN [plural limbs]
1 a leg or an arm (**membro**)
2 a large branch of a tree (**galho**)
lime /laɪm/ ▶ NOUN [plural limes]
1 a small, sour fruit that looks like a green lemon □ *Add the juice of two limes.* (**lima**)
2 a large tree with yellow flowers (**visgo**)
3 no plural a white substance that is used to help plants grow and to make cement (= substance used in building) (**cal**)
4 no plural a bright green colour (**verde-limão**)
▶ ADJECTIVE having a bright green colour □ *a lime green shirt* (**verde-limão**)
limelight /'laɪmlaɪt/ NOUN, NO PLURAL **the limelight** attention that famous people get from the public □ *She liked being in the limelight.* (**publicidade**)
limerick /'lɪmərɪk/ NOUN [plural limericks] a funny poem with five lines (**poema leve**)
limestone /'laɪmstəʊn/ NOUN, NO PLURAL a type of rock that is used in building and in making cement (= grey powder mixed with water and used for building) (**calcário**)

limit /'lɪmɪt/ ▶ NOUN [plural limits]

1 the largest or smallest amount or level that is allowed (limite) ⬜ There's a time limit for this test (limite de tempo) ⬜ She had above the legal limit of alcohol in her blood. (limite legal) ⬜ Each person is allowed 10 kg of luggage, and you are over the limit (acima do limite)

2 the largest amount or level of something that is possible ⬜ + to There's a limit to how much I can help her. (limite, extremo)

3 the outside edge of an area ⬜ the city limits (limite, fronteira)

▶ VERB [limits, limiting, limited]

1 to keep someone or something below a particular amount or level ⬜ Places on the course are limited, so book early. ⬜ People covered their windows to limit damage from the storm. ⬜ + to I shall have to limit you to one cake each. (limitar)

2 if something is limited to a particular place or group of people, it only happens or exists in that place or group ⬜ + to These beliefs are not limited to rural communities. (restringir)

• **limitation** /ˌlɪmɪ'teɪʃən/ NOUN [plural limitations]

1 something that stops something from reaching the highest possible amount or level ⬜ We have to work within the limitations of the law. ⬜ The government has placed limitations on their freedom to demonstrate. (restrição)

2 an area in which someone or something is not good ⬜ Life in the country has its limitations. (limitação)

• **limited** /'lɪmɪtɪd/ ADJECTIVE small in amount or number ⬜ a limited choice (limitado)

limousine /'lɪməzi:n/ NOUN [plural limousines]
a large expensive car with a driver ⬜ a chauffeur-driven limousine (limusine)

limp /lɪmp/ ▶ VERB [limps, limping, limped]
to walk with difficulty because your leg or foot hurts ⬜ Beckham limped off the pitch. (mancar)

• NOUN, NO PLURAL a way of walking that is not even and shows that someone's leg or foot hurts ⬜ He walked with a limp. (manqueira)

• ADJECTIVE [limper, limpest] not stiff or firm ⬜ This lettuce has gone a bit limp. (murcho) ⬜ a limp handshake (aperto de mão frouxo)

limpet /'lɪmpɪt/ NOUN [plural limpets]
a small sea creature with a shell shaped like a cone that fastens itself to rocks (lapa)

line /laɪn/ ▶ NOUN [plural lines]

1 a long thin mark ⬜ There are white lines in the middle of the road. (linha) ⬜ Draw a straight line from A to B. (linha reta) ⬜ Sign on the dotted line (linha pontilhada) ⬜ The first runners have already crossed the finishing line (linha de chegada)

2 a row of things or people ⬜ The children formed an orderly line. ⬜ There is a line of fine oak trees by the road. (fila)

3 a border between two areas or two situations ⬜ They crossed the state line that morning. (limite, fronteira) ⬜ There can be a fine line (= a very small difference) between humour and rudeness. (sutil limite)

4 a row of words on a page ⬜ Look at the first line of the poem. (verso)

5 a piece of rope, wire, etc. used for a particular purpose ⬜ I was hanging the washing on the line. (fio, cordão)

6 a telephone connection ⬜ There's a strange noise on this line. (conexão)

7 a mark on an older person's face (ruga)

8 a part of a railway ⬜ Flooding has closed the line between Edinburgh and Glasgow. (via)

9 an opinion or a way of thinking about something ⬜ + on What's your company's line on flexible working hours? (linha, direção) ⬜ Her line of argument was that more families should receive financial help. (linha de discussão)

10 the US word for queue (ver queue)

11 along the lines of something similar to something ⬜ I wrote a letter along the lines of the one I sent to Bob. (semelhante a algo)

⇨ go to draw the line, read between the lines

▶ VERB [lines, lining, lined]

1 to be in a row along the sides of something ⬜ Police officers will line the route of the procession. (alinhar)

2 to cover the inside of a piece of clothing or a container with something ⬜ The cloak is lined with fur. (encapar)

♦ PHRASAL VERB **line (someone/something) up** to stand in a row or to put people or things in a row ⬜ Line up by the door. ⬜ All the spice jars were lined up on the shelf. (dispor algo/alguém em fila)

linear /'lɪnɪə(r)/ ADJECTIVE

1 connected with or using lines or length ⬜ linear measurements (linear)

2 able to be represented by a straight line. A maths word. ⬜ a linear equation (linear)

lined /laɪnd/ ADJECTIVE

1 a lined piece of clothing has material sewn on the inside ⬜ a lined jacket (forrado)

2 lined skin has a lot of marks because of age (marcado)

3 lined paper has lines on it to write on (pautado)

linen /'lɪnɪn/ NOUN, NO PLURAL

1 a type of cloth like a heavy, slightly rough, cotton that is made from a plant ⬜ a linen jacket (linho)

2 things made of cloth used to cover beds or tables ⬜ table linen (roupa branca)

liner /'laɪnə(r)/ NOUN [plural liners]

1 a large ship that carries passengers (navio de cruzeiro)

2 something that is put inside a container to keep it clean ⬜ a bin liner (revestimento)

linesman /'laɪnzmən/ NOUN [plural linesmen]
a man whose job is to decide whether a ball has

linger

crossed a line during a game such as tennis or football (**juiz de linha**)

linger /ˈlɪŋgə(r)/ VERB [**lingers, lingering, lingered**] to stay somewhere for a long time □ *Fans were still lingering at the stage door.* □ *The smell of fish seemed to linger for days.* (**subsistir**)

lingerie /ˈlænʒəri/ NOUN, NO PLURAL women's underwear □ *expensive silk lingerie* (**lingerie, roupa íntima feminina**)

linguist /ˈlɪŋgwɪst/ NOUN [*plural* **linguists**] someone who speaks a lot of languages, or someone who teaches linguistics (**linguista**)

• **linguistic** /lɪŋˈgwɪstɪk/ ADJECTIVE to do with language or linguistics (**linguístico**)

• **linguistics** /lɪŋˈgwɪstɪks/ NOUN, NO PLURAL the scientific study of language (**linguística**)

lining /ˈlaɪnɪŋ/ NOUN [*plural* **linings**] a covering on the inside of a piece of clothing or a container □ *a jacket lining* □ *a silver box with a velvet lining* (**forro**)

link /lɪŋk/ ▶ NOUN [*plural* **links**]

1 a relationship between two people or things □ *+ between Research soon proved the link between smoking and lung cancer.* □ *+ with It is thought that the group has links with terrorist organizations.* (**elo, vínculo**)

2 a way of travelling between two places □ *There's a new rail link between the airport and the city centre.* (**conexão**)

3 a connection between two files, especially on a website. A computing word. □ *Click on the link to reserve your tickets.* (**conexão**)

4 one of the rings of a chain (**elo**)

▶ VERB [**links, linking, linked**]

1 if two people or things are linked, they are connected to each other in some way □ *The two murders are not thought to be linked.* □ *Were these two events linked in any way?* (**unir**) 🔁 *Diet and health are closely linked.* (**fortemente unidos**)

2 to provide a way of travelling between two places □ *A walkway links the two buildings.* (**ligar**)

♦ PHRASAL VERB **link (something/someone) up** to form a connection □ *Other stores have linked up with designers to produce more collections.* (**unir-se a algo/alguém**)

lint /lɪnt/ NOUN, NO PLURAL a soft type of cloth for covering cuts or small injuries (**retalho fino, compressa**)

lion /ˈlaɪən/ NOUN [*plural* **lions**] a large, wild animal of the cat family, the male of which has thick hair around its head (**leão**)

lioness /ˈlaɪənes/ NOUN [*plural* **lionesses**] a female lion (**leoa**)

lip /lɪp/ NOUN [*plural* **lips**]

1 either the upper or the lower outside edge of your mouth □ *He kissed her lightly on the lips.* (**lábio**)

list

2 the edge of a container that liquid is poured out of (**aba, orla**)

liposuction /ˈlɪpəʊˌsʌkʃən/ NOUN, NO PLURAL a medical treatment in which fat is sucked out of someone's body to make them look thinner (**lipoaspiração**)

lip-read /ˈlɪp riːd/ VERB [**lip-reads, lip-reading, lipread**] to watch the way someone's lips move in order to understand what they are saying because you cannot hear them (**leitura labial**)

• **lip-reading** /ˈlɪpˌriːdɪŋ/ NOUN, NO PLURAL when someone lip-reads (**leitura labial**)

lipstick /ˈlɪpstɪk/ NOUN [*plural* **lipsticks**] make--up that women put on their lips to make the lips a different colour □ *She was wearing bright red lipstick.* (**batom**)

liqueur /lɪˈkjʊə(r)/ NOUN [*plural* **liqueurs**] a strong, sweet alcoholic drink, usually drunk at the end of a meal □ *an orange liqueur* (**licor**)

liquid /ˈlɪkwɪd/ ▶ NOUN [*plural* **liquids**] a substance that can flow, such as water or oil □ *In hot weather make sure you drink plenty of liquids.* (**líquido**)

▶ ADJECTIVE in the form of a liquid □ *a liquid detergent* (**líquido**)

• **liquidize** or **liquidise** /ˈlɪkwɪdaɪz/ VERB [**liquidizes, liquidizing, liquidized**] to make something into a liquid □ *Add 300 ml of water and liquidize the ingredients.* (**liquidificar**)

• **liquidizer** or **liquidiser** /ˈlɪkwɪdaɪzə(r)/ NOUN [*plural* **liquidizers**] a machine for making solid food into a smooth liquid (**liquidificador**)

liquor /ˈlɪkə(r)/ NOUN, NO PLURAL a US word for alcoholic drink (**licor**)

liquorice /ˈlɪkərɪs/ NOUN, NO PLURAL a black sweet made using the root of a plant (**alcaçuz**)

lisp /lɪsp/ ▶ NOUN [*plural* **lisps**] a way of speaking in which 's' sounds like 'th' (**ceceio**) 🔁 *Al has a slight lisp.* (**fala com ceceio**)

▶ VERB [**lisps, lisping, lisped**] to speak with a lisp (**cecear**)

list /lɪst/ ▶ NOUN [*plural* **lists**] a group of things such as names, numbers or prices, written one below the other □ *His name is on the list* (**lista**) 🔁 *a shopping list* (**lista de compras**) 🔁 *I've added your name to the list.* (**adicionei à lista**) 🔁 *You should make a list of things to do.* (**fazer uma lista**)

> ➤ Notice the preposition. Something is on a list and not 'in' a list:
> ✓ *I'll put your name on the list.*
> ✗ *I'll put your name in the list.*

▶ VERB [**lists, listing, listed**] to write a list, or to give information in the form of a list □ *The players are listed alphabetically.* (**listar**)

listen

listen /ˈlɪsən/ VERB [listens, listening, listened]
1 to pay attention to a sound so that you can hear it □ **+ to** *Listen to me when I'm talking!* □ *Do you ever listen to classical music?* □ *I often listen to the radio.* (ouvir)
2 to pay attention to someone's advice and do what they suggest □ *I told you to wear a coat but you wouldn't listen!* (ouvir)
♦ PHRASAL VERBS **listen (out) for something** to try to hear something □ *Will you listen out for the baby while I'm in the shower?* (prestar atenção a algo) **listen in (on something)** to secretly listen to other people speaking □ *The police had been listening in on his calls.* (ouvir algo em segredo)
• **listener** /ˈlɪsənə(r)/ NOUN [plural listeners]
1 someone who listens to a radio show □ *listeners to the breakfast show* (ouvinte)
2 a good listener someone who listens when people speak to them and concentrates on what they are saying (um bom ouvinte)

listless /ˈlɪstlɪs/ ADJECTIVE tired and without energy □ *She had felt listless all day.* (lânguido)

lit /lɪt/ PAST TENSE AND PAST PARTICIPLE OF **light** □ *She lit the fire.* □ *I haven't lit the candles yet.* (ver **light**)

liter /ˈliːtə(r)/ NOUN [plural liters] the US spelling of **litre** (ver **litre**)

literacy /ˈlɪtərəsi/ NOUN, NO PLURAL the ability to read and write □ *There are concerns over levels of literacy and numeracy.* (alfabetização)

literal /ˈlɪtərəl/ ADJECTIVE meaning exactly what the word says (literal) 🔹 *That's the literal translation.* (tradução literal) 🔹 *The hole in the ozone layer isn't a hole in the literal sense.* (em sentido literal)
• **literally** /ˈlɪtərəli/ ADVERB
1 used to emphasize that something surprising is true □ *One side was literally two centimetres lower than the other.* (literalmente)
2 in a literal way □ *The word literally translates as chief or leader.* (literalmente)

literary /ˈlɪtərəri/ ADJECTIVE to do with books, writers and literature (literário) 🔹 *a literary critic* (crítica literária) □ *a literary magazine*

literate /ˈlɪtərət/ ADJECTIVE able to read and write □ *He had no education and was barely literate.* (alfabetizado)

literature /ˈlɪtrətʃə(r)/ NOUN, NO PLURAL
1 stories, poetry and plays □ *He's studying English literature.* □ *20th-century children's literature* (literatura)
2 all the written information about a subject □ *Most scientific literature supports the theory.* (literatura)

litigation /ˌlɪtɪˈɡeɪʃən/ NOUN, NO PLURAL a formal word meaning the use of the legal system to make a decision about a disagreement □ *We hope to avoid litigation.* (litígio)

litmus /ˈlɪtməs/ NOUN, NO PLURAL a substance that shows whether something is acid or alkaline. A chemistry word. (tornassol)

litmus paper /ˈlɪtməs ˌpeɪpə(r)/ NOUN, NO PLURAL a type of paper containing litmus, used to show whether something is acid or alkaline. A chemistry word. (papel de tornassol)

litre /ˈliːtə(r)/ NOUN [plural litres] a unit for measuring liquid, equal to 100 centilitres □ **+ of** *a litre of water* □ *Petrol now costs more than £1 per litre.* (litro)

litter /ˈlɪtə(r)/ ▶ NOUN [plural litters]
1 paper and other rubbish that people have thrown on the ground in a public place (lixo) 🔹 *You can be fined for dropping litter.* (jogar lixo)
2 a group of animals born to the same mother at the same time □ *a litter of puppies* (ninhada)
▶ VERB [litters, littering, littered]
1 to be spread around a place in an untidy way □ *Children's toys littered the floor.* (espalhar)
2 be littered with something to include a lot of something bad □ *The article was littered with errors.* (estar repleto de algo ruim)

little /ˈlɪtəl/ ▶ DETERMINER, PRONOUN, ADVERB [**less**, **least**]
1 not much □ *There is little hope of finding them alive.* □ *She cares so little for other people's opinions.* □ *It costs very little to go on a camping holiday.* □ **+ of** *I remember very little of what he said.* (pouco)
2 a little a small amount or to a small degree □ *I added a little salt.* □ *'Would you like milk?' 'Just a little, please.'* □ *Jump up and down a little to keep warm.* □ *I'm feeling a little cold.* (um pouco)
▶ ADJECTIVE [**littler**, **littlest**]
1 small □ *They stuck little pieces of cardboard all over it.* □ *He's got his own little bicycle* (pequeno, pouco) 🔹 *Can I have a little bit of butter?* (um pouco)
2 short in time or distance (um pouco) 🔹 *It's only a little way to the hotel.* (caminho curto) 🔹 *He'll be here in a little while.* (pouco tempo)
3 young (pequeno, novo) 🔹 *a little boy/girl* (menininho/menininha) 🔹 *my little brother/sister* (meu irmãozinho/irmãzinha)
4 not important or serious (insignificante) 🔹 *She worries about every little thing.* (coisa insignificante)

live[1] /lɪv/ VERB [lives, living, lived]
1 to be alive □ *Cats don't usually live for much more than twenty years.* □ *People are living longer these days.* (viver)
2 to have your home in a certain place □ *How long have you lived in Madrid?* □ *I live next door to Sam.* (morar)
3 to pass your life in a certain way □ *She's used to living alone.* (viver)
♦ PHRASAL VERBS **live something down** to make people forget something embarrassing that you

live 461 **loan**

did □ *Fancy forgetting my own birthday – I'll never live it down!* (fazer esquecer de algo) **live on something** 1 to eat a particular type of food □ *They live on nuts and insects.* (viver de) 2 money you live on is money you use for the things you need □ *We managed to live on our savings for two years.* (viver com) **live up to something** to be as good as you hoped or expected □ *The restaurant didn't really live up to my expectations.* (viver à altura de algo)

live² /laɪv/ ADJECTIVE
1 not dead □ *We bought some live oysters.* (vivo)
2 connected to an electricity supply □ *a live socket* (carregado)
3 a live broadcast is happening as you watch or hear it (vivo)
▶ ADVERB if something is broadcast live, it is happening as you watch or hear it □ *We are going live to our correspondent in Berlin.* (ao vivo)

livelihood /ˈlaɪvlihʊd/ NOUN [plural **livelihoods**] the way you earn enough money to live □ *Many families lost their homes and their livelihoods as a result of the floods.* (sustento)

lively /ˈlaɪvli/ ADJECTIVE [**livelier, liveliest**] full of activity, interest or energy □ *a group of lively children* (vivo) ▣ *There was a lively debate on the issue.* (debate ao vivo) □ *The café has great food and a lively atmosphere.*

liver /ˈlɪvə(r)/ NOUN [plural **livers**] a large organ in your body that is very important for cleaning your blood. A biology word. (fígado)

livestock /ˈlaɪvstɒk/ NOUN, NO PLURAL farm animals (gado)

livid /ˈlɪvɪd/ ADJECTIVE extremely angry □ *I told Ian and he was livid.* (lívido, pálido)

living /ˈlɪvɪŋ/ ▶ NOUN [plural **livings**]
1 the money you earn from working and that you live on (sustento) ▣ *I make my living as a professional actor.* (consigo meu sustento) ▣ *He earns a living by teaching the piano.* (ganha o sustento) ▣ *I make a decent living* (= enough money). (sustento decente) ▣ *What do you do for a living?* (= What is your job?) (faz como sustento)
2 the way you live □ *We want to encourage healthy living.* (subsistência)
▶ ADJECTIVE
1 alive □ *a living organism* □ *She has no living relatives.* (vivo)
2 to do with the way people live (vida) ▣ *Living standards have improved.* (padrões de vida)

living room /ˈlɪvɪŋ ruːm/ NOUN [plural **living rooms**] a room in a house for sitting and relaxing in □ *I was in the living room, watching television.* (sala de estar)

lizard /ˈlɪzəd/ NOUN [plural **lizards**] a reptile with four legs, a long body and a tail (lagarta)

llama /ˈlɑːmə/ NOUN [plural **llamas**] a large South American animal with a long neck, that is kept for its wool and to carry things (lhama)

load /ləʊd/ ▶ VERB [**loads, loading, loaded**]
1 to put something into a vehicle, especially a ship or a truck □ *+ up* *We loaded up the van with furniture.* □ *+ onto* *The boxes are loaded onto a truck.* □ *+ with* *A tanker loaded with oil has sunk off the coast.* (carregar)
2 to put something into a machine or piece of equipment □ *Have you loaded the dishwasher?* (carregar)
3 to put a program into a computer's memory so you can use it □ *The laptop comes loaded with anti-virus software.* (carregar)
4 to put bullets in a gun (carregar)
▶ NOUN [plural **loads**]
1 the things that a vehicle or person is carrying or can carry (carga) ▣ *The ship was carrying a load of new cars.* □ *There were two lorry loads of rubbish.* □ *Take another load upstairs.* (levando uma carga)
2 **loads/a load** an informal word meaning a large amount □ *We have loads to talk about.* □ *+ of* *He brought a load of food with him.* (um monte)
3 the amount of work that someone has to do (carga) ▣ *We can't handle the current work load.* (carga de trabalho)
4 the amount of something that a machine can deal with at one time □ *We had to do several loads of laundry.* (fardo, carregamento)
5 **a load of something** an informal phrase used to emphasize that something is completely stupid, wrong, etc. □ *What a load of rubbish!* (uma grande quantidade de algo)
• **loaded** /ˈləʊdɪd/ ADJECTIVE
1 if a gun is loaded, it has bullets in it (carregado) ▣ *a loaded gun* (arma carregada)
2 carrying a load □ *a fully loaded plane* (carregado)
3 with a second or hidden meaning (capcioso) ▣ *That's a loaded question, isn't it?* (pergunta capciosa) □ *a loaded term*
4 an informal word meaning very rich □ *He's absolutely loaded.* (muito rico)

loaf /ləʊf/ NOUN [plural **loaves**] a large piece of bread for cutting into smaller pieces □ *+ of* *a loaf of bread* □ *a brown sliced loaf* (pão)
◆ PHRASAL VERB [**loafs, loafing, loafed**] **loaf about/around** to spend time doing very little (vadiar)

loan /ləʊn/ ▶ NOUN [plural **loans**]
1 money that you borrow (empréstimo) ▣ *He wasn't able to repay the loan.* (pagar o empréstimo) ▣ *They took out a loan* (= arranged to borrow money) *to extend the house.* (fizeram um empréstimo) ▣ *a bank loan* (empréstimo bancário)
2 **on loan** borrowed from someone □ *The painting is on loan from the National Gallery.* (por empréstimo)

loathe

▶ VERB [**loans, loaning, loaned**] to lend something to someone ◻ *My brother loaned me the money to buy a new car.* (**emprestar**)

loathe /ləʊð/ VERB [**loathes, loathing, loathed**] to hate someone or something ◻ *I loathe shopping.* (**abominar**)
• **loathing** /ˈləʊðɪŋ/ NOUN, NO PLURAL a feeling of great dislike (**abominação**)

loaves /ləʊvz/ PLURAL OF **loaf** (*ver* **loaf**)

lob /lɒb/ ▶ VERB [**lobs, lobbing, lobbed**] to throw or hit something high into the air ◻ *The men lobbed grenades into the building.* (**arremessar**)
▶ NOUN [*plural* **lobs**] when you lob something (**arremesso**)

lobby /ˈlɒbɪ/ ▶ NOUN [*plural* **lobbies**]
1 a room inside the entrance to a building (**saguão**) ◻ *I'll meet you in the hotel lobby.* (**saguão do hotel**)
2 a group of people who try to persuade politicians about something (**grupo que influencia legisladores, lobistas**) ◻ *an environmental lobby group* (**grupo de lobistas**) ◻ *America's powerful gun lobby*
▶ VERB [**lobbies, lobbying, lobbied**] to try to persuade politicians about a particular subject ◻ *Small businesses are lobbying for a change in the rules.* (**tentar influenciar**)

lobe /ləʊb/ NOUN [*plural* **lobes**]
1 the soft round part at the bottom of your ear (**lóbulo da orelha**)
2 one part of a body organ that has several parts, like the brain. A biology word. (**lóbulo**)

lobster /ˈlɒbstə(r)/ NOUN [*plural* **lobsters**] a sea animal with a hard shell, two large claws (= hard curved parts) and eight legs (**lagosta**)

local /ˈləʊkəl/ ▶ ADJECTIVE to do with the area near to you ◻ *our local library* ◻ *a local newspaper* (**local**) ◻ *local government* (**governo local**) ◻ *Local residents are unhappy about the plans.* (**moradores**)
▶ NOUN [*plural* **locals**]
1 someone who lives in a particular area ◻ *If you want to know the way, you'd better ask a local.* (**habitante**)
2 an informal word meaning the pub nearest to your home (**bar local, do bairro**)

local anaesthetic /ˌləʊkəl ˌænɪsˈθetɪk/ NOUN [*plural* **local anaesthetics**] a drug that makes part of your body lose feeling before you have medical treatment (**anestesia local**)

locality /ləˈkælətɪ/ NOUN [*plural* **localities**] a formal word meaning a particular place and the area around it ◻ *There are higher rates of crime in rural localities.* (**localidade**)

locally /ˈləʊkəlɪ/ ADVERB in or from the area near to you ◻ *Most of our vegetables are grown locally.* ◻ *The hill is known locally as Old Misty.* (**localmente**)

locate /ləʊˈkeɪt/ VERB [**locates, locating, located**]
1 to find out exactly where something or someone is ◻ *He was trying to locate the school on the map.* ◻ *Police have now located the girl's mother.* (**localizar**)
2 be located by/in/near, etc. to be in a particular place ◻ *Their headquarters are located in Paris.* ◻ *The camps are mostly located near the border.* (**estar situado em...**)
• **location** /ləʊˈkeɪʃən/ NOUN [*plural* **locations**]
1 a place or position ◻ *Nobody knows the exact location of the meeting.* ◻ *We have over 200 staff at 40 locations across the country.* (**localização**)
2 on location if a film is made on location, it is filmed in a real place and not in a studio (= special building where films are recorded) (**no local**)

loch /lɒx/ NOUN [*plural* **lochs**] a lake in Scotland (**lago na Escócia**)

lock /lɒk/ ▶ NOUN [*plural* **locks**]
1 a device that fastens things such as doors and drawers, usually opened and closed using a key ◻ *There was no lock on the door.* ◻ *We had to change the lock on the front door.* (**fechadura**)
2 under lock and key in a place which is locked ◻ *The weapons are kept safely under lock and key.* (**guardado a sete chaves**)
3 a small part of a river or canal (= artificial river) with gates that allows boats to move to a higher or lower level (**comporta, dique**)
4 a piece of someone's hair ◻ *a lock of blonde hair* (**mecha de cabelo**)
▶ VERB [**locks, locking, locked**]
1 to fasten something such as a door with a key, or to be fastened this way (**trancar com chave**) ◻ *Lock the door when you leave.* (**tranque a porta**) ◻ *This door doesn't lock.*
2 to put something or someone in a place that is locked ◻ **+ up** *He's a dangerous criminal who should be locked up.* ◻ **+ away** *I locked all my jewellery away in a box.* ◻ **+ in** *The medicines are locked in a cupboard.* (**encerrar**)
3 to become fixed in a position ◻ *The wheels locked and the car skidded off the road.* (**travar**)

locker /ˈlɒkə(r)/ NOUN [*plural* **lockers**] a small cupboard, especially one that can be locked ◻ *I left my suitcase in a luggage locker at the station.* (**compartimento com chave**)

locomotion /ˌləʊkəˈməʊʃən/ NOUN, NO PLURAL a formal word meaning the power to move or the way something moves (**locomoção**)
• **locomotive** /ˌləʊkəˈməʊtɪv/ NOUN [*plural* **locomotives**] a railway engine that pulls trains (**locomotiva**)

locust /ˈləʊkəst/ NOUN [*plural* **locusts**] a large insect that flies in large groups that eat and destroy plants (**gafanhoto**)

lodge /lɒdʒ/ ▶ VERB [**lodges, lodging, lodged**]

loft   463   **long**

1 to officially make a complaint, say that you should be given something, etc. (**apresentar queixa**) ▢ *The team lodged a complaint with the FIA.* (**apresentou uma queixa**) ▢ *We have lodged a planning application with the council.*
2 to become fixed somewhere, often when this is not wanted ▢ *A piece of apple had lodged between his front teeth.* ▢ *He has a bullet lodged in his brain.* (**alojar-se**)
3 to live in a room in someone else's house and pay them rent (**hospedar-se**)
▶ NOUN [*plural* **lodges**] a small house in the countryside ▢ *a hunting lodge* ▢ *a ski lodge* (**chalé**)

• **lodger** /ˈlɒdʒə(r)/ NOUN [*plural* **lodgers**] a person who lives in rooms that they rent in someone else's house (**inquilino**)

• **lodging** /ˈlɒdʒɪŋ/ NOUN [*plural* **lodgings**] a place to stay, especially for a short time (**alojamento**)

loft /lɒft/ NOUN [*plural* **lofts**] the space between the roof of a house and the rooms ▢ *Our suitcases are stored in the loft.* (**sótão**)

log /lɒg/ ▶ NOUN [*plural* **logs**]
1 a part of a branch or tree that has been cut up (**tora**)
2 an official written record of what happens, especially on a journey (**agenda, diário**)
▶ VERB [**logs, logging, logged**] to make an official written record of something (**registrar no diário**)

◆ PHRASAL VERBS **log in/on** to start using a computer, website, etc. by typing in a word or code (= series of letters or numbers) (**iniciar uma sessão**) **log off/out** to stop using a computer, website, etc. by clicking on something on the screen (**encerrar uma sessão**)

logarithm /ˈlɒgərɪðəm/ NOUN [*plural* **logarithms**] one of a series of numbers in lists that are used to make multiplying and dividing easier. A maths word. (**logaritmo**)

loggerheads /ˈlɒgəhedz/ PLURAL NOUN **be at loggerheads** if you are at loggerheads with someone, you argue or disagree with them strongly ▢ *They are at loggerheads over plans to cut down the trees.* (**brigar, discutir com alguém**)

logic /ˈlɒdʒɪk/ NOUN, NO PLURAL a way of thinking using facts and reason ▢ *I could see the logic of his argument.* (**lógica**) ▢ *This decision just defies logic* (= does not seem reasonable). (**despreza a lógica**)

• **logical** /ˈlɒdʒɪkəl/ ADJECTIVE based on or using logic ▢ *What's the logical thing to do next?* (**lógico**) ▢ *There is only one logical conclusion.* (**conclusão lógica**)

• **logically** /ˈlɒdʒɪkəli/ ADVERB in a logical way ▢ *Logically, there was no other alternative.* ▢ *We need to think logically about this.* (**logicamente**)

login /ˈlɒgɪn/ NOUN [*plural* **logins**] the letters or numbers that you type into a box on the computer screen in order to start using a system. A computing word. (**senha de acesso**)

logo /ˈləʊgəʊ/ NOUN [*plural* **logos**] a design that is the symbol of a company or a product ▢ *The company has launched a new logo.* (**logotipo**)

loiter /ˈlɔɪtə(r)/ VERB [**loiters, loitering, loitered**] to stand or wait in a place doing nothing ▢ *Her friends loitered at the door.* (**perder tempo**)

loll /lɒl/ VERB [**lolls, lolling, lolled**]
1 to lie or sit in a lazy, relaxed way ▢ *Pete's been lolling about watching football all afternoon.* (**relaxar**)
2 if your head or your tongue lolls, it hangs loosely ▢ *Her head lolled to one side.* (**balançar, cair**)

lollipop /ˈlɒlipɒp/ NOUN [*plural* **lollipops**] a hard sweet on a stick (**pirulito**)

lolly /ˈlɒli/ NOUN [*plural* **lollies**]
1 a lollipop (**pirulito**)
2 an ice lolly (**picolé**)

lone /ləʊn/ ADJECTIVE alone, single or only ▢ *He was killed by a lone gunman.* (**sozinho**) ▢ *She's a lone parent with two young children.* (**mãe solteira**)

loneliness /ˈləʊnlinɪs/ NOUN, NO PLURAL
1 when you are unhappy because you are alone ▢ *He felt a growing sense of loneliness.* (**solidão**)
2 the state of being a long way from anything or anyone else (**isolamento**)

lonely /ˈləʊnli/ ADJECTIVE [**lonelier, loneliest**]
1 unhappy because you are alone, with no friends around you (**solitário**) ▢ *She suddenly felt very lonely.* (**sentiu-se solitária**) ▢ *I get lonely at the weekends.* (**me sinto solitário**)
2 far from other places and with very few people ▢ *He lived in a lonely cottage on the hillside.* (**isolado**)

loner /ˈləʊnə(r)/ NOUN [*plural* **loners**] a person who prefers to be alone and who avoids close relationships ▢ *Steve's always been a loner.* (**solitário**)

long¹ /lɒŋ/ ▶ ADJECTIVE [**longer, longest**]
1 lasting a lot of time (**longo**) ▢ *It took a long time to persuade her to come.* (**longo tempo**) ▢ *There were long delays on the trains.*
2 measuring a long distance from one end to the other ▢ *She has very long hair.* ▢ *We went on a long journey.* ▢ *How long is the rope?* (**longo**) ▢ *It's a long way home from here.* (**caminho longo**)
3 a long book or document has a lot of pages or words (**extenso**)
4 having a certain length ▢ *The garden is 50 m long.* ▢ *The film was three hours long.* (**de duração**)

⇨ go to **in the long/short run**
▶ ADVERB [**longer, longest**]
1 for a long time ▢ *Have you been waiting long?* ▢ *It won't be long till she starts school.* ▢ *The concert didn't last long.* (**muito tempo**)
2 much earlier or later than the time you are talking about (**muito tempo**) ▢ *The house was*

knocked down long ago. (há muito tempo) *He was a vegetarian long before I met him.* (muito tempo atrás)

3 as long as used for saying that something must happen or be true before something else can happen or be true □ *You can borrow my jacket as long as you bring it back tomorrow.* (contanto que)

4 before long soon □ *Before long, we were all singing songs.* (sem muita demora)

5 no longer not now □ *I no longer wish to see her.* (não agora)

long² /lɒŋ/ VERB [longs, longing, longed] to want something very much □ *I was longing to sit down.* □ *They were longing for a chance to rest.* (ansiar por, desejar ardentemente)

long division /ˌlɒŋ dɪˈvɪʒən/ NOUN, NO PLURAL a method of dividing one number, usually a long one, by another, in which all the calculations are written down. A maths word. (divisão longa)

longevity /lɒnˈdʒevɪti/ NOUN, NO PLURAL when someone lives for a long time. A formal word □ *Improvements in diet have led to an increase in longevity.* (longevidade)

longing /ˈlɒŋɪŋ/ NOUN, NO PLURAL a feeling of wanting something very much □ *They were looking at the food with longing.* (saudade, ânsia)

• **longingly** /ˈlɒŋɪŋli/ ADVERB in a way that shows that you want something very much (com saudade, ansiosamente)

longitude /ˈlɒndʒɪtjuːd/ NOUN [plural longitudes] the position of a place east or west of an imaginary line that passes from north to south through Greenwich, London. A geography word. (longitude)

long jump /ˈlɒŋ ˌdʒʌmp/ NOUN, NO PLURAL a sports event where you run up to a line and then jump forward as far as possible (salto a distância)

long-life /ˌlɒŋˈlaɪf/ ADJECTIVE made or designed to last longer than usual (longa vida) *long-life batteries* (baterias de longa vida) *a carton of long-life milk* (leite longa vida)

long-range /ˌlɒŋˈreɪndʒ/ ADJECTIVE
1 able to reach a great distance (de longo alcance) *long-range missiles* (mísseis de longo alcance)
2 looking a long way into the future (longo alcance) *a long-range weather forecast* (previsão de tempo de longo alcance)

long-sighted /ˌlɒŋˈsaɪtɪd/ ADJECTIVE able to see objects that are far away more clearly than things closer to you (presbita)

long-standing /ˌlɒŋˈstændɪŋ/ ADJECTIVE having existed for a long time □ *She is in a long-standing relationship.* (duradouro)

long-suffering /ˌlɒŋˈsʌfərɪŋ/ ADJECTIVE accepting the trouble and problems that someone has caused in a patient way over a long period time □ *She played the part of his long-suffering wife.* (resignação)

long-term /ˌlɒŋˈtɜːm/ ADJECTIVE
1 continuing to exist or have an effect a long time into the future □ *We know nothing about the long-term effects of this medicine.* □ *What are your long-term plans?* (longo prazo)
2 having existed for a long time □ *She was in a long-term relationship.* (longo período)

long-winded /ˌlɒŋˈwɪndɪd/ ADJECTIVE if a piece of writing or speech is long-winded, it is much longer than necessary □ *a long-winded explanation* (prolixo)

loo /luː/ NOUN [plural loos] an informal word for a toilet □ *I need to go to the loo.* (toalete)

look /lʊk/ VERB [looks, looking, looked]
1 to turn your eyes to see something □ + **at** *She was looking at the view.* □ *Look behind you.* □ *Oh look, there's a deer over there!* □ *Look where you're going!* (olhar)
2 to try to find something or someone □ + **for** *I'm looking for my passport.* (procurar)
3 to have a particular appearance □ *You look a bit tired.* □ *Kate looked fine when I saw her yesterday.* (parecer)
4 to seem □ *It looks as if Joe won't be coming.* □ *His job prospects are looking good.* (parecer)

♦ IDIOM **look on the bright side** to think about the good parts of a situation that is mostly bad □ *'The power's been cut off again.' 'Oh well, look on the bright side – you'll be saving on your electricity bills!'* (ver o lado bom das coisas)

> Notice the prepositions that are used with look. When you turn your eyes to see something (sense 1), you look at something:
> ✓ I looked at the clock.
> ✗ I looked the clock.

⇨ go to **look down your nose at someone/something**, **look the part**

♦ PHRASAL VERBS **look after someone** to take care of someone or something □ *Her husband looks after the baby during the day.* (cuidar de alguém)
look at something to think about something in order to make a decision about it □ *We're looking at ways of making the road safer.* (considerar algo)
look down on someone/something to think that you are better than someone or too good for something □ *She never looked down on poor people.* (desprezar alguém/algo)
look forward to something to feel pleased and excited about something that is going to happen □ *I'm really looking forward to meeting his family.* (esperar ansiosamente por algo)

> When look forward to is followed by a verb, the verb is in the -ing form:
> ✓ We're looking forward to seeing you!
> ✗ We're looking forward to see you.

look into something to try to find information about something □ *I'm looking into the possibility of having solar panels.* (investigar

look-alike

algo) **look out** to be careful because something might be dangerous ◻ *Look out! The path is very slippery.* **(cuidado)** **look something up** to look in a book, on a computer, etc. to find information about something ◻ *I looked up the word 'digest' in the dictionary.* **(procurar)** **look up** if things are looking up, a situation is getting better **(melhorar)** **look up to someone** to admire someone ◻ *I always looked up to my older brother.* **(admirar alguém)**

▶ NOUN [*plural* **looks**]

1 when you look at something or someone **(olhada)** 🔊 *May I have a look at your watch?* **(dar uma olhada)** 🔊 *Take a look at these documents.* **(dê uma olhada)** 🔊 *I had a good look round their house.* **(boa olhada)**

2 when you try to find something or someone **(olhada)** 🔊 *I had a look outside, but I couldn't see her.* **(dei uma olhada)**

3 an expression on someone's face ◻ *She gave me a warning look.* ◻ *There was a look of disgust on his face.* **(olhar)**

4 the appearance of someone or something **(aspecto)** 🔊 *I don't like the look of those black clouds.* ◻ *The house had a neglected look about it.*

5 **someone's looks** how attractive someone is ◻ *She is worried that she is losing her looks.* **(beleza de alguém)**

look-alike /ˈlʊkəˌlaɪk/ NOUN [*plural* **look-alikes**] a person who looks very like someone else ◻ *a Prince Charles look-alike* **(sósia)**

lookout /ˈlʊkaʊt/ NOUN [*plural* **lookouts**]

1 a person who watches for danger ◻ *The lookout spotted a boat on the horizon.* **(guarda)**

2 a place where someone can watch from, especially for danger ◻ *a lookout tower* **(vigilância)**

3 **keep a lookout/be on the lookout** to watch carefully for something ◻ *I'll keep a lookout for the missing books.* ◻ *We're always on the lookout for opportunities to expand.* **(estar à espreita de algo)**

4 **your (own) lookout** your problem or worry and nobody else's. An informal phrase ◻ *If you do not study for the exam, that's your own lookout.* **(é problema seu)**

loom¹ /luːm/ NOUN [*plural* **looms**] a machine for making cloth **(tear)**

loom² /luːm/ VERB [**looms, looming, loomed**]

1 to appear over or in front of you, especially in a frightening way ◻ *A shadowy figure loomed towards us.* **(surgir)**

2 if an unpleasant or difficult event or situation looms, it is likely to happen soon ◻ *A big decision is looming before us.* **(aproximar)**

loop /luːp/ ▶ NOUN [*plural* **loops**] a circle of something such as a thread, a piece of string or a narrow piece of cloth ◻ *Make a loop and pull one end through it.* **(laçada)**

▶ VERB [**loops, looping, looped**] to form a loop ◻ *She had a scarf looped around her neck.* **(laçar)**

loophole /ˈluːphəʊl/ NOUN [*plural* **loopholes**] something that allows people to avoid doing what they should do without breaking a rule or the law ◻ *She found a loophole in her contract.* **(brecha)**

lord

loose /luːs/ ADJECTIVE [**looser, loosest**]

1 not tight or firmly fixed ◻ *a loose knot* ◻ *Wear loose, comfortable clothing.* **(frouxo)** 🔊 *One of the screws had come loose.* **(veio frouxo)**

2 not tied up or shut in ◻ *Her hair was hanging loose.* ◻ *Let the dogs run around loose.* **(solto, livre)**

3 not exact or detailed ◻ *a loose translation* ◻ *The descriptions were very loose.* **(vago)**

4 not carefully organized or official ◻ *The organization was a loose alliance of political groups.* **(descuidado)**

◆ IDIOMS **at a loose end** having free time but nothing to do ◻ *I found myself at a loose end.* **(sem ter o que fazer)** **loose ends** the last details or parts of something that need to be dealt with ◻ *There are still a few loose ends to tie up.* **(pendências)**

▶ NOUN, NO PLURAL **on the loose** if a criminal or a wild animal is on the loose, they have escaped and are free ◻ *A dangerous killer is on the loose.* **(estar à solta)**

• **loosely** /ˈluːsli/ ADVERB

1 not firmly or tightly ◻ *She had a silk scarf tied loosely around her neck.* ◻ *His arms hung loosely at his sides.* **(de maneira livre)**

2 not exactly or in detail ◻ *The book is loosely based on a true story.* ◻ *I'm using the term loosely.* **(vagamente)**

3 not in an organized or official way ◻ *They are loosely connected to the Conservative Party.* **(imprecisamente)**

• **loosen** /ˈluːsən/ VERB [**loosens, loosening, loosened**] to make something less firm, fixed or tight ◻ *I had to loosen my belt.* ◻ *She loosened her grip on Frank's arm.* **(afrouxar)**

loot /luːt/ ▶ NOUN stolen goods or money **(roubo)**

▶ VERB [**loots, looting, looted**] to steal things from shops or houses, especially during times of violence ◻ *Shops were looted during the riot.* **(roubar, saquear)**

• **looter** /ˈluːtə(r)/ NOUN [*plural* **looters**] a person who loots from shops or houses **(ladrão)**

• **looting** /ˈluːtɪŋ/ NOUN, NO PLURAL when people loot from shops or houses ◻ *There were reports of widespread looting in the city.* **(roubo, saque)**

lopsided /ˌlɒpˈsaɪdɪd/ ADJECTIVE with one side higher or lower than the other ◻ *a lopsided smile* **(torto)**

lord /lɔːd/ NOUN [*plural* **lords**]

1 used as the title of a man with a high social rank in the UK, or a man with this title □ *Lord Asquith* □ *the Lord Mayor of London* (**Lorde**)
2 Lord used in prayers as a way of addressing God (**o Senhor**)
3 the Lords one of the two parts of the British government, with members who are not elected (**nobres, aristocratas**)

lordship /ˈlɔːdʃɪp/ NOUN [plural **lordships**] **your lordship** used to address or refer to some men with a high social rank in the UK □ *May we express our gratitude to your lordship?* (**senhorio**)

lore /lɔː(r)/ NOUN, NO PLURAL the traditional knowledge, stories and beliefs of a group of people (**doutrina, sabedoria**)

lorry /ˈlɒrɪ/ NOUN [plural **lorries**] a large vehicle for carrying heavy goods by road (**caminhão**) ▣ *a lorry driver* (**caminhoneiro**)

lose /luːz/ VERB [**loses, losing, lost**]
1 to not be able to find someone or something □ *I've lost my keys.* (**perder**)
2 to have something taken away from you (**perder**) ▣ *Fifty people have lost their jobs.* (**perderam seus empregos**) ▣ *He was willing to lose his life for his beliefs.* (**perder a vida**)
3 to have less of something than you had before ▣ *She has lost weight recently.* (**perdeu peso**) ▣ *The children soon lost interest in the animals.* (**perderam interesse**) ▣ *The business is losing money.* (**perdendo dinheiro**)
4 to not have something you had before (**perder**) ▣ *I was so angry, I lost control and started shouting.* (**perdi o controle**) ▣ *I would hate to lose contact with my friends.* (**perder contato**) ▣ *I lost sight* (= stopped being able to see) *of the train.* (**perdi de vista**)
5 to be beaten in a competition, election, etc. □ + **by** *I lost by 4 games to 6.* (**perder**) ▣ *We narrowly lost* (= only just lost) *the match.* (**perdemos por um triz**)
6 a clock or watch loses time when it goes too slowly □ *My watch is losing about a minute a day.* (**atrasar**)

◆ IDIOMS **lose count of something** used for emphasizing that something has happened many times □ *I've lost count of the number of times I've been in hospital.* (**perder a conta de algo**) **lose the plot** to start behaving strangely. An informal phrase. □ *I keep forgetting things – I think I'm losing the plot!* (**perder a razão**) **lose sight of something** to forget about an important fact or aim because you are thinking about other things □ *We must not lose sight of the fact that the club is supposed to be fun.* (**perder a noção de algo**)
⇨ go to **lose the thread, lose sleep over something**

◆ PHRASAL VERB **lose out** to not get something that other people get □ *Bill lost out when his father gave the business to his brothers.* (**sair perdendo**)

• **loser** /ˈluːzə(r)/ NOUN [plural **losers**]
1 the person who does not win a competition, election, etc. □ *Even the loser will win a huge amount of money.* (**perdedor**)
2 an informal word meaning someone who never seems to succeed at anything (**fracassado**)

loss /lɒs/ NOUN [plural **losses**]
1 when you lose something □ *She was sacked over the loss of confidential documents.* □ + **of** *He spoke about the loss of his home in a fire.* (**perda**) ▣ *There will be some job losses.* (**perdas de emprego**)
2 when you have less of something than you had before (**perda**) ▣ *She gives advice about weight loss.* (**perda de peso**) ▣ *He seemed to suffer a loss of confidence.* (**sofrer uma perda**) □ *Many older people are affected by hearing loss.*
3 when a business spends more money than it earns, or this amount of money □ + **of** *The company announced a pre-tax loss of £2 million.* (**prejuízo**)
4 the death of someone (**perda**) ▣ *I was still mourning the loss of my brother.* (**chorando pela perda**) ▣ *It's surprising that there wasn't a greater loss of life.* (**perda de vida**)
5 be at a loss (to do something) when you do not know what to do or to say in a situation □ *They're still at a loss to explain what went wrong.* (**estar desorientado**)
6 a disadvantage □ *It'll be your loss if you do not buy this wonderful car.* (**desvantagem**)
7 when you lose a race, competition etc. □ *This is the team's sixth loss in a row.* (**fracasso, perda**)

lost /lɒst/ ▶ ADJECTIVE
1 if something is lost, nobody knows where it is □ *The painting has been lost for centuries.* (**perdido**)
2 someone who is lost does not know where they are ▣ *How did you get lost when you had a map?* (**se perdeu**) ▣ *We were hopelessly lost.* (**irremediavelmente perdido**)
3 confused and not able to understand something □ *I'm sorry – can you explain that last bit again?* (**desorientado, desnorteado**)
4 no longer existing or available □ *a lost opportunity* (**desperdiçado, perdido**) ▣ *I never travelled when I was younger, but now I'm making up for lost time.* (**compensando o tempo perdido**)
5 be lost without someone/something to be unable to manage without someone or something □ *I'd be lost without my mobile phone.* (**estar perdido sem algo/alguém**)
▶ PAST TENSE OF **lose** (**ver lose**)

lot /lɒt/ NOUN [plural **lots**]
1 a lot/lots a large number or amount □ + **of** *There were a lot of people there.* □ *I bought lots of food.* □ *She doesn't eat a lot.* □ *We've got a lot to talk about.* (**muitos**)
2 a lot better/happier/quicker, etc. much better/happier/quicker, etc. □ *You'd keep a lot warmer if you wore a hat.* (**muito mais**)

lotion | lovely

3 a group of things or people □ *Another lot of visitors will arrive tomorrow.* (grupo)
4 the lot everything □ *He had fifteen paintings and sold the lot.* (tudo)

> Notice (sense 1) that *a* only goes before *lot* and not before *lots* □ *She has a lot of friends.* □ *She has lots of friends.*

♦ IDIOM **draw lots** to make a decision by pulling out one of several pieces of paper □ *They drew lots to decide who would jump first.* (tentar a sorte)

lotion /ˈləʊʃən/ NOUN [plural **lotions**] a thick liquid for putting on your skin or hair (loção) 🔊 *a bottle of suntan lotion* (loção bronzeadora) □ *a moisturizing lotion*

lottery /ˈlɒtəri/ NOUN [plural **lotteries**]
1 a game where people win money or prizes when their number or ticket is chosen by chance from many others (loteria) 🔊 *He looked like he'd won the lottery.* (ganhou na loteria)
2 a situation where something depends on chance, usually in an unfair way (loteria)

loud /laʊd/ ▶ ADJECTIVE [**louder**, **loudest**]
1 making a lot of sound (alto) 🔊 *a loud noise* (ruído alto) 🔊 *She asked again in a louder voice.* (voz mais alta) □ *The music was too loud for me.*
2 a loud colour is very bright (espalhafatoso)
▶ ADVERB [**louder**, **loudest**]
1 making a lot of sound □ *Could you speak a little louder please?* □ *I screamed as loud as I could.* (alto)
2 out loud so that other people can hear you □ *I read the letter out loud.* □ *She laughed out loud.* (em voz alta)

♦ IDIOM **loud and clear** in a way that is clear and easy to understand □ *The message came across loud and clear.* (alto e claro)

loudhailer /ˌlaʊdˈheɪlə(r)/ NOUN [plural **loudhailers**] a device that you hold and speak into to make your voice much louder (amplificador)

loudly /ˈlaʊdli/ ADVERB making a lot of sound □ *The crowds cheered loudly.* □ *I knocked again more loudly.* (ruidosamente)

loudspeaker /ˌlaʊdˈspiːkə(r)/ NOUN [plural **loudspeakers**] a piece of electrical equipment that makes voices and sounds louder (alto-falante)

lounge /laʊndʒ/ ▶ NOUN [plural **lounges**]
1 a room in a house where you sit and relax □ *I was watching TV in the lounge.* (sala de estar)
2 a room in a public building where people can sit to relax or to wait □ *a hotel lounge* (saguão) 🔊 *an airport lounge* (saguão de aeroporto)
▶ VERB [**lounges**, **lounging**, **lounged**] to sit or to lie somewhere in a lazy way □ *The students were lounging around the common room.* (passar o tempo de modo ocioso)

louse /laʊs/ NOUN [plural **lice**] a small insect that lives on a person or an animal (piolho)

lousy /ˈlaʊzi/ ADJECTIVE [**lousier**, **lousiest**] an informal word that means very bad □ *lousy weather* □ *I've had a lousy day.* □ *I'm feeling lousy.* (mal, ruim)

lout /laʊt/ NOUN [plural **louts**] a young man who behaves in a rude and unpleasant way (grosseiro)

♦ **loutish** /ˈlaʊtɪʃ/ ADJECTIVE rude, unpleasant and violent □ *loutish behaviour* (rude, grosso)

lovable /ˈlʌvəbəl/ ADJECTIVE easy to love or to like a lot □ *a lovable child* □ *She's such a lovable character.* (cativante)

love /lʌv/ ▶ VERB [**loves**, **loving**, **loved**]
1 to have a strong romantic feeling for someone □ *I love you.* (amar)
2 to have a strong emotional feeling for a friend or family member who you like and care about □ *I loved my mother very much.* (amar)
3 to like or enjoy something very much □ *I love Chinese food.* □ *+ ing* *He loves teasing the children.* □ *+ to do something* *I'd love to be able to play the piano.* (adorar, gostar de)
▶ NOUN [plural **loves**]
1 *no plural* a strong romantic feeling for someone (amor) 🔊 *She fell in love with him at university.* (apaixonou-se) 🔊 *Within days, they were madly in love* (= loved each other very much). (loucamente apaixonados) □ *+ for* *My love for him did not survive.*
2 *no plural* a strong emotional feeling for a friend or family member who you like and care about □ *+ for* *Her love for her children kept her going.* (amor)
3 *no plural* a feeling of liking or enjoying something very much □ *+ of* *I did not share her love of opera.* (paixão)
4 something or someone that you love □ *Her great love was music.* □ *Robert was her first love.*
5 *no plural* used at the end of a letter □ *Hope to see you soon. Love, Emma.* □ *Have a great birthday. Lots of love, Mum.* (com amor)
6 give/send someone your love to ask someone to pass on a message of affection to someone □ *'I'm going to see Fiona next week.' 'Really? Do give her my love.'* (mandar a alguém suas lembranças)

♦ **loveless** /ˈlʌvlɪs/ ADJECTIVE without love (sem amor) 🔊 *He felt trapped in a loveless marriage.* (casamento sem amor)

loveliness /ˈlʌvlinɪs/ NOUN, NO PLURAL the quality of being attractive or pleasant (delicadeza, amabilidade)

lovely /ˈlʌvli/ ADJECTIVE [**lovelier**, **loveliest**]
1 beautiful or attractive □ *She has lovely eyes.* (encantador) 🔊 *You look lovely in that dress.* (está encantadora)
2 enjoyable or pleasant □ *It was lovely to see you again.* □ *It was a lovely evening.* (encantador, gracioso)

3 kind and friendly ☐ *She's a really lovely woman.* (adorável)

lover /ˈlʌvə(r)/ NOUN [plural **lovers**]
1 a person who is having a romantic relationship with someone else (amante, namorado)
2 someone who is very interested in or enthusiastic about something ☐ *an art lover* ☐ *a music lover* ☐ *I've always been an animal lover.* (adorador)

loving /ˈlʌvɪŋ/ ADJECTIVE
1 showing or expressing love ☐ *a loving look* ☐ *She has a very loving family.* (amoroso)
2 **in loving memory** used to remember someone who has died ☐ *In loving memory of my father, John.* (em memória)
• **lovingly** /ˈlʌvɪŋli/ ADVERB in a loving way ☐ *He gazed lovingly at her.* (com amor)

low /loʊ/ ▶ ADJECTIVE, ADVERB [**lower, lowest**]
1 near to the ground or short in height ☐ *a low hedge* ☐ *I can reach the lowest branches.* (baixo)
2 less than usual in amount or level ☐ *We are experiencing very low temperatures.* ☐ *I try to look for the lowest prices.* ☐ *The risk of frost is very low now.* ☐ **+ in** *Skimmed milk is low in fat.* (baixo)
3 a low sound or musical note is near the bottom of the range of sounds (baixo)
4 quiet ☐ *He spoke in a low voice.* (baixo)
5 not bright ☐ *low lighting* (baixo)
6 unhappy (para baixo) ☐ *He was feeling low.* (sentindo-se para baixo, triste)
▶ ADVERB [**lower, lowest**] in or to a low position or level ☐ *Their supplies began to run low.* ☐ *They flew low over the desert.* (baixo)
▶ NOUN [plural **lows**] a very low level (baixo) ☐ *Unemployment is at an all-time low.* (um nível mais baixo de todos os tempos)

low-cost /ˌloʊˈkɒst/ ADJECTIVE charging a low price for something ☐ *low-cost airlines* (custo baixo)

lowdown /ˈloʊdaʊn/ NOUN, NO PLURAL **the lowdown** the most important or interesting facts about someone or something (verdade pura) ☐ *Daniel gave me the lowdown on the market research project.* (me deu a pura verdade)

lower /ˈloʊə(r)/ ▶ VERB [**lowers, lowering, lowered**]
1 to move something to a position nearer the bottom of something or nearer the ground ☐ **+ into** *They lowered the boat into the water.* ☐ *She lowered her head slightly.* (abaixar)
2 to reduce something in amount or degree ☐ *They have lowered their prices.* (abaixar) ☐ *A good diet can lower your risk of heart disease.* (abaixar o risco) ☐ *She lowered her voice to a whisper.* (abaixou sua voz)
▶ ADJECTIVE below something else or nearer the bottom of something ☐ *the lower jaw* ☐ *a lower back problem* (inferior, mais baixo)

lower class /ˌloʊə(r) ˈklɑːs/ NOUN [plural **lower classes**] people with the lowest position in a society, with the least money ☐ *The lower classes have a poorer standard of living.* ☐ *lower class families* (classe inferior, classe baixa)

low-key /ˌloʊˈkiː/ ADJECTIVE quiet and with little activity or attention ☐ *We had a low-key wedding with only six guests.* (reservado)

lowly /ˈloʊli/ ADJECTIVE [**lowlier, lowliest**] having a job or position that is not important ☐ *Don't ask me, I'm just a lowly assistant.* (humilde, modesto)

loyal /ˈlɔɪəl/ ADJECTIVE always supporting or being a friend to someone (leal, fiel) ☐ *a loyal fan* (fã leal) ☐ *We want to reward loyal customers.* (clientes fiéis) ☐ *He remained loyal to the party.* (permaneceu fiel)
• **loyally** /ˈlɔɪəli/ ADVERB in a loyal way ☐ *She has stood loyally by her husband throughout the troubles.* (lealmente, fielmente)
• **loyalty** /ˈlɔɪəlti/ NOUN, NO PLURAL being loyal to someone (lealdade, fidelidade) ☐ *You always have a sense of loyalty to your home town.* (senso de lealdade) ☐ **+ to** *The fans have demonstrated their loyalty to the team.*

lozenge /ˈlɒzɪndʒ/ NOUN [plural **lozenges**]
1 a sweet that you suck to help a sore throat (pastilha)
2 a diamond shape (losango)

LP /ˌelˈpiː/ NOUN [plural **LPs**] a record which plays for 20 to 30 minutes on each side (LP, abreviatura de *long-play*)

L-plate /ˈelpleɪt/ NOUN [plural **L-plates**] a small white sign with a red letter L on it, put on a car that is driven by someone learning to drive (placa branca com a letra L em vermelho, colocado em carros de autoescola)

Ltd ABBREVIATION Limited; used in the names of companies ☐ *Joe Bloggs Shoes Ltd* (Ltda., abreviação de limitada)

lubricate /ˈluːbrɪkeɪt/ VERB [**lubricates, lubricating, lubricated**] to put oil or another substance on a machine to make it run smoothly (lubrificar)
• **lubrication** /ˌluːbrɪˈkeɪʃən/ NOUN, NO PLURAL when you lubricate something, or a substance used to lubricate (lubrificação)

lucid /ˈluːsɪd/ ADJECTIVE
1 clear and easily understood ☐ *She gave a lucid explanation of the differences.* (lúcido)
2 thinking and speaking clearly ☐ *There are only short periods when she is lucid.* (lúcido)
• **lucidity** /luːˈsɪdəti/ NOUN, NO PLURAL the quality of being lucid (lucidez)
• **lucidly** /ˈluːsɪdli/ ADVERB in a lucid way (lucidamente)

luck /lʌk/ NOUN, NO PLURAL
1 when something good happens by chance (sorte, acaso) ☐ *With a bit of luck, we'll be there by lunch time* (um pouco de sorte) ☐ *Meeting*

lucrative / lunar

Tim was a real *piece of luck*. (um pouco de sorte) ▪ When I heard I had won, I *couldn't believe my luck*. (não conseguia acreditar na minha sorte) ▪ I *wished* him any *luck* selling your house? (teve alguma sorte) □ I've been trying to buy a wedding dress, but without any luck so far.
2 the way things happen by chance (**sorte**) ▪ *bad/ good luck* (má/boa sorte) □ Whether or not you'll get on the course depends on your luck.
3 when you are successful at something (**sorte**) ▪ Have you *had* any *luck* selling your house? (teve alguma sorte) □ I've been trying to buy a wedding dress, but without any luck so far.
4 Good luck! used to tell someone that you hope they will succeed □ Good luck with your exams. (**boa sorte!**)
5 Bad luck! used to say that you are sorry about something bad that has happened to someone □ You broke your arm? Oh, bad luck! (**Que azar!**)
6 Hard/Tough luck! used to say that you do not have any sympathy for someone □ She missed the train? Well that's tough luck – she should have got up earlier. (**Bem feito!**)
♦ IDIOM **try your luck** to see if you will be successful at something □ She went to Hollywood to try her luck in the movies. (**tentar a sorte**)
⇨ go to **push your luck**
• **luckily** /ˈlʌkɪli/ ADVERB because of good luck □ The car hit us, but luckily nobody was badly hurt. □ Luckily for me, the door was unlocked. (**por sorte, afortunadamente**)
• **lucky** /ˈlʌki/ ADJECTIVE [**luckier, luckiest**]
1 a lucky person has good luck □ + *to do something* You're lucky to live so near the school. □ + *that* It's lucky that they didn't discover the truth. (**sortudo**)
2 bringing good luck □ a lucky charm (**que traz sorte, afortunado**)
3 You'll be lucky! used to say that you do not think someone has a chance of success □ Get the children to wash up? You'll be lucky! □ You'll be lucky if you manage to see her – she's off to Paris in ten minutes. (**Sorte sua se conseguir...!**)

lucrative /ˈluːkrətɪv/ ADJECTIVE making a lot of money □ a lucrative business (**lucrativo**)

ludicrous /ˈluːdɪkrəs/ ADJECTIVE completely silly or unreasonable □ It's a ludicrous idea! (**ridículo**)

lug /lʌg/ VERB [**lugs, lugging, lugged**] to pull or to carry something with difficulty. An informal word. □ He lugged the suitcases up the stairs. (**puxar, arrastar**)

luggage /ˈlʌgɪdʒ/ NOUN, NO PLURAL a traveller's bags and cases (**bagagem**) ▪ I was only travelling with *hand luggage*. (bagagem de mão) ▪ Each passenger can check in *two pieces of luggage*. (duas bagagens) ▪ a *luggage rack* (uma prateleira de bagagens)

> Remember that the noun luggage is not used in the plural:
> ✓ I had so much luggage.
> ✗ I had so many luggages.

lukewarm /ˈluːkwɔːm/ ADJECTIVE
1 describes liquid that is slightly warm □ The water in the shower was only lukewarm. (**morno**)
2 only slightly interested or enthusiastic □ We got a fairly lukewarm welcome. (**indiferente**)

lull /lʌl/ ▶ VERB [**lulls, lulling, lulled**]
1 to make someone feel calm and relaxed □ She rocked the pram gently, lulling the baby to sleep. (**embalar**)
2 to make someone feel relaxed and confident, often when they should not □ We were lulled into a false sense of security. (**acalmar**)
▶ NOUN [plural **lulls**] a time when something noisy, busy or violent stops for a while □ There was a lull in the fighting.

lullaby /ˈlʌləbaɪ/ NOUN [plural **lullabies**] a gentle song to help a child to sleep (**canção de ninar**)

lumber /ˈlʌmbə(r)/ VERB [**lumbers, lumbering, lumbered**] to move in a slow, heavy and awkward way □ We saw a bear lumbering through the forest. (**mover-se com dificuldades**)
♦ PHRASAL VERB **lumber someone with something** to give someone something that they do not want, especially a task □ I got lumbered with the clearing up. (**empurrar algo para cima de alguém**)

lumberjack /ˈlʌmbədʒæk/ NOUN [plural **lumberjacks**] someone whose job is cutting down trees for wood (**lenhador**)

luminous /ˈluːmɪnəs/ ADJECTIVE bright enough to be seen in the dark □ a luminous jacket (**luminoso, reluzente**)

lump /lʌmp/ NOUN [plural **lumps**]
1 a small piece of something without a clear shape □ + *of* a lump of coal □ a bowl of sugar lumps (**grumo, caroço**)
2 a hard piece of tissue growing on or in your body □ She found a lump in her breast. (**nódulo**)
♦ IDIOM **a lump in your throat** a feeling in your throat when you are going to cry □ There was a lump in my throat as I waved goodbye. (**um nó na garganta**)
♦ PHRASAL VERB [**lumps, lumping, lumped**] **lump something together** to think about or to deal with a number of different people or things all in the same way □ You can't just lump all old people together. (**juntar algo indiscriminadamente**)

lump sum /ˈlʌmp ˌsʌm/ NOUN [plural **lump sums**] a large amount of money all paid at one time □ He got a lump sum when he retired. (**soma total, bruta**)

lumpy /ˈlʌmpi/ ADJECTIVE [**lumpier, lumpiest**] full of lumps □ a lumpy sauce (**encaroçado**)

lunacy /ˈluːnəsi/ NOUN, NO PLURAL stupid and possibly dangerous behaviour □ It would be lunacy to travel in this weather. (**loucura**)

lunar /ˈluːnə(r)/ ADJECTIVE to do with the moon □ a lunar eclipse (**lunar**)

lunatic /ˈluːnətɪk/ NOUN [plural **lunatics**] someone who behaves in a stupid or dangerous way □ *He was driving like a lunatic.* (lunático)

lunch /lʌntʃ/ NOUN [plural **lunches**] the meal that you eat in the middle of the day (almoço) 🔊 *I had a sandwich for lunch.* (no almoço) 🔊 *I had lunch with a friend.* (almocei) 🔊 *We ate lunch in a small café.* (almoçamos) 🔊 *We took a packed lunch.* (almoço pronto) 🔊 *I'll call you during my lunch break.* (pausa de almoço)

lunchtime /ˈlʌntʃtaɪm/ NOUN [plural **lunchtimes**] the time in the middle of the day when you have lunch □ *I'll meet you at lunchtime.* □ *They arrived yesterday lunchtime.* (horário de almoço)

lung /lʌŋ/ NOUN [plural **lungs**] one of the two organs inside your chest like bags that you use for breathing. A biology word. (pulmão)

lunge /lʌndʒ/ ▶ VERB [**lunges, lunging, lunged**] to make a sudden strong or violent movement forwards □ *He suddenly lunged forward and grabbed the bag from her.* (empurrar com força)
▶ NOUN [plural **lunges**] a sudden violent movement forwards (empurrão) 🔊 *An angry customer made a lunge at the manager.* (deu um empurrão)

lurch /lɜːtʃ/ ▶ VERB [**lurches, lurching, lurched**]
1 to move along in an uncontrolled way □ *The boat lurched and we fell over.* □ *The van lurched forward, then stopped again.* (cambalear)
2 if your heart or your stomach lurches, you have a sudden, uncomfortable feeling of surprise, excitement, fear etc. (agitar)
▶ NOUN [plural **lurches**] a sudden, uncontrolled movement □ *The bus stopped with a lurch.* (guinada)

lure /ljʊə(r)/ ▶ VERB [**lures, luring, lured**] to persuade a person or an animal to do something using a reward □ *Scraps of food are used to lure the animals out of their burrows.* □ *They're offering special deals to lure customers back.* (atrair)
▶ NOUN [plural **lures**] something that lures an animal or person to do something □ *Few people can resist the lure of a big salary.* (chamariz)

lurk /lɜːk/ VERB [**lurks, lurking, lurked**] to wait secretly where you cannot be seen, especially because you are going to do something bad □ *Someone was lurking in the bushes.* (esconder-se)

luscious /ˈlʌʃəs/ ADJECTIVE looking, smelling or tasting very good □ *a luscious peach* (cheiroso)

lush /lʌʃ/ ADJECTIVE [**lusher, lushest**] lush plants are green, healthy and growing well □ *Cows graze on the lush farmland.* (viçoso)

luster /ˈlʌstə(r)/ NOUN, NO PLURAL the US spelling of **lustre** (brilho)

lustre /ˈlʌstə(r)/ NOUN, NO PLURAL
1 a shiny appearance □ *the dazzling lustre of white marble* (brilho)
2 the quality which makes something special (resplendor) 🔊 *The brand has lost its lustre in recent years.* (perdeu seu resplendor)
• **lustrous** /ˈlʌstrəs/ ADJECTIVE shiny and healthy looking □ *her long, lustrous hair* (lustroso, brilhante)

luxuriant /lʌɡˈʒʊəriənt/ ADJECTIVE growing in a thick and healthy way □ *luxuriant forest* (exuberante)

luxurious /lʌɡˈʒʊəriəs/ ADJECTIVE very comfortable and expensive □ *The hotel room was very luxurious.* □ *She enjoyed a luxurious lifestyle.* (luxuoso)
• **luxury** /ˈlʌkʃəri/ NOUN [plural **luxuries**]
1 a situation in which you are very comfortable, with expensive or beautiful things □ *They live in luxury.* □ *We stayed in five-star luxury.* □ *a luxury hotel* □ *luxury goods* (luxo)
2 something that is pleasant, and often expensive, but not necessary □ *We couldn't afford luxuries such as chocolate.* (luxo)
3 something that is very special because you cannot do it often □ *A day on my own is such a luxury.* (luxo)

-ly /li/ SUFFIX
1 -ly is added to the end of words to make adverbs describing the way that something is or is done □ *carefully* (-mente)
2 -ly is added to the end of words to mean 'happening every particular amount of time' □ *weekly* (-mente)

lymph /lɪmf/ NOUN, NO PLURAL a clear liquid containing white blood cells that helps keep the blood healthy. A biology word. (linfa)
• **lymphatic** /lɪmˈfætɪk/ ADJECTIVE connected to the system that produces lymph. A biology word. □ *the lymphatic system* (linfático)

lymph gland /ˈlɪmf ˌɡlænd/ or **lymph node** /ˈlɪmf nəʊd/ NOUN [plural **lymph glands** or **lymph nodes**] one of many small organs in the body that help to fight infection. A biology word. (glândula linfática)

lyric /ˈlɪrɪk/ NOUN [plural **lyrics**]
1 lyrics the words of a song □ *He wrote the lyrics for most of their songs.* (letra de música)
2 a short poem about feelings and emotions (poema lírico)
• **lyrical** /ˈlɪrɪkəl/ ADJECTIVE sounding like poetry or music □ *a lyrical description of the scenery* (poético, lírico)

Mm

M or **m** /em/ the 13th letter of the alphabet (a décima terceira letra do alfabeto)

m /em/ ABBREVIATION **metre** or **metres**, or **million** (abreviação de metro ou milhão)

mac /mæk/ NOUN [plural **macs**] a coat you wear when it is raining (capa de chuva)

macabre /məˈkɑːbrə/ ADJECTIVE strange and unpleasant, often to do with death □ *a macabre painting of skulls and bones* (macabro)

macaroni /ˌmækəˈrəʊni/ NOUN, NO PLURAL pasta in the shape of short tubes (macarrão)

machine /məˈʃiːn/ NOUN [plural **machines**] a piece of equipment that uses power to do a particular job □ *a washing machine* □ *a coffee machine* (máquina) ▣ *He used a fax machine in the office.* (usou uma máquina) □ *Cows are usually milked by machine.*

machine gun /məˈʃiːn ˌɡʌn/ NOUN [plural **machine guns**] an automatic gun that fires a lot of bullets very quickly (metralhadora)

machinery /məˈʃiːnəri/ NOUN, NO PLURAL big machines □ *farm machinery* (maquinaria) ▣ *Cranes and other heavy machinery were used to remove the debris.* (maquinaria pesada)

macho /ˈmætʃəʊ/ ADJECTIVE describes a man who behaves in a typically male way, for example by being strong and not showing his feelings (machista)

mackerel /ˈmækərəl/ NOUN [plural **mackerels** or **mackerel**] a small sea fish which you can eat (cavala)

mad /mæd/ ADJECTIVE [**madder**, **maddest**]
1 an informal word meaning stupid □ *Swimming where you know there are sharks is a mad thing to do.* □ *I thought he was mad wanting to climb Everest.* (louco, maluco)
2 mentally ill (louco) ▣ *The poor woman went mad with grief.* (ficou louca)
3 a mainly US word meaning very angry □ *I got mad at him for lying to me.* (louco da vida)
4 go mad an informal phrase meaning to become very angry or behave in a way that is not controlled □ *She'll go mad if she finds out you tricked her.* (ficar louco)
5 be mad about/on someone/something to like someone or something very much □ *He's mad about football.* (ser louco por algo)
6 like mad (a) as quickly as possible and using a lot of energy □ *She was pedalling like mad to keep up with the others.* (b) a lot □ *My arms were hurting like mad.* (como louco)

madam /ˈmædəm/ NOUN [plural **madams**]
1 *no plural* a formal and polite word used for talking to a woman, for example when serving her in a shop or restaurant □ *Can I help you, madam?* (senhora)
2 Dear Madam a way of beginning a formal letter to a woman when you do not know her name □ *Dear Madam, I'm writing to enquire about the job which was advertised in the newspaper.* (prezada senhora)

mad cow disease /ˌmæd ˈkaʊ dɪˌziːz/ NOUN, NO PLURAL an informal phrase for **BSE** (doença da vaca louca)

madden /ˈmædən/ VERB [**maddens**, **maddening**, **maddened**] to make someone feel very annoyed (enlouquecer)

• **maddening** /ˈmædənɪŋ/ ADJECTIVE very annoying □ *a maddening attitude* (enlouquecedor)

made /meɪd/ ▶ PAST TENSE AND PAST PARTICIPLE OF **make** (ver **make**)
▶ ADJECTIVE
1 be made from/of something to consist of something, or to be built from something □ *a necklace made of shells* □ *The carpet is made from recycled materials.* (ser feito de algo)
2 be made for someone/something to be perfect for a person or situation □ *The role was just made for him.* (ser perfeito para alguém/algo)

madly /ˈmædli/ ADVERB
1 using a lot of energy or enthusiasm □ *We were rushing about madly trying to get ready in time.* (loucamente)
2 extremely □ *He was madly jealous.* (loucamente) ▣ *They're madly in love.* (loucamente apaixonados)

madness /ˈmædnɪs/ NOUN, NO PLURAL stupid or dangerous behaviour (loucura) ▣ *In a moment of madness he hit the other man.* (momento de loucura)

magazine /ˌmæɡəˈziːn/ NOUN [plural **magazines**] a thin book with pictures in it which is usually published every week or every month (revista) ▣ *Amy was reading a magazine.* (lendo uma revista) □ *a fashion magazine* □ *a magazine article*

maggot /ˈmæɡət/ NOUN [plural **maggots**] an insect with a soft body, which becomes a fly (**larva**)

magic /ˈmædʒɪk/ ▶ NOUN, NO PLURAL

1 a strange power that some people believe exists, causing strange things to happen that you cannot explain (**magia**) 🔂 *Wizards use magic.* (**usam magia**)

2 tricks, such as making things disappear, which are done to entertain people □ *Children love watching magic.* (**mágica**)

3 a beautiful and attractive quality which makes something or someone seem special □ *The island's special magic attracts thousands of tourists each year.* □ *+ of the magic of Christmas* (**magia**)

4 as if by magic in a surprising way that you cannot explain □ *Helen saw a bird fly up, and then, as if by magic, disappear.* (**como mágica**)

▶ ADJECTIVE

1 involving tricks such as making things disappear 🔂 *magic tricks* (**truques de mágica**) □ *a magic show*

2 able to make impossible things happen 🔂 *a magic wand* (**uma varinha mágica**) □ *a magic potion*

• **magical** /ˈmædʒɪkəl/ ADJECTIVE

1 special and exciting or attractive □ *a magical atmosphere* □ *a magical place* (**mágico**)

2 done using magic, or having magic powers □ *magical powers* □ *magical healing* (**mágico**)

• **magically** /ˈmædʒɪkəli/ ADVERB using magic, or in a way that seems to be magic □ *The next morning, the missing books had magically reappeared on the shelf.* (**magicamente**)

• **magician** /məˈdʒɪʃən/ NOUN [plural **magicians**]

1 someone who does magic tricks to entertain people (**mágico**)

2 someone who has magic powers, especially in stories (**mágico**)

magistrate /ˈmædʒɪstreɪt/ NOUN [plural **magistrates**] a judge who deals with crimes which are not of the most serious type (**magistrado**)

magma /ˈmæɡmə/ NOUN, NO PLURAL hot, liquid rock inside the Earth. A geography word. (**magma**)

magnanimous /mæɡˈnænɪməs/ ADJECTIVE kind or generous in a situation in which you could be angry, jealous, etc. A formal word. □ *In a magnanimous gesture, he congratulated his opponent.* (**magnânimo**)

magnesium /mæɡˈniːziəm/ NOUN, NO PLURAL a light, silver-white metal element that burns with a very bright flame. A chemistry word. (**magnésio**)

magnet /ˈmæɡnɪt/ NOUN [plural **magnets**]

1 a piece of iron which makes other metal objects move towards it (**ímã**)

2 be a magnet for someone to be a person or place which attracts a lot of people □ *Paris is a magnet for artists.* (**ser atraente para alguém**)

• **magnetic** /mæɡˈnetɪk/ ADJECTIVE

1 having the power of a magnet □ *Iron has magnetic properties.* □ *The satellite will measure the sun's magnetic field.* (**magnético**)

2 able to attract people □ *Sara had a magnetic personality.* (**magnético**)

• **magnetism** /ˈmæɡnɪtɪzəm/ NOUN, NO PLURAL

1 the power that a magnet has to attract metals. A physics word. (**magnetismo**)

2 the power some people have to attract or influence other people (**magnetismo**)

magnification /ˌmæɡnɪfɪˈkeɪʃən/ NOUN [plural **magnifications**]

1 *no plural* making things seem bigger or closer than they really are (**ampliação**)

2 the amount, shown by a number, by which an instrument like a microscope or a telescope makes things seem bigger (**ampliação**)

magnificence /mæɡˈnɪfɪsəns/ NOUN, NO PLURAL being magnificent □ *the magnificence of a cathedral* (**magnificência**)

• **magnificent** /mæɡˈnɪfɪsənt/ ADJECTIVE extremely beautiful or skilful, making you feel great admiration □ *The apartment has magnificent views of the lake.* □ *It was a truly magnificent performance by this team.* (**magnífico**)

• **magnificently** /mæɡˈnɪfɪsəntli/ ADVERB in a magnificent way □ *The team played magnificently.* (**de modo magnífico**)

magnify /ˈmæɡnɪfaɪ/ VERB [**magnifies, magnifying, magnified**]

1 to make something seem more important or serious than it really is □ *The problems are magnified because of his age.* (**exaltar**)

2 to make something seem bigger or closer than it really is □ *The lens magnifies the image.* (**ampliar**)

magnifying glass /ˈmæɡnɪfaɪɪŋ ˌɡlɑːs/ NOUN [plural **magnifying glasses**] a piece of glass that you hold in your hand which makes small writing and small objects look bigger (**lupa**)

magnitude /ˈmæɡnɪtjuːd/ NOUN, NO PLURAL the great size or degree of something □ *The government has failed to understand the magnitude of the problem.* (**magnitude**)

magnolia /mæɡˈnəʊliə/ NOUN [plural **magnolias**] a bush with large white or pink flowers that smell sweet (**magnólia**)

magpie /ˈmæɡpaɪ/ NOUN [plural **magpies**] a large black and white bird (**pássaro pega**)

mahogany /məˈhɒɡəni/ NOUN, NO PLURAL a hard dark wood used for making furniture (**mogno**)

maid /meɪd/ NOUN [plural **maids**] a woman whose job is to keep the rooms clean and tidy in a hotel or house (**empregada doméstica, arrumadeira**)

maiden /ˈmeɪdən/ ▶ NOUN [plural **maidens**] an old-fashioned word for a young woman who is not married (**donzela, virgem**)

maiden name

▶ ADJECTIVE **maiden voyage/flight** the first journey that a ship or plane makes (**primeira viagem de um avião/navio**)

maiden name /ˈmeɪdən ˌneɪm/ NOUN [plural **maiden names**] the family name that a married woman had when she was born (**nome de solteira**)

mail /meɪl/ ▶ NOUN, NO PLURAL

1 letters and packages which are sent by post □ *Mail was being delivered to the wrong address.* (**correspondência**)

2 the system of sending and delivering letters and packages □ *His passport had been sent in the mail.* (**correio**)

> ➤ Remember that the noun *mail* is not used in the plural:
> ✓ We get a lot of mail.
> ✗ We get a lot of mails.

▶ VERB [**mails, mailing, mailed**]

1 to send a letter or package in the post (**enviar por correio**)

2 to e-mail someone □ *I'll mail you some photos.* (**enviar e-mail**)

mailbox /ˈmeɪlbɒks/ NOUN [plural **mailboxes**]

1 the place on a computer where e-mails are stored. A computing word □ *I had eight messages in my mailbox.* (**caixa de correio/e-mail**)

2 especially in the US, a box outside someone's house where their letters are delivered (**caixa de correio**)

3 the US word for **postbox** (**caixa-postal**)

mailing list /ˈmeɪlɪŋ ˌlɪst/ NOUN [plural **mailing lists**] a list of people that an organization or business regularly sends information to (**lista de destinatários**)

mail order /ˌmeɪl ˈɔːdə(r)/ NOUN, NO PLURAL a system of buying things, in which you choose something at home and it is delivered to you (**pedido com entrega em domicílio**)

maim /meɪm/ VERB [**maims, maiming, maimed**] to injure someone badly and permanently □ *Many soldiers were maimed or killed in the war.* (**mutilar**)

main /meɪn/ ▶ ADJECTIVE

1 biggest or most important □ *The main reason I do sport is to improve my health.* □ *a main road* □ *Police guarded the main entrance of the building.* (**principal**)

2 the main thing the most important part of a situation □ *The baby is healthy and that's the main thing.* (**o mais importante**)

main course /ˌmeɪn ˈkɔːs/ NOUN [plural **main courses**] the main part of a meal □ *For my main course I had fish.* (**prato principal**)

mainframe /ˈmeɪnfreɪm/ NOUN [plural **mainframes**] a large, powerful computer that is used by many people. A computing word. (**computador de grande porte**)

maisonette

mainland /ˈmeɪnlənd/ ▶ NOUN, NO PLURAL **the mainland** the main part of a country and not the islands around it □ *The island is 25 miles off the Scottish mainland.* (**continente**)

▶ ADJECTIVE used for describing the main part of a country and not the islands around it □ *mainland China* (**continental**)

mainly /ˈmeɪnli/ ADVERB mostly or in most cases □ *Her job mainly involves organizing conferences.* □ *We chose Spain mainly because of the weather.* □ *The spice is used mainly in Indian cooking.* (**principalmente**)

mains /meɪnz/ PLURAL NOUN

1 the pipes or wires that carry water or electricity into a building □ *Some of the houses don't have mains electricity.* (**encanamento**)

2 the mains the place inside a building where you connect something to the electricity supply □ *Plug this into the mains.* (**tronco principal de eletricidade, água etc.**)

mainstream /ˈmeɪnstriːm/ ▶ ADJECTIVE involving or using ordinary ideas or methods which most people accept □ *the mainstream media* □ *a mainstream school* (**tendência atual**)

▶ NOUN, NO PLURAL **the mainstream** the most ordinary ideas or methods which most people accept □ *The party is not in the political mainstream.* (**corrente principal**)

maintain /meɪnˈteɪn/ VERB [**maintains, maintaining, maintained**]

1 to make something continue at the same level or in the same way as before □ *Players need to maintain their fitness levels.* □ *The Republican Party has maintained control of the country.* (**manter**)

2 to keep a house or piece of equipment in good condition □ *The car hadn't been maintained properly.* (**manter**)

3 a formal word meaning to keep saying that something is true even if other people do not believe you (**afirmar, sustentar**) 🔳 *Robinson maintained his innocence* (= said he was innocent) *throughout the trial.* (**afirmou inocência**) □ *Geddings maintained that he had not intended to mislead anyone.*

• **maintenance** /ˈmeɪntənəns/ NOUN, NO PLURAL

1 regular cleaning or repairs done to keep something in good condition (**manutenção**) 🔳 *The bridge has been closed for routine maintenance work.* (**trabalho de manutenção**)

2 making something continue at the same level or in the same way as before □ *Our school is committed to the maintenance of high standards.* (**manutenção**)

3 money that someone pays regularly to their former wife or husband (**pensão alimentícia**)

maisonette /ˌmeɪzəˈnet/ NOUN [plural **maisonettes**] an apartment which has stairs in it (**duplex**)

maize /meɪz/ NOUN, NO PLURAL a tall plant with yellow seeds that you eat as a vegetable (milho)

majestic /məˈdʒestɪk/ ADJECTIVE very big and beautiful, making you feel great admiration □ *majestic mountains* □ *a majestic cathedral* (majestoso, suntuoso)

majesty /ˈmædʒəsti/ NOUN [plural **majesties**]
1 His/Her/Your Majesty a title used when speaking to or about a king or queen □ *Her Majesty will be attending a Thanksgiving service next week.* (Sua/Vossa Majestade)
2 no plural a formal word meaning the quality of being great and beautiful □ *the majesty of the mountains* (majestade)

major /ˈmeɪdʒə(r)/ ▶ ADJECTIVE very big, serious or important □ *a major problem* □ *major changes* □ *The company has offices in all major cities.* (principal)
▶ NOUN [plural **majors**] an army officer above the rank of captain (major)

majority /məˈdʒɒrəti/ ▶ NOUN [plural **majorities**]
1 no plural most of the people or things in a group □ *+ of The study showed that a majority of people have access to the Internet.* □ *The illness is linked to diet in the majority of cases.* (maioria) ▣ *The vast majority of students agreed with the proposal.* (grande maioria)
2 be in the majority to form the largest group □ *In the nursing profession, women are in the majority.* (ser a maioria)
3 the number of votes by which one person or group wins an election (maioria) ▣ *Harper won a comfortable majority.* (venceu pela maioria dos votos) □ *+ of He won by a majority of 120.*
▶ ADJECTIVE to do with most people in a group □ *a majority decision* (majoritária)

make /meɪk/ ▶ VERB [**makes, making, made**]
1 to create something □ *I'll make dinner.* □ *She makes all the children's clothes.* □ *They've made a film of the book.* (fazer)
2 to cause someone to feel a particular emotion □ *It made me so angry.* □ *That film makes me cry.* (fazer)
3 to force someone to do something □ *My parents made me do my homework.* □ *No one is going to make you go if you don't want to.* (fazer)
4 make an appointment/date to arrange to see someone at a particular time □ *I've made a doctor's appointment.* (marcar consulta/compromisso)
5 used with some nouns to do with speech □ *May I make a suggestion?* □ *He made a very strange comment.* □ *I've made a complaint.* □ *He made an interesting point.* (fazer)
6 make a decision to decide something □ *Have you made a decision yet?* (tomar uma decisão)
7 make a mistake to do something wrong □ *Everyone makes mistakes.* (cometer um erro)
8 make progress to develop or improve □ *The children are all making progress.* (progredir)
9 make a noise/sound to cause there to be a noise or sound □ *The children were making so much noise.* (fazer barulho/ruído)
10 to earn money □ *He makes about $90,000 a year.* □ *You can make a lot of money in banking.* (ganhar dinheiro)
11 to be the total amount of two or more numbers added together □ *Six and six makes twelve.* (perfazer)
12 to manage to go somewhere or manage to arrive somewhere in time to do something □ *I don't think I'm going to make the party tonight.* □ *If we hurry, we might just make the earlier train.* (conseguir ir/chegar a tempo)
13 make do to accept or use something although it is not exactly what you wanted □ *If we can't borrow Andrew's van we'll have to make do with the car.* (quebrar o galho)
14 make it to manage to go somewhere or manage to arrive somewhere in time to do something □ *If we run we might just make it before the train leaves.* (conseguir)
⇨ go to **make the best of something, make a clean breast of something**
◆ PHRASAL VERBS **make something into something** to change something so that it becomes something else □ *We've made the back room into an office.* (tornar/transformar) **make something of someone/something** to think of someone or something in a particular way □ *What do you make of his girlfriend?* (achar, concluir) **make something/someone out** to be able to see or hear something or someone although with difficulty □ *His voice was very low but I could just make out what he said.* (conseguir entender, distinguir) **make out something** to pretend something is true □ *He made out that he was rich.* (aparentar) **make it up to someone** to do something nice for someone so that they will forgive you □ *I know I haven't been home much this week but I'll make it up to you – I'll take you out for dinner.* (compensar) **make up** to become friendly again after an argument (fazer as pazes) **make up something** to give an explanation that is not true □ *He made up some excuse about the train being late.* (inventar uma desculpa) **make up for something** to make someone feel less upset or angry about something you have done by doing something nice □ *He was late but made up for it by bringing me a present.* (compensar)
▶ NOUN [plural **makes**] the name of a company that produces a particular product □ *What make is your washing machine?* (marca)

make-believe /ˈmeɪk bɪˌliːv/ NOUN, NO PLURAL things that someone pretends are real (faz de conta)

makeover /ˈmeɪkəʊvə(r)/ NOUN [plural **makeovers**] a number of changes that are made

maker

to someone or something in order to improve their appearance (renovação, reformulação) 🔲 *She looks like she's had a makeover.* (passou por uma renovação)

maker /ˈmeɪkə(r)/ NOUN [plural **makers**] a person, business or machine that makes a particular type of thing 🔲 *a filmmaker* 🔲 *a coffee maker* (produtor, fabricante)

makeshift /ˈmeɪkʃɪft/ ADJECTIVE temporary and made from whatever is available 🔲 *a makeshift refugee camp* (provisório)

make-up /ˈmeɪkʌp/ NOUN, NO PLURAL

1 coloured substances that you put on your face to improve or change your appearance (maquiagem) 🔲 *A lot of women wear make-up.* (usam maquiagem) 🔲 *She was putting on her make-up.* (passando maquiagem)
2 the combination of characteristics or qualities that form a person or their character (constituição) 🔲 *You can't change your genetic make-up.* (constituição genética)
3 the people or things that form a group 🔲 + *of* *There has been a change in the make-up of the audience.* (composição)

making /ˈmeɪkɪŋ/ NOUN, NO PLURAL

1 the process or business of producing something 🔲 *decision making* 🔲 *He was involved in the making of the film.* (criação, produção)
2 have the makings of something to have all the qualities needed to become something 🔲 *Olivia has the makings of a very good singer.* (ter as qualidades essenciais)
3 of your own making done or caused by yourself 🔲 *The problems are all of his own making.* (causado pela própria pessoa)

malaria /məˈleəriə/ NOUN, NO PLURAL a serious tropical disease which people can get if they are bitten by a mosquito (= type of insect) (malária)

male /meɪl/ ▶ ADJECTIVE

1 belonging to the sex that does not have babies 🔲 *male students* 🔲 *a male swan* 🔲 *The group's members are mostly male.* (macho)
2 to do with men or boys 🔲 *He heard a male voice in the next room.* 🔲 *male hormones* (masculino)

▶ NOUN [plural **males**] a male person or animal 🔲 *Thirty thousand adult males disappear every year.* (macho)

malevolent /məˈlevələnt/ ADJECTIVE a formal word meaning wanting to harm someone 🔲 *his malevolent influence* (malévolo)

malfunction /ˌmælˈfʌŋkʃən/ ▶ NOUN [plural **malfunctions**] a fault that causes something to stop working correctly 🔲 *a technical malfunction* (mau funcionamento)

▶ VERB [**malfunctions, malfunctioning, malfunctioned**] to not work correctly 🔲 *The automatic gates were malfunctioning.* (não funcionar corretamente)

manage M

malice /ˈmælɪs/ NOUN, NO PLURAL a feeling of wanting to harm or upset someone 🔲 *I have no malice towards her.* (malícia)

• **malicious** /məˈlɪʃəs/ ADJECTIVE

1 deliberately trying to harm or upset someone 🔲 *malicious rumours* (maldoso)
2 designed to cause damage to someone's computer 🔲 *malicious software* (maligno)

malignant /məˈlɪɡnənt/ ADJECTIVE a malignant lump in the body is caused by cancer (maligno)

mall /mɔːl, mæl/ NOUN [plural **malls**] a shopping centre that is indoors (shopping center)

mallet /ˈmælɪt/ NOUN [plural **mallets**] a wooden hammer (marreta)

malnutrition /ˌmælnjuːˈtrɪʃən/ NOUN, NO PLURAL a medical condition in which someone is ill because they have not eaten enough healthy food for a long time (desnutrição)

malt /mɔːlt/ NOUN, NO PLURAL grain that is used in making beer and whisky (= strong alcoholic drink) (malte)

maltreat /ˌmælˈtriːt/ VERB [**maltreats, maltreating, maltreated**] to treat a person or animal cruelly (maltratar)

• **maltreatment** /ˌmælˈtriːtmənt/ NOUN, NO PLURAL cruel treatment of a person or animal 🔲 *the maltreatment of prisoners* (maus-tratos)

mammal /ˈmæməl/ NOUN [plural **mammals**] an animal that feeds its babies on milk from its own body 🔲 *Humans, cows and dogs are mammals.* (mamífero)

mammoth /ˈmæməθ/ ▶ ADJECTIVE very large 🔲 *a mammoth task* (gigantesco)

▶ NOUN [plural **mammoths**] a type of elephant with hair on its skin that lived a very long time ago (mamute)

man /mæn/ ▶ NOUN [plural **men**]

1 an adult male human 🔲 *a young man* 🔲 *an old man* 🔲 *a married man* 🔲 *I work mainly with men.* (homem)
2 *no plural* humans considered as a group 🔲 *Man is closely related to the ape.* (homem)

▶ VERB [**mans, manning, manned**] to be the person who is in charge of a particular machine or a particular place at work 🔲 *Bernhard was manning the information desk.* (ser encarregado de)

manage /ˈmænɪdʒ/ VERB [**manages, managing, managed**]

1 to succeed in doing something 🔲 + *to do something* *The prisoners managed to escape.* 🔲 *We couldn't manage without your help.* 🔲 *Emma managed a smile even though she didn't feel very happy.* (conseguir)
2 to be in charge of a business, team, etc. 🔲 *Who manages the business for you?* 🔲 *Alan is managing the new project.* (administrar)
3 to live on very little money 🔲 *I don't know how he manages on his student grant.* (sobreviver financeiramente)

4 to use money, time, etc. in a sensible way □ *The scheme helps families to manage their finances.* (administrar)

- **manageable** /ˈmænɪdʒəbəl/ ADJECTIVE easy to control or deal with □ *With more staff, the workload will be more manageable.* □ *manageable hair* (controlável)

- **management** /ˈmænɪdʒmənt/ NOUN, NO PLURAL **1** the job of controlling a business or activity □ *a job in management* (gestão, administração) ▣ *The report criticized his management style.* (estilo de administração) ▣ *management skills* (habilidades de gestão)
2 the people who control a company □ *The management has agreed to further talks.* □ *The restaurant is under new management.* (gerente, diretor) ▣ *senior management* (diretor executivo)
3 the way that something is controlled □ + *of The government's successful management of the economy continues.* (administração)

- **manager** /ˈmænɪdʒə(r)/ NOUN [plural **managers**] someone who is in charge of a company, team, etc. □ *a project manager* □ *a football manager* (gerente, diretor) ▣ *She's a senior manager for a law firm.* (diretor executivo) □ + *of Can I speak to the manager of the hotel, please?*

- **manageress** /ˌmænɪdʒəˈres/ NOUN [plural **manageresses**] a woman who is in charge of a restaurant, shop, etc. (dirigente, diretora)

- **managerial** /ˌmænɪˈdʒɪəriəl/ ADJECTIVE to do with managing a company □ *He doesn't have much managerial experience.* (gerencial)

managing director /ˌmænɪdʒɪŋ dɪˈrektə(r)/ NOUN [plural **managing directors**] someone who is in charge of a big company (diretor administrativo)

mandarin /ˈmændərɪn/ NOUN [plural **mandarins**] a type of small orange (tangerina)

mandatory /ˈmændətəri/ ADJECTIVE a formal word meaning necessary because of a rule or law □ *The mandatory retirement age for judges was 70.* (obrigatório, compulsório)

mane /meɪn/ NOUN [plural **manes**] the long hair on a horse's or lion's neck (juba, crina)

maneuver /məˈnuːvə(r)/ NOUN [plural **maneuvers**], VERB [**maneuvers, maneuvering, maneuvered**] the US spelling of **manoeuvre** (manobra)

mangled /ˈmæŋɡəld/ ADJECTIVE crushed and twisted □ *Rescuers searched through the mangled wreckage of the train.* (destroçado)

mango /ˈmæŋɡəʊ/ NOUN [plural **mangos** or **mangoes**] a tropical fruit with a green skin and yellow flesh (manga)

manhandle /ˈmænhændəl/ VERB [**manhandles, manhandling, manhandled**] to move someone or something roughly □ *He had been manhandled by security guards.* (levar à força)

manhole /ˈmænhəʊl/ NOUN [plural **manholes**] a covered hole in a road which someone goes down to examine pipes (poço de inspeção)

manhood /ˈmænhʊd/ NOUN, NO PLURAL
1 the period of time when someone is a man □ *A ceremony is held when a boy reaches manhood.* (idade adulta)
2 qualities which are typical of a man (virilidade)

manhunt /ˈmænhʌnt/ NOUN [plural **manhunts**] a search for a criminal (perseguição) ▣ *Police have launched a massive manhunt for the killer.* (lançou uma perseguição)

mania /ˈmeɪniə/ NOUN [plural **manias**]
1 a very strong enthusiasm for something □ *World Cup mania was sweeping the country.* (mania)
2 a type of mental illness (mania)

- **maniac** /ˈmeɪniæk/ NOUN [plural **maniacs**] someone who behaves in a dangerous or stupid way □ *Slow down, you maniac!* (maníaco)

- **manic** /ˈmænɪk/ ADJECTIVE
1 extremely excited and active and not able to relax □ *He sounded slightly manic when we spoke.* (agitado)
2 involving a lot of uncontrolled activity □ *Children's parties are always a bit manic.* (agitado)
3 suffering from mania (maníaco)

manicure /ˈmænɪkjʊə(r)/ ▶ NOUN [plural **manicures**] a treatment in which someone makes your hands and nails look attractive, for example by cutting the nails (manicure)
▶ VERB [**manicures, manicuring, manicured**] to give someone a manicure (fazer as unhas)

manifesto /ˌmænɪˈfestəʊ/ NOUN [plural **manifestos** or **manifestoes**] a written statement of what a political party intends to do (manifesto)

manipulate /məˈnɪpjʊleɪt/ VERB [**manipulates, manipulating, manipulated**]
1 to control someone or something so that they do what you want, often in a dishonest way □ *He knew how to manipulate the media.* (manipular)
2 to move or use something in a skilful way □ *The software allows you to manipulate information and images.* (manejar)

- **manipulation** /məˌnɪpjʊˈleɪʃən/ NOUN, NO PLURAL manipulating something or someone (manipulação)

- **manipulative** /məˈnɪpjʊlətɪv/ ADJECTIVE controlling people so that they do what you want, in a dishonest way (manipulador)

mankind /mænˈkaɪnd/ NOUN, NO PLURAL all humans □ *This is one of the most deadly diseases in the history of mankind.* (espécie humana)

manly /ˈmænli/ ADJECTIVE [**manlier, manliest**] having typical male qualities, such as strength (varonil)

man-made /ˌmæn ˈmeɪd/ ADJECTIVE made or caused by people and not natural □ *a man-made lake* □ *man-made disasters* (artificial)

manner /ˈmænə(r)/ NOUN [plural **manners**]
1 the way in which a person behaves towards other people □ *He had a very aggressive manner.* (jeito, modo)

manoeuvre 477 manouvre marathon M

2 the way in which something happens or is done □ *The boys behaved in a very responsible manner.* □ **+ of** *The manner of his death was extremely shocking.* (**maneira, modo**)
3 manners polite ways of behaving in a social situation (**modos, maneiras**) □ *His parents had taught him good manners.* (**boas maneiras**) □ *It's bad manners* (= it is not polite) *to talk when your mouth is full of food.* (**maus modos**) □ *She needs to learn some manners.* (**aprender bons modos**)
4 all manner of many different types of person or thing □ *The shop stocks all manner of things.* (**todos os tipos**)

• **mannerism** /ˈmænərɪzəm/ NOUN [plural **mannerisms**] the way in which a particular person speaks or behaves □ *John's mannerisms are very much like his father's.* (**peculiaridade**)

manoeuvre /məˈnuːvə(r)/ ▶ NOUN [plural **manoeuvres**]
1 a difficult movement that needs skill and attention □ *The ice skaters performed a perfect manoeuvre.* (**manobra**)
2 something clever which you do to get something you want □ *political manoeuvres* (**manobra**)
3 a movement of a lot of soldiers and military equipment (**manobra**)
▶ VERB [**manoeuvres, manoeuvring, manoeuvred**] to move something somewhere carefully or skilfully □ *She manoeuvred the car into a very small space.* (**manobrar**)

manpower /ˈmænpaʊə(r)/ NOUN, NO PLURAL the workers who are needed for a particular job □ *We don't have the manpower to cope with such a heavy workload.* (**mão de obra**)

mansion /ˈmænʃən/ NOUN [plural **mansions**] a very large, expensive house (**mansão**)

manslaughter /ˈmænslɔːtə(r)/ NOUN, NO PLURAL the crime of killing someone but not intentionally (**homicídio culposo**)

mantelpiece /ˈmæntəlpiːs/ NOUN [plural **mantelpieces**] the shelf above a fireplace (= a space for a fire in the wall of a room) (**consolo de lareira**)

manual /ˈmænjuəl/ ▶ ADJECTIVE
1 involving your hands or physical strength (**manual**) □ *manual work* (**trabalho manual**) □ *manual labour* (**trabalho manual**)
2 done by a person and not automatic □ *The car has a manual gearbox.* (**manual**)
▶ NOUN [plural **manuals**] a book that tells you how to do something such as use a machine (**manual**)

manufacture /ˌmænjuˈfæktʃə(r)/ ▶ VERB [**manufactures, manufacturing, manufactured**] to make something in a factory □ *The company manufactures car parts* (**fabricar**)
▶ NOUN, NO PLURAL the process of making something in a factory □ *These chemicals are used in the manufacture of explosives.* (**manufatura, fabricação**)

• **manufacturer** /ˌmænjuˈfæktʃərə(r)/ NOUN [plural **manufacturers**] a company that makes something in a factory □ *food manufacturers* (**fabricante**)

• **manufacturing** /ˌmænjuˈfæktʃərɪŋ/ NOUN, NO PLURAL the business of making things in factories □ *More than 30,000 manufacturing jobs have been lost.* (**fabricação**)

manure /məˈnjʊə(r)/ NOUN, NO PLURAL solid waste from animals that you put on soil to make plants grow better (**esterco**)

manuscript /ˈmænjuskrɪpt/ NOUN [plural **manuscripts**]
1 the original copy of a book or document, written or typed by the writer (**manuscrito**)
2 a very old book or document that someone wrote before printing was invented (**manuscrito**)

many /ˈmeni/ DETERMINER, PRONOUN [plural **more, most**]
1 a lot or a large number □ *Were there many people at the party?* □ *We've had so many problems.* □ *There are too many people here.* □ *She doesn't have many friends.* (**muitos**)
2 how many used to ask about the number of something □ *How many chairs will you need?* (**quantos?/quantas?**)

> Remember that many is used with the plural forms of countable nouns. It is not used with uncountable nouns:
> ✓ How many plates do we need?
> ✗ How many food do we need?
> With uncountable nouns, the word much is used: □ How much food do we need?

map /mæp/ ▶ NOUN [plural **maps**] a drawing of an area which shows things such as roads, rivers and hills □ *Where's Tokyo on this map?* (**mapa**) □ *Emma stopped the car and looked at the map.* (**olhar no mapa**) □ *She drew a little map to show where her house was.* (**desenhou um mapa**) □ *a road map* (**mapa de rodovias**) □ **+ of** *Have you got a map of France?*
▶ VERB [**maps, mapping, mapped**] to make a map of an area (**mapear**)
♦ PHRASAL VERB **map something out** to plan exactly how something will happen □ *His parents had mapped out his life for him.* (**planejar**)

maple /ˈmeɪpəl/ NOUN [plural **maples**] a tree that produces a sweet substance (**bordo de árvore**)

mar /mɑː(r)/ VERB [**mars, marring, marred**] to spoil something □ *The argument had marred the evening for her.* (**estragar**)

marathon /ˈmærəθən/ ▶ NOUN [plural **marathons**]
1 a race in which people run approximately 26 miles or 42 kilometres (**maratona**) □ *She ran her first marathon last year.* (**correu sua primeira maratona**)

2 a long and difficult activity ▢ *He defeated Federer after a five-set marathon.* (maratona)
▶ ADJECTIVE very long and difficult ▢ *The agreement was reached after marathon talks.* (maratona)

marble /ˈmɑːbəl/ NOUN [plural **marbles**]
1 no plural a type of smooth stone used for making things ▢ *a marble statue* (**mármore**)
2 a small glass ball that children play with (**bola de gude**)

March /mɑːtʃ/ NOUN the third month of the year, after February and before April ▢ *I'm going to Chile in March.* (**março**)

march /mɑːtʃ/ ▶ VERB [**marches, marching, marched**]
1 to walk with many other people in order to protest (= show that you disagree) about something ▢ + *through Anti-war protesters marched through the streets.* ▢ + *on Around 1,000 workers marched on* (= marched towards) *Parliament.* (**marchar**)
2 if soldiers march, they walk together with the same, regular steps (**marchar**)
3 to walk somewhere quickly in an angry, confident or determined way ▢ *into/out of He marched into the office and demanded to speak to the manager.* (**caminhar com determinação ou intensidade**)
▶ NOUN [plural **marches**]
1 an event in which a large group of people walk somewhere to protest (= show that they disagree) about something ▢ + *against 2,000 people took part in a march against the new employment laws.* (**marcha**)
2 a walk with regular steps done by soldiers ▢ *a slow march* (**marcha**)
• **marcher** /ˈmɑːtʃə(r)/ NOUN [plural **marchers**] a person who is marching in order to show that they disagree about something (**manifestante**)

mare /meə(r)/ NOUN [plural **mares**] a female horse (**égua**)

margarine /ˌmɑːdʒəˈriːn, ˌmɑːɡəˈriːn/ NOUN, NO PLURAL a soft yellow food that you spread on bread and use in cooking (**margarina**)

margin /ˈmɑːdʒɪn/ NOUN [plural **margins**]
1 the amount by which someone wins an election or competition (**margem**) ▣ *Republicans won the election by a wide margin* (= by a lot of votes). (**ampla margem**)
2 the empty space at the side of a page ▢ *The teacher had written some comments in the margin.* (**margem**)
3 an extra amount of something that you include to be sure that you will be safe or successful (**margem**) ▣ *There is very little margin for error in these calculations.* (**margem de erro**)
• **marginal** /ˈmɑːdʒɪnəl/ ADJECTIVE small and not important ▢ *a marginal improvement* (**marginal**)
• **marginally** /ˈmɑːdʒɪnəli/ ADVERB slightly ▢ *This product is marginally better.* (**levemente**)

marina /məˈriːnə/ NOUN [plural **marinas**] an area of water where small boats are kept (**marina**)

marine /məˈriːn/ ▶ ADJECTIVE
1 to do with the sea and the animals that live there ▢ *marine animals* ▢ *the marine environment* (**marinho**)
2 to do with ships ▢ *marine engineers* (**náutico**)
▶ NOUN [plural **marines**] a soldier who fights on land and at sea (**fuzileiro naval**)

marital /ˈmærɪtəl/ ADJECTIVE to do with marriage ▢ *They were having marital problems.* (**marital**) ▣ *Are employers allowed to ask about your marital status* (= whether you are married or not)? (**estado civil**)

mark /mɑːk/ ▶ NOUN [plural **marks**]
1 an area of something that is a different colour from the thing it is on ▢ *There's a dirty mark on the sofa.* ▢ *The rabbit's fur is brown, with black marks.* ▢ *The bite marks have faded now.* (**marca**)
2 a number or letter that says how well you have done a piece of school work, exam, etc. (**nota**) ▣ *a high/low mark* (**nota alta/baixa**) ▣ *He got top marks* (= the best possible marks) *in all his exams.* (**as notas mais altas**)
3 the halfway/high-water/100-point, etc. mark used to show the level or amount of something (**marca de metade do caminho/maré alta/dos 100 pontos etc.**)
4 a mark of something a sign that something exists or is true ▢ *They were silent for a minute as a mark of respect.* (**sinal de**)
5 leave a mark on something to have a continuing effect on someone or something ▢ *He really left his mark on the Australian community.* (**deixar marcas**)
▶ VERB [**marks, marking, marked**]
1 to happen in order to celebrate something ▢ *A concert was held to mark the anniversary of his birth.* (**marcar**)
2 to show that something is happening or true ▢ *The protest marked the beginning of a campaign for democracy.* ▢ *This film marks his return to adventure stories.* (**marcar**)
3 to judge the quality of and correct a student's work, exam, etc. (**avaliar**)
4 to make a mark on the surface of something ▢ *Shoes with black soles may mark this floor.* (**manchar**)
5 to write words or a symbol on something ▢ *I've marked on the list the people I want to see.* ▢ *Go along the path marked 'exit'.* (**marcar**)
• **marked** /mɑːkt/ ADJECTIVE obvious (**marcante, notável**) ▣ *There has been a marked improvement in her work.* (**melhora notável**)
• **marker** /ˈmɑːkə(r)/ NOUN [plural **markers**]
1 something used to mark the position of something (**marcador**)
2 a pen with a thick point that is used to write on several surfaces (**marcador**)

market

market /'mɑːkɪt/ ▶ NOUN [plural markets]
1 a building or outside area where people sell things □ *a street market* □ *an outdoor market* □ *a fish market* (feira, mercado) 🔲 *a market stall* (uma banca de mercado)
2 the buying and selling of a particular thing (mercado) 🔲 *The housing market is not as strong as it was.* (mercado de moradias) 🔲 *The company has increased its market share.* (participação no mercado)
3 the market the business of buying and selling stocks and shares (= parts of companies that can be bought and sold) □ *The New York market closed higher yesterday.* (mercado de ações)
4 the number of people who want to buy something □ *There is a huge market for mobile phones.* (mercado)
5 the typical place or group of people that a product is sold to □ *The magazine is aimed at the teenage market.* □ *Our main market is in Europe.* (mercado)
6 on the market available for people to buy □ *The house has been on the market for six months.* (estar à venda)
▶ VERB [markets, marketing, marketed] to advertise something in order to persuade people to buy it □ *The company markets the drug in the US.* □ *+ as It was marketed as a sugar-free drink.* (vender)

• **marketing** /'mɑːkɪtɪŋ/ NOUN, NO PLURAL the job of deciding how to advertise a product and what price to sell it for (marketing) 🔲 *a marketing campaign* (campanha de marketing) □ *Paul's the marketing manager for an electronics company.*

marketplace /'mɑːkɪtpleɪs/ NOUN [plural marketplaces]
1 the marketplace the business of buying and selling products □ *Companies need to be able to compete in the global marketplace.* (o mercado)
2 an area outdoors where there is a market (praça do mercado)

market research /ˌmɑːkɪt rɪˈsɜːtʃ/ NOUN, NO PLURAL the work of finding out what products people buy and what they like about them (pesquisa de mercado)

markings /'mɑːkɪŋz/ PLURAL NOUN
1 the colours and patterns on an animal or bird □ *The bird has beautiful yellow and white markings on its wings.* (cores e padrões do corpo dos animais)
2 things which are painted or written on something □ *The road markings were very unclear.* (marcas)

marmalade /'mɑːməleɪd/ NOUN, NO PLURAL jam made from oranges or lemons (geleia de frutas)

maroon /məˈruːn/ ▶ ADJECTIVE having a dark, purplered colour □ *a maroon T-shirt* (grená)
▶ NOUN, NO PLURAL a dark purple-red colour (cor de grená)

marshal

marooned /məˈruːnd/ ADJECTIVE left in a place that you cannot escape from □ *He was marooned on a desert island.* (abandonado)

marquee /mɑːˈkiː/ NOUN [plural marquees] a very large tent used for parties, weddings or shows □ *They've hired a marquee for their wedding reception.* (tenda ao ar livre, toldo)

marriage /'mærɪdʒ/ NOUN [plural marriages]
1 the legal relationship of being husband and wife □ *My parents had a long and happy marriage.* (casamento)
2 the ceremony in which a man and woman become husband and wife □ *The marriage took place in St Paul's Cathedral.* (casamento)

> ▶ Notice that a marriage is a ceremony in which a man and woman become husband and wife. The occasion when two people become husband and wife, when friends and family dance and eat, etc. is called a wedding:
> ✓ *I was invited to the wedding.*
> ✗ *I was invited to the marriage.*

married /'mærɪd/ ADJECTIVE
1 having a husband or wife □ *a married man* □ *a married couple* □ *+ to Miranda is married to John.* (casado) 🔲 *They are getting married in June.* (vão se casar)
2 to do with marriage □ *married life* (casado)

marrow /'mærəʊ/ NOUN [plural marrows]
1 the soft substance inside long bones such as the ones in your leg. A biology word. (medula, tutano)
2 a large vegetable that has a thick green skin and is white inside (abóbora-menina)

marry /'mæri/ VERB [marries, marrying, married]
1 to make someone your husband or wife in a special ceremony □ *Andrew has asked me to marry him.* □ *Her brother never married.* (casar-se)
2 to officially perform the ceremony that makes two people become husband and wife □ *They were married by the bishop.* (casar)

marsh /mɑːʃ/ NOUN [plural marshes] an area of land that is soft and wet all the time (pântano)

marshal /'mɑːʃəl/ ▶ NOUN [plural marshals]
1 an official who controls the crowds at big public events such as pop concerts □ *The marshals at football matches usually wear yellow jackets.* (mestre de cerimônia)
2 in the US, a police officer or fire officer with a high rank (chefe de polícia ou de bombeiros)
▶ VERB [marshals, marshalling/US marshaling, marshalled/US marshaled] to bring together or organize people or things in order to achieve a particular aim □ *The rebels were marshalling their forces for an attack.* (organizar)

marshmallow /ˌmɑːʃˈmæləʊ/ NOUN [plural marshmallows] a very soft pink or white sweet (marshmallow)

marshy /ˈmɑːʃɪ/ ADJECTIVE marshy ground is very wet and soft (pantanoso)

marsupial /mɑːˈsuːpɪəl/ NOUN [plural marsupials] an animal such as the kangaroo whose babies are carried in a pouch (= pocket) on the mother's front. A biology word. (marsupial)

martial /ˈmɑːʃəl/ ADJECTIVE to do with military organizations or war (marcial) ▪ The city is now under martial law (= being controlled by the army). (lei marcial)

martial art /ˌmɑːʃəl ˈɑːt/ NOUN [plural martial arts] a fighting sport such as karate or judo in which you use your hands and feet (arte marcial)

Martian /ˈmɑːʃən/ NOUN [plural Martians] in stories, a creature from the planet Mars (marciano)

martyr /ˈmɑːtə(r)/ ▶ NOUN [plural martyrs] someone who is killed because of their beliefs (mártir)
▶ VERB [martyrs, martyring, martyred] to kill someone because of their beliefs ▪ Hundreds were brutally martyred for their faith. (martirizar)
• **martyrdom** /ˈmɑːtədəm/ NOUN, NO PLURAL when someone is martyred (martírio)

marvel /ˈmɑːvəl/ ▶ NOUN [plural marvels] someone or something that is extremely effective and surprising ▪ the marvels of modern medicine (maravilha)
▶ VERB [marvels, marvelling/US marveling, marvelled/US marveled] to admire something very much ▪ We could only marvel at Ronaldo's skills. (maravilhar-se)
• **marvellous** /ˈmɑːvələs/ ADJECTIVE extremely good ▪ That's marvellous news! (maravilhoso, ótimo)

marvelous /ˈmɑːvələs/ ADJECTIVE the US spelling of marvellous (maravilhoso)

mascara /mæsˈkɑːrə/ NOUN, NO PLURAL make-up that you put on your eyelashes (= hairs around your eyes) to make them look darker and longer (rímel)

mascot /ˈmæskət/ NOUN [plural mascots] a person or object that a person or team thinks brings them good luck (mascote)

masculine /ˈmæskjulɪn/ ADJECTIVE
1 to do with men, or having qualities that are typical of a man ▪ a deep, masculine voice (masculino)
2 in English grammar, masculine forms of words refer to males. For example, he is a masculine pronoun. (masculino)
• **masculinity** /ˌmæskjuˈlɪnɪtɪ/ NOUN, NO PLURAL being like a man (masculinidade)

mash /mæʃ/ VERB [mashes, mashing, mashed] to crush something, especially food, until it is soft ▪ I'll mash the potatoes. (triturar, esmagar)

mask /mɑːsk/ ▶ NOUN [plural masks] something that you wear over your face in order to protect it, to hide or for decoration ▪ a carnival mask ▪ The surgeon removed his mask to speak to her. (máscara)
▶ VERB [masks, masking, masked] to prevent something such as a feeling or smell from being noticed ▪ She sprayed air freshener to mask the cooking smells. (mascarar)

mason /ˈmeɪsən/ NOUN [plural masons] someone whose job is to make things from stone (pedreiro)
• **masonry** /ˈmeɪsənrɪ/ NOUN, NO PLURAL the parts of a building that are made of stone ▪ He was hit by a piece of falling masonry. (alvenaria)

mass /mæs/ ▶ NOUN [plural masses]
1 a large lump or quantity of something with no clear shape ▪ + of The car was reduced to a mass of tangled metal. ▪ The little girl had a mass of blonde curls. (massa)
2 masses a lot of something. An informal word. ▪ He's got masses of toys. (montes)
3 no plural in science, a measure of the quantity of material in something (massa)
4 the masses the ordinary people in a society and not the rich, powerful people (as massas)
5 Mass a ceremony in some Christian churches in which people eat bread and drink wine (missa)
▶ ADJECTIVE involving a very large number of people ▪ a mass meeting (em massa) ▪ mass unemployment (desemprego em massa)
▶ VERB [masses, massing, massed] to come together or bring people together in large numbers ▪ Soldiers are massing on the border. (juntar-se)

massacre /ˈmæsəkə(r)/ ▶ NOUN [plural massacres] the killing of a large number of people (massacre)
▶ VERB [massacres, massacring, massacred] to kill a large number of people ▪ Hundreds of villagers were massacred in the attack. (massacrar)

massage /ˈmæsɑːʒ/ ▶ VERB [massages, massaging, massaged] to rub parts of a person's body in order to make them relax or to make the muscles less painful ▪ Could you massage my shoulders? (massagear)
▶ NOUN [plural massages] when someone massages you (massagem) ▪ I gave her a foot massage. (fiz massagem nos pés dela)

massive /ˈmæsɪv/ ADJECTIVE very big ▪ She earns a massive amount of money. (maciço)
• **massively** /ˈmæsɪvlɪ/ ADVERB extremely ▪ She was massively overweight. (extremamente)

mass media /ˌmæs ˈmiːdɪə/ PLURAL NOUN newspapers, radio, television and the Internet (mídia de massa)

mass-produce /ˌmæs prəˈdjuːs/ VERB [mass-produces, mass-producing, mass-produced] to

mast

make large numbers of things cheaply in a factory □ *mass-produced goods* (**produzir em massa**)

• **mass production** /ˌmæs prəˈdʌkʃən/ NOUN, NO PLURAL when things are mass-produced (**produção em massa**)

mast /mɑːst/ NOUN [plural **masts**]
1 a tall pole used for sending out radio, television or mobile phone signals (**torre**)
2 a tall pole for holding the sails of a boat or ship (**mastro**)

master /ˈmɑːstə(r)/ ▶ NOUN [plural **masters**]
1 a man who has control over something □ *a dog and its master* (**dono**)
2 someone who is very good at a particular activity □ *a master of disguise* (**mestre**)
3 an original document, film or recording from which you can make copies □ *the master file* (**master**)
4 Master a formal title for a boy, used before his name □ *Master Teddy Smith* (**Senhor, título formal para meninos utilizado antes do nome**)
5 Master's (degree) a university qualification that you can study for after you have got a degree (= first university qualification) □ *a Master's in law* (**mestre**)
▶ ADJECTIVE very skilled in a particular job or activity □ *a master craftsman* (**mestre**)
▶ VERB [**masters, mastering, mastered**]
1 to learn how to do something well □ *Juggling needs quite a lot of practice before you master it.* (**dominar**)
2 to control a feeling □ *I've never managed to master my fear of heights.* (**dominar**)

• **masterful** /ˈmɑːstəfʊl/ ADJECTIVE very skilful □ *a masterful performance* (**de mestre**)

mastermind /ˈmɑːstəmaɪnd/ ▶ NOUN [plural **masterminds**] the person who plans and organizes a complicated activity □ *Waterman was the musical mastermind behind her career.* (**mentor, cabeça**)
▶ VERB [**masterminds, masterminding, masterminded**] to plan and organize all the details of a complicated activity □ *It is thought that he also masterminded the bomb attack on the Metro last year.* (**planejar**)

masterpiece /ˈmɑːstəpiːs/ NOUN [plural **masterpieces**] a book, painting, piece of music or other work of art that is one of the greatest of its type (**obra-prima**)

mastery /ˈmɑːstərɪ/ NOUN, NO PLURAL
1 great skill at something □ *her mastery of the language* (**maestria**)
2 control over something □ *mastery of the seas* (**domínio**)

mat /mæt/ NOUN [plural **mats**]
1 a flat piece of material for covering or protecting part of a floor □ *a doormat* (**capacho, tapete**)
2 a small piece of material for putting under something to protect a table's surface □ *a table mat* (**descanso de panela**)

material M

match /mætʃ/ ▶ NOUN [plural **matches**]
1 a sports competition between two players or two teams (**partida**) ▣ *a football match* (**partida de futebol**) ▣ *Who won the match?* (**ganhou a partida**)
2 a short, thin piece of wood with a substance on the end that produces fire when it is rubbed on a rough surface (**fósforo**) ▣ *He struck a match to light a candle.* (**riscou um fósforo**)
3 something that is similar to another thing or suitable to be worn with another thing, especially in its colour or pattern □ *This isn't the same make of paint but it's a very good match.* (**combinação**)
4 a person or animal who is as good as another (**páreo**) ▣ *I could beat him over a mile, but I was no match for him when it came to the 100 metres.* (**não era páreo**)
▶ VERB [**matches, matching, matched**]
1 to be the same colour or style □ *Her handbag matched her shoes.* □ *His handwriting matched that on the letter.* (**combinar com**)
2 to be as good or as large as someone or something else □ *I can't match Joe's strength.* □ *The company will match* (= give the same amount) *any sum of money you donate.* (**equiparar**)
3 to put two people or things together because they are suitable for each other □ *+ to Match the word on the left to its meaning on the right.* (**ligar, relacionar**)

♦ PHRASAL VERBS **match up** if two pieces of information match up, they are the same □ *The police found that their stories didn't match up.* (**igualar-se**) **match up to something** to be as good as someone or something else □ *The holiday didn't match up to our expectations.* (**equiparar-se**)

matchbox /ˈmætʃbɒks/ NOUN [plural **matchboxes**] a small cardboard box that contains matches (**caixa de fósforos**)

matching /ˈmætʃɪŋ/ ADJECTIVE the same in colour or design □ *She wore a dress with a matching jacket.* (**combinação**)

mate /meɪt/ ▶ NOUN [plural **mates**]
1 an informal word for a friend □ *He's a good mate of mine.* (**amigo**) ▣ *She's my best mate.* (**melhor amiga**)
2 an informal, friendly word used for talking to someone □ *You all right, mate?* □ *Thanks, mate.* (**companheiro**)
3 the male or female that an animal breeds with (**macho ou fêmea**)
▶ VERB [**mates, mating, mated**] animals and birds mate when they have sex to produce babies □ *Swans mate for life.* (**acasalar**)

material /məˈtɪərɪəl/ NOUN [plural **materials**]
1 cloth □ *The jacket was made of a very thick material.* (**tecido**)
2 a substance used for making something else □ *building materials* □ *raw materials for the steel industry* (**material**)

3 information and ideas in a piece of writing □ *She used her experiences as material for her new book.* □ *publicity material* (**material**)

materialistic /mə.tɪərɪə'lɪstɪk/ ADJECTIVE
believing that money and possessions are the most important things in life □ *We live in a materialistic society.* (**materialista**)

materialize *or* **materialise** /mə'tɪərɪəlaɪz/ VERB [**materializes, materializing, materialized**] to happen □ *Did the promised pay rise ever materialize?* (**materializar-se**)

maternal /mə'tɜːnəl/ ADJECTIVE
1 to do with, or typical of, a mother □ *maternal feelings* (**materno**) 🔁 *a maternal instinct* (**instinto materno**)
2 related through your mother's side of your family □ *your maternal grandmother* (**materno**)

maternity /mə'tɜːnəti/ ADJECTIVE to do with pregnancy and giving birth (**maternidade**) 🔁 *maternity clothes* (**roupas de maternidade**) □ *a maternity hospital*

math /mæθ/ NOUN, NO PLURAL the US word for **maths** (**matemática**)

mathematical /ˌmæθə'mætɪkəl/ ADJECTIVE to do with or using mathematics □ *a mathematical genius* □ *a mathematical calculation* (**matemático**)

mathematician /ˌmæθəmə'tɪʃən/ NOUN [plural **mathematicians**] someone who studies mathematics or is an expert in mathematics (**matemático**)

mathematics /ˌmæθə'mætɪks/ NOUN, NO PLURAL the study of measurements, numbers, quantities and shapes. A formal word. (**matemática**)

maths /mæθs/ NOUN, NO PLURAL a short way to say and write **mathematics** (**matemática**)

matinée /'mætɪneɪ/ NOUN [plural **matinées**] a performance at a theatre or cinema in the afternoon (**matinê**)

matrices /'meɪtrɪsiːz/ PLURAL OF **matrix** (**matrizes**)

matrimony /'mætrɪməni/ NOUN, NO PLURAL the state of being married. A formal word. (**matrimônio**)

matrix /'meɪtrɪks/ NOUN [plural **matrixes** or **matrices**] an arrangement of numbers or symbols in lines that go up and down, used in maths. A maths word. (**matriz**)

matron /'meɪtrən/ NOUN [plural **matrons**] an old-fashioned word for an important nurse in a hospital (**enfermeira-chefe**)

matt *or* **matte** /mæt/ ADJECTIVE not shiny □ *photos with a matt finish* □ *matt paint* (**fosco**)

matted /'mætɪd/ ADJECTIVE in a thick mass because of being wet or dirty □ *matted hair* (**emaranhado**)

matter /'mætə(r)/ ▶ NOUN [plural **matters**]
1 a subject or situation □ *He wants to see you to discuss a personal matter.* □ *We need to think about all the practical matters.* □ **+ for** *This is a matter for the police.* (**assunto**) 🔁 *To make matters worse, I had forgotten my phone.* (**para piorar as coisas**)
2 the matter used to talk about something that is wrong with something or causing a problem (**o problema**) 🔁 *What's the matter with Rachel? She's very quiet.* (**qual é o problema com**) 🔁 *I know something's the matter with Eve.* (**alguma coisa é o problema com**) □ *What's the matter with these tomatoes? They look brown.*
3 *no plural* any substance that takes up space and is part of the physical universe (**matéria**)
4 *no plural* a particular type of substance □ *We added plenty of organic matter to the soil* (**substância**)
5 as a matter of fact used to add information or to say that something that has just been said is wrong □ *As a matter of fact, he's one of the richest men in the country.* (**na verdade**)
6 a matter of something used to talk about what is needed for something to happen □ *He'll be fine in the exam – it's just a matter of confidence.* □ *It's a matter of making sure the foundations are deep enough.* (**uma questão de**)
7 a matter of days/hours, etc. used to say that something will happen in a short time □ *The symptoms should improve in a matter of days.* (**uma questão de dias/horas etc.**)
▶ VERB [**matters, mattering, mattered**] to be important (**importar**) 🔁 *It doesn't matter if you're late – we can save you some food.* □ *Does it matter if the door isn't completely closed?* (**não importa**) □ *Winning matters to him more than it should.*

• **matter-of-fact** /ˌmætər əv 'fækt/ ADJECTIVE dealing with or talking about an unusual or upsetting situation in a calm way, as if it were normal □ *She tried hard to be matter-of-fact about it all.* (**simples, prático**)

mattress /'mætrɪs/ NOUN [plural **mattresses**] the thick, soft part of a bed, that you lie on (**colchão**)

mature /mə'tjʊə(r)/ ▶ ADJECTIVE
1 completely grown or developed □ *a mature male elephant* □ *mature trees* (**maduro**)
2 behaving in a sensible way, like an adult □ *He's a very mature 13-year-old.* (**maduro**)
▶ VERB [**matures, maturing, matured**]
1 to become completely grown or developed (**amadurecer**)
2 to start to behave in a sensible way, like an adult (**amadurecer**)

• **maturity** /mə'tjʊərəti/ NOUN, NO PLURAL
1 when someone behaves in a sensible way, like an adult □ *I've never known such maturity in a child of her age.* (**maturidade**)

maul / **mean**

2 when someone or something is completely grown or developed □ *These animals reach maturity after two years.* (maturidade)

maul /mɔːl/ VERB [mauls, mauling, mauled] if you are mauled by a wild animal, it attacks you and badly injures you □ *The zoo keeper was mauled by one of the lions.* (lacerar)

mauve /məʊv/ ▶ ADJECTIVE having a pale purple colour (cor de malva)
▶ NOUN, NO PLURAL a pale purple colour

maximum /ˈmæksɪməm/ ▶ NOUN, NO PLURAL the greatest amount or degree that is possible or allowed □ *The maximum I'm prepared to pay is £200.* □ *The car will hold a maximum of five people.* (máximo)
▶ ADJECTIVE being the greatest amount or degree that is possible or allowed □ *The maximum speed limit is 40 mph on this road.* □ *The crime carries a maximum penalty of five years' imprisonment.* (máximo)

May /meɪ/ NOUN the fifth month of the year, after April and before June □ *The weather was awful in May.* (maio)

may /meɪ/ MODAL VERB
1 used to talk about the possibility that something is true or something will happen □ *I may apply for the job, but I'm not sure yet.* □ *He thinks she may be lying.* (ser possível)
2 a formal word used for asking for or giving permission □ *May I ask what you're doing in my room?* □ *You may leave the table now.* (poder)
3 may ... but used to show that although one thing is true, there is another thing that is more important □ *You may not enjoy studying, but qualifications are important.* (pode..., mas)
4 may as well used to say that you should probably do something because there is nothing better to do □ *We may as well wait inside.* (o melhor a fazer)

maybe /ˈmeɪbi/ ADVERB
1 possibly □ *Maybe she called earlier.* □ *Maybe they're not coming.* □ *It'll take two, maybe three, days to paint the room.* (talvez)
2 used for suggesting something that you are not sure about □ *Maybe we should tell him.* (talvez)

mayhem /ˈmeɪhem/ NOUN, NO PLURAL a confused or noisy situation in which no one is in control □ *The accident caused mayhem on the motorway.* (confusão e destruição)

mayonnaise /ˌmeɪəˈneɪz/ NOUN, NO PLURAL a thick white sauce made with oil and eggs □ *prawn mayonnaise sandwiches* (maionese)

mayor /meə(r)/ NOUN [plural mayors] a man or woman elected as the official leader of a town or city (prefeito)

maze /meɪz/ NOUN [plural mazes] a complicated system of paths that you have to try to find your way out of (labirinto)

MB /ˌem ˈbiː/ ABBREVIATION **megabyte** (megabyte)

MD /ˌem ˈdiː/ ABBREVIATION **managing director** (MD)

me /miː/ PRONOUN used as the object in a sentence to talk or write about yourself □ *Would you make me a cup of tea, please?* □ *Are there any letters for me?* □ *Hi, it's me. Sorry, but I'm going to be late.* (eu, me, mim)

▶ Remember that me is used after a verb or preposition. In a sentence in which you are doing the action, use I before the verb: □ *I gave her some flowers.* □ *He gave me some flowers.*

meadow /ˈmedəʊ/ NOUN [plural meadows] a field of grass (prado, campina)

meager /ˈmiːɡə(r)/ ADJECTIVE the US spelling of **meagre** (insuficiente, escasso)

meagre /ˈmiːɡə(r)/ ADJECTIVE very small in amount □ *How can you survive on such a meagre diet?* (insuficiente, escasso)

meal /miːl/ NOUN [plural meals] food that you eat at one time, for example, breakfast, lunch or dinner (refeição) □ *We're going out for a meal on Saturday night.* (sair para comer) □ *I have my main meal in the evening.* (refeição principal)

mean[1] /miːn/ VERB [means, meaning, meant]
1 to have a particular meaning □ *What does 'intrepid' mean?* □ *Her name means 'lucky' in Arabic.* (significar)
2 to try to express an opinion or a fact □ *I didn't know what she meant when she told me to speak like a lady.* □ *What did she mean by 'too academic'?* (querer dizer) □ *I see what you mean about his bad temper.* (sei o que você quer dizer)
3 to intend to do something □ + **to do something** *I'm sorry. I didn't mean to upset you.* □ *Did you mean to take this turning?* (intencionar)
4 to be a sign that something will happen, or to have a particular result □ + **that** *Higher wages meant that more people could afford cars.* □ *Dark clouds usually mean rain.* □ *The right equipment can mean the difference between life and death.* (significar)
5 to be serious about what you have said (falar sério) □ *If you don't tidy your room, you won't have dinner, and I mean it this time!* □ *She keeps threatening to leave, but she doesn't really mean it.*
6 to be important to someone □ + **to** *That puppy means such a lot to her.* □ *Fame meant nothing to him.* (importar para alguém)
7 to be intended for someone or something □ *The sweets were meant for the children.* (destinar-se a)
8 be meant to do something if you are meant to do something, someone has said that you must do it □ *I'm meant to do my homework before I watch TV.* (dever fazer alguma coisa)

9 I mean used to correct something you have said □ *He was born in 1948 – I mean 1958.* (**quero dizer**)

mean² /miːn/ ▶ ADJECTIVE [meaner, meanest]
1 a mean person does not like spending money or giving things to other people □ *She's too mean to pay to have her hair cut.* (**mesquinho**)
2 unkind □ *Mum, Adam's being mean to me!* (**malvado**)
3 a US word meaning violent and frightening □ *a mean dog* (**bravo**)
4 average. A maths word. □ *The mean income was £400 per week.* (**média**)
▶ NOUN [plural **means**] the average. A maths word.
⇨ go to **means**

meander /mɪˈændə(r)/ VERB [meanders, meandering, meandered]
1 if a river or road meanders, it turns many times (**serpear**)
2 to walk or move slowly in no particular direction □ *We spent the day meandering around the village.* (**vaguear**)

meaning /ˈmiːnɪŋ/ NOUN [plural **meanings**]
1 what a word or action expresses □ *The music conveys the meaning of the text.* □ *I didn't understand the meaning of his words.* □ *We searched for a hidden meaning in his letter.* (**sentido, significado**)
2 importance or purpose □ *We all want to understand the meaning of life.* □ *He helped me understand the meaning of these events.* (**sentido, significado**)

• **meaningful** /ˈmiːnɪŋfʊl/ ADJECTIVE
1 useful or important □ *meaningful discussions* (**significativo**)
2 intended to express something □ *a meaningful look* (**significativo**)
3 showing a meaning that can be understood □ *a meaningful comparison* (**significativo**)

• **meaningless** /ˈmiːnɪŋlɪs/ ADJECTIVE
1 having no purpose or importance □ *He felt as if his life was meaningless.* (**sem sentido**)
2 having no meaning □ *It's a fairly meaningless phrase.* (**sem sentido**)

meanness /ˈmiːnnɪs/ NOUN, NO PLURAL
1 when someone does not like spending money or giving things to other people (**mesquinharia**)
2 unpleasant or unkind behaviour (**maldade**)

means /miːnz/ NOUN [plural **means**]
1 a way or method of doing something □ *a means of transport* □ *a means of payment* (**meios**)
2 money □ *Does he have the means to buy a car?* (**meios**)
3 by all means used to politely give someone permission to do something □ *'Can I have a look at your magazine?' 'By all means.'* (**sem dúvida**)
4 by no means not at all or in no way □ *It was by no means the worst talk I'd heard.* (**de jeito nenhum, nem um pouco**)

meant /ment/ PAST TENSE AND PAST PARTICIPLE OF **mean** □ *I meant every word I said.* □ *She had meant to tell him but had forgotten.* (**ver mean**)

meantime /ˈmiːntaɪm/ NOUN, NO PLURAL **in the meantime** in the time before something happens □ *We're having the car repaired but in the meantime we're borrowing my sister's.* (**nesse ínterim**)

meanwhile /ˈmiːnwaɪl/ ADVERB
1 in the time before something happens □ *I'll start the report once the sales figures are in. Meanwhile I've got plenty of work to be getting on with.* (**enquanto isso**)
2 at the same time □ *Tom was enjoying himself with his friends. Meanwhile, I was working like crazy back here.* (**enquanto isso**)

measles /ˈmiːzəlz/ NOUN, NO PLURAL an infectious disease, especially among children, in which you feel very hot and your skin is covered in red spots (**sarampo**)

measly /ˈmiːzli/ ADJECTIVE [measlier, measliest] too small in amount. An informal word. □ *All I had to eat was one measly little biscuit.* (**mísero**)

measurable /ˈmeʒərəbəl/ ADJECTIVE big enough to be measured or noticed □ *There's no measurable difference between them.* (**mensurável**)

measure /ˈmeʒə(r)/ ▶ VERB [measures, measuring, measured]
1 to find how tall, long, wide, fast, etc. something is □ *She was measuring the window for some new curtains.* (**medir**)
2 to judge how good or bad something is □ *How do you measure success?* □ *This is the only way we know of measuring the performance of such schemes.* (**medir**)
3 to be a particular size □ *The room measures 3.5 metres from the door to the window.* (**medir**)
▶ NOUN [plural **measures**]
1 an official action done to achieve something or deal with something (**medida**) ▣ *The school is being closed as a temporary measure.* (**uma medida temporária**) ▣ *The government is introducing new measures to combat obesity.* (**introduzir novas medidas**)
2 a unit used in measuring □ *A kilogram is a measure of weight, while a kilometre is a measure of distance or length.* (**medida**)

• **measurement** /ˈmeʒəmənt/ NOUN [plural **measurements**]
1 a size or amount found by measuring □ *Can you write down the exact measurements of the floor?* (**dimensão**)
2 *no plural* the act of measuring something (**medição**)

meat /miːt/ NOUN [plural **meats**] the flesh of animals eaten as food (**carne**) ▣ *red meat* such as beef (**carne vermelha**) ▣ *white meat* such as chicken (**carne branca**)

mechanic · meditate

- **meaty** /ˈmiːti/ ADJECTIVE [**meatier, meatiest**] containing a lot of meat □ *The food tends to be quite meaty.* (carnudo)

mechanic /mɪˈkænɪk/ NOUN [plural **mechanics**] someone whose job is to repair vehicles and machines (**mecânico**) ▣ *a car mechanic* (um mecânico de carros)

- **mechanical** /mɪˈkænɪkəl/ ADJECTIVE
1 to do with machines □ *There must have been a mechanical failure.* □ *a mechanical device* (mecânico)
2 done without thinking or without showing emotion □ *He moved his hands in an almost mechanical way.* (mecânico)

- **mechanics** /mɪˈkænɪks/ PLURAL NOUN
1 the study of how machines work and how physical forces act on objects (**mecânica**)
2 the mechanics of something the way something is done □ *I don't understand the mechanics of their financial arrangements.* (o mecanismo de algo)

- **mechanism** /ˈmekənɪzəm/ NOUN [plural **mechanisms**] a working part of a machine, or its system of working parts □ *The cogs and springs are part of the clock's mechanism.* (mecanismo)

medal /ˈmedəl/ NOUN [plural **medals**] a metal disk given as a prize in a competition or for brave actions (**medalha**) ▣ *an Olympic medal* (medalha olímpica) ▣ *a gold/silver/bronze medal* (medalha de ouro/prata/bronze) ▣ *He was awarded a medal* for bravery. (recebeu uma medalha)

- **medallist** /ˈmedəlɪst/ NOUN [plural **medallists**] someone who has won a medal in a competition (agraciado com medalha) ▣ *an Olympic gold medallist* (ganhador de medalha de ouro)

meddle /ˈmedəl/ VERB [**meddles, meddling, meddled**] to become involved in things that are not your responsibility, in an annoying way □ *They should stop meddling in other countries' affairs.* (interferir)

media /ˈmiːdɪə/ ▶ PLURAL NOUN **the media** newspapers, television and radio or other means of communicating information to the public □ *There was nothing in the media about his speech.* (meio de comunicação) ▣ *The event received a lot of media coverage.* (cobertura da mídia)
▶ PLURAL OF **medium** (ver **medium**)

mediaeval /ˌmedɪˈiːvəl/ ADJECTIVE another spelling of **medieval** (medieval)

median /ˈmiːdɪən/ ▶ NOUN [plural **medians**] the middle number or amount in a series of numbers or amounts. A maths word. (média)
▶ ADJECTIVE being the median. A maths word □ *the median price/age* (médio)

mediate /ˈmiːdɪeɪt/ VERB [**mediates, mediating, mediated**] to try to find an agreement between two people or groups who are arguing about something □ *An independent committee has been set up to mediate between the two companies.* (mediar)

- **mediation** /ˌmiːdɪˈeɪʃən/ NOUN, NO PLURAL when you mediate between people or groups □ *All attempts at mediation have so far failed.* (mediação)

- **mediator** /ˈmiːdɪeɪtə(r)/ NOUN [plural **mediators**] someone who mediates between people or groups □ *United Nations mediators are trying to secure a lasting peace.* (mediador)

medic /ˈmedɪk/ NOUN [plural **medics**] an informal word for a doctor or a medical student (**médico**)

medical /ˈmedɪkəl/ ▶ ADJECTIVE to do with medicine or doctors and their work (**médico**) ▣ *He did not need further medical treatment.* (tratamento médico) ▣ *She's receiving the best medical care.* (cuidados médicos) ▣ *the medical staff* (equipe médica) ▣ *a serious medical condition* (condição médica)
▶ NOUN [plural **medicals**] a general examination by a doctor to find out about a person's health □ *The new player passed a medical yesterday.* (exame médico)

medical certificate /ˈmedɪkəl səˈtɪfɪkət/ NOUN [plural **medical certificates**] a document from a doctor that gives information about your health, for example if you are too ill to work (atestado médico)

medically /ˈmedɪkəli/ ADVERB by or to do with medicine □ *The illness can be treated medically.* □ *She is not medically qualified.* (medicamente)

medication /ˌmedɪˈkeɪʃən/ NOUN, NO PLURAL medicine □ *He is on medication for his epilepsy.* (medicação)

medicinal /məˈdɪsɪnəl/ ADJECTIVE to do with medicine or having an effect like medicine □ *medicinal plants* (medicinal)

medicine /ˈmedɪsɪn/ NOUN [plural **medicines**]
1 a substance used to treat or prevent illnesses □ *cough medicine* (remédio) ▣ *Have you taken your medicine?* (tomou seu remédio?)
2 no plural the science of treating and preventing illnesses (medicina) ▣ *He studied medicine at the University of Melbourne.* (cursou Medicina) □ *traditional Chinese medicine*

medieval /ˌmedɪˈiːvəl/ ADJECTIVE to do with the period of history from about AD 1000 to AD 1500 □ *a medieval castle* (medieval)

mediocre /ˌmiːdɪˈəʊkə(r)/ ADJECTIVE not of very good quality □ *a mediocre performance* (medíocre)

- **mediocrity** /ˌmiːdɪˈɒkrəti/ NOUN, NO PLURAL the state of being mediocre (mediocridade)

meditate /ˈmedɪteɪt/ VERB [**meditates, meditating, meditated**]
1 to try to empty your mind or to concentrate on only one thing in order to relax or for religious reasons □ *He was sitting cross-legged, meditating.* (meditar)

2 to think about something carefully □ *She was meditating on her future.* (refletir)

- **meditation** /ˌmedɪˈteɪʃən/ NOUN, NO PLURAL when you meditate (meditação)

medium /ˈmiːdiəm/ ▶ ADJECTIVE in the middle of a group of amounts or sizes □ *He is dark and of medium height.* □ *Heat a large pan over a medium heat.* (médio) *Small and medium sized businesses will be affected.* (de tamanho médio)

▶ NOUN [plural **mediums** or **media**]
1 a way of expressing or communicating information □ + *for The Internet is a popular medium for advertising.* □ + *of SMS is a cheap medium of communication.* (meio)

2 something that is used for a particular purpose □ *Memory Sticks are now a popular storage medium.* (meio)

▶ NOUN [plural **mediums**] someone who believes they can communicate with the dead (médium)

medley /ˈmedli/ NOUN [plural **medleys**]
1 a piece of music combining several other pieces of music □ *He played a medley of Scottish tunes.* (pot-pourri)

2 a mixture of different things □ *a medley of exotic fruit* (mistura)

meek /miːk/ ADJECTIVE [**meeker, meekest**] gentle and not likely to complain or argue with other people □ *He's portrayed as being very meek and mild.* (dócil)

- **meekly** /ˈmiːkli/ ADVERB without complaining or arguing □ *'Sorry,' said Lily meekly.* (docilmente)
- **meekness** /ˈmiːknɪs/ NOUN, NO PLURAL the quality of being meek (docilidade)

meet /miːt/ VERB [**meets, meeting, met**]
1 to come to the same place as someone else by chance □ *Guess who I met in town!* (encontrar)
2 to come to the same place as someone else because you have arranged to see them □ *Let's meet for a coffee next week.* □ *Is there anywhere we can meet privately?* □ *The committee meets once a month.* (encontrar-se)
3 to wait for someone at a particular place where they will arrive □ *We'll meet her at the airport.* (encontrar)
4 to be with and speak to someone for the first time □ *Have you met my big sister, Jane?* (conhecer) *I'm very pleased to meet you at last.* (satisfeito em conhecê-lo)
5 two things meet when they come together or touch □ *Turn right where the road meets a track.* (encontrar-se)
6 to achieve something or to be big enough, good enough, etc. to do something (satisfazer) *There is no play area to meet the needs of children.* (satisfazer às necessidades) □ *Extra funding will help us meet the challenge.*
7 to experience something □ *We met a lot of resistance to our plans for a new airport.* (encontrar)

8 to meet the cost of something is to pay for it (enfrentar os custos de)

◆ PHRASAL VERBS **meet up** to come together with other people in order to do something □ *We meet up about once a week for a chat.* (encontrar-se) **meet with something** to get a particular reaction □ *My suggestion that we go for a walk met with groans from the others.* (encontrar)

- **meeting** /ˈmiːtɪŋ/ NOUN [plural **meetings**] a time when people come together, especially to discuss something □ *We need to arrange a meeting to discuss this matter.* □ *Anne's in a meeting at the moment.* (reunião)

mega- /ˈmegə/ PREFIX
1 mega- is added to the beginning of words to mean 'a million' □ *megabyte* (mega-)
2 mega- is added to the beginning of words to mean 'very large or great' □ *a Hollywood megastar* (= extremely famous person) (mega-)

megabyte /ˈmegəbaɪt/ NOUN [plural **megabytes**] a unit used to measure computer memory or data, equal to approximately a million bytes. This is often written MB. A computing word. (megabyte)

megahertz /ˈmegəhɜːts/ NOUN [plural **megahertz**] a unit of measurement of radio waves and the speed of a computer. A physics and computing word. (mega-hertz)

megaphone /ˈmegəfəʊn/ NOUN [plural **megaphones**] a device shaped like a cone that someone speaks through to make their voice sound louder (megafone)

meiosis /maɪˈəʊsɪs/ NOUN, NO PLURAL when a cell divides twice to make four cells, each with half the number of chromosomes of the original cell. A biology word. (meiose)

melancholy /ˈmelənkəli/ ▶ ADJECTIVE sad, or making you feel sad □ *The dog gave a melancholy howl.* (melancólia)

▶ NOUN, NO PLURAL a feeling of sadness (melancolia)

mellow /ˈmeləʊ/ ▶ ADJECTIVE [**mellower, mellowest**]
1 soft and pleasant in sound, colour, taste, etc. □ *We listened to the mellow sound of the clarinet.* (suave)
2 calm and relaxed □ *He was in a mellow mood.* (afável)

▶ VERB [**mellows, mellowing, mellowed**] to become more gentle and relaxed, especially as you get older □ *I think he's mellowed with age.* (suavizar)

melodic /mɪˈlɒdɪk/ ADJECTIVE having a pleasant tune or pleasant to listen to □ *a simple, melodic tune* □ *a melodic voice* (melódico)

melodious /mɪˈləʊdiəs/ ADJECTIVE pleasant to listen to □ *He had a deep, melodious voice.* (melodioso)

melodrama 487 menace

melodrama /ˈmeləˌdrɑːmə/ NOUN [plural **melodramas**] a story, play, etc. with a lot of exciting action that is more extreme than in real life (**melodrama**)

- **melodramatic** /ˌmelədrəˈmætɪk/ ADJECTIVE making things seem more shocking or exciting than they really are ▢ *Stop being so melodramatic.* (**melodramático**)

melody /ˈmelədi/ NOUN [plural **melodies**] a tune, especially one that is pleasant to listen to ▢ *The song had a catchy melody.* (**melodia**)

melon /ˈmelən/ NOUN [plural **melons**] a large round fruit with a thick green or yellow skin and sweet, yellow or orange flesh (**melão**)

melt /melt/ VERB [**melts, melting, melted**]
1 to become soft or liquid when heated ▢ *By mid-afternoon the snow had melted.* ▢ *Salt is used to melt ice on roads.* ▢ *Stir in the melted butter.* (**derreter**)
2 to make someone feel kindness, affection or sympathy (**comover**) 🔾 *He's got a smile that will melt your heart.* (**comover seu coração**)
♦ PHRASAL VERBS **melt away** to disappear ▢ *The tension soon melted away.* (**desaparecer**) **melt something down** to heat metal until it becomes liquid (**derreter**) **melt into something** to become part of something so that people cannot see you any more ▢ *He got past the guards and melted into the crowd.* (**desaparecer**)

melting point /ˈmeltɪŋ ˌpɔɪnt/ NOUN [plural **melting points**] the temperature at which a particular substance melts when it is heated (**ponto de fusão**)

member /ˈmembə(r)/ NOUN [plural **members**] a person who belongs to a group or organization ▢ **+ of** *He's the youngest member of the team.* (**membro**) 🔾 *They celebrated with friends and family members.* (**membros da família**) 🔾 *It was reported by a member of the public.* (**membro do público**) 🔾 *The restaurant is open to members of staff.* (**membros da equipe**)

- **membership** /ˈmembəʃɪp/ NOUN [plural **memberships**]
1 no plural being a member ▢ **+ of** *Membership of the gym costs £600 a year.* (**associação**)
2 all the people who are members of a group or club ▢ *The union membership voted to reject the offer.* (**sociedade**)

membrane /ˈmembreɪn/ NOUN [plural **membranes**] a thin layer that covers or separates some parts of the body. A biology word. (**membrana**)

memento /mɪˈmentəʊ/ NOUN [plural **mementos**] something that you keep to help you remember something you have done or a place you have visited ▢ *Take this as a memento of your visit.* (**recordação**)

memo /ˈmeməʊ/ NOUN [plural **memos**] a short note that you send to someone who works in the same company or organization as you (**memorando**)

memoirs /ˈmemwɑːz/ PLURAL NOUN someone's memoirs are a book that they write about their life (**memórias**)

memorable /ˈmemərəbəl/ ADJECTIVE a memorable event is one that you remember because it is special or important ▢ *Their kiss was the most memorable moment of the film.* (**memorável**)

- **memorably** /ˈmemərəbli/ ADVERB in a way that will not be forgotten (**memoravelmente**)

memorial /mɪˈmɔːriəl/ NOUN [plural **memorials**] a statue (= stone object) or other structure built to remember a person or an event ▢ *a war memorial* (**memorial**)

memorize or **memorise** /ˈmeməraɪz/ VERB [**memorizes, memorizing, memorized**] to learn something so that you are able to remember it ▢ *Memorize your password, don't write it down.* (**memorizar**)

memory /ˈmeməri/ NOUN [plural **memories**]
1 the ability to remember things ▢ *There are several ways to improve your memory.* ▢ **+ for** *I've got an awful memory for names* (= I don't remember them). (**memória**) 🔾 *He suffers from short-term memory loss.* (**perda de memória**)
2 something you remember ▢ **+ of** *He has happy memories of his school days.* (**recordação**) 🔾 *The pictures brought back painful memories.* (**trouxeram recordações**)
3 no plural the part of a computer where information is stored. A computing word ▢ *6GB of memory* (**memória**)
4 in living memory from a time that people who are alive now can still remember ▢ *Last month's storm was the worst in living memory.* (**memória viva**)
5 in memory of someone as a way of remembering someone who has died ▢ *There will be a minute's silence in memory of the accident victims.* (**em memória de alguém**)

Memory Stick /ˈmeməri ˌstɪk/ NOUN [plural **Memory Sticks**] a small piece of electronic equipment that you use for storing information which you can then copy onto a computer. A trademark. (**cartão de armazenamento de memória**)

men /men/ PLURAL OF **man** (**ver man**)

menace /ˈmenəs/ ▶ NOUN [plural **menaces**]
1 something that causes or might cause trouble or danger ▢ *These biting flies are a real menace.* (**ameaça**)
2 when something seems threatening ▢ *His voice was full of menace.* (**ameaça**)
▶ VERB [**menaces, menacing, menaced**] to threaten someone or something ▢ *They were*

menaced by gangs of young men as they walked home. (ameaçar)

- **menacing** /ˈmenəsɪŋ/ ADJECTIVE threatening or frightening □ *a menacing look* (ameaçador)

mend /mend/ ▶ VERB [mends, mending, mended]

1 to repair something that is broken or damaged □ *We need to mend the hole in the tent.* □ *I took my watch to be mended.* (consertar)

2 to end an argument or disagreement between people □ *They tried to mend relations with their neighbours.* (consertar)

♦ IDIOMS **mend fences** to improve a relationship with someone after an argument or disagreement **mend your ways** to improve your behaviour that has been bad in the past □ *He promised he would mend his ways.* (melhorar um relacionamento)

▶ NOUN, NO PLURAL **be on the mend** to be getting better or improving after an illness or problems (em recuperação)

menial /ˈmiːniəl/ ADJECTIVE menial jobs need little skill or training and are boring to do (desinteressante) ▣ *She had a series of menial jobs.* (empregos desinteressantes)

meningitis /ˌmenɪnˈdʒaɪtɪs/ NOUN, NO PLURAL a serious illness which affects the brain (meningite)

menopause /ˈmenəpɔːz/ NOUN, NO PLURAL the time in a woman's life when her loss of blood each month stops and she can no longer get pregnant (menopausa)

menstrual /ˈmenstruəl/ ADJECTIVE to do with menstruation. A biology word. (menstrual)

menstruation /ˌmenstruˈeɪʃən/ NOUN, NO PLURAL the regular flow of blood that a woman has from her womb (= place where baby grows) each month. A biology word. (menstruação)

-ment /mənt/ SUFFIX -ment is added to the end of verbs to make nouns relating to the results of the actions or processes of the verb □ *accomplishment* (-mento, -ção)

mental /ˈmentəl/ ADJECTIVE to do with the mind or thinking □ *mental arithmetic* □ *Does she have the mental strength to be a top player?* (mental) ▣ *mental illness* (doença mental) ▣ *mental health services* (saúde mental)

- **mentality** /menˈtælɪti/ NOUN [plural **mentalities**] the attitudes and opinions that someone has □ *I don't understand the mentality of people who do these things.* (mentalidade)

- **mentally** /ˈmentəli/ ADVERB in or with the mind □ *You must commit yourself mentally and physically when you practice yoga.* (mentalmente)

mention /ˈmenʃən/ ▶ VERB [mentions, mentioning, mentioned]

1 to talk or to write about something, but not in detail □ *Nobody mentioned it before.* □ *+ in His name was mentioned in the report.* □ *+ to Don't mention it to Jonathan.* □ *+ that You mentioned that he's got a new car.* (mencionar) ▣ *As I mentioned earlier, I hadn't met him before.* (como mencionei)

2 not to mention used to add and to emphasize something extra □ *It means more demand on energy and water, not to mention the extra waste and pollution.* (sem contar, além de)

3 don't mention it something you say to be polite when someone thanks you for something (não há de quê)

▶ NOUN [plural **mentions**] when you mention something (menção) ▣ *He made no mention of marriage.* (não fez menção) ▣ *She got a special mention in the front of the book.* (obteve uma menção)

menu /ˈmenjuː/ NOUN [plural menus]

1 a list of the food available in a restaurant □ *Would you like to look at the menu?* □ *We have a three course set menu.* (cardápio)

2 on a computer, a list of choices on the screen that you can choose from. A computing word. (menu) ▣ *a drop-down menu* (lista suspensa)

menu bar /ˈmenjuː ˌbɑː(r)/ NOUN [plural **menu bars**] the part at the top of a computer screen that has instructions such as 'file' and 'edit'. A computing word. (barra de menu)

menu option /ˈmenjuː ˌɒpʃən/ NOUN [plural **menu options**] one of the instructions such as 'file' or 'edit' at the top of a computer screen. A computing word. (opção do menu)

MEP /ˌemiːˈpiː/ ABBREVIATION Member of the European Parliament; someone who has been elected to represent people in the European Parliament (abreviação de Membro do Parlamento Europeu)

mercenary /ˈmɜːsɪnəri/ ▶ NOUN [plural **mercenaries**] a soldier who fights for any army or country that will pay him (mercenário)

▶ ADJECTIVE interested only in getting money for yourself □ *He's become very mercenary.* (mercenário)

merchandise /ˈmɜːtʃəndaɪs/ NOUN, NO PLURAL goods that are bought and sold □ *They sell sports merchandise.* (mercadoria)

- **merchandising** /ˈmɜːtʃənˌdaɪzɪŋ/ NOUN, NO PLURAL selling products related to a film, book, sports team, etc. □ *The team earns millions from merchandising and sponsorship.* (propaganda)

merchant /ˈmɜːtʃənt/ ▶ NOUN [plural **merchants**] someone who has a business buying and selling goods □ *a wine merchant* (comerciante)

▶ ADJECTIVE to do with buying, selling and transporting goods □ *a merchant ship* (mercante)

merchant bank /ˌmɜːtʃənt ˈbæŋk/ NOUN [plural **merchant banks**] a bank that provides services to companies (banco mercantil)

- **merchant banker** /ˌmɜːtʃənt ˈbæŋkə(r)/ NOUN [plural **merchant bankers**] someone who works for a merchant bank (funcionário de banco mercantil)

merchant navy

merchant navy /ˌmɜːtʃənt ˈneɪvi/ NOUN [*plural* **merchant navies**] ships that are used to transport goods, not for military purposes (**marinha mercante**)

merciful /ˈmɜːsɪfʊl/ ADJECTIVE
1 willing to forgive and show kindness □ *They begged the king to be merciful.* (**misericordioso**)
2 something that is merciful is lucky for you because it ends a bad situation □ *For him, death was a merciful release.* (**misericordioso**)

• **mercifully** /ˈmɜːsɪfʊli/ ADVERB
1 used to say you are pleased or grateful for something □ *After the heat outside, the room was mercifully cool.* (**misericordiosamente**)
2 in a merciful way □ *He was treated mercifully.* (**com misericórdia, misericordiosamente**)

merciless /ˈmɜːsɪlɪs/ ADJECTIVE cruel and not willing to forgive or be kind □ *a merciless attack* (**impiedoso**)

• **mercilessly** /ˈmɜːsɪlɪsli/ ADVERB in a merciless way □ *They mocked her mercilessly.* (**impiedosamente**)

mercury /ˈmɜːkjʊri/ NOUN, NO PLURAL a silver chemical element, used in liquid form in thermometers (= devices to measure temperature). A chemistry word. (**mercúrio**)

mercy /ˈmɜːsi/ NOUN [*plural* **mercies**]
1 the quality of being kind and willing to forgive someone, especially someone you have power over (**misericórdia**) 🔁 *The judge showed no mercy to the killers.* (**não mostrou misericórdia**) □ *He ignored their pleas for mercy.*
2 at the mercy of someone/something in a situation that is controlled by someone or something else that could harm you □ *The little fishing boat was at the mercy of the weather.* (**estar à mercê de algo/alguém**)
3 something you are grateful for (**algo pelo qual se é grato**) 🔁 *It was a small mercy at the end of a terrible day.* (**algo de bom**)

mere /mɪə(r)/ ADJECTIVE [**merest**]
1 used to emphasize that something is small or not important □ *The flight from London to Madrid cost a mere £25.* □ *A mere handful of people turned up.* □ *There was the merest hint of a smile on his face.* (**mero, reles**)
2 used to emphasize that something is important even though it seems small (**simples**) 🔁 *The mere fact that I could walk was amazing after all my injuries.* (**o simples fato**)

• **merely** /ˈmɪəli/ ADVERB only or simply □ *I asked him again but he merely shrugged his shoulders.* (**meramente**)

merge /mɜːdʒ/ VERB [**merges, merging, merged**] if two things or organizations merge, they combine or join with each other □ *Her work life seemed to be increasingly merging with her home life.* □ *The two companies merged in 1999.* (**fundir-se**)

• **merger** /ˈmɜːdʒə(r)/ NOUN [*plural* **mergers**] when two or more businesses join to form a single company (**fusão de empresas**)

meridian /məˈrɪdiən/ NOUN [*plural* **meridians**] an imaginary line around the Earth passing through the North Pole and the South Pole (**meridiano**)

meringue /məˈræŋ/ NOUN [*plural* **meringues**] a sweet food made from a mixture of egg whites and sugar and baked (**merengue**)

merit /ˈmerɪt/ ▶ NOUN [*plural* **merits**] a quality that makes something or someone valuable or important □ *The film lacks artistic merit.* □ *Players are picked for the team on merit.* (**mérito**)
▶ VERB [**merits, meriting, merited**] to deserve something □ *His idea merits serious consideration.* (**merecer**)

mermaid /ˈmɜːmeɪd/ NOUN [*plural* **mermaids**] in stories, a beautiful creature who lives in the sea and is half a woman and half a fish (**sereia**)

merrily /ˈmerɪli/ ADVERB
1 in a happy way □ *They laughed and chattered merrily.* (**alegremente**)
2 without thinking enough about what you are doing □ *He was merrily helping himself to all our food.* (**irresponsavelmente**)

merry /ˈmeri/ ADJECTIVE [**merrier, merriest**] happy and showing that you are enjoying yourself □ *He whistled a merry tune.* (**alegre**)

Merry Christmas /ˌmeri ˈkrɪsməs/ EXCLAMATION something that people say or write to wish people a happy time at Christmas (**Feliz Natal**)

merry-go-round /ˈmerigəʊraʊnd/ NOUN [*plural* **merry-go-rounds**] a large machine with models of animals and vehicles that children sit on as it goes round and round (**carrossel**)

mesh /meʃ/ ▶ NOUN [*plural* **meshes**] wire or thread formed into a net □ *a fine wire mesh* (**malha**)
▶ VERB [**meshes, meshing, meshed**] to fit or to work together well □ *This new theory meshes well with existing evidence.* (**entrosar-se**)

mesmerize or **mesmerise** /ˈmezməraɪz/ VERB [**mesmerizes, mesmerizing, mesmerized**] to be very attractive or interesting and take all your attention □ *Audiences all over the country have been mesmerized by their performance.* (**fascinar, hipnotizar**)

mess /mes/ NOUN [*plural* **messes**]
1 an untidy or dirty state □ *The kitchen's in a mess.* (**bagunça**)
2 someone or something that is dirty or untidy □ *I'd been gardening and I looked a right mess.* □ *Your room's a complete mess.* (**bagunça**)
3 something that is in a confused state or that involves a lot of problems □ *His whole life was in a mess.* (**bagunça**) 🔁 *He made a complete mess of the accounts.* (**fez bagunça**)

◆ PHRASAL VERBS [**messes, messing, messed**] **mess about/around 1** to waste time with silly behaviour □ *Stop messing about and get on with your work!* **(fazer bobagem)** **2** to spend time in a relaxed way doing something that does not need much effort □ *I've just been messing around in the garden.* **(ficar à toa)** **mess someone about/ around** to treat someone badly by not doing something you said you would do or by changing your plans. An informal word. □ *I'm really sorry to mess you around, but I won't be able to meet you today after all.* **(atrapalhar)** **mess something up 1** to do something badly or to spoil something □ *I messed up my French exam.* **(estragar)** **2** to make something untidy □ *She messed up all my carefully arranged papers.* **(bagunçar)**

message /'mesɪdʒ/ ▶ NOUN [plural **messages**]
1 a piece of written or spoken information sent from one person to another **(recado)** 🔁 *I sent a message wishing him luck.* **(mandei um recado)** 🔁 *I left a message on her phone.* **(deixei um recado)** 🔁 *a text message* **(mensagem de texto)** □ + *from She's received thousands of messages from well-wishers.* □ + *of messages of support*
2 the most important idea that you want people to understand from a book, speech, action, etc. **(mensagem)** 🔁 *This sends a clear message that this behaviour is not acceptable.* **(manda uma mensagem)**
▶ VERB [**messages, messaging, messaged**] to send someone a message using a mobile phone or computer **(enviar mensagem)**

message board /'mesɪdʒ ˌbɔːd/ NOUN [plural **message boards**] a place on a website where you can read messages from other people and write messages to other people. A computing word. **(fórum de discussão on-line)**

messaging /'mesɪdʒɪŋ/ NOUN, NO PLURAL sending and receiving messages using mobile phones or computers **(envio de mensagens)**

messenger /'mesɪndʒə(r)/ NOUN [plural **messengers**] someone who carries messages from one person to another **(mensageiro)**

messiah /mɪ'saɪə/ NOUN [plural **messiahs**]
1 someone who comes to save people from unhappiness or evil **(messias)**
2 the Messiah in the Christian religion, Jesus Christ **(o Messias)**

Messrs /'mesəz/ PLURAL OF **Mr**; often used in the name of a company or business □ *Messrs Stein and Goldsmith, jewellers to the rich and famous.* **(senhores)**

messy /'mesi/ ADJECTIVE [**messier, messiest**]
1 untidy or dirty □ *a messy room* □ *He had long, messy hair.* **(sujo)**
2 complicated and unpleasant to deal with □ *a messy divorce* **(complicado)**

met /met/ PAST TENSE AND PAST PARTICIPLE OF **meet** **(ver met)**

metabolism /mɪ'tæbəlɪzəm/ NOUN, NO PLURAL the process that changes food in your body into energy. A biology word. **(metabolismo)**

metal /'metəl/ NOUN [plural **metals**] a hard shiny material such as iron, steel, gold or silver □ *The car was now a heap of twisted metal* **(metal)** 🔁 *precious metals* **(metais preciosos)** 🔁 *The car was sold for scrap metal.* **(ferro-velho)**

• **metallic** /mə'tælɪk/ ADJECTIVE
1 looking, sounding or tasting like metal □ *It shut with a metallic click.* □ *I had a horrible metallic taste in my mouth.* **(metálico)**
2 made of or to do with metal □ *a small metallic object* **(metálico)**
3 shiny like metal □ *metallic paint* **(metálico)**

metallurgy /mə'tælədʒi/ NOUN, NO PLURAL the study of metals **(metalurgia)**

metamorphose /ˌmetə'mɔːfəʊz/ VERB [**metamorphoses, metamorphosing, metamorphosed**] a formal word meaning to change completely in appearance or form **(metamorfosear)**

• **metamorphosis** /ˌmetə'mɔːfəsɪs, ˌmetəmɔː'fəʊsɪs/ NOUN [plural **metamorphoses**]
1 a complete change in the appearance of something **(metamorfose)**
2 when some animals and insects change from one form to another as they develop. A biology word. **(metamorfose)**

metaphor /'metəfə(r)/ NOUN [plural **metaphors**] a way of describing something by comparing it to something else □ *To use a boxing metaphor, the minister got knocked out in the first round.* **(metáfora)**

• **metaphorical** /ˌmetə'fɒrɪkəl/ ADJECTIVE using a metaphor **(metafórico)**

meteor /'miːtɪə(r)/ NOUN [plural **meteors**] a piece of rock travelling through space very fast **(meteoro)**

• **meteoric** /ˌmiːtɪ'ɒrɪk/ ADJECTIVE
1 happening or developing very fast, in a surprising way **(meteórico)** 🔁 *He enjoyed a meteoric rise to fame in the 1980s.* **(ascensão meteórica)**
2 to do with meteors **(meteórico)**

• **meteorite** /'miːtɪəraɪt/ NOUN [plural **meteorites**] a meteor that has fallen to Earth **(meteorito)**

meteorologist /ˌmiːtɪə'rɒlədʒɪst/ NOUN [plural **meteorologists**] someone who studies the weather and says whether it will rain, be sunny, etc. in the near future **(meteorologista)**

• **meteorology** /ˌmiːtɪə'rɒlədʒi/ NOUN, NO PLURAL the study of weather **(meteorologia)**

meter /'miːtə(r)/ NOUN [plural **meters**]
1 a device that measures and records the amount of something **(registro, contador)** 🔁 *a gas meter* **(registro de gás)** □ *Take a meter reading on the day you move in.*
2 the US spelling of **metre** **(metro)**

methane /'miːθeɪn/ NOUN, NO PLURAL a gas that is produced when plant material decays. A biology and chemistry word. **(metano)**

method

method /'meθəd/ NOUN [plural **methods**] a way of doing something, especially a planned or organized way □ + *of* methods of disease prevention □ + *for* We need to develop new methods for dealing with the problem. (**método**) 🔊 *Artists here use traditional methods.* (**usam métodos**) □ *teaching methods* □ *farming methods*

• **methodical** /mə'θɒdɪkəl/ ADJECTIVE well-organized and using a system for doing something □ *a methodical approach* (**metódico**)

• **methodically** /mə'θɒdɪkəli/ ADVERB in a methodical way (**metodicamente**)

meths /meθs/ NOUN, NO PLURAL a short way to say and write methylated spirits (ver **methylated spirits**) or methamphetamine (**metanfetamina**)

methylated spirits /ˌmeθɪleɪtɪd 'spɪrɪts/ NOUN, NO PLURAL a type of alcohol which is used as a fuel and not drunk (**etanol**)

meticulous /mə'tɪkjʊləs/ ADJECTIVE paying careful attention to every detail □ *It took weeks of meticulous planning.* (**meticuloso**)

• **meticulously** /mə'tɪkjʊləsli/ ADVERB very carefully □ *The event was meticulously planned.* (**meticulosamente**)

metre /'miːtə(r)/ NOUN [plural **metres**]

1 a unit for measuring length, equal to 100 centimetres. □ + *of* *Almost two metres of snow had fallen.* □ *It's suitable for boats up to three metres in length.* □ *He fell just ten metres from the finish line.* □ *a 400 metre runner* (**metro**) 🔊 *2500 square metres of office space* (**metros quadrados**)

2 the regular rhythm of poetry or music (**métrica**)

• **metric** /'metrɪk/ ADJECTIVE to do with a system of measuring that uses units such as litres and grams, based on tens (**métrico**)

metro /'metrəʊ/ NOUN [plural **metros**] an underground train system □ *the Moscow metro* (**metrô**) 🔊 *Where's the nearest metro station?* (**estação de metrô**)

metropolis /mə'trɒpəlɪs/ NOUN [plural **metropolises**] a large city, especially a capital city (**metrópole**)

• **metropolitan** /ˌmetrə'pɒlɪtən/ ADJECTIVE to do with a large city (**metropolitana**) 🔊 *a metropolitan area* (**área metropolitana**) □ *the Metropolitan Police Force*

mettle /'metəl/ NOUN, NO PLURAL a formal word meaning courage and determination (**determinação**) 🔊 *It was a hard match but the team showed their mettle.* (**mostrou determinação**)

mg /ˌem 'dʒiː/ ABBREVIATION milligram (**abreviação de miligrama**)

miaow /miː'aʊ/ C NOUN [plural **miaows**] the sound that a cat makes (**miado**)

▶ VERB [**miaows, miaowing, miaowed**] a cat miaows when it makes this sound (**miar**)

mid-

mice /maɪs/ PLURAL OF **mouse** (**camundongos**)

micro- /'maɪkrəʊ/ PREFIX **micro-** is added to the beginning of words to mean 'very small' □ *microchip* □ *microorganism* (**micro-**)

microbe /'maɪkrəʊb/ NOUN [plural **microbes**] an extremely small living thing, such as a virus or bacterium. A biology word. (**microrganismo**)

microbiology /ˌmaɪkrəʊbaɪ'ɒlədʒi/ NOUN, NO PLURAL the study of very small living things (**microbiologia**)

microchip /'maɪkrəʊtʃɪp/ NOUN [plural **microchips**] a very small part in a computer or other electronic equipment that contains a circuit (= system of wires) and stores information (**microchip**)

microclimate /'maɪkrəʊˌklaɪmət/ NOUN [plural **microclimates**] the weather in a particular area that is different from the area around it (**microclima**)

microcosm /'maɪkrəʊkɒzəm/ NOUN [plural **microcosms**] something small that has all the features or qualities of something larger that it is part of. A formal word. □ *The city is sometimes seen as a microcosm of US society.* (**microcosmo**)

microorganism /ˌmaɪkrəʊ'ɔːɡənɪzəm/ NOUN [plural **microorganisms**] an extremely small living thing, such as a virus or bacterium. A biology word. (**microrganismo**)

microphone /'maɪkrəfəʊn/ NOUN [plural **microphones**] an electronic device used for recording sound or making sound louder □ *Speak into the microphone.* □ *She took the microphone to address the crowd.* (**microfone**)

microprocessor /ˌmaɪkrəʊ'prəʊsesə(r)/ NOUN [plural **microprocessors**] the part inside a computer that makes it work. A computing word. (**microprocessador**)

microscope /'maɪkrəskəʊp/ NOUN [plural **microscopes**] a piece of equipment with lenses (= curved pieces of glass) that makes very small objects look much larger so that you can study them closely (**microscópio**)

• **microscopic** /ˌmaɪkrə'skɒpɪk/ ADJECTIVE microscopic objects are so small they can only be seen using a microscope (**microscópico**)

microwave /'maɪkrəweɪv/ NOUN [plural **microwaves**]

1 a very short radio wave. A physics word. (**micro-ondas**)

2 a microwave oven (**forno de micro-ondas**)

microwave oven /ˌmaɪkrəweɪv 'ʌvən/ NOUN [plural **microwave ovens**] an oven that cooks food very quickly using electrical and magnetic waves instead of heat (**forno de micro-ondas**)

mid- /mɪd/ PREFIX **mid-** is added to the beginning words to mean 'to do with the middle of something' □ *midsummer* (= in the middle of summer)

midday /ˌmɪdˈdeɪ/ NOUN, NO PLURAL
twelve o'clock in the middle of the day, or around this time ☐ *She arrived at midday yesterday.* 🔁 *We waited in the hot midday sun.* 🔁 *They had bread and cheese for their midday meal.* (**meio-dia**)

middle /ˈmɪdəl/ ▶ NOUN [plural middles]
1 the middle the point, position or part furthest from the sides or edges of something ☐ *Let me sit in the middle.* ☐ **+ of** *They live on an island in the middle of the ocean.* (**centro**)
2 the point in a period of time that is half way through that period of time ☐ **+ of** *I woke up in the middle of the night.* ☐ *He stood up and asked a question in the middle of the meeting.* (**meio**)
3 be in the middle of doing something to be busy doing something ☐ *I can't come to the phone – I'm in the middle of bathing the children.* (**no meio de uma atividade**)
4 your stomach
◆ IDIOM **the middle of nowhere** somewhere that is far away from houses, towns, etc. ☐ *She has a little cottage in the middle of nowhere.* (**no meio do nada, no fim do mundo**)
▶ ADJECTIVE
1 in the central point or position of something ☐ *I liked the middle section of the book.* ☐ *I was driving in the middle lane.* ☐ *He's the middle child of a family of five boys.* (**meio**)
2 at a level that is in the centre of a range of levels ☐ *They are a middle income family.* ☐ *a soldier of middle rank* (**médio**)

middle-aged /ˌmɪdəlˈeɪdʒd/ ADJECTIVE
approximately between the ages of 45 and 60 ☐ *a middle-aged man* (**meia-idade**)

Middle Ages /ˌmɪdəl ˈeɪdʒɪz/ NOUN, NO PLURAL
the Middle Ages the period of history, especially European history, approximately between the years 1100 and 1450 ☐ *The monastery was built in the Middle Ages.* (**Idade Média**)

middle class /ˌmɪdəl ˈklɑːs/ ▶ NOUN [plural middle classes]
the social class that consists mainly of educated people who have a good standard of living (**classe média, burguesia**)
▶ ADJECTIVE to do with the middle class ☐ *a middle class family*

Middle East /ˌmɪdəl ˈiːst/ NOUN, NO PLURAL
the Middle East all the countries in the area where Europe, Asia and Africa meet, including Egypt, Israel, Jordan, Lebanon, Syria, Iran and Iraq (**Oriente Médio**)

• **Middle-Eastern** /ˌmɪdəl ˈiːstən/ ADJECTIVE in or to do with the Middle East ☐ *Middle-Eastern countries*

midget /ˈmɪdʒɪt/ NOUN [plural midgets]
a very small person (**anão**)

Midlands /ˈmɪdləndz/ PLURAL NOUN
the Midlands the area in the middle of England (**região central da Inglaterra**)

midnight /ˈmɪdnaɪt/ NOUN, NO PLURAL
twelve o'clock at night ☐ *The competition closes at midnight tonight.* ☐ *It was past midnight when we finally got home.* (**meia-noite**)

midriff /ˈmɪdrɪf/ NOUN [plural midriffs]
the area around the middle of your body, above your waist (**diafragma, ventre**)

midst /mɪdst/ NOUN, NO PLURAL
1 in the midst of something in the middle of a situation ☐ *The whole country is in the midst of an economic crisis.* (**meio**)
2 in your midst among a group of people ☐ *They didn't realize there was a celebrity in their midst.* (**no meio, entre**)

midsummer /ˌmɪdˈsʌmə(r)/ NOUN, NO PLURAL
the period in the middle of the summer (**solstício de verão**)

midway /ˌmɪdˈweɪ/ ADVERB, ADJECTIVE
1 in the middle point between two times ☐ *He scored midway through the second half* 🔁 *He has reached the midway point of his four-year term.* (**ponto médio, no meio do caminho**)
2 at the middle point between two places ☐ *It's a small town midway between Glasgow and Edinburgh.* (**a meio do caminho**)

midweek /ˌmɪdˈwiːk/ ADJECTIVE, ADVERB
in the middle of the week, on or around Wednesday ☐ *We tend to do the shopping midweek.* ☐ *The midweek match has been cancelled.* (**meio da semana**)

midwife /ˈmɪdwaɪf/ NOUN [plural midwives]
a nurse who is specially trained to help women when they are having babies (**parteira**)

might¹ /maɪt/ MODAL VERB
1 used to talk about the possibility that something is true or something will happen ☐ *He might stay.* ☐ *It might rain.* (**poder = possibilidade**)
2 you might like/want to do something used to make polite suggestions ☐ *You might want to take some extra food with you.* (**poder = sugestão**)
3 used to ask permission in a polite and slightly formal way ☐ *Might I borrow your dictionary?* (**permitir**)
4 might as well used to say that you should probably do something because there is nothing better to do ☐ *If you can't be bothered to practise, you might as well give up the piano.* (**poder também, poder muito bem**)

might² /maɪt/ NOUN, NO PLURAL
a formal word meaning power or strength 🔁 *He pulled with all his might.* (**força**)

might've /ˈmaɪtəv/
a short way to say and write might have (**poderia ter**)

mighty /ˈmaɪti/ ADJECTIVE [mightier, mightiest]
a formal word meaning big and powerful ☐ *the mighty Mississippi River* (**poderoso**)

migraine /ˈmiːɡreɪn, ˈmaɪɡreɪn/ NOUN [plural migraines]
a very bad headache that lasts a long time (**enxaqueca**)

migrant /ˈmaɪɡrənt/ NOUN [plural migrants]
someone who goes to live in a different country to find work ☐ *skilled migrants* (**migrante, emigrante**)

migrate

migrate /maɪˈɡreɪt/ VERB [migrates, migrating, migrated]
1 if birds or animals migrate, they travel to a different part of the world at the same time each year ☐ *The birds migrate northwards in spring.* (migrar)
2 to move to a different country to find work ☐ *His family migrated to Australia in 1918.* (migrar)
• **migration** /maɪˈɡreɪʃən/ NOUN, NO PLURAL when birds, animals or people migrate (migração)

mike /maɪk/ NOUN [*plural* mikes] an informal word for **microphone** (microfone)

mild /maɪld/ ADJECTIVE [milder, mildest]
1 mild weather is quite warm ☐ *The weather was unusually mild for November.* ▣ *The mild winter had prevented ice from forming on the lake.* (ameno)
2 not severe or not serious ☐ *The virus causes a relatively mild illness.* ☐ *She looked at him with mild annoyance.* (leve)
3 having a flavour that is not strong ☐ *mild cheese* ☐ *Chicken has a mild flavour.* (suave)
4 a mild person is gentle and quiet (sereno)

mildew /ˈmɪldjuː/ NOUN, NO PLURAL a substance that grows on plants and walls if they are slightly wet (mofo, bolor)

mildly /ˈmaɪldli/ ADVERB
1 slightly ☐ *Eric looked mildly surprised at my comments.* (ligeiramente)
2 **to put it mildly** said after you have said something which you could have expressed in a much stronger way ☐ *It was a bit of a shock, to put it mildly.* (para ser indulgente)

mile /maɪl/ NOUN [*plural* miles]
1 a unit for measuring distance, equal to 1760 yards ☐ *The ship was 20 miles off the coast.* ▣ *His car was travelling at a speed of 110 miles per hour.* ▣ *The traffic jam was six miles long.* (milhas/por hora)
2 **miles** an informal word meaning a long way ☐*They live miles away.* ☐ *We walked for miles.* (milhas, quilômetros)
• **mileage** /ˈmaɪlɪdʒ/ NOUN, NO PLURAL the number of miles that a vehicle has travelled since it was new ▣ *high/low mileage* (milhagem, quilometragem)

mileometer /maɪˈlɒmɪtə(r)/ NOUN [*plural* mileometers] an instrument in a car that shows how many miles the car has travelled (marcador de milhas)

milestone /ˈmaɪlstəʊn/ NOUN [*plural* milestones] an important event in someone's life or in the development of something ☐ *The game was a milestone in British sporting history.* (marco)

militant /ˈmɪlɪtənt/ ▶ ADJECTIVE willing to do extreme or violent things to achieve political or social changes (militante)
▶ NOUN [*plural* militants] someone who is militant

military /ˈmɪlɪtəri/ ▶ ADJECTIVE to do with the army, navy or air force ▣ *Military forces invaded the country.* ▣ *Many soldiers were injured in military operations.* ▣ *a military base* ☐ *a military commander* (militar/forças militares/base militar)
▶ NOUN, NO PLURAL the military a country's army, navy and air force ☐ *the US military* ☐ *All men have to serve two years in the military.* (exército)

militia /mɪˈlɪʃə/ NOUN [*plural* militias] a group of people who are not soldiers for their job, but who are trained to fight if necessary (milícia)

milk /mɪlk/ ▶ NOUN, NO PLURAL a white liquid produced by female animals, which people drink or which is used to feed babies ☐ *Would you like a glass of milk?* ☐ *Breast milk contains important nutrients for babies.* (leite)
▶ VERB [milks, milking, milked]
1 to take milk from a cow or goat ☐ *The cows are milked by machine.* (ordenhar)
2 to get every advantage you can from someone or something ☐ *He claimed she was milking the tragedy for publicity.* (tirar proveito)

milkman /ˈmɪlkmən/ NOUN [*plural* milkmen] a man whose job is delivering milk to people's houses (leiteiro)

milkshake /ˈmɪlkʃeɪk/ NOUN [*plural* milkshakes] a sweet drink made of milk mixed with a flavoured liquid ☐ *a banana milkshake* (milkshake)

milk tooth /ˈmɪlk ˌtuːθ/ NOUN [*plural* milk teeth] one of the first set of teeth that grow in a child's mouth (dente de leite)

milky /ˈmɪlki/ ADJECTIVE [milkier, milkiest]
1 containing a lot of milk ☐ *a hot milky drink* (lácteo, com leite)
2 looking like milk ☐ *a milky liquid* (leitoso)

mill /mɪl/ ▶ NOUN [*plural* mills]
1 a building with machinery for crushing corn and other grain (moinho)
2 a factory that produces a particular material such as cotton, paper or wool ☐ *a paper mill* (fábrica)
3 a machine in your kitchen for crushing pepper (= black spice) or coffee ☐ *a pepper mill* (moedor)
▶ VERB [mills, milling, milled] to crush grain, pepper, etc. in a mill (moer)
◆ PHRASAL VERB **mill around/about (something)** if people are milling around, they are moving around a place ☐ *Crowds of people were milling around St Mark's Square.* (dar voltas em torno de)

millennium /mɪˈleniəm/ NOUN [*plural* millennia] a period of a thousand years (milênio)

milligram *or* **milligramme** /ˈmɪlɪɡræm/ NOUN [*plural* milligrams *or* milligrammes] a unit for measuring weight, equal to one thousandth of a gram. This is often written **mg**. (miligrama)

milliliter /ˈmɪlɪliːtə(r)/NOUN [*plural* millilitres] the US spelling of **millilitre** (mililitro)

millilitre /ˈmɪlɪliːtə(r)/ NOUN [*plural* millilitres] a unit for measuring liquid, equal to one thousandth of a litre. This is often written **ml**. (mililitro)

millimeter /ˈmɪlɪmiːtə(r)/ NOUN [plural **millimeters**] the US spelling of **millimetre** (milímetro)

millimetre /ˈmɪlɪmiːtə(r)/ NOUN [plural **millimetres**] a unit for measuring length, equal to one thousandth of a metre. This is often written **mm** (milímetro)

million /ˈmɪljən/ NUMBER [plural **millions**]
1 the number 1,000,000 (milhão)
2 millions a very large number. An informal word □ **+ of** There were millions of flies crawling on the food. (milhões)

millionaire /ˌmɪljəˈneə(r)/ NOUN [plural **millionaires**] someone who has a million pounds or a million dollars or more (milionário)

millionth /ˈmɪljənθ/ ▶ NUMBER 1,000,000th written as a word (milionésimo)
▶ NOUN [plural **millionths**] 1/1,000,000; one of a million equal parts of something (milionésimo)

millipede /ˈmɪlɪpiːd/ NOUN [plural **millipedes**] a small insect with a long body and a lot of legs (centopeia)

mime /maɪm/ ▶ VERB [**mimes, miming, mimed**]
1 to tell a story or show an action using only movements and not words or real objects □ Ella mimed chopping vegetables. (fazer mímica)
2 to pretend to sing or play a musical instrument while a piece of recorded music is played □ The band were accused of miming during their concert. (dublar, imitar)
▶ NOUN, NO PLURAL the use of movements only and not words or real objects to tell a story or show an action □ a mime artist (mímica)

mimic /ˈmɪmɪk/ ▶ VERB [**mimics, mimicking, mimicked**]
1 to copy the way someone speaks or behaves as a joke (imitar)
2 to behave or react in the same way as someone or something else □ Scientists are working on a drug that will mimic the effects of exercise. (imitar)
▶ NOUN [plural **mimics**] someone who copies the way people talk or behave □ Joe's a good mimic. (imitador)

• **mimicry** /ˈmɪmɪkri/ NOUN, NO PLURAL the action of mimicking someone (imitação)

min /mɪn/ ABBREVIATION
1 minute, used in writing (minuto)
2 minimum, used in writing (mínimo)

mince /mɪns/ ▶ NOUN, NO PLURAL meat that has been cut into very small pieces using a machine (picadinho de carne)
▶ VERB [**minces, mincing, minced**] to cut food into very small pieces using a machine □ minced beef (moer)

mind /maɪnd/ ▶ NOUN [plural **minds**]
1 your brain, or your ability to think, understand, remember, etc. □ All sorts of thoughts went through my mind. (mente)
2 bear/keep something in mind to remember something □ Bear in mind that the shops shut at 6:00. (lembrar-se de)
3 make up your mind to decide □ I couldn't make up my mind whether to go to Paris or not. (decidir)
4 on your mind if something is on your mind, you are thinking about it a lot and usually worrying about it □ I've got a lot on my mind at the moment. (ter algo/alguém em mente)
5 come/spring to mind to be something that you think of □ He wants the name of a good restaurant, but nothing springs to mind. (vir à mente/à lembrança)
6 have someone/something in mind to be thinking of a particular person or thing □ Do you have any particular colour in mind for the curtains? (ter alguém/algo em mente)
7 all in the mind if something is all in the mind, you are imagining it □ He thinks people are laughing at him, but it's all in the mind. (é tudo imaginação)

♦ IDIOMS **be/go out of your mind** to become extremely worried or upset □ We were out of our minds with worry for them. (perder a razão) **have a good mind to do something** to want to do something because you are angry □ I've a good mind to complain to his boss! (ter bons motivos para fazer algo) **put your mind to something** to try very hard to achieve something by thinking hard and giving it all your attention □ I could probably do this crossword if I put my mind to it. (concentrar-se) **put/set someone's mind at rest** to make someone stop being worried □ I'm going to go back to check that the door's locked – just to put my mind at rest. (parar de se preocupar com alguém/algo) **take your mind off something** to stop you thinking about something bad by making you think about something else □ I'm in a lot of pain, but going dancing takes my mind off it. (distrair, desviar a atenção)

⇨ go to **cross your mind**, **be in two minds**, **speak your mind**, **slip your mind**
▶ VERB [**minds, minding, minded**]
1 to be upset or annoyed by something □ Do you mind if I smoke? □ I'm sure Sue wouldn't mind you borrowing her car. (incomodar-se, importar-se)
2 would you mind doing something used to ask someone politely to do something □ Would you mind opening the window? (você se importaria em fazer algo)
3 to look after someone or something □ She was at home, minding the children. (tomar conta)
4 used to tell someone to be careful not to get hurt □ Mind your head on that branch. (cuidado)
5 never mind used to say that something is not important □ 'I haven't finished my homework.' 'Never mind, you can hand it in tomorrow.' (não tem importância)

mine 495 mine minister M

6 mind you used to start part of a sentence that is the opposite to what you said before □ *I'm shocked to hear that Mick's in prison. Mind you, he was always in trouble at school.* (**por outro lado, entretanto**)

♦ PHRASAL VERB **mind out** used to tell someone to be careful not to get hurt □ *Mind out – there's a car coming!* (**cuidado**)

- **minder** /'maɪndə(r)/ NOUN [plural **minders**] someone who looks after another person and protects them from harm (**protetor**)

- **mindless** /'maɪndlɪs/ ADJECTIVE
1 a mindless job is boring and does not need any thought or imagination (**tedioso**)
2 mindless violence, damage, etc. is done for no reason (**estúpido**)

mine[1] /maɪn/ PRONOUN used to talk or write about things belonging to or to do with you □ *Is this book yours or mine?* □ *Jan is a friend of mine.* (**meu, minha, meus, minhas**)

mine[2] /maɪn/ ▶ NOUN [plural **mines**]
1 a place where people dig something such as coal or gold from the ground □ *a coal mine* (**mina**)
2 a bomb that is hidden in the ground or in water, which explodes when someone touches it (**mina**)
▶ VERB [**mines, mining, mined**]
1 to dig into the ground in order to get something such as coal or gold □ *Diamonds are mined from the rocks.* (**extrair**)
2 to put bombs under the ground or in water (**minar, colocar minas**)

minefield /'maɪnfiːld/ NOUN [plural **minefields**]
1 a situation that has many possible problems □ *This is a political minefield for the government.* (**campo minado**)
2 an area of land with explosive mines in it (**campo minado**)

miner /'maɪnə(r)/ NOUN [plural **miners**] someone who works in a mine (**mineiro**)

mineral /'mɪnərəl/ NOUN [plural **minerals**]
1 a natural substance in the earth, such as coal, salt or gold □ *Our mineral resources are not infinite.* (**mineral**)
2 a natural substance such as iron or zinc that your body needs to stay healthy (**mineral**) □ *Some vegetables contain a lot of vitamins and minerals.* (**vitaminas e minerais**)

mineral water /'mɪnərəl ˌwɔːtə(r)/ NOUN [plural **mineral waters**] water that you buy in bottles, which comes from under the ground □ *a bottle of mineral water* (**água mineral**)

mingle /'mɪŋɡəl/ VERB [**mingles, mingling, mingled**]
1 to meet and talk to a lot of people, moving from one person to another □ *The players mingled with the crowd and posed for photographs.* (**misturar-se**)
2 if substances, smells, feelings, etc. mingle, they mix □ *The smoke mingled with the mist.* (**misturar-se**)

mini- /'mɪni/ PREFIX mini- is added to the beginning of words to mean 'small' or 'short' □ *minibus* □ *miniskirt* (**mini-**)

miniature /'mɪnətʃə(r)/ ▶ ADJECTIVE very much smaller than normal □ *a miniature camera* (**miniatura**)
▶ NOUN [plural **miniatures**]
1 a very small model of something bigger (**miniatura**)
2 a very small painting of someone (**miniatura**)

mini-break /'mɪnibreɪk/ NOUN [plural **mini-breaks**] a short holiday □ *We've just booked a two-night minibreak in Amsterdam.* (**miniférias**)

minibus /'mɪnibʌs/ NOUN [plural **minibuses**] a small bus for about 12 people (**micro-ônibus**)

minimal /'mɪnɪməl/ ADJECTIVE very small in amount or degree □ *The fire caused minimal damage.* (**mínimo**)

- **minimize** or **minimise** /'mɪnɪmaɪz/ VERB [**minimizes, minimizing, minimized**] to reduce something to the smallest amount or degree possible □ *Good hygiene minimizes the risk of infection.* (**minimizar**)

- **minimum** /'mɪnɪməm/ ▶ ADJECTIVE being the smallest amount or degree that is possible or allowed (**mínimo**) □ *The minimum age for driving in the UK is 17.* (**idade mínima**) □ *£250 was the minimum needed to open a bank account.*
▶ NOUN, NO PLURAL the smallest amount or degree that is possible or allowed (**mínimo**) □ *At college he did the bare minimum of work.* (**somente o mínimo**) □ *We need to keep costs to a minimum.* (**manter os custos no mínimo**) □ + *of He did his duties with the minimum of fuss.* □ *The hotel costs a minimum of £200 a night.*

mining /'maɪnɪŋ/ NOUN, NO PLURAL the job of digging something such as coal or gold from the ground □ *the mining industry* (**mineração**)

miniskirt /'mɪnɪskɜːt/ NOUN [plural **miniskirts**] a very short skirt (**minissaia**)

minister /'mɪnɪstə(r)/ NOUN [plural **ministers**]
1 a politician who is in charge of a government department (**ministro**) □ *Government ministers will visit China next week.* (**ministros do governo**) □ + *of/for the Minister for Education*
2 a priest in some Christian churches □ *a Methodist minister* (**ministro, pastor**)

♦ PHRASAL VERB [**ministers, ministering, ministered**] **minister to someone** a formal word meaning to help someone, especially someone who is ill, old or poor □ *Houk has ministered to the sick and needy for over 20 years.* (**atender, dar assistência a alguém**)

- **ministerial** /ˌmɪnɪ'stɪəriəl/ ADJECTIVE to do with government ministers □ *a ministerial meeting* (**ministerial**)

- **ministry** /'mɪnɪstri/ NOUN [plural **ministries**]
1 a government department □ *the Ministry of Defence* □ *ministry officials* (**ministério**)

2 the job of a church minister (**ministério**)

mink /mɪŋk/ NOUN [plural **mink**]
1 a small animal with very valuable fur (**visom**)
2 no plural the dark brown fur of a mink □ *a mink coat* (**visom**)

minor /'maɪnə(r)/ ▶ ADJECTIVE not serious or important (**menor, sem importância**) 🔁 *He suffered minor injuries in the accident.* (**ferimentos leves**) □ *I've made a few minor changes to the report.* 🔁 *The problems were relatively minor.* (**relativamente sem importância**)
▶ NOUN [plural **minors**] someone who is legally a child (**menor de idade**)

minority /maɪ'nɒrəti/ ▶ NOUN [plural **minorities**]
1 a small group of people which is part of a much larger group (**minoria**) 🔁 *A small minority of our students are from Africa.* (**uma pequena minoria**)
2 be in the minority to form less than half of a group □ *In this country, people without Internet access are in the minority.* (**ser ou estar em minoria**)
3 a group of people of a different race or religion than most people in a country (**minoria**) 🔁 *ethnic minorities* (**minorias étnicas**)
▶ ADJECTIVE
1 to do with less than half of a group of people □ *This is very much a minority view.* (**da minoria**)
2 to do with groups that are of a different race or religion from most people in a country □ *minority communities* □ *minority faiths* (**da minoria**)

mint /mɪnt/ NOUN [plural **mints**]
1 no plural a plant with strong-smelling leaves, used in cooking (**menta, hortelã**)
2 a type of sweet with a strong flavour (**bala de menta**)
3 a factory which makes coins (**casa da moeda**)

minus /'maɪnəs/ ▶ PREPOSITION
1 used for showing that one number is taken away from another number □ *8 minus 2 is 6* (**menos**)
2 without □ *He came home covered in mud and minus one shoe.* (**menos**)
▶ ADJECTIVE
1 less than zero □ *minus ten degrees* (**negativo**)
2 used after a letter to show that a score for a piece of work is slightly less than the score represented by the letter alone □ *I got an A minus for my essay.* (**menos**)
▶ NOUN [plural **minuses**]
1 a sign (–) used in maths to show that you should take one number away from another number, or that a number is less than zero (**sinal de subtração**)
2 something bad about a situation (**contra**) 🔁 *There are plusses and minuses* (= advantages and disadvantages) *to having brothers and sisters.* (**prós e contras**)

minuscule /'mɪnəskjuːl/ ADJECTIVE extremely small □ *minuscule differences* (**minúsculo**)

minute¹ /'mɪnɪt/ NOUN [plural **minutes**]
1 a period of sixty seconds □ *The journey only lasted a few minutes.* □ *I loved every minute of my visit.* □ *Rendell scored in the eighth minute.* (**minuto**)
2 a short time □ *Wait a minute while I look for my keys.* □ *Just a minute – I need to phone Clara.* (**minuto**)
3 the exact time □ *I knew something was wrong the minute I saw him.* □ *At that very minute there was a loud explosion.* (**minuto**)
4 any minute very soon □ *Paul will be here any minute now.* □ *The bomb could explode at any minute.* (**imediatamente**)
5 this minute immediately □ *Come here this minute!* (**neste momento**)
⇨ go to **minutes**

minute² /maɪ'njuːt/ ADJECTIVE
1 extremely small □ *Minute traces of blood were found on his clothes.* (**minúsculo**)
2 in minute detail considering or giving all the details □ *The report examines the event in minute detail.* (**em detalhes minuciosos**)

minute³ /'mɪnɪt/ VERB [**minutes, minuting, minuted**] to make an written record of something that was said in a meeting □ *I'd like it minuted that I oppose the plan.* (**minutar**)

minutes /'mɪnɪts/ PLURAL NOUN a written record of a meeting (**ata**) 🔁 *Who is going to take the minutes?* (**fazer a ata**)

miracle /'mɪrəkəl/ NOUN [plural **miracles**]
1 something extremely lucky that happens and that no one would expect □ *It's a miracle that no one was killed in the accident.* □ *a miracle cure* (**milagre**)
2 something that happens which seems impossible and that people think God has done (**milagre**)
• **miraculous** /mɪ'rækjʊləs/ ADJECTIVE extremely lucky and not expected (**milagroso**) 🔁 *He made a miraculous recovery.* (**recuperação milagrosa**)
• **miraculously** /mɪ'rækjʊləsli/ ADVERB in a lucky way which you did not expect □ *Miraculously, he survived the accident.* (**milagrosamente**)

mirage /mɪ'rɑːʒ/ NOUN [plural **mirages**] an image of water which does not exist, caused by very hot air (**miragem**)

mirror /'mɪrə(r)/ ▶ NOUN [plural **mirrors**] a piece of special glass that you look at to see an image of yourself □ *Ben was looking at himself in the mirror.* (**espelho**) 🔁 *There was a full-length mirror in the bedroom.* (**espelho de corpo inteiro**)
▶ VERB [**mirrors, mirroring, mirrored**] to be the same as something else or show what something else is like □ *The film mirrors his life very closely.* (**espelhar**)

mirth /mɜːθ/ NOUN, NO PLURAL a literary word meaning laughter (**alegria, riso**)

mis- /mɪs/ PREFIX **mis-** is added to the beginning of words to mean 'bad' or 'badly', or 'wrong' or 'wrongly' □ *misbehave* □ *misunderstand* (**má qualidade ou erro**)

misadventure /ˌmɪsədˈventʃə(r)/ NOUN [plural **misadventures**]

1 a formal word meaning something bad that happens to you □ *After a series of misadventures, he was glad to be at home.* (**desventura, infortúnio**)

2 *no plural* a word used in British law when someone dies because of an accident (**infortúnio**) 🔁 *The verdict was death by misadventure.* (**homicídio acidental**)

misapprehension /ˌmɪsæprɪˈhenʃən/ NOUN [plural **misapprehensions**] a formal word meaning a belief that is wrong □ *Police shot him under the misapprehension that he was a terrorist.* (**mal-entendido**)

misbehave /ˌmɪsbɪˈheɪv/ VERB [**misbehaves, misbehaving, misbehaved**] to behave badly □ *Players who misbehave are fined.* (**comportar-se mal**)

• **misbehavior** /ˌmɪsbɪˈheɪvjə(r)/ NOUN, NO PLURAL the US spelling of **misbehaviour** (**mau comportamento**)

• **misbehaviour** /ˌmɪsbɪˈheɪvjə(r)/ NOUN, NO PLURAL bad behaviour (**mau comportamento**)

miscalculate /mɪsˈkælkjʊleɪt/ VERB [**miscalculates, miscalculating, miscalculated**]

1 to judge a situation wrongly □ *The government miscalculated the public reaction.* (**calcular mal**)

2 to calculate an amount wrongly □ *The doctor had miscalculated how much of the drug to give him.* (**calcular mal**)

• **miscalculation** /ˌmɪskælkjʊˈleɪʃən/ NOUN [plural **miscalculations**] when someone miscalculates something □ *It was a serious miscalculation.* (**erro de cálculo**)

miscarriage /mɪsˈkærɪdʒ/ NOUN [plural **miscarriages**]

1 when a baby comes out of its mother's body so early that it is not developed and dies (**aborto espontâneo**)

2 *a miscarriage of justice* when someone is punished for a crime they did not commit (**erro judicial**)

miscellaneous /ˌmɪsəˈleɪniəs/ ADJECTIVE of many different types □ *There was a box containing miscellaneous items.* (**misto, variado**)

mischief /ˈmɪstʃɪf/ NOUN, NO PLURAL slightly bad behaviour that does not cause serious harm □ *I hope you children haven't been getting up to mischief.* (**travessura**)

• **mischievous** /ˈmɪstʃɪvəs/ ADJECTIVE enjoying causing trouble, but in a way that does not cause serious harm □ *a mischievous boy* □ *a mischievous smile* (**travesso**)

misconception /ˌmɪskənˈsepʃən/ NOUN [plural **misconceptions**] a belief that is wrong, showing that you do not understand something (**concepção errônea**) 🔁 *It's a common misconception that cancer only affects older people.* (**erro comum**)

misconduct /mɪsˈkɒndʌkt/ NOUN, NO PLURAL a formal word meaning bad or unacceptable behaviour (**má conduta**) 🔁 *The doctor was found guilty of professional misconduct.* (**má conduta profissional**)

misconstrue /ˌmɪskənˈstruː/ VERB [**misconstrues, misconstruing, misconstrued**] to understand something in the wrong way □ *His shyness had been misconstrued as rudeness.* (**interpretar mal**)

misdemeanor /ˌmɪsdɪˈmiːnə(r)/ NOUN [plural **misdemeanors**] the US spelling of **misdemeanour** (**má conduta**)

misdemeanour /ˌmɪsdɪˈmiːnə(r)/ NOUN [plural **misdemeanours**] a formal word meaning something bad that someone has done □ *He has learned from his past misdemeanours.* (**má conduta**)

miser /ˈmaɪzə(r)/ NOUN [plural **misers**] someone who keeps all their money because they hate spending it (**avarento**)

miserable /ˈmɪzərəbəl/ ADJECTIVE

1 very unhappy □ *She's miserable because all her friends are away.* □ *Dan looked pretty miserable.* (**infeliz**)

2 making you feel unhappy □ *What miserable weather!* □ *She'd had a miserable childhood.* (**miserável**)

3 in a bad mood □ *Smile! Don't be so miserable!* (**desanimado**)

4 small in amount, and not enough □ *I got a miserable £5.50 for three hours' work!* (**miséria**)

• **miserably** /ˈmɪzərəbli/ ADVERB

1 in an unhappy way □ *Alyssa nodded miserably.* (**tristemente**)

2 completely and in a disappointing way (**miseravelmente**) 🔁 *His attempt to win had failed miserably.* (**falhou miseravelmente**)

miserly /ˈmaɪzəli/ ADJECTIVE very unwilling to spend money (**de modo avarento**)

misery /ˈmɪzəri/ NOUN [plural **miseries**]

1 *no plural* great unhappiness or suffering □ *Bad weather has caused misery for thousands of air travellers.* (**sofrimento**)

2 someone who is in a bad mood □ *Come and join us, you misery!* (**desanimado**)

3 *put someone out of their misery* to make someone stop worrying by telling them something they are waiting to hear □ *Come on, put me out of my misery. Did you pass your driving test or not?* (**acabar com o tormento de alguém, contando-lhe algo**)

misfit /ˈmɪsfɪt/ NOUN [plural **misfits**] someone who is very different from other people in a group and is not accepted by them □ *I felt like a social misfit.* (**desajustado**)

misfortune /mɪsˈfɔːtʃuːn/ NOUN [plural **misfortunes**] bad luck (**azar**) ▣ *I had the misfortune of sitting next to a very noisy group of people.* (**tive o azar de**)

misgivings /mɪsˈgɪvɪŋz/ PLURAL NOUN doubts or worries (**dúvidas, apreensões**) ▣ *I have serious misgivings about some of the decisions he has made.* (**tenho dúvidas**)

misguided /ˌmɪsˈgaɪdɪd/ ADJECTIVE based on beliefs or ideas that are not correct □ *The scheme was a misguided attempt to help students.* (**equivocado**)

mishandle /ˌmɪsˈhændəl/ VERB [**mishandles, mishandling, mishandled**] to deal with a situation badly, causing problems □ *The government has mishandled the crisis.* (**lidar de modo errado**)

mishap /ˈmɪshæp/ NOUN [plural **mishaps**] a slight accident or mistake (**percalço**)

misinterpret /ˌmɪsɪnˈtɜːprɪt/ VERB [**misinterpret, misinterpreting, misinterpreted**] to understand something wrongly □ *They misinterpreted the results of the study.* (**interpretar erroneamente**)

misjudge /mɪsˈdʒʌdʒ/ VERB [**misjudges, misjudging, misjudged**]
1 to have the wrong opinion about a person or situation □ *I realize now that I had misjudged him.* (**julgar mal**)
2 to judge an amount or distance wrongly □ *They misjudged the amount of time needed to get to the airport.* (**subestimar**)

mislay /mɪsˈleɪ/ VERB [**mislays, mislaying, mislaid**] to lose something for a short time □ *Em had mislaid her keys.* (**perder**)

mislead /mɪsˈliːd/ VERB [**misleads, misleading, misled**] to make someone believe something that is not true □ *The government deliberately misled the public about the state of the economy.* (**enganar**)

• **misleading** /mɪsˈliːdɪŋ/ ADJECTIVE making someone believe something that is not true □ *misleading information* (**enganador**)

misprint /ˈmɪsprɪnt/ NOUN [plural **misprints**] a mistake made in printing □ *That's definitely a misprint. It should be 10, not 100.* (**erro de impressão**)

Miss /mɪs/ NOUN [plural **Misses**]
1 a word used before the name of a girl or a woman who is not married □ *Miss Smith* □ *Miss Zoe Arnison* (**senhorita**)
2 a word children use for talking to a female teacher □ *I haven't done my homework, Miss.* (**moça, senhorita**)

miss /mɪs/ ▶ VERB [**misses, missing, missed**]
1 to fail to hit or catch something you are aiming at (**errar**) ▣ *A bullet narrowly missed (= only just missed) his spine.* (**errou por pouco**) □ *He missed the penalty.*
2 to not go to something or experience something □ *I had to miss my daughter's school concert.* □ *Don't miss their new show!* (**perder**)
3 to miss a train, bus, plane, etc. is to not arrive in time to catch it (**perder**)
4 to feel sad because of someone you can no longer be with or something you can no longer have or do (**sentir saudade, falta**) ▣ *I missed my family terribly when I lived abroad.* (**senti uma terrível falta de minha família**) □ *+ ing I miss being able to walk on the beach.*
5 to be too late for something □ *I missed the first few minutes of the concert.* □ *Kate? You've just missed her, I'm afraid.* (**perder**)
6 to not notice something ▣ *Our house has a pink front door – you can't miss it!* □ *Why is he so angry? Did I miss something?* (**perder**)
7 to not take an opportunity □ *If you don't take this job, you'll be missing the best chance of your life.* (**perder**)
8 to not achieve something □ *He always misses his sales targets.* (**não atingir**)
9 to discover that you have lost something or someone □ *When did you first miss your purse?* (**sentir falta**)

◆ PHRASAL VERBS **miss someone/something out** to not include someone or something □ *He read us the book, but he missed out all the rude words.* (**omitir, deixar alguém/algo de fora**) **miss out** to not get something that other people get □ *I was away at school, so I missed out on all the fun.* (**perder**)

▶ NOUN [plural **misses**] when you do not hit something you are aiming at □ *His miss cost his team the match.* (**falha**)

◆ IDIOM **give something a miss** to decide not to do something □ *I was feeling tired, so I decided to give the party a miss.* (**não fazer algo, dar um tempo**)

missile /ˈmɪsaɪl/ NOUN [plural **missiles**]
1 a weapon that travels long distances and explodes when it hits something □ *long-range missiles* (**míssil**)
2 an object that someone throws to hit someone or something □ *Police were hit by bottles, stones and other missiles.* (**projétil**)

missing /ˈmɪsɪŋ/ ADJECTIVE
1 if someone or something is missing, they are not where you expect them to be and you do not know where they are (**desaparecido**) ▣ *Some important documents had gone missing* (**desapareceram**) □ *Rescue teams are looking for three missing climbers.*
2 not included in something □ *Kewell was missing from the team because of injury.* (**faltando**)

mission /ˈmɪʃən/ NOUN [plural **missions**]
1 an important job that someone has been sent to do by a government or organization □ *He visited Baghdad on a fact-finding mission.* (**missão**)
2 a military operation □ *He had been killed during a combat mission.* (**missão**)

misspell

3 a space flight □ *The astronauts were on a mission to Mars.* (**missão**)
4 a group of people who are sent to do something by their government □ *members of the diplomatic mission* (**missão**)
5 something that you very much want to achieve (**missão**) ▣ *It was my father's mission in life to protect these birds.* (**missão na vida**)

• **missionary** /ˈmɪʃənəri/ NOUN [plural **missionaries**] someone who goes to another country to teach people about Christianity (**missionário**)

misspell /ˌmɪsˈspel/ VERB [misspells, misspelling, misspelt or misspelled] to spell something in the wrong way □ *You've misspelt my name. It should be 'Jayne' not 'Jane'.* (**pronunciar errado**)

• **misspelling** /ˌmɪsˈspelɪŋ/ NOUN [plural **misspellings**] a word that is spelt the wrong way (**erro de pronúncia**)

mist /mɪst/ ▶ NOUN [plural **mists**] very small drops of water in the air that make it difficult for you to see (**névoa**) ▣ *A fine mist hung over the city.* (**névoa fina**) ▣ *The morning mist had lifted.* (**névoa da manhã**)
▶ VERB [mists, misting, misted] if your eyes mist, they fill with tears □ *Chrissy's eyes misted as she thought about her mother.* (**cobrir-se de lágrimas**)
◆ PHRASAL VERB **mist up/over** to become covered with small drops of water □ *The windows misted up while she was cooking.* (**embaçar, enevoar**)

mistake /mɪˈsteɪk/ ▶ NOUN [plural **mistakes**]
1 something wrong that you do (**erro**) ▣ *We've all made mistakes.* (**cometemos erros**) ▣ *She knew that inviting him would be a big mistake.* (**grande erro**) ▣ *There were lots of spelling mistakes in his writing.* (**erros de grafia**) □ + *to do something It was a mistake to come here.*
2 by mistake by accident □ *He deleted the file by mistake.* □ *The letter had been delivered to the wrong house by mistake.* (**por engano**)
▶ VERB [mistakes, mistaking, mistook, mistaken]
1 to understand something in the wrong way □ *No one could mistake his meaning.* (**enganar-se sobre**)
2 there is no mistaking something used for saying that something is very obvious □ *There was no mistaking the pride in his voice.* (**não há como negar**)
◆ PHRASAL VERB **mistake someone/something for someone/something** to think wrongly that a person or thing is someone or something else □ *People often mistake Clare for her sister.* (**confundir alguém/algo com alguém/algo**)

• **mistaken** /mɪˈsteɪkən/ ADJECTIVE if you are mistaken, you are wrong about something □ *If they thought that was the end of their problems, they were mistaken.* (**confundido**) ▣ *He was shot in the mistaken belief that he was a terrorist.* (**crença errada**)

499

mitten

• **mistakenly** /mɪˈsteɪkənli/ ADVERB wrongly □ *She mistakenly believed that their love would last.* (**equivocadamente**)

mistletoe /ˈmɪsəltəʊ/ NOUN, NO PLURAL a plant with white berries which is used as a decoration inside houses at Christmas (**visco**)

mistook /mɪˈstʊk/ PAST TENSE OF **mistake** (**ver mistake**)

mistreat /ˌmɪsˈtriːt/ VERB [mistreats, mistreating, mistreated] to treat a person or animal cruelly □ *The prisoners had been mistreated.* (**maltratar**)

• **mistreatment** /ˌmɪsˈtriːtmənt/ NOUN, NO PLURAL cruel treatment □ *the mistreatment of animals* (**maus-tratos**)

mistrust /ˌmɪsˈtrʌst/ ▶ NOUN, NO PLURAL a feeling that you cannot trust someone or something □ *The public has a deep mistrust of this government.* (**desconfiança**)
▶ VERB [mistrusts, mistrusting, mistrusted] to not trust someone or something (**desconfiar**)

misty /ˈmɪsti/ ADJECTIVE [mistier, mistiest] with a lot of small drops of water in the air □ *a misty morning* (**enevoado**)

misunderstand /ˌmɪsʌndəˈstænd/ VERB [misunderstands, misunderstanding, misunderstood] to understand something in the wrong way □ *I'm sorry, I misunderstood your question.* (**entender mal**)

• **misunderstanding** /ˌmɪsʌndəˈstændɪŋ/ NOUN [plural **misunderstandings**]
1 a problem caused by not understanding something correctly □ *I think there's been a misunderstanding.* (**mal-entendido**)
2 a slight disagreement or argument (**desentendimento**)

misuse ▶ VERB /ˌmɪsˈjuːz/ [misuses, misusing, misused] to use something in the wrong way □ *He is accused of misusing public money.* (**mau uso**)
▶ NOUN, NO PLURAL /ˌmɪsˈjuːs/ when you use something in the wrong way □ *the misuse of power* (**abuso**)

mite /maɪt/ NOUN [plural **mites**]
1 a very small insect (**ácaro**)
2 an informal word for a child who you feel sorry for □ *The poor little mite looked terrified.* (**coitadinho**)
3 a mite an informal phrase meaning slightly □ *She looked a mite annoyed.* (**ligeiramente**)

mitigating /ˈmɪtɪɡeɪtɪŋ/ ADJECTIVE making a crime or mistake seem less serious (**atenuante**) ▣ *His age was a mitigating factor in the crime.* (**fator atenuante**)

mitosis /maɪˈtəʊsɪs/ NOUN, NO PLURAL when a cell divides into two cells, each with the same number of chromosomes as the original cell. A biology word. (**mitose**)

mitten /ˈmɪtən/ NOUN [plural **mittens**] a glove (= something you wear on your hand) without separate parts for each finger (**luva sem divisões para os dedos**)

mix

mix /mɪks/ ▶ VERB [mixes, mixing, mixed]
1 to combine two or more substances ☐ *If you mix black paint and white paint, you get grey.* (misturar) ☐ *In a small bowl, mix together the garlic and butter.* (misturar tudo) ☐ + **with** *Mix the powder with water.* (misturar com)
2 to combine ☐ *Oil and water don't mix.* (misturar)
3 to combine two or more styles, activities, feelings, etc. ☐ *The President believed it was wrong to mix religion and politics.* ☐ + **with** *The villa successfully mixes modern architecture with antique-style furniture.* (misturar, combinar)
4 to talk to people and spend time with them socially ☐ *Marija was very shy and found it difficult to mix.* ☐ + **with** *My Mum doesn't like the people I mix with.* (relacionar-se)
♦ PHRASAL VERBS **mix someone/something up** to think that a person or thing is someone or something else ☐ *The twins are very alike and the teacher often mixes them up.* (confundir algo/alguém) **mix something up** to put a group of things in the wrong order ☐ *Somehow the pages have all got mixed up.* (misturar)
▶ NOUN [plural **mixes**]
1 a combination of people or things ☐ + **of** *The film was an odd mix of comedy and horror.* (mistura)
2 a powder that you combine with liquid to make a particular food ☐ *a cake mix* (mistura)

• **mixed** /mɪkst/ ADJECTIVE
1 involving many different types ☐ *We live in a racially mixed society.* ☐ *a mixed salad* (misto)
2 partly good and partly bad ☐ *The film has had mixed reviews.* ☐ *The strategy produced mixed results.* (misto)
3 for both girls and boys, or men and women ☐ *a mixed school* (misto)
4 mixed feelings when you are happy and unhappy about something at the same time ☐ *I have mixed feelings about going back to work.* (sentimentos confusos)

mixed-race /ˌmɪkst ˈreɪs/ ADJECTIVE having one parent from one race (= group of people with the same skin colour, type of hair, etc.) and the other parent from a different race (miscigenado)

mixed up /ˌmɪkst ˈʌp/ ADJECTIVE
1 confused (confuso) ☐ *I got mixed up and thought the meeting was on Thursday rather than Friday.* (fiquei confuso)
2 be mixed up in something if you are mixed up in something illegal or bad, you are involved in it ☐ *He had been mixed up in a credit card fraud.* (estar envolvido em algo)
3 having a lot of emotional problems. An informal word ☐ *He's a very mixed up little boy.* (confuso)

mixer /ˈmɪksə(r)/ NOUN [plural **mixers**] a machine used for mixing something ☐ *a cement mixer* (misturador)

mixture /ˈmɪkstʃə(r)/ NOUN [plural **mixtures**]
1 a combination of different things (mistura) ☐ *The city is a strange mixture of old and new buildings.* ☐ + **of** *I felt a mixture of anger and sadness.* (mistura estranha)
2 a substance that you get by combining two or more things ☐ *Stir the mixture until the sugar dissolves.* (mistura)

mix-up /ˈmɪksʌp/ NOUN [plural **mix-ups**] a mistake that happens because someone is confused about something (confusão, desordem)

ml /ˌem ˈel/ ABBREVIATION **millilitre** or **millilitres** (abreviação de mililitro)

mm /ˌem ˈem/ ABBREVIATION **millimetre** or **millimetres** (abreviação de milímetro)

mnemonic /nɪˈmɒnɪk/ NOUN [plural **mnemonics**] a word, phrase or poem that helps you remember something (mnemônico)

moan /məʊn/ ▶ VERB [moans, moaning, moaned]
1 to complain about something, often in a way that annoys other people ☐ *Oh stop moaning!* ☐ *Tim was moaning about the weather.* (lamentar-se, gemer)
2 to make a long, low sound, usually because you are in pain ☐ *I could hear the injured passengers moaning in pain.* (gemer)
▶ NOUN [plural **moans**]
1 when you complain about something, often in a way that annoys other people (reclamação) ☐ *She was having a moan about the cost of everything.* (estava reclamando)
2 a long, low sound you make, usually when you are in pain (gemido)

moat /məʊt/ NOUN [plural **moats**] a deep hole around a castle, designed to prevent attacks (fosso)

mob /mɒb/ ▶ NOUN [plural **mobs**] an angry crowd ☐ *A mob attacked his house with petrol bombs.* (multidão)
▶ VERB [mobs, mobbing, mobbed] if a crowd of people mobs someone, they surround them ☐ *The singer was mobbed by fans.* (rodear)

mobile /ˈməʊbaɪl/ ▶ ADJECTIVE
1 able to move or be moved ☐ *He was older and less mobile than his wife.* ☐ *a mobile home* (móvel)
2 socially mobile able to move from a lower social class to a higher one (socialmente móvel)
▶ NOUN [plural **mobiles**]
1 a telephone that you carry with you ☐ *Is your mobile switched on?* (celular) ☐ *Have you got my mobile number?* (número do celular)
2 a decoration that you hang from a ceiling (móbile)

mobile phone /ˌməʊbaɪl ˈfəʊn/ NOUN [plural **mobile phones**] a telephone that you carry with you (telefone celular)

mobility /məˈbɪləti/ NOUN, NO PLURAL
1 being able to move around ☐ *These exercises will help improve mobility.* (mobilidade)
2 social mobility the ability to move from a lower social class to a higher one (mobilidade social)

mobilize

mobilize or **mobilise** /ˈməʊbɪlaɪz/ VERB [mobilizes, mobilizing, mobilized]
1 to organize a group of people to support something □ *The party were trying to mobilize voters.* (**mobilizar**)
2 to prepare to fight a war, or prepare soldiers to fight a war □ *Troops were quickly mobilized.* (**mobilizar**)

moccasin /ˈmɒkəsɪn/ NOUN [plural **moccasins**] a soft leather shoe (**mocassim**)

mock /mɒk/ ▶ VERB [mocks, mocking, mocked] to be unkind to someone by making jokes about them or by copying what they say or do □ *Other people might mock David's voice, but I love it.* (**zombar**)
▶ ADJECTIVE not real but made to look real □ *a mock leather sofa* (**simulado**)

• **mockery** /ˈmɒkəri/ NOUN, NO PLURAL
1 make a mockery of something to make something seem stupid or not useful □ *This judgment makes a mockery of the whole legal system.* (**fazer zombaria de algo**)
2 when someone mocks someone or something (**zombaria**)

modal verb /ˌməʊdəl ˈvɜːb/ NOUN [plural **modal verbs**] a verb such as 'ought' or 'might' that is used to show ideas such as being possible, necessary, certain, etc. (**verbo modal**)

mode /məʊd/ NOUN [plural **modes**]
1 a formal word meaning a method of doing something □ *a mode of transport* (**modo**)
2 the value that appears most often in a series of numbers. A maths word. (**modo**)

model /ˈmɒdəl/ ▶ NOUN [plural **models**]
1 a small copy of something bigger □ *+ of On display was a model of the ship.* (**modelo**) ⊞ *He enjoys making models of aeroplanes.* (**montar modelos**)
2 a person whose job is to wear clothes at fashion shows and for magazine photographs (**modelo**) ⊞ *a fashion model* (**modelo de passarela**) □ *a male model*
3 a particular type of car, machine, etc. that a company makes (**modelo**) ⊞ *The latest model allows you to download video podcasts.* (**modelo mais recente**)
4 a way of doing something, for example a way of operating a business (**modelo**) ⊞ *They have developed a very successful business model.* (**modelo de negócios**)
▶ VERB [models, modelling/US modeling, modelled/US modeled]
1 to work as a model, wearing clothes at fashion shows and for magazine photographs (**trabalhar como modelo**)
2 if something is modelled on something else, it copies it □ *The programme is modelled on a popular US game show.* (**modelar-se em**)
♦ PHRASAL VERB **model yourself on someone** to try to be like someone else □ *He has modelled himself on the former president.* (**espelhar-se em alguém**)
▶ ADJECTIVE
1 a model car, building, etc. is a small copy of a real one □ *He enjoys making model planes.* (**modelo**)
2 behaving perfectly □ *She was a model student.* (**exemplar**)

• **modelling** /ˈmɒdəlɪŋ/ NOUN, NO PLURAL the job of working as a model, wearing clothes at fashion shows and for magazine photographs □ *She had a very successful modelling career.* (**de modelo**)

modem /ˈməʊdem/ NOUN [plural **modems**] a device that connects a computer to a telephone line. A computing word. (**modem**)

moderate /ˈmɒdərət/ ▶ ADJECTIVE
1 not extreme □ *He was recommended to take moderate exercise.* □ *moderate heat* (**moderado**)
2 having political or religious beliefs that are not extreme (**moderado**)
▶ NOUN /ˈmɒdərət/ [plural **moderates**] someone whose political or religious beliefs are not extreme (**moderado**)
▶ VERB /ˈmɒdəreɪt/ [moderates, moderating, moderated] to make something less extreme □ *The organization has moderated its position.* (**moderar**)

• **moderately** /ˈmɒdərətli/ ADVERB quite but not very □ *The campaign was moderately successful.* (**moderadamente**)

moderation /ˌmɒdəˈreɪʃən/ NOUN, NO PLURAL
1 in moderation if you do something in moderation, you do it only a little □ *It's fine to eat sugar in moderation.* (**com moderação**)
2 when beliefs or actions are not extreme (**moderação**)

modern /ˈmɒdən/ ADJECTIVE
1 to do with the present time and not the past (**moderno**) ⊞ *In the modern world, most women go out to work.* (**mundo moderno**) ⊞ *Modern life is very busy.* (**vida moderna**)
2 using the most recent ideas, styles, etc. (**moderno**) ⊞ *modern art* (**arte moderna**) ⊞ *modern technology* (**tecnologia moderna**)

• **modernity** /mɒˈdɜːnɪti/ NOUN, NO PLURAL being modern □ *There was a conflict between modernity and tradition.* (**modernidade**)

• **modernization** or **modernisation** /ˌmɒdənaɪˈzeɪʃən/ NOUN, NO PLURAL making something more modern □ *economic modernization* (**modernização**)

• **modernize** or **modernise** /ˈmɒdənaɪz/ VERB [modernizes, modernizing, modernized] to become more modern, or to make something more modern (**modernizar**)

modern languages /ˌmɒdən ˈlæŋɡwɪdʒɪz/ PLURAL NOUN languages that are spoken now, such as German or Spanish, which you study at school or university (**línguas modernas**)

modest /ˈmɒdɪst/ ADJECTIVE
1 quite small ☐ *a modest increase* ☐ *a modest apartment* (**modesto**)
2 not talking about your skills and achievements even when you have been successful ☐ *Paul is very modest.* (**modesto**)
• **modesty** /ˈmɒdɪsti/ NOUN, NO PLURAL the quality of not being too proud of your abilities and achievements ☐ *With characteristic modesty, he never spoke about his work.* (**modéstia**)

modicum /ˈmɒdɪkəm/ NOUN, NO PLURAL **a modicum of something** a formal phrase meaning a little of something ☐ *Anyone with a modicum of intelligence could see that he would fail.* (**quantidade módica**)

modification /ˌmɒdɪfɪˈkeɪʃən/ NOUN [plural **modifications**] a small change, or the process of changing something (**modificação**) 🔁 *They've made some modifications to the boat.* (**fizeram modificações**)
• **modify** /ˈmɒdɪfaɪ/ VERB [**modifies, modifying, modified**] to change something slightly ☐ *We've had to modify our plans.* (**modificar**)

module /ˈmɒdjuːl/ NOUN [plural **modules**]
1 a separate part of a college or university course ☐ *We're doing a module on English grammar.* (**módulo**)
2 a separate unit that is part of something larger ☐ *the space station's escape module* (**módulo**)

mohair /ˈməʊheə(r)/ NOUN, NO PLURAL soft wool that comes from a type of goat (**pelo de cabra angorá**)

Mohammed /məˈhæmɪd/ NOUN the Arab holy man on whose ideas the religion of Islam is based (**Maomé**)

moist /mɔɪst/ ADJECTIVE [**moister, moistest**] slightly wet ☐ *moist air* (**úmido**)
• **moisten** /ˈmɔɪsən/ VERB [**moistens, moistening, moistened**] to make something slightly wet ☐ *He licked his lips to moisten them.* (**umedecer**)
• **moisture** /ˈmɔɪstʃə(r)/ NOUN, NO PLURAL a small amount of liquid in or on something ☐ *This helps keep the moisture in the soil.* (**umidade**)
• **moisturize** or **moisturise** /ˈmɔɪstʃəraɪz/ VERB [**moisturizes, moisturizing, moisturized**] to put cream on your skin to make it soft and not dry (**hidratar**)
• **moisturizer** or **moisturiser** /ˈmɔɪstʃəraɪzə(r)/ NOUN [plural **moisturizers**] a cream you put on your skin to make it soft and not dry (**hidratante**)

molar /ˈməʊlə(r)/ NOUN [plural **molars**] one of the large teeth that you chew with at the back of your mouth. A biology word. (**dente molar**)

mole /məʊl/ NOUN [plural **moles**]
1 a small brown spot on your skin which is permanent (**verruga, pinta**)
2 a small animal which lives underground and is almost blind (**toupeira**)
3 someone who works for an organization and gives secret information to its competitors (**espião**)

molecular /məˈlekjʊlə(r)/ ADJECTIVE to do with molecules ☐ *molecular structure* (**molecular**)

molecule /ˈmɒlɪkjuːl/ NOUN [plural **molecules**] the smallest unit that a chemical element or compound can be divided into. Molecules are made up of two or more atoms. A chemistry or physics word. (**molécula**)

molehill /ˈməʊlhɪl/ NOUN [plural **molehills**] a pile of earth that a mole pushes up while it is digging underground (**monte de terra feito por toupeiras**)

mollycoddle /ˈmɒlɪkɒdəl/ VERB [**mollycoddles, mollycoddling, mollycoddled**] to treat someone too kindly and protect them from unpleasant things too much (**mimar**)

molten /ˈməʊltən/ ADJECTIVE molten rock or metal is liquid because it is very hot (**derretido**)

mom /mɒm/ NOUN [plural **moms**] the US word for mum (**mamãe**)

moment /ˈməʊmənt/ NOUN [plural **moments**]
1 a short period of time ☐ *Stop what you're doing for a moment.* (**momento, instante**) 🔁 *Wait a moment – I'm not ready.* (**espere um momento**) 🔁 *Please take a moment* (= use a short period of time) *to read this information.* (**leve um instante**)
2 a particular point in time ☐ *Just at that moment, she heard a door slam.* ☐ *Winning this competition has been the proudest moment in my athletics career.* (**momento**)
3 at the moment now ☐ *The house is empty at the moment.* (**no momento**)
4 at any moment at any time soon ☐ *Doctors have said he could die at any moment.* (**a qualquer momento**)
5 in a moment very soon ☐ *I'll explain what I mean in a moment.* ☐ *I'll be back in a moment.* (**em um instante**)
6 the moment (that) as soon as ☐ *The moment I met him I knew we'd be friends.* (**no momento em que**)
• **momentarily** /ˈməʊməntərɪli/ ADVERB for a short period of time ☐ *He was momentarily suspended in the air.* (**momentaneamente**)
• **momentary** /ˈməʊməntəri/ ADJECTIVE continuing for only a very short time ☐ *There was a momentary pause, and then everyone started talking.* (**momentâneo**)

momentous /məˈmentəs/ ADJECTIVE very important, causing big changes ☐ *a momentous occasion* ☐ *a momentous decision* (**significativo**)

momentum /məˈmentəm/ NOUN, NO PLURAL
1 when something continues to develop, increase or become more successful (**impulso**) 🔁 *The idea is gaining political momentum.* (**ganhar impulso**)
2 the force that makes a moving object continue to move. A physics word. (**impulso**)

monarch /ˈmɒnək/ NOUN [plural **monarchs**] a king or queen (**monarca**)
• **monarchy** /ˈmɒnəki/ NOUN [plural **monarchies**]

monastery — month

1 a system in which a country has a king or queen □ *The Greek monarchy was abolished in 1973.* (**monarquia**)

2 a country that has a king or queen □ *Britain is a monarchy.* (**monarquia**)

monastery /ˈmɒnəstəri/ NOUN [plural **monasteries**] a building where monks (= religious men) live (**mosteiro**)

• **monastic** /məˈnæstɪk/ ADJECTIVE to do with monasteries or monks (= religious men) (**monástico**)

Monday /ˈmʌndɪ/ NOUN [plural **Mondays**] the day of the week after Sunday and before Tuesday □ *On Monday, I went to London.* □ *See you next Monday.* (**segunda-feira**)

monetary /ˈmʌnɪtəri/ ADJECTIVE to do with money, especially the money in a country's economy □ *The government is tightening its monetary policy.* (**monetário**)

money /ˈmʌnɪ/ NOUN, NO PLURAL

1 coins and paper notes that you use for buying things □ *We don't have the money for a new car.* (**dinheiro**) ▣ *Dan spends most of his money on computer games.* (**gasta dinheiro**) ▣ *I'm trying to save some money.* (**poupa dinheiro**) ▣ *She earns a lot of money.* (**ganha dinheiro**)

2 make money to earn money or to make a profit □ *He had never made much money from writing.* □ *She made a lot of money from the sale of the house.* (**ganha dinheiro**)

mongrel /ˈmʌŋɡrəl/ NOUN [plural **mongrels**] a dog that is a mixture of different breeds (**vira-lata**)

monitor /ˈmɒnɪtə(r)/ ▶ VERB [**monitors, monitoring, monitored**] to check something regularly to see how it changes □ *The school monitors the progress of all its students.* (**monitorar, controlar**)

▶ NOUN [plural **monitors**]

1 a screen that is attached to a computer. A computing word □ *a computer monitor* (**monitor**)

2 a piece of equipment which measures something continuously □ *a heart monitor* (**monitor**)

monk /mʌŋk/ NOUN [plural **monks**] one of a group of religious men who live together (**monge**)

monkey /ˈmʌŋkɪ/ NOUN [plural **monkeys**] an animal with a long tail that lives in trees in hot countries □ *The monkeys were trained to perform simple tasks.* (**macaco**)

mono- /ˈmɒnəʊ/ PREFIX **mono-** is added to the beginning of words to mean 'one' or 'single' □ *monologue* □ *monorail* (**mono-**)

monologue /ˈmɒnəlɒɡ/ NOUN [plural **monologues**] a long speech by one person, especially in a play (**monólogo**)

monopolize or **monopolise** /məˈnɒpəlaɪz/ VERB [**monopolizes, monopolizing, monopolized**] to control something completely so that other people or organizations cannot take part in it or share it □ *He monopolized the conversation and no one had the chance to speak.* □ *The company had for a long time monopolized the software business.* (**monopolizar**)

• **monopoly** /məˈnɒpəlɪ/ NOUN [plural **monopolies**]

1 when a company or government controls a particular business or industry so that other companies cannot compete □ *The law ended the state's monopoly on broadcasting.* (**monopólio**)

2 a big company that controls a particular industry or business □ *He was the manager of an electricity monopoly.* (**monopólio**)

monorail /ˈmɒnəreɪl/ NOUN [plural **monorails**] a railway on which the trains run on one rail (= long piece of metal), instead of two rails (**monotrilho**)

monotone /ˈmɒnətəʊn/ NOUN, NO PLURAL a way of speaking in which your voice never changes □ *He spoke in a low monotone.* (**em um único tom**)

• **monotonous** /məˈnɒtənəs/ ADJECTIVE boring because of never changing □ *monotonous work* (**monótono**)

• **monotony** /məˈnɒtənɪ/ NOUN, NO PLURAL when something is boring because it never changes □ *the monotony of the task* (**monotonia**)

monsoon /mɒnˈsuːn/ NOUN [plural **monsoons**] the season when it rains a lot in some hot countries (**monção**)

monster /ˈmɒnstə(r)/ ▶ NOUN [plural **monsters**]

1 in stories, a very big and frightening creature □ *My little boy thinks there are monsters under his bed.* (**monstro**)

2 a cruel and evil person (**monstro**)

▶ ADJECTIVE an informal word meaning extremely big □ *a monster truck* (**monstro**)

monstrosity /mɒnˈstrɒsətɪ/ NOUN [plural **monstrosities**] something that is big and very ugly □ *The building was a monstrosity.* (**monstruosidade**)

monstrous /ˈmɒnstrəs/ ADJECTIVE

1 morally very bad □ *a monstrous crime* (**monstruoso**)

2 big and very ugly (**monstruoso**)

month /mʌnθ/ NOUN [plural **months**]

1 one of twelve periods that a year is divided into □ *the month of May* □ *the winter months* (**mês**) ▣ *I went to France last month.* (**mês passado**) ▣ *It's my birthday next month.* (**próximo mês**)

2 any period of approximately four weeks or 30 days □ *We spent a few months in Melbourne.* □ *People often wait several months for an appointment.* (**mês**)

3 a long time □ *Police spent months investigating the case.* (**mês**)

• **monthly** /ˈmʌnθlɪ/ ADJECTIVE, ADVERB happening once a month □ *a monthly meeting* □ *He is paid monthly.* (**mensalmente**)

monument /ˈmɒnjumənt/ NOUN [plural monuments]

1 something that has been built in memory of a person or event □ *They built a monument to Sir Walter Scott.* (**monumento**)

2 a building or structure that is important in history □ *The Parthenon is one of Greece's ancient monuments.* (**monumento**)

- **monumental** /ˌmɒnjuˈmentəl/ ADJECTIVE extremely big or important □ *a monumental task* (**monumental**)

moo /muː/ ▶ VERB [moos, mooing, mooed] a cow moos when it makes a long low sound (**mugir**)
▶ NOUN [plural moos] the long low sound a cow makes

mood /muːd/ NOUN [plural moods]

1 someone's feelings at a particular time (**humor**) 🔄 *I woke up in a bad mood this morning.* (**mau humor**) 🔄 *You're in a good mood today!* (**bom humor**) 🔄 *The government has misjudged the public mood.* (**sentimento público**) □ + *of There was a mood of optimism in Europe at the time.*

2 be in a mood to feel angry or unhappy □ *He was still in a mood after their argument that morning.* (**de mau humor, zangado**)

3 be/feel in the mood to feel as if you want to do something □ *I didn't feel in the mood for going out.* (**estar a fim**)

- **moodiness** /ˈmuːdɪnɪs/ NOUN, NO PLURAL when someone is moody (**mau humor**)
- **moody** /ˈmuːdɪ/ ADJECTIVE [moodier, moodiest] often becoming angry or unhappy □ *moody teenagers* (**instável**)

moon /muːn/ NOUN [plural moons]

1 the moon the round object that you see in the sky at night and which moves around the Earth (**Lua**) 🔄 *The moon shone brightly.* (**lua brilhou**) 🔄 *Neil Armstrong made the first moon landing.* (**pouso na Lua**)

2 full/half/crescent/new moon used for talking about the shape of the moon at a particular time □ *There was a full moon* (= the moon looked like a complete circle) *that night.* □ *He watched the new moon* (= a moon that looks like a thin curve) *rising.* (**lua cheia/minguante/crescente/nova**)

3 a similar object that moves around another planet □ *Saturn's moons* (**lua**)

◆ IDIOM **be over the moon** an informal phrase meaning to be very happy about something that has happened □ *He was over the moon when he passed his driving test.* (**ficar nas nuvens, eufórico**)

moonlight /ˈmuːnlaɪt/ NOUN, NO PLURAL light that comes from the moon □ *His eyes shone in the moonlight.* (**luar**)

- **moonlit** /ˈmuːnlɪt/ ADJECTIVE lit by the moon □ *a clear moonlit night* (**enluarado**)

moor¹ /mɔː(r)/ NOUN [plural moors] a large high area of land that is covered with grass and bushes. A geography word. (**charneca**)

moor² /mɔː(r)/ VERB [moors, mooring, moored] to fasten a boat to something (**atracar**)

moorland /ˈmɔːlənd/ NOUN [plural moorlands] a large high area of land that is covered with grass and bushes. A geography word. (**charneca**)

moose /muːs/ NOUN [plural moose] a large deer with big, flat horns which lives in North America (**alce**)

mop /mɒp/ ▶ NOUN [plural mops]

1 something with a long handle that you use for washing floors (**esfregão**)

2 a lot of thick, often untidy, hair □ *He had a mop of black hair.* (**cabeleira**)

▶ VERB [mops, mopping, mopped]

1 to clean a floor with a mop (**limpar com esfregão**)

2 to remove a liquid from something using a cloth □ *He mopped his sweaty face with a handkerchief.* (**enxugar com pano**)

◆ PHRASAL VERB **mop something up** to clean a liquid from a surface using a cloth or mop □ *The waiter mopped up the spilled tea.* (**limpar, secar**)

mope /məʊp/ VERB [mopes, moping, moped] to spend time feeling bored or unhappy and doing little □ *Ben spent most of the day moping around in his pyjamas.* (**vaguear com tristeza**)

moped /ˈməʊped/ NOUN [plural mopeds] a light motorcycle with a small engine (**bicicleta motorizada**)

moraine /mɒˈreɪn/ NOUN, NO PLURAL earth and stones that have been carried along by glaciers (= large masses of ice). A geography word. (**moreia, acúmulo de pedras e barro**)

moral /ˈmɒrəl/ ▶ ADJECTIVE

1 to do with right and wrong and the way people should behave (**moral**) 🔄 *She had high moral standards.* (**padrões morais**) □ *He objected to the war for moral reasons.*

2 behaving in a way that is right and good (**moral**)

▶ NOUN [plural morals] something that a story or experience teaches you about how to behave (**moral**) 🔄 *The moral of the story is never give up.* (**moral da história**)

⇨ *go to* **morals**

morale /məˈrɑːl/ NOUN, NO PLURAL how confident or happy a person or group of people feel □ *Morale in the office is fairly low.* (**moral, ânimo**) 🔄 *Pay rises usually improve morale.* (**melhora o ânimo**)

morality /məˈrælətɪ/ NOUN, NO PLURAL beliefs about what is right or wrong behaviour (**moralidade**)

moralize or **moralise** /ˈmɒrəlaɪz/ VERB [moralizes, moralizing, moralized] to say what is the right way to behave, especially in a way that criticizes other people's behaviour (**moralizar**)

morally /'mɒrəlɪ/ ADVERB to do with what is right or wrong behaviour □ *Not paying your taxes is morally wrong.* (moralmente)

morals /'mɒrəlz/ PLURAL NOUN the beliefs someone has about what is right and wrong behaviour □ *His remarks have started a public debate on the nation's morals.* (moral, moralidade)

morbid /'mɔːbɪd/ ADJECTIVE too interested in death or other subjects that most people think are sad or unpleasant (mórbido) ▣ *He had developed a morbid fascination with the murders.* (fascinação mórbida)

more /mɔː(r)/ ▶ DETERMINER, PRONOUN

1 a larger number or amount □ *He has more friends than anyone else I know.* (mais) ▣ *The bill was more than £10,000.* (mais do que) ▣ *He knows more about elephants than anyone else in the UK.* ▣ *More and more people are buying organic food.* (cada vez mais)

2 something in addition to what you have, what is there, or what you have talked about (mais) ▣ *Is there any more cake?* (mais bolo) ▣ *Would you like some more coffee?* (um pouco mais de café) □ *You need to do more to help.* □ *8 people died, and at least twenty more were injured.*

▶ ADVERB

1 used to make comparative forms of adjectives and adverbs, especially ones with 2 or more syllables (mais) ▣ *He's more patient than I am.* (mais do que) □ *More recently, I have begun to enjoy crime novels.* ▣ *Harry's a lot more emotional than his sister.* (muito mais)

2 to a greater degree (mais) ▣ *I exercise more than I used to.* (mais do que) ▣ *I like her more and more.* (cada vez mais)

3 more or less almost, but not exactly □ *We've more or less finished decorating the kitchen.* □ *She more or less said she didn't trust us.* (mais ou menos)

4 the more ... the more/less used to say that if one thing increases, another thing will increase or decrease □ *The more I read about Cuba, the more I want to go there.* (quanto mais ..., mais/menos)

• **moreish** /'mɔːrɪʃ/ ADJECTIVE moreish food makes you want to eat more of it. An informal word. (com "gosto de quero mais")

moreover /mɔːˈrəʊvə(r)/ ADVERB a formal word for also □ *We do not have the facilities for this project. Moreover, we do not have enough staff.* (além disso)

morgue /mɔːɡ/ NOUN [plural **morgues**] a place where dead bodies are kept until they are buried or burned (necrotério)

morning /'mɔːnɪŋ/ NOUN [plural **mornings**]

1 the early part of the day from when the sun rises to the middle of the day □ *He takes the dog for a walk every morning.* (manhã) ▣ *He was late this morning.* (esta manhã)

2 the period from the middle of the night to the middle of the day □ *Adam didn't get to bed till 3 o'clock in the morning.* (de manhã)

3 in the morning (a) in the early part of the day □ *I'm usually quite tired in the morning.* (b) tomorrow morning □ *See you in the morning.* (de manhã)

4 Good morning! used to say 'hello' when you meet someone in the morning (Bom dia!)

moron /'mɔːrɒn/ NOUN [plural **morons**] an informal word for a very stupid person □ *Some moron left the fridge door open all night.* (idiota)

• **moronic** /məˈrɒnɪk/ ADJECTIVE an informal word that means very stupid (idiota)

morose /məˈrəʊs/ ADJECTIVE bad-tempered and speaking little (rabugento)

morphine /'mɔːfiːn/ NOUN, NO PLURAL a powerful drug used to make pain less strong (morfina)

morsel /'mɔːsəl/ NOUN [plural **morsels**] a small piece of food □ *Joe finished off every morsel of the pie.* (bocado)

mortal /'mɔːtəl/ ▶ ADJECTIVE

1 unable to live forever and sure to die one day □ *We are all mortal.* (mortal)

2 very great or extreme (mortal) ▣ *She lived in mortal fear of being discovered.* (medo mortal) ▣ *The two men became mortal enemies.* (inimigos mortais)

3 causing someone to die (mortal) ▣ *He was dealt a mortal blow* (= He was injured so badly that he died). (golpe mortal)

▶ NOUN [plural **mortals**] a human being. A literary word. (mortal)

• **mortality** /mɔːˈtælətɪ/ NOUN, NO PLURAL

1 the fact that you will not live forever □ *He was well aware of his own mortality.* (mortalidade)

2 the number of deaths in a particular group or at a particular time (mortalidade) ▣ *Infant mortality is still very high in the region.* (mortalidade infantil) ▣ *The mortality rate from the war continues to rise.* (taxa de mortalidade)

• **mortally** /'mɔːtəlɪ/ ADVERB causing death (mortalmente) ▣ *The soldier was mortally wounded.* (ferido mortalmente)

mortar /'mɔːtə(r)/ NOUN [plural **mortars**]

1 a type of large gun that fires explosives up into the air □ *a mortar attack* (morteiro)

2 a substance that is put between bricks in order to hold the bricks in place (argamassa)

mortgage /'mɔːɡɪdʒ/ NOUN [plural **mortgages**] money that you borrow from a bank or financial organization in order to buy a house or land (hipoteca) ▣ *They've taken out a huge mortgage on the flat.* (fizeram uma hipoteca)

mortified /'mɔːtɪfaɪd/ ADJECTIVE extremely embarrassed □ *She was mortified when she realized her mistake.* (mortificado)

mortuary /'mɔːtʃʊərɪ/ NOUN [plural **mortuaries**] a place where dead bodies are kept until they are buried or burned (necrotério)

mosaic /məʊˈzeɪɪk/ NOUN [plural **mosaics**] a picture made by fitting together many small pieces of coloured glass or stone □ *Roman mosaics* (**mosaico**)

Moslem /ˈmɒzləm/ NOUN [plural **Moslems**], ADJECTIVE another spelling of **Muslim** (*ver* **Muslim**)

mosque /mɒsk/ NOUN [plural **mosques**] a place where Muslims meet and pray (**mesquita**)

mosquito /məˈskiːtəʊ/ NOUN [plural **mosquitoes** *or* **mosquitos**] an insect which feeds by biting people or animals and sucking their blood (**mosquito**)

moss /mɒs/ NOUN [plural **mosses**] a small green plant that grows on rocks, trees, or the ground, in slightly wet places (**musgo**)

• **mossy** /ˈmɒsi/ ADJECTIVE [**mossier, mossiest**] covered with moss □ *a mossy bank by the river* (**musgoso**)

most /məʊst/ ▶ DETERMINER, PRONOUN

1 the largest number or amount □ *Most people support the policy.* □ *Which club has spent most money on new players this season?* □ *All three children eat a lot but Tom eats the most.* (**mais**)

2 almost all □ *Most of my friends are people I know from work.* □ *I like most types of fruit.* (**a maioria**)

3 at the most and not more □ *The trip should cost £500 at the most.* (**no máximo**)

4 make the most of something to get as much advantage as possible from something that may not continue □ *Make the most of the good weather while it lasts.* (**aproveitar ao máximo**)

▶ ADVERB

1 used to make superlative forms of adjectives and adverbs, especially ones with two or more syllables □ *Paul was the most intelligent boy in the class.* □ *Most importantly, he has learned to pay more attention in class.* (**o, a, os, as mais**)

2 more than anyone or anything else □ *What kind of music do you like most?* (**mais**)

• **mostly** /ˈməʊstli/ ADVERB in most cases or most of the time □ *They mostly play indoors.* □ *The band plays mostly '70s music.* (**principalmente, quase sempre**)

MOT /ˌeməʊˈtiː/ NOUN [plural **MOTs**] in Britain, a test done on cars more than three years old to make sure they are safe to drive (**teste de segurança em carros usados**)

motel /məʊˈtel/ NOUN [plural **motels**] a hotel near a main road for people who are travelling by car (**hotel à beira da estrada**)

moth /mɒθ/ NOUN [plural **moths**] an insect with large wings that flies at night (**mariposa**)

mother /ˈmʌðə(r)/ ▶ NOUN [plural **mothers**]

1 the female parent of a person or animal □ *My mother was very tall.* □ *The cubs learn to hunt from their mother.* (**mãe**)

2 Mother the title of some nuns (= religious women who live together) □ *Mother Teresa* (**madre**)

▶ VERB [**mothers, mothering, mothered**] to be kind to someone and look after them □ *Zoe has always mothered her little brother.* (**cuidar como mãe**)

• **motherhood** /ˈmʌðəhʊd/ NOUN, NO PLURAL the state of being a mother (**maternidade**)

mother-in-law /ˈmʌðərɪnˌlɔː/ NOUN [plural **mothers-in-law**] the mother of your husband or wife (**sogra**)

motherly /ˈmʌðəli/ ADJECTIVE kind and often looking after other people (**maternalmente**)

Mother's Day /ˈmʌðəz ˌdeɪ/ NOUN, NO PLURAL a Sunday in the spring when children give their mothers cards and presents □ *a Mother's Day card* (**Dia das Mães**)

mother tongue /ˌmʌðə ˈtʌŋ/ NOUN [plural **mother tongues**] the first language you learn to speak as a child □ *English is not her mother tongue.* (**língua nativa**)

motif /məʊˈtiːf/ NOUN [plural **motifs**] a shape or design that is repeated in a pattern (**tema, motivo**)

motion /ˈməʊʃən/ ▶ NOUN [plural **motions**]

1 movement or how something moves □ *The motion of the waves made him sleepy.* (**movimento**) □ *Do not attempt to get off while the ride is in motion.* (**em movimento**)

2 one movement that you make □ *He flicked the fly away with a quick motion of his wrist.* (**movimento**)

3 a suggestion that is voted on at a formal meeting or in a court of law (**moção**) □ *The motion was passed unanimously.* (**a moção foi aceita**)

♦ IDIOM **go through the motions** to do something because you have to, but with little effort or enthusiasm (**limitar-se a fazer a obrigação**)

▶ VERB [**motions, motioning, motioned**] to make a movement with your hand in order to show someone that you want them to do something □ *He motioned for her to come forward.* (**acenar**)

• **motionless** /ˈməʊʃənlɪs/ ADJECTIVE not moving at all (**imóvel**)

motivate /ˈməʊtɪveɪt/ VERB [**motivates, motivating, motivated**]

1 to make someone feel interested and enthusiastic so that they want to do something □ *A good coach knows how to motivate his team.* (**motivar**)

2 to cause someone to act in a particular way □ *He had been motivated by greed.* (**motivar**)

• **motivation** /ˌməʊtɪˈveɪʃən/ NOUN [plural **motivations**]

1 *no plural* enthusiasm and interest in doing something □ *At university, he lacked motivation.* (**motivação**)

2 something that makes you want to do something □ *Pregnancy was her motivation to stop smoking.* (**motivação**)

motive /ˈməʊtɪv/ NOUN [plural **motives**] the reason someone has for doing something □ *There seemed to be no motive for the attack.* (**motivo**)

motor

motor /ˈməʊtə(r)/ ▶ NOUN [plural **motors**] the part of a machine that uses petrol, electricity, etc. to produce movement and make the machine work □ *an electric motor* (**motor**)

▶ ADJECTIVE

1 to do with vehicles that have engines □ *motor racing* □ *the motor industry* (**motor**)
2 using the power of an engine □ *a motor mower* (**motor**)

motorbike /ˈməʊtəbaɪk/ NOUN [plural **motorbikes**] a vehicle with two wheels and an engine. You sit on it like a bicycle. (**motocicleta**)

motor car /ˈməʊtə ˌkɑː/ NOUN [plural **motor cars**] a car. An old-fashioned phrase. (**automóvel**)

motorcycle /ˈməʊtəˌsaɪkəl/ NOUN [plural **motorcycles**] a motorbike or moped (**motocicleta**)
• **motorcyclist** /ˈməʊtəˌsaɪklɪst/ NOUN [plural **motorcyclists**] someone who rides a motorbike or moped (**motociclista**)

motorist /ˈməʊtərɪst/ NOUN [plural **motorists**] someone who drives a car (**motorista**)

motor racing /ˈməʊtə ˌreɪsɪŋ/ NOUN, NO PLURAL the sport of driving cars very fast around a track (**corrida automobilística**)

motorway /ˈməʊtəweɪ/ NOUN [plural **motorways**] a wide road for vehicles travelling fast over long distances (**rodovia, autoestrada**)

mottled /ˈmɒtəld/ ADJECTIVE covered with small areas of different colour and different shapes (**mosqueado**)

motto /ˈmɒtəʊ/ NOUN [plural **mottoes** or **mottos**] a short sentence or phrase that states the beliefs or purpose of a person or organization □ *The motto of the Scouts is 'Be prepared'.* (**lema**)

mould /məʊld/ ▶ NOUN [plural **moulds**]
1 a hollow container which a liquid is poured into so that the liquid has the same shape as the container when it is cool and firm □ *a jelly mould* (**molde, fôrma**)
2 a soft green or black substance that grows on old food or in wet conditions □ *The bathroom ceiling was covered in mould.* (**mofo, bolor**)

▶ VERB [moulds, moulding, moulded] to shape something with your hands or in a mould □ *She moulded the icing into pretty flower shapes.* (**modelar**)

• **mouldy** /ˈməʊldɪ/ ADJECTIVE [**mouldier**, **mouldiest**] covered with mould □ *The bread has gone mouldy.* (**mofado, embolorado**)

moult /məʊlt/ VERB [**moults, moulting, moulted**] birds and animals moult when they lose their feathers or hair (**mudar**)

mound /maʊnd/ NOUN [plural **mounds**]
1 a pile or large amount of something □ *a mound of ironing* (**montículo, pilha**)
2 a small hill or pile of earth or stones □ *a burial mound* (**montículo**)

Mount /maʊnt/ NOUN [plural **Mounts**] used before the names of mountains □ *the top of Mount Everest* (**Monte**)

mount /maʊnt/ VERB [**mounts, mounting, mounted**]

1 to organize something in order to achieve a particular aim (**preparar**) 🔲 *Local residents are mounting a protest against the plans.* (**preparar um protesto**)
2 if a feeling among a group of people mounts, it increases in level □ *Fears are mounting for the safety of the young climbers.* (**aumentar**)
3 to fix an object onto something □ *They've mounted the speakers on the wall.* (**instalar**)
4 to go up steps or get onto something □ *The audience applauded as she mounted the stage.* (**subir**)
5 to get on a horse or bicycle (**montar**)
♦ PHRASAL VERB **mount up** to gradually increase □ *The cost soon mounts up.* (**crescer, aumentar**)

mountain /ˈmaʊntɪn/ NOUN [plural **mountains**] a very high hill □ *the Rocky Mountains* □ *We spent our holiday walking in the mountains.* □ *a mountain range* (**montanha**)

mountain bike /ˈmaʊntɪn ˌbaɪk/ NOUN [plural **mountain bikes**] a bicycle with thick tyres and a strong frame, for riding on rough ground (**bicicleta de montanha**)
• **mountain biking** /ˈmaʊntɪn ˌbaɪkɪŋ/ NOUN, NO PLURAL the sport or activity of riding a mountain bike (**ciclismo de montanha**)

mountaineer /ˌmaʊntɪˈnɪə(r)/ NOUN [plural **mountaineers**] someone who climbs mountains (**montanhismo**)
• **mountaineering** /ˌmaʊntɪˈnɪərɪŋ/ NOUN, NO PLURAL the sport or activity of climbing mountains (**montanhismo, alpinismo**)

mountainous /ˈmaʊntɪnəs/ ADJECTIVE having a lot of mountains □ *mountainous countries like Nepal* (**montanhoso**)

mounted /ˈmaʊntɪd/ ADJECTIVE riding a horse □ *mounted policemen* (**montado**)

mourn /mɔːn/ VERB [**mourns, mourning, mourned**] to be very sad because someone you love has died □ *She was still mourning for her husband.* (**prantear**)
• **mourner** /ˈmɔːnə(r)/ NOUN [plural **mourners**] someone who is at a funeral □ *The church was packed with mourners.* (**enlutado, acompanhante de enterro**)
• **mournful** /ˈmɔːnfʊl/ ADJECTIVE full of sadness □ *mournful music* (**pesaroso**)
• **mourning** /ˈmɔːnɪŋ/ NOUN, NO PLURAL when someone mourns for someone who has died (**luto**) 🔲 *a period of mourning* (**período de luto**)

mouse

mouse /maʊs/ NOUN [plural **mice**]
1 a small animal with grey or brown fur and a long tail (**rato**)

2 a small device that you move with your hand in order to make a computer do things. A computing word. (**mouse**)

mouse mat /ˈmaʊs ˌmæt/ NOUN [plural **mouse mats**] a small piece of material that you move a computer mouse on (**mousepad, apoio para mouse**)

mousse /muːs/ NOUN [plural **mousses**]
1 a soft, cold, sweet food that is made with cream and eggs □ *chocolate mousse* (**musse**)
2 a substance that you put in your hair to keep it in a particular style □ *a styling mousse* (**musse**)

moustache /məˈstɑːʃ/ NOUN [plural **moustaches**] a line of hair that some men grow above their top lip (**bigode**)

mousy /ˈmaʊsɪ/ ADJECTIVE [**mousier, mousiest**]
1 a mousy person is shy and nervous (**tímido**)
2 mousy hair is light brown (**marrom-claro**)

mouth ▶ NOUN /maʊθ/ [plural **mouths**]
1 the part of your face that you use for speaking and eating and which contains your tongue and teeth (**boca**)
2 the place where a river flows into the sea (**boca, embocadura**)
3 the entrance to a cave, tunnel (= passage through the earth), etc. (**boca, entrada**)
▶ VERB /maʊð/ [**mouths, mouthing, mouthed**] to make the shapes of words with your mouth without making the sounds □ *She mouthed something at me but I didn't understand.* (**pronunciar palavras sem emitir som**)

• **mouthful** /ˈmaʊθfʊl/ NOUN [plural **mouthfuls**]
1 an amount of food or drink that you put in your mouth at one time □ *She ate a few mouthfuls of soup.* (**bocado**)
2 a word or phrase that is difficult to say □ *Her surname's a bit of a mouthful.* (**palavra difícil de pronunciar**)

mouthpiece /ˈmaʊθpiːs/ NOUN [plural **mouthpieces**]
1 the part of a musical instrument or telephone that you put in or close to your mouth (**bocal, embocadura**)
2 a person, newspaper, etc. that states the opinions of a particular group □ *a mouthpiece of the government* (**porta-voz**)

mouthwash /ˈmaʊθwɒʃ/ NOUN, NO PLURAL a liquid that you use for cleaning your mouth and teeth (**colutório**)

mouth-watering /ˈmaʊθˌwɔːtərɪŋ/ ADJECTIVE mouth-watering food looks or smells very good and makes you want to eat it (**de dar água na boca**)

movable /ˈmuːvəbəl/ ADJECTIVE able to be moved (**móvel**)

move /muːv/ ▶ VERB [**moves, moving, moved**]
1 to change position, or to change the position of something □ *Please move your bag off the kitchen table.* □ *He moved forwards to kick the ball.* □ *Nobody moved as the clock struck.* □ *I'm sure I saw the curtain move.* (**mover, mexer**)
2 if a person or an organization moves, they go to live or work in a different place □ **+ to** *We moved to London in 2003.* (**mudar**) 🔑 *We moved house over ten times while I was a child.* (**mudamos de casa**) □ *Our office is moving to Bristol.*
3 to change the time of something □ *The meeting has been moved to next Monday.* (**mudar**)
4 to make you feel a strong, usually sad, emotion (**comover, emocionar**) 🔑 *I was moved to tears by her story.* (**emocionado às lágrimas**)
5 to make progress □ *The building work is moving ahead well.* □ *Now we've got the money, we can get moving with the project.* (**avançar**)
6 to take action to do something □ **+ to do something** *Police moved quickly to control the riot.* (**agir**)

◆ PHRASAL VERBS **move in** to begin to live in a new home or work in a new place □ *We moved in last year.* (**mudar-se para**) **move on**
1 to leave the place where you have been and go somewhere else □ *We stayed in Venice for 2 weeks before moving on.* (**mudar-se**)
2 to start to do something different or to talk about something different □ *The job was getting boring, so I decided it was time to move on.* □ **+ to** *I think we've made a decision about the hall – shall we move on to the playing fields?* (**mudar-se**) **move out** to leave the place where you have been living or working □ *I moved out of my parents' house when I was 18.* (**mudar-se**) **move over/up** to change your position in order to make space for someone or something □ *Can you move up a bit so we can get the door closed?* (**mudar de opinião, dar espaço**)

▶ NOUN [plural **moves**]
1 an action that achieves something (**movimento, atitude**) 🔑 *Buying a house turned out to be a good move.* (**boa atitude**) 🔑 *They made no move to help her.* (**não fizeram nada**) 🔑 *I've given him my phone number – it's up to him to make the next move.* (**próximo passo**)
2 a move towards/away from something a change in a situation or in people's opinions which makes something more/less common or popular □ *There has been a move towards providing more care for patients at home.* (**mudança que facilite/dificulte o acesso das pessoas a algo**)
3 when you go to live or work in another place □ *I've packed all my files ready for the office move.* □ *They split up after her move to London.* (**mudança**)
4 a change of position □ *The slightest move was painful.* (**movimento**)
5 when you move a piece in a game such as chess □ *Come on, it's your move.* (**jogada**)

◆ IDIOMS **get a move on** an informal phrase meaning to hurry □ *Get a move on – we're going to be late!* (**apressar-se**) **make a move** an informal

movie

word meaning to leave a place, especially where you have been a guest □ *We'd better make a move – our train leaves at six.* (**sair**)

• **movement** /'mu:vmənt/ NOUN [plural **movements**]
1 a change of position or place □ *I saw a slight movement of the curtain.* □ *Aim for slow, graceful movements of the arms.* □ *The police tracked the movements of all the suspects.* (**movimento**)
2 a group of people with the same interests or aims □ *the anti-war movement* (**movimento**)
3 movement towards/away from something a change in a situation or in people's opinions that makes something more/less common or popular □ *There has been some movement towards accepting the peace proposals.* (**avanço/ retrocesso**)
4 a part of a long piece of classical music (**movimento**)

movie /'mu:vɪ/ NOUN [plural **movies**]
1 a film □ *Do you have a favourite movie?* □ *a movie star* □ *a horror movie* (**filme**)
2 the movies a cinema □ *Let's go to the movies.* (**cinema**)

moving /'mu:vɪŋ/ ADJECTIVE making you feel emotional □ *She made a moving speech about her son.* (**emocionante**)
• **movingly** /'mu:vɪŋlɪ/ ADVERB in a moving way (**emocionantemente**)

mow /məʊ/ VERB [**mows, mowing, mowed, mown** or **mowed**] to cut grass with a machine (**cortar a grama**) 🔁 *Simon's mowing the lawn.* (**está cortando a grama**)
• **mower** /'məʊə(r)/ NOUN [plural **mowers**] a machine for cutting grass (**cortador de grama**)

MP /ˌem'pi:/ ABBREVIATION Member of Parliament; someone who has been elected to the British parliament (**abreviação de Membro do Parlamento**)

MP3 /ˌempi:'θri:/ NOUN [plural **MP3s**] a computer file that stores music and recorded speech (**MP3**)

MP3 player /ˌempi:'θri: ˌpleɪə(r)/ NOUN [plural **MP3 players**] a small piece of computer equipment for storing and playing music and recorded speech (**aparelho de MP3**)

mph /ˌempi:'eɪtʃ/ ABBREVIATION miles per hour; a unit for measuring speed □ *The maximum speed on this road is 30 mph.* (**milhas por hora**)

MPV /ˌempi:'vi:/ ABBREVIATION multi-purpose vehicle; a large car that carries more people than a normal car (**minivan**)

Mr /'mɪstə(r)/ NOUN a title used before a man's name □ *My art teacher is called Mr Jackson.* □ *Hello, Mr Rose.* (**abreviação de Mister, senhor**)

MRI /ˌemɑ:'raɪ/ ABBREVIATION magnetic resonance imaging; a system that produces images of the organs inside the body □ *an MRI scan* (**abreviação de ressonância magnética nuclear**)

Mrs /'mɪsɪz/ NOUN a title used before a married woman's name □ *That's my neighbour, Mrs Baker.* □ *Good morning, Mrs Clarke.* (**abreviação de senhora**)

MRSA /ˌemɑ:res'eɪ/ ABBREVIATION methicillin resistant straphylococcus aureus; a type of bacteria that is found in hospitals and that makes people seriously ill (**tipo de bactéria**)

MS /ˌem 'es/ ABBREVIATION **multiple sclerosis** (**abreviação de esclerose múltipla**)

Ms /mɪz, məz/ NOUN a title sometimes used before a woman's name, whether she is married or not □ *Ms Duggan* (**abreviação de senhora ou senhorita**)

much /mʌtʃ/ ▶ DETERMINER, PRONOUN
1 how much used in questions about amounts □ *How much fruit do you eat each day?* □ *The pay depends on how much responsibility you take on.* □ *How much are* (= what is the price) *of these apples?* (**quanto?**)
2 used in negative sentences to say that there is not a large amount of something □ *A few more days won't make much difference.* □ *She doesn't say much.* □ *There isn't much to laugh about.* □ *'Do you have any money?' 'Not much.'* (**muito**)
3 too much (a) more than is wanted, needed or acceptable □ *We bought far too much food.* □ *She has missed too much of the course to do the exam.* □ *We've got too much work.* (b) too difficult, upsetting, etc. for someone to accept or deal with □ *Her rudeness was too much for me, and I burst into tears.* (**demais**)
4 so much used to emphasize the large amount of something □ *I have so much work to do.* □ *Why did you give me so much food?* (**tanto**)
5 as much used to talk about amounts that are as large as something else □ *I hope I can give you as much support as you've given me.* (**tanto quanto**)
6 a lot or a lot of □ *Much of what was said was irrelevant.* □ *There was much laughter coming from the girls' room.* (**muito**)
7 not much of a used to say that something or someone is not good in quality □ *It's not much of a home – more like a shed really.* □ *I'm not much of a musician.* (**não exatamente**)

> ➤ Remember that much is only used with nouns that are not used in the plural:
> ✓ I've eaten too much food.
> ✗ There are too much cars on the road.
> ➤ With nouns that are in the plural, the word many is used: □ How many dogs do they have?

▶ ADVERB
1 often or a lot □ *Do you miss your old school much?* (**muito**) 🔁 *Thanks very much – you've*

been a great help. (muito obrigado) ▪ He doesn't love her *as much* as she loves him. (tanto quanto) ▪ I had to work away from home *too much* in my last job. (demais)

2 used to emphasize comparative adjectives □ He's much taller than his brother. □ She's much more beautiful now she's older. (muito)

muck /mʌk/ NOUN

1 an informal word that means dirt □ You've trodden muck all over the carpet. (sujeira)
2 waste from farm animals □ The farmer was spreading muck on the fields. (esterco)

♦ PHRASAL VERBS [mucks, mucking, mucked] **muck about/around** to behave in a silly way or to waste time. An informal phrase. □ We haven't time to muck about. (vadiar) **muck something up** to do something badly. An informal phrase. □ I mucked up the last paper of the exam. (estragar, fazer de modo errado)

• **mucky** /'mʌki/ ADJECTIVE [muckier, muckiest] an informal word that means dirty □ Get your mucky feet off the sofa! (sujo)

mucus /'mju:kəs/ NOUN, NO PLURAL a thick sticky liquid that is produced by some parts of your body, for example, your nose (muco)

mud /mʌd/ NOUN, NO PLURAL soft wet soil □ His football boots were covered in mud. (lama)

muddle /'mʌdəl/ ▶ NOUN [plural **muddles**] a confused situation or state □ He is in such a muddle financially. (desordem)
▶ VERB [muddles, muddling, muddled] to put things in the wrong order □ She'd muddled all the papers. (desorganizar, atrapalhar)

♦ PHRASAL VERBS **muddle something up** to put things in the wrong order □ Please don't muddle up my revision notes. (desorganizar) **muddle someone/something up** to confuse two things or people with each other □ I often get Klaus muddled up with his brother. (confundir duas coisas ou pessoas)

muddy /'mʌdi/ ADJECTIVE [muddier, muddiest] covered or filled with mud □ The track through the woods was very muddy. □ Take off your muddy boots. (enlameado)

mudguard /'mʌdgɑːd/ NOUN [plural **mudguards**] a curved piece of plastic or metal over the wheel of a bicycle or motorcycle, which stops mud and water from hitting the rider (para-lama)

muesli /'mju:zli/ NOUN, NO PLURAL a mixture of grains, nuts and dried fruit eaten with milk for breakfast □ a bowl of muesli (müsli)

muffin /'mʌfɪn/ NOUN [plural **muffins**]

1 a small cake for one person □ a blueberry muffin (muffin)

2 a small round piece of bread that is cut in two and eaten hot with butter □ toasted muffins (pão inglês arredondado e tostado)

muffle /'mʌfəl/ VERB [muffles, muffling, muffled] to make a sound quieter (abafar)

• **muffled** /'mʌfəld/ ADJECTIVE a muffled sound is not loud or clear □ A muffled scream came from the garden. (abafado)

• **muffler** /'mʌflə(r)/ NOUN [plural **mufflers**] the US word for silencer (silenciador)

mug /mʌg/ ▶ NOUN [plural **mugs**] a cup with straight sides and a handle □ a mug of hot chocolate (caneca)

▶ VERB [mugs, mugging, mugged] to attack someone in a public place and steal their money or something they are carrying □ John was mugged just outside the station. (assaltar)

• **mugger** /'mʌgə(r)/ NOUN [plural **muggers**] someone who mugs people (assaltante)

• **mugging** /'mʌgɪŋ/ NOUN [plural **muggings**] when someone is mugged (assalto)

muggy /'mʌgi/ ADJECTIVE [muggier, muggiest] in muggy weather, the air is hot and slightly wet in a way that is unpleasant (abafado)

mule /mju:l/ NOUN [plural **mules**]

1 an animal that is used to carry heavy things and whose parents are a male donkey and a female horse (mula)

2 a type of woman's shoe with no part to cover the back of your foot (sandália)

mull /mʌl/

♦ PHRASAL VERB [mulls, mulling, mulled] **mull something over** to spend time thinking about something carefully □ I sat down to mull over what she had said. (ponderar sobre alguma coisa)

multi- /'mʌlti/ PREFIX multi- is added to the beginning of words to mean 'many' □ multicultural studies □ a multinational company (multi-)

multicultural /ˌmʌltiˈkʌltʃərəl/ ADJECTIVE involving or including people from many races and religions □ a multicultural society (multicultural)

multilateral /ˌmʌltiˈlætərəl/ ADJECTIVE involving more than two countries or groups □ Both countries have agreed to take part in multilateral talks on the crisis. (multilateral)

multimedia /ˌmʌltiˈmiːdɪə/ ADJECTIVE using sound, images and film in computers □ multimedia content (multimídia)

multinational /ˌmʌltiˈnæʃənəl/ ▶ ADJECTIVE

1 operating in many different countries □ a multinational company (multinacional)
2 with people from many different countries □ a multinational force (multinacional)

▶ NOUN [plural **multinationals**] a big company that operates in many different countries □ He works for one of the big multinationals. (multinacional)

multiple /'mʌltɪpəl/ ▶ ADJECTIVE many □ She suffered multiple injuries in the crash. (múltiplo)
▶ NOUN [plural **multiples**] a number that contains another number an exact number of times. A maths word □ 9 and 12 are multiples of 3. (múltiplo)

multiple-choice /ˌmʌltɪpəl ˈtʃɔɪs/ ADJECTIVE a multiple-choice exam or question gives you different answers from which you choose the answer that you think is correct **(múltipla escolha)**

multiple sclerosis /ˌmʌltɪpəl skləˈrəʊsɪs/ NOUN, NO PLURAL a serious illness that gradually stops a person from being able to walk and speak **(esclerose múltipla)**

multiplex /ˈmʌltɪpleks/ NOUN [plural **multiplexes**] a large cinema with many rooms for showing different films at the same time **(multiplex)**

multiplication /ˌmʌltɪplɪˈkeɪʃən/ NOUN, NO PLURAL the process of multiplying one number by another. A maths word. **(multiplicação)**
• **multiply** /ˈmʌltɪplaɪ/ VERB [**multiplies, multiplying, multiplied**]
1 to increase a number by adding it to itself a particular number of times. A maths word ☐ *13 multiplied by 3 is 39.* **(multiplicar)**
2 to increase or make something increase by a large amount ☐ *The number of coffee bars on our high streets has multiplied in recent years.* **(multiplicar)**

multiracial /ˌmʌltɪˈreɪʃəl/ ADJECTIVE involving or including people from many races ☐ *Britain is a multiracial society.* **(multirracial)**

multi-storey /ˌmʌltɪˈstɔːri/ ADJECTIVE a multi-storey building has a lot of floors ☐ *a multi-storey car park* **(de vários andares)**

multitasking /ˈmʌltɪˌtɑːskɪŋ/ NOUN, NO PLURAL when you do many things at the same time ☐ *Multitasking is a normal feature of office life.* **(realização simultânea de váreas tarefas)**

multitude /ˈmʌltɪtjuːd/ NOUN a **multitude of something** a very large number of something. A formal phrase. ☐ *The new system has introduced a whole multitude of problems.* **(multidão)**

mum /mʌm/ NOUN [plural **mums**] an informal word for mother ☐ *Can I have another cake, Mum?* ☐ *How's your mum?* **(mamãe)**

mumble /ˈmʌmbəl/ VERB [**mumbles, mumbling, mumbled**] to speak quietly or without opening your mouth enough, so that people cannot understand you ☐ *He mumbled something about not having enough money.* **(resmungar)**

mummy /ˈmʌmi/ NOUN [plural **mummies**]
1 a child's word for mother ☐ *Mummy, can we go now?* ☐ *Where's your mummy, Jake?* **(mamãe)**
2 a dead body that is rubbed with special substances and covered with cloth to stop it decaying ☐ *an Egyptian mummy* **(múmia)**

mumps /mʌmps/ NOUN, NO PLURAL an infectious disease that children get, in which the neck becomes swollen and sore **(caxumba)**

munch /mʌntʃ/ VERB [**munches, munching, munched**] to eat something, especially noisily ☐ *Claire was happily munching her chocolate bar.* **(mastigar)**

mundane /mʌnˈdeɪn/ ADJECTIVE ordinary, happening often, and not exciting ☐ *mundane tasks* **(mundano)**

municipal /mjuːˈnɪsɪpəl/ ADJECTIVE to do with a city or town and its local government ☐ *the municipal elections* **(municipal)**

munitions /mjuːˈnɪʃənz/ PLURAL NOUN weapons and military equipment ☐ *a munitions factory* **(munição)**

mural /ˈmjʊərəl/ NOUN [plural **murals**] a picture that is painted directly onto a wall **(mural)**

murder /ˈmɜːdə(r)/ ▶ NOUN [plural **murders**] the crime of killing someone deliberately **(assassinato, homicídio)** ☐ *He admitted committing the murder.* ☐ *He was charged with attempted murder* (= trying to kill someone). **(tentativa de homicídio)**
▶ VERB [**murders, murdering, murdered**] to kill someone deliberately ☐ *She denies murdering her husband.* **(assassinar)**
• **murderer** /ˈmɜːdərə(r)/ NOUN [plural **murderers**] someone who has murdered another person **(assassino)**
• **murderous** /ˈmɜːdərəs/ ADJECTIVE likely or intended to kill someone ☐ *a murderous attack* **(assassino)**

murky /ˈmɜːki/ ADJECTIVE [**murkier, murkiest**]
1 dark or dirty and difficult to see through ☐ *murky pond water* **(obscuro)**
2 dishonest and secret ☐ *the murky world of arms dealing* **(desonesto)**

murmur /ˈmɜːmə(r)/ ▶ VERB [**murmurs, murmuring, murmured**] to speak very quietly ☐ *He murmured something in her ear.* **(sussurrar)**
▶ NOUN [plural **murmurs**]
1 something that is said very quietly **(sussurro)**
2 a low, continuous noise made by voices or sounds far away ☐ *We could hear the murmur of traffic in the distance.* **(murmúrio)**

muscle /ˈmʌsəl/ NOUN [plural **muscles**] one of the parts in the body that are connected to bones and that cause the body to move by becoming shorter or longer ☐ *stomach muscles* **(músculo)** ☐ *Joe has pulled a muscle* (= injured the muscle) *in his leg.* **(rompeu um músculo)**
◆ PHRASAL VERB [**muscles, muscling, muscled**] **muscle in** to get involved in an activity that the people doing it do not want you to be involved in ☐ *Jane's trying to muscle in on the book club now.* **(intrometer-se)**
• **muscular** /ˈmʌskjʊlə(r)/ ADJECTIVE
1 having big, strong muscles ☐ *muscular arms* **(musculoso)**
2 to do with the muscles ☐ *muscular pain* **(muscular)**

museum /mjuːˈziːəm/ NOUN [plural **museums**] a building where collections of interesting things are arranged for people to see □ *the Natural History Museum* (museu)

mush /mʌʃ/ NOUN, NO PLURAL food that is soft and wet □ *Don't overcook the vegetables or they'll turn to mush.* (papa, mingau)

mushroom /ˈmʌʃrʊm/ ▶ NOUN [*plural* **mushrooms**] a type of fungus (= plant with no leaves or flowers) that you can eat, with a stem and a flat or round top □ *mushroom risotto* (cogumelo)
▶ VERB [**mushrooms, mushrooming, mushroomed**] to increase in size or number very quickly □ *The use of mobile phones has mushroomed over the past decade.* (crescer como cogumelo)

mushy /ˈmʌʃi/ ADJECTIVE [**mushier, mushiest**]
1 soft and wet (semelhante a um mingau)
2 too romantic or emotional in a way that seems silly □ *mushy love songs* (piegas)

music /ˈmjuːzɪk/ NOUN, NO PLURAL
1 sounds arranged in patterns, sung or played by instruments (música) 🔊 *Do you like classical music?* (música clássica) 🔊 *I've been listening to a lot of dance music recently.* (ouvindo música) □ *a music teacher*
2 the written sounds that represent a piece of music (música) 🔊 *I wish I could read music.* (interpretar música)

> ➤ Remember that the noun *music* is not used in the plural:
> ✓ *He listens to a lot of music.*
> ✗ *He listens to a lot of musics.*

• **musical** /ˈmjuːzɪkəl/ c ADJECTIVE
1 to do with music □ *She has no musical training.* (musical) 🔊 *Do you play a musical instrument?* (instrumento musical)
2 good at playing or singing music □ *The whole family is very musical.* (musical)
3 having a sound that is pleasant to listen to □ *a musical voice* (musical)
▶ NOUN [*plural* **musicals**] a play or film in which there is a lot of singing and dancing □ *He loves all the old Hollywood musicals.* (musical)
• **musician** /mjuːˈzɪʃən/ NOUN [*plural* **musicians**] someone who plays a musical instrument □ *She's one of our most talented young musicians.* (músico)

Muslim /ˈmʊzlɪm/ *or* **Moslem** /ˈmɒzləm/
▶ NOUN [*plural* **Muslims** *or* **Moslems**] someone who believes in Islam (muçulmano)
▶ ADJECTIVE to do with Islam □ *Friday is the Muslim holy day.*

muslin /ˈmʌzlɪn/ NOUN, NO PLURAL a thin cotton cloth (musselina)

mussel /ˈmʌsəl/ NOUN [*plural* **mussels**] a small sea creature that has two joined black oval shells and can be eaten (mexilhão)

must /məs, məst, stressed mʌst/ MODAL VERB
1 used to say that something is necessary □ *You must arrive for your interview on time.* □ *We mustn't be late.* (precisar)
2 used to say that you think something is true □ *You must be very tired after such a long journey.* □ *They must have known about the money.* (dever)
3 used to make an offer or a suggestion □ *You must come over for dinner.* □ *We must meet up soon.* (dever)
4 used to say that you intend to do something □ *I must phone my mother this evening.* (dever, ter de)

mustache /ˈmʌstæʃ/ NOUN [*plural* **mustaches**] an American spelling of **moustache** (bigode)

mustard /ˈmʌstəd/ NOUN, NO PLURAL a cold yellow or brown sauce used to give food a hot taste (mostarda)

muster /ˈmʌstə(r)/ VERB [**musters, mustering, mustered**] to feel or make other people feel enough courage, enthusiasm or energy to do something □ *I'm trying to muster up the energy to go out.* (juntar forças, criar coragem, encorajar)

mustn't /ˈmʌsənt/ a short way to say and write must not □ *I mustn't forget.* (forma negativa e abreviada de *must*)

> ➤ Note that *mustn't* means it is necessary not to do something. To say that it is not necessary to do something, use *don't need/ have to*:
> ✓ *Come if you like but you don't need to.*
> ✗ *Come if you like but you mustn't to.*

musty /ˈmʌsti/ ADJECTIVE [**mustier, mustiest**] having a slightly wet, unpleasant smell □ *a musty old library* (bolorento)

mutate /mjuːˈteɪt/ VERB [**mutates, mutating, mutated**] when living things mutate, their genes (= parts that control characteristics) change so they develop a different form. A biology word. (mutar)
• **mutation** /mjuːˈteɪʃən/ NOUN [*plural* **mutations**] when a living thing mutates. A biology word. (mutação)

mute /mjuːt/ ADJECTIVE not speaking or not able to speak (mudo)
• **muted** /ˈmjuːtɪd/ ADJECTIVE
1 not bright or loud □ *The room was tastefully decorated in muted colours.* □ *We could hear muted voices outside.* (de baixa intensidade ou volume)
2 not showing strong feelings □ *He gave a cautious and slightly muted response.* (calado)

mutilate /ˈmjuːtɪleɪt/ VERB [**mutilates, mutilating, mutilated**] to damage someone's body badly, especially by cutting off a part of it □ *a mutilated body* (mutilar)
• **mutilation** /ˌmjuːtɪˈleɪʃən/ NOUN, NO PLURAL when a body is mutilated (mutilação)

mutiny 513 myth

mutiny /ˈmjuːtɪni/ ▶ NOUN [plural **mutinies**] when a group of people refuses to obey someone in authority, especially when sailors on a ship refuse to obey orders (**motim**)
▶ VERB [**mutinies, mutinying, mutinied**] to refuse to obey the orders of someone in authority ▫ *The crew mutinied against the captain.* (**amotinar-se**)

mutter /ˈmʌtə(r)/ VERB [**mutters, muttering, muttered**] to speak quietly, often when you are complaining ▫ *He muttered something about people never listening to him.* (**murmurar**)

mutton /ˈmʌtən/ NOUN, NO PLURAL meat from an adult sheep (**carne de carneiro**)

mutual /ˈmjuːtʃuəl/ ADJECTIVE
1 a mutual feeling is one that two or more people feel for each other ▫ *mutual admiration* ▫ *It's a relationship based on mutual respect.* (**mútuo, recíproco**) ▣ *I don't like Maria and I'm sure the feeling's mutual.* (**o sentimento é recíproco**)
2 shared by two people ▫ *Peter and Ahmed have a mutual friend who works at the library.* (**mútuo**)
• **mutually** /ˈmjuːtʃuəli/ ADVERB relating to both sides in a situation ▫ *We hope to come to a mutually acceptable agreement.* (**mutuamente, reciprocamente**)

muzzle /ˈmʌzəl/ ▶ NOUN [plural **muzzles**]
1 the nose and mouth of an animal such as a dog (**focinho**)
2 a cover put over a dog's nose and mouth to stop it biting people (**focinheira**)
3 the open end of a gun, where the bullet comes out (**broca**)
▶ VERB [**muzzles, muzzling, muzzled**]
1 to put a muzzle on a dog (**pôr focinheira**)
2 to stop someone from saying what they want to say (**calar alguém**)

my /maɪ/ DETERMINER belonging to or to do with me ▫ *There's my son.* ▫ *Have you seen my boots anywhere?* (**meu, minha, meus, minhas**)

myriad /ˈmɪriəd/ ▶ NOUN **a myriad of something** a formal word meaning a very large number of things ▫ *We have a myriad of options now at the supermarket.* (**imensa quantidade**)
▶ ADJECTIVE a formal word meaning very many ▫ *society's myriad problems* (**incontáveis**)

myself /maɪˈself/ PRONOUN
1 the reflexive form of I ▫ *I was washing myself.* ▫ *I cut myself on the glass.* ▫ *I felt really proud of myself.* (**eu mesmo, de mim mesmo**)
2 used to show that you do something without any help from other people ▫ *I suppose I'll have to do it myself if no one else can be bothered.* (**eu mesmo**) ▣ *I can't take care of him all by myself.* (**sozinho**)
3 used to emphasize the pronoun I ▫ *I have not seen the film myself.* (**eu mesmo**)

4 by myself not with or near other people ▫ *I live by myself.* (**sozinho**)
5 to myself without having to share with anyone else ▫ *I had the whole swimming pool to myself.* (**só para mim**)

mysterious /mɪˈstɪəriəs/ ADJECTIVE
1 strange and difficult to understand or explain (**misterioso**) ▣ *He died in mysterious circumstances.* (**circunstâncias misteriosas**) ▫ *No one knows why she left – it's very mysterious.*
2 keeping something secret ▫ *Why are you being so mysterious about where you went last night?* (**misterioso**)
• **mysteriously** /mɪˈstɪəriəsli/ ADVERB in a mysterious way ▫ *Both documents disappeared mysteriously one evening.* (**misteriosamente**)
• **mystery** /ˈmɪstəri/ NOUN [plural **mysteries**]
1 something strange which you do not understand and which cannot be explained (**mistério**) ▣ *She set out to solve the mystery of his disappearance.* (**solucionar o mistério**) ▣ *What happened to her remains a mystery.* (**continua a ser um mistério**)
2 no plural the quality of being strange, interesting and not completely understood (**mistério**) ▣ *She has an air of mystery about her.* (**um ar de mistério**)
3 a film, book etc. with a story in which strange events are not explained until the end (**mistério**) ▣ *a murder mystery* (**mistério de assassinato**)

mystic /ˈmɪstɪk/ NOUN [plural **mystics**] someone who tries to understand things to do with religion or the spirit by praying or meditating (= removing all thoughts from the mind) (**místico**)
• **mystical** /ˈmɪstɪkəl/ ADJECTIVE
1 to do with mystics (**místico**)
2 involving magical or religious powers (**místico**)

mystify /ˈmɪstɪfaɪ/ VERB [**mystifies, mystifying, mystified**] if you are mystified by something, you do not understand or cannot explain it ▫ *Doctors were mystified by her symptoms.* ▫ *Helena looked mystified.* (**ficar/deixar perplexo**)

myth /mɪθ/ NOUN [plural **myths**]
1 a story about ancient gods, heroes (= brave people) and monsters (= frightening creatures) ▫ *Greek and Roman myths* (**mito**)
2 something that many people believe, but which is not true (**mito**) ▣ *The study dispels the myth* (= proves the myth wrong) *that late-night eating causes weight gain.* (**destruir o mito**)
• **mythical** /ˈmɪθɪkəl/ ADJECTIVE existing only in myths ▫ *mythical creatures like dragons and unicorns* (**mítico**)
• **mythological** /ˌmɪθəˈlɒdʒɪkəl/ ADJECTIVE to do with myth or mythology (**mitológico**)
• **mythology** /mɪˈθɒlədʒi/ NOUN, NO PLURAL stories about ancient gods and heroes (= brave people) (**mitologia**)

N*n*

N¹ or **n** /en/ the 14th letter of the alphabet (**a décima quarta letra do alfabeto**)

N² /en/ ABBREVIATION north (**abreviação de Norte**)

n/a /ˌen ˈeɪ/ ABBREVIATION not applicable; something you write on a form when it asks a question that you do not need to answer (**sigla: nenhuma alternativa correta**)

nab /næb/ VERB [**nabs, nabbing, nabbed**]
1 an informal word meaning to take something quickly □ *The best seats had all been nabbed when we arrived.* (**agarrar**)
2 an informal word meaning to catch someone who has done something wrong □ *The police nabbed me parking on a yellow line.* (**flagrar**)

naff /næf/ ADJECTIVE [**naffer, naffest**] an informal word meaning not good or not fashionable □ *a rather naff website* (**inferior, de mau gosto**)

nag /næɡ/ VERB [**nags, nagging, nagged**]
1 to keep criticizing someone or complaining because they have not done something □ *I keep nagging him to go to the dentist's.* (**aborrecer**)
2 if worry or doubts nag you, you cannot stop thinking about them □ *The thought that he might not contact me has been nagging at the back of my mind.* (**atormentar**)
• **nagging** /ˈnæɡɪŋ/ ADJECTIVE causing you worry or pain for a long time □ *I had nagging doubts about the safety of the expedition.* (**preocupante**)

nail /neɪl/ ▶ NOUN [plural **nails**]
1 the hard covering on top of the ends of your fingers and toes □ *You need to cut your nails.* (**cortar as unhas**) □ *a pair of nail scissors* (**cortador de unhas**)
2 a thin pointed piece of metal, used to join things together, especially pieces of wood (**prego**)
▶ VERB [**nails, nailing, nailed**] to attach or join something with a nail or nails □ *Nail the number on the door.* (**pregar**)

naïve /naɪˈiːv/ ADJECTIVE too ready to trust other people because of not having much experience of life □ *He had taken advantage of her naïve belief in his honesty.* (**ingênuo**)
• **naïvely** /naɪˈiːvlɪ/ ADVERB in a naïve way □ *I naïvely thought that he really loved me.* (**ingenuamente**)

naked /ˈneɪkɪd/ ADJECTIVE
1 not wearing any clothes □ *He stripped naked to the waist to cut the grass.* (**nu**) □ *The children were running around stark naked in the sun.* (**completamente nu**)
2 not covered or protected □ *a naked flame* □ *a naked light bulb* (**desprotegido**)
3 a naked feeling or emotion is not hidden although it may be shocking □ *There was naked hostility in his eyes.* (**exposto**)
4 the naked eye if you can see something with the naked eye, you can see it without the help of any special equipment □ *House mites are too small to be seen with the naked eye.* (**olho nu**)

name /neɪm/ ▶ NOUN [plural **names**] (**nome**)
1 the word or words that you use to refer to a person, animal, place or thing □ *What's your name?* □ *Write your name and address here.* (**nome e endereço**) □ *I can't remember the name of the street.* □ *She changed her name when she got married.*
2 by name using your name □ *He asked for you by name.* (**pelo nome**)
3 the reputation that a person or an organization has (**fama**) □ *The company has a name for quality.* □ *He made his name as an international footballer* (**fazer o nome**). □ *This kind of behaviour gives football fans a bad name* (**causar má fama**). □ *He is going to court to try to clear his name* (= prove that bad things that have been said about him are not true) (**limpar o nome**)
4 in the name of something if something is done in the name of something, it is done to help that thing be successful □ *Many wars have been fought in the name of religion.* □ *He led 15 Arctic expeditions in the name of science.* (**em nome de**)
▶ VERB [**names, naming, named**]
1 to give someone or something a name □ *They've named their son Samuel.* □ *The ship has not been named yet.* (**nomear**)
2 to say what the name of someone or something is □ *The dead men will not be named until their families have been informed.* (**nomear**)
3 to choose someone for a job or a position in an organization □ **+ as** *She was named as the next chief executive.* (**nomear**)

> ➤ Note that to **name** someone is to give someone (often a baby) or something a name. To say the name of someone or something, use **be called**:
> ✓ *She is called Justina.*
> ✗ *She is named Justina.*

namely

♦ PHRASAL VERB **name someone after someone** to give someone the same name as someone else to show respect or love for that person ☐ *She was named after her grandmother.*

• **nameless** /ˈneɪmləs/ ADJECTIVE
1 with no name, or with a name that is not known ☐ *a nameless soldier* (**sem nome**)
2 with a name that is not given (**anônimo**) 🔂 *A person who shall remain nameless has eaten all the chocolate.* (**continuar anônimo**)

namely /ˈneɪmli/ ADVERB used to give more detail about what you have just mentioned ☐ *Two of our members, namely the Grimes brothers, have won medals this term.* (**isto é**)

namesake /ˈneɪmseɪk/ NOUN [*plural* **namesakes**] someone who has the same name as you (**homônimo**)

nanny /ˈnæni/ NOUN [*plural* **nannies**] a person whose job is to look after someone's child or children, usually in their own home (**babá, ama**)

nano- /ˈnænəʊ/ PREFIX nano- is added to the beginning of words from an 'extremely small' ☐ *nano-technology* (**nano-**)

nap /næp/ ▶ NOUN [*plural* **naps**] a short sleep during the day 🔂 *The baby usually has a nap in the afternoon.* (**soneca**)

▶ VERB [**naps, napping, napped**] to have a nap (**tirar uma soneca**)

nape /neɪp/ NOUN [*plural* **napes**] the back of your neck (**nuca**)

napkin /ˈnæpkɪn/ NOUN [*plural* **napkins**] a piece of cloth or paper that you can use during a meal to protect your clothes or clean your mouth or fingers ☐ *white linen napkins* (**guardanapo**)

nappy /ˈnæpi/ NOUN [*plural* **nappies**] a thick piece of soft cloth or paper that you fasten around a baby's bottom (**fralda**) 🔂 *Could you change the baby's nappy?* (**trocar a fralda**)

narcotic /nɑːˈkɒtɪk/ ▶ NOUN [*plural* **narcotics**]
1 any illegal drug (**qualquer tipo de droga**)
2 a drug that makes you want to sleep or stops you feeling pain (**narcótico**)

▶ ADJECTIVE making you want to sleep or feel less pain ☐ *Alcohol can have a narcotic effect.* (**narcótico**)

narrate /nəˈreɪt/ VERB [**narrates, narrating, narrated**] to speak the words of a story ☐ *The story was narrated by Stephen Fry.* (**narrar**)

• **narration** /nəˈreɪʃən/ NOUN [*plural* **narrations**] the process of speaking the words of a story (**narração**)

• **narrative** /ˈnærətɪv/ NOUN [*plural* **narratives**] a story or a description of events ☐ *Too much description slows down the narrative.* (**narrativa**)

• **narrator** /nəˈreɪtə(r)/ NOUN [*plural* **narrators**] the person who speaks the words of a story (**narrador**)

nationalism

narrow /ˈnærəʊ/ ▶ ADJECTIVE [**narrower, narrowest**]
1 not very wide ☐ *She found a narrow door in the garden wall.* ☐ *The road was too narrow for overtaking.* (**estreito**)
2 only just achieved (**apertado**) ☐ *The Democrats won by a narrow margin.* 🔂 *We had a narrow escape when our car went off the road* (**escapamos por pouco**)
3 limited in range ☐ *We have a narrow range of options.* (**estreito**)

▶ VERB [**narrows, narrowing, narrowed**] to become narrower or to make something narrower ☐ *The road narrows as you leave the village.* (**estreitar-se**)

♦ PHRASAL VERB **narrow something down** to reduce the number of possibilities ☐ *We've narrowed the candidates down to three.* (**reduzir**)

• **narrowly** /ˈnærəʊli/ ADVERB by a small amount ☐ *United were narrowly defeated by 6 goals to 5.* ☐ *The bullet narrowly missed his heart.* (**por um triz**)

narrow-minded /ˌnærəʊˈmaɪndɪd/ ADJECTIVE not willing to accept new ideas or other people's opinions (**tacanho**)

nasal /ˈneɪzəl/ ADJECTIVE to do with the nose ☐ *a nasal spray* (**nasal**)

nastiness /ˈnɑːstɪnəs/ NOUN, NO PLURAL being nasty (**ruindade**)

nasty /ˈnɑːsti/ ADJECTIVE [**nastier, nastiest**]
1 very unpleasant or unkind ☐ *The drug left a nasty taste in my mouth.* ☐ *He's always saying nasty things about everybody.* (**desagradável**)
2 serious ☐ *a nasty accident* (**sério**)

nation /ˈneɪʃən/ NOUN [*plural* **nations**]
1 a country with its own government ☐ *the African nations* (**nação**)
2 the people of a country ☐ *Today the nation is voting for a new government.* (**povo**)

• **national** /ˈnæʃənəl/ ▶ ADJECTIVE (**nacional**)
1 to do with the whole of a country ☐ *They report local, national and international news.* 🔂 *National security is a priority.* (**segurança nacional**) 🔂 *House prices in the south-east are well above the national average.* (**média nacional**)
2 typical of a particular country ☐ *Paella is the national dish of Spain.* ☐ *Dancers in national costume greeted the president.* (**nacional**)

▶ NOUN [*plural* **nationals**] someone who officially lives in a particular country ☐ *UK nationals require a visa to visit China.* (**cidadão**)

national anthem /ˌnæʃənəl ˈænθəm/ NOUN [*plural* **national anthems**] the official song of a country (**hino nacional**)

nationalism /ˈnæʃənəlɪzəm/ NOUN, NO PLURAL
1 the belief that the people of a country should have their own government ☐ *Irish nationalism* (**nacionalismo**)

2 a great love for your own country (nacionalismo)

• **nationalist** /ˈnæʃənəlɪst/ ▶ NOUN [plural **nationalists**]

1 someone who wants their country to have its own government □ *Scottish nationalists* (nacionalista)

2 someone with a great love for their own country (nacionalista)

▶ ADJECTIVE wanting your country to have its own government □ *nationalist beliefs* (nacionalista)

nationality /ˌnæʃəˈnælətɪ/ NOUN [plural **nationalities**] the state of being a legal member of a particular country □ *Omar has British nationality.* (nacionalidade) 🔂 *Louis has dual nationality because his mother is French and his father is American.* (dupla nacionalidade)

nationalize or **nationalise** /ˈnæʃənəlaɪz/ VERB [**nationalizes, nationalizing, nationalized**] if an industry or company is nationalized, the government takes control of it □ *In Britain the railways were nationalized for years.* (nacionalizar)

national park /ˌnæʃənəl ˈpɑːk/ NOUN [plural **national parks**] an area of countryside that the government protects so that the public can enjoy it (parque nacional)

national service /ˌnæʃənəl ˈsɜːvɪs/ NOUN, NO PLURAL a period of time that young people have to spend in the army in some countries □ *He did his national service in Northern Greece.* (serviço militar)

nationwide /ˌneɪʃənˈwaɪd/ ADJECTIVE, ADVERB in every part of a country □ *The party is planning a nationwide drive to crack down on crime.* □ *The scheme will be launched nationwide next year.* (por todo o país)

native /ˈneɪtɪv/ ▶ ADJECTIVE

1 to do with the place you were born in □ *His native language is French.* □ *In 1965 he left his native Austria.* (natal)

2 to do with the first people who lived in a place □ *the native inhabitants of New Zealand* □ *native art* (nativo)

3 native animals and plants live or grow naturally in a place and were not brought there from another place □ *These plants are native to the west coast.* (nativo)

▶ NOUN [plural **natives**] someone who was born in a particular place □ *She's a native of New South Wales.* (nativo)

Native American /ˌneɪtɪv əˈmerɪkən/ NOUN [plural **Native Americans**] a person from the race of people who lived in North or South America before the Europeans arrived there (americano nativo)

NATO /ˈneɪtəʊ/ ABBREVIATION North Atlantic Treaty Organization; an organization of North American and European countries that give each other military support (OTAN – Organização do Tratado do Atlântico Norte)

natter /ˈnætə(r)/ ▶ VERB [**natters, nattering, nattered**] an informal word meaning to talk with someone about things that are not important □ *We left them nattering about the wedding.* (tagarelar, "bater papo")

▶ NOUN, NO PLURAL an informal word meaning a conversation about things that are not important 🔂 *They were having a natter about last night's match.* (papo, conversa sem compromisso)

natural /ˈnætʃərəl/ ADJECTIVE

1 to do with or made by nature, not by people or machines □ *the natural world* □ *an area of outstanding natural beauty* (natural) 🔂 *An earthquake is an example of a natural disaster.* (desastre natural) 🔂 *The old man had died of natural causes.* (causas naturais)

2 normal or to be expected □ *It's only natural to be a little nervous before a test.* (natural)

3 a natural characteristic or ability is something you have from when you are born □ *She has a natural flair for languages.* □ *His hair has a natural curl.* (natural)

natural gas /ˌnætʃərəl ˈgæs/ NOUN, NO PLURAL gas that comes from under the ground and can be used for heating and cooking (gás natural)

natural history /ˌnætʃərəl ˈhɪstərɪ/ NOUN, NO PLURAL the study of plants and animals (história natural)

naturalist /ˈnætʃərəlɪst/ NOUN [plural **naturalists**] someone who studies plants and animals (naturalista)

naturalize or **naturalise** /ˈnætʃərəlaɪz/ VERB [**naturalizes, naturalizing, naturalized**] (naturalizar) **be naturalized** to become an official member of a country you were not born in (naturalizado)

naturally /ˈnætʃərəlɪ/ ADVERB

1 as would be expected □ *Naturally, we were annoyed not to win.* (naturalmente)

2 in a way that is normal □ *Joe began to relax and act a bit more naturally.* (naturalmente)

3 having been born with a particular characteristic □ *She has a naturally bubbly personality.* (naturalmente)

4 without help from anything artificial □ *Let the skin heal naturally.* (naturalmente)

natural resources /ˌnætʃərəl rɪˈsɔːsɪz/ PLURAL NOUN substances that people use and that exist naturally, like wood, oil and water (recursos naturais)

natural selection /ˌnætʃərəl sɪˈlekʃən/ NOUN, NO PLURAL the way that plants and animals that are strong and suitable for the place where they live have more young and live longer than others. A biology word. (seleção natural)

nature /ˈneɪtʃə(r)/ NOUN [plural **natures**]
1 no plural everything in the world that was not made or changed by people, such as animals, trees, the sea, etc. □ *I love watching programmes about nature.* □ *the forces of nature* (**natureza**)
2 a person's character or qualities ▣ *It's human nature to protect one's family.* (**natureza humana**) ▣ *It's not in her nature to be unkind.* (**em sua natureza**)
3 the type of a particular thing □ *What is the nature of your complaint?* ▣ *I like crime novels and books of that nature.* (**dessa natureza**)

> Note that **nature** (sense 1) is never used with **the**:
> ✓ *I've always loved nature.*
> ✗ *I've always loved the nature.*

nature reserve /ˈneɪtʃə rɪˌzɜːv/ NOUN [plural **nature reserves**] an area of land where plants and animals are protected (**reserva natural**)

naughtiness /ˈnɔːtɪnɪs/ NOUN, NO PLURAL bad behaviour or not doing what you are told to do (**desobediência**)

naughty /ˈnɔːti/ ADJECTIVE [**naughtier, naughtiest**] behaving badly or not doing what you are told to do □ *You've been a very naughty little boy.* (**malcriação**)

nausea /ˈnɔːziə/ NOUN, NO PLURAL the feeling that you are going to vomit □ *The drug may cause nausea in some patients.* (**náusea**)

• **nauseating** /ˈnɔːzieɪtɪŋ/ ADJECTIVE making you feel as if you are going to vomit □ *a nauseating smell* (**nauseante**)

• **nauseous** /ˈnɔːziəs/ ADJECTIVE feeling as if you are going to vomit (**nauseado**)

nautical /ˈnɔːtɪkəl/ ADJECTIVE to do with ships, sailors and the sea □ *The pub has a nautical theme.* (**náutico**)

naval /ˈneɪvəl/ ADJECTIVE to do with the navy □ *an important naval base* (**naval**)

navel /ˈneɪvəl/ NOUN [plural **navels**] the small hollow in the centre of your stomach where you were connected to your mother before you were born (**umbigo**)

navigate /ˈnævɪgeɪt/ VERB [**navigates, navigating, navigated**]
1 to use a map or other equipment to find your way somewhere in a vehicle □ *My mother always drove and my father had to navigate.* (**navegar**)
2 to find your way around or through a difficult place □ *There were several flights of stairs to navigate with our luggage.* (**percorrer**)
3 to deal with a complicated system or situation □ *We had to navigate the legal system.* (**lidar, navegar**)

• **navigation** /ˌnævɪˈgeɪʃən/ NOUN, NO PLURAL
1 the process of using maps or other equipment to find your way somewhere (**navegação**)
2 when ships or aircraft travel on a journey (**navegação**)
3 a way to understand and use a complicated system □ *The website has clear navigation tools.* (**navegação**)

• **navigator** /ˈnævɪgeɪtə(r)/ NOUN [plural **navigators**] someone who navigates in a vehicle (**piloto, navegador**)

navy /ˈneɪvi/ NOUN [plural **navies**]
1 the navy military ships and the soldiers that work on them (**marinha**) ▣ *Matt is hoping to join the navy.* (**se alistar na marinha**)
2 a very dark blue colour (**azul-marinho**)

• **navy** /ˈneɪvi/ ADJECTIVE of a very dark blue colour □ *a navy jacket* (**azul-marinho**)

navy blue /ˌneɪvi ˈbluː/ ▶ NOUN, NO PLURAL a very dark blue colour

▶ ADJECTIVE of a very dark blue colour □ *navy blue trousers* (**azul-marinho**)

NB /ˌen ˈbiː/ ABBREVIATION written at the start of a sentence to make someone pay particular attention to it □ *NB Latecomers will not be admitted.* (**nota bene = note bem**)

near /nɪə(r)/ ▶ PREPOSITION, ADVERB [**nearer, nearest**]
1 a short distance away □ *I live quite near Tom.* □ **+ to** *We rented a house near to the beach.* □ *Stand a little nearer and you'll be able to see better.* □ *They took him to the nearest hospital.* (**perto**)
2 a short time in the future □ *I don't want to take on extra work so near my exams.* ▣ *It's a bit early to plan the food – let's talk about it nearer the time.* (**próximo**)
3 nowhere near not at all close in distance, time or a quality □ *The station is nowhere near here.* □ *He's nowhere near as handsome as his brother.* (**próximo**)
4 near to something close to having achieved something or finished something □ *We're near to completing the plans for our journey.* (**perto de**)
5 close to an amount or level □ *Their estimate was near our budget of £2 million.* □ *Temperatures were near freezing point.* (**próximo**)
6 almost □ *It's near impossible to see that it's a fake.* □ *Her performance was near perfect.* (**quase**)
7 almost in a particular state □ *Sarah was near tears.* (**quase**)

▶ ADJECTIVE [**nearer, nearest**] not far away in distance or time (**próximo**) ▣ *Will you be seeing Kate in the near future?* □ *He is a near neighbour of mine.* □ *The ball struck the near post.* (**futuro próximo**)

▶ VERB [**nears, nearing, neared**] to come close to something in distance or time □ *As we neared the building, the faces at the window became clearer.* □ *The building work is nearing completion.* □ *She is nearing the end of her time as president.* (**aproximar-se, chegar perto**)

nearby /ˌnɪəˈbaɪ/ ADJECTIVE, ADVERB quite close to where you are or the place you are talking about □ *We went to a nearby restaurant for dinner.* □ *Is there a bank nearby?* (**perto**)

> Note that **nearby** is not a preposition. The preposition with the same meaning is **near**:
> ✓ *Their apartment is very near the office.*
> ✗ *Their apartment is very nearby the office.*

nearly /ˈnɪəli/ ADVERB almost but not completely □ *We're nearly there.* □ *Nearly everyone had a good time.* □ *They've lived there for nearly three years.* (**quase**)

neat /niːt/ ADJECTIVE [**neater, neatest**]
1 tidy and arranged carefully □ *Your handwriting's very neat.* (**arrumado**) *Anna always keeps her room neat and tidy.* (**limpo e arrumado**)
2 done in a clever or skilful way □ *Rooney scored with a neat shot into the corner of the goal.* (**correto, preciso**)
3 a neat alcoholic drink is not mixed with another liquid □ *She was drinking neat whisky.* (**puro**)
4 a US word for good or nice □ *What a neat car!* (**ótimo**)
▶ **neatly** /ˈniːtli/ ADVERB in a tidy way □ *The papers were stacked neatly in the corner.* (**caprichosamente**)

necessarily /ˌnesəˈserɪli/ ADVERB **not necessarily** not in every case □ *Men aren't necessarily stronger than women.* (**necessariamente**)

necessary /ˈnesəsəri/ ADJECTIVE needed in order to do something, get something or make something happen □ *The website lists the necessary skills for each job.* (**necessário**) *I can work late if necessary.* (**se necessário**) □ **+ to do something** *Is it necessary to come early?* □ **+ for** *Good English is necessary for this job.*

necessitate /nɪˈsesɪteɪt/ VERB [**necessitates, necessitating, necessitated**] a formal word meaning to make something necessary □ *A manufacturer's fault necessitated the recall of the toys.* (**requerer, tornar necessário**)

necessity /nɪˈsesɪti/ NOUN [plural **necessities**]
1 the need for something □ *There's absolutely no necessity for you to stay.* (**necessidade**) *She went back to work out of necessity.* (**sem necessidade**)
2 something that is needed □ *A warm coat is a necessity in this weather.* (**necessidade**)

neck /nek/ NOUN [plural **necks**]
1 the part of your body between your head and your shoulders □ *She had her headphones slung around her neck.* (**pescoço**)
2 the opening in a piece of clothing that you put your head through □ *This T-shirt is too baggy around the neck.* (**gola**)
3 the narrow part of a bottle near its opening (**gargalo**)

◆ IDIOMS **be up to your neck (in something)** to be very busy □ *Sue's up to her neck in work this week* (**estar até o pescoço**). **neck and neck** if two people in a race or competition are neck and neck they are level with each other and either of them could win (**cabeça com cabeça**)
▶ go to **stick your neck out**

necklace /ˈneklɪs/ NOUN [plural **necklaces**] a piece of jewellery you wear around your neck □ *a diamond necklace navy* (**colar**)

nectar /ˈnektə(r)/ NOUN, NO PLURAL the sweet liquid that bees collect from flowers to make honey. A biology word. (**nectar**)

nectarine /ˈnektərɪn/ NOUN [plural **nectarines**] a soft round fruit with a smooth red and yellow skin and yellow flesh with a lot of juice (**nectarina**)

née /neɪ/ ADJECTIVE a word used in front of the family name that a woman had before she got married □ *Mrs Janet Carter, née Tindale* (**nascida, nome de solteira**)

need /niːd/ ▶ VERB [**needs, needing, needed**]
1 if you need something, you must have it in order to exist or to do something □ *I need a sharp knife.* □ *I need your advice.* □ *Do you need any help?* □ *This provides the energy needed to heat the building.* (**necessitar**)
2 if you need to do something, you must do it, and if you need to have a particular quality, you must have it □ **+ to do something** *We all need to eat and drink.* □ *You need to make more effort with your studies.* □ *You need to be tough to be a doctor.* (**precisar**)
3 someone doesn't need to do something/ needn't do something it is not necessary for someone to do something □ *She doesn't need to pay me.* □ *You needn't hurry.* (**não precisar fazer algo**)
4 if something needs to be done, someone should do it □ **+ ing** *The dogs need feeding.* □ *These clothes need a wash.* (**precisar**)
▶ NOUN [plural **needs**]
1 something that it is necessary to have (**necessidade**) □ **+ for** *There is an urgent need for more nurses.* *These new buses meet the needs of wheelchair users.* (**atender as necessidades**)
2 something that it is necessary to do (**necessidade**) □ **+ to do something** *He recognizes the need to invest more money.* *There is no need to wait for me.* (**não precisa**)
3 be in need of something to need something □ *This house is in need of a thorough clean.* (**necessitar de algo**)
4 no plural the state of not having enough food, money, etc. □ *We were shocked at the levels of need in the area.* (**carência**)

> Remember that the noun **need** takes the preposition **for**:
> ✓ *There is a need for more housing.*
> ✗ *There is a need of more housing.*

needle

needle /'ni:dəl/ NOUN [plural **needles**]
1 a small, pointed piece of metal used for sewing (**agulha**) 🔲 *a needle and thread* (agulha e linha) 🔲 *Can you thread this needle for me?* (enfiar o fio na agulha)
2 the thin, sharp metal part of a medical instrument for putting a drug into someone's body or taking blood out (**agulha**)
3 a thin part on a piece of equipment that moves to point to a measurement 🔲 *The needle on the dial was showing 80 mph.* (**agulha**)
4 a long thin piece of wood, metal or plastic that is used for knitting (= making something with wool and two long sticks) 🔲 *a pair of knitting needles* (agulha de tricô)

needless /'ni:dlɪs/ ADJECTIVE not necessary 🔲 *a needless waste of money* 🔲 *Needless to say, we never saw him again.* (**inútil**)

needn't /'ni:dənt/ a short way to say and write need not (**need not = ver need**)

needy /'ni:di/ ▶ ADJECTIVE [**needier, neediest**] not having enough money 🔲 *We hope to provide help for needy families who have lost their homes.* (**necessitado**)
▶ NOUN **the needy** people who do not have enough money 🔲 *The charity does a lot of work to help the needy.* (**os necessitados**)

negative

negative /'negətɪv/ ▶ ADJECTIVE
1 not feeling hope or enthusiasm 🔲 *Since his illness he's been feeling very negative.* (**negativo**) 🔲 *You'll never win until you lose that negative attitude.* (atitude negativa)
2 bad or harmful 🔲 *The drug has a number of negative effects.* (**negativo**)
3 if the result of a test is negative, it shows that something has not happened or been found 🔲 *The result of the pregnancy test was negative.* (**negativo**)
4 a negative word or phrase expresses the meaning 'not' or 'no' 🔲 *a negative sentence* 🔲 *We got a negative reply to our request.* (**negativo**)
5 a negative number is less than zero, for example 25. A maths word. (**negativo**)
▶ NOUN [plural **negatives**]
1 a film before it is printed, where light objects appear dark and dark objects appear light (**negativo**)
2 a word or phrase that expresses the meaning 'not' or 'no' **negative equity** /ˌnegətɪv 'ekwəti/ NOUN, NO PLURAL the situation when your house is worth less than the amount you owe to the organization that lent you the money for it (**negativa**)

negative equity /ˌnegətɪv 'ekwəti/ NOUN, NO PLURAL the situation when your house is worth less than the amount you owe to the organization that lent you the money for it (**patrimônio líquido negativo**)

neigh

neglect /nɪ'glekt/ ▶ VERB [**neglects, neglecting, neglected**]
1 to not give someone or something enough care and attention 🔲 *I've been neglecting the housework because I've been so busy.* 🔲 *The couple are accused of neglecting their children.* (**negligenciar**)
2 neglect to do something to not do something, often deliberately 🔲 *She neglected to mention she had been sacked from her previous job.* (**negligenciar**)
▶ NOUN, NO PLURAL when someone or something does not get enough care or attention 🔲 *The poor garden has suffered years of neglect.* (**negligência**)

negligence /'neglɪdʒəns/ NOUN, NO PLURAL when someone does not take enough care with something, especially if it harms someone 🔲 *They sued their GP for medical negligence.* (**negligência**)

• **negligent** /'neglɪdʒənt/ ADJECTIVE not careful enough in a job or activity that affects someone else 🔲 *The court decided the train company had not been negligent.* (**negligente**)

negligible /'neglɪdʒəbəl/ ADJECTIVE very small and not important 🔲 *The extra money has had a negligible effect so far.* (**desprezível**)

negotiable /nɪ'gəʊʃəbəl/ ADJECTIVE a negotiable price, offer, etc. can be discussed and changed % *The price of the house was not negotiable.* (**negociável**)

negotiate /nɪ'gəʊʃieɪt/ VERB [**negotiates, negotiating, negotiated**]
1 to try to make an agreement with someone by having discussions with them 🔲 *Employees are currently negotiating with managers over a pay rise.* 🔲 *The two parties are hoping to negotiate a settlement to the conflict.* (**negociar**)
2 to successfully move over, along or through something 🔲 *He had trouble negotiating the last fence and came in third.* (**transpor**)

• **negotiation** /nɪˌgəʊʃi'eɪʃən/ NOUN [plural **negotiations**] when people discuss a subject in order to come to an agreement on it 🔲 *Negotiations had reached a difficult stage.* 🔲 *We will not enter into negotiations with terrorists.* (**negociação**)

• **negotiator** /nɪ'gəʊʃieɪtə(r)/ NOUN [plural **negotiators**] someone who tries to make people come to an agreement by having discussions 🔲 *a peace negotiator* (**negociador**)

Negro /'ni:grəʊ/ NOUN [plural **Negroes**] an old fashioned word for a black person, that many people now think is offensive (**negro**)

neigh /neɪ/ ▶ VERB [**neighs, neighing, neighed**] to make the long high noise that a horse makes (**relinchar**)
▶ NOUN [plural **neighs**] the noise that a horse makes (**relincho**)

neighbor /ˈneɪbə(r)/ NOUN [plural **neighbors**] the US spelling of **neighbour** (vizinho)

• **neighborhood** /ˈneɪbəhʊd/ NOUN [plural **neighborhoods**] the US spelling of **neighbourhood** (bairro)

• **neighboring** /ˈneɪbərɪŋ/ ADJECTIVE the US spelling of **neighbouring** (vizinho)

neighbour /ˈneɪbə(r)/ NOUN [plural **neighbours**]
1 someone who lives near you or in the next house to you (vizinho) □ We asked a neighbour to feed the cat. ▣ Cecilia was our next-door neighbour for twelve years. (vizinho ao lado)
2 a person or country that is near another person or country □ Britain's nearest neighbour is France. (vizinho)

• **neighbourhood** /ˈneɪbəhʊd/ NOUN [plural **neighbourhoods**] an area of a town or city □ This is a pretty neighbourhood with a lot of trees and parks. (bairro)

• **neighbouring** /ˈneɪbərɪŋ/ ADJECTIVE next to or near □ We spent the afternoon shopping in a neighbouring town. (vizinho)

neither /ˈnaɪðə(r)/ ▶ DETERMINER, PRONOUN not either of two people or things □ Neither woman seemed to understand English. □ Neither of us can go. □ CONJUNCTION **neither ... nor** used when something negative is true of two people or things □ Neither Peter nor Michael turned up. □ I neither know, nor care, where he is. (nem um nem outro, nenhum dos dois)
▶ ADVERB used to say that a negative statement is also true about someone or something else □ I can't go and neither can Fay. □ 'I don't like garlic.' 'Neither does Richard.' (nem, também não) □ 'I'm not working today.' 'Me neither, let's go out.' (nem eu, também não)

neon /ˈniːɒn/ NOUN, NO PLURAL a gas that shines very brightly when electricity passes through it. A chemistry word (neon) ▣ the neon lights of the city (luzes neon)

nephew /ˈnefjuː/ NOUN [plural **nephews**] the son of your brother or sister, or the son of your wife's or husband's brother or sister (sobrinho)

nerve /nɜːv/ NOUN [plural **nerves**]
1 one of the connections like threads that carry messages between your brain and other parts of your body. A biology word □ the optic nerve □ nerve endings (nervo)
2 the courage you need to do something difficult or dangerous □ **+ to do something** I didn't have the nerve to jump. (coragem)
3 a way of behaving that is rude or likely to annoy people (atrevimento) ▣ You've got a nerve talking to me like that! (ser atrevido) □ **+ to do something** I don't know how she had the nerve to criticize my driving.
4 nerves nervous feelings (nervos) ▣ She went for a walk to calm her nerves. (acalmar os nervos)

♦ IDIOM **get on someone's nerves** to annoy someone, especially by doing the same thing many times □ His constant complaints were getting on my nerves. (dar nos nervos de alguém, irritar)

nerve-racking /ˈnɜːvˌrækɪŋ/ ADJECTIVE making you feel very nervous □ Driving in Rome was nerve-racking, to say the least. (enervante)

nervous /ˈnɜːvəs/ ADJECTIVE
1 worried or frightened □ I get terribly nervous just before I go on stage. □ a nervous laugh □ **+ about** She was very nervous about her interview. (nervoso)
2 to do with the nerves in your body. A biology word □ nervous disorders (nervoso)

nervous breakdown /ˌnɜːvəs ˈbreɪkdaʊn/ NOUN [plural **nervous breakdowns**] a mental illness in which someone is so worried, unhappy and tired that they cannot deal with their normal life □ He had a nervous breakdown when he was only 17. (esgotamento nervoso)

nervously /ˈnɜːvəsli/ ADVERB in a worried, slightly frightened, way □ She giggled nervously. (nervosamente)

nervousness /ˈnɜːvəsnəs/ NOUN, NO PLURAL a worried, slightly frightened feeling □ He struggled to hide his nervousness. (nervosismo)

nervous system /ˈnɜːvəs ˌsɪstəm/ NOUN [plural **nervous systems**] all the nerves in your body and the way they connect to your brain to send messages about feeling and movement. A biology word. (sistema nervoso)

-ness /nɪs/ SUFFIX -ness is added to the end of adjectives to make nouns relating to the qualities or states of the adjectives □ sadness (-ade, -ismo, -eza etc.)

nest /nest/ ▶ NOUN [plural **nests**] a place where birds or some kinds of insects and animals live and have their babies □ We found a wasps' nest in a tree. (ninho)
▶ VERB [**nests, nesting, nested**] to build a nest (nidificar)

nestle /ˈnesəl/ VERB [**nestles, nestling, nestled**]
1 to press yourself into a warm and comfortable place or position □ She nestled her head against his chest. (aconchegar-se)
2 to be in a protected, partly hidden place □ We rented a cottage that nestled at the foot of the hill. (abrigar-se)

net /net/ ▶ NOUN [plural **nets**]
1 a material made of crossed string or rope with holes between, or something made from this and used for a particular purpose (rede) ▣ a fishing net (rede de pesca) ▣ a mosquito net (rede de mosquito) ▣ The trapeze artists performed without a safety net (rede de segurança).

2 a thin material made of crossed threads with holes between ◻ *net curtains* (**rede**)
3 the Net the Internet 🔁 *She spends hours surfing the Net*. (**navegar na rede**)
▶ VERB [**nets, netting, netted**]
1 to get something, especially a profit ◻ *The sale of his company netted him over $4 million.* (**render**)
2 to kick or throw a ball into a net in a sport ◻ *Roberto netted his fifth goal in three matches.* (**lançar para a rede**)
▶ ADJECTIVE
1 a net amount of money has had all the costs such as tax taken off it (**líquido**) 🔁 *We made a net profit of over £3,000.* (**lucro líquido**)
2 the net result or effect of something is its result or effect when you consider all the parts of it (**líquido**)
3 the net weight of something is its weight without its container (**líquido**)

netball /'netbɔːl/ NOUN, NO PLURAL a game where two teams of players throw a ball to each other and try to score goals by throwing the ball through a high net (**basquetebol**)

netting /'netɪŋ/ NOUN, NO PLURAL material made of crossed threads, ropes or wires with holes between. 🔁 *Wire netting surrounds the old church.* (**tule, filé**)

nettle /'netəl/ NOUN [plural **nettles**] a wild plant that has leaves which hurt you if you touch them ⇨ *go to* **grasp the nettle** (**urtiga**)

network /'netwɜːk/ NOUN [plural **networks**]
1 a system of roads, railways lines, etc. that cross and connect with one another ◻ *A strike has shut down the railway network.* (**rede**)
2 a group of people or companies that work together or help each other ◻ *She is lucky to have the support of a wide network of friends.* ◻ *The company has a network of dealers throughout the country.* (**rede**)
3 a system of computers that are all connected together so that they can share information (**rede**)
4 a group of television or radio companies that broadcast the same programmes ◻ *The show went out on a big cable network.* (**rede**)
• **networking** /'netwɜːkɪŋ/ NOUN, NO PLURAL
1 when someone uses social events to meet people who might help their job or business (**rede de contatos**)
2 when computers are connected together. A computing word. (**rede**)

neural /'njʊərəl/ ADJECTIVE to do with your nerves. A biology word. (**neural**)

neurologist /njʊə'rɒlədʒɪst/ NOUN [plural **neurologists**] a doctor who treats diseases which affect the nerves in your body (**neurologista**)
• **neurology** /njʊə'rɒlədʒɪ/ NOUN, NO PLURAL the study of the nerves in your body and the way they send messages to your brain, and of the diseases that affect them (**neurologia**)

neuron /'njʊərɒn/ or **neurone** /'njʊərəʊn/ NOUN [plural **neurons** or **neurones**] a nerve cell that sends messages between the brain and the body. A biology word. (**neurônio**)

neurotic /njʊə'rɒtɪk/ ADJECTIVE worrying about things too much ◻ *She is becoming neurotic about what she eats.* (**neurótico**)

neuter /'njuːtə(r)/ ▶ VERB [**neuters, neutering, neutered**] to do a medical operation on an animal so that it cannot have babies (**esterilizar**)
▶ ADJECTIVE in the grammar of some languages, words that are neuter are not masculine or feminine and may have special pronouns, different endings for their adjectives, etc. (**neutro**)

neutral /'njuːtrəl/ ▶ ADJECTIVE
1 not supporting either side in an argument, war or competition ◻ *The referee must remain neutral.* (**neutro**)
2 a neutral colour is not strong or bright (**neutro**)
▶ NOUN, NO PLURAL when the gears in a vehicle are not connecting the power of the engine to the wheels ◻ *She put the car in neutral and put the handbrake on.* (**ponto morto**)
• **neutrality** /njuː'træləti/ NOUN, NO PLURAL the state of being neutral in an argument, war or competition (**neutralidade**)
• **neutralize** or **neutralise** /'njuːtrəlaɪz/ VERB [**neutralizes, neutralizing, neutralized**] to prevent something from having an effect ◻ *Extra soldiers are intended to neutralize the threat of attack.* (**neutralizar**)

neutron /'njuːtrɒn/ NOUN [plural **neutrons**] a part of the nucleus of an atom with no electrical charge. A physics word. (**nêutron**)

never /'nevə(r)/ ADVERB
1 not ever ◻ *I've never been abroad.* ◻ *It's never too late to learn.* ◻ *I promise never to say that again.* ◻ *I would never do anything to hurt you.* (**nunca**)
2 used to express surprise ◻ '*Chris is getting married.*' '*Never! I don't believe it.*' (**Nossa!**)

> ► Note that **never** usually goes before a 'to infinitive'. It does not go between 'to' and the verb:
> ✓ *I promise never to do it again.*
> ✗ *I promise to never do it again.*

never-ending /,nevər'endɪŋ/ ADJECTIVE continuing for a long time or for ever ◻ *There was a never-ending stream of traffic outside our window.* (**infindável**)

nevertheless /,nevəðə'les/ ADVERB despite that ◻ *The car isn't perfect, but it's very good nevertheless.* (**entretanto, apesar de tudo**)

new /njuː/ ADJECTIVE [**newer, newest**]
1 not existing before, or only recently made, found, invented, etc. ◻ *A new hospital is being*

built in the city. □ *We are creating entirely new online materials.* □ *These accusations are not new.* (novo) 🔹 *New technology has improved international communications.* (nova tecnologia)

2 only recently bought or received □ *He bought a new jacket.* □ *I got a new bike for my birthday.* (novo)

3 different □ *I met my new boss today.* □ *He showed me a new way to make cheese sauce.* (novo)

4 not familiar □ *Working in a team is a new experience for me.* □ **+ to** *The business world is still new to her.* (novo)

5 new to something if you are new to an area or an activity, you have only recently come there or started to do it □ *She's still quite new to the job.* (novato em)

newborn /ˈnjuːbɔːn/ ADJECTIVE a newborn baby has just been born (recém-nascido)

newcomer /ˈnjuːkʌmə(r)/ NOUN [plural **newcomers**] a person who has recently arrived □ *Catriona's family are newcomers to the village.* (recém-chegado)

newfangled /ˌnjuːˈfæŋɡəld/ ADJECTIVE new and complicated in a way that annoys you □ *I can't get used to this newfangled mobile phone.* (novidade tecnológica complicada)

newly /ˈnjuːli/ ADVERB recently □ *the newly appointed London Mayor* (recém, recentemente)

news /njuːz/ NOUN, NO PLURAL

1 new information □ **+ about** *Have you heard the news about Raj?* □ **+ of** *News of her safe return was greeted with joy.* □ **+ on** *Is there any news on the completion date yet?* (novidade, notícia) 🔹 *We've had some good news: Beth is pregnant.* (notícias boas) 🔹 *I'm afraid I've got some bad news* (notícias ruins)

2 the news information about important events on the radio or television, or in newspapers, etc. (noticiário) 🔹 *the local/national news* (noticiário local/nacional) □ *They always watch the news at 10 o'clock.*

> Remember that news is used with a singular verb:
> ✓ *The news is so bad at the moment.*
> ✗ *The news are so bad at the moment.*

newsagent /ˈnjuːzeɪdʒənt/ NOUN [plural **newsagents**]

1 someone who sells newspapers and magazines (jornaleiro)

2 newsagent's a shop that sells newspapers and magazines and usually other things like sweets and cigarettes (banca de jornal com loja de conveniência)

newsgroup /ˈnjuːzɡruːp/ NOUN [plural **newsgroups**] a place on the Internet where people who are interested in a particular subject can leave messages. A computing word. (fóruns de discussão)

newsletter /ˈnjuːzletə(r)/ NOUN [plural **newsletters**] a short report about a club or organization that is regularly sent to its members □ *the monthly newsletter* (circular)

newspaper /ˈnjuːzpeɪpə(r)/ NOUN [plural **newspapers**]

1 large folded pieces of paper printed with reports and pictures about recent events and sold every day or every week □ *I saw your picture in the newspaper.* (jornal) 🔹 *He started out on the local newspaper.* (jornal local)

2 *no plural* the paper that newspapers are printed on □ *Wrap the glasses in newspaper and pack them carefully.* (jornal)

New Testament /ˌnjuː ˈtestəmənt/ NOUN, NO PLURAL **the New Testament** the second part of the Christian Bible, written after Jesus Christ was born (Novo Testamento)

New Year /ˌnjuː ˈjɪə(r)/ NOUN, NO PLURAL the first few days of January, when people often celebrate □ *They're having a New Year's party.* □ *Happy New Year!* (Ano-Novo)

New Year's Day /ˌnjuː jɪəz ˈdeɪ/ NOUN, NO PLURAL 1 January, the first day of the year (dia de ano novo)

New Year's Eve /ˌnjuː jɪəz ˈiːv/ NOUN, NO PLURAL 31 December, the last day of the year (véspera de ano novo)

next /nekst/ ▶ ADJECTIVE

1 following or happening immediately after □ *What's the next name on the list?* □ *I need to phone hi in the next hour or so.* □ *The next morning he felt much better.* □ *Next time I see Sally, I'll ask her.* (próximo, seguinte)

2 next week/Saturday/year, etc. the week/Saturday/year, etc. after this one □ *Do you want to come round next weekend?* (próxima semana, sábado, ano etc.)

3 nearest to the place where you are now □ *Take the next left.* □ *The next town is five miles away.* (próximo, seguinte)

▶ ADVERB

1 immediately after something else □ *What will happen next?* □ *Next we need to paint the walls.* (a seguir, em seguida)

2 the next best/most important, etc. the second best/most important, etc. □ *Cycling was the next most popular form of exercise.* (o mais/a seguir)

3 the time when you next do something is the first time you do it again □ *When are you likely to next see Julie?* (na próxima vez)

4 Whatever next? something you say when you are surprised about something that exists or has happened □ *Blue roses? Whatever next?* (O que mais vem/pode acontecer a seguir?)

▶ PREPOSITION

next door

1 next to (a) in a position at the side of someone or something ☐ *I put the book down next to her.* (**ao lado de**) 🔁 *Nobody wants to live right next to a motorway* (**bem ao lado**). (b) in the second position of importance, quality, etc. ☐ *Next to France, Ireland is my favourite place for a holiday.*
2 next to nothing almost nothing ☐ *I earn next to nothing from my writing.* (**quase nada**)

▶ PRONOUN

1 the person or thing that follows or happens immediately after someone or something else ☐ *Who's next to see the doctor?* ☐ *They've already sacked 20 staff – who's going to be next?* (**próximo**)
2 the week/Saturday/year, etc. after next two weeks/Saturdays/years, etc. from the present ☐ *I'm going to New York the week after next.* (**daqui a duas semanas/sábados/anos etc.**)

next door /ˌnekst ˈdɔː(r)/ ADJECTIVE, ADVERB in the next house, building or room (**vizinho**) 🔁 *We have very nice next door neighbours.* (**vizinhos**) ☐ *Our office is next door to the station.* ☐ *We get on well with the people next door.*

next of kin /ˌnekst əv ˈkɪn/ NOUN [*plural* **next of kin**] your closest relation ☐ *The army will inform his next of kin of his death.* (**parente mais próximo**)

NHS /ˌenˈeɪtʃˈes/ ABBREVIATION **the NHS** the National Health Service; the system which provides free medical treatment for people in the UK ☐ *He had the operation done on the NHS.* (**abrev. Serviço Nacional de Saúde**)

nib /nɪb/ NOUN [*plural* **nibs**] the point of a pen where the ink comes out (**ponta, pena**)

nibble /ˈnɪbəl/ VERB [**nibbles, nibbling, nibbled**] to eat something with little bites ☐ *A mouse had nibbled right through the wires.* (**mordiscar**)

nice /naɪs/ ADJECTIVE [**nicer, nicest**]

1 pleasant, good or attractive ☐ *If the weather's nice, we can go for a walk.* ☐ *She took me to a really nice restaurant.* (**bonito, agradável**) 🔁 *Have a nice time in Germany!* (**divertir-se**)
2 kind or friendly ☐ *That wasn't a very nice thing to do.* ☐ **+ to** *She's always nice to the children.* ☐ **+ of** *It was very nice of Rob to give me a lift.* ☐ **+ about** *My tutor was really nice about my work.*
3 nice and... used to emphasize a positive quality (**enfatiza uma qualidade**) ☐ *It was nice and warm in the kitchen.* (**agradavelmente quente etc.**)
• **nicely** /ˈnaɪsli/ ADVERB
1 well ☐ *My carrots are coming along nicely this year.* ☐ *She played the piano very nicely.* (**bem, agradavelmente**)
2 in a polite way (**gentilmente**) 🔁 *Ask the lady nicely.* (**pedir gentilmente**)
• **niceness** /ˈnaɪsnɪs/ NOUN, NO PLURAL being pleasant or attractive (**gentileza, encanto**)

niche /niːʃ/ NOUN [*plural* **niches**]
1 a situation or job that you feel very comfortable and happy in (**nicho**) 🔁 *She seems to have found her niche in life.* (**encontrar seu lugar**)

523

night N

2 a hollow space in a wall where objects can be put (**nicho**)
3 an opportunity for a business or a product ☐ *We realized that there was a niche for a women--only decorating service.* (**nicho**)

niche market /ˌniːʃ ˈmɑːkɪt/ NOUN [*plural* **niche markets**] when a product or a service is produced for only a small number of people who want it (**nicho de mercado**)

nick /nɪk/ ▶ NOUN [*plural* **nicks**]
1 a small cut ☐ *He had a nick on his chin.* (**talho, corte**)
2 the nick an informal word for a prison or a police station (**a prisão ou a delegacia**)
3 in good/bad nick an informal phrase meaning in good or bad condition ☐ *My car's six years old but in pretty good nick.* (**em boa ou má condição**)
♦ IDIOM **in the nick of time** just before it is too late ☐ *We got out of the burning house in the nick of time.* (**na hora H**)

▶ VERB [**nicks, nicking, nicked**]
1 an informal word meaning to steal something ☐ *Who's nicked my pen?* (**roubar**)
2 an informal word meaning to arrest someone ☐ *Connor got nicked for speeding last night.* (**prender**)
3 to make a very small cut in something ☐ *I nicked my finger on a tin can.* (**fazer um corte**)

nickel /ˈnɪkəl/ NOUN [*plural* **nickels**]
1 a white metal that is often mixed with other metals. A chemistry word. (**níquel**)
2 an American or Canadian coin worth five cents (**moeda de cinco centavos**)

nickname /ˈnɪkneɪm/ ▶ NOUN [*plural* **nicknames**] a name that you use for someone that is not their real name ☐ *His nickname at school was 'President' because his real name's Kennedy.* (**apelido**)

▶ VERB [**nicknames, nicknaming, nicknamed**] to call someone by a nickname ☐ *They nicknamed him 'Scottie'.* (**apelidar**)

nicotine /ˈnɪkəti:n/ NOUN, NO PLURAL the poisonous substance in tobacco (**nicotina**)

niece /niːs/ NOUN [*plural* **nieces**] the daughter of your brother or sister, or the daughter of your wife's or husband's brother or sister (**sobrinha**)

nifty /ˈnɪfti/ ADJECTIVE [**niftier, niftiest**] an informal word meaning effective and designed in a clever way ☐ *a nifty little gadget* (**estiloso**)

niggle /ˈnɪgəl/ VERB [**niggles, niggling, niggled**] to worry or annoy you slightly but for a long time ☐ *The question was niggling at the back of her mind.* (**incomodar**)
• **niggling** /ˈnɪglɪŋ/ ADJECTIVE not very serious but not going away ☐ *a niggling back injury* ☐ *She still had some niggling doubts about his suitability for the job.* (**insistente**)

night /naɪt/ NOUN [*plural* **nights**]
1 the time when it is dark and when people usually sleep (**noite**) 🔁 *I hardly slept last night.*

(noite passada) 🔁 *I spent the night at my sister's.* (passar a noite) 🔁 *The dog woke me up in the middle of the night.* (no meio da noite) 🔁 *He's been having sleepless nights worrying about work.* (noites de insônia)
2 at night during the time when it is dark □ *I don't walk the streets on my own at night.* (à noite)
3 the part of the evening before you go to bed (noite) 🔁 *I went out with David last night.* (noite passada) □ *Are you doing anything on Saturday night?* (sábado à noite) □ *I'm having a night out with my friends on Friday.*
4 Good night. Something you say when you leave someone in the evening, or when you or they go to bed (boa noite)
5 have an early/a late night to go to bed early/late (ir dormir cedo/tarde)

> ▶ Notice that we usually say **at night** to mean 'during the time when it is dark':
> ✓ *I never drive at night.*
> ✗ *I never drive in the night.*

nightclub /ˈnaɪtklʌb/ NOUN [plural **nightclubs**] a place where people can dance and drink late at night (casa noturna)

nightdress /ˈnaɪtdres/ NOUN [plural **nightdresses**] a loose dress that a woman or girl sleeps in (camisola)

nightfall /ˈnaɪtfɔːl/ NOUN, NO PLURAL the time when it starts to get dark in the evening □ *They set off at nightfall.* (anoitecer, crepúsculo)

nightingale /ˈnaɪtɪŋgeɪl/ NOUN [plural **nightingales**] a small bird that sings beautifully (rouxinol)

nightly /ˈnaɪtli/ ADJECTIVE, ADVERB every night □ *He makes nightly visits to the park with the dog.* □ *Episodes of the show are broadcast nightly.* (todas as noites)

nightmare /ˈnaɪtmeə(r)/ NOUN [plural **nightmares**]
1 a frightening dream □ *Older children often have nightmares.* (pesadelo)
2 a very unpleasant experience □ *The drive home was a complete nightmare.*

night shift /ˈnaɪt ˌʃɪft/ NOUN [plural **night shifts**]
1 a period of time when people work during the night □ *I'm doing night shifts this week.* (turno da noite)
2 the group of people who work in a place at night (turno da noite)

nightshirt /ˈnaɪtʃɜːt/ NOUN [plural **nightshirts**] a long loose shirt for sleeping (camiseta de dormir)

nil /nɪl/ NOUN, NO PLURAL
1 a score of zero in a game or sport □ *The score was eight-nil.* (zero)
2 used to mean that something does not exist □ *Their chances of survival are virtually nil.* (nulo)

nimble /ˈnɪmbəl/ ADJECTIVE [**nimbler**, **nimblest**]
1 able to move quickly and easily □ *She darted around with nimble movements.* (ágil)
2 able to react quickly to a situation □ *The more nimble companies have been able to make big profits.* (ágil)

• **nimbly** /ˈnɪmbli/ ADVERB in a nimble way □ *He jumped nimbly aside to let the bike pass.* (agilmente)

nine /naɪn/ NUMBER [plural **nines**] the number 9 (nove)

nineteen /ˌnaɪnˈtiːn/ NUMBER [plural **nineteens**] the number 19 (dezenove)

nineteenth /ˌnaɪnˈtiːnθ/ NUMBER 19th written as a word (décimo nono)

ninetieth /ˈnaɪntiəθ/ NUMBER 90th written as a word (nonagésimo)

ninety /ˈnaɪnti/ NUMBER [plural **nineties**]
1 the number 90 (noventa)
2 the nineties the years between 1990 and 1999 (os anos 1990)

ninth /naɪnθ/ ▶ NUMBER 9th written as a word (nono)
▶ NOUN [plural **ninths**] 1/9; one of nine equal parts of something (nona parte)

nip /nɪp/ ▶ VERB [**nips**, **nipping**, **nipped**]
1 an informal word meaning to go somewhere quickly or for a short time □ *I must just nip to the shops.* (dar um pulo)
2 to bite someone or to press someone's skin in a quick, sharp way □ *The dog was nipping at his ankles.* (morder ou beliscar)
♦ IDIOM **nip something in the bud** to stop something before it can develop or grow □ *These problems should be nipped in the bud.* (cortar pela raiz)
▶ NOUN [plural **nips**]
1 a small bite or sharp pressing movement □ *The insects can give you a nasty nip.* (mordida, beliscão)
2 a cold feeling 🔁 *There's a nip in the air today.* (frio cortante)

nipple /ˈnɪpəl/ NOUN [plural **nipples**] the darker, pointed part on a woman's breasts or a man's chest (mamilo)

nippy /ˈnɪpi/ ADJECTIVE [**nippier**, **nippiest**]
1 an informal word meaning cold □ *It's a bit nippy out today.* (frio)
2 an informal word meaning able to move quickly □ *a nippy little car* (ágil)

nitrate /ˈnaɪtreɪt/ NOUN [plural **nitrates**] a chemical that is used to make crops grow better. A chemistry word. (nitrato)

nitrogen /ˈnaɪtrədʒən/ NOUN, NO PLURAL a colourless gas that is found in air. A chemistry word. (nitrogênio)

no /nəʊ/ ▶ EXCLAMATION
1 used to refuse, disagree or give a negative answer □ *'Can you give me a lift to the station?'*

'No, sorry, I need to get straight home.' □ 'Tim's really stupid.' 'No he isn't!' □ 'Can I have some more cake?' 'No, you've had more than enough already.' □ 'Are you all right?' 'No, I've got my foot stuck.' (não)
2 used to agree with a negative statement □ 'The weather's not very good today.' 'No, it's a bit cold.' (não)
3 used to express shock or surprise ▣ *Oh no! I've left my passport at home!* □ 'Chris and Alice are getting married.' 'No! They've only known each other a few weeks!' (oh, não)

♦ IDIOM **not take no for an answer** to refuse to accept that someone will not do something or does not want something (não aceitar um não como resposta)

▶ DETERMINER
1 not any □ *They have no money.* □ *There is no need to bring a coat.* □ *It is no secret that he hates his job.* □ *No decisions have been taken yet.* (nenhum)
2 used to say that something is not allowed □ *No smoking.* (proibido)

▶ ADVERB not any □ *She's no better this morning.* (não) ▣ *No fewer than four players were sent off during the match.* □ *Payment is due no later than the 15th.* (não menos que, no mais tardar)

No. or **no.** /nəʊ/ ABBREVIATION number (número, nº)

nobility /nəˈbɪləti/ NOUN, NO PLURAL
1 the nobility people in the highest social groups of society □ *the Italian nobility* (a nobreza)
2 the quality of being noble □ *There was a certain nobility about him.* (nobreza)

noble /ˈnəʊbəl/ ADJECTIVE [**nobler, noblest**]
1 brave and honest, or helping other people in a way that people admire □ *We are doing important work for a noble cause.* (nobre)
2 belonging to a high social class □ *He comes from a noble family.* (nobre)

nobleman /ˈnəʊbəlmən/ NOUN [plural **noblemen**] a man who belongs to one of the highest social groups in a society (nobre)

noblewoman /ˈnəʊbəlwʊmən/ NOUN [plural **noblewomen**] a woman who belongs to one of the highest social groups in a society (nobre)

nobly /ˈnəʊbli/ ADVERB in a way that is brave and honest or helps other people in a way that people admire □ *He went nobly into battle.* (nobremente)

nobody /ˈnəʊbədi/ ▶ PRONOUN not any person □ *Nobody tells me what to do!* □ *There was nobody at home.* (ninguém) ▣ *Nobody else noticed it.* (ninguém mais)

> Note that **nobody** is always followed by a singular verb:
> ✓ *Nobody has said anything.*
> ✗ *Nobody have said anything.*

▶ NOUN [plural **nobodies**] a person who is not at all important □ *He's just a nobody.*

nocturnal /nɒkˈtɜːnəl/ ADJECTIVE
1 nocturnal animals are active at night. A biology word □ *Lemurs are nocturnal animals.*
2 happening at night (noturno)

nod /nɒd/ ▶ VERB [**nods, nodding, nodded**]
1 to move your head up and down, especially to agree or to say 'yes' (acenar com a cabeça em concordância) ▣ *He nodded his head enthusiastically.* (acenou a cabeça) ▣ *His wife nodded in agreement.* (acenou a cabeça em concordância)
2 to move your head in a particular direction to point to something □ *She nodded towards the door.* (indicar com a cabeça)

♦ PHRASAL VERB **nod off** an informal word meaning to start sleeping □ *Grandma nodded off in her chair.* (cair no sono)

▶ NOUN [plural **nods**] when you nod your head (aceno de cabeça) ▣ *He gave a small nod.* (acenou com a cabeça)

noise /nɔɪz/ NOUN [plural **noises**]
1 a sound (barulho) ▣ *Did you hear a noise outside?* (ouviu um barulho) ▣ *The bird was making screeching noises.* (fazer barulhos) ▣ *There was a sudden, loud noise.* (barulho alto)
2 *no plural* sound that is loud or unpleasant □ *+ of He shouted over the noise of the engine.* (barulho) ▣ *Could you please make a little less noise?* (fazer barulho) ▣ *The background noise made it difficult to hear.* (barulho no fundo)

• **noisily** /ˈnɔɪzɪli/ ADVERB in a way that makes a lot of noise □ *A helicopter circled noisily overhead.* (ruidosamente)

• **noisy** /ˈnɔɪzi/ ADJECTIVE [**noisier, noisiest**] making a lot of noise □ *a noisy party* □ *Some people complain about noisy neighbours.* □ *The fridge seems very noisy – is there something wrong with it?* (barulhento)

nomad /ˈnəʊmæd/ NOUN [plural **nomads**] a member of a group of people, usually with animals, who move from place to place instead of living in the same place all the time (nômade)

• **nomadic** /nəʊˈmædɪk/ ADJECTIVE to do with or like a nomad □ *nomadic tribes* (nômade)

nominate /ˈnɒmɪneɪt/ VERB [**nominates, nominating, nominated**] to suggest someone for a job, position or prize □ *Charles nominated Peter as leader of the group.* □ *She was nominated for an Oscar.* (nomear)

• **nomination** /ˌnɒmɪˈneɪʃən/ NOUN [plural **nominations**] when someone or something is nominated for something (nomeação) ▣ *He's seeking the Republican nomination for governor.* (tentar a indicação para) ▣ *She received a Grammy nomination for her debut album.* (receber indicação para)

- **nominee** /ˌnɒmɪˈniː/ NOUN [plural **nominees**] a person who has been nominated for a job, position or prize □ *a presidential nominee* (**pessoa nomeada**)

non- /nɒn/ PREFIX non- is added to the beginning of words to mean 'not' □ *a non-smoker* (= someone who does not smoke) (**não**)

nonchalance /ˈnɒnʃələns/ NOUN, NO PLURAL the quality of being nonchalant □ *We were impressed by his nonchalance.* (**indiferença**)

nonchalant /ˈnɒnʃələnt/ ADJECTIVE calm and not worried or excited □ *He tried to sound nonchalant.* (**indiferente**)

non-committal /ˌnɒnkəˈmɪtəl/ ADJECTIVE avoiding giving a clear opinion or decision □ *The minister gave a typically non-committal reply.* (**descomprometido, sem compromisso**)

nondescript /ˈnɒndɪskrɪpt/ ADJECTIVE very ordinary and boring, with no noticeable qualities □ *They live in a rather nondescript bungalow.* (**indefinido**)

none /nʌn/ ▶ PRONOUN not any □ + *of None of them are going to admit to being wrong.* □ *We looked for more biscuits but there were none left.* (**nenhum**) 🔁 *Most people there ate little food, or none at all.* (**nenhum**)
▶ ADVERB
1 none the less nonetheless (**apesar disso**)
2 not at all or not very (**nada ou não muito**) 🔁 *I heard the answer but I'm none the wiser* (= I still do not understand). (**não mais informado**) 🔁 *His feet were none too clean.* (**nada limpos**)

nonentity /nɒnˈentəti/ NOUN [plural **nonentities**] someone who is not important or interesting □ *Most of the other candidates are political nonentities.* (**pessoa sem importância**)

nonetheless /ˌnʌnðəˈles/ ADVERB despite that □ *It would not be easy; nonetheless, he intended to try his best.* □ *There have been one or two delays; the road will open on time, nonetheless.* (**apesar disso**)

non-existent /ˌnɒnɪɡˈzɪstənt/ ADJECTIVE not existing □ *Medical facilities are almost non-existent in this area.* (**inexistente**)

non-fiction /ˌnɒnˈfɪkʃən/ NOUN, NO PLURAL writing that is about real facts, not invented stories (**não ficção**)

nonplussed /ˌnɒnˈplʌst/ ADJECTIVE surprised and confused □ *For a moment, Sylvia looked nonplussed.* (**perplexo**)

nonsense /ˈnɒnsəns/ NOUN, NO PLURAL
1 something that is not true or sensible (**disparate, bobagem**) 🔁 *His theory is a load of nonsense.* (**um monte de disparates**) 🔁 *You're talking nonsense.* (**falar asneiras**) 🔁 *These reports are absolute nonsense.* (**disparate absoluto**)
2 silly behaviour □ *Stop your nonsense now please.* (**bobagem**)

3 make a nonsense of something to make something seem stupid or unreasonable □ *It made a complete nonsense of all my plans.* (**parecer bobagem, sem sentido**)

- **nonsensical** /nɒnˈsensɪkəl/ ADJECTIVE not true or reasonable □ *It would be nonsensical to pay someone to do the work and then do it yourself.* (**disparatado**)

non-stop /ˌnɒnˈstɒp/ ADJECTIVE, ADVERB without a rest or a pause □ *There was non-stop hammering from the room above.* □ *It's rained non-stop for three days.* (**direto, ininterrupto**)

non-toxic /ˌnɒnˈtɒksɪk/ ADJECTIVE not poisonous □ *We only use non-toxic plastics.* (**atóxico**)

noodle /ˈnuːdəl/ NOUN [plural **noodles**] a long thin piece of pasta (**macarrão**)

nook /nʊk/ NOUN [plural **nooks**] a small corner or space, especially where something can be hidden (**recanto**)
♦ IDIOM **every nook and cranny/all the nooks and crannies** every part of a place □ *I've cleaned every nook and cranny of the flat.* (**em todos os cantinhos**)

noon /nuːn/ NOUN, NO PLURAL twelve o'clock in the middle of the day □ *We'll have our lunch at noon.* □ *It was a few minutes past noon.* (**meio-dia**)

no one or **no-one** /ˈnəʊwʌn/ PRONOUN not any person □ *No one's in at the moment.* □ *No one knows what happened.* □ *There was no one to ask.* (**ninguém**) 🔁 *There was no one else in the building.* (**ninguém mais**)

> ▶ Note that **no one** is always followed by a singular verb:
> ✓ *No one tells me anything.*
> ✗ *No one tell me anything.*

noose /nuːs/ NOUN [plural **nooses**] a circle of rope that becomes tighter when the end is pulled, used to kill people or catch animals (**nó corrediço**)

nor /nɔː(r)/ CONJUNCTION
1 neither ... nor used when something negative is true of two people or things □ *Neither Jack nor Jenny is at home.* □ *Neither the teachers nor the parents are happy with the situation.* (**nem... nem**)
2 used after a negative statement to say that the same is true for someone else □ *He didn't see anything unusual, and nor did any of his friends.* □ *I'm sure Jack wouldn't like that and nor would I.* (**nem**)

norm /nɔːm/ NOUN [plural **norms**] what people usually do or what usually happens 🔁 *It has become the norm to send young children to nursery school.* □ *He wrote about changing social norms.* (**norma**)

normal /ˈnɔːməl/ ADJECTIVE

north

1 usual and expected □ + *to do something* *It's normal to feel hungry at lunchtime.* □ + *for* *This temperature is normal for August.* (normal) 🔁 *He just wants to live a normal life.* (vida normal) 🔁 *There's been a lot of building work, but we should be back to normal soon.* (voltar ao normal)
2 *as normal* in the usual and expected way □ *Conditions were tough, but we just carried on as normal.* (como o normal, normalmente)
• **normality** /nɔːˈmælətɪ/ NOUN, NO PLURAL when things are normal □ *After all the excitement it was good to return to normality.* (normalidade)
• **normally** /ˈnɔːməlɪ/ ADVERB
1 usually □ *We normally go to bed pretty early.* □ *Normally, I drive to work.* □ *I don't normally do this kind of thing.* (normalmente)
2 in the usual and expected way □ *This plant has developed normally, but the other one is diseased.* (normalmente)

north /nɔːθ/ ▶ NOUN, NO PLURAL

1 the direction that is to your left when you are facing the rising sun (norte)
2 the part of a country or the world that is in the north □ *He lives in the north of England.* (norte)
▶ ADJECTIVE, ADVERB in or towards the north □ *the cold north wind* □ *We were travelling north on the motorway.* (do norte ou para o norte)
• **northbound** /ˈnɔːθbaʊnd/ ADJECTIVE moving or going towards the north (do norte ou para o norte) 🔁 *northbound traffic* (trânsito do norte)

north-east /ˌnɔːθˈiːst/ ▶ NOUN, NO PLURAL

1 the direction between north and east (nordeste)
2 the part of a country between the north and the east □ *the north-east of Scotland* (nordeste)
▶ ADJECTIVE, ADVERB in or towards the north-east □ *The north-east region of Spain.* (do/para o nordeste)

northerly /ˈnɔːðəlɪ/ ADJECTIVE coming from, or going towards, the north □ *a northerly breeze* □ *going in a northerly direction* □ *the island's most northerly point* (do/para o norte)

northern /ˈnɔːðən/ ADJECTIVE in or from the north □ *the cold northern climate* □ *Northern districts will have some rain.* (do/para o norte)
• **northerner** /ˈnɔːðənə(r)/ NOUN [plural **northerners**] a person from the north (nortista)

North Pole /ˌnɔːθ ˈpəʊl/ NOUN, NO PLURAL the North Pole the point on the Earth that is furthest north (polo Norte)

northward /ˈnɔːθwəd/ or **northwards** /ˈnɔːθwədz/ ADVERB to or towards the north □ *We cycled northwards for several miles.* (para o norte)

north-west /ˌnɔːθˈwest/ ▶ NOUN, NO PLURAL

1 the direction between north and west (noroeste)
2 the part of a country between the north and the west □ *the north-west of England* (noroeste)
▶ ADJECTIVE, ADVERB in or towards the north-west (do/para o noroeste)

nose /nəʊz/ NOUN [plural **noses**]

1 the part of your face that you breathe and smell through (nariz) 🔁 *I need to blow my nose.* (assoar o nariz) 🔁 *I had sore eyes and a runny nose.* (nariz escorrendo)
2 the front part of something that sticks out, for example, the front of an aircraft (nariz)
♦ IDIOMS **get up someone's nose** an informal phrase meaning to annoy someone □ *He really gets up my nose with his constant boasting* (irritar). **look down your nose at someone/something** to act as if you think that someone or something is not good enough □ *I saw the way she looked down her nose at our staff* (menosprezar). **poke/stick your nose in/into something** an informal phrase meaning to be too interested in something that does not involve you □ *I don't want him poking his nose into my business* (intrometer-se). **put someone's nose out of joint** to offend someone □ *He talked to Ally all evening, and I could see that Anna had her nose put out of joint* (ofender). **turn your nose up at something** to refuse to accept something because you do not think it is good enough for you □ *She turned her nose up at my soup* (torcer o nariz para). **under someone's nose** if something happens under someone's nose, they are there when it happens, but they do not notice □ *He was rescued from under the noses of his guards* (debaixo do nariz de alguém, bem à vista).

⇨ go to **have/keep your nose to the grindstone**
♦ PHRASAL VERB [noses, nosing, nosed] **nose about/around (somewhere)** to look around a place, often in order to find information □ *I found him nosing around in my office.* (bisbilhotar)

nosedive /ˈnəʊzdaɪv/ ▶ VERB [nosedives, nosediving, nosedived]

1 to fall very quickly in value or quality □ *His career nosedived.* (despencar, cair subitamente)
2 to fall very quickly towards the ground □ *The two-seater plane nosedived into a field.* (cair subitamente)
▶ NOUN [plural **nosedives**]
1 a sudden loss of value or quality (queda súbita) 🔁 *The company's shares took a nosedive.* (despencar)
2 when an aircraft falls very quickly towards the ground (mergulho de ponta) 🔁 *The plane went into a nosedive.* (mergulhar de ponta)

nosey /ˈnəʊzɪ/ ADJECTIVE another spelling of **nosy** (ver nosy)

nostalgia /nɒˈstældʒə/ NOUN, NO PLURAL a feeling of mixed happiness and sadness when you remember times in the past □ *The programme prompted a wave of nostalgia for his youth.* (nostalgia)
• **nostalgic** /nɒˈstældʒɪk/ ADJECTIVE thinking of or making you remember happy times in the past □ *We enjoyed a nostalgic evening of black and white movies.* (nostálgico)

nostril /ˈnɒstrɪl/ NOUN [plural **nostrils**] one of the two openings in your nose that you breathe and smell through (**narina**)

nosy /ˈnəʊzi/ ADJECTIVE [**nosier**, **nosiest**] always wanting to find out about other people and what they are doing ☐ *I shut the garage door because of the nosy neighbours.* ☐ *I'm sorry for being so nosy.* (**curioso, intrometido**)

not /nɒt/ ADVERB

1 used after verbs like be and do and modal verbs to make negative sentences. It often becomes **n't** when it is added to verbs ☐ *I'm not going.* ☐ *They have not made a decision yet.* ☐ *It isn't fair.* ☐ *I can't hear you.* (**não**)

2 used to give the next words or phrase a negative meaning ☐ *I told her not to look.* ☐ *Not everyone was happy with the decision.* ☐ *'Are you ready?' 'Not yet.'* ☐ *'Did it upset you?' 'Not at all.'* ☐ *Let's not go there again.* (**não**)

3 used with verbs like hope and suspect or adverbs like certainly or definitely to make a negative reply ☐ *'Will you be much longer?' 'I hope not.'* ☐ *'Can I borrow £5?' 'Certainly not.'* (**não, que não**)

4 or not used to express a negative possibility ☐ *I don't know if he'll be there or not.* (**ou não**)

5 not only ... but used to say that more than one thing has happened or is true ☐ *Not only was he rude, but he left without paying the bill.* (**não só... como também**)

6 not a/one used to emphasize that there is or was no thing or person ☐ *Not one of his students passed the exam.* ☐ *There was not a drop of water to drink.* (**nenhum**)

> ► Note that **not** usually goes before a 'to infinitive'. It does not go between 'to' and the verb:
> ✓ He told me **not to** be late
> ✗ He told me to not be late.

notable /ˈnəʊtəbəl/ ADJECTIVE important and worth remembering ☐ *The most notable part of the evening was the music.* (**notável**) ☐ *The whole family were there, with one notable exception.* (**exceção notável**)

• **notably** /ˈnəʊtəbli/ ADVERB especially ☐ *I loved the old buildings, notably the palace.* (**especialmente**)

notch /nɒtʃ/ NOUN [plural **notches**]
1 a small, V-shaped cut in something ☐ *We cut notches in a stick as the days passed.* (**entalhe**)
2 a level of quality or amount ☐ *He'll have to raise his game a few notches.* (**pontos, graus etc.**)
♦ PHRASAL VERB [**notches, notching, notched**]
notch something up to achieve something ☐ *He notched up the 85th win of his career.* (**atingir pontos, votos etc.**)

note /nəʊt/ ► NOUN [plural **notes**]

1 a short piece of writing to help you remember something (**nota, anotação**) ☐ *I made a note of his phone number.* ☐ *I've got a note of all their names.* (**fazer uma anotação**)
2 a short letter (**bilhete**) ☐ *I wrote her a note to say how sorry I was.* (**escrever um bilhete**) ☐ *He scribbled a note to his wife.* (**rabiscou um bilhete**)
3 notes information that you write down when you are reading a book, in a lesson, etc. (**anotações**) ☐ *There is a handout, so you don't need to take notes.* (**fazer anotações**)
4 take note to notice something or to pay attention to something ☐ *We failed to take note of the speed regulations.* ☐ *Cyclists take note: a helmet could save your life.* (**tomar nota, prestar atenção**)
5 a short explanation of something in a book ☐ *There are notes at the end of each chapter.* (**nota**)
6 a feeling or quality (**nota**) ☐ *His speech struck just the right note of optimism.* (**atingiu uma nota**) ☐ *On a happier note, I am pleased to welcome our new assistant.*
7 a piece of paper money ☐ *a five pound note* (**nota, cédula**)
8 a single musical sound or the written sign for it ☐ *I can't reach the high notes.* (**nota musical**)
► VERB [**notes, noting, noted**]
1 to notice something or to pay attention to something ☐ *+ that I noted that she always wore red, and wondered why.* ☐ *We noted the absence of the prince.* (**notar**)
2 to say or write something ☐ *+ that He also noted that the building seemed in need of repair.* ☐ *She noted sadly that most of the trees have been cut down.* (**observar, mencionar**)
♦ PHRASAL VERB **note something down** to write something down so that you will not forget it ☐ *I noted down the train times.* (**anotar**)

notebook /ˈnəʊtbʊk/ NOUN [plural **notebooks**]
1 a small book that you use to write things down in (**caderno**)
2 a very small computer that you can carry around. A computing word. (**computador portátil**)

notepad /ˈnəʊtpæd/ NOUN [plural **notepads**]
1 several pieces of paper joined together at one end, used for writing (**bloco de notas**)
2 a small computer that you can carry around. A computing word. (**editor básico de texto**)

notepaper /ˈnəʊtpeɪpə(r)/ NOUN, NO PLURAL
plain paper that you use for writing letters on ☐ *a sheet of headed notepaper* (**papel de carta**)

nothing /ˈnʌθɪŋ/ PRONOUN
1 not anything ☐ *There's nothing to eat.* ☐ *There's nothing wrong with me.* ☐ *He carried on as if nothing had happened.* (**nada**) ☐ *There was nothing else we could do.* (**nada mais**) ☐ *I've heard nothing but (= only) praise for her work.* (**nada além**)

notice

2 not something important or valuable □ *'What are you writing?' 'Oh, it's nothing – just a little poem.'* (**nada**)

3 be/have nothing to do with someone if something is nothing to do with you, there is no reason for you to know about it or be involved with it □ *It's nothing to do with you what I spend my money on.* (**não ter nada a ver com**)

4 for nothing (a) without being paid □ *He mended my car for nothing.* (**de graça**) (b) with no successful result □ *You mean we did all that work for nothing?* (**a troco de nada**)

5 have nothing to do with something to not be involved in something □ *I had nothing to do with the decision.* (**não ter nada a ver com**)

6 have nothing to lose to be in a situation where it is worth taking a risk because even if you fail, it will not be worse □ *I had nothing to lose, so I told him exactly what I thought.* (**não ter nada a perder**)

7 nothing like (a) not at all similar □ *He's nothing like his brother.* (b) *not almost* □ *The water's nothing like hot enough yet.* (**nada parecido**)

8 nothing much not a lot or nothing important □ *'What did you have for lunch?' 'Nothing much.'* (**nada de mais, não muito**)

9 there's nothing like used to say that something is the best thing □ *There's nothing like a bit of sunshine to cheer you up.* (**não há nada como**)

10 There's nothing to it. used to say that something is easy to do □ *Just slip the rope over the hook – there's nothing to it.* (**não ter nada de mais**)

11 stop at nothing if someone would stop at nothing to achieve something, they would do anything, even something bad, to achieve it (**sem limites**)

> Remember that **nothing** is not used with other negative words, such as 'not' and 'never':
> ✓ *She said nothing.*
> ✗ *She didn't say nothing.* □ *She didn't say anything.*

• **nothingness** /'nʌθɪŋnɪs/ NOUN, NO PLURAL a state where nothing exists (**nada**)

notice /'nəʊtɪs/ ▶ VERB [notices, noticing, noticed]
to become aware of something because you see, hear, feel, smell or taste it □ *I noticed a funny smell in the hall.* □ *Did you notice the way George was looking at Emily?* □ *+ that* I noticed that the kitchen window was open. □ *+ question word* He noticed how she kept checking her mobile. (**perceber, notar**)

> Note that the verb **notice** is not used with the verbs 'can' and 'could':
> ✓ *I noticed that she was thinner.*
> ✗ *I could notice that she was thinner.*

▶ NOUN [plural **notices**]

1 a written sign □ *a notice pinned on the board* □ *A handwritten notice on the door said 'Closed'.* □ *The council has put up warning notices next to the river.* (**aviso, anúncio**)

2 *no plural* attention (**atenção**) ▣ *No one took any notice of* (= paid attention to) *her.* (**prestar atenção**) ▣ *It's come to our notice that you are always late.* (**chegar ao conhecimento**) ▣ *It didn't escape my notice that Jo left early.* (**deixar de perceber**)

3 *no plural* a warning about something that is going to happen (**notificação**) ▣ *Please give me notice if you plan to visit.* (**avisar**) ▣ *We have to be ready to leave at a moment's notice.* (**a qualquer momento**) ▣ *The schedule was changed at short notice.* (**de repente**)

4 your notice when you officially tell your employer that you are going to leave your job, or the time you work after this (**demissão**) ▣ *Cathy's handed in her notice.* (**entregar a demissão**)

5 until further notice until someone says that the situation has changed □ *The museum is closed until further notice.* (**até novo aviso**)

noticeable /'nəʊtɪsəbəl/ ADJECTIVE
obvious or easy to see □ *There was a noticeable difference in his appearance.* □ *The most noticeable feature was the smell.* (**visível**)

• **noticeably** /'nəʊtɪsəbli/ ADVERB in a way that is obvious □ *We were all noticeably more relaxed after dinner.* (**visivelmente**)

notification /ˌnəʊtɪfɪ'keɪʃən/ NOUN [plural notifications]
when someone officially tells you something ▣ *You will receive notification of any changes to the payments.* (**notificação**)

notify /'nəʊtɪfaɪ/ VERB [notifies, notifying, notified]
to officially tell someone about something □ *You will be notified of the date.* (**notificar**)

notion /'nəʊʃən/ NOUN [plural notions]
an idea or a belief □ *This goes against the whole notion of free speech.* (**noção**)

notoriety /ˌnəʊtə'raɪəti/ NOUN, NO PLURAL
the quality of being notorious ▣ *They had gained notoriety as one of the most violent gangs in Chicago.* (**notoriedade**)

notorious /nəʊ'tɔːriəs/ ADJECTIVE
famous for something bad □ *a notorious criminal* (**notório**)

• **notoriously** /nəʊ'tɔːriəsli/ ADVERB well known in a bad way □ *That model is notoriously unreliable.* (**notoriamente**)

nought /nɔːt/ NOUN [plural noughts]

1 the number 0 □ *The code is a series of ones and noughts.* □ *It's nought point five centimetres long.* □ *The car can go from nought to sixty in four seconds.* (**zero**)

2 nothing (**nada**) ▣ *All their efforts had come to nought* (= produced nothing). (**resultar em nada**)

noun /naʊn/ NOUN [plural nouns]
a word that refers to a person, a thing, or a quality. For example, tree, Sue, air and happiness are nouns. (**nome, substantivo**)

nourish /ˈnʌrɪʃ/ VERB [**nourishes, nourishing, nourished**] to provide people, animals or plants with the food they need to grow or stay healthy (nutrir)

• **nourishing** /ˈnʌrɪʃɪŋ/ ADJECTIVE containing the substances you need to stay healthy □ *a nourishing meal* (nutritivo)

• **nourishment** /ˈnʌrɪʃmənt/ NOUN, NO PLURAL the food you need to stay healthy □ *Eggs provide a vital source of nourishment.* (alimento)

novel
/ˈnɒvəl/ ▶ NOUN [*plural* **novels**] a book that tells an invented story □ *a historical/romantic novel* (romance)
▶ ADJECTIVE completely new and different from anything else □ *What a novel idea!* 🔁 *They take a novel approach to education.* (insólito)

• **novelist** /ˈnɒvəlɪst/ NOUN [*plural* **novelists**] a person who writes novels (romancista)

• **novelty** /ˈnɒvəlti/ NOUN [*plural* **novelties**]
1 the quality of being novel (novidade) 🔁 *At first I enjoyed living abroad, but the novelty soon wore off.* (perdeu o interesse pela novidade)
2 something that is novel or that you have not experienced before □ *In this part of the world, mothers who work full-time are still a bit of a novelty.* (novidade)
3 a small novelty toy or other object with no practical use (novidade)

November /nəʊˈvembə(r)/ NOUN, NO PLURAL the eleventh month of the year, after October and before December □ *What's the weather like in November?* (novembro)

novice /ˈnɒvɪs/ NOUN [*plural* **novices**] someone who is only just learning how to do something □ *a novice rider* (principiante, noviço)

now
/naʊ/ ▶ ADVERB

1 at the present time □ *It is now five o'clock.* □ *I'm working as a teacher now.* (agora) 🔁 *He has refused to speak until now.* (até agora)
2 from this moment, though not before □ *Now I can see him.* □ *You can look at the answers now.* (agora) 🔁 *From now on, I'll be giving you homework every day.* (de agora em diante)
3 from this moment, as a result of something □ *Now I can afford to go on holiday.* □ *Now will you try to be more careful?* (agora)
4 immediately □ *I'll do it now.* (agora) 🔁 *I want to see you in my office right now!* (agora mesmo)
5 used to start a sentence □ *Now, can anyone tell me the last two kings of England?* (Bem) 🔁 *Now then, I gather there has been some bad behaviour in class.* (agora, então)
6 any day/moment/time, etc. now used to say that something will happen very soon □ *The weather should change any day now.* (a qualquer dia/hora/momento/hora agora)
7 (every) now and then sometimes, but not often □ *Every now and then I treat myself to a really hot curry.* (de vez em quando)
8 for now for the present time, though the situation might change □ *She's working part time for now.* (por enquanto)
9 just now a very short time ago □ *I saw Jim outside just now.* (agora mesmo)
▶ CONJUNCTION as a result of something or after something has happened □ *Now that I've thought about it more, I've decided not to go.* □ *It's very quiet now Jon has gone.* (agora que)

nowadays
/ˈnaʊədeɪz/ ADVERB at the present time, usually when compared to the past □ *Nowadays, women usually have their babies in hospital.* □ *There's much more for youngsters to do nowadays than there was 20 years ago.* (atualmente)

nowhere
/ˈnəʊweə(r)/ ADVERB

1 not anywhere □ *We've got nowhere to go.* (em nenhum lugar) 🔁 *These birds are found nowhere else in the world.* (em nenhum outro lugar)
2 get/go nowhere to not make any progress or be successful □ *This is useless – we're getting nowhere.* □ *The talks have been going nowhere.* (chegar/ir a lugar algum)
3 nowhere to be found/seen impossible to see or find anywhere □ *Her son was nowhere to be found.* □ *The cat was nowhere to be seen.* (que não se consegue encontrar/ver)
4 from/out of nowhere appearing or happening suddenly or in a way that is not expected □ *The storm had appeared from nowhere.* □ *The car just came out of nowhere.* (do nada)
5 nowhere near not at all close in distance, time or a quality □ *Paris is nowhere near Marseilles.* □ *The stadium was nowhere near full.* (nada perto, sequer perto de)

noxious /ˈnɒkʃəs/ ADJECTIVE harmful or poisonous □ *noxious gases* (nocivo)

nozzle /ˈnɒzəl/ NOUN [*plural* **nozzles**] a part at the end of a pipe that controls a liquid or gas that comes out of it (esguicho)

nuance /ˈnjuːɒns/ NOUN [*plural* **nuances**] a slight difference in meaning, appearance, etc. □ *They don't understand the nuances of the language.* (nuança)

nuclear
/ˈnjuːklɪə(r)/ ADJECTIVE

1 to do with the reaction that happens when atoms are divided or forced together (nuclear) 🔁 *nuclear power* (energia nuclear) 🔁 *a nuclear bomb* (bomba nuclear)
2 to do with the central part of an atom. A physics word. (nuclear, do núcleo)

nucleus /ˈnjuːklɪəs/ NOUN [*plural* **nuclei**]
1 the central part of an atom. A physics word. (núcleo)
2 the central part of a living cell. A biology word. (núcleo)
3 the central or most important part of something □ *The nucleus of the team hasn't changed.* (núcleo)

nude /njuːd/ ▶ ADJECTIVE not wearing any clothes □ *a nude woman* (**nu**)
▶ NOUN [*plural* **nudes**] a picture of someone without clothes on (**nu**)

nudge /nʌdʒ/ ▶ VERB [**nudges, nudging, nudged**]
1 to push someone or something gently, especially with your elbow □ *I nudged him and he began to speak.* (**cutucar**)
2 to move or to change gradually by small amounts □ *The unemployment rate nudged up to 4.8%.* (**atingir**)
▶ NOUN [*plural* **nudges**] a gentle push, especially with your elbow 🔂 *Give him a nudge or he'll fall asleep.* (**sinal com o cotovelo, cutucada**)

nudity /ˈnjuːdətɪ/ NOUN, NO PLURAL not having any clothes on □ *The state has laws against public nudity.* (**nudez**)

nugget /ˈnʌgɪt/ NOUN [*plural* **nuggets**]
1 a small lump of something □ *a gold nugget* (**pepita**)
2 a piece of information or advice □ *He gave me some useful nuggets of information.* (**informação ou conselho**)

nuisance /ˈnjuːsəns/ NOUN [*plural* **nuisances**] a person, thing or situation that annoys you or causes problems for you □ *The rabbits have become a nuisance to local gardeners.* (**amolação**) 🔂 *'I've locked myself out.' 'Oh, what a nuisance!'* (**que amolação!**) 🔂 *He was making a nuisance of himself, shouting and singing loudly.* (**constrangimento**)

numb /nʌm/ ▶ ADJECTIVE [**number, numbest**]
1 if a part of your body is numb, you cannot feel it (**dormente**) 🔂 *I was so cold my hands had gone completely numb.* (**ficar dormente**)
2 so shocked that you cannot think clearly or show any emotion □ *I was numb with grief.* (**estarrecido**)
▶ VERB [**numbs, numbing, numbed**]
1 to cause a pain to become less or to stop someone feeling strong emotions □ *They took drugs to numb their feelings.* (**entorpecer**)
2 to cause a part of the body to lose feeling □ *The cold numbed our fingers.* (**adormecer**)

number /ˈnʌmbə(r)/ ▶ NOUN [*plural* **numbers**]
1 a word or a symbol showing how many of something there are or in what position something is in a series □ *the number four* □ *Please write down any three figure number.* □ *I was number eight on the list.* (**número**)
2 a quantity of things or people □ + *of We hope to increase the number of customers.* (**número**) 🔂 *He keeps a large number of animals.* (**grande número**) □ *A number of* (= several) *people have complained.*
3 a number that represents something or someone, for example to show what they are or who they belong to □ *a membership number* □ *What is your account number?* (**número**)
4 a telephone number □ *I'll give you my number.* (**número**) 🔂 *I must have dialled the wrong number.* (**número errado**)

5 a song or a piece of music □ *a catchy number* (**número musical**)
▶ VERB [**numbers, numbering, numbered**]
1 to give a thing or a person a number as part of a series □ *The boxes are all clearly numbered.* □ *Have you numbered the pages?* (**numerar**)
2 to be a particular quantity □ *The crowd numbered many thousands.* (**totalizar**)
3 someone's/something's days are numbered someone or something will not exist or be in a particular situation for much longer □ *His days as chief of the organization are numbered.* (**seus dias estão contados**)

number plate /ˈnʌmbəpleɪt/ NOUN [*plural* **number plates**] a metal sign on the front and the back of a vehicle, showing the letters and numbers that represent that vehicle (**chapa, placa**)

numbness /ˈnʌmnɪs/ NOUN, NO PLURAL when you lose feeling in a part of your body □ *Their sting can cause slight numbness.* (**entorpecimento**)

numeracy /ˈnjuːmərəsɪ/ NOUN, NO PLURAL the ability to use numbers and to do basic mathematics □ *Some school-leavers lack basic literacy and numeracy skills.* (**habilidade com números**)

numeral /ˈnjuːmərəl/ NOUN [*plural* **numerals**] a symbol that represents a number □ *a Roman numeral* (**algarismo**)

numerate /ˈnjuːmərət/ ADJECTIVE able to use numbers and to do basic mathematics (**hábil com números**)

numerator /ˈnjuːməreɪtə(r)/ NOUN [*plural* **numerators**] the number above the line in a fraction. A maths word. (**numerador**)

numerical /njuːˈmerɪkəl/ ADJECTIVE to do with numbers or using numbers □ *Put the cards into numerical order.* (**numérico**)

numerous /ˈnjuːmərəs/ ADJECTIVE many □ *Numerous people have had the same experience.* (**numeroso**) 🔂 *I've met him on numerous occasions.* (**em inúmeras ocasiões**)

nun /nʌn/ NOUN [*plural* **nuns**] a member of a religious group of women who live away from other people (**freira**)

nurse /nɜːs/ ▶ NOUN [*plural* **nurses**] a person whose job is to look after people when they are ill or injured, especially in a hospital □ *She works as a nurse at the hospital.* (**enfermeiro**)
▶ VERB [**nurses, nursing, nursed**] to look after someone when they are ill or injured □ *He had nursed her back to health over several weeks.* (**cuidar**)

nursery /ˈnɜːsərɪ/ NOUN [*plural* **nurseries**]
1 a place where babies and young children are looked after while their parents are at work □ *Lizzie goes to a local nursery three days a week.* (**creche**)
2 a place where plants are grown and sold (**viveiro**)

3 a room in a house for young children (**quarto de criança**)

nursery rhyme /'nɜːsəri ˌraɪm/ NOUN [plural **nursery rhymes**] a short simple traditional poem or song for children (**rimas infantis**)

nursery school /'nɜːsəri ˌskuːl/ NOUN [plural **nursery schools**] a school for children between about three and five years old (**escola maternal**)

nursing /'nɜːsɪŋ/ NOUN, NO PLURAL the job of being a nurse (**enfermagem**)

nursing home /'nɜːsɪŋ həʊm/ NOUN [plural **nursing homes**] a place where people live when they are too old or ill to look after themselves (**clínica de repouso**)

nurture /'nɜːtʃə(r)/ VERB [**nurtures, nurturing, nurtured**]
1 to look after a person, animal or plant so that they grow in a healthy way □ *After birth, all mammals nurture their offspring.* (**criar**)
2 to help and encourage someone or something to develop □ *The scholarship was set up to nurture young talent.* (**estimular**)

nut /nʌt/ NOUN [plural **nuts**]
1 the fruit of some trees that has a hard shell and an inside part that can often be eaten □ *a cashewnut* □ *a bag of mixed nuts* (**noz**)
2 a small piece of metal with a hole in the middle which fits onto the end of a bolt (= thin piece of metal) to hold things together □ *a wheel nut* (**porca**)
3 an informal word for someone who is very interested in or enthusiastic about something □ *He's a bit of a fitness nut.* (**maluco**)
♦ IDIOM **the nuts and bolts** the basic parts or details of a job or an activity □ *I knew nothing about the nuts and bolts of running a business.* (**porcas e parafusos**)

nutmeg /'nʌtmeg/ NOUN [plural **nutmegs**] a hard brown seed that is made into a powder and used as a spice to flavour food (**noz-moscada**)

nutrient /'njuːtriənt/ NOUN [plural **nutrients**]
1 any substance in food that gives you energy and makes you healthy □ *Iron is an essential nutrient for many animals.* (**nutriente**)
2 any substance in soil that helps plants to grow (**nutriente**)

nutrition /njuˈtrɪʃən/ NOUN, NO PLURAL
1 food and the way it affects your health □ *Good nutrition is necessary for a quick recovery.* □ *information about nutrition* (**nutrição**)
2 the study of food and how it affects health □ *a nutrition expert* (**nutrição**)

• **nutritional** /njuˈtrɪʃənəl/ ADJECTIVE to do with nutrition (**alimentar, nutricional**) 🔁 *These drinks offer no nutritional value.* □ *a nutritional supplement* (**valor alimentar nutricional**)

• **nutritious** /njuˈtrɪʃəs/ ADJECTIVE healthy for you to eat or drink □ *a nutritious meal* (**nutritivo**)

nutshell /'nʌtʃel/ NOUN [plural **nutshells**] the hard shell around a nut (**casca de noz**)
♦ IDIOM **in a nutshell** expressed in as few words as possible □ *To put it in a nutshell, we must stop spending so much money.* (**em poucas palavras**)

nutty /'nʌti/ ADJECTIVE [**nuttier, nuttiest**]
1 containing nuts or tasting of nuts □ *a nutty flavor* (**de noz**)
2 an informal word meaning silly or very strange □ *a nutty idea* (**pirado**)

nuzzle /'nʌzəl/ VERB [**nuzzles, nuzzling, nuzzled**] to rub your face or nose gently against something □ *The dog nuzzled his face.* (**focinhar**)

nylon /'naɪlɒn/ NOUN, NO PLURAL a strong, light artificial material used for example to make clothes and rope □ *a black nylon bag* (**náilon**)

Oo

O or **o** /əʊ/ the 15th letter of the alphabet (**a décima quinta letra do alfabeto**)

oak /əʊk/ NOUN [plural **oaks**] a large tree with seeds called acorns, or the wood from this tree (**carvalho**)

OAP /ˌəʊeɪˈpiː/ ABBREVIATION **old age pensioner** (**aposentado por idade**)

oar /ɔː(r)/ NOUN [plural **oars**] a long piece of wood with a flat end, used for making a boat move (**remo**)

oasis /əʊˈeɪsɪs/ NOUN [plural **oases**]
 1 a place in a desert where there are plants and water (**oásis**)
 2 a calm, pleasant place that is surrounded by noise and activity □ *The hotel is an oasis of calm in a busy city.* (**oásis**)

oath /əʊθ/ NOUN [plural **oaths**] a formal promise (**juramento**) 🔁 *Members swear an oath of secrecy about the group.* (**fazer um juramento**)

oats /əʊts/ PLURAL NOUN a type of grain that people and animals eat (**aveia**)

obedience /əˈbiːdɪəns/ NOUN, NO PLURAL the quality of being willing to do what a person or rule tells you to do □ *Teachers expect obedience from their pupils.* (**obediência**)
• **obedient** /əˈbiːdɪənt/ ADJECTIVE doing what a person or rule tells you to do □ *an obedient child* (**obediente**)

obese /əʊˈbiːs/ ADJECTIVE extremely fat (**obeso**)
• **obesity** /əʊˈbiːsəti/ NOUN, NO PLURAL when someone is obese □ *childhood obesity* (**obesidade**)

obey /əˈbeɪ/ VERB [**obeys**, **obeying**, **obeyed**] to do what a person or rule tells you to do □ *He was taught to obey his parents.* (**obedecer**) 🔁 *Drivers must obey the law.* (**obedecer às leis**) 🔁 *He refused to obey a court order.* (**recusar obedecer**)

obituary /əˈbɪtʃʊəri/ NOUN [plural **obituaries**] an announcement in a newspaper that someone has died, with a short description of their life (**obituário**)

object¹ /ˈɒbdʒɪkt/ NOUN [plural **objects**]
 1 a thing that you can see or touch but not a person or animal □ *There were various objects on the table.* □ *Keep sharp objects away from children.* (**objeto**)
 2 an aim or purpose □ *His main object in life was to become rich.* □ **+ of** *The object of the exercise is to improve teaching standards.* (**objetivo**)
 3 **object of something** someone or something that people have a particular feeling about □ *The Prime Minister became an object of ridicule.* (**objeto**)
 4 in grammar, the person or thing that a verb affects □ *In the sentence 'I ate the apple', 'apple' is the object.* (**objeto gramatical**)

object² /əbˈdʒekt/ VERB [**objects**, **objecting**, **objected**] to say that you do not want something to happen □ *Nobody objected to the original proposal.* (**objetar**)
• **objection** /əbˈdʒekʃən/ NOUN [plural **objections**] a reason you do not want something to happen □ *My only objection is that he is too young.* (**objeção**) 🔁 *I have no objections to the changes.* (**não ter objeções**)
• **objectionable** /əbˈdʒekʃənəbəl/ ADJECTIVE offensive □ *I find his attitude thoroughly objectionable.* (**repreensível**)

objective /əbˈdʒektɪv/ ▶ NOUN [plural **objectives**] an aim or purpose (**objetivo**) 🔁 *They achieved their main objective of raising money for the hospital.* (**objetivo principal**)
▶ ADJECTIVE telling facts which are not influenced by opinions or feelings □ *We make an objective assessment of each student's progress.* (**objetivo**)

obligation /ˌɒblɪˈɡeɪʃən/ NOUN [plural **obligations**] a duty to do something (**obrigação**) 🔁 *Schools have a legal obligation to take good care of students.* (**obrigação legal**)
• **obligatory** /əˈblɪɡətəri/ ADJECTIVE
 1 something that is obligatory must be done because of a law or rule □ *Voting is obligatory in Peru.* (**obrigatório**)
 2 if something is obligatory in a particular situation, it is done so often that people expect it □ *After the wedding ceremony there were the obligatory photographs.* (**obrigatório**)
• **oblige** /əˈblaɪdʒ/ VERB [**obliges**, **obliging**, **obliged**]
 1 if you are obliged to do something, you must do it □ *Banks are obliged to list the names of their directors.* (**obrigar**)
 2 to help someone by doing something they have asked you to (**atender uma solicitação**) 🔁 *He asked me to speak at the conference and I was happy to oblige.* (**feliz em atender**)

- **obliged** /əˈblaɪdʒd/ ADJECTIVE (**obrigado**) **feel obliged to do something** to feel that you must do something for someone □ *I felt obliged to ask her to the party as she had invited me to hers.* (**sentir-se obrigado a**)
- **obliging** /əˈblaɪdʒɪŋ/ ADJECTIVE willing to help □ *He's very obliging.* (**prestativo, obsequioso**)

oblique /əˈbliːk/ ADJECTIVE saying something in a way that is not direct. A formal word □ *He made an oblique reference to the problem.* (**oblíquo**)

obliterate /əˈblɪtəreɪt/ VERB [**obliterates, obliterating, obliterated**] to destroy something completely □ *The house was obliterated by an earthquake.* (**arrasar**)

oblivion /əˈblɪviən/ NOUN, NO PLURAL
1 when someone or something has been completely forgotten □ *Many television presenters slide into oblivion.* (**esquecimento**)
2 a state in which you are not aware of what is happening around you □ *The sleeping pill brings almost instant oblivion.* (**desligamento**)

- **oblivious** /əˈblɪviəs/ ADJECTIVE not aware of what is happening □ *He seemed oblivious to the chaos around him.* (**esquecido, distraído**)

oblong /ˈɒblɒŋ/ ▶ NOUN [plural **oblongs**] a rectangle (**retângulo**) ▶ ADJECTIVE in the shape of a rectangle □ *an oblong table* (**retangular**)

obnoxious /əbˈnɒkʃəs/ ADJECTIVE rude and unpleasant □ *obnoxious behavior* (**detestável**)

oboe /ˈəʊbəʊ/ NOUN [plural **oboes**] a musical instrument shaped like a long tube that you play by blowing through it (**oboé**)

obscene /əbˈsiːn/ ADJECTIVE
1 unpleasant and shocking □ *obscene language* (**obsceno**)
2 too large and morally wrong □ *He earns an obscene amount of money.* (**imoral**)

- **obscenity** /əbˈsenəti/ NOUN [plural **obscenities**]
1 a word that is very rude □ *The youths shouted obscenities at the police.* (**palavrão**)
2 behaviour or language that is unpleasant or shocking (**obscenidade**)

obscure /əbˈskjʊə(r)/ ▶ ADJECTIVE only known by a few people □ *an obscure artist* (**obscuro**)
▶ VERB [**obscures, obscuring, obscured**]
1 to cover something so that you cannot see it □ *Thick clouds obscured the sun.* (**obscurecer**)
2 to hide a fact or make it difficult to understand □ *The article deliberately obscures some vital facts.* (**obscurecer**)

- **obscurity** /əbˈskjʊərəti/ NOUN, NO PLURAL the state when people do not know about or do not remember someone or something □ *After years of obscurity, he suddenly found himself famous.* (**obscuridade**)

obsequious /əbˈsiːkwiəs/ ADJECTIVE a formal word meaning too eager to agree with someone or do things for them □ *an obsequious manner* (**subserviente**)

observant /əbˈzɜːvənt/ ADJECTIVE good at noticing things (**observador**)

observation /ˌɒbzəˈveɪʃən/ NOUN [plural **observations**]
1 a remark (**observação**) 🔁 *She made some interesting observations about their relationship.* (**fazer observações**)
2 no plural when you watch someone or something very carefully □ *He has been kept in hospital for observation.* (**observação**)

observatory /əbˈzɜːvətəri/ NOUN [plural **observatories**] a building with equipment for people to look at the stars and planets (**observatório**)

observe /əbˈzɜːv/ VERB [**observes, observing, observed**]
1 to watch someone or something very carefully □ *Police continued to observe his actions with interest.* (**observar**)
2 a formal word meaning to notice someone or something □ *Scientists observed no serious side effects of the drug.* (**notar**)
3 to obey a rule, agreement or religious tradition □ *The older members of the community still observe this tradition.* (**observar**)
4 a formal word meaning to say something that you notice □ *'You're very smartly dressed,' he observed.* (**fazer uma observação, reparar**)

- **observer** /əbˈzɜːvə(r)/ NOUN [plural **observers**]
1 someone who sees something (**observador**) 🔁 *A casual observer* (= someone who sees something but does not pay close attention to it) *would not have realized that anything was wrong.* (**observador casual**)
2 someone who watches something as a job □ *political observers* (**observador**)

obsess /əbˈses/ VERB [**obsesses, obsessing, obsessed**] to think about someone or something too much of the time □ *I don't have time to obsess about eating and fitness any more.* (**obcecar**)

- **obsessed** /əbˈsest/ ADJECTIVE thinking about someone or something too much of the time □ *He became obsessed with football.* (**obcecado**)

- **obsession** /əbˈseʃən/ NOUN [plural **obsessions**]
1 a person or thing that you cannot stop thinking about □ *Horse-racing had become an obsession for him.* (**obsessão**)
2 no plural when you cannot stop thinking about something □ *David's tidiness borders on obsession.* (**obsessão**)

- **obsessive** /əbˈsesɪv/ ADJECTIVE unable to stop thinking about something or behaving in a particular way □ *obsessive jealousy* (**obsessivo**)

obsolescent /ˌɒbsəˈlesənt/ ADJECTIVE being replaced by something newer and better. A formal word □ *obsolescent technology* (**obsolescente**)

obsolete

obsolete /ˈɒbsəliːt/ ADJECTIVE no longer used because there is now something newer and better □ *Much of this technology is now obsolete.* (obsoleto)

obstacle /ˈɒbstəkəl/ NOUN [plural **obstacles**]
1 something that stops you from doing what you want to do □ *He had overcome a lot of obstacles in his life.* (obstáculo)
2 an object that is in front of you and that you must move or go around in order to go forward (obstáculo)

obstetrician /ˌɒbstəˈtrɪʃən/ NOUN [plural **obstetricians**] a doctor who deals with pregnant women and the birth of babies (obstetra)

• **obstetrics** /ɒbˈstetrɪks/ NOUN, NO PLURAL the area of medicine to do with pregnant women and the birth of babies (obstetrícia)

obstinacy /ˈɒbstɪnəsi/ NOUN, NO PLURAL when someone is obstinate (obstinação)

• **obstinate** /ˈɒbstənət/ ADJECTIVE refusing to change your ideas or behaviour □ *an obstinate child* (obstinado)

obstruct /əbˈstrʌkt/ VERB [**obstructs, obstructing, obstructed**]
1 to block somewhere such as a road, door or path, so that people cannot move along or through it □ *The road was obstructed by a fallen tree.* (obstruir)
2 to stop someone from seeing something □ *Her hat was obstructing his vision.* (obstruir)
3 to try to prevent something from happening □ *He was arrested for obstructing the police investigation.* (obstruir)

• **obstruction** /əbˈstrʌkʃən/ NOUN [plural **obstructions**]
1 when something blocks somewhere such as a road, door or path, so that people cannot move along or through it □ *A badly parked car was causing an obstruction.* (obstrução)
2 when something prevents something else from happening □ *the obstruction of justice* (obstrução)

obtain /əbˈteɪn/ VERB [**obtains, obtaining, obtained**] a formal word meaning to get something □ *Clients can obtain information from our website.* (obter)

> Note that the word obtain is used mainly in formal situations and is not common. The usual word is get:
> ✓ Where did you get your jacket?
> ✗ Where did you obtain your jacket?

obtuse /əbˈtjuːs/ ADJECTIVE
1 a formal word meaning stupid (tolo)
2 an obtuse angle is more than 90°C. A maths word. (obtuso)

obvious /ˈɒbvɪəs/ ADJECTIVE easy to see or understand (óbvio) □ + **that** *It was obvious that she was unhappy.* 🔊 *It was blindingly obvious* (= very obvious) *that the project would fail.* (completamente óbvio) 🔊 *He started crying for no obvious reason.* (razão óbvia) □ + **to** *It was obvious to anyone in the room that he was lying.*

• **obviously** /ˈɒbvɪəsli/ ADVERB
1 used for giving information that you expect other people will already know or will agree with □ *Obviously, I'll need some help.* □ *Obviously we're not happy with this situation.* (obviamente)
2 in a way that is easy to see or understand □ *Lara was so obviously disappointed.* (obviamente)

occasion /əˈkeɪʒən/ NOUN [plural **occasions**]
1 a particular time when something happens □ *I've met him on several occasions.* 🔊 *He has run in the race on three previous occasions.* (ocasião)
2 an important event (ocasião) 🔊 *She only wore the shoes for special occasions.* (ocasiões especiais) 🔊 *The shop has been trading for 50 years and is offering free drinks to mark the occasion.* (comemorar a ocasião)
3 on occasion(s) sometimes □ *We've had arguments on occasion.* (ocasionalmente)

• **occasional** /əˈkeɪʒənəl/ ADJECTIVE happening sometimes but not often □ *They made occasional visits to Scotland.* (ocasional, eventual) 🔊 *Eating the occasional ice cream won't make you fat.* (eventual)

• **occasionally** /əˈkeɪʒənəli/ ADVERB sometimes but not often □ *I occasionally go to the theatre.* 🔊 *Very occasionally I've felt lonely.* (ocasionalmente)

occult /ɒˈkʌlt/ NOUN, NO PLURAL (oculto) **the occult** things which are to do with magic or mysterious powers that cannot be explained (práticas sobrenaturais)

occupant /ˈɒkjʊpənt/ NOUN [plural **occupants**] a formal word meaning someone who is in a building or vehicle □ *the occupants of the flat* (ocupante)

occupation /ˌɒkjuˈpeɪʃən/ NOUN [plural **occupations**]
1 a formal word meaning job □ *Firefighting is a dangerous occupation.* □ *professional occupations* (ocupação, profissão)
2 no plural when an army enters a country or area and takes control of it 🔊 + **of** *the Roman occupation of Britain* (ocupação)
3 a formal word meaning something you like doing in your free time □ *Reading is his favourite occupation.* (ocupação)

• **occupational** /ˌɒkjuˈpeɪʃənəl/ ADJECTIVE to do with your job (ocupacional, profissional) 🔊 *For bank workers, robbery is an occupational hazard* (= something bad that sometimes happens in a particular job). (riscos ocupacionais) □ *occupational pensions*

occupied /ˈɒkjʊpaɪd/ ADJECTIVE
1 already being used by someone □ *Are these buildings occupied?* (ocupado)

2 busy doing something (ocupado) 🔲 *This book should keep you occupied for a while.* (**manter ocupado**)
3 controlled by the army of another country 🔲 *occupied territories* (**ocupado**)

occupier /'ɒkjupaɪə(r)/ NOUN [plural **occupiers**] a formal word meaning the person who lives in a particular house or flat (**ocupante**)

occupy /'ɒkjupaɪ/ VERB [**occupies, occupying, occupied**]
1 to occupy a space is to fill it 🔲 *A table occupied the centre of the room.* (**ocupar**)
2 if someone occupies a building, they live or work there 🔲 *The building is occupied by several small companies.* (**ocupar**)
3 to keep someone busy 🔲 *She has more than enough to occupy her.* 🔲 *He occupied himself with the garden.* (**ocupar**)
4 to enter a country or area and take control of it with an army 🔲 *Soldiers were occupying the town.* (**ocupar**)
5 a formal word meaning to have a particular job or position 🔲 *It was the first time a woman had occupied the position of Prime Minister.* (**ocupar**)

occur /ə'kɜː(r)/ VERB [**occurs, occurring, occurred**]
1 a formal word meaning to happen 🔲 *The accident occurred last night.* (**ocorrer**)
2 to exist or be present 🔲 *Dragons only occur in fairy tales.* (**acontecer, existir**)
♦ PHRASAL VERB **occur to someone** if something occurs to you, you suddenly think it 🔲 *It never occurred to me that I should see a doctor about it.* (**ocorrer**)
• **occurrence** /ə'kʌrəns/ NOUN [plural **occurrences**] something that happens 🔲 *Shark attacks are a very rare occurrence.* (**ocorrência, acontecimento**)

ocean /'əʊʃən/ NOUN [plural **oceans**]
1 one of the 5 large areas of sea in the world 🔲 *the Atlantic Ocean* (**oceano**)
2 the ocean the salt water that covers most of the Earth's surface 🔲 *ocean currents* (**o oceano**)

o'clock /ə'klɒk/ ADVERB used after the numbers one to twelve to say what time of day it is 🔲 *School starts at nine o'clock.* 🔲 *'What time is it?' 'It's nearly 12 o'clock.'* (**hora, horas**)

octagon /'ɒktəgən/ NOUN [plural **octagons**] a shape with eight sides. A maths word. (**octágono**)
• **octagonal** /ɒk'tægənəl/ ADJECTIVE in the shape of an octagon. A maths word. (**octagonal**)

octave /'ɒktɪv/ NOUN [plural **octaves**] a range of eight musical notes, for example from one C to the next C above or below it (**oitava**)

October /ɒk'təʊbə(r)/ NOUN, NO PLURAL the tenth month of the year, after September and before November 🔲 *He retired in October.* (**outubro**)

octopus /'ɒktəpəs/ NOUN [plural **octopuses**] a sea animal with eight long arms (**polvo**)

odd /ɒd/ ADJECTIVE [**odder, oddest**]
1 strange 🔲 *It seems an odd choice.* 🔲 *He's very odd.* (**estranho**)
2 happening sometimes but not often 🔲 *There has been the odd occasion when we've disagreed.* (**ocasional**)
3 without the other one of a pair 🔲 *an odd shoe* (**avulso**)
4 of different types, sizes, shapes, etc. 🔲 *Have you got any odd bits of wood I could use?* (**de sobra**)
5 an odd number is a number that you cannot divide exactly by two 🔲 *5 and 7 are odd numbers.* (**ímpar**)
6 20 odd/50 odd, etc. approximately 20, 50, etc. 🔲 *He's lived here 30 odd years.* (**por volta de**)
• **oddity** /'ɒdətɪ/ NOUN [plural **oddities**] a strange or unusual person or thing 🔲 *He's always been a bit of an oddity.* (**pessoa ou coisa estranha**)
• **oddly** /'ɒdlɪ/ ADVERB
1 strangely 🔲 *He's behaving very oddly.* (**estranhamente**)
2 oddly enough used for saying that something seems surprising or strange 🔲 *Oddly enough, he didn't seem disappointed that he'd lost.* (**curiosamente**)

odds /ɒdz/ PLURAL NOUN
1 the chances of something happening 🔲 *The odds are that he will win.* (**probabilidades**)
2 against all odds if something happens against all odds, it happens even though it did not seem possible 🔲 *Against all odds, she made a full recovery.* (**contra todas as possibilidades**)
3 at odds with someone/something disagreeing with someone or something 🔲 *The countries are at odds with each other on many issues.* (**em desacordo com alguém/algo**)
♦ IDIOM **it makes no odds** an informal way of saying that it is not important to you what happens 🔲 *It makes no odds to me whether he comes or not.* (**não tem importância**)

odds and ends /,ɒdz ən 'endz/ PLURAL NOUN different small objects which are not valuable 🔲 *I keep various odds and ends in that drawer.* (**bugigangas**)

odious /'əʊdɪəs/ ADJECTIVE a formal word meaning extremely unpleasant 🔲 *an odious man* (**odioso**)

odor /'əʊdə(r)/ NOUN [plural **odors**] the US spelling of **odour** (**odor**)

odour /'əʊdə(r)/ NOUN [plural **odours**] a smell, especially a bad one 🔲 *There was a strong odour of rotting fish.* (**odor**)

oesophagus /iː'sɒfəgəs/ NOUN [plural **oesophaguses** or **oesophagi**] the tube that takes food from the mouth to the stomach. A biology word. (**esôfago**)

oestrogen /'iːstrədʒən/ NOUN, NO PLURAL a chemical substance that causes female characteristics to develop. A biology word. (**estrogênio**)

of /əv/ PREPOSITION

1 used to show an amount or measurement □ *hundreds of people* □ *a pint of milk* □ *an increase of 13* 🔁 *I'm part of a team.* □ *I left home at the age of 16.* (**de**)

2 used to show which members of a group are affected or being talked about □ *I have some bananas, but none of themare ripe.* □ *Many of our members are over 60.* □ *All of the children will receive a present.* (**de**)

3 used to talk about the characteristics or qualities that someone or something has □ *Did you notice the size of their offices?* (**de**)

4 used after a noun to show a particular example of that thing □ *There have been several cases of cholera.* □ *I grew up in the town of Aylesbury.* □ *We worked together for a short period of time.* (**de**)

5 made from or caused by something □ *They constructed a building of ice.* □ *There was a large pile of newspapers in the corner.* □ *The whole house smelled of garlic.* □ *We could hear their shouts of joy.* □ *He died of hunger.* (**de**)

6 about something, showing something or to do with something □ *He told us stories of his adventures in India.* □ *I need a map of Berlin.* □ *I always carry a photograph of my children.* □ *You remind me of my sister.* □ *He was frightened of bees.* (**de**)

7 containing something □ *I gave her a box of chocolates.* □ *Would you like a glass of water?* □ *I read a book of his poems.* (**de**)

8 belonging to or experienced by someone or something □ *The furniture is the property of the school.* □ *I lost the lid of the box.* □ *We must consider the needs of the patients.* (**de**)

9 used to show the position of something or someone □ *We live just south of Edinburgh.* □ *I sat at the side of the bed.* □ *There is a large garden to the rear of the property.* (**de**)

off /ɒf/ ▶ ADVERB, PREPOSITION

1 away from the top or surface of something □ *I took the book off the shelf.* □ *Keep off the grass.* □ *I'm trying to get the mud off my shoes.* □ *Make sure you don't fall off!* (**distante, afastado de, para fora de alguma superfície**)

2 no longer attached to something □ *The petals have all dropped off.* □ *Some tiles have come off the roof.* (**separar-se de**)

3 away from a place □ *He walked off and left me.* (**distante**)

4 if you take clothes off, you stop wearing them □ *I took off my jacket.* □ *He had his shoes off.* (**tirar uma roupa/sapato**)

5 out of a public vehicle □ *I got off the train in Padua.* □ *Take the number 7 bus and get off at the station.* (**descer**)

6 not operating □ *I switched the heating off.* □ *Make sure your phones are off.* (**desligar, desligado**)

7 if a price has a particular amount off, it is reduced by that amount □ *All computer games are 20% off this week.* (**desconto**)

8 not at work or at school □ *Why don't you take the day off?* □ *She's off work today.* (**de folga, livre**)

9 away in distance or time □ *We were drifting a few miles off the coast.* □ *The holiday seems a long way off.* (**distante**)

10 near to something, and usually connected to it □ *My office is off the main corridor.* □ *Our road is just off the main road.* (**próximo de**)

▶ ADJECTIVE

1 if food is off, it is rotten and cannot be eaten □ *This milk is off.* (**estragado**)

2 not at work or school □ *Lulu is off on Fridays.* (**de folga**)

3 not going to happen now □ *The holiday is off.* (**cancelado**)

4 not correct □ *The figures were off by a large amount.* (**errado**)

5 if a particular food is off in a restaurant, they have sold it all and you cannot now have it □ *The salmon is off.* (**esgotado**)

▶ go to **badly-off, well-off**

offal /'ɒfəl/ NOUN, NO PLURAL animal organs such as the liver, heart, etc. which people eat (**miúdos**)

off-chance /'ɒftʃɑːns/ NOUN, NO PLURAL **on the off-chance** if you do something **on the off-chance**, you do it because you hope something good might happen even though it does not seem likely □ *I don't suppose they'll have any tickets left, but I'll ring up on the off chance.* (**possibilidade remota**)

offence /ə'fens/ NOUN [plural **offences**]

1 a crime □ *The police charged him with three offences.* (**transgressão**) 🔁 *He has committed several violent offences.* (**cometer transgressões**) 🔁 *Burning the flag is a criminal offence in some countries.* (**transgressão criminal**)

2 *no plural* when you upset someone by saying or doing something (**ofensa**) 🔁 *His comments certainly caused offence.* (**causou ofensa**) 🔁 *Philip took offence* (= felt offended) *at the suggestion.* (**ficar ofendido**)

offend /ə'fend/ VERB [offends, offending, offended]

1 to make someone feel upset or angry by something you say or do □ *I hope I didn't offend anyone.* (**ofender**)

2 a formal word meaning to commit a crime □ *Prisons are full of people who have offended more than once.* (**transgredir**)

• **offended** /ə'fendɪd/ ADJECTIVE angry or upset because of something that someone has said or done □ *I felt very offended that he hadn't invited me to the wedding.* (**ofendido**)

• **offender** /ə'fendə(r)/ NOUN [plural **offenders**] a person who has committed a crime □ *young offenders* (**transgressor**)

offense

offense /əˈfens/ NOUN [plural **offenses**] the US spelling of **offence** (repulsivo)

offensive /əˈfensɪv/ ▶ ADJECTIVE

1 rude and insulting □ *offensive remarks* (ofensivo) ▣ *He found the question deeply offensive.* (profundamente ofensivo)
2 very unpleasant □ *an offensive smell* (repulsivo)
3 used for or to do with attacking (ofensivo) ▣ *offensive weapons* (arma de ataque)
▶ NOUN [plural **offensives**] a military attack (ofensiva) ▣ *The army launched a major offensive against the rebels.* (lançar uma ofensiva)

offer /ˈɒfə(r)/ ▶ VERB [**offers, offering, offered**]

1 to ask someone if they want something □ *She offered me another drink.* □ *+ to He offered the sweets to all the children in the class.* (oferecer)
2 to say that you will do something for someone □ *+ to do something She offered to carry my bag for me.* (oferecer)
3 to provide something □ *The college offers a wide variety of courses.* □ *An accountant might be able to offer you some advice.* (oferecer)
4 to say that you will pay a particular amount of money for something □ *I'll offer you £50 for the picture.* (oferecer)
▶ NOUN [plural **offers**]
1 when you ask someone if they want something or if you can do something for them (oferta, proposta) ▣ *It was a very generous offer.* (proposta generosa) ▣ *I've had several job offers.* (propostas de emprego) ▣ *She accepted his offer to drive her home.* □ *+ of an offer of help* (aceitar uma proposta)
2 an amount of money offered (oferta) ▣ *They made an offer of £300,000 for the house.* (fazer uma oferta)
3 when something is sold at a lower price than usual ▣ *Check the company's website for special offers.* (oferta)
4 on offer (a) available □ *There's a free lunch on offer for anyone who helps.* (b) being sold at a lower price than usual □ *These chocolates were on offer.* (em oferta)
• **offering** /ˈɒfərɪŋ/ NOUN [plural **offerings**] something that you give to someone □ *This is the television channel's latest offering.* (presente)

offhand /ˌɒfˈhænd/ ▶ ADJECTIVE slightly rude and unfriendly □ *You were a bit offhand with her at the meeting.* (brusco, rude)
▶ ADVERB now and without thinking about something □ *Can you tell me offhand how much it might cost?* (improviso)

office /ˈɒfɪs/ NOUN [plural **offices**]

1 a building where people work for a company (escritório) ▣ *Our head office (= main office) is in London.* (matriz) ▣ *an office building* (prédio de escritórios) ▣ *office workers* (funcionários de escritório)
2 the room in which a particular person works □ *The manager is in her office.* (escritório)
3 a room or building used for a particular purpose □ *the tourist information office* □ *The ticket office opens at 8 o'clock.* (gabinete)
4 an important job or position □ *He's only been in office for a year.* ▣ *She held office for several years.* □ *+ of the office of President* (função)

officer /ˈɒfɪsə(r)/ NOUN [plural **officers**]

1 a person in the army, navy or air force who is in charge of ordinary soldiers □ *senior army officers* (oficial)
2 someone who has a particular job in a government or organization □ *a prison officer* □ *immigration officers* □ *He's the chief executive officer of the company.* (funcionário)
3 a police officer □ *Armed officers shot the man.* (oficial)

official /əˈfɪʃəl/ ▶ ADJECTIVE

1 done or approved by a government or someone in authority □ *an official announcement* □ *Canada has two official languages.* □ *Official figures show that crime has risen by 10%.* (oficial)
2 to do with an important job □ *The Queen has cancelled her official engagements due to illness.* □ *The President will make an official visit to Moscow.* (oficial)
3 an official reason, explanation, etc. is one that people are told, but it may not be true □ *The official explanation was that he was ill.* (oficial)
▶ NOUN [plural **officials**] someone who has an important job in an organization, especially a government (funcionário graduado) ▣ *government officials* (funcionários graduados do governo)
• **officially** /əˈfɪʃəli/ ADVERB
1 publicly and formally □ *The new library is now officially open.* □ *He will officially retire next week.* (oficialmente)
2 according to the information that people have been given, although it may not be true □ *Officially the company is saying that he chose to resign.* (oficialmente)

officious /əˈfɪʃəs/ ADJECTIVE too eager to tell other people what to do □ *An officious little man told us to move our bicycles.* (intrometido)

offing /ˈɒfɪŋ/ NOUN, NO PLURAL **be in the offing** to be going to happen soon □ *Apparently there's a deal in the offing.* (iminente)

off-licence /ˈɒflaɪsəns/ NOUN [plural **off-licences**] a shop that sells alcohol (licença para venda de bebida alcoólica)

offline /ˌɒfˈlaɪn/ ADJECTIVE a computer which is offline is not connected to the Internet. A computing word. (sem conexão)

offload /ɒfˈləʊd/ VERB [**offloads, offloading, offloaded**] to sell or give something that you do not want to someone else □ *The company is trying to offload its troubled restaurant business.* (desfazer-se de)

off-peak /ˌɒfˈpiːk/ ADJECTIVE, ADVERB at the cheapest, least popular times ☐ *I always travel off-peak.* (fora da hora de pico)

off-putting /ˈɒfˌpʊtɪŋ/ ADJECTIVE making you not want to go somewhere, have something, etc. ☐ *His description of the hotel was a bit off-putting.* (desencorajador)

offset /ˈɒfset/ VERB [**offsets, offsetting, offset**] one thing offsets another thing when it has the opposite effect and creates a balance ☐ *The price rises will be offset by tax cuts.* (contrabalançar)
• **offsetting** /ˈɒfsetɪŋ/ NOUN, NO PLURAL when you do something that reduces the amount of carbon dioxide in the air, such as paying for someone to plant trees, because you are doing something that puts more carbon dioxide in the air, such as flying by aeroplane (redução na emissão de dióxido de carbono)

offshoot /ˈɒfʃuːt/ NOUN [plural **offshoots**] a company or group that has developed from a larger one ☐ *The company is an offshoot of a large American multinational.* (ramificação)

offshore /ˌɒfˈʃɔː(r)/ ADJECTIVE
1 in the sea, not far from the land ☐ *offshore oil rigs* (costeiro)
2 an offshore wind is blowing away from the land towards the sea ☐ *offshore breezes* (costeiro)

offside /ˌɒfˈsaɪd/ ADJECTIVE in a position that is not allowed by the rules of a game such as football ☐ *The goal was disallowed because Rodriguez was offside.* (em impedimento)

offspring /ˈɒfsprɪŋ/ NOUN [plural **offspring**] a formal word for the child of a person or animal ☐ *Parents are responsible for their offspring.* (prole)

off-white /ˌɒfˈwaɪt/ ▶ NOUN, NO PLURAL a white colour that is slightly yellow or slightly grey (quase branco, branco não puro)
▶ ADJECTIVE having a white colour that is slightly yellow or slightly grey ☐ *an off-white wedding dress*

often /ˈɒfən, ˈɒftən/ ADVERB
1 many times ☐ *I often go to the cinema.* ☐ *I don't play tennis very often now.* (com frequência) ▣ *How often do you see Jess?* (com que frequência) ▣ *I wish I could travel more often.* (com mais frequência) ▣ *He visits the area quite often.* (com muita frequência)
2 in many situations or cases ☐ *Jokes are often difficult to translate.* ☐ *Often, schools are unable to deal with problem students.* (com frequência)

ogre /ˈəʊɡə(r)/ NOUN [plural **ogres**]
1 a frightening person ☐ *Her father was a bit of an ogre.* (ogro)
2 a big, ugly and frightening man in children's stories (ogro)

oh /əʊ/ EXCLAMATION
1 used when you have just understood something ☐ *Oh, I see.* ☐ *Oh, so that's why she isn't here.* (oh)
2 used when you are disappointed or annoyed ☐ *Oh, that's a shame!* ☐ *Oh no, the computer has just crashed!* (ah)
3 used when you are very pleased or surprised ☐ *Oh, that's very kind!* ☐ *Oh, that's fantastic!* (ah)

oil /ɔɪl/ ▶ NOUN, NO PLURAL
1 a thick, dark liquid under the ground that is used for making petrol ☐ *Oil prices have increased.* ☐ *the oil industry* ☐ *US oil production* (petróleo)
2 a thick liquid from plants or animals, used in cooking ☐ *olive oil* ☐ *vegetable oil* ☐ *Heat the oil in a pan and fry the onions until soft.* (óleo)
▶ VERB [**oils, oiling, oiled**] to put oil on something (lubrificar, olear)

oilfield /ˈɔɪlfiːld/ NOUN [plural **oilfields**] a place where there is oil under the ground or under the sea (campo petrolífero)

oil paint /ˈɔɪl ˌpeɪnt/ NOUN [plural **oil paints**] paint made with oil (tinta a óleo)
• **oil painting** /ˈɔɪl ˌpeɪntɪŋ/ NOUN [plural **oil paintings**] a picture painted with oil paints (pintura a óleo)

oil rig /ˈɔɪl ˌrɪɡ/ NOUN [plural **oil rigs**] a large structure with equipment for getting oil from under the ground or under the sea (plataforma petrolífera)

oil well /ˈɔɪl ˌwel/ NOUN [plural **oil wells**] a hole that is made to get oil from under the ground or under the sea (poço de petróleo)

oily /ˈɔɪli/ ADJECTIVE [**oilier, oiliest**] like oil, or covered with oil ☐ *an oily liquid* ☐ *an oily cloth* (oleoso)

oink /ɔɪŋk/ NOUN [plural **oinks**] the sound that a pig makes (som do porco)

ointment /ˈɔɪntmənt/ NOUN [plural **ointments**] a substance that you rub onto your skin as a medical treatment (pomada)

OK or **okay** /ˌəʊˈkeɪ/ ▶ EXCLAMATION
1 an informal way of agreeing or asking someone if they agree ☐ *'I'll come over after work.' 'OK'.* ☐ *OK! I'll do it!* ☐ *You need to do your homework before Friday, OK?* (tudo bem)
2 used before you start talking, especially to many people ☐ *OK, first of all I'd like to welcome you all to the school.* (tudo bem)
▶ ADJECTIVE, ADVERB
1 an informal word meaning allowed or acceptable (tudo bem) ▣ *Is it OK if I get there a bit later?* (tudo bem) ▣ *'I'm really sorry I forgot your birthday.' 'That's OK.'* (tudo bem) ☐ **+ to do something** *Is it OK to open the window?*
2 an informal word meaning good enough ☐ *Do I look OK in this dress?* ☐ *I think I did OK in the exam.* (bem)
3 an informal word meaning healthy and happy ☐ *'How are you?' 'I'm OK, thanks.'* ☐ *Are you feeling OK now?* (bem)

old /əʊld/ ADJECTIVE [older, oldest]

1 used to talk about someone's age (**de idade**) 🔁 *How old are you?* □ *He's nine years old.* (**qual sua idade**)

2 having lived or existed for a long time (**velho**) 🔁 *an old man/ woman* □ *an old church* (**homem/mulher velho (a)**) □ *She's not old enough to vote.* □ *I'm too old to go out partying all night.* □ *My older brother* (= older than me) *is a builder.* (**velho**)

3 having been owned or used for a long time □ *I wore a pair of old shoes.* (**velho**)

4 used to talk about something or someone from a time before now □ *My old car didn't have air conditioning.* □ *The old road went through the town centre.* □ *I saw one of my old teachers yesterday.* (**antigo**)

5 an old friend someone who has been your friend for a long time (**velho amigo**)

6 the old days a period in history, or earlier in your life □ *In the old days, we never locked our doors.* (**antigamente**)

old age /ˌəʊld ˈeɪdʒ/ NOUN, NO PLURAL
the time when someone is old □ *He wrote poems in his old age.* (**velhice**)

old age pensioner /ˌəʊld eɪdʒ ˈpenʃənə(r)/
NOUN [plural old age pensioners] an old person who has stopped working (**aposentado**)

old-fashioned /ˌəʊldˈfæʃənd/ ADJECTIVE
not modern or fashionable □ *old-fashioned clothes* □ *His ideas are very old-fashioned.* □ *He contacted her in the old fashioned way, by writing a letter.* (**fora de moda**)

Old Testament /ˌəʊld ˈtestəmənt/ NOUN, NO PLURAL
the Old Testament the first part of the Christian Bible, which deals with the time before Christ was born (**Antigo Testamento**)

O level /ˈəʊ ˌlevəl/ NOUN [plural O levels]
an exam in a particular subject that students in England, Wales and Northern Ireland took in the past at about age 16. The exam has been replaced by GCSEs □ *She's got* (= has been successful in) *an O level in French.* (**antigo exame inglês de qualificação do ensino médio**)

olive /ˈɒlɪv/ ▶ NOUN [plural olives]

1 a small black or green fruit that is not sweet. It is eaten and is used to make oil for cooking. (**oliva, azeitona**)

2 a dark yellow-green colour (**cor oliva**)

▶ ADJECTIVE having a dark yellow-green colour □ *an olive carpet* (**oliva**)

olive oil /ˌɒlɪv ˈɔɪl/ NOUN, NO PLURAL
oil from olives, used in cooking (**azeite de oliva**)

Olympic /əˈlɪmpɪk/ ADJECTIVE
to do with the Olympic Games □ *an Olympic athlete* □ *an Olympic medal* (**olímpico**)

Olympic Games /əˌlɪmpɪk ˈɡeɪmz/ or Olympics /əˈlɪmpɪks/ (**Jogos Olímpicos / Olimpíadas**) PLURAL NOUN
the Olympic Games/the Olympics the international sports competition that takes place every four years in a different country (**os Jogos Olímpicos/as Olimpíadas**)

ombudsman /ˈɒmbʊdzmən/ NOUN [plural ombudsmen]
a person who deals with complaints that people make about a government or other official organization (**ombudsman**)

omelet /ˈɒmlɪt/ NOUN [plural omelets]
the US spelling of **omelette** (**omelete**)

omelette /ˈɒmlɪt/ NOUN [plural omelettes]
a food made by mixing eggs and frying them, often with other food inside □ *a cheese omelette* (**omelete**)

omen /ˈəʊmen/ NOUN [plural omens]
a sign showing you that something good or bad is going to happen (**presságio, agouro**) 🔁 *It was a sunny day, which he took as a good omen.* (**bom presságio**)

ominous /ˈɒmɪnəs/ ADJECTIVE
giving a warning that something bad is going to happen □ *There are ominous signs that the Earth's weather pattern is changing dramatically.* (**agourento**)

omission /əˈmɪʃən/ NOUN [plural omissions]

1 something that has not been included but should have been (**omissão**) 🔁 *There are some glaring omissions* (= very obvious things missing) *in his report.* (**flagrante omissão**)

2 when something is not included □ *the omission of his name from the list* (**omissão**)

omit /əˈmɪt/ VERB [omits, omitting, omitted]

1 to not include something □ *This detail was omitted from the documents.* (**omitir**)

2 omit to do something a formal phrase meaning to not do something, often because you forget □ *I omitted to tell him about the meeting.* (**deixar de fazer**)

omni- /ˈɒmnɪ/ PREFIX
omni- is added to the beginning of words to mean 'all', 'every' or 'everywhere' □ *omnivore* (**oni- = tudo, todos, totalmente**)

omnivore /ˈɒmnɪvɔː(r)/ NOUN [plural omnivores]
an animal that eats meat and plants. A biology word. (**onívoro**)

• **omnivorous** /ɒmˈnɪvərəs/ ADJECTIVE eating meat and plants. A biology word □ *Humans are omnivorous.* (**onívoro**)

on /ɒn/ ▶ PREPOSITION

1 touching or supported by the top surface of something □ *The books are on the table.* □ *We built our house on a hill.* □ *I was standing on one leg.* (**sobre**)

2 onto something □ *Rain was falling on the crowd.* □ *I jumped on the bike.* (**em, sobre**)

3 sticking to or hanging from something □ *There were lots of pictures on the walls.* □ *Put your coat on the peg.* (**em**)

4 used to say what day or date something happens □ *He's coming to see us on Friday.* (**em**)

5 about □ *He gave me a book on Scottish history.* □ *I can't comment on her views.* (**sobre**)

6 using a particular form of transport □ *I came on the bus.* (**de**)
7 being performed or broadcast □ *The programme will be on TV next week.* (**em**)
8 used to say how much time or money you use for a particular thing □ *We spent £300 on flowers.* (**em**)
9 as a result of touching or hitting something □ *I tripped on a loose stone.* □ *She hit her head on the shelf.* (**em**)
10 using a particular machine or piece of equipment □ *He's on the phone at the moment.* □ *The letter was written on a typewriter.* (**em**)
11 affecting someone or something □ *This is an attack on our freedom.* □ *I don't have any influence on their decisions.* (**sobre**)
12 have something on you to be carrying something □ *Have you got a pen on you?* (**ter consigo**)
▶ ADVERB
1 if you have a piece of clothing on, you are wearing it □ *Put your coat on.* (**usar no corpo**)
2 if a machine or a piece of equipment is on, it is working or being used □ *Switch the light on.* □ *Shall we have the heating on?* (**ligado**)
3 used to show that an action continues □ *We worked on into the night.* □ *We all became bored as he droned on about football.* (**continuar**)
4 onto a vehicle □ *I got on at Cambridge station.* (**em (um veículo)**)
5 being performed or broadcast □ *What's on at the cinema?* (**passando na TV, no cinema etc.**)
6 going to take place □ *Is the party still on?* (**acontecer**)
7 forward □ *They moved on.* □ *We went on until we came to a river.* (**adiante**)
8 happening or planned □ *I've got a lot on at the moment.* □ *Have you got anything on this weekend?* (**coisas planejadas ou acontecendo**)
9 on and on continuing for a long time □ *The speeches went on and on.* (**continuamente**)
10 on and off sometimes □ *I've been going to the gym on and off for months.* (**de vez em quando**)
◆ IDIOMS **be/go on about someone/something** to talk a lot about someone or something □ *He's always going on about his dogs.* (**ficar falando sobre**) **go on at someone** to complain to someone repeatedly, or to repeatedly ask someone to do something □ *She's always going on at me to get my hair coloured.* (**ficar falando sobre**)

once /wʌns/ ▶ ADVERB
1 one time only □ *He only did it once.* □ *It's the kind of opportunity you get once in your life.* □ *I only met him once.* (**uma vez**)
2 once a/every one time in every period of time □ *I wash my car once a week.* □ *We meet about once every four or five months.* (**uma vez a cada**)
3 at a time in the past □ *People once lived in caves.* □ *They once owned the whole town.* □ *I was a communist once.* (**outrora**)

4 once again/more again, or one more time □ *I found myself alone once more.* □ *He is once again in prison.* □ *Basic errors have once again cost lives.* (**mais uma vez**)
5 at once (a) immediately □ *Miss Peters wants to see you at once.* (b) at the same time □ *I can't do two things at once.* (**imediatamente**)
6 all at once (a) suddenly □ *All at once, the crowd started to move.* (**de repente**) (b) at the same time □ *The movie was funny and inspiring all at once.* (**ao mesmo tempo**)
7 once in a while sometimes, but not often □ *I like to go to the opera once in a while.* (**de vez em quando**)
8 once or twice a few times □ *I've met him once or twice.* (**poucas vezes**)
▶ CONJUNCTION as soon as □ *Once you've finished, you can go.* □ *Once I started getting into debt, I was always anxious.* (**assim que**)

oncoming /ˈɒnkʌmɪŋ/ ADJECTIVE oncoming vehicles are moving towards you □ *the oncoming traffic* (**em sentido contrário**)

one /wʌn/ ▶ NUMBER [*plural* **ones**] the number 1 (**um**)
▶ PRONOUN [*plural* **ones**]
1 used to avoid repeating a word □ *These plums are delicious – would you like one?* □ *My fridge broke and I had to buy a new one.* □ *Our house is one of the ones with a yellow door.* (**um, daquele**)
2 a formal word meaning anyone or you □ *One can see the sea from here.* (**qualquer pessoa**)
3 one another each other □ *They embraced one another.* □ *They have great respect for one another.* (**um ao outro, mutuamente**)
4 one at a time separately □ *I spoke to the children one at a time.* (**um de cada vez**)
5 one by one one after the other □ *One by one, people began to get up and leave.* (**um por um**)
▶ DETERMINER
1 used to talk about one particular person or thing □ *We've only had one reply.* □ **+ of** *One of my friends came round.* (**um**) 🔒 *One or two of the apples were rotten.* (**uns poucos**)
2 one day/evening, etc. on a day/evening, etc. in the future that has not been decided □ *We must meet up for lunch one day.* (**um dia/uma noite etc.**)

one-off /ˌwʌnˈɒf/ ▶ ADJECTIVE happening only once □ *a one-off payment* (**por uma vez**)
▶ NOUN [*plural* **one-offs**] something that happens only once □ *The meeting was just a one-off.* (**por uma vez**)

onerous /ˈəʊnərəs/ ADJECTIVE a formal word meaning difficult to do and needing a lot of effort □ *an onerous task* (**difícil**)

oneself /wʌnˈself/ PRONOUN the reflexive form of 'one' used for talking about yourself or people in general. A formal word □ *One can lie to oneself as well as to other people.* (**si, si mesmo**)

one-sided /ˌwʌnˈsaɪdɪd/ ADJECTIVE
1 with one person or team having a lot more skill than the other □ *a one-sided game* (**unilateral**)
2 showing or considering only one opinion, in a way that is unfair □ *It was a very one-sided account of what happened.* (**parcial**)

one-to-one /ˌwʌntəˈwʌn/ ADJECTIVE between only two people □ *Seriously ill patients need one-to-one care.* (**individualizado**)

one-way /ˌwʌnˈweɪ/ ADJECTIVE
1 allowing cars to travel in one direction only (**de mão única**) □ *It was a narrow one-way street.* (**rua de mão única**) □ *The town had a very complicated one-way system.* (**sistema de mão única**)
2 a one-way ticket, price, etc. is for travelling to a place but not coming back □ *The airline is offering one-way fares to Paris for £25.* (**de ida**)

ongoing /ˌɒnˈgəʊɪŋ/ ADJECTIVE continuing now □ *an ongoing investigation* (**em curso**)

onion /ˈʌnjən/ NOUN [plural **onions**] a round vegetable with many layers that makes your eyes hurt when you cut it □ *Fry the onions until they are soft.* □ *onion soup* (**cebola**)

online /ˌɒnˈlaɪn/ ADJECTIVE, ADVERB using the Internet □ *online advertising* □ *online videos* (**on-line**) □ *Younger people are more likely to go online for the news.* (**ficar on-line**) □ *Many people now shop online.* (**compras on-line**)

onlooker /ˈɒnˌlʊkə(r)/ NOUN [plural **onlookers**] someone who watches something happening □ *A crowd of onlookers had gathered.* (**espectador**)

only /ˈəʊnli/ ▶ ADVERB
1 used to emphasize how small an amount, number, etc. is □ *There are only two weeks left.* □ *Only one of us can win.* □ *She left the job after only a week.* □ *This is only the beginning.* (**apenas, somente**)
2 nobody or nothing else □ *Only you can do it.* □ *I only use the best quality ingredients.* □ *She would only say that she was disappointed.* (**só**)
3 used to say that something is not important or not intended to be harmful □ *'What's that noise?' 'Oh, it's only the children.'* □ *I was only trying to help.* (**apenas**)
4 only just (a) a very short time ago □ *I've only just finished my essay.* (b) by a very small amount □ *He only just beat me.* (**acabar de, só**)
5 not only used to say that one thing is true and another, often surprising, thing is true too □ *Not only did he apologise, he bought everyone a present.* □ *We will not only save money, but we'll get the job done quicker.* (**não só**)

▶ ADJECTIVE without any others of the same type □ *It was the only book on keeping goats that I could find.* □ *His only son was killed in the war.* (**único**) □ *She was an only child* (= had no brothers or sisters). (**filho único**)

▶ CONJUNCTION used to say that something cannot happen or is not true □ *I'd like to come, only I have to work.* (**só que**)

onomatopoeia /ˌɒnəmætəˈpiːə/ NOUN, NO PLURAL when words sound like the thing they describe, for example 'splash' (**onomatopeia**)

onset /ˈɒnset/ NOUN, NO PLURAL (**início**) **the onset of something** the start of something □ *The onset of symptoms occurs 48 hours after infection.* (**início de alguma coisa**)

onslaught /ˈɒnslɔːt/ NOUN [plural **onslaughts**] an attack □ *a verbal onslaught* (**ataque**)

onto /ˈɒntə/ PREPOSITION
1 used for showing movement into a position in or on something □ *I climbed onto the roof.* □ *Jim got onto the bus.* □ *The dog rolled onto its side.* (**para, em**)
2 if you are onto someone, you know who has done something bad. An informal word □ *It looks like the police are onto him.* (**ciente**)
3 be onto something to have discovered something useful or important □ *The scientists soon realized that they were onto something.* (**ciente de alguma coisa**)

onus /ˈəʊnəs/ NOUN, NO PLURAL **the onus is on someone to do something** it is someone's responsibility to do something □ *The onus is on schools to ensure that bullying is dealt with properly.* (**responsabilidade**)

onward /ˈɒnwəd/ ADJECTIVE going forward, or continuing □ *Train passengers transferred to buses for their onward journey.* (**ver on**)

• **onwards** /ˈɒnwədz/ or **onward** /ˈɒnwəd/ ADVERB
1 from ... onwards from a particular time and continuing □ *The rule will apply from 2010 onwards.* (**de ... em diante**)
2 a formal word meaning forwards □ *They rode onwards.* (**para diante**)

ooze /uːz/ VERB [oozes, oozing, oozed]
1 to flow slowly □ *The glue oozed out of the tube.* (**escoar-(se)**)
2 an informal word meaning to have a lot of a quality □ *He oozes confidence.* (**exalar, transparecer**)

opal /ˈəʊpəl/ NOUN [plural **opals**] a white stone used in jewellery (**opala**)

opaque /əʊˈpeɪk/ ADJECTIVE difficult to see through □ *opaque glass* (**opaco**)

open /ˈəʊpən/ ▶ ADJECTIVE
1 not shut or fastened (**aberto**) □ *The window was wide open.* □ *An open book lay on the table.* □ *The door burst open and Ella ran in. His eyes were open and he was still breathing.* (**bem aberto**)
2 if a shop or a business is open, people can go there and use it □ *We are open from 9–5.* □ *Is the restaurant open on Mondays?* (**aberto**)
3 not covered, surrounded or blocked (**aberto**) □ *She had a love of open spaces* □ *I like to walk in*

the open countryside. □ He had an open wound on his leg. □ The Oxford road is open again. **(espaços abertos)**

4 if a computer program or document is open, it is ready to be used. A computing word. **(aberto)**

5 available to be visited or used **(aberto)** 🔁 The meeting is *open to the public*. **(aberto ao público)** □ She declared the hospital officially open. □ The new road will be open in June.

6 honest and not keeping secrets □ He was very open with me about his work. □ We would like to see a more open style of government. □ We need open debate on the subject. **(aberto)**

7 open emotions are not hidden □ They showed open hostility to the strangers. **(aberto, franco)**

8 not yet decided □ The matter is still open for discussion. **(aberto)**

9 if you are open to something, you are willing to consider it **(aberto a)** 🔁 I've got some ideas about the new building, but I'm *open to suggestions*. □ We are open to the challenge that a new business brings. **(aberto a sugestões)**

10 if something or someone is open to problems or difficulties, there is a risk that they will get them □ You must not leave yourself open to criticism. **(aberto)**

◆ IDIOM **have/keep an open mind** to not form an opinion until you know all the facts about something □ He hasn't been here long, so I'm keeping an open mind about the quality of his work. **(ter a mente aberta)**

▶ VERB [**opens, opening, opened**]

1 to move to a position that is not shut or fastened, or to make something do this □ He opened the door. □ I opened my eyes. □ Open your books on page 34. **(abrir)**

2 to remove the cover from a package, letter, etc. □ I opened my birthday presents this morning. □ Have you opened the letter from the bank yet? **(abrir)**

3 if a shop or business opens, you can start to go there and use it □ What time does the surgery open? □ We don't open on Sundays. **(abrir)**

4 to become available to be visited or used, or to make something available to be visited or used □ The new supermarket opened last week. □ They will be opening the new road in December. **(abrir)**

5 to make a computer program or document ready to use. A computing word □ Open the spreadsheet and click at the top of the column. **(abrir)**

6 to begin something □ He opened the meeting with a speech of welcome. □ Police have opened an enquiry into the shooting. **(abrir)**

7 if you open a bank account, you make an arrangement with a bank to keep your money there **(abrir)**

8 open fire to start to shoot □ Gunmen opened fire on the building. **(abrir fogo)**

◆ PHRASAL VERBS **open something up** to create new opportunities □ My qualifications opened up the chance to travel. **(abrir) open up** to start to be willing to talk about yourself and your feelings □ He opened up to the nurse and confessed his fears. **(abrir-se, desabafar)**

▶ NOUN, NO PLURAL

1 in the open outside □ We slept in the open. **(fora, ao ar livre)**

2 in/into the open not secret □ It's time their financial affairs were brought into the open. **(do conhecimento público)**

• **opener** /'əʊpənə(r)/ NOUN [plural **openers**] something that opens a container such as a bottle or a can □ a tin opener **(abridor)**

• **opening** /'əʊpənɪŋ/ NOUN [plural **openings**]

1 a hole or space □ There was an opening in the fence. **(abertura)**

2 the beginning of something □ The opening of the film was very violent. **(abertura)**

3 an opportunity, especially to get a job □ There is an opening in the sales team. **(oportunidade)**

4 an event to mark the start of a place, building, etc. being available to visit or use □ We all went to the opening of the new museum. **(inauguração)**

▶ ADJECTIVE happening at the beginning of something **(abertura)** 🔁 I'd like to make a few *opening remarks*. **(observações de abertura)** □ The opening chapter is rather technical.

• **openly** /'əʊpənlɪ/ ADVERB without trying to hide anything **(abertamente)** 🔁 She *talked openly* about her illness. **(conversar abertamente)**

open-minded /ˌəʊpənˈmaɪndɪd/ ADJECTIVE willing to consider new and different ideas □ My doctor's quite open-minded about alternative therapies. **(liberal)**

openness /'əʊpənnɪs/ NOUN, NO PLURAL when someone is willing to tell people things □ We need more openness in government. **(sinceridade)**

open-plan /ˌəʊpənˈplæn/ ADJECTIVE open-plan rooms or buildings are not divided into smaller areas by walls □ an open-plan office **(de área livre)**

opera /'ɒpərə/ NOUN [plural **operas**] a musical play in which the words are sung □ an opera singer **(ópera)**

operate /'ɒpəreɪt/ VERB [**operates, operating, operated**]

1 if machinery or equipment operates, it works, and if you operate it, you make it work □ The radio operates on batteries. □ My job was to operate the switchboard. **(funcionar)**

2 if a system or service operates, it exists and can be used, and if you operate a system or service, you organize it and make it work □ The train service only operates in the summer months. □ The organization operates a complaints procedure. **(operar)**

3 if a business or an organization operates, it does its work, and if someone operates a business or organization, they manage it □ Some prisons are operated by private security firms. **(operar)**

4 to cut into someone's body to repair or remove a part when someone is ill □ **+ on** *They operated on the boy to save his sight.* (operar)

operating system /ˈɒpəreɪtɪŋ ˌsɪstəm/ NOUN [*plural* **operating systems**] a set of programs that control how a computer works. A computing word. (sistema operacional)

operating theater /ˈɒpəreɪtɪŋ ˌθɪətə(r)/ NOUN [*plural* **operating theaters**] the US spelling of operating theatre

operating theatre /ˈɒpəreɪtɪŋ ˌθɪətə(r)/ NOUN [*plural* **operating theatres**] a room in a hospital where doctors do operations (sala de cirurgia)

operation /ˌɒpəˈreɪʃən/ NOUN [*plural* **operations**]
1 when a doctor cuts into someone's body in order to repair or remove part of it (operação) 🔁 *He has to have an operation on his heart.* (fazer uma operação) 🔁 *a minor operation* (uma pequena cirurgia)
2 a carefully planned and organized action □ *a rescue operation* □ *It was a joint operation between British and Spanish troops.* (operação)
3 a business or organization □ *The company is combining two of its existing operations.* (operadora)
4 *no plural* when something is working or being used □ *The operation of the machine is controlled by computer.* □ *The hotel has just completed its first year of operation.* (funcionamento)
5 in/into operation when something is in operation, it is working or being used, and when something comes into operation, it starts working or being used □ *The new tax scheme is now in operation.* □ *When will the new trains be coming into operation?* (em funcionamento)
• **operational** /ˌɒpəˈreɪʃənəl/ ADJECTIVE
1 working or able to be used □ *The new terminal is now fully operational.* (operacional)
2 to do with how a system, machine or business works □ *operational costs* (operacional)

operator /ˈɒpəreɪtə(r)/ NOUN [*plural* **operators**]
1 someone whose job is to work a machine □ *a lift operator* (operador)
2 someone whose job is to connect telephone calls □ *Ask the operator to put you through to his extension.* (telefonista)
3 a person or company that does a particular type of business □ *a tour operator* (operador)

ophthalmic /ɒfˈθælmɪk/ ADJECTIVE to do with the eye □ *an ophthalmic optician* (oftálmico)

opinion /əˈpɪnjən/ NOUN [*plural* **opinions**]
1 what you think or believe □ **+ of** *What's your opinion of the new arts centre?* □ **+ about** *My opinions about education have changed.* (opinião) 🔁 *She has strong opinions about the war.* (opiniões fortes) 🔁 *In my opinion, you did the right thing.* (na minha opinião) 🔁 *She didn't give* (= say) *her opinion of the film.* (dar opinião) 🔁 *I have a very high/low* (= good/bad) *opinion of most of my colleagues.* (opinião boa ou ruim)
2 public opinion what most people think or believe □ *Public opinion has turned against the party.* (opinião pública)

> ➤ Note that you **give** (or **express**) an opinion. You do not 'say' an opinion:
> ✓ *Did she give her opinion of Claudia's work?*
> ✗ *Did she say her opinion of Claudia's work?*

• **opinionated** /əˈpɪnjəneɪtɪd/ ADJECTIVE having very strong opinions, and often refusing to accept that you are wrong □ *I found him arrogant and opinionated.* (teimoso)

opinion poll /əˈpɪnjən ˌpəʊl/ NOUN [*plural* **opinion polls**] when a number of people are asked questions to find out what they think about a particular subject □ *The latest opinion polls show the president's popularity is falling.* (pesquisa de opinião)

opponent /əˈpəʊnənt/ NOUN [*plural* **opponents**]
1 someone you compete against in a game or a competition □ *He beat his opponent by four points.* (adversário)
2 someone who disagrees with an idea, action, etc. and tries to stop or change it □ *She is a fierce opponent of the war.* □ *He threw his political opponents in jail.* (adversário)

opportune /ˈɒpətjuːn/ ADJECTIVE happening at a useful or lucky time 🔁 *He chose an opportune moment to make the announcement.* (oportuno)

opportunity /ˌɒpəˈtjuːnəti/ NOUN [*plural* **opportunities**]
1 a chance to do something or a situation when you can do something □ *She saw the trip as the opportunity of a lifetime.* □ **+ for** *There will be an opportunity for questions later.* □ **+ to do something** *I had the opportunity to travel a lot in Europe.* (oportunidade) 🔁 *I took the opportunity to speak to the senator in private.* (aproveitar a oportunidade)
2 a job or something that is worth doing □ *We can give you information about employment opportunities.* □ *There are a lot of opportunities in the army.* (em oposição a, ao contrário de)

oppose /əˈpəʊz/ VERB [**opposes, opposing, opposed**] to disagree with someone's ideas, plans or actions and try to change or stop them □ *Local people opposed the plan to expand the airport.* (opor-se a)
• **opposed** /əˈpəʊzd/ ADJECTIVE
1 opposed to something disagreeing with someone's ideas, plans or actions □ *He's always been opposed to battery farming.* (oposto a)
2 as opposed to used to emphasize the difference between two things □ *I'm interested in European*

cinema, as opposed to the Hollywood variety. (em oposição a, ao contrário de)

• **opposing** /əˈpəʊzɪŋ/ ▶ ADJECTIVE
1 playing or fighting against each other □ The two brothers fought on opposing sides in the war. □ A penalty was awarded to the opposing team. (oposto)
2 opposing ideas or beliefs are completely different □ My husband and I have opposing views on education. (oposto)

opposite /ˈɒpəzɪt/ ▶ ADJECTIVE

1 facing something or on the other side of something □ The answers are on the opposite page. □ She lives on the opposite side of town. (contrário)
2 completely different □ Her remarks had the opposite effect to what she intended. □ They walked off in opposite directions. (oposto, contrário)

▶ PREPOSITION, ADVERB facing something or on the other side of something □ The house opposite mine is up for sale. □ Who lives in the house opposite? □ I was sitting opposite my brother at the table. (defronte)

▶ NOUN [plural **opposites**] someone or something that is completely different from someone or something else □ Hot is the opposite of cold. □ My sister and I are complete opposites. (oposto)

opposition /ˌɒpəˈzɪʃən/ NOUN, NO PLURAL
1 strong disagreement with something and efforts to change it □ The plan has met with opposition from the medical profession. (oposição)
2 the people you are fighting or competing against □ United come up against tough opposition this afternoon. (adversário)
3 the Opposition the main political party that opposes the party in government □ the leader of the Opposition (a oposição)

oppress /əˈpres/ VERB [**oppresses, oppressing, oppressed**]
1 to treat a group of people cruelly or unfairly, often by limiting what they can do □ These laws oppress women. (oprimir)
2 to make someone feel worried or unhappy □ The silence in the room oppressed her. (oprimir)

• **oppression** /əˈpreʃən/ NOUN, NO PLURAL cruel or unfair treatment, often limiting what people can do □ They fought against the oppression of the working classes. (opressão)

• **oppressive** /əˈpresɪv/ ADJECTIVE
1 cruel and unfair, often limiting what people can do □ an oppressive regime (opressivo)
2 making you feel worried and uncomfortable □ Her husband's presence was oppressive. (opressivo)
3 oppressive weather is hot and uncomfortable, with no wind □ the oppressive heat of the desert (sufocante)

opt /ɒpt/ VERB [**opts, opting, opted**] to make a choice or a decision to do something □ I opted for the strawberry gateau. □ She opted to stay on at college. (optar)

◆ PHRASAL VERB **opt out** to decide not to do something □ I opted out of the trip. (desistir)

optic /ˈɒptɪk/ ADJECTIVE to do with the eye. A biology word □ the optic nerve (ótico)

optical /ˈɒptɪkəl/ ADJECTIVE to do with the eyes, sight or light □ an optical instrument (ótico)

optical illusion /ˌɒptɪkəl ɪˈluːʒən/ NOUN [plural **optical illusions**] something which tricks your eyes, making you think you can see something that is not really there (ilusão de ótica)

optician /ɒpˈtɪʃən/ NOUN [plural **opticians**] someone whose job is to test your eyes and make and sell glasses (oculista)

optimism /ˈɒptɪmɪzəm/ NOUN, NO PLURAL when you believe that good things will happen □ She was full of optimism about her new job. (otimismo)

• **optimist** /ˈɒptɪmɪst/ NOUN [plural **optimists**] someone who usually believes that good things will happen (otimista)

• **optimistic** /ˌɒptɪˈmɪstɪk/ ADJECTIVE hoping or believing that good things will happen □ I'm not feeling very optimistic about this exam. (otimista)

• **optimistically** /ˌɒptɪˈmɪstɪkəli/ ADVERB in an optimistic way □ 'She might still come,' he said optimistically. (com otimismo)

optimum /ˈɒptɪməm/ ADJECTIVE the best or most suitable □ The flat is small but optimum use is made of the space. (ótimo, o melhor)

option /ˈɒpʃən/ NOUN [plural **options**]

1 something that you can choose or decide to do □ There are several options open to me. □ Is there a vegetarian option on the menu? □ Our only option was to accept his offer. □ **+ of doing something** We have the option of buying or leasing a car. (opção, escolha)
2 keep/leave your options open to arrange a situation so that you still have choices about it in the future □ They're pressing me to accept the job, but I want to keep my options open a bit longer. (deixar, manter as opções abertas)

• **optional** /ˈɒpʃənəl/ ADJECTIVE if something is optional, you can have it or do it if you want to, but you do not have to □ Music was an optional subject at my school. (opcional) 🔁 The car has a lot of optional extras. (opcionais)

or /ɔː(r)/ CONJUNCTION

1 used to show possibilities or choices □ Would you prefer tea or coffee? □ We could see a film or go for a walk. □ Their little girl must be seven or eight. □ Shall we have pizza, pasta or risotto? (ou)
2 used after a negative verb to say not any of a list of things or people □ I don't like him or his sister. (nem)

3 used for saying what will happen if something is not done □ *I'd better go or I'll miss the last bus.* (senão)

4 used to explain or correct something you have just said □ *30% of the population, or three out of ten people, voted.* □ *There were ten of us, or rather nine.* (ou)

-or /-ə(r)/ SUFFIX another way of spelling –er (ver –er)

oral /ˈɔːrəl/ ▶ ADJECTIVE

1 spoken, not written □ *an oral examination* (oral)

2 to do with the mouth □ *oral hygiene* (oral)

▶ NOUN [plural **orals**] an examination where you have to speak □ *I've got my Spanish oral tomorrow.* (exame oral)

• **orally** /ˈɔːrəli/ ADVERB

1 by speaking □ *I prefer to communicate orally rather than by e-mail.* (oralmente)

2 by swallowing □ *This medicine must be taken orally.* (por via oral)

orange /ˈɒrɪndʒ/ ADJECTIVE having the colour you get if you mix red and yellow □ *This bush has tiny orange flowers in summer.* (alaranjado)

▶ NOUN [plural **oranges**]

1 a round fruit with orange skin and a lot of juice □ *orange juice* (laranja)

2 no plural the colour you get if you mix red and yellow (laranja, alaranjado)

orang-utan /ɒˈræŋətæn/ NOUN [plural **orang-utans**] an animal like a monkey with long arms and orange or brown hair (orangotango)

orator /ˈɒrətə(r)/ NOUN [plural **orators**] a person who is good at making public speeches □ *a great orator* (orador)

orbit /ˈɔːbɪt/ ▶ NOUN [plural **orbits**] the circular path along which something moves around a sun, moon or planet □ *The spaceship is in orbit round the moon.* (órbita)

▶ VERB [**orbits**, **orbiting**, **orbited**] to go round a sun, moon or planet □ *The spacecraft is orbiting Earth.* (orbitar)

orchard /ˈɔːtʃəd/ NOUN [plural **orchards**] an area of land where fruit trees are grown □ *a cherry orchard* (pomar)

orchestra /ˈɔːkɪstrə/ NOUN [plural **orchestras**] a large group of musicians playing together □ *a symphony orchestra* (orquestra)

• **orchestral** /ɔːˈkestrəl/ ADJECTIVE written for or played by an orchestra □ *orchestral music* (orquestral)

orchestrate /ˈɔːkɪstreɪt/ VERB [**orchestrates**, **orchestrating**, **orchestrated**] to organize or arrange a complicated event or activity so that you get the result you want □ *He was responsible for orchestrating the whole presidential campaign.* (orquestrar)

orchid /ˈɔːkɪd/ NOUN [plural **orchids**] a flower with an unusual shape (orquídea)

ordain /ɔːˈdeɪn/ VERB [**ordains**, **ordaining**, **ordained**] to make someone a priest in a special ceremony □ *Some Christian churches have decided to ordain women.* (ordenar)

ordeal /ɔːˈdiːl/ NOUN [plural **ordeals**] a very unpleasant experience □ *He spent ten years in prison, but survived the ordeal with great courage.* (provação)

order /ˈɔːdə(r)/ ▶ NOUN [plural **orders**]

1 an instruction to do something (ordem) □ *The soldier was given the order to shoot.* (dar a ordem) □ *I refuse to take orders from that man.* (receber ordens) □ *They obeyed the order to retreat.* (obedecer à ordem)

2 under orders if you are under orders, you have been told to do something or to behave in a particular way □ *We were under orders not to speak to anyone.* (sob ordens)

3 when you ask for food or goods that you will pay for. (pedido) □ *The waiter came to take our order.* (atender nosso pedido) □ *The government has placed an order for ten new helicopters.* (fazer um pedido)

4 the way things are arranged (ordem) □ *The books are in alphabetical order of their authors.* (ordem alfabética) □ *List the options in your order of preference.*

5 when people are calm and obeying the law (ordem) □ *Troops were called in to restore order to the region.* (restaurar a ordem)

6 a state where everything is tidy or in its correct state □ *I need to get my accounts in order.* (ordem)

7 in order to do something so that something can happen or be done □ *She took the money in order to buy food.* □ *I phoned him in order to arrange a meeting.* (a fim de)

8 out of order not working correctly □ *The toilets are out of order today.* (enguiçado)

▶ VERB [**orders**, **ordering**, **ordered**]

1 to tell someone to do something □ *+ to do something The doctor ordered her to rest for a few days.* (ordenar)

2 to say that something must happen or be done □ *The government has ordered an enquiry into the incident.* □ *I can prove that he ordered the killing.* (ordenar)

3 to ask for food or goods that you will pay for □ *I ordered some magazines from the newsagent.* □ *I ordered the pizza.* (encomendar)

4 to arrange things in a particular way □ *I ordered the CDs according to the type of music.* (ordenar)

• **orderly** /ˈɔːdəli/ ADJECTIVE

1 controlled and behaving well □ *Please form an orderly queue.* (ordenado, organizado)

2 in a tidy or correct arrangement □ *He kept orderly records of all his expenses.* (ordenado)

ordinal /ˈɔːdɪnəl/ ADJECTIVE ordinal numbers are numbers like first, second, third. A maths word. (ordinal)

ordinarily

ordinarily /ˈɔːdənərəli/ ADVERB usually ☐ *I don't ordinarily drink wine.* (**comumente**)

- **ordinary** /ˈɔːdənəri/ ADJECTIVE
  1 normal and not unusual or different ☐ *It was just an ordinary Monday morning.* ☐ *Ordinary people don't buy designer clothes.* (**comum**)
  2 out of the ordinary unusual or different from normal ☐ *Your tests show nothing out of the ordinary.* (**excepcional**)

ordination /ˌɔːdɪˈneɪʃən/ NOUN [plural **ordinations**] the act or ceremony of making someone a priest ☐ *His parents attended his ordination.* (**ordenação**)

ore /ɔː(r)/ NOUN [plural **ores**] rock or earth which contains a metal ☐ *iron ore* (**minério**)

organ /ˈɔːgən/ NOUN [plural **organs**]
1 a part of your body that has a special purpose ☐ *an organ donor* (= someone who lets their organs be used after they die) (**órgão**)
2 a large musical instrument with keys like a piano and several long pipes that air is pushed through, often found in churches ☐ *She played the organ at our wedding.* (**órgão**)

organic /ɔːˈgænɪk/ ADJECTIVE
1 organic food is produced without using chemicals ☐ *I only buy organic vegetables.* (**orgânico**)
2 found in or made by living things ☐ *organic fertilizers* (**orgânico**)
3 containing carbon. A chemistry word ☐ *organic compounds* (**orgânico**)

- **organically** /ɔːˈgænɪkəli/ ADVERB without using chemicals ☐ *Organically grown vegetables are often more expensive.* (**organicamente**)

organism /ˈɔːgənɪzəm/ NOUN [plural **organisms**] any living thing, especially one that is very small. A biology word ☐ *Samples of marine organisms were collected from the sea bed.* (**organismo**)

organist /ˈɔːgənɪst/ NOUN [plural **organists**] someone who plays the organ (= large instrument like a piano that is played in a church) (**organista**)

organization or **organisation** /ˌɔːgənaɪˈzeɪʃən/ NOUN [plural **organizations**]
1 a group of people who work together for a purpose ☐ *He's working for a voluntary organization that helps ex-prisoners.* (**organização**)
2 no plural the activity of arranging or preparing for an event or an activity ☐ *The festival took months of organization.* (**organização**)
3 no plural the way in which something is arranged or organized ☐ *Paul's essays show a lack of organization.* (**organização**)

- **organize** or **organise** /ˈɔːgənaɪz/ VERB [**organizes, organizing, organized**]
  1 to arrange and prepare an event or an activity ☐ *We've organized a surprise party for his birthday.* (**organizar**)

origin

2 to make something tidy or to put something in order ☐ *He organized all the papers into neat piles.* (**organizar**)

- **organized** or **organised** /ˈɔːgənaɪzd/ ADJECTIVE
  1 involving a group of people who plan and do something together ☐ *We went on an organized tour of the vineyard.* ☐ *organized crime* (**organizado**)
  2 an organized person is good at planning and arranging things ☐ *I'm just not very organized.* (**organizado**)

- **organizer** or **organiser** /ˈɔːgənaɪzə(r)/ NOUN [plural **organizers**] someone who organizes an event or an activity ☐ *a conference organizer* (**organizador**)

Orient /ˈɔːrɪənt/ NOUN, NO PLURAL **the Orient** an old fashioned word for the countries in eastern Asia such as China and Japan ☐ *spices from the Orient* (**Oriente**)

oriental /ˌɔːrɪˈentəl/ ADJECTIVE from or to do with the countries of eastern Asia such as China and Japan ☐ *oriental cuisine* (**oriental**)

orienteering /ˌɔːrɪənˈtɪərɪŋ/ NOUN, NO PLURAL a sport in which you run across countryside, finding your way with a map (**esporte de orientação**)

origin /ˈɒrɪdʒɪn/ NOUN [plural **origins**]
1 the cause of something or place where something starts ☐ *There are many theories about the origin of our solar system.* ☐ *The English language contains many words of Anglo-Saxon origin.* (**origem**)
2 the country, race, class etc. that someone comes from ☐ *Her family are Italian in origin.* (**origem**) 🔁 *Please state your ethnic origin on the form.* (**origem étnica**)

- **original** /əˈrɪdʒɪnəl/ ▶ ADJECTIVE
  1 existing from the beginning, or not having been changed ☐ *The original story had been changed over the centuries.* ☐ *Our house still has the original fireplaces.* (**original**)
  2 new and interesting, and not like others of its type ☐ *a novel full of original ideas* (**original**) 🔁 *Her paintings are highly original.* (**altamente original**)
  3 done by the artist himself or herself ☐ *He own an original drawing by Picasso.* (**original**)
  ▶ NOUN [plural **originals**] a piece of art that is in the form in which it was first created and is not a copy ☐ *The original of this painting is in Florence.* (**original**)

- **originality** /əˌrɪdʒɪˈnælɪti/ NOUN, NO PLURAL the quality of being new and interesting and not like others of its type ☐ *I admire the originality of his paintings.* (**originalidade**)

- **originally** /əˈrɪdʒɪnəli/ ADVERB
  1 in the beginning ☐ *His family comes from Scotland originally.* (**originalmente**)
  2 before something changed or was changed ☐ *The building was originally used as a store.* (**originalmente**)

- **originate** /əˈrɪdʒɪneɪt/ VERB [originates, originating, originated] to start to happen or exist □ *This style of painting originated in China.* (dar origem a, nascer, surgir)

ornament ▶ NOUN /ˈɔːnəmənt/ [plural ornaments] an object used to decorate a room, building or place □ *Every surface was covered with china ornaments.* (ornamento)
▶ VERB /ˈɔːnəment/ [ornaments, ornamenting, ornamented] to decorate something □ *The ceiling was richly ornamented.* (ornamentar)
- **ornamental** /ˌɔːnəˈmentəl/ ADJECTIVE having no purpose except decoration □ *an ornamental pond* (ornamental)

ornate /ɔːˈneɪt/ ADJECTIVE decorated with a complicated design □ *A huge mirror with an ornate surround hung over the fire.* (floreado, rebuscado)

ornithologist /ˌɔːnɪˈθɒlədʒɪst/ NOUN [plural ornithologists] someone who studies or is an expert on birds (ornitólogo)
- **ornithology** /ˌɔːnɪˈθɒlədʒɪ/ NOUN, NO PLURAL the study of birds (ornitologia)

orphan /ˈɔːfən/ ▶ NOUN [plural orphans] a child whose parents are both dead (órfão)
▶ VERB [orphans, orphaning, orphaned] if you are orphaned, you become an orphan □ *Sadie was orphaned at the age of six.* (tornar-se órfão)
- **orphanage** /ˈɔːfənɪdʒ/ NOUN [plural orphanages] a home for orphans (orfanato)

orthodox /ˈɔːθədɒks/ ADJECTIVE
1 having ideas that most people accept and think are correct □ *orthodox medical treatment* (ortodoxo, convencional)
2 keeping the traditional customs and beliefs of Judaism or some types of Christianity □ *orthodox Jews* (ortodoxo)

orthopaedic /ˌɔːθəˈpiːdɪk/ ADJECTIVE to do with the treatment or study of bones and muscles (ortopédico)

orthopedic /ˌɔːθəˈpiːdɪk/ ADJECTIVE the US spelling of orthopaedic (ortopédico)

oscillate /ˈɒsɪleɪt/ VERB [oscillates, oscillating, oscillated]
1 to keep changing between two feelings, opinions or types of behaviour □ *His mood oscillated between elation and depression.* (oscilar)
2 to move between one position and another regularly and repeatedly □ *The magnetic field oscillates to create magnetic waves.* (oscilar)

osmosis /ɒzˈməʊsɪs/ NOUN, NO PLURAL when a liquid goes through a thin layer, for example water into the roots of a plant. A biology word. (osmose)

ostensible /ɒˈstensəbəl/ ADJECTIVE an ostensible reason for something is one that people state but that may not be true □ *The ostensible purpose of the meeting was to promote good community relations.* (aparente)

- **ostensibly** /ɒˈstensəblɪ/ ADVERB if something is ostensibly the reason for something, people say it is the reason but it may not be □ *His arrest was ostensibly for theft but was really for political reasons.* (aparentemente)

ostentatious /ˌɒstenˈteɪʃəs/ ADJECTIVE intended to attract attention or admiration, often by showing how rich or powerful someone is □ *Martins was wearing the ostentatious jewellery of a hip-hop singer.* (ostentatório)
- **ostentatiously** /ˌɒstenˈteɪʃəslɪ/ ADVERB in a very ostentatious or obvious way □ *She ostentatiously ignored his comments.* (ostentosamente)

osteopath /ˈɒstɪəpæθ/ NOUN [plural osteopaths] someone whose job is to treat pain in the bones and muscles by moving and rubbing them with their hands (osteopata)
- **osteopathy** /ˌɒstɪˈɒpəθɪ/ NOUN, NO PLURAL a form of treatment for pain in the bones and muscles in which an osteopath moves and rubs them with their hands (osteopatia)

osteoporosis /ˌɒstɪəʊpəˈrəʊsɪs/ NOUN, NO PLURAL a disease in which the bones become weak and break easily (osteoporose)

ostracize or **ostracise** /ˈɒstrəsaɪz/ VERB [ostracizes, ostracizing, ostracized] to deliberately leave someone out of a group by refusing to speak to them or be friendly with them □ *He was ostracized by his former workmates for refusing to join the strike.* (colocar no ostracismo)

ostrich /ˈɒstrɪtʃ/ NOUN [plural ostriches] a large bird which cannot fly but runs very fast (avestruz)

other /ˈʌðə(r)/ ▶ ADJECTIVE
1 used to talk about something or someone else of a similar type □ *Do you have any other news to tell me?* □ *I have lots of other questions.* (outro) 🔲 *I prefer living with other people.* (outras pessoas) 🔲 *There were lots of other things to do.* (outras coisas)
2 different from the thing or person you have been talking about □ *There must be some other reason.* □ *Does this dress come in any other colours?* (outro) 🔲 *I thought Kate would be taller than Jo, but it was the other way round* (= the opposite). (é o oposto)
3 used to talk about the second of two things or people, when the first has already been mentioned □ *Where is my other glove?* □ *I live on the other side of town.* (outro) 🔲 *This vase is Chinese, and the other one is Japanese.* (o outro)
4 used to talk about the remaining people or things □ *The other team members will arrive tomorrow.* (outro)

5 the other day/week, etc. a few days/weeks, etc. ago □ *I saw Adam a few days ago.* (outro dia, semana etc.)

6 every other day/Sunday, etc. on one of each two days/Sundays, etc. □ *I try to run every other*

otherwise

day. (dia sim, dia não/domingo sim, domingo não etc.)

7 other than except □ *I had no food other than a bar of chocolate I found in my bag.* □ *Other than Charlie, nobody was interested in my news.* (a não ser, exceto)

8 somewhere/someone, etc. or other used to say somewhere/someone, etc. when it is not important exactly where or who □ *I ought to give him something or other for his birthday.* (um lugar ou outro, uma pessoa ou outra etc.)

▶ PRONOUN

1 the second of two □ *Here's one sock, but where is the other?* (o outro)

2 others things or people of a similar type □ *I really enjoyed that book. Do you have any others by her?* (outros)

3 the others the remaining people or things □ *I've found some of her letters, but where are the others?* □ *Wait for the others to arrive.* (os demais)

4 others other people □ *I find her amusing. Others might disagree.* (outros)

otherwise /ˈʌðəwaɪz/ ADVERB

1 used to say what will happen if something is not done or is not true □ *You need to get up, otherwise you'll be late.* □ *I hope it won't be cold. Otherwise we'll need to take coats.* (senão)

2 if the thing that has just been mentioned is not true □ *He must have seen the letter, otherwise how could he have known the truth?* (senão)

3 except for the thing that has just been mentioned □ *I've got a cold, but I'm fine otherwise.* □ *One person raised his hand. Otherwise, nobody moved.* (em outros aspectos, por outro lado)

4 different from what has been said □ *Unless I hear otherwise, I'll be there at ten.* □ *I thought the food was fine, but Des thought otherwise.* (de outra maneira)

otter /ˈɒtə(r)/ NOUN [*plural* **otters**] a small animal with brown fur that lives by rivers, swims well and eats fish (lontra)

ouch /aʊtʃ/ EXCLAMATION a word that people say when they feel a sudden pain (ai!)

ought /ɔːt/ MODAL VERB

1 ought to do something (a) used to say what is the best or right thing to do □ *I think we ought to call the police.* □ *He ought to wear glasses.* (b) used to say that you expect something to be true □ *They ought to reach Berlin by tomorrow.* □ *Three loaves ought to be enough.* (dever)

2 ought to have used to say what would have been the right thing to do when you have done something different □ *They ought to have travelled by train.* □ *He ought to have had more sense.* (deveria ter)

oughtn't /ˈɔːtənt/ a short way to say and write ought not □ *You really oughtn't to see him again.* (forma negativa de ought)

out

ounce /aʊns/ NOUN [*plural* **ounces**] a unit for measuring weight, equal to 1/16 of a pound. This is often written oz. (onça)

our /ˈaʊə(r)/ ADJECTIVE belonging to or to do with us □ *That is our car.* (nosso)

ours /ˈaʊəz/ PRONOUN used to talk or write about things belonging to or to do with us □ *That car is ours.* □ *These books are ours.* (nosso)

ourselves /aʊəˈselvz/ PRONOUN

1 the reflexive form of we □ *We saw ourselves in the mirror.* □ *We should keep some of the money for ourselves.* (nos)

2 used to show that we do something without any help from other people □ *We painted the room ourselves.* (nós mesmos) 🔂 *We built the house all by ourselves.* (absolutamente sozinhos)

3 used to emphasize the pronoun we □ *We ourselves played no part in this.* (nós mesmos)

4 by ourselves not with or near other people □ *They left us by ourselves in a cold room.* (sozinhos)

5 to ourselves without having to share with anyone else □ *We had the whole hotel to ourselves.* (só para nós)

-ous /-əs/ SUFFIX -ous is added to the end of words to mean 'having a particular quality' □ *adventurous* (-oso)

oust /aʊst/ VERB [**ousts, ousting, ousted**] to force someone out of their position or job □ *She was ousted from her position on the board.* (expulsar, desalojar)

out /aʊt/ ADVERB, PREPOSITION

1 from inside a container, hole, vehicle, etc. □ *She opened her bag and took out an umbrella.* □ **+ of** *He got out of the car.* (fora, para fora) 🔂 *I opened the cupboard and a bag of rice fell out.* (cair fora)

2 away from your home or work for a social activity (fora) 🔂 *Are you going out tonight?* □ *I was out with Gerry last night.* (sair)

3 away from your home or work □ *I phoned, but you were out.* (fora)

4 away from a building or place □ *I stood out in the garden.* □ **+ of** *She was dragged out of the room by armed guards.* □ *He is not allowed to go out of the country.* (fora)

5 out of used to say what something is made from □ *The shelter was made out of sticks.* (de)

6 used to talk about places that are far away □ *My brother lives in Florida. I'd love to spend some time out there with him.* (lá)

7 if a fire or light is out, it is not shining □ *When we reached the house, all the lights were out.* (apagado)

8 no longer in a game or competition because you have lost □ *The batsman is out.* □ **+ of** *England are out of the World Cup.* (eliminado)

9 available to be bought or seen □ *His latest film will be out next week.* (disponível)
10 out of because of □ *I only went to see her out of curiosity.* (por)
11 out of something with no more of something remaining □ *The printer's out of ink.* (sem algo)
12 two/six, etc. out of ten/a hundred, etc. used to say how many people or things in a group are involved in or affected by something (dois/seis etc. entre dez/cem etc.)
13 not accurate □ *I think my measurements were a bit out.* □ **+ by** *His estimate was out by over £1,000.* (errado)

out-and-out /ˌaʊtənˈaʊt/ ADJECTIVE in every way □ *an out-and-out liar* (absoluto, completo)

outback /ˈaʊtbæk/ NOUN, NO PLURAL **the outback** the areas in Australia that are far away from towns and cities (interior)

out-box /ˈaʊtbɒks/ NOUN [plural **out-boxes**] the place on a computer which stores e-mail messages that you are going to send. A computing word. (caixa de saída)

outbreak /ˈaʊtbreɪk/ NOUN [plural **outbreaks**] when something such as war or a disease starts □ *There's been a fresh outbreak of measles in the area.* (eclosão)

outbuilding /ˈaʊtbɪldɪŋ/ NOUN [plural **outbuildings**] a building that is separate from but near to a main building, for example for keeping tools, animals or vehicles in (anexo, dependência)

outburst /ˈaʊtbɜːst/ NOUN [plural **outbursts**] when someone suddenly says something that shows strong emotion, especially anger □ *Her outburst shocked her colleagues.* (explosão)

outcast /ˈaʊtkɑːst/ NOUN [plural **outcasts**] someone who is not accepted by society or by other members of a group □ *The defendant was described as a social outcast with a history of drug abuse.* (marginal, excluído)

outcome /ˈaʊtkʌm/ NOUN [plural **outcomes**] the final result of something □ *What was the outcome of your discussion?* (resultado)

outcrop /ˈaʊtkrɒp/ NOUN [plural **outcrops**] a rock or group of rocks that sticks out above the surface of the ground (afloramento)

outcry /ˈaʊtkraɪ/ NOUN [plural **outcries**] a strong reaction of anger or disapproval by a large number of people □ *The decision caused a public outcry.* (protesto)

outdated /ˌaʊtˈdeɪtɪd/ ADJECTIVE old-fashioned and no longer suitable □ *They are using terribly outdated systems for their customer records.* (antiquado, obsoleto)

outdo /ˌaʊtˈduː/ VERB [**outdoes, outdoing, outdid, outdone**] to do something better than someone else □ *The girls tried to outdo each other in their kindness.* (sobrepujar)

outdoor /ˌaʊtˈdɔː(r)/ ADJECTIVE happening or done outside or for use outside □ *an outdoor swimming pool* □ *outdoor shoes* (de sair)

• **outdoors** /ˌaʊtˈdɔːz/ ADVERB outside □ *She sat outdoors in the sun.* □ *Don't go outdoors if it's raining.* (fora, ao ar livre)

outer /ˈaʊtə(r)/ ADJECTIVE
1 on or near the outside of something □ *Peel off the outer layers of the onion.* (exterior)
2 furthest away from the centre □ *the outer suburbs of Paris* (distante)

outer space /ˌaʊtə ˈspeɪs/ NOUN, NO PLURAL the area outside the Earth's atmosphere where the other planets and stars are □ *Many people long to meet visitors from outer space.* (espaço sideral)

outfit /ˈaʊtfɪt/ NOUN [plural **outfits**]
1 a set of clothes that are worn together □ *I've bought myself a new outfit for the wedding.* □ *Jake got a cowboy outfit for his birthday.* (traje)
2 an organization or business □ *He runs a small transport outfit.* (empresa)

outgoing /ˌaʊtˈɡəʊɪŋ/ ADJECTIVE
1 friendly and liking to talk to other people □ *Sally's quite a confident, outgoing girl.* (sociável, expansivo)
2 leaving a position of authority □ *The outgoing president gave his final speech.* (que deixa o poder)
3 going out of or away from a place □ *We can't make outgoing calls from this phone.* (de saída)

• **outgoings** /ˈaʊtɡəʊɪŋz/ PLURAL NOUN money that you have to spend on regular costs like rent, food, travelling etc. □ *I'm trying to cut down on my monthly outgoings.* (despesas)

outgrow /ˌaʊtˈɡrəʊ/ VERB [**outgrows, outgrowing, outgrew, outgrown**]
1 to become too big for something □ *She has outgrown all her clothes.* (crescer demais para)
2 to lose your interest in something as you get older □ *I think I might be outgrowing my obsession with fantasy novels.* (passar da idade para)

outing /ˈaʊtɪŋ/ NOUN [plural **outings**] a short journey made for pleasure □ *I took the kids on an outing to the seaside.* (saída, passeio)

outlandish /aʊtˈlændɪʃ/ ADJECTIVE very strange and unusual □ *As a student, he wore the most outlandish clothes.* (estranho, bizarro)

outlast /ˌaʊtˈlɑːst/ VERB [**outlasts, outlasting, outlasted**] to last or live longer than someone or something else □ *I think these shoes will outlast us all.* (sobreviver)

outlaw /ˈaʊtlɔː/ ▶ VERB [**outlaws, outlawing, outlawed**] to make something illegal □ *Should computer hacking be outlawed completely?* (ilegal)
▶ NOUN [plural **outlaws**] a criminal, especially one who moves from place to place to avoid being caught (fora da lei)

outlay

outlay /ˈaʊtleɪ/ NOUN [plural **outlays**] an amount of money that is spent, especially in order to start a business or something that you want to do ☐ *The scheme required an initial outlay of £50,000.* (**despesa**)

outlet /ˈaʊtlet/ NOUN [plural **outlets**]
1 a way of expressing or using strong feelings or ideas ☐ *Sports like boxing are seen as an outlet for male aggression.* ☐ *What Becky needs is an outlet for her creativity.* (**vazão**)
2 a shop or business that sells goods made by a particular company or of a particular type ☐ *The number of fast food outlets in the town has rocketed.* (**loja de produtores com venda direta ao público**)
3 a place where a gas or liquid can flow out of something (**escoadouro**)

outline /ˈaʊtlaɪn/ ▶ VERB [**outlines, outlining, outlined**]
1 to explain the main ideas and facts about something ☐ *The headmaster outlined the planned changes to the school.* (**resumir**)
2 to draw or make a line around the outside of something ☐ *She drew a red square, outlined in blue.* (**delinear, esboçar**)
▶ NOUN [plural **outlines**]
1 a line that shows the shape of something ☐ *First he drew the outline of a church seen against the sky.* (**contorno**)
2 a short description of the main parts of something ☐ *Just give me an outline of the facts.* (**resumo**)

outlive /ˌaʊtˈlɪv/ VERB [**outlives, outliving, outlived**] to live or exist longer than someone or something else ☐ *He outlived his older brother by fifteen years.* (**sobreviver**)

outlook /ˈaʊtlʊk/ NOUN [plural **outlooks**]
1 someone's attitude to life ☐ *He has a strange outlook on life.* (**perspectiva**)
2 what is likely to happen in the future ☐ *The outlook for the economy is poor.* (**previsão**)
3 a view ☐ *From the top there is a wonderful outlook over the valley.* (**panorama**)

outlying /ˈaʊtˌlaɪɪŋ/ ADJECTIVE at the edges of or a short distance away from a particular place ☐ *They moved to the town from one of the outlying villages.* (**distante, afastado**)

outmoded /ˌaʊtˈmoʊdəd/ ADJECTIVE not modern or fashionable ☐ *The doctor has some outmoded ideas about bringing up children.* (**antiquado, obsoleto**)

outnumber /ˌaʊtˈnʌmbə(r)/ VERB [**outnumbers, outnumbering, outnumbered**] to be more in number than another group of people or things ☐ *The boys outnumber the girls by three to two.* (**exceder em número**)

out-of-date /ˌaʊtəvˈdeɪt/ ADJECTIVE old and often no longer useful or suitable ☐ *Our computer systems are becoming rather out-of-*

551

outshine O

date. ☐ *I have an out-of-date list of addresses.* (**ultrapassado**)

outpatient /ˈaʊtpeɪʃənt/ NOUN [plural **outpatients**] someone who comes to a hospital for treatment but does not sleep there at night (**paciente ambulatorial**)

outpost /ˈaʊtpoʊst/ NOUN [plural **outposts**]
1 part of a business or organization that is far away from its main part ☐ *His restaurant empire includes outposts in Dubai, Tokyo and New York.* (**posto avançado**)
2 a small military camp (= place where people live in tents) far away from the main army, built especially to protect it from a surprise attack (**pequeno acampamento militar para defesa**)

outpouring /ˈaʊtˌpɔːrɪŋ/ NOUN [plural **outpourings**] a public expression of a strong emotion ☐ *There was an outpouring of grief at her death.* (**efusão, expansão**)

output /ˈaʊtpʊt/ ▶ NOUN [plural **outputs**]
1 a quantity of goods produced or an amount of work done ☐ *The output of this factory increased last year.* (**produção**)
2 the information produced by a computer (**informações produzidas pelo computador**)
3 the power produced by an engine or a piece of equipment (**potência**)
▶ VERB [**outputs, outputting, output**] to produce information from a computer ☐ *The data is output in the form of a spreadsheet.* (**produzir informação em um computador**)

outrage /ˈaʊtreɪdʒ/ ▶ NOUN [plural **outrages**]
1 a strong feeling of anger or shock ☐ *Her remarks caused outrage among animal lovers.* (**ultraje**)
2 a shocking or cruel action ☐ *The decision to close the hospital is an outrage.* (**ultraje**)
▶ VERB [**outrages, outraging, outraged**] to make someone feel shocked and angry ☐ *Fay was outraged by his behaviour.* (**ultrajar**)

• **outrageous** /aʊtˈreɪdʒəs/ ADJECTIVE shocking or very unreasonable ☐ *His behaviour was absolutely outrageous.* ☐ *This restaurant charges outrageous prices.* (**abusivo**)

• **outrageously** /aʊtˈreɪdʒəsli/ ADVERB in an outrageous way ☐ *It's outrageously expensive to go to the opera.* (**abusivamente**)

outright ▶ ADVERB /ˌaʊtˈraɪt/ in a clear and complete way ☐ *We won outright.* (**imediatamente**)
🔟 *When the bomb exploded, they were killed outright* (= immediately). (**matar de imediato**).
▶ ADJECTIVE /ˈaʊtraɪt/ clear and complete ☐ *Many people want an outright ban on public smoking.* (**total**)

outset /ˈaʊtset/ NOUN **at/from the outset** at or from the beginning (**início**) ☐ *The project was in difficulty from the outset.* (**de início**)

outshine /ˌaʊtˈʃaɪn/ VERB [**outshines, outshining, outshone**] to do something much better than someone else □ *Jo easily outshone the other candidates.* (eclipsar)

outside ▶ ADVERB /ˌaʊtˈsaɪd/ not inside a building □ *Let's eat outside.* □ *He went outside for a cigarette.* (fora)
▶ PREPOSITION

1 not inside a building, room or area, but near it □ *He was standing outside our house.* □ *I come from a small village just outside York.* (fora de)

2 not part of something □ *Nursery schools are outside our area of responsibility.* □ *Catering for large weddings is outside my experience.* (fora de)

▶ ADJECTIVE /ˈaʊtsaɪd/

1 not inside a building □ *We painted the outside walls of the shed.* □ *Gran's old house used to have an outside toilet.* (exterior) 🔲 *He wanted the outside world* (= people in other places) *to know of his suffering.* (o mundo exterior)

2 not belonging to a group or organization □ *We've had to get in some outside support to help with the conference.* (externo)

3 an outside chance a very small possibility □ *City still have an outside chance of winning the trophy.* (possibilidade remota)

▶ NOUN /ˌaʊtˈsaɪd, ˈaʊtsaɪd/ [*plural* **outsides**] **the outside** the outer surface or part of something □ *The outside of the house was painted white.* □ *The cake was burnt on the outside.* (exterior)

• **outsider** /ˌaʊtˈsaɪdə(r)/ NOUN [*plural* **outsiders**]

1 someone who does not belong to a particular group or place □ *I have lived here for ten years, but I still feel like an outsider.* (forasteiro, estranho)

2 a horse or person that is not expected to win a race or competition (azarão)

outsize /ˈaʊtsaɪz/ ADJECTIVE bigger than the largest usual size □ *outsize clothing* (extragrande)

outskirts /ˈaʊtskɜːts/ PLURAL NOUN **the outskirts** the outer parts of a town or city □ *He lives on the outskirts of Edinburgh.* (arredores, periferia)

outspoken /ˌaʊtˈspəʊkən/ ADJECTIVE saying exactly what you mean, even if it upsets people □ *She is an outspoken critic of the government.* (franco, sem papas na língua)

outstanding /ˌaʊtˈstændɪŋ/ ADJECTIVE

1 excellent □ *an outstanding student* (notável)

2 not yet paid or done □ *You must complete all your outstanding assignments.* □ *This bill for your mobile phone is still outstanding.* (pendente)

outstretched /ˌaʊtˈstretʃt/ ADJECTIVE if part of your body is outstretched, it is stretched out as far as possible, usually in order to reach something □ *She stood with outstretched arms waiting to welcome them.* (esticado, distendido)

out-tray /ˈaʊttreɪ/ NOUN [*plural* **out-trays**] the container in your office where you put letters or papers ready for posting or passing to someone else (caixa de entrada e saída)

outward /ˈaʊtwəd/ ADJECTIVE

1 to do with how things appear □ *She shows no outward sign of unhappiness.* (exterior, aparente)

2 away from a place □ *The outward flight was severely delayed.* (de ida)

• **outward** /ˈaʊtwəd/ or **outwards** /ˈaʊtwədz/ ADVERB towards the outside □ *Most windows open outward.* (para fora)

• **outwardly** /ˈaʊtwədli/ ADVERB in the way that something seems, which may not be the truth □ *Outwardly they were cheerful.* (aparentemente)

outweigh /ˌaʊtˈweɪ/ VERB [**outweighs, outweighing, outweighed**] to be more important than something else □ *The advantages outweigh the disadvantages.* (exceder)

outwit /ˌaʊtˈwɪt/ VERB [**outwits, outwitting, outwitted**] to get an advantage over someone by doing something clever, often to trick them □ *She outwitted the police and managed to escape.* (passar a perna em, despistar)

oval /ˈəʊvəl/ ▶ ADJECTIVE shaped like a circle with the edges pressed slightly together □ *an oval table* (oval)
▶ NOUN [*plural* **ovals**] an oval shape □ *He drew an oval.* (oval)

ovary /ˈəʊvəri/ NOUN [*plural* **ovaries**]

1 the part of a woman's body where eggs are formed. A biology word. (ovário)

2 the part of a flower where seeds are formed. A biology word. (ovário)

oven /ˈʌvən/ NOUN [*plural* **ovens**] the part of a cooker that is shaped like a box with a door and is used for cooking and heating food □ *Bake the cake in the centre of the oven for 30 minutes.* (forno)

oven glove /ˈʌvən ˌglʌv/ NOUN [*plural* **oven gloves**] a special glove (= covering for your hand) made of a thick material that you use when you take hot food out of an oven (luva para forno)

ovenproof /ˈʌvənpruːf/ ADJECTIVE ovenproof dishes do not break when they are put into a hot oven (refratário)

over /ˈəʊvə(r)/ ▶ PREPOSITION

1 above someone or something, or moving across the place above someone or something □ *His photograph hung over the fireplace.* □ *An eagle flew right over our heads.* (acima de)

2 about a particular subject □ *They quarrelled over the children.* □ *He was in court over a dispute with a neighbour.* (sobre)

3 more than □ *He's over 90 years old.* □ *She left school just over three years ago.* (acima de)

4 across □ *We ran over the bridge.* (atravessar)

5 covering something or someone □ *I put a blanket over her legs.* □ *There was snow over the hills.* (sobre) 🔲 *You've got mud all over your clothes.* (sobre toda a)

6 on the other side of something □ *There is a house just over that hill.* □ *The sun set over the* horizon. □ My house is just over the road. (do outro lado)

7 be/get over something to feel better after being ill or unhappy □ He never got over the disappointment. □ I had the flu, but I'm over it now. (recuperar-se, superar, curar)

8 used to talk about controlling or defeating someone or something □ Chelsea celebrated their win over Leeds. □ He ruled over the entire country. (sobre)

▶ ADVERB

1 moving across the place above someone or something □ An aeroplane flew over. (por sobre)

2 from one side to the other □ That bridge isn't safe – I'm not going over. (atravessar)

3 higher in number or amount □ Children aged seven and over may swim alone. (acima)

4 onto the other side □ The dog rolled over in the mud. □ Turn your papers over. (ao contrário, para cima)

5 to a particular place □ He walked over to speak to them. □ Would you like to come over for lunch? (para lá, para cá)

6 towards the side □ Could you stand a bit further over to the right? □ I moved over to make room for him. (para o lado)

7 remaining □ There were two cakes left over. (de sobra)

8 all over again again, from the beginning □ My computer crashed, and I had to do my essay all over again. (tudo outra vez)

9 over and over again and again □ I told her over and over not to talk to strangers. (repetidas vezes)

▶ ADJECTIVE

1 finished □ The match is already over. (acabado)

2 over and done with if you get an unpleasant task over and done with, you complete it so that you do not have to worry about it any more (acabado e enterrado)

over- /ˈəʊvə(r)/ PREFIX **over-** is added to the beginning of words to mean 'too' or 'too much' □ Be careful not to get overconfident. □ an overcrowded train (em excesso, muito, demais)

overall ▶ ADJECTIVE /ˈəʊvərɔːl/ including everything □ The overall cost of the holiday has gone up. (no total)

▶ ADVERB /ˌəʊvərˈɔːl/ considering or including everything or everyone □ Overall, I'm very pleased with the film. (no geral)

▶ NOUN /ˈəʊvərɔːl/ [plural **overalls**]

1 a piece of clothing like a thin coat worn over ordinary clothes to protect them □ She wears an overall when cleaning the house. (avental, jaleco)

2 overalls a piece of clothing that covers the legs and body, worn to protect clothing during dirty work (macacão)

overawed /ˌəʊvərˈɔːd/ ADJECTIVE frightened or nervous because something is so big or powerful, or because you admire it so much □ He was completely overawed by the splendid surroundings of the palace. (apavorado, intimidado)

overbearing /ˌəʊvəˈbeərɪŋ/ ADJECTIVE trying to control other people without thinking about their feelings □ I can't stand his overbearing manner. (dominante, autoritário)

overboard /ˈəʊvəbɔːd/ ADVERB over the side of a ship or boat and into the water □ He jumped overboard to save the drowning man. □ Man overboard! (ao mar, pela borda fora)

♦ IDIOM **go overboard** to do something too much, often because you are excited about something □ I think you've gone a bit overboard with the decorations. (exagerar, passar dos limites)

overcame /ˌəʊvəˈkeɪm/ PAST TENSE OF **overcome**

overcast /ˌəʊvəˈkɑːst/ ADJECTIVE dark and with a lot of clouds □ The sky was overcast but it didn't rain. (nublado)

overcharge /ˌəʊvəˈtʃɑːdʒ/ VERB [**overcharges**, **overcharging**, **overcharged**] to charge someone too much money for something □ I think you've overcharged me for the wine. (cobrar preço alto demais)

overcoat /ˈəʊvəkəʊt/ NOUN [plural **overcoats**] a long warm coat □ a cashmere overcoat (sobretudo)

overcome /ˌəʊvəˈkʌm/ VERB [**overcomes**, **overcoming**, **overcame**, **overcome**]

1 to manage to deal successfully with a problem □ She has struggled to overcome her depression (superar).

2 if you are overcome by an emotion, it has a very strong effect on you and you cannot control it □ He shut himself away, overcome with grief. (dominado)

3 if you are overcome by an illness, or by smoke, heat, etc., it makes you very ill, weak or unconscious □ One fireman was overcome by the fumes. (dominado)

overcook /ˌəʊvəˈkʊk/ VERB [**overcooks**, **overcooking**, **overcooked**] to cook food for too long □ overcooked vegetables (cozinhar demais)

overcrowded /ˌəʊvəˈkraʊdɪd/ ADJECTIVE an overcrowded place has too many people or things in it □ our overcrowded prisons (superlotado)

• **overcrowding** /ˌəʊvəˈkraʊdɪŋ/ NOUN, NO PLURAL when there are too many people or things in one place □ There is severe overcrowding on our rail network. (superlotação)

overdo /ˌəʊvəˈduː/ VERB [**overdoes**, **overdoing**, **overdid**, **overdone**] to do something too much or to use too much of something (exagerar) □ It's good to work hard, but don't overdo it. (não exagere)

• **overdone** /ˌəʊvəˈdʌn/ ADJECTIVE cooked too much □ He gave us an overdone steak. (cozido demais)

overdose ▶ NOUN /ˈəʊvədəʊs/ [plural **overdoses**] more of a drug or medicine than is safe □ an overdose of sleeping pills (overdose)

▶ VERB /ˌəʊvəˈdəʊs/ [overdoses, overdosing, overdosed] to take too much of a drug or medicine (tomar uma overdose)

overdraft /ˈəʊvədrɑːft/ NOUN [plural **overdrafts**] when a bank allows you to take more money out of your account than you have put in □ *I have a £500 overdraft limit.* (saque a descoberto)

• **overdrawn** /ˌəʊvəˈdrɔːn/ ADJECTIVE when you have taken more money out of your bank account than you have put in (a descoberto) 🔁 *I don't want to go overdrawn.* (ficar no vermelho)

overdrive /ˈəʊvədraɪv/ NOUN, NO PLURAL an extra gear in some motor vehicles for travelling fast □ *She put the car into overdrive.* (sobremarcha, marcha extra)

♦ IDIOM **go/move into overdrive** to be come very active or to start making a lot of effort □ *As soon as I asked her to help with the wedding, Mum went into overdrive.* (fazer algo com exagero, exagerar)

overdue /ˌəʊvəˈdjuː/ ADJECTIVE if something is overdue, it should have happened, been done, been paid, etc. before now □ *Our library books are overdue.* □ *He received a long overdue promotion.* (atrasado, vencido)

overestimate /ˌəʊvərˈestɪmeɪt/ VERB [overestimates, overestimating, overestimated] to think that something is larger or better than it really is □ *Geologists overestimated the amount of gold to be found in the rock.* (superestimar)

overflow /ˌəʊvəˈfləʊ/ VERB [overflows, overflowing, overflowed]

1 if a container overflows, liquid flows over its edges, and if a liquid overflows, it flows over the edges of a container □ *The sink overflowed and flooded the bathroom.* (transbordar)

2 if a river or a lake overflows, it becomes too full and water flows out of it (transbordar)

3 if a place is overflowing with people or things, there are too many of them to fit there □ *There were boxes overflowing with toys.* □ *The crowd overflowed into the street.* (abarrotar)

overgrown /ˌəʊvəˈɡrəʊn/ ADJECTIVE full of plants that have grown too large and thick □ *The back garden is completely overgrown with weeds.* (cheio de vegetação)

overhang /ˌəʊvəˈhæŋ/ VERB [overhangs, overhanging, overhung] to hang over something □ *The stream was overhung by the branches of a tree.* (pender, pendurar)

overhaul ▶ VERB /ˌəʊvəˈhɔːl/ [overhauls, overhauling, overhauled]

1 to examine a machine and repair any damage □ *He had his car overhauled at the garage.* (revisar, inspecionar)

2 to change a system a lot in order to make it more effective □ *There are plans to overhaul the tax system.* (revisar)

▶ NOUN /ˈəʊvəhɔːl/ [plural **overhauls**] when you overhaul something □ *The mechanic gave the car a complete overhaul.* (revisão)

overhead /ˌəʊvəˈhed/ ADVERB, ADJECTIVE above your head or high above the ground □ *A plane was flying overhead.* □ *overhead cables* (aéreo)

overheads /ˈəʊvəhedz/ PLURAL NOUN the money that a business has to spend regularly on things like rent and electricity (despesas gerais)

overhear /ˌəʊvəˈhɪə(r)/ VERB [overhears, overhearing, overheard] to hear what someone says when they are not talking to you □ *I overheard them talking about me.* (ouvir por acaso)

overjoyed /ˌəʊvəˈdʒɔɪd/ ADJECTIVE very happy □ *We were overjoyed to hear that he was safe.* (radiante)

overland /ˈəʊvəlænd/ ADVERB, ADJECTIVE across land, instead of by sea or air □ *They travelled overland across America.* □ *an overland safari* (por terra, por via terrestre)

overlap ▶ VERB /ˌəʊvəˈlæp/ [overlaps, overlapping, overlapped]

1 if objects overlap, part of each one is covered by part of another one □ *Each roof tile overlaps the one below it.* □ *The curtains should be wide enough to overlap.* (sobrepor-se)

2 if two things overlap, they include some of the same parts, ideas, etc. □ *The categories often overlap.* (sobrepor-se)

▶ NOUN /ˈəʊvəlæp/ [plural **overlaps**]

1 when two things overlap □ *There's some overlap between the two company's markets.* (sobreposição)

2 the amount by which something overlaps □ *There's an overlap of half an hour between the two programmes.* (sobreposição)

overload /ˌəʊvəˈləʊd/ VERB [overloads, overloading, overloaded]

1 when something is overloaded, it has too many people or things in it or on it □ *The car was overloaded and dangerously close to the ground.* (sobrecarregar)

2 if you are overloaded with work or problems, you have more than you can deal with □ *Many social workers are overloaded with cases.* (sobrecarregar)

3 to give a machine or system more information, work, etc. than it can deal with □ *The mobile phone network was overloaded.* (sobrecarregar)

4 to cause too much electricity to pass through an electrical system (sobrecarregar)

overlook /ˌəʊvəˈlʊk/ VERB [overlooks, overlooking, overlooked]

1 to fail to notice or consider something □ *You have overlooked one important detail.* (deixar passar)

2 to ignore a fault or mistake □ *I shall overlook your lateness this time.* (fechar os olhos para, fazer vista grossa)

3 to have a view over a place □ *The house overlooks the river.* (contemplar do alto)

overly

overly /ˈəʊvəlɪ/ ADVERB too much or very much □ *The figures were overly optimistic.* □ *He didn't seem overly concerned.* (**excessivamente**)

overnight /ˌəʊvəˈnaɪt/ ADJECTIVE, ADVERB
1 for or during the night □ *an overnight train* □ *The centre provides overnight accommodation.* (**noturno, de pernoite**) ▣ *We stayed overnight in London.* (**pernoitar**)
2 sudden or suddenly (**da noite para o dia**) ▣ *an overnight success* □ *He became a hero overnight.* (**sucesso da noite para o dia**)

overpower /ˌəʊvəˈpaʊə(r)/ VERB [**overpowers, overpowering, overpowered**]
1 to defeat someone because you are stronger than them □ *He was overpowered by two policemen.* (**subjugar**)
2 to affect you so strongly that you cannot think or behave normally □ *They were overpowered by the smell.* (**subjugar**)
• **overpowering** /ˌəʊvəˈpaʊərɪŋ/ ADJECTIVE very strong □ *an overpowering smell* (**irresistível, esmagador**)

overran /ˌəʊvəˈræn/ PAST TENSE OF overrun (*ver* overrun)

overrated /ˌəʊvəˈreɪtɪd/ ADJECTIVE not as good or as important as people believe □ *His new film is overrated.* (**superestimado**)

overreact /ˌəʊvərɪˈækt/ VERB [**overreacts, overreacting, overreacted**] to react in a way that is too extreme to be reasonable □ *When I burst into tears, he accused me of overreacting.* (**reagir descontroladamente, de modo exagerado**)

overriding /ˌəʊvəˈraɪdɪŋ/ ADJECTIVE more important than anything else □ *a matter of overriding importance* □ *Their overriding consideration is the need to maintain peace in the area.* (**prioritário**)

overrule /ˌəʊvəˈruːl/ VERB [**overrules, overruling, overruled**] to officially change a decision □ *The President has the power to overrule parliament in certain circumstances.* (**anular**)

overrun /ˌəʊvəˈrʌn/ VERB [**overruns, overrunning, overran, overrun**]
1 if a place is overrun with something, there are very large numbers of that thing there □ *The house is overrun with mice.* (**infestado**)
2 to continue for longer than planned or to cost more than planned □ *The concert overran by half an hour.* (**exceder**)

oversaw /ˌəʊvəˈsɔː/ PAST TENSE OF oversee (*ver* oversee)

overseas /ˌəʊvəˈsiːz/ ADJECTIVE, ADVERB in, to or from another country □ *an overseas job* □ *overseas students* □ *They went overseas.* (**além-mar**)

oversee /ˌəʊvəˈsiː/ VERB [**oversees, overseeing, oversaw, overseen**] to watch something being done to check that it is done correctly □ *His job is to oversee the factory workers.* (**supervisionar**)

overturn

overshadow /ˌəʊvəˈʃædəʊ/ VERB [**overshadows, overshadowing, overshadowed**]
1 if an unpleasant thing overshadows an event, it makes it less enjoyable □ *The race was overshadowed by the death of a competitor.* (**ofuscar**)
2 to seem much more successful or important than someone or something else □ *Clare was always overshadowed by her brilliant sister.* (**ofuscar**)

oversight /ˈəʊvəsaɪt/ NOUN [*plural* **oversights**] a mistake that you make because you have not noticed something □ *It was a serious oversight on his part.* (**descuido**)

oversleep /ˌəʊvəˈsliːp/ VERB [**oversleeps, oversleeping, overslept**] to sleep for longer than you planned to □ *I was late for the lecture because I overslept.* (**dormir demais**)

overt /ˈəʊvɜːt, əʊˈvɜːt/ ADJECTIVE not secret or hidden □ *He was taken aback by the overt hostility of the locals.* (**declarado**)

overtake /ˌəʊvəˈteɪk/ VERB [**overtakes, overtaking, overtook, overtaken**]
1 to move past a vehicle that is travelling in the same direction □ *He overtook a police car.* (**ultrapassar**)
2 to become more successful than someone or something else □ *China has overtaken Germany as the world's biggest exporter.* (**ultrapassar**)

overthrow /ˌəʊvəˈθrəʊ/ ▶ VERB [**overthrows, overthrowing, overthrew, overthrown**] to take power away from a leader or a government by force □ *They are plotting to overthrow the current regime.* (**derrubar**)
▶ NOUN, NO PLURAL /ˈəʊvəθrəʊ/ when a leader or a government is overthrown (**derrubar**)

overtime /ˈəʊvətaɪm/ NOUN, NO PLURAL extra time spent working in addition to your normal working hours (**horas extras**) ▣ *We had to work overtime to get everything finished.* (**fazer horas extras**)

overtly /əʊˈvɜːtlɪ/ ADVERB in an overt way □ *The newspaper article was overtly critical of the regime.* (**publicamente, abertamente**)

overtook /ˌəʊvəˈtʊk/ PAST TENSE OF overtake (*ver* overtake)

overture /ˈəʊvətjʊə(r)/ NOUN [*plural* **overtures**]
1 a piece of music played at the start of an opera or ballet (**abertura**)
2 a friendly attempt to start a discussion or a relationship (**preliminares**) ▣ *They have started to make overtures to neighbouring governments.* (**fazer aproximações**)

overturn /ˌəʊvəˈtɜːn/ VERB [**overturns, overturning, overturned**]
1 to officially change a decision □ *The ruling was overturned by the court of appeal.* (**derrubar**)
2 to turn something upside down or to turn upside down □ *Chairs were overturned and*

glasses were broken. □ *The bus overturned in wet conditions.* (virar, emborcar)

overweight /ˌəʊvəˈweɪt/ ADJECTIVE an overweight person is too heavy □ *I'm about four kilos overweight.* (acima do peso)

overwhelm /ˌəʊvəˈwelm/ VERB [overwhelms, overwhelming, overwhelmed]

1 to have a very strong and sudden effect on someone □ *We were overwhelmed with joy.* (esmagar)

2 to be too much for someone or something to deal with □ *I'm overwhelmed with work at the moment.* □ *Heavy rain overwhelmed the drainage system.* (atolado)

3 to defeat someone completely □ *Our soldiers were overwhelmed by the enemy.* (subjugado)

• **overwhelming** /ˌəʊvəˈwelmɪŋ/ ADJECTIVE
1 very large or important □ *They won an overwhelming victory over their rivals.* (esmagador)
🔲 *An overwhelming majority of workers voted to strike.* (uma maioria esmagadora)

2 overwhelming emotions and feelings are very strong □ *There's an overwhelming feeling of relief.* □ *The temptation was almost overwhelming.* (forte, sufocante)

• **overwhelmingly** /ˌəʊvəˈwelmɪŋli/ ADVERB used to emphasize that something is very strong or very large □ *They voted overwhelmingly in favour of the reform.* (esmagadoramente)

overwork ▶ VERB /ˌəʊvəˈwɜːk/ [overworks, overworking, overworked] to work too hard or to make someone work too hard (trabalhar excessivamente)

▶ NOUN, NO PLURAL /ˈəʊvəwɜːk/ when you work too hard □ *Overwork made him ill.* (excesso de trabalho)

• **overworked** /ˌəʊvəˈwɜːkt/ ADJECTIVE made to work too hard □ *The staff are overworked.* (sobrecarregado)

overwrite /ˌəʊvəˈraɪt/ VERB [overwrites, overwriting, overwrote, overwritten] to replace information in a computer file with different information. A computing word. (escrever novos dados apagando os anteriores)

ovulate /ˈɒvjuleɪt/ VERB [ovulates, ovulating, ovulated] when a woman or female animal ovulates, she produces eggs. A biology word. (ovular)

• **ovulation** /ˌɒvjuˈleɪʃən/ NOUN, NO PLURAL the process of ovulating. A biology word. (ovulação)

owe /əʊ/ VERB [owes, owing, owed]

1 to have to pay money to someone □ *I owe Val £10.* □ *+ to He owes money to suppliers.* (dever)

2 used to say that someone deserves something from someone (dever) 🔲 *I think you owe Simon an apology.* □ *We owe it to future generations to protect the planet.* (dever desculpas)

3 to have something only because of someone or something □ *+ to He owes his success to his family.* □ *The college owes its existence to a small group of wealthy individuals.* (dever)

• **owing to** /ˈəʊɪŋ tə/ PREPOSITION because of □ *He withdrew from the competition owing to a back injury.* □ *The club closed down owing to lack of funding.* (devido a)

owl /aʊl/ NOUN [plural owls] a large bird that hunts at night (coruja)

own /əʊn/ ▶ ADJECTIVE belonging to or done by the person mentioned □ *I need to spend more time with my own family.* □ *The rules are for your own safety.* □ *Is this all your own work?* (próprio)
🔲 *I'd love to have a horse of my very own.* (meu próprio cavalo)

▶ PRONOUN

1 used to show that something belongs to someone or something □ *I lent him a pencil, because he forgot to bring his own.* □ *There are plenty of showers – each bedroom has its own.* (próprio)

2 on your own (a) without help from anyone else □ *He managed to finish the work on his own.* □ *Did you do this all on your own?* (b) alone □ *I live on my own in a small flat.* (completamente só)

3 of your own if someone or something has something of its own, it belongs only to them □ *I'd love a bedroom of my own.* □ *Each apartment has a small garden of its own.* (próprio)

♦ IDIOMS **get your own back** to do something unpleasant to someone who has done something unpleasant to you (dar o troco) **get/have your own** way to make things happen in the way you want them to, often when other people disagree □ *We all wanted to go to Greece, but Maria got her own way as usual, so we're going to Florida.* (impor sua vontade) **hold your own** to be as confident or successful as other people in a situation □ *She did well to hold her own with all those experienced politicians.* (permanecer firme)

▶ VERB [owns, owning, owned] you own something if it belongs to you, especially if you have bought it □ *I own a car.* □ *He doesn't own a single book.* (possuir)

♦ PHRASAL VERB **own up** to admit that you did something wrong □ *Nobody owned up to breaking the chair.* (admitir)

• **owner** /ˈəʊnə(r)/ NOUN [plural owners] a person who owns something (proprietário)

• **ownership** /ˈəʊnəʃɪp/ NOUN, NO PLURAL when someone owns something □ *He retained ownership of the firm.* (propriedade) 🔲 *Home ownership has risen.* (propriedade residencial)

own goal /ˌəʊn ˈɡəʊl/ NOUN [plural own goals]

1 a goal that someone scores by mistake against their own team (gol contra)

2 something you do that harms yourself (contra si mesmo)

ox /ɒks/ NOUN [plural oxen] a large, male cow used for pulling farm machines (boi)

oxbow lake /ˌɒksbəʊ ˈleɪk/ NOUN [plural **oxbow lakes**] a lake that is formed when part of a river curves so much that it separates from the rest of the river. A geography word. (**lagoa marginal**)

oxide /ˈɒksaɪd/ NOUN [plural **oxides**] a chemical that is made of oxygen and another substance. A chemistry word. (**óxido**)

oxygen /ˈɒksɪdʒən/ NOUN, NO PLURAL a gas that has no taste, colour or smell, and forms part of the air. A chemistry word. (**oxigênio**)

oxymoron /ˌɒksɪˈmɔːrɒn/ NOUN [plural **oxymorons**] when two words that seem to be opposites are used together, for example 'deafening silence' (**oxímoro**)

oyster /ˈɔɪstə(r)/ NOUN [plural **oysters**] a type of sea creature in a shell that can be eaten (**ostra**)

oz ABBREVIATION ounce (**medida**)

ozone /ˈəʊzəʊn/ NOUN, NO PLURAL a form of oxygen with a strong smell. A chemistry word. (**ozônio**)

ozone layer /ˈəʊzəʊn ˌleɪə(r)/ NOUN, NO PLURAL the layer of ozone that is around the Earth and that protects the planet from the harmful effects of the sun (**camada de ozônio**)

P p

P or **p** /piː/ the 16th letter of the alphabet (a décima sexta letra do alfabeto)

p /piː/ ABBREVIATION **page** or **pence** (abrev. de página ou pence)

p & p /ˌpiːənˈpiː/ ABBREVIATION postage and packing; the price that you must pay for someone to send something to you by post (custos de postagem e embalagem)

PA /ˌpiːˈeɪ/ ABBREVIATION **personal assistant** (assistente pessoal)

pace /peɪs/ ▶ NOUN [plural **paces**]
1 the speed at which something happens or at which someone does something □ *the pace of change* □ *He was walking at a very slow pace.* (ritmo)
2 a step 🔲 *Take four paces forward.* (passo)
3 keep pace with someone/something to move at the same speed as someone or change at the same speed as someone or something □ *Manufacturers are struggling to keep pace with demand for the product.* (acompanhar o ritmo de)
▶ VERB [**paces, pacing, paced**]
1 to walk backwards and forwards because you are worried □ *She was pacing up and down, waiting for the phone to ring.*
2 pace yourself to do something at a sensible speed so that you are not too tired □ *You need to pace yourself because there are a lot of things to see in New York.* (vá com calma)

pacemaker /ˈpeɪsmeɪkə(r)/ NOUN [plural **pacemakers**] a small device that is put in someone's body to keep their heart beating correctly (marca-passo)

pachyderm /ˈpækɪdɜːm/ NOUN [plural **pachyderms**] an animal with very thick skin, for example a rhinoceros or an elephant. A biology word. (paquiderme)

pacifism /ˈpæsɪfɪzəm/ NOUN, NO PLURAL the belief that all wars are wrong (pacifismo)

• **pacifist** /ˈpæsɪfɪst/ NOUN [plural **pacifists**] someone who believes that all wars are wrong (pacifista)

• **pacify** /ˈpæsɪfaɪ/ VERB [**pacifies, pacifying, pacified**] to make someone calm after they have been upset or angry □ *'That's a pretty dress,' he said in an attempt to pacify her.* (apaziguar)

pack /pæk/ ▶ VERB [**packs, packing, packed**]
1 to put things in a bag or case ready for a journey □ *She packed hurriedly and caught the next train.* □ *Ben packed his bag for the holiday.* □ *Make sure you pack your swimming costume.* (empacotar, acondicionar)
2 to put something into a box so it can be moved, sold or stored □ *She has a job packing chocolates in a factory.* (empacotar) □ **+ in** *The food was packed in brown paper bags.* (interromper) □ **+ up** *They packed up all their furniture ready for the house move.*
3 if people pack a place, a lot of them go there and fill it □ *Reporters packed the courtroom.* □ **+ into** *More then 15,000 fans packed into the sports stadium.*

◆ PHRASAL VERBS **pack something in**
1 an informal phrase meaning to stop doing something □ *She had been forced to pack her job in because of illness.* (interromper)
2 an informal phrase meaning to do a lot of things in a short time □ *I managed to pack in three trips to the cinema this week.* (realizar muita coisa em pouco tempo) **pack someone off** an informal word meaning to send someone away suddenly □ *He was packed off to boarding school at the age of eight.* (mandar alguém embora) **pack up** an informal word meaning to stop working □ *My printer has packed up again.* (enguiçar) **pack (something) up** to put things into bags or boxes so that they can be moved □ *He packed up his belongings and left.* □ *We decided to pack up and go home.* (empacotar)

▶ NOUN [plural **packs**]
1 a set of documents that have been put together (documentação) 🔲 *All new students will receive an information pack.* (conjunto de informações) □ *If you are interested in the job, you can download an application pack.*
2 a set of products that are sold together □ *I bought a pack of 6 cakes.* (pacote)
3 a small container that something is sold in □ **+ of** *a pack of chewing gum* (caixinha)
4 a set of 52 cards that you play games with □ **+ of** *a pack of cards* (baralho)
5 a group of animals that live and hunt together □ **+ of** *a pack of wolves* (bando, alcateia)
6 a group of similar people, especially people you do not like □ **+ of** *There was a pack of kids standing outside the shop.* (bando, quadrilha)

package /ˈpækɪdʒ/ ▶ NOUN [plural **packages**]
1 something that has been wrapped in paper or put in a box, especially so it can be sent by post

□ *He sent the package to his brother.* □ *Police will destroy any suspicious packages.* (**embrulho**)
2 a group of products or services that are sold together □ *The company has launched a new broadband package.* □ *The hotel offers a wedding package.* (**pacote**)
3 a set of plans that are designed to deal with something □ *The government announced a new aid package for some of the world's poorest countries.* (**pacote**)
4 a US word for a container or a box that a product is sold in (**embalagem**)
▶ VERB [**packages, packaging, packaged**]
1 to put something in a box or bag or to wrap them up in order to be sold □ *The sweets are packaged in pretty boxes.* (**empacotar**)
2 to sell a product or service together with other products or services □ *A small instruction book is packaged with the DVD.* (**pacote de produtos ou serviços**)
3 to try to make someone or something appear to have particular qualities □ *The cosmetic surgery is packaged as a holiday.* (**vender como**)

• **packaged** /ˈpækɪdʒd/ ADJECTIVE sold in a container or bag □ *packaged fruit and vegetables* (**empacotado**)

package holiday /ˈpækɪdʒ ˌhɒlɪdeɪ/ NOUN [*plural* **package holidays**] a holiday in which a company arranges everything such as your travel and your hotel (**pacote de férias/pacote de viagem**)

packaging /ˈpækɪdʒɪŋ/ NOUN, NO PLURAL the material that a product is sold in □ *Supermarkets are asking suppliers to reduce packaging.* (**embalagem**)

packed /pækt/ ADJECTIVE
1 very crowded □ *The train was packed.* (**abarrotado**)
2 containing a lot of something □ *Bananas are packed with vitamins and minerals.* (**repleto de**)

packed lunch /ˌpækt ˈlʌntʃ/ NOUN [*plural* **packed lunches**] food in a container that you take to eat at school, work, etc. (**refeição para viagem**)

packet /ˈpækɪt/ NOUN [*plural* **packets**] a box or bag containing several of the same things □ *There were a lot of seeds in the packet.* (**pacote**) ▣ *He opened the packet and offered me some peanuts.* (**abriu o pacote**) □ *+ of a packet of biscuits* □ *a packet of crisps*

packing /ˈpækɪŋ/ NOUN, NO PLURAL
1 the process of putting things into bags or boxes so that you can take them somewhere ▣ *Have you done your packing for the holiday?* (**empacotamento**)
2 the material you use for wrapping and protecting objects, especially when you send them somewhere ▣ *There will be a small extra charge for postage and packing.* (**postagem e empacotamento**)

pact /pækt/ NOUN [*plural* **pacts**] an agreement between two people, groups or countries (**pacto**) ▣ *We made a pact never to tell anyone what happened.* (**fazer um pacto**)

pad /pæd/ ▶ NOUN [*plural* **pads**]
1 a thick piece of soft material, used for protecting something or for making it more comfortable □ *I always wear knee pads and elbow pads when I'm roller skating.* (**almofada**)
2 a book of pieces of paper, used for writing or drawing on □ *a sketch pad* (**bloco**)
3 a special place where helicopters (= type of aircraft) can fly from or land, or where a spacecraft leaves the ground (**plataforma**) ▣ *They sent a satellite into space from the launch pad.* (**plataforma de lançamento**)
▶ VERB [**pads, padding, padded**]
1 to walk somewhere very quietly □ *He padded into the kitchen in his pyjamas.* (**andar silenciosamente**)
2 to fill or wrap something with a soft material □ *The horses' hooves had been padded with cloth to muffle the sound.* (**rechear, forrar**)
♦ PHRASAL VERB **pad something out** to add information to a speech or piece of writing in order to make it longer, often when this is not necessary □ *The book had been padded out with old material.* (**rechear**)

• **padded** /ˈpædɪd/ ADJECTIVE filled or covered with a soft material □ *a padded envelope* □ *a padded jacket* (**forrado**)

• **padding** /ˈpædɪŋ/ NOUN, NO PLURAL
1 soft material used for filling something (**enchimento**)
2 unnecessary information that has been added to a speech or piece of writing, in order to make it longer (**informações desnecessárias**)

paddle /ˈpædəl/ ▶ VERB [**paddles, paddling, paddled**]
1 to move a boat through water using a paddle □ *She paddled the canoe down the river.* (**utilizar remo, remar suavemente**)
2 to walk in water that is not deep □ *The children were paddling in the sea.* (**patinhar**)
▶ NOUN [*plural* **paddles**] a short piece of wood with a flat end, used for rowing a boat (**tipo de remo**)

paddock /ˈpædək/ NOUN [*plural* **paddocks**] a field where someone keeps horses (**padoque**)

paddy field /ˈpædi ˌfiːld/ NOUN [*plural* **paddy fields**] a field where rice is grown (**arrozal**)

padlock /ˈpædlɒk/ ▶ NOUN [*plural* **padlocks**] a lock with a curved metal part on top and a key that goes in the bottom, used for locking things such as bicycles or gates (**cadeado**)
▶ VERB [**padlocks, padlocking, padlocked**] to fasten something using a padlock □ *I padlocked my bike to the railings.* (**fechar com cadeado**)

paediatric /ˌpiːdɪˈætrɪk/ ADJECTIVE to do with the medical treatment of children ◻ *a paediatric nurse* (**pediátrico**)

- **paediatrician** /ˌpiːdɪəˈtrɪʃən/ NOUN [plural **paediatricians**] a doctor who treats children (**pediatria**)

- **paediatrics** /ˌpiːdɪˈætrɪks/ NOUN, NO PLURAL the area of medicine to do with children (**pediatra**)

pagan /ˈpeɪɡən/ ▶ NOUN [plural **pagans**] someone who believes in a religion that is not one of the world's main religions (**pagão**)
▶ ADJECTIVE to do with pagans or paganism ◻ *a pagan festival* (**pagão**)

- **paganism** /ˈpeɪɡənɪzəm/ NOUN, NO PLURAL pagan beliefs and customs (**paganismo**)

page /peɪdʒ/ ▶ NOUN [plural **pages**]

1 a piece of paper in a book, newspaper or magazine, or one side of it ◻ *The information can be found on page 135.* (**página**) ▣ *His picture was on the front page of the newspaper.* (**página do frontispício**) ▣ *She turned the pages very slowly.* (**virou as páginas**)

2 the writing or pictures that you see on a computer screen, especially as part of a website ◻ *You need to refresh the page to see the information.* (**página**) ▣ *Visit our information page to find out more.* (**visite a nossa página**)
▶ VERB [**pages, paging, paged**] to call someone by sending a message to their pager (= small piece of electronic equipment) ◻ *Nurses paged the doctor.* (**enviar mensagem via pager**)

pageant /ˈpædʒənt/ NOUN [plural **pageants**] a show outdoors, especially one that tells a historical or religious story (**quadro vivo, espetáculo**)

- **pageantry** /ˈpædʒəntri/ NOUN, NO PLURAL special clothes, music, decorations, etc. which are used in formal ceremonies ◻ *He loved the colour and pageantry of the festival.* (**pompa**)

pager /ˈpeɪdʒə(r)/ NOUN [plural **pagers**] a small electronic device that makes a noise to tell you to telephone someone or go somewhere (**pager**)

paid /peɪd/ ▶ PAST TENSE AND PAST PARTICIPLE OF **pay**
▶ ADJECTIVE

1 paid work is work for which you get money (**pago**) ▣ *Have you had any paid employment in the last six months?* (**emprego contratado**) ▣ *She has a highly paid job.*

2 paid holiday or paid leave is time when your employer pays you although you are not working ◻ *I have six weeks paid leave a year.* (**licença remunerada**)

pail /peɪl/ NOUN [plural **pails**] an open container with a handle, used for carrying liquids (**balde**)

pain /peɪn/ ▶ NOUN [plural **pains**]

1 the unpleasant feeling you have when part of your body hurts (**dor**) ◻ *stomach pains* ▣ *He felt a stinging pain.* (**sentiu dor**) ▣ *Aspirin is used to relieve pain* (= make pain less bad). (**aliviar a dor**) ▣ *Ann felt a sharp pain in her leg.* (**dor aguda**) ◻ + *in* *He had pains in his chest.*

2 be in pain to have an unpleasant feeling because part of your body hurts ◻ *Amy was in constant pain from a broken shoulder.* ◻ *He was obviously in great pain.* (**com dor**)

3 *no plural* sadness (**dor**) ▣ *She felt that seeing him would cause her too much pain.* (**causar-lhe dor**) ▣ *Nothing I can say will ease the pain* (= make it less bad). (**amenizar a dor**) ◻ + *of* *The pain of leaving his wife behind was almost too much to bear.*

4 an informal word meaning someone or something that is annoying ◻ *Sometimes she can be a real pain.* (**pessoa ou coisa insuportável, mala**)

♦ IDIOM **be at/take pains to do something** to make a lot of effort to do something ◻ *He took great pains to be fair to everyone.* (**esforçar-se**)
▶ VERB [**pains, paining, pained**] to make someone feel sad or upset ◻ *It pained him to see food wasted.* (**chatear**)

- **pained** /peɪnd/ ADJECTIVE showing that you feel sad, upset or angry ▣ *He stared at the damage with a pained expression.* (**dolorido**)

- **painful** /ˈpeɪnfʊl/ ADJECTIVE

1 making you feel unhappy or ashamed (**doloroso**) ▣ *painful memories* ◻ *His time in prison had been a very painful experience.* (**memórias dolorosas**) ◻ + *for* *It is painful for parents to see their child so unhappy.* ◻ + *to do something* *It was too painful to think about his failed marriage.*

2 causing physical pain ◻ *Is your knee still painful?* ◻ *She had a painful lump on her arm.* (**doendo**)

- **painfully** /ˈpeɪnfʊli/ ADVERB (**dolorosamente**)

1 used to emphasize that something is bad ◻ *It was a painfully slow process.* ◻ *She was painfully thin.* (**terrivelmente**)

2 in a painful way ◻ *This type of poison would kill an animal slowly and painfully.* (**dolorosamente**)

painkiller /ˈpeɪnkɪlə(r)/ NOUN [plural **painkillers**] a drug that reduces pain (**analgésico**)

painless /ˈpeɪnləs/ ADJECTIVE

1 causing no physical pain ◻ *a painless death* (**indolor**)

2 not unpleasant or difficult ◻ *Checking in at the airport was relatively painless.* (**sem grandes problemas**)

painstaking /ˈpeɪnzteɪkɪŋ/ ADJECTIVE done very carefully and slowly ◻ *painstaking research* (**meticuloso**)

paint /peɪnt/ ▶ NOUN [plural **paints**] a coloured substance that you put on a surface to change its colour or to make a picture ◻ *a tin of red paint* (**tinta**) ▣ *The ceiling needs a new coat of paint.* (**demão de tinta**) ◻ *a box of oil paints*
▶ VERB [**paints, painting, painted**]

paintbrush

1 to put paint on a surface □ *Dan was painting the front door.* □ *The dining room was painted red.* (pintar)
2 to make a picture using paint □ *He painted a portrait of the queen.* (pintar)

paintbrush /ˈpeɪntbrʌʃ/ NOUN [*plural* **paintbrushes**] a brush you use for painting (pincel)

painter /ˈpeɪntə(r)/ NOUN [*plural* **painters**]
1 an artist who makes pictures using paint (pintor)
2 someone whose job is to paint buildings and rooms (pintor) ▣ *My Dad is a painter and decorator.* (pintor e decorador)

painting /ˈpeɪntɪŋ/ NOUN [*plural* **paintings**]
1 a picture that someone has made using paint □ *They sold a painting by Monet.* (pintura)
2 *no plural* the activity of painting walls or pictures □ *I enjoy painting.* (pintura)

pair /peə(r)/ ▶ NOUN [*plural* **pairs**]
1 two things of the same kind that you use or keep together □ + *of a pair of socks* □ *a pair of shoes* □ *a pair of china dogs* (par)
2 a single thing made up of two parts □ *I bought a pair of jeans.* □ *a pair of glasses* □ *a pair of scissors* (par)
3 two people who do something together, or who are friends □ *The Australian pair won the game.* □ *The teacher asked us to work in pairs.* (fazer par)
▶ VERB [**pairs, pairing, paired**] to put two people or things together □ + *with The T-shirt looks great paired with jeans*
◆ PHRASAL VERB **pair up** if two people pair up, they join together to do something □ *The two singers will pair up again for a new album.* (formar dupla)

pajamas /pəˈdʒɑːməz/ PLURAL NOUN the US spelling of **pyjamas** (pijama)

pal /pæl/ NOUN [*plural* **pals**] an informal word meaning friend □ *My Mum met one of her old school pals.* (amigo)

palace /ˈpælɪs/ NOUN [*plural* **palaces**] a big, grand house where a king, queen or president lives □ *the presidential palace* □ *Crowds of people stood outside the palace gates.* (palácio)

palatable /ˈpælətəbəl/ ADJECTIVE
1 acceptable □ *The policy was changed to make it more palatable to voters.* (agradável)
2 having a pleasant flavour □ *The cheese is very palatable.* (gostoso)

palate /ˈpælət/ NOUN [*plural* **palates**]
1 the top part of the inside of your mouth. A biology word. (palato)
2 your ability to taste and judge flavours □ *The restaurant serves dishes to suit every palate.* (paladar)

palaver /pəˈlɑːvə(r)/ NOUN, NO PLURAL an informal word meaning a situation that causes a lot of work or worry □ *He'd had to go through the palaver of applying for a new passport.* (transtorno)

pale /peɪl/ ▶ ADJECTIVE [**paler, palest**]
1 light in colour □ *She was wearing a pale blue T-shirt.* □ *the pale light of dawn* (pálido)
2 having very white skin, especially because you are ill or because you have had a shock □ *She looked very pale and thin.* (pálido) ▣ *He suddenly went very pale.* (ficou muito pálido)
3 less important, less good etc. when compared with something else (pálido) ▣ *After the illness, he was a pale imitation of his former self.* (uma pálida imitação)
▶ VERB [**pales, paling, paled**] to seem less important, less good, etc. when compared with something else □ *The amount she earns pales in comparison with the £500,000 a year that her sister earns.* (inferiorizar-se)

palette /ˈpælət/ NOUN [*plural* **palettes**] a board that artists mix paints on (paleta)

pall /pɔːl/ ▶ VERB [**palls, palling, palled**] to become less interesting or less enjoyable □ *Life as a manager was beginning to pall.* (perder a graça)
▶ NOUN [*plural* **palls**] *a pall of smoke/dust* a thick cloud of smoke or dust (uma nuvem de fumaça/poeira)
⇨ go to **cast a pall over something**

pallet /ˈpælɪt/ NOUN [*plural* **pallets**] a wooden base used for moving or storing heavy things (paleta)

pallid /ˈpælɪd/ ADJECTIVE pale and unhealthy □ *There were tears running down his pallid cheeks.* (pálido)

pallor /ˈpælə(r)/ NOUN, NO PLURAL the pale colour that someone's skin has when they are unhealthy or afraid (palidez)

palm /pɑːm/ NOUN [*plural* **palms**]
1 the inside surface of your hand (palma) ▣ *She kept wiping the palms of her hands on her skirt.* (as palmas das mãos)
2 a tree that grows in hot, dry places (palmeira)
◆ PHRASAL VERB [**palms, palming, palmed**] **palm something off** to get rid of something that you do not want by persuading someone else to take it or buy it □ *She palms all her old clothes off on me.* (impingir)

palpable /ˈpælpəbəl/ ADJECTIVE easy to notice □ *There was a palpable sense of relief when the boy was found.* (evidente)

palpitations /ˌpælpɪˈteɪʃənz/ PLURAL NOUN if you have palpitations, your heart beats quickly and with an irregular rhythm (palpitações)

paltry /ˈpɔːltri/ ADJECTIVE a paltry amount is very small and often not enough □ *a paltry sum of money* (irrisório)

pamper /ˈpæmpə(r)/ VERB [**pampers, pampering, pampered**] to look after someone very well and do nice things for them □ *We spent the day being pampered at a spa.* (mimar)

- **pampered** /'pæmpəd/ ADJECTIVE getting a lot of care and attention, often too much, which makes you unpleasant □ *The report describes pampered teenagers who never have to do any chores.* (mimado)

pamphlet /'pæmflɪt/ NOUN [plural **pamphlets**] a thin book with a paper cover, which has information in it (folheto)

pan /pæn/ ▶ NOUN [plural **pans**] a metal container with a handle, used for cooking food □ *Cover the pan with a lid.* (panela)
▶ VERB [**pans, panning, panned**]
1 an informal meaning to criticize something a lot □ *Critics panned the film.* (criticar ferrenhamente)
2 if a television or film camera pans somewhere, it moves in that direction □ *The camera panned around the room.* (panoramizar)
♦ PHRASAL VERB **pan out** to develop in a particular way □ *He had no regrets about the way his career had panned out.* (vingar, lograr)

panache /pə'næʃ/ NOUN, NO PLURAL confidence and skill □ *They danced with great panache.* (altivez)

pancake /'pænkeɪk/ NOUN [plural **pancakes**] a thin food made by frying a mixture of milk, flour and eggs (panqueca)

pancreas /'pæŋkriəs/ NOUN [plural **pancreases**] a small organ in the body which produces substances that help you digest food. A biology word. (pâncreas)

panda /'pændə/ NOUN [plural **pandas**] a large animal from China which is black and white, and looks like a bear (panda)

pandemonium /,pændɪ'məʊniəm/ NOUN, NO PLURAL a lot of noise and confusion □ *There was pandemonium on the street after the explosion.* (pandemônio)

pander /'pændə(r)/
♦ PHRASAL VERB [**panders, pandering, pandered**] **pander to someone** to do everything that someone wants, even if it is wrong, in order to please them □ *The government was accused of pandering to large companies.* (favorecer de maneira ilícita)

pane /peɪn/ NOUN [plural **panes**] a piece of glass used in a window or door □ *a pane of glass* (vidro de janela)

panel /'pænəl/ NOUN [plural **panels**]
1 a usually rectangular piece of wood, glass, etc. that is part of a door, wall, etc. (painel, almofada de porta)
2 a group of people who are chosen to discuss or judge something, or to answer questions □ *A panel of judges will decide on the winner.* (painel, grupo de participantes de um debate)
3 the part of a machine where the switches are □ *a control panel* (painel)

- **paneling** /'pænəlɪŋ/ NOUN, NO PLURAL the US spelling of **panelling** (ver panelling)
- **panelist** /'pænəlɪst/ NOUN [plural **panelists**] the US spelling of **panellist** (ver panellist)
- **panelling** /'pænəlɪŋ/ NOUN, NO PLURAL wood or other material used for panels in walls, doors, etc. (apainelamento)
- **panellist** /'pænəlɪst/ NOUN [plural **panellists**] one of the members of a panel (participante de um debate)

pang /pæŋ/ NOUN [plural **pangs**] a sudden strong feeling □ *a pang of guilt* (pontada, angústia)

panic /'pænɪk/ ▶ NOUN, NO PLURAL a sudden strong feeling of fear or worry that makes you unable to think calmly (pânico) ▣ *The fire caused panic.* (causou pânico) □ *People ran into the streets in panic when the earthquake struck.*
▶ VERB [**panics, panicking, panicked**] to be so frightened or worried that you cannot think calmly (entrar em pânico) □ *There's no need to panic. We've got plenty of time.*

- **panicky** /'pænɪki/ ADJECTIVE frightened, worried and unable to think calmly (apavorado, em pânico)

panic-stricken /'pænɪkstrɪkən/ ADJECTIVE extremely frightened (apavorado, em pânico)

pannier /'pæniə(r)/ NOUN [plural **panniers**] a bag on the side of a bicycle or an animal such as a horse (bagageiro, cesto de vime para transporte, caçuá)

panorama /,pænə'rɑːmə/ NOUN [plural **panoramas**] a view of a wide area of land (panorama)

pansy /'pænzi/ NOUN [plural **pansies**] a garden plant with bright flowers (amor-perfeito)

pant /pænt/ VERB [**pants, panting, panted**]
1 to breathe quickly and noisily, especially because you have been using a lot of physical effort □ *He was sweating and panting.* (ofegar)
2 to say something while breathing quickly and noisily □ *'I've just run two miles to catch this train,' he panted.* (falar de maneira ofegante)

panther /'pænθə(r)/ NOUN [plural **panthers**] a large, wild, black cat (pantera)

panties /'pæntiz/ PLURAL NOUN underwear that a woman or girl wears to cover her bottom □ *a pair of panties* (calcinha)

pantihose /'pæntɪhəʊz/ PLURAL NOUN another spelling of **pantyhose** (ver pantyhose)

pantomime /'pæntəmaɪm/ NOUN [plural **pantomimes**] a Christmas play for children, based on a traditional story with jokes and singing (pantomima de Natal)

pantry /'pæntri/ NOUN [plural **pantries**] a small room near a kitchen, used for storing food (despensa)

pants /pænts/ PLURAL NOUN
1 a piece of underwear that covers your bottom (cueca) ▣ *a clean pair of pants* (cueca)
2 the US word for **trousers** (calça)

pantyhose   563   paragon

pantyhose /ˈpæntɪhəʊz/ PLURAL NOUN the US word for **tights** (meia-calça)

papal /ˈpeɪpəl/ ADJECTIVE to do with the Pope (= leader of the Catholic Church) ▫ *a papal visit* (papal)

paper /ˈpeɪpə(r)/ ▶ NOUN [*plural* **papers**]
1 *no plural* the thin material that you write on or draw on, or that you wrap things in (papel) 🔊 *I wrote his address on a piece of paper*. (pedaço de papel) ▫ *The present was wrapped in pretty pink paper.*
2 a newspaper (jornal) 🔊 *Have you read today's paper?* (leu o jornal de hoje) 🔊 *I saw the article in the local paper.* (jornal local)
3 a piece of writing or a talk on a subject that you have studied (ensaio, estudo) 🔊 *He has written many influential papers.* (tem escrito estudos/ensaios influentes) ▫ + *on She published a research paper on the disease.*
4 an exam ▫ *an exam paper* ▫ *He showed me last year's maths paper.* (exame escrito)
5 *no plural* (a) used when you are judging something from written information but the real situation may be different ▫ *The deal had seemed good on paper.* (b) if you put information or ideas on paper, you write them down ▫ *It sometimes helps to put your feelings down on paper.* (no papel)
⇨ *go to* **papers**
▶ ADJECTIVE made from paper or cardboard ▫ *a paper bag* ▫ *paper cups* (de papel)
▶ VERB [**papers, papering, papered**] to cover the walls of a room with paper (empapelar)

paperback /ˈpeɪpəbæk/ NOUN [*plural* **paperbacks**] a book with a cover made from thick paper (brochura)

paper clip /ˈpeɪpə ˌklɪp/ NOUN [*plural* **paper clips**] a piece of bent wire, used for holding pieces of paper together (clipe)

papers /ˈpeɪpəz/ PLURAL NOUN official documents ▫ *legal papers* ▫ *He's signed the divorce papers.* (documentos, papéis)

paperweight /ˈpeɪpəweɪt/ NOUN [*plural* **paperweights**] a heavy object that you put on top of pieces of paper to stop them moving (peso de papel)

paperwork /ˈpeɪpəwɜːk/ NOUN, NO PLURAL work such as writing letters or reports, or keeping records ▫ *The job involves a lot of paperwork.* (trabalho de escrita)

par /pɑː(r)/ NOUN, NO PLURAL
1 be on a par (with something) to be the same size, standard, etc. as something else ▫ *The city is on a par with London in terms of size.* (estar no mesmo nível de)
2 below par not as good as usual, or not the expected standard ▫ *The team are performing below par.* (abaixo da média)

parable /ˈpærəbəl/ NOUN [*plural* **parables**] a story, especially from the Bible, that teaches people a moral or religious lesson (parábola)

parabola /pəˈræbələ/ NOUN [*plural* **parabolas**] a curve like the one made by an object being thrown up and dropping down again. A maths word. (parábola)

paracetamol /ˌpærəˈsiːtəmɒl/ NOUN [*plural* **paracetamols**] a drug that reduces pain (paracetamol)

parachute /ˈpærəʃuːt/ ▶ NOUN [*plural* **parachutes**] a large piece of cloth attached to a person's body by strings that they use to help them fall safely if they jump from an aircraft (paraquedas)
▶ VERB [**parachutes, parachuting, parachuted**] to jump from an aircraft using a parachute (saltar de paraquedas)
• **parachutist** /ˈpærəʃuːtɪst/ NOUN [*plural* **parachutists**] someone who parachutes (paraquedista)

parade /pəˈreɪd/ ▶ NOUN [*plural* **parades**]
1 an event in which people or vehicles move through an area to celebrate something, often with music, decorations, etc. ▫ *Hundreds of people took part in the carnival parade.* (desfile)
2 on parade if soldiers are on parade, they march together (parada militar)
▶ VERB [**parades, parading, paraded**]
1 to walk with a lot of other people in order to celebrate something or to complain about something ▫ *Demonstrators paraded through the streets of the city.* (desfilar)
2 to walk somewhere so that people will admire you ▫ *She was parading round the room in her new dress.* (desfilar)
3 to show people something such as a skill or your possessions, in order to make them admire you ▫ *He enjoyed parading his wealth and power.* (exibir)

paradise /ˈpærədaɪs/ NOUN, NO PLURAL
1 in some religions, the place good people go when they die (paraíso)
2 a perfect place or situation ▫ *The island is a paradise for birdwatchers.* (paraíso)

paradox /ˈpærədɒks/ NOUN [*plural* **paradoxes**] a person, thing or situation that is strange because it has features which seem impossible to have together ▫ *It's a paradox of western society that rising wealth seems to come together with rising unhappiness.* (paradoxo)
• **paradoxical** /ˌpærəˈdɒksɪkəl/ ADJECTIVE combining two qualities or ideas that seem to be the opposite of each other ▫ *He finds himself in a paradoxical situation – a pacifist arguing for war.* (paradoxal)

paraffin /ˈpærəfɪn/ NOUN, NO PLURAL a type of oil used for heating, and in lights (querosene)

paragon /ˈpærəgən/ NOUN [*plural* **paragons**] someone who is perfect (paradigma) 🔊 *She has* always been a *paragon of virtue* (= very good, honest, etc.).

paragraph /'pærəgrɑːf/ NOUN [plural **paragraphs**] a part of a piece of writing that starts on a new line and contains one or more sentences □ *I read the first paragraph of the article.* (**parágrafo**)

parallel /'pærəlel/ ▶ ADJECTIVE
1 parallel lines have the same distance between them all the way along (**paralela**) 🔲 *She drew two parallel lines.* (**linhas paralelas**) 🔲 *Lockwood Road runs parallel to Hollies Road.* (**é paralela a**)
2 happening at the same time and in a similar way □ *Parallel studies have been carried out in Japan and the US.*
▶ NOUN [plural **parallels**] a way in which things, people or situations are similar (**paralelo**) 🔲 *The author drew parallels between the situation now and the situation in the 1980s* (= showed how the two situations are similar). (**traçou paralelos**) □ + **between** *There are striking parallels between the two bridges.*
▶ VERB [**parallels, paralleling, paralleled**] a formal word meaning to be similar to something else, or to happen at the same time as something else □ *Their findings parallel work done by scientists in the US.* (**igualar-se a**)

parallelogram /ˌpærə'leləgræm/ NOUN [plural **parallelograms**] a shape with four straight sides, with the opposite sides parallel. A maths word. (**paralelogramo**)

paralyse /'pærəlaɪz/ VERB [**paralyses, paralysing, paralysed**]
1 if someone is paralysed by something, they are unable to move their body, or are unable to move part of their body □ *He was paralysed by a skiing accident in which he broke his neck.* (**paralisar**)
2 to make something unable to work or continue normally □ *Heavy snow falls paralysed the road and rail network.* (**paralisar**)
• **paralysed** /'pærəlaɪzd/ ADJECTIVE unable to move your body or unable to move part of your body □ *The accident left him paralysed.* (**paralisado**)
• **paralysis** /pə'rælɪsɪs/ NOUN, NO PLURAL when someone cannot move their body or cannot move a part of their body (**paralisia**)

paralyze /'pærəlaɪz/ VERB [**paralyzes, paralyzing, paralyzed**] the US spelling of **paralyse** (*ver* **paralyse**)
• **paralyzed** /'pærəlaɪzd/ ADJECTIVE the US spelling of **paralysed** (*ver* **paralysed**)

paramedic /ˌpærə'medɪk/ NOUN [plural **paramedics**] someone who works in an ambulance (= medical emergency vehicle) and is trained to help ill or injured people (**paramédico**)

paramilitaries /ˌpærə'mɪlɪtəriz/ PLURAL NOUN soldiers who are part of a paramilitary group (**paramilitares**)
• **paramilitary** /ˌpærə'mɪlɪtəri/ ADJECTIVE operating like an army but not an official army □ *a paramilitary organization* (**paramilitar**)

paramount /'pærəmaʊnt/ ADJECTIVE more important than anything else □ *The children's safety is paramount.* (**supremo**)

paranoia /ˌpærə'nɔɪə/ NOUN, NO PLURAL when someone believes that people are trying to harm them or that people do not like them although there is no proof of this (**paranoia**)
• **paranoid** /'pærənɔɪd/ ADJECTIVE believing that people do not like you and are trying to harm you although there is no proof of this □ *He was paranoid about someone stealing his money.* (**paranoico**)

parapet /'pærəpet/ NOUN [plural **parapets**] a low wall along the edge of a bridge or roof (**parapeito**)

paraphernalia /ˌpærəfə'neɪliə/ NOUN, NO PLURAL all the different objects that you need for doing something □ *Kevin packed all his fishing paraphernalia into the back of the car.* (**parafernália**)

paraphrase /'pærəfreɪz/ ▶ VERB [**paraphrases, paraphrasing, paraphrased**] to say or write something in a different way, usually in order to explain it more clearly (**parafrasear**)
▶ NOUN [plural **paraphrases**] a different and usually clearer way of saying or writing something (**paráfrase**)

parasite /'pærəsaɪt/ NOUN [plural **parasites**]
1 an animal or plant that lives on or in another animal or plant in order to get food from it. A biology word. (**parasita**)
2 someone who gets the things they need to live from other people's effort □ *He's just a parasite – he should go and get a job.* (**parasita**)
• **parasitic** /ˌpærə'sɪtɪk/ ADJECTIVE
1 a parasitic animal or plant is a parasite. A biology word □ *a parasitic worm* (**parasita**)
2 a parasitic disease is caused by a parasite. A biology word. (**parasitário**)

paratrooper /'pærətruːpə(r)/ NOUN [plural **paratroopers**] a soldier who jumps out of aircraft using a parachute (= large piece of cloth attached to the body by strings) (**paraquedista**)
• **paratroops** /'pærətruːps/ PLURAL NOUN a group of paratroopers (**paratropa**)

parcel /'pɑːsəl/ NOUN [plural **parcels**] something wrapped in paper and sent somewhere □ *A parcel arrived for you this morning.* (**pacote**) 🔲 *She opened the parcel and there were three books inside.* (**abriu o pacote**)

parched /pɑːtʃt/ ADJECTIVE
1 an informal word meaning very thirsty (**sedento**)
2 parched land is extremely dry (**ressecado**)

parchment /'pɑːtʃmənt/ NOUN [plural **parchments**] a material made from animal skin and used for writing on in the past, or a document written on this (**pergaminho**)

pardon /'pɑːdən/ ▶ EXCLAMATION
1 used to ask someone to repeat what they have just said because you did not hear it □ *'We're*

parent 565 **part**

going to be late.' 'Pardon?' 'I said, we're going to be late.' (como?)

2 pardon me used when you have just made a rude noise with your body (desculpe-me)

▶ VERB [**pardons, pardoning, pardoned**] to officially forgive someone who has committed a crime □ *He was pardoned by President Clinton in 2001.* (perdoar, indultar)

▶ NOUN [*plural* **pardons**] (indulto)

1 an official order to forgive someone for a crime □ *Although he died in 1998, his family are still campaigning for a full pardon.*

2 I beg your pardon (a) a formal way of saying sorry when you have made a mistake □ *Oh, I beg your pardon – I thought you meant I should sit here.* (b) a formal way of asking someone to repeat what they have just said because you did not hear it (queira desculpar)

parent /ˈpeərənt/ NOUN [*plural* **parents**] your mother or father □ *My parents divorced last year.* □ *Her proud parents watched as she received the award.* (pai/mãe)

• **parentage** /ˈpeərəntɪdʒ/ NOUN, NO PLURAL used for talking about who your parents are, where they come from, what their religion is, etc. □ *He was born in Vienna of Jewish parentage.* (ascendência)

• **parental** /pəˈrentəl/ ADJECTIVE to do with a parent or parents □ *parental responsibilities* (parental)

parenthesis /pəˈrenθɪsɪs/ NOUN [*plural* **parentheses**] one of the two signs ( ) which you use in writing □ *The children's ages are in parentheses after their names.* (parêntese)

parenthood /ˈpeərənthʊd/ NOUN, NO PLURAL being a parent □ *the joys of parenthood* (parentalidade)

parenting /ˈpeərəntɪŋ/ NOUN, NO PLURAL the activity of looking after your own children 🔳 *parenting skills* (cuidados paternais/maternais)

parish /ˈpærɪʃ/ NOUN [*plural* **parishes**] an area that has its own church □ *a parish priest* (paróquia)

• **parishioner** /pəˈrɪʃənə(r)/ NOUN [*plural* **parishioners**] someone who lives in a parish, especially someone who goes to the church (paroquiano)

park /pɑːk/ ▶ NOUN [*plural* **parks**] an area of grass and trees in a town where people can go to relax □ *I went for a walk in the park.* (parque) 🔳 *They were sitting on a park bench.* (banco de praça)

▶ VERB [**parks, parking, parked**] to leave a vehicle in a place, for example by the side of the road or in a car park (estacionar) 🔳 *She parked the car outside the house.* □ *Dad drove into town but couldn't find anywhere to park.* (estacionou o carro)

• **parking** /ˈpɑːkɪŋ/ NOUN, NO PLURAL

1 space where you can park your vehicle □ *There is free parking for museum visitors.* (estacionamento) 🔳 *She drove round, looking for a parking space.* (vaga de estacionamento)

2 the process of putting a vehicle into a space and leaving it there □ *Many learner drivers find parking very difficult.* (estacionar)

parking lot /ˈpɑːkɪŋ ˌlɒt/ NOUN [*plural* **parking lots**] the US word for **car park** (área de estacionamento)

parking meter /ˈpɑːkɪŋ ˌmiːtə(r)/ NOUN [*plural* **parking meters**] a piece of equipment at the side of a road that you put money in so you can park your car near to it (parquímetro)

parking ticket /ˈpɑːkɪŋ ˌtɪkɪt/ NOUN [*plural* **parking tickets**] a piece of paper telling you that you must pay money because you have parked your vehicle illegally (multa por estacionamento irregular)

parliament /ˈpɑːləmənt/ NOUN [*plural* **parliaments**] a group of people who make the laws for a country □ *the Scottish parliament* (parlamento) 🔳 *He entered parliament* (= was elected to a parliament) *in 1981.* (foi eleito ao parlamento)

• **parliamentary** /ˌpɑːləˈmentəri/ ADJECTIVE to do with a parliament □ *a parliamentary debate* (parlamentar)

parlor /ˈpɑːlə(r)/ NOUN [*plural* **parlors**] the US spelling of **parlour** (ver **parlour**)

parlour /ˈpɑːlə(r)/ NOUN [*plural* **parlours**] a shop selling a particular product or service □ *an ice cream parlour* □ *a beauty parlour* (loja ou salão)

parmesan /ˌpɑːmɪˈzæn/ NOUN, NO PLURAL a type of hard Italian cheese (parmesão)

parochial /pəˈrəʊkɪəl/ ADJECTIVE interested only in things which affect the area where you live □ *a parochial attitude* (paroquial)

parody /ˈpærədɪ/ ▶ NOUN [*plural* **parodies**] a piece of music, a book, etc. that copies the style of another one in a funny way □ *Their act contained parodies of TV advertisements.* (paródia)

▶ VERB [**parodies, parodying, parodied**] to copy the style of another writer, musician, etc. in a funny way (parodiar)

parole /pəˈrəʊl/ NOUN, NO PLURAL an arrangement in which someone is allowed to leave prison early but must go back to prison if they do not behave well (liberdade condicional) 🔳 *Roberts was released on parole in 2005.* (em liberdade condicional)

parrot /ˈpærət/ NOUN [*plural* **parrots**] a tropical bird with brightly coloured feathers that can copy what people say (papagaio)

parsley /ˈpɑːslɪ/ NOUN, NO PLURAL a herb with green leaves, used in cooking (salsa)

parsnip /ˈpɑːsnɪp/ NOUN [*plural* **parsnips**] a long, pale yellow vegetable that grows under the ground (pastinaca)

part /pɑːt/ ▶ NOUN [*plural* **parts**]

1 one of the pieces, areas, amounts, etc. that together make something □ *The pizza is cut into six equal parts.* □ *She lives in a remote part of*

Scotland. □ *I spent part of the day working in the garden.* □ *They made me feel part of the family.* (parte)

2 take part to be involved in an activity with other people □ *Everyone can take part in the competition.* □ *She took part in a run for charity.* (tomar parte)

3 some, but not all of something □ **+ of** *Part of the problem is that he works such long hours.* □ *Part of me thinks we should just forget about her.* (parte)

4 in part to some degree □ *I still feel that he's in part to blame.* (em parte)

5 the way in which someone is involved in a situation or an activity (parte) 🗖 *He played an important part in postwar politics.* (desempenhar um papel importante) □ *I had no part in the arrangements.*

6 a character in a play, film, etc. or the words or actions that the character has to say or do (papel) 🗖 *He's playing the part of Othello.* (representando o papel de Otelo) □ *I need to learn my part.*

7 a piece of a machine or a piece of equipment (parte) 🗖 *We took plenty of spare parts for the van.* (partes sobressalentes)

♦ IDIOM **look the part** to look the way someone is expected to look in a particular situation or for a particular activity □ *In her neat blouse and glasses, she really looked the part of a strict headmistress.* (parecer adequado)

▶ ADVERB to some degree 🗖 *The creature is part man, part beast.* □ *She is part German.*

▶ VERB [**parts, parting, parted**]

1 when people part, they go away from each other □ *We parted at the end of the street.* (separar(-se)) 🗖 *They parted company in Toronto.* (separaram a companhia) □ *After ten years of marriage, they agreed to part.*

2 when two things part, they move away from each other to leave a space, and if you part two things, you make a space between them □ *Suddenly, the clouds parted and we had a wonderful view.* □ *We parted the curtains slightly.* (separar(-se))

3 if you part your hair, you make a line in it and brush the hair away from that line on both sides (dividir, fazer a risca)

♦ PHRASAL VERB **part with something** to give something away, often when you do not want to □ *I couldn't bear to part with my books.* (desfazer-se de)

partial /ˈpɑːʃəl/ ADJECTIVE
1 not complete □ *a partial success* (parcial)
2 be partial to something to like something □ *She's very partial to chocolate.* (apreciar)
• **partially** /ˈpɑːʃəli/ ADVERB not completely □ *a partially eaten biscuit* (parcialmente)

participant /pɑːˈtɪsɪpənt/ NOUN [*plural* **participants**] someone who takes part in an event or activity with other people □ *She was an active participant in the debate.* (participante)

participate /pɑːˈtɪsɪpeɪt/ VERB [**participates, participating, participated**] to take part in an event or activity □ *The programme aims to encourage more children to participate in sport.* (participar)
• **participation** /pɑːˌtɪsɪˈpeɪʃən/ NOUN, NO PLURAL taking part in an event or activity □ *In the 19th century, participation in politics was very rare for women.* (participação)

participle /ˈpɑːtɪsɪpəl/ NOUN [*plural* **participles**] a word formed from a verb and used as an adjective, or to form different tenses of the verb. The present participle usually ends in '-ing' and the past participle usually ends in '-ed'. (particípio)

particle /ˈpɑːtɪkəl/ NOUN [*plural* **particles**] a very small piece of something □ *a particle of dust* □ *tiny carbon particles* (partícula)

particular /pəˈtɪkjʊlə(r)/ ▶ ADJECTIVE
1 used to show that you are talking about one person or thing and not others □ *On that particular day I was early.* □ *Is there a particular person I should speak to about this?* (particular)
2 especially great □ *He took particular care when writing the letter.* □ *Aircraft safety is an area of particular concern.* (especial, particular)
3 if a person is particular, they have strong opinions about what they like and dislike and are not easy to please □ **+ about** *She's very particular about what she eats.* (exigente)
▶ NOUN [*plural* **particulars**]
1 in particular (a) especially □ *I enjoy reading novels, romantic fiction in particular.* □ *There's a lot of pressure on young women in particular.* (b) special or important (especialmente) 🗖 *We just chatted about nothing in particular.* (nada de especial) 🗖 *Did you notice anything in particular?* (alguma coisa em especial?)
2 particulars details about a person or situation □ **+ of** *I don't know all the particulars of the case.*
• **particularly** /pəˈtɪkjʊləli/ ADVERB
1 very, or more than usual □ *The noise was particularly loud.* □ *Young babies are particularly vulnerable.* (particularmente) 🗖 *They were not particularly helpful.* (não particularmente)
2 used to show that something is true for one person or thing more than others □ *Temperatures were very high this summer, particularly in July.* □ *The changes will affect those on low incomes, particularly the elderly.* (particularmente, especialmente)

parting /ˈpɑːtɪŋ/ NOUN [*plural* **partings**]
1 when you leave someone or say goodbye (despedida, separação)
2 a line in your hair where you brush the hair in opposite directions (risca (cabelo))

partition /pɑːˈtɪʃən/ ▶ NOUN [*plural* **partitions**]
1 a thin wall that divides a room into parts □ *The bank clerk sits behind a glass partition.* (divisória)

partly — 567 — **pass**

2 when you divide a country into separate areas or countries □ *Pakistan was formed at the partition of India in 1947.* (divisão)
▶ VERB [partitions, partitioning, partitioned]
1 to divide a country into areas or countries □ *The only solution was to partition the country into two separate states.* (dividir)
2 to divide a room using a partition (dividir)

partly /ˈpɑːtlɪ/ ADVERB
in some ways or to some degree, but not completely □ *I was partly to blame for the mix-up.* □ *He had to leave his job, partly because of his health.* □ *That's only partly true.* (em parte)

partner /ˈpɑːtnə(r)/ NOUN [plural partners]
1 one of two people who do something together, such as dancing or playing a game (parceiro) ▣ *a dance partner* (parceiro de dança) □ *a tennis partner*
2 one of two or more people who own a business together (sócio) ▣ *She's a senior partner in a law firm.* (sócio sênior) ▣ *his former business partner* (sócio da empresa)
3 someone you are married to or have a sexual relationship with □ *She lives with her long-term partner and their two children.* (parceiro (relacionamento))
4 a country or an organization that works with or has an agreement with another (parceiro) ▣ *Brazil is one of our largest trading partners.* (parceiros comerciais)

• **partnership** /ˈpɑːtnəʃɪp/ NOUN [plural partnerships]
1 a relationship between two or more people or groups working together (parceria) ▣ *The company has formed partnerships with several universities.* (formar parcerias)
2 a business owned by two or more partners (sociedade)

part of speech /ˌpɑːt əv ˈspiːtʃ/ NOUN [plural parts of speech]
in grammar, one of the groups that words belong to depending on the job they do, such as noun, verb, adjective or adverb (categoria gramatical)

partridge /ˈpɑːtrɪdʒ/ NOUN [plural partridges]
a small round grey and brown wild bird that is hunted for sport and food (perdiz)

part-time /ˌpɑːtˈtaɪm/ ADJECTIVE, ADVERB
working for only part of a full working day or week (meio expediente) ▣ *a part-time job* (emprego de meio período) ▣ *She works part-time for the local newspaper.* (trabalha meio expediente)

party /ˈpɑːtɪ/ ▶ NOUN [plural parties]
1 an event where people celebrate something or enjoy themselves together eating, drinking, dancing, etc. (festa) ▣ *a birthday party* (festa de aniversário) ▣ *We're having a party next week.* (fazendo uma festa) ▣ *He threw a huge party to celebrate.* (deu uma festa)
2 an organized group of people who share the same political beliefs and try to get elected to the government (partido) ▣ *a political party* (partido político) ▣ *the party leader* (líder do partido) □ *He joined the Labour Party in 1936.*
3 a group of people travelling or doing something together □ **+ of** *The museum was busy with several parties of schoolchildren.* (excursão)
4 a formal word for a person or group involved in a legal agreement or disagreement □ *Interested parties have been asked to submit proposals.* □ *He isn't the only guilty party.* (parte)
▶ VERB [parties, partying, partied] to enjoy yourself at a party □ *He was out partying with friends at a nightclub.* (divertir-se em uma festa)

> ► Note that you **have** or **throw** a party (noun, sense 1): You do not 'make' a party:
> ✓ We're having a party for Celia's 21ˢᵗ birthday.
> ✗ We're making a party for Celia's 21ˢᵗ birthday.

pass /pɑːs/ ▶ VERB [passes, passing, passed]
1 to go past something □ *The lorry passed us on a bend.* □ *I pass her house every morning.* (passar por)
2 to move in a particular direction or to a particular place □ *The procession passed in front of the town hall.* □ *The road passes through a forest.* (passar)
3 to be successful in an exam □ *She passed her entrance exams.* □ *I've got my driving test tomorrow, but I don't think I'll pass.* (passar em provas, exames)
4 to give someone something with your hand □ *Pass me the butter, please.* □ **+ to** *He passed a note to his colleague.* (entregar, passar às mãos de)
5 if time passes, it goes by □ *A whole year passed and she did not receive a letter from him.* □ *The morning passed slowly.* (passar)
6 pass the time to do something to use a period of time □ *I passed the time reading a book.* (passar)
7 to kick, hit or throw the ball to someone else on your team in a sport □ *He passed the ball to Edwards.* (passar)
8 to go higher than a particular level or amount □ *Donations have passed the £1 million mark.* (ultrapassar)
9 to officially accept a law (sancionar, aprovar) ▣ *The government has passed new legislation to deal with Internet fraud.* (aprovou nova legislação)
10 to come to an end or go away □ *The storm passed and the sun came out again.* □ *The pain soon passed.* (passar)
11 pass sentence when judges pass sentence, they say what someone's punishment will be (proferir)

> Remember that you **spend** a period of time somewhere. You do not 'pass' a period of time: □ *I spent the summer in Barcelona.* □ *I've spent all morning cleaning.* □ *We spent the holidays at my grandparents.*

⇨ go to **pass the buck**

♦ PHRASAL VERBS **pass something around/round** to offer something to everyone in a group □ *She passed round the biscuits.* (circular) **pass away/on** to die (morrer) **pass something down** to give something or teach something to someone younger than you □ *The stories were passed down from generation to generation.* (passar, legar) **pass for someone/something** to look enough like someone or something that people could believe that you were that person or thing □ *She's nearly fifty, but she could pass for a thirty-year-old.* (passar-se por) **pass something on**
1 to give someone something that has been given to you □ *Can you pass on a message for me?* □ *When you've finished with the book, could you pass it on to Paola?* (passar adiante)
2 to give someone an illness □ *I don't want to pass on my cold to anyone.* (passar) **pass out** to become unconscious □ *When I saw the blood, I passed out.* (desmaiar)

▶ NOUN [*plural* **passes**]
1 a successful result in an exam or on a course (aprovação (prova, exame))
2 a ticket or document that allows you to go into a place or to travel on a vehicle (passe) 🔳 *Have you got your bus pass?* (passe de ônibus)
3 when you kick, hit or throw the ball to someone else on your team in a sport (passe de bola)
4 a narrow path between mountains (desfiladeiro)

passable /ˈpɑːsəbəl/ ADJECTIVE
1 of quite a good standard but not the best □ *He does a passable imitation of Elvis.* (tolerável)
2 if a road is passable, it is not blocked and can be travelled along (transitável)

passage /ˈpæsɪdʒ/ NOUN [*plural* **passages**]
1 a long narrow room or area that connects rooms or places □ *He ran down a narrow passage between buildings.* □ *a secret underground passage* (passagem)
2 a part of a piece of writing or music □ *Read the next passage aloud.* □ **+ from** *He quoted a passage from the Bible.* (passagem (bíbl.))
3 a tube in the body that air or liquid passes through 🔳 *Your nasal passages are connected to your nose.* (via)
4 a journey or a route through a place □ *Huge icebergs blocked our passage.* (passagem)
5 when something or someone makes progress from one stage to another □ *We are watching the passage of this legislation through parliament.* (passagem)
6 the passage of time when time passes (passagem)

passageway /ˈpæsɪdʒweɪ/ NOUN [*plural* **passageways**] a passage between rooms or places □ *She led us through a long narrow passageway.* (corredor)

passenger /ˈpæsɪndʒə(r)/ NOUN [*plural* **passengers**] someone travelling in a vehicle who is not the driver or someone who works on it (passageiro) 🔳 *an airline passenger* (passageiro de avião) 🔳 *I sat in the passenger seat.* (assento do passageiro)

passer-by /ˌpɑːsəˈbaɪ/ NOUN [*plural* **passers-by**] someone who is passing a place when something happens □ *Several passers-by were injured in the explosion.* (passante)

passing /ˈpɑːsɪŋ/ ▶ ADJECTIVE
1 lasting only for a short time and not important or serious □ *For many children, it's just a passing phase.* (passageiro)
2 moving, walking, driving, etc. past somewhere □ *A passing motorist stopped to help.* (passante)
▶ NOUN, NO PLURAL
1 when something ends or no longer exists □ *They regret the passing of old traditions.* (desaparecimento)
2 when time passes □ *With each passing day, their hopes faded.* (passagem)
3 in passing if you say something in passing, you mention it quickly while you are talking about something else □ *He only mentioned Foster in passing.* (de passagem)

passion /ˈpæʃən/ NOUN [*plural* **passions**]
1 very strong beliefs and opinions about something □ *He spoke with real passion.* (paixão) 🔳 *Passions are running high* (= people are very angry and upset) *in the city.* (ânimos exaltados)
2 *no plural* a very strong feeling of love □ *He kissed her in a moment of passion.* (paixão)
3 something you are very interested in and enthusiastic about □ *They share a passion for the countryside.* (paixão)

• **passionate** /ˈpæʃənɪt/ ADJECTIVE
1 showing strong emotions or beliefs □ *She's a passionate advocate of animal rights.* □ *I feel very passionate about this issue.* (apaixonado)
2 having a strong feeling of love □ *They had a very passionate relationship.* (apaixonado)
• **passionately** /ˈpæʃənɪtli/ ADVERB in a passionate way □ *He spoke passionately about the need for action.* (apaixonadamente)

passive /ˈpæsɪv/ ADJECTIVE
1 allowing things to happen to you without reacting or doing anything to change them □ *These people are not just passive victims.* □ *He had a largely passive role.* (passivo)
2 a passive verb is used when the person or thing that is the subject of the verb does not do the

action but has something done to them, for example in the sentence The leaves are being eaten by caterpillars. (voz passiva)

- **passively** /ˈpæsɪvlɪ/ ADVERB in a passive way □ He just sat passively and listened. (passivamente)

passive smoking /ˌpæsɪv ˈsməʊkɪŋ/ NOUN, NO PLURAL when you breathe in the smoke from other people's cigarettes (fumante passivo)

Passover /ˈpɑːsəʊvə(r)/ NOUN, NO PLURAL a Jewish celebration in March or April, remembering the escape of the ancient Jews from Egypt (páscoa judaica)

passport /ˈpɑːspɔːt/ NOUN [plural **passports**]
1 an official document with your photograph and personal details that you carry when you travel to a foreign country □ a British passport (passaporte) ▣ You have to show your passport. (mostrar seu passaporte) □ passport control
2 something that makes it possible to do or achieve something □ She saw education as a passport to a better life.

password /ˈpɑːswɜːd/ NOUN [plural **passwords**] a secret word that you have to know before you are allowed into a place, or before you can use a computer or system (senha) ▣ Please enter your password. (digite sua senha)

past /pɑːst/ ▶ PREPOSITION, ADVERB
1 up to and further than □ She dashed past me, gasping as she ran. □ He just walked past without saying hello. □ Bullets flew past my head. □ Follow the road past a cottage. (adiante)
2 further than □ Turn right just past the bridge. □ A few miles past the farm, we came to a turning. (depois de)
3 used for saying the time up to 30 minutes after an hour □ It's ten past three. □ I'll meet you at half past ten. (passados (minutos))
4 later than □ It's past eight o'clock. □ It's well past my bedtime. (mais tarde do que)
5 after a particular stage or level □ This bread is past its best. (passado do melhor prazo de consumo)
6 used for talking about a period of time passing □ Days went past and still there was no news. (passar)
7 past it an informal phrase meaning too old to do the things you used to do □ He thinks anyone over 30 is past it. (velho demais)
8 wouldn't put something past someone used to say that you think it is possible that someone has done something, especially something bad □ I wouldn't put it past her to leave without paying back the money. (não pôr a mão no fogo por alguém)

▶ NOUN, NO PLURAL
1 the past the time before the present □ I have met him a few times in the past. □ When we meet, we never talk about the past. (passado)
2 someone's past is their life and experiences until now, and a country's past is what has happened there and what its people have done □ I don't know much about her past. □ The country is trying to forget its military past. (o passado de)
3 the past the form of a verb that is used for talking about things that happened before the present (tempo pretérito do verbo)

▶ ADJECTIVE
1 having happened or existed in the time before the present □ I have admitted my past mistakes. (passado) ▣ They know from past experience that free food will attract a crowd. (experiência anterior)
2 used to talk about a period of time just before the present □ The past few days have been very difficult for all of us. (o(s) último(s))
3 having had a particular position in a country or an organization □ Paintings of past presidents hang on the walls. (anterior)
4 finished □ I used to mix with movie stars, but that's all past now. (passado)

pasta /ˈpæstə/ NOUN, NO PLURAL a food made from flour, water and eggs and formed into different shapes □ pasta with tomato sauce (massa)

paste /peɪst/ ▶ NOUN [plural **pastes**]
1 a soft, slightly wet mixture, often of food □ tomato paste □ Mix until you have a smooth, thick paste. (pasta)
2 no plural a type of glue for sticking paper (cola)
▶ VERB [**pastes, pasting, pasted**]
1 to stick something onto a surface with glue □ There were posters pasted all over the wall. (cola)
2 to move words or a picture from one place on a computer screen to another. A computing word ▣ You can cut and paste the text into your own document. (colar (transferir conteúdo digital de uma origem a um destino))

pastel /ˈpæstəl/ ▶ ADJECTIVE pastel colours are pale and contain a lot of white □ pastel blue
▶ NOUN [plural **pastels**]
1 a soft stick used to draw with (pastel)
2 a pale colour (cor/tom pastel)

pasteurization or **pasteurisation** /ˌpɑːstʃəraɪˈzeɪʃən/ NOUN, NO PLURAL the process of heating milk to kill all the bacteria in it (pasteurização)

- **pasteurize** or **pasteurise** /ˈpɑːstʃəraɪz/ VERB [**pasteurizes, pasteurizing, pasteurized**] to heat milk so that all the bacteria in it are killed (pasteurizar)

pastime /ˈpɑːstaɪm/ NOUN [plural **pastimes**] something you enjoy doing for fun □ Reading is one of my favourite pastimes. (passatempo)

pastor /ˈpɑːstə(r)/ NOUN [plural **pastors**] a priest in some churches (pastor)

pastoral /ˈpɑːstərəl/ ADJECTIVE
1 to do with giving people help or advice about personal problems, especially by a teacher or a

priest (**pastoral**) 🔲 *The college provides excellent pastoral care.* (**aconselhamento pastoral**)
2 to do with the countryside or country life 🔲 *a pastoral scene* (**pastoral, bucólico**)

past participle /ˌpɑːst ˈpɑːtɪsɪpəl/ NOUN [*plural* **past participles**] a form of a verb that usually ends with '-ed' and is used to form the perfect tense, passive forms and sometimes adjectives (**particípio passado**)

pastry /ˈpeɪstri/ NOUN [*plural* **pastries**]
1 *no plural* a mixture of flour and fat made into a flat piece and baked with food inside (**tipo de massa para doces ou salgados**)
2 a cake made with pastry (**doces e salgados feitos com tipo específico de massa**)

past tense /ˌpɑːst ˈtens/ NOUN [*plural* **past tenses**] a form of a verb that you use when you are talking about what has happened in the past. For example, *relaxed* in *I relaxed after the race* is a past tense. (**pretérito**)

pasture /ˈpɑːstʃə(r)/ NOUN [*plural* **pastures**] a field with grass for cows and other animals to eat (**pasto**)

pasty¹ /ˈpeɪsti/ ADJECTIVE [**pastier, pastiest**] having skin that is pale and looks unhealthy (**pálido, descorado**)

pasty² /ˈpæsti/ NOUN [*plural* **pasties**] a piece of pastry folded around food such as meat and vegetables (**torta, pastelão**)

pat /pæt/ ▶ VERB [**pats, patting, patted**] to touch or to hit someone or something gently with your flat hand in a friendly way 🔲 *Celia patted his shoulder kindly.* 🔲 *He patted the horse's neck.* (**afagar**)
◆ IDIOMS **pat someone on the back** to praise someone for something they have done 🔲 *I patted myself on the back for a job well done.* (**congratular, elogiar**)
▶ NOUN [*plural* **pats**] when you pat someone or something 🔲 *He gave the dog a pat on the head.* (**tapinha**)
◆ IDIOMS **a pat on the back** praise for doing something 🔲 *She deserves a pat on the back.* (**um tapinha nas costas**)

patch /pætʃ/ ▶ NOUN [*plural* **patches**]
1 a small area of something, especially that is different from what is around it 🔲 *a patch of grass* (**canteiro**) 🔲 *a vegetable patch* (= area of ground where you grow vegetables) 🔲 *There's a damp patch on the wall.* (**canteiro de hortaliças**)
2 a piece of material used to cover a hole 🔲 *a jacket with patches on the elbows* (**remendo**)
3 a period of time with a particular quality (**período**) 🔲 *He's been going through a rough patch in his career.* (**período difícil**)
4 a piece of material used to cover a damaged eye 🔲 *She had to wear a patch over her right eye.* (**venda de olhos**)

5 a piece of software used to fix a computer problem. A computing word. 🔲 *You can download a patch from the website.* (**programa de computação**)
◆ IDIOM **not a patch on someone/something** much less good than someone or something else 🔲 *He's a good player, but not a patch on Gordon.* (**não ser páreo para**)
▶ VERB [**patches, patching, patched**] to repair a hole using a patch 🔲 *We patched the hole in the roof.* (**remendar**)
◆ PHRASAL VERBS **patch something up**
1 to become friendly with someone again after an argument 🔲 *The two men have patched things up now.* (**apaziguar, reconciliar**)
2 to repair something, often not very carefully 🔲 *We tried to patch up the wall.* (**remendar**) **patch someone up** to give someone who is injured basic medical treatment 🔲 *The nurse patched them up and sent them home.* (**prestar cuidados médicos**)

patchwork /ˈpætʃwɜːk/ NOUN, NO PLURAL
1 small pieces of cloth sewn together in a decorative pattern (**retalhos**) 🔲 *a patchwork quilt* (**colcha de retalhos**)
2 something that is made up of different pieces 🔲 *a green patchwork of fields* (**trabalho de retalhos**)

patchy /ˈpætʃi/ ADJECTIVE [**patchier, patchiest**]
1 existing in some places but not in others (**irregular**) 🔲 *patchy fog* (**nevoeiro irregular**)
2 good sometimes but not always 🔲 *The standard of cooking can be a bit patchy.* (**irregular**)

paté /ˈpæteɪ/ NOUN [*plural* **patés**] a smooth mixture of meat, fish or vegetables that you eat on bread (**patê**)

patent /ˈpeɪtənt/ ▶ NOUN [*plural* **patents**] an official document that gives one person or company the right to make and sell a product and stops others from copying it (**patente**)
▶ VERB [**patents, patenting, patented**] to get a patent for something 🔲 *She patented her design.* (**patentear**)
▶ ADJECTIVE obvious 🔲 *His patent lack of enthusiasm annoyed his colleagues.* (**óbvio**)
• **patently** /ˈpeɪtəntli/ ADVERB very clearly 🔲 *It's patently obvious he had no intention of doing it.* (**evidentemente**)

paternal /pəˈtɜːnəl/ ADJECTIVE
1 to do with being a father 🔲 *He showed off his daughter's trophy with paternal pride.* (**paternal**)
2 from your father's side of the family 🔲 *my paternal grandparents* (**paterno**)
• **paternity** /pəˈtɜːnəti/ ▶ NOUN, NO PLURAL the state of being a father 🔲 *There were some doubts over the baby's paternity.* (**paternidade**)
▶ ADJECTIVE to do with being or becoming a father 🔲 *paternity leave* (**licença paternidade**)

path

path /pɑːθ/ NOUN [plural **paths**]
1 a narrow route across a piece of ground that people walk or ride a bicycle along ▫ *We walked along a narrow path through the woods.* ▫ *Dad was coming up the garden path.* (**caminho, trilha**) 🔉 *There's a cycle path beside the canal.* (**ciclovia**)
2 the direction in which something travels or moves ▫ *+ of People living in the path of the storm were evacuated.* (**trajetória**)
3 a particular way of doing or achieving something (**caminho**) 🔉 *She took an unusual career path.* (**trajetória professional**)
♦ IDIOM **cross paths (with someone)** if you cross paths with someone or your paths cross, you meet each other by chance ▫ *I'd crossed paths with Stevens before.* (**cruzar o caminho de**)

pathetic /pəˈθetɪk/ ADJECTIVE
1 an informal word meaning not at all useful, skilful or effective ▫ *This knife is pathetic. It won't cut anything!* (**patético**) 🔉 *She made a pathetic attempt to deny it.* (**tentativa patética**)
2 causing you to feel sympathy or sadness ▫ *She's a rather pathetic figure these days.* (**patético**)

pathetic fallacy /pəˌθetɪk ˈfæləsi/ NOUN, NO PLURAL when animals or objects are described as having human feelings (**falácia patética**)

pathogen /ˈpæθədʒən/ NOUN [plural **pathogens**] a microorganism that causes disease. A biology word. (**patógeno**)

pathologist /pəˈθɒlədʒɪst/ NOUN [plural **pathologists**] an expert in diseases, especially one who examines people who have died to discover the reason for their deaths (**patologista**)

• **pathology** /pəˈθɒlədʒi/ NOUN, NO PLURAL the study of diseases (**patologia**)

pathway /ˈpɑːθweɪ/ NOUN [plural **pathways**]
1 a path that you can walk along ▫ *Paved pathways lead through the garden.* (**trilha**)
2 a route from one place to another that things such as electricity or signals move along ▫ *pathways to the brain* (**caminho**)
3 a way that something can be done or achieved ▫ *There is no established pathway for women to enter this profession.* (**caminho, modelo, modo de proceder**)

patience /ˈpeɪʃəns/ NOUN, NO PLURAL
1 the ability to stay calm, especially when waiting for something, doing something for a long time or dealing with something or someone annoying ▫ *You need to have a lot of patience when dealing with young children.* (**paciência**) 🔉 *I'm losing my patience with her silly behaviour.* (**perder a paciência**)
2 a card game played by one person (**paciência (jogo de cartas)**)

• **patient** /ˈpeɪʃənt/ ▶ ADJECTIVE showing patience ▫ *+with I'm a slow learner and he's been very patient with me.* ▫ *I'm not a very patient person.* (**paciente**)

patronize

▶ NOUN [plural **patients**] someone who is being treated by a doctor or a nurse (**paciente**) 🔉 *The clinic treats patients with eye problems.* (**trata pacientes**) ▫ *Every patient receives advice about healthy eating.*

• **patiently** /ˈpeɪʃəntli/ ADVERB in a patient way 🔉 *We waited patiently for a bus.* (**pacientemente**)

patio /ˈpætiəʊ/ NOUN [plural **patios**] a flat area covered in stone at the back of a house, where people can sit (**pátio**)

patriot /ˈpætriət/ NOUN [plural **patriots**] someone who loves and is loyal to his or her country (**patriota**)

• **patriotic** /ˌpætriˈɒtɪk/ ADJECTIVE showing love and loyalty to your country ▫ *a patriotic song* ▫ *He's very patriotic.* (**patriótico**)

• **patriotism** /ˈpætriətɪzəm/ the quality of being patriotic (**patriotismo**)

patrol /pəˈtrəʊl/ ▶ VERB [**patrols, patrolling**/US **patroling, patrolled**/US **patroled**] to go around an area or building watching for any trouble or problems ▫ *Troops patrol the border.* (**patrulhar**)
▶ NOUN [plural **patrols**] (**patrulha**)
1 a group of soldiers or police officers who patrol an area 🔉 *a police patrol* (**patrulha de polícia**)
2 when someone patrols an area 🔉 *The soldiers were on a routine patrol when they were attacked.* (**patrulha de rotina**)

patron /ˈpeɪtrən/ NOUN [plural **patrons**]
1 someone who supports the work of an artist, musician, etc. ▫ *He was a great patron of the arts.* (**patrocinador**)
2 a famous person who gives their public support to an organization ▫ *She became patron of the Multiple Sclerosis Society.* (**patrono**)
3 a customer of a shop, restaurant or business ▫ *The restaurant offers discounts to regular patrons.* (**cliente, freguês**)

• **patronage** /ˈpætrənɪdʒ/ NOUN, NO PLURAL support or money given by a patron to a person or an organization ▫ *He was known for his patronage of the arts.* (**patrocínio**)

patronize *or* **patronise** /ˈpætrənaɪz/ VERB [**patronizes, patronizing, patronized**]
1 to treat someone in a way that shows you think you are better than them or think that they are stupid ▫ *Since his promotion, he thinks he can patronize all the junior clerks.* ▫ *Don't patronize me!* (**menosprezar**)
2 a formal word meaning to be a customer in a shop, restaurant, etc. ▫ *He and his family have patronized our shop for as long as we can remember.* (**frequentar**)

• **patronizing** /ˈpætrənaɪzɪŋ/ ADJECTIVE behaving in a way that shows you think you are better than someone or think that they are stupid ▫ *I hate his patronizing manner.* ▫ *a patronizing tone of voice* (**depreciativo**)

- **patronizingly** /ˈpætrənaɪzɪŋlɪ/ ADVERB in a patronizing way □ *She remarked patronizingly that the work was very good for a beginner.* (depreciativamente)

patron saint /ˌpeɪtrən ˈseɪnt/ NOUN [plural **patron saints**] a saint (= very holy person in the Christian religion) who is believed to protect a place, activity or trade □ *St Andrew is the patron saint of Scotland.* (padroeiro)

patter /ˈpætə(r)/ ▶ VERB [**patters, pattering, pattered**] to make quick, light sounds by hitting or falling on something □ *The rain was pattering on the windows.* (tamborilar)

▶ NOUN, NO PLURAL

1 a series of quick, light sounds of something hitting something □ *I heard the patter of feet in the room above.* (sequência de ruídos leves)
2 fast, confident speech, especially by someone selling something □ *He started on his usual sales patter.* (tagarelice)

pattern /ˈpætən/ NOUN [plural **patterns**]
1 the way in which something normally happens or is organized □ + **of** *the pattern of the seasons* (padrão) ▣ *The game followed a familiar pattern.* (seguiu um padrão) ▣ *When we analyzed the data, a clear pattern emerged.* (surgiu um padrão) ▣ *annual weather patterns* (padrões do clima)
2 a design of shapes, colours, etc. repeated on a surface □ *The room was decorated in floral patterns.* □ *The boxes are carved with intricate patterns.* (estampa)
3 a set of instructions and shapes used for making something □ *a sewing pattern* (modelo)

- **patterned** /ˈpætənd/ ADJECTIVE having a design of shapes, colours, etc. □ *a patterned dress* (estampado)

paunch /pɔːntʃ/ NOUN [plural **paunches**] a fat stomach □ *You're getting a bit of a paunch.* (pança)

pauper /ˈpɔːpə(r)/ NOUN [plural **paupers**] an old-fashioned word for a very poor person □ *He was buried in a pauper's grave.* (indigente)

pause /pɔːz/ ▶ VERB [**pauses, pausing, paused**]
1 to stop what you are doing for a short time □ + **to do something** *The actor paused to speak to fans.* □ *He paused for a moment before replying.* (fazer uma pausa)
2 to stop a CD, DVD, etc. for a short time by pressing a button (pausar)

▶ NOUN [plural **pauses**]

1 a short stop or rest (pausa) ▣ *There was a long pause before anyone spoke.* (longa pausa) □ + **for** *He kept going with hardly a pause for breath.*
2 a button that you press to pause a CD, DVD, etc. □ *Press pause.* (botão de pausa)

pave /peɪv/ VERB [**paves, paving, paved**] to make a layer of stones, bricks etc. on an area of ground □ *The courtyard is paved with local stone.* (calçar)

♦ IDIOM **pave the way for something** to do something that makes it possible for something else to happen □ *This decision could pave the way for other legal cases.* (preparar o caminho para algo)

pavement /ˈpeɪvmənt/ NOUN [plural **pavements**] a path next to a road which people walk along □ *He waited on the pavement in front of the shop.* (calçada)

pavilion /pəˈvɪljən/ NOUN [plural **pavilions**]
1 a building at a sports ground where players change their clothes (pavilhão)
2 a large building or tent, especially at an event (pavilhão)

paving stone /ˈpeɪvɪŋ ˌstəʊn/ NOUN [plural **paving stones**] a piece of flat stone used to cover a path or an outside area (laje)

paw /pɔː/ ▶ NOUN [plural **paws**] the foot of some animals, such as cats and dogs (pata)

▶ VERB [**paws, pawing, pawed**] to touch something with a paw □ *The horse pawed the ground.*

pawn /pɔːn/ NOUN [plural **pawns**]
1 one of the small, least important pieces in the game of chess (peão)
2 someone who is used and controlled by someone more powerful □ *These people are being used as political pawns.* (fantoche)

pay /peɪ/ ▶ VERB [**pays, paying, paid**]
1 to give money in order to buy something or because you owe someone (pagar) □ + **for** *I'll pay for the meal.* ▣ *He offered to pay the bill.* (pagar a conta) □ *I don't pay tax in this country.* □ + **by** *Can I pay by credit card?*
2 to give someone money for work that they do □ *I need the money to pay the builder.* □ *I get paid on the 15th of each month.* (remunerar)
3 to give you an advantage □ + **to do something** *It pays to book in advance.* □ *Crime does not pay.* (recompensar)
4 to suffer because of something you have done (pagar) ▣ *She paid dearly* (= suffered a lot) *for her carelessness.* (pagou caro) □ + **for** *I'll make you pay for what you did.*
5 pay attention to concentrate on something □ *She paid great attention to his words.* (prestar atenção, homenagem)
6 pay someone a compliment to say something nice about someone (elogiar)
7 pay tribute to someone to say or do something to show your respect and admiration for someone (homenagear)
8 pay someone/something a visit to visit someone or something (retribuir uma visita)

> Note that you pay **for** the thing that you are buying: □ *Camille paid for the watch.*
> ✓ *Camille paid £120 for the watch.*
> ✗ *Camille paid the watch.*

pay-as-you-go

♦ PHRASAL VERBS **pay someone back** to do something bad to someone because of something bad they have done to you (**pagar na mesma moeda**) **pay off** if an action pays off, it gives you an advantage □ Giving up my job was a risk, but it really paid off. **pay off something** to pay all of the money that you owe for something □ In a couple of years, we'll have paid off the mortgage. (**compensar**) **pay up** to pay money that you owe, especially when you do not want to (**saldar dívida**)
▶ NOUN, NO PLURAL someone's pay is the amount of money they are paid by their employer □ The job's boring, but the pay's good. 🔳 I asked him for a *pay rise*. (**aumento na remuneração**) 🔳 Many workers are facing *pay cuts*. (**cortes na remuneração**)

• **payable** /'peɪəbəl/ ADJECTIVE
1 that must be paid □ The second instalment is payable on or before 1 July. (**pagável**)
2 a cheque that is payable to someone has their name written on it 🔳 Cheques should be *made payable to* 'Smith Mills Limited'. (**nominal a**)

pay-as-you-go /ˌpeɪ əzjʊˈɡəʊ/ ADJECTIVE paying for a service just before you use it, not after you have used it □ *pay-as-you-go mobile phones* (**pré-pago**)

payee /ˌpeɪˈiː/ NOUN [*plural* payees] someone who money or a cheque is paid to (**pessoa a quem se paga**)

payment /'peɪmənt/ NOUN [*plural* payments]
1 money paid for something (**pagamento**) 🔳 We *make* monthly *payments*. (**fazer pagamentos**) □ All payments will be made to your bank account. 🔳 He received a *cash payment* of £200. (**pagamento em dinheiro**)
2 no plural when you pay for something □ + *of* He was involved with the payment of bribes. (**pagamento**)

payout /'peɪaʊt/ NOUN [*plural* payouts] a large amount of money that is paid to someone (**dividendos**)

pay-per-view /ˌpeɪpəˈvjuː/ NOUN, NO PLURAL a system in which you pay an amount of money to watch a particular television programme (**taxa para a transmissão de um programa**)

payroll /'peɪrəʊl/ NOUN [*plural* payrolls] a list of all the people that a company employs and the money that they earn □ The company has 500 people on the payroll. (**folha de pagamento**)

payslip /'peɪslɪp/ NOUN [*plural* payslips] a piece of paper from your employer that shows details of money you have earned, tax you have paid, etc. (**contracheque**)

PC /ˌpiːˈsiː/ ABBREVIATION (**abrev. personal computer**)
1 personal computer (**computador pessoal**)
2 police constable; used before a police officer's name □ *PC Evans* (**título e identificação da polícia**)

peak

PDA /ˌpiːdiːˈeɪ/ ABBREVIATION personal digital assistant; a small computer that you can hold in your hand. A computing word. (**abrev. assistente pessoal digital: palmtop**)

PDF /ˌpiːdiːˈef/ ABBREVIATION portable document format; a type of computer file that you can send from one computer to another. A computing word. (**tipo de arquivo de computador, abrev. formato de arquivo transferível**)

PE /ˌpiːˈiː/ ABBREVIATION physical education; a school subject in which children learn sports, games and exercise. (**educação física**)

pea /piː/ NOUN [*plural* peas] a small round green vegetable (**ervilha**)

peace /piːs/ NOUN, NO PLURAL
1 a situation in which there is no war or violence □ The two countries have been at peace for 50 years. (**paz**) 🔳 We are seeking to *bring peace* to the region. (**trazer paz**) 🔳 The police were at the demonstration to *keep the peace*. (**manter a paz**) 🔳 *peace talks* (**discursos, negociações de paz**) 🔳 a *peace deal* (**acordo de paz**)
2 a situation which is quiet and calm □ I want a little peace to get on with my homework. (**paz**) 🔳 She goes to the library for a bit of *peace and quiet*. (**paz e tranquilidade**)

• **peaceful** /'piːsfʊl/ ADJECTIVE
1 not involving war or violence □ a peaceful protest (**pacífico**) 🔳 It says its nuclear programme is for *peaceful purposes*. (**fins pacíficos**)
2 quiet and calm □ She felt more peaceful than she had all day. □ a peaceful seaside town (**tranquilo**)
3 not wanting to be involved in war or violence □ a peaceful nation (**pacífico**)

• **peacefully** /'piːsfʊli/ ADVERB
1 quietly and calmly (**tranquilamente**) 🔳 She died *peacefully* in her sleep. (**morreu em paz**) □ The baby was sleeping peacefully.
2 without any violence □ The demonstration began peacefully. □ The two groups live peacefully together. (**pacificamente**)

peacetime /'piːstaɪm/ NOUN, NO PLURAL a period of time when there is no war (**época de paz**)

peach /piːtʃ/ ▶ NOUN [*plural* peaches] a round fruit with a soft skin, pale orange flesh and a large stone inside (**pêssego**)
▶ ADJECTIVE having a pale orange colour like a peach

peacock /'piːkɒk/ NOUN [*plural* peacocks] a large, male bird with a long tail with colourful feathers (**pavão**)

peak /piːk/ ▶ NOUN [*plural* peaks]
1 the highest, greatest or most successful level (**apogeu, pico**) □ the peak of the holiday season 🔳 She *reached the peak* of her career in the 1990s. (**atingiu o apogeu**) 🔳 The trains are packed at *peak times*. (**horas de pico**)

2 the pointed top of a mountain or hill (**pico**) ▣ *snow covered mountain peaks* (**picos da montanha**)

3 the flat part at the front of a cap (= soft hat) that sticks out (**aba**)

▶ VERB [**peaks, peaking, peaked**] to reach the highest, greatest or most successful level ▫ *Traffic usually peaks about 5 or 6 o'clock.* (**chegar ao ponto máximo**)

▶ ADJECTIVE when the largest number of people are using or doing something ▫ *I try to travel outside peak periods.*

peal /piːl/ ▶ NOUN [*plural* **peals**]

1 a sound made by one or more large bells ringing together (**repique**)

2 a loud sound of laughter ▣ *They burst into peals of laughter.* (**gargalhada**)

3 a loud sound of thunder (**estrondo**)

▶ VERB [**peals, pealing, pealed**] if bells peal, they ring loudly together (**repicar, estrondear**)

peanut /ˈpiːnʌt/ NOUN [*plural* **peanuts**] a type of nut that grows underground in a shell and can be eaten (**amendoim**)

peanut butter /ˌpiːnʌt ˈbʌtə(r)/ NOUN, NO PLURAL a thick, soft mixture made with crushed peanuts that you spread on bread (**pasta de amendoim**)

pear /peə(r)/ NOUN [*plural* **pears**] a fruit with green, yellow or brown skin and white flesh which is round at the bottom and narrower at the top (**pera**)

pearl /pɜːl/ NOUN [*plural* **pearls**]

1 a round, white object, formed inside the shell of an oyster (= sea creature), and used for making jewellery ▫ *a pearl necklace* (**pérola**)

2 a pearl of wisdom a useful piece of information (**uma pérola de sabedoria**)

peasant /ˈpezənt/ NOUN [*plural* **peasants**] a poor person who works on the land in a poor country ▫ *a peasant farmer* (**camponês**)

peat /piːt/ NOUN, NO PLURAL a substance formed in the ground over many years from decayed plants, used for growing plants or as a fuel for burning (**turfa**)

pebble /ˈpebəl/ NOUN [*plural* **pebbles**] a small stone that has been made smooth by water (**pedregulho**)

peck /pek/ ▶ VERB [**pecks, pecking, pecked**] if a bird pecks, it hits something or picks something up with its beak ▫ *Birds pecked at the crumbs.* (**bicar**)

♦ IDIOM **pecking order** the order of power or importance of people or animals within a group ▫ *He's dropped down the pecking order under the new coach.* (**ordem hierárquica**)

▶ NOUN [*plural* **pecks**]

1 when a bird pecks (**bicada**)

2 a quick, light kiss ▫ *He gave me a peck on the cheek.* (**beijoca**)

peckish /ˈpekɪʃ/ ADJECTIVE an informal word meaning slightly hungry ▫ *I'm a bit peckish.* (**faminto**)

peculiar /pɪˈkjuːliə(r)/ ADJECTIVE

1 strange or not expected, sometimes in an unpleasant way ▫ *a very peculiar smell* ▫ *It seems peculiar that no one noticed.* ▫ *That would explain his peculiar behaviour recently.* (**estranho**)

2 peculiar to someone/something typical of a particular person, place or thing ▫ *It's a phenomenon peculiar to this region.* (**típico**)

• **peculiarity** /pɪˌkjuːliˈærəti/ NOUN [*plural* **peculiarities**]

1 a peculiar thing, habit or quality ▫ *She put up with her grandmother's peculiarities.* (**excentricidade**)

2 a feature or characteristic typical of one person, thing or place ▫ *We have to respond to the peculiarities of the market.* (**particularidades**)

• **peculiarly** /pɪˈkjuːliəli/ ADVERB

1 in a strange way ▫ *He's been behaving very peculiarly.* (**estranhamente**)

2 in way that is typical of a particular person, thing or place ▫ *a peculiarly British habit* (**tipicamente**)

pedal /ˈpedəl/ ▶ NOUN [*plural* **pedals**] a part that you push with your foot, such as on a bicycle, in a car or on a machine (**pedal**) ▣ *the brake pedal* (**pedal do freio**)

▶ VERB [**pedals, pedalling/US pedaling, pedalled/US pedaled**] to push the pedals on a bicycle or to ride a bicycle ▫ *We hired bikes and pedalled along the coast road.* (**pedalar**)

pedantic /pɪˈdæntɪk/ ADJECTIVE thinking too much about correct details or rules ▫ *Oh, don't be so pedantic; you know what I meant!* (**pedante**)

peddle /ˈpedəl/ VERB [**peddles, peddling, peddled**]

1 to sell something illegal or of bad quality ▫ *They peddle cigarettes to kids.* (**vender produtos ilegais ou bugigangas, mascatear**)

2 to try to persuade people to believe a story, idea, etc., especially one that is not true ▫ *Don't believe the propaganda peddled by the industry.* (**forjar**)

pedestal /ˈpedɪstəl/ NOUN [*plural* **pedestals**] a base that something stands on, especially a statue (= stone model of a person) (**pedestal**)

♦ IDIOM **put/place someone on a pedestal** to admire someone so much that you think they are perfect ▫ *We tend to put sportsmen on a pedestal.* (**venerar alguém**)

pedestrian /pɪˈdestriən/ ▶ NOUN [*plural* **pedestrians**] someone who is walking and not travelling in a vehicle ▫ *Pedestrians and cyclists are given priority in the city centre.* (**pedestre**)

▶ ADJECTIVE a formal word meaning ordinary and boring ▫ *The main dishes were rather pedestrian.*

pedestrian crossing 575 pelt

pedestrian crossing /pɪˌdestrɪən 'krɒsɪŋ/ NOUN [plural **pedestrian crossings**] a place marked on a road where vehicles must stop to allow people to cross (**faixa de pedestre**)

pediatric /ˌpiːdiˈætrɪk/ ADJECTIVE the US spelling of **paediatric** (ver **paediatric**)

• **pediatrician** /ˌpiːdɪəˈtrɪʃən/ NOUN [plural **pediatricians**] the US spelling of **paediatrician** (**pediatra**)

• **pediatrics** /ˌpiːdiˈætrɪks/ NOUN, NO PLURAL the US spelling of **paediatrics** (**pediatria**)

pedigree /ˈpedɪɡriː/ ▶ NOUN [plural **pedigrees**]
1 a record of the family history of an animal, especially with all members of the same breed (**pedigree**)
2 the past experiences or achievements of a person or an organization ☐ He has an impressive pedigree as a manager. (**realizações**)
3 your family history (**ascendência**)
▶ ADJECTIVE a pedigree animal has a family history with all members of the same breed ☐ a pedigree dog

pedlar /ˈpedlə(r)/ NOUN [plural **pedlars**] a person who travels around selling small things (ver **peddle**)

peek /piːk/ ▶ VERB [**peeks, peeking, peeked**]
1 to look at something quickly, especially when you should not be looking ☐ He peeked inside the box. (**espiar**)
2 to be just seen behind something ☐ A blue book was peeking out of her bag. (**ser visto, aparecer**)
▶ NOUN [plural **peeks**] a quick look ☐ He took a peek inside the room. (**espiada**)

peel /piːl/ ▶ VERB [**peels, peeling, peeled**]
1 to remove the skin of a vegetable or a piece of fruit ☐ She was peeling potatoes. ☐ + **off** Let the peppers cool then peel off the skin. (**descascar**)
2 to remove something from a surface by pulling it carefully ☐ + **off** He carefully peeled off the label. ☐ + **away** I opened the box and peeled away the layers of tissue paper. (**puxar**)
3 if paint or skin peels, it comes off in small pieces ☐ The paint was peeling off the walls. (**descamar**)
◆ PHRASAL VERB **peel something off** to remove clothes that are tight or wet ☐ We peeled off our wet suits. (**tirar uma roupa apertada ou molhada**)
▶ NOUN, NO PLURAL the skin of some fruit and vegetables ☐ orange peel (**casca**)

• **peeler** /ˈpiːlə(r)/ NOUN [plural **peelers**] a kitchen tool used to peel vegetables ☐ a potato peeler (**descascador**)

peep /piːp/ ▶ VERB [**peeps, peeping, peeped**]
1 to be just seen from behind something ☐ The sun peeped out from behind the clouds. (**aparecer**)
2 to look at something quickly and usually secretly, through or from behind something ☐ He peeped over the top of the wall. (**espreitar**)

▶ NOUN [plural **peeps**]
1 a slight sound ☐ You won't hear a peep out of us. (**pio**)
2 a quick look at something ☐ I had a peep into next door's garden. (**espiadela**)

peer /pɪə(r)/ ▶ VERB [**peers, peering, peered**] to look at something carefully, usually because it is difficult to see ☐ He peered through a downstairs window. (**espreitar**)
▶ NOUN [plural **peers**]
1 people of a similar age or social position to you ☐ She was popular with her peers and teachers. (**par**)
2 in the UK, someone who has a high social position and a special title, for example 'Lord' (**nobre**)

peer group /ˈpɪə ˌɡruːp/ NOUN [plural **peer groups**] all the people of a similar age or social position to you ☐ Children are greatly influenced by their peer groups. (**grupo de colegas**)

peer pressure /ˈpɪə ˌpreʃə(r)/ NOUN, NO PLURAL the influence that people of a similar age or social position have on you ☐ There's a lot of peer pressure on teenagers to wear the latest fashions. (**pressão dos colegas**)

peeved /piːvd/ ADJECTIVE annoyed ☐ I was a bit peeved because she was late. (**irritado**)

peg /peɡ/ NOUN [plural **pegs**]
1 a small object used for fastening wet clothes to a string to dry (**prendedor/pregador de roupas**)
2 a bent piece of metal or plastic for hanging coats, hats or jackets on (**cabide**) ☐ a coat peg (**cabide de casaco**)
3 a piece of wood or metal used to fix something in place ☐ a tent peg (**pino**)

pejorative /pɪˈdʒɒrətɪv/ ADJECTIVE a pejorative word or phrase is offensive or expresses criticism ☐ a pejorative term (**pejorativo, depreciativo**)

• **pejoratively** /pɪˈdʒɒrətɪvlɪ/ ADVERB in a pejorative way ☐ The word is used pejoratively. (**pejorativamente**)

pelican /ˈpelɪkən/ NOUN [plural **pelicans**] a large white bird with a large part that hangs down under its beak where it stores fish (**pelicano**)

pelican crossing /ˌpelɪkən ˈkrɒsɪŋ/ NOUN [plural **pelican crossings**] a place where people can cross the road with lights that you use by pressing a button to make the traffic stop (**sinal luminoso para travessia de pedestres**)

pellet /ˈpelɪt/ NOUN [plural **pellets**]
1 a small hard round piece of a substance ☐ pet food pellets (**bolinha**)
2 a small round piece of metal used in some guns ☐ a shotgun pellet (**chumbinho**)

pelt /pelt/ ▶ VERB [**pelts, pelting, pelted**]
1 to throw things at someone or something with force ☐ The minister's car was pelted with eggs. (**arremessar**)
2 if rain pelts down, it falls with force ☐ Rain pelted down outside. (**chover forte**)

3 to run or to move very fast □ *He came pelting down the road on his bike.* (correr a toda velocidade)

▶ NOUN [*plural* **pelts**]

1 the skin from an animal □ *beaver pelts* (pele)

2 (at) full pelt moving very fast □ *He was running at full pelt.* (a toda velocidade)

pelvic /'pelvɪk/ ADJECTIVE to do with the pelvis. A biology word □ *the pelvic bone* (pélvico)

pelvis /'pelvɪs/ NOUN [*plural* **pelvises**] the large round bones that connect the bottom of your back to your legs. A biology word. (pélvis)

pen /pen/ ▶ NOUN [*plural* **pens**]

1 an object used for writing with ink (caneta, pena) 🔲 *a ballpoint pen* □ *Have you got a pen and paper?* (caneta esferográfica)

2 a small area surrounded by a fence and used for keeping animals in (cercado)

▶ VERB [**pens, penning, penned**]

1 to put an animal in a pen (cercar)

2 to write something □ *Tom Martin will pen the script for the new film.* (escrever)

◆ PHRASAL VERB **pen someone in** to prevent someone from moving or escaping □ *Supporters were penned in behind barriers.*

penal /'pi:nəl/ ADJECTIVE to do with the punishment of criminals □ *penal reform* □ *a penal code* (penal)

penalize *or* **penalise** /'pi:nəlaɪz/ VERB [**penalizes, penalizing, penalized**]

1 to punish someone for breaking a rule or law □ *Players can be penalized for swearing.* (penalizar, punir)

2 to give someone a disadvantage □ *Rises in fuel prices penalize families with big cars.* (penalizar)

• **penalty** /'penəlti/ NOUN [*plural* **penalties**]

1 a punishment for breaking a rule or law 🔲 *He faces a maximum penalty of 10 years in jail.* 🔲 *The regulator has imposed a penalty of £20,000 on the bank.* (multa, penalidade)

2 a free shot at the goal in some sports, given because a player in the other team has broken a rule 🔲 *Henry scored a penalty.* 🔲 *Rooney will take the penalty.* (pênalti, penalidade máxima)

penance /'penəns/ NOUN, NO PLURAL punishment that you accept to show you are sorry for doing something wrong (penitência)

pence /pens/ PLURAL OF **penny** □ *a ten pence coin penchant* (ver **penny**)

penchant /'pãʃã/ NOUN, NO PLURAL **have a penchant for something** to like something very much (predileção, propensão)

pencil /'pensəl/ NOUN [*plural* **pencils**] a long thin wooden object for writing or drawing, with a black or coloured substance in the centre □ *coloured pencils* □ *a pencil drawing* (lápis)

◆ PHRASAL VERB [**pencils, pencilling/**US **penciling, pencilled/**US **penciled**] **pencil something in** to plan or to arrange something which may be changed later □ *The meeting is pencilled in for 10 March.* (agendar provisoriamente)

pencil sharpener /'pensəl ˌʃɑːpənə(r)/ NOUN [*plural* **pencil sharpeners**] a device for making the point of a pencil sharp (apontador de lápis)

pendant /'pendənt/ NOUN [*plural* **pendants**] a piece of jewellery that hangs from a long chain around your neck (pingente)

pending /'pendɪŋ/ ▶ PREPOSITION a formal word meaning waiting for something else to happen first □ *He was held in prison pending trial.* (até)

▶ ADJECTIVE a formal word meaning waiting to be decided or dealt with □ *The court's decision is still pending.* (pendente)

pendulum /'pendjʊləm/ NOUN [*plural* **pendulums**] a weight at the end of a long bar that moves from side to side, especially inside a large clock (pêndulo)

penetrate /'penɪtreɪt/ VERB [**penetrates, penetrating, penetrated**]

1 to get into or through something □ *Rain could not penetrate those thick trees.* □ *The knife penetrated his heart.* (penetrar)

2 to successfully join a group or to be successful in a particular area □ *Our company has begun to penetrate new markets in South America.* (introduzir-se)

• **penetrating** /'penɪtreɪtɪŋ/ ADJECTIVE

1 a penetrating look seems to be reading your thoughts □ *a penetrating gaze/stare* (penetrante)

2 a penetrating sound is loud and can be heard through other sounds (penetrante)

3 intelligent and understanding something very well □ *a penetrating analysis* (penetrante)

• **penetration** /ˌpenɪ'treɪʃən/ NOUN, NO PLURAL when something penetrates something else (penetração)

pen friend /'pen ˌfrend/ NOUN [*plural* **pen friends**] a friend you write letters to, but do not meet (correspondente)

penguin /'peŋgwɪn/ NOUN [*plural* **penguins**] a black and white bird that cannot fly but uses its wings to swim under water (pinguim)

penicillin /ˌpenɪ'sɪlɪn/ NOUN, NO PLURAL a drug used for treating infections caused by bacteria (penicilina)

peninsula /pə'nɪnsjʊlə/ NOUN [*plural* **peninsulas**] a long area of land that sticks out from a larger area of land, and has water around most of it. A geography word. (península)

penis /'pi:nɪs/ NOUN [*plural* **penises**] the male organ for urinating and producing babies. A biology word. (pênis)

penknife /'pennaɪf/ NOUN [*plural* **penknives**] a small knife with blades that fold into the handle (canivete)

pennant /'penənt/ NOUN [*plural* **pennants**] a long flag with a point at one end (flâmula)

penniless /ˈpenɪlɪs/ ADJECTIVE having no money □ *penniless refugees* (sem um tostão)

penny /ˈpenɪ/ NOUN [plural **pence** or **pennies** or **p**]
1 a small British coin worth one hundredth of £1 □ *Crisps cost 40 pence.* (pêni)
2 every penny all of someone's money □ *He spends every penny he earns on computer games.* (todo o dinheiro)
3 not pay/not cost a penny to not pay or not cost any money at all □ *The great thing about this food is that it doesn't cost a penny.* (não custa nada)

➤ Note that when you are saying how much something costs, the plural **pence** is used. When you are talking about the coins themselves, use the plural **pennies**: □ *It cost me fifty pence.* □ *I only had a few pennies left in my purse.*

pension /ˈpenʃən/ NOUN [plural **pensions**] an amount of money that a government or company regularly gives someone when they are too old to work (pensão) □ *My grandma gets a state pension* (= a pension that a government gives people). (pensão do governo) □ *a company pension* (= a pension that a company gives to former employees) (pensão da empresa) □ *The company has a good pension scheme.* (plano de aposentadoria)

• **pensioner** /ˈpenʃənə(r)/ NOUN [plural **pensioners**] someone who gets a pension (pensionista)

pensive /ˈpensɪv/ ADJECTIVE thinking about something in a serious way □ *He was in a pensive mood.* (pensativo)

pentagon /ˈpentəgən/ NOUN [plural **pentagons**] a solid shape with five sides. A maths word. (pentágono)

pentathlon /penˈtæθlən/ NOUN [plural **pentathlons**] a sports competition in which you must do five different sports (pentatlo)

pent-up /ˌpentˈʌp/ ADJECTIVE a pent-up feeling is one which you feel strongly but have not expressed □ *pent-up frustration* (reprimido)

penultimate /pəˈnʌltɪmət/ ADJECTIVE coming not last in a series of things but next to last □ *the penultimate game of the competition* (penúltimo)

people /ˈpiːpəl/ ▶ PLURAL NOUN
1 men, women and children □ *young people* □ *How many people have you invited to your party?* □ *People don't like being criticized.* (pessoas)
2 the people the ordinary people in a country who do not have important positions □ *The Prime Minister must listen to the people if he wants to get re-elected.* (povo)
3 *plural* **peoples** a formal word meaning a race or group of people in a particular country □ *+ of all the peoples of the world* □ *the Russian people* (povos)

▶ VERB [**peoples, peopling, peopled**] if a place is peopled by a particular type of person, they live there. A formal word □ *It's an area that's peopled by very poor families* (povoar)

➤ Remember that the noun **people** always takes a plural verb: □ *People are generally happy with the government.*

➤ Remember also that you do not say 'all people' or 'every people'. Instead you say **everyone** or **everybody**:
✓ *Everyone feels sad sometimes.*
✗ *All people feel sad sometimes.*

people carrier /ˈpiːpəl ˌkærɪə(r)/ NOUN [plural **people carriers**] a large, high car which carries up to eight people (minivan)

pepper /ˈpepə(r)/ ▶ NOUN [plural **peppers**]
1 *no plural* a powder with a strong taste which is added to food (pimenta) □ *He sprinkled salt and pepper on his food.* (sal e pimenta) □ *freshly ground black pepper* (pimenta-do-reino)
2 a hollow red, green or yellow vegetable which is eaten raw or cooked □ *a sliced red pepper* (pimentão)

▶ VERB [**peppers, peppering, peppered**] if something is peppered with things, it includes a lot of them □ *The article was peppered with references to the attack.* (apimentar)

peppercorn /ˈpepəkɔːn/ NOUN [plural **peppercorns**] a very small dried fruit that is crushed to make pepper (grão de pimenta)

pepper mill /ˈpepə ˌmɪl/ NOUN [plural **pepper mills**] a piece of kitchen equipment used for crushing peppercorns (moedor de pimenta)

peppermint /ˈpepəmɪnt/ NOUN [plural **peppermints**]
1 a strong, fresh taste that comes from a herb and is used in food (hortelã-pimenta)
2 a sweet that tastes of peppermint (bala de hortelã)

peppery /ˈpepərɪ/ ADJECTIVE tasting of pepper □ *a peppery sauce* (apimentado)

pep talk /ˈpep ˌtɔːk/ NOUN [plural **pep talks**] a talk that is intended to encourage someone to work harder □ *The players were given a pep talk by their manager before the game.* (discurso de motivação)

per /pɜː(r)/ PREPOSITION for each □ *The meal will cost £20 per person.* □ *He was driving at 65 miles per hour when the crash happened.* □ *How much are the apples per kilo?* (por)

perceive /pəˈsiːv/ VERB [**perceives, perceiving, perceived**]
1 to understand or think about something in a particular way □ *He was perceived as a threat to the state.* (considerar)

2 a formal word meaning to notice something □ *I perceived that something was not right.* (perceber)

percent /pə'sent/ or per cent /pə 'sent/
ADVERB, ADJECTIVE, NOUN in or for every 100, shown by the symbol □ *Sales have increased by ten percent.* □ *There has been a five percent fall in the number of people who are unemployed.* □ *Sixty percent of schoolchildren felt that they got too much homework.* (porcento)

- **percentage** /pə'sentɪdʒ/ NOUN [plural **percentages**] a number that is expressed as a number in 100 (porcentagem) □ *A high percentage of students got top grades.* □ *What percentage of children have a television in their bedrooms?* (porcentagem alta)

perceptible /pə'septəbəl/ ADJECTIVE a formal word meaning able to be noticed □ *The change was barely perceptible.* (perceptível)

- **perception** /pə'sepʃən/ NOUN [plural **perceptions**]
1 the way you see or understand something □ *The visit changed my perception of the city.* (percepção)
2 the ability to see, hear or feel something □ *Anxiety can affect a person's perception of pain.* (percepção)

- **perceptive** /pə'septɪv/ ADJECTIVE good at noticing and understanding things □ *She's very perceptive for a child.* (perspicaz)

perch /pɜːtʃ/ ▶ VERB [**perches, perching, perched**]
1 if something is perched somewhere, it is on the top or edge of something □ *The house is perched on a hillside overlooking the lake.* (situar-se no topo)
2 to sit on the edge of something □ *She perched on a stool next to me.* (sentar-se à beira de)
▶ NOUN [plural **perches**] something that a bird sits on (poleiro)

percussion /pə'kʌʃən/ NOUN, NO PLURAL musical instruments that you hit or shake, such as drums (percussão)

- **percussionist** /pə'kʌʃənɪst/ NOUN [plural **percussionists**] someone who plays percussion instruments (percussionista)

perennial /pə'reniəl/ c ADJECTIVE never ending □ *Then there is the perennial problem of how to dispose of toxic waste.* (perene)
▶ NOUN [plural **perennials**] a plant that lives for more than one year

perfect ▶ ADJECTIVE /'pɜːfɪkt/
1 without any mistakes or faults □ *Emma has perfect teeth.* □ *Your English is perfect.* (perfeito)
2 exactly right for something □ *Jones was the perfect choice for the role.* □ *South Beach is the perfect place for a holiday.* (perfeito)
3 very good □ *The shoes were a perfect fit.* □ *This building is a perfect example of 1930s architecture.* (perfeito)
4 complete □ *a perfect stranger* (perfeito) □ *Ed's idea made perfect sense to me.* (fazer total sentido)
▶ VERB /pə'fekt/ [**perfects, perfecting, perfected**] to make something perfect □ *The hills are ideal for skiers determined to perfect their technique.* (perfeito = tempo verbal em inglês)
▶ NOUN, NO PLURAL /'pɜːfɪkt/ **the perfect** the tense of a verb that in English is formed with has/have/had and the past participle □ *'He has played tennis for years'* is in the perfect. (aperfeiçoar)

- **perfection** /pə'fekʃən/ NOUN, NO PLURAL the state of being perfect □ *Some people try to achieve physical perfection.* □ *The meat was cooked to perfection* (= it was cooked perfectly). (perfeição)

- **perfectionist** /pə'fekʃənɪst/ NOUN [plural **perfectionists**] someone who tries to do everything perfectly (perfeccionista)

- **perfectly** /'pɜːfɪktli/ ADVERB
1 in an extremely good way □ *The children behaved perfectly.* □ *His arrival was perfectly timed because the meal was just ready.* (perfeitamente)
2 completely □ *It was perfectly obvious that he was lying.* □ *The equipment is old but it's perfectly safe.* (perfeitamente)

perforate /'pɜːfəreɪt/ VERB [**perforates, perforating, perforated**] to make a small hole in something (perfurar, picotar)

- **perforated** /'pɜːfəreɪtɪd/ ADJECTIVE having a small hole, or many small holes □ *a perforated eardrum*

- **perforation** /ˌpɜːfə'reɪʃən/ NOUN [plural **perforations**] a small hole in something, especially many small holes in paper that help you to tear it (perfuração)

perform /pə'fɔːm/ VERB [**performs, performing, performed**]
1 to do a task □ *Surgeons perform operations.* □ *He found it difficult to perform simple tasks after the accident.* (executar)
2 to act in a play, sing a song, etc. with people watching you □ *It was the first time we'd performed the song.* □ *I love performing in front of a live audience.* (representar)
3 perform well/poorly/badly etc. to do something well or badly □ *His team performed poorly in both games.* □ *The business has performed well* (= it has been successful) *in difficult circumstances.* (desempenhar (bem, mal etc.))

- **performance** /pə'fɔːməns/ NOUN [plural **performances**]
1 an occasion when someone acts in a play, sings a song, etc. with people watching them (apresentação, atuação) □ *The show included a live performance by several bands.* (apresentação ao vivo) □ *Kylie gave an impromptu performance.* (fez uma apresentação) □ **+ of** *We went to a performance of Mozart's 'Magic Flute'.*

perfume — permissible

2 the level of success that someone or something has (**desempenho**) 🔹 The team needs to improve its *performance*. (**melhorar seu desempenho**) 🔹 Her *poor performance* in the exams was very disappointing. (**desempenho ruim**)

- **performer** /pəˈfɔːmə(r)/ NOUN [plural **performers**]
  1 a singer, actor, etc. who performs ◻ She's a great performer. ◻ a circus performer (**intérprete**)
  2 someone or something who does something with a particular level of success (**executor**) 🔹 He is one of the team's *top performers*. ◻ The school has been rated as a poor performer. (**melhores realizadores**)

perfume /ˈpɜːfjuːm/ NOUN [plural **perfumes**] a liquid that women put on their skin to make them smell nice (**perfume**) 🔹 She always *wears perfume*. ◻ I could smell her perfume. (**usa perfume**)

- **perfumed** /ˈpɜːfjuːmd/ ADJECTIVE containing perfume ◻ a perfumed body lotion (**perfumado**)

perhaps /pəˈhæps/ ADVERB
1 possibly ◻ I can't find Leo. Perhaps he's left. ◻ Perhaps I shouldn't have told him. (**talvez**)
2 used when you are suggesting something ◻ Perhaps we should invite Lisa. What do you think? (**talvez**)

peril /ˈperɪl/ NOUN [plural **perils**] a formal word meaning danger ◻ He describes the perils of the open sea. ◻ The business's future was in peril. (**perigo**)

- **perilous** /ˈperɪləs/ ADJECTIVE a formal word meaning dangerous ◻ It was a perilous journey across miles of desert. (**perigoso**)

perimeter /pəˈrɪmɪtə(r)/ NOUN [plural **perimeters**] the edge of an area ◻ Guards patrol the perimeter of the military camp. ◻ a perimeter fence (**perímetro**)

period /ˈpɪəriəd/ ▶ NOUN [plural **periods**]
1 an amount of time ◻ The work was done over a two year period. (**período**) 🔹 Rachel has learned a lot in a short *period of time*. (**período**) 🔹 He had spent *long periods* in prison. (**longos períodos**) ◻ + of He lived there for a period of several years.
2 a time in history ◻ the Regency period ◻ one of the earliest geological periods (**período**)
3 one of the parts that a day at school is divided into ◻ We had history first period. (**período**)
4 the flow of blood each month from a woman's body (**menstruação**)
5 the US word for **full stop** (**ponto-final**)
▶ ADJECTIVE in the style of a time in history ◻ period costumes (**de época**)

- **periodic** /ˌpɪəriˈɒdɪk/ ADJECTIVE happening sometimes but not often ◻ periodic attacks (**periódico**)
- **periodical** /ˌpɪəriˈɒdɪkəl/ NOUN [plural **periodicals**] a magazine about a particular subject that is published regularly (**periódico**)

periodic table /ˌpɪəriɒdɪk ˈteɪbəl/ NOUN, NO PLURAL **the periodic table** a list of all the chemical elements, arranged by the structure of their atoms. A chemistry word. (**tabela periódica**)

peripheral /pəˈrɪfərəl/ ADJECTIVE
1 not as important as other things ◻ a peripheral role (**secundário**)
2 to do with the outer edge of something ◻ peripheral nerves (**periférico**)

- **periphery** /pəˈrɪfəri/ NOUN [plural **peripheries**] the outer edge of something ◻ Land on the periphery of the city is very expensive now. (**periferia**)

perish /ˈperɪʃ/ VERB [**perishes, perishing, perished**] a formal word meaning to die ◻ Four children perished in the fire. (**perecer**)

- **perishable** /ˈperɪʃəbəl/ ADJECTIVE perishable food does not stay fresh for long ◻ Fresh meat, milk and other perishable foods should be kept in a refrigerator. (**perecível**)

perjury /ˈpɜːdʒəri/ NOUN, NO PLURAL the crime of telling a lie in a court (**perjúrio, juramento falso**)

perk /pɜːk/ NOUN [plural **perks**] something extra that someone's employer gives them such as free meals or a free car ◻ Free train travel is one of the perks of working for a railway company. (**mordomia**)

- ◆ PHRASAL VERB [**perks, perking, perked**] **perk (someone) up** to feel happier, or to make someone feel happier ◻ The children perked up when I mentioned getting an ice cream. (**animar-se**)
- **perky** /ˈpɜːki/ ADJECTIVE [**perkier, perkiest**] happy and full of energy ◻ He seemed perky enough. (**animado**)

perm /pɜːm/ ▶ NOUN [plural **perms**] a chemical treatment that makes your hair curly for a long time (**permanente**) 🔹 My grandmother *had a perm*. (**fez permanente**)
▶ VERB [**perms, perming, permed**] to make someone's hair curly for a long time by putting chemicals on it

permanence /ˈpɜːmənəns/ NOUN, NO PLURAL the state of lasting forever or for a very long time (**permanência**)

- **permanent** /ˈpɜːmənənt/ ADJECTIVE lasting forever or for a very long time ◻ The accident left him with permanent brain damage. ◻ Ella has been offered a permanent job. ◻ We need a permanent solution to the problem. (**permanente**)
- **permanently** /ˈpɜːmənəntli/ ADVERB in a way that lasts forever or for a very long time ◻ Her sight had been permanently damaged. ◻ Many new mothers feel permanently tired. (**permanentemente**)

permeable /ˈpɜːmiəbəl/ ADJECTIVE permeable substances allow liquid or gas to pass through them. A biology or physics word. (**permeável**)

permissible /pəˈmɪsəbəl/ ADJECTIVE a formal word meaning allowed by a rule ◻ Some cities have pollution levels that are higher than the permissible limits. (**permissível**)

permission /pəˈmɪʃən/ NOUN, NO PLURAL if you have permission to do something, someone says you can do it (**permissão, autorização**) 🔄 *A doctor can't operate on you unless you give permission.* (**der permissão**) 🔄 *You need to get permission from your teacher if you want to leave the class early.* (**conseguir autorização de**) 🔄 *Rob had taken his Dad's car without permission.* (**sem permissão**) ☐ + *to do something* *I asked her permission to use the phone.*

> ► Remember that you **get permission** or **give permission** to do something. You do not 'get/ give a permission':
> ✓ I **got permission** from my teacher to leave early.
> ✗ I got a permission from my teacher to leave early.

permit ► VERB /pəˈmɪt/ [**permits, permitting, permitted**] a formal word meaning to allow something ☐ *Smoking is not permitted anywhere in the building.* (**permitir**)
► NOUN /ˈpɜːmɪt/ [*plural* **permits**] an official document that allows you to do something ☐ *a work permit* (**licença, permissão**)

perpendicular /ˌpɜːpənˈdɪkjʊlə(r)/ ADJECTIVE at an angle of 90° to something. A maths word ☐ *a perpendicular line* (**perpendicular**)

perpetrate /ˈpɜːpɪtreɪt/ VERB [**perpetrates, perpetrating, perpetrated**] a formal word meaning to do something bad or illegal ☐ *They perpetrated one of the largest frauds in legal history.* (**perpetrar**)

• **perpetrator** /ˈpɜːpɪtreɪtə(r)/ NOUN [*plural* **perpetrators**] a formal word meaning someone who has done something bad or illegal (**perpetrador**)

perpetual /pəˈpetʃuəl/ ADJECTIVE never ending or happening too often ☐ *They live in perpetual fear of attacks.* (**perpétuo**)

• **perpetuate** /pəˈpetʃueɪt/ VERB [**perpetuates, perpetuating, perpetuated**] to make something continue for a long time, especially something that is bad or wrong. A formal word ☐ *Stories like this perpetuate the myth that women are bad drivers.* (**perpetuar**)

perplex /pəˈpleks/ VERB [**perplexes, perplexing, perplexed**] to confuse someone (**deixar perplexo**)

• **perplexed** /pəˈplekst/ ADJECTIVE confused because you do not understand something ☐ *a perplexed expression* (**perplexo**)

persecute /ˈpɜːsɪkjuːt/ VERB [**persecutes, persecuting, persecuted**] to treat someone badly and unfairly, especially because of their religion, race or beliefs ☐ *Christians were persecuted in the Roman Empire.* (**perseguir**)

• **persecution** /ˌpɜːsɪˈkjuːʃən/ NOUN, NO PLURAL when someone is persecuted (**perseguição**)

• **persecutor** /ˈpɜːsɪkjuːtə(r)/ NOUN [*plural* **persecutors**] someone who persecutes other people (**perseguidor**)

perseverance /ˌpɜːsɪˈvɪərəns/ NOUN, NO PLURAL determination to continue with something although it is difficult (**perseverança**)

persevere /ˌpɜːsɪˈvɪə(r)/ VERB [**perseveres, persevering, persevered**] to continue doing something although it is difficult ☐ *It's not an easy task but she perseveres.* (**perseverar**)

persist /pəˈsɪst/ VERB [**persists, persisting, persisted**]
1 if something bad persists, it continues ☐ *If the problem persists, talk to your doctor.* (**persistir**)
2 to continue to do or say something ☐ *'Why can't I go, Mum?' he persisted.* (**insistir**)

• **persistence** /pəˈsɪstəns/ NOUN, NO PLURAL when someone continues to do something in a determined way ☐ *I admire your persistence.* (**persistência**)

• **persistent** /pəˈsɪstənt/ ADJECTIVE
1 continuing to do something even when it is difficult or when someone tells you to stop ☐ *I said I wasn't interested but the salesman was quite persistent.* (**persistente**)
2 if something unpleasant is persistent, it continues for a long time ☐ *persistent rain* (**persistente, contínuo**)

person /ˈpɜːsən/ NOUN [*plural* **people**]
1 a man, woman or child ☐ *Heather's a really nice person.* ☐ *Tatsuya was the first person in his family to go to university.* ☐ *How many people were at the party?* (**pessoa**) 🔄 *Jeremy is the kind of person who knows everything.* (**tipo de pessoa**)
2 in person if you do something in person, you do it by going somewhere instead of by writing or by sending someone else to do it ☐ *He apologized to her in person.* (**pessoalmente**)

> ► Note that the plural of person is usually **people**. The plural 'persons' is sometimes used in formal writing but it is not used generally:
> ✓ *Most people here own a car.*
> ✗ Most persons here own a car.

personal /ˈpɜːsənəl/ ADJECTIVE
1 belonging to, or to do with one particular person ☐ *a personal opinion* ☐ *personal belongings* (**pessoal**) 🔄 *I know from personal experience that the exam is very difficult.* (**por experiência própria**)
2 private and to do with your health, relationships, etc. (**pessoal**) 🔄 *The singer's personal life has been quite troubled.* ☐ *Never give out personal information to a company on the phone.* (**vida pessoal**)
3 done by someone and not by a person

representing them □ *The Prime Minister wrote a personal reply to her letter.* (**pessoal**)

personal assistant /ˌpɜːsənəl əˈsɪstənt/ NOUN [*plural* **personal assistants**] someone whose job is to help another person, for example by writing e-mails and letters, organizing meetings, etc. (**assistente pessoal**)

personal computer /ˌpɜːsənəl kəmˈpjuːtə(r)/ NOUN [*plural* **personal computers**] a small computer that is designed to be used by one person (**computador pessoal**)

personality /ˌpɜːsəˈnælətɪ/ NOUN [*plural* **personalities**]
1 someone's character and the qualities they have (**personalidade**) 🔁 *Artie has a very outgoing personality.* (**tem personalidade**) □ *The accident had changed his personality.*
2 a famous person (**personalidade**) 🔁 *He's one of America's best known TV personalities.* (**celebridades da TV**)
3 *no plural* qualities that make people notice you and want to be with you □ *He's got a lot of personality.* (**personalidade**)

personalized /ˈpɜːsənəlaɪzd/ ADJECTIVE
1 marked with your name or with a particular decoration to show that it is yours □ *personalized notepaper* (**personalizado**)
2 done or made in a way that is suitable for a particular person □ *We offer personalized treatment.* (**personalizado**)

personally /ˈpɜːsənəlɪ/ ADVERB
1 used when stating your own opinion □ *Personally, I don't like him.* (**pessoalmente**)
2 done by you and not by anyone else □ *He wrote to everyone personally.* (**pessoalmente**)
3 take something personally to think that someone is saying something bad about you and feel upset □ *He was criticizing the organization and not you – I wouldn't take it personally.* (**levar para o lado pessoal**)

personal pronoun /ˌpɜːsənəl ˈprəʊnaʊn/ NOUN [*plural* **personal pronouns**] one of the pronouns such as 'I', 'she', 'they', or 'him' that refers to a particular person, thing or group of people or things (**pronome pessoal**)

personnel /ˌpɜːsəˈnel/ NOUN, NO PLURAL
1 the people who work for a particular company or organization □ *army personnel* (**pessoal**)
2 the department in a company that finds new people to work for the company and keeps records of employees □ *Mel works in personnel.* (**departamento pessoal**)

perspective /pəˈspektɪv/ NOUN [*plural* **perspectives**]
1 a way of thinking about or judging something □ *Try thinking about the problem from a different perspective.* (**perspectiva**)
2 put/keep something in perspective to think about something in a sensible way and not think it is more important than it really is (**colocar/manter em perspectiva**)

perspiration /ˌpɜːspəˈreɪʃən/ NOUN, NO PLURAL a formal word meaning sweat (**transpiração, suor**)

perspire /pəˈspaɪə(r)/ VERB [**perspires, perspiring, perspired**] a formal word meaning to sweat (**transpirar**)

persuade /pəˈsweɪd/ VERB [**persuades, persuading, persuaded**]
1 to make someone agree to do something by telling them why they should do it □ **+ to do something** *I tried to persuade Tanya to come with us.* (**persuadir**)
2 to make someone believe something □ **+ that** *I managed to persuade her that I was telling the truth.* □ **+ of** *He tried to persuade the jury of his innocence.* (**convencer**)

• **persuasion** /pəˈsweɪʒən/ NOUN [*plural* **persuasions**]
1 *no plural* when you persuade someone (**persuasão**) 🔁 *After a little gentle persuasion, he agreed to come with us.* (**um pouco de persuasão/conversa**)
2 a formal word meaning a political or religious belief □ *The course is intended for people of all religious persuasions.* (**crença**)

• **persuasive** /pəˈsweɪsɪv/ ADJECTIVE able to make people do what you want, or able to make people change their opinions □ *She can be very persuasive.* □ *a persuasive argument* (**persuasivo**)

pertain /pəˈteɪn/
♦ PHRASAL VERB [**pertains, pertaining, pertained**] (**pertencer, ser pertinente**) **pertain to something** if one thing pertains to another thing, it is to do with it. A formal word. □ *Documents pertaining to the case have been stolen.* (**pertinente a**)

perturb /pəˈtɜːb/ VERB [**perturbs, perturbing, perturbed**] a formal word meaning to make someone feel worried (**perturbar**)

• **perturbed** /pəˈtɜːbd/ ADJECTIVE a formal word meaning worried □ *She didn't see mat all perturbed by the news.* (**perturbado**)

peruse /pəˈruːz/ VERB [**peruses, perusing, perused**] a formal word meaning to read or look at something □ *His lawyer perused the documents.* (**ler atentamente, examinar**)

pervade /pəˈveɪd/ VERB [**pervades, pervading, pervaded**] a formal word meaning to be in every part of a place □ *The smell of sweat pervaded the room.* (**impregnar**)

• **pervasive** /pəˈveɪsɪv/ ADJECTIVE a formal word meaning existing everywhere □ *a pervasive feeling of despair* (**penetrante**)

perverse /pəˈvɜːs/ ADJECTIVE strange and the opposite of what you expect or consider reasonable □ *He takes a perverse pleasure in upsetting his mother.* (**perverso**)

pessimism /ˈpesɪmɪzəm/ NOUN, NO PLURAL the belief that the future will be bad □ *There is* general pessimism about the state of the economy. (pessimismo)

• **pessimist** /'pesɪmɪst/ NOUN [plural **pessimists**] someone who usually expects bad things to happen (pessimista)

• **pessimistic** /ˌpesɪ'mɪstɪk/ ADJECTIVE expecting that bad things will happen □ *a pessimistic outlook* (pessimista)

pest /pest/ NOUN [plural **pests**]
1 an animal or insect that destroys crops (praga)
2 an informal word for an annoying person, often a child (peste)

pester /'pestə(r)/ VERB [**pesters, pestering, pestered**] to annoy someone by asking them for something many times □ *The children were pestering me to buy them ice creams.* (importunar)

pesticide /'pestɪsaɪd/ NOUN [plural **pesticides**] a chemical used for killing insects which destroy crops (pesticida)

pet /pet/ ▶ NOUN [plural **pets**] an animal that you keep in your home (animal de estimação) □ *Do you have any pets?* (tem algum animal de estimação?) □ *Dogs and cats are very popular pets.* □ *Adam has a pet rabbit.*
▶ VERB [**pets, petting, petted**] to touch and move your hand along an animal's fur (acariciar o pelo do animal)

petal /'petəl/ NOUN [plural **petals**] one of the coloured parts of a flower □ *rose petals* (pétala)

peter /'piːtə(r)/
♦ PHRASAL VERB [**peters, petering, petered**] **peter out** to gradually end □ *Her voice petered out.* (desaparecer gradualmente)

petite /pə'tiːt/ ADJECTIVE a girl or woman who is petite is attractively small and thin (delicada)

petition /pɪ'tɪʃən/ ▶ NOUN [plural **petitions**] a piece of paper that a lot of people sign to try to get a government or someone in authority to do something (petição) □ *We signed a petition against the closure of the post office.* (assinamos uma petição)
▶ VERB [**petitions, petitioning, petitioned**] to officially ask a government or someone in authority to do something by giving them a petition □ *They're petitioning the local council for better street lighting.* (requerer)

Petri dish /'piːtrɪ ˌdɪʃ/ NOUN [plural **Petri dishes**] a flat dish used by scientists for growing bacteria or other cells. A chemistry word. (placa de Petri)

petrified /'petrɪfaɪd/ ADJECTIVE extremely frightened (petrificado)

petrol /'petrəl/ NOUN, NO PLURAL a fuel for cars, made from oil □ *I've just filled the car up with petrol.* □ *petrol prices* (gasolina)

petrol cap /'petrəl ˌkæp/ NOUN [plural **petrol caps**] the small part of a car that you take off to put petrol in (tampa do tanque de gasolina)

petroleum /pɪ'trəʊlɪəm/ NOUN, NO PLURAL oil from under the ground, used for making petrol (petróleo)

petrol station /'petrəl ˌsteɪʃən/ NOUN [plural **petrol stations**] a place where you buy petrol for a car (posto de gasolina)

petticoat /'petɪkəʊt/ NOUN [plural **petticoats**] a piece of clothing like a thin skirt or dress that a woman wears under her skirt or dress (anágua)

petty /'petɪ/ ADJECTIVE [**pettier, pettiest**]
1 not serious, or not important □ *petty details* □ *petty crimes* (insignificante)
2 unpleasant to other people because of something that is not important (mesquinho)

petulance /'petjʊləns/ NOUN, NO PLURAL the quality of being petulant (petulância)

• **petulant** /'petjʊlənt/ ADJECTIVE bad-tempered because you cannot do or have what you want (petulante)

pew /pjuː/ NOUN [plural **pews**] a long wooden seat in a church (banco de igreja)

pewter /'pjuːtə(r)/ NOUN, NO PLURAL a grey metal that is a mixture of the metals lead and tin (estanho, liga de estanho)

pH /ˌpiː'eɪtʃ/ NOUN, NO PLURAL a number that says how acid or alkaline a substance is. A chemistry word. (abrev. potential hydrogen = potencial de hidrogênio)

phantom /'fæntəm/ ▶ NOUN [plural **phantoms**] the spirit of a dead person which some people think they can see (fantasma)
▶ ADJECTIVE imagined and not existing □ *phantom pains*

pharaoh /'feərəʊ/ NOUN [plural **pharaohs**] a king in ancient Egypt (faraó)

pharmaceutical /ˌfɑːmə'sjuːtɪkəl/ ADJECTIVE to do with the making and selling of medicines (farmacêutico) □ *the pharmaceutical industry*

pharmacist /'fɑːməsɪst/ NOUN [plural **pharmacists**] someone who prepares and sells medicines (farmacêutico)

• **pharmacy** /'fɑːməsɪ/ NOUN [plural **pharmacies**]
1 a shop where medicines are prepared and sold □ *You can get most medicines at your local pharmacy.* (farmácia)
2 no plural the study of medicines and how they work (curso de farmácia)

phase /feɪz/ NOUN [plural **phases**] a stage in the development of a thing or person □ *The first phase of the project was to interview 100 students.* □ *Children go through so many phases.* (fase)
♦ PHRASAL VERBS [**phases, phasing, phased**] **phase something in** to gradually start using a new law, system, etc. □ *The changes will be phased in over two years* (iniciar gradualmente). **phase something out** to gradually stop using something □ *The one-cent coins were phased out a few years ago.* (terminar gradualmente)

PhD

PhD /ˌpiːeɪtʃˈdiː/ ABBREVIATION Doctor of Philosophy; the highest university degree ☐ *He's doing a PhD in applied mathematics.* (**grau de doutorado**)

pheasant /ˈfezənt/ NOUN [plural **pheasants**] a large bird with a long tail, that is hunted for sport and eaten (**faisão**)

phenomenal /fɪˈnɒmɪnəl/ ADJECTIVE very great ☐ *The show was a phenomenal success.* (**fenomenal**)

• **phenomenon** /fɪˈnɒmɪnən/ NOUN [plural **phenomena**] something that happens or exists, especially something that is unusual and difficult to explain ☐ *The researchers are studying natural phenomena such as storms and tornadoes.* (**fenômeno**)

phew /fjuː/ EXCLAMATION a way of writing the sound that people make when they are hot or tired, or when they are happy because they have avoided an unpleasant situation ☐ *'Phew, it's hot in there!'* ☐ *Phew, what a relief!* (**ufa!**)

philosopher /fɪˈlɒsəfə(r)/ NOUN [plural **philosophers**] someone who studies philosophy (**filósofo**)

• **philosophical** /ˌfɪləˈsɒfɪkəl/ ADJECTIVE
1 to do with philosophy ☐ *a philosophical debate* (**filosófico**)
2 calmly accepting a bad situation because you cannot change it ☐ *He was very philosophical about not getting the job.* (**filosófico**)

• **philosophy** /fɪˈlɒsəfi/ NOUN [plural **philosophies**]
1 no plural the study of ideas about life ☐ *She did philosophy at university.* (**filosofia**)
2 a set of beliefs about how you should live ☐ *My philosophy is to work hard and play hard.* (**filosofia**)

phlegm /flem/ NOUN, NO PLURAL the thick yellow substance produced in your nose and throat when you have a cold (**muco, catarro**)

phobia /ˈfəʊbiə/ NOUN [plural **phobias**] a very strong fear of something that you cannot explain or control ☐ *Maria's got a phobia about spiders.* (**fobia**)

phone /fəʊn/ ▶ NOUN [plural **phones**] (**telefone**)
1 a telephone ☐ *Here's my phone number.* (**número de telefone**) ☐ *The phone was ringing.* (**o telefone estava tocando**) ☐ *Can you answer the phone please?* (**atenda o telefone**) ☐ *You can order a pizza by phone.*
2 on the phone using the telephone ☐ *Mum's on the phone at the moment.* ☐ *I talk to my cousins on the phone every week.* (**ao telefone**)
▶ VERB [**phones, phoning, phoned**] to speak to someone using a telephone ☐ *I phoned my grandma last night.* ☐ **+ up** *I'll phone up and find out when the library opens.* (**telefonar**)

> Note that you **phone** a person or place. You do not 'phone to' a person or place:
> ✓ *I'll phone Javier.*
> ✗ *I'll phone to Javier.*
> ✓ *I'll phone the hospital.*
> ✗ *I'll phone to the hospital.*

◆ PHRASAL VERB **phone (someone) back** to call someone again using a telephone, because you could not talk to them the first time ☐ *I'm busy just now. I'll phone you back later.* (**retornar a ligação**)

phone box /ˈfəʊn ˌbɒks/ NOUN [plural **phone boxes**] a small structure in a public place containing a telephone which you can pay to use ☐ *There's a phone box outside the station.* (**cabine telefônica**)

phone call /ˈfəʊn ˌkɔːl/ NOUN [plural **phone calls**] when you speak to someone using a telephone (**telefonema**) ☐ *I'm just going to make a quick phone call.* (**fazer um telefonema**)

phone-in /ˈfəʊnɪn/ NOUN [plural **phone-ins**] a television or radio programme in which people can telephone to give their opinions or to ask questions (**programa com participação do público por telefone**)

phone number /ˈfəʊn ˌnʌmbə(r)/ NOUN [plural **phone numbers**] the series of numbers that you use to call a particular telephone ☐ *What's your phone number?* (**número do telefone**)

phonetic /fəˈnetɪk/ ADJECTIVE to do with the sounds people make when they talk (**fonético**)

• **phonetics** /fəˈnetɪks/ NOUN, NO PLURAL the study of the sounds that people make when they talk (**fonética**)

phoney /ˈfəʊni/ or **phony** /ˈfəʊni/ ADJECTIVE [**phonier, phoniest**]
1 not real ☐ *He'd given us a phony address.* (**falso**)
2 not sincere ☐ *phoney laughter* (**falso**)

phosphorus /ˈfɒsfərəs/ NOUN, NO PLURAL a chemical element that burns if air touches it. A chemistry word. (**fósforo**)

photo /ˈfəʊtəʊ/ NOUN [plural **photos**] a photograph ☐ *digital photos* ☐ *Who's that woman in the photo?* (**foto**) ☐ *She took a photo of Clare and me on the beach.* (**tirou uma foto**) ☐ *They showed us their wedding photos.* (**fotos do casamento**) ☐ **+ of** *There were photos of the children all over the house.*

photo- /ˈfəʊtəʊ/ PREFIX photo- is added to the beginning of words to mean 'to do with light' or 'to do with photographs' ☐ *photosynthesis* ☐ *photocopier* (**foto-**)

photocopier /ˈfəʊtəʊkɒpiə(r)/ NOUN [plural **photocopiers**] a machine that copies a document by taking a photograph of it (**fotocopiadora**)

- **photocopy** /ˈfəʊtəʊkɒpɪ/ C NOUN [plural **photocopies**] a copy of a document that you make using a photocopier (**fotocópia**) 🔊 *He made a photocopy of the instructions.* (**tirou uma fotocópia**)
  ▶ VERB [**photocopies, photocopying, photocopied**] to make a copy of a document using a photocopier □ *Why don't you photocopy the map?* (**fotocopiar**)

photogenic /ˌfəʊtəʊˈdʒenɪk/ ADJECTIVE always looking attractive in photographs □ *Suki is very photogenic.* (**fotogênico**)

photograph /ˈfəʊtəɡrɑːf/ ▶ NOUN [plural **photographs**] a picture made with a camera (**fotografia**) 🔊 *I took a photograph using my new camera.* (**tirei uma fotografia**) □ + *of a photograph of Lake Geneva*
  ▶ VERB [**photographs, photographing, photographed**] to make a picture of something using a camera □ *She photographed me in the school play.* (**fotografar**)
- **photographic** /ˌfəʊtəʊˈɡræfɪk/ ADJECTIVE to do with photographs or photography □ *We have photographic evidence of the damage.* (**fotográfico**)
- **photographer** /fəˈtɒɡrəfə(r)/ NOUN [plural **photographers**] someone who takes photographs, especially as their job □ *He's a professional photographer.* □ *a press photographer* (= photographer for a newspaper) □ *a fashion photographer* (**fotógrafo**)
- **photography** /fəˈtɒɡrəfɪ/ NOUN, NO PLURAL the art of taking photographs (**fotografia**) 🔊 *digital photography* (**fotografia digital**) □ *John teaches photography at the college.*

Photostat /ˈfəʊtəʊstæt/ NOUN [plural **Photostats**] a copy of a document made on a particular type of machine. A trademark. (**marca registrada, fazer cópias com essa máquina**)

photosynthesis /ˌfəʊtəʊˈsɪnθəsɪs/ NOUN, NO PLURAL the process by which plants make their food from the sun. A biology word. (**fotossíntese**)

phrasal verb /ˌfreɪzəl ˈvɜːb/ NOUN [plural **phrasal verbs**] a verb that you use with an adverb or preposition, which has a different meaning from the verb used alone □ *'Give up' and 'get on' are examples of phrasal verbs.* (**verbo frásico**)

phrase /freɪz/ ▶ NOUN [plural **phrases**] a group of words that have a particular meaning (**frase**) 🔊 *She used the phrase 'unwelcome attention' several times.* (**usou a frase**)
  ▶ VERB [**phrases, phrasing, phrased**] to express something using particular words □ *He phrased the question very carefully to avoid upsetting her.* (**expressar, exprimir**)

phrase book /ˈfreɪz bʊk/ NOUN [plural **phrase books**] a book that shows you useful words and phrases in a foreign language, which you use when you are travelling □ *an Italian phrase book* (**guia de conversação**)

physical /ˈfɪzɪkəl/ ADJECTIVE
1 to do with the body □ *These children have low levels of physical activity.* (**físico (exercício)**)
2 to do with real things that you can see or touch, and not things that exist only in your mind □ *There was no physical evidence to link him to the crime.* (**físico (matéria física)**)
- **physically** /ˈfɪzɪkəlɪ/ ADVERB
1 in a way that is to do with the body (**fisicamente**) 🔊 *I'm trying to get physically fit.*
2 in the real world, according to the laws of physics □ *It's physically impossible to get this work done by Friday.* (**fisicamente**)

physicist /ˈfɪzɪsɪst/ NOUN [plural **physicists**] someone who studies physics, usually as their job (**físico**)

physics /ˈfɪzɪks/ NOUN, NO PLURAL the scientific study of natural forces, for example, heat, light, sound and electricity (**física**)

physiological /ˌfɪzɪəˈlɒdʒɪkəl/ ADJECTIVE to do with the way the bodies of living things work □ *They are attempting to study the physiological effects of vitamins.* (**fisiológico**)

physiology /ˌfɪzɪˈɒlədʒɪ/ NOUN, NO PLURAL
1 the scientific study of the bodies of living things (**fisiologia**)
2 the way in which the body of a particular animal or plant works □ *He is studying the physiology of sharks.* (**fisiologia**)

physiotherapist /ˌfɪzɪəʊˈθerəpɪst/ NOUN [plural **physiotherapists**] someone whose job is to give people physiotherapy (**fisioterapeuta**)
- **physiotherapy** /ˌfɪzɪəʊˈθerəpɪ/ NOUN, NO PLURAL the treatment of injuries and diseases by moving parts of the body (**fisioterapia**)

physique /fɪˈziːk/ NOUN [plural **physiques**] the shape and size of someone's body □ *He has a slim physique.* (**físico**)

pi /paɪ/ NOUN, NO PLURAL a number that is used to show the relationship between the distance around a circle and the distance across it. A maths word. (**a letra grega pi**)

pianist /ˈpɪənɪst/ NOUN [plural **pianists**] someone who plays the piano □ *a concert pianist* (**pianista**)

piano /pɪˈænəʊ/ NOUN [plural **pianos**] a musical instrument that you play by pressing the black and white keys on a long keyboard (**piano**)

piccolo /ˈpɪkələʊ/ NOUN [plural **piccolos**] a type of small flute (= a musical instrument that you blow into) with a high sound (**flautim**)

pick /pɪk/ ▶ VERB [**picks, picking, picked**]
1 to choose a person or thing from a group □ *Jones has been picked for the England team.* □ *Pick any card from the pack.* (**escolher**)

picket | 585 | picture

2 to take fruit, flowers or vegetables from the plant or tree they are growing on □ *The children picked a bunch of wild flowers for their mum.* □ *I picked a few strawberries for tea.* (**colher**)

3 to remove a small piece of something, using your finger and thumb □ *She carefully picked the fluff off her jacket.* (**pegar com os dedos**)

4 pick an argument/a fight to deliberately start an argument or a fight with someone (**arranjar briga**)

5 pick someone's pocket to steal something from someone's pocket (**bater carteira**)

6 pick a lock to use a piece of wire to open a lock (**arrombar um cofre**)

◆ PHRASAL VERBS **pick on someone** to treat one particular person unkindly or unfairly □ *Please stop picking on your brother.* (**provocar**) **pick up** to increase or improve □ *Sales have picked up since summer.* (**melhorar**) **pick someone/something up** to go and collect someone or something from somewhere □ *Could you pick me up at the airport tomorrow?* □ *I need to pick up my dry cleaning.* (**ir e buscar**) **pick something up** 1 to lift something □ *She picked up the phone and started to dial.* □ *They asked us to pick up the litter.* (**pegar**) 2 to learn something by watching or listening instead of having lessons □ *I just picked the language up while I was living in Mexico.* (**aprender naturalmente, captar**) 3 to find or get something □ *We're hoping to pick up some bargains in the sales.* □ *I picked up a tummy bug on holiday.* (**pegar, conseguir**)

▶ NOUN [plural **picks**]

1 have/take your pick to choose what you want from a group □ *You can take your pick from a wide range of cheeses.* (**faça uma escolha**)

2 the pick of something the best in a group □ *See page 29 for the pick of this season's new styles.* (**item(ns) selecionado(s)**)

3 a tool with a wooden handle and curved metal end for breaking hard ground (**picareta**)

picket /ˈpɪkɪt/ ▶ VERB [**pickets, picketing, picketed**] to stand outside a place, usually a place of work, to try to stop other people going in, as a way of showing your anger about something □ *Striking postmen picketed outside the sorting office.* (**fazer piquete**)

▶ NOUN [plural **pickets**] a group of people who are picketing □ *Unions organized a picket in front of the factory.* (**piquete**)

pickle /ˈpɪkəl/ ▶ NOUN [plural **pickles**] food made from fruit or vegetables that are put in vinegar (= liquid with a sour taste) or water with salt so that they can be kept for a long time □ *We had a cheese and pickle sandwich.* (**picles**)

▶ VERB [**pickles, pickling, pickled**] to put fruit, vegetables or meat in vinegar or water with salt to make them last for a long time □ *We use these onions for pickling.* (**pôr em conserva**)

• **pickled** /ˈpɪkəld/ ADJECTIVE kept in vinegar or water with salt □ *pickled herrings* (**em conserva**)

pickpocket /ˈpɪkpɒkɪt/ NOUN [plural **pickpockets**] a criminal who steals things from people's pockets or bags (**batedor de carteira**)

picky /ˈpɪki/ ADJECTIVE [**pickier, pickiest**] difficult to please and only liking a few things. An informal word (**exigente**) 🔁 *Our first child was a really picky eater.* (**comedor exigente**)

picnic /ˈpɪknɪk/ ▶ NOUN [plural **picnics**] a meal that you take with you to eat outdoors (**piquenique**) 🔁 *We had a picnic on the beach.* (**fizemos um piquenique**) 🔁 *There's a beautiful picnic area in the forest.* (**área para piquenique**)

> Note that you **have** a picnic. You do not 'make' a picnic:
> ✓ We had a picnic in the park.
> ✗ We made a picnic in the park.

▶ VERB [**picnics, picnicking, picnicked**] to have a picnic (**fazer piquenique**)

• **picnicker** /ˈpɪknɪkə(r)/ NOUN [plural **picnickers**] someone who is having a picnic (**aquele que faz piquenique**)

pictogram /ˈpɪktəɡræm/ NOUN [plural **pictograms**] a diagram where amounts are represented by simple pictures. A maths word. (**pictograma**)

pictorial /pɪkˈtɔːriəl/ ADJECTIVE to do with pictures or using pictures to show something □ *a pictorial encyclopaedia* (**ilustrado**)

picture /ˈpɪktʃə(r)/ ▶ NOUN [plural **pictures**]

1 a painting, drawing or photograph □ *The walls were covered with pictures of her family.* (**pintura, desenho ou retrato**) 🔁 *Draw a picture of your house.* (**faça um desenho**) 🔁 *Can I take a picture* (= take a photograph) *of your garden?* (**tire uma foto**)

2 an idea or description of what something or someone is like □ *Police psychologists have built up a picture of a likely suspect.* □ *He had a picture in his mind of what he wanted to do.* □ *The report provides an accurate picture of services for the disabled.* (**descrição, quadro, retrato**)

3 the big/bigger/wider picture the whole situation, not just one part of it □ *I know that job losses are hard to accept, but we have to look at the bigger picture.* (**contexto geral, cenário completo**)

4 an image on a screen □ *The picture is rather poor on TVs in this area.* (**imagem**)

5 the pictures an old-fashioned word for the cinema □ *We went to the pictures last night.* (**cinema**)

6 a film □ *'Titanic' won the award for best picture.* (**filme**)

◆ IDIOM **keep/put someone in the picture** to make sure someone knows what is happening □ *There*

have been lots of changes in the organization – I'll put you in the picture over lunch. (colocar a par da situação)
▶ VERB [pictures, picturing, pictured]
1 to form an image of something in your mind □ *I just couldn't picture my mother as a young girl.* (imaginar)
2 to show someone in a picture □ *Angelina is pictured here with her father.* (identificar alguém em uma fotografia)

picture messaging /ˈpɪktʃə ˌmesɪdʒɪŋ/ NOUN, NO PLURAL when you send and receive pictures on a mobile phone (mandar mensagens com imagens)

picturesque /ˌpɪktʃəˈresk/ ADJECTIVE a picturesque place is attractive to look at □ *a picturesque old castle* (pitoresco)

pie /paɪ/ NOUN [plural **pies**] food such as meat, vegetables or fruit, baked in a covering of pastry □ *apple pie and custard* □ *chicken and mushroom pie* (torta)

piece /piːs/ NOUN [plural **pieces**]
1 an amount or example of something of a particular type □ *a piece of wood* □ *Use a fresh piece of paper for each answer.* □ *Let me give you a piece of advice.* (pedaço, fragmento)
2 one of the parts that join together to make a particular thing □ *a jigsaw with 300 pieces* □ *Cut the pizza into eight pieces.* (peça, pedaço) ▣ *He took the clock to pieces to repair it.* (desmontou) ▣ *I just touched the stool and it fell to pieces.* (caiu em pedaços)
3 a single story, report, piece of music etc. □ *There's a short piece in the paper about our company.* □ *They played one of Schubert's pieces for violin and piano.* (peça, nota)
4 one of the objects you move in games like chess (peça)
5 a coin of a particular value □ *a 50p piece* (moeda)
♦ IDIOMS **a piece of cake** something that is a piece of cake is very easy to do □ *The driving test should be a piece of cake for you.* (moleza, muito fácil) **give someone a piece of your mind** to speak angrily to someone because of something they have done (dar bronca) **go to pieces** to be unable to work normally or think clearly because you are in a very difficult situation □ *I just went to pieces after my husband left me.* (ficar em pedaços)
♦ PHRASAL VERB [pieces, piecing, pieced] **piece something together** to discover the truth about something by putting together all the separate pieces of information you have □ *Forensic experts have pieced together the last moments of her life.* (reconstituir)

piecemeal /ˈpiːsmiːl/ ADJECTIVE done a little at a time and in no particular order □ *The party was criticized for having a piecemeal approach to policy making.* (pouco a pouco, por partes)

pier /pɪə(r)/ NOUN [plural **piers**] a long wooden or metal structure built out over the sea that people can walk along (cais)

pierce /pɪəs/ VERB [pierces, piercing, pierced]
1 if a sharp object pierces something, it makes a hole in it (perfurar) ▣ *I've just had my ears pierced.* (furei as orelhas)
2 if light or sound pierces something, it can be seen or heard through it □ *A shaft of sunlight managed to pierce the clouds.* (trespassar)
• **piercing** /ˈpɪəsɪŋ/ ADJECTIVE
1 very strong, loud or unpleasant □ *A piercing wind was blowing off the sea.* □ *a piercing scream* (penetrante)
2 seeming to know what you are thinking □ *The detective gave her a piercing look.* (penetrante)

pig /pɪg/ NOUN [plural **pigs**] a farm animal with a fat body, small eyes and a curly tail, kept for meat (porco)

pigeon /ˈpɪdʒɪn/ NOUN [plural **pigeons**] a grey bird that is often seen in towns or kept for racing (pombo)

pigeon-hole /ˈpɪdʒɪnhəʊl/ ▶ NOUN [plural **pigeon-holes**] one of a series of open boxes attached to a wall, used to put people's letters in (caixa de correio)
▶ VERB [pigeon-holes, pigeon-holing, pigeon-holed] to judge what type of person someone is without knowing much about them

piggyback /ˈpɪgibæk/ NOUN [plural **piggybacks**] a way of carrying someone on your back with your arms supporting their legs (passeio nos ombros de alguém) ▣ *I gave Katie a piggyback home.*

pig-headed /ˌpɪgˈhedɪd/ ADJECTIVE unwilling to change your opinions even if it is obvious that you are wrong (cabeçudo, teimoso)

piglet /ˈpɪglɪt/ NOUN [plural **piglets**] a baby pig (leitão, porquinho)

pigment /ˈpɪgmənt/ NOUN [plural **pigments**] a substance that gives something a colour □ *He used natural pigments in his paints.* (pigmento)

pigsty /ˈpɪgstaɪ/ NOUN [plural **pigsties**]
1 a small building where pigs are kept (chiqueiro)
2 an informal word for a dirty or very untidy place □ *Your room's a complete pigsty.* (chiqueiro, lugar sujo)

pigtail /ˈpɪgteɪl/ NOUN [plural **pigtails**] a piece of hair that has been plaited (= had three pieces twisted together) (tranças, maria-chiquinha)

pike /paɪk/ NOUN [plural **pike** or **pikes**] a large fish that lives in lakes or rivers and can be eaten (lúcio)

Pilates /pɪˈlɑːteɪz/ NOUN, NO PLURAL a way of exercising in which you stretch your body and make your muscles stronger (pilates)

pile

pile /paɪl/ ▶ NOUN [plural **piles**]
1 a number of things one on top of the other □ *a pile of leaves* □ *Dirty dishes were stacked in piles around the room.* (**pilha**)
2 piles of something an informal phrase meaning a lot of something □ *I've got piles of work to do.* (**pilha(s) de, monte(s) de**)
▶ VERB [**piles, piling, piled**] to put things on top of each other in a pile □ *They pile all the chairs against the wall.* (**empilhar**)
◆ PHRASAL VERB **pile up** to increase in amount □ *Work has started to pile up in the office.* (**amontoar-se**)

pile-up /'paɪlʌp/ NOUN [plural **pile-ups**] when several vehicles crash into each other □ *Two people were killed in a pile-up involving six vehicles.* (**engavetamento**)

pilfer /'pɪlfə(r)/ VERB [**pilfers, pilfering, pilfered**] to steal things which are not worth much money □ *Everyone pilfers the occasional envelope from work.* (**roubar, furtar**)

pilgrim /'pɪlgrɪm/ NOUN [plural **pilgrims**] a person who is travelling to a holy place (**peregrino**)

• **pilgrimage** /'pɪlgrɪmɪdʒ/ NOUN [plural **pilgrimages**] a journey to a holy place □ *They went on a pilgrimage to Mecca* (**peregrinação**)

pill /pɪl/ NOUN [plural **pills**] a small piece of solid medicine that you swallow □ *antihistamine pills* (**pílula**)

pillage /'pɪlɪdʒ/ ▶ VERB [**pillages, pillaging, pillaged**] to steal things from a place during a war (**saquear**)
▶ NOUN, NO PLURAL stealing things from a place during a war (**produto de saque, saqueado**)

pillar /'pɪlə(r)/ NOUN [plural **pillars**] a tall, strong structure, usually made of stone, used to support something □ *The statue is on top of a stone pillar.* (**pilar**)

pillow /'pɪləʊ/ NOUN [plural **pillows**] a bag full of feathers or other soft material that you rest your head on when you are in bed (**travesseiro**)

pillowcase /'pɪləʊkeɪs/ or **pillowslip** /'pɪləʊslɪp/ NOUN [plural **pillowcases** or **pillowslips**] a cover for a pillow (**fronha**)

pilot /'paɪlət/ ▶ NOUN [plural **pilots**]
1 someone who flies a plane or other aircraft □ *an airline pilot* □ *a pilot's licence* (**piloto**)
2 a single television programme that is made and shown to find out if people would watch a whole series (**piloto, programa-teste**)
▶ VERB [**pilots, piloting, piloted**]
1 to fly a plane or other aircraft (**pilotar**)
2 to arrange for a small group of people to try a new product in order to find out if it will be successful □ *The software is being piloted in a major supermarket.* (**teste de aceitação de produto**)

pine

pimple /'pɪmpəl/ NOUN [plural **pimples**] a small pink lump on your skin (**espinha**)

PIN /pɪn/ ABBREVIATION personal identification number; a secret number that you press on a machine in order to use a bank card □ *I forgot my PIN.* (**abrev. número de identificação pessoal, senha**)

pin /pɪn/ ▶ NOUN [plural **pins**]
1 a very thin, pointed piece of metal used for holding together pieces of cloth when you are sewing (**alfinete**)
2 a thin piece of metal or wood, used for holding things together □ *He's had a pin in his leg since the accident.* (**pino**)
▶ VERB [**pins, pinning, pinned**]
1 to fasten something in place with a pin □ *She pinned the flower to her dress.* (**prender com alfinete**)
2 to hold someone somewhere firmly so that they cannot move □ *The policemen pinned him against the wall.* (**prender**)
◆ PHRASAL VERB **pin someone down**
1 to make someone decide about something □ *I need to pin her down about a date for the meeting.* (**obrigar a uma definição**)
2 to hold someone on the ground so that they cannot move (**deixar preso no chão**)

pinafore /'pɪnəfɔː(r)/ NOUN [plural **pinafores**] a loose dress with no sleeves that you wear over a shirt (**salopete, avental**)

pincer /'pɪnsə(r)/ NOUN [plural **pincers**] one of the strong front legs of some sea animals, used for holding things (**pinça**)

pinch /pɪntʃ/ ▶ VERB [**pinches, pinching, pinched**]
1 to press someone's skin or flesh tightly between your thumb and finger, especially in order to hurt them □ *Tom pinched me, Mum!* (**beliscar**)
2 if a shoe or piece of clothing pinches, it hurts you because it is too small or tight □ *This jacket pinches a little under the arms.* (**apertar**)
3 an informal word that means to steal something □ *Have you pinched my magazine?* (**roubar**)
▶ NOUN [plural **pinches**]
1 a small amount of something that you pick up between your finger and thumb (**pitada**) 🔅 *Add a pinch of salt.* (**pitada de sal**)
2 when you pinch someone □ *She gave him a pinch on the arm.* (**beliscão**)
◆ IDIOM **feel the pinch** to not have enough money □ *Consumers are beginning to feel the pinch as prices rise.* (**apertar-se financeiramente**)

• **pinched** /pɪntʃt/ ADJECTIVE if someone's face is pinched, it looks thin and pale because they are ill or cold

pine¹ /paɪn/ NOUN [plural **pines**]
1 a tall tree with needles (= thin pointed leaves) (**pinheiro**)

2 no plural the light coloured wood of a pine tree (pinho)

pine² /paɪn/ VERB [pines, pining, pined] to feel sad, usually because you are not with a person that you love (ter saudades)

pineapple /ˈpaɪnæpəl/ NOUN [plural pineapples] a large fruit with sweet yellow flesh and a thick brown skin with sharp points on it □ pineapple juice (abacaxi)

ping /pɪŋ/ ▶ VERB [pings, pinging, pinged] to make a short high noise like a small hard object hitting against metal □ Did you hear the microwave ping? (tinir)
▶ NOUN [plural pings] a pinging noise □ an electronic ping (tinido)

pink /pɪŋk/ ▶ ADJECTIVE having the colour you get if you mix red and white □ She wore a pink dress. □ His cheeks were pink from running. (rosa)
▶ NOUN, NO PLURAL the colour you get if you mix red and white (cor-de-rosa)

pinnacle /ˈpɪnəkəl/ NOUN [plural pinnacles]
1 the time in someone's life when they are most successful □ Playing King Lear was the pinnacle of his acting career. (apogeu, auge)
2 a high pointed rock or mountain (pico)

pinpoint /ˈpɪnpɔɪnt/ VERB [pinpoints, pinpointing, pinpointed]
1 to find out exactly what something is □ Doctors were unable to pinpoint the cause of death. (indicar com precisão)
2 to find out exactly where something is □ With this system police can instantly pinpoint the location of a mobile phone. (localizar)

pins and needles /ˌpɪnz ən ˈniːdəlz/ NOUN, NO PLURAL a feeling of sharp little pains in a part of your body after you have been in the same position for too long (formigamento)

pint /paɪnt/ NOUN [plural pints] a unit for measuring liquid, equal to 20 fluid ounces (pinta = unidade de medida para líquidos, variável de acordo com o país) □ a pint of milk/beer (uma pinta de leite/cerveja)

pioneer /ˌpaɪəˈnɪə(r)/ ▶ NOUN [plural pioneers]
1 one of the first people to develop a new idea, skill or method □ Charles Babbage was one of the pioneers of computer technology. (pioneiro)
2 one of the first people to go to a new country to live and work there □ the American pioneers (pioneiro)
▶ VERB [pioneers, pioneering, pioneered] to be one of the first people to do or make something □ The hospital is pioneering new surgical techniques. (ser o pioneiro de)

pious /ˈpaɪəs/ ADJECTIVE following religious rules very carefully in your life (piedoso)

pip /pɪp/ NOUN [plural pips] a small seed in a fruit such as an apple or lemon (semente)

pipe /paɪp/ ▶ NOUN [plural pipes]
1 a metal or plastic tube through which water or gas can flow (cano) □ A pipe had burst and there was water everywhere. (um cano rompeu)
2 a tube with a hollow bowl at one end used for smoking tobacco (cachimbo) □ Grandpa used to smoke a pipe. (fumar um cachimbo)
3 a musical instrument which is a tube or many tubes stuck together that you play by blowing through (flauta)
▶ VERB [pipes, piping, piped] to carry liquid or gas from one place to another through pipes □ Water is piped from the reservoir to the nearby cities. (canalizar)
◆ PHRASAL VERB **pipe up** to suddenly say something after you have been quiet for a time (falar de uma vez, desembuchar)

pipeline /ˈpaɪplaɪn/ NOUN [plural pipelines] a long pipe that crosses the land or sea and carries oil or gas (duto (oleoduto, aqueduto))
◆ IDIOM **in the pipeline** being planned or organized, or about to happen □ Further job losses are in the pipeline. (estar prestes a ser implementado)

pipette /pɪˈpet/ NOUN [plural pipettes] a small, glass tube used by scientists for sucking up small amounts of liquid. A chemistry word. (pipeta)

piping hot /ˌpaɪpɪŋ ˈhɒt/ ADJECTIVE food or drink that is piping hot is very hot □ She brought me a bowl of piping hot soup. (escaldante)

piracy /ˈpaɪrəsi/ NOUN, NO PLURAL
1 the illegal copying and selling of things such as DVDs, books and computer software (pirataria)
2 stealing things from ships while they are at sea (pirataria)

• **pirate** /ˈpaɪrət/ ▶ NOUN [plural pirates]
1 someone who steals things from ships while they are at sea □ As a boy, he loved stories about pirates and smugglers. (pirata)
2 someone who makes and sells illegal copies of things such as DVDs, books and computer software (pirata, comerciante ilegal)
▶ ADJECTIVE illegally copied □ pirate DVDs (copiado ilegalmente)

pistol /ˈpɪstəl/ NOUN [plural pistols] a small gun that is held in one hand (pistola)

piston /ˈpɪstən/ NOUN [plural pistons] a round piece of metal that fits inside a tube in an engine and moves up and down to produce power (pistão)

pit /pɪt/ NOUN [plural pits]
1 a large, deep hole dug in the ground □ The dead animals were buried in a pit. (cova)
2 a deep mine, especially a coal mine □ His father and grandfather had both worked at the pit. (poço de mina, mina)
3 **the pits** the place at the side of a race track where the cars stop to get fuel or have their tyres changed (box)

pitch

◆ PHRASAL VERB [**pits, pitting, pitted**] **pit someone against someone** to make two people or teams fight or compete with each other □ *The semi-final pits Wigan against Hull.* (**fazer com que pessoas ou times se enfrentem, colocar um contra outro**)
▶ go to **pit your wits against someone**

pitch /pɪtʃ/ ▶ NOUN [*plural* **pitches**]
1 an area of ground, often with lines marked on it, where people play games like football, rugby or cricket □ *a football pitch* (**campo**)
2 the level of activity or excitement ▣ *The excitement reached fever pitch in the last five minutes of the game.* (**grau de intensidade**)
3 when you try to persuade someone to buy something ▣ *It was the usual sales pitch.* (**conversa de vendedor**)
4 how high or low a sound is (**volume de som**)
▶ VERB [**pitches, pitching, pitched**]
1 to create something for people of a particular age, level of understanding, etc. □ *The talk was pitched just right for the audience.* (**adequar algo a determinado grupo**)
2 to make a sound at a particular level □ *The next song was pitched very high.* (**executar um som em tom específico**)
3 to throw or fall suddenly in a particular direction □ *The boat rocked violently and Joe pitched forward into the lake.* (**capotar, cair de repente**)
4 pitch a tent to put up a tent so that it is ready to use (**armar uma barraca**)
5 in baseball, to be the player who throws the ball at the person with the stick (**atirar, cair**)
◆ PHRASAL VERB **pitch in** to work with other people on something □ *We can get the job done if we all pitch in.* (**colaborar**)

pitch-black /ˌpɪtʃˈblæk/ *or* **pitch-dark** /ˌpɪtʃˈdɑːk/ ADJECTIVE very dark □ *It was pitch-dark in the forest.* (**preto como breu**)

pitcher /ˈpɪtʃə(r)/ NOUN [*plural* **pitchers**]
1 in baseball, the player who throws the ball at the person with the stick (**lançador**)
2 the US word for **jug** (**jarro**)

pitfall /ˈpɪtfɔːl/ NOUN [*plural* **pitfalls**] a difficulty or danger that a particular action might cause □ *You should be aware of the pitfalls of buying a secondhand car.* (**armadilha, cilada**)

pitiful /ˈpɪtɪfʊl/ ADJECTIVE
1 very bad □ *It was a pitiful performance by the national team.* (**lamentável**)
2 making you feel sad □ *The dog – thin and dirty after weeks of neglect – was a pitiful sight.* (**entristecedor**)

pitta bread /ˈpɪtə ˌbred/ NOUN [*plural* **pitta breads**] a type of flat bread originally from the Middle East (**pão sírio**)

pittance /ˈpɪtəns/ NOUN, NO PLURAL a very small amount of money □ *She works so hard and gets paid a pittance.* (**ninharia**)

pity

pity /ˈpɪti/ ▶ NOUN, NO PLURAL
1 sadness you feel for other people who are suffering or in trouble □ *She felt a wave of pity for the poor old man, abandoned by his family.* (**pena**)
2 it's a pity... used for saying that you feel sorry or disappointed about a situation □ *It's a pity that John couldn't come.* (**é uma pena**)
3 take pity on someone to feel so sorry for someone that you help them □ *Mark took pity on me and gave me a lift home.* (**ficar com pena de alguém**)
▶ VERB [**pities, pitying, pitied**] to feel pity for someone □ *I really pity her, having a mother like that.* (**sentir pena**)

pivot /ˈpɪvət/ ▶ NOUN [*plural* **pivots**]
1 a pin or central point on which something balances and turns (**eixo, centro**)
2 the most important part of something on which everything else is based □ *These policies are the pivot of the government's strategy.* (**pivô**)
▶ VERB [**pivots, pivoting, pivoted**] to turn while balancing on a central point (**girar**)

pixel /ˈpɪksəl/ NOUN [*plural* **pixels**] one of the very small parts that form pictures on a computer or television screen (**pixel**)

pixie /ˈpɪksi/ NOUN [*plural* **pixies**] in stories, a creature like a small man with pointed ears who can do magic (**duende ou elfo**)

pizza /ˈpiːtsə/ NOUN [*plural* **pizzas**] a flat round piece of bread with cheese, vegetables or meat on top that is baked in an oven (**pizza**) □ *a mushroom pizza* ▣ *Would you like another slice of pizza?* (**fatia de pizza**)

placard /ˈplækɑːd/ NOUN [*plural* **placards**] a large sign with a message on it that someone carries in a public place, often to show that they disagree with something □ *Students holding placards marched through the town.* (**cartaz**)

placate /pləˈkeɪt/ VERB [**placates, placating, placated**] to say or do things to make someone less angry or offended (**aplacar, apaziguar**)

place

place /pleɪs/ ▶ NOUN [*plural* **places**]
1 a particular area, position, town, building, etc. □ *We rented a place by the sea.* □ *I imagine Beijing is a very interesting place.* □ *She broke her arm in three places.* (**lugar**) ▣ *Make sure you keep the money in a safe place.* (**lugar seguro**) ▣ *Smoking is not allowed in public places.* (**lugares públicos**)
2 the position where something should be, or where something or someone usually is □ *Put the books back in their proper place on the shelf.* (**lugar**)
3 take place to happen □ *The election is due to take place next month.* □ *The wedding took place in secret.* (**acontecer**)

4 all over the place (a) in or to many different places □ *You see lovely buildings all over the place.* □ *We travelled all over the place.* (**em todos os lugares**) (b) in an untidy state □ *She left her books all over the place.* (**bagunçado**)
5 the opportunity to be in a team, go on a course, take part in a competition, etc. □ *She has a place to study English at Cambridge University.* (**lugar**) 🔁 *That win has secured Liverpool a place in the final.* (**assegurou o lugar**)
6 a seat on a public vehicle or in a public building □ *Please go back to your places and sit down.* (**lugar**) 🔁 *Would you save my place while I get a coffee?* (**guardar meu lugar**)
7 a position in a queue (= line of people waiting) (**lugar**) 🔁 *Now I've lost my place in the queue.* (**perdi meu lugar**)
8 in first/third/last, etc. place used to show someone's position at the end of a race or competition (**colocação, lugar**)
9 in place (a) in the correct position □ *Make sure the safety harness is in place.* (b) if rules, systems, etc. are in place, they exist and can be used □ *They have put measures in place to combat theft.* (**no lugar**)
10 in place of someone/something instead of someone/something □ *Pat is here today, in place of Marc, who is ill.* (**no lugar de**)
11 out of place (a) not suitable for or comfortable in a particular situation □ *I felt a bit out of place wearing jeans at such a glamorous party.* (**sentir-se deslocado**) (b) not in the correct position □ *She never has a hair out of place.* (**fora do lugar**)

◆ IDIOMS **fall/fit into place**
1 if things fall into place, you suddenly understand them □ *When I learned that Zoe was his daughter, things fell into place.* (**fazer sentido**)
2 to start to happen in a successful way □ *After months of trying to organize the trip, everything is starting to fall into place.* (**começar a dar certo**)
put someone in their place to make someone aware that they are not as important or clever as they think they are (**colocar alguém em seu devido lugar**)

▶ VERB [**places, placing, placed**]
1 to put something somewhere, usually with care □ *He placed his hand on her shoulder.* □ *She placed a flower on the grave.* (**colocar**)
2 to cause someone or something to be in a particular situation or state □ *He had placed me in a very awkward spot by promising that I would go to the party.* □ *Money worries placed a great strain on their marriage.* □ *The government has placed restrictions on public pay rises.* (**colocar**)
3 to have a particular opinion about something or someone □ *He placed a lot of faith in his staff.* □ *She placed great importance on personal morality.* (**colocar**)
4 if you place an advertisement somewhere, you arrange for it to be shown there (**colocar**)
5 place a call to make a telephone call □ *At 6.15 he placed a call to the emergency services.* (**telefonar**)

placebo /pləˈsiːbəʊ/ NOUN [*plural* **placebos**] a substance with no effect on the body, used in testing medicines or given to people who think they need medicine but do not (**placebo**)

placement /ˈpleɪsmənt/ NOUN [*plural* **placements**] a temporary job that allows someone to get experience of working □ *I got a work placement in a school last summer.* (**colocação**)

placenta /pləˈsentə/ NOUN [*plural* **placentas**] the organ inside the mother that provides food for a growing baby. A biology word. (**placenta**)

place value /ˈpleɪs ˌvæljuː/ NOUN, NO PLURAL the value of a number decided by its position, for example if it is a one, a ten, a hundred, etc. A maths word. (**valor posicional**)

placid /ˈplæsɪd/ ADJECTIVE gentle and calm □ *a placid baby* (**plácido, calmo**)

plague /pleɪɡ/ ▶ NOUN [*plural* **plagues**]
1 a serious disease that spreads very quickly and causes many people to die □ *The plague struck London in the 17th century.* (**epidemia**)
2 a large number of insects or other animals that suddenly appear and cause damage or problems □ *a plague of red ants* (**praga, peste**)
▶ VERB [**plagues, plaguing, plagued**] to cause someone a lot of pain or trouble for a long time □ *The squad has been plagued by injuries this season.* (**atormentar**)

plaice /pleɪs/ NOUN [*plural* **plaice**] a type of flat sea fish that people eat (**solha**)

plain /pleɪn/ ▶ ADJECTIVE [**plainer, plainest**]
1 obvious (**evidente**) 🔁 *She made it quite plain that she didn't like me.* (**deixou evidente**)
2 in one colour or without any decoration or pattern □ *a plain white tablecloth* (**liso**)
3 simple or ordinary □ *He likes fairly plain cooking.* (**comum**)
4 a plain person is not attractive (**comum**)
▶ NOUN [*plural* **plains**] a large flat area of land (**planície**)
▶ ADVERB completely □ *Leaving her kids alone in the house was just plain wrong.* (**completamente**)

plait /plæt/ ▶ NOUN [*plural* **plaits**] a piece of hair that is formed by twisting three thinner pieces of hair over and under each other □ *She wears her hair in plaits.* (**trança**)
▶ VERB [**plaits, plaiting, plaited**] to make a plait

plan /plæn/ ▶ VERB [**plans, planning, planned**]
1 to decide what you are going to do and how you are going to do it □ *We spent months planning the wedding.* □ *Always plan your essay before you start writing.* (**planejar**)
2 to hope and expect to do something in the future □ **+ to do something** *Natasha is planning to go to university next year.* □ **+ on doing**

plane — 591 — **plate**

something They're planning on taking a year off to travel. (planejar)
3 to draw a design of something such as a building □ We got a designer in to plan the garden. (projetar)
▶ NOUN [*plural* plans]
1 an idea or arrangement for something you hope to do in the future □ What are your plans for the future? (plano) □ + *to do something* We have no plans to move house at the moment. ▣ There's been a change of plan. We're going out on Friday instead. (uma mudança de plano) ▣ If everything goes according to plan, she'll arrive at 11. (sai como planejado)
2 a drawing that shows how a building, town, machine, etc. will be built (planta) ▣ The council is drawing up plans to redevelop the town centre.

plane /pleɪn/ ▶ NOUN [*plural* planes]
1 an aeroplane (avião)
2 a flat or level surface □ A cube has six planes. (plano)
3 a tool with a sharp blade in the bottom, used for making a wooden surface smooth (cepilho, desbastador)
▶ VERB [planes, planing, planed] to make wood smooth and level using a plane (desbastar)

planet /ˈplænɪt/ NOUN [*plural* planets] any of the large objects in space that move around a sun or star □ the planet Venus (planeta)

planetarium /ˌplænɪˈteərɪəm/ NOUN [*plural* planetariums] a building with a curved ceiling where you can look at lights that represent the positions of the stars and planets (planetário)

plank /plæŋk/ NOUN [*plural* planks] a long flat piece of wood (tábua)

planning /ˈplænɪŋ/ NOUN, NO PLURAL
1 the process of deciding what you are going to do and how you are going to do it □ The festival has taken weeks of planning. (planejamento)
2 control over what people build in towns and other areas □ town planning (planejamento urbano)

plant /plɑːnt/ ▶ NOUN [*plural* plants]
1 any living thing that grows from the ground and has a stem, roots and leaves □ Young plants must be protected from frost. □ a tobacco plant (planta)
2 a factory or industrial building □ a power plant (fábrica)
▶ VERB [plants, planting, planted]
1 to put seeds or plants in soil so that they grow □ They're planting trees along the roadside. (plantar)
2 to secretly put something illegal or stolen in a place that will make someone appear guilty of a crime □ Pete claims the drugs were planted on him. (plantar uma prova, forjar uma prova para incriminar alguém)

3 plant a bomb to hide a bomb somewhere (esconder uma bomba)
4 to put something firmly in a place or position □ He planted his feet on either side of the rope and pulled. (firmar)

• **plantation** /plænˈteɪʃən/ NOUN [*plural* plantations]
1 a large area of land where tea, cotton, coffee, etc. is grown □ a sugar plantation (plantação, plantio)
2 an area of land where trees are grown to be used as wood (plantação)

plaque /plɑːk/ NOUN [*plural* plaques]
1 a metal plate with writing on it, fixed to a wall in memory of a famous person or event (placa)
2 *no plural* a substance that forms on teeth and can cause tooth decay (placa)

plasma /ˈplæzmə/ NOUN, NO PLURAL the clear liquid part of blood. A biology word. (plasma)

plasma screen /ˈplæzmə ˌskriːn/ NOUN [*plural* plasma screens] a television screen that is made up of two sheets of glass with special gases between them and produces very clear pictures (tela de plasma)

plaster /ˈplɑːstə(r)/ ▶ NOUN [*plural* plasters]
1 a piece of soft sticky cloth that you put over a cut to keep it clean (emplastro, adesivo)
2 *no plural* a substance that is put on walls and dries to form a hard, smooth surface (gesso)
3 in plaster if your arm, leg etc. is in plaster, it has a hard cover around it to protect a broken bone (engessado)
▶ VERB [plasters, plastering, plastered]
1 to cover a lot of a surface with one thing or many things □ We plastered ourselves in sun cream before going out. □ Her bedroom walls are plastered with posters. (lambuzar)
2 to put plaster on walls (colocar gesso na parede)

plaster cast /ˈplɑːstə ˌkɑːst/ NOUN [*plural* plaster casts] a hard cover put around a broken arm or leg to protect it while it gets better (atadura de gesso)

plastic /ˈplæstɪk/ ▶ NOUN [*plural* plastics] a light strong substance made from chemicals and used to make many different things □ toys made of plastic (plástico)
▶ ADJECTIVE made of plastic □ plastic bags (plástico)

Plasticine /ˈplæstɪsiːn/ NOUN, NO PLURAL a soft substance that children use for making small models and shapes. A trademark. (marca registrada de massa de modelar)

plastic surgery /ˌplæstɪk ˈsɜːdʒəri/ NOUN, NO PLURAL medical operations to improve someone's appearance or to repair damage to skin (cirurgia plástica)

plate /pleɪt/ NOUN [*plural* plates]
1 a flat dish for eating or serving food from □ a paper/ plastic plate □ Pass your plates. (prato)

plateau

2 a thin flat piece of metal or another hard substance □ *a steel plate* (chapa)
3 one of the large areas of rock that make up the Earth's surface. A geography word. (placa)
4 a large picture or photograph in a book □ *a colour plate* (ilustração)

plateau /ˈplætəʊ/ NOUN [plural **plateaus** or **plateaux**]
1 a wide, flat area of high land. A geography word. (planalto)
2 a period when the level of something does not change (patamar) 🔁 *Sales of computers have reached a plateau.* (alcançou o patamar)

platelet /ˈpleɪtlɪt/ NOUN [plural **platelets**] a small part of a cell in the blood that makes it go thick if you have a cut. A biology word. (plaqueta)

platform /ˈplætfɔːm/ NOUN [plural **platforms**]
1 the area next to the tracks at a railway station, where passengers get on and off trains □ *The 9:45 service to Leeds will leave from platform 4.* (plataforma)
2 a raised area of floor where performers and speakers stand so that the audience can see them (plataforma)
3 the main changes a political party promises to make if it is elected □ *He campaigned on a platform of low taxation.* (plataforma)

platinum /ˈplætɪnəm/ NOUN, NO PLURAL a very valuable silver metal that is used to make jewellery (platina)

platoon /pləˈtuːn/ NOUN [plural **platoons**] a small group of soldiers (pelotão)

platter /ˈplætə(r)/ NOUN [plural **platters**] a large plate used for serving food (travessa)

plausible /ˈplɔːzəbəl/ ADJECTIVE seeming to be reasonable and true □ *It was a plausible excuse.* (plausível)

play /pleɪ/ ▶ VERB [**plays**, **playing**, **played**]
1 to spend time enjoying yourself with games or toys □ *The children were playing in the garden.* (brincar)
2 to take part in a sport or game □ *He plays cricket on Saturdays.* □ *Luke played well in the last match.* □ *+ for He used to play for the national team.* (jogo)
3 to make music with a musical instrument, or to perform a piece of music □ *Do you play the piano?* □ *He played all the Beethoven sonatas.* (tocar instrumento)
4 if you play a CD, DVD, etc., you put it in a machine to make it produce sound or images (colocar CD, DVD etc. para tocar)
5 to act as a character in a film, play, etc. (representar) 🔁 *She plays the part of Harry's daughter.* (faz o papel de)
6 play a part in something to be involved in something □ *Money played no part in her decision.* (ter participação em)
7 play a joke/trick on someone to do something to trick someone or make them laugh (pregar uma peça em alguém)

♦ IDIOM **play safe** to not take any risks □ *I decided to play safe and cook something I'd done before.* (não arriscar)

▶ go to **play it by ear**, **play devil's advocate**

♦ PHRASAL VERBS **play about/around** to behave in a silly way □ *Stop playing about and get on with your work!* (fazer gracinhas, não levar as coisas a sério) **play along** to pretend to agree with someone, or to pretend that something is true □ *She likes to imagine she's a princess, and the rest of us just play along with her.* (concordar, cooperar, fingir, entrar no jogo) **play (around) with something** to think of ideas and ways of doing things □ *We are playing around with the idea of charging entrance fees.* (desenvolver uma ideia) **play at something** to do something in a way that is not serious □ *She only has four cows – she's just playing at farming.* (não levar a sério) **play something down** to try to make something seem less important □ *He always plays down his health problems.* (subestimar) **play up**
1 if children play up, they behave in a silly way (comportar-se mal)
2 if a machine or a piece of equipment plays up, it does not work correctly □ *Sorry, I can't hear you – my phone's playing up.* (estar com problemas)
3 if a part of your body is playing up, you are having problems with it □ *My ears are playing up again.* (estar com problemas) **play with something** to touch or move something repeatedly, usually because you are bored or nervous □ *Stop playing with your food!* (brincar com)

▶ NOUN [plural **plays**]
1 a story that is performed by actors in a theatre (peça) 🔁 *Our school is putting on a play.* (apresentando uma peça)
2 no plural the activity of taking part in a sport or game □ *Play was stopped because of the rain.* (jogo)
3 no plural the activity of enjoying yourself with games and toys □ *Young children learn best through play.* (brincadeira)

playdate /ˈpleɪdeɪt/ NOUN [plural **playdates**] an arrangement made by parents for children to play together □ *Emily and Molly have a playdate on Saturday.* (encontro para brincar)

player /ˈpleɪə(r)/ NOUN [plural **players**]
1 someone who plays a sport or game (jogador)
2 someone who plays a musical instrument (músico)
3 a machine for playing DVDs, CDs, etc. (aparelho de som, DVD, CD etc.)

playful /ˈpleɪfʊl/ ADJECTIVE
1 full of fun or wanting to play □ *a playful puppy* (brincalhão)
2 not intended to be serious □ *a playful remark* (brincalhão)

playground

playground /ˈpleɪɡraʊnd/ NOUN [plural **playgrounds**] an area, often next to a school or in a public park, where children play □ *Harry fell and hurt his knee in the playground.* (parquinho, playground)

playgroup /ˈpleɪɡruːp/ NOUN [plural **playgroups**] an organized group where very young children can go to play and learn together (grupo de recreação)

playing card /ˈpleɪɪŋ ˌkɑːd/ NOUN [plural **playing cards**] one of a set of 52 rectangular pieces of card used for playing games (carta de baralho)

playing field /ˈpleɪɪŋ ˌfiːld/ NOUN [plural **playing fields**] an area of land used for playing sports such as football □ *the school playing fields* (quadra, campo)

playmate /ˈpleɪmeɪt/ NOUN [plural **playmates**] a child who plays with another child (colega)

play-off /ˈpleɪɒf/ NOUN [plural **play-offs**] an extra game played to decide the winner from two players or teams with equal points in a competition (jogo para desempate)

playschool /ˈpleɪskuːl/ NOUN [plural **playschools**] another word for **playgroup** (jardim de infância)

playwright /ˈpleɪraɪt/ NOUN [plural **playwrights**] someone who writes plays (dramaturgo)

plc /ˌpiːelˈsiː/ ABBREVIATION public limited company; a company in the UK with shares that people can buy (sociedade anônima)

plea /pliː/ NOUN [plural **pleas**]
1 a statement that someone makes in a law court to say if they have committed a crime or not □ *a plea of guilty/not guilty* (objeção, alegação)
2 when someone asks for something in a serious and emotional way □ *I couldn't ignore this plea for help.* (apelo)

plead /pliːd/ VERB [pleads, pleading, pleaded]
1 to ask for something in a serious, emotional way because you want it very much □ *She pleaded with her boss to give her one last chance.* (suplicar)
2 to say whether you are guilty or not guilty of a crime in a law court (alegar) ▣ *He pleaded guilty to all three charges.* (declarou-se culpado)
3 plead ignorance to pretend that you did not know about something (alegar ignorância)

pleasant

pleasant /ˈplezənt/ ADJECTIVE
1 nice or enjoyable □ *We had a very pleasant evening at Sarah's.* □ *It was very pleasant, sitting out in the garden.* (agradável)
2 friendly and easy to talk to □ *Our new neighbours seem very pleasant.* (amigável, amistoso)

• **pleasantly** /ˈplezəntli/ ADVERB in a pleasant way □ *She smiled very pleasantly at us.* (agradavelmente) ▣ *I was pleasantly surprised by his attitude.* (agradavelmente surpreso)

please

please /pliːz/ ▶ EXCLAMATION
1 used as a polite way of asking for something □ *Could I have a glass of water, please?* □ *Please could you turn the music down?* □ *Would you please leave?* (por favor)
2 yes, please used as a polite way of accepting an offer □ *'Would you like another biscuit?' 'Yes, please.'* (sim, por favor)
▶ VERB [**pleases, pleasing, pleased**]
1 to make someone happy by doing what they want □ *You can't please everyone.* □ *My mother is quite hard to please.* (agradar)
2 as/anything/whatever, etc. you please in any way or at any time you want □ *You can come and go as you please.* □ *You can do whatever you please in your own home.* (como/quando quiser)
3 please yourself used to tell someone you do not care what they do (faça o que achar melhor)

• **pleased** /pliːzd/ ADJECTIVE
1 happy or satisfied with something □ + **with** *He was pleased with the way the garden looked.* □ + **at** *We were all pleased at the result.* □ + **to do something** *She looked pleased to see him.* □ *She wasn't pleased when he told her he'd lost the tickets.* (contente)
2 pleased with yourself proud of what you have done, often in an annoying way (orgulhoso)
3 (I'm) pleased to meet you something you say to be polite when you meet someone for the first time (prazer em conhecê-lo)

• **pleasing** /ˈpliːzɪŋ/ ADJECTIVE
1 making you feel happy or satisfied □ *a pleasing result* (agradável)
2 enjoyable □ *a visually pleasing design* (agradável)

• **pleasingly** /ˈpliːzɪŋli/ ADVERB in an enjoyable way □ *a pleasingly rich chocolate cake* (agradavelmente)

pleasurable /ˈpleʒərəbəl/ ADJECTIVE giving pleasure or enjoyment □ *a pleasurable sensation* (aprazível)

pleasure

pleasure /ˈpleʒə(r)/ NOUN [plural **pleasures**]
1 *no plural* a feeling of enjoyment or satisfaction (prazer) ▣ *She took pleasure in cooking.* (sentiu prazer) ▣ *It gives me great pleasure to be here today.* (me dá prazer)
2 something that you enjoy □ *He enjoys the simple pleasures of life.* (prazer) ▣ *It's a great pleasure to welcome you back.* (grande prazer)
3 *no plural* time spent enjoying yourself and not working □ *Is your trip business or pleasure?* □ *We encourage students to read for pleasure.* (lazer)
4 it's my pleasure used when someone thanks you. A formal phrase. □ *'Thank you so much for all your help.' 'It's my pleasure.'* (o prazer é meu)

pleat /pliːt/ NOUN [plural **pleats**] a fold made or sewn in a piece of cloth (dobra, prega, plissê)

• **pleated** /ˈpliːtɪd/ ADJECTIVE having folds or folded lines □ *a pleated skirt* (plissado)

plectrum /ˈplektrəm/ NOUN [plural **plectrums**] a small piece of plastic or metal used to play the strings of a guitar (palheta)

pledge /pledʒ/ ▶ NOUN [plural **pledges**] a serious promise (promessa) ▣ *The government has made a pledge to improve school food.* (fez uma promessa) □ *He has received pledges of support from all over the world.*
▶ VERB [**pledges, pledging, pledged**] to promise seriously to do or to give something □ *The prime minister pledged to increase spending.* □ *The US has pledged $6 million in aid.* (prometer)

plentiful /ˈplentɪfʊl/ ADJECTIVE existing or available in large amounts (abundante, fértil) ▣ *There was a plentiful supply of fresh fish.* (estoque abundante) □ *Food was cheap and plentiful.*

plenty /ˈplenti/ PRONOUN, ADVERB
1 a lot of something, as much as you need or more than you need □ + *of You'll have plenty of time to complete the test.* □ *Remember to drink plenty of water.* (bastante, suficiente) ▣ *There's plenty more bread in the freezer if we run out.* (mais que o suficiente)
2 **plenty big/long, etc. enough** easily big/long, etc. enough □ *The dress is plenty big enough for you.* (suficientemente grande, longo, etc.)

pliable /ˈplaɪəbəl/ ADJECTIVE easy to bend without breaking □ *The material is strong and pliable.* (maleável)

pliers /ˈplaɪəz/ PLURAL NOUN a tool used for holding and pulling small things or for cutting wire (alicate)

plight /plaɪt/ NOUN, NO PLURAL a very bad or difficult situation □ *She talked about the plight of refugees.* (situação difícil)

plinth /plɪnθ/ NOUN [plural **plinths**] a block of stone on which a statue (= model made from stone or metal) stands (plinto)

plod /plɒd/ VERB [**plods, plodding, plodded**]
1 to walk slowly with heavy steps □ *He plodded back up the hill.* (caminhar pesadamente)
2 to work slowly, especially doing a job that you find boring □ *I'm still plodding along with the project.* (labutar)

plonk /plɒŋk/ VERB [**plonks, plonking, plonked**] an informal word meaning to put something down in a careless or noisy way □ *She plonked a couple of glasses on the table.* (arriar, baixar ruidosamente)

◆ PHRASAL VERB **plonk yourself down** an informal phrase meaning to sit down somewhere in a careless way □ *He plonked himself down on the sofa and turned on the TV.* (jogar-se sobre)

plop /plɒp/ ▶ NOUN [plural **plops**] the sound of a small object dropping into water □ *The frog jumped back into the pond with a plop.* (chape)
▶ VERB [**plops, plopping, plopped**]
1 to fall or to drop making this sound (cair fazendo chape)
2 an informal word meaning to drop something or to sit somewhere carelessly □ *Jenny plopped down on an armchair.* (jogar ou jogar-se fazendo chape)

plot /plɒt/ ▶ NOUN [plural **plots**]
1 the story of a play, book or film □ *the plot of a novel* □ *The film's plot is based on a true story.* (trama)
2 a secret plan, especially to do something bad □ *an alleged plot to kidnap a soldier* (trama)
3 a piece of land to be used for a particular purpose □ *a vegetable plot* □ *a plot of land* (lote)
▶ go to **lose the plot**
▶ VERB [**plots, plotting, plotted**]
1 to plan to do something bad or illegal □ *The group are thought to be plotting more attacks.* (tramar)
2 to mark points on a map or a graph (= mathematical picture showing changes or comparing things) □ *He used a map to plot his route across the mountains.* (traçar)

plough /plaʊ/ ▶ NOUN [plural **ploughs**] a farm tool with a heavy blade which is pulled through the soil to turn the soil over (arado)
▶ VERB [**ploughs, ploughing, ploughed**] to turn over soil with a plough (arar)

◆ PHRASAL VERBS **plough into something** to hit something with force □ *The car lost control and ploughed into a group of people.* (lançar-se em)
plough something into something to spend a lot of money on something in order to improve it □ *They are ploughing more money into education.*
plough through something
1 to work slowly and with difficulty until you finish something □ *We ploughed through hundreds of documents searching for information.* (resolver)
2 to hit something with force and go through it □ *The car ploughed through a wall and into a garden.* (atravessar)

plover /ˈplʌvə(r)/ NOUN [plural **plovers**] a small bird that finds food in water (lavadeira)

ploy /plɔɪ/ NOUN [plural **ploys**] a clever plan or method to achieve something, often by tricking people □ *This is just a marketing ploy.* (estratagema)

pluck /plʌk/ VERB [**plucks, plucking, plucked**]
1 to quickly take something or someone from a place □ *Five survivors were plucked from the sea.* (arrancar)
2 to remove the feathers from a dead bird before cooking it (depenar)
3 to take hold of something and to pull it firmly so that it comes out or off □ *He plucked a leaf from the tree.* (apanhar)

◆ IDIOM **pluck up (the) courage (to do something)** to find the courage to do something difficult □ *It took me ages to pluck up the courage to talk to her.* (tomar coragem)

plug

plug /plʌg/ ▶ NOUN [plural **plugs**]
1 an object attached to a piece of electrical equipment by a wire which connects it to an electricity supply (**plugue**)
2 an object that you use for blocking a hole, especially in a bath or sink □ *a bath plug* (**tampão**)
3 when someone talks about a new book, film, etc. in public to make people interested in it □ *The interview was just a plug for his new book.* (**fazer a divulgação pessoal de um trabalho na mídia**)
◆ IDIOMS **pull the plug (on something)** to stop an activity from continuing □ *The channel announced that it is pulling the plug on the programme.* (**interromper**)
▶ VERB [**plugs, plugging, plugged**]
1 to push something into a hole to block it □ *We need to plug the leak in the boat.* (**tampar**)
2 to talk about a new film, book, etc. to make people interested in it □ *The author plugged his new book during the interview.* (**fazer a divulgação pessoal de um trabalho na mídia**) **plug a gap/hole** to provide something that is missing and needed □ *They need new players to plug the gaps left by those who went in the summer.* (**preencher a falta**)
◆ PHRASAL VERBS **plug away** to keep working or doing something for a long time. An informal phrase. □ *He plugs away in his studio every day.* (**trabalhar ou fazer uma atividade por horas a fio**) **plug something in** to connect a piece of electrical equipment to the electricity supply □ *I plugged in my laptop.* (**ligar**) **plug something into something** (**ligar algo em algum lugar**)
1 to connect one piece of electrical equipment to another □ *Plug the camera into your computer to download pictures.* (**conectar cabos/equipamentos um ao outro**)
2 to connect a piece of electrical equipment to the electricity supply □ *Don't leave your phone charger plugged into a socket when you're not using it.* (**conectar à fonte de energia**)

plughole /ˈplʌghəʊl/ NOUN [plural **plugholes**] the hole in a sink or a bath that water flows out of (**ralo da pia**)

plum /plʌm/ NOUN [plural **plums**] a soft red, purple or yellow fruit with a smooth skin and a large seed in the middle (**ameixa**)

plumage /ˈpluːmɪdʒ/ NOUN, NO PLURAL a bird's feathers □ *exotic birds with bright plumage* (**plumagem**)

plumb /plʌm/ VERB [**plumbs, plumbing, plumbed**] **plumb the depths/ plumb new depths** to reach the worst point in something □ *Relations between the countries have plumbed new depths.* (**atingir o pior nível, chegar ao fundo do poço**)
◆ PHRASAL VERB **plumb in something** to connect something such as a washing machine to a water supply (**conectar**)

plunge

• **plumber** /ˈplʌmə(r)/ NOUN [plural **plumbers**] someone whose job is to connect and repair water and gas pipes (**encanador**)
• **plumbing** /ˈplʌmɪŋ/ NOUN, NO PLURAL
1 the system of pipes that carry water and gas in a building (**encanamento**)
2 the work of a plumber (**encanação**)

plume /pluːm/ NOUN [plural **plumes**]
1 a long feather □ *ostrich plumes* (**pluma**)
2 a tall cloud of dust or smoke moving up in the air (**nuvem**) 🖼 *a plume of smoke* (**de fumaça, de poeira**)

plummet /ˈplʌmɪt/ VERB [**plummets, plummeting, plummeted**]
1 to quickly become much lower in value or amount □ *Temperatures plummeted to minus five degrees.* (**cair rapidamente**)
2 to fall straight down very fast □ *They plummeted to the ground.* (**cair verticalmente**)

plump /plʌmp/ ADJECTIVE [**plumper, plumpest**] fat or round in a pleasant way □ *She squeezed the baby's plump little legs.* (**rechonchudo**)
◆ PHRASAL VERB [**plumps, plumping, plumped**] **plump for something** an informal phrase meaning to choose something □ *I finally plumped for the green dress.* (**escolher, decidir-se por**)

plunder /ˈplʌndə(r)/ ▶ VERB [**plunders, plundering, plundered**] to steal everything valuable from a place, often causing a lot of damage □ *Buildings were set on fire and shops were plundered.* (**saquear**)
▶ NOUN, NO PLURAL
1 when someone plunders a place (**saqueador**)
2 things stolen in this way (**saque**)

plunge /plʌndʒ/c VERB [**plunges, plunging, plunged**]
1 to fall suddenly and with force □ *The bus plunged off a mountain road.* (**despencar**)
2 to quickly become much lower in value or amount □ *The share price has plunged.* □ *Temperatures plunged below freezing.* (**despencar**)
3 to jump, especially into water □ *They plunged into the cool water.* (**mergulhar, afundar**)
4 to push something, such as a knife, violently into something □ *He plunged a knife into her stomach.* (**cravar**)
◆ PHRASAL VERB **plunge something into something** to cause something to be suddenly in a particular, often bad, state □ *The violence threatens to plunge the country into civil war.* □ *The building was plunged into darkness.* (**mergulhar**)
▶ NOUN [plural **plunges**]
1 a fall □ *He survived a 20-metre plunge.* (**queda**)
2 a sudden fall in value or amount □ *a plunge in oil prices* (**queda repentina**)
◆ IDIOM **take the plunge** to do something important or difficult after considering it for a long time □ *He took the plunge and quit his job.* (**aventurar-se**)

pluperfect /ˌpluːˈpɜːfɪkt/ NOUN, NO PLURAL the tense of a verb that shows that an action finished before a particular time or event in the past, formed using had and a past participle (**mais-que-perfeito**)

plural /ˈplʊərəl/ ▶ NOUN [*plural* **plurals**] the form of a noun, pronoun or verb that you use when there is more than one of something (**plural**)
▶ ADJECTIVE in the plural form □ *a plural noun* (**plural**)

plus /plʌs/ ▶ PREPOSITION
1 added to □ *8 plus 2 is 10.* □ *He charges $50 an hour, plus travel expenses.* (**mais**)
2 as well as □ *There are six children, plus two adults.* (**mais**)
▶ ADJECTIVE
1 used to describe a measurement or temperature that is greater than zero □ *plus ten degrees centigrade* (**positivo, acima de zero**)
2 used after a number to show that the real amount may be more than that number □ *You have to be 60 plus to join the club.* (**maior de**)
▶ NOUN [*plural* **pluses**]
1 a mathematical symbol (+) showing that a number is to be added to another (**símbolo de adição**)
2 an advantage (**vantagem**) 🔲 *Being near to the beach is a big plus.* (**grande vantagem**)

plush /plʌʃ/ ADJECTIVE [**plusher, plushest**] expensive and comfortable □ *a plush hotel* □ *plush carpets* (**requintado**)

plutonium /pluːˈtəʊniəm/ NOUN, NO PLURAL a very poisonous radioactive element. A chemistry word. (**plutônio**)

ply /plaɪ/ VERB [**plies, plying, plied**]
1 a formal word meaning to travel along a particular route □ *The liners plied between England and South Africa.* (**cobrir um percurso**)
2 ply your trade to work, especially in a particular place □ *He's now plying his trade in New York.* (**exercer sua profissão**)
◆ PHRASAL VERB **ply someone with something** to keep giving someone a lot of something □ *They plied me with coffee and cake.* (**suprir alguém com alguma coisa**)

plywood /ˈplaɪwʊd/ NOUN, NO PLURAL thick board made up of thin layers of wood glued together (**madeira compensada**)

PM /ˌpiːˈem/ ABBREVIATION **prime minister** (**primeiro-ministro**)

pm or **p.m.** /ˌpiːˈem/ ABBREVIATION added after the time to show that it is in the afternoon or the evening (**abrev. inserida depois da hora: depois do meio-dia**)

pneumatic /njuːˈmætɪk/ ADJECTIVE
1 filled with air □ *pneumatic tyres* (**pneumático**)
2 worked using air pressure □ *a pneumatic drill* (**pneumático**)

pneumonia /njuːˈməʊniə/ NOUN, NO PLURAL a serious infection of the lungs which makes breathing difficult and painful (**pneumonia**)

poach /pəʊtʃ/ VERB [**poaches, poaching, poached**]
1 to cook food by heating it gently in water or another liquid □ *poached eggs* (**escaldar, cozer**)
2 to hunt and kill fish, birds or animals on someone else's land without permission (**caçar ou pescar ilegalmente**)
3 to persuade someone to leave one job or organization to join another □ *He was poached by a private company.* (**ser sondado e convencido a mudar para outra empresa**)
• **poacher** /ˈpəʊtʃə(r)/ NOUN [*plural* **poachers**] someone who poaches animals, birds or fish (**caçador/pescador ilegal**)

PO box /ˌpiːˈəʊ ˌbɒks/ NOUN [*plural* **PO boxes**] post office box; a numbered box at a post office where letters can be sent for you to collect (**caixa postal**)

pocket /ˈpɒkɪt/ ▶ NOUN [*plural* **pockets**]
1 an extra piece of cloth sewn into a piece of clothing or a bag, used for keeping small things in □ *It was in my jeans pocket.* □ *He pulled his wallet from his back pocket.* (**bolso**)
2 the amount of money you are able to spend on something □ *There are presents to suit every pocket.* (**bolso, condição financeira**)
3 a small area or group which is separate and different from others □ + **of** *pockets of mist* □ *There are still pockets of resistance in the south.* (**foco**)
4 out of pocket having lost money as the result of something □ *Nobody will be left out of pocket.* (**sem dinheiro**)
▶ VERB [**pockets, pocketing, pocketed**]
1 to steal money □ *It was said that she pocketed the proceeds.* (**roubar dinheiro**)
2 to put something in your pocket □ *He pocketed his keys.* (**guardar no bolso**)
3 to earn or to win money □ *Senior managers will pocket huge bonuses.* (**embolsar**)
▶ ADJECTIVE small enough to fit in a pocket □ *a pocket calculator* (**de bolso**)

pocketbook /ˈpɒkɪtbʊk/ NOUN [*plural* **pocketbooks**]
1 a US word for **wallet** (**carteira**)
2 a US word for **handbag** (**bolsa**)

pocket money /ˈpɒkɪt ˌmʌni/ NOUN, NO PLURAL money that parents regularly give their children to buy small things □ *They spent all their pocket money on sweets.* (**mesada**)

pod /pɒd/ NOUN [*plural* **pods**] a long narrow part that grows on plants and has seeds inside (**vagem**)

podcast /ˈpɒdkɑːst/ NOUN [*plural* **podcasts**] a recording that you get from a website and then listen to on a computer or MP3 player (= small

podgy /ˈpɒdʒi/ ADJECTIVE [podgier, podgiest] an informal word meaning slightly fat □ *podgy little hands* (rechonchudo)

podium /ˈpəʊdiəm/ NOUN [plural podiums] a small raised area that someone stands on, often to speak to a lot of people (pódio) 🔲 *The chairman took the podium (= stood on the podium) to open the conference.*

poem /ˈpəʊɪm/ NOUN [plural poems] a piece of writing using interesting language, arranged in short lines, often using words with the same sounds □ *a love poem* (poema) 🔲 *He wrote a poem for her.* (escreveu um poema)

• **poet** /ˈpəʊɪt/ NOUN [plural poets] someone who writes poems □ *He was a poet and novelist.* (poeta)

• **poetic** /pəʊˈetɪk/ ADJECTIVE
1 expressing ideas with beauty and imagination □ *a poetic account of his childhood* (poético)
2 to do with poems □ *poetic language* (poético)

• **poetry** /ˈpəʊɪtri/ NOUN, NO PLURAL poems in general □ *a book of poetry* (poesia)

poignant /ˈpɔɪnjənt/ ADJECTIVE making you feel sadness or sympathy (comovente) 🔲 *There is that poignant moment in the film when the mother sees her son for the last time.*

point /pɔɪnt/ ▶ NOUN [plural points]

1 an idea, opinion, or thing you want to say (opinião) 🔲 *He made the point that some people wouldn't be able to afford the service.* (colocou a questão) 🔲 *I do take your point (= understand your opinion) about the high fence.* (entendi sua opinião) 🔲 *'Meg says it's not fair for the girls to do all the work.' 'Well, she does have a point (= her opinion is worth considering).* (a opinião dela é válida).

2 the reason for something or the purpose of something (razão) 🔲 *What's the point of going home if you just have to go straight back out again?* (qual é a razão de) 🔲 *I can't really see the point of exercising.* (ver a razão) 🔲 *There's no point in asking her – she won't come.* (não há razão para)

3 the most important thing about what has been said (questão) 🔲 *The point is, we can't afford a holiday.* (a questão é) 🔲 *She talked for so long, I thought she'd never get to the point.* (chegar à questão) 🔲 *He missed the point entirely – it's about fun, not making money.*

4 a particular time in an event or process (instante, ponto) 🔲 *At that point, we decided to leave.* (naquele ponto) 🔲 *I've reached the point with my studies where I'd like to specialize more.* (alcançou o ponto) 🔲 *At some point today, I need to phone Miriam.* (em algum momento)

5 a particular place □ *Drinks are available at several points along the route.* 🔲 *This is the highest point in England.* (ponto)

6 a feature or characteristic (característica) 🔲 *I know you don't like Mike, but he does have some good points.* (qualidades)

7 the sharp end of something □ *Make a small hole with the point of a needle.* (ponta)

8 the mark '.' that is used in decimal numbers that have a part less than one, e.g. 5.34 (ponto)

9 a unit for showing the score in a game or a competition □ *Who got the highest number of points?* (ponto) 🔲 *You score 2 points for each correct answer.* (marca dois pontos)

10 be at the point of doing something to be going to do something very soon □ *We were at the point of signing the contract when the buyers pulled out.* (estar prestes a fazer algo)

11 up to a point in part □ *I agree with you up to a point.* (até certo ponto)

▶ VERB [points, pointing, pointed]

1 to show someone something by holding your finger or a thin object towards it □ *+ at He pointed at a man in black.* □ *She pointed towards the exit with her umbrella.* (apontar)

2 to face in a particular direction, or to make something face a particular direction □ *+ at He pointed the gun at the target.* □ *The sign pointed north.* □ *What time is it when the little hand points to the three?* (apontar)

♦ PHRASAL VERBS **point something/someone out** to show someone a person or thing □ *I pointed out his mother, sitting in the crowd.* □ *He pointed out the damage to the wood.* (apontar, mostrar)
point something out to make someone aware of a fact □ *He pointed out that he had been waiting for over an hour.* (ressaltar) **point to something** to show that something is probably true (apontar para) □ *All the evidence points to his guilt.*

point-blank /ˌpɔɪntˈblæŋk/ ADJECTIVE, ADVERB
1 in a direct or rude way □ *She refused point-blank to come.* (sem rodeios, à queima-roupa)
2 very close 🔲 *The gun was fired at point-blank range.* (à queima-roupa)

pointed /ˈpɔɪntɪd/ ADJECTIVE
1 with a sharp end □ *a pointed stick* (pontudo)
2 direct and showing that you disagree □ *He made a few pointed comments.* □ *pointed criticism* (afiado)

pointer /ˈpɔɪntə(r)/ NOUN [plural pointers]
1 an informal word for a piece of advice 🔲 *She gave me a few pointers on how to dress.* (dica)
2 something which tells you about a situation or how something is developing □ *This result is an important pointer to future success.* (indicador)
3 a long stick you use to point to things (apontador)

pointless /ˈpɔɪntləs/ ADJECTIVE having no purpose or meaning □ *a pointless argument* □ *It's pointless asking him – he'll never come.* (inútil)

point of view /ˌpɔɪnt əv ˈvjuː/ NOUN [plural points of view]

poise

1 a way of considering or judging a situation ◻ *From an ethical point of view, I see nothing wrong.* (**ponto de vista**)
2 an opinion about something ◻ *They have different points of view.* (**ponto de vista**)

poise /pɔɪz/ NOUN, NO PLURAL
1 a calm, confident way of behaving ◻ *He recovered his poise to win the second game.* (**equilíbrio**)
2 a controlled and attractive way of standing or moving ◻ *She had the poise of a dancer.* (**equilíbrio, postura**)

• **poised** /pɔɪzd/ ADJECTIVE
1 waiting and ready to do something ◻ *She looks poised to be the first female winner of the award.* ◻ *He stood poised on the edge of the diving board.* (**aprumado**)
2 calm, confident and controlled (**equilibrado**)

poison /ˈpɔɪzən/ ▶ NOUN [*plural* **poisons**] a substance that causes death or illness when you eat, drink or breathe it ◻ *a deadly poison* ◻ *rat poison* (**veneno**)

▶ VERB [**poisons, poisoning, poisoned**]
1 to kill or harm someone with poison ◻ *They were poisoned by carbon monoxide fumes.* (**envenenar**)
2 to add poison or another dangerous substance to something ◻ *These chemicals are poisoning the water.* (**envenenar**)

• **poisoning** /ˈpɔɪzənɪŋ/ NOUN, NO PLURAL an illness caused by a poison or other harmful substance (**intoxicação**) ⬚ *She had mild food poisoning.* (**intoxicação alimentar**)

• **poisonous** /ˈpɔɪzənəs/ ADJECTIVE
1 containing poison ◻ *This cleaning liquid is poisonous.* (**venenoso**)
2 a poisonous animal can produce poison ◻ *a poisonous snake* (**venenoso, peçonhento**)

poke /pəʊk/ ▶ VERB [**pokes, poking, poked**]
1 to quickly push something or someone with your finger or with something sharp ◻ *He poked me in the ribs.* (**cutucar**)
2 to appear through a hole or from behind something ◻ *She poked her head through the curtains.* ◻ *His hair was poking out from under his hat.* (**aparecer**)

♦ PHRASAL VERB **poke around** to look for something, especially by moving things ◻ *He was poking around in my drawers, looking for the photo.* (**fuçar**)

♦ IDIOM **poke fun at someone** to make jokes about someone or something in an unkind way ◻ *He was poking fun at my hat.* (**caçoar, tirar sarro**)

▶ go to **poke your nose in/into something**

▶ NOUN [*plural* **pokes**] when you poke someone or something ◻ *She gave me another poke in the arm.*

• **poker** /ˈpəʊkə(r)/ NOUN [*plural* **pokers**]
1 a heavy metal stick used for moving wood or coal in a fire (**tiçoeiro**)
2 *no plural* a card game played for money (**pôquer**)

poky /ˈpəʊki/ ADJECTIVE [**pokier, pokiest**] a poky place is too small ◻ *a poky little kitchen* (**pequeno demais, apertado**)

polar /ˈpəʊlə(r)/ ADJECTIVE to do with the north or south pole (= areas at the top and bottom of the Earth) ◻ *a polar region* ◻ *polar ice* (**polar**)

polar bear /ˈpəʊlə ˌbeə(r)/ NOUN [*plural* **polar bears**] a large white bear that lives near the North Pole (**urso polar**)

pole /pəʊl/ NOUN [*plural* **poles**]
1 a long thin stick made of metal or wood, often used for supporting something ◻ *an aluminium tent pole* (**poste, estaca, vara**)
2 one of the two areas at the most northern and southern points of the Earth (**polo**)
3 one of the two ends of a magnet (= piece of iron that makes metal objects move towards it). A physics word. (**polo**)
4 the front position at the start of a motor race (**posição na primeira fila**) ⬚ **pole position** ◻ *The Ferrari is in on pole for tomorrow's race.* (**primeiro lugar na largada da corrida**)

♦ IDIOM **poles apart** completely different or opposite ◻ *Their styles are poles apart.* (**opostos**)

polecat /ˈpəʊlkæt/ NOUN [*plural* **polecats**] a small wild animal with a long body (**doninha**)

pole vault /ˈpəʊl vɔːlt/ NOUN, NO PLURAL a sports event in which you get yourself over a high bar using a long pole (**salto com vara**)

• **pole vaulter** NOUN [*plural* **pole vaulters**] someone who takes part in a pole vault competition (**saltador com vara**)

police /pəˈliːs/ ▶ NOUN, NO PLURAL the people whose job is to make people obey the law and to catch people who break the law (**polícia**) ⬚ *One of his neighbours called the police.* (**chamou a polícia**) ◻ *Last night police were questioning four men.* ⬚ *the police force* (**força policial**) ⬚ *a police investigation* (**investigação policial**)

▶ VERB [**polices, policing, policed**]
1 to make sure an event or area is safe by using police officers ◻ *It was a huge operation to police the demonstration.* (**policiar**)
2 to make people obey laws or rules ◻ *But how do we police the Internet?* (**policiar**)

policeman /pəˈliːsmən/ NOUN [*plural* **policemen**] a male police officer (**policial**)

police officer /pəˈliːs ˌɒfɪsə(r)/ NOUN [*plural* **police officers**] a member of the police ◻ *an armed police officer* (**policial, comandante**)

police station /pəˈliːs ˌsteɪʃən/ NOUN [*plural* **police stations**] a building where the police have their offices (**delegacia**)

police woman

police woman /pəˈliːswʊmən/ NOUN [plural **policewomen**] a female police office (**policial feminina**)

policy /ˈpɒləsɪ/ NOUN [plural **policies**]
1 a plan about how to deal with something by a government, political party, business, etc. ◻ *government policies* (**política**) ▣ *US foreign policy* (**política externa**) ◻ *the party's policy on immigration*
2 an arrangement you have with an insurance company (= company that gives you money if you damage something, etc.) (**apólice**) ▣ *a home insurance policy* (**apólice de seguro**)

polio /ˈpəʊlɪəʊ/ NOUN, NO PLURAL a serious disease that affects the nerves and muscles (**poliomielite**)

polish /ˈpɒlɪʃ/ ▶ VERB [**polishes, polishing, polished**]
1 to rub something until it shines ◻ *Remember to polish your shoes.* (**polir**)
2 to improve a skill by doing something many times ◻ *I've had plenty of opportunities to polish my public speaking skills.* (**aperfeiçoar**)
◆ PHRASAL VERB **polish something off** to eat or to drink all of something ◻ *She polished off the chocolate cake.* (**raspar o prato (fig.), acabar com**)
▶ NOUN [plural **polishes**]
1 a substance used to polish something (**polidor**) ▣ *shoe polish* ◻ *furniture polish* (**polidor de sapatos**)
2 when you polish something ◻ *He gave the car a good polish.* (**polida**)
• **polished** /ˈpɒlɪʃt/ ADJECTIVE (**polido**)
1 clean and shiny ◻ *a polished wooden floor*
2 showing great skill ◻ *He's a polished performer.*

polite /pəˈlaɪt/ ADJECTIVE [**politer, politest**] behaving in a pleasant way towards other people, for example, saying 'thank you' and 'please' ◻ *Her children are very polite.* ◻ **+ to** *She was polite to hospital staff.* ◻ **+ to do something** *He was too polite to interrupt.* (**educado, polido**)
• **politely** /pəˈlaɪtlɪ/ ADVERB in a polite way ◻ *'Would you like a seat?' he asked her politely.* ◻ *She politely declined the invitation.* (**polidamente**)
• **politeness** /pəˈlaɪtnɪs/ NOUN, NO PLURAL the quality of being polite ◻ *I agreed to go out of politeness.* (**polidez, educação**)

political /pəˈlɪtɪkəl/ ADJECTIVE to do with politics, politicians or government (**político**) ▣ *a political party* (**partido político**) ▣ *a political leader* (**líder político**) ◻ *a political and economic crisis*
• **politically** /pəˈlɪtɪkəlɪ/ ADVERB in a way that is to do with politics ◻ *Politically, she was very naive.* (**politicamente**)

politically correct /pəˈlɪtɪkəlɪ kəˈrekt/ ADJECTIVE said or done so that no one is offended, especially so that women and people of a different race are not offended (**politicamente correto**)

pollute

politician /ˌpɒləˈtɪʃən/ NOUN [plural **politicians**] someone whose job is politics, especially someone who has been elected to a parliament ◻ *People don't seem to trust politicians.* (**politico**)
• **politics** /ˈpɒlətɪks/ NOUN, NO PLURAL
1 ideas or activities to do with governing a country ◻ *He's very interested in politics.* (**política**)
2 the job of being a politician ▣ *He entered politics after leaving university.* (**entrou na política**)
3 the things that people in a group do in order to get more power than other members of the group ▣ *I'm fed up with office politics.* (**política do escritório**)
4 someone's beliefs about politics ◻ *I don't know about his politics.* (**opinião política**)

polka /ˈpɒlkə/ NOUN [plural **polkas**] a fast traditional dance, or music for this dance (**polca**)

poll /pəʊl/ ▶ NOUN [plural **polls**]
1 when a number of people are asked their opinion on a particular subject (**pesquisa de opinião**) ▣ *The poll showed that about 55% of people are against the war.* (**a pesquisa de opinião mostrou**) ▣ *The poll was conducted for a local newspaper.* (**a pesquisa de opinião foi conduzida**)
2 a political election in which people vote (**eleição**) ▣ *Voters go to the polls* (= vote) *on 24 November.* (**vão às urnas**)
▶ VERB [**polls, polling, polled**] to ask a number of people their opinion on a particular subject ◻ *Over half the people polled said they were unhappy with the government.* (**fazer pesquisa de opinião**)

pollen /ˈpɒlən/ NOUN, NO PLURAL the powder that a flower releases and which can make new seeds. A biology word. (**pólen**)

pollinate /ˈpɒlɪneɪt/ VERB [**pollinates, pollinating, pollinated**] to put the pollen from one plant on another plant, causing seeds to start to form. A biology word. (**polinizar**)
• **pollination** /ˌpɒlɪˈneɪʃən/ NOUN, NO PLURAL the process of pollinating plants. A biology word. (**polinização**)

polling station /ˈpəʊlɪŋ ˌsteɪʃən/ NOUN [plural **polling stations**] the building where you vote in an election (**local de votação**)

pollutant /pəˈluːtənt/ NOUN [plural **pollutants**] a substance that causes harm to the air, soil or water ◻ *pollutants from vehicle exhausts* (**poluente**)

pollute /pəˈluːt/ VERB [**pollutes, polluting, polluted**] to let harmful substances go into the air, soil or water ◻ *We need to find energy sources which don't pollute the environment.* (**poluir**)

- **pollution** /pəˈluːʃən/ NOUN, NO PLURAL
1 substances which pollute (**poluição**) ▣ *the health effects of* air pollution (**poluição do ar**) ▣ *a major* source of pollution (**fonte de poluição**) □ + *from We need to reduce pollution from traffic.*
2 when harmful substances pollute a place (**poluição**) □ + *of We need to take action against the pollution of the oceans.*

polo /ˈpəʊləʊ/ NOUN, NO PLURAL a game played by two teams of players on horses who hit a ball along the ground using hammers with long handles (**polo**)

polo neck /ˈpəʊləʊ ˌnek/ NOUN [*plural* **polo necks**] a sweater (= top made from wool) with a high round neck (**gola alta**)

poly- /ˈpɒli/ PREFIX poly- is added to the beginning of words to mean 'many' (**poli**)

polyester /ˌpɒliˈestə(r)/ NOUN, NO PLURAL a light, artificial cloth used for making clothes (**poliéster**)

polygon /ˈpɒlɪɡɒn/ NOUN [*plural* **polygons**] a shape with three or more sides. A maths word. (**polígono**)

polymer /ˈpɒlɪmə(r)/ NOUN [*plural* **polymers**] a chemical compound made of small molecules of the same type joined together to form large molecules. A chemistry word. (**polímero**)

polystyrene /ˌpɒlɪˈstaɪriːn/ NOUN, NO PLURAL a very light plastic material used for making containers and for protecting delicate objects (**poliestireno**)

polythene /ˈpɒlɪθiːn/ NOUN, NO PLURAL a very thin plastic material used for making bags, etc. (**polietileno**)

pomegranate /ˈpɒmɪˌɡrænɪt/ NOUN [*plural* **pomegranates**] a round fruit with a thick brown skin and a lot of small red parts inside containing seeds (**romã**)

pomp /pɒmp/ NOUN, NO PLURAL formal, traditional ceremony with special clothes, music, etc. □ *the traditional pomp and ceremony of the state opening of Parliament* (**pompa**)

pompous /ˈpɒmpəs/ ADJECTIVE too serious and thinking you are very important □ *That sounds terribly pompous.* (**pomposo**)

poncho /ˈpɒntʃəʊ/ NOUN [*plural* **ponchos**] a loose piece of clothing covering the shoulders and top half of the body which has a hole for your head to go through (**poncho**)

pond /pɒnd/ NOUN [*plural* **ponds**] a small area of water, smaller than a lake □ *a garden pond* □ *a fish pond* (**lagoa**)

ponder /ˈpɒndə(r)/ VERB [**ponders, pondering, pondered**] to think about something carefully and for a long time □ *He'd pondered the question all day.* (**ponderar, considerar**)

pong /pɒŋ/ ▶ NOUN, NO PLURAL an informal word meaning a strong unpleasant smell □ *There's a bit of a pong coming from the bin.* (**fedor**)

▶ VERB [**pongs, ponging, ponged**] an informal word meaning to have a strong unpleasant smell □ *The changing room pongs of stale sweat.*

pony /ˈpəʊni/ NOUN [*plural* **ponies**] a small horse (**pônei**)

ponytail /ˈpəʊniteɪl/ NOUN [*plural* **ponytails**] a hairstyle with your hair tied at the back of your head and hanging down (**rabo de cavalo**)

pony-trekking /ˈpəʊniˌtrekɪŋ/ NOUN, NO PLURAL the activity of riding ponies over long distances in the countryside (**cavalgada**)

poodle /ˈpuːdəl/ NOUN [*plural* **poodles**] a type of dog with curly hair (**poodle**)

pool /puːl/ ▶ NOUN [*plural* **pools**]
1 an area of water made for swimming in □ *The hotel has an indoor pool.* □ *a heated pool* (**piscina**)
2 a small area of liquid □ *There was a small pool of blood on the floor.* (**poça**)
3 *no plural* a game in which two players try to hit coloured balls into holes around the edge of a table using a long, wooden stick (**jogo de bilhar**)
4 a group of people or things that are available or are shared by several people □ *There's a growing pool of candidates for the leadership role.* □ *a car pool* (**grupo de pessoas ou recursos compartilhados, consórcio, cooperativa**)

▶ VERB [**pools, pooling, pooled**] to put things together so that everyone can use them (**juntar**) ▣ *We should all work together and* pool *our resources.* (**juntar nossos recursos**)

poor /pʊə(r)/ ADJECTIVE [**poorer, poorest**]
1 having little money and owning few things □ *a poor country* □ *His family were very poor.* (**pobre**)
2 of a low standard (**fraco**) ▣ *The paper was of* poor quality. (**qualidade inferior**) ▣ *He's in very* poor health. (**saúde fraca**) □ *It was a poor performance by the team generally.*
3 used to show that someone or something deserves sympathy □ *Poor you! You sound so ill.* □ *The poor little thing is all wet.* (**coitado, pobre**)

• **poorly** /ˈpʊəli/ ▶ ADVERB badly or not well enough □ *a poorly paid job* □ *He performed fairly poorly in both matches.* (**mal**)

▶ ADJECTIVE [**poorlier, poorliest**] an informal word meaning ill □ *Grant's feeling a bit poorly today.* (**mal de saúde, doente**)

pop /pɒp/ ▶ NOUN [*plural* **pops**]
1 *no plural* modern music with short, simple songs and a strong beat (**música popular**) ▣ *pop* music (**música popular**) ▣ *a* pop star (**celebridade**) ▣ *a catchy* pop song (**canção popular**)
2 a short sound like something exploding □ *They heard a loud pop.* □ *The bottle opened with a pop.* (**estouro**)
3 *no plural* a sweet drink with bubbles (**bebida gasosa, refrigerante**)

▶ VERB [**pops, popping, popped**]

popcorn

1 to go somewhere quickly, for a short time □ + *out* *I just popped out for a few minutes.* □ + *into* *I need to pop into the office.* (sair precipitadamente)
2 to put something somewhere quickly □ *I'll just pop the pizza in the oven.* □ *Karen popped her head around the door.* (enfiar)
3 to make a short sound like something exploding □ *The fire crackled and popped.* (estourar) 🔲 *I could hear the sound of corks popping.* (rolhas estourando)
4 to suddenly tear, making a loud noise, or to make something do this (estourar) 🔲 *I could hear balloons popping in the background.* (balões estourando)

♦ IDIOM **pop the question** to ask someone to marry you. An informal phrase. (pedir alguém em casamento)

♦ PHRASAL VERB **pop up** to suddenly appear □ *Bars and café's are popping up all over the place.* (surgir)

popcorn /'pɒpkɔːn/ NOUN, NO PLURAL a food made from seeds of grain which break open when they are heated (pipoca)

Pope /pəʊp/ NOUN [plural **Popes**] the leader of the Catholic Church (papa)

poplar /'pɒplə(r)/ NOUN [plural **poplars**] a type of tall, thin tree (álamo)

poppy /'pɒpi/ NOUN [plural **poppies**] a tall, red flower that grows in fields (papoula)

popular /'pɒpjʊlə(r)/ ADJECTIVE

1 liked by a lot of people □ *a popular tourist destination* □ *She was a very popular student.* □ + *with* *The beach is popular with tourists.* 🔲 *Podcasts are becoming increasingly popular.* (tornando-se popular) 🔲 *The new resort has proved hugely popular.* (provaram ser populares)
2 believed or felt by many people 🔲 *According to popular belief, cutting your hair will help it to grow.* (crença popular) 🔲 *You can't change popular opinion overnight.* (opinião popular) □ *As a leader he has enormous popular support.*
3 to do with ordinary people, not experts 🔲 *popular culture* (cultura popular) □ *a popular science book*

• **popularity** /ˌpɒpjʊ'lærəti/ NOUN, NO PLURAL when a lot of people like something or someone □ *The popularity of the sport has increased in recent years.* (popularidade)

• **popularize** or **popularise** /'pɒpjʊləraɪz/ VERB [**popularizes, popularizing, popularized**] to make something popular □ *YouTube has popularized the idea of sharing videos.* (popularizar)

• **popularly** /'pɒpjʊləli/ ADVERB by many or most people □ *The Academy Awards are popularly known as the Oscars.* (popularmente)

populate /'pɒpjʊleɪt/ VERB [**populates, populating, populated**] if people or animals populate an area, they live there □ *The area is mostly populated by recent immigrants.* (povoar)

• **populated** /'pɒpjʊleɪtɪd/ ADJECTIVE a populated area has people living there (povoado) 🔲 *a populated area* (área povoada) 🔲 *Pollution is worse in densely populated* (= with many people) *urban areas.* (densamente povoada)

• **population** /ˌpɒpjʊ'leɪʃən/ NOUN [plural **populations**]
1 all the people who live in an area, country, etc. (população) 🔲 *The troops are there to protect the local population.* (população local) 🔲 *More than half the world's population live in cities.*
2 the number of people who live in an area, country, etc. □ + *of* *The city has a population of around two million.* (população)
3 the people or animals of a particular type who live in an area □ + *of* *a large population of seabirds* □ *the elderly population* (população)

pop-up /'pɒpʌp/ ADJECTIVE
1 a pop-up book has pictures which stick up when you open the book (livro cujos recortes criam efeitos tridimensionais nas ilustrações)
2 describes something on a computer screen which suddenly appears when you click the mouse or press a key. A computing word □ *a pop-up menu* (item que aparece de repente na tela do computador)

porcelain /'pɔːsəlɪn/ ▶ NOUN, NO PLURAL a hard, white substance used to make good quality plates, cups, etc. (porcelana)
▶ ADJECTIVE made from porcelain □ *a porcelain doll*

porch /pɔːtʃ/ NOUN [plural **porches**] a small covered entrance to a house (pórtico)

porcupine /'pɔːkjʊpaɪn/ NOUN [plural **porcupines**] a small animal that has long sharp needles on its back (porco-espinho)

pore /pɔː(r)/ NOUN [plural **pores**] one of the very small holes in your skin that sweat comes out of. A biology word. (poro)

♦ PHRASAL VERB [**pores, poring, pored**] **pore over something** to read things very carefully, examining them in detail □ *We spent the day poring over papers.* (ler minuciosamente)

pork /pɔːk/ NOUN, NO PLURAL meat from a pig □ *a pork chop* (carne de porco)

porous /'pɔːrəs/ ADJECTIVE allowing liquids and gases to pass through □ *porous soil* (poroso)

porpoise /'pɔːpəs/ NOUN [plural **porpoises**] a large sea mammal, similar to a dolphin (toninha)

porridge /'pɒrɪdʒ/ NOUN, NO PLURAL a food made by cooking oats (= a type of grain) in water or milk, often eaten for breakfast (mingau de aveia)

port /pɔːt/ NOUN [plural **ports**]

1 a place where ships can stop on the coast, and the town or city around it □ *the Israeli port of Haifa* □ *a major shipping port* □ *It's a small fishing port on the south coast.* (porto)
2 a hole in a computer which another piece of equipment can be connected to. A computing

word □ *a USB port* (entrada de computador, p. ex., a USB)
3 *no plural* a strong, sweet type of red wine (vinho do porto)
4 *no plural* the left side of a ship or aircraft when you are facing the front (bombordo)

portable /'pɔːtəbəl/ ADJECTIVE small enough to be carried easily □ *a portable television* □ *a portable DVD player* (portátil)

porter /'pɔːtə(r)/ NOUN [plural **porters**]
1 someone whose job is to carry bags for people at a station, hotel, etc. □ *The porter will take your bags up to your room.* (carregador)
2 someone whose job is to look after a building □ *the night porter at the hotel* (porteiro)
3 someone whose job is to move people and things around in a hospital □ *a hospital porter* (carregador)

portfolio /ˌpɔːtˈfəʊliəʊ/ NOUN [plural **portfolios**]
1 a collection of pictures, photographs, etc. that you show to people so they can see what your work is like (portfólio)
2 a flat case for carrying large drawings, paintings, etc. (pasta de documentos, portfólio)

porthole /'pɔːthəʊl/ NOUN [plural **portholes**] a round window in the side of a ship or plane (vigia)

portion /'pɔːʃən/ NOUN [plural **portions**]
1 a part of a total amount □ *She spends a large portion of her income on clothes.* (porção)
2 how much food one person eats at a meal □ *Try eating smaller portions.* (porção)

portly /'pɔːtlɪ/ ADJECTIVE [portlier, portliest] quite fat (corpulento)

portrait /'pɔːtreɪt/ NOUN [plural **portraits**]
1 a painting or photograph of a person, especially of their face □ *a portrait of the prince* (retrato) 🔹 *a portrait painter* (pintor de retratos)
2 a description of something □ *The novels provide a vivid portrait of India during this period.* (descrição)

portray /pɔːˈtreɪ/ VERB [portrays, portraying, portrayed]
1 to make someone or something seem a particular way by writing things about them or by showing particular pictures of them □ *He was portrayed in the media as a hero.* (retratar)
2 to act the part of a character or to show an emotion in a film or play □ *He is portrayed in the film by actor, Guy Pearce.* (representar)
• **portrayal** /pɔːˈtreɪəl/ NOUN [plural **portrayals**] when you portray someone or something □ *She won an Oscar for her portrayal of Queen Elizabeth II.* (representação)

pose /pəʊz/ ▶ VERB [poses, posing, posed]
1 to cause a danger or a problem (causar) 🔹 *Air pollution poses a serious threat to health.* (causa uma ameaça à saúde) 🔹 *Discarded plastic bottles pose an environmental risk.* (causam risco ao meio ambiente)
2 to sit or stand still while someone takes a photograph or paints a picture of you □ *They posed for pictures with their arms around each other.* (posar)
3 to ask a question (apresentar) 🔹 *The report poses more questions than it answers.* (propôs perguntas)
♦ PHRASAL VERB **pose as something** to pretend to be someone you are not □ *The thief posed as a gas repair man.* (fazer se passar por)
▶ NOUN [plural **poses**]
1 a position you put your body in, especially for a picture (pose)
2 when someone behaves in a way that is not natural or sincere so that other people will admire them □ *He's not intellectual at all. It's just a pose.* (pose)
• **poser** /'pəʊzə(r)/ NOUN [plural **posers**]
1 someone who behaves in a way to make people admire them (pessoa afetada, superficial)
2 a question that is difficult to answer (pergunta embaraçosa)

posh /pɒʃ/ ADJECTIVE [posher, poshest]
1 an informal word meaning expensive and comfortable □ *a posh hotel* □ *a posh London restaurant* (chique)
2 an informal word meaning from a high social class □ *a posh accent* (chique)

position /pəˈzɪʃən/ ▶ NOUN [plural **positions**]
1 a way of standing, sitting or lying □ *I must have been sleeping in an awkward position.* (posição (em pé, sentado, deitado etc.))
2 the place where something is, or the way in which it has been put there □ *His pipe was in its usual position, beside his chair.* □ *Push the lever to the 'on' position.* (localização)
3 the situation that someone is in (situação) 🔹 *Our team is in a strong position to win the championship.* (situação boa) 🔹 *Her demands put me in a very difficult position.* (situação difícil) □ *Unfortunately, I am not in a position* (= I am not able) *to help you.* □ *In her position, I'd hire a really good lawyer.*
4 an opinion □ **+ on** *This statement explains the government's position on immigration.* □ *He thinks organic farming is stupid, and he'll never change his position.* (posicionamento, opinião)
5 a person or organization's level of power, importance, or influence (posição) 🔹 *This new office will strengthen the position of our business in the area.* (fortalecer a posição de) 🔹 *She is struggling to maintain her position as a leading expert on Renaissance art.* (manter sua posição)
6 a job or post (posto, cargo) 🔹 *What is the percentage of women holding senior positions here?* (mulheres atuando nos cargos superiores) 🔹 *Our marketing manager left, and we have not yet filled his position.* □ *He applied for a teaching position.* (preenchemos sua vaga)

positive

▶ VERB [**positions, positioning, positioned**]
1 to put someone or something in a particular place, often to be ready to do something □ *A camera was positioned above the door.* □ *Masked gunmen positioned themselves around the grounds.* (**posicionar**)
2 to try to make people think about a person or an organization in a particular way □ *He positioned the party as the true champion of family values.* (**posicionar**)
3 to put a person or an organization in a particular situation, in order to achieve something □ *The company is well positioned for growth.* (**posicionar**)

positive /'pɒzɪtɪv/ ADJECTIVE

1 completely certain □ **+ that** *Are you absolutely positive that he's German?* □ **+ about** *Jack has seen the letter. I'm positive about that.* (**seguro, certo**)
2 feeling happy about a situation and believing that the future will be good (**positivo**) 🔁 *He has a very positive attitude to life.* (**atitude positiva**) 🔁 *It can be difficult to remain positive when you have so many problems.* (**permanecer positivo**)
3 if an experience or the result of an action is positive, you get a good result from it □ *I have had a very positive experience with acupuncture.* (**positivo**) 🔁 *The currency rate had a positive effect on our business.* (**efeito positivo**)
4 if someone's reaction to something is positive, they like it or agree to it (**positivo**) 🔁 *I am not expecting a positive response to my request for more money.* (**resposta positiva**) 🔁 *Feedback from the show's audiences has been overwhelmingly positive.* (**incontestavelmente positivo**)
5 if you take positive action, you do something to try to achieve something (**positivo**) 🔁 *He took positive steps to improve his education.* (**tomou atitudes positivas**)
6 if the result of a test is positive, it shows that something has happened or been found 🔁 *The athlete tested positive for banned substances.* (**teve teste positivo**)
7 a positive number is one that is greater than zero. A maths word. (**positivo**)

• **positively** /'pɒzɪtɪvli/ ADVERB
1 in a positive way □ *People usually respond positively to encouragement.* □ *She talks positively about her childhood experiences.* (**positivamente**)
2 used to emphasize your description of someone or something □ *He was positively furious.* (**positivamente**)

posse /'pɒsi/ NOUN [plural **posses**] a group of people who are standing together, doing the same thing □ *There was a posse of journalists waiting outside the house.* (**grupo organizado**)

possess /pə'zes/ VERB [**possesses, possessing, possessed**] a formal word meaning to have something □ *He was charged with possessing an illegal weapon.* □ *Candidates should possess strong communication skills.* (**possuir**)

• **possessed** /pə'zest/ ADJECTIVE controlled by an evil spirit (**possuído**)

• **possession** /pə'zeʃən/ NOUN [plural **possessions**]
1 something you possess (**posse**) 🔁 *They packed up their personal possessions.* (**posses pessoais**) 🔁 *The ring was her most prized possession.* (**posse estimada**)
2 *no plural* when you possess something □ **+ of** *He was charged with possession of a firearm.* □ *Illegal drugs were found in his possession.* (**posse**) 🔁 *The bank took possession of the apartment.* (**tomou posse**)

• **possessive** /pə'zesɪv/ ▶ ADJECTIVE
1 wanting someone to give only you their love and attention □ *He's very jealous and possessive.* (**possessivo**)
2 not wanting to share your things with other people □ *Children are very possessive with their toys.* (**possessivo**)
3 in grammar, showing who or what a person or thing belongs to □ *a possessive pronoun such as 'mine'* (**possessivo**)
▶ NOUN [plural **possessives**] in grammar, a word that shows who or what a person or thing belongs to (**possessivo**)

possibility /ˌpɒsə'bɪlɪti/ NOUN [plural **possibilities**]
1 the chance that something might happen □ **+ of** *We were warned about the possibility of flooding.* □ **+ that** *There's a strong possibility that the tour will be cancelled.* (**possibilidade**) 🔁 *The minister raised the possibility of military action.* (**levantou a possibilidade de**)
2 something that might happen (**possibilidade**) 🔁 *Civil war is now a real possibility.* (**possibilidade real**) 🔁 *Storms are a distinct possibility.* (**possibilidade diferente**)
3 one choice from things which are all possible □ **+ of** *We discussed the possibility of moving abroad.* (**possibilidade**) 🔁 *Have you considered other possibilities?* (**considerar outras possibilidades**)

possible /'pɒsəbəl/ ADJECTIVE

1 something that is possible can happen or be done □ **+ to do something** *It isn't possible to see the doctor today.* (**possível**) 🔁 *Try to avoid the area if possible.* (**se possível**) 🔁 *Several advances have been made possible by new technology.* (**tornaram-se possíveis**)
2 something that is possible may be true □ **+ that** *It's possible that I made a mistake.* □ *That doesn't seem possible.* (**possível**) 🔁 *There are several possible explanations.* (**explicações possíveis**)

3 as soon/quickly, etc. as possible as soon, quickly, etc. as you can □ *We need the work doing as quickly as possible.* (assim que possível, o mais rápido possível)

4 the best/highest, etc. possible used to say that something is the best, highest, etc. that exists □ *He's receiving the best possible care.* □ *I'll speak to him at the earliest possible opportunity.* (o melhor, o mais alto etc. possível)

• **possibly** /ˈpɒsəblɪ/ ADVERB

1 perhaps □ *It could take about 5 days, possibly longer.* (possivelmente)

2 used with can and could for emphasis □ *It was worse than we could possibly imagine.* □ *He can't possibly need more money!* (possivelmente)

3 used when you ask someone politely to do something that might cause problems for them □ *Could you possibly get there a little earlier?* (por acaso, possivelmente)

post /pəʊst/ ▶ NOUN [plural **posts**]

1 *no plural* the service which collects and deliver letters and packages, or the letters and packages sent □ *I sent it by post.* □ *Has the post arrived yet?* (correio)

2 a job □ *the post of finance director* □ *a teaching post* (cargo, função) 🔲 *He held a senior post at the bank.* (mantinha uma função superior)

3 a long piece of wood fixed into the ground (poste) 🔲 *a fence post* (poste de cerca) 🔲 *a goal post* (trave)

4 a message which has been put on a website. A computing word □ *a blog post* □ *She announced the tour in a post on her website.* (mensagem em um site)

5 a place where a soldier or guard stands □ *a police border post* (posto)

▶ VERB [**posts, posting, posted**]

1 to send a letter or package by post 🔲 *I posted the letter yesterday.* (enviar)

2 to put a message, video, picture, etc. on a website. A computing word □ *He posted a message to fans on his website.* □ *A video of the interview was posted on the Internet.* (postar, publicar)

3 to send someone to another place to work for a while □ *He was posted to the BBC's New York office.* (enviar)

♦ IDIOM **keep someone posted** to tell someone if a situation changes, especially someone in a different place □ *Keep me posted if there are any developments.* (manter informado)

post- /pəʊst/ PREFIX post- is added to the beginning of words to mean 'after' □ *postwar* (= after a war) (pós)

postage /ˈpəʊstɪdʒ/ NOUN, NO PLURAL the cost of sending a letter or package (taxa postal) 🔲 *That's £35 plus £4 postage and packing.* (taxa de postagem e empacotamento)

postage stamp /ˈpəʊstɪdʒ ˌstæmp/ NOUN [plural **postage stamps**] a formal word for a **stamp** (= a printed piece of paper that you buy and stick on letters before you post them) (selo postal)

postal /ˈpəʊstəl/ ADJECTIVE to do with the service that collects and delivers letters and packages □ *a postal worker* (postal)

postal order /ˈpəʊstəl ˌɔːdə(r)/ NOUN [plural **postal orders**] a document you buy at a post office as a safe way of sending money by post (selo postal)

postbox /ˈpəʊstbɒks/ NOUN [plural **postboxes**] a container in a public place where letters can be posted (caixa de correio)

postcard /ˈpəʊstkɑːd/ NOUN [plural **postcards**] a card with a picture on one side. You write on the other side and send the card by post without an envelope □ *a picture postcard* □ *I'll send you a postcard from Tokyo.* (cartão-postal)

post code /ˈpəʊst ˌkəʊd/ NOUN [plural **post codes**] a series of letters and numbers at the end of an address (código postal)

postdate /ˌpəʊstˈdeɪt/ VERB [**postdates, postdating, postdated**] to write a date on something such as a cheque or document, which is later than the date when you are writing it (pós--datar)

poster /ˈpəʊstə(r)/ NOUN [plural **posters**] a large notice or picture used for advertising, for decorating a wall, or for giving information □ *She has posters of movie stars all over her bedroom walls.* (cartaz)

posterior /pɒˈstɪərɪə(r)/ ▶ ADJECTIVE a formal word meaning at the back □ *the posterior area of the brain* (posterior)

▶ NOUN [plural **posteriors**] a formal word meaning the back of something

posterity /pɒˈsterətɪ/ NOUN, NO PLURAL the people who will live in the future □ *These works of art should be preserved for posterity.* (posteridade)

postgraduate /ˌpəʊstˈgrædʒuət/ ▶ NOUN [plural **postgraduates**] a person who already has a university qualification and who is studying for an advanced qualification (estudante de pós--graduação)

▶ ADJECTIVE to do with postgraduates □ *postgraduate students* □ *a postgraduate course* (de pós-graduação)

posthumous /ˈpɒstjʊməs/ ADJECTIVE to do with something that happens after a person's death □ *He received a posthumous award for bravery.* (póstumo)

• **posthumously** /ˈpɒstjʊməslɪ/ ADVERB after someone's death □ *Butler's novel was published posthumously in 1903.* (postumamente)

postman /ˈpəʊstmən/ NOUN [plural **postmen**] someone whose job is to deliver letters and packages to houses or offices □ *Has the postman been yet?* (carteiro)

postmark

postmark /ˈpəʊstmɑːk/ NOUN [plural **postmarks**] an official mark put on a letter showing the date and place it was posted (**carimbo postal**)

postmaster /ˈpəʊstmɑːstə(r)/ NOUN [plural **postmasters**] someone whose job is managing a post office (**o chefe do correio**)

postmistress /ˈpəʊstmɪstrɪs/ NOUN [plural **postmistresses**] a woman whose job is managing a post office (**a chefe do correio**)

post mortem /ˌpəʊst ˈmɔːtəm/ NOUN [plural **post mortems**] a medical examination of a dead body to find out the cause of death (**autópsia**)

postnatal /ˌpəʊstˈneɪtəl/ ADJECTIVE to do with the time just after a woman has given birth to a baby □ *postnatal depression* (**pós-natal**)

post office /ˈpəʊst ˌɒfɪs/ NOUN [plural **post offices**] a shop where you can post letters and packages, and buy stamps (**agência do correio**)

postpone /ˌpəʊstˈpəʊn/ VERB [**postpones, postponing, postponed**] to decide to do something at a later time than planned □ *We had to postpone our trip to Paris.* (**adiar**)

• **postponement** /ˌpəʊstˈpəʊnmənt/ NOUN [plural **postponements**] when you postpone something □ *the postponement of the elections* (**adiar**)

postscript /ˈpəʊstskrɪpt/ NOUN [plural **postscripts**] an extra message written at the end of a letter, usually after the abbreviation *PS* (**pós-escrito**)

posture /ˈpɒstʃə(r)/ NOUN [plural **postures**] the position of your body when you stand, sit or walk, especially the position of your back and shoulders □ *Back pain can be caused by poor posture.* (**postura**)

postwar /ˌpəʊstˈwɔː(r)/ ADJECTIVE to do with the period after a war, especially the Second World War □ *postwar rebuilding* □ *the postwar period* (**pós-guerra**)

posy /ˈpəʊzi/ NOUN [plural **posies**] a few small flowers which have been tied together (**ramalhete, buquê**)

pot /pɒt/ ▶ NOUN [plural **pots**] a round container used for cooking, for storing things in, or for growing plants in □ *+ of a pot of paint* (**panela, pote, vaso**) 🖼 *a pile of dirty pots and pans* (= containers used for cooking) (**potes e panelas**) 🖼 *a flower pot* (= container for growing plants) (**vaso de flores**)
▶ VERB [**pots, potting, potted**]
1 to put a plant into a pot (**plantar em um vaso**)
2 to hit a ball into a hole in a game of pool, snooker or billiards (**mandar a bola para a caçapa**)

potassium /pəˈtæsiəm/ NOUN, NO PLURAL A soft, white metal. A chemistry word. (**potássio**)

potato /pəˈteɪtəʊ/ NOUN [plural **potatoes**] a very common white, round vegetable that grows underground with a brown or yellow skin □ *mashed potato* □ *roast potatoes* (**batata**)

potato chip /pəˈteɪtəʊ ˌtʃɪp/ NOUN [plural **potato chips**] the US phrase for **crisp** (= very thin piece of potato cooked in oil) (**batatinha frita**)

potency /ˈpəʊtənsi/ NOUN, NO PLURAL how strong something is □ *the potency of the drug* (**potência**)

• **potent** /ˈpəʊtənt/ ADJECTIVE powerful, strong or effective □ *a potent poison* □ *a potent mix of frustration and resentment* (**potente**)

potential /pəˈtenʃəl/ ▶ ADJECTIVE able to become something in the future □ *a potential customer* □ *a potential risk* □ *This technology has many other potential uses.* (**potencial**)
▶ NOUN, NO PLURAL
1 qualities that could be developed successfully in the future □ *She's a player with great potential.* 🖼 *He hasn't reached his full potential yet.*
2 the possibility that something may happen or develop □ *There's a lot of potential for economic growth.*

• **potentially** /pəˈtenʃəli/ ADVERB possibly true in the future □ *potentially dangerous side effects* □ *This is potentially bad news for workers.* (**potencialmente**)

pothole /ˈpɒthəʊl/ NOUN [plural **potholes**] a hole in a road (**caldeirão**)

potion /ˈpəʊʃən/ NOUN [plural **potions**] a drink containing medicine or poison, or one that people believe has a magical effect (**poção**)

pot plant /ˈpɒt ˌplɑːnt/ NOUN [plural **pot plants**] a plant grown inside the house in a container (**planta de vaso**)

potter /ˈpɒtə(r)/ ▶ VERB [**potters, pottering, pottered**] to move about in a relaxed way, especially at home, doing small jobs □ *Jenny pottered around in the kitchen.* (**vaguear, ocupando-se com pequenos trabalhos**)
▶ NOUN [plural **potters**] someone who makes things from clay (**oleiro, ceramista**)

pottery /ˈpɒtəri/ NOUN [plural **potteries**]
1 *no plural* objects such as bowls and cups made from clay (**louça de cerâmica**)
2 *no plural* the job or activity of making things from clay (**atividade cerâmica**)
3 a place where things are made from clay (**olaria, fábrica de cerâmica**)

potty /ˈpɒti/ ▶ NOUN [plural **potties**] a container that a small child sits on to go to the toilet (**troninho, penico**)
▶ ADJECTIVE [**pottier, pottiest**] an informal word meaning stupid or strange □ *He has some fairly potty ideas.* (**pirado, biruta**)

pouch /paʊtʃ/ NOUN [plural **pouches**]
1 a small soft bag (**bolsa**)
2 the fold of skin that some female animals carry their babies in (**bolsa**)

pouffe /puːf/ NOUN [plural **pouffes**] a low soft seat with no back or arms (**pufe**)

poultry /ˈpəʊltri/ NOUN, NO PLURAL

pounce

1 birds such as chickens and turkeys that are kept for people to eat (**aves domésticas**)
2 the meat from these birds (**aves**)

pounce /paʊns/ VERB [**pounces, pouncing, pounced**] to jump or move forward suddenly to attack or catch someone or something □ *The cat pounced on the mouse.* (**saltar, dar o bote**)

◆ PHRASAL VERB **pounce on something** to criticize someone for something very quickly □ *Critics pounced on the Senator's comments.* (**investir contra**)

pound /paʊnd/ ▶ NOUN [plural **pounds**]

1 the main unit of money in Britain. The written symbol is £. □ *They cost just a few pounds each.* □ *a multi-million pound contract* (**libra esterlina**)
2 a coin worth one pound (**moeda de uma libra**)
3 a unit for measuring weight, equal to 16 ounces. This is often written lb. (**libra**)

▶ VERB [**pounds, pounding, pounded**]

1 to hit something hard repeatedly □ *Someone was pounding at the door, trying to get in.* (**bater**)
2 if your heart pounds, it beats quickly, usually because you are afraid □ *My heart was pounding before the interview.* (**bater acelerado**)
3 to walk or run with heavy steps □ *He came pounding up behind me.* (**andar pesadamente**)

pour /pɔː(r)/ VERB [**pours, pouring, poured**]

1 to make a liquid flow out of a container □ + *into* She poured the orange juice into a glass. □ + *out* She poured out the tea. □ + *over* Pour the sauce over the chicken. (**verter, colocar um líquido**)
2 to rain very hard (**chover torrencialmente**) 🔁 *It's pouring with rain outside.* □ *The rain was pouring down.* (**está chovendo torrencialmente**)
3 to flow out of something fast and in large quantities □ *Water was pouring through the ceiling.* □ *The sweat poured down his face.* (**escorrer**)
4 to go into or leave somewhere in large numbers □ *Crowds of people poured out of the stadium.* (**entrar ou sair em grande quantidade**)

◆ PHRASAL VERB **pour something out** to talk about your feelings suddenly and with emotion □ *He poured out his troubles to me.* (**desabafar**)

pout /paʊt/ ▶ VERB [**pouts, pouting, pouted**] to push your lips out because you are angry or in order to look attractive (**fazer beiço**)
▶ NOUN [plural **pouts**] when someone pouts

poverty /ˈpɒvəti/ NOUN, NO PLURAL the state of being poor □ *Many families are living in poverty.* □ *a campaign to reduce global poverty* (**pobreza**)

powder /ˈpaʊdə(r)/ NOUN [plural **powders**] a substance in the form of very small dry pieces, like dust □ *chilli powder* □ *washing powder* □ *She sprinkled some cocoa powder on the top.* (**pó**)

• **powdered** /ˈpaʊdəd/ ADJECTIVE dried and made into a powder □ *powdered milk* (**em pó**)

• **powdery** /ˈpaʊdəri/ ADJECTIVE made of very small pieces, like powder □ *powdery snow* (**constituído de pequenas partículas ou pó**)

power /ˈpaʊə(r)/ ▶ NOUN [plural **powers**]

1 the ability to control or influence people or things □ *economic/military power* □ + *over* The big factory owners had a lot of power over local people. □ *They really understand the power of the media.* (**poder, capacidade**)
2 energy used for working machines, or the supply of this energy (**energia**) 🔁 *nuclear power* (**energia nuclear**) 🔁 *We are looking at new ways to generate power.* (**gerar energia**) 🔁 *Electricity companies are working day and night to restore power to the area.* (**restaurar a energia**)
3 political control □ *His government was in power* (= ruling the country) *for over 10 years.* (**poder**) 🔁 *The army seized power last year.* (**tomou o poder**) 🔁 *Tony Blair came to power in 1997.* (**chegou ao poder**)
4 a country with a lot of influence in the world □ *He says that Western powers are failing to deal with climate change.* (**potência**)
5 strength or force □ *The power of the blast knocked me over.* (**poder**)
6 the official right to do something □ + *to do something* We don't have the power to issue visas. □ *The committee's powers are limited.* (**autoridade**)
7 do everything in your power to do everything that you can to achieve something □ *Doctors did everything in their power to save her.* (**fazer tudo ao seu alcance**)
8 the number of times a number has to be multiplied by itself. For example, '10 to the power of 4' is 10 x 10 x 10 x 10. A maths word. (**potência**)

▶ VERB [**powers, powering, powered**]

1 to provide something with the energy to work □ *Batteries are used to power the telescope.* (**fornecer energia**)
2 to move very quickly and with force, or to make something move very quickly and with force □ *He powered the ball into the net.* (**impulsionar**)

power cut /ˈpaʊə kʌt/ NOUN [plural **power cuts**] a period when there is no electricity because of a problem with the supply (**corte de energia**)

powerful /ˈpaʊəfʊl/ ADJECTIVE

1 having the ability to control or influence people or things □ *a powerful politician* □ *a powerful nation* (**poderoso**)
2 having a lot of physical force □ *a powerful earthquake* □ *a powerful backhand* (**poderoso**)
3 very effective, being able to do a lot □ *Computers have become more powerful.* (**poderoso**)
4 having a very strong effect on the body or mind □ *a powerful drug* (**poderoso**)
5 a person's body is powerful if it has big, strong muscles (**poderoso**)

powerless

- **powerfully** /'pauəfuli/ ADVERB in a powerful way □ *a tall, powerfully built man* (**poderosamente**)

powerless /'pauələs/ ADJECTIVE not able to control or to affect things 🔁 *She felt powerless to stop him.* (**impotente**)

power outage /'pauər ˌautɪdʒ/ NOUN [plural **power outages**] the US phrase for **power cut** (**corte de energia**)

power station /'pauə ˌsteɪʃən/ NOUN [plural **power stations**] a building where electricity is produced □ *a nuclear power station* (**central elétrica**)

PR /ˌpiːˈɑː(r)/ ABBREVIATION **public relations** (**relações públicas**)

practical /'præktɪkəl/ ▶ ADJECTIVE

1 to do with real situations, not ideas (**prático**) 🔁 *This research has no practical applications.* (**aplicações práticas**) 🔁 *They provide practical advice.* (**conselhos práticos**)
2 useful and suitable (**prático**) 🔁 *It's the most practical solution to the problem.* (**solução prática**) □ *It's not practical to cycle in a long skirt.*
3 good at repairing things and doing things with your hands □ *He's not a very practical person.* (**prático**)
4 able to make sensible decisions □ *She's much more practical than her sister.* (**prático**)
▶ NOUN [plural **practicals**] a lesson or an examination in which students learn or use practical skills (**aula ou exame prático**)

practical joke /ˌpræktɪkəl ˈdʒəuk/ NOUN [plural **practical jokes**] a trick that makes someone look silly and makes other people laugh (**trote**)

practically /'præktɪkəli/ ADVERB
1 almost □ *It was practically full.* □ *Practically everything was destroyed.* (**praticamente**)
2 in a way that is to do with real situations (**praticamente**) 🔁 *Practically speaking, it won't have much effect.* (**falando praticamente**)

practice /'præktɪs/ ▶ NOUN [plural **practices**]

1 no plural when you do something often so that you get better at it □ *He'll soon learn to play the violin with a bit more practice.* □ *He goes to choir practice on Mondays.* (**prática**)
2 an activity, especially one that people have been doing for a long time □ *They campaigned to end the practice of torture.* □ *She studied their religious practices.* (**prática**)
3 put something into practice to do something which was an idea or a plan □ *We formed a community to put our ideas about society into practice.* (**pôr em prática**)
4 in practice used for saying what really happens when it is different from what you think will happen □ *Making bicycles freely available seemed a good idea, but in practice they just got stolen.* (**na prática**)

607

praise P

5 be out of practice to not have done something for a long time □ *I'd love to play in your hockey team, but I'm a bit out of practice.* (**estar fora de forma**)
6 good/best practice a good/the best way to do something □ *It's good practice to consult with patients' relatives.* (**boa prática, a melhor prática**)
7 the place where a doctor, lawyer, etc. works □ *She set up a medical practice in the town.* (**consultório**)
▶ VERB [**practices, practicing, practiced**] the US spelling of **practise**
- **practiced** /'præktɪst/ ADJECTIVE the US spelling of **practised**
- **practicing** /'præktɪsɪŋ/ ADJECTIVE the US spelling of **practising**

practise /'præktɪs/ VERB [practises, practising, practised]

1 to do something again and again so that you get better at it 🔁 *Practise breathing through your nose.* □ *To become a good musician, you must practise regularly.* (**treinar, exercitar**)
2 to do something, especially as part of a tradition or a religion □ *He practises yoga.* □ *They are free to practise their religion.* (**praticar**)
3 to work as a doctor, lawyer, etc. □ *to practice medicine/law* (**praticar**)
- **practised** /'præktɪst/ ADJECTIVE skilful because of having a lot of experience □ *He stretched the pizza dough with practised ease.* (**prático**)
- **practising** /'præktɪsɪŋ/ ADJECTIVE
1 a practising member of a religion believes in that religion and follows its rules □ *He is a practising Catholic.* (**praticante**)
2 working in a particular job □ *She is a practising lawyer.* (**praticante**)

> ► Remember that in British English, **practise** with an **s** is a verb. **Practice** with a **c** is a noun: □ *This gave me a chance to practise my language skills.* □ *I have football practice tonight.*

pragmatic /præɡˈmætɪk/ ADJECTIVE sensible and possible in a particular situation (**pragmático**) 🔁 *He has a pragmatic approach to politics.* □ *a pragmatic solution*
- **pragmatically** /præɡˈmætɪkəli/ ADVERB in a pragmatic way (**de modo pragmático**)
- **pragmatism** /'præɡmətɪzəm/ NOUN, NO PLURAL a pragmatic way of dealing with things (**pragmatismo**)
- **pragmatist** /'præɡmətɪst/ NOUN [plural **pragmatists**] a person who is pragmatic (**pragmatista**)

prairie /'preəri/ NOUN [plural **prairies**] a large area of flat land covered with grass in North America. A geography word. (**pradaria**)

praise /preɪz/ ▶ VERB [praises, praising, praised]

1 to say how well someone has done and how you admire them □ **+ for** He was widely praised for his work. □ The prime minister praised the rescue effort. (elogiar)
2 to express thanks to God □ Praise the Lord! (louvar)
▶ NOUN, NO PLURAL when you praise someone □ **+ for** She received praise for her handling of the incident. (elogio) 🔲 He **won praise** from the team coach. (ganhou elogio)

praiseworthy /ˈpreɪzwɜːði/ ADJECTIVE good and deserving praise □ a praiseworthy effort (louvável)

pram /præm/ NOUN [plural prams] a small vehicle with wheels that a baby lies in and which you push (carrinho de bebê)

prance /prɑːns/ VERB [prances, prancing, pranced] to dance or to jump about, especially because you want people to look at you □ The singer pranced around the stage. (saltitar ou dançar para chamar a atenção)

prank /præŋk/ NOUN [plural pranks] a trick you play on someone as a joke (peça)

prawn /prɔːn/ NOUN [plural prawns] a small sea animal you can eat that has a curved shaped and is pink when cooked (camarão grande)

pray /preɪ/ VERB [prays, praying, prayed]
1 to speak to a god □ **+ for** She knelt down and prayed for forgiveness. □ **+ to** He prayed to Allah. (rezar, orar)
2 to hope very much that something will happen □ **+ for** We were praying for a nice sunny day. □ **+ that** They prayed that someone would find them. (em oração)
• **prayer** /preə(r)/ NOUN [plural prayers]
1 the words that you use when you pray to a god □ the Lord's prayer (oração, reza) 🔲 He **said a prayer** of thanks. □ They went to the mosque for Friday prayers. (fez uma oração)
2 no plural when you pray to a god □ They knelt in prayer. (em oração)

pre- /priː/ PREFIX pre- is added to the beginning of words to mean 'before' □ prehistoric (= before the time when history was written down) □ pre-dinner drinks (pré-)

preach /priːtʃ/ VERB [preaches, preaching, preached]
1 to talk to a group of people about a religious subject, usually as part of a church service (pregar) 🔲 Father Andrew will **preach the sermon**. (pregou o sermão)
2 to speak about something to persuade people to accept it □ He preached patience and understanding. (pregar)
3 to give someone advice in an annoying way □ He's always preaching to me about studying hard. (pregar)
• **preacher** /ˈpriːtʃə(r)/ NOUN [plural preachers] someone who preaches at a religious service (pregador)

precarious /prɪˈkeəriəs/ ADJECTIVE
1 dangerous or full of risks (precário) 🔲 With the manager now against him, he's in a very **precarious position**.
2 likely to fall □ The tree was leaning over at a precarious angle.
• **precariously** /prɪˈkeəriəsli/ ADVERB in a precarious way □ He was standing precariously close to the edge. (precariamente)

precaution /prɪˈkɔːʃən/ NOUN [plural precautions] something you do to avoid an accident or a problem happening (precaução) 🔲 We're **taking** all necessary **precautions**. (tomando precauções) 🔲 They stopped work on the site as a **safety precaution**. (prevenção de segurança)
• **precautionary** /prɪˈkɔːʃənəri/ ADJECTIVE done as a precaution 🔲 He was taken to hospital as a **precautionary measure**. (preventivo)

precede /prɪˈsiːd/ VERB [precedes, preceding, preceded] to come or to happen before something else □ They were involved in the protests that preceded last week's election. (preceder)
• **precedence** /ˈpresɪdəns/ NOUN, NO PLURAL when one person or thing is more important than another (precedência) 🔲 Public health must **take precedence over** economic considerations.
• **precedent** /ˈpresɪdənt/ NOUN [plural precedents]
1 something that happened in the past and now provides a rule for what should happen in future (precedente) 🔲 a **legal precedent** (precedente legal) 🔲 This decision **sets a precedent**. (estabelecer um precedente)
2 something that happened in the past that is similar to something now (precedente) 🔲 The scale of the book's success is **without precedent**. (sem precedentes)
• **preceding** /prɪˈsiːdɪŋ/ ADJECTIVE coming or happening before □ He hadn't seen his family during the preceding year. (precedente)

precinct /ˈpriːsɪŋkt/ NOUN [plural precincts] (área de pedestres)
1 an area of shops in the centre of a town where cars are not allowed 🔲 a **shopping precinct** (área de compras para pedestres)
2 precincts the area around a large building □ the cathedral precincts (precinto, recinto)

precious /ˈpreʃəs/ ▶ ADJECTIVE
1 very valuable and rare □ precious stones □ In many parts of the world, water is a precious resource. (precioso)
2 very important to someone □ His books are very precious to him. (precioso)
▶ ADVERB **precious little/few** used to emphasize there is very little or very few of something □ There's precious little evidence. (muito pouco)

precipice /ˈpresɪpɪs/ NOUN [plural precipices] a high, steep side of a piece of land (precipício)

precise /prɪˈsaɪs/ ADJECTIVE

1 exact □ *the precise location* □ *He didn't give any precise details.* (preciso) 🔁 *At that precise moment, the bell rang.* (no momento preciso)
2 careful and accurate □ *Her work is very precise.* (preciso)

• **precisely** /prɪˈsaɪslɪ/ ADVERB
1 exactly or accurately □ *We need to find out precisely what happened.* □ *It arrived at precisely 12.34.* (precisamente)
2 used to emphasize the reason for something (precisamente) 🔁 *He explained that his books are strange precisely because his own life is so ordinary.* (precisamente porque)
3 used to strongly agree with someone's opinion (exatamente)

• **precision** /prɪˈsɪʒən/ NOUN, NO PLURAL the quality of being exact and accurate □ *He hit the target again and again with precision.* (precisão)

precocious /prɪˈkəʊʃəs/ ADJECTIVE a precocious child is more advanced than is usual for his or her age (precoce)

pre-date /ˌpriːˈdeɪt/ VERB [pre-dates, pre-dating, pre-dated] to have existed or been built before something else □ *Balloons pre-date aircraft.* (preceder)

predator /ˈpredətə(r)/ NOUN [plural predators] an animal that hunts and eats other animals (predador)

• **predatory** /ˈpredətərɪ/ ADJECTIVE hunting and eating other animals □ *predatory birds* (predatório, predador)

predecessor /ˈpriːdɪsesə(r)/ NOUN [plural predecessors]
1 the person who did a particular job before someone else got that job □ *My predecessor was in this job for twenty years.* (predecessor)
2 something that existed before something else and was replaced by the new thing □ *The European Economic Community was a predecessor of the European Union.* (predecessor)

predicament /prɪˈdɪkəmənt/ NOUN [plural predicaments] a difficult situation in which you do not know what to do □ *I found myself in a predicament.* (apuro, enrascada)

predict /prɪˈdɪkt/ VERB [predicts, predicting, predicted] to say that you think something will happen in the future □ *They're predicting snow for next week.* (predizer)

• **predictable** /prɪˈdɪktəbəl/ ADJECTIVE expected or easy to predict □ *The ending of the film was entirely predictable.* (previsível)

• **predictably** /prɪˈdɪktəblɪ/ ADVERB in a way that is easy to predict □ *Predictably, Josh arrived late.* (previsivelmente)

• **prediction** /prɪˈdɪkʃən/ NOUN [plural predictions] when you predict something, or something that is predicted (previsão) 🔁 *I don't want to make any predictions yet.* (fazer previsões)

predictive texting /prɪˌdɪktɪv ˈtekstɪŋ/ NOUN, NO PLURAL the way that words appear on a mobile phone when you type in the first letter of the words in a text message (digitação inteligente)

predominant /prɪˈdɒmɪnənt/ ADJECTIVE main or most common □ *The predominant colour in his paintings is blue.* (predominante)

• **predominantly** /prɪˈdɒmɪnəntlɪ/ ADVERB mostly or mainly □ *The trains are predominantly old, out-of-date models.* (predominantemente)

pre-empt /prɪˈempt/ VERB [pre-empts, pre-empting, pre-empted]
1 to do something in order to prevent something else happening □ *We must take action to pre-empt any potential terrorist attacks.* (prevenir)
2 to do or to say something before someone else is able to □ *I don't want to pre-empt anything the Minister is going to say.* (antecipar)

• **pre-emptive** /prɪˈemptɪv/ ADJECTIVE done in order to prevent something (preventivo) 🔁 *The actor launched a pre-emptive strike against film critics yesterday.* (ataque preventivo)

preen /priːn/ VERB [preens, preening, preened]
1 if a bird preens, it cleans its feathers (limpar as penas)
2 to spend a lot of time improving your appearance □ *Sasha was preening herself in front of the mirror.* (arrumar-se)

preface /ˈprefɪs/ ▶ NOUN [plural prefaces] a short introduction at the start of a book (prefácio) ▶ VERB [prefaces, prefacing, prefaced] to say or to write something before the main thing you want to say or write (prefaciar)

prefect /ˈpriːfekt/ NOUN [plural prefects] an older student in a school who has some responsibilities over younger students (monitor, chefe)

prefer /prɪˈfɜː(r)/ VERB [prefers, preferring, preferred] to like or to want one thing more than something else □ *I prefer the red dress to the black one.* □ **+ to do something** *We'd prefer to stay near the beach.* □ *He prefers not to talk about his family in public.* □ **+ ing** *I prefer working from home.* □ *You can bring you own food if you prefer.* (preferir)

• **preferable** /ˈprefərəbəl/ ADJECTIVE better than something else □ *A sandwich would be preferable to any of the food in that café.* (preferível)

• **preferably** /ˈprefərəblɪ/ ADVERB used to show what you would prefer □ *We're looking for a two-bedroom flat, preferably near the town centre.* (preferivelmente)

• **preference** /ˈprefərəns/ NOUN [plural preferences] when you prefer one thing to another, or something that you like or prefer (preferência) 🔁 *The choice is down to personal preference.* □ *The children showed a preference for sweet foods.* (preferência pessoal)

prefix /ˈpriːfɪks/ NOUN [plural prefixes] a group of letters that is added to the beginning of a word to make another word (prefixo)

pregnancy /ˈpreɡnənsi/ NOUN [plural **pregnancies**] the period when a woman or a female animal carries a developing baby inside her □ *Smoking during pregnancy can harm the baby.* (gravidez)

• **pregnant** /ˈpreɡnənt/ ADJECTIVE if a woman or a female animal is pregnant, she is carrying a developing baby inside her (grávida) ▣ *a pregnant woman* (mulher grávida) □ + *with She was pregnant with twins.* ▣ *She got pregnant again quite quickly.* (ficar grávida)

preheat /ˌpriːˈhiːt/ VERB [**preheats, preheating, preheated**] to turn an oven on so it reaches a particular temperature before you put the food in it □ *Preheat the oven to 180°.* (preaquecer)

prehistoric /ˌpriːhɪˈstɒrɪk/ ADJECTIVE to do with the time in the past before history was written down □ *prehistoric times* □ *prehistoric animals* (pré-histórico)

prejudice /ˈpredʒudɪs/ ▶ NOUN [plural **prejudices**] when someone has an unfair opinion or dislike of someone or something without knowing or understanding them (preconceito) ▣ *racial prejudice* (preconceito racial) □ *There is still prejudice against people with mental disabilities.*

▶ VERB [**prejudices, prejudicing, prejudiced**]
1 to cause someone to have an unfair opinion about someone or something □ *She said the publicity could prejudice the jury against her client.* (predispor contra)
2 a formal word meaning to have a harmful effect on something □ *I don't want to say anything that might prejudice the investigation.* (prejudicar, causar dano)

• **prejudiced** /ˈpredʒudɪst/ ADJECTIVE having a prejudice against someone or something □ *prejudiced attitudes* □ *He's prejudiced against female writers.* (preconceituoso)

preliminary /prɪˈlɪmɪnəri/ ▶ ADJECTIVE done or said before the main event or activity (preliminar) ▣ *The preliminary results are promising, but more work is needed.* □ *This process is at a very preliminary stage.* (resultados preliminares)

▶ NOUN [plural **preliminaries**] something said or done to prepare for a main event (preliminar)

premature /ˈprematjuə(r)/ ADJECTIVE
1 a premature baby is born before the time it should have been born (prematuro)
2 happening or done too early or before the usual time □ *It's a bit premature to talk about wedding plans.* □ *premature deaths from cancer* (prematuro)

• **prematurely** /ˈprematjuəli/ ADVERB early or before the usual time □ *His playing career ended prematurely.* (prematuramente)

premier /ˈpremɪə(r)/ ▶ ADJECTIVE best, most successful or most important □ *France's premier resort* □ *one of the world's premier sports events* (principal)

▶ NOUN [plural **premiers**] the political leader of a country □ *the Chinese premier* (primeiro--ministro)

premiere /ˈpremɪeə(r)/ ▶ NOUN [plural **premieres**] the first public showing or performance of a film, play, etc. (estreia) ▣ *the world premiere of the new James Bond film* (estreia mundial)

▶ VERB [**premieres, premiering, premiered**] to be shown or performed in public for the first time □ *The film will premiere at the Cannes Film Festival.* (estrear)

premise /ˈpremɪs/ NOUN [plural **premises**]
1 a formal word meaning an idea or a theory that something is based on □ *The basic premise of the programme is to encourage exercise.* (premissa)
2 premises the buildings and land owned and used by an organization □ *The fire affected several shops and other business premises.* (locais, instalações)

premium /ˈpriːmiəm/ ▶ NOUN [plural **premiums**]
1 a regular amount of money that you pay for insurance (= arrangement in which a company gives you money if you have an accident or are ill) (prêmio) ▣ *an insurance premium* (prêmio de seguro)
2 an extra amount that you have to pay for something (bonificação) ▣ *Companies will pay a premium for advertising during popular shows.* (pagar bonificação)
3 at a premium difficult to get and so often expensive □ *Hotel space is at a premium during the festival.* (com alta demanda e preço elevado)
4 put/place a premium on something to think that something is very important or valuable □ *We put a premium on fresh, local ingredients.* (valorizar)

▶ ADJECTIVE of the highest quality and often expensive □ *premium food products* (da mais alta qualidade) ▣ *a premium rate call* (plano especial de tarifa elevada)

premonition /ˌpreməˈnɪʃən/ NOUN [plural **premonitions**] a feeling you have that something is going to happen (premonição) ▣ *She had a premonition that her sister was going to have an accident.* (ter uma premonição)

preoccupation /priːˌɒkjuˈpeɪʃən/ NOUN [plural **preoccupations**] something that you think about too much of the time □ *She has an unhealthy preoccupation with food.* (preocupação)

• **preoccupied** /priːˈɒkjupaɪd/ ADJECTIVE thinking so much about one thing that you do not pay enough attention to other things □ *He had become preoccupied with work.* (preocupado)

• **preoccupy** /priːˈɒkjupaɪ/ VERB [**preoccupies, preoccupying, preoccupied**] if something preoccupies you, you think about it a lot (preocupar(-se))

prepaid /ˌpriːˈpeɪd/ ADJECTIVE paid for before you need or use it □ *prepaid postage* (pré-pago)

preparation

preparation /ˌprepəˈreɪʃən/ NOUN [plural preparations]
1 no plural when you get ready for something □ + *for* This is ideal preparation for next week's tournament. (**preparação**) 🔹 We did some shopping *in preparation for* the trip. (**como preparação para**) □ Make sure the food preparation area is clean.
2 something you do to get ready for something □ How are the wedding preparations going? (**preparativo**) 🔹 We're *making* the final *preparations for* the opening. (**fazer os preparativos**)

preparatory /prɪˈpærətəri/ ADJECTIVE preparing for something □ Some preparatory work is needed before building can start. (**preparatório**)

prepare /prɪˈpeə(r)/ VERB [prepares, preparing, prepared]
1 to get ready for something or to make something ready □ + *for* We need to prepare for the long journey. □ + *to do something* They are preparing to open a new shop. □ He prepared a report on the company. □ We have to prepare students for working life. (**preparar**) 🔹 *Prepare yourself* for a shock when you see him. (**preparar(-se)**)
2 to make food ready for eating □ Mum was in the kitchen, preparing dinner. (**preparar**)

• **prepared** /prɪˈpeəd/ ADJECTIVE
1 ready to do something (**preparado**) 🔹 We're *much better prepared* this year. (**mais bem preparado**)
2 made before you need or use it (**preparado**) 🔹 His lawyer read a *prepared statement*. (**discurso preparado**) □ They sell ready prepared meals.
3 prepared to do something willing to do something □ How much are you prepared to pay? (**preparado, disposto**)

preposition /ˌprepəˈzɪʃən/ NOUN [plural prepositions] a word or phrase used before a noun or a pronoun to show things like position, time or method. For example, in, by and out of are prepositions. (**preposição**)

prepossessing /ˌpriːpəˈzesɪŋ/ ADJECTIVE a formal word meaning attractive □ It's not a very prepossessing building. (**atraente, fascinante**)

preposterous /prɪˈpɒstərəs/ ADJECTIVE stupid and unreasonable □ That's a preposterous suggestion! (**absurdo, despropositado**)

prescribe /prɪˈskraɪb/ VERB [prescribes, prescribing, prescribed]
1 to tell a patient to take a particular medicine □ Doctors often prescribe antibiotics for infections. (**prescrever**)
2 a formal word meaning to say officially that something must be done (**prescrever**)

• **prescription** /prɪˈskrɪpʃən/ NOUN [plural prescriptions]
1 a written instruction from a doctor saying that someone needs a particular medicine □ + *for* a prescription for sleeping pills (**prescrição, receita**) 🔹 a *prescription drug* (= medicine that must be prescribed by a doctor) (**prescrição médica**)
2 on prescription if a medicine is on prescription, you can only get it if you have a written instruction from a doctor saying that you need it (**receita obrigatória**)

• **prescriptive** /prɪˈskrɪptɪv/ ADJECTIVE a formal word meaning telling people exactly what to do □ There is a very prescriptive approach to teaching reading. (**prescritivo**)

presence /ˈprezəns/ NOUN, NO PLURAL
1 the fact of someone or something being somewhere □ Tests indicated the presence of the disease. (**presença**) 🔹 He was questioned *in the presence of* a lawyer. (**na presença de**)
2 a group of soldiers or police officers who are in a place for a particular reason (**presença de espírito**) 🔹 the US *military presence* in the region (**presença militar**) 🔹 There was a heavy *police presence* outside the stadium. (**presença policial**)
3 make your presence felt to make people notice you and listen to you □ The protesters really made their presence felt. (**fazer sentir sua presença**)
4 presence of mind the ability to think and act in a calm and sensible way □ She had the presence of mind to call an ambulance. (**presença de espírito**)

present¹ /ˈprezənt/ ▶ NOUN [plural presents]
1 something you give to someone, for example for their birthday □ I've got a present for you. (**presente**) 🔹 a *birthday present* (**presente de aniversário**) 🔹 The children opened their *Christmas presents*. (**presentes de Natal**)
2 the present the time now (**o tempo presente**)
3 at present now □ He doesn't have a job at present. (**atualmente**)

▶ ADJECTIVE
1 being in a particular place □ Both men were present at the meeting. □ Vitamin D is present in small quantities in food. (**estar presente**)
2 to do with the time now □ The present system isn't working. (**atual**) 🔹 We'll look at fashion from the 50s to *the present day*. (**nos dias de hoje**)

present¹ /prɪˈzent/ VERB [presents, presenting, presented]
1 to give something to someone formally, often at a ceremony □ She presented the best actor award. □ The captain was presented with the trophy. (**presentear**)
2 to tell facts to people, especially in a formal way □ They presented new evidence in court. (**apresentar**)
3 to cause something (**apresentar**) 🔹 This will *present problems* for some schools. (**apresentar problemas**)
4 to show someone or something in a particular way □ We want to present a more modern image. (**apresentar**)

5 to introduce a radio or television show □ *She presents the news on the BBC.* (apresentar)
6 to introduce one person to another in a formal way (apresentar)

• **presentable** /prɪˈzentəbəl/ ADJECTIVE clean or tidy enough to be seen in public □ *He got up, washed, and made himself as presentable as possible.* (apresentável)

• **presentation** /ˌprezənˈteɪʃən/ NOUN [plural **presentations**]
1 a talk to a group of people explaining or describing something (apresentação) 🔁 *She gave a presentation on her research.* (fazer uma apresentação)
2 when you show something to people or the way in which it is shown or arranged □ *The presentation of food is very important.* (apresentação)
3 when something, such as a prize, is formally given to someone □ *a presentation ceremony* (apresentação)

• **presenter** /prɪˈzentə(r)/ NOUN [plural **presenters**]
1 someone who introduces the parts of a radio or television programme □ *the presenter of Radio 4's Today Programme* (apresentador)
2 someone who gives a presentation (apresentador)

presently /ˈprezəntli/ ADVERB
1 a formal word meaning now □ *Are you employed presently?* (atualmente)
2 an old-fashioned word meaning 'soon' □ *The bus should be here presently.* (em breve)

present participle /ˌprezənt ˈpɑːtɪsɪpəl/ NOUN [plural **present participles**] the form of a verb ending in *-ing*, usually used after the verb *be*. For example, *going* in *I was going*. (particípio presente)

present tense /ˌprezənt ˈtens/ NOUN [plural **present tenses**] a form of a verb used to show that the action is happening now (tempo presente)

preservation /ˌprezəˈveɪʃən/ NOUN, NO PLURAL when you preserve something □ *The preservation of the rainforests is extremely important.* (preservação)

preservative /prɪˈzɜːvətɪv/ NOUN [plural **preservatives**] a substance that is put in food or on wood to stop it decaying □ *The drink contains no artificial colourings or preservatives.* (conservante)

preserve /prɪˈzɜːv/ ▶ VERB [**preserves, preserving, preserved**] to keep something the same, stopping it from being lost or destroyed □ *We try to preserve our traditions and culture.* □ *ancient fossils preserved in rocks* (preservar)
▶ NOUN [plural **preserves**]
1 a food such as jam that is made by cooking fruit with sugar □ *strawberry preserve* (conserva)
2 an activity that is thought to be suitable only for a particular type of person □ *Sailing should not be the preserve of the rich.* (atividade reservada, privilégio)
3 a safe area for plants and animals (reserva)

preside /prɪˈzaɪd/ VERB [**presides, presiding, presided**] to be in charge of a meeting or a formal event □ *Reverend Williams presided over the ceremony.* □ *the presiding judge* (presidir)

presidency /ˈprezɪdənsi/ NOUN [plural **presidencies**] the position of being a president or the time when someone is a president □ *He won the presidency again in 1980.* □ *It was the most serious crisis of Mr Chirac's presidency.* (presidência)

president /ˈprezɪdənt/ NOUN [plural **presidents**]
1 the elected leader of a country that has no king or queen □ *the Russian president* □ + *of the president of Pakistan* □ *President Bush* (presidente)
2 the person with the highest position in a company or an organization □ + *of He became president of General Motors in 1920.* (presidente)

• **presidential** /ˌprezɪˈdenʃəl/ ADJECTIVE to do with the president of a country (presidencial) 🔁 *the presidential election* (eleição presidencial) 🔁 *a presidential candidate* (candidato presidencial)

press /pres/ ▶ VERB [**presses, pressing, pressed**]
1 to push something, or to push something firmly against something else □ *Press the red button.* □ *Orla pressed her lips together.* □ *Nothing's happening – try pressing harder.* (apertar(-se))
2 to try to persuade someone to do something or agree to something □ + *to do something They pressed us to decide a date for the meeting.* □ + *on I tried to press him on his promise to visit.* □ + *for We are pressing for an official enquiry into the accident.* (pressionar) 🔁 *She is taking legal advice in order to press her claim for compensation.* (pressionar um direito/reivindicação)
3 press a point to repeat what you have said in order to try to make someone accept your opinion □ *I suggested she might pay for the damage, but she was so upset, I didn't press the point.* (insistir no assunto)
4 press charges to make someone be officially accused of a crime in a court □ *Having looked at the evidence, the police decided not to press charges against her.* (apresentar acusações)
5 to make clothes flat by ironing them (passar a ferro)
6 to move in a particular direction in a close group □ *The crowd pressed forward to see the princess.* (comprimir-se)

♦ PHRASAL VERB **press ahead/on** to continue with something, even if there are difficulties □ *We were all tired, but we decided to press ahead and finish the job.* (persistir)

▶ NOUN [plural **presses**]
1 the press newspapers and magazines, and the people who write for them □ *He issued a*

statement to the press. □ *Press reports suggested that he was sacked from the post.* □ *She was mocked in the press.* (**imprensa**)

2 a bad/good press criticism/praise from newspapers, magazines, television, etc. □ *Their new family car received a very bad press.* (**crítica (negativa ou positiva)**)

3 a push against something □ *I gave the panel a press and it opened.* (**pressão, aperto**)

4 a machine that prints books, newspapers, etc. (**impressora, prelo**)

5 a company that makes and prints books □ *He published his book with one of the academic presses.* (**editora**)

press conference /ˈpres ˌkɒnfərəns/ NOUN [plural **press conferences**] an official meeting at which someone gives information to people who work in television and on newspapers and answers their questions *The police are holding a press conference this afternoon.* (**dar uma entrevista coletiva**)

pressing /ˈpresɪŋ/ ADJECTIVE important and needing to be dealt with now □ *There is a pressing need for more judges in our courts.* (**urgente**)

press office /ˈpres ˌɒfɪs/ NOUN [plural **press offices**] a department of an organization that deals with the people who work on newspapers (**assessoria de imprensa**)

press-up /ˈpresʌp/ NOUN [plural **press-ups**] an exercise in which you lie on your front and use your hands to push the top half of your body up off the floor □ *He does 20 press-ups every morning.* (**flexão**)

pressure /ˈpreʃə(r)/ NOUN [plural **pressures**]
1 no plural when someone tries to persuade or force someone to do something □ **+ to do something** *The government are under pressure to change the law.* (**pressão**) *Her father put pressure on her to study medicine.* (**colocar pressão**) *I don't want to put you under pressure.* (**sob pressão**)
2 no plural the force on or against a surface from something pressing on it □ *Applying pressure to the wound will stop the bleeding.* (**pressão**)
3 the force that a liquid or gas has when it is inside something □ *air pressure* □ *high blood pressure* (**pressão**)
4 difficulties and problems that cause you to worry □ *the pressures of work* (**pressão**)

• **pressurize** or **pressurise** /ˈpreʃəraɪz/ VERB [**pressurizes, pressurizing, pressurized**]
1 to persuade or force someone to do something □ *I felt I had been pressurized into leaving.* (**pressionar**)
2 to control the air pressure inside something (**pressurizar**)

• **pressurized** or **pressurised** /ˈpreʃəraɪzd/ ADJECTIVE with a high air pressure inside □ *a pressurized container* (**pressurizado**)

prestige /preˈstiːʒ/ NOUN, NO PLURAL respect and admiration □ *There's a certain prestige attached to working for such a company.* (**prestígio**)

• **prestigious** /preˈstɪdʒəs/ ADJECTIVE generally admired and respected □ *She teaches at one of the most prestigious universities in Canada.* (**prestigiado**)

presumably /prɪˈzjuːməblɪ/ ADVERB used for saying something that you think is probably true □ *Presumably the picnic will be cancelled if it rains.* (**presumivelmente**)

presume /prɪˈzjuːm/ VERB [**presumes, presuming, presumed**] to believe that something is true without having any proof (**presumir**) □ *I presume you've invited Sophie to the party?* *Six soldiers are missing, presumed dead.* (**supostamente falecido**)

• **presumption** /prɪˈzʌmpʃən/ NOUN [plural **presumptions**] when you presume something, or something that is presumed □ *The presumption is that you are innocent until you are proved guilty.* (**presunção**)

• **presumptuous** /prɪˈzʌmptʃuəs/ ADJECTIVE being too confident with someone in a way that does not show respect for them □ *It's a bit presumptuous giving advice to your teacher!* (**presunçoso**)

pre-tax /ˌpriːˈtæks/ ADJECTIVE before tax has been paid (**bruto**) *pre-tax profits* (**rendimento bruto**)

pretence /prɪˈtens/ NOUN, NO PLURAL when you behave in a way that makes people believe something that is not true (**fingimento, simulação**) *She was struggling to keep up the pretence that she still loved her husband.* (**manter a simulação**)
▶ go to **under false pretences**

pretend /prɪˈtend/ VERB [**pretends, pretending, pretended**]
1 to try to make someone believe something that is not true □ **+ that** *She closed her eyes and pretended that she was asleep.* □ **+ to do something** *Chris was sitting at the table, pretending to do his homework.* (**fingir**)
2 to imagine that something is true as part of a game □ **+ to do something** *The children were pretending to be robots.* (**fingir**)

pretense /prɪˈtens/ NOUN [plural **pretenses**] the US spelling of **pretence** (ver **pretence**)

pretentious /prɪˈtenʃəs/ ADJECTIVE trying to sound more clever or interesting than you really are in order to make people admire you □ *Jim found her pretentious.* (**pretensioso**)

pretext /ˈpriːtekst/ NOUN [plural **pretexts**]
1 a false reason that you give for doing something (**pretexto**)
2 on the pretext of If you do something on the pretext of doing something else, you pretend that you are doing the first thing in order to do the

prettiness /ˈprɪtɪnɪs/ NOUN, NO PLURAL being pretty □ *the prettiness of the garden* (**beleza**)

pretty /ˈprɪti/ ▶ ADJECTIVE [prettier, prettiest]
1 a pretty woman or girl is attractive □ *His girlfriend is very pretty.* (**lindo, bonito**)
2 things that are pretty are attractive, often in a delicate way □ *She was wearing a pretty white dress.* □ *What pretty flowers!* (**lindo, bonito**)
▶ ADVERB
1 quite □ *Eight out of ten is a pretty good mark.* (**muito, bastante**)
2 very □ *That's a pretty good salary, if you ask me!* (**muito bom**)
3 pretty much/well almost □ *The building work is pretty much finished.* (**quase**)

prevail /prɪˈveɪl/ VERB [prevails, prevailing, prevailed] to be the main quality or influence in a situation. A formal word. □ *Let's hope that common sense will prevail.* □ *He was brought up in an area where violence prevailed.* (**prevalecer**)
• **prevailing** /prɪˈveɪlɪŋ/ ADJECTIVE
1 most common at a particular time or among a particular group of people □ *That is the prevailing attitude among young people.* (**predominante**)
2 most common in a particular area □ *The prevailing winds blow from the south.* (**predominante**)

prevalence /ˈprevələns/ NOUN, NO PLURAL how prevalent something is (**prevalência**)
• **prevalent** /ˈprevələnt/ ADJECTIVE common in a particular place or among a particular group of people □ *The disease is becoming increasingly prevalent in some parts of the UK.* (**prevalecente**)

prevent /prɪˈvent/ VERB [prevents, preventing, prevented] to stop something happening or someone doing something □ *Police are working hard to prevent gun crime.* □ + from *They were prevented from leaving the building.* (**impedir**)
• **preventable** /prɪˈventəbəl/ ADJECTIVE able to be prevented □ *preventable illnesses* (**evitável**)
• **prevention** /prɪˈvenʃən/ NOUN, NO PLURAL when you prevent something (**prevenção**) □ *crime prevention* (**prevenção de crime**) □ *the prevention of infection*
• **preventive** /prɪˈventɪv/ ADJECTIVE done in order to make sure that something bad, such as illness or crime, does not start □ *preventive medicine* □ *preventive measures* (**preventivo**)

preview /ˈpriːvjuː/ NOUN [plural previews]
1 a showing or performance of a film, play, etc. to a small group of people before it is shown to everyone □ *Previews of the musical start this week.* (**pré-estreia**)
2 a short piece of a film, programme, etc. used to advertise it (**apresentação parcial com fins de propaganda**)

previous /ˈpriːviəs/ ADJECTIVE happening or existing before □ *Please write down your previous address.* □ *I have some previous experience of working with children.* (**anterior**)
• **previously** /ˈpriːviəsli/ ADVERB before □ *I'd met Sven a few months previously.* □ *He previously worked in a bank.* (**anteriormente**)

prey /preɪ/ NOUN, NO PLURAL an animal or bird that another animal hunts, kills and eats (**presa**)
◆ PHRASAL VERBS [preys, preying, preyed] **prey on something** to hunt something and kill it □ *Wolves prey on small mammals.* (**apresar, caçar e matar**)
prey on someone to use someone who is weak or easy to trick in order to get what you want, for example money □ *These people prey on the elderly.* (**fazer alguém de vítima**)
◆ IDIOM **prey on someone's mind** if something preys on your mind, you cannot stop thinking or worrying about it □ *Her comments were preying on my mind.* (**atormentar**)

price /praɪs/ ▶ NOUN [plural prices]
1 the amount of money that something costs (**preço**) □ *Food prices continue to rise.* (**preços continuam a subir**) □ *House prices are falling.* (**preços estão caindo**)
2 a disadvantage that you experience as a result of doing something bad or trying to achieve something (**preço**) □ *He committed a crime and he paid the price.* (**pagar o preço**) □ *the price of fame*
▶ VERB [prices, pricing, priced]
1 to set a price for something □ *The new flats are priced at £250,000.* (**avaliar**)
2 to mark a price on something (**pôr preço em**)
• **priceless** /ˈpraɪsləs/ ADJECTIVE
1 extremely valuable □ *priceless works of art* (**inestimável**)
2 an informal word meaning very funny □ *The look on his face was priceless.* (**impagável**)
• **pricey** /ˈpraɪsi/ ADJECTIVE [pricier, priciest] an informal word for expensive □ *It's a nice club but the drinks are a bit pricey.* (**caro**)

prick /prɪk/ ▶ VERB [pricks, pricking, pricked] to make a very small hole in something with a sharp object □ *Diane pricked her finger on a rose bush.* (**picar**)
▶ NOUN [plural pricks] a sudden short pain you feel when something pricks your skin □ *I felt a slight prick as the nurse gave me the injection.* (**picada**)

prickle /ˈprɪkəl/ ▶ NOUN [plural prickles] one of the many thin sharp points on some animals and plants □ *Be careful of the prickles.* (**espinho**)
▶ VERB [prickles, prickling, prickled] to feel something unpleasant on your skin as if many sharp points are pressing against it, or to cause this feeling □ *She felt her skin prickle in the heat.* (**alfinetar**)

pride — principle

- **prickly** /ˈprɪklɪ/ ADJECTIVE [pricklier, prickliest]
  1 covered in prickles or feeling like many sharp points □ *a prickly bush* □ *I find wool next to my skin very prickly.* (espinhoso)
  2 becoming annoyed easily □ *She's rather prickly.* (irritadiço)

pride /praɪd/ NOUN, NO PLURAL
1 a feeling of pleasure because you have achieved something or because someone such as your child has achieved something □ *There was such pride in his face as he looked at his baby daughter.* (orgulho)
2 respect for yourself (orgulho) ▣ *Jenny always took pride in her appearance.* (ter orgulho de)
3 a feeling of being better or more important than other people
4 someone's pride and joy something or someone that makes you very happy □ *That garden is her pride and joy.*

priest /priːst/ NOUN [plural priests] someone who performs religious services in some religions □ *a Roman Catholic priest* (padre)

- **priestess** /ˌpriːstˈes/ NOUN [plural priestesses] a female priest in some ancient or non-Christian religions (sacerdotisa)

- **priesthood** /ˈpriːsthʊd/ NOUN, NO PLURAL the job and responsibilities of being a priest, or priests as a group (sacerdócio)

prim /prɪm/ ADJECTIVE [primmer, primmest] shocked by anything rude (afetado)

primarily /ˈpraɪmərɪlɪ/ ADVERB mainly □ *These free newspapers are targeted primarily at young people.* (principalmente)

primary /ˈpraɪmərɪ/ ▶ ADJECTIVE main □ *Heart disease is still one of the primary causes of early death.* (principal)
▶ NOUN [plural primaries] in the US, a vote in each state in which a political party chooses who will represent them in a general election □ *the New Hampshire primary* (primária)

primary colour /ˌpraɪmərɪ ˈkʌlə(r)/ NOUN [plural primary colours] one of the colours red, blue and yellow which make other colours when they are mixed together (cor primária)

primary school /ˈpraɪmərɪ ˌskuːl/ NOUN [plural primary schools] a school for children between the ages of four and eleven (escola primária)

primate /ˈpraɪmeɪt/ NOUN [plural primates] an animal that belongs to the group that includes monkeys and humans (primata)

prime /praɪm/ ▶ ADJECTIVE
1 main □ *Good health care is a matter of prime importance.* (principal) ▣ *He is the prime suspect in the investigation.* (suspeito principal)
2 best □ *a prime cut of beef* (de primeira qualidade) ▣ *houses in a prime location* (localização privilegiada)

▶ NOUN, NO PLURAL the time of someone's life when they are at their best and most successful (plenitude) ▣ *In his prime, Muhammad Ali was the most famous man in the world.* (em sua melhor época)
▶ VERB [primes, priming, primed]
1 to prepare someone with the information they need for an event such as a meeting □ *We were all primed with questions to ask the guest speaker.* (instruir)
2 to prime a bomb is to make it ready to explode (preparar)

prime minister /ˌpraɪm ˈmɪnɪstə(r)/ NOUN [plural prime ministers] the leader of the government in Britain and in many other countries of the world □ *the Irish prime minister* (primeiro-ministro)

prime number /ˌpraɪm ˈnʌmbə(r)/ NOUN [plural prime numbers] a number that can only be divided exactly by 1 or itself. A maths word. (número primo)

primitive /ˈprɪmɪtɪv/ ADJECTIVE
1 belonging to the earliest stages of development □ *primitive man* □ *a primitive computer* (primitivo)
2 simple and not modern or comfortable □ *The accommodation was fairly primitive.* (primitivo)

primrose /ˈprɪmrəʊz/ NOUN [plural primroses] a wild plant with small pale yellow flowers (prímula)

prince /prɪns/ NOUN [plural princes] the son or grandson of a king or queen, or the male ruler of a small state or country □ *Prince Charles* (príncipe)

princess /ˌprɪnˈses/ NOUN [plural princesses] the daughter or grand-daughter of a king or queen, or the wife of a prince □ *Princess Caroline of Monaco* (princesa)

principal /ˈprɪnsɪpəl/ ▶ ADJECTIVE main □ *Steel-making was the principal industry in the area.* (principal)
▶ NOUN [plural principals] the person in charge of a school, college or university (diretor escolar)

- **principally** /ˈprɪnsɪpəlɪ/ ADVERB mainly or mostly □ *She collects old toys, principally dolls.* (principalmente)

principle /ˈprɪnsɪpəl/ NOUN [plural principles]
1 a general rule or idea about how something is done □ *We follow the principle of first come, first served.* □ *The government has drawn up principles of good practice for landlords.* (princípio)
2 a general rule that you base your behaviour on because you think it is morally right (princípio) ▣ *It was against his principles to borrow money.* (contra seus princípios)
3 in principle in general although not in all the details □ *The president has agreed in principle to hold democratic elections.* (em princípio)

4 on principle if you do something on principle, you do it because you believe it is morally right □ *He doesn't eat meat on principle.* (por princípio)

print /prɪnt/ ▶ VERB [prints, printing, printed]
1 to produce words, pictures, etc. on paper or another surface using a machine □ *We printed 500 copies of the letter.* □ *Cooking instructions are printed on the back of the label.* □ *All our reference books are printed in Italy.* □ *Is this document ready to print?* (imprimir)
2 to publish writing in a newspaper, magazine, etc. □ *They did not print my letter.* (publicar)
3 to write words without joining the letters together □ *Print your name at the top of the form.* (escrever com letra de forma)

◆ PHRASAL VERB **print something out** to make a printed copy of a document or image from a computer □ *I printed out the map.* (imprimir)
▶ NOUN [*plural* **prints**]
1 words, pictures, etc. that are produced on paper or another surface using a machine □ *She can only read books with large print.* □ *I was so excited to see my name in print.* (impressão)
2 in/out of print still/not still published □ *His novels went out of print years ago.* (à venda/esgotado)
3 a mark that is left when something has pressed on a surface □ *Prints from his boots could still be seen in the mud.* (impressão)
4 a fingerprint (= mark left when someone has touched something) (impressão digital)
5 a copy of an original picture by an artist □ *He has a print of the Mona Lisa on his wall.* (impressão)
6 a type of picture made by pressing a raised image into ink and then onto paper (chancela)
7 a pattern on a piece of paper or material □ *Floral prints are popular for summer dresses.* (estampa)

• **printer** /'prɪntə(r)/ NOUN [*plural* **printers**]
1 a machine that prints words and pictures from a computer (impressora)
2 a person or company whose business is printing books, newspapers, etc. (impressor)

printout /'prɪntaʊt/ NOUN [*plural* **printouts**] information from a computer that is printed on paper (impressão)

prior /'praɪə(r)/ ADJECTIVE
1 happening or existing before □ *I couldn't go because I had a prior engagement.* (anterior)
2 prior to something before something □ *Little is known about the days prior to his death.* (anterior)

prioritize or **prioritise** /praɪˈɒrɪtaɪz/ VERB [**prioritizes, prioritizing, prioritized**] to decide which task is most important and must be done first □ *He's not very good at prioritizing his work.* (priorizar)

• **priority** /praɪˈɒrəti/ NOUN [*plural* **priorities**]
1 the most important thing, which has to be dealt with before other things (prioridade) ⬚ *The environment is a top priority for the government.* (prioridade principal)* ⬚ *The football club has made it a priority to wipe out racism at matches.* (fazer disso uma prioridade)
2 the quality of being more important than anything else (prioridade) ⬚ *The university aims to give priority to students from state schools.* (dar prioridade a)* ⬚ *Families who are homeless must take priority on housing lists.* (ter prioridade)

prise /praɪz/ VERB [**prises, prising, prised**] to force something open, off or out, often using a flat tool □ *He prised open the lid with a screwdriver.* (forçar)

prism /'prɪzəm/ NOUN [*plural* **prisms**]
1 an object made of clear glass that separates a beam of white light into seven colours (prisma)
2 a solid shape with sides that are parallel and ends that are the same shape, e.g. a triangle. A maths word (prisma)

prison /'prɪzən/ NOUN [*plural* **prisons**]
a building where criminals are kept □ *Her father is in prison.* (prisão) ⬚ *If he commits another crime he will be sent to prison.* (mandar para a prisão) ⬚ *He was released from prison last month.* (libertar da prisão)

• **prisoner** /'prɪzənə(r)/ NOUN [*plural* **prisoners**]
1 someone who is kept in prison as a punishment □ *Four prisoners share each cell.* (preso, prisioneiro)
2 someone who is kept in a place and cannot get out (prisioneiro) ⬚ *Her father had kept her prisoner in the cellar for over 20 years.* (a manteve como prisioneira)

pristine /'prɪstiːn/ ADJECTIVE in perfect condition, like new □ *Charlie was wearing a pair of pristine white trainers.* (imaculado)

privacy /'prɪvəsi, 'praɪvəsi/ NOUN, NO PLURAL being alone where people cannot see or hear you □ *A higher fence will give us a bit more privacy.* (privacidade)

private /'praɪvɪt/ ▶ ADJECTIVE
1 belonging to or used by only one person, or a small group of people □ *a private beach* □ *The prince flew in on his private plane.* (privado)
2 where other people cannot see or hear you □ *Can we find somewhere more private?* (privado)
3 owned and managed by people or companies, not by the government □ *private industry* □ *a private hospital* (privado)
4 to do with relationships, family and the things that people do when they are not working (privado, particular) ⬚ *He never discusses his private life in interviews* □ *I never make private calls from the office.* (vida privada)
5 if someone is private, they talk very little about their feelings □ *He was a very private man.* (reservado)

private school   617   problem

▶ NOUN [plural **privates**]
1 an ordinary soldier in the army (**soldado raso**)
2 in private with no one else present □ *Could I speak to you in private for a moment?* (**em particular**)

• **privately** /'praɪvɪtli/ ADVERB
1 away from other people □ *Can we talk privately?* (**particularmente**)
2 a privately owned company is owned by a person or business and not by the government (**empresa privada**)
3 secretly □ *Privately, he thought they were all fools.* (**particularmente**)

private school /ˌpraɪvɪt 'skuːl/ NOUN [plural **private schools**] a school which parents must pay to send their children to (**escola particular**)

privatization *or* **privatisation**
/ˌpraɪvɪtaɪ'zeɪʃən/ NOUN, NO PLURAL the process by which a business or industry that is owned and controlled by the government is sold to private companies □ *the privatization of the rail network* (**privatização**)

• **privatize** *or* **privatise** /'praɪvɪtaɪz/ VERB [**privatizes, privatizing, privatized**] to sell a business or industry that is owned by the government to private companies (**privatizar**)

privet /'prɪvɪt/ NOUN, NO PLURAL a plant that is often used to make hedges (= lines of bushes that separate areas of land) (**alfena**)

privilege /'prɪvɪlɪdʒ/ NOUN [plural **privileges**]
1 a special right or advantage given to only one person, or to only a few people □ *The directors have special privileges such as their own dining room.* (**privilégio**)
2 a special experience that makes you feel very lucky □ *It's been a great privilege to work with you all.* (**privilégio**)

• **privileged** /'prɪvɪlɪdʒd/ ADJECTIVE having advantages that most people do not have □ *She comes from a very privileged background.* □ *I felt privileged to work with such a great director* (**privilegiado**)

prize /praɪz/ ▶ NOUN [plural **prizes**] something won in a competition or given as a reward for good work (**prêmio**) 🔁 *The first prize was a trip to France.* (**primeiro prêmio**) 🔁 *Adam won a prize in the raffle.* (**ganhar um prêmio**)
▶ ADJECTIVE a prize animal, vegetable or flower is good enough to win a prize (**digno de prêmio**)
▶ VERB [**prizes, prizing, prized**] to consider something to be very valuable or important □ *Gold has always been prized for its beauty and rarity.* (**apreciar**)

pro /proʊ/ NOUN [plural **pros**] someone who is paid for playing a sport □ *a golf pro* (**profissional**)
♦ IDIOM **pros and cons** the advantages and disadvantages of something □ *We discussed the pros and cons of moving abroad.* (**prós**)

pro- /proʊ/ PREFIX
1 pro- is added to the beginning of words to mean something to do with 'beginning' or 'forward' □ *prologue* □ *proceed*
2 pro- is also added to the beginning of words to mean 'supporting someone or something' □ *Henry's always been pro-Europe.* (**pró-**)

probability /ˌprɒbə'bɪləti/ NOUN [plural **probabilities**] (**probabilidade**)
1 how probable it is that something will happen □ *This has a 40 per cent probability of success.*
2 something that will probably happen □ *Redundancies are now a probability.*

probable /'prɒbəbəl/ ADJECTIVE likely to be true or to happen □ *A lit cigarette was the probable cause of the fire.* □ *It now seems probable that we will go to war.* (**provável**)

• **probably** /'prɒbəbli/ ADVERB used for saying that something is likely to happen or be true □ *I'll probably be late.* □ *He'll probably lose it anyway.* (**provavelmente**)

probation /prə'beɪʃən/ NOUN, NO PLURAL
1 a period of time during which someone who committed a crime must not do anything wrong or they will go to prison □ *He was put on probation for six months.* (**liberdade condicional**)
2 a period of time when someone in a new job is watched to make sure they can do the job well (**período de experiência**)

• **probationary** /prə'beɪʃənəri/ ADJECTIVE to do with probation □ *I have to work a probationary period of three months.* (**experimental**)

probation officer /prə'beɪʃən ˈɒfɪsə(r)/ NOUN [plural **probation officers**] someone whose job is to help criminals who are on probation and check that they are doing nothing wrong (**oficial da condicional**)

probe /proʊb/ ▶ VERB [**probes, probing, probed**] to ask questions in order to find out information about someone or something (**investigar, sondar**) 🔁 *She asked some very probing questions.* (**perguntas investigativas**)
▶ NOUN [plural **probes**]
1 when someone asks questions in order to find out facts about someone or something (**investigação**)
2 a long thin medical tool that is used for looking at things inside the body (**sonda**)
3 a spacecraft with no people that is sent into space to collect information (**sonda espacial**)

probiotic /ˌproʊbaɪ'ɒtɪk/ ▶ NOUN [plural **probiotics**] a food or pill that contains bacteria of the type that some people think makes you healthy (**probiótico**)
▶ ADJECTIVE containing probiotics □ *probiotic yoghurt*

problem /'prɒbləm/ NOUN [plural **problems**]
1 a situation that is causing difficulties □ *financial problems* □ **+ with** *There's a problem with the car.* (**problema**) 🔁 *He's having problems*

with someone at work. (**ter problemas com**) / *I don't want to cause any problems for you.* (**causar nenhum problema**) □ *We had problems finding a hotel.*

2 no problem (a) used for agreeing to do something for someone □ *'Could you get some milk on the way home, please?' 'Sure, no problem.'* (b) used when someone thanks you for something □ *'Thanks for lending me your bike.' 'No problem.'* (**sem problemas**)

3 have a problem with something/someone to not like something or someone or to not approve of them (**ter problemas com algo/alguém**)

4 a question that you have to answer or solve □ *maths problems* (**problema**)

> Note that you 'have problems **doing** something'. You do not have problems 'to do something':
> ✓ *We had problems finding the house.*
> ✗ *We had problems to find the house.*

> A very bad problem is a **serious** problem and not an 'important' problem:
> ✓ *Debt is a very serious problem.*
> ✗ *Debt is a very important problem.*

- **problematic** /ˌprɒbləˈmætɪk/ ADJECTIVE causing problems □ *The arrangements were problematic.* (**problemático**)

proboscis /prəʊˈbɒsɪs/ NOUN [plural **proboscises** or **proboscess**] a long, thin tube that some insects have for sucking. A biology word. (**probóscide**)

procedure /prəˈsiːdʒə(r)/ NOUN [plural **procedures**] a way of doing something or the order in which things are done (**procedimento**) □ *There are standard procedures for customers making complaints.* (**procedimentos padronizados**)

proceed /prəˈsiːd/ VERB [**proceeds, proceeding, proceeded**]

1 to continue something. A formal word. □ *She has decided not to proceed with her application.* (**seguir, prosseguir**)

2 proceed to do something to do something next, especially something annoying □ *He said he wasn't hungry and proceeded to eat two slices of cake.* (**continuar a fazer algo**)

3 to go somewhere. A formal word. □ *Passengers for flight 394 to Madrid should proceed to gate 21.*

- **proceedings** /prəˈsiːdɪŋz/ PLURAL NOUN
1 things that are done or said, especially in a formal situation □ *A power cut interrupted the proceedings.* (**procedimentos**)
2 legal action □ *She has started proceedings against the company.* (**ação legal**)

- **proceeds** /ˈprəʊsiːdz/ PLURAL NOUN the money made from a sale or other event □ *All the proceeds from the concert will go to famine relief.* (**dinheiro apurado**)

process /ˈprəʊses/ ▶ NOUN [plural **processes**]
1 a series of actions or events that have a particular result □ *the production process* □ *Getting a visa is a lengthy process.* (**processo**)
2 a series of changes □ *the ageing process* (**processo**)
3 in the process while doing something □ *He won the cup, breaking the course record in the process.* (**no processo**)
4 in the process of (doing) sth in the middle of doing something □ *We're in the process of buying a house in France.* (**em processo de**)
▶ VERB [**processes, processing, processed**]
1 to deal with information in several official stages or on a computer □ *We will process your order as quickly as possible.* (**processar**)
2 to treat something with chemicals to make it last longer □ *processed food* □ *Cocoa butter is processed to remove the fat.* (**processar**)

- **procession** /prəˈseʃən/ NOUN [plural **processions**] a line of people or vehicles moving along slowly, one behind the other □ *a funeral procession* (**cortejo, desfile**)

proclaim /prəˈkleɪm/ VERB [**proclaims, proclaiming, proclaimed**] to state something publicly or officially □ *He proclaimed his innocence.* (**proclamar**)

- **proclamation** /ˌprɒkləˈmeɪʃən/ NOUN [plural **proclamations**] a public announcement of something important □ *the proclamation of independence* (**proclamação**)

procure /prəˈkjʊə(r)/ VERB [**procures, procuring, procured**] a formal word meaning to succeed in getting something □ *It was impossible to procure funding for the project.* (**conseguir**)

prod /prɒd/ ▶ VERB [**prods, prodding, prodded**]
1 to press something with a finger or pointed object □ *She prodded him in the back.* (**cutucar**)
2 to encourage someone to do something, especially something they have agreed to do □ *He'll get the information for you but you have to prod him.* (**estimular**)
▶ NOUN [plural **prods**]
1 when you press something with a finger or pointed object (**cutucão, picada**)
2 when you encourage someone to do something, especially something they have agreed to do (**empurrãozinho, estímulo**) □ *Give her a prod if she forgets.* (**dar um empurrãozinho**)

prodigious /prəˈdɪdʒəs/ ADJECTIVE very great □ *prodigious talent* □ *prodigious wealth* (**prodigioso**)

- **prodigiously** /prəˈdɪdʒəsli/ ADVERB extremely □ *She is prodigiously talented.* (**prodigiosamente**)

prodigy /ˈprɒdɪdʒi/ NOUN [plural **prodigies**] a young person who is extremely clever or extremely good at something (**prodígio**) □ *a child prodigy* (**criança prodígio**)

produce

produce ▶ VERB /prəˈdjuːs/ [produces, producing, produced]
1 to make, grow or create something □ *The new factory will produce goods for export.* □ *The plum tree didn't produce much fruit last year.* □ *The sun produces both light and heat.* (**produzir**)
2 to have a particular effect □ *This style of teaching produces better results.* (**produzir**)
3 to show something so that people can see it □ *The conjuror produced a rabbit from a hat.* □ *The diary was produced as evidence at the trial.* (**produzir**)
4 to organize the actors, equipment and money, etc. that are needed for a film, programme, play or musical recording □ *a film produced by George Lucas* (**apresentar, produzir**)
▶ NOUN, NO PLURAL /ˈprɒdjuːs/ things that are grown or produced on farms, especially food (**produto, produção**) 🔊 *The village shop sells local produce.* (**produção local**)

• **producer** /prəˈdjuːsə(r)/ NOUN [*plural* **producers**]
1 someone who organizes the actors, equipment and money, etc. that are needed for a film, programme or musical recording □ *an independent producer* (**produtor**)
2 someone who makes products or grows produce to be sold □ *a major wine producer* (**produtor**)

product /ˈprɒdʌkt/ NOUN [*plural* **products**]
1 something that is produced in large numbers for selling (**produto**) 🔊 *dairy products* (**produtos de laticínio**) □ *household cleaning products*
2 the result of something □ *We are all the products of our environment.* (**produto**)

• **production** /prəˈdʌkʃən/ NOUN [*plural* **productions**]
1 *no plural* making, growing or producing something, or the amount that is produced □ *the production of organic food* □ *We now have two of these types of car in production.* □ *We have increased production by 30%.* (**produção**)
2 a performance or number of performances of a play or show □ *He played the lead in the school production of 'Grease'.* (**produção**)
3 *no plural* the process of organizing the actors, equipment and money, etc. needed for a film, programme, play or musical recording □ *a TV production company* (**de produções**)

• **productive** /prəˈdʌktɪv/ ADJECTIVE
1 having useful results □ *I had a very productive day at work.* □ *a productive meeting* (**produtivo**)
2 producing a lot of something □ *This was the most productive period of his writing career.* (**produtivo**)

• **productivity** /ˌprɒdʌkˈtɪvəti/ NOUN, NO PLURAL the rate at which goods are produced, or the rate at which one person works to produce something □ *The company introduced measures designed to increase productivity.* (**produtividade**)

profile

prof /prɒf/ ABBREVIATION **professor** □ *Prof Cale* (abreviatura de professor universitário)

profession /prəˈfeʃən/ NOUN [*plural* **professions**]
1 a type of job that needs special qualifications and training, for example, medicine, law and teaching □ *He is considering going into the legal profession.* (**profissão**)
2 all the people who work in a particular profession □ *The medical profession has been angered by her remarks.* (**profissão**)

• **professional** /prəˈfeʃənəl/ ADJECTIVE
1 to do with a profession □ *professional training* (**profissional**)
2 doing something for money instead of as a hobby or for pleasure □ *a professional footballer* (**profissional**)
3 doing a job with great skill and care □ *She is always very calm and professional.* (**profissional**)

• **professionalism** /prəˈfeʃənəlɪzəm/ NOUN, NO PLURAL a way of doing something that shows great skill and care (**profissionalismo**)

• **professionally** /prəˈfeʃənəli/ ADVERB
1 with the special qualifications and training needed for a particular job □ *a professionally qualified accountant* (**profissionalmente**)
2 in a way that shows great skill or care □ *He managed a difficult situation very professionally.* (**profissionalmente**)
3 for money and not as a hobby □ *He never played football professionally.* (**profissionalmente**)
4 in a way that is to do with your work □ *I've known him professionally for ten years or more.* (**profissionalmente**)

professor /prəˈfesə(r)/ NOUN [*plural* **professors**]
1 in the UK, the most important teacher in a university department (**professor universitário**)
2 in the US, a teacher in a university or college (**professor universitário**)

proficiency /prəˈfɪʃənsi/ NOUN, NO PLURAL the level of skill you have achieved in doing something □ *proficiency in a second language* (**proficiência**)

• **proficient** /prəˈfɪʃənt/ ADJECTIVE good at something that needs skill or practice □ *a proficient diver* (**proficiente**)

profile /ˈprəʊfaɪl/ NOUN [*plural* **profiles**]
1 a short description of someone or something □ *We have drawn up a profile of our ideal candidate.* (**perfil**)
2 the idea or opinion that most people have about someone or something □ *The company's profile has changed over the years.* (**projeção**)
🔊 *The case has had a very high profile* (= has had a lot of attention) *in the British press.* (**elevada projeção**)
3 the shape of someone's face seen from the side □ *The photo shows Jessica in profile.* (**perfil**)

profit /ˈprɒfɪt/ ▶ NOUN [plural **profits**] money you make by selling something for more than you paid for it □ *The company is looking for ways to increase its profits.* (lucro) 🔂 *We made a profit when we sold the house.* (ter lucro) 🔂 *Many farmers find it hard to sell their meat at a profit.* (vender com lucro)

> ➤ Note that you **make** a profit. You do not 'gain' a profit:
> ✓ *We made a big profit on the sale.*
> ✗ *We gained a big profit on the sale.*

▶ VERB [**profits, profiting, profited**] to get an advantage from something □ *Convicted criminals are not allowed to profit from their crimes.* (lucrar)

- **profitable** /ˈprɒfɪtəbəl/ ADJECTIVE
1 making a profit □ *a profitable business* (lucrativo)
2 useful and valuable □ *This might be a more profitable use of your time.* (lucrativo)

profound /prəˈfaʊnd/ ADJECTIVE
1 very great □ *profound changes* (profundo) 🔂 *Losing her mother as a child had a profound effect on Anna.* (efeito profundo)
2 profound feelings are very strong □ *He had a profound sense of guilt about his past.* (profundo)
3 showing a lot of knowledge and understanding □ *profound comments* (profundo)

- **profoundly** /prəˈfaʊndli/ ADVERB in a profound way □ *I was profoundly shocked by what she said.* (profundamente)

profuse /prəˈfjuːs/ ADJECTIVE produced or given in large amounts □ *profuse bleeding* □ *profuse apologies* (profuso, abundante)

- **profusely** /prəˈfjuːsli/ ADVERB very much (profusamente) 🔂 *He apologized profusely.* □ *The wound was bleeding profusely.* (desculpar-se profusamente)

progesterone /prəˈdʒestərəʊn/ NOUN, NO PLURAL a substance produced in the bodies of women and female animals which makes the womb (= organ where the baby grows) ready for pregnancy. A biology word. (progesterona)

program /ˈprəʊɡræm/ ▶ NOUN [plural **programs**]
1 a set of instructions put into a computer to make it perform a task. A computing word. □ *a word processing program* (programa)
2 the US spelling of **programme** (programa)
▶ VERB [**programs, programming, programmed**]
1 to put a set of instructions into a computer or piece of electronic equipment to make it do something. A computing word. (programar)
2 the US spelling of **programme** (programar)

programme /ˈprəʊɡræm/ NOUN [plural **programmes**]
1 a television or radio show □ *an arts programme* (programa)
2 a list of planned events or activities □ *the government's education programme* □ *a programme of reform* (programa)
3 a thin book that gives information about an event or performance (programa)

programmer /ˈprəʊɡræmə(r)/ NOUN [plural **programmers**] someone whose job is to write computer programs (programador)

- **programming** /ˈprəʊɡræmɪŋ/ NOUN, NO PLURAL the work of writing computer programs (programação)

progress ▶ NOUN, NO PLURAL /ˈprəʊɡres/
1 improvement of skills or knowledge (progresso) 🔂 *Freya has made a lot of progress in the last year.* (fez progresso)
2 in progress happening or being done now (em curso) □ *Work is currently in progress to develop the site.*
3 movement forward or towards something □ *The bus made very slow progress through the crowds.*
▶ VERB /prəˈɡres/ [**progresses, progressing, progressed**]
1 to develop □ *The work is progressing well.* □ *As the disease progresses, the patient requires more care.*
2 if a period of time progresses, it continues □ *As the evening progressed, I felt more and more tired.*
3 to go forward □ *They progressed slowly up the icy ridge.* (avanço)

- **progression** /prəˈɡreʃən/ NOUN, NO PLURAL
1 development from one stage to the next □ *the progression of a disease* (progressão)
2 movement forward (avanço)

- **progressive** /prəˈɡresɪv/ ADJECTIVE
1 using very modern ideas □ *a progressive school* (progressista)
2 happening gradually □ *The disease causes progressive damage to the immune system.* (progressivo)

- **progressively** /prəˈɡresɪvli/ ADVERB gradually □ *Dad's sight is getting progressively worse.* (progressivamente)

prohibit /prəˈhɪbɪt/ VERB [**prohibits, prohibiting, prohibited**] to not allow people officially to do something □ *Smoking is prohibited in most public places.* (proibir)

- **prohibition** /ˌprəʊɪˈbɪʃən/ NOUN [plural **prohibitions**] an official order that people are not allowed to do something □ *a prohibition on drinking outside* (proibição)

- **prohibitive** /prəˈhɪbətɪv/ ADJECTIVE so expensive that you cannot buy something □ *Property prices in the south-east are prohibitive.* (inatingíveis)

project ▶ NOUN /ˈprɒdʒekt/ [plural **projects**]
1 a piece of work that is planned with a particular aim □ *a research project* □ *a major construction project* (projeto)
2 a piece of work done by a student, often involving collecting information on a subject and

proletariat

writing about it (projeto) 🔲 *Hannah's doing a project on Henry VIII.* (fazer um projeto sobre)
▶ VERB /prəˈdʒekt/ [projects, projecting, projected]
1 to calculate an amount in the future, using information that you have now □ *Sales are projected to rise in the spring.* (projetar)
2 to make light or an image from a film fall onto a flat surface or screen □ *The concert was projected live onto a big screen in the square.* (projetar)
3 if you project a particular quality, you make everyone believe that you have that quality □ *He's trying to project himself as a caring politician.* (projetar-se)
4 to make your voice loud enough to be heard a long way away (projetar-se)
5 to stick out from a surface (projetar-se)
• **projection** /prəˈdʒekʃən/ NOUN [plural projections] (projeção)
1 a calculation about an amount in the future, using information that you have now □ *Economists have to make projections about future sales.*
2 when light or an image from a film falls onto a flat surface or screen
3 something that sticks out
• **projectionist** /prəˈdʒekʃənɪst/ NOUN [plural projectionists] someone who operates a film projector, especially in a cinema (projecionista)
• **projector** /prəˈdʒektə(r)/ NOUN [plural projectors] a machine used to project films on to a screen □ *an overhead projector* (projetor)

proletariat /ˌprəʊlɪˈteərɪət/ NOUN, NO PLURAL the proletariat the workers in a society, who do not own property (proletariado)

proliferate /prəˈlɪfəreɪt/ VERB [proliferates, proliferating, proliferated] to quickly increase in number □ *Companies such as these have proliferated in the last few years.* (proliferar)

• **proliferation** /prəˌlɪfəˈreɪʃən/ NOUN, NO PLURAL when something increases quickly □ *Recent years have seen the proliferation of leisure facilities in the town.* (proliferação)

prolific /prəˈlɪfɪk/ ADJECTIVE a prolific writer, artist, etc. produces a lot of work □ *a prolific composer* (prolífico)

prologue /ˈprəʊlɒg/ NOUN [plural prologues] a short introduction at the beginning of a play, story or poem (prólogo)

prolong /prəˈlɒŋ/ VERB [prolongs, prolonging, prolonged] to make something continue for longer □ *drugs to prolong life* (prolongar)

• **prolonged** /prəˈlɒŋd/ ADJECTIVE continuing for a long time or for longer than expected □ *a prolonged absence from school* (prolongado)

prom /prɒm/ NOUN [plural proms] in the US, a formal party for students at a high school (= school for children between 14 and 18) at the end of a school year (baile)

promote

promenade /ˌprɒməˈnɑːd/ NOUN [plural promenades] a wide path for people to walk along by the sea (passeio público)

prominence /ˈprɒmɪnəns/ NOUN, NO PLURAL being prominent (proeminência)

• **prominent** /ˈprɒmɪnənt/ ADJECTIVE
1 important and known by a lot of people □ *a prominent member of the government* (proeminente, notável)
2 sticking out or easily seen □ *a prominent landmark* (proeminente)

• **prominently** /ˈprɒmɪnəntli/ ADVERB in a prominent way □ *Long skirts feature prominently in all the fashion shows.* (proeminentemente)

promise /ˈprɒmɪs/ ▶ VERB [promises, promising, promised]
1 to tell someone that you will certainly do something □ + *to do something* *I've promised to help Rebecca with the food.* □ + *that* *I promise that I'll pay you back.* □ *But you promised me you'd come!* (prometer)
2 to say that you will certainly give something to someone □ *I've promised my copy of the book to Mila.* (prometer)
3 promise to be to show signs of being good or successful □ *It promises to be another lovely day tomorrow.* (prometer ser)
▶ NOUN [plural promises]
1 something that someone promises to do (promessa) 🔲 *I'm not making any promises.* (fazer promessas) 🔲 *I try to keep my promises* (= do what I have said I will do). (manter promessas) 🔲 *The unions accused the government of breaking its promise to them* (= not doing what it said it would). (quebrar promessa)
2 no plural signs that someone or something will be good or successful in the future (promessa) 🔲 *She shows great promise as a gymnast.* (prometer ser sucesso)

• **promising** /ˈprɒmɪsɪŋ/ ADJECTIVE showing signs of being good or successful in the future □ *She's one of our most promising young tennis players.* (promissor)

promontory /ˈprɒməntəri/ NOUN [plural promontories] an area of land that sticks out into the sea. A geography word. (promontório)

promote /prəˈməʊt/ VERB [promotes, promoting, promoted]
1 to help something to happen more □ *Our aim is to promote peace amongst nations.* □ *We must do more to promote recycling.* (promover)
2 to give someone a more important job or a job that earns more money in the same organization □ *Jack's been promoted to store manager.* (promover)
3 to tell people about something in order to persuade them to buy it or use it □ *The book stores are all promoting her latest novel.* (promover)

prompt — proper noun

- **promotion** /prəˈməʊʃən/ NOUN [plural promotions]
1 a move to a more important job or a job that earns more money in the same organization (promoção) 🔲 *Let's hope she gets her promotion.* (conseguir promoção)
2 when you help something to happen more 🔲 *the promotion of green issues* (promoção)
3 activities and materials which tell people about something in order to persuade them to buy it or use it (promoção)

prompt /prɒmpt/ ▶ ADJECTIVE doing something or happening without delay or at exactly the right time 🔲 *Thank you for your prompt reply to my letter.* (breve, imediato, pontual)
▶ VERB [prompts, prompting, prompted]
1 to cause someone to do something 🔲 *The scandal in the newspapers prompted his resignation.* 🔲 *What prompted you to tell him?* (induzir, mover)
2 to tell someone, especially an actor, what they should say next (soprar, servir de ponto)

- **promptly** /ˈprɒmptli/ ADVERB without delay or at exactly the right time 🔲 *All complaints must be dealt with promptly.* 🔲 *The concert started promptly at 7.30.* (pontualmente)

- **promptness** /ˈprɒmptnɪs/ NOUN, NO PLURAL being prompt (pontualidade, prontidão)

prone /prəʊn/ ADJECTIVE
1 often suffering from something 🔲 *He's always been prone to headaches.* 🔲 *an injury-prone football player* (propenso)
2 lying flat, especially with your face down. A formal word. (deitado de bruços)

prong /prɒŋ/ NOUN [plural prongs] one of the points of a fork (dente)

pronoun /ˈprəʊnaʊn/ NOUN [plural pronouns] a word that can be used in place of a noun. For example, in the sentence Sara ate the ice cream, Sara and the ice cream could be changed to pronouns and the sentence would be She ate it. (pronome)

pronounce /prəˈnaʊns/ VERB [pronounces, pronouncing, pronounced]
1 to say the sound of a word or letter 🔲 *The two 'z's in pizza are pronounced 'tz'.* 🔲 *How do you pronounce your surname?* (pronunciar)
2 to state something formally and publicly 🔲 *He was pronounced dead at the scene of the accident.* 🔲 *I now pronounce you man and wife.* (declarar)

- **pronounced** /prəˈnaʊnst/ ADJECTIVE noticeable 🔲 *He walks with a very pronounced limp.* (pronunciado)

pronto /ˈprɒntəʊ/ ADVERB an informal word that means quickly or soon 🔲 *Could you do it pronto?* (imediatamente)

pronunciation /prəˌnʌnsiˈeɪʃən/ NOUN [plural pronunciations] the way that a word is pronounced 🔲 *The pronunciation of some Arabic words is very difficult for English speakers.* (pronúncia)

proof /pruːf/ NOUN, NO PLURAL facts or objects which prove that something is true 🔲 + *that Do we have any proof that she was actually there?* (prova) 🔲 *I was asked to provide proof of identity.* (prova de identidade)

-proof /pruːf/ SUFFIX -proof is added to the end of words to mean 'protected against' (à prova de) 🔲 *waterproof*

prop /prɒp/ ▶ NOUN [plural props]
1 something such as a piece of wood used to hold a structure up (escora)
2 a piece of furniture or other object used in a play or film 🔲 *the props department* (acessório)
▶ VERB [props, propping, propped] if you prop something against a wall or other surface you let it rest against it 🔲 *He propped his bicycle against the wall and came in.* (escorar, apoiar)
◆ PHRASAL VERBS **prop something up** to use a prop or props to stop something falling down (escorar, apoiar) 🔲 *The roof had been propped up with metal posts.* **prop yourself up** to support yourself with your arms or with an object 🔲 *She propped herself up with a pillow.* (apoiar-se)

propaganda /ˌprɒpəˈgændə/ NOUN, NO PLURAL ideas, information or opinions that are spread by a political group or by one side in a war, in order to influence people (propaganda)

propel /prəˈpel/ VERB [propels, propelling, propelled] to push something forward, often using an engine or some other form of power 🔲 *a jet propelled engine* (propelir)

- **propeller** /prəˈpelə(r)/ NOUN [plural propellers] an object with blades that turn and make a ship or aeroplane move forward (propulsor)

proper /ˈprɒpə(r)/ ADJECTIVE
1 correct and suitable 🔲 *The staff hadn't received proper training.* 🔲 *The proper procedures were followed.* (correto, adequado)
2 real or good enough 🔲 *This is my first proper meal for days.* (adequado, apropriado)
3 behaving in a way that is socially accepted 🔲 *She wanted to know the proper way to address him.* (adequado, apropriado)

- **properly** /ˈprɒpəli/ ADVERB correctly or suitably 🔲 *You're not properly dressed for the cold.* 🔲 *Come on, children, sit up properly.* (corretamente)

proper fraction /ˌprɒpə ˈfrækʃən/ NOUN [plural proper fractions] a fraction where the number below the line is bigger than the number above the line. A maths word. (fração própria)

proper noun /ˌprɒpə ˈnaʊn/ NOUN [plural proper nouns] a noun that is the name of a particular person, place or thing and begins with a capital letter (nome próprio)

property

property /'prɒpəti/ NOUN [plural **properties**]
1 a house and the land it is on (**propriedade**) 🔲 *Private property – keep off!* 🔲 *property prices* (**propriedade privada**)
2 no plural the things that belong to you (**propriedade**) 🔲 *Customers must look after their personal property.* (**propriedade pessoal**)
3 a quality or ability to do something 🔲 *The substance is said to have unique properties.* (**propriedade**)

> ► Remember that **property** meaning 'the things that belong to you' is not used in the plural:
> ✓ *Stolen property is returned to the rightful owners.*
> ✗ *Stolen properties are returned to the rightful owners.*

prophecy /'prɒfɪsi/ NOUN [plural **prophecies**] a statement that something will happen in the future (**profecia**)

• **prophesy** /'prɒfɪsaɪ/ VERB [**prophesies, prophesying, prophesied**] to say that something will happen in the future (**profetizar**)

prophet /'prɒfɪt/ NOUN [plural **prophets**] in some religions, a man chosen by God to teach people and give them his messages 🔲 *the Prophet Isaiah* (**profeta**)

proportion /prə'pɔːʃən/ NOUN [plural **proportions**]
1 a part of a whole amount or total 🔲 *A small proportion of old people live in care homes.* (**proporção**)
2 the number or amount of two groups or things when compared with each other 🔲 *The proportion of women to men in the company has risen.* (**proporção**)
3 in proportion at the right size compared with other parts 🔲 *Her legs are short but they're in proportion.* (**proporcional**)
4 out of proportion (a) at the wrong size compared with something else 🔲 *The cat is surely out of proportion with the people in the picture.* (b) seeming too important or serious 🔲 *You've been thinking about the problem for too long and got it out of proportion.* (**desproporcional**)
5 in proportion to something at the same rate or by the same amount as something 🔲 *Salaries should rise in proportion to experience.* (**em proporção a**)
6 proportions (a) the size of something 🔲 *a house of generous proportions* (= a large house) (b) the level of something 🔲 *The problem has now reached alarming proportions.* (**proporções**)

• **proportional** /prə'pɔːʃənəl/ ADJECTIVE of the correct size, amount or level in relation to something else 🔲 *Tax is proportional to income.* (**proporcional**)

prospect

proposal /prə'pəʊzəl/ NOUN [plural **proposals**]
1 a plan or suggestion 🔲 *The council has come up with a proposal to ease traffic congestion.* (**proposta**)
2 when someone asks another person to marry them (**proposta de casamento**)

• **propose** /prə'pəʊz/ VERB [**proposes, proposing, proposed**]
1 to suggest a plan or idea 🔲 *I propose that we hold the meeting at a later date.* (**propor**)
2 to intend to do something. A formal word. 🔲 *I don't propose to tell him about the matter.* (**propor**)
3 to ask someone to marry you (**propor casamento**)

> ► Note that **propose** meaning 'to suggest a plan or idea' is followed by **that** and not 'to do something':
> ✓ *I propose that we discuss this with Maria tomorrow.*
> ✗ *I propose to discuss this with Maria tomorrow.*

• **proposition** /ˌprɒpə'zɪʃən/ NOUN [plural **propositions**]
1 an offer or suggestion 🔲 *an interesting proposition* (**proposta**)
2 a statement expressing an opinion or judgment 🔲 *We have no evidence to support the proposition that he is lying.* (**proposição**)

proprietor /prə'praɪətə(r)/ NOUN [plural **proprietors**] the owner of a shop or business (**proprietário**)

prose /prəʊz/ NOUN, NO PLURAL writing that is not a poem (**prosa**)

prosecute /'prɒsɪkjuːt/ VERB [**prosecutes, prosecuting, prosecuted**] to accuse someone of a crime and take them to court 🔲 *She is being prosecuted for fraud.* (**processar**)

• **prosecution** /ˌprɒsɪ'kjuːʃən/ NOUN [plural **prosecutions**]
1 the lawyer or team of lawyers who try to prove that someone is guilty in a court of law 🔲 *She was called as a witness for the prosecution.* (**acusação**)
2 the process of prosecuting someone 🔲 *He faces prosecution for assault.* (**denúncia**)

prospect /'prɒspekt/ ► NOUN [plural **prospects**]
1 the possibility of something happening 🔲 *And is there no prospect of promotion?* (**perspectiva**)
2 the thought or idea of something that will happen in the future 🔲 *The prospect of a three--hour exam filled him with dread.* (**perspectiva**)
3 prospects chances of success in the future 🔲 *Employment prospects are not good at present.* (**chances de sucesso**)

► VERB /prə'spekt/ [**prospects, prospecting, prospected**] to search for gold or other valuable metals in the earth (**prospectar**)

- **prospective** /prəˈspektɪv/ ADJECTIVE likely to be or become something □ *We've found a prospective buyer for the house.* □ *The college had applications from nearly 200 prospective students.* (potencial)

prospectus /prəˈspektəs/ NOUN [plural **prospectuses**] a small book that gives you information about a school, college or university and the courses it offers (prospecto, folheto)

prosper /ˈprɒspə(r)/ VERB [**prospers, prospering, prospered**] to succeed, especially by making a lot of money (prosperar)

- **prosperity** /prɒsˈperəti/ NOUN, NO PLURAL success, especially having a lot of money (prosperidade)
- **prosperous** /ˈprɒspərəs/ ADJECTIVE successful, especially by making a lot of money (próspero)

prostrate /ˈprɒstreɪt/ ADJECTIVE lying flat with your face down. A formal word (prostrado)

protagonist /prəˈtæɡənɪst/ NOUN [plural **protagonists**] the main person in a play, film or story (protagonista)

protect /prəˈtekt/ VERB [**protects, protecting, protected**] to keep someone or something safe from harm or danger □ *A mother will always protect her children.* □ *+ from Protect the young plants from frost.* (proteger, amparar)

- **protection** /prəˈtekʃən/ NOUN, NO PLURAL when someone or something is protected □ *+ against A good diet provides protection against some diseases.* (proteção)
- **protective** /prəˈtektɪv/ ADJECTIVE
  1 providing protection □ *protective equipment* (protetor)
  2 wanting to protect someone □ *She is very protective of her children.* (protetor)
- **protector** /prəˈtektə(r)/ NOUN [plural **protectors**] someone who protects another person (protetor)

protégé or **protégée** /ˈprɒteʒeɪ/ NOUN [plural **protégés** or **protégées**] someone who is helped and advised by an older, more experienced person (protegido)

> This word is spelt **protégée** when the person helped or advised is a woman.

protein /ˈprəʊtiːn/ NOUN [plural **proteins**] a substance in foods such as eggs, meat and milk that is necessary for strength and growth (proteína)

protest ▶ VERB /prəˈtest/ [**protests, protesting, protested**] to march or stand with a group of other people to show that you disagree with something □ *Thousands took to the streets to protest about the war.* (protestar)

▶ NOUN /ˈprəʊtest/ [plural **protests**] a strong statement saying that something is wrong, or an organized action against something □ *Several MPs resigned in protest at the cuts.* □ *Students organized a peaceful protest against the regime.* (protesto)

Protestant /ˈprɒtɪstənt/ ▶ NOUN [plural **Protestants**] a member of one of the Christian churches that separated from the Catholic Church in the 1500s (protestante)

▶ ADJECTIVE to do with Protestants or their church

protester /prəˈtestə(r)/ NOUN [plural **protesters**] someone who does something to show that they do not agree with something □ *Anti-airport protesters blocked the roads.* (protestante)

proton /ˈprəʊtɒn/ NOUN [plural **protons**] one of the parts of a nucleus of an atom which has a positive electrical charge. A physics word. (próton)

protoplasm /ˈprəʊtəʊplæzəm/ NOUN, NO PLURAL the transparent liquid inside living cells. A biology word. (protoplasma)

prototype /ˈprəʊtətaɪp/ NOUN [plural **prototypes**] the first model of a new design, for example of a car, used to test how well it works before it is produced in large numbers (protótipo)

protractor /prəˈtræktə(r)/ NOUN [plural **protractors**] an object like half a circle, used for measuring angles. A maths word. (transferidor)

protrude /prəˈtruːd/ VERB [**protrudes, protruding, protruded**] to stick out from something □ *A pen was protruding from his pocket.* (salientar-se)

- **protrusion** /prəˈtruːʒən/ NOUN [plural **protrusions**] something that sticks out from something (protuberância)

proud /praʊd/ ADJECTIVE [**prouder, proudest**]
1 feeling pleased about your achievements or about the achievements of someone such as your child (orgulhoso) □ *She felt very proud when her son got the award.* ⃞ *Holding the winner's trophy was a really proud moment for me.* (momento de orgulho) □ *+ of I'm proud of the fact that I carried on and didn't give up.* □ *+ to do something He was very proud to play for the national team.*
2 not wanting to ask for help although you need it □ *She's too proud to let anyone pay her bills.* (orgulhoso)
3 thinking that you are better than other people, in a way that annoys people (orgulhoso)

- **proudly** /ˈpraʊdli/ ADVERB in a proud way □ *She proudly showed me her medal.* (orgulhosamente)

prove /pruːv/ VERB [**proves, proving, proved**]
1 to show that something is true (provar) ⃞ *Carter was determined to prove his innocence.* (provar sua inocência) □ *+ that DNA tests proved that he was guilty.*
2 if something proves useful, impossible, etc., you find that it is useful, etc. (provar) □ *The business proved to be so successful that we had to take on more staff.*
3 prove yourself to show people that you can do something well □ *When you start a new job you feel you have to prove yourself.* (provar ser capaz)

- **proven** /ˈpruːvən/ ADJECTIVE shown to be true or good □ *There is no scientifically proven cure for colds.* (demonstrado)

proverb /ˈprɒvɜːb/ NOUN [plural **proverbs**] an old phrase that most people know which gives you advice about life □ *There is a legendary Chinese proverb which states 'A journey of a thousand miles starts with a single step'.* (provérbio)

- **proverbial** /prəˈvɜːbiəl/ ADJECTIVE used when you are using all or part of a proverb □ *The last few days have been like the proverbial calm before the storm.* (proverbial)

provide /prəˈvaɪd/ VERB [**provides, providing, provided**] to give or supply something □ *The hospital provides information on the treatments available.* □ *School provides an opportunity for children to learn and develop.* □ **+ with** *The refugees were provided with food and shelter.* (suprir)

- PHRASAL VERB **provide for someone** to give someone the money, food, etc. that they need □ *She worked all hours to provide for her family.* (sustentar)

- **provided** /prəˈvaɪdɪd/ or **providing** /prəˈvaɪdɪŋ/ CONJUNCTION used when saying that one thing will happen only if another thing happens □ *Providing you have no objection, I'd like you to work next Sunday.* □ *You'll do well in the test, provided that you work hard.* (contanto que)

province /ˈprɒvɪns/ NOUN [plural **provinces**]
1 one of the parts that some countries are divided into □ *Sichuan province in China* (província)
2 **the provinces** the parts of a country that are not near the capital city (o interior)

- **provincial** /prəˈvɪnʃəl/ ADJECTIVE
1 to do with a province or the provinces □ *a provincial government* (interiorano, provinciano)
2 old-fashioned and not typical of people in a capital city □ *provincial attitudes* (provinciano)

provision /prəˈvɪʒən/ NOUN, NO PLURAL
1 when someone provides something □ *the provision of healthcare* (provisão)

2 **make provision for someone/something** to make arrangements for something that you will need □ *Many people aren't making sufficient provision for their retirement.* (fazer provisões para alguém/algo)

- **provisional** /prəˈvɪʒənəl/ ADJECTIVE not certain, and possibly going to change (provisório) *They've set a provisional date for the meeting.* (data provisória)

- **provisions** /prəˈvɪʒənz/ PLURAL NOUN supplies of food (provisões)

provocation /ˌprɒvəˈkeɪʃən/ NOUN [plural **provocations**] something that makes you feel angry □ *He used to hit people at the slightest provocation.* (provocação)

provocative /prəˈvɒkətɪv/ ADJECTIVE intended to make someone angry □ *provocative questions* (provocativo)

provoke /prəˈvəʊk/ VERB [**provokes, provoking, provoked**]
1 to cause a particular reaction or feeling, often an angry one □ *His remarks have provoked a lot of criticism.* (provocar)
2 to make someone angry deliberately □ *The children are always provoking each other.* (provocar)

prowl /praʊl/ VERB [**prowls, prowling, prowled**] to walk around somewhere slowly and secretly □ *The murderer prowled the streets looking for his next victim.* (rondar)

- **prowler** /ˈpraʊlə(r)/ NOUN [plural **prowlers**] someone who walks around secretly somewhere, intending to do something bad (gatuno)

proximity /prɒkˈsɪmɪti/ NOUN, NO PLURAL the quality of being near to something or someone (proximidade) *People living in close proximity to the factory have complained about the noise.*

proxy /ˈprɒksi/ NOUN [plural **proxies**] someone who has the authority to do something for you, especially to vote (procurador)

prude /pruːd/ NOUN [plural **prudes**] someone who is too easily shocked (puritano)

prudence /ˈpruːdəns/ NOUN, NO PLURAL a formal word meaning the quality of being prudent (prudência)

- **prudent** /ˈpruːdənt/ ADJECTIVE a formal word meaning careful and sensible □ *prudent advice* (prudente)

prudish /ˈpruːdɪʃ/ ADJECTIVE too easily shocked □ *My parents are very prudish.* (puritano)

prune /pruːn/ ▶ VERB [**prunes, pruning, pruned**] to cut bits off a plant (podar)
▶ NOUN [plural **prunes**] a dried plum (= fruit with a smooth skin and a big seed in the middle) (ameixa seca)

pry /praɪ/ VERB [**pries, prying, pried**] to try to find out things that people do not want you to know □ *She didn't want to answer questions from prying journalists.* (espreitar)

PS /ˌpiːˈes/ ABBREVIATION postscript. You write PS when you want to add something to the end of a letter □ *PS Say hi to David from me.* (pós-escrito)

psalm /sɑːm/ NOUN [plural **psalms**] a song in the Bible (salmo)

pseudo- /ˈsjuːdəʊ/ PREFIX pseudo- is added to the beginning of words to mean 'pretending to be something' □ *pseudonym* □ *pseudo-scientific language* (pseudo)

pseudonym /ˈsjuːdənɪm/ NOUN [plural **pseudonyms**] a name that someone, especially a writer, uses instead of their real name (pseudônimo)

psyche /ˈsaɪki/ NOUN [plural **psyches**] your mind and feelings □ *the female psyche* (psique)

psychiatric /ˌsaɪkiˈætrɪk/ ADJECTIVE to do with mental illness □ *a psychiatric hospital* (psiquiátrico)

- **psychiatrist** /saɪˈkaɪətrɪst/ NOUN [plural **psychiatrists**] a doctor who treats mentally ill people (psiquiatra)
- **psychiatry** /saɪˈkaɪətri/ NOUN, NO PLURAL the study and treatment of mental illness (psiquiatria)

psychic /ˈsaɪkɪk/ ▶ ADJECTIVE having special powers such as knowing what people are thinking, and what will happen in the future (vidente)
▶ NOUN [plural **psychics**] someone who is psychic

psychoanalysis /ˌsaɪkəʊəˈnæləsɪs/ NOUN, NO PLURAL a form of treatment for people with mental problems where the patient talks about their life to help them understand their feelings (psicanálise)
- **psychoanalyst** /ˌsaɪkəʊˈænəlɪst/ NOUN [plural **psychoanalysts**] someone who is trained to do psychoanalysis (psicanalista)
- **psychoanalyze** or **psychoanalyse** /ˌsaɪkəʊˈænəlaɪz/ VERB [**psychoanalyzes, psychoanalyzing, psychoanalyzed**] to treat someone or study someone by using psychoanalysis (psicanalisar)

psychological /ˌsaɪkəʊˈlɒdʒɪkəl/ ADJECTIVE to do with the mind □ *psychological damage* (psicológico)
- **psychologist** /saɪˈkɒlədʒɪst/ NOUN [plural **psychologists**] someone who has studied psychology and human behavior (psicólogo)
- **psychology** /saɪˈkɒlədʒi/ NOUN, NO PLURAL the study of the mind and how it affects the way we behave (psicologia)

psychopath /ˈsaɪkəʊpæθ/ NOUN [plural **psychopaths**] someone who is very violent and dangerous (psicopata)
- **psychopathic** /ˌsaɪkəʊˈpæθɪk/ ADJECTIVE to do with a psychopath □ *psychopathic behaviour* (psicopático)

PTO /ˌpiːtiːˈəʊ/ ABBREVIATION please turn over; written at the bottom of a page to show that someone should turn the page and read the other side (vide verso)

pub /pʌb/ NOUN [plural **pubs**] a place where people buy and drink alcoholic drinks, especially in the UK (pub, bar)

puberty /ˈpjuːbəti/ NOUN, NO PLURAL the time when a child's body changes into an adult's body (puberdade) ▣ *Girls usually reach puberty earlier than boys.* (alcançar a puberdade)

public /ˈpʌblɪk/ ▶ ADJECTIVE
1 to do with the people generally of a country (público) ▣ *There has been a change in public opinion on this issue.* (opinião pública) ▣ *There is a lot of public support for the idea.* (apoio público)
2 available for everyone □ *a public park* □ *public libraries* □ *public events* (público)
3 to do with the government and not private companies □ *public funding* □ *public employees* (público)
4 known by everyone (público) ▣ *It's public knowledge that they're getting married.* (de conhecimento público) ▣ *They refused to make the investigation's findings public.* (o público geral)
▶ NOUN, NO PLURAL
1 the public people generally (o público) ▣ *A member of the public called the police* (membro do público) ▣ *The product will go on sale to the general public tomorrow.* (o público geral)
2 in public in a place where anyone can see □ *He was embarrassed when his parents kissed in public.* (em público)
- **publicly** /ˈpʌblɪkli/ ADVERB
1 in a way that the public can hear or see □ *He has said publicly that he supports communism.* (publicamente)
2 by the public □ *publicly owned companies* (público)

publication /ˌpʌblɪˈkeɪʃən/ NOUN [plural **publications**]
1 no plural the process of printing and selling a book, magazine, etc. □ *The publication of the images provoked a strong reaction.* (publicação)
2 something such as a magazine or newspaper that is printed and sold (publicação)

publicity /pʌbˈlɪsɪti/ NOUN, NO PLURAL
1 attention that something gets from newspapers, television, etc. (publicidade) ▣ *The affair attracted a lot of publicity.* (atrair publicidade)
2 the activity of making people aware of a new product, film, etc. (publicidade) ▣ *He took part in a publicity campaign for the new film.* (campanha de publicidade)

publicize or **publicise** /ˈpʌblɪsaɪz/ VERB [**publicizes, publicizing, publicized**] to tell people about a new book, film, etc., or about an event that is going to happen □ *The event was well publicized.* (divulgar, dar publicidade)

public relations /ˌpʌblɪk rɪˈleɪʃənz/ NOUN, NO PLURAL the job of making a company, famous person, product, etc. seem good to the public (relações públicas)

public school /ˌpʌblɪk ˈskuːl/ NOUN [plural **public schools**]
1 in the UK, a school that you pay to go to, often where you stay as well as study (escola particular)
2 in the US, a school that the government pays for (escola pública)

public transport /ˌpʌblɪk ˈtrænspɔːt/ NOUN, NO PLURAL trains and buses that people can use □ *We need to encourage more people to use public transport.* (transporte coletivo)

public transportation /ˈpʌblɪk trænspɔːˈteɪʃən/ NOUN, NO PLURAL the US phrase for **public transport** (transporte coletivo)

publish /ˈpʌblɪʃ/ VERB [**publishes, publishing, published**]
1 to print a book, magazine, etc. so that people can buy it □ *The book was published in September.* (publicar)

2 if a newspaper or magazine publishes an article, photograph, etc., it prints it □ *The newspaper published her letter.* □ *The magazine published photos of the Princess on the beach.* (**publicar**)
3 to make information available to people generally □ *The company does not publish sales information.* (**divulgar, tornar público**)

• **publisher** /ˈpʌblɪʃə(r)/ NOUN [*plural* **publishers**] a person or company that publishes books, newspapers or magazines (**editor**)

• **publishing** /ˈpʌblɪʃɪŋ/ NOUN, NO PLURAL the work or business of producing books, newspapers and magazines so people can buy them □ *Isabella works in publishing.* □ *a publishing company* (**publicação**)

puck /pʌk/ NOUN [*plural* **pucks**] the hard flat object that players hit in the game of ice hockey (**disco do jogo de hóquei**)

pudding /ˈpʊdɪŋ/ NOUN [*plural* **puddings**] sweet food eaten at the end of a meal □ *We've got ice cream for pudding.* (**sobremesa**)

puddle /ˈpʌdəl/ NOUN [*plural* **puddles**] a small pool of rain on the ground □ *Young children love splashing in puddles.* (**poça**)

puerile /ˈpjʊəraɪl/ ADJECTIVE a formal word meaning silly and like a young child □ *a puerile sense of humour* (**pueril**)

puff /pʌf/ ▶ VERB [**puffs, puffing, puffed**] to breathe quickly because you have been exercising (**ofegar**) 🔁 *John was puffing and panting as he came up the hill.* (**ofegante, esbaforido**)
♦ PHRASAL VERBS **puff something out** if you puff out your cheeks or your chest, you make them bigger by filling them with air (**inflar**) **puff up** if part of your body puffs up, it swells, because you are ill or injured □ *His face had puffed up where he'd been hit.* (**inchar**)
▶ NOUN [*plural* **puffs**] a small breath of air, wind, air or smoke □ *a puff of air* (**baforada**)

puffin /ˈpʌfɪn/ NOUN [*plural* **puffins**] a big, black and white sea bird with a brightly coloured beak (**papagaio-do-mar**)

puffy /ˈpʌfɪ/ ADJECTIVE [**puffier, puffiest**] swollen □ *His eyes were puffy because he'd been crying.* (**inchado**)

pull /pʊl/ ▶ VERB [**pulls, pulling, pulled**]
1 to hold something and move it towards you □ *He pulled the door open.* (**puxar**) 🔁 *Stop pulling my hair!* (**puxar o cabelo**) 🔁 *He pointed the gun at her and pulled the trigger.* □ + *at* *He kept pulling at my sleeve.*
2 if a machine, vehicle, etc. pulls something, it is attached to it and moves it □ *We had to get a tractor to pull our car out of the mud.* □ *The gliders are pulled up into the air by a winch.* (**puxar**)
3 to separate the pieces of something or to damage something (**despedaçar, demolir, arrancar**) □ + *apart* *We pulled apart the curtains and looked inside.* □ + *down* *The old houses will be pulled down.* □ + *off* *He pulled off the insect's wings.*
4 if you pull a muscle you hurt it by stretching it too much (**romper**)
5 to suddenly produce a weapon and threaten someone with it □ *Then he pulled a gun on us.* (**apontar**)
6 pull a face to twist your face into an ugly or funny shape (**fazer caretas**)
7 pull yourself together to manage to become calm after having been upset □ *I managed to pull myself together enough to call the police.* (**recompor-se**)
⇨ go to **pull someone's *leg*, pull your *socks* up, pull *strings*, pull the *wool* over *someone's* eyes, pull the *plug* (on something)**
♦ PHRASAL VERBS **pull ahead**
1 to get in front of someone by moving faster than them □ *The other runners started to pull ahead.* (**ultrapassar**)
2 to make more progress than someone else □ *The Democrats seem to be pulling ahead in the polls.* (**sair-se melhor**) **pull something apart** to criticize something in detail □ *He just pulled my argument apart.* (**despedaçar**) **pull away**
1 if a vehicle pulls away, it moves away (**retirar-se**)
2 to move away from someone who is trying to hold you or touch you □ *She pulled away when he tried to kiss her.* (**afastar-se**) **pull back** to decide not to do something, often because of the risk □ *They have pulled back from investing any more money in the company.* (**voltar atrás**) **pull in/into somewhere**
1 if a vehicle pulls in, it stops at the side of the road or goes into a place □ *We'll pull in at the next lay-by.* (**encostar**)
2 if train pulls in, it arrives at a station (**chegar**) **pull something off** to be successful at doing something, often something that was a risk □ *Providing food for a thousand guests was a huge challenge, but we pulled it off.* (**realizar**) **pull something on** if you pull on clothes, you put them on quickly (**realizar**) □ *I pulled on an old pair of jeans.* (**enfiar**) **pull out** (**abandonar**)
1 to stop being involved in an event or an activity □ *She had to pull out of the race because of injury.*
2 if a car or truck pulls out, it moves onto a road or moves in front of something □ *A huge lorry pulled out right in front of me.* (**arrancar, sair**)
3 if a train pulls out, it leaves a station (**arrancar, sair**) **pull (something) out** if an army pulls out of an area, it leaves it □ *They have pulled their forces out of the region.* [**remover, retirar**] **pull over** if a vehicle pulls over, it moves to the side of the road and often stops (**parar, estacionar**) **pull through** to stay alive after a serious illness or injury □ *He has major head injuries, and doctors don't know if he will pull through.* (**sobreviver**) **pull together** to work hard together to achieve something □ *The whole team pulled together to*

win the cup. (cooperar) **pull up** if a vehicle pulls up, it stops (parar)
▶ NOUN [plural **pulls**]
1 when you hold something and move it towards you ◻ *give the handle a pull* (puxão)
2 no plural the force that causes something to move in a particular direction ◻ *the pull of gravity* (atração)

pull-down menu /ˈpʊldaʊn ˌmenjuː/ NOUN [plural **pull-down menus**] a list of instructions on a computer screen which only appears when you click on a button. A computing word. (comandos do menu)

pulley /ˈpʊli/ NOUN [plural **pulleys**] a piece of equipment for lifting heavy things which consists of a rope and a wheel (roldana)

pullover /ˈpʊlˌəʊvə(r)/ NOUN [plural **pullovers**] a piece of clothing for the top part of your body made of wool that you pull over your head (pulôver)

pulmonary /ˈpʌlmənəri/ ADJECTIVE to do with the lungs. A biology word. (pulmonar)

pulp /pʌlp/ NOUN, NO PLURAL
1 a soft wet substance that you make by crushing something ◻ *paper made from wood pulp* (pasta)
2 the soft flesh of some fruits and vegetables (polpa)

pulpit /ˈpʊlpɪt/ NOUN [plural **pulpits**] the high place in a church where a priest stands to talk to people (púlpito)

pulsate /pʌlˈseɪt/ VERB [**pulsates, pulsating, pulsated**] to move or make sounds with a strong regular rhythm (pulsar)

pulse /pʌls/ ▶ NOUN [plural **pulses**]
1 your pulse is the regular movement that you feel on your lower arm or neck, caused by your heart pushing blood through your body (pulso) ◻ *The nurse took my pulse* (= counted the number of movements in one minute). (verificar o pulso)
2 pulses seeds that you can eat, for example peas and beans (grãos de leguminosas)
▶ VERB [**pulses, pulsing, pulsed**] to move or change with a regular rhythm ◻ *The lights were pulsing from blue to pink.* (pulsar)

pulverize or **pulverise** /ˈpʌlvəraɪz/ VERB [**pulverizes, pulverizing, pulverized**] to crush something into many small pieces or into a powder ◻ *The rock had been pulverized.* (triturar)

puma /ˈpjuːmə/ NOUN [plural **pumas**] a large, wild cat that lives in America (puma)

pummel /ˈpʌməl/ VERB [**pummels, pummelling, pummelled**] to hit something or someone several times with your closed hand ◻ *He started pummelling on the door.* (esmurrar)

pump /pʌmp/ ▶ NOUN [plural **pumps**] a piece of equipment that makes a gas or liquid move into or out of something ◻ *She got a bicycle pump and put some air in the tyres.* (bomba) ◻ *a petrol pump* (= for putting petrol into a car) (bomba de gasolina) ◻ *a water pump*
▶ VERB [**pumps, pumping, pumped**] to force liquid or gas to move somewhere ◻ *Your heart pumps blood around your body.* ◻ *Water is pumped from the well.* (bombear)
◆ PHRASAL VERBS **pump something into something** to spend a lot of money on a business or piece of work ◻ *They have pumped millions of pounds into the business.* (injetar boa quantia de dinheiro em algo) **pump something up** to put air into something using a pump ◻ *Ellie was pumping her bike tyres up.* (encher)

pumpkin /ˈpʌmpkɪn/ NOUN [plural **pumpkins**] a large, round, orange vegetable with a thick skin (abóbora)

pun /pʌn/ NOUN [plural **puns**] a joke using words that sound the same but have different meanings (trocadilho)

punch /pʌntʃ/ ▶ VERB [**punches, punching, punched**]
1 to hit someone or something with your closed hand ◻ *He punched the man in the face.* (dar socos)
2 to make a small hole in something using a special tool (furar) ◻ *The tool is used for punching holes in metal.* (furar buracos)
▶ NOUN [plural **punches**]
1 a hit using your closed hand (soco)
2 a tool for making a hole in something (perfurador)

punchline /ˈpʌntʃlaɪn/ NOUN [plural **punchlines**] the last line of a joke which is the funny part (conclusão de uma piada)

punch-up /ˈpʌntʃʌp/ NOUN [plural **punch-ups**] a fight in which people punch each other. An informal word. (pancadaria)

punchy /ˈpʌntʃi/ ADJECTIVE [**punchier, punchiest**] powerful and effective ◻ *a punchy performance* (vigoroso)

punctual /ˈpʌŋktʃuəl/ ADJECTIVE arriving at exactly the arranged time and not late ◻ *Robert was always very punctual.* ◻ *Switzerland has punctual and reliable trains.* (pontual)
• **punctuality** /ˌpʌŋktʃuˈæləti/ NOUN, NO PLURAL the quality of being punctual (pontualidade)
• **punctually** /ˈpʌŋktʃuəli/ ADVERB at exactly the right time ◻ *They arrived punctually* (pontualmente)

punctuate /ˈpʌŋktʃueɪt/ VERB [**punctuates, punctuating, punctuated**]
1 to put marks such as , . ! in a piece of writing (pontuar)
2 if something is punctuated with things, these things happen several times in it ◻ *Her story was punctuated by little squeaks and giggles.* (pontuar)
• **punctuation** /ˌpʌŋktʃuˈeɪʃən/ NOUN, NO PLURAL the use of marks such as , . ! in writing ◻ *Children find punctuation difficult.* (pontuação)

punctuation mark /ˌpʌŋktʃuˈeɪʃən ˌmɑːk/ NOUN [plural **punctuation marks**] one of the marks such as , . ! which are used in writing (**sinal de pontuação**)

puncture /ˈpʌŋktʃə(r)/ c NOUN [plural **punctures**] a small hole made by something sharp, especially in a tyre (**furo**)

▶ VERB [**punctures, puncturing, punctured**] to make a small hole in something □ *A bullet had punctured the fuel tank.* (**furar**)

pungent /ˈpʌndʒənt/ ADJECTIVE a pungent smell is very strong and sometimes not pleasant □ *the pungent smell of fish* (**picante, penetrante**)

punish /ˈpʌnɪʃ/ VERB [**punishes, punishing, punished**] to make someone suffer because they have done something wrong □ +*for* He was punished for his crimes. □ + *by/with* People who drop litter will be punished with fines. (**punir**)

• **punishable** /ˈpʌnɪʃəbəl/ ADJECTIVE having a particular punishment □ *The crime of murder is punishable by death in many countries.* (**punível**)

• **punishing** /ˈpʌnɪʃɪŋ/ ADJECTIVE involving a lot of work or activity and making you feel extremely tired 🔁 *The Prime Minister has had a punishing schedule in recent weeks.* (**agenda extenuante**)

• **punishment** /ˈpʌnɪʃmənt/ NOUN [plural **punishments**] something that is done to punish someone (**punição**) 🔁 *He had to stay behind after school as a punishment.* (**como punição**) □ + *for* The maximum punishment for murder was life sentence in prison. 🔁 *The old man escaped punishment after promising never to drive again.* (**escapar da punição**)

punk /pʌŋk/ NOUN [plural **punks**]
1 *no plural* a type of loud music that was especially popular in the 1970s and 1980s (**punk**)
2 someone who likes punk music and often has brightly coloured hair (**punk**)

punnet /ˈpʌnɪt/ NOUN [plural **punnets**] a small box that fruit is sold in (**caixinha**)

punt /pʌnt/ ▶ NOUN [plural **punts**] a boat with a flat bottom that you move by pushing a pole against the bottom of a river (**tipo de barco impelido por vara**)

▶ VERB [**punts, punting, punted**] to travel on a river in a punt (**navegar nesse tipo de barco**)

punter /ˈpʌntə(r)/ NOUN [plural **punters**] an informal word meaning customer □ *He's one of our regular punters.* (**freguês**)

puny /ˈpjuːni/ ADJECTIVE [**punier, puniest**] small and weak □ *a puny boy* (**frágil**)

pup /pʌp/ NOUN [plural **pups**] a young dog or a young seal (= large animal that lives on land and in the sea) (**filhote de cachorro, filhote de foca**)

pupa /ˈpjuːpə/ NOUN [plural **pupae**] an insect in the stage of development before it becomes an adult. A biology word. (**pupa, crisálida**)

pupil /ˈpjuːpəl/ NOUN [plural **pupils**]
1 a student in a school □ *primary school pupils* □ *former pupils of the school* (**aluno**)
2 the small black circle in the middle of your eye (**pupila**) 🔁 *Pupils dilate to let in more light.* (**pupilas**)

puppet /ˈpʌpɪt/ NOUN [plural **puppets**] a toy in the shape of an animal or person that you move by pulling strings or by putting it on your hand □ *The children enjoyed the puppet show.* (**fantoche, títere**)

puppy /ˈpʌpi/ NOUN [plural **puppies**] a young dog (**filhote de cachorro**)

purchase /ˈpɜːtʃəs/ ▶ VERB [**purchases, purchasing, purchased**] a formal word meaning to buy something □ *Tickets may be purchased in advance.* (**comprar**)

▶ NOUN [plural **purchases**]
1 a formal word meaning something you have bought □ *I was admiring your purchases.* (**compra**)
2 *no plural* a formal word meaning the act of buying something □ *There has been an increase in the purchase of household goods.* (**compra**)

• **purchaser** /ˈpɜːtʃəsə(r)/ NOUN [plural **purchasers**] a formal word meaning someone who buys something (**comprador**)

pure /pjʊə(r)/ ADJECTIVE [**purer, purest**]
1 not mixed with anything else □ *pure gold* □ *pure oxygen* (**puro**)
2 complete □ *There was a look of pure joy on his face.* (**completo**) 🔁 *It was pure chance that we met.* (**completo acaso**)
3 clean (**puro**) □ *pure water*

puree /ˈpjʊəreɪ/ NOUN, NO PLURAL a thick substance made by crushing fruit or vegetables □ *tomato puree* (**purê**)

purely /ˈpjʊəli/ ADVERB only or simply □ *She is criticized purely because of her appearance.* (**puramente**)

purge /pɜːdʒ/ ▶ VERB [**purges, purging, purged**] to get rid of people or things that are not wanted □ *He had tried to purge his political opponents.* (**livrar-se de algo/alguém**)

▶ NOUN [plural **purges**] the act of getting rid of people or things that are not wanted (**eliminação**)

purify /ˈpjʊərɪfaɪ/ VERB [**purifies, purifying, purified**] to make something pure by taking out the bad or dirty substances □ *The water is then purified.* (**purificar**)

purity /ˈpjʊərəti/ NOUN, NO PLURAL the quality of being pure (**pureza**)

purple /ˈpɜːpəl/ ▶ ADJECTIVE having the colour you get if you mix red and blue □ *The carpet was dark purple.* □ *His face was purple with rage.* (**púrpura**)

▶ NOUN, NO PLURAL the colour you get if you mix red and blue (**cor púrpura**)

purpose

purpose /'pɜːpəs/ NOUN [plural **purposes**]
1 what you intend to achieve when you do something □ + *of* *The main purpose of the trip was to improve students' French.* (**propósito**) 🔁 *He had entered the building with the sole purpose of stealing something.* (**com o único propósito de**) □ *The website can be used for educational purposes too.*
2 on purpose deliberately □ *He broke the vase on purpose to annoy me.* (**de propósito**)
3 *no plural* a feeling of knowing what you want to achieve (**propósito**) 🔁 *I lack a sense of purpose.* (**sentimento de propósito**)

- **purposeful** /'pɜːpəsfʊl/ ADJECTIVE showing that you know what you want to achieve □ *He walked into the office with a purposeful stride.* (**determinado**)
- **purposely** /'pɜːpəslɪ/ ADVERB deliberately □ *She had purposely embarrassed him.* (**propositadamente**)

purr /pɜː(r)/ ▶ VERB [**purrs, purring, purred**] a cat purrs when it makes a long, low noise because it is happy (**ronronar**)
▶ NOUN [plural **purrs**] the long, low noise that a cat makes when it is happy (**rom-rom**)

purse /pɜːs/ ▶ NOUN [plural **purses**]
1 a small container that women carry money in □ *She had a lot of money in her purse.* □ *Mary opened her purse and got out some coins.* (**porta-níquel**)
2 the US word for **handbag** (**bolsa**)
▶ VERB [**purses, pursing, pursed**] **purse your lips** to bring your lips together tightly in a round shape □ *Billy pursed his lips thoughtfully.*

pursue /pə'sjuː/ VERB [**pursues, pursuing, pursued**]
1 to do something or try to achieve something over a period of time □ *She wanted to pursue a career in the media.* (**seguir**)
2 to continue discussing something or trying to find out about something (**insistir no assunto, tentar descobrir**) 🔁 *She looked a bit embarrassed so I didn't pursue the matter.*
3 to chase someone or something in order to catch them □ *Should the police pursue stolen cars at high speed?* (**perseguir**)

- **pursuer** /pə'sjuːə(r)/ NOUN [plural **pursuers**] someone who is chasing someone or something in order to catch them (**perseguidor**)
- **pursuit** /pə'sjuːt/ NOUN [plural **pursuits**]
1 *no plural* the act of chasing someone or something (**perseguição**) 🔁 *The dogs were in pursuit of a hare.* (**em perseguição de**)
2 *no plural* when you try to achieve something, usually over a period of time □ *the pursuit of happiness* (**busca**)
3 pursuits a formal word meaning hobbies (**atividade**) 🔁 *She enjoys walking, climbing and other outdoor pursuits.*

push

pus /pʌs/ NOUN, NO PLURAL a thick yellow substance that forms in an infected part of your body (**pus**)

push /pʊʃ/ ▶ VERB [**pushes, pushing, pushed**]
1 to press against someone or something with your hands or body, so that they move □ *I had to push him up the hill in his wheelchair.* □ *The new tooth is pushing the old one out.* □ *She pushed the door open.* □ *He pushed back his chair.* (**empurrar**)
2 to go in a particular direction, moving people out of your way □ *He pushed to the front of the queue.* □ *I tried to push closer to the stage.* (**abrir passagem**)
3 to try to make someone do something they do not want to do □ + *into He was pushed into accepting the job.* □ + *to do something They pushed me to agree to the plan.* (**impelir**)
4 to make someone work very hard □ *Our teachers pushed us to the limit.* □ *In this sport, you really have to push yourself.* (**forçar**)
5 to make something reach a particular level, value, etc. □ *Inflation is pushing prices up.* (**empurrar**)
◆ IDIOM **push your luck** to take a big risk that may result in failure or trouble □ *They offered us a bed for the night, but we thought that asking for a car as well would be pushing our luck.* (**abusar da sorte**)
◆ PHRASAL VERBS **push someone about/around** to force someone to do what you want them to do □ *I'm fed up with letting my family push me around.* (**dominar, humilhar**) **push ahead/forward** to continue with something, even if there are difficulties □ *The government is pushing ahead with tax reforms.* (**resistir**) **push for something** to try to achieve something or get something □ *We are pushing for better working conditions.* (**pressionar por**) **push in** to join a queue (= line of people waiting) in front of people who were there before you (**entrar na fila**) **push on**
1 to make an effort to make progress with something □ *We need to push on and finish the digging.* (**esforçar-se**)
2 to continue a journey □ *We decided to push on to Tokyo.* (**continuar**) **push someone/something over** to push someone or something so that they fall □ *He pushed his friend over in the playground.* (**derrubar, fazer cair**) **push something through** to get a law, plan, etc. accepted □ *The government is pushing through new legislation on hunting.* (**forçar a aceitação**)
▶ NOUN [plural **pushes**]
1 when you press against someone or something with your hands or body, so that it moves □ *The door's a bit stiff – give it a good push.* (**empurrão**)
2 an effort to achieve something □ + *for He is stepping up his training in a final push for a gold medal.* (**esforço**)
3 if you give someone a push, you encourage them to do something □ *He's capable of passing*

pushchair

his exams, but he'll need a push. (**empurrãozinho, uma força**)
4 the push if you get the push, you have to leave your job. An informal phrase. (**demissão**)
5 at a push if you say that something is possible at a push, it is possible but not easy □ *I can get five people in my car, or six at a push.* (**com esforço**)

pushchair /ˈpʊʃtʃeə(r)/ NOUN [plural **pushchairs**] a chair on wheels used for pushing a young child around (**carrinho de bebê**)

pushy /ˈpʊʃɪ/ ADJECTIVE [**pushier, pushiest**] behaving in an unpleasant way because you are determined to get what you want or determined to make someone do something □ *The school often has to deal with pushy parents.* (**agressivo**)

pussy /ˈpʊsɪ/ or **pussycat** /ˈpʊsɪkæt/ NOUN [plural **pussies** or **pussycats**] an informal word meaning cat, which is often used by children (**gatinho, bichano**)

put /pʊt/ VERB [**puts, putting, put**]

1 to move something to a place or position □ *Put the shopping on the table.* □ *He put his hands in the air.* □ *She put her arms around me.* (**pôr**)
2 to cause someone or something to be in a particular situation or state □ *Your actions put lives at risk.* □ *He put pressure on me to agree to the proposal.* □ *He was put to death.* □ *Plans for the office move have been put in place.* (**pôr**)
3 put something into effect/practice, etc. to make something start to work or be used □ *We learned some new exercise techniques, which I'll be putting into practice next week.* (**pôr em prática**)
4 put a stop/end to something to make something stop □ *We must put a stop to this bad behaviour in class.* (**pôr um fim**)
5 to say or write something in a particular way □ *She described him as 'unusual', which is a polite way of putting it.* (**modo de dizer**)
6 to write something □ *Where do I put my address?* □ *I need to leave her a message, but I'm not sure what to put.* (**escrever**)
⇨ go to **put your *feet* up, put your *foot* down, put your *foot* in it, put your *mind* to something, put your *mind* at rest, put someone in their *place*, put *two* and two together**

◆ PHRASAL VERBS **put something across/over** to explain something □ *They used computer graphics to help put across their ideas.* (**comunicar, fazer entender**) **put something aside**
1 to keep something so that it can be used later □ *We put aside a bit of money each month to use for birthdays.* (**reservar**)
2 to not allow yourself to be affected by an emotion, opinion or problem □ *In a disaster situation, governments must put aside politics and work together.* (**deixar de lado, ignorar**) **put something away**
1 to put something in the place where it is kept □ *He never puts his clothes away.* (**guardar**)

2 if you put money away, you save it, usually in a bank (**guardar no banco**) **put something back** to put something in the place where it came from □ *Could you put the milk back in the fridge?* (**colocar de volta**) **put someone/something down** to put someone or something onto a surface □ *He put down the gun.* (**abaixar, colocar sobre uma superfície**) **put someone down** to criticize someone and make them feel stupid or not important (**criticar, humilhar**) **put something down** if a protest (= when people complain publicly about something) or an attempt to take control of a country or area is put down, it is stopped with force □ *Troops were sent in to put down the uprising.* (**subjugar**) **put someone down for something** to put someone's name on a list to do something or to become a member of an organization □ *We've put James down to do karate.* (**inscrever para**) **put something down to something** to think that something is the reason for a situation □ *He puts his poor performance down to a knee injury.* (**atribuir a**) **put forward something** to state an idea, opinion, etc. for other people to consider □ *They put forward a proposal to get the club out of debt.* (**propor**) **put in something/put something into something** to spend money, time or energy doing something □ *They put a lot of effort into the play.* (**investir**) **put off something** to delay doing something □ *I know I'll need an operation on my shoulder, but I'm trying to put it off as long as possible.* (**adiar**) **put someone off** to prevent someone from concentrating (**desconcentrar**) **put someone off (something)** to make someone not want to do something or not want to have something □ *That fall put me off climbing for ever.* (**desestimular**) **put something on**
1 to start wearing something □ *You'd better put on a coat.* (**vestir**)
2 to make a machine or piece of equipment start working □ *Shall we put the heating on?* (**ligar**)
3 put on weight to become fatter (**engordar**) **put something out**
1 to make a fire stop burning □ *Firefighters were called to put out the blaze.* (**apagar**)
2 to turn a light off (**apagar**) **put someone through** to connect someone to the person they want to speak to on the telephone □ *Just a moment, I'll put you through to the accounts department.* (**passar a ligação para**) **put someone through something** to make someone experience something unpleasant □ *The job would have meant moving house every six months, and I couldn't put my family through that.* (**passar por**) **put something to someone** to suggest something to someone □ *I'll put your offer to him and see what he thinks.* (**sugerir**) **put something up**
1 to build something such as a wall or fence □ *They put up a barrier between the two areas.* (**erguer**)
2 to fasten something to a wall □ *We put up signs advertising the concert.* (**afixar**)

3 put up the price/cost of something to increase the price of something (aumentar o preço/custo de algo) **put someone up** to let someone stay in your home for a few days ☐ *I put her up while she looked for a job.* (acolher) **put up with someone/something** to accept a situation or someone's behaviour although you do not like it ☐ *I can't put up with his laziness any longer!* (tolerar)

putrid /ˈpjuːtrɪd/ ADJECTIVE rotten and smelling bad ☐ *putrid meat* (podre)

putt /pʌt/ ▶ VERB [putts, putting, putted] in golf, to hit a ball gently so that it rolls towards the hole (tacar a bola de leve)
▶ NOUN [*plural* putts] in golf, a gentle hit of the ball that you make so that it will go into the hole (tacada suave)

putty /ˈpʌti/ NOUN, NO PLURAL a soft substance used for fixing glass in window frames (betume)

puzzle /ˈpʌzəl/ ▶ NOUN [*plural* puzzles]
1 a game or toy that gives you a problem to solve (quebra-cabeça) 🔄 *Ben was doing a jigsaw puzzle.* (quebra-cabeça)
2 something that is difficult to understand (enigma) 🔄 *Researchers hope to solve the puzzle of why some children develop the disease.* (solucionar o enigma)
▶ VERB [**puzzles, puzzling, puzzled**] if something puzzles you, you feel confused because you do not understand it ☐ *Their unexplained deaths puzzled police for years.* (confundir)

♦ PHRASAL VERB **puzzle over something** to think about something carefully and for a long time in order to understand it ☐ *Doctors have puzzled over why women are more likely to suffer from the disease.* (quebrar a cabeça a respeito)

• **puzzled** /ˈpʌzəld/ ADJECTIVE confused and not understanding something ☐ *She had a puzzled look on her face.* (confuso)

• **puzzling** /ˈpʌzlɪŋ/ ADJECTIVE difficult to understand ☐ *puzzling behavior* (intrigante)

PVC /ˌpiːviːˈsiː/ ABBREVIATION polyvinyl chloride; a type of plastic (PVC, tipo de plástico)

pyjamas /pəˈdʒɑːməz/ PLURAL NOUN loose trousers and a shirt that you wear in bed (pijama) 🔄 *He was wearing a pair of pyjamas.* (um pijama) ☐ *silk pyjamas*

pylon /ˈpaɪlən/ NOUN [*plural* pylons] a tall metal structure that supports electric wires (torre)

pyramid /ˈpɪrəmɪd/ NOUN [*plural* pyramids] a solid shape with a square base and triangular sides which form a point at the top (pirâmide)

pyre /ˈpaɪə(r)/ NOUN [*plural* pyres] a pile of wood for burning dead bodies on (pira)

Pyrex /ˈpaɪreks/ NOUN, NO PLURAL a type of glass used for making dishes that can be used in an oven. A trademark. ☐ *a Pyrex bowl* (fôrma de vidro, pirex)

python /ˈpaɪθən/ NOUN [*plural* pythons] a large snake that kills animals by winding itself around them (jiboia)

Q q

Q or **q** /kjuː/ the 17th letter of the alphabet (**a décima sétima letra do alfabeto**)

quack /kwæk/ ▶ NOUN [plural **quacks**] the sound made by a duck (= a common water bird)
▶ VERB [**quacks, quacking, quacked**] to make the sound of a duck (**grasnar**)

quadrant /ˈkwɒdrənt/ NOUN [plural **quadrants**] a shape that is a quarter of a circle. A maths word. (**quadrante**)

quadrilateral /ˌkwɒdrɪˈlætərəl/ NOUN [plural **quadrilaterals**] any shape with four sides. A maths word. (**quadrilátero**)

quadruped /ˈkwɒdruped/ NOUN [plural **quadrupeds**] an animal that has four feet. A biology word. (**quadrúpede**)

quadruple /kwɒˈdruːpəl/ ▶ VERB [**quadruples, quadrupling, quadrupled**] to become four times bigger or to make something four times bigger ☐ *The shopkeeper had quadrupled the price.* (**quadruplicar**)
▶ ADJECTIVE made up of four parts or events, or four times more than usual ☐ *a quadruple murder* (**quádruplo**)

quadruplet /ˈkwɒdruplɪt/ NOUN [plural **quadruplets**] one of four children born at one time to the same mother (**quadrigêmeos**)

quagmire /ˈkwæɡmaɪə(r)/ NOUN [plural **quagmires**]
1 an area of soft, very wet ground ☐ *Heavy rain had turned the garden into a quagmire.* (**charco, pântano**)
2 a difficult and complicated situation ☐ *He has become bogged down in a political quagmire.* (**situação difícil**)

quail /kweɪl/ NOUN [plural **quail** or **quails**] a small brown bird that is hunted for food (**recuar, acovardar-se**)

quaint /kweɪnt/ ADJECTIVE [**quainter, quaintest**] old fashioned in a pleasant or attractive way ☐ *a quaint little fishing village* (**singular**)

quake /kweɪk/ ▶ VERB [**quakes, quaking, quaked**]
1 to be very frightened or nervous so that your body shakes ☐ *She was quaking in fear.* (**estremecer**)
2 to shake violently ☐ *The ground quaked under their feet.* (**tremer**)
▶ NOUN [plural **quakes**] a short way to say and write earthquake (**terremoto**)

qualification /ˌkwɒlɪfɪˈkeɪʃən/ NOUN [plural **qualifications**]
1 an exam you have passed or a course you have completed (**qualificação**) ☐ *He lacks formal academic qualifications.* (**qualificações acadêmicas**) ☐ *She gained her teaching qualification at Leeds University.* (**obter qualificação**)
2 a skill or quality you have that makes you suitable for a job or position ☐ + *for His only qualification for the job was some experience in journalism.* (**qualificação**)
3 no plural when you do what is needed to get something such as a place in a competition ☐ + *for They missed out on qualification for the World Cup.* (**classificação**)
4 something you add to what you say to make it less strong or less certain ☐ *He welcomed the proposals, but with one qualification.* (**restrição**)

• **qualified** /ˈkwɒlɪfaɪd/ ADJECTIVE
1 having the qualifications needed for a job ☐ *a qualified teacher* ☐ *He was the most qualified candidate.* (**qualificado**)
2 having the skills or knowledge needed to do something ☐ *Alison would be better qualified to comment on that.* (**qualificado**)
3 not completely certain or positive because of some doubts or limits ☐ *Unions gave their qualified backing to the proposals.* (**limitado**)

• **qualifier** /ˈkwɒlɪfaɪə(r)/ NOUN [plural **qualifiers**]
1 a game that someone must win to enter the main part of a sports competition ☐ *His next game will be the European Championship qualifier against Italy.* (**classificatório**)
2 a person or a team that has won a game to enter the main part of a competition (**classificado**)

• **qualify** /ˈkwɒlɪfaɪ/ VERB [**qualifies, qualifying, qualified**]
1 to have the qualities that make you suitable for something or give you the right to something ☐ + *for They qualify for free legal advice.* ☐ + *as The family do not qualify as refugees.* (**qualificar-se**)
2 to pass an exam or to complete a course needed to do a job ☐ + *as He qualified as a lawyer.* ☐ + *in She qualified in medicine in London.* (**habilitar-se**)
3 to do what is needed to enter a competition or the next stage of a competition ☐ + *for Australia qualified for the finals.* (**classificar-se**)

4 to add something to what you have said to make it less strong or less certain ☐ *He qualified his comment by adding that he didn't expect much progress this year.* (**atenuar**)

quality /'kwɒlɪtɪ/ ▶ NOUN [*plural* **qualities**]
1 how good or bad something is (**qualidade**) 🔳 *All our courses are of a very high quality.* (**alta qualidade**) ☐ + *of The quality of her work is much better now.* 🔳 *Your health affects your quality of life.* (**qualidade de vida**) 🔳 *We are taking measures to improve air quality.* (**melhorar a qualidade**)
2 *no plural* when something is of a very good standard ☐ *The company has a reputation for quality.* (**qualidade**)
3 a part of someone's character ☐ *Her best qualities are her kindness and honesty.* (**qualidade**)
4 a feature of something ☐ + *of The unique qualities of the soil here produce excellent grapes.* (**qualidade**)
▶ ADJECTIVE of a high standard ☐ *a quality brand* ☐ *There's a need for more quality childcare facilities.* (**de qualidade**)

qualms /kwɑːmz/ NOUN, NO PLURAL doubts about whether something is right, especially morally (**hesitação**) 🔳 *He has no qualms about dismissing staff who can't do the job.*

quandary /'kwɒndərɪ/ NOUN [*plural* **quandaries**] a situation in which it is very difficult to make a decision ☐ *Ann was in a quandary over whether to move to Australia.* (**dilema, dúvida**)

quantity /'kwɒntɪtɪ/ NOUN [*plural* **quantities**] the amount or number of something ☐ + *of We only need a small quantity of paper.* ☐ *People throw away huge quantities of food.* 🔳 *It can be produced cheaply and in large quantities.* (**quantidades grandes**) 🔳 *We need to improve both the quantity and quality of facilities.* (**quantidade e qualidade**)

quarantine /'kwɒrəntiːn/ ▶ NOUN, NO PLURAL when a person or an animal is kept away from other people or animals because they have or might have a disease ☐ *The animals were being held in quarantine.* (**quarentena**)
▶ VERB [**quarantines, quarantining, quarantined**] to put a person or an animal in quarantine (**ficar em quarentena**)

quarrel /'kwɒrəl/ ▶ VERB [**quarrels, quarrelling/** US **quarreling, quarrelled/** US **quarreled**] to argue about something, usually with someone you know well ☐ *I've quarrelled with my brother.* (**discutir, brigar**)
▶ NOUN [*plural* **quarrels**] an argument, usually with someone you know well ☐ *I've had a quarrel with the manager.* (**discussão, briga**)

quarry /'kwɒrɪ/ ▶ NOUN [*plural* **quarries**]
1 a place where stone is dug out of the ground ☐ *a limestone quarry* (**pedreira**)
2 an animal that is being hunted ☐ *He caught sight of his quarry a few metres away.* (**presa**)
▶ VERB [**quarries, quarrying, quarried**] to dig stone out of the ground (**extrair pedras**)

quart /kwɔːt/ NOUN [*plural* **quarts**] a unit for measuring liquids, equal to 2 pints (**quarto de litro**)

quarter /'kwɔːtə(r)/ ▶ NOUN [*plural* **quarters**]
1 1/4 ; one of four equal parts of something ☐ *We cut the cake into quarters.* (**quarto**)
2 quarter past/to 15 minutes after/before the hour ☐ *He arrived at quarter past three.* (**quinze minutos depois/antes da hora**)
3 quarter after/of the US phrase for 15 minutes after/before the hour (**quinze minutos depois/ antes da hora**)
4 one of four equal parts of a year ☐ *In the first quarter, the company made a profit.* (**trimestre**)
5 a coin with the value of 25 cents (**moeda de 25 centavos de dólar**)
▶ VERB [**quarters, quartering, quartered**] to divide something into four equal parts ☐ *She quartered the melon.* (**dividir em quatro partes**)

quarter-final /ˌkwɔːtə'faɪnəl/ NOUN [*plural* **quarter-finals**] the part of a competition involving the last eight teams or players ☐ *She reached the quarterfinals of the French Open.* (**quarta de final**)

quarterly /'kwɔːtəlɪ/ ADJECTIVE, ADVERB happening, done or produced every three months ☐ *quarterly payments* (**trimestral**)

quarters /'kwɔːtəz/ PLURAL NOUN rooms to stay in, especially for soldiers (**alojamentos**) 🔳 *He showed them to their sleeping quarters.* (**alojamentos para dormir**)

quartet /kwɔː'tet/ NOUN [*plural* **quartets**]
1 a group of four musicians or singers ☐ *a string quartet* (**quarteto**)
2 a piece of music written for four musicians or singers (**quarteto**)

quartz /kwɔːts/ NOUN, NO PLURAL a hard substance found in rocks that can be used in clocks and watches (**quartzo**)

quash /kwɒʃ/ VERB [**quashes, quashing, quashed**]
1 to stop something you do not like from continuing (**aniquilar**) 🔳 *He was keen to quash the rumours.*
2 to officially change a legal decision (**anular**) 🔳 *An appeal court quashed his conviction.*

quasi- /'kweɪzaɪ/ PREFIX quasi- is added to the beginning of words to mean 'almost, but not quite' ☐ *She has a quasi-official role.* (**quase**)

quaver /'kweɪvə(r)/ ▶ VERB [**quavers, quavering, quavered**] if your voice quavers, it shakes slightly ☐ *Her voice quavered with fright as she spoke.* (**tremular**)
▶ NOUN [*plural* **quavers**] when your voice quavers (**tremido**)

quay /kiː/ NOUN [plural **quays**] a hard area built next to the water where things are put onto and taken off ships (**cais**)

queasy /ˈkwiːzɪ/ ADJECTIVE [**queasier, queasiest**] feeling like you might vomit □ *The motion of the boat made her queasy.* (**enjoado**)

queen /kwiːn/ NOUN [plural **queens**]
1 a woman who rules a country which has a royal family □ *Queen Elizabeth II* □ + *of the Queen of Denmark* (**rainha**)
2 the wife of a king (**rainha**)
3 a woman who is the most successful or most important in a particular area □ + *of Madonna, the queen of pop* (**rainha**)
4 a playing card with a picture of a queen on it □ *the queen of hearts* (**rainha**)
5 in the game of chess, the piece that has a crown and can move in any direction (**rainha**)
6 the largest female insect in a group, that produces eggs □ *a queen bee* (**rainha**)

queer /kwɪə(r)/ ADJECTIVE [**queerer, queerest**] strange or unusual □ *queer behaviour* (**estranho**)

quench /kwentʃ/ VERB [**quenches, quenching, quenched**] **quench your thirst** to drink until you no longer feel thirsty (**saciar a sede**)

query /ˈkwɪərɪ/ ▶ NOUN [plural **queries**] a question □ *Please phone me if you have any queries.* (**pergunta**)
▶ VERB [**queries, querying, queried**] to question whether something is correct or true □ *I rang the gas company to query my bill.* (**questionar**)

quest /kwest/ NOUN [plural **quests**] a search for something or an attempt to do something, especially a long and difficult one □ *He vowed to continue his quest for justice* (**busca**)

question /ˈkwestʃən/ ▶ NOUN [plural **questions**]
1 the words you say or write when you want to ask something (**pergunta**) 🔁 *After the talk, some people asked questions.* (**fazer perguntas**) 🔁 *He refused to answer my question.* (**responder perguntas**) 🔁 *She faced some tough questions about how the money was spent.* (**enfrentar perguntas**)
2 a situation or problem that needs to be discussed or solved □ *There is the question of how much to pay him.* (**questão**) 🔁 *We need to address the question of funding.* (**dirigir a pergunta**) 🔁 *Toni raised the question of transport.* (**levantar a questão**)
3 a doubt about something □ + *over There is still a question over ownership of the building.* (**questão**) 🔁 *Staffing difficulties have called into question their ability to do the work.* (**questionar**) 🔁 *This incident has raised questions about airport security.* (**levantar dúvidas**)
4 no question of something no possibility that something will happen or be agreed to □ *There's no question of him leaving.* (**fora de questão**)
5 be a question of something used to talk about the most important fact in a situation □ *It's a question of cost.* (**ser uma questão de**)
6 in question the person or thing being talked about □ *The patient in question has a history of mental illness.* (**em questão**)
7 out of the question if you say that something is out of the question, you are emphasizing that it is not possible □ *A pay rise is out of the question at the moment.* (**fora de questão**)
▶ VERB [**questions, questioning, questioned**]
1 to ask someone questions, often officially □ *She was questioned by the military police.* □ *He questioned me about where I had found the jewels.* □ *He questioned why I had decided to leave my job.* (**perguntar, interrogar**)
2 to express doubts about something □ *They questioned the truth of his statement.* (**questionar**) 🔁 *I would question the wisdom of buying a house at the moment.* (**questionar a ideia, opinião geral**)

• **questionable** /ˈkwestʃənəbəl/ ADJECTIVE (**questionável**)
1 possibly not true or completely correct □ *The official government statistics look questionable to me.*
2 possibly not honest or legal □ *They were involved in some highly questionable deals.*

• **questioning** /ˈkwestʃənɪŋ/ NOUN, NO PLURAL when someone is asked questions, especially by the police □ *He was brought in for questioning over the robbery.* (**interrogatório**)

question mark /ˈkwestʃən ˌmɑːk/ NOUN [plural **question marks**] the mark '?' that you write after a sentence which is a question (**ponto de interrogação**)

questionnaire /ˌkwestʃəˈneə(r)/ NOUN [plural **questionnaires**] a list of questions to be answered by several people to get information (**questionário**) 🔁 *The students were asked to complete a short questionnaire.* (**completar um breve questionário**)

queue /kjuː/ ▶ NOUN [plural **queues**] a line of people waiting for something □ +*of There was a long queue of people waiting for taxis.* (**fila**) 🔁 *We joined the queue for tickets.* (**pegar a fila**)
▶ VERB [**queues, queuing, queued**] to stand in a queue □ *We had to queue for three hours to get the tickets.* (**fazer/ficar na fila**)

quibble /ˈkwɪbəl/ ▶ VERB [**quibbles, quibbling, quibbled**] to argue or to complain about details that are not important □ *They were quibbling over who should pay for what.* (**discutir ou reclamar de ninharias**)
▶ NOUN [plural **quibbles**] a complaint or criticism about a detail that is not important (**reclamação ou crítica por ninharias**)

quiche /kiːʃ/ NOUN [plural **quiches**] an open pastry case filled with eggs and cheese, often with vegetables or meat (**quiche**)

quick /kwɪk/ ▶ ADJECTIVE [**quicker, quickest**]
1 taking a short time □ Can we take a quick break? □ I had a quick look at the website. (**rápido**)
2 fast □ He's very quick on his feet. (**rápido**)
3 quick to do something doing something immediately or very soon □ She's always quick to help. □ He was quick to see the business opportunity. (**prestes a fazer alguma coisa**)
▶ ADVERB an informal word meaning quickly □ Come quick! □ It all happened so quick. (**rapidamente**)
• **quickly** /'kwɪklɪ/ ADVERB
1 in a short time or immediately □ I get bored quickly. □ He quickly realized his mistake. (**depressa, imediatamente**) 🔲 I need to sort this out as quickly as possible. (**o mais depressa possível**)
2 fast □ He had to move quickly. □ The fire quickly spread. (**depressa, imediatamente**)
• **quickness** /'kwɪknɪs/ NOUN, NO PLURAL the quality of being quick □ I was surprised by the quickness of his reply. (**rapidez**)

quicksand /'kwɪksænd/ NOUN, NO PLURAL loose wet sand that things sink into (**areia movediça**)

quick-tempered /ˌkwɪk'tempəd/ ADJECTIVE getting angry easily □ He was unfriendly and quick-tempered. (**irritadiço, irascível**)

quid /kwɪd/ NOUN [plural **quid**] an informal word for a pound (£1) □ He paid fifty quid for the jacket. (**libra**)

quiet /'kwaɪət/ ▶ ADJECTIVE [**quieter, quietest**]
1 making little noise or no noise □ a quiet voice (**quieto**) 🔲 He asked everyone to be quiet. (**ficar quieto**) 🔲 He kept quiet, not wanting to disturb her. (**permanecer quieto**)
2 calm and without much activity □ It was a quiet street with little traffic. □ It had been a relatively quiet week. (**tranquilo**)
3 not saying very much □ He was quite quiet and shy. (**calado**)
4 felt, but not expressed □ There was a quiet confidence about him. (**reservada**)
5 keep (something) quiet to not speak about something because it is a secret □ He was told to keep quiet about the payments. (**deixar quieto**)
▶ NOUN, NO PLURAL a quiet situation or time □ She returned to the quiet of her room. (**quietude**) 🔲 All he wanted was a bit of peace and quiet. (**paz e tranquilidade**)
▶ VERB [**quiets, quieting, quieted**] to make someone calm and quiet □ He raised a hand to quiet the crowd. (**aquietar**)
• **quieten** /'kwaɪətən/ VERB [**quietens, quietening, quietened**] to become quiet and calm or to make someone or something quiet and calm □ Things seem to have quietened down. □ Her mother was trying to quieten her. (**acalmar-se, acalmar**)
• **quietly** /'kwaɪətlɪ/ ADVERB
1 with little or no noise □ She slipped quietly from the room. □ 'It's okay,' she said quietly. (**quietamente**)
2 in a calm way that is not obvious □ He was quietly confident. (**calmamente**)
• **quietness** /'kwaɪətnɪs/ NOUN, NO PLURAL the state or quality of being quiet □ I like the quietness of early morning. (**quietude**)

quill /kwɪl/ NOUN [plural **quills**] a large feather made into a pen (**pena de escrever**)

quilt /kwɪlt/ NOUN [plural **quilts**] a warm cover for a bed, filled with feathers or another soft material (**acolchoado**)
• **quilted** /'kwɪltɪd/ ADJECTIVE made of two layers of cloth with a soft material between them □ a quilted jacket (**acolchoado**)

quintet /ˌkwɪn'tet/ NOUN [plural **quintets**]
1 a group of five musicians or singers (**quinteto**)
2 a piece of music written for five musicians or singers (**quinteto**)

quintuplet /ˌkwɪn'tjuːplɪt/ NOUN [plural **quintuplets**] one of five children born at one time to the same mother (**quíntuplos**)

quip /kwɪp/ ▶ NOUN [plural **quips**] a clever and funny remark or reply (**ironia, gracejo**)
▶ VERB [**quips, quipping, quipped**] to make a quip □ 'Flattery will get you everywhere,' she quipped. (**gracejar**)

quirk /kwɜːk/ NOUN [plural **quirks**]
1 something strange or unusual in a person's behaviour □ Wearing odd socks is just one of his little quirks. (**peculiaridade**)
2 something strange or unexpected that happens 🔲 By a quirk of fate, they met again years later. (**por ironia do destino**)
• **quirky** /'kwɜːkɪ/ ADJECTIVE [**quirkier, quirkiest**] strange and unusual □ a quirky sense of humour (**peculiar**)

quit /kwɪt/ VERB [**quits, quitting, quit**]
1 to leave a job, school, etc. □ He's quit his job. □ She quit university to become a singer. (**abandonar**)
2 to stop doing something □ I'm going to quit smoking. (**abandonar**)

quite /kwaɪt/ ADVERB
1 to some degree but not very or completely □ I'm quite hungry but I don't mind waiting. □ I'm quite nervous about it. □ They're quite likely to win. (**bastante, razoavelmente**)
2 completely □ I'm afraid I'm not quite ready. □ She made her position quite clear. □ It had quite the opposite effect. (**completamente**)
3 quite a bit/a few/a while, etc. a large amount, a long time, etc. compared to what is normal or expected □ He lost quite a bit of money. □ It took us quite a while. (**um tanto**)

quits | 637 | **Qur'an**

4 used for emphasis ☐ *It was really quite amazing.* ☐ *It was quite an experience.* (**realmente**)
5 used to agree with something someone has just said ☐ *'If he's twenty, he shouldn't expect his mother to cook for him.' 'Quite.'* (**realmente**)

quits /kwɪts/ ADJECTIVE if two people are quits, they do not owe each other anything, especially money ☐ *I've paid for the damage to your car – now we're quits.* (**quite**)

quitter /'kwɪtə(r)/ NOUN [*plural* **quitters**] an informal word meaning someone who stops trying to do something too easily (**molenga**)

quiver /'kwɪvə(r)/ ▶ VERB [**quivers, quivering, quivered**] to shake slightly ☐ *Her lip quivered and her eyes filled with tears.* (**estremecer**)
▶ NOUN [*plural* **quivers**] when something quivers ☐ *There was a slight quiver in his voice.* (**tremor**)

quiz /kwɪz/ ▶ NOUN [*plural* **quizzes**] a competition in which you have to answer questions ☐ *a general knowledge quiz* (**jogo de perguntas**)
▶ VERB [**quizzes, quizzing, quizzed**] to ask someone a lot of questions ☐ *He was quizzed by police.* (**questionar**)

quizzical /'kwɪzɪkəl/ ADJECTIVE showing that you do not understand or believe something (**zombeteiro**) *She gave him a quizzical look.*

quota /'kwəʊtə/ NOUN [*plural* **quotas**] an amount that someone is allowed to have or has to do ☐ *EU fishing quotas* ☐ *We all have to achieve our quota of sales.* (**cota**)

quotation /kwəʊ'teɪʃən/ NOUN [*plural* **quotations**]
1 a set of words taken from a speech or piece of writing ☐ *a quotation from Shakespeare* (**citação**)
2 a price which someone gives you for doing a job ☐ *I'd like a quotation for replacing these missing roof tiles.* (**orçamento**)

quotation marks /kwəʊ'teɪʃən ˌmɑːks/ PLURAL NOUN the symbols ' ' or " " used in writing to show that someone's words are being repeated exactly (**aspas**)

quote /kwəʊt/ ▶ VERB [**quotes, quoting, quoted**]
1 to repeat someone's words exactly as they said or wrote them ☐ *He quoted a passage from the Bible.* ☐ *One newspaper quoted him as saying: 'People are only interested in price.'* (**citar**)
2 to say how much money you will charge for doing something ☐ *He quoted a price for repairing the bicycle.* (**fazer orçamento**)
▶ NOUN [*plural* **quotes**]
1 words which are quoted ☐ *a famous quote from Adam Smith* (**citação**)
2 a price quoted for a job (**orçamento**) *He gave me a quote for the repairs.* (**deu um orçamento**)

Qur'an /kəˈrɑːn/ NOUN another spelling of Koran (*ver* **Koran**)

R r

R or **r** /ɑː(r)/ the 18th letter of the alphabet (a décima oitava letra do alfabeto)

rabbi /ˈræbaɪ/ NOUN [plural **rabbis**] a Jewish religious leader (**rabino**)

rabbit /ˈræbɪt/ NOUN [plural **rabbits**] a small animal with long ears and soft fur, which people keep as a pet, or which lives in holes in the ground □ *She let me stroke her pet rabbit.* (**coelho**)

rabble /ˈræbəl/ NOUN, NO PLURAL a noisy group of people who are behaving badly (**turba**)

rabid /ˈræbɪd, ˈreɪbɪd/ ADJECTIVE
1 having extremely strong opinions, or behaving in an extreme and often unpleasant way □ *My brother is a rabid fan of rap music.* (**fanático**)
2 suffering from rabies □ *a rabid dog* (**raivoso**)

rabies /ˈreɪbiːz/ NOUN, NO PLURAL a serious disease caused by being bitten by an infected animal (**raiva**)

race /reɪs/ ▶ NOUN [plural **races**]
1 a competition to see who can get somewhere fastest or do something fastest □ *I'm running in a race this weekend.* (**corrida**) *Lewis won the race.* (**ganhou a corrida**)
2 one of the groups that people can be divided into according to their skin colour and physical characteristics □ *It's our hope that people of all races can live together in peace.* (**raça, etnia**)
3 a competition to get a position of power *Kerry was defeated in the US presidential race of 2004.* (**disputa presidencial**) □ + **for** *Johnson won the race for mayor of London.* (**disputa para**)
4 no plural a situation in which a person or group tries to be the first to do something □ + **to do something** *Scientists were involved in the race to find a cure for AIDS.* (**corrida**)
5 a race against time/the clock a situation in which something must be done in a very short time □ *Paterson is facing a race against time to be fit for Friday's game.* (**uma corrida contra o tempo**)
▶ VERB [**races, racing, raced**] (**correr**)
1 to compete against someone in a race □ *I'll race you to the postbox.* □ + **against** *His horse will be racing against some of the best horses in the country.* (**apostar corrida, correr contra**)
2 to go somewhere very quickly, or to move someone or something very quickly □ + **to** *Ambulances raced to the scene of the accident.* □ *Emma raced down the stairs to answer the door.* □ *He was raced to hospital with a suspected heart attack.* (**correr**)
3 if your heart or mind races, it works at a faster speed than normal □ *I could feel my heart racing with excitement.* □ *My mind was racing after such a busy and eventful day.* (**disparar**)
4 to use an animal or a vehicle to compete in races □ *My Grandad raced horses for more than 40 years.* (**correr com**)

racecourse /ˈreɪskɔːs/ NOUN [plural **racecourses**] the track that horses race on (**hipódromo**)

racehorse /ˈreɪshɔːs/ NOUN [plural **racehorses**] a horse that competes in races (**cavalo de corrida**)

racial /ˈreɪʃəl/ ADJECTIVE to do with a person's race □ *racial discrimination* (**racial**)
• **racially** /ˈreɪʃəli/ ADVERB in a way that is to do with someone's race □ *They consider themselves racially distinct from their neighbours.* (**racialmente**)

racing /ˈreɪsɪŋ/ NOUN, NO PLURAL the sport of racing animals or vehicles (**corrida**) *Dad watches horse racing on television.* (**corrida de cavalo**) *He's one of the most famous people in motor racing.* (**corrida de automóvel**) *a racing driver* (**piloto de corrida**)

racism /ˈreɪsɪzəm/ ▶ NOUN, NO PLURAL unfair treatment of someone or dislike of someone because they belong to a different race □ *The scheme aims to tackle racism in schools.* □ *He was a victim of racism.* (**racismo**)
• **racist** /ˈreɪsɪst/ ADJECTIVE to do with racism □ *racist remarks* (**racista**)
▶ NOUN [plural **racists**] someone who dislikes people or treats them unfairly because they belong to a different race

rack /ræk/ ▶ NOUN [plural **racks**] a place where things are kept, usually made of narrow pieces of wood or metal □ *I put my bag in the luggage rack.* (**estante, prateleira**)
▶ VERB [**racks, racking, racked**] (**atormentar**)
1 if you are racked with pain or with a feeling, you suffer a lot because of it □ *She was racked with guilt that she hadn't done more to save his life.* (**afligido**)
2 rack your brains an informal phrase meaning to try very hard to think of something □ *I've racked my brains but I can't think of an answer to the problem.* (**quebrar a cabeça**)

racket /'rækɪt/ NOUN [plural **rackets**]
1 a piece of equipment that you use for hitting the ball in games such as tennis ▫ *a tennis racket* (**raquete**)
2 an informal word meaning a loud and unpleasant noise 🔊 *They were making a terrible racket.* (**fazer algazarra**)
3 an informal word meaning an illegal way of making money ▫ *He had been involved in a smuggling racket.* (**crime**)

radar /'reɪdɑː(r)/ NOUN [plural **radars**] a system or piece of equipment that uses radio waves to find the position of aeroplanes, ships, etc. (**radar**)

radiance /'reɪdiəns/ NOUN, NO PLURAL
1 happiness that shows on your face (**resplendor**)
2 how bright something is (**brilho**)

• **radiant** /'reɪdiənt/ ADJECTIVE
1 showing that you are very happy ▫ *a radiant smile* (**irradiante**)
2 bright ▫ *radiant sunshine* (**brilhante**)

radiate /'reɪdieɪt/ VERB [**radiates, radiating, radiated**]
1 to show an emotion or quality in your face or behaviour ▫ *Wendi radiated confidence.* (**irradiar**)
2 to send out heat or light ▫ *She was enjoying the warmth radiating from the log fire.* (**irradiar**)
3 to spread out in different directions from a central point ▫ *Secret alleyways radiate from the harbour.* (**espalhar-se**)

• **radiation** /ˌreɪdi'eɪʃən/ NOUN, NO PLURAL
1 energy from a nuclear reaction which can harm or kill people. A physics word ▫ *radiation sickness* ▫ *They were exposed to high levels of radiation.* (**irradiação**)
2 heat or light in the form of waves which you cannot see. A physics word ▫ *solar radiation* (**radiação**)

• **radiator** /'reɪdieɪtə(r)/ NOUN [plural **radiators**]
1 a metal object that is filled with hot water to heat a room (**aquecedor**)
2 part of an engine that keeps it cool (**radiador**)

radical /'rædɪkəl/ ▶ ADJECTIVE
1 believing that there should be big political and social changes ▫ *radical views* (**radical**)
2 big and important ▫ *radical changes* (**radical**)
▶ NOUN [plural **radicals**] someone who believes that there should be big political and social changes

• **radically** /'rædɪkəli/ ADVERB in a big and important way (**radicalmente**) 🔊 *The new system is radically different from what we had before.*

radio /'reɪdiəʊ/ ▶ NOUN [plural **radios**]
1 a piece of equipment that you use for listening to programmes which are broadcast (**rádio**) 🔊 *Raj switched the radio on to hear the news.* (**ligou o rádio**) ▫ *He bought a digital radio.*
2 no plural programmes that you listen to using a radio (**ouvir rádio**) 🔊 *I enjoy listening to the radio.* 🔊 *The local radio station broadcasts travel news.* (**estação de rádio**) 🔊 *a radio show* (**programa de rádio**) ▫ *James is a radio presenter.* (**locutor de rádio**)
3 no plural a system of broadcasting that uses sound waves instead of wires to send messages ▫ *He gave orders by radio.* (**rádio**) 🔊 *They lost radio contact with the crew.* (**perder contato com o rádio**)
4 a piece of electrical equipment, for example on a ship or plane, that receives or sends messages as sound waves (**rádio**)
▶ VERB [**radios, radioing, radioed**] to communicate with someone by radio ▫ *The captain of the ship radioed for help.* (**mandar mensagens pelo rádio**)

radioactive /ˌreɪdiəʊ'æktɪv/ ADJECTIVE sending out harmful radiation (= energy from a nuclear reaction). A physics word ▫ *radioactive substances* (**radioativo**)

• **radioactivity** /ˌreɪdiəʊæk'tɪvəti/ NOUN, NO PLURAL harmful energy that is produced by a radioactive substance. A physics word. (**radioatividade**)

radiographer /ˌreɪdi'ɒɡrəfə(r)/ NOUN [plural **radiographers**] someone whose job is to do X-rays (= pictures of the inside of someone's body) in a hospital (**radiologista**)

• **radiography** /ˌreɪdi'ɒɡrəfi/ NOUN, NO PLURAL the job or science of doing X-rays (**radiografia**)

radiotherapy /ˌreɪdiəʊ'θerəpi/ NOUN, NO PLURAL the use of radiation (= energy from a nuclear reaction) to treat diseases such as cancer (**radioterapia**)

radish /'rædɪʃ/ NOUN [plural **radishes**] a small round vegetable with a red skin and strong taste that is eaten raw in salads (**rabanete**)

radius /'reɪdiəs/ NOUN [plural **radii**]
1 within a 15 mile/10 km, etc. radius less than 15 miles, 10 kilometres, etc. from a particular place ▫ *We deliver anywhere within a ten-mile radius of the store.* (**raio**)
2 the distance from the centre of a circle to the edge. A maths word. (**raio**)

raffle /'ræfəl/ ▶ NOUN [plural **raffles**] a competition in which people buy a ticket with a number on, and win a prize if their number is chosen (**rifa**) 🔊 *Would you like to buy a raffle ticket?* (**bilhete de rifa**)
▶ VERB [**raffles, raffling, raffled**] to offer something as a prize in a raffle (**rifar**)

raft /rɑːft/ NOUN [plural **rafts**]
1 a flat boat made from long pieces of wood tied together (**jangada**)
2 a raft of something a lot of things ▫ *They have a raft of issues to deal with.* (**um montão de coisas**)

rafter /'rɑːftə(r)/ NOUN [plural **rafters**] one of the sloping pieces of wood that form the frame of a roof (**viga, caibro**)

rag /ræɡ/ NOUN [plural **rags**] an old piece of cloth ▫ *an oily rag* (**trapo**)
⇨ go to **rags**

rage /reɪdʒ/ ▶ NOUN, NO PLURAL
1 extreme anger that you cannot control □ *He killed his wife in a fit of jealous rage.* (**fúria**) 🔄 *I've never seen him fly into a rage* (= become extremely angry) *like that before.* (**ficar com tanta fúria**)
2 all the rage an informal phrase meaning fashionable or popular □ *These tiny bags are all the rage.* (**em grande moda**)
▶ VERB [**rages, raging, raged**]
1 to continue with a lot of force, violence or anger □ *The fire raged for almost a week.* □ *Debate is still raging over whether he should be prosecuted.* (**espalhar, propagar**)
2 to speak in an angry way □ *'Don't you touch her!' John raged.* (**enfurecer-se, exasperar**)

ragged /ˈrægɪd/ ADJECTIVE
1 torn and untidy □ *ragged clothes* (**maltrapilho**)
2 having a rough edge □ *a ragged hole* (**furos irregulares em uma roupa**)

rags /rægz/ PLURAL NOUN (**trapos**)
1 clothes which are old and torn □ *The children were dressed in rags.*
2 rags to riches used for describing a situation in which someone who is very poor becomes very rich □ *Her life had been a rags to riches story.*

raid /reɪd/ ▶ NOUN [plural **raids**] (**ataques, incursões**)
1 a sudden military attack □ *a bombing raid* (**ataque**)
2 a sudden unexpected visit from the police, who enter a building and search it □ *Guns were found during a police raid on the house.* (**batida policial**)
3 a violent attack on a bank, shop, etc. to steal things □ *He was arrested for a £250,000 raid on a jeweller's shop.* (**assalto**)
▶ VERB [**raids, raiding, raided**]
1 to attack a place using weapons □ *Troops raided villages.* (**invadir**)
2 to use force to enter a place in order to search it □ *Police raided the premises and questioned staff.* (**efetuar batida policial**)
3 to attack a place in order to steal things □ *Armed robbers raided her home.* (**assaltar**)
• **raider** /ˈreɪdə(r)/ NOUN [plural **raiders**] someone who attacks a place, especially to steal something (**assaltante**)

rail /reɪl/ NOUN [plural **rails**] (**trens, vigas, barras, trilhos**)
1 *no plural* the railway system □ *Travelling by rail is more relaxing than driving.* (**trem**) 🔄 *Rail fares have increased again.* (**preço da passagem de trem**)
2 a bar for hanging things on (**viga, barra**) 🔄 *a towel rail*
3 a bar that you hold to stop you falling □ *Hold onto the rail.* (**corrimão, grade, parapeito**)
4 one of the two long metal bars that form a track for trains (**trilho**)
• **railing** /ˈreɪlɪŋ/ NOUN [plural **railings**] a fence made of vertical metal bars, or the bar that goes along the top of a fence like this □ *He was leaning on the railings.* (**grade**)

railroad /ˈreɪlrəʊd/ NOUN [plural **railroads**] the US word for **railway** (**estrada de ferro, ferrovia**)

railway /ˈreɪlweɪ/ ▶ NOUN [plural **railways**] (**estrada de ferro, ferrovia**)
1 a track for trains to travel on □ *Glasgow has Scotland's only underground railway.* (**estrada de ferro, ferrovia**)
2 the railway the system and organizations to do with trains □ *We need to encourage more people to use the railway.* (**companhia de estrada de ferro, transporte ferroviário**)
▶ ADJECTIVE to do with trains and the tracks they use (**férreo, ferroviário**) 🔄 *I'll meet you at the railway station.* (**estação férrea**) 🔄 *Children should be told about the danger of playing on railway lines.* (**linha férrea**) □ *a railway bridge*

rain /reɪn/ ▶ NOUN, NO PLURAL water that falls from the sky □ *The children didn't want to go out in the rain.* (**chuva**) 🔄 *Heavy rain* (= a large amount of rain) *has caused flooding in the area.* (**chuva pesada**) 🔄 *500mm of rain fell last month.* (**queda de chuva**) 🔄 *It was pouring with rain* (= a lot of rain was falling) *outside.* (**chovendo muito**)
▶ VERB [**rains, raining, rained**] when it rains, water falls from the sky (**chover**) 🔄 *It's raining so take an umbrella.* 🔄 *It rained heavily* (= a lot of rain fell) *all night.* (**choveu muito**)
♦ PHRASAL VERB **be rained off** if an event is rained off, it has to stop because there is too much rain □ *The game was rained off.* (**ser interrompido por causa da chuva**)

rainbow /ˈreɪnbəʊ/ NOUN [plural **rainbows**] a curved line of colours that you see in the sky when it is raining and sunny at the same time (**arco-íris**)

raincoat /ˈreɪnkəʊt/ NOUN [plural **raincoats**] a light coat that you wear when it rains □ *She was wearing a blue raincoat.* (**capa de chuva**)

rainfall /ˈreɪnfɔːl/ NOUN, NO PLURAL the amount of rain that falls in a particular place over a particular period of time (**precipitação, índice pluviométrico**) 🔄 *Heavy rainfall lead to widespread flooding.*

rainforest /ˈreɪnfɒrɪst/ NOUN [plural **rainforests**] a tropical forest with very tall trees which are close together, in an area where it rains a lot. A geography word □ *the Amazon rainforest* (**mata tropical**)

rainy /ˈreɪni/ ADJECTIVE [**rainier, rainiest**] raining a lot □ *a rainy day* (**chuvoso**)

raise /reɪz/ ▶ VERB [**raises, raising, raised**]
1 to lift something to a higher position □ *Raise your hand if you know the answer.* □ *The wreck was slowly raised from the sea bed.* □ *She raised her eyebrows in surprise.* (**levantar**)
2 to increase the amount or level of something □ *They've raised the rent again.* □ *We are trying to raise standards in the school.* □ *This case has raised awareness of the disease.* (**elevar**)

raisin / rancid

3 to mention a new subject in a discussion □ *I want to raise a matter that we all care very much about.* ▣ *His teachers have raised concerns about his health.* (**levantar uma questão**)
4 to cause a particular emotion or reaction (**provocar reações**) ▣ *The accident raised questions over safety standards.* ▣ *The drop in oil prices has raised fears of a recession.*
5 to collect money for a particular purpose □ *We're raising money for charity.* (**angariar**)
6 if you raise children, you look after them until they are adults □ *My wages are not enough to raise a family.* (**criar, educar**)
7 raise your voice to speak more loudly than normal (**aumentar**)
8 if you raise crops, you grow them, and if you raise animals, you keep them (**criar**)

> ➤ Note that **raise** is always followed by an object: □ *She raised her hand.* □ *They have raised taxes.*
> ➤ The verb **rise** has the same meaning but is used without an object:
> ✓ *Taxes have risen.*
> ✗ *Taxes have raised.*

▶ NOUN [*plural* **raises**] the US word for **rise** (= increase in the amount of money you earn) (**aumento**)

raisin /ˈreɪzən/ NOUN [*plural* **raisins**] a dried grape (= small round fruit) (**uva-passa**)

rake /reɪk/ ▶ NOUN [*plural* **rakes**] a garden tool with a long handle and thin metal pieces on the end, used for making the soil level and smooth, or for collecting up dead leaves, etc. (**ancinho**)
▶ VERB [**rakes, raking, raked**] to use a rake to collect dead leaves or to make soil smooth (**ancinhar**)
◆ PHRASAL VERB **rake something in** to earn a large amount of money. An informal phrase (**ganhar muito dinheiro**) ▣ *His book has sold really well – he must be raking it in.*

rally /ˈræli/ ▶ NOUN [*plural* **rallies**]
1 a large public meeting to support something or to complain about something □ *Over 1000 people attended an anti-war rally.* (**assembleia**)
2 a car race on public roads □ *a rally driver* (**rali**)
▶ VERB [**rallies, rallying, rallied**]
1 to join other people in order to support someone or something, especially when they are having problems □ *Parents rallied behind the head teacher.* (**juntar-se**)
2 to improve or to become higher or stronger again □ *The team rallied and went on to win the game.* (**recuperar-se**)
◆ PHRASAL VERB **rally round (someone)** if people rally round, they try to help someone who is having problems □ *Friends rallied round and offered to do the shopping and drive me to hospital appointments.* (**juntar-se para ajudar**)

RAM /ræm/ ABBREVIATION Random Access Memory; a type of computer memory. A computing word. (**RAM**)

ram /ræm/ ▶ VERB [**rams, ramming, rammed**]
1 to hit something with a lot of force □ *The boat was clearly going to ram the pier.* (**bater contra**)
2 to push something somewhere using a lot of force □ *Boyd rammed the ball into the net.* (**forçar**)
▶ NOUN [*plural* **rams**] a male sheep (**carneiro**)

Ramadan /ˌræməˈdæn/ NOUN, NO PLURAL the ninth month of the Islamic year, when Muslims do not eat anything during the day (**Ramadã**)

ramble /ˈræmbəl/ ▶ VERB [**rambles, rambling, rambled**]
1 to talk for a long time in a confusing or boring way □ *He rambled on about his horses.* (**perambular**)
2 to walk in the countryside for pleasure (**passear**)
▶ NOUN [*plural* **rambles**] a long walk in the countryside
• **rambler** /ˈræmblə(r)/ NOUN [*plural* **ramblers**] someone who walks in the countryside (**passeador**)
• **rambling** /ˈræmblɪŋ/ ADJECTIVE
1 a rambling building or garden is big and has an irregular shape □ *a rambling house* (**irregular**)
2 long and confusing □ *a rambling speech* (**desconexo**)

ramp /ræmp/ NOUN [*plural* **ramps**]
1 a sloping surface that joins two places that are at different levels □ *We should be able to get the wheelchair up the ramp quite easily.* (**rampa**)
2 the US word for **slip road** (**via de acesso**)

rampage /ræmˈpeɪdʒ/ ▶ VERB [**rampages, rampaging, rampaged**] to run around a place, causing a lot of damage □ *Protestors rampaged through the streets, attacking shops and government buildings.* (**mover-se furiosamente**)
▶ NOUN **go on the rampage** if a group of people go on the rampage, they run around an area, behaving violently and causing damage □ *English football fans went on the rampage after their team lost.* (**tumulto, rebuliço, de caráter violento**)

rampant /ˈræmpənt/ ADJECTIVE increasing or spreading very fast □ *rampant inflation* (**desenfreado**)

rampart /ˈræmpɑːt/ NOUN [*plural* **ramparts**] a pile of earth or a wall that was built around a castle or city to protect it in the past (**baluarte**)

ramshackle /ˈræmʃækəl/ ADJECTIVE a ramshackle building is in very bad condition (**decrépito**)

ran /ræn/ PAST TENSE OF **run** (*ver* **run**)

ranch /rɑːntʃ/ NOUN [*plural* **ranches**] a large farm where cows or horses are kept (**rancho**)

rancid /ˈrænsɪd/ ADJECTIVE rancid food tastes or smells unpleasant because the fat in it is no longer fresh □ *rancid butter* (**rançoso**)

random

random /ˈrændəm/ ADJECTIVE
1 done without a plan or a system □ *a random selection* (**casual**)
2 at random without a plan or system □ *The killer had chosen his victims at random.* (**ao acaso**)
• **randomly** /ˈrændəmlɪ/ ADVERB in a random way □ *Numbers are chosen randomly.* (**aleatoriamente**)

rang /ræŋ/ PAST TENSE OF **ring** (*ver* **ring**)

range /reɪndʒ/ ▶ NOUN [*plural* **ranges**]
1 a group of things of a similar type □ *+ of The shop stocks a huge range of toys and games.* (**variedade**) 🔳 *There is a wide range of courses to choose from.* (**grande variedade**)
2 all the ages, numbers, etc. that are included within fixed limits (**faixa, extensão**) 🔳 *Most of the sofas we sell are in the £500–£1,000 price range.* (**faixa de preço**) 🔳 *The programme is aimed at children in the 10–13 age range.* (**faixa de idade**)
3 the distance from which something can be seen, heard or reached (**alcance**) 🔳 *Spectators have to stand well out of range of the arrows.* (**fora de alcance**) 🔳 *He shot the man at close range* (= from a position that is very close). (**a pouca distância**)
4 an area where you can practise hitting golf balls or shooting □ *a firing range* (**área ou campo de golfe, de tiro**)
5 a group of hills or mountains 🔳 *a mountain range* (**cadeia de montanhas**)

▶ VERB [**ranges, ranging, ranged**]
1 to include both things that are mentioned, and other things between them □ *+ from The company has accommodation ranging from hostels to luxury hotels.* (**variar de... até...**) □ *Prices range from £70–£150 per night.* (**variação de preço**) □ *+ between The dancers' ages ranged between 16 and 40.* (**variar entre**)
2 to deal with a lot of different subjects □ *+ over The articles range over many topics.* (**abranger**)
• **ranger** /ˈreɪndʒə(r)/ NOUN [*plural* **rangers**] someone whose job is to look after a forest or an area of countryside (**guarda-florestal**)

rank /ræŋk/ ▶ NOUN [*plural* **ranks**]
1 someone's level in an organization or in society (**nível, posto, classe**) 🔳 *A private is the lowest rank in the British army.* (**menor posto**) 🔳 *A duchess has a very high social rank.* (**na alta sociedade**) □ *+ of He held the rank of colonel.* □ *There are now more women in the senior ranks of the profession.*
2 ranks the people who belong to a particular group □ *He has now joined the ranks of the world's richest people.* □ *There is corruption within the party's own ranks.* (**categoria, grupo**)
3 break ranks to show publicly that you disagree with a group that you belong to □ *He broke ranks with party leaders on the issue.* (**discordar publicamente de seu grupo**)

▶ VERB [**ranks, ranking, ranked**] to have a certain position that shows how good, bad, important, etc someone or something is (**classificar(-se)**) □ *+ as He ranks as one of the world's best actors.* (**classificar-se como**) 🔳 *+ among The country ranks among the world's poorest.* (**classificar-se entre**)
• **ranking** /ˈræŋkɪŋ/ NOUN [*plural* **rankings**] a position on a list that shows how good or bad someone or something is □ *The player is 44ᵗʰ in the official world tennis rankings.* (**classificação**)

ransack /ˈrænsæk/ VERB [**ransacks, ransacking, ransacked**] to search a place in an untidy way and steal things □ *The house had been ransacked.* (**vasculhar**)

ransom /ˈrænsəm/ NOUN [*plural* **ransoms**] an amount of money that is paid to a criminal so that they will give back a person they have taken as a prisoner (**resgate**) 🔳 *They paid a ransom of over $1 million.* (**pagaram um resgate**)

rant /rænt/ ▶ VERB [**rants, ranting, ranted**] to talk or write a lot in an angry way □ *He was ranting about the disgusting state of the country.* (**discursar agressivamente**)
▶ NOUN [*plural* **rants**] a long, angry speech or piece of writing □ *He phoned me up to have a rant about the legal system.* (**discurso agressivo, reclamação enfática**)

rap /ræp/ ▶ VERB [**raps, rapping, rapped**] to hit something quickly and hard □ *Lisa rapped on the door.* (**golpes secos**)
▶ NOUN [*plural* **raps**]
1 a quick hard hit □ *There was a rap on the window.* (**golpe seco**)
2 a type of pop music with words that are spoken in rhythm (**rap**)

rapid /ˈræpɪd/ ADJECTIVE done, happening or moving quickly □ *There has been a rapid growth in air travel.* (**rápido**)
• **rapidly** /ˈræpɪdlɪ/ ADVERB quickly □ *The town is expanding rapidly.* (**rapidamente**)
• **rapids** /ˈræpɪdz/ PLURAL NOUN parts of a river where the water flows very quickly, usually over dangerous rocks (**corredeiras**)

rapport /ræˈpɔː(r)/ NOUN, NO PLURAL a feeling of understanding someone and liking them (**empatia**) 🔳 *The teachers at the school have a very good rapport with the students.*

rapture /ˈræptʃə(r)/ NOUN, NO PLURAL
1 great happiness □ *There was an expression of rapture on his face.* (**êxtase**)
2 in rapture(s) in a state of great happiness and enthusiasm □ *The audience was in raptures over her singing.* (**em delírio**)
• **rapturous** /ˈræptʃərəs/ ADJECTIVE showing happiness and enthusiasm (**delirante**) 🔳 *There was rapturous applause at the end of the performance.*

rare /reə(r)/ ADJECTIVE [**rarer, rarest**]
1 not happening or existing often □ *This type of attack is extremely rare.* □ *This is a rare example*

rarity

of a blue diamond. □ *On rare occasions, errors are made.* □ **+ to do something** *It's rare to find a vase like this in perfect condition.* (**raro**)
2 rare meat is cooked for a short time and often still has blood in it □ *I like my steak rare.* (**malpassado**)

• **rarely** /ˈreəli/ ADVERB not often □ *I rarely see him.* □ *He's a keen football fan and rarely misses a game.* (**raramente**)

rarity /ˈreərəti/ NOUN [plural **rarities**]
1 something that is not common or does not happen very often □ *Rain is a rarity in that part of the world.* (**raridade**)
2 the quality of being rare □ *The jewel is very expensive because of its rarity.* (**raridade**)

rascal /ˈrɑːskəl/ NOUN [plural **rascals**] a child who behaves badly but who you still feel affection for (**travesso**)

rash /ræʃ/ ▶ NOUN [plural **rashes**]
1 an area of red spots on your skin, often caused by an illness (**erupção cutânea**) 🔹 *I came out in a rash* (= developed a rash). (**surgiu uma erupção**)
2 a rash of something several unpleasant things that suddenly start happening □ *There has been a rash of kidnappings recently.* (**onda de acontecimentos**)

▶ ADJECTIVE [**rasher**, **rashest**] done without careful thought □ *It was a rash promise.* (**precipitado**)

rasher /ˈræʃə(r)/ NOUN [plural **rashers**] a thin piece of bacon (= meat from a pig) (**fatia de toucinho, presunto**)

raspberry /ˈrɑːzbəri/ NOUN [plural **raspberries**] a small soft red fruit that grows on bushes (**framboesa**)

rat /ræt/ NOUN [plural **rats**] an animal that looks like a large mouse with a long tail (**rato**)

rate /reɪt/ ▶ NOUN [plural **rates**]
1 how often something happens, or the number of people or things it happens to □ *Unemployment rates have fallen.* □ *We need to lower crime rates.* □ *The birth rate has risen.* (**índice**)
2 the speed at which something happens □ *The rate of progress has been very slow.* □ *The disease is spreading at a tremendous rate.* (**velocidade**) 🔹 *At this rate, we'll have eaten all the food before lunch time.* (**a essa velocidade**)
3 an amount of money that is paid for something (**taxa**) □ *They charge very high rates for their services.* □ *Rates of pay have risen.* □ *The exchange rate is in our favour at the moment.* (**taxa de câmbio**) 🔹 *The banks have raised interest rates.* (**taxas de juros**)
4 at any rate used to say that at least one part of what you have said is certain □ *He's gone to see his cousin or someone – a relative at any rate.* (**de qualquer modo**)
⇨ go to **first-rate**, **second-rate**, **third-rate**

▶ VERB [**rates**, **rating**, **rated**]
1 to judge the quality or level of someone or something □ *How do you rate him as a tennis player?* □ *Patients were asked to rate their pain on a scale of 1–5.* (**avaliar**)
2 to deserve something □ *The incident rated a mention in the national news.* (**merecer alguma coisa**)

rather /ˈrɑːðə(r)/ ADVERB
1 slightly □ *It's rather cold in here, isn't it?* □ *He felt rather tired after such a long journey.* (**um tanto**)
2 **rather than** instead of □ *Many people choose to rent rather than buy houses.* □ *Rather than punishment, some children need support to improve their behaviour.* (**em vez de**)
3 **would rather** used when saying what you would prefer to do □ *I would rather talk about this later if you don't mind.* □ *I'd rather go swimming.* (**preferir**)
4 **or rather** used when giving more accurate information about what you have said □ *I've already agreed; or rather, I haven't said 'no'.* (**ou melhor**)

ratio /ˈreɪʃiəʊ/ NOUN [plural **ratios**] the relationship between two numbers or amounts that shows how much bigger one is than the other □ *Our nursery has a ratio of one member of staff to three children.* (**proporção**)

ration /ˈræʃən/ ▶ NOUN [plural **rations**] a limited amount of something that you are allowed to have □ *I ate my ration of biscuits for the day before lunchtime.* (**ração**)

▶ VERB [**rations**, **rationing**, **rationed**] to limit the amount of something that people are allowed to have because there is not a lot available □ *Sugar was rationed during the war.* (**racionar**)

rational /ˈræʃənəl/ ADJECTIVE reasonable and sensible □ *a rational decision* (**racional**)

• **rationale** /ˌræʃəˈnɑːl/ NOUN, NO PLURAL the reasons for a decision or belief □ *He challenged the government's rationale for going to war.* (**razões, argumentação lógica**)

• **rationalize** or **rationalise** /ˈræʃənəlaɪz/ VERB [**rationalizes**, **rationalizing**, **rationalized**] to think of reasons to explain your behaviour □ *People often try to rationalize their bad habits.* (**refletir**)

rat race /ˈræt ˌreɪs/ NOUN, NO PLURAL **the rat race** the unpleasant situation in life when people have to work too much and compete with each other (**rotina exaustiva**)

rattle /ˈrætəl/ ▶ VERB [**rattles**, **rattling**, **rattled**]
1 if something rattles, it makes a noise by hitting against something else repeatedly □ *The windows were rattling in the wind.* (**chocalhar**)
2 to shake something so that it makes a noise □ *She rattled the door but it was locked.* (**chocalhar**)
3 an informal word meaning to make someone feel worried or less confident □ *A police warning had rattled the gang.* (**abalar a confiança**)

◆ PHRASAL VERB **rattle something off** to quickly say something you have learned, especially a list □

He rattled off the names of all the US presidents. (falar na ponta da língua)
▶ NOUN [plural **rattles**] (chocalhos, barulheiras)
1 the noise that something hard and loose makes when it is shaken □ *There's a bad rattle coming from the engine.* (barulheira)
2 a baby's toy that makes a noise when you shake it (chocalho)

rattlesnake /ˈrætəlsneɪk/ NOUN [plural **rattlesnakes**] a poisonous snake that makes a noise with its tail (cascavel)

ratty /ˈræti/ ADJECTIVE [**rattier**, **rattiest**] an informal word meaning bad-tempered □ *By the end of the day the children are ratty.* (ranzinza)

raucous /ˈrɔːkəs/ ADJECTIVE loud and unpleasant □ *raucous laughter* (rouco)

ravage /ˈrævɪdʒ/ VERB [**ravages**, **ravaging**, **ravaged**] to damage something very badly □ *The area has been ravaged by drought.* (devastação)
• **ravages** /ˈrævɪdʒɪz/ PLURAL NOUN **the ravages of something** the bad effects of something □ *Some people have cosmetic surgery to stop the ravages of old age.* (danos)

rave /reɪv/ ▶ VERB [**raves**, **raving**, **raved**]
1 to talk about something very enthusiastically □ *He's been raving about a new computer game he's bought.* (falar com entusiasmo)
2 to talk in an angry and confused way (delirar)
▶ NOUN [plural **raves**] a very large party where people dance to loud music (rave)

raven /ˈreɪvən/ NOUN [plural **ravens**] a large black bird (corvo)

ravenous /ˈrævənəs/ ADJECTIVE very hungry (voraz)

ravine /rəˈviːn/ NOUN [plural **ravines**] a deep narrow valley with steep sides. A geography word. (ravina)

ravioli /ˌræviˈəʊli/ NOUN, NO PLURAL a type of pasta in the shape of squares with meat, cheese or vegetables inside (raviólli)

ravishing /ˈrævɪʃɪŋ/ ADJECTIVE extremely beautiful (encantador)

raw /rɔː/ ADJECTIVE [**rawer**, **rawest**]
1 raw food is not cooked □ *raw vegetables* □ *raw meat* (cru)
2 a raw substance is still in its natural state (bruto) ▣ *raw materials* (matéria-prima) ▣ *Raw sewage had been pumped into the river.* (água de esgoto sem tratamento)
3 a raw feeling or quality is strong and natural ▣ *raw emotions* □ *Her grief at her father's death was still raw.* (sentimentos intensos não controlados)
4 having no experience or training ▣ *He was only 16 and a raw recruit in the army.* (inexperiente)
5 raw skin is red and sore (pele ferida/em carne viva)
◆ IDIOM **hit/touch a raw nerve** to upset or offend someone by something that you say □ *Powell's comments hit a raw nerve.* (atingir um ponto fraco)

ray /reɪ/ NOUN [plural **rays**]
1 a beam of light □ *a ray of sunlight* (raio)
2 **a ray of hope** a small amount of hope □ *This research offers a ray of hope for asthma sufferers.* (raio de esperança)

razor /ˈreɪzə(r)/ NOUN [plural **razors**] a sharp tool that you use for shaving hair from your face and body □ *He uses an electric razor.* (navalha, barbeador) ▣ *a razor blade* (lâmina de barbear)

Rd /rəʊd/ ABBREVIATION **Road** (estrada)

re- /riː/ PREFIX re- is added to the beginning of words to mean 'again' □ *reappear* □ *rearrange* (re-)

reach /riːtʃ/ ▶ VERB [**reaches**, **reaching**, **reached**]
1 to arrive somewhere □ *We didn't reach the cottage till long after dark.* □ *The train reached London at 10.34.* □ *My letter never reached him.* (chegar a)
2 to be able to touch or hold something □ *I can't reach the top shelf.* (alcançar)
3 to stretch out your arm to touch or hold something □ *He reached over me to get some bread.* □ **+ for** *As I reached for the fruit, I fell off the ladder.* (estender o braço)
4 to be long enough to touch something □ *The ladder didn't reach to the top window.* □ *Charlotte's hair reaches right down her back.* (tentar alcançar)
5 to get to a particular amount, level or situation □ *Temperatures have reached 35°.* □ *We have nearly reached our target of £1,000.* (atingir) ▣ *I've reached a point where I don't care what happens to him any more.* (chegar a um ponto)
6 **reach an agreement/a decision, etc.** to agree/decide, etc. about something □ *The jury failed to reach a verdict.* (chegar a um acordo/a uma decisão)
7 to contact someone, especially by telephone □ *I've been trying to reach you all day.* (entrar em contato)

> ➤ Note that **reach** meaning 'to arrive somewhere' is never followed by 'to':
> ✓ *It was midnight by the time we reached London.*
> ✗ *It was midnight by the time we reached to London.*

▶ NOUN, NO PLURAL
1 **beyond/out of (someone's) reach** (a) too far away to touch or hold □ *Keep all medicines out of reach.* (b) not possible for someone to have or achieve □ *They feel that a university education is beyond their reach.* (fora do alcance)
2 **within (someone's) reach** (a) close enough for someone to touch or hold □ *I made sure all his equipment was within reach.* (b) possible for someone to get or achieve □ *Suddenly, the gold medal seems within her reach.* (ao alcance)

3 within reach of something close enough to get to a place □ *The house is within easy reach of the beach.* (perto, de fácil acesso)

react /rɪˈækt/ VERB [**reacts, reacting, reacted**]
1 to behave or feel a particular way because of something that has happened or something someone has said □ *How did Helen react when she heard the news?* (reagir) □ **+ to** *He reacted angrily to their criticism.* (reagir a) □ **+ by** *He reacted by sacking 10 workers.*
2 if a substance reacts with another substance, it changes when they are put together. A chemistry word. (reagir)
3 to experience unpleasant effects because of something you have eaten or put on your skin □ **+ to** *My eyes reacted to the chlorine in the pool.* (reagir a)

- **reaction** /rɪˈækʃən/ NOUN [*plural* **reactions**]
1 behaviour or feelings that are a result of something that has happened or something someone has said □ *Did you see his reaction when he found out?* □ **+ to** *There has been a huge reaction to his death.* □ *The news provoked angry reactions from members of the public.* (reação)
2 the change that happens when two substances are put together. A chemistry word. □ *a chemical reaction* (reação química)
3 an unpleasant effect caused by something you have eaten or put on your skin □ *He had an allergic reaction to the drug.* (reação alérgica)
4 reactions the ability to move quickly when something happens □ *You need very fast reactions to play tennis well.* (reações)

read /riːd/ ▶ VERB [**reads, reading, read**]
1 to look at words and understand them □ *He was reading a novel.* □ **+ about** *I read about the court case in the papers.* □ **+ that** *I read that they were going to open a new store.* (ler)
2 to look at words and say them aloud □ *I always read a story to the children at bedtime.* (ler em voz alta)
3 to understand the meaning of symbols, numbers, etc. (entender os símbolos) 🔈 *Can you read music?* □ *The man came to read the electricity meter.*
4 to show an amount or level on a piece of equipment □ *The thermometer reads 31 degrees.* (registrar)
5 if a computer or a piece of equipment reads something, it understands and uses the information on it □ *A scanner reads the bar codes.* (ler)

♦ IDIOM **read between the lines** to guess a meaning that is not expressed in a direct way □ *He wrote saying he understood our decision, but reading between the lines, I could tell he was upset.* (ler nas entrelinhas)

♦ PHRASAL VERBS **read something into something** to think that an action or someone's words have a particular extra meaning, often when they do not □ *She only said that she was feeling tired – you shouldn't read too much into that.* (tirar conclusões) **read something out** to read something aloud □ *He read out the list of names.* (ler em voz alta) **read something through** to read the whole of something, often to check for mistakes □ *Make sure you read through your essay and correct your spelling.* (ler do começo ao fim) **read up about/on something** to read about a subject or to get more information about it □ *I need to read up on the Romans before my next class.* (ler a respeito)

▶ NOUN [*plural* **reads**]
1 a good/difficult, etc. read something that is good/difficult, etc. to read (leitura)
2 an act of reading □ *Have a read and see what you think.* (lida)

- **readable** /ˈriːdəbəl/ ADJECTIVE easy or enjoyable to read (agradável de ler)
- **reader** /ˈriːdə(r)/ NOUN [*plural* **readers**] a person who reads □ *Regular readers will recognize this name.* (leitor)

readily /ˈredɪli/ ADVERB
1 quickly and easily 🔈 *The fruit is readily available in most supermarkets.* (facilmente)
2 in a willing way □ *The whole family readily agreed to help.* (de bom grado)

readiness /ˈredɪnəs/ NOUN, NO PLURAL
1 being ready and prepared for something □ *The car had been filled with petrol in readiness for the journey.* (pronto)
2 being willing to do something □ *The country has signalled its readiness to negotiate.* (boa vontade)

reading /ˈriːdɪŋ/ NOUN [*plural* **readings**]
1 no plural the activity of looking at and understanding written words □ *How does the school teach reading?* □ *The course will help you improve your reading skills.* (leitura)
2 *no plural* something that you read □ *This book is essential reading for anyone who is interested in Spanish history.* (leitura)
3 a measurement made by an instrument □ *The instrument provides you with an accurate blood sugar reading.* (medição)
4 an event at which someone reads something to people, or the thing they read □ *We went to a poetry reading.* □ *a reading from Shakespeare* (leitura)
5 the way that someone understands a particular situation or event □ **+ of** *His reading of the situation was more optimistic.* (entendimento)

ready /ˈredi/ ADJECTIVE
1 prepared for something (pronto, preparado) 🔈 *He was getting ready to leave.* (preparando-se) □ **+ for** *Are the children ready for bed?*
2 prepared and available to use, eat, etc. □ *Dinner's ready.* □ *The report should be ready by the end of the year.* (pronto)

3 willing □ + *to do something* *He was always ready to help.* (**disposto a**)

ready meal /ˈredɪ ˌmiːl/ NOUN [*plural* **ready meals**] a complete meal which you buy already cooked from a shop and heat and eat at home (**comida pronta**)

real /rɪəl/ ADJECTIVE

1 existing, and not invented or imaginary (**real, verdadeiro**) 🔲 *In real life the actor is a quiet family man.* (**na vida real**) □ *The story is based on real events.*

2 true and not pretended □ *Everyone calls her 'Sunny' but her real name is Barbara.* □ *The real reason he missed the class was that he had forgotten to bring his homework.* (**verdadeiro**)

3 not artificial □ *The seats are made of real leather.* □ *The diamond looked real.* (**verdadeiro**)

4 used for emphasizing something □ *The death of my mother was a real shock.* (**verdadeiro**)

5 get real an informal way of of telling someone that they are being silly and unreasonable about something □ *It's time to get real and do something to stop the damage to the environment.* (**cair na real**)

real estate /ˈrɪəl ɪˌsteɪt/ NOUN, NO PLURAL buildings and land □ *real estate investors* (**imóveis**)

realism /ˈrɪəlɪzəm/ NOUN, NO PLURAL
1 the ability to accept the real situation and deal with it in a sensible way (**realismo**)
2 a style of art or writing which shows things as they really are (**realismo**)

• **realist** /ˈrɪəlɪst/ NOUN [*plural* **realists**] someone who accepts situations as they really are, instead of pretending that they are different (**realista**)

• **realistic** /ˌrɪəˈlɪstɪk/ ADJECTIVE
1 accepting or based on the true facts of a situation (**realista**) 🔲 *The team has a realistic chance of winning the competition.* (**chance realista**) □ + *about Navarez seems realistic about his future.* (**realista sobre**)
2 looking or sounding real □ *The fight scenes were very realistic.* □ *In the film, they used a doll for the baby but it looked very realistic.* (**realista**)

• **realistically** /ˌrɪəˈlɪstɪkəli/ ADVERB
1 considering the true facts of a situation □ *Realistically, there was no chance of success.* (**de modo realista**)
2 in a way that looks real □ *The grapes were realistically painted.* (**de modo realista**)

reality /rɪˈælətɪ/ NOUN [*plural* **realities**]
1 the true facts of a situation □ *We must face reality.* (**realidade**)
2 in reality used when saying what the true situation is, especially when it seems different □ *Everyone thought she was very successful, but in reality she was almost bankrupt.* (**na verdade**)
3 become a reality to start to exist or happen □ *I dreamt of playing in the world championship, but never thought it would become a reality.* (**tornar-se realidade**)

reality TV /rɪˌælətɪ tiːˈviː/ NOUN, NO PLURAL television programmes with real people in real situations, not actors pretending to do things (**programa televisivo com pessoas em situações reais**)

realization *or* **realisation** /ˌrɪəlaɪˈzeɪʃən/ NOUN, NO PLURAL when you suddenly realize something □ *The realization that they were sinking caused instant panic.* (**percepção**)

realize *or* **realise** /ˈrɪəlaɪz/ VERB [**realizes, realizing, realized**]
1 to know and understand something that you did not know or understand before 🔲 *I suddenly realized that he wasn't joking.* □ *I didn't realize he was so ill.* (**compreender, perceber**)
2 to achieve something □ *He never realized his ambition to become a professional footballer.* (**realizar**)

really /ˈrɪəlɪ/ ADVERB

1 very or very much □ *I really like Dan.* □ *I'm really excited about the holiday.* □ *I don't really like fish.* (**muito, muitíssimo**)
2 used for saying what the true situation is □ *Did you really mean what you said?* □ *He doesn't really have much choice.* (**realmente**)
3 not really no or not completely □ *'Are you ready for your trip?' 'Not really, there's still a lot of things I need to do.'* (**não completamente**)
4 Really? used when you are surprised or interested by what someone has just said □ *'Mrs Robinson is leaving the school in July.' 'Really?'* (**é mesmo?**)

realm /relm/ NOUN [*plural* **realms**]
1 an area of knowledge or activity □ *Within the realms of political commentators, he is considered highly.* (**setor**)
2 a literary word for a country that has a king or queen (**reino**)

real-time /ˈrɪəltaɪm/ ADJECTIVE describes computer systems that deal with new information exactly at the time when the information arrives. A computing word. (**tempo real**)

reap /riːp/ VERB [**reaps, reaping, reaped**]
1 to get something good as a result of something you have done (**colher**) 🔲 *He passed the exam so he's reaped the benefits of all that hard work.*
2 to cut and collect a crop (**colher, ceifar**)

reappear /ˌriːəˈpɪə(r)/ VERB [**reappears, reappearing, reappeared**] to appear again after not being seen for a period of time □ *Weeds keep reappearing if they are not removed at the root.* (**reaparecer**)

• **reappearance** /ˌriːəˈpɪərəns/ NOUN [*plural* **reappearances**] when someone or something reappears □ *His sudden reappearance surprised everyone.* (**reaparecimento**)

rear /rɪə(r)/ ▶ NOUN, NO PLURAL **the rear** the back part of something □ *They were sitting at the rear of the plane.* (**fundos, retaguarda**)

rearrange

▶ ADJECTIVE at the back of something □ *The rear wheels of the car were stuck in mud.* (traseiro)
▶ VERB [**rears, rearing, reared**]
1 if you rear children or animals, you look after them as they grow (criar)
2 if a horse or other animal rears, it lifts its front legs into the air (empinar-se)

rearrange /ˌriːəˈreɪndʒ/ VERB [**rearranges, rearranging, rearranged**]
1 to change the position of things □ *They had rearranged the furniture in the room.* (reorganizar, mudar de lugar)
2 to change the time when something will happen □ *The president has rearranged his schedule so he can attend the service.* (remarcar)

reason /ˈriːzən/ ▶ NOUN [plural **reasons**]
1 the reason for something is why it happened, exists or is done □ **+ for** *No one knows the reason for his disappearance.* □ **+ that** *The reason that I phoned was to see if you want to meet for lunch.* (razão) ▣ *There are many good reasons for taking up a sport.* (boas razões) ▣ *He did not give any reason for his lateness.* (não deu nenhuma razão ou motivo) ▣ *That is the reason why I moved to Paris.* (razão por que)
2 *no plural* a good cause for something □ **+ to do something** *We have reason to suspect he is guilty.* (motivo) ▣ *He has good reason to be happy.* ▣ *There is no reason to be afraid.* (não há razão) ▣ *She could see no reason to apologize.* (não viu razão para)
3 *no plural* the ability to think clearly and behave in a sensible way □ *Will you please listen to reason?* (raciocinar claramente) ▣ *We all tried to make him see reason.* (enxergar a razão) ▣ *Order whatever food you'd like, within reason.* (dentro do razoável)
▶ VERB [**reasons, reasoning, reasoned**] to consider the facts about something and decide what you think is true □ *I reasoned that he might have missed the train.* (raciocinar)
◆ PHRASAL VERB **reason with someone** to try to persuade someone to change their actions or beliefs by telling them what is true or sensible □ *He waved a gun around as police tried to reason with him.* (argumentar com alguém)

• **reasonable** /ˈriːzənəbəl/ ADJECTIVE
1 sensible and fair (sensato) □ *I suppose it's a reasonable decision.* □ *Any reasonable person would agree with that.* (qualquer pessoa sensata) ▣ *We proved beyond reasonable doubt that she was guilty.* (acima de qualquer dúvida)
2 if something is reasonable, there are good reasons why you think it is true or correct □ *They made the reasonable assumption that we would be late.* □ *These figures seem reasonable to me.* (razoável)
3 quite large but not very large (boa quantidade) ▣ *We have a reasonable chance of winning the competition.* (boas chances) ▣ *I eat a reasonable amount of vegetables.* (quantidade razoável)
4 of quite high quality but not very high quality □ *He's a reasonable swimmer.* (razoável)
5 not very expensive □ *Their clothes are very reasonable.* (preço acessível)

• **reasonably** /ˈriːzənəbli/ ADVERB
1 in a sensible and fair way □ *He has behaved very reasonably towards us.* (razoavelmente)
2 to quite a high level or standard □ *I'm reasonably good at the piano.* □ *He is in a reasonably paid job.* (satisfatório)

• **reasoned** /ˈriːzənd/ ADJECTIVE having been considered carefully □ *a reasoned argument/decision* (pensado, avaliado)

• **reasoning** /ˈriːzənɪŋ/ NOUN, NO PLURAL the process of thinking about the facts about something and making a judgment about it □ *He tried to explain the reasoning behind his decision.* (raciocínio)

reassurance /ˌriːəˈʃɔːrəns/ NOUN [plural **reassurances**] something that stops someone from feeling worried □ *Young children need reassurance from their parents.* (tranquilização)

reassure /ˌriːəˈʃɔː(r)/ VERB [**reassures, reassuring, reassured**] to say or do something to make someone feel less worried □ *He tried to reassure me that everything would be all right.* (tranquilizar)

• **reassuring** /ˌriːəˈʃɔːrɪŋ/ ADJECTIVE making you feel less worried □ *a reassuring look* (tranquilizador)

rebate /ˈriːbeɪt/ NOUN [plural **rebates**] an amount of money that is paid back to someone because they have paid too much (reembolso) ▣ *a tax rebate*

rebel ▶ NOUN /ˈrebəl/ [plural **rebels**]
1 someone who fights against a government □ *Rebels have clashed with government troops.* (rebelde)
2 someone who refuses to obey rules or people in authority □ *He was always a bit of a rebel at school.* (rebelde)
▶ VERB /rɪˈbel/ [**rebels, rebelling, rebelled**] (rebelar-se)
1 to fight against a government (rebelar-se contra o governo)
2 to refuse to obey rules or someone in authority □ *It's not unusual for teenagers to rebel against their parents.* (não seguir regras)

• **rebellion** /rɪˈbeljən/ NOUN [plural **rebellions**]
1 when people refuse to obey their leader or people in authority □ *teenage rebellion* (rebeldia)
2 the use of violence to try to change a government □ *The government tried to crush the rebellion.* (rebelião)

• **rebellious** /rɪˈbeljəs/ ADJECTIVE difficult to control and not wanting to obey rules or people in authority □ *rebellious teenagers* (rebelde)

reboot /ˌriːˈbuːt/ VERB [**reboots, rebooting, rebooted**] to start a computer again. A computing word □ *You'll have to reboot to save these changes.* (reiniciar)

rebound /rɪˈbaʊnd/ VERB [rebounds, rebounding, rebounded] to move back after hitting a surface □ *The ball rebounded off the edge of the goal.* (**ricochetear**)

♦ PHRASAL VERB **rebound on someone** if something you have done rebounds on you, it has a bad effect on you □ *His comments may rebound on him.* (**recair**)

rebuild /ˌriːˈbɪld/ VERB [rebuilds, rebuilding, rebuilt]
1 to build something again when it has been destroyed □ *Engineers have been called in to rebuild the bridge.* (**reconstruir**)
2 to make something strong and successful again after it has been damaged □ *It will take a long time to rebuild trust between them.* (**recuperar**) 🔲 *Charities are helping these people to rebuild their lives after the flood.* (**reconstruir sua vida**)

rebuke /rɪˈbjuːk/ ▶ VERB [rebukes, rebuking, rebuked] to speak angrily to someone because they have done something wrong (**repreender**)
▶ NOUN [plural **rebukes**] something that is said in an angry way to someone who has done something wrong (**repreensão**) 🔲 *The President's comments earned him a sharp rebuke from environmentalists.* (**forte reprovação**)

recall /rɪˈkɔːl/ VERB [recalls, recalling, recalled]
1 to remember □ *Do you recall how we used to play here as children?* (**lembrar-se**)
2 to order someone to come back □ *The government has recalled all its diplomats.* (**chamar de volta**)
3 if a store or company recalls a product, they ask people to return it because there is something wrong with it (**retornar um produto**)

recap /ˈriːkæp/ ▶ VERB [recaps, recapping, recapped] to repeat the most important points of what has been said □ *To recap, this button switches it on, and this one controls volume.* (**recapitular**)
▶ NOUN [plural **recaps**] when you recap something □ *Could you give us a brief recap, please?* (**recapitulação**)

recapture /ˌriːˈkæptʃə(r)/ VERB [recaptures, recapturing, recaptured]
1 to bring back a feeling or experience from the past □ *The film perfectly recaptures the atmosphere of 1940s Hollywood.* (**retomar**)
2 to catch a person or animal that has escaped (**recapturar**)

recede /rɪˈsiːd/ VERB [recedes, receding, receded]
1 to move backwards □ *The flood water is starting to recede.* (**recuar, afastar-se**)
2 to become less □ *His fear had receded a little.* (**diminuir**)
3 if a man's hair is receding, he is starting to lose hair at the front of his head (**começar a ter entradas no cabelo, ficar careca**)

receipt /rɪˈsiːt/ NOUN [plural **receipts**]
1 a piece of paper you get when you buy something or when you have paid money to someone □ *Make sure you keep the receipt.* □ *a credit card receipt* (**nota fiscal**) □ + *for The receipt for the clothes was still in the bag.* (**nota fiscal das roupas**)
2 *no plural* a formal word meaning the fact that you have received something (**recebimento**) 🔲 *On receipt of the debit card, you must sign it.* (**no recebimento**) □ + *of He confirmed receipt of the letter.*

receive /rɪˈsiːv/ VERB [receives, receiving, received]
1 to get or be given something □ + *from She received a letter from her aunt.* □ *She has been receiving treatment for cancer.* □ *The story received a lot of attention.* □ *He received an award for his work.* (**receber**)
2 if something is received in a particular way, that is how people react to it (**receber**) 🔲 *The idea was well received* (= people liked it). □ *The new policy was received badly.*
3 to welcome guests at a formal occasion □ *The mayor stood near the door and received his guests personally.* (**receber**)
4 be on/at the receiving end of something to be the person who is affected by something, especially something unpleasant □ *He had been on the receiving end of her bad temper.* (**sofrer as consequências**)

• **receiver** /rɪˈsiːvə(r)/ NOUN [plural **receivers**]
1 the part of a telephone that you hear and speak through □ *'Goodbye,' he said, and replaced the receiver.* (**fone**)
2 a piece of equipment that receives electronic, radio or television signals □ *All new televisions have a digital receiver.* (**receptor**)

recent /ˈriːsənt/ ADJECTIVE
1 happening only a short time ago □ *recent events* □ *The most recent figures show that violent crimes are increasing.* □ *These changes are relatively recent.* (**recente**)
2 in recent years/months/weeks, etc. in the years, months, etc. just before now □ *They've won the competition twice in recent years.* (**anos/meses/semanas etc. recentes**)

• **recently** /ˈriːsəntlɪ/ ADVERB a short time ago □ *I saw Ann quite recently.* □ *He recently bought a new car.* □ *Recently, the situation became worse.* (**recentemente**)

receptacle /rɪˈsɛptəkəl/ NOUN [plural **receptacles**] a formal word meaning container (**receptáculo**)

reception /rɪˈsɛpʃən/ NOUN [plural **receptions**]
1 a big, formal party (**recepção**) 🔲 *The wedding reception was at a hotel.* (**recepção de casamento**) 🔲 *Government leaders will attend a reception hosted by the Queen.* (**comparecer a uma recepção**) □ + *for a reception for the French president*

2 *no plural* the place where people go when they arrive at a hotel, office building, etc. □ *He was checking in at reception.* (recepção) 🔊 *She walked up to the reception desk.* (balcão de recepção) 🔊 *The hotel has a large reception area.* (área de recepção)

3 the way someone reacts to something (recepção) 🔊 *The Prime Minister got a very friendly reception when he visited the factory.*

4 *no plural* the quality of the sound or pictures that you get on a radio, television, mobile phone, etc. □ *There's poor mobile phone reception in some rural areas.* (recepção, sinal)

• **receptionist** /rɪˈsepʃənɪst/ NOUN [*plural* **receptionists**] someone whose job is to welcome and help people who arrive at a hotel, office building, etc. (recepcionista)

receptive /rɪˈseptɪv/ ADJECTIVE willing to accept suggestions and new ideas □ *They've become more receptive to change.* (receptivo)

recess /rɪˈses/ NOUN [*plural* **recesses**]
1 a space where a wall is further back than the rest of the wall □ *The vase was placed in a small recess.* (recanto)
2 a time when parliament or law courts do not work (recesso)

recession /rɪˈseʃən/ NOUN [*plural* **recessions**] a time when a country's economy is not successful □ *The rise in oil prices could trigger a recession.* (recessão)

recessive /rɪˈsesɪv/ ADJECTIVE a recessive gene is only passed on to a child if both parents have it. A biology word. (recessivo)

recipe /ˈresɪpi/ NOUN [*plural* **recipes**]
1 a set of instructions for how to cook something (receita) 🔊 *a recipe book* (livro de receitas) □ *+ for This is a delicious recipe for chocolate cake.*
2 **a recipe for disaster/success, etc.** something that will probably have a very bad/good, etc. result □ *Exercising on a hot day and not drinking anything is a recipe for disaster.* (receita para um desastre/sucesso etc.)

recipient /rɪˈsɪpiənt/ NOUN [*plural* **recipients**] a formal word meaning a person who receives something □ *He has been the recipient of several awards.* (recebedor)

reciprocal /rɪˈsɪprəkəl/ ADJECTIVE involving two people or groups who each do the same for each other □ *a reciprocal arrangement* (recíproco)

• **reciprocate** /rɪˈsɪprəkeɪt/ VERB [**reciprocates, reciprocating, reciprocated**] to do the same thing for someone as they have done for you, or to have the same feelings for someone that they have for you □ *His affection was not reciprocated.* (reciprocar)

recital /rɪˈsaɪtəl/ NOUN [*plural* **recitals**] a performance of music, songs or poetry, usually by one person □ *an organ recital* (recital)

recite /rɪˈsaɪt/ VERB [**recites, reciting, recited**] to say something that you have learned, such as a poem (recitar)

reckless /ˈrekləs/ ADJECTIVE doing something without caring or thinking about the results of your actions (irresponsável, imprudente) □ *reckless driving* (direção imprudente)

• **recklessly** /ˈrekləsli/ ADVERB in a reckless way □ *He was accused of recklessly endangering the life of others.* (de maneira imprudente)

reckon /ˈrekən/ VERB [**reckons, reckoning, reckoned**]
1 to think that something is true □ *I reckon we'll win.* (considerar)
2 to calculate □ *The cost of restoring the painting is reckoned at £8,000.* (calcular)

♦ IDIOM **a force/power to be reckoned with** someone or something that can have a strong effect on a situation □ *The new party is a force to be reckoned with.* (ter força/poder considerável)

♦ PHRASAL VERBS **reckon on something** to expect something to happen, and to base your plans on it □ *I hadn't reckoned on getting stuck in traffic.* (confiar que algo vá acontecer) **reckon with something/someone** to consider the possible effect of something or someone □ *They hadn't reckoned with the anger of his fans.* (contar com algo/alguém)

reclaim /rɪˈkleɪm/ VERB [**reclaims, reclaiming, reclaimed**]
1 to get back something that you have lost or that has been taken from you □ *Luggage that is not reclaimed by passengers at the airport is sold.* (recuperar)
2 to improve an area of land so that it can be used (recuperar a terra)

recline /rɪˈklaɪn/ VERB [**reclines, reclining, reclined**]
1 to lie in a relaxed way □ *Ginny was reclining on the sofa.* (reclinar)
2 if a chair reclines, you can move the back to a lower position (reclinar)

recluse /rɪˈkluːs/ NOUN [*plural* **recluses**] a person who lives alone and does not like being with other people (recluso)

• **reclusive** /rɪˈkluːsɪv/ ADJECTIVE living alone and not wanting to be with other people (recluso)

recognition /ˌrekəɡˈnɪʃən/ NOUN, NO PLURAL
1 the fact of knowing someone or something because you have seen them before □ *a smile of recognition* (reconhecimento)
2 respect and admiration □ *She has earned international recognition for her work.* (reconhecimento)
3 agreement that something is true or important □ *There is a growing recognition that play is important in children's development.* (reconhecimento)

recognizable or recognisable
/ˈrekəgnaɪzəbəl/
ADJECTIVE easy to recognize ☐ *He is barely recognizable since he shaved off his beard.* (reconhecível)

• **recognize** or **recognise** /ˈrekəgnaɪz/ VERB [recognizes, recognizing, recognized]
1 to know who or what someone or something is because you have seen them before ☐ *I recognized his face but couldn't remember his name* ☐ *Emma hadn't seen him for 50 years, but recognized him immediately.* (reconhecer)
2 to accept that something is true ☐ *We recognize the importance of research.* ☐ *+ that Most people recognize that there is no easy solution to the problem of global warming.* (reconhecer)
3 to officially accept that something is legal ☐ *Other countries have refused to recognize the new state.* (reconhecer)
4 to show that you respect and admire what someone has done ☐ *His scientific achievements were recognized when he was awarded the Nobel Prize.* (reconhecer)

recoil /rɪˈkɔɪl/ VERB [recoils, recoiling, recoiled]
1 to move back suddenly from someone or something that frightens you or that you do not like ☐ *She recoiled from his touch.* (recuar)
2 to feel that something is unpleasant or morally wrong ☐ *Most people recoil from the idea of torture.* (recuar)

recollect /ˌrekəˈlekt/ VERB [recollects, recollecting, recollected] a formal word meaning to remember ☐ *He could clearly recollect events of 35 years ago.* (lembrar-se de)

• **recollection** /ˌrekəˈlekʃən/ NOUN [plural **recollections**] something that you remember ☐ *I have absolutely no recollection of what happened.* (lembrança)

recommend /ˌrekəˈmend/ VERB [recommends, recommending, recommended]
1 to advise someone to do something ☐ *+ that Health experts recommend that you eat at least five portions of fruit or vegetables every day.* ☐ *We don't recommend the use of this drug.* (recomendar)
2 to suggest to someone that they would like something ☐ *+ to My sister recommended this book to me.* (recomendar)

> Note that **recommend**, meaning 'to advise' is followed by a noun or is followed by **that**...
> It is not followed by 'to do something':
> ☐ *She recommended new glasses.*
> ✓ *She recommended that I buy new glasses.*
> ✗ *She recommended me to buy new glasses.*

• **recommendation** /ˌrekəmenˈdeɪʃən/ NOUN [plural **recommendations**]
1 something that someone advises you to do ☐ *The school will implement the inspector's recommendations.* (recomendação)
2 something that a person suggests you would like ☐ *I bought the game on my friend's recommendation.* (recomendação)

reconcile /ˈrekənsaɪl/ VERB [reconciles, reconciling, reconciled]
1 to find a way in which two very different situations, beliefs, etc. can both exist together ☐ *She couldn't reconcile her religious faith with the feelings of hatred she had for her attackers.* (reconciliar)
2 if you are reconciled with someone, you are friendly with them again after an argument (reconciliar)

♦ PHRASAL VERB **reconcile yourself to something** to accept that you will have to do or deal with something unpleasant ☐ *He has reconciled himself to the idea of spending six weeks in hospital.* (reconciliar-se com)

• **reconciliation** /ˌrekənsɪliˈeɪʃən/ NOUN, NO PLURAL
1 when two people or groups form a friendly relationship again after an argument ☐ *There is no prospect of a reconciliation.* (reconciliação)
2 a way in which two very different situations, beliefs, etc. can both exist together (reconciliação)

reconsider /ˌriːkənˈsɪdə(r)/ VERB [reconsiders, reconsidering, reconsidered] to think again about a decision, to decide if you should change it ☐ *We have agreed to reconsider the policy.* (reconsiderar)

reconstruct /ˌriːkənˈstrʌkt/ VERB [reconstructs, reconstructing, reconstructed]
1 to build something again ☐ *Many of the buildings had to be reconstructed following the earthquake.* (reconstruir)
2 to be able to describe or copy a situation or event by using information that you have ☐ *Police used computer technology to reconstruct the crash scene.* (reconstruir)

• **reconstruction** /ˌriːkənˈstrʌkʃən/ NOUN [plural **reconstructions**]
1 when you describe or copy a situation or an event using information that you have ☐ *The film shows a reconstruction of the battle.* (reconstrução)
2 the act of building something again ☐ *The reconstruction of the city is still not complete.* (reconstrução)

record ▶ NOUN /ˈrekɔːd/ [plural **records**]
1 a piece of information that has been stored in a document or on a computer (registro, documentação) ☐ *They keep records of all overseas sales.* (mantêm registros) ☐ *Records show that crime has risen.* (registros mostram) ☐ *medical/dental records* (registros médicos/dentários) ☐ *She now has a criminal record.* (antecedentes criminais)
2 the things that a person or an organization has achieved or done ☐ *She has an excellent record on motivating staff.* (histórico) ☐ *The company has a very poor safety record.* (histórico de segurança)

recoup /rɪˈkuːp/ VERB [recoups, recouping, recouped] to get back money that you have spent or lost □ *The initial investment of £50,000 is unlikely to be recouped.* (**recuperar**)

3 the best achievement ever in a particular activity, especially a sport (**recorde**) 🔊 *He holds the record for the high jump.* (**possui o recorde**) 🔊 *She broke the previous record by 2 seconds.* (**quebrou o recorde**) 🔊 *He has set a new record for sailing the Atlantic.* (**estabeleceu novo recorde**)
4 the highest/lowest/most expensive, etc. on record the highest/lowest/most expensive, etc. thing that has ever happened or been recorded □ *It was the hottest summer on record.* (**o maior/mais baixo/mais caro... registrado**)
5 off the record if you say something off the record, you do not say it in public □ *Several MPs have told me off the record that they think the prime minister should resign.* (**confidencialmente**)
6 on (the) record if you say something on the record, you say it officially and publicly □ *He went on the record as a supporter of independence.* (**oficialmente**)
7 a round flat piece of plastic that music and speech can be stored on □ *I found a pile of old jazz records.* (**disco**)
◆ IDIOM **put/set the record straight** to make sure that people know the truth about something □ *People are accusing me of disloyalty, and I want to set the record straight.* (**dirimir dúvidas**)
▶ VERB /rɪˈkɔːd/ [records, recording, recorded]
1 to put sounds or images on a CD, video, etc. (**gravar**) 🔊 *I phoned her, but all I got was a recorded message.* □ *The band recorded their first album in 1982.*
2 to keep information about something in a document or on a computer □ *All their addresses are recorded in a central database.* (**registrar**)
3 to measure the amount or level of something □ *The meter records how much electricity is being produced.* (**medir**)
4 to achieve something □ *Liverpool recorded another victory today.* (**conquistar, alcançar**)
▶ ADJECTIVE /ˈrekɔːd/ bigger, better, faster, etc. than has ever happened or existed before □ *Record temperatures have led to water shortages.* (**recorde**) 🔊 *I finished my meal in record time.* (**em tempo recorde**)
• **recorder** /rɪˈkɔːdə(r)/ NOUN [plural **recorders**]
1 a machine that copies and stores sounds or images (**gravador**)
2 a simple musical instrument made from a wooden pipe with holes that you cover with your fingers as you blow (**flauta**)
• **recording** /rɪˈkɔːdɪŋ/ NOUN [plural **recordings**]
1 sounds or images that have been recorded □ *I have a recording of the poet's own voice.* (**gravação**)
2 no plural the process of recording sounds or images □ *They argued a lot during recording.* (**gravação**)

recover /rɪˈkʌvə(r)/ VERB [recovers, recovering, recovered]
1 to get better after being ill, injured or upset □ *The doctor says I am recovering very well.* □ + *from He is recovering from a stress-related illness.* □ *Most parents never recover from the death of a child.* (**recuperar-se**)
2 to return to a normal condition after problems or damage □ *The sea can take years to recover after an oil spillage.* □ *There are signs that the economy is recovering.* (**recuperar-se**)
3 to get something back that has been lost, stolen, etc. □ + *from They recovered several bodies from the wreckage of the plane.* □ *Police recovered several weapons from the apartment.* (**recuperar**)
4 to get back control over something (**recuperar**) □ *I paused for a moment to recover my breath.* (**recuperar o fôlego**) □ *Dudley recovered his composure and apologized.* (**recompôs-se**)
• **recovery** /rɪˈkʌvəri/ NOUN [plural **recoveries**]
1 the process of getting better after being ill, injured or upset (**recuperação**) 🔊 *He made a miraculous recovery.* (**teve uma recuperação**) 🔊 *She is expected to make a full recovery from her injuries.* (**recuperação completa**)
2 the process of returning to a normal condition after problems or damage □ *economic recovery* (**recuperação**)
3 when someone gets something back that has been stolen or lost □ *the recovery of stolen goods* (**recuperação**)

recreate /ˌriːkriˈeɪt/ VERB [recreates, recreating, recreated] to make something so that it is the same as it was in the past or the same as it is in another place □ *The play successfully recreates the atmosphere of wartime London.* (**recriar**)

recreation /ˌrekriˈeɪʃən/ NOUN, NO PLURAL a formal word meaning enjoyable things that you do in your free time □ *outdoor recreation* (**recreação**)
• **recreational** /ˌrekriˈeɪʃənəl/ ADJECTIVE to do with recreation □ *recreational activities* (**recreativo**)

recreation ground /ˌrekriˈeɪʃən ˌɡraʊnd/ NOUN [plural **recreation grounds**] an area of land where people can play sports and games (**área de recreação**)

recrimination /rɪˌkrɪmɪˈneɪʃən/ NOUN [plural **recriminations**] when two people criticize and blame each other (**recriminação**) 🔊 *The talks broke up with bitter recriminations on both sides.* (**ásperas recriminações**)

recruit /rɪˈkruːt/ ▶ VERB [recruits, recruiting, recruited] to find new people to work for a company or join an organization □ *The company recruits a few school-leavers each year.* (**recrutar**)
▶ NOUN [plural **recruits**] someone who has recently joined a company or organization

(recruta) 🔹 *New recruits are given a tour of the building.* (recrutas novatos)

- **recruitment** /rɪˈkruːtmənt/ NOUN, NO PLURAL the process of recruiting people □ *We'd like to see the recruitment of more women.* (recrutamento)

rectangle /ˈrektæŋɡəl/ NOUN [*plural* **rectangles**] a shape with four straight sides and four angles of 90°. The opposite sides are of the same length, but two sides are longer than the other two. (retângulo)

- **rectangular** /rekˈtæŋɡjʊlə(r)/ ADJECTIVE having the shape of a rectangle □ *a rectangular table* (retangular)

rectify /ˈrektɪfaɪ/ VERB [**rectifies, rectifying, rectified**] a formal word meaning to correct something such as a mistake or problem □ *The mistake was soon rectified.* (retificar)

recuperate /rɪˈkuːpəreɪt/ VERB [**recuperates, recuperating, recuperated**] to spend time getting better after an illness or injury □ *He is at home recuperating from a knee injury.* (recuperar)

- **recuperation** /rɪˌkuːpəˈreɪʃən/ NOUN, NO PLURAL the process of getting better after an illness or injury (recuperação)

recur /rɪˈkɜː(r)/ VERB [**recurs, recurring, recurred**] to happen again □ *There is a possibility that the situation will recur.* (repetir-se)

- **recurrence** /rɪˈkʌrəns/ NOUN [*plural* **recurrences**] when something happens again □ *There has been a recurrence of the same problem.* (recorrência)

- **recurrent** /rɪˈkʌrənt/ or **recurring** /rɪˈkɜːrɪŋ/ ADJECTIVE happening several times □ *Bad weather was a recurrent problem.* (recorrente)

recycle /ˌriːˈsaɪkəl/ VERB [**recycles, recycling, recycled**] to save something so that it can be used again or to do something to a substance so that it can be used again □ *I keep the bags in this drawer and recycle them.* □ *Most plastics can be recycled.* (reciclar)

- **recycled** /ˌriːˈsaɪkəld/ ADJECTIVE made from something which has been used before □ *recycled paper* (reciclado)

- **recycling** /ˌriːˈsaɪklɪŋ/ NOUN, NO PLURAL the process of dealing with things which have been used so that they can be used again □ *We need to encourage recycling.* (reciclagem)

red /red/ ▶ ADJECTIVE

1 having the colour of blood □ *She drives a red car.* (vermelho) 🔹 *He was wearing a bright red shirt.* (vermelho vivo) 🔹 *The carpet was dark red.* (vermelho escuro)

2 go red if you go red, your cheeks become red because you are embarrassed □ *He went bright red when he saw me.* (corar, ficar corado)

3 red hair is an orange colour (ruivo)

▶ NOUN [*plural* **reds**] the colour of blood □ *The walls were painted a deep red.* (vermelho)

red blood cell /ˌred ˈblʌd ˌsel/ NOUN [*plural* **red blood cells**] Red blood cells have no nucleus and they give the blood its red colour. A biology word. (eritrócitos)

redeem /rɪˈdiːm/ VERB [**redeems, redeeming, redeemed**]

1 to make something seem less bad □ *The show was partly redeemed by the excellent music.* (redimir)

2 redeem yourself to do something which makes people have a better opinion of you after you have done something bad □ *He had been given a chance to redeem himself.* (redimir-se)

3 to exchange something for something else □ *The voucher can be redeemed for a free swimming lesson at any local pool.* (trocar)

- **redemption** /rɪˈdempʃən/ NOUN, NO PLURAL

1 beyond redemption too badly damaged to be saved or improved □ *The cake was burned beyond redemption.* (sem salvação)

2 when a person is saved from the power of evil, especially according to the Christian religion (redenção)

redevelop /ˌriːdɪˈveləp/ VERB [**redevelops, redeveloping, redeveloped**] to improve an area by repairing buildings or building new ones □ *The area by the river has been redeveloped.* (remodelar)

- **redevelopment** /ˌriːdɪˈveləpmənt/ NOUN, NO PLURAL when an area is redeveloped □ *The city centre is due for redevelopment next year.* (renovação)

red-handed /ˌredˈhændɪd/ ADVERB (em flagrante)

◆ IDIOM **catch someone red-handed** an informal phrase meaning to see someone at the moment when they are doing something bad (pegar alguém em flagrante)

red herring /ˌred ˈherɪŋ/ NOUN [*plural* **red herrings**] a fact that is not important but which takes your attention from something that is important (pista falsa)

red tape /ˌred ˈteɪp/ NOUN, NO PLURAL official rules and processes which seem unnecessary and which make things happen very slowly □ *There is a lot of red tape involved in adopting children.* (burocracia, papelada)

reduce /rɪˈdjuːs/ VERB [**reduces, reducing, reduced**]

1 to make something smaller or less □ *Eating a healthy diet significantly reduces your risk of heart disease.* □ *We need to reduce pollution.* □ **+ to** *We have reduced the number of classes from six to four.* (reduzir)

2 reduce someone to tears to make someone start crying □ *His comments had reduced her to tears.* (fazer chorar)

◆ PHRASAL VERB **reduce someone to doing something** to make someone do something which is worse than they did before □ *He was a*

redundancy

famous actor who had been reduced to doing television advertisements for toilet paper. (rebaixar alguém)

- **reduction** /rɪˈdʌkʃən/ NOUN [plural **reductions**] a decrease in the size, number, or amount of something (**redução**) 🔲 *We're offering massive price reductions.* (**redução de preços**) 🔲 + *in* *There has been a significant reduction in the number of deaths on our roads.*

redundancy /rɪˈdʌndənsi/ NOUN [plural **redundancies**]
1 when someone must leave their job because there is not enough work 🔲 *There have been a lot of redundancies in the company.* (**redução**)
2 the fact of being no longer needed or used because better, newer or similar things already exist (**redundância**)

- **redundant** /rɪˈdʌndənt/ ADJECTIVE
1 redundant workers no longer have a job because their company does not have enough work for them (**excedente**) 🔲 *820 people were made redundant when the factory closed.* (**tornar-se excedente**)
2 not needed or used because there are better, newer or similar things 🔲 *Floppy disks have become virtually redundant.* (**redundante**)

reed /riːd/ NOUN [plural **reeds**] a tall plant which looks like grass and grows in water (**junco**)

reef /riːf/ NOUN [plural **reefs**] a line of rocks, sand or coral (= hard substance made from small sea creatures) near the surface of the sea. A geography word. (**recife**)

reek /riːk/ VERB [**reeks, reeking, reeked**] to smell very unpleasant 🔲 *His clothes reeked of fish.* (**cheirar mal**)

reel /riːl/ ▶ NOUN [plural **reels**] an object that you wind something such as film, thread, etc. around (**carretel**)

▶ VERB [**reels, reeling, reeled**]
1 be reeling from something to feel very shocked by something 🔲 *The area is still reeling from a tropical storm which killed over 600 people.* (**abalar-se, chocar-se**)
2 to walk in a way that looks as if you might fall over (**cambalear**)

◆ PHRASAL VERB **reel something off** to say a long list of things very quickly 🔲 *She reeled off the names of everyone she had invited to the party.* (**listar rapidamente**)

re-elect /ˌriːɪˈlekt/ VERB [**re-elects, re-electing, re-elected**] to elect someone again 🔲 *He hopes to be re-elected next year.* (**reeleger**)

- **re-election** /ˌriːɪˈlekʃən/ NOUN, NO PLURAL when someone is re-elected 🔲 *I will not be standing for re-election.* (**reeleição**)

ref /ref/ NOUN [plural **refs**] a short way to say and write referee (**abrev. árbitro**)

refer /rɪˈfɜː(r)/
◆ PHRASAL VERBS [**refers, referring, referred**] **refer to someone/something** to mention someone or

refine

something 🔲 *She referred to the wedding several times.* (**referir-se a alguém/algo**) 🔲 + *as* *He referred to the man as 'Robert'.* (**referir-se como**)
refer to something
1 a formal word meaning to look at something in order to get information 🔲 *Please refer to the catalogue for more details.* (**consultar**)
2 to be about something 🔲 *The figures refer to the period between 1990 and 2000.* (**referir-se**)
refer someone/something to someone/ something to send someone or something to another place to be dealt with 🔲 *My doctor referred me to the hospital to get an X-ray.* 🔲 *The matter has been referred to the police.* (**encaminhar alguém/algo a alguém/algo**)

- **referee** /ˌrefəˈriː/ ▶ NOUN [plural **referees**] the person in a game such as football, who makes sure the players obey the rules 🔲 *The referee blew his whistle to end the game.* (**árbitro**)
▶ VERB [**referees, refereeing, refereed**] to be a referee during a game 🔲 *Dixon refereed the match.* (**arbitrar**)

- **reference** /ˈrefrəns/ NOUN [plural **references**]
1 a remark that mentions someone or something (**referência**) 🔲 *She made no reference to what had happened the day before.* (**não fez referência a**)
2 the process of looking at something to get information, or the thing you look at (**referência**) 🔲 *He filed the documents away for future reference.* (**para referência futura**)
3 a written report on your character that someone reads before offering you a job 🔲 *You'll need a reference from your previous employer.* (**referência**)
4 with/in reference to something a formal phrase, used to show what a remark, letter, etc. is referring to 🔲 *With reference to your letter of June 4th, I am pleased to inform you that your application has been successful.* (**com referência a**)

reference book /ˈrefrəns bʊk/ NOUN [plural **reference books**] a book that you look in for information (**obra de referência**)

referendum /ˌrefəˈrendəm/ NOUN [plural **referenda** or **referendums**] when the people of a country vote on a political question (**referendo**) 🔲 *We promise to hold a referendum on the issue.* (**apoiar um referendo**)

referral /rɪˈfɜːrəl/ NOUN [plural **referrals**] when someone sends you to another person for help or information 🔲 *The doctor can make a referral to a cancer specialist.* (**encaminhamento, indicação**)

refill ▶ VERB /ˌriːˈfɪl/ [**refills, refilling, refilled**] to fill something again 🔲 *We'll need to refill the tank before we go much further.* (**reabastecer**)
▶ NOUN /ˈriːfɪl/ [plural **refills**] something used to refill an empty container 🔲 *Can you buy refills for that kind of pen?* (**refil**)

refine /rɪˈfaɪn/ VERB [**refines, refining, refined**]
1 to make a substance pure 🔲 *Oil is refined into petrol.* (**refinar**)

2 to improve something gradually □ *We are refining the technique.* (aprimorar)

- **refined** /rɪˈfaɪnd/ ADJECTIVE
1 a refined substance has been made pure by removing material that is not wanted from it □ *refined sugar* (refinado)
2 polite and understanding style and culture □ *a refined gentleman* (refinado)

- **refinement** /rɪˈfaɪnmənt/ NOUN [plural **refinements**]
1 a small change you make to improve something, or the process used to do this □ *The system needs further refinement.* (aprimoramento)
2 polite behaviour and knowledge of style and culture □ *She was a woman of great refinement.* (refinamento)

- **refinery** /rɪˈfaɪnəri/ NOUN [plural **refineries**] a factory where substances such as oil or foods are refined (refinaria) 🔲 *an oil refinery* (refinaria de petróleo)

refit ▶ VERB /ˌriːˈfɪt/ [**refits, refitting, refitted**] to repair and put new equipment, furniture, etc. into a vehicle, a room or a building □ *The ship has been refitted.* (reformar)
▶ NOUN /ˈriːfɪt/ [plural **refits**] when something is refitted □ *The stadium has undergone a major refit.* (restauração, reforma)

reflect /rɪˈflekt/ VERB [**reflects, reflecting, reflected**]
1 if something is reflected, you can see an image of it in a surface like a mirror □ *+ in She caught sight of herself reflected in a shop window.* (refletir)
2 to be a sign of something □ *+ question word Her face reflected how she felt inside.* (refletir) 🔲 *The price reflects the fact that the house is in a very popular area.* (reflete o fato de que)
3 to send back heat, light etc. from a surface □ *The surface reflects light.* □ *The sunlight reflected off the pond.* (refletir)
4 to think carefully about something, especially something that has happened □ *+ on I need time to reflect on my experiences.* (refletir, pensar com cuidado)
5 reflect well/badly, etc. on someone/ something to cause people to have a good/bad, etc. opinion of someone or something □ *This sort of behaviour reflects badly on the school.* (refletir bem/mal em alguém/algo)

- **reflection** /rɪˈflekʃən/ NOUN [plural **reflections**]
1 an image that you can see in a surface like a mirror □ *He stared at his own reflection in the mirror.* (reflexo)
2 a sign that shows what something is like □ *The match wasn't an accurate reflection of his ability.* (reflexo)
3 a reflection on someone/something when something creates a good or bad opinion of someone or something □ *His bad manners are a reflection on his parents.* (reflexo em alguém/algo)
4 your thoughts about things that have happened or the process of thinking like this □ *We all need some time for quiet reflection.* (reflexão)

- **reflective** /rɪˈflektɪv/ ADJECTIVE
1 thinking carefully about things □ *He was in a reflective mood.* (reflexivo)
2 a reflective surface sends back light and can be seen easily when light shines on it □ *They wear reflective jackets.* (refletivo)

- **reflector** /rɪˈflektə(r)/ NOUN [plural **reflectors**] a piece of metal or plastic which reflects light, especially on a vehicle or a bicycle (refletor)

reflex /ˈriːfleks/ ▶ NOUN [plural **reflexes**] a physical movement that is an automatic reaction to something □ *He had quick reflexes* (= reacted very quickly). (reflexo)
▶ ADJECTIVE a reflex action is one that is done automatically and without thinking (reflexo)

reflexive /rɪˈfleksɪv/ ADJECTIVE
1 to do with words that show that the subject of a verb is the same as its object □ *'Hurt yourself' is a reflexive verb.* □ *'Himself' is a reflexive pronoun.* (reflexivo)
2 done automatically and without thinking □ *a reflexive action* (reflexo)

reflexologist /ˌriːflekˈsɒlədʒɪst/ NOUN [plural **reflexologists**] someone who treats medical conditions by pressing on particular places on the bottom of your feet (reflexologista)

- **reflexology** /ˌriːflekˈsɒlədʒi/ NOUN, NO PLURAL the work of a reflexologist (reflexologia)

reform /rɪˈfɔːm/ ▶ VERB [**reforms, reforming, reformed**]
1 to make changes to something in order to improve it □ *There are plans to reform the exams system.* (reformar)
2 to improve your behaviour or to help someone do this (corrigir(-se), regenerar) □ *a reformed smoker* (fumante regenerado)
▶ NOUN [plural **reforms**] changes that are made to improve something, or the process of making these changes □ *There were calls for reform of the tax system.* (reforma)

- **reformer** /rɪˈfɔːmə(r)/ NOUN [plural **reformers**] someone who tries to achieve changes to improve something □ *a social reformer* (reformador)

refract /rɪˈfrækt/ VERB [**refracts, refracting, refracted**] if light is refracted, it changes direction when it hits the surface of something like water or glass. A physics word. (refratar)

- **refraction** /rɪˈfrækʃən/ NOUN, NO PLURAL when light refracts. A physics word. (refração)

refrain /rɪˈfreɪn/ ▶ VERB [**refrains, refraining, refrained**] a formal word meaning to stop yourself from doing something □ *Please refrain from talking in the library.* (abster-se)
▶ NOUN [plural **refrains**]
1 a part of a song that is repeated (refrão)
2 a remark or a complaint that is often repeated □ *'No more roads' has become a common refrain.* (refrescar a memória de alguém)

refresh

refresh /rɪˈfreʃ/ VERB [refreshes, refreshing, refreshed]

1 to make you feel cooler or less tired □ *The cool air refreshed him a bit.* □ *She woke up feeling refreshed and rested.* (refrescar a memória)

2 **refresh someone's memory** to make someone remember something □ *Maybe this photo will refresh your memory.* (atualizar)

3 to change what is on a computer screen so that you can see the latest information. A computing word. (atualizar)

- **refreshing** /rɪˈfreʃɪŋ/ ADJECTIVE
1 making you feel cooler or less tired □ *a refreshing drink* (refrescante)
2 new and different in a pleasant way (renovador) ▣ *The series made a refreshing change from the usual crime shows.* (mudança revigorante)

- **refreshments** /rɪˈfreʃmənts/ PLURAL NOUN food and drink □ *Are refreshments available inside the park?* (lanche, refeição rápida) ▣ *Light refreshments will be provided.* (lanches leves)

refrigerate /rɪˈfrɪdʒəreɪt/ VERB [refrigerates, refrigerating, refrigerated] to put food or drink in a fridge to keep it cold □ *Cover the mixture and refrigerate overnight.* (refrigerar)

- **refrigeration** /rɪˌfrɪdʒəˈreɪʃən/ NOUN, NO PLURAL when you refrigerate things □ *It will keep for several days without refrigeration.* (refrigeração)

- **refrigerator** /rɪˈfrɪdʒəreɪtə(r)/ NOUN [plural refrigerators] a machine that you can store food or drink in to keep it cold and fresh (geladeira)

refuel /ˌriːˈfjuːəl/ VERB [refuels, refuelling/US refueling, refuelled/US refueled] to fill a vehicle with fuel again □ *We stopped to refuel at a petrol station.* (reabastecer)

refuge /ˈrefjuːdʒ/ NOUN [plural refuges]

1 protection from danger (refúgio) ▣ *The family took refuge from the fighting in a church.* (usou como refúgio)

2 a place where someone can go to be safe from danger □ *They run a refuge for homeless people.* (abrigo)

- **refugee** /ˌrefjuːˈdʒiː/ NOUN [plural refugees] a person who goes to another country because they are not safe in their own country (refugiado) ▣ *a refugee camp* (campo de refugiados)

refund ▶ VERB /rɪˈfʌnd/ [refunds, refunding, refunded] to give someone back some money that they have paid (reembolsar) ▣ *We'll refund your money if you're not completely satisfied.* (reembolsar seu dinheiro)

▶ NOUN /ˈriːfʌnd/ [plural refunds] money that is refunded (reembolso) ▣ *He got a refund from the airline.* (conseguir reembolso)

refusal /rɪˈfjuːzəl/ NOUN [plural refusals] when you refuse to accept or to do something □ *His refusal to discuss the problem led to more bad feeling.* (recusa)

regenerate

refuse[1] /rɪˈfjuːz/ VERB [refuses, refusing, refused]

1 to say that you will not do something □ *He refused to help me.* □ *She refused a request for an interview.* (recusar(-se) a)

2 to say that you will not accept something you are offered □ *Gerry refused a cup of tea but took a glass of water.* (recusar)

refuse[2] /ˈrefjuːs/ NOUN, NO PLURAL a formal word for rubbish that people throw away □ *household refuse* (lixo, refugo)

regain /rɪˈgeɪn/ VERB [regains, regaining, regained] to get something back that you had before □ *Boston regained the lead in the second half.* (recuperar, recobrar) ▣ *He regained consciousness in hospital.* (recuperou a consciência)

regal /ˈriːgəl/ ADJECTIVE like or suitable for a king or queen (régio)

regard /rɪˈgɑːd/ ▶ VERB [regards, regarding, regarded]

1 to think about someone or something in a particular way □ *My mother still regards me as a child.* □ *He was regarded with suspicion by many.* (considerar)

2 a formal word meaning to look at someone or something □ *He regarded me thoughtfully.* (olhar)

▶ NOUN, NO PLURAL

1 respect or care for someone or something (consideração, respeito) ▣ *They went ahead without regard for our opinion.* (sem consideração com) ▣ *The professor's work is held in high regard.* (alta consideração)

2 **in/with regard to something** a formal phrase meaning to do with something □ *I am writing in regard to your recent advertisement.* □ *Where do they stand with regard to the law?* (com respeito a)

3 **in that/this regard** in the way already mentioned □ *No one was injured, so we're lucky in that regard.* (a esse respeito)

- **regarding** /rɪˈgɑːdɪŋ/ PREPOSITION about □ *I'd like to talk to you regarding next weekend.* □ *Police have appealed for information regarding the incident.* (com respeito a)

- **regardless** /rɪˈgɑːdləs/ ADVERB without paying any attention to something □ *Regardless of the cost, I'm determined to take this holiday.* □ *We warned them, but they carried on regardless.* (independentemente de)

- **regards** /rɪˈgɑːdz/ PLURAL NOUN
1 used when sending good wishes to someone (saudações) ▣ *Give my regards to Fiona when you see her.* (dê minhas saudações/lembranças)
2 used at the end of a friendly but polite letter or e-mail (saudações)

regatta /rɪˈgætə/ NOUN [plural regattas] an event with several boat races (regata)

regenerate /rɪˈdʒenəreɪt/ VERB [regenerates, regenerating, regenerated] to improve something so that it returns to its original good state □ *The council is regenerating old housing.* (restaurar)

- **regeneration** /rɪˌdʒenəˈreɪʃən/ NOUN, NO PLURAL when something is regenerated ☐ *urban regeneration projects* (**restauração**)

reggae /ˈreɡeɪ/ NOUN, NO PLURAL a style of music that has strong rhythms, originally from Jamaica (**reggae**)

regime /reɪˈʒiːm/ NOUN [*plural* **regimes**]
1 a system of government, especially one you disapprove of ☐ *There have been attempts to topple the repressive regime.* (**regime**)
2 a system of rules ☐ *The hospital has a strict regime of hygiene.* (**regulamento**)

regiment /ˈredʒɪmənt/ NOUN [*plural* **regiments**] a large group of soldiers in an army (**regimento**)

- **regimental** /ˌredʒɪˈmentəl/ ADJECTIVE to do with an army regiment (**regimental**)

- **regimented** /ˈredʒɪmentɪd/ ADJECTIVE organized in a very controlled way ☐ *She runs the school in a very regimented manner.* (**disciplinado**)

region /ˈriːdʒən/ NOUN [*plural* **regions**]
1 a large area of land such as a part of a country with a particular characteristic ☐ *We visited some of the wine-making regions of Spain.* ☐ *The region's economy is growing steadily.* (**região**)
2 a part of the body ☐ *He had a pain in the chest region.* ☐ *The injury affected the region of her brain responsible for language.* (**região**)
3 in the region of approximately ☐ *Repairs will cost in the region of £500.* (**por volta de**)

- **regional** /ˈriːdʒənəl/ ADJECTIVE to do with a particular region of a country ☐ *a regional accent* ☐ *a regional newspaper* (**regional**)

register /ˈredʒɪstə(r)/ ▶ VERB [**registers, registering, registered**]
1 to put your name on an official list ☐ **+ for** *We registered for the new term's swimming class.* ☐ **+ with** *Make sure you register with the embassy.* ☐ *You must register your son's birth in the next week.* (**matricular-se, inscrever-se em, registrar-se**)
2 to express an opinion or to show a feeling ☐ *The fans registered their protest by staying away.* ☐ *Her face registered her disappointment.* (**registrar, expressar**)
3 if a device registers a measurement, it shows it ☐ *The earthquake registered 8.6 on the Richter scale.* (**registrar**)
4 to notice and understand something ☐ *She certainly heard the news but I don't know if it really registered.* (**registrar**)
▶ NOUN [*plural* **registers**]
1 an official list of names ☐ *Our teacher takes the register every morning.* ☐ *a register of births and deaths* (**lista ou registro**)
2 a style of language used in a particular situation, for example whether it is formal or informal (**registro linguístico**)

- **registrar** /ˌredʒɪˈstrɑː(r)/ NOUN [*plural* **registrars**] a person whose job is to keep official records, especially of births, marriages and deaths (**escrivão**)

- **registration** /ˌredʒɪˈstreɪʃən/ NOUN [*plural* **registrations**] when you put your name on an official list ☐ **+ for** *Registration for next term's classes starts on the 20th.* (**registro**) 🔲 *a registration fee* (**taxa de inscrição**) 🔲 *You need to complete a registration form.* (**formulário de inscrição**)

- **registry** /ˈredʒɪstri/ NOUN [*plural* **registries**] an office or building where official records are kept (**arquivo**)

registration number /ˌredʒɪˈstreɪʃən ˌnʌmbə(r)/ NOUN [*plural* **registration numbers**] the set of numbers and letters on the front and back of a vehicle (**número de licença, placa**)

registry office /ˈredʒɪstri ˌɒfɪs/ or **register office** /ˈredʒɪstə(r) ˌɒfɪs/ NOUN [*plural* **registry offices** or **register offices**] the place where you go to register a birth, marriage or death, or to have a marriage ceremony (**cartório de registro civil**)

regret /rɪˈɡret/ ▶ VERB [**regrets, regretting, regretted**]
1 to wish that something had not happened and to feel sorry about it ☐ *He regretted his decision bitterly.* ☐ **+ ing** *Yes I'm sorry, I regret saying that.* % *I regret not working harder at school.* ☐ **+ that** *He now regrets that he didn't do more.* (**lamentar, arrepender-se**)
2 a formal word used to say politely that you are sorry about something ☐ **+ that** *We regret that the rest of the tour will be cancelled.* ☐ **+ to do something** *We regret to inform you that the flight has been delayed.* (**lamentar**)
▶ NOUN [*plural* **regrets**] a sad feeling about something that has happened (**pesar, arrependimento**) 🔲 *Marion had no regrets about leaving home.* (**não teve arrependimentos**) 🔲 *He expressed regret for his actions.* (**expressou arrependimento**) 🔲 *It is with great regret that I am leaving the club.* (**grande pesar**)

- **regretful** /rɪˈɡretfʊl/ ADJECTIVE feeling regret about something that has happened ☐ *He sounded regretful.* (**pesaroso, arrependido**)

- **regretfully** /rɪˈɡretfʊli/ ADVERB in a way that shows regret ☐ *She shook her head regretfully.* (**lamentavelmente**)

- **regrettable** /rɪˈɡretəbəl/ ADJECTIVE if something is regrettable, you wish it had not happened ☐ *a regrettable accident* ☐ *It's very regrettable that things turned out this way.* (**lamentável**)

- **regrettably** /rɪˈɡretəbli/ ADVERB used to show that you wish something had not happened ☐ *Regrettably, a number of mistakes were made.* (**lamentavelmente**)

regular /ˈreɡjʊlə(r)/ ▶ ADJECTIVE
1 happening often or doing something often (**regular**) 🔲 *We all know the benefits of regular exercise.* (**exercício regular**) 🔲 *I keep in regular contact with my family.* (**contato regular**) 🔲 *He writes to me on a regular basis.* (**de modo regular**) ☐ *She was a regular visitor to the museum.*

regulate — rein

2 having the same amount of time or space between each thing ▫ *He has a regular heartbeat.* (**regular**) ▫ *I still see the doctor at regular intervals.* (**em intervalos regulares**)
3 of a standard size or quality ▫ *I'll have a regular coffee, please.* (**comum**)
4 following the usual rules of grammar ▫ *'Cat' has a regular plural.* (**regular**) ▫ *'Pick' is a regular verb.* (**verbo regular**)
5 a US word meaning usual ▫ *My regular doctor was away.* (**habitual**)
▶ NOUN [*plural* **regulars**] someone who often goes to the same bar, shop, etc. ▫ *He's a regular in our restaurant.* (**cliente habitual, freguês**)

• **regularity** /ˌreɡjuˈlærəti/ NOUN, NO PLURAL
1 when something often happens or is often done ▫ *She began to get lost with alarming regularity.* (**regularidade**)
2 the state of having the same amount of time or space between each thing ▫ *The trees are arranged with a pleasing regularity.* (**frequência**)

• **regularly** /ˈreɡjuləli/ ADVERB
1 often ▫ *We regularly have to call the police on a Saturday night.* ▫ *Patients are regularly denied medical care.* (**frequentemente**)
2 with the same amount of time or space between each thing ▫ *The flowers were planted regularly along the border.* ▫ *All the equipment is regularly checked.* (**regularmente**)

regulate /ˈreɡjuleɪt/ VERB [**regulates, regulating, regulated**]
1 to control an organization, a process, an activity, etc. using rules ▫ *These companies are regulated by the Financial Services Authority.* (**regulamentar**)
2 to control a machine so that it works how you want it to ▫ *You can regulate the temperature of the heating.* (**regular**)
3 to control a process within the body ▫ *Hormones regulate appetite.* (**regular**)

• **regulation** /ˌreɡjuˈleɪʃən/ NOUN [*plural* **regulations**]
1 a rule or a law ▫ *We can't allow that – it's against the regulations.* (**regulamento**) ▫ *There are strict safety regulations.*
2 the process of regulating something ▫ *the regulation of greenhouse emissions* (**regulação**)

• **regulator** /ˈreɡjuleɪtə(r)/ NOUN [*plural* **regulators**] a person whose job is to regulate something ▫ *There were complaints to the media regulator.* (**regulador**)

• **regulatory** /ˈreɡjulətəri/ ADJECTIVE to do with regulating organizations, processes or activities ▫ *The industry has its own regulatory authority.* (**regulador**)

rehabilitate /ˌriːəˈbɪlɪteɪt/ VERB [**rehabilitates, rehabilitating, rehabilitated**] to help someone to have a normal life again after they have had serious problems ▫ *We want to rehabilitate young criminals.* (**reabilitar**)

• **rehabilitation** /ˌriːəˌbɪlɪˈteɪʃən/ NOUN, NO PLURAL the process of rehabilitating someone ▫ *a drug rehabilitation centre* ▫ *He's continuing his rehabilitation from a knee injury.* (**reabilitação**)

rehearsal /rɪˈhɜːsəl/ NOUN [*plural* **rehearsals**] a practice for a performance ▫ *We are starting rehearsals for the new show.* (**ensaio**)

rehearse /rɪˈhɜːs/ VERB [**rehearses, rehearsing, rehearsed**] to practise performing something ▫ *Can we rehearse that last bit again?* (**ensaiar**)

reheat /ˌriːˈhiːt/ VERB [**reheats, reheating, reheated**] to make food or drink hot again ▫ *Once cooked, do not reheat.* (**reaquecer**)

rehouse /ˌriːˈhaʊz/ VERB [**rehouses, rehousing, rehoused**] to provide someone with somewhere else to live ▫ *Hundreds of people need to be rehoused following the flood.* (**realojar**)

reign /reɪn/ ▶ VERB [**reigns, reigning, reigned**]
1 to rule over a country as a king or queen ▫ *Queen Victoria reigned for over sixty years.* (**reinar**)
2 to be very important, successful etc. at a particular time (**reinar**) ▫ *It's clear that the actress still reigns supreme in Hollywood.*
3 to be the main feature or feeling of a situation ▫ *Confusion reigns over when he is due to arrive.* (**predominar**)
▶ NOUN [*plural* **reigns**]
1 the time when someone is the king or queen of a country ▫ *in the reign of King John* (**reinado**)
2 a time when someone is important, successful or powerful ▫ *The defeat ended his reign as world champion.* (**reinado**)

reimburse /ˌriːɪmˈbɜːs/ VERB [**reimburses, reimbursing, reimbursed**] to give someone back the money they have paid for something ▫ *The theatre will reimburse everyone who had tickets for the cancelled performance.* (**reembolsar**)

rein /reɪn/ NOUN [*plural* **reins**]
1 a long piece of leather which goes around a horse's neck and is used to control it ▫ *He held the horse's reins tightly.* (**rédea**)
2 the reins control of something (**as rédeas, o controle**) ▫ *He took the reins of the bank last July.* (**assumiu o controle**)
3 free rein freedom to do what you want ▫ *They are given free rein to read what they want.* (**permissão, liberdade para**)
♦ IDIOMS **give full rein to something** to allow something to happen or develop in a way that is not controlled ▫ *We want you to give full rein to your artistic powers.* (**desenfrear**) **keep a tight rein on something** to control something a lot ▫ *She keeps a tight rein on her feelings.* (**manter controle**)

♦ PHRASAL VERB [**reins, reining, reined**] **rein someone/something in** to start to control something that has got out of control ▫ *The party leader must try to rein in his more extreme supporters.* (**puxar as rédeas, assumir o controle**)

reincarnation /ˌriːɪnkɑːˈneɪʃən/ NOUN, NO PLURAL the idea that the spirit of a dead person is born again in a new body □ *Do they believe in reincarnation?* (reencarnação)

reindeer /ˈreɪndɪə(r)/ NOUN [plural **reindeer**] a type of large deer with large horns that lives in northern areas (rena)

reinforce /ˌriːɪnˈfɔːs/ VERB [**reinforces, reinforcing, reinforced**]
1 to make an idea, a feeling, etc. stronger □ *Parents need to reinforce these healthy eating messages.* □ *Magazines reinforce the idea that girls have to be very thin.* (reforçar)
2 to make something stronger □ *reinforced glass* □ *The concrete walls have been reinforced with steel.* (reforçar)

• **reinforcement** /ˌriːɪnˈfɔːsmənt/ NOUN [plural **reinforcements**]
1 when something is reinforced □ *Teachers use positive reinforcement to encourage good behaviour.* (reforço)
2 reinforcements extra soldiers, police officers, etc. sent somewhere □ *The army has sent reinforcements to the area.* (reforços)

reinstate /ˌriːɪnˈsteɪt/ VERB [**reinstates, reinstating, reinstated**]
1 to give someone back the job or position they had before □ *His supporters want him reinstated as Chairman.* (restabelecer)
2 to bring back something that existed before □ *The ban has been reinstated.* (reinstalar)

reiterate /riːˈɪtəreɪt/ VERB [**reiterates, reiterating, reiterated**] a formal word meaning to say something again to make people understand it □ *In answer to your question, I can only reiterate my organization's position on the matter.* (reiterar)

reject ▶ VERB /rɪˈdʒekt/ [**rejects, rejecting, rejected**]
1 to refuse to accept something □ *The machine rejected my coin.* □ *Unions rejected the offer.* (rejeitar) 🔁 *Graham rejected the idea out of hand* (= without considering it). (sem avaliar)
2 to decide not to accept someone for a job, a course, etc. □ *He was rejected for the job.* □ *Her application was rejected.* (rejeitar)
3 to not give someone enough love or attention □ *He felt rejected by his family.* (rejeitar)
4 if the body rejects an organ that has been put into it from another person, it does not accept it (rejeitar)
▶ NOUN /ˈriːdʒekt/ [plural **rejects**] someone or something that has been rejected because they are not good enough (rejeitado)

• **rejection** /rɪˈdʒekʃən/ NOUN [plural **rejections**]
1 when someone or something is not accepted □ *They are challenging the rejection of their building application in court.* □ *I received a rejection letter.* (rejeição)
2 the feeling of not being loved or wanted □ *She struggled with feelings of rejection.* (rejeição)
3 when the body rejects a new organ (rejeição)

rejoice /rɪˈdʒɔɪs/ VERB [**rejoices, rejoicing, rejoiced**] to feel or to show great happiness □ *His family rejoiced at the news.* (regozijar)

relapse /rɪˈlæps/ ▶ NOUN [plural **relapses**]
1 when someone becomes ill again after a period of improvement (recaída) 🔁 *She suffered a relapse.* (sofreu uma recaída)
2 when a situation or someone's behaviour becomes worse again after a period of improvement □ *At home, there was a relapse into arguments and bitterness.* (recaída)
▶ VERB [**relapses, relapsing, relapsed**]
1 to become worse again after a period of improvement □ *By that time, the whole country had relapsed into chaos.* (recair)
2 to go back to the state you were in before □ *He relapsed into silence.* (recair)
3 to become ill again after a period of improvement □ *She relapsed after the holiday, and died soon after.* (ter uma recaída)

relate /rɪˈleɪt/ VERB [**relates, relating, related**]
1 to show a connection between two things □ *The study attempted to relate mobile phone use to headaches.* (relacionar)
2 to tell a story or to say what happened □ *They related their strange experience to their friends.* (relatar)
♦ PHRASAL VERB **relate to someone/something**
1 to be connected with someone or something □ *The charges relate to the death of a man last November.* □ *The figures relate to the period 2004–2005.* (referir-se a)
2 to understand or to feel sympathy for someone or something □ *I couldn't relate to any of the characters.* (relacionar-se a)

• **related** /rɪˈleɪtɪd/ ADJECTIVE
1 connected □ *Is violent crime related to violence on TV?* □ *They published a series of related articles.* (relacionado)
2 belonging to the same family as someone else □ *We have the same surname, but we're not related.* (aparentado)

> ➤ Remember that one thing is **related to** another thing. It is not 'related with' another thing:
> ✓ *Health is very much related to diet.*
> ✗ *Health is very much related with diet.*

• **relation** /rɪˈleɪʃən/ NOUN [plural **relations**]
1 a connection between things □ *+ between Scientists established the relation between smoking and lung cancer.* (relação) 🔁 *Most movies bear no relation to* (= are nothing like) *reality.* (não ter relação com)
2 relations the way in which people, groups or countries deal with each other (relações) 🔁 *international relations* (relações internacionais)

☐ + *between* Relations between the two organizations are friendly. ☐ + *with* They have good relations with their neighbours.

3 someone in your family (**parente**) 🔁 All our *friends and relations* were there. (**amigos e parentes**) ☐ + *of* He's a distant relation of Tolstoy.

4 in relation to (a) a formal phrase meaning to do with ☐ They might have important information in relation to this incident. (b) when compared to something else ☐ It's a measure of your weight in relation to your height. (**em relação a**)

- **relationship** /rɪˈleɪʃənʃɪp/ NOUN [plural **relationships**]

1 the way people or groups feel about each other and deal with each other ☐ + *with* Anne felt she had a good relationship with her brother. ☐ + *between* There's a close relationship between our two countries. (**relação**) 🔁 They *had a father-son relationship*. (**tiveram uma relação**)

2 the connection between things ☐ + *between* What's the relationship between these numbers? ☐ There seems to be little relationship between how hard I work and how much I achieve. (**relação, conexão**)

3 the situation when people spend time together and have romantic feelings for each other ☐ He's having a relationship with a younger woman. (**relacionamento**)

relative /ˈrelətɪv/ ▶ NOUN [plural **relatives**] a member of your family (**parente**) 🔁 We invited all our *friends and relatives*. (**amigos e parentes**) 🔁 She has no *close relatives*. (**parentes próximos**) 🔁 He's a *distant relative* of the prime minister. (**parentes distantes**)

▶ ADJECTIVE

1 compared with similar people or things ☐ We are in a period of relative calm. ☐ It compares the relative merits of the two education systems. (**relativo**)

2 relative to compared with ☐ Housing costs are low relative to those of London. ☐ The situation has improved relative to 12 months ago. (**comparado a**)

- **relatively** /ˈrelətɪvli/ ADVERB quite, compared with similar people or things ☐ It's a relatively easy journey. (**relativamente**)

relax /rɪˈlæks/ VERB [relaxes, relaxing, relaxed]

1 to rest and become calmer and less worried ☐ We spent the afternoon relaxing by the pool ☐ Relax – the children are quite safe. ☐ A holiday will help to relax you. (**relaxar**)

2 to let your muscles become less tight ☐ Feel your shoulders relax. (**relaxar**)

3 to make a rule less severe ☐ The government has relaxed the immigration rules. (**flexibilizar**)

- **relaxation** /ˌriːlækˈseɪʃən/ NOUN, NO PLURAL

1 when you relax or relax a part of your body ☐ We practised relaxation techniques. (**relaxamento**) 🔁 I need a little *rest and relaxation*. (**descanso e relaxamento**)

2 when a rule is relaxed ☐ a relaxation of security restrictions (**flexibilização**)

- **relaxed** /rɪˈlækst/ ADJECTIVE

1 feeling calm, comfortable and not worried ☐ People are relaxed and enjoying themselves. ☐ a relaxed atmosphere (**relaxado, calmo**)

2 not worrying much about rules, details, etc. ☐ We take a relaxed approach to discipline.

- **relaxing** /rɪˈlæksɪŋ/ ADJECTIVE making you feel relaxed ☐ We had a relaxing break in the country. ☐ a relaxing massage (**relaxante**)

relay /ˈriːleɪ/ ▶ VERB [relays, relaying, relayed]

1 to pass a message from one person to another ☐ She relayed the information to the others. (**retransmitir**)

2 to broadcast something on television or radio ☐ His speech was relayed across the world. (**retransmitir**)

▶ NOUN [plural **relays**] a relay race (**uma corrida de revezamento**)

relay race /ˈriːleɪ ˌreɪs/ NOUN [plural **relay races**] a race for teams in which each person in the team does part of the race, one after the other (**corrida de revezamento**)

release /rɪˈliːs/ ▶ VERB [releases, releasing, released]

1 to let a person or an animal go free ☐ Three more prisoners have been released. ☐ + *from* He was released from prison in 2004. (**liberar**)

2 to stop holding something ☐ Release the handbrake slowly. ☐ We released the balloons and they floated into the air. (**soltar**)

3 to let a substance spread into an area ☐ + *into* Carbon dioxide is released into the atmosphere. (**liberar**)

4 to make something available to the public ☐ The film is released in cinemas on December 1. ☐ She released her first album last year. ☐ The company released a statement yesterday. (**lançar**)

▶ NOUN [plural **releases**]

1 when someone or something is allowed to go free ☐ + *of* The government demanded the release of the hostages. ☐ + *from* I met him just after his release from prison. (**liberação**)

2 when something is made available to the public or the thing made available ☐ + *of* The tour follows the release of her latest album. (**lançamento**) 🔁 a *news release* (**lançamento de uma notícia**)

3 when a substance is allowed to spread into an area (**liberação**)

relegate /ˈrelɪɡeɪt/ VERB [relegates, relegating, relegated] to move someone or something down to a less important or successful position or level ☐ My team has been relegated to the third division. (**relegar**)

- **relegation** /ˌrelɪˈɡeɪʃən/ NOUN, NO PLURAL when someone is relegated (**relegação**)

relent /rɪˈlent/ VERB [relents, relenting, relented]

1 to agree to something or allow something after refusing before ☐ She is hoping they might relent and allow her to visit her son. (**ceder**)

2 to become less strong or severe □ *The rain relented slightly.* (amenizar)

- **relentless** /rɪ'lentlɪs/ ADJECTIVE never stopping or becoming less strong □ *We stood all day in the relentless heat.* (implacável) 🔳 *He was under relentless pressure at work.*
- **relentlessly** /rɪ'lentlɪsli/ ADVERB in a relentless way □ *Her comments were relentlessly critical.* (implacavelmente)

relevance /'reləvəns/ NOUN, NO PLURAL the way that something is connected to or important for something else □ *What possible relevance can this have to me?* □ *He explained the relevance of the findings.* (relevância)

- **relevant** /'reləvənt/ ADJECTIVE connected to or important for a subject, situation, etc. □ *Is this answer relevant to the question?* (relevante) 🔳 *They sent us all the relevant information.* (informações relevantes)

reliability /rɪˌlaɪə'bɪlɪti/ NOUN, NO PLURAL how much you can trust or believe someone or something □ *This will improve the reliability of the system.* □ *He questioned the reliability of the witness.* (confiabilidade)

reliable /rɪ'laɪəbəl/ ADJECTIVE
1 a reliable person can be trusted to do what they say they will do or to do something well □ *We need to find a reliable supplier of spare parts.* □ *He's one of the team's most reliable players.* (confiável)
2 a reliable system, piece of equipment, vehicle, etc. works well and does not often stop working □ *I need a reliable car to get me to work.* □ *The trains aren't very reliable.* (confiável)
3 reliable information can be believed and is probably true or correct □ *Her letters are a reliable source of information.* □ *There are no reliable estimates of the number of people affected.* (confiável)

- **reliably** /rɪ'laɪəbli/ ADVERB in a way that can be trusted or believed □ *The service operates reliably and efficiently.* 🔳 *I'm reliably informed that she's planning to leave.* (por fonte segura)

reliance /rɪ'laɪəns/ NOUN, NO PLURAL when you need someone or something and cannot manage without them □ *We need to reduce our reliance on cars.* (dependência)

- **reliant** /rɪ'laɪənt/ ADJECTIVE **reliant on someone/ something** needing someone or something and not able to manage without them □ *The charity is totally reliant on donations from the public.* (dependente de alguém/alguma coisa)

relic /'relɪk/ NOUN [*plural* **relics**] an important object from the past □ *a religious relic* (relíquia)

relief /rɪ'li:f/ NOUN, NO PLURAL
1 a good feeling because something bad or unpleasant stops or does not happen (alívio) 🔳 *He gave a sigh of relief.* □ *It was a relief to be outside in the fresh air again.* □ *To my relief, no one was hurt.* (suspiro de alívio)
2 food, medicine, etc. to help a large group of people in need □ *The agency provides relief for flood victims.* (auxílio) 🔳 *You can help the disaster relief effort.* (auxílio a calamidades)
3 when you stop pain or suffering or make it less (alívio) 🔳 *Talk to your doctor about pain relief.* (alívio da dor) □ *This cream can provide relief from the symptoms of eczema.*

- **relieve** /rɪ'li:v/ VERB [**relieves, relieving, relieved**]
1 to stop pain, suffering or a problem or to make it less □ *The drug is used to relieve pain.* □ *The new clinic will relieve pressure on the hospital.* □ *He read magazines to relieve the boredom.* (aliviar)
2 to replace someone who is working so they can stop working □ *Wallis came up to relieve him for his lunch break.* (substituir)

♦ PHRASAL VERB **relieve someone of something**
1 a formal word meaning to take a problem or something heavy from someone □ *Let me relieve you of that heavy suitcase.* (aliviar)
2 a formal word meaning to tell someone to leave a job □ *He was relieved of his duties.* (desobrigar)

- **relieved** /rɪ'li:vd/ ADJECTIVE feeling relief □ *I'm so relieved that you're home safely.* □ *She looked relieved.* (aliviado)

religion /rɪ'lɪdʒən/ NOUN [*plural* **religions**] belief in a god or gods, and the activities and traditions to do with this belief □ *What is the role of religion in our society?* □ *We teach respect for different religions and cultures.* (religião)

- **religious** /rɪ'lɪdʒəs/ ADJECTIVE
1 to do with religion □ *a religious service* (religioso) 🔳 *a religious leader* (líder religioso) 🔳 *religious beliefs* (crenças religiosas)
2 having strong beliefs about a god or gods (religioso) 🔳 *He was a deeply religious man.* (profundamente religioso) □ *I'm not particularly religious.*

relinquish /rɪ'lɪŋkwɪʃ/ VERB [**relinquishes, relinquishing, relinquished**] a formal word meaning to give up something or your right to something □ *She relinquished the chairmanship to let a younger person take over.* (desistir, renunciar a)

relish /'relɪʃ/ ▶ VERB [**relishes, relishing, relished**] to enjoy something very much □ *He relished the prospect of living alone.* (apreciar)
▶ NOUN [*plural* **relishes**]
1 no plural great enjoyment □ *He told them about his experiences with great relish.* (satisfação)
2 a cold, thick sauce eaten with other food to add flavour (tempero, molho) □ *onion relish* (molho de alho)

relive /ˌriː'lɪv/ VERB [**relives, reliving, relived**] to remember an experience very clearly □ *She was forced to relive her ordeal in court.* (reviver)

relocate /ˌriː'ləʊ'keɪt/ VERB [**relocates, relocating, relocated**] to move to another place □ *My firm relocated to Edinburgh.* (transferir-se)

reluctance   661   remember

reluctance /rɪˈlʌktəns/ NOUN, NO PLURAL when someone is unwilling to do something □ *She was disappointed by their reluctance to help.* (**relutância**)

- **reluctant** /rɪˈlʌktənt/ ADJECTIVE unwilling to do something □ *She seemed reluctant to talk about it.* □ *He was a rather reluctant participant.* (**relutante**)

- **reluctantly** /rɪˈlʌktəntli/ ADVERB in a way that shows that you are unwilling □ *Nick reluctantly agreed.* (**com relutância**)

rely /rɪˈlaɪ/

♦ PHRASAL VERB [relies, relying, relied] **rely on someone/something** (**depender de, contar com, confiar**)

1 to need someone or something in order to exist or be successful □ *We rely on the help of parents and friends.* (**depender de alguém/algo**) 🔁 *The system relies heavily on computer technology.* (**depende muito de**)

2 to trust someone or something to do what they say they will do or what they should do □ *You can rely on our support.* □ *We can rely on Alan to sort it out.* □ *You can't rely on the trains in this country.* (**contar com, confiar**)

remain /rɪˈmeɪn/ VERB [remains, remaining, remained]

1 to continue to be in the same state or condition □ *He remained silent on the issue.* □ *His location remains a mystery.* □ *I won't vote for them while he remains leader.* (**permanecer**)

2 to stay in the same place or position □ *She is expected to remain in hospital for another week.* (**permanecer**)

3 to be left when everything or everyone else has gone □ *All that remains in the fireplace is a pile of ash.* □ *The chemotherapy kills the cancer cells that remain after surgery.* (**restar**)

4 to continue to exist 🔁 *Several questions remain about the details of the plan.* (**dúvidas permanecem**) 🔁 *The fact remains that she shouldn't have been there.* (**o fato permanece**)

5 it remains to be seen it is not yet known, but will be known in the future □ *It remains to be seen whether he'll be able to persuade his parents.* (**resta saber**)

- **remainder** /rɪˈmeɪndə(r)/ NOUN, NO PLURAL the remainder what is left of something after some of it has gone □ *He spent the remainder of his life in London.* □ *I tipped the remainder of the liquid away.* (**o resto**)

- **remaining** /rɪˈmeɪnɪŋ/ ADJECTIVE continuing to be there after other people or things have gone, been used, etc. □ *The remaining contestants will perform tonight.* □ *We can use the remaining time to tidy up.* (**restantes**)

- **remains** /rɪˈmeɪnz/ PLURAL NOUN

1 parts of something that are left after the main part has gone □ *People returned to the remains of their burnt homes.* □ *the remains of a Roman temple* (**restos**)

2 the body of a dead person □ *Her remains will be flown back to this country for burial.* (**restos**) 🔁 *Human remains were found.* (**restos mortais humanos**)

remake /ˈriːmeɪk/ NOUN [plural **remakes**] a new film that has the same story and title as an earlier film □ *a remake of the classic 1950s horror movie* (**refilmagem**)

remark /rɪˈmɑːk/ ▶ VERB [**remarks, remarking, remarked**] to express an opinion or a thought □ + *that* Tim remarked that he liked Di's hat. □ + *on* She didn't remark on the new painting. (**comentar, expressar opinião**)

▶ NOUN [plural **remarks**] something you say when expressing an opinion or a thought (**comentário**) □ + *about* He made a nasty remark about my writing. □ + *on* The President's remarks on immigration caused controversy. 🔁 *He made a racist remark.* (**fez um comentário**)

- **remarkable** /rɪˈmɑːkəbəl/ ADJECTIVE surprising or noticeable, usually in a way that you admire □ *It's a remarkable story.* □ *It's remarkable how quickly she recovered.* (**notável**)

- **remarkably** /rɪˈmɑːkəbli/ ADVERB in a very surprising or noticeable way □ *Remarkably, there were no injuries.* □ *They looked remarkably similar.* (**notavelmente**)

remaster /ˌriːˈmɑːstə(r)/ VERB [**remasters, remastering, remastered**] to make a new and better recording of an old recording (**remasterizar**) 🔁 *The record has recently been digitally remastered.* (**remasterizado digitalmente**)

remedial /rɪˈmiːdiəl/ ADJECTIVE

1 intended to improve something that is in a bad state (**corretivo**) 🔁 *Urgent remedial action is needed to save the business.* (**ação corretiva**)

2 intended to help people who have difficulty learning skills such as reading and writing □ *She attends a remedial maths class.* (**de reforço**)

remedy /ˈremədi/ ▶ NOUN [plural **remedies**]

1 something that treats an illness (**remédio**) 🔁 *a herbal remedy* (**remédio de ervas**) □ *Cloves are a traditional remedy for toothache.*

2 something that solves a problem □ *Their policies are seen as a remedy for the country's economic crisis.* (**solução**)

▶ VERB [**remedies, remedying, remedied**] to deal with a problem or a bad situation (**consertar**) 🔁 *People are without homes and nothing has been done to remedy the situation.* (**consertar a situação**)

remember /rɪˈmembə(r)/ VERB [**remembers, remembering, remembered**]

1 to have something from the past in your mind or to bring something back to your mind □ *I couldn't remember her name.* □ + *question word* I don't remember why we chose it. □ + *that* She

suddenly remembered that she'd left the window open. □ **+ ing** He remembered seeing a young girl outside. □ **+ as** He will be remembered as a great player. (**lembrar, lembrar-se de**)
2 not to forget to do something □ **+ to do something** Remember to take your key with you. (**lembrar-se de**)

• **remembrance** /rɪˈmembrəns/ NOUN, NO PLURAL when you show that you have not forgotten someone who has died □ *a service of remembrance* (**lembrança**) 🔲 *There was a minute's silence in remembrance of the victims.*

remind /rɪˈmaɪnd/ VERB [**reminds, reminding, reminded**] to make someone remember something □ **+ to do something** Remind me to close the window before I go out. □ *She reminded herself why she was there.* □ **+ that** *I want to remind everybody that the bus will leave at four o'clock.* □ **+ of** *She sent an email reminding students of the new timetable.* (**lembrar, fazer lembrar**)

♦ PHRASAL VERB **remind someone of someone/ something** (**lembrar alguém de algo/alguém**)
1 to make you think about someone or something from the past □ *That picture reminds me of our holiday last year.* (**fazer lembrar**)
2 to make you think about someone or something because of being similar to them □ *Thomas reminded her of her father.* (**fazer lembrar**)

> Note that if someone or something makes you think about someone or something from the past, they **remind** you **of** them. Remind in this sense is always followed by to:
> ✓ *She **reminds** me **of** my sister.*
> ✗ *She reminds me my sister.*

• **reminder** /rɪˈmaɪndə(r)/ NOUN [plural **reminders**]
1 something that makes you remember someone or something (**lembrança**) 🔲 *His scars are a constant reminder of the accident.* (**lembrança constante**) □ *This serves as a reminder of why we need to be careful.*
2 something that helps someone remember to do something □ *She received a reminder from the gas company that the bill was due.* (**lembrete**)

reminisce /ˌremɪˈnɪs/ VERB [**reminisces, reminiscing, reminisced**] to think, talk or write about things you remember from the past, usually happy times □ *Most of the meal was spent reminiscing about our school days.* (**lembrar o passado**)

• **reminiscence** /ˌremɪˈnɪsəns/ NOUN [plural **reminiscences**] when you remember things from the past or the things you remember □ *The speech was mostly reminiscences about his childhood.* (**reminiscência**)

• **reminiscent** /ˌremɪˈnɪsənt/ ADJECTIVE **reminiscent of someone/something** similar to something else and making you think of it □ *Her paintings use colours and shapes reminiscent of children's TV programmes.* (**reminiscente**)

remission /rɪˈmɪʃən/ NOUN, NO PLURAL a period of time when a serious illness does not affect you □ *His cancer is in remission.* (**remissão**)

remittance /rɪˈmɪtəns/ NOUN [plural **remittances**] a formal word meaning money that you send to pay for something (**remessa de valores**)

remnant /ˈremnənt/ NOUN [plural **remnants**] a small piece of something that is left after the rest has been used, lost or destroyed □ *Police found remnants of fireworks in the building.* (**retalho, resíduo**)

remorse /rɪˈmɔːs/ NOUN, NO PLURAL a strong guilty feeling about something bad or wrong that you have done □ *She was full of remorse for her actions.* (**remorso**)

• **remorseful** /rɪˈmɔːsful/ ADJECTIVE feeling very guilty and sorry □ *She was genuinely remorseful.* (**cheio de remorso**)

• **remorsefully** /rɪˈmɔːsfuli/ ADVERB in a way that shows remorse (**com remorso**)

• **remorseless** /rɪˈmɔːslɪs/ ADJECTIVE
1 not feeling guilty or sorry for what you have done □ *a remorseless killer* (**impiedoso, sem remorso**)
2 never stopping □ *the remorseless heat* (**incessante**)

• **remorselessly** /rɪˈmɔːslɪsli/ ADVERB in a way that never stops (**incessantemente**)

remote /rɪˈməʊt/ ▶ ADJECTIVE [**remoter, remotest**]
1 a remote place is very far away from other places □ *a remote village* (**remoto**)
2 a remote chance is very slight (**remoto**) 🔲 *There's not even a remote possibility that we'll win.* (**possibilidade remota**)
3 able to be used from a distance □ *The system allows remote access to staff working from home.* (**remoto**)
▶ NOUN [plural **remotes**] a remote control (**controle remoto**)

remote control /rɪˌməʊt kənˈtrəʊl/ NOUN [plural **remote controls**]
1 a device for operating equipment such as a television from a distance (**controle remoto**)
2 a system for operating something from a distance □ *The bomb was detonated by remote control.* (**controle remoto**)

remotely /rɪˈməʊtli/ ADVERB
1 slightly 🔲 *I'm not even remotely interested.* □ *We weren't doing anything remotely dangerous.* (**remotamente**)
2 from a distance □ *a remotely operated vehicle* (**a distância**)

removal /rɪˈmuːvəl/ NOUN [plural **removals**] when something is removed □ *He called for the removal of foreign troops.* □ *Doctors advised the removal of the tumour.* (**remoção**)

remove /rɪˈmuːv/ VERB [removes, removing, removed]

1 to take something away or to get rid of something ▫ *The police have removed the car.* ▫ *Doctors removed the tumour.* ▫ **+ from** *Remove the pan from the heat and stir in the cream.* (remover)

2 to take clothes off ▫ *Please remove your shoes at the door.* (tirar)

3 to make someone leave a job or position ▫ **+ from** *He was removed from office after corruption charges.* (destituir)

4 be removed from something to be completely different from something ▫ *The dream is very far removed from reality.* (ser completamente diferente)

renal /ˈriːnəl/ ADJECTIVE to do with the kidneys. A biology word. (renal)

rename /ˌriːˈneɪm/ VERB [renames, renaming, renamed] to give something or someone a new name ▫ *I renamed all the files in that folder.* (renomear)

render /ˈrendə(r)/ VERB [renders, rendering, rendered]

1 a formal word meaning to put someone or something into a particular state or condition ▫ *His rudeness rendered me speechless.* ▫ *Snow had rendered the road impassable.* (deixar em uma condição ou estado)

2 a formal word meaning to do something for someone ▫ *They attempted to render medical assistance.* (prestar assistência, auxílio)

rendezvous /ˈrɒndɪvuː/ NOUN [plural **rendezvous**] an arranged meeting, especially a secret one (encontro)

rendition /renˈdɪʃən/ NOUN [plural **renditions**] a performance of something such as a song ▫ *We had to listen to my uncle's rendition of 'White Christmas'.* (apresentação)

renew /rɪˈnjuː/ VERB [renews, renewing, renewed]

1 to start doing something again after a break, often with more energy ▫ *We'll renew our attempt to get the rules changed.* (renovar)

2 to make or to pay for something to continue for another period of time ▫ *You can renew your bus pass at the office.* (renovar)

renewable /rɪˈnjuːəbəl/ ADJECTIVE describes a type of natural energy such as power from the sun which can be replaced quickly and which will not end (renovável)

• **renewables** /rɪˈnjuːəbəlz/ PLURAL NOUN types of energy which are renewable (energias renováveis)

renewal /rɪˈnjuːəl/ NOUN [plural **renewals**]

1 when something starts again or you start something again after a break ▫ *There has been a renewal of interest in his novels.* (renovação)

2 when you make or pay for something to continue for another period of time ▫ *My contract is due for renewal in August.* (renovação)

renewed /rɪˈnjuːd/ ADJECTIVE starting again after a break, sometimes with more energy ▫ *Renewed fighting has broken out.* ▫ *There have been renewed efforts to find the killer.* (renovado)

renounce /rɪˈnaʊns/ VERB [renounces, renouncing, renounced]

1 a formal word meaning to say publicly that you no longer agree with or believe in something ▫ *They are trying to persuade the rebels to renounce violence.* (renunciar a)

2 a formal word meaning to officially give up a right to something ▫ *He renounced his claim to the land.* (renunciar a)

renovate /ˈrenəveɪt/ VERB [renovates, renovating, renovated] to repair and improve an old building so that it can be used again ▫ *We've completely renovated the house.* (restaurar, reformar)

• **renovation** /ˌrenəˈveɪʃən/ NOUN [plural **renovations**] when you renovate a building ▫ *The museum is undergoing renovation.* (restauração)

renown /rɪˈnaʊn/ NOUN, NO PLURAL a formal word meaning when someone is known and respected by many people ▫ *a man of great renown* (renome)

• **renowned** /rɪˈnaʊnd/ ADJECTIVE famous and respected ▫ *She was renowned for her stirring political speeches.* (renomado)

rent /rent/ ▶ VERB [rents, renting, rented]

1 to pay someone money so that you can use a house or other building ▫ *We rented a villa near the beach.* (alugar)

2 a mainly US word meaning to pay someone money to use something such as a car or tools for a short time ▫ *She rented a car for the week.* (alugar)

3 to let other people pay to use something you own ▫ **+ out** *They rent out the building for weddings.* ▫ **+ to** *We'll rent the house to students while we're away.* (alugar)

> Note that in British English, **rent** is mainly used for houses and other buildings. The verb **hire** means 'to pay someone money to use something such as a car or tools for a short time'.

▶ NOUN [plural **rents**] money you pay to the owner of a house or other building to use it (aluguel) ▫ *He's struggling to pay the rent.* (pagar o aluguel)

• **rental** /ˈrentəl/ NOUN [plural **rentals**]

1 when you rent something ▫ *a car rental business* (aluguel)

2 the amount of rent you pay (aluguel)

reorganization or **reorganisation** /riːˌɔːɡənaɪˈzeɪʃən/ NOUN, NO PLURAL when something is reorganized ▫ *He was moved to a new department as part of the company's reorganization.* (reorganização)

reorganize or **reorganise** /riːˈɔːɡənaɪz/ VERB [reorganizes, reorganizing, reorganized] to organize something again in a different way in order to make it better □ *We have reorganized our adult classes.* (**reorganizar**)

rep /rep/ NOUN [plural **reps**] an informal word for someone who sells the products and services of a company (**representante, vendedor**) 🔁 *She's a sales rep for a computer firm.* (**representante de vendas**)

repaid /rɪˈpeɪd/ PAST TENSE AND PAST PARTICIPLE OF **repay** (*ver* **repay**)

repair /rɪˈpeə(r)/ ▶ VERB [**repairs, repairing, repaired**]

1 to fix something that is damaged or not working □ *Can the washing machine be repaired?* (**consertar**) 🔁 *It will cost millions to repair the damage done by the storms.* (**consertar o dano**)

2 to try to improve a bad situation □ *It will take time to repair the damage caused by the scandal.* (**consertar, reparar**)

▶ NOUN [plural **repairs**]

1 something you do to repair something □ *The ship needed extensive repairs.* (**reparo**)

2 in good/bad repair in good or bad condition □ *The car is in remarkably good repair for its age.* (**em bom/mau estado**)

reparations /ˌrepəˈreɪʃənz/ PLURAL NOUN money paid by a country that has lost a war (**reparação**)

repartee /ˌrɑːpɑːˈtiː/ NOUN, NO PLURAL conversation in which people make clever or humorous remarks (**resposta ou diálogo espirituoso**)

repay /rɪˈpeɪ/ VERB [**repays, repaying, repaid**]

1 to pay back money that you have borrowed □ *They are struggling to repay the loans.* (**pagar**)

2 to do something for someone because they did something kind for you □ *How can we ever repay this kindness?* (**pagar**)

• **repayment** /rɪˈpeɪmənt/ NOUN [plural **repayments**] money you repay □ *monthly mortgage repayments* (**reembolso**)

repeat /rɪˈpiːt/ ▶ VERB [**repeats, repeating, repeated**]

1 to say something again □ *Could you repeat your name please?* □ *She repeated her request.* □ *I don't want to repeat myself* (= say the same thing again). (**repetir**)

2 to do something again or to happen again □ *I hope this mistake will never be repeated.* □ *The programme is repeated on Friday at 10pm.* (**repetir**)

3 to tell someone something you were told by someone else □ *Don't you dare repeat this to your friends.* (**repetir**)

▶ NOUN [plural **repeats**]

1 something that happens again □ *She wants to avoid a repeat of what happened last year.* (**repetição, reprise**) 🔁 *He's hoping for a repeat performance of last month's win.* (**reprise da apresentação, bis**)

2 a television or radio programme that is broadcast again □ *They were watching repeats of old comedy shows.* (**reprise**)

• **repeated** /rɪˈpiːtɪd/ ADJECTIVE done or happening several times □ *After repeated attempts to phone him, I finally went round to his office.* (**repetido**)

• **repeatedly** /rɪˈpiːtɪdli/ ADVERB again and again □ *The victim had been stabbed repeatedly.* (**repetidamente**)

repel /rɪˈpel/ VERB [**repels, repelling, repelled**]

1 to keep someone or something away □ *This material repels water.* □ *Use a spray to repel mosquitoes.* (**repelir**)

2 to force someone who is attacking you to move back □ *Soldiers were ready to repel any attack.* (**repelir**)

3 if something repels you, you find it very unpleasant □ *People are both fascinated and repelled by the terrible images.* (**repugnar**)

• **repellent** /rɪˈpelənt/ ▶ ADJECTIVE very unpleasant □ *a repellent sight* (**repelente**)

▶ NOUN [plural **repellents**] a substance that you use to keep something away □ *an insect repellent* (**repelente**)

repent /rɪˈpent/ VERB [**repents, repenting, repented**] to be sorry for something that you have done □ *He repented of his crimes.* (**arrepender-se**)

• **repentance** /rɪˈpentəns/ NOUN, NO PLURAL when you repent (**arrependimento**)

• **repentant** /rɪˈpentənt/ ADJECTIVE sorry for something you have done □ *She looked ashamed and repentant.* (**arrependido**)

repercussions /ˌriːpəˈkʌʃənz/ PLURAL NOUN the bad effects of an action or an event that follow later □ *This attack could have serious repercussions for the tourist industry.* (**repercussões**)

repertoire /ˈrepətwɑː(r)/ NOUN [plural **repertoires**] all the music, songs, etc. that a performer knows and can perform (**repertório**)

repetition /ˌrepɪˈtɪʃən/ NOUN [plural **repetitions**] when something is repeated □ *We don't want a repetition of yesterday's argument.* □ *learning by repetition* (**repetição**)

• **repetitive** /rɪˈpetɪtɪv/ ADJECTIVE boring because the same thing is repeated many times □ *They have to do lots of simple, repetitive tasks.* (**repetitivo**)

replace /rɪˈpleɪs/ VERB [**replaces, replacing, replaced**]

1 to take the place of another thing or person □ *The company bought new computers to replace the old ones.* □ *The cinema was demolished and replaced by a supermarket.* □ *+ with The phone has been replaced with a newer version.* □ *+ as He was replaced as chairman last year.* (**substituir, recolocar**)

2 to put something back where it was before or in its correct position □ *Make sure you replace the books in exactly the right order.* (**recolocar**)

replay

- **replacement** /rɪˈpleɪsmənt/ NOUN [plural **replacements**] a person or thing that replaces another one ☐ *This is broken so I'd like a replacement, please.* (**substituto**) ☐ *They will have to find a replacement for the injured goalkeeper.* (**encontrar um substituto**)

replay ▶ NOUN /ˈriːpleɪ/ [plural **replays**]
1 a sports match that is played again because nobody won the first time ☐ *He scored in the second-round replay.* (**partida para desempate**)
2 an important moment in a sports match that is shown again on television (**retransmissão na TV**)
▶ VERB /ˌriːˈpleɪ/ [**replays, replaying, replayed**] to play a sports match again because there was no winner the first time (**partida para desempate**)

replenish /rɪˈplenɪʃ/ VERB [**replenishes, replenishing, replenished**] to get more of something to replace what has been used ☐ *Health officials are appealing for blood donors to help replenish supplies.* (**reabastecer**)

- **replenishment** /rɪˈplenɪʃmənt/ NOUN, NO PLURAL when you replenish something (**reabastecimento**)

replica /ˈreplɪkə/ NOUN [plural **replicas**] an accurate copy of something ☐ *a replica football shirt* (**réplica**)

replicate /ˈreplɪkeɪt/ VERB [**replicates, replicating, replicated**] to do something or make something again so that it is exactly the same ☐ *The company is hoping to replicate the success it had in Japan.* (**duplicar**)

reply /rɪˈplaɪ/ ▶ VERB [**replies, replying, replied**] to answer ☐ *'No, I don't!' he replied angrily.* ☐ *+ that He replied that he was planning to stay another week.* ☐ *+ to You haven't replied to my question yet.* (**responder**)
▶ NOUN [plural **replies**] an answer ☐ *+ to We've had a number of replies to our advertisement.* ☐ *In reply, Phoebe gave a nod.* (**resposta**) ▣ *He received no reply to his letters.* (**não recebeu resposta**)

report /rɪˈpɔːt/ ▶ NOUN [plural **reports**]
1 a description of something that has happened ☐ *+ of Reports of an accident are just coming in.* (**relatório, informação**) ▣ *a television news report* (**reportagem**)
2 a written description of a situation or the results of a study ☐ *+ on a UN report on climate change* ☐ *+ into the police report into the accident* (**relatório**) ▣ *The organization will publish its annual report tomorrow.* (**relatório anual**)
3 a teacher's written description of a student's progress (**relatório escolar, boletim**) ▣ *a school report* (**boletim escolar**)
▶ VERB [**reports, reporting, reported**]
1 to tell people about an event or situation on television, on radio, in newspapers, etc. ☐ *The whole story was reported in the papers.* ☐ *+ on Tonight we'll be reporting on religious education.* (**relatar, fazer relatório**)

represent

2 to give information about a situation or an event ☐ *+ ing Witnesses reported seeing the bus lose control.* ☐ *+ on There were regular meetings to report on progress.* ☐ *The company reported a record annual profit.* (**declarar, anunciar**)
3 to tell someone officially that something has happened ☐ *+ to Did you report the incident to the police?* (**denunciar**)
4 to make a complaint about someone's behaviour ☐ *I reported the bus driver for not stopping.* (**dar parte, queixar-se**)
5 to go to a place and tell them that you have arrived ☐ *+ to Please report to reception when you enter the building.* ☐ *+ for He didn't report for work yesterday.* (**apresentar-se**)

- **reportedly** /rɪˈpɔːtɪdli/ ADVERB used to show that you have heard information but cannot be sure it is true ☐ *She reportedly threatened to resign.* (**conforme boatos**)

reported speech /rɪˌpɔːtɪd ˈspiːtʃ/ NOUN, NO PLURAL the words you use when you say what someone has said without using their exact words (**discurso indireto**)

reporter /rɪˈpɔːtə(r)/ NOUN [plural **reporters**] a person whose job is to describe events for newspapers, television or radio news programmes, etc. (**repórter**) ▣ *a newspaper reporter* (**repórter de jornal**)

repossess /ˌriːpəˈzes/ VERB [**repossesses, repossessing, repossessed**] to take back something that someone has bought, for example a car or a house, because they cannot finish paying for it ☐ *He lost his job and his house was repossessed.* (**retomar**)

- **repossession** /ˌriːpəˈzeʃən/ NOUN [plural **repossessions**] when something is repossessed (**retomada**)

represent /ˌreprɪˈzent/ VERB [**represents, representing, represented**]
1 to speak or to act officially for someone else ☐ *Our MPs represent us in the government.* ☐ *He was represented by a lawyer.* (**representar**)
2 be something or to be equal to something ☐ *The virus represents a major threat to public health.* ☐ *This figure represents an increase of 8* ☐ (**representar**)
3 to be a symbol or an example of something ☐ *The crown represents the king or queen.* (**representar**)
4 to take part in a competition for your country, school, etc. ☐ *She has represented her country at the highest level.* (**representar**)
5 to show or to describe something in a particular way ☐ *+ as The children in the picture were all represented as angels.* (**representar**)

- **representation** /ˌreprɪzenˈteɪʃən/ NOUN [plural **representations**]
1 when someone is represented by someone else (**representação**) ▣ *You are entitled to legal representation.* (**representação legal**)

2 when someone or something is shown in a particular way ☐ *It was not an accurate representation of his views.* (representação)
3 representations a formal word for something you officially ask for or complain about (representação) ☐ *He made representations to the Foreign Office.* (apresentar reclamações)

• **representative** /ˌreprɪˈzentətɪv/ ▶ NOUN [plural representatives]
1 someone who represents someone else ☐ *a union representative* ☐ *There were representatives of several international organizations at the meeting.* (representante)
2 someone whose job is to sell the products of the company they work for (representante) ☐ *a sales representative* (representante de vendas)
▶ ADJECTIVE typical of a group of people or things ☐ *a representative sample* ☐ *These statistics are representative of the overall population.* (representativo)

repress /rɪˈpres/ VERB [represses, repressing, repressed]
1 to try not to show or to express a feeling ☐ *She repressed a smile.* (reprimir)
2 to control people by force ☐ *The regime represses any dissent.* (reprimir)

• **repressed** /rɪˈprest/ ADJECTIVE
1 not able or willing to show your feelings ☐ *She plays a repressed housewife.* (reprimido)
2 if a feeling is repressed, you do not show it ☐ *repressed emotions* (reprimido)

• **repression** /rɪˈpreʃən/ NOUN, NO PLURAL when someone or something is repressed ☐ *There have been allegations of political repression.* (repressão)

• **repressive** /rɪˈpresɪv/ ADJECTIVE controlling people by force ☐ *a repressive regime* (repressivo)

reprieve /rɪˈpriːv/ ▶ NOUN [plural reprieves] when a punishment or an unpleasant event is stopped or delayed ☐ *She won a last-minute reprieve from being deported.* (comutação, adiamento ou perdão de pena)
▶ VERB [reprieves, reprieving, reprieved] to stop or to delay a punishment or an unpleasant event (comutar/adiar/perdoar pena)

reprimand /ˈreprɪmɑːnd/ ▶ VERB [reprimands, reprimanding, reprimanded] to officially criticize someone for doing something wrong ☐ *She was reprimanded for unprofessional conduct.* (repreender)
▶ NOUN [plural reprimands] when someone is reprimanded ☐ *He received a written reprimand.* (reprimenda)

reprint ▶ VERB /ˌriːˈprɪnt/ [reprints, reprinting, reprinted]
1 to print more copies of a book (reimprimir)
2 to print a copy of a piece of writing, a photograph, etc. (imprimir uma cópia)
▶ NOUN /ˈriːprɪnt/ [plural reprints] a new copy of a book (reimpressão)

reprisal /rɪˈpraɪzəl/ NOUN [plural reprisals] something unpleasant you do to someone because of something bad they have done to you ☐ *The country will suffer reprisals for their attacks.* (represália)

reproach /rɪˈprəʊtʃ/ ▶ NOUN [plural reproaches]
1 an expression of criticism or disappointment about someone's behaviour ☐ *He gave her a look of reproach.* (reprovação, censura)
2 above/beyond reproach very good and not able to be criticized ☐ *His behaviour was beyond reproach.* (irreensível)
▶ VERB [reproaches, reproaching, reproached] to criticize someone for their behaviour ☐ *The teacher reproached the pupils for being noisy.* (reprovar)

• **reproachful** /rɪˈprəʊtʃfʊl/ ADJECTIVE showing criticism ☐ *reproachful words* (reprovador)

reproduce /ˌriːprəˈdjuːs/ VERB [reproduces, reproducing, reproduced]
1 to make something again or to copy something ☐ *The child had reproduced his father's signature.* ☐ *Other scientists failed to reproduce the same results.* (reproduzir)
2 to produce babies, young animals or plants. A biology word. ☐ *The virus reproduces quickly.* (reproduzir-se)

• **reproduction** /ˌriːprəˈdʌkʃən/ NOUN [plural reproductions]
1 a copy of something ☐ *a reproduction of the painting* (reprodução)
2 the process of producing babies or young animals or plants. A biology word. ☐ *human reproduction* (reprodução)

• **reproductive** /ˌriːprəˈdʌktɪv/ ADJECTIVE to do with the process of reproduction. A biology word. ☐ *the reproductive organs* (reprodutivo)

reptile /ˈreptaɪl/ NOUN [plural reptiles] an animal with cold blood that lays eggs, such as a snake or lizard. A biology word. (réptil)

republic /rɪˈpʌblɪk/ NOUN [plural republics] a country with no king or queen, but with an elected government and usually a president (= elected leader) (república)

• **republican** /rɪˈpʌblɪkən/ ADJECTIVE
1 belonging to a republic or wanting your country to be a republic (republicano)
2 Republican someone who supports the Republican Party in the US (republicano)

repulsive /rɪˈpʌlsɪv/ ADJECTIVE very unpleasant ☐ *She found the images repulsive.* (repulsivo)

reputable /ˈrepjʊtəbəl/ ADJECTIVE considered to be of good quality, honest, etc. ☐ *a reputable company* (respeitável)

reputation /ˌrepjʊˈteɪʃən/ NOUN [plural reputations] the opinion that most people have of someone or something based on experience ☐ *The restaurant has a very good reputation* ☐ + for *He has a reputation for being a very tough player.*

request | 667 | **reservation**

□ + *as* The country has built a reputation as a tourist destination. ⮕ He gained an *international reputation*. (**reputação**)

- **reputed** /rɪ'pju:tɪd/ ADJECTIVE used to say that people in general consider something to be true □ She is reputed to be earning over £500,000 a year. (**considerado como**)

- **reputedly** /rɪ'pju:tɪdli/ ADVERB according to what most people believe □ She is reputedly the most talented member of the government. (**supostamente**)

request /rɪ'kwest/ ▶ NOUN [plural **requests**]

1 when someone politely asks for something (**pedido**) ⮕ I've got a *request* to make. (**fazer um pedido**) □ + *for* There were hundreds of requests for information. □ + *to do something* The man refused repeated requests to leave.

2 on request if something is available on request, it is available to people who ask for it (**a pedido**)

▶ VERB [**requests, requesting, requested**] to ask politely for something □ The committee requested additional information. □ The pilot requested permission to land. □ + *that* She requested that the case be delayed. (**pedir**)

> Note that you **request** something. You do not 'request for' something:
> ✓ He requested an invitation.
> ✗ He requested for an invitation.

requiem /'rekwɪəm/ NOUN [plural **requiems**] a religious piece of music that is played at a Christian service for someone who has died (**réquiem**)

require /rɪ'kwaɪə(r)/ VERB [**requires, requiring, required**]

1 to need something □ Do you require any further information? □ He required treatment for an ankle injury. (**precisar**)

2 be required to do something to officially have to do something □ All staff are required to dress appropriately. ⮕ All passengers are *required by law* to wear seat belts. (**exigido por lei**)

- **requirement** /rɪ'kwaɪəmənt/ NOUN [plural **requirements**]

1 something you have to have or to do in order to do something else (**exigência**) ⮕ There is no *legal requirement* to notify the parents. (**exigência legal**) ⮕ It *meets* the safety *requirements*. (**satisfazer as exigências**)

2 something that you need or want ⮕ Each kitchen is designed to *meet* customer *requirements*. (**satisfazer as exigências**)

rerun /'ri:rʌn/ NOUN [plural **reruns**] a television programme that is repeated (**reprise**)

resat /ˌri:'sæt/ PAST TENSE AND PAST PARTICIPLE OF resit (**ver resit**)

reschedule /ˌri:'ʃedju:l/ VERB [**reschedules, rescheduling, rescheduled**] to arrange for something to happen at a different time □ My meeting has been rescheduled. (**reprogramar**)

rescue /'reskju:/ ▶ VERB [**rescues, rescuing, rescued**] to save someone from danger □ + *from* Firefighters rescued the people from the burning house. (**salvar, resgatar**)

▶ NOUN [plural **rescues**] when someone is rescued □ They were stranded with no hope of rescue. (**salvamento**) ⮕ Fire fighters made several *rescue attempts*. (**tentativas de salvamento**) ⮕ A passing driver *came to her rescue*. (**vieram em seu salvamento**)

- **rescuer** /'reskjuə(r)/ NOUN [plural **rescuers**] a person who rescues someone (**salvador**)

research /rɪ'sɜ:tʃ, 'ri:sɜ:tʃ/ ▶ NOUN [plural **researches**] when you study a subject carefully to find new information □ + *into* They fund research into causes of cancer. (**pesquisa**) ⮕ The *research was carried out* in 2005. (**a pesquisa foi conduzida**) ⮕ The *research shows* little educational benefit to homework. (**as pesquisas mostram**)

▶ VERB [**researches, researching, researched**] to study a subject carefully to find new information □ She is researching her family history. □ I was researching a book about Einstein. (**pesquisar**)

- **researcher** /rɪ'sɜ:tʃə(r)/ NOUN [plural **researchers**] a person who researches something (**pesquisador**)

resemblance /rɪ'zembləns/ NOUN [plural **resemblances**] when things or people look or seem similar in some way □ Can you see the resemblance between the brothers? (**semelhança**) ⮕ The film *bears little resemblance to* (= is quite different from) the original book. (**não tem semelhança com**)

- **resemble** /rɪ'zembəl/ VERB [**resembles, resembling, resembled**] to look similar or to seem similar in some way □ Tom resembles his father. □ The website resembles the front page of a newspaper. (**parecer-se com**)

resent /rɪ'zent/ VERB [**resents, resenting, resented**] to feel angry or unhappy about something you think is unfair □ She resented being interrupted. □ He resented his sister because of the attention she received. (**ressentir-se de**)

- **resentful** /rɪ'zentfʊl/ ADJECTIVE feeling angry and unhappy about something you think is unfair □ a resentful look (**ressentido**)

- **resentment** /rɪ'zentmənt/ NOUN, NO PLURAL the feeling of resenting something (**ressentimento**) ⮕ There is *deep resentment* towards the authorities. (**profundo ressentimento**)

reservation /ˌrezə'veɪʃən/ NOUN [plural **reservations**]

1 an arrangement to keep a place for you in a restaurant, hotel, plane, etc. □ + *for* We have a reservation for dinner. (**reserva**) ⮕ I'd like to *make a reservation* for two double rooms, please. (**fazer uma reserva**)

2 a feeling of doubt about something □ + *about* Some people expressed reservations about the

plans. (reservas) ▣ *Peter had reservations about moving abroad.* (ter dúvidas)
• **reserve** /rɪˈzɜːv/ ▶ VERB [**reserves, reserving, reserved**]
1 to ask a hotel, restaurant, etc. to keep a place for you □ *I'd like to reserve a table for dinner tonight, please.* □ *We reserved seats in a no-smoking section.* (reservar)
2 to keep something for a particular use or person □ **+ for** *Some seats are reserved for elderly or disabled passengers.* □ *Mix in half the sugar, reserving the rest for the icing.* (reservar)
3 to wait before expressing your opinion about something ▣ *I'll reserve judgment until I see it for myself.* (reservar o julgamento)
4 reserve the right to do something a formal phrase meaning to keep the right to do something in the future □ *The management reserves the right to refuse entry.* (reservar-se o direito de)
▶ NOUN [*plural* **reserves**]
1 an amount of something you have available to use in the future □ *the world's oil reserves* □ *She seems to have amazing reserves of energy and patience.* (reserva)
2 someone or something available to be used if another person or thing is not available □ *He was a reserve in the England team.* □ *He managed to open his reserve parachute.* (reserva)
3 in reserve available to be used if needed □ *It's always wise to keep some money in reserve.* (de reserva)
4 an area of land where plants or animals are protected (reserva) ▣ *a nature reserve* (reserva natural)
5 *no plural* the quality of being quiet and not showing your feelings □ *Despite his initial reserve, he soon started to make friends.* (reserva)
• **reserved** /rɪˈzɜːvd/ ADJECTIVE quiet and not showing your feelings □ *He's a reserved man.* (reservado)

reservoir /ˈrezəvwɑː(r)/ NOUN [*plural* **reservoirs**] a large lake where water is collected and stored in order to be used by people in an area (reservatório)

reset button /ˌriːset ˈbʌtən/ NOUN [*plural* **reset buttons**] a switch on a computer that lets you turn the computer off and then on again if the computer is not working (botão de reinicializar)

reshuffle /ˌriːˈʃʌfəl/ NOUN [*plural* **reshuffles**] when people within a group are given different jobs, especially in the government (alterações em cargos, atividades) ▣ *There's been another cabinet reshuffle by the Prime Minister.* (mudanças no gabinete)

reside /rɪˈzaɪd/ VERB [**resides, residing, resided**] a formal word meaning to live in a place (residir)
• **residence** /ˈrezɪdəns/ NOUN [*plural* **residences**] a formal word meaning where someone lives □ *Buckingham Palace is one of the queen's official residences.* □ *What is your country of residence?* (residência)
• **resident** /ˈrezɪdənt/ ▶ NOUN [*plural* **residents**] someone who lives in a place (residente) ▣ *Local residents are opposed to the plans.* (residentes locais)
▶ ADJECTIVE living in a place □ *How long have you been resident in this country?* (residente)
• **residential** /ˌrezɪˈdenʃəl/ ADJECTIVE
1 a residential area has mostly houses, not offices or factories (residencial)
2 a residential activity is one where you stay at the place where you are working or studying □ *a residential course for teachers* (residencial)

residue /ˈrezɪdjuː/ NOUN [*plural* **residues**] an amount left after the rest of a substance has gone or been used □ *It left a sticky residue.* (resíduo)

resign /rɪˈzaɪn/ VERB [**resigns, resigning, resigned**] to officially say that you are leaving your job □ *She resigned from her post as finance director.* (demitir-se)
♦ PHRASAL VERB **resign yourself to something** to accept something unpleasant that you cannot change % *He had resigned himself to defeat.* □ *They're resigned to losing the house.* (resignar-se a)
• **resignation** /ˌrezɪgˈneɪʃən/ NOUN [*plural* **resignations**]
1 when you resign from your job □ *a letter of resignation* □ *There have been calls for the minister's resignation.* (demissão) ▣ *He's handed in his resignation.* (entregou sua demissão)
2 a feeling of accepting something unpleasant that you cannot change □ *a look of resignation* (resignação)
• **resigned** /rɪˈzaɪnd/ ADJECTIVE accepting a bad situation that you cannot change % *a resigned sigh* □ *I'm resigned to the fact that I will never be rich.* (resignado)

resilience /rɪˈzɪliəns/ NOUN, NO PLURAL the quality of being able to deal with hard treatment or difficult situations without being badly affected □ *She showed great resilience in coming back to win the match.* (resiliência)
• **resilient** /rɪˈzɪliənt/ ADJECTIVE able to deal with hard treatment or difficult situations without being badly affected □ *She's a strong and resilient woman.* (resiliente)

resin /ˈrezɪn/ NOUN, NO PLURAL a sticky substance produced by some trees (resina)

resist /rɪˈzɪst/ VERB [**resists, resisting, resisted**]
1 to try to stop something from happening or to refuse to accept something □ *The bank resisted pressure to cut interest rates.* (resistir a)
2 to stop yourself from doing or having something you want (resistir a) ▣ *She resisted the temptation to take a look.* (resistiu à tentação) □ *The opportunity was too good to resist.*
3 to fight against someone or something, especially when they are attacking you. (resistir a) □ *They couldn't resist the attackers.* ▣ *He resisted arrest.* (resistiu à prisão)

resit

- **resistance** /rɪˈzɪstəns/ NOUN, NO PLURAL
1 when you refuse to accept something (resistência) 🔹 *The plans have met stiff resistance.* (encontrar resistência)
2 when you fight against someone or something (resistência) □ *armed resistance* 🔹 *The rebels put up fierce resistance.* (manter grande resistência)
3 the ability to not be affected by something □ *the body's resistance to disease* (resistência)
4 the amount by which a substance can stop or slow down an electric current. A physics word. (resistência)

- **resistant** /rɪˈzɪstənt/ ADJECTIVE
1 not harmed or affected by something □ *a water resistant watch* □ *The bacteria have become resistant to antibiotics.* (resistente)
2 not accepting something □ *They are stubbornly resistant to change.* (resistente)

resit /ˌriːˈsɪt/ ▶ VERB [resits, resitting, resat] to take an exam again (refazer um exame)
▶ NOUN /ˈriːsɪt/ [plural resits] when you take an exam again (repetição de um exame)

resolute /ˈrezəluːt/ ADJECTIVE very determined not change your opinions or decisions □ *Jim remained resolute in his refusal to sing.* (resoluto)

- **resolutely** /ˈrezəluːtli/ ADVERB in a determined way □ *We have resolutely refused to do extra work.* (decididamente)

- **resolution** /ˌrezəˈluːʃən/ NOUN [plural resolutions]
1 an official decision which a group of people vote for (resolução) 🔹 *The UN passed a resolution imposing sanctions.* (aprovar uma resolução)
2 a firm decision to do something (decisões, resoluções) 🔹 *I made several New Year's resolutions.* (resoluções de Ano Novo)
3 when you solve a problem or a disagreement □ *We are hoping for a diplomatic resolution of the dispute.* (resolução)
4 the quality of being determined (resolução)

- **resolve** /rɪˈzɒlv/ ▶ VERB [resolves, resolving, resolved]
1 to solve or successfully deal with a problem or a disagreement □ *He tried to resolve the dispute peacefully.* (resolver)
2 to make a firm decision to do something □ *We have resolved to try harder next time.* (decidir)
▶ NOUN, NO PLURAL determination □ *I have always admired his resolve.* (determinação)

resort /rɪˈzɔːt/
♦ PHRASAL VERB [resorts, resorting, resorted]
resort to something to do something you do not want to do in order to solve a problem □ *The worst thing would be to resort to violence.* (recorrer a alguma coisa)
▶ NOUN [plural resorts]
1 a place where people go on holiday □ *a popular seaside resort* □ *a ski resort* (local de férias, resort)
2 a last resort something you do only when everything else has failed □ *I suppose we could borrow the money as a last resort.* (último recurso)

respect

resound /rɪˈzaʊnd/ VERB [resounds, resounding, resounded] to make a loud sound that fills a place, or to be filled with a loud sound □ *The scream resounded through the building.* (ressoar)

- **resounding** /rɪˈzaʊndɪŋ/ ADJECTIVE
1 complete or very great 🔹 *a resounding victory* 🔹 *The tour has been a resounding success.* (ressonante)
2 loud and filling a place with sound □ *It hit the floor with a resounding crash.* (ressonante)

resource /rɪˈzɔːs/ NOUN [plural resources] something that you have and are able to use (recurso) 🔹 *the country's natural resources* (recursos naturais) □ *He blamed a lack of resources for the delays.*

- **resourceful** /rɪˈzɔːsfʊl/ ADJECTIVE good at finding ways of doing things and solving problems □ *We had little to work with so we had to be resourceful.* (engenhoso)

- **resourcefulness** /rɪˈzɔːsfʊlnɪs/ NOUN, NO PLURAL the quality of being resourceful (engenhosidade)

respect /rɪˈspekt/ ▶ NOUN [plural respects]
1 the feeling of admiring someone or something because of their behaviour or their achievements □ *+ of She earned the respect of her colleagues.* □ *+ for I have the utmost respect for Mr Williams.* (respeito)
2 polite behaviour towards someone □ *+ for Their behaviour shows a lack of respect for others.* (respeito) 🔹 *He treats everyone with respect.* (tratar com respeito)
3 a feeling that something is important or powerful and should be treated carefully (respeito) 🔹 *The sea can be very dangerous – you must treat it with respect.* (tratar com respeito)
4 a part of something or a way of thinking about it □ *In many respects, the two boys are very similar.* □ *The plan was good in every respect.* (aspecto)
5 with respect to someone/something a formal phrase meaning to do with someone or something □ *No decision has yet been made with respect to the new stadium.* (a respeito de alguém/algo)
▶ VERB [respects, respecting, respected]
1 to admire someone or something because of their behaviour or achievements □ *I respect her enormously.* (respeitar) 🔹 *He was highly respected in the local community.* (altamente respeitado)
2 to treat someone politely and show care for their beliefs, rights, etc. □ *We ask the media to respect her privacy.* □ *They have failed to respect the human rights of the refugees.* (respeitar)
3 to agree to obey a rule, a decision, etc. □ *We will respect their decision.* (respeitar)

- **respectability** /rɪˌspektəˈbɪlɪti/ NOUN, NO PLURAL the quality of being accepted by society as good, correct, honest, etc. □ *His writing has only recently achieved mainstream respectability.* (respeitabilidade)

- **respectable** /rɪˈspektəbəl/ ADJECTIVE
  1 accepted by society as good, correct, honest, etc. □ *Simon comes from a respectable family.* (**respeitável**)
  2 quite good □ *a perfectly respectable score* (**respeitável**)
- **respectably** /rɪˈspektəblɪ/ ADVERB
  1 in a socially acceptable way □ *She was respectably dressed.* (**respeitavelmente**)
  2 quite well □ *He played very respectably.* (**respeitavelmente**)
- **respected** /rɪˈspektɪd/ ADJECTIVE admired by many people □ *She was a respected lawyer.* (**respeitado**)
- **respectful** /rɪˈspektfʊl/ ADJECTIVE showing respect for someone or something □ *a respectful attitude* □ *I stayed a respectful distance away.* (**respeitador**)
- **respectfully** /rɪˈspektfʊlɪ/ ADVERB in a way that shows respect □ *Everyone respectfully bowed their heads as the coffin went past.* (**respeitosamente**)

respective /rɪˈspektɪv/ ADJECTIVE to do with each person or thing that has been mentioned separately □ *David and Diane are each good at their respective jobs.* (**respectivo**)

- **respectively** /rɪˈspektɪvlɪ/ ADVERB in the same order as the things already mentioned □ *Colin, Jane and Ian were given £5, £3 and £1 respectively.* (**respectivamente**)

respiration /ˌrespəˈreɪʃən/ NOUN, NO PLURAL
1 a formal word for breathing (**respiração**)
2 when living things make energy from food. A biology word. (**respiração**)

- **respirator** /ˈrespəreɪtə(r)/ NOUN [*plural* **respirators**] a machine that helps someone to breathe when they are too ill to do it naturally (**respirador**)
- **respiratory** /rɪˈspɪrətərɪ/ ADJECTIVE to do with breathing (**respiratório**) 🔁 *the respiratory system*

respite /ˈrespaɪt/ NOUN, NO PLURAL a period of rest from something unpleasant or difficult □ *The pain continued without respite for about two hours.* (**pausa**)

resplendent /rɪˈsplendənt/ ADJECTIVE very bright and attractive in a grand way □ *She was resplendent in a red satin dress.* (**resplandecente**)

respond /rɪˈspɒnd/ VERB [**responds, responding, responded**]
1 to answer or to react □ *If someone hits you, you tend to respond by hitting back.* □ *'That's not my problem,' Gina responded.* □ *Police responded quickly to the call.* (**responder**)
2 to improve as a result of treatment □ *She is responding well to treatment.* (**reagir**)

- **response** /rɪˈspɒns/ NOUN [*plural* **responses**] an answer or a reaction □ *His response was a shake of his head.* □ *What was the response of his colleagues to his announcement?* (**resposta**)

responsibility /rɪˌspɒnsəˈbɪlɪtɪ/ NOUN [*plural* **responsibilities**]
1 something that you must do or deal with □ + **for** *The manager has responsibility for all the business.* □ + **of** *The first responsibility of a government is to protect its citizens.* □ + **to do something** *It's my responsibility to make sure all the doors are locked.* □ *They share the childcare responsibilities.* (**responsabilidade**)
2 blame for doing something, usually something bad (**responsabilidade**) 🔁 *I take full responsibility for the mistake.* (**assumir toda a responsabilidade**) 🔁 *No one has yet claimed responsibility for the bombing.* (**assumir a responsabilidade**)

- **responsible** /rɪˈspɒnsəbəl/ ADJECTIVE
  1 if you are responsible for something, you are the person who must do it or deal with it □ + **for** *Who is responsible for keeping the money?* □ *the minister responsible for transport* (**responsável**)
  2 if you are responsible for something which happens, you are to blame for it □ + **for** *Is human activity directly responsible for global warming?* (**responsável**) 🔁 *He felt partly responsible for the mess.* (**sentir-se responsável**) 🔁 *We hold the company responsible for her death.* (**considerar responsável**)
  3 sensible and able to be trusted □ *I'm looking for a responsible teenager to babysit.* (**responsável**)
  4 involving important jobs or decisions □ *He holds a responsible position within the company.* (**de responsabilidade**)
- **responsibly** /rɪˈspɒnsɪblɪ/ ADVERB in a sensible way, showing good judgment □ *Drivers must act responsibly.* □ *He called on industry to behave more responsibly.* (**com responsabilidade**)

responsive /rɪˈspɒnsɪv/ ADJECTIVE
1 reacting in a quick and positive way □ *The disease was much more responsive to the second drug.* □ *Then steering on this car is much more responsive.* (**responsivo**)
2 willing to talk or answer questions □ *I tried to make conversation, but he wasn't very responsive.* (**correspondente**)

rest /rest/ ▶ NOUN [*plural* **rests**]
1 the rest the part of something that is left, or the people or things that are left □ *I don't want to spend the rest of my life here.* □ *The rest of the country will have showers.* □ *I want half of you in this room and the rest outside.* (**resto**)
2 a time when you relax or sleep (**descanso**) 🔁 *Why don't you have a rest before dinner?* (**tirar um descanso**)
3 come to rest to stop moving □ *The coin rolled off the table and came to rest under his feet.* □ *Her eyes came to rest on the letter.* (**parar, ficar parado**)

▶ VERB [**rests, resting, rested**]
1 to relax or sleep after an activity □ *You should rest every few minutes when you're lifting such heavy weights.* (**descansar**)

restart

2 if you rest part of your body, you stop using it so that it becomes less tired ◻ *Let's stop and rest our legs for a minute.* (descansar)
3 to be supported by something, or to put something on something else for support ◻ *He left his spade resting against a wall.* ◻ *Mo rested her hands on the piano keys for a moment.* (apoiar, pousar)
♦ PHRASAL VERB **rest on something** to depend on something ◻ *The success of the business rests on one product.* (depende de)

restart /ˌriːˈstɑːt/ VERB [restarts, restarting, restarted]
1 to turn a computer off and then on again ◻ *Have you tried restarting your computer?* (reinicializar o computador)
2 to start again or to start something again ◻ *The course restarts in September.* (reiniciar)

restaurant /ˈrestərɒnt/ NOUN [plural restaurants] a place where you can buy and eat a meal ◻ *a Chinese restaurant* (restaurante)

restful /ˈrestfʊl/ ADJECTIVE making you feel calm and relaxed ◻ *restful music* (repousante)

restless /ˈrestlɪs/ ADJECTIVE not able to stay still or quiet because you are nervous, worried or bored ◻ *The audience began to get restless after about an hour.* (inquieto, impaciente)
• **restlessly** /ˈrestlɪsli/ ADVERB in an restless way ◻ *The horses stamped restlessly.* (inquietamente)
• **restlessness** /ˈrestlɪsnɪs/ NOUN, NO PLURAL a feeling of being restless (inquietação)

restoration /ˌrestəˈreɪʃən/ NOUN, NO PLURAL when you make something the way it was before ◻ *After the fire, the restoration of the church took three years.* ◻ *the restoration of democracy* (restauração)

• **restore** /rɪˈstɔː(r)/ VERB [restores, restoring, restored]
1 to bring something back that existed before 🔵 *Police struggled to restore order.* ◻ *He's trying to restore public confidence in the government.* (restaurar)
2 to repair something so it is like it was before ◻ *The house had been restored to its former glory.* (restaurar)
3 a formal word meaning to give something back to the person it belongs to ◻ *The necklace has now been restored to its grateful owner.* (instituir)

restrain /rɪˈstreɪn/ VERB [restrains, restraining, restrained]
1 to stop someone from doing something, often using force ◻ *He attacked the man as friends tried to restrain him.* (conter)
2 to control your emotions or behaviour ◻ *We had to restrain ourselves from laughing.* (conter, controlar-se)
3 a formal word meaning to stop something increasing ◻ *The government needs to restrain spending.* (conter)

671

result

• **restrained** /rɪˈstreɪnd/ ADJECTIVE calm and not showing much emotion ◻ *I expected him to be furious, but he was very restrained.* (contido)
• **restraint** /rɪˈstreɪnt/ NOUN [plural restraints]
1 no plural when you control your emotions or behaviour ◻ *She behaved with amazing restraint.* (controle) 🔵 *He urged both sides in the dispute to show restraint.* (controlar-se)
2 something that prevents you from doing something or stops something from increasing ◻ *Wage restraints have angered unions.* (repressão)
3 something that limits someone's physical movement ◻ *Police used restraints to keep him on the bed.* (conter)

restrict /rɪˈstrɪkt/ VERB [restricts, restricting, restricted] to limit something ◻ *We are restricting people to one ticket each.* ◻ *Parents can restrict children's access to certain websites.* (restringir)
• **restriction** /rɪˈstrɪkʃən/ NOUN [plural restrictions] a limit on something ◻ *Are there any parking restrictions on this road?* (restrição) 🔵 *Airlines imposed restrictions on hand luggage.* (impor restrições)
• **restrictive** /rɪˈstrɪktɪv/ ADJECTIVE limiting something, often too much ◻ *restrictive laws* (restritivo)

restroom /ˈrestrʊm/ NOUN [plural restrooms] a US word for a room with a toilet, especially for public use (banheiro)

restructure /ˌriːˈstrʌktʃə(r)/ VERB [restructures, restructuring, restructured] to change the way a company, system, etc. is organized ◻ *They have radically restructured the business.* (reestruturar)
• **restructuring** /ˌriːˈstrʌktʃərɪŋ/ NOUN, NO PLURAL when you restructure something (reestruturação)

result /rɪˈzʌlt/ ▶ NOUN [plural results]
1 what happens because of something else ◻ *+ of This could be another result of global warming.* (resultado) 🔵 *He died as a result of the accident.* (como resultado de) 🔵 *He tried to play again too quickly, with the result that he made the injury worse.* (como resultado)
2 the score or the winner at the end of a competition, an election, etc. ◻ *the election result* ◻ *+ of Do you know the result of yesterday's match?* (resultado)
3 the information you get at the end of a study or an experiment ◻ *+ of the results of the survey* (resultado) 🔵 *the test results* (resultados do teste)
4 the score that you get in an exam (resultado) 🔵 *She got good exam results.* (resultados do exame)
5 results success in something you do (resultados) 🔵 *His methods get results.* (dar resultado)
▶ VERB [results, resulting, resulted] to happen because of something else ◻ *The fire apparently resulted from a dropped cigarette.* (resultar)
♦ PHRASAL VERB **result in something** to cause something ◻ *The changes will result in the loss of 300 jobs.* (resultar em alguma coisa)

resume /rɪˈzjuːm/ VERB [resumes, resuming, resumed] a formal word meaning to start again □ *Normal services will resume next week.* (recomeçar, retomar)

résumé /ˈrezjuːmeɪ/ NOUN [plural résumés]
1 a mainly US word for a list of your qualifications and the jobs you have done, that you show to someone you want to work for (currículo)
2 a short explanation or description of something □ *I gave them a brief résumé of what had been discussed.* (resumo)

resumption /rɪˈzʌmpʃən/ NOUN, NO PLURAL a formal word meaning when something resumes (= starts again) □ *the resumption of peace talks* (retomada)

resurgence /rɪˈsɜːdʒəns/ NOUN, NO PLURAL when something begins to happen again, often in a stronger way than before □ *There was a resurgence of violence in the area.* (ressurgimento)

resurrect /ˌrezəˈrekt/ VERB [resurrects, resurrecting, resurrected] to bring something back into use after a long time □ *They've resurrected plans for a tram system.* (ressuscitar)
• **resurrection** /ˌrezəˈrekʃən/ NOUN, NO PLURAL
1 when you resurrect something (ressurreição)
2 the Resurrection the Christian belief that Jesus Christ came back to life after his death (Ressurreição de Cristo)

resuscitate /rɪˈsʌsɪteɪt/ VERB [resuscitates, resuscitating, resuscitated] to make someone start breathing again when they have stopped □ *Doctors were unable to resuscitate him.* (ressuscitar)
• **resuscitation** /rɪˌsʌsɪˈteɪʃən/ NOUN, NO PLURAL when you resuscitate someone (ressuscitação) *Someone gave him mouth-to-mouth resuscitation.* (ressuscitação boca a boca)

retail /ˈriːteɪl/ ▶ NOUN, NO PLURAL the selling of goods to the public, usually in shops □ *I work in retail.* (varejo)
▶ VERB [retails, retailing, retailed] to be sold at a particular price □ *The device will retail at £48.* (vender a varejo/a retalho)
• **retailer** /ˈriːteɪlə(r)/ NOUN [plural retailers] a person or company that sells goods to the public, usually in a shop □ *a clothing retailer* (varejista)
• **retailing** /ˈriːteɪlɪŋ/ NOUN, NO PLURAL the business of selling goods to the public (comércio varejista)

retain /rɪˈteɪn/ VERB [retains, retaining, retained] to keep something □ *A smaller house would retain heat better in the winter.* (reter)

retaliate /rɪˈtælieɪt/ VERB [retaliates, retaliating, retaliated] to do something bad to someone because they have done something bad to you □ *He retaliated by pushing the other player in the chest.* (retaliar, revidar)
• **retaliation** /rɪˌtæliˈeɪʃən/ NOUN, NO PLURAL when someone retaliates (retaliação) *The bombing was in retaliation for recent killings of rebel fighters.* (em retaliação)

retch /retʃ/ VERB [retches, retching, retched] to almost vomit □ *The smell made me retch.* (ânsia de vômito)

retention /rɪˈtenʃən/ NOUN, NO PLURAL when something is kept or not allowed to leave or escape □ *Pay is a key factor in the recruitment and retention of staff.* (retenção)

rethink /riːˈθɪŋk/ ▶ VERB [rethinks, rethinking, rethought] to think about something again and decide what changes to make □ *We urge the government to rethink its policy on immigration.* (repensar)
▶ NOUN, NO PLURAL /ˈriːθɪŋk/ the act of rethinking something □ *The policy needs a complete rethink.* (reconsideração)

reticence /ˈretɪsəns/ NOUN, NO PLURAL the quality of being reticent (discrição)

reticent /ˈretɪsənt/ ADJECTIVE giving little information □ *He was very reticent about his plans.* (discreto)

retina /ˈretɪnə/ NOUN [plural retinas or retinae] the area at the back of your eye that receives light and sends signals to your brain. A biology word. (retina)

retinue /ˈretɪnjuː/ NOUN [plural retinues] a group of people who travel with an important or famous person (comitiva)

retire /rɪˈtaɪə(r)/ VERB [retires, retiring, retired]
1 to stop working because you are old □ *Many people retire at 65.* □ *+ from She had just retired from a career in nursing.* □ *+ as He retired as director in 2005.* (aposentar(-se))
2 a formal word meaning to go to a quiet place □ *+ to He retired to his bedroom.* (retirar-se)
• **retired** /rɪˈtaɪəd/ ADJECTIVE no longer working because you are old □ *a retired teacher* (aposentado)
• **retirement** /rɪˈtaɪəmənt/ ▶ NOUN [plural retirements]
1 the period of time after you stop working because you are old □ *I hope you enjoy your retirement.* (aposentadoria)
2 the act of stopping work because you are old □ *He announced his retirement from politics.* (aposentadoria) *Tom had taken early retirement* (= stopped working before the usual age). (obter aposentadoria antecipada)
▶ ADJECTIVE to do with the time when you stop working because you are old (referente à aposentadoria) *He is close to retirement age.* (idade de se aposentar) □ *a retirement party*
• **retiring** /rɪˈtaɪərɪŋ/ ADJECTIVE shy and talking little (retraído)

retort /rɪˈtɔːt/ ▶ VERB [retorts, retorting, retorted] to answer quickly in an angry or humorous way □ *'You don't scare me,' she retorted.* (replicar, retorquir)
▶ NOUN [plural retorts] a quick and angry or humorous answer □ *an angry retort* (réplica, retorção)

retrace

retrace /rɪˈtreɪs/ VERB [retraces, retracing, retraced] (retroceder) **retrace your steps** to walk back exactly the same way that you came □ *I retraced my steps but there was no sign of my wallet.* (voltar para trás)

retrain /ˌriːˈtreɪn/ VERB [retrains, retraining, retrained] to learn new skills for a different job □ *He retrained as a plumber.* (fazer treinamento para exercer nova atividade)

• **retraining** /ˌriːˈtreɪnɪŋ/ NOUN, NO PLURAL learning new skills so that you can get a different job (treinamento para exercer nova atividade)

retreat /rɪˈtriːt/ ▶ NOUN [plural **retreats**]
1 when you go to a place which is safer or quieter (retirada, fuga (para se proteger)) 🖫 *When they had gone, I beat a hasty retreat* (= went very quickly) *back into the house.* (bater em retirada)
2 a quiet place where people go to rest and relax □ *He spent the weekend at the presidential retreat at Camp David.* (retiro)
3 when an army moves back because it does not want to fight □ *a strategic retreat* (retirada)
▶ VERB [retreats, retreating, retreated]
1 to go somewhere safer or quieter □ *He retreated to the car and phoned the police.* (retirar-se)
2 if an army retreats, it moves back because it does not want to fight (retirar-se)

retrieve /rɪˈtriːv/ VERB [retrieves, retrieving, retrieved]
1 to find something and bring it back □ *He retrieved his pen from under the sofa.* (recuperar)
2 to get information that is stored on a computer (recuperar)

• **retriever** /rɪˈtriːvə(r)/ NOUN [plural **retrievers**] a type of dog (raça de cachorro)

return /rɪˈtɜːn/ ▶ VERB [returns, returning, returned]
1 to go or come back to a place □ *We fly out on Friday and return the following Wednesday.* □ + *to We all returned to our classrooms.* □ + *from He returned from his skiing holiday with a broken leg.* (voltar, retornar) 🖫 *All the air crew have returned safely.* (voltar a salvo)
2 to start to happen or exist again □ *When we reached the town, our fears returned.* □ *Her cancer has returned.* (voltar, retornar)
3 to take, put or send something back □ *Please return your books by Friday.* □ + *to All sports equipment should be returned to the gym.* (devolver)
4 to do something to someone that they have done to you (devolver) 🖫 *She never returns my calls* (= telephones me back). 🖫 *The soldiers immediately returned fire* (= shot at the people who were shooting them). (devolver tiros) □ *He returned my smile.*
5 return a verdict to say whether someone is guilty of a crime or not (proferir o veredicto)
◆ PHRASAL VERB **return to something**

1 to go back to the condition or situation that someone or something was in before (retornar, voltar) 🖫 *Life in the city is beginning to return to normal.* (voltar ao normal)
2 to start doing something again (retornar) 🖫 *The miners were forced to return to work.* □ *He turned away and returned to his gardening.* (retornar ao trabalho)
3 to start talking again about a subject that has already been discussed □ *Can we return to the issue of safety?* (voltar)
▶ NOUN [plural **returns**]
1 when someone comes or goes back to a place □ + *to On my return to the house, I found the door wide open.* □ + *from After his return from Africa, he settled in London.* (volta, retorno) 🖫 *They celebrated the safe return of the climbers.* (retorno a salvo)
2 when something starts to happen or exist again □ + *of Police ensured the return of order to the area.* □ + *to The opposition has demanded a return to democracy.* (retorno)
3 when something is taken, put or sent back □ + *of We are delighted at the safe return of the stolen paintings.* (retorno)
4 in return in exchange for something □ *When we're away, she walks our dog, and in return I water her plants.* □ *He gave me some CDs in return for the book.* (em troca de)
5 when someone starts doing something again □ + *to We are expecting her return to work next week.* (retorno)
6 a key on a computer keyboard that starts a new line or makes the computer do something (tecla para voltar) 🖫 *Type your password and press return.* (apertar a tecla de retorno)
7 a ticket that allows you to travel to a place and back again □ *I'd like a return to Glasgow, please.* (bilhete de ida e volta)
8 something that has been taken back, especially to a shop □ *All the tickets have been sold, but there may be some returns later.* (devolução)
9 a profit □ + *of The shares generated a return of over 20%.* □ + *on We were hoping for a higher return on our investment.* (retorno, lucro)
10 an official form that you have to complete, especially to do with tax (devolução) 🖫 *I haven't filled in my tax return yet.* (restituição do imposto de renda)
▶ ADJECTIVE
1 to do with a journey to and from a place (de ida e volta) 🖫 *a return ticket/trip* (passagem de ida e volta)
2 to do with the part of a journey when you are coming back (de volta) 🖫 *The return journey took over 4 hours.* □ *Our return flight was delayed.* (viagem de volta)
3 a return match or game is the second one of two between the same people (revanche)

reunion /riːˈjuːnjən/ NOUN [plural **reunions**] a meeting of people such as friends or family members who have not seen each other for a long time □ *a family reunion* (reunião)

• **reunite** /ˌriːjuːˈnaɪt/ VERB [**reunites, reuniting, reunited**] people are reunited when they meet again after not seeing each other for a long time □ *The injured soldiers were flown home and were reunited with their families.* (reunir)

Rev /rev/ ABBREVIATION Reverend, used in writing □ *Rev Pat Green* (reverendo)

rev /rev/ VERB [**revs, revving, revved**] to make an engine go faster (acelerar)

reveal /rɪˈviːl/ VERB [**reveals, revealing, revealed**]
1 to tell someone something that is secret or surprising □ *He refused to reveal details of the project.* (revelar)
2 to show something that you could not see before □ *The mobile phone has a screen which slides back to reveal the keyboard.* (revelar)

• **revealing** /rɪˈviːlɪŋ/ ADJECTIVE
1 telling you something that you did not know □ *a revealing interview* (revelador)
2 revealing clothes show a part of the body that is usually covered □ *a revealing dress* (revelador)

revel /ˈrevəl/
♦ PHRASAL VERB [**revels, revelling/US reveling, revelled/US reveled**] **revel in something** to enjoy a situation very much □ *Maxine revelled in all the attention she got.* (divertir-se com)

revelation /ˌrevəˈleɪʃən/ NOUN [plural **revelations**]
1 a surprising fact which was secret □ *The article was full of revelations about his private life.* (revelação)
2 a good experience which surprises you very much □ *Seeing them in concert was a revelation.* (revelação)

reveler /ˈrevələ(r)/ NOUN [plural **revelers**] the US spelling of reveller (*ver* reveller)

reveller /ˈrevələ(r)/ NOUN [plural **revellers**] someone who is having fun in a noisy way at a party (folião, farrista)

revenge /rɪˈvendʒ/ NOUN, NO PLURAL when you hurt or upset someone because they have hurt or upset you or someone that you love (vingança) ▣ *Ben had ruined her life and she was determined to get revenge.* (conseguir vingança) ▣ *a revenge attack* (ataque de vingança)

revenue /ˈrevənjuː/ NOUN, NO PLURAL money that a business or government gets □ *Most of the government's revenue comes from taxes.* (rendimento)

reverberate /rɪˈvɜːbəreɪt/ VERB [**reverberates, reverberating, reverberated**] if a sound reverberates, it comes back and you hear it again □ *The sound of gunfire reverberated along the valley.* (repercutir)

• **reverberation** /rɪˌvɜːbəˈreɪʃən/ NOUN [plural **reverberations**] when a sound reverberates (repercussão)

revere /rɪˈvɪə(r)/ VERB [**reveres, revering, revered**] a formal word meaning to respect and admire someone or something very much □ *It's a holy site revered by Jews and Muslims.* (reverenciar)

• **reverence** /ˈrevərəns/ NOUN, NO PLURAL great respect and admiration (reverência)

• **Reverend** /ˈrevərənd/ NOUN [plural **Reverends**] a title used before the name of some Christian priests □ *Reverend Ian Black* (reverendo)

reversal /rɪˈvɜːsəl/ NOUN [plural **reversals**] a change so that something becomes the opposite of what it was before □ *The win was a dramatic reversal of fortune for the team.* (inversão)

reverse /rɪˈvɜːs/ ▶ VERB [**reverses, reversing, reversed**]
1 if a vehicle reverses, it moves backwards □ *A car was reversing.* (dar ré, voltar)
2 to make a vehicle move backwards □ *She reversed the car into the parking space.* (dar ré)
3 to change something so that it is the opposite of what it was before (revogar) ▣ *The government has reversed its decision.* (revogar sua decisão)

▶ NOUN, NO PLURAL
1 the reverse the opposite □ *It's not bad news – in fact, the reverse.* (o oposto)
2 in reverse in the opposite order □ *We visited the same places as them but in reverse.* (ao contrário)
3 the position which you put a car's controls in to make it move backwards □ *I put the car in reverse.* (em marcha a ré)

▶ ADJECTIVE opposite to what you expect □ *The policy had the reverse effect.* (oposto)

• **reversible** /rɪˈvɜːsəbəl/ ADJECTIVE
1 able to be changed back □ *This is not a reversible process.* (reversível)
2 reversible clothes can be worn with the inside part on the outside □ *a reversible jacket* (reversível, de dupla face)

revert /rɪˈvɜːt/ VERB [**reverts, reverting, reverted**] to go back to the way something was before □ *Many exprisoners revert to a life of crime.* (reverter)

review /rɪˈvjuː/ ▶ VERB [**reviews, reviewing, reviewed**]
1 to examine something again, often in order to decide if changes should be made □ *The company is reviewing its safety procedures following the accident.* □ *Lawyers are reviewing the case.* (rever)
2 to write your opinion of a new book, play, etc. □ *She reviewed the book for the New York Times.* (resenhar)
3 the US word for revise (= study) (revisar)

▶ NOUN [plural **reviews**]
1 when something is examined again, often in order to decide if changes need to be made □ + *of* *The government is conducting a review of the policy.* (revisão)

revise — rhetoric

2 under review being examined again □ *All our contracts are under review.* (**em revisão**)

3 an article which gives someone's opinion of a new book, play, etc. □ *a film review* (**críticas**) □ *The play got some good reviews.* □ *+ of He wrote a review of the book.* (**obter críticas**)

- **reviewer** /rɪˈvjuːə(r)/ NOUN [plural **reviewers**] someone who writes their opinion of new books, plays, etc. (**crítico**)

revise /rɪˈvaɪz/ VERB [**revises, revising, revised**]
1 to change something, often in order to improve it □ *The revised edition of the dictionary has hundreds of new words in it.* □ *We've had to revise our plans.* (**rever**)
2 to study for an exam by looking again at the work you have done □ *+ for Guy was busy revising for his Chinese exam.* (**rever**)

- **revision** /rɪˈvɪʒən/ NOUN [plural **revisions**]
1 change made in order to improve something □ *The law needs revision.* (**revisão**)
2 work that you do before an exam, by looking at work you have already done (**revisão**) □ *I need to do some revision for my history test.* (**fazer revisão**)

revival /rɪˈvaɪvəl/ NOUN [plural **revivals**]
1 a performance of something that has not been performed for many years □ *a revival of an old musical* (**renascimento**)
2 an increase in how popular or successful something is □ *There has been a revival of interest in his music.* (**renascimento**)

revive /rɪˈvaɪv/ VERB [**revives, reviving, revived**]
1 to make someone conscious again □ *Doctors were unable to revive him.* (**reanimar, ressuscitar**)
2 to make something popular or successful again □ *He was trying to revive his career.* (**reviver**)
3 to make someone feel better and less tired □ *A cool shower should revive you.* (**reanimar**)

revolt /rɪˈvəʊlt/ ▶ NOUN [plural **revolts**]
1 when a group of people use violence in order to change a government (**revolta**)
2 when people refuse to accept the authority of a leader □ *The leader is facing a revolt by members of his party.* (**revolta, rebelião**)
▶ VERB [**revolts, revolting, revolted**]
1 to use violence in order to change a government (**rebelar-se contra**)
2 to refuse to accept the authority of a leader (**rebelar-se contra**)
3 if you are revolted by something, it shocks you or makes you feel ill □ *I was revolted by the thought of eating worms.* (**enojar-se**)

- **revolting** /rɪˈvəʊltɪŋ/ ADJECTIVE extremely unpleasant □ *a revolting smell* (**nojento**)

revolution /ˌrevəˈluːʃən/ NOUN [plural **revolutions**]
1 a time when people use violence to change a government □ *the French Revolution of 1789* (**revolução**)
2 a complete change in something such as an industry or society □ *Computers have led to a revolution in the way we work.* (**revolução**)
3 a complete turn of something such as a wheel (**revolução**)

- **revolutionary** /ˌrevəˈluːʃənəri/ ▶ ADJECTIVE
1 completely new and different □ *revolutionary technology* (**revolucionário**)
2 to do with a political revolution □ *Castro's revolutionary movement* (**revolucionário**)
▶ NOUN [plural **revolutionaries**] someone who is involved in a political revolution (**revolucionário**)

- **revolutionize** or **revolutionise** /ˌrevəˈluːʃənaɪz/ VERB [**revolutionizes, revolutionizing, revolutionized**] to completely change something and make it better □ *The drug could revolutionize the way that cancer is treated.* (**revolucionar**)

revolve /rɪˈvɒlv/ VERB [**revolves, revolving, revolved**] to move in a circle around something □ *The Earth revolves around the sun.* (**girar**)
◆ PHRASAL VERB **revolve around someone/something** to have something as the main part □ *The film revolves around two teenage criminals.* (**girar em torno de, tratar-se de**)

- **revolver** /rɪˈvɒlvə(r)/ NOUN [plural **revolvers**] a type of small gun (**revólver**)
- **revolving** /rɪˈvɒlvɪŋ/ ADJECTIVE moving in a circle □ *a revolving door* (**giratório**)

reward /rɪˈwɔːd/ ▶ NOUN [plural **rewards**] something you get for doing something good or useful □ *financial rewards* □ *+ for The victim's family are offering a £5,000 reward for any information that helps catch the killer.* □ *He got his reward for all his hard work when the team scored a goal.* (**recompensa**)
▶ VERB [**rewards, rewarding, rewarded**] to give someone something good for something they have done □ *+ for He was rewarded for all his hard work.* □ *+ with The baby rewarded me with a smile as I picked her up.* (**recompensar**)

- **rewarding** /rɪˈwɔːdɪŋ/ ADJECTIVE giving you a feeling of satisfaction □ *Nursing can be a very rewarding job.* (**compensador**)

rewind /riːˈwaɪnd/ VERB [**rewinds, rewinding, rewound**] to make a tape (= long strip on which pictures and sound are recorded) move back towards the beginning (**rebobinar**)

rewrite /riːˈraɪt/ ▶ VERB [**rewrites, rewriting, rewrote, rewritten**] to write something again, making changes to it □ *You'll have to rewrite this because it is full of mistakes.* (**reescrever**)
▶ NOUN /ˈriːraɪt/ [plural **rewrites**] something which has been written again (**texto reescrito**)

rhetoric /ˈretərɪk/ NOUN, NO PLURAL words that are intended to make people believe or admire you, but which are not sincere □ *political rhetoric* (**retórica**)

- **rhetorical** /rɪˈtɒrɪkəl/ ADJECTIVE a rhetorical question is one that is not a real question because you do not intend anyone to answer it (**retórica**)

rheumatism /ˈruːmətɪzəm/ NOUN, NO PLURAL a disease that makes your knees, hips, etc. and muscles painful (**reumatismo**)

rhino /ˈraɪnəʊ/ NOUN [plural **rhinos**] an informal word for rhinoceros (**rinoceronte**)

rhinoceros /raɪˈnɒsərəs/ NOUN [plural **rhinoceroses**] a large, grey animal from Africa and Asia that has thick skin and a horn on its nose (**rinoceronte**)

rhizome /ˈraɪzəʊm/ NOUN [plural **rhizomes**] a thick stem of a plant that grows along or under the ground. A biology word.

rhododendron /ˌrəʊdəˈdendrən/ NOUN [plural **rhododendrons**] a large bush with big flowers (**rododendro, azálea**)

rhombus /ˈrɒmbəs/ NOUN [plural **rhombuses** or **rhombi**] a shape with four straight sides and four angles that are not 90°. A maths word. (**rombo**)

rhubarb /ˈruːbɑːb/ NOUN, NO PLURAL a plant that has red stems which you cook and eat as fruit (**ruibarbo**)

rhyme /raɪm/ ▶ VERB [**rhymes, rhyming, rhymed**] if words rhyme, they end with the same sound □ 'Ghost' rhymes with 'toast'. (**rimar**)
▶ NOUN [plural **rhymes**]
1 a word that sounds like another, or a pair of words that have a similar sound □ I don't think there is a rhyme for 'orange'. (**rima**)
2 a short poem or song using words which rhyme □ a book of children's rhymes (**poema, poesia**)
3 poetry that uses words which sound similar at the end of each line □ The story was written in rhyme. (**rima**)

rhythm /ˈrɪðəm/ NOUN [plural **rhythms**] a repeated pattern of sounds or movements □ He had an irregular heart rhythm. □ + **of** Amy's foot was tapping to the rhythm of the music. (**ritmo**) 🔁 She has a good *sense of rhythm*. (**noção de ritmo**)
• **rhythmic** /ˈrɪðmɪk/ ADJECTIVE a rhythmic sound or movement has a repeated pattern (**rítmico**)

rib /rɪb/ NOUN [plural **ribs**] one of the curved bones in your chest, around your heart and lungs (**costela**)

ribbon /ˈrɪbən/ NOUN [plural **ribbons**] a long, narrow piece of cloth, used for example to tie your hair up, or as a decoration on a present (**fita**)

rib cage /ˈrɪb ˌkeɪdʒ/ NOUN [plural **rib cages**] the set of bones that form your chest (**caixa torácica**)

rice /raɪs/ NOUN, NO PLURAL brown or white grains that you cook and eat as food □ *boiled rice* (**arroz**) 🔁 a *grain of rice* (**grão de arroz**) □ *brown rice* □ *rice fields*

rich /rɪtʃ/ ▶ ADJECTIVE [**richer, richest**]
1 having a lot of money □ Her Dad's very rich. □ rich countries (**rico**) 🔁 He was looking for ways to *get rich* (= become rich). (**ficar rico**)
2 full of something good (**rico**) 🔁 Nuts and seeds are a particularly *rich source of* iron. (**fonte rica de**) □ + **in** Oranges are rich in vitamin C.
3 full of interesting events, ideas, etc. □ The city has a very rich history. □ The area is home to a rich variety of wildlife. (**rico**)
4 rich food contains a lot of butter or cream □ The cake was very rich so I only managed a small piece. (**rico**)
5 rich colours are strong and bright □ The carpet was a rich red. (**forte**)
▶ NOUN, NO PLURAL **the rich** people who have a lot of money □ She enjoyed reading about the lifestyles of the rich and famous. (**rico**)
• **riches** /ˈrɪtʃɪz/ PLURAL NOUN a literary word meaning a lot of money and expensive things (**riquezas**)
• **richly** /ˈrɪtʃli/ ADVERB
1 in a beautiful way, often using expensive and brightly coloured materials □ The rooms were richly decorated. (**ricamente**)
2 if something is richly deserved, you deserve it very much (**ricamente**)
3 with a lot of money □ She was richly rewarded. (**ricamente**)

Richter scale /ˈrɪktə ˌskeɪl/ NOUN, NO PLURAL the Richter scale a way of measuring how strong earthquakes (= the ground suddenly moving) are. A geography word. (**escala Richter**)

rickshaw /ˈrɪkʃɔː/ NOUN [plural **rickshaws**] a type of vehicle used in East Asia, in which passengers are pulled by someone who is walking or riding a bicycle (**riquixá**)

ricochet /ˈrɪkəʃeɪ/ VERB [**ricochets, ricocheting, ricocheted**] if a bullet or stone ricochets off something, it hits it and moves away from it (**ricochetear**)

rid /rɪd/ ADJECTIVE
1 get rid of something (a) to throw something away or give it to someone else □ My parents got rid of the old sofa and bought a new one. (b) to make something go away that you do not want □ I opened the window to get rid of the smell. □ I can't seem to get rid of this cold. (**livrar-se de, desembaraçar-se**)
2 get rid of someone to make someone go away □ He arrived at 7 o'clock and we couldn't get rid of him. (**livrar-se de**)
◆ PHRASAL VERB [**rids, ridding, rid**] **rid someone/ something of something** to get rid of something bad □ Scientists are working to rid the world of this virus. (**livrar alguém/algo de algo**)
• **riddance** /ˈrɪdəns/ NOUN, NO PLURAL (**livramento**) **Good riddance!** said when you are pleased that someone or something has gone (**já vai tarde!**)

ridden /ˈrɪdən/ PAST PARTICIPLE OF **ride** (**ver ride**)

riddle /ˈrɪdəl/ NOUN [plural **riddles**]
1 a strange or confusing question with a clever answer that you have to work out (**charada**)

riddled

2 a mystery that is difficult to solve □ *How the burglar got into the house is a bit of a riddle.* (enigma)

riddled /'rɪdəld/ ADJECTIVE riddled with something (**crivado**) (a) full of something bad □ *The letter was riddled with errors.* (b) full of a lot of small holes □ *The glass was riddled with holes where the bullets had hit it.*

ride /raɪd/ ▶ VERB [rides, riding, rode, ridden] **1** to travel on a bicycle, motorcycle or horse □ *I learned to ride a bike when I was six.* □ *Do you ride* (= ride a horse)? □ *He turned and rode off.* (**montar, andar de**)

2 to travel in or on a vehicle □ *She had been riding around in the car all day.* (**passear**)

◆ PHRASAL VERBS **ride on something** if one thing rides on something else, it depends on it in order to be successful □ *The whole future of the team is riding on this game.* (**depender de**) **ride something out** to get to the end of a difficult situation without being harmed □ *The business is confident it can ride out the economic recession.* (**sobreviver a**)
▶ NOUN [plural **rides**]

1 a journey in or on a vehicle □ *It was a short bus ride from the airport to the hotel.* (**passeio, volta**) 🔁 *We went for a bike ride.* (**saiu para um passeio de bicicleta**) □ + *in* I had a ride in her new car. □ + *on* Can I have a ride on your bike?

2 a machine that people ride on for fun which moves them up and down or moves them very fast, etc. (**brinquedos de parques de diversões**) 🔁 *We went on all the rides at the fair.* (**fomos a todos os brinquedos**)

3 a bumpy/rough, etc. ride used for talking about how difficult a situation is □ *It's likely to be a fairly rough ride for the school over the next few months.* (**um tormento**)

• **rider** /'raɪdə(r)/ NOUN [plural **riders**] someone sitting on and controlling a bicycle, motorcycle or horse □ *horse riders* (**ciclista, motociclista, cavaleiro**)

ridge /rɪdʒ/ NOUN [plural **ridges**]
1 a long narrow piece of high land □ *mountain ridges* (**cadeia, serrania**)
2 a narrow raised line on the surface of something (**aresta**)

ridicule /'rɪdɪkjuːl/ ▶ VERB [ridicules, ridiculing, ridiculed] to say unkind things about someone or something in order to make them seem silly □ *His accent was ridiculed by the other children.* (**ridicularizar**)

▶ NOUN, NO PLURAL unkind remarks that people make in order to make someone or something seem silly □ *The minister faced public ridicule over his comments.* (**escárnio**)

• **ridiculous** /rɪ'dɪkjʊləs/ ADJECTIVE very silly □ *It's a ridiculous idea!* (**ridículo**)

riding /'raɪdɪŋ/ NOUN, NO PLURAL the activity or sport of riding horses (**equitação**) 🔁 *Mia goes riding every week.* (**cavalga**) □ *riding lessons*

rife /raɪf/ ADJECTIVE if something bad is rife, it exists or happens often □ *Crime is rife in this area.* (**abundante**)

rifle /'raɪfəl/ NOUN [plural **rifles**] a type of long gun (**rifle**)

◆ PHRASAL VERB [rifles, rifling, rifled] **rifle through something** to search a lot of things quickly, especially in order to steal something □ *I caught him rifling through the papers on my desk.* (**vasculhar**)

rift /rɪft/ NOUN [plural **rifts**]
1 a situation in which two people or groups have argued with each other (**desavença**) 🔁 *The talks were an attempt to heal the rift between the two countries.*
2 a large long crack in the land (**fenda**)

rift valley /ˌrɪft 'væli/ NOUN [plural **rift valleys**] a valley with steep sides that is formed when the ground moves. A geography word. (**vale em região de falhas tectônicas**)

rig /rɪg/ ▶ VERB [rigs, rigging, rigged] to do something dishonest so that a competition or election has the result that you want □ *The election must have been rigged.* (**fraude**)

◆ PHRASAL VERB **rig something up** to make something quickly using things that you have □ *We rigged up a new aerial using a wire coat hanger.* (**improvisar**)

▶ NOUN [plural **rigs**] a large structure, used for getting oil or gas from under the sea □ *an oil rig* (**torre de petróleo ou gás**)

• **rigging** /'rɪgɪŋ/ NOUN, NO PLURAL the ropes that support a ship's sails (**cordame**)

right /raɪt/ ▶ ADJECTIVE

1 correct □ + *about* He was right about the train being late. □ *Make sure you sign in the right place.* □ *Are we going in the right direction?* (**correto**) 🔁 *I got most of the answers right.* (**acertei**) 🔁 *'I hear you're leaving.' 'That's right, I've got a new job.'* (**está correto**)

2 suitable or in the condition that you want or expect □ + *for* He is not the right person for the job. □ *We didn't have the right clothes for the weather.* (**certo**) 🔁 *I need a new table, and this one looks just right.* (**adequado**) □ *As soon as I saw her, I knew that something wasn't right.*

3 fair or acceptable □ *It doesn't seem right that so many people in the world are hungry.* □ + *to do something* It's not right to tax the poor. (**certo**)

4 on or to the side that is towards the east when you are facing north □ *I write with my right hand.* □ *We sat on the right side of the church.* (**lado direito, à direita**)

▶ ADVERB

1 towards the direction that is to the east when you are facing north □ *Now turn right.* (**à direita**)
2 exactly □ *Don't move – stay right there.* □ *We were right in the middle of dinner.* □ *Stay right behind me.* (**exatamente**)

3 immediately □ *I'll come right after lunch.* (**imediatamente**) 🔲 *I want the work done right now.* (**já, agora**)
4 all the way □ *This road goes right round the outside of the park.* □ *I watched the film right to the end.* (**totalmente**)
5 correctly □ *Can't you do anything right?* (**corretamente**)
6 used to get someone's attention before you speak or start to do something □ *Right, shall we go outside?* (**certo, bem**)

▶ NOUN [*plural* **rights**]
1 something that you are allowed to do or have, either officially or because it is acceptable □ + **to** *Everyone has a right to a decent education.* □ *These laws protect their religious rights.* (**direito**) 🔲 *You have no right to speak to me like that.* (**não tem direito**) 🔲 *What gives her the right to tell us what to do?* (**dá direito a ela**)
2 *no plural* the side or direction that is on or towards the right side of your body □ *There's a chemist over there on the right.* (**direita**)
3 *no plural* behaviour that is morally good □ *These children do not know right from wrong.* (**certo**)
4 **the right** people or groups with political opinions that support ideas such as having private owners of companies and people taking responsibility for their own lives (**à direita**)

> ▶ Note (noun, sense 1) that you have a **right to** something or the **right to do** something. You do not have the 'right of' something:
> ✓ *Everybody has a right to healthcare.*
> ✗ *Everybody has a right of healthcare.*

▶ VERB [**rights, righting, righted**]
1 to put something back in a vertical position □ *He righted the glass and filled it again.* (**endireitar**)
2 to do something to make a bad or unfair situation better □ *We cannot right the mistakes of the past.* (**corrigir**)

right angle /ˌraɪt ˈæŋɡəl/ NOUN [*plural* **right angles**] an angle of 90°, like the corner of a square. A maths word. (**ângulo reto**)

right click /ˌraɪt ˈklɪk/ VERB [**right clicks, right clicking, right clicked**] to press the right button on a computer mouse so that the computer will do something. A computing word. (**clicar com o botão direito do mouse**)

righteous /ˈraɪtʃəs/ ADJECTIVE
1 morally good □ *a righteous man* (**justo**)
2 righteous indignation/anger strong angry feelings when you think that something is not fair or not morally right (**indignação (moralista)**)

rightful /ˈraɪtfəl/ ADJECTIVE considered as legally or morally correct 🔲 *The stolen goods were returned to their rightful owners.* (**legítimo**)

right-hand /ˌraɪtˈhænd/ ADJECTIVE
1 on the right side of something □ *Take the right-hand turn.* (**do lado direito**) 🔲 *The post office is on the right-hand side of the road.* (**do lado direito**)
2 someone's right-hand man or woman is the person they depend on to work with and help them (**braço direito**)

right-handed /ˌraɪtˈhændɪd/ ADJECTIVE using your right hand to do things, especially to write □ *Are you right-handed?* □ *a right-handed tennis player* (**destro**)

rightly /ˈraɪtli/ ADVERB
1 correctly or fairly □ *Phil has rightly pointed out that Monday 12th is a bank holiday.* (**corretamente**)
2 in a way that is reasonable in a situation □ *People are rightly concerned about this decision.* (**justificadamente**)

right of way /ˌraɪt əv ˈweɪ/ NOUN [*plural* **rights of way**]
1 the right to drive onto a road or across a road before other vehicles □ *Who has right of way at the roundabout?* (**preferência**)
2 a path that people can walk on which crosses land that someone owns (**via pública**)

right wing /ˌraɪt ˈwɪŋ/ NOUN **the right wing** the members of a political party who do not like change □ *the right wing of the Conservative Party* (**ala direita**)
• **right-wing** /ˌraɪtˈwɪŋ/ ADJECTIVE supporting the ideas of the political right □ *right-wing politicians* (**direitista**)

rigid /ˈrɪdʒɪd/ ADJECTIVE
1 unwilling to change or impossible for someone to change □ *a rigid schedule* □ *The rules are very rigid.* (**rígido**)
2 stiff and impossible to bend □ *a rigid frame* (**rígido**)

rigmarole /ˈrɪɡməroʊl/ NOUN, NO PLURAL a process that is annoying because it is so long and complicated □ *I had to go through the whole rigmarole of reapplying for the licence.* (**processo desnecessariamente complicado**)

rigorous /ˈrɪɡərəs/ ADJECTIVE very careful and dealing with every detail □ *We make rigorous safety checks on all the equipment.* (**rigoroso**)

rim /rɪm/ NOUN [*plural* **rims**]
1 the top edge of a container such as a cup or bowl (**borda**)
2 the outside edge of something like a wheel (**aro**)

rind /raɪnd/ NOUN [*plural* **rinds**] the thick skin on some foods such as lemons, cheese or bacon (**casca**)

ring¹ /rɪŋ/ ▶ NOUN [*plural* **rings**]
1 a round piece of jewellery that you wear on your finger (**anel**) 🔲 *a wedding ring* (**anel de casamento, aliança**) □ *I was wearing a diamond ring.*

ring

2 something in the shape of a circle □ *The children sat in a ring around the story-teller.* □ *The house was surrounded by a ring of fire.* (**círculo**)
3 a group of people involved in an illegal activity □ *a spy ring* (**quadrilha**)
4 an area where people do the sport of boxing (**ringue**)
5 an area where people perform in a circus (= show where people and animals perform) (**picadeiro**)
▶ VERB [**rings, ringing, ringed**]
1 to surround someone or something □ *The area is ringed with trees.* (**circundar**)
2 to draw a circle around something □ *Ring any items that you are interested in.* (**circular**)

ring² /rɪŋ/ ▶ VERB [**rings, ringing, rang, rung**]
1 if a bell rings, it produces a sound, and if you ring a bell, you make it produce a sound □ *I think I heard the doorbell ring.* (**tocar**)
2 to telephone someone □ *I'm ringing about the car you have for sale.* (**telefonar**)
3 if the telephone rings, it makes a sound so that you know someone is telephoning you (**tocar**)

> ➤ Note that you **ring** (= telephone) a person or place. You do not 'ring to' a person or place:
> ✓ *I'll just ring my sister.*
> ✗ *I'll just ring to my sister.*

◆ PHRASAL VERBS **ring (someone) back** to telephone someone after they have telephoned you □ *I'm a bit busy – can I ring you back later?* (**retornar a ligação**) **ring out** to make a loud, clear noise □ *Suddenly, shots rang out.* (**soar**) **ring someone up** to telephone someone □ *She rang me up in the middle of the night.* (**telefonar para alguém**)
▶ NOUN [*plural* **rings**] (**telefonar**)
1 give someone a ring to telephone someone □ *I'll give you a ring tomorrow.* (**dar um telefonema para alguém**)
2 the sound a bell makes □ *Did I hear a ring at the door?* (**toque**)

ringleader /ˈrɪŋliːdə(r)/ NOUN [*plural* **ringleaders**] the leader of a group of people who are doing something bad (**chefe do grupo**)

ringlet /ˈrɪŋlɪt/ NOUN [*plural* **ringlets**] a long curl of hair (**um cacho de cabelo**)

ring road /ˈrɪŋ ˌrəʊd/ NOUN [*plural* **ring roads**] a road that goes around a town or city (**anel viário**)

ringtone /ˈrɪŋtəʊn/ NOUN [*plural* **ringtones**] the sound that a mobile phone makes when you call it (**toque de sinal**)

rink /rɪŋk/ NOUN [*plural* **rinks**] a large area of ice where people skate (= move wearing boots with metal blades on the bottom) (**rinque**)

rinse /rɪns/ ▶ VERB [**rinses, rinsing, rinsed**] to remove dirt or soap from something by putting it in clean water □ *Rinse your hair well after shampooing it.* (**enxaguar**)
▶ NOUN [*plural* **rinses**] a wash with clean water □ *He gave the cup a rinse.* (**enxágue**)

rip-off

riot /ˈraɪət/ ▶ NOUN [*plural* **riots**]
1 a time when a large crowd of people behave violently in a public place (**tumulto**) 🔁 *His election sparked riots in the capital.* (**despertou tumultos**) 🔁 *Riot police were brought in to control the crowd.* (**tropa de choque**)
2 run riot (a) to become impossible to control □ *Her emotions were running riot.* (b) to behave in a noisy and uncontrolled way □ *Too many parents allow their children to run riot.* (**desenfrear-se**)
▶ VERB [**riots, rioting, rioted**] if a crowd of people riot, they behave violently in a public place (**participar de tumultos**)

• **rioter** /ˈraɪətə(r)/ NOUN [*plural* **rioters**] someone who takes part in a riot □ *Rioters threw stones and bottles at police.* (**arruaceiro, participante de tumulto**)

• **rioting** /ˈraɪətɪŋ/ NOUN, NO PLURAL violent behavior in a public place by a crowd of people (**tumulto, confusão**) 🔁 *Rioting broke out in the streets of the city.* (**um tumulto ocorreu**)

• **riotous** /ˈraɪətəs/ ADJECTIVE
1 involving a lot of noise and excitement □ *a riotous celebration* (**tumultuado**)
2 noisy and violent □ *riotous behaviour* (**tumultuoso**)

rip /rɪp/ ▶ VERB [**rips, ripping, ripped**]
1 to tear something roughly □ *She ripped sheets into strips and used them as bandages.* □ *Steve had ripped his trousers on the barbed wire.* (**rasgar**)
2 to remove something quickly and forcefully □ *The storm ripped the roof off their house.* (**arrancar**)
◆ PHRASAL VERBS **rip someone off** to charge someone too much money for something. An informal phrase. □ *Some of the taxi drivers rip tourists off.* (**cobrar preço alto, superfaturar, meter a faca**) **rip something up** to tear something into small pieces □ *I ripped the letter up and put it in the bin.* (**picar**)
▶ NOUN [*plural* **rips**] a rough tear □ *There was a rip in my sleeve where the handlebars had caught it.* (**rasgão**)

ripe /raɪp/ ADJECTIVE [**riper, ripest**]
1 ripe fruit is ready to be picked or eaten □ *The plums were ripe and juicy.* □ *ripe tomatoes* (**maduro**)
2 be ripe for something to be ready for something to happen, especially when it should have happened sooner □ *The company is ripe for a takeover.* (**estar preparado para**)
3 ripe old age an old age □ *He lived to the ripe old age of 98.* (**idade avançada**)

• **ripen** /ˈraɪpən/ VERB [**ripens, ripening, ripened**] when fruit ripens, it becomes ready to pick or eat □ *The apples are ripening quickly this year.* (**amadurecer**)

rip-off /ˈrɪpɒf/ NOUN [*plural* **rip-offs**] something that is much too expensive. An informal word. □ *At £100 a ticket, the show is a complete rip-off.* (**roubo, exploração**)

ripple /ˈrɪpəl/ ▶ NOUN [plural ripples]
1 a small movement on the surface of water □ *Tiny fish were causing ripples in the water.* (ondulação)
2 a feeling or sound that spreads gradually through a place □ *A ripple of nervous laughter followed his comments.* (agitação)
▶ VERB [ripples, rippling, rippled] to move like waves □ *The curtains rippled in the breeze.* (ondular)

rise /raɪz/ ▶ VERB [rises, rising, rose, risen]
1 to go up □ *A column of smoke rose above the village.* □ *+ up The balloon rose up into the air.* □ *The sun rises in the east.* □ *Ahead, the ground rose steeply.* (elevar-se, levantar-se)
2 to increase in level □ *Prices have risen this year.* (aumentar) 🔁 *Profits rose sharply in the second half of the year.* (aumentaram rapidamente) □ *The government has tried to calm rising panic about fuel costs.*
3 to be come successful or powerful □ *+ to She rose to the position of chief executive.* (subir, destacar-se, ganhar poder) 🔁 *He is a rising star in the government.* (estrela em ascensão)
4 rise to the challenge/occasion to manage to deal with a difficult situation successfully (mostrar-se à altura da situação)
5 to stand up □ *We all rose when the judge entered.* (ficar em pé)
6 to get out of bed □ *His habit was to rise early for breakfast.* (levantar-se da cama)
7 to fight against a government or someone in power □ *+ up The people rose up to protest about food shortages.* (levantar-se)

> Note that **rise** has no object after it. If you want to say 'to make something go up' or 'to make something increase in level', use the verb **raise**. Raise is always followed by an object:
> ✓ *She raised her hand.*
> ✗ *She rose her hand.*
> ✓ *They raised prices.*
> ✗ *They rose prices.*

◆ PHRASAL VERB **rise above something** to not let an unpleasant situation affect you □ *The group is constantly arguing, but he manages to rise above all that.* (lidar bem com a situação)
▶ NOUN [plural rises]
1 an increase in level □ *There has been a rise in the number of homeless people.* (aumento)
2 when a person or a business becomes successful or powerful □ *The firm's rise from a small operation in Mick's bedroom to a multinational company shows that anyone can be successful.* (crescimento) 🔁 *The programme looks at her sudden rise to fame.* (ascensão à fama)
3 give rise to something to cause something to happen or exist □ *The accident has given rise to worries about safety.* (dar início a)
4 an increase in pay □ *I'm going to ask my boss for a rise.* (aumento)

risk /rɪsk/ ▶ NOUN [plural risks]
1 a possibility that something bad will happen □ *+ of We face the risk of losing our homes.* □ *+ that There's a risk that the whole project might be called off.* (risco) 🔁 *If you give up your job, you will be taking a big risk.* (assumindo um grande risco) 🔁 *Without advertising, they run the risk of being ignored.* (correr o risco)
2 something that could cause problems or danger in the future □ *+ to These laws are a risk to free speech.* □ *Smoking is a well known health risk.* (risco, perigo)
3 at risk in a situation where something bad might happen □ *Their traditional way of life is at risk.* □ *These children are at risk of violence.* (em risco)
4 at your own risk if you do something at your own risk, you take responsibility for anything bad that might happen to you □ *Bags can be left here at the customer's own risk.* (por conta e risco de)
▶ VERB [risks, risking, risked]
1 to do something although you know there is a possibility that something bad will happen □ *I risked a glance at the document.* □ *+ ing She couldn't risk phoning him.* (arriscar(-se) a)
2 to put yourself in a situation where something bad could happen to you □ *He risked punishment by entering the room.* □ *+ ing She risked failing her exams.* (arriscar-se)
3 to take the chance of damaging or losing something (arriscar) 🔁 *Soldiers are risking their lives every day.* □ *We have risked a lot of money on this business.* (arriscando sua vida)

> Note that the verb **risk** is followed by **doing something** and never by 'to do something':
> ✓ *I wouldn't risk telling him.*
> ✗ *I wouldn't risk to tell him.*

• **risky** /ˈrɪski/ ADJECTIVE [riskier, riskiest] dangerous □ *It's too risky to wait any longer.* (arriscado)

risotto /rɪˈzɒtəʊ/ NOUN [plural risottos] an Italian dish of rice, often with meat or fish (risoto)

risqué /ˈriːskeɪ/ ADJECTIVE risqué jokes, stories, remarks, etc. are slightly rude (malicioso)

rite /raɪt/ NOUN [plural rites] a ceremony, especially one to do with a religion □ *funeral rites* (rito)

ritual /ˈrɪtʃuəl/ ▶ NOUN [plural rituals]
1 a series of formal actions that are part of a ceremony □ *religious rituals* (ritual)
2 something that you often do at the same time or in the same way □ *Reading stories to your child should be part of the bedtime ritual.* (ritual)
▶ ADJECTIVE to do with a ritual □ *ritual dances* (ritual)

rival /ˈraɪvəl/ ▶ NOUN [plural rivals] a person or organization that competes against another □ *The two teams are bitter rivals.* (rival)
▶ ADJECTIVE competing against each other □ *rival gangs* □ *rival political parties* (rival)

river · robin

▶ VERB [rivals, rivalling/US rivaling, rivalled/US rivaled] to be as good, as something or someone else □ Shop-bought vegetables can't rival the ones you grow yourself. (rivalizar)

- **rivalry** /ˈraɪvəlri/ NOUN, NO PLURAL when people or organizations compete against each other □ There's a lot of rivalry between the twins. (rivalidade)

river /ˈrɪvə(r)/ NOUN [plural rivers] a large stream of water that flows across land □ There were several boats on the river. (rio) 🔁 He crossed the river using the main bridge. (cruzou o rio) □ the River Nile

rivet /ˈrɪvɪt/ ▶ VERB [rivets, riveting, riveted] if you are riveted by something, you find it very interesting and cannot stop looking at it (fascinado)
▶ NOUN [plural rivets] a type of large pin used for holding pieces of metal together (rebite)

- **riveting** /ˈrɪvɪtɪŋ/ ADJECTIVE extremely interesting, keeping all your attention □ It's a riveting story. (fascinante)

road /rəʊd/ NOUN [plural roads]
1 a hard, level surface for vehicles to travel along □ There were a lot of cars parked in the road. (estrada) 🔁 Children need to learn how to cross the road safely. (atravessaram a estrada) 🔁 The accident happened on the main road between Pula and Porec. (estrada principal) 🔁 We live on a very busy road. (estrada movimentada) 🔁 He died in a road accident. (acidente na estrada)
2 over/across the road on the opposite side of a road □ Mark and Carrie live across the road from us. (do outro lado da rua/estrada)
3 down/along the road further on the same road □ My school is just down the road. (à frente na estrada)
4 by road in a vehicle that travels on the road □ The journey to London is three hours by road. (por estrada)
5 Road used in the name of some roads □ They live at 12 Lockwood Road. (rua)

road rage /ˈrəʊd ˌreɪdʒ/ NOUN, NO PLURAL angry or violent behaviour between drivers on the road □ He was arrested following a road rage incident. (briga de trânsito)

roadside /ˈrəʊdsaɪd/ ADJECTIVE happening or placed by the side of a road □ roadside bombings (beira da estrada)

roadworks /ˈrəʊdwɜːks/ PLURAL NOUN the work of repairing a road surface □ Roadworks are causing delays on the motorway. (obras em estrada)

roadworthy /ˈrəʊdˌwɜːði/ ADJECTIVE if a vehicle is roadworthy, it is in good enough condition to drive on the roads (em condições de rodar)

roam /rəʊm/ VERB [roams, roaming, roamed] to walk or travel around a place without a particular aim (vaguear) 🔁 You see youths roaming the streets at night. (vagueando pela rua)

roar /rɔː(r)/ ▶ VERB [roars, roaring, roared]
1 to make a continuous loud sound □ Planes roared overhead. (rugir, urrar)
2 if a vehicle roars somewhere, it moves there quickly, making a loud sound □ Cars roared past as we sat at the roadside. (roncar)
3 to say something in a loud, angry voice □ 'Get out!' he roared. (esbravejar)
4 when a lion roars, it makes a loud sound (rugir)
▶ NOUN [plural roars]
1 a loud deep sound □ the roar of the engine (ronco, ruído)
2 the call or sound that a lion makes (rugido)

roast /rəʊst/ ▶ VERB [roasts, roasting, roasted]
1 to cook meat or vegetables in an oven or over a fire □ Roast the potatoes at the same time as the turkey. (assar)
2 meat or vegetables roast when they cook in an oven or over a fire □ The sauce can be made while the vegetables are roasting. (assar)
▶ ADJECTIVE cooked in the oven □ roast potatoes □ roast beef (assado)
▶ NOUN [plural roasts] a piece of meat that has been cooked in the oven □ We're having a roast tonight. (assado)

- **roasting** /ˈrəʊstɪŋ/ ADJECTIVE an informal word meaning very hot □ It was roasting outside today. (muito quente)

rob /rɒb/ VERB [robs, robbing, robbed]
1 to steal something from a place or person (roubar) 🔁 They robbed a bank. (roubaram um banco) □ + of The family were robbed of jewellery worth at least £1 million.
2 rob someone of something to take something important from someone □ He was robbed of the chance to compete by an injury. (privar alguém de algo)

▶ Remember that thieves **rob** people and places. They **steal** money and objects: □ My parents were robbed in the street. □ They had robbed a bank. □ They stole my father's wallet. □ They stole five hundred pounds from her.

- **robber** /ˈrɒbə(r)/ NOUN [plural robbers] a person who steals (ladrão) 🔁 Armed robbers broke into his house. (ladrões armados) 🔁 a bank robber (ladrão de banco)
- **robbery** /ˈrɒbəri/ NOUN [plural robberies] the crime of stealing something from a person or place (roubo) 🔁 He committed several robberies. (cometeu roubos) 🔁 a bank robbery (roubo de banco) 🔁 He was in prison for armed robbery. (roubo armado) 🔁 Parvez was shot during an attempted robbery. (atentado de roubo)

robe /rəʊb/ NOUN [plural robes] a long loose piece of clothing □ a priest's robes (manto, toga, roupão)

robin /ˈrɒbɪn/ NOUN [plural robins] a small brown bird with a red chest (papo-roxo)

robot /ˈrəʊbɒt/ NOUN [plural **robots**] a machine that can do things like a person (robô)

• **robotic** /rəʊˈbɒtɪk/ ADJECTIVE to do with or similar to a robot □ *Robotic devices are used in performing some types of surgery.* (robótico)

robust /rəʊˈbʌst/ ADJECTIVE strong □ *a robust economy* □ *He was in robust health.* (robusto)

rock /rɒk/ ▶ NOUN [plural **rocks**]
1 the hard stone substance that the Earth is made of □ *volcanic rock* □ *The team were digging a tunnel through solid rock.* (rocha)
2 a large stone □ *Protesters threw rocks at the police.* (pedra)
3 a type of music with a strong beat that is played on electric guitars and drums □ *He played in a rock band.* (rock)
▶ VERB [**rocks, rocking, rocked**]
1 to move or move something gently backwards and forwards or from side to side □ *She was rocking the baby in her arms.* □ *The boats rocked gently in the harbour.* (embalar, balançar(-se))
2 to make a place shake □ *Three bombs rocked the capital, killing at least 20 people.* (abalar)
3 to shock a lot of people □ *Several corruption scandals have rocked the government.* (abalar)
4 if something or someone rocks, they are extremely good. An informal word. □ *This place rocks!* (arrasar)
♦ IDIOM **rock the boat** to cause problems by criticizing something or by trying to change something which other people are satisfied with. An informal phrase □ *I don't want to rock the boat.* (criar caso)

rock and roll or **rock 'n' roll** /ˌrɒk ən ˈrəʊl/ NOUN, NO PLURAL a type of pop music with a strong beat that was popular in the 1950s (rock and roll)

rocket /ˈrɒkɪt/ ▶ NOUN [plural **rockets**]
1 a long thin weapon with a bomb in it which is fired from a plane or ship □ *Rockets were fired across the border.* □ *a rocket attack* (foguete)
2 a long thin spacecraft □ *The Ariane rocket was launched from the EU space centre.* (foguete)
3 something which explodes high in the sky and makes bright lights for entertainment (rojão)
▶ VERB [**rockets, rocketing, rocketed**] to increase very quickly □ *Oil prices have rocketed.* (subir como um foguete)

rocking chair /ˈrɒkɪŋ ˌtʃeə(r)/ NOUN [plural **rocking chairs**] a chair which moves backwards and forwards when you sit on it (cadeira de balanço)

rocking horse /ˈrɒkɪŋ ˌhɔːs/ NOUN [plural **rocking horses**] a child's toy horse that they can sit on and rock backwards and forwards (cavalo de balanço)

rock music /ˈrɒk ˌmjuːzɪk/ NOUN, NO PLURAL a type of music with a strong beat that is played on electric guitars and drums (rock)

rocky /ˈrɒki/ ADJECTIVE [**rockier, rockiest**]
1 made of rock, or covered with rocks □ *the rocky slopes of the mountains* (rochoso)
2 a relationship or situation that is rocky is difficult and may not be successful □ *Their marriage has been going through a rocky patch.* (difícil)

rod /rɒd/ NOUN [plural **rods**] a long thin pole (vara, haste) 🔁 *a fishing rod* (vara de pesca)

rode /rəʊd/ PAST TENSE OF **ride** (ver **ride**)

rodent /ˈrəʊdənt/ NOUN [plural **rodents**] a small animal with long sharp front teeth, such as a rabbit or a mouse (roedor)

rodeo /ˈrəʊdɪəʊ/ NOUN [plural **rodeos**] a show of riding and other skills by cowboys (= men who ride horses and look after cows in the US) (rodeio)

roe /rəʊ/ NOUN, NO PLURAL the eggs of a fish, eaten as food (ova)

rogue /rəʊɡ/ ▶ NOUN [plural **rogues**] a dishonest or badly behaved man or boy (vigarista, maroto) 🔁 *He's a lovable rogue* (= someone who behaves badly but you still like them). (adorável vigarista)
▶ ADJECTIVE not behaving in the same way as other people or things, and likely to cause problems □ *rogue nations* (insubordinado, traidor)

role /rəʊl/ NOUN [plural **roles**]
1 the character that an actor is in a play or film (papel) 🔁 *Daniel Radcliffe played the role of Harry Potter in the film.* (interpretou o papel de) 🔁 *It was his first starring role* (= important role) *in a Hollywood movie.* (papel principal)
2 the job or purpose that someone or something has (papel) 🔁 *Diet plays an important role in maintaining good health.* (faz um papel) □ + *of The role of women has changed greatly over the last century.*

roll /rəʊl/ ▶ VERB [**rolls, rolling, rolled**]
1 to move along like a ball, or to make something move in this way □ + ***down/along, etc.*** *Rocks sometimes rolled down the hills.* □ *She rolled the ball along the ground.* (rolar)
2 to move on wheels, or to make something on wheels move □ *Take the brake off and let the car roll forwards.* □ + ***into*** *The train rolled into the station.* □ *I rolled the bike into the yard.* (rodar)
3 to turn your body when you are lying down, or to turn someone else's body when they are lying down □ + ***over*** *My back hurts every time I roll over in bed.* □ *She rolled the baby onto his tummy.* (virar-se)
4 if a small amount of liquid rolls, it moves smoothly down a surface □ + ***down*** *Tears were rolling down her cheeks.* (rolar)
5 to fold something so that it forms the shape of a ball or a tube □ *She rolled her clothes in tissue paper before packing them.* □ + ***up*** *Roll the sleeping bag up tightly and tie the string around it.* (enrolar)
6 roll your eyes to move your eyes upwards, especially to show that you are annoyed □ *He just rolled his eyes when I told him what had happened.* (virar os olhos)

roll call

◆ IDIOM **be rolling in it** an informal phrase meaning to be very rich (**estar rolando/nadando em dinheiro**)

◆ PHRASAL VERBS **roll something up**

1 to make a piece of clothing shorter by folding it □ *She rolled her sleeves up so they didn't get wet.* (**dobrar**)

2 to fold something so that it forms the shape of a ball or tube □ *The carpet had been rolled up.* (**enrolar**) **roll up** an informal word meaning to arrive, especially late □ *John rolled up just as the others were leaving.* (**chegar de carro**)

▶ NOUN [*plural* **rolls**]

1 a small loaf of bread for one person, often with something such as meat or cheese in it □ *I had a cheese roll for lunch.* (**pãozinho**)

2 something that has been rolled into the shape of a tube □ **+ of** *a roll of toilet paper* □ *We'll need 12 rolls of wallpaper for this room.* (**rolo**)

3 an official list of names, for example the names of students at a school or the people who can vote in an election (**lista**) 🔁 *He's not on the electoral roll.* (**lista de eleitores**)

4 a long deep sound □ *a drumroll* □ *a roll of thunder* (**ressoo, reboo**)

5 be on a roll an informal phrase meaning to be in a period in which you are having a lot of success □ *The team are on a roll at the moment having won the last five games.* (**estar em boa fase**)

roll call /'rəʊl ˌkɔːl/ NOUN [*plural* **roll calls**] when someone calls out the names from a list (**chamada**)

roller /'rəʊlə(r)/ NOUN [*plural* **rollers**] something in the shape of a tube, used for spreading something or for making something flat □ *She was painting the room with a roller.* (**rolo**)

Rollerblades /'rəʊləbleɪdz/ PLURAL NOUN boots with a row of wheels on the bottom, used for skating. A trademark. (**patins (marca registrada)**)

roller coaster /ˈrəʊlə ˌkəʊstə(r)/ NOUN [*plural* **roller coasters**]

1 a steep track on which people ride for fun in a very fast train (**montanha-russa**)

2 a situation which changes often and suddenly, causing strong emotions □ *Pregnancy had been an emotional roller coaster.* (**montanha-russa de emoções**)

roller skate /'rəʊlə ˌskeɪt/ ▶ NOUN [*plural* **roller skates**] a boot with two pairs of wheels on the bottom, used for skating (**patins**)

▶ VERB [**roller skates, roller skating, roller skated**] to move using roller skates

• **roller skating** /ˈrəʊlə ˌskeɪtɪŋ/ NOUN, NO PLURAL the activity of moving on roller skates (**andar de patins**)

rolling pin /ˈrəʊlɪŋ ˌpɪn/ NOUN [*plural* **rolling pins**] a thick stick that you roll over pastry to make it flat (**rolo de massa**)

ROM /rɒm/ ABBREVIATION Read Only Memory; a type of memory in a computer that allows you to see information, but not change it. A computing word. (**Memória Somente de Leitura**)

Roman Catholic /ˌrəʊmən ˈkæθlɪk/ ▶ NOUN [*plural* **Roman Catholics**] a member of the part of the Christian church that has the Pope for a leader (**católico**)

▶ ADJECTIVE to do with, or belonging to, the Roman Catholic Church (**católico**)

romance /rəʊˈmæns/ NOUN [*plural* **romances**]

1 *no plural* the feelings connected with being in love □ *They met at college and romance soon blossomed* (**romance**)

2 a short relationship between people who are in love (**romance**) 🔁 *The couple had a whirlwind romance* (= short and exciting relationship). (**romance rápido/passageiro**)

3 *no plural* a feeling of excitement and mystery connected with something □ *He loved the romance of long-distance train travel.* (**romantismo**)

4 a love story □ *She read mainly romances.* (**romance**)

Roman numeral /ˌrəʊmən ˈnjuːmərəl/ NOUN [*plural* **Roman numerals**] one of the letters used to represent numbers in the system used by the ancient Romans, in which, for example I = 1 and V = 5 (**algarismo romano**)

romantic /rəʊˈmæntɪk/ ADJECTIVE

1 to do with feelings of love (**romântico**) 🔁 *a romantic relationship* (**relacionamento romântico**) 🔁 *His latest film is a romantic comedy.* (**comédia romântica**) □ *a romantic dinner for two*

2 thinking of or showing things as better and more exciting than they are in real situations □ *I had this romantic idea of life as an actor.* (**romântico**)

• **romantically** /rəʊˈmæntɪkəli/ ADVERB in a way that is to do with love □ *She's not romantically involved with anyone just now.* (**romanticamente**)

• **romanticize** or **romanticise** /rəʊˈmæntɪsaɪz/ VERB [**romanticizes, romanticizing, romanticized**] to think of or show something as better and more exciting than it really is, ignoring all the bad things □ *It was said that the film romanticized crime.* (**romantizar**)

romp /rɒmp/ VERB [**romps, romping, romped**]

1 to play with a lot of energy and movement □ *The children can romp around outside in the sun.* (**brincar livremente, fazer bagunça**)

2 an informal word meaning to win a game or a race very easily (**vencer facilmente**) 🔁 *His horse romped home in the Gold Cup.* (**venceu facilmente**) □ *They romped to a 6-1 win.*

roof /ruːf/ NOUN [*plural* **roofs**]

1 the part that covers the top of a building or vehicle □ *The house has a red tiled roof.* □ **+ of** *He climbed onto the roof of the building.* (**teto**)

2 the roof of your mouth the top inside surface of your mouth (palato, céu da boca)

♦ IDIOMS **go through the roof** an informal phrase meaning to reach an extremely high level □ *Prices have gone through the roof.* (disparar, atingir nível alto) **hit the roof** an informal phrase meaning to become very angry (perder as estribeiras) **a roof over your head** a house, flat, etc. to live in □ *At least we have food and a roof over our heads.* (um teto para morar)

roof rack /ˈruːf ˌræk/ NOUN [plural **roof racks**] a metal frame that you can fix to the roof of a car, for carrying things (bagageiro)

rook /rʊk/ NOUN [plural **rooks**]
1 a large black bird (gralha)
2 in the game of chess, a piece which is shaped like a castle (torre)

room /ruːm, rʊm/ NOUN [plural **rooms**]
1 one of the areas a building is divided into inside □ *We have three rooms downstairs and four upstairs.* □ *She got up and left the room.* (cômodo) ▣ *He went back to his hotel room.* (quarto de hotel)
2 *no plural* space for something □ + *for Is there room for another chair?* □ *There wasn't enough room in the car for everyone.* □ + *to do something They had no room to move.* (espaço)
3 *no plural* an opportunity or possibility that something can happen □ + *for I feel there's still a lot of room for improvement.* (lugar)

roommate /ˈruːmmeɪt/ NOUN [plural **roommates**]
1 in the UK, a person you share a room with, for example as a student (colega de quarto)
2 in the US, a person you share a house or flat with (pessoa com quem se divide a casa ou o apartamento)

roomy /ˈruːmi/ ADJECTIVE [**roomier**, **roomiest**] having a lot of space □ *a roomy cabin* (espaçoso)

roost /ruːst/ ▶ NOUN [plural **roosts**] the place where a bird rests at night (poleiro)
▶ VERB [**roosts**, **roosting**, **roosted**] if a bird roosts somewhere, it sits or sleeps there at night (empoleirar-se)

• **rooster** /ˈruːstə(r)/ NOUN [plural **roosters**] a male chicken (galo)

root /ruːt/ ▶ NOUN [plural **roots**]
1 the part of a plant that grows underground □ + *of the roots of the tree* (raiz)
2 the basic cause of a problem □ + *of The root of all our troubles is that we don't have enough money.* (raiz) ▣ *We must address the root causes of the violence.* (raiz do problema)
3 the part of a tooth or hair that holds it to your body (raiz)
4 roots the origin of someone or something □ *his working class roots* □ *The company traces its roots back to 1830.* (raízes)

♦ IDIOMS **take root**

1 to start to be believed or to develop □ *His ideas now seem to have taken root in the UK.* (criar raízes)
2 to start growing roots (enraizar)
▶ VERB [**roots**, **rooting**, **rooted**]
1 to grow roots □ *The plants root very easily in compost.* (enraizar)
2 be rooted in something to come from or to be caused by something □ *His art is rooted in the folk tradition.* (originar-se em, basear-se em) **rooted to the spot** an informal phrase (paralisado de medo ou de surpresa) meaning not able to move because you are surprised or afraid

♦ PHRASAL VERBS **root around** to search for something, especially in an untidy way □ *Who's been rooting around in my desk?* (fuçar) **root for someone** to support someone and want them to win □ *I'll be rooting for the local team.* (torcer para alguém) **root something out** to find something and get rid of it □ *He promised to root out corruption.* (extirpar)

rope /rəʊp/ ▶ NOUN [plural **ropes**]
1 very thick strong string (corda)
2 the ropes the things someone needs to know to do a job (pegar o jeito) ▣ *She's still learning the ropes.* (pegando o jeito) ▣ *Matthew will show you the ropes.* (mostrará o caminho das pedras, o funcionamento das coisas)

♦ IDIOM **on the ropes** having problems and likely to lose or fail □ *After last week's defeat in parliament, the party are on the ropes.* (em situação delicada)
▶ VERB [**ropes**, **roping**, **roped**] to tie something with rope □ *The climbers are roped together.* (convencer alguém a fazer algo)

♦ PHRASAL VERBS **rope someone in/into something** to persuade someone to do something, especially when they do not want to □ *I got roped into playing.* (convencer alguém a fazer algo) **rope something off** to separate part of an area using rope, especially to stop people going there

ropy *or* **ropey** /ˈrəʊpi/ ADJECTIVE [**ropier**, **ropiest**] an informal word meaning of fairly bad quality □ *a ropy performance* (de má qualidade)

rosary /ˈrəʊzəri/ NOUN [plural **rosaries**] a string with beads (= small balls) on it that people in some religions use to count prayers as they say them (rosário)

rose[1] /rəʊz/ ▶ NOUN [plural **roses**] a garden plant with sharp points on the stems and flowers that smell sweet (rosa)
▶ ADJECTIVE having a pale pink colour (cor-de-rosa)

rose[2] /rəʊz/ PAST TENSE OF **rise** □ *The temperature rose steadily as the day wore on.* (ver **rise**)

rosemary /ˈrəʊzməri/ NOUN, NO PLURAL a plant with thin leaves that are used in cooking (alecrim)

rosette /rəʊˈzet/ NOUN [plural **rosettes**] a round decoration made of ribbon (= long, narrow piece

roster /ˈrɒstə(r)/ NOUN [plural **rosters**] the US word for **rota** (lista de escala)

rostrum /ˈrɒstrəm/ NOUN [plural **rostrums**] a small raised area that someone stands on to make a speech (tribuna)

rosy /ˈrəʊzɪ/ ADJECTIVE [**rosier**, **rosiest**]
1 pink in colour ☐ *rosy cheeks* (rosado)
2 positive or likely that good things will happen ☐ *The future certainly looks rosy for Hugh.* (cor-de-rosa)

rot /rɒt/ ▶ VERB [**rots, rotting, rotted**] to decay or to make something decay ☐ *The leaves fall on the forest floor and gradually rot into the soil.* ☐ *Sugar rots the teeth.* (apodrecer)
▶ NOUN, NO PLURAL ☐ *They've discovered some rot in the roof timbers.* (podridão)
♦ IDIOM **stop the rot** to stop a bad situation from becoming worse (evitar o pior)

rota /ˈrəʊtə/ NOUN [plural **rotas**] a list of jobs to be done that shows who must do them and when they must be done ☐ *a cleaning rota* (rodízio)

rotary /ˈrəʊtərɪ/ ADJECTIVE moving round and round like a wheel (rotativo)

rotate /rəʊˈteɪt/ VERB [**rotates, rotating, rotated**]
1 to turn around like a wheel, or to make something turn around like a wheel ☐ *Each wheel rotates on its own axle.* (girar, rodar)
2 to replace one person or thing with another in a particular order ☐ *Rotating the different kinds of vegetables we grow keeps the soil healthy.* (revezar)
• **rotation** /rəʊˈteɪʃən/ NOUN [plural **rotations**]
1 a rotating movement ☐ *The rotation of the blades keeps the air moving.* (rotação)
2 when people or things rotate (rotação)

rotor /ˈrəʊtə(r)/ NOUN [plural **rotors**] a part of a machine that turns round a point ☐ *a helicopter rotor blade* (rotor)

rotten /ˈrɒtən/ ADJECTIVE
1 decayed or decaying ☐ *rotten eggs* ☐ *a rotten floorboard* (podre)
2 an informal word meaning very bad or unpleasant ☐ *We had a rotten meal there.* ☐ *I felt rotten when I woke up.* (péssimo)

rough /rʌf/ ▶ ADJECTIVE [**rougher, roughest**]
1 not smooth ☐ *We drove along a rough track.* ☐ *I get very rough skin on my feet.* (áspero)
2 not gentle ☐ *Rugby is a rough game.* (bruto, rude)
3 a rough sea has a lot of big waves because the wind is strong ☐ *The sea was too rough for swimming in.* (turbulento)
4 not exact ☐ *a rough guess/estimate* (aproximado)
5 full of problems and causing unhappiness ☐ *She had quite a rough time in her first job.* (período difícil)
6 ill (indisposto) ☐ *I felt rough the next day.* (eu me senti indisposto)
7 a rough place or area is unpleasant and often dangerous (desagradável)
8 done quickly and not completely finished ☐ *a rough sketch* (rústico)
▶ ADVERB if people live rough or sleep rough, they sleep outside because they do not have homes (viver ou morar na rua)

roughage /ˈrʌfɪdʒ/ NOUN, NO PLURAL a substance in food which your body cannot digest, and which helps your bowels work well (fibra alimentar)

roughen /ˈrʌfən/ VERB [**roughens, roughening, roughened**] to make something less smooth (tornar áspero)

roughly /ˈrʌflɪ/ ADVERB
1 approximately ☐ *There were roughly ten thousand people in the stadium.* (aproximadamente) ☐ *They're roughly the same size.* ☐ *Her name roughly translates as 'white flower'.* (aproximadamente o mesmo)
2 in a quick way, without being careful or gentle ☐ *If you handle the flowers roughly, you'll damage them.* ☐ *roughly chopped onions* (brutalmente)

roughness /ˈrʌfnɪs/ NOUN, NO PLURAL
1 the quality of not being smooth ☐ *the roughness of his skin* (aspereza)
2 when someone or something is not gentle (aspereza)

roulette /ruːˈlet/ NOUN, NO PLURAL a game in which a ball is dropped onto a turning wheel marked with numbers and people guess where the ball will stop (roleta)

round /raʊnd/ ▶ ADVERB, PREPOSITION
1 on all sides ☐ *We sat round the table.* ☐ *We tied a rope round the tree.* (em volta de)
2 moving in a circle or along the edges of something ☐ *The Moon goes round the Earth.* (em círculo, em volta de) ☐ *We drove round and round in circles.* (em volta de)
3 to face the opposite direction ☐ *If you look round, you can see the clock.* (em sentido oposto) ☐ *He turned round and waved.* (ele se virou)
4 to the other side of something ☐ *We were allowed to go round the back of the theatre.* (em volta de) ☐ *I saw Jo coming round the corner.* (na virada da esquina)
5 in or to different parts of a place ☐ *We travelled all round Spain.* (por)
6 to someone's home (em visita) ☐ *Why don't you come round for supper?* (vir em visita) ☐ *I'm going round to Fred's after school.* (ir em visita)
7 near (perto) ☐ *Do you live round here?*
8 from one person or place to another ☐ *The news got round pretty quickly.* ☐ *Please pass the books round to everyone.* (de pessoa em pessoa)
9 round about approximately ☐ *They pay round about £10 per hour.* (aproximadamente)
⇨ go to **be/go round the** *bend*, **drive someone round the** *bend*

roundabout

▶ ADJECTIVE [rounder, roundest]
1 having the shape of a circle or a ball □ *a round table* □ *The Earth is round.* (redondo)
2 a round number is shown as the nearest unit, for example 1, 10, 100, 1,000 (número redondo)
▶ NOUN [plural **rounds**]
1 a part of a competition □ *They lost in the second round of the cup.* □ *The Swedish team is through to the next round.* (rodada, assalto)
2 when someone goes to several people or houses as part of their job □ *Our postman usually finishes his round by midday.* (ronda)
3 a group of events □ *We're doing the next round of interviews tomorrow.* □ *His life is just one long round of parties.* (série, sucessão)
4 drinks that you buy for several people □ *It's my round – what would you like?* (rodada)
5 a single bullet or similar object fired from a weapon (cartucho de bala)
6 a round of applause when people clap (salva de palmas)
7 a round of golf a game of golf (rodada)
▶ VERB [**rounds, rounding, rounded**] to go around something □ *As I rounded the corner, I came face to face with Sharon.* (virar, contornar)
◆ PHRASAL VERBS **round something down** to reduce a number to the nearest suitable unit. A maths word. (arredondar um número para menos) **round something off** to end an event or an activity in a suitable way □ *We rounded off the evening with some dancing.* (fechar (um evento)) **round on someone** to suddenly speak angrily to someone or about someone □ *The minister rounded on his critics, accusing them of lying.* (voltar-se contra) **round someone/something up** to bring a group of animals or people together □ *Farmers are rounding the animals up for the winter.* □ *Police are trying to round up all the suspects.* (reunir) **round something up** to increase a number to the nearest suitable unit. A maths word. □ *The fare was £4.50, so I rounded it up to £5.* (arredondar um número para mais)

roundabout /ˈraʊndəbaʊt/ NOUN [plural **roundabouts**]
1 a place where several roads meet and the traffic must go around a circle in the same direction before turning onto the next road □ *Turn left at the roundabout.* (praça circular)
2 a round structure that children sit on while it turns round (carrossel)

rounders /ˈraʊndəz/ PLURAL NOUN a team game in which players try to hit a ball then run around four sides of a square (jogo semelhante ao beisebol)

roundly /ˈraʊndli/ ADVERB clearly and completely or by many people (claramente) 🔁 *We were roundly criticized for failing to finish.* □ *He was roundly defeated.*

round-the-clock /ˌraʊndðəˈklɒk/ ADJECTIVE during all the day and all the night (durante 24 horas)

round trip /ˈraʊnd ˌtrɪp/ NOUN [plural **round trips**] when you go to a place and come back again □ *It's a round trip of nearly five hundred miles.* (viagem de ida e volta)

round-up /ˈraʊndʌp/ NOUN [plural **round-ups**] an short description of information or events □ *Let's go back to the studio for the latest news round-up.* (resumo)

rouse /raʊz/ VERB [**rouses, rousing, roused**]
1 to cause an emotion □ *It's a topic that always rouses passions.* (despertar)
2 a formal word meaning to wake someone up (despertar)
• **rousing** /ˈraʊzɪŋ/ ADJECTIVE exciting and making people feel enthusiastic □ *rousing music* □ *a rousing speech* (vibrante)

rout /raʊt/ ▶ NOUN [plural **routs**] a complete defeat (derrota)
▶ VERB [**routs, routing, routed**] to defeat someone completely (derrotar)

route /ruːt/ NOUN [plural **routes**]
1 a way of getting from one place to another (caminho) 🔁 *Which route do you take to work?* (qual caminho você pega) □ *a bus route* □ + *of There were police all along the route of the march.* □ *It's the main route between London and Bristol.*
2 a way of achieving something □ *He went down a fairly traditional career route.* (trajeto, caminho)

routine /ruːˈtiːn/ ▶ NOUN [plural **routines**]
1 the usual things that you do and they way you do them (rotina) 🔁 *Exercise should be part of your daily routine.* (rotina diária) □ *They settled into a routine of family life.*
2 a performance that someone does in the same way many times (apresentação) 🔁 *a dance routine* (coreografia de dança)
▶ ADJECTIVE normal and done regularly □ *a routine inspection* (rotineiro)

rove /rəʊv/ VERB [**roves, roving, roved**] to move or to travel around from one place to another □ *His eyes roved around the room.* (vaguear)
• **roving** /ˈrəʊvɪŋ/ ADJECTIVE moving or travelling from place to place □ *a roving reporter* (ambulante)

row¹ /rəʊ/ NOUN [plural **rows**]
1 a number of people or things arranged next to each other in a line □ *the front row of seats* □ *Sow the seeds in a straight row.* □ *a row of figures* (fila, fileira)
2 in a row happening one after another □ *They've lost five matches in a row.* (em fila)

row² /rəʊ/ VERB [**rows, rowing, rowed**] to pull a boat through water using oars (= long wooden poles) (remar)

row³ /raʊ/ ▶ NOUN [plural **rows**]
1 a noisy argument or strong disagreement (briga) 🔁 *Tom had a row with his girlfriend.* (teve uma briga) □ *The incident caused a political row.* □ *They went on strike in a row over pay.*

2 a loud unpleasant noise □ *Why are the children making such a row?* (**barulheira**)
▶ VERB [**rows, rowing, rowed**] to argue noisily □ *They were always rowing and falling out.* (**brigar**)

> Notice the different pronunciations. **row¹** and **row²** are pronounced the same and rhyme with low. **row³** is pronounced differently and rhymes with how.

rowboat /ˈrəʊbəʊt/ NOUN [plural **rowboats**] the US word for **rowing boat** (**barco a remo**)

rowdy /ˈraʊdi/ ADJECTIVE [**rowdier, rowdiest**] noisy and likely to cause trouble □ *a rowdy party* (**turbulento**)

rowing boat /ˈrəʊɪŋ ˌbəʊt/ NOUN [plural **rowing boats**] a small boat that you pull through the water using oars (= long wooden poles) (**barco a remo**)

royal /ˈrɔɪəl/ ADJECTIVE to do with a king or queen or their family (**real**) 🔁 *the Danish royal family* (**família real**) □ *a royal wedding*
• **royalty** /ˈrɔɪəlti/ NOUN, NO PLURAL all the members of the king or queen's family (**realeza, membro da família real**)

RSVP /ˌɑːresviːˈpiː/ ABBREVIATION written on an invitation in order to ask for a reply (**favor responder**)

rub /rʌb/ ▶ VERB [**rubs, rubbing, rubbed**]
1 to move your hand or an object backwards and forwards over a surface □ *He was rubbing his eyes.* □ *She rubbed her cheek against the velvet.* (**esfregar**)
2 to spread a substance on something and move it backwards and forwards with your fingers so that it covers it or goes into its surface □ *She rubbed cream onto the red skin.* (**friccionar**)
3 to press and move against something, often causing pain or damage □ *My shoes are rubbing and giving me blisters.* (**apertar**)
♦ IDIOM **rub it in** to say something which makes someone feel even worse about something which has embarrassed or upset them. An informal phrase □ *OK, he knows he did badly in the exam – there's no need to rub it in.* (**repisar, insistir em assunto desagradável**)
♦ PHRASAL VERBS **rub off** if a characteristic or feeling rubs off on someone, they get it from someone else □ *I wish some of her enthusiasm would rub off on her sisters.* (**contagiar**) **rub something out** to remove words or pictures by rubbing them with a piece of rubber or a cloth □ *Copy these words off the board before I rub them out.* (**apagar**)
▶ NOUN [plural **rubs**] a movement of your hand or an object over a surface □ *Let me give your neck a rub where it's aching.* (**esfregadura, fricção**)

rubber /ˈrʌbə(r)/ NOUN [plural **rubbers**]
1 *no plural* a strong substance that stretches and bends easily, made from tree juices □ *shoes with rubber soles* □ *a pair of rubber gloves* (**borracha**)
2 a small block that you rub on paper in order to remove pencil marks (**borracha**)

rubber band /ˌrʌbə ˈbænd/ NOUN [plural **rubber bands**] a small thin circle of rubber you put around things to hold them together (**elástico**)

rubber stamp /ˌrʌbə ˈstæmp/ NOUN [plural **rubber stamps**] a small tool for printing numbers or short words on paper (**carimbo**)
• **rubber-stamp** VERB [**rubber-stamps, rubberstamping, rubber-stamped**] to officially agree to a plan or a decision without giving it attention □ *The minister rubber-stamped the decision.* (**aprovar oficialmente**)

rubbish /ˈrʌbɪʃ/ ▶ NOUN, NO PLURAL
1 things that have been thrown away because they are no longer wanted □ *Put the rubbish in the bin.* □ *More household rubbish could be recycled.* (**lixo**) 🔁 *a rubbish bin* (**cesto de lixo**)
2 an informal word for something someone says that is not true or is stupid (**bobagem**) 🔁 *He's talking rubbish.* (**falando bobagem**)
3 an informal word for something of very bad quality □ *Her new chat show is absolute rubbish.* (**porcaria**)
▶ ADJECTIVE an informal word meaning of very bad quality or stupid □ *That was a rubbish suggestion!* (**idiota**)

rubble /ˈrʌbəl/ NOUN, NO PLURAL the broken pieces that are left when a building falls down □ *a pile of rubble* (**entulho, pedregulho**)

ruby /ˈruːbi/ NOUN [plural **rubies**] a dark red stone that is used in jewellery (**rubi**)

rucksack /ˈrʌksæk/ NOUN [plural **rucksacks**] a bag that you carry on your back (**mochila**)

rudder /ˈrʌdə(r)/ NOUN [plural **rudders**] the flat piece at the back of a boat or an aeroplane that moves to control its direction (**leme**)

ruddy /ˈrʌdi/ ADJECTIVE [**ruddier, ruddiest**] pink and healthy looking □ *a ruddy complexion* (**corado**)

rude /ruːd/ ADJECTIVE [ruder, rudest]
1 insulting and not polite □ + *to* *She was very rude to hotel staff.* □ *I don't mean to be rude, but isn't it a bit old?* □ + *to do something* *It would be rude to ignore them.* (**rude, grosseiro**)
2 embarrassing or offensive and not acceptable in a polite situation □ *rude jokes* □ *a rude word* (**grosseiro**)
3 **rude awakening** something shocking that happens suddenly (**choque repentino**)

> Note that someone is **rude to** someone else and not 'rude with' someone else:
> ✓ He was very rude to my mother.
> ✗ He was very rude with my mother.

• **rudely** /ˈruːdli/ ADVERB in a way that is rude (**grosseiramente**) 🔁 *She was rudely interrupted in the middle of her speech.* (**interrompida grosseiramente**)

- **rudeness** /'ruːdnɪs/ NOUN, NO PLURAL when someone is rude □ *I apologize for my friend's rudeness.* (**grosseria**)

rueful /'ruːfʊl/ ADJECTIVE showing that you are slightly sorry or sad about something □ *She gave a rueful smile.* (**pesaroso**)
- **ruefully** /'ruːfʊli/ ADVERB in a rueful way □ *He shrugged ruefully.* (**pesarosamente**)

ruff /rʌf/ NOUN [plural **ruffs**] a piece of cloth in many folds that was worn around the neck in the past (**rufo**)

ruffle /'rʌfəl/ VERB [**ruffles, ruffling, ruffled**]
1 to rub something, usually hair, so that it is not smooth □ *She ruffled the child's hair.* (**desarranjar**)
2 to annoy or upset someone □ *She never seems to get ruffled.* (**irritar**)

rug /rʌg/ NOUN [plural **rugs**] a cover for the floor which is not fixed □ *a sheepskin rug* (**tapete**)

rugby /'rʌgbi/ NOUN, NO PLURAL a sport played by two teams in which the players throw and run with an oval ball (**rúgbi**) ▣ *a rugby player* (**jogador de rúgbi**) ▣ *He plays rugby.* (**joga rúgbi**)

rugged /'rʌgɪd/ ADJECTIVE
1 rough with a lot of rocks □ *a rugged coastline* (**acidentado**)
2 with strong but attractive features □ *He has rugged good looks.* (**rústico**)

ruin /'ruːɪn/ ▶ VERB [**ruins, ruining, ruined**]
1 to spoil something completely □ *The rain had ruined my hair style.* □ *The injury threatens to ruin her athletics career.* (**estragar, arruinar**)
2 to cause someone to lose all their money (**arruinar**)
▶ NOUN [plural **ruins**]
1 something such as an old building that has fallen down □ *a Roman ruin* □ *the ancient Inca ruins of Machu Picchu* (**ruína**)
2 when someone loses everything they have (**ruína**) ▣ *He faced financial ruin.* (**ruína financeira**)
3 in ruins destroyed or completely spoilt □ *The city was in ruins after the earthquake.* (**em ruínas**)
- **ruined** /'ruːɪnd/ ADJECTIVE destroyed □ *a ruined castle* (**arruinado**)

rule /ruːl/ ▶ NOUN [plural **rules**]
1 an instruction about what is allowed or what is not allowed □ *It's against the rules to move your feet when you're holding the ball.* (**regra, regulamento**) ▣ *She was disqualified from the competition for breaking the rules.* (**quebrar as regras**) ▣ *You must follow* (= obey) *all the rules carefully.* (**seguir as regras**) ▣ *There are strict rules about employing staff.* (**regras rigorosas**)
2 the person or group that controls a country or an area (**governo, poder, controle**) ▣ *The country is under military rule.* (**controle militar**)
3 a principle that shows how something happens, especially in language or science □ *The rule for forming plurals is fairly simple.* □ *What you described would not follow the rules of physics.* (**regra**)
4 as a rule usually □ *I have my hair cut every six weeks as a rule.* (**via de regra**)
⇨ go to **a rule of thumb**
▶ VERB [**rules, ruling, ruled**]
1 to control a country or an area □ *He ruled France in the 18th century.* □ *She is a minister in the ruling socialist party.* (**governar**)
2 to make an official decision □ + *that The judge has ruled that the prisoner can go free.* (**decretar**)
◆ PHRASAL VERB **rule something/someone out** to decide that something is not possible or that something or someone cannot be used or chosen □ *The police have ruled out murder.* □ *His injury rules him out of the next match.* (**excluir alguém/algo**)
- **ruler** /'ruːlə(r)/ NOUN [plural **rulers**]
1 a person who controls a country or an area □ *Gandhi never became ruler of India.* (**dirigente**)
2 a flat strip of wood, plastic or metal, used to draw straight lines or for measuring short lengths (**régua**)
- **ruling** /'ruːlɪŋ/ [plural **rulings**] an official decision, often by a judge □ *They plan to challenge the judge's ruling in the European Court.* (**despacho, decisão oficial**)

rum /rʌm/ NOUN, NO PLURAL a strong alcoholic drink made from sugar (**rum**)

rumble /'rʌmbəl/ ▶ VERB [**rumbles, rumbling, rumbled**]
1 to make a low continuous sound □ *Thunder rumbled in the distance.* (**estrondar**)
2 to move along making a long, low sound □ *A truck rumbled down the street.* (**movimentar barulhento de um veículo**)
▶ NOUN [plural **rumbles**] a long low sound □ *the distant rumble of traffic* (**estrondo**)

rummage /'rʌmɪdʒ/ VERB [**rummages, rummaging, rummaged**] to search for something by moving things in an untidy way □ *She rummaged in her handbag for a pen.* (**remexer em busca de algo**)

rummy /'rʌmi/ NOUN, NO PLURAL a card game where each player has seven cards and tries to collect sets of similar cards (**jogo de cartas**)

rumor /'ruːmə(r)/ ▶ NOUN [plural **rumors**] the US spelling of **rumour** (**rumor, boato**)
▶ VERB [**rumors, rumoring, rumored**] the US spelling of **rumour**

rumour /'ruːmə(r)/ ▶ NOUN [plural **rumours**] information that people tell each other, although it may not be true □ *I heard a rumour that Jen was leaving.* (**rumor, boato**) ▣ *Someone has been spreading rumours.* (**espalhando boatos**)
▶ VERB [**rumours, rumouring, rumoured**] if something is rumoured, people say it is true, although it may not be □ *The player is rumoured to be joining Chelsea.*

rump /rʌmp/ NOUN [plural **rumps**] the area around an animal's tail or above its back legs (**garupa**)

rumpus

rumpus /'rʌmpəs/ NOUN, NO PLURAL a noisy situation where people are arguing or complaining □ *His comments caused a rumpus outside the courtroom.* (**algazarra**)

run /rʌn/ ▶ VERB [runs, running, ran, run]

1 to move with very fast steps □ *We had to run for the bus.* □ *They ran down the street screaming.* (**correr**)

2 to run in a race or as a sport □ *I'm hoping to run a marathon.* □ *He runs every morning.* (**correr**)

3 to control or organize an organization, event or activity □ *She runs a successful transport business.* □ *The college runs part-time courses.* □ *The party is not ready to run the country.* (**dirigir**)

4 if an activity or event runs for a particular time that is when or how long it takes place □ *The course runs over the summer.* □ *The movie ran for over four hours.* (**durar**)

5 if a machine or a piece of equipment is running, it is being used □ *I left the engine running while I ran into the house.* □ **+ on** *The heating runs on solar energy.* (**funcionar**)

6 to use a computer program □ *We run Windows in the office.* □ *I ran a grammar check on the document.* (**usar um programa**)

7 if a liquid runs somewhere, it flows in that direction □ *I had tears running down my face.* □ *Water ran over the side of the bath.* (**escorrer**)

8 if your nose is running, liquid is coming out of it (**escorrer**)

9 if buses and trains are running, they are travelling and people can use them □ *The number 5 bus runs every 10 minutes.* (**circular**) 🔁 *The trains never run on time.* (**circulam na hora**)

10 to take someone somewhere in a car □ *I run the children to school if it's raining.* (**levar com o carro**)

11 to move something through or across something □ *Grace ran her finger down the list.* □ *He ran his fingers through his hair.* (**passar**)

12 if something runs in a particular direction or position, that is where it is □ *A path ran behind the house.* □ *Wires ran overhead.* (**estender-se**)

13 to be at a particular level □ **+ at** *Sales are running at around 150 per month.* (**atingir**) 🔁 *Food supplies were running low.* (**atingindo um nível baixo**)

♦ PHRASAL VERBS **run across someone/something** to meet someone or find something by chance □ *I ran across Kelly in the library the other day.* (**cruzar com alguém/algo**) **run around** to be busy doing things □ *I've been running around preparing for his visit.* (**ocupar-se, ficar para lá e para cá**) **run around after someone** to be busy doing things for someone □ *I've been running around after the children.* (**ficar para lá e para cá atrás de alguém**) **run away**

1 to leave a place secretly (**fugir**) 🔁 *I ran away from home several times.* (**fugi de casa**)

2 to try to get away from an unpleasant situation □ *You can't just run away from your responsibilities.* (**esquivar-se**) **run someone/something down**

run

1 to knock someone or something over with a vehicle □ *The lorry driver simply ran him down.* (**atropelar**)

2 to criticize someone or something repeatedly □ *He is constantly trying to run down his colleagues.* (**menosprezar**) **run for something** to try to be elected for a position □ *She is running for president.* (**candidatar-se**) **run into someone** to meet someone by chance □ *I ran into Jake at the supermarket.* (**encontrar-se por acaso com alguém**) **run into something**

1 to drive a vehicle into an object □ *I lost control and ran into a wall.* (**colidir com algo**)

2 to reach a particular level □ *His legal costs ran into thousands of dollars.* (**atingir**)

3 to begin to experience problems □ *The project ran into financial difficulties.* (**entrar em dificuldades**) **run off** to suddenly leave a place or a person □ *My father ran off when I was 3.* (**fugir**) **run out**

1 to use the whole amount of something □ *We have run out of money.* (**ficar sem ter**)

2 to be completely used □ *The milk has run out.* (**terminar**) **run someone/something over** to drive over someone or something in a vehicle □ *I reversed and ran over his bike.* (**examinar rapidamente**) **run through something** (**passar rapidamente**)

1 to quickly read something or tell someone about something □ *Let me run through the rules again.*

2 to quickly practise something □ *Can we run through the last act?* **run something up** if you run up debts or bills (= money you owe for things you have bought), you owe that amount □ *I ran up huge debts at college.* (**acumular**) **run up against something** if you run up against a problem or a difficult situation, you experience it □ *We ran up against a lot of prejudice against women.* (**enfrentar**)

▶ NOUN [plural **runs**]

1 when you run in a race or as a sport (**corrida**) 🔁 *I always go for a run before breakfast.* □ *That run was fast enough to give him a place in the Olympic team.* (**dar uma corrida**)

2 when you move with very fast steps (**corrida**) 🔁 *When she saw Terry, she broke into a run* (= started running). (**começou a correr/saiu em disparada**)

3 make a run for it to try to escape by running away □ *He spotted the open door and made a run for it.* (**tentar escapar correndo**)

4 on the run trying to escape, especially from the police □ *While he was on the run, he had contact with his sister.* (**em fuga**)

5 a series of similar events □ *a run of bad luck* (**série**)

6 the length of time a show, television programme, etc, continues □ *The musical had a long Broadway run.* (**temporada**)

7 a journey in a vehicle □ *We chatted on the run down to Devon.* (**passeio**)

8 a point that a player wins in a game like cricket or baseball (**pontos**) 🔁 *He scored 58 runs.*

9 an area with a fence where animals are kept □ *a chicken run* (cercado)
10 a practice/trial run when you do something in order to practise it, before doing it in a real situation (treino)
♦ IDIOM **in the long/short run** at or during the time that is far away/near □ *In the short run, you can expect some financial losses.* (a longo/curto prazo)

runaway /'rʌnəweɪ/ ▶ NOUN [plural **runaways**] someone who has left their home secretly □ *a teenage runaway* (fugitivo)
▶ ADJECTIVE
1 happening or succeeding very quickly and easily (fácil) 🔸 *Their latest product has been a runaway success.* (sucesso fácil) 🔸 *Ellis was the runaway winner.* (vencedor fácil)
2 having left your home secretly □ *a runaway school girl* (fugitivo)
3 a runaway vehicle is out of control and moving very fast (descontrolado)

run-down /ˌrʌn'daʊn/ ADJECTIVE
1 not kept in good condition □ *a run-down neighbourhood* (precário)
2 tired and not healthy (abatido)

rung¹ /rʌŋ/ NOUN [plural **rungs**] a step on a ladder (= a piece of equipment with steps you climb up to reach a high place) (degrau)

rung² /rʌŋ/ PAST PARTICIPLE OF **ring²** □ *Have you rung your mother?* (ver **ring²**)

run-in /'rʌnɪn/ NOUN [plural **run-ins**] an informal word for an argument or a fight 🔸 *I had a bit of a run-in with one of the directors.* (desentendimento, discussão)

runner /'rʌnə(r)/ NOUN [plural **runners**]
1 a person or animal that runs □ *He's a very fast runner.* □ *a marathon runner* (corredor)
2 someone who carries something illegally from one place to another □ *a drug runner* (contrabandista)
3 a blade on the bottom of something that it slides along on (lâmina de patim de gelo)

runner-up /ˌrʌnər'ʌp/ NOUN [plural **runners-up**] the person who finishes in second place in a competition (segundo colocado) 🔸 *She finished runner-up in last year's race.* (terminou em segundo lugar)

running /'rʌnɪŋ/ ▶ NOUN, NO PLURAL
1 the sport or activity of moving with very fast steps (corrida) 🔸 *She gets up early to go running.* (fazer uma corrida) □ *He took up marathon running.* (corrida)
2 the organization and management of something (administração) □ **+ of** *You'll be responsible for the running of the shop.* 🔸 *She's still involved with the day-to-day running of the company.* (gerenciamento diário)
3 in/out of the running an informal phrase meaning having/not having a chance of winning something □ *He's still in the running for the championship.* (com/sem chance de)

▶ ADJECTIVE
1 used to say that something happens a number of times, one directly after another □ *The album is at number one for the third week running.* (consecutivo)
2 continuing without stopping □ *a running commentary on the events* (contínuo)
3 running water water which comes through pipes from a water supply □ *The cottage has no running water or electricity.* (água corrente)

runny /'rʌni/ ADJECTIVE [**runnier**, **runniest**]
1 in a liquid state □ *runny honey* (líquido)
2 if you have a runny nose or eyes, they are producing a lot of liquid (gotejante) 🔸 *I had a cough and a runny nose.* (nariz escorrendo)

run-of-the-mill /ˌrʌnəvðə'mɪl/ ADJECTIVE ordinary or average, not special in any way □ *They offer a fairly run-of-the-mill range of pub food.* (comum, médio)

run-up /'rʌnʌp/ NOUN, NO PLURAL the period of time or events immediately before an important event □ *the run-up to the competition* (momentos que antecedem um evento)

runway /'rʌnweɪ/ NOUN [plural **runways**] the long, wide road at an airport that aeroplanes take off from and land on (pista)

rupture /'rʌptʃə(r)/ ▶ VERB [**ruptures, rupturing, ruptured**] to tear or to break open, or to cause this □ *He ruptured a knee ligament.* □ *A gas pipeline ruptured.* (romper)
▶ NOUN [plural **ruptures**] a break or tear, especially in a muscle or an organ (ruptura)

rural /'rʊərəl/ ADJECTIVE to do with the countryside (rural) 🔸 *She grew up in a rural area.* (área rural) □ *a rural community*

rush /rʌʃ/ ▶ NOUN [plural **rushes**]
1 a sudden, strong movement or feeling □ *a rush of cold air* (ímpeto, onda) 🔸 *She felt a rush of excitement.* (sentiu um ímpeto) 🔸 *an adrenaline rush* (onda de adrenalina)
2 a hurry □ *It was a bit of a rush but we got there in time.* (pressa)
3 be in a rush to be hurrying □ *I was in a rush to get to the airport on time.* (na correria, com pressa)
4 when a large number of people try to go somewhere or do something at the same time □ *There was a sudden rush for the door.* □ *a rush for tickets* (corrida)
▶ VERB [**rushes, rushing, rushed**]
1 to move or to do something quickly and suddenly □ *Firefighters rushed to the scene.* □ *Several colleagues rushed to help the woman.* (correr, apressar-se)
2 to take someone or something somewhere very quickly (levar com pressa) 🔸 *He was rushed to hospital in an ambulance.* (levar às pressas ao hospital)
3 to do something too quickly and without enough care □ *I don't want to rush things.* (precipitar)

rush hour /ˈrʌʃ ˌaʊə(r)/ NOUN [plural **rush hours**] the time when there is most traffic because people are travelling to or from work (**hora do rush**) 🔁 the morning rush hour (**hora do rush da manhã**) 🔁 Trains are packed during the evening rush hour. (**hora do rush da noite**)

rusk /rʌsk/ NOUN [plural **rusks**] a hard dry biscuit that babies eat (**torrada**)

russet /ˈrʌsɪt/ NOUN, NO PLURAL a red-brown colour (**ruivo**)

rust /rʌst/ ▶ NOUN, NO PLURAL a brown substance that forms on iron and other metals if they are in air and water (**ferrugem**)
▶ VERB [**rusts, rusting, rusted**] to become covered in rust ◻ The equipment was just left to rust. (**enferrujar**)

rustic /ˈrʌstɪk/ ADJECTIVE simple, in a way that is typical of the countryside ◻ The house had a certain rustic charm. (**rústico**)

rustle /ˈrʌsəl/ ▶ VERB [**rustles, rustling, rustled**] to make a soft dry sound when moving, or to make something do this ◻ Trees rustled in the breeze. ◻ They rustled their papers. (**farfalhar**)
◆ PHRASAL VERB **rustle something up** to make something quickly from what you have available ◻ I could rustle up an omelette.
▶ NOUN [plural **rustles**] when something rustles ◻ the rustle of a silk dress

rusty /ˈrʌsti/ ADJECTIVE [**rustier, rustiest**]
1 covered in rust (= a reddish-brown substance that forms on metal) ◻ rusty nails (**enferrujado**)
2 if a skill is rusty, it is not as good as it was before ◻ My Spanish is a bit rusty these days. (**enferrujado**)

rut /rʌt/ NOUN [plural **ruts**]
1 a boring situation where nothing changes (**rotina**) 🔁 I was getting stuck in a rut and I needed a change. (**preso a uma rotina**)
2 a deep track made by a wheel ◻ There were deep ruts in the road. (**sulco**)

ruthless /ˈruːθlɪs/ ADJECTIVE cruel and trying to achieve what you want without caring how your behaviour affects others ◻ a ruthless dictator (**impiedoso**)
• **ruthlessly** /ˈruːθlɪsli/ ADVERB in a ruthless way ◻ ruthlessly ambitious (**impiedosamente**)
• **ruthlessness** /ˈruːθlɪsnɪs/ NOUN, NO PLURAL the quality of being ruthless (**crueldade**)

rye /raɪ/ NOUN, NO PLURAL a type of grain that is used for making flour (**centeio**)

Ss

S¹ or **s** /es/ the 19th letter of the alphabet (a décima nona letra do alfabeto)

S² /es/ ABBREVIATION **south** (ver **south²**)

Sabbath /ˈsæbəθ/ NOUN **the Sabbath** the day of the week for rest and prayer in some religions (Sabá)

sabbatical /səˈbætɪkəl/ NOUN [plural **sabbaticals**] a period when a university teacher does not teach because they are studying away from the university (sabático)

sabotage /ˈsæbətɑːʒ/ ▶ NOUN, NO PLURAL
1 deliberate damage that someone does to an enemy's property or equipment □ an act of sabotage (sabotagem)
2 secret action that is intended to stop someone or something from succeeding (sabotagem)
▶ VERB [**sabotages, sabotaging, sabotaged**]
1 to deliberately damage an enemy's property or equipment □ Rebels had sabotaged the electricity supply lines. (sabotar)
2 to do something to stop someone or something from being successful (sabotar)

sac /sæk/ NOUN [plural **sacs**] any part of a plant or animal that is like a bag, especially one that contains liquid. A biology word. (bolsa)

saccharin /ˈsækərɪn/ NOUN, NO PLURAL a very sweet chemical that is used instead of sugar (sacarina)

• **saccharine** /ˈsækərɪn/ ADJECTIVE too romantic, in a way that is annoying □ a saccharine romantic comedy (sacarina, piegas)

sachet /ˈsæʃeɪ/ NOUN [plural **sachets**] a small flat bag that contains a little of a liquid or powder □ a sachet of shampoo (sachê)

sack /sæk/ ▶ NOUN [plural **sacks**]
1 a large bag made of strong material used for carrying or storing things □ a sack of potatoes (saco)
2 the sack when you lose your job (ser despedido) 🔹 He got the sack for being late all the time. (foi despedido) 🔹 They'll give her the sack if she doesn't work harder. (será despedida)
▶ VERB [**sacks, sacking, sacked**] to tell someone they can no longer have their job □ He was sacked for stealing. (despedir)

sacrament /ˈsækrəmənt/ NOUN [plural **sacraments**] any of several important Christian ceremonies such as marriage or baptism (= naming a child) (sacramento)

sacred /ˈseɪkrɪd/ ADJECTIVE
1 holy, or to do with God □ a sacred shrine (sagrado)
2 to do with religion □ sacred music (sagrado)
3 very important and not to be changed □ I'm standing on the sacred turf of this world-famous football ground. (sagrado)

sacrifice /ˈsækrɪfaɪs/ ▶ NOUN [plural **sacrifices**]
1 giving up something important to you in order to achieve something that is more important, or the thing that you give up in this way (sacrifício) 🔹 We had to make sacrifices in order to be able to buy a house. (fazer sacrifícios)
2 the act of killing someone or something and offering them to a god, or the person or animal that is killed in this way (sacrifício)
▶ VERB [**sacrifices, sacrificing, sacrificed**]
1 to give up something that is important to you in order to achieve something that is more important □ He sacrificed his life to save his fellow soldiers. (sacrificar)
2 to kill someone or something and offer them to a god (sacrificar)

sacrilege /ˈsækrɪlɪdʒ/ NOUN, NO PLURAL treating something that is holy or admired without respect (sacrilégio)

• **sacrilegious** /ˌsækrɪˈlɪdʒəs/ ADJECTIVE not showing respect for something that is holy or admired (sacrílego)

sad /sæd/ ADJECTIVE [**sadder, saddest**]
1 unhappy (triste) 🔹 I felt sad saying goodbye to them. (me senti triste) □ + **to do something** I'll be sad to leave the company after so many years.
2 making you feel unhappy □ a sad film □ a sad story (triste)
3 if something is sad, it is bad and you wish it was different (triste) 🔹 It's a sad fact that some people think there is nothing wrong with violence. (triste fato)
4 boring and not fashionable □ I'm so sad, I spent my holiday working. (péssimo)

• **sadden** /ˈsædən/ VERB [**saddens, saddening, saddened**] to make someone feel unhappy □ We were greatly saddened by the news. (entristecer)

saddle /ˈsædəl/ ▶ NOUN [plural **saddles**]
1 a leather seat for putting on a horse's back (sela)
2 a seat on a bicycle or motorcycle (selim, assento)
▶ VERB [**saddles, saddling, saddled**] to put a saddle on a horse so that you can ride it (sobrecarregar, encarregar)

◆ PHRASAL VERB **saddle someone with something** to give someone a difficult job or responsibility (sobrecarregar alguém com alguma coisa)

sadism /'seɪdɪzəm/ NOUN, NO PLURAL when someone enjoys being cruel and hurting other people (sadismo)

• **sadist** /'seɪdɪst/ NOUN [plural **sadists**] someone who enjoys being cruel and hurting other people (sádico)

• **sadistic** /sə'dɪstɪk/ ADJECTIVE enjoying being cruel and hurting other people ▫ *a sadistic attack* (sádico)

sadly /'sædli/ ADVERB
1 used for saying that you wish something was not true ▫ *Sadly, she can't be here with us today.* (infelizmente)
2 in an unhappy way ▫ *She waved sadly.* (tristemente)

sadness /'sædnɪs/ NOUN, NO PLURAL a feeling of unhappiness ▫ *It is with great sadness that we announce the death of our mother, Nancy.* (tristeza)

sae /es eɪ 'iː/ ABBREVIATION stamped addressed envelope; an envelope with your name, address and a stamp on it (envelope com nome e endereço do remetente e selo pago)

safari /sə'fɑːri/ NOUN [plural **safaris**] a journey to watch wild animals living in their natural home, especially in Africa (safári)

safari park /sə'fɑːri pɑːk/ NOUN [plural **safari parks**] a large area of land where wild animals are kept for visitors to see (parque safári)

safe /seɪf/ ▶ ADJECTIVE [**safer**, **safest**]
1 not likely to cause harm or damage ▫ *That ladder doesn't look very safe to me.* ▫ **+ to do something** *Is it safe to drink the water?* (seguro) 🔂 *We need a safe place to rest.* (local seguro)
2 not in danger of being harmed, damaged, lost, etc. ▫ *You must keep these documents safe.* ▫ **+ from** *Nobody is safe from the disease.* (seguro, a salvo)
3 not damaged, harmed, stolen, etc ▫ *Thank goodness you're safe!* (salvo, seguro) 🔂 *They are celebrating the safe return of the paintings.* (retorno seguro)
▶ NOUN [plural **safes**] a strong box with a lock, where money or valuable objects are kept (cofre)

safeguard /'seɪfgɑːd/ ▶ NOUN [plural **safeguards**] something that protects against danger or harm (salvaguarda) ▫ *The double lock is a safeguard against theft.*
▶ VERB [**safeguards**, **safeguarding**, **safeguarded**] to protect someone or something from danger or harm ▫ *These vaccinations safeguard our children against deadly diseases.* (proteger, salvaguardar)

safekeeping /ˌseɪf'kiːpɪŋ/ NOUN, NO PLURAL **for safekeeping** in order to stop something being lost or damaged ▫ *The documents are in the file for safekeeping.* (proteção, custódia)

safely /'seɪfli/ ADVERB without risk or danger ▫ *Drive safely.* ▫ *We got everyone home safely.* ▫ *The children were safely tucked up in bed.* (em segurança)

safety /'seɪfti/ NOUN, NO PLURAL
1 being safe, not being in danger or dangerous ▫ *The safety of passengers is our first concern.* ▫ *Tests will ensure the safety of the drugs.* (segurança)
2 a safe place ▫ *Everyone dived for safety.*

safety belt /'seɪfti belt/ NOUN [plural **safety belts**] a strong belt in a car or plane that goes across your body 🔂 *Fasten your safety belt.* (cinto de segurança)

safety pin /'seɪfti pɪn/ NOUN [plural **safety pins**] a pin with a cover that fits over the sharp point when it is closed (alfinete de segurança)

safety valve /'seɪfti vælv/ NOUN [plural **safety valves**] a device on a piece of equipment that lets gas or liquid escape if the pressure is too high (válvula de segurança)

saffron /'sæfrən/ NOUN, NO PLURAL thin yellow threads from a plant that are used to add colour and flavour to food (açafrão)

sag /sæg/ VERB [**sags**, **sagging**, **sagged**] to hang down or not be firm ▫ *The mattress has begun to sag in the middle.* (ceder, arquear, vergar)

saga /'sɑːgə/ NOUN [plural **sagas**]
1 a long story, especially one about a group of people over many years ▫ *a family saga* (saga)
2 a series of events that take a long time to tell someone about ▫ *We were delayed coming home – actually it's a bit of a saga.* (saga)

sage /seɪdʒ/ NOUN [plural **sages**]
1 a herb that is used in cooking to add flavor (sálvia)
2 a literary word for a wise man (sábio)

said /sed/ PAST TENSE AND PAST PARTICIPLE OF **say** ▫ *She said she was coming.* ▫ *They have said I can come back any time.* (ver **say**)

sail /seɪl/ ▶ VERB [**sails**, **sailing**, **sailed**]
1 to travel somewhere in a ship or a boat ▫ *They're sailing off the coast of Sweden.* (navegar)
2 to start a journey in a ship ▫ *The ferry sails at noon.* (zarpar)
◆ PHRASAL VERB **sail through something** to do something quickly and easily ▫ *Amy sailed through her exams with no bother.* (conseguir com facilidade)
▶ NOUN [plural **sails**]
1 a sheet of strong cloth attached to a boat, which catches the wind and carries the boat along (vela)
2 a wide flat blade that turns on a windmill (= a building where flour is made) (asa)

• **sailing** /'seɪlɪŋ/ NOUN, NO PLURAL the sport or activity of sailing small boats (navegação)

sailing boat /'seɪlɪŋ bəʊt/ NOUN [plural **sailing boats**] a small boat with sails (barco a vela)

sailor /ˈseɪlə(r)/ NOUN [plural sailors]

1 someone who works on a ship □ *a merchant sailor* (marinheiro)

2 someone who goes sailing □ *Joe's a keen sailor.* (marinheiro)

saint /seɪnt/ NOUN [plural saints]

1 a dead person that the Christian church believes was especially holy □ *Saint Francis* (santo)

2 a very good and kind person □ *She's an absolute saint, looking after her mother like that.* (santo)

• **saintly** /ˈseɪntli/ ADJECTIVE very good or very holy (santo)

sake /seɪk/ NOUN [plural sakes]

1 for someone's sake in order to help someone □ *For his mother's sake, he wanted to be there.* □ *Please don't go to any trouble just for my sake.* (por causa de)

2 for the sake of something in order to get or achieve something □ *I gave in for the sake of peace.* (por amor a)

salad /ˈsæləd/ NOUN [plural salads] a mixture of usually raw vegetables that sometimes includes other food, such as fish or cheese □ *a mixed salad* □ *rice salad* (salada)

salami /səˈlɑːmi/ NOUN [plural salamis] a type of sausage made from cooked meat and usually eaten cold (salame)

salary /ˈsæləri/ NOUN [plural salaries] an amount of money that a person is paid for doing their job each month or year □ *The job offers an annual salary of £35,000.* (salário)

sale /seɪl/ NOUN [plural sales] (vendas, liquidações)

1 *no plural* the process of selling things for money □ *the sale of houses* (venda)

2 the act of selling one thing (venda) ▣ *Have you made any sales yet?* (fez uma venda)

3 an event at which things are sold for money □ *a sale of antique furniture* (venda)

4 for sale available for someone to buy □ *Are these paintings for sale?* (à venda) ▣ *They've just put their house up for sale.* (pôr à venda)

5 a time when goods are sold at cheaper prices than usual □ *the January sales* (liquidação)

6 on sale (a) offered for sale □ *The DVD is on sale now.* (b) available to buy for less than the usual price □ *Designer dresses now on sale on the 5th floor.* (em liquidação)

7 sales (a) how many things a company sells □ *Sales are down for last month.* (vendas) ▣ *sales figures* (b) the department of a company whose work is selling things □ *She works in sales.* (resultados das vendas)

sales assistant /ˈseɪlz əˌsɪstənt/ NOUN [plural sales assistants] someone whose job is to sell things in a shop (vendedor)

sales clerk /ˈseɪlz klɜːrk/ NOUN [plural sales clerks] the US phrase for **sales assistant** (vendedor)

salesman /ˈseɪlzmən/ NOUN [plural salesmen] a man whose job is to sell goods or services to customers (vendedor)

sales rep /ˈseɪlz rep/ NOUN [plural sales reps] someone who travels to different places, selling things for a company (representante de vendas)

saleswoman /ˈseɪlzˌwʊmən/ NOUN [plural saleswomen] a woman whose job is to sell goods or services to customers (vendedora)

salient /ˈseɪliənt/ ADJECTIVE being the most important or noticeable. A formal word. □ *These are the salient features of the proposed legislation.* (proeminente, de destaque)

saline /ˈseɪlaɪn/ ADJECTIVE containing salt □ *a saline solution* (salino)

saliva /səˈlaɪvə/ NOUN, NO PLURAL the liquid that your mouth produces (saliva)

sallow /ˈsæləʊ/ ADJECTIVE [sallower, sallowest] sallow skin is pale, slightly yellow, and does not look healthy □ *a sallow complexion* (pálido)

salmon /ˈsæmən/ NOUN [plural salmon]

1 a large silver fish that swims up rivers to produce its eggs (salmão)

2 the orange-pink flesh from this fish eaten as food (carne de salmão)

3 an orange-pink colour (cor salmão)

salmonella /ˌsælməˈnelə/ NOUN, NO PLURAL a type of bacteria found in food that can make you very ill (salmonela)

salon /ˈsælɒn/ NOUN [plural salons] a shop where people will cut your hair or improve the appearance of a part of your body (salão de beleza)

saloon /səˈluːn/ NOUN [plural saloons] a car with front and back seats and a separate space for carrying things (carro estilo sedã)

salsa /ˈsælsə/ NOUN [plural salsas]

1 a type of Latin-American music, or a dance for this music (salsa)

2 a cold sauce with tomatoes and spices in it (molho)

salt /sɔːlt, sɒlt/ ▶ NOUN, NO PLURAL a white substance that comes from the ground or the sea and is used often for giving flavour to food (sal) ▣ *salt and pepper* (sal e pimenta) ▣ *Add a pinch of salt.* (pitada de sal)

▶ VERB [salts, salting, salted] to add salt to food (salgar)

• **salted** /ˈsɔːltɪd/ ADJECTIVE with salt added □ *salted peanuts* (com sal)

• **salty** /ˈsɔːlti/ ADJECTIVE [saltier, saltiest] containing salt or tasting very strongly of salt □ *I thought the soup was too salty.* (salgado)

salubrious /səˈluːbriəs/ ADJECTIVE a salubrious place is pleasant, clean and crime does not happen often there □ *This is not the most salubrious part of London.* (salubre)

salutary /ˈsæljʊtəri/ ADJECTIVE a salutary experience is difficult but has a good effect on

salute your future behaviour. A formal word. □ *Criticism is often salutary.* (**salutar**)

salute /səˈluːt/ ▶ VERB [**salutes, saluting, saluted**]
1 to show respect to someone, especially a military officer, by touching your head with your right hand (**continência**)
2 to praise someone or something that someone has done, often publicly □ *The newspapers all salute her efforts to restore peace.* (**saudar**)
▶ NOUN [*plural* **salutes**]
1 a movement that shows respect to someone you meet, especially a military officer □ *The Queen returned the salute.* (**saudação**)
2 an event, speech etc. that shows respect for someone □ *His first words were a salute to the people of South Africa.* (**saudação**)

salvage /ˈsælvɪdʒ/ ▶ VERB [**salvages, salvaging, salvaged**]
1 to save what you can after a building or ship has been damaged or destroyed □ *We managed to salvage a few belongings after the fire.* (**salvar**)
2 to succeed in achieving one good thing in a situation where you have failed generally (**salvar**)
▶ NOUN, NO PLURAL when things are salvaged or the things that are salvaged □ *a salvage operation* (**salvamento, salvos**)

salvation /sælˈveɪʃən/ NOUN, NO PLURAL
1 in the Christian religion, when God saves you from evil (**salvação**)
2 someone or something that saves you in a bad situation □ *Once again, Rooney was England's salvation, scoring in the final minute of the game.* (**salvação**)

same /seɪm/ ▶ ADJECTIVE, PRONOUN
1 the same (a) the person or thing mentioned, not a different one □ *He won the lottery and left his job on the same day.* (**o mesmo, igual**) ▣ *We both started speaking at the same time.* (**ao mesmo tempo**) (b) exactly like someone or something else ▣ *I was wearing the same jacket as Barbara.* (**igual à/ao de**) ▣ *He broke his own mobile phone and now he's done the same thing to mine!* (**a mesma coisa**) □ *You know I'd do the same for you.* (c) not changed □ *I thought she might have grown up a bit since leaving home, but she's just the same.*
2 same here used to say that something is also true for you. An informal phrase. □ *'I'm always late for work.' 'Same here – my boss gets really angry!'* (**o mesmo aqui, aqui também**)
3 at the same time used to say that another thing is also true □ *He needs to keep active, but at the same time he should be careful of his knees.* (**ao mesmo tempo**)
▶ ADVERB in the same way □ *We tend to dress the same.* □ *We treat all our children the same.* (**do mesmo modo**)

sample /ˈsɑːmpəl/ ▶ NOUN [*plural* **samples**] a small amount or number of something that shows what the rest is like (**amostra**) ▣ *The magazine came with a free sample of chocolate.* (**amostra grátis**) ▣ *This was a random sample of consumers.* (**amostra aleatória**)
▶ VERB [**samples, sampling, sampled**] to try a small amount of food or drink to find out what it is like □ *Would you like to sample our new yoghurt?* (**provar uma amostra**)

sanatorium /ˌsænəˈtɔːrɪəm/ NOUN [*plural* **sanatoriums** *or* **sanatoria**] a hospital that cares for people who need treatment or rest for a long time (**sanatório**)

sanction /ˈsæŋkʃən/ ▶ NOUN [*plural* **sanctions**]
1 an official order to stop speaking with or doing trade with a country that has broken international law (**sanção**) ▣ *international sanctions* (**sanções internacionais**) ▣ *trade sanctions* (**sanções comerciais**)
2 official permission or approval for an action □ *The proposed changes to the Act will require the sanction of Parliament.* (**sanção**)
3 a punishment for breaking a rule or law (**sanção**)
▶ VERB [**sanctions, sanctioning, sanctioned**] to give official permission for something (**sancionar**)

sanctity /ˈsæŋktɪtɪ/ NOUN, NO PLURAL the quality or condition of being holy or of deserving respect □ *the sanctity of marriage* (**santidade**)

sanctuary /ˈsæŋktʃʊərɪ/ NOUN [*plural* **sanctuaries**]
1 a place that officially protects someone (**refúgio**) ▣ *Many refugees seek sanctuary in these countries.* (**buscar refúgio**)
2 a safe place where animals can live in a natural environment and not be hunted □ *a bird sanctuary* (**reserva**)

sand /sænd/ ▶ NOUN, NO PLURAL very small grains of rock that are found on beaches and in deserts (**areia**)
▶ VERB [**sands, sanding, sanded**] to make a surface, especially wood, smooth by rubbing it with something rough (**lixar**)

sandal /ˈsændəl/ NOUN [*plural* **sandals**] a light open shoe for wearing when the weather is warm (**sandália**)

sandbag /ˈsændbæg/ NOUN [*plural* **sandbags**] a strong bag filled with sand that is used to build walls in order to keep out flood water or bullets (**saco de areia**)

sandcastle /ˈsændˌkɑːsəl/ NOUN [*plural* **sandcastles**] a pile of sand made to look like a castle, usually built by children playing on a beach (**castelo de areia**)

sand dune /ˈsænd djuːn/ NOUN [*plural* **sand dunes**] a hill of sand near a beach or in the desert (**duna de areia**)

sandpaper /ˈsændˌpeɪpə(r)/ NOUN, NO PLURAL strong paper with a layer of sand stuck to one side, used for making wood smooth (**lixa, papel de lixa**)

sandstone /'sændstəʊn/ NOUN, NO PLURAL a type of light-coloured stone that is used in building (**arenito**)

sandwich /'sænwɪdʒ/ ▶ NOUN [plural **sandwiches**] two pieces of bread with food between them □ *a ham sandwich* □ *a toasted sandwich* (**sanduíche**)
▶ VERB **be sandwiched between someone/something** to be in a small space between two bigger things or people □ *I was sandwiched between two huge men on the Metro.* (**ficar entalado entre pessoas/coisas**)

sandy /'sændɪ/ ADJECTIVE [**sandier, sandiest**]
1 covered with sand, or with sand inside □ *a sandy beach* □ *sandy shoes* (**arenoso**)
2 sandy hair is a light red-brown colour (**castanho-avermelhado**)

sane /seɪn/ ADJECTIVE [**saner, sanest**]
1 not mad or mentally ill □ *The judge was told that Foster was sane at the time of the murder.* (**são de espírito**)
2 sensible and showing good judgment □ *Reducing the stress in your life seems like a very sane thing to do.* (**sensato**)

sang /sæŋ/ PAST TENSE OF **sing** (**ver sing**)

sanitary /'sænɪtərɪ/ ADJECTIVE to do with keeping clean and healthy □ *Diseases spread quickly where sanitary conditions are poor.* (**sanitário**)

sanitation /,sænɪ'teɪʃən/ NOUN, NO PLURAL ways of protecting people's health by providing clean water and taking dirty water and waste away from buildings (**saneamento**)

sanity /'sænɪtɪ/ NOUN, NO PLURAL not being mad or mentally ill (**sanidade**)

sank /sæŋk/ PAST TENSE OF **sink** □ *The ship sank in rough waters.* (**ver sink**)

Santa Claus or **Santa** /'sæntə/ NOUN an imaginary old man with a white beard in a red coat who children believe brings presents on Christmas Eve □ *What did Santa bring you?* (**Papai Noel**)

sap /sæp/ ▶ NOUN, NO PLURAL the liquid inside plants and trees (**seiva**)
▶ VERB [**saps, sapping, sapped**] to make someone feel weak and tired (**consumir**) 🔁 *The heat saps my energy.* (**sugar energia**)

sapling /'sæplɪŋ/ NOUN [plural **saplings**] a young tree (**árvore nova**)

sapphire /'sæfaɪə(r)/ NOUN [plural **sapphires**] a dark blue stone that is used in jewellery (**safira**)

sarcasm /'sɑːkæzəm/ NOUN, NO PLURAL saying one thing when you mean the opposite, in order to criticize someone or make them feel stupid □ *'Nice jacket,' said Max, with heavy sarcasm.* (**sarcasmo**)

• **sarcastic** /sɑː'kæstɪk/ ADJECTIVE using sarcasm □ *I didn't know if he really liked it or if he was being sarcastic.* (**sarcástico**)

sardine /sɑː'diːn/ NOUN [plural **sardines**] a type of small sea fish that people eat (**sardinha**)

sardonic /sɑː'dɒnɪk/ ADJECTIVE showing no respect for what someone has said □ *a sardonic smile* (**sardônico**)
• **sardonically** /sɑː'dɒnɪkəlɪ/ ADVERB in a sardonic way □ *He laughed sardonically.* (**sardonicamente**)

sari /'sɑːrɪ/ NOUN [plural **saris**] a long piece of cloth that is wrapped round the body and worn as a dress especially by women in South Asia (**sári**)

sarong /sə'rɒŋ/ NOUN [plural **sarongs**] a wide piece of cloth that is wrapped round the lower part of the body and worn as a skirt (**sarongue**)

sash /sæʃ/ NOUN [plural **sashes**] a strip of cloth worn around the waist or over one shoulder, usually as part of a uniform (**faixa**)

sat /sæt/ PAST TENSE AND PAST PARTICIPLE OF **sit** □ *He sat down.* □ *I've sat here for an hour waiting for you!* (**ver sit**)

Satan /'seɪtən/ NOUN another name for the Devil (= the most powerful evil spirit in some religions) (**Satã**)

satchel /'sætʃəl/ NOUN [plural **satchels**] a bag that you wear over your shoulder, used by children for carrying books to school (**mochila escolar**)

satellite /'sætəlaɪt/ NOUN [plural **satellites**]
1 a piece of equipment that is put in space to travel around the Earth in order to send and receive information □ *a satellite link* □ *a weather/communications satellite* (**satélite**)
2 a natural object in space, such as the moon, that moves around a planet or star (**satélite**)

satellite dish /'sætəlaɪt dɪʃ/ NOUN [plural **satellite dishes**] a circular piece of equipment that is attached to the side of a building to receive signals for satellite television (**parabólica**)

satellite television /'sætəlaɪt 'telɪˌvɪʒən/ NOUN, NO PLURAL television programmes that are sent to people's televisions using satellites (**programação via satélite**)

satin /'sætɪn/ NOUN, NO PLURAL a type of cloth with a shiny surface (**cetim**)

satire /'sætaɪə(r)/ NOUN [plural **satires**]
1 the use of humour to criticize stupid or bad behaviour (**sátira**)
2 any book, film, play or television programme using this type of humour □ *a political satire* (**sátira**)
• **satirical** /sə'tɪrɪkəl/ ADJECTIVE using satire □ *He writes for a satirical magazine.* □ *a satirical cartoon* (**satírico**)
• **satirize** or **satirise** /'sætəraɪz/ VERB [**satirizes, satirizing, satirized**] to criticize someone or something using satire □ *Her first play satirized the political system.* (**satirizar**)

satisfaction /,sætɪs'fækʃən/ NOUN, NO PLURAL a feeling of pleasure at having achieved something or got something good □ *She looked at the finished work with satisfaction.* □ *+ from doing*

satisfactory

something I get a lot of satisfaction from cooking. **(satisfação)** ▣ *Job satisfaction is extremely important.* **(satisfação profissional)**

satisfactory /ˌsætɪsˈfæktəri/ ADJECTIVE of a good enough standard ※ *Her progress in maths was described as satisfactory.* □ *We are still waiting for a satisfactory outcome to the situation.* **(satisfatório)**

satisfied /ˈsætɪsfaɪd/ ADJECTIVE
1 pleased because you have achieved something or got something good □ + **with** *Are you satisfied with the progress on the project?* □ *You're never satisfied – that's your problem.* □ *a satisfied customer* **(satisfeito)**
2 if you are satisfied that something is true, you are certain that it is true □ + **that** *I am satisfied that they did all they could to help her.* **(convencido)**

• **satisfy** /ˈsætɪsfaɪ/ VERB [**satisfies, satisfying, satisfied**]
1 to make someone pleased by giving them what they want or need □ *The resort should satisfy even the most experienced skiers.* □ *This proposal is unlikely to satisfy campaigners.* **(satisfazer)**
2 if something satisfies a rule or condition, it has or does what is necessary for it **(satisfazer)** ▣ *Are you sure you satisfy the entry requirements for law school?*
3 to provide proof that something is true □ + **that** *The defendant was unable to satisfy the police that his dog was not dangerous.* **(convencer)**

• **satisfying** /ˈsætɪsˌfaɪɪŋ/ ADJECTIVE
1 making you feel pleased because you have achieved something or got something good □ *I find my work as a doctor very satisfying.* □ *It's very satisfying to see the results of your cooking.* **(satisfatório)**
2 a satisfying meal is one in which there is enough food to make you feel full **(satisfatório)**

SATNAV /ˈsætnæv/ ABBREVIATION satellite navigation; a piece of equipment especially used in cars to tell the driver how to get to a place **(sistema usado no GPS)**

satsuma /ˌsætˈsuːmə/ NOUN [*plural* **satsumas**] a fruit like a small orange **(tangerina)**

saturate /ˈsætʃəreɪt/ VERB [**saturates, saturating, saturated**] to make something extremely wet □ *His shirt was saturated with sweat.* **(saturar)**

Saturday /ˈsætədi/ NOUN [*plural* **Saturdays**] the day of the week after Friday and before Sunday □ *On Saturday, we went shopping.* □ *What are you doing next Saturday?* **(sábado)**

sauce /sɔːs/ NOUN [*plural* **sauces**] a liquid food with a particular flavour that you put on other food □ *She had spaghetti with tomato sauce.* □ *ice cream with chocolate sauce* **(molho)**

save

saucepan /ˈsɔːspən/ NOUN [*plural* **saucepans**] a round metal container with a handle, used for cooking food on top of an oven **(caçarola)**

saucer /ˈsɔːsə(r)/ NOUN [*plural* **saucers**] a small plate that goes under a cup □ *a cup and saucer* **(pires)**

sauna /ˈsɔːnə/ NOUN [*plural* **saunas**]
1 a hot room where you sit and sweat **(sauna)**
2 a period of time inside a sauna **(banho de sauna)** ▣ *I had a sauna at the health club.* **(fazer um banho de sauna)**

saunter /ˈsɔːntə(r)/ ▶ VERB [**saunters, sauntering, sauntered**] to walk slowly for pleasure □ *We were just sauntering round the park.* **(passear a pé)**
▶ NOUN [*plural* **saunters**] a slow walk for pleasure □ *We went for a saunter along the seafront.* **(passeio a pé)**

sausage /ˈsɒsɪdʒ/ NOUN [*plural* **sausages**] a long tube of meat mixed with spices **(linguiça ou salsicha)**

sausage roll /ˈsɒsɪdʒ ˈrəʊl/ NOUN [*plural* **sausage rolls**] a small amount of meat mixed with spices inside a tube of pastry **(rolinho de linguiça/salsicha)**

sauté /ˈsəʊteɪ/ ▶ VERB [**sautés, sautéing, sautéed or sautéd**] to fry food quickly in a little butter or oil □ *Lightly sauté the mushrooms.* **(saltear)**
▶ ADJECTIVE fried quickly in a little butter or oil □ *sauté potatoes* **(sauté)**

savage /ˈsævɪdʒ/ ▶ ADJECTIVE
1 very violent and cruel □ *savage beatings* **(feroz, selvagem)**
2 criticizing someone or something very strongly □ *He launched a savage attack on his former employer.* **(feroz)**
▶ VERB [**savages, savaging, savaged**]
1 to attack and badly injure someone □ *A young child had been savaged by a dog.* **(atacar ferozmente)**
2 to criticize something or someone very strongly □ *The film was savaged by the critics.* **(atacar ferozmente)**

• **savagely** /ˈsævɪdʒli/ ADVERB in a violent and cruel way □ *The 78-year-old woman was savagely attacked on her way home.* **(selvagemente)**

• **savagery** /ˈsævɪdʒri/ NOUN, NO PLURAL extreme violence □ *Police were shocked by the savagery of the attack.* **(selvageria)**

savanna or **savannah** /səˈvænə/ NOUN, NO PLURAL a large area in a hot country, with grass and not many trees. A geography word. **(savana)**

save /seɪv/ ▶ VERB [**saves, saving, saved**]
1 to stop someone or something being harmed, killed or destroyed □ *The firefighters saved everyone in the building.* □ *Switch off lights and*

help save the planet. □ + *from* *A shelter of branches and leaves saved them from freezing.* (salvar) 🔁 *The correct equipment could save your life.* (salvar sua vida)

2 to avoid using something, or to use less of it than usual □ *You can save 40 minutes by taking the motorway.* (economizar)

3 to keep something so that you can use it later □ *Save any food that's left over and heat it up later.* □ *We're saving our energy for tomorrow's walk.* (economizar)

4 to keep money, usually in a bank, so that you can use it later □ *We have saved regularly all our lives.* (poupar)

5 to make it possible to avoid doing something □ *Plastic window frames will save you a lot of work in the future.* □ + *ing* *If you all write your names on a piece of card, it will save me having to ask every time.* (evitar)

6 to make a computer store information. A computing word □ *Make sure you save your work regularly.* (salvar no computador)

7 to not let the ball go in the net in sports such as football □ *He saved a penalty.* (defender)

◆ PHRASAL VERBS **save on something** to not spend the money that something would cost if you bought it or used it □ *With better insulation you can save on your heating bills.* (economizar em) **save up** to keep money so that you can use it in the future (economizar) □ + *for* *I'm saving up for a new car.*

▶ NOUN [*plural* **saves**] when someone stops the ball going into the net in a sport such as football (defesa) 🔁 *He made two brilliant saves.* (fazer uma defesa)

• **saver** /ˈseɪvə(r)/ NOUN [*plural* **savers**] someone who is saving money, usually in a bank (poupador)

• **saving** /ˈseɪvɪŋ/ NOUN [*plural* **savings**]
1 an amount that you have avoided spending □ *There are big savings to be made in the summer sales.* □ *That is a saving of £35 on the normal price.* (economia)
2 **savings** money that you have saved in a bank □ *Joe's going to spend all his savings on a drum kit.* (economias)

• **saviour** /ˈseɪvjə(r)/ NOUN [*plural* **saviours**]
1 someone who saves something from harm or danger (salvador)
2 **Saviour** in Christian religions, Jesus Christ (Salvador)

savior /ˈseɪvjə(r)/ NOUN [*plural* **saviors**] the US spelling of **saviour**

savour /ˈseɪvə(r)/ VERB [**savours, savouring, savoured**] to eat or drink something slowly in order to enjoy it for longer □ *We ate the cake slowly, savouring every mouthful.* (saborear)

• **savoury** /ˈseɪvəri/ ADJECTIVE not sweet or not containing sugar □ *I much prefer savoury snacks to sweets.* (condimentado)

saw¹ /sɔː/ ▶ NOUN [*plural* **saws**] a tool with a thin blade used for cutting through wood or metal (serra)

▶ VERB [**saws, sawing, sawed, sawn**] to cut through wood or metal using a saw (serrar)

saw² /sɔː/ PAST TENSE OF **see** □ *I saw Paolo last week.* (*ver* see)

sawdust /ˈsɔːdʌst/ NOUN, NO PLURAL the thick dust that is produced when wood is cut with a saw (serragem)

sawn /sɔːn/ PAST PARTICIPLE OF **saw** (particípio passado de saw)

sax /sæks/ NOUN [*plural* **saxes**] a saxophone □ *a tenor sax* (abreviação de saxophone)

saxophone /ˈsæksəfəʊn/ NOUN [*plural* **saxophones**] a long curved musical instrument made of metal that you play by blowing into it and pressing different keys (saxofone)

• **saxophonist** /ˌsækˈsɒfənɪst/ NOUN [*plural* **saxophonists**] someone who plays the saxophone (saxofonista)

say /seɪ/ ▶ VERB [**says, saying, said**]
1 to express something in words □ *I asked her about the rumours, but she wouldn't say anything.* □ *I asked for more money, but my boss said no.* □ + *that* *Officials say that the death toll has reached 30.* □ + *about* *Did she say anything about the wedding?* (dizer)
2 to give information in words or signs □ *What does the notice say?* □ *My watch said six.* (dizer)
3 to mean something □ *They seem to be saying that the building is not suitable.* □ *I'm not saying she's mean – it's just that she never shares her things.* (querer dizer)
4 to show what something or someone is like □ + *about* *The state of the offices said a lot about the company.* □ *What do your clothes say about you?* (dizer)
5 used to give a possibility □ *Say we were to print the book in India – could we be sure of getting it on time?* □ *We only need a few more people – 20 say – to get the job done.* (digamos, vamos dizer)

> ➤ Remember that you **say** something but you do not 'say someone something':
> ✓ *She said she was leaving.*
> ✗ *She said me she was leaving.*

▶ NOUN, NO PLURAL
1 when you are involved in making a decision (participar da decisão) 🔁 *I had no say in how the money was spent.* (não participar da decisão)
2 **have your say** to be allowed to give your opinion about something □ *Let Mark finish speaking, then you can have your say.* (dar sua opinião)

• **saying** /ˈseɪɪŋ/ NOUN [*plural* **sayings**] a phrase or sentence that people often use, giving advice or saying something that many people believe is true □ *Gran's favourite saying was 'an apple a day keeps the doctor away'.* (dito, ditado)

scab

scab /skæb/ NOUN [plural **scabs**] a hard covering of dried blood that forms over a cut (**casca de ferida**)

• **scabby** /'skæbɪ/ ADJECTIVE [**scabbier, scabbiest**] covered in scabs □ *a scabby knee* (**sarnento**)

scaffold /'skæfəʊld/ NOUN [plural **scaffolds**] in the past, a structure where criminals were killed by hanging them by the neck or cutting off their head (**cadafalso**)

• **scaffolding** /'skæfəldɪŋ/ NOUN, NO PLURAL a structure of long metal poles and wooden boards for people to stand on when they are working on the outside of a building (**andaime**)

scald /skɔːld/ ▶ VERB [**scalds, scalding, scalded**] to burn someone with very hot liquid or steam (**escaldar**)

▶ NOUN [plural **scalds**] a burn caused by hot liquid or steam (**escaldadura**)

scale /skeɪl/ ▶ NOUN [plural **scales**]

1 the general size or level of something □ *The cyclone has caused destruction on a huge scale.* □ *Experts warn that the scale of the problem is increasing.* (**escala**)

2 a series of numbers or marks used for measuring the level of something □ *The earthquake measured 3.2 on the Richter scale.* □ *Patients are asked to grade the pain they feel on a scale of one to ten.* (**escala**)

3 the size of something such as a model or a map, compared to the real size of the thing it represents □ *What's the scale of the map?* (**escala**)

4 scales an instrument for weighing things (**balança**) 🔲 *a set of* kitchen scales (**balança de cozinha**) 🔲 *I weighed myself on the* bathroom scales. (**balança de banheiro**)

5 a series of musical notes that goes up in order (**escala musical**) □ *the scale of G major* 🔲 *I try to* practise *my* scales *each day.* (**praticar a escala**)

6 one of the small thin pieces covering the skin of a fish or snake (**escama**)

▶ VERB [**scales, scaling, scaled**] to climb up something □ *People were scaling the wall, singing and shouting.* (**escalar**)

♦ PHRASAL VERB **scale something up/down** to increase/lower the size, level or importance of something □ *The massive police operation is slowly being scaled down.* (**aumentar ou diminuir**)

scallion /'skælɪən/ NOUN [plural **scallions**] the US word for spring onion (**cebolinha, cebolinha-verde**)

scallop /'skɒləp/ NOUN [plural **scallops**] a sea animal that lives in a shell and that you can eat (**vieira**)

scalp /skælp/ NOUN [plural **scalps**] the skin on the part of the head where the hair grows (**couro cabeludo**)

scalpel /'skælpəl/ NOUN [plural **scalpels**] a small sharp knife, used especially by doctors who do medical operations (**bisturi**)

scapegoat

scaly /'skeɪlɪ/ ADJECTIVE [**scalier, scaliest**] scaly skin has small pieces falling off it because it is very dry (**escameado, escamoso**)

scam /skæm/ NOUN [plural **scams**] an illegal way of making money. An informal word. □ *Don't fall for it – it's a scam.* (**fraude**)

scamper /'skæmpə(r)/ VERB [**scampers, scampering, scampered**] to run quickly and lightly, taking short steps □ *The puppy scampered around the garden.* (**safar-se, fugir apressadamente**)

scampi /'skæmpɪ/ NOUN, NO PLURAL large prawns (= small sea animals) that are fried (**camarão-lagosta**)

scan /skæn/ ▶ VERB [**scans, scanning, scanned**]

1 to use a piece of equipment to copy a picture of something onto a computer □ *Scan the photo and then e-mail it to me.* (**escanear**)

2 to use a piece of equipment to produce an image of inside someone's body or inside a piece of luggage □ *All bags are scanned at the airport.* (**escanear corpo/bagagem**)

3 to read something very quickly □ *Lou scanned the jobs section of the paper, looking for anything suitable.* (**correr os olhos por**)

4 to look all around an area from one position □ *The police were scanning the crowd for signs of trouble.* (**esquadrinhar**)

▶ NOUN [plural **scans**] a medical process in which a special machine produces an image of the inside of your body □ *a brain scan* (**exame com escâner**)

scandal /'skændəl/ NOUN [plural **scandals**]

1 a situation in which important people behave in a way that is morally very wrong □ *a political/financial scandal* (**escândalo**)

2 talk or writing in the newspapers, etc. about behaviour that shocks people (**escândalo**)

• **scandalize** or **scandalise** /'skændəlaɪz/ VERB [**scandalizes, scandalizing, scandalized**] to make people feel extremely shocked or offended □ *The family was scandalized by the marriage.* (**escandalizar**)

• **scandalous** /'skændələs/ ADJECTIVE shocking or wrong □ *It's a scandalous waste of public money.* (**escandaloso**)

scanner /'skænə(r)/ NOUN [plural **scanners**]

1 a machine that copies a picture or document into a computer. A computing word. (**escâner**)

2 a machine that produces a picture of the inside of a part of someone's body as part of a medical test □ *an MRI scanner* (**escâner**)

3 a machine that can read information using light □ *a bar code scanner* (**escâner**)

scant /skænt/ ADJECTIVE [**scanter, scantest**] very little or not enough □ *There is scant evidence for any of these claims.* (**escasso, insuficiente**) □ *She paid scant attention to the teacher's words.*

• **scanty** /'skæntɪ/ ADJECTIVE [**scantier, scantiest**] very small □ *a scanty nightshirt* (**escasso**)

scapegoat /'skeɪpɡəʊt/ NOUN [plural **scapegoats**] someone who is blamed for something that they did not do so that someone else will not be blamed 🔲 *The manager was made a scapegoat for the team's poor performance.* (bode expiatório)

scar /skɑː(r)/ ▶ NOUN [plural **scars**]

1 a mark that is left on skin from an injury (cicatriz) 🔲 *The surgery left a small scar.* (deixar uma cicatriz)

2 a bad feeling that you have for a long time after a bad experience (cicatriz) 🔲 *The accident also left some psychological scars.* (cicatrizes psicológicas) 🔲 *He still bears the mental scars of the ordeal.* (carregar cicatrizes)

▶ VERB [**scars, scarring, scarred**] to cause a scar 🔲 *He was badly scarred by the fire.* (deixar cicatriz)

scarce /skeəs/ ADJECTIVE [**scarcer, scarcest**] only available in small amounts 🔲 *Food was scarce in wartime.* 🔲 *scarce resources* (raro)

• **scarcely** /ˈskeəsli/ ADVERB almost not at all 🔲 *The place had scarcely changed.* 🔲 *I could scarcely believe it.* (mal, quase não)

• **scarcity** /ˈskeəsɪti/ NOUN [plural **scarcities**] when something is scarce 🔲 *There was a scarcity of clean water.* (falta, carência)

scare /skeə(r)/ ▶ VERB [**scares, scaring, scared**]

1 to frighten or to worry someone 🔲 *We don't want to scare people.* 🔲 *The reports are intended to scare us into driving more carefully.* (assustar)

2 scare the daylights/life, etc. out of someone to frighten someone very much. An informal phrase. (assustar muito, apavorar)

◆ PHRASAL VERB **scare someone away/off**

1 to make someone worried so that they decide not to do something 🔲 *Recent attacks in the region have scared away the tourists.* (espantar)

2 to frighten someone so that they leave 🔲 *He scared the thieves off.* (espantar)

▶ NOUN [plural **scares**]

1 a situation in which a lot of people are frightened or worried about something 🔲 *a public health scare* (ameaça) 🔲 *There was a bomb scare at the airport.* (ameaça de bomba)

2 when something frightens or worries you for a short time (susto) 🔲 *It gave us all a bit of a scare when Maria fainted.* (dar um susto)

scarecrow /ˈskeəkrəʊ/ NOUN [plural **scarecrows**] a simple model of a person in a field intended to frighten birds away (espantalho)

scared /skeəd/ ADJECTIVE frightened 🔲 *I'm scared of spiders.* 🔲 *She's scared of her teacher.* 🔲 *She lay in bed, too scared to move.* (que tem medo, medroso) 🔲 *I'm scared stiff* (= very frightened) *of heights.* (duro ou paralisado de medo) 🔲 *I was scared to death* (= very frightened) *of messing it up.* (morto de medo)

scarf /skɑːf/ NOUN [plural **scarves**] a piece of cloth that you wear around your neck or head to keep warm or to look attractive 🔲 *a silk scarf* 🔲 *a thick woolen scarf* (cachecol)

scarlet /ˈskɑːlət/ NOUN, NO PLURAL a bright red colour (escarlate)

scarper /ˈskɑːpə(r)/ VERB [**scarpers, scarpering, scarpered**] an informal word meaning to run away 🔲 *They scarpered without paying the bill.* (fugir)

scarves /skɑːvz/ PLURAL OF **scarf** (plural de scarf)

scary /ˈskeəri/ ADJECTIVE [**scarier, scariest**] making you feel frightened or very worried 🔲 *a scary film* 🔲 *The scary thing is how quickly the disease spreads.* (assustador)

scathing /ˈskeɪðɪŋ/ ADJECTIVE criticizing severely 🔲 *a scathing comment* 🔲 *He was scathing about the government's economic policy.* (mordaz)

• **scathingly** /ˈskeɪðɪŋli/ ADVERB in a scathing way (com mordacidade)

scatter /ˈskætə(r)/ VERB [**scatters, scattering, scattered**]

1 to spread something in a lot of places over a wide area 🔲 *Scatter the seeds evenly over the prepared soil.* (espalhar)

2 if people or animals scatter, they suddenly run away in different directions 🔲 *The crowd scattered with the arrival of the police.* (dispersar-se)

scatterbrain /ˈskætəbreɪn/ NOUN [plural **scatterbrains**] an informal word for someone who often forgets things (pessoa dispersa)

• **scatterbrained** /ˈskætəbreɪnd/ ADJECTIVE often forgetting things. An informal word. (dispersivo)

scattered /ˈskætəd/ ADJECTIVE in a lot of places over a wide area or over a period of time (disperso) 🔲 *Some scattered showers are expected later.* (chuvas dispersas) 🔲 *About 20 people were killed in scattered violence across the country.*

• **scattering** /ˈskætərɪŋ/ NOUN [plural **scatterings**] a small number or quantity, spread over a wide area 🔲 *There was a thin scattering of snow.* (difuso, disperso)

scavenge /ˈskævɪndʒ/ VERB [**scavenges, scavenging, scavenged**]

1 to search in rubbish for things that can be used or eaten 🔲 *Stray dogs scavenged for food from the dustbins.* (revirar lixo)

2 if a wild bird or animal scavenges, they eat dead animals that have already been killed by something else 🔲 *scavenging vultures* (alimentar-se de carniça)

• **scavenger** /ˈskævɪndʒə(r)/ NOUN [plural **scavengers**] a person or an animal that scavenges (vasculhador de lixo)

scenario /sɪˈnɑːriəʊ/ NOUN [plural **scenarios**] a situation that might happen 🔲 *We're prepared for all possible scenarios.* (cenário) 🔲 *The worst-case scenario* (= worst possible situation) *is that we get no money for the project.* (a pior situação)

scene /siːn/ NOUN [plural **scenes**]

1 the place where an event happens 🔲 *+ of the scene of the accident* (cena) 🔲 *a crime scene* (cena do crime) 🔲 *An ambulance was very quickly on the scene.*

scent

2 part of a play, a book or a film that happens in one place □ *We'll have to film the scene on the beach next.* (**cena**) 🔁 *the opening scene of Othello* (**a cena de abertura**) □ **+ from** *It was like a scene from a Hollywood movie.*

3 a place or situation as someone sees it □ **+ of** *Before me was a scene of celebration.* □ *Rescuers described a scene of utter devastation.* □ *There were chaotic scenes as fights broke out.* (**cena**)

4 a loud and embarrassing argument in a public place (**cena**) 🔁 *There's no need to make a scene.* (**fazer uma cena**)

5 the people and things to do with a particular activity or way of living (**cenário**) 🔁 *They burst onto the music scene in 2004.* (**cena musical**) 🔁 *The city's arts scene is flourishing.* (**cenário artístico**)

6 behind the scenes not seen by the public □ *He prefers to work behind the scenes.* (**nos bastidores**)

7 set the scene (for something) (a) to create a situation which shows what might happen next or makes something likely □ *His speech set the scene for a hard-fought election campaign.* (b) to describe a general situation before talking about a particular event □ *First, let me set the scene.* (**criar uma situação**)

- **scenery** /ˈsiːnəri/ NOUN, NO PLURAL

1 what you see around you, especially the countryside □ *You get to see some wonderful scenery from the train.* □ *We stopped to take in the stunning scenery.* (**cenário**) 🔁 *He needed a change of scenery* (= to go somewhere different). (**mudança de cenário**)

2 the large pictures used in the theatre behind the actors (**cenário**)

- **scenic** /ˈsiːnɪk/ ADJECTIVE with attractive things to look at, especially the countryside □ *a scenic route* □ *a scenic area* (**cênico**)

scent /sent/ ▶ NOUN [*plural* **scents**]

1 a good smell □ *The scent of lilies can fill a whole room.* (**perfume, aroma**)

2 a liquid that women put on their skin to make them smell nice (**perfume**)

3 the smell of an animal that other animals can follow (**cheiro farejado por animais**)

▶ VERB [**scents, scenting, scented**]

1 to find something by smell □ *A hungry animal will scent food long before it sees it.* (**farejar**)

2 to have a feeling that something exists or might happen □ *Two guards, scenting trouble, hurried over.* (**farejar**)

- **scented** /ˈsentɪd/ ADJECTIVE with a pleasant smell □ *a scented candle* □ *scented oils* (**perfumado**)

sceptic /ˈskeptɪk/ NOUN [*plural* **sceptics**] a person who doubts whether something is true or as good as other people believe □ *Where alternative medicine is concerned, I'm a sceptic.* (**cético**)

- **sceptical** /ˈskeptɪkəl/ ADJECTIVE doubting that something is true □ *Yuko thinks it will work, but I'm still sceptical.* □ *She's sceptical about the benefits the Olympics will bring.* (**cético**)

sceptre /ˈseptə(r)/ NOUN [*plural* **sceptres**] a pole that a king or queen carries at official ceremonies (**cetro**)

schedule /ˈʃedjuːl/ ▶ NOUN [*plural* **schedules**] a plan that shows when things should happen or be done □ *a flight schedule* □ *He has a very busy work schedule.* □ *The building work finished on schedule* (= when planned). □ *The project is already six months behind schedule.* (**programa**)

▶ VERB [**schedules, scheduling, scheduled**] to plan that something will happen at a particular time □ *The meeting has been scheduled for next Wednesday.* (**programar**)

scheme /skiːm/ ▶ NOUN [*plural* **schemes**]

1 a plan or system for doing something □ *a national training scheme* □ *a pension scheme* (**projeto**)

2 a plan to get money, usually by tricking people □ *a fraudulent tax scheme* (**trama**)

3 in the scheme of things as part of the general situation or the way things are organized □ *In the scheme of things, it's a small amount of money.* (**no esquema geral**)

▶ VERB [**schemes, scheming, schemed**] to make secret plans, especially to cause harm or damage □ *He was scheming to push Willis out of his job.* (**tramar**)

- **scheming** /ˈskiːmɪŋ/ ADJECTIVE clever at getting what you want in a dishonest way □ *She plays a scheming politician.* (**maquiavélico, oportunista, ardiloso**)

schizophrenia /ˌskɪtsəˈfriːniə/ NOUN, NO PLURAL a severe mental illness in which someone cannot always understand what is real and what is not (**esquizofrenia**)

- **schizophrenic** /ˌskɪtsəˈfrenɪk/ ▶ ADJECTIVE to do with schizophrenia (**esquizofrênico**)

▶ NOUN [*plural* **schizophrenics**] someone who is suffering from schizophrenia (**pessoa esquizofrênica**)

scholar

scholar /ˈskɒlə(r)/ NOUN [*plural* **scholars**] a person who studies a particular subject and has a lot of knowledge of it □ *a scholar of Greek* (**erudito, conhecedor**)

- **scholarly** /ˈskɒləli/ ADJECTIVE showing a deep knowledge of a subject (**erudito**) 🔁 *a scholarly work about Victorian art* (**um trabalho profundo**)

- **scholarship** /ˈskɒləʃɪp/ NOUN [*plural* **scholarships**]

1 money given to a student to pay for their studies at a school or university □ *There are several scholarships available for very bright students.* (**bolsa de estudos**)

2 serious study of a subject (**erudição**)

- **scholastic** /skəˈlæstɪk/ ADJECTIVE a formal word meaning to do with schools and education □ *scholastic achievements* (**escolar**)

school /skuːl/ ▶ NOUN [plural schools]

1 a place where children go to learn (escola) 🔹 *You'll go to school when you're five years old.* (ir para a escola) □ *We walked home from school together.*
2 *no plural* the time when you are at school □ *He plays football after school on a Wednesday.* (escola) 🔹 *She left school at sixteen.* (abandonar a escola)
3 *no plural* all the students and teachers in a school □ *The whole school was in the playground.* (escola)
4 in the US, a college or university □ *Where did you go to school?* (faculdade, universidade)
5 a part of a college or a university □ *+ of the Stanford University school of medicine* (instituto, departamento)
6 a place where people go to learn a particular skill (curso) 🔹 *a language school* (um curso de idioma)
7 a large number of fish or dolphins (= sea mammals) that swim together in a group □ *a large school of fish* (cardume)
8 school of thought a particular opinion or way of thinking about something □ *There are two schools of thought regarding its origin.* (escola de pensamento)

▶ VERB [schools, schooling, schooled] a formal word meaning to educate a child □ *The brothers are being schooled at home.* (educar, disciplinar)

school age /ˈskuːl eɪdʒ/ NOUN, NO PLURAL the age when a child must go to school □ *children of school age* (idade escolar)

schoolboy /ˈskuːlbɔɪ/ NOUN [plural schoolboys]
a boy who goes to school (aluno, colegial)

schoolchild /ˈskuːltʃaɪld/ NOUN [plural schoolchildren] a child who goes to school □ *a large party of schoolchildren* (aluno, colegial)

schooldays /ˈskuːldeɪz/ PLURAL NOUN the time in your life when you go to school □ *His schooldays were the happiest days of his life.* (tempos de escola)

schoolgirl /ˈskuːlɡɜːl/ NOUN [plural schoolgirls]
a girl who goes to school (aluna, colegial)

schooling /ˈskuːlɪŋ/ NOUN, NO PLURAL education, especially at school □ *He had no formal schooling.* (instrução, educação escolar)

school-leaver /ˈskuːlˌliːvə(r)/ NOUN [plural school-leavers] a young person who is leaving or has recently left school □ *a training scheme for unemployed school-leavers* (aluno em fim de curso)

schoolteacher /ˈskuːlˌtiːtʃə(r)/ NOUN [plural schoolteachers] a teacher in a school (professor)

schoolwork /ˈskuːlwɜːk/ NOUN, NO PLURAL the work that a child does at school or for school (lição, trabalho escolar)

science /ˈsaɪəns/ NOUN [plural sciences]

1 *no plural* the study and knowledge of the physical world and the way things happen in it (ciência) 🔹 *He studied science and mathematics.* □ *Few now question the science behind climate change.* (estudar ciência)
2 a particular part of science, especially chemistry, physics or biology □ *biological science* □ *environmental science* □ *+ of the science of genetics* (ciência)
3 the organized study of something □ *a degree in political science* □ *the School of Social Sciences* (ciências)

science fiction /ˈsaɪəns ˈfɪkʃən/ NOUN, NO PLURAL stories and films that take place in an imagined future or in other parts of the universe □ *a science fiction novel* (ficção científica)

scientific /ˌsaɪənˈtɪfɪk/ ADJECTIVE

1 to do with science (científico) 🔹 *scientific research* (pesquisa científica) 🔹 *a paper in a scientific journal* (revista científica)
2 based on an organized system of rules, methods or tests □ *The survey wasn't very scientific, but it gives a rough picture.* (científico)

• **scientifically** /ˌsaɪənˈtɪfɪkəlɪ/ ADVERB according to the rules of science □ *a scientifically proven law* (cientificamente)

scientist /ˈsaɪəntɪst/ NOUN [plural scientists]
someone who studies science or who works in science □ *Scientists believe the condition is genetic.* □ *a team of forensic scientists* (cientista)

scissor /ˈsɪzəz/ PLURAL NOUN a cutting tool that you hold in one hand that has two blades joined in the middle (tesoura) 🔹 *a pair of scissors* (tesoura) □ *She cut them up using kitchen scissors.*

> ➤ Remember that **scissors** is a plural noun:
> ✓ *You'll need some scissors.*
> ✗ *You'll need a scissors.*

scoff /skɒf/ VERB [scoffs, scoffing, scoffed]

1 to show you think that someone or something is stupid and does not deserve respect, sometimes by laughing □ *Many MPs scoffed at the idea.* (zombar)
2 an informal word meaning to eat something very fast □ *If you leave those crisps near Nick he'll scoff the lot.* (engolir, comer ansiosamente)

scold /skəʊld/ VERB [scolds, scolding, scolded]
to criticize someone angrily for doing something wrong. An old-fashioned word. (ralhar)
• **scolding** /ˈskəʊldɪŋ/ NOUN [plural scoldings] when someone is scolded. An old-fashioned word. (repreensão)

scone /skɒn, skəʊn/ NOUN [plural scones] a small, round, plain cake that is often eaten with butter and jam (bolinho inglês)

scoop /skuːp/ ▶ VERB [scoops, scooping, scooped]

1 to lift or to remove something in your curved hands or with a large spoon or similar tool □ *She scooped up a handful of water.* □ *Scoop out the seeds with a teaspoon.* (pegar com concha, com as mãos em concha etc.)

scooter

2 an informal word meaning to win something such as money or a prize ▫ *He scooped the Best Actor award for the role.* (embolsar)
▶ NOUN [*plural* scoops]
1 a tool like a large spoon for lifting liquid or soft substances, or the amount that this tool holds ▫ *an ice cream scoop* ▫ *Serve chilled with a scoop of cream.* (concha, colher)
2 a news story that a newspaper prints before other newspapers do (furo jornalístico)

scooter /ˈskuːtə(r)/ NOUN [*plural* scooters]
1 a smaller and less powerful motorcycle (lambreta) ▣ *Young men ride by on motor scooters.* (lambretas)
2 a child's toy with two wheels at either end of a board and a tall handle, which you stand on and push yourself along (patinete)

scope /skəʊp/ NOUN, NO PLURAL
1 the whole range of matters that something deals with ▫ *That whole question falls outside the scope of this meeting.* (alcance)
2 an opportunity or possibility that something can happen ▫ *There's plenty of scope for improving these plans.* ▫ *There's a lot of scope for growth.* (oportunidade)

scorch /skɔːtʃ/ VERB [scorches, scorching, scorched] to burn the surface of something ▫ *The flames had scorched his clothes.* (queimar, chamuscar)
• **scorched** /skɔːtʃt/ ADJECTIVE dried by heat or slightly burnt ▫ *an area of scorched grass* (queimado, chamuscado)
• **scorching** /ˈskɔːtʃɪŋ/ ADJECTIVE very hot ▫ *It was a scorching day.* (ardente) ▣ *The game was played in scorching heat.* (um calor ardente)

score /skɔː(r)/ ▶ VERB [scores, scoring, scored]
1 to get a point in a game, test or competition (marcar pontos) ▣ *Ronaldo scored the winning goal.* (marcar o gol) ▣ *Drivers score 10 points for a win.* (marcar 10 pontos) ▫ + *for* Hamilton has scored again for the Rovers. ▫ + *against* He scored against Brazil in the World Cup.
2 to keep a record of the points that are won in a game or competition ▫ *Who's scoring?* (marcar a pontuação)
3 to scratch a surface with something sharp (arranhar)
▶ NOUN [*plural* scores]
1 the number of points that you get in a game, test or competition (contagem, escore, placar) ▣ *What was the final score?* (placar final) ▣ *What's the highest score you can get?* (maior pontuação) ▣ *Katie's test scores weren't very good.* (pontuações da prova)
2 scores of something a lot of something ▫ *We've received scores of e-mails about this.* (um monte de)
3 on this/that score to do with the subject or thing mentioned ▫ *We have plenty of food so we'll have no worries on that score.* (sobre esse assunto)

4 a piece of written music (partitura) ▣ *a musical score* (partitura) ▣ *Stein wrote the score for the film.* (escreveu a partitura)

scoreboard /ˈskɔːbɔːd/ NOUN [*plural* scoreboards] a board on which the score in a game is shown (marcador)

scorer /ˈskɔːrə(r)/ NOUN [*plural* scorers] someone who scores points in a game or competition (marcador de pontos) ▣ *He was the team's top scorer last season.* (o maior marcador de pontos)

scorn /skɔːn/ ▶ VERB [scorns, scorning, scorned] a formal word meaning to refuse to accept something because you think it is stupid or nor worth your attention ▫ *He initially scorned the idea.* (desdenhar, desprezar)
▶ NOUN, NO PLURAL a formal word for a feeling that someone or something is stupid or not worth your attention (desprezo, desdém) ▣ *She poured scorn on the suggestion* (= said it was stupid). (desdenhou)
• **scornful** /ˈskɔːnfʊl/ ADJECTIVE showing scorn ▫ *He was scornful of the minister's claims.* (desprezador)
• **scornfully** /ˈskɔːnfʊli/ ADVERB in a way that shows scorn (desdenhosamente)

scorpion /ˈskɔːpɪən/ NOUN [*plural* scorpions] an animal that looks like a large insect and has a curved, poisonous tail (escorpião)

scoundrel /ˈskaʊndrəl/ NOUN [*plural* scoundrels] an old-fashioned word that means a man who behaves badly and dishonestly (patife)

scour /ˈskaʊə(r)/ VERB [scours, scouring, scoured]
1 to search a large area carefully ▫ *Teams of villagers scoured the hillside for the missing climber.* (esquadrinhar)
2 to clean a surface by rubbing hard with something rough ▫ *The saucepans needed scouring.* (esfregar)

scourge /skɜːdʒ/ NOUN [*plural* scourges] a cause of great suffering or harm to many people or to a particular group of people ▫ *Cancer is the scourge of Western society.* (flagelo)

scout /skaʊt/ ▶ NOUN [*plural* scouts]
1 the Scouts an organization for young people that encourages activities outdoors and practical skills (os Escoteiros)
2 a member of the Scouts (escoteiro) ▣ *a boy scout* (escoteiro)
3 someone whose job is going to different places, looking for people who are very good at particular things, for example sport (caçador de talentos) ▣ *The young player was spotted by a talent scout last year.* (caçador de talentos)
▶ VERB [scouts, scouting, scouted] to search for something, especially in many places ▫ *I'll scout around for a chair that matches the others.* (fazer reconhecimento, vasculhar)

scowl /skaʊl/ ▶ VERB [scowls, scowling, scowled] to look at someone or something in an angry way (franzir a sobrancelha)
▶ NOUN [*plural* scowls] an angry look (carranca)

scrabble /ˈskræbəl/ VERB [scrabbles, scrabbling, scrabbled] to try to find or to get hold of something with your fingers ▫ He was on his knees, scrabbling about in the sand trying to find his glasses. (tatear com os dedos)

scramble /ˈskræmbəl/ ▶ VERB [scrambles, scrambling, scrambled]
1 to climb or to move using your hands and feet, especially with difficulty ▫ We scrambled up the side of the hill. (trepar, escalar)
2 to push other people out of the way to get to something ▫ People were scrambling to get to the bargains before anyone else. (engalfinhar-se, disputar)
3 to mix eggs together and cook them (preparar ovos mexidos)
4 to change a message or broadcast so that it can only be understood using special equipment (codificar uma mensagem a ser decifrada com equipamento próprio)
▶ NOUN [plural **scrambles**]
1 a difficult climb over rough ground (escalada dificultosa)
2 when you push other people out of the way to get to something first (disputa)
3 a race on motorcycles over rough ground (competição de motocicleta)

scrambled egg /ˈskræmbəld ˈeg/ NOUN [plural **scrambled eggs**] eggs mixed together and cooked in a pan (ovos mexidos)

scrap /skræp/ ▶ NOUN [plural **scraps**]
1 a small piece or amount of something (pedaço) ▣ I have his address written on a *scrap of paper*. (pedaço de papel) ▫ There isn't a scrap of evidence against us.
2 old or broken vehicles and machines that can be taken apart and their parts used again (sucata) ▣ *scrap metal* (ferro velho)
3 an informal word for a fight (luta)
▶ VERB [scraps, scrapping, scrapped]
1 to decide not to use something or to stop using it ▫ Let's just scrap the whole idea now. (descartar) ▣ The *plan has been scrapped*. (descartar um plano)
2 to get rid of a machine, vehicle, etc. (descartar)
3 an informal word meaning to fight with someone (lutar)

scrapbook /ˈskræpbʊk/ NOUN [plural **scrapbooks**] an empty book you can fill with pictures, articles, etc. (álbum)

scrape /skreɪp/ ▶ VERB [scrapes, scraping, scraped]
1 to get something off a surface by using something sharp or rough ▫ Scrape the mud off your shoes before you come in. (raspar)
2 to damage something slightly by rubbing it against something rough ▫ Eva fell off her bike and scraped her knee. (arranhar)
3 to manage to achieve something with difficulty ▫ They scraped a win in the last few minutes of the game. (conseguir por pouco)
4 *scrape a living* to manage to live on a small amount of money (viver com dificuldade)
♦ PHRASAL VERBS *scrape by* to manage to live on a small amount of money ▫ Millions of people scrape by on less than a dollar a day. (sobreviver financeiramente) *scrape through (something)* to only just achieve something ▫ They scraped through to the semi-finals. (passar raspando) *scrape something together* to manage to collect enough of something, especially money, with difficulty ▫ We scraped together enough money for a deposit. (juntar)
▶ NOUN [plural **scrapes**]
1 a mark or injury caused by scraping something ▫ They suffered only minor scrapes and bruises. (raspão, esfoladura)
2 a difficult situation (enrascada) ▣ I *got into a few scrapes* when I was travelling. (meter-se em enrascadas)

scrap heap /ˈskræp hiːp/ NOUN [plural **scrap heaps**]
1 a place where objects, machines and vehicles that have been thrown away are left in a pile (ferro-velho)
2 *on the scrap heap* not wanted or considered useful any longer (para o lixo)

scrappy /ˈskræpi/ ADJECTIVE [scrappier, scrappiest] performed or organized badly ▫ a scrappy game (agressivo)

scratch /skrætʃ/ ▶ VERB [scratches, scratching, scratched]
1 to make a mark on a surface with something sharp or pointed ▫ The car was quite badly scratched. ▫ Students had scratched their names on the desks. (arranhar, riscar)
2 to rub your nails on your skin, usually because it feels uncomfortable ▫ She scratched her nose. ▫ Try not to scratch the spots. (coçar)
♦ IDIOMS *scratch your head* to not be able to understand or think of something (não conseguir entender ou pensar) *scratch the surface (of something)* **1** to only understand or deal with a small part of something much larger ▫ These changes barely scratch the surface of the problem. (ser superficial)
2 to start looking at something more carefully ▫ But scratch the surface and you find the situation is more complicated. (olhar com mais atenção para uma situação)
▶ NOUN [plural **scratches**]
1 a mark left on a surface or your skin by something sharp ▫ He looked for scratches on the car. ▫ They escaped with minor scratches. (arranhão)
2 when you rub your nails on your skin (arranhadura)
3 *from scratch* from the beginning ▫ They learn to cook simple, healthy meals from scratch. (do zero)
4 *up to scratch* good enough ▫ The work wasn't up to scratch. (à altura)

scrawl /skrɔːl/ ▶ VERB [scrawls, scrawling, scrawled] to write in a very untidy way ▫ People had scrawled messages on the wall. (rabiscar, escrever de maneira ilegível)
▶ NOUN, NO PLURAL very untidy writing (garrancho)

scrawny

scrawny /ˈskrɔːnɪ/ ADJECTIVE [**scrawnier, scrawniest**] very thin, in an unhealthy way □ *a few scrawny chickens* (esquelético)

scream /skriːm/ ▶ VERB [**screams, screaming, screamed**]

1 to make a high, loud sound because you are frightened, excited or in pain □ + *out* *The woman screamed out and the man ran off.* □ + *in* *The children screamed in terror.* □ + *with* *He was screaming with pain.* (berrar, gritar) 🔁 *She screamed at the top of her voice.* (berrou o mais alto que pôde)

2 to shout words in a high voice because you are frightened, angry or in pain □ + *at* *Fans screamed abuse at the referee.* □ *'Run!' he screamed.* (berrar, gritar) 🔁 *They heard someone screaming for help.* (gritar pedindo socorro)

▶ NOUN [plural **screams**] a loud, high noise or shout □ + *of* *a scream of agony* □ *She let out a high-pitched scream.* (berro, grito)

◆ IDIOM **be a scream** to be very funny. An informal phrase. (ser uma piada)

scree /skriː/ NOUN, NO PLURAL small pieces of broken rock, for example on the side of a mountain. A geography word. (pedras, seixos)

screech /skriːtʃ/ ▶ NOUN [plural **screeches**] a sudden, unpleasant, high sound □ *the screech of an owl* □ *There was a screech of tyres as the car sped away.* (som estridente, guincho, urro)
▶ VERB [**screeches, screeching, screeched**] to make a screech (urrar, guinchar, soar estridente) 🔁 *The car screeched to a halt* (= stopped while making a loud, high sound).

screen /skriːn/ ▶ NOUN [plural **screens**]

1 the part of a computer, television or cinema that you watch images on (tela) 🔁 *a computer screen* (tela de computador) 🔁 *a 17-inch screen* 🔁 *Fans watched on giant TV screens.* (telas de TV)

2 *no plural* cinema films in general (telão, cinema) □ *the screen adaptation of the novel* 🔁 *She made her big screen* (= cinema and not television) *début last year.* (filme)

3 a piece of wood, cloth, metal, etc. that divides one area from another or prevents something from being seen □ *We were separated by a glass screen.* (divisória, tela, biombo, cortina etc.)

▶ VERB [**screens, screening, screened**]

1 to test a lot of people for a particular illness □ *All the workers here are screened for the virus.* (triar)

2 to check someone to make sure they are suitable for something □ *They screen applicants for any criminal convictions.* □ *All passengers are screened for weapons.* (passar por uma avaliação ou inspeção)

3 to show a television programme or film □ *They are screening the whole series for the third time.* (projetar, exibir)

4 to hide something □ *This part of the garden is screened by a high fence.* (esconder)

screen dump /ˈskriːn dʌmp/ NOUN [plural **screen dumps**] an image of what you can see on a computer screen at a particular time. A computing word. (captura de tela)

screenplay /ˈskriːnpleɪ/ NOUN [plural **screenplays**] the written text for a film, including the actors' words and directions (roteiro)

screen saver /ˈskriːn ˌseɪvə(r)/ NOUN [plural **screen savers**] a picture that appears on a computer screen when the computer has not been used for some time. A computing word. (protetor de tela)

screw /skruː/ ▶ NOUN [plural **screws**] a small, pointed, metal object used to fix things together by turning it around into a hole (parafuso)
▶ VERB [**screws, screwing, screwed**]

1 to fix a screw into something □ *Screw the bits of wood together.* (parafusar)

2 to attach or to fasten something with a turning movement □ *Screw the lid on tightly.* (rosquear, parafusar)

◆ PHRASAL VERBS **screw (something) up** an informal word meaning to make a mistake or to do something badly (estragar, atrapalhar tudo) **screw something up 1** to crush something, especially paper □ *He screwed up her letter and dropped it in the bin.* (amassar) **2** **screw up your eyes/face** to twist your face because you are in pain, concentrating, etc. (contrair os olhos/rosto, contorcer(-se))

screwdriver /ˈskruːˌdraɪvə(r)/ NOUN [plural **screwdrivers**] a tool with a long, thin metal part used for turning screws (chave de fenda)

scribble /ˈskrɪbəl/ ▶ VERB [**scribbles, scribbling, scribbled**]

1 to write very quickly and in an untidy way □ *I scribbled his name down before I forgot it.* (rabiscar)

2 to draw untidy lines and shapes □ *The baby had a pen and was scribbling on the wall.* (rabiscar)

▶ NOUN [plural **scribbles**]

1 writing that is very untidy (garrancho)

2 untidy lines and shapes that someone has drawn (rabisco)

scrimp /skrɪmp/ VERB [**scrimps, scrimping, scrimped**] to spend as little money as possible by living cheaply (economizar) 🔁 *After scrimping and saving for a year, we had enough money for a short holiday.* (pechinchar e economizar)

script /skrɪpt/ ▶ NOUN [plural **scripts**]

1 the words of a film, play, speech, etc. (script, texto, roteiro) 🔁 *a film script* (um roteiro de filme) □ *She writes scripts for TV series.*

2 the type of letters used to write a language □ *Cyrillic script* (escrita, tipo de letra)

▶ VERB [**scripts, scripting, scripted**] to write a script for a performance or speech □ *The film version was scripted by Bob Goldberg.* (preparar um roteiro)

scripture /ˈskrɪptʃə(r)/ NOUN [plural **scriptures**] the holy writings of a religion, for example the Bible (**escritura**)

scriptwriter /ˈskrɪptˌraɪtə(r)/ NOUN [plural **scriptwriters**] a person who writes scripts for films (**roteirista**)

scroll /skrəʊl/ ▶ NOUN [plural **scrolls**] a long roll of paper with writing on it (**rolo de pergaminho**)
▶ VERB [**scrolls, scrolling, scrolled**] to move text up or down on a computer screen so that you can see different parts of it. A computing word. □ *Scroll down to the bottom of the page.* (**mover a tela rolando**)

scroll bar /ˈskrəʊl ˈbɑː(r)/ NOUN [plural **scroll bars**] a long, thin area on the side or bottom of a computer screen that allows you to move text so that you can see different parts of it. A computing word. (**barra de rolagem**)

scrounge /skraʊndʒ/ VERB [**scrounges, scrounging, scrounged**] an informal word meaning to get something from someone else and not buy it yourself □ *He was trying to scrounge a drink off me.* (**filar**)

• **scrounger** /ˈskraʊndʒə(r)/ NOUN [plural **scroungers**] an informal word for someone who scrounges things (**aquele que fila, aproveitador**)

scrub /skrʌb/ ▶ VERB [**scrubs, scrubbing, scrubbed**] to rub something hard to get it clean □ *We'll need to scrub these stains off the floor.* (**esfregar**)
▶ NOUN, NO PLURAL
1 a dry area of land with small trees and bushes (**mato ralo**)
2 when you scrub something (**esfregação**)

scruff /skrʌf/ NOUN [plural **scruffs**]
1 someone who looks very untidy (**desleixado**)
2 by the scruff of the neck by holding the collar or the back of a person's or an animal's neck □ *The mother cat lifts her kittens in her mouth by the scruff of the neck.* (**segurar pelo colarinho ou pela nuca**)

• **scruffy** /ˈskrʌfɪ/ ADJECTIVE [**scruffier, scruffiest**] untidy and dirty □ *scruffy clothes* □ *She was looking scruffy.* (**desleixado**)

scrum /skrʌm/ NOUN [plural **scrums**] a time in the game of rugby when players from both teams form a circle by joining arms with their heads down and try to win the ball (**luta pela bola no rúgbi**)

scrumptious /ˈskrʌmpʃəs/ ADJECTIVE tasting very good *a scrumptious dessert* (**delicioso**)

scrunch /skrʌntʃ/ ▶ VERB [**scrunches, scrunching, scrunched**]
1 to crush or press something □ *She scrunched up the empty packet in her hand.* (**apertar, esmagar**)
2 to make the noise of something hard being crushed □ *The gravel scrunched under our feet.* (**ranger, estalar**)
▶ NOUN, NO PLURAL the noise of something hard being crushed (**rangido, barulho de esmagar**)

• **scrunchie** /ˈskrʌntʃɪ/ NOUN [plural **scrunchies**] a circular piece of cloth with rubber inside which girls and women use to hold their hair together at the back of their head (**prendedor de cabelo**)

scruples /ˈskruːpəlz/ PLURAL NOUN moral beliefs which make you unwilling to do something that you believe is wrong □ *He had no scruples about taking money from his elderly mother.* (**escrúpulos**)

scrupulous /ˈskruːpjʊləs/ ADJECTIVE
1 careful not to do anything that is unfair, dishonest or morally wrong □ *A less scrupulous individual would have kept the money.* (**escrupuloso**)
2 paying careful attention to even the smallest details □ *He's scrupulous about keeping accurate accounts.* (**meticuloso**)

• **scrupulously** /ˈskruːpjʊləslɪ/ ADVERB in a scrupulous way □ *scrupulously honest* □ *The room was scrupulously clean.* (**escrupulosamente**)

scrutinize or **scrutinise** /ˈskruːtɪnaɪz/ VERB [**scrutinizes, scrutinizing, scrutinized**] to examine or look at something carefully □ *She scrutinized his face for any sign of emotion.* (**inspecionar**)

• **scrutiny** /ˈskruːtɪnɪ/ NOUN, NO PLURAL close and careful examination □ *The president's personal life came under close public scrutiny.* (**inspeção**)

scuba diving /ˈskuːbə ˈdaɪvɪŋ/ NOUN, NO PLURAL the sport of swimming under the surface of water using special equipment to help you breathe (**mergulho**)

scuff /skʌf/ VERB [**scuffs, scuffing, scuffed**] to make marks on something by rubbing it against something rough □ *I've scuffed my new boots already.* (**arranhar, arrastar os pés**)

scuffle /ˈskʌfəl/ NOUN [plural **scuffles**] a short fight involving a small number of people □ *There was a scuffle outside the club.* (**luta**)

sculpt /skʌlpt/ VERB [**sculpts, sculpting, sculpted**] to make an object using a material such as clay, stone or wood (**esculpir**)

• **sculptor** /ˈskʌlptə(r)/ NOUN [plural **sculptors**] an artist who makes sculptures (**escultor**)

• **sculpture** /ˈskʌlptʃə(r)/ NOUN [plural **sculptures**]
1 an object that an artist makes using a material like clay, stone or wood □ *'The Kiss' is a famous sculpture by Rodin.* (**escultura**)
2 *no plural* the art of making objects using materials like clay, stone or wood (**escultura**)

scum /skʌm/ NOUN, NO PLURAL a layer of dirt or an unpleasant substance on the surface of a liquid (**espuma de sujeira**)

scurry /ˈskʌrɪ/ VERB [**scurries, scurrying, scurried**] to move quickly □ *The mouse scurried back into its hole.* (**correr**)

scuttle /ˈskʌtəl/ VERB [**scuttles, scuttling, scuttled**] to move quickly with short, fast steps (**disparar**)

scuzzy /ˈskʌzɪ/ ADJECTIVE [**scuzzier, scuzziest**] dirty and unpleasant. An informal word. (**imundo**)

scythe

scythe /saɪð/ NOUN [plural **scythes**] a tool with a long curved blade that is used for cutting long grass or crops (**espécie de foice, alfanje**)

sea /siː/ NOUN [plural **seas**]
1 no plural the salt water that covers most of the Earth's surface □ They live by the sea. □ I love swimming in the sea. □ Australia is completely surrounded by sea. (**mar**)
2 a large area of salt water □ the Dead Sea (**mar**)

seabed /ˈsiːbed/ NOUN, NO PLURAL the ground under the sea (**fundo do mar**)

seabird /ˈsiːbɜːd/ NOUN [plural **seabirds**] any bird that lives on or near the sea and finds its food in it (**ave marinha**)

seafood /ˈsiːfuːd/ NOUN, NO PLURAL fish and sea animals that you can eat, especially animals in shells (**frutos do mar**)

seafront /ˈsiːfrʌnt/ NOUN, NO PLURAL the area of a town next to the sea □ We walked down by the seafront. (**orla marítima**)

seagull /ˈsiːgʌl/ NOUN [plural **seagulls**] a large bird that lives near the sea and has grey and white feathers (**gaivota**)

seahorse /ˈsiːhɔːs/ NOUN [plural **seahorses**] a type of small fish that swims vertically and has a head and neck that look like a horse's (**cavalo-marinho**)

seal /siːl/ ▶ NOUN [plural **seals**]
1 a large animal with shiny fur that spends its time both in the sea and on land (**foca**)
2 a piece of plastic or paper, etc. around part of a container that you must break in order to open the container (**lacre**)
3 something that keeps something firmly closed so that air or water cannot get in or out □ The washing machine needs a new seal. (**vedação**)
4 an official mark printed on or pressed into a document to show that it is legal □ the presidential seal (**selo**)

▶ VERB [**seals, sealing, sealed**]
1 to stick the top part of an envelope down so that it is closed (**colar**)
2 to close a container or an area by covering it completely with something so that air or liquid cannot get into it or get out of it (**vedar**)

♦ PHRASAL VERB **seal off something** to prevent people from entering or leaving a place □ After the bomb scare, police sealed off the city centre. (**interditar**)

sea level /ˈsiː ˈlevəl/ NOUN, NO PLURAL the average level of the sea's surface, used as the point from which the height of land is measured □ The summit is 4000 feet above sea level. (**nível do mar**)

sea lion /ˈsiː ˈlaɪən/ NOUN [plural **sea lions**] a type of large seal (= animal with shiny fur that lives in the sea and on land) (**leão-marinho**)

seam /siːm/ NOUN [plural **seams**]
1 a line of sewing that joins two pieces of cloth □ The seam has split. (**costura**)
2 a layer of coal in the ground (**veio**)

seashore

seaman /ˈsiːmən/ NOUN [plural **seamen**] a sailor (**marujo, marinheiro**)

seaplane /ˈsiːpleɪn/ NOUN [plural **seaplanes**] a type of aircraft that is designed to take off from and land on water (**hidroavião**)

sear /sɪə(r)/ VERB [**sears, searing, seared**] to burn the surface of something (**selar, cauterizar**)

search /sɜːtʃ/ ▶ VERB [**searches, searching, searched**]
1 to look carefully for something or someone □ + for I'm still searching for my keys. □ + through Firefighters searched through the wreckage for survivors. (**procurar**)
2 if police search someone or something, they examine the min order to find something such as drugs or weapons □ Both men were arrested and searched. □ Police searched his flat. (**revistar**)
3 to look for information on the Internet. A computing word □ Have you tried searching the Net? (**procurar, pesquisar**)

▶ NOUN [plural **searches**]
1 an attempt to find someone or something (**procura, busca, investigação**) ▣ The police made a thorough search for the missing child. (**busca completa**) □ + for We will stop at nothing in our search for her.
2 in search of in order to find □ They went off in search of somewhere to eat. (**à procura de**)
3 an attempt to achieve something □ the search for happiness (**busca, procura**)
4 an attempt to find information on the Internet. A computing word (**busca**) ▣ Have you done a search on his name? (**fazer uma busca/pesquisa**)

• **searchable** /ˈsɜːtʃəbəl/ ADJECTIVE searchable computer files are organized in a way that allows you to look for particular information, words, etc. A computing word. (**que possibilita busca**)

search engine /ˈsɜːtʃ ˈendʒɪn/ NOUN [plural **search engines**] a computer program that helps you to search for something on the Internet. A computing word. (**buscador**)

searching /ˈsɜːtʃɪŋ/ ADJECTIVE showing that you want to find out the truth □ a searching question (**investigador**)

searchlight /ˈsɜːtʃlaɪt/ NOUN [plural **searchlights**] a strong light that can be turned in different directions (**holofote**)

search party /ˈsɜːtʃ ˈpɑːti/ NOUN [plural **search parties**] a group of people who make an organized search for someone who is missing (**expedição de busca**)

search warrant /ˈsɜːtʃ ˈwɒrənt/ NOUN [plural **search warrants**] an official document giving the police permission to search a building (**mandado de busca**)

seashell /ˈsiːʃel/ NOUN [plural **seashells**] an empty shell that a sea creature used to live in (**concha**)

seashore /ˈsiːʃɔː(r)/ NOUN, NO PLURAL the area of land next to the sea (**praia**)

seasick /ˈsiːsɪk/ ADJECTIVE feeling like you will vomit when you are on a boat, because of its movement (**mareado**)

- **seasickness** /ˈsiːsɪknɪs/ NOUN, NO PLURAL the feeling of being seasick (**mareagem**)

seaside /ˈsiːsaɪd/ NOUN, NO PLURAL a place near the sea where people go on holiday □ *Let's have a day at the seaside.* (**litoral**) 🔁 *a seaside resort* (**resort litorâneo**)

season /ˈsiːzən/ ▶ NOUN [plural **seasons**]
1 one of the four main periods that the year is divided into, each having different weather □ *Spring is my favourite season.* (**estação**)
2 a period of the year when a particular thing happens □ *the football season* □ *This hotel will be packed in the holiday season.* (**temporada**)
3 in season growing now and available in large quantities □ *Strawberries are in season for most of the summer.* (**na estação**)
4 out of season (a) not growing now so not available in large quantities □ *I try not to buy vegetables that are out of season.* (b) at the time of year when most people do not visit a place □ *Holidays are much cheaper out of season.* (**fora de estação**)
▶ VERB [**seasons, seasoning, seasoned**] to add flavor to food by putting salt, herbs or spices into it (**temperar**)

- **seasonal** /ˈsiːzənəl/ ADJECTIVE
1 happening only at particular times of the year □ *The farm offers seasonal employment to fruit-pickers.* (**sazonal**)
2 growing now so fresh and full of flavor □ *Our main courses are served with a selection of seasonal vegetables.* (**da estação**)

- **seasoning** /ˈsiːzənɪŋ/ NOUN [plural **seasonings**] salt, herbs and spices that you use to add flavour to food (**tempero**)

season ticket /ˈsiːzən ˌtɪkɪt/ NOUN [plural **season tickets**] a ticket that you can use as often as you like for a particular period of time (**assinatura**)

seat /siːt/ ▶ NOUN [plural **seats**]
1 a piece of furniture for sitting on □ *a garden seat* □ *He was in the passenger seat of the car.* (**banco, cadeira, poltrona**)
2 a chair that you pay to sit on in a vehicle or in a theatre □ *I've booked three seats for the theatre.* □ *I prefer window seats in aeroplanes.* (**lugar**)
3 the part of a chair that you sit on (**assento**)
4 a position in a parliament or committee (= group of people chosen to make decisions about something) (**cadeiras, membros**) 🔁 *The party lost three seats in the election.* (**perder integrantes**)
▶ VERB [**seats, seating, seated**]
1 to have enough room for a particular number of people to sit down □ *The new theatre seats 600 people.* (**acomodar**)
2 to give someone a place to sit. A formal word. (**oferecer lugar para sentar**)
3 be seated to be sitting down (**estar sentado**)

seat belt /ˈsiːt ˌbelt/ NOUN [plural **seat belts**] a strong belt in a car or plane that goes across your body □ *Please fasten your seat belts now.* (**cinto de segurança**)

seating /ˈsiːtɪŋ/ NOUN, NO PLURAL the type or number of seats available in a place, or the way that they are arranged □ *The hotel dining room has seating for 70 guests.* (**disposição de lugares**)

seaweed /ˈsiːwiːd/ NOUN, NO PLURAL a type of plant that grows in the sea (**alga**)

seaworthy /ˈsiːˌwɜːði/ ADJECTIVE a boat that is seaworthy is in good enough condition to be sailed on the sea (**em condições de navegar**)

sec /sek/ NOUN [plural **secs**] an informal word meaning a very short time □ *I'll be back in a sec.* (**segundo**)

secateurs /ˌsekəˈtɜːz/ PLURAL NOUN a tool used for cutting plants (**tesoura de jardinagem**)

secluded /sɪˈkluːdɪd/ ADJECTIVE a secluded place is quiet and private □ *a secluded beach* (**recluso**)

- **seclusion** /sɪˈkluːʒən/ NOUN, NO PLURAL when you are alone, away from other people □ *He has spent much of the last two years in seclusion.* (**reclusão**)

second[1] /ˈsekənd/ ▶ NUMBER 2nd written as a word □ *Julia is their second daughter.* □ *Marta came second in the race.* □ *This programme is the second in a series of three.* (**segundo**)
▶ VERB [**seconds, seconding, seconded**] to second an idea or plan is to support it when someone suggests it (**apoiar**)

second[2] /ˈsekənd/ NOUN [plural **seconds**]
1 one of 60 parts that a minute is divided into □ *He ran the race in 57 seconds.* (**segundo**)
2 a very short time □ *Just wait a second.* (**um segundo/momento**)

secondary /ˈsekəndəri/ ADJECTIVE
1 secondary education is for students between the age of 11 and 18 (**ensinos fundamental II e médio**)
2 less important than something else □ *Your health comes first. Money is secondary.* (**secundário**)
3 being something that develops from something else □ *a secondary infection* (**secundário**)

secondary school /ˈsekəndəri ˌskuːl/ NOUN [plural **secondary schools**] a school for students between the ages of 11 and 18 (**escola de ensinos fundamental II e médio**)

second best /ˌsekənd ˈbest/ ▶ NOUN, NO PLURAL
1 the person or thing that is next after the best □ *He was the second best in his class at maths.* (**segundo melhor**)
2 something that is not as good as you would like it to be □ *I'm not going to settle for second best.* (**segundo melhor**)
▶ ADJECTIVE not best but next best □ *She's the team's second best scorer.* (**segundo melhor**)

second-class /ˌsekəndˈklɑːs/ ▶ ADJECTIVE
1 describes the less expensive way of travelling that most people choose and the less expensive

second cousin 709 **section** S

way of sending post that is slower □ *a second-class compartment* □ *a second-class stamp* (**de segunda classe**)

2 not as good or not as important as other people or things (**de segunda classe, inferior**) 🔁 *Some of the immigrants were treated like second-class citizens.* (**cidadãos de classe inferior**)

▶ ADVERB using the cheapest type □ *I sent the letter second-class.* (**do tipo mais barato**)

second cousin /ˈsekənd ˈkʌzən/ NOUN [*plural* **second cousins**] the son or daughter of one of your parent's cousins (**primo de segundo grau**)

second-hand /ˌsekəndˈhænd/ ADJECTIVE, ADVERB
1 used for describing things which someone else has owned before you □ *a second-hand car* □ *Kathryn buys all her clothes second-hand.* (**de segunda mão**)

2 told to you by someone who got the information from another person □ *I only heard the news secondhand.* (**em segunda mão**)

secondly /ˈsekəndlɪ/ ADVERB used for introducing the second thing you want to mention □ *And secondly, I'd like to thank Mrs Ambrose for all her help.* (**em segundo lugar**)

second nature /ˈsekənd ˈneɪtʃə(r)/ NOUN, NO PLURAL something that you do without thinking because it seems so normal or natural □ *Texting is second nature to young people now.* (**hábito**)

second person /ˈsekənd ˈpɜːsən/ NOUN, NO PLURAL in grammar, the form of a word that is used for the person you are talking or writing to □ *'You' is a second person pronoun.* (**segunda pessoa**)

second-rate /ˈsekəndˈreɪt/ ADJECTIVE not of good quality □ *a second-rate hotel* (**inferior**)

second thoughts /ˈsekənd ˈθɔːts/ PLURAL NOUN
1 have second thoughts to start to have doubts about a decision you have made □ *She seems to be having second thoughts about getting married.* (**mudança de opinião**)

2 on second thoughts used for saying that you have changed your mind about something □ *You can come with me. On second thoughts, it might be best if you wait here.* (**pensando melhor**)

secrecy /ˈsiːkrəsɪ/ NOUN, NO PLURAL the quality of being secret (**sigilo**)

secret /ˈsiːkrɪt/ ▶ NOUN [*plural* **secrets**]
1 a piece of information that must not be told to other people (**segredo**) 🔁 *I'll tell you a little secret.* (**contar um segredo**) 🔁 *She can't keep a secret* (= not tell someone a secret). (**guardar segredo**) 🔁 *The birthday party was a well-kept secret.* (**segredo bem guardado**)

2 *no plural* a way of achieving something □ *Her hair always looks so good. I wish I knew her secret.* □ **+ of** *The secret of success is hard work.* (**segredo**)

3 in secret without other people knowing □ *They began to meet in secret.* (**em segredo**)

4 make no secret of something to make your feelings clear to other people □ *She made no secret of her desire to have a child.* (**não fazer segredos**)

5 the secrets of something the things that people do not yet understand or know about □ *These images could help reveal the secrets of the universe.* (**os segredos de**)

▶ ADJECTIVE not told or shown to other people □ *secret information* (**secreto**) 🔁 *The facts of the case were kept secret.* (**mantido secreto**) □ *The talks were held at a secret location.*

secretarial /ˌsekrəˈteərɪəl/ ADJECTIVE to do with the job of a secretary □ *secretarial skills* (**de secretário**)

secretary /ˈsekrətərɪ/ NOUN [*plural* **secretaries**]
1 someone whose job is to type letters, arrange meetings and take notes at business meetings, etc. □ *Please leave a message with my secretary if I'm out.* (**secretário**)

2 someone who is in charge of a government department □ *the education secretary* □ *He's the former British foreign secretary.* (**secretário**)

Secretary of State /ˈsekrətərɪ əv ˈsteɪt/ NOUN [*plural* **Secretaries of State**]
1 in the UK, someone who is in charge of one of the main government departments such as education, health or defence (**Secretário de Estado**)

2 in the US, the person who is in charge of the government department which deals with matters that involve other countries (**Secretário de Estado**)

secrete /sɪˈkriːt/ VERB [**secretes, secreting, secreted**] if a plant or animal secretes a substance, it produces it. A biology word. □ *The plant secretes a sticky liquid that attracts flies.* (**secretar**)

• **secretion** /sɪˈkriːʃən/ NOUN [*plural* **secretions**] a substance that a plant or animal produces. A biology word. (**secreção**)

secretive /ˈsiːkrətɪv/ ADJECTIVE not wanting to tell people about something □ *Logan was very secretive about his past.* (**reservado**)

secretly /ˈsiːkrɪtlɪ/ ADVERB in a secret way □ *They met secretly.* (**secretamente**)

secret service /ˈsiːkrɪt ˈsɜːvɪs/ NOUN [*plural* **secret services**]
1 a government department that tries to discover information about other countries □ *a secret service agent* (**serviço secreto**)

2 in the US, the government department that protects the President (**serviço secreto**)

sect /sekt/ NOUN [*plural* **sects**] a group of people who have different beliefs from a larger group, especially in a religion (**seita**)

• **sectarian** /sekˈteərɪən/ ADJECTIVE to do with religious differences between groups □ *sectarian violence* (**sectário**)

section /ˈsekʃən/ NOUN [*plural* **sections**] one of the parts that together make up something □ *The table has three sections that fit together.* □ *the fiction section of the library* □ *the arts section of the newspaper* (**seção**)

sector /ˈsektə(r)/ NOUN [plural **sectors**]
1 one of the parts that an area is divided into □ *the American sector of the city* (setor)
2 one of the parts that a country's economy is divided into □ *the retail sector* (setor)

secular /ˈsekjʊlə(r)/ ADJECTIVE not religious or not to do with religion (secular, profano) 🔁 *a secular state* (estado secular) □ *secular music*

secure /sɪˈkjʊə(r)/ ▶ ADJECTIVE
1 not likely to fail or change □ *a secure job* □ *They are financially secure.* (seguro)
2 safe, confident and not worried □ *Children need to feel secure.* (seguro)
3 safe against attack or harm □ *You can make your home more secure by installing a burglar alarm.* (seguro)
4 a secure place is guarded so that only particular people can go into it or leave it □ *Police have taken the family to a secure location.* □ *a secure area of the airport* (seguro)
5 firmly fixed or fastened □ *Check that the ropes are secure.* (seguro)
▶ VERB [**secures, securing, secured**]
1 to get something important □ *She has secured a place at the best college in the country.* (obter)
2 to fix or fasten something firmly □ *The tent was secured with ropes and pegs.* (prender)
3 to make something safe from being attacked or harmed □ *Soldiers were brought in to secure the border.* (proteger)

• **security** /sɪˈkjʊərəti/ ▶ NOUN, NO PLURAL
1 safety from danger or crime and the things that are done to achieve this (segurança) 🔁 *We need to tighten airport security.* (aumentar a segurança) 🔁 *The policy was a threat to national security.* (segurança nacional)
2 the people in an organization whose job is to protect the buildings and workers □ *Call security if you see anything suspicious.* (segurança)
3 a feeling of safety and confidence or a situation that provides this (segurança) 🔁 *A stable family background can give children a sense of security.* (sentimento de segurança)
4 the situation when something is not likely to fail or change (segurança) 🔁 *Job security is very important for most people.* (segurança do trabalho) 🔁 *A lot of people are worried about financial security.* (segurança financeira)
5 property or goods that you legally promise to give someone if you cannot pay back the money you have borrowed from them □ *He used his house as security on the loan.* (garantia)
▶ ADJECTIVE to do with the safety of someone or something (de segurança) 🔁 *a security guard* (um guarda de segurança) 🔁 *The airport needs to improve security measures.* (medidas de segurança) □ *a security risk*

sedate /sɪˈdeɪt/ ▶ VERB [**sedates, sedating, sedated**] to give someone a drug to make them feel calmer (dar sedativo, sedar)
▶ ADJECTIVE calm and slow □ *Pedro walked at a more sedate pace.* (sedado)

• **sedation** /sɪˈdeɪʃən/ NOUN, NO PLURAL when someone is sedated (sedação)

• **sedative** /ˈsedətɪv/ NOUN [plural **sedatives**] a drug that someone is given to sedate them (sedativo)

sedentary /ˈsedəntəri/ ADJECTIVE a sedentary job or way of life is one in which you sit down most of the time and do very little exercise (sedentário)

sediment /ˈsedɪmənt/ NOUN, NO PLURAL a solid substance that forms at the bottom of a liquid (sedimento)

• **sedimentary** /ˌsedɪˈmentəri/ ADJECTIVE sedimentary rock is formed from the sand and stones at the bottom of rivers or the sea. A geography word. (sedimentário)

seduce /sɪˈdjuːs/ VERB [**seduces, seducing, seduced**] to cause someone to do something that they would not usually do □ *The prospect of making a quick profit seduced him into buying the shares.* (seduzir)

• **seductive** /sɪˈdʌktɪv/ ADJECTIVE attractive and making you want to do something □ *a seductive idea* (sedutor)

see /siː/ VERB [**sees, seeing, saw, seen**]
1 to look at someone or something and notice them □ *The dog goes mad whenever he sees a cat.* □ *I saw you coming.* □ *Can you see where the switch is?* (ver)
2 to meet someone or spend time with them □ *Have you seen Peter much lately?* □ *I'm seeing Billie at the weekend.* (ver, encontrar)
3 to watch a film, television programme, etc. □ *Did you see 'Pride and Prejudice'?* (assistir)
4 to understand something (compreender) 🔁 Now *I see what you mean.* (compreendo o que você quer dizer) 🔁 *I don't see why I should tidy up your mess.* (não compreendo por que) 🔁 *'He couldn't come because he didn't have a ticket.' 'Oh, I see.'* (eu compreendo)
5 to find out something by waiting for something to happen □ *I'll see what she says.* □ *Let's see how today's lesson goes.* □ *See if you can arrange a taxi.* (ver)
6 to find out information about something □ *Can you see what time the bank opens?* □ *As we have seen, Cromwell was hated by the Irish.* (saber)
7 to imagine something or to believe that something will happen □ *I can't see him as a father.* □ *I can't see the building being ready by June.* (ver, imaginar)
8 if you see someone somewhere, you go there with them □ *I'll see you to the door.* (acompanhar)
9 if you see that something happens, you make sure that it happens □ *+ that I'll see that he's back before eight.* (certificar-se)

seed 711 **seize**

10 if a place or a period of time sees something, that is where or when it happens □ *The town saw mass unemployment in the eighties.* (**ver**)

11 I'll see/We'll see used to say that you will consider agreeing to what someone has asked, but will not decide immediately □ *'Can I have a new bike for my birthday?' 'We'll see.'* (**vamos ver**)

12 let me see used when you are trying to remember something □ *It must have been – let me see – at least fifteen years ago.* (**deixe-me ver**)

13 See you. an informal way of saying goodbye (**Até mais!**)

14 you see used when you are explaining something □ *We didn't have a car then, you see.* (**veja, entenda**)

⇨ go to **not see eye to eye**

♦ PHRASAL VERBS **see about something** to deal with something or to organize something □ *We need to see about the lighting.* (**cuidar de**) **see something in someone/ something** to believe that someone or something has particular, usually good, qualities □ *She's always hanging round with Rob – I don't know what she sees in him.* (**ver alguma qualidade em alguém/algo**) **see someone off** to go with someone to say goodbye to them (**ir ao embarque**) **see someone/something off** to defeat or get rid of someone or something that is threatening you □ *He saw off over twenty other artists to win the prize.* (**derrotar, eliminar**) **see someone out** to go to the door with someone who is leaving (**acompanhar até a porta**) **see out something** to finish spending a period of time in a particular place or doing a particular thing □ *He saw out the decade in London.* (**passar**) **see through someone/ something** to understand that someone or something is trying to trick you □ *I knew they only wanted my money – I could see through their flattery.* (**perceber, não se deixar enganar**) **see something through** to finish doing something, even if it is difficult □ *We're determined to see this job through.* (**perceber, não se deixar enganar**) **see to something** to deal with something □ *Don't worry about the travel arrangements – I'll see to all that.* (**providenciar, lidar com**)

seed /siːd/ NOUN [plural **seeds**]
1 a thing that a plant produces and that new plants grow from (**semente**) 🔲 *Sow the seeds about two inches deep in the soil.* (**plantar as sementes**) □ *sunflower seeds*
2 the seeds of something something that makes a new situation start to develop (**as sementes de**)
• **seedless** /ˈsiːdləs/ ADJECTIVE seedless fruit has no seeds in it □ *seedless grapes* (**sem semente**)
• **seedling** /ˈsiːdlɪŋ/ NOUN [plural **seedlings**] a very young plant (**muda**)

seeing /ˈsiːɪŋ/ CONJUNCTION **seeing as/that** used for saying a reason (**visto que**) □ *We thought we'd visit you, seeing as we were in the area.*

seek /siːk/ VERB [**seeks, seeking, sought**]
1 a formal word meaning to try to find or achieve something □ *They were seeking a long-term solution.* (**buscar, tentar**)
2 a formal word meaning to ask for something □ *You should seek the advice of a doctor.* (**procurar**)

> Note that **seek**, meaning 'to try to find' is only used in formal English. The usual phrase for this meaning is **look for**:
> ✓ I'm looking for a good hairdresser.
> ✗ I'm seeking a good hairdresser.

seem /siːm/ VERB [**seems, seeming, seemed**] to appear to be something □ *He seemed very pleased to see you.* (**parecer**) 🔲 *She seemed like a very nice young woman.* (**parecer**) 🔲 *It seems likely that he will be in hospital for several weeks.* (**parece que**) □ *It seems strange we haven't heard from him.* □ *+ to do something Nothing seems to worry him.*
• **seemingly** /ˈsiːmɪŋli/ ADVERB used for saying what seems true although it is probably not true □ *The queue to get in was seemingly endless.* (**aparentemente**)

seen /siːn/ PAST PARTICIPLE OF **see** (*ver* **see**)

seep /siːp/ VERB [**seeps, seeping, seeped**] to flow through something in small amounts □ *Blood was seeping through his shirt.* (**vazar, infiltrar(-se)**)

seesaw /ˈsiːsɔː/ NOUN [plural **seesaws**] a long board that two children sit on, one at each end, and when one child moves high into the air, the other child moves down towards the ground (**gangorra**)

seethe /siːð/ VERB [**seethes, seething, seethed**] to be extremely angry, often without shouting or showing your anger (**ferver de raiva**)

see-through /ˈsiːθruː/ ADJECTIVE made of plastic or cloth that you can see through □ *a see-through dress* (**transparente**)

segment /ˈsɛgmənt/ NOUN [plural **segments**] one of several parts of something □ *Divide the orange into segments.* □ *The policy will affect many segments of society.* (**segmento**)

segregate /ˈsɛgrɪgeɪt/ VERB [**segregates, segregating, segregated**] to separate different groups of people □ *Police segregated the fans from rival football teams.* (**segregar**)
• **segregation** /ˌsɛgrɪˈgeɪʃən/ NOUN, NO PLURAL the act of separating groups of people (**segregação**)

seismic /ˈsaɪzmɪk/ ADJECTIVE to do with earthquakes (= sudden movements of the Earth's surface). A geography word. (**sísmico**)
• **seismograph** /ˈsaɪzməɡrɑːf/ NOUN [plural **seismographs**] a piece of equipment for measuring earthquakes (= sudden movements of the Earth's surface). A geography word. (**sismógrafo**)

seize /siːz/ VERB [**seizes, seizing, seized**]
1 to take something into your hand quickly and firmly □ *Joel seized my hand and shook it.* (**agarrar**)

2 to use an opportunity enthusiastically and effectively (**agarrar**) 🔃 *He seized the opportunity to join the team.* (**agarrar a oportunidade**) □ *She seized her chance to escape.*

3 to take control of a place, especially using force (**tomar**) 🔃 *Rebels seized control of the city.* (**tomar o controle**)

4 if the police or government officers seize something, they take it away from someone □ *Police raided his home and seized several computers.* (**apreender**)

◆ PHRASAL VERBS **seize on something** to use something quickly and enthusiastically in order to get an advantage for yourself □ *He seized on the figures as evidence that the government is failing.* (**apossar-se/aproveitar-se de algo**) **seize up** to stop moving or working correctly □ *My back seized up and I couldn't move.* □ *The car's engine seized up.* (**encrencar**)

• **seizure** /ˈsiːʒə(r)/ NOUN [plural **seizures**]
1 when police or government officers take something away from someone □ *the seizure of illegal weapons* (**apreensão**)
2 a sudden attack of an illness, which makes your brain not work correctly for a short time □ *A few hours after birth, he suffered a seizure.* (**convulsão**)
3 the act of taking control of a place, especially using force □ *the seizure of power* (**tomada**)

seldom /ˈseldəm/ ADVERB not often □ *He seldom travelled abroad.* □ *A teacher's job is seldom an easy one.* (**raramente**)

select /sɪˈlekt/ ▶ VERB [**selects, selecting, selected**] to choose someone or something □ *She selected some items and went to pay for them.* □ **+ for** *Hawthorne has been selected for the Olympic hockey team.* (**selecionar**)
▶ ADJECTIVE
1 a select group is a small group of people who have been chosen carefully □ *He agreed to speak to a select group of journalists.* (**selecionado**)
2 of very good quality, or expensive □ *select wines* (**seleto**)

• **selection** /sɪˈlekʃən/ NOUN [plural **selections**]
1 a range of things that you can choose from (**seleção**) 🔃 *The shop has a wide selection of boots and shoes.* (**seleção ampla**)
2 something that you have chosen □ *Bring your selection to the cash desk at the door.* (**escolha**)
3 the process of choosing someone or something □ *Jury selection for the trial began yesterday.* (**seleção**)

• **selective** /sɪˈlektɪv/ ADJECTIVE
1 careful about who or what you choose □ *The club is very selective about its members.* (**seletivo**)
2 involving only the people or things which have been chosen □ *The marketing campaign is aimed at a selective group of donors.* (**seletivo**)

self /self/ NOUN [plural **selves**] your character (**si mesmo**) 🔃 *He was worried about revealing his true self to her.* (**eu verdadeiro**)

self- /self/ PREFIX self- is added to the beginning of words to mean 'relating to or done by yourself or by itself' □ *self-control* □ *self-imposed* □ *self-raising flour* (**auto-**)

self-appointed /ˈselfəˈpɔɪntɪd/ ADJECTIVE giving yourself a responsibility or job without getting other people's agreement □ *self-appointed community leaders* (**autonomeado**)

self-assurance /ˈselfəˈʃʊərəns/ NOUN, NO PLURAL the quality of being confident about your own abilities (**autoconfiança**)

• **self-assured** /ˈselfəˈʃʊəd/ ADJECTIVE confident about your own abilities (**seguro**)

self-catering /ˈselfˈkeɪtərɪŋ/ ADJECTIVE cooking your own meals on a holiday, or allowing someone to do this □ *a self-catering holiday/apartment* (**preparo das próprias refeições, cozinha disponível**)

self-centred /ˈselfˈsentə(r)d/ ADJECTIVE thinking only about yourself and not about other people (**egocêntrico**)

self-confessed /ˈselfkənˈfest/ ADJECTIVE admitting that you have a bad habit or that you are a particular type of bad person □ *a self-confessed chocolate addict* □ *a self-confessed thief* (**assumido**)

self-confidence /ˈselfˈkɒnfɪdəns/ NOUN, NO PLURAL being sure of yourself and your own abilities (**autoconfiança**)

• **self-confident** /ˈselfˈkɒnfɪdənt/ ADJECTIVE sure of yourself and your own abilities (**seguro**)

self-conscious /ˈselfˈkɒnʃəs/ ADJECTIVE nervous because you think other people are looking at you and criticizing you □ *She felt very self-conscious dancing in public.* (**tímido, constrangido**)

self-contained /ˈselfkənˈteɪnd/ ADJECTIVE
1 a self-contained flat has its own kitchen and bathroom (**autossuficiente**)
2 not needing help from other people □ *She's very self-contained.* (**autossuficiente**)

self-control /ˈselfkənˈtrəʊl/ NOUN, NO PLURAL your ability to control your behaviour when you are angry, excited, etc. □ *I lost my self-control, and hit him.* (**autocontrole**)

self-defence /ˈselfdɪˈfens/ NOUN, NO PLURAL the process of trying to defend yourself when someone is attacking you □ *classes in self-defence* □ *He said he fired the gun in self-defence.* (**autodefesa**)

self-defense /ˈselfdɪˈfens/ NOUN, NO PLURAL the US spelling of **self-defence** (**autodefesa**)

self-destructive /ˈselfdɪˈstrʌktɪv/ ADJECTIVE often doing things that harm you (**autodestrutivo**)

self-discipline /ˈselfˈdɪsɪplɪn/ NOUN, NO PLURAL the ability to keep making yourself do difficult or hard things in order to achieve something □ *She lacks self-discipline.* (**autodisciplina**)

• **self-disciplined** /ˈselfˈdɪsɪplɪnd/ ADJECTIVE having self-discipline (**autodisciplinado**)

self-drive

self-drive /ˈselfdraɪv/ ADJECTIVE a self-drive holiday is one in which you drive to the place you are going (**com carro próprio**)

self-employed /ˌselfɪmˈplɔɪd/ ADJECTIVE having your own business instead of being employed by someone else ☐ *a self-employed painter and decorator* (**autônomo**)

- **self-employment** /ˌselfɪmˈplɔɪmənt/ NOUN, NO PLURAL the situation when you have your own business and are not employed by someone else (**firma própria**)

self-esteem /ˌselfɪˈstiːm/ NOUN, NO PLURAL the belief that you are a nice and successful person ☐ *She's always had low self-esteem.* (**autoestima**)

self-evident /ˌselfˈevɪdənt/ ADJECTIVE obvious ☐ *It is self-evident that the world's resources cannot cope with an increasing population.* (**óbvio**)

self-explanatory /ˌselfɪkˈsplænətri/ ADJECTIVE easy to understand, and needing no more explanation ☐ *The title is self-explanatory.* (**que dispensa explicação**)

self-help /ˌselfˈhelp/ NOUN, NO PLURAL ways of dealing with your own problems instead of depending on other people ☐ *a self-help manual* (**autoajuda**)

self-importance /ˌselfɪmˈpɔːtəns/ NOUN, NO PLURAL behaviour that shows that you think you are more important than other people (**presunção**)

- **self-important** /ˌselfɪmˈpɔːtənt/ ADJECTIVE behaving as if you are more important than other people (**presunçoso**)

self-imposed /ˌselfɪmˈpəʊzd/ ADJECTIVE a self-imposed rule, punishment, etc. is one you have chosen yourself ☐ *The school has a self-imposed deadline of August 24 for completion of the project.* (**autoimposto**)

self-indulgent /ˌselfɪnˈdʌldʒənt/ ADJECTIVE doing too many things for your own pleasure or interest (**indulgente com relação a si mesmo**)

self-inflicted /ˌselfɪnˈflɪktɪd/ ADJECTIVE caused by yourself ☐ *self-inflicted wounds* (**causado por si próprio**)

self-interest /ˌselfˈɪntrəst/ NOUN, NO PLURAL interest only in what will help you ☐ *He acted purely out of self-interest.* (**interesse pessoal**)

- **self-interested** /ˌselfˈɪntrəstɪd/ ADJECTIVE interested only in what will help you (**interessado pessoalmente**)

selfish /ˈselfɪʃ/ ADJECTIVE thinking only about yourself and not about what other people might want or need ☐ *He's a very selfish person.* ☐ *I decided to stay for purely selfish reasons.* (**egoísta**)

- **selfishly** /ˈselfɪʃli/ ADVERB in a selfish way ☐ *He acted very selfishly.* (**egoisticamente**)
- **selfishness** /ˈselfɪʃnɪs/ NOUN, NO PLURAL the state of being selfish (**egoísmo**)

selfless /ˈselfləs/ ADJECTIVE thinking about other people and not about yourself ☐ *Her selfless acts saved a young man's life.* (**desinteressado**)

sell

self-made /ˌselfˈmeɪd/ ADJECTIVE rich because you have worked hard ☐ *a self-made woman* ☐ *a self-made millionaire* (**feito com o próprio esforço**)

self-pity /ˌselfˈpɪti/ NOUN, NO PLURAL the feeling that your situation is worse than other people's and that you deserve sympathy (**autopiedade**)

self-portrait /ˌselfˈpɔːtreɪt/ NOUN [*plural* **self-portraits**] a drawing or painting of you that you have done yourself (**autorretrato**)

self-raising flour /ˌselfreɪzɪŋ ˈflaʊə(r)/ NOUN, NO PLURAL flour that makes cakes rise when you cook them (**farinha com fermento**)

self-reliance /ˌselfrɪˈlaɪəns/ NOUN, NO PLURAL the ability to do things by yourself without help (**autoconfiança**)

- **self-reliant** /ˌselfrɪˈlaɪənt/ ADJECTIVE able to do things by yourself without help (**autoconfiante**)

self-respect /ˌselfrɪˈspekt/ NOUN, NO PLURAL the feeling that you are as good as anyone else and should treat yourself and other people well (**respeito próprio**)

- **self-respecting** /ˌselfrɪˈspektɪŋ/ ADJECTIVE feeling self-respect ☐ *No self-respecting teenager would want their parents to come with them on a night out.* (**que se respeita**)

self-righteous /ˌselfˈraɪtʃəs/ ADJECTIVE believing that you are morally a very good person, in a way that annoys another people (**convencido**)

self-sacrifice /ˌselfˈsækrɪfaɪs/ NOUN, NO PLURAL when you choose not to do or have something that you want, in order to help someone else ☐ *It was an act of courage and self-sacrifice.* (**abnegação**)

self-satisfied /ˌselfˈsætɪsfaɪd/ ADJECTIVE too pleased with yourself and your achievements ☐ *a self-satisfied grin* (**convencido**)

self-service /ˌselfˈsɜːvɪs/ ADJECTIVE involving customers getting or doing something themselves ☐ *a self-service restaurant* ☐ *The airline provides a self-service check-in.* (**self-service, em que cada um se serve**)

self-sufficient /ˌselfsəˈfɪʃənt/ ADJECTIVE able to provide everything you need for yourself (**autossuficiente**)

sell /sel/ VERB [**sells, selling, sold**]
1 to give someone something in exchange for money ☐ **+ for** *They sold the house for £450,000.* ☐ **+ to** *She sold the business to a Chinese company.* ☐ *He sold me his bike.* (**vender**)
2 to have something available for people to buy ☐ *The shop sells handmade chocolates.* ☐ *Do you sell batteries?* (**vender**)
3 if something sells, people buy it ☐ *Tickets sold quickly for both shows.* (**vender**) ☐ *T-shirts sell well* (= a lot of people buy T-shirts) *at this time of year.* (**vender bem**) ☐ *The album sold 350,000 copies in Australia.*
4 sell for/at £300/£60, etc. used for saying what price someone pays for something ☐ *Apartments in this area sell for around £200,000.* (**vender por**)

5 if you sell an idea, you try to make people accept it □ *You'll need to sell the idea to your employer.* (vender a ideia, convencer)

◆ PHRASAL VERBS **sell something off** to sell something quickly for a low price □ *The company has sold off eight of its stores.* (liquidar) **sell out 1** if a shop sells out of something, there is none of it left for people to buy □ *I'm sorry, we've sold out of milk.* **2** if something sells out, there is none left for people to buy □ *When I got there, all the tickets had sold out.* (esgotado/esgotar) **sell up** to sell your house or business □ *We sold up and moved to France.* (vender a casa ou um negócio)

sell-by date /'selbaɪ ˌdeɪt/ NOUN [plural **sell-by dates**] a date on a food package, which shows when shops should stop selling the food (data de validade) 🔊 *The sausages were past their sell-by date.* (data de validade vencida)

seller /'selə(r)/ NOUN [plural **sellers**]
1 someone who is selling something □ *ticket sellers* (vendedor)
2 top/big seller a product that a lot of people buy □ *The toy was a top seller last Christmas.* (campeão de vendas)

Sellotape /'seləteɪp/ NOUN, NO PLURAL a long, narrow piece of sticky plastic that you use for sticking paper together. A trademark. (fita adesiva (marca registrada))

sellout /'selaʊt/ NOUN [plural **sellouts**] an event for which all the tickets have been sold □ *The concert was a sellout.* (lotação esgotada)

semblance /'sembləns/ NOUN, NO PLURAL (aparência) **a/some semblance of something** when something seems to have a particular quality □ *He tried to bring some semblance of order to the proceedings.* (alguma semelhança)

semen /'siːmən/ NOUN, NO PLURAL the liquid produced by the male sex organs. A biology word. (sêmen)

semester /sɪ'mestə(r)/ NOUN [plural **semesters**] the US word for **term** (= period that a school or college year is divided into) (semestre)

semi /'semɪ/ NOUN [plural **semis**] a house that is joined to another house on one side (geminada)

semi- /'semɪ/ PREFIX semi- is added to the beginning of words to mean 'half' or 'partly' □ *semicircle* □ *semiprecious* (semi-)

semicircle /'semɪˌsɜːkəl/ NOUN [plural **semicircles**] half a circle (semicírculo)

semicolon /ˌsemɪ'kəʊlən/ NOUN [plural **semicolons**] a punctuation mark (;) used to separate different parts of a sentence or list (ponto e vírgula)

semiconductor /ˌsemɪkən'dʌktə(r)/ NOUN [plural **semiconductors**] a substance that allows some electricity to go through it. A physics word. (semicondutor)

semi-detached /ˌsemɪdɪ'tætʃt/ ADJECTIVE a semidetached house is joined to another house on one side (geminado)

semi-final /ˌsemɪ'faɪnəl/ NOUN [plural **semi-finals**] one of the two games in a competition which are played just before the last game (semifinal) 🔊 *Sweden reached the semi-final of the 1994 World Cup.* (chegou à semifinal)

seminar /'semɪnɑː(r)/ NOUN [plural **seminars**] a meeting to discuss and learn about a particular subject □ *a marketing seminar* (seminário)

semi-precious /ˌsemɪˈpreʃəs/ ADJECTIVE a semiprecious stone is used for making jewellery but is not as valuable as some other stones (semiprecioso)

senate /'senɪt/ NOUN [plural **senates**] the smaller but more powerful part of a government which has two parts, for example in countries such as the US and France □ *The French senate approved the bill.* □ *a senate committee* (senado)

• **senator** /'senətə(r)/ NOUN [plural **senators**] a member of a senate □ *Democratic senator, Hillary Clinton* (senador)

send /send/ VERB [**sends, sending, sent**]
1 to arrange for something to go somewhere □ *He sent me an e-mail.* □ *Sophia sent him a birthday card.* □ *+ to I sent a text message to my Dad.* (mandar, enviar)
2 to make someone go somewhere (mandar) 🔊 *He was sent home from school because he was sick.* (mandado para casa) □ *+ to The doctor took one look and sent me straight to hospital.* □ *The government sent a team of rescue workers to the area.*
3 to cause someone to be in a particular state □ *The loneliness was sending me crazy.* □ *The warmth sent me to sleep.* (deixar)

◆ PHRASAL VERBS **send something back** to return something to the person who sent it to you □ *He filled in the questionnaire and sent it back.* (mandar de volta) **send for someone** to ask for someone to come to you □ *They sent for a doctor.* (mandar buscar) **send someone in** to send a large group of soldiers or police officers to deal with a situation □ *The government has sent in troops to restore calm.* (mandar, enviar) **send something in** to send something to an organization □ *Hundreds of readers have sent in stories of their own experiences.* (mandar, enviar) **send off for something** to write to an organization and ask them to send you something □ *I sent off for a catalogue.* (fazer uma solicitação a uma firma) **send someone off** to make a player leave a sports game because they have done something wrong □ *He was sent off for swearing at the referee.* (expulsar) **send something out** to send something to a lot of people □ *Have you sent out the party invitations yet?* (mandar, enviar)

• **sender** /'sendə(r)/ NOUN [plural **senders**] the person who sent a letter, e-mail, etc. □ *If this letter is not delivered, please return it to the sender.* (remetente)

senile

senile /ˈsiːnaɪl/ ADJECTIVE very confused and often forgetting things because of old age (**senil**)

• **senility** /sɪˈnɪləti/ NOUN, NO PLURAL the state of being senile (**senilidade**)

senior /ˈsiːniə(r)/ ▶ ADJECTIVE

1 having a higher position in an organization □ *senior government officials* □ *She has a very senior position in the company.* (**superior, mais antigo**)

2 older □ *senior members of the family* □ *senior players* (**mais velho**)

▶ NOUN [plural **seniors**]

1 be 5/10 etc. years someone's senior to be 5/10 etc. years older than someone □ *My brother is six years my senior.* (**ser 5, 10 etc. anos mais velho que alguém**)

2 a US word for **senior citizen** (**idoso**)

senior citizen /ˌsiːniə ˈsɪtɪzən/ NOUN [plural **senior citizens**] an older person who does not work anymore (**idoso**)

seniority /ˌsiːniˈɒrəti/ NOUN, NO PLURAL how old or powerful a person is □ *We sat along the table in order of seniority.* (**superioridade de idade**)

sensation /senˈseɪʃən/ NOUN [plural **sensations**]

1 a physical feeling, or the ability to have physical feelings □ *He had a burning sensation in his chest.* (**sensação**) ⬛ *She lost all sensation in the right side of her face.* (**perder toda a sensação**)

2 a feeling that you cannot explain □ *I had a strange sensation that I had been there before.* (**sensação**)

3 a state of excitement or shock □ *The announcement caused quite a sensation.* (**sensação**)

• **sensational** /senˈseɪʃənəl/ ADJECTIVE

1 extremely good or exciting □ *Kate looked sensational in her new dress.* (**sensacional**)

2 causing a lot of excitement or shock □ *sensational news* (**sensacional**)

sense /sens/ ▶ NOUN [plural **senses**]

1 *no plural* a feeling or belief about someone or something □ *People need work that gives them a sense of achievement.* □ *They have created a sense of calm in the building.* □ *I got the sense that he was worried about something.* (**senso**)

2 one of the five abilities of sight, touch, taste, hearing and smell □ *Janet lost her sense of smell after an illness.* (**sentido**)

3 *no plural* a natural quality (**senso**) ⬛ *I don't think he has much of a sense of humour.* (**senso de humor**) □ *She has a great sense of style.*

4 *no plural* the ability to understand things and make sensible decisions (**sensatez**) ⬛ *Someone had the sense to call an ambulance.* (**teve a sensatez**) ⬛ *We were grateful for her good sense.* (**bom senso**)

5 *no plural* a good reason □ *+ in I can't see the sense in buying another computer.* (**sentido**)

6 the meaning of a word or of speech or writing □ *A single English word can have lots of different senses.* □ *You only have to understand the general sense of the passage.* (**significado**)

7 make sense (a) to have a clear meaning □ *Her explanations didn't make sense.* (b) to be a sensible thing to do □ *It makes sense to switch to low energy light bulbs.* (**fazer sentido**)

8 make sense of something to understand something that is difficult to understand □ *I couldn't make sense of all the different types of pension schemes.* (**entender, concordar**)

▶ VERB [**senses, sensing, sensed**] to become aware of something without being told □ *+ that I sensed that not many people agreed with what I was saying.* (**sentir**)

• **senseless** /ˈsensləs/ ADJECTIVE

1 stupid and with no purpose □ *senseless violence* (**insensato**)

2 unconscious □ *A firemen was knocked senseless by a falling lamppost.* (**inconsciente**)

• **senselessness** /ˈsensləsnɪs/ NOUN, NO PLURAL when something is stupid and has no purpose □ *the senselessness of war* (**insensatez**)

sense of humour /ˌsens əv ˈhjuːmə(r)/ NOUN, NO PLURAL your ability to understand things that are funny and to say funny things yourself □ *She's got a good sense of humour.* (**senso de humor**)

sensible /ˈsensəbəl/ ADJECTIVE

1 showing good judgment and the ability to make good decisions □ *Lizzie's a very sensible girl.* (**sensato**) ⬛ *a sensible decision* (**decisão sensata**) ⬛ *He did the sensible thing and called the police.* (**fazer a coisa sensata**) ⬛ *It's sensible to have insurance when you travel.* (**ser sensato**)

2 sensible shoes and clothes are comfortable instead of fashionable □ *a good sensible pair of walking shoes* (**confortável**)

> ➤ Note that **sensible** when used to describe a person does not mean 'very easily offended or upset'. For this, use the word **sensitive**.

• **sensibly** /ˈsensəbli/ ADVERB in a way that shows good judgment □ *Jeff very sensibly kept the receipt.* (**sensatamente**)

sensitive /ˈsensɪtɪv/ ADJECTIVE

1 a sensitive situation or subject needs to be dealt with or spoken about carefully in order to avoid offending people □ *Mental health is a sensitive issue.* (**delicado**)

2 very quickly and easily affected by something □ *Fair skin is usually very sensitive to the sun.* (**sensível**)

3 being aware of other people's feelings and careful not to upset them □ *He's a very sensitive, caring young man.* (**sensível**)

4 very easily offended or upset □ *Jamie's very sensitive about being bald.* □ *She was very sensitive to criticism.* (**suscetível**)

5 a sensitive piece of equipment can measure very small changes □ *The alarm is very sensitive and is sometimes set off by birds or cats.* (**sensível**)

- **sensitively** /ˈsensɪtɪvli/ ADJECTIVE in a way that carefully considers how people are feeling □ *The matter has been dealt with very sensitively.* (sensivelmente)
- **sensitivity** /ˌsensɪˈtɪvɪti/ NOUN, NO PLURAL
  1 the quality of always being aware of other people's feelings and careful not to upset them (sensibilidade)
  2 when something is very quickly and easily affected by something □ *This increases the skin's sensitivity to sunlight.* (suscetibilidade)

sensor /ˈsensə(r)/ NOUN [plural **sensors**] a device that notices things such as heat, light or movement □ *A sensor on the front of the camera measures how much light is available.* (sensor)

- **sensory** /ˈsensəri/ ADJECTIVE to do with sight, hearing, smell, taste and touch □ *sensory nerves* (sensorial)

sensual /ˈsensjuəl/ ADJECTIVE to do with physical feelings □ *sensual experiences* (sensual)

- **sensuous** /ˈsensjuəs/ ADJECTIVE giving you physical pleasure □ *She loved the sensuous feeling of silk against her skin.* (sensual)

sent /sent/ PAST TENSE AND PAST PARTICIPLE OF **send** (ver **send**)

sentence /ˈsentəns/ ▶ NOUN [plural **sentences**]
1 a group of words that usually includes a verb and expresses a statement or question □ *He hadn't finished his sentence before she interrupted him.* (sentença)
2 the punishment that a judge gives to someone who has committed a crime (sentença) ▣ *Floyd received a five year prison sentence.* (sentença de prisão) ▣ *He is serving a life sentence* (= in prison for the rest of his life) *for killing a police officer.* (prisão perpétua) ▣ *Two of the killers were given a death sentence* (= a punishment of death). (sentença de morte)
▶ VERB [**sentences, sentencing, sentenced**] when a judge sentences a criminal, he or she tells them what their punishment will be □ + **to** *The whole gang was sentenced to life imprisonment.* (sentenciar, condenar)

sentiment /ˈsentɪmənt/ NOUN [plural **sentiments**]
1 a formal word meaning opinion or feeling □ *Several other people share these sentiments.* (sentimento)
2 feelings such as sympathy or love □ *There's no place for sentiment in professional sport.* (sentimento)

- **sentimental** /ˌsentɪˈmentəl/ ADJECTIVE
  1 showing too many emotions such as sympathy or love □ *a sentimental love story* (sentimental)
  2 to do with emotions (sentimental) ▣ *The necklace is not worth much but it has a lot of sentimental value because it was my mother's.* (valor sentimental)

sentry /ˈsentri/ NOUN [plural **sentries**] a soldier who guards an entrance (sentinela)

separable /ˈsepərəbəl/ ADJECTIVE able to be separated from each other or from the main part of something □ *a coat with a separable hood* (separável)

separate ▶ ADJECTIVE /ˈsepərət/
1 different and not the same (distinto) ▣ *This is a completely separate matter.* (completamente distinto) ▣ *The children have separate bedrooms.*
2 not touching something else or not joined to it □ + **from** *Cycle paths keep bikes separate from traffic.* (separado)
▶ VERB /ˈsepəreɪt/ [**separates, separating, separated**]
1 to divide something into different parts □ + **into** *The class was separated into two teams.* □ + **from** *This article about his life separates fact from fiction.* (separar)
2 to be between two things so that they do not touch each other □ *The north and the south are separated by a range of high mountains.* □ + **from** *Only a thin camping mat separated me from the hard ground.* (separar)
3 to keep people apart from each other □ *A teacher had to separate the boys who were fighting.* (separar)
4 to stop living with your husband or wife □ *My parents separated last year.* □ + **from** *He had recently separated from his wife.* (separa-se)

- **separately** /ˈsepərətli/ ADVERB not together □ *Each of the suspects was interviewed separately by the police.* (separadamente)
- **separation** /ˌsepəˈreɪʃən/ NOUN [plural **separations**]
  1 when people are apart from each other □ + **from** *Lily found the long separation from her family very difficult while she was working abroad.* (separação)
  2 keeping things apart □ + **of** *They wanted a strict separation of church and state.* □ *I firmly believe in the separation of work from family life.* (separação)
  3 when a husband and wife decide to stop living with each other □ *The couple announced their separation in May.* (separação)

September /sepˈtembə(r)/ NOUN the ninth month of the year, after August and before October □ *School starts again in September.* (setembro)

septic /ˈseptɪk/ ADJECTIVE infected with bacteria □ *a septic wound* (infectado)

sequel /ˈsiːkwəl/ NOUN [plural **sequels**] a book, play or film that continues an earlier story (sequência)

sequence /ˈsiːkwəns/ NOUN [plural **sequences**]
1 a series of things that happen one after the other (sequência) ▣ *It was a remarkable sequence of events.* (sequência de eventos)
2 the order in which something happens or exists □ *Put these numbers in the correct sequence.* (sequência)

sequin

3 a part of a film □ *The film's opening sequence was filmed in Geneva.* □ *She choreographed the film's dance sequences.* (**sequência**)

sequin /ˈsiːkwɪn/ NOUN [plural **sequins**] a small shiny circle that you sew onto clothes as a decoration (**lantejoula**)

serenade /ˌserəˈneɪd/ ▶ NOUN [plural **serenades**] a song that someone sings for someone they love (**serenata**)

▶ VERB [**serenades, serenading, serenaded**] to sing or play music for someone you love (**fazer uma serenata**)

serene /sɪˈriːn/ ADJECTIVE calm and peaceful □ *a serene smile* (**sereno**)

• **serenely** /sɪˈriːnli/ ADVERB in a calm and peaceful way (**serenamente**)

• **serenity** /sɪˈrenɪti/ NOUN, NO PLURAL the quality of being calm and peaceful (**serenidade**)

sergeant /ˈsɑːdʒənt/ NOUN [plural **sergeants**]
1 an officer of middle rank in the police □ *Sergeant Adam Cragg was the officer in charge.* (**sargento**)

2 an officer of middle rank in the army (**sargento**)

sergeant-major /ˈsɑːdʒəntˈmeɪdʒə(r)/ NOUN [plural **sergeant-majors**] an army rank above sergeant (**primeiro-sargento**)

serial /ˈsɪəriəl/ ▶ NOUN [plural **serials**] a story that is printed or broadcast in several parts □ *'Cranford Chronicles' is a five-part television drama serial.* (**seriado**)

▶ ADJECTIVE **serial killer/murderer/offender, etc.** someone who commits the same type of crime many times (**em série**)

serial number /ˈsɪəriəl ˈnʌmbə(r)/ NOUN [plural **serial numbers**] a different number that is printed on each product or on paper money (**número de série**)

series /ˈsɪəriːz/ NOUN [plural **series**]
1 **a series of something** several similar things that happen or are done one after the other □ *a series of accidents* □ *They held a series of meetings.* (**série**)

2 a set of television or radio programmes with the same subject or the same characters (**série**) □ *They're filming a new TV series.* (**séries de TV**) □ *a comedy series* □ *+ of an old series of 'Cheers'*

serious /ˈsɪəriəs/ ADJECTIVE
1 important and needing attention (**sério**) □ *The report raises serious questions about the quality of education.* (**questões sérias**) □ *Obesity is becoming a serious health issue.* (**questão séria**)
2 very bad (**sério, grave**) □ *a serious accident* (**acidente grave**) □ *serious injuries* (**ferimentos sérios**) □ *Noy was involved in several killings and other serious crimes.* (**crime sério**)
3 meaning what you are saying and not joking or pretending □ *I can never tell when he's joking and when he's being serious.* □ *+ about Are you serious about becoming a teacher?* (**sério**)

serve

4 a serious person is sensible, quiet, and does not laugh much □ *William was a very serious little boy.* (**sério**)

• **seriously** /ˈsɪəriəsli/ ADVERB
1 very badly (**seriamente, gravemente**) □ *Her father is seriously ill.* (**gravemente doente**) □ *Jan was seriously injured in the accident.* (**gravemente ferido**)

2 in a way that shows you think something is important (**seriamente**) □ *We're taking these threats very seriously.* (**considerar essas ameaças muito seriamente**) □ *We're seriously considering moving to Japan.* (**considerar seriamente**)
3 used to emphasize that you are not joking, or to ask someone whether they are joking □ *Seriously, I didn't sleep for three nights because I was so worried.* □ *'John said he would pay.' 'Seriously?'* (**É sério?**)
4 an informal word meaning very □ *They sell seriously expensive clothes.* (**muitíssimo**)

sermon /ˈsɜːmən/ NOUN [plural **sermons**] a speech that a priest makes in a church (**sermão**)

serpent /ˈsɜːpənt/ NOUN [plural **serpents**] an old word for a snake (**serpente**)

serrated /sɪˈreɪtɪd/ ADJECTIVE having an edge with sharp points in the shape of Vs □ *a serrated knife* (**serrilhado**)

servant /ˈsɜːvənt/ NOUN [plural **servants**] someone who works in a big house and does jobs such as cooking and cleaning for the person who owns the house (**empregado**)

serve /sɜːv/ ▶ VERB [**serves, serving, served**]
1 to give someone food or drink □ *I'll serve the soup and you can give out the spoons.* □ *Serve the cheese with crusty bread.* (**servir**)
2 to sell things to customers in a shop □ *Are you being served?* (**atender**)
3 to work for a person or an organization □ *Brown had served the family for fifty years.* □ *As a soldier, he served in Egypt.* □ *+ as He served as treasurer for three years.* (**servir a**)
4 to be used for a particular purpose (**servir**) □ *+ as The cave served as a shelter for the night.* □ *+ to do something This news serves to remind us of all we owe to our soldiers.* □ *These new regulations serve no useful purpose.* (**servir para nada**)
5 to provide something for people or an area □ *This hospital serves nearly a million local people.* □ *There is no bus network serving these villages.* (**prestar serviço**)
6 to be in prison for a period of time □ *She's serving 6 months for fraud.* (**cumprir**) □ *After he has served his sentence, he hopes to become an actor.* (**cumprir sua sentença**)
7 to start playing by throwing the ball up and hitting it in sports such as tennis (**servir**)
8 if an amount of food serves a certain number of people, it is enough for that number □ *The recipe says the pie serves six.* (**serviço, dar o saque inicial**)

9 serve someone right if a bad situation or result serves you right, you deserve it □ *If you're sick, it serves you right for eating too much chocolate.* (**benfeito para**)

▶ NOUN [*plural* **serves**] throwing the ball up and hitting it to start playing a point in tennis (**serviço ou saque**) 🔁 *a very fast serve* (**saque rápido**)

• **server** /'sɜːvə(r)/ NOUN [*plural* **servers**]

1 a computer that stores information or does work for other computers that are connected to it. A computing word. (**servidor**)

2 the person who serves in sports such as tennis (**jogador que dá o saque**)

service /'sɜːvɪs/ ▶ NOUN [*plural* **services**]

1 a system to provide something that people need, or an organization that provides it □ *There have been cuts in mental health services.* □ *The firm has promised to improve the bus service.* (**serviço**) 🔁 *The charity provides basic services to homeless people.* (**fornece serviços**) 🔁 *We are offering a free e-mail service.* (**oferecendo serviço**)

2 *no plural* the help that someone gives you in a place such as a hotel or shop □ *I love the things they sell, but the service is awful.* (**serviço**)

3 *no plural* the period of time that you work for a business or organization □ *She resigned after 25 years' service in the company.* (**serviço**) 🔁 *He has 30 years of military service.* (**serviço militar**)

4 something that you do to help someone □ *Can I be of any service to you?* □ *He was given an award for services to the community.* (**serviço**)

5 when a car or machine is checked and repaired □ *I'm taking my car in for a service.* (**manutenção**)

6 the services a country's military organizations (**forças armadas**)

7 a religious ceremony (**cerimônia**) 🔁 *The queen attended a service to remember the dead.* (**assistir à cerimônia**)

8 when you throw the ball up and hit it to start playing a point in tennis □ *a terrible first service* (**serviço, saque**)

9 in service/out of service being used/no longer being used □ *These aircraft have now been taken out of service.* (**em uso/fora de uso**)

▶ VERB [**services, servicing, serviced**] to check and repair a car or a machine □ *We need to get the boiler serviced.* (**fazer revisão e conserto**)

service charge /'sɜːvɪs ˌtʃɑːdʒ/ NOUN [*plural* **service charges**] in a restaurant, an amount of money that is added to the bill (= piece of paper showing what you must pay) and given to the person who brought the food and drink to your table (**taxa de serviço**)

service industry /'sɜːvɪs ˌɪndʌstri/ NOUN [*plural* **service industries**] an industry that provides a service but does not make products (**indústria de serviços**)

service station /'sɜːvɪs ˌsteɪʃən/ NOUN [*plural* **service stations**] a place where you can buy petrol, especially a place on a motorway where you can also buy food (**posto de gasolina**)

serviette /ˌsɜːviˈet/ NOUN [*plural* **serviettes**] a piece of cloth or paper that you use during a meal to protect your clothes or clean your mouth or fingers (**guardanapo**)

servile /'sɜːvaɪl/ ADJECTIVE too eager to obey and please someone (**servil**)

serving /'sɜːvɪŋ/ NOUN [*plural* **servings**] an amount of food enough for one person □ *The packet says it contains four servings.* (**porção**)

sesame /'sesəmi/ NOUN, NO PLURAL a plant whose seeds and oil are used in cooking □ *sesame seeds* (**sésamo, gergelim**)

session /'seʃən/ NOUN [*plural* **sessions**]

1 a period of time that is used for doing something □ *He missed last night's training session.* (**sessão**)

2 a meeting or a series of meetings of a court or parliament □ *He called a special session of parliament to deal with the crisis.* (**sessão**)

set /set/ ▶ VERB [**sets, setting, set**]

1 to decide on a level for something □ *Prices were set too high.* (**colocar, estabelecer**) 🔁 *We need to set a limit on what we will spend.* (**estabelecer um limite**) 🔁 *The company has set new targets for growth.* (**estabelecer novos alvos**)

2 to decide the time or date of something (**estabelecer**) 🔁 *Have they set a date for the meeting?* (**estabelecer uma data**) □ *The government has set a timetable for change.*

3 to put something somewhere □ *Set the tray down on the table.* (**pôr, colocar**)

4 to be in a particular position □ *The house is well back from the road.* (**pôr, colocar**)

5 to cause something or someone to happen or to do something (**provocar**) □ + *ing Her remarks set me thinking.* 🔁 *My accident set in motion a whole chain of events.* (**provocar**)

6 to make a piece of equipment ready to work at a particular time □ *Don't forget to set the DVD to record.* (**ajustar, estabelecer**) 🔁 *Did you set the alarm?* (**acertar o alarme**)

7 if a substance sets, it becomes solid □ *Wait an hour or so for the jelly to set.* (**endurecer**)

8 if a book, film, etc. is set somewhere, that is where the story happens □ *Her first novel is set in Berlin.* (**situar-se**)

9 the sun sets when it goes down (**pôr-se**)

10 if a teacher sets work or sets an exam, they tell the students to do it □ *The teacher doesn't set my children enough homework.* (**estabelecer**)

11 set an example to behave in a way that other people may copy □ *I try to set the children a good example by wearing my cycle helmet.* (**dar um exemplo**)

12 set a record to achieve the best result ever in an activity, especially a sport □ *She set a new world record for the 100 m.* (**marcar um recorde**)

setback — **settle**

13 set someone/something free to let a person or an animal out of the place where they are being kept (**libertar**)

⇨ go to **set** *eyes* **on something/someone**, **set** your *mind* **at rest**, **put/set the** *record* **straight**, **set your** *sights* **on something**, **set the** *stage* **for something**

◆ PHRASAL VERBS **set about something** to start doing something ☐ *They set about the cooking with enthusiasm.* ☐ **+ ing** *He set about cleaning the car.* (**começar**) **set something aside 1** to save something for a particular purpose ☐ *I set aside part of my wages each week.* ☐ *We set aside a whole evening to talk.* (**reservar**) **2** to not consider something or not be affected by something ☐ *We tried to set aside our differences and work together.* ☐ *She set aside her usual caution.* (**deixar de lado**) **set something down 1** to write something down ☐ *He set down his evidence in a 50 page document.* (**escrever**)

2 to officially decide rules, systems, etc. ☐ *They have set down new guidelines on dealing with challenging behaviour.* (**estabelecer**) **set in** if something, usually something bad, sets in, it starts to exist ☐ *Tiredness had begun to set in.* **set off** to start a journey ☐ *We need to set off early tomorrow.* (**instalar-se**) **set something off** to make something start working or happening ☐ *The smoke set off the fire alarm.* (**partir**) **set someone/something on someone** to make a person or animal attack someone ☐ *I'll set my dogs on you!* (**fazer um animal/alguém atacar alguém**) **set out 1 + to do something** to intend to do something ☐ *I set out to prove him wrong.* (**pretender**) **2** to start a journey ☐ *We set out after breakfast.* **set something out** to explain something to someone ☐ *He set out his plans for future development.* (**esclarecer**) **set something up 1** to start a business, organization or group ☐ *A tribunal was set up to hear the case.* ☐ *He set up his firm in 2003.* (**estabelecer**)

2 to make something ready to be used ☐ *I set up a bank account for my son.* ☐ *We have set up a new website.* ☐ *I need to set up my equipment.* (**preparar**)

3 to arrange for something to happen ☐ *We need to set up a meeting.* (**organizar**) **set upon someone/something** to attack someone or something ☐ *He was set upon and robbed.* (**atacar, assaltar alguém/algo**)

▶ NOUN [*plural* **sets**]

1 a group of people or things that belong together or are used together ☐ *a set of chairs* ☐ *a chess set* (**conjunto, coleção**)

2 a radio or television ☐ *We have a technical problem; please do not adjust your set.* (**aparelho**)

3 the place where actors perform in a play, film, etc. ☐ *He had to wear the wig all the time on set.* (**cenário**)

4 a series of games that form part of a tennis match (**set**)

5 a group of people with similar interests ☐ *He is part of a very sporty set.* (**grupo, conjunto**)

6 a group of numbers. A maths word. (**conjunto**)

▶ ADJECTIVE

1 fixed ☐ *We meet at set times each week.* (**estabelecido**)

2 set menu a menu with a limited choice of food for a fixed price (**cardápio econômico**)

3 ready or prepared ☐ **+ to do something** *Are we all set to go?* (**pronto**)

4 not willing to change your opinions or behavior (**fixo**) ☐ *She has very set ideas about how to cook fish.* (**ideia fixa**)

◆ IDIOM **set in stone/concrete** if a decision or a plan is set in stone/concrete, it cannot be changed ☐ *We're thinking of selling the house, but nothing's set in stone yet.* (**concreto**)

setback /'setbæk/ NOUN [*plural* **setbacks**] a problem that stops you making progress (**atraso**) ☐ *The project suffered a major setback when the manager resigned.* (**sofrer um atraso**)

set square /'set ˌskweə(r)/ NOUN [*plural* **set squares**] a plastic object shaped like a triangle, used for measuring angles. A maths word. (**esquadro**)

settee /se'tiː/ NOUN [*plural* **settees**] a comfortable chair for two or more people ☐ *Guy and Anna were sitting on the settee.* (**tipo de sofá/divã**)

setting /'setɪŋ/ NOUN [*plural* **settings**]

1 the place where something is or where something happens ☐ *The hotel is the perfect setting for a wedding reception.* (**cenário**)

2 the place or period of time in which the events in a film, book, etc. happen ☐ *She chose Los Angeles as the setting for her novels.* (**cenário**)

3 the position of the controls on a piece of equipment ☐ *What setting did you have the oven on?* (**ajuste**)

settle /'setəl/ VERB [**settles, settling, settled**]

1 if you settle an argument, you end it by agreeing something ☐ *I wish they would settle their differences.* ☐ *The case was settled out of court.* (**resolver, acertar**)

2 to decide on something or to arrange something ☐ *Have you settled a date for the wedding?* (**resolver, acertar**) ☐ *That settles it – I'm leaving!* (**isso resolve**) ☐ *That's settled – we'll all meet next Tuesday.* (**Está combinado!**)

3 to pay money that you owe ☐ *The bill can be settled in cash or with a cheque.* (**saldar, quitar**) ☐ *This money helped us settle our debts.* (**saldar nossos débitos**)

4 to become relaxed and comfortable in a situation ☐ *Harry settled into his armchair and fell asleep.* ☐ *Settle back and enjoy the show!* (**acomodar-se**)

5 to make someone feel calm and relaxed □ *I need to settle the kids before they go to bed.* □ *I need something to settle my nerves.* **(acalmar)**
6 to go somewhere and make your home there □ *The family settled in New South Wales.* □ *They may not settle permanently in the UK.* **(estabelecer(-se))**
7 to land on a surface or on the bottom of something and stay there □ *A fly settled on the picture frame for a moment.* □ *The snow's too wet to settle.* **(permanecer pousado)**

◆ PHRASAL VERBS **settle down** to start to live a life with less change, for example by staying somewhere for a long time or staying in a relationship □ *I'm not ready to settle down and have kids yet.* **(manter estabilidade)** **settle (someone) down** to become calm or make someone calm after being nervous or excited □ *Settle down now, it's time to do some work.* **(acalmar(-se))** **settle for something** to accept something that is not exactly what you wanted □ *I was hoping for £1,000, but in the end I settled for £800.* **(conformar-se com)** **settle in** to start to feel happy and confident in a new situation □ *She's finding it difficult to settle in at her new school.* **(ajustar-se)** **settle up** to pay someone the money that you owe them □ *I'll settle up with you at the end of the evening.* **(saldar)**

• **settled** /'setəld/ ADJECTIVE
1 happy and confident in a situation, and not wanting to change □ *Now I've got a flat, I feel much more settled.* **(acomodado, com estabilidade)**
2 good, and not likely to change □ *The weather is quite settled at the moment.* **(estável)**

• **settlement** /'setəlmənt/ NOUN [plural **settlements**]
1 an agreement that ends an argument **(acordo)** 🔲 *The two sides have failed to reach a settlement.* **(chegar a um acordo)** 🔲 *a divorce settlement* **(acordo de divórcio)**
2 a place where people have come and built homes □ *New settlements have grown up in the desert.* **(colônia)**
3 the payment of an amount of money that is owed □ *Please accept this cheque as settlement of the bill.* **(quitação)**

• **settler** /'setlə(r)/ NOUN [plural **settlers**] someone who goes with other people to a place and builds a home there **(colono, colonizador)**

seven /'sevən/ NUMBER [plural **sevens**] the number 7 **(sete)**

seventeen /,sevən'ti:n/ NUMBER the number 17 **(dezessete)**

seventeenth /,sevən'ti:nθ/ NUMBER 17ᵗʰ written as a word **(décimo sétimo)**

seventh /'sevənθ/ ▶ NUMBER 7ᵗʰ written as a word □ *the seventh day of the week* **(sétimo)**
▶ NOUN [plural **sevenths**] 1/7; one of seven equal parts of something **(um sétimo)**

seventieth /'sevəntɪəθ/ NUMBER 70ᵗʰ written as a word **(septuagésimo)**

seventy /'sevəntɪ/ NUMBER [plural **seventies**]
1 the number 70 **(setenta)**
2 the seventies the years between 1970 and 1979 **(os anos 1970)**

sever /'sevə(r)/ VERB [**severs, severing, severed**]
1 to cut through something □ *He bled to death after a piece of glass severed an artery in his neck.* **(cortar)**
2 to end a relationship or connection □ *She had severed all links with her parents several years ago.* **(romper)**

several /'sevərəl/ DETERMINER, PRONOUN more than a few but not a lot □ *I met him several years ago.* □ *Several people admired her dress.* □ **+ of** *Several of my friends have dogs.* □ *Would you like one of these leaflets? I've got several.* **(vários)**

> If you want to say 'a very small number' do not use the word **several**. Instead, use the phrase **a few**:
> ✓ *I've got a lot of friends but only a few close friends.*
> ✗ *I've got a lot of friends but only several close friends.*

severe /sɪ'vɪə(r)/ ADJECTIVE
1 very bad □ *severe weather conditions* □ *He suffered severe head injuries in the accident.* □ *She has severe health problems.* **(grave)**
2 extreme □ *severe punishments* □ *There were severe restrictions on the sale of weapons.* □ *severe criticism* **(severo, sério)**
3 not friendly or kind □ *a severe expression* **(severo)**

• **severely** /sɪ'vɪəlɪ/ ADVERB in a way that is extreme □ *Two of the passengers were severely injured.* **(severamente)**

• **severity** /sɪ'verɪtɪ/ NOUN, NO PLURAL the quality of being severe □ *I don't think you understand the severity of the situation.* **(severamente)**

sew /səʊ/ VERB [**sews, sewing, sewed, sewn**] to use a needle and thread to join things together □ *He sewed the button back on his shirt.* **(costurar)**

sewage /'su:ɪdʒ/ NOUN, NO PLURAL the waste from people's bodies that is taken away from houses in underground pipes □ *the sewage system* **(água de esgoto)**

sewer /'su:ə(r)/ NOUN [plural **sewers**] an underground pipe for taking sewage away from buildings **(esgoto)**

sewing /'səʊɪŋ/ NOUN, NO PLURAL
1 the skill or activity of making or repairing things using a needle and thread □ *I'm not very good at sewing.* **(costura)**
2 something that you are making using a needle and thread □ *She put down her sewing and looked at him over her glasses.* **(costura)**

sewing machine /ˈsəʊɪŋ məˈʃiːn/ NOUN [plural **sewing machines**] a machine that you use for sewing cloth together (**máquina de costura**)

sewn /səʊn/ PAST PARTICIPLE OF **sew** (ver **sew**)

sex /seks/ NOUN [plural **sexes**]
1 no plural the act in which a man puts his penis into a woman's vagina ◻ sex education (**sexo**)
2 no plural the fact of being male or female ◻ It is now technically possible for couples to choose the sex of their baby. ◻ There are laws against sex discrimination. (**sexo**)
3 the group that includes girls and women, or the group that includes boys and men (**sexo**) 🔁 Some teenagers feel very embarrassed about talking to members of the opposite sex. (**sexo oposto**) ◻ The classes are intended for both sexes.

• **sexism** /ˈseksɪzəm/ NOUN, NO PLURAL unfair treatment of someone because they are a woman or because they are a man ◻ The scheme aims to tackle sexism in the workplace. (**sexismo, preconceito de sexo**)

• **sexist** /ˈseksɪst/ ▶ ADJECTIVE to do with sexism ◻ sexist attitudes ◻ sexist remarks (**sexista, preconceituoso**)
▶ NOUN [plural **sexists**] someone who treats another person unfairly because they are a woman or because they are a man (**sexista, preconceituoso**)

• **sexual** /ˈsekʃuəl/ ADJECTIVE
1 to do with or involving the activity of sex ◻ a sexual relationship ◻ sexual behavior (**sexual**)
2 to do with the differences between men and women ◻ sexual equality (**sexual**)

• **sexy** /ˈseksi/ ADJECTIVE sexually attractive (**sexy**)

sh /ʃ/ EXCLAMATION used to show that you want someone to be quiet ◻ Shh! You'll wake the baby. (**shh!**)

shabby /ˈʃæbi/ ADJECTIVE [**shabbier, shabbiest**]
1 old and slightly damaged ◻ shabby clothes (**gasto**)
2 bad and not fair ◻ He complained about the shabby treatment he had received. (**mesquinho, desrespeitoso**)

shack /ʃæk/ NOUN [plural **shacks**] a small building made of wood or metal (**cabana, barraco**)

shackle /ˈʃækəl/ VERB [**shackles, shackling, shackled**]
1 to put metal rings around a prisoner's hands or feet to stop them from moving (**algemar**)
2 if you are shackled by something, it prevents you from doing what you want ◻ I was shackled by my guilt. (**algemar**)

• **shackles** /ˈʃækəlz/ PLURAL NOUN
1 chains that are used to fasten a prisoner's hands or feet together (**algemas**)
2 things which limit your freedom ◻ He wanted to throw off the shackles of anxiety and self-doubt. (**algemas**)

shade /ʃeɪd/ ▶ NOUN [plural **shades**]
1 no plural an area which is cooler and darker because there is no light from the sun ◻ He was lying in the shade of a tree. ◻ On hot days I prefer sitting in the shade. ◻ This plant prefers shade. (**sombra**)
2 an object that goes around a light and prevents the light being too bright ◻ a lamp with a purple shade (**quebra-luz, guarda-sol**)
3 a particular type of a colour ◻ + of The wall was painted in a deep shade of green. (**matiz**)
4 a shade slightly ◻ Can you make it a shade looser? ◻ He was a shade under 1.80 m tall. (**um pouquinho**)
5 shades an informal word for **sunglasses** (**óculos escuros**)
▶ VERB [**shades, shading, shaded**] to protect something from the sun ◻ A row of trees shaded the path. (**sombrear, proteger da luz**)

shadow /ˈʃædəʊ/ ▶ NOUN [plural **shadows**]
1 a dark shape on a surface caused when an object is between the surface and a bright light ◻ There was a shadow on the wall. (**sombra**) 🔁 The candle cast shadows around the room. (**projeta sombras**)
2 no plural an area that is dark because light cannot reach it ◻ I couldn't see his face because it was in shadow. (**escuro**)
3 a bad effect or influence (**sombra**) 🔁 Many people are living under the shadow of war. (**sob a sombra de**) 🔁 Her son's death cast a shadow over (= had a bad effect on) the rest of her life. (**lançou uma sombra em**)
4 beyond/without a shadow of doubt used for emphasizing that you are certain about something ◻ Without a shadow of doubt, that man saved my life. (**sem sombra de dúvida**)
▶ VERB [**shadows, shadowing, shadowed**] to follow someone and watch what they are doing ◻ She noticed the bodyguard shadowing him. (**seguir de perto**)
▶ ADJECTIVE having a particular job in the main political party which competes against the party that rules the country ◻ the shadow education minister (**oposição**)

• **shadowy** /ˈʃædəʊi/ ADJECTIVE
1 like a shadow and not easy to see clearly ◻ Shadowy figures moved in and out of the trees. (**vago**)
2 mysterious and secret ◻ a shadowy organization (**sombrio**)

shady /ˈʃeɪdi/ ADJECTIVE [**shadier, shadiest**]
1 a shady place has little light because it is covered by something ◻ The plant will grow best in a shady spot. (**sombreado**)
2 slightly illegal or dishonest ◻ shady business deals (**obscuro**)

shaft /ʃɑːft/ NOUN [plural **shafts**]
1 a long hole down into the ground or down a building ◻ a lift shaft ◻ a mine shaft (**poço**)
2 a long handle of a tool or weapon (**cabo**)
3 a shaft of light a line of light (**raio de luz**)

shaggy /ˈʃægɪ/ ADJECTIVE [shaggier, shaggiest]
shaggy hair or fur is long and untidy (**desgrenhado**)

shake /ʃeɪk/ ▶ VERB [shakes, shaking, shook, shaken]

1 to make many quick small movements from side to side or up and down □ *The whole area shook when the bomb landed.* □ *Mina was shaking with fear.* □ *His hands were shaking as he tried to sign his name.* (**tremer**)

2 to make something move quickly from side to side or up and down several times □ *The wind was shaking the trees and rattling the windows.* □ *A huge explosion shook the building.* □ *Shake the bottle before opening.* (**sacudir, agitar**)

3 to shock or upset someone □ *It was an event that shook the world.* □ *He was still very shaken by the news.* (**abalar**)

4 shake your head to move your head from side to side as a way of saying 'no' □ *I asked if she was coming and he just shook his head.* (**abanar a cabeça**)

5 shake hands to hold someone's hand and move it up and down when you meet them for the first time or when making an agreement □ *He shook hands with the Prime Minister.* □ *We shook hands and the deal was done.* (**apertar as mãos**)

6 if your voice shakes, you sound nervous □ *'What shall I do?' she said, her voice shaking slightly.* (**tremer**)

♦ PHRASAL VERBS **shake something off** to get rid of an illness, injury or problem □ *I can't seem to shake off this cold.* (**livrar-se de**) **shake something out** to shake something so that any dust or dirt comes out of it □ *He shook out the rug and folded it up.* (**sacudir**) **shake someone up** to shock or upset someone □ *The accident shook me up a bit.* (**abalar**) **shake something up** to make big changes in an organization □ *The new leader was serious about shaking up the party.*

▶ NOUN [plural **shakes**]

1 a quick movement from side to side or backwards and forwards (**sacudida**) 🔷 *Give the bottle a quick shake.* (**dar uma sacudida**)

2 an informal word for **milkshake** (**milk-shake**)

shake-up /ˈʃeɪkʌp/ NOUN [plural shake-ups] a big change in an organization or system □ *The report led to a shake-up in security procedures.* (**reviravolta**)

shaky /ˈʃeɪkɪ/ ADJECTIVE [shakier, shakiest]

1 not very good or certain (**vacilante, trôpego**) 🔷 *The team recovered after a slightly shaky start.* (**começo incerto**) □ *The future of the project looks very shaky.*

2 making small quick movements from side to side or up and down □ *shaky hands* (**que se agita**)

3 physically weak □ *My legs felt a little shaky when I got out of bed.* (**fraco, trêmulo**)

shall /ʃəl/ MODAL VERB

1 used to make a suggestion or an offer □ *Shall we play chess?* □ *Shall I open the window?* (**que tal...?**)

2 how/what/when, etc. shall used to ask someone what to do □ *What shall I cook for dinner?* □ *When shall we phone him?* (**como/o que/quando dever fazer algo**)

3 used as a formal way of saying what you will do in the future □ *I shall make an official complaint.* □ *I shall never forget this moment.* (**determinação de fazer algo**)

shallow /ˈʃæləʊ/ ADJECTIVE [shallower, shallowest]

1 not deep (**raso**) 🔷 *shallow water* (**água rasa**) 🔷 *The children were playing in the shallow end of the pool.* (**na parte rasa**) □ *The lake was quite shallow.* □ *a shallow dish*

2 never thinking about things which are important or serious □ *I found her very shallow.* (**superficial**)

sham /ʃæm/ NOUN, NO PLURAL something that is done to make people believe something that is not true □ *The trial was a sham.* (**farsa, imitação**)

shamble /ˈʃæmbəl/ VERB [shambles, shambling, shambled] to walk slowly and awkwardly without lifting your feet very much □ *The old man shambled along, leaning on his stick.* (**andar sem firmeza**)

shambles /ˈʃæmbəlz/ NOUN, NO PLURAL **a shambles** something that is organized very badly or is very untidy □ *The education system is a shambles.* (**bagunça**)

shame /ʃeɪm/ ▶ NOUN

1 it's/what a shame used when saying that you are disappointed about something □ *What a shame that you can't come to the party.* □ *It's a shame we can't stay longer.* □ *It would be a great shame if you had to give up playing the violin.* (**é uma vergonha!/que vergonha!**)

2 no plural the embarrassing feeling you have when you know you have done something wrong (**vergonha**) 🔷 *Emma felt a sense of shame about the things she had done.* (**vergonha**) 🔷 *His crimes had brought shame on his whole family.* (**trazer desonra**) □ + *of He had suffered the shame of being arrested in front of his friends.*

3 have no shame to not feel embarrassed or guilty although you have done something bad □ *These young criminals have no shame.* (**não ter vergonha**)

4 put someone to shame to be much better than someone or something □ *Their results put ours to shame.* (**envergonhar**)

▶ VERB [**shames, shaming, shamed**] to make someone feel ashamed (**envergonhar**)

♦ PHRASAL VERB **shame someone into (doing) something** to make someone feel so ashamed that they do something □ *The government has been shamed into action.* (**agir por vergonha**)

• **shameful** /ˈʃeɪmfʊl/ ADJECTIVE so bad that you should be ashamed □ *shameful behaviour* (**vergonhoso**)

• **shameless** /ˈʃeɪmlɪs/ ADJECTIVE not feeling embarrassed or guilty although you should do □ *It was a shameless attempt to win votes.* (**desavergonhado**)

shampoo 723 sharp

shampoo /ʃæmˈpuː/ ▶ NOUN [plural **shampoos**] liquid soap used especially for washing your hair □ *a bottle of shampoo* (**xampu**)
▶ VERB [**shampoos, shampooing, shampooed**] to wash something using shampoo (**lavar com xampu**)

shan't /ʃɑːnt/ a short way to say and write shall not □ *I shan't be late.* (**forma abreviada de shall not**)

shanty town /ˈʃænti taʊn/ NOUN [plural **shanty towns**] an area where poor people live in small, basic houses built from pieces of wood or metal (**favela**)

shape /ʃeɪp/ ▶ NOUN [plural **shapes**]
1 the form that is made by the outer edge of something □ *She made a cake in the shape of a piano.* □ *His body has changed shape dramatically.* □ *The children stuck coloured shapes onto the card.* □ *What shape is the window?* (**forma, formato**)
2 the health or condition of someone or something (**forma**) 🔹 *The team is in good shape for Saturday's match.* (**em boa forma**) 🔹 *He leaves the company in better shape than he found it.* (**em forma melhor**) 🔹 *I'm getting a bit out of shape* (= not strong and healthy). (**fora de forma**) 🔹 *He runs every day to keep in shape* (= stay strong and healthy) (**manter a forma**).
3 take shape to develop so that you can see what the end result will be □ *Gradually, the novel started to take shape in my mind.* (**tomar forma**)
▶ VERB [**shapes, shaping, shaped**]
1 to influence the development of something or someone □ *Her views were shaped by her experiences in China.* □ *He wants to use his power to shape the future.* (**modelar**)
2 to make something a particular shape □ *He shapes the clay pots on the potter's wheel.* (**melhorar**)
◆ PHRASAL VERB **shape up**
1 to develop, usually in a satisfactory way □ *This is shaping up to be a really exciting match.* (**desenvolver-se**)
2 an informal word meaning to improve your work or your behaviour □ *We'll have to sack him if he doesn't shape up.*
• **shapeless** /ˈʃeɪpləs/ ADJECTIVE having no particular shape □ *a shapeless old cardigan* (**informe**)
• **shapely** /ˈʃeɪpli/ ADJECTIVE a shapely body or part of a body has an attractive shape □ *shapely legs* (**bem torneado**)

share /ʃeə(r)/ ▶ VERB [**shares, sharing, shared**]
1 to divide something between two or more people □ *+ between* *We had two pizzas to share between 7 people.* □ *+ among* *I shared the sweets among the children.* (**partilhar**)
2 to have or use something at the same time as someone else □ *There aren't enough books to go round so some of you will have to share.* □ *She shares a home with her elderly mother.* □ *We must all share the blame for the accident.* (**compartilhar**)
3 to allow someone to have part of something that is yours or to use something that is yours □ *She kindly shared her lunch with me.* □ *William wouldn't share his toys.* (**partilhar**)
4 to have the same feelings, opinions or experiences as someone else □ *They shared her interest in antique furniture.* □ *I share your concerns about the level of debt.* (**partilhar**)
5 to tell someone something □ *She shared her tips on growing roses.* (**revelar**)
◆ PHRASAL VERB **share something out** to divide something between each person in a group □ *We shared out the food between us.* (**repartir**)
▶ NOUN [plural **shares**]
1 a part of a total number or amount of something that is divided between people □ *I took my share of the cake.* (**porção**) 🔹 *We hope to increase our share of the market.* (**aumentar nossa porção**) 🔹 *She wants a larger share of the profits.* (**porção maior**)
2 a reasonable amount of something, often something unpleasant □ *I've done my share of hard work.* (**ação**) 🔹 *He's had more than his fair share of tragedy.*
3 one of the equal parts of the value of a company that you can buy or sell □ *+ in* *She has shares in the bank.* (**ação**) 🔹 *I bought shares in his business.* (**comprei ações**) 🔹 *Shares rose/fell* (= increased/lost value) *at the news.* (**subiram/caíram**)

shareholder /ˈʃeəˌhəʊldə(r)/ NOUN [plural **shareholders**] someone who owns shares in a company (**acionista**)

shark /ʃɑːk/ NOUN [plural **sharks**] a large sea fish with very sharp teeth (**tubarão**)

sharp /ʃɑːp/ ▶ ADJECTIVE [**sharper, sharpest**]
1 having a thin edge or a pointed end that can cut things easily □ *a sharp knife* □ *sharp teeth* (**afiado**)
2 a sharp decrease or increase is sudden and large (**acentuado**) 🔹 *There has been a sharp rise in crime.* (**aumento acentuado**)
3 a sharp contrast/difference, etc. a very big difference □ *There is a sharp contrast in their lifestyles.* (**brusco**)
4 a sharp pain is sudden, short and painful (**agudo**)
5 a sharp bend or turn is one that changes direction suddenly (**brusco**)
6 a sharp image is clear □ *I can get a really sharp focus with this camera.* (**nítido**)
7 clever and quick to notice things (**perspicaz, esperto**)
8 if your hearing or eyesight (= how well you can see) is sharp, you can hear or see very well (**aguçado**)
9 showing anger □ *She received a sharp rebuke from her mother.* (**ríspido**)
10 a sharp taste is quite sour or bitter (**aguçado**)
11 in music, higher by half a note (**sustenido**)
▶ ADVERB
1 5 o'clock, 6.15, etc. sharp at exactly 5 o'clock, 6.15, etc. (**em ponto**)

2 with a sudden change of direction □ *Turn sharp left at the next set of traffic lights.* (abruptamente)

▶ NOUN [plural **sharps**] in written music, a sign (#) that makes a note higher by half a note (sustenido)

• **sharpen** /ˈʃɑːpən/ VERB [**sharpens, sharpening, sharpened**]
1 to make something sharp or sharper □ *The leopard was sharpening its claws on a tree.* □ *I need to sharpen this pencil.* (apontar, afiar)
2 to make an image clearer □ *How do you sharpen the focus?* (clarear)

• **sharpener** /ˈʃɑːpənə(r)/ NOUN [plural **sharpeners**] a device that you use to sharpen pencils or knives (apontador, afiador)

• **sharply** /ˈʃɑːpli/ ADVERB
1 suddenly and by a large amount (agudamente)
🔁 *Temperatures fall sharply at night.* (caem drasticamente)
2 in a strong and angry way □ *The report sharply criticized his handling of the affair.* (rispidamente)
3 if you turn sharply, you turn suddenly in a completely different direction (bruscamente)

shatter /ˈʃætə(r)/ VERB [**shatters, shattering, shattered**]
1 to break into lots of very small pieces or to break something into lots of very small pieces □ *He dropped the glass and it shattered.* □ *The explosion shattered windows.* (estilhaçar)
2 to completely destroy a feeling, a belief or a state □ *His confidence was shattered.* □ *The early morning calm was shattered by the sound of gunfire.*

• **shattered** /ˈʃætəd/ ADJECTIVE
1 very shocked or upset by something that has happened □ *He was completely shattered when his brother died.* (abalado)
2 an informal word meaning very tired □ *I must get some sleep – I'm shattered.* (exausto, quebrado)

shave /ʃeɪv/ ▶ VERB [**shaves, shaving, shaved**]
1 to use a razor (= thin, sharp piece of metal) to cut away hair that is growing on your face or body □ *He shaved and showered, then got dressed.* □ **+ off** *He shaved off his beard.* (barbear-se, fazer a barba)
2 to cut very thin layers from something with a sharp blade □ *Shave off thin slices of cheese.* (barbear)

▶ NOUN [plural **shaves**] when you shave □ *You need a shave and a haircut.* (fazer a barba)

♦ IDIOM **a close shave** a situation in which you only just avoid something bad or dangerous □ *The crew had a close shave when the boat's engine caught fire.* (ficar por um fio, prestes a sofrer algo)

• **shaven** /ˈʃeɪvən/ ADJECTIVE if part of someone's body is shaven, it has been shaved □ *We saw monks with shaven heads.* (barbeado)

• **shaver** /ˈʃeɪvə(r)/ NOUN [plural **shavers**] an electrical tool for shaving hair (aparelho de barbear elétrico)

• **shavings** /ˈʃeɪvɪŋz/ PLURAL NOUN very thin strips of wood or metal that have been cut off a surface with a sharp tool (apara)

shawl /ʃɔːl/ NOUN [plural **shawls**] a large piece of cloth for covering a woman's shoulders (xale)

she /ʃiː/ PRONOUN used to talk or write about a woman, girl or female animal that has already been mentioned □ *Madeleine is funny. She really makes me laugh.* (ela)

sheaf /ʃiːf/ NOUN [plural **sheaves**]
1 many pieces of paper that are tied or held together □ *He carried a thick sheaf of papers.* (maço)
2 pieces of a crop such as wheat which have been cut and tied together (maço)

shear /ʃɪə(r)/ VERB [**shears, shearing, sheared, sheared** or **shorn**]
1 to cut wool from a sheep (tosar, tosquiar)
2 if a piece of metal shears, it breaks off □ *The bolt had sheared off.* (cisalhar)

• **shears** /ʃɪəz/ PLURAL NOUN a cutting tool with two large sharp blades (cisalhas)

sheath /ʃiːθ/ NOUN [plural **sheaths**] a long narrow case for a knife (bainha)

• **sheathe** /ʃiːð/ VERB [**sheathes, sheathing, sheathed**] to cover something in order to protect it (embainhar)

shed /ʃed/ ▶ NOUN [plural **sheds**] a simple wooden or metal building used for working in or for storing things (barracão) 🔁 *a garden shed* (barracão de jardim)

▶ VERB [**sheds, shedding, shed**]
1 to get rid of something that you do not need □ *I've managed to shed a few pounds* (= lose some weight). □ *The company is trying to shed its traditional image.* (livrar-se de algo, eliminar)
2 to let clothes, skin, leaves etc. fall or drop off □ *Snakes shed their skin.* (mudar, soltar)
3 shed tears to cry (derramar lágrimas, chorar)
4 shed blood used to mean that someone is injured or killed □ *The army is ready to shed its blood to defend the country.* (derramar sangue, matar)
⇨ go to **shed light on something** (lançar luz sobre algo, esclarecer)

she'd /ʃiːd/ a short way to say and write she had or she would □ *She'd forgotten her umbrella.* □ *She'd rather not say.* (abreviação de *she had* ou de *she would*)

shedload /ˈʃedləʊd/ NOUN [plural **shedloads**] an informal word that means a lot of something □ *They've made shedloads of money.* (grande quantidade, um monte)

sheen /ʃiːn/ NOUN, NO PLURAL a soft shine on a surface □ *a grey silk suit with a metallic sheen* (brilho)

sheep

sheep /ʃiːp/ NOUN [plural **sheep**] a farm animal with a thick wool coat (**carneiro**) *a flock of sheep* (**rebanho de carneiros**)

> Remember that the plural form of **sheep** is the same as the singular form □ *He has a lot of sheep.*

sheepdog /ˈʃiːpdɒɡ/ NOUN [plural **sheepdogs**] a dog trained to control sheep (**cão pastor**)

sheepish /ˈʃiːpɪʃ/ ADJECTIVE if someone looks sheepish, they look slightly embarrassed □ *a sheepish grin* (**encabulado**)

- **sheepishly** /ˈʃiːpɪʃli/ ADVERB in a way that shows you are slightly embarrassed □ *He smiled sheepishly.* (**de modo encabulado**)

sheepskin /ˈʃiːpskɪn/ NOUN, NO PLURAL leather made from the skin of a sheep, usually with the wool left on it □ *a sheepskin rug* (**couro de carneiro**)

sheer /ʃɪə(r)/ ADJECTIVE
1 used to emphasize the degree, size, strength, etc. of something □ *The sheer scale of the building is breathtaking.* □ *The first problem is the sheer size of the city.* (**absoluto, completo**)
2 complete or only □ *It was sheer luck that no one was hurt.* □ *He ate four bags of crisps. It was just sheer greed.* (**pura**)
3 very steep or vertical □ *There were sheer cliffs on either side.* (**íngreme**)
4 sheer cloth is so thin you can see through it (**fino**)

sheet /ʃiːt/ NOUN [plural **sheets**]
1 a large, flat piece of cloth used to cover a bed □ *I'll just change the sheets on your bed.* (**lençol**)
2 a single piece of paper or a document on a single piece of paper □ + *of* an A4 sheet of paper □ *She gave him a fact sheet about diabetes.* (**folha**)
3 a large thin flat piece of metal, plastic, glass, etc. □ + *of* a sheet of aluminium foil □ *They covered it with a plastic sheet.* (**lâmina**)

sheikh /ʃeɪk/ NOUN [plural **sheikhs**] a leader in an Arab country (**xeique**)

shelf /ʃelf/ NOUN [plural **shelves**]
1 a flat piece of wood, metal, etc. fixed horizontally to a wall or as part of a cupboard, used for putting things on □ *She stood on a chair to reach the top shelf of the kitchen cupboard.* (**prateleira**) *He got a job stacking supermarket shelves.* (**prateleiras de supermercado**)
2 an area of land or the bottom of the sea that is like a shelf, with a flat top. A geography word. □ *the coastal shelf* (**banco de areia, recife**)

shell /ʃel/ ▶ NOUN [plural **shells**]
1 a hard covering on an egg or a nut □ *Remove the hard outer shell of the nut.* (**concha, casca, carapaça**)
2 a hard covering that protects the body of some sea creatures or other animals □ *a snail shell* (**carcaça**)

sherbet

3 a metal case filled with explosives which is fired from a large gun □ *The building was hit by a mortar shell.* □ *Tanks fired shells.* (**carapaça**)
4 the outer parts of a building, vehicle or other structure (**carcaça**)
▶ VERB [**shells, shelling, shelled**]
1 to fire an explosive shell □ *The enemy were shelling the area.* (**bombardear**)
2 to remove nuts, eggs or vegetables from their shells □ *freshly shelled peas* (**descascar**)
◆ PHRASAL VERB **shell out** an informal word meaning to pay a lot of money to buy something □ *They shelled out £120 each for tickets.* (**desembolsar**)

she'll /ʃiːl/ a short way to say and write she will □ *She'll be back in a minute.* (**abreviação de she will**)

shellfish /ˈʃelfɪʃ/ NOUN [plural **shellfish**] animals with a hard outer shell that live in the sea, rivers or lakes (**molusco, marisco**)

shelter /ˈʃeltə(r)/ ▶ NOUN [plural **shelters**]
1 a building or other structure that provides protection from harm or bad weather □ *an underground bomb shelter* □ *Earthquake victims are living in makeshift shelters.* (**abrigo**)
2 no plural protection from danger or bad weather (**abrigo**) *It was pouring with rain, so we took shelter in a shop doorway.* (**procuramos abrigo**) □ *The explosion sent people running for shelter.*
▶ VERB [**shelters, sheltering, sheltered**]
1 to stay in a place where you are protected from harm or bad weather □ *We sheltered from the rain under a tree.* □ *Thirty people sheltered in the basement.* (**abrigar(-se)**)
2 to protect someone from harm □ *The family were accused of sheltering criminals.* (**abrigar**)
- **sheltered** /ˈʃeltəd/ ADJECTIVE
1 protected from wind and rain □ *We found a sheltered spot to stop for a picnic.* (**área protegida do clima**)
2 protected from the difficult or unpleasant things in life (**superprotegido**) *She had a very sheltered upbringing.* (**educação superprotetora**)
3 **sheltered accommodation/housing** places where old or ill people live alone but there is someone to help them if they need it (**acomodação adaptada para deficientes físicos, idosos etc., casa de repouso**)

shelve /ʃelv/ VERB [**shelves, shelving, shelved**] to decide not to do something that had been planned □ *The company shelved plans to expand into Asia.* (**ver shelf**)

shelves /ʃelvz/ PLURAL OF **shelf** (**plural de shelf**)

shepherd /ˈʃepəd/ ▶ NOUN [plural **shepherds**] someone whose job is to look after sheep (**pastor**)
▶ VERB [**shepherds, shepherding, shepherded**] to control the direction of a group of people □ *She shepherded the children into a side room.* (**conduzir**)

sherbet /ˈʃɜːbət/ NOUN [plural **sherbets**] a powder with a fruit flavour and a sharp taste (**tipo de pó doce usado em drinques efervescentes**)

sheriff /'ʃerɪf/ NOUN [plural **sheriffs**]
1 in the US, the person who is in charge of the police in a particular area (**xerife**)
2 in England and Wales, the person who represents the king or queen in a particular area (**oficial civil de um condado**)
3 in Scotland, a judge (**juiz supremo de um condado**)

sherry /'ʃerɪ/ NOUN, NO PLURAL a type of strong Spanish wine (**xerez**)

she's /ʃiːz/ a short way to say and write she is or she has □ *She's my friend.* □ *She's always been my friend.* (**abreviação de** *she is* **ou de** *she has*)

shield /ʃiːld/ ▶ NOUN [plural **shields**]
1 a large, flat object that is carried to protect someone's body from an attack □ *They were faced by police carrying riot shields.* (**escudo**)
2 a prize for winning a competition in the shape of a shield (**troféu**)
3 something that protects someone or something from harm or danger □ *a heat shield* (**escudo**)
▶ VERB [**shields, shielding, shielded**] to protect someone or something from harm or danger □ *He had his hand over his eyes, shielding them from the strong sun.* (**proteger**)

shift /ʃɪft/ ▶ VERB [**shifts, shifting, shifted**]
1 to move something or to change position □ *Tom shifted uncomfortably in his seat.* □ *She shifted her weight from foot to foot.* (**transferir**)
2 to change something from one state, subject, etc. to another □ *Aid workers are shifting their attention from emergency help to long-term planning.* (**mudar**)
▶ NOUN [plural **shifts**]
1 a change from one thing to another □ *This represents a major shift in policy.* (**mudança**)
2 the period of time when one group of people works (**turno**) 🔁 *The miners worked 12-hour shifts.* (**trabalharam em turno**) 🔁 *Who's on the night shift this week?* (**turno da noite**)
3 a simple, loose dress (**vestido simples e sem mangas**)

shift key /'ʃɪft kiː/ NOUN [plural **shift keys**] the key on a computer that lets you write capital letters (= large letters, for example at the beginning of sentences). A computing word. (**tecla shift**)

shifty /'ʃɪfti/ ADJECTIVE [**shiftier, shiftiest**] looking or behaving in a way that seems dishonest □ *The younger man looked a little shifty.* (**velhaco**)

shilling /'ʃɪlɪŋ/ NOUN [plural **shillings**] an old British coin worth five pence (**xelim**)

shimmer /'ʃɪmə(r)/ VERB [**shimmers, shimmering, shimmered**] to shine with a moving light □ *The sea shimmered in the afternoon sun.* (**tremeluzir**)

shin /ʃɪn/ NOUN [plural **shins**] the front part of your leg below your knee (**canela**)

shine /ʃaɪn/ ▶ VERB [**shines, shining, shone**]
1 to send out or reflect light (**brilhar**) 🔁 *The sun's shining – let's eat outside.* □ *We could see the lights of the city shining below us.* (**sol está brilhando**)
2 to point a light on something □ *Don't shine your torch in my face.* (**brilhar**)
3 to be bright and shiny □ *She had polished the copper pans until they shone.* (**brilhar**)
4 to be very good at something □ *Lorna really shone in the gymnastics competition.* (**brilhar**)
▶ NOUN, NO PLURAL
1 a bright and shiny appearance □ *Julie's hair had a beautiful shine.* (**brilho**)
2 the act of rubbing something until it is shiny □ *Do you want me to give your shoes a shine?* (**polimento**)

shingle /'ʃɪŋɡəl/ NOUN, NO PLURAL a lot of small stones on a beach or near a river (**cascalho**)

shingles /'ʃɪŋɡəlz/ NOUN, NO PLURAL a disease that causes painful red spots on an area of your skin (**herpes zóster, cobrelo**)

shining /'ʃaɪnɪŋ/ ADJECTIVE a shining example of something someone or something that is very good at something □ *She's a shining example of growing old gracefully.* (**brilhante**)

shiny /'ʃaɪni/ ADJECTIVE [**shinier, shiniest**] with a smooth surface that reflects light □ *shiny hair* □ *a shiny new bicycle* (**brilhante**)

ship /ʃɪp/ ▶ NOUN [plural **ships**] a large boat that carries passengers or goods on sea journeys □ *Her ship sails from Southampton tomorrow.* □ *They travelled from South Africa by ship.* (**navio**)
▶ VERB [**ships, shipping, shipped**] to carry something somewhere on a ship or in another vehicle □ *The waste is shipped abroad for disposal.* □ *You order was shipped this morning.* (**expedir por via marítima**)

• **shipment** /'ʃɪpmənt/ NOUN [plural **shipments**]
1 a quantity of goods sent by ship □ *We're expecting another shipment of the consoles next week.* (**carga**)
2 the sending of goods from one place to another □ *I'll organize shipment of your order.* (**expedição por via marítima**)

• **shipping** /'ʃɪpɪŋ/ NOUN, NO PLURAL
1 the business of sending goods from one place to another □ *a shipping company* (**navegação**)
2 ships and boats considered as a group □ *The rocks are a danger to shipping.* (**frota**)

-ship /ʃɪp/ SUFFIX -ship is added to the end of words to make nouns relating to the relationships between people □ *friendship* (**sufixo indicativo de cargo, grau, qualidade, estado, condição, força, prática, relação**)

shipshape /'ʃɪpʃeɪp/ ADJECTIVE tidy and in order (**bem-arrumado**)

shipwreck

shipwreck /'ʃɪprek/ NOUN [plural **shipwrecks**] a ship that has been destroyed or sunk, especially by hitting rocks (**naufrágio**)

- **shipwrecked** /'ʃɪprekt/ ADJECTIVE involved in a shipwreck ☐ *shipwrecked sailors* ☐ *a shipwrecked tanker* (**náufrago**)

shipyard /'ʃɪpjɑːd/ NOUN [plural **shipyards**] a place where ships are built and repaired (**estaleiro**)

shirk /ʃɜːk/ VERB [**shirks, shirking, shirked**] to avoid doing something that you should do ☐ *Bill never shirked his responsibilities as a father.* (**esquivar-se de**)

- **shirker** /'ʃɜːkə(r)/ NOUN [plural **shirkers**] someone who avoids work, a responsibility or a duty (**malandro**)

shirt /ʃɜːt/ NOUN [plural **shirts**] a piece of clothing for the top half of your body, often made from cotton, with long or short sleeves, a collar, and buttons down the front (**camisa**)

shiver /'ʃɪvə(r)/ ▶ VERB [**shivers, shivering, shivered**] to shake slightly because you are cold or frightened ☐ *She shivered in her flimsy cotton dress.* (**estremecer, arrepiar-se**)
▶ NOUN [plural **shivers**] a shake that goes through your body when you are cold or frightened ☐ *A shiver of terror went down his spine.* (**arrepio**)

- **shivery** /'ʃɪvəri/ ADJECTIVE shivering, because you are cold or ill ☐ *Daisy's hot and shivery and has a nasty cough.* (**arrepiante**)

shoal /ʃəʊl/ NOUN [plural **shoals**] a large group of fish swimming together (**cardume**)

shock /ʃɒk/ ▶ NOUN [plural **shocks**]

1 no plural a strong and unpleasant reaction you have when something bad happens that you do not expect ☐ *The whole town is in shock at the news of the closures.* (**choque**) 🔁 *You gave me such a shock bursting in like that!* (**deu-me um choque**) 🔁 *I got quite a shock when I saw the bill.* (**fiquei em choque**)

2 something that happens and makes you very surprised or upset ☐ *The news of his arrest was a terrible shock to his family.* (**abalo**)

3 no plural a serious medical condition when you feel very weak because of an injury to your body (**choque**) 🔁 *He had lost so much blood that he went into shock.* (**estado de choque**)

4 a sudden violent shake or movement, for example caused by a crash or an explosion ☐ *The shock of the impact threw us all forward.* (**choque**)

5 a current of electricity that passes through your body (**choque**) 🔁 *I got an electric shock when I unplugged the iron.* (**choque elétrico**)
▶ VERB [**shocks, shocking, shocked**]

1 to surprise and upset someone very much ☐ *I was shocked to see how ill he looked.* (**abalar**)

2 to say or do something to embarrass or disgust someone ☐ *Some young artists deliberately set out to shock the public.* (**chocar**)

shoot

shock absorber /'ʃɒk əbˌsɔːbə(r)/ NOUN [plural **shock absorbers**] a device fitted to a car's wheels to make travelling over rough ground more comfortable (**amortecedor**)

shocking /'ʃɒkɪŋ/ ADJECTIVE

1 making you feel surprised and upset ☐ *The news report contained some shocking scenes of the war.* (**chocante**)

2 very bad ☐ *The weather's been shocking this summer.* (**horrível**)

shoddy /'ʃɒdi/ ADJECTIVE [**shoddier, shoddiest**] not very well made or made with poor quality materials ☐ *shoddy workmanship* (**ordinário**)

shoe /ʃuː/ NOUN [plural **shoes**] something made of leather or a similar material that you wear on your foot (**sapato**) ☐ *high-heeled shoes* 🔁 *a pair of shoes* (**par de sapatos**) ☐ *a shoe shop*

shoelace /'ʃuːleɪs/ NOUN [plural **shoelaces**] a thin piece of material or leather tied through holes in a shoe to fasten it ☐ *He bent down to fasten his shoelace.* (**cordão de sapato**)

shoestring /'ʃuːstrɪŋ/ (**ter ou gastar muito pouco dinheiro**) NOUN **on a shoestring** spending or having very little money ☐ *They manage to run the youth club on a shoestring.* (**com o dinheiro contado**)

shone /ʃɒn/ PAST TENSE AND PAST PARTICIPLE OF **shine** (**ver shine**)

shoo /ʃuː/ EXCLAMATION used when you want to chase a person or animal away (**xô!**)

shook /ʃʊk/ PAST TENSE OF **shake** (**ver shake**)

shoot /ʃuːt/ ▶ VERB [**shoots, shooting, shot**]

1 to fire a gun or other weapon ☐ *I shot an arrow in the air.* ☐ *Stop or I'll shoot!* (**atirar**)

2 to kill or injure a person or animal with a gun ☐ *He had been shot three times in the chest.* (**abater a tiros, fuzilar**) 🔁 *A passer-by was shot dead in the incident.* (**fuzilado**)

3 to go somewhere very quickly ☐ *The rocket shot up into the air.* ☐ *Pain shot through his body.* (**lançar**)

4 in games like football, basketball, etc., to kick, hit or throw the ball to try to score a point or points ☐ *He shot at goal but the ball went wide.* ☐ *'Shoot!' the crowd shouted.* (**lançar**)

5 to make a film or video, or take a photograph ☐ *They're shooting some scenes at Alnwick Castle.* (**fotografar, filmar**)

◆ PHRASAL VERB **shoot up** if a price, rate or amount shoots up, it increases a lot very quickly ☐ *Food prices have shot up in the last six months.* (**saltar, subir rapidamente**)
▶ NOUN [plural **shoots**]

1 a new part of a plant or a very young plant ☐ *bamboo shoots* (**broto**)

2 when someone takes photographs or makes a film ☐ *a fashion shoot* (**sessão de fotos ou filmagem**)

- **shooting** /ˈʃuːtɪŋ/ NOUN [plural **shootings**]
1 a situation when someone is shot with a gun ☐ *There's been a fatal shooting in South London.* (tiro)
2 the sport of hunting animals or birds with a gun ☐ *grouse shooting* (caça)

shooting star /ˈʃuːtɪŋ ˈstɑː(r)/ NOUN [plural **shooting star**] a piece of rock that burns in the Earth's atmosphere, making a line of bright light in the night sky (meteoro)

shop /ʃɒp/ ▶ NOUN [plural **shops**] a place where goods are sold or a particular service is provided ☐ *a flower shop* ☐ *We spent the afternoon going around the shops at the mall.* (loja)
▶ VERB [**shops, shopping, shopped**] to buy things in shops ☐ *I hate shopping for clothes.* (fazer compras)

shopaholic /ˌʃɒpəˈhɒlɪk/ NOUN [plural **shopaholics**] someone who loves shopping and spends too much time and money on it (comprador compulsivo, consumista)

shop assistant /ˈʃɒp əˌsɪstənt/ NOUN [plural **shop assistants**] someone who sells things and looks after customers in a shop (vendedor, balconista)

shopkeeper /ˈʃɒpˌkiːpə(r)/ NOUN [plural **shopkeepers**] someone who owns or manages a shop (lojista)

shoplifter /ˈʃɒpˌlɪftə(r)/ NOUN [plural **shoplifters**] someone who steals things from shops (ladrão de loja, gatuno)

- **shoplifting** /ˈʃɒpˌlɪftɪŋ/ NOUN, NO PLURAL the crime of stealing things from shops (roubo em loja)

shopper /ˈʃɒpə(r)/ NOUN [plural **shoppers**] someone who goes to shops or is shopping ☐ *We had to push through crowds of Saturday shoppers.* (comprador)

shopping /ˈʃɒpɪŋ/ NOUN, NO PLURAL
1 the activity of going around shops to buy things (compra) ☐ *Let's go shopping tomorrow.* (fazer compras)
2 the things you buy at the shops ☐ *Can you get the shopping out of the boot?* (compra)

shopping center /ˈʃɒpɪŋ ˈsentə(r)/ NOUN [plural **shopping centers**] the US phrase for **shopping centre** (shopping center)

shopping centre /ˈʃɒpɪŋ ˈsentə(r)/ NOUN [plural **shopping centres**] an area or large building with a lot of different shops (shopping center)

shore /ʃɔː(r)/ NOUN [plural **shores**] the area of land next to the sea or next to a lake (praia)

shorn /ʃɔːn/ PAST PARTICIPLE OF **shear**

short /ʃɔːt/ ▶ ADJECTIVE [**shorter, shortest**]
1 small in height, length or distance ☐ *a short skirt* ☐ *The school is a short walk from here.* ☐ *She has short hair.* ☐ *My brother is very short.* (baixo, curto)
2 continuing for a small period of time ☐ *We watched a short film about whales.* ☐ *We'll take a short break now.* (curto)
3 not having many words or pages ☐ *Can you give us a short description of the house?* ☐ *It's quite a short book.* (curto)
4 not having enough of something ☐ + *of The troops are short of equipment.* (desprovido) ☐ *Water was in short supply.* (suprimento em falta)
5 if someone is short with you, they speak in a rude, angry way, not using many words (rude)
6 be short for something to be a shorter way of saying or writing something ☐ *'Jon' is short for 'Jonathan'.* (abreviação de)
⇨ go to **a short fuse, in the long/short run**
▶ ADVERB
1 not having enough of something ☐ *We are three players short.* (aquém) ☐ *I won't let my children go short.* ☐ *Our supplies were beginning to run short.* (estar no fim)
2 not reaching a particular level, quality or position (não alcançar, ficar aquém) ☐ *My ball stopped slightly short of the last hole.* (parou perto) ☐ *His behaviour fell short of the standards required.* (não atingiu)
3 short of something without doing something ☐ *Short of locking him in his room, I don't know how to stop him staying out late.* (perto de)
4 cut something short to end something before it is finished ☐ *We cut short our holiday to go and help her.* (antecipar, encurtar, abreviar)
⇨ go to **stop short of something**
▶ NOUN
1 in short something you say before you say the main fact or facts about something you have been talking about ☐ *In short, the whole holiday was a disaster.* (em resumo)
2 for short being a short form of a word ☐ *I'm Alistair, but you can call me Al for short.* (como abreviação)

- **shortage** /ˈʃɔːtɪdʒ/ NOUN [plural **shortages**] when there is not enough of something ☐ *People in the region face severe food shortages.* (escassez, falta)

- **shortness** /ˈʃɔːtnɪs/ NOUN, NO PLURAL **shortness of breath** when you feel that you cannot breathe in enough air (brevidade, escassez)

shortbread /ˈʃɔːtbred/ NOUN, NO PLURAL a rich sweet biscuit made from flour, sugar and butter (biscoito amanteigado)

short circuit /ˈʃɔːt ˈsɜːkɪt/ NOUN [plural **short circuits**] when a bad connection in a piece of electrical equipment stops it from working (curto-circuito)

- **short-circuit** VERB [**short-circuits, short circuiting, short-circuited**] to have a short-circuit

shortcoming /ˈʃɔːtˌkʌmɪŋ/ NOUN [plural **shortcomings**] a fault in someone or something ☐ *Whatever his shortcomings as a teacher, the children love her.* (falha)

short cut

short cut /ʃɔːt ˈkʌt/ NOUN [plural **short cuts**]
1 a quicker way of travelling between two places (**atalho**) 🔊 *I took a short cut home across the fields.* (**pegou um atalho**)
2 a way of doing something that saves time and effort ◻ *I'm afraid it must be done this way; there are no short cuts.* (**simplificar**)
3 a picture or a group of keys on a computer that allow you to do something quickly. A computing word. (**atalho**)

shorten /ˈʃɔːtən/ VERB [**shortens, shortening, shortened**] to make something shorter or to become shorter ◻ *We're working hard to shorten the waiting list for the operation.* ◻ *The days are shortening.* (**encurtar**)

shortfall /ˈʃɔːtfɔːl/ NOUN [plural **shortfalls**]
1 a failure to reach the level or amount expected or needed ◻ *A shortfall in the grain harvest has caused prices to rise.* (**deficiência**)
2 the amount by which something is less than you expected or needed it to be ◻ *There's a shortfall of £3 million which can't be accounted for.* (**complemento**)

short form /ˈʃɔːt ˈfɔːm/ NOUN [plural **short forms**] a word made from two words that have been joined together and some letters missed out. An apostrophe replaces the missing letters. For example, don't is a short form of 'do not'. (**abreviação**)

shorthand /ˈʃɔːthænd/ NOUN, NO PLURAL a fast way of writing what someone is saying by using symbols ◻ *He's taking a shorthand and typing course.* (**estenografia, taquigrafia**)

shortlist /ˈʃɔːtlɪst/ ▶ NOUN [plural **shortlists**] a list of the people or things that are being considered for a job, prize, etc., chosen from a much larger number ◻ *He made the shortlist but didn't get the job.* (**lista de aprovados, indicados**)
▶ VERB [**shortlists, shortlisting, shortlisted**] to put someone on a shortlist ◻ *He has been shortlisted for the post of chief executive.* (**selecionado**)

short-lived /ˈʃɔːtˈlɪvd/ ADJECTIVE lasting only for a short time ◻ *Their joy was short-lived.* (**efêmero**)

shortly /ˈʃɔːtli/ ADVERB
1 soon ◻ *We'll shortly be arriving at Waverley Station.* (**logo**)
2 shortly before/after within a short period of time before or after something ◻ *The bomb exploded shortly before midday.* (**logo antes/depois**)
3 in a rude, angry way ◻ *'I can't help you,' the manager said shortly.* (**de modo seco, rude**)

shorts /ʃɔːts/ PLURAL NOUN
1 short trousers that stop above your knees ◻ *a pair of shorts* (**shorts**)
2 a mainly US word for underwear for men (**calção**)

short-sighted /ˈʃɔːtˈsaɪtɪd/ ADJECTIVE
1 unable to see things clearly unless they are very close to you ◻ *The clinic offers laser treatment to short-sighted patients.* (**míope**)

2 not thinking about what is likely to happen in the future ◻ *The company was criticized for its shortsighted planning.* (**falta de visão**)

short-tempered /ˈʃɔːtˈtempəd/ ADJECTIVE a short-tempered person gets angry very easily (**irritadiço**)

short-term /ˈʃɔːtˈtɜːm/ ADJECTIVE lasting for only a short time ◻ *Dad's short-term memory is poor.* ◻ *Borrowing a striker from another club provided a short-term solution to the problem.* (**de curto prazo**)

shot /ʃɒt/ ▶ NOUN [plural **shots**]
1 the act of firing a gun or the sound of it being fired ◻ *I heard a shot out in the alley.* (**tiro**) 🔊 *Someone took a shot at me!* (**me deu um tiro**)
2 an informal word meaning a chance or attempt to do something ◻ *It's Murray's first shot at the Wimbledon title.* (**tentativa**) 🔊 *I didn't think I'd get the job, but I gave it a shot anyway.*
3 a kick, hit or throw of the ball to try to score a point or points ◻ *It was an excellent shot that just missed the goal.* (**jogada**)
4 a photograph or an image in a film ◻ *I managed to get some good shots of the mountains.* (**fotografia, tomada**)
5 a small amount of medicine that is put into your body through a needle ◻ *a shot of morphine* (**injeção**)
6 a heavy metal ball that is thrown in a sports event (**chumbo, projétil**)
7 like a shot very quickly ◻ *If they offered me the right price, I'd sell the house like a shot.* (**como um raio, num instante**)
▶ PAST TENSE AND PAST PARTICIPLE OF **shoot** (**ver shoot**)

shotgun /ˈʃɒtɡʌn/ NOUN [plural **shotguns**] a type of long gun used for hunting animals and birds (**espingarda**)

shot put /ˈʃɒt ˌpʊt/ NOUN, NO PLURAL **the shot** put a sports event in which people throw a heavy metal ball as far as possible (**arremesso de peso**)
• **shot putter** /ˈʃɒt ˌpʊtə(r)/ NOUN [plural **shot putters**] someone who puts the shot (**arremessador de peso**)

should

should /ʃʊd/ MODAL VERB
1 used to say what is the best or right thing to do ◻ *He said that we should all go home.* ◻ *Should I write her a letter?* ◻ *You shouldn't eat too much chocolate.* (**dever (fazer algo)**)
2 should have used to say what would have been the right thing to do when you have done something different ◻ *I should have helped him.* ◻ *I'm late – I should have taken a taxi.* (**deveria ter**)
3 used to say that you expect something to be true ◻ *The train should be arriving in a couple of minutes.* ◻ *The children should be asleep by eight.* (**dever (probabilidade)**)
4 why should/shouldn't someone do something used to ask in an angry way for a reason ◻ *Why should I be the one to apologize?* (**por que é que alguém deveria/não deveria fazer algo?**)

shoulder

shoulder /ˈʃəʊldə(r)/ ▶ NOUN [plural **shoulders**]
1 one of the two parts of your body between your neck and your arms (**ombro**)
2 a piece of meat that includes the top of the animal's front leg ◻ *a shoulder of lamb* (**quarto dianteiro**)
▶ VERB [**shoulders, shouldering, shouldered**] to take responsibility for something ◻ *Kath had to shoulder the burden of caring for her mother.* (**arcar com**)

shoulder bag /ˈʃəʊldə ˈbæɡ/ NOUN [plural **shoulder bags**] a bag that you can put over your shoulder (**bolsa a tiracolo**)

shoulder blade /ˈʃəʊldə ˈbleɪd/ NOUN [plural **shoulder blades**] either of the two flat bones at the top of your back below each shoulder (**omoplata**)

shoulder strap /ˈʃəʊldə ˈstræp/ NOUN [plural **shoulder straps**]
1 a thin piece of cloth that goes over your shoulder to hold up clothes such as a dress ◻ *Katie was wearing a black dress with thin shoulder straps.* (**tira**)
2 a thin piece of leather or cloth attached to a bag, that you can carry over your shoulder (**alça**)

shouldn't /ˈʃʊdənt/ a short way to say and write should not ◻ *You shouldn't have waited out in the rain.* (**abreviação de should not**)

should've /ˈʃʊdəv/ a short way to say and write should have ◻ *You should've seen him!* (**abreviação de should have**)

shout /ʃaʊt/ ▶ VERB [**shouts, shouting, shouted**] to say something very loudly or to make a loud noise with your voice ◻ *Someone was shouting my name.* ◻ *There's no need to shout.* ◻ + *at She's always shouting at the children.* (**gritar**)
◆ PHRASAL VERB **shout something out** to say something loudly ◻ *Don't all shout out the answers at once!* (**gritar**)
▶ NOUN [plural **shouts**] a loud cry or call ◻ *There were shouts of approval from the crowd.* (**grito**)

shove /ʃʌv/ ▶ VERB [**shoves, shoving, shoved**]
1 to push someone or something hard or roughly ◻ *Someone shoved me in the back.* (**empurrar**)
2 to put something somewhere quickly and without care ◻ *I shoved a few clothes in a suitcase and left.* (**atirar, jogar**)
▶ NOUN [plural **shoves**] a hard or rough push (**empurrão**) ◻ *I gave him a shove and he fell into the pool.* (**deu um empurrão**)

shovel /ˈʃʌvəl/ ▶ NOUN [plural **shovels**] a tool for digging or moving earth, sand, snow, etc. ◻ *a garden shovel* (**pá**)
▶ VERB [**shovels, shovelling** or US **shoveling, shovelled** or US **shoveled**] to move earth, sand, snow, etc. using a shovel ◻ *I helped Dad shovel the snow off the drive.* (**revolver com pá**)

show

show /ʃəʊ/ ▶ VERB [**shows, showing, showed, shown**]
1 to prove that something exists or is true (**mostrar**) ◻ + *that The evidence shows that he could not have committed the crime.* ◻ *Polls show an increase in support for the president.* ◻ *This incident shows why it is important to follow safety regulations.* (**mostra por que**)
2 to allow someone to see something or to cause them to see it ◻ *Show me your new bike.* ◻ *Young people were shown images of knife wounds.* ◻ *His website shows pictures of him with his family.* (**mostrar**)
3 to allow someone to watch you doing something so that they learn how to do it ◻ *Can you show me how to work the DVD player?* (**mostrar**)
4 to tell someone where to go or where someone is, by explaining, pointing or taking them there ◻ *I showed her where to put her coat.* ◻ + *to I'll show you to your room.* (**mostrar**)
5 to give information about something ◻ *This timetable shows all the trains to London.* (**mostrar**)
6 to express your feelings ◻ *I try to show an interest in his work.* ◻ *The man showed no emotion as the judge read his sentence.* (**demonstrar**)
7 to be able to be noticed ◻ *The scar hardly shows.* ◻ *I tried not to let my disappointment show.* (**aparecer**)
◆ PHRASAL VERBS **show someone around/round (something)** to take someone to all the parts of a place so that they can see it for the first time ◻ *The children showed me around the gardens.* (**levar para conhecer**) **show someone in** to bring someone into a room, usually to meet people (**trazer alguém ao recinto**) **show off** to behave in a way that makes people notice you, or to talk a lot about something that you own, because you want people to admire you ◻ *He's always showing off about his cars.* (**exibir(-se), aparecer**) **show something/someone off** to show something or someone to other people because you are proud of them ◻ *She likes to show off her legs in short skirts.* (**exibir algo/alguém**) **show someone out** to take someone to the door when they are going to leave (**acompanhar à porta**) **show up** to arrive ◻ *She showed up an hour late.* (**aparecer, chegar**) **show someone up** to do something that embarrasses someone ◻ *My Dad always shows me up in front of my friends.* (**envergonhar alguém**)
▶ NOUN [plural **shows**]
1 a performance in the theatre or on radio or television ◻ *He is starring in a new comedy show on the BBC.* (**espetáculo**)
2 an event where people or businesses can show things to the public ◻ *We went to a boat show.* ◻ *a fashion show* (**exposição**)
3 when people express their feelings or opinions ◻ *All the workers walked out in a show of*

support for their sacked colleagues. □ *Six ships were sent to the region in a show of force.* (demonstração)
4 on show able to be seen □ *Some of her statues are on show in New York.* (exposto)
5 for show (a) in order for people to look at, not to use □ *The antique glasses are just for show.* (apenas para olhar) (b) in order to create a particular, often false, appearance □ *All that sports gear is just for show – she never does any exercise.* (só aparência)

showbiz /ˈʃəʊbɪz/ NOUN, NO PLURAL an informal way of saying or writing show business □ *a showbiz magazine* (ver **show business**)

show business /ˈʃəʊ ˌbɪznɪs/ NOUN, NO PLURAL the entertainment business, including films, theatre, music and television □ *Thousands of kids dream of a career in show business.* (indústria de espetáculos)

showcase /ˈʃəʊkeɪs/ ▶ NOUN [plural **showcases**] a situation or event that shows the qualities and skills of a person or thing □ *The fair is a showcase for local arts and crafts.* □ *The competition offers a showcase of British talent.* (amostra, exibição)
▶ VERB [**showcases, showcasing, showcased**] to be designed to show the qualities and skills of a person or thing □ *The concert will showcase new local bands.* (servir como amostra, vitrine)

showdown /ˈʃəʊdaʊn/ NOUN [plural **showdowns**] a big argument or meeting to end a disagreement □ *Management and unions seem to be heading for a showdown.* (pôr as cartas na mesa)

shower /ˈʃaʊə(r)/ ▶ NOUN [plural **showers**]
1 a piece of bathroom equipment that produces a flow of water that you stand under to wash yourself □ *Adam's in the shower.* (chuveiro)
2 an act of washing yourself under a shower (banho de chuveiro) □ *I had a shower to cool off.* (tomei uma ducha)
3 a short period of rain □ *We got caught in a shower.* (aguaceiro)
4 a lot of small things falling through the air □ *The fire sent out a shower of sparks.* (chuva de algo)
▶ VERB [**showers, showering, showered**]
1 to wash your body under a shower □ *Alex quickly showered and got ready for the party.* (tomar banho de chuveiro)
2 to give someone a large number or amount of things □ *He showered her with expensive gifts.* (encher alguém de)
3 to cover someone or something with a lot of falling pieces □ *The square was showered with debris after the blast.* (cobrir algo/alguém de)

• **showery** /ˈʃaʊəri/ ADJECTIVE with short periods of rain □ *Tomorrow it will be showery in the south.* (chuvoso)

showjumping /ˈʃəʊdʒʌmpɪŋ/ NOUN, NO PLURAL a competitive sport in which people go over series of jumps on horses (prova de saltos)

shown /ʃəʊn/ PAST PARTICIPLE OF **show** (ver **show**)

show-off /ˈʃəʊɒf/ NOUN [plural **show-offs**] someone who behaves in a way that makes people notice them, or talks a lot about something that they own, because they want people to admire them □ *I can't stand her. She's such a show-off.* (exibir(-se))

showroom /ˈʃəʊrʊm/ NOUN [plural **showrooms**] a place where people can look at the things that are on sale □ *a car showroom* (salão de exposição)

showy /ˈʃəʊi/ ADJECTIVE [**showier, showiest**] attracting attention, for example by being big and bright, often in a way that people disapprove of (ostentoso)

shrank /ʃræŋk/ PAST TENSE OF **shrink** (ver **shrink**)

shrapnel /ˈʃræpnəl/ NOUN, NO PLURAL pieces of metal that fly out in all directions when a bomb explodes □ *A piece of shrapnel hit him in the thigh.* (estilhaço)

shred /ʃred/ ▶ NOUN [plural **shreds**]
1 a small, thin piece that has been cut or torn from something □ *shreds of paper* (farrapo) □ *His shirt was torn to shreds.* (ficou em fiapos, rasgou toda)
2 a very small amount of something □ *They didn't have a shred of evidence to link him to the crime.* (pedaço, um mínimo de algo)
3 in shreds badly damaged or completely destroyed □ *By this time her marriage was in shreds.* (arruinado, em pedaços)
▶ VERB [**shreds, shredding, shredded**] to tear or cut something into very small, thin pieces □ *Shred the lettuce finely.* (retalhar)

shrewd /ʃruːd/ ADJECTIVE [**shrewder, shrewdest**] clever and showing good judgment □ *a shrewd guess* □ *He was a shrewd politician.* (astuto)

shriek /ʃriːk/ ▶ VERB [**shrieks, shrieking, shrieked**] to make a loud high noise or speak in a loud high voice because you are afraid, excited, etc. □ *She shrieked when she saw the mouse.* □ *'Watch out!' he shrieked.* (guinchar, gritar)
▶ NOUN [plural **shrieks**] the noise of a person or animal shrieking □ *Shrieks of laughter came from the games room.* (guincho, grito estridente)

shrill /ʃrɪl/ ADJECTIVE a shrill sound is high, loud and unpleasant □ *a shrill voice* (estridente)

shrimp /ʃrɪmp/ NOUN [plural **shrimps** or **shrimp**] a small sea creature with a shell that turns pink when it is cooked (camarão)

shrine /ʃraɪn/ NOUN [plural **shrines**] a religious place where people go to pray, often because it has something to do with a holy person □ *a shrine to the Virgin Mary* (santuário)

shrink /ʃrɪŋk/ VERB [**shrinks, shrinking, shrank, shrunk**]
1 to get smaller or to make something smaller in size, amount or value □ *My sweater shrank in the*

wash. □ *The number of honey bees has shrunk dramatically.* (**encolher**)

2 to move away from something because you are shocked or frightened □ *She shrank back, terrified of the snarling animal.* (**esquivar-se**)

◆ PHRASAL VERB **shrink from something** to avoid doing something because you find it unpleasant □ *He did not shrink from his duty.* (**fugir de, ter pavor de**)

shrivel /ˈʃrɪvəl/ VERB [**shrivels, shrivelling** or US **shriveling, shrivelled** or US **shriveled**] to become smaller and drier □ *The leaves of the plant will shrivel in strong sunlight.* (**murchar**)

shroud /ʃraʊd/ ▶ NOUN [*plural* **shrouds**] a cloth wrapped around a dead body □ *the Turin shroud* (**mortalha**)

▶ VERB [**shrouds, shrouding, shrouded**] to cover something completely □ *The hills were shrouded in mist.* (**velar**)

shrub /ʃrʌb/ NOUN [*plural* **shrubs**] a small bush (**arbusto**)

• **shrubbery** /ˈʃrʌbəri/ NOUN [*plural* **shrubberies**] an area in a garden where shrubs are grown (**moita de arbustos**)

shrug /ʃrʌɡ/ ▶ VERB [**shrugs, shrugging, shrugged**] to raise and lower your shoulders in a movement that shows you do not know something or that you do not care about it (**dar de ombros**) 🔁 *She shrugged her shoulders and said, 'I don't mind.'* (**deu de ombros**)

◆ PHRASAL VERB **shrug something off**
1 to show that something does not worry you □ *He shrugged off claims that he had lost the support of the party.* (**ignorar, não ligar**)
2 to deal with something easily □ *He soon managed to shrug off his injury.* (**lidar bem com**)

▶ NOUN [*plural* **shrugs**] a quick up and down movement of your shoulders □ *'If you like,'* she said with a shrug. (**meneio de ombros**)

shrunk /ʃrʌŋk/ PAST PARTICIPLE OF **shrink** (**ver shrink**)

shrunken /ˈʃrʌŋkən/ ADJECTIVE smaller than before or than normal □ *a shrunken old man* (**encolhido**)

shudder /ˈʃʌdə(r)/ ▶ VERB [**shudders, shuddering, shuddered**]

1 to shake suddenly, usually because of shock or disgust □ *She shuddered when she thought of his injuries.* (**estremecer**)

2 to shake violently □ *The whole house shuddered as the lorry passed.* (**sacudir, estremecer**)

▶ NOUN [*plural* **shudders**] a sudden shaking movement □ *'Don't remind me!'* she said with a shudder. (**estremecimento**)

shuffle /ˈʃʌfəl/ VERB [**shuffles, shuffling, shuffled**]

1 to walk slowly, sliding your feet along the ground without lifting them □ *The old woman shuffled slowly into the hall.* (**arrastar os pés**)

2 to move your body because you feel nervous, bored or uncomfortable □ *The audience were beginning to shuffle around in their seats.* (**inquietar-se**)

3 to mix up a set of playing cards before playing a game □ *Whose turn is it to shuffle?* (**embaralhar**)

shun /ʃʌn/ VERB [**shuns, shunning, shunned**] to deliberately ignore or avoid someone or something □ *He's a great actor but has always shunned the limelight.* (**evitar**)

shunt /ʃʌnt/ VERB [**shunts, shunting, shunted**]

1 to move people or things to another place, especially to avoid having to deal with them □ *Toxic waste was shunted all around Europe.* (**remover, pôr de lado**)

2 to move a train from one track to another (**desviar**)

shush /ʃʊʃ/ EXCLAMATION used to tell someone to be quiet □ *'Shush! There's someone coming!'* (**Shhh!, Pssst!**)

shut /ʃʌt/ ▶ VERB [**shuts, shutting, shut**]

1 to close something or to become closed □ *Could you please shut the window?* □ *I heard the door shut as he left.* □ *She shut her eyes and tried to remember his face.* (**fechar**)

2 to close a business for the day or for a short period of time □ *The shop shuts at 6 every evening.* (**fechar**)

3 to put someone or something in a place so that they cannot go anywhere else □ *Can you shut the dogs outside?* (**fechar, encerrar**)

◆ PHRASAL VERBS **shut someone/something away** to put someone or something in a place they cannot get out of □ *He should be shut away in prison.* (**prender, aprisionar (pessoa ou coisa)**) **shut (something) down 1** if a business, factory, shop etc. shuts down, or if someone shuts it down, it closes □ *The factory shut down several years ago.* (**fechar**) **2** to stop a machine from working (**parar uma máquina**) **shut someone/something in (something)** to put a person or an animal in a place they cannot get out of □ *We shut the rabbit in its cage.* (**prender, aprisionar (pessoa ou animal)**) **shut something off** to stop a machine from working or power or water from flowing □ *Shut off the electricity at the mains.* (**fechar parar uma máquina, impedir pó/água de levantar/fluir**) **shut someone/something out** to close a door, gate, etc. to stop a person or animal entering a place □ *I had to close the window to shut out the flies.* (**fechar, impedir a entrada**) **shut (someone) up** an informal word meaning to stop talking or make someone stop talking □ *I wish he'd shut up for once.* □ *Once she gets on to the old days, nothing will shut her up.* (**calar**) **shut someone/something up** to keep a person or animal in a place □ *I've been shut up in the house all day.* (**manter uma pessoa/um animal em certo local**)

▶ ADJECTIVE

1 closed □ *All the windows were shut.* (**fechado**)

2 if a business is shut, it has closed for the day or for a short period of time □ *The swimming pool is shut for repairs.* (**fechado**)

shutter

shutter /'ʃʌtə(r)/ NOUN [plural **shutters**]
1 a wooden or metal cover for a window that can be opened or closed (**veneziana**)
2 the moving part inside a camera, which opens for a moment when a photograph is taken (**obturador**)

shuttle /'ʃʌtəl/ ▶ NOUN [plural **shuttles**] an air, train or other transport service that goes backwards and forwards between two places □ *There's a shuttle bus to the airport.* (**viagem curta de ida e volta, ponte aérea**)
▶ VERB [**shuttles, shuttling, shuttled**] to go backwards and forwards between two places (**fazer viagem de ida e volta**)

shuttlecock /'ʃʌtəlkɒk/ NOUN [plural **shuttlecocks**] the object that is hit in the sport of badminton (**peteca**)

shy /ʃaɪ/ ▶ ADJECTIVE [**shyer, shyest**]
1 nervous and not confident when meeting and speaking to people (**tímido**) 🔲 *My brother is painfully shy.*
2 embarrassed or nervous about doing something □ **+ of/about doing something** *Oliver's never been shy of saying what he thinks.* (**retraído**)
▶ VERB [**shies, shying, shied**] if a horse shies, it turns to the side suddenly because it has been frightened (**refugar**)
◆ PHRASAL VERB **shy away from something** to avoid something or avoid doing something because you are frightened or nervous □ *She had always shied away from talking about her childhood.* (**esquivar--se de algo**)

• **shyly** /'ʃaɪli/ ADVERB in a shy way □ *She smiled shyly.* (**timidamente**)

• **shyness** /'ʃaɪnɪs/ NOUN, NO PLURAL the state of being shy (**timidez**)

SI /ˌes'aɪ/ ABBREVIATION an abbreviation used to describe units of measurement. A maths and physics word. □ *SI units* (**unidade de medida**)

sibling /'sɪblɪŋ/ NOUN [plural **siblings**] a brother or sister □ *Most younger children tend to copy their older siblings.* (**irmão e irmã**)

sick /sɪk/ ▶ ADJECTIVE [**sicker, sickest**]
1 feel sick to feel as if you are going to vomit □ *The smell made me feel physically sick.* (**enjoado**)
2 be sick to vomit (**enjoado**) 🔲 *He was violently sick.* (**violentamente enjoado**)
3 sick people or animals are ill □ *He looks after his sick mother.* (**doente**) 🔲 *I got sick on holiday.* (**fiquei doente**)
4 off sick not at work because you are ill (**ausente por doença**)
5 to do with time when you are not at work because you are ill (**relacionado a doença e trabalho**) □ *sick leave* (**licença por doença**) □ *sick pay* (**auxílio-doença**)
6 sick of something/someone an informal phrase meaning angry about something/someone or bored with something/someone □ *I'm sick of having to do all his work for him.* □ *I'm sick of salad – can't we have a hot meal?* (**farto, cansado**)
7 make someone sick (a) to make someone angry and upset □ *It makes me sick the way she expects everyone to do what she wants all the time.* (b) to make someone very jealous □ *She does everything well – it makes me sick!* (**deixar doente/irritado/aborrecido**)
8 very unpleasant and cruel □ *a sick joke* (**mórbido**)
▶ NOUN **the sick** people who are ill □ *The sick were taken to hospital.* (**os doentes**)

• **sicken** /'sɪkən/ VERB [**sickens, sickening, sickened**]
1 to make someone feel upset and shocked □ *I was sickened by their cruelty.* (**chocar, decepcionar**)
2 to become ill □ *The child began to sicken.* (**adoecer**)

• **sickening** /'sɪkənɪŋ/ ADJECTIVE very unpleasant and shocking □ *sickening violence* (**nojento**)

sick leave /'sɪk ˌliːv/ NOUN, NO PLURAL a period when you do not go to work because you are ill □ *Natasha's on sick leave at the moment.* (**licença por doença**)

sickly /'sɪkli/ ADJECTIVE [**sicklier, sickliest**]
1 if food is sickly, it makes you feel ill because it contains too much sugar, cream, etc. □ *The cake was a bit sickly.* (**enjoativo**)
2 someone who is sickly is often ill or gets ill easily □ *a sickly child* (**doentio**)

sickness /'sɪknɪs/ NOUN, NO PLURAL
1 when someone is ill □ *He had a lot of time off work due to sickness.* (**doença**)
2 an illness in which you vomit □ *These tablets may cause sickness.* (**enjoo, náusea**)

side

side /saɪd/ NOUN [plural **sides**]
1 the outer surface or edge of something, especially one that is not the top, bottom, front or back □ *He built a house by the side of the river.* □ *Go round the side of the building.* □ *Write on both sides of the paper.* □ *We sat on opposite sides of the table.* (**lado**) 🔲 *The two soldiers stood on either side of (= both sides of) the king.* (**ambos os lados de**)
2 one of the parts or areas of something when it is divided □ *In the UK, people drive on the left hand side of the road.* □ *We live in the north side of town.* (**lado**) 🔲 *Australia is on the other side of the world.* (**outro lado**)
3 the area of something that is near the edge □ *Could you move to the side, please?* □ *He put the pasta to one side and started making the sauce.* (**lado**)
4 an edge or flat surface of a shape □ *How many sides does a hexagon have?* (**face**)
5 the left or right part of someone's body □ *She stood by his side all day.* □ *Could you lie on your side, please?* (**lado**)
6 side by side next to each other □ *They sat side by side on the sofa.* (**lado a lado**)

7 one of the people or groups who are arguing □ *Both sides agree that discussions are needed.* (ambos os lados)

8 if you are on someone's side, you support the m in an argument (lado) 🔵 *Why do you always take Mum's side?*

9 one of the teams in a competition □ *He was chosen to captain the England side.* (lado)

10 a quality, characteristic or part of a situation □ *I look after the legal side of the business.* □ *There's a nasty side to him.* □ *We could see the funny side of the situation.* (lado, aspecto)

♦ PHRASAL VERB [**sides, siding, sided**] **side with someone** to support someone in an argument □ *Dad always sides with my sister when we argue.* (tomar partido de alguém)

sideboard /'saɪdbɔːd/ NOUN [*plural* **sideboards**] a piece of furniture with cupboards and drawers, used for storing plates and glasses (bufê, aparador)

sideburns /'saɪdbɜːnz/ PLURAL NOUN hair that grows on a man's face, in front of his ears (costeletas)

sidecar /'saɪdkɑː(r)/ NOUN [*plural* **sidecars**] a small vehicle that is attached to the side of a motorcycle for a passenger (carro acoplado a motocicletas)

side effect /'saɪd ɪˌfekt/ NOUN [*plural* **side effects**]
1 an unpleasant effect of a drug 🔵 *The drug can have serious side effects.* (efeito colateral)
2 an extra result of a situation □ *Traffic jams, noise and pollution are the worst side effects of increasing the number of tourists.* (efeito secundário)

sidekick /'saɪdkɪk/ NOUN [*plural* **sidekicks**] someone who helps or spends time with a more powerful or important person. An informal word. □ *I couldn't speak to the boss, but I spoke to one of his sidekicks.* (aliado, braço direito)

sidelight /'saɪdlaɪt/ NOUN [*plural* **sidelights**] one of the small lights on the front of a car, next to the main lights (luz lateral)

sideline /'saɪdlaɪn/ ▶ NOUN [*plural* **sidelines**]
1 an extra job in addition to your main job □ *She's a hairdresser with a sideline as a children's entertainer.* (atividade paralela)
2 the line along each side of a sports field which marks the edge of the playing area (linha lateral)
3 the **sidelines** (a) the area behind the line marking the edge of a playing field □ *The coach was frantically shouting instructions from the sidelines.* (b) a situation where you are not involved in what is happening and do not try to influence it □ *The government were accused of sitting on the sidelines and watching people die of starvation.* (lado de fora)

▶ VERB [**sidelines, sidelining, sidelined**]
1 to stop someone taking part in something or being involved in something, often in an unfair way. □ *Employers were accused of sidelining the unions.* (deixar alguém para escanteio/de lado)

2 to stop someone being able to play in a sport □ *For the last three months she has been sidelined by a knee injury.* (tirar de campo, ficar impedido de jogar)

sidelong /'saɪdlɒŋ/ ADJECTIVE **a sidelong look/glance** a quick look from the corner of your eye □ *He started to speak, after a sidelong glance at his mother.* (olhar de esguelha)

sideshow /'saɪdʃəʊ/ NOUN [*plural* **sideshows**] a small show or entertainment that is part of a larger, more important show (atração secundária de um show)

sidestep /'saɪdstep/ VERB [**sidesteps, sidestepping, sidestepped**]
1 to avoid dealing with something difficult or unpleasant □ *The minister deftly sidestepped the journalist's question.* (evitar)
2 to avoid someone or something by moving to one side □ *Ronaldo sidestepped the defender and sent a perfect cross to Rooney.* (desviar-se)

sidetrack /'saɪdtræk/ VERB [**sidetracks, sidetracking, sidetracked**] to make someone forget what they were talking about or doing and start talking about or doing something else □ *Sorry, I got sidetracked by all this talk of food.* (desviar)

sidewalk /'saɪdwɔːk/ NOUN [*plural* **sidewalks**] the US word for **pavement** (calçada)

sideways /'saɪdweɪz/ ADJECTIVE, ADVERB
1 to, towards or from the side □ *The train lurched and I fell sideways onto the man in the next seat.* □ *I saw him cast a sideways glance at the clock.* (para o lado, de lado)
2 with one side facing forward □ *I think the table will go through the door sideways.* (com um lado para a frente, de lado)

siding /'saɪdɪŋ/ NOUN [*plural* **sidings**] a short length of railway track where trains are kept when they are not being used (desvio de trilho usado para estacionar trens quando não em uso)

sidle /'saɪdəl/ VERB [**sidles, sidling, sidled**] to move somewhere quietly because you do not want to be noticed □ *He sidled up to her and handed her a drink.* (esgueirar-se)

SIDS /sɪdz/ ABBREVIATION sudden infant death syndrome; when a baby suddenly dies in its sleep and the reason is not known (Síndrome da Morte Súbita Infantil)

siege /siːdʒ/ NOUN [*plural* **sieges**]
1 a situation in which an army surrounds a place and stops supplies from getting in or people from getting out □ *The port was under siege.* (cerco)
2 a situation in which people surround a building to complain about something or to force the people inside to come out □ *Police shot the gunman after a 12-hour armed siege of the property.* (cerco, sítio)

siesta /sɪ'estə/ NOUN [*plural* **siestas**] a short sleep in the afternoon, especially in hot countries

sieve

(sesta) ◨ *I decided to take a siesta in my room.* (fazer uma sesta)

sieve /sɪv/ ▶ NOUN [plural **sieves**] a round kitchen tool with a bottom made of a wire or plastic net, used to separate larger pieces of a substance, especially food, from liquids or powders (peneira, crivo)

▶ VERB [**sieves, sieving, sieved**] to put something through a sieve ▢ *Sieve the stock carefully.* (peneirar)

sift /sɪft/ VERB [**sifts, sifting, sifted**]

1 to pass a substance such as flour or sugar through a sieve to remove larger pieces ▢ *Sifting the flour will help make a lighter cake.* (peneirar)

2 to look at every part of a place or in every part of documents, etc. in order to find something ▢ *Investigators are sifting through the rubble to find the cause of the fire.* (inspecionar)

sigh /saɪ/ ▶ VERB [**sighs, sighing, sighed**] to breathe out noisily, because you feel tired, disappointed, unhappy, etc. ▢ *She sighed wearily as she looked at the pile of ironing she had to do.* (suspirar)

▶ NOUN [plural **sighs**] a long noisy breath out, often because you are tired, disappointed, unhappy, etc. ▢ *'I'm afraid there's still no news,' he said with a sigh.* (suspiro) ◨ *When Phil finally got home we all breathed a huge sigh of relief.* (suspiro de alívio)

sight /saɪt/ NOUN [plural **sights**]

1 *no plural* the ability to see ▢ *He lost his sight in an explosion.* (vista)

2 *no plural* when you see something ▢ *He fainted at the sight of blood.* (visão, vista) ◨ *I caught sight of him, hurrying round a corner.* (tive a visão)

3 *no plural* the place or area you are able to see ▢ *We watched the ship until it disappeared from sight.* (vista) ◨ *We were soon within sight of land.* ◨ *We waved until their car was out of sight.* (fora de vista)

4 something that you see ▢ *Foxes are a familiar sight round here.* ▢ *I'll never forget the sight of all those people waving flags.* ▢ *Joe and Ben can't stand the sight of each other.* (vista)

5 the sights interesting places to visit in a country or area ▢ *He offered to show me the sights of Hong Kong.* (pontos turísticos)

6 an informal word for a person or thing that looks ugly, shocking, silly, untidy, etc. ▢ *What a sight she is with that bright blue hair!* (visão)

♦ IDIOM **set your sights on something** to try to achieve something ▢ *She has set her sights on Olympic gold.* (ter como meta)

⇨ go to **lose sight of something** (perder algo de vista)

• **sighted** /ˈsaɪtɪd/ ADJECTIVE sighted people can see ▢ *the partially sighted* (aquele que vê)

• **sighting** /ˈsaɪtɪŋ/ NOUN [plural **sightings**] when someone sees something, especially something that is hard to find ▢ *There have been several sightings of the bear.* (descoberta)

sight-read /ˈsaɪtˌriːd/ VERB [**sight-reads, sight-reading, sight-read**] to play or sing music by reading the notes, without having heard or seen the music before (cantar ou tocar por partitura)

sightseeing /ˈsaɪtˌsiːɪŋ/ NOUN, NO PLURAL

travelling around looking at interesting things and places ▢ *The hotel organized a sightseeing trip to the Roman amphitheatre.* (circuito turístico)

• **sightseer** /ˈsaɪtˌsiːə(r)/ NOUN [plural **sightseers**] someone who goes sightseeing ▢ *In August the city is full of sightseers.* (turista)

sign /saɪn/ ▶ NOUN [plural **signs**]

1 something that shows that something is happening or will happen or that something exists ▢ **+ of** *There is no sign of spring arriving yet.* ▢ **+ that** *There are signs that the economy is recovering.* (sinal) ◨ *My boss is showing signs of stress.* (mostrando sinais) ◨ *I can't see much sign of progress.* (ver muito sinal) ◨ *The fact that he is eating well is a good sign.* (bom sinal)

2 an object in a public place with words, symbols or pictures that give information ▢ *The sign said 'No smoking'.* ▢ *Follow the signs to the car park.* (tabuleta, placa)

3 a movement or a sound that tells someone something, or tells them to do something ▢ *A glance towards the door was our sign to leave.* (sinal)

4 a symbol with a particular meaning ▢ *a dollar sign* (tabuleta, placa)

▶ VERB [**signs, signing, signed**]

1 to write your name on something, for example to agree officially to something, or to prove that something was done by you ▢ *Please sign the contract and return it to us.* ▢ *The letter was not signed.* ▢ *The painting is a signed original.* (assinar)

2 if a sports team signs a player, they make an official agreement for that person to play for them (contratar jogador)

♦ PHRASAL VERB **sign up** to agree to join an activity, course, etc. ▢ *I've signed up for a week's rock climbing course.* (inscrever-se)

signal /ˈsɪɡnəl/ ▶ NOUN [plural **signals**]

1 a sign, action or sound that sends a message to someone (sinal) ◨ *When I give the signal, turn on the music.* (der o sinal) ◨ **+ to do something** *The troops waited for the signal to attack.*

2 a fact, event or action that shows what someone is going to do or what is probably going to happen ▢ **+ of** *The government is accused of ignoring the signals of a recession.* (sinal)

3 a piece of equipment that gives information to the driver of a vehicle, especially to tell them whether to stop or go ▢ *traffic signals* (sinal)

4 a series of waves of sound or light received by a radio or television ▢ *We picked up a strong signal from another ship.* (sinal)

▶ VERB [**signals, signalling** or US **signaling, signalled** or US **signaled**]

1 to make a sign, sound or movement to tell someone something □ *You must signal well before the junction.* □ **+ to** *Jo was signalling to us from across the room.* (**fazer sinal**)

2 to show that you are ready or willing to do something □ *The unions have signalled that they will accept the new offer.* (**sinalizar**)

3 to mark or show something that is happening or will happen □ *The birth of her first child signalled a complete change in her life.* (**marcar**)

signature /ˈsɪɡnətʃə(r)/ NOUN [*plural* **signatures**] your name, written by you, for example on the bottom of a letter or on a document □ *Someone had forged my signature on the form.* (**assinatura**)

signature tune /ˈsɪɡnətʃə(r) ˈtjuːn/ NOUN [*plural* **signature tunes**] a piece of music that is always played before and after a particular television or radio programme (**vinheta**)

significance /sɪɡˈnɪfɪkəns/ NOUN, NO PLURAL the meaning or importance of something □ *I didn't appreciate the significance of what he said at the time.* (**significado**)

• **significant** /sɪɡˈnɪfɪkənt/ ADJECTIVE

1 large or important □ *A significant number of children are failing to reach the required standard.* □ *She is now recognized as one of the most significant novelists of the 20th century.* (**significativo, considerável**)

2 having a particular meaning □ *Do you think it's significant that he left no note for his wife?* (**significativo, importante**)

• **significantly** /sɪɡˈnɪfɪkəntli/ ADVERB

1 by a large amount or in a way that is noticeable □ *Standards of health are significantly better nowadays.* (**significativamente**)

2 in a way that has a particular meaning □ *Significantly, the company has not denied the reports.* (**significativamente**)

• **signify** /ˈsɪɡnɪfaɪ/ VERB [**signifies, signifying, signified**] to have a particular meaning □ *A symbol of a skull and crossbones signifies a poison.* (**significar**)

sign language /ˈsaɪn ˌlæŋɡwɪdʒ/ NOUN, NO PLURAL a set of movements made with the hands that is used to communicate with deaf people (**linguagem de sinais, libras**)

signpost /ˈsaɪnpəʊst/ NOUN [*plural* **signposts**] a sign by a road showing which direction to go to get to a particular place (**placa de sinalização**)

• **signposted** /ˈsaɪnpəʊstɪd/ ADJECTIVE shown with signposts □ *The route is clearly signposted.* (**sinalizado**)

Sikh /siːk/ ▶ NOUN [*plural* **Sikhs**] someone whose religion is Sikhism (**sique, adepto do siquismo**)
▶ ADJECTIVE to do with Sikhs or Sikhism □ *We visited the Sikh temple at Amritsar.* (**sique, relativo ao siquismo**)

• **Sikhism** /ˈsiːkɪzəm/ NOUN, NO PLURAL a religion in which people believe in one God, started by Guru Nanak in Punjab in North India (**siquismo**)

silence /ˈsaɪləns/ ▶ NOUN [*plural* **silences**]

1 *no plural* when it is completely quiet and no sound can be heard □ *For a moment there was absolute silence in the theatre.* (**silêncio**)

2 a period when there is no sound or no one speaks □ *The players observed two minutes' silence for their former teammate.* (**silêncio**)

3 when someone refuses to talk about something □ *At last she has broken her silence about her divorce.* (**silêncio**)

▶ VERB [**silences, silencing, silenced**]

1 to stop someone speaking or something making a noise □ *Her father silenced her with a glare.* (**silenciar**)

2 to prevent someone from giving their opinion or criticizing you □ *The regime has failed to silence all of its opponents.* (**calar**)

• **silencer** /ˈsaɪlənsə(r)/ NOUN [*plural* **silencers**]

1 an object put on a gun to reduce the noise it makes when it is fired (**silenciador**)

2 an object fitted to a car to reduce the noise of the engine

• **silent** /ˈsaɪlənt/ ADJECTIVE

1 not speaking or making any noise (**calado**) 🔲 *The crowd fell silent.* (**ficou calada**) □ *They sat in silent contemplation.*

2 completely quiet □ *the silent churchyard* (**silencioso**)

3 not giving any information about something (**calado**) 🔲 *'You have the right to remain silent,' said the police officer.*

4 a silent letter is one that is written as part of a word, but has no sound when the word is spoken, for example the 'b' in 'lamb' (**letra muda**)

• **silently** /ˈsaɪləntli/ ADVERB without speaking or making any noise □ *He put the phone down silently.* (**silenciosamente**)

silhouette /ˌsɪluːˈet/ NOUN [*plural* **silhouettes**] the dark shape of something seen when there is something light behind it □ *Robert drew the city in silhouette.* (**silhueta**)

• **silhouetted** /ˌsɪluːˈetɪd/ ADJECTIVE seen in the form of a silhouette □ *I saw a figure approaching, silhouetted against the setting sun.* (**silhuetado, visto em silhueta**)

silicon /ˈsɪlɪkən/ NOUN, NO PLURAL a chemical element used in electronic devices and for making glass. A chemistry word. (**silício**)

silicon chip /ˌsɪlɪkən ˈtʃɪp/ NOUN [*plural* **silicon chips**] a very small piece of silicon used in computers and other electronic devices (**chip de silício**)

silicone /ˈsɪlɪkəʊn/ NOUN, NO PLURAL a substance formed from silicon and other substances, used in many things such as paints and rubbers. A chemistry word. (**silicone**)

silk

silk /sɪlk/ NOUN [plural **silks**] a soft smooth cloth made from the very soft thin threads produced by a silkworm □ *The dress was made of ivory silk.* □ *a silk kimono* (**seda**)

• **silken** /'sɪlkən/ ADJECTIVE like silk or made from silk □ *silken thread* (**de seda**)

silkworm /'sɪlkwɜːm/ NOUN [plural **silkworms**] a type of caterpillar (= small soft creature) which produces threads that are used to make silk (**bicho-da-seda**)

silky /'sɪlki/ ADJECTIVE [**silkier, silkiest**] soft and smooth, like silk □ *silky hair* (**sedoso**)

sill /sɪl/ NOUN [plural **sills**] a horizontal shelf made of wood or stone at the bottom of the opening for a window (**peitoril, soleira**)

silliness /'sɪlinɪs/ NOUN, NO PLURAL silly behaviour (**estupidez**)

• **silly** /'sɪli/ ADJECTIVE [**sillier, silliest**]
1 showing that you are not intelligent or not thinking about something carefully or seriously □ *a silly mistake* □ *How could you be so silly?* (**bobo, estúpido**)
2 not important or serious □ *She gets so upset over silly little things.* (**estupidez**)
3 making you look stupid or funny □ *a silly hat* (**bobo, estúpido**)

silt /sɪlt/ NOUN, NO PLURAL sand and mud that are carried along and left behind by flowing water (**sedimento**)

silver /'sɪlvə(r)/ ▶ NOUN [plural **silvers**]
1 *no plural* a valuable shiny grey metal, used to make jewellery, etc. □ *This tray is made of solid silver.* (**prata**)
2 a silver medal (= prize for coming second in a competition or race) (**medalha de prata**)
▶ ADJECTIVE
1 made of silver □ *a pair of silver earrings* (**de prata, prateado**)
2 having the colour of silver □ *silver paint* (**prateado**)

silver lining /ˌsɪlvə 'laɪnɪŋ/ NOUN, NO PLURAL a positive or good part of a bad or unpleasant situation □ *She's very good at finding the silver lining to any setback.* (**consolo, lado positivo**)

silver wedding /ˌsɪlvə 'wedɪŋ/ NOUN [plural **silver weddings**] a celebration of 25 years of marriage (**bodas de prata**)

silvery /'sɪlvəri/ ADJECTIVE looking like silver or silver in colour □ *Birch trees have silvery bark.* (**prateado**)

SIM card /'sɪm kɑːd/ NOUN [plural **SIM cards**] a plastic card inside a mobile phone that stores information such as names and telephone numbers (**cartão de memória para celular**)

similar /'sɪmɪlə(r)/ ADJECTIVE two things are similar when they are like each other but not exactly the same □ + *to An alligator is similar to a crocodile, but smaller.* (**similar, semelhante**)

simplistic

• **similarity** /ˌsɪmɪ'lærəti/ NOUN [plural **similarities**]
1 the degree to which one thing is like another □ + *to Her similarity to her sister is uncanny.* (**similitude, semelhança**) 🔁 *This painting bears no similarity to Waldorf's other work.*
2 a characteristic that two people or things share □ *There are several similarities between the two novels.* (**similaridade**)

• **similarly** /'sɪmɪləli/ ADVERB in the same or a similar way □ *The report makes a comparison of similarly priced MP3 players.* (**similarmente, semelhantemente**)

simile /'sɪmɪli/ NOUN [plural **similes**] a sentence or phrase in which one thing is described by being compared with another, using as or like. For example, *Its fleece was white as snow* and *He ran like a hare* are similes (**símile**)

simmer /'sɪmə(r)/ VERB [**simmers, simmering, simmered**] to cook food slowly by boiling it very gently (**aferventar**)
♦ PHRASAL VERB **simmer down** to become calm after being angry or excited □ *It's best to leave him alone until he simmers down.* (**acalmar-se**)

simper /'sɪmpə(r)/ VERB [**simpers, simpering, simpered**] to smile in a way that looks silly and is not natural (**dar um sorriso forçado**)

simple /'sɪmpəl/ ADJECTIVE [**simpler, simplest**]
1 easy to do, solve or understand □ *a simple sum* □ *The dishwasher came with a set of simple instructions.* □ *This mobile phone is very simple to use.* (**simples, fácil**)
2 plain or without any decoration □ *a simple design* □ *I like simple home cooking.* (**simples**)
3 basic or not complicated □ *Stone Age men could make simple tools.* □ *The simple truth is he's too old for the job.* (**simples**)

• **simplicity** /sɪm'plɪsəti/ NOUN, NO PLURAL
1 being plain, natural or not complicated □ *His work reflects the simplicity of Japanese painting.* (**simplicidade**)
2 being easy to do, solve or understand (**simplicidade**)

simplification /ˌsɪmplɪfɪ'keɪʃən/ NOUN, NO PLURAL the act of simplifying something (**simplificação**)

• **simplify** /'sɪmplɪfaɪ/ VERB [**simplifies, simplifying, simplified**] to make something easier to do or understand □ *We have tried to simplify the testing process.* (**simplificar**)

simplistic /sɪm'plɪstɪk/ ADJECTIVE making a problem or situation seem less complicated or difficult than it really is □ *a simplistic argument* (**simplista**)

• **simplistically** /sɪm'plɪstɪkəli/ ADVERB in a simplistic way □ *I think the play has been interpreted too simplistically.* (**simplisticamente**)

simply /ˈsɪmplɪ/ ADVERB

1 only □ *Now, it's simply a question of waiting until something happens.* (**simplesmente**)
2 used to emphasize what you are saying □ *I simply don't understand him!* (**de maneira simples, simplesmente**)
3 in a way that is not difficult or complicated □ *I'll explain it simply so that you all understand.* (**simplesmente, com simplicidade**)
4 with no decorations or extra details □ *a simply furnished apartment* (**simplista**)

simulate /ˈsɪmjʊleɪt/ VERB [simulates, simulating, simulated]

1 to make something that seems real but is not □ *The emergency services simulated a major disaster.* (**simular**)
2 to pretend to feel a particular emotion □ *He simulated disgust.* (**fingir**)

- **simulation** /ˌsɪmjʊˈleɪʃən/ NOUN [plural simulations]
1 the process of simulating something (**simulação**)
2 something that simulates something □ *computer simulations* (**imitação**)

- **simulator** /ˈsɪmjʊleɪtə(r)/ NOUN [plural simulators] a machine that simulates real conditions, used especially to train people to operate aircraft □ *a flight simulator* (**simulador**)

simultaneous /ˌsɪməlˈteɪnɪəs/ ADJECTIVE

happening or done at exactly the same time □ *a simultaneous translation* (**simultâneo**)

- **simultaneously** /ˌsɪməlˈteɪnɪəslɪ/ ADVERB at exactly the same time □ *The commentary was broadcast simultaneously on the radio.* (**simultaneamente**)

sin /sɪn/ NOUN [plural sins]

a very bad thing to do, especially one that breaks a religious law □ *the sin of pride* (**pecado**) 🔹 *He felt that he had committed a sin.* (**cometeu um pecado**)

since /sɪns/ ▶ CONJUNCTION

1 from a particular time or event in the past until the present □ *Ann's been a lot happier since she changed jobs.* □ *He's put on weight since I saw him last.* (**desde que**)
2 because □ *I decided to go shopping, since I had some free time.* (**já que**)

▶ PREPOSITION

1 from a particular time in the past until the present □ *The little girl has been missing since Christmas.* □ *We've been living here since 1986.* □ *I haven't spoken to Gretta since last week.* (**desde**)
2 since when? used to show that you are surprised or annoyed about something □ *Since when did he have the right to tell us what to do?* (**desde quando?**)

▶ ADVERB

1 from the time that has already been mentioned until the present □ *She joined the choir last month and has been going to practice regularly since.* (**desde então**) 🔹 *I came to London in 1995, and I've lived here ever since.* (**desde então**)
2 at a later time than the time first mentioned □ *They met last year and have since become friends.* (**desde então**)

sincere /sɪnˈsɪə(r)/ ADJECTIVE

1 honest and saying what you really think □ *I'm never sure he's being sincere with me.* (**sincero**)
2 used to emphasize that the feeling you are expressing is real □ *We'd like to offer our sincere thanks to our hosts.* (**sincero**)

- **sincerely** /sɪnˈsɪəlɪ/ ADVERB
1 in a way that is sincere □ *I sincerely hope you're right about this.* (**sinceramente**)
2 Yours sincerely used at the end of a letter when you have used the name of the person you are writing to (**atenciosamente**)

- **sincerity** /sɪnˈserətɪ/ NOUN, NO PLURAL being sincere □ *Nobody could doubt his sincerity.* (**sinceridade**)

sine /saɪn/ NOUN [plural sines]

in a triangle with one angle of 90°, the sine is the length of the side opposite one of the angles of less than 90° divided by the hypotenuse (= longest side). A maths word. (**seno**)

sinew /ˈsɪnju:/ NOUN [plural sinews]

a type of strong body tissue that joins your muscles to your bones (**tendão, nervo**)

- **sinewy** /ˈsɪnju:ɪ/ ADJECTIVE a sinewy body is thin with strong muscles (**musculoso**)

sinful /ˈsɪnfʊl/ ADJECTIVE

morally wrong or breaking a religious law □ *It's sinful to throw so much food away.* (**pecaminoso**)

- **sinfulness** /ˈsɪnfʊlnɪs/ NOUN, NO PLURAL being sinful (**pecado**)

sing /sɪŋ/ VERB [sings, singing, sang, sung]

1 to make musical sounds with your voice □ *She sings in a Gospel choir.* □ *I asked him to sing my favourite song.* (**cantar**)
2 birds sing when they make musical sounds (**cantar**)

singe /sɪndʒ/ VERB [singes, singeing, singed]

to burn the surface or edge of something slightly by touching it with something hot □ *I singed the tablecloth with the iron.* (**chamuscar**)

singer /ˈsɪŋə(r)/ NOUN [plural singers]

a person who sings, especially as their job □ *a folk singer* (**cantor**)

singing /ˈsɪŋɪŋ/ NOUN, NO PLURAL

the activity of making musical sounds with your voice □ *a singing teacher* (**canto**)

single /ˈsɪŋɡəl/ ▶ ADJECTIVE

1 only one □ *I didn't get a single card on my birthday.* □ *A single shelf held all her belongings.* (**único**)
2 talking about each thing in a group separately 🔹 *He rang me every single day while he was away.* (**cada dia**)

3 not married ☐ *a club for single women* (**solteiro**)
4 for use by one person ☐ *a single room* ☐ *a pair of single sheets* (**de solteiro**)
5 a single ticket is used for a journey in one direction (**de ida**)
6 a single parent looks after their children on their own ☐ *a single mother* (**pai solteiro, mãe solteira**)
▶ NOUN [plural **singles**]
1 a ticket for a journey you make in one direction but not back again ☐ *How much is a single to York?* ☐ *Two singles to Kings Cross.* (**bilhete de ida**)
2 a musical CD or record with only one or two songs on it (**CD ou gravação musical**) 🔂 *a hit single* (= very popular song) (**gravação musical de sucesso**)
3 singles in sports like tennis and badminton, a game when one player plays against another ☐ *The men's singles final is this afternoon.* (**partida de tênis ou badminton com dois competidores**)
◆ PHRASAL VERB [**singles, singling, singled**] **single someone/something out** to choose one person or thing from a group to say good or bad things about ☐ *Jamie felt he had been singled out for criticism.* (**escolher, selecionar alguém/algo**)

single bed /ˈsɪŋɡəl ˈbed/ NOUN [plural **single beds**] a bed for one person (**cama de solteiro**)

single file /ˈsɪŋɡəl ˈfaɪl/ ▶ NOUN, NO PLURAL a line of people or vehicles one behind the other ☐ *The soldiers marched in single file.* (**fila**)
▶ ADVERB in one line ☐ *They walked single file along the narrow ridge.* (**fila única**)

single-handed /ˈsɪŋɡəlˈhændɪd/ ADJECTIVE, ADVERB without anyone else's help ☐ *He carried out the rescue single-handed.* (**sozinho, sem ajuda**)
• **single-handedly** /ˈsɪŋɡəlˈhændɪdli/ ADVERB without anyone else's help ☐ *He transformed the organization single-handedly.* (**fazer algo sem ajuda**)

single-minded /ˈsɪŋɡəlˈmaɪndɪd/ ADJECTIVE being determined to achieve something (**determinado, focado**)

singly /ˈsɪŋɡli/ ADVERB one at a time or separately ☐ *The flowers grow singly or in clusters.* (**um a um**)

singsong /ˈsɪŋsɒŋ/ ADJECTIVE a singsong voice goes up and down like someone singing (**voz oscilante**)

singular /ˈsɪŋɡjʊlə(r)/ ▶ ADJECTIVE
1 in grammar, a singular form of a word is the form used to talk about one person, thing or group ☐ *'Child' is the singular form of 'children'.* (**singular**)
2 very noticeable or unusual ☐ *He has produced a poem of singular beauty.* (**singular**)
▶ NOUN **the singular** the form of a noun, pronoun, adjective or verb that you use to talk about one person, thing or group ☐ *The singular is 'sheep' and the plural is also 'sheep'.* (**o singular**)
• **singularly** /ˈsɪŋɡjʊləli/ ADVERB extremely or in a noticeable way ☐ *He was singularly unprepared for life in the outback.* (**singularmente**)

sinister /ˈsɪnɪstə(r)/ ADJECTIVE making you feel that something harmful or evil will happen ☐ *a sinister black figure* (**sinistro**)

sink /sɪŋk/ ▶ VERB [**sinks, sinking, sank, sunk**]
1 to drop below the surface of water and move down to the bottom, or to make something do this ☐ *The boat sank in a storm.* ☐ *She fell in and sank below the surface of the water.* (**afundar(-se) na água**)
2 to move to a lower position or level ☐ *The sun was sinking towards the horizon.* ☐ + *into* *He sank to his knees.* (**baixar**)
3 to go into or to push something into the surface of something soft ☐ + *into* *Our feet sank deep into the mud.* ☐ *The dog sank its teeth into the postman's leg.* (**afundar(-se) em algo macio**)
4 if your heart sinks, you feel sad or disappointed (**deprimir-se**)
◆ PHRASAL VERBS **sink in** if a fact sinks in, you understand it completely ☐ *It took a moment for the news to sink in.* (**ser compreendido**) **sink something into something** to spend a large amount of money on an activity or a business ☐ *All her cash was sunk into the company.* (**investir bastante dinheiro em algo**)
▶ NOUN [plural **sinks**] a bowl fixed to the wall in a kitchen or bathroom, used for washing in (**pia**) 🔂 *She put the dirty cups in the* kitchen sink. (**pia da cozinha**)

sinner /ˈsɪnə(r)/ NOUN [plural **sinners**] someone who has committed a sin (**ver sin**)

sinuous /ˈsɪnjuəs/ ADJECTIVE with a lot of curves ☐ *the sinuous movement of a snake* (**sinuoso**)

sinus /ˈsaɪnəs/ NOUN [plural **sinuses**] one of the hollow spaces in the bones in your head that are connected to your nose (**seio da face**)
• **sinusitis** /ˌsaɪnəˈsaɪtɪs/ NOUN, NO PLURAL an illness in which your sinuses become very painful (**sinusite**)

sip /sɪp/ ▶ VERB [**sips, sipping, sipped**] to drink something slowly taking only a small amount at a time ☐ *Russell sipped his coffee.* (**sorver**)
▶ NOUN [plural **sips**] when you sip a drink (**pequeno gole**) 🔂 *She* took *a* sip *of water.* (**tomou um pequeno gole**)

siphon /ˈsaɪfən/ ▶ NOUN [plural **siphons**] a tube used to move a liquid from one container into another (**sifão**)
▶ VERB [**siphons, siphoning, siphoned**]
1 to take something, especially money, from somewhere dishonestly, a small amount at a time ☐ *They siphoned cash from victims' bank accounts.* ☐ *They allegedly siphoned off $10 million from aid funds.* (**desviar recursos, dinheiro**)
2 to move liquid using a siphon ☐ *Two men were caught siphoning diesel from a lorry.* (**extrair com sifão**)

sir /sɜː(r)/ NOUN [plural **sirs**]
1 a polite way of speaking or writing to a man, especially one you do not know ☐ *Excuse me, sir. Can I help you?* (**senhor, cavalheiro**)

2 Dear Sir a way of beginning a formal letter to a man when you do not know his name (**Prezado senhor**)

3 a title used before the name of a knight (= a man with a high social rank) □ *Sir Paul McCartney*. (**sir**)

siren /ˈsaɪərən/ NOUN [plural **sirens**] a device that makes a very loud noise to warn people of something □ *I heard police sirens outside.* (**sirene**)

sirloin /ˈsɜːlɔɪn/ NOUN [plural **sirloins**] a piece of beef (= meat from a cow) cut from the top of the back leg (**lombo**)

sister /ˈsɪstə(r)/ NOUN [plural **sisters**]

1 a girl or a woman who has the same parents as you (**irmã**) 🔹 *He had two older sisters.* (**irmã mais velha**) 🔹 *She was walking to school with her younger sister.* (**irmã mais nova**)

2 a female nurse who is in charge of part of a hospital □ *a ward sister* (**enfermeira-chefe**)

3 a nun (= a member of a female religious group), often used as a title □ *Sister Dorothy* (**freira**)

• **sisterhood** /ˈsɪstəhʊd/ NOUN [plural **sisterhoods**]
1 a friendly feeling among women and girls (**irmandade**)
2 a group of women, especially nuns

sister-in-law /ˈsɪstərɪnlɔː/ NOUN [plural **sisters-in-law**] your brother's wife, or your husband or wife's sister (**cunhada**)

sit /sɪt/ VERB [**sits, sitting, sat**]

1 to be in a position where your weight is supported on your bottom, not your legs □ *I sat next to my friend.* (**sentar(-se)**) 🔹 *Would you please sit still while I get the books out?* □ + **on** *He was sitting on the sofa.* □ + **down** *They were sitting down waiting for me.*

2 to move your body into a position where your weight is supported on your bottom □ *He came in and sat on the floor.* □ + **down** *Sit down now, and get on with your work, please.* (**sentar(-se)**)

3 to make someone sit somewhere □ *We sat the children on extra cushions.* (**fazer sentar, pôr sentado, acomodar**)

4 to be in a particular place without moving or being used □ *There was a big parcel sitting on the kitchen table.* □ *This jam's been sitting on the shelf for months.* (**estar/permanecer em certo lugar**)

5 if you sit an exam, you do an exam □ *She's sitting her GCSEs next term.* (**realizar um exame/teste**)

6 if an official group of people sits, it has a meeting □ *The committee sits on the second Tuesday of each month.* (**reunir-se**)

♦ PHRASAL VERBS **sit about/around** to spend time sitting down and not doing much □ *We've been sitting about chatting all morning.* (**ficar à toa, relaxar**) **sit back** to relax and wait for something to happen □ *Just sit back and enjoy the show.* (**apreciar o momento, despreocupar-se**) **sit up 1** to move from a lying position to a sitting position □ *Can you manage to sit up?* (**erguer-se de posição deitada para sentar-se**) **2** to sit with your back straight (**sentar-se de modo ereto**) 🔹 *Sit up straight and pay attention!* (**sente-se direito**)

sitcom /ˈsɪtkɒm/ NOUN [plural **sitcoms**] a television comedy programme that is always in the same place and has the same characters (**série televisiva**)

site /saɪt/ ▶ NOUN [plural **sites**]

1 a place where something happens or happened, or a place used for a certain purpose □ + **of** *the site of a battle* (**local, sítio**) 🔹 *He works on a construction site.* (**local de construção**) □ *It is one of the most visited archaeological sites in Europe.* □ *The minister visited the crash site.*

2 a website. A computing word (**website**) 🔹 *an Internet site* (**site da internet**) □ *The footage is posted on video sharing sites like YouTube.*

3 on site available or happening in an office, factory, etc., not in another place □ *He was treated by the company doctor on site.* □ *There's a small shop on site.* (**no local**)

▶ VERB [**sites, siting, sited**] to build something in a particular place □ *The factory is sited next to a large housing development.* (**localizar-se**)

sitting room /ˈsɪtɪŋruːm/ NOUN [plural **sitting rooms**] a room, usually in a house, for sitting and relaxing in (**sala de estar**)

situate /ˈsɪtjueɪt/ VERB [**situates, situating, situated**] if something is situated somewhere, it is in that place or position □ *The university is situated on the outskirts of Dallas.* □ *The farm is situated in a remote area.* (**situar**)

• **situation** /ˌsɪtjuˈeɪʃən/ NOUN [plural **situations**]
1 the things that are happening in a place or affecting someone at a particular time (**situação**) 🔹 *We're in a difficult situation.* (**situação difícil**) 🔹 *She handled the situation very well.* (**lidou com a situação**) □ *They're trying to improve the situation for migrant workers.*
2 a formal word for the place or position where something is □ *Plant the sunflowers in a sunny situation.* (**localização**)

six /sɪks/ NUMBER [plural **sixes**] the number 6 (**seis**)

sixteen /sɪksˈtiːn/ NUMBER the number 16 (**dezesseis**)

sixteenth /sɪksˈtiːnθ/ NUMBER 16th written as a word (**décimo sexto**)

sixth /sɪksθ/ ▶ NUMBER 6th written as a word (**sexto**)

▶ NOUN [plural **sixths**] 1/6; one of six equal parts of something (**sexto**)

sixth form /ˈsɪksθ fɔːm/ NOUN [plural **sixth forms**] in British schools, the classes in which students aged 16 to 18 study □ *Melanie's in the sixth form.* (**grau equivalente ao ensino médio na Grã-Bretanha**)

- **sixth-former** /'sɪksθə'fɔː(r)/ NOUN [plural **sixth formers**] a student in the sixth form at a British school (estudante do grau equivalente ao ensino médio na Grã-Bretanha)

sixth sense /'sɪksθ 'sens/ NOUN, NO PLURAL an ability that means you seem to be aware of things that cannot be seen, heard, touched, smelled or tasted □ *She always knows when there is going to be a storm – she seems to have a sixth sense about it.* (sexto sentido)

sixtieth /'sɪkstɪəθ/ NUMBER 60th written as a word (sexagésimo)

sixty /'sɪkstɪ/ NUMBER [plural **sixties**]
1 the number 60 (sessenta)
2 **the sixties** the years between 1960 and 1969 (os anos 1960)

size /saɪz/ NOUN [plural **sizes**]
1 how big, small, long, wide, etc. something is, □ + *of The hole was the size of a tennis ball.* □ *They are less than 2 centimetres in size.* □ *We were disappointed by the small size of the bedrooms.* (tamanho, dimensão) *It's about the same size as a credit card.* (o mesmo tamanho) *There were boats of every size and shape.* (tamanho e forma) □ *The government wants to reduce class sizes.*
2 one of the measurements that clothes, shoes and other objects are made in □ *Can I try a smaller size?* □ *I'm a size 12.* (tamanho)

◆ PHRASAL VERB [**sizes, sizing, sized**] **size something/ someone up** to study someone or something to decide what they are like □ *He quickly sized up the situation.* □ *She sized up the two men.* (avaliar)

- **sizeable** /'saɪzəbəl/ or **sizable** ADJECTIVE quite big □ *a sizeable crowd* □ *He made a sizeable income from renting his land.* (considerável)
- **-sized** /saɪzd/ SUFFIX -sized is added to the end of words to describe how big something is □ *a medium sized company* (sufixo que determina tamanho, dimensão)

sizzle /'sɪzəl/ VERB [**sizzles, sizzling, sizzled**] to make a noise like food frying □ *Steaks were sizzling on the grill.* (crepitar, estalar)

skate /skeɪt/ □ NOUN [plural **skates**]
1 an ice skate (patim de gelo)
2 a roller skate (patim de roda)

◆ IDIOM **get your skates on** an informal phrase used to tell someone to hurry □ *If you want to go, you'll need to get your skates on.* (ande logo!)

▶ VERB [**skates, skating, skated**] to move wearing skates □ *The Russian pair skated well.* (patinar)

skateboard /'skeɪtbɔːd/ NOUN [plural **skateboards**] a long narrow board with wheels on the bottom which you ride by standing on it (skate)

- **skateboarding** /'skeɪtbɔːdɪŋ/ NOUN, NO PLURAL the activity of riding on a skateboard (andar de skate)

skater /'skeɪtə(r)/ NOUN [plural **skaters**] someone who skates on ice (patinador)

skating /'skeɪtɪŋ/ NOUN, NO PLURAL the sport or activity of moving over ice wearing skates (patinação)

skeletal /'skelɪtəl/ ADJECTIVE
1 extremely thin (esquelético)
2 to do with a skeleton (relacionado ao esqueleto)

skeleton /'skelɪtən/ NOUN [plural **skeletons**]
1 the frame of bones inside the body of a person or an animal □ *They found a nearly complete dinosaur skeleton.* (esqueleto)
2 **a skeleton staff/crew, etc.** fewer people than normal, but just enough to continue working □ *A skeleton staff will continue to maintain the building.* (equipe enxuta)

◆ IDIOM **a skeleton in the cupboard/closet** a secret from your past that you do not want people to know about □ *He claims to have no skeletons in his cupboard.* (um esqueleto no armário: um segredo escondido)

skeleton key /'skelɪtən 'kiː/ NOUN [plural **skeleton keys**] a key that will open several different locks (chave mestra)

skeptic /'skeptɪk/ NOUN [plural **skeptics**] the US spelling of **sceptic** (cético)

- **skeptical** /'skeptɪkəl/ ADJECTIVE the US spelling of **sceptical**

sketch /sketʃ/ □ NOUN [plural **sketches**]
1 a drawing that is done quickly □ *a pencil sketch* □ *He drew a rough sketch of the house.* (esboço, croqui)
2 a short, funny piece of acting (esquete) *a comedy sketch* (esquete cômico)
3 a short description of something without a lot of details □ *The book consists of biographical sketches of famous scientists.* (resumo)
▶ VERB [**sketches, sketching, sketched**] to draw something quickly □ *She had sketched some designs.* (esboçar)

◆ PHRASAL VERB **sketch something out** to describe something quickly and without a lot of details □ *He sketched out the challenges ahead.* (resumir)

- **sketchy** /'sketʃɪ/ ADJECTIVE [**sketchier, sketchiest**] not complete and without many details □ *Because the area is so remote, details of the incident are sketchy.* (incompleto)

skew /skjuː/ VERB [**skews, skewing, skewed**]
1 to change or to influence facts or amounts so that they are not fair or accurate □ *This could skew the results.* (distorcer)
2 if something is skewed, it is not straight □ *His hat was skewed at an angle.* (enviesar)

skewer /'skjuːə(r)/ NOUN [plural **skewers**] a long thin pointed piece of metal or wood that you can cook small pieces of food on (espeto)

ski /skiː/ ▶ NOUN [plural **skis**] one of two long narrow strips of wood or metal that you attach to boots and use for moving over snow (**esqui**) *a pair of skis* (**par de patins**)

▶ ADJECTIVE to do with the sport or activity of skiing □ *a ski resort* □ *the ski slopes* (**relacionado ao esqui**)

▶ VERB [**skis, skiing, skied**] to move over snow on skis □ *They skied down together.* □ *I'm just learning to ski.* (**esquiar**)

skid /skɪd/ VERB [**skids, skidding, skidded**] to slide over a surface in a way that is not controlled □ *The plane skidded off the runway in heavy rain.* (**derrapar**)

skier /ˈskiːə(r)/ NOUN [plural **skiers**] someone who skis (**esquiador**)

skies /skaɪz/ PLURAL NOUN the sky, used especially when talking about the weather □ *The forecast is for sunny skies and warm temperatures.* (**clima**)

skiing /ˈskiːɪŋ/ NOUN, NO PLURAL the sport or activity of moving over snow on skis (**esqui**) *I would love to go skiing.* (**esquiar**) *a skiing holiday* (**férias na neve**)

skilful /ˈskɪlfʊl/ ADJECTIVE showing the ability to do something well □ *He's a very skilful player.* □ *She's very skilful at handling the media.* (**habilidoso**)

• **skilfully** /ˈskɪlfʊli/ ADVERB in a skilful way □ *They had skilfully avoided being caught.* □ *a skilfully edited programme* (**habilmente**)

• **skilfulness** /ˈskɪlfʊlnɪs/ NOUN, NO PLURAL the quality of being skillful (**habilidade**)

skill /skɪl/ NOUN [plural **skills**]

1 an ability to do something that you develop through training and practice (**habilidade, experiência, competência**) *It helps children develop their social skills.* (**desenvolvem suas habilidades**) *Effective communication skills are essential.* (**habilidades de comunicação**) *They lack basic computer skills.* (**competências básicas**)

2 no plural the ability to do something very well □ *His skill as a writer is in creating believable characters.* □ **+ in** *He showed great skill in handling the situation.* □ **+ at** *She was known for her skill at motivating workers.* (**habilidade**)

• **skilled** /skɪld/ ADJECTIVE

1 a skilled person is very good at what they do □ *Amanda's a skilled pianist.* (**especializado, perito**) *a highly skilled workforce* (**altamente especializado**)

2 a skilled job needs special training and practice (**especializado**)

skillful /ˈskɪlfʊl/ ADJECTIVE the US spelling of **skilful**
• **skillfully** /ˈskɪlfʊli/ ADVERB the US spelling of **skilfully**

skim /skɪm/ VERB [**skims, skimming, skimmed**]

1 to move just above or just touching the surface of something □ *The birds flew low, skimming across the water.* (**deslizar**)

2 to remove something floating on the top of a liquid □ *Skim off any fat that floats to the surface.* (**escumar**)

3 to read something quickly without paying attention to details □ *He quickly skimmed through the file.* (**ler superficialmente**)

skimmed milk /ˈskɪmd ˈmɪlk/ NOUN, NO PLURAL milk from which the cream has been removed (**leite desnatado**)

skim milk /ˈskɪm ˈmɪlk/ NOUN, NO PLURAL the US word for **skimmed milk** (**leite desnatado**)

skimp /skɪmp/ VERB [**skimps, skimping, skimped**] to buy or to use not enough of something □ *Don't skimp on the cream in the recipe.* (**economizar, evitar o uso**)

• **skimpy** /ˈskɪmpi/ ADJECTIVE [**skimpier, skimpiest**] skimpy clothes do not cover much of your body (**decotado**)

skin /skɪn/ ▶ NOUN [plural **skins**]

1 the outside layer of your body (**pele**) *She had blonde hair and very pale skin.* (**pele clara**) *People with dark skin don't burn as easily in the sun.* (**pele escura**) *A moisturizing cream will help prevent dry skin.* (**pele seca**) □ *skin cancer* (**câncer de pele**)

2 the outside layer of a dead animal which is used for making something □ *the illegal trade in tiger skins* (**pele de animal**)

3 the outside layer of some fruits and vegetables □ *banana skins* □ *grape skin* (**casca**)

4 a layer that forms on the top of some liquids □ *Warm milk develops a skin as it cools.* (**película**)

◆ IDIOMS **do something by the skin of your teeth** an informal phrase meaning to only just succeed in doing something □ *She caught the train by the skin of her teeth.* (**conseguir por um triz**) **make your skin crawl** to make you feel very uncomfortable because you are shocked or frightened □ *That noise makes my skin crawl* (**de arrepiar a pele**)

▶ VERB [**skins, skinning, skinned**] to remove the skin from something □ *I've skinned the tomatoes.* (**esfolar, descascar**)

skincare /ˈskɪnkeə(r)/ NOUN, NO PLURAL keeping your skin in good condition □ *skincare products* (**cuidados com a pele**)

skinflint /ˈskɪnflɪnt/ NOUN [plural **skinflints**] an informal word meaning someone who does not like spending money (**pão-duro**)

skinhead /ˈskɪnhed/ NOUN [plural **skinheads**] a man who has extremely short hair, especially one who also behaves violently (**skinhead**)

skinny /ˈskɪni/ ADJECTIVE [**skinnier, skinniest**]

1 very thin □ *She's too skinny.* (**magricela**)

2 skinny clothes fit your body very tightly □ *skinny jeans* (**justo**)

3 low in fat □ *a skinny latte* (**com baixo teor de gordura**)

skint /skɪnt/ ADJECTIVE having no money. An informal word □ *I can't afford the ticket. I'm totally skint.* (**sem dinheiro, duro**)

skin-tight

skin-tight /ˌskɪnˈtaɪt/ ADJECTIVE skin-tight clothes fit your body very tightly (**justo, agarrado**)

skip /skɪp/ ▶ VERB [**skips, skipping, skipped**]
1 to move forward by jumping from one foot to the other □ *He skipped down the road.* (**saltitar**)
2 to jump over a rope that you are turning □ *The girls were skipping in the playground.* (**pular corda**)
3 to not do something that you should do □ *Children who skip breakfast find it more difficult to concentrate in class.* □ *He was being bullied and regularly skipped school.* (**pular**)
4 to avoid reading or mentioning something □ *The report skips over some essential issues.* (**pular item, trecho, página**)
▶ NOUN [*plural* **skips**]
1 a large container for waste □ *We put a lot of broken furniture and bricks in the skip.* (**caçamba**)
2 a skipping movement (**pulo**)

skipper /ˈskɪpə(r)/ NOUN [*plural* **skippers**]
1 the person in charge of a boat or ship (**capitão**)
2 an informal word for the leader of a team □ *the former England skipper Alan Shearer* (**capitão**)

skipping rope /ˈskɪpɪŋ ˌrəʊp/ NOUN [*plural* **skipping ropes**] a rope that you jump over as you are turning it (**corda de pular**)

skirmish /ˈskɜːmɪʃ/ ▶ NOUN [*plural* **skirmishes**] a short fight or argument (**discussão**)
▶ VERB [**skirmishes, skirmishing, skirmished**] to take part in a skirmish (**participar de uma discussão**)
• **skirmishing** /ˈskɜːmɪʃɪŋ/ NOUN, NO PLURAL fighting or arguments that are not very serious (**argumentação fraca**)

skirt /skɜːt/ ▶ NOUN [*plural* **skirts**] a piece of clothing for girls or women that hangs from the waist (**saia**) 🔲 *Anja was wearing a black skirt.* (**usando uma saia**) □ *a short skirt*
▶ VERB [**skirts, skirting, skirted**]
1 to go around the edge of something □ *A small canal skirts the field.* (**beirar**)
2 to avoid talking about something □ *He skirted the issue of immigration.* (**esquivar-se de**)

skirting board /ˈskɜːtɪŋ ˌbɔːd/ NOUN [*plural* **skirting boards**] a narrow piece of wood fixed to the bottom of an inside wall where it meets the floor (**rodapé**)

skittle /ˈskɪtəl/ NOUN [*plural* **skittles**] an object in the shape of a bottle that you try to knock down with a ball as a game (**pino**)
• **skittles** /ˈskɪtəlz/ NOUN, NO PLURAL a game in which you use a ball to knock down objects in the shape of a bottle (**boliche**)

skive /skaɪv/ VERB [**skives, skiving, skived**] an informal word meaning to not be at school or work when you should be □ *He skived off work to go and see a film.* (**cabular**)

743

• **skiver** /ˈskaɪvə(r)/ NOUN [*plural* **skivers**] an informal word meaning someone who avoids work (**aquele que cabula**)

skulduggery /skʌlˈdʌɡəri/ NOUN, NO PLURAL activities that are intended to trick people (**fraude, trapaça**)

skulk /skʌlk/ VERB [**skulks, skulking, skulked**] to hide somewhere or move quietly in a way that makes you look guilty □ *He was skulking behind a parked car to avoid seeing her.* (**mover-se furtivamente**)

skull /skʌl/ NOUN [*plural* **skulls**]
1 the structure of bones that form your head □ *He fell out of a tree and fractured his skull.* (**crânio**)
2 **skull and crossbones** a picture of two crossed bones and a skull, often used as a warning sign, for example on poison

skull cap /ˈskʌl ˌkæp/ NOUN [*plural* **skull caps**] a small round hat that some men wear for religious reasons (**solidéu**)

skunk /skʌŋk/ NOUN [*plural* **skunks**] a small animal that produces an unpleasant smell if it is attacked (**gambá**)

sky /skaɪ/ NOUN [*plural* **skies**] the area above the Earth where you can see the sun, moon, stars and clouds □ *There was a beautiful clear blue sky.* □ *She looked up at the cloudy sky.* □ *There were several stars in the sky.* (**céu**)
⇨ go to **skies**

skydiving /ˈskaɪˌdaɪvɪŋ/ NOUN, NO PLURAL a sport in which people jump out of aeroplanes (**queda-livre**)

skylight /ˈskaɪlaɪt/ NOUN [*plural* **skylights**] a window in a roof (**claraboia**)

skyline /ˈskaɪlaɪn/ NOUN [*plural* **skylines**] the shape made by buildings against the sky □ *the London skyline* (**linha do horizonte**)

Skype /skaɪp/ NOUN, NO PLURAL an Internet system used for making telephone calls. A trademark. (**Skype**)

skyscraper /ˈskaɪˌskreɪpə(r)/ NOUN [*plural* **skyscrapers**] a very tall building (**arranha-céu**)

slab /slæb/ NOUN [*plural* **slabs**] a thick flat piece of something □ *a slab of concrete* (**laje, fatia grossa**)

slack /slæk/ ▶ ADJECTIVE [**slacker, slackest**]
1 loose or not pulled tight □ *The rope was too slack.* (**frouxo**)
2 not caring enough about doing something well □ *a slack attitude* (**folgado**)
3 if business is slack, not many people are buying things (**vagaroso**)
▶ VERB [**slacks, slacking, slacked**] to do less work than you should (**folgar**)
• **slacken** /ˈslækən/ VERB [**slackens, slackening, slackened**]
1 to make something looser, or to become looser □ *His grip on her arm slackened.* (**afrouxar**)
2 to become slower or less active, or to make something become slower or less active □ *The pace of economic growth has slackened.* (**desacelerar, diminuir a velocidade**)

slacks

slacks /slæks/ PLURAL NOUN an old-fashioned word for an informal style of trousers (**tipo de calça**)

slain /sleɪn/ PAST PARTICIPLE OF **slay** (**ver slay**)

slalom /ˈslɑːləm/ NOUN [plural **slaloms**] a race in which people move from side to side between poles (**corrida de esqui com obstáculos**)

slam /slæm/ ▶ VERB [**slams, slamming, slammed**]
1 to shut quickly with a loud noise, or to shut something quickly with a loud noise (**bater**) ▣ She walked angrily out of the room and slammed the door. (**bater a porta**) ▣ The gate slammed shut. (**bater com tudo**)
2 to put something somewhere with a loud noise ▫ He slammed the books down on the table. (**bater, trombar**)
▶ NOUN [plural **slams**] the noise of something being slammed (**pancada**)

slander /ˈslɑːndə(r)/ ▶ NOUN [plural **slanders**] the crime of saying bad things about someone which are not true (**calúnia, difamação**)
▶ VERB [**slanders, slandering, slandered**] to say bad things about someone which are not true (**caluniar, difamar**)

• **slanderous** /ˈslɑːndərəs/ ADJECTIVE not true, and with the intention of making people have a bad opinion of someone ▫ slanderous remarks (**caluniador**)

slang /slæŋ/ NOUN, NO PLURAL very informal words and phrases ▫ 'Brass' is a slang word for money. (**gíria, jargão**)

• **slangy** /ˈslæŋi/ ADJECTIVE [**slangier, slangiest**] using slang ▫ slangy language (**em gíria**)

slant /slɑːnt/ ▶ VERB [**slants, slanting, slanted**] to slope or to move in a sloping line ▫ Sunlight slanted through the window. (**inclinar-se**)
▶ NOUN [plural **slants**]
1 a way of writing or talking about something which shows a particular opinion ▫ This was a new slant on an old argument. (**inclinação**)
2 a slope (**ladeira**)

slap /slæp/ ▶ VERB [**slaps, slapping, slapped**] to hit something or someone with the flat part of your hand ▫ She slapped him across the face. (**estapear**)
♦ PHRASAL VERB **slap something on** to quickly put something on a surface ▫ Rachel slapped on some sun cream. (**espalhar rapidamente**)
▶ NOUN [plural **slaps**] a hit made with the flat part of your hand (**tapa**)
♦ IDIOM **a slap in the face** something someone does which upsets or insults you ▫ The fare increases are a slap in the face for commuters. (**um tapa na cara**)

slap-bang /ˈslæpˈbæŋ/ ADVERB
1 exactly in a particular place ▫ The theatre is slap-bang in the middle of Milan. (**bem no/na, exatamente no/na**)
2 directly and with force ▫ He drove slap-bang into the wall. (**de uma vez, brusca e diretamente**)

slapdash /ˈslæpdæʃ/ ADJECTIVE careless ▫ slapdash work (**desleixado**)

slapstick /ˈslæpstɪk/ NOUN, NO PLURAL a type of comedy in which the actors do silly things such as falling over or throwing things at each other (**palhaçada**)

slash /slæʃ/ ▶ VERB [**slashes, slashing, slashed**]
1 to cut something quickly and violently ▫ Vandals had slashed the car's tyres. (**talhar**)
2 an informal word meaning to reduce something by a large amount ▫ Many stores are slashing the price of TVs. (**reduzir drasticamente**)
▶ NOUN [plural **slashes**]
1 a long deep cut (**talho**)
2 one of two punctuation marks (/) or (\), used especially in computing and in website addresses (**barra**)

slat /slæt/ NOUN [plural **slats**] one of several thin flat pieces of wood or plastic which are used for making furniture or for making a blind (= covering for a window) (**lâmina**)

slate /sleɪt/ ▶ NOUN [plural **slates**]
1 a type of grey stone that can be broken into thin layers (**ardósia**)
2 a piece of this stone used for making a roof (**telha de ardósia**)
3 a piece of this stone that was used in the past to write on (**lousa**)
▶ VERB [**slates, slating, slated**] an informal word meaning to criticize someone or something ▫ The film was slated by critics. (**criticar asperamente**)

slate PC /ˈsleɪt ˌpiːˈsiː/ NOUN [plural **slate PCs**] a small computer that you write on with a special pen (**slate PC: tipo de tablet**)

slaughter /ˈslɔːtə(r)/ ▶ VERB [**slaughters, slaughtering, slaughtered**]
1 to kill an animal, usually for its meat (**abater**)
2 to kill a lot of people very violently (**massacrar**)
3 an informal word meaning to defeat someone completely in a game or competition (**derrotar**)
▶ NOUN, NO PLURAL the act of slaughtering people or animals ▫ Officials carried out a mass slaughter of cows to prevent the spread of the disease. ▫ The war has seen the slaughter of innocent civilians. (**massacre, abate**)

slaughterhouse /ˈslɔːtəhaʊs/ NOUN [plural **slaughterhouses**] a place where animals are killed for their meat (**matadouro**)

slave /sleɪv/ ▶ NOUN [plural **slaves**]
1 someone who is owned by another person and has to work for them without being paid ▫ My parents treat me like a slave. (**escravo**)
2 **be a slave to something** to be influenced by something too much ▫ He was a slave to money. (**ser escravo de algo**)
▶ VERB [**slaves, slaving, slaved**] an informal word meaning to work very hard ▫ Don was slaving away in the kitchen making dinner. (**trabalhar como escravo**)

slay 745 **sleigh**

- **slavery** /ˈsleɪvəri/ NOUN, NO PLURAL
  1 the system of having slaves □ *The US did not abolish slavery until 1865.* (escravatura)
  2 the state of being a slave □ *He had been sold into slavery.* (escravatura)

slay /sleɪ/ VERB [**slays, slaying, slew, slain**] a literary word meaning to kill a person or animal □ *The dragon was slain by Saint George.* (matar)

sleaze /sliːz/ NOUN, NO PLURAL behaviour in business or politics that is dishonest or morally bad □ *The government is facing allegations of sleaze and corruption.* (desonestidade)

- **sleazy** /ˈsliːzi/ ADJECTIVE [**sleazier, sleaziest**]
  1 dirty, and attracting unpleasant people □ *a sleazy nightclub* (sujo, decadente, baixo)
  2 dishonest or morally bad □ *a sleazy businessman* (desonesto)

sledge /sledʒ/ or **sled** /sled/ ▶ NOUN [plural **sledges** or **sleds**]
1 a small vehicle with a flat bottom or long metal or wooden pieces under it, that you sit on to slide over snow (trenó)
2 a larger vehicle that is pulled over snow by dogs or horses (trenó)
▶ VERB [**sledges, sledging, sledged**] to ride on a sledge

sledgehammer /ˈsledʒˌhæmə(r)/ NOUN [plural **sledgehammers**] a large heavy hammer that you hold with both hands (marreta)

sleek /sliːk/ ADJECTIVE [**sleeker, sleekest**]
1 smooth, soft and shiny □ *A mink has sleek dark brown fur.* (macio)
2 looking fashionable and expensive (glamouroso, elegante)
◆ PHRASAL VERB [**sleeks, sleeking, sleeked**] **sleek something back/down** to push something back or down to make it look smooth and shiny □ *She sleeked back her hair.* (alisar, lustrar)

sleep /sliːp/ ▶ NOUN [plural **sleeps**]
1 *no plural* the state when you are resting with your eyes closed and are naturally unconscious □ *I really need some sleep.* (sono) 🔲 *I couldn't get to sleep.* (pegar no sono)
2 a period of time when you are sleeping □ *I managed to have a sleep this morning.* (sono, soneca) 🔲 *She fell into a deep sleep.* (sono profundo)
3 go to sleep (a) to begin to sleep (b) if part of your body goes to sleep, you lose the feeling in it (ir dormir/adormecer)
4 put something to sleep to kill an animal because it is old or ill (sacrificar um animal)
◆ IDIOM **lose sleep over something** to worry about something (perder o sono, preocupar-se)
▶ VERB [**sleeps, sleeping, slept**]
1 to become naturally unconscious and rest with your eyes closed □ *I hardly slept at all last night.* □ *She slept through the fire alarm* (= did not wake up). (dormir) 🔲 *After their long walk, they slept soundly* (= slept well). (dormiram bem)
2 if a place sleeps a particular number of people, it has enough space for that many people to sleep there (comportar para dormir)
◆ PHRASAL VERB **sleep in** to sleep later than usual in the morning (dormir até tarde)

- **sleeper** /ˈsliːpə(r)/ NOUN [plural **sleepers**]
  1 someone who is sleeping (pessoa que dorme)
  2 a light/heavy sleeper someone who wakes easily/does not wake easily after they are asleep (aquele que tem sono leve/pesado)
  3 a train with beds for passengers to sleep in (dormitório)

sleepily /ˈsliːpɪli/ ADVERB in a tired way □ *'What time is it?' she asked sleepily.* (morosamente, sonolento)

- **sleepiness** /ˈsliːpinɪs/ NOUN, NO PLURAL when you feel tired and want to sleep (sonolência)

sleeping bag /ˈsliːpɪŋ bæɡ/ NOUN [plural **sleeping bags**] a large bag made of thick, warm cloth, used for sleeping in, especially when you are camping (saco de dormir)

sleeping pill /ˈsliːpɪŋ pɪl/ NOUN [plural **sleeping pills**] a pill containing a drug that makes you sleep (sonífero)

sleepless /ˈsliːpləs/ ADJECTIVE if you have a sleepless night, you are unable to sleep (insone)

- **sleeplessness** /ˈsliːpləsnɪs/ NOUN, NO PLURAL being unable to sleep (insônia)

sleepover /ˈsliːpəʊvə(r)/ NOUN [plural **sleepovers**] when a child stays at a friend's house for the night (dormir na casa de um amigo)

sleepwalk /ˈsliːpwɔːk/ VERB [**sleepwalks, sleepwalking, sleepwalked**] to walk around while you are still asleep (andar dormindo)

- **sleepwalker** /ˈsliːpˌwɔːkə(r)/ NOUN [plural **sleepwalkers**] someone who sleepwalks (sonâmbulo)
- **sleepwalking** /ˈsliːpˌwɔːkɪŋ/ NOUN, NO PLURAL when someone sleepwalks (sonambulismo)

sleepy /ˈsliːpi/ ADJECTIVE [**sleepier, sleepiest**] feeling tired and wanting to sleep (sonolento)

sleet /sliːt/ ▶ NOUN, NO PLURAL a mixture of rain and snow (saraiva)
▶ VERB [**sleets, sleeting, sleeted**] if it is sleeting, sleet is falling (saraivar)

sleeve /sliːv/ NOUN [plural **sleeves**] the part of a piece of clothing that covers your arm or part of your arm □ *a dress with wide sleeves* (manga)
◆ IDIOM **have something up your sleeve** to have a secret plan □ *I haven't persuaded them to come yet, but I've still got a few things up my sleeve.* (guardar na manga)

- **sleeved** /sliːvd/ ADJECTIVE having sleeves of a particular length □ *a long-sleeved dress* (de mangas)
- **sleeveless** /ˈsliːvləs/ ADJECTIVE having no sleeves □ *a sleeveless top* (sem mangas)

sleigh /sleɪ/ NOUN [plural **sleighs**] a vehicle that is pulled over snow by horses or other animals (trenó)

sleight of hand /ˌslaɪt əv ˈhænd/ NOUN, NO PLURAL
1 the skill of moving your hands in a quick and clever way so that other people cannot see what you are doing, for example when doing a magic trick (**agilidade nas mãos, prestidigitação**)
2 if something is done by sleight of hand it is done in a skilful but slightly dishonest way (**habilidade em enganar, iludir**)

slender /ˈslendə(r)/ ADJECTIVE
1 thin in an attractive way □ *a slender figure* (**esguio**)
2 small or slight □ *His chances of winning are extremely slender.* (**escasso**)

slept /slept/ PAST TENSE AND PAST PARTICIPLE OF **sleep** (*ver* **sleep**)

sleuth /sluːθ/ NOUN [plural **sleuths**] a word sometimes used in books and films for someone who tries to solve crimes (**detetive**)

slew /sluː/ PAST TENSE OF **slay** (*ver* **slay**)

slice /slaɪs/ ▶ NOUN [plural **slices**]
1 a thin or smaller piece cut from a larger piece of food □ *He cut himself a thick slice of chocolate cake.* □ *a slice of ham* (**fatia**)
2 apart of something □ *He wanted to get a slice of the profits.* (**fatia**)
▶ VERB [**slices, slicing, sliced**]
1 to cut something into slices □ *Slice the onions thinly.* □ *a tin of sliced peaches* (**fatiar**)
2 to cut something easily with a sharp blade or knife □ *He had the top of his finger sliced off in the accident.* (**talhar**)

slick /slɪk/ ▶ ADJECTIVE [**slicker, slickest**]
1 done well and without seeming to involve much effort □ *a slick dance routine* □ *a slick election campaign* (**inteligente**)
2 clever at persuading people but probably not completely honest □ *a slick sales pitch* (**dissimulado**)
▶ NOUN [plural **slicks**] a layer of oil that has been left on the surface of the sea (**mancha de óleo**)
• **slickly** /ˈslɪkli/ ADVERB skilfully and looking as if taking little effort □ *He passed the ball slickly forward.* (**de modo inteligente**)

slide /slaɪd/ ▶ VERB [**slides, sliding, slid**]
1 to move over a surface quickly and smoothly, or to make something do this □ *The kids enjoyed sliding on the ice.* □ *a sliding door* □ *We slid the poles into place.* (**escorregar, deslizar**)
2 to move quietly or make something move quietly □ *He slowly slid the gun out of his pocket.* □ *Karen slid into the back of the room without anyone noticing.* (**mover-se ou mover algo furtivamente**)
3 to gradually become worse or get into a worse situation □ *We found ourselves gradually sliding into debt.* (**entrar em declínio, piorar**) 🔄 *The restaurant had let standards slide since we were last there.* (**deixar cair/piorar**)
▶ NOUN [plural **slides**]

1 a piece of play equipment on which children climb up steps and slide down a smooth sloping surface □ *Megan loves playing on the slide.* (**escorregador**)
2 a sliding movement □ *The car went into a slide on the wet road.* (**área escorregadia**)
3 a slow fall in level, price, quality etc. □ *the dollar's slide against the euro* □ *The film charts the family's gradual slide into poverty.* (**queda**)
4 a small transparent photograph that you shine light through to look at an image on a screen □ *a slide show* (**slide**)
5 a small clear piece of glass or plastic which you put something on so that you can look at it using a microscope (= scientific instrument for examining things) (**lâmina**)

slight /slaɪt/ ADJECTIVE [**slighter, slightest**]
1 small or not important □ *a slight increase in temperature* □ *There's a slight problem with your application.* □ *Lewis has a slight cold.* (**leve, ligeiro**)
2 a slight person is thin and light □ *He has a slight build.* (**leve**)
3 not in the slightest not at all □ *I'm not worried in the slightest by the news.* (**nem um pouco**)
• **slightly** /ˈslaɪtli/ ADVERB by only a small amount □ *Adam is slightly taller than Alex.* □ *I only know her slightly.* (**ligeiramente**)

slim /slɪm/ ▶ ADJECTIVE [**slimmer, slimmest**]
1 thin in an attractive way □ *His sister's a tall, slim girl with blonde hair.* (**esbelto**)
2 small □ *The chances of winning the lottery are very slim.* (**pequeno**)
▶ VERB [**slims, slimming, slimmed**] to become or try to become thinner □ *I can't have any cake, I'm slimming.* (**emagrecer**)
◆ PHRASAL VERBS **slim down** to become slimmer □ *He's slimmed down a lot in the last year.* (**emagrecer**) **slim something down** to make an organization or business smaller, especially by employing fewer people

slime /slaɪm/ NOUN, NO PLURAL a thick, sticky, unpleasant liquid □ *When the flood subsided the carpets were covered in slime.* (**lama**)

slimmer /ˈslɪmə(r)/ NOUN [plural **slimmers**] someone who is trying to become thinner (**aquele que tenta emagrecer**)
• **slimming** /ˈslɪmɪŋ/ NOUN, NO PLURAL the process of trying to become thinner □ *a slimming club* (**regime de emagrecimento**)

slimness /ˈslɪmnɪs/ NOUN, NO PLURAL being attractively thin □ *A wide belt accentuated the slimness of her waist.* (**magreza**)

slimy /ˈslaɪmi/ ADJECTIVE [**slimier, slimiest**] covered with, or feeling like, slime (= thick, unpleasant liquid) □ *a slimy substance* (**malacento, viscoso**)

sling /slɪŋ/ ▶ VERB [**slings, slinging, slung**]
1 to throw something somewhere in a careless way □ *Just sling your rucksack in the corner.* (**arremessar**)

slink … slobber

2 to put something in a position where it hangs down □ *She slung her bag over her shoulder and stalked out.* (**pendurar**)

▶ NOUN [*plural* **slings**] a wide piece of cloth that is hung from someone's neck or shoulder to support an injured arm □ *Ken had his arm in a sling.* (**tipoia**)

slink /slɪŋk/ VERB [**slinks, slinking, slunk**] to move quietly, trying not to be noticed, often because you have done something wrong □ *He came slinking in well past midnight.* (**esgueirar-se**)

slinky /ˈslɪŋki/ ADJECTIVE [**slinkier, slinkiest**] slinky clothing fits your body well and makes you look attractive □ *a slinky black top* (**provocante**)

slip /slɪp/ ▶ VERB [**slips, slipping, slipped**]
1 to slide and lose your balance or fall □ *Gran had slipped on the ice and broken her hip.* (**escorregar**)
2 to fall out of position or out of your hands □ *The knife slipped and I nearly cut myself.* □ *I'm sorry, the cup just slipped out of my hands.* (**escorregar**)
3 to put something somewhere quickly □ *Dad slipped a £10 note in my pocket.* (**enfiar**)
4 to go somewhere quietly and without anyone noticing you □ *I saw Polly slip out of the room.* □ *They must have slipped away while we were watching the show.* (**escapar**)
5 to become worse or lower in value, level, etc. □ *Profits have been slipping for months.* □ *I think support for the strike has slipped.* (**diminuir, piorar**)
6 if you slip a piece of clothing on or off, you put it on or take it off quickly and easily □ *I'll just slip on a jacket.* □ *Slip off your shoes.* (**colocar ou tirar rapida/facilmente**)

◆ IDIOMS **let something slip** to tell someone something that is a secret by mistake □ *Annie let it slip that she'd been left a lot of money.* (**deixar escorregar, contar um segredo sem querer**) **slip your mind** if something slips your mind, you forget about it or forget to do it □ *I'm so sorry about missing lunch yesterday – it completely slipped my mind.* (**esquecer**)

◆ PHRASAL VERBS **slip out** if something slips out, you say it without meaning to □ *I wasn't going to mention it but it just slipped out.* (**deixar escapar**) **slip up** to make a mistake or do something wrong □ *I'm afraid you slipped up on the first question.* (**errar**)

▶ NOUN [*plural* **slips**]
1 a small piece of paper □ *a slip of paper* □ *Fill in the green slip and give it back to me.* (**pedaço de papel**)
2 a small mistake (**lapso**) 🔼 *She made a couple of slips in her dance routine* (**cometeu alguns lapsos**)
3 a slip of the tongue something that you say by mistake (**algo dito sem querer**)
4 an act of sliding or falling (**escorregar ou cair**)
5 a piece of thin clothing that a girl or woman wears under her dress or skirt (**combinação**)

◆ IDIOM **give someone the slip** to escape from someone who is following you □ *He gave the police the slip near the tube station.* (**esquivar--se, escapar, dar uma rasteira**)

slip-on /ˈslɪpɒn/ NOUN [*plural* **slip-ons**] a shoe that is easy to put on because it does not fasten □ *I prefer slip-ons to shoes with laces.* (**sapato de enfiar o pé, mocassim**)

slippage /ˈslɪpɪdʒ/ NOUN, NO PLURAL
1 the amount that something has slipped (= slid down) (**quantidade de queda/perda de algo**)
2 the amount of time by which something that is being done has been delayed □ *There must not be any slippage on this project.* (**atraso**)

slipped disc /slɪpt ˈdɪsk/ NOUN [*plural* **slipped discs**] a painful injury in which one of the layers of body tissue between the bones in your back moves out of place (**deslocamento de disco**)

slipper /ˈslɪpə(r)/ NOUN [*plural* **slippers**] a soft shoe for wearing indoors (**chinelo**)

slippery /ˈslɪpəri/ ADJECTIVE a slippery surface is smooth, wet or shiny and not easy to walk on or hold □ *The floor was slippery with grease.* (**escorregadio**)

slip road /ˈslɪp ˌrəʊd/ NOUN [*plural* **slip roads**] a narrow road used by traffic going on to or leaving a motorway (**via de acesso**)

slipshod /ˈslɪpʃɒd/ ADJECTIVE careless and untidy □ *He's begun to demonstrate a slipshod approach to his work.* (**desmazelado**)

slipstream /ˈslɪpstriːm/ NOUN [*plural* **slipstreams**] the flow of air behind someone or something that is moving very fast (**rajada de vento provocada por algo em movimento**)

slip-up /ˈslɪpʌp/ NOUN [*plural* **slip-ups**] a small mistake □ *I made an embarrassing slip-up when I addressed him as 'Madam Chairman'.* (**errar**)

slit /slɪt/ ▶ NOUN [*plural* **slits**] a long cut or narrow opening □ *Her tight black skirt had a slit up the side.* (**cortar**)

▶ VERB [**slits, slitting, slit**] to make a long narrow cut in something □ *He quickly slit the letter open.* (**corte**)

slither /ˈslɪðə(r)/ VERB [**slithers, slithering, slithered**] to slide over a surface □ *The ice cubes slithered off the table.* □ *She saw a snake slithering through the grass.* (**escorregar, deslizar**)
• **slithery** /ˈslɪðəri/ ADJECTIVE unpleasantly smooth and difficult to hold (**deslizante, ondulante**)

sliver /ˈslɪvə(r)/ NOUN [*plural* **slivers**] a long thin piece cut or broken from something □ *slivers of glass* □ *The cake was topped with slivers of chocolate.* (**lasca**)

slob /slɒb/ NOUN [*plural* **slobs**] an informal word meaning a lazy, untidy person (**relaxado, descuidado**)

slobber /ˈslɒbə(r)/ VERB [**slobbers, slobbering, slobbered**] to have saliva (= liquid from the mouth) coming out of your mouth □ *a slobbering bulldog* (**babão, com saliva escorrendo**)
• **slobbery** /ˈslɒbəri/ ADJECTIVE slobbery kisses or lips are unpleasantly wet (**babado, cheio de saliva**)

slog /slɒg/ ▶ VERB [**slogs, slogging, slogged**]
1 to work very hard for a long time ☐ *Tom spent hours slogging away at his revision.* (**trabalhar duramente**)
2 to walk or travel somewhere using a lot of effort ☐ *We slogged up the mountain.* (**andar penosamente**)
▶ NOUN, NO PLURAL
1 a period of hard or boring work ☐ *It was such a slog moving that piano.* (**trabalho duro**)
2 a difficult walk or journey ☐ *The climb up the hill was quite a slog.* (**caminhada ou jornada árdua**)

slogan /ˈsləʊgən/ NOUN [*plural* **slogans**] a phrase that is easy to remember and is used to advertise something or to emphasize the opinions of political parties, etc. ☐ *advertising slogans* (**slogan**)

slop /slɒp/ VERB [**slops, slopping, slopped**] liquid slops when it moves around or comes out of its container ☐ *You've managed to slop soup down your front.* (**transbordar**)

slope /sləʊp/ ▶ VERB [**slopes, sloping, sloped**] to have one end higher than the other ☐ *The garden slopes upwards.* ☐ *a sloping roof* (**inclinar(-se)**)
▶ NOUN [*plural* **slopes**]
1 a surface that slopes ☐ *a steep slope* ☐ *a ski slope* (**declive**)
2 the amount that a surface slopes ☐ *a slope of 30 degrees* (**declive**)
3 the side of a hill or mountain ☐ *Sheep graze on the lower slopes of the mountains.* (**declive**)

sloppy /ˈslɒpi/ ADJECTIVE [**sloppier, sloppiest**]
1 careless or untidy ☐ *a sloppy piece of work* (**desleixado**)
2 showing emotions in a way that seems silly and embarrassing ☐ *a sloppy love story* (**piegas**)
3 a sloppy substance has too much liquid in it (**aguado**)
4 sloppy clothes are loose and do not have a clear shape ☐ *a sloppy jumper* (**folgado, sem forma**)

slosh /slɒʃ/ VERB [**sloshes, sloshing, sloshed**]
1 if you slosh a liquid, you throw it somewhere in a careless way ☐ *He sloshed cold water on his face.* (**espirrar**)
2 liquid sloshes when it moves around noisily in a container or over the edge of something ☐ *Water sloshed over the side of the boat.* (**bater com vigor em algo líquido**)

slot /slɒt/ ▶ NOUN [*plural* **slots**]
1 a small narrow opening, especially one that you put coins or bank cards into ☐ *There's a pound coin stuck in the slot.* (**fenda**)
2 a period of time in an event or an activity when something particular is planned to happen ☐ *The new chat show will fill the early evening slot.* (**faixa de horário**)
▶ VERB [**slots, slotting, slotted**] to go into a slot or to put something into a slot ☐ *Slot the metal token in here.* (**abertura**)
♦ PHRASAL VERBS **slot something in** to find a time to do something or be with someone ☐ *We can slot in an extra lesson after lunch.* (**encaixar (horário)**)
slot together to fit together easily ☐ *The pieces of the storage unit just slot together.* (**encaixar**)

sloth /sləʊθ/ NOUN [*plural* **sloths**]
1 a South American animal that lives mostly in trees and moves very slowly (**bicho-preguiça**)
2 a literary word meaning being lazy (**preguiça**)
• **slothful** /ˈsləʊθfʊl/ ADJECTIVE a literary word meaning lazy (**preguiçoso**)

slot machine /ˈslɒt məˌʃiːn/ NOUN [*plural* **slot machines**] a machine that you operate by putting in coins to try to win more money (**caça-níqueis**)

slouch /slaʊtʃ/ VERB [**slouches, slouching, slouched**] to move, stand or sit with your back curved and your head hanging forward (**andar encurvado, ter postura encurvada**)

slovenly /ˈslʌvənli/ ADJECTIVE careless or untidy and dirty ☐ *The landlady was a plump, slovenly woman.* (**desleixado**)

slow /sləʊ/ ▶ ADJECTIVE [**slower, slowest**]
1 not fast or not moving or acting quickly ☐ *a slow march* ☐ *a slow reader* ☐ *We made slow progress through the crowds.* (**lento, vagaroso**)
2 not doing something immediately ☐ + **to do something** *Social services had been slow to take any action to protect the child.* ☐ + **in** *He was very slow in coming to the phone.* (**lento, vagaroso**)
3 not clever ☐ *She was put in a group with the slower students.* (**atrasado**)
4 not busy or not exciting ☐ *Business was slow in the restaurant last night.* (**fraco (negócio, movimento)**)
5 not exciting ☐ *I found the film very slow.* (**devagar, sem graça**)
6 if a clock or watch is slow, it shows a time earlier than the correct time ☐ *I think your clock's five minutes slow.* (**atrasado**)
▶ VERB [**slows, slowing, slowed**]
1 to become slower or to make something slower ☐ *The train slowed as we approached Birmingham.* ☐ *Increased hygiene has slowed the spread of the disease.* (**reduzir a velocidade**)
2 to become lower in amount or level, or to make something do this ☐ *Profit growth has slowed in recent months.* (**diminuir**)
♦ PHRASAL VERBS **slow down** to become less active ☐ *I've had to slow down a bit since my illness.* (**pegar leve, diminuir o ritmo**) **slow (something) down** to become slower or to make something slower ☐ *You should slow down as you approach the bend.* (**tornar mais lento**)

slowcoach /ˈsləʊkəʊtʃ/ NOUN [*plural* **slowcoaches**] an informal word for someone who takes a long time to do something (**lento, tartaruga**)

slowdown /ˈsləʊdaʊn/ NOUN [*plural* **slowdowns**] when an economy becomes less successful (**diminuição do ritmo**) 🔲 *Experts predict an economic slowdown.* (**desaquecimento econômico**)

slowly /ˈsləʊli/ ADVERB

1 at a slow speed □ *He drove slowly past the house.* □ *She speaks very slowly.* (**lentamente**)
2 gradually □ *She is slowly recovering from her ordeal.* (**gradualmente**)

slow motion /ˌsləʊ ˈməʊʃən/ NOUN, NO PLURAL

a way of filming actions to make them seem much slower than in real life □ *The bomb blast seemed to happen in slow motion.* (**câmera lenta**)

• **slow-motion** ADJECTIVE shown in slow motion □ *a slow-motion replay* (**em câmera lenta**)

sludge /slʌdʒ/ NOUN, NO PLURAL thick soft mud or any similar substance □ *Sludge can build up in your radiators over time.* (**lodo**)

slug¹ /slʌg/ NOUN [plural slugs] a creature with a long soft body and no legs, like a snail with no shell □ *Slugs had attacked our bean plants.* (**lesma**)

slug² /slʌg/ VERB [slugs, slugging, slugged] to hit someone or something very hard (**bater, atingir**)

sluggish /ˈslʌgɪʃ/ ADJECTIVE not reacting or moving as quickly as usual □ *The heat made me feel tired and sluggish.* □ *There was only a sluggish flow of water from the tap.* (**lerdo**)

• **sluggishly** /ˈslʌgɪʃli/ ADVERB in a sluggish way □ *The engine started rather sluggishly.* (**lerdamente**)

slum /slʌm/ ▶ NOUN [plural slums] a part of a town or city where the buildings are dirty and in bad condition □ *She sang about her childhood in the slums of Naples.* (**bairro pobre, periferia**)

▶ VERB [slums, slumming, slummed] **slum it** an informal phrase meaning to live without the good conditions you are used to (**viver em condições inferiores às quais se está acostumado, de modo mais simples**)

slumber /ˈslʌmbə(r)/ ▶ VERB [slumbers, slumbering, slumbered] a literary word meaning to sleep (**dormir**)

▶ NOUN [plural slumbers] a literary word meaning sleep (**sono**)

slump /slʌmp/ ▶ VERB [slumps, slumping, slumped]

1 to quickly go down to a much lower level □ *Business has slumped in the last few months.* (**baixar repentinamente**)
2 to fall or sit down suddenly because you feel weak, ill or tired □ *He was slumped over his desk, fast asleep.* □ *She suddenly slumped back in her chair.* (**despencar**)

▶ NOUN [plural slumps]
1 a big fall in sales, values, etc. □ *a slump in property prices* (**baixa repentina**)
2 a period when businesses are not selling many goods and a lot of people do not have jobs □ *The economy is facing a slump.* (**depressão, recessão**)

slung /slʌŋ/ PAST TENSE AND PAST PARTICIPLE OF sling (ver sling)

slunk /slʌŋk/ PAST TENSE AND PAST PARTICIPLE OF slink (ver slink)

slur /slɜː(r)/ ▶ VERB [slurs, slurring, slurred] to pronounce words in way that is not clear, usually because you are drunk or ill □ *The poor man was staggering and slurring his speech.* (**balbuciar**)

▶ NOUN [plural slurs] an insult or remark that is likely to damage someone's reputation □ *racial slurs* (**insulto**)

slurp /slɜːp/ VERB [slurps, slurping, slurped] to drink very noisily □ *The little boy was slurping his milkshake through a straw.* (**beber fazendo barulho**)

slush /slʌʃ/ NOUN, NO PLURAL snow on the ground that is dirty and partly melted □ *By evening the thick snow had turned to slush.* (**neve semiderretida**)

• **slushy** /ˈslʌʃi/ ADJECTIVE [slushier, slushiest]
1 soft and almost liquid, like partly melted snow □ *the slushy pavement* (**cheio de neve semiderretida**)
2 romantic in a silly way □ *a slushy novel* (**pieguice**)

sly /slaɪ/ ▶ ADJECTIVE [slyer or slier, slyest or sliest]

1 clever and good at tricking others □ *a sly and manipulative politician* (**malicioso, dissimulado**)
2 showing that you know something that other people do not know □ *a sly smile* (**malicioso**)

▶ NOUN, NO PLURAL **on the sly** if you do something on the sly you do it in secret because you should not be doing it □ *She was still texting her old boyfriend on the sly.* (**às escondidas**)

• **slyly** /ˈslaɪli/ ADJECTIVE in a sly way (**maldosamente**)

• **slyness** /ˈslaɪnɪs/ NOUN, NO PLURAL being sly (**maldade, malícia**)

smack /smæk/ ▶ VERB [smacks, smacking, smacked]

1 to hit someone with your hand flat □ *It is wrong to smack children.* (**dar uma palmada**)
2 smack your lips to show that you are enjoying some food by making a loud noise with your lips or tongue (**estalar a boca para demonstrar apreciação por um prato**)
3 to hit something hard with a loud noise □ *The car smacked into a wall.* (**atingir com estrondo**)

♦ PHRASAL VERB **smack of something** to seem to have an unpleasant quality □ *His reaction smacks of hypocrisy.* (**cheirar a**)

▶ NOUN [plural smacks] a hit with a flat hand, or the sound made by this □ *I'll give you a smack if you aren't careful!* (**palmada**)

▶ ADVERB exactly in a particular place □ *The ball landed smack in the middle of the pond.* (**em cheio**)

small /smɔːl/ ADJECTIVE [smaller, smallest]

1 little □ *a small country* (**pequeno**) 🔁 *This coat is too small for you now.* (**muito pequeno**) □ *We're only interviewing a small number of applicants.*
2 very young □ *a playground for small children* □ *I used to love these books when I was small.* (**pequeno**)
3 not important or serious □ *a small problem* (**pequeno**)

4 feel/look small to feel or look silly and not important ☐ *He always made me feel small.* (sentir-se insignificante)

small ad /'smɔːl 'æd/ NOUN [plural **small ads**] a short advertisement about something for sale, in a newspaper (pequeno anúncio)

small change /'smɔːl 'tʃeɪndʒ/ NOUN, NO PLURAL coins that are of low value ☐ *Can you lend me 10 pence? I don't have any small change.* (trocado)

smallholder /'smɔːlˌhəʊldə(r)/ NOUN [plural **smallholders**] someone who has an area of land that they use as a very small farm (chacareiro)

• **smallholding** /'smɔːlˌhəʊldɪŋ/ NOUN [plural **smallholdings**] an area of land that is used as a very small farm (chácara)

small intestine /'smɔːl ɪnˈtestɪn/ NOUN [plural **small intestines**] the upper part of the body's system for digesting food where food is digested and taken into the body. A biology word. (intestino delgado)

small-minded /'smɔːlˈmaɪndɪd/ ADJECTIVE having a limited view of the world and not wanting to learn about different ideas or ways of doing things (mente fechada)

smallness /'smɔːlnɪs/ NOUN, NO PLURAL how small something is when compared to other things (pequenez, insignificância)

smallpox /'smɔːlpɒks/ NOUN, NO PLURAL a serious infectious disease which causes fever and marks on the skin ☐ *smallpox vaccination* (varíola)

small print /'smɔːl 'prɪnt/ NOUN, NO PLURAL the details of a contract (= written legal agreement) that are often printed in very small letters (letras miúdas de um contrato) ☐ *You should always read the small print before signing anything.* (ler as entrelinhas)

small-scale /'smɔːlˈskeɪl/ ADJECTIVE not very large or important ☐ *a small-scale operation* (de pouca importância, em escala reduzida)

small talk /'smɔːl 'tɔːk/ NOUN, NO PLURAL polite conversation about things that are not important, such as the weather (falar sobre amenidades) ☐ *Danny's useless at making small talk.* (jogar conversa fora)

smarmy /'smɑːmɪ/ ADJECTIVE [**smarmier, smarmiest**] too pleasant and polite, in a way that is false ☐ *The head waiter has a very smarmy manner.* (bajulador)

smart /smɑːt/ ▶ ADJECTIVE [**smarter, smartest**]
1 clean and tidy ☐ *a pair of smart black shoes* ☐ *She looked really smart in her uniform.* (elegante)
2 clever ☐ *a smart answer* ☐ *He's one of the smartest guys I know.* (esperto)
3 fashionable and expensive ☐ *It's the smartest club in town.* ☐ *a smart flat on the river* (chique, elegante)
4 fast or strong ☐ *We walked at a smart pace.* (vigoroso)

5 smart weapons, machines, etc. use computers to make them work ☐ *smart bombs* (inteligente)
▶ VERB [**smarts, smarting, smarted**] to feel a sharp, burning pain ☐ *The thick smoke made my eyes smart.* (arder)

smart card /'smɑːt 'kɑːd/ NOUN [plural **smart cards**] a small plastic card which stores information about a person ☐ *Swipe your smart card to get into the building.* (cartão de crédito inteligente)

smarten /'smɑːtən/
♦ PHRASAL VERBS [**smartens, smartening, smartened**] **smarten something up** to make something look better, for example by cleaning it or painting it ☐ *A coat of paint would smarten this room up.* (embelezar, enfeitar) **smarten (someone) up** to make someone look cleaner and tidier ☐ *I'd like to smarten up before we go out.* (tornar-se elegante)

smartly /'smɑːtlɪ/ ADVERB
1 in a way that is tidy and fashionable ☐ *smartly dressed businessmen* (de modo elegante, moderno)
2 quickly or strongly ☐ *She tapped him smartly on the back.* ☐ *He marched smartly out of the room.* (vigorosamente)

smartness /'smɑːtnɪs/ NOUN, NO PLURAL being smart (elegância)

smash /smæʃ/ ▶ VERB [**smashes, smashing, smashed**]
1 to break something into pieces, for example by dropping it ☐ *She smashed one of our best glasses.* ☐ *Mum, I've smashed a window.* ☐ *Police had to smash the door down.* (estraçalhar)
2 to break into pieces ☐ *The vase fell off the table and smashed.* (estraçalhar)
3 to hit something, or hit against it, with great force ☐ *The car smashed into a traffic island and overturned.* (esmagar, colidir)
4 to completely destroy a group or an organization ☐ *Police have smashed a drugs ring in South London.* (arrasar, detonar)
5 smash a record to do something better, faster, etc. than anyone has ever done it before (quebrar um recorde)
▶ NOUN [plural **smashes**]
1 the sound of something breaking (ruído de algo quebrando)
2 a road accident in which two vehicles hit each other and are damaged ☐ *There's been a bad smash on the M62.* (colisão, ruína)

smash hit /'smæʃ 'hɪt/ NOUN [plural **smash hits**] a show, play, film, etc. that is very successful ☐ *This new musical is sure to be a smash hit.* (sucesso esmagador)

smashing /'smæʃɪŋ/ ADJECTIVE an old-fashioned word that means very good or very enjoyable ☐ *That was a smashing meal.* (magnífico, esmagado)

smattering

smattering /ˈsmætərɪŋ/ NOUN **a smattering** a small amount of something ☐ *George speaks German, Italian, and a smattering of French.* (**alguma noção de, conhecimento superficial**)

smear /smɪə(r)/ ▶ VERB [**smears, smearing, smeared**]

1 to spread a soft or dirty substance on a surface ☐ *Her face was smeared with mascara.* (**lambuzar**)
2 if a liquid such as paint or ink smears, it spreads in a way that is not intended (**borrar, manchar**)
3 to say things about someone that are unpleasant and not true (**difamar**)

▶ NOUN [*plural* **smears**]

1 a dirty mark made by spreading something sticky on something ☐ *smears of paint* (**mancha**)
2 something unpleasant and not true that is said about someone ☐ *a smear campaign* (**difamação**)

smear test /ˈsmɪə 'test/ NOUN [*plural* **smear tests**] a medical test for a woman, in which cells are taken from the entrance of the womb (= part where a baby grows) to check for cancer (**exame de Papanicolau**)

smell /smel/ ▶ VERB [**smells, smelling, smelled** or **smelt**]

1 to notice or recognize something by using your nose ☐ *Can you smell burning?* ☐ *I could smell his sweaty trainers from across the room.* (**cheirar**)
2 to have a particular smell ☐ *Those scones smell delicious.* ☐ *+ of The sheets smelled of lavender.* ☐ *This chicken smells funny.* (**cheirar**)
3 to have a bad smell ☐ *His breath smells.* (**cheirar**)

▶ NOUN [*plural* **smells**] (**cheiro**)

1 *no plural* the ability to smell things (**olfato**) 🔁 *The virus made him lose his* sense of smell. (**sentido do olfato**)
2 the quality you notice by smelling ☐ *a strong smell of garlic* ☐ *These lilies have a lovely smell.*
3 the act of smelling something ☐ *Have a smell of this soup.* (**sinta o cheiro**)

• **smelly** /ˈsmelɪ/ ADJECTIVE [**smellier, smelliest**] having a strong or bad smell ☐ *smelly feet* (**malcheiroso**)

smelt¹ /smelt/ VERB [**smelts, smelting, smelted**] to melt rock to remove the metal it contains (**fundir**)

smelt² /smelt/ PAST TENSE AND PAST PARTICIPLE OF **smell** (*ver* **smell**)

smile /smaɪl/ ▶ VERB [**smiles, smiling, smiled**] to show you are happy or think something is funny by making the corners of your mouth go up ☐ *The little girl smiled happily up at him.* (**sorrir**)

➤ Remember that you **smile at** someone. You do not 'smile to' someone:
✓ *She turned and smiled at me.*
✗ *She turned and smiled to me.*

751

smoke

▶ NOUN [*plural* **smiles**] an expression in which the corners of your mouth go up to show you are happy ☐ *a broad smile* ☐ *'Can I help you?' she said with a smile.* (**sorriso**)

smiley /ˈsmaɪlɪ/ NOUN [*plural* **smileys**] an emoticon (= image of a face made with keyboard symbols), used in e-mails to express emotions (**smiley, emoticon: ícone que representa emoções no texto digital**)

smirk /smɜːk/ ▶ VERB [**smirks, smirking, smirked**] to smile in an unpleasant or unkind way ☐ *He sat smirking at her in his new sports car.* (**sorrir tolamente**)

▶ NOUN [*plural* **smirks**] an unpleasant or unkind smile (**sorriso tolo**)

smithereens /ˌsmɪðəˈriːnz/ PLURAL NOUN **smash/ blow something to smithereens** to break something into very small pieces in a violent way ☐ *The building was blown to smithereens by a bomb.* (**despedaçar algo**)

smitten /ˈsmɪtən/ ADJECTIVE very much in love with someone (**apaixonado**)

smock /smɒk/ NOUN [*plural* **smocks**] a loose piece of clothing worn over other clothes to protect them ☐ *an artist's smock* (**bata**)

smog /smɒg/ NOUN, NO PLURAL a mixture of smoke and fog which hangs over some cities and towns (**névoa pesada**)

smoke /sməʊk/ ▶ NOUN, NO PLURAL

1 the grey or black gas that something produces when it is burning ☐ *I can smell smoke.* ☐ *cigarette smoke* (**fumaça**) 🔁 *Firefighters battled* thick smoke *to rescue the children.* (**fumaça espessa**) 🔁 *A* cloud of smoke *rose into the air.* (**nuvem de fumaça**)
2 the act of smoking a cigarette ☐ *My grandmother enjoys a smoke.* (**fumar cigarro**)

▶ VERB [**smokes, smoking, smoked**]

1 someone who smokes sucks smoke from cigarettes ☐ *My parents don't smoke.* ☐ *Dan was smoking a cigarette.* (**fumar**)
2 to produce smoke ☐ *The chimney was smoking.* (**fumegar**)

• **smoked** /sməʊkt/ ADJECTIVE smoked foods have been given a special flavour by being hung in smoke ☐ *smoked salmon* (**defumado**)

• **smoker** /ˈsməʊkə(r)/ NOUN [*plural* **smokers**] someone who smokes cigarettes (**fumante, tabagista**) 🔁 *He used to be a* heavy smoker (= someone who smokes a lot of cigarettes). (**fumante compulsivo**)

• **smoking** /ˈsməʊkɪŋ/ NOUN, NO PLURAL the habit of smoking cigarettes (**ato de fumar**) 🔁 *My Dad wants to* stop smoking. (**parar de fumar**) ☐ *In England smoking is banned in public buildings.*

• **smoky** /ˈsməʊkɪ/ ADJECTIVE [**smokier, smokiest**]
1 filled with smoke ☐ *a smoky bar* (**enfumaçado**)
2 like smoke ☐ *a smoky grey colour* (**fumacento**)

smolder

smolder /ˈsmoʊldə(r)/ VERB [smolders, smoldering, smoldered] the US spelling of **smoulder** (ver smoulder)

smooth /smuːð/ ▶ ADJECTIVE [smoother, smoothest]

1 having an even surface ☐ *She ran her fingers along the smooth surface of the wood.* ☐ *Babies have beautifully smooth, soft skin.* (**liso**)
2 a smooth substance has no lumps ☐ *Stir the ingredients until a smooth paste is formed.* (**homogêneo**)
3 happening without any problems (**suave**) ☐ *Young people want a smooth transition from school to work.* (**transição suave**) ☐ *His recovery from the operation was relatively smooth.*
4 having no sudden movements ☐ *Larger boats provide a smoother ride than rowing boats.* ☐ *In one smooth movement, he climbed onto the horse.* (**suave**)
5 too polite and confident in a way that makes people not trust you ☐ *He is a very smooth talker.* (**pessoa que causa desconfiança por ser excessivamente segura e gentil**)

▶ VERB [smooths, smoothing, smoothed]

1 to move your hand across something in order to make it flat or smooth ☐ *She smoothed the bed covers and tidied her bedroom.* (**alisar**)
2 to make something happen more easily ☐ *Schools are working to smooth the transition from primary school to high school.* (**facilitar, suavizar**)

♦ PHRASAL VERB **smooth something over** to end a disagreement or problem, especially by talking to someone ☐ *She invited Antonio to dinner to try and smooth things over.* (**passar suavemente**)

• **smoothie** /ˈsmuːði/ NOUN [plural **smoothies**] a thick drink made by crushing fruit (**smoothie, bebida natural à base de frutas**)

• **smoothly** /ˈsmuːðli/ ADVERB
1 without any problems (**tranquilamente**) ☐ *The event went very smoothly.* (**ocorreu com tranquilidade**) ☐ *The organization was running very smoothly.*
2 without any sudden movements ☐ *He pulled the knife smoothly out of its case.* (**suavemente**)
3 in a way that is too polite and confident ☐ *'Not at all, sir,' he replied smoothly.* (**calmamente**)

smother /ˈsmʌðə(r)/ VERB [smothers, smothering, smothered]

1 to cover something with a substance ☐ *The little boy's hands were smothered in chocolate.* ☐ *She smothered him with kisses.* (**cobrir, sufocar**)
2 to kill someone by putting something over their nose and mouth (**sufocar**)
3 to give someone too much love and attention ☐ *I felt she was smothering me.* (**sufocar emocionalmente**)
4 to stop something from happening ☐ *Maya smothered the urge to laugh.* (**segurar, controlar**)
5 to stop a fire from burning by covering it (**abafar**)

snack bar

smoulder /ˈsmoʊldə(r)/ VERB [smoulders, smouldering, smouldered]

1 to burn slowly, without a flame (**arder sem chama**)
2 to feel a strong emotion but not express it ☐ *He was smouldering with rage.* (**emoção latente**)

SMS /ˌes em ˈes/ ABBREVIATION short message service; a system for sending text messages between mobile phones (**abrev. Short Message Service, mensagem de texto de celular**)

smudge /smʌdʒ/ ▶ NOUN [plural **smudges**] a dirty mark where someone has touched something and it has spread (**borrão**)
▶ VERB [smudges, smudging, smudged] to spoil the appearance of something by touching it and making it spread ☐ *She had smudged her lipstick.* (**manchar, borrar**)

smug /smʌɡ/ ADJECTIVE [smugger, smuggest] too pleased with your abilities and achievements ☐ *a smug smile* ☐ *Jack looked very smug.* (**convencido**)

smuggle /ˈsmʌɡəl/ VERB [smuggles, smuggling, smuggled]

1 to bring something into a country illegally ☐ *The weapons had been smuggled into the country.* (**contrabandear**)
2 to take something somewhere secretly ☐ *He smuggled the puppy into his room.* (**fazer entrar/ sair clandestinamente**)

• **smuggler** /ˈsmʌɡlə(r)/ NOUN [plural **smugglers**] someone who brings something into a country illegally (**contrabandista**)

• **smuggling** /ˈsmʌɡlɪŋ/ NOUN, NO PLURAL the activity of bringing something into a country illegally ☐ *drug smuggling* ☐ *a smuggling operation* (**contrabando**)

smugly /ˈsmʌɡli/ ADVERB in a way that shows you are too pleased with your own abilities and achievements ☐ *He smiled smugly when he heard he had won.* (**convencidamente**)

• **smugness** /ˈsmʌɡnɪs/ NOUN, NO PLURAL when you are too pleased with your own abilities and achievements (**convencimento**)

smutty /ˈsmʌti/ ADJECTIVE [smuttier, smuttiest] slightly rude ☐ *He was telling smutty jokes.* (**obsceno**)

snack /snæk/ ▶ NOUN [plural **snacks**] a small meal, or a small amount of food that you eat between meals (**refeição ligeira**) ☐ *She had a snack during the morning.* (**fez uma refeição ligeira**) ☐ *Some people eat too many snack foods such as crisps and biscuits.* (**petiscos**)
▶ VERB [snacks, snacking, snacked] to eat food between your meals ☐ *Eating a big breakfast will help you not to snack.* ☐ *+ on You should try snacking on healthy food such as fruit and nuts.* (**lanchar, beliscar**)

snack bar /ˈsnæk bɑː(r)/ NOUN [plural **snack bars**] a place where you can buy snacks (**lanchonete**)

snag /snæg/ ▶ NOUN [*plural* **snags**] an informal word meaning a small problem □ *The process hit a snag.* (empecilho)
▶ VERB [**snags, snagging, snagged**] to become stuck on something sharp, or to damage something by getting it stuck on something sharp □ *Ellie had snagged her tights on a thorn.* (ficar preso/rasgar/danificar alguma coisa em algo pontiagudo)

snail /sneɪl/ NOUN [*plural* **snails**]
1 a small creature with a soft body and a shell on its back (caracol, lesma)
2 at a snail's pace very slowly □ *He was driving at a snail's pace.* (a passo de tartaruga, muito lento)

snail mail NOUN, NO PLURAL a humorous phrase for letters sent by post instead of by computer (correio tradicional)

snake /sneɪk/ ▶ NOUN [*plural* **snakes**] a long thin animal with no legs, which slides along the ground □ *There are several poisonous snakes in the region.* (cobra, serpente)
▶ VERB [**snakes, snaking, snaked**] to move in a thin, curved line □ *The queue snaked round the building.* (serpentear)

snap /snæp/ ▶ VERB [**snaps, snapping, snapped**]
1 to break with a sudden, sharp noise or to break something with a sudden, sharp noise □ *The twig snapped.* □ *He snapped off a piece of his biscuit.* (quebrar com estalo)
2 to move into a particular position with a sudden, sharp noise, or to move something like this □ *She snapped the book shut.* □ *The two plastic parts snap together.* (mover(-se) de forma brusca)
3 snap your fingers to rub your finger and thumb together in a quick movement to make a sudden, sharp noise (estalar os dedos)
4 to speak to someone in an angry way □ *When I asked for a break, he snapped at me.* (falar bruscamente)
5 to suddenly be unable to control your emotions, especially your anger □ *I put up with his untidiness, but when he flooded the bathroom, I just snapped.* (explodir)
6 if an animal snaps, it tries to bite someone or something (tentar morder)
7 an informal word meaning to take a photograph □ *He was snapped leaving the restaurant.* (fotografar)
♦ PHRASAL VERBS **snap out of something** to stop feeling angry or upset □ *Come on, snap out of it – you're ruining everyone's day.* (parar de se aborrecer, sair dessa) **snap something up** to take or buy something quickly and enthusiastically □ *The new handbags were snapped up within days of getting into the shops.* (agarrar)
▶ NOUN [*plural* **snaps**]
1 a sudden, short sound □ *She shut her purse with a snap.* (estalo)
2 an informal word for a photograph (fotografia instantânea) 🔁 *holiday snaps* (fotos de férias)
▶ ADJECTIVE done or decided very quickly, without much thought (súbito) 🔁 *a snap decision/judgment*

• **snappy** /ˈsnæpi/ ADJECTIVE [**snappier, snappiest**]
1 clever and interesting, and usually not using many words □ *It's a very snappy title for a book.* (inteligente, sacado)
2 fashionable □ *He was wearing a very snappy suit.* (elegante)
3 if someone is snappy, they speak to people in a bad tempered way (mal-humorado)
4 quick (rápido) 🔁 *Get me a coffee, and make it snappy!* (vamos logo!)

snapshot /ˈsnæpʃɒt/ NOUN [*plural* **snapshots**]
1 a photograph that you take quickly □ *There was a snapshot of him on the beach.* (instantâneo)
2 something which gives you an idea of what something else is like □ *His songs were a snapshot of his life.* (panorama)

snare /sneə(r)/ ▶ NOUN [*plural* **snares**] a device for catching animals (armadilha)
▶ VERB [**snares, snaring, snared**]
1 to catch an animal using a snare (capturar com armadilha)
2 to get someone or something which is difficult to get □ *He snared a gold medal in the competition.* (conquistar)
3 to get someone in a situation or place they do not want to be in by using tricks □ *They use these special offers to snare customers.* (atrair de modo ardiloso)

snarl /snɑːl/ ▶ VERB [**snarls, snarling, snarled**]
1 to say something in an angry or threatening way □ *'I have no comment,' he snarled.* (rosnar)
2 if an animal snarls, it makes an angry sound and shows its teeth □ *The dog snarled every time he tried to move.* (rosnar)
3 to stop traffic from moving easily □ *The accident snarled traffic along the highway.* (bagunçar, causar confusão)
▶ NOUN [*plural* **snarls**] an angry sound or expression in which a person or animal shows their teeth (rosnado)

snatch /snætʃ/ ▶ VERB [**snatches, snatching, snatched**]
1 to take something from someone suddenly and roughly □ *She snatched the book out of my hand.* (agarrar, arrebatar)
2 to quickly get or do something when you do not have much time □ *I managed to snatch an hour's sleep before the party.* (agarrar a oportunidade)
▶ NOUN [*plural* **snatches**] **a snatch of something** a short part of something such as a piece of music or a conversation □ *I only heard snatches of their conversation.* (fragmento)

sneak /sniːk/ ▶ VERB [**sneaks, sneaking, sneaked**]
1 to go somewhere quietly and secretly □ *Maggie sneaked out of the house.* (esgueirar-se)

2 to take something somewhere secretly ☐ *He had sneaked his mobile phone into the exam room.* (**surrupiar**)

3 sneak a look/glance at something to look at something quickly and secretly ☐ *Archie sneaked a look at his watch.* (**olhar de relance/arriscar uma olhada**)

4 to tell someone in authority something bad that another person has done (**delatar**)

♦ PHRASAL VERB **sneak up on someone**

1 to walk towards someone without them seeing or hearing you ☐ *You scared me sneaking up on me like that.* (**andar furtivamente até alguém**)

2 if an event sneaks up on you, it happens before you are ready for it (**pegar de surpresa**)

▶ NOUN [*plural* **sneaks**] someone who tells people in authority when someone else has done something bad (**delator**)

• **sneaker** /ˈsniːkə(r)/ NOUN [*plural* **sneakers**] a US word for a type of sports shoe (**tênis**) ☐ *Farooq was wearing a pair of sneakers.* (**par de tênis**)

• **sneaking** /ˈsniːkɪŋ/ ADJECTIVE

1 have a sneaking feeling/suspicion to think that something is probably true ☐ *I had a sneaking suspicion that she was lying.* (**ter um pressentimento de algo**)

2 have a sneaking admiration/regard, etc. for someone/something to like someone or something secretly although you do not want to admit it (**ter uma admiração secreta por alguém/algo**)

• **sneaky** /ˈsniːki/ ADJECTIVE [**sneakier, sneakiest**] clever but slightly unfair or dishonest ☐ *It was a very sneaky way of making money.* (**vil**)

sneer /snɪə(r)/ ▶ VERB [**sneers, sneering, sneered**] to talk about someone or behave towards someone in an unpleasant way that shows that you do not admire them ☐ *John sneered at my attempt to write a story.* ☐ *'You're going to need lots of luck,' he sneered.* (**falar de/tratar alguém com descaso, zombar**)

▶ NOUN [*plural* **sneers**] a sneering expression or remark (**zombaria**)

sneeze /sniːz/ ▶ VERB [**sneezes, sneezing, sneezed**] to suddenly blow out air from your nose and mouth in a way that you cannot control ☐ *Dust always makes me sneeze.* (**espirrar**)

▶ NOUN [*plural* **sneezes**] the action and sound of sneezing (**espirro**)

snide /snaɪd/ ADJECTIVE criticizing someone in a way that is unkind and not direct (**sarcástico**) ☐ *He kept making snide remarks about my cooking.*

sniff /snɪf/ ▶ VERB [**sniffs, sniffing, sniffed**]

1 to breathe in air through your nose noisily ☐ *He was crying and sniffing.* (**fungar**)

2 to breathe in through your nose in order to smell something ☐ *Tess sniffed the air.* (**farejar**)

▶ NOUN [*plural* **sniffs**] a quick loud breath through your nose (**fungada**)

sniffle /ˈsnɪfəl/ ▶ VERB [**sniffles, sniffling, sniffled**] to sniff several times, especially because you have a cold or are crying (**fungar**)

▶ NOUN [*plural* **sniffles**] a slight cold (**resfriado**)

snigger /ˈsnɪɡə(r)/ ▶ VERB [**sniggers, sniggering, sniggered**] to laugh quietly in an unkind way (**rir em silêncio com escárnio ou desrespeito**)

▶ NOUN [*plural* **sniggers**] a quiet unkind laugh (**riso dissimulado**)

snip /snɪp/ ▶ VERB [**snips, snipping, snipped**] to cut something with a quick small cut using scissors ☐ *She snipped the ends off.* (**cortar com tesoura**)

▶ NOUN [*plural* **snips**] a quick small cut with scissors (**corte de tesoura**)

snipe /snaɪp/ ▶ VERB [**snipes, sniping, sniped**]

1 to criticize someone in an unpleasant way ☐ *She's always sniping at her colleagues.* (**criticar com malícia**)

2 to shoot at someone from a hidden place (**atirar de tocaia**)

▶ NOUN [*plural* **snipers**] someone who shoots at people from a hidden place (**franco-atirador**)

snippet /ˈsnɪpɪt/ NOUN [*plural* **snippets**] a small piece of something such as news, information or conversation ☐ *a snippet of information* (**trecho, fragmento**)

snivel /ˈsnɪvəl/ VERB [**snivels, snivelling, snivelled**] to cry and complain in a way that annoys other people (**choramingar**)

snob /snɒb/ NOUN [*plural* **snobs**] someone who thinks they are better than other people because they belong to a higher social class or because they know more ☐ *Don't be such a snob!* (**esnobe**)

• **snobbery** /ˈsnɒbəri/ NOUN, NO PLURAL the attitude or behaviour of a snob (**esnobismo**)

• **snobbish** /ˈsnɒbɪʃ/ also **snobby** /ˈsnɒbi/ ADJECTIVE behaving like a snob (**esnobe**)

snog /snɒɡ/ VERB [**snogs, snogging, snogged**] if people snog, they kiss each other for a long time. An informal word. (**beijação**)

snooker /ˈsnuːkə(r)/ NOUN, NO PLURAL a game played on a table, in which two players try to hit coloured balls into pockets ☐ *a snooker player* (**sinuca**)

snoop /snuːp/ VERB [**snoops, snooping, snooped**]

1 to look around a place secretly in order to find something ☐ *Jane was snooping around to try to find my diary.* (**bisbilhotar**)

2 to try to find out information about someone in a secret way ☐ *Mobile phone records allow officials to snoop on innocent citizens.* (**espionar**)

• **snooper** /ˈsnuːpə(r)/ NOUN [*plural* **snoopers**] someone who snoops (**bisbilhoteiro**)

snooty /ˈsnuːti/ ADJECTIVE [**snootier, snootiest**] behaving in a rude and unfriendly way because you think you are better than other people (**esnobe, arrogante**)

snooze /snuːz/ ▶ NOUN [*plural* **snoozes**] a short light sleep (**cochilo**) ☐ *Grandad was having a snooze in his chair.*

▶ VERB [**snoozes, snoozing, snoozed**] to sleep for a short time (**cochilar**)

snore /snɔː(r)/ ▶ VERB [snores, snoring, snored] to make a loud noise when you breathe while you are sleeping □ *My Dad snores and you can hear it all round the house.* (roncar)
▶ NOUN [plural snores] a loud noise that someone makes when they snore (ronco)

snorkel /ˈsnɔːkəl/ ▶ NOUN [plural snorkels] a tube that allows you to breathe when you are swimming under water (tubo snorkel)
▶ VERB [snorkels, snorkelling/US snorkeling, snorkelled/US snorkeled] to swim under water using a snorkel (snorkeling, mergulhar com snorkel)

snort /snɔːt/ ▶ VERB [snorts, snorting, snorted] to make a noise through your nose □ *The horses snorted, stamping their hooves.* □ *He snorted with laughter.* (bufar)
▶ NOUN [plural snorts] a loud noise made through your nose □ *a snort of laughter* (bufo)

snout /snaʊt/ NOUN [plural snouts] a pig's nose (focinho)

snow /snəʊ/ ▶ NOUN, NO PLURAL soft white pieces that fall from the sky when it is very cold (neve) ▣ *15 centimetres of snow fell in many areas.* ▣ *Heavy snow affected much of the country.* (muita neve) ▣ *The snow was starting to melt.*
▶ VERB [snows, snowing, snowed]
1 if it snows, snow falls from the sky □ *It's been snowing all night.* (nevar)
2 be snowed in to be unable to leave your house because there is so much snow (ficar preso em casa por causa da neve)
♦ IDIOM **be snowed under** to have too much work □ *I'm snowed under with all my college work.* (estar atolado de trabalho)

snowball /ˈsnəʊbɔːl/ ▶ NOUN [plural snowballs] a ball of snow that children make and throw at each other (bola de neve) ▣ *The children were throwing snowballs.* (atirando bolas de neve) ▣ *a snowball fight* (guerra de bola de neve)
▶ VERB [snowballs, snowballing, snowballed] if a situation or a problem snowballs, it grows or develops quickly □ *The strike snowballed and soon all the post offices were closed.* (virar uma bola de neve)

snowboarding /ˈsnəʊbɔːdɪŋ/ NOUN, NO PLURAL a sport in which you move over snow while standing on a board (snowboarding)

snowbound /ˈsnəʊbaʊnd/ ADJECTIVE unable to go anywhere because there is too much snow (ficar preso por causa da neve)

snow-capped /ˈsnəʊkæpt/ ADJECTIVE snow-capped mountains have snow on the top (coroado de neve)

snowdrift /ˈsnəʊdrɪft/ NOUN [plural snowdrifts] a pile of snow which the wind has blown (neve acumulada pelo vento)

snowdrop /ˈsnəʊdrɒp/ NOUN [plural snowdrops] a small white flower that grows at the end of winter (galanto)

snowfall /ˈsnəʊfɔːl/ NOUN [plural snowfalls] an occasion when snow falls from the sky, or the amount of snow which falls (nevada) ▣ *There was a heavy snowfall overnight.*

snowflake /ˈsnəʊfleɪk/ NOUN [plural snowflakes] one of the soft white pieces that fall from the sky when it is very cold (floco de neve)

snowman /ˈsnəʊmæn/ NOUN [plural snowmen] a model of a person which children make from snow (boneco de neve) ▣ *The children have built a snowman.* (fizeram um boneco de neve)

snowplough /ˈsnəʊplaʊ/ NOUN [plural snowploughs] a vehicle that moves snow off the roads (máquina de limpar neve)

snowstorm /ˈsnəʊstɔːm/ NOUN [plural snowstorms] a storm with a lot of snow (tempestade de neve)

snowy /ˈsnəʊi/ ADJECTIVE [snowier, snowiest] covered with snow, or involving snow □ *snowy hills* □ *snowy weather* (nevoado)

snub /snʌb/ ▶ VERB [snubs, snubbing, snubbed] to treat someone in a rude way, especially by ignoring them □ *I tried to speak to him but he just snubbed me and turned away.* (ofender)
▶ NOUN [plural snubs] an act of snubbing someone □ *The government saw the move as a deliberate snub.* (ofensa)
▶ ADJECTIVE a snub nose is small and turns up at the end (arrebitado)

snuff /snʌf/
♦ PHRASAL VERB [snuffs, snuffing, snuffed] **snuff something out**
1 an informal word meaning to end something in a sudden way □ *Injury snuffed out his hopes of winning the competition.* (extinguir)
2 to stop a candle burning (apagar)

snuffle /ˈsnʌfəl/ VERB [snuffles, snuffling, snuffled] to breathe noisily through your nose (fungar)

snug /snʌg/ ADJECTIVE [snugger, snuggest]
1 warm and comfortable □ *We were all quite snug in our sleeping bags.* (aconchegante)
2 snug clothes fit quite tightly □ *The jacket was a snug fit.* (justo)

snuggle /ˈsnʌgəl/ VERB [snuggles, snuggling, snuggled] to get into a warm and comfortable position □ *Sam snuggled up to his mother and soon fell asleep.* (aconchegar-se)

snugly /ˈsnʌgli/ ADVERB
1 in a warm and comfortable way □ *They were all snugly dressed in thick coats.* (aconchegantemente)
2 tightly □ *The jacket fits quite snugly.* (justamente)

so /səʊ/ ▶ ADVERB

1 used to emphasize the word that follows □ *I was so happy to see her.* □ *I've never seen so many children.* □ *Thank you so much for all your help.* (**tão, tanto, muito**)

2 used to avoid repeating something that has just been said □ *'Are you coming to the party?' 'I hope so.'* □ *'How do you know Emma's going camping?' 'Because she said so.'* (**isso**) 🔁 *When she won the competition, she was the first person over 40 to do so.* (**a fazer isso**)

3 used to say that something is true for something or someone else □ *She's tired and so am I.* □ *The accommodation was dreadful, and so was the food.* (**também**)

4 so far until now □ *I'm enjoying the job so far.* (**por enquanto, até agora**)

5 or so used to show that a number or amount is not exact □ *There were forty people or so at the party.* □ *I've been feeling ill for the last week or so.* (**mais ou menos**)

6 used to get someone's attention when you want to talk about something □ *So, who's ready for some food?* (**e assim por diante**)

7 So what? used to show that you do not think something is important □ *'Sam will be cross if we're late.' 'So what? He can't do anything to us.'* (**E daí?**)

8 and so on used to show that other similar things could be added to what you have just said □ *Make sure you have plenty of pens, pencils, paper and so on.* (**e assim por diante**)

9 so as to in order to □ *We got there early so as to get good seats.* (**a fim de**)

10 used to agree with something that you have just been shown or told □ *'Look, our tomato seeds are coming up.' 'Oh, so they are!'* (**de fato**)

11 used, often with a hand movement, to describe a size, position, etc. □ *I saw a little boy about so high.* □ *Stretch your leg out so.* (**assim (demonstrando com as mãos)**)

▶ CONJUNCTION

1 used to show that something was the reason for something else □ *He asked me to come, so I did.* □ *So they got married and lived happily ever after.* (**então**)

2 so (that) in order to make something happen □ *I've washed my jeans so that I can wear them tomorrow.* (**para que**)

soak /səʊk/ VERB [soaks, soaking, soaked]

1 to put something in liquid for a period of time □ *If you soak your blouse, the stain might come out.* (**pôr/ficar de molho**)

2 to make someone or something very wet □ *Torrential rain soaked the city.* (**encharcar**)

◆ PHRASAL VERB **soak something up**

1 if something soaks up a liquid, it takes it in □ *I used a towel to soak up the spilt milk.* (**absorver**)

2 to enjoy experiencing something (**aproveitar, curtir**) 🔁 *We just sat there, soaking up the atmosphere.* (**curtindo o clima**)

• **soaked** /səʊkt/ ADJECTIVE very wet (**encharcado**) 🔁 *It was raining and I was getting soaked.*

• **soaking** /ˈsəʊkɪŋ/ or **soaking wet** /ˈsəʊkɪŋ ˈwet/ ADJECTIVE very wet □ *Take your clothes off – they're soaking.* (**encharcado**)

so-and-so /ˈsəʊənˌsəʊ/ NOUN [plural so-and-sos]

1 used when referring to a person or thing without saying exactly which person or thing □ *She's always gossiping about so-and-so getting married or so-and so's new job.* (**fulano**)

2 used instead of calling someone a rude name □ *She can be a real so-and-so!* (**você-sabe-o-quê**)

soap /səʊp/ NOUN [plural soaps]

1 *no plural* a substance that you use for washing (**sabão**) 🔁 *a bar of soap* (**barra de sabão**) □ *He washed his face with soap and water.*

2 a television programme about the lives of a group of people which is broadcast regularly □ *Do you watch any of the soaps?* (**ensaboar**)

soap opera /ˈsəʊp ˌɒpərə/ NOUN [plural soap operas] a formal word for **soap** (= television programme) (**novela**)

soap powder /ˈsəʊp ˌpaʊdə(r)/ NOUN, NO PLURAL soap in the form of a powder, used for washing clothes (**sabão em pó**)

soapy /ˈsəʊpi/ ADJECTIVE [soapier, soapiest] covered in, full of, or similar to soap □ *soapy water* (**ensaboado**)

soar /sɔː(r)/ VERB [soars, soaring, soared]

1 to increase very quickly to a high level □ *The price of petrol has soared over the last ten years.* (**subir, elevar-se**)

2 to fly high in the air □ *An eagle soared high above their heads.* (**voar alto**)

• **soaring** /ˈsɔːrɪŋ/ ADJECTIVE increasing very quickly □ *soaring prices* (**elevar-se rapidamente**)

sob /sɒb/ ▶ VERB [sobs, sobbing, sobbed] to cry noisily □ *Lisa lay on her bed, sobbing.* (**soluçar**)
▶ NOUN [plural sobs] the sound of someone sobbing (**soluço**)

sober /ˈsəʊbə(r)/ ADJECTIVE

1 not drunk (**sóbrio**)

2 serious □ *a sober man* (**sóbrio**)

3 plain and not brightly coloured □ *sober colours* (**sóbrio**)

• **sobering** /ˈsəʊbərɪŋ/ ADJECTIVE making you become serious and think about a situation □ *The accident is a sobering reminder of how dangerous motorbikes can be.* (**grave, sério**)

sob story /ˈsɒb ˌstɔːri/ NOUN [plural sob stories] an informal word meaning a story that you tell someone to make them feel sorry for you □ *He gave me some sob story about his mother being ill.* (**drama**)

so-called /ˌsəʊˈkɔːld/ ADJECTIVE used for showing that you think a word used for describing someone or something is wrong □ *My so-called friend has stolen some money from me.* (**suposto, pretenso**)

soccer /'sɒkə(r)/ NOUN, NO PLURAL football □ *The children were playing soccer.* □ *a soccer ball* (**futebol**)

sociable /'səʊʃəbəl/ ADJECTIVE someone who is sociable enjoys being with other people □ *I'm quite a sociable person.* (**sociável**)

social /'səʊʃəl/ ADJECTIVE

1 to do with society □ *The programme is designed to tackle crime and other social problems.* □ *The school attracts students from all social backgrounds.* (**social**)

2 to do with meeting and being friendly with other people □ *I always feel nervous in social situations.* (**social**) □ *a social club* □ *He didn't have very good social skills.* (**habilidades sociais**)

• **socialism** /'səʊʃəlɪzəm/ NOUN, NO PLURAL the political belief that a country's main industries should be owned by the government, and that people should have equal opportunities (**socialismo**)

• **socialist** /'səʊʃəlɪst/ ▶ NOUN [plural **socialists**] someone who believes in socialism (**socialista**)
▶ ADJECTIVE to do with socialism □ *socialist principles*

• **socialize** or **socialise** /'səʊʃəlaɪz/ VERB [**socializes, socializing, socialized**] to spend time with other people for fun □ *He doesn't socialize much.* (**participar de atividades sociais**)

social life /'səʊʃəl 'laɪf/ NOUN [plural **social lives**] the time when you do things with friends □ *She has a busy social life.* (**vida social**)

socially /'səʊʃəli/ ADVERB

1 in a way that is to do with society □ *This is a socially conservative country.* (**socialmente**)

2 in a way that is connected with people meeting each other and being friendly □ *He never mixes socially with his colleagues.* (**socialmente**)

social networking /'səʊʃəl 'netwɜːkɪŋ/ NOUN, NO PLURAL using websites to meet people and talk to them (**rede social**)

social science /'səʊʃəl 'saɪəns/ NOUN [plural **social sciences**] the study of society and the way it is organized (**ciências sociais**)

social security /'səʊʃəl sɪ'kjʊərəti/ NOUN, NO PLURAL money that the government pays to people who are old, ill, or unemployed (**seguro social**)

social services /'səʊʃəl 'sɜːvɪsɪz/ PLURAL NOUN the government department that provides help to people who have problems with their lives (**assistência social**)

social work /'səʊʃəl 'wɜːk/ NOUN, NO PLURAL work that the government pays for to help people who are poor, ill, or have problems (**serviço social**)

• **social worker** /'səʊʃəl 'wɜːkə(r)/ NOUN [plural **social workers**] someone whose job is to help people who are poor, ill, or have problems (**assistente social**)

society /sə'saɪəti/ NOUN [plural **societies**]

1 all the people who live in a group or in a particular country or area □ *Racism still exists in British society.* □ *Australia is a more multicultural society.* (**sociedade**) □ *We have a responsibility to support the weaker members of society.* (**membros da sociedade**)

2 an organization for people with a particular interest □ *She joined the university's debating society.* (**sociedade**)

sociologist /ˌsəʊsi'ɒlədʒɪst/ NOUN [plural **sociologists**] someone who studies how human societies are organized and how people behave (**sociólogo**)

• **sociology** /ˌsəʊsi'ɒlədʒi/ NOUN, NO PLURAL the study of societies and the way people behave (**sociologia**)

sock /sɒk/ NOUN [plural **socks**] a covering for your foot that you wear inside your shoe (**meia**) □ *a pair of socks* (**par de meias**) □ *She was wearing black socks.* (**usando meias**)

♦ IDIOM **pull your socks up** to try to improve your behaviour or work □ *You'll have to pull your socks up if you want to pass the exam.* (**melhorar o rendimento**)

socket /'sɒkɪt/ NOUN [plural **sockets**]

1 the place on a wall where you connect electrical equipment to the electricity supply □ *an electric socket* (**tomada, embocadura**)

2 a hollow place that something fits into □ *She nearly pulled my arm out of its socket.* (**cavidade**)

soda /'səʊdə/ NOUN, NO PLURAL water with bubbles in it that you mix with other drinks (**soda**)

sodden /'sɒdən/ ADJECTIVE very wet □ *The ground's sodden after all that rain.* (**encharcado**)

sodium /'səʊdiəm/ NOUN, NO PLURAL a chemical element found in salt. A chemistry word. (**sódio**)

sofa /'səʊfə/ NOUN [plural **sofas**] a long, comfortable seat for more than one person □ *Dan and Clare were sitting on the sofa watching television.* (**sofá**)

sofa bed /'səʊfə 'bed/ NOUN [plural **sofa beds**] a sofa that you can pull out to make into a bed (**sofá-cama**)

soft /sɒft/ ADJECTIVE [**softer, softest**]

1 not hard or firm □ *a nice soft cushion* □ *soft ground* (**macio**)

2 smooth and pleasant to touch □ *She had soft silky hair.* □ *soft leather* (**macio**)

3 not severe enough with other people when they have done something wrong □ *He's far too soft with his children.* □ **+ on** *I think the government is too soft on crime.* (**suave**)

4 not loud □ *a soft voice* (**suave**)

5 not bright □ *Her bedroom is decorated in soft pastel colours.* □ *a soft light* (**suave, claro**)

6 an informal word meaning easy and not involving much work (leve) 🔲 *The subject isn't a soft option.* (opção leve)

♦ IDIOM **have a soft spot for someone** an informal phrase meaning to like someone 🔲 *I've always had a soft spot for Jenny.* (ter uma queda por alguém)

soft drink /ˌsɒft ˈdrɪŋk/ NOUN [plural **soft drinks**] a cold drink that does not contain alcohol (bebida não alcoólica)

soften /ˈsɒfən/ VERB [**softens, softening, softened**]
1 to become soft or to make something soft 🔲 *Soften the clay by working it with your hands.* 🔲 *The cream softens the skin.* (suavizar)
2 to make the effect of something unpleasant slightly easier (atenuar) 🔲 *They tried to soften the blow of job losses by helping staff to retrain.* (minimizar o choque)
3 to become more friendly, gentle or kind 🔲 *Her face softened and she smiled.* 🔲 *He appears to have softened his stance on the issue.* (demonstrar suavidade, suavizar)
4 to become or to make something become less strong, less bright, etc. 🔲 *Her voice softened as she looked at the baby.* (suavizar)

soft fruit /ˌsɒft ˈfruːt/ NOUN [plural **soft fruits** or **soft fruit**] a small fruit with no stone, for example a strawberry or a blackcurrant (fruta pequena sem caroço)

softly /ˈsɒftli/ ADVERB gently or quietly 🔲 *Snow was falling softly in the moonlight.* 🔲 *She stroked the cat softly.* (suavemente)

softness /ˈsɒftnɪs/ NOUN, NO PLURAL the quality of being soft, gentle or quiet 🔲 *the softness of the pillows* (suavidade)

soft-spoken /ˌsɒftˈspəʊkən/ ADJECTIVE having a quiet, gentle voice 🔲 *his shy, soft-spoken manner* (afável, brando)

soft toy /ˌsɒft ˈtɔɪ/ NOUN [plural **soft toys**] a toy made from cloth, usually in the form of an animal (brinquedo macio para bebê)

software /ˈsɒftweə(r)/ NOUN, NO PLURAL computer programs. A computing word. (software) 🔲 *We've installed new software.* (instalamos novo software) 🔲 *Users need to download a piece of software.* (parte do software)

soggy /ˈsɒɡi/ ADJECTIVE [**soggier, soggiest**] unpleasantly wet and soft 🔲 *soggy ground* 🔲 *I had to walk back in soggy shoes.* (encharcado)

soil /sɔɪl/ ▶ NOUN, NO PLURAL
1 the top layer of the ground, that you can grow plants in 🔲 *a soil sample* 🔲 *Rice and corn grow well in the rich soil.* 🔲 *He brushed the red, sandy soil off his trousers.* (terra)
2 used to talk about the land belonging to a particular country 🔲 *It was his first win on American soil.* (solo)

▶ VERB [**soils, soiling, soiled**] a formal word meaning to make something dirty 🔲 *soiled linen* (sujar)

solace /ˈsɒləs/ NOUN, NO PLURAL a formal word meaning comfort from very sad feelings or disappointment (consolo) 🔲 *She found some solace in writing poetry.* (encontrou conforto)

solar /ˈsəʊlə(r)/ ADJECTIVE
1 to do with the sun 🔲 *a solar eclipse* (solar)
2 to do with energy from the sun 🔲 *solar panels* (solar)

solar energy /ˌsəʊlə(r) ˈenədʒi/ or **solar power** /ˌsəʊlə(r) ˈpaʊə(r)/ NOUN, NO PLURAL electricity that is made using the sun's light and heat (energia solar)

solar system /ˈsəʊlə(r) sɪstəm/ NOUN [plural **solar systems**] the sun and the planets that move around it (sistema solar)

sold /səʊld/ PAST TENSE AND PAST PARTICIPLE OF **sell** (ver **sell**)

solder /ˈsəʊldə(r)/ ▶ VERB [**solders, soldering, soldered**] to join two pieces of metal with metal that has been melted (soldar)
▶ NOUN, NO PLURAL melted metal used to join pieces of metal together (solda)

soldier /ˈsəʊldʒə(r)/ NOUN [plural **soldiers**] someone who is in the army 🔲 *Two soldiers from the same regiment were captured.* (soldado)

sole[1] /səʊl/ ADJECTIVE
1 only 🔲 *Her sole ambition was to be famous.* 🔲 *A young boy was the sole survivor of the accident.* (único)
2 belonging to only one person 🔲 *He has sole ownership of the company.* (exclusivo)

sole[2] /səʊl/ NOUN [plural **soles**] the bottom part of your foot or of a shoe 🔲 *The sand was hot on the soles of her feet.* (sola do pé dela)

sole[3] /səʊl/ NOUN [plural **sole**] a flat fish that people can eat (linguado)

solely /ˈsəʊlli/ ADVERB only or alone 🔲 *You are solely responsible for your own actions.* 🔲 *The centre is run solely by volunteers.* (unicamente, único)

solemn /ˈsɒləm/ ADJECTIVE
1 serious and sometimes sad 🔲 *a solemn expression* 🔲 *a rather solemn little boy* (sério)
2 happening in a serious, formal way (solene) 🔲 *a solemn ceremony* (cerimônia solene) 🔲 *It was a solemn occasion.*
3 done or said in a serious and sincere way (sério) 🔲 *You've got to make me a solemn promise.* (promessa séria)

• **solemnity** /səˈlemnəti/ NOUN, NO PLURAL the quality of being solemn (solenidade)
• **solemnly** /ˈsɒləmli/ ADVERB in a solemn way 🔲 *Joe nodded solemnly.* (solenemente)

solicit /səˈlɪsɪt/ VERB [**solicits, soliciting, solicited**] a formal word meaning to ask someone for advice, help or money 🔲 *The government is trying to solicit aid from other countries.* (solicitar)

solicitor

solicitor /sə'lɪsɪtə(r)/ NOUN [plural **solicitors**] someone whose job is to give advice to people about the law and help them with legal work □ *a firm of solicitors* (**advogado**)

solicitous /sə'lɪsɪtəs/ ADJECTIVE a formal word meaning showing that you care a lot about someone's comfort and happiness □ *She talked about you constantly and seemed most solicitous for your welfare.* (**solícito**)

solid /'sɒlɪd/ ▶ ADJECTIVE

1 firm and with a fixed shape, not in the form of a liquid or a gas (**sólido**) 🔂 *They scrambled through the mud to more solid ground.* (**terra sólida**) □ *The river froze solid.*

2 not hollow or with no spaces inside □ *a solid chocolate egg* (**maciço, compacto**) 🔂 *They had to cut through solid rock.* (**pedra maciça**)

3 able to be trusted □ *He's a solid and dependable leader.* (**maciço**) 🔂 *We don't have any solid evidence.* (**prova concreta**)

4 strong and well made □ *a solid piece of furniture* (**sólido**)

5 solid gold, silver, etc. made only of gold, silver, etc. □ *a solid gold pendant* (**de ouro puro, prata pura etc.**)

6 with no pauses in between □ *I've been working for six solid hours.* (**consecutivo**)

7 good, but not excellent or special □ *I think it was a pretty solid performance.* (**razoavelmente bom**)

8 a solid shape has length, width, and height. A maths word. □ *A cube is a solid figure.* (**sólido**)

▶ NOUN [plural **solids**]

1 something that is not a liquid or a gas □ *This element changes from a solid to a gas when heated.* (**sólido**)

2 a shape that has length, width, and height. A maths word. (**sólido**)

3 solids food in the form of solid substances, not liquids □ *Do not eat any solids for 24 hours.* (**sólidos**)

solidarity /ˌsɒlɪ'dærəti/ NOUN, NO PLURAL loyal support and agreement between members of a group (**solidariedade**) 🔂 *The Scandinavian countries showed solidarity with Norway.* (**demonstrou solidariedade com**)

solid fuel /'sɒlɪd 'fjuːəl/ NOUN [plural **solid fuels**] a type of fuel that is made from something solid, such as coal or wood (**combustível sólido**)

solidify /sə'lɪdɪfaɪ/ VERB [**solidifies, solidifying, solidified**]

1 to become solid or to make something solid □ *Let the butter cool and solidify slightly.* (**solidificar(-se)**)

2 a formal word meaning to become stronger or clearer □ *He has solidified his position as the group's spokesman.* (**solidificar(-se)**)

solution

solidly /'sɒlɪdli/ ADVERB

1 strongly or firmly (**solidez**) 🔂 *a solidly built structure* (**estrutura solidificada**) □ *He struck it solidly with his fist.*

2 continuously □ *We've been working solidly since nine o'clock this morning.* □ *It had been raining solidly for a week.* (**continuamente**)

3 supporting or believing something strongly □ *Public opinion is solidly against the move.* (**firme**)

4 well, but not in a special way □ *Hicks played solidly.* (**razoavelmente bem**)

solitary /'sɒlɪtəri/ ADJECTIVE

1 lonely or alone □ *She saw a solitary figure standing near the door.* □ *He lived a solitary existence.* (**solitário**)

2 used to emphasize that there is only one person or thing □ *He could not remember a single solitary fact from the previous lesson.* (**único**)

solitary confinement /'sɒlɪtəri kən'faɪnmənt/ NOUN, NO PLURAL if a prisoner is in solitary confinement, they are kept by themselves and are not allowed to communicate with others (**prisão em solitária**)

solitude /'sɒlɪtjuːd/ NOUN, NO PLURAL when you are alone □ *She enjoyed the solitude of her little cottage by the lake.* (**solidão**)

solo /'səʊləʊ/ ▶ NOUN [plural **solos**] a piece of music or a song for one person to play or sing □ *a guitar solo* □ *Emma sang a solo in the Christmas concert.* (**solo**)

▶ ADJECTIVE done or performed by one person alone □ *a solo flight* □ *a solo album* □ *He went on to have a career as a solo artist.* (**de solo**)

▶ ADVERB alone □ *It's the first time he's flown solo.*

• **soloist** /'səʊləʊɪst/ NOUN [plural **soloists**] someone who sings or plays a solo (**solista**)

solstice /'sɒlstɪs/ NOUN [plural **solstices**] one of the two days in the year when there are the most hours of light or darkness (**solstício**) 🔂 *the summer/winter solstice*

soluble /'sɒljʊbəl/ ADJECTIVE

1 a soluble substance will dissolve in a liquid. A chemistry word □ *soluble aspirin* □ *The drug is soluble in water.* (**solúvel**)

2 a soluble problem can be solved (**solúvel**)

solution /sə'luːʃən/ NOUN [plural **solutions**]

1 an answer to a problem or a question □ *+ to It's difficult to offer simple solutions to a complex problem.* (**solução**) 🔂 *We must try to find a peaceful solution.* (**encontrar uma solução**)

2 a liquid with a substance dissolved in it. A chemistry word. □ *a salt water solution* □ *a bottle of contact lens solution* (**solução**)

> ► Remember that 'solution' meaning 'an answer to a problem' is followed by the preposition **to**:
> ✓ *There is no easy solution **to** the problem.*
> ✗ *There is no easy solution of the problem.*

solve /sɒlv/ VERB [solves, solving, solved]

1 to find an answer to a problem or a difficult question □ *Solve the puzzle to win a prize.* (resolver) ■ *A new bridge won't solve the traffic problem.* (resolverá o problema)

2 to understand and explain how a mystery happened or a crime took place ■ *Scientists believe they have solved the mystery.* ■ *This information could help us to solve the crime.* (resolver)

solvent¹ /'sɒlvənt/ NOUN [plural solvents]
something that dissolves another substance. A chemistry word. (solvente)

solvent² /'sɒlvənt/ ADJECTIVE
having enough money to pay what you owe □ *At last they were financially solvent.* (solvente)

somber /'sɒmbə(r)/ ADJECTIVE
the US spelling of sombre (sombrio)

• **somberly** /'sɒmbəlɪ/ ADVERB the US spelling of sombrely (sombriamente)

sombre /'sɒmbə(r)/ ADJECTIVE

1 serious and sad □ *I found him in a sombre mood.* □ *a sombre ceremony* (escuro)

2 dark in colour □ *sombre colours* □ *a sombre suit* (sombrio)

• **sombrely** /'sɒmbəlɪ/ ADVERB in a serious and sad way □ *'It's a great shame,' he said sombrely.* (sombriamente)

sombrero /sɒm'breərəʊ/ NOUN [plural sombreros]
a Mexican hat with a wide brim (sombrero, chapéu mexicano)

some /sʌm/ DETERMINER, PRONOUN

1 used to talk about a number or an amount without saying exactly how many or how much □ *It's all right; I've got some money.* □ *Would you like some more milk?* □ *I've made a cake – would you like some?* (algum, um pouco)

2 used to talk about part of a larger amount or number of things or people □ + *of Some of the apples were rotten.* □ *Some people have brought rain coats and some haven't.* (algum)

3 a fairly large amount of something, especially time or distance □ *It was some time before I noticed.* □ *We've still got some way to go.* (algum)

4 used to talk about a person or a thing when you do not know exactly who or what they are □ *He mentioned some letter that he had received.* □ *Some silly person forgot to close the gate.* (alguém/algo)

somebody /'sʌmbədɪ/ PRONOUN

1 used to talk about a person when you do not know who they are or it is not necessary to say their name □ *Somebody knocked at the door.* □ *They get money every time somebody downloads a song.* □ *She's somebody who's popular at school.* (alguém) ■ *Let somebody else* (= another person) *do it for a change.* (outro alguém)

2 an important person □ *He really thinks he's somebody in that big car.* (alguém importante)

some day or someday /'sʌmdeɪ/ ADVERB
at a time in the future although you are not sure exactly when □ *Prince William will be king some day.* □ *We'll go and visit them someday soon.* (algum dia)

somehow /'sʌmhaʊ/ ADVERB
in a way that is not known or that you do not understand □ *Don't worry, we'll manage somehow.* □ *She'd somehow managed to get her finger caught in the mechanism.* □ *Somehow, it didn't seem very important.* (de algum jeito) ■ *He'll succeed in the end, somehow or other.* (de um jeito ou de outro)

someone /'sʌmwʌn/ PRONOUN
used to talk about a person when you do not know who they are or it is not necessary to say their name □ *We'll have to find someone to replace him.* □ *I was having a conversation with someone at work about it.* (alguém) ■ *It's good to have someone else* (= another person) *to blame.* (outro alguém)

someplace /'sʌmpleɪs/ ADVERB
a US word for somewhere □ *Are you going someplace?* □ *I left my glasses someplace around here.* (algum lugar)

somersault /'sʌməsɔːlt/ ▶ NOUN [plural somersaults]
when you turn your body over in the air so that your feet go over your head (salto mortal)

▶ VERB [somersaults, somersaulting, somersaulted] to do a somersault □ *She somersaulted neatly into the water.* (dar um salto mortal)

something /'sʌmθɪŋ/ PRONOUN

1 used to talk about a thing or a fact when you do not know what it is, or when it is not necessary to say what it is □ *I've got something in my eye.* □ *Let's have something to eat before we go.* □ *She told me something else as well.* □ *The roof's leaking and we need to do something about it.* (alguma coisa)

2 used to show that what you have said is only a guess or an example □ *I think he's an actor or something like that.* □ *She speaks something like ten different languages.* (algo assim) ■ *We could take her some flowers or something.* (algo assim)

3 have something to do with something to be connected with something, or to be the cause of something □ *I think Alison had something to do with organizing the party.* □ *I'm not sure why they came home early, but the weather might have had something to do with it.* (ter alguma coisa a ver com algo)

sometime /'sʌmtaɪm/ ▶ ADVERB
used to talk about a time when you do not know when it is or it is not necessary to say exactly when it is □ *I'll talk to you about it sometime when you aren't so busy.* □ *They should arrive sometime soon.* □ *They left this neighbourhood sometime last year.* (em algum momento)

sometimes

▶ ADJECTIVE

1 used to talk about someone who had a particular position in the past, but not any longer □ *Dr Wilson, sometime member of Trinity College* (**então**)

2 used to talk about someone who does something only part of the time, not always □ *He's a writer and sometime actor.* (**esporádico**)

sometimes /ˈsʌmtaɪmz/ ADVERB at times, but not always □ *I still see him sometimes.* □ *Sometimes I feel like giving up my job and moving away.* (**às vezes**)

somewhat /ˈsʌmwɒt/ ADVERB quite or slightly □ *The wind had died down somewhat.* □ *It came as somewhat of a surprise.* (**um pouco**)

somewhere /ˈsʌmweə(r)/ ADVERB

1 used to talk about a place when you do not know where it is, or when it is not necessary to say where it is □ *Let's go away somewhere for a few days.* □ *They live somewhere near Oxford.* □ *It must be around here somewhere.* □ *Put it somewhere safe.* (**em algum lugar**) 🔁 *If you don't like it, we can go somewhere else* (= to another place). (**para algum outro lugar**)

2 used to talk about an approximate amount, time, or number □ + *between* *She must be somewhere between 35 and 40.* □ + *around* *They generally cost somewhere around $30.* (**por volta de**)

3 get somewhere to make progress □ *I think we're getting somewhere with them.* (**chegar a algum lugar, fazer progresso**)

son /sʌn/ NOUN [plural sons] someone's male child (**filho**) 🔁 *They have two young sons.* (**filhos jovens**) 🔁 *Her eldest son, Dave, is at university.* (**filho mais velho**) □ + *of* *He's the son of Algerian immigrants.*

sonar /ˈsəʊnɑː(r)/ NOUN, NO PLURAL equipment that uses sound waves to find out where things are under water (**sonar**)

sonata /səˈnɑːtə/ NOUN [plural sonatas] a piece of classical music, in several parts, for one musical instrument (**sonata**)

song /sɒŋ/ NOUN [plural songs]

1 a piece of music with words that you sing □ *a pop song* □ *This is one of my favourite songs.* (**canção**) 🔁 *She mostly sings folk songs.* (**canta canções**)

2 no plural songs in general or the activity of singing □ *A blackbird suddenly burst into song.* □ *a song and dance routine* (**canto**)

◆ IDIOM **make a song and dance about something** an informal phrase meaning to treat something as being more difficult or more annoying than it really is □ *I don't want to make a big song and dance about it.* (**fazer onda, dar muita importância a algo**)

songbird /ˈsɒŋbɜːd/ NOUN [plural songbirds] a bird that sings (**ave que canta**)

sonic /ˈsɒnɪk/ ADJECTIVE to do with sound. A physics word □ *a sonic boom* (**sônico**)

son-in-law /ˈsʌnɪnlɔː/ NOUN [plural sons-in-law] your daughter's husband (**genro**)

sonnet /ˈsɒnɪt/ NOUN [plural sonnets] a type of poem that has 14 lines (**soneto**)

soon /suːn/ ADVERB [sooner, soonest]

1 in a short time from now □ *It will soon be summer.* □ *I hope to see you soon.* □ *Soon we'll be reaching Liverpool* □ *I'd like the work done by Friday, or sooner if you can.* (**logo**) 🔁 *I'll do it as soon as I can.* (**logo que**)

2 too soon too early □ *It's too soon to tell whether she'll recover.* □ *Help arrived not a moment too soon.* (**cedo demais**)

3 as soon as immediately □ *As soon as I saw her, I knew something was wrong.* □ *He started shouting at us as soon as we arrived.* (**logo que**)

4 sooner or later used to say that you are certain that something will happen at some time in the future □ *Sooner or later there's going to be an accident.* (**mais cedo ou mais tarde**)

5 no sooner ... than used to talk about something that happens immediately after something else □ *No sooner had we eaten than we were sent off to work again.* (**tão logo, assim que**)

soot /sʊt/ NOUN, NO PLURAL the black powder that is produced when wood, coal, etc. burns (**fuligem**)

soothe /suːð/ VERB [soothes, soothing, soothed]

1 to make someone feel calmer or happier □ *She was unable to soothe her crying baby.* (**acalmar**)

2 to make pain less strong □ *I had a bath to soothe my sore muscles.* (**aplacar, aliviar**)

• **soothing** /ˈsuːðɪŋ/ ADJECTIVE

1 making you feel calmer or happier □ *soothing music* (**calmante**) 🔁 *She had a soft, soothing voice.*

2 making pain less strong □ *a soothing massage* (**calmante**)

sooty /ˈsʊti/ ADJECTIVE [sootier, sootiest] covered in soot or like soot (**ver soot**)

sophisticated /səˈfɪstɪkeɪtɪd/ ADJECTIVE

1 knowing a lot about the world, culture, fashion, etc. □ *a highly sophisticated audience* □ *It's a sophisticated and cosmopolitan city.* (**sofisticado, refinado**)

2 using new and clever ideas (**elaborado, complexo**) 🔁 *highly sophisticated software* (**altamente complexo**)

• **sophistication** /səˌfɪstɪˈkeɪʃən/ NOUN, NO PLURAL the quality of being sophisticated □ *a level of technical sophistication* □ *She preferred the sophistication of the French capital.* (**sofisticação**)

sopping /ˈsɒpɪŋ/ ADJECTIVE an informal word meaning very wet □ *a sopping towel* (**ensopado, encharcado**) 🔁 *They pulled off their sopping wet clothes.* (**ensopadas**)

soppy /ˈsɒpi/ ADJECTIVE [soppier, soppiest] showing too much emotion in a way that seems silly □ *a soppy love song* (**piegas**)

soprano /səˈprɑːnəʊ/ NOUN [plural sopranos]
1 a very high singing voice (**soprano**)
2 a woman or young boy with a high singing voice (**soprano**)

sorbet /ˈsɔːbeɪ/ NOUN [plural sorbets] a sweet food made with crushed ice, sugar and fruit (**sorbet, sorvete de frutas**)

sorcerer /ˈsɔːsərə(r)/ NOUN [plural sorcerers] a man in stories who can do magic (**feiticeira**)
• **sorceress** /ˈsɔːsərɪs/ NOUN [plural sorceresses] a woman in stories who can do magic (**feiticeiro**)
• **sorcery** /ˈsɔːsəri/ NOUN, NO PLURAL magic, or the ability to do magic (**feitiçaria**)

sordid /ˈsɔːdɪd/ ADJECTIVE to do with behaviour which is dishonest or morally bad □ *a sordid secret* □ *What was his role in this sordid affair?* (**sórdido**)

sore /sɔː(r)/ ▶ ADJECTIVE [sorer, sorest]
1 if a part of your body is sore, it is painful □ *a sore finger* (**dolorido**) 🔊 *She woke up with a sore throat.* (**dor de garganta**) 🔊 *My legs feel sore today.* (**estão doloridos**)
2 a sore point something which you are angry or upset about and do not want to talk about □ *His job situation is a bit of a sore point at the moment.* (**um assunto delicado**)
▶ NOUN [plural sores] a red, painful place on your skin □ *The horse had a nasty sore on its leg.* (**ferida**)
• **sorely** /ˈsɔːli/ ADVERB very much or a lot (**penosamente**) 🔊 *He was sorely disappointed.* (**muito decepcionado**) 🔊 *Mr Watson will be sorely missed by his colleagues.* (**fará muita falta**)
• **soreness** /ˈsɔːnɪs/ NOUN, NO PLURAL when something is sore □ *He has a lot of muscle soreness.* (**irritação, dor**)

sorrow /ˈsɒrəʊ/ NOUN [plural sorrows]
1 a feeling of great sadness □ *The President expressed his great sorrow.* □ *I couldn't find the words to comfort her in her sorrow.* (**pesar**)
2 something that makes you feel sad □ *the joys and sorrows of parenthood* (**tristeza**)
• **sorrowful** /ˈsɒrəfʊl/ ADJECTIVE very sad □ *a long, sorrowful face* (**pesaroso**)
• **sorrowfully** /ˈsɒrəfəli/ ADVERB in a sorrowful way □ *She stared sorrowfully at the broken pieces.* (**pesarosamente**)

sorry /ˈsɒri/ ADJECTIVE [sorrier, sorriest]
1 (I'm) sorry (a) something that you say when you have done something wrong, hurt someone, upset someone, etc. □ *Sorry, I didn't mean to hurt you.* □ *I'm so sorry – I've spilt tea on your carpet.* (**desculpa, perdão**) 🔊 *He broke my chair and he never even said sorry.* (**pediu desculpas**) (b) something you say to be polite when you have to tell someone something they may not like □ *Sorry, the shop's closing now.* □ *I'm sorry, but the tickets have all been sold.* (c) something you say when you disagree or argue with someone □ *I'm sorry, but this work just isn't good enough.* □ *I'm sorry, but I am not clearing up after you any more!*
2 ashamed about something that you have done and wishing you had not done it □ *She knows how much she upset us, and she's not even sorry.* □ **+ that** *I'm really sorry that I lied to you.* □ **+ about** *I'm sorry about forgetting your birthday.* □ **+ for** *He's truly sorry for spoiling your party.* (**arrependido**)
3 feeling sympathy for someone □ *I was sorry to hear about your father.* □ **+ for** *I feel really sorry for Anna, having to travel on her own.* □ **+ that** *I was sorry that you didn't get the job.* 🔊 *It's time to stop feeling sorry for yourself and get on with your life.* (**triste, ter pena de**)
4 used to say that you wish a situation could have been different □ **+ that** *I was sorry that I never met her.* □ **+ to do something** *I think they were sorry to leave.* 🔊 *I'm sorry to say that I was not impressed by the restaurant.* (**desolado**)

sort /sɔːt/ ▶ NOUN [plural sorts]
1 a type of thing or person □ **+ of** *What sort of books do you read?* □ *We won't tolerate that sort of behaviour here.* □ *It's the sort of shop that might sell matches.* (**tipo**) 🔊 *There were all sorts of people there.* (**todos os tipos de**) 🔊 *She needs to take up a hobby of some sort.* (**de algum tipo**) 🔊 *He enjoys skiing and that sort of thing.* (**esse tipo de coisa**)
2 sort of similar, but not exactly what has been said □ *I think she'd sort of forgotten about us by then.* □ *The house was sort of cut out of the rock.* (**meio**)
3 of sorts used to describe something that acts as a particular thing, but is not as good as the usual thing □ *We made a bed of sorts from dried grass.* □ *He was able to claim a victory of sorts.* (**sofrível**)
▶ VERB [sorts, sorting, sorted]
1 to arrange things or people into groups or into a particular order □ **+ into** *We sorted the books into piles by subject.* (**separar, classificar**)
2 an informal word meaning to arrange or deal successfully with something □ *'What about accommodation?' 'Already sorted!'* (**reservado, resolvido**)
♦ PHRASAL VERBS **sort something out** to arrange or deal successfully with something □ *We've sorted out a new system for feeding the cattle.* □ *Did you manage to sort out Jackie's problem with her computer?* (**cuidar de**) **sort through something** to look at a number of things in order to look for something or to organize them □ *It took us ages to sort through his correspondence.* (**arrumar**)

SOS /ˌes əʊ ˈes/ NOUN, NO PLURAL a signal that a ship or aircraft sends to ask for help (**SOS**)

so-so /ˈsəʊ səʊ/ ADJECTIVE not very good but not very bad □ *The restaurant looked nice but the meal was so-so.* (**mais ou menos**)

sought

sought /sɔːt/ PAST TENSE AND PAST PARTICIPLE OF **seek** (ver **seek**)

sought-after /ˈsɔːtɑːftə(r)/ ADJECTIVE if something is sought-after, many people want to have it and try hard to get it ☐ *His watercolours are now much sought-after.* (**desejado, procurado**)

soul /səʊl/ NOUN [plural **souls**]
1 the part of a person that is not their body but which some people believe continues to exist after they die ☐ *the souls of the dead* ☐ *God rest his soul.* (**alma**)
2 your inner feelings and character (**alma**) 🔁 *She isn't one to bare her soul* (= express her inner feelings) *and rarely gives interviews.* 🔁 *I searched my soul, but I could not agree to her wishes.*
3 a type of pop music that expresses strong emotions, especially played by Black Americans (**soul**) 🔁 *a soul singer* (**cantor de soul**) 🔁 *He grew up listening to soul music.* (**música soul**)
4 a person ☐ *The poor old soul got an awful shock.* ☐ *A few brave souls waited in the rain.* (**alma**)
5 the special character of something ☐ *The market place is the soul of the city.* (**alma, espírito, essência**)

soul-destroying /ˈsəʊldɪstrɔɪɪŋ/ ADJECTIVE very boring or upsetting, especially because of continuing for a long time ☐ *The work is absolutely soul destroying.* (**embrutecedor**)

soulful /ˈsəʊlfʊl/ ADJECTIVE having or expressing deep feelings of sadness ☐ *The dog has large soulful eyes.* (**comovente**)

• **soulfully** /ˈsəʊlfəlɪ/ ADVERB in a soulful way ☐ *He sang soulfully of the lost days of his youth.* (**comoventemente**)

soulless /ˈsəʊlɪs/ ADJECTIVE
1 having no interesting or attractive features ☐ *a soulless modern hotel* (**desinteressante**)
2 showing no emotion ☐ *She met my gaze with her soulless eyes.* (**desalmado**)

sound /saʊnd/ ▶ NOUN [plural **sounds**]
1 something that you can hear (**som, barulho**) 🔁 *I could hear a faint sound.* (**ouvir um som**) ☐ *+ of We heard the sound of breaking glass.* 🔁 *Elspeth made a sound of disgust.* (**fez um som**) ☐ *There isn't a sound coming from the children's bedroom.*
2 the sound of something the way that something you read or hear about seems to you ☐ *I don't much like the sound of your new boss.* (**modo como algo soa**) 🔁 *You need a holiday, by the sound of it.* (**pelo jeito, ao que parece**)
▶ VERB [**sounds, sounding, sounded**]
1 if something sounds good, bad, etc., it seems that way from what you have heard or read ☐ *Tom's holiday sounds wonderful.* ☐ *I don't want to sound too negative.* ☐ *I don't think that sounds right. Are you sure?* (**parecer**) 🔁 *You sound as though you know a lot about it.* 🔁 *You sound as if you're not certain.* 🔁 *That sounds like a good idea.* (**parecer como**)
2 used to talk about a noise that you hear ☐ *His voice sounded shaky.* ☐ *All their songs sound exactly the same.* (**soar**) 🔁 *That sounds like Zoe's voice in the kitchen.* (**soa como**)
3 to make a noise ☐ *Sound your horn before you turn the corner.* ☐ *If the fire alarm sounds, leave the building immediately.* (**tocar**)

◆ PHRASAL VERBS **sound off** an informal phrase meaning to express your feelings and opinions, often loudly and angrily ☐ *I shouldn't have sounded off at you like I did this morning.* (**expressar-se rudemente**) **sound someone out** to ask for someone's opinion about something ☐ *Could you sound John out about my suggestion?* (**sondar**)

▶ ADJECTIVE [**sounder, soundest**]
1 strong, firm or healthy ☐ *The walls of the old church were still sound.* ☐ *Her health was pretty sound.* (**forte**)
2 good, sensible and that you can trust (**sólido, consistente**) 🔁 *It seemed like sound advice.* (**conselho consistente**) ☐ *The recommendations are based on scientifically sound evidence.*
3 a sound sleep is deep and difficult to wake up from (**sono pesado**)
4 good and complete ☐ *He has a sound knowledge of French.* (**profundo**)
▶ ADVERB **sound asleep** if someone is sound asleep, they are sleeping and it is difficult to wake them ☐ *At ten o'clock I was still sound asleep.* (**profundamente adormecido**)

sound barrier /ˈsaʊnd ˌbæriə(r)/ NOUN, NO PLURAL the point at which an aircraft is travelling at the same speed as sound 🔁 *The jets can break the sound barrier.* (**barreira do som**)

sound bite /ˈsaʊndbaɪt/ NOUN [plural **sound bites**] a short statement made by a politician or someone famous that is reported in newspapers, on television, etc. because it is interesting, funny or clever (**frase de efeito**)

sound card /ˈsaʊndkɑːd/ NOUN [plural **sound cards**] a small part in a computer that allows it to play sounds. A computing word. (**placa de som**)

sound effect /ˈsaʊnd ɪˌfekt/ NOUN [plural **sound effects**] the sounds that are used in films and plays which are made artificially (**efeito sonoro**)

soundly /ˈsaʊndlɪ/ ADVERB
1 sleep soundly if you sleep soundly, you sleep well and nothing wakes you ☐ *Within a few minutes she was sleeping soundly.* (**dormir bem**)
2 completely (**completamente**) 🔁 *The party was soundly defeated in recent elections.* (**totalmente derrotado**)
3 in a way that is good, strong or sensible ☐ *The business is soundly managed.* (**firmemente**)

soundproof /ˈsaʊndpruːf/ ADJECTIVE a soundproof material, structure, or room is made so that sound cannot pass through it (**à prova de ruído**)

soundtrack

soundtrack /'saʊndtræk/ NOUN [plural **soundtracks**] a recording of the music from a film or television programme (**trilha sonora**)

soup /suːp/ NOUN [plural **soups**] a liquid food made from meat, fish or vegetables □ *a bowl of chicken soup* (**sopa**)

sour /'saʊə(r)/ ▶ ADJECTIVE [**sourer, sourest**]
1 sour food has a bitter taste like a lemon, sometimes because it is bad □ *sour plums* □ *a sour taste* (**azedo, ácido**) 🔄 *The milk had gone sour in the sun.* (**azedou**)
2 unfriendly and unpleasant □ *He wore a sour expression.* (**azedo**) 🔄 *The day started on a sour note.*
♦ IDIOM **sour grapes** used to say that someone is criticizing something because they are jealous or disappointed □ *I'm not going to question the referee's decisions, because that would be sour grapes.* (**dor de cotovelo, inveja**)
▶ VERB [**sours, souring, soured**] to become unfriendly or unpleasant □ *The whole mood had soured.* (**azedar**) 🔄 *The incident soured relations between the two countries.*

source /sɔːs/ NOUN [plural **sources**]
1 where something begins or comes from (**fonte, origem**) 🔄 *renewable energy sources* (**fonte de energia**) □ *Nuts are a rich source of protein.* □ *Tourism is the island's main source of income.*
2 a person, book, etc. that you get information from □ *Police sources said that the attack was a suicide bombing.* (**fonte**)
3 the original cause of something, especially a problem □ *Money is a major source of tension in many families.* (**origem**)
4 the place where a river starts (**nascente**)

south /saʊθ/ ▶ NOUN
1 the direction that is to your right when you are facing towards the rising sun (**sul**)
2 the part of a country or the world that is in the south □ *We went on holiday to the south of France.* (**sul**)
▶ ADJECTIVE, ADVERB in or towards the south □ *the south coast* □ *The river flows south into the sea.* (**sul, meridional**)

• **southbound** /'saʊθbaʊnd/ ADJECTIVE moving or going towards the south (**para o sul**) 🔄 *southbound traffic*

south-east /ˌsaʊθˈiːst/ ▶ NOUN
1 the direction between south and east (**sudeste**)
2 the part of a country between the south and the east □ *It's another sunny day in the south-east.* (**sudeste**)
▶ ADJECTIVE, ADVERB in or towards the south-east □ *the south-east coast* (**do sudeste**)

southerly /'sʌðəli/ ADJECTIVE coming from or going towards the south □ *Southerly gales are forecast.* □ *They were travelling in a southerly direction.* (**sul**)

southern /'sʌðən/ ADJECTIVE in or from the south □ *the southern states of the USA* (**meridional, sul**)
• **southerner** /'sʌðənə(r)/ NOUN [plural **southerners**] a person from the south (**sulista**)

South Pole /ˌsaʊθ ˈpəʊl/ NOUN **the South Pole** the point on the Earth that is furthest South (**polo Sul**)

southward /'saʊθwəd/ or **southwards** /'saʊθwədz/ ADVERB to or towards the south □ *We were soon heading southward down the motorway.* (**para o sul**)

south-west /ˌsaʊθˈwest/ ▶ NOUN
1 the direction between south and west (**sudoeste**)
2 the part of a country between the south and the west □ *the south-west of France* (**sudoeste**)
▶ ADJECTIVE, ADVERB in or towards the south-west (**do sudoeste**)

souvenir /ˌsuːvəˈnɪə(r)/ NOUN [plural **souvenirs**] something that you buy to help you remember a particular place or occasion □ + *of* *We brought back some shells as souvenirs of our holiday.* (**lembrança**) 🔄 *a souvenir shop* (**loja de lembrancinhas**)

sovereign /'sɒvrɪn/ ▶ NOUN [plural **sovereigns**]
1 a king or queen (**soberano**)
2 an old gold coin (**soberano**)
▶ ADJECTIVE a sovereign state has its own independent government
• **sovereignty** /'sɒvrɪnti/ NOUN, NO PLURAL a formal word meaning when a country has independent political power to govern itself (**soberania**)

sow¹ /səʊ/ VERB [**sows, sowing, sowed, sown**] to put seeds on or in the ground so that they will grow (**semear**)

sow² /saʊ/ NOUN [plural **sows**] a female pig (**porca**)

> This meaning of **sow** rhymes with **how**.

soya bean /ˌsɔɪə ˈbiːn/ NOUN [plural **soya beans**] a type of bean that can be cooked and eaten or used to make milk, oil and other foods (**soja**)

soya milk /ˌsɔɪə ˈmɪlk/ NOUN, NO PLURAL a type of milk made from soya beans (**leite de soja**)

soy sauce /ˌsɔɪ ˈsɔːs/ NOUN, NO PLURAL a dark brown sauce made from soya beans, put on food to add flavour (**molho de soja**)

spa /spɑː/ NOUN [plural **spas**]
1 a place where people can drink or bath in water that comes from the ground and is believed to be good for you (**balneário**)
2 a place where people go to relax and have beauty treatments (**spa**)

space /speɪs/ ▶ NOUN [plural **spaces**]
1 no plural the area available to be used □ *There isn't enough space to hold a party here.* (**espaço**) 🔄 *Can you make space for one more person?* (**abrir espaço**) 🔄 *We created more space by removing all the shelves.* (**criamos espaço**) 🔄 *I don't have enough disk space.* (**espaço no disco**)

space bar — spare

2 an empty area □ *Write your name in the space at the top of the sheet.* (lugar) 🔁 *I couldn't find a parking space.* (lugar para estacionar) 🔁 *It is important for cities to have plenty of open spaces.* (lugares abertos)

3 no plural the area outside the Earth's atmosphere, where the planets and stars are □ *Another rocket was launched into space yesterday.* (espaço)

4 a period of time □ *In the space of a month, he had completely reorganized the business.* 🔁 *She has achieved a lot in a short space of time.* (espaço)

> ► Remember that when you say 'space' meaning 'the area outside the Earth's atmosphere', you do not use the word 'the' before it:
> ✓ *He's always been very interested in space.*
> ✗ *He's always been very interested in the space.*

▶ VERB [**spaces, spacing, spaced**] to arrange things so that they have a particular distance or amount of time between them □ *Helpers were spaced at intervals of roughly 5 kilometres.* □*The journeys were spaced over a five year period.* (espaçar)

space bar /ˈspeɪs bɑː(r)/ NOUN [plural **space bars**] the long, narrow key at the front of a computer keyboard that lets you make a space between words. A computing word. (barra de espaço)

spacecraft /ˈspeɪskrɑːft/ NOUN [plural **spacecraft** or **spacecrafts**] a vehicle that can travel into space (nave espacial)

spaceship /ˈspeɪsʃɪp/ NOUN [plural **spaceships**] a vehicle that can travel into space (nave espacial)

space shuttle /ˈspeɪs ˌʃʌtəl/ NOUN [plural **space shuttles**] a vehicle like a plane that can travel into space and come back to Earth to be used again (ônibus espacial)

space station /ˈspeɪs ˌsteɪʃən/ NOUN [plural **space stations**] a place in space where people can live and do experiments (estação espacial)

spacesuit /ˈspeɪssuːt/ NOUN [plural **spacesuits**] a set of clothes worn by someone in space (traje espacial)

spacious /ˈspeɪʃəs/ ADJECTIVE large and with a lot of room □ *a spacious apartment* (espaçoso)

spade /speɪd/ NOUN [plural **spades**]
1 a tool with a wide flat part that you use for digging (pá)
2 spades one of the four types of playing card, which have the symbol (♠) printed on them □ *the ace of spades* (espadas)

◆ IDIOM **call a spade a spade** to say exactly what you think, without worrying about whether you are being polite (sem papas na língua)

spaghetti /spəˈɡeti/ NOUN, NO PLURAL a type of pasta that is like long thin string □ *spaghetti with tomato sauce* (espaguete)

spam /spæm/ NOUN, NO PLURAL e-mails that you do not want, especially e-mails trying to sell you things. A computing word. (spam)
▶ VERB [**spams, spamming, spammed**] to send spam to someone. A computing word. (enviar spam)

span /spæn/ ▶ NOUN [plural **spans**]
1 the length of time that something lasts □ *The country had changed completely within a span of twenty years.* (período) 🔁 *Most toddlers have a very short attention span.* (período de atenção)
2 the width of something □ *Its wings have a span of over 3 metres.* (vão)
▶ VERB [**spans, spanning, spanned**]
1 to go across an area □ *An old wooden bridge spans the river.* (atravessar)
2 to go all over an area □ *The company's dealers now span the whole world.* (atravessar)
3 to last for a particular period of time □ *His singing career spanned three decades.* (durar)

spangle /ˈspæŋɡəl/ NOUN [plural **spangles**] a small shiny piece of metal or plastic used as a decoration on clothes (lantejoula)
• **spangly** /ˈspæŋɡli/ ADJECTIVE covered with spangles □ *a spangly scarf* (coberto de lantejoulas)

spaniel /ˈspænjəl/ NOUN [plural **spaniels**] a type of dog with long ears that hang down □ *a golden spaniel* (cocker spaniel)

spank /spæŋk/ VERB [**spanks, spanking, spanked**] to hit someone on the bottom with your hand flat, especially as a punishment (estapear)

spanner /ˈspænə(r)/ NOUN [plural **spanners**] a metal tool used for turning nuts (= small pieces of metal holding things together) to take them off or make them tighter (chave-inglesa)
◆ IDIOM **put/throw a spanner in the works** to cause a big problem in the progress of something □ *We were due to fly to New York, but the airline strike put a spanner in the works.* (estragar um plano)

spar /spɑː(r)/ VERB [**spars, sparring, sparred**]
1 to practise fighting with someone (praticar boxe)
2 to argue with someone (discutir)

spare /speə(r)/ ▶ ADJECTIVE
1 extra and available to be used □ *I stayed in Fiona's spare room.* □ *I've got a spare ticket for Saturday's concert, if you'd like it.* □ *Neither of us had any spare cash.* (de reserva)
2 spare time time when you do not have to work and can do what you want □ *What do you do in your spare time?* (disponível)
▶ VERB [**spares, sparing, spared**]
1 to be able to give or lend something to someone because you do not need it yourself □ *Could you spare me a few pounds?* □ *We can't spare anyone to help out today.* (dispensar)
2 if you can spare the time to do something, you have enough time to do it □ *I'd love to come with you, but I just can't spare the time.* (dispor de)

3 to prevent someone from experiencing something unpleasant ☐ *I tried to spare him the embarrassment of a public apology.* (**poupar**)
4 to spare if you have something to spare, you have more of it than you need ☐ *We fed all 50 people and still had supplies to spare.* (**de sobra**)
5 to not harm or kill someone or something ☐ *In the violence that followed, not even the children were spared.* (**poupar**)
6 spare no expense/effort to spend as much money/make as much effort as is needed to achieve something ☐ *We spared no expense to make the party a wonderful occasion.* (**não poupar gastos/esforço**)
7 spare a thought for someone to think about someone who is in a difficult situation ☐ *When you sit down to dinner, spare a thought for some of the children who will not have anything to eat today.* (**pensar em alguém necessitado**)
▶ NOUN [*plural* **spares**]
1 an extra thing that can be used if the one you are using or usually use is lost, broken, etc. ☐ *If you lose your compass, I've got a spare.* (**peça de reserva**)
2 a part of a machine or a vehicle that can be used to replace a broken part ☐ *It's not easy to get spares for these old cars.* (**estepe**)

spare part /ˌspeə ˈpɑːt/ NOUN [*plural* **spare parts**] a part for a machine or car that is used to replace a part that is broken (**peça sobressalente**)

sparing /ˈspeərɪŋ/ ADJECTIVE using a very small amount ☐ *He is very sparing with his praise.* (**frugal**)
• **sparingly** /ˈspeərɪŋli/ ADVERB in very small amounts ☐ *These chillies are very hot, so use them sparingly.* (**frugalmente**)

spark /spɑːk/ ▶ NOUN [*plural* **sparks**]
1 a very small burning piece that is sent out from a fire or made by rubbing two hard surfaces together ☐ *A shower of sparks shot out of the bonfire.* (**faísca**)
2 a small amount of something such as enthusiasm or interest ☐ *There seemed to be no spark of life in the old woman.* (**centelha**)
▶ VERB [**sparks, sparking, sparked**]
1 to make a spark (**faiscar**)
2 to cause something, especially anger or a fight ☐ *Her remark sparked off a huge argument.* (**provocar**)

sparkle /ˈspɑːkəl/ ▶ VERB [**sparkles, sparkling, sparkled**] to shine, sending out a lot of points of bright light ☐ *Her jewels sparkled in the candlelight.* (**brilhar**)
▶ NOUN [*plural* **sparkles**] points of bright light ☐ *the sparkle of the sea* (**brilho**)
• **sparkling** /ˈspɑːklɪŋ/ ADJECTIVE
1 sending out points of bright light ☐ *sparkling eyes* (**faiscante, cintilante**)
2 a sparkling drink has bubbles of gas in it ☐ *I'll have sparkling mineral water.* (**espumante**)
3 full of energy and fun ☐ *sparkling conversation* (**vivo**)

spark plug /ˈspɑːk ˌplʌɡ/ NOUN [*plural* **spark plugs**] a small part in a car engine that produces an electrical spark (= very small flame) to make the fuel burn (**vela de ignição**)

sparrow /ˈspærəʊ/ NOUN [*plural* **sparrows**] a small brown bird (**pardal**)

sparse /spɑːs/ ADJECTIVE [**sparser, sparsest**] if something is sparse, there is not much or not enough of it ☐ *sparse vegetation* ☐ *Information from the battle front is sparse.* (**esparso**)

spasm /ˈspæzəm/ NOUN [*plural* **spasms**] a sudden movement of your muscles that you cannot control ☐ *The muscles of his leg had gone into spasm.* (**espasmo**)

spat /spæt/ PAST TENSE AND PAST PARTICIPLE OF **spit** (*ver* **spit**)

spate /speɪt/ NOUN, NO PLURAL a sudden large number or amount ☐ *There's been a spate of burglaries in the suburbs.* (**onda**)

spatter /ˈspætə(r)/ VERB [**spatters, spattering, spattered**] to cover something with small drops of liquid ☐ *His hair was spattered with paint.* (**salpicar, borrifar**)

spatula /ˈspætjʊlə/ NOUN [*plural* **spatulas**] a kitchen tool with a wide, flat blade, used for spreading or mixing soft substances or lifting pieces of food (**espátula**)

spawn /spɔːn/ ▶ VERB [**spawns, spawning, spawned**]
1 to cause or produce something ☐ *The children's cartoon spawned a multi-million pound empire.* (**produzir**)
2 to lay eggs ☐ *The salmon return to the same places to spawn.* (**desovar**)
▶ NOUN, NO PLURAL the eggs of frogs, toads or fish ☐ *frog spawn* (**ova**)

speak /spiːk/ VERB [**speaks, speaking, spoke, spoken**]
1 to say something ☐ + **to** *Could I speak to you for a moment?* ☐ + **about** *He never spoke publicly about his marriage.* ☐ *She was so tired she could hardly speak.* ☐ *We all sat there, and nobody spoke.* (**falar**)
2 to be able to talk in a particular language ☐ *Do you speak Greek?* (**falar**)
3 to make a speech ☐ + **about** *She spoke for almost an hour about her work with lions.* (**falando**)
4 generally/strictly, etc. speaking used to show that you are talking in a general/exact, etc. way ☐ *They disapprove of parents helping with homework, generally speaking.* ☐ *Strictly speaking a spider is an animal.* (**falando de maneira geral, específica etc.**)
5 Speaking. something you say when someone on the telephone asks to speak to you ☐ *'May I speak to Mrs Kennedy?' 'Speaking.'* (**É (fulano) quem fala!**)
♦ IDIOMS **speak volumes** to show a lot about someone or something ☐ *After such a major injury, this performance speaks volumes for the type of*

character he is. (dar uma aula sobre) **speak your mind** to say what you really think □ *She's not afraid to speak her mind.* (dizer o que pensa)

♦ PHRASAL VERBS **speak out** to speak about something in public, especially something that you have strong opinions about □ *He has spoken out against building wind farms in the area.* (falar francamente) **speak up 1** to say something more loudly □ *Could you speak up, please?* (falar alto) **2** to tell people your opinion about something □ *We all thought our boss was being unfair, but nobody was brave enough to speak up.* (pronunciar-se) **speak up for someone/ something** to say something to support someone or something □ *I was grateful to Jenny for speaking up for me.* (falar em favor de alguém/algo)

• **speaker** /ˈspiːkə(r)/ NOUN [plural **speakers**]
1 a piece of equipment that the sound from a radio, CD player, etc. comes out of (alto-falante)
2 someone who gives a speech (orador, locutor) 🔾 *Our guest speaker tonight is from Oxfam.* (orador convidado)
3 someone who is speaking (aquele que fala)
4 someone who is able to speak a particular language □ *We need an Arabic speaker to work in our sales department.* (falante da língua, aquele que fala determinado idioma)

spear /spɪə(r)/ ▶ NOUN [plural **spears**] a long thin weapon with a sharp metal point (lança, arpão)
▶ VERB [**spears, spearing, speared**] to push a thin, sharp point into something □ *He speared a piece of meat with his fork.* (arpoar)

spearmint /ˈspɪəmɪnt/ NOUN, NO PLURAL a herb whose leaves are used to produce a flavour used in sweets and toothpaste (= substance for cleaning your teeth) (hortelã)

special /ˈspeʃəl/ ADJECTIVE
1 unusual, and usually better than what is normal (especial) 🔾 *We've been saving this wine for a special occasion.* (ocasião especial) □ *My boyfriend always makes me feel really special.* 🔾 *We've all been making a special effort to be friendly.* (esforço especial)
2 meant for or having a particular purpose □ *Special trains will take fans to the match.* □ *a special tool for making rugs* (especial)

• **specialist** /ˈspeʃəlɪst/ NOUN [plural **specialists**] someone who knows a lot about a particular subject □ *My GP has referred me to a heart specialist.* (especialista)

• **speciality** /ˌspeʃiˈælɪti/ NOUN [plural **specialities**] something that someone does very well □ *Birthday cakes are my speciality.* (especialidade)

specialization *or* **specialisation** /ˌspeʃəlaɪˈzeɪʃən/ NOUN, NO PLURAL when someone studies or works at one particular subject or job or one part of a subject or job □ *The new A levels were originally designed to reduce academic specialization.* (especificação)

• **specialize** *or* **specialise** /ˈspeʃəlaɪz/ VERB [**specializes, specializing, specialized**] to study or work at one particular subject or job or one part of a subject or job □ *Judy specializes in counselling the bereaved.* □ *Next door there's a little shop which specializes in old theatre posters.* (especializar)

specially /ˈspeʃəli/ ADVERB for one particular purpose □ *Jo's had her costume specially made for the party.* (especialmente)

special needs /ˌspeʃəl ˈniːdz/ PLURAL NOUN the needs of people who have physical or mental problems □ *special needs students* (necessidades especiais)

species /ˈspiːʃiːz/ NOUN [plural **species**] a group of animals or plants whose members have similar features and that can produce young together □ *a rare species of orchid* (espécie)

specific /spəˈsɪfɪk/ ADJECTIVE
1 giving all the details about something in a clear way □ *Sarah's directions weren't very specific.* (específico)
2 exactly as has been stated or described □ *Each child has his own specific jobs to do.* (específico)

• **specifically** /spəˈsɪfɪkəli/ ADVERB
1 for one particular purpose and no other □ *These flats were designed specifically for the elderly.* (especificamente)
2 clearly and exactly □ *I specifically told you not to go out tonight.* (especificamente)

specification /ˌspesɪfɪˈkeɪʃən/ NOUN [plural **specifications**] a clear description of how something should be made or done □ *The car was built to his own specifications.* (especificação)

specify /ˈspesɪfaɪ/ VERB [**specifies, specifying, specified**] to state something clearly or in detail □ *Please specify the colour and size you require on the order form.* (especificar)

specimen /ˈspesɪmən/ NOUN [plural **specimens**]
1 a small amount of blood, etc. that can be tested by doctors or scientists □ *a specimen of urine* (espécime)
2 an example of a particular type of animal or plant □ *The specimens were arranged in cases, clearly labelled.* (espécime)

speck /spek/ NOUN [plural **specks**]
1 a very small piece of something □ *a speck of dust* (partícula, grão)
2 a small spot or mark □ *a speck of paint* (respingo)

speckle /ˈspekəl/ NOUN [plural **speckles**] one of several small spots □ *The egg was covered with speckles.* (pinta, salpico)

• **speckled** /ˈspekəld/ ADJECTIVE covered in speckles □ *a speckled hen* (pintado, salpicado)

specs /speks/ PLURAL NOUN an informal word meaning glasses □ *Has anyone seen my specs?* (óculos)

spectacle /ˈspektəkəl/ NOUN [plural **spectacles**]
1 something that is interesting, exciting or surprising to see □ *The opening ceremony of the games was a wonderful spectacle.* (espetáculo)
2 make a spectacle of yourself to do something silly or embarrassing that a lot of people see (fazer um papelão)
• **spectacles** /ˈspektəkəlz/ PLURAL NOUN an old fashioned word for glasses □ *a pair of spectacles* (óculos)

spectacular /spekˈtækjʊlə(r)/ ADJECTIVE very interesting, exciting or surprising □ *a spectacular firework display* □ *The scenery was absolutely spectacular.* (espetacular)
• **spectacularly** /spekˈtækjʊləlɪ/ ADVERB in a spectacular way or to a very great degree □ *a spectacularly successful film* (espetacular)

spectator /spekˈteɪtə(r)/ NOUN [plural **spectators**] someone who is watching an event □ *United won the match in front of more than 60,000 spectators.* (espectador)

specter /ˈspektə(r)/ NOUN [plural **specters**] the US spelling of **spectre** (ver **spectre**)

spectre /ˈspektə(r)/ NOUN [plural **spectres**]
1 something unpleasant that people are frightened might happen again □ *The thunderstorms have raised the spectre of more flooding.* (fantasma)
2 a ghost (= spirit of a dead person) (espectro)

spectrum /ˈspektrəm/ NOUN [plural **spectra** or **spectrums**]
1 a range of possible ideas, opinions or qualities 🔹 *The conference brings together people with a wide spectrum of views.* (espectro)
2 all the different colours produced when light passes through glass or water (espectro)

speculate /ˈspekjʊleɪt/ VERB [**speculates, speculating, speculated**]
1 to make a guess about something that you do not know much about □ *I wouldn't like to speculate about who might be the next president.* (especular)
2 to buy and sell things with the aim of making money but with the possibility of losing it □ *Many firms speculated on the financial markets rather than building factories.* (especular)
• **speculation** /ˌspekjʊˈleɪʃən/ NOUN [plural **speculations**]
1 guesses about what will happen or why something happened □ *There's been a lot of speculation about how she died.* (especulação)
2 buying and selling things such as houses or shares in companies in order to make a large profit □ *The rewards of financial speculation can be enormous.* (especulação)
• **speculative** /ˈspekjʊlətɪv/ ADJECTIVE based on speculation □ *The link between the virus and mental illness is purely speculative.* (especulativo)

sped /sped/ PAST TENSE AND PAST PARTICIPLE OF **speed** □ *A bullet sped past his ear.* (ver **speed**)

speech /spiːtʃ/ NOUN [plural **speeches**]
1 a talk that you give in front of a group of people (discurso) 🔹 *The bride's father usually makes a speech.* (faz um discurso)
2 *no plural* the ability to speak (habilidade de falar) 🔹 *He seemed to have lost the power of speech.* (poder da palavra)
3 *no plural* the particular way that someone speaks □ *She was so tired that her speech was slurred.* (modo de falar)
4 a set of words that one person says in a play □ *The old king's final speech is very moving.* (fala)

> Note that when you speak formally in front of a group of people, you **make a speech**. You can also **give a speech**:
> ✓ *I had to make/give a speech at the wedding.*
> ✗ *I had to do a speech at the wedding.*

• **speechless** /ˈspiːtʃlɪs/ ADJECTIVE unable to talk because you are so angry, shocked, upset, etc. □ *The unfairness of his remarks left her speechless.* (mudo, sem fala)

speed /spiːd/ ▶ NOUN [plural **speeds**]
1 how quickly someone or something moves □ *He was driving at a speed of about 30 miles per hour.* □ *The train was travelling at speed when it hit the debris on the track.* (rapidez) 🔹 *What's the top speed of this model?*
2 how quickly someone or something works or something happens □ *Our new programs offer accuracy and speed.* □ *The managers are very pleased with the speed of her progress.* (velocidade) 🔹 *You'll gradually pick up speed as you learn the job.*
▶ VERB [**speeds, speeding, sped** or **speeded**]
1 to move, go or pass quickly □ *He sped off down the road on his bike.* □ *The hours sped by as we sat and chatted.* (ir em alta velocidade)
2 to drive faster than the law says you can □ *I really didn't think I was speeding until I saw the police car.* (exceder a velocidade)
♦ PHRASAL VERB **speed (something) up** to go faster or make something faster □ *Accepting online applications should speed up the recruitment process.* (acelerar)

speedboat /ˈspiːdbəʊt/ NOUN [plural **speedboats**] a small boat with a powerful engine that can go very fast (barco de corrida)

speed-dial /ˈspiːddaɪəl/ NOUN, NO PLURAL a feature on a telephone that allows you to telephone a number by pressing only one button (discagem rápida)

speeding /ˈspiːdɪŋ/ NOUN, NO PLURAL the offence of driving faster than the law says you can □ *He's* been fined for speeding three times. (**excesso de velocidade**)

speed limit /'spiːd ˌlɪmɪt/ NOUN [plural **speed limits**] the fastest speed at which you are legally allowed to drive a vehicle on a particular road □ He was over the speed limit. (**limite de velocidade**)

speedometer /spɪ'dɒmɪtə(r)/ NOUN [plural **speedometers**] a piece of equipment in a car that measures how fast you are travelling (**velocímetro**)

speedway /'spiːdweɪ/ NOUN, NO PLURAL the sport of motorcycle racing, or the track that is used for this (**corrida de motos, pista para esse tipo de corrida**)

speedy /'spiːdi/ ADJECTIVE [**speedier, speediest**] quick or fast □ Thanks for the speedy reply to my letter. (**rápido**)

spell /spel/ ▶ VERB [**spells, spelling, spelt** or **spelled**]
1 to say or write the letters of a word in the correct order □ Could you spell your name for me? □ Adam was always good at spelling. (**soletrar**)
2 to make up a word □ L-i-g-h-t spells 'light'. (**formar**)
3 to mean that something bad is going to happen (**significar**) 🔄 A heavy fine will spell disaster for the company. (**significará um desastre**)
▶ NOUN [plural **spells**]
1 a short period of time □ The weather will be dull, with sunny spells. (**temporada**)
2 a set of words that are used to make something magic happen (**fórmula mágica**) 🔄 The wicked witch cast a spell on Snow White.

spellbound /'spelbaʊnd/ ADJECTIVE if you are spellbound by something, it is so interesting and good that all your attention is held by it □ The audience was spellbound for the whole two hours. (**fascinado**)

spellcheck /'speltʃek/ or **spellchecker** /'spelˌtʃekə(r)/ NOUN [plural **spellchecks** or **spellcheckers**] a computer program that checks whether you have spelled words correctly. A computing word. (**verificador de pronúncia**)
• **spellcheck** /'speltʃek/ VERB [**spellchecks, spellchecking, spellchecked**] to use a spellcheck on a document. A computing word. (**usar o verificador de pronúncia em um documento**)

spelling /'spelɪŋ/ NOUN [plural **spellings**]
1 the way that a word is spelt □ 'Donut' is the American spelling of 'doughnut'. (**ortografia**)
2 no plural the ability to spell □ His spelling is terrible. (**ortografia, habilidade de soletrar**)

spend /spend/ VERB [**spends, spending, spent**]
1 to use money to buy things (**gastar**) 🔄 We spent a lot of money on our holiday. □ Try to cut down how much you spend.
2 to pass time doing something 🔄 Do you spend much time on the computer? 🔄 I used to spend hours reading in my room. 🔄 I spent ages decorating that cake. □ We spent the weekend at my sister's. (**passar (tempo)**)

> ➤ Note that you spend money **on** someone or something:
> ✓ She spends a lot of money on clothes.
> ✗ She spends a lot of money for clothes.

• **spending** /'spendɪŋ/ NOUN, NO PLURAL the amount of money that a government, organization or person spends □ The government are taking steps to cut spending on prisons. (**despesas**)

sperm /spɜːm/ NOUN [plural **sperm** or **sperms**] a cell from a man that joins with the egg from a woman to make a baby. A biology word. (**esperma**)

spew /spjuː/ VERB [**spews, spewing, spewed**] to come out in large amounts, or to make something do this □ Great clouds of smoke and ash spewed from the volcano. (**expelir**)

sphere /sfɪə(r)/ NOUN [plural **spheres**]
1 a solid object that is the shape of a ball (**esfera**)
2 a particular area or subject of interest, activity, work, etc. □ He is well known within the political sphere. (**esfera, setor, área**)
• **spherical** /'sferɪkəl/ ADJECTIVE having the shape of a Sphere (**esférico**)

spice /spaɪs/ ▶ NOUN [plural **spices**]
1 a substance made from a plant that adds flavour to food □ herbs and spices □ Ginger is a spice. (**tempero, especiaria**)
2 something that adds excitement to a situation □ She took up hang-gliding to add a little spice to her life. (**animar**)
▶ VERB [**spices, spicing, spiced**] to add spice to food or drink □ apples spiced with cinnamon (**condimentar**)
◆ PHRASAL VERB **spice something up** to make something more exciting □ Producers decided to spice up the show with a live debate. (**incrementar, apimentar**)
• **spiciness** /'spaɪsɪnɪs/ NOUN, NO PLURAL being spicy □ I would reduce the spiciness of the sauce. (**qualidade de condimentado**)
• **spicy** /'spaɪsi/ ADJECTIVE [**spicier, spiciest**] tasting hot on your tongue □ spicy food (**condimentado**)

spider /'spaɪdə(r)/ NOUN [plural **spiders**] a small creature with eight legs that uses very thin threads to make a web for catching insects (**aranha**)
• **spidery** /'spaɪdəri/ ADJECTIVE spidery writing is untidy with long, thin lines (**desleixado, com linhas soltas**)

spike /spaɪk/ NOUN [plural **spikes**] a hard, sharp point, usually made of metal or wood □ There were sharp spikes on top of the wall. (**ponta, espigão**)

- **spiky** /'spaɪki/ ADJECTIVE [**spikier, spikiest**] with sharp points □ *a spiky hairstyle* (**pontudo**)

spill /spɪl/ VERB [**spills, spilling, spilt** *or* **spilled**]
1 to come out of a container by accident or to make something, especially a liquid, do this □ *Careful! You're going to spill your tea.* □ *She spilt a can of paint all over the carpet.* □ *The sack burst and the rice spilled out onto the floor.* (**derramar**)
2 if people spill out of a place they all leave it together □ *Crowds were spilling out of the football ground and heading off home.* (**sair aos montes**)
◆ IDIOM **spill the beans** to tell someone a secret □ *Come on, spill the beans. What's going on?* (**dar com a língua nos dentes, espalhar a notícia, contar um segredo**)
◆ PHRASAL VERB **spill over** to spread from one place to another □ *By now the rioting had spilled over into the neighbouring streets.* (**espalhar de um lugar a outro**)
- **spillage** /'spɪlɪdʒ/ NOUN [*plural* **spillages**]
1 the act of spilling something □ *The spillage of the lorry's load caused long tailbacks.* (**derramamento**)
2 an amount that has been spilled □ *Put a tray under the freezer to catch any spillages.* (**resto derramado, quantidade derramada**)

spin /spɪn/ ▶ VERB [**spins, spinning, spun**]
1 to turn round and round very quickly or make something do this □ *The ballerina spun round and round on her toes.* □ *He can spin the basketball on his finger.* (**girar, rodopiar**)
2 to make long, thin threads out of cotton, wool, or other material by pulling it and twisting it (**fiar**)
3 to remove water from clothes after washing them by turning them round and round very fast in a machine (**centrifugar**)
◆ PHRASAL VERB **spin something out** to make something last a long time, often longer than is necessary □ *She had to spin the story out till the end of the lesson.* (**prolongar**)
▶ NOUN [*plural* **spins**]
1 when you make something spin □ *Some tennis players can put a lot of spin on the ball.* (**giro**)
2 a way of talking about something that makes it seem less bad than it really is □ *political spin* (**dourar a pílula**) 🔁 *It was impossible to put a positive spin on such a bad result.* (**favorecer, ser tendencioso**)
3 an informal and slightly old-fashioned word for a short journey in a car (**rodopio**) 🔁 *We went for a spin in Joe's new car.*

spinach /'spɪnɪdʒ/ NOUN, NO PLURAL a vegetable with large dark green leaves (**espinafre**)

spinal /'spaɪnəl/ ADJECTIVE to do with your spine. A biology word. □ *a spinal injury* (**espinhal**)

spinal column /'spaɪnəl 'kɒləm/ NOUN [*plural* **spinal columns**] the bones and nerves that form your spine. A biology word. (**coluna vertebral**)

spinal cord /'spaɪnəl 'kɔːd/ NOUN [*plural* **spinal cords**] the nerve cells inside your spine. A biology word. (**medula espinhal**)

spindly /'spɪndli/ ADJECTIVE long, thin and not very strong (**esguio**) 🔁 *spindly legs*

spin doctor /'spɪn 'dɒktə(r)/ NOUN [*plural* **spin doctors**] a politician who finds ways of talking about mistakes or problems in a positive way (**político com habilidade em manipular notícias ruins**)

spin drier *or* **spin dryer** /'spɪn 'draɪə(r)/ NOUN [*plural* **spin driers** *or* **spin dryers**] a machine that dries clothes by turning them round and round very fast (**secadora**)

spine /spaɪn/ NOUN [*plural* **spines**]
1 the line of bones down the back of a person or animal (**coluna vertebral, espinha**)
2 a stiff point that grows on some plants or animals such as a hedgehog □ *the spines of a cactus* (**espinho**)
3 the narrow part of a book's cover that you can see when it is on a shelf (**lombada de livro**)

spine-chilling /'spaɪntʃɪlɪŋ/ ADJECTIVE a spine chilling story, film or book is very frightening (**de arrepiar**)

spineless /'spaɪnlɪs/ ADJECTIVE weak and not brave enough to deal with something well □ *The union was accused of being completely spineless.* (**sem pulso firme**)

spinning wheel /'spɪnɪŋ 'wiːl/ NOUN [*plural* **spinning wheels**] a piece of equipment for making thread, with a large wheel that turns round (**roca**)

spin-off /'spɪnɒf/ NOUN [*plural* **spin-offs**] a new product that is based on an older one, or something that is created as the result of something else □ *The rapid commercial development of computers was one of the spin-offs of the space programme in the 1960s.* (**subproduto**)

spinster /'spɪnstə(r)/ NOUN [*plural* **spinsters**] an old-fashioned word for a woman who is not married (**solteira**)

spiral /'spaɪərəl/ ▶ NOUN [*plural* **spirals**]
1 a shape formed by a line that curves round and round a centre point □ *The shell formed a perfect spiral.* (**espiral**)
2 a situation that gets worse in a way that is not controlled □ *They were caught in a spiral of violence.* (**espiral**)
▶ ADJECTIVE in the shape of a spiral (**espiralado**) 🔁 *a spiral staircase*
▶ VERB [**spirals, spiralling**/US **spiraling, spiralled**/US **spiraled**]
1 to increase, fall or get worse very quickly □ *House prices have spiralled recently.* (**subir ou cair rapidamente**)
2 to move in a spiral □ *The smoke spiralled up through the trees.* (**mover em espiral**)

spire 771 splint

spire /ˈspaɪə(r)/ NOUN [plural **spires**] a tall pointed roof on a church tower (**pináculo**)

spirit /ˈspɪrɪt/ ▶ NOUN [plural **spirits**]
1 your attitude or the attitude of a group of people □ + *of* *The celebration was held in a spirit of friendship.* □ *Her adventurous spirit took her all over the world.* □ *Our town has a strong community spirit.* (**espírito**)
2 *no plural* enthusiasm and determination □ *He showed real spirit during his illness.* (**espírito**)
3 enter/get into the spirit of something to take part in an event or activity in an enthusiastic and suitable way □ *Everyone was dancing and getting into the spirit of the evening.* (**entrar no espírito da coisa**)
4 spirits your mood 🔁 *She was in really high/low spirits* (= a happy/sad mood). (**humor, ânimo**)
5 the part of a person that some people believe continues to live after the body dies (**espírito**)
6 a creature without a physical body that some people believe can influence our lives (**espírito**) 🔁 *evil spirits*
7 a strong alcoholic drink, for example brandy or gin (**bebida alcoólica forte**)
▶ VERB [**spirits, spiriting, spirited**] to take someone or something somewhere without people noticing □ *He was spirited into a waiting taxi.* (**dar um sumiço em alguém**)
• **spirited** /ˈspɪrɪtɪd/ ADJECTIVE enthusiastic and determined (**vigoroso**) 🔁 *She mounted a spirited defence of her husband's actions.*

spirit level /ˈspɪrɪt ˌlevəl/ NOUN [plural **spirit levels**] a tool that you use to check whether a surface is level (**nível de bolha**)

spiritual /ˈspɪrɪtʃuəl/ ADJECTIVE
1 to do with someone's spirit, emotions and thoughts and not their body □ *an intensely spiritual experience* (**espiritual**)
2 to do with religion □ *The poor looked to the church for spiritual leadership.* (**espiritual**)

spit /spɪt/ ▶ VERB [**spits, spitting, spat**]
1 to force liquid or food out of your mouth □ *She took one mouthful and then spat it out on to her plate.* (**cuspir**)
2 if it is spitting, it is raining a little (**garoa**)
▶ NOUN [plural **spits**]
1 the liquid inside your mouth (**saliva**)
2 a thin metal bar that you put me a ton to cook over a fire □ *The ox was roasted on a spit.* (**espeto**)

spite /spaɪt/ NOUN, NO PLURAL
1 a feeling of wanting to hurt or upset someone □ *He threw my picture away out of spite.* (**rancor**)
2 in spite of used to say that a fact or event makes something else that happens surprising □ *We decided to go to the seaside in spite of the rain.* □ *He passed his exam in spite of doing no revision.* (**apesar de**)
• **spiteful** /ˈspaɪtfʊl/ ADJECTIVE doing or saying something unpleasant or cruel just to upset or hurt someone □ *a spiteful remark* (**rancoroso**)

• **spitefully** /ˈspaɪtfʊli/ ADVERB in a spiteful way (**rancorosamente**)
• **spitefulness** /ˈspaɪtfʊlnɪs/ NOUN, NO PLURAL being spiteful (**rancor**)

spitting image /ˌspɪtɪŋ ˈɪmɪdʒ/ NOUN **be the spitting image of someone** to look exactly like someone else □ *Tara's the spitting image of her mother.* (**ser "a imagem cuspida" de alguém, ter a mesma aparência**)

splash /splæʃ/ ▶ VERB [**splashes, splashing, splashed**]
1 to put liquid on something with a quick movement □ *Kate splashed some cold water on her face.* (**espirrar**)
2 if a liquid splashes somewhere, it moves there and makes a noise □ *The water splashed over the edge of the pan.* (**espirrar, bater**)
3 to move water around in a noisy way □ *The baby was splashing happily in his bath.* (**espirrar, bater na água**)
◆ PHRASAL VERB **splash out** to spend a lot of money on something □ *The singer has just splashed out on a mansion in Malibu.* (**esbanjar dinheiro**)
▶ NOUN [plural **splashes**]
1 the sound that water makes when something hits it □ *Kurt fell into the pool with a loud splash.* (**splash**)
2 a mark made on something where a liquid has hit it □ *Her jeans were covered in splashes of paint.* (**mancha**)
3 a splash of colour an area of colour that makes something look brighter □ *A beautiful Chinese rug provided a splash of colour.* (**um toque de cor**)
◆ IDIOM **make a splash** an informal phrase meaning to get a lot of attention □ *The group made a huge splash in Canada.* (**chamar a atenção**)

splatter /ˈsplætə(r)/ VERB [**splatters, splattering, splattered**] if a liquid splatters, drops of it fall all over something, and if you splatter a liquid, you make drops fall all over something □ *Blood was splattered on the walls.* (**borrifar, espirrar**)

splay /spleɪ/ VERB [**splays, splaying, splayed**] to spread your legs, arms or fingers wide apart □ *He sat on the floor with his legs splayed.* (**abrir/estender braços, pernas ou dedos**)

spleen /spliːn/ NOUN [plural **spleens**] an organ in your body which controls the quality of your blood. A biology word. (**baço**)

splendid /ˈsplendɪd/ ADJECTIVE very good □ *a splendid idea* (**esplêndido**)
• **splendour** /ˈsplendə(r)/ NOUN, NO PLURAL the quality of being very beautiful and grand □ *the splendour of the royal palaces* (**esplendor**)

splint /splɪnt/ NOUN [plural **splints**] a piece of wood used to keep a broken bone in the right position (**tala**)
• **splinter** /ˈsplɪntə(r)/ ▶ NOUN [plural **splinters**] a very small sharp piece of wood or glass □ *I got a splinter in my hand.* (**lasca**)

split

▶ VERB [splinters, splintering, splintered] to break into very small sharp pieces □ *The wood had splintered.* (espatifar-se)

split /splɪt/ ▶ VERB [splits, splitting, split]
1 to break or tear apart □ *Your trousers have split down the back.* (rachar)
2 to break something or tear it apart □ *The lightning had split the tree in two.* (rachar)
3 to share something □ *We drove to Edinburgh and split the cost of the petrol.* (dividir)
4 to cause a group to disagree and divide into smaller groups □ *The issue could split the Labour Party.* (dividir)
5 to divide a group of people into smaller groups □ *I split the children into two groups.* (dividir)
6 to end a marriage or relationship □ *I was three when my parents split.* □ *I've just split up with my boyfriend.* (separar)
♦ IDIOM **split hairs** to argue about small details that are not important (discutir por bobagem)
▶ NOUN [plural **splits**]
1 a tear or break in something □ *There's a long split in the wood.* (rachadura)
2 a disagreement that divides a group □ *This may leave a lasting split in the Republican Party.* (divisão)

split second /ˌsplɪt ˈsekənd/ NOUN, NO PLURAL a very short time □ *For a split second I thought something awful had happened.* (fração de segundo)
• **split-second** ADJECTIVE taking a very short time □ *a split-second decision* (levar muito pouco tempo para fazer algo)

splutter /ˈsplʌtə(r)/ VERB [splutters, spluttering, spluttered] to say something with difficulty because you are so angry or shocked □ *'I don't know what you're talking about!' he spluttered.* (gaguejar)

spoil /spɔɪl/ VERB [spoils, spoiling, spoilt or spoiled]
1 to make something less good □ *I had an argument with Adrian and it spoilt the whole evening.* □ *Low cloud spoilt the view of the mountains.* □ *The weather was fairly awful but we didn't let it spoil our fun.* (estragar, piorar as coisas)
2 to always allow a child to have or do what they want and cause them to become badly behaved □ *She spoils those children.* (mimar)
3 to treat someone in a very nice way and give them nice things □ *Breakfast in bed! You're spoiling me!* (mimar)
4 if food spoils, it starts to decay. A formal word. (estragar)

spoilsport /ˈspɔɪlspɔːt/ NOUN [plural **spoilsports**] someone who does something that stops someone else enjoying themselves □ *Don't be such a spoilsport!* (estraga prazeres)

spoilt /spɔɪlt/ ▶ PAST TENSE AND PAST PARTICIPLE OF **spoil** (ver **spoil**)

▶ ADJECTIVE behaving badly because you have always been allowed to have or do what you want (mimado) □ *You're behaving like a spoilt child!* (criança mimada)

spoke¹ /spəʊk/ PAST TENSE OF **speak** (ver **speak**)

spoke² /spəʊk/ NOUN [plural **spokes**] one of the thin metal pieces that connect the centre of a wheel with the edge (raio)

spoken /ˈspəʊkən/ PAST PARTICIPLE OF **speak** (ver **speak**)

spokesman /ˈspəʊksmən/ NOUN [plural **spokesmen**] a man who speaks officially for someone else (o porta-voz)

spokesperson /ˈspəʊksˌpɜːsən/ NOUN [plural **spokespeople**] someone who speaks officially for someone else □ *an army spokesperson* (porta-voz)

spokeswoman /ˈspəʊksˌwʊmən/ NOUN [plural **spokeswomen**] a woman who speaks officially for someone else (a porta-voz, oradora)

sponge /spʌndʒ/ ▶ NOUN [plural **sponges**]
1 a soft object, made from natural or artificial material, that you use to wash your body (esponja)
2 a light cake (pão de ló)
▶ VERB [sponges, sponging, sponged]
1 to wash something with a sponge □ *A nurse was sponging his face.* (limpar com esponja)
2 an informal word meaning to try to get money from people without doing anything to help them □ *At 35, he's still sponging off his parents.* (viver à custa de)

sponge bag /ˈspʌndʒ bæɡ/ NOUN [plural **sponge bags**] a bag that you carry things such as soap and a toothbrush in when you are travelling (nécessaire)

sponge cake /ˈspʌndʒ keɪk/ NOUN [plural **sponge cakes**] a light cake (pão de ló)

spongy /ˈspʌndʒɪ/ ADJECTIVE [**spongier**, **spongiest**] something that is spongy feels soft when you press it □ *spongy ground* (esponjoso)

sponsor /ˈspɒnsə(r)/ ▶ VERB [sponsors, sponsoring, sponsored]
1 to pay for something such as an event or television programme, often as a way of advertising your company □ *A local company sponsors our football team.* (patrocinador)
2 to agree to give someone money for a school, organization, etc. if they do something difficult □ *Will you sponsor me to run in the race?* (apadrinhar, financiar)
▶ NOUN [plural **sponsors**] a person or company that sponsors someone or something □ *The company is the official sponsor of the 2008 European Cup.* (patrocinador)
• **sponsored** /ˈspɒnsəd/ ADJECTIVE (em prol de uma causa) **a sponsored swim/walk, etc.** a swim or walk, etc. that you do to get money for a school or charity (= organization that helps people), in which people agree to give you money

spontaneity — spotlight

if you are successful (nado/corrida etc. em prol de uma causa)

- **sponsorship** /ˈspɒnsəʃɪp/ NOUN, NO PLURAL when someone sponsors someone or something (patrocínio) ▣ *Toyota announced a five-year sponsorship deal with the American Football League.* (acordo de patrocínio)

spontaneity /ˌspɒntəˈneɪəti/ NOUN, NO PLURAL the quality of being spontaneous (espontaneidade)

- **spontaneous** /spɒnˈteɪniəs/ ADJECTIVE happening naturally and not planned or organized □ *spontaneous applause* (espontâneo)

spoof /spuːf/ NOUN [plural **spoofs**] a television programme, advertisement, etc. which copies the style of a serious one and makes it seem silly and funny (paródia)

spooky /ˈspuːki/ ADJECTIVE [**spookier**, **spookiest**] an informal word that means frightening □ *The forest is really spooky at night.* (fantasmagórico)

spool /spuːl/ NOUN [plural **spools**] an object that you wind thread, film, etc. around □ *a spool of cotton* (carretel, bobina)

spoon /spuːn/ ▶ NOUN [plural **spoons**] an object with a handle and a curved part at one end that you use for lifting liquid food to your mouth □ *a soup spoon* □ *a wooden spoon* (colher)
▶ VERB [**spoons**, **spooning**, **spooned**] to lift up food on a spoon □ *She was slowly spooning the cereal into the baby's mouth.* (dar com colher)

- **spoonful** /ˈspuːnfʊl/ NOUN [plural **spoonfuls**] the amount a spoon will hold □ *Jamila put a spoonful of sugar in her coffee.* (colherada)

sporadic /spəˈrædɪk/ ADJECTIVE happening in a few places, or happening sometimes but not regularly □ *Sporadic violence continued across the country.* (esporádico)

spore /spɔː(r)/ NOUN [plural **spores**] a cell that is produced by some plants, for example mushrooms, that develops into a new plant. A biology word. (esporo)

sport /spɔːt/ ▶ NOUN [plural **sports**]
1 *no plural* games and physical activities like football, tennis and swimming □ *Adam loves all kinds of sport.* □ *She watches a lot of sport on the television.* (esporte)
2 a particular game or activity □ *Football is a very popular sport.* (esporte) ▣ *My Dad has played sports all his life.* ▣ *We have very good sports facilities at our school.*
▶ VERB **be sporting something** to be wearing something, especially something unusual which people notice □ *He arrived sporting a bright red shirt and orange shoes.* (vestir algo chamativo, arriscar-se no visual, ostentar)

- **sporting** /ˈspɔːtɪŋ/ ADJECTIVE to do with sport (esportivo) ▣ *sporting events* □ *David Beckham was his sporting hero.*

sports car /ˈspɔːts kɑː(r)/ NOUN [plural **sports cars**] a small fast car that has two seats and no roof (carro esporte)

sportsman /ˈspɔːtsmən/ NOUN [plural **sportsmen**] a man who takes part in sport (o esportista)

sportswoman /ˈspɔːtsˌwʊmən/ NOUN [plural **sportswomen**] a woman who takes part in sport (a esportista)

sporty /ˈspɔːti/ ADJECTIVE [**sportier**, **sportiest**]
1 good at sport □ *She's very sporty.* (bom nos esportes)
2 designed to go fast and look attractive □ *a sporty car* (chamativo e rápido, com design esportivo)

spot /spɒt/ ▶ NOUN [plural **spots**]
1 a place or position □ *This is a lovely spot for a picnic.* □ *X marks the spot where the treasure is buried.* □ *She hopes to retain her number one spot in the championship.* (lugar)
2 a round shape that is often part of a pattern □ *She wore a pink dress with white spots.* (bolinhas)
3 a small dirty mark on something □ *There were spots of oil all over the table.* (mancha)
4 a red raised mark on your skin □ *Teenagers often suffer from spots.* (sinal, espinha, acne)
5 on the spot (a) immediately □ *She threatened to sack me on the spot.* (imediatamente) (b) in the place where something happens □ *There were several reporters on the spot when the plane landed.* (no local) (c) in one place, without moving away □ *We had to jog on the spot for ten minutes.*

♦ IDIOM **put someone on the spot** to try to make someone answer a difficult or embarrassing question □ *When I put him on the spot, he denied having met her.* (colocar contra a parede)
▶ VERB [**spots**, **spotting**, **spotted**] to see or notice something or someone □ *I suddenly spotted Ian over by the window.* □ *Social workers spotted signs of neglect in the girl.* (avistar)

spot check /ˈspɒt tʃek/ NOUN [plural **spot checks**] a check that is done without warning to make sure something is good enough □ *The organization does spot checks on nursing homes.* (inspeção ao acaso)

spotless /ˈspɒtləs/ ADJECTIVE completely clean □ *a spotless white tablecloth* (imaculado, impecável)

- **spotlessly** /ˈspɒtləsli/ ADVERB **spotlessly clean** completely clean □ *She keeps the house spotlessly clean.* (impecavelmente)

spotlight /ˈspɒtlaɪt/ ▶ NOUN [plural **spotlights**]
1 a very bright light which you can direct at something (farolete)
2 the spotlight a lot of attention that someone or something gets from newspapers, television, etc. □ *Health care is in the spotlight again.* (centro das atenções, destaque na mídia)

spot-on

▶ VERB [spotlights, spotlighting, spotlighted] to make people give a lot of attention to something □ *The report spotlighted failures in the police investigation.* (chamar a atenção, destacar)

spot-on /ˈspɒtˈɒn/ ADJECTIVE an informal word meaning completely right □ *His judgement has always been spot-on.* (exato)

spotted /ˈspɒtɪd/ ADJECTIVE having a pattern of spots □ *a spotted handkerchief* (manchado, sarapintado)

spotty /ˈspɒti/ ADJECTIVE [spottier, spottiest]
1 having a lot of spots on your skin □ *a spotty face* (sarapintado)
2 having a pattern of spots □ *a spotty scarf* (com estampa de bolinhas, sarapintado)

spouse /spaʊs/ NOUN [plural spouses] a formal word meaning your husband or wife (cônjuge)

spout /spaʊt/ ▶ NOUN [plural spouts] the long thin part of a container, which you pour liquid out of □ *The spout on the teapot was cracked.* (bico)
▶ VERB [spouts, spouting, spouted]
1 if a liquid spouts, it comes out quickly with a lot of force □ *The oil came spouting up out of the ground.* (jorrar)
2 to talk a lot about something which other people think is boring or silly. An informal word □ *He was spouting a lot of nonsense about politics again.* (declamar)

sprain /spreɪn/ ▶ VERB [sprains, spraining, sprained] to twist and injure a part of your body such as your ankle □ *Kelly fell and sprained her wrist.* (torcer)
▶ NOUN [plural sprains] a painful injury when you twist a part of your body such as your ankle (entorse)
• **sprained** /spreɪnd/ ADJECTIVE with a sprain □ *a sprained ankle* (distendido, com torção)

sprang /spræŋ/ PAST TENSE OF **spring** (ver **spring**)

sprawl /sprɔːl/ ▶ VERB [sprawls, sprawling, sprawled]
1 to lie or sit with your legs and arms spread out in a relaxed way □ *The cat was sprawled on the grass in the sunshine.* (esparramar-se)
2 if a town sprawls, it covers a large area with no clear shape (expandir-se, alastrar-se)
▶ NOUN, NO PLURAL a large area of town without a clear shape □ *urban sprawl* (área expandida)
• **sprawling** /ˈsprɔːlɪŋ/ ADJECTIVE built over a large area with no clear shape □ *Sydney's sprawling suburbs* (esparramado)

spray /spreɪ/ ▶ VERB [sprays, spraying, sprayed] to cause a liquid to come out of a container in many very small drops □ *She sprayed herself with perfume.* (borrifar, pulverizar, aspergir)
▶ NOUN [plural sprays]
1 many very small drops of liquid in the air □ *The spray from the waterfall wet their hair.* (borrifo)
2 liquid in a container which is forced out in very small drops □ *a perfume spray* (borrifo)

spread /spred/ ▶ VERB [spreads, spreading, spread]
1 to cover a larger area or to affect more and more people, or to make something do this □ *The cancer has spread to his lungs.* □ *The virus spread rapidly in the crowded conditions.* □ *I don't want to spread alarm.* □ *Fire spread throughout the building.* (cobrir)
2 to arrange something so that it covers a large area □ **+ out** *I spread the map out on the table.* □ *The bird spread its wings and flew off.* □ *Bits of machinery were spread all over the floor.* (estender)
3 if information spreads, or you spread it, it becomes known by more and more people □ *Rumours spread very quickly in this little village.* (espalhar) 🔊 *News of his death spread rapidly.* (notícias se espalharam) 🔊 *I always try to spread the word* (= tell people in a positive way) *about green energy.* (divulgar a causa)
4 to put a layer of a soft substance onto a surface □ *She spread her toast thickly with butter.* (passar uma camada de algo)
5 to separate something into parts so that it can be shared or so that it does not happen all at once □ **+ out** *Luckily, the exams were spread out over two whole weeks.* □ *They invested in several companies in order to spread the risk.* (dividir, segmentar)
6 if people or things are spread over an area, they are in several parts of that area □ *We have a dozen offices spread throughout Europe.* (espalhar)
◆ PHRASAL VERB **spread out** if people spread out, they move away from a group to cover a larger area □ *We all spread out to search for the boy.* (espalhar)
▶ NOUN [plural spreads]
1 when something covers a larger area or affects more and more people □ *We need to stop the spread of cholera.* □ *There has been a rapid spread of violence in the area.* (difusão, propagação)
2 the area that something covers □ *You need to consider the geographical spread of these people.* (extensão)
3 a type of soft food that you spread on bread □ *cheese/chocolate spread* (alimento pastoso para passar no pão)

spreadsheet /ˈspredʃiːt/ NOUN [plural spreadsheets] a computer program that shows and calculates financial information. A computing word. (programa de planilha de cálculos)

spree /spriː/ NOUN [plural sprees] a time when you do a lot of something that you enjoy □ *a shopping spree* (farra, diversão)

sprig /sprɪɡ/ NOUN [plural sprigs] a small stem of a plant that has leaves on it □ *a sprig of holly* (broto)

sprightly /ˈspraɪtli/ ADJECTIVE an old person who is sprightly is very active □ *She's very sprightly for 85.* (**ativo**)

spring /sprɪŋ/ ▶ NOUN [plural **springs**]
1 the season between winter and summer when plants start to grow □ *Daffodils flower in spring.* □ *There will be an election next spring.* □ *spring sunshine.* (**primavera**)
2 a twisted piece of wire which goes back to its original shape after you have pushed or pulled it □ *The chair had some broken springs in it.* (**mola**)
3 a place where water flows out of the ground □ *a mountain spring* □ *spring water* (**fonte**)
4 a jump or quick movement □ *With a spring, the frog landed right in front of them.* (**pulo**)
▶ VERB [**springs, springing, sprang, sprung**]
1 to move or jump quickly □ *He sprang out of bed to answer the door.* (**saltar, pular**)
2 spring to mind if something springs to mind, you immediately think of it □ *'Honest' isn't the first word that springs to mind when describing him.* (**vir à lembrança**)
3 spring to life to suddenly become active, or to suddenly start doing something □ *Suddenly the fax machine sprang to life.* (**ganhar vida, ficar ativo**)
◆ PHRASAL VERBS **spring from something** to develop from something else □ *His confidence springs from his loving family background.* (**ter origem em algo**) **spring something on someone** to suddenly tell someone something or ask them to do something that they are not expecting □ *I'm sorry to spring this on you, but could we come and stay at your house tonight?* (**surpreender alguém, revelar algo surpreendente**) **spring up** to appear or start to exist very suddenly □ *New office buildings are springing up all over the city.*

springboard /ˈsprɪŋbɔːd/ NOUN [plural **springboards**]
1 something that helps another thing to happen (**trampolim**)
2 a board that you jump from into water (**trampolim**)

spring cleaning /ˌsprɪŋ ˈkliːnɪŋ/ NOUN, NO PLURAL the process of cleaning a house with great care, which people sometimes do in spring (**limpeza de primavera**)

spring onion /ˌsprɪŋ ˈʌnjən/ NOUN [plural **spring onions**] a thin white onion with a green stem that is often eaten raw (**cebolinha**)

springtime /ˈsprɪŋtaɪm/ NOUN, NO PLURAL the season of spring □ *The bulbs flower in springtime.* (**primavera**)

springy /ˈsprɪŋi/ ADJECTIVE [**springier, springiest**] something that is springy is not hard and returns to its original shape after being pressed □ *springy grass* (**elástico, flexível**)

sprinkle /ˈsprɪŋkəl/ VERB [**sprinkles, sprinkling, sprinkled**] to put small drops or pieces of something over a surface □ *She sprinkled chocolate chips onto the cake.* (**borrifar, salpicar**)
• **sprinkler** /ˈsprɪŋklə(r)/ NOUN [plural **sprinklers**]
1 a piece of equipment in the ceiling of a room that water comes out of if a fire starts (**irrigador**)
2 a piece of equipment that spreads small drops of water over an area □ *He was using a sprinkler to water the lawn.* (**regador**)
• **sprinkling** /ˈsprɪŋklɪŋ/ NOUN, NO PLURAL **a sprinkling of something** a small amount of something spread on a surface □ *There was a sprinkling of snow on top of the mountain.* (**pequena quantidade**)

sprint /sprɪnt/ ▶ VERB [**sprints, sprinting, sprinted**] to run fast for a short distance □ *He sprinted down the street after her.* (**correr a toda**)
▶ NOUN [plural **sprints**] a short running race □ *the 100 metre sprint* (**corrida**)
• **sprinter** /ˈsprɪntə(r)/ NOUN [plural **sprinters**] someone who runs in a sprint (**corredor**)

sprout /spraʊt/ ▶ VERB [**sprouts, sprouting, sprouted**] to start to grow, or to produce new leaves or flowers □ *Buds were sprouting on the sycamore tree.* (**brotar**)
◆ PHRASAL VERB **sprout up** to suddenly appear or start to exist □ *New café's are sprouting up everywhere.* (**crescer**)
▶ NOUN [plural **sprouts**]
1 a round green vegetable that looks like a very small cabbage (**broto**)
2 a part of a plant that is just starting to grow □ *bean sprouts* (**broto**)

spruce¹ /spruːs/ NOUN [plural **spruces**] a tall tree with leaves that look like needles (**abeto**)

spruce² /spruːs/
◆ PHRASAL VERBS [**spruces, sprucing, spruced**] **spruce something/someone up** to make someone or something look cleaner and nicer □ *They had spent a lot of money sprucing up the hotel.* (**arrumar-se**)
ADJECTIVE [**sprucer, sprucest**] clean and tidy □ *You're looking very spruce in your new suit.*

sprung /sprʌŋ/ PAST PARTICIPLE OF **spring** (**ver spring**)

spud /spʌd/ NOUN [plural **spuds**] an informal word for potato (**batata**)

spun /spʌn/ PAST PARTICIPLE OF **spin** (**ver spin**)

spur /spɜː(r)/ ▶ NOUN [plural **spurs**]
1 something which encourages something else □ *Hosting the Olympic Games was a spur to improve the city.* (**incitação**)
2 a sharp metal piece on a horse rider's boot that the rider presses against the horse to make it move faster (**espora**)
3 on the spur of the moment suddenly and without planning □ *It was a decision that was made on the spur of the moment.* (**no calor do momento**)
▶ VERB [**spurs, spurring, spurred**]
1 to encourage someone to do something □ *Winning the prize spurred her on to try even harder.* (**incentivar, estimular**)

2 to make something happen □ *The increase in sales was spurred by rising wages.* (**impulsionar**)

spurious /'spjʊərɪəs/ ADJECTIVE a formal word meaning based on facts or reasons that are not correct □ *The company had made spurious claims about the health benefits of its products.* (**improcedente, falso, incorreto**)

spurn /spɜːn/ VERB [**spurns, spurning, spurned**] a formal word meaning to refuse to accept something □ *He spurned all her efforts to be friendly.* (**refutar**)

spurt /spɜːt/ ▶ VERB [**spurts, spurting, spurted**] to flow quickly and forcefully □ *Blood was spurting from a wound on his head.* (**jorro**)
▶ NOUN [*plural* **spurts**]
1 a sudden forceful flow of a liquid □ *a spurt of blood* (**jorrar**)
2 a sudden increase in something such as speed or development (**aumento repentino**) ▣ *Children often have a growth spurt around this age.* (**crescimento repentino**)

sputter /'spʌtə(r)/ VERB [**sputters, sputtering, sputtered**]
1 to make several noises like very small explosions □ *The engine sputtered and stopped.* (**estalar**)
2 to say something with difficulty because you are so angry or shocked □ *'You're a fool!' he sputtered.* (**gaguejar, falar de modo confuso**)

spy /spaɪ/ ▶ NOUN [*plural* **spies**] someone whose job is to discover secret information about another country or company □ *a former Russian spy* (**espião**)
▶ VERB [**spies, spying, spied**]
1 to work as a spy □ *Both men had been spying for the government.* (**espionar**)
2 a formal word meaning to notice someone or something □ *He suddenly spied a man hiding behind the door.* (**notar, avistar**)
◆ PHRASAL VERB **spy on someone** to secretly watch what someone is doing □ *Hetty spent a lot of time spying on her neighbours.* (**vigiar**)

squabble /'skwɒbəl/ ▶ VERB [**squabbles, squabbling, squabbled**] to argue about something that is not important □ *The children were squabbling over who was going to sit in the front seat.* (**brigar**)
▶ NOUN [*plural* **squabbles**] an argument about something that is not important (**briga**)

squad /skwɒd/ NOUN [*plural* **squads**]
1 a part of a police force that tries to stop a particular type of crime □ *the police fraud squad* (**equipe**)
2 a small group of soldiers who work together as a team (**equipe**)
3 a sports team □ *the England squad for the World Cup* (**equipe**)

squad car /skwɒd 'kɑː(r)/ NOUN [*plural* **squad cars**] a car that police officers use (**carro de polícia**)

squadron /'skwɒdrən/ NOUN [*plural* **squadrons**] a group of soldiers or military vehicles □ *a squadron of fighter planes* (**esquadrão**)

squalid /'skwɒlɪd/ ADJECTIVE dirty and unpleasant □ *The refugees were living in squalid camps.* (**esquálido**)

squall /skwɔːl/ NOUN [*plural* **squalls**] a sudden very strong wind (**rajada**)

squalor /'skwɒlə(r)/ NOUN, NO PLURAL very dirty and unpleasant conditions □ *The old man had been living alone in squalor.* (**ver squalid**)

squander /'skwɒndə(r)/ VERB [**squanders, squandering, squandered**] to waste something that is very valuable, especially time or money □ *He squandered all his money on fast cars.* (**esbanjar**)

square /skweə(r)/ ▶ NOUN [*plural* **squares**]
1 a flat shape with four equal sides and four angles of 90 degrees (**quadrado**)
2 an open space with buildings on all four sides □ *a tree-lined square* □ *There was a clock in the market square.* □ *Trafalgar Square* (**praça**)
3 the result of multiplying a number by itself. A maths word □ *The square of 4 is 16.* (**quadrado**)
◆ IDIOM **be back to square one** to be back in the same situation as you were at the start of something □ *I wasted all the money I won, and now I'm back to square one.* (**recomeçar do zero**)
▶ ADJECTIVE
1 shaped like a square □ *a square table* (**quadrado**)
2 measuring a particular amount on each side □ *The room was about 3 metres square.* (**quadrado**)
3 a square metre/foot/mile, etc. the area of a square which has sides which are a metre, a foot, a mile, etc. long □ *The tiles cost £20 a square metre.* □ *The building offers 65,000 square metres of office space.* (**metro/pé/milha etc. quadrado**)
4 (all) square (a) having the same number of points as someone else in a game □ *The two teams were all square at half-time, at 3-3.* (**empatar**) (b) not owing each other any money □ *If you pay for the coffee this week, we'll be square.* (**estar quite**)
5 straight or level □ *Keep the paper square with the edge of the table.* (**alinhar**)
▶ VERB [**squares, squaring, squared**] to multiply a number by itself. A maths word □ *Three squared is nine.* (**elevar ao quadrado**)
◆ PHRASAL VERBS **square with something** if two facts, ideas, reasons, etc. square with each other, they agree with each other □ *These policies don't square with the government's claims to be concerned about the environment.* (**concordante, de acordo**) **square up** to pay someone money that you owe □ *If you buy the drinks, I'll square up with you later.*
• **squarely** /'skweəli/ ADVERB directly □ *The judge's comments were aimed squarely at Ms Cisero.* □ *Susan looked at him squarely.* (**diretamente**)

square meal

square meal /ˈskweə ˈmiːl/ NOUN [plural **square meals**] a large meal of healthy food (**refeição nutritiva e substancial**)

square root /ˈskweə ˈruːt/ NOUN [plural **square roots**] the number which makes another number when multiplied by itself. A maths word □ *The square root of nine is three.* (**raiz quadrada**)

squash /skwɒʃ/ ▶ VERB [**squashes, squashing, squashed**]
1 to press something until it is flat □ *Juliet squashed the empty can.* (**espremer**) *All the strawberries got squashed at the bottom of the bag.*
2 to put a lot of people or things into a small space □ *I was squashed in the back seat of the car with three other people.* □ **+ into** *12 of us squashed into two cars to travel into town.* (**espremer**)
▶ NOUN [plural **squashes**]
1 **a squash** a situation in which there are too many people or things in a place □ *It was a bit of a squash fitting everything in the suitcase.* (**aglomeração/concentração de pessoas/coisas**)
2 *no plural* a game in which you hit a small rubber ball against the walls of a court (**squash**)
3 *no plural* a sweet cold drink with a fruit flavour □ *a glass of orange squash* (**suco de...**)
4 a hard vegetable that grows on the ground (**abóbora**)
• **squashy** /ˈskwɒʃi/ ADJECTIVE soft and easy to press □ *a big, squashy sofa* (**mole**)

squat /skwɒt/ ▶ VERB [**squats, squatting, squatted**]
1 to bend your legs so that your bottom is close to the ground and balance on your feet □ *He squatted down to talk to the child.* (**agachar(-se)**)
2 to live in a building without permission (**morar em um local sem permissão, ocupação irregular**)
▶ ADJECTIVE short and fat □ *a rather squat little man* (**atarracado**)
▶ NOUN [plural **squats**] a building that people are living in without permission (**local de ocupação irregular**)
• **squatter** /ˈskwɒtə(r)/ NOUN [plural **squatters**] someone who is living in a building without permission (**morador irregular**)

squawk /skwɔːk/ ▶ VERB [**squawks, squawking, squawked**] if a bird squawks, it makes a loud noise □ *Seagulls were squawking.* (**grasnar, estrilhar**)
▶ NOUN [plural **squawks**] a loud noise that a bird makes (**grasnado**)

squeak /skwiːk/ ▶ VERB [**squeaks, squeaking, squeaked**] to make a very high sound □ *The door squeaked when he opened it.* (**ranger, guinchar**)
▶ NOUN [plural **squeaks**] a very high sound (**guincho**)
• **squeaky** /ˈskwiːki/ ADJECTIVE [**squeakier, squeakiest**]
1 making a noise like a squeak □ *a squeaky floorboard* (**rangente, guinchante**)
2 **squeaky clean** very clean (**muito limpo**)

squirrel

squeal /skwiːl/ ▶ VERB [**squeals, squealing, squealed**] to make a long, loud, high sound □ *The baby squealed with delight when he saw his mother.* (**guinchar**)
▶ NOUN [plural **squeals**] a long, loud, high sound that someone makes □ *a squeal of excitement* (**guincho**)

squeamish /ˈskwiːmɪʃ/ ADJECTIVE not liking to see unpleasant things, especially blood □ *I couldn't be a nurse – I'm so squeamish.* (**melindroso, sensível, molenga**)

squeeze /skwiːz/ ▶ VERB [**squeezes, squeezing, squeezed**]
1 to press something tightly □ *She squeezed my hand encouragingly.* (**apertar**)
2 to try to move somewhere where there is very little space □ *The cat tried to squeeze itself under the sofa.* □ *He was trying to squeeze into some very tight jeans.* (**comprimir**)
3 to press something in order to get something out □ *He squeezed the last of the toothpaste out of the tube.* □ *Emma was squeezing a lemon.* (**espremer**)
▶ NOUN [plural **squeezes**]
1 the action of squeezing or pressing something (**aperto**) *She gave my hand a friendly squeeze.*
2 **a (tight) squeeze** a situation in which there is only just enough space □ *We all got into the car, but it was a tight squeeze.* (**bem apertado**)

squelch /skweltʃ/ ▶ VERB [**squelches, squelching, squelched**] to make a noise when you move through something soft and wet like mud □ *The wet ground squelched under his feet.* (**fazer barulho ao chapinhar**)
▶ NOUN [plural **squelches**] the noise you make when you move through something soft and wet like mud (**chapinhar**)

squid /skwɪd/ NOUN [plural **squids**] a sea animal with a soft body and ten arms that is eaten as food (**lula**)

squiggle /ˈskwɪɡəl/ NOUN [plural **squiggles**] an informal word meaning a short, curly written line (**til, pequeno rabisco curvo**)

squint /skwɪnt/ ▶ VERB [**squints, squinting, squinted**]
1 to close your eyes slightly when you are looking at something □ *She looked up at him, squinting in the sunlight.* (**olhar com os olhos semicerrados**)
2 to have eyes that look in different directions (**ser estrábico**)
▶ NOUN [plural **squints**] a problem with your eyes that makes them look in different directions (**estrabismo**)

squirm /skwɜːm/ VERB [**squirms, squirming, squirmed**] to move and twist your body because you are embarrassed, in pain, etc. □ *She squirmed when she remembered how rude she had been.* (**contorcer-se**)

squirrel /ˈskwɪrəl/ NOUN [plural **squirrels**] a small grey or red animal with a long, thick tail that lives in trees and eats nuts (**esquilo**)

squirt /skwɜːt/ VERB [squirts, squirting, squirted] to force out a stream of liquid □ He squirted some ketchup on his fries. □ The kids were squirting each other with water. (esguichar)

Sr /'siːnɪə(r)/ ABBREVIATION Senior; used after someone's name to show they are the older of two men in a family with the same name (sênior)

St /seɪnt, striːt/ ABBREVIATION
1 Saint (Santo)
2 street (rua)

stab /stæb/ ▶ VERB [stabs, stabbing, stabbed] to kill or to injure someone by pushing a knife or other sharp object into them □ The woman was stabbed with a knife. (apunhalar)
▶ NOUN [plural stabs]
1 when you stab someone or something (punhalada, facada) 🔵 a stab wound (ferida por golpe)
2 a sudden, strong feeling □ She felt a stab of pain in her leg. (pontada)
♦ IDIOM **have/make/take a stab at something**
1 an informal phrase meaning to try to do something you have not done before □ I'd love to have a stab at running my own business. (tentativa)
2 an informal phrase meaning to guess the answer to something □ Go on, take a stab at it. (arriscar um palpite, tentar adivinhar)
• **stabbing** /'stæbɪŋ/ ▶ NOUN [plural stabbings] a crime in which someone is stabbed (apunhalamento)
▶ ADJECTIVE a stabbing pain is a sudden, strong pain (lancinante)

stability /stə'bɪlɪti/ NOUN, NO PLURAL
1 when a situation stays the same and there are no sudden changes (estabilidade) 🔵 a period of economic stability (estabilidade econômica) □ Children need stability.
2 when something is firm and strong and does not move (estabilidade)

stabilize or **stabilise** /'steɪbəlaɪz/ VERB [stabilizes, stabilizing, stabilized]
1 to stop changing, or to make something do this □ She's been very ill but her condition has stabilized. (estabilizar)
2 to make something firm and strong and not move □ Put a book under the table leg to stabilize it. (estabilizar)

stable /'steɪbəl/ ▶ ADJECTIVE
1 firm, strong and not moving □ This bracket will help to keep the shelf stable. (estável)
2 not changing over a period of time (estável) 🔵 The price has remained relatively stable over recent years. (permaneceu estável) 🔵 He's in a stable condition in hospital. (quadro estável)
3 sensible and calm □ She's a happy, emotionally stable young woman. (emocionalmente estável)
▶ NOUN [plural stables] a building to keep horses in (estábulo)

stack /stæk/ ▶ NOUN [plural stacks]
1 a pile of things □ a stack of books (pilha)
2 stacks of something an informal phrase meaning a lot of something □ The phone has stacks of new features. (pilhas de algo)
▶ VERB [stacks, stacking, stacked] to put things into a stack □ Stack the dishes in the sink and I'll wash them later. (empilhar) 🔵 He got a job stacking shelves in a supermarket.

stadium /'steɪdiəm/ NOUN [plural stadiums or stadia] a large open area for playing sports, with seats around it 🔵 a football stadium □ They will face Real Madrid at the Bernabeu Stadium in the semi-finals. (estádio)

staff /stɑːf/ ▶ NOUN, NO PLURAL the people who work for a particular organization (pessoal) 🔵 Six new members of staff are joining the school this term. (membros da equipe) □ The company has a staff of 150. □ There is a shortage of medical staff in many hospitals.
▶ VERB [staffs, staffing, staffed] to work at a place or to provide workers for somewhere □ More nurses are needed to staff these clinics. (prover de pessoal)

stag /stæg/ NOUN [plural stags] a male deer (veado)

stage /steɪdʒ/ ▶ NOUN [plural stages]
1 the raised area in a theatre where the actors and other performers perform □ This is their first appearance on stage together. 🔵 As the band took the stage, the audience went wild. 🔵 I loved the stage show. (palco)
2 one part of a process, or a period of time in the development of something □ + of The designs are at various stages of development. 🔵 The work is still in its early stages. 🔵 It's hard to predict what will happen at this stage. (estágio, fase)
♦ IDIOM **set the stage for something** to make something possible □ Hamilton's win last week sets the stage for a thrilling end to the season. (tornar algo viável)
▶ VERB [stages, staging, staged]
1 to organize a performance □ They staged a charity pop concert in Rome. (encenar)
2 to organize and take part in something, especially a meeting to complain about something (organizar) 🔵 Students staged a noisy protest against his visit.

stage fright /'steɪdʒ ˌfraɪt/ NOUN, NO PLURAL strong feelings of fear or nervousness about performing in front of an audience (medo de palco)

stagger /'stægə(r)/ VERB [staggers, staggering, staggered]
1 to walk moving from side to side in a way that looks as if you might fall □ He staggered across the room and fell into a chair. (cambalear)
2 if you are staggered, you are very surprised □ I was staggered when they got married. (abalar)
3 to arrange events so that they do not all happen at the same time □ We have to stagger our lunch breaks so that there's always someone in the office. (escalonar)

stagnant | stall

- **staggering** /ˈstæɡərɪŋ/ ADJECTIVE very surprising □ *The amount of money collected was absolutely staggering.* (abalador)

stagnant /ˈstæɡnənt/ ADJECTIVE
1 stagnant water is dirty because it does not flow □ *a stagnant pond* (estagnado)
2 not developing or changing □ *The economy remains stagnant.* (estagnado)

- **stagnate** /stæɡˈneɪt/ VERB [**stagnates, stagnating, stagnated**] to become stagnant □ *His career has stagnated.* (estagnar)

stag party /ˈstæɡ ˌpɑːtɪ/ or **stag night** /ˈstæɡ ˌnaɪt/ NOUN [*plural* **stag parties** or **stag nights**] a party that a man has with his male friends just before he gets married (despedida de solteiro)

staid /steɪd/ ADJECTIVE serious and not willing to try new things □ *The organization is trying to get rid of its staid image.* (sóbrio, sério)

stain /steɪn/ ▶ VERB [**stains, staining, stained**]
1 to leave a mark that is difficult to remove □ *The coffee you spilt has stained the carpet.* □ + *with His uniform was stained with blood.* (manchar)
2 to paint wood with a special substance in order to change its colour (tingir, pintar)
▶ NOUN [*plural* **stains**]
1 a dirty mark on something that is difficult to remove □ *His overalls were covered in oil stains.* (mancha)
2 a substance you put on wood to change its colour (envernizar)

stained glass /ˌsteɪnd ˈɡlɑːs/ NOUN, NO PLURAL pieces of coloured glass used for making pictures in windows (vitral)

stainless steel /ˌsteɪnləs ˈstiːl/ NOUN, NO PLURAL a type of steel (= strong metal) that does not rust (= become damaged by water) □ *stainless steel cutlery* (aço inoxidável)

stair /steə(r)/ NOUN [*plural* **stairs**]
1 stairs a set of steps that go from one level in a building to another (escadaria) 🔁 *I climbed the stairs to the second floor.* (subir a escadaria) 🔁 *I always take the stairs instead of the lift.* (ir de escada) 🔁 *A flight of stairs led down to the cellar.* (lance de escada)
2 one of these steps □ *Alice sat on the bottom stair.* (escada, degrau)

staircase /ˈsteəkeɪs/ NOUN [*plural* **staircases**] a set of stairs (escadaria) 🔁 *a spiral staircase* (= stairs which curl round and round) (escada em espiral)

stairway /ˈsteəweɪ/ NOUN [*plural* **stairways**] a set of stairs inside or outside a building (escadaria)

stairwell /ˈsteəwel/ NOUN [*plural* **stairwells**] the tall space in a building that contains the stairs (poço de escada)

stake /steɪk/ ▶ NOUN [*plural* **stakes**]
1 at stake if something is at stake, you risk losing it □ *There's a lot at stake for both teams.* □ *There are people's lives at stake here.* (em jogo)
2 part of a business that you own □ *He bought a 24% stake in the company.* (ação)
3 a strong pointed stick, for example to support a fence □ *a wooden stake* (estaca)
4 an amount of money that you risk by trying to guess the result of a competition □ *a £5 stake* (aposta)
5 stakes the things you could lose in a situation or competition □ *The threat of a nuclear attack has raised the stakes in the dispute between the two countries.* (riscos)
▶ VERB [**stakes, staking, staked**]
1 to risk losing something as a result of a situation or competition □ *He has staked his political future on this plan.* □ *I'll stake £10 on Paul winning.* (apostar)
2 stake a/your claim to say publicly that something should belong to you □ *He's already staked his claim to be captain next year.* (reivindicar)
♦ PHRASAL VERB **stake something out** to watch a place to see whether anyone leaves or enters □ *Police staked out the building.* (vigiar)

stale /steɪl/ ADJECTIVE [**staler, stalest**]
1 not fresh □ *stale bread* □ *The air smelt stale inside the room.* (velho)
2 not new or interesting □ *The jokes seemed stale.* (velho)

stalemate /ˈsteɪlmeɪt/ NOUN, NO PLURAL
1 a situation in which progress is impossible because the people or groups involved do not agree (impasse) 🔁 *The talks are designed to break the stalemate between the two sides.*
2 a situation in a game of chess in which neither player can make a move so neither player can win (empate)

stalk /stɔːk/ ▶ NOUN [*plural* **stalks**] the stem of a flower, leaf or fruit □ *an apple stalk* (haste)
▶ VERB [**stalks, stalking, stalked**]
1 to follow an animal quietly, in order to catch and kill it □ *The tigress stalked her prey.* (tocaiar)
2 to follow and watch someone in a way that they find threatening □ *She is stalked by press photographers.* (perseguir)
3 to walk in a proud, often angry, way □ *She had offended him so much that he stalked out of the room.* (andar com arrogância)

- **stalker** /ˈstɔːkə(r)/ NOUN [*plural* **stalkers**] someone who stalks another person (tocaieiro)

stall /stɔːl/ ▶ NOUN [*plural* **stalls**] a table or a small open shop where people sell things (banca) 🔁 *a market stall* (tenda de mercado) □ *a roadside food stall* □ *The stalls sell fresh fruit and vegetables.*
⇨ go to **stalls**
▶ VERB [**stalls, stalling, stalled**]
1 if a vehicle stalls, its engine suddenly stops while you are driving □ *The car stalled at traffic lights and she couldn't get it started again.* (enguiçar)
2 to delay someone or to delay doing something □ *I'll try and stall her for a few minutes.* (protelar)

3 to stop making progress ▢ *Peace talks have stalled again.* (estagnar-se, paralisar)

stallion /ˈstælɪən/ NOUN [plural **stallions**] a male horse (garanhão)

stalls /stɔːlz/ PLURAL NOUN **the stalls** the seats nearest to the stage in a theatre (primeira fila)

stalwart /ˈstɔːlwət/ ▶ NOUN [plural **stalwarts**] a strong, loyal supporter ▢ *a meeting of the party stalwarts* (apoiador/partidário firme e leal, esteio)

▶ ADJECTIVE supporting someone or something in a strong and loyal way (apoio firme, esteio) *He's always been one of our most stalwart supporters.* (engajados apoiadores/partidários)

stamen /ˈsteɪmən/ NOUN [plural **stamens**] the male part of a flower that makes pollen. A biology word. (estame)

stamina /ˈstæmɪnə/ NOUN, NO PLURAL the strength and energy to keep doing something for a long time ▢ *You need to do exercises to increase your stamina.* (resistência)

stammer /ˈstæmə(r)/ ▶ VERB [**stammers, stammering, stammered**]
1 to have a speech problem that makes you stop or repeat some letters when you speak (gaguejar)
2 to speak like this because you are frightened or nervous ▢ *'I'm s-s-sorry,' he stammered.* (gaguejar)
▶ NOUN [plural **stammers**] a speech problem that makes you stammer (gagueira)

stamp /stæmp/ NOUN [plural **stamps**]
1 a small printed piece of paper that you buy and stick on letters before you post them (selo) *a first-class stamp* ▢ *I noticed the Canadian stamp on the envelope.*
2 a tool that you use to stamp words, numbers or a design on something, or the mark it makes *a rubber stamp* ▢ *a date stamp* (carimbo)
3 stamp of approval when someone publicly says they approve of something ▢ *The president gave his personal stamp of approval to the scheme.* (selo/carimbo de aprovação)
4 when you stamp your foot (batida de pé)

♦ IDIOM **put your stamp on something** to make changes to something in a way that shows your character ▢ *In his time as director, Murray has put his stamp on this organization.* (deixar sua marca)

▶ VERB [**stamps, stamping, stamped**]
1 to bring your foot down firmly on the ground ▢ **+ on** *He stamped on the brake.* *She stamped her feet to keep them warm.* (pisar)
2 to print letters, numbers, or a design on something ▢ *The official stamped her passport.* ▢ **+ with** *Each letter is stamped with the date we receive it.* (carimbar)
3 to put a stamp on a letter (selar)

♦ PHRASAL VERB **stamp something out** to stop something unpleasant or harmful from happening ▢ *We are determined to stamp out corruption.* (erradicar)

stamped addressed envelope /ˈstæmpt əˈdrestˈenvələʊp/ NOUN [plural **stamped addressed envelopes**] an envelope that you write your name and address on and stick a stamp on, so that someone can send you a reply (envelope com nome e endereço do remetente e selo pago)

stampede /stæmˈpiːd/ ▶ NOUN [plural **stampedes**] when a large group of people or animals suddenly go somewhere very quickly ▢ *The bell went and there was a stampede for the door.* (estouro, debandada)
▶ VERB [**stampedes, stampeding, stampeded**] if a large group of people or animals stampede, they suddenly go somewhere very quickly (causar debandada)

stance /stæns/ NOUN [plural **stances**]
1 someone's opinion about something ▢ *What's the company's stance on working from home?* *They are taking a tough stance against illegal immigration.* (postura)
2 a formal word meaning the way someone is standing ▢ *He had a stiff, upright stance.* (postura)

stand /stænd/ ▶ VERB [**stands, standing, stood**]
1 to be in a vertical position on your feet, not sitting or lying ▢ *I was so tired I could barely stand.* ▢ *I stood on a chair to reach the shelf.* ▢ *He was standing next to his brother.* (ficar em pé)
2 to get up onto your feet after sitting or lying ▢ *Everyone stood when the queen entered.* ▢ **+ up** *Stand up and let me look at you.* (levantar)
3 to put your foot on something, often by accident ▢ **+ on** *You stood on my finger.* (pisar)
4 to be in a particular position ▢ *The train stood outside Waterloo for nearly an hour.* ▢ *Durham stands on the River Wear.* (ficar)
5 to put something in a particular position ▢ *I stood the jug on the table.* (posicionar)
6 to be able to accept someone or something *I can't stand her brother, Mark.* ▢ *Marie couldn't stand hearing her parents arguing any more.* (aguentar, submeter-se a)
7 to continue to exist or to be used ▢ *The judge ordered that the sentence should stand.* *His offer of money still stands.* (permanecer)
8 to be in a particular condition or situation *As things stand* (= the way things are now), *we can't take on any more work.* *At least with Tom you always know where you stand* (= know what he thinks and what he expects you to do). (ficar)
9 to be strong enough to deal with something or not to be damaged by something ▢ *I left my last job because I couldn't stand the pressure.* ▢ *That dish won't stand the heat of an oven.* (suportar)
10 to try to be elected ▢ **+ for** *She's standing for parliament at the next election.* (candidatar-se)
11 stand a chance to have a chance of achieving something ▢ *I think he stands a good chance of winning.* (ter boas chances)

12 stand trial if someone stands trial, they go to a court where it is decided if they are guilty of a crime (**ser submetido a julgamento**)
⇨ go to **stand your ground**

♦ PHRASAL VERBS **stand about/around** to stand somewhere and not do much □ *They've been standing around doing nothing all morning.* (**ficar à toa**) **stand aside 1** to leave a position in a business or an organization so that someone else can do it □ *I have decided to stand aside to allow one of my younger colleagues to take over.* (**ficar de lado**) **2** to move a short distance to the side □ *We stood aside to let him pass.* (**sair do caminho**) **stand at something** to be at a particular level or amount □ *Unemployment stands at over 4 million.* (**estar por volta de**) **stand back** to move a short distance away from someone □ *Stand back, please, so that the doctors can get through.* (**afastar-se**) **stand by 1** to be ready to do something □ *Teams of doctors are standing by with medical equipment.* (**ficar alerta**) **2** to do nothing to prevent an unpleasant action or situation □ *The government is just standing by while its people starve.* (**permanecer parado, inativo**) **stand by someone** to continue to support someone □ *My parents stood by me all through the trial.* (**ficar ao lado, apoiar**) **stand by something** to continue to have the same opinion, or to not change a promise or an agreement □ *I stand by everything I said yesterday.* □ *I think they will stand by their promises.* (**manter a palavra, postura**) **stand down** to leave a position in a business or an organization so that someone else can have it □ **+ as** *He offered to stand down as chairman.* (**retirar-se**) **stand for something 1** if letters stand for something, that thing begins with those letters □ *What does BBC stand for?* (**significar**) **2** to support a particular idea □ *Our party stands for freedom and democracy.* (**apoiar uma ideia**) **3** to be willing to accept a situation or someone's behaviour □ *I won't stand for laziness!* (**aceitar algo**) **stand in** to do someone else's job while they are not able to do it, for example because they are on holiday □ **+ for** *I'm standing in for their usual teacher, who's off sick.* (**substituir**) **stand out 1** to be very easy to see or notice □ *The yellow flowers really stood out against the green background.* (**destacar-se**) **2** to be better than other similar people or things □ **+ from** *He stood out from the other students because of his original mind.* (**destacar-se**)
⇨ go to **stand out like a sore thumb stand up** to get up onto your feet after sitting or lying □ *She stood up and left the room.* (**levantar-se**) **stand up for someone/something** to support someone or something that is being criticized or attacked □ *My brother always stands up for me when my parents tell me off.* (**defender alguém/algo**) **stand up to someone** to not allow yourself to be controlled or treated badly by someone, usually someone more powerful than you □ *Our manager is awful, but nobody dares to stand up to her.* (**enfrentar alguém**)

▶ NOUN [plural **stands**]

1 someone's opinion about something □ **+ on** *What's your head teacher's stand on school uniform?* (**opinião**) 🔁 *He takes a tough stand on crime.* (**tem uma posição**)

2 make a stand to act in a strong way in order to achieve something or to prevent something □ *By refusing to buy battery farmed eggs, we are making a stand against cruelty.* (**oferecer resistência/opor-se**)

3 something that an object stands on □ *a large mirror on a stand* (**base**)

4 a small shop with an open front, often that can be moved from place to place □ *There were lots of food stands at the fair.* (**banca, tenda**)

5 rows of seats where people sit to watch sports □ *Spectators were cheering from the stands.* (**arquibancada**)

6 the stand the place in a court where people stand when they are being asked questions (**banco das testemunhas**) 🔁 *Her husband is due to take the stand* (= be questioned) *tomorrow.*

standard /ˈstændəd/ ▶ NOUN [plural **standards**]

1 a level of quality □ **+ of** *We hope to improve the standard of medical care.* (**padrão**) 🔁 *The club has set high standards for itself this season.* (**alto padrão**) 🔁 *Living standards have risen dramatically.* (**padrão de vida**) 🔁 *The facilities do not meet basic safety standards.* (**atingir padrões**) 🔁 *Standards have been slipping* (= getting worse) *recently.* (**padrões vêm caindo**)

2 standards principles about what is acceptable behaviour □ *Standards aren't what they used to be.* □ *He has high moral standards.* (**princípios morais**)

3 an official rule or system for measuring things □ *The kilogram is the international standard of weight.* (**unidade de medida**)

▶ ADJECTIVE normal or usual □ *the standard charge for postage* 🔁 *All of this is standard police procedure.* □ *Chemotherapy is now a standard treatment for cancer.* (**padrão**)

• **standardize** or **standardise** /ˈstændədaɪz/ VERB [**standardizes, standardizing, standardized**] to make or to keep things all the same □ *We're trying to standardize the filing system.* (**padronizar**)

standby /ˈstændbaɪ/ NOUN [plural **standbys**]

1 something or someone that you can use if you need them □ *I always keep some long-life milk as a standby.* (**pronto para uso**)

2 on standby ready to travel or ready to do something if needed □ *Ambulance crews were on standby to treat any injuries.* (**de prontidão**)

standing /ˈstændɪŋ/ ▶ NOUN [plural **standings**]

1 your position or people's opinion of you in a group or society □ *This affair has damaged his international standing.* (**reputação**)

2 the period of time that something continues or exists for □ *a relationship of several years standing* (**duração**)

▶ ADJECTIVE

1 to do with actions that are done standing up (**em pé**) ▣ *His speech received a standing ovation* (= when an audience stands and claps). (**aplausos em pé**) □ *She pulled herself up to a standing position.*
2 permanent, regularly used, or continuing (**estabelecido, permanente**) ▣ *It's a standing joke around the office.* (**piada costumeira**) □ *We have a standing invitation to visit.*

standing order /ˈstændɪŋ ˈɔːdə(r)/ NOUN [*plural* **standing orders**] an instruction to your bank to regularly pay a particular amount of money from your account to someone else (**débito automático**)

standing ovation /ˈstændɪŋ əʊˈveɪʃən/ NOUN [*plural* **standing ovations**] when everyone stands up and claps at the end of a performance, speech, etc. (**aplausos em pé**)

stand-off /ˈstændɒf/ NOUN [*plural* **stand-offs**] a situation in which an argument or a fight stops because no one can win or achieve their aim □ *a political stand-off* (**impasse**)

standpoint /ˈstændpɔɪnt/ NOUN [*plural* **standpoints**] a particular way of thinking about a situation □ *From a political standpoint, it was a difficult decision.* (**ponto de vista**)

standstill /ˈstændstɪl/ NOUN, NO PLURAL a complete stop (**paralisado**) ▣ *Icy roads brought traffic to a standstill.* (**levaram à paralisação do tráfego**)

stank /stæŋk/ PAST TENSE OF **stink** (**ver stink**)

staple¹ /ˈsteɪpəl/ ▶ NOUN [*plural* **staples**] a type of food or product that you use a lot of □ *staples such as milk and bread* (**gêneros de primeira necessidade**)

▶ ADJECTIVE a staple food or product is one of the most basic and important ones ▣ *Their staple diet is rice.* (**básico, principal**)

staple² /ˈsteɪpəl/ ▶ NOUN [*plural* **staples**] a bent piece of wire that you push through papers to fasten them together (**grampo**)

▶ VERB [**staples, stapling, stapled**] to fasten papers together with a staple □ *Staple the pages together.* (**grampear**)

• **stapler** /ˈsteɪplə(r)/ NOUN [*plural* **staplers**] a small tool for stapling papers together (**grampeador**)

star /stɑː(r)/ ▶ NOUN [*plural* **stars**]

1 a mass of burning gas in the sky that you can see at night as a point of light □ *the brightest star in the night sky* □ *There are billions of stars in our galaxy.* (**estrela**)

2 a famous person, especially a performer ▣ *a film star* ▣ *a pop star* ▣ *He became one of Hollywood's biggest stars.* □ + **of** *He was married to Jennifer Aniston, star of the TV show 'Friends'.* (**estrela**)

3 a shape with five or more points □ *a six--pointed star* □ *The EU symbol is a circle of gold stars on a blue background.* (**estrela**)

4 used to show the standard of something, especially a hotel, restaurant, etc. □ *a three-star hotel* □ *The resort received a top rating of four stars.* (**estrela**)

▶ ADJECTIVE to do with a famous person or the best, most famous, etc. person in a group □ *a star performance* □ *the club's star player* (**de estrela**)

▶ VERB [**stars, starring, starred**] to have the main part in a film □ *Tom Cruise is to star in the sequel.* □ *a new film starring Kate Winslet* (**estrelar**)

starboard /ˈstɑːbəd/ NOUN, NO PLURAL the right side of a ship or aircraft when you are facing the front (**estibordo**)

starch /stɑːtʃ/ ▶ NOUN [*plural* **starches**]
1 a substance in foods such as potatoes, pasta and bread (**amido**)
2 a powder used to make clothes stiff (**goma de amido**)

▶ VERB [**starches, starching, starched**] to make clothes stiff using starch □ *a starched white shirt* (**engomar**)

• **starchy** /ˈstɑːtʃi/ ADJECTIVE containing a lot of starch □ *Avoid sugary and starchy foods.* (**amiláceo**)

stardom /ˈstɑːdəm/ NOUN, NO PLURAL when someone is very famous □ *She achieved international stardom as a supermodel.* (**estrelato**)

stare /steə(r)/ ▶ VERB [**stares, staring, stared**] to look at someone or something for a long time □ *What are you staring at?* (**fitar**)

▶ NOUN [*plural* **stares**] when you look at someone or something for a long time ▣ *Tony gave him a blank stare.* (**olhar vazio**)

starfish /ˈstɑːfɪʃ/ NOUN [*plural* **starfish**] a sea animal with five arms (**estrela-do-mar**)

stark /stɑːk/ ▶ ADJECTIVE [**starker, starkest**]
1 unpleasant, clear and impossible to avoid (**desolador**) ▣ *Scientists issued a stark warning about global warming.* (**aviso desolador**) ▣ *She was faced with a stark choice.*
2 complete and clear □ *There were stark differences in the quality of service.* (**completo**)
3 plain and empty □ *a stark, barren landscape* (**desolado**)

▶ ADVERB **stark naked** wearing no clothes (**nu em pelo**)

• **starkly** /ˈstɑːkli/ ADVERB in a stark way □ *a starkly furnished room* □ *The figures starkly show the financial problems we are facing.* (**completamente**)

starry /ˈstɑːri/ ADJECTIVE [**starrier, starriest**] full of stars □ *a starry sky* (**estrelado**)

starry-eyed /ˈstɑːriˈaɪd/ ADJECTIVE full of dreams or hopes, especially ones that are not sensible □ *She is starry-eyed about her future.* (**sonhador**)

start /stɑːt/ ▶ VERB [**starts, starting, started**]
1 to begin doing something □ + **to do something** *Suddenly, a bird started to sing.* □ + **ing** *What time did you start working this morning?* □ *I'm starting a new job next week.* (**começar**)

startle   783   state

2 to begin to happen or exist, or to make something happen or exist □ *Work on the new bridge has started at last.* □ *He started an online art gallery.* □ *The fire started in the kitchen.* (**começar**)

3 to begin an event, activity or period of time in a particular way □ *My day started very badly.* □ **+ by** *Shall we start by introducing ourselves?* □ **+ with** *I'd like everyone to give their opinion. Let's start with Mel.* (**começar**)

4 to start with (a) at the beginning of a period □ *To start with, I wasn't sure if I'd get on with him.* (b) used before you say the first thing in a list of things □ *Why did I leave my job? Well, to start with, the money was awful.* (**para começo**)

5 to begin to work or to make a machine or a vehicle begin to work □ *The car wouldn't start.* □ *I couldn't start the engine.* (**dar a partida, funcionar**)

6 to be the lowest amount or level of something □ **+ at** *Prices start at £5.* (**começar**)

◆ PHRASAL VERBS **start (something) off** to begin an activity or an event □ *Let's start off with some gentle exercises.* (**começar**) **start on something** to begin doing something □ *Have you started on the cleaning yet?* (**começar com**) **start out 1** to begin as a particular thing or in a particular way □ **+ as** *I started out as a junior assistant.* □ **+ ing** *He started out selling his photographs on a market stall.* (**iniciar**) **2** to begin a journey □ *We started out after dinner.* (**pôr-se a caminho**) **start over** a US word meaning to begin something again □ *I burned the onions and had to start over.* (**recomeçar**) **start something up 1** to begin a business, organization or activity □ *She started up a school for bullied children.* (**pôr em funcionamento**) **2** to make a machine or a vehicle begin to work □ *He started up the engine and off we went.* (**pôr em funcionamento**)

▶ NOUN [plural **starts**]

1 the beginning of something (**início**) 🔁 *Right from the start, I knew I'd be happy here.* (**logo de início**) □ **+ of** *The runners lined up for the start of the race.*

2 the way something begins (**começo**) 🔁 *The business got off to a good start.* (**começar bem**) □ *After a shaky start, his performance was very good.*

3 make a start to begin doing something □ *I'm going to make a start on the cooking.* (**iniciar**)

4 for a start used to give the first of a list of reasons □ *For a start, I'm fed up with sharing a room with my sister.* (**para começar**)

5 the beginning of a journey (**começo, início**) 🔁 *I must go to bed – we've got an early start tomorrow.* (**começar cedo**)

6 the place where a race begins (**local de partida**)

● **starter** /'staːtə(r)/ NOUN [plural **starters**] the first part of a meal, eaten before the main part □ *We had soup as a starter.* (**entrada**)

startle /'staːtəl/ VERB [**startles, startling, startled**] to suddenly frighten or shock someone □ *He was startled by a loud noise.* (**assustar**)

● **startled** /'staːtəld/ ADJECTIVE shocked or surprised by something unexpected □ *a startled expression* (**assustado**)

● **startling** /'staːtlɪŋ/ ADJECTIVE shocking because of being unusual or unexpected □ *Dr Jones made a startling discovery.* (**chocante**)

starvation /staː'veɪʃən/ NOUN, NO PLURAL when people are very hungry and have not got enough to eat □ *Thousands of people die of starvation every year.* (**fome, inanição**)

starve /staːv/ VERB [**starves, starving, starved**] to die or to suffer because you have not got enough to eat (**morrer de fome, sofrer por fome**) 🔁 *If they don't get food aid, these people are going to starve to death.* (**morrer de fome**)

◆ PHRASAL VERB **starve someone/something of something** if someone or something is starved of something they need, they do not have enough of it □ *His brain had been starved of oxygen.* (**sofrer falta, carecer de**)

● **starving** /'staːvɪŋ/ ADJECTIVE
1 an informal word meaning very hungry □ *What's for dinner? I'm starving.* (**estar faminto**)
2 dying because you do not have enough to eat □ *pictures of starving children* (**morrendo de fome**)

stash /stæʃ/ ▶ VERB [**stashes, stashing, stashed**] an informal word meaning to hide something in a secret place □ *He had thousands of pounds stashed away under the floorboards.* (**esconder**)
▶ NOUN [plural **stashes**] an informal word for an amount of something hidden in a secret place □ *He showed me his stash of secret files and photographs.* (**secreto, oculto, aquilo que é escondido**)

state /steɪt/ ▶ NOUN [plural **states**]

1 the condition that someone or something is in □ *The house was in a very poor state.* □ **+ of** *She's always complaining about the state of our public transport.* (**estado**) 🔁 *I'm still in a state of shock.*

2 a country (**Estado**) □ *the state of Israel* 🔁 *There was a meeting between heads of state* (= leaders of countries).

3 the state the government of a country □ *The state should provide for the sick and elderly.* (**o governo**)

4 a part of a country that has its own government □ *New York state* □ **+ of** *the southern Indian state of Andhra Pradesh* (**estado**)

5 the States the US □ *He spent six weeks in the States.* (**os Estados Unidos**)

6 in a state very upset and worried □ *There's no point getting in a state about things.* (**em pânico**)

▶ ADJECTIVE

1 to do with the government of a country □ *a state pension* □ *a state school* (**estadual**)

2 to do with a part of a country that has its own government □ *the state governor* □ *It's an offence under California state law.* (**estado**)

3 official and involving political leaders (**de Estado**) 🔁 *The Prince was on a state visit to India.* (**visita de Estado**)

▶ VERB [**states, stating, stated**] to formally say or write something □ *The letter clearly states that you must bring some identification with you.* □ *They were given an opportunity to state their views.* (**declarar**)

• **stately** /'steɪtli/ ADJECTIVE
1 slow and formal □ *a stately procession* □ *The vehicle was moving at a stately pace.* (**pomposo**)
2 large and formal □ *We were shown into a stately living room.* (**pomposo**)

stately home /ˌsteɪtli 'həʊm/ NOUN [*plural* **stately homes**] a large, old house in the countryside where a rich, important family live or lived (**casarão**)

statement /'steɪtmənt/ NOUN [*plural* **statements**]
1 something that you say or write, especially formally or officially ⚞ *The police asked me to make a written statement of what I saw.* □ *A statement on his website said he had no plans to leave the band.* (**declaração**)
2 a document showing how much money you have in your bank account and what you have spent ⚞ *Check your bank statements regularly.* (**extrato**)

state of affairs /ˌsteɪt əv ə'feəz/ NOUN, NO PLURAL a situation, especially one that is bad □ *This is a sorry state of affairs.* (**conjuntura**)

state-of-the-art /ˌsteɪt əv ðɪ 'ɑːt/ ADJECTIVE using the newest designs, ideas, technology, etc. □ *state-of-the-art medical facilities* (**de ponta, atual**)

statesman /'steɪtsmən/ NOUN [*plural* **statesmen**] an important political leader (**estadista**)

static /'stætɪk/ ▶ ADJECTIVE not moving or changing □ *Crime levels have remained static.* (**estática**)
▶ NOUN, NO PLURAL electricity caused by rubbing two surfaces together □ *You get static when you comb your hair with a plastic comb.* (**estática**)

station /'steɪʃən/ ▶ NOUN [*plural* **stations**]
1 a building where trains or buses stop to let people get on and off (**estação**) ⚞ *a railway station* ⚞ *a bus station* □ *I'll meet you at the station.*
2 a building where some types of work take place ⚞ *He was taken to the local police station.* (**delegacia de polícia**) ⚞ *a fire station* (**corpo de bombeiros**) ⚞ *We stopped at a petrol station* (= a place that sells petrol). (**posto de gasolina**) ⚞ *a nuclear power station* (**usina elétrica**)
3 a company which makes and broadcasts television or radio programmes ⚞ *a local radio station* ⚞ *The interview was broadcast by a Spanish television station.* (**estação**)
▶ VERB [**stations, stationing, stationed**] to put or to send someone to a particular position or place □ *They stationed a guard at each door.* (**estacionar**)

stationary /'steɪʃənəri/ ADJECTIVE not moving □ *a line of stationary traffic* (**estacionário**)

stationery /'steɪʃənəri/ NOUN, NO PLURAL paper, pens, and other things you use to write with (**artigos de papelaria**)

statistical /stə'tɪstɪkəl/ ADJECTIVE to do with statistics □ *All the statistical evidence supports our case.* (**estatístico**)

• **statistically** /stə'tɪstɪkəli/ ADVERB using statistics □ *His views have not been statistically proven.* (**estatisticamente**)

statistics /stə'tɪstɪks/ PLURAL NOUN
1 information about something which is represented by numbers □ *the official crime statistics* (**estatística**) ⚞ *Statistics show that the number of births has increased by 2% over the last five years.*
2 the study of information in the form of numbers (**estatística**)

statue /'stætʃuː/ NOUN [*plural* **statues**] a large model of a person or animal made out of stone, metal or wood □ + *of a huge statue of the Buddha* □ *a life size bronze statue* (**estátua**)

statuesque /ˌstætʃu'esk/ ADJECTIVE tall and attractive □ *a statuesque model and film star* (**belo, atraente**)

stature /'stætʃə(r)/ NOUN, NO PLURAL
1 a formal word meaning importance and respect □ *He is a political figure of international stature.* (**estatura**)
2 a formal word meaning size or height □ *He was small in stature but had a strong personality.* (**estatura**)

status /'steɪtəs/ NOUN [*plural* **statuses**]
1 someone's position in a society or group compared to other people ⚞ *Is success at school determined by social status?* (**posição social**)
2 the legal position of someone or something ⚞ *The legal status of many websites is unclear.* ⚞ *There are questions about age, marital status* (= whether you are married or not), *etc.* (**condição**)
3 the situation or condition of something at a particular time □ *Call your airline to check on the status of your flight.* (**condição**)

status quo /ˌsteɪtəs 'kwəʊ/ NOUN, NO PLURAL the situation as it is now, used especially when you are talking about possible changes □ *Most countries want to maintain the status quo.* (**status quo**)

status symbol /'steɪtəs ˌsɪmbəl/ NOUN [*plural* **status symbols**] something you own that shows you are rich or important (**símbolo de status**)

statute /'stætʃuːt/ NOUN [*plural* **statutes**] a formal word meaning a law (**estatuto**)

• **statutory** /'stætʃutəri/ ADJECTIVE necessary or controlled by law □ *statutory employment rights* (**estatutário**)

staunch /stɔːntʃ/ ADJECTIVE [**stauncher, staunchest**] loyal □ *a staunch supporter of the government* (**leal**)

stave /steɪv/
◆ PHRASAL VERB [staves, staving, staved] **stave something off** to delay something happening □ *We had a packet of crisps to stave off our hunger.* (**adiar**)

stay /steɪ/ ▶ VERB [stays, staying, stayed]
1 to remain in a place □ *Make sure you stay inside the house.* □ *Would you like to stay for dinner?* (**ficar**) ▣ *He agreed to stay home and look after the children.* (**ficar em casa**) ▣ *Stay there/here!* (**Fique aí/aqui!**) □ *I stayed in the same job for nearly twenty years.*
2 to continue to be in a particular condition □ *She tried to stay calm as they waited.* □ *I could hardly stay awake.* □ *Things can't stay the same for ever.* (**manter-se**) ▣ *At the moment we are very happy together, and I hope it will stay that way.* (**permanecer desse jeito**)
3 to spend a period of time in a place □ + *with I'm going to stay with my sister for a few days.* □ + *in We stayed in a wonderful hotel.* (**permanecer**) ▣ *I stayed the night at a friend's house.* (**passei a noite**)
◆ IDIOMS **stay put** to remain in the same place □ *My mother has decided to stay put because she has so many friends where she lives now.* (**permanecer no mesmo lugar**) **stay the course** to continue doing something, even if it is difficult □ *Do you think you will stay the course?* (**continuar, seguir em frente**)
◆ PHRASAL VERBS **stay away** to not go somewhere □ *The gardens are open to the public, but so far the crowds have stayed away.* (**ficar longe**) **stay behind** to remain in a place after other people have left □ *I stayed behind to tidy up.* (**ficar por mais tempo**) **stay in** to remain in your house □ *I stayed in on Saturday and watched TV.* (**ficar em casa**) **stay on** to remain at a place, course, job, etc. for another period of time □ *He's staying on at school to do his A levels.* (**permanecer por mais algum tempo**) **stay out** to not come home at night, or to come home very late □ *My parents don't like me staying out late.* (**ficar fora de casa**) **stay out of something** to not become involved with an argument or in a difficult situation □ *My brothers are always fighting, but I try to stay out of it.* (**ficar de fora**) **stay together** if two people in a relationship stay together, they continue to live together (**continuar juntos**) **stay up** to not go to bed until later than usual □ *We stayed up to watch the election results.* (**ficar acordado**)
▶ NOUN [plural **stays**] a period of time that you spend at a place □ *The trip includes an overnight stay in Bangkok.* (**estada**)

steadfast /ˈstedfɑːst/ ADJECTIVE
a formal word meaning not changing your opinion or what you are doing □ *He remained steadfast in his refusal to negotiate.* (**constante**)

steadily /ˈstedɪli/ ADVERB
1 in a continuous and gradual way □ *His performance has improved steadily.* □ *Costs have risen steadily.* (**regularmente**)
2 without changing □ *It's been raining steadily all week.* (**regularmente**)

steady /ˈstedi/ ▶ ADJECTIVE [steadier, steadiest]
1 firm and not shaking □ *You need a steady hand.* □ *Can you hold it steady for me?* (**firme**)
2 continuous and gradual (**constante**) ▣ *We're making steady progress.* (**contínuo**)
3 not changing □ *I tried to keep a steady pace.* (**constante**)
▶ VERB [steadies, steadying, steadied]
1 to stop something from moving or shaking □ *She tried to steady the tray.* (**parar**)
2 to become calmer, or to make someone become calmer □ *She waited until her voice had steadied.* (**equilibrar**) ▣ *I took several deep breaths to steady my nerves.*
3 steady yourself to stop yourself from falling, especially by holding onto something □ *Helen steadied herself against the wall.* (**firmar-se**)

steak /steɪk/ NOUN [plural steaks]
a thick piece of meat or fish, especially meat from a cow □ *He was eating steak and chips.* □ *tuna steaks* (**bife**)

steal /stiːl/ VERB [steals, stealing, stole, stolen]
1 to take something without the owner's permission □ *The thieves stole money and jewellery.* □ *It's wrong to steal.* □ + *from Several valuable paintings were stolen from the house.* □ *a stolen car* (**roubar**)
2 to move quietly □ *He stole out of the house to meet his girlfriend.* (**furtar**)

> Remember that thieves **steal** money and objects. They rob people and places: □ *They stole his money and his watch.* □ *They were robbed in the street.* □ *They robbed a bank.*

stealth /stelθ/ NOUN, NO PLURAL
a secret or quiet way of doing something □ *The government is introducing new taxes by stealth.* (**procedimento furtivo**)

• **stealthy** /ˈstelθi/ ADJECTIVE [stealthier, stealthiest] doing something secretly or quietly □ *a stealthy killer* (**furtivo**)

steam /stiːm/ ▶ NOUN, NO PLURAL
1 the gas that is formed when you heat water □ *Steam was rising from the coffee pot.* (**vapor**)
2 a steam train/engine etc. a train, engine, etc. that uses power from steam (**trem, máquina etc. a vapor**)
◆ IDIOMS **let off steam** to say how angry you are feeling in a way that makes you feel better (**desabafar**) **run out of steam** to lose your energy or enthusiasm for something (**desanimar**) **under your own steam** without anyone else's help □ *He wanted to explore the city under his own steam.* (**por seu próprio esforço**)
▶ VERB [steams, steaming, steamed]
1 to produce steam □ *A kettle was steaming on the stove.* □ *a steaming bowl of soup* (**fumegante**)

steamroller

2 to cook food in steam □ *steamed vegetables* (cozer no vapor)
◆ PHRASAL VERB **steam (something) up** to become covered in steam, or to cover something in steam □ *My glasses steamed up and I couldn't see a thing.* (embaçar)
• **steamer** /ˈstiːmə(r)/ NOUN [plural **steamers**]
1 a pan used for cooking food in steam (panela a vapor)
2 a ship that uses steam for power (navio a vapor)

steamroller /ˈstiːmˌrəʊlə(r)/ NOUN [plural **steamrollers**] a vehicle used for making road surfaces flat (rolo compressor)

steamy /ˈstiːmɪ/ ADJECTIVE [**steamier, steamiest**] full of or covered in steam □ *a steamy rainforest* (cheio de vapor)

steel /stiːl/ ▶ NOUN, NO PLURAL a very hard metal that is a mixture of iron and carbon (aço) 🔂 *Many knives and forks are made from stainless steel* (= steel that stays shiny). (aço inoxidável)
▶ ADJECTIVE
1 made from steel □ *steel knives* (de aço)
2 to do with making steel and steel objects □ *the steel industry* (relacionado a aço)
▶ VERB [**steels, steeling, steeled**] **steel yourself** to prepare yourself for something difficult or bad □ *She steeled herself for the test results.* (encher-se de coragem)
• **steely** /ˈstiːlɪ/ ADJECTIVE [**steelier, steeliest**] determined and strong □ *a steely gaze* □ *Her steely determination impressed many people.* (de aço)

steep /stiːp/ ▶ ADJECTIVE [**steeper, steepest**]
1 a steep hill or slope goes up or down very quickly □ *a steep hill* □ *The path was too steep for me to cycle up.* (íngreme) 🔂 *It was a steep climb to the top of the hill.* (subida íngreme)
2 a steep increase or decrease is very big (abruptamente) 🔂 *There has been a steep rise in oil prices.* (aumento abrupto) 🔂 *The company suffered a steep decline in sales.* (diminuição abrupta)
3 an informal word for expensive □ *Three pounds for a cup of coffee? That's a bit steep.* (exorbitante)
▶ VERB **be steeped in history/tradition/culture, etc.** to have a lot of a particular quality □ *China is a beautiful country, steeped in tradition and history.* (aprofundar-se em história/tradição/cultura etc.)

steeple /ˈstiːpəl/ NOUN [plural **steeples**] a pointed tower on a church (campanário)

steeply /ˈstiːplɪ/ ADVERB in a way that is steep (abruptamente) 🔂 *Oil prices have risen very steeply.*

steer /stɪə(r)/ VERB [**steers, steering, steered**]
1 to control the direction that a vehicle moves in □ *He steered the car through the narrow streets.* □ *The captain steered out of the harbour.* (dirigir, conduzir)

2 to influence what someone does or the way something develops □ *He intended to steer the country from anarchy to peace.* (conduzir)
3 to put your hand on someone's arm or back and show them where to go □ *Penny steered me towards the house.* (conduzir)
4 steer clear of someone/something to avoid someone or something □ *It's best to steer clear of Dad when he's angry.* (evitar)

steering wheel /ˈstɪərɪŋ ˌwiːl/ NOUN [plural **steering wheels**] the wheel a driver holds to control a car's direction (volante)

stem /stem/ ▶ NOUN [plural **stems**] the long thin part of a plant, which the leaves grow on (caule, haste)
▶ VERB [**stems, stemming, stemmed**] to stop something from continuing (estancar) 🔂 *He used his scarf to stem the flow of blood.* (estancar o sangue) □ *The government has failed to stem the violence.*
◆ PHRASAL VERB **stem from something** to happen or develop as a result of something □ *The charges stem from an incident in which he spat at a police officer.* (originar-se de)

stench /stentʃ/ NOUN [plural **stenches**] a strong bad smell □ *the stench of rotting meat* (fedor)

stencil /ˈstensəl/ ▶ NOUN [plural **stencils**] a piece of card with shapes cut out of it, which you paint over in order to make a pattern on something (estêncil)
▶ VERB [**stencils, stencilling, stencilled**] to use a stencil to decorate a surface (produzir por meio de estêncil)

step /step/ ▶ NOUN [plural **steps**]
1 one of a series of actions involved in doing or achieving something (passo) 🔂 *These talks are an important step in bringing peace to the region.* (passo importante) 🔂 *For me, that school play was the first step towards becoming an actor.* (primeiro passo) 🔂 *I shall take steps to prevent this happening again.* (tomar providências) 🔂 *Step by step* (= gradually) *she is learning to speak again.* (passo a passo)
2 in step (a) having similar opinions or ways of doing things as someone else, or changing at the same speed as something else □ *Wages have not stayed in step with inflation.* (equiparar(-se)) (b) walking at the same speed as someone else □ *He fell in step with Daniel and they walked together.* (no mesmo passo)
3 out of step having different opinions or ways of doing things from someone else, or changing at a different speed from something else (em desacordo, fora do compasso)
4 the action of lifting your foot off the ground and putting it down again in walking, running or dancing (passo) 🔂 *He took a step forward.* (deu um passo) □ *I'm sure I heard steps* (= the sound that steps make) *outside.*

5 a flat surface that you walk on to go up or down to a different level, often one of a series □ *The postman left the parcel on the front step.* □ *We climbed the steep steps to the monastery.* (**degrau**)
6 a particular movement of the feet, for example in dancing □ *Try to learn these simple steps.* (**passo**)

♦ IDIOM **one step ahead** slightly more successful than someone else, or having done something just before someone else □ *I like to stay one step ahead of the competition.* (**um passo à frente**)

▶ VERB [**steps, stepping, stepped**]
1 to take a step □ *He opened the door and stepped out.* (**caminhar**)
2 to put your foot on something, often by accident □ + **on** *He stepped on my toe!* □ + **in** *I stepped in some mud.* (**pisar**)

♦ PHRASAL VERBS **step aside**
1 to leave a position in a business or an organization so that someone else can do it □ *She decided to step aside and let her daughters run the firm.* (**desviar-se**)
2 to move a short distance away from someone □ *He stepped aside to let us past.* (**afastar-se**)
step down to leave a position in a business or an organization so that someone else can have it □ *He stepped down as president in 2007.* (**demitir-se**) **step in** to become involved in a situation in order to try to deal with it □ *The army had to step in to halt the violence.* (**intervir**) **step something up** to increase something that is being used or done □ *Security has been stepped up following the bomb scares.* □ *They stepped up his dose of painkillers.* (**intensificar**)

step- /step/ PREFIX step- is added to the beginning of words to show that people are related to you by a second marriage □ *stepfather* □ *stepdaughter* (**por casamento**)

stepbrother /'step,brʌðə(r)/ NOUN [plural **stepbrothers**] the son of a person who has married your mother or father, but who is not your brother (**meio-irmão (filho do padrasto ou madrasta)**)

stepchild /'step.tʃaɪld/ NOUN [plural **stepchildren**] someone who is the child of your husband or wife, but is not your child (**enteado(a)**)

stepdaughter /'step,dɔːtə(r)/ NOUN [plural **stepdaughters**] the daughter of your husband or wife, who is not your daughter (**enteada**)

stepfather /'step,fɑːðə(r)/ NOUN [plural **stepfathers**] the man who is married to your mother but is not your father (**padrasto**)

stepladder /'step,lædə(r)/ NOUN [plural **stepladders**] a small ladder (= something you use for reaching high places) that folds (**escada**)

stepmother /'step,mʌðə(r)/ NOUN [plural **stepmothers**] the woman who is married to your father but is not your mother (**madrasta**)

steppe /step/ NOUN **the steppes** a large area of hot, dry land with grass in Russia and Asia. A geography word. (**estepe**)

stepping stone /'stepɪŋ 'stəʊn/ NOUN [plural **stepping stones**]
1 something which helps you achieve something else □ *Think of the job as a stepping stone to greater things.* (**trampolim**)
2 one of a line of stones that people walk on to cross a stream (**alpondra**)

stepsister /'step,sɪstə(r)/ NOUN [plural **stepsisters**] the daughter of a person who has married your mother or father, but who is not your sister (**meia-irmã (filha do padrasto ou madrasta)**)

stepson /'stepsʌn/ NOUN [plural **stepsons**] the son of your husband or wife, who is not your son (**enteado**)

stereo /'steriəʊ/ NOUN [plural **stereos**]
1 a piece of equipment for playing music which plays the sound through two speakers (= pieces of equipment that sound comes out of) (**aparelho de som**)
2 in stereo using a system that sends sound out through two speakers (= pieces of equipment that sound comes out of) (**som estereofônico**)

stereotype /'steriətaɪp/ ▶ NOUN [plural **stereotypes**] an idea about what a particular type of person is like, which may be wrong or unfair □ *The programme aims to challenge racial stereotypes.* (**estereótipo**)

▶ VERB [**stereotypes, stereotyping, stereotyped**] to think that all women, all rich people, all white people, etc. have particular qualities (**estereotipar, generalizar**)

• **stereotypical** /,steriəʊ'tɪpɪkəl/ ADJECTIVE involving a stereotype □ *Many people have a very stereotypical view of old people.* (**relacionado a estereótipo**)

sterile /'steraɪl/ ADJECTIVE
1 completely clean, with no bacteria □ *A surgeon's instruments must be sterile.* (**estéril**)
2 unable to have babies (**estéril**)

• **sterilization** or **sterilisation** /,sterəlaɪ'zeɪʃən/ NOUN, NO PLURAL the treatment of something to destroy bacteria (**esterilização**)

• **sterilize** or **sterilise** /'sterəlaɪz/ VERB [**sterilizes, sterilizing, sterilized**] to make something clean by getting rid of bacteria □ *You need to sterilize babies' milk bottles.* (**esterilizar**)

sterling /'stɜːlɪŋ/ ▶ NOUN, NO PLURAL the money used in Great Britain □ *She changed her euros into sterling.* (**libra esterlina**)
▶ ADJECTIVE very good □ *He has done some sterling work.* (**excelente**)

stern /stɜːn/ ▶ ADJECTIVE [**sterner, sternest**] very serious and slightly angry □ *He had a stern expression on his face.* □ *a stern warning* (**severo**)
▶ NOUN [plural **sterns**] the back part of a ship (**popa**)

steroid /'stɪərɔɪd/ NOUN [plural **steroids**] a drug that doctors give people to treat swelling, or one that some people take illegally to improve their sports performance (**esteroide**)

stethoscope /'steθəskəʊp/ NOUN [plural **stethoscopes**] an instrument that a doctor uses to listen to your heart or breathing (**estetoscópio**)

stew /stju:/ ▶ NOUN [plural **stews**] a mixture of vegetables and meat cooked slowly together in liquid □ *beef stew* (**ensopado**)
▶ VERB [**stews, stewing, stewed**] to cook something slowly in liquid □ *I stewed the apples.* (**guisar**)

steward /'stjuəd/ NOUN [plural **stewards**]
1 a man whose job is to look after passengers on an aeroplane or a ship (**comissário**)
2 an official at events such as races and concerts (**organizado**)

stewardess /'stjuədɪs/ NOUN [plural **stewardesses**] an old-fashioned word for a woman whose job is to look after passengers on an aeroplane (**aeromoça**)

stick¹ /stɪk/ VERB [**sticks, sticking, stuck**]
1 to push something thin or sharp into something, or to be pushed into something □ *We stuck pins into the cushion.* □ *Stop sticking your elbows into me!* □ *There was a thorn sticking in my skin.* □ *He stuck his fingers in his ears.* (**espetar**)
2 to fix something to something else, or to become fixed to something □ *Never mind, we can always stick the pieces back together.* □ *We stuck labels on the jam jars.* □ *He had a piece of paper stuck on his back.* (**colar**)
3 to become unable to move □ *The car stuck in the mud.* □ *This drawer keeps sticking.* (**emperrar**)
4 an informal word meaning to put something somewhere □ *Just stick the shopping on the floor.* □ *He stuck his head round the door to say hello.* (**colocar**)

♦ IDIOMS **stick to your guns** to refuse to change your decisions about something □ *Kat stuck to her guns and refused to sell the house.* (**manter sua posição, manter-se firme**) **stick your neck out** to decide to do or say something although it might be wrong or make people angry □ *I'm going to stick my neck out here and say that this vase is worth at least £30,000.* (**arriscar a pele**)
⇨ go to **stick your nose in/into something**

♦ PHRASAL VERBS **stick around** an informal word meaning to stay in a place □ *He didn't stick around long enough to see his children grow up.* (**ficar por perto**) **stick at something** to continue to try to do something difficult □ *She found reading difficult, but she stuck at it and now she really enjoys it.* (**perseverar**) **stick by someone** to continue to support someone, especially when they are having problems □ *My parents stuck by me when I was in prison.* (**permanecer leal**) **stick out 1** to come out further than a surface or an edge □ *His ears stickout.* □ *I could see an umbrella sticking out of her bag.* (**ressaltar, aparecer**) **2** to be easy to notice □ *The thing that stuck out most was the way they dressed.* □ *His work stuck out from all the rest.* (**destacar(-se)**)
⇨ go to **stick out like a sore thumb**

stick something out to stretch a part of your body forward □ *They stuck out their hands for food.* (**esticar-se**) 🔁 *She stuck her tongue out at me.* (**mostrou a língua**) **stick to something 1** if you stick to a plan, decision, etc., you do not change it □ *They promised to stick to our original agreement.* (**ficar preso a, restringir-se a, seguir**)
2 to continue using or doing something □ *They offered me a new car, but I prefer to stick to my bike.* □ *I've never been able to stick to a diet.* (**continuar**) **stick together** to continue to stay together and support each other □ *We women have to stick together!* (**manter-se juntos**) **stick up** to come up above a surface □ *My hair was sticking up.* (**ficar em pé**) **stick up for someone** to support someone who is asking for something or being criticized □ *If I ask the boss for a pay rise, I want you all to stick up for me.* (**tomar a defesa de**) **stick with someone/something** to continue using, doing or being with someone or something □ *The manager decided to stick with the same team.* (**continuar com alguém/algo**)

stick² /stɪk/ NOUN [plural **sticks**]
1 a thin piece of wood that has come from a tree □ *We searched for sticks to make a fire.* (**graveto**)
2 a long thin piece of wood used for a particular purpose □ *a walking stick* □ *a hockey stick* (**vara**)
3 a long thin piece of something □ *a stick of rhubarb* (**haste**)

sticker /'stɪkə(r)/ NOUN [plural **stickers**] a sticky piece of paper with a picture or writing on it □ *There were lots of stickers on the back window of the car.* (**adesivo**)

sticking plaster /'stɪkɪŋ ˌplɑːstə(r)/ NOUN [plural **sticking plasters**] something that you stick on your skin to cover a cut (**esparadrapo**)

stick insect /'stɪk ˌɪnsekt/ NOUN [plural **stick insects**] an insect with a long thin body and legs (**insetos da ordem** *Phasmatodea*: **bicho-pau, bicho-folha**)

stickler /'stɪklə(r)/ NOUN [plural **sticklers**] someone who thinks that a particular thing is very important and that other people should think it is important too □ *Rosie's a stickler for doing things properly.* (**defensor veemente de uma causa**)

sticky /'stɪki/ ADJECTIVE [**stickier, stickiest**]
1 designed or likely to stick to another surface 🔁 *Mend the book with some sticky tape.* (**fita adesiva**) 🔁 *sticky fingers* (**grudento, adesivo, pegajoso**)
2 difficult to deal with (**difícil de lidar**) 🔁 *They found themselves in a sticky situation.* (**saia justa**)
3 sticky weather is hot with slightly wet air (**abafado**)

stiff /stɪf/ ▶ ADJECTIVE [**stiffer, stiffest**]
1 difficult to bend □ *stiff cardboard* □ *stiff material* (**duro, rígido**)

2 if something is stiff, it is difficult or impossible to move it in the usual way □ *I can't turn the tap on – it's too stiff.* (**rijo**)
3 if part of your body is stiff, it hurts when you move it (**rígido**) 🔁 *I've got a stiff neck.* (**pescoço duro**) □ *stiff joints*
4 extreme □ *a stiff challenge* (**difícil**) 🔁 *The company is facing stiff competition from its Japanese rivals.* (**competição difícil**) 🔁 *People who break the law will face stiff penalties.* (**penalidades duras**)
5 a stiff wind is very strong □ *a stiff breeze* (**forte, intenso**)
6 not relaxed or friendly □ *She replied with stiff politeness.* □ *Baldwin gave a stiff nod.* (**duro, rígido**)
7 a stiff substance is thick □ *Whisk the cream until stiff.* (**engrossar**)
▶ ADVERB **bored/worried/scared stiff** an informal phrase meaning extremely bored, worried or frightened □ *I was bored stiff in the English lesson.* (**extremamente entediado/preocupado/assustado**)

• **stiffen** /ˈstɪfən/ VERB [**stiffens, stiffening, stiffened**]
1 to suddenly stop moving because you are frightened, angry, etc. □ *She suddenly stiffened with fright.* (**enrijecer(-se)**)
2 to make something stiff □ *You can stiffen cotton with starch.* (**endurecer**)

• **stiffly** /ˈstɪfli/ ADVERB in a stiff way □ *Grandad got up stiffly from his chair.* □ *'No thank you,' she replied stiffly.* (**rigidamente**)

• **stiffness** /ˈstɪfnɪs/ NOUN, NO PLURAL the quality of being stiff □ *Massage can ease muscle stiffness.* (**rigidez**)

stifle /ˈstaɪfəl/ VERB [**stifles, stifling, stifled**] to stop something from happening or developing (**abafar, reprimir**) 🔁 *She stifled a yawn.* (**segurou um bocejo**)

• **stifling** /ˈstaɪflɪŋ/ ADJECTIVE very hot □ *stifling heat* (**sufocante**)

stigma /ˈstɪɡmə/ NOUN [**plural stigmas**] a feeling that something is bad or embarrassing, especially when this is wrong (**estigma**) 🔁 *There used to be a stigma attached to being unemployed.*

• **stigmatize** or **stigmatise** /ˈstɪɡmətaɪz/ VERB [**stigmatizes, stigmatizing, stigmatized**] to think that something is bad or embarrassing, especially when this is wrong (**estigmatizar**)

stile /staɪl/ NOUN [**plural stiles**] a set of steps for climbing over a wall or fence in the countryside (**escada**)

stiletto /stɪˈletəʊ/ NOUN [**plural stilettos**]
1 a shoe with a thin, high heel (= part of a shoe under the back of the foot) □ *a pair of stilettos* (**sapato com salto stiletto**)
2 a thin, high heel on a shoe (**salto**)

still /stɪl/ ▶ ADVERB
1 up to a particular time and continuing □ *Are you still living in Tokyo?* □ *By Sunday she still hadn't replied to the invitation.* □ *I'm still hungry.* (**ainda**)

2 despite what you have just said or done □ *She's treated me badly but she's still my daughter and I love her.* □ *It was raining but we still decided to go.* (**ainda**)
3 used for saying that something is possible even now □ *You can still catch the bus if you leave now.* (**ainda**)
4 better/worse/larger, etc. still used for emphasizing that something is even better, worse, etc. □ *You could come over tomorrow. Better still, why don't you bring Jane too?* (**melhor/pior/maior ainda**)
▶ ADJECTIVE [**stiller, stillest**]
1 not moving (**quieto**) 🔁 *Keep still while I brush your hair!* (**manter quieto**)
2 calm □ *The city seems very still in the early morning.* □ *the still night air* (**quieto**)
3 a still drink is without bubbles □ *still lemonade* (**sem gás**)

stillborn /ˈstɪlbɔːn/ ADJECTIVE a stillborn baby is born dead (**natimorto**)

still life /ˌstɪl ˈlaɪf/ NOUN [**plural still lifes**] a painting of objects such as flowers or fruit (**natureza-morta**)

stillness /ˈstɪlnɪs/ NOUN, NO PLURAL the quality of being still □ *the stillness of early morning* (**quietude**)

stilted /ˈstɪltɪd/ ADJECTIVE a stilted way of talking or writing is formal and not natural □ *a stilted conversation* (**afetado**)

stilts /stɪlts/ PLURAL NOUN
1 a pair of long poles that you stand on and walk on (**pernas de pau**)
2 poles that support a building, raising it above the ground or water (**estacas**)

stimulant /ˈstɪmjʊlənt/ NOUN [**plural stimulants**] a drug that gives you more energy □ *The caffeine in coffee is a stimulant.* (**estimulante**)

stimulate /ˈstɪmjʊleɪt/ VERB [**stimulates, stimulated, stimulating**]
1 to encourage something to grow and develop □ *The policy helped to stimulate economic growth.* (**estimular**)
2 to encourage someone or make them feel excited □ *Good teaching should stimulate children and get them interested in a subject.* (**estimular**)

• **stimulating** /ˈstɪmjʊleɪtɪŋ/ ADJECTIVE interesting, and making you think about new ideas □ *a stimulating discussion* (**estimulante**)

• **stimulation** /ˌstɪmjʊˈleɪʃən/ NOUN, NO PLURAL the act of stimulating someone or something □ *stimulation of the senses* (**estimulação**)

• **stimulus** /ˈstɪmjʊləs/ NOUN [**plural stimuli**] something that causes something else to happen or develop □ *Light is the stimulus that causes a flower to open.* (**estímulo**)

sting /stɪŋ/ ▶ VERB [**stings, stinging, stung**]
1 if an insect or plant stings you, it hurts your skin when it touches you □ *I was badly stung by nettles.* □ *Bees can sting.* (**picar**)

stingy

2 to feel a sudden pain in your eyes or skin, or to make someone feel a sudden pain in their eyes or skin □ *The shampoo made her eyes sting.* □ *Smoke stung his eyes.* (**picar, arder**)
3 to make someone feel upset □ *He was stung by her criticism.* (**magoar**)
▶ NOUN [plural **stings**]
1 the sudden pain you feel when an insect or plant stings you □ *a wasp sting* (**picada**)
2 a sudden pain in your eyes or skin (**arder**)
• **stinging** /ˈstɪŋɪŋ/ ADJECTIVE criticizing someone a lot □ *stinging criticism* (**provocar**)

stingy /ˈstɪndʒi/ ADJECTIVE [**stingier, stingiest**] an informal word meaning not liking to spend money □ *He's very stingy with money.* (**mesquinho, avarento**)

stink /stɪŋk/ ▶ NOUN [plural **stinks**] a bad smell □ *the stink of rotting fish* (**fedor**)
♦ IDIOM **cause/create/kick up a stink** an informal phrase meaning to complain a lot about something □ *You should kick up a stink if they won't give you your money back.* (**reclamar, rodar a baiana**)
▶ VERB [**stinks, stinking, stank** or **stunk, stunk**]
1 to have a bad smell □ *The house stinks of cats.* (**feder**)
2 an informal word meaning to be unfair or dishonest □ *The deal stinks.* (**feder**)

stint /stɪnt/ NOUN [plural **stints**] a period of time that you spend doing something □ *He did a five-year stint as party chairman.* (**atividade com prazo determinado**)

stipulate /ˈstɪpjʊleɪt/ VERB [**stipulates, stipulating, stipulated**] a formal word meaning to say that something should be done □ *The rules stipulate that all products must display a label showing country of origin.* (**estipular**)
• **stipulation** /ˌstɪpjʊˈleɪʃən/ NOUN [plural **stipulations**] something that has been stipulated □ *He was given a temporary visa with the stipulation that he left the country when it ran out.* (**estipulação**)

stir /stɜː(r)/ ▶ VERB [**stirs, stirring, stirred**]
1 to mix something with a circular movement □ *He put sugar in his tea and stirred it.* (**mexer**)
2 to move slightly, or to make something move slightly □ *The baby stirred in its sleep.* □ *The breeze stirred her hair.* (**mexer(-se) levemente**)
3 to cause an emotion in someone □ *The poem stirred powerful emotions in him.* (**tocar, mexer com as emoções**)
♦ PHRASAL VERB **stir something up**
1 to deliberately cause problems □ *He was always trying to stir up trouble.* (**criar confusão**)
2 to make someone remember something, often something bad □ *The meeting had stirred up some painful memories for her.* (**trazer à tona, provocar**)
▶ NOUN, NO PLURAL

1 an act of stirring (**agitação, comoção**) □ *Now give the paint a stir.*
2 cause/create a stir to make people feel excited or interested □ *Their arrival caused quite a stir.* (**animar, agitar**)

stir-fry /ˈstɜːfraɪ/ ▶ VERB [**stir-fries, stir-frying, stirfried**] to cook small pieces of food very quickly in hot oil □ *stir-fried vegetables* (**fritar**)
▶ NOUN [plural **stir-fries**] a meal made by cooking small pieces of food very quickly in hot oil (**fritura**)

stirring /ˈstɜːrɪŋ/ ADJECTIVE making you feel very strong emotions □ *a stirring speech* (**comovente**)

stirrup /ˈstɪrəp/ NOUN [plural **stirrups**] a metal ring that you put your foot in when you are riding a horse (**estribo**)

stitch /stɪtʃ/ ▶ NOUN [plural **stitches**]
1 a piece of thread on cloth that has been sewn □ *She sewed the hem with small neat stitches.* (**ponto**)
2 a piece of thread that a doctor uses to repair injuries to your skin □ *He cut his hand and needed stitches in it.* (**ponto**)
3 a bad pain in your side that you get when you are running □ *I've got a stitch.* (**pontada**)
4 in stitches laughing a lot □ *We were all in stitches when we heard what had happened.* (**às gargalhadas**)
▶ VERB [**stitches, stitching, stitched**] to sew □ *I stitched the button on to my coat.* (**costurar**)
♦ PHRASAL VERB **stitch something up** to repair a hole in something by sewing (**costurar, suturar**)

stoat /stəʊt/ NOUN [plural **stoats**] a small wild animal with a long thin body (**arminho**)

stock /stɒk/ ▶ NOUN [plural **stocks**]
1 the goods that a shop has available □ *Buy now while stocks last!* (**estoque**)
2 out of/in stock not available/available to buy in a particular shop □ *I'm sorry but the item is out of stock at the moment.* (**indisponível/disponível em estoque**)
3 a supply of something □ *a secret stock of weapons* □ *Fish stocks have declined in many seas.* (**estoque, sortimento**)
4 stocks shares in a company, which you can buy (**ações**)
5 a liquid in which meat or vegetables have been cooked □ *chicken stock* (**caldo**)
6 take stock of something to think carefully about a situation □ *I needed time to take stock of my life.* (**avaliar algo**)
▶ VERB [**stocks, stocking, stocked**]
1 to have something available to buy □ *Most supermarkets now stock organic products.* (**ter em estoque**)
2 to fill a place with something so that you can use it later □ *He stocked the fridge with plenty of drinks.* (**abastecer**)
♦ PHRASAL VERB **stock up** to buy a lot of something □ *We stocked up on food for our trip.* (**estocar**)

stockade

▶ ADJECTIVE a stock answer or phrase is one that someone always uses (**comum**)

stockade /stɒˈkeɪd/ NOUN [plural **stockades**] a fence of strong posts put up round an area or building to protect or defend it (**paliçada**)

stockbroker /ˈstɒkˌbrəʊkə(r)/ NOUN [plural **stockbrokers**] someone whose job is to buy and sell company shares for other people (**corretor de ações**)

stock exchange /ˈstɒk ɪksˌtʃeɪndʒ/ NOUN [plural **stock exchanges**] a place where company shares are bought and sold (**bolsa de valores**)

stocking /ˈstɒkɪŋ/ NOUN [plural **stockings**] a very thin piece of clothing for a woman's foot and leg □ *a pair of stockings* (**meia**)

stock market /ˈstɒk ˌmɑːkɪt/ NOUN [plural **stock markets**]
1 a place where company shares are bought and sold (**bolsa de valores**)
2 the business of buying and selling shares (**mercado de ações**)

stockpile /ˈstɒkpaɪl/ ▶ VERB [**stockpiles, stockpiling, stockpiled**] to collect a lot of things that you can use later □ *There are reports that weapons are being stockpiled.* (**armazenar**)
▶ NOUN [plural **stockpiles**] a large supply of something (**armazenamento**)

stocktaking /ˈstɒkˌteɪkɪŋ/ NOUN, NO PLURAL the process of counting all the goods in a shop or factory □ *The shop is closed for stocktaking.* (**levantamento de estoque**)

stocky /ˈstɒki/ ADJECTIVE [**stockier, stockiest**] a stocky person is wide and strong-looking but usually short (**atarracado**)

stodgy /ˈstɒdʒi/ ADJECTIVE [**stodgier, stodgiest**]
1 stodgy food is heavy and makes you feel full very quickly □ *a stodgy pudding* (**pesado**)
2 serious and boring (**enfadonho**)

stoical /ˈstəʊɪkəl/ *or* **stoic** /ˈstəʊɪk/ ADJECTIVE not complaining when bad things happen to you □ *She's clearly suffering but she's very stoical about it.* (**estoico**)
• **stoicism** /ˈstəʊɪsɪzəm/ NOUN, NO PLURAL the quality of being stoical □ *I admire her stoicism.* (**estoicismo**)

stoke /stəʊk/ VERB [**stokes, stoking, stoked**]
1 to put coal, wood, etc. on a fire (**atiçar fogo**)
2 to make something increase, especially something bad □ *There are fears that this will stoke more violence.*

stole[1] /stəʊl/ PAST TENSE OF **steal** (*ver* **steal**)

stole[2] /stəʊl/ NOUN [plural **stoles**] a long piece of fur or cloth that a woman wears around her shoulders (**estola**)

stolen /ˈstəʊlən/ PAST PARTICIPLE OF **steal**

stomach /ˈstʌmək/ ▶ NOUN [plural **stomachs**]
1 the part inside your body where food goes when you have eaten it (**estômago**)
2 the front part of your body below your chest □ *a flat stomach* (**barriga**)

791 **stool** S

3 on an empty stomach without first eating something □ *You shouldn't take the pills on an empty stomach.* (**com o estômago vazio**)
4 not have the stomach for something to not be brave enough to do something □ *I don't have the stomach for dangerous sports.* (**não ter estômago para algo**)
▶ VERB **can't stomach something** used for saying that someone does not like something □ *I can't stomach TV programmes that show real operations.* (**não conseguir engolir algo, não ter estômago para algo**)

stomach ache /ˈstʌmək ˌeɪk/ NOUN [plural **stomach aches**] a pain in the stomach (**dor de barriga**)

stomach bug /ˈstʌmək ˌbʌg/ NOUN [plural **stomach bugs**] an infectious illness that affects the stomach (**infecção no estômago**)

stomp /stɒmp/ VERB [**stomps, stomping, stomped**] to walk in a heavy and noisy way □ *He shouted at us and stomped out of the room.* (**pisar duro, pisão**)

stone /stəʊn/ ▶ NOUN [plural **stones**]
1 a small piece of rock (**pedregulho**) 🔊 *The boys were throwing stones into the water.* (**atirando pedregulhos**)
2 *no plural* the hard substance that rocks are made of □ *The house was built of stone.* (**pedra**)
3 a small piece of valuable rock, used for making jewellery 🔊 *The necklace was made of gold and precious stones* (= valuable and rare stones). (**pedra preciosa**)
4 a unit for measuring weight, equal to 6.35 kilograms (14 pounds) □ *I weigh nine stone.* (**unidade de medida de peso**)
5 the hard piece in the middle of some fruits □ *a peach stone* (**caroço**)
⇨ go to **set in stone/concrete**
▶ ADJECTIVE made of stone □ *stone walls* □ *a stone floor* (**de pedra**)
▶ VERB [**stones, stoning, stoned**]
1 to throw stones at someone □ *They had been stoned to death.* (**apedrejar**)
2 to take the stones out of fruit (**descaroçar**)

stone cold /ˌstəʊn ˈkəʊld/ ADJECTIVE very cold □ *The soup was stone cold.* (**frio como o gelo, frio demais**)

stone deaf /ˌstəʊn ˈdef/ ADJECTIVE completely deaf (**surdo como uma porta**)

stony /ˈstəʊni/ ADJECTIVE [**stonier, stoniest**]
1 full of, or covered with, stones □ *a stony beach* (**pedregoso**)
2 unfriendly 🔊 *They sat in stony silence.* □ *a stony expression* (**empedernido, duro**)

stood /stʊd/ PAST TENSE AND PAST PARTICIPLE OF **stand** (*ver* **stand**)

stool /stuːl/ NOUN [plural **stools**] a seat without a back □ *She was sitting on a stool in the kitchen.* (**tamborete, banco**)

stoop /stu:p/ ▶ VERB [**stoops, stooping, stooped**] to bend your body forwards and down □ *The doorway was so low that she had to stoop to get through it.* **(abaixar-se)**

♦ PHRASAL VERB **stoop to doing something** to do something bad in order to get or achieve something □ *Surely he wouldn't stoop to stealing from his own mother!* **(prestar-se a)**

▶ NOUN, NO PLURAL a position in which your body is bent forwards □ *The old man walked with a stoop.* **(inclinado, inclinação)**

stop /stɒp/ ▶ VERB [**stops, stopping, stopped**]
1 to prevent something happening or existing or someone from doing something □ + *ing He'll never succeed but that won't stop him trying.* □ + *from The barriers stop the crowd from pouring into the street.* □ *Nothing seems to stop the violence.* **(impedir, deter)**
2 to no longer do something □ + *ing The wound has stopped bleeding.* □ *Please stop this nonsense.* **(parar)** 🔊 *Stop it! I'm trying to concentrate.* **(Pare com isso!)**
3 to not happen or exist any more □ *It was lovely when the noise stopped.* □ *We're waiting for the rain to stop.* **(parar)**
4 to no longer move or to make something finish moving □ *A car stopped outside the house.* □ *He stopped the ball with his foot.* **(parar um movimento)**
5 if a public vehicle stops somewhere, it stays there for a short time for people to get on and off □ *Does this train stop at Chester?* **(parar)**
6 to no longer work □ *My watch has stopped.* **(parar de funcionar)**
7 stop at nothing if someone will stop at nothing, they will do anything possible to achieve what they want **(não ser impedido por nada, ir até o fim)**

♦ IDIOM **stop short of something** to not do something, although you almost do it □ *His remarks stopped short of calling the minister a liar.* **(parar de repente, segurar-se)**
⇨ go to **stop the rot**

♦ PHRASAL VERB **stop off** to go to a place on your way to somewhere else □ *We stopped off at my son's house for a few days.* **(fazer uma parada)**

▶ NOUN [*plural* **stops**]
1 a place where someone spends some time, often during a journey 🔊 *Our first stop was Las Vegas.* 🔊 *Next stop, Rome.* **(parada)**
2 a place where a public vehicle stops 🔊 *This train calls at all stops to Glasgow.* **(parar)**
3 a period of time when you stop somewhere 🔊 *We made a brief stop in Moscow.* **(interrupção)**
4 come to a stop to stop moving □ *The train came to a stop just outside Hull.* **(parar o movimento)**

stopgap /ˈstɒpgæp/ NOUN [*plural* **stopgaps**] something that is temporary 🔊 *This is a stopgap measure until a new headteacher can be found.* **(tapa-buraco)**

stoplight /ˈstɒplaɪt/ NOUN [*plural* **stoplights**] the US word for **traffic lights** **(luz vermelha do semáforo)**

stopover /ˈstɒpˌəʊvə(r)/ NOUN [*plural* **stopovers**] a short stay somewhere on a long plane journey □ *They are flying from London to Sydney with a stopover in Singapore.* **(fazer uma parada)**

stoppage /ˈstɒpɪdʒ/ NOUN [*plural* **stoppages**]
1 a time when people stop working because they are angry about something □ *Taxi drivers are staging a nationwide stoppage in protest at the new fare system.* **(interrupção)**
2 a time when a game stops because a player is injured or because of bad weather □ *Injury stoppages added six minutes to the end of the game.* **(interrupção)**

stopper /ˈstɒpə(r)/ NOUN [*plural* **stoppers**] something that you push into the top of a bottle in order to close it **(tampão)**

stopwatch /ˈstɒpwɒtʃ/ NOUN [*plural* **stopwatches**] a watch used for measuring exactly how long it takes someone to do something **(cronômetro)**

storage /ˈstɔːrɪdʒ/ NOUN, NO PLURAL
1 the act of keeping things in a place until you need them □ *the storage of goods* 🔊 *The apartment has plenty of storage space* (= places where you can store things). **(armazenagem)**
2 in storage if you put something in storage, you pay for it to be stored somewhere **(reserva)**

store /stɔː(r)/ ▶ NOUN [*plural* **stores**]
1 a shop □ *the village store* □ *an online store* 🔊 *The company opened its first store in 1930.* 🔊 *The store sells cards and gifts.* **(loja)**
2 a supply of something which you keep to use when you need it □ + *of Squirrels keep a store of food.* **(provisão)**
3 in store (for someone) going to happen to someone □ *There may be some good news in store for her soon.* **(reservado (para alguém))**

▶ VERB [**stores, storing, stored**]
1 to keep something somewhere □ *Store the chocolate in a cool dry place.* □ + *away The books had been carefully stored away.* **(armazenar)**
2 to keep information electronically □ *All the information is stored on computers.* **(guardar)**
3 store up problems/trouble to do something that will cause problems in the future □ *You're storing up health problems if you don't do any exercise.* **(criar/provocar problemas)**

storey /ˈstɔːri/ NOUN [*plural* **storeys**] one of the levels in a building □ *a four-storey carpark* **(andar)**

stork /stɔːk/ NOUN [*plural* **storks**] a bird with long legs and a long beak which walks in water **(cegonha)**

storm /stɔːm/ ▶ NOUN [*plural* **storms**]
1 a time when there is suddenly a lot of wind and rain **(tempestade)** 🔊 *A huge storm hit New*

Orleans. (a tempestade atingiu) ◨ She waited indoors until the storm had passed. (até a tempestade passar) ◨ a tropical storm (tempestade tropical)

2 no plural a situation in which a lot of people disagree about something and are very angry □ **+ of** The decision provoked a storm of protest. (tumulto)

▶ VERB [**storms, storming, stormed**]

1 to enter a place using force □ Troops stormed the embassy. □ Police stormed the building. (tomar de assalto)

2 to walk somewhere in a very angry way □ She stormed out of the room. (precipitar-se)

- **stormy** /ˈstɔːmɪ/ ADJECTIVE [**stormier, stormiest**]
1 with a lot of strong winds and rain ◨ stormy weather □ a stormy night (tempestuoso)
2 involving a lot of arguments □ a stormy relationship (tempestuoso)

story /ˈstɔːrɪ/ NOUN [plural **stories**]

1 a description of events, which can be real or invented (história) ◨ The teacher was reading a story to the class. (lendo uma história) ◨ The film is based on a true story. (história verídica) ◨ The children were telling each other ghost stories. (contando histórias) □ **+ of** The book is the story of his life. □ **+ about** It's a story about a Jewish boy growing up in London.

2 a report in a newspaper or on television about something that has happened (notícia) ◨ The paper published a front-page story about the singer's private life. (notícia de primeira página) ◨ The murder was a big news story. (reportagem)

3 an explanation of what has happened, which may not be true (relato) ◨ I don't think he's telling me the full story. (a história completa) ◨ The police didn't believe her story. (não acreditou na versão dela)

4 the US spelling of **storey** (ver **storey**)

stout /staʊt/ ADJECTIVE [**stouter, stoutest**]

1 fat □ He was a rather stout middle-aged man. (corpulento)

2 thick and strong □ stout boots (resistente)

stove /stəʊv/ NOUN [plural **stoves**]

1 a piece of equipment for cooking on □ There was a pan on the stove. (fogão)

2 a piece of equipment that burns wood or coal and heats a room (estufa)

stow /stəʊ/ VERB [**stows, stowing, stowed**] to put something in a place until you need it (arrumar)

stowaway /ˈstəʊəweɪ/ NOUN [plural **stowaways**] someone who hides on a ship or aeroplane in order to travel secretly (passageiro clandestino)

straddle /ˈstrædəl/ VERB [**straddles, straddling, straddled**]

1 to stand or sit with one leg on each side of something □ Lori straddled the fence. (montar)

2 to be on both sides of a place □ The village straddles the border of Israel and Lebanon. (estar posicionado em dois locais ao mesmo tempo, ter posição neutra)

straggle /ˈstrægəl/ VERB [**straggles, straggling, straggled**] to walk more slowly than other people in a group □ Some of the younger children were straggling behind. (desgarrar-se)

- **straggler** /ˈstræɡlə(r)/ NOUN [plural **stragglers**] a person who walks more slowly than the other people in a group (retardatário)

- **straggly** /ˈstræɡlɪ/ ADJECTIVE [**stragglier, straggliest**] growing in an untidy way □ straggly hair (em desalinho)

straight /streɪt/ ▶ ADJECTIVE [**straighter, straightest**]

1 not bent or curved □ a straight line □ straight hair (reto)

2 completely horizontal or vertical □ That picture isn't straight. (reto)

3 honest (verdadeiro) ◨ Give me a straight answer! (resposta sincera)

4 tidy (em ordem) ◨ I need to get this room straight before the students arrive. (deixar arrumado)

5 one after another with nothing in between □ Juventus have now had five straight wins. (seguido)

♦ IDIOMS **get something straight** to make sure that you understand a situation correctly □ Now let's get this straight. You want to borrow £3,000? (vamos esclarecer as coisas) **keep a straight face** to manage to stop yourself laughing □ When I saw her hat, I could hardly keep a straight face. (ficar sério)

▶ ADVERB

1 in a straight line □ I was so tired, I couldn't walk straight. □ The lion ran straight towards him. □ She was looking straight at me. (em linha reta)

2 straight on without changing direction □ Go straight on at the traffic lights. (seguir em linha reta)

3 immediately □ I came straight here. (imediatamente)

4 straight away immediately □ Could you come to my office straight away, please? (imediatamente)

5 if you sit up straight, or stand up straight, you sit or stand with your back completely vertical (com postura reta)

6 not think straight to be unable to think clearly, often because you are very tired, upset or excited (não pensar com clareza)

7 tell someone straight to tell someone something in a direct and honest way, even if it may upset them □ I told him straight that if he didn't work harder he'd fail his exams. (dizer abertamente)

- **straighten** /ˈstreɪtən/ VERB [**straightens, straightening, straightened**] to become straight or to make something straight □ The road curved then straightened. □ He straightened his tie. (endireitar(-se))

♦ PHRASAL VERBS **straighten something out** to deal with a problem or a complicated situation □ *I spent the whole day trying to straighten out my finances.* (**resolver algo**) **straighten up** to stand up straight (**endireitar-se**)

straightforward /ˌstreɪtˈfɔːwəd/ ADJECTIVE
1 easy □ *a straightforward task* (**simples**)
2 honest □ *He's fairly straightforward.* (**franco**)

strain /streɪn/ ▶ VERB [strains, straining, strained]
1 to injure part of your body by using it too much □ *You'll strain your eyes reading in the dark.* (**forçar**)
2 to try hard to do something □ *He strained to look through a small hole in the wall.* (**forçar**)
3 to spoil a relationship by causing problems □ *The move has strained political relations with the US.* (**prejudicar**)
4 to separate solid parts from a liquid □ *Now strain the pasta.* (**filtrar, coar**)
▶ NOUN [plural **strains**]
1 an injury to part of your body because you have used it too much □ *a muscle strain* (**estiramento, distensão**)
2 the bad effects on your mind and body when you have too much work or too many worries □ *The strain of looking after four young children was too much for her.* □ *He's been under a lot of strain recently.* (**tensão**)
3 when something has a lot of pressure on it □ *The dam had burst under the strain.* (**pressão**)
4 a type of a particular disease □ *a deadly strain of bird flu* (**estirpe de algum vírus**)

• **strained** /streɪnd/ ADJECTIVE
1 not friendly or relaxed □ *At that time relations between the two countries were very strained.* (**tenso**)
2 injured by being used too much □ *a strained knee ligament* (**luxado**)

• **strainer** /ˈstreɪnə(r)/ NOUN [plural **strainers**] a kitchen tool used for separating solids from a liquid (**coador**)

strait /streɪt/ NOUN [plural straits] a narrow area of sea that joins two larger seas. A geography word. □ *the Straits of Gibraltar* (**estreito**)

straitjacket /ˈstreɪtˌdʒækɪt/ NOUN [plural straitjackets] a special jacket that is put on a violent person to stop them from moving their arms (**camisa de força**)

strait-laced /ˌstreɪtˈleɪst/ ADJECTIVE old-fashioned and easy to shock □ *Her parents were very straitlaced.* (**austero**)

strand /strænd/ NOUN [plural strands]
1 a thin piece of something such as hair or thread □ *a strand of hair* (**fio, cordão**)
2 one of many parts to something □ *one strand of the business* (**ramo**)

stranded /ˈstrændɪd/ ADJECTIVE being in a place that you cannot leave (**ficar aprisionado, retido**) 🔁 *She was left stranded without money or passport.* (**ficou retida**)

strange /streɪndʒ/ ADJECTIVE [stranger, strangest]
1 unusual □ *She's a very strange woman.* □ + *that* *It's strange that he hasn't called.* (**estranho**) 🔁 *The strange thing is that the burglars ignored all her jewellery.* (**o estranho é que...**) 🔁 *That's strange – I wonder why she didn't tell you?* (**isso é estranho**)
2 not familiar □ *Being ill in a strange country was quite frightening.* (**estranho**)

• **strangely** /ˈstreɪndʒli/ ADVERB
1 in a strange way □ *She looked at me strangely.* (**estranhamente**)
2 used for saying that something is surprising (**estranhamente**) 🔁 *Strangely enough, some actors are quite shy.* (**por mais estranho que pareça**)

• **stranger** /ˈstreɪndʒə(r)/ NOUN [plural **strangers**]
1 someone who you do not know □ *Children should never talk to strangers.* (**estranho**) 🔁 *How many people would give £5000 to a complete stranger?* (**completo estranho**)
2 someone who is in a place they do not know □ *I'm afraid I don't know where the station is. I'm a stranger here myself.* (**forasteiro**)
3 **be no stranger to something** to have a lot of experience of something □ *She is no stranger to public attention.* (**estar acostumado a**)

> Remember that a **stranger** is a person you do not know. It is not a person from another country. (The word for this is **foreigner**.)
> ✓ *Foreigners are usually very welcome in this region.*
> ✗ *Strangers are usually very welcome in this region.*

strangle /ˈstræŋgəl/ VERB [strangles, strangling, strangled] to kill someone by putting something around their throat □ *She had been strangled with a piece of rope.* (**estrangular**)

strap /stræp/ ▶ NOUN [plural straps] a long narrow piece of leather or cloth used to hold things, fasten things or hang things on □ *a watch strap* □ *The bag had a shoulder strap.* (**correia**)
▶ VERB [straps, strapping, strapped] to fasten something with a strap □ *I usually strap my bag to my bike.* (**prender em correia**)

• **strapless** /ˈstræpləs/ ADJECTIVE a strapless dress or top has no pieces of material over the shoulders (**tomara que caia, sem alças**)

strapping /ˈstræpɪŋ/ ADJECTIVE tall and strong □ *a strapping young man* (**robusto**)

stratagem /ˈstrætədʒəm/ NOUN [plural stratagems] a formal word meaning a plan for achieving something □ *political stratagems* (**estratagema**)

strategic /strəˈtiːdʒɪk/ ADJECTIVE
1 done as part of a plan □ *strategic marketing decisions* (**estratégico**)
2 to do with fighting a war □ *The country was considered to be a strategic threat.* (**estratégico**)

strategy

3 a strategic position is one that is good for doing something □ *Cameras were installed at strategic locations.* (estratégico)

strategy /ˈstrætɪdʒɪ/ NOUN [plural **strategies**] a plan for achieving something □ *a business strategy* □ *He had developed his own strategies for dealing with stress.* (estratégia)

straw /strɔː/ ▶ NOUN [plural **straws**]
1 long dried stems of crops which animals eat or sleep on □ *The cows need fresh straw.* (palha)
2 a thin tube used for sucking up a drink (canudo)
♦ IDIOM **the last/final straw** the last in a series of unpleasant events, which makes you feel angry or makes you want to stop doing something □ *They all started laughing at her, and it was the last straw.* (a gota-d'água)
▶ ADJECTIVE made of straw □ *a straw hat* (de palha)

strawberry
/ˈstrɔːbərɪ/ NOUN [plural **strawberries**] a soft red fruit with many very small seeds on its surface □ *fresh strawberries* □ *strawberry ice cream* (morango)

stray /streɪ/ ▶ VERB [**strays, straying, strayed**] to go away from the place where you should be □ *Be careful not to stray from the path.* □ *The farmer was searching for some sheep that had strayed.* (perder-se, desviar-se, desgarrar-se)
▶ ADJECTIVE
1 a stray animal is lost or has no home □ *stray dogs* (desgarrado)
2 separated from the rest □ *a stray bullet* (isolado, perdido)
▶ NOUN [plural **strays**] a cat or dog that has no home (abandonado)

streak /striːk/ ▶ NOUN [plural **streaks**]
1 a long thin line or mark □ *hair with blonde streaks* □ *There were dirty streaks on the window.* (mecha, linha, risco)
2 a part of someone's character, especially a bad one □ *He has a cowardly streak.* (traço)
3 a winning/losing streak a time when someone always wins/loses at a game □ *The team are on a winning streak at the moment.* (sequência de vitórias/derrotas)
▶ VERB [**streaks, streaking, streaked**]
1 to mark something with streaks □ *His face was streaked with black grease.* (riscar)
2 to run or move very quickly □ *He streaked off down the hill.* (correr, mover-se com rapidez)

stream
/striːm/ ▶ NOUN [plural **streams**]
1 a very narrow river □ *The children were paddling in the stream.* (riacho)
2 a flow of something (fluxo) 🔹 *The museum had a steady stream of visitors.* (fluxo regular) 🔹 *There was a constant stream of traffic.* (fluxo constante)
▶ VERB [**streams, streaming, streamed**] to flow □ + **down** *Tears streamed down her face* □ *The workers streamed out of the factory gates.* (rolar, fluir, circular)

strength

• **streamer** /ˈstriːmə(r)/ NOUN [plural **streamers**] a long narrow piece of coloured paper, used as a decoration (fita, faixa)

streamline /ˈstriːmlaɪn/ VERB [**streamlines, streamlining, streamlined**]
1 to change something so that it happens more quickly and effectively □ *The company streamlined its production methods.* (modernizar)
2 to change the shape of something so that it moves through air or water as easily as possible (dar forma aerodinâmica a)

• **streamlined** /ˈstriːmlaɪnd/ ADJECTIVE
1 effective and wasting no time or money □ *a streamlined process* (organizado)
2 designed to move through air or water as easily as possible □ *a streamlined jet* (com forma aerodinâmica a)

street
/striːt/ ▶ NOUN [plural **streets**] a road with buildings such as houses and shops on one or both sides (rua) 🔹 *Lincoln's main street was full of shoppers.* (rua principal) □ *There are a lot of shops on this street.* □ *She walked down the street to the library.* □ *I live at 32 Montgomery Street.*
♦ IDIOMS **be right up someone's street** an informal phrase meaning to be exactly what someone wants or likes □ *The course will be right up your street.* (ser moldado por alguém) **be streets ahead** to be much better than other people or things □ *The company is streets ahead of its rivals in terms of customer service.* (ser muito superior a) **on the streets** without a home □ *With no family and no money, he ended up on the streets.* (de rua)
▶ ADJECTIVE to do with a street, or happening on a street (relacionado a rua) 🔹 *A group of teenagers were standing on the street corner* (= the place where one street joins another street). □ *Street crime has increased.* (esquina)

street lamp /ˈstriːt ˌlæmp/ or **street light** /ˈstriːt ˌlaɪt/ NOUN [plural **street lamps** or **street lights**] a light at the top of a pole in the street (poste de luz)

strength
/streŋθ/ NOUN [plural **strengths**]
1 *no plural* when someone or something is strong (força) 🔹 *He didn't have the strength to lift the box.* (ter força) □ *The soup gave her a little more strength.* □ *They tested the strength of the metal.*
2 *no plural* when someone is brave and determined (força, determinação) 🔹 *During her time in prison, she showed great strength of character.* (força de caráter)
3 *no plural* how strong someone's beliefs and feelings are □ *I was shocked by the strength of opposition to the plans.* (convicção, determinação)
4 a good quality or the ability to do something well □ *Her greatest strength is her sense of humour.* (força, virtude)

5 *no plural* how successful, good or powerful something is □ *The strength of the dollar has caused problems for some companies.* □ *The government should not underestimate the strength of the army.* (**força, poder**)

6 full strength when the correct number of people are present □ *The team will be back to full strength for next week's match.* (**completo**)

• **strengthen** /ˈstreŋθən/ VERB [**strengthens, strengthening, strengthened**] to become stronger or to make something stronger □ *He did exercises to strengthen his muscles.* □ *The wind strengthened.* (**fortalecer**)

strenuous /ˈstrenjuəs/ ADJECTIVE

1 using a lot of effort or energy (**pesado, intenso**) ▣ *You should avoid strenuous exercise for six weeks after the operation.*

2 very strong and determined □ *strenuous objections to the proposal* (**fervoroso**)

stress /stres/ ▶ NOUN [*plural* stresses]

1 the bad effect on your mind or body when you have too much work or too many worries □ *A lot of headaches are caused by stress.* (**estresse**) ▣ *He was suffering from stress and exhaustion.* (**estar estressado**) ▣ *Exercise is an effective way to reduce stress.* (**reduzir o estresse**) ▣ *Students often have high stress levels around the time of exams.* (**níveis de estresse**)

2 be under stress to have too much work or too many worries □ *I've been under a lot of stress recently.* (**estar sob pressão, estressado**)

3 *no plural* special importance that is given to something (**dar muita importância a algo**) ▣ *The school lays great stress on the behaviour of its students.* (**dá importância**)

4 *no plural* physical pressure □ *The metal bends under stress.* □ *Jogging puts a lot of stress on your knee joints.* (**pressão física**)

5 the emphasis of a particular part of a word when you are saying it □ *In the word 'bedroom' the stress is on 'bed'.* (**ênfase em determinada pronúncia**)

▶ VERB [**stresses, stressing, stressed**]

1 to say that something is important (**enfatizar**) ▣ *Her speech stressed the need for change.* (**enfatizou a necessidade de**) □ *+ that She stressed that she did not blame her father.*

2 to emphasize part of a word □ *When 'object' is a noun you stress the 'ob'.* (**enfatizar determinada pronúncia**)

3 to worry about something □ *The meeting will be fine – you really mustn't stress over it!* (**preocupar-se, estressar-se**)

• **stressed** /strest/ ADJECTIVE feeling extremely worried and tired □ *I'm really stressed at the moment.* □ *I get really stressed out when I do exams.* (**estressado**)

• **stressful** /ˈstresfʊl/ ADJECTIVE making you feel very worried and tired □ *Starting a new job can be very stressful.* (**estressante**)

stress mark /ˈstres ˌmɑːk/ NOUN [*plural* **stress marks**] a mark that shows which part of a word you should emphasize (**acento**)

stretch /stretʃ/ ▶ VERB [stretches, stretching, stretched]

1 to make something longer or wider, especially by pulling □ *Stretch this rope between the two posts.* (**esticar**)

2 to become longer or wider □ *This material stretches.* □ *New shoes usually stretch a little.* (**esticar**)

3 to push your arms or legs as far as you can □ *Amy got out of bed and stretched.* □ *She stretched her arms over her head.* □ *+ over/ across, etc. He stretched across me to get the book.* (**estender, alongar**)

4 to cover a large area □ *The mountains stretch from the north to the south of the country.* (**estender-se**)

5 to continue for a period of time □ *+ into The trial stretched into its third week.* (**estender-se**)

♦ IDIOM **stretch your legs** to go for a walk after sitting for a long time (**alongue as pernas**)

▶ NOUN [*plural* **stretches**]

1 an area of land or water □ *+ of This is a very dangerous stretch of road.* □ *It's a deserted stretch of beach.* (**trecho**)

2 a continuous period of time □ *+ of You can't learn to drive in such a short stretch of time.* (**período de tempo**)

3 at a stretch continuously □ *He had been working for 14 hours at a stretch.* (**continuamente**)

4 the action of stretching (**espreguiçar-se**) ▣ *I always have a good stretch when I get out of bed.* (**espreguiçar-se**)

• **stretcher** /ˈstretʃə(r)/ NOUN [*plural* **stretchers**] a bed for carrying an ill or injured person □ *The stretcher was put into the back of the ambulance.* (**maca**)

• **stretchy** /ˈstretʃi/ ADJECTIVE [**stretchier, stretchiest**] able to stretch □ *stretchy fabric* (**elástico**)

strew /struː/ VERB [**strews, strewing, strewed, strewn**] to drop a lot of things in an untidy way □ *Toys were strewn all over the floor.* (**espalhar**)

strict /strɪkt/ ADJECTIVE [stricter, strictest]

1 expecting people to obey your rules □ *a strict teacher* □ *+ with He's very strict with the students.* (**rigoroso**)

2 something that is strict must be obeyed (**rigoroso**) ▣ *The airport has strict rules on what you can and can't take on a plane.* (**regras rigorosas**) ▣ *There is a strict limit on the number of places available on the course.* (**limite rigoroso**)

3 following all the rules of a particular belief or way of living □ *He's a strict vegetarian.* (**estrito**)

4 exact □ *She's not depressed in the strict sense of the word.* (**exato**)

- **strictly** /ˈstrɪktlɪ/ ADVERB
1 exactly (**exatamente**) ▪ *It's not strictly true.* (**exatamente verdadeiro**) ▪ *They are not refugees, strictly speaking* (= used for emphasizing that you are being exact). (**no sentido exato da palavra**)
2 in a way in which you are expected to obey rules □ *He was brought up very strictly.* (**de maneira rígida**)
3 *strictly prohibited/forbidden/banned* used to emphasize that something is not allowed □ *Smoking is strictly prohibited.* (**rigorosamente proibido**)
4 for a particular purpose or person □ *The spa was strictly women only.* (**estritamente**)

stride /straɪd/ ▶ VERB [**strides, striding, strode, stridden**] to walk with long steps □ *He strode up the path.* (**caminhos a passos largos**)
▶ NOUN [*plural* **strides**] a long step you take when you walk (**entrar no ritmo, adquirir prática**)
◆ IDIOMS *get into your stride* to start to do something well and confidently after a period of time □ *You'll soon get into your stride.* *take something in your stride* to deal with something difficult and not allow it to affect you □ *She's had a lot of health problems but she's taken them all in her stride.* (**lidar com facilidade, tirar de letra**)

strident /ˈstraɪdənt/ ADJECTIVE
1 expressed in a forceful way □ *strident criticism* (**contundente**)
2 loud and not pleasant to hear □ *a strident voice* (**estridente, agudo**)

strife /straɪf/ NOUN, NO PLURAL a formal word meaning fighting or disagreement (**conflito**)

strike /straɪk/ ▶ VERB [**strikes, striking, struck**]
1 to hit someone or something □ *The missile struck its target.* □ *My head struck the table.* □ *The house was struck by lightning.* (**atingir**)
2 to attack someone or something suddenly □ *The enemy troops struck at dawn.* □ *Who knows when the terrorists may strike again?* (**atacar**)
3 if a thought strikes you, you suddenly think of it □ *+ that It suddenly struck me that the road would be closed.* (**ocorrer**)
4 if you are struck by something, you notice it and think it is unusual, interesting, or good □ *He was struck by her beauty.* (**impressionar**)
5 if something unpleasant strikes, it happens suddenly □ *The earthquake struck in the evening.* (**ocorrer de repente**) ▪ *Just as they reached the city, disaster struck.* (**o desastre ocorreu**)
6 if you strike a match, you rub it against a rough surface to make it burn (**riscar, acender**)
7 if you strike an agreement, you make an agreement with someone (**fazer acordo**) ▪ *Unions have struck a deal over pay.* (**entrar em um acordo**)
8 to refuse to work because of an argument with your employer □ *+ for They were striking for higher wages.* □ *+ over They are striking over their working conditions.* (**fazer greve**)
9 if a clock strikes, it makes a number of sounds to show the time □ *The clock struck three.* (**bater, badalar**)
◆ PHRASAL VERBS *strike someone as something* to seem to someone to have a particular quality □ *He didn't strike me as particularly shy.* (**ser considerado por alguém de determinada maneira**) *strike back* to attack or criticize someone who has attacked or criticized you □ *The minister struck back at her critics, saying they did not know all the facts.* (**devolver o ataque**) *strike someone down* if you are struck down by a disease, you are made very ill by it (**derrubar**) *strike something out* to draw a line through a word or phrase to remove it □ *She struck out the names of all those who had offended her.* (**riscar**) *strike up something* to start something such as a conversation or a relationship □ *The two men struck up a friendship when they were in the army.* (**iniciar algo**)
▶ NOUN [*plural* **strikes**]
1 a period of time when workers refuse to work because of an argument with their employer (**greve**) ▪ *The train drivers are threatening to go on strike.* (**entrar em greve**)
2 a sudden attack, especially a military one □ *The city has suffered repeated air strikes.* (**ataque**)

- **striker** /ˈstraɪkə(r)/ NOUN [*plural* **strikers**]
1 a worker who is refusing to work because of an argument with their employer (**grevista**)
2 in football, a player whose job is to try to score goals (**striker**)

- **striking** /ˈstraɪkɪŋ/ ADJECTIVE
1 very noticeable (**perceptível**) ▪ *There are some striking similarities between the two boys.* (**similaridades evidentes**)
2 attractive in an unusual way that gets people's attention □ *She's a very striking woman.* (**cativante, admirável**)

string /strɪŋ/ ▶ NOUN [*plural* **strings**]
1 *no plural* strong thread, used for tying things (**barbante**) ▪ *a ball of string* (**rolo de barbante**)
2 *a string of something* (a) a series of things or a group of things □ *a string of disasters* □ *They have opened a string of nightclubs across Europe.* (**série de coisas**) (b) several things which are on a piece of string □ *a string of beads* (**colar**)
3 a piece of wire used to make a sound on a musical instrument (**corda**)
4 *the strings* the people in an orchestra (= group of musicians) who play instruments with strings (**família de cordas**)
5 *strings* special conditions that limit an offer or agreement (**cordas**) ▪ *The gift came with no strings attached.* (**sem compromisso**)
◆ IDIOM *pull strings* to use influence that you have with important people to get something done □ *I pulled a few strings to get him a job in the ministry.* (**mexer os pauzinhos**)

stringent

▶ VERB [**strings, stringing, strung**] to hang something somewhere using string □ *Coloured lights were strung across the ceiling.* (**pendurar em cordão**)

♦ PHRASAL VERBS **string someone along** to make someone believe something that is not true for a long time, especially something about your plans □ *He's never going to marry her – he's just stringing her along until he finds someone better.* (**enganar alguém**) **string something together** to use words in a way that other people can understand (**encadear ideias/frases**) 🔁 *He can barely string a sentence together.* (**formar uma frase**)

stringent /ˈstrɪndʒənt/ ADJECTIVE stringent rules, laws or limits are very severe or strongly controlled □ *stringent security measures* (**rigoroso**)

stringy /ˈstrɪŋɪ/ ADJECTIVE [**stringier, stringiest**]
1 looking like string □ *stringy hair* (**fino e pegajoso**)
2 stringy meat is hard and difficult to chew (**fibroso**)

strip /strɪp/ ▶ NOUN [*plural* **strips**] a long narrow piece of something □ *+ of a strip of paper* □ *a narrow strip of land* □ *Slice the peppers into strips.* (**tira, faixa**)

▶ VERB [**strips, stripping, stripped**]
1 to remove a layer or covering from something □ *+ off You need to strip off the old paint first.* (**retirar a camada**)
2 to remove your clothes □ *He stripped and dived into the water.* □ *+ off They stripped off their jackets.* (**tirar a roupa**)

♦ PHRASAL VERB **strip someone of something** to take something away from someone as a punishment □ *The officer was stripped of his rank.* (**provar alguém de algo**)

stripe /straɪp/ NOUN [*plural* **stripes**] a line of colour □ *a T-shirt with black and white stripes* (**listra**)
• **striped** /straɪpt/ *or* **stripy** /ˈstraɪpɪ/ ADJECTIVE having stripes □ *a stripy shirt* (**listrado**)

strive /straɪv/ VERB [**strives, striving, strove, striven**] a formal word meaning to try very hard to achieve something □ *The airline must strive to remain competitive.* (**empenhar-se**)

strode /strəʊd/ PAST TENSE OF **stride** (*ver* **stride**)

stroke /strəʊk/ ▶ NOUN [*plural* **strokes**]
1 a sudden illness in the brain that affects someone's ability to move and speak (**derrame cerebral**) 🔁 *She had a stroke in August.* (**teve um derrame**)
2 the way you hit the ball in games such as tennis or golf □ *Both players produced a range of strokes.* (**rebatida, golpe**)
3 a way of moving your arms and legs when you swim □ *I usually do breast stroke.* (**braçada**)
4 a stroke of luck something you are not expecting which is lucky □ *Police solved the crime by an incredible stroke of luck.* (**um golpe de sorte**)
5 a mark made by moving a pen or a brush across a surface (**traço**) 🔁 *His work is done with short brush strokes and intense colours.* (**pinceladas**)
6 the sound made by a clock each hour □ *We arrived on the stroke of midnight.* (**badalada**)

▶ VERB [**strokes, stroking, stroked**] to rub something gently with your hand □ *She was stroking the cat.* (**acariciar, afagar**)

stroll /strəʊl/ ▶ VERB [**strolls, strolling, strolled**] to walk in a slow, relaxed way □ *We strolled down to the beach.* (**passear**)

▶ NOUN [*plural* **strolls**] a relaxed walk □ *They went for a stroll in the park.* (**passeio**)

strong /strɒŋ/ ADJECTIVE [**stronger, strongest**]
1 physically powerful □ *He is very strong.* □ *I have strong legs from cycling.* (**forte**)
2 not easy to damage or break □ *We tied the branches together with a strong rope.* □ *They have a very strong relationship.* (**resistente**)
3 believed, felt or expressed in a deep and forceful way □ *He has very strong opinions about climate change.* □ *There has been strong opposition to the new airport.* (**sólido, forte**)
4 very noticeable (**evidente**) 🔁 *There was a strong smell of fish in the room.* (**forte cheiro**) □ *She speaks with a strong French accent.*
5 successful and of good quality □ *We all benefit from a strong economy.* □ *There is strong evidence of his guilt.* (**forte**) 🔁 *We are in a strong position to win the contract* (= we are likely to win it). (**posição vantajosa**)
6 if there is a strong chance or possibility of something, that thing is very likely (**grande, forte**)
7 having or using a lot of power or force □ *I felt a strong pull on the rope.* (**forte, intenso**) 🔁 *strong winds* (**ventos fortes**)
8 brave and determined □ *Life is hard, but I try to stay strong for the sake of the children.* (**forte, firme**)
9 a strong drink has a lot of a particular substance in it □ *He drinks really strong coffee.* (**forte**)

stronghold /ˈstrɒŋhəʊld/ NOUN [*plural* **strongholds**]
1 a place where a lot of people support a particular idea or political party □ *a Republican stronghold* (**comitê**)
2 an area that is defended by a military group (**fortaleza**)

strongly /ˈstrɒŋlɪ/ ADVERB
1 very much □ *I strongly recommend that you follow the instructions.* □ *He felt very strongly that there had been an error.* □ *We are strongly opposed to the plans.* (**muitíssimo**)
2 tasting or smelling of something a lot □ *The cheese is strongly flavoured.* (**fortemente**)

strong-willed /ˈstrɒŋˈwɪld/ ADJECTIVE determined □ *Young children can be very strong-willed.* (**determinado, enérgico**)

stroppy /ˈstrɒpɪ/ ADJECTIVE [**stroppier, stroppiest**] an informal word meaning bad-

strove /strəʊv/ PAST TENSE OF **strive** (ver **strive**)

struck /strʌk/ PAST TENSE AND PAST PARTICIPLE OF **strike** (ver **strike**)

structural /ˈstrʌktʃərəl/ ADJECTIVE to do with the structure of something □ *High winds caused structural damage to many buildings.* (**estrutural**)

• **structurally** /ˈstrʌktʃərəli/ ADVERB in a way that is to do with the structure of something □ *The building is structurally sound.* (**estruturalmente**)

structure /ˈstrʌktʃə(r)/ ▶ NOUN [plural **structures**]
1 the way that the parts of something are arranged or organized □ **+ of** *the structure of the story* □ *Crick and Watson discovered the structure of DNA.* □ *a new management structure* (**estrutura**)
2 something that has been built □ *The bridge was a massive steel structure.* (**estrutura**)
▶ VERB [**structures, structuring, structured**] to arrange or to plan something in an organized way □ *Many students have difficulty in structuring their essays.* (**estruturar**)

struggle /ˈstrʌɡəl/ ▶ VERB [**struggles, struggling, struggled**]
1 to try hard to do something that is difficult □ *She struggled to finish the work on time.* (**lutar para**)
2 to move somewhere with difficulty □ *She struggled up the stairs with her heavy suitcase.* (**mover-se com dificuldade**)
3 to turn and twist your body in order to try to escape □ *The child struggled in his arms.* (**debater-se**)
▶ NOUN [plural **struggles**]
1 when something is difficult to do or to achieve □ *It was a struggle, but I managed to get everything finished.* (**luta, grande esforço**)
2 a fight □ *the country's armed struggle for independence* (**luta**)

strum /strʌm/ VERB [**strums, strumming, strummed**] to play a musical instrument such as a guitar by moving your fingers across the strings (**dedilhar**)

strung /strʌŋ/ PAST TENSE AND PAST PARTICIPLE OF **string** (ver **string**)

strut /strʌt/ ▶ VERB [**struts, strutting, strutted**] to walk in a proud way (**pavonear-se**)
▶ NOUN [plural **struts**]
1 a proud way of walking (**andar pomposamente**)
2 a long piece made of wood or metal which supports something (**suporte**)

stub /stʌb/ ▶ NOUN [plural **stubs**] a short piece of something which is left when the rest has been used □ *cigarette stubs* (**toco**)
▶ VERB [**stubs, stubbing, stubbed**] **stub your toe** to hit your toe against something (**dar uma topada**)

◆ PHRASAL VERB **stub something out** to stop a cigarette burning by pressing it against something (**apagar**)

stubble /ˈstʌbəl/ NOUN, NO PLURAL
1 short hairs on a man's face when he has not shaved (**barba por fazer**)
2 short stems of a crop such as corn left in the fields after it has been cut (**restolho**)

stubborn /ˈstʌbən/ ADJECTIVE refusing to change your mind or do what other people tell you □ *a stubborn man* □ *I was frustrated by Tom's stubborn refusal to make any changes.* (**teimoso**)

• **stubbornly** /ˈstʌbənli/ ADVERB in a stubborn way □ *She stubbornly refused to listen to my advice.* (**teimosamente**)

• **stubbornness** /ˈstʌbənnɪs/ NOUN, NO PLURAL the quality of being stubborn (**teimosia**)

stuck /stʌk/ ▶ PAST TENSE AND PAST PARTICIPLE OF **stick** (ver **stick**)
▶ ADJECTIVE
1 unable to move (**emperrado, preso**) 🔊 *The van got stuck in deep snow.*
2 in a situation that you do not like but cannot change □ *She was stuck at home looking after her younger brother.* (**preso**)
3 unable to do something because it is too difficult (**empacado**) 🔊 *Ask the teacher to help you if you get stuck.*

stuck-up /ˌstʌkˈʌp/ ADJECTIVE an informal word that describes someone who thinks they are better than other people (**convencido, orgulhoso**)

stud /stʌd/ NOUN [plural **studs**]
1 a small, round piece of metal, used for decorating something such as clothes (**tacha**)
2 a small, round earring (= jewellery for the ears) (**brinco**)
3 a place where people keep and breed Horses (**haras**)

student /ˈstjuːdənt/ ▶ NOUN [plural **students**] someone who is studying, especially at a college or university □ *a law student* □ *a part-time university student* □ **+ at** *He's a student at Harvard University.* (**estudante**)
▶ ADJECTIVE
1 to do with students □ *student loans* □ *student accommodation* (**estudantil**)
2 studying to become something □ *a student nurse* (**estudante**)

studio /ˈstjuːdɪəʊ/ NOUN [plural **studios**]
1 a room from which radio or television programmes are broadcast 🔊 *a TV studio* □ *The programme's recorded in front of a live studio audience.* (**estúdio**)
2 a place where films are made, or a company that makes films (**estúdio**) 🔊 *an independent film studio* (**estúdio de cinema**) □ *Hollywood studios*
3 the room that an artist or photographer works in □ *She set up her own photographic studio.* (**estúdio**)

4 a small apartment with only one main room ◨ *He moved into a tiny studio apartment.* (**studio**)

studious /ˈstjuːdɪəs/ ADJECTIVE spending a lot of time reading and studying ☐ *a studious young man* (**estudioso**)

study /ˈstʌdi/ ▶ NOUN [plural **studies**]
1 when you spend time examining something to find out more about it ☐ *a scientific study* (**estudo**) ◨ *Researchers conducted a study on the effects of mobile phones.* (**conduzir um estudo**) ☐ *A new study shows coffee-drinking does not increase the risk of heart disease.* (**um estudo mostra**)
2 when you spend time learning about a subject ☐ + **of** *the study of history* ☐ *He completed his undergraduate studies.* (**estudo**)
3 a room used for studying or quiet work ☐ *She sat reading in her study.* (**escritório**)
▶ VERB [**studies, studying, studied**]
1 to spend time learning about a subject ☐ *I'm studying French.* ☐ + **for** *Sophie is studying for a degree in politics.* ☐ + **to do something** *She's studying to be a teacher.* (**estudar**)
2 to spend time examining something to find out more about it ☐ *Researchers studied the effects of heat on the body.* ☐ *We must study the problem in detail.* (**estudar**)
3 to look at something carefully ☐ *He studied the railway timetable.* (**estudar**)

stuff /stʌf/ ▶ NOUN, NO PLURAL
1 used to talk about a substance, material or a group of objects ☐ *What's that black oily stuff on the beach?* ☐ *I've got too much stuff to carry.* ☐ *I need to buy some stuff for the party.* (**substância, coisa, coisas**)
2 used to talk about information, situations or things that people do, think or say ☐ *He told me all this stuff about his childhood.* ☐ *His book has some interesting stuff about India in it.* (**assunto, histórias, informações**)
♦ IDIOMS **know your stuff** to know a lot about a subject ☐ *When it comes to European law, he really knows his stuff.* (**entender do assunto**)
▶ VERB [**stuffs, stuffing, stuffed**]
1 to push something into a space, often in a quick, careless way ☐ *He stuffed the letter into his pocket.* ☐ *I stuffed tissue in my ears to block out the noise.* ☐ *All his old letters were stuffed into drawers.* (**socar, abarrotar, entupir**)
2 to fill something completely ☐ *She used feathers to stuff the cushions.* ☐ *Her suitcase was stuffed with clothes.* (**encher**)
3 to fill food such as meat, fish or vegetables with another kind of food, often a mixture of small pieces ☐ *peppers stuffed with rice* (**rechear**)
4 to fill the body of a dead animal with a substance so that it looks as if it is still alive (**empalhar**)
♦ IDIOM **stuff your face** a very informal phrase meaning to eat a lot (**empanturrar-se**)
• **stuffing** /ˈstʌfɪŋ/ NOUN, NO PLURAL
1 material used for putting inside things such as cushions (= soft, filled bags to sit on) or soft toys (**recheio**)
2 food used for putting inside other food ☐ *We had turkey with an apricot stuffing.* (**recheio**)

stuffy /ˈstʌfi/ ADJECTIVE [**stuffier, stuffiest**]
1 a stuffy place has no fresh air ☐ *How can you sit in this stuffy classroom all day?* (**abafado**)
2 formal, boring and old-fashioned ☐ *The university has a very stuffy image.* (**enfadonho**)

stumble /ˈstʌmbəl/ VERB [**stumbles, stumbling, stumbled**]
1 to almost fall while you are walking ☐ *He stumbled along the track in the dark.* (**tropeçar**)
2 to make mistakes or to pause when you are speaking ☐ *She stumbled over the difficult words.* (**tropeçar**)
♦ PHRASAL VERB **stumble across/on/upon something** to find something by chance ☐ *I stumbled across this book today.* (**tropeçar em, topar com**)

stumbling block /ˈstʌmblɪŋ ˌblɒk/ NOUN [plural **stumbling blocks**] a problem that makes it difficult to do something ☐ *High fees are the major stumbling block for many students.* (**empecilho**)

stump /stʌmp/ ▶ NOUN [plural **stumps**]
1 the part of something left after the main part has been taken away (**toco**) ◨ *She sat on a tree stump.* (**toco da árvore**)
2 in cricket, one of the three wooden sticks that you throw the ball at (**stump**)
▶ VERB [**stumps, stumping, stumped**] an informal word meaning to be too difficult to answer or to understand ☐ *The problem has stumped scientists for years.* (**desafiar**)
♦ PHRASAL VERB **stump up (something)** to pay for something, slightly unwillingly ☐ *We had to stump up cash to pay the medical bills.* (**desembolsar**)
• **stumpy** /ˈstʌmpi/ ADJECTIVE [**stumpier, stumpiest**] short and thick ☐ *The dog had a stumpy tail.* (**curto e grosso**)

stun /stʌn/ VERB [**stuns, stunning, stunned**]
1 if you are stunned by something, it surprises or shocks you very much ☐ *We were all stunned by the news of the accident.* (**atordoar**)
2 to make someone unconscious, usually by hitting them on the head (**deixar sem sentidos**)

stung /stʌŋ/ PAST TENSE AND PAST PARTICIPLE OF **sting** (*ver* **sting**)

stunk /stʌŋk/ PAST TENSE AND PAST PARTICIPLE OF **stink** (*ver* **stink**)

stunning /ˈstʌnɪŋ/ ADJECTIVE
1 extremely attractive ☐ *She looked stunning.* (**estonteante**)
2 extremely surprising or shocking ☐ *a stunning announcement* (**assombroso**)
• **stunningly** /ˈstʌnɪŋli/ ADVERB in a stunning way ☐ *She was a stunningly beautiful woman.* ☐ *a stunningly simple idea* (**surpreendentemente**)

stunt /stʌnt/ ▶ NOUN [plural **stunts**]
1 something exciting or unusual that someone does to attract attention (façanha) 🔲 *The whole event was a big publicity stunt.* (golpe publicitário)
2 something dangerous and exciting that someone does, especially in a film ☐ *The actor performs all his own stunts.* (façanha)
▶ VERB [**stunts, stunting, stunted**] to stop something growing or developing normally ☐ *Lack of water stunted the plants.* (retardar, deter o crescimento)
• **stunted** /'stʌntɪd/ ADJECTIVE smaller than normal and often badly shaped ☐ *There were just a few stunted trees.* (atrofiado)

stuntman /'stʌntˌmæn/ *or* **stuntwoman** /'stʌntˌwʊmən/ NOUN [plural **stuntmen** *or* **stuntwomen**] a man or woman who does dangerous things instead of an actor in a film (dublê)

stupefied /'stju:pɪfaɪd/ ADJECTIVE so shocked or bored that you cannot think ☐ *He stood there with a stupefied look on his face.* (estupefato)
• **stupefying** /'stju:pɪfaɪɪŋ/ ADJECTIVE making you so shocked or bored that you cannot think (espantoso)

stupendous /stju:'pendəs/ ADJECTIVE extremely good or large ☐ *The hotel is surrounded by stupendous mountains.* (estupendo)

stupid /'stju:pɪd/ ADJECTIVE
1 silly and not clever ☐ *It was a stupid thing to do!* ☐ *a stupid idea* ☐ *I felt rather stupid.* (estúpido, bobo)
2 used to show that you are annoyed ☐ *What's wrong with this stupid thing?* ☐ *What are you doing, you stupid idiot?* (abobalhado)
• **stupidity** /stju:'pɪdɪti/ NOUN, NO PLURAL the quality of being stupid (estupidez)
• **stupidly** /'stju:pɪdli/ ADVERB in a stupid way ☐ *I'd rather stupidly forgotten to bring a coat.* ☐ *Stupidly, I agreed to do it.* (estupidamente)

sturdy /'stɜ:di/ ADJECTIVE [**sturdier, sturdiest**] strong ☐ *sturdy shoes* (resistente)

stutter /'stʌtə(r)/ ▶ VERB [**stutters, stuttering, stuttered**] to repeat some letters when you speak ☐ *'H-hello,' he stuttered.* (gaguejar)
▶ NOUN [plural **stutters**] a speech problem that makes you repeat letters when you speak (gagueira)

sty¹ /staɪ/ NOUN [plural **sties**] a place where pigs are kept (pocilga, chiqueiro)

sty² *or* **stye** /staɪ/ NOUN [plural **sties** *or* **styes**] an infection near your eye that makes it painful and swollen (terçol)

style /staɪl/ ▶ NOUN [plural **styles**]
1 a particular way of doing something ☐ *a mix of musical styles* ☐ *+ of She has a wonderful style of writing.* (estilo)
2 the design of something, especially clothes or buildings ☐ *+ of a new style of shoe* ☐ *We stayed in a traditional style chalet.* (estilo)
3 no plural the quality of being attractive, fashionable, wearing nice clothes, etc. (estilo) 🔲 *She has a real sense of style.* (senso de estilo)
4 in style in an attractive, exciting way, often spending a lot of money ☐ *They celebrated the New Year in style at a top hotel.* (em grande estilo, com classe)
▶ VERB [**styles, styling, styled**] to arrange or to design something, such as clothes or hair, in a particular style ☐ *I'm having my hair cut and styled.* (arrumar com estilo)
• **stylish** /'staɪlɪʃ/ ADJECTIVE attractive and fashionable ☐ *It's one of the city's most stylish hotels.* ☐ *She looked stylish in a simple black dress.* (estiloso, elegante)
• **stylishly** /'staɪlɪʃli/ ADVERB in a stylish way ☐ *He was dressed very stylishly.* (elegantemente)

suave /swɑ:v/ ADJECTIVE a suave man is very polite and confident (afável)

sub /sʌb/ NOUN [plural **subs**]
1 an informal word for **submarine** (submarino)
2 an informal word for **substitute** (substituto)

sub- /sʌb/ PREFIX sub- is added to the beginning of words to mean 'below' or 'under' ☐ *submarine* ☐ *subzero* (sub-)

subatomic particle /ˌsʌbə'tɒmɪk 'pɑ:tɪkəl/ NOUN [plural **subatomic particles**] a piece of matter that is smaller than an atom. A physics word. (partícula subatômica)

subconscious /ˌsʌb'kɒnʃəs/ ▶ NOUN, NO PLURAL the part of your mind that contains thoughts and feelings which you are not aware of (subconsciente)
▶ ADJECTIVE to do with your subconscious ☐ *subconscious fears* (subconsciente)
• **subconsciously** /ˌsʌb'kɒnʃəsli/ ADVERB in a subconscious way (subconscientemente)

subdivide /ˌsʌbdɪ'vaɪd/ VERB [**subdivides, subdividing, subdivided**] to divide something into smaller parts ☐ *Each class is subdivided into groups according to ability.* (subdividir)
• **subdivision** /ˌsʌbdɪ'vɪʒən/ NOUN [plural **subdivisions**] a part made by subdividing (subdivisão)

subdue /səb'dju:/ VERB [**subdues, subduing, subdued**] to control someone or something, especially using force ☐ *Police used tear gas to subdue the crowd.* (subjugar)
• **subdued** /səb'dju:d/ ADJECTIVE
1 quieter than usual, especially because you are unhappy ☐ *You seem very subdued today.* (deprimido)
2 not very loud or bright ☐ *subdued voices* (brando)

subheading /'sʌbˌhedɪŋ/ NOUN [plural **subheadings**] a title of one part of a text, not the main title (subtítulo)

subject

subject ▶ NOUN /'sʌbdʒɪkt/ [plural **subjects**]
1 the person or thing that a story, a conversation, etc. is about ☐ **+ of** The affair has been the subject of many rumours. (**assunto**) ☐ He raised the subject of (= started talking about) security at the jail. (**levantar o assunto**) ☐ Can we change the subject (= talk about something different), please?
2 something that you study and learn about at school, university, etc. ☐ French is my favourite subject at school. ☐ Fewer students are now studying science subjects. (**matéria**)
3 in grammar, the subject of a sentence is the person or thing that does something ☐ In the sentence 'John plays tennis.', 'John' is the subject. (**sujeito**)
▶ ADJECTIVE /'sʌbdʒɪkt/ **subject to something** (a) affected or controlled by something ☐ The soldiers there are not subject to Czech law. (b) only possible if something else or happens ☐ The plans are subject to approval by the government. (**sujeito a**)
▶ VERB /səb'dʒekt/ [**subjects, subjecting, subjected**] **subject someone to something** a formal word meaning to make someone suffer something unpleasant ☐ He was subjected to cruel treatment. (**sujeitar, submeter**)
• **subjective** /səb'dʒektɪv/ ADJECTIVE based on your own thoughts and feelings, and not facts ☐ a subjective opinion (**subjetivo**)

subject matter /'sʌbdʒɪkt 'mætə(r)/ NOUN, NO PLURAL the person or thing that you are talking about, writing about, painting, etc. ☐ His films varied in style and subject matter. (**assunto**)

subjunctive /səb'dʒʌŋktɪv/ NOUN, NO PLURAL a verb form used to express a doubt, a wish or something uncertain. For example, in English, we say 'if I were you', using were instead of was after I. (**subjuntivo**)

sublet /ˌsʌb'let/ VERB [**sublets, subletting, sublet**] to rent a house or a flat to someone when you are renting it from someone else (**sublocar**)

sublime /sə'blaɪm/ ADJECTIVE very great or beautiful ☐ a sublime performance (**sublime**)

subliminal /ˌsʌb'lɪmɪnəl/ ADJECTIVE a formal word meaning affecting your thoughts or behaviour in a way that you are not aware of (**subliminar**) ☐ Are there subliminal messages hidden in the programme? (**mensagens subliminares**)

submarine /ˌsʌbmə'ri:n/ ▶ NOUN [plural **submarines**] a ship that travels under water (**submarino**)
▶ ADJECTIVE a formal word meaning to do with things under the sea ☐ submarine cables (**submarino**)

submerge /səb'mɜ:dʒ/ VERB [**submerges, submerging, submerged**] to cover something with water, or to go under water ☐ Entire villages had been submerged. (**submergir**)
• **submergence** /səb'mɜ:dʒəns/ or **submersion** /səb'mɜ:ʃən/ NOUN, NO PLURAL when something submerges (**submersão**)

subside

submission /səb'mɪʃən/ NOUN [plural **submissions**]
1 when someone is completely controlled by someone else ☐ They were beaten into submission. (**submissão**)
2 something such as a plan or document that you give to someone so they can make a decision about it (**submissão**)

submissive /səb'mɪsɪv/ ADJECTIVE always willing to obey other people (**submisso**)

submit /səb'mɪt/ VERB [**submits, submitting, submitted**]
1 to give a plan, a document, etc. to someone so they can make a decision about it ☐ All competition entries must be submitted by Friday. (**apresentar**)
2 to agree to something or to accept someone's control, especially when you are being forced to ☐ The rebels were ordered to submit. (**submeter**)

subnormal /ˌsʌb'nɔ:məl/ ADJECTIVE less intelligent than most other people (**abaixo do normal**)

subordinate /sə'bɔ:dɪnət/ ▶ ADJECTIVE a formal word meaning lower in position or less important ☐ his subordinate officers (**subordinado**)
▶ NOUN [plural **subordinates**] a formal word meaning someone who has a less important position (**subordinado**)

subordinate clause /sə'bɔ:dɪnət 'klɔ:z/ NOUN [plural **subordinate clauses**] in grammar, a part of a sentence which adds information but cannot exist on its own ☐ In the sentence 'The book that I got for my birthday was boring.', 'that I got for my birthday' is a subordinate clause. (**oração subordinada**)

subscribe /səb'skraɪb/ VERB [**subscribes, subscribing, subscribed**] to get a product or service by regularly paying money ☐ One in three Americans subscribe to cable television. (**assinar, subscrever**)
♦ PHRASAL VERB **subscribe to something** a formal phrase meaning to agree with something ☐ I don't subscribe to that view. (**apoiar uma ideia**)
• **subscriber** /səb'skraɪbə(r)/ NOUN [plural **subscribers**] someone who gets a product or service by regularly paying money (**assinante**)
• **subscription** /səb'skrɪpʃən/ NOUN [plural **subscriptions**] money that you pay regularly to get a product or service or to be a member of an organization (**assinatura**)

subsequent /'sʌbsɪkwənt/ ADJECTIVE happening after something else ☐ The story is about the soldier's capture and subsequent escape. (**subsequente**)
• **subsequently** /'sʌbsɪkwəntlɪ/ ADVERB later ☐ She ate the shellfish and subsequently became ill. (**subsequentemente**)

subside /səb'saɪd/ VERB [**subsides, subsiding, subsided**]
1 to become less strong ☐ The pain gradually subsided. (**ceder, baixar**)

2 if land or a building subsides, it starts to sink gradually into the ground (**ceder**)

• **subsidence** /səbˈsaɪdəns, ˈsʌbsɪdəns/ NOUN, NO PLURAL when land or a building subsides (**abaixamento**)

subsidiary /səbˈsɪdjərɪ/ NOUN [plural **subsidiaries**] a company that is controlled by a larger company (**subsidiário**)

subsidize or **subsidise** /ˈsʌbsɪdaɪz/ VERB [**subsidizes, subsidizing, subsidized**] to pay part of the cost of something in order to help a person or an organization ◻ *The government subsidizes the mining industry.* (**subsidiar**)

• **subsidy** /ˈsʌbsɪdɪ/ NOUN [plural **subsidies**] money given to help someone or something or to keep prices low ◻ *farming subsidies* (**subsídio**)

subsist /səbˈsɪst/ VERB [**subsists, subsisting, subsisted**] a formal word meaning to live with only just enough food or money ◻ *They subsisted on a diet of potatoes and milk.* (**subsistir**)

• **subsistence** /səbˈsɪstəns/ NOUN, NO PLURAL when someone has or produces just enough for their needs ◻ *subsistence farming* (**subsistência**)

substance /ˈsʌbstəns/ NOUN [plural **substances**]
1 a liquid, a solid or a gas ◻ *Glue is a sticky substance.* ◻ *a toxic substance* (**substância**)
2 *no plural* a formal word meaning the quality of being true or important (**substância**) ▣ *There's no substance to the allegations.* (**sem consistência**) ◻ *He said nothing of substance.*
3 *no plural* the general or most important ideas of what someone says or writes ◻ + *of The substance of her argument was that women are more intelligent than men.* (**essência**)

substandard /ˌsʌbˈstændəd/ ADJECTIVE not as good as it should be ◻ *substandard housing* (**abaixo do padrão**)

substantial /səbˈstænʃəl/ ADJECTIVE
1 large in amount ◻ *a substantial sum of money* ◻ *We have made substantial progress.* (**substancial**)
2 large and strong ◻ *The leather bag was more substantial.* (**substancial**)

• **substantially** /səbˈstænʃəlɪ/ ADVERB
1 by a large amount ◻ *Profits have increased substantially.* (**substancialmente**)
2 a formal word meaning in most ways ◻ *The two reports are substantially the same.* (**essencialmente**)

substantiate /səbˈstænʃɪeɪt/ VERB [**substantiates, substantiating, substantiated**] a formal word meaning to give facts that show that something is true ◻ *There was no evidence to substantiate the claims.* (**fundamentar**)

substitute /ˈsʌbstɪtjuːt/ ▶ VERB [**substitutes, substituting, substituted**] to use one thing or person instead of something or someone else ◻ *I substituted your name for mine on the list.* (**substituto**)

▶ NOUN [plural **substitutes**]
1 a person or thing used instead of another (**substituto**) ▣ *Use lemons as a substitute for limes.* (**como substituto de**)
2 a player who replaces another player in a team during a game ◻ *James came on as a substitute at halftime.* (**substituto**)

• **substitution** /ˌsʌbstɪˈtjuːʃən/ NOUN [plural **substitutions**] when someone or something is substituted (**substituição**)

subterranean /ˌsʌbtəˈreɪnɪən/ ADJECTIVE a formal word meaning under the ground ◻ *subterranean passages* (**subterrâneo**)

subtitles /ˈsʌbˌtaɪtəlz/ PLURAL NOUN words at the bottom of a screen which show what the actors are saying in a film ◻ *a French film with English subtitles* (**legenda**)

subtle /ˈsʌtəl/ ADJECTIVE [**subtler, subtlest**]
1 slight and difficult to notice or to describe (**sutil**) ▣ *There have been subtle changes.* (**mudanças sutis**) ▣ *There is a subtle difference between the two birds.* (**diferença sutil**)
2 a subtle flavour, smell, colour, etc. is pleasant and not very strong ◻ *a subtle shade of green* (**sutil**)
3 clever ◻ *They are finding more subtle ways of selling their products.* (**engenhoso**)

• **subtlety** /ˈsʌtəltɪ/ NOUN [plural **subtleties**] the quality of being subtle ◻ *I love the subtlety of the colours in the painting.* (**sutileza**)

• **subtly** /ˈsʌtlɪ/ ADVERB in a subtle way ◻ *The picture has been subtly altered.* (**sutilmente**)

subtotal /ˈsʌbˌtəʊtəl/ NOUN [plural **subtotals**] the total of one set of numbers, but not the final total (**subtotal**)

subtract /səbˈtrækt/ VERB [**subtracts, subtracting, subtracted**] to take one number away from another. A maths word. ◻ + *from If you subtract 4 from 6, you get 2.* (**subtrair**)

• **subtraction** /səbˈtrækʃən/ NOUN [plural **subtractions**] when you subtract one number from another. A maths word. (**subtração**)

subtropical /ˌsʌbˈtrɒpɪkəl/ ADJECTIVE connected to the parts of the Earth near the tropics (= very hot parts near the equator). A geography word. (**subtropical**)

• **subtropics** /ˌsʌbˈtrɒpɪks/ PLURAL NOUN **the subtropics** the subtropical areas of the Earth. A geography word. (**regiões subtropicais**)

suburb /ˈsʌbɜːb/ NOUN [plural **suburbs**] an area of houses at the edge of a town or city ◻ *a suburb of Liverpool* (**subúrbio**)

• **suburban** /səˈbɜːbən/ ADJECTIVE to do with suburbs ◻ *suburban housing* (**suburbano**)

• **suburbia** /səˈbɜːbɪə/ NOUN, NO PLURAL the people who live in suburbs and the way they live (**subúrbio**)

subversive /səbˈvɜːsɪv/ ▶ ADJECTIVE intended to harm a government or political system ◻ *a subversive organization* (**subversivo**)

▶ NOUN [plural **subversives**] a subversive person (**subversivo**)

subvert /səbˈvɜːt/ VERB [subverts, subverting, subverted] a formal word meaning to destroy a government or political system ◻ *This is clearly an attempt to subvert democracy.* (**subverter**)

subway /ˈsʌbweɪ/ NOUN [plural **subways**]
1 a path under a busy road or railway (**passagem subterrânea**)
2 the US word for underground (= a railway under the ground) (**metrô**)

sub-zero /ˌsʌb ˈzɪərəʊ/ ADJECTIVE sub-zero temperatures are lower than 0° (**abaixo de zero**)

succeed /səkˈsiːd/ VERB [succeeds, succeeding, succeeded]
1 to achieve something, or to have the effect you want ◻ *If you try hard, I'm sure you'll succeed.* ◻ *Ravana's devious plan had succeeded.* ◻ **+ in** *She succeeded in getting the job.* (**ter êxito**)
2 to do an important job after someone else ◻ **+ as** *She succeeded her father as manager of the company.* ◻ *He was succeeded by Lois Gallois.* (**suceder**)

> Note that **succeed**, meaning 'to achieve something' is followed by '**in doing** something':
> ✓ *She finally succeeded in persuading him.*
> ✗ *She finally succeeded to persuade him.*

success /səkˈses/ NOUN [plural **successes**]
1 *no plural* the achievement of what you tried to achieve ◻ *Her success is due to determination and hard work.* (**sucesso**) ◻ *He tried, without success, to pull her out of the water.* (**sem sucesso**) ◻ *The project had little chance of success.* (**chance de sucesso**) ◻ **+ in** *Have you had any success in finding a job?*
2 something that is popular or has the result that you want (**sucesso**) ◻ *The party had been a great success.* ◻ *The film was a huge success.* (**enorme sucesso**)

• **successful** /səkˈsesfʊl/ ADJECTIVE
1 earning or achieving a lot in your work ◻ *a successful businessman* (**bem-sucedido**) ◻ *Houlahan had a highly successful career training horses.* (**extremamente bem-sucedido**)
2 having the result you wanted ◻ *a successful election campaign* ◻ *The policy has been very successful.* ◻ **+ in** *He was successful in his attempt to buy the business.* (**bem-sucedido**)
3 very popular and making a lot of money (**de muito sucesso**) ◻ *He starred in the hugely successful action film 'Die Hard'.* (**de enorme sucesso**)

• **successfully** /səkˈsesfʊli/ ADVERB in a successful way ◻ *Surgeons successfully removed a blood clot from his brain.* ◻ *She successfully completed all six races.* (**com sucesso**)

• **succession** /səkˈseʃən/ NOUN, NO PLURAL
1 a series of things that happen one after the other ◻ *He's suffered a succession of injuries recently.* (**sucessão**)
2 in quick/rapid succession happening very quickly after each other ◻ *She sneezed three times in quick succession.* (**em rápida sucessão**)
3 when someone has an official job after someone else ◻ *Some people challenged Brown's succession as Labour Party leader.* (**sucessão**)

• **successive** /səkˈsesɪv/ ADJECTIVE happening one after the other ◻ *The team won three successive games.* (**sucessivo**)

• **successor** /səkˈsesə(r)/ NOUN [plural **successors**] someone who has an important job after someone else ◻ *The head teacher's successor will be Carolyn Robinson.* (**sucessor**)

succinct /səkˈsɪŋkt/ ADJECTIVE expressing something clearly using very few words ◻ *His remarks were succinct and to the point.* (**sucinto**)

• **succinctly** /səkˈsɪŋktli/ ADVERB in a way that is succinct (**sucintamente**)

succulent /ˈsʌkjʊlənt/ ADJECTIVE full of juice, and good to eat ◻ *succulent peaches* (**suculento**)

succumb /səˈkʌm/ VERB [succumbs, succumbing, succumbed]
1 to be unable to stop something from affecting you. A formal word ◻ *She succumbed to temptation and took the money.* (**sucumbir**)
2 to become very ill or to die from an illness. A formal word. (**sucumbir**)

such /sʌtʃ/ DETERMINER, PRONOUN
1 such a used before a phrase with a noun for emphasizing a statement ◻ *I was such a fool to believe him.* ◻ *This is such a waste of time.* ◻ *She's such a nice person.* (**tão, tanto**)
2 such as used for giving an example ◻ *Citrus fruits such as oranges and lemons contain a lot of vitamin C.* (**como**)
3 similar to someone or something that has already been mentioned ◻ *Such things are difficult to find.* (**tal, tais**)
4 such ... that used for saying what the result of something is ◻ *It was such an awful hotel that we decided to leave.* (**tão... que**)
5 as such used in negative statements to say that the word you are using is not exactly correct ◻ *He doesn't have a job as such, but he helps in the shop sometimes.* (**desse tipo**)
6 there's no such thing/person used for saying that something or someone does not exist ◻ *There are no such things as monsters.* (**não existe esse tipo de coisa/pessoa**)

such-and-such /ˈsʌtʃəndsʌtʃ/ DETERMINER, PRONOUN used for referring to something without saying exactly which thing ◻ *Let's suppose that you go into such-and-such a shop.* (**tal e tal**)

suck /sʌk/ ▶ VERB [sucks, sucking, sucked]
1 to take something into your mouth by pulling in air ◻ *She was sucking lemonade through a straw.* ◻ **+ in** *Gerald sucked in his breath.* (**sugar, sorver**)
2 to hold something in your mouth while making pulling movements with your lips and tongue ◻

My sister still sucks her thumb. □ *She was sucking a sweet.* □ **+ on** *The baby was sucking on a dummy.* (chupar)

3 if water or air sucks someone somewhere, it pulls them as it moves □ **+ under** *He was sucked under by a wave.* (puxar)

◆ PHRASAL VERB **suck someone into something** if someone is sucked into something bad, they become involved it □ *He had been sucked into a life of crime.* (envolver alguém em alguma atividade)

▶ NOUN [plural **sucks**] the action of sucking □ *She took a suck of her lollipop.* (chupada)

• **sucker** /'sʌkə(r)/ NOUN [plural **suckers**]
1 an informal word for someone who is easy to trick because they believe everything that people tell them (otário)
2 a piece of rubber that sticks on a surface (ventosa)

• **suckle** /'sʌkəl/ VERB [**suckles, suckling, suckled**] to feed a baby or young animal milk from the body □ *The cow suckled her calf.* (amamentar)

• **suction** /'sʌkʃən/ NOUN, NO PLURAL when air or liquid is removed from a space or container (sucção)

sucrose /'su:krəʊz/ NOUN, NO PLURAL a type of sugar that is found in most plants. A biology word. (sacarose)

sudden /'sʌdən/ ADJECTIVE
1 happening quickly and unexpectedly □ *The sudden death of his mother changed everything.* □ *Pat felt a sudden urge to laugh.* □ *The attack was so sudden that he hadn't been able to defend himself.* (súbito)
2 all of a sudden suddenly □ *All of a sudden, he started to run towards the door.* (de repente)

• **suddenly** /'sʌdənli/ ADVERB quickly and unexpectedly □ *Suddenly a woman ran into the room, shouting.* □ *I suddenly felt very tired.* (subitamente)

• **suddenness** /'sʌdənnɪs/ NOUN, NO PLURAL the quality of being sudden □ *We were shocked by the suddenness of his death.* (subitaneidade)

Sudoku /suːˈdəʊkuː/ NOUN [plural **Sudokus**] a number game in which you write a number in every small square of a larger 9 x 9 square (Sudoku)

suds /sʌdz/ PLURAL NOUN soap bubbles (espuma de sabão)

sue /suː/ VERB [**sues, suing, sued**] to start a law case to try to get money from a person or organization that has harmed you □ *He sued the company for racial discrimination.* (processar, acionar)

suede /sweɪd/ ▶ NOUN, NO PLURAL a type of leather with a rough surface (camurça)
▶ ADJECTIVE made of suede □ *a suede jacket* (de camurça)

suet /'suːɪt/ NOUN, NO PLURAL a hard fat from an animal used in cooking (sebo)

suffer /'sʌfə(r)/ VERB [**suffers, suffering, suffered**]
1 to feel pain or unpleasant feelings (sofrer) *She suffered a lot of pain after the accident.* (sofrer de dor) □ *I couldn't bear to see him suffering like that.*
2 to be injured or suddenly have a health problem □ *He suffered a heart attack at the age of 47.* (sofrer) *She suffered serious head injuries in the accident.* (sofrer ferimentos)
3 to have a bad experience, such as a defeat, loss of money, etc. (sofrer) *The team suffered a defeat in the first round of the competition.* (sofrer uma derrota) □ *The company suffered massive financial losses.*
4 suffer from something to have a particular illness □ *Her brother suffers from depression.* (sofrer de)
5 to become worse □ *If you don't get enough sleep, your work will start to suffer.* (sofrer)

• **sufferance** /'sʌfərəns/ NOUN, NO PLURAL (tolerância) **on sufferance** if you do something on sufferance, you are allowed to do it by someone who would prefer that you did not do it. A formal phrase □ *I was allowed to use his new camera but only on sufferance.* (por condescendência)

• **sufferer** /'sʌfərə(r)/ NOUN [plural **sufferers**] someone who suffers from a particular illness □ *asthma sufferers* (sofredor)

• **suffering** /'sʌfərɪŋ/ NOUN, NO PLURAL pain or unpleasant feelings *Years of civil war and drought have caused widespread human suffering.* (sofrimento)

suffice /səˈfaɪs/ VERB [**suffices, sufficing, sufficed**] a formal word meaning to be enough □ *£50 should suffice.* (bastar)

sufficiency /səˈfɪʃənsi/ NOUN, NO PLURAL a formal word meaning enough of something □ *There is a sufficiency of teachers in those subjects.* (suficiência)

• **sufficient** /səˈfɪʃənt/ ADJECTIVE enough □ *There is sufficient evidence to charge him with murder.* (suficiente)

• **sufficiently** /səˈfɪʃəntli/ ADVERB in a way that is enough □ *He has a sufficiently large number of supporters to win the election.* (suficientemente)

suffix /'sʌfɪks/ NOUN [plural **suffixes**] a group of letters that is added to the end of a word to make another word (sufixo)

suffocate /'sʌfəkeɪt/ VERB [**suffocates, suffocating, suffocated**]
1 to kill someone by preventing them from getting enough oxygen □ *The thick black smoke was suffocating him.* (sufocar)
2 to die because of not getting enough oxygen □ *Babies can suffocate if they sleep with a pillow.* (sufocar-se)

• **suffocation** /ˌsʌfəˈkeɪʃən/ NOUN, NO PLURAL suffocating or being suffocated □ *The cause of death was suffocation.* (sufocamento)

suffrage /ˈsʌfrɪdʒ/ NOUN, NO PLURAL a formal word meaning the right to vote (**direito de voto, sufrágio**)

• **suffragette** /ˌsʌfrəˈdʒet/ NOUN [plural **suffragettes**] a woman who fought for women's right to vote (**sufragista**)

suffuse /səˈfjuːz/ VERB [**suffuses, suffusing, suffused**] if a place is suffused with light or colour, there is a lot of it all around. A literary word. □ *The room was suffused with light.* (**cobrir de, encher de**)

sugar /ˈʃʊɡə(r)/ NOUN [plural **sugars**]
1 *no plural* white or brown grains that you add to food and drink to make them taste sweeter (**açúcar**) ▫ *Do you take sugar in your tea?* (**pôr açúcar**)
2 the amount of sugar that a small spoon holds □ *I have two sugars in coffee.* (**colher de açúcar**)

sugar beet /ˈʃʊɡə ˌbiːt/ NOUN, NO PLURAL a plant that grows under the ground which sugar comes from (**beterraba**)

sugar cane /ˈʃʊɡə ˌkeɪn/ NOUN, NO PLURAL a tall tropical plant with stems that sugar comes from (**cana-de-açúcar**)

sugary /ˈʃʊɡəri/ ADJECTIVE sweet □ *sugary snacks* (**doce**)

suggest /səˈdʒest/ VERB [**suggests, suggesting, suggested**]
1 to mention something as a possibility □ *He suggested a picnic.* □ + *that* *I suggest that we have lunch now.* □ + *ing* *She suggested meeting outside the theatre.* (**sugerir**)
2 to show that something may be true (**sugerir**) ▫ *The study suggests that drinking green tea could be good for your health.* (**o estudo sugere que**) ▫ *Recent evidence suggests that this may not be true.* (**evidência sugere que**)
3 to say something in a way that is not direct □ + *that* *Are you suggesting that I'm too old for the job?* (**sugerir**)
4 to tell someone about something that they might like or find useful □ *Can you suggest a nice place to stay in Paris?* □ + *for* *She suggested me for the job.* (**sugerir**)

> Notice the examples in 'suggest' (sense 1). You **suggest that** someone **does** something, or you **suggest doing** something. You do not suggest 'to do' something. □ *I suggest that we start now.*
> ✓ *I suggest starting now.*
> ✗ *I suggest to start now.*

• **suggestion** /səˈdʒestʃən/ NOUN [plural **suggestions**]
1 an idea that you mention (**sugestão**) ▫ *He made several helpful suggestions.* (**fazer/dar uma sugestão**) ▫ *Do you have any suggestions about where we could go for a holiday?* (**ter alguma sugestão**) □ + *that* *He rejected suggestions that he had lied.*
2 *no plural* a sign that something is true □ + *of* *There was no suggestion of improper behaviour.* □ + *that* *There was some suggestion that he had been involved in the fraud.* (**sugestão**)
3 *a suggestion of something* a very small amount of something □ *There was a suggestion of anger in her voice.* (**um traço de**)

• **suggestive** /səˈdʒestɪv/ ADJECTIVE *suggestive of something* a formal phrase meaning making you think of something □ *There was a smell suggestive of onions.* (**sugestivo**)

suicidal /suːɪˈsaɪdəl/ ADJECTIVE
1 wanting to kill yourself □ *He'd been feeling suicidal for several weeks.* (**suicida**)
2 likely to cause death □ *He was driving at a suicidal speed.* (**suicida**)
3 likely to cause serious problems or damage □ *The policy will be politically suicidal.* (**suicida**)

suicide /ˈsuːɪsaɪd/ NOUN [plural **suicides**]
1 the act of killing yourself deliberately (**suicídio**) ▫ *He committed suicide by jumping off a bridge.* (**cometer suicídio**)
2 an action that is likely to cause serious problems for you (**suicídio**) ▫ *This sort of confession is political suicide.* (**suicídio político**)

suit /suːt/ ▶ NOUN [plural **suits**]
1 a jacket and trousers or a jacket and skirt which are made of the same cloth and are worn together (**terno, conjunto, tailleur**) ▫ *He was wearing a suit and tie.*
2 pieces of clothing that you wear for a particular activity □ *a jogging suit* (**conjunto**)
3 one of the four types of cards in a set used for playing games □ *The four suits are hearts, diamonds, clubs and spades.* (**naipe**)
4 a case in a law court (**processo**) ▫ *She filed a suit* (= started a case) *against the bank.*
▶ VERB [**suits, suiting, suited**]
1 if something suits you, it makes you look nice □ *Blue really suits her.* □ *That dress suits you.* (**cair bem, combinar com**)
2 to be convenient for someone □ *Would it suit you if I called round this evening?* (**convir a**) ▫ *Another year here would suit me fine.* (**seria conveniente**)
3 *be well/ideally etc. suited to something* to have the right qualities for something □ *She's very well suited to the job.* (**apropriado**)
4 *Suit yourself!* used for telling someone in an annoyed way that they can do what they want □ *Suit yourself! I'm going out now anyway.* (**Como preferir!**)

◆ IDIOM *suit someone down to the ground* to be extremely suitable for someone □ *Being a model suits her down to the ground.* (**cair como uma luva**)

• **suitability** /ˌsuːtəˈbɪləti/ NOUN, NO PLURAL the quality of being suitable □ *I am not sure of his suitability for the role.* (**conveniência**)

• **suitable** /ˈsuːtəbəl/ ADJECTIVE right for a purpose, person or occasion □ *Finding suitable accommodation wasn't easy.* □ + *for* *High-heeled shoes aren't suitable for walking in the country.* (**conveniente**)

suitcase

- **suitably** /ˈsuːtəblɪ/ ADVERB in a way that is suitable □ *Are you suitably dressed for the cold weather?* (**convenientemente**)

suitcase /ˈsuːtkeɪs/ NOUN [*plural* **suitcases**] a big case with a handle, that you carry your clothes in when you are travelling (**mala**) ◘ *He packed his suitcase and went to the airport.* (**arrumou a mala**) ◘ *I unpacked my suitcase as soon as I arrived.* (**desfazer a mala**)

suite /swiːt/ NOUN [*plural* **suites**]
1 a set of expensive rooms in a hotel □ *a hotel suite* (**suíte**)
2 a set of furniture □ *a bathroom suite* (**conjunto**)

suitor /ˈsuːtə(r)/ NOUN [*plural* **suitors**] an old-fashioned word for a man who wants to marry a woman (**pretendente**)

sulfur /ˈsʌlfə(r)/ NOUN, NO PLURAL the US spelling of **sulphur** (*ver* **sulphur**)

sulfuric acid /sʌlˈfjʊərɪk ˈæsɪd/ NOUN, NO PLURAL the US spelling of **sulphuric acid** (**ácido sulfúrico**)

sulk /sʌlk/ ▶ VERB [**sulks, sulking, sulked**] to show that you are angry by being silent □ *He's sulking because I said he couldn't go out.* (**amuar, ficar de mau humor**)
▶ NOUN [*plural* **sulks**] a time when someone is sulking □ *He's in a sulk because his Dad said he couldn't have an ice cream.* (**mau humor**)

- **sulky** /ˈsʌlkɪ/ ADJECTIVE [**sulkier, sulkiest**]
1 sulking □ *She's in a sulky mood.* (**amuado, de mau humor**)
2 often sulking □ *a sulky child* (**mal-humorado**)

sullen /ˈsʌlən/ ADJECTIVE angry and silent □ *a sullen young man* (**emburrado**)

sulphur /ˈsʌlfə(r)/ NOUN, NO PLURAL a yellow chemical element which burns with a blue flame and has an unpleasant smell. A chemistry word. (**enxofre**)

sulphuric acid /sʌlˈfjʊərɪk ˈæsɪd/ NOUN, NO PLURAL a strong, colourless acid. A chemistry word. (**ácido sulfúrico**)

sultan /ˈsʌltən/ NOUN [*plural* **sultans**] a ruler in some Muslim countries □ *the Sultan of Brunei* (**sultão**)

sultana /səlˈtɑːnə/ NOUN [*plural* **sultanas**]
1 a raisin (= dried grape) which is light in colour (**sultana**)
2 a sultan's wife (**sultana**)

sultry /ˈsʌltrɪ/ ADJECTIVE [**sultrier, sultriest**] sultry weather is unpleasantly hot (**abafado**)

sum /sʌm/ NOUN [*plural* **sums**]
1 an amount of money (**soma**) ◘ *Huge sums were spent on repairing the building.* (**somas enormes**) ◘ *Some footballers earn vast sums of money.* (**somas de dinheiro**)
2 the total when you add numbers together □ *+ of The sum of 2, 3 and 4 is 9.* (**soma total**)
3 a simple calculation □ *I was never any good at sums.* (**cálculo, conta**)

summon

◆ PHRASAL VERBS [**sums, summing, summed**] **sum (something) up** to end a discussion, speech, etc. by mentioning the main pieces of information in it (**resumir**) □ *So to sum up, more money needs to be spent on education.* **sum someone up** if something that someone does sums them up, it is typical of their, usually bad, behaviour (**resumir**)

summarize or **summarise** /ˈsʌməraɪz/ VERB [**summarizes, summarizing, summarized**] to give the main pieces of information about something □ *He summarized the arguments.* (**resumir**)

- **summary** /ˈsʌmərɪ/ NOUN [*plural* **summaries**] a short statement which gives the main pieces of information about something □ *A summary of her speech was printed in the newspaper.* (**sumário, resumo**)

summer /ˈsʌmə(r)/ NOUN [*plural* **summers**] the season between spring and autumn when the weather is warmest □ *People buy more ice cream in summer.* □ *My sister got married last summer.* □ *summer clothes* □ *summer holidays* □ *Summers are getting hotter.* (**verão**)

summer camp /ˈsʌmə(r) ˌkæmp/ NOUN [*plural* **summer camps**] a place where children can stay with other children in the summer holiday and do different activities (**acampamento de verão**)

summer holiday /ˈsʌmə(r) ˈhɒlɪdeɪ/ NOUN [*plural* **summer holidays**] a period of time in the summer when children do not go to school (**férias de verão**)

summer school /ˈsʌmə(r) ˌskuːl/ NOUN [*plural* **summer schools**] a course that you do in the summer at a school, college or university □ *He had attended a summer school for writers.* (**curso de férias**)

summertime /ˈsʌmətaɪm/ NOUN, NO PLURAL the season of summer □ *The garden looks beautiful in summertime.* (**verão**)

summer vacation /ˈsʌmə(r) vəˈkeɪʃən/ NOUN [*plural* **summer vacations**] the period of time in the summer when people do not go to classes at university (**férias de verão**)

summery /ˈsʌmərɪ/ ADJECTIVE right for summer □ *summery weather* (**veranil**)

summit /ˈsʌmɪt/ NOUN [*plural* **summits**]
1 the top of a hill or mountain ◘ *He reached the summit of Mount Everest in 1970.* (**cume, auge**)
2 a meeting between leaders of governments □ *The Prime Minister travelled to Brussels for an EU summit.* (**de cúpula**)

summon /ˈsʌmən/ VERB [**summons, summoning, summoned**]
1 to order someone to come □ *The headteacher summoned me to her office.* (**intimação**)
2 to find enough strength, courage, etc. to do something, although it is difficult □ *At last I summoned up the courage to ask her for a date.* (**convocar**)

- **summons** /ˈsʌmənz/ NOUN [plural **summonses**] a letter that says you must go to a court □ *He received a summons for a driving offence.* (**criar coragem**)

sumptuous /ˈsʌmptʃʊəs/ ADJECTIVE very expensive and of very high quality □ *a sumptuous meal* (**suntuoso**)

- **sumptuously** /ˈsʌmptʃʊəsli/ ADVERB in a way that is sumptuous □ *a sumptuously decorated room* (**suntuosamente**)

sun /sʌn/ ▶ NOUN, NO PLURAL

1 the sun the yellow thing in the sky which gives light and heat to the Earth (**o sol**) □ *The sun shone brightly into the room.* (**o sol brilhou**) □ *The sun rose at 7.12 am.* (**o sol nasceu**) □ *The sun set at 8.24 pm.* (**o sol se pôs**) □ *The Earth goes round the sun.*

2 the light and heat from the sun □ *We sat in the sun.* (**sol**)

▶ VERB [**suns, sunning, sunned**] **sun yourself** to sit or lie outside in the sun (**tomar sol**)

sunbathe /ˈsʌnbeɪð/ VERB [**sunbathes, sunbathing, sunbathed**] to lie or sit in the sun so that your skin becomes darker □ *Lots of people were sunbathing on the beach.* (**tomar banho de sol**)

- **sunbathing** /ˈsʌnbeɪðɪŋ/ NOUN, NO PLURAL the activity of lying or sitting in the sun so that your skin becomes darker (**banho de sol**)

sunbeam /ˈsʌnbiːm/ NOUN [plural **sunbeams**] a beam of light from the sun (**raio de sol**)

sunbed /ˈsʌnbed/ NOUN [plural **sunbeds**]
1 a piece of equipment that you lie on to make your skin darker (**cama de bronzeamento artificial**)
2 a comfortable chair used for sitting or lying outside in the sun (**espreguiçadeira**)

sunblock /ˈsʌnblɒk/ NOUN [plural **sunblocks**] a cream that you put on your skin to stop the sun from burning it (**protetor solar**)

sunburn /ˈsʌnbɜːn/ NOUN, NO PLURAL an area of sore, red skin caused by being in the sun for too long (**queimadura de sol**)

- **sunburnt** /ˈsʌnbɜːnt/ ADJECTIVE having sore, red skin because you have been in the sun for too long □ *a sunburnt nose* (**bronzeado**)

suncream /ˈsʌnkriːm/ NOUN, NO PLURAL cream that you put on your skin to protect it from the sun (**protetor solar**)

sundae /ˈsʌndeɪ/ NOUN [plural **sundaes**] a dish of ice cream served with fruit, nuts and a sweet sauce (**sundae**)

Sunday /ˈsʌndi/ NOUN [plural **Sundays**] the day of the week after Saturday and before Monday □ *I always go to church on Sundays.* (**domingo**)

Sunday school /ˈsʌndi ˌskuːl/ NOUN [plural **Sunday schools**] a class on Sundays at a church, where children learn about the Christian religion (**escola dominical**)

sundial /ˈsʌndaɪəl/ NOUN [plural **sundials**] an instrument that uses light from the sun and shadow to show you what time it is (**relógio de sol**)

sundry /ˈsʌndri/ ADJECTIVE
1 of many different types □ *sundry items* (**vários, diversos**)
2 all and sundry everyone (**tudo e todos**)

sunflower /ˈsʌnˌflaʊə(r)/ NOUN [plural **sunflowers**] a tall yellow flower with seeds that you can eat (**girassol**)

sung /sʌŋ/ PAST PARTICIPLE OF **sing** (**ver sing**)

sunglasses /ˈsʌnˌglɑːsɪz/ PLURAL NOUN dark glasses that protect your eyes from the sun □ *She was wearing a pair of sunglasses.* (**óculos escuros**)

sunk /sʌŋk/ PAST PARTICIPLE OF **sink** (**ver sink**)

- **sunken** /ˈsʌŋkən/ ADJECTIVE
1 under water □ *sunken treasure* (**submerso**)
2 lower than the surrounding area □ *a sunken bath* (**afundado**)

sunlight /ˈsʌnlaɪt/ NOUN, NO PLURAL the light from the sun (**luz do sol**) □ *Driving can be difficult in bright sunlight* (**luz forte do sol**) □ *Keep babies out of direct sunlight.* (**luz do sol direta**)

- **sunlit** /ˈsʌnlɪt/ ADJECTIVE lit up by the sun □ *a sunlit room* (**ensolarado**)

sunny /ˈsʌni/ ADJECTIVE [**sunnier, sunniest**]

1 full of light from the sun (**ensolarado**) □ *It's sunny outside.* (**está ensolarado**) □ *It's a lovely sunny day.* (**dia ensolarado**) □ *sunny weather*
2 happy □ *She has a very sunny nature.* □ *a sunny smile* (**radiante**)

sunrise /ˈsʌnraɪz/ NOUN [plural **sunrises**]
1 the time when the sun appears in the morning □ *I was up at sunrise.* (**nascer do sol**)
2 the appearance of the sky at sunrise □ *There was a spectacular sunrise this morning.* (**nascer do sol**)

sunroof /ˈsʌnruːf/ NOUN [plural **sunroofs**] a window in the roof of a car that you can open (**teto solar**)

sunscreen /ˈsʌnskriːn/ NOUN [plural **sunscreens**] a cream that you put on your skin to stop the sun from burning it (**filtro solar**)

sunset /ˈsʌnset/ NOUN [plural **sunsets**]

1 the time when the sun starts to disappear in the evening □ *We left the beach at sunset.* (**pôr do sol**)
2 the appearance of the sky at sunset □ *There was a beautiful golden sunset.* (**ocaso**)

sunshine /ˈsʌnʃaɪn/ NOUN, NO PLURAL the light and heat of the sun □ *He was squinting in the bright sunshine.* (**luz do sol**)

sunstroke /ˈsʌnstrəʊk/ NOUN, NO PLURAL an illness caused by spending too long in the sun (**insolação**)

suntan /ˈsʌntæn/ NOUN [plural **suntans**] a brown skin colour that you get because you have been in the sun (**bronzeamento**)

suntan lotion

- **sun-tanned** /'sʌntænd/ ADJECTIVE having a suntan □ She came back from holiday looking very suntanned. (bronzeado)

suntan lotion /'sʌntæn ˌləʊʃən/ NOUN [plural **suntan lotions**] a cream that you put on your skin to stop the sun from burning it (loção bronzeadora)

super /'su:pə(r)/ C ADJECTIVE an old-fashioned word meaning extremely good □ We had a super time at the fair. (super)

▶ ADVERB an informal word meaning very □ I exercise a bit but I'm not super fit. (super)

super- /'su:pə(r)/ PREFIX super- is added to the beginning of words to mean 'above' or 'extreme' □ superhuman □ superpower (super-)

superb /su:'pɜ:b/ ADJECTIVE extremely good □ a superb performance (magnífico)

- **superbly** /su:'pɜ:bli/ ADVERB in a way that is extremely good □ They played superbly in the first-half. (magnificamente)

superbug /'su:pəˌbʌg/ NOUN [plural **superbugs**] a type of bacteria that is very difficult to kill (superbactéria)

supercilious /ˌsu:pə'sɪliəs/ ADJECTIVE a formal word meaning treating other people as if they are not important □ a supercilious smile (desdenhoso)

superconductor /ˌsu:pəkən'dʌktə(r)/ NOUN [plural **superconductors**] a substance that allows an electrical current to pass through it easily at very low temperatures. A physics word. (supercondutor)

superficial /ˌsu:pə'fɪʃəl/ ADJECTIVE
1 affecting the surface only □ The wound is only superficial. □ The building suffered superficial damage. (superficial)
2 without details □ He had only a superficial knowledge of history. (superficial)
3 never thinking about things which are important or serious □ He's very superficial. (leviano, superficial)

superfluous /su:'pɜ:fluəs/ ADJECTIVE a formal word meaning not necessary □ superfluous equipment (supérfluo)

superhuman /ˌsu:pə'hju:mən/ ADJECTIVE superhuman strength or effort is much greater than ordinary human strength or ability □ A superhuman effort will be needed if we are going to finish the project on time. (sobre-humano)

superintendent /ˌsu:pərɪn'tendənt/ NOUN [plural **superintendents**]
1 a police officer with a fairly high rank (comandante)
2 someone who is in charge of something such as a building (diretor)

superior /su:'pɪərɪə(r)/ ▶ ADJECTIVE
1 better than something else (superior) ■ This product is far superior to earlier versions. (de longe superior)

supper

2 thinking that you are better than other people □ I can't stand her superior attitude. (superior)
3 having a higher rank than someone else (superior)

▶ NOUN [plural **superiors**] a person who has a higher rank than you at work □ He made complaints to his superiors. (superior)

- **superiority** /su:ˌpɪərɪ'ɒrəti/ NOUN, NO PLURAL being superior □ his superiority over others (superioridade)

superlative /su:'pɜ:lətɪv/ ▶ ADJECTIVE in grammar, the superlative form of an adjective or adverb is the form that usually ends with -est or is formed with most. For example, hardest, worst and most difficult are superlative forms. (superlativo)

▶ NOUN [plural **superlatives**] a superlative form of an adjective or adverb (superlativo)

supermarket /'su:pəˌmɑ:kɪt/ NOUN [plural **supermarkets**] a large shop that sells food and other goods (supermercado)

supermodel /'su:pəˌmɒdəl/ NOUN [plural **supermodels**] a very successful model (= person who wear clothes to advertise them) who earns a lot of money (supermodelo)

supernatural /ˌsu:pə'nætʃərəl/ ▶ ADJECTIVE mysterious and impossible to explain □ supernatural powers (sobrenatural)

▶ NOUN the supernatural mysterious events or creatures that are impossible to explain (o sobrenatural)

superpower /'su:pəˌpaʊə(r)/ NOUN [plural **superpowers**] a country which has a lot of political and military power (superpotência)

supersonic /ˌsu:pə'sɒnɪk/ ADJECTIVE faster than the speed of sound □ a supersonic aeroplane (supersônico)

superstar /'su:pəˌstɑ:(r)/ NOUN [plural **superstars**] a very famous actor, singer, person who plays sport, etc. (estrela)

superstition /ˌsu:pə'stɪʃən/ NOUN [plural **superstitions**] a belief that some things or actions are lucky or unlucky (superstição)

- **superstitious** /ˌsu:pə'stɪʃəs/ ADJECTIVE believing in superstitions (supersticioso)

supervise /'su:pəvaɪz/ VERB [**supervises**, **supervising**, **supervised**] to be in charge of a person or an activity □ Someone has to be there to supervise the children. □ He was supervising the road repair work. (supervisionar)

- **supervision** /ˌsu:pə'vɪʒən/ NOUN, NO PLURAL the act of supervising □ The prisoner was kept under close supervision. (supervisão)

- **supervisor** /ˌsu:pəvaɪzə(r)/ NOUN [plural **supervisors**] someone whose job is to make sure that other people do their work correctly (supervisor)

supper /'sʌpə(r)/ NOUN [plural **suppers**] a meal that you eat in the evening □ He ate his supper and went to bed. (jantar, ceia)

supple /'sʌpəl/ ADJECTIVE able to bend and stretch easily □ *Yoga is great for keeping you fit and supple.* □ *supple leather* (**flexível**)

supplement ▶ NOUN /'sʌplɪmənt/ [plural **supplements**]
1 a pill or liquid that you take when your food does not contain everything you need (**suplemento**) 🖼 *I always take a vitamin supplement.* (**suplemento de vitaminas**)
2 something extra that makes something better or bigger □ *They depended on this money as a supplement to their income.* (**suplemento**)
3 a separate part of a newspaper, magazine or book □ *The magazine published a special supplement on the Awards Ceremony.* (**suplemento**)
▶ VERB /'sʌplɪment/ [**supplements, supplementing, supplemented**] to add something in order to improve something or make it bigger □ *He supplements his wages by working in the evening.* (**suplementar**)
• **supplementary** /ˌsʌplɪ'mentəri/ ADJECTIVE extra □ *a supplementary charge* (**suplementar**)

suppleness /'sʌpəlnɪs/ NOUN, NO PLURAL the ability to bend and stretch easily (**elasticidade**)

supplier /sə'plaɪə(r)/ NOUN [plural **suppliers**] a company or country which supplies a product □ *In the 1990s, Australia was the world's largest supplier of coal.* (**fornecedor**)

supply /sə'plaɪ/ ▶ NOUN [plural **supplies**]
1 an amount of something that you can use (**abastecimento, suprimento**) 🖼 *The lack of rain is threatening the city's water supply.* (**abastecimento de água**) 🖼 *There is a limited supply of housing in the area.* (**suprimento limitado**) 🖼 *A plentiful supply of restaurants and bars mean that tourists are well catered for.* (**abundante oferta**) □ **+ of** *a supply of food*
2 no plural the process of providing something □ **+ of** *The company is involved in the supply of weapons to the Middle East.* (**fornecimento**)
3 supplies food, clothes, medicines, etc. that you need to live or to do something □ *A military plane landed with medical supplies for the refugees.* (**suprimentos**)
4 be in short/plentiful supply to have little/a lot of something available □ *Food was in short supply.* (**estar com falta de suprimentos/ter bastante estoque**)
▶ VERB [**supplies, supplying, supplied**] to provide something □ *Wind power could supply up to 20% of the country's electricity.* □ **+ with** *The farm supplies several major supermarkets with milk.* □ **+ to** *He supplied information to the police.* (**fornecer**)
▶ ADJECTIVE *a supply teacher* takes another teacher's place for a time (**substituto**)

support /sə'pɔːt/ ▶ VERB [**supports, supporting, supported**]
1 to agree with an idea, a person, etc. and want them to succeed □ *I support the idea in principle.* □ *Teachers did not support the proposal.* (**apoiar**)
2 to be under something and stop it from falling □ *The roof was supported by wooden beams.* (**apoiar, escorar**)
3 to show that a theory or statement is true □ *All the latest research supports this theory.* □ *There was no evidence to support his claim.* (**confirmar**)
4 to provide money for someone or something □ *She supports her family on a very low wage.* (**sustentar**)
5 to like a particular sports team and want them to win □ *Which football team do you support?* (**torcer**)
▶ NOUN [plural **supports**]
1 no plural agreement with an idea or a person and wanting them to succeed (**apoio**) 🖼 *The idea has received strong support from all the parties.* (**forte apoio**) 🖼 *Klinsmann eventually won massive public support in Germany.* (**apoio público**) □ **+ for** *There was not much support for the war.*
2 no plural encouragement and help (**ajuda**) 🖼 *He called to offer support as soon as he heard about my accident.* (**oferecer ajuda**)
3 no plural money provided for someone (**apoio**) 🖼 *A lack of financial support means that many students do not complete their courses.* (**apoio financeiro**) □ **+ from** *The treatment costs £2000 a month but she receives no support from the government.*
4 an object under something, which stops it from falling □ *One of the supports of the bridge collapsed.* (**suporte**)
• **supporter** /sə'pɔːtə(r)/ NOUN [plural **supporters**]
1 someone who agrees with an idea or person and wants them to succeed (**defensor, partidário**) 🖼 *He was a strong supporter of government policy.*
2 someone who likes a sports team and wants them to win □ *a Liverpool supporter* (**torcedor**)
• **supportive** /sə'pɔːtɪv/ ADJECTIVE giving help and encouragement □ *Parents have been very supportive of the school.* (**apoiador**)

suppose /sə'pəʊz/ VERB [**supposes, supposing, supposed**]
1 to think that something is probably true □ **+ that** *I suppose that all the tickets have been sold now?* (**supor**) 🖼 *I don't suppose we'll see him again.* □ *I suppose you'll be going to the concert.*
2 be supposed to do something (a) to be expected to do something, especially because of a rule □ *I'm supposed to look after my little sister on Saturdays.* □ *You're not supposed to walk on the grass.* (**dever**) (b) to be intended or expected to have a particular result or to happen in a particular way □ *The belts are supposed to support your back.* □ *He wasn't supposed to arrive until next week.* (**dever, ser esperado**)
3 I suppose used to say that you think something is possible, true or correct, although you are not sure or happy about it □ *We could get a taxi, I suppose.* □ *I suppose I deserve his criticism.* □ *I suppose the weather might improve.* (**eu suponho/acho**)

suppress

4 I suppose so (a) used to agree to something that you do not want to do or to happen □ *'Could you do the shopping this week?' 'I suppose so.'* (b) used to agree that something is possible, true or correct, but in a way that shows that you are not sure or happy about it □ *'We could always hire a gardener.' 'I suppose so, but it would be rather expensive.'* (**creio que sim**)
5 be supposed to be something to be considered by many people to have a particular quality □ *That area is supposed to be really beautiful.* □ *He's supposed to be good at maths.* (**ser considerado**)
6 used to tell someone to imagine that something is true so that a situation can be considered □ *Suppose you had £500,000 – what would you buy?* □ **+ that** *Supposing that you get the job – where will you live?* (**supor**)

• **supposed** /səˈpəʊzd/ ADJECTIVE believed by some people to exist or be true, although you think it may not □ *Why did none of her supposed friends help her?* □ *These people are a supposed threat to our security.* (**suposto**)

• **supposedly** /səˈpəʊzɪdli/ ADVERB according to what some people say, although you think it may not be true □ *He is supposedly one of the best doctors in the country.* □ *He charged me an extra £5, supposedly to cover postage.* (**supostamente**)

suppress /səˈpres/ VERB [suppresses, suppressing, suppressed]
1 to control a feeling so that you do not show it □ *She suppressed a smile.* (**reprimir**)
2 to stop people from complaining about a government, especially by using force □ *The rebellion was suppressed by government forces.* (**reprimir**)
3 to stop people from finding out about something important □ *The police were accused of trying to suppress evidence.* (**suprimir**)
4 to stop a physical process □ *The drug suppresses the growth of the tumour.* (**paralisar**)

• **suppression** /səˈpreʃən/ NOUN, NO PLURAL the act of suppressing something □ *the suppression of protests* (**repressão, contenção**)

supremacy /suˈpreməsi/ NOUN, NO PLURAL the state of being the most powerful □ *the supremacy of the president* (**supremacia**)

supreme /suːˈpriːm/ ADJECTIVE
1 most powerful □ *the supreme ruler* (**supremo**)
2 extreme □ *supreme courage* (**supremo**)

• **supremely** /suːˈpriːmli/ ADVERB extremely □ *She's supremely confident of her abilities.* (**supremamente**)

surcharge /ˈsɜːtʃɑːdʒ/ NOUN [plural surcharges] an extra amount of money that you have to pay □ *There's a surcharge if you exceed the airline's baggage limit.* (**sobretaxa**)

sure /ʃʊə(r)/ ▶ ADJECTIVE
1 certain □ **+ that** *I'm sure that we've met before.* □ **+ about** *Alex is coming, but I'm not sure about*

surface

Dan. □ **+ question word** *I'm not sure why he was so angry.* □ **+ of** *I'll phone you when I'm sure of the date.* □ *Are you sure you want to leave?* (**certo, seguro**)
2 make sure (a) to do something to make it certain that something happens □ *Can you make sure all the doors are locked?* (**certificar-se**) (b) to check that something is true □ *I think his birthday's on Saturday, but I'll just look in the diary to make sure.* (**certificar-se**)
3 sure to do something certain to happen or be the result of something □ *He's sure to win.* (**ter certeza de**)
4 be sure to do something used to tell someone that they must do something □ *Be sure to take plenty of water with you.* (**não deixe/esqueça de**)
5 certain to be successful □ *A spoonful of sugar is a sure way to cure hiccups.* (**certo**)
6 certain to be true (**com certeza**) 🔍 *Well kept gardens are a sure sign of a good neighbourhood.* (**sinal seguro**)

▶ ADVERB
1 used to agree to something □ *'Could I borrow your hammer?' 'Sure!'* (**É claro!/Claro que sim!**)
2 for sure without any doubts □ *I think he's Polish, but I don't know for sure.* (**com certeza**)
3 sure enough as was expected □ *I had an X-ray and sure enough, the bone was broken.* (**de fato**)

• **surely** /ˈʃʊəli/ ADVERB
1 used to show surprise about something □ *Surely you're going to wash that fruit before you eat it!* □ *Surely he didn't just leave her there!* (**certamente/é claro que**)
2 used to show that you think something is very likely □ *Surely they'll phone if they're not coming.* (**com certeza**)
3 surely not used to show that you do not think something can be true □ *Sam punched someone? Surely not!* (**é claro que não**)

surf /sɜːf/ ▶ VERB [surfs, surfing, surfed]
1 to ride on a board on waves on the sea □ *Australia has some of the best places to surf.* (**surfar**)
2 to look at a lot of different websites. A computing word. □ *He surfed the Internet for the best deals.* (**navegar**)
▶ NOUN, NO PLURAL the white part at the top of waves on the sea (**espuma**)

surface /ˈsɜːfɪs/ ▶ NOUN [plural surfaces]
1 the outside or top layer of something □ *The leaves had a rough surface.* □ *The temperature of the Earth's surface has risen.* □ **+ of** *A light wind rippled the surface of the lake.* (**superfície**)
2 no plural what someone or something seems to be like, especially when this is different from what they are really like □ *Beneath his calm surface there was a lot of anger.* (**aparência**)
▶ VERB [surfaces, surfacing, surfaced]
1 to appear or become known about □ *The allegations of assault surfaced last week.* (**tornar-se público**)

2 to come up to the surface of water □ *The submarine surfaced close to the ship.* (emergir)
3 to put a hard top layer on a road or path □ *Workmen were surfacing the road.* (revestir)

surface area /'sɜːfɪs 'eərɪə/ NOUN, NO PLURAL the total area of the outside surface of something. A maths word. (área de superfície)

surfboard /'sɜːfbɔːd/ NOUN [plural **surfboards**] a long board that you balance on and use for moving on the sea's waves (prancha de surfe)

surfer /'sɜːfə(r)/ NOUN [plural **surfers**] a person who surfs the waves (surfista)

surfing /'sɜːfɪŋ/ NOUN, NO PLURAL the sport of balancing on a board and moving on the sea's waves ▣ *We went surfing in Cornwall.* (surfe)

surge /sɜːdʒ/ ▶ VERB [**surges, surging, surged**]
1 to move in a particular direction with a lot of force □ *The crowd surged towards the fire exit.* □ *The storm surged up the coast.* (arremessar-se)
2 to increase very quickly □ *Oil prices surged.* (aumentar rapidamente)
▶ NOUN [plural **surges**]
1 a surge of excitement/anger, etc. a sudden, strong feeling □ *He felt a surge of affection for her.* (surto)
2 a sudden, large increase □ *There's been a surge in gang violence.* (aumento repentino)
3 a sudden movement in a particular direction (arremesso)

surgeon /'sɜːdʒən/ NOUN [plural **surgeons**] a doctor who does operations (cirurgião)

surgery /'sɜːdʒəri/ NOUN [plural **surgeries**]
1 medical treatments which involve cutting into someone's body □ *heart surgery* (cirurgia)
2 a place where you go to see a doctor or a dentist (consultório)

surgical /'sɜːdʒɪkəl/ ADJECTIVE to do with medical operations □ *surgical techniques* (cirúrgico)

• **surgically** /'sɜːdʒɪkəli/ ADVERB involving an operation □ *The lump will have to be surgically removed.* (cirurgicamente)

surly /'sɜːli/ ADJECTIVE [**surlier, surliest**] bad--tempered and rude □ *surly staff* (rispidez)

surname /'sɜːneɪm/ NOUN [plural **surnames**] your last name or family name □ *Smith is a common English surname.* □ *What's your surname?* (sobrenome)

surpass /sə'pɑːs/ VERB [**surpasses, surpassing, surpassed**]
1 a formal word meaning to be better than someone or something (ultrapassar) ▣ *His work surpassed my expectations.* (ultrapassar expectativas)
2 to be greater than a particular limit or amount □ *Donations have surpassed the 100,000 mark.* (superar)

surplus /'sɜːpləs/ C NOUN [plural **surpluses**] an extra amount that is more than you need □ *This country produces a surplus of grain.* (excedente)
▶ ADJECTIVE extra and more than you need □ *We have surplus food.* (excedente)

surprise /sə'praɪz/ ▶ NOUN [plural **surprises**]
1 *no plural* the feeling caused by something sudden or unexpected □ *He stared at her in surprise.* (surpresa) ▣ *To my surprise, I passed my driving test first time.* (para minha surpresa)
2 something sudden or unexpected □ *Your letter was a nice surprise.* (surpresa) ▣ *The news of their engagement came as a big surprise.* (chegar como uma grande surpresa)
3 take/catch someone by surprise to happen unexpectedly, and make you feel surprised □ *The message had taken her by surprise.* (pegar alguém de surpresa)
▶ ADJECTIVE unexpected (de surpresa) ▣ *I organized a surprise party for my Mum's 40th birthday.* (festa surpresa) ▣ *The President made a surprise visit to Baghdad.* (visita surpresa)
▶ VERB [**surprises, surprising, surprised**]
1 to make someone feel surprise □ *He surprised me by turning up without calling.* (surpreender) ▣ *It wouldn't surprise me if he'd committed other similar crimes.* (não me surpreenderia se...)
2 to attack someone suddenly and without warning □ *They surprised the enemy from the rear.* (surpreender)

• **surprised** /sə'praɪzd/ ADJECTIVE having a feeling of surprise (surpreso) ▣ *Anna looked surprised when I told her.* (parecer surpreso) □ + *that I'm surprised that he agreed to come.* □ + *to do something I was very surprised to hear that he had left.* □ + *at/by She was surprised by the news.*

> Notice the prepositions that follow the word **surprised**. You are **surprised at** or **by** something:
> ✓ *I was surprised at/by his decision.*
> ✗ *I was surprised about his decision.*

• **surprising** /sə'praɪzɪŋ/ ADJECTIVE making you feel surprise □ *A surprising number of people voted for him.* (surpreendente) ▣ *It's surprising how many people believe in ghosts.* (é surpreendente como) ▣ *It's hardly surprising that* (= it is not surprising that) *people sometimes have arguments when they live together.* (raramente é uma surpresa)

• **surprisingly** /sə'praɪzɪŋli/ ADVERB in a way that surprises you □ *She's surprisingly strong for such a small woman.* (surpreendentemente)

surreal /sə'rɪəl/ or **surrealistic** /sə,rɪə'lɪstɪk/ ADJECTIVE strange, and like something from a dream □ *It was a surreal experience finding myself in a room full of people wearing 18th--century clothes.* (surreal/surrealista)

• **surrealism** /sə'rɪəlɪzəm/ NOUN, NO PLURAL a style of art or literature in which different ideas

surrender

or images are connected in a strange way (surrealismo)

- **surrealist** /səˈrɪəlɪst/ ADJECTIVE to do with surrealism □ *surrealist paintings* (surrealista)

surrender /səˈrendə(r)/ ▶ VERB [**surrenders, surrendering, surrendered**]

1 to stop fighting or trying to escape because you know you will not be successful □ *They surrendered to the enemy.* (render-se)

2 a formal word meaning to give something to someone in authority because they demand it □ *He was forced to surrender his passport.* (devolver, desistir de)

▶ NOUN, NO PLURAL an act of surrendering (rendição)

surreptitious /ˌsʌrəpˈtɪʃəs/ ADJECTIVE secret so that other people do not notice □ *He took a surreptitious glance at his watch.* (secreto, clandestino)

- **surreptitiously** /ˌsʌrəpˈtɪʃəsli/ ADVERB in a secret way □ *He surreptitiously put it in his pocket.* (secretamente)

surrogate /ˈsʌrəɡət/ ▶ ADJECTIVE taking the place of someone or something else (substituto) 🔲 *a surrogate mother* (= a woman who has a baby for another woman) (mãe de aluguel)

▶ NOUN [plural **surrogates**] a person or thing that takes the place of someone or something □ *Robots are already used as surrogates for humans in some industrial processes.* (substituto)

surround /səˈraʊnd/ VERB [**surrounds, surrounding, surrounded**]

1 to be or go all around something or someone □ *Fans surrounded the players.* □ *The city is surrounded by hills.* (rodear)

2 if you are surrounded by something or someone, you have a lot of them near you □ *I'm surrounded by good friends who will help me.* □ *Losing weight is not easy when you are surrounded by food.* (cercar)

3 if a feeling or quality surrounds something, it is connected with it □ *There is a lot of secrecy surrounding the organization.* (cercar)

- **surrounding** /səˈraʊndɪŋ/ ADJECTIVE all around a place □ *People from the surrounding villages come to the market.* □ *Brisbane and the surrounding area became the fastest growing region in Australia.* (circundante)

- **surroundings** /səˈraʊndɪŋz/ PLURAL NOUN the area around a person or place □ *The hotel is set in beautiful surroundings.* □ *He was glad to be back in his own surroundings.* (cercanias)

surveillance /sɜːˈveɪləns/ NOUN, NO PLURAL when people such as the police watch someone very closely □ *The FBI had been keeping him under surveillance for several months.* (vigilância)

survey ▶ NOUN /ˈsɜːveɪ/ [plural **surveys**]

1 a set of questions designed to find out people's opinions (levantamento, pesquisa) 🔲 *We conducted a survey of students.* (conduzir uma pesquisa) 🔲 *The survey showed that parents and children both want more time together.* (a pesquisa mostrou que)

2 an examination of a building in order to see its condition and value, especially when someone wants to buy it (vistoria, inspeção)

▶ VERB /səˈveɪ/ [**surveys, surveying, surveyed**]

1 to ask people a set of questions in order to find out their opinions □ *60% of people surveyed felt that television was a bad influence on children.* (pesquisar)

2 to look at something carefully (fazer levantamento) 🔲 *Residents surveyed the damage which the storm had caused to their homes.* (verificar os prejuízos)

3 to examine a building or land (inspecionar)

- **surveyor** /səˈveɪə(r)/ NOUN [plural **surveyors**] someone whose job is to examine the condition of a building or to look at the details of an area of land (inspetor, topógrafo)

survival /səˈvaɪvəl/ NOUN, NO PLURAL the fact of continuing to live or exist □ *His survival depended on finding fresh water.* (sobrevivência)

survive /səˈvaɪv/ VERB [**survives, surviving, survived**]

1 to continue to live after something bad has happened □ *He didn't survive long after the accident.* □ *Amazingly, the diver survived the shark attack.* (sobreviver a)

2 to continue to exist or live normally (sobreviver) 🔲 *Many companies are struggling to survive.* (lutando para sobreviver) □ *They survive on only £100 a week.*

- **surviving** /səˈvaɪvɪŋ/ ADJECTIVE still alive or existing after others have died or been destroyed □ *He is the last surviving soldier from the war.* (sobrevivente)

- **survivor** /səˈvaɪvə(r)/ NOUN [plural **survivors**] someone who continues to live after something bad has happened to them □ *He was the only survivor of the crash which killed the princess.* (sobrevivente)

susceptible /səˈseptəbəl/ ADJECTIVE likely to be affected by something □ *Children are more susceptible to colds.* (suscetível)

suspect ▶ NOUN /ˈsʌspekt/ [plural **suspects**] someone who may have committed a crime □ *terrorist suspects* (suspeito) 🔲 *He's the prime suspect in the murder of Rachel Smith.* (principal suspeito)

▶ VERB /səˈspekt/ [**suspects, suspecting, suspected**]

1 to think that someone may have committed a crime □ *He's suspected of murdering two women.* (suspeitar)

2 to think that something might be true □ *I suspect that she is hiding her true feelings.* (suspeitar)

▶ ADJECTIVE /ˈsʌspekt/

1 difficult to trust (suspeito) 🔲 *The country's election process is highly suspect.* (altamente suspeito)

2 looking dangerous or illegal (**suspeito**) 🔲 *Four suspect packages were blown up by bomb squad officers.* (**pacotes suspeitos**)

suspend /səˈspend/ VERB [**suspends, suspending, suspended**]
1 to stop something for a period of time ☐ *All business will be suspended until after New Year.* (**suspender**)
2 to make someone leave their job or a school for a short time because they have done something wrong ☐ *He was suspended from his job after allegations that he had bullied his staff.* (**suspender**)
3 to hang something ☐ *The meat was suspended from a hook.* (**pendurar**)

• **suspenders** /səˈspendə(r)z/ PLURAL NOUN
1 a piece of underwear that a woman wears to hold up her stockings (= very thin leg coverings) (**cinta-liga**)
2 the US word for braces (**suspensório**)

suspense /səˈspens/ NOUN, NO PLURAL excitement and nervousness because you are waiting for something to happen ☐ *We waited in suspense for the result.* (**suspense**)

suspension /səˈspenʃən/ NOUN [plural **suspensions**]
1 when something stops for a period of time ☐ *This could lead to a suspension of the talks.* (**suspensão**)
2 when someone must leave a job, school or team for a period of time because they have done something wrong ☐ *He faces a two-match suspension for dangerous play.* (**suspensão**)
3 the parts that are attached to a vehicle's wheels, and make it more comfortable to ride in (**suspensão**)

suspension bridge /səˈspenʃən ˌbrɪdʒ/ NOUN [plural **suspension bridges**] a type of bridge that hangs from cables (= very thick, strong wires) attached to towers (**ponte pênsil**)

suspicion /səˈspɪʃən/ NOUN [plural **suspicions**]
1 a feeling or a belief that someone has done something wrong or illegal (**suspeita**) 🔲 *He was arrested on suspicion of drink-driving.* (**sob suspeita de**) 🔲 *His odd behaviour raised suspicions.* (**levantar suspeita**)
2 a feeling that something is true (**suspeita**) 🔲 *I had a strong suspicion that it was broken.* (**ter uma suspeita**)

• **suspicious** /səˈspɪʃəs/ ADJECTIVE
1 feeling or showing that you do not completely trust someone ☐ *She gave him a suspicious glance.* (**desconfiado**)
2 making you think that a crime might be involved ☐ *He died in suspicious circumstances.* (**suspeitoso**)

• **suspiciously** /səˈspɪʃəsli/ ADVERB in a suspicious way ☐ *She looked at him suspiciously.* ☐ *The boys were acting suspiciously.* (**suspeitosamente**)

sustain /səˈsteɪn/ VERB [**sustains, sustaining, sustained**]
1 to make something continue ☐ *It would be difficult to sustain such a fast pace.* (**manter**)
2 a formal word meaning to suffer something, such as an injury, damage, etc. (**sofrer**) 🔲 *He sustained head injuries in the accident.* (**sofrer ferimentos**)
3 to keep someone healthy and strong ☐ *They don't have enough food to sustain them through the winter.* (**sustentar, manter**)

• **sustainable** /səˈsteɪnəbəl/ ADJECTIVE
1 able to continue in the same way for a long time ☐ *sustainable economic growth* (**sustentável**)
2 not damaging the environment and so able to continue in the same way ☐ *sustainable farming practices* (**sustentável**)

• **sustainably** /səˈsteɪnəbli/ ADVERB in a sustainable way ☐ *a sustainably managed forest* (**sustentavelmente**)

• **sustained** /səˈsteɪnd/ ADJECTIVE continuing in the same way ☐ *a sustained period of success* (**mantido**)

• **sustenance** /ˈsʌstɪnəns/ NOUN, NO PLURAL a formal word meaning food and drink (**sustento**)

swab /swɒb/ ▶ NOUN [plural **swabs**] a piece of material used, for example, to clean injuries (**cotonete**)
▶ VERB [**swabs, swabbing, swabbed**] to clean something using a swab (**limpar com cotonete**)

swagger /ˈswægə(r)/ ▶ VERB [**swaggers, swaggering, swaggered**] to walk in a proud and confident way, moving your body from side to side ☐ *He swaggered along the street in his new suit.* (**fanfarronear**)
▶ NOUN [plural **swaggers**] a proud and confident way of walking (**andar fanfarrão**)

swallow /ˈswɒləʊ/ ▶ VERB [**swallows, swallowing, swallowed**]
1 to make food or drink go down your throat ☐ *Try to swallow the pill.* ☐ *She swallowed a large mouthful of water.* (**engolir**)
2 to make a movement in your throat as if you are eating something ☐ *My throat hurts when I swallow.* ☐ *He swallowed hard and cleared his throat.* (**engolir**)
3 to accept something difficult or unpleasant (**aceitar**) 🔲 *Being told you are losing your job is pretty hard to swallow.* (**duro de engolir**)
4 an informal word meaning to accept what someone tells you, especially when it is not true ☐ *She'll never swallow that story!* (**engolir**)
5 to hide a feeling and not allow it to affect your behaviour (**engolir**) 🔲 *He swallowed his pride and accepted the offer of help.* (**engolir seu orgulho**)

♦ PHRASAL VERB **swallow something up** to make something disappear or to use all of something ☐ *The increase in profits has been swallowed up by rising wage bills.* (**tragar**)
▶ NOUN [plural **swallows**]

swam

1 when you swallow food or drink (gole)
2 a small bird with long pointed wings and a tail with two points (andorinha)

swam /swæm/ PAST TENSE OF swim (ver swim)

swamp /swɒmp/ ▶ NOUN [plural **swamps**] an area of land that is always very wet (pântano)
▶ VERB [**swamps, swamping, swamped**]
1 to give someone more of something than they can deal with □ *I'm swamped with work.* (atolar-se em)
2 to cover something with water □ *A great wave swamped the deck.* (inundar)

swan /swɒn/ NOUN [plural **swans**] a large white bird with a long neck which lives on rivers and lakes (cisne)

swap /swɒp/ ▶ VERB [**swaps, swapping, swapped**] to exchange one thing for another thing □ *I took the dress back to the shop and swapped it for a bigger size.* (trocar)
▶ NOUN [plural **swaps**] when you swap one thing for another (troca) 🔲 *He suggested that we do a swap.* (fazer uma troca)

swarm /swɔːm/ ▶ NOUN [plural **swarms**] a large group of insects which are flying or moving together □ *a swarm of bees* (enxame)
▶ VERB [**swarms, swarming, swarmed**]
1 if a lot of people swarm somewhere, they quickly move there □ *Reporters swarmed around her as she left court.* (formigar, aglomerar-se)
2 if a place is swarming with people or insects, there are a lot of them there □ *The area was swarming with police.* (formigar, aglomerar-se)

swarthy /'swɔːði/ ADJECTIVE [**swarthier, swarthiest**] with dark skin (escuro, moreno)

swashbuckling /'swɒʃˌbʌklɪŋ/ ADJECTIVE full of adventure and excitement □ *a swashbuckling drama* (fanfarrice)

swat /swɒt/ VERB [**swats, swatting, swatted**] to hit and kill an insect (matar um inseto)

sway /sweɪ/ ▶ VERB [**sways, swaying, swayed**]
1 to move from side to side □ *The trees swayed in the wind.* (balançar-se)
2 to persuade someone to change their opinion or decision □ *He wasn't swayed by threats.* (influenciar)
▶ NOUN, NO PLURAL (influência) **hold sway** a formal phrase meaning to have power or influence □ *He still holds sway in the party.* (mantém influência)

swear /sweə(r)/ VERB [**swears, swearing, swore, sworn**]
1 to use words that are offensive □ *He was sent off for swearing at the referee.* (jurar)
2 to promise □ *She swore never to do it again.* (prometer)
3 used to say that you are certain about something (jurar) 🔲 *I could have sworn I left the book on my desk.* (eu poderia ter jurado)
4 **swear someone to secrecy** to make someone promise that they will not tell people something (jurar segredo)

◆ PHRASAL VERBS **swear by something** to believe that something is very good and effective □ *She swears by her grandmother's recipe.* (jurar por)
swear someone in if someone is sworn in, they make a public promise before they start an important job □ *The country's first elected female leader was sworn in last month.* (prestar juramento)

• **swearing** /'sweərɪŋ/ NOUN, NO PLURAL the use of offensive words (xingamento)

swear word /'sweə ˌwɜːd/ NOUN [plural **swear words**] a word that is offensive (xingamento)

sweat /swet/ ▶ NOUN, NO PLURAL the salty liquid that comes out of your skin when you are hot □ *He was dripping with sweat after his run.* (suor)
▶ VERB [**sweats, sweating, sweated**] to give out sweat □ *Exercise makes you sweat.* (suar)

• **sweater** /'swetə(r)/ NOUN [plural **sweaters**] a piece of clothing for the top part of your body that you pull over your head □ *He was wearing a blue sweater and jeans.* (suéter, pulôver)

sweatshirt /'swetʃɜːt/ NOUN [plural **sweatshirts**] a piece of clothing for the top part of your body, made of thick, soft cotton (casaco de moletom)

sweaty /'swetɪ/ ADJECTIVE [**sweatier, sweatiest**] wet with sweat □ *sweaty hands* (suado)

swede /swiːd/ NOUN [plural **swedes**] a large round yellow vegetable that grows under the ground (nabo)

sweep /swiːp/ ▶ VERB [**sweeps, sweeping, swept**]
1 to clean something using a brush □ *He swept the floor.* □ *+ up She swept up the broken glass.* (varrer)
2 to move someone or something somewhere with a quick, strong movement □ *+ away Whole villages were swept away by the flood.* □ *Tonnes of mud were swept down the hillside.* (varrer, ser arrastado)
3 to quickly affect a large area □ *The disease is sweeping through the country.* (estender-se)
4 to go somewhere quickly and confidently □ *She swept into my room without knocking.* (mover-se impetuosamente)

◆ IDIOM **sweep someone off their feet** to quickly make someone love you (fazer alguém se apaixonar de repente)
▶ NOUN [plural **sweeps**]
1 when you sweep something clean □ *She gave the room a sweep.* (varrição)
2 a sweeping movement □ *He indicated the damage with a sweep of his hand.* (movimento impetuoso)

• **sweeper** /'swiːpə(r)/ NOUN [plural **sweepers**] in football, a player who stays behind the other players to stop the other team scoring (zagueiro)

• **sweeping** /'swiːpɪŋ/ ADJECTIVE
1 affecting many people or things 🔲 *The system has undergone sweeping changes.* (abrangente)

2 too general to be true 🔂 *That seems a rather sweeping statement.* (genérico)

sweepstake /'swi:psteɪk/ NOUN [plural **sweepstakes**] a system in which several people give money to guess the result of something and the person who guesses correctly wins all the money (loteria)

sweet /swi:t/ ▶ ADJECTIVE [**sweeter, sweetest**]
1 tasting like sugar ☐ *He loves sweet food.* (doce)
2 pleasant in smell or sound ☐ *the sweet smell of flowers* (doce)
3 attractive and making you feel affection ☐ *a sweet little boy* (doce)
4 kind and friendly ☐ *She seems very sweet.* (gentil) 🔂 *It was sweet of him to offer.* (foi gentileza de)
▶ NOUN [plural **sweets**]
1 a small piece of sweet food, for example chocolate ☐ *a packet of sweets* (doce)
2 something sweet that people eat at the end of a meal (doce)

sweetcorn /'swi:tkɔ:n/ NOUN, NO PLURAL yellow grains of the maize plant, that you eat as a vegetable (milho doce)

sweeten /'swi:tən/ VERB [**sweetens, sweetening, sweetened**] to make something sweet ☐ *Sweeten the raspberries with sugar.* (adoçar)
• **sweetener** /'swi:tənə(r)/ NOUN [plural **sweeteners**]
1 a substance used instead of sugar to sweeten food and drinks (adoçante)
2 something that you offer to someone in order to persuade them to do something (suborno)

sweetheart /'swi:thɑ:t/ NOUN [plural **sweethearts**]
1 a word used when talking to someone you love ☐ *Sleep well, sweetheart.* (querido/a)
2 a slightly old-fashioned word meaning a boyfriend or girlfriend (namorado) 🔂 *They were childhood sweethearts.* (namoradinhos de infância)

sweetie /'swi:tɪ/ NOUN [plural **sweeties**]
1 an informal word meaning a nice, kind person ☐ *She's a real sweetie.* (doçura)
2 a word used for talking to someone you love ☐ *There you are, sweetie.* (doçura)
3 a word used by children meaning a sweet ☐ *Mum, can I have a sweetie?* (doce)

sweetly /'swi:tlɪ/ ADVERB in an attractive or friendly way ☐ *She smiled sweetly.* (docemente, gentilmente)

sweetness /'swi:tnɪs/ NOUN, NO PLURAL
1 the quality of being sweet in taste or smell (doçura)
2 the quality of being kind and friendly (amabilidade)

sweet tooth /'swi:t 'tu:θ/ NOUN, NO PLURAL if you have a sweet tooth, you like sweet food (queda por doces)

swell /swel/ ▶ VERB [**swells, swelling, swelled, swollen**]
1 to become bigger in size ☐ *The wasp sting made her finger swell.* ☐ **+ up** *My feet swelled up.* (inchar)
2 to increase in number ☐ *The population has swelled by thirty percent.* (aumentar)
▶ NOUN, NO PLURAL the movement of the sea as it goes up and down (movimento ondulante)
• **swelling** /'swelɪŋ/ NOUN [plural **swellings**] a swollen part of the body (inchaço)

swelter /'sweltə(r)/ VERB [**swelters, sweltering, sweltered**] to be too hot ☐ *Bus passengers sweltered in temperatures that hit 100 degrees.* (calor sufocante)
• **sweltering** /'sweltərɪŋ/ ADJECTIVE unpleasantly hot ☐ *It's sweltering today.* (sufocante)

swept /swept/ PAST TENSE AND PAST PARTICIPLE OF **sweep** (ver **sweep**)

swerve /swɜ:v/ ▶ VERB [**swerves, swerving, swerved**] to suddenly move to the right or left when you are driving ☐ *The driver had to swerve to avoid hitting a dog.* (desviar)
▶ NOUN [plural **swerves**] when you swerve (desvio)

swift /swɪft/ ADJECTIVE [**swifter, swiftest**] quick ☐ *I hope she makes a swift recovery.* (rápido, veloz)
• **swiftly** /'swɪftlɪ/ ADVERB quickly (rapidamente)
• **swiftness** /'swɪftnɪs/ NOUN, NO PLURAL the quality of being quick (rapidez)

swig /swɪg/ ▶ VERB [**swigs, swigging, swigged**] to drink something by taking a large amount into your mouth. An informal word. ☐ *He was swigging from a bottle of water.* (beber em grandes goles)
▶ NOUN [plural **swigs**] when you swig something. An informal word. (gole, trago)

swill /swɪl/ ▶ VERB [**swills, swilling, swilled**] to wash something by moving water around quickly inside it ☐ *He swilled out the cups.* (lavar)
▶ NOUN, NO PLURAL waste food which pigs eat (lavagem)

swim /swɪm/ ▶ VERB [**swims, swimming, swam, swum**]
1 to move through water using your arms and legs ☐ *Can you swim?* ☐ *He swam across the river.* (nadar)
2 if your head swims, you feel confused or as if everything is moving around ☐ *He felt sick and his head was swimming.* (girar)
3 if something is swimming in a liquid, it is covered with it ☐ *The food was swimming in oil.* (nadar)
▶ NOUN [plural **swims**] when you swim 🔂 *I think I'll go for a swim.* (nado)
• **swimmer** /'swɪmə(r)/ NOUN [plural **swimmers**] someone or something that swims ☐ *an Olympic swimmer* (nadador) 🔂 *She was a strong swimmer* (= able to swim well).
• **swimming** /'swɪmɪŋ/ NOUN, NO PLURAL the activity or sport of moving through water using your arms and legs ☐ *Swimming is excellent exercise.* 🔂 *We went swimming at the local pool.* (natação)

swimming baths

swimming baths /'swɪmɪŋ ˌbɑːðz/ PLURAL NOUN a building with a pool inside which people can swim in (**piscina**)

swimming costume /'swɪmɪŋ ˌkɒstjuːm/ NOUN [plural **swimming costumes**] a piece of clothing that women and girls wear for swimming (**traje de banho**)

swimming pool /'swɪmɪŋ ˌpuːl/ NOUN [plural **swimming pools**] an area of water made for swimming in (**piscina**)

swimming trunks /'swɪmɪŋ ˌtrʌŋks/ PLURAL NOUN a piece of clothing that men and boys wear for swimming (**sunga ou calção de banho**)

swimsuit /'swɪmsuːt/ NOUN [plural **swimsuits**] a piece of clothing that women and girls wear for swimming (**maiô**)

swindle /'swɪndəl/ ▶ VERB [**swindles, swindling, swindled**] to trick someone in order to take their money ☐ That shopkeeper has swindled me out of £2! (**trapacear**)
▶ NOUN [plural **swindles**] when someone is swindled (**trapaça**)
• **swindler** /'swɪndlə(r)/ NOUN [plural **swindlers**] a person who swindles other people (**trapaceiro**)

swine /swaɪn/ NOUN [plural **swine**]
1 a rude word for someone who treats others people badly (**porco**)
2 an old word for a pig (**porco**)

swing /swɪŋ/ ▶ VERB [**swings, swinging, swung**]
1 to move backwards and forwards through the air, or to make something do this ☐ You swing your arms when you walk. ☐ The children were swinging on a rope hanging from a tree. (**balançar**)
2 to move in a smooth, wide curve, or to make something do this (**gingar**) ☐ The door swung open. ☐ She sat up and swung her legs over the side of the bed. (**gingar, oscilar, bascular**)
3 to try to hit something or someone ☐ + **at** She swung at the ball. ☐ Craig turned round and swung at my brother. (**virar-se para bater**)
4 to turn suddenly ☐ + **round** He swung round and stared at us. (**virar-se de repente**)
5 if moods, opinions, etc. swing, they suddenly change ☐ Public opinion has swung against the war. (**oscilar**)
6 swing into action to suddenly start doing something ☐ A major rescue operation swung into action last night. (**entrar em ação**)
▶ NOUN [plural **swings**]
1 a seat hanging from ropes or chains, that children sit on and move backwards and forwards (**balanço**)
2 a sudden and big change (**alterações**) ☐ She experienced dramatic mood swings. (**alterações de humor**) ☐ They recorded extreme swings in temperature.
3 a swinging movement, especially to hit someone or something (**giro para bater**) ☐ Simon took a swing at him and missed. (**virou-se para atingi-lo**) ☐ He's been practising his golf swing.
4 in full swing if an event or process is in full swing, it is happening and full of activity ☐ The party was in full swing. (**em pleno vapor**)

swipe /swaɪp/ ▶ VERB [**swipes, swiping, swiped**]
1 an informal word meaning to hit or to try to hit someone or something ☐ She swiped me across the face. (**bater com violência**)
2 to pull a plastic card through a device so electronic details can be read ☐ You have to swipe your card in order to get into the building. (**passar o cartão**)
3 an informal word meaning to steal something ☐ The tapes had been swiped from his office. (**roubar**)
▶ NOUN [plural **swipes**]
1 an informal word meaning when you try to hit someone or something ☐ He took a swipe at the ball. (**golpe violento**)
2 an informal word meaning when you criticize someone ☐ The president took a swipe at his critics. (**ataque verbal**)

swipe card /'swaɪp ˌkɑːd/ NOUN [plural **swipe cards**] a plastic card with electronic information on it which you pull through a device, especially to open a door (**cartão de acesso**)

swirl /swɜːl/ ▶ VERB [**swirls, swirling, swirled**] to move quickly round in circles ☐ Leaves swirled along the ground. (**rodopiar**)
▶ NOUN [plural **swirls**] a swirling movement (**redemoinho**)

swish /swɪʃ/ ▶ VERB [**swishes, swishing, swished**] to move with a sound like cloth moving ☐ Her long skirt swished as she danced. (**farfalhar**)
▶ NOUN [plural **swishes**] a swishing sound (**farfalhar, barulho de tecidos**)

switch /swɪtʃ/ ▶ VERB [**switches, switching, switched**]
1 to change from one thing to another thing ☐ We switched channels to watch the news. ☐ + **from** She switched from English to French effortlessly. ☐ + **to** Many families have switched to cheaper gas suppliers. (**mudar**)
2 to exchange two things ☐ Someone had switched the name tags. (**trocar**)
◆ PHRASAL VERBS **switch (something) on/off** to turn something on or off using a switch ☐ I switched the light on. ☐ He'd forgotten to switch off the microphone. (**ligar/desligar**) **switch off** an informal phrase meaning to stop giving your attention to something ☐ If it's boring, students just switch off. (**desviar a atenção**) **switch over 1** to change from one radio or television programme to another ☐ I switched over to CNN. (**mudar de canal**) **2** to start using a different system, product, etc. ☐ Many airlines have switched over to electronic ticketing systems. (**mudar**)

► NOUN [plural switches]
1 a device that you press to make something work or stop working (**interruptor**) 🗣 *I can't find the light switch.* (**interruptor da luz**) 🗣 *He flicked the switch on the kettle.*
2 a change from one thing to another □ *+ of/in We're considering a switch of location.* (**mudança**) 🗣 *People are making the switch from CDs to digital downloads.* (**fazer a mudança**)

switchboard /ˈswɪtʃbɔːd/ NOUN [plural **switchboards**] equipment for connecting telephone calls in an office building, a hospital, etc. (**painel de controle**)

swivel /ˈswɪvəl/ VERB [**swivels, swivelling**/US **swiveling, swivelled**/US **swiveled**] to turn round quickly, or to turn something round quickly □ *I swivelled round to look at him.* (**giro, movimento giratório**)

swollen /ˈswəʊlən/ ► ADJECTIVE bigger than usual □ *He had a swollen ankle after falling downstairs.* □ *Several swollen rivers burst their banks.* (**inchado**)
► PAST PARTICIPLE OF **swell** (ver **swell**)

swoon /swuːn/ ► VERB [**swoons, swooning, swooned**] an old-fashioned word meaning to faint (= suddenly become unconscious) (**desmaiar**)
► NOUN [plural **swoons**] an old-fashioned word meaning when you swoon (**desmaio**)

swoop /swuːp/ ► VERB [**swoops, swooping, swooped**]
1 to suddenly and quickly move down □ *The owl swooped down on its prey.* (**mergulhar sobre**)
2 if police officers swoop, they go somewhere without warning, in order to find someone or something □ *More than twenty police officers swooped on the house.* (**lançar-se em ataque**)
► NOUN [plural **swoops**] when something or someone swoops (**arremetida**)

swop /swɒp/ ► VERB [**swops, swopping, swopped**] another spelling of **swap** (**trocar**)
► NOUN [plural **swops**] another spelling of **swap** (**troca**)

sword /sɔːd/ NOUN [plural **swords**] a weapon with a long blade (**espada**)

swordfish /ˈsɔːdfɪʃ/ NOUN [plural **swordfish** or **swordfishes**] a large fish with a long pointed face (**peixe-espada**)

swore /swɔː(r)/ PAST TENSE OF **swear** (ver **swear**)

sworn /swɔːn/ ► PAST PARTICIPLE OF **swear** (ver **swear**)
► ADJECTIVE
1 made or given after you have officially promised that it is true □ *a sworn statement* (**jurado**)
2 sworn enemies are people who will always hate each other (**jurado, declarado**)

swot /swɒt/ ► NOUN [plural **swots**] an informal word for someone who studies too much (**CDF, estudioso**)
► VERB [**swots, swotting, swotted**] an informal word meaning to study hard (**estudar muito**)
♦ PHRASAL VERB **swot up on something** an informal phrase meaning to learn as much as you can about something (**estudar ao máximo**)

swum /swʌm/ PAST PARTICIPLE OF **swim** (ver **swim**)

sycamore /ˈsɪkəmɔː(r)/ NOUN [plural **sycamores**] a tree with seeds in the shape of two wings (**sicômoro**)

syllable /ˈsɪləbəl/ NOUN [plural **syllables**] a word or part of a word that is a single sound. For example, pen has one syllable and pen-cil has two syllables. (**sílaba**)

syllabus /ˈsɪləbəs/ NOUN [plural **syllabuses** or **syllabi**] a list of what students will learn in a subject (**plano de curso**)

symbiosis /ˌsɪmbɪˈəʊsɪs/ NOUN, NO PLURAL when two living things live together and depend on each other. A biology word. (**simbiose**)

symbol /ˈsɪmbəl/ NOUN [plural **symbols**]
1 something that represents a more general idea □ *+ of The dove is a symbol of peace.* (**símbolo**) 🗣 *The statue became a symbol of freedom.* (**tornar-se um símbolo**)
2 a written sign or a letter that represents something □ *+ for H is the chemical symbol for hydrogen* (**símbolo**)
• **symbolic** /sɪmˈbɒlɪk/ ADJECTIVE representing something 🗣 *The gift was a symbolic gesture of friendship.* (**simbólico**)
• **symbolism** /ˈsɪmbəlɪzəm/ NOUN, NO PLURAL the use of symbols to represent ideas, especially in art and literature □ *He uses a lot of religious symbolism in his work.* (**simbolismo**)
• **symbolize** or **symbolise** /ˈsɪmbəlaɪz/ VERB [**symbolizes, symbolizing, symbolized**] to be a symbol of something □ *A ring symbolizes everlasting love.* (**simbolizar**)

symmetrical /sɪˈmetrɪkəl/ ADJECTIVE having two halves which are exactly the same □ *The two sides of a person's face are never completely symmetrical.* (**simétrico**)
• **symmetry** /ˈsɪmətri/ NOUN, NO PLURAL the quality of being symmetrical □ *the symmetry of the building* (**simetria**)

sympathetic /ˌsɪmpəˈθetɪk/ ADJECTIVE
1 feeling or showing sympathy □ *a sympathetic smile* (**simpático**)
2 showing someone or something in an attractive or positive way □ *It's a sympathetic portrait of the former president.* (**simpático**)
3 supporting a person or idea □ *He was not sympathetic to their arguments.* (**concordante**)
• **sympathetically** /ˌsɪmpəˈθetɪkəli/ ADVERB in a sympathetic way (**simpaticamente**)

sympathize or **sympathise** /ˈsɪmpəθaɪz/ VERB [**sympathizes, sympathizing, sympathized**]
1 to feel or to show sympathy for someone □ *I really sympathize with his family.* (**simpatizar**)

2 to support someone's ideas or actions □ *She had sympathized with the aims of the French Revolution.* (concordar, simpatizar)

sympathy /'sɪmpəθɪ/ NOUN [plural **sympathies**]
1 when you feel sorry for someone who is unhappy or suffering □ **+ for** *I have great sympathy for the victims.* □ *She received many letters of sympathy when her husband died.* □ *He expressed his sympathies to the family.* (simpatia)
2 support for a group, an organization or a belief (concordância) ▣ *Are you in sympathy with the strikers?* (em concordância com) □ *He's an actor with left-wing sympathies.*

symphony /'sɪmfənɪ/ NOUN [plural **symphonies**] a long piece of music for an orchestra (= large group of musicians) (sinfonia)

symptom /'sɪmptəm/ NOUN [plural **symptoms**]
1 a sign that someone has a particular illness □ *Sore throat, blocked nose, and sneezing are the usual symptoms of a cold.* (sintoma)
2 a sign that a serious problem exists □ *Crime is often a symptom of problems in society.* (sintoma)
• **symptomatic** /ˌsɪmptəˈmætɪk/ ADJECTIVE
1 showing that a more serious problem exists □ *His situation is symptomatic of a legal system which is failing to protect children.* (sintomático)
2 to do with the symptoms of an illness (sintomático)

synagogue /'sɪnəgɒg/ NOUN [plural **synagogues**] a building where Jewish people go to pray (sinagoga)

synchronization /ˌsɪŋkrənaɪˈzeɪʃən/ NOUN, NO PLURAL when things are synchronized (sincronização)

synchronize or **synchronise** /'sɪŋkrənaɪz/ VERB [**synchronizes, synchronizing, synchronized**] to make two things move or happen at the same time or speed (sincronizar)

syndicate /'sɪndɪkət/ NOUN [plural **syndicates**] a group of people or organizations that work together □ *a banking syndicate* (sindicato)

syndrome /'sɪndrəʊm/ NOUN [plural **syndromes**] a medical condition which has a particular set of physical or mental problems □ *irritable bowel syndrome* (síndrome)

synonym /'sɪnənɪm/ NOUN [plural **synonyms**] a word that has the same meaning as another word (sinônimo)
• **synonymous** /sɪˈnɒnɪməs/ ADJECTIVE
1 having the same meaning as another word (sinônimo)
2 used to mean that two things are closely connected and people think of them together □ *Diamonds have always been synonymous with Hollywood glamour.* (sinônimo)

synopsis /sɪˈnɒpsɪs/ NOUN [plural **synopses**] a short description of a book, play, etc. (sinopse)

syntax /'sɪntæks/ NOUN, NO PLURAL the set of grammatical rules about how words are arranged to make sentences (sintaxe)

synthesis /'sɪnθəsɪs/ NOUN [plural **syntheses**]
1 a combination of things □ *His latest plan is a synthesis of old and new ideas.* (síntese)
2 the production of something by a chemical or biological reaction. A chemistry or biology word. (síntese)
• **synthesizer** or **synthesiser** /'sɪnθəsaɪzə(r)/ NOUN [plural **synthesizers**] an electronic musical instrument that makes the sounds of other musical instruments (sintetizador)
• **synthetic** /sɪnˈθetɪk/ ADJECTIVE not made from natural substances □ *synthetic fabrics* (sintético)

syphon /'saɪfən/ ▶ NOUN [plural **syphons**] another spelling of **siphon** (sifão)
▶ VERB [**syphons, syphoning, syphoned**] another spelling of **siphon** (tirar com sifão)

syringe /sɪˈrɪndʒ/ NOUN [plural **syringes**] a tube used with a needle for taking blood out of your body or for putting drugs into your body (seringa)

syrup /'sɪrəp/ NOUN [plural **syrups**] a thick, sticky substance made from sugar (calda)

system /'sɪstəm/ NOUN [plural **systems**]
1 an way of organizing or doing something (sistema) ▣ *the country's education system* (sistema educacional) ▣ *the US legal system* (sistema legal) □ **+ of** *There's a system of checks already in place.* □ **+ for** *We have a new system for processing applications.*
2 pieces of equipment that work together □ *a computer operating system* □ *There's a problem with the central heating system.* (sistema, aparelho)
3 parts of the body that work together to do something ▣ *the body's immune system* (sistema imunológico) ▣ *The virus attacks the nervous system.* (sistema nervoso)
• **systematic** /ˌsɪstəˈmætɪk/ ADJECTIVE using a particular method which you have planned carefully □ *Police carried out a systematic search of the area.* (sistemático)
• **systematically** /ˌsɪstəˈmætɪkəlɪ/ ADVERB in a way that you have planned carefully □ *He systematically killed his enemies.* (sistematicamente)

Tt

T or t /tiː/ the 20th letter of the alphabet (a vigésima letra do alfabeto)

ta /tɑː/ EXCLAMATION an informal word for **thank you** (muito obrigado)

tab /tæb/ NOUN [plural **tabs**] a small piece of paper, metal, etc., used for opening something or marking the place of something ☐ *She pulled the tab on the drinks can.* (aba, tira, alça)

♦ IDIOM **keep (close) tabs on someone/something** an informal phrase meaning to watch someone or something to find out what they are doing or what is happening ☐ *Parents often give their children a mobile phone as a way of keeping tabs on them.* (manter controle sobre)

tabby /ˈtæbi/ NOUN [plural **tabbies**] a cat with grey or brown stripes (gato malhado)

tab key /ˈtæb ˌkiː/ NOUN [plural **tab keys**] a key on a computer keyboard that you press to move several spaces forward in a line of text. A computing word. (tabulador)

table /ˈteɪbəl/ ▶ NOUN [plural **tables**]

1 a piece of furniture with a flat surface that you put things on (mesa) ☐ *They were sitting at the dining room/kitchen table.* (mesa de jantar/de cozinha) ☐ *There was an alarm clock on the bedside table.*

2 lay/set the table to put the knives, forks, glasses, etc. on a table so that you are ready for a meal ☐ *The children offered to lay the table.* (pôr/estender a mesa)

3 a set of numbers or words that are arranged in rows ☐ *The table below shows which schools have the best results.* (tabela)

♦ IDIOM **turn the tables on someone** to change a situation so that you have an advantage over someone after they had an advantage over you (virar o jogo)

▶ VERB [**tables, tabling, tabled**] to ask for something to be discussed at a formal meeting ☐ *They tabled proposals calling for the tax to be cut.* (colocar na pauta)

tablecloth /ˈteɪbəlklɒθ/ NOUN [plural **tablecloths**] a cloth for covering a table (toalha)

table manners /ˈteɪbəl ˌmænəz/ PLURAL NOUN the way you behave when you are eating a meal at a table ☐ *He had terrible table manners.* (comportamento à mesa)

tablespoon /ˈteɪbəlspuːn/ NOUN [plural **tablespoons**] a large spoon, often used for measuring things when you are cooking (colher de sopa)

• **tablespoonful** /ˈteɪbəlˌspuːnfʊl/ NOUN [plural **tablespoonfuls**] the amount that a tablespoon will hold (colher de sopa)

tablet /ˈtæblɪt/ NOUN [plural **tablets**]

1 a pill (comprimido) ☐ *She took a vitamin tablet.* ☐ *She takes sleeping tablets.* (tomar um comprimido)

2 a small, flat device attached to a computer that you write on with a special pen. A computing word. (tablet)

table tennis /ˈteɪbəl ˌtenɪs/ NOUN, NO PLURAL a game in which people hit a ball over a net which is attached to a table (tênis de mesa, pingue-pongue)

tabloid /ˈtæblɔɪd/ NOUN [plural **tabloids**] a small newspaper with lots of pictures and not much serious news (tabloide)

taboo /təˈbuː/ ▶ NOUN [plural **taboos**] something that people must not do or talk about because it might be offensive to other people ☐ *Divorce used to be a social taboo in Britain.* (tabu)

▶ ADJECTIVE not allowed because it might be offensive to other people ☐ *a taboo subject* (tabu, proibido)

tabulate /ˈtæbjʊleɪt/ VERB [**tabulates, tabulating, tabulated**] to arrange numbers or information in rows (organizar em tabelas)

tacit /ˈtæsɪt/ ADJECTIVE understood although not said directly ☐ *They have given tacit approval for the plan.* (tácito)

tack /tæk/ ▶ NOUN [plural **tacks**]

1 a way of achieving something (rumo) ☐ *We aren't getting anywhere, so we need to try a different tack.* (rumo diferente)

2 a short nail with a flat top (tacha)

3 the US word for **drawing pin** (percevejo)

▶ VERB [**tacks, tacking, tacked**] to fasten something with tacks ☐ *She had a poster of David Beckham tacked to her wall.* (prender com tachas ou percevejos)

♦ PHRASAL VERB **tack something on** to add something, often something not planned or expected ☐ *The bank tacked on interest payments to the bill.* (incluir)

tackle /ˈtækəl/ ▶ VERB [**tackles, tackling, tackled**]

1 to deal with something difficult (atacar,

enfrentar) *The policy is designed to tackle the problem of pollution.* (atacar o problema) □ *The government has failed to tackle poverty.*
2 to try to get the ball from another player in games such as football and hockey (**desarmar**)
3 to talk to someone because you are not happy with their behaviour □ *I decided to tackle him about the mess in the office.* (**tentar resolver**)
▶ NOUN [*plural* **tackles**]
1 an attempt to get the ball from another player in games such as football and hockey □ *He was sent off after his tackle on Higgins.* (**desarmar**)
2 special equipment used for something □ *fishing tackle* (**equipamento**)

tacky /ˈtækɪ/ ADJECTIVE [**tackier, tackiest**]
1 an informal word meaning of bad quality, or showing no style □ *The shop sold tacky souvenirs.* (**brega, inferior**)
2 slightly wet or sticky □ *The paint is still tacky.* (**pegajoso**)

tact /tækt/ NOUN, NO PLURAL the ability to be careful in what you do or say so that you do not upset or offend someone □ *She showed great tact in dealing with their complaints.* (**tato**)

• **tactful** /ˈtæktfʊl/ ADJECTIVE careful in what you do or say so that you do not upset or offend someone □ *She was trying to think of a tactful way of asking him to leave.* (**cuidadoso**)

• **tactfully** /ˈtæktfʊli/ ADVERB in a tactful way □ *He handled the situation very tactfully.* (**com discernimento**)

tactic /ˈtæktɪk/ NOUN [*plural* **tactics**] a way of doing something to achieve what you want (**tática**) *The companies had used the same tactics for promoting their products.* (**usar as mesmas táticas**) □ *I've got a new tactic for persuading the children to walk.*

• **tactical** /ˈtæktɪkəl/ ADJECTIVE to do with the methods you use to achieve what you want (**tático**) *The government has made several tactical errors.* (**erros táticos**)

tactless /ˈtæktlɪs/ ADJECTIVE doing or saying something that might offend or upset someone □ *a tactless remark* (**falta de tato, falta de educação**)

tadpole /ˈtædpəʊl/ NOUN [*plural* **tadpoles**] a small creature that will become a frog (= a small green or brown animal that jumps, and lives near water)

taffeta /ˈtæfɪtə/ NOUN, NO PLURAL a type of stiff shiny cloth □ *She was wearing a black taffeta dress.* (**tafetá**)

tag /tæɡ/ ▶ NOUN [*plural* **tags**] a small piece of paper, plastic, etc. with information on it which is attached to something else (**rótulo, etiqueta**) *She looked at the price tag on the jacket.* (**etiqueta de preço**)
▶ VERB [**tags, tagging, tagged**] to put a tag on something (**etiquetar**)

♦ PHRASAL VERB **tag along** an informal word meaning to go somewhere with someone, especially when they have not asked you to go □ *Do you mind if I tag along with you?* (**acompanhar**)

tail /teɪl/ ▶ NOUN [*plural* **tails**]
1 the part that sticks out from the end of an animal's body (**rabo**) *The dog wagged its tail.* (**abanar o rabo**)
2 the back part of an aeroplane □ *The aeroplane had a red and black symbol painted on its tail.* (**cauda**)
3 the tail end of something the last part of something □ *It was the tail end of their holiday.* (**final**)
⇨ go to **tails**
▶ VERB [**tails, tailing, tailed**] to follow someone in order to watch what they do or where they go □ *The police were tailing him.* (**seguir**)

♦ PHRASAL VERB **tail off** to gradually become quieter or weaker or to happen less often □ *Her voice tailed off and her eyes filled with tears.* (**enfraquecer, minguar**)

tailback /ˈteɪlbæk/ NOUN [*plural* **tailbacks**] a line of traffic that has stopped or is moving slowly □ *There are long tailbacks at junction 10.* (**uma fila de veículos parados**)

tailor /ˈteɪlə(r)/ ▶ NOUN [*plural* **tailors**] someone whose job is making men's clothes such as suits (**alfaiate**)
▶ VERB [**tailors, tailoring, tailored**] to design something so that it is exactly what someone wants □ *The teaching is tailored to your child's particular needs.* (**confeccionar, adaptar**)

tails /teɪlz/ PLURAL NOUN the side of a coin that is opposite the side that has the head on it □ *Heads or tails?* (**coroa**)

taint /teɪnt/ VERB [**taints, tainting, tainted**]
1 if a person or organization is tainted by something, it makes people have a bad opinion of them □ *The government has been tainted by corruption.* (**estragar**)
2 to spoil something by adding a harmful substance □ *The main river running through the town is tainted with chemicals.* (**estragar**)

take /teɪk/ VERB [**takes, taking, took, taken**]
1 to get something and often move it from one place to another □ *I took him some food.* □ *Make sure you take a coat with you.* □ *Who's taken all the milk?* □ **+ away** *His passport was taken away from him.* □ **+ back** *I must take Jo's book back.* □ **+ out** *He opened the case and took out a cloak.* (**pegar, tirar, levar de volta**)
2 to accept something that you have been offered □ *She took a biscuit.* □ *Are you going to take the job?* □ *Do you take credit cards?* (**aceitar**)
3 to go somewhere with someone, especially to look after them or to provide transport for them □ *I took my mother to the hospital.* □ *I take my son swimming every week.* (**levar**)
4 to do or have a particular thing □ *Take a deep breath.* □ *Take a look at his work.* □ *She won't*

take any responsibility for the business. □ *Sometimes, you have to take a chance.* (**fazer, dar, tomar**)

5 to need a particular amount of time to be done □ *I just need to finish this letter – it won't take long.* □ *It took him five years to finish his novel.* (**demorar**)

6 to need something □ **+ to do something** *It takes a lot of courage to oppose your friends.* □ *It took five people to lift the piano.* (**necessitar**)

7 to travel somewhere using a particular form of transport □ *I took a ferry to Stockholm.* (**tomar, pegar**)

8 to swallow medicine □ *I have to take these antibiotics for a week.* (**tomar**)

9 to use something of a particular size or type □ *The printer only takes A4 paper.* □ *I take size 12 trousers.* (**usar**)

10 if you take a photograph, you use your camera to make a picture (**tirar**)

11 if a space or container takes a certain amount, it has enough room for it □ *This jug takes nearly two pints.* (**caber**)

⇨ go to **take your breath away, take the bull by the horns, take your eye off something/someone, take your mind off something**

◆ PHRASAL VERBS **take after someone** to be like an older person in your family □ *She's so emotional – she takes after her father.* (**ser parecido com**) **take something apart** to separate something into pieces □ *He took the bike apart and cleaned all the parts.* (**desmontar**) **take something down 1** to write something □ *He took down our names.* (**anotar**) **2** to remove something from a wall or a position □ *They took down the posters.* (**remover**) **3** to remove something from a website □ *He had to take down those pages for legal reasons.* (**remover**) **take something forward** to make something develop or continue successfully □ *He is the best person to take our business forward.* (**levar adiante**) **take something in** to understand something □ *I enjoyed the course but there was an awful lot to take in.* (**assimilar**) **take someone in 1** to allow someone to live with you □ *The children were taken in by a neighbour.* (**acolher**) **2** if you are taken in by someone or something, they trick you □ *They used a very similar brand name, and a lot of customers were taken in.* (**enganar**) **take something off** to remove a piece of clothing □ *He took off his jacket.* (**tirar**) **take off 1** if an aircraft takes off, it leaves the ground at the beginning of a flight (**decolar**) **2** to suddenly become successful □ *With all the extra publicity, our business really took off.* (**deslanchar**) **take on something** to accept work, responsibility, etc. □ *We've taken a lot of work this winter.* (**admitir**) **take someone on 1** to begin to employ someone □ *We've had to take on more staff.* (**admitir**) **2** to compete against someone □ *England are taking on France in the rugby.* (**desafiar**) **take someone out** to go somewhere with someone and pay for them □ *He's taking me out for a meal tonight.* (**levar para passear**) **take something out on someone** to behave badly towards someone because you are upset, especially when it is not their fault □ *I know you had a bad day at work, but there's no need to take it out on me!* (**descarregar em, descontar em**) **take over (something) 1** to start doing something that someone else was doing □ *Could you take over the cooking while I make a phone call?* □ **+ from** *She took over from Annie as treasurer.* (**assumir o lugar**) **2** to take control of something □ *The business was taken over by a French company.* (**assumir o controle**) **take to someone/something** to start to like someone or something □ *I took to Paul as soon as I met him.* (**começar a simpatizar com**) **take something up 1** to start doing an activity □ *I've taken up judo.* (**começar a**) **2** to use a particular amount of time or space □ *His piano takes up most of the front room.* (**ocupar**) **take someone up on something** to accept someone's offer □ *May I take you up on your offer of accommodation?* (**aceitar um oferecimento**)

takeaway /'teɪkəweɪ/ NOUN [plural **takeaways**]

1 a meal that you buy at a restaurant and take to eat somewhere else (**prato para viagem**) 🔊 *We got a Chinese takeaway.*

2 a shop that sells meals that you can take and eat somewhere else (**restaurante que fornece pratos para viagem**)

taken /'teɪkən/ PAST PARTICIPLE OF **take** (*ver* **take**)

take-off /'teɪkɒf/ NOUN [plural **take-offs**] the time when an aeroplane leaves the ground and goes up into the air □ *Please keep your seat belt fastened during take-off.* (**decolagem**)

takeover /'teɪkˌəʊvə(r)/ NOUN [plural **takeovers**] when a company takes control of another company (**aquisição**) 🔊 *The company accepted a takeover bid.* (**proposta de aquisição**)

takers /'teɪkəz/ PLURAL NOUN people who want to buy, do or accept something □ *She sent her work to several publishers, but there weren't any takers.* (**pessoa que aceita**)

takings /'teɪkɪŋz/ PLURAL NOUN the money that a shop or organization gets for selling things □ *Cinema takings have increased.* (**receita**)

talc /tælk/ *or* **talcum powder** /'tælkəm ˌpaʊdə(r)/ NOUN, NO PLURAL a powder that smells pleasant, which people put on their bodies after having a bath (**talco**)

tale /teɪl/ NOUN [plural **tales**] a story, often one that is difficult to believe □ *tales of great adventures* (**história, narração**)

talent /'tælənt/ NOUN [plural **talents**] a natural ability to do something well □ *Sarah had a talent for acting.* (**talento**)

• **talented** /'tæləntɪd/ ADJECTIVE having the ability to do something well □ *She's a talented young artist.* (**talentoso**)

talk

talk /tɔːk/ ▶ VERB [talks, talking, talked]
1 to say words in order to communicate ☐ + *to* I talked to Molly on the phone yesterday. ☐ + *about* He's always talking about football. ☐ I like him, but he talks too much. (**conversar**)
2 to discuss something, especially to try to plan something or solve an argument ☐ + *about* We need to talk about the housework. ☐ We agreed to meet to talk about the expedition. (**discutir**)
3 talk rubbish/nonsense, etc. to say things that are silly or not true (**falar bobagens, asneiras**)
4 talk politics/sport, etc. to talk about a particular subject (**conversar sobre política/esportes etc.**)
◆ PHRASAL VERBS **talk about something** if people are talking about something, they are saying that they might do it or it might happen ☐ They're talking about raising the school-leaving age. (**falar em**) **talk at someone** to talk to someone in a forceful way without allowing them to reply (**falar sem escutar ou permitir que o outro fale**) **talk down to someone** to talk to someone in a way that shows that you think you are more important or more clever than them (**falar com simplismo deliberado**) **talk someone into/out of something** to persuade someone to do/not to do something ☐ I never wanted to go skiing, but Ralf talked me into it. (**persuadir a fazer/não fazer**) **talk something over** to discuss something, especially a problem or a plan ☐ There are a lot of issues to do with the business – we really need to talk things over. (**discutir sobre**) **talk someone round** to persuade someone to agree to something ☐ She didn't want to play in the concert, but her teacher talked her round. (**convercer a**) **talk someone through something** to explain all the parts of a process to someone ☐ I think I know how to set the fire alarm, but could you just talk me through it one more time? (**explicar um processo**) **talk up someone/something** to talk about someone or something in a way that makes them seem successful or important ☐ He was busy talking up his party's chances in the election. (**contar vantagem**)
▶ NOUN [plural **talks**]
1 a conversation (**conversa**) 🔲 I need to *have a talk* with Julie. ☐ + *about* We had a brief talk about school. (**ter uma conversa**)
2 talks formal meetings between people such as politicians, especially to try to make plans or solve arguments (**discussões**) 🔲 Ministers will be *holding talks* in Geneva. ☐ + *between* Talks between unions and employers have broken down. (**manter discussões**)
3 when someone talks to a group of people about a particular subject (**discurso, conferência**) 🔲 He *gave a talk* about his work with gorillas. (**fazer uma palestra**)
4 no plural when people talk about what might happen or be true ☐ + *of* There was talk of an election in June. (**conversa**)

◆ IDIOM **be all talk (and no action)** to talk about what you are going to do, but never do it ☐ I know he promised to resign, but he's all talk – he'll never do it. (**é só conversa**)
• **talkative** /ˈtɔːkətɪv/ ADJECTIVE a talkative person talks a lot (**falador**)
• **talker** /ˈtɔːkə(r)/ NOUN [plural **talkers**] (**conversador**) a smooth talker someone who is good at persuading people by saying nice things (**bom de conversa**)

tall /tɔːl/ ADJECTIVE [taller, tallest]
1 bigger in height than most people or things (**alto, grande**) 🔲 a *tall building* (**edifício alto**) ☐ He's tall for his age. ☐ tall trees
2 used when talking about the height of someone or something ☐ She's less than five feet tall. (**de altura**)

tally /ˈtæli/ ▶ NOUN [plural **tallies**] a record of how many points you have won, how much money you have spent, etc. (**registro**) 🔲 He *kept a tally* of how many people had used the service. (**manter um registro**)
▶ VERB [tallies, tallying, tallied] if statements or numbers tally, they are the same ☐ His answer tallied with mine. (**combinar**)
◆ PHRASAL VERB **tally something up** to add things together ☐ I tried to tally up everything we had spent. (**registrar**)

Talmud /ˈtælmʊd/ NOUN, NO PLURAL **the Talmud** a holy book of the Jewish religion (**Talmude**)

talon /ˈtælən/ NOUN [plural **talons**] a strong, curved nail of some birds (**garra**)

tambourine /ˌtæmbəˈriːn/ NOUN [plural **tambourines**] a flat, round musical instrument with small metal discs that make a noise when you shake it (**pandeiro**)

tame /teɪm/ ▶ ADJECTIVE [tamer, tamest]
1 a tame animal is no longer wild, and has been trained to be near people (**domesticado, manso**)
2 not exciting enough ☐ The film was very tame. (**entediante**)
▶ VERB [tames, taming, tamed]
1 to train a wild animal so that it can be near people ☐ They had tried to tame the horse. (**domesticar**)
2 to control something or someone that is difficult to control ☐ She had spent a long time trying to tame her hair. (**controlar**)

tamper /ˈtæmpə(r)/ (**alterar**)
◆ PHRASAL VERB [tampers, tampering, tampered] **tamper with something** to make changes to something, especially in a way that stops it working correctly ☐ Someone had tampered with the lock. (**adulterar**)

tan /tæn/ ▶ NOUN [plural **tans**]
1 a brown colour on your skin because you have been in the sun (**bronzeado**) 🔲 Many people want to *get a tan* even though it is bad for your skin. (**pegar um bronzeado**)

2 a light brown colour (marrom-claro)
▶ VERB [tans, tanning, tanned] to get darker skin because you have been in the sun □ *She tans very easily.* (bronzear(-se))
▶ ADJECTIVE of a light brown colour □ *tan shoes* (marrom-claro)

tandem /ˈtændəm/ NOUN [plural **tandems**] (um com o outro)
1 **in tandem** together with someone or something else □ *The two drugs work in tandem to fight the disease.* (os dois juntos)
2 a bicycle for two people (bicicleta com dois assentos)

tang /tæŋ/ NOUN [plural **tangs**] a strong and pleasant taste or smell □ *He breathed in the salty tang of the sea air.* (sabor/cheiro forte)

tangent /ˈtændʒənt/ NOUN [plural **tangents**]
1 a straight line that touches a curve but does not go through it. A maths word. (tangente)
2 in a triangle with one angle of 90°, the tangent is the length of the side opposite one of the angles of less than 90° divided by the length of the side next to it. A maths word. (tangente)
♦ IDIOM **go off at a tangent** to start talking or thinking about a completely different subject (sair pela tangente)

tangerine /ˌtændʒəˈriːn/ NOUN [plural **tangerines**] a type of small orange (tangerina)

tangible /ˈtændʒəbəl/ ADJECTIVE real enough to be seen, touched or measured □ *The policies were beginning to produce tangible results.* (tangível)

tangle /ˈtæŋɡəl/ ▶ NOUN [plural **tangles**] a mass of wires, hair, string, etc. which are twisted together (emaranhado, bagunça)
▶ VERB [tangles, tangling, tangled] to become twisted together (emaranhar)
• **tangled** /ˈtæŋɡəld/ ADJECTIVE twisted together □ *She ruffled his tangled hair.* (emaranhado)

tango /ˈtæŋɡoʊ/ NOUN [plural **tangoes**] an energetic dance from South America, where the two dancers hold each other very tightly (tango)

tank /tæŋk/ NOUN [plural **tanks**]
1 a large container for liquids or gases (tanque, reservatório) *The car's fuel tank was empty.* □ *an oxygen tank* (tanque de gasolina)
2 a large military vehicle with a gun on top, which moves on metal belts over wheels (tanque de guerra)

tankard /ˈtæŋkəd/ NOUN [plural **tankards**] a large metal cup (caneca)

tanker /ˈtæŋkə(r)/ NOUN [plural **tankers**] a ship or truck which carries liquids or gases (petroleiro, navio-tanque, caminhão-tanque) *an oil tanker* (petroleiro)

tanned /tænd/ ADJECTIVE having brown skin because you have been in the sun □ *She came back from Spain looking fit and tanned.* (bronzeado)

tantalizing *or* **tantalising** /ˈtæntəˌlaɪzɪŋ/ ADJECTIVE attractive and making you want something □ *She passed the bakery with its tantalizing smells of fresh bread and cakes.* (tentador)

tantamount /ˈtæntəmaʊnt/ ADJECTIVE (equivalente) **be tantamount to something** to be as bad as something else (ser equivalente a) □ *His actions are tantamount to cheating.*

tantrum /ˈtæntrəm/ NOUN [plural **tantrums**] when someone, especially a young child, behaves in a very angry way, often shouting (acesso de raiva, chilique) *Small children often have temper tantrums.* (ataques de birra)

tap /tæp/ ▶ NOUN [plural **taps**]
1 a device you use for controlling the flow of water or gas from a pipe (torneira) *She turned on the tap to wash her hands.* (abrir a torneira) *The tap is dripping.* (a torneira está pingando) *I always drink tap water rather than bottled water.* (água de torneira) □ *the hot/cold tap*
2 a light knock □ *He felt a tap on his shoulder.* (batida leve)
3 **on tap** if something is on tap, it is easily available □ *Spain offers excellent leisure facilities and sunshine on tap.* (à disposição)
4 a device that is put on someone's telephone so someone can listen to what they are saying (grampo)
▶ VERB [taps, tapping, tapped]
1 to knock gently □ + **on** *He tapped on the window.* □ *She tapped me on the arm.* (bater de leve)
2 to hit your fingers or feet gently against something *He tapped his foot in time with the music.*
3 to secretly put a device on someone's telephone so someone can listen to what they are saying □ *The police had tapped his phone.* (grampear)
♦ PHRASAL VERB **tap into something** to use something to help you □ *They tapped into this enthusiasm and made the project a success.* (aproveitar)

tap dancing /ˈtæp ˌdɑːnsɪŋ/ NOUN, NO PLURAL a type of dancing in which you wear shoes that make a noise on the floor (sapateado)

tape /teɪp/ ▶ NOUN [plural **tapes**]
1 a long, thin piece of plastic for recording sounds or pictures, or the case that it is kept in (fita de gravação) *They played a tape of the police interview.*
2 no plural a long, thin piece of plastic that is sticky on one side, used for fastening things □ *The door was sealed with yellow police tape.* (fita adesiva)
3 a thin piece of material used for tying things or for sewing onto things □ *I sewed name tapes into their clothes.* (fita)

tape measure 825 **taste**

4 the tape the strip of material that shows where a race finishes ▫ *She was the first through the tape.* (**fita de chegada**)

▶ VERB [**tapes, taping, taped**]

1 to record sounds and pictures onto tape ▫ *I taped the show to watch later.* (**gravar**)

2 to fasten something somewhere using tape ▫ *The note was taped to the car's windscreen.* (**prender com fita**)

tape measure /ˈteɪp ˌmeʒə(r)/ NOUN [plural **tape measures**] a long thin piece of cloth, plastic or metal with measurements on it, used for measuring things (**fita métrica**)

taper /ˈteɪpə(r)/ VERB [**tapers, tapering, tapered**] to become gradually narrower at one end ▫ *The blade tapered to a sharp point.* (**afilar**)

◆ PHRASAL VERB **taper off** to decrease gradually ▫ *Demand for the product has tapered off.* (**diminuir gradualmente**)

tape recorder /ˈteɪp rɪˌkɔːdə(r)/ NOUN [plural **tape recorders**] a piece of equipment that records and plays sounds on tape (**gravador**)

tapestry /ˈtæpɪstri/ NOUN [plural **tapestries**] a piece of cloth with a design woven into it with coloured threads (**tapeçaria**)

tar /tɑː(r)/ NOUN, NO PLURAL a thick, black sticky substance which is used for covering roads (**alcatrão, piche**)

tarantula /təˈræntjʊlə/ NOUN [plural **tarantulas**] a large spider which is poisonous (**tarântula**)

target /ˈtɑːɡɪt/ ▶ NOUN [plural **targets**]

1 a person or thing that someone attacks (**alvo**) ▫ *Old people are an easy target for thieves.* (**um alvo fácil**) ▫ *It is believed that the White House was the intended target of the terrorist attack.*

2 a person or thing that people criticize or joke about ▫ *Fletcher has been a constant target of criticism.* ▫ *He was the target of everyone's jokes.* (**alvo**)

3 a level that you are trying to achieve (**alvo**) ▫ *The company won't reach its sales targets.* (**atingir seu alvo**)

4 be on target to be making progress at the expected rate ▫ *The project is on target to finish in May.* (**dentro da previsão**)

5 a mark or object that people aim at when they are shooting (**alvo**) ▫ *I practised until I could hit the target.* (**atingir o alvo**)

6 target audience/market the people that something is designed for ▫ *The magazine's target market is young men.* (**público-alvo, mercado-alvo**)

▶ VERB [**targets, targeting, targeted**]

1 to try to attack a particular person or place ▫ *The attacker mainly targets young women.* (**alvejar**)

2 to put bombs or other weapons in a particular position ▫ *Two roadside bombs were targeted at police patrols.* (**alvejar**)

3 to be designed for a particular group ▫ *The programme is targeted at teenagers.* (**alvejar**)

tariff /ˈtærɪf/ NOUN [plural **tariffs**]

1 a list of prices ▫ *The website compares mobile phone tariffs.* (**tabela de preços**)

2 a tax on goods which come into a country ▫ *import tariffs* (**taxa alfandegária**)

Tarmac /ˈtɑːmæk/ NOUN, NO PLURAL a mixture of tar and small stones, used for covering a road. A trademark. (**asfalto, macadame**)

tarmac /ˈtɑːmæk/ NOUN, NO PLURAL (**asfalto**) **the tarmac** the area at an airport where the planes take off and land ▫ *They walked out on to the tarmac towards the plane.* (**pista**)

tarnish /ˈtɑːnɪʃ/ VERB [**tarnishes, tarnishing, tarnished**]

1 to make people have a worse opinion of someone or something (**deslustrar**) ▫ *The affair tarnished his reputation.* (**denegrir uma reputação**)

2 if metal tarnishes or something tarnishes it, it stops being shiny (**embaçar**)

tarpaulin /tɑːˈpɔːlɪn/ NOUN [plural **tarpaulins**] a piece of strong material which is used to cover things and protect them from rain (**encerado**)

tart /tɑːt/ ▶ NOUN [plural **tarts**] a pastry case with no top, filled with fruit, vegetables, etc. ▫ *a jam tart* (**torta**)

▶ ADJECTIVE tasting sour ▫ *The apples were tart.* (**azedo**)

tartan /ˈtɑːtən/ NOUN [plural **tartans**] a traditional Scottish cloth with a pattern of coloured squares and lines (**xadrez**)

task /tɑːsk/ NOUN [plural **tasks**] a job that you have to do (**tarefa**) ▫ *The school is facing the difficult task of trying to raise money.* (**tarefa difícil**) ▫ *He was so ill that he couldn't even perform simple tasks.* (**executar tarefas simples**) ▫ **+ of** *I was given the task of helping the teacher carry the books to the office.*

◆ IDIOM **take someone to task** to criticize someone ▫ *The government has been taken to task for closing hospitals.* (**criticar**)

taskbar /ˈtɑːskbɑː(r)/ NOUN [plural **taskbars**] on a computer screen, a row of words or pictures that shows you the different programs you have already opened. A computing word. (**barra de tarefas**)

task force /ˈtɑːsk ˌfɔːs/ NOUN [plural **task forces**] a group of people or soldiers who work together to do a particular thing ▫ *She headed a task force which was set up to deal with world pollution.* (**força-tarefa**)

tassel /ˈtæsəl/ NOUN [plural **tassels**] a lot of threads tied together at one end, used as decoration (**borla**)

taste /teɪst/ ▶ NOUN [plural **tastes**]

1 the flavour of something, especially food or drink ▫ *The seeds have a bitter taste.* (**gosto**)

2 *no plural* the ability to recognize flavours □ *Smoking can affect your sense of taste.* (paladar)
3 the things that you like, for example clothes, music or food □ *+ for She developed a taste for luxury.* □ *+ in He has unusual tastes in music.* (gosto) 🔁 *She has rather expensive tastes.* (gostos caros)
4 *no plural* the ability to judge whether something such as clothing, art or behaviour is good and suitable for a situation (gosto) 🔁 *He has extremely good taste.* (bom gosto)
5 a small amount of food or drink to try 🔁 *Can I have a taste of your cheese?* (prova)
6 an experience of something □ *+ of They got a taste of what life is really like here.* (experiência)

♦ IDIOM **leave a bad/bitter/nasty, etc. taste in your mouth** if an experience leaves a bad taste in your mouth, you are upset or angry about it afterwards (deixar um gosto amargo etc. na boca)

▶ VERB [**tastes, tasting, tasted**]
1 to have a particular flavor □ *This sauce tastes salty.* (ter gosto de)
2 to experience the flavour of something □ *Can you taste the herbs in this?* (sentir o gosto)
3 to try a small amount of food or drink to judge its flavour □ *Have you tasted this cheese?* (experimentar)
4 to experience something for a short time □ *They'd tasted victory for the first time and wanted more.* (experimentar)

• **tasteful** /ˈteɪstful/ ADJECTIVE attractive or showing good judgment □ *The ceremony was very tasteful.* (de bom gosto)
• **tastefully** /ˈteɪstfuli/ ADVERB in a tasteful way □ *tastefully decorated* (com gosto)
• **tasteless** /ˈteɪstlɪs/ ADJECTIVE
1 showing bad judgment and likely to offend people □ *a tasteless remark* (mau gosto)
2 having no flavour (insípido)
3 not attractive □ *cheap, tasteless decorations* (de mau gosto)
• **tasting** /ˈteɪstɪŋ/ NOUN [*plural* **tastings**] an event at which you can try a particular food or drink □ *The shop offers free cheese tastings.* (degustação)
• **tasty** /ˈteɪsti/ ADJECTIVE [**tastier, tastiest**] having a good flavour (saboroso)

tattered /ˈtætəd/ ADJECTIVE old and torn □ *a tattered photograph* □ *tattered clothes* (esfarrapado)

tatters /ˈtætəz/ PLURAL NOUN (farrapos) **in tatters** (a) very badly damaged or spoilt □ *His career was in tatters.* (b) badly torn □ *Her dress was in tatters.* (em farrapos)

tattoo /təˈtuː/ ▶ NOUN [*plural* **tattoos**] a permanent picture made on someone's skin with ink (tatuagem)
▶ VERB [**tattoos, tattooing, tattooed**] to put a tattoo on someone's skin (tatuar)

tatty /ˈtæti/ ADJECTIVE [**tattier, tattiest**] untidy, old and in bad condition □ *a tatty old coat* (surrado, esfarrapado)

taught /tɔːt/ PAST TENSE AND PAST PARTICIPLE OF **teach** (*ver* **teach**)

taunt /tɔːnt/ ▶ VERB [**taunts, taunting, taunted**] to say unkind things to someone to make them upset or angry □ *Opposing football fans taunted each other.* (escarnecer, zombar)
▶ NOUN [*plural* **taunts**] something you say to taunt someone □ *Some refugees suffered racist taunts.* (insulto)

taut /tɔːt/ ADJECTIVE [**tauter, tautest**] pulled or stretched tight □ *Check that the rope is taut.* (esticado)

tavern /ˈtævən/ NOUN [*plural* **taverns**] an old word for a pub (taverna)

tawdry /ˈtɔːdri/ ADJECTIVE [**tawdrier, tawdriest**]
1 unpleasant and not moral □ *The whole tawdry tale has now become public.* (vergonhoso)
2 cheap and of bad quality □ *tawdry ornaments* (de qualidade inferior)

tax /tæks/ ▶ NOUN [*plural* **taxes**] money you pay to the government from your income or that is added to the price of goods you buy to pay for public services (taxa, imposto) 🔁 *Most pensioners don't pay tax.* (pagar imposto) □ *+ on A company pays tax on its profits.* 🔁 *income tax rates* (imposto de renda)
▶ VERB [**taxes, taxing, taxed**]
1 to charge tax on something □ *There are plans to tax the profits of oil companies.* □ *Their income will be taxed at 40%.* (taxar)
2 if something taxes you, you find it difficult or tiring □ *The matches so far haven't really taxed her physically.* (sobrecarregar)

• **taxable** /ˈtæksəbəl/ ADJECTIVE if something is taxable, you have to pay tax on it □ *taxable income* (tributável)
• **taxation** /tækˈseɪʃən/ NOUN, NO PLURAL the system of tax or the amount of money the government gets in taxes (taxação)

tax disc /ˈtæks dɪsk/ NOUN [*plural* **tax discs**] a small round document on the window of a vehicle, that shows the owner has paid road tax (selo de imposto sobre automóvel)

taxi /ˈtæksi/ ▶ NOUN [*plural* **taxis**] a car with a driver that you pay to take you from one place to another (táxi) 🔁 *They took a taxi to the airport.* 🔁 *Don't worry, I'll get a taxi home.* (pegar um táxi) 🔁 *a taxi driver* (motorista de táxi)
▶ VERB [**taxis, taxiing, taxied**] an aeroplane taxis when it moves slowly along the ground after landing or before leaving (taxiar)

taxing /ˈtæksɪŋ/ ADJECTIVE difficult or needing a lot of effort □ *He has a taxing schedule.* (desgastante)

taxi rank /ˈtæksi ˌræŋk/ NOUN [*plural* **taxi ranks**] a place where taxis wait until people need them (ponto de táxi)

taxonomy

taxonomy /tækˈsɒnəmɪ/ NOUN [plural **taxonomies**] a system of organizing things in groups of similar things, for example plants and animals. A biology word. (taxonomia)

taxpayer /ˈtæksˌpeɪə(r)/ NOUN [plural **taxpayers**] someone who has to pay tax on the money they earn (contribuinte)

tax year /ˈtæks ˌjɪə(r)/ NOUN [plural **tax years**] a period of twelve months that is used for calculating the tax you have to pay (ano fiscal)

TB /ˌtiːˈbiː/ ABBREVIATION **tuberculosis** (tuberculose)

tbsp /ˈteɪbəlspuːn/ ABBREVIATION **tablespoon** (colher de sopa)

tea /tiː/ NOUN [plural **teas**]
1 a drink made by pouring boiling water on dried leaves, or the leaves you use to make this drink (chá) ▣ Can I have a *cup of tea*? (xícara de chá) ▣ *She sat and drank her tea.* (tomar chá) □ *Two teas and a coffee, please.* □ *Do you serve peppermint tea?*
2 a light meal with tea that some people have in the afternoon ▣ *We stopped in a café for afternoon tea.* (chá da tarde)
3 used by some people to refer to the meal they have in the early evening (jantar)

teabag /ˈtiːbæg/ NOUN [plural **teabags**] a small bag of thin paper containing tea leaves that you pour boiling water over to make tea (saquinho de chá)

teach /tiːtʃ/ VERB [**teaches, teaching, taught**]
1 to give lessons at a school, college or university □ *She taught at the local school.* □ *He teaches maths.* □ *Students are taught in small classes.* (ensinar)
2 to pass your knowledge, skills or experience on to another person □ + *to do something* *Parents should teach their children to behave properly.* □ + *question word* *Will you teach me how to sail a dinghy?* □ + *about* *They are taught about healthy eating.* (ensinar)
3 if an experience teaches you something, you learn something new because of it □ *Recent experience had taught him to be cautious.* (ensinar)
• **teacher** /ˈtiːtʃə(r)/ NOUN [plural **teachers**] someone who teaches, usually as their job □ *She's an English teacher.* □ *He's the head teacher at the local school.* (professor)
• **teaching** /ˈtiːtʃɪŋ/ NOUN, NO PLURAL the work of a teacher □ *teaching methods* □ *language teaching materials* □ *We want to improve the quality of teaching in state schools.* (ensino)
• **teachings** /ˈtiːtʃɪŋz/ PLURAL NOUN the ideas and beliefs of a particular person or group, especially about religion or politics (ensinamentos)

teacup /ˈtiːkʌp/ NOUN [plural **teacups**] a cup used for drinking tea (xícara de chá)

teak /tiːk/ NOUN, NO PLURAL a type of hard yellow brown wood (teca)

tear

tea leaf /ˈtiː ˌliːf/ NOUN [plural **tea leaves**] a dried leaf from a tea plant □ *Pour hot water over the tea leaves.* (folha de chá)

team /tiːm/ ▶ NOUN [plural **teams**]
1 a group of people who play together against another group in a game or a sport □ *the England cricket team* □ *Which football team do you support?* (time) ▣ *He was selected for the national team.* (time nacional)
2 a group of people who work together □ + *of* *a team of engineers* □ *the senior management team* (equipe)
▶ VERB [**teams, teaming, teamed**] to put people or things together □ *She wore a dress teamed with boots.* (juntar)
♦ PHRASAL VERB **team up (with someone)** to join with other people to achieve something by working together □ *He has teamed up with Nicole Kidman for two recent film projects.* (juntar-se)

teammate /ˈtiːmmeɪt/ NOUN [plural **teammates**] someone who is in the same team as you (companheiro de equipe)

teamwork /ˈtiːmwɜːk/ NOUN, NO PLURAL when people work together effectively □ *The aim of the project is to encourage teamwork.* (trabalho de equipe)

teapot /ˈtiːpɒt/ NOUN [plural **teapots**] a container for making tea in with a spout (= tube which the tea comes out of) and a handle (bule de chá)

tear¹ /teə(r)/ ▶ VERB [**tears, tearing, tore, torn**]
1 to damage paper, cloth, etc. by pulling it apart or making a hole in it □ *You've torn your sleeve on that barbed wire.* □ *The cat tore a hole in the curtain.* (rasgar, arrancar)
2 to pull or to remove something using force □ *a page torn from a notebook* □ *Liz tore open the envelope.* □ *He tore off a large chunk of bread.* (rasgar, arrancar)
3 an informal word meaning to go somewhere very fast □ *Ellis tore down the left wing and scored.* (correr a toda)
4 be torn between something if you are torn between two things or people, you do not know which one to choose or to support □ *She found herself torn between her family and her career.* (ficar dividido/indeciso entre)
♦ PHRASAL VERBS **tear something apart**
1 to cause a group of people to argue or to fight with each other □ *The civil war is tearing the country apart.* (dilacerar)
2 to badly damage or to destroy something □ *The explosion tore the building apart.* (destruir) **tear someone apart** to make someone feel extremely upset or worried □ *Not knowing where she is is tearing me apart.* (acabar com alguém) **tear someone away** to force someone to leave a place or to stop doing something □ *I'd like to talk to*

you if you can tear yourself away from the television for a minute. (**forçar alguém a sair ou a parar de**) **tear something down** to knock down a building or a wall ☐ *The old buildings are being torn down.* (**derrubar um prédio ou uma parede**) **tear off something** if you tear off your clothes, you take them off very quickly and without care (**tirar afobadamente**) **tear through something** if an explosion, a storm, etc. tears through a place, it causes a lot of damage there ☐ *A tornado tore though the town.* (**causar estragos**) **tear something up** to pull a piece of paper into many small pieces ☐ *She tore up the letter.* (**picar**)
▶ NOUN [*plural* **tears**] the place where something has been torn ☐ *There was a large tear in the fabric.* (**rasgo, rasgão**)

tear² /tɪə(r)/ NOUN [*plural* **tears**]
1 a drop of liquid that comes from your eyes when you cry (**lágrima**) 🔳 *His mum burst into tears* (= started crying). ☐ *They cried tears of joy.* (**pôr-se a chorar**)
2 in tears crying ☐ *We were all in tears at the end of the film.* (**aos prantos**)

teardrop /'tɪədrɒp/ NOUN [*plural* **teardrops**] a single tear (**gota de lágrima**)

tearful /'tɪəfʊl/ ADJECTIVE crying or with people crying ☐ *We said a tearful goodbye.* (**choroso**)
• **tearfully** /'tɪəfʊli/ ADVERB in a tearful way ☐ *She apologized tearfully.* (**chorosamente, lacrimosamente**)

tear gas /'tɪə(r) ˌɡæs/ NOUN, NO PLURAL a gas which hurts people's eyes, especially used to control crowds (**gás lacrimogêneo**)

tear-stained /'tɪəˌsteɪnd/ ADJECTIVE covered in tears ☐ *her tear-stained face* (**manchado de lágrimas**)

tease /tiːz/ VERB [**teases, teasing, teased**] to say or do something to make someone angry or embarrassed, or to make them believe something that is not true, either as a joke or to make them angry ☐ *I didn't mean what I said. I was only teasing.* ☐ *Stop teasing the dog!* (**provocar, irritar, caçoar**)
• **teaser** /'tiːzə(r)/ NOUN [*plural* **teasers**] a difficult problem or question (**problema intrigante**)

teaspoon /'tiːspuːn/ NOUN [*plural* **teaspoons**] a small spoon used for mixing sugar in tea or for measuring small amounts (**colher de chá**)
• **teaspoonful** /'tiːˌspuːnfʊl/ NOUN [*plural* **teaspoonfuls**] the amount a teaspoon will hold (**colher de chá**)

teat /tiːt/ NOUN [*plural* **teats**]
1 the part of a female animal that its babies suck to get milk (**teta, úbere**)
2 the rubber part on a feeding bottle that a baby sucks to get milk (**bico da mamadeira**)

teatime /'tiːtaɪm/ NOUN, NO PLURAL the time in the early evening when people have a meal (**hora do chá**)

tea towel /'tiː ˌtaʊəl/ NOUN [*plural* **tea towels**] a cloth for drying dishes after they have been washed (**pano de prato**)

technical /'teknɪkəl/ ADJECTIVE
1 to do with science and technology ☐ *Does he have any technical training?* (**técnico**)
2 to do with the way a machine or a system works (**técnico**) 🔳 *We're having some technical problems with our computers.* (**problemas técnicos**)
3 to do with special knowledge or skills in a particular subject or job (**técnico**) 🔳 *a highly technical legal issue* (**altamente técnico**) 🔳 *What is the technical term for your hip bone?* (**termo técnico**)
4 according to the details of a rule or the law ☐ *This is a technical breach of the regulations.* (**técnico**)
• **technicality** /ˌteknɪˈkælətɪ/ NOUN [*plural* **technicalities**] a detail of the law or a rule ☐ *He was acquitted on a legal technicality.* (**formalidade jurídica**)
• **technically** /'teknɪkli/ ADVERB
1 to do with technology or practical skills ☐ *The project is technically challenging.* ☐ *a technically gifted player* (**tecnicamente**)
2 according to the details of a rule or the law ☐ *Technically, it's not illegal.* ☐ *Technically speaking, he's right.* (**tecnicamente**)

technician /tek'nɪʃən/ NOUN [*plural* **technicians**] someone whose job is to do practical work in a laboratory or to use special equipment (**técnico**)

technique /tek'niːk/ NOUN [*plural* **techniques**] a particular method of doing something ☐ *traditional painting techniques* (**técnica**) 🔳 *We've been using a new technique.* (**usar uma técnica nova**) ☐ + **for** *There are improved techniques for DNA testing.*

techno- /'teknəʊ/ PREFIX techno- is added to the beginning of words to mean 'to do with technology' (**tecno-**)

technological /ˌteknəˈlɒdʒɪkəl/ ADJECTIVE to do with technology ☐ *technological advances* (**tecnológico**)
• **technologically** /ˌteknəˈlɒdʒɪkli/ ADVERB in a way that is to do with technology ☐ *technologically advanced* (**tecnologicamente**)

technology /tek'nɒlədʒɪ/ NOUN [*plural* **technologies**] scientific knowledge, methods or equipment used in practical ways (**tecnologia**) 🔳 *The system uses wireless technology.* (**usar tecnologia**) 🔳 *The company is investing in new technology.* (**nova tecnologia**)

teddy /'tedɪ/ NOUN [*plural* **teddies**] a toy in the shape of a bear with soft fur (**urso de pelúcia**)

tedious /'tiːdɪəs/ ADJECTIVE long and boring ☐ *It was slow, tedious work.* (**tedioso**)

- **tedium** /'ti:dɪəm/ NOUN, NO PLURAL when something is tedious (**tédio**)

tee /ti:/ NOUN [*plural* **tees**]
1 the place where a golf ball is hit from to start part of a game of golf (**local da primeira tacada do golfe**)
2 a small plastic stick that you rest a golf ball on to hit it (**pino que levanta a bola**)
◆ PHRASAL VERB [**tees, teeing, teed**] **tee off** to hit a golf ball from a tee (**bater a bola, começar**)

teem /ti:m/ VERB [**teems, teeming, teemed**] if it is teeming with rain, rain is falling very heavily □ *Rain was teeming down.* (**repleto de**)
◆ PHRASAL VERB **teem with something** if a place teems with people or animals, there are many of them moving around there □ *The seafront was teeming with tourists.* (**repleto de**)

teenage /'ti:neɪdʒ/ ADJECTIVE
1 aged between 13 and 19 (**adolescente**) 🔁 *a teenage girl* (**a adolescente**) 🔁 *a group of teenage boys* (**os adolescentes**) □ *They have a teenage son.*
2 to do with people of this age □ *teenage magazines*

- **teenager** /'ti:n,eɪdʒə(r)/ NOUN [*plural* **teenagers**] someone who is aged between 13 and 19 □ *She's just a typical teenager.* □ *The site's popular with teenagers and young adults.* (**adolescente**)

- **teens** /ti:nz/ PLURAL NOUN the years of your life between the ages of 13 and 19 □ *He was in his teens when the family moved.* (**adolescência**) 🔁 *The audience were mostly in their late teens and early twenties.* (**final da adolescência**)

teeny /'ti:ni/ ADJECTIVE [**teenier, teeniest**] an informal word meaning very small (**minúsculo**)

tee-shirt /'ti:ʃɜ:t/ NOUN [*plural* **tee-shirts**] another spelling of **T-shirt** (**camiseta**)

teeter /'ti:tə(r)/ VERB [**teeters, teetering, teetered**]
1 if something or someone teeters, they stand or move as if they are going to fall □ *The vase was teetering on the edge of the shelf.* (**oscilar, balançar**)
2 teeter on the brink/edge of something to be in a situation where it is possible that something bad could happen at any moment □ *The country is teetering on the brink of civil war.* (**oscilar à beira de**)

teeth /ti:θ/ PLURAL OF **tooth** □ *Look after your teeth.* (**dentes**)

teethe /ti:ð/ VERB [**teethes, teething, teethed**] a baby teethes when its first teeth start to grow (**iniciar a dentição**)

teething troubles /'ti:ðɪŋ 'trʌbəlz/ PLURAL NOUN problems that happen at the beginning of a piece of work, or with a new piece of equipment □ *We're having teething troubles with the new computer system.* (**problemas iniciais**)

teetotal /ti:'təʊtəl/ ADJECTIVE someone who is teetotal does not drink any alcohol (**abstinente**)

- **teetotaller** /ti:'təʊtələ(r)/ NOUN [*plural* **teetotallers**] someone who does not drink alcohol (**pessoa abstinente**)

TEFL /'tefəl/ ABBREVIATION teaching English as a foreign language (**Ensino do Inglês como Língua Estrangeira**)

tele- /'telɪ/ PREFIX
1 tele- is added to the beginning of words to mean 'over a long distance' □ *telepathic* (**indica longa distância**)
2 tele- is added to the beginning of words to mean 'using a telephone, radio, etc.' □ *telebanking* (**indica o uso de telefone, rádio etc.**)
3 tele- is added to the beginning of words to mean 'to do with the television' □ *teletext* (**referente à televisão**)

telebanking /'telɪˌbæŋkɪŋ/ NOUN, NO PLURAL a system in which you move money into and out of your bank account by telephone (**atendimento bancário via telefone**)

telecommunications /'telɪkəˌmju:nɪ'keɪʃənz/ PLURAL NOUN sending information over long distances by telephone, radio or television □ *a telecommunications company* (**telecomunicações**)

telegram /'telɪgræm/ NOUN [*plural* **telegrams**] a message sent by telegraph, used especially in the past for short, urgent messages (**telegrama**)

telegraph /'telɪgrɑ:f/ NOUN [*plural* **telegraphs**] a system used especially in the past for sending messages over long distances using radio signals (**telégrafo**)

- **telegraphic** /ˌtelɪ'græfɪk/ ADJECTIVE using telegraph (**telegráfico**)

telemarketing /'telɪˌmɑ:kɪtɪŋ/ NOUN, NO PLURAL another word for **telesales** (**televendas**)

telepathic /ˌtelɪ'pæθɪk/ ADJECTIVE able to know another person's thoughts without speaking or writing (**telepático**)

- **telepathy** /tɪ'lepəθɪ/ NOUN, NO PLURAL the ability to know another person's thoughts without speaking or writing (**telepatia**)

telephone /'telɪfəʊn/ ▶ NOUN [*plural* **telephones**]
1 *no plural* a system for speaking to someone in another place, using equipment connected by wires □ *I spoke to him by telephone yesterday.* (**telefone**) 🔁 *Kennedy made a telephone call.* (**chamada telefônica**)
2 a piece of equipment that you use to make telephone calls (**telefone**) 🔁 *The telephone rang.* (**telephone tocou**) 🔁 *Isabelle answered the telephone.* (**atendeu o telefone**) 🔁 *Can I use your telephone?* (**usar seu telefone**)
▶ VERB [**telephones, telephoning, telephoned**] to contact someone using the telephone □ *Her mother telephoned the police when she didn't return home.* (**telefonar**)

telephone box /ˈtelɪfəʊn ˌbɒks/ NOUN [plural **telephone boxes**] a small structure in a public place containing a telephone which you can pay to use (**cabine telefônica**)

telephone number /ˈtelɪfəʊn ˈnʌmbə(r)/ NOUN [plural **telephone numbers**] the series of numbers that you use to call a particular telephone □ *Give me your telephone number, and I'll ring you tonight.* (**número do telefone**)

telephoto lens /ˌtelɪˈfəʊtəʊ ˈlenz/ NOUN [plural **telephoto lenses**] a camera lens (= piece of curved glass) which produces large images of small objects or objects which are far away (**teleobjetiva**)

telesales /ˈtelɪseɪlz/ NOUN, NO PLURAL the selling of goods and services by telephone (**televendas**)

telescope /ˈtelɪskəʊp/ NOUN [plural **telescopes**] a piece of equipment with lenses (= curved pieces of glass) and mirrors inside that makes objects that are far away seem closer or larger (**telescópio**)

• **telescopic** /ˌtelɪˈskɒpɪk/ ADJECTIVE
1 to do with telescopes (**telescópico**)
2 with parts that can be pushed inside each other (**de encaixar**)

teletext /ˈtelɪtekst/ NOUN, NO PLURAL a service that provides news and information in written form on your television screen. A trademark. (**teletexto (marca registrada)**)

televise /ˈtelɪvaɪz/ VERB [**televises, televising, televised**] to broadcast something on television □ *The event is being televised live.* (**televisionar**)

television /ˈtelɪˌvɪʒən/ NOUN [plural **televisions**]
1 *no plural* a system for sending images and sounds in the form of electrical signals, or programmes broadcast in this way (**televisão**) ▣ *Children watch too much television.* (**assistir à televisão**) □ *It was her first appearance on television.* ▣ *a commercial television station* (**estação de TV**)
2 the equipment which receives these pictures and sounds □ *a new flat-screen television* (**televisão**) ▣ *an old black-and-white television set* (**televisor**) ▣ *He switched on the television.* (**mudar o canal da televisão**)

> Remember that people and things appear **on** television:
> ✓ *He's often on television these days.*
> ✗ *He's often in television these days.*

tell /tel/ VERB [**tells, telling, told**]
1 to give someone information by speaking □ *Don't tell Mum I've lost my key.* □ + **that** *He told the court that he was abroad at the time.* □ + **question word** *Can you tell us why you disagree?* (**contar, dizer**) ▣ *He promised to tell the truth.* (**contar, dizer a verdade**) ▣ *She accused us of telling lies about her.* (**contar mentiras**)

2 to order someone to do something □ + **to do something** *He told me to sit down.* (**mandar**) ▣ *I wish you would do as you are told!* (**fazer o que mandaram**)
3 if you can tell something, you know that it is true or recognize the characteristics of someone or something (**dizer**) ▣ *I couldn't tell if he was joking or not.* (**dizer se**) □ + **that** *I could tell that she was upset.* ▣ *Can you tell the difference between butter and margarine?* (**dizer a diferença**)
4 **tell the time** to be able to understand the information on a clock or watch (**dizer a hora**)

> Note that when you use the word **tell**, meaning 'to speak to someone', you must say the person that you are speaking to □ *I told Peter I would come.*
> ✓ *I told him I would come.*
> ✗ *I told that I would come.*

♦ PHRASAL VERBS **tell someone/something apart** to be able to see the difference between two people or things □ *There are two sisters, and I can never tell them apart.* (**diferenciar**) **tell someone off** to speak angrily to someone who has done something wrong □ + **for** *He told me off for wasting water.* (**repreender**)

• **telling** /ˈtelɪŋ/ ADJECTIVE
1 showing the truth about something □ *Perhaps the most telling remark came from his brother.* (**revelador**)
2 important or effective (**eficaz**)

• **telling-off** /ˌtelɪŋ ˈɒf/ NOUN, NO PLURAL when you tell someone off □ *His teacher gave him a telling--off for being late again.* (**reprimenda**)

telltale /ˈtelteɪl/ ADJECTIVE showing that something certainly exists or is true (**revelador**) ▣ *The doctor spotted the telltale signs of the disease.* (**os sinais reveladores**)

telly /ˈtelɪ/ NOUN [plural **tellies**] an informal word for television (**tela, televisão**)

temp /temp/ ▶ NOUN [plural **temps**] someone who has a job for a short period of time, especially in an office □ *She was working as a temp.* (**temporário**)
▶ VERB [**temps, temping, temped**] to do a job for a short period of time □ *I was temping at a law firm.* (**trabalhar temporariamente**)

temper /ˈtempə(r)/ NOUN [plural **tempers**]
1 when someone becomes angry very easily (**gênio forte**) ▣ *My father had a really bad temper.* (**gênio muito forte**) □ *He was known for his violent temper.* ▣ *The little boy had a temper tantrum.*
2 **lose/keep your temper** to become angry/control your feeling □ *I'm afraid I lost my temper and shouted at him.* □ *He was trying to keep his temper.* (**perder/manter o controle**)

temperament 831 tend

3 a person's mood □ *Don't ask him until he's in a better temper.*

temperament /ˈtempərəmənt/ NOUN [plural **temperaments**] your character, which affects the way you think and behave □ *Alex has a calm temperament.* □ *His fiery temperament often got him into trouble.* (**temperamento**)

• **temperamental** /ˌtempərəˈmentəl/ ADJECTIVE
1 a temperamental person changes their mood suddenly and gets upset easily □ *Actors are notoriously temperamental.* (**temperamental**)
2 a temperamental machine, vehicle, etc. does not always work well □ *The shower's a bit temperamental.* (**temperamental**)

temperate /ˈtempərət/ ADJECTIVE with weather that is never quite very cold or very hot. A geography word □ *a temperate climate* □ *a temperate region* (**temperado**)

temperature /ˈtemprətʃə(r)/ NOUN [plural **temperatures**]
1 how hot or cold a place or a thing is □ *Average temperatures in spring are a pleasant 19-24 °C.* □ *+ of a temperature of minus 10 °C* (**temperatura**) 🔊 *The furnace is heated to very high temperatures.* (**temperaturas altas**) 🔊 *Serve at room temperature.* (**temperatura ambiente**)
2 how hot or cold a person's body is (**temperatura**) 🔊 *Flora woke up with a headache and a high temperature.* (**temperatura alta**) 🔊 *A nurse came in to take his temperature* (= to measure it). (**medir a temperatura dele**)
3 have a temperature if someone has a temperature, their body is hotter than it should be because they are ill (**estar com febre**)

tempest /ˈtempɪst/ NOUN [plural **tempests**] a violent storm with very strong wind (**tempestade**)

• **tempestuous** /temˈpestjuəs/ ADJECTIVE full of very strong emotions □ *a tempestuous relationship* (**tempestuoso**)

template /ˈtemplɪt/ NOUN [plural **templates**] something that is used as a pattern to make other things of the same kind (**modelo**) 🔊 *This policy could provide a template for other cities to copy.* (**fornecer um modelo**)

temple /ˈtempəl/ NOUN [plural **temples**]
1 a building in which the members of some religions show respect for a god by praying, having religious ceremonies, etc. □ *a Hindu temple* (**templo**)
2 the area on the side of your head between the side of your eye and your hair □ *He rubbed his temples.* (**têmpora**)

tempo /ˈtempəʊ/ NOUN [plural **tempos** or **tempi**] the speed and rhythm of a piece of music (**tempo, andamento**)

temporarily /ˈtempərərəlɪ/ ADVERB for a short or limited time only □ *The road was temporarily closed.* □ *He'd repaired the roof temporarily with a piece of plastic.* □ *The noise seems to have stopped, at least temporarily.* (**temporariamente, provisoriamente**)

• **temporary** /ˈtempərərɪ/ ADJECTIVE lasting or used only for a short or limited time □ *a temporary job* □ *The firm hires temporary workers in the summer.* (**temporário, provisório**) 🔊 *He was put in charge of the team on a temporary basis.* (**em bases provisórias**) 🔊 *Some families are living in temporary accommodation.* (**acomodações provisórias**)

tempt /tempt/ VERB [**tempts, tempting, tempted**]
1 to make someone want to do something or to have something □ *I was very tempted by their offer.* □ *Special deals are aimed at tempting people to switch banks.* (**tentar**)
2 tempt fate to be too confident or to do something that might end your good luck □ *I didn't want to tempt fate by thinking too far ahead.* (**tentar o destino**)

• **temptation** /tempˈteɪʃən/ NOUN [plural **temptations**]
1 when you are tempted by something (**tentação**) 🔊 *She resisted the temptation to open it straight away.* (**resistir à tentação**)
2 something that tempts you □ *I'm on a diet, but those cakes were too much of a temptation.* (**tentação**)

• **tempting** /ˈtemptɪŋ/ ADJECTIVE attractive and making you want to do or to have something □ *The food looks very tempting.* □ *a tempting offer* (**tentador**)

ten /ten/ NUMBER [plural **tens**] the number 10 (**dez**)

tenacious /tɪˈneɪʃəs/ ADJECTIVE determined not to stop doing something or trying to do something □ *He's a tenacious opponent.* (**tenaz**)

• **tenaciously** /tɪˈneɪʃəslɪ/ ADVERB in a tenacious way □ *She kept to her point tenaciously and would not give way.* (**tenazmente**)

• **tenacity** /tɪˈnæsətɪ/ NOUN, NO PLURAL the quality of being tenacious □ *Everyone admires her tenacity.* (**tenacidade**)

tenancy /ˈtenənsɪ/ NOUN [plural **tenancies**] the time when someone is a tenant or the agreement that makes someone a tenant (**locação**)

tenant /ˈtenənt/ NOUN [plural **tenants**] someone who pays rent to the owner of a house, building or land to use it □ *The table was left by the previous tenants.* (**inquilino**)

tend /tend/ VERB [**tends, tending, tended**] (**tender**)
1 tend to do something to often do something, happen, or be a particular way □ *She tends to be a bit moody.* □ *People tend not to talk about financial problems.* (**tender a**)
2 a formal word meaning to look after someone or something □ *He spends most days tending his garden.* □ *A nurse tended to the injuries to his face.* (**cuidar**)

• **tendency** /ˈtendənsɪ/ NOUN [plural **tendencies**] when someone often does something or something often happens ☐ *Teenagers often have a tendency to get up late.* (**tendência**)

tender /'tendə(r)/ ▶ ADJECTIVE

1 tender meat or vegetables are soft and easy to cut ☐ *Cook the beans until tender.* (**macio, tenro**)

2 kind and gentle ☐ *a tender smile* ☐ *They shared a tender moment.* (**terno**)

3 slightly painful when touched ☐ *The skin can be tender and red.* ☐ *My arm's quite tender to touch.* (**sensível**)

4 sensitive and not very strong ☐ *These plants are too tender to be grown outside.* (**sensível**)

▶ VERB [**tenders, tendering, tendered**]

1 to make a formal offer to do a particular job ☐ *Companies have been invited to tender for the contract.* (**oferecer propostas**)

2 to formally offer something (**oferecer formalmente**) ▣ *The minister has tendered his resignation.* (**ofereceu sua renúncia**)

▶ NOUN [*plural* **tenders**] a formal offer to do a particular job ☐ *The company recently won the tender to install phones at Sydney Airport.* (**oferta de trabalho**)

• **tenderly** /'tendəli/ ADVERB in a kind, gentle way ☐ *He smiled at her tenderly.* (**ternamente**)

• **tenderness** /'tendənɪs/ NOUN, NO PLURAL the quality of being tender (**ternura**)

tendon /'tendən/ NOUN [*plural* **tendons**] strong body tissue that connects a muscle to a bone. A biology word. (**tendão**)

tendril /'tendrəl/ NOUN [*plural* **tendrils**] a long, thin, curling stem of a plant, that winds around things (**gavinha**)

tenement /'tenəmənt/ NOUN [*plural* **tenements**] a large building with several floors divided into flats ☐ *a low-rent tenement building* (**habitação coletiva**)

tenner /'tenə(r)/ NOUN [*plural* **tenners**] an informal word for ten pounds (= £10) or a ten pound note (**dez libras**)

tennis /'tenɪs/ NOUN, NO PLURAL a game played on a court with a net across the middle in which the players hit a small ball over the net using rackets (= objects held in the hand) (**tênis**) ▣ *We play tennis every weekend.* (**jogar tênis**) ▣ *a professional tennis player* (**tenista**) ▣ *a tennis court* (**quadra de tênis**)

tenor /'tenə(r)/ NOUN [*plural* **tenors**] a male singer who has quite a high voice (**tenor**)

tenpin bowling /'tenpɪn 'bəʊlɪŋ/ NOUN, NO PLURAL a game in which you roll a heavy ball along the floor, and try to knock down ten wooden objects in the shape of bottles (**boliche**)

tense[1] /tens/ NOUN [*plural* **tenses**] a form of a verb which shows whether the action of the verb happens now (the **present tense**), in the past (the **past tense**), or in the future (the **future tense**) (**tempo**)

tense[2] /tens/ ▶ ADJECTIVE [**tenser, tensest**]

1 feeling nervous and unable to relax ☐ *He looked tense and exhausted.* (**tenso**)

2 making you feel nervous or worried ☐ *There was a tense atmosphere in the court.* (**tenso**)

3 stretched tight ☐ *tense muscles* (**retesado**)

▶ VERB [**tenses, tensing, tensed**] if you tense your muscles, you stretch them tight (**retesar**)

• **tensely** /'tensli/ ADJECTIVE in a way that is nervous and not relaxed ☐ *He stared tensely at the screen.* (**tensamente**)

• **tension** /'tenʃən/ NOUN [*plural* **tensions**]

1 the feeling when people do not trust each other (**tensão**) ▣ *racial tension* (**tensão racial**) ▣ *The two leaders are meeting in an effort to ease tensions between the countries.* (**avaliar as tensões**)

2 a nervous or worried feeling ☐ *She could sense the tension in him.* (**tensão**)

3 the state of being stretched tight (**tensão**)

tent /tent/ NOUN [*plural* **tents**] a frame covered with cloth which you sleep in when you are camping (**tenda, barraca**) ▣ *We pitched the tent (= put it up) next to the river.* (**armar a barraca**)

tentacle /'tentəkəl/ NOUN [*plural* **tentacles**] one of the long arms of a sea animal such as an octopus (**tentáculo**)

tentative /'tentətɪv/ ADJECTIVE

1 not certain yet ☐ *a tentative agreement* (**experimental**)

2 not confident ☐ *She took a few tentative steps towards him.* (**tímido, hesitante**)

tenterhooks /'tentəhʊks/ PLURAL NOUN **on tenterhooks** nervous and excited because you are waiting for something ☐ *We were on tenterhooks waiting for the exam results.* (**em suspense**)

tenth /tenθ/ ▶ NUMBER 10th written as a word (**décimo**)

▶ NOUN [*plural* **tenths**] 1/10 one of ten equal parts of something (**um décimo**)

tenuous /'tenjuəs/ ADJECTIVE something that is tenuous is so uncertain that it almost does not exist ☐ *He had some tenuous links with the Royal Family, which he was always boasting about.* (**tênue**)

tepid /'tepɪd/ ADJECTIVE tepid liquid is slightly warm (**tépido**)

term /tɜːm/ ▶ NOUN [*plural* **terms**]

1 in terms of something/in … terms used for saying which part of a situation you are talking about ☐ *In financial terms, the company has been very successful.* ☐ *Families are doing a lot for the environment in terms of recycling.* (**em termos de/em termos…**)

2 one of the periods of time that the school or college year is divided into ☐ *Students do exams in the summer term.* (**período, semestre**)

3 a limited period of time ☐ *the president's term of office* ☐ **+ of** *He was sent to prison for a term of 15 years.* (**período**)

terminal 833 **territory**

4 a word or expression with a particular meaning or used in a particular subject (**termo**) 🔊 *Patients don't understand complicated medical terms.* (**termos médicos**) ☐ *+ for What is the term for someone who collects coins?* ☐ *+ of 'Darling' is a term of affection.*
5 in the long/short term during a long/short period of time from now ☐ *Exposure to low levels of radiation increases the risk of ill health in the long term.* (**em longo/curto prazo**)
6 terms the rules of an agreement ☐ *Under the terms of his contract, he is eligible for a payout of £2 million.* (**termos**)
7 be on good/bad/friendly etc. terms with someone used for saying what type of relationship you have with someone ☐ *She remained on good terms with her husband after their divorce.* (**em boas/más/amigáveis relações**)
8 come to terms with something to accept and deal with a sad situation ☐ *The family are still coming to terms with his death.* (**adaptar-se a**)
▶ VERB [**terms, terming, termed**] to use a particular word or phrase to describe someone or something ☐ *Dogs that are used for hunting are often termed 'hounds'.* (**denominar**)

terminal /ˈtɜːmɪnəl/ ▶ NOUN [*plural* **terminals**]
1 a building where planes, boats, trains or buses arrive at and leave from 🔊 *Smoking is not allowed in the terminal building.* ☐ *Developers want to build a new terminal and runway at the airport.* (**terminal**)
2 a computer screen and keyboard. A computing word. (**terminal**)
▶ ADJECTIVE a terminal illness cannot be cured, and causes death (**terminal**) 🔊 *Jane had terminal cancer.* (**câncer terminal**)
• **terminate** /ˈtɜːmɪneɪt/ VERB [**terminates, terminating, terminated**] a formal word meaning to end, or to make something end (**terminar**) 🔊 *His employers terminated his contract.* (**terminar seu contrato**)
• **termination** /ˌtɜːmɪˈneɪʃən/ NOUN [*plural* **terminations**] a formal word meaning the act of ending something ☐ *The inquiry resulted in termination of the agreement.* (**término**)

terminology /ˌtɜːmɪˈnɒlədʒɪ/ NOUN [*plural* **terminologies**] the words and phrases that are used in a particular subject ☐ *military terminology* (**terminologia**)
terminus /ˈtɜːmɪnəs/ NOUN [*plural* **termini** or **terminuses**] the place where a bus or train ends its journey (**ponto final**)
termite /ˈtɜːmaɪt/ NOUN [*plural* **termites**] an insect that eats wood (**cupim**)
terrace /ˈterəs/ NOUN [*plural* **terraces**]
1 an area next to a building or on the roof of a building where you can sit ☐ *They sat and drank coffee on the terrace at the Hotel Duomo.* (**terraço**)
2 a row of houses that are joined to each other (**fileira de casas**)
3 one of a series of flat areas cut into the side of a hill, where crops are grown (**terraço**)
terraced house /ˈterəst ˈhaʊs/ NOUN [*plural* **terraced houses**] a house that is one of a row of houses which are joined together (**casas geminadas**)
terrain /teˈreɪn/ NOUN, NO PLURAL a particular type of land ☐ *rough terrain* (**terreno**)
terrapin /ˈterəpɪn/ NOUN [*plural* **terrapins**] a small animal that lives in water and has a hard shell on its back (**tartaruga fluvial**)
terrestrial /təˈrestrɪəl/ ADJECTIVE
1 terrestrial television, radio, etc. does not use signals from satellites (= devices in space) or cables (= thick wires) (**terrestre**)
2 to do with Earth and not space or other planets ☐ *terrestrial dust* (**terrestre**)
3 living on land and not water ☐ *terrestrial animals* (**terrestre**)

terrible /ˈterəbəl/ ADJECTIVE very bad or of very low quality (**péssimo, terrível**) ☐ *a terrible smell* ☐ *He made a terrible mistake.* ☐ *I'm terrible at remembering names.* 🔊 *I feel terrible about lying to my parents.* (**sentir-se péssimo**)
• **terribly** /ˈterəblɪ/ ADVERB
1 extremely ☐ *I'm terribly sorry I broke your vase.* ☐ *I feel terribly guilty about it.* (**extremamente**)
2 very badly ☐ *His death has affected us terribly.* (**terrivelmente**)

terrier /ˈterɪə(r)/ NOUN [*plural* **terriers**] a type of small dog (**terrier**)
terrific /təˈrɪfɪk/ ADJECTIVE
1 excellent ☐ *He's done a terrific job as team captain.* ☐ *The party was terrific.* (**esplêndido**)
2 very great ☐ *The car was travelling at terrific speed.* (**incrível, muito grande**)
• **terrifically** /təˈrɪfɪklɪ/ ADVERB extremely ☐ *We were terrifically pleased to get the award.* (**muitíssimo**)

terrified /ˈterɪfaɪd/ ADJECTIVE very frightened ☐ *I was terrified of my history teacher.* ☐ *He is absolutely terrified that someone will break into the house while he is alone.* (**aterrorizado, com medo**)
• **terrify** /ˈterɪfaɪ/ VERB [**terrifies, terrifying, terrified**] to make someone feel very frightened ☐ *The thought of dying terrifies me.* (**aterrorizar**)
• **terrifying** /ˈterɪfaɪɪŋ/ ADJECTIVE making you feel very frightened ☐ *a terrifying ordeal* (**aterrorizante**)
territorial /ˌterɪˈtɔːrɪəl/ ADJECTIVE to do with land that a particular country controls ☐ *a territorial dispute* (**territorial**)
territory /ˈterətrɪ/ NOUN [*plural* **territories**]
1 the land that a particular country controls (**território**) 🔊 *The army was in enemy territory.* (**território inimigo**) ☐ *The plane wasn't allowed to land on British territory.*

2 the area that an animal thinks is its own ◻ *Cats don't like it when other cats go into their territory.* (território)
3 an area of knowledge or experience (território, área) ⏺ *Technology was unfamiliar territory for me.* (território/área desconhecido/a)

terror /ˈterə(r)/ NOUN, NO PLURAL
1 a feeling of great fear ◻ *He ran away in terror.* (terror)
2 violence used by illegal groups to achieve political aims (terror) ⏺ *Many people were killed in the September 11th terror attacks.* (ataques terroristas) ⏺ *Police have arrested 15 terror suspects.* (suspeitos de terrorismo)

• **terrorism** /ˈterərɪzəm/ NOUN, NO PLURAL violence used by illegal groups to achieve political aims ◻ *There has been a rise in global terrorism.* (terrorismo)

• **terrorist** /ˈterərɪst/ NOUN [*plural* **terrorists**] someone who uses terrorism (terrorista) ⏺ *a terrorist organization* (organização terrorista) ◻ *a suspected terrorist*

• **terrorize** *or* **terrorise** /ˈterəraɪz/ VERB [**terrorizes, terrorizing, terrorized**] to frighten someone by threatening to use violence ◻ *Gangs of teenagers terrorized the neighbourhood.* (aterrorizar)

test /test/ ▶ NOUN [*plural* **tests**]
1 an exam, usually a short one ◻ *a spelling test* (teste, exame, prova) ⏺ *You will need to pass a simple maths test.* (passar no teste) ⏺ *I had to take a test to prove my French was good enough.* (fazer uma prova) ⏺ *He failed his driving test.* (ser reprovado no teste)
2 a medical examination of your body or part of your body ◻ *an eye/blood test* (exame médico) ⏺ *Tests showed she was suffering from a rare blood disease.* (os testes mostraram...)
3 something you do to check that something works correctly, is safe, etc. (teste) ⏺ *They will be conducting tests on the new aircraft over the next year.* (conduzir testes) ⏺ *nuclear tests* (testes nucleares)
4 a situation that proves the qualities of someone or something ◻ *+ of The election will be a test of strength for the president.* (teste) ⏺ *She faces a real test of character in the months ahead.* (enfrentar um teste)
5 **put someone/something to the test** to do something that proves how good or effective someone or something is ◻ *The system will be put to the test next week.* (testar)

> ► Remember that you **do** or **take** a test (exam). You do not 'make' a test:
> ✓ *I had to do a test in my interview.*
> ✗ *I had to make a test in my interview.*

▶ VERB [**tests, testing, tested**]
1 to do something to check that something works correctly, is safe, etc. ◻ *After driving through water, you should test the brakes.* ◻ *+ on The drugs are tested on volunteers.* ◻ *We need to design experiments to test our theories.* (testar)
2 to do a medical examination of your body or part of your body ◻ *I need to get my eyes tested.* ◻ *+ for We are testing for anaemia.* (examinar)
3 to give someone an exam, usually a short one ◻ *+ on Can you test me on my verb endings?* (testar)
4 to prove the qualities of someone or something ◻ *These problems will test her ability to lead others.* (testar)

testament /ˈtestəmənt/ NOUN [*plural* **testaments**] **testament to something** a formal phrase meaning proof of something good ◻ *Her success is testament to all her hard work.* (testamento)

testicle /ˈtestɪkəl/ NOUN [*plural* **testicles**] one of the two organs under a man's penis. A biology word. (testículo)

• **testicular** /tesˈtɪkjulə(r)/ ADJECTIVE to do with the testicles. A biology word ◻ *testicular cancer* (testicular)

testify /ˈtestɪfaɪ/ VERB [**testifies, testifying, testified**] to give information in a court ◻ *He testified at the inquest into the Princess's death.* (testemunhar)

testimonial /ˌtestɪˈməʊniəl/ NOUN [*plural* **testimonials**] a written statement about someone's character, skills and abilities (testemunho)

testimony /ˈtestɪməni/ NOUN [*plural* **testimonies**]
1 a formal statement that someone makes in a court (testemunho)
2 **testimony to something** a formal phrase meaning proof of something good ◻ *The huge profits are testimony to the confidence that people have in the company.* (testemunho de)

testosterone /teˈstɒstərəʊn/ NOUN, NO PLURAL a chemical substance that causes male characteristics to develop. A biology word. (testosterona)

test tube /ˈtest ˌtjuːb/ NOUN [*plural* **test tubes**] a thin glass tube which is closed at one end, used in scientific experiments (tubo de ensaio)

testy /ˈtesti/ ADJECTIVE [**testier, testiest**] bad--tempered (impaciente)

tetanus /ˈtetənəs/ NOUN, NO PLURAL a serious disease that makes the muscles in your neck and face stiff, caused by bacteria that get into a cut on your skin (tétano)

tetchy /ˈtetʃi/ ADJECTIVE [**tetchier, tetchiest**] getting annoyed easily ◻ *We had a rather tetchy meeting.* (maçante)

tether /ˈteðə(r)/ ▶ VERB [**tethers, tethering, tethered**] to tie an animal to a tether (amarrar um animal com corda)
▶ NOUN [*plural* **tethers**] a rope or chain used for tying up an animal so that it can walk around but not escape (corda)

text

♦ IDIOM **be at/reach the end of your tether** to feel that you cannot deal with a bad situation any more □ *Some parents reach the end of their tether with badly behaved children.* (estar no fim da corda)

text /tekst/ ▶ NOUN [plural **texts**]

1 a written message sent to a mobile phone (texto) 🔁 *I sent a text to my sister.* (mandar uma mensagem de texto) □ *She got a text from her boyfriend.*

2 *no plural* the writing in a book □ *The pictures were nice but the text wasn't very interesting.* (texto)

3 a book or piece of writing that people study □ *India's ancient texts* (texto, matéria)

▶ VERB [**texts, texting, texted**] to send a written message to someone's mobile phone □ *Text me when you get to the station.* (mandar mensagens)

textbook /'tekstbʊk/ NOUN [plural **textbooks**] a book about a subject which you use at school or college □ *a biology textbook* (livro escolar)

textile /'tekstaɪl/ NOUN [plural **textiles**] cloth □ *the textile industry* (têxtil)

text message /'tekst ˌmesɪdʒ/ NOUN [plural **text messages**] a text (= written message sent to a mobile phone) (mensagem de texto)

texture /'tekstʃə(r)/ NOUN [plural **textures**] the way something feels when you touch it □ *the smooth texture of a baby's skin* (textura)

than /ðæn/ CONJUNCTION used when comparing things □ *The test was easier than I thought it would be.* □ *He can swim better than me.* □ *The dress cost more than £200.* (que, do que)

thank /θæŋk/ VERB [**thanks, thanking, thanked**]

1 to tell someone that you are grateful for something □ **+ for** *He thanked me for the birthday present* □ *I must thank Emma for helping me.* (agradecer)

2 thank goodness/thank heavens/thank God used for saying you are pleased about something □ *Thank goodness no one was seriously hurt.* (graças a Deus)

• **thankful** /'θæŋkfʊl/ ADJECTIVE pleased or grateful that something good has happened □ *I'm just thankful that someone found my dog.* (agradecido, grato)

• **thankfully** /'θæŋkfʊli/ ADVERB used for saying that you are pleased because something good has happened □ *Thankfully, he managed to escape.* (agradecidamente)

• **thankless** /'θæŋkləs/ ADJECTIVE a thankless task is one which is difficult and you do not get any praise for doing it 🔁 *She had the thankless task of deciding which schools would have to close.* (ingrato)

• **thanks** /θæŋks/ ▶ EXCLAMATION

1 something you say to show that you are grateful □ *'I've made you a drink.' 'Thanks.'* (obrigado) 🔁

835

that

'Here's an invitation to the party.' 'Oh, thanks very much.' (muito obrigado) 🔁 *Many thanks for your letter.* (muitos agradecimentos por) □ **+ for** *Thanks for the flowers. They're beautiful.* □ *Thanks for driving me to the airport.*

2 used as a way of accepting an offer □ *'Would you like a sweet?' 'Thanks.'* (sim, obrigado)

3 no thanks used as a polite way of saying you do not want something □ *'Do you want to come with us?' 'No thanks, I'm busy on Saturday.'* (não, obrigado)

▶ PLURAL NOUN

1 something you say or do to show that you are grateful □ *He expressed his thanks to everyone who had taken part.* □ *I got no thanks for helping him.* (agradecimentos)

2 thanks to someone/something because of someone or something □ *We finished the project on time, thanks to everyone's hard work.* □ *Thanks to the strike, our flight was cancelled.* (graças a alguém/algo)

Thanksgiving /'θæŋksˌgɪvɪŋ/ NOUN, NO PLURAL a holiday in the US and Canada in autumn, when families eat a special meal together (ação de graças)

thank you /'θæŋkjuː/ EXCLAMATION

1 something you say to someone when you are grateful for something they have done or given you (obrigado) 🔁 *'I've made you a cup of coffee.' 'Oh, thank you very much.'* (muito obrigado) □ **+ for** *Thank you for the flowers. They're beautiful.* □ *Thank you for helping me yesterday.*

2 used when answering a question in a polite way □ *'How are you?' 'I'm fine, thank you.'* (obrigado)

3 used as a polite way of accepting or refusing someone's offer □ *'Would you like to come for a meal with us?' 'Thank you. That would be lovely.'* (obrigado) 🔁 *'Do you want another biscuit?' 'No, thank you.'* (não, obrigado)

> Note that you say **thank you for** something or **thank you for + doing** something □ *Thank you for your help.* □ *Thank you for helping.*

that ▶ CONJUNCTION /ðət/

1 used after some verbs, adjectives and nouns to start a new part of a sentence □ *He said that he hated sports.* □ *We must make sure that we invite enough people.* □ *The fact that he earns so much means he can afford a big house.* (que)

2 used instead of 'who' or 'which' at the beginning of a clause (= part of a sentence) □ *People that know her well say she is very ambitious.* □ *We are working with organizations that provide emergency aid.* (que)

3 used after a superlative adjective for explaining more about the adjective □ *These clothes were the best that we could find.* (que)

4 used after words to do with amounts of things, actions or people, for example 'nothing', 'anybody' and 'all' □ *We did everything that we could to help her.* □ *There was nothing that we could give him.* (**que**)

▶ DETERMINER [*plural* **those**] used to talk about a person or thing that you can see or that you have already talked about □ *Who is that girl over there?* □ *Pass me that towel, please.* □ *I left that job a year ago.* (**aquele, aquela, aquilo**)

▶ PRONOUN [*plural* **those**]

1 used to talk about something that you can see or that you have already talked about □ *I don't want to know that.* □ *Who is that at the door?* (**isso, aquilo, aquele, aquela**)

2 that's it (a) used to say that someone has done something correctly □ *Put the wire through the loop – that's it.* (b) used to show that you are angry and will not continue with something □ *That's it! You can cook your own meals from now on!* (**é isso mesmo**)

3 that's that used to say that something has happened or been decided and the situation cannot be changed □ *The taxi's broken down? Oh, well that's that then – we'll never catch our flight.* □ *He just walked out and that was that – we never saw him again.* (**é isso, chega**)

▶ ADVERB /ðæt/ to the amount or degree mentioned □ *I didn't think I'd run that far.* □ *The film wasn't that bad.* (**tão**)

thatched /θætʃt/ ADJECTIVE having a roof that is made from straw (= dried stems of crops) or reeds (= a type of tall grass that grows in water) □ *a thatched cottage* (**coberto de sapé**)

that'd /ˈðætəd/ a short way to say and write that had or that would □ *That'd never happened before.* □ *That'd be nice.* (**abreviação de *that had* ou *that would***)

that'll /ˈðætəl/ a short way to say and write that will □ *That'll be too big for you.* (**abreviação de *that will***)

that's /ðæts/ a short way to say and write that is □ *That's not what I meant.* (**abreviação de *that is***)

thaw /θɔː/ ▶ VERB [**thaws, thawing, thawed**]

1 if something that is frozen thaws, it melts □ *The ice has thawed.* (**derreter**)

2 to become more friendly □ *Relations between the two men have thawed recently.* (**tornar-se mais amistoso**)

▶ NOUN, NO PLURAL

1 a period when the weather becomes warmer and ice melts (**degelo**)

2 when people who have had a bad relationship start to be more friendly (**reconciliação**)

the /ðə/ DETERMINER

1 used before a noun to refer to a particular person or thing that has been mentioned or is known about □ *The bus arrived late, as usual.* □ *I opened the letter and read it.* □ *The men rode on horses and the women rode in carriages.* (**o, a, os, as**)

2 used before a noun when there is only one of that thing □ *The moon was shining.* □ *Balloons floated up into the air.* (**o, a, os, as**)

3 used to refer to part of a thing □ *Hold the box at the bottom.* □ *Come to the back of the building.* (**o, a, os, as**)

4 used in dates □ *the third of June* □ *July the fourth*

5 used before nouns referring to actions, especially ones followed by 'of' □ *the introduction of new rules* □ *the abolition of slavery* (**o, a, os, as**)

theater /ˈθɪətə(r)/ NOUN [*plural* **theaters**] the US spelling of **theatre** (**ver theatre**)

theatre /ˈθɪətə(r)/ NOUN [*plural* **theatres**]

1 a building where plays are performed (**teatro**) □ *We went to the theatre last night.* (**foi ao teatro**)

2 no plural the work of writing or performing plays □ *I've always wanted to work in theatre.* (**teatro**) □ *The Australian theatre company 'Back to Back' toured Europe with its production 'Small Metal Objects'.* (**companhia teatral**)

3 a room where operations are done in a hospital □ *He was in theatre for three hours.* (**sala de cirurgia**)

4 the US word for **cinema** (**cinema**)

• **theatrical** /θɪˈætrɪkəl/ ADJECTIVE

1 to do with plays or acting □ *theatrical performances* (**teatral, dramático**)

2 doing or saying things in an obvious and emotional way because you want people to notice you □ *She spread her arms in a theatrical gesture.* (**teatral, dramático**)

thee /ðiː/ PRONOUN an old-fashioned word for **you** (**te, a ti**)

theft /θeft/ NOUN [*plural* **thefts**] the crime of stealing something (**roubo**) □ *car thefts* (**roubos de carro**) □ + *of The theft of a laptop from a government employee has raised concerns about security.* □ *She was jailed for theft.*

their /ðeə(r)/ DETERMINER belonging to or to do with them □ *Do you know their address?* (**seu, deles, sua, delas**)

• **theirs** /ðeəz/ PRONOUN used to talk or write about things belonging to or to do with a group of people or things that have already been mentioned □ *They say it belongs to them, but I know it's not theirs.* (**deles, delas**)

them /ðem/ PRONOUN

1 used for talking about two or more people or things that you have already mentioned □ *The girls waved to me and I waved back to them.* □ *'Do you like strawberries?' 'Yes, I love them.'* (**eles, elas, os, as**)

2 used to avoid saying 'him' or 'her' □ *If anyone asks where I am, can you tell them I've gone to the dentist's.* (**eles, elas, os, as**)

theme /θiːm/ NOUN [*plural* **themes**]

theme park

1 the main idea or subject in a book, film, discussion, etc. (**tema, assunto**) 🔲 *The country's history is the central theme of the book.* (**tema central**)

2 theme song/tune/music the music that is played at the start and end of a television programme (**música tema**)

theme park /'θiːmˌpɑːk/ NOUN [plural **theme parks**]
a place where you go for fun, where the entertainments and machines you ride on are based on one subject □ *Disney theme parks* (**parque temático**)

themselves /ðəmˈselvz/ PRONOUN

1 the reflexive form of they □ *They'd made themselves a cosy little shelter.* (**eles/as mesmos/as, eles/elas próprios/as, a si mesmos/as**)

2 used to show that two or more people do something without any help from other people □ *They'll have to work it out themselves.* (**sozinhos**) 🔲 *They built the shelter all by themselves.* (**tudo sozinhos**)

3 used to emphasize the pronoun they □ *They themselves are innocent.* (**eles/elas próprios/próprias**)

4 by themselves not with or near other people □ *They sat by themselves and didn't talk to anyone else.* (**sozinhas**)

5 to themselves without having to share with anyone else □ *They had the hall to themselves for the morning.* (**para si**)

then /ðen/ ▶ ADVERB

1 at that time, in the past or future □ *I didn't know you then.* (**então**) 🔲 *The rest of the kids should be here by then.* (**então**) 🔲 *They can deliver the car by March, but we really need it before then.* (**antes**) 🔲 *Max and I met up in June, but I haven't seen him since then.* (**até então**)

2 after that time or next □ *I went for a swim, and then I went home.* □ *Mix in the flour and then the fruit.* (**então, depois**)

3 because of that □ *If you can't be quiet, then you'll have to leave the room.* □ *'This carpet will last longer.' 'I think we'll have that then.'* (**então**)

▶ ADJECTIVE at that time, but not now □ *I went there with my then boyfriend.* (**de então**)

theology /θiˈɒlədʒi/ NOUN, NO PLURAL the study of God and religion (**teologia**)

theorem /'θɪərəm/ NOUN [plural **theorems**]
a rule in maths that can be proved to be true. A maths word. (**teorema**)

theoretical /ˌθɪəˈretɪkəl/ ADJECTIVE

1 based on ideas and not on practical situations □ *theoretical physics* (**teórico**)

2 possible but not certain □ *The drug is not given to pregnant women because of a theoretical risk to the unborn baby.* (**teórico**)

• **theoretically** /ˌθɪəˈretɪkli/ ADVERB possibly but not yet done or proved (**teoricamente**) 🔲 *It is theoretically possible to halt the disease in its course.* (**teoricamente possível**)

theory /'θɪəri/ NOUN [plural **theories**]

1 an idea which tries to explain why something happens □ **+ about** *There are many theories about why children are getting fatter.* □ **+ of** *Newton's theory of gravity* (**teoria**)

2 in theory used for saying what should be true but may not be true □ *In theory you can get there in two hours but there's often a lot of traffic.* (**na teoria**)

3 no plural the ideas and principles of an art or science □ *economic theory* (**teoria**)

therapeutic /ˌθerəˈpjuːtɪk/ ADJECTIVE

1 making you feel more relaxed and happy □ *I've always found yoga very therapeutic.* (**terapêutico**)

2 used for treating illnesses □ *therapeutic drugs* (**terapêutico**)

therapist /'θerəpɪst/ NOUN [plural **therapists**]
someone who treats physical or mental problems without using drugs □ *a speech therapist* (**terapeuta**)

therapy /'θerəpi/ NOUN [plural **therapies**]

1 the treatment of medical problems □ *There are many effective therapies for treating depression.* (**terapia**)

2 in therapy having treatment for a mental or emotional problem (**em terapia**)

there /ðeə(r)/ ▶ PRONOUN used to start a statement about something that exists or happens □ *There is a mouse somewhere in this house.* □ *There's too much noise.* □ *There is plenty of milk in the fridge.* □ *I thought there would be more time for discussion.* (**haver**)

▶ ADVERB

1 at, in or to a place □ *I know someone who lives there.* □ *I'm going there tomorrow.* □ *When I got to work, Clive was already there.* (**lá**)

2 used to show someone something you are pointing to or want them to look at □ *You can leave your coats there.* □ *There's Dad.* (**lá**)

3 at a particular point in a process □ *Don't stop there. I was just beginning to enjoy the story.* □ *We've all worked hard – shall we leave it there for today?* (**ali, lá**)

4 there and then immediately □ *I decided there and then that I wanted to be a doctor.* (**imediatamente**)

thereabouts /ˌðeərəˈbaʊts/ ADVERB approximately 🔲 *It will cost £50 or thereabouts.* (**mais ou menos**)

thereafter /ˌðeərˈɑːftə(r)/ ADVERB a formal word meaning after a particular time □ *The cost is £40 for the first session and £30 thereafter.* (**depois disso**)

thereby /ˌðeəˈbaɪ/ ADVERB in this way □ *Exercise lowers blood pressure thereby reducing the need for medication.* (**por meio disso**)

therefore /'ðeəfɔː(r)/ ADVERB because of that □ *She had been awake all that night and therefore was very tired the next day.* (**por isso**)

thermal /ˈθɜːməl/ ADJECTIVE
1 using heat, or to do with heat. A physics word □ *thermal energy* (termal, térmico)
2 thermal clothes are made from a special cloth which keeps you warm (térmico)

thermo- /ˈθɜːməʊ/ PREFIX used at the start of words to mean 'to do with or using heat' □ *thermometer* (termo-)

thermometer /θəˈmɒmɪtə(r)/ NOUN [plural **thermometers**] an instrument for measuring the temperature of something or someone □ *The nurse used a thermometer to take his temperature.* (termômetro)

Thermos /ˈθɜːmɒs/ NOUN [plural **Thermoses**] a container that keeps drinks hot or cold. A trademark. □ *a Thermos flask* (térmico (marca registrada))

thermostat /ˈθɜːməʊstæt/ NOUN [plural **thermostats**] a device that keeps a room or a machine at a particular temperature (termostato)

thesaurus /θɪˈsɔːrəs/ NOUN [plural **thesauri** or **thesauruses**] a book that lists groups of words that have similar meanings (tesauro)

these /ðiːz/ ▶ DETERMINER used to talk about people or things that you have already talked about, or that you can see, usually near you □ *These cups are dirty.* □ *These athletes train very hard.* □ *These problems could have been avoided.* (estes, estas)
▶ PRONOUN used to talk about things that you have already talked about, or that you can see, usually near you □ *I can't eat these.* □ *Are these yours?* (estes, estas)

thesis /ˈθiːsɪs/ NOUN [plural **theses**] a long piece of writing that you do as part of an advanced university course □ *She wrote a thesis on the poetry of John Donne.* (tese)

they /ðeɪ/ PRONOUN
1 used to talk or write about two or more people or things that have already been mentioned □ *Apes are not monkeys. They don't have tails.* □ *What did they think of your idea?* (eles, elas)
2 people in general, or people in authority □ *They say it's going to be a hot summer.* □ *They've raised taxes again.* (eles, elas ou pronome indefinido)

they'd /ðeɪd/ a short way to say and write they had or they would □ *They'd all had their lunch.* □ *They'd like to come with us.* (abreviação de *they had* ou *they would*)

they'll /ðeɪl/ a short way to say and write they will or they shall □ *They'll be here tomorrow.* (abreviação de *they will* ou *they shall*)

they're /ðeə(r)/ a short way to say and write they are □ *They're going to the park after school.* (abreviação de *they are*)

they've /ðeɪv/ a short way to say and write they have □ *They've never been skating before.* (abreviação de *they have*)

thick /θɪk/ ▶ ADJECTIVE [**thicker, thickest**]
1 wide between the opposite sides or surfaces □ *Make sure you wear a thick coat.* □ *There was a thick layer of snow on the ground.* (grosso, espesso)
2 having a particular width between sides or surfaces □ *The ice was two feet thick.* (de espessura)
3 made up of many parts that are very close together □ *thick hair* (denso, abundante)
4 a thick liquid does not flow easily □ *thick gravy* (grosso, denso)
5 thick smoke, fog, etc. fills the air and is difficult to see through (cerrado, denso)
6 an informal word meaning stupid (grosso, tolo)
▶ NOUN, NO PLURAL
1 **in the thick of something** to be involved in the most busy or important part of a situation or activity □ *They were in the thick of the battle.* (no centro de)
2 **through thick and thin** in all situations, even very difficult ones □ *We've stuck together through thick and thin.* (haja o que houver)

• **thicken** /ˈθɪkən/ VERB [**thickens, thickening, thickened**] to become thick or thicker or to make something thick or thicker □ *I used flour to thicken the sauce.* (engrossar)

• **thickly** /ˈθɪkli/ ADVERB in a thick layer or into thick pieces □ *thickly sliced bread* (espessamente)

• **thickness** /ˈθɪknɪs/ NOUN, NO PLURAL how thick something is □ *The thickness of the walls means that heat stays in the building.* (espessura, densidade)

thickset /ˌθɪkˈset/ ADJECTIVE having a wide, heavy body □ *a thickset man* (encorpado)

thick-skinned /ˌθɪkˈskɪnd/ ADJECTIVE not easily upset if someone criticizes or insults you □ *Mary's very thick skinned.* (insensível)

thief /θiːf/ NOUN [plural **thieves**] someone who steals things (ladrão) ▣ *car thieves* (ladrões de carro) ▣ *Thieves stole her handbag.* (os ladrões roubaram)

thigh /θaɪ/ NOUN [plural **thighs**] the top part of your leg above your knee (coxa)

thimble /ˈθɪmbəl/ NOUN [plural **thimbles**] a small, hard cover you put on your finger to protect it when you are sewing (dedal)

thin /θɪn/ ▶ ADJECTIVE [**thinner, thinnest**]
1 not wide from one side to the other □ *He spread a thin layer of jam on the cake.* □ *Cut the potato into thin slices.* (fino)
2 a thin person or animal does not have much fat on their body (magro) ▣ *She is painfully thin.* (terrivelmente magro)
3 a thin liquid flows very easily □ *They were given a bowl of thin soup.* (ralo)
4 if you have thin hair, the hairs are not close together (ralo)

thing

5 thin air does not contain much oxygen (**rarefeito**)
6 disappear/vanish into thin air to disappear suddenly and completely ▫ *He's just vanished into thin air – no one knows where he is.* (**sumir de repente**)
⇨ go to **wear thin**
▶ VERB [**thins, thinning, thinned**]
1 to make a substance thin or thinner, for example by adding water or liquid to it (**diluir, enfraquecer**)
2 if your hair is thinning, you gradually have less of it (**escassear**)
◆ PHRASAL VERB **thin something out** if a group of people or things thins out, or if someone thins them out, some of them are removed (**desfalcar**)

thing /θɪŋ/ NOUN [plural **things**]

1 used to refer to an object without using its name ▫ *I bought a few things for the party when I was in town.* ▫ *Where's the thing for opening bottles?* (**coisa**)
2 an action or event ▫ *I hope I haven't done the wrong thing.* ▫ *The same thing happened to me once.* (**coisa**) ▣ *It was a good thing Pia arrived.* (**bom acontecimento**)
3 a fact, belief or idea ▫ *She said lots of nice things about you.* ▫ *He asked me a few things about my work.* (**coisa**)
4 things a situation ▫ *Things improved when the new manager started.* ▫ *Things are a bit difficult for me at the moment.* (**as coisas, a situação**)
5 your things the objects that belong to you ▫ *He packed up his things and left.* (**suas coisas**)
6 no such thing used to say that something does not exist ▫ *There's no such thing as ghosts.* (**não existe tal coisa**)
7 used to refer to a person or animal after an adjective that shows how you feel about them ▫ *You poor thing – you must be exhausted.* ▫ *I'm not having that filthy thing in the house!* (**coisa**)
8 first/last thing at the beginning/end of the day ▫ *I always go for a run first thing in the morning.* ▫ *I lock all the doors last thing.* (**primeira/última coisa**)

think /θɪŋk/ VERB [thinks, thinking, thought]

1 to have an opinion about someone or something ▫ *I think there's too much salt in this soup.* ▫ **+ that** *I think that you should ask him to leave.* ▫ **+ about** *What do you think about the death penalty?* ▫ **+ of** *What do you think of his new girlfriend?* (**achar**)
2 to believe that something is true, although you are not certain ▫ *I think Anna will be here soon.* ▫ **+ that** *We thought that there would be more people there.* (**achar**) ▣ *'Do the trains run on Sunday?' 'I think so.'* (**acho que sim**)
3 to consider something, especially in order to understand it or to decide what to do ▫ **+ about** *You need to think very carefully about which*

839

think

subjects to choose. ▫ **+ of** *We need to think of a way to raise money.* (**pensar**)
4 to remember someone or something ▫ **+ about** *I was just thinking about the time we went to New York.* ▫ **+ of** *I often think of my mother.* (**pensar**)
5 to express words to yourself in your mind ▫ *I just remember thinking, 'I must stay calm'.* (**pensar**)
6 if you are thinking of doing something, you are considering doing it ▫ **+ of** *I'm thinking of starting my own business.* ▫ **+ about** *They're thinking about sending their son to boarding school.* (**pensar, refletir**)
7 not think much of someone/something to have a low opinion of someone or something ▫ *I don't think much of my new manager.* (**não ter boa opinião a respeito de**)
8 think nothing of something to do something that other people would find difficult or strange in an easy and natural way ▫ *He thinks nothing of cycling 50 km to work every day.* (**achar que não é nada**)
◆ IDIOM **think twice** to consider something carefully, often deciding not to do something you had intended to do ▫ *People would think twice about weekend breaks if air travel was more expensive.* (**pensar duas vezes**)
◆ PHRASAL VERBS **think ahead** to prepare for a possible situation in the future ▫ *You need to think ahead – how many people will still want this kind of service in 10 years time?* (**pensar adiante, à frente**) **think back** to remember something from the past ▫ *If you think back to when we were children, we were just as bad.* (**relembrar**) **think something out** to consider all the parts of something carefully ▫ *He's thought it all out – the timing, the finances, everything.* (**planejar detalhadamente**) **think something over** to consider something before you make a decision ▫ *They offered him the job, but he's asked for a few days to think it over.* (**refletir sobre**) **think something through** to think about all the possible results of something ▫ *I didn't think it through properly and there were all sorts of problems with the transport.* (**considerar todas as possibilidades**) **think something up** to invent something such as an idea or a plan ▫ *We tried to think up a way to get her to come to London.* (**inventar**)

• **thinking** /ˈθɪŋkɪŋ/ NOUN, NO PLURAL
1 when you think ▫ *You must do some serious thinking before you decide on a career.* (**reflexão, pensamento**)
2 your opinion or thoughts about a particular subject ▫ *What's your thinking on this?* ▣ *This whole plan is, to my way of thinking, a serious mistake.* (**no meu modo de pensar**)
▶ ADJECTIVE intelligent and interested in serious subjects ▫ *a magazine for the thinking woman* (**reflexivo**)

thinly /ˈθɪnli/ ADVERB in a thin piece or layer □ *Slice the onions thinly.* (finalmente, em fatias finas)

third /θɜːd/ ▶ NUMBER 3rd written as a word □ *That's the third time he's called today.* □ *She came third in an art competition.* (terceiro)
▶ NOUN [*plural* **thirds**] 1/3; one of three equal parts of something □ *The bottle holds a third of a litre.* (um terço)

third party /ˌθɜːd ˈpɑːtɪ/ NOUN [*plural* **third parties**] someone who is not one of the two main people or organizations involved in something □ *There is a third party who saw the fight and can act as witness.* (terceira parte)
• **third-party** /ˌθɜːdˈpɑːtɪ/ ADJECTIVE third-party insurance protects you if you damage something belonging to someone else or injure another person (terceiros)

third person /ˌθɜːd ˈpɜːsən/ NOUN, NO PLURAL in grammar, the form of words used when you talk or write about someone who is not you and not the person you are talking or writing to □ *'He' is a third person pronoun.* (terceiro, terceira pessoa) 🔁 *The story is written in the third person.* (terceira pessoa)

third-rate /ˌθɜːdˈreɪt/ ADJECTIVE of a very bad quality or standard □ *a third-rate spy film* (de última categoria)

Third World /ˌθɜːd ˈwɜːld/ ▶ NOUN, NO PLURAL the **Third World** a slightly old-fashioned name for the countries of the world that are the poorest and least developed □ *The work aims to improve health in the Third World.* (Terceiro Mundo)
▶ ADJECTIVE to do with the countries of the Third World 🔁 *a Third World country* (o Terceiro Mundo)

thirst /θɜːst/ NOUN, NO PLURAL
1 the feeling that you need something to drink (sede) 🔁 *He paused to quench his thirst* (= have a drink) *at a café.* (saciar a sede)
2 a thirst for something a feeling of wanting something very much □ *She has a thirst for knowledge.* (sede de)
• **thirsty** /ˈθɜːsti/ ADJECTIVE [**thirstier, thirstiest**] feeling that you need something to drink □ *They were tired, hungry and thirsty.* (com sede, sedento) 🔁 *I felt incredibly thirsty.* (sentir sede)

thirteen /ˌθɜːˈtiːn/ NUMBER the number 13 (treze)

thirteenth /ˌθɜːˈtiːnθ/ NUMBER 13th written as a word (décimo terceiro)

thirtieth /ˈθɜːtɪəθ/ NUMBER 30th written as a word (trigésimo)

thirty /ˈθɜːti/ NUMBER [*plural* **thirties**]
1 the number 30 (trinta)
2 the thirties the years between 1930 and 1939 (os anos 1930)

this /ðɪs/ ▶ DETERMINER [*plural* **these**]
1 used to talk about a person or thing that you have already talked about, or something that you can see, usually near you □ *This apple is sour.* □ *I've lived in this country for five years.* □ *This argument went on for weeks.* (este, esta, isto)
2 used to refer to a present period of time, or the one that comes next □ *I went shopping this morning.* □ *I'll be seeing her this weekend.* (neste, nesta)
▶ PRONOUN
1 used to talk about something that you have already talked about, or that you can see, usually near you □ *I can't eat this.* □ *Where are you going after this?* □ *This is my bedroom.* (este, esta, isto)
2 used to say who you are on the telephone □ *Hello, this is Ollie.* (indica quem fala ao telefone: Alô, aqui é o Ollie)
3 this and that several different, usually not very important, things □ *'What have you been doing today?' 'Oh, this and that.'* (isto e aquilo)
▶ ADVERB to the amount or degree mentioned □ *It wasn't this hot yesterday.* □ *I didn't know we'd used this much fuel already.* (tão, tanto)

thistle /ˈθɪsəl/ NOUN [*plural* **thistles**] a plant with sharp leaves and large purple flowers (cardo)

thorax /ˈθɔːræks/ NOUN [*plural* **thoraxes** *or* **thoraces**]
1 the part of your body between the head and the waist. A biology word. (tórax)
2 the middle part of an insect's body, where the wings are joined. A biology word. (tórax)

thorn /θɔːn/ NOUN [*plural* **thorns**] a sharp point on the stems of some plants (espinho)
♦ IDIOM **a thorn in someone's side** a problem or something annoying for someone that continues for a long time □ *The media were a thorn in his side.* (uma pedra no caminho de alguém)
• **thorny** /ˈθɔːni/ ADJECTIVE [**thornier, thorniest**]
1 covered with thorns □ *a thorny bush* (espinhoso)
2 a thorny problem or question is difficult to deal with (espinhoso) 🔁 *the thorny issue of illegal immigration* (um problema complicado/delicado)

thorough /ˈθʌrə/ ADJECTIVE
1 done carefully, paying attention to every detail □ *He made a thorough search.* (minucioso) 🔁 *We are conducting a thorough investigation into this incident.* (investigação minuciosa)
2 used to emphasize how bad or annoying something is □ *It was a thorough nuisance.* (completo)

thoroughbred /ˈθʌrəbred/ NOUN [*plural* **thoroughbreds**] a horse that has parents of the same high quality breed (= type), usually used for racing (de sangue puro)

thoroughfare /ˈθʌrəfeə(r)/ NOUN [*plural* **thoroughfares**] a public road, especially the main road through a town (via pública)

thoroughly

thoroughly /'θʌrəlɪ/ ADVERB
1 with great care and attention to every detail □ *Clean all the kitchen surfaces thoroughly.* □ *The book has been thoroughly researched.* (**minuciosamente**)
2 completely 🔁 *We thoroughly enjoyed ourselves.* □ *She was feeling thoroughly fed up.* □ *They thoroughly deserve this victory.* (**completamente**)

those /ðəʊz/ ▶ DETERMINER used to talk about several people or things already mentioned or that you can see, usually not near you □ *Who are those two boys?* □ *In those days, people didn't have cars.* (**aqueles/as, esses/as**)
▶ PRONOUN used to talk about several things already mentioned or that you can see, usually not near you □ *What are those?* □ *Those are just some of the problems we face.* (**aqueles/as**)

thou /ðaʊ/ PRONOUN an old-fashioned word for **you** (**tu**)

though /ðəʊ/ ▶ ADVERB used to show that what you have just said is surprising or different from what you said before □ *It's a pity we didn't win. It was an exciting match, though.* (**de qualquer modo**)
▶ CONJUNCTION
1 but □ *We only waited for half an hour, though it seemed like hours.* □ *He will continue his political work, though not necessarily with the same party.* (**embora**)
2 despite the fact that □ *He went out, though I told him not to.* (**apesar de**)

thought /θɔːt/ ▶ NOUN [*plural* **thoughts**]
1 an idea, opinion, word or image that you have in your mind □ + *on Do you have any thoughts on the problem of transport?* □ + *about I had a sudden thought about the garden.* □ + *of I can't bear the thought of leaving you all.* (**pensamento**)
2 *no plural* the activity of thinking □ *This issue needs some careful thought.* (**reflexão**)
▶ PAST TENSE AND PAST PARTICIPLE of **think** (*ver* **think**)

• **thoughtful** /'θɔːtfʊl/ ADJECTIVE
1 a thoughtful person is kind and thinks of other people □ *It was very thoughtful of you to phone.* (**atencioso**)
2 if someone looks thoughtful, they look as if they are thinking (**pensativo**)

• **thoughtfully** /'θɔːtfʊlɪ/ ADVERB in a thoughtful way □ *She stared thoughtfully at the letter.* □ *She'd very thoughtfully left drinks and sandwiches on the kitchen table for us.* (**atenciosamente**)

• **thoughtless** /'θɔːtlɪs/ ADJECTIVE a thoughtless person does things without thinking about how other people will be affected by their actions (**desatencioso**)

thousand /'θaʊzənd/ NUMBER [*plural* **thousands**]
1 the number 1,000 (**mil**)
2 **thousands** a large number. An informal word □ + *of I've climbed that tree thousands of times.* (**milhares**)

841

threat

thousandth /'θaʊzəntθ/ ▶ NUMBER 1,000th written as a word (**milésimo**)
▶ NOUN [*plural* **thousandths**] 1/1,000; one of a thousand equal parts of something (**um milésimo**)

thrash /θræʃ/ VERB [**thrashes, thrashing, thrashed**]
1 an informal word meaning to beat someone very easily in a game □ *His Croatia side thrashed Iceland 4-0.* (**vencer esmagadoramente**)
2 to make uncontrolled, violent movements □ *The fish thrashed around in the shallow water.* (**debater-se**)
3 to hit someone or something very hard, often repeatedly (**surrar**)
1 PHRASAL VERB **thrash something out** to continue discussing something until you reach an agreement □ *They've been in talks to thrash out a deal.* (**discutir**)

thread /θred/ ▶ NOUN [*plural* **threads**]
1 a long, thin piece of cotton, wool, etc. used for sewing □ *fine silken threads* □ *His name was embroidered in red thread.* (**linha, fio**)
2 the main idea that joins the parts of a story, a discussion, etc. 🔁 *A common thread runs though all of her work.* (**ideia, concepção central**)
3 a series of messages on a website about a particular subject (**assunto específico em um grupo de discussão**)
♦ IDIOM **lose the thread** to stop understanding what someone is saying, usually because you are not concentrating enough (**perder o fio da meada**)
▶ VERB [**threads, threading, threaded**]
1 to push something long and thin through a hole □ *He threaded a piece of wire through a hole in the top.* (**enfiar**)
2 to push a piece of thread through the hole in the top of a needle (**enfiar**)
3 to put objects with a hole in them onto a thread, wire, etc. □ *They were threading beads onto a string.* (**enfiar**)
4 to move carefully through or between people or things (**enfiar-se**) 🔁 *He threaded his way through the crowd.* (**enfiar-se no meio**)

threadbare /'θredbeə(r)/ ADJECTIVE a threadbare carpet or piece of cloth is thin because it has been used a lot (**gasto, surrado**)

threat /θret/ NOUN [*plural* **threats**]
1 a warning that someone might hurt you or harm you, especially if you do not do what they say (**ameaça**) 🔁 *She has received death threats.* (**ameaças de morte**) □ + *against Militia leaders have issued threats against the president.* □ + *of He has a reputation for using threats of violence.*
2 something that might cause harm or problems (**ameaça**) 🔁 *The virus doesn't pose any threat to human health.* □ + *to These actions are a threat to international peace.* (**apresentar uma ameaça**)

3 the possibility that something bad might happen □ **+ of** *There's a threat of serious flooding.* (ameaça)

• **threaten** /ˈθretən/ VERB [threatens, threatening, threatened]
1 to say that someone will be harmed or hurt, especially if they do not do something □ *His wife was threatened with a knife.* □ **+ to do something** *The kidnappers have threatened to kill the hostages.* (ameaçar)
2 to be likely to cause harm or problems □ *Government cuts threaten the future of the service.* (ameaçar)
3 to seem likely to happen □ *The situation threatens to become a global crisis.* (ameaçar)

• **threatening** /ˈθretənɪŋ/ ADJECTIVE likely to hurt you or to cause harm □ *He became aggressive and threatening when the police arrived.* □ *She's been receiving threatening phone calls.* (ameaçador)

• **threateningly** /ˈθretənɪŋli/ ADVERB in a threatening way □ *He moved threateningly towards her.* (ameaçadoramente)

three /θriː/ NUMBER [plural threes] the number 3 (três)

three-dimensional /ˌθriː dɪˈmenʃənəl/ ADJECTIVE a three-dimensional shape is solid and has length, width and height that you can measure □ *a three dimensional model of the building* (tridimensional)

three-point turn /ˌθriː pɔɪnt ˈtɜːn/ NOUN [plural three-point turns] a movement to turn a car round in which you go forward, go back, and go forward again (manobra de três pontos da baliza)

threshold /ˈθreʃhəʊld/ NOUN [plural thresholds]
1 a level at which something starts to happen □ *There has been an increase in the threshold for tax.* □ *He has a high pain threshold.* (limiar)
2 on the threshold of something to be just about to start something new □ *We're on the threshold of incredible advances in technology.* (no limiar/início de)
3 the floor at a door going into a building or a room □ *He crossed the threshold of his new home.* (soleira da porta)

threw /θruː/ PAST TENSE OF **throw** (ver **throw**)

thrift /θrɪft/ NOUN, NO PLURAL the quality of being careful about spending money (economia)

• **thrifty** /ˈθrɪfti/ ADJECTIVE [thriftier, thriftiest] using money and other things carefully, without wasting any (econômico)

thrill /θrɪl/ ▶ VERB [thrills, thrilling, thrilled] to make someone feel excited and very pleased □ *He thrilled the crowd with some dramatic shots.* (emocionar, fazer vibrar)
▶ NOUN [plural thrills] a feeling of excitement and pleasure, or the thing that gives you that feeling □ *She felt a thrill of excitement.* □ *Getting this job was a real thrill.* (emoção, curtição)

• **thrilled** /θrɪld/ ADJECTIVE excited and very pleased about something □ *We're absolutely thrilled about the news.* □ *She's thrilled with the result.* (encantado, vibrante)

• **thriller** /ˈθrɪlə(r)/ NOUN [plural thrillers] a book, film or play with an exciting story, full of danger and frightening events (**suspense**) 🔄 *He stars in a new crime thriller set in New York.* (suspense policial)

• **thrilling** /ˈθrɪlɪŋ/ ADJECTIVE very exciting □ *They played a thrilling match in the final round.* (vibrante)

thrive /θraɪv/ VERB [thrives, thriving, thrived] to grow strong and healthy, or to become successful □ *The business is thriving.* □ *These guys thrive on competition.* (desenvolver(-se))

• **thriving** /ˈθraɪvɪŋ/ ADJECTIVE healthy or successful □ *The area has a thriving tourism industry.* (próspero)

throat /θrəʊt/ NOUN [plural throats]
1 the top part of the tube that goes from your mouth down to your stomach □ *My throat felt dry and I couldn't speak.* □ *He got a piece of food stuck in his throat.* (**garganta, pescoço**) 🔄 *I had a headache and a* **sore throat**. (dor de garganta) 🔄 *The teacher* **cleared her throat**. (limpar a garganta)
2 the front part of your neck □ *He put his hands round her throat.* (pescoço)

throb /θrɒb/ ▶ VERB [throbs, throbbing, throbbed]
1 to make a low sound with a strong rhythm □ *Music throbbed from passing cars.* (pulsar, bater)
2 if part of your body throbs, you feel a strong, regular pain □ *My head was throbbing.* (latejar)
3 if your heart throbs, it beats fast and hard (palpitar)
▶ NOUN [plural throbs] when something throbs □ *the throb of motorcycle engines* (barulho de pulsação/funcionamento)

throes /θrəʊz/ PLURAL NOUN (angústia) **in the throes of something** involved in a difficult or painful situation □ *He was in the throes of a divorce.* (na luta de)

thrombosis /θrɒmˈbəʊsɪs/ NOUN [plural thromboses] a lump of blood that blocks the flow of blood in someone's body, often causing serious illness (trombose)

throne /θrəʊn/ NOUN [plural thrones]
1 a special chair that a king or queen sits on (trono)
2 the throne the position of being a king or queen (**o trono**) 🔄 *The prince's daughter cannot* **take the throne**. (assumir o trono)

throng /θrɒŋ/ ▶ NOUN [plural throngs] a large crowd of people □ *She faced a throng of reporters as she came out.* (multidão)
▶ VERB [throngs, thronging, thronged] to move around in a large crowd □ *Cheering supporters thronged the streets.* (aglomerar-se)

throttle /ˈθrɒtəl/ c NOUN [plural **throttles**] the part of an engine that controls fuel going into the engine (**afogador**)

▶ VERB [**throttles, throttling, throttled**] to hold someone tightly round their neck so they cannot breath (**estrangular**)

through /θruː/ ▶ PREPOSITION

1 from one end or side of something to the other □ *He walked through the door.* □ *The pole fits through this hole.* □ *We walked through the woods.* (**através de**)

2 because of something or using something □ *He lost his home through no fault of his own.* □ *He contacted people through his website.* (**por causa de, através de**)

3 for the whole of a period of time or activity □ *We drove through the night.* □ *We left half way through the film.* □ *She has lived through some terrible events.* (**durante, ao longo de**)

4 if information comes through someone, they tell you about it □ *I heard about the club through a friend.* (**através de**)

5 a US word meaning from one time to another time □ *He's staying with us Monday through Friday.* (**de... até...**)

▶ ADVERB

1 from one end or side of something to the other □ *He opened the hatch and stuck his head through.* □ *There are yellow stains on the ceiling where the water came through.* (**por onde**)

2 connected by telephone (**fazer a ligação**) 🔂 *Can you put me through to the manager, please?* (**passar a ligação**) 🔂 *I tried to ring Molly, but I couldn't get through.* (**fazer a ligação**)

3 talk/think something through to talk/think carefully about something in order to decide what to do (**avaliar cuidadosamente**)

4 soaked/wet through very wet (**encharcado**)

▶ ADJECTIVE

1 a through train does not stop at stations between the place it starts and the place it is going to (**direto**)

2 be through with something an informal phrase meaning to have finished doing or using something □ *Are you through with the paper yet?* (**acabar de**)

throughout /θruːˈaʊt/ ▶ PREPOSITION

1 during a whole period of time □ *It rained throughout June and July.* □ *There will be regular news bulletins throughout the day.* (**durante todo o**)

2 in every part of something □ *They have stores throughout the country.* (**por todo o**)

▶ ADVERB

1 during a whole period of time □ *The show was quite long, but the children behaved themselves throughout.* (**do começo ao fim**)

2 in every part of something □ *It is a spacious apartment, with storage space throughout.* (**em todo o**)

throw /θrəʊ/ ▶ VERB [**throws, throwing, threw, thrown**]

1 to make something move through the air by pushing it with your hand □ *He threw the ball to me.* □ *They were throwing stones into the water.* (**jogar, atirar, lançar**)

2 to put something somewhere very quickly and without care □ *She threw her bag down and rushed to switch on the TV.* □ *I threw a few clothes into a case and set off.* (**jogar**)

3 to move your body or part of your body into a position quickly and with force □ *She threw herself to the floor.* □ *He threw his arms around me.* (**jogar(-se), atirar(-se), lançar(-se)**)

4 to make someone confused □ *The new road signs really threw me.* (**confundir, derrubar**)

5 if someone is thrown into prison, they are put there in a rough way (**atirar, jogar, mandar para**)

6 to put someone in a bad state □ *We were thrown into confusion by his early arrival.* (**lançar**)

⇨ go to **throw** *light* on something, **throw** your *weight* around, **throw** your *weight* behind someone/ something

◆ PHRASAL VERBS **throw something away**
1 to get rid of something you do not want □ *I threw away the rest of the food.* (**jogar fora**)
2 to waste something □ *She threw away her career to follow her boyfriend.* **throw something in** to give a customer something extra for the same price □ *If you buy two duvets, we'll throw in two pillows free.* (**dar de lambuja**) **throw something out** to get rid of something that you do not want □ *I've thrown out all my old college books.* (**livrar-se de, desfazer-se de**) **throw someone out** to force someone to leave a place □ *My parents threw me out when I was seventeen.* (**expulsar**) **throw (something) up** an informal word meaning to vomit (**vomitar**) **throw something up** to cause a particular result □ *The experiments threw up more questions than they answered.* (**resultar**)

▶ NOUN [plural **throws**] an act of throwing something □ *That was a great throw!* (**lance, lançamento**)

throwaway /ˈθrəʊəˌweɪ/ ADJECTIVE
1 intended to be thrown away after use □ *a throwaway lighter* (**descartável**)
2 a throwaway remark or act is said or done without thinking carefully □ *It was just a stupid throwaway remark.* (**descartável**)

thrush /θrʌʃ/ NOUN [plural **thrushes**] a wild bird with brown feathers and a front with spots (**tordo**)

thrust /θrʌst/ ▶ VERB [**thrusts, thrusting, thrust**] to push something somewhere quickly and with force □ *He thrust his hands into his coat pockets.* □ *Someone thrust a microphone at him.* (**enfiar, investir(-se)**)

◆ PHRASAL VERB **thrust something on/upon someone** to suddenly make someone deal with something □ *The responsibility had been thrust on him.* (**impor-se**)

▶ NOUN [plural **thrusts**]

1 a quick and forceful push forward □ *He died from a single knife thrust.* (**investida, ataque**)

2 the thrust of something the main idea in what someone says or writes □ *The main thrust of his argument was that the policy is unfair.* (**a ideia principal, a tônica**)

thud /θʌd/ ▶ NOUN [plural **thuds**] a sound made by something heavy falling or hitting something □ *He landed with a loud thud.* (**baque, batida**)
▶ VERB [**thuds, thudding, thudded**] to make a thud □ *Waves thudded against the shore.* (**baquear, bater**)

thug /θʌg/ NOUN [plural **thugs**] a violent man □ *a gang of thugs* (**brigão**)

thumb /θʌm/ ▶ NOUN [plural **thumbs**] the short, thick finger that is on the side of your hand □ *He injured his right thumb.* □ *She held it carefully between her thumb and forefinger.* (**polegar**)
♦ IDIOMS **a rule of thumb** a simple, general rule that you can follow to do something (**uma regra prática**) 🔁 *As a rule of thumb, use double the amount of flour to butter.* (**como regra prática**)
stick/stand out like a sore thumb to be very noticeable because of being different from the other people or things around □ *With her blonde hair, she stuck out like a sore thumb.* (**ser facilmente notado/diferenciado**) **the thumbs up** when someone says that they like something 🔁 *The show got the thumbs up from critics.* (**sinal de positivo feito com o polegar**) **under someone's thumb** completely controlled by someone else □ *He's entirely under her thumb.* (**sob o domínio de alguém**)
▶ VERB [**thumbs, thumbing, thumbed**] **thumb a lift/ride** to stand by the road and hold your hand out to ask cars to stop and take you somewhere (**pedir carona**)
♦ PHRASAL VERB **thumb through something** to read something, looking quickly through the pages □ *She sat thumbing through a glossy magazine.* (**folhear com os dedos**)

thump /θʌmp/ ▶ VERB [**thumps, thumping, thumped**] (**bater**)

1 to hit someone or something hard, usually with your hand □ *He thumped the table for emphasis.* (**bater fortemente**)

2 if your heart thumps, it beats very hard or quickly □ *My heart was thumping.* (**bater forte ou apressadamente**)

3 to fall or hit something with a loud, heavy noise □ *Their feet thumped on the wooden floor.* (**bater com forte barulho**)
▶ NOUN [plural **thumps**]

1 a loud, heavy noise □ *It fell to the floor with a loud thump.* (**pancada**)

2 when you hit someone or something hard □ *She gave him a thump on the nose.* (**pancada**)

thunder /ˈθʌndə(r)/ ▶ NOUN, NO PLURAL

1 the loud, deep sound that you hear in a storm after a flash of lightning (= bright light in the sky) (**trovão, trovoada**) 🔁 *thunder and lightning* (**trovão e relâmpago**) 🔁 *There was a loud clap of thunder.* (**estrondo de trovão**)

2 a loud sound like thunder □ *the thunder of horses' hooves* (**estrondo**)
▶ VERB [**thunders, thundering, thundered**]

1 if it is thundering, there is a storm with thunder (**trovejar**)

2 to make a loud sound like thunder □ *The children thundered up the stairs.* (**estrondear**)

3 to talk in a very loud, angry voice □ *'What are you doing?' thundered Morris.* (**esbravejar**)

thunderbolt /ˈθʌndəbəʊlt/ NOUN [plural **thunderbolts**] a flash of lightning (= bright light in the sky) that is followed immediately by thunder (**raio**)

thunderclap /ˈθʌndəklæp/ NOUN [plural **thunderclaps**] a sudden loud noise made by thunder (**estrondo do trovão**)

thunderous /ˈθʌndərəs/ ADJECTIVE very loud, like thunder □ *thunderous applause* (**tonitruante, ensurdecedor**)

thunderstorm /ˈθʌndəstɔːm/ NOUN [plural **thunderstorms**] a storm with thunder and lightning (= bright light in the sky) □ *Thunderstorms were forecast for the afternoon.* □ *We arrived in the middle of a thunderstorm.* (**tempestade com trovões**)

thundery /ˈθʌndəri/ ADJECTIVE if the weather is thundery, there is or is likely to be thunder □ *The forecast is for thundery showers.* (**estrondoso, tempestuoso**)

Thursday /ˈθɜːzdɪ/ NOUN [plural **Thursdays**] the day of the week after Wednesday and before Friday □ *My piano lessons are on Thursday.* (**quinta-feira**)

thus /ðʌs/ ADVERB

1 a formal word meaning as a result of that □ *The drug thins the blood, thus preventing clotting.* (**consequentemente**)

2 a formal word meaning in this or that way □ *The poem begins thus: 'I must go down to the sea again.'* (**assim, desse modo**)

3 thus far a formal phrase meaning until now □ *Thus far, the agreement seems to be working.* (**até agora**)

thwart /θwɔːt/ VERB [**thwarts, thwarting, thwarted**] to prevent someone from doing what they want to do □ *Police thwarted a car bomb attack.* (**impedir**)

thy /ðaɪ/ DETERMINER an old-fashioned word for **your** □ *Thy will be done.* (**teu**)

thyme /taɪm/ NOUN, NO PLURAL a herb using in cooking with lots of very small leaves and flowers (**tomilho**)

thyroid /ˈθaɪrɔɪd/ NOUN [plural **thyroids**] an organ in your neck that produces a substance

tiara ... which controls how your body grows and works. A biology word (**tireoide**) 🔁 *the thyroid gland* (**glândula tireoide**)

tiara /tɪˈɑːrə/ NOUN [plural **tiaras**] a piece of jewellery like a small crown (**tiara**)

tick /tɪk/ ▶ NOUN [plural **ticks**] (**tiques, tique-taques**)
1 a small written mark (✓) used to show that something is correct or to show which things on a list have been dealt with (**tique**) 🔁 *He put a tick in the box marked 'No'.* □ *The girl put a tick next to her name.* (**faça um tique**)
2 the regular noise that a clock makes □ + *of* / *could hear the tick of the clock in the hall.* (**tique-taque**)
3 an informal word meaning a very short time □ *Can you wait a tick while I get my coat?* (**um instante**)
4 a small insect that sucks the blood of animals (**carrapato**)
▶ VERB [**ticks, ticking, ticked**]
1 to write a tick (**ticar**) 🔁 *You just tick the boxes.* (**selecione os quadrinhos**)
2 to make a regular noise like a clock □ *a ticking clock* (**tiquetaquear**)
◆ IDIOM **what makes someone tick** what causes someone to behave the way they do □ *I don't understand what makes her tick.* (**o que motiva alguém a agir assim**)
◆ PHRASAL VERBS **tick away/by/down** used to say that time is passing □ *Time was ticking away fast.* □ *The clock is ticking down to Monday's deadline.* (**voar**) **tick something off** to write a tick next to something to show it has been dealt with □ *She ticked off the names on the list.* (**ticar**) **tick someone off** an informal phrase meaning to talk to someone angrily because they have done something wrong □ *He ticked off the boys for throwing stones.* (**dar bronca em**) **tick over 1** to continue or to work in a slow, regular way □ *The business is ticking over nicely.* (**funciona lenta e regularmente**) **2** if an engine is ticking over, it is working slowly while the vehicle is stopped (**funcionar em marcha lenta**)

ticket /ˈtɪkɪt/ NOUN [plural **tickets**]
1 a small piece of printed paper that shows you have paid to do something (**bilhete, passagem**) 🔁 *She bought an airline ticket to Paris.* (**passagem de avião**) 🔁 *a single/return ticket* (**bilhete único/de ida e volta**) □ + *for He's got free tickets for the match.*
2 an official notice saying that you have done something wrong while driving □ *a parking ticket* (**notificação de infração**)
• **ticketing** /ˈtɪkɪtɪŋ/ NOUN, NO PLURAL producing and selling tickets (**produção e venda de bilhetes**)

tickle /ˈtɪkəl/ ▶ VERB [**tickles, tickling, tickled**]
1 to touch someone's body lightly so that they laugh □ *She tickled him under the arms.* (**fazer cócegas**)
2 if something tickles you, it causes an uncomfortable, light feeling on your skin □ *The grass tickled her nose.* (**coçar**)
3 to make someone feel pleased or to make them laugh □ *She was tickled by the suggestion.* (**divertir-se**)
▶ NOUN [plural **tickles**] when something or someone tickles you (**cócega**)
• **ticklish** /ˈtɪklɪʃ/ ADJECTIVE if you are ticklish, you laugh when someone tickles you (**coceguento**)
• **tickly** /ˈtɪkli/ ADJECTIVE [**ticklier, tickliest**] causing a tickling feeling (**que faz cócegas**)

tidal /ˈtaɪdəl/ ADJECTIVE to do with tides (= the rise and fall of the sea) □ *a tidal current* (**de maré**)

tidal wave /ˈtaɪdəl weɪv/ NOUN [plural **tidal waves**]
1 a very large wave that sometimes comes up onto the land (**maremoto**)
2 a very large amount of something that arrives suddenly □ *There was a tidal wave of criticism.* (**onda brusca**)

tiddlywinks /ˈtɪdliwɪŋks/ NOUN, NO PLURAL a game in which you press a small coloured disc down on another one making it jump upwards and fall into a cup (**jogo de fazer saltar fichas dentro de uma caneca**)

tide /taɪd/ NOUN [plural **tides**]
1 the regular rise and fall of the level of the sea (**maré**) 🔁 *At high tide, the rocks are completely covered.* (**maré alta**) 🔁 *You can walk out to the island at low tide.* (**maré baixa**)
2 an increase in the number or amount of something □ *the rising tide of crime* (**maré**) 🔁 *We need measures to stem the tide* (= stop the increase) *of people leaving the country.* (**estancar a maré**)
3 the way that most people think or behave (**tendência**) 🔁 *He's trying to turn the tide of public opinion.* (**mudar a tendência**)
◆ PHRASAL VERB [**tides, tiding, tided**] **tide someone over** to help someone get through a difficult time, especially by providing money □ *She had just enough to tide her over until she could get another job.* (**ajudar a superar uma situação**)

tidily /ˈtaɪdɪli/ ADVERB in a tidy way □ *They stacked the boxes tidily.* □ *She tied her hair back tidily.* (**ordenadamente**)

tidiness /ˈtaɪdinɪs/ NOUN, NO PLURAL the quality of being tidy (**ordem**)

tidings /ˈtaɪdɪŋz/ PLURAL NOUN an old-fashioned word for **news** □ *glad tidings* (**notícias**)

tidy /ˈtaɪdi/ ▶ ADJECTIVE [**tidier, tidiest**]
1 carefully ordered or arranged with everything in its correct place □ *Everything looked tidy.* (**em ordem, arrumado**) 🔁 *He keeps his room tidy.* (**mantém seu quarto arrumado**)
2 a tidy person likes to keep things ordered and in their correct place □ *She's the tidiest person I know.* (**organizado**)

3 an informal word used to talk about a large amount of money (razoável) 🔲 *She's saved a tidy sum.* (soma razoável) 🔲 *The event will make a tidy profit.* (lucro razoável)

▶ VERB [**tidies, tidying, tidied**] to put things back in their correct places and to make something tidy ☐ *Anne was tidying the kitchen.* ☐ **+ up** *Are you going to tidy up the mess you've made?* ☐ **+ away** *He tidied away his tools.* (arrumar)

tie /taɪ/ ▶ VERB [**ties, tying, tied**]

1 to join or to fasten things together using string, rope, etc. ☐ **+ together** *We tied the boats together.* ☐ **+ with** *a gift box tied with white ribbon* ☐ **+ to** *The riders tied their horses to a tree.* ☐ *She tied her long hair in a ponytail.* ☐ *Their hands were tied behind their backs.* (amarrar)

2 to twist pieces of rope, string, etc. together to make a knot (amarrar) 🔲 *Tie a knot in the end of the thread.* ☐ *He bent down to tie his shoe lace.* ☐ **+ around** *She had a silk scarf tied around her neck.*

3 if two teams or players tie, they each have the same number of points ☐ **+ for** *They tied for second place.* (empatar) 🔲 *He came back to tie the score at 3-3.* (empatar)

4 if two things are tied, they are connected, often in a way that cannot be changed ☐ **+ with** *Researchers have tied ocean heating directly with global warming.* ☐ **+ into** *Customers will be tied into an 18-month contract.* (amarrar, comprometer, ligar)

◆ IDIOM **tie the knot** an informal phrase meaning to get married ☐ *The couple plan to tie the knot next summer.* (casar-se)

◆ PHRASAL VERBS **tie someone down** to limit someone's freedom ☐ *You're tied down by rules and regulations.* (limitar) **tie in with something 1** to fit well with something ☐ *Her visit will tie in nicely with our plans.* (conectar, combinar) **2** to provide more proof of something ☐ *That ties in with what we've found.* (conectar, combinar) **tie someone/something up 1** to fasten someone or something with rope, etc. so that they cannot move ☐ *The boat's tied up in the harbour.* ☐ *The kidnappers tied them both up.* (amarrar) **2** to keep someone or something busy so that they cannot be used for other things ☐ *This kind of incident ties up police resources.* (ficar, estar ocupado)

▶ NOUN [*plural* **ties**]

1 a narrow piece of cloth worn round your neck under your shirt collar and tied in a knot (gravata) 🔲 *I have to wear a suit and tie for work* ☐ *James loosened his tie.* (terno e gravata)

2 a connection between two people or things ☐ **+ between** *He spoke of the close ties between the two countries.* ☐ **+ with** *She severed all ties with her former coach.* (ligações, laços)

3 a situation in which two teams or players each have the same number of points ☐ **+ for** *There was a tie for third place.* (empate)

tie-break /ˈtaɪbreɪk/ or tie-breaker /ˈtaɪbreɪkə(r)/

NOUN [*plural* **tie-breaks** or **tie-breakers**] an extra question or test that will decide the winner in a competition where two people or teams have the same score (desempate)

tier /tɪə(r)/ NOUN [*plural* **tiers**]

1 one of several rows or layers, one above the other ☐ *a wedding cake with three tiers* ☐ *We had seats in the upper tier of the stadium.* (fileira, camada)

2 one of several layers in a system or an organization ☐ *the top tier of English football* (camada)

tiff /tɪf/ NOUN [*plural* **tiffs**] an informal word for an argument, especially one between friends (desentendimento) 🔲 *He'd had a tiff with his brother.* (ter um desentendimento)

tiger /ˈtaɪɡə(r)/ NOUN [*plural* **tigers**] a large wild animal related to the cat with yellow fur and black stripes (tigre)

tight /taɪt/ ▶ ADJECTIVE [**tighter, tightest**]

1 fitting very closely and difficult to move ☐ *I was wearing very tight jeans.* ☐ *The top on this jar is very tight.* (apertado)

2 very firm and strong ☐ *Have you got a tight grip on that rope?* ☐ *a tight knot* (apertado, firme)

3 if something such as material or string is tight, it has been pulled or stretched so that it is straight ☐ *The piece of wood was held in place by four tight wires.* (esticado)

4 controlled in a firm way ☐ *There are tight regulations about the sale of food.* (rigoroso) 🔲 *Security at the event was extremely tight.* (segurança rigorosa)

5 a tight bend is a part of a road that suddenly curves a lot and is difficult to drive round (fechado, cerrado)

6 if money, time or space is tight, you do not have much of it (apertado) 🔲 *We were on a very tight budget.* (orçamento apertado)

▶ go to **keep a tight rein on something**
▶ ADVERB

1 very firmly (com firmeza) 🔲 *Hold on tight!* (segure firme!) ☐ *Make sure the belt is pulled tight.*

2 sit tight if someone sits tight, they do not move or take any action ☐ *Just sit tight – Mr Jones will be here in a moment.* (sentar-se de modo reto)

• **tighten** /ˈtaɪtn/ VERB [**tightens, tightening, tightened**]

1 to become firmer and stronger or to make something firmer and stronger ☐ *He tightened his grip on my arm.* ☐ *I tightened up the screws.* (apertar)

2 to make something more firmly controlled ☐ *Security was tightened before the parade.* ☐ *The club rules have been tightened up.* (reforçar)

3 to pull something so that it is straighter or fits more closely ☐ *Now you can tighten the rope.* (puxar para prender, firmar)

tight-fisted

tight-fisted /ˌtaɪtˈfɪstɪd/ ADJECTIVE an informal word meaning not willing to spend or to share your money (**pão-duro**)

tightly /ˈtaɪtli/ ADVERB
1 in a firm and strong way ☐ *She held her purse tightly.* ☐ *I pulled the door tightly shut.* (**firmemente**)
2 in a firmly controlled way ☐ *Access to the stage door is tightly controlled.* (**firmemente**)
3 closely ☐ *He wore a tightly fitting shirt.* (**apertadamente**)

tightness /ˈtaɪtnɪs/ NOUN, NO PLURAL the state of feeling or being tight ☐ *He felt some tightness across his chest.* (**aperto, rigor**)

tightrope /ˈtaɪtrəʊp/ NOUN [*plural* **tightropes**] a long piece of rope stretched tightly between two places, which someone walks along (**corda bamba**)

tights /taɪts/ PLURAL NOUN a piece of women's clothing covering the feet, legs and bottom made of very thin material (**meia-calça, malha de ginástica, colante**) ▣ *a pair of tights*

tigress /ˈtaɪɡrɪs/ NOUN [*plural* **tigresses**] a female tiger (**tigresa**)

tile /taɪl/ ▶ NOUN [*plural* **tiles**] a piece of hard, flat material such as clay or stone, used for covering roofs, walls or floors ☐ *red roof tiles* ☐ *shiny ceramic floor tiles* (**telha, azulejo, ladrilho**)
▶ VERB [**tiles, tiling, tiled**] to fix tiles on a surface (**ladrilhar**)
• **tiled** /taɪld/ ADJECTIVE covered with tiles ☐ *a tiled floor* (**ladrilhado**)

till¹ /tɪl/ PREPOSITION, CONJUNCTION until ☐ *We'll probably stay here till the end.* ☐ *It doesn't get dark till 10 o'clock in the summer.* (**até**)

till² /tɪl/ NOUN [*plural* **tills**] a machine in a shop for counting what customers need to pay for and for putting money in ☐ *She works at a supermarket behind the till.* (**caixa**)

tilt /tɪlt/ VERB [**tilts, tilting, tilted**] to move something so that one side is lower than the other, or to move like this ☐ *He tilted his head to one side.* (**inclinar**)

timber /ˈtɪmbə(r)/ NOUN [*plural* **timbers**]
1 wood that is used for building things such as houses, or a piece of this wood (**madeira**)
2 trees that can be used to provide wood for building (**floresta**)

timbre /ˈtæmbrə, ˈtɪmbə(r)/ NOUN [*plural* **timbres**] the quality of sound that something makes ☐ *The timbre of his voice changed.* (**timbre**)

time /taɪm/ ▶ NOUN [*plural* **times**]
1 *no plural* the way we measure minutes, hours, days, etc. ☐ *I was hardly aware of time passing.* (**tempo**)
2 a particular moment in a day ☐ *What's the time?* ☐ *What would be a convenient time to meet?* (**hora**) ▣ *What time does the show start?*

time-consuming

(*Que hora?*) ▣ *Excuse me, have you got the time* (= can you tell me what time it is)? (**tem horas?**) ▣ *Can Dina tell the time* (= be able to read a clock) yet? (**dizer as horas**)
3 *no plural* an amount of time (**tempo**) ▣ *Do you spend a lot of time in London?* (**passar muito tempo**) ▣ *Ironing sheets is a complete waste of time.* (**perda de tempo**) ▣ *We spent a long time talking about the past.* (**longo tempo**) ▣ *It takes a lot of time to learn a language well.* (**leva tempo**)
4 a particular occasion ☐ *Do you remember the time Michael fell in the river?* ☐ *I've been to Morocco several times.* (**vez**) ▣ *Next time you see Billy, can you remind him he still has my camera?* (**da próxima vez**) ▣ *The first time we met, I thought he was really rude.* (**primeira vez**)
5 *no plural* if it is time to do something or for something to happen, it should be done or happen now ☐ *It's time the children were in bed.* ☐ *Is it time to plant the tomatoes yet?* (**hora de**)
6 in time not too late ☐ *We got there just in time to see the queen.* ☐ *I hope the present arrives in time for his birthday.* (**a tempo**)
7 on time not early or late ☐ *The trains are usually on time.* (**na hora**)
8 a long enough period (**tempo**) ▣ *We don't have time to contact everyone.* (**ter tempo**) ☐ *We can play tennis if there's time later.*
9 an experience, or a period in someone's life (**tempo, época, período**) ▣ *Did you have a nice time in Brighton?* (**tempo bom**) ☐ *I had a dreadful time when the children were young.*
10 all the time (a) continuously ☐ *We monitor our staff all the time.* (b) very often ☐ *I love Crete – we go there all the time.* (**todo o tempo, o tempo todo**)
11 one/two/five, etc. at a time one/two/five etc. on a particular occasion ☐ *He leaped up the steps three at a time.* ☐ *One at a time, we went to the front of the class.* (**um/dois etc. de cada vez**)
12 in a hour's/day's/year's, etc. time after a particular period of time ☐ *The work should be complete in three weeks' time.* (**em um período de uma hora/dias/semanas/anos etc.**)

> ▶ Note that you **have** a good/great, etc. time somewhere. You do not 'spend' a good/great, etc. time somewhere:
> ✓ *We had a great time in Paris.*
> ✗ *We spent a great time in Paris.*

▶ VERB [**times, timing, timed**]
1 to arrange for something to happen at a particular time ☐ *The meeting was timed to coincide with his visit.* (**escolher o momento de, marcar a hora**)
2 to measure how long something takes ☐ *He timed me running a mile.* (**cronometrar**)

time-consuming /ˈtaɪmkənˌsjuːmɪŋ/ ADJECTIVE taking a long time to do ☐ *Doing the washing by hand is very time-consuming.* (**demorado**)

time-honored /ˈtaɪmˌɒnəd/ ADJECTIVE the US spelling of time-honoured (*ver* **time-honoured**)

time-honoured /ˈtaɪmˌɒnəd/ ADJECTIVE a time-honoured tradition is one that has been followed for a long time and is respected (consagrado pelo tempo) ◘ *They celebrated in time-honoured fashion with champagne.* (no costume tradicional)

timeless /ˈtaɪmlɪs/ ADJECTIVE not affected by time or changing fashions ◻ *His novels are timeless.* (atemporal)

time limit /ˈtaɪm ˌlɪmɪt/ NOUN [*plural* **time limits**] a fixed length of time during which something must be done and finished ◻ *a 30-day time limit* (limite de tempo) ◘ *No time limit has been set for this project.* (estabelecer um limite de tempo)

timely /ˈtaɪmli/ ADJECTIVE happening or done at the right time (oportuno) ◘ *This serves as a timely reminder of the importance of preparation.* (lembrança oportuna)

timer /ˈtaɪmə(r)/ NOUN [*plural* **timers**] a device for measuring how long something takes ◻ *a kitchen timer* (marcador de tempo)

times /taɪmz/ PREPOSITION used in mathematics between the numbers you are multiplying ◻ *Two times four is eight.* (vezes)

time scale /ˈtaɪm ˌskeɪl/ NOUN [*plural* **time scales**] the period of time during which an event or process happens ◻ *Evolution happens over a time scale of many thousands of years.* (escala de tempo)

timetable /ˈtaɪmˌteɪbəl/ NOUN [*plural* **timetables**]
1 a list of the times when public vehicles such as trains or buses arrive or leave (horário)
2 a list of the lessons at a school, college, etc. and the times they happen (horário) ◘ *We want to see more practical subjects on the school timetable.* (horário escolar)
3 a plan for when you expect or hope that things will happen ◻ + *for We have set out a clear timetable for reform.* (programação)

time zone /ˈtaɪm ˌzəʊn/ NOUN [*plural* **time zones**] one of the areas that the world is divided into, each of which uses one standard time (fuso horário)

timid /ˈtɪmɪd/ ADJECTIVE nervous, shy and easily frightened ◻ *a timid child* ◻ *a timid smile* (tímido)

• **timidity** /tɪˈmɪdəti/ NOUN, NO PLURAL the quality of being timid (timidez)

• **timidly** /ˈtɪmɪdli/ ADVERB in a timid way ◻ *Oliver raised his hand timidly.* (timidamente)

timing /ˈtaɪmɪŋ/ NOUN, NO PLURAL
1 the ability to choose the right time to do or say something ◻ *All comedians need to learn good timing.* (timing, cronometragem) ◘ *Perfect timing – we were just about to order.* (cronometragem perfeita)
2 the time when something happens ◻ *What was surprising was the timing of the announcement.* (o horário)

timpani /ˈtɪmpəni/ PLURAL NOUN large drums that are usually used in an orchestra (= large group of musicians playing together) (tímpanos, timbales)

tin /tɪn/ NOUN [*plural* **tins**]
1 a closed metal container which food is sold in ◻ + *of a tin of tuna* ◻ *He opened a tin of tomato soup.* (lata)
2 a metal container with a lid, which you store food or other things in ◻ + *of a tin of biscuits* ◻ *a tin of paint* (lata)
3 no plural a soft, silver metal ◻ *the tin roof of the garage* ◻ *a tin bucket* (folha de flandres)

tinder /ˈtɪndə(r)/ NOUN, NO PLURAL small, dry pieces of wood that can be used to light a fire (isca de fogo, gravetos secos)

tinfoil /ˈtɪnfɔɪl/ NOUN, NO PLURAL very thin sheets of metal used for covering food (papel-alumínio)

tinge /tɪndʒ/ NOUN [*plural* **tinges**] a slight amount of something, especially a colour or a feeling ◻ *white with a tinge of pink* ◻ *There was a tinge of sadness in her voice.* (toque)

• **tinged** /tɪndʒd/ ADJECTIVE containing a slight amount of a colour, feeling, etc. ◻ *Her eyes were tinged with red where she had been crying.* (com um toque de)

tingle /ˈtɪŋɡəl/ ▶ VERB [**tingles, tingling, tingled**] to feel a sharp, slightly uncomfortable feeling, especially on your skin ◻ *My face was tingling in the cold night air.* (formigar)
▶ NOUN [*plural* **tingles**] a slight uncomfortable or excited feeling ◻ *I felt a tingle of excitement as the curtain went up.* (formigamento)

tinker /ˈtɪŋkə(r)/ VERB [**tinkers, tinkering, tinkered**] to try to repair or to improve a machine by making small changes ◻ *Phil spends hours tinkering with his motorbike.* (soldar, consertar)

tinkle /ˈtɪŋkəl/ ▶ VERB [**tinkles, tinkling, tinkled**] to make a sound like small bells ringing (tilintar)
▶ NOUN [*plural* **tinkles**] a small, repeated ringing sound (tinindo)

tinned /tɪnd/ ADJECTIVE tinned food is sold and kept in closed metal containers ◻ *tinned soup* (enlatado)

tinnitus /tɪˈnaɪtəs/ NOUN, NO PLURAL a medical condition in which you have a continuous ringing sound in your ears (zumbido no ouvido)

tinny /ˈtɪni/ ADJECTIVE [**tinnier, tinniest**]
1 a tinny sound is thin, hard and high (estridente)
2 a tinny object is made of thin or bad quality metal (de estanho)

tin opener /ˈtɪn ˌəʊpənə(r)/ NOUN [*plural* **tin openers**] a small tool for opening metal containers of food (abridor de lata)

tinsel

tinsel /'tɪnsəl/ NOUN, NO PLURAL long pieces of shiny material that are used as a decoration at Christmas (**enfeite de Natal, feito de lâminas de material brilhante**)

tint /tɪnt/ ▶ NOUN [plural **tints**] a small amount of colour □ *His skin had a yellowish tint.* (**matiz, nuance**)

▶ VERB [**tints, tinting, tinted**] to add a small amount of colour to something (**tingir**)

tiny /'taɪni/ ADJECTIVE [**tinier, tiniest**] extremely small □ *a baby's tiny hands and feet* (**minúsculo**) □ *a tiny amount of water* (**porção minúscula**)

tip /tɪp/ ▶ NOUN [plural **tips**]

1 the point at the end or the top of something □ *They used arrows with poison tips.* □ *Point to it with the tip of your finger.* (**ponta**)

2 a small extra amount of money for someone who has done a job for you (**gorjeta**) □ *Did you leave a tip?* (**deixar uma gorjeta**)

3 a piece of helpful advice □ *He gave me some useful tips on laying floor tiles.* (**sugestão, dica**)

4 a place where you can take things you want to get rid of □ *I'm going to take the old carpet to the tip.* (**depósito de lixo**)

5 an informal word meaning a very untidy place □ *Your bedroom's a tip.* (**depósito de lixo**)

♦ IDIOMS **the tip of the iceberg** a small part of something, especially a serious problem □ *We have seen six cases of the disease at our clinic, and that's just the tip of the iceberg.* (**a ponta do iceberg**) **on the tip of your tongue** if a word is on the tip of your tongue, you cannot remember it but you feel that you are almost able to remember it (**na ponta da língua**)

▶ VERB [**tips, tipping, tipped**]

1 to move something so that it is not flat or vertical, or to move in this way □ *Tip the chairs forward against the tables.* □ *The vehicle tipped onto its side.* (**inclinar**)

2 to pour something from a container □ *They just tip the rubbish over the side of the ship.* □ *She tipped a bucket of water on my head.* (**despejar**)

3 to give a small extra amount of money to someone who has done a job for you □ *She tipped the taxi driver.* (**dar uma gorjeta**)

♦ PHRASAL VERBS **tip someone off** to give someone a warning or some information, often secretly, so that they can prepare for something □ *His friends tipped him off before the police arrived.* (**avisar, dar uma informação**) **tip (something) over** to push something onto its side or to fall on one side □ *She tipped her drink over.* **tip something up** to move a container so that things come out of it more easily (**virar, tombar**)

tiptoe /'tɪptəʊ/ ▶ VERB [**tiptoes, tiptoeing, tiptoed**] to walk somewhere very quietly or carefully on your toes □ *She tiptoed along the corridor, trying not to wake the other guests.* (**andar na ponta dos pés**)

▶ NOUN **on tiptoe** standing or walking balanced on your toes □ *I can just see the sea if I stand on tiptoe.* (**ponta dos pés**)

tirade /taɪ'reɪd/ NOUN [plural **tirades**] a long angry speech that criticizes someone or something □ *She launched into a long tirade against the government.* (**longo discurso de crítica**)

tire /taɪə(r)/ VERB [**tires, tiring, tired**] to start feeling that you need a rest □ *Grandma tires easily nowadays.* (**cansar(-se)**)

♦ PHRASAL VERBS **tire of something** to become bored with something □ *We were beginning to tire of Nigel's stories.* (**cansar-se de**) **tire someone out** to make someone feel tired □ *Let's go to the park and tire the children out a bit.* (**esgotar**)

• **tired** /taɪəd/ ADJECTIVE

1 feeling that you need a rest □ *You must be tired after your journey.* (**cansado**) □ *I was getting really tired.* (**ficar cansado**) □ *He felt too tired and ill to continue.* (**sentir-se cansado**)

2 bored and often annoyed □ + *of I'm tired of wearing the same clothes every day.* (**cansado, farto**) □ *I'm sick and tired of people asking me questions.* (**farto de**)

• **tiredness** /'taɪədnɪs/ NOUN, NO PLURAL the state of being tired □ *Tiredness is the main symptom of this virus.* (**cansaço**)

• **tireless** /'taɪəlɪs/ ADJECTIVE having a lot of energy and always continuing with something □ *He was a tireless campaigner for social justice.* □ *We admired her tireless efforts to raise money for charity.* (**incansável**)

• **tirelessly** /'taɪəlɪsli/ ADVERB in a tireless way □ *They worked tirelessly for the cause.* (**incansavelmente**)

• **tiresome** /'taɪəsəm/ ADJECTIVE annoying or boring □ *Mona has a tiresome habit of finishing my sentences for me.* (**cansativo**)

• **tiring** /'taɪərɪŋ/ ADJECTIVE making you feel tired □ *It was a long and tiring trip.* (**cansativo**)

> Notice the different meanings of **tiresome** and **tiring**. Tiresome means 'annoying'. It does not mean 'making you tired'. For this meaning, use the word 'tiring':
> ✓ *Travelling is fun but it's tiring.*
> ✗ *Travelling is fun but it's tiresome.*

tissue /'tɪʃuː/ NOUN [plural **tissues**]

1 the substance that animals and plants are made of. A biology word □ *muscle tissue* □ *plant tissue* (**tecido**)

2 a thin, soft piece of paper for cleaning your nose, etc. □ *She took out a tissue to wipe her face.* (**lenço de papel**)

3 very thin paper used for wrapping objects □ *a sheet of white tissue* (**papel de seda**) □ *The* *glasses were wrapped in tissue paper.* (papel de seda)

tit /tɪt/ NOUN [plural **tits**] a type of small bird (chapim)

titbit /'tɪtbɪt/ NOUN [plural **titbits**]
1 a small piece of food (petisco)
2 a small but interesting piece of information (fofoca) □ *a titbit of gossip* (uma fofoca apetitosa)

title /'taɪtəl/ ▶ NOUN [plural **titles**]
1 the name of something such as a book, song or film □ + *of What's the title of your poem?* □ *How did you choose the book's title?* (título)
2 the position of being the winner of a sports competition (título) ⮕ *She won her first grand slam title last year.* (ganhou um título) □ *He's hoping to defend his Olympic 100-metre title.*
3 a word that you can use before your name, for example Ms or Professor □ *Her title is 'Doctor', not 'Mrs'.* (título)
▶ VERB [**titles, titling, titled**] to give something a title □ *My new book is titled 'Missing'.* (entitular)

titter /'tɪtə(r)/ ▶ VERB [**titters, tittering, tittered**] to laugh in a silly, nervous or embarrassed way (rir nervosamente)
▶ NOUN [plural **titters**] a silly, nervous laugh (risinho nervoso)

to /tuː/
1 used before a verb to make the infinitive form □ *I want to leave now.* □ *I forgot to tell him.* (indica o tempo verbal infinitivo)
2 used as part of the infinitive to show the purpose of something □ *I went to get a drink.* □ *I phoned her to invite her to the party.* (para (introduzindo o infinitivo))
▶ PREPOSITION
1 used to say where someone or something goes □ *We went to the shops.* □ *I go to work by bus.* □ *The cup fell to the floor.* (para, a, em)
2 used to say who is given something, told something, etc. □ *Give the letter to Clara.* □ *I spoke to her several times.* (para, com)
3 connected or fixed □ *The cake was stuck to the tin.* □ *We nailed the chairs to the floor.* (a)
4 facing or going in a particular direction □ *He had his back to me.* □ *Keep to the side of the woods.* □ *He pointed to the sign.* (para)
5 used to say how someone's actions affect someone or something □ *He was always kind to me.* □ *What have you done to my car?* (para, a)
6 from ... to (a) used to show a period of time □ *We are open from 9 to 6.* (b) used to show a range of something □ *Everyone was there, from young to old.* (de... até)
7 used for saying the time up to thirty minutes before an hour □ *It's ten to three.* (para)
▶ ADVERB
1 almost closed □ *Would you pull the door to?* (quase fechado, encostado)

2 to and fro backwards and forwards □ *He was rocking to and fro.* (em vaivém)

toad /təʊd/ NOUN [plural **toads**] a small brown animal that jumps using its long back legs (sapo)

toadstool /'təʊdstuːl/ NOUN [plural **toadstools**] a type of fungus (= plant with no leaves or flowers) that is often poisonous (cogumelo)

toast /təʊst/ ▶ NOUN [plural **toasts**]
1 bread that has been made hard and slightly brown by heating □ *I had toast and marmalade for breakfast.* (torrada) ⮕ *a piece of toast* (uma fatia de torrada)
2 when people lift their glasses and drink together to express good wishes to someone (brinde) ⮕ *I'd like to propose a toast to the bride and groom.* (propor um brinde)
▶ VERB [**toasts, toasting, toasted**]
1 to cook bread under a heat □ *a toasted sandwich* (tostar)
2 to drink a toast to someone □ *They were soon toasting their success.* (brindar)
• **toaster** /'təʊstə(r)/ NOUN [plural **toasters**] a machine for making toast (torradeira)

tobacco /tə'bækəʊ/ NOUN, NO PLURAL the leaves of a plant that are dried and used for smoking □ *tobacco smoke* □ *the tobacco industry* (tabaco)
• **tobacconist** /tə'bækənɪst/ NOUN [plural **tobacconists**]
1 someone whose job is selling tobacco products (negociante de tabaco)
2 tobacconist's a shop that sells tobacco products and sometimes sweets and newspapers (tabacaria)

toboggan /tə'bɒɡən/ NOUN [plural **toboggans**] a simple vehicle without wheels that you sit on to slide across snow (tobogã)

today /tə'deɪ/ ▶ ADVERB
1 on this day □ *I can't come today.* (hoje) ⮕ *I spoke to Alan earlier today.* (hoje cedo) ⮕ *My parents are coming over later today.* (hoje mais tarde)
2 at or around the present time □ *People are taller today than they were a hundred years ago.* (hoje)
▶ NOUN, NO PLURAL this day □ *Today is Tuesday.* □ *Today's announcement comes as no surprise.* (hoje)

toddle /'tɒdəl/ VERB [**toddles, toddling, toddled**]
1 if a young child toddles, it is learning to walk □ *She's just starting to toddle.* (andar vacilante)
2 an informal word meaning to walk somewhere □ *Then she toddled off to bed.* (caminhar em direção a)
• **toddler** /'tɒdlə(r)/ NOUN [plural **toddlers**] a young child who is learning to walk □ *The children range from toddlers to young teens.* □ *a mother and toddler group* (criança pequena)

toe /təʊ/ NOUN [plural **toes**]

1 one of the five parts at the end of your foot □ *Reach up high, standing on your toes.* (**dedo do pé**) ▣ *He injured his left big toe.* (**dedão**) ▣ *She stubbed* (= hit) *her toe on the end of the bed.* (**bateu seu dedo do pé**)

2 the closed end of a shoe or sock □ *a hole in the toe of my sock* (**biqueira**)

toenail /'təʊneɪl/ NOUN [plural **toenails**] the hard part at the end of each toe (**unha do pé**)

toffee /'tɒfi/ NOUN [plural **toffees**] a hard, sticky sweet made of boiled butter and sugar □ *a piece of toffee* □ *a bag of toffees* (**caramelo**)

tog /tɒg/ NOUN [plural **togs**] a measurement of how warm a duvet (= bed cover) is □ *a 10.5 tog duvet* (**medida de aquecimento de um edredom**)

together /tə'geðə(r)/ ADVERB

1 with or near each other □ *We work together.* □ *They spent the evening together watching television.* (**junto**) ▣ *The houses are quite close together.* (**bem juntos**)

2 touching, joined or mixed with each other □ *Mix the sugar and eggs together in a bowl.* □ *She pressed her hands together.* □ *Add all the numbers together.* (**junto**)

3 at the same time □ *All these things happened together.* (**juntamente, ao mesmo tempo**)

4 together with as well as or including □ *Keep the fruit, together with its juice, in the refrigerator.* (**junto com**)

toggle /'tɒgəl/ ▶ NOUN [plural **toggles**]

1 a key on a computer that allows you to move between any documents or programs that you are using. A computing word. (**alternador**)

2 a piece of wood or plastic that passes through a hole to fasten a coat or jacket (**fecho**)

▶ VERB [**toggles, toggling, toggled**] to move from one document or program to another by pressing a key. A computing word. (**alternar de um documento ou programa a outro**)

toil /tɔɪl/ ▶ VERB [**toils, toiling, toiled**] a formal word meaning to work hard for a long time □ *Farm workers toiled in the fields.* (**labutar**)

▶ NOUN, NO PLURAL a formal word meaning hard work (**labuta**)

toilet /'tɔɪlɪt/ NOUN [plural **toilets**]

1 a large bowl that you sit on to get rid of waste from your body (**vaso sanitário**) ▣ *I need to go to the toilet.* (**usar o vaso sanitário**) ▣ *He flushed the toilet and washed his hands in the sink.* (**dar descarga**)

2 a room with a toilet in it (**toalete**) ▣ *a public toilet* (**banheiro público**) □ *Excuse me, where are the ladies' toilets?*

toilet paper /'tɔɪlɪt ˌpeɪpə(r)/ NOUN, NO PLURAL thin, soft paper used for cleaning the body after using the toilet (**papel higiênico**)

toiletries /'tɔɪlɪtriz/ PLURAL NOUN products that you use to keep clean and to look and smell nice □ *She packed a toothbrush and toothpaste and a few other toiletries.* (**produtos de perfumaria**)

toilet roll /'tɔɪlɪt ˌrəʊl/ NOUN [plural **toilet rolls**] a roll of toilet paper (**rolo de papel higiênico**)

token /'təʊkən/ NOUN [plural **tokens**]

1 a plastic or metal disc used in a machine instead of money □ *You need to buy special tokens for the coffee machine.* (**ficha**)

2 a piece of paper that you can use instead of money (**vale**) ▣ *a book token worth £10* (**vale livro**) □ *Just collect the tokens to get a free gift.*

3 a sign or a symbol of something (**símbolo, sinal**) ▣ *Please accept this gift as a token of our thanks for all your hard work.* (**como um símbolo**)

told /təʊld/ PAST TENSE AND PAST PARTICIPLE OF **tell** (*ver* **tell**)

tolerable /'tɒlərəbəl/ ADJECTIVE

1 if something is tolerable, it is slightly unpleasant, but you are willing to accept it □ *Air conditioning makes the summer heat more tolerable.* (**tolerável**)

2 acceptable but not very good (**tolerável**)

• **tolerably** /'tɒlərəbli/ ADVERB in a way that is acceptable but not very good □ *The system works tolerably well.* (**regularmente**)

tolerance /'tɒlərəns/ NOUN, NO PLURAL

1 when you are willing to accept other people's ideas and behaviour, even when they are different from yours □ *Everyone needs to show tolerance.* (**tolerância**) ▣ *His speech was about religious tolerance.* (**tolerância religiosa**)

2 the ability to experience something without serious bad effects □ *She had a very low tolerance for pain.* □ *We need crops with drought tolerance.* (**tolerância**)

• **tolerant** /'tɒlərənt/ ADJECTIVE

1 showing tolerance towards different people □ *He's tolerant of different views and lifestyles.* (**tolerante**)

2 able to experience something without serious bad effects □ *Some plants are more tolerant of low temperatures.* (**tolerante**)

• **tolerate** /'tɒləreɪt/ VERB [**tolerates, tolerating, tolerated**]

1 to accept something even if you do not like it or agree with it □ *I can't tolerate this noise for much longer.* □ *We will not tolerate aggressive behaviour.* (**tolerar**)

2 to be able to experience something without serious bad effects □ *Older patients are less able to tolerate chemotherapy.* (**tolerar**)

toll /təʊl/ ▶ NOUN [plural **tolls**]

1 money you pay to cross a bridge or to use a road □ *a toll road* (**pedágio**)

2 the number of people killed or injured, or the damage caused in a bad accident or event (**perda**) ▣ *The death toll was highest in the city centre.* (**perda de vidas**)

3 take a/its toll (on someone/something) to have a bad effect on someone or something □ *The heavy workload has taken its toll on her.* (deixou marcas)
▶ VERB [**tolls, tolling, tolled**] if a bell tolls, it rings slowly (soar, dobrar o sino)

tomato /tə'mɑːtəʊ/ NOUN [plural **tomatoes**] a soft, red fruit with a lot of juice that is used like a vegetable in salads, sauces, etc. □ *pasta with tomato sauce* □ *a cheese and tomato sandwich* (tomate)

tomb /tuːm/ NOUN [plural **tombs**] a place where a dead body is buried, often with a stone structure (túmulo)

tombola /tɒm'bəʊlə/ NOUN [plural **tombolas**] a game of luck where people choose numbered tickets, some of which win prizes (tômbola)

tomboy /'tɒmbɔɪ/ NOUN [plural **tomboys**] a girl who likes energetic activities that boys usually enjoy (moleca)

tombstone /'tuːmstəʊn/ NOUN [plural **tombstones**] a piece of stone with a dead person's name written on it at the end of a grave (lápide)

tomcat /'tɒmkæt/ NOUN [plural **tomcats**] a male cat (gato macho)

tomorrow /tə'mɒrəʊ/ ▶ NOUN, NO PLURAL
1 the day after today □ *Tomorrow is Wednesday.* (amanhã) □ *He's arriving early tomorrow morning.* (amanhã de manhã) □ *Will he be fit for the game tomorrow night?* (amanhã à noite) □ *I'll be back the day after tomorrow.* (depois de amanhã)
2 the future □ *Today's children are tomorrow's taxpayers.* (amanhã)
▶ ADVERB on the day after today □ *Let's have our meeting tomorrow.* □ *We'll be here tomorrow.* (amanhã)

ton /tʌn/ NOUN [plural **tons**]
1 a unit for measuring weight, equal to 2240 pounds in Britain or 2000 pounds in America □ *a truck carrying 60 tons of coal* (tonelada)
2 tons of an informal phrase meaning a lot of something □ *She's got tons of clothes to choose from.* □ *I've got tons of things to do.* (montes de)

tone /təʊn/ ▶ NOUN [plural **tones**]
1 the quality of a sound or of someone's voice (tom) □ *I could tell she was angry from her tone of voice.* (tom de voz) □ *a cello with a soft gentle tone*
2 the general feeling or atmosphere of a situation (tom) □ *His enthusiasm set the tone for the evening.* (dar o tom de)
3 a sound made by a machine, such as a telephone (toque) □ *a mobile phone ring tone* (toque de chamada)
4 a particular type of colour □ *several tones of blue* (tom)
▶ VERB [**tones, toning, toned**]

1 to do exercises to make part of your body more healthy, stronger, etc. □ *It's a great way to tone your legs.* (tonificar)
2 to look good with something of a different colour □ *The red scarf tones in with the plum--coloured coat.* (combinar)
◆ PHRASAL VERB **tone something down** to make something less strong, less offensive, etc. □ *He had to tone down his language with young children around.* (abrandar, atenuar)

tone-deaf /'təʊn'def/ ADJECTIVE not able to hear the difference between different musical notes (sem ouvido tonal)

tongs /tɒŋz/ PLURAL NOUN a tool with two long parts that are joined at one end, which you press together to pick something up (pinça)

tongue /tʌŋ/ NOUN [plural **tongues**]
1 the soft part inside your mouth that you can move and that you use to speak, eat and taste □ *He ran his tongue across his teeth.* (língua) □ *Tim stuck his tongue out at me.* (mostrar a língua)
2 a formal word meaning a language (língua) □ *He spoke in his native tongue of Punjabi.* (língua nativa)
3 the piece of leather under the opening of a shoe or boot (língua)
◆ IDIOMS **bite/hold your tongue** to not say something, especially when you want to □ *There are times when I've had to bite my tongue.* (morder, controlar a língua) **tongue in cheek** used to talk about something that someone says as a joke □ *His comments were tongue in cheek.* (ironia)

tongue-tied /'tʌŋtaɪd/ ADJECTIVE too nervous, shy or embarrassed to speak (com a língua presa, envergonhado)

tongue twister /'tʌŋ ˌtwɪstə(r)/ NOUN [plural **tongue twisters**] a phrase or sentence that is difficult to say quickly (trava-línguas)

tonic /'tɒnɪk/ NOUN [plural **tonics**]
1 a clear drink with bubbles in it and a bitter taste □ *a glass of gin and tonic* (tônica)
2 something that makes you feel stronger or gives you energy (tônico)

tonight /tə'naɪt/ ▶ NOUN, NO PLURAL the night or evening of today □ *I'll have to miss tonight's class, I'm afraid.* (hoje à noite)
▶ ADVERB on the night or evening of today □ *I'm going to bed early tonight.* □ *The show is on BBC1 at 9pm tonight.* (nesta noite)

tonne /tʌn/ NOUN [plural **tonnes**] a unit for measuring weight, equal to 1000 kilograms (tonelada)

tonsil /'tɒnsəl/ NOUN [plural **tonsils**] one of the soft parts on either side of the back of your throat. A biology word. (amídala)
• **tonsillitis** /ˌtɒnsɪ'laɪtɪs/ NOUN, NO PLURAL an infection that causes your tonsils to swell and hurt (amidalite)

too /tu:/ ADVERB

1 more than necessary or more than is sensible □ *If the water is too hot, add some cold.* □ *The offer was too good to refuse.* □ *Don't spend too much.* (**demais**) 🔄 *You're driving much too fast!* (**rápido demais**)

2 also □ *Can I come too?* □ *I was really shocked and I think Maria was too.* (**também**)

3 not too an informal phrase meaning 'not very' □ *I hope it's not too serious.* □ *His health is not too good.* (**não muito**)

> Note that if something is **too** heavy/hot/old, etc. it is bad. It means that something is more heavy/ hot/old, etc. than you want it to be □ *It's too heavy – I can't lift it.* □ *The weather is too hot – I like it a bit cooler.*

took /tʊk/ PAST TENSE OF **take** (*ver* **take**)

tool /tu:l/ NOUN [*plural* **tools**]

1 a piece of equipment that you hold in your hand and use to do a particular job □ *a set of gardening tools* (**ferramenta**) 🔄 *Keep a basic tool kit in the car.* (**caixa de ferramentas**)

2 something that helps you to do or to achieve something □ *The guidelines are a useful tool for parents.* (**ferramenta**)

toolbar /'tu:lbɑ:(r)/ NOUN [*plural* **toolbars**] on a computer screen, a row of icons (= small pictures) that shows you all the different things you can do. A computing word. (**barra de ferramentas**)

toot /tu:t/ ▶ VERB [**toots, tooting, tooted**] to toot a horn on a vehicle is to make it sound (**buzinar**)
▶ NOUN [*plural* **toots**] the noise a horn on a vehicle makes (**buzina**)

tooth /tu:θ/ NOUN [*plural* **teeth**]

1 one of the hard, white parts in your mouth that you use for biting □ *He has one front tooth missing.* (**dente**) 🔄 *I brushed my teeth and washed my face.* (**escovar os dentes**) 🔄 *That cat's got sharp teeth.* (**dentes afiados**)

2 one of the row of sharp points that form one side of an object such as a comb (= thing used to tidy hair) (**dente**)

toothache /'tu:θeɪk/ NOUN, NO PLURAL a pain in or around your tooth (**dor de dente**) 🔄 *I had terrible toothache.* □ *He went to the dentist with toothache.* (**ter dor de dente**)

toothbrush /'tu:θbrʌʃ/ NOUN [*plural* **toothbrushes**] a small brush that you use for cleaning your teeth (**escova de dentes**)

toothpaste /'tu:θpeɪst/ NOUN, NO PLURAL a cream that you use to clean your teeth (**pasta de dentes**)

top /tɒp/ ▶ NOUN [*plural* **tops**]

1 the highest point or part of something □ *We climbed to the top of the tower.* □ *They were waiting at the top of the steps.* □ *Start reading at the top of the page.* (**topo, cume, alto, copa**)

2 the top the most successful position (**topo**) 🔄 *He's determined to get to the top of his profession.* (**chegar ao topo**)

3 on (the) top on the upper surface of something □ *I keep his photograph on top of the TV.* □ *I like pizza with lots of olives on top.* (**sobre, em cima, por cima**)

4 the lid or cover of a container □ *Screw the top back on tightly.* (**tampa**)

5 a piece of clothing for the upper half of your body □ *She was wearing green trousers and a black top.* (**blusa**)

◆ IDIOMS **off the top of your head** if you say something off the top of your head, you say the most correct thing you can without checking or thinking carefully □ *I'm not sure how many people were there, but off the top of my head I'd say around 200.* (**de memória**) **at the top of your voice** shouting, singing, etc. as loudly as possible □ *He was yelling at the top of his voice for them to come back.* (**aos gritos**) **over the top** an informal idiom meaning too extreme □ *I know you were angry, but smashing the chair was a bit over the top.* (**demais**)
▶ ADJECTIVE

1 most important or successful □ *Safety is our top priority.* (**primeiro, principal**) 🔄 *He came top in the exam.* □ *a top fashion designer* (**ficou em primeiro**)

2 in the highest part of something (**superior**) 🔄 *My office is on the top floor.* (**andar superior**)
▶ VERB [**tops, topping, topped**]

1 to cover the upper surface of something □ *Top the cake with fruit and whipped cream.* (**tampar, cobrir**)

2 to be more important or successful than other things □ *This album is expected to top the charts next week.* (**ultrapassar**)

3 to be larger than a particular amount □ *Sales of the DVD have topped 2 million.* (**ultrapassar**)

◆ PHRASAL VERBS **top something off** to finish a successful event or activity with something □ *He topped off a fine game with his third goal.* (**finalizar com**) **top (something) up 1** to add more of something to a container that already has something in it □ *Let me top up your drink.* (**completar**) **2** to add more of something so that it reaches a particular level □ *Some restaurant owners use tips to top up waiters' wages.* (**aumentar**)

topaz /'təʊpæz/ NOUN, NO PLURAL a type of valuable stone that is often yellow (**topázio**)

top hat /ˌtɒp 'hæt/ NOUN [*plural* **top hats**] a tall, formal hat with a flat top for men (**cartola**)

topic /'tɒpɪk/ NOUN [*plural* **topics**] a subject to study, write or talk about □ *+ of The storms were the main topic of conversation.* □ *A range of* topics were discussed. □ *Immigration can be a sensitive topic.* (**tópico**)

topical /ˈtɒpɪkəl/ ADJECTIVE to do with things that are happening at the present time (**atual**) *The journal deals with topical issues.* (**questões atuais**) □ *His remarks are highly topical.*

topless /ˈtɒplɪs/ ADJECTIVE without any clothes on the top half of your body (**sem a parte de cima**)

topmost /ˈtɒpməʊst/ ADJECTIVE highest □ *the topmost branches of the tree* (**o mais alto**)

top-notch /ˌtɒpˈnɒtʃ/ ADJECTIVE of excellent quality □ *We ate at a top-notch restaurant.* (**de primeira qualidade**)

topping /ˈtɒpɪŋ/ NOUN [plural **toppings**] food that covers or decorates the top of a dish of food □ *vegetable pie with cheese topping* (**cobertura**)

topple /ˈtɒpəl/ VERB [**topples, toppling, toppled**]
1 to fall over or to make something fall over □ *I knocked into a table and it toppled over.* □ *High winds toppled trees.* (**derrubar, cair**)
2 to make someone lose a position of power □ *The regime was toppled in 1932.* (**derrubar**)

top-secret /ˌtɒpˈsiːkrɪt/ ADJECTIVE very secret and important □ *This is top-secret information.* (**altamente secreto**)

topsy-turvy /ˌtɒpsiˈtɜːvi/ ADJECTIVE, ADVERB an informal word meaning turned upside-down or very confused □ *It's been a bit of a topsy-turvy week.* (**de cabeça para baixo**)

top-up /ˈtɒpʌp/ NOUN [plural **top-ups**]
1 when you put some more of a drink into someone's glass □ *Let me give you a top-up.* (**cobrir, suplementar, encher até o fim**)
2 an amount of money you pay to increase the level of another amount of money □ *a top-up loan*

top-up card /ˈtɒpʌp ˌkɑːd/ NOUN [plural **top-up cards**] a card that you have that allows you to pay money to use your mobile phone (**cartão de celular**)

Torah /ˈtɔːrə/ NOUN, NO PLURAL the holy books of the Jewish religion, especially the first five books of the Jewish Bible (**Torá**)

torch /tɔːtʃ/ ▶ NOUN [plural **torches**]
1 a small electric light that you carry in your hand (**lanterna**) *Someone shone a torch into the tent.* (**acender uma lanterna**)
2 a long stick burning at one end that is carried □ *the Olympic torch* (**tocha**)
▶ VERB [**torches, torching, torched**] an informal word meaning to burn something so that it is destroyed □ *Protesters torched cars.* (**queimar**)

tore /tɔː(r)/ PAST TENSE OF **tear** (*ver* **tear**)

torment ▶ VERB /tɔːˈment/ [**torments, tormenting, tormented**]
1 to treat someone cruelly or to annoy them in an unkind way □ *A gang of youths had been tormenting the family.* (**atormentar**)
2 if you are tormented by something, you suffer for a long time because of it □ *She is still tormented by bad dreams.* (**atormentar**)
▶ NOUN /ˈtɔːment/ [plural **torments**] a formal word meaning very great pain or worry that continues for a long time □ *There were no signs of his inner torment.* (**tormento**)

• **tormentor** /tɔːˈmentə(r)/ NOUN [plural **tormentors**] a person who torments someone (**atormentador**)

torn /tɔːn/ PAST PARTICIPLE OF **tear** (*ver* **tear**)

tornado /tɔːˈneɪdəʊ/ NOUN [plural **tornadoes**] a violent storm with a powerful wind with a circular movement that causes a lot of damage (**tornado**)

torpedo /tɔːˈpiːdəʊ/ C NOUN [plural **torpedoes**] a long thin bomb that moves quickly under water and explodes when it hits the thing it is aimed at (**torpedo**)
▶ VERB [**torpedoes, torpedoing, torpedoed**] to fire a torpedo at something (**torpedear**)

torrent /ˈtɒrənt/ NOUN [plural **torrents**]
1 a lot of water flowing or falling quickly □ *a torrent of water* (**torrente**)
2 a large amount of something unpleasant (**torrente de**) *He was subjected to a torrent of abuse.* (**uma torrente de insultos**)

• **torrential** /təˈrenʃəl/ ADJECTIVE torrential rain is very heavy rain *a day of torrential rain* (**torrencial**)

torso /ˈtɔːsəʊ/ NOUN [plural **torsos**] the main part of your body, not including your arms, legs or head (**torso**)

tortoise /ˈtɔːtəs/ NOUN [plural **tortoises**] an animal that moves slowly and has a hard shell covering its body (**tartaruga**)

torture /ˈtɔːtʃə(r)/ ▶ VERB [**tortures, torturing, tortured**] to hurt someone in a cruel way, usually as a punishment or to get information from them □ *He was interrogated and tortured by his captors.* (**torturar**)
▶ NOUN, NO PLURAL
1 when someone is tortured □ *The European Convention on Human Rights bans all forms of torture.* □ *The men showed signs of torture.* (**tortura**)
2 when something causes suffering □ *Not being able to see her children was torture.* (**tortura**)

• **torturer** /ˈtɔːtʃərə(r)/ NOUN [plural **torturers**] a person who tortures someone (**atormentador**)

Tory /ˈtɔːri/ ▶ NOUN [plural **Tories**] someone who supports or is a member of the Conservative Party in the UK (**conservador**)
▶ ADJECTIVE to do with the Conservative Party □ *Tory policies* □ *Tory councillors* (**conservador**)

toss /tɒs/ ▶ VERB [**tosses, tossing, tossed**]
1 to throw something lightly or without care □ *Toss the keys over here, would you?* □ *He tossed aside the magazine.* (**lançar**)

2 to move repeatedly from side to side (**revirar-se**) ◫ *Alice spent the night tossing and turning restlessly.* (**revirando-se**)

3 to throw a coin up in the air to see which side it falls on, in order to make a choice ◫ *We decided to toss for the front seat.* (**jogar cara ou coroa**) ◫ *Why not just toss a coin?* (**jogar a sorte na moeda**)

4 to mix food, especially so it is covered in a liquid ◫ *Toss the chicken with lemon juice and oil.* (**misturar**)

▶ NOUN, NO PLURAL when you toss a coin to make a choice (**decisão na moeda**) ◫ *It was decided by the toss of a coin.* ◫ *Williams won the toss and chose to serve first.* (**ganhar a sorte/decisão na moeda**)

toss-up /ˈtɒsʌp/ NOUN, NO PLURAL an informal word for a situation in which there are two possible choices which are difficult to decide between ◫ *It was a tossup between Alex and Jon for captain.* (**decisão entre duas escolhas difíceis**)

tot /tɒt/ NOUN [*plural* **tots**]
1 an informal word meaning a small child (**criança pequena**)
2 a small glass of a strong alcoholic drink (**dose pequena de bebida alcoólica**)
◆ PHRASAL VERB [**tots, totting, totted**] **tot something up** to add numbers together ◫ *If you tot up all the costs, it comes to £347.* (**adicionar**)

total /ˈtəʊtəl/ ▶ ADJECTIVE

1 complete ◫ *She was a total stranger.* ◫ *He showed a total lack of respect.* ◫ *The job must be done in total secrecy.* (**total**)
2 including everything (**total**) ◫ *Two more people arrived yesterday, bringing the total number of guests to 12.* (**número total**) ◫ *the total cost of the project*

▶ NOUN [*plural* **totals**] the number or amount you get when you add everything together ◫ + *of We've got a total of fifteen cats.* (**total**) ◫ *They raised a grand total of £940.* (**grandioso total**) ◫ *There were thirty people in total.*

▶ VERB [**totals, totalling**/US **totaling, totalled**/US **totaled**] to be a particular number or amount when added together ◫ *Our collection totalled £320.* (**totalizar**)

• **totally** /ˈtəʊtəlɪ/ ADVERB completely ◫ *Is she totally deaf?* ◫ *I agree with you totally.* (**totalmente**)

> **Totally** is only used before adjectives with very strong meanings. Before adjectives with less strong meanings, use **very** or **extremely** ◫ *I was totally exhausted.* ◫ *I was very tired.* ◫ *It's totally ridiculous.* ◫ *It's very silly.*

totem pole /ˈtəʊtəm ˌpəʊl/ NOUN [*plural* **totem poles**] a tall wooden pole with designs on it made by Native Americans (**totem**)

totter /ˈtɒtə(r)/ VERB [**totters, tottering, tottered**] to walk with small steps as if you are going to fall over ◫ *She tottered on high heels up the street.* (**vacilar, cambalear**)

touch /tʌtʃ/ ▶ VERB [**touches, touching, touched**]

1 to put your hand or fingers on something ◫ *Please do not touch the items on the shelf.* ◫ *Can you touch the ceiling?* (**tocar**)
2 if things touch, there is no space between them ◫ *We stood in a long line with our shoulders touching.* (**tocar-se**)
3 if you are touched by someone's actions, you feel happy and grateful because they have been kind ◫ *I was touched by your kind letter.* (**tocar, emocionar-se**)
4 if someone's words or situation touch you, you feel sad for them ◫ *Who could fail to be touched by their stories of suffering?* (**tocar, emocionar-se**)

◆ PHRASAL VERBS **touch down** if an aircraft touches down, it lands (**aterrissar**) **touch on/upon something** to mention a subject ◫ *He did briefly touch on the problems he is having.* (**mencionar**) **touch something up** to make small changes to improve something, especially its appearance ◫ *I need to touch up the paint on the windows.* (**retocar**)

▶ NOUN [*plural* **touches**]
1 when you put your hands or fingers on something ◫ *You can start the engine at the touch of a button.* ◫ *I felt a touch on my shoulder.* (**toque**)
2 *no plural* the ability to feel ◫ *The fur was smooth to the touch.* (**tato**)
3 a touch is a small detail that makes something better ◫ *Matching flowers were a nice touch.* (**um toque**) ◫ *She added the finishing touches to the display.* (**toques finais**)
4 a particular quality that something adds to a situation ◫ *The story about his father gave the speech a personal touch.* ◫ *Her presence added a touch of glamour to the occasion.* (**toque**)
5 in touch (a) if you are in touch with someone, you communicate with them ◫ *I wish Sally would get in touch with me.* ◫ *I hope we can stay in touch.* (b) if you are in touch with a subject or a situation, you know the recent information about it ◫ *I like to keep in touch with what's going on in the world.* (**em contato**)
6 lose touch to stop communicating with someone, usually not deliberately ◫ *We lost touch after we left university.* (**perder o contato**)
7 out of touch if you are out of touch with a subject or a situation, you do not know the recent information about it ◫ *I didn't know Joe had got married – I'm rather out of touch these days.* (**sem contato, fora de contato**)

touch-and-go /ˌtʌtʃənˈgəʊ/ ADJECTIVE an informal word used to mean that the result of a situation is very uncertain and could be very bad ◫

It was touch-and go whether she'd survive. **(estado de incerteza, situação arriscada)**

touchdown /ˈtʌtʃdaʊn/ NOUN [plural **touchdowns**]
1 when an aircraft or spacecraft lands on the ground □ *They announced the spacecraft's successful touchdown in the Arizona desert.* **(aterrissar)**
2 when the ball is carried over a line to score points in rugby or American football **(marcar um tento)**

touching /ˈtʌtʃɪŋ/ ADJECTIVE making you feel sympathy □ *a touching story about a lost puppy* **(tocante)**

touchpad /ˈtʌtʃpæd/ NOUN [plural **touchpads**] a small flat area on a laptop (= small computer you can carry around) that you touch to work the computer programs **(dispositivo sensível ao toque)**

touch screen /ˈtʌtʃ ˌskriːn/ NOUN [plural **touch screens**] a computer screen that you touch in order to make the computer do something **(tela de toque)**

touchy /ˈtʌtʃi/ ADJECTIVE [**touchier, touchiest**]
1 easily annoyed □ *What's she so touchy about today?* **(suscetível)**
2 needing to be dealt with carefully because people are likely to become annoyed or upset □ *a touchy subject* **(delicado)**

tough /tʌf/ ADJECTIVE [**tougher, toughest**]
1 difficult to deal with □ *It was a tough decision.* □ *He had a tough time in that job.* **(duro)**
2 very severe □ *Tough new measures have been introduced to reduce vandalism.* □ *We're very tough on students who do not work hard enough.* **(duro)**
3 physically or mentally strong □ *You need to be tough to succeed in business.* **(resistente)**
4 not easy to cut or damage □ *You'll need a tough pair of shoes for climbing.* □ *The meat was a bit tough.* **(resistente, duro)**

• **toughen** /ˈtʌfən/ VERB [**toughens, toughening, toughened**]
1 to become physically or mentally stronger, or to make someone physically or mentally stronger □ *A year in the army has really toughened him up.* **(endurecer(-se), fortalecer)**
2 to make something more severe □ *The government plans to toughen regulations on the sale of alcohol.* **(endurecer)**

• **toughness** /ˈtʌfnɪs/ NOUN, NO PLURAL being tough **(dureza)**

tour /tʊə(r)/ ▶ NOUN [plural **tours**]
1 a visit somewhere, stopping several times at places of interest □ + *of* We went on a tour of the wine region. **(viagem, excursão)** 🔁 *He takes visitors on guided tours of the city.* **(excursões guiadas)**
2 a number of performances or matches in different places by a performer or sports team □ *a cricket tour of South Africa* □ *The singer's currently on tour in Europe.* **(excursão, turnê)**

▶ VERB [**tours, touring, toured**] to go on a tour □ *We're going to tour the wine-making regions of France.* □ *We've hired a car to tour the city.* **(viajar)**

• **tourism** /ˈtʊərɪzəm/ NOUN, NO PLURAL travelling to and visiting places for enjoyment, or the business of providing holiday services **(turismo)** 🔁 *the tourism industry* □ *The program was set up to promote tourism on the island.*

• **tourist** /ˈtʊərɪst/ NOUN [plural **tourists**]
1 a person who is travelling for enjoyment or on holiday □ *a group of foreign tourists* **(turista)** 🔁 *a tourist attraction* **(atração turística)**
2 a player on a sports tour □ *The tourists won the first match in the series.* **(excursionista)**

tournament /ˈtʊənəmənt/ NOUN [plural **tournaments**] a number of sports matches that make up a big competition **(torneio)** 🔁 *a golf tournament* **(torneio de golfe)** 🔁 *the US Open tennis tournament* **(torneio de tênis)**

tour operator /ˈtʊər ˌɒpəreɪtə(r)/ NOUN [plural **tour operators**] a company that organizes holidays for people **(operador turístico)**

tousled /ˈtaʊzəld/ ADJECTIVE tousled hair is untidy **(despenteado)**

tout /taʊt/ ▶ NOUN [plural **touts**] a person who tries to sell something, especially tickets for an event, usually illegally **(cambista)** 🔁 *a ticket tout* **(cambista de ingressos)**

▶ VERB [**touts, touting, touted**]
1 to try to persuade people that something is good or important □ *White is already being touted as a possible candidate.* □ *He is touting the benefits of preventive care.* **(promover)**
2 to try to persuade people to buy something **(conquistar fregueses)**

tow /təʊ/ ▶ VERB [**tows, towing, towed**] to pull something behind you with a rope or chain □ *The car broke down and we had to be towed home.* **(rebocar)**

▶ NOUN [plural **tows**] when you tow something **(reboque)**

toward /təˈwɔːd/ PREPOSITION a mainly US word for **towards** **(ver towards)**

towards /təˈwɔːdz/ PREPOSITION
1 in the direction of someone or something □ *I ran towards her.* □ *The sign points towards the east.* □ *He moved his chair towards the window* **(para)**
2 used to talk about the way someone feels about someone or something □ *I found his attitude towards money strange.* □ *She feels a lot of bitterness towards her family.* **(para com, com respeito a)**
3 near something □ *The bit about Cromwell is towards the end of the book.* □ *I hope to finish my book towards the end of the year.* **(perto de)**
4 for the purpose of achieving something □ *Nothing has been done towards organizing the party.* **(pelo)**

towel 857 **track**

5 in order to help to pay for something □ *He made a donation towards the new roof.* (para)
6 used to talk about how a situation is developing □ *The country is sliding towards civil war.* (em direção a)

towel /'tauəl/ ▶ NOUN [plural **towels**] a piece of soft, thick cloth for drying yourself (**toalha**) 🔁 *a bath towel* (**toalha de banho**) □ *She picked up the wet towel from the bathroom floor.* 🔁 *She dried her hands using a paper towel.* (**toalha de papel**)
▶ VERB [**towels, towelling, towelled**] to dry a thing or person with a towel □ *Towel your hair dry before applying the conditioner.* (**enxugar com toalha**)
• **towelling** /'tauəlɪŋ/ NOUN, NO PLURAL thick, soft cotton cloth that is good for drying things □ *a bath robe made of toweling* (**atoalhado**)

tower /'tauə(r)/ ▶ NOUN [plural **towers**] a tall narrow building or part of a building □ *a church tower* 🔁 *the Eiffel Tower* (**torre**)
▶ VERB [**towers, towering, towered**] to be much taller than other things or people □ *William towers over all his colleagues.* (**elevar-se**)

tower block /'tauə ˌblɒk/ NOUN [plural **tower blocks**] a very tall building where people live or work □ *a 20-storey tower block* (**torre**)

towering /'tauərɪŋ/ ADJECTIVE
1 very tall □ *towering office blocks* (**elevado**)
2 very important and admired by many people □ *He was a towering literary figure.* (**elevado**)

town /taʊn/ NOUN [plural **towns**]
1 a place where people live and work, bigger than a village and smaller than a city (**cidade**) 🔁 *She comes from a small town in Ohio.* (**cidade pequena**) 🔁 *The wedding was in her home town of Hobart.* (**cidade natal**)
2 the main part of a town where many shops and businesses are (**cidade, centro da cidade**) 🔁 *I'm going into town to do some shopping.*
♦ IDIOM **go to town** an informal phrase meaning to do something with a lot of effort, energy or money □ *She really went to town on the decorations.* (**empenhar-se**)

town centre /ˌtaʊn 'sentə(r)/ NOUN [plural **town centres**] the part of a town where most of the shops, restaurants, etc. are (**centro da cidade**)

town hall NOUN [plural **town halls**] a building that contains local government offices (**prefeitura**)

towpath /'təʊpɑːθ/ NOUN [plural **towpaths**] a path next to a river or canal (= a passage filled with water, made for boats to travel on) (**caminho que circunda um canal ou rio**)

toxic /'tɒksɪk/ ADJECTIVE poisonous (**tóxico**) 🔁 *toxic chemicals* (**substâncias químicas tóxicas**) 🔁 *The river is polluted with toxic waste.* (**lixo tóxico**)

• **toxicity** /tɒk'sɪsəti/ NOUN, NO PLURAL the quality of being toxic (**toxicidade**)
• **toxin** /'tɒksɪn/ NOUN [plural **toxins**] a substance that is poisonous (**toxina**)

toy /tɔɪ/ NOUN [plural **toys**] an object made for someone, especially a child, to play with (**brinquedo**)
♦ PHRASAL VERBS [**toys, toying, toyed**] **toy with something 1** to consider an idea, but not in a very serious way □ *I'm toying with the idea of cutting my hair short.* (**brincar com a ideia de**) **2** to keep touching or moving something, usually because you are nervous or upset □ *He was just toying with his food.* (**brincar**) **toy with someone** to pretend that you love someone when you do not have serious feelings about them (**brincar com os sentimentos**)

trace /treɪs/ ▶ VERB [**traces, tracing, traced**]
1 to find someone or something by following information about where they have been □ *The man has been traced to a village in the south of the country.* (**rastrear**)
2 to discover the origin of something □ *She can trace her family back to the 13th century.* (**investigar**)
3 to describe the development of something □ *The book traces his journey from farmer's son to famous explorer.* (**descrever**)
4 to copy a picture by covering it with a sheet of thin paper and drawing over the lines you can see through it (**calcar**)
▶ NOUN [plural **traces**]
1 a mark or sign that someone or something leaves behind (**vestígio, traço**) 🔁 *He disappeared without trace.* (**desapareceu sem deixar vestígio**)
2 a very small amount of something □ *There were traces of explosives on his shoes.* (**resíduos**)

trace element /'treɪs ˌelɪmənt/ NOUN [plural **trace elements**] a chemical that an animal or plant needs very small amounts of to develop in a normal way. A biology or chemistry word. (**elementos de traço**)

trachea /trə'kiːə/ NOUN [plural **tracheas**] the tube that carries air to your lungs. A biology word. (**traqueia**)

tracing paper /'treɪsɪŋ ˌpeɪpə(r)/ NOUN, NO PLURAL very thin paper that you can see the lines of a picture through (**papel de decalque**)

track /træk/ ▶ NOUN [plural **tracks**]
1 a rough path or road □ *We followed a narrow track along the edge of the field.* (**trilha**)
2 the long metal pieces that a train moves along □ *Repairs were needed to the track.* (**trilhos**)
3 an area of ground used for racing, often with a circular path (**pista**)
4 a mark on the ground left by a person, animal or thing that has been there □ *They followed the bear's tracks through the forest.* (**rastro**)

5 one of the songs or pieces of music on a CD, record, etc. (**faixa**)
6 on track likely to be successful □ *We are on track to finish the work by next year.* (**a caminho de**)
7 on the right/wrong track trying to achieve something in a way that is likely to be successful/unsuccessful □ *If she's hoping to be a professional musician, she's certainly on the right track.* (**no caminho certo/errado**)
8 keep track to continue to have enough information about something □ *I can't keep track of all the new rules.* (**manter-se atualizado, manter o controle**)
9 lose track to no longer have enough information about something □ *I've lost track of the number of times I've had to give her money.* (**perder contato**)
▶ VERB [**tracks, tracking, tracked**]
1 to follow a person, animal or vehicle by looking for their marks or using special equipment □ *They use radar to track the aircraft's movements.* (**rastrear**)
2 to watch and record the progress or development of something □ *The report tracks the performance of several major companies.* (**rastrear**)
◆ PHRASAL VERB **track someone/something down** to find someone or something after looking for them for a long time □ *I'm trying to track down an old friend.* □ *The shop has tracked down the book you ordered.* (**localizar**)

track and field /ˈtræk ənd ˈfiːld/ NOUN, NO PLURAL a mainly US phrase for sports such as running, jumping and throwing (**atletismo**)

track record /ˈtræk ˈrekɔːd/ NOUN [*plural* **track records**] all the things you have done in the past, by which people judge you □ *He has an excellent track record as an administrator.* (**histórico**)

tracksuit /ˈtræksuːt/ NOUN [*plural* **tracksuits**] comfortable trousers and a top that you wear for sport (**agasalho esportivo**)

tract /trækt/ NOUN [*plural* **tracts**]
1 a large area of land (**extensão de terreno**)
2 a system of tubes and organs in the body. A biology word (**aparelho**) 🔲 the *digestive tract* (**aparelho digestivo**)
3 a piece of writing, especially about politics or religion (**panfleto, folheto**)

tractor /ˈtræktə(r)/ NOUN [*plural* **tractors**] a powerful vehicle with large wheels, used on farms (**trator**)

trade /treɪd/ ▶ NOUN [*plural* **trades**]
1 *no plural* the buying and selling of goods, services or shares (= parts of a company that you can sell or buy) □ *international trade* (**comércio**)
2 a particular area of business □ *She works in the diamond trade.* (**negócio**)
3 a job using your hands that involves skill and training (**ofício**) 🔲 *He learned the trade from his father.* (**aprender o ofício**)
▶ VERB [**trades, trading, traded**]

1 to buy or sell goods, services or shares (= parts of a company that you can sell or buy) □ + *with We will not trade with corrupt regimes.* (**comerciar**)
2 to exchange something for something else □ + *for I traded my waterproof coat for a camera.* (**trocar, permutar**)
◆ PHRASAL VERB **trade something in** to give something old as part of the payment for something new □ *We traded in our car for a newer model.* (**dar como parte de pagamento**)

trademark /ˈtreɪdmɑːk/ NOUN [*plural* **trademarks**] a name, word or symbol that a company uses on its products and which legally belongs to that company (**marca registrada**)

trade-off /ˈtreɪdɒf/ NOUN [*plural* **trade-offs**] a situation where the advantage of one thing brings the disadvantage of another □ *There's a trade-off between cost and convenience.* (**equilíbrio de vantagens e desvantagens**)

trader /ˈtreɪdə(r)/ NOUN [*plural* **traders**] a person or company that buys and sells things (**comerciante**)

tradesman /ˈtreɪdzmən/ NOUN [*plural* **tradesmen**]
1 a person who works with their hands in a skilled job (**técnico**)
2 a person who sells something (**comerciante**)

trade union /ˈtreɪd ˈjuːnjən/ NOUN [*plural* **trade unions**] an organization of workers that tries to get good pay and conditions for its members (**sindicato**)

trading /ˈtreɪdɪŋ/ NOUN, NO PLURAL the activity of buying and selling goods, services or shares (= parts of a company that you can sell or buy) □ *High street trading has been hit by the recession.* (**comércio, negócio**)

tradition /trəˈdɪʃən/ NOUN [*plural* **traditions**] a custom that has continued for a long time □ *Having special birthday meals is a family tradition.* □ *He does not follow any religious tradition.* (**tradição**)

• **traditional** /trəˈdɪʃənəl/ ADJECTIVE
1 based on customs that have existed for a long time □ *They wore traditional costumes.* (**tradicional**)
2 based on what usually happens or what people have usually done □ *He did not follow the traditional career path.* (**tradicional**)
• **traditionally** /trəˈdɪʃənəli/ ADVERB based on what usually happens or what people have usually done □ *Traditionally, summer is a quiet time in politics.* (**tradicionalmente**)

traffic /ˈtræfɪk/ ▶ NOUN, NO PLURAL
1 vehicles that are travelling (**tráfego**) 🔲 *We were stuck in heavy traffic* (= a lot of traffic). (**tráfego pesado**)
2 the illegal buying and selling of goods □ *the traffic of weapons* (**tráfico**)
▶ VERB [**traffics, trafficking, trafficked**] to buy and sell things illegally (**traficar**)

traffic circle

traffic circle /ˈtræfɪk ˈsɜːkəl/ NOUN [plural **traffic circles**] the US phrase for roundabout (rotatória)

traffic jam /ˈtræfɪk ˌdʒæm/ NOUN [plural **traffic jams**] a long line of vehicles that cannot move because the road is blocked (engarrafamento)

trafficker /ˈtræfɪkə(r)/ NOUN [plural **traffickers**] someone who buys or sells goods illegally □ *drug traffickers* (traficante)

• **trafficking** /ˈtræfɪkɪŋ/ NOUN, NO PLURAL buying and selling goods illegally (tráfico)

traffic lights /ˈtræfɪk laɪts/ PLURAL NOUN a set of red, yellow and green lights that tell vehicles when to stop or go (semáforo)

traffic warden /ˈtræfɪk ˌwɔːdn/ NOUN [plural **traffic wardens**] a person whose job is to check that vehicles have been parked legally (guarda)

tragedy /ˈtrædʒədi/ NOUN [plural **tragedies**]
1 a very sad event, often where people die □ *The train driver could not be blamed for the tragedy.* (tragédia)
2 a very bad situation that makes people upset □ *It is a tragedy that so many children are becoming involved in crime.* (tragédia)
3 a story that has a sad ending, especially when the main character dies (tragédia)

• **tragic** /ˈtrædʒɪk/ ADJECTIVE very sad, often because of a death (trágico) ▣ *His death was a tragic accident.* (acidente trágico) □ *Her carelessness had tragic consequences.*

• **tragically** /ˈtrædʒɪkli/ ADVERB in a way that is very sad □ *The poet died tragically young.* (tragicamente)

trail /treɪl/ ▶ NOUN [plural **trails**]
1 a series of marks or objects that someone or something leaves when they move somewhere □ *They left a trail of litter behind them.* (pista, rastro)
2 a lot of damage or a series of bad events (trilha) ▣ *Their huge trucks had left a trail of destruction.* (trilha de destruição)
3 a path through the countryside (trilha)
▶ VERB [**trails, trailing, trailed**]
1 to hang down from something or across something □ *Her long coat trailed on the floor.* □ *Roses trailed over the wall.* (arrastar-se)
2 to walk slowly because you are tired or unhappy □ *The children trailed along behind their parents.* (arrastar-se)
3 to be losing in a competition or an election □ *Their team is trailing by 5 points.* (estar perdendo)
4 to point a camera or gun in a particular
4 to leave a substance on the ground as you move □ *He's trailed mud all over the house.* (deixar um rastro)
5 to follow someone secretly □ *He was trailed by the secret police for years.* (seguir secretamente)

♦ PHRASAL VERB **trail away/off** if someone's words trail away/off, they gradually stop □ *His voice trailed off as she entered the room.* (diminuir, desaparecer, morrer)

• **trailer** /ˈtreɪlə(r)/ NOUN [plural **trailers**]
1 a container on wheels that is pulled behind another vehicle (trailer)
2 a short part of a film or programme that is used as an advertisement for it (trailer)

train¹ /treɪn/ NOUN [plural **trains**]
1 a vehicle that moves on a railway and carries passengers □ *I prefer to travel by train.* (trem) ▣ *I caught the early train.* (pegar o trem)
2 a series of thoughts or events (fluxo, série) ▣ *The sudden noise interrupted my train of thought.* (fluxo de pensamentos) ▣ *Her argument set off a terrible train of events.* (uma série de eventos)
3 the back part of a long dress that hangs on the floor

train² /treɪn/ VERB [**trains, training, trained**]
1 to teach a person or animal to do something □ + *to do something* *Veronica has trained her dog to carry her handbag.* (treinar, instruir)
2 to learn to do a particular job □ + *as* *Andrew trained as a nurse when he left school.* (treinar)
3 to prepare for a sports event □ *The team trains for three hours every day.* (treinar)
4 to point a camera or gun in a particular direction □ + *on* *The enemy's guns are trained on the airport.* (apontar em uma direção)

• **trainee** /treɪˈniː/ NOUN [plural **trainees**] someone who is being trained to do a particular job (pessoa em treinamento)

• **trainer** /ˈtreɪnə(r)/ NOUN [plural **trainers**]
1 someone who teaches people or animals to do something (treinador, adestrador)
2 trainers soft shoes that are used for sport (tênis)

• **training** /ˈtreɪnɪŋ/ NOUN, NO PLURAL
1 the process of training people or being trained □ + *in* *We received very little training in how to use the equipment.* (formação) ▣ *They run training courses for diving instructors.* (cursos de formação)
2 preparation for a sports event □ *The team will be in training for the next year.* (treinamento)

traipse /treɪps/ VERB [**traipses, traipsing, traipsed**]
1 to walk somewhere slowly □ *She traipsed up the hill carrying three heavy bags of shopping.* (passear)
2 to travel a long way □ *You can't expect them to traipse all the way to Scotland for a party.* (viajar um longo caminho)

trait /treɪt/ NOUN [plural **traits**] a particular characteristic or quality that someone or something has □ *The test is supposed to reveal major character traits.* (traço, característica)

traitor /ˈtreɪtə(r)/ NOUN [plural **traitors**] a person who is not loyal to their friends or country (traidor)

trajectory /trəˈdʒektəri/ NOUN [plural **trajectories**] the curved line which something follows when it goes or is thrown into the air (trajetória)

tram /træm/ NOUN [plural **trams**] a type of electric bus that runs on metal tracks in the street (bonde)

tramp /træmp/ ▶ NOUN [plural **tramps**] a person without a home who walks from place to place (vagabundo)
▶ VERB [**tramps, tramping, tramped**] to walk with firm, heavy steps (andar pesadamente)

trample /ˈtræmpəl/ VERB [**tramples, trampling, trampled**] to walk on something with heavy steps, often causing damage ◻ *The sheep had trampled all over the wheat.* (pisotear)

trampoline /ˈtræmpəliːn/ NOUN [plural **trampolines**] a piece of equipment that you jump up and down on for exercise or sport (cama elástica)

trance /trɑːns/ NOUN [plural **trances**] a state when you are awake but not completely conscious of what is happening or what you are doing (transe)

tranquil /ˈtræŋkwɪl/ ADJECTIVE quiet, calm and peaceful ◻ *The hotel is in a tranquil setting by a lake.* (tranquilo)

• **tranquilize** /ˈtræŋkwɪˌlaɪz/ VERB [**tranquilizes, tranquilizing, tranquilized**] the US spelling of **tranquillize** (tranquilizar)

• **tranquilizer** /ˈtræŋkwɪˌlaɪzə(r)/ NOUN [plural **tranquilizers**] the US spelling of **tranquillizer** (tranquilizante)

• **tranquillity** /trænˈkwɪlɪti/ NOUN, NO PLURAL the state of being tranquil (tranquilidade)

• **tranquillize** *or* **tranquillise** /ˈtræŋkwɪˌlaɪz/ VERB [**tranquillizes, tranquillizing, tranquillized**] to give a person or animal a drug to make them calmer and more relaxed (tranquilizar)

• **tranquillizer** *or* **tranquilliser** /ˈtræŋkwɪˌlaɪzə(r)/ NOUN [plural **tranquillizers**] a drug that makes people feel calmer and more relaxed (tranquilizante)

trans- /trænz/ PREFIX (trans-)
1 trans- is added to the beginning of words to mean 'across' ◻ *transatlantic*
2 trans- is added to the beginning of words to mean 'changing' ◻ *transformation*

transaction /trænˈzækʃən/ NOUN [plural **transactions**] when something is bought or sold (transação)

transatlantic /ˌtrænzətˈlæntɪk/ ADJECTIVE involving crossing the Atlantic Ocean ◻ *a transatlantic flight* (transatlântico)

transfer ▶ VERB /trænsˈfɜː(r)/ [**transfers, transferring, transferred**]
1 to move someone or something from one place to another ◻ *She transferred all her photos onto a CD.* ◻ *I transferred some money into his account.* (transferir)
2 to change to a different job or place of work in the same organization, or to move someone to a different job or place of work in the same organization ◻ *+ to He transferred to the New York office.* (transferir)
3 to change to a different vehicle as part of a journey ◻ *We transferred to an internal flight from Helsinki.* (transferir(-se))
4 to make someone able to speak to someone else instead of you on the telephone by connecting them ◻ *+ to I'll transfer you to our accounts department.* (transferir)
5 to sell a sports player to another team (transferir)
▶ NOUN /ˈtrænsfɜː(r)/ [plural **transfers**]
1 when someone moves to another job or place of work in the same organization ◻ *The sergeant has asked for a transfer.* (transferência)
2 the act of moving someone or something from one place to another ◻ *I am responsible for the transfer of supplies to the new base.* (transferência)
3 when a sports player is sold to another team (transferência)
4 a piece of paper with a design on one side that can be pressed on to another surface (transferência)

• **transferable** /trænsˈfɜːrəbəl/ ADJECTIVE able to be used by someone else or for a different purpose ◻ *This ticket is not transferable.* (transferência)

transfix /trænsˈfɪks/ VERB [**transfixes, transfixing, transfixed**] if you are transfixed by something, it keeps your attention ◻ *The whole nation was transfixed by the drama.* (paralisar, chocar)

transform /trænsˈfɔːm/ VERB [**transforms, transforming, transformed**] to change something completely ◻ *We could transform this room with a few tins of paint.* (transformar)

• **transformation** /ˌtrænsfəˈmeɪʃən/ NOUN [plural **transformations**] a complete change in someone or something (transformação) 🔁 *The organization has undergone a complete transformation.* (submeter-se a uma transformação completa)

• **transformer** /trænsˈfɔːmə(r)/ NOUN [plural **transformers**] a device that changes the strength of an electric current. A physics word. (transformador)

transfusion /trænsˈfjuːʒən/ NOUN [plural **transfusions**] when blood from someone else is put into the body of a person who is ill or injured (transfusão)

transient /ˈtrænzɪənt/ ADJECTIVE
1 a formal word meaning lasting for only a short time ◻ *transient pleasures* (transitório)
2 staying in one place for only a short time ◻ *a transient population* (temporário)

transistor

transistor /trænˈzɪstə(r)/ NOUN [plural **transistors**]
1 a small piece of electronic equipment used to control the flow of electricity in radios, televisions, computers, etc. A physics word. (**transistor**)
2 a small radio (**radinho de pilha**)

transit /ˈtrænsɪt/ NOUN, NO PLURAL the activity of moving someone or something from one place to another ◻ *Their luggage has been lost in transit* (= while being moved). (**trânsito**)

transition /trænˈzɪʃən/ NOUN [plural **transitions**] a change from one state, situation or system to another ◻ *The transition from childhood to adulthood was difficult for her.* ◻ *We are trying to ensure a smooth transition to the new working methods.* (**transição**)

• **transitional** /trænˈzɪʃənəl/ ADJECTIVE to do with a transition (**transitório**) 🔹 *During the transitional period either system may be used.* (**período transitório**)

transitive /ˈtrænzɪtɪv/ ADJECTIVE a transitive verb always has an object ◻ *In the sentence 'I can see Mary.', 'see' is a transitive verb.* (**transitivo**)

translate /trænsˈleɪt/ VERB [**translates, translating, translated**]
1 to change words into a different language ◻ + *into Can you translate this into French?* (**traduzir**)
2 to cause something ◻ + *into The company's success has translated into higher earnings for its staff.* (**traduzir**)

• **translation** /trænsˈleɪʃən/ NOUN [plural **translations**]
1 writing or speech that has been changed into a different language ◻ + *of This is a new translation of her novel.* (**tradução**)
2 no plural the process of translating something (**tradução**)

• **translator** /trænsˈleɪtə(r)/ NOUN [plural **translators**] someone whose job is to change words into a different language (**tradutor**)

translucent /trænzˈluːsənt/ ADJECTIVE translucent objects allow light to pass through them but are not completely transparent (**translúcido**)

transmission /trænzˈmɪʃən/ NOUN [plural **transmissions**]
1 a television or radio broadcast, or the process of broadcasting ◻ *Transmissions from outside the region have been blocked.* (**transmissão**)
2 the process of sending something out from somewhere ◻ *the transmission of data* (**transmissão**)
3 the process of spreading a disease from one person to another (**transmissão**)
4 the part of a vehicle that takes power from the engine to turn the wheels (**transmissão**)

• **transmit** /trænzˈmɪt/ VERB [**transmits, transmitting, transmitted**]
1 to broadcast programmes, information, etc. ◻ *The company plans to transmit live coverage of the match via mobile phones.* (**transmitir**)

861

transport

2 to send something out from somewhere ◻ *The device transmits a radio signal.* (**transmitir**)
3 to spread a disease ◻ *The disease is transmitted by Mosquitos.* (**transmitir**)
4 if a substance transmits light, heat, etc., it allows it to pass through (**transmitir**)

transparent /trænsˈpærənt/ ADJECTIVE
1 if something is transparent, you can see through it ◻ *The box is made of transparent plastic so that you can see all the wires inside.* (**transparente**)
2 easy to understand and not keeping anything secret ◻ *Our system of expenses must be completely transparent.* (**transparente**)
3 obviously not true ◻ *a transparent lie* (**transparente**)

transpiration /ˌtrænspɪˈreɪʃən/ NOUN, NO PLURAL when a plant transpires. A biology word. (**transpiração**)

transpire /trænˈspaɪə(r)/ VERB [**transpires, transpiring, transpired**]
1 if it transpires that something happened, people discover that it has happened. A formal word ◻ *It later transpired that he had been in Paris all the time.* (**transpirar**)
2 if a plant transpires, water from its leaves goes back into the air. A biology word. (**transpirar**)

transplant ▶ NOUN /ˈtrænsˌplɑːnt/ [plural **transplants**] an operation to put an organ from one person's body into someone else (**transplante, enxerto**) 🔹 *He had a heart transplant.* (**transplante de coração**)
▶ VERB /trænsˈplɑːnt/ [**transplants, transplanting, transplanted**]
1 to remove a part from one person's body and put it in someone else's (**transplantar**)
2 to move a plant that is growing in one place to somewhere else ◻ *The seedlings can be transplanted when they have four leaves.* (**transplantar**)

transport ▶ NOUN, NO PLURAL /ˈtrænspɔːt/
1 vehicles or a system used for taking people and goods from one place to another (**transporte**) 🔹 *Older people have free travel on public transport.* (**transporte público**) 🔹 *Paris has a very efficient transport system.* (**sistema de transporte**) 🔹 *Trains are a very safe form of transport.* (**meio de transporte**)
2 moving people or things from one place to another ◻ *The price includes the cost of transport.* ◻ + *of The transport of farm animals was banned.* (**transporte**)

> ► Remember that **transport** cannot be used in the plural:
>   ✓ *Public transport is very good in the capital.*
>   ✗ *Public transports are very good in the capital.*
> ► To talk about one particular type of transport, use the phrase **form of transport** ◻ *Train is probably the greenest form of transport.*

transpose

▶ VERB /trænsˈpɔːt/ [transports, transporting, transported] to move something from one place to another ▢ *The planes were used to transport prisoners.* ▢ *Red blood cells transport oxygen around the body.* (transportar)

• **transportation** /ˌtrænspɔːˈteɪʃən/ NOUN, NO PLURAL
1 the process of moving people or things ▢ *transportation costs* (transporte)
2 the US word for **transport** (sense 1) (transporte)

• **transporter** /trænsˈpɔːtə(r)/ NOUN [plural transporters] a long vehicle that is usually used for taking a number of large objects, such as cars, to another place (transportador)

transpose /trænsˈpəʊz/ VERB [transposes, transposing, transposed]
1 to make two things change places ▢ *The keyboarder had transposed two of the numbers.* (inverter)
2 to play music in a different key to the one it is written in (transpor)

trap /træp/ ▶ NOUN [plural traps]
1 a piece of equipment for catching animals ▢ *a mouse trap* (armadilha)
2 a clever plan that is designed to trick someone (cilada) ▣ *Police set a trap for the suspected thief.* (armou uma cilada)
3 an unpleasant situation that is very difficult to escape from (armadilha) ▣ *Many families are caught in the low pay poverty trap.* (armadilha da pobreza)

▶ VERB [traps, trapping, trapped]
1 if you are trapped in a bad place or situation, you cannot escape from it ▢ *Passengers were trapped as fire swept through the bus.* ▢ *He was trapped in a loveless marriage.* (ficar preso)
2 to trick someone into doing or saying something ▢ *The suspect was trapped into admitting that he had been there.* (ficar sem saída, cair/ser apanhado em armadilha)
3 to catch an animal in a trap ▢ *The animals were trapped for their fur.*

trapdoor /ˈtræpdɔː(r)/ NOUN [plural trapdoors] a door in a floor or a ceiling (alçapão)

trapeze /trəˈpiːz/ NOUN [plural trapezes] a short bar hanging between two ropes high up from the ground, on which someone moves backwards and forwards to entertain people (trapézio)

trapezium /trəˈpiːziəm/ NOUN [plural trapeziums or trapezia] a shape with four sides, two of which are parallel. A maths word. (trapézio)

trappings /ˈtræpɪŋz/ PLURAL NOUN the nice things that someone has because of their position ▢ *Simon had all the trappings of success – a nice house, a boat, and three children at private school.* (adornos)

trash /træʃ/ ▶ NOUN, NO PLURAL
1 an informal word meaning things that are of bad quality ▢ *There's a lot of trash on television.* (lixo)
2 the US word for **rubbish** (= things that have been thrown away) (lixo)

▶ VERB [trashes, trashing, trashed]
1 an informal word meaning to destroy something completely ▢ *Rioters trashed cars.* (destroçar)
2 an informal word meaning to criticize something badly (criticar duramente)

trashcan /ˈtræʃkæn/ NOUN [plural trashcans] the US word for **dustbin** (lata de lixo)

trashy /ˈtræʃi/ ADJECTIVE [trashier, trashiest] of very bad quality ▢ *trashy magazines* (sem valor, ordinário)

trauma /ˈtrɔːmə/ NOUN [plural traumas] a very unpleasant experience that upsets someone a lot and for a long time ▢ *She never recovered from the trauma of losing her son.* (trauma)

• **traumatic** /trɔːˈmætɪk/ ADJECTIVE very upsetting, unpleasant or frightening ▢ *a traumatic event* (traumático)

• **traumatize** or **traumatise** /ˈtrɔːmətaɪz/ VERB [traumatizes, traumatizing, traumatized] to make someone feel very upset or frightened (traumatizar)

travel /ˈtrævəl/ ▶ VERB [travels, travelling/US traveling, travelled/US traveled]
1 to go from one place to another ▢ *Holly spent the summer travelling in the United States.* ▢ *Some people have to travel long distances to get to school.* (viajar) ▣ *She travels the world in her job.* (viajar pelo mundo) ▢ + *by* *I like travelling by train.*
2 to move at a particular speed ▢ *How fast does light travel?* ▢ *The vehicle was travelling too fast.* (deslocar-se)

▶ NOUN [plural travels]
1 no plural the activity of going from one place to another (viagem) ▣ *Cheap air travel has encouraged more people to fly.* (viagem de avião) ▣ *Make sure you have travel insurance if you go abroad.* (seguro de viagem)
2 your travels the journeys you make ▢ *Did you have good weather on your travels?* (suas viagens)

travel agency /ˈtrævəl ˌeɪdʒənsi/ NOUN [plural travel agencies] a shop or business where you can buy holidays (agência de viagem)

travel agent /ˈtrævəl ˌeɪdʒənt/ NOUN [plural travel agents]
1 a person whose job is to arrange holidays for people (agente de viagem)
2 a travel agent's a travel agency (agente de viagem)

traveler /ˈtrævələ(r)/ NOUN [plural travelers] the US spelling of **traveller** (viajante)

traveler's check /ˈtrævələ(r)z tʃek/ NOUN [plural traveler's checks] the US spelling of **traveller's cheque** (cheque viagem)

traveller

traveller /ˈtrævələ(r)/ NOUN [plural **travellers**]
1 a person who is on a journey (**viajante**) ▫ *Air travellers faced delays due to bad weather.* (**viajantes de avião**)
2 a person who lives in a vehicle and does not stay in one place (**viajante**)

traveller's cheque /ˈtrævələz ˌtʃek/ NOUN [plural **traveller's cheques**] a cheque for a fixed amount that you can change for local money when you are abroad (**cheque viagem**)

traverse /ˈtrævəs, trəˈvɜːs/ VERB [**traverses, traversing, traversed**] to go from one side of a place or area to another (**atravessar**)

trawl /trɔːl/ VERB [**trawls, trawling, trawled**]
1 to search something in order to find something ▫ *Detectives trawled through old police files.* (**investigar**)
2 to catch fish by pulling a large net through the water (**pescar com rede de arrasto**)
• **trawler** /ˈtrɔːlə(r)/ NOUN [plural **trawlers**] a boat that pulls a net along the bottom of the sea in order to catch fish (**traineira**)

tray /treɪ/ NOUN [plural **trays**]
1 a flat object for carrying food, plates, cups, etc. on ▫ *The waiter was carrying a tray of drinks.* (**bandeja**)
2 a flat container ▫ *Put the paper in the paper tray.* (**caixa, recipiente plano**)

treacherous /ˈtretʃərəs/ ADJECTIVE
1 very dangerous ▫ *Snow has caused treacherous driving conditions.* ▫ *treacherous mountains* (**traiçoeiro**)
2 a treacherous person is not loyal and is willing to do things that will harm you (**traiçoeiro**)
• **treachery** /ˈtretʃəri/ NOUN, NO PLURAL when someone acts in a treacherous way (**traição**)

treacle /ˈtriːkəl/ NOUN, NO PLURAL a sweet, dark, sticky liquid made from sugar and used in cooking (**melado**)

tread /tred/ ▶ VERB [**treads, treading, trod, trodden**]
1 to put your foot on something ▫ *Don't tread on the flowers.* (**pisar em**)
2 to walk in a particular way ▫ *We trod carefully around the broken glass.* (**pisar**)
3 **tread carefully/warily** to be careful about what you say or do ▫ *We need to tread carefully.* (**ter cuidado em falar ou fazer**)
4 **tread water** to stay in one place in water by moving your legs up and down (**boiar em pé**)
▶ NOUN [plural **treads**]
1 the sound you make when you walk ▫ *He heard the heavy tread of their boots on the bridge.* (**som de passos**)
2 the raised pattern on a tyre ▫ *The tread on this tyre is completely worn away in parts.* (**banda de pneu**)

treason /ˈtriːzən/ NOUN, NO PLURAL the crime of not being loyal to your country, for example by giving away secret information (**traição**)

treble

treasure /ˈtreʒə(r)/ ▶ NOUN [plural **treasures**]
1 valuable objects, especially if they have been hidden ▫ *The children were hoping to find some buried treasure.* (**tesouro**)
2 a valuable and important object ▫ *The painting is a national treasure which must not be sold.* (**tesouro**)
▶ VERB [**treasures, treasuring, treasured**] to think that something is very special and important ▫ *These are memories which I shall always treasure.* (**estimar**)
• **treasurer** /ˈtreʒərə(r)/ NOUN [plural **treasurers**] a person who looks after the money for an organization (**tesoureiro**)
• **treasury** or **Treasury** /ˈtreʒəri/ NOUN, NO PLURAL the treasury the part of a government that is responsible for a country's money (**ministério ou departamento da fazenda**)

treat /triːt/ ▶ VERB [**treats, treating, treated**]
1 to behave in a particular way towards someone ▫ *I think Debbie treated Steve really badly.* ▫ *They treat their staff well.* (**tratar**)
2 to deal with something in a particular way ▫ + *as* *He treated my remark as a joke.* ▫ *We treat any form of racism very seriously.* (**tratar**)
3 to give medicine or medical care to someone who is ill or injured ▫ *Doctors use all the latest methods to treat their patients.* ▫ + *for* *She is being treated for shock.* (**tratar**)
4 to put a substance on something to protect it ▫ *The material is treated with a spray to make it waterproof.* (**tratamento de proteção**)
5 to buy or do something special for someone ▫ + *to* *I treated the children to a pizza on the way home.* (**oferecer, regalar**)
▶ NOUN [plural **treats**] something special that you do or buy for someone (**regalo**) ▫ *We're having dinner in front of the TV as a special treat.* (**regalo especial**)
• **treatable** /ˈtriːtəbəl/ ADJECTIVE a treatable illness can be cured by medicine or medical care (**curável**)
• **treatment** /ˈtriːtmənt/ NOUN [plural **treatments**]
1 medicine or medical care ▫ *My treatment will last for about a month.* (**tratamento**) ▫ *He is receiving treatment for a heart condition.* (**receber tratamento**) ▫ *They are trying out a new treatment for migraine.*
2 **no plural** the way you behave towards someone or deal with something ▫ *Will I get special treatment if I offer to pay more?* (**tratamento**)
3 when a substance is put on something to protect it, or the substance that is used ▫ *She recommended a wood treatment for our floorboards.* (**tratamento**)

treaty /ˈtriːti/ NOUN [plural **treaties**] an official agreement between countries (**tratado**) ▫ *The two countries have signed a peace treaty.* (**tratado de paz**)

treble /ˈtrebəl/ ▶ DETERMINER three times bigger or three times as much ▫ *House prices are treble what they were ten years ago.* (**triplo**)

▶ VERB [trebles, trebling, trebled] to become or to make something three times as big or as much □ *Her pay has trebled over the last year.* (**triplicar**)
▶ NOUN [plural **trebles**]
1 the part that controls the highest sounds on a radio or other piece of equipment for playing music (**controle de alta frequência**)
2 a boy with a high singing voice (**soprano**)

tree /triː/ NOUN [plural **trees**] a very tall plant with branches and leaves □ *an apple tree* □ *an oak tree* (**árvore**) ▣ *We planted a new tree.* (**plantar uma árvore**) ▣ *The children were climbing trees.* (**subir em árvores**) ▣ *a tree trunk* (**tronco de árvore**)

trek /trek/ ▶ VERB [**treks, trekking, trekked**] to go on a long and difficult journey by walking □ *They were trekking in the Himalayas.* (**viajar**)
▶ NOUN [plural **treks**] a long and difficult walk □ *They had to make a long trek to find water.* (**jornada**)

trellis /ˈtrelɪs/ NOUN [plural **trellises**] a wooden frame that a plant grows up (**treliça**)

tremble /ˈtrembəl/ ▶ VERB [**trembles, trembling, trembled**]
1 to shake because you are cold or frightened □ *Joe's hand trembled as he dialled the number.* (**tremer**)
2 if your voice trembles, you sound weak, nervous or upset □ *Anna's voice trembled as she spoke.* (**tremer, vacilar**)
▶ NOUN [plural **trembles**] a shaking movement in part of the body □ *She had a slight tremble in her left hand.* (**tremor**)

tremendous /trɪˈmendəs/ ADJECTIVE
1 very great □ *The car was travelling at a tremendous speed.* (**enorme**)
2 very good □ *That's tremendous news!* (**fantástico**)
• **tremendously** /trɪˈmendəsli/ ADVERB extremely □ *We're tremendously grateful to you.* (**enormemente**)

tremor /ˈtremə(r)/ NOUN [plural **tremors**]
1 a small earthquake (= when the earth shakes) □ *The tremor lasted about a minute.* (**tremor**)
2 a shaking movement in part of your body □ *There was a tremor in his hands.* (**tremor**)

trench /trentʃ/ NOUN [plural **trenches**] a long narrow hole dug in the ground (**trincheira**)

trend /trend/ NOUN [plural **trends**] a gradual change or development □ *There's a new trend towards healthier eating.* (**tendência**)
• **trendy** /ˈtrendi/ ADJECTIVE [**trendier, trendiest**] fashionable □ *a trendy restaurant* □ *trendy clothes* (**em moda**)

trepidation /ˌtrepɪˈdeɪʃən/ NOUN, NO PLURAL a formal word meaning fear about something that is going to happen □ *Smith waited for his turn to jump with considerable trepidation.* (**temor**)

trespass /ˈtrespəs/ VERB [**trespasses, trespassing, trespassed**] to go onto someone else's land without permission □ *No trespassing! This is private property.* (**invadir**)
• **trespasser** /ˈtrespəsə(r)/ NOUN [plural **trespassers**] someone who goes onto someone else's land without permission □ *Trespassers will be prosecuted.* (**intruso, invasor**)

tri- /traɪ/ PREFIX tri- is added to the beginning of words to mean 'three' □ *triangle* □ *triathlon* (**tri-**)

trial /ˈtraɪəl/ ▶ NOUN [plural **trials**]
1 a legal process in which a court has to decide whether someone is guilty of a crime □ *a murder trial* (**julgamento**) ▣ *She's on trial for the killing of her husband.* (**em julgamento por**) ▣ *The suspect will now have to stand trial.* ▣ *He had not been given a fair trial.* (**julgamento justo**)
2 a test that is done to find out how good or effective something is □ *The company is carrying out trials on new products.* (**prova, teste**) ▣ *Clinical trials of the anti-cancer drug have been successful.* (**testes clínicos**)
3 trial and error a way of achieving something by trying lots of different methods and finding out which is successful □ *They solved the problem by trial and error.* (**tentativa e erro**)
4 trials a sports competition that decides who will be included in a team □ *The Olympic trials were held last month.* (**eliminatórias**)
▶ ADJECTIVE done for a short time as a way of finding out what someone or something is like □ *The couple had a trial separation last year and have now decided to get divorced.* (**tentativa, período de experiência**) ▣ *He was hired for a six-month trial period.* (**período experimental**)

triangle /ˈtraɪæŋgəl/ NOUN [plural **triangles**]
1 a flat shape with three sides and three angles □ *a right-angled triangle* (**triângulo**)
2 a musical instrument in the shape of a triangle that you hit with a metal stick (**triângulo**)
• **triangular** /traɪˈæŋgjʊlə(r)/ ADJECTIVE in the shape of a triangle □ *a triangular shape* □ *a triangular piece of cloth* (**triangular**)

triathlon /traɪˈæθlɒn/ NOUN [plural **triathlons**] a sports competition that has three parts, usually swimming, running and cycling (= riding a bicycle) (**triatlo**)

tribal /ˈtraɪbəl/ ADJECTIVE to do with a tribe □ *tribal ceremonies* (**tribal**)

tribe /traɪb/ NOUN [plural **tribes**] a group of families who have the same culture and language and have a traditional way of living a long way from cities □ *the Christian Arab tribes of the Syrian desert* (**tribo**)

tribesman /ˈtraɪbzmən/ NOUN [plural **tribesmen**] a man who belongs to a particular tribe (**membro de tribo**)

tribulation /ˌtrɪbjʊˈleɪʃən/ NOUN [plural **tribulations**] a problem in life (**tribulação**) ▣ *She*

tribunal

told me all the trials and tribulations of her work. (provas e tribulações)

tribunal /traɪˈbjuːnəl/ NOUN [plural tribunals] an official group of people whose job is to make a judgment about a particular problem, crime or disagreement □ *an employment tribunal* □ *a war crimes tribunal* (**tribunal**)

tributary /ˈtrɪbjʊtrɪ/ NOUN [plural tributaries] a stream or river that flows into a larger river. A geography word. (**afluente**)

tribute /ˈtrɪbjuːt/ NOUN [plural tributes]
1 a speech or action that shows you admire someone □ *The film will be shown as a tribute to its star who died last week.* (**tributo**)
2 pay tribute to someone/something to praise someone or something in public (**fazer um tributo a alguém/alguma coisa**)
3 be a tribute to someone/something to show how good or effective someone or something is □ *The success of the project is a tribute to her skill and determination.* (**ser um tributo a alguém/alguma coisa**)

trick /trɪk/ ▶ NOUN [plural tricks]
1 an unfair or unpleasant thing that you do to someone as a joke, or in order to get an advantage for yourself (**ardil, truque**) 🔁 *The children were playing tricks on each other.* (**pregar peças em**) 🔁 *He accused the party of using dirty tricks in the election campaign.* (**peça suja**)
2 something that looks like magic which you do to entertain people (**truque**) 🔁 *a magic trick* (**truque de mágica**) 🔁 *Ella was doing card tricks.* (**fazer truques**)
3 an effective way of doing something □ *There's a trick to opening that door quietly.* (**truque**) 🔁 *The trick is to find the way you learn best.* (**o segredo é**)
4 do the trick if something does the trick, it does what is needed to achieve something □ *I had a headache this morning but that tablet seems to have done the trick.* (**resolver o problema**)
▶ ADJECTIVE **a trick question** a question that is designed to make you give the wrong answer (**pegadinha**)
▶ VERB [tricks, tricking, tricked] to make someone do what you want by using clever but unfair methods □ + **into** *She was tricked into signing the papers.* (**enganar**)
• **trickery** /ˈtrɪkərɪ/ NOUN, NO PLURAL the use of tricks to get what you want (**trapaça, logro**)

trickle /ˈtrɪkəl/ ▶ VERB [trickles, trickling, trickled] to flow in a slow, thin stream □ *Sweat trickled down his face.* (**pingar, respingar**)
▶ NOUN [plural trickles] a slow, thin stream of liquid □ *The waterfall has become a trickle because there's been so little rain.* (**um pingo**)

tricky /ˈtrɪkɪ/ ADJECTIVE [trickier, trickiest] difficult to do or to deal with □ *a tricky situation* (**complicado**)

trim

tricycle /ˈtraɪsɪkəl/ NOUN [plural tricycles] a bicycle with three wheels (**triciclo**)

tried /traɪd/ PAST TENSE AND PAST PARTICIPLE OF **try** (**ver try**)

trifle /ˈtraɪfəl/ NOUN [plural trifles]
1 a sweet food made from cake, fruit, cream and custard (= sauce of eggs and cream) (**pavê**)
2 a trifle a small amount □ *It's a trifle hot in here.* (**ninharia**)
♦ PHRASAL VERB [trifles, trifling, trifled] **trifle with someone/something** to treat someone in a way that is not serious □ *We played chess, but he is so good, he was just trifling with me.* (**brincar, menosprezar**)
• **trifling** /ˈtraɪflɪŋ/ ADJECTIVE not at all important □ *a trifling matter* (**insignificante**)

trigger /ˈtrɪɡə(r)/ ▶ NOUN [plural triggers]
1 the part you pull to fire a gun (**gatilho**) 🔁 *He pointed the gun and pulled the trigger.* (**puxar o gatilho**)
2 something that causes something else to happen □ *Money is one of the most common triggers for arguments.* (**gatilho**)
▶ VERB [triggers, triggering, triggered] to make something start to happen □ *The announcement triggered violent protests around the country.* (**desencadear**)

trill /trɪl/ ▶ NOUN [plural trills] in music, when two notes are played one after the other, very fast (**tremolo**)
▶ VERB [trills, trilling, trilled] to make a sound like a trill □ *Birds were trilling in the high branches.* (**gorjear**)

trillion /ˈtrɪljən/ NUMBER [plural trillions] the number 1,000,000,000,000 (**trilhão**)

trilogy /ˈtrɪlədʒɪ/ NOUN [plural trilogies] a set of three plays, books, poems, etc. that have the same subject or the same characters (**trilogia**)

trim /trɪm/ ▶ VERB [trims, trimming, trimmed]
1 to cut a small amount off something □ *Get your hair trimmed.* □ *You'll need to trim that photo to get it into the frame.* (**aparar**)
2 to decorate the edges of something □ *a coat trimmed with white fur* (**enfeitar**)
3 to reduce something □ *The company has been forced to trim the number of employees.* (**cortar, diminuir**)
▶ NOUN [plural trims]
1 the act of cutting a small amount off something □ *Ask the hairdresser for a quick trim.* (**corte**)
2 a decoration that is added to something □ *The dress had a lace trim at the neck.* (**enfeite**)
▶ ADJECTIVE a trim person has a thin but healthy and attractive body (**delgado**)
• **trimming** /ˈtrɪmɪŋ/ NOUN [plural trimmings]
1 a decoration on the edge of something (**enfeite, guarnição**)
2 all the trimmings extra things added to a meal to make it more special or traditional □ *We had a*

Christmas dinner of roast turkey and all the trimmings. (**guarnições**)

trinket /'trɪŋkɪt/ NOUN [plural **trinkets**] a piece of jewellery or a small pretty object which is not valuable (**bijuteria**)

trio /'triːəʊ/ NOUN [plural **trios**] a group of three people or things, especially musicians (**trio**)

trip /trɪp/ ▶ NOUN [plural **trips**] a journey to a place and back again ☐ *There are boat trips around Lake Geneva.* (**viagem**) 🔲 *a shopping trip* (**viagem de compras**) 🔲 *He has made several trips to Japan.* (**fez várias viagens**) ☐ *+ to We went on a trip to the zoo.*
▶ VERB [**trips, tripping, tripped**]
1 to hit your foot on something and fall, or almost fall ☐ *+ over Caroline tripped over the edge of the carpet.* ☐ *Mind you don't trip on the step.* (**tropeçar**)
2 to make someone fall by putting your foot in front of them ☐ *+ up One of the boys tripped me up.* (**fazer tropeçar**)

triple /'trɪpəl/ ▶ ADJECTIVE consisting of three parts ☐ *triple-glazed windows* ☐ *a triple somersault* (**triplo**)
▶ VERB [**triples, tripling, tripled**] to become or to make something three times bigger in size or amount ☐ *The number of students has tripled this year.* (**triplicar**)
▶ DETERMINER three times as big, as many, or as much ☐ *We had triple the number of entries this year.* (**triplicar**)

triplet /'trɪplɪt/ NOUN [plural **triplets**] one of three children born to the same mother at the same time (**trigêmeos**)

tripod /'traɪpɒd/ NOUN [plural **tripods**] a piece of equipment with three legs, used for supporting something like a camera (**tripé**)

trite /traɪt/ ADJECTIVE a trite remark, phrase, etc. is one that people have said so often that it is not interesting or original ☐ *It sounds trite to say that funerals 'bring people together', but it's true.* (**batido, banal**)

triumph /'traɪəmf/ ▶ NOUN [plural **triumphs**]
1 a great success in a competition or fight ☐ *It was another triumph for the champions.* ☐ *England's only World Cup triumph was in 1966.* (**triunfo**)
2 the feeling of happiness you get when you have won or been successful ☐ *He felt a sense of triumph.* (**triunfo**)
▶ VERB [**triumphs, triumphing, triumphed**] to win or succeed ☐ *Yeltsin triumphed over his rivals again.* (**triunfar**)

• **triumphant** /traɪˈʌmfənt/ ADJECTIVE very happy after winning or succeeding ☐ *the triumphant medal winners* (**triunfante**)

• **triumphantly** /traɪˈʌmfəntli/ ADVERB in a triumphant way ☐ *She raised her arm triumphantly.* (**triunfantemente**)

trivia /'trɪviə/ NOUN, NO PLURAL facts and details that are not important ☐ *She knew a lot of sports trivia.* (**insignificâncias**)

• **trivial** /'trɪviəl/ ADJECTIVE not important or not serious ☐ *trivial details* ☐ *a trivial problem* (**trivial**)

• **triviality** /ˌtrɪviˈælɪti/ NOUN [plural **trivialities**]
1 something that is not important ☐ *I don't want to bore you with trivialities.* (**insignificâncias**)
2 the quality of not being important (**insignificância**)

• **trivialize** or **trivialise** /'trɪviəlaɪz/ VERB [**trivializes, trivializing, trivialized**] to make something seem less important than it really is ☐ *No one should trivialize this achievement.* (**banalizar**)

trod /trɒd/ PAST TENSE OF **tread** (**ver tread**)

trodden /'trɒdən/ PAST PARTICIPLE OF **tread** (**ver tread**)

trolley /'trɒli/ NOUN [plural **trolleys**]
1 a container on wheels, used for carrying things ☐ *a supermarket trolley* (**carrinho, vagonete**)
2 a table on wheels (**mesa com rodinhas**)
3 the US word for **tram** (**bonde**)

trombone /trɒmˈbəʊn/ NOUN [plural **trombones**] a metal musical instrument that you play by blowing, and by sliding a long part up and down (**trombone**)

troop /truːp/ ▶ NOUN [plural **troops**] (**tropa**)
1 troops soldiers ☐ *The US sent troops to Darfur.* (**soldados**)
2 a group of people or animals ☐ *a troop of monkeys* (**bando**)
▶ VERB [**troops, trooping, trooped**] if a group of people troop somewhere, they go there ☐ *More than 7.5 million people trooped through the museum's doors last year.* (**reunir-se em bando**)

trophy /'trəʊfi/ NOUN [plural **trophies**] a prize such as a silver cup that you get for winning a competition ☐ *Helen won the junior tennis trophy three years running.* (**troféu**)

tropical /'trɒpɪkəl/ ADJECTIVE in or to do with the tropics ☐ *a tropical rainforest* (**tropical**)

tropics /'trɒpɪks/ PLURAL NOUN **the tropics** the hot areas near the equator (= line round the middle of the world). A geography word. (**trópicos**)

trot /trɒt/ ▶ VERB [**trots, trotting, trotted**]
1 if a horse trots, it moves more quickly than walking, but does not run ☐ *The horse trotted down the road.* (**trotar**)
2 if a person trots somewhere, they walk with short, fast steps ☐ *They all trotted off to look at his paintings.* (**trotar**)
◆ PHRASAL VERB **trot something out** to say something that has been said many times before ☐ *Politicians trot out the same old ideas at election time.* (**repetir o que já foi dito/é sabido**)
▶ NOUN [plural **trots**]
1 on the trot happening one after the other ☐ *The team have won three games on the trot.* (**em seguida**)

trouble /'trʌbəl/ ▶ NOUN [plural **troubles**]

1 problems, difficulties or worries □ + *ing* *She has trouble sleeping.* □ *He had financial troubles.* (**problema**) 🔲 *You'd have no trouble finding a better job.* (**nenhum problema**)

2 *no plural* extra effort (**esforço**) 🔲 *A washing machine would save you a lot of trouble.* 🔲 *He took the trouble to thank everyone individually.* (**ter o trabalho de**) 🔲 *They went to so much trouble to make our visit pleasant.* (**fazer um grande esforço**)

3 *no plural* the thing about something that causes problems (**problema**) 🔲 *The trouble is, I already have a meeting on that day.* □ *The trouble with Sarah is that she never stops to think.* (**o problema é**)

4 *no plural* a problem with your health or with a machine or piece of equipment □ *She has heart trouble.* □ *The car had some sort of engine trouble.* (**problema**)

5 *no plural* a difficult or dangerous situation (**problema**) 🔲 *Their ship got into trouble during a storm.* (**ter problemas**) 🔲 *The business is in deep trouble.* (**problema sério**)

6 *no plural* a situation where you will be punished or blamed (**problema**) 🔲 *We got into trouble for talking in class.* (**ficamos em apuros**) 🔲 *If I'm late home, I'll be in big trouble.* (**ter um problemão**)

7 *no plural* a situation where people are behaving badly, fighting, causing difficulties, etc. (**problema**) 🔲 *Some people at the back of the hall started to cause trouble.* (**causar problemas**) 🔲 *The trouble started when police tried to arrest the man.* (**o problema começou**)

▶ VERB [**troubles, troubling, troubled**] if something troubles you, it worries you □ *They were troubled by reports of violence in the area.* (**perturbar**)

• **troubled** /'trʌbəld/ ADJECTIVE

1 suffering because you have a lot of problems in your life □ *The troubled star returned home yesterday.* (**perturbado**)

2 having a lot of problems □ *We live in troubled times.* (**problemáticos**)

• **troublemaker** /'trʌbəl,meɪkə(r)/ NOUN [plural **troublemakers**] someone who deliberately causes problems (**encrenqueiro**)

• **troublesome** /'trʌbəlsəm/ ADJECTIVE causing worry or problems □ *He has a troublesome knee injury.* (**incômodo, transtorno**)

trough /trɒf/ NOUN [plural **troughs**] a long container that animals eat or drink from (**cocho**)

trounce /traʊns/ VERB [**trounces, trouncing, trounced**] to defeat someone very easily (**derrotar**)

troupe /tru:p/ NOUN [plural **troupes**] a group of performers who work together □ *a troupe of acrobats* (**trupe**)

trouser /'traʊzə(r)/ ADJECTIVE relating to trousers □ *He put the money in his trouser pocket.* (**da calça**)

trousers /'traʊzəz/ PLURAL NOUN a piece of clothing for the lower half of your body that covers each leg separately (**calça**) 🔲 *She was wearing a pair of black trousers.* (**uma calça**) □ *leather trousers*

trout /traʊt/ NOUN [plural **trout**] a type of fish that lives in rivers and lakes and is eaten (**truta**)

truancy /'tru:ənsi/ NOUN, NO PLURAL the act of staying away from school without permission (**cábula, vadiagem**)

• **truant** /'tru:ənt/ NOUN [plural **truants**]

1 a student who stays away from school without permission (**estudante que cabula aula**)

2 play truant to stay away from school without permission (**cabular aulas**)

truce /tru:s/ NOUN [plural **truces**] an agreement to stop fighting or arguing (**trégua**) 🔲 *The political parties called a truce.* (**pedir trégua**)

truck /trʌk/ NOUN [plural **trucks**] a large road vehicle for carrying goods □ *He drove the truck into the yard.* □ *Her Dad's a truck driver.* (**caminhão**)

trudge /trʌdʒ/ VERB [**trudges, trudging, trudged**] to walk with slow, heavy steps □ *They were trudging along in the snow.* (**arrastar-se**)

true /tru:/ ADJECTIVE [**truer, truest**]

1 real and not invented (**verdadeiro**) 🔲 *Is it a true story?* (**história verdadeira**) □ + *that* *Is it true that you're moving to Tokyo?*

2 real and not pretended □ *Ben never showed his true feelings.* □ *She's a true friend.* □ *He had finally found true love.* □ *He had a false passport to hide his true identity.* (**real, verdadeiro**)

3 come true if something comes true, the thing you have spoken about really happens □ *I never thought my wish to travel round the world would come true.* (**tornar-se real, realizar-se**)

4 be true to someone/something to be loyal to someone or something, and do what you said you would do □ *He had always been true to his principles.* (**ser verdadeiro, sincero com alguém/algo**)

truffle /'trʌfəl/ NOUN [plural **truffles**]

1 a soft sweet made of chocolate (**trufa**)

2 a rare type of fungus (= plant with no leaves or flowers) that grows under the ground, which you can eat (**túbera, tipo raro de cogumelo**)

truly /'tru:li/ ADVERB

1 really □ *Tell me what you truly want to do.* (**realmente**)

2 in a sincere way □ *I'm truly sorry.* (**sinceramente**)

trump /trʌmp/ NOUN [plural **trumps**] a card that has a higher value than other cards in some card games (**trunfo**)

◆ IDIOM **come up/turn up trumps** to do something which helps you to succeed, especially when it is not expected □ *Beckham came up trumps with a goal in the last minute of the game.* (**surgir com trunfo**)

trump card /'trʌmp ˌkɑːd/ NOUN [plural **trump cards**] a usually secret advantage that will help you succeed (**um trunfo, uma vantagem**)

trumped-up /'trʌmptʌp/ ADJECTIVE deliberately invented in order to make someone seem guilty □ *trumped-up evidence* (**forjado**)

trumpet /'trʌmpɪt/ NOUN [plural **trumpets**] a metal musical instrument that you blow into □ *Millie is learning to play the trumpet.* (**trombeta**)

truncheon /'trʌntʃən/ NOUN [plural **truncheons**] a short, thick stick that police officers carry (**cassetete**)

trundle /'trʌndəl/ VERB [**trundles, trundling, trundled**]
1 to move slowly along on wheels or to move something like this □ *Lorries were trundling through the empty streets* (**rolar**)
2 to walk in a slow, heavy way □ *Eventually, he trundled off down the road.* (**arrastar-se**)

trunk /trʌŋk/ NOUN [plural **trunks**]
1 the thick main stem of a tree (**tronco**) 🔁 *a tree trunk* (**tronco de árvore**)
2 an elephant's long nose (**tromba**)
3 a large box for storing things (**baú**)
4 the main part of a person's body, not including their head, arms or legs (**tronco**)
5 the US word for **boot** (= part of a car) (**porta-malas**)

trunk road /'trʌŋk ˌrəʊd/ NOUN [plural **trunk roads**] a main road between towns (**rodovia principal**)

trunks /trʌŋks/ PLURAL NOUN a piece of clothing that men or boys wear for swimming (**calção de banho, sunga**)

trust /trʌst/ ▶ VERB [**trusts, trusting, trusted**]
1 to believe that someone is honest and loyal □ *The colonel picked out ten men he knew he could trust.* (**confiar**)
2 to feel confident that someone will do something correctly and well or will look after something well □ **+ to do something** *I know I can trust you to choose a suitable present.* (**confiar**)
3 to allow someone to have or use something that belongs to you because you think they will be careful with it □ **+ with** *Can I trust you with my new camera?* (**confiar**)
4 Trust you/him/her, etc. used to say that a silly or annoying action is typical of someone □ *Trust Dan to be late!* (**Adivinhe se o Dan vai se atrasar!**)
▶ NOUN [plural **trusts**]
1 no plural the belief that someone is honest and loyal (**confiança**) 🔁 *The new manager will have to gain the trust of her staff.* (**ganhar a confiança**)
2 a legal arrangement in which someone looks after and controls money or property for someone else (**procurador em confiança**) 🔁 *His inheritance was held in trust until he was twenty one.* (**manter/administrar em confiança**)

• **trustee** /trʌs'tiː/ NOUN [plural **trustees**]
1 someone who looks after and controls someone else's money or property in a legal arrangement (**curador**)
2 one of a group of people who manage a company or organization such as a school or hospital (**administrador**)

• **trusting** /'trʌstɪŋ/ ADJECTIVE believing that other people are honest and good □ *She is a very trusting person.* (**confiável**)

• **trustworthy** /'trʌstˌwɜːði/ ADJECTIVE able to be trusted □ *I'm sure he's a trustworthy person.* (**digno de confiança**)

truth /truːθ/ NOUN [plural **truths**]
1 the truth the true facts (**verdade**) 🔁 *I don't think he is telling the truth.* (**dizer a verdade**) 🔁 *The simple truth is that she never really loved him.* (**a pura verdade**) □ **+ about** *I don't think we'll ever know the truth about what happened.*
2 no plural the quality of being true □ **+ in** *Do you think there's any truth in the rumours that he is planning to leave?* (**verdade**)
3 a fact that people accept is true □ *People don't like being told uncomfortable truths.* (**verdade**)

> Note that you **tell** the truth. You do not 'say the truth':
> ✓ *Tell me the truth: Do you like her?*
> ✗ *Say the truth: Do you like her?*

• **truthful** /'truːθfʊl/ ADJECTIVE honest □ *I don't think he's been completely truthful with me.* □ *a truthful answer* (**que diz a verdade**)

• **truthfully** /'truːθfʊli/ ADVERB in a truthful way □ *I don't think he answered truthfully.* (**veridicamente**)

try /traɪ/ ▶ VERB [**tries, trying, tried**]
1 to make an effort or an attempt to do something □ **+ to do something** *Please try to understand.* □ *We tried everything we could to save him.* (**tentar**) 🔁 *He failed the exam, but he can always try again next year.* (**tentar de novo**)
2 to do or use something to see if you like it or if it works or is effective □ *Try this powder for a cleaner wash.* □ *I've never tried Chinese food.* □ **+ ing** *You could try phoning him.* (**experimentar**)
3 to find out if someone committed a crime by hearing all the evidence (= facts or statements given in a court of law) □ *They will be tried in the European Court of Human Rights.* □ **+ for** *She was tried for murder.* (**julgar**)
◆ PHRASAL VERBS **try something on** to put on a piece of clothing to see if it fits or what it looks like on you □ *I tried on three summer dresses but I didn't*

tsar 869 **tumble**

like any of them. (experimentar uma roupa) **try something out** to use something to see if it works or is effective or if you like it ◻ *We're trying out a new type of carrot seed this year.* (experimentar)
▶ go to **try your luck**
▶ NOUN [plural **tries**]
1 an attempt to do something ◻ *That was a good try. Better luck next time.* (tentativa) ▣ *I couldn't get the tyre off – could you have a try?* (fazer uma tentativa)
2 when you do or use something to see if you like it or if it works or is effective ▣ *I saw an advert for a sailing course, so I thought I'd give it a try.* (fazer uma experiência)
3 in the sport of rugby, a successful attempt to put the ball over the other team's goal line (ensaio)
• **trying** /ˈtraɪɪŋ/ ADJECTIVE difficult and annoying ◻ *He can be very trying sometimes.* (desgastante)

tsar /zɑː(r)/ NOUN [plural **tsars**] a ruler of Russia before 1917 (czar)

T-Shirt /ˈtiː ʃɜːt/ NOUN [plural **T-shirts**] a piece of clothing made from soft cotton which you wear on the top part of your body ◻ *She was wearing jeans and a white T-shirt.* (camiseta)

tsp /ˈtiːspuːn/ ABBREVIATION **teaspoon** (colher de chá)

tsunami /tsuːˈnɑːmɪ/ NOUN [plural **tsunamis**] a very high, fast wave that is caused by an earthquake (= when the ground shakes) under the sea (tsunami)

tub /tʌb/ NOUN [plural **tubs**]
1 a container with a lid which has food in it ◻ *a tub of ice cream* (pote)
2 a round, deep container ◻ *The tub was full of bright red flowers.* (tina)
3 the US word for **bath** (banheira)

tuba /ˈtjuːbə/ NOUN [plural **tubas**] a large metal musical instrument that you blow which plays very low notes (tuba)

tubby /ˈtʌbɪ/ ADJECTIVE [**tubbier**, **tubbiest**] an informal word meaning slightly fat (rechonchudo)

tube /tjuːb/ NOUN [plural **tubes**]
1 a long, thin pipe ◻ *He was in hospital with a feeding tube in his stomach.* (cano, tubo)
2 a container for a soft substance which you press to get the substance out ◻ *+ of a tube of toothpaste* (tubo)
3 no plural an underground railway system, especially in London ◻ *We can easily get there by tube.* (metrô) ▣ *a tube station* (estação de metrô)

tuber /ˈtjuːbə(r)/ NOUN [plural **tubers**] a swollen underground plant root that new plants can grow from. A biology word ◻ *Potatoes are tubers that you can eat or plant again.* (tubérculo)

tuberculosis /tjuːˌbɜːkjuˈləʊsɪs/ NOUN, NO PLURAL a serious infectious disease that affects your lungs (tuberculose)

tuck /tʌk/ VERB [**tucks**, **tucking**, **tucked**]
1 to push the edge of something somewhere to make it tidy or firm ◻ *Tuck your shirt into your trousers.* ◻ *She tucked the flap into the envelope and sealed it with tape.* (enfiar)
2 to put something into a small space ◻ *She tucked the bag under her arm.* (comprimir)
◆ PHRASAL VERBS **tuck something away 1** to put something in a safe place ◻ *He quickly tucked the letter away when Ann walked into the room.* (guardar com segurança) **2** if a place is tucked away, it is difficult to find or few people go there ◻ *The studio is tucked away at the top of the house.* **tuck in/tuck into something** an informal word meaning to start eating something enthusiastically ◻ *Joe tucked into a bowl of spaghetti.* (comer com entusiasmo) **tuck someone in/up 1** to make someone comfortable in bed by putting the sheets over them ◻ *She went upstairs to tuck the children in.* (embrulhar nas cobertas) **2** if you are tucked up in bed, you are lying comfortably in bed ◻ *He was tucked up in bed by 9pm.* (deitar-se confortavelmente na cama)

Tuesday /ˈtjuːzdɪ/ NOUN [plural **Tuesdays**] the day of the week after Monday and before Wednesday ◻ *Kay's coming on Tuesday.* (terça-feira)

tuft /tʌft/ NOUN [plural **tufts**] several pieces of grass or hair that are growing from the same place ◻ *The baby had a tuft of dark hair.* (tufo)

tug /tʌɡ/ ▶ VERB [**tugs**, **tugging**, **tugged**] to pull something suddenly and firmly ◻ *She tugged her hand away from mine.* ◻ *James tugged on the rope.* (puxar)
▶ NOUN [plural **tugs**]
1 a sudden firm pull (puxão) ▣ *I gave his arm a tug and he looked at me crossly.* (dar um puxão)
2 a **tugboat** (rebocador)

tugboat /ˈtʌɡbəʊt/ NOUN [plural **tugboats**] a boat that is used for pulling other boats (rebocador)

tug-of-war /ˌtʌɡəvˈwɔː(r)/ NOUN, NO PLURAL a competition in which two teams pull each end of a rope and try to pull each other over (cabo de guerra)

tuition /tjuːˈɪʃən/ NOUN, NO PLURAL teaching something, especially to one person or a small group ◻ *His parents paid for him to have private tuition in English.* (aula, ensino) ▣ *Students have to pay tuition fees.* (remuneração de aula)

tulip /ˈtjuːlɪp/ NOUN [plural **tulips**] a type of flower in the shape of a cup that is often red or yellow (tulipa)

tumble /ˈtʌmbəl/ ▶ VERB [**tumbles**, **tumbling**, **tumbled**]
1 to fall somewhere ◻ *He tripped and tumbled down the stairs.* (levar um tombo)
2 if a price tumbles, it suddenly becomes lower ◻ *Oil prices tumbled last week.* (cair, reduzir)
▶ NOUN [plural **tumbles**] a fall (tombo) ▣ *Lucy had taken a tumble* (= fallen) *over the doorstep.* (levar um tombo)

tumbledown /'tʌmbəldaʊn/ ADJECTIVE a tumbledown building is old and in bad condition (arruinado, dilapidado)

tumble-dry /'tʌmbəl'draɪ/ VERB [tumble-dries, tumble-drying, tumble-dried] to dry clothes in a tumble-dryer (secar roupas na secadora)

- **tumble-dryer** or **tumble-drier** /'tʌmbəl'draɪə(r)/ NOUN [plural tumble-dryers or tumble-driers] a machine that dries clothes by turning them in hot air (secadora de roupas)

tumbler /'tʌmblə(r)/ NOUN [plural tumblers] a glass with straight sides that you drink from (copo)

tummy /'tʌmɪ/ NOUN [plural tummies] an informal word for stomach (estômago, barriga)

tumour /'tjuːmə(r)/ NOUN [plural tumours] a group of cells in your body which are not growing in a normal way □ He had an operation to remove a brain tumour. (tumor)

tumult /'tjuːmʌlt/ NOUN [plural tumults] a formal word meaning a situation in which there is a lot of noise, confusion, or excitement □ the tumult of battle (tumulto)

- **tumultuous** /tjuː'mʌltjʊəs/ ADJECTIVE
  1 involving a lot of activity, violence, or confusion □ It had been a tumultuous year. (tumultuoso)
  2 noisy and excited □ He walked on stage to tumultuous applause. (tumultuoso)

tuna /'tjuːnə/ NOUN [plural tuna] a large sea fish that you can eat □ a tuna sandwich (atum)

tundra /'tʌndrə/ NOUN, NO PLURAL a large area where the ground is always frozen below the surface, and not many plants can grow. A geography word. (tundra)

tune /tjuːn/ ▶ NOUN [plural tunes]
1 a series of musical notes that sound nice (melodia) 🔊 She was *playing* some *tunes* on the piano. (tocar melodias) 🔊 a *catchy tune* (= one that is easy to remember) (uma melodia cativante)
2 in tune playing or singing exactly the right sounds □ He can't sing in tune. (afinado)
3 out of tune playing or singing sounds which are slightly wrong □ The piano is out of tune. (desafinado)
4 be in tune with someone/something to understand the way someone thinks and the things that they want □ She is very in tune with the needs of her students. (em harmonia)
5 be out of tune with someone/something to not understand the way that someone thinks and the things that they want □ The government is out of tune with the people in this country. (em divergência)

◆ IDIOM **change your tune** to change your opinion in a surprising or sudden way □ You've changed your tune! (mude seu tom de voz)

▶ VERB [tunes, tuning, tuned]
1 to make small changes to a musical instrument so that it sounds right □ Ben was tuning his guitar. (afinar)
2 if a radio or television is tuned to a particular programme, it is receiving it □ You're tuned to Radio Gold. (sintonizar) 🔊 *Stay tuned* (= keep listening or watching) *for a chance to win £1,000.* (fique sintonizado)
3 to make small changes to an engine so that it works better (ajustar)

◆ PHRASAL VERB **tune in** to listen to or watch a particular radio or television programme □ Over 5 million viewers tuned in to watch the game. (sintonizar)

- **tuneful** /'tjuːnfʊl/ ADJECTIVE tuneful music is nice to listen to (melodioso)
- **tuneless** /'tjuːnlɪs/ ADJECTIVE not having a pleasant tune (desarmônico)
- **tunelessly** /'tjuːnlɪslɪ/ ADVERB in a tuneless way □ She was whistling tunelessly. (desarmonicamente)

tunic /'tjuːnɪk/ NOUN [plural tunics] a loose piece of clothing with no sleeves (túnica)

tunnel /'tʌnəl/ ▶ NOUN [plural tunnels] a long underground passage □ There is a rail tunnel linking England and France. (túnel) 🔊 There were plans to *build* a *tunnel* through the Alps. (construir um túnel)
▶ VERB [tunnels, tunnelling/US tunneling, tunnelled/US tunneled] to make an underground passage □ Will they tunnel under the river or build a bridge over it? (escavar um túnel)

turban /'tɜːbən/ NOUN [plural turbans] a long piece of cloth that some men wrap around their heads for religious reasons (turbante)

turbine /'tɜːbaɪn/ NOUN [plural turbines] a machine or engine that gets power when water or gas moves a wheel around (turbina)

turbulence /'tɜːbjʊləns/ NOUN, NO PLURAL
1 movement in the water or air that makes ships or air craft move suddenly □ There was a lot of turbulence on the flight so we had to stay in our seats. (turbulência)
2 when there are lot of sudden and confusing changes □ political turbulence (turbulência)

- **turbulent** /'tɜːbjʊlənt/ ADJECTIVE
  1 involving a lot of changes, confusion or disagreement □ It was a turbulent week for the government. □ a turbulent relationship (turbulento)
  2 turbulent air or water moves suddenly and strongly (turbulento)

turf /tɜːf/ ▶ NOUN, NO PLURAL short thick grass and the soil under it (relva, gramado)
▶ VERB [turfs, turfing, turfed] to put turf on an area of ground (gramar)

◆ PHRASAL VERB **turf someone out** an informal word meaning to make someone leave a place □ He was turfed out of the club following an argument. (obrigar a se retirar)

turkey — turnaround

turkey /'tɜːkɪ/ NOUN [plural turkeys]
1 a large bird that lives on farms and is eaten as food (**peru**)
2 *no plural* the meat from this bird ☐ *roast turkey* ☐ *a turkey sandwich* (**peru**)

turmoil /'tɜːmɔɪl/ NOUN, NO PLURAL a state of worry and confusion ☐ *Her mind was in turmoil.* ☐ *political turmoil* (**alvoroço**)

turn /tɜːn/ ▶ VERB [turns, turning, turned]
1 to move your body or part of your body to face in another direction ☐ *He turned and walked away.* ☐ + *around* *I turned around to look at them.* ☐ + *to* *She turned to her neighbour and whispered something.* ☐ *He turned his head slightly.* (**virar(-se)**)

2 to move something so that it faces in another direction, or to make like this ☐ *The car turned upside down.* ☐ + *over* *You must not turn the cards over before the game starts.* ☐ + *round* *He turned the book round so that we could see the picture.* (**virar**)

3 to make a circular movement around a central point, or to make something do this ☐ *The wheels began to turn.* ☐ *Turn the handle to the right.* (**virar**)

4 if you turn the page of a book, you move it so that you can see the next page (**virar**)

5 to change in a particular way ☐ *She took one look and turned pale.* ☐ *Things turned nasty when the police arrived.* (**tornar(-se)**)

6 if your thoughts or your conversation turn to something, you start thinking or talking about that subject ☐ *Later on, talk turned to the coming elections.* (**dirigir(-se)**) 🔁 *We need to turn our attention to the causes of these crimes.* (**dirigir nossa atenção para**)

♦ IDIOM **not turn a hair** to not show any emotion when something shocking happens (**não balançar um fio de cabelo**)

⇨ go to **turn a *blind* eye to something**, **turn your nose up at something**, **turn the *tables* on someone**

♦ PHRASAL VERBS **turn (someone) against someone/something** to start to dislike someone or something and to stop supporting them, or to make someone do this ☐ *My friends have all turned against me.* (**voltar-se contra**) **turn someone away** to say that someone cannot go into a place ☐ *When they arrived at work the next day, they were turned away.* (**impedir de entrar**) **turn (someone) back** to stop a journey and go back again, or to make someone do this ☐ *Their car was turned back at the border.* (**voltar, mandar de volta**) **turn something down** to make a machine produce less sound, heat, etc. ☐ *Could you turn the music down, please?* ☐ *I've turned down the heating.* (**abaixar, diminuir**) **turn someone/something down** to not accept an offer ☐ *He asked her to marry him but she turned him down.* ☐ *I turned down a job in his company.* (**recusar alguém/alguma coisa**) **turn (someone/something) into someone/something** to change into something different or to make someone or something do this ☐ *His book is being turned into a movie.* ☐ *The caterpillar turns into a moth.* (**tornar-se/transformar-se em...**) **turn off (something)** to leave the road or path you are travelling on to go on another road or path ☐ *Turn off the main road when you see a sign to the town hall.* (**sair da estrada**) **turn something off** to move a switch so that a machine stops working or a supply of something is stopped ☐ *Don't forget to turn off the lights.* (**desligar**) **turn something on** to move a switch so that a machine starts working or a supply of something is started ☐ *I've turned on the heating.* (**ligar**) **turn out** to be found to have a particular reason, quality or result (**revelar-se**) 🔁 *It turned out that she'd never received the letter.* (**revelou-se que**) 🔁 *Conditions in the hotel turned out to be really bad.* **turn over** to change to a different television programme (**mudar de canal**) **turn to someone** to go to someone for help ☐ *I had lots of problems at work, and I felt there was nobody to turn to.* (**voltar-se a alguém para pedir ajuda**) **turn up 1** to arrive ☐ *He didn't turn up for work this morning.* (**aparecer**) **2** to be found ☐ *My glasses turned up in the car.* (**ser encontrado**) **turn something up** to make a machine produce more sound, heat, etc. ☐ *Can you turn the volume up?* (**aumentar (volume, calor etc.)**)

▶ NOUN [plural turns]

1 the time when you can or must do something, before or after someone else (**vez**) 🔁 *It's your/my turn next.* (**sua/minha vez**) ☐ *Josh hasn't had a turn yet.*

2 take turns/take it in turns if people take turns, each person does something, one after the other (**revezar-se**)

3 in turn one after the other ☐ *He tried each of the dishes in turn.* (**alternadamente, em rodízio**)

4 a change of direction or a curve or corner in a road or path (**esquina**) 🔁 *Take the first turn on the right.* (**vire a primeira esquina**) 🔁 *a left/right turn* (**esquina à direita/à esquerda**)

5 when something is moved in a circle around a central point ☐ *I gave the screw another turn.* (**volta**)

6 when a situation changes (**mudança**) 🔁 *Events took a dramatic turn when the president announced his resignation.* (**ter uma mudança/reviravolta dramática**) 🔁 *His health has taken a turn for the better/worse.* (**mudança para melhor/pior**)

7 a good turn something helpful or kind that you do for someone (**uma boa ação**)

turnaround /'tɜːnəraʊnd/ NOUN [plural turnarounds] a situation that changes from a bad one to a good one ☐ *In a remarkable turnaround,*

the team went on to win the competition. (reviravolta)

turning /'tɜːnɪŋ/ NOUN [plural **turnings**] a place where a car can leave a road and go onto another road (rua transversal, esquina, desvio) ▭ *Take the second turning on the right.* (pegue o desvio) ▭ *We took a wrong turning and ended up on a mud track.* (uma rua transversal errada)

turning point /'tɜːnɪŋ ˌpɔɪnt/ NOUN [plural **turning points**] an important time which could change the future of something ▭ *He's reached a turning point in his career.* (ponto crítico, momento decisivo)

turnip /'tɜːnɪp/ NOUN [plural **turnips**] a hard, round, white vegetable that grows under the ground (nabo)

turnout /'tɜːnaʊt/ NOUN, NO PLURAL the number of people who go to an event or who go to vote in an election (comparecimento) ▭ *There was a low turnout in the election.* (fraco comparecimento)

turnover /'tɜːnˌəʊvə(r)/ NOUN [plural **turnovers**]
1 the value of the goods and services that a company sells during a particular time ▭ *The business has an annual turnover of more than $2.4 billion.* (movimento total)
2 the rate at which people leave and join a company or organization ▭ *The company has a high turnover of staff.* (rotatividade de empregados)
3 a piece of pastry which is folded over fruit or jam ▭ *an apple turnover* (pastel doce)

turnpike /'tɜːnpaɪk/ NOUN [plural **turnpikes**] a large road in America which drivers pay to use (rodovia expressa sujeita a pedágio)

turnstile /'tɜːnstaɪl/ NOUN [plural **turnstiles**] a gate that turns, allowing one person to go through at a time (catraca)

turpentine /'tɜːpəntaɪn/ NOUN, NO PLURAL a liquid with a strong smell, used for removing paint (aguarrás)

turquoise /'tɜːkwɔɪz/ ▶ NOUN, NO PLURAL a green-blue colour (turquesa, azul-turquesa)
▶ ADJECTIVE having a green-blue colour

turret /'tʌrɪt/ NOUN [plural **turrets**] a small tower on a castle (torreão, torre)

turtle /'tɜːtəl/ NOUN [plural **turtles**] an animal that usually lives in water and has a hard shell (tartaruga)

tusk /tʌsk/ NOUN [plural **tusks**] one of the two long teeth that stick out of the mouth of some animals, such as elephants (presa)

tussle /'tʌsəl/ ▶ NOUN [plural **tussles**] a fight or argument between two people who want the same thing ▭ *They have been involved in a legal tussle over their daughter.* (briga, contenda)
▶ VERB [**tussles, tussling, tussled**] to argue or fight with someone over something you both want ▭ *The players were tussling for the ball.* (brigar por disputa)

tut /tʌt/ or **tut-tut** /ˌtʌt'tʌt/ ▶ EXCLAMATION a sound you make with your tongue to show disapproval (tsc, tsc)
▶ VERB [**tuts, tutting, tutted**] to make a sound with your tongue to show disapproval (monitor)

tutor /'tjuːtə(r)/ ▶ NOUN [plural **tutors**]
1 a teacher who teaches one person or a small group ▭ *He hired a private tutor to help him learn Japanese.* (monitor)
2 a university teacher who works with a small group of students (orientador)
▶ VERB [**tutors, tutoring, tutored**] to teach one person or a small group ▭ *He tutored children with learning difficulties.* (ensinar)

• **tutorial** /tjuːˈtɔːrɪəl/ NOUN [plural **tutorials**] a university class in which a small group of students discuss a subject ▭ *She had no lectures or tutorials that day.* (tutoria, orientação)

TV /ˌtiːˈviː/ NOUN [plural **TVs**] television ▭ *She switched the TV on.* (ligar a TV) ▭ *What's on TV tonight?* ▭ *I think the children watch too much TV.* (assistir à TV)

twang /twæŋ/ NOUN [plural **twangs**]
1 the sound of a tight string or wire being pulled ▭ *We listened to the twang of his guitar strings.* (blém!)
2 someone's accent ▭ *His voice had a southern twang.* (sotaque)

tweak /twiːk/ ▶ VERB [**tweaks, tweaking, tweaked**]
1 to pull something quickly and suddenly ▭ *He tweaked my hair roughly.* (puxar, beliscar)
2 to make small changes to something ▭ *They had tweaked the words of the song.* (alterar levemente)
▶ NOUN [plural **tweaks**]
1 a quick and sudden pull (puxão, beliscão)
2 a small change that is made to something (pequenas alterações)

tweed /twiːd/ NOUN [plural **tweeds**] a type of thick wool cloth ▭ *a tweed jacket* (tweed)

tweezers /'twiːzəz/ PLURAL NOUN a small tool consisting of two narrow pieces of metal that are joined at one end, used for picking up very small things or for pulling out hairs (pinça)

twelfth /twelfθ/ NUMBER 12th written as a word (décimo segundo)

twelve /twelv/ NUMBER [plural **twelves**] the number 12 (doze)

twentieth /'twentɪəθ/ NUMBER 20th written as a word (vigésimo)

twenty /'twentɪ/ NUMBER [plural **twenties**]
1 the number 20 (vinte)
2 the twenties the years between 1920 and 1929 (os anos 1920)

twice /twaɪs/ ADVERB two times ▭ *He sneezed twice.* ▭ *I could eat twice that amount.* ▭ *I visit my grandmother twice a week.* (duas vezes)

twiddle

twiddle /ˈtwɪdəl/ VERB [**twiddles, twiddling, twiddled**] to move something around several times in your hands, especially because you are bored □ *He was twiddling with his wedding ring.* (**girar**)

♦ IDIOM **twiddle your thumbs** an informal phrase meaning to do nothing because you are waiting for something to happen □ *We were left twiddling our thumbs when the builder failed to arrive.* (**ficar girando os polegares por impaciência**)

twig /twɪg/ ▶ NOUN [*plural* **twigs**] a thin branch from a tree □ *We need a pile of dry twigs to start the fire.* (**ramo**)
▶ VERB [**twigs, twigging, twigged**] an informal word meaning to suddenly understand something □ *Then I twigged what he meant.* (**entender, perceber, notar**)

twilight /ˈtwaɪlaɪt/ NOUN, NO PLURAL the time in the evening just before it becomes completely dark (**lusco-fusco, luz crepuscular**)

twin /twɪn/ ▶ NOUN [*plural* **twins**] one of two children born to the same mother at the same time □ *Paul and Jo are twins.* (**gêmeo**) 🔁 *Our children are identical twins* (= they look exactly the same). (**gêmeos idênticos**)
▶ ADJECTIVE
1 twin sister/brother/daughters, etc. a sister, brother, etc. who is a twin □ *Bella's my twin sister.* (**irmã ou irmão gêmeo**)
2 belonging to a pair of things that are very similar □ *twin beds* □ *The boat is powered by twin engines.* (**do mesmo par**)
▶ VERB [**twins, twinning, twinned**] if a place is twinned with another place in a different country, the two places have a special relationship □ *Edinburgh is twinned with Munich.* (**geminar**)

twine /twaɪn/ ▶ NOUN, NO PLURAL strong string (**barbante**)
▶ VERB [**twines, twining, twined**] to twist around something □ *Roses twined round the fence posts.* (**enrolar-se**)

twinge /twɪndʒ/ NOUN [*plural* **twinges**] a sudden unpleasant feeling □ *a twinge of pain* □ *Heidi felt a twinge of guilt.* (**pontada**)

twinkle /ˈtwɪŋkəl/ ▶ VERB [**twinkles, twinkling, twinkled**]
1 if lights or stars twinkle, they shine in the dark, often in a way that looks as if their light is going on and off □ *The lights were twinkling along the shore.* (**cintilar, piscar**)
2 if someone's eyes twinkle, they look happy or as if they are joking (**cintilar, brilhar**)
▶ NOUN [*plural* **twinkles**]
1 a bright shining light (**cintilação**)
2 a look in your eyes that shows you are happy or joking □ *He had a mischievous twinkle in his eye.* (**brilho**)

twirl /twɜːl/ ▶ VERB [**twirls, twirling, twirled**] to turn around and around very quickly, or to make something turn around and around very quickly □

twitter

The leaders of the parade twirled their batons. (**enrolar, rodopiar**)
▶ NOUN [*plural* **twirls**] a fast turn around and around (**giro**)

twist /twɪst/ ▶ VERB [**twists, twisting, twisted**]
1 to turn something using your hands □ *Twist the handle hard and then pull it to open the door.* □ *She twisted the lid of the jar.* (**girar, torcer(-se)**)
2 to turn the top half of your body □ **+ round/ around** *Gregory twisted round in his chair to look at me.* (**virar-se**)
3 to bend something out of its correct shape □ *The front wheel of the bike twisted when it hit the wall.* (**torcer, retorcer**)
4 twist your ankle/knee, etc. to hurt your ankle, knee, etc. by turning it suddenly (**torcer o tornozelo/o joelho etc.**)
5 if a road or river twists, it has a lot of curves in it (**serpentear**) 🔁 *The road twisted and turned up the mountain.* (**serpentear e virar**)
6 to change what someone has said in an unfair way (**distorcer**) 🔁 *He was angry about the way the media had twisted his words.* (**distorcer as palavras**)

♦ IDIOM **twist someone's arm** an informal phrase meaning to persuade someone to do something □ *OK then, I'll come – you've twisted my arm!* (**convencer**)
▶ NOUN [*plural* **twists**]
1 a sudden and unexpected change in a story or situation □ *This announcement added a new and bizarre twist to his sudden death.* (**virada**)
2 a movement in which you turn something □ *Give the lid a twist.* (**giro**)
3 a piece of something that has been bent □ *She put a twist of lemon in the drink.* (**torção**)
4 a curve in a road or river (**virada, curva**)

• **twisted** /ˈtwɪstɪd/ ADJECTIVE
1 bent □ *The car was a wreck of twisted metal after the crash.* (**curvado, torcido**)
2 enjoying things which are cruel or shocking □ *The story looks inside a killer's twisted mind.* (**pervertido**)

twit /twɪt/ NOUN [*plural* **twits**] an informal word meaning a stupid person □ *Don't be such a twit!* (**idiota, cretino**)

twitch /twɪtʃ/ ▶ VERB [**twitches, twitching, twitched**]
1 if part of your body twitches, it moves slightly in a way you cannot control □ *Her eyelid twitched.* (**crispar-se, contrair(-se), repuxar**)
2 to make a small, sudden movement □ *I thought I saw the curtains twitch.* (**mexer-se**)
▶ NOUN [*plural* **twitches**]
1 a slight movement of your body which you cannot control (**puxão, repuxão**)
2 a small, sudden movement (**movimento rápido**)

twitter /ˈtwɪtə(r)/ VERB [**twitters, twittering, twittered**] to make several high noises □ *Birds were twittering in the trees.* (**produzir sons agudos**)

two /tu:/ NUMBER [*plural* **twos**] the number 2 (**dois**)
- IDIOMS **be in two minds** to not be able to decide between two possibilities □ *I'm in two minds about whether to sell my car.* (**estar indeciso**) **put two and two together** to guess the truth of something from things you have seen or heard □ *'How did you know she was going out with Tom?' 'Well, she seemed happier than usual, and when I saw them at the cinema, I put two and two together.'* (**somar dois com dois, descobrir a verdade**)

two-dimensional /tu:dɪˈmenʃəl/ ADJECTIVE
1 a two-dimensional shape is flat (**bidimensional**)
2 a two-dimensional character in a book, television programme, etc. does not seem real because their personality is not shown well enough (**sem consistência ou profundidade, inverossímil**)

two-faced /ˌtu:ˈfeɪst/ ADJECTIVE not sincere about your feelings or opinions, and telling people whatever will please them (**de duas caras**)

twofold /ˈtu:fəʊld/ ▶ ADJECTIVE twice as much or as many (**duplo**) 🔁 *There has been a twofold increase in crime rates.* (**aumento dobrado**)
▶ ADVERB by twice as much or as many □ *Divorce has increased twofold.* (**duas vezes mais**)

two-way /ˌtu:ˈweɪ/ ADJECTIVE
1 moving or allowing movement in two opposite directions □ *a two-way street* □ *two-way traffic* (**de duas vias**)
2 a two-way communication system is able to send and receive messages □ *a two-way radio* (**bidirecional**)

tycoon /taɪˈku:n/ NOUN [*plural* **tycoons**] a rich and successful person in business □ *She married a Texas oil tycoon.* (**magnata**)

type /taɪp/ ▶ NOUN [*plural* **types**]
1 used for talking about people or things that have similar qualities and can be considered as a group (**tipo**) 🔁 *Research of this type has never been done before.* (**deste tipo**) □ **+ of** *He's the type of person who never worries about anything.* □ *What type of dog have you got?* □ *There are many different types of cancer.*
2 someone who has particular interests or qualities □ *Kate's not the jealous type.* (**tipo**)
3 be someone's type to be the kind of person that someone is attracted to □ *Andy's nice but he's not really my type.* (**ser o tipo de alguém**)
4 *no plural* printed letters and numbers □ *The title should be in bold type.* (**letra, tipo**)
▶ VERB [**types, typing, typed**] to write something using a keyboard on a computer or typewriter □ *Type your name and then your password.* (**digitar**)

typewriter /ˈtaɪpˌraɪtə(r)/ NOUN [*plural* **typewriters**] an old-fashioned machine that prints words directly onto paper when you press keys (**máquina de escrever**)

- **typewritten** /ˈtaɪpˌrɪtən/ ADJECTIVE produced using a typewriter □ *a typewritten letter* (**escrito à máquina**)

typhoid /ˈtaɪfɔɪd/ NOUN, NO PLURAL a serious disease that you get from dirty food or water (**febre tifoide**)

typhoon /taɪˈfu:n/ NOUN [*plural* **typhoons**] a tropical storm with strong winds (**tufão**)

typical /ˈtɪpɪkəl/ ADJECTIVE having the usual qualities of a particular person or thing (**típico**) 🔁 *This is a typical example of a 17th-century cottage.* (**exemplo típico**) □ *Beth is a typical teenager.* □ *On a typical day, there are over 100,000 lorries on Britain's roads.* □ **+ of** *It was typical of Emily to offer to help.*

- **typically** /ˈtɪpɪkli/ ADVERB
1 used for saying what is usually true or what usually happens □ *An insect typically has six legs and two pairs of wings.* □ *Schools in the area typically finish around 3pm.* (**tipicamente**)
2 as you would expect from a particular person or thing □ *Typically, Tracy arrived late.* □ *He was behaving in a typically aggressive way.* (**tipicamente**)

typist /ˈtaɪpɪst/ NOUN [*plural* **typists**] someone whose job is to type letters in an office (**datilógrafo**)

tyrannical /tɪˈrænɪkəl/ ADJECTIVE using power in a cruel and unfair way □ *a tyrannical leader* (**tirânico**)

tyranny /ˈtɪrəni/ NOUN [*plural* **tyrannies**] a cruel and unfair way of using power (**tirania**)

tyrant /ˈtaɪrənt/ NOUN [*plural* **tyrants**] a ruler who uses power in a cruel and unfair way (**tirano**)

tyre /ˈtaɪə(r)/ NOUN [*plural* **tyres**] a piece of rubber around the edge of a wheel, which has air in it (**pneu**) 🔁 *We had a flat tyre.* (**pneu furado**)

Uu

U or **u** /juː/ the 21st letter of the alphabet (**a vigésima primeira letra do alfabeto**)

ubiquitous /juːˈbɪkwɪtəs/ ADJECTIVE seeming to be everywhere □ *the ubiquitous use of mobile phones* (**onipresente**)

udder /ˈʌdə(r)/ NOUN [plural **udders**] the part that hangs under a cow and produces milk (**úbere**)

UFO /ˈjuːˈefəʊ, ˈjuːˈfəʊ/ ABBREVIATION unidentified flying object; an object flying in the sky that cannot be explained and that some people think may come from another planet (**OVNI**)

ugh /ʌg/ EXCLAMATION used to express disgust □ *'Ugh! It tastes horrible.'* (**ugh!**)

ugliness /ˈʌglɪnɪs/ NOUN, NO PLURAL the state of being ugly (**feiura**)

ugly /ˈʌglɪ/ ADJECTIVE [**uglier, ugliest**]
1 not pleasant to look at □ *an ugly building* □ *a big ugly monster* (**feio**)
2 very unpleasant, and often involving violence (**ameaçador, ruim**) 🔁 *When the police arrived, things started to get ugly.*

> People do not often use the word **ugly** to describe people as it sounds unkind. Sometimes the word **plain** (which has the same meaning) is used instead as it sounds less unkind.

UHT milk /ˌjuːeɪtʃtiː ˈmɪlk/ NOUN, NO PLURAL milk that has been heated to a very high temperature to make it stay fresh for longer (**leite longa vida**)

UK /ˌjuːˈkeɪ/ ABBREVIATION United Kingdom (**abrev. Reino Unido**)

ulcer /ˈʌlsə(r)/ NOUN [plural **ulcers**] a small sore area on your skin or inside your body (**úlcera**) 🔁 *a mouth ulcer* (**úlcera na boca**)

ulterior /ʌlˈtɪərɪə(r)/ ADJECTIVE **ulterior motive** a secret reason for doing something or behaving in a particular way (**oculto**) □ *He's started being very helpful, but I'm sure he's got an ulterior motive.* (**razão oculta**)

ultimate /ˈʌltɪmət/ ▶ ADJECTIVE
1 happening at the end of a process □ *Our ultimate aim was to give up work.* (**por último**)
2 better, worse, greater, etc. than all others □ *He made the ultimate sacrifice for his country.* (**o maior, melhor**)

▶ NOUN, NO PLURAL **the ultimate in something** the best or greatest example of something □ *This sofa is the ultimate in luxury.* (**referência em alguma coisa**)

• **ultimately** /ˈʌltɪmətlɪ/ ADVERB at the end of a process □ *Ultimately, they were forced to admit defeat.* (**finalmente**)

ultimatum /ˌʌltɪˈmeɪtəm/ NOUN [plural **ultimatums** or **ultimata**] if you give someone an ultimatum, you threaten something bad if they do not what you want (**ultimato**) 🔁 *I gave her an ultimatum – either get rid of the dog or I'm leaving.*

ultra- /ˈʌltrə/ PREFIX ultra- is added to the beginning of words to mean 'extremely' □ *ultra-careful* (**ultra-**)

ultrasound /ˈʌltrəsaʊnd/ NOUN, NO PLURAL sound waves that are used to make a picture of the inside of someone's body 🔁 *Many pregnant women have an ultrasound scan.* (**ultrassom**)

ultraviolet /ˌʌltrəˈvaɪələt/ ADJECTIVE ultraviolet light is light you cannot see and which turns the skin darker. A physics word. (**ultravioleta**)

umbilical cord /ʌmˈbɪlɪkəl ˈkɔːd/ NOUN [plural **umbilical cords**] the tube that connects a baby to its mother while it is inside its mother's body. A biology word. (**cordão umbilical**)

umbrella /ʌmˈbrelə/ NOUN [plural **umbrellas**] a frame with cloth over it that you hold above you for shelter when it rains (**guarda-chuva**)

umpire /ˈʌmpaɪə(r)/ NOUN [plural **umpires**] the person in a game such as cricket, who makes sure the players obey the rules (**árbitro**)

umpteen /ˌʌmpˈtiːn/ DETERMINER an informal word meaning a large number 🔁 *We've been there umpteen times.* (**um monte**)

• **umpteenth** /ˌʌmpˈtiːnθ/ DETERMINER an informal word meaning the latest in a long number of things 🔁 *For the umpteenth time, don't put banana skins in the waste paper basket!* (**enésimo**)

UN /ˌjuːˈen/ ABBREVIATION United Nations (**abrev. Nações Unidas**)

un- /ʌn/ PREFIX un- is used at the beginning of words to mean 'not' □ *untidy* □ *unkind* (**prefixo de negação**)

unable /ʌnˈeɪbəl/ ADJECTIVE **unable to do something** not able to do something □ *He stood completely still, unable to take his eyes off the bear.* (**incapaz**)

unacceptable /ˌʌnəkˈseptəbəl/ ADJECTIVE
something unacceptable cannot be allowed to happen, exist or continue because it is wrong or not of a high enough standard (**inaceitável**) His behaviour is totally unacceptable. (**totalmente inaceitável**) ☐ The bank decided that the financial risk was unacceptable.
• **unacceptably** /ˌʌnəkˈseptəblɪ/ ADVERB of an unacceptable level or standard ☐ There is an unacceptably high level of pollution in the river. (**inaceitavelmente**)

unaccompanied /ˌʌnəˈkʌmpənɪd/ ADJECTIVE not having anyone with you ☐ Unaccompanied children are not permitted at this event. (**desacompanhado**)

unaccountable /ˌʌnəˈkaʊntəbəl/ ADJECTIVE
1 impossible to explain (**inexplicável**) For some unaccountable reason, he decided to wear a velvet suit. (**razão inexplicável**)
2 someone who is unaccountable does not have to explain the reasons for their actions ☐ Many of Scotland's services are run by people who are unaccountable to the public. (**o que não responde por, não é responsável por**)
• **unaccountably** /ˌʌnəˈkaʊntəblɪ/ ADVERB without an explanation ☐ She was feeling unaccountably depressed. (**inexplicavelmente**)

unaccounted for /ˌʌnəˈkaʊntɪd fɔː(r)/ ADJECTIVE if someone or something is unaccounted for, you do not know what has happened to them or how they have been used ☐ Eight people were killed in the explosion and four people are still unaccounted for. (**estar desaparecido, não ser encontrado**)

unaccustomed /ˌʌnəˈkʌstəmd/ ADJECTIVE
1 not usual ☐ We were in the unaccustomed position of having plenty of money. (**incomum**)
2 unaccustomed to something not used to something ☐ I was unaccustomed to such luxury. (**desacostumado a algo**)

unadulterated /ˌʌnəˈdʌltəreɪtɪd/ ADJECTIVE
1 pure, with nothing added ☐ unadulterated drinking water. (**puro**)
2 used to emphasize how good or bad something is ☐ The holiday was two weeks of unadulterated pleasure. (**puro**)

unaffected /ˌʌnəˈfektɪd/ ADJECTIVE not affected or changed by something ☐ Most people working here have been unaffected by the changes in company policy. (**indiferente, inalterado**)

unaided /ˌʌnˈeɪdɪd/ ADJECTIVE without help ☐ She is now able to walk unaided. (**sem ajuda**)

unambiguous /ˌʌnæmˈbɪɡjuəs/ ADJECTIVE having only one, clear meaning ☐ The law is quite unambiguous on this point. (**sem ambiguidade, evidente**)

unanimity /ˌjuːnəˈnɪmətɪ/ NOUN, NO PLURAL the state of being unanimous (**unanimidade**)

unanimous /juːˈnænɪməs/ ADJECTIVE agreed by everyone ☐ a unanimous decision (**unânime**)
• **unanimously** /juːˈnænɪməslɪ/ ADVERB in a way that is unanimous ☐ He was elected unanimously. (**unanimamente**)

unannounced /ˌʌnəˈnaʊnst/ ADJECTIVE, ADVERB if you arrive somewhere unannounced, you have not told anyone you are coming (**inesperado, de surpresa**)

unanswered /ˌʌnˈɑːnsəd/ ADJECTIVE
1 not having been answered or solved (**não respondido**) There are a lot of unanswered questions about the origins of the universe. (**questões não respondidas**)
2 unanswered letters, telephone calls, etc. have not been replied to (**não respondido/retornado**)

unapproachable /ˌʌnəˈprəʊtʃəbəl/ ADJECTIVE difficult to talk to because of being formal and unfriendly (**inacessível, frio**)

unarmed /ˌʌnˈɑːmd/ ADJECTIVE without weapons ☐ They attacked a group of unarmed civilians. (**desarmado, sem armas**)

unassuming /ˌʌnəˈsjuːmɪŋ/ ADJECTIVE having a pleasant, quiet manner, and not wanting to be noticed (**discreto, despretensioso**)

unattainable /ˌʌnəˈteɪnəbəl/ ADJECTIVE impossible to get or to achieve (**inacessível**)

unattended /ˌʌnəˈtendɪd/ ADJECTIVE not being looked after ☐ Passengers are asked not to leave their luggage unattended. (**desacompanhado, abandonado**)

unattractive /ˌʌnəˈtræktɪv/ ADJECTIVE
1 not pleasant to look at ☐ a rather unattractive modern house (**não atraente**)
2 not pleasant or not enjoyable ☐ Pride is one of his more unattractive qualities. (**desagradável**)

unauthorized or **unauthorised** /ˌʌnˈɔːθəraɪzd/ ADJECTIVE done or produced without official permission ☐ an unauthorized biography (**não autorizado**)

unavailable /ˌʌnəˈveɪləbəl/ ADJECTIVE
1 not able to be somewhere or to speak to someone ☐ I'm sorry, Dr Hughes is unavailable at the moment. (**indisponível**)
2 impossible to get or buy ☐ His book is unavailable in the UK. (**indisponível**)

unavoidable /ˌʌnəˈvɔɪdəbəl/ ADJECTIVE impossible to avoid or prevent ☐ I'm sorry to give you extra work, but I'm afraid it's unavoidable. (**inevitável**)
• **unavoidably** /ˌʌnəˈvɔɪdəblɪ/ ADVERB for reasons that could not be avoided ☐ I was unavoidably delayed. (**inevitavelmente**)

unaware /ˌʌnəˈweə(r)/ ADJECTIVE not knowing about something ☐ We were unaware of the danger. (**desconhecer, não estar ciente**)
• **unawares** /ˌʌnəˈweəz/ ADVERB **catch/take someone unawares** to happen when someone does not expect it ☐ Their arrival caught me unawares. (**pegar desprevenido**)

unbearable

unbearable /ʌnˈbeərəbəl/ ADJECTIVE too painful or unpleasant to deal with ☐ *The pain was unbearable.* (**insuportável**)

• **unbearably** /ʌnˈbeərəbli/ ADVERB in a way that is impossible to accept or deal with ☐ *It is unbearably hot outside.* (**insuportavelmente**)

unbeatable /ʌnˈbiːtəbəl/ ADJECTIVE better than all others ☐ *Our catalogue offers unbeatable value for money.* (**imbatível**)

• **unbeaten** /ʌnˈbiːtən/ ADJECTIVE never having been beaten in a game or competition (**invicto**) 🔂 *Can United maintain its unbeaten record?*

unbelievable /ˌʌnbɪˈliːvəbəl/ ADJECTIVE
1 used to emphasize how bad, good, extreme, etc. something is ☐ *For me, seeing the whales was an unbelievable experience.* (**inacreditável**)
2 difficult to believe ☐ *an unbelievable story* (**inacreditável**)

• **unbelievably** /ˌʌnbɪˈliːvəbli/ ADVERB used to emphasize how bad, good, extreme, etc. something is ☐ *She's unbelievably rich.* (**inacreditavelmente**)

unblock /ʌnˈblɒk/ VERB [**unblocks, unblocking, unblocked**] to remove something that is blocking something such as a pipe ☐ *I had to unblock the sink.* (**desbloquear, desimpedir, desentupir**)

unborn /ʌnˈbɔːn/ ADJECTIVE not yet born (**por nascer**) 🔂 *an unborn child*

unbroken /ʌnˈbrəʊkən/ ADJECTIVE continuous ☐ *He has the longest unbroken run of wins in the sport.* (**ininterrupto**)

unbutton /ʌnˈbʌtən/ VERB [**unbuttons, unbuttoning, unbuttoned**] to open the buttons, especially on a piece of clothing ☐ *He unbuttoned his shirt.* (**desabotoar**)

uncalled for /ʌnˈkɔːld fɔː(r)/ ADJECTIVE offensive and not fair ☐ *That remark was completely uncalled for.* (**inoportuno**)

uncanny /ʌnˈkæni/ ADJECTIVE strange and difficult to explain ☐ *He had an uncanny ability to know what I was thinking.* (**estranho**)

uncaring /ʌnˈkeərɪŋ/ ADJECTIVE not kind and not caring about bad things that happen to people (**insensível, sem empatia**)

uncertain /ʌnˈsɜːtən/ ADJECTIVE
1 not sure what to decide ☐ + ***about*** *I was uncertain about what to do next.* (**incerto**)
2 not known (**incerto**) 🔂 *The future is uncertain.* (**futuro é incerto**) ☐ + ***question word*** *It is still uncertain whether he will be fit enough to play.*

• **uncertainty** /ʌnˈsɜːtənti/ NOUN [plural **uncertainties**] when something is uncertain ☐ *There is a lot of uncertainty surrounding the event.* (**incerteza**)

unchanged /ʌnˈtʃeɪndʒd/ ADJECTIVE staying the same (**imutável, inalterado**) 🔂 *Her condition remained unchanged overnight.* (**permanecer inalterado**)

uncharacteristic /ˌʌnˌkærəktəˈrɪstɪk/ ADJECTIVE not typical of someone or something ☐ *He spoke with uncharacteristic anger.* (**atípico**)

uncharitable /ʌnˈtʃærɪtəbəl/ ADJECTIVE not kind ☐ *He made some rather uncharitable remarks about their work.* (**rude**)

uncivilized or **uncivilised** /ʌnˈsɪvɪlaɪzd/ ADJECTIVE
1 rude and offensive ☐ *Do you think it's uncivilized to eat with your fingers?* (**rude**)
2 an offensive word meaning not having a developed society or culture (**ignorante**)
3 an uncivilized time is a time that is not convenient, especially very early in the morning (**horário inapropriado**)

uncle /ˈʌŋkəl/ NOUN [plural **uncles**]
1 the brother of one of your parents ☐ *My aunt and uncle live in Scotland.* ☐ *Uncle Douglas came to visit.* (**tio**)
2 your aunt's husband (**tio**)

unclean /ʌnˈkliːn/ ADJECTIVE
1 not morally good ☐ *After the experience, she felt unclean.* (**impuro**)
2 dirty ☐ *unclean conditions* (**sujo**)

unclear /ʌnˈklɪə(r)/ ADJECTIVE
1 not obvious or easy to understand ☐ *It's unclear why she left her job.* ☐ *The writing was rather unclear.* (**obscuro, incerto**)
2 if you are unclear about something, you do not completely understand it ☐ *I'm sorry; I'm still unclear on that point – could you explain it again?* (**inseguro, confuso**)

uncomfortable /ʌnˈkʌmftəbəl/ ADJECTIVE
1 not feeling comfortable ☐ *We were uncomfortable in the heat.* (**desconfortável**)
2 causing you to feel uncomfortable ☐ *The seats were really uncomfortable.* (**desconfortável**)
3 slightly embarrassed or slightly embarrassing ☐ + ***about*** *I feel uncomfortable about accepting money from her.* ☐ *There were a lot of uncomfortable silences.* (**constrangido**)

• **uncomfortably** /ʌnˈkʌmftəbli/ ADVERB
1 in an uncomfortable way ☐ *Tom shifted uncomfortably in his seat.* (**desconfortavelmente**)
2 in a way that makes you feel worried or embarrassed ☐ *Inflation is still uncomfortably high.* (**incomodamente**)

uncommon /ʌnˈkɒmən/ ADJECTIVE unusual or rare 🔂 *It is not uncommon for luggage to go missing.* (**incomum**)

uncompromising /ʌnˈkɒmprəmaɪzɪŋ/ ADJECTIVE determined not to change your opinions or decisions ☐ *He has been uncompromising in his opposition to the government's plans.* (**intransigente**)

unconcerned /ˌʌnkənˈsɜːnd/ ADJECTIVE not worried about something ☐ *She was unconcerned* about the prospect of months of unemployment. (**indiferente**)

unconditional /ˌʌnkənˈdɪʃənəl/ ADJECTIVE not limited in any way □ *an unconditional surrender* □ *My mother gave us unconditional love.* (**incondicional**)

- **unconditionally** /ˌʌnkənˈdɪʃənəli/ ADVERB without any limits □ *It is required that you agree to these terms unconditionally.* (**incondicionalmente**)

unconfirmed /ˌʌnkənˈfɜːmd/ ADJECTIVE unconfirmed information may not be true because there is no official proof yet □ *There were unconfirmed reports that the man had been seen in Paris.* (**não confirmado**)

unconnected /ˌʌnkəˈnektɪd/ ADJECTIVE not related in any way □ *His decision to resign was entirely unconnected to his illness.* (**desconectado**)

unconscious /ʌnˈkɒnʃəs/ ADJECTIVE
1 in a state like sleep where you are not aware of what is happening around you, because you are seriously ill or injured (**inconsciente**) □ *A brick hit his head and he was knocked unconscious.* (**ficou inconsciente**)
2 an unconscious thought or feeling is one that you are not aware of having □ *I think I must have had an unconscious desire to hurt my brother.* (**inconsciente**)
3 if you are unconscious of something, you do not notice it □ *He was unconscious of the danger.* (**sem consciência**)

- **unconsciously** /ʌnˈkɒnʃəsli/ ADVERB if you do something unconsciously, you are not aware that you are doing it □ *I must have been copying her unconsciously.* (**inconscientemente**)
- **unconsciousness** /ʌnˈkɒnʃəsnɪs/ NOUN, NO PLURAL the state of being unconscious (**inconsciência, perda de consciência**)

uncontrollable /ˌʌnkənˈtrəʊləbəl/ ADJECTIVE not possible to control (**incontrolável**) □ *She suddenly had an uncontrollable urge to kick something.* (**desejo incontrolável**)

- **uncontrollably** /ˌʌnkənˈtrəʊləbli/ ADVERB in an uncontrollable way □ *She sobbed uncontrollably at the funeral.* (**incontrolavelmente**)

unconventional /ˌʌnkənˈvenʃənəl/ ADJECTIVE different from what most people think is normal □ *He uses unconventional methods to train his animals.* □ *My parents were very unconventional.* (**não convencional**)

- **unconventionally** /ˌʌnkənˈvenʃənəli/ ADVERB in an unconventional way □ *She likes to dress unconventionally.* (**de modo não convencional**)

unconvincing /ˌʌnkənˈvɪnsɪŋ/ ADJECTIVE
1 if something is unconvincing, you do not believe it or do not think it is correct □ *He produced a somewhat unconvincing excuse for being late.* (**não convincente**)
2 not seeming real □ *The plot and the characters are unconvincing.* (**não convincente**)

uncooperative /ˌʌnkəʊˈɒpərətɪv/ ADJECTIVE not willing to help someone or to work with other people □ *He was being deliberately uncooperative.* (**não cooperativo**)

uncoordinated /ˌʌnkəʊˈɔːdɪneɪtɪd/ ADJECTIVE
1 an uncoordinated person moves their body in an awkward way □ *I'm too uncoordinated to be good at games.* (**descoordenado**)
2 badly organized so that the parts of something do not work well together □ *The publicity campaign had been run in a hasty, uncoordinated fashion.* (**sem combinar, não harmônico**)

uncount noun /ˈʌŋ kaʊnt ˈnaʊn/ or uncountable noun /ʌnˈkaʊntəbəl ˈnaʊn/ NOUN [plural **uncount nouns** or **uncountable nouns**] in grammar, a noun that does not have a plural form, e.g. happiness, water or advice (**substantivo incontável**)

uncouth /ʌnˈkuːθ/ ADJECTIVE rude and unpleasant □ *He is aggressive and uncouth.* (**desagradável**)

uncover /ʌnˈkʌvə(r)/ VERB [**uncovers, uncovering, uncovered**]
1 to discover something that had been secret or hidden (**descobrir**) □ *Police have uncovered new evidence relating to the murder.* (**descobriu novas evidências**)
2 to remove a cover from something (**descobrir**)

undecided /ˌʌndɪˈsaɪdɪd/ ADJECTIVE not having made a decision about something (**indeciso**)

undelete /ˌʌndɪˈliːt/ VERB [**undeletes, undeleting, undeleted**] on a computer, to make something that has been deleted (= removed) appear again (**recuperar algo excluído**)

undeniable /ˌʌndɪˈnaɪəbəl/ ADJECTIVE certainly true □ *It is undeniable that the Earth goes round the sun.* (**inegável**)

- **undeniably** /ˌʌndɪˈnaɪəbli/ ADVERB in a way that is certainly true (**de modo inegável**)

under /ˈʌndə(r)/ ▶ PREPOSITION
1 below something □ *The bag is under the table.* □ *We walked under the bridge.* (**sob, embaixo de**)
2 covered by something □ *I found my glasses under a cushion.* □ *The mountains were under a thick layer of snow.* (**sob, embaixo de**)
3 less than an amount, level or age □ *All the clothes are under £20.* □ *The competition is open to anyone under 30.* (**menos de**)
4 having a particular thing done, or affected by a particular thing (**sob**) □ *Our troops came under attack.* (**sob ataque**) □ *He was under pressure to resign.* (**sob pressão**) □ *I think you should show her some sympathy under the circumstances* (= because of the situation). (**sob as circunstâncias**)
5 controlled by a particular person, government, organization, etc. □ *The country was under military control.* □ *This issue does not come under my authority.* (**sob as ordens de**)

6 according to a rule, law, etc. □ *Under the proposal, people would pay to have their rubbish removed.* □ *He will be allowed to continue on the course under certain conditions.* (**segundo, de acordo com**)

7 used to show where to find or put information, books, documents, etc. □ *You'll find her books under 'history'.* (**em**)

▶ ADVERB

1 in or to a lower place □ *We watched the divers go under.* (**abaixo, para baixo**)

2 less than an amount, level or age □ *The play equipment is for children aged 6 and under.* (**abaixo, para baixo**)

under- /ˈʌndə(r)/ PREFIX
1 under- is added to the beginning of words to mean 'below' □ *underfoot* □ *underground* (**sub-**)
2 under- is added to the beginning of words to mean 'not enough' □ *underdeveloped* □ *undernourished* (**sub-**)

under-age /ˈʌndər ˈeɪdʒ/ ADJECTIVE not old enough to do something legally (**menor de idade**)

underarm /ˈʌndərɑːm/ ▶ ADJECTIVE, ADVERB if you throw a ball underarm, you start with your hand in a low position and facing up (**de baixo para cima**)

▶ NOUN [plural **underarms**] the area of your body under your arm (**axila**)

undercover /ˈʌndəˌkʌvə(r)/ ADJECTIVE working or done secretly □ *an undercover police operation* (**clandestino**)

underdeveloped /ˌʌndədɪˈveləpt/ ADJECTIVE an underdeveloped country or area is not modern and does not have much industry (**subdesenvolvido**)

underdog /ˈʌndədɒɡ/ NOUN [plural **underdogs**] the person or team that will probably lose a competition (**azarão**)

underdone /ˌʌndəˈdʌn/ ADJECTIVE not cooked enough (**malpassado**)

underestimate /ˌʌndərˈestɪmeɪt/ VERB [**underestimates, underestimating, underestimated**]
1 to think that something or someone is less important, valuable, powerful, etc. than they really are □ *You should not underestimate the importance of a good education.* (**subestimar**)
2 to think that an amount will be less than it is □ *The builder underestimated the number of bricks needed.* □ *I completely underestimated how much work the course would be.* (**subestimar**)

underfoot /ˌʌndəˈfʊt/ ADVERB on the ground where you are walking □ *The stones underfoot grew slippery in the rain.* (**no chão**)

undergo /ˌʌndəˈɡəʊ/ VERB [**undergoes, undergoing, underwent, undergone**] to experience something □ *He underwent an operation to mend his broken leg.* (**passar por**)

undergraduate /ˌʌndəˈɡrædʒuət/ NOUN [plural **undergraduates**] someone who is studying at a university and has not yet done their degree (= qualification) (**estudante não graduado**)

underground ▶ ADJECTIVE /ˈʌndəɡraʊnd/
▶ ADVERB /ˌʌndəˈɡraʊnd/
1 below the surface of the ground □ *Moles live underground.* □ *an underground stream* (**subterrâneo**)
2 existing or done secretly and often illegally □ *an underground organization* (**na clandestinidade**)
▶ NOUN /ˈʌndəɡraʊnd/ [plural **undergrounds**] a railway that is under the ground, usually in a large city □ *the London Underground* (**metrô**)

undergrowth /ˈʌndəɡrəʊθ/ NOUN, NO PLURAL bushes and plants that cover the ground (**vegetação rasteira**)

underhand /ˌʌndəˈhænd/ ADJECTIVE secret and not honest □ *Some players use underhand tactics to confuse their opponents.* (**escuso**)

underline /ˌʌndəˈlaɪn/ VERB [**underlines, underlining, underlined**]
1 to draw a line under something □ *Underline all the adjectives in these sentences.* (**sublinhar**)
2 to emphasize that something is important or true □ *She underlined the need to be careful crossing the road.* (**sublinhar**)

underlying /ˌʌndəˈlaɪɪŋ/ ADJECTIVE underlying reasons, problems, etc. are basic and important, but not easy to notice at first (**oculto**) □ *The underlying cause of these diseases is poverty.* (**causa por trás**)

undermine /ˌʌndəˈmaɪn/ VERB [**undermines, undermining, undermined**] to make someone or something weaker, less confident or less effective □ *Her colleagues are always trying to undermine her.* □ *Reduced funding threatens to undermine our work.* (**minar**)

underneath /ˌʌndəˈniːθ/ ADVERB, PREPOSITION
1 under something □ *Look underneath the table!* □ *He was wearing a jumper with a shirt underneath.* (**sob, debaixo de**)
2 used to describe what someone or something is really like, when they seem different □ *Underneath the fierce exterior, he's a really kind person.* (**por trás de**)

undernourished /ˌʌndəˈnʌrɪʃt/ ADJECTIVE not healthy because of not eating enough good food (**subnutrido**)

underpants /ˈʌndəpænts/ PLURAL NOUN underwear that men and boys wear under their trousers (**cueca**)

underpass /ˈʌndəpɑːs/ NOUN [plural **underpasses**] a road or path under another road (**túnel**)

underprivileged /ˌʌndəˈprɪvɪlɪdʒd/ ADJECTIVE having less money and fewer opportunities than other people (**desprivilegiado**)

underrate /ˌʌndəˈreɪt/ VERB [**underrates, underrating, underrated**] to think that someone or something is less good than they really are ☐ *We should not underrate Australia's football team.* (subestimar)

• **underrated** /ˌʌndəˈreɪtɪd/ ADJECTIVE of a higher quality than people think ☐ *He's a very underrated composer.* (subestimado)

understand /ˌʌndəˈstænd/ VERB [**understands, understanding, understood**]
1 to know what something means ☐ *I can't understand the instructions.* ☐ *Do you understand German?* (compreender)
2 to know why something happens, how something works, or the effect or importance of something ☐ + *question word Doctors still don't understand how the disease is spread.* ☐ *We didn't understand the significance of his words at the time.* (compreender, entender)
3 to know why someone behaves and feels the way they do ☐ *I'll never understand him.* ☐ *I understood her anger.* ☐ *I don't understand what you are trying to achieve.* (entender)
4 to think that something is true ☐ + *that I understood that you weren't coming.* (interpretar como sendo fato, verdade)

• **understandable** /ˌʌndəˈstændəbəl/ ADJECTIVE reasonable in a particular situation ☐ *His disappointment at not being in the football team was understandable.* (compreensível)

• **understandably** /ˌʌndəˈstændəblɪ/ ADVERB in a way that is reasonable in a particular situation ☐ *She was understandably upset.* (compreensivelmente)

• **understanding** /ˌʌndəˈstændɪŋ/ C NOUN [plural **understandings**]
1 no plural knowledge about something (conhecimento) ▣ *Scientists are trying to gain a better understanding of the origins of the universe.* (obter mais conhecimento)
2 no plural when someone shows that they accept that your behaviour and feelings are reasonable, or when someone shows sympathy ☐ *My teachers showed great understanding when my father died.* (entendimento)
3 an agreement between two people, often one that is not spoken or written ☐ *We have an understanding. I cut his grass and he gives me apples.* (trato)
4 my/his/their, etc. understanding what I/he/ they, etc. think is true ☐ *My understanding was that the meeting would still take place.* (no meu entendimento/no entendimento dele/deles)
5 on the understanding that used to say that you will do something if someone agrees to something ☐ *I will accept the post of chairman on the understanding that it will be for one year only.* (desde que)

▶ ADJECTIVE able to understand other people's feelings or to forgive someone because of their situation ☐ *The illness makes me bad-tempered at times, but my family have been very understanding.* (compreensivo)

understatement /ˌʌndəˈsteɪtmənt/ NOUN [plural **understatements**] when you describe something in a way that makes it seem less extreme than it really is ☐ *To say that his work is inadequate is an understatement.* (atenuação, meia verdade)

understood /ˌʌndəˈstʊd/ PAST TENSE AND PAST PARTICIPLE OF **understand** (ver **understand**)

understudy /ˈʌndəˌstʌdɪ/ NOUN [plural **understudies**] someone who learns the part of another actor so they can play that part if the actor is ill (substituto, suplente)

undertake /ˌʌndəˈteɪk/ VERB [**undertakes, undertaking, undertook, undertaken**]
1 to start to do a job or an activity, usually one that will take a long time ☐ *We all had to undertake extensive training.* (assumir, empreender)
2 undertake to do something a formal word meaning to promise to do something ☐ *I undertook to ensure their safety.* (comprometer-se a)

undertaker /ˈʌndəˌteɪkə(r)/ NOUN [plural **undertakers**] someone whose job is to arrange funerals (agente funerário)

undertaking /ˌʌndəˈteɪkɪŋ/ NOUN [plural **undertakings**]
1 a difficult or long job or activity ☐ *It will be an enormous undertaking to equip every member of staff with their own terminal.* (empreendimento)
2 a promise to do something ▣ *The company has given an undertaking to protect jobs.* (compromisso)

undervalue /ˌʌndəˈvæljuː/ VERB [**undervalues, undervaluing, undervalued**] to not understand how valuable, important, useful, etc. someone or something is ☐ *Sometimes we undervalue the contribution of artists to society.* (subestimar)

• **undervalued** /ˌʌndəˈvæljuːd/ ADJECTIVE if something or someone is undervalued, people do not understand how valuable, important, useful, etc. they are ☐ *She felt undervalued in her last job.* (subestimado)

underwater /ˌʌndəˈwɔːtə(r)/ ADJECTIVE, ADVERB under the surface of water ☐ *an underwater creature* ☐ *Can you swim underwater?* (subaquático, embaixo da água)

underway /ˌʌndəˈweɪ/ ADJECTIVE happening or having started (encaminhado, em andamento) ▣ *Work on the new motorway got underway last week.* (foi encaminhado)

underwear /ˈʌndəweə(r)/ NOUN, NO PLURAL clothes you wear next to your skin and under your other clothes (roupa de baixo)

underweight /ˌʌndəˈweɪt/ ADJECTIVE not heavy enough (abaixo do peso)

underwent /ˌʌndəˈwent/ PAST TENSE OF **undergo** (ver **undergo**)

underworld   881   unenviable

underworld /ˈʌndəˌwɜːld/ NOUN, NO PLURAL
1 the criminals in a society and the lives they have (**submundo**)
2 in stories, the place where people go when they die (**inferno**)

undesirable /ˌʌndɪˈzaɪərəbəl/ ADJECTIVE
unpleasant or harmful ☐ *She's mixing with some very undesirable friends.* ☐ *The drugs have undesirable side effects.* (**indesejável**)

undetected /ˌʌndɪˈtektɪd/ ADJECTIVE not discovered or seen (**não detectado**) ◘ *The fraud went undetected for years.* (**permaneceu não detectada**)

undid /ʌnˈdɪd/ PAST TENSE of undo (**ver undo**)

undignified /ʌnˈdɪɡnɪfaɪd/ ADJECTIVE
embarrassing or making you look silly ☐ *She landed in an undignified heap at the bottom of the steps.* (**indigno, ridículo**)

undisguised /ˌʌndɪsˈɡaɪzd/ ADJECTIVE
undisguised feelings are not hidden ☐ *She watched her son receive his certificate with undisguised pride.* (**indisfarçável**)

undisputed /ˌʌndɪˈspjuːtɪd/ ADJECTIVE not questioned or doubted by anyone ☐ *She is the undisputed leader in this area of research.* (**incontestável**)

undivided /ˌʌndɪˈvaɪdɪd/ ADJECTIVE complete ◘ *You must give me your undivided attention.* (**inteiro**)

undo /ʌnˈduː/ VERB [undoes, undoing, undid, undone]
1 to open something that is fastened ☐ *He undid his jacket.* (**desfazer**)
2 to get rid of the effect of something that has been done, so that something goes back to its original state ☐ *She's undone all the good work of the previous manager.* (**desfazer**)

undoing /ʌnˈduːɪŋ/ NOUN, NO PLURAL the thing that causes someone to fail ☐ *He's clever enough but greed was his undoing.* (**ruína**)

undone /ʌnˈdʌn/ ▶ PAST PARTICIPLE OF undo
▶ ADJECTIVE
1 not fastened, closed or tied (**solto, desamarrado ou aberto**) ◘ *One of your shoelaces has come undone.* (**está desamarrado**)
2 not done ☐ *The kitchen was filthy and the washing had been left undone.* (**inacabado, por fazer**)

undoubted /ʌnˈdaʊtɪd/ ADJECTIVE certain ☐ *Ellie has undoubted talent as a singer.* (**indubitável**)
• **undoubtedly** /ʌnˈdaʊtɪdli/ ADVERB certainly ☐ *He is undoubtedly one of the best players.* (**indubitavelmente**)

undress /ʌnˈdres/ VERB [undresses, undressing, undressed] to take your clothes off, or to take someone's clothes off (**despir(-se)**)
• **undressed** /ʌnˈdrest/ ADJECTIVE not wearing any clothes (**despido**) ◘ *He was getting undressed.* (**despindo-se**)

undue /ʌnˈdjuː/ ADJECTIVE more than is necessary ☐ *undue alarm* (**indevido, desmedido**)
• **unduly** /ʌnˈdjuːli/ ADVERB more than is necessary ☐ *He did not seem unduly worried.* (**indevidamente, desmedidamente**)

unearth /ʌnˈɜːθ/ VERB [unearths, unearthing, unearthed]
1 to discover something, especially something secret or hidden ☐ *Someone had unearthed some unpleasant facts about him.* (**descobrir, revelar**)
2 to find something by digging in the ground (**desenterrar**)

unearthly /ʌnˈɜːθli/ ADJECTIVE strange and a bit frightening ☐ *an unearthly sound* (**sobrenatural**)

unease /ʌnˈiːz/ NOUN, NO PLURAL a feeling of being worried that something bad might happen ☐ *There is growing unease about the military situation.* (**apreensão**)
• **uneasily** /ʌnˈiːzɪli/ ADVERB in a way that shows you are worried ☐ *John looked uneasily at his watch.* (**apreensivamente**)
• **uneasiness** /ʌnˈiːzɪnɪs/ NOUN, NO PLURAL another word for unease (**apreensão**)
• **uneasy** /ʌnˈiːzi/ ADJECTIVE
1 worried that something bad might happen ☐ *I felt uneasy about walking home so late at night.* (**apreensivo**)
2 an uneasy situation or relationship could change and become worse at any time ☐ *At the moment, there is an uneasy peace in the area.* (**inquietante, incômodo**)

unemployed /ˌʌnɪmˈplɔɪd/ ▶ ADJECTIVE
without a job ☐ *My Dad's unemployed at the moment.* ☐ *unemployed miners* (**desempregado**)
▶ NOUN the unemployed people who are unemployed (**os desempregados**)
• **unemployment** /ˌʌnɪmˈplɔɪmənt/ NOUN, NO PLURAL
1 the number of people who do not have a job (**desemprego**) ◘ *Unemployment has risen again.* (**o desemprego aumentou**)
2 not having a job (**desemprego**)

unemployment benefit /ˌʌnɪmˈplɔɪmənt ˈbenɪfɪt/ NOUN, NO PLURAL money that the government pays to people who do not have jobs (**seguro-desemprego**)

unending /ʌnˈendɪŋ/ ADJECTIVE seeming to continue forever ☐ *Today was just an unending succession of interruptions.* (**interminável**)

unenthusiastic /ˌʌnɪnθjuːziˈæstɪk/ ADJECTIVE
not wanting to do something or not thinking that something is good ☐ *She was very unenthusiastic about the trip.* (**desanimado**)
• **unenthusiastically** /ˌʌnɪnθjuːziˈæstɪkli/ ADVERB in an unenthusiastic way ☐ *They agreed unenthusiastically to stay another day.* (**desanimadamente**)

unenviable /ʌnˈenvɪəbəl/ ADJECTIVE difficult and not pleasant (**invejável**) ◘ *I had the unenviable* *task* of telling her that her work was not good enough. (**tarefa inevitável, difícil tarefa**)

unequal /ˌʌnˈiːkwəl/ ADJECTIVE
1 different in size, amount or position □ *an unequal share of money* (**desigual**)
2 not fair because of not being the same for everyone □ *The report claims that old people receive unequal treatment from doctors.* (**desigual**)

unequivocal /ˌʌnɪˈkwɪvəkəl/ ADJECTIVE clearly stated so that there can be no doubt about what is meant □ *He has the party's unequivocal support.* (**inequívoco**)

• **unequivocally** /ˌʌnɪˈkwɪvəkli/ ADVERB in an unequivocal way □ *She has stated quite unequivocally that she will not resign.* (**inequivocadamente**)

unerring /ʌnˈɜːrɪŋ/ ADJECTIVE always correct or accurate □ *She had an unerring talent for spotting promising youngsters.* (**infalível**)

unethical /ʌnˈeθɪkəl/ ADJECTIVE morally wrong □ *He has acted in a most unethical manner.* (**antiético**)

uneven /ʌnˈiːvən/ ADJECTIVE
1 not level or smooth □ *an uneven road* (**irregular**)
2 not the same in size or amount □ *There is an uneven distribution of cancer cases in the country.* (**irregular**)
3 not all of the same quality □ *Your work has been uneven this year.* (**irregular**)

• **unevenly** /ʌnˈiːvənli/ ADVERB in an uneven way □ *The paint was applied unevenly.* (**irregularmente**)

uneventful /ˌʌnɪˈventfʊl/ ADJECTIVE without anything interesting, surprising or important happening □ *The holidays were pretty uneventful.* (**rotineiro**)

unexpected /ˌʌnɪkˈspektɪd/ ADJECTIVE surprising because of not being expected □ *an unexpected visitor* □ *an unexpected development* (**inesperado**)

• **unexpectedly** /ˌʌnɪkˈspektɪdli/ ADVERB in a way that you were not expecting □ *He was unexpectedly delayed.* (**inesperadamente**)

unexplained /ˌʌnɪkˈspleɪnd/ ADJECTIVE not yet having an explanation □ *unexplained deaths* (**inexplicado**)

unfailing /ʌnˈfeɪlɪŋ/ ADJECTIVE an unfailing quality is always present and strong □ *Thanks to her unfailing good humour and encouragement we managed to get the crisis sorted out.* (**infalível**)

unfair /ʌnˈfeə(r)/ ADJECTIVE
1 not right or reasonable □ *Some of her criticism was very unfair.* (**injusto**)
2 when a situation is unfair, people are not treated in an equal way, or do not have equal opportunities (**injusto, desleal**) ▣ *His father's fame gives him an unfair advantage.* (**vantagem injusta**)

• **unfairly** /ʌnˈfeəli/ ADVERB in a way that is unfair □ *We have been very unfairly treated.* (**injustamente**)

• **unfairness** /ʌnˈfeənɪs/ NOUN, NO PLURAL being unfair (**injustiça**)

unfaithful /ʌnˈfeɪθfʊl/ ADJECTIVE not loyal or not keeping your promises (**infiel**)

unfamiliar /ˌʌnfəˈmɪliə(r)/ ADJECTIVE
1 not known or seen before □ *an unfamiliar feeling* □ *an unfamiliar face* (**desconhecido, estranho**)
2 unfamiliar with something not having any knowledge or experience of something □ *I was unfamiliar with the British legal system.* (**pouco versado em**)

unfashionable /ʌnˈfæʃənəbəl/ ADJECTIVE not fashionable or popular □ *Wide ties were becoming unfashionable.* (**fora de moda, antiquado**)

unfasten /ʌnˈfɑːsən/ VERB [**unfastens, unfastening, unfastened**] to open something that was fastened □ *She unfastened her coat.* (**desprender, desatar**)

unfavorable /ʌnˈfeɪvrəbəl/ ADJECTIVE the US spelling of **unfavourable**

unfavourable /ʌnˈfeɪvrəbəl/ ADJECTIVE
1 not positive, or criticizing something □ *They came back with unfavourable reports of the resort.* (**desfavorável**)
2 likely to cause problems or make it difficult to succeed □ *The company did well despite unfavourable economic conditions.* (**desfavorável**)

unfeeling /ʌnˈfiːlɪŋ/ ADJECTIVE not feeling sympathy for other people □ *I'm sorry to seem unfeeling, but I can't solve your problems for you.* (**insensível**)

unfinished /ʌnˈfɪnɪʃt/ ADJECTIVE not completed □ *The builders left the house unfinished when the money ran out.* (**incompleto, não terminado**)

unfit /ʌnˈfɪt/ ADJECTIVE
1 not suitable or not good enough □ *The water is unfit to drink.* (**inapto, incapacitado**)
2 not in good physical condition, especially because of not doing enough exercise (**fora de forma**)

unfold /ʌnˈfəʊld/ VERB [**unfolds, unfolding, unfolded**]
1 to spread out something that was folded (**desdobrar**)
2 if a situation unfolds, it develops and people start to know about it □ *The details of what happened began to unfold.* (**revelar**)

unforeseen /ˌʌnfɔːˈsiːn/ ADJECTIVE not expected (**inesperado**) ▣ *The flight has been cancelled due to unforeseen circumstances.* (**circunstâncias inesperadas**)

unforgettable /ˌʌnfəˈgetəbəl/ ADJECTIVE impossible to forget, usually because of being enjoyable, interesting, etc. □ *Seeing the lions up close was a truly unforgettable experience.* (**inesquecível**)

unforgivable /ˌʌnfəˈɡɪvəbəl/ ADJECTIVE unforgivable behaviour is so bad that you cannot forgive it (**imperdoável**)
• **unforgivably** /ˌʌnfəˈɡɪvəblɪ/ ADVERB in a way that is unforgivable □ *She was unforgivably rude.* (**imperdoavelmente**)

unfortunate /ʌnˈfɔːtʃənət/ ADJECTIVE
1 caused by bad luck □ *an unfortunate accident* (**infeliz**)
2 if something is unfortunate, you wish it had not happened or been true □ *It was an unfortunate choice of words.* (**infeliz**)
• **unfortunately** /ʌnˈfɔːtʃənətlɪ/ ADVERB used to show that you wish something had not happened or been true □ *Unfortunately, I lost the ring.* (**infelizmente**)

unfounded /ʌnˈfaʊndɪd/ ADJECTIVE not based on facts □ *The accusations against him have been proved to be unfounded.* (**infundado**)

unfriendly /ʌnˈfrendlɪ/ ADJECTIVE not friendly □ *His sister was very unfriendly.* (**antipático**)

unfurnished /ʌnˈfɜːnɪʃt/ ADJECTIVE with no furniture □ *We rented an unfurnished flat in Oxford.* (**desmobiliado**)

ungainly /ʌnˈɡeɪnlɪ/ ADJECTIVE moving in a way that is awkward and not attractive (**desajeitado**)

ungrateful /ʌnˈɡreɪtfʊl/ ADJECTIVE not grateful □ *He was so ungrateful, I wished I hadn't helped him.* (**ingrato**)
• **ungratefully** /ʌnˈɡreɪtfʊlɪ/ ADVERB in a way that is ungrateful (**de maneira ingrata**)

unhappily /ʌnˈhæpɪlɪ/ ADVERB in a way that is not happy □ *He waited unhappily while the others played outside.* (**com ar infeliz**)

unhappiness /ʌnˈhæpɪnɪs/ NOUN, NO PLURAL the state of being unhappy (**infelicidade**)

unhappy /ʌnˈhæpɪ/ ADJECTIVE [**unhappier, unhappiest**]
1 sad or causing sadness (**triste, infeliz**) 🔁 *Ben has been feeling unhappy for a long time.* (**sentindo-se infeliz**) □ *an unhappy marriage*
2 not pleased or not satisfied (**descontente**) □ + *about He was unhappy about the result of the meeting.* 🔁 *We were deeply unhappy about the quality of their work.* (**profundamente descontente**)

unhealthy /ʌnˈhelθɪ/ ADJECTIVE [**unhealthier, unhealthiest**]
1 someone who is unhealthy is ill, or does not have good health □ *He looks very unhealthy.* (**doentio**)
2 harmful for your health □ *an unhealthy lifestyle* (**insalubre, mórbido**)

3 harmful for your mental state □ *She has an unhealthy obsession with death.*

unheard /ʌnˈhɜːd/ ADJECTIVE ignored or not heard by anyone (**ignorado, desconhecido**) 🔁 *Their pleas for help went unheard.*

unheard-of /ʌnˈhɜːd ɒv/ ADJECTIVE if something is unheard-of, it has never happened before and is often shocking □ *Divorce was almost unheard-of in 19th-century England.* (**incomum, sem precedente**)

unhurt /ʌnˈhɜːt/ ADJECTIVE not injured □ *The passengers were unhurt.* (**ileso**)

uni- /ˈjuːnɪ/ PREFIX uni- is used at the beginning of words to mean 'having or being only one of something' □ *unilateral* (**prefixo uni-**)

unicorn /ˈjuːnɪkɔːn/ NOUN [*plural* **unicorns**] in stories, an animal like a white horse with a horn on its head (**unicórnio**)

unidentified /ˌʌnaɪˈdentɪfaɪd/ ADJECTIVE not recognized, known or named □ *An unidentified man was seen leaving the house.* (**não identificado**)

unification /ˌjuːnɪfɪˈkeɪʃən/ NOUN, NO PLURAL when two countries join together to form one country (**unificação**)

unified /ˈjuːnɪfaɪd/ ADJECTIVE
1 with all people and groups working together and having the same opinions □ *We need a unified response to this threat.* (**unir, unificar**)
2 a unified country, organization, etc. has been formed by more than one country, organization, etc. joining together □ *The new unified company will employ hundreds of local people.* (**unificado**)
3 the same in all places and situations □ *There is a unified system of registration for electricians.* (**único**)

uniform /ˈjuːnɪfɔːm/ ▶ NOUN [*plural* **uniforms**] a set of clothes that shows you belong to a particular organization, job or school □ *a bus driver's uniform* (**uniforme**) 🔁 *school uniform* (**uniforme escolar**)
▶ ADJECTIVE the same size, shape, standard, etc. □ *The company is trying to achieve uniform standards of training for all staff.* (**uniforme**)
• **uniformed** /ˈjuːnɪfɔːmd/ ADJECTIVE wearing a uniform □ *He was accompanied by two uniformed policemen.* (**uniformizado**)
• **uniformity** /ˌjuːnɪˈfɔːmətɪ/ NOUN, NO PLURAL the state of being the same size, shape, standard, etc. □ *We need to bring some uniformity to the laws in the region.* (**uniformidade**)
• **uniformly** /ˈjuːnɪfɔːmlɪ/ ADVERB in a way that is the same in all situations □ *The school has achieved uniformly high standards.* (**uniformemente**)

unify /ˈjuːnɪfaɪ/ VERB [**unifies, unifying, unified**]
1 to make people, groups, countries, etc. feel that they belong together □ *A sporting event like this can really unify a nation.* (**unificar**)

2 if groups, organizations, countries, etc. unify, they join together (**unificar**)

3 to make something the same in all places and situations (**unificar**)

unilateral /ˌjuːnɪˈlætərəl/ ADJECTIVE a unilateral action or decision is one done or made by only one of the people or groups involved □ *They agreed to a unilateral withdrawal of their troops.* (**unilateral**)

• **unilaterally** /ˌjuːnɪˈlætərəli/ ADVERB in a unilateral way □ *Canada has acted unilaterally in banning fishing in this part of the Atlantic.* (**unilateralmente**)

unimaginable /ˌʌnɪˈmædʒɪnəbəl/ ADJECTIVE impossible to imagine because of being so extreme or so unusual (**inimaginável**) □ *This is a disaster of an almost unimaginable scale.*

unimaginative /ˌʌnɪˈmædʒɪnətɪv/ ADJECTIVE not thinking of or not using new and interesting ideas □ *Her house is decorated in a tasteful but unimaginative style.* (**sem imaginação/criatividade**)

unimportance /ˌʌnɪmˈpɔːtəns/ NOUN, NO PLURAL the fact of not being important (**insignificância**)

• **unimportant** /ˌʌnɪmˈpɔːtənt/ ADJECTIVE not important (**insignificante**)

uninhabitable /ˌʌnɪnˈhæbɪtəbəl/ ADJECTIVE if a place or a building is uninhabitable, it is impossible for people to live there □ *Pollution is making parts of the planet uninhabitable.* (**inabitável**)

uninhabited /ˌʌnɪnˈhæbɪtɪd/ ADJECTIVE an uninhabited place does not have people living in it (**inabitado**)

uninspired /ˌʌnɪnˈspaɪəd/ ADJECTIVE

1 not exciting or interesting □ *It was an uninspired performance.* (**entediante**)

2 not having any new or interesting ideas □ *I'm supposed to be writing a poem, but I feel completely uninspired.* (**sem inspiração**)

• **uninspiring** /ˌʌnɪnˈspaɪərɪŋ/ ADJECTIVE something that is uninspiring does not make you feel excited, enthusiastic or interested □ *Despite being one of London's most expensive restaurants, the food was pretty uninspiring.* (**sem graça**)

uninstall /ˌʌnɪnˈstɔːl/ VERB [**uninstalls, uninstalling, uninstalled**] to remove a program from a computer. A computing word. (**desinstalar**)

unintelligible /ˌʌnɪnˈtelɪdʒəbəl/ ADJECTIVE impossible to understand (**ininteligível**)

unintentional /ˌʌnɪnˈtenʃənəl/ ADJECTIVE done by accident and not planned □ *Any offence caused was entirely unintentional.* (**não intencional**)

• **unintentionally** /ˌʌnɪnˈtenʃənəli/ ADVERB in an unintentional way □ *The film is unintentionally funny.* (**sem querer**)

uninterested /ˌʌnˈɪntrəstɪd/ ADJECTIVE not interested □ *I am totally uninterested in sport.* (**desinteressado**)

• **uninteresting** /ˌʌnˈɪntrəstɪŋ/ ADJECTIVE boring (**desinteressante**)

uninterrupted /ˌʌnˌɪntəˈrʌptɪd/ ADJECTIVE

1 continuous □ *We have had ten years of uninterrupted economic growth.* (**ininterrupto**)

2 an uninterrupted view is not blocked by anything (**desimpedido**)

uninvited /ˌʌnɪnˈvaɪtɪd/ ADJECTIVE an uninvited guest has not been invited (**não convidado**)

union /ˈjuːnɪən/ NOUN [plural **unions**]

1 another word for a **trade union** (**sindicato**)

2 a group of countries, organizations, etc. that join together (**união**)

3 the process of joining people or things together (**unir**)

• **unionist** /ˈjuːnjənɪst/ NOUN [plural **unionists**] a member of a trade union (**membro de sindicato**)

unique /juːˈniːk/ ADJECTIVE

1 completely different from anyone or anything else (**único**)

2 very special and unusual □ *a unique opportunity* (**único**)

3 unique to something only happening or existing in one place □ *The species is unique to this island.* (**único, ímpar**)

• **uniquely** /juːˈniːkli/ ADVERB in a unique way □ *Is love a uniquely human emotion?* □ *He is uniquely placed to lead the party to victory.* (**exclusivamente**)

unisex /ˈjuːnɪseks/ ADJECTIVE intended for either men or women □ *unisex clothes* (**unissex**)

unison /ˈjuːnɪsən/ NOUN **in unison** if people do something in unison, they all do it together (**uníssono**)

unit /ˈjuːnɪt/ NOUN [plural **units**]

1 a measure used to show an amount or level □ *A metre is a unit of length.* □ *What is the unit of currency in Ecuador?* (**unidade**)

2 an organization or a part of an organization with a particular purpose, or the people that work in it □ *They set up a specialist burns unit at the hospital.* □ *He is a member of an elite police unit.* (**unidade**)

3 a single thing that can be part of a larger group of things □ *The book is divided into ten units.* (**unidade**)

4 a piece of furniture (**módulo**) □ *They bought new kitchen units.* (**módulos de armário para cozinha**) □ *They stock a range of storage units.*

5 a building or part of a building □ *Two hundred new residential units are to be built on the land.* (**unidade**)

6 a machine or part of a machine □ *We had to put in an air conditioning unit.* (**unidade, item**)

unite /juːˈnaɪt/ VERB [**unites, uniting, united**]

1 if people or groups unite, they join together, often to achieve something □ *Workers in the area have united to oppose the pay cuts.* (**unir-se**)

United Kingdom 885 **unloved**

2 to join people or groups together, often making them them feel that they belong together and have the same opinions □ *We need a new leader to unite the party.* (unir(-se))

• **united** /juːˈnaɪtɪd/ ADJECTIVE
1 if people are united about something, they agree about it □ *They are united in their opposition to the proposals.* (unido)
2 with all the parts joined together □ *Shall we see a united Ireland one day?* (unido)

United Kingdom /juːˌnaɪtɪd ˈkɪŋdəm/ NOUN **the United Kingdom** England, Scotland, Wales and Northern Ireland (Reino Unido)

United Nations /juːˌnaɪtɪd ˈneɪʃənz/ NOUN **the United Nations** an organization of people from most countries of the world, that works to try to solve world problems (Nações Unidas)

United States of America /juːˌnaɪtɪd ˌsteɪts əv əˈmerɪkə/ NOUN **the United States of America** the 50 states that make the country of North America (Estados Unidos da América)

unity /ˈjuːnɪti/ NOUN, NO PLURAL when people agree on things and act together □ *She has called for unity within the party.* (unidade)

universal /ˌjuːnɪˈvɜːsəl/ ADJECTIVE
1 affecting or including everyone in the world □ *English may become a universal language that everyone can learn and use.* (universal)
2 relating to everyone in a group □ *He performed to universal applause.* (universal)

• **universally** /ˌjuːnɪˈvɜːsəli/ ADVERB by everyone in a group or in the world □ *He was universally admired.* (universalmente)

universe /ˈjuːnɪvɜːs/ NOUN **the universe** everything that exists anywhere, including the Earth, the sun and all the other planets and stars in space □ *Somewhere in the universe there might be another world like ours.* (universo)

university /ˌjuːnɪˈvɜːsəti/ NOUN [plural **universities**] a place where you go to study at the highest level after leaving school (universidade) 🔁 *I am hoping to go to university.* (entrar na universidade) □ *university students*

unjust /ˌʌnˈdʒʌst/ ADJECTIVE not fair □ *an unjust punishment* (injusto)

• **unjustifiable** /ˌʌndʒʌstɪˈfaɪəbəl/ ADJECTIVE if something is unjustifiable, you cannot say that it is right or fair □ *All acts of terrorism are morally unjustifiable.* (injustificável)

• **unjustified** /ˌʌnˈdʒʌstɪfaɪd/ ADJECTIVE not fair or having no good reason □ *Her criticism was completely unjustified.* (injustificado)

• **unjustly** /ˌʌnˈdʒʌstli/ ADVERB not fairly □ *He was treated very unjustly.* (injustamente)

unkempt /ˌʌnˈkempt/ ADJECTIVE not tidy □ *unkempt hair* (desalinhado, bagunçado)

unkind /ʌnˈkaɪnd/ ADJECTIVE [**unkinder, unkindest**] cruel and not kind □ *It was unkind of you to tease her.* (cruel, duro)

• **unkindly** /ʌnˈkaɪndli/ ADVERB in an unkind way □ *They treated me unkindly.* (cruelmente)
• **unkindness** /ʌnˈkaɪndnɪs/ NOUN, NO PLURAL being unkind (indelicadeza)

unknown /ˌʌnˈnəʊn/ ADJECTIVE
1 not known □ *The man's whereabouts are unknown.* (desconhecido)
2 not famous □ *an unknown actor* (desconhecido)

unlawful /ˌʌnˈlɔːfʊl/ ADJECTIVE illegal □ *A verdict of unlawful killing was reached.* (ilegal, ilícito)

unleaded /ˌʌnˈledɪd/ ADJECTIVE unleaded petrol does not have lead (= a soft, grey metal) added to it and so causes less harm to the environment (sem chumbo)

unleash /ʌnˈliːʃ/ VERB [**unleashes, unleashing, unleashed**] to do something or cause something that has a strong and often violent effect □ *She unleashed a furious outburst against the media.* (descontrolar, soltar)

unless /ənˈles/ CONJUNCTION except when, or except if □ *We always go for a walk on Sundays, unless it's raining.* □ *Don't come unless I phone you.* (a menos que, a não ser que)

unlike /ʌnˈlaɪk/ PREPOSITION
1 different from □ *I never saw twins who were so unlike each other.* (diferente)
2 not usual for someone □ *It's unlike her to be so bad tempered.* (que não é característico de)

unlikely /ʌnˈlaɪkli/ ADJECTIVE
1 not likely or expected to happen (improvável) □ + *that It's unlikely that she'll come.* □ + *to do something We're unlikely to finish the work today.* 🔁 *A victory for England now seems highly unlikely.* (altamente improvável)
2 probably not true □ *an unlikely tale* (improvável)

unlimited /ʌnˈlɪmɪtɪd/ ADJECTIVE if something is unlimited, you can have or use as much of it as you want □ *This ticket allows unlimited travel on all train services for two months.* □ *The country does not have an unlimited amount of money to spend on health care.* (ilimitado)

unload /ˌʌnˈləʊd/ VERB [**unloads, unloading, unloaded**]
1 to take things off or out of a vehicle □ *After we got back from the trip, our first job was to unload the car.* (descarregar)
2 if a vehicle unloads, things are taken off or out of it □ *The ship unloaded in Marseilles.* (descarregar)

unlock /ˌʌnˈlɒk/ VERB [**unlocks, unlocking, unlocked**] to open something that is locked □ *Unlock this door now!* (destrancar)

unloved /ˌʌnˈlʌvd/ ADJECTIVE not loved or liked □ *They have at last got rid of their unloved president.* (não amado)

unlucky /ʌnˈlʌki/ ADJECTIVE having bad luck, causing bad luck or caused by bad luck □ *I'm very unlucky at cards.* □ *It was an unlucky defeat.* (**azarado**)

unmade /ʌnˈmeɪd/ ADJECTIVE an unmade bed has not had its covers arranged in a tidy way after being slept in (**desfeito, não arrumado**)

unmanageable /ʌnˈmænɪdʒəbəl/ ADJECTIVE very difficult to use or control □ *Her son has become completely unmanageable.* (**incontrolável**)

unmanned /ʌnˈmænd/ ADJECTIVE unmanned vehicles or machines are controlled automatically, and do not have people in or near them to operate them □ *They use unmanned aircraft to gather information.* (**sem seres humanos**)

unmarried /ʌnˈmærɪd/ ADJECTIVE not married □ *unmarried couples* (**solteiro**)

unmask /ʌnˈmɑːsk/ VERB [unmasks, unmasking, unmasked] to show the truth about someone or something, especially something bad □ *He was unmasked as a liar and a cheat.* (**desmascarar**)

unmistakable /ˌʌnmɪˈsteɪkəbəl/ ADJECTIVE if something is unmistakable, you could not think that it was anything else □ *I heard the unmistakable sound of a Ferrari.* (**inequívoco**)

• **unmistakably** /ˌʌnmɪˈsteɪkəblɪ/ ADVERB in an unmistakable way □ *It was unmistakably his handwriting.* (**inconfundivelmente**)

unmitigated /ʌnˈmɪtɪgeɪtɪd/ ADJECTIVE used to emphasize how extreme something is (**completo, absoluto**) □ *The performance was an unmitigated disaster.* (**desastre completo**)

unmoved /ʌnˈmuːvd/ ADJECTIVE not affected emotionally □ *He appeared unmoved as the judge read out the sentence.* (**impassível**)

unnatural /ʌnˈnætʃərəl/ ADJECTIVE not natural or not normal □ *The animals were being fed an unnatural diet.* (**artificial**)

• **unnaturally** /ʌnˈnætʃərəli/ ADVERB in a strange or unusual way □ *The building was unnaturally silent.* (**artificialmente**)

unnecessarily /ʌnˈnesəsərɪli/ ADVERB in a way that is not necessary □ *We spent all that money unnecessarily.* □ *I thought you were unnecessarily rude.* (**desnecessariamente**)

unnecessary /ʌnˈnesəsəri/ ADJECTIVE
1 something unnecessary is possible to avoid □ *These measures will cause unnecessary suffering.* □ *We can't afford any unnecessary expense.* (**desnecessário**)
2 not needed □ *Any unnecessary clothing can be given to charity.* (**desnecessário**)

unnerve /ʌnˈnɜːv/ VERB [unnerves, unnerving, unnerved] to make someone feel worried or nervous □ *His silence unnerved me.* (**enervar**)

• **unnerving** /ʌnˈnɜːvɪŋ/ ADJECTIVE causing you to feel worried or nervous (**enervante**)

unnoticed /ʌnˈnəʊtɪst/ ADJECTIVE not noticed by anyone (**despercebido**) ▣ *His strange clothes did not go unnoticed.* (**passar despercebido**)

unobtrusive /ˌʌnəbˈtruːsɪv/ ADJECTIVE not attracting much attention □ *He tried to be as unobtrusive as possible.* (**discreto**)

• **unobtrusively** /ˌʌnəbˈtruːsɪvli/ ADVERB in an unobtrusive way □ *She slipped unobtrusively into the room.* (**discretamente**)

unoccupied /ʌnˈɒkjupaɪd/ ADJECTIVE not being used or lived in □ *These houses have been unoccupied for years.* (**desocupado**)

unofficial /ˌʌnəˈfɪʃəl/ ADJECTIVE not done or allowed by anyone in authority □ *Unofficial estimates suggest unemployment is still rising.* (**extraoficial**)

• **unofficially** /ˌʌnəˈfɪʃəli/ ADVERB in an unofficial way □ *Unofficially, I can tell you that you've passed your exams.* (**extraoficialmente**)

unorthodox /ʌnˈɔːθədɒks/ ADJECTIVE unorthodox behaviour or opinions are different from what is usual □ *She used unorthodox methods of treating depression.* (**não convencional**)

unpack /ʌnˈpæk/ VERB [unpacks, unpacking, unpacked] to take things out of a case, bag, box, etc. □ *I've unpacked my case.* □ *Have you unpacked yet?* (**desempacotar**)

unpaid /ʌnˈpeɪd/ ADJECTIVE
1 not paid for doing work (**trabalho não remunerado**) ▣ *We are expected to do unpaid overtime.* (**horas extras não remuneradas**)
2 not yet paid for (**de pagamento pendente**) □ *unpaid debts* (**débitos pendentes**)

unpleasant /ʌnˈplezənt/ ADJECTIVE
1 if something is unpleasant, you do not like it or enjoy it □ *an unpleasant smell* □ *I found skiing a thoroughly unpleasant experience.* (**desagradável**)
2 not polite, friendly or kind □ + *to He was rather unpleasant to his students.* (**desagradável**)

• **unpleasantly** /ʌnˈplezəntli/ ADVERB in an unpleasant way □ *The weather was unpleasantly hot.* □ *She laughed rather unpleasantly when I asked for a cold drink.* (**desagradavelmente**)

• **unpleasantness** /ʌnˈplezəntnɪs/ NOUN, NO PLURAL
1 a situation in which people are angry, violent, upset, etc. □ *His behaviour caused a great deal of unpleasantness at work.* (**desentendimento**)
2 being unpleasant (**aborrecimento, desagrado**)

unplug /ʌnˈplʌg/ VERB [unplugs, unplugging, unplugged] to stop a piece of equipment from being connected to its supply of electricity by pulling out its plug (= device with small metal parts) □ *I've unplugged the printer.* (**desligar, deixar sem conexão elétrica**)

unpopular /ʌnˈpɒpjʊlə(r)/ ADJECTIVE disliked by many people □ *His attitude makes him very unpopular at school.* (**impopular**)

unprecedented /ʌnˈpresɪdəntɪd/ ADJECTIVE if something is unprecedented, it has never happened or existed before □ *Researchers have been given unprecedented access to the files.* (**sem precedente**)

unpredictable /ˌʌnprɪˈdɪktəbəl/ ADJECTIVE if someone or something is unpredictable, they change a lot, so you cannot guess what they are going to be like or what they are going to do □ *The weather can be pretty unpredictable.* (**imprevisível**)

unprepared /ˌʌnprɪˈpeəd/ ADJECTIVE not prepared for something or not expecting something □ *We were unprepared for the racism we encountered there.* (**despreparado**)

unprofessional /ˌʌnprəˈfeʃənəl/ ADJECTIVE not behaving in a way that is suitable for work or for a particular job □ *Talking about her clients was extremely unprofessional.* (**sem profissionalismo**)

unprofitable /ʌnˈprɒfɪtəbəl/ ADJECTIVE not making a profit □ *We were forced to close our unprofitable branches.* (**não lucrativo**)

unprovoked /ˌʌnprəˈvəʊkt/ ADJECTIVE an unprovoked attack is when someone is attacked for no reason (**não provocado**)

unqualified /ʌnˈkwɒlɪfaɪd/ ADJECTIVE
1 without the qualifications to do a particular job □ *Concern was expressed about the increasing number of unqualified people offering medical treatment.* (**sem qualificação**)
2 without the necessary experience to do something □ *I am unqualified to advise you.* (**sem qualificação**)
3 complete and not limited in any way (**irrestrito**)
🔒 *His performance was an unqualified success.*

unquestionably /ʌnˈkwestʃənəblɪ/ ADVERB without any doubt □ *He is, unquestionably, a great actor.* (**indiscutivelmente**)

unravel /ʌnˈrævəl/ VERB [unravels, unravelling/ US unraveling, unravelled/US unraveled]
1 to understand something complicated □ *She was determined to unravel the mystery.* (**desvendar, elucidar**)
2 if complicated plans, arrangements, etc. unravel, they start to fail □ *All my plans started to unravel.* (**destruir**)
3 if threads in a piece of cloth unravel, they stop being twisted together, and if you unravel them, you stop them from being twisted together (**desembaraçar**)

unreal /ʌnˈrɪəl/ ADJECTIVE not seeming to be true or real □ *All this success still feels a bit unreal.* (**irreal**)

• **unrealistic** /ˌʌnrɪəˈlɪstɪk/ ADJECTIVE based on hopes or wishes that are not likely to be possible □ *It's unrealistic to think that sales will go up.* (**fantasioso**)

• **unreality** /ˌʌnrɪˈælɪtɪ/ NOUN, NO PLURAL the state of being unreal □ *All the time I was at the palace, I had a feeling of unreality.* (**fantasia**)

unreasonable /ʌnˈriːzənəbəl/ ADJECTIVE
1 not fair, often because of wanting too much □ *It's unreasonable to expect students to do so much homework.* □ *The unions were accused of making unreasonable demands.* (**irracional**)
2 not based on good reasons □ *Their conclusions were not unreasonable.* (**injusto**)

• **unreasonably** /ʌnˈriːzənəblɪ/ ADVERB
1 in an unfair way □ *I think you're behaving really unreasonably.* (**injustamente**)
2 in a way that is not based on good reasons □ *She believed, not unreasonably, that she would be paid for her work.* (**sem razão**)

unrelated /ˌʌnrɪˈleɪtɪd/ ADJECTIVE if situations or events are unrelated, there is no connection between them □ *The police say the murders are probably unrelated.* (**não relacionado**)

unreliable /ˌʌnrɪˈlaɪəbəl/ ADJECTIVE
1 not able to be trusted to do something □ *He's totally unreliable.* □ *My car's a bit unreliable.* (**não confiável**)
2 unreliable information may not be true (**não confiável**)

unremitting /ˌʌnrɪˈmɪtɪŋ/ ADJECTIVE never stopping or getting better □ *We've had a year of unremitting gloom.* (**ininterrupto**)

unrepresentative /ˌʌnreprɪˈzentətɪv/ ADJECTIVE not typical of a group of people or things □ *The research was based on an unrepresentative sample.* (**atípico**)

unrest /ʌnˈrest/ NOUN, NO PLURAL when people are angry about something and may cause trouble □ *The new tax sparked unrest all over the country.* (**incômodo**)

unrestrained /ˌʌnrɪˈstreɪnd/ ADJECTIVE not limited or controlled in any way □ *People were dancing with unrestrained joy.* (**irrestrito**)

unripe /ʌnˈraɪp/ ADJECTIVE unripe fruit is not ready to eat (**não amadurecido**)

unroll /ʌnˈrəʊl/ VERB [unrolls, unrolling, unrolled] to open out something that has been rolled up and make it flat □ *He unrolled the map and put it on the ground.* (**desenrolar**)

unruly /ʌnˈruːlɪ/ ADJECTIVE
1 badly behaved and difficult to control □ *an unruly child* (**incontrolável**)
2 unruly hair is untidy and difficult to control (**rebelde**)

unsafe /ʌnˈseɪf/ ADJECTIVE dangerous □ *unsafe practices* (**perigoso, inseguro**)

unsaid /ʌnˈsed/ ADJECTIVE thought but not said (**não dito**) 🔒 *Some things are better left unsaid.* (**é melhor não dizer**)

unsatisfactory /ˌʌnsætɪsˈfæktərɪ/ ADJECTIVE not good enough (**insatisfatório**)

unsavoury /ʌnˈseɪvərɪ/ ADJECTIVE unpleasant and morally bad □ *an unsavoury character* (**de mau gosto**)

unscathed /ʌnˈskeɪðd/ ADJECTIVE without being harmed □ *They escaped from the burning building unscathed.* (ileso)

unscrew /ʌnˈskruː/ VERB [unscrews, unscrewing, unscrewed]
1 to remove something with a turning movement □ *Joe unscrewed the lid from the bottle and took a drink.* (desenroscar)
2 to remove something by taking out a screw (= small pointed metal object) or screws □ *She unscrewed the cupboard door.* (desparafusar)

unscrupulous /ʌnˈskruːpjʊləs/ ADJECTIVE willing to do dishonest or illegal things in order to make money, get an advantage, etc. (inescrupuloso)

unseemly /ʌnˈsiːmlɪ/ ADJECTIVE embarrassing and not suitable □ *unseemly behavior* (inconveniente)

unseen /ʌnˈsiːn/ ADJECTIVE, ADVERB not seen or not noticed □ *He managed to leave the house unseen.* (não visto)

unselfish /ʌnˈselfɪʃ/ ADJECTIVE thinking of other people's needs and feelings and not your own (altruísta)
• **unselfishly** /ʌnˈselfɪʃlɪ/ ADVERB in an unselfish way (altruisticamente)
• **unselfishness** /ʌnˈselfɪʃnɪs/ NOUN, NO PLURAL being unselfish (altruísmo)

unsettled /ʌnˈsetəld/ ADJECTIVE
1 if the weather is unsettled, it changes a lot (incerto)
2 worried or upset in a situation (inquieto)

unshaven /ʌnˈʃeɪvən/ ADJECTIVE with hair growing on the face after not shaving recently (sem barbear)

unsightly /ʌnˈsaɪtlɪ/ ADJECTIVE not nice to look at □ *unsightly office blocks* (feio, mal-ajeitado)

unskilled /ʌnˈskɪld/ ADJECTIVE
1 without special skills or training (inexperiente) ▣ *unskilled workers* (trabalhadores inexperientes)
2 unskilled work does not need special skills or training (que não exige prática)

unsociable /ʌnˈsəʊʃəbəl/ ADJECTIVE not wanting to be with other people (não sociável)

unsolicited /ˌʌnsəˈlɪsɪtɪd/ ADJECTIVE given to you without you asking for it (não solicitado) ▣ *unsolicited advice* (conselho não solicitado)

unsolved /ʌnˈsɒlvd/ ADJECTIVE having no solution or explanation □ *an unsolved murder* (não resolvido)

unsound /ʌnˈsaʊnd/ ADJECTIVE
1 not safe □ *The building is structurally unsound.* (não seguro)
2 based on facts or ideas that cannot be trusted □ *unsound evidence* (não confiável)

unspeakable /ʌnˈspiːkəbəl/ ADJECTIVE too bad to describe in words □ *unspeakable rudeness* (indizível)

unspoiled /ʌnˈspɔɪld/ or **unspoilt** /ʌnˈspɔɪlt/ ADJECTIVE not spoiled or damaged in any way □ *the unspoiled beauty of the countryside* (intacto)

unspoken /ʌnˈspəʊkən/ ADJECTIVE understood, although not said in words □ *an unspoken agreement* (não dito)

unstable /ʌnˈsteɪbəl/ ADJECTIVE
1 changing or likely to change over a period □ *a politically unstable region* (instável)
2 not firm or strong □ *This chair seems a bit unstable.* (instável)
3 not calm and having moods that change suddenly □ *She seems a little unstable.* (instável)

unsteadily /ʌnˈstedɪlɪ/ ADVERB in an unsteady way (irregularmente)

unsteady /ʌnˈstedɪ/ ADJECTIVE likely to fall and not firm □ *After the operation she was very unsteady on her feet.* (oscilante)

unstoppable /ʌnˈstɒpəbəl/ ADJECTIVE not able to be stopped or prevented □ *an unstoppable force* (inevitável)

unstuck /ʌnˈstʌk/ ADJECTIVE **come unstuck** to stop making progress, or to fail □ *I came unstuck with the last stage of the recipe.* (dar errado)

unsubscribe /ˌʌnsəbˈskraɪb/ VERB [unsubscribes, unsubscribing, unsubscribed] to remove your name from an Internet mailing list (= all the people that an organization sends information to) (cancelar o recebimento de e-mail marketing)

unsubstantiated /ˌʌnsəbˈstænʃɪeɪtɪd/ ADJECTIVE not proved true □ *unsubstantiated rumours* (sem base/provas)

unsuccessful /ˌʌnsəkˈsesfʊl/ ADJECTIVE not managing to do something you are trying to do (malsucedido) ▣ *Thieves made an unsuccessful attempt to steal the car.* □ *I tried to contact him but was unsuccessful.* (tentativa malsucedida)
• **unsuccessfully** /ˌʌnsəkˈsesfʊlɪ/ ADVERB in an unsuccessful way □ *I tried unsuccessfully to persuade her.* (em vão)

unsuitable /ʌnˈsuːtəbəl/ ADJECTIVE not right for a purpose or occasion □ *unsuitable clothing* (impróprio, inoportuno)

unsung /ʌnˈsʌŋ/ ADJECTIVE not praised or not famous although you have done something very good (não celebrado) ▣ *an unsung hero*

unsure /ʌnˈʃɔː(r)/ ADJECTIVE
1 not certain □ *I was unsure of the spelling.* □ *I asked if she was coming but he seemed unsure.* (inseguro)
2 **be unsure of yourself** to not be confident (ter baixa autoestima)

unsuspecting /ˌʌnsəˈspektɪŋ/ ADJECTIVE not aware that something bad is happening or going to happen (que não desconfia)

unsustainable /ˌʌnsəˈsteɪnəbəl/ ADJECTIVE

unsympathetic

1 not able to continue in the same way for a long time □ *unsustainable economic growth* (insustentável)
2 damaging the environment and so not able to continue in the same way □ *unsustainable farming practices* (não sustentável)

unsympathetic /ˌʌn.sɪmpəˈθetɪk/ ADJECTIVE
1 not caring about other people's problems □ *She was fairly unsympathetic when I had my accident.* (insensível)
2 not showing support for a group or belief (que não manifesta apoio)

untangle /ʌnˈtæŋɡəl/ VERB [untangles, untangling, untangled]
1 to separate something that is twisted together or has knots in it (desembaraçar)
2 to try to solve a difficult problem (esclarecer)

unthinkable /ʌnˈθɪŋkəbəl/ ADJECTIVE too bad or strange for you to be able to imagine (impensável)

untidiness /ʌnˈtaɪdɪnɪs/ NOUN, NO PLURAL being untidy (desordem)

untidy /ʌnˈtaɪdɪ/ ADJECTIVE [untidier, untidiest]
1 not carefully ordered or arranged □ *His flat is always untidy.* (desarrumado)
2 an untidy person does not keep their home, office, etc. tidy (desleixado)

untie /ʌnˈtaɪ/ VERB [unties, untying, untied] to unfasten something that is tied in a knot □ *He untied his shoelaces.* (desamarrar)

until /ənˈtɪl/ PREPOSITION, CONJUNCTION
1 continuing to a particular time but not after that □ *He'll be here until midday.* □ *I waited until she'd gone.* (até)
2 continuing as far as somewhere □ *Carry on walking until you get to a bridge.* (até)
3 not…until not before □ *I won't start until you tell me.* (não… até)

untimely /ʌnˈtaɪmlɪ/ ADJECTIVE
1 happening too soon □ *his untimely death* (prematuro)
2 happening at a time that is not convenient □ *her untimely return* (inoportuno)

untold /ʌnˈtəʊld/ ADJECTIVE too great to be counted or measured □ *untold riches* □ *untold misery* (imensurável)

untoward /ˌʌntəˈwɔːd/ ADJECTIVE unexpected and not convenient. A formal word. (adverso)

untrue /ʌnˈtruː/ ADJECTIVE false, not true □ *His story was completely untrue.* (falso)

untrustworthy /ʌnˈtrʌstˌwɜːðɪ/ ADJECTIVE not able to be trusted (que não merece confiança)

untruth /ʌnˈtruːθ/ NOUN [plural untruths] a formal word meaning a lie (inverdade)

unused¹ /ʌnˈjuːzd/ ADJECTIVE not having been used or not used now □ *unused stamps* (não usado)

unwise

unused² /ʌnˈjuːst/ ADJECTIVE **be unused to sth** to have little experience of something □ *I'm unused to cooking my own meals.* (não acostumado a)

unusual /ʌnˈjuːʒəl/ ADJECTIVE
1 not normal or not ordinary (incomum) □ *It's unusual for him to arrive late.* (é incomum para) □ *Police took the unusual step of issuing a photograph of the suspect.*
2 not like other things or people in a way that is interesting or attractive □ *They make some lovely, quite unusual jewellery.* (original, incomum)

• **unusually** /ʌnˈjuːʒəlɪ/ ADVERB to a degree that is not normal or ordinary □ *It has been unusually cold for the time of year.* (incomumente)

unveil /ʌnˈveɪl/ VERB [unveils, unveiling, unveiled]
1 to announce a new plan to the public □ *The minister unveiled the plans at the conference this morning.* (anunciar)
2 to take a cover off something as part of a ceremony (desvelar)

unwanted /ʌnˈwɒntɪd/ ADJECTIVE not wanted □ *unwanted gifts* (não desejado)

unwarranted /ʌnˈwɒrəntɪd/ ADJECTIVE not deserved and not fair □ *unwarranted criticism* (injustificado)

unwary /ʌnˈweərɪ/ ADJECTIVE not aware of the dangers or risks in a situation □ *the unwary traveller* (descuidado, imprudente)

unwelcome /ʌnˈwelkəm/ ADJECTIVE not wanted □ *unwelcome attention* □ *unwelcome news* □ *unwelcome visitors* (indesejável)

unwell /ʌnˈwel/ ADJECTIVE not healthy. A formal word. (indisposto, doente)

unwieldy /ʌnˈwiːldɪ/ ADJECTIVE
1 large and awkward to carry (desajeitado)
2 large, complicated and difficult to work with □ *an unwieldy system* (complexo, de difícil controle)

unwilling /ʌnˈwɪlɪŋ/ ADJECTIVE not wanting to do something □ + **to do something** *They seem unwilling to help.* (relutante)

• **unwillingly** /ʌnˈwɪlɪŋlɪ/ ADVERB in an unwilling way (relutantemente)

• **unwillingness** /ʌnˈwɪlɪŋnɪs/ NOUN, NO PLURAL being unwilling □ + **to do something** *His apparent unwillingness to discuss the problem made the situation very difficult.* (relutância)

unwind /ʌnˈwaɪnd/ VERB [unwinds, unwinding, unwound]
1 to relax □ *Having a bath is a good way to unwind.* (relaxar)
2 to remove something that is wrapped around something else □ *He unwound the bandage.* (desenfaixar)

unwise /ʌnˈwaɪz/ ADJECTIVE not sensible □ *It would be unwise to spend all the money now.* (insensato)

unworthy

unworthy /ˌʌnˈwɜːði/ ADJECTIVE
1 to be unworthy of something is to not deserve it □ *I felt I was unworthy of his love.* (**indigno**)
2 if behaviour is unworthy of someone, it is bad and they would not do it for that reason (**vergonhoso, inconveniente, injustificado**)

unwound /ˌʌnˈwaʊnd/ PAST TENSE AND PAST PARTICIPLE OF **unwind** (*ver* **unwind**)

unwrap /ˌʌnˈræp/ VERB [unwraps, unwrapping, unwrapped] to open something that is wrapped □ *She carefully unwrapped the present.* (**desembrulhar**)

unzip /ˌʌnˈzɪp/ VERB [unzips, unzipping, unzipped]
1 to unfasten something using its zip (= fastening device with two rows of small parts that fit tightly together) □ *He unzipped his bag and took out a book.* (**abrir o zíper**)
2 to make a computer file bigger again after it has been made smaller. A computing word. (**descompactar**)

up /ʌp/ ▶ ADVERB, PREPOSITION
1 towards or in a higher position □ *I walked up the stairs.* □ *We went up in a helicopter.* □ *He looked up and saw her.* □ *She threw the ball up in the air.* (**para cima**)
2 to a greater amount or level □ *Prices have gone up again.* □ *Could you turn the volume up a bit?* (**para cima**)
3 if you stand up or sit up, you move your body to a vertical position (**para cima**)
4 up to less than or as much as a particular amount or level □ *The hall can hold up to 200 people.* (**até**)
5 up to him/you, etc. if an action or decision is up to you, you are responsible for doing it or making it □ *It's up to you whether you come or not.* (**você é quem decide**)
6 used after verbs to show that something is finished or completely used □ *Eat up all your vegetables.* (**tudo ou completamente**)
7 if you go up to someone, you move close to them, often in order to speak to them □ *He came up to me and asked if I needed any help.* (**aproximar-se**)
8 further along a road, river, etc. □ *He lives just up the road from me.* (**mais adiante**)
9 in or towards the north of a country □ *She lives up in Glasgow.* (**norte do país**)
10 be up to something to be doing something, usually something wrong or secret □ *The children are very quiet – what are they up to?* (**aprontar**)
▶ ADJECTIVE
1 not in bed □ *He's not up yet.* □ *I've been up half the night.* (**levantado da cama**)
2 if an amount or level is up, it is higher □ *Profits are up by 25% this year.* □ *They were two goals up at the end of the first half.* (**acima de**)
3 if the sun is up, it has risen (**alto no céu**)
4 if a period of time that something lasts for is up, it has finished □ *Bring the boats in now – your time is up.* (**acabado, terminado**)
5 if something is up, there is a problem. An informal word (**haver algo errado**) 🔄 *What's up with you today?* (**O que há de errado com?**) □ *As soon as we reached the house, I knew something was up.*
6 if a computer is up, it is working. A computing word. (**ligado**)
▶ NOUN [plural ups] **ups and downs** good experiences and situations and bad experiences and situations □ *We've been married over 30 years, and we've certainly had our ups and downs.* (**altos e baixos**)
▶ VERB [ups, upping, upped] to increase something □ *The doctors have upped his dose of painkillers.* (**elevar, aumentar**)

up-and-coming /ˌʌpəndˈkʌmɪŋ/ ADJECTIVE starting to become successful and famous □ *an up-and coming young actor* (**despontar**)

upbeat /ˈʌpbiːt/ ADJECTIVE positive and feeling hope □ *He seemed quite upbeat about his health.* (**otimista**)

upbringing /ˈʌpbrɪŋɪŋ/ NOUN, NO PLURAL the way that your parents treat you when you are a child □ *We had a strict upbringing.* (**criação**)

update ▶ VERB /ʌpˈdeɪt/ [updates, updating, updated]
1 to add the latest information to something □ *When did we last update the website?* (**atualizar**)
2 to change something to make it more modern □ *I need to update my wardrobe.* (**atualizar**)
◆ PHRASAL VERB **update someone on something** to tell someone the latest information □ *Could you update me on any recent developments?* (**atualizar alguém de algo**)
▶ NOUN /ˈʌpdeɪt/ [plural updates] the latest information about a subject (**informação atualizada**) 🔄 *Dan gave me an update on the situation.* (**me deu informações atualizadas**)

upgrade ▶ VERB /ʌpˈgreɪd/ [upgrades, upgrading, upgraded]
1 to improve a computer or machine, especially by adding or replacing parts (**upgrade, atualização**)
2 to give someone a more important job in the same organization (**promoção**)
▶ NOUN /ˈʌpgreɪd/ [plural upgrades] a piece of software that makes a computer more powerful (**upgrade**)

upheaval /ʌpˈhiːvəl/ NOUN [plural upheavals] a great change, involving activity and often problems □ *I can't face the upheaval of moving house.* (**transtorno**)

upheld /ʌpˈheld/ PAST TENSE AND PAST PARTICIPLE OF **uphold** (*ver* **uphold**)

uphill ▶ ADJECTIVE /ˈʌphɪl/
1 going upwards ▫ *an uphill part of the track* (**íngreme, elevado**)
2 very difficult (**difícil**) ▫ *We face an uphill struggle getting people to change their habits.* (**luta difícil**)
▶ ADVERB /ˌʌpˈhɪl/ up a slope ▫ *We travelled uphill for several miles.* (**ascendente, íngreme**)

uphold /ʌpˈhəʊld/ VERB [**upholds, upholding, upheld**] to support or agree with a decision, especially in a court of law ▫ *The court upheld his complaint.* (**sustentar, manter**)

upholstery /ʌpˈhəʊlstəri/ NOUN, NO PLURAL the cloth and soft parts of a chair or other seat ▫ *car upholstery* (**estofamento**)

upkeep /ˈʌpkiːp/ NOUN, NO PLURAL the process or cost of keeping something such as a house or car in good condition (**manutenção**)

uplifting /ʌpˈlɪftɪŋ/ ADJECTIVE making you feel happy and full of hope ▫ *an uplifting film* (**edificante**)

upload /ʌpˈləʊd/ VERB [**uploads, uploading, uploaded**] to copy computer programs or files from a small computer to a larger one or to the Internet. A computing word. (**transferência de dados**)

upmarket /ˈʌpmɑːkɪt/ ADJECTIVE expensive and of high quality ▫ *an upmarket hotel* (**produto/serviço exclusivo/luxuoso**)

upon /əˈpɒn/ PREPOSITION on. A formal word ▫ *a castle upon a high cliff* (**sobre**)

upper /ˈʌpə(r)/ ADJECTIVE
1 being the higher of two things that are the same ▫ *my upper lip* (**superior**)
2 at the top or towards the top ▫ *the upper floors of the building* (**superior**)
3 of a higher social class or rank (**superior**)

upper class /ˌʌpə ˈklɑːs/ NOUN [*plural* **upper classes**] people with the highest social class in a society (**classe alta, aristocracia**)
• **upper-class** /ˌʌpəklɑːs/ ADJECTIVE being from or typical of the upper class ▫ *an upper-class accent* (**pertencente à alta sociedade**)

uppermost /ˈʌpəməʊst/ ADJECTIVE
1 be uppermost in someone's mind to be the main thing that someone is thinking about
2 highest ▫ *the uppermost floors of the building* (**superior**)

upright /ˈʌpraɪt/ ▶ ADVERB vertical ▫ *He was sitting upright in his cot.* (**ereto, vertical**)
▶ ADJECTIVE
1 vertical ▫ *Make sure your seat is in an upright position and fasten your seat belt.* (**vertical**)
2 honest ▫ *an upright citizen* (**correto**)

uprising /ˈʌpˌraɪzɪŋ/ NOUN [*plural* **uprisings**] when a lot of people in a country use violence to try to change their government (**levante, insurreição**)

uproar /ˈʌprɔː(r)/ NOUN, NO PLURAL when a lot of people criticize something very angrily (**alvoroço, tumulto**)

uproot /ˌʌpˈruːt/ VERB [**uproots, uprooting, uprooted**]
1 to make people move away from their homes ▫ *Thousands of people were uprooted by the war.* (**desapropriar**)
2 to pull a plant and its roots out of the ground (**arrancar**)

upset ▶ VERB /ʌpˈset/ [**upsets, upsetting, upset**]
1 to make someone sad or worried ▫ *I didn't mean to upset you.* (**perturbar**)
2 to stop something from happening in the right way ▫ *I don't want to upset your plans.* (**contrariar**)
3 to knock something over by accident (**derrubar**)
4 upset your stomach to cause an illness in your stomach (**causar indigestão**)
▶ ADJECTIVE /ʌpˈset/
1 sad or worried about something that has happened ▫ *He looked upset.* ▫ *+ that She's upset that no one invited her.* (**incomodado, contrariado**) ▫ *She got upset looking at his photos.* (**ficou incomodado**)
2 upset stomach/tummy an illness affecting the stomach (**indigestão**)
▶ NOUN /ˈʌpset/ [*plural* **upsets**]
1 when a very good team or player is defeated by a less good team or player (**derrubar**)
2 stomach/tummy upset an illness affecting the stomach (**indigestão**)
3 when someone feels sad or worried (**aflito, perturbado, desconcertado**)
• **upsetting** /ʌpˈsetɪŋ/ ADJECTIVE making you feel upset ▫ *I found the whole experience very upsetting.* ▫ *upsetting news* (**inquietante**)

upshot /ˈʌpʃɒt/ NOUN **the upshot (of something)** the final result of something ▫ *The upshot of the discussion is that we've decided not to go.* (**desfecho**)

upside down /ˌʌpsaɪd ˈdaʊn/ ADJECTIVE, ADVERB with the top part where the bottom should be and the bottom part where the top should be ▫ *He was holding the book upside down.* (**de cabeça para baixo**)

upstage /ʌpˈsteɪdʒ/ VERB [**upstages, upstaging, upstaged**] to do something that makes people look at you instead of someone else (**tirar a atenção de alguém, chamar a atenção para si**)

upstairs ▶ ADVERB /ʌpˈsteəz/ to or on a higher level of a building ▫ *I went upstairs to get changed.* (**no andar de cima**)
▶ ADJECTIVE /ˈʌpsteəz/ on a higher level of a building ▫ *an upstairs bedroom* (**andar de cima**)

uptake /ˈʌpteɪk/ NOUN **be slow/quick on the uptake** to be slow/quick to understand what someone means (**rápido para entender**)

uptight /ˌʌpˈtaɪt/ ADJECTIVE nervous and often becoming angry □ *You seem a bit uptight today.* (nervoso)

up-to-date /ˌʌptəˈdeɪt/ ADJECTIVE
1 having the latest information □ *an up-to-date news story* (atualizado, em dia)
2 new or modern □ *up-to-date technology* □ *up-to-date fashions* (na moda)

upward /ˈʌpwəd/ ADJECTIVE
1 towards a higher place or position □ *an upward climb* (ascendente)
2 towards a higher level □ *an upward trend* (para cima)

• **upwards** /ˈʌpwədz/ or **upward** /ˈʌpwəd/ ADVERB
1 towards a higher place or position □ *He looked upwards and saw the sun.* (para cima, para um lugar mais alto)
2 towards a higher level (um nível acima)

uranium /jʊˈreɪniəm/ NOUN, NO PLURAL a metal that is used for making nuclear energy. A chemistry word. (urânio)

urban /ˈɜːbən/ ADJECTIVE to do with a town or city □ *urban areas* □ *urban planning* (urbano)

urge /ɜːdʒ/ ▶ VERB [**urges, urging, urged**] to advise someone strongly to do something □ *If you haven't already filled in the form, I urge you to do so.* (insistir em)

♦ PHRASAL VERB **urge someone on** to encourage someone as they are doing something □ *I could hear the crowds urging me on as I ran the last few metres.* (instigar)

▶ NOUN [*plural* **urges**] a sudden, strong feeling of wanting to do something □ *I felt an urge to shake him.* (ímpeto) 🔲 *I resisted the urge to tell her* (= did not tell her although I wanted to). (resisti ao ímpeto)

urgency /ˈɜːdʒənsi/ NOUN, NO PLURAL when something is very serious and needs action now □ *I didn't realize the urgency of the situation.* (urgência)

• **urgent** /ˈɜːdʒənt/ ADJECTIVE very serious and needing action now (urgente) 🔲 *There is an urgent need for water and food supplies in the region.* (necessidade urgente) 🔲 *He has called for urgent action to stop the killing.* (ação urgente)

• **urgently** /ˈɜːdʒəntli/ ADVERB in an urgent way □ *Medical supplies are needed urgently.* (urgentemente)

urinal /jʊəˈraɪnəl/ NOUN [*plural* **urinals**] a toilet, often fitted to a wall, that men and boys can urinate into (mictório)

urinate /ˈjʊərɪneɪt/ VERB [**urinates, urinating, urinated**] to pass urine out of your body. A formal word. (urinar)

• **urine** /ˈjʊərɪn/ NOUN, NO PLURAL the waste liquid passed out of the bodies of people and animals (urina)

URL /ˌjuːɑːrˈel/ ABBREVIATION Uniform Resource Locator; an Internet address. A computing word. (endereço eletrônico)

urn /ɜːn/ NOUN [*plural* **urns**]
1 a container for holding a dead person's ashes (= a powder that remains after a body is burnt) (urna)
2 a large metal container used for making large amounts of tea or coffee (cafeteira, chaleira)

US /ˌjuːˈes/ ABBREVIATION the United States of America (Estados Unidos)

us /ʌs/ PRONOUN used as the object in a sentence to talk or write about yourself and at least one other person □ *Do you want to come with us?* □ *They gave us coffee.* □ *The news surprised all of us.* (nos, nós)

USA /ˌjuːesˈeɪ/ ABBREVIATION the United States of America (EUA)

usage /ˈjuːzɪdʒ/ NOUN [*plural* **usages**]
1 the way that words are used when they are spoken or written □ *a book on English usage.* (uso)
2 the way that something is used or how much of something is used □ *Energy usage is at its highest at around 9pm.* (uso)

use ▶ VERB /juːz/ [**uses, using, used**]
1 to do something with something for a particular purpose □ *Use a knife to open it.* □ *He used words like 'disappointing' and 'shocking'.* □ + *for I use these boxes for storing apples.* □ + *as Dad uses this room as his office.* (usar)
2 to take an amount of something from a supply in order to do something with it □ *I've used all the milk now.* □ *You can use the logs from the shed.* (usar)
3 to treat someone in an unfair or unkind way in order to get something you want □ *He just used her to get to know her rich relatives.* (usar/aproveitar-se de alguém)

♦ PHRASAL VERB **use something up** to use all of a supply of something □ *We've used up all the paper.* (esgotar, acabar)

▶ NOUN /juːs/ [*plural* **uses**]
1 *no plural* when you use something □ + *of We do not allow the use of calculators in the exam.* (uso) 🔲 *We were able to make use of the sports facilities.* (faça uso de)
2 the purpose for which something is used □ *This knife has a lot of uses.* □ *They deny that the uranium is for military use.* (uso)
3 *no plural* if something is of use, it is useful or effective □ *Is this coat of any use to you?* (utilidade) 🔲 *What's the use of leaving messages when he never replies?* 🔲 *It's no use asking him for help – he's always busy.* (não tem utilidade)
4 *no plural* the right or ability to use something □ + *of He offered me the use of his car while he's away.* □ *She lost the use of her legs.* (uso)

• **used** /juːzd/ ADJECTIVE something that is used has been owned and used by someone else □ *He sells used cars.* (usado)

used to[1] /ˈjuːst tuː/ MODAL VERB used to talk about things that happened regularly in the past or things

used to that were true in the past, especially when they no longer happen or are true □ *I used to visit her a lot when she lived in Germany.* □ *The fence used to be painted white.* □ *I used to be a teacher.* (**costumava, havia**)

> If you use **used to** in a question or a negative, you should use the form use to □ *Did you use to play the piano?* □ *I didn't use to like many vegetables.*

used to² /'juːst tuː/ ADJECTIVE if you are used to something, you have often seen it or experienced it before, so it does not seem strange, difficult, etc. □ *I'm used to living on my own.* (**acostumado**) 🔁 *Working nights is difficult, but you get used to it.* (**fica acostumado/acaba se acostumando**)

useful /'juːsfʊl/ ADJECTIVE helpful for doing something or achieving something □ *The book gave me some useful information.* □ **+ for** *These little pots are useful for growing seedlings.* (**útil**) 🔁 *The contacts I made in that job proved useful later.* (**revelou-se útil**)

• **usefully** /'juːsfʊli/ ADVERB in a way that is helpful □ *How can we spend the money most usefully?* □ *There was nothing I could usefully do.* (**utilmente**)

• **usefulness** /'juːsfʊlnɪs/ NOUN, NO PLURAL being useful □ *He questioned the usefulness of their research.* (**utilidade**)

useless /'juːslɪs/ ADJECTIVE
1 having no purpose, or not effective or working correctly □ *This knife's useless – it's completely blunt.* □ *It's useless trying to explain to them.* □ *She wastes her money on useless ornaments.* (**inútil**)
2 an informal word meaning without skill □ *I'm useless at maths.* (**inútil**)
• **uselessly** /'juːslɪsli/ ADVERB in a useless way □ *The cord flapped uselessly in the wind.* (**inutilmente**)

user /'juːzə(r)/ NOUN [*plural* **users**] a person who uses something □ *users of public transport* (**usuário**)

user-friendly /'juːzə'frendli/ ADJECTIVE easy for anyone to use or understand □ *a user-friendly system* (**fácil de usar**)

username /'juːzəneɪm/ NOUN [*plural* **usernames**] a name that you type, together with a password (= secret word), so that you can use a computer system. A computing word. (**nome de usuário**)

usher /'ʌʃə(r)/ ▶ NOUN [*plural* **ushers**] someone who shows people where to sit, especially at a theatre or wedding (**lanterninha**)

▶ VERB [**ushers, ushering, ushered**] to go with someone and show them the way □ *The waiter ushered him to a table.* (**conduzir**)

usual /'juːʒəl/ ADJECTIVE
1 done or happening most often □ *I had my usual coffee this morning.* □ *'What did you talk about?' 'Oh, the usual things.'* □ *My walk to work took longer than usual.* (**habitual, costumeiro**)
2 as usual as happens most often □ *He was late as usual.* (**como de costume**)
• **usually** /'juːʒəli/ ADVERB normally, on most occasions □ *I usually drink tea.* □ *We usually go on holiday in August.* □ *Usually I'm in bed by ten o'clock.* (**habitualmente, em geral**)

utensil /juː'tensəl/ NOUN [*plural* **utensils**] a tool that you use in the kitchen (**utensílio**) 🔁 *kitchen utensils* (**utensílios de cozinha**)

uterus /'juːtərəs/ NOUN [*plural* **uteri**] the organ inside a woman's or female animal's body where her babies grow until they are ready to be born. A biology word. (**útero**)

utility /juː'tɪlɪti/ NOUN [*plural* **utilities**] a company which supplies gas, electricity, water or another basic service (**serviço**)

utilize or **utilise** /'juːtɪlaɪz/ VERB [**utilizes, utilizing, utilized**] a formal word for use □ *Old newspapers are utilized in the production of recycled paper.* (**utilizar**)

utmost /'ʌtməʊst/ ▶ ADJECTIVE greatest possible □ *I have the utmost respect for both players.* (**extremo**)
▶ NOUN **do your utmost** to make the greatest possible effort □ *She did her utmost to help him.* (**fazer o melhor possível**)

utter¹ /'ʌtə(r)/ VERB [**utters, uttering, uttered**] to say something □ *She didn't utter a single word.* (**pronunciar**)

utter² /'ʌtə(r)/ ADJECTIVE complete □ *utter silence* (**absoluto, total**)
• **utterly** /'ʌtəli/ ADVERB completely □ *I feel utterly exhausted.* (**totalmente**)

U-turn /'juːtɜːn/ NOUN [*plural* **U-turns**]
1 a turn in the shape of a U, made by a driver to go back the way he or she has just come (**retorno em U**)
2 a complete change of plan or ideas □ *a U-turn in government policy* (**virada de 180°**)

UV /juː'viː/ ABBREVIATION **ultraviolet** ; a type of light from the sun which turns the skin darker (**UV, ultravioleta**)

Vv

V¹ or **v** /vi:/ the 22nd letter of the alphabet (a vigésima segunda letra do alfabeto)

V² /vi:/ ABBREVIATION
1 versus; used for saying which two players or teams are competing against each other □ *Arsenal v Manchester United* (abrev. de *versus*)
2 very □ *v good* (= very good) (abrev. de *very* = muito)

V³ /vi:/ ABBREVIATION **volt**; a unit for measuring how strong an electric current is (volt)

vacancy /'veɪkənsɪ/ NOUN [plural **vacancies**]
1 an available room in a hotel □ *Sorry, no vacancies.* (vaga)
2 an available job (vaga)

• **vacant** /'veɪkənt/ ADJECTIVE
1 if something is vacant, it is available because no one else is using it □ *a vacant seat* □ *a vacant office* (vago)
2 if a job is vacant, it is available because no one is doing it (vaga)
3 looking as if you are not thinking about anything (vago) ▣ *a vacant expression* (uma expressão vaga)

• **vacate** /və'keɪt/ VERB [**vacates, vacating, vacated**] to leave somewhere or something so that it is available for someone else. A formal word □ *Hotel guests must vacate their rooms by midday.* (desocupar)

vacation /və'keɪʃən/ NOUN [plural **vacations**]
1 the US word for **holiday** (férias) ▣ *We're taking a vacation in the mountains this summer.* (tirar férias)
2 **on vacation** taking a holiday. A US phrase. (em férias)
3 a part of the year when a university is closed □ *the summer vacation* (férias)

vaccinate /'væksɪneɪt/ VERB [**vaccinates, vaccinating, vaccinated**] to put a vaccine into someone's body to protect them from a disease (vacinar)

• **vaccination** /ˌvæksɪ'neɪʃən/ NOUN [plural **vaccinations**] the process of vaccinating someone (vacinação)

vaccine /'væksi:n/ NOUN [plural **vaccines**] a substance containing bacteria or a virus, which is put into someone's body in order to protect them against a disease (vacina)

vacuum¹ /'vækjʊəm/ NOUN [plural **vacuums**]
1 a space with no air or other gases in it (vácuo)
2 when something very important is missing from a situation (vácuo)

vacuum² /'vækjʊəm/ VERB [**vacuums, vacuuming, vacuumed**] to clean a floor using a vacuum cleaner (passar aspirador de pó)

vacuum cleaner /'vækjʊəm ˌkli:nə(r)/ NOUN [plural **vacuum cleaners**] an electrical machine that sucks dust up from the floor (aspirador)

vacuum flask /'vækjʊəm ˌflɑ:sk/ NOUN [plural **vacuum flasks**] a container for keeping drinks hot or cold (garrafa térmica)

vacuum-packed /'vækjʊəm'pækt/ ADJECTIVE in a container from which all the air has been removed □ *These nuts are vacuum-packed for freshness.* (embalado a vácuo)

vagina /və'dʒaɪnə/ NOUN [plural **vaginas**] the passage in a woman's body that connects her womb (= organ where a baby grows) to the outside of her body. A biology word. (vagina)

vagrant /'veɪgrənt/ NOUN [plural **vagrants**] a person without a home who walks from place to place. A formal word. (andarilho)

vague /veɪg/ ADJECTIVE [**vaguer, vaguest**]
1 not clear and without details (vago) ▣ *I have a vague idea of where he lives.* (ideia vaga) ▣ *He had a vague memory of seeing her there.* (memória vaga)
2 explaining something in a way that is not clear and has no details (vago) □ *He was a bit vague about their plans.*

• **vaguely** /'veɪglɪ/ ADVERB
1 in a way that is not clear and has no details (vagamente) ▣ *I vaguely remember saying that.* (lembrar-se vagamente)
2 slightly ▣ *He looked vaguely familiar.* (vagamente familiar)

vain /veɪn/ ADJECTIVE [**vainer, vainest**]
1 very pleased with your appearance and paying too much attention to it (vaidoso)
2 unsuccessful (vão) ▣ *I made a vain attempt to get her to stay.* (tentativa vã)
3 **in vain** without achieving what you want to □ *I tried in vain to persuade him.* (em vão)

• **vainly** /'veɪnlɪ/ ADVERB without achieving what you want to do □ *I turned over, vainly trying to get comfortable.* (inutilmente)

⇨ go to **vanity**

valentine

valentine /'væləntaɪn/ NOUN [plural **valentines**]
1 a card that you send on Valentine's Day (14 February) to show that you love someone (**cartão de Dia dos Namorados**)
2 the person you send a valentine to (**a pessoa a quem se manda o cartão de namorados**)

valet ▶ NOUN /'væleɪ/ [plural **valets**]
1 a male servant who works for another man and looks after his clothes (**camareiro**)
2 someone who parks customers' cars at a hotel, restaurant, etc. (**manobrista**)
▶ VERB /'vælɪt/ [**valets, valeting, valeted**] to clean out someone's car for payment (**lavar carros em troca de dinheiro**)

valiant /'væljənt/ ADJECTIVE a formal word meaning brave (**valente**) 🔲 She made *a valiant attempt* to rescue the cat. (**uma tentativa corajosa**)
• **valiantly** /'væljəntli/ ADVERB in a brave way (**corajosamente**)

valid /'vælɪd/ ADJECTIVE
1 legally or officially acceptable and able to be used 🔲 *a valid passport* 🔲 *a valid ticket* (**válido**)
2 reasonable and acceptable 🔲 *a valid excuse* 🔲 *a valid argument* (**válido**)
• **validate** /'vælɪdeɪt/ VERB [**validates, validating, validated**] to prove that something is true 🔲 *Have these claims ever been validated?* (**validar**)
• **validity** /və'lɪdəti/ NOUN, NO PLURAL the quality of being valid (**validade**)

Valium /'væliəm/ NOUN, NO PLURAL a drug that people take to make them feel calm and less nervous. A trademark. (**nome comercial do fármaco diazepam**)

valley /'væli/ NOUN [plural **valleys**] an area of low land between hills, often with a river running through it (**vale**)

valour /'vælə(r)/ NOUN, NO PLURAL a literary word that means courage, especially in a war (**bravura**)

valuable /'væljuəbəl/ ADJECTIVE
1 worth a lot of money 🔲 *valuable jewellery* (**valioso**)
2 very useful 🔲 *valuable advice* 🔲 *She's a valuable member of the team.* (**valioso**)

> Note that **valuable** does not have the same meaning as 'expensive'. If something is valuable, you could sell it for a lot of money. If something is expensive, it costs a lot of money: 🔲 *valuable antiques/paintings* 🔲 *expensive food/clothes*

• **valuables** /'væljuəbəlz/ PLURAL NOUN things, especially things that you own, that are worth a lot of money (**valores**)

valuation /ˌvælju'eɪʃən/ NOUN [plural **valuations**]
1 the act of deciding how much money something is worth (**valor**)
2 the amount of money that someone decides something is worth (**valor**)

value /'vælju:/ ▶ NOUN [plural **values**]
1 the amount of money that something is worth 🔲 *The paintings had an estimated value of $1.4 billion.* 🔲 *The house has increased in value.* (**valor**)
2 how useful and important something is 🔲 *This food has very little nutritional value.* (**valor**)
3 the quality or amount of something compared to its price (**custo-benefício**) 🔲 *I thought the hotel was very good value.* (**bom custo-benefício**)
▶ VERB [**values, valuing, valued**]
1 to think something is important and worth having 🔲 *I really value my free time.* 🔲 *I value your advice on the matter.* (**valorizar**)
2 to say how much something is worth 🔲 *The jewels were valued at three thousand dollars.* (**avaliar**)
• **values** /'vælju:z/ PLURAL NOUN the things that you consider to be most important in life and that influence the way you treat other people (**valores**)

valve /vælv/ NOUN [plural **valves**] something that opens and shuts to control the flow of liquid, air or gas through a pipe (**válvula**)

vampire /'væmpaɪə(r)/ NOUN [plural **vampires**] in stories, a dead person who comes out at night and sucks blood from people's necks (**vampiro**)

van /væn/ NOUN [plural **vans**] a road vehicle, like a small truck, used for carrying goods (**furgão**)

vandal /'vændəl/ NOUN [plural **vandals**] someone who deliberately damages things in public places (**vândalo**)
• **vandalism** /'vændəlɪzəm/ NOUN, NO PLURAL the crime of deliberately damaging something such as a public building (**vandalismo**)
• **vandalize** or **vandalise** /'vændəlaɪz/ VERB [**vandalizes, vandalizing, vandalized**] to deliberately damage something in a public place (**vandalizar**)

vanguard /'væŋgɑ:d/ NOUN, NO PLURAL **in the vanguard of something** creating new and original ideas and methods 🔲 *They are very much in the vanguard of cancer research.* (**vanguarda**)

vanilla /və'nɪlə/ NOUN, NO PLURAL a flavour that is used in a lot of sweet foods 🔲 *vanilla ice cream* (**baunilha**)

vanish /'vænɪʃ/ VERB [**vanishes, vanishing, vanished**] to disappear suddenly, leaving nothing behind 🔲 *He was standing in front of me a moment ago and suddenly he vanished.* (**sumir**)

vanity /'vænəti/ NOUN, NO PLURAL when someone is very pleased with their own appearance and pays too much attention to it (**vaidade**)

vapor /'veɪpə(r)/ NOUN, NO PLURAL the US spelling of **vapour** (*ver* **vapour**)

vapour /'veɪpə(r)/ NOUN, NO PLURAL many very small drops of liquid in the air 🔲 *water vapour* (**vapor**)

variable /ˈveərɪəbəl/ ADJECTIVE changing often and never staying the same □ *work of variable quality* (**variável**)

variant /ˈveərɪənt/ NOUN [*plural* **variants**] a different type of the same thing (**variante**)

• **variation** /ˌveərɪˈeɪʃən/ NOUN [*plural* **variations**] a change in the amount or level of something □ *variations in temperature* (**variação**)

varied /ˈveərɪd/ ADJECTIVE of many different types □ *He has varied interests, from comic books to bird watching.* (**variado**)

variety /vəˈraɪətɪ/ NOUN [*plural* **varieties**]
1 *no plural* a lot of different types □ + *of The chairs are available in a variety of colours.* (**variedade**)
2 *no plural* the quality of having many different things □ *You need variety in your diet.* (**variedade**)
3 a type that is different from other similar things □ *a new variety of rose* (**variedade**)

various /ˈveərɪəs/ ADJECTIVE many different □ *There were various types of cheese.* □ *There's been flooding in various parts of the country.* (**vários**)

varnish /ˈvɑːnɪʃ/ ▶ NOUN [*plural* **varnishes**] a liquid that you paint on wood to protect it and to give it a shiny surface (**verniz**)
▶ VERB [**varnishes, varnishing, varnished**] to put varnish on wood (**envernizar**)

vary /ˈveərɪ/ VERB [**varies, varying, varied**]
1 if things of the same type vary, they are all different in some way □ *Prices vary from shop to shop.* (**variar**)
2 if something varies, it changes at different times □ *Snowfall varies throughout the season.* (**variar**)
3 to change something slightly □ *You can vary the quantity that you order depending on your requirements at any given time.* (**variar**)

vase /vɑːz/ NOUN [*plural* **vases**] a decorative container for flowers (**vaso**)

vast /vɑːst/ ADJECTIVE extremely big □ *a vast area of land* (**vasto**)
• **vastly** /ˈvɑːstlɪ/ ADVERB very much □ *His work has improved vastly.* (**imensamente**)

VAT /væt, ˌviːeɪˈtiː/ ABBREVIATION value added tax; a tax on goods and services in the UK (**imposto sobre bens e serviços no Reino Unido**)

vat /væt/ NOUN [*plural* **vats**] a large container for liquids (**barril, tonel**)

vault /vɔːlt/ NOUN [*plural* **vaults**]
1 a room in a bank for storing valuable things (**caixa-forte**)
2 a room under a church where dead bodies are buried (**câmara mortuária**)

VCR /ˌviːsiːˈɑː(r)/ ABBREVIATION video cassette recorder; a machine used for watching and recording videos (**gravador de videocassete**)

VDU /ˌviːdiːˈjuː/ ABBREVIATION visual display unit; a computer screen. A computing word. (**unidade de exibição visual**)

veal /viːl/ NOUN, NO PLURAL meat from a baby cow (**vitela**)

veer /vɪə(r)/ VERB [**veers, veering, veered**] to suddenly change direction, especially when moving fast □ *The car suddenly veered to the left.* (**guinar**)

veg /vedʒ/ ABBREVIATION **vegetables** (**hortaliças, verduras**) ⬚ *fruit and veg* (**frutas e hortaliças**)

vegan /ˈviːgən/ ▶ NOUN [*plural* **vegans**] someone who does not eat anything that comes from an animal, such as meat, eggs or milk (**vegano**)
▶ ADJECTIVE not eating or containing foods from an animal □ *a vegan restaurant* (**vegano**)

vegetable /ˈvedʒtəbəl/ NOUN [*plural* **vegetables**] a plant that you can eat, especially one that is not sweet □ *vegetables such as potatoes and carrots* (**hortaliça**)

> Note that although the word 'fruit' cannot be used in the plural, the word **vegetable** can:
> ✓ Eat more fruit and vegetables.
> ✗ Eat more fruit and vegetable.

vegetarian /ˌvedʒɪˈteərɪən/ ▶ NOUN [*plural* **vegetarians**] someone who does not eat meat or fish (**vegetariano**)
▶ ADJECTIVE not eating or containing meat or fish □ *vegetarian cookery* (**vegetariano**)

vegetation /ˌvedʒɪˈteɪʃən/ NOUN, NO PLURAL plants and trees (**vegetação**)

veggie /ˈvedʒɪ/ ▶ NOUN [*plural* **veggies**] an informal word that means **vegetarian** □ *You're not a veggie, are you?* (**vegetariano**)
▶ ADJECTIVE not eating or containing meat or fish. An informal word. □ *veggie food* (**vegetariano**)

vehement /ˈviːɪmənt/ ADJECTIVE expressing your opinion forcefully □ *She was vehement in her condemnation of the practice.* (**veemente**)
• **vehemently** /ˈviːɪməntlɪ/ ADVERB forcefully □ *She argued vehemently in support of the government.* (**veementemente**)

vehicle /ˈviːɪkəl/ NOUN [*plural* **vehicles**] something that carries people or goods, especially on roads, for example a car or a truck (**veículo**)

veil /veɪl/ NOUN [*plural* **veils**] a piece of material that covers a woman's head or face (**véu**)
• **veiled** /veɪld/ ADJECTIVE
1 wearing a veil (**com véu**)
2 not directly expressed □ *veiled threats* □ *veiled criticism* (**velado**)

vein /veɪn/ NOUN [*plural* **veins**] one of the thin tubes inside the body that carry blood back to the heart (**veia**)

Velcro /ˈvelkrəʊ/ NOUN, NO PLURAL a sticky material that is used to fasten clothes. A trademark. (velcro)

velocity /vɪˈlɒsəti/ NOUN, NO PLURAL the speed at which something moves. A physics word. (velocidade)

velvet /ˈvelvɪt/ NOUN, NO PLURAL a thick cloth that feels very soft on one side (veludo)
- **velvety** /ˈvelvɪti/ ADJECTIVE feeling like velvet (aveludado)

vendetta /venˈdetə/ NOUN [plural **vendettas**] when someone tries to harm someone else over a long period of time because they are angry about something that they did in the past (vendeta)

vending machine /ˈvendɪŋ məˌʃiːn/ NOUN [plural **vending machines**] a machine that you can buy things from such as drinks and sweets (máquina de venda automática)

vendor /ˈvendɔː(r)/ NOUN [plural **vendors**] someone who is selling something □ *an ice cream vendor* (camelô, vendedor)

veneer /vəˈnɪə(r)/ NOUN [plural **veneers**]
1 a thin layer of wood that provides an attractive surface to something (madeira folheada)
2 a pleasant manner that is not sincere and that hides someone's real character (verniz)

venetian blind /vɪˌniːʃən ˈblaɪnd/ NOUN [plural **venetian blinds**] a covering for a window that is made of long, horizontal pieces of metal or wood that you turn to allow in or keep out light (veneziana)

vengeance /ˈvendʒəns/ NOUN, NO PLURAL punishment that you give to someone who has harmed you (vingança)
- **vengeful** /ˈvendʒfʊl/ ADJECTIVE wanting to punish someone because they have hurt you. A formal word. (vingativo)

venison /ˈvenɪsən/ NOUN, NO PLURAL meat from a deer (carne de veado)

Venn diagram /ˈven ˌdaɪəɡræm/ NOUN [plural **Venn diagrams**] a mathematical picture using circles which go over each other where the things in them share the same characteristics. A maths word. (diagrama de Venn)

venom /ˈvenəm/ NOUN, NO PLURAL
1 the poison that some snakes produce (peçonha)
2 very strong hate and anger □ *His letters were full of venom.* (malignidade)
- **venomous** /ˈvenəməs/ ADJECTIVE
1 poisonous □ *a venomous snake* (peçonhento)
2 full of hate and anger □ *a venomous attack* (maligno)

vent /vent/ ▶ NOUN [plural **vents**] a small opening to allow air, gas or smoke to pass through (respiradouro)
♦ IDIOM **give vent to something** to express a feeling strongly, especially anger (dar vazão a)
▶ VERB [**vents, venting, vented**] to express your anger or other bad feeling strongly □ *He was just venting his frustration with the situation.* (descarregar)

ventilate /ˈventɪleɪt/ VERB [**ventilates, ventilating, ventilated**] to allow fresh air into a room or building (ventilar)
- **ventilation** /ˌventɪˈleɪʃən/ NOUN, NO PLURAL when you allow fresh air into a room or building (ventilação)
- **ventilator** /ˈventɪˌleɪtə(r)/ NOUN [plural **ventilators**]
1 a machine that helps someone to breathe by forcing air into and out of their lungs (respirador mecânico)
2 an opening or piece of equipment that allows air into a room or building (respirador, ventilador, exaustor)

ventricle /ˈventrɪkəl/ NOUN [plural **ventricles**] one of the two lower parts of the heart. A biology word. (ventrículo)

ventriloquism /venˈtrɪləkwɪzəm/ NOUN, NO PLURAL the skill of speaking without moving your lips and making it look as if a puppet (= toy in the shape of a person) is speaking (ventriloquismo)
- **ventriloquist** /venˈtrɪləkwɪst/ NOUN [plural **ventriloquists**] someone who has the skill of ventriloquism (ventríloquo)

venture /ˈventʃə(r)/ ▶ NOUN [plural **ventures**] an activity, often a business activity 🔁 *It's his latest business venture.* (empreendimento)
▶ VERB [**ventures, venturing, ventured**] to go somewhere that involves a risk □ *The weather was so bad I didn't venture out of the hotel for two days.* (aventurar-se a)

venue /ˈvenjuː/ NOUN [plural **venues**] the place where an event happens □ *The castle is used as a wedding venue.* (local, lugar)

veranda /vəˈrændə/ NOUN [plural **verandas**] a covered area next to a building where you can sit (varanda)

verb /vɜːb/ NOUN [plural **verbs**] a word that says what someone or something does. For example, eat, speak and be are verbs. (verbo)

verbal /ˈvɜːbəl/ ADJECTIVE (verbal)
1 spoken and not written □ *a verbal agreement*
2 to do with words □ *verbal communication*

verdict /ˈvɜːdɪkt/ NOUN [plural **verdicts**] a decision made in a court of law saying whether someone is guilty or not guilty of committing a crime (veredito) 🔁 *Eventually the jury reached a verdict.* (chegar a um veredito)

verge /vɜːdʒ/ NOUN [plural **verges**] the area at the edge of a road, usually covered in grass (orla)
♦ IDIOM **on the verge of something** going to do something very soon □ *The company is on the verge of collapse.* (prestes a fazer/à beira de)

verify /ˈverɪfaɪ/ VERB [**verifies, verifying, verified**] to prove that something is true (verificar)

veritable /ˈverɪtəbəl/ ADJECTIVE a formal word meaning real □ *The meal when it came was a veritable feast.* (**autêntico**)

vermin /ˈvɜːmɪn/ PLURAL NOUN animals or insects that destroy crops or cause disease (**animais ou insetos daninhos**)

verruca /vəˈruːkə/ NOUN [plural **verrucas**] a small hard lump on the bottom of someone's foot (**verruga**)

versatile /ˈvɜːsətaɪl/ ADJECTIVE (**versátil**)
1 useful for many different things □ *versatile clothes*
2 able to do many different things □ *a versatile actor*
• **versatility** /ˌvɜːsəˈtɪlɪti/ NOUN, NO PLURAL when someone or something is versatile (**versatilidade**)

verse /vɜːs/ NOUN [plural **verses**]
1 a set of lines that form one part of a song or poem (**estrofe**)
2 poetry and not ordinary writing (**poesia**)

version /ˈvɜːʃən/ NOUN [plural **versions**]
1 one form of something when other forms of it exist □ *I know three versions of this song.* (**versão**)
2 one person's description of something that happened (**versão**) 🔁 *I've only heard Debbie's version of events.* (**versão dos eventos**)

versus /ˈvɜːsəs/ PREPOSITION used for saying which two players or teams are competing against each other □ *It's Scotland versus France tonight.* (**versus**)

vertebra /ˈvɜːtɪbrə/ NOUN [plural **vertebrae**] one of the row of small bones down the middle of your back. A biology word. (**vértebra**)

vertebrate /ˈvɜːtɪbreɪt/ NOUN [plural **vertebrates**] an animal that has a bone down the middle of its back. A biology word. (**vertebrado**)

vertical /ˈvɜːtɪkəl/ ADJECTIVE pointing straight up, at an angle of 90° to the ground □ *vertical lines* (**vertical**)

vertigo /ˈvɜːtɪɡəʊ/ NOUN, NO PLURAL a feeling as if everything around you is moving when you are in a very high place (**vertigem**)

verve /vɜːv/ NOUN, NO PLURAL excitement and energy (**verve**)

very /ˈveri/ ▶ ADVERB
1 to a great degree □ *I'm very tired.* □ *She was very pleased.* □ *It all happened very quickly.* (**muito**)
2 not very good/nice/pleased, etc. not good/nice/pleased, etc. □ *She wasn't very pleased.* (**não muito**)

> ▶ **Very** is not used before adjectives which have a strong meaning:
> ✓ *I was very tired.*
> ✗ *I was very exhausted.*
> ▶ If you are using an adjective with a strong meaning, put an adverb such as **completely** or **absolutely** before it □ *I was completely exhausted.*

▶ ADJECTIVE exact □ *At that very moment, the telephone rang.* (**exato**)

vessel /ˈvesəl/ NOUN [plural **vessels**]
1 a formal word that means a large boat or ship (**navio**)
2 a formal word that means a container for liquids (**recipiente**)
3 a tube that carries blood through your body. A biology word. (**vaso**)

vest /vest/ NOUN [plural **vests**]
1 a piece of underwear without sleeves that covers the top part of the body (**camiseta**)
2 the US word for **waistcoat** (**colete**)

vested interest /ˌvestɪd ˈɪntrəst/ NOUN [plural **vested interests**] a feeling of wanting something to happen or succeed because you will get an advantage from it (**interesse pessoal**)

vestige /ˈvestɪdʒ/ NOUN [plural **vestiges**] a very small amount of something that remains. A formal word. (**vestígio**)

vet /vet/ NOUN [plural **vets**] someone whose job is to treat animals that are ill or injured (**veterinário**)

veteran /ˈvetərən/ NOUN [plural **veterans**]
1 someone who has a lot of experience of something over many years (**veterano**)
2 someone who fought in a war (**veterano de guerra**)

veterinarian /ˌvetərɪˈneərɪən/ NOUN [plural **veterinarians**] the US word for **vet** (**veterinário**)

veterinary surgeon /ˈvetərɪnri ˈsɜːdʒən/ NOUN [plural **veterinary surgeons**] a formal way of saying vet (**cirurgião veterinário**)

veto /ˈviːtəʊ/ ▶ VERB [**vetoes, vetoing, vetoed**] to officially stop something from happening □ *The president vetoed the plan to lower taxes.* (**vetar**)
▶ NOUN [plural **vetoes**] when someone officially stops something from happening (**veto**)

via /ˈvaɪə/ PREPOSITION
1 travelling through a place □ *The train goes to London via Birmingham.* (**por**)
2 using a particular method or person to communicate □ *We keep in touch via e-mail.* (**via**)

viable /ˈvaɪəbəl/ ADJECTIVE able to succeed □ *a viable option* (**viável**)

viaduct /ˈvaɪədʌkt/ NOUN [plural **viaducts**] a bridge that takes a railway over a road or river (**viaduto**)

vibrant /ˈvaɪbrənt/ ADJECTIVE
1 exciting and full of life □ *a vibrant city* (**vibrante**)
2 colourful and bright (**vibrante**)

vibrate /vaɪˈbreɪt/ VERB [**vibrates, vibrating, vibrated**] to make small, quick shaking movements □ *The floor was vibrating with the music.* (**vibrar**)
• **vibration** /vaɪˈbreɪʃən/ NOUN [plural **vibrations**] when something vibrates (**vibração**)

vicar /ˈvɪkə(r)/ NOUN [plural **vicars**] in the Church of England, a priest (**pároco**)

vicarious — view

- **vicarage** /ˈvɪkərɪdʒ/ NOUN [plural **vicarages**] a house where a vicar lives (**casa paroquial**)
- **vicarious** /vɪˈkeərɪəs/ ADJECTIVE a vicarious feeling is one that you get when someone else does something and not when you do something yourself (**vicário**)
- **vicariously** /vɪˈkeərɪəslɪ/ ADVERB experienced when someone else does something (**vicariamente**)

vice /vaɪs/ NOUN [plural **vices**]
1 a bad habit □ vices such as smoking (**vício**)
2 a crime that shows low moral standards (**vício**)
3 a tool for holding an object while you cut it, put glue on it, etc. (**torno**)

vice- /vaɪs/ PREFIX vice- is added to the beginning of words that refer to very important jobs to mean 'next in importance' □ the vice-president of the company (**vice-**)

vice-president /ˌvaɪsˈprezɪdənt/ NOUN [plural **vice-presidents**] the person who is next in rank after a country's president □ the vice-president of the United States (**vice-presidente**)

vice versa /ˌvaɪsə ˈvɜːsə/ ADVERB used for saying that the opposite of what you have said is also true □ I needed his help and vice versa. (**vice-versa**)

vicinity /vɪˈsɪnɪtɪ/ NOUN, NO PLURAL the area around a place □ There are no schools in the vicinity. (**vizinhança, adjacência**)

vicious /ˈvɪʃəs/ ADJECTIVE
1 extremely cruel and violent □ a vicious attack (**cruel, feroz**)
2 extremely unkind □ She could be vicious. (**grosseiro**)

vicious circle /ˌvɪʃəs ˈsɜːkəl/ NOUN, NO PLURAL a situation in which one problem causes another problem which then makes the first problem even worse (**círculo vicioso**)

victim /ˈvɪktɪm/ NOUN [plural **victims**] someone who is harmed or killed by something bad, such as a crime, disease, flood, etc. □ victims of crime □ victims of the bombing □ murder victims (**vítima**)
- **victimize** or **victimise** /ˈvɪktɪmaɪz/ VERB [**victimizes, victimizing, victimized**] to treat one person unfairly because you do not like something about them (**vitimar**)

victor /ˈvɪktə(r)/ NOUN [plural **victors**] a formal word that means the person who has won a competition or fight (**vencedor**)

Victorian /vɪkˈtɔːrɪən/ ▶ ADJECTIVE from the period between 1837 and 1901, when Queen Victoria ruled the UK (**vitoriano**)
▶ NOUN [plural **Victorians**] a person who lived during the time of Queen Victoria (**vitoriano**)

victorious /vɪkˈtɔːrɪəs/ ADJECTIVE successful in a fight or competition (**vitorioso**)
- **victory** /ˈvɪktərɪ/ NOUN [plural **victories**] success in a fight or competition □ victory in the Cup Final □ + **for** The game ended in victory for France. (**vitória**)

video /ˈvɪdɪəʊ/ ▶ NOUN [plural **videos**]
1 a recording of a film or television programme made on videotape (**vídeo (gravação de programas)**)
2 a recording of an event that has been made using a video camera (**filmagem**)
3 a machine for playing videos (**aparelho de vídeo, videocassete**)
▶ VERB [**videos, videoing, videoed**]
1 to record a television programme onto videotape (**gravar um programa**)
2 to film an event using a video camera (**filmar um evento**)

video camera /ˈvɪdɪəʊ ˌkæmərə/ NOUN [plural **video cameras**] a piece of equipment that you use to record events onto videotape (**câmera de vídeo**)

video card /ˈvɪdɪəʊ kɑːd/ NOUN [plural **video cards**] a small part in a computer that allows it to play video. A computing word. (**placa de vídeo**)

video game /ˈvɪdɪəʊ ˌɡeɪm/ NOUN [plural **video games**] an electronic game in which players move images on a computer or television screen (**videogame**)

videotape /ˈvɪdɪəʊteɪp/ NOUN [plural **videotapes**] magnetic tape that pictures and sounds can be recorded on (**videoteipe**)

vie /vaɪ/ VERB [**vies, vying, vied**] to compete with other people to do something better or get more of something □ Children vie with each other for their mother's attention. (**competir**)

view /vjuː/ ▶ NOUN [plural **views**]
1 your opinion □ + **on** What's your view on wind farms? □ + **about** He made his views about the government very clear. (**opinião, visão**) □ I take the view that smacking children is wrong. (**ponto de vista**)
2 your ability to see things from a place □ The pillar spoilt my view of the concert. (**visão**) □ Eventually, the lion came into view. (**aparecer**) □ She tore up her work in full view of her teachers. (**na frente de**)
3 the things you can see from a place □ There's a fantastic view from the top of the hill. (**vista**)
4 **in view of something** because of something □ In view of the weather, we have cancelled the game. (**por causa de**)
5 **on view** if something is on view, it is in a place where people can go to look at it □ Several classic cars will be on view at the event. (**em exibição**)
6 **with a view to doing something** in order to make it possible to do something □ He's moving to London with a view to finding a job. (**com a finalidade de**)
▶ VERB [**views, viewing, viewed**]
1 to have a particular opinion about something or someone □ + **as** His ideas were viewed as a threat to society. (**ser visto como**)

2 to look at something ▫ *People came from all over the country to view his work.* (ver)
- **viewer** /'vju:ə(r)/ NOUN [*plural* **viewers**] someone who watches television ▫ *The programme attracted more than a million viewers.* (telespectador)

viewpoint /'vju:pɔɪnt/ NOUN [*plural* **viewpoints**] an opinion, especially one based on your situation ▫ *Try to see the situation from her viewpoint.* (ponto de vista)

vigil /'vɪdʒɪl/ NOUN [*plural* **vigils**] when someone stays quietly somewhere for a period, often in order to be with an ill person or to show their beliefs about something (vigília)

vigilance /'vɪdʒɪləns/ NOUN, NO PLURAL being careful to notice any trouble or problems (vigilância)
- **vigilant** /'vɪdʒɪlənt/ ADJECTIVE watching things carefully in order to notice any trouble or problems ▫ *Police have urged the public to be vigilant after a series of bomb attacks in the region.* (vigilante)

vigorous /'vɪɡərəs/ ADJECTIVE very active and energetic ▫ *vigorous exercise* (vigoroso)
- **vigorously** /'vɪɡərəsli/ ADVERB in an active and energetic way (vigorosamente)
- **vigour** /'vɪɡə(r)/ NOUN, NO PLURAL energy and strength (vigor)

vile /vaɪl/ ADJECTIVE [**viler**, **vilest**] extremely unpleasant ▫ *a vile taste* (vil)

villa /'vɪlə/ NOUN [*plural* **villas**] a large house, especially one used for holidays (casa de passeio)

village /'vɪlɪdʒ/ NOUN [*plural* **villages**] an area where people live in the countryside, which is smaller than a town ▫ *She lives in a village just outside Stratford.* (aldeia, povoado)
- **villager** /'vɪlɪdʒə(r)/ NOUN [*plural* **villagers**] someone who lives in a village (aldeão)

villain /'vɪlən/ NOUN [*plural* **villains**] a bad person in a story, film, etc. (vilão)
- **villainous** /'vɪlənəs/ ADJECTIVE behaving like a villain (desprezível)

vindicate /'vɪndɪkeɪt/ VERB [**vindicates**, **vindicating**, **vindicated**] to prove that something someone said or did is true or right after most people thought it was wrong (provar, demonstrar)
- **vindication** /ˌvɪndɪ'keɪʃən/ NOUN, NO PLURAL when someone is vindicated (vindicação, defesa)

vindictive /vɪn'dɪktɪv/ ADJECTIVE deliberately trying to harm or upset someone who has harmed or upset you (vingativo)

vine /vaɪn/ NOUN [*plural* **vines**] a plant that grapes (= small green or red fruit that grows in groups) grow on (videira)

vinegar /'vɪnɪɡə(r)/ NOUN, NO PLURAL a sour liquid that is used for giving flavour to food (vinagre)

vineyard /'vɪnjəd/ NOUN [*plural* **vineyards**] a place where grapes (= small green or red fruit that grows in groups) are grown to produce wine (vinha, vinhedo)

vintage /'vɪntɪdʒ/ ▶ NOUN [*plural* **vintages**] the wine that was produced in a particular year (safra de bom vinho)
▶ ADJECTIVE
1 typical of a particular time in the past ▫ *vintage clothing* (vintage)
2 vintage wine is of the best quality and was produced several years ago (vintage, de qualidade superior)

vintage car /'vɪntɪdʒ 'kɑ:(r)/ NOUN [*plural* **vintage cars**] a car made between 1917 and 1930 that is still in very good condition (carro antigo)

vinyl /'vaɪnɪl/ NOUN, NO PLURAL a type of strong plastic used for making furniture and floor coverings (vinil)

viola /vɪ'əʊlə/ NOUN [*plural* **violas**] a musical instrument like a big violin (= instrument with four strings, which you hold under your chin) (viola)

violate /'vaɪəleɪt/ VERB [**violates**, **violating**, **violated**] to break a law or rule (violar)
- **violation** /ˌvaɪə'leɪʃən/ NOUN [*plural* **violations**] when a law or rule is broken (violação)

violence /'vaɪələns/ NOUN, NO PLURAL
1 actions intended to hurt or kill someone or to damage something ▫ *Something must be done to stop the violence.* ▫ + **against** *violence against women* (violência)
2 force and strength, often causing damage ▫ *The violence of the storm shocked everyone.* (violência)
- **violent** /'vaɪələnt/ ADJECTIVE
1 involving actions intended to hurt or kill someone or to damage something ▫ *violent crime* ▫ *a violent film* (violento)
2 with a lot of force and strength, causing damage ▫ *a violent storm* ▫ *a violent explosion* (violento)
3 extreme and impossible to control ▫ *a violent coughing fit* (violento)
- **violently** /'vaɪələntli/ ADVERB in a violent way (violentamente)

violet /'vaɪələt/ ▶ NOUN [*plural* **violets**] a small purple flower (violeta)
▶ ADJECTIVE having a pale purple colour (violeta)

violin /ˌvaɪə'lɪn/ NOUN [*plural* **violins**] a musical instrument with four strings, which you hold under your chin and play by pulling a bow (= long, thin piece of wood with hair stretched along it) across the strings (violino)
- **violinist** /ˌvaɪə'lɪnɪst/ NOUN [*plural* **violinists**] someone who plays the violin (violinista)

VIP /ˌvi:aɪ'pi:/ ABBREVIATION very important person; someone who is treated very well because they are powerful or famous (abrev. Very Important Person)

viper

viper /ˈvaɪpə(r)/ NOUN [plural **vipers**] a small poisonous snake (**víbora**)

viral /ˈvaɪrəl/ ADJECTIVE caused by a virus □ *a viral infection* (**viral**)

virtual /ˈvɜːtʃuəl/ ADJECTIVE
1 almost a particular thing □ *He was a virtual prisoner in his own home.* (**praticamente**)
2 using computer images to make something that is not real seem real □ *a virtual tour of the museum* (**virtual**)

• **virtually** /ˈvɜːtʃuəli/ ADVERB almost □ *Virtually all her friends have left.* (**praticamente**)

virtual reality /ˌvɜːtʃuəl riˈæləti/ NOUN, NO PLURAL the use of computer images and sounds to make something that is not real seem real (**realidade virtual**)

virtue /ˈvɜːtjuː/ NOUN [plural **virtues**]
1 a good quality in a person's character □ *Patience is a virtue.* (**virtude**)
2 an advantage □ *The virtue of this approach is that it is quicker.* (**virtude**)
3 a way of behaving that is morally good. A formal word. □ *a woman of virtue* (**virtudes**)
4 by virtue of something because of something, especially something good (**por virtude de**)

virtuoso /ˌvɜːtjuˈəʊzəʊ/ NOUN [plural **virtuosos**] someone who is excellent at something, especially playing a musical instrument □ *a virtuoso pianist* (**excelente, virtuose**)

virtuous /ˈvɜːtʃuəs/ ADJECTIVE behaving well, in a way that is morally good (**virtuoso**)

virus /ˈvaɪrəs/ NOUN [plural **viruses**]
1 a very small living thing that can enter the body and cause disease. A biology word. (**vírus**)
2 an illness caused by a virus □ *He's been off work all week with a virus.* (**vírus**)
3 a computer program that can send itself to many computers, for example by e-mail, and can destroy files on those computers. A computing word. (**vírus**)

visa /ˈviːzə/ NOUN [plural **visas**] a document that you need to travel to and work in some countries (**visto de passaporte**)

vis-à-vis /ˌviːzɑːˈviː/ PREPOSITION
1 to do with something □ *I spoke to Michael vis-à-vis the price increases.* (**a respeito de**)
2 when compared with something (**face a face**)

viscous /ˈvɪskəs/ ADJECTIVE a viscous liquid is thick. A biology word. (**viscoso**)

visibility /ˌvɪzɪˈbɪlɪti/ NOUN, NO PLURAL
1 how far and well you can see, for example in bad weather □ *poor visibility caused by heavy rain* (**visibilidade**)
2 the fact of being easy to see □ *Visibility is important for cyclists.* (**visibilidade**)

• **visible** /ˈvɪzəbəl/ ADJECTIVE able to be seen □ *Is the house visible from the road?* (**visível**)

• **visibly** /ˈvɪzɪbli/ ADVERB in a way that you can see or notice □ *She was visibly upset by his remarks.* (**visivelmente**)

vision /ˈvɪʒən/ NOUN [plural **visions**]
1 your ability to see □ *poor vision* (**visão**)
2 an idea of how something should be in the future □ *He talked about his vision for the school.* (**visão**)
3 the ability to think about the future and make plans that are clever and show imagination (**visão**)
4 have visions of doing something to imagine something happening □ *I had visions of turning up late and missing the train.* (**ter visões de fazer alguma coisa**)
5 an image that appears in front of someone during a religious experience (**visão**)

visit /ˈvɪzɪt/ ▶ VERB [**visits, visiting, visited**]
1 to go and see a place or person □ *We're going to visit my aunt while we're in York.* □ *We visited a couple of museums.* (**visitar**)
2 to look at a website □ *It's one of the most visited websites in the UK.* (**visitar**)
▶ NOUN [plural **visits**] the act of visiting a place or person (**visita**) ▣ *I'm going to pay him a visit.* (**pagar uma visita**)

• **visitor** /ˈvɪzɪtə(r)/ NOUN [plural **visitors**] someone who visits a place or person (**visitante, visita**) ▣ *She had two visitors yesterday.* (**teve dois visitantes**)

visor /ˈvaɪzə(r)/ NOUN [plural **visors**]
1 the clear part of a helmet (= hard hat) that covers someone's face (**viseira**)
2 a hat for protecting your eyes from the sun which consists of a piece of plastic attached to a strip that goes around the head (**viseira**)

visual /ˈvɪʒjuəl/ ADJECTIVE to do with seeing □ *visual signals* (**visual**)

visual aid /ˈvɪʒjuəl ˈeɪd/ NOUN [plural **visual aids**] a picture, film, etc. that helps you to understand a subject that you are learning about (**recurso visual**)

visualize or **visualise** /ˈvɪʒjuəlaɪz/ VERB [**visualizes, visualizing, visualized**] to form a picture in your mind □ *I remember his name, but I can't visualize him.* (**visualizar**)

visually /ˈvɪʒjuəli/ ADVERB in a way that is to do with seeing □ *Visually, it's a beautiful film.* (**visualmente**)

vital /ˈvaɪtəl/ ADJECTIVE necessary or extremely important □ *vital information* □ *He played a vital role in the project.* (**vital**)

• **vitality** /vaɪˈtæləti/ NOUN, NO PLURAL energy and interest □ *A better diet will restore lost vitality.* (**vitalidade**)

• **vitally** /ˈvaɪtəli/ ADVERB extremely (**vitalmente**) ▣ *vitally important* information (**vitalmente importante**)

vitamin /ˈvɪtəmɪn/ NOUN [plural **vitamins**] a substance in food that you need to stay healthy □ *Oranges contain vitamin C.* (**vitamina**)

viva /ˈvaɪvə/ NOUN [plural **vivas**] a spoken exam at university (**exame oral de universidades**)

vivacious /vɪˈveɪʃəs/ ADJECTIVE full of energy, and enjoying meeting and speaking to people □ *a vivacious young woman* (**vivaz**)

vivid /ˈvɪvɪd/ ADJECTIVE
1 producing very clear ideas and pictures in your mind □ *a vivid description* □ *vivid memories* (**vívido**)
2 very bright □ *vivid colours* (**vivo**)
• **vividly** /ˈvɪvɪdli/ ADVERB in a very clear way □ *I vividly remember meeting him.* (**vividamente**)

vivisection /ˌvɪvɪˈsekʃən/ NOUN, NO PLURAL when experiments are done on animals that are alive, usually for scientific reasons (**vivisseção**)

vixen /ˈvɪksən/ NOUN [plural **vixens**] a female fox (= wild animal like a dog with red fur) (**raposa fêmea**)

V-neck /ˈviːnek/ NOUN [plural **V-necks**]
1 a neck opening in a piece of clothing formed to make a point at the front (**gola ou decote em V**)
2 a piece of clothing for the upper half of the body with this neck opening (**roupa com decote em V**)
• **V-necked** ADJECTIVE having a V-neck □ *a V-necked sweater* (**com decote em V**)

vocabulary /vəˈkæbjʊləri/ NOUN [plural **vocabularies**]
1 the range of words that someone knows and uses □ *She has a good vocabulary for a child of her age.* (**vocabulário**)
2 all the words in a language (**vocabulário**)

vocal /ˈvəʊkəl/ ADJECTIVE
1 to do with your voice □ *vocal quality* (**vocal**)
2 saying your opinions strongly □ *her vocal opposition to the plan* (**franco, enérgico**)

vocal cords /ˈvəʊkəl ˌkɔːdz/ PLURAL NOUN the part at the top of the throat that produces the voice (**pregas vocais**)

vocalist /ˈvəʊkəlɪst/ NOUN [plural **vocalists**] a singer, especially a singer of pop music (**vocalista**)

vocation /vəʊˈkeɪʃən/ NOUN [plural **vocations**] a job that you feel you must do because you have the skills for it and because the work is very important □ *For Dan, teaching is a vocation.* (**vocação**)
• **vocational** /vəʊˈkeɪʃənəl/ ADJECTIVE providing the skills needed for a particular job □ *vocational training* (**vocacional**)

vociferous /vəˈsɪfərəs/ ADJECTIVE saying your opinions in a strong, loud way □ *a vociferous group of protesters.* (**vociferante**)

vodka /ˈvɒdkə/ NOUN, NO PLURAL a strong clear alcoholic drink (**vodca**)

vogue /vəʊɡ/ NOUN, NO PLURAL when something is very fashionable or popular □ *There is a current vogue for Spanish films.* (**moda**)

voice /vɔɪs/ ▶ NOUN [plural **voices**]
1 the sound you make when you speak or sing □ *She has quite a low voice.* □ *Her singing voice is beautiful.* □ *I thought I heard voices.* (**voz**)
2 lose your voice to stop being able to speak for a while, because you are ill (**perder a voz**)
3 no plural the chance to say your opinions □ *Poor people like this have no voice.* (**voz**)
4 no plural a person who says the opinions of a particular group □ *the voice of the people* (**voz**)
▶ VERB [**voices, voicing, voiced**] to express an opinion (**expressar(-se)**) *Many people have voiced their concerns.* (**expressar preocupações**)

void /vɔɪd/ ▶ ADJECTIVE not legally or officially acceptable and unable to be used □ *The contract was declared void.* (**nulo**)
▶ NOUN, NO PLURAL
1 when something very important is missing from a situation □ *Her death had left a void in his life.* (**vazio**)
2 a very large space with nothing in it (**vácuo**)

volatile /ˈvɒlətaɪl/ ADJECTIVE
1 a volatile person is likely to change their mood very quickly (**volúvel**)
2 a volatile situation could change very suddenly (**volúvel**)
3 a volatile liquid or substance changes quickly to a gas. A chemistry word. (**volátil**)

volcanic /vɒlˈkænɪk/ ADJECTIVE to do with a volcano □ *volcanic activity* (**vulcânico**)

volcano /vɒlˈkeɪnəʊ/ NOUN [plural **volcanoes**] a mountain that sometimes sends out hot lava (= liquid rock) through a hole in its top (**vulcão**)

vole /vəʊl/ NOUN [plural **voles**] a small animal similar to a mouse (**rato silvestre**)

volley /ˈvɒli/ ▶ NOUN [plural **volleys**]
1 in some sports, for example tennis, when a ball is hit before it reaches the ground (**voleio**)
2 a lot of bullets or weapons that are fired or thrown at the same time (**salva de tiros**)
▶ VERB [**volleys, volleying, volleyed**] in a sport such as tennis, to hit a ball before it reaches the ground (**rebater a bola antes de ela bater no chão**)

volleyball /ˈvɒlibɔːl/ NOUN, NO PLURAL a game in which two teams hit a ball over a high net with their hands (**voleibol**)

volt /vəʊlt/ NOUN [plural **volts**] a unit for measuring the strength of an electric current (**volt**)
• **voltage** /ˈvəʊltɪdʒ/ NOUN [plural **voltages**] the amount of electrical force something has (**voltagem**)

volume /ˈvɒljuːm/ NOUN [plural **volumes**]
1 the level of sound that something makes (**volume**) *Can you turn the volume down on the TV, please?* (**diminuir o volume**)
2 the space that something takes up or the amount of space that a container has (**volume**)

3 the amount of something ☐ *+ of The volume of trade has increased.* (**volume**)
4 a book, especially a book that is part of a set (**volume**)
➪ go to *speak* volumes

voluntary /ˈvɒləntrɪ/ ADJECTIVE
1 done by choice and not because you have to ☐ *She took voluntary redundancy.* (**voluntário**)
2 done without payment (**voluntário**) 🔁 *voluntary work* (**trabalho voluntário**)

volunteer /ˌvɒlənˈtɪə(r)/ ▶ NOUN [*plural* **volunteers**]
1 someone who offers to do something ☐ *Do I have any volunteers to help me tidy up?* (**voluntário**)
2 someone who does work for no payment (**voluntário**)
3 someone who chooses to join the armed forces (**voluntário**)
▶ VERB [**volunteers, volunteering, volunteered**]
1 to offer to do something ☐ *Dana volunteered to take the children swimming.* (**oferecer-se como voluntário**)
2 to choose to join the armed forces (**servir voluntariamente**)
3 to give information or make a suggestion without being asked for it (**oferecer-se para**)

vomit /ˈvɒmɪt/ ▶ VERB [**vomits, vomiting, vomited**] to bring food back up from your stomach through your mouth (**vomitar**)
▶ NOUN, NO PLURAL food that someone has brought back from their stomach through their mouth (**vômito**)

vote /vəʊt/ ▶ VERB [**votes, voting, voted**] to make a formal choice by secretly marking a piece of paper or putting your hand up to be counted ☐ *+ for Which candidate did you vote for in the local elections?* ☐ *+ to do something They voted to reject the offer.* (**votar**)

▶ NOUN [*plural* **votes**]
1 a choice you make by marking a piece of paper or putting your hand up to be counted (**voto**) 🔁 *The party offering to lower taxes will get my vote.*
2 the vote the right to vote in elections ☐ *They campaigned to be given the vote.* (**direito a voto**)
• **voter** /ˈvəʊtə(r)/ NOUN [*plural* **voters**] someone who votes in an election (**votante, eleitor**)

vouch /vaʊtʃ/ (**garantir**)
◆ PHRASAL VERB [**vouches, vouching, vouched**]
vouch for someone to say that you know from experience that someone is good and can be trusted (**responsabilizar-se por**)

voucher /ˈvaʊtʃə(r)/ NOUN [*plural* **vouchers**]
1 a piece of paper that can be used instead of money to pay for something (**vale**)
2 a piece of paper that allows you to pay less than usual for something (**cupom de desconto**)

vow /vaʊ/ ▶ VERB [**vows, vowing, vowed**] to promise in a very serious way (**jurar**)
▶ NOUN [*plural* **vows**] a serious promise ☐ *marriage vows* (**juramento**)

vowel /ˈvaʊəl/ NOUN [*plural* **vowels**]
1 one of the letters a, e, i, o or u (**vogal**)
2 a speech sound you make that does not use your lips, teeth, or tongue to stop the flow of air (**vogal**)

voyage /ˈvɔɪɪdʒ/ NOUN [*plural* **voyages**] a long journey by sea or in space (**viagem**)

vulgar /ˈvʌlgə(r)/ ADJECTIVE very rude (**vulgar**)
vulnerable /ˈvʌlnərəbəl/ ADJECTIVE easily hurt, upset or made ill ☐ *the protection of vulnerable children* ☐ *After surgery, people are more vulnerable to infection.* (**vulnerável**)
vulture /ˈvʌltʃə(r)/ NOUN [*plural* **vultures**] a large bird that eats dead animals (**abutre, urubu**)

Ww

W or **w**[1] /ˈdʌbəlju:/ the 23rd letter of the alphabet (a vigésima terceira letra do alfabeto)

W[2] /west/ ABBREVIATION **west** (oeste)

wad /wɒd/ NOUN [plural **wads**]
1 a thick piece of soft material □ *She cleaned the wound with a wad of cotton wool.* (chumaço)
2 a pile of thin pieces of paper or paper money (maço)

waddle /ˈwɒdəl/ VERB [**waddles, waddling, waddled**] to walk moving from side to side, like a duck (= water bird with short legs) (andar gingando)

wade /weɪd/ VERB [**wades, wading, waded**] to walk through water or mud □ *We waded across the stream.* (avançar penosamente)
◆ PHRASAL VERB **wade through something** to read or deal with a lot of complicated information □ *We had to wade through all his old files.* (ler ou lidar com informações complicadas)

wafer /ˈweɪfə(r)/ NOUN [plural **wafers**] a very thin biscuit, often eaten with ice cream (wafer)

waffle /ˈwɒfəl/ ▶ NOUN [plural **waffles**]
1 a type of flat cake with a pattern of deep squares on it (waffle, tipo de massa doce)
2 talk or writing that does not say anything useful or interesting (conversa ou texto vazio)
▶ VERB [**waffles, waffling, waffled**] to talk or write a lot without saying anything useful or interesting (encher linguiça, enrolar na conversa)

waft /wɑːft, wɒft/ VERB [**wafts, wafting, wafted**] to float through the air □ *The smell of freshly baked bread came wafting out of the window.* (espalhar-se pelo ar)

wag /wæg/ VERB [**wags, wagging, wagged**]
1 if an animal wags its tail, it moves it from side to side □ *The dog ran backwards and forwards, wagging its tail.* (abanar)
2 if you wag your finger, you move it from side to side, often when you are talking in an angry way or telling someone not to do something (mover de um lado para o outro)
3 if tongues wag, people talk together about a situation, often about someone's private life (falar dos outros)

wage /weɪdʒ/ ▶ NOUN [plural **wages**] money that someone is paid for doing their job □ *They pay our wages on Fridays.* □ *a wage increase/cut* □ *What's the average wage?* (salário)
▶ VERB [**wages, waging, waged**]
1 to try hard to achieve something or fight against something □ *We are waging war on litter.* (travar uma luta)
2 to start a war or a fight (iniciar uma guerra ou luta)

wager /ˈweɪdʒə(r)/ ▶ NOUN [plural **wagers**] an agreement to risk money on the result of a competition or situation (aposta)
▶ VERB [**wagers, wagering, wagered**] to make a wager (apostar)

waggle /ˈwægəl/ VERB [**waggles, waggling, waggled**] to move something quickly from side to side or up and down, or to move in this way □ *Can you waggle your ears?* (sacudir)

wagon /ˈwægən/ NOUN [plural **wagons**]
1 a vehicle with four wheels that is pulled by horses □ *a hay wagon* (carroça)
2 a container that is pulled by a train, used for carrying goods □ *a coal wagon* (vagão)

waif /weɪf/ NOUN [plural **waifs**] someone, especially a child, who looks thin and poor and often has no home (criança abandonada)

wail /weɪl/ ▶ VERB [**wails, wailing, wailed**]
1 to cry loudly □ *A small child was wailing in the next room.* (chorar alto)
2 to make a long, loud, high noise □ *The sirens wailed all night.* (soar sirene)
▶ NOUN [plural **wails**] a loud cry or a long, loud, high noise (choro ou barulho alto e longo)

waist /weɪst/ NOUN [plural **waists**] the middle part of your body, where you wear a belt (cintura)

waistband /ˈweɪstbænd/ NOUN [plural **waistbands**] the top part of a pair of trousers or a skirt that goes around your waist (cós, cintura)

waistcoat /ˈweɪskəʊt/ NOUN [plural **waistcoats**] a short jacket with no sleeves and usually with buttons up the front that is worn over a shirt (colete)

waistline /ˈweɪstlaɪn/ NOUN [plural **waistlines**] (cintura)
1 the shape or size that you are round the waist □ *My waistline has expanded over the years.*
2 the part of a piece of clothing, especially a dress, that goes around your waist

wait /weɪt/ ▶ VERB [**waits, waiting, waited**]
1 to stay in a place until something happens, something or someone is ready, etc. □ *+ for*

Several people were already waiting for the bus. □ *He asked us to wait outside.* □ *We waited patiently for the show to begin.* (esperar)
2 to not do something until something happens, someone arrives, etc. □ *I will wait until it stops raining before I leave.* □ **+ for** *We'd better wait for Jasmine before we start.* (esperar)
3 to not do something or get something for a particular period of time □ *I had to wait 6 months for my operation.* □ *You'll have to wait a bit longer before you are old enough to be left alone.* □ *I decided to wait a while before making a decision.* (esperar)
4 to expect that something will happen □ *We're all waiting for her to announce her engagement.* (esperar)
5 can't wait/can hardly wait if you can't wait to do something or for something to happen, you are very excited about it □ *I can't wait for our holiday!* (não ver a hora de)
6 wait a minute/second (a) used to tell someone to stop what they are doing or stay where they are for a short time □ *Wait a minute – I just need to get my keys.* (espere um minuto/segundo) (b) used for saying that you disagree with something or are angry about something □ *Wait a minute – I'm the boss round here, not you!*
♦ PHRASAL VERBS **wait on someone 1** to bring food to a customer in a restaurant (servir) **2** to do everything for someone that they ask you to □ *I'm not going to wait on my children.* (servir) **wait up** to not go to bed until someone comes home □ *I'll be late tonight – don't wait up for me.* (permanecer/ficar acordado)
▶ NOUN [plural **waits**] a period of time when you are waiting (espera) 🔲 *We had a long wait for the bus.*
• **waiter** /ˈweɪtə(r)/ NOUN [plural **waiters**] someone who brings food to customers in a restaurant (garçom)

waiting list /ˈweɪtɪŋ ˌlɪst/ NOUN [plural **waiting lists**] a list of people who are waiting to get or do something □ *hospital waiting lists* (lista de espera)

waiting room /ˈweɪtɪŋ ˌruːm/ NOUN [plural **waiting rooms**] a room where people can wait, for example in a railway station or at the doctor's (sala de espera)

waitress /ˈweɪtrɪs/ NOUN [plural **waitresses**] a woman who brings food to customers in a restaurant (garçonete)

waive /weɪv/ VERB [**waives, waiving, waived**]
1 to choose not to take or use something that is your right □ *He waived his right to remain anonymous.* (desistir de)
2 to allow someone not to obey a rule or not to pay money they owe you (abrir mão de) 🔲 *His solicitor agreed to waive his fee.* (abrir mão dos honorários)

wake¹ /weɪk/ VERB [**wakes, waking, woke, woken**] to stop sleeping, or to make someone stop sleeping □ *We woke the children early and set off.* (acordar, despertar)
♦ PHRASAL VERBS **wake (someone) up** to stop sleeping, or to make someone stop sleeping □ *We were woken up by the dogs barking.* (acordar) **wake up to something** to become aware of something □ *We need to wake up to the fact that global warming is getting worse.* (conscientizar-se)

wake² /weɪk/ NOUN [plural **wakes**]
1 in the wake of something after something has happened and as a result of it □ *Many airlines went bankrupt in the wake of the disaster.* (como consequência de)
2 the raised lines of water behind a moving boat (rastro, esteira)

waken /ˈweɪkən/ VERB [**wakens, wakening, wakened**] to stop sleeping, or to make someone stop sleeping □ *A loud sound wakened me.* (despertar, acordar)

walk /wɔːk/ ▶ VERB [**walks, walking, walked**]
1 to move by putting one foot in front of the other □ *The door opened and Simon walked in.* □ *I think I'll walk to work today.* (andar, caminhar, passear)
2 to go somewhere with someone on foot, to make sure they are safe □ *Dad will walk you home.* (levar a pé)
3 if you walk a dog, you take it to get exercise (levar para caminhar)
♦ IDIOMS **walk all over someone** to make someone do what you want, in a way that does not respect them (tratar desrespeitosamente) **walk on eggshells** to be very careful not to upset or offend someone (ser muito cuidadoso para não ofender)
♦ PHRASAL VERBS **walk off with something 1** to steal something □ *Someone's walked off with my umbrella.* (roubar) **2** to win a prize □ *She walked off with first prize for her oil painting.* **walk out 1** to leave a place because you are angry or upset □ *Many of the audience walked out after what they described as racist jokes.* (retirar-se zangado) **2** to leave a person you are in a relationship with, or a job or a group of people you are working with □ *My father walked out on us when we were little.* (abandonar)
▶ NOUN [plural **walks**]
1 a journey made by walking □ *It's just a short walk to the newsagent's.* □ *I need to take the dog for a walk.* (passeio, caminhada)
2 the way someone walks □ *I recognized Ann by her walk.* (andar)
3 a route that you can walk for enjoyment □ *There is a lovely walk by the lake.* (caminho)
4 from all walks of life if people in a group come from all walks of life, they have many different jobs, social positions, etc. (de diferentes origens)

- **walker** /'wɔːkə(r)/ NOUN [plural **walkers**] someone who walks, especially for enjoyment (caminhante)

walkie-talkie /ˌwɔːkɪˈtɔːki/ NOUN [plural **walkie-talkies**] a radio that you can carry with you to send and receive messages from someone with a similar radio (walkie-talkie)

walking /'wɔːkɪŋ/ NOUN, NO PLURAL the activity of going for walks for enjoyment □ *walking boots* (caminhada)

walking stick /'wɔːkɪŋ ˌstɪk/ NOUN [plural **walking sticks**] a stick that you use for support when you walk (bengala)

walkover /'wɔːkˌəʊvə(r)/ NOUN [plural **walkovers**] a game, competition, etc. that has been won easily (vitória fácil)

walkway /'wɔːkweɪ/ NOUN [plural **walkways**] a path that connects two places or buildings, especially one that is above the ground (passagem)

wall /wɔːl/ NOUN [plural **walls**]
1 any of the sides of a room or building □ *She hung the new clock on the kitchen wall.* (parede)
2 a structure made of brick or stone that separates two areas or goes around an area □ *A high wall surrounds the school.* (muro, muralha)
♦ IDIOM **drive someone up the wall** an informal phrase meaning to make someone very angry □ *The children were driving me up the wall.* (enfurecer)

wallaby /'wɒləbi/ NOUN [plural **wallabies**] an animal like a small kangaroo (canguru de raça pequena)

walled /wɔːld/ ADJECTIVE surrounded by a wall □ *a walled garden* (murado)

wallet /'wɒlɪt/ NOUN [plural **wallets**] a flat container for money and credit cards, usually made of leather (carteira)

wallflower /'wɔːlˌflaʊə(r)/ NOUN [plural **wallflowers**]
1 someone who does not have anyone to dance with at a social event (moça que ninguém tira para dançar)
2 a plant which has flowers with a sweet smell (goivo amarelo)

wallop /'wɒləp/ ▶ VERB [**wallops, walloping, walloped**] an informal word meaning to hit someone or something hard □ *He walloped his head on the door as he came into the room.* (bater forte)
▶ NOUN [plural **wallops**] an informal word meaning a hard hit (pancada, soco)

wallow /'wɒləʊ/ VERB [**wallows, wallowing, wallowed**]
1 to spend too much time feeling sad □ *He did not wallow in self-pity but simply worked even harder.* (consumir-se de tristeza)
2 to roll around in mud or water □ *The hippos were wallowing in the mud.* (chafurdar)

wallpaper /'wɔːlˌpeɪpə(r)/ ▶ NOUN [plural **wallpapers**]
1 paper that you can use to cover and decorate the walls of a room (papel de parede)
2 a pattern or picture that you choose to have on your main computer screen. A computing word. (pano de fundo, wallpaper)
▶ VERB [**wallpapers, wallpapering, wallpapered**] to put wallpaper onto the walls of a room (colocar papel de parede)

walnut /'wɔːlnʌt/ NOUN [plural **walnuts**] a large nut that you can eat, with many deep, curved lines in its surface (noz)

walrus /'wɔːlrəs/ NOUN [plural **walruses**] a large sea animal with tusks (= large curved teeth that come out of its mouth) (morsa)

waltz /wɔːls/ ▶ NOUN [plural **waltzes**] a dance for two people, with a rhythm of three repeated beats (valsa)
▶ VERB [**waltzes, waltzing, waltzed**]
1 to dance a waltz (dançar uma valsa)
2 to walk somewhere in a confident way that annoys other people □ *She just waltzed in and helped herself to our food.* (andar com arrogância)

WAN /wæn/ ABBREVIATION wide area network; a system that connects the computers of people who are in different places (rede de longa distância)

wan /wɒn/ ADJECTIVE someone who is wan looks pale and tired (pálido)

wand /wɒnd/ NOUN [plural **wands**] a long thin stick used for doing magic (varinha mágica)

wander /'wɒndə(r)/ ▶ VERB [**wanders, wandering, wandered**]
1 to go from one place to another without any clear plan or purpose □ *We spent the summer wandering all around southern Italy.* (vaguear)
2 if your mind or your thoughts wander, you start to think about other things instead of the thing you should be thinking about (vaguear)
♦ PHRASAL VERB **wander off** to go away from a place, especially from the place you should be □ *The children have wandered off again.* (perder-se, desaparecer do lugar)
▶ NOUN [plural **wanders**] a short walk that has no plan or purpose □ *Shall we go for a wander in the garden?* (passeio)

wane /weɪn/ ▶ VERB [**wanes, waning, waned**]
1 to become less strong □ *Support for the government is waning fast.* (minguar)
2 if the moon wanes, it seems to become smaller (minguar)
▶ NOUN **on the wane** becoming less strong or successful □ *Her career was on the wane.* (em declínio)

wangle /'wæŋgəl/ VERB [**wangles, wangling, wangled**] to get something by persuading

wanly

someone in a clever way □ *Do you think you could wangle me a couple of free tickets to the concert?* (arranjar)

wanly /'wɒnli/ ADJECTIVE in a tired, sad way □ *She smiled wanly.* (palidamente)

want /wɒnt/ ▶ VERB [wants, wanting, wanted]
1 to feel that you would like to have something or do something, or to wish that something will happen □ *Do you want some cake?* □ *Nobody wants higher taxes.* □ **+ to do something** *I didn't want anyone to know.* (querer)
2 to need something □ *Your hands want a good wash.* (precisar de)
3 if something wants doing, it needs to be done □ *The tomato plants want watering.* (precisar de)
4 used to give someone advice or a warning □ *Maps? You want to try the library.* □ *She has a lot of influence. You don't want to upset her.* (dever)
▶ NOUN [plural wants]
1 no plural the state of being very poor or not having the things you need to live □ *Many families are living in severe want.* (carência, necessidade)
2 **for want of something** because of something that is not done or not available □ *He failed the test, but not for want of trying.* (por falta de alguma coisa)
3 your wants are the things you need or would like to have □ *The local shops are sufficient for our wants.* (necessidades)

• **wanted** /'wɒntɪd/ ADJECTIVE
1 someone who is wanted is being searched for by the police (procurado) 🔲 *Pictures of the wanted man appeared in all the newspapers.* (o homem procurado)
2 loved, needed, and cared for (querido) 🔲 *Make your pet feel wanted by giving it plenty of attention.* (sentir-se querido, amado)

• **wanting** /'wɒntɪŋ/ ADJECTIVE not of a high enough quality or standard (a desejar) 🔲 *Against a much better side, the team was found wanting.* (encontrar-se deficiente, a desejar)

wanton /'wɒntən/ ADJECTIVE causing violence or damage for no reason □ *We have seen the wanton destruction of our cities.* (injustificado, gratuito)

WAP /wæp/ ABBREVIATION wireless application protocol; a system that connects mobile phones to the Internet. A computing word. (protocolo para aplicações sem fio)

war /wɔː(r)/ NOUN [plural wars]
1 fighting between two countries or groups, involving armies (guerra) 🔲 *War broke out* (= started) *between the two countries.* (a guerra eclodiu) 🔲 *That was the year that war was declared* (= announced). (a guerra foi declarada) □ **+ between** *the war between Britain and Argentina*
2 **at war** fighting a war □ *The two countries had been at war for years.* (em guerra)

3 a series of activities intended to stop something bad from happening □ **+ on** *the war on drugs* (guerra)

warble /'wɔːbəl/ VERB [warbles, warbling, warbled] if a bird warbles, it sings (gorjear)

ward /wɔːd/ NOUN [plural wards] a room with beds in a hospital □ *the children's ward* (ala, enfermaria)
♦ PHRASAL VERB [wards, warding, warded] **ward something off** to stop something bad from happening (prevenir)

warden /'wɔːdn/ NOUN [plural wardens] someone who is in charge of a building and the people in it (guardião)

warder /'wɔːdə(r)/ NOUN [plural warders] someone who guards the prisoners in a prison (carcereiro)

wardrobe /'wɔːdrəʊb/ NOUN [plural wardrobes]
1 a tall cupboard that you hang clothes inside (guarda-roupa)
2 all of the clothes someone owns □ *my summer wardrobe* (guarda-roupa)

warehouse /'weəhaʊs/ NOUN [plural warehouses] a big building where businesses store large amounts of things □ *a furniture warehouse* (depósito, armazém)

wares /weəz/ PLURAL NOUN an old-fashioned word meaning things that are for sale (mercadorias)

warfare /'wɔːfeə(r)/ NOUN, NO PLURAL fighting in a war □ *modern warfare* (guerra)

warhead /'wɔːhed/ NOUN [plural warheads] the front part of a missile (= weapon that travels) that contains the explosive □ *a nuclear warhead* (ogiva)

warily /'weərɪli/ ADVERB in a nervous way as if you do not trust someone □ *She eyed him warily.* (desconfiadamente, cautelosamente)

warlike /'wɔːlaɪk/ ADJECTIVE often starting wars (belicoso)

warm /wɔːm/ ▶ ADJECTIVE [warmer, warmest]
1 quite hot in a way that is pleasant □ *a nice warm bath* □ *Are you warm enough?* (quente) 🔲 *I tried to keep warm by jumping up and down.* (manter quente)
2 warm clothes make you feel warm □ *a warm winter coat* (quente)
3 friendly and showing good feelings towards other people (caloroso) 🔲 *a warm welcome* (recepção calorosa) □ *She's a very warm person.*
▶ VERB [warms, warming, warmed] to make someone or something warm □ *She warmed her hands on the radiator.* □ *I'll just warm the sauce.* (aquecer, esquentar)
♦ PHRASAL VERBS **warm to someone/something** to start to like someone or something after not liking them at the beginning □ *I've warmed to*

him over the months. (começar a gostar) **warm (someone/something) up** to become warm, or to make someone or something warm □ *Put a sweater on and you'll soon warm up.* □ *Could you warm up the soup?* (aquecer(-se)) **warm up** to make your body ready to do a sport by doing gentle exercises □ *It's important to warm up before a run.* (fazer aquecimento)

warm-blooded /wɔːmˈblʌdɪd/ ADJECTIVE a warm blooded animal's temperature stays the same and does not change according to the temperature of the air around it. A biology word. (de sangue quente)

warm-hearted /wɔːmˈhɑːtɪd/ ADJECTIVE kind and showing good feelings towards other people (afetuoso)

warmly /ˈwɔːmli/ ADVERB
1 in a warm way □ *Make sure you're warmly dressed for the walk.* (calorosamente)
2 showing good feelings □ *She spoke very warmly of him.* (calorosamente)

warmth /wɔːmθ/ NOUN, NO PLURAL
1 pleasant heat, or the state of being pleasantly warm □ *the warmth of the fire* (calor)
2 when someone is friendly and shows good feelings towards other people □ *the warmth of her welcome* (calor)

warm-up /ˈwɔːmʌp/ NOUN [plural **warm-ups**] a set of gentle exercises that make your body ready to do a sport (aquecimento)

warn /wɔːn/ VERB [**warns, warning, warned**] to tell someone about a possible danger or something bad that may happen so that they can avoid it or prepare for it □ **+ about** *I warned her about the icy roads.* □ **+ that** *He warned me that it would be expensive.* □ **+ to do something** *I warned you to be careful!* (prevenir, advertir, avisar)

• **warning** /ˈwɔːnɪŋ/ NOUN [plural **warnings**]
1 a statement that tells you about a possible danger or something bad that may happen (aviso) 🔍 *There are health warnings on all bottles of alcohol.* (alertas sobre saúde) □ *There are flood warnings for the region.*
2 without warning if something bad happens without warning, it happens suddenly so that you do not know it is going to happen □ *The volcano erupted without any warning.* (sem aviso)
3 when someone tells you that they will punish you if you do something again □ *Isabel got a warning from the teacher.* (advertência)

warp /wɔːp/ VERB [**warps, warping, warped**] to become bent or twisted, or to make something do this □ *The wet weather had warped the door.* (entortar, empenar)

warpath /ˈwɔːpɑːθ/ NOUN **be on the warpath** to be angry about something and wanting to punish the person who is responsible for it (em pé de guerra, furioso, ficar furioso)

warrant /ˈwɒrənt/ ▶ NOUN [plural **warrants**] a document that gives the police the right to arrest someone or search their property (mandato)
▶ VERB [**warrants, warranting, warranted**] to be a good reason for an action □ *He made a mistake but it didn't warrant such a harsh punishment.* (justificar, assegurar)

warranty /ˈwɒrənti/ NOUN [plural **warranties**] a promise by a company that it will repair or replace its product if it breaks or stops working (garantia)

warren /ˈwɒrən/ NOUN [plural **warrens**]
1 a group of underground passages where rabbits live (galerias subterrâneas de coelhos)
2 a place where you can easily get lost because there are so many passages (área residencial superpovoada)

warring /ˈwɔːrɪŋ/ ADJECTIVE fighting against each other □ *the warring factions* (em guerra, rivais)

warrior /ˈwɒrɪə(r)/ NOUN [plural **warriors**] especially in the past, a soldier (guerreiro)

warship /ˈwɔːʃɪp/ NOUN [plural **warships**] a ship with guns, used for fighting at sea (navio de guerra)

wart /wɔːt/ NOUN [plural **warts**] a small hard lump on the skin (verruga)

wartime /ˈwɔːtaɪm/ NOUN, NO PLURAL a period when there is a war (período de guerra)

wary /ˈweəri/ ADJECTIVE not wanting to do something or trust someone because you think it might cause problems □ *I'd be very wary of lending her money.* (cauteloso)

was /wɒz/ VERB the past tense of the verb **be** when it is used with I, he, she or it □ *I was surprised to see Rosie there.* □ *Mr Brock was my favourite teacher.* (ver **be**)

wash /wɒʃ/ ▶ VERB [**washes, washing, washed**]
1 to clean something with water and soap □ *His mum still washes his clothes.* (lavar)
2 to clean a part of your body □ *I washed before breakfast.* (lavar(-se)) 🔍 *Wash your hands before dinner.* (lave suas mãos)
3 if water washes against something, it flows against it □ *Gentle waves were washing against the boat.* (marulhar)
♦ PHRASAL VERBS **wash something away** if something such as a building, tree or car is washed away, the force of the water carries it away □ *Whole trees were washed away in the storm.* (arrastar) **wash something down** to have a drink when you eat food or take medicine □ *I had a hamburger washed down with a milkshake.* (beber para engolir) **wash out** to disappear when you wash something □ *Luckily the coffee stains washed out.* (lavar) **wash something out** to wash the inside of something (lavar por dentro) **wash (something) up** to wash the plates, dishes, etc. that you have used for eating □ *It's my turn to wash up.* (lavar louças)

washbasin

▶ NOUN [plural **washes**]

1 when you wash yourself or wash something (banho, lavagem) 🔹 *I'll just have a wash.* (dar uma lavada) ▫ *Could you give this shirt a wash?*
2 all the clothes that need to be washed ▫ *Your red shirt is in the wash.* (roupas para lavar)
3 the waves that a boat causes as it moves (marulho)

• **washable** /ˈwɒʃəbəl/ ADJECTIVE able to be washed (lavável)

washbasin /ˈwɒʃˌbeɪsən/ NOUN [plural **washbasins**] a bowl with taps (= objects you turn to get water) for washing your hands and face in (pia)

washer /ˈwɒʃə(r)/ NOUN [plural **washers**]
1 a flat ring made of metal or rubber that you put between a nut and a bolt (= objects used for fastening things) (arruela)
2 an informal word for **washing machine** (máquina de lavar)

washing /ˈwɒʃɪŋ/ NOUN, NO PLURAL all the clothes that need to be washed (roupa para lavar)

washing machine /ˈwɒʃɪŋ məˌʃiːn/ NOUN [plural **washing machines**] a piece of electrical equipment that you wash clothes in (máquina de lavar roupa)

washing powder NOUN, NO PLURAL a powder that you use for washing clothes (sabão em pó)

washing-up /ˌwɒʃɪŋˈʌp/ NOUN, NO PLURAL
1 all the dishes, plates, etc. that need to be washed after cooking or eating (louça para lavar)
2 the activity of washing dishes and plates, etc. after cooking or eating (lavagem da louça) 🔹 *I'll do the washing-up.* (lavar a louça)

washout /ˈwɒʃaʊt/ NOUN, NO PLURAL an event that fails completely, often because no one goes to it. An informal word. (fiasco)

wasn't /ˈwɒzənt/ a short way to say and write was not ▫ *He wasn't there.* (abreviação de *was not*)

wasp /wɒsp/ NOUN [plural **wasps**] an insect with a thin black and yellow body that can sting you (= hurt you when it touches your skin) (vespa)

waste /weɪst/ ▶ VERB [**wastes, wasting, wasted**]
1 to use too much of something, often in a way that means some of it is thrown away ▫ *I'm trying not to waste any paper.* ▫ *We waste far too much food.* (desperdiçar)
2 to use something, especially time or money, in a way that does not have good results (desperdiçar) 🔹 *You're wasting your time.* (desperdiçar tempo) 🔹 *He wastes so much money.* (desperdiçar dinheiro)
3 be wasted on someone if something of good quality is wasted on someone, they do not understand how good it is (ser desperdiçado com)
♦ PHRASAL VERB **waste away** to become very thin (definhar-se)

▶ NOUN [plural **wastes**]

1 *no plural* when too much of something is used, often so that some of it is thrown away ▫ *You should never throw away food – it's such a waste.* (desperdício)
2 *no plural* when something, especially time or money, is used in a way that does not have good results (desperdício) 🔹 *I'm not going to clean this area – it's just a waste of time.* (desperdício de tempo) 🔹 *The whole course was a complete waste of money.* (desperdício de dinheiro)
3 *no plural* rubbish or material that cannot be used for anything ▫ *industrial waste* (refugo, resíduo)
4 *usually plural* a large area of land where no crops grow ▫ *the frozen wastes of Siberia* (deserto)

▶ ADJECTIVE

1 waste products or materials have no use now and can be thrown away ▫ *waste paper* (residual)
2 waste land has no buildings or crops on it (desolado)

waste bin /ˈweɪst ˌbɪn/ NOUN [plural **waste bins**] a container for putting rubbish in (lata de lixo)

wasted /ˈweɪstɪd/ ADJECTIVE
1 achieving nothing ▫ *a wasted morning* (desperdiçado)
2 very thin, usually because of illness ▫ *her wasted arms* (definhado)

wasteful /ˈweɪstfʊl/ ADJECTIVE causing things to be thrown away ▫ *It's so wasteful to use disposable plates.* (desperdiçador)

wasteland /ˈweɪstlænd/ NOUN [plural **wastelands**] an area of empty land where crops cannot grow (terra improdutiva)

watch /wɒtʃ/ ▶ VERB [**watches, watching, watched**]
1 to look at someone or something for a while ▫ *Max is watching the football.* ▫ *I watched the children dancing.* (assistir, olhar)
2 to be careful about something ▫ *Watch you don't trip over that step.* (tomar cuidado)
3 to look after someone or something ▫ *Could you watch the baby for me while I go and wash my hands?* (vigiar, tomar conta)
♦ IDIOM **watch your step** to make sure you behave well or in a sensible way (ter cuidado)
♦ PHRASAL VERB **watch out** used for telling someone to be careful ▫ *Watch out! Don't bang your head!* (tomar cuidado)

▶ NOUN [plural **watches**]

1 a small clock that you wear on your lower arm (relógio)
2 keep a watch on something/someone to pay attention to something or someone, often to make sure that nothing bad happens (ficar de olho)

• **watchful** /ˈwɒtʃfʊl/ ADJECTIVE careful to notice what is happening (vigilante) 🔹 *Molly kept a watchful eye on her little sister.* (manter os olhos em)

water /ˈwɔːtə(r)/ ▶ NOUN, NO PLURAL
1 a clear liquid that falls from the sky as rain and is used for drinking, washing, etc. ▫ *a glass of water* (água)

2 an area of water such as a part of a sea □ *I didn't go into the water.* (**água**)

▶ VERB [**waters, watering, watered**]

1 to water a plant is to pour water on it so it will live and grow (**regar**)

2 if your eyes water, they produce tears □ *The smoke made her eyes water.* (**lacrimejar**)

3 if your mouth waters, it produces liquid because you see or smell something good to eat (**ficar com água na boca**)

◆ PHRASAL VERB **water something down** to add water to a liquid so that it is weaker (**diluir em água**)

watercolour /ˈwɔːtəˌkʌlə(r)/ NOUN [*plural* **watercolours**]

1 a type of paint that is mixed with water, not oil (**aquarela**)

2 a painting done with watercolour paints (**pintura de aquarela**)

water cooler /ˈwɔːtə ˈkuːlə(r)/ NOUN [*plural* **water coolers**] a machine which provides cool water for people to drink (**refrigerador de água**)

watercress /ˈwɔːtəkres/ NOUN, NO PLURAL a plant with round leaves that is eaten in salads (**agrião**)

waterfall /ˈwɔːtəfɔːl/ NOUN [*plural* **waterfalls**] a place where a river or stream falls over a high rock onto rocks below (**cascata, cachoeira**)

waterfront /ˈwɔːtəfrʌnt/ NOUN [*plural* **waterfronts**] the area along the edge of a lake, river or sea □ *waterfront apartments* (**beira-mar**)

watering can /ˈwɔːtərɪŋ kæn/ NOUN [*plural* **watering cans**] a container with a handle, used for pouring water on plants (**regador**)

waterlogged /ˈwɔːtəlɒgd/ ADJECTIVE waterlogged ground is so wet that you can see water on the surface □ *a waterlogged pitch* (**alagado**)

watermark /ˈwɔːtəmɑːk/ NOUN [*plural* **watermarks**] a design on a piece of paper or a banknote (= piece of paper money) that you can only see when you hold it up against the light (**marca-d'água**)

watermelon /ˈwɔːtəˌmelən/ NOUN [*plural* **watermelons**] a large round fruit with a hard green skin and red flesh (**melancia**)

waterproof /ˈwɔːtəpruːf/ ▶ ADJECTIVE waterproof material does not allow water through it (**impermeável**)

▶ NOUN [*plural* **waterproofs**] a coat or other piece of clothing made of waterproof material (**pano impermeável**)

waters /ˈwɔːtəz/ PLURAL NOUN used for talking about large areas of water, especially areas of the sea which belong to a particular country □ *The boat had entered Australian waters.* (**mares**)

watershed /ˈwɔːtəʃed/ NOUN [*plural* **watersheds**] a very important time which changes the future of something □ *a watershed in India's history* (**divisor de águas**)

water-ski /ˈwɔːtəskiː/ VERB [**water-skis, waterskiing, water-skied**] to travel over water on skis, pulled by a boat with a motor (**praticar esqui aquático**)

• **water-skiing** /ˈwɔːtəskiːɪŋ/ NOUN, NO PLURAL the activity of travelling over water on skis, pulled by a boat with a motor (**esporte de esqui aquático**)

water sports /ˈwɔːtəspɔːtz/ PLURAL NOUN sports that are played on water or in water (**esportes aquáticos**)

water table /ˈwɔːtəˌteɪbəl/ NOUN [*plural* **water tables**] the area under the Earth's surface where there is water. A geography word. (**lençol freático**)

watertight /ˈwɔːtətaɪt/ ADJECTIVE

1 not allowing liquid in or out (**estanque**)

2 a watertight excuse is a very good one that no one can say is not true (**infalível**)

waterway /ˈwɔːtəweɪ/ NOUN [*plural* **waterways**] a river or canal (= artificial water passage) that a boat can travel along (**via navegável**)

watery /ˈwɔːtəri/ ADJECTIVE

1 containing too much water □ *watery soup* (**aguado**)

2 filled with water □ *watery eyes* (**cheio de água**)

watt /wɒt/ NOUN [*plural* **watts**] a unit of electrical power. This is often shortened to W. (**watt**)

• **wattage** /ˈwɒtɪdʒ/ NOUN, NO PLURAL electric power measured in watts (**voltagem**)

wave /weɪv/ ▶ NOUN [*plural* **waves**]

1 a raised line of water that moves across the sea or other area of water □ *The waves were huge.* (**onda**)

2 a movement of the hand to say hello or goodbye or to attract someone's attention (**aceno**) 🔁 *She gave a cheery wave as the train left the station.* (**acenar, fazer um aceno**)

3 a sudden, strong emotion or feeling □ *The pain comes in waves.* □ + *of A wave of sadness came over me.* (**onda**)

4 a lot of similar events happening in a short period of time, often bad events □ + *of the recent wave of violence* □ *a new wave of bombings* (**onda**)

5 a large group of people arriving somewhere together □ + *of Waves of protesters surrounded the building.* (**onda**)

6 the form that sound or light takes as it travels through the air □ *sound waves* (**onda**)

7 a curving shape in your hair □ *Your hair has a natural wave.* (**onda**)

▶ VERB [**waves, waving, waved**]

1 to move your hand in the air to say hello or goodbye or to attract someone's attention (**acenar**) 🔁 *She waved goodbye and then got on the train.* (**acenar adeus**)

2 to move in the wind □ *Flags were waving in the breeze.* (**ondular**)

3 to move something from side to side in the air □ *She waved a hanky at me.* (**ondular**)

wavelength

4 hair that waves is slightly curly ☐ *Mel's hair waves naturally.* (ondular-se)

♦ PHRASAL VERB **wave someone off** to wave your hand to someone who is leaving ☐ *I felt so sad waving him off at the station.* (despedir-se com aceno)

wavelength /ˈweɪvleŋθ/ NOUN [plural **wavelengths**]

1 the distance between one sound or light wave and the next (comprimento de onda)

2 the length of radio wave that a radio station uses to broadcast programmes (comprimento de onda)

♦ IDIOM **be on the same wavelength** to think in the same way as someone else so you are able to understand them (estar em sintonia)

waver /ˈweɪvə(r)/ VERB [**wavers, wavering, wavered**]

1 to start to feel uncertain about a decision or belief ☐ *She has never wavered in this belief.* (hesitar)

2 to shake slightly ☐ *His voice wavered, and tears filled his eyes.* (tremular)

wavy /ˈweɪvi/ ADJECTIVE [**wavier, waviest**]

1 a wavy line goes up and down in gentle curves (ondulado)

2 wavy hair has slight curls in it (ondulado)

wax /wæks/ ▶ NOUN, NO PLURAL
a solid substance such as bees make, which becomes liquid when you heat it (cera)

▶ VERB [**waxes, waxing, waxed**]

1 to put wax on the surface of something (encerar)

2 to remove hair from a part of the body by putting hot wax on the skin ☐ *I had my legs waxed.* (depilar com cera)

3 if the moon waxes, it seems to become bigger (crescer)

waxwork /ˈwæksˌwɜːk/ NOUN [plural **waxworks**] a model of a person, made of wax (figura de cera)

• **waxworks** /ˈwæksˌwɜːks/ PLURAL NOUN a place where you can see models of famous people, made of wax (museu de cera)

waxy /ˈwæksi/ ADJECTIVE [**waxier, waxiest**] like wax ☐ *a waxy substance* (semelhante a cera)

way /weɪ/ ▶ NOUN [plural **ways**]

1 a method of doing something, or how someone does something ☐ + *of* *We are trying out new ways of working.* ☐ + *to do something* *The best way to make new friends is to join a club.* ☐ + *that* *I like the way that she sings.* (jeito, maneira) 🔁 *I've found a way to make cakes without eggs.* (encontrar uma maneira)

2 used to talk about a particular feature or characteristic of something (aspectos) 🔁 *He's like his father in many ways.* (em muitos aspectos) 🔁 *In some ways I'd prefer it if I could work full time.* (em alguns aspectos)

3 a route from one place to another ☐ + *to* *Do you know the way to the station?* (caminho) 🔁 *Sorry I'm late – I lost my way.* (perder meu caminho) 🔁 *Can you manage to find your way to the main hall?* (encontrar seu caminho)

4 a distance, or a journey or movement from one place to another (distância) 🔁 *It's quite a long way to the coast.* (longa distância) 🔁 *They have come all the way from Brazil* (toda a distância) 🔁 *We made our way to the party on bikes.*

5 an amount of time (longe) 🔁 *The wedding still seems a long way off.* (muito longe)

6 on his/its/my, etc. way coming towards a place ☐ *Karen just phoned to say she's on her way.* ☐ *Dinner is on its way.* (a caminho)

7 in/out of the way in/not in a position that stops someone seeing something or being able to move easily ☐ *I couldn't see the stage – there was a pillar in the way.* ☐ *Could you get out of the way while I'm trying to cook, please?* (ficar/sair do caminho, atrapalhar)

8 used to talk about how much of something has happened or been done (caminho) 🔁 *We were half way through our dinner when the phone rang.* (a meio caminho de)

9 by the way used to add a piece of information ☐ *By the way, have you heard the news about Alex?* (aliás, a propósito)

10 no way (a) certainly not. An informal phrase. ☐ *'Are you giving any money towards Carlo's present?' 'No way!'* (b) no possibility ☐ *There's no way we'll be finished before June.* (c) used to show surprise. An informal phrase. ☐ *They're getting married? No way!* (nem pensar, de jeito nenhum)

11 under way happening or being done now ☐ *Plans are under way to modernize the centre.* (em curso)

12 way of life the things that someone usually does ☐ *Marriage had changed his whole way of life.* (estilo de vida)

▶ ADVERB used to emphasize the amount or level of something ☐ *We have gone way over our budget.* ☐ *It was way too hot for running.* (muito além, de longe, excessivamente)

way out /ˈweɪ ˈaʊt/ NOUN [plural **ways out**]

1 a door you go through to leave a public building (saída)

2 an excuse not to do something that you do not want to do (desculpa, saída)

wayward /ˈweɪwəd/ ADJECTIVE behaving badly and not obeying other people (desobediente)

WC /ˌdʌbəljuːˈsiː/ NOUN [plural **WCs**]
a toilet (abrev. water closet: WC, banheiro)

we /wiː/ PRONOUN

1 used to talk or write about yourself and at least one other person ☐ *We left home at about nine o'clock.* (nós)

2 people in general ☐ *We need to do more about global warming.* (nós, as pessoas)

weak /wi:k/ ADJECTIVE [weaker, weakest]

1 not physically strong □ *His illness has left him feeling very weak.* □ *She suffers from a weak heart.* (fraco)

2 not powerful □ *a weak government/leader* (fraco)

3 not strong in character □ *She's too weak to stand up to her boss.* (fraco)

4 likely to break □ *The metal bolts were too weak to hold the structure.* □ *a weak bridge* (fraco)

5 not of a high quality or standard □ *Her written work is very weak.* □ *The company's still weak on customer care.* (fraco)

6 weak liquids contain a lot of water, do not have a strong taste, or do not contain much alcohol □ *a cup of weak tea* (fraco)

7 a weak argument, excuse, etc. is one that other people are not likely to believe or accept □ *She put forward a very weak case against the plans.* (fraco)

8 a weak economy or currency (= system of money in a country) is not worth as much when compared with others □ **+ against** *The dollar is weak against the pound.* (fraco)

9 a weak light or sound is difficult to see or hear (fraco)

• **weaken** /'wi:kən/ VERB [weakens, weakening, weakened]

1 to become weak or to make someone or something weak □ *The metal had weakened because of rain and age.* □ *The illness weakened her heart.* (enfraquecer(-se), gastar(-se))

2 to become less determined, or to make someone less determined □ *Dad said I couldn't have a new phone, but he's beginning to weaken.* (amolecer)

• **weakling** /'wi:klɪŋ/ NOUN [plural weaklings] a physically weak person (fracote)

• **weakly** /'wi:klɪ/ ADVERB without much strength or force □ *She smiled weakly at his joke.* (fracamente)

• **weakness** /'wi:knɪs/ NOUN [plural weaknesses]

1 *no plural* when something or someone is not strong or forceful □ *The weakness of the frame meant that the building was dangerous.* □ *I was ashamed of my weakness.* (fraqueza, fragilidade)

2 a feature of something that is not of a high quality or standard □ *His main weakness is that he does not react quickly enough.* □ *The plan has several major weaknesses.* (fraqueza)

3 something that you like very much, often something that you think you should not have □ *Chocolate is my only weakness.* □ **+ for** *I have a weakness for expensive shoes.* (fraqueza)

wealth /welθ/ NOUN, NO PLURAL

1 when someone has a lot of money and expensive things □ *The wealth of these people is amazing.* (fortuna)

2 a wealth of something a lot of a good quality or thing □ *There's a wealth of talent in the team.* (abundância de)

• **wealthy** /'welθɪ/ ADJECTIVE [wealthier, wealthiest] rich □ *a wealthy businessman* (rico)

wean /wi:n/ VERB [weans, weaning, weaned] to gradually start feeding a baby on food and stop feeding it on its mother's milk (desmamar)

weapon /'wepən/ NOUN [plural weapons]
something that is used for fighting, such as a gun or a knife □ *The murder weapon was never found.* (arma)

wear /weə(r)/ ▶ VERB [wears, wearing, wore, worn]

1 to have clothes, jewellery, etc. on your body □ *Ann was wearing a red hat.* □ *How long have you worn glasses?* □ *He doesn't wear a wedding ring.* (usar)

2 to arrange your hair in a particular style □ *She usually wears her hair in a ponytail.* (usar)

3 to have a particular expression on your face □ *Ted wore an angry frown.* (apresentar certa expressão)

4 if a material or surface wears, it gradually becomes thinner because of being used or rubbed, and if something wears it, it makes it thinner □ *His sleeves had worn through at the elbows.* (gastar(-se)) □ *My chair has worn a hole in the carpet.* (abrir um buraco, gastar)

> Note that to **wear** clothes is to have them on your body. To say 'to start to wear clothes', use the phrasal verb **put on**:
> ✓ *I put on my coat and left.*
> ✗ *I wore my coat and left.*

♦ IDIOM **wear thin** to become less strong or less effective □ *He warned them that his patience was wearing thin.* □ *Her jokes were beginning to wear thin.* (diminuir, gastar(-se), ficar esgotado)

♦ PHRASAL VERBS **wear (something) away** to disappear because of being used or rubbed, or to make something do this □ *Over the years, the sea has worn away the rocks.* (gastar, desgastar) **wear someone down** to gradually make someone less strong or less determined □ *She keeps phoning me and writing me letters, trying to wear me down.* (amolecer) □ *They were worn down by years of struggle.* **wear off** if a feeling or the effect of something wears off, it gradually disappears □ *The an aesthetic should soon wear off.* (desaparecer) **wear on** if time wears on, it passes □ *As the day wore on, we got more and more bored.* (passar) **wear (something) out** to use something so much that it becomes damaged and cannot be used any more, or to become damaged in this way □ *These shoes are completely worn out already.* (gastar(-se)) **wear someone out** to make someone very tired □ *Walking so far completely wore me out.* (esgotar)

▶ NOUN, NO PLURAL

wearily

1 the amount that you use something over a period of time □ *The quality of carpet you need depends on how much wear it will have.* (uso)
2 damage caused by being used □ *There are signs of wear on the cables.* (desgastar)
3 clothes used in a particular situation or by particular people □ *evening wear* (roupas)
4 wear and tear damage caused by being used (desgaste)

• **wearer** /'weərə(r)/ NOUN [*plural* **wearers**] someone who is wearing something (pessoa que veste)

wearily /'wɪərɪlɪ/ ADVERB in a weary way □ *He sighed wearily.* (com cansaço)

wearing /'weərɪŋ/ ADJECTIVE making you tired or making you lose your patience □ *Kids can be very wearing.* (cansativo)

weary /'wɪərɪ/ ADJECTIVE [**wearier**, **weariest**]
1 tired □ *He finally got home, weary after a long day.* (cansado)
2 annoyed or bored with something that has been happening for a long time □ *I'm rather weary of the whole situation.* (aborrecido)

weasel /'wɪːzəl/ NOUN [*plural* **weasels**] a small wild animal with a long thin body (doninha)

weather /'weðə(r)/ ▶ NOUN, NO PLURAL the conditions outside, for example how hot, cold, wet or dry it is (tempo, clima) ▣ *cold/hot weather* (clima quente/frio) ▣ *bad weather* (tempo ruim) □ *The weather's very warm for October.*
▶ VERB [**weathers**, **weathering**, **weathered**] to continue despite a bad situation □ *Somehow she managed to weather the crisis.* (resistir a)

weather-beaten /'weðə,biːtən/ ADJECTIVE having a rough, dark skin caused by being often in the sun and wind □ *a weather-beaten face* (maltratado pelo tempo)

weather forecast /'weðə ˈfɔːkɑːst/ NOUN [*plural* **weather forecasts**] a description of what the weather will be like during the next day, few days, etc. (previsão do tempo)

weave /wiːv/ VERB [**weaves**, **weaving**, **wove**, **woven**]
1 to make cloth by passing threads under and over each other on a frame called a loom (tecer)
2 to make something by twisting long pieces of things together □ *She taught me how to weave baskets.* (trançar)
3 to move in and out between objects □ *The motorbike was weaving through the traffic.* (ziguezaguear)

• **weaver** /'wiːvə(r)/ NOUN [*plural* **weavers**] someone who weaves cloth (tecelão)

web /web/ NOUN [*plural* **webs**]
1 a very thin net that a spider makes for catching insects (teia)
2 the Web the World Wide Web all the websites on the Internet (a rede mundial de computadores via internet)

• **webbed** /webd/ ADJECTIVE webbed feet have skin joining the toes together (com membrana interdigital)

webcam /'webkæm/ NOUN [*plural* **webcams**] a camera which allows you to see and hear on the Internet moving pictures and sounds as they are happening. A computing word. (câmera de vídeo conectada a um computador com acesso à internet)

webcast /'webkɑːst/ NOUN [*plural* **webcasts**] something that is broadcast on the Internet as it happens. A computing word. (transmissão via web)

web page /'web ˌpeɪdʒ/ NOUN [*plural* **web pages**] a page on a website. A computing word. (página da internet)

website /'websaɪt/ NOUN [*plural* **websites**] a group of connected pages on the Internet about a particular company, organization, subject, etc. A computing word. □ *Rowling's official website* □ *He has his own website.* (conjunto de páginas da internet)

we'd /wiːd/ a short way to say and write we had or we would □ *We'd better hurry up.* □ *We'd buy a new car if we had the money.* (abreviação de *we had* ou *we would*)

wedding /'wedɪŋ/ NOUN [*plural* **weddings**] a marriage ceremony □ *I met her at Lucy and John's wedding.* □ *a wedding present* (casamento)

wedge /wedʒ/ ▶ NOUN [*plural* **wedges**]
1 a piece of hard material that is thick at one end and thin at the other and is used to hold something in place □ *a door wedge* (cunha, calço)
2 something shaped like a wedge □ *He cut himself a thick wedge of cake.* (em forma de cunha)
▶ VERB [**wedges**, **wedging**, **wedged**]
1 to hold something, often a door, in place with a wedge □ *She wedged the door open with a piece of cardboard.* (calçar)
2 to push something firmly into a small space (entalar)

wedlock /'wedlɒk/ NOUN, NO PLURAL the state of being married. An old-fashioned word. (matrimônio)

Wednesday /'wenzdɪ/ NOUN [*plural* **Wednesdays**] the day of the week after Tuesday and before Thursday □ *Shall we meet again on Wednesday?* (quarta-feira)

wee /wiː/ ADJECTIVE an informal word used especially by Scottish people, meaning small □ *a wee boy* (pequenino)

weed /wiːd/ ▶ NOUN [*plural* **weeds**] a wild plant that is growing where you do not want it to □ *The garden was overgrown with weeds.* (erva daninha)
▶ VERB [**weeds**, **weeding**, **weeded**] to remove the weeds from a place □ *I spent an hour weeding the garden.* (remover ervas daninhas)

- **weedy** /ˈwiːdɪ/ ADJECTIVE [**weedier, weediest**] an informal word meaning thin and weak (**fraco**)

week /wiːk/ NOUN [plural **weeks**]

1 a period of seven days □ *Debbie teaches aerobics twice a week.* □ *I'll see you next week.* (**semana**)

2 in/during the week on the five days from Monday to Friday when many people go to work □ *I don't go out much during the week.* (**na/durante a semana**)

weekday /ˈwiːkˌdeɪ/ NOUN [plural **weekdays**]
any of the days from Monday to Friday □ *The office is only open on weekdays.* (**dia de semana, dia útil**)

weekend /ˌwiːkˈend/ NOUN [plural **weekends**]
Saturday and Sunday □ *We're going to Oxford for the weekend.* □ *I like to go cycling at the weekend.* (**fim de semana**)

weekly /ˈwiːklɪ/ ▶ ADJECTIVE happening or produced once every week □ *a weekly magazine* (**semanal**)

▶ ADVERB once every week □ *In those days I used to get paid weekly.* (**semanalmente**)

weep /wiːp/ VERB [**weeps, weeping, wept**] to cry □ *She wept when she heard the terrible news.* (**chorar**)

weigh /weɪ/ ▶ VERB [**weighs, weighing, weighed**]

1 to measure how heavy something is □ *Brenda weighs herself every day.* □ *Weigh the ingredients carefully.* (**pesar**)

2 to have a particular weight □ *My suitcase weighed 15 kilograms.* (**pesar**)

3 to consider something carefully □ *We need to weigh all the facts before reaching a decision.* (**pesar, considerar**)

♦ PHRASAL VERBS **weigh someone down**

1 to be heavy and make it difficult for someone to move □ *He was weighed down with luggage.* (**curvar com o peso**)

2 to make someone feel worried or unhappy □ *He is weighed down with responsibility.* (**pressionar**) **weigh on someone** to make someone feel worried or unhappy (**pressionar**) 🔁 *Her fans' expectations weigh heavily on her.* (**pressionar fortemente**) **weigh something out** to measure an amount of something □ *I weighed out the flour and the sugar.* (**pesar**) **weigh something up** to consider the advantages and disadvantages of something □ *We spent a long time weighing up the pros and cons of moving.* (**ponderar**)

- **weight** /weɪt/ NOUN [plural **weights**]

1 *no plural* how heavy someone or something is □ *My luggage was above the weight limit.* (**peso**) 🔁 *He has lost a lot of weight* (= got thinner) *recently.* (**perdeu peso**) 🔁 *I've put on weight* (= got fatter) *since I stopped cycling.* (**ganhar peso, engordar**)

2 *no plural* the quality of being heavy □ *The shelf bent under the weight of all those books.* (**peso**) 🔁 *I wasn't sure if the branch would bear my weight* (= not break). (**aguentar meu peso**)

3 *no plural* importance or influence (**peso**) 🔁 *His opinions carry a lot of weight in political circles.* (**ter peso, influência**) 🔁 *The letters that have been found add weight to the argument that he was planning to leave.* (**dar peso**)

4 a heavy object □ *I put a 200 g weight on the scales.* (**peso**)

5 weights heavy objects that you lift to make your muscles stronger □ *I spend the first ten minutes lifting weights.* (**pesos**)

♦ IDIOMS **a weight off your mind** a problem or a worry that has been solved □ *Having someone to help me with the work is a weight off my mind.* (**um peso a menos**) **throw your weight around** to try to make people do what you want in a rude and forceful way, especially when you have some power over them □ *Since he was been promoted, he's been throwing his weight around a bit.* (**pressionar**) **throw your weight behind someone/something** to support a plan □ *The government is throwing its weight behind a campaign to reduce knife crime.* (**apoiar, usar influência**)

▶ VERB [**weights, weighting, weighted**] to put something heavy into or onto something □ *We weighted the sheet down with rocks.* (**pôr lastro em**)

- **weightless** /ˈweɪtlɪs/ ADJECTIVE having no weight (**leve, sem importância**)

weightlifter /ˈweɪtˌlɪftə(r)/ NOUN [plural **weightlifters**] someone who competes in the sport of weightlifting (**levantador de peso**)

- **weightlifting** /ˈweɪtˌlɪftɪŋ/ NOUN, NO PLURAL a sport in which people compete to lift the heaviest weight (**levantamento de peso**)

weight training /ˈweɪt ˌtreɪnɪŋ/ NOUN, NO PLURAL a form of exercise in which people lift weights to make their muscles strong (**exercícios com pesos**)

weighty /ˈweɪtɪ/ ADJECTIVE [**weightier, weightiest**]

1 serious and important □ *They are discussing some weighty matters.* (**de peso, importantes**)

2 heavy □ *a weighty volume of magic spells* (**pesado**)

weir /wɪə(r)/ NOUN [plural **weirs**] a low wall across a river to control its flow (**represa**)

weird /wɪəd/ ADJECTIVE [**weirder, weirdest**] very strange □ *Something really weird just happened.* (**estranho**)

- **weirdly** /ˈwɪədlɪ/ ADVERB in a weird way □ *The horses stood weirdly still and silent.* (**de modo estranho**)

- **weirdness** /ˈwɪədnɪs/ NOUN, NO PLURAL being weird (**estranheza**)

welcome /ˈwelkəm/ ▶ ADJECTIVE

1 if someone or something is welcome, you are pleased about it □ *This fall in inflation is welcome news to home owners.* □ *We stopped for a very welcome rest.* (**bem-vindo**)

2 if you are welcome somewhere, people like you being there and make you feel happy and comfortable (**bem-vindo**) 🔁 *They made us very welcome in their home.* (**nos fez sentir bem-vindos**) □ *He is no longer welcome at his parents' house.*

3 welcome to do something if someone is welcome to do something, you are happy to allow them to do it □ *You're welcome to borrow my bike when I'm not using it.* (**ter liberdade para**)

4 You're welcome. used as a polite reply when someone has thanked you for something □ *'Thank you for all your help.' 'You're welcome.'* (**de nada, não há de que**)

5 welcome to something if you say that someone is welcome to something, you mean that they can have it because you do not want it □ *She stole my boyfriend, and frankly, she's welcome to him!* (**pode ficar com**)

▶ VERB [**welcomes, welcoming, welcomed**]

1 to meet someone and make them feel that you are happy to see them □ *The whole family turned out to welcome us at the airport.* (**dar boas-vindas**)

2 to be pleased about something □ *I would welcome the chance of a different job.* □ *We welcome these new reforms.* (**dar boas-vindas**)

3 to be pleased to accept something □ *We would welcome suggestions from others.* □ *Applications from older people are welcomed.* (**ser bem-vindo**)

▶ NOUN [plural **welcomes**] the way that people treat someone when they arrive somewhere (**acolhida, boas-vindas**) 🔁 *We received a very warm welcome in Berlin.* (**calorosa acolhida**)

▶ EXCLAMATION used for welcoming someone who has arrived somewhere □ + **to** *Welcome to London!* (**bem-vindo a...!**)

• **welcoming** /ˈwelkəmɪŋ/ ADJECTIVE friendly and kind to someone who has just arrived □ *All the staff were very welcoming.* (**acolhedor**)

weld /weld/ VERB [**welds, welding, welded**] to join together pieces of metal by heating them (**soldar**)

• **welder** /ˈweldə(r)/ NOUN [plural **welders**] someone whose job is to weld metals (**soldador**)

• **welding** /ˈweldɪŋ/ NOUN, NO PLURAL the activity of joining metal by heat (**solda**)

welfare /ˈwelfeə(r)/ NOUN, NO PLURAL

1 health, happiness and safety □ *The police were concerned for the child's welfare.* (**bem-estar**)

2 a US word for money given by the government to people who do not have enough money and cannot earn it (**auxílio-desemprego**)

welfare state /ˈwelfeə(r) ˌsteɪt/ NOUN, NO PLURAL a system in which a government provides services such as free health care and money for people who do not have enough money and cannot earn it (**bem-estar estatal**)

we'll /wiːl/ a short way to say and write we will □ *I'm sure we'll meet again.* (**forma abreviada de we will**)

well¹ /wel/ ▶ ADVERB [**better, best**]

1 in a satisfactory, successful or correct way □ *Janet speaks French very well.* □ *Federer played really well.* (**bem**) 🔁 *My students are all doing well.* (**sair-se bem**) 🔁 *Our meetings went well.* (**ir bem**)

2 completely □ *Mix the butter and sugar well before adding the flour.* □ *I know Marie really well.* □ *He was well aware of the situation.* (**bem**)

3 as well in addition □ *I'd like an ice cream as well.* □ *As well as his family, a lot of his colleagues were there.* (**também**)

4 by a large amount □ *Profits are well up on last year.* □ *We need to be there well before the show starts.* (**bem**)

5 may as well/might as well used to make a suggestion because of a situation □ *If you're spending that much on rent, you might as well buy a flat.* □ *We may as well talk to them.* (**também**)

6 well done used to praise someone for something they have done □ *You passed? Oh, well done!* □ *Well done for remembering the map!* (**parabéns**)

7 used to form compound adjectives (= adjectives in two parts). When they are used before nouns, they usually have hyphens, e.g. a well-paid job □ *The business was very well run.* □ *Their staff are well paid.* (**bem**)

▶ ADJECTIVE [**better, best**]

1 healthy (**bem**) 🔁 *I don't feel very well.* (**sentir-se bem**) 🔁 *You're looking well.* (**melhorar**) 🔁 *Get well soon!*

2 just as well used to say that something is lucky or convenient □ *It's just as well that I live so close to work, otherwise I'd be late every day.* (**sorte que**)

3 all is well everything about a situation is good or satisfactory □ *I hope all is well with you and your family.* (**que tudo esteja bem**)

▶ EXCLAMATION

1 used at the beginning of a statement, especially a reply, often when you are explaining something, or expressing slight doubt or disagreement □ *'How did you make the sofa?' 'Well, I started with an old bed frame.'* □ *'Do you think he's suitable for the job?' 'Well, I've never worked with him, so it's hard to say.'* □ *'It's a great book, isn't it?' 'Well, I didn't enjoy it as much as you.'* (**bem**)

2 oh well used for accepting a bad situation □ *'Kiera is going to be late.' 'Oh well, we'll have to start without her.'* (**bem, paciência**)

well² /wel/ NOUN [plural **wells**] a deep hole in the ground where you can get water, oil or gas □ *an oil well* (**poço**)

♦ PHRASAL VERB [**wells, welling, welled**] **well up**

1 if a liquid wells up, it comes to the surface and almost flows over it □ *Tears welled up in his eyes.* (**verter**)

2 if an emotion wells up, it becomes stronger □ *A feeling of rage welled up inside her.* (**cresceu**)

well-balanced /ˌwelˈbælənst/ ADJECTIVE

1 containing a lot of things or parts that make a good combination □ *a well-balanced diet* (**bem equilibrado**)
2 in a calm and happy mental state

well-behaved /ˌwelbɪˈheɪvd/ ADJECTIVE a well-behaved child is polite and behaves in a way that pleases people (**bem-comportado**)

well-being /ˌwelˈbiːɪŋ/ NOUN, NO PLURAL the state of being happy, safe, healthy, etc. □ *I'm only thinking of your well-being.* (**bem-estar**)

well-built /ˌwelˈbɪlt/ ADJECTIVE having a large, strong body □ *He was tall and well-built.* (**bem estruturado**)

well-dressed /ˌwelˈdrest/ ADJECTIVE wearing attractive clothes of good quality (**bem-vestido**)

well-earned /ˌwelˈɜːnd/ ADJECTIVE if something I well-earned, you deserve it □ *She was enjoying a well-earned rest in Cyprus after several months' hard work.* (**descanso bem merecido**)

well-heeled /ˌwelˈhiːld/ ADJECTIVE an informal word meaning rich (**endinheirado**)

wellie /ˈwelɪ/ NOUN [plural **wellies**] an informal word for a wellington (**ver wellington**)

well-informed /ˌwelɪnˈfɔːmd/ ADJECTIVE having a lot of knowledge about something (**bem-informado**)

wellington /ˈwelɪŋtən/ or **wellington boot** NOUN [plural **wellingtons** or **wellington boots**] a rubber boot that you wear to protect your feet from mud and water (**galocha**)

well-intentioned /ˌwelɪnˈtenʃənd/ ADJECTIVE trying to help, but sometimes causing problems □ *Well-intentioned offers of help just made me feel more depressed.* (**bem-intencionado**)

well-known /ˌwelˈnəʊn/ ADJECTIVE famous or known by many people □ *a well-known writer* (**conhecido**)

well-meaning /ˌwelˈmiːnɪŋ/ ADJECTIVE a well-meaning person wants to be helpful and kind, but sometimes causes problems □ *Well-meaning visitors gave the animals unsuitable food.* (**bem-intencionado**)

well-off /ˌwelˈɒf/ ADJECTIVE [**better-off**, **best-off**]
1 having a lot of money □ *Only the better-off kids had bicycles.* (**próspero**)
2 in a good situation □ *The trouble is, you don't realize when you're well-off.* (**feliz**)

well-read /ˌwelˈred/ ADJECTIVE a well-read person has read a lot of books (**versado**)

well-spoken /ˌwelˈspəʊkən/ ADJECTIVE having a way of speaking that sounds educated and polite (**bem-falante**)

well-timed /ˌwelˈtaɪmd/ ADJECTIVE done at a good or suitable moment □ *A few well-timed jokes kept the atmosphere friendly.* (**oportuno**)

well-to-do /ˌweltəˈduː/ ADJECTIVE rich □ *Our customers are mostly quite well-to-do.* (**abastado**)

well-wisher /ˈwelˌwɪʃə(r)/ NOUN [plural **well-wishers**] someone who wants someone to be happy, successful, etc. □ *Her dressing room was filled with flowers from admirers and well-wishers.* (**simpatizantes**)

well-worn /ˌwelˈwɔːn/ ADJECTIVE
1 used or worn a lot □ *a well-worn dictionary* (**gasto**)
2 having been said many times before □ *a well-worn phrase* (**repetição, ladainha**)

Welsh /welʃ/ ▶ ADJECTIVE
1 belonging to or from Wales (**galês**)
2 to do with the Welsh language (**galês**)
▶ NOUN, NO PLURAL
1 the Celtic language of Wales (**galês**)
2 the Welsh the people of Wales (**o povo galês, os galeses**)

went /went/ PAST TENSE OF **go** (**ver go**)

wept /wept/ PAST TENSE AND PAST PARTICIPLE OF **weep** (**ver weep**)

we're /wɪə(r)/ a short way to say and write we are □ *We're so pleased you could come.* (**abreviação de we are**)

were /wɜː(r)/ PAST TENSE OF **be** when it is used with you, we or they □ *We were so relieved to see him.* (**ver be**)

weren't /wɜːnt/ a short way to say and write were not □ *Weren't the acrobats amazing?* (**abreviação de were not**)

werewolf /ˈwɪəwʊlf/ NOUN [plural **werewolves**] in stories, a person who changes into a wolf (= animal like a fierce dog) when there is a full (= completely round) moon (**lobisomem**)

west /west/ ▶ NOUN, NO PLURAL
1 the direction in which the sun goes down (**oeste**)
2 the countries in Europe and North America □ *The family moved to the West in 1998.* (**oeste**)
3 the area of a country that is in the west □ *the west of Scotland* (**oeste**)
▶ ADJECTIVE, ADVERB in or towards the west □ *the west coast of America* □ *We travelled west as far as the motorway.* (**no/para o oeste**)

• **westerly** /ˈwestəlɪ/ ADJECTIVE to or towards the west □ *a westerly breeze* (**no/para o oeste**)

• **western** /ˈwestən/ ▶ ADJECTIVE in or from the west □ *the western hills* (**no/do oeste, ocidental**)
▶ NOUN [plural **westerns**] a book or film about cowboys (= men who ride horses and look after cows) in North America (**gênero de histórias sobre cowboys**)

• **westernized** or **westernised** /ˈwestənaɪzd/ ADJECTIVE influenced by what is typical in America and Western Europe (**ocidentalizado**)

• **westward** /ˈwestwəd/ or **westwards** /ˈwestwədz/ ADVERB to or towards the west □ *We travelled westwards.* (**para o oeste, em direção oeste**)

wet

wet /wet/ ▶ ADJECTIVE [**wetter, wettest**]
1 full of water or covered with water ◻ *wet clothes* ◻ *It's easy to skid on wet roads.* (molhado) ◻ *My trousers are soaking wet!* (encharcado)
2 not dried ◻ *wet paint* (molhado)
3 raining ◻ *a wet afternoon* (chuvoso)
4 an informal word meaning having a weak character and not being brave ◻ *Just jump – don't be so wet!* (medroso)
▶ VERB [**wets, wetting, wet**] to make something wet ◻ *He wet his hair to flatten it down.* (molhar)

wetlands /ˈwetləndz/ PLURAL NOUN a large area of very wet land, often by a lake or river. A geography word. (pantanal)

wet suit /ˈwet ˌsuːt/ NOUN [plural **wet suits**] a rubber suit that you wear to keep you warm when you swim in cold water (roupa de mergulho)

we've /wiːv/ a short way to say and write we have ◻ *We've got something to tell you.* (abreviação de *we have*)

whack /wæk/ ▶ VERB [**whacks, whacking, whacked**] to hit someone or something hard ◻ *He whacked his brother on the head with a book.* (bater)
▶ NOUN [plural **whacks**] a hard hit

whale /weɪl/ NOUN [plural **whales**] a very large mammal that lives in the sea (baleia)
◆ IDIOM **have a whale of a time** to enjoy yourself very much (divertir-se muito)
• **whaler** /ˈweɪlə(r)/ NOUN [plural **whalers**] a ship used for hunting whales (navio baleeiro)
• **whaling** /ˈweɪlɪŋ/ NOUN, NO PLURAL the activity of hunting and killing whales (pesca de baleia)

wharf /wɔːf/ NOUN [plural **wharfs** or **wharves**] a place by the sea or by a river, where goods can be put on or taken off ships (cais)

what /wɒt/ ▶ DETERMINER, PRONOUN
1 used for asking for information about something ◻ *What day is it today?* ◻ *What's your brother's name?* ◻ *What did that man want?* ◻ *What shall we do this evening?* (que, o que, qual)
2 used for referring to something ◻ *This bag is just what I wanted.* ◻ *I saw what you did.* ◻ *I had no idea what to do.* (o que)
3 what for used to ask about the purpose of something or the reason for something ◻ *What's this handle for?* ◻ *What did you do that for?* (para que)
4 an informal word used when you have not heard someone and want them to repeat what they have said ◻ *'Could you pass the bread?' 'What?'* (o quê?, como?)
5 an informal word used to ask what someone wants when they speak to you or call to you ◻ *'Kate!' 'Yes, what?'* (sim, pois não)
6 what if used to make people think about the result of a possible event or action ◻ *What if nobody comes?* ◻ *What if it rains all day?* (e se...?)
7 so what? used to show that you do not think something is important ◻ *'You'll be late for school.' 'So what?'* (E daí?)
8 used to emphasize your feelings about something ◻ *What a beautiful view!* (Que...!)
▶ EXCLAMATION used to express surprise or shock ◻ *'The car repairs cost £400.' 'What! I had no idea it would be that much.'* (O quê?!)

whatever /wɒtˈevə(r)/ PRONOUN, DETERMINER
1 any, anything or any amount ◻ *I can give you whatever money you need.* ◻ *Choose whatever you like from the menu.* (tudo o que/qualquer coisa que)
2 used to say that something will always be true and will not be affected by anything else ◻ *You know we'll always love you, whatever happens.* ◻ *We'll be going, whatever the weather.* (o que quer que)
3 used at the beginning of a question, especially to show that you are surprised, upset or shocked ◻ *Whatever are you doing?* ◻ *Whatever does this thing do?* (o que)
4 or whatever used after a list or an example to mean other things of the same type ◻ *The children will be watching TV or whatever.* (qualquer coisa assim)
5 used when you do not know what something is ◻ *I have one of those things for pulling nails out, whatever it's called.* ◻ *I'm talking to you, whatever your name is!* (seja o que for, seja qual for)

what'll /ˈwɒtəl/ a short way to say and write what will ◻ *What'll happen to him?* (abreviação de *what will*)

what's /wɒts/ a short way to say and write what is or what has ◻ *What's that noise?* ◻ *What's she got in her hand?* (abreviação de *what is*)

whatsoever /ˌwɒtsəʊˈevə(r)/ ADJECTIVE used to emphasize a negative statement ◻ *Your problems are nothing whatsoever to do with me.* (em absoluto)

what've /ˈwɒtəv/ a short way to say and write what have (abreviação de *what have*)

wheat /wiːt/ NOUN, NO PLURAL a plant that produces grain that is used to make flour (trigo)

wheedle /ˈwiːdəl/ VERB [**wheedles, wheedling, wheedled**] to try to persuade someone to do something, often by saying nice things to them ◻ *I managed to wheedle some money out of my dad.* (persuadir)

wheel

wheel /wiːl/ ▶ NOUN [plural **wheels**]
1 a round object under a vehicle that turns to make the vehicle move (roda) ◻ *There's a spare wheel in the boot.* (estepe)
2 at/behind the wheel driving a vehicle (na direção, no volante)
3 a round part in a piece of machinery ◻ *The wheels began to turn.* (maquinismo, maquinaria)
▶ VERB [**wheels, wheeling, wheeled**]

1 to push something along on wheels □ *He got a puncture and had to wheel his bike home.* (rodar, girar)
2 to move in a wide curve in the air □ *Vultures were wheeling overhead.* (voar em círculo)

♦ PHRASAL VERBS **wheel around/round** to turn round quickly, often because you are surprised or angry □ *She wheeled around and slapped him.* (virar-se)
wheel something out to show, use, or say something that has been shown, used or said many times before □ *He wheeled out some of his famous friends to say nice things about him.* (tirar do baú)

wheelbarrow /ˈwiːlˌbærəʊ/ NOUN [plural **wheelbarrows**] a container with a wheel at the front and handles at the back, used especially for carrying things in a garden (carrinho de mão)

wheelchair /ˈwiːlˌtʃeə(r)/ NOUN [plural **wheelchairs**] a seat with wheels, used by people who cannot walk (cadeira de rodas)

wheeze /wiːz/ ▶ VERB [**wheezes, wheezing, wheezed**] to breathe with a rough noise, usually because you are ill (resfolegar)
▶ NOUN [plural **wheezes**] the noise someone makes when they wheeze (respirar com dificuldade)

when /wen/ ADVERB, CONJUNCTION
1 used for asking about the time something happened or will happen □ *When did you get home?* □ *When do you think they will arrive?* □ *When will the cakes be ready?* (quando)
2 used for talking about the time at which something happens or will happen □ *I'll go when I've had a shower.* □ *I'm not sure when the new store will open.* (quando)
3 used for talking about something that happens at the same time as something else □ *I was just going out when the phone rang.* □ *When I heard the news, I went straight to the airport.* □ *I was with her when she died.* (quando)
4 despite the fact that □ *Why do you need to buy the books when all the information is available online?* □ *How can you be busy when you don't have a job?* (quando, uma vez que)

whenever /wenˈevə(r)/ CONJUNCTION, ADVERB
1 at any time □ *You can borrow my book whenever you want to.* (sempre que)
2 every time □ *They go swimming whenever they get the chance.* (sempre que)
3 used at the beginning of a question, especially to show that you are surprised □ *Whenever did you do all this?* (quando, afinal)

when's /wenz/ a short way to say and write when is □ *When's Layla coming?* (**when is**)

where /weə(r)/ ADVERB, CONJUNCTION
1 used for asking about a place or position □ *Where are we going?* □ *Where did you get that hat?* □ *Where can I park my car?* □ *Where do you come from?* (onde)
2 used for talking about a place or position □ *I know where you can buy really good fish.* □ *He told me where he lives.* □ *That is the place where I lost my camera.* (onde)
3 used for talking about a particular point in a process or event □ *I'm afraid this is where we must stop for today.* □ *I liked the part in the play where he murdered his wife.* (onde)

whereabouts ▶ ADVERB /ˌweərəˈbaʊts/ used to ask where someone or something is □ *Whereabouts in Texas do you come from?* (onde)
▶ NOUN, NO PLURAL /ˈweərəbaʊts/ the whereabouts of a person or thing is the place where they are □ *Do you know the whereabouts of your cousin?* (paradeiro)

whereas /weərˈæz/ CONJUNCTION used for comparing two things □ *He likes going out and meeting people, whereas I'm quite shy.* (enquanto, ao passo que)

whereby /weəˈbaɪ/ ADVERB using or according to which □ *We have an agreement whereby I look after the house and she looks after the garden.* (pelo qual, com o qual)

where's /weəz/ a short way to say and write where is or where has □ *Where's the cat?* □ *Where's he gone?* (abreviação de **where is** ou **where has**)

whereupon /ˌweərəˈpɒn/ CONJUNCTION a formal word meaning immediately after which □ *She interrupted him again, whereupon he stood up and walked out of the room.* (ao que, quando)

where've /weəv/ a short way to say and write where have □ *Where've the children gone?* (abreviação de **where have**)

wherever /weərˈevə(r)/ CONJUNCTION, ADVERB
1 to or in any place □ *Wherever he is, I am sure he will come back soon.* (em qualquer lugar que, onde quer que)
2 to or in every place □ *He follows me wherever I go.* (seja onde for)
3 used to ask where someone or something is, especially when you are surprised or angry □ *Wherever did you get that hat?* (onde, onde foi que)
4 used to say that it does not matter where something is, where you go, etc., the result will be the same □ *Wherever I hide the biscuits, the children still find them.* (onde quer que)
5 used to show that you do not know where something or someone is □ *He lives in Greenham, wherever that is.* (seja onde for)

wherewithal /ˈweəwɪðɔːl/ NOUN **the wherewithal** the money or things that are needed to do something □ *We don't have the wherewithal to complete the project.* (com o que)

whet /wet/ VERB [**whets, whetting, whetted**]
whet your appetite to make you feel that you want something or want to do something □ *He'd*

seen a clip of the film, which had whetted his appetite to see more. (**despertar a vontade**)

whether /ˈweðə(r)/ CONJUNCTION

1 used to show that there is a choice between two possibilities □ *Whether we like it or not, we have to get up early.* □ *I couldn't decide whether to have the salmon or the pork.* (**se... ou**) 🔁 *I wasn't sure whether or not to tell her.* (**se falo para ela ou não**)

2 if □ *I'm not sure whether they're coming.* (**se**)

which /wɪtʃ/ ADJECTIVE, DETERMINER

1 used for asking or talking about a choice between two or more people or things □ *Which hand do you think the coin is in?* □ *Which person is tallest?* □ **+ Of** *Which of these books is yours?* (**qual, que**)

2 used for referring to something □ *I saw the letter which was lying on the table.* □ *These are the rules which we have all agreed to.* (**que**)

3 used for giving extra information about something □ *The cars, which were all luxury models, were available for us to use.* □ *I went to her party, which was very pleasant.* (**que, o que**)

whichever /wɪtʃˈevə(r)/ DETERMINER, PRONOUN

1 used to say that it is not important which thing or person happens, is chosen, etc., because the result will be the same □ *He'll be pleased, whichever one you give him.* (**qualquer um que**)

2 any of a group of things or people □ *Come on whichever day suits you.* (**qualquer que**)

3 used to talk about the thing or person that has been chosen, has happened, etc. □ *You can come round on Monday or Tuesday, whichever suits you.* □ *Whichever person gets most points is the winner.* (**qualquer um que**)

whiff /wɪf/ NOUN [plural **whiffs**] a smell which you notice for a short time □ *a whiff of garlic* (**baforada**)

while /waɪl/ ▶ CONJUNCTION

1 during the time that □ *Will you be going to Disneyland while you are in Florida?* □ *I had a cup of coffee while I was waiting.* (**enquanto, quando**)

2 although □ *While I understand why you got angry, I think you should try to control your temper.* (**embora**)

3 used to compare two people or things □ *Bob is quite intellectual, while his brothers are more sporty.* (**enquanto**)

> Note that the word **while**, meaning 'during the time that' is never followed by a noun:
> ✓ *She got ill while we were on holiday.*
> ✗ *She got ill while the holiday.*

▶ NOUN **a while** a period of time □ *We waited inside for a while, but the rain didn't stop.* (**um tempo**) 🔁 *I haven't seen her for quite a while* (= a long time). (**muito tempo**)

◆ PHRASAL VERB [**whiles, whiling, whiled**] **while something away** if you while away time, you do pleasant things to make the time pass, especially when you are waiting for something □ *We whiled away the evening chatting.* (**passar o tempo**)

whilst /waɪlst/ CONJUNCTION while □ *You could look at these magazines whilst you're waiting.* (**enquanto, quando**)

whim /wɪm/ NOUN [plural **whims**] a sudden feeling that you want to have something or do something, usually something not very important □ *I phoned her on a whim.* (**por capricho, à toa**)

whimper /ˈwɪmpə(r)/ ▶ VERB [**whimpers, whimpering, whimpered**] to make a quiet crying sound because of pain or fear (**choramingar**)
▶ NOUN [plural **whimpers**] a quiet crying sound

whimsical /ˈwɪmzɪkəl/ ADJECTIVE slightly strange and humorous □ *Her pictures are detailed and whimsical.* (**extravagante**)

whine /waɪn/ ▶ VERB [**whines, whining, whined**]
1 to talk in a complaining voice □ *She's always whining about her job.* (**lamuriar-se**)
2 a dog or other animal whines when it makes a long high sound (**choramingar**)
▶ NOUN [plural **whines**]
1 when someone whines □ *I had to listen to his whines about not having any money.* (**lamúria**)
2 the sound a dog or animal makes when it whines (**choramingo**)

whinge /wɪndʒ/ ▶ VERB [**whinges, whingeing, whinged**] to complain about things that are not important in a way that other people find annoying. An informal word. (**ficar reclamando**)
▶ NOUN [plural **whinges**] an informal word meaning when someone whinges 🔁 *She was having a whinge about her neighbours.* (**fazer um carnaval, escarcéu**)

whinny /ˈwɪni/ ▶ NOUN [plural **whinnies**] the high sound that a horse makes (**relincho**)
▶ VERB [**whinnies, whinnying, whinnied**] if a horse whinnies, it makes a high sound (**relinchar**)

whip /wɪp/ ▶ NOUN [plural **whips**] a piece of leather or other material fastened to a handle and used to hit animals or people (**chicote, açoite**)
▶ VERB [**whips, whipping, whipped**]
1 to hit someone or something with a whip (**açoitar**)
2 to move something very quickly □ *He whipped out a piece of paper and waved it at us.* □ *They whipped off the covers.* (**tirar, arrancar**)
3 to mix food, especially cream, very quickly to make it become thick (**bater**)

◆ PHRASAL VERB **whip something up**
1 to make people feel strong motions □ *His speeches whipped up anger amongst the workers.* (**suscitar, provocar**)
2 to produce a meal very quickly □ *I can whip up some soup if you like.* (**preparar rapidamente**)

whir /wɜː(r)/ ▶ VERB [**whirs, whirring, whirred**] a mainly US spelling of **whirr** (**zumbir**)

▶ NOUN [*plural* whirs] a mainly US spelling of whirr (**zumbido**)

whirl /wɜːl/ ▶ VERB [whirls, whirling, whirled]
1 to turn round and round very quickly or to make someone or something do this ▫ *He picked up the boy and whirled him round.* (**rodopiar**)
2 if your mind or thoughts are whirling, you feel confused or excited and not calm (**turbilhonar, agitar-se**)
♦ PHRASAL VERB **whirl around/round** to turn round very quickly, often because of surprise or anger ▫ *He whirled around and punched the man in the face.* (**virar-se rapidamente**)
▶ NOUN [*plural* whirls]
1 a confused or excited situation, with a lot happening ▫ *The whole town was in a whirl of excitement.* (**turbilhão**)
2 a very fast turning movement (**virada, redemoinho**)
♦ IDIOM **give something a whirl** to try an activity ▫ *She invited me to go sailing with her, so I thought I'd give it a whirl.* (**fazer uma tentativa**)

whirlpool /ˈwɜːlpuːl/ NOUN [*plural* whirlpools] an area of water where a strong current moves the water in circles, often pulling things down into it (**redemoinho de água**)

whirlwind /ˈwɜːlwɪnd/ cNOUN [*plural* whirlwinds] a powerful wind that has a circular movement and can damage things (**redemoinho de vento**)
▶ ADJECTIVE
1 a whirlwind tour/trip a quick visit to a place (**viagem muito rápida**)
2 a whirlwind romance a romantic relationship that starts very suddenly and develops very quickly (**romance relâmpago**)

whirr /wɜː(r)/ ▶ VERB [whirrs, whirring, whirred] to make a continuous, low sound (**zumbir**)
▶ NOUN [*plural* whirrs] a continuous, low sound (**zumbido**)

whisk /wɪsk/ ▶ NOUN [*plural* whisks] a kitchen tool with curved wire parts, used for mixing things like cream or eggs and getting a lot of air into them (**batedor de ovos**)
▶ VERB [whisks, whisking, whisked]
1 to mix food with a whisk (**bater**)
2 to make someone or something move somewhere quickly ▫ *They whisked us off to meet their cousins.* ▫ *She whisked away the plates.* (**tirar/mover/levar rapidamente**)

whisker /ˈwɪskə(r)/ NOUN [*plural* whiskers]
1 one of the long stiff hairs that grow on the faces of animals like mice, cats and dogs (**bigode**)
2 a whisker an extremely small amount or distance ▫ *He missed the ball by a whisker.* (**por um fio**)

whisky /ˈwɪski/ NOUN [*plural* whiskies] a strong alcoholic drink made from grain, or a glass of this drink (**uísque**)

whisper /ˈwɪspə(r)/ ▶ VERB [whispers, whispering, whispered] to talk very quietly so that other people cannot hear ▫ *My friend whispered the answer to me.* (**sussurrar, cochichar**)
▶ NOUN [*plural* whispers] something said in a very quiet voice ▫ *She answered in a whisper.* (**murmúrio, sussurro**)

whistle /ˈwɪsəl/ ▶ VERB [whistles, whistling, whistled]
1 to make a high sound or musical notes by blowing air through your lips ▫ *She was whistling a merry tune.* (**assobiar**)
2 to make a high sound using a whistle ▫ *The train whistled as it entered the tunnel.* ▫ *The referee whistled for the end of the game.* (**apitar**)
3 to make a high sound, often caused by air blowing ▫ *The wind whistled round our legs.* (**assoprar, assobiar**)
4 to move very quickly ▫ *A bullet whistled past his ear.* (**passar raspando**)
▶ NOUN [*plural* whistles]
1 a small object that makes a high sound when you blow in it (**apito**)
2 a piece of equipment that makes a loud, high sound, for example on a train (**apito**)
3 the sound made when someone or something whistles (**assobio**)

white /waɪt/ ▶ ADJECTIVE
1 having the colour of snow ▫ *He served the soup in large, white bowls.* ▫ *This powder will get your washing really white.* (**branco**)
2 white people are of a race that have pale skin ▫ *He married a white woman.* (**branco**)
3 white tea or coffee has milk in it (**com leite**)
4 white wine is a pale yellow colour (**branco**)
▶ NOUN [*plural* whites]
1 the colour of snow ▫ *The white of the walls reflected the sunlight.* (**branco**)
2 the white of an egg is the clear substance around the yolk (= yellow part) which turns white if it is cooked (**clara de ovo**)

white blood cell /waɪt ˈblʌd ˌsel/ NOUN [*plural* white blood cells] white blood cells have a nucleus and many of them fight disease. A biology word. (**leucócitos, glóbulos brancos**)

whiteboard /ˈwaɪtbɔːd/ NOUN [*plural* whiteboards] a big white screen which is connected to a computer. You write on it using a special pen which controls the computer. (**lousa digital**) ▣ *an interactive whiteboard* (**lousa digital interativa**)

white-collar /ˌwaɪtˈkɒlə(r)/ ADJECTIVE white-collar workers have jobs in offices, not jobs involving physical work (**de gabinete**)

white lie /ˌwaɪt ˈlaɪ/ NOUN [*plural* white lies] a lie that is not very serious, especially one used to avoid upsetting someone (**mentira inofensiva**)

whiten /ˈwaɪtən/ VERB [whitens, whitening, whitened] to make something white or whiter ▫ *She had her teeth whitened.* (**branquear**)

whitewash

whitewash /ˈwaɪtwɒʃ/ ▶ NOUN, NO PLURAL
1 something that is done to try to stop people discovering the truth about something □ *This report is just a whitewash – it doesn't answer the most important questions.* (**dissimulador**)
2 a type of thin, white paint (**cal**)
▶ VERB [**whitewashes, whitewashing, whitewashed**] to paint whitewash on something (**caiar**)

whizz /wɪz/ ▶ VERB [**whizzes, whizzing, whizzed**] to move somewhere very quickly □ *We whizzed down the hill on our bikes.* (**sair em disparada**)
▶ NOUN [*plural* **whizzes**] an informal word meaning someone who is extremely good at doing something □ *She's a whizz at crosswords.* (**gênio**)

who /huː/ PRONOUN
1 used for asking about a person or people □ *Who is your favourite actor?* □ *Who left the door open?* □ *Who are you going to London with?* (**quem**)
2 used for referring to a person or people □ *It was Malcolm who told me the news.* □ *It was the Italians who invented pizza.* □ *I know who has been offered the job.* (**que**)
3 used for giving extra information about a person or people □ *Emily, who lives next door, is 12 years old.* (**que**)

who'd /huːd/ a short way to say and write who had or who would □ *It was my Dad who'd told him.* □ *Who'd like another biscuit?* (**abreviação de *who had* ou *who would***)

whodunit *or* **whodunnit** /ˌhuːˈdʌnɪt/ NOUN [*plural* **whodunits** *or* **whodunnits**] a book, play or film in which the story is about finding the person who did a murder (**novela policial, história de detetive**)

whoever /huːˈevə(r)/ PRONOUN, CONJUNCTION
1 the person that has done something □ *Would whoever it was that left the gate open please go and close it.* (**quem, aquele que, quem quer que**)
2 any person □ *Bring whoever you like to the party.* (**quem**)
3 used to say that it does not matter who does something, who is chosen, etc., because the result will be the same □ *It'll take a long time, whoever does it.* (**seja quem for**)
4 used at the beginning of a question to show that you are surprised □ *Whoever told you I was a doctor?* (**quem**)
5 used to show that you do not know who someone is □ *We need to talk to Mr Buckley, whoever he is.* (**seja quem for**)

whole /həʊl/ ▶ ADJECTIVE
1 containing or including every part of something □ *We spent the whole day on the beach.* □ *I drank a whole bottle of milk.* □ *Half the guests were late, and the whole thing was a disaster.* (**inteiro**)
2 not broken into parts □ *The cake is decorated with whole hazelnuts.* (**inteiro**)
3 the whole point the most important reason for something □ *For him, the whole point of owning a smart car is to be seen as successful.* (**o ponto/motivo principal**)
▶ NOUN, NO PLURAL
1 a complete thing, especially one that is made up of different parts □ *Two halves make a whole.* (**inteiro**)
2 the whole of something all of something □ *She spent the whole of her life in Wales.* □ *The Olympics will benefit the whole of the country.* (**todo o**)
3 on the whole used to talk about what something is usually or mostly like □ *On the whole, I enjoy school.* □ *People were very kind to us on the whole.* (**no conjunto**)
4 as a whole considering all the parts of something, especially a group of people or an organization □ *These scandals affect the industry as a whole.* (**como um todo**)
▶ ADVERB
1 in one complete piece □ *He swallowed the egg whole.* (**inteiro**)
2 an informal word meaning completely □ *We are trying a whole new approach to the problem.* (**completamente**)

wholefood /ˈhəʊlfuːd/ NOUN [*plural* **wholefoods**] a food that has not been changed to take away any part of it, and has not had any artificial substances added (**alimento integral**)

wholehearted /ˌhəʊlˈhɑːtɪd/ ADJECTIVE enthusiastic and complete (**sincero**) □ *He gave Clinton his wholehearted support.* (**apoio integral**)

wholemeal /ˈhəʊlmiːl/ ADJECTIVE made from flour which has been made from whole grains (**farinha integral**) 🔁 *wholemeal bread/flour* (**farinha de trigo integral**)

wholesale /ˈhəʊlseɪl/ ADJECTIVE
1 wholesale goods are bought in large amounts, often by businesses that sell them again (**no atacado**)
2 affecting every person or every part of something (**abrangente**) 🔁 *We need to make wholesale changes to our education system.* (**mudanças completas**)

wholesome /ˈhəʊlsəm/ ADJECTIVE
1 healthy and good for you □ *wholesome food* (**saudável**)
2 having characteristics that people think are pleasant and morally good □ *She had the image of a wholesome country girl.* (**sadia**)

who'll /huːl/ a short way to say and write who will □ *Who'll help me to carry this box?* (**abreviação de *who will***)

wholly /ˈhəʊli/ ADVERB completely □ *They were wholly committed to the team.* (**completamente**)

whom /huːm/ PRONOUN a formal word, used instead of 'who' when it is the object of a verb or a preposition □ *He phoned his friend Andrew, whom he hadn't seen for years.* □ *To whom should I address the letter?* (**quem, a quem**)

whoop /wu:p/ ▶ VERB [whoops, whooping, whooped] to give a loud shout of excitement (bradar)
▶ NOUN [plural whoops] a loud shout of excitement (brado)

whooping cough /'hu:pɪŋ ˌkɒf/ NOUN, NO PLURAL a disease which makes it difficult to breathe and causes a loud, painful cough (coqueluche)

whoops /wups/ EXCLAMATION something you say when you make a mistake or have a small accident (Opa! Ops!)

whopper /'wɒpə(r)/ NOUN [plural whoppers]
1 an informal word meaning something that is extremely big ▢ That fish was an absolute whopper. (colosso)
2 an informal word meaning a lie (grande mentira)

whopping /'wɒpɪŋ/ ADJECTIVE an informal word meaning extremely big ▢ a whopping 20% pay rise (gritante)

who're /'hu:ə(r)/ a short way to say and write who are ▢ Who're you going with? (abreviação de who are)

who's /hu:z/ a short way to say and write who is or who has ▢ Who's coming for a walk? ▢ Who's got the TV guide? (abreviação de who has ou who is)

whose /hu:z/ ADJECTIVE, PRONOUN
1 used to say that something or someone belongs to someone or is connected to them ▢ This is the boy whose family owns the farm. ▢ Cheeky, whose real name was Robert Ritchie, lived in Glasgow. (cujo)
2 used to ask who something belongs to or is connected with ▢ Whose bike is this? ▢ Whose is this coat? ▢ Whose fault was it that we were late? (de quem)

who've /hu:v/ a short way to say and write who have ▢ These are the members who've already paid their subscriptions. (abreviação de who have)

why /waɪ/ ADVERB
1 used for asking and talking about the reason for something ▢ Why were you late? ▢ Why didn't they phone us? ▢ She explained why she had made the decision. ▢ I have no idea why he was so angry. (por que)
2 used for making a suggestion ▢ Why don't you ask Claire to come with you? ▢ Why doesn't he ask a doctor about it? (por que)
3 why not …? (a) used for making a suggestion ▢ Why not make some soup with the vegetables you have left? (por que…?) (b) used for agreeing to a suggestion ▢ 'Shall we invite Peter?' 'Yes, why not?' (por que não?)

why's /waɪz/ a short way to say and write why is or why has ▢ Why's she crying? (abreviação de why is ou why has)

why've /waɪv/ a short way to say and write why have ▢ Why've we got to wait? (abreviação de why have)

wicked /'wɪkɪd/ ADJECTIVE
1 evil or morally wrong ▢ a wicked old witch ▢ Separating children from their parents is wicked. (mau, ruim)
2 slightly unkind or badly behaved, but in a way that makes people laugh ▢ He had a wicked sense of humour. ▢ a wicked grin (travesso, ferino)
3 an informal word meaning very good ▢ He scored a wicked goal. (ótimo)
• **wickedly** /'wɪkɪdli/ ADJECTIVE
1 in a way that is slightly unkind or badly behaved, but makes people laugh ▢ He told some wickedly funny jokes. (maliciosamente)
2 in an evil way ▢ She treated them wickedly. (maldosamente)
• **wickedness** /'wɪkɪdnɪs/ NOUN, NO PLURAL evil ▢ There is so much wickedness in the world. (maldade)

wicker /'wɪkə(r)/ NOUN, NO PLURAL long, thin pieces of wood that are twisted together to make furniture, baskets, etc. ▢ a wicker chair (vime)

wicket /'wɪkɪt/ NOUN [plural wickets] in cricket, three vertical wooden sticks with two horizontal parts across the top (conjunto de três varas fincadas no solo no jogo de críquete)

wide /waɪd/ ▶ ADJECTIVE [wider, widest]
1 a large distance from side to side ▢ a wide river ▢ Floods affected a wide area. (largo, amplo)
2 having a particular width ▢ The river is nearly a mile wide at some points. (de largura)
3 including many different things (amplo) 🔂 They sell a wide range of products. (ampla gama) ▢ The college offers a wide choice of subjects.
4 very large ▢ She has a wide circle of friends. ▢ They won the contest by a wide margin. (enorme)
5 if your eyes are wide, they are open as far as possible (escancarado)
6 if something that is aimed, for example a ball, is wide, it goes to the side of the thing it was aimed at ▢ His shot was wide. (fora do alvo)
▶ ADVERB [wider, widest]
1 with a large distance from top to bottom or side to side ▢ The tiger opened his mouth wide, showing his enormous fangs. (completamente, amplamente) 🔂 The door was wide open. (escancarado) 🔂 She stood with her feet wide apart. (amplamente separado)
2 wide awake completely awake (bem acordado)
3 if something that is aimed, for example a ball, goes wide, it goes to the side of the thing it is aimed at (fora do alvo)
4 far and wide over a large area ▢ They travelled far and wide. (por toda parte)
• **widely** /'waɪdli/ ADVERB
1 by many people or in many places ▢ He was widely considered to be the best poet of his

generation. □ *The tour was widely advertised.* (amplamente, muito)

2 by a large amount □ *Standards vary widely.* (largamente, extensamente)

• **widen** /ˈwaɪdən/ VERB [widens, widening, widened]

1 to make something wider or to become wider □ *The river widens as it reaches the sea.* (alargar(-se))

2 to become bigger or to make something bigger □ *We hope to widen the scope of our operation.* (ampliar-se)

• **widening** /ˈwaɪdənɪŋ/ ADJECTIVE becoming wider or bigger □ *There is a widening gap between rich and poor.* (que se alarga)

wide-ranging /ˌwaɪdˈreɪndʒɪŋ/ ADJECTIVE dealing with many subjects or affecting many people or things □ *In a wide-ranging interview, she talks about her life and work.* (abrangente)

widespread /ˈwaɪdspred/ ADJECTIVE found in a lot of places or among a lot of people □ *There is widespread use of these drugs.* □ *There has been widespread criticism of the law.* (muito difundido)

widow /ˈwɪdəʊ/ NOUN [plural widows] a woman whose husband has died (viúva)

• **widowed** /ˈwɪdəʊd/ ADJECTIVE if someone is widowed, their husband or wife has died (enviuvar)

• **widower** /ˈwɪdəʊə(r)/ NOUN [plural widowers] a man whose wife has died (viúvo)

width /wɪdθ/ NOUN [plural widths] the width of something is how much it measures from side to side □ *This curtain material comes in several different widths.* (largura)

wield /wiːld/ VERB [wields, wielding, wielded]

1 if you wield a tool or a weapon, you hold it as if you are going to use it □ *There is a portrait of him wielding a sword.* (manejar)

2 to have power or influence (controlar)

wife /waɪf/ NOUN [plural wives] the woman that a man is married to (esposa)

WiFi /ˈwaɪˌfaɪ/ NOUN, NO PLURAL a system for connecting computers to the Internet that does not use wires (Wi-Fi, sistema de conexão à internet sem fio)

wig /wɪg/ NOUN [plural wigs] a covering of artificial hair that is worn on the head (peruca)

wiggle /ˈwɪgəl/ ▶ VERB [wiggles, wiggling, wiggled] to make small movements from side to side, or to make something do this □ *Harriet was wiggling her loose tooth.* (balançar levemente)
▶ NOUN [plural wiggles] a small movement from side to side (meneio, movimento)

• **wiggly** /ˈwɪglɪ/ ADJECTIVE [wigglier, wiggliest] a wiggly line has lots of small curves (tortuoso)

wigwam /ˈwɪgwæm/ NOUN [plural wigwams] a tall tent shaped like a cone, used in the past by Native Americans (tenda)

wild /waɪld/ ▶ ADJECTIVE [wilder, wildest]

1 wild animals or plants live in natural conditions and are not kept by human beings □ *wild salmon* □ *wild flowers* (selvagem)

2 a wild area of land is in a natural state and has not been used for houses, farming, etc. (selvagem)

3 not controlled, and often expressing strong emotions or a lot of energy and excitement (louco) ▣ *When he came on stage, the audience went wild.* (ficar louco) □ *The children were wild with excitement.* ▣ *wild parties* (festas loucas)

4 not based on facts or careful thought □ *He was making wild accusations.* (irrefletido)

5 with strong wind and storms □ *It was a wild night.* (tempestuoso)

6 wild about something very enthusiastic about something or liking something very much □ *I'm not wild about the idea of camping.* (maluco por)

7 run wild to not be controlled □ *The children were allowed to run wild.* (brincar à vontade)
▶ NOUN [plural wilds]

1 in the wild in a natural environment, not in a farm, zoo, etc. □ *These birds will not be able to survive in the wild.* (na natureza)

2 the wilds of somewhere the areas of a place that are very natural and far away from where people live (nos confins de algum lugar)

wild card /ˈwaɪld ˌkɑːd/ NOUN [plural wild cards] a symbol used to represent any letter or number on a computer. A computing word. (curinga)

wilderness /ˈwɪldənɪs/ NOUN [plural wildernesses] a wild area of a country with no roads, houses, etc. (selva, selvageria)

wildfire /ˈwaɪldˌfaɪə(r)/ NOUN, NO PLURAL **spread like wildfire** if a story, information, etc. (fogo selvagem) spreads like wildfire, many people hear about it very quickly (espalha-se rapidamente)

wild-goose chase /ˌwaɪldˈguːs ˌtʃeɪs/ NOUN [plural wild-goose chases] a search for something that is impossible to find (busca inútil)

wildlife /ˈwaɪldlaɪf/ NOUN, NO PLURAL wild animals, birds, insects and plants (fauna selvagem)

wildly /ˈwaɪldlɪ/ ADVERB

1 in a way that is not controlled □ *Everyone was cheering wildly.* (selvagemente)

2 extremely □ *They were wildly excited.* (extremamente)

wiles /waɪlz/ PLURAL NOUN tricks used to make people do what you want (artimanhas)

wilful /ˈwɪlfʊl/ ADJECTIVE

1 a wilful person is determined to do what they want □ *a wilful child* (determinado)

2 deliberate □ *wilful damage* (proposital)

• **wilfully** /ˈwɪlfʊlɪ/ ADVERB in a wilful way (propositalmente)

will[1] /wɪl/ MODAL VERB

1 used to talk about the future □ *It will be winter soon.* □ *Will Tom be at the party?* □ *It won't take* long to mend the hole. (**indicação do futuro verbal**)

2 used to talk about whether someone is willing to do something □ *Will you hold this for me?* □ *I'll carry that bag for you.* □ *He won't lend me any money.* (**solicitação ou indicação de ação a ser realizada**)

3 used to talk about whether someone or something is able to do something □ *The car won't start.* □ *See if a drop of oil will help.* (**indicação de possibilidade**)

4 used in conditional sentences that start with 'if' □ *If he is rude, I will leave straight away.* □ *If it rains, they will have to work indoors.* (**indicação de futuro verbal em orações condicionais**)

5 used to show that you think something is true □ *Many of you will have seen me before.* (**afirmação de uma possibilidade**)

> Notice that instead of **will not**, people often say or write the short form **won't** □ *I won't tell her.*

will² /wɪl/ ▶ NOUN [plural **wills**]

1 the mental strength needed to achieve something □ *She has the will to succeed.* (**vontade**) 🔁 *He had a very strong will.* (**força de vontade**)

2 what you want to do or to happen □ *He signed the document against my will.* □ *We must listen to the will of the people.* (**vontade**)

3 a legal document that says what you want to happen to your money and possessions when you die (**testamento**) 🔁 *Have you made a will?* (**fazer um testamento**)

▶ VERB [**wills, willing, willed**] if you will something to happen, you try to make it happen by wishing for it very much □ *We were willing our team to win.* (**desejar**)

willful /ˈwɪlfʊl/ ADJECTIVE the US spelling of **wilful**

willing /ˈwɪlɪŋ/ ADJECTIVE

1 willing to do something if you are willing to do something, you will do it if you are asked to □ *He will do well if he's willing to work hard.* □ *She wasn't willing to accept responsibility.* (**disposto a**)

2 eager and happy to do something □ *a willing helper* (**disposto, ansioso para**)

• **willingly** /ˈwɪlɪŋli/ ADVERB if you do something willingly, you do it in a happy and eager way (**de boa vontade**)

• **willingness** /ˈwɪlɪŋnɪs/ NOUN, NO PLURAL the state of being willing □ *I was impressed by his willingness to listen.* (**boa vontade**)

willow /ˈwɪləʊ/ NOUN [plural **willows**] a tree with long thin branches and leaves that often grows near water (**salgueiro**)

willpower /ˈwɪlˌpaʊə(r)/ NOUN, NO PLURAL the mental strength needed to achieve something difficult, especially to stop yourself doing something bad □ *I know I should lose weight, but I haven't got any willpower.* (**força de vontade**)

wilt /wɪlt/ VERB [**wilts, wilting, wilted**]

1 if a plant wilts, it hangs down towards the ground because it needs water or is dying (**murchar**)

2 if a person wilts, they become weak or tired (**abater-se**)

wily /ˈwaɪli/ ADJECTIVE [**wilier, wiliest**] able to trick people in a clever way (**astuto**)

wimp /wɪmp/ NOUN [plural **wimps**] an informal and insulting word for someone who is not strong or brave (**inseguro**)

win /wɪn/ ▶ VERB [wins, winning, won]

1 to beat everyone else in a game, competition, election, etc. (**ganhar, vencer**) 🔁 *We played tennis, and Sam won easily.* (**ganhar com facilidade**) □ *They won the championship three times.*

2 to defeat the other side in a war, argument, etc. (**vencer**)

3 to get something because of your skill or effort □ *It took a long time to win their trust.* □ *The company has won a major contract.* (**conquistar**)

4 to get something because you have been successful in a game, competition, etc. □ *She won a gold medal at the 2008 Olympics.* □ *The film won two Oscars.* (**conquistar**)

5 you can't win used to say that nothing you do will be successful or please people □ *I can't win – if I offer to help with his homework he says I'm interfering, and if I don't, he says I don't care about him.* (**não tem jeito, impossível acertar**)

♦ PHRASAL VERB **win someone over/round** to persuade someone to agree with you or to like you □ *They won over their critics with offers of extra money.* (**conquistar**)

▶ NOUN [plural **wins**] when someone wins a game, competition, etc. □ *This is the team's third consecutive win.* (**vitória**)

wince /wɪns/ VERB [**winces, wincing, winced**] to make a small, quick movement with your face because of sudden pain or thinking about something unpleasant □ *He winced when I reminded him of his mistake.* (**estremecer**)

winch /wɪntʃ/ ▶ NOUN [plural **winches**] a piece of equipment with a rope or chain, used for lifting or pulling something heavy (**guincho**)

▶ VERB [**winches, winching, winched**] to use a winch to lift or pull something (**guinchar**)

wind¹ /wɪnd/ NOUN [plural winds]

1 a current of air (**vento**) 🔁 *Strong winds prevented the aircraft from landing.* (**ventos fortes**) 🔁 *The wind blew and snow fell.* (**o vento soprou**)

2 no plural if someone has wind, they have gas in their stomach, which makes them feel uncomfortable (**gás**)

wind² /waɪnd/ VERB [winds, winding, wound]

1 to twist or wrap something around something else □ **+ round** *A turban is a long piece of cloth that is wound round the head.* (**enrolar**)

windfall

2 if a road, path or river winds somewhere, it has a lot of curves or turns □ *+ through A narrow path wound through the valley.* (serpentear)
3 to turn a part of a machine or piece of equipment in order to make it work □ *This watch has a battery, so you don't need to wind it.* □ *+ up He has a toy car that you wind up to make it go.* (dar corda)

◆ PHRASAL VERBS **wind down** to gradually become less busy or active □ *We're winding down for the summer break.* (diminuir o ritmo) **wind (something) down** to end gradually, or to make something end gradually □ *I've decided to wind down the business.* (encerrando) **wind up** to end in a particular state or position □ *+ ing He wound up having to apologize.* □ *You could wind up unemployed.* (acabar) **wind someone up 1** an informal word meaning to try to make someone believe something that is not true, usually for a joke □ *He isn't really going to charge you – he's just winding you up.* (provocar) **2** an informal word meaning to make someone upset or angry □ *It really winds me up when he's late.* (aborrecer) **wind something up** to end something □ *He wound up the interview and left.* □ *She decided to wind up the company.* (encerrar)

windfall /ˈwɪndfɔːl/ NOUN [plural **windfalls**] money that you get without expecting it (ganho inesperado)

wind farm /ˈwɪnd ˌfɑːm/ NOUN [plural **wind farms**] a group of wind turbines (= tall, thin structures with long parts that turn in the wind) that produce electricity (parque eólico)

winding /ˈwaɪndɪŋ/ ADJECTIVE a winding road, river, etc. has a lot of turns in it (sinuoso)

wind instrument /ˈwɪnd ˌɪnstrʊmənt/ NOUN [plural **wind instruments**] an instrument in an orchestra (= large group of musicians) that is played by blowing air into it (instrumento de sopro)

windmill /ˈwɪndmɪl/ NOUN [plural **windmills**] a building with large parts on the outside which are turned by the wind and provide power for crushing grain (moinho de vento)

window /ˈwɪndəʊ/ NOUN [plural **windows**]
1 an opening in the wall of a building or in a vehicle, with glass fitted in it (janela) 🔁 *Could you open/close the window, please?* (abrir/fechar a janela)
2 an area on a computer screen where you can work or see information. A computing word (janela) 🔁 *I opened a new window.* (abrir uma nova janela)

window pane /ˈwɪndəʊ ˌpeɪn/ NOUN [plural **window panes**] a piece of glass in a window (vidro)

window shopping /ˈwɪndəʊ ˌʃɒpɪŋ/ NOUN, NO PLURAL looking at things for sale in shop windows but not buying them (olhar vitrines)

wing

windowsill /ˈwɪndəʊsɪl/ NOUN [plural **windowsills**] a shelf at the bottom of a window (peitoril)

windpipe /ˈwɪndpaɪp/ NOUN [plural **windpipes**] the tube that goes from your mouth down your throat and into your lungs (traqueia)

windscreen /ˈwɪndskriːn/ NOUN [plural **windscreens**] the window at the front of a car or other vehicle (para-brisa)

windscreen wiper /ˈwɪndskriːn ˌwaɪpə(r)/ NOUN [plural **windscreen wipers**] one of two long parts with a rubber edge that move across the windscreen of a vehicle to remove rain from it (limpador de para-brisa)

windshield /ˈwɪndʃiːld/ NOUN [plural **windshields**] the US word for **windscreen** (para-brisa)

windsurfing /ˈwɪndˌsɜːfɪŋ/ NOUN, NO PLURAL the sport of moving across the surface of water standing on a narrow board with a sail attached to it (windsurfe)

windswept /ˈwɪndswept/ ADJECTIVE
1 a windswept place often has strong winds (varrido por ventos)
2 looking untidy from being in the wind (desalinhado pelo vento)

wind turbine /ˈwɪnd ˌtɜːbaɪn/ NOUN [plural **wind turbines**] a tall, thin structure with long parts that turn in the wind, used for producing electricity (turbina eólica)

windy /ˈwɪndi/ ADJECTIVE [**windier**, **windiest**] with a lot of wind □ *a windy day* (ventoso)

wine /waɪn/ NOUN [plural **wines**] an alcoholic drink usually made from grapes (= small green or purple fruits) (vinho) 🔁 *a glass of wine* (taça de vinho) 🔁 *red/white wine* (vinho tinto/branco)

wine bar /ˈwaɪn ˌbɑː(r)/ NOUN [plural **wine bars**] a place where people go to drink wine and often have a meal (bar de vinhos)

wine glass /ˈwaɪn ˌglɑːs/ NOUN [plural **wine glasses**] a glass with a long stem, used for drinking wine (taça de vinho)

wing /wɪŋ/ NOUN [plural **wings**]
1 one of the parts of a bird or an insect's body that it uses to fly with (asa) 🔁 *The owl flapped its wings.* (bateu as asas)
2 one of the two long flat parts that stick out at either side of an aircraft (asa)
3 a part that sticks out from a main building □ *They are repairing the east wing of the house.* (ala)
4 one of the sides of a sports field, or a player who plays on this part in sports like football □ *He's dribbling the ball down the wing.* (ala)
5 a part of a political party or other organization with its own responsibilities or opinions □ *He's a member of the party's military wing.* (ala)

6 the wings the areas on either side of the stage in a theatre that are hidden from the audience (**bastidores**)

♦ IDIOM **take someone under your wing** to look after someone who has less experience of something than you (**por debaixo da asa, proteger**)

• **winged** /wɪŋd/ ADJECTIVE having wings □ *a winged insect* (**alado**)

• **winger** /'wɪŋə(r)/ NOUN [*plural* **wingers**] a player in a sports team whose place is on one of the wings (**ponta**)

wink /wɪŋk/ ▶ VERB [winks, winking, winked]

1 to shut one of your eyes and open it again quickly, as a friendly or secret sign to someone (**piscar, dar uma piscadela**)

2 if a light winks, it goes off and on again quickly (**piscar**)

▶ NOUN [*plural* **winks**] the action of winking (**piscadela, piscada**)

winner /'wɪnə(r)/ NOUN [*plural* winners]

someone who wins a race, competition, election, etc. □ *This year's winner gets a £3,000 prize.* (**vencedor**)

winning /'wɪnɪŋ/ ADJECTIVE

1 describes the person, team, etc. that wins (**vitorioso**) 🖻 *the winning entry* (**participante vitorioso**)

2 a winning smile, manner, etc. is very attractive and makes people like you or do what you want (**cativante**)

winnings /'wɪnɪŋz/ PLURAL NOUN the money that someone wins (**ganhos**)

winter /'wɪntə(r)/ NOUN [*plural* winters] the

coldest season of the year, between autumn and spring □ *the winter months* □ *a winter coat* (**inverno**)

wintertime /'wɪntətaɪm/ NOUN, NO PLURAL the period of winter □ *In wintertime these cottages get no sun at all.* (**inverno**)

wintry /'wɪntri/ ADJECTIVE cold, like winter (**invernal**)

wipe /waɪp/ ▶ VERB [**wipes, wiping, wiped**]

1 to rub the surface of something to clean it or dry it □ *I wiped my face with a tissue.* □ *We wiped all the tables.* (**limpar, enxugar**) 🖻 *Please wipe your feet* (= clean the dirt off your shoes) *before you come in.* (**limpar seus pés**)

2 to remove something, for example dirt or water, from the surface of something by rubbing it □ *Wipe any mud off the potatoes.* (**limpar**)

3 if you wipe a computer disk, video tape, etc., you remove all the information from it (**apagar**)

♦ PHRASAL VERBS **wipe something down** to clean the surface of something by rubbing it □ *We wiped down all the cupboard doors.* (**limpar esfregando**) **wipe something off** something to reduce the amount that something is worth by a lot □ *Millions of dollars were wiped off shares yesterday.* (**desvalorizar**) **wipe something out 1** to destroy something completely □ *These elephants were in danger of being wiped out by hunters.* (**exterminar**) **2** to clean the inside surface of something by rubbing it □ *Please wipe the bath out after you have used it.* (**limpar o interior**) **wipe someone out** to make someone feel very tired □ *The journey wiped him out.* (**exaurir**) **wipe something up** to clean away a substance, often a liquid, with a cloth (**limpar alguma coisa com pano**)

▶ NOUN [*plural* **wipes**]

1 an act of wiping something □ *I need to give my glasses a wipe.* (**limpadela**)

2 a piece of wet cloth or soft paper used to wipe things with (**esfregão**)

• **wiper** /'waɪpə(r)/ NOUN [*plural* **wipers**] a windscreen wiper (**limpador de para-brisa**)

wire /'waɪə(r)/ ▶ NOUN [plural wires]

1 *no plural* metal that has been made into long, thin pieces, used for fastening things together, or for fences, etc. □ *a wire fence* (**arame**)

2 a piece of wire used for carrying electricity or telephone signals (**fio**)

♦ IDIOM **get your wires crossed** to become confused because you and the person you are talking to are talking about different things (**cruzar as linhas, falar assuntos diferentes**)

▶ VERB [**wires, wiring, wired**]

1 to connect wires to a piece of electrical equipment □ *Do you know how to wire a plug?* (**fazer instalação elétrica**)

2 to fasten things together with wire (**prender com fio**)

wireless /'waɪələs/ ▶ ADJECTIVE not connected with wires □ *a wireless Internet connection* (**conexão sem fio**)

▶ NOUN [*plural* **wirelesses**] an old-fashioned word for a radio (**rádio**)

wiring /'waɪərɪŋ/ NOUN, NO PLURAL the wires that form the electrical system in a building or piece of equipment (**instalação elétrica**)

wiry /'waɪəri/ ADJECTIVE [**wirier, wiriest**]

1 someone who is wiry has a thin, strong body (**rijo**)

2 wiry hair is strong and stiff (**duro, espetado**)

wisdom /'wɪzdəm/ NOUN, NO PLURAL when someone understands a lot about life and is able to make good decisions and give good advice (**sabedoria**)

wisdom tooth /'wɪzdəm ˌtuːθ/ NOUN [*plural* **wisdom teeth**] one of the big teeth at the back of your mouth that grow when you are an adult (**dente do siso**)

wise /waɪz/ ADJECTIVE [wiser, wisest]

1 a wise person understands a lot about life and is able to make good decisions and give good advice (**sábio**)

2 showing good judgment □ *a wise decision* (**sábio**)

3 be none the wiser to still not understand something even when you have tried to find out or when someone has tried to explain it (**ficar na mesma**)

4 wise to something knowing about something, especially a trick or something bad □ *We are wise to all the tricks the photographers use.* (**ter conhecimento de**)

wisecrack /ˈwaɪzkræk/ NOUN [plural **wisecracks**] a clever joke (**gracejo**)

wish /wɪʃ/ ▶ VERB [**wishes, wishing, wished**]

1 to want something to happen, especially to want a situation to change □ *I wish it would stop raining.* □ **+ that** *I wish that I could go with you.* □ *I wish you wouldn't work so hard.* (**desejar**)

2 wish to do something a formal word meaning to want to do something □ *Do you wish to pay now or later?* (**desejar**)

3 used to say that you hope someone will have something or enjoy something (**desejar**) 🔲 *We all wish you luck.* (**desejamos sorte a você**) □ *I wished her a happy birthday.*

4 to make a magic wish □ **+ for** *I wished for a new bicycle.* (**desejar**)

▶ NOUN [plural **wishes**]

1 what you want to do or to happen (**desejo**) 🔲 *We must respect his wishes* (= do what he wants). (**respeitar seus desejos**) 🔲 *I have no wish to see the document.* (**não ter nenhum desejo**)

2 something that you want to happen by magic (**pedido**) 🔲 *Blow out the candles and make a wish!* (**faça um pedido**)

3 best wishes a polite way of ending a letter or e-mail (**saudações cordiais**)

wishful thinking /ˌwɪʃfʊl ˈθɪŋkɪŋ/ NOUN, NO PLURAL a belief that is based on what you want to be true and not what is likely to be true □ *I thought the rain was stopping, but I think it was just wishful thinking.* (**ilusão, esperança**)

wishy-washy /ˈwɪʃɪˌwɒʃɪ/ ADJECTIVE an informal word meaning weak □ *a wishy-washy approach to discipline* (**insosso**)

wisp /wɪsp/ NOUN [plural **wisps**] a small, thin amount of something □ *a wisp of cloud* □ *a wisp of hair* (**fio, filete**)

• **wispy** /ˈwɪspɪ/ ADJECTIVE [**wispier, wispiest**] in the form of wisps (**fino**) 🔲 *She had rather wispy hair.* (**cabelo em mechas**)

wistful /ˈwɪstfʊl/ ADJECTIVE

1 slightly sad, because you are remembering something good from the past □ *a wistful smile* (**melancólico**)

2 slightly sad because you cannot have something you want (**melancólico**)

• **wistfully** /ˈwɪstfʊlɪ/ ADVERB in a wistful way □ *She gazed wistfully at the beautiful sports car.* (**melancolicamente**)

wit /wɪt/ NOUN, NO PLURAL the ability to say funny and clever things (**senso de humor**)
▶ go to **wits**

witch /wɪtʃ/ NOUN [plural **witches**] a woman in stories who has evil magic powers (**bruxa, feiticeira**)

• **witchcraft** /ˈwɪtʃkrɑːft/ NOUN, NO PLURAL the use of magic, especially for evil purposes (**bruxaria, feitiçaria**)

witch doctor /ˈwɪtʃ ˌdɒktə(r)/ NOUN [plural **witch doctors**] in some cultures, a man who uses magic to try to cure illness (**feiticeiro, pajé, curandeiro**)

witch-hunt /ˈwɪtʃhʌnt/ NOUN [plural **witch-hunts**] an unfair attempt to punish a person or a group of people □ *The communist witch-hunt of the 1950s ruined many Hollywood careers.* (**caça às bruxas**)

with /wɪð/ PREPOSITION

1 if something or someone is in a place with something or someone else, or doing something with someone or something else, they are together □ *Come with me.* □ *She keeps her diary on the shelf with her other books.* □ *He was playing football with his friends.* (**com**)

2 holding or carrying □ *He arrived with a huge bunch of roses.* (**com**)

3 using □ *The board was stuck down with glue.* □ *I chopped up the wood with an axe.* (**com**)

4 having □ *Who is that man with the curly hair?* □ *The meeting was in the room with the large table.* (**de**)

5 used to show what something refers to □ *What's wrong with your eye?* □ *I'm really pleased with my new computer.* (**com**)

6 as the result of □ *He was doubled up with pain.* (**com**)

7 against □ *I'm always arguing with my parents.* □ *He was killed in the war with Spain.* (**com**)

8 used to describe how something happens or is done □ *It is with great pleasure that I can announce the winner.* □ *She agreed with a smile.* □ *He stood with his hands behind his back.* (**com**)

9 used after verbs to do with covering, filling or mixing □ *He covered the table with a sheet.* □ *Mix the dry ingredients with the milk in a large bowl.* (**com**)

10 used after verbs to do with separating or finishing □ *I parted with them at the station.* □ *Have you finished with this magazine?* (**usado com certos verbos no sentido de separação ou término**)

withdraw /wɪðˈdrɔː/ VERB [**withdraws, withdrawing, withdrew, withdrawn**]

1 to take something away or to stop providing something □ *The council has withdrawn funding for the day centre.* □ *His father has withdrawn consent for the treatment.* (**retirar(-se)**)

2 to not take part in something, or to say that someone cannot take part in something □ *The* king's advisers have withdrawn from the negotiations. ☐ He began to withdraw from public life. (retirou-se)

3 to take money out of a bank account ☐ I withdrew £100 for the weekend. (sacar)

4 if an army withdraws or is withdrawn, it leaves an area (retirar) ▣ We plan to withdraw our forces from the area. (retirar forças militares)

5 to say that something you said earlier was not correct or true ☐ I hope that he will withdraw these allegations.

- **withdrawal** /wɪðˈdrɔːəl/ NOUN [plural **withdrawals**]

1 when something is taken away or not provided any more ☐ The withdrawal of her support was a blow to the campaign. (retirar(-se))

2 when someone does not take part in something ☐ A knee injury forced her withdrawal from the tournament. (retirou-se)

3 an amount of money that you take out of your bank account, or the process of taking it out (saque) ▣ You can make a withdrawal at any bank. (fazer um saque)

4 when an army leaves an area ☐ We are hoping for a withdrawal of our troops by May. (retirar forças militares)

- **withdrawn** /wɪðˈdrɔːn/ ADJECTIVE a person who is withdrawn is shy and finds it difficult to communicate with other people (retraído)

wither /ˈwɪðə(r)/ VERB [**withers, withering, withered**] if a plant withers, it becomes dry and starts to die (murchar)

withhold /wɪðˈhəʊld/ VERB [**withholds, withholding, withheld**] to refuse to give something to someone (recusar, reter) ▣ She was accused of withholding information from the police. (reter informações)

within /wɪˈðɪn/ ▶ PREPOSITION

1 in less than a particular amount of time, or during a particular period of time ☐ The police were called within minutes of the discovery. ☐ We'll be home within the hour. ☐ Within the last week there have been reports of fighting in the area. (dentro de)

2 less than a particular distance or amount away from something (a menos de, ao alcance de) ▣ A box of tissues was placed within reach. (ao alcance) ☐ I have always lived within 20 miles of York. ☐ They are within two points of the championship.

3 inside a place, group, organization or system ☐ They took cover within the castle walls. ☐ I moved to another job within the same company. (dentro)

4 in the range that is possible because of a particular limit (dentro do limite) ▣ We completed the project well within budget. ☐ This job should be well within his capability. (bem no limite)

5 if something is within the law, rules, etc., it is allowed ☐ The court decided that he had been acting within the law. ☐ We are within our rights to ask for compensation. (dentro)

▶ ADVERB

1 inside a place, organization, group or system ☐ The notice on the restaurant window said: 'Waiters wanted. Apply within.' (dentro do local)

2 inside a person ☐ Reading her poems, you could tell they truly came from within. (de dentro)

without /wɪˈðaʊt/ ▶ PREPOSITION

1 not having something ☐ I prefer my coffee without milk. ☐ It's a kind of bicycle without pedals. (sem) ☐ They left us without any food or water. ▣ We had to do without cutlery. (ajeitar--se sem)

2 not with someone or something ☐ Don't leave without me! (sem)

3 not doing something ☐ + **ing** He left without saying goodbye. (sem)

▶ ADVERB **do/go without** to manage when you do not have something ☐ We only have two blankets, so the children will have to do without. (passar, ajeitar-se sem)

withstand /wɪðˈstænd/ VERB [**withstands, withstanding, withstood**] to not be harmed by something ☐ The buildings are specially designed to withstand earthquakes. (resistir)

witness /ˈwɪtnɪs/ ▶ NOUN [plural **witnesses**]

1 someone who sees an event such as an accident or a crime happening, and can tell other people about it ☐ + **to** Were there any witnesses to the accident? (testemunha)

2 someone who answers questions in a court about what they know about a crime (testemunha)

3 someone who watches somebody sign (= write their name on) an important document and writes their name there too (testemunha)

▶ VERB [**witnesses, witnessing, witnessed**]

1 to see something happening ☐ Several people witnessed the shooting. (testemunhar)

2 to be a witness when someone signs (= writes their name on) an important document (ser testemunha)

witness box /ˈwɪtnɪs ˌbɒks/ NOUN [plural **witness boxes**] the place where a witness stands in a court (banco das testemunhas)

wits /wɪts/ PLURAL NOUN the ability to think quickly and make good decisions (sagacidade, sabedoria) ▣ She made a fortune from her quick wits. (raciocínio rápido) ▣ There are thieves about so you need to keep your wits about you (= pay attention and be ready to react quickly). (ficar atento)

♦ IDIOMS **be at your wits end** to be so upset or worried about something that you do not know what to do ☐ I'm at my wits end trying to feed the family on my wages. (não saber mais o que fazer) **frighten/scare the wits out of someone** to frighten someone very much (apavorar) **pit your**

witter

wits against someone to try to defeat someone by using your intelligence (tentar ser mais esperto que alguém)

witter /ˈwɪtə(r)/ VERB [witters, wittering, wittered] to talk a lot about things that are not important (falar muito e sobre coisas bobas)

witticism /ˈwɪtɪsɪzəm/ NOUN [plural witticisms] a funny and clever remark (observação sensata e espirituosa)

wittily /ˈwɪtɪli/ ADVERB in a funny and clever way (de modo sensato e engraçado)

witty /ˈwɪti/ ADJECTIVE [wittier, wittiest] clever and funny □ My brother is very witty. □ a witty remark (inteligente e engraçado)

wives /waɪvz/ PLURAL OF wife (esposas)

wizard /ˈwɪzəd/ NOUN [plural wizards]
1 in stories, a man with magic powers (mágico)
2 someone who is very good at something □ a computer wizard (gênio)
• **wizardry** /ˈwɪzədri/ NOUN, NO PLURAL a high level of skill at a difficult thing, or something that is made using a high level of skill □ technical wizardry (genialidade)

wizened /ˈwɪzənd/ ADJECTIVE having a lot of lines because of being old □ a wizened face (encarquilhado)

WMD /ˌdʌbəljuːemˈdiː/ ABBREVIATION weapons of mass destruction; weapons which kill many people and cause a lot of damage (armas de destruição em massa)

wobble /ˈwɒbəl/ ▶ VERB [wobbles, wobbling, wobbled]
1 to move from side to side, or to make something move from side to side □ This table wobbles. (oscilar, balançar)
2 to become less strong or less confident □ The dollar wobbled yesterday. (oscilar)
3 if your voice wobbles, you sound as if you are going to cry (oscilar)
▶ NOUN [plural wobbles]
1 a movement from side to side (oscilação)
2 an informal word meaning a period of feeling less strong or less confident □ I had prepared my speech, but I had a bit of a wobble when I saw how many people were there. (vacilo)
• **wobbly** /ˈwɒbli/ ADJECTIVE [wobblier, wobbliest]
1 moving from side to side □ a wobbly tooth (oscilante)
2 an informal word meaning not strong or not confident □ He's still feeling a bit wobbly after his defeat last week. (inseguro)

wodge /wɒdʒ/ NOUN [plural wodges] an informal word meaning a thick piece or amount of something □ a wodge of papers (montão)

woe /wəʊ/ NOUN [plural woes]
1 sadness (angústia)
2 woes the things that make you sad or cause you problems □ He told me all his woes. (aflições)
• **woeful** /ˈwəʊfʊl/ ADJECTIVE
1 very bad and unsuccessful □ a woeful attempt to be funny (infeliz)
2 sad □ a woeful sigh (angustioso)
• **woefully** /ˈwəʊfʊli/ ADVERB
1 used to emphasize how bad or unsuccessful something is □ The building is woefully inadequate. (lamentavelmente)
2 in an unhappy way □ She stared woefully at the mess. (de modo infeliz)

wok /wɒk/ NOUN [plural woks] a type of large pan shaped like a bowl, used to cook food in a Chinese style (panela usada na culinária chinesa)

woke /wəʊk/ PAST TENSE OF wake (ver wake)

woken /ˈwəʊkən/ PAST PARTICIPLE OF wake (ver wake)

wolf /wʊlf/ NOUN [plural wolves] a wild animal like a large dog (lobo)
♦ PHRASAL VERB [wolfs, wolfing, wolfed] wolf something down to eat something very quickly because you are very hungry (comer esfomeado)

woman /ˈwʊmən/ NOUN [plural women] an adult female person □ There were three other women in the office. (mulher)
• **womanhood** /ˈwʊmənhʊd/ NOUN, NO PLURAL the state of being a woman □ When they reach womanhood, they are expected to marry. (condição de mulher)
• **womanly** /ˈwʊmənli/ ADJECTIVE having the qualities that people expect a woman to have (feminino)

womb /wuːm/ NOUN [plural wombs] the organ inside a woman's or female animal's body where her babies grow. A biology word. (útero)

wombat /ˈwɒmbæt/ NOUN [plural wombats] an Australian animal like a small bear (vombate)

won /wʌn/ PAST TENSE AND PAST PARTICIPLE OF win (ver win)

wonder /ˈwʌndə(r)/ ▶ VERB [wonders, wondering, wondered]
1 to want to know something □ + *question word* I wonder what Jack has bought me for Christmas. □ I wonder whether Susie is coming? (interrogar(-se), querer saber)
2 used to ask someone something in a polite way □ I wonder if you could tell me where the post office is? □ I was wondering if you would like to have dinner with me? (gostaria de saber)
▶ NOUN [plural wonders]
1 no plural a feeling of great admiration and surprise □ The comet filled people who saw it with wonder. □ We stared in wonder at the castle. (maravilhamento, assombro)
2 something that makes you feel admiration and surprise □ Now we can keep in touch all the time, with the wonders of modern technology. (maravilha)
3 no wonder used to say that something does not surprise you □ It's no wonder she gets cross if you behave like that. (não é de admirar que)

- **wonderful** /'wʌndəfʊl/ ADJECTIVE extremely good □ We had a wonderful view of the mountains. □ This job is a wonderful opportunity for her. (maravilhoso)
- **wonderfully** /'wʌndəfʊli/ ADVERB in a wonderful way □ They played wonderfully well. (maravilhosamente)
- **wondrous** /'wʌndrəs/ ADJECTIVE if something is wondrous, you like and admire it very much □ a wondrous sight (maravilhoso)

wonky /'wɒŋki/ ADJECTIVE [wonkier, wonkiest] an informal word meaning not level or firm □ Is that table safe? It looks a bit wonky. (cambaleante)

won't /wəʊnt/ a short way to say and write will not □ He won't tell me what he saw. (abreviação de will not)

woo /wu:/ VERB [woos, wooing, wooed] to try to persuade someone to support you or to buy something from you □ The policy was intended to woo young voters. (cortejar, conquistar)

wood /wʊd/ NOUN [plural woods]
1 the hard substance that trees are made of □ a piece of wood □ a wood floor □ They were chopping wood for the fire. (madeira)
2 also **woods** an area where a lot of trees grow closely together □ We went for a walk in the woods. (bosque)
- **wooded** /'wʊdɪd/ ADJECTIVE a wooded area has trees growing on it (arborizado)
- **wooden** /'wʊdən/ ADJECTIVE
1 made of wood □ wooden toys □ a wooden chair (de madeira)
2 a wooden actor does not look natural and does not express enough emotion (enfadonho)

woodland /'wʊdlənd/ NOUN [plural woodlands] land covered with trees (arvoredo)

woodlouse /'wʊdlaʊs/ NOUN [plural woodlice] an insect that lives in rotten wood or slightly wet areas (tatuzinho)

woodpecker /'wʊd,pekə(r)/ NOUN [plural woodpeckers] a bird that uses its beak to make holes in trees (pica-pau)

woodwind /'wʊdwɪnd/ NOUN, NO PLURAL the group of musical instruments that you play by blowing, for example flutes and clarinets (instrumentos de sopro)

woodwork /'wʊdwɜ:k/ NOUN, NO PLURAL
1 the activity of making things from wood (carpintaria, marcenaria)
2 the parts of a building that are made from wood

woodworm /'wʊdwɜ:m/ NOUN [plural woodworm] an insect that eats wood, or the damage that it causes (larva de caruncho)

woody /'wʊdi/ ADJECTIVE [woodier, woodiest]
1 covered with trees (arborizado)
2 woody plants have a thick, hard stem (lenhoso)

woof /wʊf/ NOUN [plural woofs] the sound that a dog makes (au-au)

wool /wʊl/ NOUN, NO PLURAL cloth or thread made from the hair of sheep (lã) ▣ a ball of wool (bola de lã) □ a wool coat
◆ IDIOM **pull the wool over someone's eyes** to trick someone (enganar)
- **woollen** /'wʊlən/ ADJECTIVE made of wool □ a woollen blanket (de lã)
- **woolly** /'wʊli/ ADJECTIVE [woollier, woolliest] made of wool or a material similar to wool □ a woolly hat (de lã)

woolen /'wʊlən/ ADJECTIVE the US spelling of woollen (ver **woollen**)
- **wooly** /'wʊli/ ADJECTIVE the US spelling of woolly (ver **woolly**)

word /wɜ:d/ c NOUN [plural words]
1 a unit of language that is written as a group of letters with spaces on either side □ She asked me how to pronounce the word 'catastrophe'. □ He always uses lots of long words. (palavra)
2 **words** something that someone says □ What were her exact words? (palavras) ▣ Tell us what happened in your own words. (com suas próprias palavras) ▣ Her last words were 'Always believe.' (últimas palavras)
3 no plural a short conversation (palavra) ▣ I'll have a word with my Dad and see if we can borrow the car. (ter uma palavra) ▣ I want a word with you. (quero uma palavra)
4 no plural a promise (palavra, promessa) ▣ He gave me his word that he would be there. (deu sua palavra) ▣ I will always keep my word. (manter minha palavra)
5 no plural news or information about someone or something □ Have you had any word of Danielle since she left? □ + **from** There's been no word from Suki. (notícias, alguma palavra) ▣ We're having a party. Can you spread the word (= tell everyone)? (espalhar a notícia)
6 **in other words** used when you say something in a different way in order to explain it □ Our expenditure is exceeding our income at the moment. In other words, we need more money. (em outras palavras)
7 **not believe/understand, etc. a word** to not believe/understand, etc. any of what is said or written □ I couldn't hear a word of what he was saying. □ She doesn't speak a word of English (acreditar (em)/ não entender uma palavra).
8 **take someone's word for it** to believe what someone says about something □ The movie's great, but you don't have to take my word for it – go and see it yourself. (acreditar na palavra de alguém)
9 **a word of advice/warning, etc.** something that someone says to advise/warn, etc. you about something □ Let me give you a word of advice – don't believe everything she tells you. (uma palavra de aconselhamento/de aviso)
10 **word for word** using exactly the same words □ He copied the essay word for word from the Internet. (palavra por palavra)

word-perfect

▶ VERB [words, wording, worded] to choose particular words to express something ▫ *I wrote him a strongly worded letter of complaint.* (**escolher as palavras, exprimir em palavras**)

• **wording** /'wɜːdɪŋ/ NOUN, NO PLURAL the words that are used to express something ▫ *We argued about the precise wording of the letter.* (**redação, formulação**)

word-perfect /'wɜːd'pɜːfɪkt/ ADJECTIVE able to say something you have learnt, such as your part in a play, without any mistakes (**textual**)

word processing /'wɜːd 'prəʊsesɪŋ/ NOUN, NO PLURAL using a word processor to write documents (**processamento de texto**)

• **word processor** /'wɜːd 'prəʊsesə(r)/ NOUN [plural **word processors**] software or a computer that you use for writing documents (**processador de texto**)

wordy /'wɜːdɪ/ ADJECTIVE [wordier, wordiest] using too many words ▫ *a wordy reply* (**prolixo**)

wore /wɔː(r)/ PAST TENSE OF wear (ver **wear**)

work /wɜːk/ c VERB [works, working, worked]

1 to do something that needs effort or energy (**trabalhar**) ▫ + **on** *She's working on another novel.* ▫ + **to do something** *We have been working to improve awareness of homelessness.* ▣ *We all need to work hard to make this event a success.* (**trabalhar duro**)

2 to have a job that you are paid to do ▫ + **for** *He works for a shipping company.* ▫ + **as** *I was working as a nurse at the time.* (**trabalhar**)

3 to operate correctly ▫ *My e-mail isn't working at the moment.* (**funcionar**)

4 to be successful or effective ▫ *The new treatment seems to be working.* (**funcionar, dar certo**) ▣ *Our plan to trick him worked well.* (**funcionou bem**)

5 to operate a machine or a piece of equipment ▫ *I don't know how to work the heating.* (**trabalhar, fazer funcionar**)

6 to gradually move into a different position (**mover-se em uma direção**) ▣ *These tiny particles can work their way into your lungs.* (**avançar**) ▣ *All the knots had begun to work loose.* (**soltar-se**)

7 work your way to achieve something gradually ▫ *He worked his way up to the position of chairman.* ▫ *They have worked their way back into the competition.* (**avançar com esforço**)

◆ PHRASAL VERBS **work at something** to try to improve something ▫ *I'm working at staying calm.* (**tentar melhorar**) **work off something** to get rid of something such as an emotion or food you have eaten ▫ *I went for a walk to work off my lunch.* (**descarregar uma emoção, trabalhar a digestão**) **work on something** to try to improve something ▫ *He needs to work on his spoken English.* (**aprimorar**) **work out 1** if a plan or a situation works out, it is successful ▫ *I hope everything works out for you.* (**dar certo**) **2** to end

worker

in a particular way ▫ *The arrangement worked out well for me.* (**terminar, acabar**) **3** to do exercises to make your body stronger ▫ *I work out four times a week.* (**treinar**) **work something out 1** to be able to understand something or make a decision about something ▫ + **question word** *There was a message on the back, but I couldn't work out what it said.* ▫ *I worked out how to put the tent up.* (**entender, decidir**) **2** to calculate something ▫ *I've worked out how much tax I owe.* ▫ *The doctors have worked out the correct dose for me.* (**calcular**) **work out at something** to be the result of a calculation ▫ *The cost works out at £150 per person.* (**resultar**) **work up something** to create something, especially a feeling ▫ *I can't work up the enthusiasm to phone him.* ▫ *Let's go for a walk to work up a bit of an appetite.* (**despertar**) **work up to something** to gradually prepare yourself to do something difficult ▫ *It took me over two years to work up to running a marathon.* (**preparar-se para**)

▶ NOUN [plural **works**]

1 no plural an activity that needs effort (**trabalho**) ▣ *It was hard work clearing up after the party.* (**trabalho pesado**) ▣ *There's still a lot of work to do before the website will be ready.* (**trabalho para fazer**)

2 no plural someone's job, or the place they go to do it (**trabalho**) ▣ *I go to work at 8.* ▫ *I usually go to the gym before work.* (**vou para o trabalho**) ▫ *My work involves talking to doctors.*

3 no plural the things that you create or do when you are working ▫ *I've done a lot of work with young people.* ▫ *Hand your work in to the teacher.* (**trabalho**)

4 something produced by an artist, musician, writer etc. ▫ *Her early works are quite different.* (**obra**)

5 get/set to work to start working ▫ *We set to work on the garden.* (**iniciar o trabalho/pôr mãos à obra**)

• **workable** /'wɜːkəbəl/ ADJECTIVE a workable system or plan is practical and will be effective (**viável**)

workbench /'wɜːkbentʃ/ NOUN [plural **workbenches**] a table where you work with tools (**bancada de trabalho**)

workbook /'wɜːkbʊk/ NOUN [plural **workbooks**] am book for students which has questions, and spaces to write the answers (**livro de exercícios**)

worked-up /'wɜːkt'ʌp/ ADJECTIVE very excited or upset (**muito aborrecido ou animado**)

worker /'wɜːkə(r)/ NOUN [plural **workers**]

1 someone who works for a company or organization, but who is not a manager ▫ *steel workers* (**trabalhador**)

2 someone who works in a particular way ▫ *a fast/ good worker* (**trabalhador**)

workforce /ˈwɜːfɔːs/ NOUN, NO PLURAL all the people who work in a country or in a particular company (**mão de obra**)

working /ˈwɜːkɪŋ/ ▶ ADJECTIVE

1 to do with your job (**de trabalho**) ▣ *They campaigned for better working conditions.* (**condições de trabalho**) ▣ *He'd spent his whole working life in the same job.* (**anos de trabalho**) ▣ *He wanted to reduce his working hours.* (**horas de trabalho**)

2 having a job □ *working mothers* (**ativo**)

3 a working knowledge of something a basic knowledge of something which is enough for you to do something effectively □ *She had acquired a working knowledge of most European languages.* (**conhecimento prático**)

4 in working order working correctly, and not broken □ *The clock isn't in working order.* (**funcionando bem**)

▶ NOUN

1 no plural a particular way of working □ *Parents of young children are allowed to request flexible working.* (**trabalho**)

2 workings the way in which something works □ *She tried to explain to me the mysterious workings of the stock market.* (**sistema de funcionamento**)

working class /ˈwɜːkɪŋ ˈklɑːs/ C NOUN [plural working classes] the social class that consists mainly of people who do physical work and do not have much money (**classe operária**)

▶ ADJECTIVE to do with the working class □ *working class families* (**operário**)

workload /ˈwɜːkləʊd/ NOUN [plural workloads] the amount of work that you have to do □ *The workload of most teachers has increased.* (**carga de trabalho**)

workman /ˈwɜːkmən/ NOUN [plural workmen] a man who does work such as building or repairing things (**operário**)

• **workmanship** /ˈwɜːkmənʃɪp/ NOUN, NO PLURAL the skill that is used for making something □ *The workmanship was poor.* (**habilidade**)

workmate /ˈwɜːkmeɪt/ NOUN [plural workmates] someone who you work with (**colega de trabalho**)

works of art NOUN [plural works of art] something which an artist has painted or made □ *The gallery houses the country's best-known works of art.* (**obra de arte**)

workout /ˈwɜːkaʊt/ NOUN [plural workouts] an occasion when you do exercises to make you stronger (**treino**)

work permit /ˈwɜːk ˈpɜːmɪt/ NOUN [plural work permits] a document that gives you the right to work in a country (**permissão de trabalho**)

workplace /ˈwɜːkpleɪs/ NOUN [plural workplaces] a building or room where people work (**local de trabalho**)

workshop /ˈwɜːkʃɒp/ NOUN [plural workshops]

1 a meeting to learn more about something by discussing it and doing practical exercises □ *a drama workshop* (**oficina**)

2 a place where things are built or repaired (**oficina**)

workstation /ˈwɜːkˌsteɪʃən/ NOUN [plural workstations] a computer and the desk and area around it in an office (**local de trabalho com o computador**)

work surface or **worktop** /ˈwɜːktɒp/ NOUN [plural work surfaces or worktops] a flat surface in a kitchen for working on (**bancada**)

world /wɜːld/ ▶ NOUN [plural worlds]

1 the world the Earth or all the people living on it □ *He is the tallest man in the world.* □ *The whole world is affected by global warming.* □ *He longed to travel the world.* □ *She really wants to change the world.* (**mundo**)

2 the people and things involved in a particular activity □ *He is famous in the world of antiques.* (**mundo**)

3 an area of the world or a group of countries with a particular characteristic □ *the Arab world* □ *Many of the goods we import are from the developing world.* (**mundo**)

4 a planet □ *a creature from another world* (**mundo**)

5 a life or a place that has been invented □ *His stories take us to a mysterious world of talking animals.* (**mundo**) ▣ *You're living in a fantasy world.* (**mundo da fantasia**)

♦ IDIOM **out of this world** of extremely good quality □ *The cream cakes are out of this world.* (**do outro mundo**)

▶ ADJECTIVE relating to the whole world □ *world peace* □ *a world record* (**mundial**)

world-class /ˈwɜːldˈklɑːs/ ADJECTIVE being one of the best in the world □ *world-class tennis players* (**classe mundial**)

world-famous /ˈwɜːldˈfeɪməs/ ADJECTIVE famous in many parts of the world □ *a world-famous writer* (**mundialmente famoso**)

worldly /ˈwɜːldli/ ADJECTIVE [worldlier, worldliest]

1 a worldly person has a lot of experience of life (**experiente**)

2 your worldly goods/possessions everything that you own (**bens mundanos**)

worldwide /ˈwɜːldwaɪd/ ADJECTIVE, ADVERB everywhere in the world □ *The incident attracted worldwide attention.* □ *The virus has killed 144 people worldwide.* (**mundial**)

World Wide Web /ˈwɜːld waɪd ˈweb/ NOUN, NO PLURAL all the websites that exist on the Internet (**rede mundial de sites**)

worm /wɜːm/ ▶ NOUN [plural worms] a long, thin, soft creature with no bones or legs which lives in soil (**verme**)

worn

▶ VERB [worms, worming, wormed] **worm your way into something** a disapproving phrase meaning to get into a situation by gradually making people like and trust you □ *She had wormed her way into the job.* (insinuar-se)

♦ PHRASAL VERB **worm something out of someone** to persuade someone to tell you something (conseguir saber com artimanhas)

worn /wɔːn/ ▶ PAST PARTICIPLE OF **wear** (ver **wear**)
▶ ADJECTIVE old and slightly damaged □ *The carpet is worn and dirty.* (usado, desgastado)

worn-out /ˌwɔːnˈaʊt/ ADJECTIVE
1 very tired (exausto)
2 too old or damaged to use □ *worn-out trousers*

worried /ˈwʌrɪd/ ADJECTIVE thinking a lot about problems or bad things that could happen □ + *about* *I'm worried about what will happen if I fail my exams.* □ + *that* *He was worried that Amy wouldn't like him.* (preocupado) 🔁 *She's worried sick about her son.* (doente de preocupação)
• **worrier** /ˈwʌrɪə(r)/ NOUN [plural **worriers**] a person who worries a lot (pessoa que vive preocupada)

worry /ˈwʌri/ ▶ VERB [worries, worrying, worried]
1 to keep thinking about a problem or something bad that might happen □ + *about* *A lot of young people worry about the future.* □ + *that* *She worried that her children might be unhappy.* (preocupar(-se))
2 to make someone feel worried (preocupar(-se)) 🔁 *It worries me that I might not be able to find a job.* (preocupa-me que)
3 Don't worry (a) said when trying to make someone feel less worried □ *Don't worry. I'm sure things will improve.* (b) used to tell someone that they do not need to do something □ *Don't worry about getting the milk. I can get it on my way home from school.* (não se preocupe)
▶ NOUN [plural **worries**]
1 something that makes you worried (preocupação) 🔁 *Lack of money is a real worry at the moment.* (preocupação real)
2 no plural the feeling of being worried □ *Some medical tests can lead to unnecessary worry or anxiety.* (preocupação)
• **worrying** /ˈwʌriɪŋ/ ADJECTIVE making you feel worried □ *a worrying development* (preocupante)
• **worryingly** /ˈwʌriɪŋli/ ADVERB □ *in a way that is worrying* □ *Water supplies are worryingly low.* (preocupantemente)

worse /wɜːs/ ▶ ADJECTIVE
1 of a lower standard, or more unpleasant (pior) 🔁 *The situation will get worse.* (ficar pior) □ + *than* *The damage was worse than expected.*
2 more ill □ *I felt worse yesterday.* (pior)
▶ ADVERB
1 more badly, or more severely □ + *than* *His headache had returned worse than ever.* (pior)
2 not as well □ + *than* *Some of the children were treated worse than others.* (pior)

▶ NOUN, NO PLURAL
1 something more unpleasant □ *Worse was still to come.* (o pior)
2 for the worse if a situation changes for the worse, it becomes more difficult or more unpleasant □ *He warned that things could change for the worse.* (para o pior)
• **worsen** /ˈwɜːsən/ VERB [worsens, worsening, worsened] to become worse, or to make something become worse □ *Increased traffic jams will worsen pollution.* □ *The situation is likely to worsen.* (piorar)

worse off /ˌwɜːs ˈɒf/ ADJECTIVE
1 poorer or in a worse situation □ *Students are worse off than they were ten years ago.* (mais pobre, em pior situação)
2 in a worse situation □ *You'd be even worse off without your car.* (em pior situação)

worship /ˈwɜːʃɪp/ ▶ VERB [worships, worshipping, worshipped]
1 to show respect for a god by praying, having religious ceremonies, etc. (adorar, cultuar)
2 to admire someone so much that you do not see their faults (adorar)
▶ NOUN, NO PLURAL religious services and other ways of worshipping (culto, adoração) 🔁 *a place of worship* (= a church, mosque, etc.) (local de culto, adoração)
• **worshipper** /ˈwɜːʃɪpə(r)/ NOUN [plural **worshippers**] someone who is worshipping in a religious building (adorador)

worst /wɜːst/ ▶ ADJECTIVE **the worst** most severe, most unpleasant, or most difficult □ *It was the worst storm we'd ever seen.* (o pior)
▶ ADVERB most badly □ *I scored worst in the test.* □ *The area worst affected by the floods was the North.* (pior)
▶ NOUN
1 the worst the person or thing that is worse than all the others □ *I've had some pretty bad exams but this was the worst.* (o pior)
2 at (the) worst used for saying what the most unpleasant or difficult situation would be □ *At worst, you might have to wait an hour for the bus.* (na pior das hipóteses)
3 if the worst comes to the worst if a situation develops in the most unpleasant or difficult way □ *If the worst comes to the worst, I'll just have to work at the weekend too.* (se o pior dos piores acontecer)

worst-case /ˌwɜːstˈkeɪs/ ADJECTIVE (pior caso) **worst-case scenario** the worst thing that could possibly happen in a situation □ *The worst-case scenario is that we lose our home.* (no pior cenário)

worth /wɜːθ/ ▶ ADJECTIVE
1 having a particular value □ *The ring is worth £1000.* (valor de)

2 used for saying that something is useful, important or enjoyable □ *The museum is worth a visit.* □ **+ ing** *It would be worth asking a solicitor for advice.* (vale a pena, digno de) 🔁 *The project was hard work but it was* worth it. (vale a pena)

▶ NOUN, NO PLURAL

1 £10, $50, etc. worth of something an amount of something that costs £10, $50, etc. to buy □ *About £10,000 worth of jewellery was stolen in the robbery.* (o valor de $10, $50 em)

2 a week's/a month's, etc. worth of something an amount for a week/month, etc. □ *A month's worth of rain fell in less than 24 hours.* (o valor de uma semana/um mês etc. em)

3 how useful someone or something is (valor) 🔁 *Since joining the team, he has* proved *his* worth. (provar seu valor)

• **worthless** /ˈwɜːθlɪs/ ADJECTIVE

1 not important or not useful □ *He felt worthless.* (sem valor, desvalorizado)

2 having no financial value □ *The necklace is worthless.* (sem valor, imprestável)

worthwhile /ˌwɜːθˈwaɪl/ ADJECTIVE if something is worthwhile, it is useful or enjoyable although you have to spend time or effort doing it □ *a worthwhile project* (que vale a pena)

worthy /ˈwɜːði/ ADJECTIVE [**worthier, worthiest**]

1 deserving respect or support □ *The German team were worthy winners.* (merecedor) 🔁 *She gives a lot of money to* worthy causes. (causas merecedoras)

2 be worthy of something a formal phrase meaning to deserve something □ *The offer is certainly worthy of consideration.* (digno de consideração)

would /wʊd/ MODAL VERB

1 used to say what might happen in a particular situation □ *What would you do if you won a million dollars?* □ *What would happen if there was a fire?* (usado como futuro do pretérito)

2 used as the past tense of will to talk about what was going to happen □ *I didn't think she would agree.* □ *He said he would come later.* (passado de will)

3 used as the past tense of will to talk about whether someone or something was willing or able to do something □ *My camera wouldn't work.* □ *She wouldn't help me.* (passado de will)

4 used for talking about what you think is true, or what you think the reason for something is □ *You would find it very hard to get another job.* □ *It would be difficult to manage without a car.* □ *Why would he want to hurt them?* (indicação de hipóteses)

5 would you used in polite questions and offers □ *Would you like a drink?* □ *Would you mind helping me with these boxes?* (você gostaria/se importaria de)

6 would like/prefer, etc. used to say what you want or what you want to do □ *I would like to see a different doctor.* □ *I would really like a hot shower.* (gostaria, preferiria)

would-be /ˈwʊdbiː/ ADJECTIVE describes what people would like to be or become □ *a group of would-be astronauts* (que pretende ser/suposto)

wouldn't /ˈwʊdənt/ a short way to say and write would not □ *She wouldn't go.* (abreviação de would not)

would've /ˈwʊdəv/ a short way to say and write would have □ *It would've been nice to see her.* (abreviação de would have)

wound¹ /waʊnd/ PAST TENSE AND PAST PARTICIPLE OF **wind** (ver wind)

wound² /wuːnd/ C NOUN [plural **wounds**]

1 an injury, especially where the skin is broken □ *gunshot wounds* (ferimento)

2 harm to someone's emotions, a relationship, etc. (ferimento, ferida) 🔁 *The party has tried to* heal the wounds *caused by the leadership contest.* (curar as feridas)

▶ VERB [**wounds, wounding, wounded**]

1 to injure a person or an animal, especially in a way that breaks their skin □ *She was seriously wounded in the attack.* (ferir, machucar)

2 to make someone feel very upset □ *He was deeply wounded by the criticism of his work.* (magoar, ferir)

• **wounded** /ˈwuːndɪd/ ADJECTIVE a wounded soldier or animal has been injured (ferido)

wove /wəʊv/ PAST TENSE OF **weave** (ver weave)

woven /ˈwəʊvən/ PAST PARTICIPLE OF **weave** (ver weave)

wow /waʊ/ EXCLAMATION an informal word used to express surprise or admiration □ *Wow! You look great!* (uau!)

WPC /ˌdʌbəljuːpiːˈsiː/ ABBREVIATION woman police officer; used before a female police officer's name □ *WPC Hobbs* (policial feminina)

wrangle /ˈræŋɡəl/ ▶ VERB [**wrangles, wrangling, wrangled**] to argue with someone for a long time, often about something complicated □ *They're still wrangling over the divorce settlement.* (discutir)

▶ NOUN [plural **wrangles**] an argument that goes on for a long time, often about something complicated (discussão) 🔁 *The club faces a* legal wrangle *over the sale of its ground.* (disputa legal)

wrap /ræp/ VERB [**wraps, wrapping, wrapped**] to cover something by putting paper or another material around it □ *Would you like the chocolates wrapped?* □ *We wrapped all the glasses in tissue paper.* (embrulhar)

◆ PHRASAL VERBS **wrap something around/round something 1** to put something such as paper or cloth around something to cover it □ *I wrapped an old shirt around the wound.* (embrulhar em) **2** if you wrap your arms, fingers or legs around

wrapping paper

something, you put them tightly around it (**envolver em**) **wrap up** to put on warm clothes (**agasalhar-se**) 🔄 *Make sure you wrap up warm.* (**agasalhar-se bem**) **wrap something up**

1 to cover something with paper or another material, especially a present ☐ *We wrapped up the toys.* (**embrulhar**)

2 to finish an activity ☐ *We need to wrap up the meeting now.* (**terminar**)

3 be wrapped up in something to give a lot of attention to something, so that you do not have time for other things (**estar envolvido em**)

• **wrapper** /ˈræpə(r)/ NOUN [*plural* **wrappers**] a piece of paper or other material that something is wrapped in (**invólucro**) 🔄 *sweet wrappers* (**papéis de bala**)

wrapping paper /ˈræpɪŋ ˌpeɪpə(r)/ NOUN, NO PLURAL decorated paper used for wrapping presents (**papel de presente/embrulho**)

wrath /rɒθ/ NOUN, NO PLURAL a formal word meaning great anger (**ira**)

wreak /riːk/ VERB [**wreaks, wreaking, wreaked**] to cause a lot of damage or harm (**causar**) 🔄 *Rabbits can wreak havoc in your garden.* (**causar uma devastação**)

wreath /riːθ/ NOUN [*plural* **wreaths**] an arrangement of flowers and leaves in the shape of a ring, used as a decoration at Christmas or for a coffin (= container someone is buried in) or grave (= place someone is buried) (**guirlanda, coroa de flores**)

wreathe /riːð/ VERB [**wreathes, wreathing, wreathed**]

1 if something is wreathed in smoke, mist (= very small drops of water in the air), etc., it is surrounded by it (**cobrir, coroar, envolver**)

2 if someone is wreathed in smiles, they are smiling a lot (**coberto, envolvido**)

wreck /rek/ ▶ VERB [**wrecks, wrecking, wrecked**]

1 to destroy or badly damage something ☐ *He wrecked all our new furniture.* ☐ *A knee injury has wrecked his chance of playing in the final.* (**destroçar**)

2 if a ship is wrecked, it is damaged and sinks (**naufragar**)

▶ NOUN [*plural* **wrecks**]

1 a ship that has sunk (**naufrágio**)

2 a badly damaged vehicle that has crashed (**destroço**)

3 someone who looks or feels very tired and untidy (**estar um caco**)

• **wreckage** /ˈrekɪdʒ/ NOUN, NO PLURAL the damaged pieces left after a vehicle has been wrecked ☐ *He was trapped in the wreckage for over an hour.* (**destroço**)

wren /ren/ NOUN [*plural* **wrens**] a small bird with brown feathers and a short tail (**corruíra**)

wrench /rentʃ/ ▶ VERB [**wrenches, wrenching, wrenched**]

wrinkle

1 to pull or twist something very hard so that it comes out of its position ☐ *I managed to wrench the knife out of his hand.* (**arrancar**)

2 to hurt part of your body by twisting it ☐ *He fell and wrenched his ankle.* (**luxou**)

▶ NOUN [*plural* **wrenches**]

1 when you feel sad because you must leave something or someone you like or love ☐ *Leaving Cambridge was a real wrench.*

2 a hard pull or twist (**luxação**)

3 a tool used to turn things (**chave-inglesa**)

wrestle /ˈresəl/ VERB [**wrestles, wrestling, wrestled**] to fight with someone by holding them and trying to throw them to the ground (**lutar corpo a corpo**)

♦ PHRASAL VERB **wrestle with something** to try to deal with a difficult problem, situation or emotion ☐ *Some football clubs are still wrestling with the issue of racism.* (**enfrentar um problema**)

• **wrestler** /ˈreslə(r)/ NOUN [*plural* **wrestlers**] someone who wrestles as a sport (**lutador**)

• **wrestling** /ˈreslɪŋ/ NOUN, NO PLURAL the sport of fighting by holding someone and trying to throw them to the ground (**luta**)

wretch /retʃ/ NOUN [*plural* **wretches**] someone you feel sorry for because they are having problems ☐ *The poor wretch did not even own a pair of shoes.* (**infeliz, desgraçado**)

• **wretched** /ˈretʃɪd/ ADJECTIVE

1 annoying ☐ *Where's that wretched cat?* (**miserável**)

2 very unpleasant or of bad quality ☐ *It was a wretched start to the day.* (**miserável**)

3 very unhappy or ill ☐ *I felt wretched, knowing I had let her down.* (**miserável**)

wriggle /ˈrɪɡəl/ VERB [**wriggles, wriggling, wriggled**] to make short, twisting movements ☐ *Stop wriggling about in your chair and sit still!* (**remexer(-se), esquivar(-se)**)

♦ PHRASAL VERB **wriggle out of something** to avoid doing something you should do ☐ *She managed to wriggle out of the cooking.* (**esquivar-se**)

wring /rɪŋ/ VERB [**wrings, wringing, wrung**]

1 to twist a wet cloth or piece of clothing so that most of the water is forced out (**torcer**)

2 wring your hands to twist your hands together because you are upset or nervous (**contorcer as mãos**)

3 wring someone's neck if you say you will wring someone's neck, you mean that you are very angry with them and want to punish them (**torcer o pescoço de alguém**)

wrinkle /ˈrɪŋkəl/ ▶ NOUN [*plural* **wrinkles**]

1 a line in your skin, caused by getting older (**ruga**)

2 a line where something such as a piece of cloth is slightly folded (**vinco, prega, dobra**)

▶ VERB [**wrinkles, wrinkling, wrinkled**] to move part of your face, especially your nose, so that lines appear on your skin (**enrugar**)

- **wrinkly** /ˈrɪŋklɪ/ ADJECTIVE [**wrinklier, wrinkliest**] having a lot of wrinkles (**enrugado**)

wrist /rɪst/ NOUN [plural **wrists**] the part of your body where your arm joins your hand (**pulso**)

wristband /ˈrɪstbænd/ NOUN [plural **wristbands**]
1 a piece of thick material that you wear around your wrist when you play sport (**munhequeira**)
2 a thin piece of material, usually plastic, that you wear around your wrist to show that you have particular opinions or support a particular person or group of people with problems (**pulseira**)

wristwatch /ˈrɪstwɒtʃ/ NOUN [plural **wristwatches**] a watch that you wear on your wrist (**relógio de pulso**)

write /raɪt/ VERB [**writes, writing, wrote, written**]

1 to form letters, words or numbers, usually on paper using a pen or pencil □ *Write your name and address on the top of the paper.* (**escrever**)
2 to use words to make a story, essay, book, letter, song, etc. □ *She has written four novels.* □ *I wrote a note and left it on the table.* □ **+ about** *She writes about gardening.* (**escrever**)
3 to send a letter or a message to someone □ **+ to** *I wrote to the manager to complain.* □ *We'll write in a week or two.* (**escrever**)
4 if you write music, you put the symbols for the notes on special paper □ *He wrote his second symphony when he was fifteen.* (**compor**)
5 if you write a computer program, you create it (**criar**)

♦ PHRASAL VERBS **write something down** to write something on a piece of paper, especially so that you do not forget it □ *I wrote down his phone number.* (**anotar**) **write off** to write to an organization in order to get something from it □ *We wrote off for tickets.* (**escrever solicitando um produto**) **write something/someone off** to think that something or someone is not useful or successful □ *When you get to fifty, most employers just write you off.* (**descartar**) **write something off 1** to say officially that an amount of money does not have to be paid or will not be paid □ *The company had to write off large debts.* (**dar por perdido**) **2** to damage a vehicle so badly that it cannot be used again (**dar por perdido**) **write something up** to write an article, a report, etc. using notes that you have made □ *We have to write up the results of our experiments.* (**relatar, descrever**)

write-off /ˈraɪtɒf/ NOUN [plural **write-offs**] a vehicle that has been so badly damaged in an accident that it cannot be repaired (**perda total**)

writer /ˈraɪtə(r)/ NOUN [plural **writers**]

1 someone who writes books, plays, newspaper articles, etc. as a job (**escritor**)
2 someone who has written something (**escritor**)

write-up /ˈraɪtʌp/ NOUN [plural **write-ups**] an article in a newspaper, magazine, etc. about something such as a new performance, product, etc. □ *The Evening Herald gave the show an enthusiastic write-up.* (**destaque**)

writhe /raɪð/ VERB [**writhes, writhing, writhed**] to twist your body because you feel uncomfortable or in pain □ *He lay writhing in agony.* (**contorcer-se**)

writing /ˈraɪtɪŋ/ NOUN [plural **writings**]
1 the forming of letters and words on paper or other surfaces so that they can be read (**escrita**)
2 your writing is the way you write (**escrita**)
3 the things that a writer has written (**escritos**)

writing paper /ˈraɪtɪŋ ˈpeɪpə(r)/ NOUN, NO PLURAL good quality paper for writing letters on (**papel de carta**)

written /ˈrɪtən/ ▶ PAST PARTICIPLE OF **write** (**ver write**)

▶ ADJECTIVE

1 using writing □ *He received a written warning.* (**por escrito**)
2 a written exam is one in which you have to write something (**exame escrito**)

wrong /rɒŋ/ ▶ ADJECTIVE

1 if something is wrong, there is a problem □ **+ with** *Is there something wrong with David? He doesn't look happy.* □ *What's wrong? I thought you'd be pleased to see me.* (**errado**)
2 not correct □ *That was the wrong answer.* □ *We made the wrong decision.* □ *You're looking in the wrong place.* □ **+ about** *He was wrong about Helen.* (**errado**)
3 not morally right □ *She has done nothing wrong.* □ **+ to do something** *It would be wrong to deceive him.* (**errado**)
4 not suitable □ **+ with** *If you want flowers, what's wrong with roses?* □ **+ for** *The dress was wrong for a wedding.* (**impróprio, errado**)

♦ IDIOM **get (hold of) the wrong end of the stick** to think that something is true when it is not □ *I think you've got the wrong end of the stick – you don't need to pay any extra.* (**entender mal**)

▶ ADVERB

1 in a way that is not correct □ *I think I have spelt your name wrong.* □ *He guessed wrong.* (**erroneamente**)
2 **go wrong** (a) to stop working correctly □ *My watch has gone wrong.* (b) to stop being successful □ *Everything went wrong after Nik left.* (**funcionar mal; dar errado**)

▶ NOUN, NO PLURAL

1 behaviour that is not morally correct (**errado**) □ *He doesn't seem to know the difference between right and wrong.* (**certo e errado**) □ *I accept that I did wrong.*
2 **be in the wrong** to be the person who is responsible for a mistake or doing something bad □ *The way she tells it, you'd think it was us that were in the wrong.* (**ser culpado**)

- **wrongdoing** /ˈrɒŋˌduːɪŋ/ NOUN, NO PLURAL bad or illegal behaviour (**transgressão**) 🔁 *He denied any wrongdoing.* (**negar qualquer crime**)
- **wrongful** /ˈrɒŋfʊl/ ADJECTIVE not correct, especially because of being unfair or illegal □ *He spent three years in jail following his wrongful conviction for murder.* (**ilegal, injusto**)
- **wrongly** /ˈrɒŋlɪ/ ADVERB not correctly □ *The plug had been fitted wrongly so the machine did not work.* □ *She was wrongly accused of fraud.* (**incorretamente**)

wrote /rəʊt/ PAST TENSE OF **write** (*ver* **write**)

wrung /rʌŋ/ PAST TENSE AND PAST PARTICIPLE OF **wring** (*ver* **wring**)

wry /raɪ/ ADJECTIVE [**wryer, wryest**] showing that you think a bad situation is slightly funny too □ *a wry smile* □ *a wry comment* (**irônico**)

WWW /ˌdʌbəljuːdʌbəljuːˈdʌbəljuː/ *or* www ABBREVIATION World Wide Web; the Internet (**internet**)

X

X or **x** /eks/
 1 the 24th letter of the alphabet (**a vigésima quarta letra do alfabeto**)
 2 used when you do not know or do not want to say the name of a person or thing □ *The man was referred to as Mr X.* (**representa o nome de uma pessoa ou coisa desconhecida**)
 3 used for representing a number or quantity that is not known. A maths word. (**símbolo matemático**)
 4 used for representing a kiss at the end of a letter (**símbolo para "beijo"**)

xenophobia /ˌzenəˈfəʊbɪə/ NOUN, NO PLURAL a dislike of foreign people and things (**xenofobia**)

Xerox /ˈzɪərɒks/ ▶ NOUN [*plural* **Xeroxes**] a copy of a document made with a Xerox machine. A trademark. (**fotocópia (marca registrada)**)
 ▶ VERB [**Xeroxes, Xeroxing, Xeroxed**] to make a copy of a document with a Xerox machine (**xerocar**)

Xmas /ˈeksməs/ NOUN an informal short way of writing **Christmas** (**abrev. Natal**)

XML /ˌeksemˈel/ ABBREVIATION extensible mark up language; a way of organizing information on a computer which makes the information easy to use in different programs. A computing word. (**linguagem de marcação extensível**)

X-ray /ˈeksreɪ/ ▶ NOUN [*plural* **X-rays**] a special kind of photograph that shows the inside parts of someone's body (**radiografia, raios X**)
 ▶ VERB [**X-rays, X-raying, X-rayed**] to make a picture of the inside of someone's body (**fazer uma radiografia, fazer raios X**)

xylophone /ˈzaɪləfəʊn/ NOUN [*plural* **xylophones**] a musical instrument made up of a set of wooden or metal bars that make different notes when you hit them with hammers (**xilofone**)

Y y

Y or **y** /waɪ/ the 25th letter of the alphabet (**a vigésima quinta letra do alfabeto**)

yacht /jɒt/ NOUN [plural **yachts**] a boat with sails that you use for racing or for pleasure (**iate**)

yachtsman /ˈjɒtsmən/ NOUN [plural **yachtsmen**] a man who sails a yacht (**o iatista**)

yachtswoman /ˈjɒtsˌwʊmən/ NOUN [plural **yachtswomen**] a woman who sails a yacht (**a iatista**)

yak /jæk/ NOUN [plural **yaks**] an animal like a cow with long hair and horns (**iaque**)

yam /jæm/ NOUN [plural **yams**] a vegetable like a potato that grows in tropical countries (**inhame**)

Yank /jæŋk/ NOUN [plural **Yanks**] an informal and slightly offensive word for someone from the United States (**ianque**)

yank /jæŋk/ VERB [**yanks, yanking, yanked**] to suddenly pull something hard □ He yanked the book out of my hand. (**arrancar, puxar**)

yap /jæp/ ▶ VERB [**yaps, yapping, yapped**] if a dog yaps, it makes a quick, high sound (**ganir**)
▶ NOUN [plural **yaps**] a quick, high sound that a dog makes (**ganido**)

yard¹ /jɑːd/ NOUN [plural **yards**] a unit for measuring length, equal to 3 feet (**jarda**)

yard² /jɑːd/ NOUN [plural **yards**]
1 an area of land, often with a fence or wall around it, and often used for a particular purpose □ The dogs have a large exercise yard. (**pátio, quintal, terreiro**)
2 a US word for a garden next to a house (**jardim**)

yarn /jɑːn/ NOUN [plural **yarns**]
1 thread made from wool, cotton, etc. used for making cloth (**fio**)
2 an exciting story, which may not be true □ He told us some great yarns about life in the army. (**fábula**)

yashmak /ˈjæʃmæk/ NOUN [plural **yashmaks**] a piece of cloth that some Muslim women use to cover their face (**véu**)

yawn /jɔːn/ ▶ VERB [**yawns, yawning, yawned**] to open your mouth very wide and breathe in, because you are feeling tired or bored (**bocejar**)
▶ NOUN [plural **yawns**] the sound or action of someone yawning (**bocejo**)

• **yawning** /ˈjɔːnɪŋ/ ADJECTIVE a **yawning gap** (a) a very large hole or place where something is missing □ There are yawning gaps in his knowledge. (**escancarado**) (b) a very big difference □ the yawning gap between rich and poor (**imensa lacuna**)

yeah /jeə/ EXCLAMATION an informal way of saying yes (**sim**)

year /jɪə(r)/ NOUN [plural **years**]
1 a period of 365 or 366 days, marking the length of time it takes for the Earth to go around the sun, especially the period from 1 January to 31 December □ We're going to America next year. □ I spent a year working in Paris. □ In recent years, the building has not been used much. (**ano**)
2 three/sixteen/fifty, etc. years old used to talk about the age of someone or something □ He's only twelve years old. □ Our house is almost three hundred years old. (**anos de idade**)
3 a three/sixteen/fifty year-old a person who is a particular age □ You're acting like a five year-old! (**com ... anos**)
4 the academic/financial, etc. year a period of twelve months used by a particular organization, system, etc. (**ano acadêmico, financeiro etc.**)
5 years a long period of time 🔁 I haven't been to Madrid for years. (**durante/há muitos anos**)
6 the students at a school, college, etc. who start in the same year □ He was in my year at school. □ We studied the Egyptians in year 3. (**ano**)

> ▶ When saying how old someone is, do not say 'years'. Say only the number or a number + 'years old': □ She is eight.
> ✓ She is eight years old.
> ✗ She is eight years.

• **yearly** /ˈjɪəlɪ/ ADJECTIVE, ADVERB happening or done every year □ our yearly holiday □ Accounts must be prepared yearly. (**anual, anualmente**)

yearn /jɜːn/ VERB [**yearns, yearning, yearned**] to want something very much □ As a teenager, I yearned for the big city. (**ansiar**)

yeast /jiːst/ NOUN, NO PLURAL a substance that is used to make bread rise (**fermento**)

yell /jel/ ▶ VERB [**yells, yelling, yelled**] to shout something loudly □ 'Let me go!' she yelled. (**berrar**)
▶ NOUN [plural **yells**] a loud shout

yellow /ˈjeləʊ/ ▶ ADJECTIVE
having the colour of the sun or a lemon □ *The garden was full of bright yellow flowers.* (amarelo)
▶ NOUN [*plural* **yellows**] the colour of the sun or a lemon (amarelo)

yelp /jelp/ ▶ VERB [**yelps, yelping, yelped**]
to make a short, high sound because of pain or excitement (latir)
▶ NOUN [*plural* **yelps**] a short, high sound (latido)

yes /jes/ EXCLAMATION
1 used to agree with someone, agree to do something, or to give a positive answer □ *'Are these shoes all right?' 'Yes, they're lovely.'* □ *'Could you help me with my homework?' 'Yes, no problem.' 'Would you like a cup of coffee?' 'Yes, please.'* (sim)

2 used to disagree with a negative statement □ *'You haven't washed your hair.' 'Yes I have.'* (sim)

yesterday /ˈjestədeɪ/ ADVERB, NOUN
the day before today □ *I saw Kim yesterday.* □ *He called me yesterday morning.* □ *Yesterday was her birthday.* (ontem)

yet /jet/ ▶ ADVERB
1 used in questions or negative statements to mean before now or before the time you are talking about □ *Have you read her new book yet?* □ *No money has changed hands yet.* □ *I have not yet had the courage to challenge her.* (ainda, já, até agora)

2 used in questions and negative statements to mean that something will not happen immediately but will happen in the future □ *Please don't leave yet.* □ *You can't go in yet.* (ainda)

3 used to emphasize how often something exists or happens (outra vez, novamente) 🔁 *Yet again, they have let us down.* (outra vez) 🔁 *Apparently, Richard has bought yet another bicycle.* (novamente outra)

4 the best/biggest/worst, etc. yet the best/biggest/worst, etc. that has ever happened or existed (o melhor, maior, pior etc. que já existiu)

5 used to say that something might happen in the future □ *Don't be too upset – she might yet turn up.* (ainda)

6 used to show how long it will be until something happens □ *It'll be a few months yet before the new road is open.* (ter ainda que fazer alguma coisa)

7 be/have yet to do something to have not done something, especially something you were expected to do □ *He has yet to apologize.*
▶ CONJUNCTION used to say something surprising after what has been said before □ *He was pleasant, yet failed to offer any real help.* □ *We claim to live in a civilized society, and yet we allow children to live in poverty.* □ *The decorations were colourful yet tasteful.* (no entanto)

yew /juː/ NOUN [*plural* **yews**]
a tree with very dark green leaves, or the wood from this tree (teixo)

Y-fronts /ˈwaɪfrʌnts/ PLURAL NOUN
a piece of underwear for men and boys that covers the bottom and has a Y-shaped opening at the front. A trademark. (cueca (marca registrada))

yield /jiːld/ ▶ VERB [**yields, yielding, yielded**]
1 to produce something useful □ *Negotiations have failed to yield results.* □ *The investment yielded a good profit.* (produzir)

2 to produce a particular amount of a crop (produzir)

3 to be forced to do something or agree to something, or to be defeated □ *The government yielded to pressure and delayed the tax rise.* □ *The army yielded to enemy forces.* (ceder)
▶ NOUN [*plural* **yields**] the amount of something that is produced □ *Farmers want cows with a high milk yield.* (produção, rendimento)

yippee /jɪˈpiː/ EXCLAMATION
a word that children use when they are pleased or excited about something (interjeição de alegria: oba! eba!)

yob /jɒb/ NOUN [*plural* **yobs**]
a young man who behaves in a rude and sometimes violent way (jovem grosseiro)

yoga /ˈjəʊɡə/ NOUN, NO PLURAL
a type of exercise for the body and the mind, which involves stretching your body and doing breathing exercises (ioga)

yogurt or yoghurt /ˈjɒɡət/ NOUN [*plural* **yogurts** or **yoghurts**]
a thick, slightly sour liquid made from milk, often with fruit added (iogurte) 🔁 *natural yoghurt* (= with no sugar or fruit added) (iogurte natural)

yolk /jəʊk/ NOUN [*plural* **yolks**]
the yellow part in the middle of an egg (gema de ovo)

Yom Kippur /ˌjɒmkɪˈpʊə(r)/ NOUN, NO PLURAL
a Jewish religious day when people do not eat or drink (Yom Kippur)

yonder /ˈjɒndə(r)/ ADVERB, DETERMINER
an old fashioned word meaning in or towards a place far away from you □ *Take my sword, and go with it to yonder river.* (longínquo)

you /juː/ PRONOUN
used to talk or write about the person or people that you are talking to □ *Do you like pizza?* □ *I'll ring you tomorrow night.* □ *Max is taller than you.* (você, tu, vocês, vós)

you'd /juːd/
a short way to say and write you had or you would □ *You'd better be careful.* □ *You'd be sorry if she left.* (abreviação de you had ou de you would)

you'll /juːl/
a short way to say and write you will □ *You'll never guess what happened next!* (abreviação de you will)

young /jʌŋ/ ▶ ADJECTIVE [**younger, youngest**]
not old □ *a young boy* □ *You're too young to stay up so late.* (jovem)

your

▶ PLURAL NOUN
1 the babies that an animal or bird has □ *a sparrow feeding its young* (**filhote**)
2 the young young people (**os jovens**)

• **youngster** /'jʌŋstə(r)/ NOUN [*plural* **youngsters**] a young person (**jovem**)

your /jɔː(r)/ DETERMINER

1 belonging to or to do with you □ *Can I borrow your pen?* (**seu, teu, vosso**)
2 belonging to or to do with people in general □ *Your school days are the happiest days of your life.* (**seu, teu, vosso**)

you're /jɔː(r)/ a short way to say and write you are □ *You're early!* (**abreviação de you are**)

yours /jɔːz/ PRONOUN

1 used to talk or write about things belonging to or to do with the person or people you are talking to □ *Which glass is yours?* (**o seu, o teu, o vosso**)
2 used at the end of a letter, before your name □ *I look forward to hearing from you. Yours, Amy.* (**atenciosamente**)

yourself /jɔːˈself/ PRONOUN [*plural* **yourselves**]

1 the reflexive form of you □ *Careful you don't cut yourself on that knife.* □ *You'll have to dry yourselves on your T-shirts.* (**você mesmo**)
2 used to show that you do something without any help from other people □ *Did you really make that skirt yourself?* (**sozinho**) 🔳 *Have you done this work all by yourself?* (**completamente sozinho**)
3 used to emphasize the pronoun you □ *You cannot film it yourselves, but you can buy a video.* (**sozinho**)
4 by yourself not with or near other people □ *It can be lonely living by yourself.* (**sozinho, só para você**)
5 to yourself without having to share with anyone else □ *You've got the house to yourself today.* (**para si mesmo**)

youth /juːθ/ NOUN [*plural* **youths**]

1 a young man □ *a gang of youths* (**jovem, rapaz**)
2 *no plural* the time in your life when you are young □ *She spent most of her youth abroad.* (**juventude**)
3 *no plural* young people □ *the youth of today* (**juventude**)

youth club /ˈjuːθ klʌb/ NOUN [*plural* **youth clubs**] a place where young people go for social activities (**clube de jovens**)

youthful /ˈjuːθfʊl/ ADJECTIVE typical of young people or seeming young □ *youthful energy* (**jovial**)

youth hostel /ˈjuːθ ˈhɒstəl/ NOUN [*plural* **youth hostels**] a simple, quite cheap hotel for travellers, especially young people (**albergue da juventude**)

you've /juːv/ a short way to say and write you have □ *You've left the door open again.* (**abreviação de you have**)

yo-yo /ˈjəʊjəʊ/ NOUN [*plural* **yo-yos**] a small, round toy that goes up and down a piece of string (**ioiô**)

yummy /ˈjʌmɪ/ ADJECTIVE yummy food tastes very good. An informal word. (**delicioso**)

yuppie or **yuppy** /ˈjʌpɪ/ NOUN [*plural* **yuppies**] a disapproving word for someone who has a good job, is young, and has a high standard of life □ *Then came the yuppies with their designer ski wear and new fast cars* (**yuppie**)

Zz

Z or **z** /zed/ the 26th letter of the alphabet (**a vigésima sexta letra do alfabeto**)

zany /ˈzeɪni/ ADJECTIVE [**zanier, zaniest**] funny and unusual □ *She's full of zany ideas.* (**maluco**)

zap /zæp/ VERB [**zaps, zapping, zapped**]
1 to destroy something quickly, often with a weapon □ *The game involves zapping aliens.* (**zapear**)
2 to move quickly between television programmes using a remote control (= device you hold in your hand to change programmes) □ *She zapped to Channel One.* (**zapear**)

zeal /ziːl/ NOUN, NO PLURAL great enthusiasm □ *The government is attacking poverty with zeal.* (**ardor**)

• **zealous** /ˈzeləs/ ADJECTIVE very enthusiastic □ *He is one of the team's most zealous supporters* (**ardoroso**)

zebra /ˈzebrə, ˈziːbrə/ NOUN [**plural zebras**] an animal like a horse with black and white stripes (**zebra**)

zebra crossing /ˈzebrə ˈkrɒsɪŋ, ˈziːbrə ˈkrɒsɪŋ/ NOUN [**plural zebra crossings**] a place where you can cross a road, marked with black and white stripes (**faixa para pedestres**)

zenith /ˈzenɪθ/ NOUN, NO PLURAL the most successful point of something □ *Scoring those five goals was the zenith of his career.* (**zênite**)

zero /ˈzɪərəʊ/ NOUN [**plural zeros**]
1 nothing or the number 0 □ *There are six zeros in one million.* (**zero**)
2 *no plural* the temperature at which water freezes □ *It was three degrees below zero.* (**zero**)
3 *no plural* no amount at all □ *Politicians have zero job security.* (**zero**)

zest /zest/ NOUN, NO PLURAL enjoyment and enthusiasm □ *Joe had a great zest for life.* (**deleite**)

zigzag /ˈzɪɡzæɡ/ ▶ NOUN [**plural zigzags**] a line with many sharp angles where it changes direction □ *a zigzag pattern* (**zigue-zague**)
▶ VERB [**zigzags, zigzagging, zigzagged**] to have or make a zigzag pattern □ *The path zigzagged up the hillside.* (**ziguezaguear**)

zinc /zɪŋk/ NOUN, NO PLURAL a blue-white metal. A chemistry word. (**zinco**)

zip /zɪp/ ▶ NOUN [**plural zips**] a device for fastening clothes or bags that has two rows of small metal or plastic parts that fit tightly together when a sliding piece is pulled along them (**zíper, fechar**)
▶ VERB [**zips, zipping, zipped**]
1 to fasten something with a zip □ *Zip up your jacket; it's cold.* (**fechar com zíper**)
2 to make the information on a computer file fit into a much smaller space, so that it can be sent or stored more easily. A computing word. □ *I'll zip the file before I send it to you.* (**compactar, zipar**)
3 to move somewhere very quickly, or to do something very quickly □ *The bullet zipped by his head.* □ *He zipped through the answers.* (**sair correndo, mover com energia**)

zip code /ˈzɪp ˌkəʊd/ NOUN [**plural zip codes**] the US phrase for post code (**código postal**)

zipper /ˈzɪpə(r)/ NOUN [**plural zippers**] the US word for zip (**zíper**)

zodiac /ˈzəʊdiæk/ NOUN, NO PLURAL the zodiac the twelve signs of the groups of stars that some people believe influence your life (**zodíaco**) □ *What sign of the zodiac are you?* (**signo do zodíaco**)

zombie /ˈzɒmbi/ NOUN [**plural zombies**]
1 in some religions or stories, a dead body that looks as if it is alive because of magic (**zumbi**)
2 someone who seems to be very slow or stupid, often because they are very tired (**zumbi**)

zone /zəʊn/ NOUN [**plural zones**] an area that has a particular feature or where a particular thing happens (**zona**) □ *This is a danger zone because of landslides.* (**zona perigosa**) □ *a smoke-free zone* □ *a war zone*

zoo /zuː/ NOUN [**plural zoos**] a place where wild animals are kept for people to look at (**jardim zoológico**)

zoological /ˌzəʊəˈlɒdʒɪkəl/ ADJECTIVE to do with animals (**zoológico**)

• **zoology** /zəʊˈɒlədʒi/ NOUN, NO PLURAL the study of animals (**zoologia**)

zoom /zuːm/ VERB [**zooms, zooming, zoomed**] to go somewhere very fast, especially with a loud noise □ *The rocket zoomed up into the air.* (**passar zunindo**)

- PHRASAL VERBS **zoom in** if a camera zooms in, it makes the thing being photographed look bigger **(dar um zoom em) zoom out** if a camera zooms out, it fits more into the picture **(tirar do close)**

zoom lens /'zu:m lenz/ NOUN [*plural* **zoom lenses**] a lens (= curved piece of glass) on a camera that can make things look bigger or smaller **(lentes de aproximação)**

zucchini /zu:'ki:nɪ/ NOUN [*plural* **zucchini**] the US word for **courgette** **(abobrinha)**

zygote /'zaɪgəʊt/ NOUN [*plural* **zygotes**] a cell which is formed when a male and a female cell join in reproduction (= process of producing babies). A biology word. **(zigoto)**